D1709532

A Portrait of the Stars and Stripes Volume II

Chronology U.S. Armed Forces 1919-1945

This book is presented to _____

From _____

Designed and typesetting by Folio Typographers, Inc.
Pennsauken, NJ

Published by Seniram Inc.
P.O. Box 432, Glenside, PA 19038

Printed by Philadelphia Press
Burlington, NJ

Hardcover bound by
Hoster Bindery, Ivyland, PA

Library of Congress Card Number   88-92574

ISBN 0-922564-01-9

A Portrait of the Stars and Stripes Volume II – 1919-1945

By Bud Hannings

Editors:
Warren W. Patton
Edna P. Nelson

SENIRAM PUBLISHING INC.
P.O. Box 432
Glenside, PA 19038

Acknowledgements

I would like to take this time to thank everyone who contributed to the successful completion of A Portrait of the Stars and Stripes, Volume II. There are many people who lent their time and expertise and I will always be grateful. Without their patience and understanding, this manuscript could never have been completed.

I owe special thanks to the United States Marine Corps Historical Division, especially Mr. Henry "Bud" Shaw (retired), his successor, Mr. Ben Frank, Mr. Dan Crawford and General E.H. Simmons, for checking the manuscript for accuracy (reference Marine actions). In addition, my continuing gratitude to Major M.K. Robb, U.S.M.C. and Major David Driegert, U.S.M.C., Marine Public Relations, Washington, D.C.

Continued special thanks to Vice Admiral William P. Lawrence, U.S.N. retired, and his wife Diane, for their unwavering support and encouragement. In addition, my sincere thanks to the Naval Historical Foundation, Washington, D.C., especially Captain Ken Coskey, retired for his tremendous assistance in providing me with many of the photographs depicting the U.S. Navy in action. Special thanks also go out to the U. S. Naval Historical Center, Washington, D.C., especially John Vajda and Paula Murphy and to the U.S. Coast Guard, Groton Ct.

Thanks also go out to the U.S. Army Historical Division, Washington, D.C., especially Mr. Karl Cocke and to the U.S. Army War College, Carlisle, Pa., especially to Lt. Col. Martin Andreson, Randy Rakers and Louise Arnold at the War College for their assistance. Also, special thanks to Corporal Gene Tomlinson, U.S.A. and Sergeant Cammie Brown (Pentagon) for their assistance.

During the course of reading this manuscript, you will notice much information concerning the recipients of the Medal of Honor. It is with great pride that I can thank Sister Maria Veronica, IHM, retired archivist at the Valley Forge Freedoms Foundation, Valley Forge, Pa.

Special thanks is also due Kathy Lisiewski, at the Traveler Restaurant in Union, Ct. for providing me with generous amounts of research material from their unique library.

Special thanks to Sean Timoney and Danielle Hannings for their endless hours of tedious typing and research.

Special thanks is also due, Mr. Warren W. Patton and Mrs. Edna Purvis Nelson for their countless hours of editing the manuscript.

Special thanks to Walt Lynch (Folio Typographers, Inc.) for the typesetting, and without his extraordinary support, there would be no book.

The following people have also been extremely helpful, offering both time and encouragement in many ways to bring this manuscript to a successful conclusion.

— Walt Lynch
— John and Jane Ewan
— Joe and Linda Venetucci
— John Graff
— William J. and Denise Graham
— Eugenia Kielar
— Tom "Murph" and Joanne Murphy
— Downey and Norma Hoster
— Don and Kathleen Kirkland
— Erik and Chris Schada
— Frederick and Barbara Loefler
— Viorel Minda
— Justin Grecescu
— Bill and Chris Ernst
— Bill and Peggy Ellis
— Sean and Rosemarie Timoney
— John Sr. and Constance Lehman
— Edith Distel
— Terri H. and Robert Mitros
— Joseph and Danielle Hannings
— Chris Hannings
— Lori Hannings
— John O'Donnell
— Tim Lynch
— Charles and Jean Haggerty

— Frank and Louise Hannings
— Bud and Jane Stocklin
— Jim and Mary Dugan
— The staff of the Abington Library, especially Mary Lou Ginsburg, Anne Morrison, Judy Platt, and Nancy Posel.
— Brent Vollrath
— Ard Gallman
— Frank Santo
— Pat McMenamin
— Butch and Karen Beal
— Vera Gallagher
— Ann and Lou Fetscher
— Ann and Al Lohr
— Eileen and John Marks
— John Kirk (Bison Books)
— Kirkland Printing, Glenside, Pa.
— Frank L. Rizzo (his untimely death prevented him from being here for the finished product, but his encouragement helped push us over the top.)
— Franciscan Nuns, St. Bonaventure's, Parochial School, Phila., PA.
— Special thanks to my patron Saint, Saint Jude and to my wife Barbara for her patience and support.

The Eternal Flag

By Bud Hannings

Flags have come and flags have gone, but the American Flag is here to stay. As each crisis evolves, our flag always waves a little prouder in the wind. Just as a new wave in the ocean appears to take the place of the one that disappeared on the beach, a new American Flag will blow in the breeze more proudly than the one that some tyrant will burn or tear.

Our flag has always flown as a beacon of freedom in the wind for all the world to see, and even as they saw it burning in Tehran, they must have seen the majestic beauty of its disappearance in the wind, only to be reappearing a few feet to the left or right to be burned again. At first I felt resentment, but after seeing it again and again, I can look back and almost thank those inconsiderate, supposed, Iranian students for helping bring together Americans of all ages.

Their barbaric burning of the greatest flag of them all, has sent sparks flying that have welded the American people into one. Almost as if the smoke from their fires traveled across the ocean and reassembled the flags to fly higher and prouder than ever before.

It is time to stop trying to please everyone in the world. Americans have helped at one time or another almost every country in the world, and did so because they wanted to help, not because they needed any glory. Many Americans have literally given their lives to liberate thousands upon thousands of imprisoned people throughout our history. We have not only helped people, but entire nations, and how quickly they forget.

Even while we were held at bay by a small and almost uncivilized band of revolutionaries, using Americans as hostages, the Americans as usual were holding their heads high, and acting in a way that all nations should act, but it was difficult to watch helplessly as the hostages had their dignity trampled, and their lives endangered.

America, you should be commended for your brave restraint. It would have been easy to unleash your unimaginable strength on our adversaries, but that would have harmed many innocent people, and that is not the American way. Your respect for the lives of many people has once again shown the American way as the best way. We can be assured of a much greater love of country, freedom, and the foresight to realize that the Iranians and anyone else who have not learned from history what great things America has done unselfishly for the rest of the world, are no longer important, but that it is important that we as Americans be aware of it.

Maybe now, the people in the rest of the world will realize that the American flag can be wounded, but never fatally. Neither burning or tearing will ever eradicate the Eternal Flag of the United States of America or the unequalled acts of valor and bravery of its countless deeds in defense of freedom throughout the world. The American Flag is an indelible mark, for us and our posterity, that possesses the unique ability to shine brighter under stress and the durability to withstand intimidation by adversaries anywhere in the world.

America I salute you and I thank God that the American Flag in the proud American tradition will always be here to help those in need.

By God, it really does feel good to be an American.

Prominent Comments

Several prominent Americans have been asked to take the time to review the manuscript. It is with a sincere amount of deep appreciation that I thank these kind gentlemen, both for taking the time out of their busy schedules to review the book and for their most gracious comments which are included for your review.

— GENERAL P.X. KELLEY, 28th Commandant, U.S. Marine Corps, retired:

"A Portrait of the Stars and Stripes II is a superb chronological memorial to those men and women of every race, creed, color, and country of national origin who have selflessly served under the Stars and Stripes."

— GENERAL WILLIAM C. WESTMORELAND (retired), Chief of Staff, United States Army, July 3rd 1968-June 30th 1972:

"A Portrait of the Stars and Stripes II is an accurate depiction of the U.S. Military during WWII. It will serve a worthy purpose for all Americans interested in a factual history of the U.S. Armed Forces."

Left to Right. General P.X. Kelley, U.S.M.C. retired, Former Secretary of the Navy, John Lehman and Mr. John Lehman Sr. (a Naval Officer in the Pacific during WWII). Photo courtesy of Kelley & the Lehman family.

— Mr. JOHN F. LEHMAN, Secretary of the Navy, former:

"A Portrait of the Stars and Stripes II cements Bud Hannings' unique position as 'citizen historian'. There is no other compilation that accomplishes what these unique volumes have achieved. They are a record of inspiration for every American and are all the more remarkable because they have been published without the help of a large organization."

— COLONEL BILL WHITE, U.S.M.C., retired, Editor Leatherneck Magazine:

"Bud Hannings' two extraordinary works (Portrait of the Stars and Stripes) belong in every library in America, particularly in our schools. Every serious student of military history should also own them. In addition to being great reading, the books are excellent research tools."

— VICE ADMIRAL WILLIAM P. LAWRENCE, Superintendent, United States Naval Academy and former Chief of Naval Personnel, retired:

"A Portrait of the Stars and Stripes II, is another unique and highly valuable contribution to our military history. Like its predecessor, it is a rare one-of-a-kind book. The book provides a painstakingly factual detailed chronological account of the key operations during World War II, which enables the uninformed reader to obtain a broad knowledge of this most significant war in our history. In addition, it provides a channel for serious researchers to effectively focus their efforts. The author deserves the strongest praise for his tireless dedication to his fellow man."

— MR. FRANK L. RIZZO, Mayor City of Philadelphia, Pa. (1972-1979):

"A Portrait of the Stars and Stripes II, like Volume I, is another excellent achievement, which should be in the collection of every historian. The book's comprehensive coverage of WWII, makes it another great reference tool for teachers and students alike. The book captures the essence of the American fighting man and makes one proud to be an American."

— MAJOR GENERAL GEORGE S. PATTON, USA, retired:

"A Portrait of the Stars and Stripes, Volume II is magnificent. I consider it a unique contribution to the history of this nation, and you are to be congratulated by all Americans for the tremendous research you have applied to this fine history."

—Mr. BILL D. ROSS, author of Iwo Jima, and Peleliu, Tragic Triumph:

"A Portrait of the Stars and Stripes II is not only monumental in size, but one whose scope is a day-by-day chronicle of the historic events of WWII. For military students and analysts, history buffs, and those who write about the 'Great War,' it is a unique 'must' for their research and libraries."

— HENRY I. (BUD) SHAW, JR., Chief Historian, United States Marine Corps (1962-1990), retired:

"A Portrait of the Stars and Stripes is a great work, which encompasses so much and with understanding of what transpired. As with Volume I, the author has done a superlative job that shows incredible research stamina and drive."

From the Author

A Portrait of the Stars and Stripes II, is exactly that, a portrait, accentuated by the gallant exploits of the men who flocked to the Colors, following the attack against Pearl Harbor. This astounding saga of the American Armed Forces begins well in advance of the call to the Colors during 1941, in essence exhibiting the unpreparedness of the U.S. Government to meet the lethal threat. Undaunted, the U.S. fighting forces must overcome a potent group of enemies and simultaneously maneuver around the political obstacles to conclude the massive conflagration that nearly destroyed the world as we know it.

The purpose of this book is not to glorify war, nor to lessen the severity of the results of warfare, but rather, to place the contributions of the individuals above politics and exhibit the zest, zeal and extraordinary courage and internal fortitude of the American Soldier without prejudice. In keeping with the tone of Volume I (1775-1918), this book maintains its fundamental task of illuminating the struggles of the American Military, while simultaneously manifesting the glorious exploits of the best this country has to offer, to insure Liberty for those of us who have been privileged to bear the sometimes envied title, "American."

Soldiers have never started wars. They are simply called upon to fight them. Since our Declaration of Independence in 1776, this nation's finest have been called upon on many occasions to insure the free flight of our magnificent Stars and Stripes, the symbol of our nation. Stalwart men and women, Americans all, have thrashed all adversarial attempts to dislodge the Stars and Stripes. This new breed of Yanks, although momentarily stunned by the arrogance of the attack on Pearl Harbor, mobilize to defeat Japan and its Axis partners.

The American dream for most people at home is derailed by this immense conflict. On the battlefields, the grim realities of war shatter the dreams forever, for many of them, but they serve with distinction, proclaiming their unabashed allegiance to their country, that we who have inherited the legacy can continue to live in the greatest country in the world.

Historians will inevitably continue to argue various decisions of the world leaders, the strategies of the Admirals and Generals and undoubtedly, the political motives behind the struggle. This book cannot answer all the questions, nor capture the entire scope of the conflict. However, the boundless heroism, and undaunted valor of the U.S. Armed Forces during World War II is indisputable and proudly presented in this book in their honor.

It is our responsibility to remember those great Americans and pay them fair tribute, for without their sacrifices and those of the mothers who bore them, there would be no Stars and Stripes waving overhead, insuring our children's dreams. This is a humble tribute to those gallant American Patriots and to their families, a tribute to those who never had time to think of themselves as Patriots, a word seldom heard on the battlefield. They simply thought of themselves as Americans. This is their incredible story.

Enjoy This Book

Bud Hannings

Bud Hannings

Table of Contents

Introduction

"A Portrait of the Stars and Stripes II is an outstanding straightforward testimonial to each and every man and woman who served Old Glory selflessly during World War II.

The book continues the magnificent saga of the U.S. Armed Forces as they march in cadence toward and through the violent sound of the guns to uphold the noble traditions and spirit of the American military profession.

It is a rapid paced and gripping chronicle, which focuses on the individual acts of bravery and heroism, while maintaining a factual depiction of the U.S. Military on all fronts in every corner of the world.

American resolve and determination are displayed from the descent of the first enemy plane at Pearl Harbor and the early setbacks in the Pacific. Gallantry, courage and extraordinary valor become commonplace as viewed through the bold deeds of our American warriors. From the Coral Sea to Midway, from North Africa to Berlin, and from Guadalcanal to Tokyo, the Stars and Stripes never faltered.

The use of present tense adds a unique touch, giving the reader a sense of being in the midst of the anguish of battle, to experience the trials and tribulations of the troops and share in the ultimate victorious triumph.

Every American can be extremely proud of our Airmen, Soldiers, Sailors, Coastguardsmen and Marines. We should also be proud of their families, loved ones, and the civilian personnel who supported them. Their enduring sacrifices ensured that the Stars and Stripes and her Allies would prevail at the conclusion of the conflict."

General Al M. Gray, U.S.M.C.
29th Commandant

Foreword

A Portrait of the Stars and Stripes II, is another unique and highly valuable contribution to our military history. Like its predecessor, it is a rare one-of-a-kind book. The book provides a painstakingly factual detailed account of the key operations during World War II, which enables the uninformed reader to obtain a broad knowledge of this most significant war in our history. In addition, it provides a channel for serious researchers to effectively focus their efforts.

The book maintains a straight-forward account of the courageous actions of our fighting forces on land, sea and in the air, capturing the stark realism of warfare with all its consequences. Again, the reader has instant access to every U.S. military action on land and sea. However, in this book, the Army, Navy and Marine Airmen add to the glory of the cause, and speed the victory process.

You will experience the sensation of crossing the vast oceans with the fleets, exchanging broadsides with the enemy, being cramped on Submarines as they maneuver through the sea to eliminate enemy warships. And you will feel the excrutiating tension as enemy planes attack the fleet. You will move across barren torrid deserts, prod through knee-deep mud, trudge along icy roads and climb rigid mountain peaks, as our fighting men plant the colors and liberate the oppressed. You will feel the pressure of the sailors as the landing craft crash through the waves to deliver the invasion forces to the beaches, and become aware of the danger as the troops come under intense artillery bombardments. You will advance with the armor and ground forces as they blast their way through the dense caves or face a deadly sniper. Also, you will experience the aura of the gallant pilots who blanket the skies to destoy the enemy's war machines and acquire air supremacy. The road to victory is full of anguish, but ultimately, the American spirit reaches its pinnacle and applies a mighty thrust to the Allied cause to bring victory.

Preeminently, the book accentuates the innumerable individual acts of courage and valor, but retains its grasp on the overall view of the great global conflict. This, the second in a trilogy of volumes, continues to pay grand tribute to all of our men and women who served Old Glory selflessly to terminate the ominous conflagration. The book is another inspiring and heartwarming story of the American Flag and its defenders; unequivocally, Volume II, continues to objectively chronicle the American military and provide a combination of enjoyable reading that makes one anxious to turn the next page.

I recommend this superb book to everyone; that they might become better acquainted with the grand nature of our national heritage.

William P. Lawrence
Vice Admiral, United States Navy, Retired

MAPS

THE STARS AND STRIPES GOES TO WAR

The years following the conclusion of the Great War, are both bitter and sweet for the United States. The people pick up on the great American dream with hope and a prayer, that peace is here to stay. They believe in their hearts that the War to end all Wars has extinguished their fear of world war forever. The ensuing years see America rush through the Roaring Twenties and then begin a near crippling crawl of desperation during the Great Depression which creates excessive poverty in the country, but at the same time strengthens most American families while they pull together as a unit to survive. While most Americans are attempting to pull their country from the brink of financial disaster, the world around them is quickly descending into another period of grave uncertainty, which not only threatens world peace, but also thoroughly jeopardizes Liberty and the Freedom of the entire world.

Between the World Wars, the United States maintains Military presence around the globe. Marines are sent to assist Haiti, Nicaragua, the Dominican Republic and Honduras to insure government stability and to protect American interests. Small contingents of Marines are also stationed in Shanghai and China. The amount of United States Soldiers stationed in countries other than America or its territories remains very small during the twenties and thirties. Quite frankly, if war erupts, the United States is ill-prepared to cope. As the United States leans toward a policy of isolationism, the clandestine veil of war begins to hover over the Far East and Europe, signaling the imminent appalling atrocities of both the Japanese and Germans, who are obsessed with expansion and world conquest at any price.

On September 18th 1931, Japanese swarm into Manchuria in a blatant act of aggression which propels them into World War II. The chain of events for the world continues to deteriorate, as Hitler assumes the position of Chancellor of Germany during January of 1933 and immediately begins to push his National Socialist Party into power. One American with foresight, Colonel Billy Mitchell, argues tirelessly for American Airpower, in a near futile attempt to convince his superiors that Aircraft Carriers must become the vanguard of the U.S. Navy to ensure command of the sea in the event of war. His dream comes to fruition on February 25th 1933, when the United States launches its first Aircraft Carrier, the *Ranger*, christened in honor of John Paul Jones' Ship. This Carrier and those that soon follow, will turn the tide of battle in a few short years. Without them and their gallant Sailors, all might have been lost.

As America slumbers, Germany and Japan are meticulously and methodically lubricating their war machinery, corroborating on a master scheme, which if successful, will lead to world conquest. Danger signals are ringing throughout the world, but America does not take sufficient precautions. During August 1935, the U.S. Congress prohibits the shipments of arms to the warring nations (Japan and China). This is followed by President Roosevelt signing a third Neutrality Act during May of 1937. America's heart says neutrality, but subsequent events will bring her to the conclusion, that once again, her brave men must bear arms, or her freedom will be gone forever.

On December 12th 1937, the U.S.S. *Panay* is destroyed without provocation on the Yangtze River by Japanese Aircraft, while throngs of people including Americans watch in disbelief along the banks. The United States takes no retaliatory measures, accepting Japan's superficial apology for the aggressive act on the 14th. In Europe, the Germans file into Austria during mid-March, raising the Nazi ensign and claiming unification. This act of German belligerence is followed by an appeasement by both France and England, who agree during September of 1938 to hand Germany possession of the Sudetenland portion of Czechoslovakia. The Germans promptly seize the remainder of Czechoslovakia during March 1939. The Italians seize diminutive Albania during the following month. Foreboding war clouds are expanding unharnessed around the globe.

Hitler storms into Poland on September 1st 1939. This profane maneuver finally provokes France and England to declare war against Germany two days later. Ironically, on the same day, a British liner, the *Athenia* is destroyed by a German Vessel. Twenty-eight American passengers go down with the British passenger Ship, but even this does not compel America to declare war. The Russians invade Poland from the east during mid-September and subsequently sign an agreement with Germany, sealing the fate of the Polish people. The Russians, holding a tremendously superior numbered Army, invade Finland during the latter part of November. They are met by a gallant, but overmatched Finnish Army, which is forced to capitulate within a couple of desperate months. The battleground of this lopsided conflict in Europe, transfers to the sea during January 1940, in what becomes known as the Battle of the Atlantic.

German U-boats devastate Allied Convoys, costing the Allies over a half million tons of Shipping within a few months. As the German Wolf Packs escalate their acts of terror, the Allies initiate Warship escorts, which gradually eliminate the enemy threat, but it becomes a vicious and gruesome struggle with staggering losses of both men and equipment, before the Allies finally exterminate the German terror on the high seas.

The German onslaught continues unchecked, as Denmark falls during April of 1940. Norway fights on until the ninth of June, when the King of Norway orders a surrender. The Germans vanquish Belgium, Luxembourg and the Netherlands, in a solitary day, the 10th of May. The French and British have been compressed at Dunkirk and face annihilation at the hands of the Germans. As the Germans close for the kill, they discover their prey have outwitted imminent disaster and are escaping across the English Channel. With only the sea to their backs, the defiant Allies are masterfully evacuated by a massive array of Vessels, which range from cumbersome fishing boats to giant Warships, operating under the spectacular supervision of the Royal Navy. The improvised rescue Armada sustains severe losses, but maneuvers into the dangerous waters off Dunkirk and after the harrowing experience, embarks with over 300,000 British, French and Belgian troops that had been trapped. This valiant undertaking sparks new life into the bloodline of the Allies. British Prime Minister Winston Churchill, on June 4th 1940, the last day of this marvelous rescue, electrifies his nation and the free world with the will and resolve to fight until victory, with these inspirational words: "WE SHALL FIGHT ON THE BEACHES, WE SHALL FIGHT ON THE LANDING GROUNDS, WE SHALL FIGHT IN THE FIELDS AND IN THE STREETS. WE SHALL NEVER SURRENDER." Germany soon initiates the Battle of Britain, delivering countless bombing raids against English cities, beginning on July 10th. The Britains refuse to succumb and by late October 1940 these steadfast Britains have held, their smaller but more determined Air Force had expelled the German Air Force from the skies over England, ending Hitler's proposed invasion.

Subsequently, Germany, Japan and Italy will sign the Tripartite Treaty. As the Allies continue to take a thrashing, France is invaded during early June of 1940 by the Germans. The country surrenders by the 22nd. This is followed by the Russians seizing Estonia, Latvia and Lithuania. The fall of France causes consternation in the United States, but war is still not declared. The U.S. does however; dispatch Marines to the French Colony of Martinique in the Western Hemisphere, to prevent German occupation.

The United States begins to bolster its forces in the Pacific during 1941, because it is apparent that it is no longer a question of whether America will be drawn into the conflict but when? During the previous year, the U.S. had given England 50 American Destroyers in exchange for Bases. The U.S. helps the Allies in other ways also, but does not enter the conflict

directly. Circumstances are beginning to change. The Germans sink an American Merchant Vessel, the *Robin Moor*, off the coast of Brazil on the 25th of May. On May 27th 1941, President Roosevelt declares "a state of unlimited emergency." It is now known within the higher echelon of the government, that when America does enter the war, she will have to bear responsibility for the entire Pacific Theater. The U.S. is also expected to play a major role in the European Theater. The Axis, seize Crete, Yugoslavia and Greece by the First of June 1941. Japanese troops shortly thereafter burst into French Indo-China on the 24th of July.

During July of 1941, U.S. Marines are dispatched to Iceland to protect that country from the Germans. Tensions continue to mount while America waits for an aggressor to make the first move. On the 17th of October 1941, a German vessel attacks the U.S.S. *Kearney* (Destroyer) off the coast of Iceland, inflicting 11 casualties. Soon after this insolent attack, the U.S.S. *Reuben James*, another Destroyer is attacked, costing the lives of 100 Americans, yet, there is no retaliation. The U.S. War Department, during the latter part of November 1941, informs all Naval Commanders in the Pacific Region that war is imminent. The message is unmistakably clear: "AN AGGRESSIVE MOVE BY JAPAN IS EXPECTED WITHIN THE NEXT FEW DAYS" "EXECUTE APPROPRIATE DEPLOYMENT." Simultaneously, General MacArthur, reactivated into the Army after retirement, because of the impending conflict, receives word at his headquarters in the Philippines, from General Marshall: "HOSTILE ACTION POSSIBLE AT ANY MOMENT" "IF HOSTILITIES CANNOT BE AVOIDED. THE UNITED STATES DESIRES THAT JAPAN COMMIT THE FIRST OVERT ACT."

Japanese diplomats are pretentiously negotiating with Washington to seek a solution for peace, while simultaneously destroying all records at the embassy, with full knowledge on the 3rd of December 1941, that a Japanese Fleet has departed the Kurile Islands to attack Pearl Harbor and destroy the American Fleet with its Carriers. This gigantic Task Force of 33 ships, including six Carriers, maintains strict radio silence, managing to sail undetected to a rendezvous point within 200 miles from Oahu, Hawaii. The Armada commences an unmerciful attack on the unsuspecting Americans at Pearl Harbor on the 7th of December 1941.

On a tranquil Sunday morning, the complacent Americans are jolted from their racks as hundreds of enemy aircraft swoop down on the base at Pearl. The Americans must first break the locks to get to the ammunition, before returning fire. Gallant men are fighting with their rifles and pistols, against Planes. Explosions occur all around them. Carnage is everywhere. Some of these valiant Americans, their bodies scorched to the bones, are trapped in the burning Ships, unable to fight back. Murderous enemy machine guns, mounted on the Planes, pound the barracks area, while other enemy Planes drop bombs on Battleship row, causing fires and ripping these men to pieces. It is a gruesome blood filled sight, etched eternally in the minds of those lucky enough to survive the vicious ordeal. Old Glory peers through the death and destruction, sneering at the Japs, while still flying briskly atop her fallen troops and mangled fleet. The tattered Stars and Stripes, scorched by crimson fire and riddled by enemy guns, bears testimony for her slain heroes, some of whom will rest until the end of time in steel caskets, such as the U.S.S. *Arizona*, on the bottom of the harbor. Many will soon die a slow agonizing death by fire, intense smoke, and drowning in the water filled chambers of the Vessels. The heroism of these gallant men at Pearl Harbor is exemplified by the dying words of Machinist Mate Robert R. Scott, who steadfastly refuses to leave his trapped companions on the U.S.S. *California*: "THIS IS MY DUTY STATION AND I WILL STAY AND GIVE THEM AIR AS LONG AS THE GUNS ARE GOING."

Japan's first blow is destructive, but not mortal. Miraculously, the American Carriers are not in port and escape the wrath of the sneak attack. The Japanese depart, assuming they had destroyed the American Fleet, but of the numerous Vessels damaged or destroyed, most will be reincarnated to retaliate against the Japanese. The *Arizona, Utah,* and the *Oklahoma* are lost forever, along with 2,334 American fighting men, on this tragic day. The Japanese lose less than 100 men during the massacre. By 1300 hours, the Japanese Fleet is embarking back to Japan. The staggered Yanks cannot pursue. On the following day, President Roosevelt, informs a stunned American populace of the deceitful act: "YESTERDAY, DECEMBER 7TH, A DATE WHICH WILL LIVE IN INFAMY, THE UNITED STATES WAS SUDDENLY AND DELIBERATELY ATTACKED BY NAVAL AND AIR FORCES OF JAPAN." The United States and England both declare war on Japan because of the unprovoked sneak attack.

America has been humiliated and many of her brave men have been lost to a foe, which chose a sneak attack before declaring war. Germany and Italy initiate hostilities against the United States within a few days, declaring war against America on the 11th of December. The U.S. reciprocates immediately, giving the Americans the ultimate challenge of fighting a victorious war against several foes in three major Theaters around the world. Japan, unconcerned about repercussions, continues to ravage the Pacific, her Planes pummeling the American positions in the Philippines, where the understrengthed defenders are bracing for an invasion. Small American Garrisons in China are forced to capitulate on the Eighth. Japanese Warships steam toward thinly garrisoned Wake Island and Guam. Japanese troops land on Bataan in the Philippines. These enemy storm troopers overrun Malaya and Thailand on the eighth. Guam is seized on the 10th. In addition, Makin and Tarawa are taken. The situation is extremely grave. The U.S. Asiatic Fleet receives orders to withdraw from Manila Bay as soon as possible and seek safer waters in the East Indies. The Japanese unsuccessfully attempt to take Wake Island on the 11th, from a force of Marines numbering less than 400 men. This valiant Garrison withstands constant air assaults, until the 23rd of December. With only 85 Marines and one operational Plane remaining, this defiant American contingent holds off a 1,500 man invasion force for several hours, until ordered to surrender. In one instance, a few Marines fire furiously, stopping over 200 Japs in their tracks. The Base Commander orders the island surrendered, but the valiant 16 day stand on Wake Island becomes an inspiration to the entire country.

The Japanese continue transporting men into the Philippines to crush the resistance. On Christmas Eve, 7,000 Japanese land 70 miles southeast of Manila. On the following day, the Japanese overrun Hong Kong. Reinforcements heading to the Philippines and Wake Island are diverted to other duty stations after it is ascertained that they will not change the desperate situation. There is little hope for the men on Bataan, but these outnumbered defenders compel the Japanese to pay an enormous price for the real estate. The Japs take

Manila easily on the second of January, while the defenders head for Bataan, where they make a defiant stand. On the 11th of January, 1942, Japan declares war against the Netherlands, dispatching troops to the Netherlands East Indies, to seize the sparsely garrisoned Dutch bases. More bad news develops when the Japanese invade Burma, during mid-January, followed by the storming of Rabaul and Kavieng, New Ireland. In addition, Allied positions in New Guinea are under vicious attack.

The Allied situation in Europe is similar. At this time, there are no American Divisions in Europe to aid the British. An Axis offensive is rolling across North Africa, east through Libya. The British are subsequently ordered to hold Tobruk. While the Germans are pushing through North Africa, they are also heavily involved on the Eastern Front against the Russians. Hitler had attacked Russia during June of 1941, with over 100 Divisions. The United States has offered its arsenal of democracy to the Russians and will contribute greatly to the eventual victory of the Red Army over the Germans. The Germans are rebuffed at the steps of Moscow during the latter part of 1941 and again at Stalingrad during late 1942. Stalin agrees to assist with the war in the Pacific, after the defeat of Germany, but his word is worthless. The Russians take all the supplies offered by the Allies, but do not keep their word too well and in fact, give the Allies a terrible time at Berlin after the close of hostilities in Europe. The Russians finally declare war on Japan, subsequent to the Atom bombs being dropped on Japan. The Red Army then invades Manchuria, while preparing to join the Allies at the surrender ceremony at Tokyo Bay, during September of 1945.

Back in the Pacific, the Australian Garrison at Rabaul, New Britain, falls to the Japanese. This disaster is followed by the capture of New Ireland, jeopardizing both New Guinea and Australia. The Allies finally score a small Naval success over the Japanese off the coast of Borneo in the Macassar Strait. The Japanese lose four Troop Transports and a Patrol Boat during the brief encounter. This is the first of several successful Naval operations against the Japanese. On February 1st, 1942, two American Naval Task Forces assault enemy positions in the Gilbert and Marshall Islands, inflicting substantial damage; thus informing Japan that its positions are not invincible. These small Allied conquests over Japan cannot override the Allied failure to halt the overall Japanese thrust in the Pacific. On February 15th, approximately 64,000 British troops surrender their Garrison at Singapore. On the same day, the Allies hurriedly evacuate Palembang, Netherlands, East Indies, narrowly escaping another Japanese invasion force. The Allies are dealt another punishing blow at Darwin, Australia, as they are once again caught completely offguard, when enemy Planes rake the crowded runways and destroy many of the Aircraft, which had been crammed closely together. The Australians also lose several Warships. This enemy attack on the 19th of February, gives the Japanese their greatest single success since Pearl Harbor.

In the Philippines, the defenders have earned themselves the nickname, "Battling Bastards of Bataan," for their tenacity and resolve. The odds are insurmountable without supplies and reinforcements, but the defenders continue to pound the Japanese, inflicting severe casualties. Toward the end of February 1942, General MacArthur is ordered to depart the Philippines and proceed to Australia. General Wainwright is to command the troops in MacArthur's absence, but Bataan falls on April 9th. This Allied setback permits the infamous "Ba-taan Death March," which costs the lives of approximately 6,000 men, Filipino and American, who are forced to walk 80 miles in the deadly tropic heat without sufficient food or rest. Organized resistance continues on the Philippines until the 10th of May, when General Wainwright surrenders all Allied Forces in the Philippines. Japan scores another success and America has yet to strike back.

In the sometimes forgotten campaign, raging feverishly in the China-Burma-India Theater, American General Joseph Stil-well assumes responsibility for the American effort. Stilwell is to work with Chiang Kai-Shek to bolster the fighting ability of the Chinese. The task is arduous. General Stilwell has no American combat troops under his command and none com-ing. The Japanese take Rangoon on the 6th of March. The undermanned British are easily forced back. General Stilwell, the General with no American combat troops or Planes, is forced to evacuate toward India. During the final days in Burma, Stilwell's command is scheduled to take the last train out of Burma, but it had been confiscated by a Chinese Gen-eral for himself and his friends. The pirated train, running along a one track railroad, inadvertently crashes head on into another train. Stilwell gets his sparse force out of Burma, but not before a murderous trek through dense jungle, without losing a man (except one who had remained behind with the Chinese). Stilwell is fuming when he gets to India, pledging to return to drive out the Japs. He does return, but Chinese poli tics finally win out and he is replaced before the campaign is finished. General Stilwell, a disciplined fighting General, often calls Kai-shek, "the peanut." On one occasion, Stilwell had been told by Kai-shek that "watermelons were good for the troops" and that he must supply "one watermelon for every four Chinese troops. In another instance, Stilwell is informed that all Chinese, killed in battle, are to be buried in pine boxes and shipped back to China. There is little pine wood in Burma jungles.

Supplies for the Allies have to be flown over the Hump (Hima-layas), by American Pilots. It is during the spring of 1944, that approximately 3,000 American troops (volunteers) under the command of General Merrill (Merrill's Marauders), move through Burma to capture Myitkyina Airfield, a primary Jap-anese strongpoint. The Marauders are the only U.S. Infantry Troops standing between the Japanese and India. These troops are supplied by air as they creep hundreds of miles through the enemy territory, guided by OSS Agents and Ka-chin natives, toward the objective (700 mile march). The trek takes a tremendous toll on the Marauders, but they continue against heavy odds and hook up with the Chinese troops to take the coveted Airfield, which falls after a brutalizing strug-gle, on the 2nd of August, 1944. The Allies finally secure Burma, during April of 1945, when the Japanese pull back to prepare to defend their homeland against an Allied assault.

May of 1942, marks the beginning of the demise of the Impe-rial Japanese Empire, induced by an enduring hard-fought and bloody series of campaigns. The Japanese Fleet has been invincible, with no major defeats. Unquestionably, they con-trol the Pacific. This Japanese superiority is about to be shat-tered by the United States Navy. The U.S. Fleet, protecting the ground troops engaged in furious combat on New Guinea, discover and intercept a Japanese Task Force in the Coral Sea, compelling the Yanks to implement immediate actions to in-sure the destruction of the Japanese Naval force, which is

threatening the success of Allied land operations.

The Naval confrontation becomes a classic sea duel, setting a new precedent for Naval warfare. The American Pilots initiate a swift takeoff from their Carriers and bludgeon the enemy Fleet. The enemy, in turn, locates and inflicts heavy damage to the U.S. Fleet, but at battle's end, the Yank Pilots have decimated the enemy. This forces the hostile assault force to abort the intended invasion of Allied positions at Port Mor-esby, New Guinea. The opposing Fleets never fired a shot at each other, leaving the entire battle to their respective Air Forces. This American victory of great magnitude is followed by another Naval conquest over the Japanese at Midway Is-land. Thanks to the American code-breakers who have the mastered the enemy code system, the U.S. is prepared for the Japanese Task Force, which is steaming toward Midway. The Japanese attempt a diversionary maneuver, by landing troops in the North Pacific on the Aleutian Islands, but the American Fleet doesn't move, choosing to wait and spring their own surprise on the Japanese.

On June 2nd 1942, the Japanese Fleet nears Midway. The U.S. Spotter Planes detect the enemy Armada as they had antici-pated. American Planes are catapulted from their Carriers to seek and destroy the invasion force. The Yanks attack with all available Planes, punishing the enemy thoroughly. This gruesome battle rages until the sixth of June, culminating with a brilliant American victory. The Japanese Planes inflict damage to the United States Fleet, but the Americans wreck the Japanese Task Force, sinking four Carriers and destroying a massive amount of enemy Planes. The Japanese, with only two Carriers remaining in their entire Navy, make a desperate run for Japan. However; the U.S. Navy pursues the humiliated Imperial Navy, dispatching Carrier and Land-based Planes to inflict further damage. The tide had changed in the Pacific. The two recent Naval victories preserve both Hawaii and the West Coast of the United States, which would have become vulnerable, if Midway had fallen. The Navy, with this magnifi-cent effort, has confiscated the momentum from the Jap-anese. Old Glory reigns triumphantly at Midway and elation will prompt the confidence of the Americans to surge to new heights. Following the Naval conquest at Midway, the Amer-icans prepare for their first land offensive, which is expected to prove American intent to fight until every enemy-held is-land between Hawaii and Japan is in American possession.

During the preliminary stages of the Battle of Midway in June of 1942, the Japs strike the Aleutian Islands, a portion of Alaska. The confrontation is known as the Battle of Dutch Harbor. American Planes, striking from secret Bases, devas-tate the enemy Fleet, which had been approaching behind a storm. The Aleutians, which control the fate of the U.S. West Coast, contain the closest Military outpost to Japan. The Jap-anese sustain great losses at the hands of the Americans, including two Transports, two Destroyers, three Heavy Cruisers and an Aircraft Carrier. The Yanks fly under terrible conditions and lose many Pilots, but they chose their fate, rather than lose contact with the enemy. After the heated contest, Japanese troops manage to land on Attu and Kiska, both of which have no U.S. troops. The ruse, does not distract the U.S. Navy, presently maintaining its positions off Midway, but the Japs now possess a Base on U.S. Territory. The Jap-anese are frequented on a daily basis by Yank Bombers and Fighters, while American Combat Troops prepare to retake the islands. The U.S. 7th Division is subsequently dispatched to rid the Aleutians of Japanese. They storm the beaches at

Attu, catching the Japanese by surprise. The enemy offers obstinate resistance, but the 7th is well suited for the task and in quick fashion, darts ashore on the 11th of May, 1943. The 7th, meets stiff opposition as it attempts to advance. The Japanese hold tight until a breakthrough occurs on the 16th. The Yanks then make splendid progress, driving the Japs back and proudly restoring Old Glory to the area. This North Pacific island falls to the Americans by the 31st of May, 1943. After the successful capitulation of Attu, the Americans prepare to capture Kiska, but the Japanese evacuate, undetected by the Americans. A large U.S. invasion force debarks on the 15th of August, but the island is free of enemy troops. Preparations are continuing, with the effort to push the Axis Powers out of North Africa and to drive the Japanese back to their homeland. There is still the perilous task of getting supplies to all necessary locations. In one incident, during June of 1942, an ill-fated Convoy, PQ-17, consisting of 33 Merchant Vessels, escorted by an array of Allied Warships, embarks from Iceland, making its way across the North Atlantic, toward Russia, with desperately needed supplies. Enemy surveillance Vessels discover the Convoy and receive instructions to destroy it. The confrontation, which occurs between the First and Fourth of July, culminates with near suicidal results. Following several days of brilliant fighting on the part of the Allies, the German Wolf Packs, aided by Planes, inflict heavy damage to the Convoy. On the Fourth of July, when orders from London reach the Warships, the losses turn to catastrophic. Based on the presumption that another German Fleet, including heavily armed Battleships, was approaching the Convoy, orders direct the Warships to evacuate the area. This abandonment forces the defenseless Merchant Vessels to scatter and attempt to make it on their own.

The Allied Warships disperse from Convoy PQ 17 and the shooting gallery begins. The deadly U-Boats attack, decimating the supply Ships. Survivors grasp for lifeboats. Some survivors, who assume they are lucky to be pulled from the deadly waters, by the remaining Vessels, are soon shocked again, as additional torpedoes pound the few remaining Ships. A few of the Vessels survive the ordeal, reaching Murmansk, Russia. The Allies who reach Russia, anticipating some sense of appreciation for the ungodly ordeal they have undergone, are unpleasantly surprised when they raise a cheer to the Russian workers on the docks, only to receive a response of silence. The subsequent explanation is somewhat self-explanatory. The workers are political prisoners. The Russians receive guns, ammunition, Tanks and supplies from the surviving Vessels of Convoy PQ-17. Its crew, because of extreme weather conditions, is compelled to spend the winter with the Russians. Future Allied Convoys are spared the fate of PQ-17, as armed escorts remain with them, regardless of impending enemy activity. A new invention, radar, begins to play a significant part in the conflict. Its effectiveness will eventually neutralize the enemy Warships. This and other types of advanced technology, in addition to the improved efficiency of American Submarines, will totally eliminate the threat to Allied Convoys by the end of 1943.

The United States commences its first land offensive of the war, when the First Marine Division storms the beaches at Guadalcanal, on the 7th of August, 1942, spearheading the American thrust into the Pacific. This invasion rapidly educates the Marines about jungle warfare and the fighting ability of their cunning foe. The Marines drive punishingly inland, fighting relentlessly. By September, 17,000 Marines control a 4

by 7 mile strip of Guadalcanal. The 164th U.S. Infantry arrives during mid-October to assist. These reinforcements will be further bolstered when the balance of the Americal Division arrives. U.S. Troops advance yard by bloody yard, destroying enemy fortifications with bullets, bayonets and fists if no artillery is available. On the 9th of February 1943, the Yanks take control. Japan has been humbled, suffering its first land defeat of the war. America, meanwhile, celebrates her first ground victory of the conflict. Simultaneously, the ground war being waged by the Australians and their American counterparts in New Guinea, against the Japanese on Papua, is also closing victoriously, further depressing the Japanese, whose thoughts of invincibility now turn to defense, against this unyielding American opponent.

On November 8th 1942, the Allies take another bold step, invading North Africa to crush the Axis powers. At first, the French decide to fire upon the Allies. They eventually sign an armistice, rather than face annihilation. By November 11th, the area is secure. Algiers and Oran capitulate quickly, but Casablanca holds out. American planes, ordered by Patton, are airborne, prepared to level Casablanca. The French Commander, who had refused to capitulate, changes his mind and signals for a surrender. At the last moment, General Patton calls off the air assault. The entire area is secure by November 11th. Patton allows the French to bear arms, enabling them to keep their image with the citizenry. Heavy fighting continues in North Africa through December, with the Allies getting thrashed by the Germans. General Patton will soon make the difference. Patton inspects the front lines in Tunisia, determining that Allied equipment is inferior to that of the Axis troops. The Allies get pummeled at the Kasserine Pass; however, total disaster is prevented when the Germans withdraw back into the pass. General Patton assumes command of the American II Corps, during March of 1943 and a remarkable transformation occurs. These same American men who had been severely defeated earlier, are turned into a mighty fighting machine under Patton. Omar Bradley, another astute American General, assumes command of the II Corps when Patton returns to Morocco during April 1943 to prepare for Sicily. The Axis troops are thoroughly beaten by mid-May, with formal surrender occurring on the 11th, culminating the North Africa campaign.

The Allies continue their aggressive advances in the Pacific, commencing an offensive to destroy enemy resistance on Rabaul. During the night of the 29th-30th June, 1943, three Allied invasion forces land in the Central Solomons, the Trobriands and New Guinea. This daring action unleashes a relentless campaign, which includes a brutalizing sea duel in the Kula Gulf on the 12th of July, which causes severe damage to an American Fleet. The Japanese, however, are repulsed and reinforcements do not reach New Georgia. The grueling campaign ceases on the 6th of October, 1943, when the bewildered Japanese withdraw from Vella LaVella, ending their occupation of the Central Solomons. The violent struggle for the remainder of New Guinea continues, with the Australians and Americans closing on Lae, prompting the Japanese to evacuate hurriedly on the 12th of September. The Australians occupy the town without opposition on the 16th and immediately set their sights on Dumpu and Kaiapit, another step toward Rabaul.

Generals Eisenhower, Lloyd R. Fredendall and Lucian Truscott.

ATTACK, ATTACK, ATTACK!

THE INVASION OF SICILY, ITALY, FRANCE AND THE
CONTINUING RETALIATORY ACTIONS IN THE PACIFIC.

The Allies invade Sicily on the 10th of July, 1943. It will take the Allies a mere 38 days to push the Axis troops from the island. Patton's troops move at such speed that it is difficult for the supplies to keep pace with the Infantry and Armor. The impressive campaign comes to a close as Regimental Combat Team 7, U.S. Third Division, rolls into Messina on the 17th of August, 1943. The Americans are joined shortly thereafter by British units. The Axis Troops evacuate to Italy. Allied guns, placed strategically along the coast of Sicily, soon begin to bombard enemy positions in Italy itself. The Allies, in hot pursuit of the Germans, commence an invasion of the Italian mainland on the 9th of September, 1943. This campaign will be conducted much differently than the one in Sicily. The Allies will sustain grievous punishment from the staunch German defenders as they attempt to drive the enemy up the mountainous boot. The campaign is rugged from the onset. Supply problems are terrible; the weather ungodly, and the villainous mountain roads, for the most part, are impassable by motorized Vehicles, especially during the freezing winter months.

The hardships endured by the Allies are dreadful. They face impregnable enemy positions, both natural and man-made as they fight their way toward Rome. One is an ominous Monastery Fortress, high in the mountains standing between Naples and Rome, surrounded by elite German troops. The Allies continuously assault the fortress called Cassino, but each time the effort fails and the casualty list soars. The gusty winter winds, supported by blinding blizzards that covet the paths leading to the Fortress, prevail, aided further by op-

pressive, frigid rain storms. The Allies initiate an invasion against Anzio, on January 22nd, 1944, which is intended to strike fast and close in from behind enemy lines, in conjunction with a massive assault against Cassino. The invasion of Anzio is nearly perfect, with the Allies receiving almost no resistance. The joint American British assault force quickly seizes a seven mile beachhead, but does not capitalize. American General Lucas, in command at Anzio, chooses extreme caution and does not advance. He wants the beachhead secure and the resupply system in tact in case of enemy counterattack. This decision allows the Germans enough time to reinforce the area and pin the Americans and British on the beaches until mid-May. In one instance, on the 30th of January, two U.S. Ranger Battalions, attempting to spearhead an assault of the VI Corps against the Germans at Anzio are slaughtered by an ambush as they move toward Cisterna. The Germans, had taken note of the Allied movements and laid a deadly trap. The U.S. 4th Ranger Battalion and elements of the Third Division attempt a rescue, but it is in vain. In another instance at Anzio, Sgt. Truman Olson, Infantry, 3rd Division, sees most of his Company become casualties during a German counterattack in the vicinity of Cisterna. Olson's Machine Gun Crew moves up to halt the assault, but every member except Olson is killed. Olson singlehandedly holds off 200 Germans for over a half hour, before becoming severely wounded. Olson refuses to quit, firing at the attackers for another hour and a half, when he is killed. His actions save the balance of Company B and the Germans retire. The fierce fighting continues at Anzio, but although there are innumerable acts of courage on the part of the Yanks, a breakout does not occur. The Germans continue to assault the beachhead, but the Yanks fight ferociously, turning back the repetitive assaults. The momentum begins to change to the side of the Yanks after the gallant counterattack by General Harmon on the 19th of February, and followed by a devastating victory for the VI Corps on the 20th, ending the German attempt to annihilate the beachhead. The Allies are still stymied at Cassino and a joint Allied decision to level the monastery by air is reached, with the hope that although the cultural and historical monastery will be destroyed, consolation will be achieved by the destruction of the impenetrable Nazi stronghold. That fateful decision eliminates the monastery on the 15th of March, 1944, after the airdrop of more than 1,000 tons of bombs, but it accomplishes little more than giving the Germans added defenses. An intriguing irony is that although the monastery has been totally devastated, the tomb of St. Benedict comes through the ordeal unscathed. The Germans who had not fortified the monastery after all, now permeate the rubble and wait in ambush for the next Allied attack. During mid-May, French troops assigned to General Clark's U.S. Fifth Army, break through a weak link in the German defenses, allowing Cassino to be overrun. The Germans begin to withdraw on all Italian fronts, allowing a breakout from the beachhead at Anzio, after being stalled there since the 22nd of January over 100 days. Finally on June 4th 1944, two days before the invasion of Normandy, troops of the U.S. 3rd Division pour into Rome to the jubilant cheers of the Italian citizens.

The Japanese, no longer invincible in the Pacific, are about to be struck again. During November of 1943, the Marines assault Bougainville, situated in the Solomons. This murderous operation rages in full fury through the remainder of the year. On December 18th, the Marines capture the infamous "Helzapoppin Ridge." U.S. Army troops arrive to relieve the Marines by mid-January. They hold steadfastly, repulsing repeated heavy enemy counterattacks, exterminating resistance on Bougainville by the end of April 1944. Another joint operation takes place when the Marines, in conjunction with the Army, strike the Japs again. The Army storms Makin, meeting nominal opposition, but the Marines at Betio and Tarawa, receive incessant withering fire that in some instances, virtually shatters Landing Crafts, which are hung up on the coral reefs. The sea is consumed by wounded and dying Marines. The enemy defenses had survived the Allied preinvasion bombardment, virtually unmolested. The Marines, who make it to shore, are threatened with annihilation.

For the first time in their history, the U.S. Marines might be thrown back to the sea in defeat. During the first night, the enemy infiltrates the Marine perimeter and commandeers empty Vehicles which are laying dead in the water. They wait in ambush for the next wave of American reinforcements, rushing to save their buddies, who are stranded on the beach, pinned down by intense enemy fire. On the 21st, reinforcements move into the sights of the Japanese gunners perched on the reefs. The unsuspecting Landing Crafts receive more fierce enemy fire, sustaining severe casualties. The besieged Marines onshore rise up to draw enemy fire upon themselves to prevent another massacre. Just in the nick of time, the tides begin to change and intrepid American Pilots dive in at dangerously low altitudes, pouring concentrated fire upon the Japs who had seized the stranded Landing Crafts. Although their bombs miss the mark, their machine guns score devastating damage and Marine Artillery joins in, killing off the

enemy threat. The Landing Crafts in timely fashion, rush the reinforcements ashore. The desperate plight is not over, but the once jeopardized Americans are now ashore awaiting further orders.

Colonel Shoup, the Commanding Officer, realizing the depth of the predicament, orders his men to advance. They inch their way forward, against fortified bunkers, using their bayonets and rifles. When the smoke clears and the guns cease firing on the 23rd of November, 1943, the Marines prevail. The Marines sustain 1,027 men killed and 2,200 wounded, while the Japanese defenders have been whittled down to 17 men out of an initial force of 4,500. Colonel Shoup, after the tenacious battle on this island of death, would remark: "THE REASON THIS VICIOUS STRUGGLE WAS WON WAS THESE GREAT AMERICAN MEN WERE DETERMINED THAT THEIR NATION WOULD NOT GO DOWN IN DEFEAT."

The Americans continue to pummel the Japanese in the Pacific. On December 15th 1943, the Allies unload a massive Naval bombardment against enemy positions at Arawe in New Britain. The U.S. Cavalry hits the beaches and quickly captures the objective. The Americans then set Cape Gloucester as the next objective in the process of pounding the Japanese into submission at the hands of Old Glory. Christmas passes in the Pacific and on the following day, the 7th Marines, 1st Marine Division, charge ashore against enemy positions, initiating another bloody struggle toward winning the Pacific. During the next three weeks, the Marines withstand fanatical enemy counterattacks, which are mounted on Cape Gloucester. The Americans hold and raise the Flag in victory on the 16th of January, 1944.

The Americans continue encroaching closer to Japan. Another joint Army-Marine operation, occurs on the 31st of January, 1944, when they descend upon Kwajalein in the Marshalls. The objective is quickly secured by the 8th of February, allowing the Marines to jump off for the next assignment. The Army remains on the island, insuring American domination. The Japanese had previously received orders on the 21st of January to withdraw their forces, which had been holding at Western New Britain. They proceed to Iboki, from where they are to make a further withdrawal to Talasea. The overpowering strength of the Americans is forcing the enemy to recoil all over the Pacific. In New Guinea, the Allies declare the Huon Peninsula secure as the Australians and Americans converge on Saidor from two different directions. The Japanese, holding Los Negros in the Admiralties, are struck by a devastating blow when U.S. Cavalry Troops assault the island on the 27th of February 1944, scoring great successes. The campaign ends with a stupendous victory for the U.S. Cavalry. With Old Glory firmly entrenched at Los Negros, the Yanks set their sights on seizing the balance of the Admiralty chain, accomplishing the mission by May the 18th, 1944. During this heated struggle, the U.S. sustains 326 killed, 1,189 wounded and four men missing in action. The Japanese suffer 3,280 killed, 75 captured and an indeterminable number of wounded. Old Glory is roaring across the Pacific; island hopping her way toward the Japanese mainland.

Back in the Atlantic Theater, the momentum has tilted greatly to the Allies. The British Isles have been inundated with American equipment and men. The troops are ready for the most expensive gamble in the history of amphibious warfare. The Invasion of Normandy is upon the world. As usual, the weather is not co-operating, but General Eisenhower makes the decision to attack. Thousands of Allied Warships venture silently across the English Channel, through an eerie darkness on the night June 5th, prepared to unleash countless legions of fighting men who will storm the beaches and rekindle the dimming beacon of freedom on the continent. These courageous Allied Soldiers will open the door to Liberty with the key of blood and guts. General Eisenhower had proclaimed in January of 1944: "AN AROUSED DEMOCRACY IS THE MOST FORMIDABLE FIGHTING MACHINE THAT CAN BE DEVISED. His observations prove correct. Prior to the main invasion, three Divisions of American and British Paratroopers are cautiously dropped behind enemy lines to cut off German reinforcements who will be rushing to the beaches. They sustain tremendous difficulties, costing precious lives, but still maintain great discipline and accomplish most of their mission.

The main invasion commences at 06:30 on June 6th, with the U.S. 4th Division quickly securing Utah Beach. The British and Canadians seize Gold, Juno and Sword Beaches, against nominal opposition, but the situation at Omaha is critical. Every solitary Soldier from the rank of Private to General is forced to exceed the bounds of human endurance and they do. In spite of the walls of fire, the crashing surf and the near invincible man made obstacles at Omaha, the Americans prevail, overcoming all adversity. By the end of the first day of gruesome fighting, the Americans have landed in excess of 50,000 men on the shores of France, many of whom are forced to sacrifice their lives, that France might be saved and the Nazis destroyed. These particular gallant sentinels of freedom, still rest under humble white crosses in that sacred burial ground at Normandy. The Germans can only mount one serious counterattack and that is against the British, who have dug in firmly, allowing them to handily repulse the enemy. The fighting continues incessantly, with the Allies suffering a total of 10,000 casualties on the first day, slightly less than had been anticipated. By the 27th of June, Cherbourg and its strategic port are secure. By the end of June, the Allies have landed over 1,000,000 Troops on French soil, spelling doom to the Germans. Toward the end of July, the Allies have broken out completely by cracking through the German defenses. Old Glory and the U.S. Army are heading for Berlin.

The Canadian First Army sprints toward Falaise, while the 1st and 3rd U.S. Armies begin to surround Argentan, a maneuver which compresses the Germans into a huge pocket. Many of the enemy troops escape the net, but in excess of 60,000 Germans are killed or captured. Patton's bold 3rd Army, darts toward the Seine River to prevent the Germans from building defenses at that point. His other reason for rushing to the Seine is to cut off the Germans, who escaped the trap at Argentan. Both endeavors succeed, causing the Germans to virtually lose the majority of two Armies. To add to the dismay of the Germans, another invasion force, commanded by Lt. General Alexander Patch, comprising three American Divisions and French Commandos, storms ashore in southern France, on the 15th of August and quickly joins the fray. At day's end, over 86,000 men and 12,000 Vehicles are ashore. On the following day, French Troops seize the Ports of Marseille and Toulon. Allied advances force the battle weary Germans to begin withdrawing toward the German Frontier, with the Allies in hot pursuit. By mid-September, Patch's troops are able to hook up with Patton's Third Army. Paris is entered by American and French troops on the 25th of August, 1944. By a predetermined decision, the German Commander officially surrenders the city to French Brigadier General Jacques Phi-

lippe LeClerc at 15:15 hours.

The Germans continue their retreat, but fight tough rear actions to forestall capitulation. Antwerp, a coveted seaport in Belgium, is seized by the British on the 4th of September, but the Germans temporarily prevent its usage as a port, by lining the banks with troops who rain fire upon Allied Vessels attempting to sail the 60 mile long journey through the estuary. The first Allied Vessel to use the port facilities drops anchor on the 28th of November. In the beginning of November 1944, the Allies begin another major offensive, sending troops on a forced march, toward the Rhine. Previous to this action, the U.S. 82nd and 101st Airborne Divisions and the British 1st Airborne Division are dropped in the Netherlands on September 17th, in spectacular fashion, initiating an undertaking to secure the routes to Antwerp, which pits 20,000 elite Paratroopers against two Panzer Divisions. The Germans (who capture a copy of Allied operation plans get it to German General Student within several hours of the beginning of the attack) mount fierce opposition, bogging down the British attempt to seize the bridge at Arnhem, however, the U.S. forces gain the bulk of their objectives. Casualties for the operation are high, but the Allies drive through fifty rugged miles of enemy territory, where the operation is finally halted, just short of its primary objective.

Hitler masterminds a massive counterattack plan, intended to crash through a weakened portion of the American lines in the vicinity of the Ardennes. The endeavor, if successful, will cost the Allies Antwerp, ostracize the British 21st Army Group and the First and Ninth U.S. Armies. The Americans are stunned by this assault on this cold miserable day of December 16th, when the darkened forests in the vicinity of Eifel come alive, bristling with twenty-five German Divisions. Their clanking Armor and unmuffled Infantry bolt toward the Meuse River, extending this offensive on a front that stretches 60 miles. The bulk of the Americans stationed at these points are relatively new and inexperienced, especially the recently arrived 106th Division, giving the Germans a temporary advantage. They punish the 106th, inflicting severe casualties and capturing thousands of the newly organized Division, which takes the brunt of the attack, and they push the 28th Division back on the 18th. Meanwhile, the First Army repulses the Germans under Dietrich at Malmedy, and the 7th Armored holds off the S.S. Panzers at St. Vith. The Germans confidently speed to Bastogne, where the Americans have decided to make their stand. The Ninth Armored holds control of Bastogne and the 10th Armored is speeding to reinforce them. The 101st U.S. Airborne, races haphazardly to Bastogne and the fighting 82nd Airborne charges to the aid of the defenders between St. Vith and Malmedy.

The Allied command, fearing a breakdown in communications between the Americans and the British, splits the command. General Bradley reluctantly relinquishes command of the U.S. First and Ninth Armies as General Eisenhower places them under British General Montgomery on the nineteenth. By this time, the Americans have the German offensive neutralized. General Bradley now has under his command only Patton's Army. Montgomery prepares to "tidy up his front," before attacking. The Germans had not been prepared for the determination of the individual American units, who refuse to budge. At Monschau, the stand is steadfast and no ground is given, not one blessed yard. The Americans stand firm for six days at St. Vith, costing the Germans valuable time and at Bastogne the story is legendary.

The Germans close on Bastogne from three sides and demand surrender. American Brigadier General Anthony C. McAuliffe responds, "NUTS." During this incredible confrontation, the Germans sustain heavy casualties, as do the Americans. However, the beleaguered Americans hold, waiting for reinforcements. General Patton is in the process of coming to their rescue. The outnumbered American Force is comprised of the able 101st Airborne, elements of the 10th Armored, a couple of Companies of Tank Destroyers and Colored Artillery. Patton commences a forced march through a blustery winter storm to relieve Bastogne and crush the German juggernaut. General Patton's disciplined and determined fighting men tramp over frozen snowbound roads, amidst falling trees and other obstacles, sprung by the Germans. In an amazing Military endeavor, Patton's 3rd Army, without the benefit of hot food, rest or sleep, advances 100 miles and prepares to attack, fighting close to the beleaguered troops by Christmas day. This U.S. Third Army, presently hindered by terrible inclement weather, has marched further and engaged more enemy Divisions during this endeavor than any other, in the history of the United States.

The horrendous weather which has hampered the march and caused additional American casualties by preventing Air cover causes much concern to the Americans. Undaunted, Patton instructs the chaplain to prepare a prayer, pleading for Divine intervention to clear the skies. Father James O'Neil pens the request and it is distributed to every man in the outfit on Christmas day, along with a Christmas greeting from Patton. The skies clear and American Planes soar overhead.

Patton's incredible troops advance and the 18,000 troops surrounded at Bastogne are saved, when elements of the Third Army, commanded by Colonel Wendell Blanchard, spearhead the liberation of Bastogne in spectacular fashion on the day after Christmas. This triumph spells certain doom to the Third Reich. Patton has broken the German stranglehold on Bastogne, but tenacious fighting would continue between the Germans and the Americans for some time.

During the operation to save Bastogne, repeated pleas were made by General Bradley, to General Eisenhower, requesting that Montgomery attack, but the pleas were in vain. In addition, the First and Ninth U.S. Armies, temporarily under the command of Montgomery, are issued orders to pull back. The words between the Allies were frequently heated. At one point, Bradley informs U.S. General Hodges: "ALTHOUGH YOU ARE NO LONGER IN MY COMMAND, I WOULD VIEW WITH SERIOUS MISGIVINGS THE SURRENDER OF ANY-MORE GROUND." General Montgomery, during a press conference on the 7th of January, infuriates the American Commanders when he erroneously takes credit for saving the Bulge. Montgomery does not attack until the 3rd of January. Both Bradley and Patton are fed up with the antics of Montgomery and so inform Eisenhower. Bradley emphatically states that if Montgomery is to be in charge of all ground troops, then he (Bradley) should be sent home. Patton tells Bradley: "IF YOU QUIT BRAD, THEN I'LL BE QUITTING WITH YOU." General Eisenhower does not place any American troops under Montgomery in the future. By the end of January 1945, the Allies recover all lost ground and it is clear that the war in Europe is nearly finished.

Hitler, during one of his fiery speeches.

Reinforcements speeding to Bastogne (Dec. 1944).

Old Glory at St. Malo with the 83rd Division, Third Army, (Aug. 1944).

U.S. Seventh Army troops advancing — hitting opposition from German Officer candidates.

VICTORY IN EUROPE AND THE PACIFIC

The Americans, operating in the Pacific Theater are not idle during June of 1944. The U.S. Navy is preparing to take another giant leap across the Pacific, narrowing the distance between the Yanks and the mainland of Japan. The next designated objective for the Marines is the strongly fortified island of Saipan, which is strategically located and must be secured. On the 15th of June, 1944, the enemy positions on the coveted island are struck with incessant lethal doses of surface and Air bombardments, intended to soften resistance for the mud Marines. After the bombardment ceases, the 2nd and 4th Marine Divisions charge the beach and begin to establish a secure beachhead, in order to withstand anticipated enemy counterattacks. Unfortunately, the Naval bombardment is insufficient, in terms of enemy destruction, making the Marines task more difficult. As expected, the Japanese initiate successive night Banzai attacks, that are in vain, against the firmly entrenched Marines, who are determined to hold the perimeter. The close quartered combat is costly, as the Marines suffer approximately 2,000 casualties throughout the day, but they have landed over 20,000 men, who will be in place to greet the U.S. 27th Division, when they arrive at the beachhead. The ground will become hallowed by the spilling of more American blood on the following day. Some difficulties arise during the campaign, as the 27th Division gets bogged down, but a quick change of Commanders gets the 27th rolling again, keeping pace with the Marines, who are operating on the flanks. The southern portion of the island is taken by the Americans, after a week of intense fighting.

The Navy begins operations against a Japanese Fleet, which had been diverted to engage the American Task Force operating in the vicinity of Saipan. During a violent sea battle in the Philippine Sea, Task Force 58 repulses the Japanese Imperial 1st Mobil Fleet on the 19th-20th of June. This engagement, quickly dubbed the "Great Turkey Shoot," once again demonstrates the ability of the individual American fighting man. The Japanese dispatch Carrier-based Planes to destroy the American Fleet, but succeed only in damaging a Heavy Cruiser, two Battleships and two Carriers, the *Bunker Hill* and the *Wasp*. However, the Japanese lose over three hundred Planes the first day. In addition, American Submarines sink two Japanese Carriers, the *Shokaku* and *Taiho*. On the second day of battle, the Japanese are badly beaten again. They lose another Carrier, the *Hiyo*, at the hands of the U.S. Fifth Fleet Task Force of Admiral Mitscher. Pilots launched from the Carriers wipe out the majority of the remaining Planes of the Japanese assault force, including over fifty Land-based Planes which the Japanese had dispatched from their base at Guam. After the "Turkey Shoot," the Japanese who had been

sent to intercept and destroy the American Fleet at Saipan, count over 450 Planes lost. The United States loses 130 Planes, including 73 which are ditched in the water, because of empty fuel tanks, or the inability to locate their Carriers in the darkness. The United States loses a total of 76 Pilots during the operation. The battered Japanese Fleet abandons the area, while the battered but intact United States Navy begins to pick up its downed Pilots. The Japanese Imperial Command has a vivid reminder of the infamous Japanese quote at the beginning of hostilities: "WE HAVE AWAKENED A SLEEPING GIANT." The U.S. Navy removes all doubts, concerning the outcome of the war, after this spectacular victory. Japan, realizing the cause is lost, begins preparations to defend its mainland.

On the ground in Saipan, the fighting is vicious, continuing at close quarters. At one point, Banzai attackers rush into the deadly Artillery of the 77th Division, which is struck by the full strength of the assault force. When the Americans cease fire, after the unsuccessful charge on the 7th of July, piles of dead Japanese are strewn about. Twenty-nine thousand Japanese die on Saipan, by a combination of being killed and by suicide. Japanese Admiral Chuichi Nagumo (Carrier Commander at both Pearl Harbor and Midway), presently commanding at Saipan, and Army Commander Lt. General Yoshitsugu Saito, both commit suicide. Many other Japanese, including civilians, choose to jump to their deaths, rather than be captured. By the ninth of July, the island is declared secure and Old Glory is less than 1,500 miles from Japan. American casualties total 14,000 including 3,400 killed. The Japanese defense force numbering approximately 30,000 is totally eliminated.

While the U.S. Army and its Allies are driving through France, the Navy is preparing to debark invasion forces against the remaining strategic Japanese-held islands. Following a huge Naval bombardment, the U.S. 77th Division lands on Guam, in conjunction with the Third Marine Division and the 1st Provisional Marine Brigade. The 3rd Marines drive south toward the Airfield at Agat, while the Army and the Marine Brigade push north to capture the Airfield at the Orote Peninsula, pinching the Japs. The fighting for control of the Airstrip on the Peninsula is ruthless and continues until the 25th, with the 77th Division and the Marine Brigade, victorious, after fired up enemy troops charge directly into point blank range of Yankee Artillery. The Japanese attempt to break out of the stranglehold by charging the Marine positions, making slight penetration, however, the 3rd Marine Division holds the beachhead, at a cost of 3,500 Japs. U.S. troops raise the Stars and Stripes triumphantly on the island of Guam, where 400 Japanese Soldiers based in Saipan had removed her on 10

December, 1941. The U.S. 77th Division and the Marines mop up the island, with the 306th Infantry, U.S.A., capturing Mount Mataguao on the 11th of August.

The invasion of Tinian follows immediately after the landings at Guam. Defiant Japanese defenders at Tinian wait confidently on the 24th of July, as the American Naval bombardment ceases. Marines advance in Landing Craft against deadly shore batteries, then begin to wallow offshore, to the amazement of the jubilant defenders, who suspect the Marines are fearful of being slaughtered and are going to abort the invasion. As the bewildered Japanese stare at the drifting 2nd Marine Division, the 4th Marine Division, 15,000 strong, have been methodically, squeezing through two minute openings along the jagged coral reefs at the reverse side of the island. The 2nd Marine Division follows suit and comes into the secure beachhead. The enemy mounts a crazed Banzai assault against the Marines during the night, but it is a futile endeavor, costing the Japanese nearly 1,500 dead. The island will be secure in one week, with Old Glory getting closer to Japan, as she is unfurled officially on the 3rd of August 1944. The capture of Tinian insures a Base for B-29 Bombers, giving the U.S. the capability to strike Japan with Land-based Bombers.

In related Pacific combat, the Australians and Americans make steady progress in New Guinea, to the pleasure of General MacArthur, who so eagerly awaits his return to the Philippines, to avenge the atrocities committed by the Japanese at Bataan and Corregidor.

Army Task Forces Reckless and Persecution, have exerted tremendous pressure against the Japanese, since their vigorous invasion of Hollandia and Aitape in April of 1944. The Japanese Airfield at Biak is secure by the early part of July, as U.S. Army assault forces advance to Noemfoor Island, claiming another island junction for MacArthur.

On the 15th of September, the Marines invade Peleliu, against intense enemy opposition, costing more precious lives. U.S. Army Regimental Combat Teams, 321 and 322, assault Angaur, Palaus, a distance of about 100 miles from Peleliu on the 17th. These assault troops wipe out nearly all enemy resistance by the 20th of September. The lone exception is a large pocket on the northwestern edge of the island. The Army and Marines combine operations on Peleliu on the 23rd and the two finally clear the northwest portion of the northern peninsula by the 2nd of October.

October 19th 1944, becomes the eve of the day of reckoning for the stoic Japanese in the Philippines. At precisely 06:00 hours on the 20th, the U.S. Naval guns unleash a massive Naval bombardment which lasts for nearly three hours, before yielding to a heavy Air strike against enemy positions at Dulag. These Carrier-based Planes fly sorties throughout the day, in support of three Divisions of the Sixth Army that land at Leyte. The Army establishes General Headquarters for Lieutenant General Walter Krueger by noon.

Admiral Halsey, who reports to Admiral Nimitz, rather than General MacArthur, pulls up anchor and moves out to engage the remnants of the Japanese Northern Force. Admiral Kinkaid's Fleet, temporarily in a precarious position, holds firm in the waters of Leyte Gulf. On the 23rd of October, two U.S. Submarines, lurking in the vicinity of Palawan, Island, spot the Japanese Armada which is moving toward Leyte. In quick time, torpedoes destroy two enemy Cruisers. Carrier

Planes attached to Vice Admiral Mitscher's Fleet discover the Japanese on the following day, in the Sibuyan Sea. In addition, these same American Planes locate the Japanese Southern Force, racing through the Sulu Sea. The U.S. prepares for action and the Japanese begin to counterattack. By dawn on the 25th, the U.S.S. Light Carrier *Princeton* is sunk by enemy Planes. In turn, the Japanese Battleship *Musashi* is destroyed by American Aircraft.

On the 25th, the Japanese Center Force enters the Philippine Sea and engages a small American Armada, commanded by Rear Admiral Sprague, inflicting heavy damage upon the Americans. However, the Japanese do not follow through toward Leyte where they can impede the land forces; instead, they withdraw by dawn. Simultaneously, Halsey's Third Fleet encounters the Northern Force of the enemy and catapults Planes toward Cape Engano, where four Japanese Carriers are destroyed. In addition to these battles, another vicious contest had ensued between the Fleet of Rear Admiral J.B. Oldendorf, whose battle Armada demolishes the Japanese Southern Force at the Battle of Surigao Bay. The Japanese make a speedy retreat on the 26th. The American Carrier Planes, supported by Land-based Army Aircraft, pursue the beaten Japs, and sink an additional six Vessels.

The American ground forces are now able to continue their advance toward Manila. By December, the atrocious weather improves slightly, allowing Air cover to be afforded the ground troops. The U.S. 77th Division, which had just fought alongside the Marines on Guam, storms ashore on the western coast of Leyte. By the 15th of December, the American advance troops seize an Airfield within 150 miles of Manila. Subsequently, additional troops land on the ninth of January 1945, in the vicinity of Luzon, from where they can drive through the Central Plains to Manila. The Japanese, lacking major Naval strength, increase their suicide attacks against the U.S. Fleet, which sustains damage, but does not relent. MacArthur's GI's advance to Manila by early February.

The Japanese hold the Americans off for a month, until the Sixth Army takes the city on the third of March 1945. MacArthur, debarks the U.S. 38th Division at Subic Bay, with instructions to speed across the Bataan Peninsula, MacArthur, drops a contingent of the 11th Airborne from the sky over Southern Luzon and has the remainder come in by sea. MacArthur has kept his promise, returning in grand fashion with 10 American Divisions and Marine Artillery units and Air units operating in support of the Army operations. The Yanks extinguish organized Japanese resistance in the Philippines by the end of July 1945.

Back in Europe, the Allies commence the final thrust toward the Rhine, against a beleaguered German Army. In addition, the Germans have taken a thrashing on the Eastern Front. German Field Marshal von Rundstedt prefers to make a disciplined withdrawal, for the purpose of a concentrated stand against the Americans and their Allies at the Rhine, but the request is forbidden by Hitler, who decides that the Germans will hold at the Roer River and the West Wall. The decision costs the German Army approximately 250,000 casualties prior to their withdrawal.

The Allies close toward the Rhine with endless caravans of motorized Vehicles and legions of men. The Russians also advance toward Berlin. It was now a case of not only defeating the Germans, but also considering the consequences if the Russians get to Berlin before the Allies. The Germans destroy all bridges as they flee, impeding the progress of the Allies, who are searching for a means of crossing the Rhine. Finally, on the 7th of March 1945, the Germans receive some bad luck. In what was expected to be just another demolition operation, the explosives set at the Ludendorff Railroad Bridge at Remagen fail to work. The explosives are detonated by the demolition teams, but the insolent railway span, rocks and quivers, then instead of falling into the river, remains in place. U.S. Infantrymen probe cautiously, then begin an impetuous dash across the bridge in the face of bewildered Germans who had anticipated the destruction of the bridge. Enemy fire opens up, but the Yank Infantry continues to gain ground, followed shortly thereafter by Armor. Satisfied the bridge will sustain the weight of the Armor Units, the U.S. Ninth Armored speeds across the Rhine, en route to destroy the Germans. One Army Officer, William C. Westmoreland (9th Infantry Division; 1st full Division to cross the Rhine) explains later, how he had laid prone on the hood of a lead Vehicle, cautiously guiding a Convoy across the battered darkened bridge. Subsequently, the U.S. Third Division, crosses the Rhine on assault boats, on March 22nd. The U.S. Seventh Army, complemented by the 1st French Army, 6th Army Group, crosses successfully toward the end of the month, against nominal resistance.

April of 1945, brings monumental decisions to the Allies and General Eisenhower. The final stance of the once proud German Army is futile. The Russians have overrun and decimated countless towns, ravaging the civilians and are within forty miles of Berlin. The U.S. Military Command, aware that Russia will reach Berlin first, and concerned with the fact that a political agreement had been previously agreed upon, concerning the fate of Berlin, concentrates on the permanent disintegration of the remnants of the German forces. The British 21st Army Group closes off the Netherlands and heads for the Jutland Peninsula. The U.S. Sixth Army Group is dispatched toward the southern portion of Germany and Austria to destroy the German resistance in the Alps. The Allies continue on course to the Elbe and Mulde Rivers, a pre-determined point of contact between themselves and the Russians, who are closing from the east. In the final days of the war in Europe, Hitler selects Admiral Karl Doenitz as his successor, then, commits suicide. The Germans begin surrendering in hordes and finally, Berlin falls. The German Government representatives arrive at General Eisenhower's Headquarters at Reims, France on the 7th of May, with the surrender becoming effective at midnight on the 8th. The war in Europe ends officially on the 8th, V.E. Day. The Allied Press Corps, in attendance at the official ceremony, is asked to sit on the story until the Russians hold another surrender exhibition, on the 9th, in Berlin. General Eisenhower, believing that this second surrender ceremony "should be a Russian affair," designates British Air Chief Marshal Tedder to represent him.

As the war effort in Europe comes to a close, the fighting continues to rage in the Pacific. The U.S. Army Air Corps, an unsung hero during the conflict in Europe and the Pacific, has been relentlessly bombing enemy positions on all fronts throughout the war. During the latter part of 1944, in addition to flying dangerous missions on all fronts, including the China Burma India Theater, they dispatch the great "Flying Fortresses" against the Japanese mainland. The 21st Bomber Command, based in Saipan, departs on November 24th, 1944,

with a force exceeding 110 Fortresses, to execute the first long range strategic bombing mission over Japan. The Planes inherit unfamiliar wind currents along the way, which push the Flying Fortresses too fast, causing the Bombardiers to misjudge the targets. The mission is not a total failure, as some of the bombs strike the targets, but it is now realized that another island must be captured, to cut down the distance of these raids, in order that Medium Bombers can be committed.

That chosen island is called Iwo Jima, consisting of less than eight square miles, including prominent Mt. Suribachi. Iwo Jima has two coveted Airfields, which can be used for Fighter escorts for the B-29s. It also contains a third field, under construction. The enemy-held island is situated in a strategic location, halfway between Saipan and Japan, making it a perfect refueling station, on the return trip from flights over Japan.

United States Naval Vessels begin bombarding the island months before the assault troops are to land. During mid-February, the Navy initiates a thunderous two day bombardment of Iwo Jima, just preceding the debarkation of United States Marines. On the 19th of February, after the cessation of an Air and Naval bombardment, the 4th and 5th Marine Divisions storm the southeast coast of the island, landing abreast on four separate beaches, without opposition, initiating the bloodiest struggle of the Pacific war. The Fourth Marine Division is to move toward the Airfield, while the 5th Marine Division advances west, to ostracize Mr. Suribachi.

The defending Japanese are basically unscathed by the numerous Naval and Air bombardments, while hiding in over a thousand caves. The Japs suddenly open fire, ringing shells down on the Marines. Naval Surface Vessels move in precariously close to shore and fire from point blank range. Tanks are quickly brought to shore, but their effectiveness is minimal, due to the rocky terrain. The Marines have to take it the difficult way, pillbox by pillbox and cave by cave.

The order to advance is given and the Marines begin the sobering task of climbing over their fallen comrades, grinding their way toward Suribachi, the ominous strongpoint. The Yanks, after five days of ruthless combat at close quarters, claim Mt. Suribachi. A war photographer, Joe Rosenthal, receives a piece of fortuitous luck, capturing a shot of Old Glory being raised, that later becomes one of the most famous photographs of the American Flag.

The Marines, after the capture of Suribachi, advance against the enemy held plateau and are again hit by intense resistance. The Japanese continue incessant fire from their fortifications and the Marines keep advancing, until the enemy is wiped out. Heavy casualties are incurred, however, thousands of U.S. Airmen, will be saved in the future, because of the sacrifices on Iwo. On the 16th of March, 1945. The Stars and Stripes arise triumphantly, terminating the bloodiest campaign in the history of the Marine Corps. The U.S.A. 147th Regimental Combat Team replaces a contingent of the Marines on the 20th of March. They will now share responsibility of the island with Regimental Combat Team 9, 3rd Marine Division. The Army Combat Team is confronted within a week by a frenzied Banzai assault, mounted by over 200 fanatical attackers. A contingent of Soldiers, attached to the VII Fighter Command and the 5th Pioneer Battalion, meet the assault with deadly force, racking the advance in quick fashion, exterminating the attackers. The Japanese defending Iwo Jima numbered approximately 23,000, however, at the close of fighting, few survive. Admiral Nimitz remarks, after the vicious battle for Iwo Jima: "UNCOMMON VALOR WAS A COMMON VIRTUE." The Americans sustain 6,800 killed 19,000 wounded.

The Japanese have been thrashed throughout the Pacific, causing the interchanging of positions between them and the Americans, who now dominate the Pacific sea lanes with their Fast Carrier Forces and Submarines. These Fleets include Cruisers, Destroyers, and Battlewagons. Okinawa, the final bastion of Japanese resistance, standing between the Yanks and Tokyo, is inhabited by over 100,000 Japanese defenders. More than 200,000 American fighting men are aboard these Vessels, awaiting the orders "to hit the beach."

Previous combined actions involving the Navy, supported by Army and Marine Corps Planes, has caused the Japanese Navy to become a battered relic. Japan's best Air weapon is the Kamikaze, the disposable Pilot. On Okinawa, Soldiers lay in ambush for the Americans in vast tunnels. The showdown is set for mid-March. In a prelude to the main event, American Aircraft, attached to Admiral Mitscher's Fast Carrier Fleet, are sprung against Japan's mainland on consecutive days, but the Japanese manage to score damage to the Fleet on the 18th and 19th. Japan initiates suicidal missions of its youthful Pilots, with instructions to strike the American Fleet with their bomb-laden craft for the honor of the Emperor. Admiral Mitscher's force, astonished at the insanity of the suicide attacks by the Japanese, is able to fight off the assaults, but these death flights inflict serious damage to the Americans during the closing months of the campaign.

On the 26th of March, the Americans commence a secondary attack on the Kerama Islands lying 15 miles from Okinawa. The U.S. 77th Division debarks with orders to secure a Naval base to facilitate Naval operations in the area and to establish a hold on Keise Shima Island from where 155mm guns can support the main invasion. On April 1st, legions of men begin boarding the assault boats for the final sprint to the beach. The U.S. 10th Army, which includes three Marine Divisions, is sped to the landing zone after the cessation of the usual Naval and Air bombardment. For the next week, the Yanks progress without heavy opposition, but there is still great caution, because they realize the Japanese are elusive and cunning. At week's end, the Americans sever the island by dispatching the Army in a northern direction, while the Marines move south, with each seeking out and destroying the enemy.

It will be a monumental blood-filled campaign before resistance is crushed. The Japanese have constructed sinister stretches of cavernous fortifications and reinforced bunkers, from which they will make their stand with over 100,000 defending troops. The 10th Army attacks yard by yard to root out the entrenched enemy in one of the most gruesome battles of the war. As the land campaign progresses, Japanese suicide Pilots strike the Fleet offshore. Naval gunners fire dead ahead, crashing shells into the water at times, to impede the flight paths. The Navy takes many destructive hits, but repulses the assault on the 6th of April. On the following day, a Japanese Armada is discovered as it steams toward Okinawa with reinforcements. It is intercepted by Mitscher's Carrier Fleet, which inflicts severe damage, sinking a Cruiser, four Destroyers and the Battleship Yamato.

America receives a stunning blow on the 12th of April, with the death of President Roosevelt. Vice President Harry S. Truman is sworn in and the death of the President does not deter the will of the 10th Army. The Yanks use Tanks, flamethrowers, grenades and dynamite to flush out the enemy. By the end of May, the Americans have destroyed approximately 50,000 enemy defenders. Soon after, the Japanese get a glimpse of hope when a devastating typhoon moves across the island, jolting the American Fleet. Japan will proclaim that the American Fleet has been destroyed by the Divine Wind, but the report is premature. The crews fight out the destructive storm and regroup to finish the enemy.

Okinawa, less than 375 miles from Japan, falls to the exhausted Yanks after a vicious 82-day battle, on the 19th of June, 1945. One Naval Officer, John Lehman, who had been on board one of the besieged ships, when asked how he thought the Americans had been able to withstand the Kamikazes responded: "GOOD GUNNERS!" The Japanese have lost approximately 110,000 killed to the Americans, who had landed on Easter Sunday. In addition, 7,400 Japanese Troops are captured with the fall of the island. On the 22nd of June, an official Flag-raising ceremony occurs and Old Glory rises triumphantly, one short stepping stone from Japan. The Americans lose 12,520 killed or missing during this campaign. Nearly 5,000 of these losses are sustained by the Navy. The Americans sustain 36,631 wounded, including nearly 5,000 Sailors offshore. The Japanese suicide Planes have destroyed and sunk 36 American Vessels and an additional 368 are damaged. In the process, the Japanese lose 7,800 Planes.

July 1945, becomes mop-up month in the Pacific. Japanese pockets of resistance are disintegrating. The unopposed U.S. Fleets begin bombarding the Japanese mainland. On the 26th of July, Japan, which still has approximately two million men under arms on the mainland, receives an ultimatum to surrender or face total destruction. The Japanese reject the proposal for surrender. President Truman is aware that an American invasion against the mainland could result in staggering losses of men. He also realizes the war could continue for a long time. After all the ramifications are considered, President Truman makes the decision to end the war, by dropping the Atom Bomb. On the 6th of August, a B-29 (Enola Gay) is launched and while in mid-air, the bomb is triggered as the crew apprehensively approaches Hiroshima. Hiroshima is devastated under one dynamic mushroom cloud, that will terminate the war in four days and change the world for all time. The Russians declare war against Japan on the eighth of August, becoming effective on the 9th of August. Japan will be struck with another Atomic explosion on the 9th at Nagasaki and surrender on the 10th.

Tokyo Bay will be enveloped by Allied Vessels on the 2nd of September, when the Allies accept the official surrender of the Japanese Empire aboard the U.S.S. Missouri. Close by are the reincarnated Vessels that had been devastated by the sneak attack at Pearl Harbor. They had won and Victory seems to pay the ultimate tribute to the thousands of American fighting men who had shed their blood to defeat the enemy. The Stars and Stripes had vanquished the Rising Sun and the endless rows of White Crosses spanning three continents, along with the battered wreckage of the steel Ships of Liberty, and the downed Planes of the gallant Airmen seem to hallow the decks of the Missouri as the instrument of surrender is signed.

As the year 1945 closes, the world is again at peace. Germany and Japan have been defeated. England, and France have again been spared, because of the enormous efforts of the United States. Some Eastern European nations have not been so lucky; they are now governed by the Soviet Union, which had carved out a good deal of Europe at the political sessions at Yalta in July. The Russians soon forget that the Allies had inadvertently kept their revolution alive and almost immediately become adversaries, igniting the Cold War of tension between the Russians and the West. Meanwhile, the Yanks are returning home to their families to reclaim the American dream of peace, tranquility, and prosperity. Old Glory has again proven that the United States of America is truly "THE LAND OF THE FREE AND THE HOME OF THE BRAVE." The Stars and Stripes will continue to maintain a keen vigil as she is catapulted into the Jet Age as the leader of the Free World. Subsequently, President Truman issues a proclamation on the 31st of December 1946, officially announcing the end of World War II.

General MacArthur returning to the Philippines, fulfilling his pledge (Oct 1944).

U.S. Marines off Iwo Jima — the ominous Mt. Suribachi in background (Feb. 1945).

Old Glory comes ashore at Okinawa (April 45).

U.S. Seventh and Fifth Armies converge at Nauders, Austria — (May 1945).

U.S. Troops observing Japanese troops in Japan laying down their arms for the final time.

January 1919 — The war to end all wars had just ended on November 11th, 1918. Since the waning days of the "Great War" until the close of 1918 Germany's Kaiser Wilhelm flees to Holland, Emperor Charles I vacates the throne of Austria and Hungary, ending the Hapsburg reign. In addition, Russia, disavows its Brest-Litovsk Treaty with defeated Germany, and Latvia declares its independence, which will be acknowledged by Russia and Germany during 1920. The Allies move into the Rhineland. Germany, having no choice in the matter, retires from Finland, turns over Kiev in the Ukraine to revolutionary troops and removes its troops from Estonia, which is then occupied by Bolshevik forces. Before the end of the year, the Allies become concerned about the gaining power of the Bolsheviks and decide to send in troops to assist the White Russians with their struggle to destroy the Bolsheviks.

Hardly enough time has passed for the smoke to clear or for the resounding echo of the massive guns to subside, nor sufficient time for the combatants to grieve their losses, and now as the people around the globe ring in the New Year, sinister and subdued sounds of war are already beginning to whisper mildly, cloaking malicious violence, which is simmering throughout Europe. The Allies, including Japan and the United States, send troops to assist the present Russian government in hopes of crushing the revolution, and ending the threat of possible world revolution as espoused by the Communists under Lenin.

Out of the flames of revolution in Russia, the Bolshevik government will attempt to instigate world revolution to eradicate capitalism and place the world under Socialist Totalitarian government. Europe becomes gripped with fear of the Bolsheviks, giving rise to another Socialist movement, led by Adolf Hitler, a presently unknown personality. Hitler, like many other German Soldiers who had fought in World War 1, dwells on the humiliating defeat and deepens his contempt for the Bolshevik leanings, which are beginning to overtake Germany. Hitler, in his quest to rid the world of the Bolsheviks and the Jews, for which he blames the rise of Bolshevism, soon initiates his Socialism on the world.

Hitler's plans are clearly spelled out in his book, Mein Kampf, which emphasizes his hate for the Jews. He blames them for all the immorality in books and advertising and claims they control the press. Hitler soon claims to: "CEASE BEING A WEAK-KNEED COSMOPOLITAN AND BECOME AN ANTI-SEMITE." However, his thoughts are not just on the Jews. The enslavement of the Slavs is another high priority, and in addition, Hitler intends to eventually eliminate Catholic priests and confiscate the property of the church. In fact, Himmler states that the "Lord's Day Bandits" are to be eliminated after the close of war and that he will personally settle with the Pope. Gypsies and Homosexuals are also scheduled for extinction by the Third Reich, as well as anyone else considered to be against Hitler.

As the power struggles commence in Germany and Russia, blood begins to trickle in drops, then forms a steady flow, which is soon followed by a profane and ghastly sea of blood at the hands of Stalin and Hitler as Europe is consumed by despicable violence and murder. Intertwined in this catastrophic global-nightmare is the greed of many other nations. Geographic boundaries are dis-regarded, as countries confiscate portions of lesser strengthed nations, almost at will.

Other and stronger tyrants, such as the Japanese, who are equally determined to dominate the world, initiate their expansion plans by ravaging the Pacific, ensuring that the world bleeds more profusely, tilting the balance of sanity, almost to the point of no return. Japan had fought with the Allies during World War 1, making it a World Power. Japan, feels comfortable with the Bolshevik Revolution as it releases pressure against them from the Russians, who now become Japan's Number two threat. The Japanese Imperial Defense Policy defines the U.S. as the Number 1 threat.

As the 1920's and 1930's progress, the Socialist Dictator movements of Hitler and Stalin, traveling on a collision course, combined with the aggression and pillage by Japan in the Pacific, plummet the world into war. While the Bolshevik leaders in Russia quarrel among themselves for survival and absolute power, the National Socialists in Germany encounter a similar internal conflict. While the National Socialists under Hitler are exterminating opposition in their controlled areas, Stalin is implementing mass murder against anyone suspected of opposing his regime. Under the rule of Stalin, mass executions of Gentiles occur, however; these deaths are not widely known, as the information is suppressed by the Soviets. In one instance, subsequent to Hitler and Stalin seizing Poland, Stalin executes about 15,000 Polish Army Officers to ensure they can not reform and oppose him; these murders and many more are blamed on Hitler.

During 1936, the prelude for world war erupts in Spain, when a revolution raises against the Republican government, in what eventually becomes the first clash between Communists and non-Communists on a large scale. The rebels, led by General Franco, receive aid from both Hitler and Mussolini, not for the propagation of capitalism, but rather for their own future purposes. The Republican government is backed by Stalin. The rebels have the backing of the church, which refers to the revolution as a "legitimate plebiscite." After three years of struggle and hundreds of thousands of deaths, including savage killing by both sides, the Nationalists under Franco prevail. Spain does not enter the Second World War, remaining neutral for the duration.

Shortly after the Spanish Civil War ceases (1939), the conflagration begins, consuming large parts of Europe in brutalizing and often barbaric warfare. The uncontrollable fires of war rage across Europe and the Pacific, however; the United States remains neutral until it is bombed without warning by the Empire of Japan, on 7 December 1941. Three days later, the 11th of December, Germany and Italy declare war against the United States. Once again, the Yanks are on their way to bring peace to Europe, however; this time, they must also defeat the Japanese in the Pacific. The following pages will bring the ultimate conclusion of World War II, with the victors and the vanquished, as the Stars and Stripes gives another preeminent performance in Three Theaters of War. The Victory Buttons, given to every Veteran during 1919, are dusted off and begin to reappear on the lapels of the Vets, as the U.S. again mobilizes to save Europe, and the world from absolute tyranny.

January 6th 1919 — Theodore Roosevelt, who had been the 26th President of the United States, dies at the age of sixty.

January 19th 1919 — A U.S. Soldier holding a Long Russian Rifle, while standing guard duty in Russia during the Archangel Expedition (January 1919).

January 1919 — Ireland declares its independence from Great Britain, subsequent to Sinn Fein, gaining many of the Irish seats in British Parliament. These newly elected representatives refuse to go to England, choosing to hold Congress in Dublin. The move by the Irish provokes war (Anglo-Irish War), which lasts until 1921.

February 1919 — (United States) The U.S. Senate appoints a committee to investigate the depth of Bolshevik penetration throughout the U.S. In addition, over fifty "Reds" are brought to Ellis Island by the Department of Justice to deport them.

February 16th 1919 — (Atlantic-France) A group of American Officers meet in Paris to formulate plans to establish the American Legion. Its spirit is "ONE HUNDRED PERCENT AMERICANISM," coined by Theodore Roosevelt, who had succumbed the previous month. The Legion is being formed to counteract several ongoing endeavors, notably a revolution in Russia, Communists mingling with U.S. troops in Germany after the Armistice, calling them comrade and attempting to convince them to "RAISE A CHEER FOR THE INTERNATIONAL." In addition, the Communists are gaining many followers in France, Italy, and at an alarming rate in Germany. During the middle of March, a larger complement of about 1,500, including Officers and enlisted men gather to further the foundation, and during May, the American Legion is officially founded in St. Louis. Colonel Theodore Roosevelt, the President's son, declines the position of Commander, due partly to rumors that he had been making a "grandstand play." Major Henry Lindsley receives the nomination. The strong anti-Bolshevik feeling in the U.S. forges strength during the early days of the Legion.

February 20th 1919 — In the Dominican Republic, A Marine Patrol, commanded by Captain William C. Byrd, springs an attack against a bandit stronghold in the mountains, killing about twelve of the band of fifty, and capturing their supplies.

February 26th 1919 — An advance detachment of Marines attached to the 15th Regiment, lands at San Pedro de Marcoris, Dominican Republic. They will assist the 4th Marine Regiment which is battling bandits on the island. The re-

mainder of the Regiment and the First Marine Air Squadron will arrive at Santo Domingo, Dominican Republic in the beginning of March. This will be the initiation of Infantry and Air units (Marine) working in coordination for the first time. The Air contingent, commanded by Captain Walter E. McCaughtry, consists of six JN-6 (Jenny) Biplanes and will operate from the jungle Airstrip, near Consuelo. The Marines will institute many small Patrols, usually mounted, as a tactic to eradicate the bandits.

Marines in the Dominicon Republic.

February 1919 — (Russia) Attempts are continuing to overthrow the Bolshevik government, which seized power during 1917. A provisional government had been established in Western Siberia. These White Russians in opposition to the Reds receive help from such nations as Britain, U.S. and Japan, however; the Bolsheviks retain power and hold to the creed of spreading revolution throughout the world. **(Germany)** The Weimar Republic is formed; its President is Freidrich Ebert. The German people give little support to this government, which is pledged to abide by the Versailles Treaty. In **Italy,** Mussolini establishes the Fasci del Combattimento (Black Shirts).

March 22nd 1919 — In the Dominican Republic, bandits ambush a Marine Patrol composed of nineteen men (44th Company). Marine Riflemen and an accompanying machine gun routs the bandits. The bandits sustain about fifteen dead. The Marines suffer no casualties.

March 31st 1919 — Marines (Squadron E) land at Port au Prince, Haiti to assist Marine ground forces fighting bandits on the island. Four Companies of the 7th Marine Regiment based at Guantanamo, Cuba had arrived about a week earlier. The Marines will engage a band of bandits at Hinche, Haiti on the 4th of April.

March 1919 — (Korea) declares its independence from Japan. Japan reacts violently and crushes the movement. **(Russia)** Lenin forms the Third International; its purpose is world revolution. The followers are bound by strict observance to the movement and must follow orders from Moscow. This is a primary reason for the rise of men such as Hitler, however; the entire world becomes disturbed by the threat.

Spring 1919 — In Hungary, a Soviet Republic is established under the dictatorship of Bela Kun, a heavy handed Jewish Communist. Kun's government has 32 Commissars; twenty-five of the thirty-two are Jewish, prompting the London Times to call it the "Jewish Mafia." The regime is violent, but short-lived, as Rumanian troops enter Hungary and occupy Budapest, prompting Kun to flee to Russia. The Rumanians are persuaded by the Allies to leave Hungary by November.

April 1919 — **(France)** Germany's hold on China's Shantung Province is given to Japan, infuriating China, which is the solitary nation that attends the conference but refuses to sign the Versailles Treaty. This action by the Allies sparks the rise of Mao Tse-tung's Marxist Communist Revolution in China. **(Ireland)** Eamon de Valera becomes president of the Sinn Fein (organization for a united Ireland and independence from Britain). **(Montenegro)** King Nicholas abdicates the throne. This nation will become known as Yugoslavia during 1929.

May 14th 1919 — The United States lands a detachment of Marines, attached to the U.S.S. *Arizona*, at Constantinople, Turkey for the protection of the American Consulate after Greeks occupy the city.

May 1919 — **(United States)** The Governor of New York State, Alfred Smith, signs a Legislative Bill, forbidding the display of Red flags (Soviet) in the state. **(International)** Fighting erupts in Afghanistan. The Afghans engage British and Indian troops, however; the hostilities cease by mutual agreement during August.

June 2nd 1919 — **(United States)** The home of U.S. Attorney General, Palmer is demolished by a bomb. Palmer is deeply involved with the search to root out Bolsheviks within the perimeter of the U.S. Palmer's thoughts on Bolshevism, in part: "BY STEALING, MURDER AND LIES, BOLSHEVISM HAS LOOTED RUSSIA NOT ONLY OF ITS MATERIAL STRENGTH, BUT OF ITS MORAL FORCE. A SMALL FORCE OF OUTCASTS FROM THE EAST SIDE OF NEW YORK HAS ATTEMPTED THIS WITH WHAT SUCCESS WE ALL KNOW." "MY INFORMATION SHOWED THAT COMMUNISM IN THIS COUNTRY WAS AN ORGANIZATION OF THOUSANDS OF ALIENS, WHO WERE DIRECT ALLIES OF TROTSKY." During November, the Justice Department makes a wide sweep of the U.S. to arrest "Reds," and before the end of the year, 249 suspected persons will be deported.

June 28th 1919 — The Treaty of Versailles is signed, ending World War I. The Germans and their Allies are not in attendance. President Wilson will present it to the U.S. Senate on the 10th of July. The issue comes to a vote during November, but political differences will prevent ratification on this date. Some of the points of the treaty: Germany receives full blame for World War 1; Alcace-Lorraine is given to France and Germany is not permitted to belong to the newly established League of Nations. During the conference, the Allies had agreed to support the White Russians in the fight against the Bolsheviks. China, which had been a participating member, does not sign the agreement. It had withdrawn from the conference, subsequent to being informed that the Allies would give Shantung Province to Japan. Subsequently, international pressure compels the Japanese to concede the territory to China during February 1922.

June 30th 1919 — The active duty strength of the Marine Corps stands at 48,834 and is composed of 2,270 Officers and 46,564 men. On the 11th of July, Congress depletes this strength, authorizing a peacetime Marine Corps consisting of 1,093 Officers and 27,400 men.

July 10th 1919 — The U.S. Navy turns over the Submarine Chaser No. 542 to the Marine Corps; it is to be commanded by Captain Charles M. Jones and utilized for trips between Quantico, Virginia and Washington, D.C.

July 22nd 1919 — Two Companies of Marines, stationed at Quantico, participate with other branches of the Service and civil authorities in quelling serious race riots in Washington, D.C.

July 23th 1919 — Haitian bandits, located at Mata de la Palma, Haiti, are strafed and bombed by Marine Aircraft. Planes play a small part in the operation against bandits and are used more often to ferry supplies and remove wounded. The Aircraft prove valuable for the ground operations in many support roles.

July 30th 1919 — The U.S.S. *New Orleans* arrives at Vladivostok, Russia. Marines debark to protect American interests. At present, the White Russians under General Denikin and Admiral Kolchak are attempting to overthrow the Bolshevik government of Lenin.

August 13th 1919 — In the Dominican Republic, a group of bandits ambush a Marine Patrol, composed of four men, under Corporal Bascome Breedon. The superior force charges with machetes and guns, killing three of the defenders. Private Thomas Rushfort, both hands rendered useless from wounds, mounts his horse and rides through the enemy to get reinforcements, however; it is too late to save the other men.

August 28th 1919 — The Treasury Department is again given responsibility for the United States Coast Guard.

September 10th 1919 — The Allies, including China, conclude a peace treaty with Austria (Treaty of St Germain), greatly reducing the size of Austria.

October 7th 1919 — U.S. Marines engage bandits led by Charlemagne Peralte, at Port au Prince, Haiti. Peralte escapes capture.

October 27th 1919 — The Marine Corps Band and a Marine Battalion render honors to King Albert of Belgium, Queen Elizabeth, and the Prince of Wales upon their arrival at Washington, D.C.

October 31st-November 1st 1919 — A Marine Patrol, including Gendarmerie (Haitian Soldiers), infiltrates the Cacos headquarters of Chief Charlemagne Peralte. The Marines are discovered, but still manage to disperse the attackers and kill the leader. This daring act would earn both Sergeant Herman H. Hanneken and Corporal William R. Button the Medal of Honor. This Patrol kills captures or disperses approximately 1,200 bandits. By June of the following year, thousands of bandits surrender or are captured, allowing the Marines to begin to transfer the duties of policing the island to the Gendarmerie.

November 11th 1919 — **(United States)** A parade marking the first anniversary of the end of World War 1 is held in Centralia, Washington, a northwestern community composed of about

11,000 people. The American Legion Post Commander, Warren Grimm, recently home from Siberia as part of the Archangel Expedition, leads the march. Leftists, called "Wobblies," anticipating a confrontation, had deployed sharpshooters in their "citadel," the I.W.W. hall, and in the nearby heights. The parade stalls near the building and bullets ring out, killing Grimm and two other Legionnaires. The building is stormed, however; the alleged killer escapes with Legionnaires on his tail. Subsequently, upon being trapped at the bank of the Skookumchuck River, the assailant, Wesley Everest, succeeds in killing another Legionnaire. He is captured and turned over to the authorities, but later in the night, he is taken from the jail and hung. At the National Convention, the American Legion recommends: "DEPORTATION OF ALL WOBBLIES AND COMMUNISTS, TO RID OUR COUNTRY OF THIS SCUM WHO HATE OUR GOD, OUR COUNTRY, OUR FLAG. The American Legion also passes a resolution against recognition of the Soviet Republic. The I.W.W. had called for lumber strikes during October to protest American Soldiers being in Russia. The I.W.W. had also used signs during the war which read: "DON'T BE A SOLDIER, BE A MAN."

November 19th 1919 — The U.S. Senate defeats ratification of the Versailles Treaty. There are strong differences of opinion, concerning the treaty. Many Senators favor the majority of points specified in the treaty, but insist that Congress may withdraw the U.S. from the League of Nations. Others are against a pledge (Article 10) that specifies that members must defend one another and yet others are totally against the treaty. President Wilson favors the treaty in its entirety and a two thirds majority fails to materialize because of the dissension.

December 17th 1919 — The 8th Marine Regiment is reactivated, to assist the Marines in Haiti in ridding the island of outlaws. The Regiment will be commanded by Lt. Col. L. McCarty Little.

December 1919 — **(United States)** A converted Army Transport Vessel, the *Buford* embarks from America, carrying almost 250 Reds and Anarchists to Russia.

January 1920 — The American Civil Liberties Union is formed in the United States. Its founder, Roger Baldwin, a Harvard Graduate, had been director of the Bureau of the American Union against Militarism and receives a jail sentence for refusing to serve in the military. Baldwin remains the ACLU's director until 1950, and then serves as an advisor until his death at 97, during 1981. During 1934, Baldwin states his position regarding civil liberties: "I TOO TAKE A CLASS POSITION. IT IS ANTI-CAPITALIST AND PRO REVOLUTIONARY ... I CHAMPION CIVIL LIBERTIES AS THE BEST NON-VIOLENT MEANS OF BUILDING THE POWER ON WHICH WORKER'S RULE MUST BE BASED ... WHEN THAT POWER OF THE WORKING CLASS IS ONCE ACHIEVED, AS IT HAS BEEN ONLY IN THE SOVIET UNION, I AM FOR MAINTAINING IT BY ANY MEANS WHATSOEVER ... THE SOVIET UNION HAS ALREADY CREATED LIBERTIES FAR GREATER THAN EXIST ELSEWHERE IN THE WORLD. Baldwin, during 1935, although stating that he had never belonged to the Communist Party says that "COMMUNISM IS THE GOAL."

March 1920 — **(Atlantic-Great Britain)** Parliament passes the Home Rule Charter Act, which bisects Ireland. The six northern counties accept the action, however; the twenty-six southern counties find the action unacceptable; the ongoing Anglo-Irish War continues into the following year. **(Atlantic-Germany)** A Putsch (rebellion) by disgruntled Army Officers

fails. Orders to demobilize, handed down by the Versailles Treaty, are ignored as some Officers attempt to seize Berlin. The revolt ceases due to a major strike called by the Socialists, however; the Soldiers are not punished. **(Atlantic-Russia)** Bolshevik forces overpower the White Russian forces at Novorossisk on the Black Sea. General Denikan manages to escape capture. Allied troops including U.S. forces (Archangel Expedition) are withdrawn from Siberia by early April. Some Japanese troops remain. By the end of November, the Bolsheviks will take Sebastopol, terminating the opposition of the anti-communists.

Sailors attached to the U.S.S. Olympia after returning from the front in Russia are greeted by troops of the U.S. 339th Regiment (Photo taken during 1918).

April 1920 — The Supreme Allied Council places Mesopotamia (portion of present day Iraq) and Palestine, under British mandate. Meanwhile, Lebanon and Syria come under French rule. In Europe, tensions are climbing along the Polish-Russian border. The Poles, reacting to a Soviet buildup of forces, mount an attack in the Ukraine. By June, the Poles are moving against Kiev (Russian Ukraine), igniting heavy fighting between the two antagonists. The Russians counterattack and drive toward Warsaw.

May 19th 1920 — Marine encounters with outlaws continue. A Patrol led by Captain Jesse Perkins surprises Cacos bandits in Haiti and the bandit leader, Benoit Batraville, successor to Charlemagne Peralte, is killed during the engagement.

May 20th 1920 — The U.S. Congress, after declining to ratify the Versailles Treaty, passes a resolution, declaring an end to World War I. President Wilson, who had sought ratification of the treaty, does not sign the resolution.

June 4th 1920 — The Treaty of Trianon is accepted by the Hungarian government which assumed power during 1919, subsequent to the flight of Bela Kun (August). This treaty greatly diminishes the size and population of Hungary. Two new states, Czechoslovakia and Yugoslavia are created from the ceded territory, the former from Bohemia, Moravia and Silesia, and the latter from the southern portion of Hungary. The settlement brings big dividends to Rumania, which receives Transylvania from Hungary and Bessarabia from Russia., doubling its size and bringing an infusion of an additional ten million people.

June 30th 1920 — Major General Commandant George Barnett is relieved "for reasons mostly political." His successor is Major General John A. Lejeune (13th Commandant). At this time active duty strength of the Marine Corps is 17,165; 1,104 Officers and 16,061 men.

July 1920 — (Europe) Russian troops have advanced against the Polish defenses and begin closing against Warsaw by the latter part of the month. In Germany, a plebiscite results in East and West Prussia deciding to become part of Germany, however; Poland, will be given a portion of West Prussia, ensuring it a path to the sea. An agreement settling a border dispute is reached between the Soviet Union and Lithuania, the latter being guaranteed independence.

August 1920 — The Treaty of Sevres, which cuts away the southern portion of the Arab nations south of Anatolia, is signed by Turkey's Sultan Mohammed VI, and is subsequently signed by the government, however; it is renounced by Mustafa Kemal and the Turkish National Assembly. Constantinople remains part of Turkey, but Bosphorus and Dardanelles transfer to international supervision. In addition, Adrianople, Gallipoli and Smyrna are ceded to Greece. In other activity, Latvia and Russia settle differences and an accord is reached that affords Latvia independence.

August 20th 1920 — A U.S. Marine Guard is established at the American mission in Tungchow, China.

August 20th 1920 — In Poland, the defense of Warsaw does not relent. Although the Communists are poised for victory, they are vanquished at the Battle of Vistula. French intervention, on the side of Poland, contributes to the great victory which results in an advantageous treaty with the Russians during 1921.

October 2nd 1920 — A U.S. Military Aircraft crashes in the vicinity of Hartford, Ct. Lt. Commander William Merrill Corry is thrown clear of the wreckage, however; he returns to the Plane, in an attempt to save another man, only to be badly burned. Corry loses his life several days later and he becomes the recipient of the Medal of Honor.

November 2nd 1920 — Warren G. Harding is elected the 29th President of the United States and secures over 60 percent of the popular vote. He will be inaugurated on March 4th, 1921.

November 12th 1920 — A Treaty is signed at Rapallo Italy, which cedes the Dalmation coast, between Italy and Yugoslavia, to Yugoslavia. Istria, a peninsula between Fiume and Trieste is given to Italy, and Fiume (Rijeka) is scheduled to become an independent state.

December 1920 — In the Dominican Republic, Major Alfred A. Cunningham, who had commanded the 1st Marine Aviation Force in France, assumes command of the 1st Aviation Squadron, which is now using DH-4bs, a more modern Biplane. Captain Cunningham remains in command until 1922, when he is succeeded by Major Edwin A. Brainard. The Squadron maintains a strength of about 130 enlisted men and nine Officers and six operational Planes. In addition, a new Airfield had been established around Santo Domingo City.

January 1921 — (Atlantic-France) The bodies of 45,000 Americans are exhumed from their graves at Romagne and other cemetery sites, at the request of American loved-ones and returned to the U.S. for burial. About 15,000 Americans remain in French cemeteries; their families had requested they remain where they had fallen. Previously, 100 Soldiers (from Michigan) who had lost their lives in Russia had arrived in Detroit during November 1919.

February 11th 1921 — A U.S. Seaplane crashes near the Marine barracks at Pensacola, Florida. The quick thinking of Pvt. Joseph Smith, a sentry on duty, saves the Pilot's life and he receives the Medal of Honor for his bravery.

February 1921 — A peace treaty (Riga) is signed by the Soviet Union and Poland. Terms include termination of Russian incursions into middle-Europe. It also stipulates that Poland will relinquish its claim on the Ukraine. The Soviet Union also signs pacts with Afghanistan and Persia. In other international activity, Mongolia proclaims its independence from China.

March 1921 — The U.S. informs the Soviet Union it will not consummate a trade agreement, however; a trade agreement is reached between the Soviet Union and Great Britain. The Soviets also conclude an agreement with Turkey's Mustapha Kemal. In other activity, Upper Silesia (along the Oder River in southwest Poland), in a plebiscite vote, agrees to join Germany, however; subsequent intervention on the part of the League of Nations, dictates a boundary settlement which is accepted reluctantly, by both Poland and Germany.

April 1921 — In China, Sun Yet-sen is elected President. In other activity, Tirol, in the Alps where Northern Italy and Western Austria meet, a plebiscite occurs which proposes joining Germany, however; the territory is subsequently given to Italy by the Allies.

May 1921 — Germany, which had previously suspended reparation installments, relents and reinitiates payment, upon an ultimatum by the Allies that the Ruhr Valley will be occupied by the Allies if payment is not forthcoming.

June 1921 — The Imperial Conference convenes in London. It concludes with the United Kingdom, her Dominions and India, forming the British Commonwealth of Nations.

July 2nd 1921 — Congress declares an end to World War I which had been waged against Germany and the Triple Entente. President Harding signs the joint resolution and the Treaty will be signed during August (Germany, Austria and Hungary).

July 21st 1921 — In a demonstration to emphasize the potential of Air Power, Planes attack and sink two Ships: the U.S.S. *Alabama* (decommissioned) and a captured German Vessel, the *Ostfriesland*. Colonel William Mitchell U.S. Army, is a steadfast advocate of Airpower and continually presses for Aircraft Carriers. His staunch belief in this idea leads to his court martial. In subsequent years, his efforts are finally rewarded, when the U.S. Government awards him the Medal of Honor posthumously. The Medal is presented to his son.

July 21st 1921 — The U.S.S. Alabama (decommissioned) under attack by U.S. Planes during a demonstration to emphasize the potential of Air Power.

19

July 1921 — (Asia Minor) During early July, fighting erupts between the Greeks under King Constantine and the Turks under Mustafa Kemal for control of Asia Minor. The hostilities continue until the defeat of the Greeks during 1922. **(Germany)** Hitler becomes President of the National Socialist Party (Nazi Party).

August 1921 — The U.S. officially terminates the war with the Triple Entente, signing treaties with Austria, Germany and Hungary.

September 1921 — The nations of Guatemala, Honduras, and San Salvador, conclude a pact which establishes the Central American Union. In other international activity, Latvia, Estonia and Lithuania are admitted to the League of Nations.

October 1921 — The Soviet Union proclaims it will give independence to the Crimea, a peninsula in the southwestern portion of the Soviet Union on the Black Sea.

November 7th 1921 — President Harding orders the Marine Corps to assist with the protection of the U.S. Mail.

November 11th 1921 — President Harding attends a service at Arlington National Cemetery. He solemnly places the Medal of Honor on the Flag draped coffin of the Unknown Soldier. Special Congressional legislation, passed on the 4th of May, had also approved Medals of Honor for the unknown Soldiers of Belgium, Great Britain, France, Italy and Rumania.

Tomb of the Unknown Soldier at Arlington National Cemetery (Officially dedicated November 11th 1932).

November 12th 1921-February 6th 1922 — The Washington Disarmament Conference convenes in the United States. The meeting is called to set limits on armaments and in order to reach agreement between all powers, concerning the situation in the Pacific and the Far East. Participating nations: the United States, Belgium, China, France, Great Britain, Italy, Japan, Portugal, and the Netherlands. The Bolshevik government of the Soviet Union is not invited. Agreements reached, include the Pacific Treaty, between the U.S., Great Britain, France, and Japan, concerning their mutual respect for each others island possessions (December 21st). The meeting concludes with agreement between the nations of Great Britain, France, Japan, Italy and the United States, concerning growths of their respective Navies and stipulating that no additional principal Ships be constructed for the following ten years. Another of the pacts guarantees the independence of China and the reaffirming of its Open Door Policy.

November 1921 — The Soviets sign an accord with Mongolia, which lends support to the government against Chinese and Japanese encroachment.

December 1921 — Great Britain gives recognition to the Irish Free State, granting it Dominion status within the British Commonwealth. Meanwhile, the Ulster Government (Northern Ireland), decides to remain with Britain. Irish Parliament (Southern Ireland) and Great Britain consummate the Anglo-Irish Treaty during January 1922. President Eamon De Valera resigns in a display of opposition to the treaty and is succeeded by Arthur Griffith. The duration of peace and tranquility is short lived. Griffith succumbs to natural causes during August 1922. Shortly thereafter, the Irish Commander in Chief, Michael Collins is assassinated by Irish Republicans (under De Valera) formed to unite Ireland as one country. This action ignites civil war.

January 25th 1922 — Anti-American feelings are escalating in Nicaragua. Marines, attached to the U.S.S. *Galveston* will land at Corinto to reinforce Marines positioned there.

February 11th 1922 — Marines continue to train Haitian troops to rid Haiti of the bandits, which are still terrorizing the people. The United States appoints Brigadier General John A. Russell as American High Commissioner and personal representative of the President to the Government of Haiti. He retains the position until 12 November 1930.

February 1922 — Great Britain's protectorate policy over Egypt is terminated, and by agreement, both countries administer the Sudan.

April 16th 1922 — (Germany) Walther Rathenau, the Foreign Minister, signs a treaty (Rapallo) with the Soviet Union. Great Britain and France are unhappy with this, because they had not been consulted. Hitler and other anti-Bolsheviks are infuriated. Hitler's subsequent speeches calling the treaty a "JEWISH SELL-OUT" of Germany to the Bolsheviks, brings about Rathenau's assassination during June.

April 28th 1922 — Civil disturbances occur in Peking, China. Marines led by Captain Charles H. Martin would debark the U.S.S. *Albany* at Peking, to bolster the American legation guard.

May 5th 1922 — U.S. Marines, attached to the Asiatic Fleet, are landed at Tienstin, China, positioned to move against Peking if necessary, to protect American lives during the ongoing political crisis. Another contingent of Marines lands at Taku, China and is positioned to move into Shanghai to protect American interests if necessary.

May 31st 1922 — In the Dominican Republic, General Lee, U.S.M.C., reports that organized banditry has been terminated in the eastern district. Most of the remaining notorious bandits had taken advantage of an amnesty arrangement. Seven leaders and about 169 followers surrender (April) and receive suspended sentences.

June 24th 1922 — In Germany, the Foreign Minister, Walther Rathenau (Jewish), is assassinated by members of the Nationalist Party. He had engineered the Treaty of Rapallo (April 16th, 1922), between Germany and Russia, without consulting with the Allies. The execution is incited by Hitler, who is calling for the termination of the Treaty of Versailles and simultaneously proclaiming that the Jews had been attempting to turn Germany over to the Bolsheviks (Russians). Hitler, although not in power, is already making plans to eliminate all Jews in Germany. During a conversation with Josef Hell (a friend), Hitler states "IF I AM EVER REALLY IN POWER, THE DESTRUCTION OF THE JEWS WILL BE MY FIRST AND MOST IMPORTANT JOB. AS SOON AS I HAVE THE POWER, I SHALL HAVE GALLOWS AFTER GALLOWS ERECTED, FOR EXAMPLE, IN MUNICH ON THE MARIENPLATZ-AS MANY OF THEM AS THE TRAFFIC ALLOWS."

July 1922 — In Turkey, the Greek Army nears Constantinople by the end of the month. Allied pressure forbids the seizure of the city and subsequent assistance given to the Turks by France and Italy, bolsters a Turkish counterattack to save the region.

August 1st 1922 — The 3rd and 15th Regiments stationed in the Dominican Republic are disbanded and its personnel reassigned to the newly reestablished 1st Marine Regiment.

September 4th 1922 — The first Transcontinental flight to be accomplished in less than twenty four hours is completed by *Lieutenant James H. Doolittle.* The flight originates in Pablo Beach, Florida and lands in San Diego, California in just over three and a half hours. The flight covers 2,163 miles (actual air time is just under twenty one and a half hours).

September 9th 1922 — The Turkish forces storm Smyrna and vanquish the Greeks, culminating Greek presence in Asia Minor.

Late October 1922 — Mussolini, in his quest to assume power in Italy, issues an ultimatum to the government, declaring that his forces will march into Rome and seize power if the government does not resign. Luigi Facta takes the threat seriously and his cabinet resigns. On the 31st, Mussolini enters Rome to become Prime Minister.

November 1922 — In Turkey, the Ottoman Empire comes to an end, as Kepal seizes Constantinople and proclaims that Turkey is a Republic.

December 16th 1922 — A French Vessel, the *Vinh-Long,* becomes severely disabled, while in the Sea of Marmora, Turkey. The U.S.S. *Bainbridge* pulls alongside the struggling Vessel, amidst violent explosions, rescuing 482 of the 495 people on board. Lieutenant Commander Walter A. Edwards, Commanding Officer of the *Bainbridge* becomes the recipient of the Medal of Honor for his courageous actions during the rescue operation.

January 10th 1923 — President Harding withdraws all remaining American troops from Germany.

January 11th 1923 — In Germany, French troops occupy the Ruhr Valley on the 11th, seizing the opportunity when Germany is late with delivery of reparation payments. German resentment spirals and Hitler soon takes advantage as the turmoil unfolds. Huge demonstrations are instigated by the National Socialist Party. Meanwhile, the financial situation in Germany is horrendous, and becoming worse as the Mark plummets steadily.

February 14th 1923 — The U.S.S. *Ashville* arrives at Masu Island, China. Marines debark to protect Americans from Chinese bandits.

March 1923 — Vilna, which had belonged to Russia until World War 1 when it was taken by Germany, now reverts to Poland (given by the Allies). In addition, East Galicia, (southeastern Poland), is also given back to Poland.

July 1923 — The Treaty of Union which had been signed in Moscow during 1922 is agreed upon by the Central Executive Committee; this establishes the Union of Soviet Socialist Republic, replacing the Russian Empire. The original constitution of the union calls for democracy, however, the Communists have absolute control and democracy is thrown to the wind, in favor of Totalitarian government and a subsequent reign of terror. In other international activity, Turkey and the Allies sign an accord (Treaty of Lausanne). The treaty modifies the Treaty of Sevres. In addition, the Dodecanese Islands in the Aegean Sea are to be returned to Italy by Greece.

August 2nd 1923 — President Warren G. Harding suffers a heart attack and dies, while in San Francisco. Vice President Calvin Coolidge, is in Vermont, visiting his family. He is sworn into office by his father (a Notary Public), on the 3rd of August and becomes our nation's 30th President.

August 11th 1923 — The Marine Corps Recruit Depot, Mare Island, California, is moved to San Diego.

Marine Corps Recruit Depot, San Diego, California.

September 1st 1923 — The Navy works on land also. The Grand Hotel in Yokahama, Japan, becomes engulfed in flames and Ensign Thomas J. Ryan, recklessly enters the burning building and rescues a woman. Ryan would become the recipient of the Medal of Honor for his actions. Japan had been struck by a grievous earthquake that wipes out thousands of people in Tokyo and Yokohama.

September 14th 1923 — In Spain, a successful coup (condoned by King Alphonso) occurs. The leader, Miguel Primo de Rivera governs for seven years.

October 28th 1923 — A collision occurs between the Steamship *Abangarez* and a Submarine, the U.S.S. 05. The Submarine sinks in less than one minute. Torpedoman 2nd class, Henry Brealt, decides to remain on board to aid a wounded Seaman, instead of jumping to safety. Brealt seals the hatch and remains submerged for 31 hours with the wounded man, until they are successfully rescued. Brealt receives the Medal of Honor at a ceremony in the White House on March 8th, 1923.

November 8th 1923 — In Germany, Adolf Hitler, who has previously been arrested for his activities, attempts a coup, however it fails and he is sentenced to prison for five years (serves about nine months). While in prison, he pens Mein Kampf, which clearly spells out his determination to conquer Europe and eliminate the Jews. It is said that Hitler received some inspiration from a book entitled, The International Jew, authored by Henry Ford during 1920.

November 15th 1923 — A detachment of Marines debarks at Tungshan, China to protect fifty American mission aries, endangered after the defeat of the forces under Sun Yat-sen at Sheklung.

January 11th 1924 — In Greece, King George II (successor to King Constantine who abdicated during the latter part of 1922) is deposed and a Republic is formed. The Greek Eleutherios Venizelos becomes Prime Minister. This government will be overthrown during 1925 by Theodore Pangalos.

January 21st 1924 — Nikolai Lenin dies. He had helped found the Bolsheviks, which had overthrown the Russian government during the revolution of 1917. Lenin had been a "pupil" of George Plekhanov, the father of Russian Marxism, who had fled Russia during 1881. Plekhanov founded "Osvobozhdenie Truda (Emancipation of Labor). Lenin, who proclaimed world revolution and the disintegration of capitalism, will be succeeded by Stalin, whose policies will become even more radical. Purges begin, to exterminate all challengers to Stalin's power.

January 1924 — In China, Sun Yat-sen's Kuomintang Congress establishes a government at Canton in coalition with Communist factions.

February 1st 1924 — Great Britain opens diplomatic relations with the Bolshevik government of the Soviet Union.

February 3rd 1924 — Woodrow Wilson, the 28th President of the U.S. dies in Washington D.C. at the age of 68.

February 27th 1924 — The United States and the Dominican Republic enter into a new treaty, which would subsequently allow the Marines to be withdrawn from the island. In other activity, a U.S. Flotilla arrives at La, Ceiba, Honduras. Political turmoil is causing additional defensive action to be taken by

the U.S. to protect American citizens. Marines led by Lt. Theodore Cartwright debark the U.S.S. *Denver*, to fortify the Marine contingents already there. Additional Marines land during the following week.

Marines and Sailors during the occupation of the Dominicon Republic (Photo taken during 1916).

March 1924 — Italy's Mussolini begins annexing territory along the Adriatic coast.

May 1924 — China recognizes the Bolshevik government of the Soviet Union. During the following month, Stalin will send advisors to help train Chinese troops at Canton.

June 15th 1924 — American Indians receive citizenship by Congressional action.

August 6th 1924 — Political stability is returning to the Dominican Republic. The U.S. Marines, 4th Regiment, depart the island and return to duty in the States. A small detachment remains behind to complete the transition.

September 7th 1924 — Additional Marines, attached to the U.S.S. *Rochester*, debark at La Ceiba, Honduras to comply with the American Consul's request for more protection.

September 9th 1924 — The U.S.S. *Huron* disembarks a detachment of Marines to guard a portion of the boundary at Shanghai, China. Marines would also be rushed to reinforce the legations at both Tientsin and Peking, to deal with the continuing political instability.

September 16th 1924 — The Dominican Republic now has the responsibility of policing itself, as the last Contingent of the 4th Marines returns to the United States.

October 6th 1924 — The U.S. Navy is pressed into Shanghai to protect American interests. Other Marine contingents, positioned at Canton, China will be reinforced toward the end of the month to assist efforts to contain the ongoing political unrest.

October 20th 1924 — The U.S.S. *Trenton* is struck by a terrible fire at 3:35 pm. Powder would ignite, causing twenty men to be trapped in a twin gun mount. Fourteen men die and six others are severely burned. Boatswain's Mate George R. Cholister and Ensign Henry C. Drexler exemplify extraordinary courage during their futile efforts to extinguish the flames and both men receive the Medal of Honor posthumously.

November 4th 1924 — Calvin Coolidge is elected President of the U.S. He is inaugurated on March 4th, 1925 (30th President. He had previously assumed office on August 3rd 1923, upon death of President Harding).

November 4th 1924 — The American 1st Expeditionary Force is transferred from Shanghai to Tientsin, China, to give added protection to American interests during the ongoing political turmoil.

November 1924 — In China, a noted Warlord, General Feng Yu-hsiang, breaks with his Allies and seizes Peking. General Yu-hsiang dies during February of 1925 and will be succeeded by Chiang Kai-shek, an ardent anti-communist. Kai-shek will soon send the Russian advisors home.

December 1924 — Toward the latter part of December, Ahmed Beg Zogu takes control of Albania, proclaiming it a dictatorship. Zogu subsequently designates himself, King Zog I.

January 15th 1925 — Political turmoil continues in China. U.S. Marines attached to the U.S.S. *Sacramento* land at Shanghai to defend American interests. The second Marine Expeditionary Force, commanded by Captain James J. Schwerin, debarks the U.S.S. *Barker*, U.S.S. *Borie* and the U.S.S. *Whipple* ten days later, to reinforce the defensive posture already there. On this day, General Pershing promotes General Douglas MacArthur to Major General. At 45, MacArthur becomes the youngest Major General in the U.S. Army.

January 1925 — The power struggle between Trotsky and Stalin, two of Lenin's hatchet men, is tilting toward Stalin. Trotsky resigns his post as chairman of the Russian Revolutionary Military Council. Stalin will succeed in ridding himself of Trotsky and another challenger, Grigori Zinoviev during 1926; both are driven from the country.

February 28th 1925 — Congress authorizes the Marine Corps Reserve. The Marine Corps will begin to organize the Reserves on July 1st.

March 13th 1925 — The U.S. Navy participates with the Army in joint maneuvers around Oahu, Hawaii. About 750 Marines from Quantico also participate.

April 20th 1925 — The U.S. Navy finds itself once again ferrying Marines to trouble spots around the globe. The U.S.S. *Denver* dispatches its contingent of Marines to La Ceiba, Honduras to protect Americans in the area.

April 25th 1925 — German Field Marshal Paul von Hindenburg, now 77 years of age, is elected President of Germany. Before the end of the year, Germany will apply for membership in the League of Nations (admitted September 1926), and Hindenburg will concentrate on solving border problems with France.

April 1925 — The native Moroccans under Abd-el-Krim, bolstered by a victorious struggle against Spanish troops which have been driven back to Spain, concentrate their efforts against the French in French Morocco.

June 5th 1925 — The U.S.S. *Huron* arrives at Shanghai. Marines are sent ashore to assist in the protection of the International Settlement. The U.S.S. *Aberenda* would arrive on the 9th and dispatches her contingent of Marine reinforcements to bolster those forces already there.

July 1st 1925 — The U.S.S. *Huron* anchors at Shanghai with another contingent of Marines. These Marines, commanded by Captain William Richards, debark. In other activity, the Marine Corps Reserve, authorized by Congress on February 28th, is established.

August 1st 1925 — The Marines which were needed to protect the American Legation at Managua, Nicaragua, withdraw. They will depart the country on U.S. Naval Ships in a few days. Several weeks after the departure of the Marines, a group of Conservatives barge into a celebration being held by some Liberal Cabinet members, accuse them of treason and throw them into jail. On the 25th of October, the fortifications at La Loma are overtaken by Emiliano Chamorro's followers. Soon after, President Solorzano and Vice President Sacasa flee the country.

October 5th 1925 — The Locarno Conference convenes. A result of the meeting is that Germany agrees to recognize their frontiers with France and Belgium.

Mid-October 1925 — Germany signs a trade agreement (Rapallo) with the Soviet Union. German troops, are already being secretly trained by Russians, in violation of the Versailles Treaty.

October 28th 1925 — The Marine Garrison stationed at Tientsin, China is further bolstered by the arrival of more reinforcements.

October 28th-December 17th 1925 — Brigadier General William "Billy" Mitchell, U.S.A., is court martialled. Mitchell, a zealous supporter of air power, has been continually pounding the Army and Navy to put heavy emphasis on Aircraft as a primary weapon. He publicly proclaims his dissatisfaction with the General Staff, which brings about a highly publicized court martial for insubordination. General MacArthur serves on the panel. Mitchell would be found guilty and be suspended from duty for five years. He resigns shortly thereafter. Mitchell, is considered by many to be a martyr for Airpower. His dream later becomes reality, when Carriers and their Planes become crucial factors during the upcoming conflict (World War II). On August 8th, 1946, by an act of Congress, the Nation would pay its belated gratitude to Mitchell and posthumously awards him the Medal of Honor. It would be presented to his son, William Mitchell Jr.

Brigadier General William "Billy" Mitchell.

October 31st 1925 — (Persia) An Army Officer, Reza Khan, becomes Shah. This action ends the Kajar Dynasty which has ruled Persia since the 18th Century. Reza Khan had established his dictatorship during 1921.

November 9th 1925 — Marines, led by Captain A. Wilson, are shifted from Shanghai to Tientsin, China, to protect Americans. This type of checkerboard movement would continue as the instability in China remains constant. On the 30th of December, additional Marines debark Naval Vessels at Shanghai.

Early January 1926 — In Greece, the Prime Minister, Theodore Pangalos, proclaims himself dictator. The Prime Minister, who seized power in a coup, will be deposed later in the year and sent to Crete for imprisonment. A new government will be formed, however, stability does not return immediately. The government will resign during 1928.

January 1926 — In the Middle East, the Kingdom of Hejaz, ruled by King Hussein is overthrown by Ibn Saud, who becomes King of Hejaz, then changes its name to Saudi Arabia.

January 16th 1926 — In Nicaragua, Emiliano Chamorro assumes the Presidency. The U.S. does not recognize his government which had been organized subsequent to purging all Liberal members of congress. Riots will begin to sweep the nation.

February 16th 1926 — The United States Coast Guard Academy site is established at New London, Connecticut.

During the 1920's, the U.S. Coast Guard spends a great deal of time enforcing prohibition laws. Photo shows Coast Guardsmen seizing contraband liquor near Seattle.

May 6th 1926 — The U.S.S. *Galveston* arrives and drops Marines at Blue Fields, Nicaragua to protect U.S. citizens after revolution erupts. The sole purpose of the Marines is to prevent riots or fighting in the city. They do not interfere with the dispute. This detachment of Marines will be relieved on October 31st, when fresh reinforcements arrive aboard the U.S.S. *Rochester.*

May 8th-9th 1926 — The U.S. Navy completes the first flight over the North Pole. Commander Richard E. Byrd and Machinist Floyd Bennett negotiate the 1,545 mile journey in a Fokker Aircraft using a special compass, which had been invented by Albert Bumstead for use during sub-zero temperatures. Both Byrd and Bennett would become recipients of the Medal of Honor for their dangerous mission.

May 1926 — In Poland, the government is overthrown by Marshal Joseph Pilsudski. In Morocco, the French finally vanquish the Moroccans, under Abd-el-Krim, ending the Riff War, which has lasted for about two years. Subsequent to the French victory, the Spanish return to Morocco and both regain control of their respective territories.

July 2nd 1926 — Today, the Army Air Service, which had been established in 1920, becomes the Army Air Corps by an Act of Congress.

July 26th 1926 — Robert Todd Lincoln, oldest son of Abraham Lincoln, dies at the age of 83.

September 26th 1926 — In Nicaragua, the warring factions are in stalemate. The U.S. enlarges the neutral zone (Blue Fields) across the bay to El Bluff where the Liberals and Conservatives are involved in vicious fighting. The U.S. will arrange a cease fire which commences on October 1st.

October 10th 1926 — The U.S.S. *Denver* arrives at Corinto, Nicaragua. Her contingent of Marines would be put ashore to protect American lives as the revolution continues. The U.S.S. *Denver* delivers additional Marines at Blue Fields on November 30th, relieving those who had arrived on the U.S.S. *Rochester.*

October 20th 1926 — President Calvin Coolidge authorizes the use of 2,500 Marines to guard the U.S. Mail.

October 30th 1926 — Nicaraguan President Chamorro resigns. A 30 day cease fire ends today. Subsequently, Congress reconvenes and selects Adolfo Diaz as the President of Nicaragua. The government is legitimate and will be recognized by the U.S. on November 14th. Mexico will argue that Sacasa, exiled in California, is the rightful ruler.

November 15th 1926 — Nicaraguan President Diaz requests all-out American intervention to quell the revolt. General Moncada has refused to give up the struggle unless ordered by the former Vice President, Sacasa.

December 23rd 1926 — The U.S.S. *Rochester* arrives at Rio Grande, Nicaragua to dispatch a contingent of Marines and Sailors to protect Americans on shore. The U.S.S. *Cleveland* would see her contingent of Marines debark at Bragman's Bluff for the same purpose.

December 25th 1926 — Hirohito becomes Emperor of Japan, subsequent to the death of his father. The Emperor's voice is never heard by the citizens, as he is considered to be a god. The first time he speaks to the Japanese public, is when he announces that Japan has surrendered to the United States, following the total defeat of Japan during 1945.

January 5th 1927 — Marines, attached to the U.S.S. *Denver*, debark at Pearl Cay, Nicaragua and establish an outpost. On the following day, additional Marines stationed on the U.S.S. *Galveston* land at Corinto, from where they will move to Managua, Nicaragua to protect the American Legation.

January 7th 1927 — The U.S.S. *Denver* arrives at Rio Grande, Nicaragua to land Marine reinforcements. Two days later, Marines attached to the U.S.S. *Cleveland* debark at Prinzapolca, Nicargua to initiate a neutral zone.

January 10th 1927 — Nicaragua continues to see the arrival of U.S. Marines, as the 2nd Battalion, 5th Marines arrives at

Blue Fields. More reinforcements will arrive shortly. In the U.S., President Coolidge informs Congress that he will initiate full measures to protect American citizens in Nicaragua. He will authorize the sale of 3,000 Krag Rifles, 200 Browning machine guns and 3,000,000 rounds of ammunition to the government of President Diaz.

January-December 1927 — Chiang Kai-shek continues the drive to unify China. His forces advance to Hankow during January and by March, the Kuomintang forces swarm into Shanghai and Nanking, however; Kai-shek's ideas start to get sidetracked. Troops that seize Nanking begin to rape and pillage. Their uncivilized behavior against foreign citizens compels American and British Warships to commence a bombardment of Nanking; the British and American citizens are rescued. In addition, the Communist factions cause friction with Kai-shek's plans, and by August, Mao Tse-tung, an upcoming Communist leader, aborts the Nationalist cause and moves to the mountains to begin to plot his own strategy for gaining power in China. By the end of the year, the Soviet Union breaks diplomatic relations with China.

February 1st 1927 — Through the request of Diaz, U.S. Marines relieve government troops and deploy to protect the city of Managua, Nicaragua.

February 9th 1927 — A detachment of U.S. Marines, commanded by Major Samuel P. Budd, debark the U.S.S. *Pecos*, to reinforce the Marine force protecting the International Settlement in Shanghai during the ongoing civil war.

February 19th 1927 — The U.S.S. *Galveston* dispatches Marines to establish an outpost along the railroad at Leon, Nicaragua. In two days, the Marine detachment aboard the U.S.S. *Trenton* arrives at Corinto, where they will set up a defensive stance to protect American citizens in the vicinity of Chinandega and Leon. The government troops had lost and resecured Chinandega, but it had been reduced to rubble.

Chinese citizens performing at the U.S. Compound at Tientsin, China for the U.S. 15th Infantry Regiment.

March 4th 1927 — The *Meifoo XIV*, an American Vessel which had been captured by Chinese rebels, is recaptured by a joint Marine-Navy assault unit. The Americans had been transported by the U.S.S. *Pittsburgh*.

March 1927 — During March, the turmoil continues in Nicaragua. On the 7th, Brigadier General Logan Feland, U.S.M.C., arrives at Corinto to assume control of the 2,000 Marines in the country. During the beginning of the month, an American diplomat is assaulted and injured, prompting additional Marines to deploy at Matagalpa. Incidents have caused Belgium and Italy to ask for protection of its citizens by the U.S. and the Chinese make the same request.

March 16th 1927 — Political turmoil fuels further instability in China, forcing the U.S. to send in additional troops. Twelve hundred men arrive in Shanghai aboard the U.S.S. *Chaumont*. More Marines arrive in May, which initiates the forming of the 3rd Marine Brigade.

May 4th 1927 — The U.S.S. *Grant* arrives at Olongapo, Philippines, where she will land Marine units including Aviation Contingents.

May 16th 1927 — Marines participate at the Battle of La Paz Centro, Nicaragua.

May 20th-21st 1927 — Captain Charles A. Lindbergh (U.S.A. Air Corps Reserve), completes the first successful flight across the Atlantic Ocean, traveling 3,600 miles from New York City to Paris, France. Lindbergh's flight in the *Spirit of St. Louis*, lasts a little over 39 and a half hours and dispels the notion that Planes cannot cross the ocean. He becomes a recipient of the Medal of Honor for this feat.

May 21st 1927 — Marines garrisoned in the Philippines begin to arrive at Shanghai. They bring a contingent of Light Tanks with them. Additional units, the 6th Regiment and 1st Battalion, 10th Marines, further bolster the force when they arrive on the 21st.

May 22nd 1927 — Henry L. Stimson, sent to Nicaragua by President Coolidge to bring an end to the fighting, has negotiated a settlement which includes both sides disarming and a U.S. supervised election in 1928. He returns to the U.S. today.

June 10th 1927 — U.S. Marines occupy the town of Ocotal, Nicaragua. At the end of June, total Marine Corps strength stands at 19,198 men — 18,000 enlisted men and 1,198 officers (active duty).

July 15th 1927 — The revolution in Nicaragua continues. The U.S.S. *Tulsa* arrives at El Gallo and lands a contingent of Marines to set up an outpost. On the following day, Marine Infantry engages approximately 700 Nicaraguan rebels, led by Augusto C. Sandino in the vicinity of Ocatal. The Marines receive Air Support from Aviation Units that swoop low, dive bombing the rebels. This is the first time that Marine Aircraft and Infantry units coordinate in battle (first Marine Dive-Bombing attack in support of ground troops). The rebels had demanded surrender, but Captain Gilbert D. Hatfield ignores the request. Successive assaults are beaten back before the arrival of the Planes. The Marines lose 1 dead and 5 wounded. The rebels lose 56 dead (recovered) and over 100 wounded. Two days later, rebels ambush a Marine Patrol near San Fernando. Of the 40 bandits, 11 are killed. One Marine is wounded. The Patrol encounters another bandit force, but advances to Jicaro and occupies it without incident.

September 17th 1927 — Marines attached to the U.S.S. *Tulsa* land and occupy the town of Bragman's Bluff, Nicaragua. The U.S.S. *Cleveland* arrives on the 23rd with reinforcements to relieve the contingent, which had landed earlier.

September 19th 1927 — In Nicaragua, at Telpaneca, a group of Sandino's rebels about 200 strong, attempt to surprise a contingent of 20 Marines and 25 Guardia Nacional troops. Dynamite is thrown near the Marines' barracks, but the startled troops recover quickly. By dawn, the rebels had lost about 25 killed and approximately 50 wounded. One Marine is killed and another succumbs later in the day. One of the Guardia troopers is wounded.

December 18th 1927 — The U.S.S. *S-4* (Submarine), collides with a Coast Guard Destroyer off Providencetown, Massachusetts and capsizes with all men aboard. Chief Gunners' Mate Thomas Eadie and Chief Torpedoman Michels dive, in attempts to hook up air hoses to save the trapped Seamen. Michels, however, becomes entrapped between lines and after two hours of dangerous diving maneuvers, Michels is rescued by Eadie and brought to the surface. Eadie is awarded the Medal of Honor for his actions.

January 1st 1928 — Marines assist Nicaraguan troops engaged against a band of rebels at Sapotillal Ridge, Nicaragua. The Marines and government troops take the crest after a bitter fight, and pause to await reinforcements. They subsequently make it to Quilali.

January 6th-8th 1928 — Marines come under heavy rebel fire in Quilali, Nicaragua. Lieutenant Christian F. Schilt braves the enemy fire, taking off ten times to evacuate the wounded and return with supplies and allow the besieged Marines to hold their positions. His Plane has no brakes and Marines grab its wings upon landing to slow the Aircraft. Schilt would become a recipient of the Medal of Honor for his courage. The operation to destroy the rebel leader Sandino and his fortress at El Chipote fails. The Patrols which had initiated the quest on December 19th, 1927, return to San Albino.

April 25th 1928 — Lt. Schilt, U.S.M.C., receiving the Medal of Honor from President Calvin Coolidge for his heroism in Nicaragua.

January 14th 1928 — Marine Aircraft successfully dive bomb rebel positions at El Chipote, Nicaragua. On the following day, the Navy puts additional Marine reinforcements ashore at Corinto.

January 15th 1928 — Three hundred Marines, commanded by General Logan Peland, arrive at Corinto, Nicaragua.

January 16th-February 20th 1928 — A meeting known as the Pan American Conference convenes in Havana, Cuba. It is the sixth International Conference of American States. The tone calls for co-operation among Western Hemisphere nations, however; discussions turn toward the U.S., and its right to intervene in the internal affairs of its neighboring countries, as claimed by the Monroe Doctrine and the Roosevelt edict in 1904.

January 18th 1928 — The force of U.S. Marines in Shanghai now stands at 1,200. In addition, there are 3,354 deployed at Tientsin and another 521 at Peking.

February 6th 1928 — An arbitration treaty is signed by France and the U.S. in Washington, D.C.

February 27th 1928 — Nicaraguan troops, with the assistance of Marines, battle rebels at Bromaderos, Nicaragua. Two attacks are repulsed before reinforcements arrive at dawn. Lt. O'Day's Patrol loses three killed and ten wounded. Two additional men die before they can be evacuated. The rebels lose 10 dead and 30 wounded.

March 10th 1928 — The Alien Property Act is signed by President Coolidge. It provides $300,000,000 in compensation to German companies and nationals, which had property confiscated from them at the onset of war during 1917.

March 25th 1928 — The U.S.S. *Rochester* anchors at Corinto, Nicaragua to place Marines ashore to assist Nicaraguan troops which are attempting to drive the rebels out and restore order in the area.

April 19th 1928 — About 5,000 Japanese Soldiers seize Shantung, China. By May approximately 20,000 additional troops occupy the city. The Chinese react by implementing a successful boycott and although the League of Nations does not intervene directly, outside pressure does facilitate the withdrawal of the Japanese intruders who initiate a pull-out toward the latter part of May 1929.

May 22nd 1928 — The Merchant Marine Act is passed by Congress. The legislation provides for an increase in the amount of money to build new Ships and authorizes the sale of U.S. Ships to private enterprise (when surplus is available). In addition, Congress had also authorized subsidized mail contracts for the Merchant Marine.

June 11th 1928 — The U.S.S. *Bruce* catches fire while at Norfolk, Virginia. Machinist Mate William R. Huber dashes into the blazing boiler room, at great peril to his own life and successfully rescues Seaman Charles H. Bryan. Huber's disregard for his safety earns him the Medal of Honor for bravery.

May-December 1928 — United States Marines continue to assist the Nicaraguan Army in their efforts to defeat the rebels. Marines participate in skirmishes including the battles at the Cua River, the Coco River and the battle of Cuje.

June-December 1928 — During June, Nationalist troops enter Peking (renamed Peiping), and a Nationalist Government is established, giving Chiang Kai-shek more control of the country. The United States recognizes the Nationalist Government during late September, and on October 6th, Kai-shek becomes president. His power as dictator is secure by the end of the year and he refuses to acknowledge the Communist Chinese. Manchuria, under Chang Hsueh-liang, will pledge its allegiance to him by the end of the year.

August 27th 1928 — The Kellogg-Briand Act (Pact of Paris) is signed in Paris by the U.S. and fourteen other nations. The act denounces and forbids war. Forty seven additional nations sign it subsequently, bringing the total to 62 countries that subscribe to diplomacy as opposed to war. The U.S. Senate ratifies the pact during January of 1929. The agreement is named after French Foreign Minister Aristide Briand and U.S. Secretary of State Frank B. Kellogg.

November 4th 1928 — An election is held in Nicaragua. U.S. troops are at each polling place to prevent cheating and rioting. The Liberal Party wins and both sides consider the election fair (each had requested U.S. troops).

November 6th 1928 — Herbert Hoover is elected President of the U.S., defeating Alfred E. Smith. He will be inaugurated on March 4th, 1929. Within a few weeks, he departs the U.S. on an American Battleship and tours South America.

December 10th 1928 — The Pan American Conference on Conciliation and Arbitration meets in Washington, D.C.

January 5th 1929 — In Yugoslavia, the constitution is abolished. King Alexander 1st, assumes dictatorial powers and bans opposition parties. At the present time, it is called the Serbo-Croat-Slovene Kingdom and will be renamed Yugoslavia on the 3rd of October, 1929.

January 14th 1929 — Civil war erupts in Afghanistan. King Amanullah abdicates his throne.

January 19th 1929 — The 3rd Marine Brigade, commanded by Smedley Butler, is disbanded at Tientsin, China. The Marines pull out by the end of January and are reassigned. With Chiang Kai-shek in power the political situation in China stabilizes, however; the rift between the Nationalists and the Communists does not end. Mao Tse-tung will emerge as the Communist leader.

January 31st 1929 — Leon Trotsky, one of the founding Bolsheviks who had overthrown the Russian government, is exiled from Russia as Stalin continues to purge his competitors and seize uncontested control of the Soviet Union. Subsequently, Trotsky will be assassinated by one of Stalin's henchmen in Mexico (1940).

February 9th 1929 — Estonia, Latvia, Poland, Rumania, and Russia, sign a pact (Litvinov Protocol), which is similar to that signed by the 62 Western countries previously. The nations denounce war. The agreement is subsequently signed by Turkey during the latter part of the month.

February 11th 1929 — Italy, under Mussolini, acknowledges the Vatican as a state and accepts the Pope as its temporal ruler. Italy agrees to compensate the Catholic church for land which it had seized. The agreement is known as the Lateran Treaty.

March 5th 1929 — Major General Wendell C. Neville becomes the fourteenth Commandant of the Marine Corps, succeeding Major General John A. Lejeune who retires to assume the post of Superintendent of Virginia Military Institute.

April 16th 1929 — The United States, through its Secretary of State Henry L. Stimson, notifies the Soviet Union that America will not recognize its Bolshevik Government.

August 31st 1929 — The 11th Marine Regiment, based in Nicaragua, receives notification that it will be disbanded. The Marines head back to Quantico, Virginia to be reassigned.

November 18th 1929 — Manchuria is invaded without provocation by Russian troops and when the fighting subsides the Chinese sustain heavy casualties.

November 29th 1929 — Lieutenant Commander Richard E. Byrd, who had made the first flight over the North Pole, becomes the first person to successfully fly over the South Pole. Byrd and Bernt Balchen depart from Little America in Antarctica and complete the flight in under 20 hours, stopping only once to refuel. Captain Alton N. Parker, U.S.M.C.R., as a member of the expedition becomes the first Pilot to fly over the Antarctic Continent.

December 1929 — Tensions are rising in India. Hostilities are erupting between the Hindus and Moslems. Discussions between British and Indian leaders are initiated in an effort to give India Dominion status and in order to avoid a possible rebellion. During the early part of 1930, Mohandas Gandhi initiates his anti-government activities.

January 2nd 1930 — The U.S. and England agree on U.S. ownership of the Turtle Islands, located in the Sulu Sea, Philippines. The conference also clarifies the boundary between British North Borneo and the Philippines.

Late January 1930 — An International Naval Conference convenes in London to expand upon previous agreements which had begun during the Washington Conferences of 1921-22. The U.S., Great Britain and Japan agree on ratios, sizes and schedules for enlarging their Navies. Italy and France refuse to accept the terms. The treaty is ratified by the U.S. Senate on July 30th.

January 28th 1930 — In Spain, Primo de Rivera, the dictator, accedes to King Alfonso's request to resign. He departs the country and dies in France shortly thereafter.

June 30th 1930 — An aviation distance record for instrument (blind) flight is set by Captain Arthur H. Page, U.S.M.C. His plane travels from Omaha, Nebraska to Anacostia, Washington, D.C.

July 31st 1930 — (Atlantic-Germany) The final elements of Allied troops depart the Rhineland. Meanwhile, the National Socialists Party under Hitler, continues to gain strength in the government. After September elections, they capture over 100 seats in the Reichstag. Similarly to the economic situation in the U.S., Germany is undergoing a severe depression of its own and Hitler's party is seizing the opportunity.

August 6th 1930 — Major General Ben H. Fuller becomes the fifteenth Commandant of the Marine Corps.

September 14th 1930 — The National Socialists score a landslide victory in the elections. Even Hitler is astounded by the results which gain him 107 seats in the Reichstag, making the National Socialists the 2nd largest party in Germany, behind the Social Democrats. The Communists gain three additional seats going from 54 to 57 and the Social Democrats go from 152 to 143. Hitler's best showing arises in the Protestant sections in northern Germany, however; the Catholic sections and working-class districts, although not as great, are still strong. Tensions begin to arise as the possibility now exists that Marxist and Nazi riots could begin simultaneously.

October 30th 1930 — Greece and Turkey sign an agreement of friendship at Ankara.

November 2nd 1930 — In Ethiopia, Haile Selassie proclaims himself Emperor. His name had been Ras Tafari while he shared power with Empress Zauditu, who succumbed during April.

November 21st 1930 — General Douglas MacArthur, becomes the Chief of Staff, United States Army. At 50, he is the youngest man to hold the post in the history of the Army.

U.S. Marines giving a performance at Fort McHenry under a replica of the Star Spangled Banner. The original Flag is displayed at the Smithsonian Institute, Washington, D.C.

December 12th 1930 — The remaining Allied forces withdraw from the Saar, a coal mining area in the Saar Basin, between France and Germany. Germany will retake the ground from France subsequent to Hitler taking power.

February 21st 1931 — The State Department revamps its Nicaraguan policy by withdrawing the Marine outposts in northern Nicaragua in order to concentrate in the area of Managua. Marines continue to assist the Guardia in ridding the country of rebels, but they change plans temporarily at the end of March, after a tremendous earthquake strikes Managua. The Marines are used to guard against looting and to set up first aid stations.

March 1931 — An agreement is reached between Turkey and Russia, whereby neither will increase their Fleet in the Black Sea without giving six months notice.

March 3rd 1931 — The Star Spangled Banner, written by Francis Scott Key during the bombardment of Fort McHenry in 1812, becomes the official United States National Anthem.

April 13th 1931 — Nicaraguan Guardia troops assisted by Marine Aircraft, repulse bandit attacks in the vicinity of Puerta Cabezas.

April 14th 1931 — Subsequent to elections in Spain two days prior, the Republican leader, Niceto Alcala Zamora, insists that King Alfonso XIII abdicate. The King departs Spain, however; he does not vacate the throne. Zamora names himself leader and establishes a provisional government. Elections occur during June, resulting in a huge majority for the Republican-Socialist coalition.

April 22nd 1931 — A treaty is agreed upon by Egypt and Persia, which results in the first such alliance between Egypt and another Moslem state.

September 18th 1931 — The Japanese march into Manchuria and propel World War II. The Japanese accuse Chinese of destroying some railroad track on the South Manchuria Railroad which belongs to Japan. The Japanese, by launching this invasion, become in strict violation of the Kellogg Briand Act of 1928 forbidding such expansion. The Council League of Nations, meeting in Geneva the following month, will request American representation to assist in the crisis.

October 1931 — In Germany, a wealthy and prominent publisher, Alfred Hugenberg, gives Hitler his support. Hugenberg, disgruntled since Germany's loss of World War 1 and his contempt for Communism, convinces him to support Hitler both financially and with his massive communications network which he had accumulated by buying newspapers, film companies, movie theaters and wire services. Now Hitler has access to the media, which has been ignoring him for years. Hugenberg owns three major newspapers in Berlin. Other German industrialists including Emil Kirdorf and Fritz Thyssen also begin lending support. Kirdorf, an elderly man who is a coal tycoon had infused much capital into the efforts of Hugenberg's ventures.

November 1931 — In Spain, the assembly alleges King Alfonso guilty of treason; it confiscates Royal property. In China, Mao Tse-tung who had taken to the hills after the Nationalists assumed control of the country, now establishes the first Chinese Soviet Republic in Kiangsi Province.

December 1931 — In Spain, a new constitution is adopted on the ninth. It permits religious freedom. On the 10th, Alcala Zamora is elected Spain's first president. In Germany, the economic situation is deteriorating rapidly and unemployment now runs rampant, fueling the fires of dissent. The Communists take advantage of the crisis and their numbers begin to swell. In Austria, banks are also sustaining large losses. Financial help has arrived from Britain, however; financial ruin is possible. During the summer, a government coalition is formed between the Christian Socialists and Agrarians. It will last under a year. Although the U.S. is undergoing a severe depression of its own, it had extended large credits to the Bank of England during the summer to shore it up.

January 7th 1932 — Secretary of State Stimson informs China and Japan that the U.S. will not recognize any territory gained outside of the limits of the Kellogg-Briand Act of 1928.

February 3rd 1932 — The U.S.S. *Houston* arrives at Shanghai and Marines are debarked to bolster the 4th Marines in the face of rising Sino-Japanese hostilities and to protect American interests.

March 13th 1932 — National elections are held in Germany. Paul von Hindenburg emerges the winner, with Hitler coming in second with about 11 million votes, and the Communist candidate, Ernst Thalmann follows with about five million votes. Von Hindenburg captures eighteen million votes, however; it is an insufficient majority and another election is scheduled.

April 24th 1932 — Marines and Guardia troops, on patrol for bandits around Costancia, Nicaragua, encounter some trouble as a live grenade becomes loose. Corporal LeRoy Truesdale grasps the grenade, losing his hand in the process, but his actions save the Patrol.

May 20th 1932 — Amelia Earhart flies from Newfoundland to Ireland, 2026 miles distant in less than fourteen hours, becoming the first woman to solo across the Atlantic. Engine trouble prevents her from reaching France.

July 15th 1932 — (Pacific-Japan) About 200 Communists are being tried in Tokyo courts.

July 25th 1932 — The Soviet Union signs non-aggression pacts with Estonia, Finland, Latvia, and Poland.

July 28th-29th 1932 — The U.S. Army, under the personal command of General Douglas MacArthur, expels the Bonus Army (World War I veterans) from Washington D.C. The remaining 2,000 or so men who had come to demand their Veteran bonus are reluctantly driven away with tear gas after the Washington D.C. police attempted to remove them without success. MacArthur is assisted by Majors Dwight D. Eisenhower and George S. Patton. The "Bonus Army" had exceeded 15,000 Veterans plus women and children during early June. Between the 15th and 17th of June, the House approves payment and the Senate declines. The bonus is subsequently approved by Congress during 1936. There is no doubt that the Veterans desperately needed the bonus as many were close to poverty, however it was thought by some that Communist instigation had been involved with the legitimate movement, however; the Veterans had driven the few Communist instigators from their ranks and professed the movement to be all American. General MacArthur would maintain throughout the years that he had "NARROWLY AVERTED A COMMUNIST REVOLUTION." He also states that criticisms of his actions are "THE BEGINNING OF A DEFINITE AND CEASELESS CAMPAIGN BY THE COMMUNISTS AND THEIR FRIENDS" (INTENDED TO DESTROY HIM).

July 31 1932 — In Germany, elections are held and the National Socialists capture 230 seats, the Socialist Democrats 133, the Catholic Center Party 97 and the Communists secure 89. No majority emerges, as neither the Communists nor the National Socialists agree to co-operating with a coalition government.

August 10th 1932 — In Spain, the liberal socialist programs of Alcala Zamora ignites a short lived coup. Loyal troops quickly extinguish the attempt by overpowering the forces under General Jose Sanjurjo, which had seized Seville.

August 13th 1932 — In Germany, Hitler refuses to accept the position of vice-chancelor under Papen. On September 12th, the Reichstag will dissolve.

September 10th 1932 — **(Pacific-Japan)** The National City Bank in New York had issued instructions for its foreign branch officers to take pictures of their respective banks throughout the Far East to exhibit the method of modernization. In Osaka, Japan, the Japanese stop the effort. Subsequently, the Japanese press, throughout the entire country, run sensational stories stating that the pictures are for the U.S. to detect the exact locations of the banks in order to bomb them.

September 25th 1932 — In Spain, Catalonia is granted autonomy by the Republican government and will be authorized to have its own president and government as well as a flag and in addition, Catalan is to be the official language.

October 4th 1932 — In Hungary, Julius Gombos assumes power, subsequent to the resignation of Count Stephan Bethlen.

November 8th 1932 — Franklin Delano Roosevelt is elected President of the U.S., defeating President Hoover. He will be inaugurated on March 4th, 1933. The grievous depression with its chronic unemployment had not helped Hoover's cause. Roosevelt captures over 22,000,000 votes to Hoover's 15,000,000. In addition, the Socialist candidate, Norman Thomas receives 882,000 votes and the Communist, William Foster, receives over 100,000.

During the early 1920's the U.S. Navy converts some Colliers into Carriers. Above, is the U.S.S. Langley, the first Vessel to be transformed.

November 11th 1932 — The Tomb of the Unknown Soldier is officially dedicated at Arlington National Cemetery.

November 17th-24th 1932 — German Chancellor von Papen resigns, subsequent to the recently held elections, which failed to gain a clear majority. On the 24th, von Hindenburg offers a limited chancellorship to Hitler, however; he again turns it down, demanding full powers. Von Hindenburg refuses to relent.

November 29th 1932 — The Soviets sign a non-aggression pact with France.

January 1st 1933 — Nicaraguans inaugurate Juan B. Sacasa as President. U.S. Marines participate in the ceremony and within two days, the final remnants of the 2nd Marine Brigade depart the country.

January 8th 1933 — Revolution starts to erupt in Spain. Dissidents in Barcelona instigate an uprising. Government troops crush the revolt, however; civil war is brewing. Barcelona will be the site of another attempted revolt during December.

January 30th 1933 — The ascent of the National Socialists under Adolf Hitler is complete when aging German President Von Hindenburg names him Chancellor. Hitler has been against the Versailles Treaty and his views concerning the elimination of the Bolsheviks (Communists) are steadfast. Hitler also intends to restore Germany to a position of strength.

February 15th 1933 — An assassination attempt on the life of President elect Franklin D. Roosevelt in a Miami motorcade fails. The quick actions of a spectator, foils the plot, but Chicago Mayor Anton Cermak is mortally wounded and dies on the 6th of March. President elect Roosevelt escapes harm. The assassin, Giuseppe Zangara, will be executed on March 20th.

February 16th 1933 — At a conference in Geneva, the nations of Czechoslovakia, Rumania and Yugoslavia (Little Entente) modify their initial treaties by establishing a permanent governing body and placing no time limit on termination in an effort to fortify themselves during the rise of National Socialist power in Germany.

February 25th 1933 — The United States Navy launches its first Aircraft Carrier. The Vessel will be named the U.S.S. *Ranger*, in honor of John Paul Jones' Vessel.

The Carrier U.S.S. Saratoga (CV-3), in the background as viewed from the deck of the U.S.S. Ranger (CV-4).

February 27th 1933 — In Germany, the Reichstag building is destroyed by fire. Hitler blames the fire on the Communists and the Communists blame it on Hitler's followers. Emergency measures are quickly taken, including the suspension of civil liberties. Storm troops take great advantage. Communist leaders are systematically rounded up and arrested; the Communist Party is disbanded. In autumn, a court finds the Communist defendants innocent, however; the arsonist, named Marinus van der Lubbe (from Holland), who had quit the Communist Party to join the International Communists, is executed.

March 4th 1933 — Franklin Roosevelt, who had escaped death the month before, is inaugurated as the 32nd President of the United States. He would state: "LET ME ASSERT MY FIRM BELIEF THAT THE ONLY THING WE (AMERICANS) HAVE TO FEAR IS FEAR ITSELF."

March 5th 1933 — In Germany, new elections are held. No majority is reached, but the National Socialist hold is becoming more firm as the opposition is becoming unorganized. In Austria, on the previous day, Englebert Dollfuss reacts to the National Socialist ascension to power in Germany and dissolves parliamentary government. During March, he restricts the free press.

March 23rd 1933 — In Germany, Hitler's rise to power is becoming meteoric. The Reichstag gives him the right to rule for four years. Hitler, who had originally intended to seize power by revolution, ascends without any violence. The Social Democrats are opposed to this action, however; the Catholic Center Party supplies the necessary votes.

March 27th 1933 — Subsequent to the League of Nations adopting the Lytton Report, which condemns the Japanese invasion of Manchuria, Japan notifies the League that it will abandon the organization in two years.

April 4th 1933 — The U.S. Navy suffers a tragic loss of men as the *Akron*, a Navy Dirigible (Blimp) sinks off the coast of New Jersey, taking the lives of all but two of the 74 man crew.

May 2nd 1933 — **(Atlantic-Germany)** Subsequent to the annual May Day celebrations, the National Socialists take the headquarters of the various independent trade unions and intern their leaders. The unions are replaced by a National Socialist (Nazi) controlled labor front and by about mid-month, all strikes and lockouts are forbidden.

May 3rd 1933 — In Dublin, Ireland, the legislature abolishes the loyalty oath to the British Crown. It will subsequently vote to eliminate the political authority of the British Governor-General.

May 10th 1933 — In Berlin, throngs of German students initiate a huge book burning, destroying thousands of books which the National Socialists, under Hitler, believe are contrary to German interests. Hitler is now striking against the Jews. Many of the books have been written by Jews. Hitler begins eliminating Jewish businesses and Jewish Doctors, and Jewish Lawyers will be prohibited from practicing. Himmler, one of Hitler's henchmen, dislikes all lawyers, regardless of religion. When war eventually breaks out, he wants to send them all to the front. Other religions will subsequently receive the wrath of Hitler. Hitler, who had been baptized a Catholic, and spent time as a child in a Benedictine Monastery where he sung in the choir, does not show much mercy to the Poles either. The Socialist parties are banned and their assets are seized by the National Socialists.

May 17th 1933 — **(In Spain)** The government begins to regulate religion. Church property is nationalized and Church schools are forbidden, bringing strong protests from the Vatican.

May 28th 1933 — The National Socialists win a victory in elections in the free city of Danzig. On June 20th, the city government is taken over by local National Socialists, however; subsequent action by the League of Nations and the Polish government working together, protects the Polish residents and ensures the city's independence.

June 14th 1933 — Hitler's inspector for Austria, Theodor Habicht, is expelled by the Austrian government as feelings between the two countries continue to deteriorate.

June 27th 1933 — In Germany, the Social Democratic party is dissolved, due to the prompting of Hitler. It had been deemed "HOSTILE TO THE NATION AND STATE." The Catholic parties follow suit on the 5th of July, as Hitler continues to eliminate all threats to his dictatorial powers. With many Communist leaders residing in concentration camps, Hitler's National Socialism seems enticing to many rank and file party members who start to accept Hitler's comparison between Socialism and Marxism. Hitler's comparison: "GERMAN SOCIALISM IS DIRECTED BY GERMANS; INTERNATIONAL SOCIALISM IS AN INSTRUMENT OF THE JEWS."

July 14th 1933 — The National Socialist Party is declared the only legitimate political party in Germany.

July 15th 1933 — France, Germany, Great Britain, and Italy, sign what is known as the Four-Power Pact, instigated by Mussolini who seeks to ensure a major power block to replace the influence of the smaller countries in the League of Nations.

Late July 1933 — **(Germany)** Hitler visits friends in Bayreuth and discloses that after he attains full power, he intends to "DISSOLVE THE MONASTERIES AND CONFISCATE THEIR PROPERTY."

October 10th 1933 — The nations of the Western Hemisphere meet in Rio de Janeiro, Brazil. A pact known as the Treaty of Non-aggression and Conciliation is signed. The Senate ratifies it on June 15th, 1934.

October 14th 1933 — Germany withdraws from the Disarmament Conference in Geneva. It also proclaims it will withdraw from the League of Nations. Japan had previously announced it was pulling out of the League. The session, convening since February, culminates today.

November 12th 1933 — It is fifteen years and one day after the end of World War 1. Today, Germany elects National Socialist candidates (against no opposition) and over 90 percent of the voters concur with the decision to withdraw from the League of Nations. Several million voters who do not subscribe to Hitler's brand of Socialism cast invalid ballots. His Gleichschaltung policy is now complete.

November 16th 1933 — President Roosevelt meets with Soviet Commissar for Foreign Affairs, Maxim Litvinov. Subsequent to the meeting, an announcement is made that the United States is re-establishing diplomatic relations with the Soviet Union. The U.S. had broken relations during 1919 due to the Bolsheviks seizure of power. The Russians are given trade status and they promise not to spread Communist propaganda in the United States. Marines arrive at Moscow on March 1st, 1934 to assume Embassy duty. The staff consists of 1 Officer and 6 enlisted men.

November 19th 1933 — **(Spain)** The first elections for the Cortez (Parliament) occurs. No clear majority is captured, however; the Clericals, Conservative Republicans and Monarchists gain 44 percent of the vote, while the Leftists gain 21 percent. Coalitions are formed, but the results are not encouraging for the country.

December 8th 1933 — This day marks the establishment of the Fleet Marine Force. The Navy and Marines have been working together as a formidable team for some time and now emphasis would be placed on quick reaction to hostilities against Americans.

January 1934 — The U.S.S. *Tulsa* arrives off Foochow, China to afford protection to the U.S. Consulate until Nationalist troops are able to gain access to the city and restore order.

January 26th 1934 — Germany and Poland agree to a ten year non-aggression pact which ensures that Germany will not attempt to take the Polish Corridor by force.

February 6th 1934 — Riots, instigated by actions of Facists and Royalists, erupt in Paris and several other French cities. The Republican government subsequently forms a coalition composed of leaders from all parties except the Communist, Royalist, and Socialist, in an attempt to avoid civil war.

February 9th 1934 — The nations of Greece, Rumania, Turkey, and Yugoslavia, sign an agreement known as the Balkan Pact, which parallels the Little Entente. Bulgaria chooses not to participate.

February 11th-15th 1934 — In Austria, the government of Dollfuss issues a decree that prohibits all political parties except the Fatherland Front. Government troops and the Heimwehr seize Socialist Headquarters. The leaders who avoid capture, abscond.

February 28th 1934 — Major General Ben H. Fuller retires from the Marine Corps, having reached the statutory age of 64. He is succeeded on the following day by Major General John N. Russell, Jr. who becomes the 16th Commandant.

March 17th 1934 — As the National Socialists under Hitler continue to move toward hostile posturing, additional nations begin to seek new alliances. The Rome Protocols are signed by Austria, Hungary, and Italy. The agreement is similar to that signed by the French supported, Little Entente.

March 24th 1934 — Congress passes legislation (Tydings-McDuffie Act) granting the Philippines commonwealth status effective 1935, and will provide for total independence in 1946

The vanguard of the U.S. Navy; Battleships on parade.

April 9th 1934 — The newly established Fleet Marine Force flexes its strength. Units from both the East and West coasts converge off the coast of Culebra, Puerto Rico to hold joint maneuvers. The Marines are now strengthened by Armor units and their expanding Air Force.

April 27th 1934 — A Pan American conference convenes at Montevideo, Uruguay. Thirteen countries including the U.S., sign an anti-war pact.

April 30th 1934 — In Austria, a new constitution is endorsed by the assembly, which in essence, gives Dollfuss dictatorial powers.

May 5th 1934 — Russia, along with Poland, Finland, Latvia, Estonia and Finland, extend their pact signed on July 25th, 1932, making it a ten year agreement of non-aggression. The Russians, aware of German activity, sign similar agreements with Rumania and Czechoslovakia during the following month.

May 29th 1934 — The U.S. and Cuba sign a treaty whereby Cuba is no longer a U.S. protectorate, a status it has held since the conclusion of the Spanish American War (1898). During August, a reciprocal trade agreement will be signed between the two countries.

June 15th 1934 — Congress passes the National Guard Act which places the National Guard under the jurisdiction of the U.S. Army during periods of National emergency or in time of war.

June 23rd 1934 — Mussolini has an Italian Fleet move into Albania, mooring at the port of Durazzo, encountering mild resistance from the government; the Italians subsequently tighten control of the country's Army and are given authorization to establish colonies in Albania.

June 30th 1934 — Hitler directs another power play. Over 75 people considered anti-Hitler are murdered, subsequent to being accused of plotting against Hitler and his regime. The executed men include General Kurt von Schleicher, the Catholic leader Erich Klauserer, and the National Socialist Gregor Strasser.

July 1st 1934 — Germany halts payment of all its international debt installments. The country is bankrupt, however; Hitler manages to continue with his arms buildup.

July 25th 1934 — A band of National Socialists seize a Vienna radio station and proclaim the resignation of Dollfuss, who is then assassinated, however; troops of the Heimwehr subdue the National Socialists. Hitler's troops are poised along the border, but Italian and Yugoslavian assistance prompts the Germans to yield for the present. Hitler and Mussolini had met previously, however; the two men are not yet amicable toward each other. At the end of the month, the government of Austria is taken over by Kurt von Schuschnigg, a close ally of Dollfuss.

August 1st 1934 — In Germany, President von Hindenburg dies at the age of 87, one day after a law had been passed, which combines the positions of Chancellor and President. In essence, Hitler, who will be addressed as Der Fuhrer, will be endorsed as president on the 19th of August.

August 1st-15th 1934 — A formal ceremony ends United States occupation of Haiti. The responsibility of protecting the island from bandits is turned over to the Haitian Army. Marines withdraw from the island by the 15th. Their presence had been due to a treaty signed with Haiti in 1915.

September 18th 1934 — In Russia, a growing concern over the rise of Hitler and his National Socialist Party, convinces Stalin, who has previously shown contempt for the League of Nations, to have the Soviet Union join the organization.

September 12th 1934 — Estonia, Latvia, and Lithuania sign what is known as the Baltic Pact, initiated because of their concerns regarding the rapid rise of the National Socialist Party and the potential threat to their existence. At the time of the pact, all three nations are governed by dictators; Konstantin Paets (Estonia), Karlis Ulmanis (Latvia) and Anatanos Smetona in Lithuania.

October 6th 1934 — In Spain, tension continues to rise as the country slides toward a civil war. Catalan President Companys proclaims the independence of Catalonia. In other activity in Spain, Communists, which have seized power in Astoria, instigate a miners revolt. The miners proclaim a Socialist Republic, however; Soldiers are rushed from Madrid to crush the insurrection. The government doles out severe punishment and the Communists maintain their course of seizing the government at the first opportunity.

October 8th 1934 — In France, at Marseilles, King Alexander of Yugoslavia and French Foreign Minister Louis Barthou are assassinated by revolutionaries, which operate out of Hungary. War is almost declared between Yugoslavia and Hungary because of the murders, however; the League of Nations intervenes and a conflict is averted.

October 16th 1934 — Chinese Communist forces under Mao Tse-tung, faced with enormous pressure from Nationalist troops of Chiang Kai-shek, abandon positions at Kiangsi Province and head toward Shensi Province, 6,000 miles distant. The arduous journey takes a heavy toll. Approximately 30,000 troops begin the march, however; due to the hardships endured during the one year journey, only about 7,000 troops reach the destination.

November 2nd 1934 — (Pacific-Japan) Information is received by the American Ambassador concerning an anti-American meeting held by the Young Men's and Ex-Soldier's Association in Kobe. Some of Lieutenant Colonel Matsumoto's remarks: AMERICA IS THE ONE NATION THAT STANDS IN THE WAY OF JUSTICE AND THE LONG LIST OF INSULTS FROM THAT COUNTRY MUST BE WIPED OUT, AND TO ESTABLISH JAPAN AS THE JUST RULER OF THE WORLD, AMERICA MUST BE CRUSHED." "WAR IS SURELY COMING . . . JAPAN HAS NEVER LOST A WAR AND NEVER WILL."

December 5th 1934 — Mussolini's Italian troops skirmish with Ethiopian forces along the Ethiopian-Somaliland border at Ualual. The Italian leader, who has eyed Ethiopia as a potential conquest for Italian expansion, will use this clash as a reason to subsequently invade the diminutive nation during 1935.

December 29th 1934 — Japan denounces the Washington Naval Treaty of 1922. It also condemns the London Naval Treaty of 1930. The agreements had limited Japan's ability to increase the size of their Navy in equal proportion to that of the U.S. and Great Britain. Japan pulls out of both treaties during 1936.

January 7th 1935 — France and Italy sign the Marseille Pact. The pact concedes some African territory to Italy, giving it a portion of French Somaliland. By the latter part of February, Mussolini sends a formidable Military force under Generals De Bono and Graziani to Eritrea to bolster Italian posture in the area.

January 13th 1935 — Under mandate of the Treaty of Versailles, an election is held in the Saar Basin. Ninety percent of the electorate choose reunion with Germany, as opposed to union with France. The area will become part of Germany on March 1st.

March 16th 1935 — The Treaty of Versailles is denounced by Hitler. He announces that Germany's Army will be built to a strength of thirty six Divisions. Actually Germany had already begun rearming and is fast increasing the size of its Air Force. During April, France calls for a conference (Stresa) to take precautions because of Hitler's intent to rearm.

March 22nd 1935 — Persia formally changes its name to Iran.

April 23rd 1935 — Poland adopts a new constitution.

April-June 1935 — The Fleet Marine Force engages in maneuvers at Midway Island in the Pacific where an American Base will be established.

May 2nd 1935 — France and the Soviet Union sign an agreement of alliance.

May 16th 1935 — Czechoslovakia and the Soviet Union sign a mutual assistance pact. If Czechoslovakia comes under attack, the agreement provides that Russia will assist, however; it stipulates that France must also support Czechoslovakia against invasion. The potential adversary is Germany. On the 19th, elections are held in Czechoslovakia and 44 seats are gained by the Sudeten Party in the German speaking section, giving it enough seats in government to become the second largest party and many of its members are National Socialists.

May 24th 1935 — In Europe and Asia, combatants are beginning to swing at each other on a consistent basis, however; in the U.S., the swinging is temporarily confined to hitting home runs. Today, the Cincinnati Reds whip the Philadelphia Phillies 2-1 in Baseball's first night game. President Roosevelt is in attendance and has the distinction of turning on the lights at Crosley Field in Cincinnati.

June 18th 1935 — Germany and Great Britain reach agreement on limiting the size of their respective Navies, with Germany suggesting it keep its Fleet at 35 percent of Great Britain's. The French express tremendous dissatisfaction with the consummation of the agreement, which in essence, condones German rearmament.

June 20th 1935 — **(Pacific-Japan)** Two life sized American Dolls (Sent by Mayor LaGuardia (N.Y.) as a good will gesture) arrive in Tokyo. They are dubbed Mr. and Mrs. America.

July 4th 1935 — Austria repeals the laws regarding anti-monarchy and restores a portion of the Habsburg property.

August 2nd 1935 — In England, the Government of India Act is passed. The legislation separates Aden and Burma from India and formulates the intended structure of the new India, which is to become an All-India Federation, composed of the provinces of British India and the Indian States. Opposition to the plan arises from both the Indian States and the Indian National Congress.

August 31st 1935 — The U.S. Congress passes legislation which prohibits the shipment of arms to all nations engaged in war. Congress also forbids the transportation of these armaments on U.S. vessels.

September 3rd 1935 — The League of Nations finds neither party at fault regarding the claims of both Italy and Ethiopia, concerning the area at Ulaula along the disputed region of the border of Italian Somaliland.

October 1st 1935 — General MacArthur, while en-route to the Philippines to act as an advisor to the newly established commonwealth, is prematurely informed that he had been replaced by Malin Craig as Chief of Staff. A previous commitment by President Roosevelt to announce the appointment on December 15th, had not been kept, to the disappointment of MacArthur. MacArthur is demoted to the rank of two star Major General.

October 2nd 1935 — The Italian Army invades Ethiopia. It captures Adua on the sixth. On the eighth, Makalle, a fortress city falls to the Italians. Both England and France try to mediate the situation. During December, the League of Nations votes to sanction Italy. Mussolini reacts by terminating ties with member nations. The British and French attempt to strike compromise, their effort resulting in the Hoare-Laval suggestions. The British maintain a Fleet at Alexandria, however; the Ethiopian situation does not convince England to declare war against Italy. Reaction in Britain against the English appeasement of Italy results in the resignation of Foreign Secretary Sir Samuel Hoare during January of 1936. He is replaced by Anthony Eden.

November 15th 1935 — Manuel Quezon, the man who had vied for MacArthur to be the U.S. advisor to the Philippines is inaugurated as Philippine President. The U.S. assumes that within ten years the Philippines will be able to withstand invasion by an adversary, such as the Japanese.

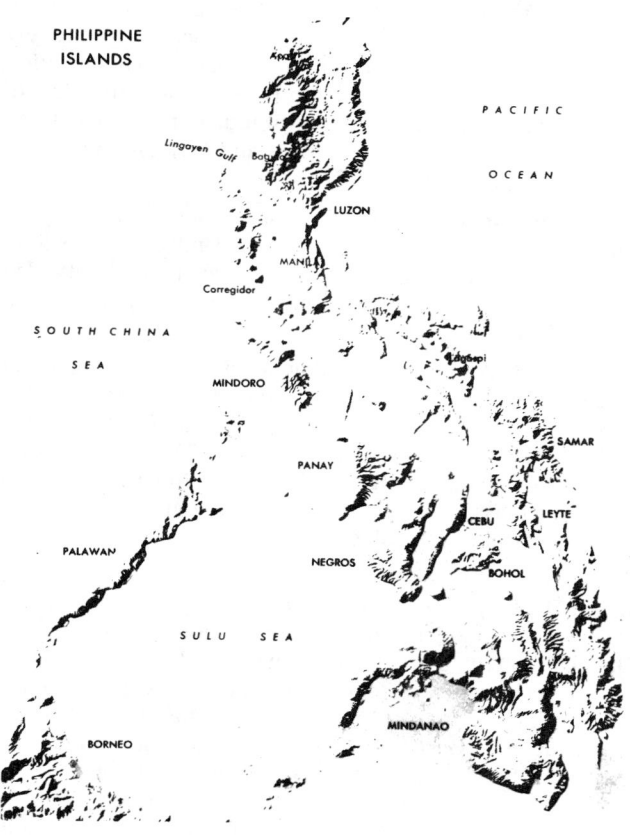

Map of the Philippine Archipelago.

Mid-December 1935 — **(Atlantic-Great Britain)** Foreign Secretary Sir Samuel Hoare, tarnished because of the Hoare-Laval proposals giving portions of Ethiopia to Italy, resigns. Anthony Eden replaces him.

January 15th 1936 — The Second London Naval Conference is in session. Japan, unwilling to agree to terms on expansion of its Fleet, quits the proceedings. Italy will follow suit. Despite the complications, France, England and the U.S. sign an agreement on the 25th.

January 16th 1936 — Spain moves closer to civil war. Election returns give a large victory to the Leftists. Soon after, Catalan autonomy is restored and the church again comes under repression, which has been sporadic for about the last forty years. Violence begins on a daily basis and churches are burned to the ground. Many of the workers feel the church is too rich and too closely associated with the upper class.

January 20th 1936 — Great Britain goes into a period of mourning as King George V dies. He is succeeded by King Edward VIII.

January 22nd 1936 — France suffers the same type of embarrassment as Great Britain had experienced, due to the controversial handling of the Ethiopian dilemma. The Laval government collapses.

February 26th 1936 — In Japan, several prominent political personalities are assassinated, in an attempt to establish a Military dictatorship. Admiral Saito, one of the victims, had spent the previous night with U.S. Ambassador Grew and other friends. General Watanabe and Finance Minister Korekiyo Takahashi are also among the victims. Thirteen Officers and four civilians receive the death penalty during July for the assassinations, however the sentences do not mention the assassinations, only that the conspirators are guilty of "employing the Imperial Army without Imperial sanction." Five Officers receive life sentences and fifty one others receive lesser punishments.

March 2nd 1936 — The United States and Panama sign a treaty, which in essence states that the United States will no longer protect the independence of Panama. The treaty also stipulates that the U.S. will no longer intervene in the internal affairs of Panama.

Early March 1936 — Great Britain invests in Air power, while bolstering its Army. Funds are committed to purchase 250 new Aircraft and establish a few Battalions of Infantry. One British Officer notes years later: "THE ARMY HAS ALWAYS BEEN ENGLAND'S CINDERELLA." Later in the month, Britain initiates a massive Naval buildup, and announces it will construct thirty eight Warships.

March 7th 1936 — Although Hitler is not quite ready for full scale war, he gambles and wins. German forces reoccupy the Rhineland, a region which had been ordered to remain demilitarized (Locarno Pacts 1925). The French and English take no action. Hitler is prepared to pull back if the Allies react aggressively. The Germans actually use the same forces repetitively to give the impression the troops are more numerous. He even utilizes a Military Band for effect. Subsequently, several additional countries, including Belgium and Italy, denounce the movement, but only with diplomatic words.

April 1st 1936 — In violation of the Saint Germain Treaty (1919), Austria's Kurt von Schuschnigg reinstates conscription for the Military, hoping to establish a superior Army than the present Heimwehr.

April 10th 1936 — In Spain, the Cortez decides to remove President Alcala Zamora from office for misuse of his power. He will be replaced in several days by Manuel Azana.

May 5th 1936 — Italian troops enter Addis Ababa, Ethiopia, the capital, subsequent to a total collapse of resistance. On the ninth, Ethiopia is annexed by Mussolini. Austria, Germany and Hungary recognize the annexation immediately and subsequently, France and England do the same (1938).

May 14th 1936 — Schuschnigg, the leader of Austria, compels Prince Stahremberg to resign from his position of vice-chancellor and Head of the Fatherland Front, eliminating the final threat to his dictatorship. On the 1st of June, Schuschnigg meets with Mussolini and by July 11th, a pact is reached between Austria and Italy.

July 4th 1936 — Ethiopia requests help from the League of Nations in forcing Italy to remove its troops from the country. Emperor Haile Selassie's plea goes unheeded and the league subsequently votes to remove sanctions against Italy. This action casts permanent doubt on the organization's ability to keep world peace and the League of Nations begins to fade away, being almost totally ignored as each additional crisis occurs.

July 17th 1936 — **Spanish Civil War** Revolution by Spanish Army units erupts in Morocco. Civil war soon overtakes Spain. By the following day, the revolt extends to the mainland. The majority of the Army and Air Force fights for the rebels. Assassinations and counter-assassinations occur and ignite the raging fires of clashing ideologies. The primary General of the overthrow attempt to restore Spain to a monarchy, is led by General Emilio Mola, whose forces are in the north, however; it becomes apparent that the rebels will need Spain's youngest General, Francisco Franco, presently exiled in the Canary Islands (in transit toward Spanish Morocco), if the revolt is to succeed against the government, which is supported by Anarchists, and Communists. The rebels are defeated in Barcelona and Madrid. As the civilians become armed, and each faction aligned to its own cause, the crisis worsens. By the latter part of July, the government controls Madrid and two thirds of Spain.

Crack troops, based in Morocco, and considered the elite of the Spanish Army, cross the straits and move to battle. Meanwhile, assistance from Germany and Italy is on the way; Planes are dispatched from both countries to aid the rebels who soon take Seville and prepare to establish their bridgehead at Andalusia. Franco arrives in Seville on the 9th of August and receives a hero's welcome, including a massive parade with a float carrying a statue of the Blessed Mother. The flag of the Republic is removed and replaced with the red and gold flag of Old Spain. The revolution receives the approval of the church, which considers it a legitimate plebiscite. The government receives aid from Stalin and the Bolsheviks in this struggle, which threatens to shred Spain into charred ruins. During August, the United States will emphasize its position of neutrality, taking no sides in the conflict, however; volunteers from the United States enter the conflict and fight for the Communists in what becomes known as the Lincoln Brigade.

The first genuine exchanges occur to the north of Madrid in the Sierras and the advantage goes to the rebels who are more disciplined. The premature enthusiasm of the government Militia becomes suspect under fire. In many instances the troops vote on whether or not to follow orders of their Officers. The Nationalists pound the government forces and initiate an offensive during the latter part of August to seize Irun. A fierce Artillery bombardment, combined with Air strikes, pummel Republican positions as the troops advance. The pressure of the bombs forces many civilians to abandon their homes and cross the international bridge to enter the tranquility of France. As the combat continues under the torrid August sun, the Republicans are pressed continually, compelling them to pull back, retreating into France. Irun is seized on the 4th of September and San Sebastian falls to the Nationalists on the eighth of October. These gains sever the Basque country (Catholic areas but aligned with Republicans) and the Asturias, from France, which leans toward the government.

After two months of struggling, the Nationalists have linked up their two Armies, and by the 5th of September are converging on Madrid, the heart of the Republican government, with expectations of a tumultuous entry on October 12th, Columbus Day. Meanwhile, in Madrid, the Marxist, Largo Caballero, becomes Prime Minister on the 4th of September. He postpones his thoughts of revolution and forms a coalition government in concert with the Socialists, Communists, and subsequently, some Anarchists. The mood in Madrid is not overly somber. Dolores Ibarruri Gomez (nicknamed La Pasionaria), a famous Spanish Communist, sings songs denouncing the "Facist" revolt and proclaims "THEY WILL NOT PASS . . . MADRID WILL BECOME THE TOMB OF FACISM."

At Toledo, a contingent of rebel Soldiers, commanded by Colonel Jose Moscardo, holding the fortress of Alcazar since the beginning of the revolution with 2,000 troops, has resisted all attempts to storm the ancient palace stronghold, virtually taunting Madrid. Government Artillery pummels the rebels. The government demands surrender. Its Commanding General urges Moscardo to capitulate, rather than force the total destruction of the Alcazar. He responds to the ultimatum: "DON'T FORCE ME TO DISHONOR MYSELF" (There are 600 women and children inside the fortress). The Republican General states: "I'LL LET YOU SPEAK WITH YOUR SON. WE'VE ARRESTED HIM." As the conversation continues, by telephone, Moscardo's son speaks: "FATHER, THEY WILL SHOOT ME IF YOU DON'T SURRENDER. WHAT SHOULD I DO?" Moscardo speaks with his seventeen year old captive son: "COMMEND YOUR SOUL TO GOD. PRAY FOR COURAGE AND LET YOUR LAST CRY BE LONG LIVE SPAIN; LONG LIVE CHRIST THE KING." A firing squad executes the boy in a few days, however; the fortress does not relent.

The ongoing siege becomes a significant symbol for both sides and great lengths are taken by the opponents. Franco diverts troops from Madrid, choosing to lift the siege before taking Madrid. The Republicans seek the aid of the Asturia miners, directing them to dig tunnels and detonate the palace. Caballaro is on site for the final assault to reduce the menacing rebels. Subsequent to an enormous explosion which plunges one of the towers into the river, the Republicans commence a full scale assault, expecting to overrun the rubble, but the fortress remains impregnable and the anticipated corpses are alive and well, under the ruins. The Republicans are repulsed and Franco's troops drive from the rear and lift the siege. The government troops retreat, rather than face possible investment. The sixty nine day saga ends on the 27th of September. Colonel Moscardo greets General Franco with the words: "GENERAL I CAN ONLY HAND YOU RUINS."

Spain is transformed into an international playground for combatants during the winter of 1936. Leon Blum, head of the French Government, had considered immediate aid to the Republican request, however; he subsequently decides on formal non-intervention, but France does send a steady flow of weapons into Spain for the Republicans. Hitler decides to send measured amounts of equipment to the Nationalists to ensure a "PREMATURE EXPLOSION IN EUROPE" does not occur. He dispatches a new unit recently formed in Germany. It is commanded by General Hugo von Sperrie and composed of Tanks, Planes and Artillery (Condor Legion). Mussolini sends over 50,000 troops to fight alongside the Nationalists. Meanwhile, Stalin enters the picture and sends enormous amounts of equipment and some troops to the Republicans. As the first Russian Ships sail into Barcelona during late October, throngs of people are waving and shouting cheers to the Sailors, however; they are not aware that Stalin has insured his investment and compelled the Republican government to ship all its gold to Moscow, prior to the arrival of the Ships and Tanks. The assistance of Stalin automatically infuses the Republican cause with volunteers from all parts of Europe and even the United States, with men who believe the fight against Facism is to begin in Spain. The Communists

units are called the International Brigades (led by Lazar Stern, a Hungarian who is called General Emilio Kleber), with each Battalion being named after a hero of the Communist cause.

During October, Madrid hears the shrill sounds of warfare as the factions exchange blows. During November, General Franco brags that he will soon attend Mass at the Cathedral. As the Republicans begin to collapse under pressure, the government leaders vacate Madrid expeditiously, accused of being traitors as they retire toward Valencia. The revolution is temporarily thrown to the wind as the Russians and Communists take the banner of Madrid and stake their reputations on being capable of holding it. The Russians roll out their Tanks and attack, however; they move too fast, making it impossible for the Republican troops to keep pace; the assault fails. Consequently, Franco's Nationalists maintain their steady advance against the city. The Communist International Brigades rush from Barcelona to stem the tide, but it is mid-November and the Communists have not fared well.

Along with the Communist Brigades, Buenaventura Durruti's Anarchists arrive to participate in what becomes the fiercest and most horrendous battleground in the history of Madrid; the battle for University City. The Nationalists close, and the Republicans resist tenaciously. Contingents of the Moroccans penetrate the city and the University area is transformed into a bloodbath. Madrid holds as heavy casualties mount on both sides, prompting Franco to change his strategy and proclaim that he would rather destroy Madrid than leave it to the Marxists. The Condor Legion drops incendiary bombs on Madrid 24 hours a day in an effort to get Madrid to capitulate, however; the citizens only intensify their hatred for the Nationalists. Russian Aircraft, piloted by Soviets, intercept the German Planes. Many of the civilians and children are evacuated, some of the children being sent to Russia. During the ferocious contest for Madrid, Durruti, leader of the Anarchists, is killed, however; the circumstances of his demise are never discovered.

Meanwhile, with Spain bisected, Franco is declared Head of State in the portion of Spain held by the Nationalists and he is called El Caudillo (a title given Christian leaders which drove the Moors out of Spain during the Middle Ages). He is also called Generalissimo in this fight to annihilate the "Reds" in Spain. As time progresses, the besieged city holds, but casualties spiral and many on both sides are executed. The Republicans gather up suspected Nationalist sympathizers and they are imprisoned and executed; over a thousand are killed by firing squads and others die in their cells. Catholic Churches are ravaged, their statues destroyed, while others are set afire. In addition, several thousand Priests and Nuns are massacred brutally. In addition ten Bishops are murdered. The Nationalists are just as vindictive and seek out the "Reds" and others, which they consider evil and persecute them.

January (1937) is another tempest with both sides pounding each other viciously. Horrendous casualties occur and both sides become exhausted. Madrid comes under another assault on February 6th, in an attempt to invest and strangle the city, rather than risk another frontal assault. Heavy fighting erupts south of the city along the Madrid-Valencia Road. The Nationalists seize Fort La Marafiosa, however; torrential rains impede progress. The Nationalists ford the Jarama River on the 10th and overrun the Andre Marty Brigade, which is nearly annihilated by the combination of storming Moroccan Cavalry and devastating Artillery fire and on the following day, the Nationalists reach the Valencia Road at Arganda del Rey. Meanwhile, the International Brigade continues to take severe losses in the absence of promised Republican volunteers. The Republicans attack steadily on the 14th, charging the Nationalists, then mount another assault on the 17th, however; the Condor Legion intervenes and the Republicans retire. Ten days later, an unwise attack against Foreign Legion troops at Pingarron, without the support of Armor, proves devastating for the Republicans. The troops including Americans (Lincoln Brigade) are struck grievously by the Foreign Legion's incessant machine gun fire. Despite the enormous losses, the International Brigade fights heroically; Madrid holds and the battle near Jarama ends in a stalemate.

On March 8th, Artillery shells precede a massive attack by four Italian Divisions, two Brigades of Italian-German Light Infantry, four Companies of Machine Gunners and about 250 Tanks and just under 200 Field Guns. Some progress is made initially, however; the Italians become disillusioned as the days pass and the weather deteriorates. By the 18th, the Republicans penetrate Italian lines solidly, and the Italians flee, abandoning their arms and ammunition as they retreat. Duce's grand scheme of glory in Spain culminates in failure and humiliation. The Republican victory at Guadalajara, which includes the disoriented retreat of the "Black Shirts" and the shredding of the Italian Legions, pumps adrenaline into the precarious cause, but it is short lived, as their first victory is also their last.

The struggle continues at a grueling pace with the edge falling toward Franco and his Nationalists. Unquestionably, the determined assistance of the Germans and Italians tilt the scales. In addition, Franco receives assistance from Portugal. During May, intense internal friction develops between the Republicans. Riots erupt in Barcelona and when the trouble subsides, the Communists are the victors. During July, the Republicans commence a large scale offensive to crush the Nationalists and drive westward from Madrid, making some progress, but the troops of Franco, recover and push the Republicans back. The intensity of battle and the pounding of Artillery and Aircraft bombardment takes a gruesome toll, with staggering amounts of casualties on both sides. Franco, sensing the kill, pivots and drives toward the sea. The tedious drive overpowers the beleaguered Republicans whose positions begin collapsing at every turn and Franco's troops reach the Mediterranean Sea during July of 1938. The Republicans, exhausted, but not prepared to capitulate, mount fierce resistance and initiate an attack which plunges 100,000 men across the Ebro River during late July, in a desperate move to turn the tide and prove the Republican cause can win. The brutality of the contest rises to a crescendo between August 1st and November 15th, however; by the 15th, the Republicans lose all ground gained since the initial assault. The Republicans had once again exhibited great courage in battle against superior forces, however; the Battle of Ebro seals the fate of the Republic. The Nationalists shatter the opposition and disintegrate the Republican Northern Army. This is followed by the effortless capitulation of Barcelona on January 26th, 1939. Madrid still breathes, but the Republican pocket is shrinking drastically. Remnant Republicans begin a flight to France, attempting to escape reprisals.

Both sides have shown little mercy during the agonizing war. The grotesque realities of warfare have been profoundly exhibited during these three years of murderous combat. The revolution ends victoriously on March 28th, 1939, when Franco accepts the Republicans unconditional surrender. White sheets are flung from nearly every window as Franco's victors enter Madrid. This menacing ordeal, which has shed oceans of blood will not subside. Purges are initiated instantaneously; about 200,000 Reds receive either prison sentences or are shot by firing squads. About 600,000 Spaniards are lost during the war. Subsequently, Spain remains at peace, while most of the world is at war. This the prelude, has decimated Spain. Her men and resources have been drained and full recovery is decades away. The U.S., which remained neutral throughout the ghastly ordeal, recognizes the Franco government on April 1st.

Opinions vary widely after the cessation of hostilities. Some say democracy is gone forever and that Spain had been deserted. Others call it a victory for Facism. And yet others are jubilant that the Anarchists and Communists failed to gain power. One thing is certain; Hitler and Mussolini had given whole hearted assistance to Franco. The Russians, under Stalin had not committed an equal amount of support to the Republicans. When war does break out on a global basis, General Franco, who owes his victory to Hitler and Mussolini, does not join their cause, choosing not to fight against the Allies, but rather, to remain neutral. Spain does not become Facist, nor Communist, but rather Frankist, and his regime lasts almost forty years with the sanction of the Army and the church. The Bourgeois (who fully realize the consequences if the Communists had vanquished Franco, also accept the Generalissimo.

July 19th 1936 — In China, Chiang Kai-shek gains control of Kwantung, despite strong Japanese opposition.

July 20th 1936 — In Portugal, Spanish General Jose Sanjurjo is killed when his Plane fails to execute a safe takeoff from a remote Airfield near Lisbon. He had been scheduled to assume the position of Spanish Head of State if the ongoing revolt succeeds.

August 7th 1936 — The United States states that it will remain neutral and provide no intervention to either side during the hostilities in Spain.

August 11th 1936 — Austria and Germany reach agreement, whereby Germany will respect Austria's independence.

August 12th 1936 — The U.S.S. *Augusta* arrives at Shanghai. A combined Navy-Marine contingent of 100 men lands to reinforce the 4th Marines. Additional Marines from the Philippines soon arrive, bringing total Marine strength in Shanghai to 2,536 men, enabling them to continue their defensive stance during the political crisis between China and Japan.

August 15th 1936 — In Spain, Badajoz falls to the rebels.

August 27th 1936 — Egypt and Great Britain reach an agreement that will permit Egyptian troops to re-enter the Sudan and permit unrestricted Egyptian emigration to the region. In addition, the pact calls for British troops to be withdrawn from Egypt, except for 10,000 troops which are to remain to protect the Suez Canal.

August 1936 — Stalin continues to purge the Soviet Union of leaders considered unloyal. Some, including Kamenev and Zinoviev are retried and subsequently executed for allegedly plotting with foreign nations to overthrow Stalin.

U.S.S. Arizona (BB-39) on duty during the 1930's.

September 4th 1936 — In Spain, a new Popular Front Government is organized in Madrid. Its leader is Largo Caballero, an ex-Socialist, turned Marxist. The Basques and Catalonians are both represented. Meanwhile, Irun is seized by the rebels. San Sebastian is seized on the eighth.

September 9th 1936 — France and Syria sign a treaty of alliance. On the 13th, France signs an agreement with Lebanon.

September 27th 1936 — In Spain, the ancient palace of Alcazar, which has been held by rebels since the beginning of the revolution is relieved, as troops under Franco arrive.

October 2nd 1936 — In France, the Socialist government, plagued by rampant inflation, devalues the franc. The U.S. and Great Britain pour economic help into France to prevent a chaotic world money market.

October 6th 1936 — (Atlantic-Germany) Captain Reinhard Gehlen is assigned to General Staff Operations. At the beginning of World War II, he is Senior General Staff Officer of the German 213th Infantry Division, however; he becomes Lt. Colonel, and during April 1942 is given control of "Foreign Armies East," and maintains thorough intelligence files on every concept of the Russian military and their strategies for post war days.

October 8th 1936 — The Popular Front Government of Spain authorizes autonomy for the Basque Provinces. Its first President will be Jose Aguirre.

October 14th 1936 — Belgium reneges on its alliance with France. The occupation of the Rhineland by the Germans prompts the action.

October 25th 1936 — Germany and Italy establish the Berlin-Rome Axis.

November 3rd 1936 — President Roosevelt wins the election in a landslide, taking almost 28,000,000 votes to his opponent's (Landon) 16,000.

November 6th 1936 — (Spain) General Franco initiates the siege of Madrid.

November 25 1936 — Germany and Japan sign the Anti-Comintern Pact. Italy joins subsequently.

December 1936 — (United States) The United States Submarines, built between 1935 and 1936 (Perch and Pike Classes), are capable of traveling at a speed of 20 knots on the surface and at 10 knots while submerged, with a cruising range of 12,000 miles. During 1938 and 1939, these Submarines, weighing in at 1,320 tons, will be surpassed by a newer Submarine (Sargo Class), 1,450 tons and formidably armed with eight torpedo tubes and either a 3" deck gun or a machine gun.

December 10th 1936 — (England) King Edward VIII abdicates the throne to marry an American woman, Wallis Warfield Simpson He is succeeded by his brother, King George VI.

January 20th 1937 — President Franklin Roosevelt is inaugurated (second term as President).

March 14th 1937 — (Vatican) Pope Pius XI issues an encyclical "On the Condition of the Church in the German Reich." Hitler initiates action to drive the clergy from their pulpits and many are sent to concentration camps. The encyclical emphasizes that racism and paganism is essential to the National Socialist Party (Nazism).

March 25th 1937 — A non-aggression pact is signed between Italy and Yugoslavia.

April 26th 1937 — (Spain) German Bombers unleash a horrendous bombardment of Guernica, a Basque village. There is no Military advantage to the raid which causes concern throughout the world. It is inhabited by civilians, many of them being killed or wounded.

May 1st 1937 — President Roosevelt signs the 3rd Neutrality Act which expands the previous Neutrality Acts of both 1935 and 1936. Though the U.S. had leaned toward isolationism, upcoming events will shift America in the other direction. The Japanese are on the move in the Pacific and the Germans are preparing to initiate new conquests in Europe.

May 6th-8th 1937 — A German Dirigible, the Hindenburg, crashes while attempting to land at Lakehurst Naval Air Station in New Jersey and rescue operations begin immediately. Thirty six of the 97 passengers are killed. A contingent of U.S. Marines, commanded by Lt. Colonel W. Galliford, assist in the rescue and also assume duty positions, to insure no rioting erupts. There is some thought that sabotage is responsible for the crash, but this theory is never substantiated.

May 17th 1937 — In Spain, the Popular Front Government of Largo Caballero is replaced by a government led by Socialist Juan Negrin. Subsequently, it takes control of the Catalan Government, stripping the area of its autonomy.

May 28th 1937 — **(Great Britian)** Neville Chamberlain becomes Prime Minister, replacing Stanley Baldwin who retires.

June 12th 1937 — In the Soviet Union, Stalin continues to purge his enemies. Marshall Michael Tukhachevesky and seven other Generals are tried and executed. Subsequently, about 35,000 Officers fade from the scene within the next several months by arrest and execution, while some simply vanish. Other high ranking officials had been executed in January, as Stalin rids the Army and Diplomatic Service of all possible adversaries.

June 18th 1937 — In Spain, the rebels take Bilbao, situated in Basque country.

July 8th 1937 — In London, a report is issued (Peel Report), calling for termination of the Palestine Mandate. It recommends partitions, containing Arab and Jewish states; Britain is to retain authority over Bethlehem and Jerusalem, in addition to controlling a path to the sea. Neither the Arabs, nor the Jews are in favor of the suggestion. During early August, the World Zionist Congress endorses the plan, however; adjustments favoring the Jews are made prior to the endorsement. The plan is still denounced by non-Zionist Jews.

July 9th 1937 — The Moslem states of Afghanistan, Iran, Iraq, and Turkey sign a non-aggression pact.

July 12th 1937 — **(Atlantic-Soviet Union)** The official Soviet newspaper Pravda announces the execution of Marshal Tukhachevsky, Generals Yakir, Uberevich, Kork, Primakov, Feldman, Putna and Eideman, the latter choosing suicide rather than arrest. Death comes as a result of being accused of overthrowing the government. Stalin's purge continues and during March of 1938 most leaders of the Old Guard will be executed as part of the wretched scheme of Stalin. His tyrannical rule virtually jails millions of innocent people (Yezhovschchina).

July 19th 1937 — In France, a new government is established by Camille Chautemps, subsequent to the resignation of the Leon Blum government. Chautemps is a Radical Socialist. Blum remains as vice-premier.

July 28th 1937 — In China, the Japanese seize Peking. On the following day, Tientsin capitulates. Chiang Kai-shek does not accept Japanese offers of settlement, however; the Chinese are poorly prepared and not yet ready to fight a full scale war. By the end of August, Japan's Imperial Navy will have the entire China coast blockaded.

August 8th 1937 — Chinese troops kill two Japanese Marines at Shanghai, prompting the Japanese to send in a Naval force, followed by Army units. Chinese, however; force them to withdraw.

August 29th 1937 — The Soviet Union and China sign a non-aggression pact.

Japanese troops moving through Shanghai.

September 8th 1937 — A Pan-Arab conference convenes at Bludan, Syria, resulting with a condemnation of the Peel Plan. The Arab nation representatives make many demands, including an end to Jewish immigration and the cessation of any thoughts of a national Jewish homeland.

October 13th 1937 — Germany informs Belgium that it is secure and safe, provided it does not enjoin any Military actions against Germany.

November 24th 1937 — The Brussells Conference ends without success. It had convened in an attempt to terminate the hostilities between China and Japan.

December 5th 1937 — In Spain, the Republicans mount an offensive to thwart Franco's Nationalists. Terulel is seized on the 19th, however; the offensive soon begins to stall.

December 7th 1937 — The Turkish Government abandons its treaty with Syria, in effect since 1926.

December 12th 1937 — Japanese Aircraft attack and sink the U.S.S. *Panay* on the Yangtze River. The *Panay*, which has Embassy Staff aboard is in transit from Nanking along with three Standard Oil Boats (also sunk). The U.S. is infuriated, but takes no retaliatory measures. Japan apologizes on the 14th.

December 13th 1937 — The Chinese lose Nanking to the Japanese after a vicious fight that drains their strength and compels a withdrawal.

January 1938 — President Roosevelt asks Congress to appropriate additional money to strengthen the Armed Forces and he seeks to emphasize the necessity of a larger and better U.S. Navy. During 1938 and continuing into 1939, the U.S. continues to modernize its Navy. The Sargo class Submarines are commissioned in 1936, followed during 1940 by the Tambor class Submarine. These travel at a speed of 21 knots, weigh 1,475 tons and carry a 3" deck gun, 2 machine guns and are equipped with ten torpedo tubes. Unfortunately, the Navy will be plagued with defective torpedoes during the first part of World War II. During 1941, the Gato class Submarine enters the scene with 1,500 tons, a surface speed of 20 knots and retaining the firepower of the Tambor class. This class Submarine continues playing a primary role against the Japanese and German Fleets.

January 4th 1938 — Great Britain suspends its plan to partition Palestine. The Jews and Arabs both increase their acts of terror. Meanwhile, British troop strength is raised to well over 25,000, to control the situation.

January 10th 1938 — In China, the Japanese seize Tsingtao.

February 2nd 1938 — A U.S. Navy Seaplane, the PBY-2, No. 0463, becomes severely damaged, while participating in tactical operations, off the coast of California. Lieutenant Carlton Hutchins buys time for the balance of the crew to bail out, by maintaining control of the Aircraft. Hutchins loses his life as the Plane crashes, but is awarded the Medal of Honor for his heroism.

February 4th 1938 — In Germany, Hitler accelerates his quest to gain absolute control. The National Socialists initiate a major reorganization, displacing various conservative leaders, which presently hold important positions. Werner von Fritsch, Commander in Chief of the German Army is replaced by Heinrich von Brauchitsch; Constantin von Neurath, Foreign Minister, is succeeded by Joachim von Ribbentrop and Hitler takes the leadership of the Ministry of War, replacing Werner von Blomberg. About a week later, Hitler confers with Schuschnigg at Berchtesgaden (Eagle's Nest) and extorts cooperation from the Austrian leader in placing National Socialists in his cabinet. Shortly afterward, Arthur Seyss Inquart is appointed Minister of the Interior.

February 15th 1938 — General Franco's Nationalists retake Teruel, then bolt for the Mediterranean Sea. His troops seize Vinaroz, isolating many Republican Soldiers at Castille. The Nationalists keep advancing, supported by the Condor Legion.

February 25th 1938 — In England, disputes concerning the government's policy toward Italy prompts the resignation of Anthony Eden. Lord Halifax succeeds him as Foreign Secretary.

February 20th 1938 — Hitler, a persuasive orator, bellows another of his speeches, detailing his intent to guarantee protection of Germans residing in other nations. Within a couple of days, his remarks land heavily in Austria. While calling for Austrian independence, Schuschnigg also emphasizes that Austria will guarantee protection to the Germans in Austria.

February 28th 1938 — A contingent of 200 Marines led by Lieutenant W.C. James departs Peiping, China, to establish an outpost at Tientsin, in conjunction with existing forces of the U.S. Army.

March 1938 — Stalin continues to exterminate opponents to his regime. Several more high ranking Bolshevik leaders are tried and executed, subsequent to being convicted of attempting to restore capitalism. The N.K.V.D. (People's Commissariat of Internal Affairs), the forerunner of the K.G.B., is responsible for the operations.

March 4th 1938 — The tone of Hitler's speeches continues to signal alarm throughout Europe. Czechoslovakia proclaims its intention to meet any adversarial intervention with force. With the seizure of Austria on the 12th, Czechoslovakia's borders are almost surrounded by German held territory. France and Russia announce their intent to respect their respective treaties with Czechoslovakia and commit support if it becomes necessary. Meanwhile, Hitler continues the facade and will proclaim his strong desires for an amicable relationship between Germany and Czechoslovakia.

March 12th-14th 1938 — Hitler dispatches troops into Austria on the 12th in the infamous "Anschluss" and proclaims on the following day that "Austria is united with Germany." About a week prior to the occupation, Kurt von Schuschnigg resigns as Chancellor of Austria (demanded by Hitler.) He will be imprisoned without trial by the National Socialists. On the 14th, Hitler arrives in Vienna. The National Socialists initiate a massive terror campaign to exterminate the opposition. Many commit suicide, while others are corralled and shipped to prison camps. Some of the more fortunate are able to escape. In addition to these atrocities against people of all faiths, the National Socialists initiate persecution of the Jews in Austria. The Jewish people are not unaccustomed to anti-Jewish sentiment, however; none expect the venom Hitler doles out because of his obsession to cleanse the world. Many of the Jews in Germany do not expect to feel the wrath as they assume his vindictiveness will only be leveled against the Jews from the east (Soviet Union).

March 1938 — The U.S. and Great Britain are startled, as Mexico seizes American and British oil companies. Attempts are made to reverse the seizure, however; Mexico refuses to relent, and subsequently consummates agreements with Germany and Italy to appropriate oil in exchange for manufactured goods.

April 16th 1938 — A premature agreement is reached between Great Britain and Italy concerning stability in the Mediterranean. It is understood that Britain will recognize the Italian seizure of Ethiopia, upon the departure of Italian forces from Spain at the conclusion of the ongoing civil strife.

April 1938 — In Czechoslovakia, disturbances develop, as German leaders in the Sudeten region demand autonomy and other concessions from the government. Prague is urged by France and England to offer some concessions, however; it remains firm. Subsequently, the situation becomes grave, but warnings from France and England to Germany, prove effective and the crisis ends temporarily. During September, street riots are reinitiated by the German speaking factions.

April 25th 1938 — In Ireland, successful negotiations between the Irish and Great Britain conclude with a three year pact which stipulates the end of tariffs between the two countries. In addition, Ireland receives England's Irish coastal defenses.

April 30th 1938 — The League of Nations receives a request from Switzerland, that it be given full neutrality. The request receives an affirmative answer, and Switzerland will not participate in any subsequent sanctions against any warring nations.

August 1938 — Mussolini initiates his method of terrorizing the Jews in Italy. His doctrine forbids inter-marriage between Gentiles and Jews. In addition, Jews are forbidden to attend or teach in schools and those that arrived in Italy subsequent to 1919 are deported. The deportation of Jews isn't entirely new. England had expelled the Jews during the year 1290 and France expelled its Jews during the year 1394. Spain and Portugal had also expelled its Jews. During March of 1492, an edict had been issued in Spain that any Jew remaining in Aragon, Castile, Sardinia or Sicily, would face death unless he becomes baptized. The expelled Jews (Spain and Portugal) find refuge in the Turkish Ottoman Empire (Balkan Peninsula from the Danube to the Peloponnesus), including such areas as Moldavia, Crimea, Mesopotamia. Despite the anti-Jewish feelings throughout the centuries, the Jews manage to survive, however; nothing they have encountered will equal Hitler's plan of total extermination. In addition to extreme hardships, the Jews have been suppressed with heavy taxes and most often forced to leave behind their wealth prior to leaving a country.

September 12th 1938 — Hitler demands the Sudeten be granted self-determination. Czechoslovakia reacts by implementing martial-law. Within about a week, British Prime Minister Chamberlain confers with Hitler at Berchtesgaden. The meeting which is supported by the French, culminates with Chamberlain offering to appease Hitler by permitting him to annex regions where more than fifty percent of the citizens speak German, however; Hitler's thirst cannot be quenched with the proposal. He insists it is insufficient. Meanwhile, while the British and French continue to find a solution and press Czechoslovakia to concede, Poland and Hungary stake claims on portions of Czechoslovakia.

September 29th 1938 — The British and French sign an agreement with Hitler and Mussolini at a conference in Munich, permitting Germany to take possession of the Sudetenland, a portion of Czechoslovakia, inhabited mainly by German speaking people. The Munich Agreement is later seen as a move to appease Hitler, who has been clamoring for self government. Chamberlain, had met with Hitler for a second time in an effort to solve the problem, but the British disagreed with Hitler's demands. This conference had been set as a compromise. No Czechoslovakians attend the meeting. Political repercussions in both France and Britain are severe.

October 1938 — Czechoslovakia is run through a shredding machine. The Germans consume about 10,000 square miles. This is followed by Poland reclaiming and occupying Teschen, which had been confiscated from them by Czechoslovakia during 1920. Slovakia and Ruthena are given autonomy on the 6th and 8th respectively, the latter under the name of Carpatho-Ukraine. In addition, with German domination, the Jews will be persecuted and the Communist Party disbanded, but many non-Jews are also killed and placed in concentration camps. Many Jews had settled in Poland centuries before, when they had been expelled from Lithuania (1495). The Jews had experienced severe treatment here during the 1600's when Sweden and the White Russians invaded Poland. It is estimated that about 100,000 Jews had lost their

lives in Great and Little Poland between 1648-1658. Now the plight of the Jews becomes even more grave. Hitler does not banish or offer an option of baptism; his solution is extinction. Unfortunately, the Jews have no homeland to seek refuge.

October 1938 — **(China)** The Japanese continue to tramp over Chinese resistance. Heavy bombardment precedes Japanese seizure of Canton. Pressure forces the Chinese to retreat toward Chungking, permitting easy access to Hankow a few days later. The successes have strangled Chinese ports and supply lines, restricting resupply to the Burma Road or by transporting the supplies from the Soviet Union.

Japanese seizing a Chinese town.

November 9th-10th 1938 — In Germany, the National Socialists instigate a massive demonstration following the assassination of a French embassy official by a Jewish refugee, a teenager, Herschel Greenspan. Throngs of National Socialists attack the Jewish areas, badgering and bludgeoning many. About one hundred are killed and thousands are sent to concentration camps. In addition, synagogues and houses are set afire. The massacre is remembered as "KRISTALLNACHT." Hundreds of thousands of European Jews had emigrated to England and the United States during the early 1900's, however; there isn't much that they can do to help the European Jews at this time. During these trying times, many countries including the U.S. are not willing to accept Jewish refugees. There will be much discussion on the subject and many will accuse the President and other leaders of the West from not doing enough for the Jews. The Pope (Pius XII) will receive harsh criticism later, however; the Catholic church is responsible for concealing more Jews than any other organization in the world.

November 14th 1938 — Tension between the United States and Germany rises, prompting the U.S. to recall its German Ambassador for consultation, which is just one step short of breaking diplomatic relations. Germany retaliates four days later by recalling its Ambassador to the United States.

November 26th 1938 — Poland and the Soviet Union renew their non-aggression pact.

December 6th 1938 — France and Germany consummate a friendship accord. Hitler claims Germany is not intending to take any adversarial steps against France. Subsequently, he makes several speeches reinforcing Germany's peaceful intentions.

December 1938 — (United States) In response to a Gallop Poll, over eighty percent of those polled respond yes to the question: "SHOULD THE UNITED STATES INCREASE THE STRENGTH OF ITS ARMY?" Americans have been watching the developments in Europe and at home where German Americans are marching throughout the U.S., carrying the American and the Nazi flags.

January 17th 1939 — Denmark, Estonia, and Latvia conclude an agreement with Germany (non-aggression), however; Finland, Norway and Sweden, professing intent to remain neutral, decline to sign the agreement.

January 26th 1939 — In Spain, the Nationalists seize Barcelona without encountering any resistance.

March 1939 — (Spain) The present Republican Premier, Juan Negrin, seeks exile in France, following a coup. Republican General Jose Miaja establishes a new government and subsequently seeks a settlement with General Franco. France and England had recognized the government of Franco as legitimate, during late February. **(Czechoslovakia)** The government in Prague ousts Premier Tiso. Hitler decides to support him and calls Czech President Emil Hacha to Berlin where the President and his Foreign Minister, Frantisek Chvalkovsky are convinced to put Czechoslovakia under the arm of Germany, with a personal guarantee of autonomy. Within days, (14th-15th) Germany overruns Czechoslovakia. In addition, Hungary will invade and annex Carpatho-Ukraine (portion of Czechoslovakia which had just received autonomy). On the 23rd, Germany annexes Memel, a portion of Lithuania.

March 28th 1939 — (Spain) The war ends as Madrid capitulates. On the following day, the U.S. recognizes the government of General Franco.

April 6th 1939 — France and Great Britain conclude a pact with Poland which guarantees its independence.

April 7th 1939 — On Good Friday, Italy, an ally of Germany, invades the tiny Balkan nation of Albania, which lies just across the Adriatic Sea. The Royal family of King Zog escapes, eventually seeking refuge in Turkey. The throne is assumed by King Victor Emmanuel. During June a Facist government is organized.

April 11th 1939 — Hungary, now closely aligned with Germany, pulls out of the League of Nations.

Late April 1939 — Adolf Hitler, speaking to a full house in the Reichstag, sarcastically reads an earlier request of President Roosevelt, for Germany to refrain from invading specific countries. Hitler's animated speech is greeted with uproarious laughter from the crowd. The applause is tumultuous when he denies Roosevelt's request.

May 13th 1939 — The U.S.S. *Squalus* sinks during a practice dive causing the loss of 26 men. Heroic rescue attempts by Chief Machinist Mate William Badders and Chief Boatswain's Mate Orson L. Crandall manage to save 33 members of the crew.

May 22nd 1939 — Germany and Italy conclude an alliance (Pact of Steel).

May 1939 — The British call for an independent state of Palestine within ten years, however; the Jews and Arabs are against the plan. Negotiations to form a Jewish state in Palestine had been ongoing for years, with a compromise struck between the British government and the Zionists (Balfour Declaration November 1917) and given to Lord Rothschild by British Secretary of State for Foreign Affairs, Arthur Balfour.

May 1939 — Admiral Nimitz, on board the U.S.S. Arizona, at San Pedro, California, relinquishing his position as Battleship Division Commander to become Chief of the Bureau of Navigation. Rear Admiral Russel Wilson (on right) succeeds him.

June 1939 — France and Turkey sign a pact of mutual aid. Turkey had signed a similar pact with Great Britain the previous month and will shortly proclaim that it will align itself with the Allies.

July 14th-26th 1939 — The U.S. cancels a trade agreement with Japan that was signed in 1911. On the 14th, Roosevelt requests that Congress repeal the Arms Embargo, which will allow the U.S. to sell war items to friendly countries such as England. On the 18th, President Roosevelt and Secretary of State Cordell Hull ask Congress to change the Neutrality Law, and on the 26th, the Secretary of State cancels the ongoing trade agreement with Japan, that had been signed during 1911, withholding war materials. Japan, however; continues expansion in China. To date, the Japanese have not lost a major sea battle in several hundred years, however; during August, in land fighting with the Russians along the Manchukuo-Outer Mongolia border, they suffer a setback when Soviet troops gain a victory, which convinces the Japanese to settle with the Russians.

August 23rd 1939 — Germany and Russia sign a non-aggression pact in Moscow. In attendance are Vyacheslav M. Molotov (Russia), von Ribbentrop (Germany), and Stalin. Hitler and Stalin make strange bedfellows, as both realize that the pact is a smoke-screen, however; it fulfills their present needs. Stalin receives a large portion of Poland during this meeting, through a clandestine agreement.

Hitler meeting with Russian Foreign Minister Vyacheslav Molotov, resulting in a non-aggression pact between Germany and Russia. An interpreter is pictured in center.

German heavy Artillery.

September 1939 — German Armor units plow through Poland.

protested by Great Britain and France, but Germany ignores demands for withdrawal. Later, the Soviet Union invades Poland from the east. These hostile invasions had been approved by the pact signed in Moscow during August.

August 29th-31st 1939 — The iron boot of Hitler is about to stomp Poland. Diplomacy is rampant, however; all measures fail, partly because Hitler is not actually seeking a solution. German ultimatums are ignored by Poland, but a short meeting occurs between the Polish Ambassador Lipsky and the Fuhrer, on the 31st. Meanwhile, Polish Aircraft are redeployed in anticipation of an imminent invasion. To further complicate the crisis, Germans, wearing Polish uniforms, storm a Gleiwitz radio station, fabricate a warning to Germany and vanish, leaving the false impression that Poland is seeking confrontation. The raiders plant a dead Pole at the scene before departing. The raid, ordered by Heydrich (Chief of Sipo and S.D., German security systems) is led by a member of the SS. Hitler uses this as his excuse to invade Poland on the following day. By the 31st, fifty three German Divisions, under the command of General von Brauchitsch, are poised for the kill. Generals von Bock and von Ronstedt, command Army Groups Heeresgruppes Nord (North) and Sud (South), respectively. Generals Guderian, Hoeppner, and von Kleist command the Armor and the Armies are commanded by Blaskowitz, von Kuchler, von Kluge, List, and von Reichenau.

September 1st 1939 — The German war machine rolls into Poland. Poland is unable to halt the advance. Polish Divisions total less than 25, and their Artillery pieces are horse drawn. Polish Cavalry Officers lead their Horseback troops in noble, but futile battle against the German Armor. In addition, their Navy is minuscule and the Air power, that which survives the onslaught, is basically obsolete. This action will be strongly

September 3rd 1939 — War is declared on Germany by both France, Great Britain and its Commonwealth nations. On the following day, England initiates bombing raids against German Shipping. In other activity, the United States suffers the loss of 28 citizens, who are passengers on the British Passenger Liner *Athena*, which is sunk by a German U-Boat in the vicinity of the Herbrides Islands. The United States does not declare war against Germany; instead, neutrality is reiterated by the President, on a casual basis and then officially within three days. The U.S. Congress takes no official action.

September 5th 1939 — President Roosevelt issues two Proclamations of Neutrality, concerning the ongoing conflict raging in Europe and the Pacific: one in reference to the Neutrality act of 1937 (forbidding shipping of arms to warring nations) and another, which reflects on International Law. The President does, however; initiate some precautionary measures, directing the U.S. Navy to initiate Neutrality Patrols to detect, report and track any enemy Aircraft or Vessels which approach the West Indies or the Atlantic coasts of the U.S.

September 6th 1939 — **(United States)** The U.S. Navy, acting upon instructions of the President, establishes the Atlantic Ocean Neutrality Patrol. It is under the jurisdiction of Rear Admiral A.W. Johnson, Commander of the Atlantic Squadron. **(Atlantic-Europe)** The 3rd, 4th (Northern Group), and the 8th and 10th (Southern Group), German Armies converge on Warsaw, Poland. The government abandons the city. Meanwhile, the 14th Army, under General List, seizes Krakow, then lunges toward the Rumanian Frontier. The Poles attempt to draw a defense line at the Vistula River.

September 8th 1939 — **(Atlantic-Poland)** Lopsided fighting at Random, slightly more than fifty miles from Warsaw, gives the Germans a victory and in excess of 60,000 prisoners. By the following day, Warsaw comes under siege, however; the courage of the Poles permits them to temporarily throw back the assault. Poland pleads for help from the Allies, and the French respond that French Divisions are now engaging the Germans. By the 11th, Upper Silesia is seized by the German troops. The German advance, both fierce and swift, continues to roll forward. By the 11th, the French abandon their effort to halt the Germans. Warsaw receives an ultimatum to surrender on the 16th, which is rejected. Meanwhile, a Polish Army, poised near the German border for a drive to Berlin, reverses its plan on the 12th, in an effort to intercept and attack the Germans. The Armies clash at the Bzura River (Battle of the Bzura River). The Poles fight bravely, however; it is a futile endeavor, costing the Poles about 170,000 prisoners by the 18th. Warsaw collapses and the government flees to Rumania, seeking political asylum. Germany intervenes and the President, Ignacy Moscicki, Marshal Smigly-Rydz, and others are interned (18th).

September 8th 1939 — (United States) President Roosevelt, realizing the situations in Europe and the Pacific are becoming even more dangerous, declares a Limited National Emergency. The proclamation increases Marine Corps strength from just over 18,000 to 25,000 men and permits the recall of retired Officers and men. In addition, Naval strength, presently at about 110,800 men, is increased to 145,00. At the present time, the U.S. Navy has 55 operational Submarines. During the 1930s, Japanese Foreign Minister Baron Kijuro expresses his sentiments of Imperial ignorance: "THE NUMBER OF SUBMARINES POSSESSED BY THE U.S. IS OF NO CONCERN TO THE JAPANESE IN AS MUCH AS JAPAN CAN NEVER BE ATTACKED BY AMERICAN SUBMARINES." Never, is a long time and the Yank Submariners will receive the opportunity to disprove this arrogant Japanese quote in due time. The American Navy has two types of Submarines; the older S-Boats, designated by numbers and the more modern type, the Fleet Submarines, which are tagged with the names of fish. The elder statesmen of the sea, the R-Boats of World War I era, will be utilized as training Ships, teaching Americans how to defend themselves against enemy Vessels and Planes, while at sea. **(Atlantic Europe)** The Allies proclaim a long-range blockade of Germany.

September 10th 1939 — Canada, which shares a border with the United States, declares war on Germany. In other activity, British troops begin arriving in France to meet the German threat. They are commanded by General John Standish Gort (later Field Marshal 1943).

September 11th 1939 — Admiral William Leahy (U.S.N. retired), begins his tenure as Governor of Puerto Rico. Shortly, he will assume the position of Ambassador to France and subsequent to the attack against Pearl Harbor (December 7th, 1941) will be asked by President Roosevelt to become his Chief of Staff. In other activity, Germany states that it will blockade the Allies.

September 16th 1939 — The British, in anticipation of the German threat to blockade their ports, initiate a system of Convoys, hoping that safety would come in numbers. On this day, the first Halifax-United Kingdom Convoy sails. On the following day, a German Submarine sinks the HMS *Courageous* off Ireland.

September 17th 1939 — Poland, a largely Catholic nation, already under siege by the Germans, is invaded by the Russian Bolsheviks on this Sunday, the Lord's day. The Soviet troops enter Poland through an undefended corridor. Warsaw will capitulate to the Germans and Russians unconditionally on Wednesday the 27th and the country is sliced up between the two invaders on the following Friday (29th). Russian Prime Minister Molotov, proclaims that the government of Poland has ceased to exist. The Bolshevik NKVD initiates its own terror against the Poles. Hundreds of thousands of Poles are arrested and sent to forced-labor camps. The amount of people who die in these hell-holes will never be known.

September 19th 1939 — Hitler enters Danzig as conqueror, yet gives a speech, which give appearances of offering conciliation with England and France. Although, it had been generally thought that the combined forces of France, which presently commands the world's largest Army, and Great Britain, which boasts the world's greatest Navy, could easily victimize the Germans, their policies of appeasement, have been supplementing Hitler's confidence. He is preparing to attack France, against the wishes of his Generals. On the Western Front, about six months will pass before heavy fighting erupts between the antagonists. Germany will tout the French and British in the media and the front will be remembered as the "PHONY WAR."

September 23rd 1939 — (Atlantic-Poland) German General von Fritsch, builder of Germany's modern Army is killed near Warsaw. He had retired prior to the Anschluss, because of his opposition, however; he is killed while with a Regiment that he doesn't command (Honorary Colonel). He will be buried in Berlin on the 26th. Neither Hitler, Ribbentrop, nor Himmler attend the service although all three had returned to Berlin.

September 26th 1939 — (Atlantic-Berlin) Rationing for food and clothing, etc., has been in effect for some time. Today, new edicts are proclaimed, including the fact that no one may get half-soles, due to the absence of leather. In addition, a bar of shaving soap or a tube of shaving cream must last a person for four months.

September 27th 1939 — Warsaw, under unmerciful siege, including the mindless bombing of civilians, finally capitulates. The National Socialist Party regime begins its reign of terror. Hitler does not discriminate. He orders the imprisonment and execution if necessary, of all persons perceived as a threat to the National Socialists. Thousands of people are persecuted, including politicians, upper class citizens, Priests, Nuns and Jews, the latter designated for extinction. The Fuehrer orders all Jews to wear a conspicuous yellow "STAR OF DAVID" for instant identification. Stalin soon joins with his indiscriminate and methodical extermination of Poles. With the fall of Warsaw, the Germans receive another 160,000 prisoners. The initial display of the "BLITZKRIEG" is successful, yet nightmarish.

Hitler in discussion with Field Marshall Walther von Brauchitsch, Commander in Chief, German High Command about the seizure of Poland.

Late September-Early October 1939 — (Atlantic-Poland) The city of Modlin, under siege for about three weeks, is forced to capitulate. This is followed by the Spartan defenders at the Garrison on Hela Peninsula, slightly outside of the vanquished Danzig. Although, a Polish exile government is formed in England, the surviving Poles are unprepared for any fighting. Poland has sustained almost 700,000 prisoners and the tragic incalculable number of dead and wounded are unknown. The Germans sustain about 10,000 killed and 30,000 wounded. The Soviets, having invaded against undefended territory avoid large amounts of casualties. Stalin will blame Hitler for the atrocities, however; Stalin, a treacherous liar, orders mass executions of Polish troops. Fifty years after the close of hostilities, the Russian government will expose the lie (Easter Saturday, 1990) and offer to show proof that Stalin ordered the massacre of 15,000 Polish troops including Officers and enlisted men (Katyn Forest). The slaughtered Polish Officers have their hands tied behind their backs, then hoisted up to their shoulders by a Russian made rope, which is then tied around their necks. In addition, their "great coats" had been strung around their heads and mouths, which are stuffed with sawdust to forbid sound. They are repeatedly struck with bayonets (unmistakably Russian because of four cornered bayonets used solely by the Russians during 1940.) Ultimately, each is shot in the head at least once; some twice and on a couple of occasions skulls are shattered by multiple shots at point blank range. The Russians plow the bodies into mass graves in the forest and plant new trees around the site. Germans stumble upon the bodies during February 1943, subsequent to seizing territory previously occupied by Soviet N.K.V.D.

October 2nd 1939 — (Atlantic-Berlin) The British Broadcasting Company announces that British Planes had launched sorties over Berlin, however; an American reporter listening in Berlin, states no Planes had been seen or heard. **(Atlantic-Panama)** A Conference of American Ministers of the American Republics confer in Panama City, Panama. The result is the Act of Panama, which leans heavily on Uncle Sam. All the Republics attend, but it is the United States Navy that gets the responsibility. The Navy is given the task of patrolling a 300 mile deep neutrality zone, to protect their shores. In other activity, Germany informs the United States that its Merchant Vessels must permit Germans to board and search them for contraband. A threat of this type has not been made against the United States since the War of 1812.

October 4th 1939 — (Atlantic-Berlin) German newspapers take a shot at Great Britain and President Roosevelt. The Nachtausgabe states in editorial: "AMERICA IS NOT NEARLY SO ANXIOUS TO JOIN THE WAR AS ARE HERR ROOSEVELT AND HIS JEWISH CAMARILLA." The 12-Uhr Blatt runs its headline in red ink: "ENGLAND'S RESPONSIBILITY — FOR THE OUTRAGEOUS PROVOKING OF WARSAW TO DEFEND ITSELF."

October 5th 1939 — The United States slowly begins to meet possible adversarial threats in the Pacific. Today, the Hawaiian Detachment of the United States Fleet is established under Vice Admiral A. Andrew, Commander Scouting Force.

October 6th 1939 — Hitler proclaims that he has no thoughts of war against Great Britain or France, stating that German actions up to this point have been carried out to rectify the injustices of the Versailles Treaty. He brags to the Danes that a non-aggression pact had been concluded with them. He tells the Norwegians: "GERMANY NEVER HAD ANY CONFLICT WITH THE NORTHERN STATES AND WE HAVE NONE TO-DAY." He bellows further, telling Holland: "THE NEW REICH HAS ENDEAVORED TO CONTINUE THE TRADITIONAL FRIENDSHIP WITH HOLLAND." He informs Belgium: "THE REICH HAS PUT FORTH NO CLAIM WHICH IN ANY WAY IS A THREAT TO BELGIUM."

October 9th 1939 — An American Freighter, the *City of Flint*, en route to England from New York, is apprehended by the German Cruiser *Deutschland* and confiscated after claiming that it is carrying contraband. The U.S. does not retaliate.

October 14th 1939 — The German U-Boat 47, commanded by Kapitan-Leutnant Gunther Prien, sinks a British Battleship, the H.M.S. *Royal Oak* in Scapa Flow. The German raid brings special joy to Hitler, because it was at Scapa Flow, that the German Navy had its demise during World War 1.

October 18th 1939 — All United States ports are closed to the warring nations who are also notified to stay out of American waters. The United States pays close attention to the movement of these Ships, especially the Submarines.

October 1939 — The German people are informed that there is a shortage of rubbers and overshoes. About five percent of the populace will be entitled to get them. In addition, there is no cotton and only sparse amounts of wool in the land, ensuring a tremendous shortage of clothes.

October 31st 1939 — (Atlantic-Moscow) Molotov, the Prime Minister of the Soviet Union proclaims: "WE STAND FOR THE SCRUPULOUS AND PUNCTILIOUS OBSERVANCE OF PACTS . . . AND WE DECLARE THAT ALL NONSENSE ABOUT SOVIETIZING THE BALTIC COUNTRIES IS ONLY TO THE INTEREST OF OUR COMMON ENEMY AND OF ALL ANTI-SOVIET PROVOCATEURS."

November 4th 1939 — The United States remains neutral, but begins moving toward the Allies. President Roosevelt, in an effort to aid the Allies, signs the Neutrality Act (of 1939), which repeals the Embargo Act of 1937 and allows the selling of arms to warring nations, provided that cash is used to procure the arms. Another stipulation is that the goods must be shipped on non-American Vessels. The act also forbids American citizens from entering combat zones, while simultaneously naming the British Isles as a combat zone. In addition, the act calls for the establishment of the National Munitions Board, which will be filled with the Secretaries of Commerce, Navy, War, and the Secretary of State.

November 30th 1939 — Finland is attacked by Soviet Union. Helsinki, the capital, is bombed and Russian troops begin to swallow the nation. Finland, with the assistance of the U.S. makes a valiant, but futile attempt to resist. Two days before, on the 28th, the Russians had scrapped the Non-Aggression pact signed with Finland during 1932. Finland would be forced to sign an Armistice on March 13th 1940. Now the Russians, who proclaim no expansion plans, are in Poland and Finland. Soon they will receive American Arms and ammunition, to hold off the Nazi hordes. Meanwhile, understrengthed U.S. troops in the Pacific are severely short of ordnance, largely because of improper weapons and lack of American reinforcement Convoys. The calls from Washington will be; Europe first and the Japanese in due time, but that is little solace to the American wives and mothers who will be receiving news that their loved ones, in the Pacific have been killed or captured. Finland solicits the help of the League of Nations and it attempts to mediate, however; the Soviets refuse the offer and are subsequently tossed out of the organization. In addition, Denmark, Norway and Sweden maintain a stance of neutrality during the invasion and conquest of Finland. Finland had been originally inhabited by Pagans, before being conquered by Sweden during the 12th Century, and then a portion (Wyborg) of it was annexed by Russia during 1721. Russia seizes the balance by conquest during the early 1800's. By 1917, Finland had driven the Bolshevik's from the country and declared itself independent of Russia.

November 1939 — Finnish forces moving on skis to intercept Russian invaders.

December 17th 1939 — A German Cruiser, the *Admiral Graf Von Spee* is scuttled off the coast of Montevideo, Uruguay after being trapped by British Warships. Captain Langsdorf, Commander of the German Vessel, commits suicide (apparently upon orders from Hitler). Two days later, on the 19th, another German Vessel, the Passenger Liner *Columbus*, is intercepted by a British Destroyer, at a distance of only 450 miles off the coast of Cape May, New Jersey. The *Columbus* is quickly scuttled by the Germans.

December 20th 1939 — America still remains neutral, while Japan becomes more entrenched in Manchuria and the Russians and Germans are slicing up Europe. Sentiment in the U.S. still leans toward neutrality, while Roosevelt realizes the crisis is only worsening. The Chief of Naval Operations instructs the Marine Corps to dispatch a unit to Midway Island, to establish a Garrison to meet a possible Japanese threat.

December 25th 1939 — (Atlantic-Europe) Although Germany and Russia are making inroads in Europe. Christmas is celebrated on all Allied fronts. Interestingly enough, many of Der Feuhrer's troops are celebrating the holiday, singing Carols and stringing signs. In Berlin, the Christmas celebration occurs as usual.

December 1939 — Canadian troops begin to arrive in England to assist with the British war efforts. Meanwhile, Indian troops are beginning to arrive in France to assist the British.

December 27th 1939 — The British who have been pestering Roosevelt to give them assistance and to join the war effort are discovered interfering with the delivery of American mail en route to Europe. The U.S. protests strongly. During early January, the U.S. protests again to the British about American Ships being delayed at Gibraltar.

Late December 1939-Early January 1940 — (Atlantic-Finland) The Finnish Army, although dwarfed by the overwhelming size of the Russian invasion force, has fought gallantly and victoriously up to now. At the onset of the heavy fighting, the excellent discipline and training of the Finns, had knocked out about seventy Tanks in one night. By Christmas day, the Russians have sustained many casualties and have been unable to vanquish Finland. As the new year approaches, the Russians will be driven back from their positions at Lake Ladoga. By the end of the first week in January, the Russians change Commanders in hopes of a victory, and on the following day, the Finns whip the Russians again, at Suomussalmi, when a force commanded by General Siilasuvo, wipes out a Russian Division and confiscates many Artillery pieces, Trucks, Tanks and equipment. Unfortunately, for Finland, the Soviet Union eventually forces a lopsided armistice (March 1940).

January 1940 — In what would be known as the Battle of the Atlantic, German Submarines begin to devastate Allied Supply lanes of the sea. The shipping losses begin to mount, costing the Allies nearly, 500,000 tons within a few months.

January 1st 1940 — San Juan, Puerto Rico, becomes the location of the newly established Tenth U.S. Naval District; Fortunately, Puerto Rico will be unmolested during the war. In a moment of jest, after the war, an American Officer, 1st Lt. Jules Isaacs, 123rd Coast Artillery, who had spent his time in Puerto Rico protecting the coast, mentioned that he had also been entrusted with preventing enemy capture of the rum supplies on the island.

January 2nd 1940 — The post of Secretary of the Navy is reactivated. Claude A. Swanson, the previous Secretary of the Navy had died during July of 1939. Charles Edison, Acting Secretary of the Navy, since the death of Swanson, assumes the position of Secretary of the Navy. After his resignation, June 24th 1940, Lewis Compton will become Acting Secretary until the position is permanently filled by the appointment of Frank Knox, on July 11th, 1940.

January 6th 1940 — Admiral C.C. Bloch, Commander of the United States Fleet, is relieved by Admiral J. O. Richardson.

January 23rd 1940 — France and Great Britain inform Germany that all German Ships operating in the Pan- American Safety Zone will be destroyed if detected.

January 10th 1940 — Hitler informs Hermann Goering, Erich Raeder, and Walther von Brauchitsch, of his intent to launch an attack against the Western Front on the 17th of January, however; two German Officers who are transporting written information concerning the imminent offensive are forced to make an emergency landing in Belgium, close to the German Frontier. This disclosure, plus deteriorating weather, convinces Hitler to delay the attack until spring. Meanwhile, the Belgium government has advance knowledge. Despite this information, within a few days, Belgium will deny France and Great Britain access to Belgium.

January 26th 1940 — The Treaty signed between the United States and Japan (Trade Treaty of 1911) expires.

January 29th-March 12th 1940 — (Atlantic-Finland) Russia has experienced unexpected setbacks due to the skill of Finland's troops. The Soviets had previously established a government of pawns in Finland, however; now it decides to request a diplomatic settlement. Talks are initiated with Sweden acting as an intermediary, but the transfer of proposals

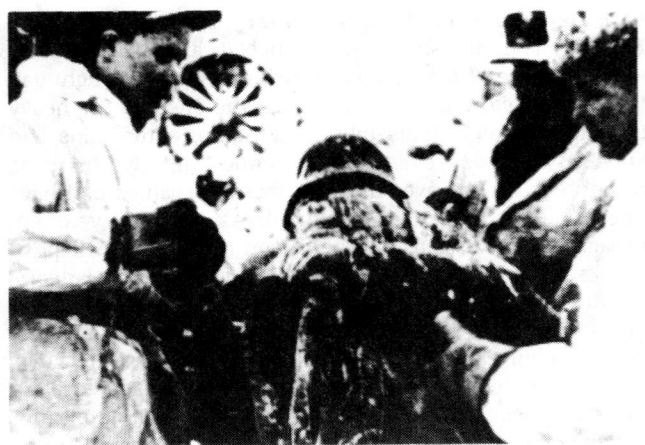

January 1939 — Finnish troops encounter a frozen Russian corpse.

prove unsatisfactory. Meanwhile, the fighting Finns are skiing rings around the Russians and shooting straight as they move, however; the procrastination of France and Great Britain, concerning aid, and the simultaneous anxiety of some Finns, who are leery of accepting their help, worsen the crisis. The greatly outnumbered Finns are pressed along the Mannerheim Line. The troops have fought valiantly, however; diminishing supplies and ammunition shortages plague the indefatigable troops and the Soviets will penetrate their defenses by the middle of the month, compelling Finland to seek an end to the hostilities.

The Russo-Finnish War ceases on March 12th. On the following day, Finland is coerced into signing an Armistice and cedes the valuable port of Vybourg to the Russians (Bolsheviks). The Russians sustain many more casualties than the Soldiers of Finland, although the Finns had a fighting force of less than a quarter of a million men matched against well over a million Soviet troops. France and England had decided to aid Finland, but the decision had been too little too late. The failure to send assistance to Finland causes the resignation of French Prime Minister Daladier about a week after the capitulation of Finland. Soon after, British Prime Minister Chamberlain suffers the same fate.

February 11th 1940 — Germany and the Soviet Union conclude a trade pact which will provide Germany with war materials such as oil and other commodities including food in exchange for the Russians receiving manufactured items including arms. This is a classic example of mutual exploitation. Neither partner trusts the other and as the agreement is consummated, Hitler already has plans to invade the Soviet Union as part of his master plan to exterminate the Bolsheviks. Stalin is willing to strike the bargain, because of lack of manufactured goods that Germany can supply.

February 1940 — (Atlantic-Germany) Himmler's personal physician, Doctor Kersten, visits a Masonic Museum, which German Officers and Party members are convinced to see. One specialist at the museum tells Kersten that World Masonry is the world's second greatest danger, after the Jews. Masonry is forbidden under Hitler. Himmler tells Kersten in part: "ONLY ONE POWER HAS NOT ALLOWED ITSELF TO BE DECEIVED, THE CATHOLIC CHURCH." Himmler then tells Kersten: "IT IS CERTAINLY KNOWN TO YOU THAT ANY CATHOLIC IS AUTOMATICALLY EXCOMMUNICATED THE MOMENT HE BECOMES A MASON ... SHE KNOWS WHAT SHE HERSELF HAS ACHIEVED WITH THIS SYSTEM AND

WILL SUFFER NO OPPOSITION LODGE." Kersten then asks Himmler why the Reich had made enemies of the Jews and Masons and also against the Catholics, instead of playing one against the other, and Himmler replies: "I CAN GIVE YOU NO ANSWER TO THAT ... THAT IS A THING WHICH THE FUHRER ALONE HAD TO DECIDE."

March 1940 — (Atlantic-Germany) Himmler speaks freely with his physician about all his inner thoughts. Today the discussion is pointed toward the Jews. Doctor Kersten mentions that he doesn't understand Anti-Semitism and tells Himmler that Jews: "HAD AT LEAST BEEN A GREAT STIMULUS IN ALMOST ALL DEPARTMENTS OF LIFE." Himmler, uninterested in the direction of the conversation bellows (IN PART): "WHEREVER THE JEW APPEARS, HE TRIES TO DO BUSINESS." KERSTEN RETORTS: "EVERYONE WANTS BUSINESS, NON-JEWISH BUSINESS PEOPLE ALSO WORK FOR THEIR PROSPERITY." Himmler, choosing not to consider the idea that Jews are simply hard working people, proclaims: "THE S0-CALLED GERMAN JEW DOESN'T WORK FOR GERMANY, BUT ONLY FOR THE JEWS." Himmler continues the tirade, accusing the Jews of controlling a "Jewish Empire" (das Judenreich) and claiming it attempts to drain all other (empires) of their materials, influence, and riches. Kersten and Himmler continue their conversation, but Himmler accepts no arguments and in fact is equal or worse than Hitler with regards to hatred of the Jews. He even claims the Catholic Church had been taken over by the Jews in the year 1077, when Pope Gregory VII became Pope. As time passes, Kersten persuades Himmler to release Jews, despite his feelings and several thousand, scheduled for death are released through Kersten's efforts.

March 18th 1940 — Italy joins with Germany and the Axis powers in the war against Great Britain and France, following a meeting between Hitler and Mussolini at a location near Brenner Pass where the Alps link Austria and Italy. Later in the month, Great Britain and France agree that neither country will attempt to seek a separate peace with Hitler.

March 28th 1940 — Great Britain and France decide to mine the waters off Norway and take offensive action to land troops in western Norway to intercept the Germans. Meanwhile, the German Kriegsmarine (German Navy) roams the seas, stalking British Convoys; some Warships prepare to debark German troops at Norway during the darkened hours of the morning of the 7th.

March 30th 1940 — In China, the Japanese establish a pawn government in Nanking.

April 2nd 1940 — The United States Fleet embarks from the West Coast, en route for Hawaii for extensive maneuvers.

April 7th 1940 — A German Naval Force embarks from their Bases, transporting an invasion force composed of several Divisions, which will land at Norway. The Fleet is protected by hundreds of Fighter Planes and Bombers. The Royal Navy discovers the enemy Armada as it sails to mine the waters. Subsequently, a British Fleet is dispatched to intercept, but not in time to halt the invasion. While the French and British prepare to land in Norway, the Germans strike with swiftness. As if it were a giant net, propelled from chutes, the landing force blankets Denmark, which capitulates within two days; Copenhagen, the capital, within hours. Simultaneously, other landings occur with lightning speed, at Bergen, Narvik, Oslo, and Trondheim, in Norway, spreading a crimson cloak upon the violated country as columns of German troops crash through Norway with swaggering arrogance. A Naval battle erupts (Battle of Narvik) off the coast, resulting in about equal losses; this is followed on the 13th by another clash that costs the British two Warships and the Germans over five.

April 1940 — Oslo, Norway after German occupation.

April 9th 1940 — Norway and Denmark are invaded by the German war machine. Germany wants to secure the inviting ports from which to strike Britain's Convoys. In addition, the acquisition of Norway will give them Airbases. At present German Planes cannot strike the British Naval facilities at Scapa Flow, which contains the British Blockade Fleet. Denmark declares war against Germany, but succumbs in one day. With the capitulation of Denmark comes the end of 1,000 years of Independence for Europe's oldest Kingdom presently ruled by King Christian X. German Bands lead a parade through the streets of what is to become the model German protectorate. Meanwhile, German troops and equipment are stowed aboard innocent appearing Merchant Vessels which creep innocently into Norway's ports, in conjunction with the invasion of Denmark. The masquerade ends as Germans pour out of the Ships, taking control of the area, virtually unopposed as Vidkun Quisling, seizes the government and instructs the fifth columnists to overpower resistance. In cadence with this operation, other Ships are steaming forward with more troops and enter the captured ports without a shot being fired against them. Bold Norwegian resistance rises and continues until the ninth of June, when the Armed Forces are ordered by King Haakon to capitulate. The Norwegians immediately begin to formulate resistance plans by establishing an underground force, which will aid the Allied cause with sabotage operations and communications to alert them about German activities. Similar activities spring up in Denmark.

April 10th 1940 — President Roosevelt, alarmed about German advances, uses the authorization of the Neutrality Act of 1939, and includes Scandinavia in the U.S. maritime danger zone.

Mid April 1940 — Allied troops debark at Narvik, Norway, to attempt neutralization of the German advance. This is followed by subsequent landing at Andalsnes and other locations, however; the German advance maintains its steady pace. Meanwhile, British units are unable to break through to Trondheim, and a later effort to reach Gudbrasndsdalen is also unsuccessful. Toward the latter part of May, France and Great

Britain (Polish troops also participate) agree to evacuate their sparse forces (no consultation with the Norwegians) from Norway. Almost 25,000 troops embark during the early part of June, leaving Norway to the German conquerors and the Norwegian resistance. The German Air Force controls the skies, however; the Royal Navy does inflict heavy damage to the German Navy during the short exchanges between the two off Normandy. When the Allies depart, they take prisoners with them for purposes of intelligence.

mid-April 1940 — Elverum, Norway, subsequent to the German advance from Oslo against British-French Forces.

April 21st 1940 — **(Atlantic-Norway)** German Planes bombard Norwegian troops which are resisting in the northern part of the country. An American Military advisor, Captain Robert M. Losey (W.P. 1929 Cadet No. 8598) is killed during the action, becoming the first American Officer to be killed in the war, which the U.S. has not yet entered.

April 25th 1940 — The United States strengthens her Naval Forces. The U.S.S. *Wasp* (CV-7), a Carrier, receives her commission at Boston, Massachusetts.

May 3rd 1940 — **(Atlantic-Greenland)** Greenland (Colony of Denmark), concerned with a possible attack by German Forces, requests that the United States provide protection. Its Governor, Eske Brun, does not adhere to Denmark's order to surrender. Greenland, composed of only 22,000 people has no Armed Forces. The U.S. is not in position to send immediate aid, prompting the Greenlanders to improvise. They raise the smallest Army in the world; fifteen volunteers (hunters), whose mission is to guard 1,600 miles of coastline. They receive the name North-East Greenland Sledge Patrol. Each man has a Sledge and a team of dogs. Greenland continues to broadcast uncoded weather reports subsequent to the capitulation of Denmark. The Allies and the Germans make good use of the information, the latter in no hurry to stop it. Greenland experiences total darkness from the end of October through the end of January, making the job of the Sledge Patrol difficult. The Germans send a detachment to Greenland during August 1942, to establish a weather station.

May 7th 1940 — The American Pacific Fleet receives explicit instructions from the President to remain in the vicinity of Hawaii.

May 9th 1940 — British troops occupy Iceland, in an effort to deter the Germans. Allied Shipping continues to receive heavy punishment in the Atlantic from German Submarines.

May 10th 1940 — **(United States)** President Roosevelt directs application of the Neutrality act to Belgium, Luxembourg and the Netherlands. **(Pacific)** Japan through its Foreign Minister Matsuoka, demands that the Netherlands East Indies maintain its economical and political status quo presently afforded Japan. **(Atlantic-Western Europe)** Without a declaration of war, the German war machine continues to advance by invading Belgium and Luxembourg, located west of France and also the Netherlands, pushing the Allies toward the sea. Swarms of Paratroopers blanket the sky, dropping near the bridges at Dordrecht, Rotterdam and Moerdijk, in Belgium. Simultaneous landings occur in Belgium near the alleged impregnable fortress of Eben Emael, while Army Groups A and B storm across the Frontier. The Germans had reconstructed an exact model of the fortress in Czechoslovakia and have practiced methodically, learning its weaknesses and seize the objective within two days.

Belgium and the Netherlands declare war against Germany, but the Dutch Army capitulates within a few days. Meanwhile the French, under Marshal Petain, anticipating the attack have fortified the Maginot Line (named for a Minister of War, Andre Maginot), to await invasion instead of attacking. Seventy Eight French Divisions are deployed along the Belgium (neutral) border, seventeen at the Maginot Line, reinforced by ten British Divisions. Ten more face Italy, while over three are stationed near the Spanish border, deployed to halt the Germans when they strike the low country. French and British troops stream across the Belgian border to intercept what they believe to be the main attack, however; the Germans implement these attacks as a ruse to fool the Allies. Bombings have driven civilians from their homes and the roads become severely clogged, hindering the advance. German Planes strafe the terrified civilians to hurry their flight.

The French disregard entrance through the Ardenne, feeling extraordinarily confident that the bridges lack sufficient strength to sustain Armor and the denseness of the forest make it near impregnable. Germans Armored Vehicles numbering 45,000 plunge through the forest, their Engineers acting as vanguard, blowing paths for the Armor to follow, reaching the Merz river effortlessly. The French order many positions to be abandoned although they are not under attack, to assist at the Meusse. Artillery supplemented by a new weapon; Dive Bombers, saturate the Allied positions on the French side of the river. The skies remain illuminated throughout the night from tracer shells and explosions, allowing the Germans to ford the river on the following day. Bridges are constructed to carry the Armor and it bolts across and rolls into the Sedan, sealing the fate of the Allies.

The German advance reaches Abbeyville on the Channel by May 21st, then diverts troops north and east to safeguard its positions along the Somme River. By the 28th of May, the Belgian Armed Forces capitulate, leaving the British and French isolated at Dunkirk.

May 11th 1940 — Winston Churchill becomes the Prime Minister of England, replacing Neville Chamberlain. He initiates communications with the U.S. and uses his charm to convince the United States to become involved with the conflict. Churchill's efforts are soon rewarded with positive help from the United States. Churchill realizes that the United States must become involved in order to defeat Germany. In other activity, British and French Troops debark at Curacao and Aruba, in the Netherlands East Indies to secure the supplies of oil.

May 12th 1940 — **(Atlantic-Netherlands-Belgium)** Clashes between German and French troops push the French across the Meusse. The Germans occupy Sedan. By the following day, the Germans push across the river.

May 14th-21st 1940 — The Germans manage to penetrate the French lines in the vicinity of Sedan, France. The motion continues and by the 21st, the British and French become threatened near Dunkirk. The Germans crash through Allied lines and reach Abbeville, France on the English Channel, encircling the Allies. German General Guderian has the majority of his Armored Divisions across the Meusse. Meanwhile, von Reichenau's 6th Army had broken through between Namur and Louvain by the 15th.

May 1940 — French troops surrendering to the German Army.

May 15th 1940 — In the Netherlands, the Dutch Army surrenders to the Germans (under threat of German Planes reducing Rotterdam). German Planes bomb the city subsequent to the surrender and about 30,000 civilians including women and children are murdered senselessly and savagely, many strewn upon the rubble in horrifying positions. The raid lasts less than two hours.

May 16th 1940 — **(United States)** President Roosevelt authorizes $1,822,000,000 for the National Defense and states the Armed Forces should receive 50,000 Aircraft per year. On the following day, the President makes clear his plan to recommission 35 Destroyers. On the 28th, the National Defense Advisory Committee will be established. **(Atlantic-Belgium)** German Armor and Infantry continue to overrun resistance. The British and French initiate a retirement toward the sea. **(Atlantic-France)** German Armor units attached to Rommel's 7th Armored Division capture throngs of Allied prisoners as they drive toward Cambrai, against disorganized French resistance. Communications between French Premier Reynaud and British Prime Minister Churchill make it clear that the Germans have vanquished the resistance and are moving against Paris.

May 17th 1940 — **(Atlantic-Belgium-France)** General von Reichenau's 6th Army enters Brussels, which is declared an "open city." The diversion of these troops from the jump against Paris, permits the French capital a reprieve. German Armor continues to overrun resistance. Elements of General Guderian's command advance toward the Oise and are met by futile French counter-attacks by the French 4th Armored Division, commanded by Colonel Charles De Gaulle.

May 18th-20th 1940 — The Germans maintain their rapid advance. Cambrai is entered on the 18th. At Le Cateau, the remaining forces of French 9th Army, now commanded by General Henri Giraud (replaced General Corap), fall into the hands of the Germans who had previously occupied the town. By the 20th, German Armor holds the high ground at Arras. In addition, Abbeville, and Amiens are taken by Germans. Meanwhile, General Weygand replaces General Gamelin as Commander-in-Chief of French Armed Forces (19th).

May 24th 1940 — The Germans push feverishly toward Boulogne and Calais, however the assault is mysteriously slowed, allowing several thousand British troops to be extricated by Warships standing off Boulogne. On the following day, the city falls. Calais follows suit soon after, and German guns will be positioned to bombard the Allies which are stranded at Dunkirk.

May 28th 1940 — King Leopold, of Belgium, concedes and agrees to surrender the Belgium Army.

May 28th-June 4th 1940 — Nearly 400,000 British and French troops are compressed on the beaches at Dunkirk, and are facing imminent annihilation. While Germany prepares for the kill, the English implement Operation Dynamo, as it is dubbed by Britain, turning disaster into a great symbol of proud determination. The English splice together a gigantic Convoy, consisting of every available Vessel; this gallant force of military and civilian Ships, scurries into the dangerous waters off Dunkirk. The Vessels suffer losses, including several Warships, but ignoring the enemy fire, successfully evacuate over 338,000 British Belgian, and French troops. Winston Churchill makes a stirring speech to further lift the hearts of the Allies and impress upon the world, England's resolve: "WE SHALL FIGHT ON THE BEACHES, WE SHALL FIGHT ON THE LANDING GROUNDS, WE SHALL FIGHT IN THE FIELDS AND IN THE STREETS . . . WE SHALL NEVER SURRENDER."

June 1940 — The United States, still committed to a stance of neutrality, begins to deliver war supplies to the British. Although America is neutral, it is clear that it would only be a matter of time before the U.S. will be drawn into the conflict. It is America's position that if war is to come, it must be provoked by an adversary.

June 1st 1940 — The U.S. Navy launches the Battleship *Washington* (BB-56) at the Philadelphia Navy Yard, becoming the first Battleship launched since the U.S.S. *West Virginia* (BB-48) launching, during November 1921 (19th).

June 4th 1940 — All British, French and Belgian troops are successfully evacuated from Dunkirk.

June 5th 1940 — **INVASION OF FRANCE** The French now feel the razor's edge of the German sword, as German troops storm into the heart of France. Paris, the capital, falls within nine days; the nation capitulates on the 22nd. Some French leaders decide to set up an exile government in England to continue the struggle. Intense political differences arise within the exiled government and the Communists infiltrate this movement. As the years pass and the Allies prepare to storm Normandy, they decline to keep Charles DeGaulle, the self-appointed French resistance leader informed, because of knowledge that his organization is infested with Communist sympathizers and German spies.

June 9th 1940 — All Allied troops have been evacuated from Norway.

June 10th 1940 — Italy, governed by Fascist, Benito Mussolini, jumps to the German cause, declaring war on both Great Britain and France. The Italians initiate hostilities, dispatching troops into France. In other activity, Canada declares war on Italy.

June 11th 1940 — President Roosevelt, once again officially embraces the Neutrality Act and proclaims the Mediterranean Sea and the mouth of the Red Sea to be designated combat zones. In other activity, Australia, New Zealand and South Africa declare war on Italy. In the Mediterranean area (North Africa), Royal Air Force Planes bombard enemy positions at Eritrea, while Italian Planes raid Aden and Port Sudan. In addition, the Italian Air Force strikes Malta. On the following day, RAF Aircraft strike Italy. In France, Paris is declared an "open city."

June 12th 1940 — The United States announces a non-aggression pact with Japan and Thailand, but awards contracts for the building of 22 new Warships.

June 14th 1940 — **(United States)** President Roosevelt signs the "11 percent Naval Expansion Act," authorizing Carriers, Submarines and Cruisers tonnage to be increased by 167,000 and simultaneously calling for auxiliary shipping to be increased by 75,000 tons in the event of hostilities. On the following day, the President authorizes the strength of the Naval Air strength to be increased up to 10,000 Planes. **(Atlantic-France)** German troops occupy Paris, France, a prelude to the total capitulation of the entire country.

June 15th-17th 1940 — Lithuania (15th), Latvia (17th) and Estonia (17th) are seized by the Soviet Union. Russia, unlike the Allies, which it will join later, liberates no one. The Communists dominate and keep everything they take, literally severing the liberty and independence of these nations that they are allegedly saving from the Germans. The Soviets actually deport the (those residing in the border regions) native populations of Estonia, Latvia, Karelia, Lithuania and inhabitants of the western Ukraine, sentencing them to miserable Siberia, replacing them with Russians which are relocated to the areas mentioned. Citizens of Georgia are also molested. By 1941, the affable Russians hold about three and a half million people in forced labor camps. This figure does not include other forced laborers which the Russians use in areas other than the camps. In addition, the populace that had been displaced from their homes and exiled without being sent to prison are not counted. The true figures of the millions of innocent people slain by the treachery of Stalin's regime will never be known.

June 17th 1940 — **(United States)** Admiral Stark, realizing the predicament the U.S. will be facing if hostilities arise, requests $4 billion to create a formidable two ocean Navy. **(Atlantic-France)** France sues for an armistice with Germany (Petain government). The armistice will be signed in a railroad car on the 22nd at Compiegne, France at the precise spot where the Germans had been forced to sign after World War 1. Hitler has the same Railroad Car transported for the occasion. This will be followed by the French armistice with Italy on the 24th.

June 18th 1940 — British Planes bombard two German cities, Bremen and Hamburg.

June 20th 1940 — (United States) The U.S. is attempting to react quickly, to the rising tensions around the globe and establishes the Bureau of Ships. Rear Admiral S.M. Robinson will assume responsibility as Chief. In unison, the U.S. decides to abolish the Bureau of Engineering and Repair. Later in the month, on the 25th, The Naval Construction Corps is abrogated and the men are reassigned to Line Officer Status, with Engineering duty only. In other activity, the position of Under Secretary of the Navy is established, to be active until the end of the emergency. **(Pacific)** The French, holding French Indo China, permit the Japanese to introduce their mission and support troops into northern Indo China.

June 22nd 1940 — Hitler arrives at Compegiegne, France for the capitulation of France. The Railroad car in the background is the original one used when Germany was compelled to submit to the Versailles Treaty at the close of World War I. Hitler had insisted the ceremony take place in the identical car.

June 22nd 1940 — (Pacific) A new Japanese cabinet is formed, with General Hideki Tojo assuming the position of Minister of War with the position of Minister of Foreign Affairs being given to Yosuke Matsuoka. **(Atlantic)** More of Europe falls to the Germans as France signs an armistice which will become effective on the 25th. The French are forced to pay the Germans 4 million francs a day for the occupation Army. A good deal of the country comes under German Military control, while about forty percent is to be governed by the puppet Vichy government. About two million prisoners of war are transported to Germany for slave labor; many die of starvation and disease. The Frenchmen are scheduled to be permanently separated from their families to cut the French birthrate, thus eliminating them as a future world power. The remaining French are given an alternative; work for Germany or face starvation. Many thousands of Frenchmen are executed for their protests.

June 24th 1940 — (Atlantic-Germany) Doctor Kersten has been at the Dresen Hotel (Bad Godesberg) along the Rhine for about a week, treating Rudolf Hess. Hess informs Kersten: "WE'LL MAKE PEACE WITH ENGLAND THE SAME WAY AS WITH FRANCE . . . GERMANY AND FRANCE MUST STAND TOGETHER WITH ENGLAND AGAINST THE ENEMY OF EUROPE, BOLSHEVISM. THAT WAS THE REASON WHY THE FUHRER ALLOWED THE ENGLISH EIGHTH ARMY TO ESCAPE DUNKIRK . . . I CAN'T IMAGINE THAT COOL, CALCULATING ENGLAND WILL RUN HER NECK INTO THE SOVIET NOOSE, INSTEAD OF SAVING IT BY COMING TO AN UNDERSTANDING WITH US." Doctor Kersten had been ar-

rested and interrogated by Heydrich during May and subsequently finds that every doctor who treats Hess is arrested by Security Police (SS). Heydrich, the head of the SS, is part Jewish and the fact is known, however; Himmler, claims Hitler picked him because he denounced his Jewish blood and further states: "THE FUHRER COULD REALLY HAVE PICKED NO BETTER MAN THAN HEYDRICH FOR THE CAMPAIGN AGAINST THE JEWS. FOR THEM HE HAD NO MERCY OR PITY."

June 27th 1940 — (United States) President Roosevelt declares a national emergency and invokes the Espionage Act of 1917, to maintain control of Shipping in the Panama Canal area and in U.S. Territorial waters. **(Atlantic)** Rumania concedes to Soviet pressure and cedes Bessarabia and northern Bukovina to Stalin.

June 1940 — Hitler stops to see Paris, while accepting the capitulation of France, however, he never returns.

July 2nd 1940 — (United States) Congress passes the Export Control Act, giving the President the power to adequately protect the national defense, prohibit or place limitations upon the exportation of Military equipment, ammunitions and other appropriate war supplies. On the 5th, Roosevelt invokes the Act against the Japanese and forbids any exportation of various commodities, including chemicals, aircraft parts and strategic minerals, without a license. Toward the end of the month, Roosevelt will forbid the export, unless licensed to do so, of aviation fuel and specific types of iron and steel, further halting the flow of needed war supplies to Japan. **(Atlantic-France)** France, the on-again off-again ally of

Great Britain, now under control of the Germans, severs diplomatic relations with the British.

July 3rd 1940 — (Atlantic-North Africa) The British attack the ports of Oran and Mers-el-Kebir, damaging French Vessels in the port. They also capture French Men-of-War which are in British ports.

July 8th 1940 — America senses danger close to its shores after France falls. The United States dispatches a force of Marines to Martinique, a French Colony in the Western Hemisphere off the coast of South America, to prevent German occupation. There is much concern over German presence in the Western Hemisphere. At present, about one million German citizens reside in Brazil and live as if they are in Germany. About 1,200 German schools exist and use National Socialist (Nazi) text books. In addition, over a quarter of a million Japanese are living in Brazil. In Ecuador, German Airlines are in operation, and the Pilots are Reserve Luftwaffe troops. German Pilots are forbidden from belonging to a Political organization, therefore, none belong to the National Socialist Party. These Planes operating from Ecuador have been modified with bomb racks and are within striking range of the Panama Canal. In Argentina, German presence is also very conspicuous, and a sturdy fifth column is poised for action if orders come from Berlin.

July 10th 1940 — (Atlantic) THE BATTLE OF BRITAIN — Germany, in preparation for an invasion of England, begins air raids in an attempt to destroy Britain's Air Fields and cities. These raids continue incessantly through August. Thanks to the resolve of the Britains and the skill of the outnumbered English Pilots in their formidable Spitfires, the German threat would be dissolved. After heavy German Air Force losses, Hitler is compelled to dismiss his plan to invade England by the end of October. England, had been badly bruised, but her Ensign still flies over Buckingham Palace.

August 1st 1940 — The United States Navy establishes the Alaskan Sector, which will be a part of the Thirteenth Naval District.

Early August 1940 — The Italians invade British Somaliland. British forces in East Africa are greatly understrengthed and will evacuate within two weeks.

August 5th 1940 — The United States is concerned about French Warships in the French West Indies, specifically about possible German confiscation and use against the Western Hemisphere. An accord to settle this problem is reached between the U.S. and France, known as the Greenslade-Robert Agreement).

July 16th 1940 — Prince Fumumaro Konoye becomes the Premier of Japan.

July 19th 1940 — (United States) President Roosevelt signs the Naval Expansion Act, which provides 1,325,000 tons of Combat Shipping, 100,000 tons of Auxiliary Shipping and 15,000 Aircraft. This action, by Roosevelt in response to the previous request by the Navy for a two Ocean Navy, will expand the Navy Fleet by 70 percent.

July 30th 1940 — (Atlantic) In a meeting held between the Foreign Ministers of the American Republics, unified action by the American Republics is mandated, the Act of Havana. Twenty-one nations attend the conference.

August 10th 1940 — England, in an effort to concentrate on the war in Europe, initiates the removal of all British troops from China and northern China.

August 15th 1940 — (Atlantic-England) Although the United States is not at war, there is still a great deal of intelligence gathering and communication with the Allies. Today, several high ranking American Officers, including Rear Admiral Ghormley and General D.C. Emmons, arrive in London for meetings with British Staff Officers.

August 18th 1940 — (United States) Sunday is normally a day off for most people in the U.S., but not for the President. He and the Prime Minister of Canada sign an agreement providing for a Permanent Joint Board to co-ordinate the defense of the U.S. and Canada, the Ogensburg Agreement.

August 19th 1940 — British Somaliland, in East Africa, is seized by Italian troops.

August 22 1940 — (United States) James Forrestal becomes the first Undersecretary of the U.S. Navy.

August 27th 1940 — (United States) President Roosevelt signs a joint resolution giving him authorization to mobilize Army Reserve Units and the National Guard into Federal service for one year. The following Saturday, President Roosevelt calls the National Guard into National Service, starting with 60,000 men whose next weekend drill will stretch for a year. The primary reason for calling up the National Guard had been the unpreparedness of the U.S. Army, because of twenty years of neglect by the United States, which had been sliding toward an isolationist position. During May of 1940, U.S. Army stands at about 185,000 men, and the Navy strength is around 120,000, including about 28,000 Marines. The Air Corps numbers about 22,000, for a grand total of approximately 300,000 men, totally inadequate to meet a genuine threat.

August 30th 1940 — (Pacific-French Indo China) The French, which have given the Japanese permission to bring their mission and support troops into northern Indo China during June, appeases them further, by granting them permission to occupy Airfields, Ports and Railroads in northern Indo China. In addition, after the Japanese move into French Indo China they request the British to close the Burma Road (6-24-40).

September 3rd 1940 — (United States) The United States, leaning heavily toward the Allied cause, agrees to transfer fifty U.S. Destroyers to England. Roosevelt fashions the agreement in this way "Destroyers for Bases." In return, England reciprocates by allowing the United States to lease strategic Military Bases for a period of 99 years. U.S. Marines are dispatched to take defensive positions at Antigua, Jamaica, Trinidad, the Bahamas and other agreed upon islands, such as St. Lucia and British Guiana. Three days later, the first eight Destroyers are transferred to the British.

September 1940 — The United States, concerned about Japan's aggressive policies, tells Japan to stay out of French Indo China. Japan pays no heed to the American warning and continues her plans of conquest.

September 9th 1940 — The Navy expansion program continues. Contracts for the construction of 12 Aircraft Carriers, Seven Battleships and 191 other Vessels are awarded to Ship Yards. **(Atlantic-Germany)** Germany gives notice that any Ships, regardless of nationality, are subject to being attacked, if spotted in waters considered to be war zones by the British.

September 1940 — German Planes en route to strike England.

London aflame following a German Air bombardment.

September 11th 1940 — German Planes bombard London again. Buckingham Palace is struck, however; the Royal family is unharmed. In other activity, Italy goes on the offensive and initiates an offensive which takes them into Egypt, however; the advance boggs down within about a week.

September 16th 1940 — (United States) President Roosevelt signs the Selective Training and Service Act making it mandatory for all males between the ages of 21 and 35 to register for the draft. Unfortunately, there is insufficient equipment and ammunition to properly train the Army. The U.S. has stripped its defenses considerably since the close of World War 1. Soldiers improvise, using stove-pipes for Cannon, bags of flour are used for bombs and Trucks have painted signs, designating them as Tanks. Incredibly, the Infantry uses mock machine guns (carved from wood). The Army possesses less than 500 genuine machine guns. The U.S. Artillery Corps is equipped with 235 Artillery pieces, and the Tank Corps comprises 10 Light and 8 Medium Tanks. In addition, the troops also implement empty beer cans as shells.

September 22nd 1940 — (French Indo China) The French meet with the Japanese in Hanoi and after signing an agreement, hand them possession of French Airfields in northern Indo China.

September 23rd-25th 1940 — (Atlantic-North Africa) British troops acting in concert with De Gaulle and his Free French force, attempt unsuccessfully to land in North Africa at Dakar. The Vichy troops fight and repulse the attempt, compelling the British to relent and withdraw on the 25th. Coastal batteries, exchanging fire with the Royal Navy,

damage two of Britain's Warships. In related activity, British Planes bombard Dakar and the French retaliate, striking Gibraltar.

September 27th 1940 — Germany, Japan and Italy sign an agreement, which will be known as the Tripartite Treaty, just after the United States issues an embargo on the export of iron and scrap steel to all nations outside of the Western Hemisphere, except Great Britain. The pact ensures that each of the three countries will "assist one another with all political economic and military means when one of the powers is attacked by a power not now involved in the European war or in the Chinese-Japanese conflict." The embargo, employed by the United States is quickly criticized by Japan. The Axis treaty, unquestionably aimed at the U.S., is celebrated in Tokyo, Berlin, and Rome, where the streets are full of cheering throngs.

Hitler and Mussolini, conferring in North Africa.

September 29th 1940 — (Pacific) The U.S. Navy arrives at Midway. A contingent of Marines and Sailors, from the Fleet Marine Force, debarks to set up defensive positions in the event of hostile actions being initiated by Japan.

September 1940 — (Atlantic-Norway) The Germans have Norway under total control by now and concentration camps are already entrenched. There are 20,000 Norwegians in one of the camps. Many of Norway's 1,500 Jews are also imprisoned here. The Gestapo has instructed all schools to begin teaching according to Nazi doctrine. The teachers (about 1,200) refuse and 10 percent are arrested and incarcerated. In addition, Catholic priests are ordered to begin teaching a new religion, as directed by Hitler; they refuse and are barred from their churches. As time passes more people join the underground, and by 1945, about 35,000 people are involved.

October 5th 1940 — (United States) The Secretary of the Navy informs the Organized Naval Reserves that they are on short notice for being called to active duty.

October 8th 1940 — (United States) The United States Government advises all American citizens to leave the Far East, due to the deteriorating conditions between the U.S. and Japan. In other activity, Japan protests to the United States, because of the American embargo on aviation fuel and scrap metal.

October 15th 1940 — General mobilization orders are issued to all Marine Corps Reserve Battalions, informing them that they shall be assigned to active duty, not later than November 9th 1940.

October 16th 1940 — (United States) Sixteen million Yanks register for the draft to comply with the Selective Training and Service Act.

October 22nd 1940 — (Atlantic-Mediterranean) Naval Task Squadron 40-T, operating in the western Mediterranean Sea area and commanded by Rear Admiral D. M. LeBreton is disbanded.

October 26th 1940 — (United States) The Marines establish a Parachute Detachment at the Naval Air Station, Lakehurst, N.J. In other activity, at the request of President Roosevelt, the Navy formulates a plan to invade Martinique. The operation calls for 2,800 Marines of the 1st Marine Brigade, reinforced by two reinforced Army Regiments, however; the assault proves unnecessary and it will be canceled.

October 28th 1940 — (Atlantic-Italy) Italy invades Greece. By the end of November, the Italians will be driven back to Albania.

October 29th 1940 — (United States) The Draft of American men for Military service is initiated. The first number to be drawn in the lottery is 158; the second lucky number is 192.

October 31st 1940 — (Atlantic) British troops debark and occupy Crete.

November 1st 1940 — (United States) The U.S. Naval Atlantic Squadron has its name changed to Patrol Force, United States Fleet. In other activity, the Navy is keeping pace with the President's plan to increase available Aircraft for the U.S. and establishes a Naval Air Station at Alameda, California.

November 8th 1940 — The United States, still neutral, loses a U.S. Merchant Vessel near Australia in the Bass Strait, off Cape Otway, after it inadvertently strikes a German mine. The Vessel, *City of Rayville*, becomes the first U.S. Merchant Vessel to be sunk during World War II. (Pacific-Japan) Admiral Nomura is appointed to the post of Ambassador to the United States.

November 1940 — (Atlantic-Germany) Himmler, speaking with Doctor Kersten states that homosexuals are to be expelled from the SS. He further states: "ITS BECAUSE WE MEAN TO GET RID OF HOMOSEXUALS ROOT AND BRANCH. THEY'RE A DANGER TO THE NATIONAL HEALTH." Himmler refers to one particular SS man which he is trying to get to change his ways. Doctor Kersten states that the individual should be given a task to prove himself, but Himmler refuses, stating: "DON'T YOU KNOW THAT THE ENEMY INTELLIGENCE MAKES GOOD USE OF HOMOSEXUALS." Doctor Kersten insinuates that Frederick the Great might have been a homosexual, however; Himmler becomes infuriated and blames those rumors on the Jews.

November 11th 1940 — The Italian Fleet at Taranto is struck by Planes of the Royal Air Force; this air assault will be followed by another attack on the following day. The Italian Fleet sustains heavy losses knocking three Battleships out.

November 20th 1940 — Germany receives another Ally, as Hungary joins the Axis Powers. On the following day, Rumania will become part of the Axis.

November 23rd 1940 — Admiral William D. Leahy is appointed Ambassador to France and will deal with the Vichy French Government.

November 30th 1940 — Chiang Kai-shek receives a bonus from Uncle Sam. The United States lends China $50 million to stabilize their currency and also gives China a $50 million dollar credit for them to buy supplies.

December 1st 1940 — (Atlantic-Alaska) The U.S. Coast Guard establishes Headquarters at Ketchikan for its Alaskan contingents.

December 9th 1940 — (Atlantic-North Africa) The British commence their offensive against the Italian Army in North Africa, rolling over the opposition and capturing thousands of prisoners and annihilating Italian Divisions, while sustaining light casualties. By mid-December, the remnant Italian forces in Italy are holding little terrain. During January, 1941, the British are attacking heavily in Libya, where they again score victory quickly, seizing Bardia on the 5th, after two days of fighting; the Italians retreat toward Tobruk, which capitulates on January 22nd, gaining the British a strategic port.

December 17th 1940 — (United States) Rear Admiral E.J. King becomes the Commander of Patrol Force, United States Fleet, replacing Rear Admiral H. Ellis.

December 19th 1940 — (Pacific) Palmyra Island, situated in the Pacific is deemed of Military importance and is put under the control of the Secretary of the Navy.

December 20th 1940 — President Roosevelt designates William A. Knudsen to head a four man Defense Board for the purpose of taking defense measures and quickening the pace of aid to England.

December 23rd 1940 — (United States) The United States Navy further expands its Air Bases by establishing a Naval Air Base at Key West, Florida.

January 1941 — (United States) The U.S. begins to bolster its Pacific defenses. The Marine 3rd Defense Battalion is ordered to Midway. Contingents of the 1st Battalion would be dispatched to Johnston and Palmyra. The Marines 6th Defense Battalion is sent to Pearl Harbor.

January 5th 1941 — William D. Leahy, Admiral U.S.N., retired, arrives in France in the capacity of U.S. Ambassador to the Vichy government. Leahy had been, until recently, the appointed Governor of Puerto Rico (11/17/1940). As the hostilities in the world continue to escalate, President Roosevelt will recall Leahy from France to become his Chief of Staff.

January 6th 1941 — (United States) President Roosevelt addresses the 77th U.S. Congress. During his speech, he emphasizes the importance of the U.S. assuming the position of "the arsenal of Democracy." He further states: "WE SHALL SEND IN EVER INCREASING NUMBERS; SHIPS, PLANES, TANKS, GUNS. THAT IS OUR PURPOSE. THAT IS OUR PLEDGE."

January 16th 1941 — (United States) President Roosevelt, intent on expanding the U.S. supply of Merchant Vessels, requests $350 million to build 200 Ships.

January 1941 — (Greece) The aging Prime Minister, General Metaxas succumbs. He is succeeded by Alexandros Korizis. (North Africa) The British seize Derna, Tripoli, and on the following day, the Italians begin retreating from Benghazi.

January 29th-March 27th 1941 — (United States) The British and Americans confer in Washington D.C. to formulate a plan which would be known as ABC-1. These mysterious meetings conclude, after agreement, that if the U.S. would enter the conflict, the priority would be to defeat Germany first, but also to allow sufficient American forces to stabilize the Japanese threat in the Pacific.

January 30th 1941 — (Atlantic-Germany) Germany proclaims that any Ships, regardless of nationality, will be destroyed if they attempt to bring aid to England.

Late January-Early April 1941 — (Atlantic-Italian East Africa) Toward the end of January, British troops (Indian 4th Division), attack and seize Jalib, Somaliland, routing the Italian troops there. Within about a week, the British initiate the battle to seize Keren, which capitulates by the end of March. By mid-February, Kismayu is taken by South African and African troops. Soon after, Free French Forces arrive, landing at Eritrea. The Italians continue to fall back and by the latter part of February, Mogadishu falls to contingents of East and West African troops, and by mid-March, additional British forces arrive in British Somaliland and drive against the Italians, pushing them toward Ethiopia. The Italians are also driven from Diredawa (Ethiopia) during the end of March. Mussolini's Armed Forces are performing poorly against the Allies. The 4th and 5th Indian Divisions seize Asmara in Eritrea on the first of April, pressing the Italians further. On the following day, five Italian Destroyers embark from Massawa to escape the encroaching British. Royal Air Force Planes bomb the Vessels. None reach Port Sudan. The Italians abandon Addis Ababa, Ethiopa, leaving the Ethiopian capital for the British to occupy by the 6th of April. By the following day, Massaway, another Italian bastion, folds ingloriously, its defenders sustaining heavy casualties. Dessie is assaulted toward the end of April, and taken effortlessly, permitting the British to move against Amba Alagi. During early May, the Italians thwart two attacks against Amba Alagi, however constant British pressure collapses the city by 16 May. The British then attack toward Gala Sidamo and the Gondar regions. This resistance is crushed by the Indian-British forces by mid-July, however; a few Italian units manage to resist until November.

February 1941 — (Atlantic-Cuba) The Marines bolster their positions at Guantanamo, Cuba, reinforce the Hawaiian Islands and fortify Midway.

February 1st 1941 — (United States) The United States Navy makes several changes. The names Atlantic Fleet and Pacific Fleet are reinitiated; the Asiatic Fleet retains its name. Admiral E.J. King becomes Commander in Chief, Atlantic Fleet, previously called Patrol Force, United States Fleet. Admiral H.E. Kimmel assumes command of the United States Pacific Fleet, but is also given responsibility of United States Fleet as a whole. Kimmel replaces Admiral J. O. Richardson as Commander in Chief of Pacific Fleet. Admiral Hart, who will be in the Philippine area when war breaks out, becomes Commander in Chief of the Asiatic Fleet.

February 6th 1941 — (Atlantic-North Africa) The British take the port of Benghazi in North Africa. The Italians are pounced upon as they continue to withdraw. Again, thousands of troops are captured (approximately 130,000 during the campaign). By the following day, all of Cyrenaica is under British control, although the Italians still control small

pockets at Jarabub and Kufra. Hitler will become concerned and send German troops under General Rommel to turn defeat into victory. Rommel arrives in Tripoli in about a week with the Africa Korps. The Germans will attempt to seize the Suez Canal.

German 88-mm, used effectively against Tanks and Planes.

February 11th-12th 1941 — (Atlantic-Great Britain) The British receive coded U.S. intelligence that several German Vessels depart Brest. The British Air Force had inflicted some damage to them in the past, but not enough to take them out of action. The R.A.F. attacks after receiving the information, but once again, the German Vessels escape total destruction, making it safely to Kiel, Germany. The BBC broadcasts the news of the escape on the 15th, to the disappointment of the Americans, listening in France.

February 12th 1941 — (Atlantic-North Africa) German General Rommel arrives in Tripoli. His Africa Korps soon follows.

February 15th 1941 — (Pacific-Hawaii) The U.S. Navy bolsters its positioning in the Pacific, establishing a Base in the Territory of Hawaii on Kaneohe, Oahu.

Mid-February 1941 — The countries of Bulgaria and Turkey conclude a friendship pact, through the effort of German duress. The agreement permits German troops passage through Bulgaria without the activity being construed as an act of war by Turkey.

February 18th 1941 — (Pacific-Hawaii) Admiral Kimmel, informed by Vice Admiral Wilson Brown that the Navy Department is unsure of whose (Naval Operations or Naval Intelligence) responsibility it is to inform the CinC Pacific with secret information, writes to Admiral Stark in part: "IF THERE IS ANY DOUBT AS TO WHOSE RESPONSIBILITY IT IS TO KEEP THE COMMANDER IN CHIEF FULLY INFORMED WITH PERTINENT REPORTS ON THE SUBJECTS THAT SHOULD BE OF INTEREST TO THE FLEET, WILL YOU KINDLY FIX THAT RESPONSIBILITY SO THAT THERE WILL BE NO MISUNDERSTANDING." Admiral Stark replies during March that ONI (Naval Intelligence) is "FULLY AWARE OF ITS RESPONSIBILITY OF KEEPING YOU INFORMED." Unknown to Kimmel is the fact that the Asiatic Fleet is capable of decoding intercepted Japanese messages on its own through "magic." This decoding equipment is also available to the Navy and War Departments in Washington, and a fourth set, destined for Hawaii and the Pacific Fleet is diverted to the British during the summer of 1941 (this information comes out during investigation subsequent to the attack on Pearl Harbor).

February 19th 1941 — The U.S. Coast Guard, begins preparations for the upcoming conflict and establishes the Coast Guard Reserve.

February 23rd 1941 — The British had recently decided to send troops to assist Greece in ridding the country of the Italian invaders. Today, the offer of about 100,000 troops is accepted by Greece.

March 1941 — The neutral American buildup continues, although the official U.S. position is to stay neutral. The 7th Defense Battalion U.S.M.C. arrives at Samoa on the 18th, being the first troops of the Fleet Marine Force to receive duty in the Southern Hemisphere during World War II.

March 1st 1941 — **(United States)** The United States Navy becomes involved in the protection of Naval Merchant Convoys in the North Pacific, a favorite hunting ground of the German Submarines. The Support Force, Atlantic Squadron, commanded by Rear Admiral A.L. Bristol, is established. The Task Force is to be comprised of Destroyers and Patrol Plane Squadrons.

March 4th 1941 — **(Atlantic-Norway)** The Royal Navy debarks Commandos at the Lofoten Islands, startling the Germans. The raid nets German prisoners and costs the Germans several Warships.

March 5th 1941 — The United States, concerned about possible hostility from Germany, requests and later receives permission from Panama to enlarge its Air Defense perimeter around the Panama Canal.

March 10th 1941 — **(China-Burma-India)** The Japanese step in between to mediate the ongoing hostilities between France and Indo China, which is in reality an undeclared war. As a result, France cedes land to Thailand and gives the Japanese authorization to use the French Airport at Saigon. In addition, the Japanese mediators convince the French to give the Japanese sole rights to the Indo Chinese rice crop.

March 11th 1941 — **(United States)** The Lend Lease Act (Bill Number 1776) becomes law and the U.S. is now authorized to give aid in the form of ammunition to the Allies, something which was forbidden under the Neutrality Act of 1939.

March 12th 1941 — **(United States)** The U.S. Navy expands in the Lone Star State. A Naval Air Base is established in Corpus Christi, Texas.

March 24th-April 15th 1941 — The Germans, led by General Erwin Rommel and assisted by Italian units, initiate an offensive against the British in North Africa. The British are forced to withdraw into Egypt. German Armor is superior against the British Armor, most of which is either obsolete or very worn. El Agheila is recaptured. Rommel drives toward the sea and invests Tobruk. The British are forced to undergo a tremendous siege by the 11th of April. The indefatigable Australian Infantry and British Artillery is up to the task. Although most of the British had retired to Egypt, the Aussies and their British cousins hold the line with their backs to the sea, until the siege is lifted during December.

March 28th 1941 — **(Atlantic)** THE BATTLE OF CAPE MATAPAN — The British Royal Navy clashes with the Italian Fleet, in what turns out to be a victory for the English. The Italian Fleet loses three Cruisers and two Destroyers to the British. In addition, several other Italian Vessels are damaged.

March 30th 1941 — **(United States)** All German, Italian and Danish Vessels presently in ports in the United States are seized. On the following day, representatives of the U.S. Government arrive in Greenland to prepare for the possible German threat. The group is there to determine proper positioning of U.S. Military bases.

April 6th-June 1st 1941 — The German Army continues to seize more of Europe. They attack Yugoslavia and Greece. Italy, following the lead of Hitler, declares war against Yugoslavia which surrenders on the 17th of April. Greece will capitulate and sign an armistice with Germany on the 23rd of April. Crete, invaded almost casually on the 20th of April, collapses totally on the 1st of June. Nations are falling faster than cartographers can revise their charts.

April 1941 — Italian troops advancing through Bulgaria.

April 7th 1941 — **(Atlantic)** The United States Navy establishes a base in Bermuda.

April 9th 1941 — The United States reaches an accord with Denmark, which will provide for American protection of Greenland, against attack by any aggressor. American troops would be sent to Greenland where Defense bases are established. In other activity, relevant to preparing for what many consider to be imminent conflict with Germany and Japan, another Battleship is ready to go to sea. The U.S.S. *North Carolina* (BB-55) is commissioned at New York, New York.

April 10th 1941 — **(United States)** President Roosevelt eliminates the Red Sea and the Gulf of Aden from the list of combat zones, opening these areas for American Shipping. **(Atlantic-Iceland)** The U.S.S. *Niblack*, a Destroyer (DD-424), operating in the vicinity of Iceland, is involved with rescuing the survivors of a Netherlands Merchant Vessel, which had been torpedoed by a German Submarine. The American Destroyer drops depth charges on the suspected position of the German Submarine. This is considered to be the first occurrence of an American Ship firing upon a German Vessel.

April 13th 1941 — The Russians and Japanese sign a non-aggression pact. This agreement stays in effect almost for the duration of the conflict. The Russians break the pact after the Americans drop the atom bomb on Japan, during August 1945, months after the cessation of the conflict in Europe and days before the surrender at Tokyo Bay.

April 14th 1941 — **(Atlantic-Yugoslavia)** King Peter flees Yugoslavia, heading for Athens. The King is seventeen years old. The Germans, under General Kleist had seized Belgrade, the capital on the 12th. On the 16th, Ante Pavelic becomes head of state. Approximately 500,000 people, predominantly Orthodox Serbs are killed, however; some Jews are also killed. These executions are carried out by Catholic followers of Pavelic. The Yugoslavians and Serbs are long standing enemies.

April 17th 1941 — **(Atlantic)** German Submarines sink an Egyptian Steamship, the *Zamzam* as it travels through the South Atlantic. Survivors, including about 150 American passengers, are rescued. The German Vessel, the *Atlantis*, had departed, searching for another target.

April 18th 1941 — American Admiral Kimmel requests high priority be given to the defenses of Wake Island, which is situated close to Japan. A Marine Defense Battalion is dispatched. **(Atlantic-Yugoslavia)** Yugoslavia surrenders to the Axis.

April 19th 1941 — **(Pacific-Hawaii)** Admiral Kimmel is informed by Admiral Stark that one Aircraft Carrier, three Battleships, four Cruisers and eighteen Destroyers are being detached from the Pacific Fleet for service in the Atlantic. This greatly depletes the fighting ability of the Pacific Fleet and endangers Pearl Harbor, the only refueling base in the Hawaiian area. In addition, other Vessels will be drained for an anticipated attack against the Azores. The plan is subsequently dropped, however; the Vessels are not returned to the Pacific Fleet. Rumors of a pending Japanese attack against Pearl Harbor have been circulating for some time. The Peruvian Ambassador had informed American Ambassador to Japan, Joseph Grew during January 1941, that Japan intended to strike Pearl Harbor with all their strength and resources. This message is sent to the State Department on January 27th 1941.

April 22nd 1941 — Congress authorizes an increase in the strength of enlisted men in the Marine Corps. The act also authorizes Marine Corps strength be placed at 20% of total Navy strength. The U.S. Navy increases its strength to 232,000 men.

April 23rd 1941 — Greece signs an armistice with Germany.

April 27th 1941 — **(Pacific-Dutch East Indies)** American and British representatives meet in Singapore to discuss future combined efforts against the Japanese if war erupts. The top U.S. representative is Captain W.R. Purnell. The Pacific Region is undermanned and understrengthed, for both the British and Americans. Neither have adequate equipment to forestall the Japanese, if they attempt to move. Time is running out and once again, the United States is about to learn what happens, when it relaxes its guard and saves money, by not properly spending on defense.

May 1941 — **(Atlantic-Iraq)** Fighting breaks out between British and Iraqi troops throughout the month, but although available British Aircraft is obsolete, its contribution aids the British greatly. By the end of the month, the leader of the Iraq forces leaves Iraq and an armistice is agreed upon.

May 12th 1941 — Japan, through Ambassador Nomura, submits a proposal to the United States, for a "just peace in the Pacific."

May 15th 1941 — **(United States)** The United States Navy commissions another Battleship, The U.S.S. *Washington* (BB-56), at the Philadelphia Navy Yard.

May 20th 1941 — The German Air Force drops Paratroopers into Crete.

May 21st 1941 — A German Submarine torpedoes and sinks an American Freighter, the *Robin Moor*, which is moving through the South Atlantic, heading toward South Africa.

May 24th 1941 — **(United States)** The U.S. Navy receives authorization to acquire an additional 550,000 tons of Auxiliary Shipping. **(Atlantic)** The H.M.S. *Hood*, a Cruiser, is sunk by the German Battleship *Bismarck* in the Denmark Strait. On the following day, the British Royal Navy will sink the Bismarck when it is intercepted in the North Atlantic.

May 27th 1941 — A state of unlimited national emergency is declared by President Roosevelt. He also extends the area that the Atlantic Neutrality Patrol is to guard. In addition, the sparse Pacific Fleet is further diminished, when President Roosevelt transfers some units to the Atlantic.

May 29th 1941 — The United States prepares to land a combined Army — Marine force, consisting of 28,000 men, led by Major General Holland Smith, U.S.M.C., on the Azore Islands, in anticipation of a German invasion. Subsequent information confirms that the Germans are not planning to attack these Portuguese Islands and President Roosevelt decides to halt the operation.

Spring 1941 — America, anticipating conflict with both Japan and Germany, begins to rethink its options in the Pacific. The United States realizes it will have to bear the responsibility of defending the area. It had become apparent that the original plans to hold on to the Philippines would not be feasible, forcing the U.S. to begin increasing Military strength there. In addition, the U.S. would contemplate the capture of the Caroline and Marshall Islands and also fix their sights on Midway, Johnston, Palmyra, Samoa and Wake Island, with Marine detachments being sent to each. General Douglas MacArthur will be returned to active duty, with the rank of Lieutenant General in July. He will be in charge of all troops (except Naval) in the Far East.

June 1st 1941 — The U.S. Coast Guard begins to patrol in the vicinity of Greenland, establishing a four Vessel Patrol Squadron. **(Atlantic-Iraq)** British troops occupy Baghdad.

June 2nd 1941 — **(United States)** The United States Navy launches its first Escort Carrier, the U.S.S. *Long Island* (AVG-1) at Newport News, Va.

June 8th 1941 — **(United States)** Congress authorizes the Government to begin requisitioning foreign Merchant Ships that are in U.S. ports and not being utilized. **(Atlantic-Syria)** British and Free French Forces, commanded by British General Henry Maitland Wilson, invade Syria. The Indian 4th Brigade and the 7th Australian Division participate with the

French. The Allies request the Vichy forces to join them, however, fighting ensues until mid July, when the Vichy Commanding Officer, General Dentz, agrees to Allied armistice terms (against the instructions of the Vichy government).

June 12th 1941 — (United States) The United States Navy calls up all Navy Reservists, except those on a deferred basis.

June 15th 1941 — (Atlantic-Alaska) A Naval Air Base is established at Kodiak, Alaska, U.S. Territory. **(Atlantic-Germany)** Over sixty-seven Officers, several civilians and about ten non-commissioned Officers and over 100 drivers report to the Intelligence Sections of the Army Groups and Armies (preparing for invasion of Russia) near Warsaw. These men are to be commanded by Major Hermann Baun, who speaks fluent Russian and Ukrainian and both English and French. Within three days, the group departs for the front lines, thus commencing a war of espionage in the east. Baun's plans are greatly flawed due to the ambitiousness of his scheme and the shortage of agents behind Russian lines, but he does succeed in getting agents into Moscow. Most Parachutists are never heard from again. Success is gained when agents convince Vladimir Minishsky, Secretary of the Central Committee of the Communist Party (White Russia) to become a German agent. Another member of Baun's secret agents is a Jewish trader named Klatt, whose information is considered too good to be true. Actually Klatt had penetrated Japanese Intelligence. Even Russian General Turgut, residing in Vienna feeds the Germans information.

June 16th-21st 1941 — (United States-Europe) The State Department urges the closing of all German Consulates within the United States. On the following day, Germany and Italy will request the closing of U.S. Consulates in their respective countries and on the 21st, the U.S. State Department requests the closure of the Italian Consulates in the U.S.

June 22nd 1941 — (United States) The Russians receive word from President Roosevelt that the United States will supply assistance to Russia to help them fight the Germans. Ironically when the Japanese declare war against the United States, the Russians do not react. They maintain their non-aggression pact with the Japanese. **(Atlantic-Europe)** Italy and Rumania declare war against Russia.

June 22nd 1941 — (Atlantic-Germany) Himmler's physician, Doctor Kersten notes: "THIS IS GERMANY'S MORTAL HOUR ... GERMANY HAS LOST THE WAR. NOBODY CAN CONQUER THE MONSTROUS SPACE THAT IS RUSSIA. RUSSIA CAN ONLY BE CONQUERED BY THE RUSSIANS THEMSELVES, NOT FROM PEOPLE BEYOND HER FRONTIERS ... HITLER COULD HAVE BEEN THE GREATEST MAN IN THE WORLD, IF HE HAD NEVER HAD STARTED A WAR. NOW HE WILL GO DOWN TO HISTORY AS GERMANY'S GRAVE DIGGER." **(Invasion Of Russia)** OPERATION BARBAROSSA — Germany, with a large portion of Europe under its control, scraps the expanded non-aggressive pact and declares war against the Soviet Union. About an hour after a train crosses the border with supplies for Germany, the invasion commences under a tumultuous bombardment of six thousand guns that send a thunderclap upon the Russians. The Germans strike along a front that stretches from the Arctic Ocean to the Black Sea. The Germans expect and receive assistance from Finland, but not enough to crush Russia. Finland, angered by the prior invasion of Russia will advance, but only to the point of retaking lost terrain. Their refusal to go further leaves the Germans alone in the bid to take Leningrad, which Hitler has ordered reduced.

Three German Army Groups roar into action striking against Leningrad, Smolensk and Kiev respectively. The Southern Group plows into the Ukraine driving toward Kiev. During this first day of combat, over 1,000 Russian Planes are destroyed and within a week, the Germans annihilate five Soviet Armies. The Russians eventually commit over three hundred Divisions against the German invasion, however, many of them are presently in the western part of the Soviet Union.

After the effortless advance into the Ukraine and the Crimea, the German Soldiers are overwhelmed by the populace which greets them as great liberators. The Ukraine detests the Russians, who have murdered and starved millions of the citizens and expect Hitler to dismember the farm collectives and allow the people to reopen their churches. Hitler has other plans and the people soon regret their short lived liberation. Hitler sends in S.S. troops who are equally as ruthless as the Russians. These death squads reinitiate mass murder. In addition the food from the area is confiscated and sent back to feed German troops.

While the S.S. troops continue their operations, the Germans maintain their advance against Moscow according to schedule. It is expected to take Moscow in short order, allowing the troops to return to Germany, while still in the summer uniforms they are wearing, however, complications develop. The German forces are ordered to split, with a portion of the Central Group's Armor diverting toward Leningrad to assist the Northern Group, while the balance turns south to help capture a large Russian force near Kiev, giving Moscow a reprieve, as the operation consumes the entire summer and unknowingly throws the attack upon the mercy of mother nature when Hitler reverses his decision and decides to reattack toward Moscow. The German Armor and other Vehicles, encounter rain and the Ukraine, unlike Germany, has few paved roads, bogging down the entire operation with absolute paralysis from impenetrable mud. This is followed by the early arrival of a Russian winter, which is always brutally vicious. Temperatures drop well below zero and the winds at times are hurricane strength. Meanwhile, the Russian civilian population digs massive Tank traps in front of Moscow, and other areas. Stalingrad is being forced to capitulate by starvation, however, the people resist despite heavy German bombing raids. By November, waterways are frozen, preventing any supplies from reaching the city.

By the 5th of December, the incredible weather conditions compel the German Commanders to inform their troops that an attack is impossible, however, on the following day, the Russians commence a full scale counter-attack along the entire front. Russian Tanks (T-34) are superior to the German Tanks and their skilled Siberian troops, well adapted to severe weather conditions, perform splendidly. The Russians crash through the minefields by stampeding cattle and to ensure that no mines have been missed, they use their own troops, sending them forward locked arm in arm with machine guns behind them.

The year ends without the Germans seizing Moscow. The Russians have suffered about 5,000,000 casualties and about 3,000,000 have been taken prisoner. The Germans suffer about twenty-five percent casualties and by the end of March 1942, the casualty list grows to about 250,000 men. With the Russian offensive continuing to build, the Germans are forced to retire as best as possible and regroup where feasible, until they can stabile the situation. By the latter part of January, the Germans have neutralized the Russian offensive. Upon arrival of Spring, the battle heats up again.

A U.S. Fleet Boat Submarine in tranquil waters.

German Soldiers crossing Russian river in Amphibious Vehicle.

A destroyed Russian Armored Vehicle and its dead crew.

June 25th 1941 — Finland declares war against Russia.

June 27th 1941 — Hungary declares war against Russia.

June 28th 1941 — Albania declares war against Russia.

June 30th 1941 — **(United States)** The United States Navy, at present, has 1,899 Vessels of all types available. Naval strength stands at approximately 284,427. Marine Corps strength is at 54,359, including 3,339 Officers. The U.S. Coast Guard strength has been built to 19,235. **(Atlantic-Europe)** France breaks off diplomatic relations with Russia.

June 1941 — Subsequent to tue invasion by Germany, Stalin unleashes the NKVD again. These Bolshevik terrorists round up all persons considered suspicious (according to Stalin's broad measures) and send them to labor camps in Siberia. The Volga-German Autonomous Republic is dissolved. After the Soviets turn back the Germans at Stalingrad, the despicable N.K.V.D. uproots and exiles entire areas, sentencing them to Siberia. National minorities are a favorite target of the terrorists. Stalin orders the dismemberment of the Crimean Autonomous Republic to punish the Crimean Tatars. All of the Karachi are forcibly taken from their lands. In addition, the entire population of the Autonomous Republic of Kalmyk receives the same fate. These atrocities occur during 1943. During March of 1944, the Chechen-Ingush Autonomous Republic is dissolved. Stalin doles out similar punishment to all of the Balkars (April 1944) who are deported from the Kabardino-Balkar Autonomous Republic, to exile in far away and desolate areas of the Soviet Union. Stalin's labor camps are not all full with German prisoners. The nation of Ukrainia is spared the evil of mass deportation only because their numbers had been too great and the Bolshevik leader has no room for them in Siberia. Some of the more fortunate are able to flee and take up arms against the Soviets. Many fight with the German Army, wearing German uniforms and they are not National Socialists (Nazis). Others form what becomes known as the Vlassov Army; all members of this group are executed upon capture.

July 1st 1941 — **(United States)** The United States establishes Naval Coastal Frontiers; 1) North Atlantic 2) Southern 3) Caribbean 4) Panama 5) Pacific Southern 6) Pacific Northern 8) Hawaiian 9) Philippine. In relevant activity, Patrol Wing Seven is commissioned at Argentia, Newfoundland. Its responsibility will be to Patrol the North Atlantic. In addition, the U.S. Coast Guard establishes its Northeast Greenland Patrol.

July 2nd 1941 — (Pacific-Japan) The Japanese, not desiring to have their Ships too far away from the Pacific, where they unquestionably have superiority, recall all Merchant Ships from the Atlantic Ocean areas.

July 3rd 1941 — (Atlantic-Indian East Africa) Italian General Pietro Gazzera, surrenders his forces to the British, ending the Italian resistance in southern Abyssinia.

July 7th 1941 — (United States) President Roosevelt informs Congress that an agreement between the U.S. and Iceland has been attained, permitting the dispatching of U.S. Troops to Iceland. The 1st Marine Brigade, which had been organized under Brigadier General John Marston, lands at Reykjavik, Iceland. They have been transported, courtesy of a Naval Task Force, commanded by Rear Admiral D.M. LeBreton. Marine presence prevents German occupation, thus denying the Germans the use of a Naval or Air Base, which could have been used against the Western Hemisphere. In other activity, the Marines establish the 1st Marine Aircraft Wing at Quantico, Va. It is commanded by Colonel Louis E. Woods. Three days later, on the 10th, the 2nd Marine Aircraft Wing will be established at San Diego, California and will be commanded by Colonel Francis P. Mulcahy.

July 8th 1941 — (United States) The U.S. Navy establishes Patrol Wing 8 at Alameda, California. Four days later, on the 12th, the Navy establishes another Naval Air Base at Quonset Point, Rhode Island. **(Atlantic-Yugoslavia)** Germany and Italy decide to slice up Yugoslavia. Croatia is to become independent. Italy is to receive a portion of Dalmatia and some of the Adriatic islands and Bosnia is slated to come under the protection of Italy. In addition, Hungary is to receive a part of the country. Germany takes Cariola, Carinthia and Montenegro.

July 10th 1941 — (Atlantic-Soviet Union) Heavy fighting continues as the Germans continue their offensive. The Soviets initiate a counterattack, but it is checked west of Kiev. In other activity, the British and Soviets conclude a mutual-assistance pact; both agree not to seek a separate peace with Germany.

July 12th 1941 — German Planes launch their first raid against Moscow.

July 15th 1941 — Another Naval Air Base is established, this time it will be at Argentia, Newfoundland, and will also be a Naval Operating Base, to further bolster U.S. Naval activity in the Atlantic.

July 16th 1941 — (Atlantic-Germany) Himmler, speaking with Doctor Kersten, turns his hatred toward Lawyers. He tells Kersten about Hitler being amused by lawyers being renamed "DEFENDERS OF JUSTICE" by Reichleiter Hans Frank, head of the National Socialist League for Defence of the Law. Himmler then gives Kersten his impression of lawyers, especially solicitors, stating that they are: "THIEVES OF THE LEGAL PROFESSION, CHEATS AND EXPLOITERS, GOING IN THE GUISE OF HONEST MEN, CALLING THEMSELVES THE FRIENDS AND HELPERS OF THE OPPRESSED, BUT REALLY SETTING THEIR WHOLE MIND AND CONDUCT ON GETTING THE VICTIM INTO THEIR NET SO THAT THEY COULD FLEECE HIM PROPERLY." Himmler's on a roll with venom today. He also tells Kersten that all lawyers and Tax consultants (he is incensed that people instruct others how to avoid taxes for the state) are to be shipped to the front lines

and that when the war ends they will be eliminated. Kersten asks how you can operate a world without attorneys and is informed that Hitler has it all worked out.

July 18th 1941 — (Pacific-Japan) Japanese Prince Konoye starts a new Cabinet. Foreign Minister Matsuoka is replaced by Admiral T. Toyoda. **(Atlantic-Great Britain)** The exile-Government of Czechoslovakia, headed by Eduard Benes, is recognized by Great Britain. The Benes government (in London) signs a mutual assistance pact with the Soviet Union.

July 19th 1941 — (United States) The Commander in Chief Atlantic Fleet, Admiral King, establishes a U.S. Task Force to serve a twofold purpose; the escorting of Convoys moving between the U.S. and Iceland and the simultaneous responsibility of protecting Iceland.

July 22nd 1941 — (United States) All Italian consulates in the United States are closed by order of President Roosevelt.

July 24th 1941 — (Pacific-Japan) Japan occupies French Indo China. Two days later, President Roosevelt places all Philippine troops under American control, with General Douglas MacArthur as Commanding General. The United States responds quickly, seizing all Japanese credits.

July 26th 1941 — (United States) The United States freezes all Chinese and Japanese assets. Two days later, the Japanese reciprocate and freeze all U.S. assets in Japan.

July 27th 1941 — (Pacific-Philippines) General Douglas MacArthur becomes Commander in Chief of the Philippine Army. He has been brought out of retirement by an act of Congress. President Roosevelt sends MacArthur a telegram, notifying him of his rank of Lieutenant General. The Philippine Government bestows upon him the title of Field Marshal. General MacArthur, while accepting the Philippine rank of Field Marshal, at the Malacanan Palace states: "THE MILITARY CODE HAS COME DOWN TO US FROM EVEN BEFORE THE AGE OF KNIGHTHOOD AND CHIVALRY . . . THE SOLDIER ABOVE ALL MEN, IS REQUIRED TO PERFORM THE HIGHEST ACT OF RELIGIOUS TEACHING . . . SACRIFICE. IN BATTLE AND IN THE FACE OF DANGER AND DEATH, HE DISCLOSES THOSE DIVINE ATTRIBUTES WHICH HIS MASTER GAVE WHEN HE CREATED MAN IN HIS OWN IMAGE. HOWEVER HORRIBLE THE INCIDENTS OF WAR MAY BE, THE SOLDIER WHO IS CALLED UPON TO OFFER AND TO GIVE HIS LIFE FOR HIS COUNTRY IS THE NOBLEST DEVELOPMENT OF MANKIND."

July 29th 1941 — (China-Burma) The Japanese, with the permission of the French, move troops into southern Indo China.

July 30th 1941 — (China-Burma) Japanese Planes launch an unprovoked attack against the U.S.S. *Tutuila* (PR-4), a River Gunboat, in the vicinity of Chungking, China. According to Ambassador to Japan, Joseph Grew, the Plane's bomb misses the Vessel by about eight yards and another just misses the Embassy. He also states the eye witnesses attest that the attack is intentional and fatalities are avoided by a miracle. Japan apologizes superficially on the following day. The U.S. does not retaliate.

August 1941 — General MacArthur keeps requesting additional troops and supplies for the defense of the Philippines against a Japanese attack. The Pacific region is not a high priority with the Chiefs of Staff or Congress and U.S. procrastination will unnecessarily cost additional American lives.

August 1st 1941 — (United States) The Naval buildup continues for the U.S. Government. The U.S. establishes a Naval Air Station at Midway Island in the Pacific and will also establish a Naval Operating Base at Trinidad.

August 5th 1941 — (Atlantic-Russia) The German advance smashes into Smolensk, seizing the city. The Soviets have sustained many casualties, prior to its capitulation.

German Tanks push toward Moscow, encountering only nominal resistance.

August 9th 1941 — (Atlantic) President Roosevelt and British Prime Minister Churchill confer at Placentia Bay, Argentia, Newfoundland (Atlantic Conference).

August 11th 1941 — (Pacific-Midway) The Marine 6th Defense Battalion, commanded by Commander Colonel Harold D. Shannon, arrives at Midway to begin preparations to relieve the 3rd Defense Battalion.

August 14th 1941 — (United States) Roosevelt and Churchill, conferring off the coast of Newfoundland, seal the Atlantic Charter (the setting of direction for post war policy). Fifteen additional countries subscribe to the charter before October. In essence, the Atlantic Charter becomes the foundation for the United Nations. President Roosevelt and Prime Minister Churchill had met discretely on Naval Vessels for several days prior to announcing their post war goals.

August 15th 1941 — (Pacific) The Pacific Ocean receives additional U.S. Naval presence. Naval Air Stations are established at Palmyra Island and Johnston Island.

August 17th 1941 — Reacting to a request from the Japanese Ambassador to the U.S., the President and the Secretary of State meet with the Japanese Ambassador to attempt to work out a plan to initiate talks on settling the Pacific situation.

August 18th 1941 — (United States) One day after meeting with the Japanese Ambassador, President Roosevelt announces that the British are to receive Aircraft from America. These new Combat Planes will be transported to the East Indies by way of Africa and Brazil.

August 19th 1941 — (Pacific-Wake Island) An advance unit of the 1st Defense Battalion arrives at Wake Island and begins to strengthen the island's defenses.

August 25th 1941 — (Atlantic) Iran is invaded by British and Russian troops to convince the Iranians to allow them to protect the oil fields. The hostilities end within two days. A subsequent agreement is reached whereby all Russian and British troops will leave Iran after the war ends. Shah Reza Pahlevi is unhappy about the intrusion. The British and the Russians agree not to occupy Teheran, however, by mid-September, they renege and occupy the city, claiming the Shah had not expelled the Axis Nationals. The Shah vacates the throne and is succeeded by his son, Crown Prince Mohammad Reza Pahlavi.

August 27th 1941 — (United States) The United States, whose Vessels have been taking supplies to the Russians in Vladivostok by way of Japanese waters, receive a strong protest from Tokyo.

August 30th 1941 — (Atlantic-Soviet Union) German troops seize Mga, severing the railroad system into Leningrad, virtually isolating the besieged city.

September 1st 1941 — (United States) The Navy takes responsibility for protecting Allied Trans-Atlantic Convoys from the meridian of Iceland to a point off Argentina. In other activity, U.S. Admiral King, Commander Atlantic Fleet, delegates a Naval Task Group, calling it a Denmark Strait Patrol and giving it responsibility to operate in waters between Greenland and Iceland. **(China-Burma-India)** The situation in the Far East continues to worsen. The American Consul and Superior Officers in Shanghai, request that all U.S. Naval forces, including Marines, be withdrawn from China; the evacuation does not occur.

September 1941 — (Atlantic) German Submarines attack and sink two U.S. Steamships, the *Montana* and *Sessa*, off the coast of Iceland. The United States then directs the Navy to destroy any Italian or German Warships spotted in U.S. protected waters, but does not declare war.

September 4th 1941 — (Atlantic) The U.S. Navy patrols the seas in the vicinity of Iceland and one of its Ships, the U.S.S. *Greer* detects a German Submarine about 175 miles off Iceland's coast. The German Submarine attacks the *Greer*, but inflicts no damage. The United States does not declare war against Germany.

September 7th 1941 — (Atlantic) German Planes attack Allied positions in the Gulf of Suez. During the attack, the American Freighter *Steel Seafarer* is sunk. No U.S. retaliation is taken.

September 9th 1941 — (United States) The United States Navy establishes Naval Coastal Frontier Forces.

September 11th 1941 — (United States) The United States begins to take additional defensive actions. President Roosevelt directs the United States Navy to protect the Ships under escort aggressively and attack any adversarial Vessel that attempts to interrupt a Convoy. **(Pacific-Midway)** The Marine 6th Defense Battalion arrives at Midway and relieves the 3rd Battalion.

September 12th 1941 — (Atlantic) The Norwegian Vessel *Buskoe*, dispatched to Greenland to establish and maintain a weather station for Germany is intercepted in Mackenzie Bay, Greenland and confiscated by the Coast Guard Cutter *Northland*, (PG-49). **(Atlantic-Soviet Union)** The Germans advance closer to Kiev, trapping hundreds of thousands of Russian troops. A new ingredient enters the fighting on the Eastern Front. The first snowfall is reported. At the time, it doesn't concern the Germans who are already convinced that the capitulation of Moscow is imminent.

September 17th 1941 — (Atlantic) The United States escorts its first British Convoy, which is heading to England.

September 19th 1941 — The Germans seize Kiev. Estimated Russian losses are about 500,000. German losses approach 100,000. Massive amounts of Russian prisoners have been taken during the siege.

September 24th 1941 — Japan directs its Consular General in Honolulu, Hawaii to give a detailed report on Vessels at Pearl Harbor, which it divides into five sectors, using the alphabet as a code: A, denotes the waters between Ford Island and the arsenal; B, the waters south and west of Ford Island; C, East Loch; D, Middle Loch; E, West Loch and the communication water routes. Other messages have been intercepted and decoded, however, Admiral Kimmel is totally unaware of the activity. Japanese Consul General Kito responds on September 29th, informing Japan that locations of Vessels would be coded; KS, repair dock; KT, Navy Dock at Navy Yard; FV, moorings near Ford Island, and FG would designate the Ships alongside Ford Island. This information is decoded and translated on October 10th, 1941, however, the information is not given to Admiral Kimmel.

September 24th 1941 — (Atlantic) The Marines (1st Provisional Brigade), are released from Naval jurisdiction to serve under Army jurisdiction while they maintain positions in Iceland. **(Atlantic-Gibraltar)** The British initiate **OPERATION HALBERD**. It sends Transports, protected by Royal Navy Warships, including a Carrier, Cruisers, Destroyers and Battleships. The Convoy delivers enough food and supplies to sustain Malta for several months.

September 26th 1941 — (United States) The United States Navy is ordered to protect all Merchant Vessels operating in American defense waters, with instructions to report and if required, to destroy German and Italian Ships when encountered. The U.S. is still not at war.

September 27th 1941 — (United States) The United States launches its first Liberty Ship, appropriately named U.S.S. *Patrick Henry*, at Baltimore, Maryland.

October 1st 1941 — (Atlantic-Russia) A meeting in Moscow, consisting of representatives of the U.S., Great Britain and Russia, which had begun on the 29th of September, ends today. The conference deals with giving the Russians aid, primarily American equipment and dollars.

October 6th 1941 — (Atlantic-Soviet Union) German troops under von Kleist take Berdyansk, capturing about 100,000 prisoners. Within two days, as the Germans inch closer to Moscow, about 600,000 Russians are captured in the regions near Bryansk and Vyazma when entire Russian Divisions are entrapped. The weather begins to change. Solid rains begin to fall along the front; the mud which it begins to create impedes the German advance. Meanwhile, the Soviet citizens continue to contribute to the cause by performing as many tasks as possible to fortify the Russian defenses.

German Horse-drawn Artillery on the advance in Russia.

October 15th 1941 — (Pacific-Wake Island) American Major James P. Devereux replaces Major Lewis A. Hohn as the Commander on Wake Island. In less than two months, this Garrison will come under heavy attack by Japanese Forces.

October 17th 1941 — (Pacific-Hawaii) The Commandant 14th Naval District, Hawaii, requests that the Navy Department send "small fast craft, equipped with listening devices and depth charges, and two Squadrons of Patrol Planes to bolster the local Naval Defenses which claim to have only the U.S.S. *Sacramento* which has "no batteries, to speak of, with which the Vessel can fight, and no speed with which she can run." On paper, the Navy Department had allocated about 100 Patrol Planes to the Commandant of the 14th Naval District, however, not a single Patrol Plane had been sent to Hawaii. The Army Air Corps fares no better. General Short has 180 Flying Fortresses in Hawaii on paper, however, only twelve are in Hawaii and of these, only six are in operating condition. **(Pacific)** The Japanese continue to tighten their grip in Indo China and move closer to war with the United States. The cabinet of Japan's Prince Konoye resigns, resulting with Konoye being replaced by General Hidaki Tojo who becomes both the Premier of Japan and its Minister of War. In other activity, all American Merchant Ships are ordered by the U.S. Navy to head for friendly ports. **(Atlantic)** The signs of war between Germany and the United States continue to erupt. German Submarines attack and badly damage the U.S.S. *Kearney*; 11 Americans are lost. Before the end of the month, another American Destroyer will be sunk by the Germans, without American retaliation.

October 19th 1941 — (Atlantic) The German U-Boats take more target practice, this time off the coast of West Africa. Their torpedoes strike and sink the American Merchant Vessel, the *Lehigh*, and the unprovoked attack once again goes unanswered.

October 20th 1941 — (United States) The U.S.S. *Hornet* (CV-8) is commissioned at Norfolk, Virginia, and will soon leave the peaceful waters of the Chesapeake, heading for the Pacific.

October 21st 1941 — (Pacific-Pearl Harbor) Two U.S. Submarines, the *Tautog* and the *Thresher*, embark from Pearl Harbor to initiate Patrols, which would simulate actual wartime conditions and in fact, are the first Navy War Patrols. After conducting the operation, the Submarines return to Pearl Harbor.

October 31st 1941 — **(Pacific)** General MacArthur futilely requests additional supplies and manpower to defend the Philippines. The average transit time for a Cargo Vessel departing the U.S. East Coast and reaching Manila is approximately 45 days. **(Atlantic)** Another German Submarine, prowling in the Atlantic, encounters and sinks the U.S.S. *Reuben James*, a Destroyer (DD-245), costing 100 American lives. On the previous day, German Submarines torpedo an Oiler, the U.S.S. *Salinas* (AO-19), approximately 700 miles east of Newfoundland, but the Vessel escapes damage and casualties. The United States still keeps alive its slackening neutrality.

German units immobilized by muddy terrain.

November 1st 1941 — **(Atlantic-Soviet Union)** By now, the weather is starting to dominate the fighting around Moscow. The mud which permeates the area forces the Germans to postpone the offensive until the colder weather arrives to allow free movement of the Armor and accompanying Vehicles. The Germans receive more cold than ever anticipated as Russia is about to be struck with one of the hardest winters in history.

November 2nd 1941 — **(Pacific)** Additional Marines arrive at Wake Island, bringing total Marine Strength, including 15 Officers, to 388 men.

November 3rd 1941 — Japanese Admiral Osami Nagano (Chief of Staff), authorizes the use of a finished attack plan, which is to be used against the American positions at Pearl Harbor.

November 5th 1941 — **(Pacific-Japan)** Tokyo sends a message to its Ambassador in Washington, D.C. giving him explicit instructions concerning the ongoing negotiations to consummate an agreement between the U.S. and Japan, that: "IT IS ABSOLUTELY NECESSARY THAT ALL ARRANGEMENTS FOR THE SIGNING OF THIS AGREEMENT BE COMPLETED BY THE 25TH OF THIS MONTH." Similar messages would be sent from Japan to Hawaii on the 11th and on the 15th, underscoring the importance of concluding an agreement by the 25th. Subsequent messages are sent and intercepted on the 16th, 22nd and 24th, which extend the deadline for consummation of an agreement with the U.S. until the 29th, while emphasizing that if no agreement is reached, the "JAPANESE PLAN WOULD AUTOMATICALLY GO INTO EFFECT." All messages are intercepted by Washington and decoded, however, the pattern remains the same; Pearl Harbor is not informed.

November 6th 1941 — **(Atlantic)** Two U.S. Warships, the U.S.S. *Omaha* (CL-4), a Cruiser and the U.S.S. *Somers* (DD-381), a Destroyer, while Patrolling in the Atlantic equatorial waters, notices a Vessel that appears suspicious. The Vessel, the German Blockade Runner *Odenwald*, is disguised as a U.S. Ship, the *Willmoto*, but the charade doesn't work and the Naval impostor is captured.

November 7th 1941 — **(United States)** Congress amends sections of the 1939 Neutrality Act, enabling U.S. Merchant Ships to be armed. They will also be permitted to transport supplies to warring nations.

November 8th 1941 — **(Atlantic)** The United States Navy establishes another Naval Operating Base, this one in Iceland, intended to bolster American Naval power in the region.

November 8th-9th 1941 — **(Atlantic-Mediterranean)** British Warships intercept an Italian Convoy as it makes its way toward Libya, sinking all Transports.

November 10th 1941 — **(Atlantic)** The United States Navy enters the Troop Transport escort business. Today, U.S. Admiral A.B. Cook's Command, escorts a Convoy on its voyage from Halifax to the Far East. The Convoy carrying 20,000 British troops is the first Convoy to be escorted by American Warships.

November 14th 1941 — **(United States)** Japanese Special Ambassador Saburo Kurusu arrives in San Francisco on an alleged mission of peace. He states that Japan is a peace loving nation and that Japan intends to establish a permanent peace in Asia, however, he maintains that U.S. aid to China is delaying Asian peace, and that America's decision not to sell Japan oil and scrap metal is also an interference with the peace. On the following day, Tojo sends a dispatch to the Japanese Consular General in Honolulu: "AS RELATIONS BETWEEN JAPAN AND THE UNITED STATES ARE MOST CRITICAL, MAKE YOUR "SHIPS IN HARBOR REPORT" IRREGULAR BUT AT THE RATE OF TWICE A WEEK. ALTHOUGH YOU ARE NO DOUBT AWARE, PLEASE TAKE EXTRA CARE TO MAINTAIN SECRECY." This dispatch is decoded and translated in Washington on December 3rd 1941.

November 15th 1941 — **(Atlantic-Germany)** Himmler visits his doctor and is visibly depressed. Doctor Kersten inquires what is wrong and Himmler informs him that he had just left the Fuhrer's Chancery and was told that the plan to destroy the Jews is being implemented. Kersten states in his diary that Himmler had wanted to simply expel the Jews, but that no countries would accept them. Kersten, a Finn, expresses horror and states that it is "FEARFUL CRUELTY TO WANT TO DESTROY MEN SIMPLY BECAUSE THEY WERE JEWS . . . THAT THEY HAD A HEART AS HE AND HIMMLER HAD." Himmler hesitates before responding and then takes a tirade, blaming the Jews for just about everything including being responsible for "overthrowing every system of government by means of wars and revolutions." He continues to rave and then says: "YOU CAN ONLY MEET THE JEWS WITH THEIR OWN METHODS AND THEIR OWN WORDS: AN EYE FOR AN EYE AND A TOOTH FOR A TOOTH." Finally, he proclaims that other nations had already partially exterminated the Jews and then compares the actions of the Americans against the Indians as a similar extermination. Doctor Kersten, unable to convince Himmler to get the policy changed, decides to begin assisting the Jews. **(Atlantic-Soviet Union)** The Germans reinitiate the attack toward Moscow. Meanwhile, the Soviet Union is rushing troops from Siberia to forestall capitulation.

December 1941 — Japanese representatives in Washington D.C. This photograph is widely used for propaganda, however, the Japanese insist they had no knowledge of the imminent attack against Pearl Harbor at the time of the photo.

November 17th 1941 — The Japanese Ambassador, Kichisaburo Nomuro, and Envoy Saburo Kurusu initiate negotiations in Washington D.C., with the intent of reestablishing unrestricted trade and to have the U.S. agree to non-interference with Japan's aggression in the Pacific. As the negotiations continue, American Code-breakers intercept Japanese Diplomatic messages, attempting to ascertain Japan's real intent. The U.S. belatedly continues to build up its stations in the Philippines and other islands in the Pacific, but it is too little, much too late. In other activity, the Neutrality Act of 1939 is amended by a joint resolution of Congress. The amendment allows the arming of U.S. Merchant Vessels and in addition, grants permission for them to enter war zones. By this time, it is perfectly clear to the U.S., that if the Axis overrun Great Britain, China, and the Soviet Union, they will control about seven eighths of the world's population which stands at about 2 billion people. In addition, the Axis would control about seventy percent of the world's resources. Projections give the North and South Americans about 30 million men (Armed), against about 200 million troops. In addition, the projection places about 500 million people in Europe and Africa under conditions of enslavement of the Nazis, and with the conquest of Russia, another 200 million people come under German domination. The Japanese, with the conquest of the Orient would control about 1,000 million people.

November 18th 1941 — **(Japan)** Tojo sends another message to the Japanese Consul General in Honolulu: "PLEASE REPORT ON THE FOLLOWING AREAS AS TO VESSELS ANCHORED THEREIN: AREA NORTH, PEARL HARBOR, MANILA BAY (HONOLULU) AND THE AREAS ADJACENT THERETO. (MAKE YOUR INVESTIGATION WITH GREAT SECRECY.)" The intercepted information is decoded and translated on December 5th 1941, however; Admiral Kimmel is not informed. In Hawaii, Consul General Kito sends a message to Tojo, explaining deployment of Vessels and schedule of entrance and departure, including the patterns of Destroyers and the distances between the Warships. This information is decoded and translated in Washington on December 6th 1941, however, again the vital information is not given to Admiral Kimmel. On the 20th, Tojo instructs the Jap Consul General to

report as much information as possible on Fleet Bases in the vicinity of the Hawaiian Military reservation, and this dispatch is intercepted and translated in Washington on the 4th of December, but not forwarded to Pearl Harbor. **(Atlantic-North Africa)** In an effort to reinforce the defenders at Tobruk, the British 8th Army launches an attack (OPERATION CRUSADER) designed to smash the German-Italian forces which have Tobruk under siege. In addition, the operation hopes to retake Cyrenaica.

November 19th 1941 — Marine Aircraft Group 21 is ordered to Midway, with instructions to modify the Base for the use of Aircraft. MacArthur continues to plead for Washington to strengthen the Philippines against attack by sending additional Aircraft and Infantry. He feels that with reinforcements and an increased Philippine Army, Japan can be stopped at the beaches.

November 20th 1941 — **(United States)** The United States Government receives Japan's final proposal to maintain peace in the Pacific. It is presented by Japanese Ambassador Nomura. The United States will give the Japanese its counter proposal on the 26th.

November 21st 1941 — **(United States)** The United States Lend-Lease program is now offered to Iceland. **(Atlantic-North Africa)** The defenders at Tobruk, acting upon orders from General Cunningham (8th Army), attack to break out of their encirclement, however anticipated British Armor does not arrive to support the endeavor. At Sidi Rezegh, the British 7th Armored Brigade is intercepted by Rommel's Tanks, and subsequent to heavy fighting, the Brigade loses over 100 Tanks. Additional British Armor is speeding to the area. On the following day, Rommel intercepts the reinforcements, forcing the remnants of the 7th Brigade, numbering about twenty Tanks and the 22nd Armored Brigade to retire from Tobruk. Another relief force, the 4th Armored Brigade is thumped by Rommel in a separate engagement, but although the Germans hold the advantage in Tanks, the British Tankers have also inflicted large losses upon Rommel forces.

November 23rd 1941 — **(South America)** Surinam (Dutch Guiana), off the coast of South America, receives U.S. troops. The government of the Netherlands requests troops to protect the bauxite (Claylike ore, used to manufacture aluminum) mines. **(Atlantic-North Africa)** The fighting near Sidi Rezegh, between the British and German Armor, combined with the vicious exchanges between Infantry continues to drain each others strength. Both sides sustain heavy losses of both men and equipment; German Tanks have been reduced to less than one hundred. The Germans dub this day the "SUNDAY OF THE DEAD." General Rommel is not at the battle. He is preoccupied with the situation at Gambut, where New Zealand troops capture the Afrika Korps Headquarters. British General Cunningham will be replaced by General Ritchie within a few days. In conjunction, with the change of British Commanders, General Auchinleck, the British Commander in Chief into the forefront to oversee the operation. Contingents of the beleaguered Garrison at Tobruk break out and encounter the British 8th Army by the end of the month, however, the Germans succeed in temporarily restoring encirclement. Determined fighting ensues, however, the German strength becomes weakened and by the 10th of December, Rommel, commanding less than fifty Tanks is forced to abort the siege of Tobruk. Meanwhile, the British continue to receive reinforcements and supplies.

November 25th 1941 — (United States) Secretary Stimson notes in his diary that he had outlined a plan of maneuvering the Japanese into striking the first blow against the United States. Admiral Kimmel makes note of this in his book and declares that neither he nor General Short had knowledge that the Roosevelt Administration was "PURSUING A COURSE OF ACTION THAT MADE WAR WITH JAPAN INEVITABLE." (Pacific) Japanese Troop Transports off Formosa are spotted cruising on a course which is taking them to Malaya. (Pacific-Hawaii) The Commandant 14th Naval District, Hawaii is informed by the Navy Department that no additional Planes are available. Pearl Harbor has been pleading for Planes since December of 1940. The response in part: "ALLOCATIONS OF NEW AIRCRAFT SQUADRONS WHICH BECOME AVAILABLE IN THE NEAR FUTURE WILL BE DETERMINED BY THE REQUIREMENTS OF THE STRATEGIC SITUATION AS IT DEVELOPS."

November 26th 1941 — The United States, through its Secretary of State Cordell Hull, informs Japan that all trade restrictions will be lifted if it pulls out of China and French Indo China. The Japanese turn the offer down on the 30th. As the diplomats are negotiating, the Japanese Task Force, which is to attack the unsuspecting Americans at Pearl Harbor, departs the Kurile Islands, maintaining radio silence to avoid detection by the United States.

November 27th 1941 — The U.S.S. *Madison* and the U.S.S. *Harrison,* depart Shanghai, evacuating the 4th Marines. Authorization had been given previously to move these troops to the Philippines. All Naval Commanders in the Pacific receive notification of the imminence of war with Japan through both the War and Navy Departments. The message reads in part "AN AGGRESSIVE MOVE BY JAPAN IS EXPECTED WITHIN THE NEXT FEW DAYS." "EXECUTE APPROPRIATE DEPLOYMENT." On the same day, General MacArthur receives similar notification from General Marshall: "HOSTILE ACTION POSSIBLE AT ANY MOMENT. IF HOSTILITIES CANNOT BE AVOIDED . . . THE UNITED STATES DESIRES THAT JAPAN COMMIT THE FIRST OVERT ACT." Pearl Harbor has not been mentioned as a specific target by the War or Navy Departments and it has been implied that Pearl Harbor hostilities are not considered "imminent or probable." At Pearl Harbor, U.S. Naval Task Force Commanders and Army Commanders are meeting with Admiral Kimmel when the word arrives. This particular conference is to determine which type of Aircraft should be dispatched to the picket fence islands of Midway, Johnston, Palmyra, and Wake, which are suspected of being the first recipients of a Japanese attack. In attendance are Lt. General Walter C. Short, Commander Hawaii; Major General Frederick L. Martin, Vice Admiral Brown; Rear Admiral Bellinger and Admiral Halsey in addition to Admiral Kimmel and Staff members. The first choice is to send Planes from General Martin's Force, but upon questioning from Halsey, it is determined that the Army Planes are unable to pursue further than 15 miles from shore. The choice becomes Marine Fighting Squadron 211 and the endeavor is to be kept strictly confidential, because of Japanese spies on Hawaii, which contains in excess of 150,000 Japanese. Major General Paul A. Putnam U.S.M.C., the Commanding Officer of Squadron 211 is one of two Officers who are aware of the assignment. Pearl Harbor, despite the constant threat of attack by the Japanese is defended by exactly six

U.S. Flying Fortresses that have the capability of locating and destroying Jap Aircraft Carriers. Admiral Kimmel had received a dispatch requesting that Marines on Midway and Wake Islands. Admiral Kimmel and General Short determine that the suggestion is impossible, because the Army has no guns, either surface or antiaircraft, and if relief occurs, the Marines would have to leave their equipment behind; there is no extra equipment to rearm the Marines upon arrival at Pearl Harbor. In addition, Admiral Kimmel receives a dispatch suggesting he remove all Carriers from the vicinity of Pearl Harbor.

November 28th 1941 — (Pacific) Marine Fighter Squadron 211 is given secret orders to depart Ewa and proceed to Ford Island (Pearl Harbor), from where the U.S.S. *Enterprise* will transport it to Wake Island. Admiral Halsey departs Pearl Harbor at 07:00 with Task Force 2, but upon passing the channel he divides the Force and creates Task Force 8 (this move had been authorized on previous day during meeting with Kimmel). Halsey also directs Task Force 8, which comprises the Enterprise, three Heavy Cruisers and nine Destroyers, to mount warheads on all torpedoes. He also instructs all Pilots to attack and sink any Ships sighted and to knock out any Planes that venture into the planned course (Halsey is aware that no Allied Vessels are in the area). Halsey's startling orders cause instant response from his staff. Commander William Buracker, unaware of the secrecy of the mission and the importance of the Japanese not discovering the Planes in transit, rushes to Halsey and states: "Admiral, did you authorize this thing?" Halsey responds "Yes" and receives another question. "Do you realize this means war?" and again the response is affirmative. Admiral Halsey is not expecting any Japanese Warships in his path, but is of the opinion that if they are around, it is to attack and if he doesn't fire first, his Force will be struck and annihilated. The order stands and the Task Force heads for Wake screening an area of a 300 mile circumference to protect the Fleet and the cargo. In other activity, Commander W.S. Cunningham, U.S.N., relieves Major Devereux as Wake Island Commander. Major James P.S. Devereux has been Island Commander since October 5th. Although Admiral Kimmel has orders not to bomb Submarines outside of the three mile limit, he issues orders to destroy any strange Submarines in the operating areas and notifies the Chief of Naval Operation of his actions. (Atlantic-East Africa) Italian General Nasi surrenders with his 22,000 troops at Gondar, terminating Italy's East African campaign, dousing Mussolini's dream of governing an African Roman Empire.

November 29th 1941 — (Pacific) U.S. strength on the Philippine Islands at this time, numbers just under 20,000 men. This force is assisted by ten Philippine Divisions (raw citizen Soldiers) numbering approximately 100,000 men, 20,000 Regular troops and more than 11,000 Filipino Scouts. Included in the U.S. strength is the Army Air Corps of about 200 Planes, including 35 new B-17s and 100 P-40s. The P-40s are inoperable, however, because they can not be utilized until the engines are broken in and there are no spare engines in the Philippines. Reinforcements are heading to various stations throughout the Pacific, but not nearly enough to withstand the fast approaching Japanese thrust. The U.S. Asiatic Fleet (reinforced) is also in the area. The Fleet is commanded by Admiral Thomas Hart. It consists of 13 Destroyers, 29 Submarines, three Cruisers, one Submarine Rescue Ship and six PT Boats. In addition, an Air Patrol Wing, comprising 30 PBYs and four Seaplane Tenders are attached to the Fleet. **(Pacific-Japan)** A message is sent from Tokyo to the Jap General Consul in Honolulu: "WE HAVE BEEN RECEIVING REPORTS FROM YOU ON SHIP MOVEMENTS, BUT IN FUTURE WILL YOU ALSO REPORT EVEN WHEN THERE ARE NO MOVE-MENTS." This message is intercepted by the U.S.; it is decoded and translated on December 5th 1941. Ironically, General MacArthur, in the Philippines and his staff are aware of the Jap messages. General Willoughby, would subsequently state that a staff report prior to the attack mentioned: "WE DREW OUR OWN CONCLUSIONS AND THE FILIPINO-AMERICAN TROOPS TOOK UP BEACH POSITIONS LONG BEFORE THE JAPANESE LANDINGS."

November 30th 1941 — The total strength of the Marine Corps reaches 65,881 men. The Americans attempt to fortify Samoa by initiating Anti-aircraft gun emplacements, to meet the threat. Although America expects an attack, it does not foresee that it will be against Pearl Harbor. The Japanese Fleet, by radio silence, has allegedly fooled U.S. intelligence to erroneously report that it is in home port. The Navy Department directs Admiral Hart, commanding Officer Asiatic Fleet to search for information on Jap movements in the China Sea as an attack on the Kra Isthmus is imminent. On the following day, Kimmel receives a dispatch from the Navy Department (copy of dispatch to Admiral Hart) emphasizing attack against Malaya; there is no mention of attack or possibility of attack against Pearl Harbor.

November 1941-Early December 1941 — **(Pacific-Philippines)** General MacArthur orders all B-17s, based at Clark Field in the Philippines to be flown south to Mindanao, where they will be immune from an enemy attack by Japanese Aircraft based on Formosa. American Planes under the command of Major General Lewis H. Brereton have been picking up increased Japanese Aircraft activity. Some Reconnaissance Missions have located Japanese Planes as close as 20 miles from the Philippines.

December 1st 1941 — **(United States)** The "Current National Situations," a publication issued by the Chief of Naval Operations states on page one: "STRONG INDICATIONS POINT TO AN EARLY JAPANESE ADVANCE AGAINST THAILAND." Further back in the same publication, regarding a headline, "Japanese Naval Situation," it states: "MAJOR CAPITAL SHIP STRENGTH IN HOME WATERS AS WELL AS THE GREATEST PORTION OF THE CARRIERS." The U.S. Navy initiates another Patrol Wing (9), at Quonset Point, Rhode Island. As 1941 closes out, Japan still pays little attention to the U.S. Submarine Service and for that matter, the rest of the U.S. Navy too, but they'll soon learn the true grit of the American Sailor, who shall imminently uphold the traditions of men like Jones, Barry, Perry, Farragut and Dewey, heroes all, but most of all Americans, determined to keep the Stars and Stripes flying forever. **(Pacific)** Marine reinforcements (2nd and 4th Defense Battalions) from the States arrive at Pearl Harbor to await further orders, which will move them to Wake Island to establish a permanent Garrison. In other activity, the Navy is still rebuilding its Vessel strength. The remaining Submarines (V-Boats) constructed during the years 1932-1934 are slowly becoming old timers, as the Navy moves towards smaller and more deadly Vessels, equipped with longer cruising ranges, more powerful diving capabilities and a more potent torpedo threat. The U.S.S. *Barracuda* (V1), *Bass* (V2), *Bonita* (V3),

maintain a crew of 75 men. The Vessels carry six torpedo tubes, a three inch deck gun and two machineguns. The U.S.S. *Argonaut* (V4) is the biggest of the V-Boats and carries a complement of 89 men, four 21" torpedo tubes, 2 six inch deck guns and weighs in at 2,710 tons. The U.S. *Narwhal* (V-5) and the *Nautilus* (V-6) each carry six torpedo tubes and two six inch deck guns. The U.S.S. *Dolphin* (V-7), *Cachalot* (V-8) the *Cuttlefish* (point Submarine at battle of Midway) are soon headed for battle. At the present time, the Pacific Submarine Fleet is headquartered at Pearl Harbor and is assigned responsibility for Midway. **(Atlantic-Soviet Union)** The Russians mount a counterattack against German positions at Tula. German General von Reichenau now commands the Southern Army Group, replacing von Runstedt who has lost Hitler's favor. On the southern front, the Russians mount another attack on the following day that pushes Von Kleist's forces back toward Mariupol.

December 2nd 1941 — **(United States)** An American Merchant Ship, the *Dunboyne*, becomes the first Merchant Vessel to receive a Naval Armed Guard crew. The U.S. maintains headquarters for its Atlantic Submarine Fleet at New London, Connecticut. The Submarines will continue to multiply and thanks is partly due to the increasing German threat in Europe. **(Pacific)** American Scout Planes have detected large concentrations of enemy Warships in Camranh Bay, situated on the southeast coast of French Indo China. Although about 50 Ships are detected, inclement weather arrives and contact is lost on the fourth. On the following day, Pilots spot the enemy Armada in the Gulf of Siam, moving in the direction of the Malay Peninsula, from where it will storm Singapore on the 8th.

December 3rd 1941 — **(Pacific)** The Japanese delegations in the United States begin to destroy all papers in the Consulates to prevent seizure by the United States. **(Atlantic)** The U.S. loses another Vessel to a German torpedo, when the Merchant Vessel *Sagadahoc* is struck and sunk in the South Atlantic.

December 4th 1941 — **(Pacific)** The Aircraft Carrier *Enterprise* arrives near Wake Island, delivering Marine Fighter Squadron 211, which takes off for Wake, on Japan's doorstep. The Fighters are to fly continuous Patrols in search of hostile Ships and Planes. Task Force 8, under Halsey, returns toward Pearl, anticipating arrival at 0730 on the 7th of December, but heavy seas hold up a refueling operation and the Carriers run behind schedule.

December 5th 1941 — **(United States)** The United States is informed by the Japanese that the recent troop movements into Indo China (With permission of the French) is to be a temporary and precautionary type movement. **(Pacific-Pearl Harbor)** Task Force 12, commanded by Admiral Newton departs Pearl Harbor heading for Midway, inadvertently taking the *Lexington*, its three Heavy Cruisers and five Destroyers out of harms way. In addition, Task Force 3, commanded by Admiral Wilson Brown embarks from Pearl, heading for Johnston Island to initiate landing exercises. At present, there are forty-nine operable Patrol Planes (PBY-5s) on Oahu; fifty-four had only recently arrived, however, some experience shakedown problems. **(Pacific-Philippines)** British Admiral Sir Thomas Phillips meets with U.S. Admiral Hart at Cavite and is seeking American Naval help in assisting the H.M.S. *Prince of Wales* and *Repulse*, both jeopardized by the

Japanese with whom the British are not yet at war. The British have only four Destroyers available for protection and request four U.S. Destroyers to augment the force. Admiral Hart declines, informing the British Admiral that the U.S. is not at war at the present time and that the loan would sap American defenses in the area. Admiral Phillips returns to Singapore on the following day. **(Atlantic-Soviet Union)** OPERATION BARBAROSSA comes to a slippery halt. The Germans, confronted by severe shortages of supplies and proper clothing, in addition to severe casualties are compelled to abort the attack against Moscow. The Germans have received a first hand education on what is known as a Russian winter. Meanwhile, with the Germans on the doorstep of Moscow, Stalin meets with Britain's Foreign Secretary, Anthony Eden and Polish General Wladyslaw Sikorski (head of exile government). Stalin and Sikorski sign a mutual aid pact.

December 6th 1941 — (United States) The "Day of Infamy" approaches. President Roosevelt makes a direct request to Japan's Emperor Hirohito, to exercise his influence to avoid war between the two countries. Meanwhile, the Japanese Task Force is closing irrevocably on Pearl Harbor. **(Atlantic-Soviet Union)** The Russians, bolstered with reinforcements, attack the Germans along the entire front which stretches for about 500 snowcovered miles. Some of the Russian Tanks drag oversize improvised sleds, which carry Soldiers over the icy route, while other troops cling precariously to the moving Armor. The assault catches the Germans completely offguard and forces the Germans to retreat. Moscow does not fall.

December 7th 1941 — (Pacific) BATTLE OF PEARL HARBOR — Japan secretly positions Vice Admiral Nagumo's Task Force of 33 Ships, including six Carriers, 200 miles north of Oahu, Hawaii. In Japan, there is a sense of anxiety concerning the secrecy of the mission. The hour in Tokyo is 01:30 as the Planes are taking off. In Washington, at 11:30 it is still just another quiet Sunday. President Roosevelt's plea to Emperor Hirohito is in transit and will be delivered by Tojo, at 03:00, Tokyo time, less than a half hour before Japanese Commander Fuchida's Planes attack Pearl Harbor. During the mere moments of a few hours, history will be drastically changed for the remainder of time. As the clock ticks away in Washington, the Japanese stall for time, as Ambassador Nomura asks the State Department for a half hour deferment of the meeting to deliver Japan's final message to the U.S., concerning the situation in the Pacific. There is an edge of a warning concerning the possible presence of an enemy Submarine in the early morning hours near Pearl, but thoughts of a major attack are not yet evident to the Americans.

The U.S.S. *Condor*, a Minesweeper, Patrolling near the entrance to Pearl Harbor, observes what appears to be a Submarine. This information is transmitted to the U.S.S. *Ward*, a Destroyer, which is moving into Pearl, after just having completed a Patrol. About seven minutes pass, between the sighting, and the crew of the *Ward*, receiving the message and taking action at a little before 04:00, but without results. The *Ward*, relaxes at about 05:00, after a serious hour of General Quarters, without locating any unidentified Vessels and the *Ward* maintains a course which takes her toward the harbor.

At 06:00, the Imperial Navy's Attack Force is commencing its assault, presumed to reach Pearl Harbor in an hour and a half. Within fifteen minutes, the Bombers and escort Fighters have been launched by the six Carriers and they are heading

south toward the unsuspecting Yanks. In advance of the main body of Aircraft, are Reconnaissance Seaplanes, which move in undetected. In addition, Japanese Cruisers acting as a vanguard of the Fleet are not detected either.

As the Planes are closing on the Harbor, the U.S.S. *Ward* is just about to enter Pearl. Its about 06:30, and the watch on the *Ward* is observing a Target Ship being towed into the harbor when they spot an uninvited periscope, trailing behind, attempting to shadow the American Target Vessel and move right through the defenses unnoticed, into the harbor. General Quarters are sounded and after making sure the intruder is foreign, the *Ward* closes, firing two shots from a distance of 100 yards, with the first shot missing and the second hitting the diminutive conning tower of the midget Submarine, at exactly 06:45. The *Ward*, follows the deck gun action with the release of four depth charges that succinctly finish the enemy Submarine, then dispatches the following message to Headquarters: "WE HAVE ATTACKED, FIRED UPON, AND DROPPED DEPTH CHARGES UPON SUBMARINE OPERATING IN DEFENSIVE SEA AREA!" Unfortunately, the dispatched message from the Destroyer to Headquarters, does not reach the Commanding Officers. There have been many reports of unidentified Submarines in waters near Pearl for about a year or so, but all had proved erroneous.

Commander Mitsuo Fuchida, leading the surprise attack against American installations at Pearl Harbor closes in. The Japanese send a total of 360 Aircraft, including Horizontal Bombers, Dive Bombers and Torpedo Bombers, to strike the unsuspecting Yanks, many of whom are sleeping late or attending church this tranquil Sunday morning. A detachment of two men, Privates George Elliot and Joseph Lockhart, working the radar station high in the hills on Oahu, pick up the enemy Planes at 07:02 and excitedly pass on the information of a large formation of Planes heading for Pearl Harbor. The person on duty at Headquarters accepts the formation of Planes as the expected B-17 Flying Fortresses, due from California and does not react, except to tell the two Privates not to worry. Japanese Planes begin flying over Kahuku Point, a little after 07:30, maneuvering around the Kodakan Peaks swarming toward Oahu from the southwest to deliver the crushing blow against its Airfields. In accordance with the prediction of a local radio station, which is being heard on the Planes' radios, Fuchida's invaders break through the clouds, entering clear skies as they approach their targets. So leisurely is the approach, Fuchida actually peers through his binoculars, scanning the area before ordering his Force to attack.

The enemy Carriers are out of harms way and full of happy Japanese, cheering their Pilots that had ascended on one of the most cowardly sneak attacks in history against the United States of America. At the slumbering harbor there are about 90 American Vessels, including nine Cruisers, eight Battleships, 28 Destroyers and five of the 22 Submarines. Many other Warships, including all Carriers are out of the Harbor and there seems to be no great thought of an invasion against Pearl Harbor, situated 4,000 miles from Japan. Most Officers have considered this possible, but not probable. Admiral Halsey's Task Force is due at Pearl Harbor at 0800, but thanks to some inclement weather he is running behind schedule. Halsey, in an effort to give his Pilots extra practice and the ground batteries an opportunity to spot live targets, dispatches Planes from the Enterprise to arrive at Pearl before the Fleet. As the Admiral is having breakfast at 0755, a terse dispatch is handed to him: "JAPANESE AIR ATTACK PEARL. THIS IS NO DRILL." Halsey, at first glance, assumes that Pearl had been firing at his Planes, but soon realizes that his Pilots are flying right into it a war without warning.

The first wave of enemy Planes strikes just prior to 0800 hours. Bombs and bullets strafe the entire area, but the Colors are raised in disciplined fashion on the U.S.S. *Nevada*, as if it is an ordinary day. As soon as the brief ceremony ends, all hands race for battle stations. As the Colors are raised on the U.S.S. *Utah*, two torpedoes interrupt the ceremony and the mighty Battleship is sent to the bottom, taking with her 58 men who have been either riddled by Jap bullets or temporarily entombed when the Vessel rolls over. In short order, the neatly parked Planes at Hickam Field and the Ships at Ford Island are set ablaze by Bombers which also blast Battleship Row, where in some instances, PBYs at the ramps on Ford Island ejaculate in the air in pieces. The Stars and Stripes lay amidst row after row of burning Ships.

On Battleship Row, the *Arizona*, *California*, *Maryland* and the *Tennessee*, along with the *Oklahoma*, *Nevada* and the *West Virginia* are besieged, their valiant crews are caught in a sudden inferno. The *Pennsylvania*, another of the Battleships, is trapped in dry dock, but her guns are operational and the Anti-aircraft crew joins with the other gunners, pouring fire into the attacking Planes. Close by, three American Destroyers are also captive in dry dock when they come under the sudden savage and relentless assault. The U.S.S. *Shaw*, isolated in a floating dry dock, is ravaged within the first 20

minutes of the assault, being struck by several bombs, one of which devastates the mess (kitchen). Fires spread and within a short time the magazine explodes. Instinctively, the dry dock is flooded to aid the fire fighters, but as the dock becomes submerged, so does the *Shaw*, and the waters around her are consumed by flaming fuel. The Destroyers *Cassin* and *Downes*, tucked near the *Pennsylvania*, are sitting ducks as their guns lack parts. The Battleship *Pennsylvania* continues to fill the sky with Anti-aircraft fire, buffering the two Destroyers, while the *Cassin's* operational machine guns direct their guns in concert.

The crew of the *Downes*, reassembles its machine guns in record time to join the fight. During the process, the crew must break the locks to get to the ammunition. As more bombs strike the dry dock area, the fuel tank of the *Downes*, is ignited, causing a huge explosion that ravages, but doesn't disable the crew. An incendiary bomb then strikes the *Downes* and flames flow like lava across the deck from a vociferous volcano. Some crewmen are instantly transformed into ashes, while others are burned beyond recognition. The *Cassin*, stranded next to the *Downes*, becomes the recipient of the rapid moving fire. Both of these Destroyers, soon resemble molten steel rubbish, but will ultimately be salvaged and join the dedicated fight in the Pacific against the Japanese. The majority, 14 out of the 17 Destroyers in port are able to avoid major damage and eventually make it out of their moorings to engage in Antisubmarine activity and join in the search for the Japanese Fleet after the morning devastation ceases.

December 7th 1941 — Wreckage of U.S. Army Planes: of 123 Planes, 63 survive the attack.

December 7th 1941 — Damage at Naval Air Station: 36 Planes out of 148 survive the attack at Pearl Harbor.

Hickam Field, Hawaii, December 7th 1941 after Japanese sneak attack.

December 7th 1941 — U.S.S. Pennsylvania (BB-38); U.S.S. Downes (DD-375) (left) and the U.S.S. Cassin (DD-372) (right).

December 7th 1941 — The U.S.S. Shaw (DD-373), exploding while under attack.

December 7th 1941 — Pearl Harbor Battleship Row: West Virginia (BB-48), Tennessee (BB-43), Arizona (BB-39), left to right.

December 7th 1941 — The U.S.S. West Virginia (BB-48) in flames at Pearl Harbor.

Japanese midget Submarine captured at Pearl Harbor during the attack on December 7th. The Vessel is now on display at the U.S. Submarine Base in Groton, Ct.

American Fighting men are coping as best as possible. Rescue operations get underway immediately to evacuate the wounded and salvage as much equipment as possible. Fortunately, many of the men are ashore when the attack occurs or the loss of life would be far worse. The *Arizona*, suffers a horrid fate as a bomb drops directly down one of her stacks, exploding the boiler room and killing all hands. The U.S.S. *Arizona*, which becomes a most hallowed shrine for these gallant American Servicemen, killed by an enemy which had not declared war until after the attack was underway. These valiant Sentinels of Freedom still sleep in the harbor as an indelible reminder of the Japanese treachery and a stirring testimony of the deeds of those Yanks at Pearl; 15 receive the Medal of Honor for their actions.

The Carriers at sea escape the ruthless assault. In addition, the Japanese curiously spare the Sub Base, although there are Five Submarines in port. The Subs manage to join in the action and also pick up survivors in the burning sea. The U.S.S. *Tautog* crewmen man their deck guns when the Jap Planes come in rapidly over Battleship Row and as the Destroyers cease fire, the *Tautog*, picks up the tempo and blasts a Plane from the sky, giving her the first Submarine unassisted kill (Plane) of the war. In addition, the *Curtiss*, a Seaplane Tender, later damaged by a crashing enemy Plane, destroys a midget Submarine. It will receive the dubious honor of being raised and cemented into the foundation of the U.S. Submarine Pier.

The Americans add to their difficulties when the overstressed ground crews, desperately engaged with the attackers, inadvertently fire upon U.S. Flying Fortresses attempting to reach Pearl Harbor. Additional Army and Naval Planes also come under attack by friendly fire. By the time the second wave of Planes appear, at just about 0840, most of the damage had been done. The second wave roars into action against the Americans, as eighty-six Dive Bombers, over fifty Horizontal Bombers and three dozen Fighters whack the already devastated defenders at Pearl. Much of the Planes' effort is concentrated on the U.S.S. *Nevada*, intentionally grounded at Waipo Point to prevent it being sunk where it might block the narrow harbor. When this attack ceases, the Navy has lost four Battleships, one Mine Layer, and a Target Ship. Three Cruisers, three Destroyers and two other Vessels are damaged. All but three, the *Oklahoma*, the *Utah* and the *Arizona*, come back to haunt the Japs in the future. In addition, 188 American Aircraft are destroyed, including eleven launched from the *Enterprise*.

By 1 P.M., the balance of the enemy Planes have returned to their Carriers. American Carriers, based at Pearl Harbor, are out of Port, saving them and giving the U.S. a sign of hope and the means to strike back. American Ships including Halsey's Fleet search for the enemy Fleet, but they disappear into the sunset, celebrating the deaths of the Yanks at Pearl. The entire West Coast could have been jeopardized if the Japanese Task Force had decided to move against it. Fortunately, the Japanese chose to return to the homeland. Only God knows the thoughts of those who perished for their country. One example of fidelity that exemplifies the actions of all Americans on this fateful day, are the final words of Machinist Mate Robert R. Scott, who steadfastly refused to leave his trapped companions on the mangled Battleship, the U.S.S. *California*: "THIS IS MY STATION AND I WILL STAY AND GIVE THEM AIR AS LONG AS THE GUNS ARE GOING." The *California* had been staggered at 08:05 by torpedoes that cause explosions and fires: the damage was so severe, that an order to abandon is given-and ignored, until further actions prove in vain. Survivors plummet into the boiling water and swim through the burning sea, as the *California* goes down. Rescue workers battle the overturned Vessel without rest, in response to the desperate taps of life, being pounded against the hull from the inside. This manifest effort saves 32 men. An additional 415 men on the *California* are lost. In a last fling with arrogance, the Japanese Commanding Officer, Fushida, makes a solitary pass over the wreckage and carnage, taking photographs of his remarkable victory.

On the following day, Admiral Halsey moves his Fleet into the battered harbor. It is a profane sight that Halsey would never forget and one that made him anxious to take the war to Japan. It will be Admiral Halsey, who ferries Colonel Doolittle's Bomber Squadron on the famous Carrier raid against Japan. The United States loss at Pearl: 2,004 Sailors, 108 Marines and 222 Soldiers killed; wounded: Army, 360; Marines, 75; Navy, 912. The Japanese lose fewer than 100 men. In addition, the Japanese lose five Midget Submarines and 28 Aircraft. The Damage to the U.S. Fleet is as follows: Sunk Battleships *Oklahoma* (BB-37), *Arizona* (BB-39), *California* (BB-44), *West Virginia* (BB-48). In addition the Minelayer *Oglala* (CM-4) and the Target Ship *Utah* (AG-16) are sunk. Damaged: Battleships *Nevada* (BB-36), *Pennsylvania* (BB-38), *Tennessee* (BB-43), *Maryland* (BB-46). Light Cruisers: *Helena* (CL-50), *Honolulu* (CL-48), *Raleigh* (CL-7). Destroyers: *Cassin* (DD-372), *Downes*

(DD-375), *Shaw* (DD-373). In addition, the Seaplane Tender *Curtiss* (AV-4) and the Repair Ship *Vestal*, (AR-4) are also damaged. THE JAPANESE DECLARATION OF WAR AGAINST THE UNITED STATES ARRIVES IN WASHINGTON D.C. AFTER THE REPREHENSIBLE ATTACK AND MASSACRE AT PEARL HARBOR.

December 7th 1941 — (Pacific-Hawaii) SEE BATTLE OF PEARL HARBOR. In other activity relating to the attack: The Americans have no exact location of the launching point of the Carrier Planes that strike Pearl Harbor. It is several days afterwards when bodies of Japanese Pilots that contain charts are retrieved from the sea that the information becomes available. **(Pacific-Japan)** The American Embassy is informed that war has broken out with the U.S. and that all personnel are to remain on Embassy grounds. In addition, all communication is severed with the outside world and any type of wireless-transmitting sets are to be surrendered. Embassy staff arrives back in the U.S. during August 42. The Swiss government will take over American interests in Japan. **(Pacific-Midway)** Two Japanese Destroyers, the *Akebono* and *Ushio* bombard American positions on Midway Island, inflicting severe damage to the installation. The Marines (6th Defense Battalion) suffer 14 casualties. Two U.S. Destroyers, the *Argonaut* and the *Trout* are on Patrol in the vicinity of Midway Island, but have no encounters with the enemy. In addition the Submarines *Tambor* and *Triton*, are operating near Wake Island, but encounter no enemy activity. **(Pacific-Philippines)** The situation for the American defenders is extremely grave. Needed supplies have not arrived in sufficient numbers. There is a drastic shortage of Anti-aircraft Guns and much of the ammunition is antiquated; many of the shells received in the Philippines are duds. The facilities for Planes are not much better. Many of the Fighter Planes are obsolete. Only one field in Luzon is capable of handling Heavy Bombers. In Mindanao, where Brereton's B-17s have been sent to avoid an attack, the situation is critical. Del Monte Airfield can accommodate the Heavy Bombers, but lacks space to accept reinforcements — if they come. In addition, of seven units recently arrived, only one is operational. **(Atlantic-North Africa)** A British offensive, which had begun in November, continues to roll forward, as the British 8th Army, under General Ritchie, engages combined German Italian Forces in the vicinity of Bir El Gubi, Libya. The Axis Powers are under superficial Italian leadership, although the genuine Commander is German Field Marshall Erwin Rommel. In other activity, the British 13 Corps pushes through El Adem Ridge, south of Tobruk.

December 8th 1941 — President Roosevelt speaks to Congress, requesting that a declaration of war be issued against Japan.

December 8th 1941 — (United States) President Roosevelt, in a historical national address, states: "YESTERDAY, DECEMBER 7th, 1941, A DATE WHICH WILL LIVE IN INFAMY, THE UNITED STATES WAS SUDDENLY AND DELIBERATELY ATTACKED BY NAVAL AND AIR FORCES OF THE EMPIRE OF JAPAN." The United States and England declare war against Japan. In Hawaii, the site of the devastating attack, the date is December 7th, since Hawaii is west of the international date line. **(Pacific-Pearl Harbor)** One Japanese Midget Submarine which had penetrated Hawaiian waters during the enemy attack, is captured after the Vessel becomes lost, then entangled on a reef near Bellows Field. The Japanese Officer, Lt. Sakamaki, chooses to swim to shore and surrender, thus receiving the dubious honor of becoming the first Japanese prisoner of war. The Submarine is confiscated in operational condition: its radio is ironically stamped, "Made in U.S.A." In other activity, Pearl Harbor's Submarine Base is commanded by Rear Admiral Thomas Withers. His command encompasses 16 modern Subs and six of the older S-Boats, all of which will operate as part of the Pacific Fleet. One of these Subs, the U.S.S. *Thresher*, gets a surprise when she surfaces, anticipating a rendezvous with the Destroyer *Litchfield*, but she is instead greeted by the Japs in an antiquated, but still deadly four piper. The Japanese shells sever the conning tower as it peeks through the water, but the *Thresher* dives deep and awaits assistance. After several more tedious hours, which also includes an accidental bombing by American Planes, the Destroyer *Thornton* finally moves out to bring in the threatened Submarine, without further incident. As the other Submarines come in later, during the coming days, nerves are less tangled and there are no more cases of mistaken identity with the U.S. Silent Service. **(Pacific)** A Japanese Naval Task Force, commanded by Vice Admiral N. Inouye, moves toward American held Guam and Wake Island. At Wake Island, the Japanese 24th Air Flotilla swings in swiftly from their Base at Roi, and deliver a devastating blow that explodes a multi-thousand gallon aviation fuel tank, causing casualties and creating fierce fires on the Airfield. The Japs also knock out seven of eight F4f-3's. Offshore, two American Submarines, the U.S.S. *Tambor* and the U.S.S. *Triton* are on patrol. The *Tambor*, within sight of the disaster, cannot reach the enemy Convoy in time. The *Triton*, lurking further south of Midway, is able to overtake the Japanese Force during the night of the 10th-11th. At Guam, in the Marianas, Jap Planes score a deadly blow, against the U.S.S. *Penguin*, a Minesweeper (AM-33), sinking her. Prior to the outbreak of hostilities, the U.S. Congress had turned down an appropriation of $5 million, intended to fortify Guam and make it an invulnerable fortress against a Japanese attack. Congress had believed that the Navy could easily defend against a Japanese attack. Japan will also head for the Gilbert Islands, soon to be remembered for the vicious campaigns fought on such places as Tarawa. Its virtually unopposed Air Force delivers lethal air raids all across the area, striking Allied positions in Hong Kong, Singapore, and British Malaya. Other Japanese Planes strike the Nauru and Ocean Islands. There are simply not enough Allied Planes to match the present superiority of the enemy. **(Pacific-Philippines)** In yet another seemingly unendless brutalizing attack, Naval Planes of the Japanese 11th Air Fleet, operating out of Formosa, swoop down with impunity, on the beleaguered American-Filipino positions at Luzon in the Philippines. American Planes on the runways at Iba and Clark Airfields are clobbered, further diminishing their numbers. Swarming enemy Army Planes had struck smaller Airstrips at Baguio and Tuguegarao, in advance of the primary attack against Clark Field. The Air raids are near synchronized, with the debarkation of land troops, who invade Bataan Island (situated between Luzon and Formosa), without opposition and initiate their quest to seize Airfields, which will stabilize the campaign to win the Philippines. U.S. Task Force 5, Asiatic Fleet, commanded by Rear Admiral William A. Glassford, begins moving away from the Philippines, departing Iloilo, heading for the Makassar Strait, Netherlands East Indies. **(Pacific-China-Burma-India)** A small contingent of Marines at Tientsin, Peiking and Camp Holcomb, China, are forced to surrender to the Japanese. Colonel William Ashurst U.S.M.C., the Senior Officer surrenders the troops. The U.S.S. *Wake* (PR-3), a River Gunboat, surrenders at Shanghai, after the crew tries unsuccessfully to destroy the Vessel. It becomes the first and only Fighting Ship to surrender to the Japanese. In other activity, the U.S.S. *President Harrison*, on a mission to evacuate the sparse contingent of Marines at Chingwangtao, China, runs aground in the vicinity of Sha Wai Shan, China and is captured by the Japanese. **(Malaya-Thailand)** Japanese troops land near the Airfield at Kota Bharu, Malaya and are met by the British Ninth Indian Division, which puts up stiff resistance, but is forced to withdraw the following night. British Lt. General Sir Lewis Heath, Commander of all British forces in Malaya north of Johore and Malacca, in addition to utilizing the Ninth Indian Division at Kota Bharu, also rushes the 11th Indian Division into Thailand, to delay the Japanese advance on Singapore. The Royal Air Force Far East Command assaults the enemy Naval Vessels and strafes the ground troops; it then departs, heading further south to the Airfield at Kuantan. **(Atlantic)** The R.A.F. strikes the Axis troops in Libya as they attempt to withdraw to Gazala. The British Eighth Army gives chase, but disciplined rear-guard actions by the Germans very effectively delay the pursuit.

December 9th 1941 — (Pacific) The Japanese approach the Gilbert Islands. On the following day, Japanese troops land on Makin and the Japanese claim occupation of the Tarawa Atoll. In addition, the American Garrison at Guam is hit by a vicious attack. Wake Island is again struck by Japanese Aircraft, which demolish buildings and the Naval Air Station at Peale Island. Anti-aircraft Batteries A and E on Peacock Point receive heavy fire, which causes much damage to these American defenses which somehow hold on. **(Pacific-Philippines)** The Japanese take another swipe at the understrengthed defenders. Enemy Planes strike Nichols Field, situated close to Manila. **(China-Burma-India)** China declares war on Japan, Germany and Italy. In other activity, the Japanese occupy Bangkok, Thailand, encountering light opposition. Additional Japanese troops strike the east coast of Thailand, landing at both Patani and Singora without incident. These combined enemy forces initiate movement across the Kra Isthmus, to assist with the seizure of Malaya. Dutch Planes rush to Singapore, to reinforce the Royal Air Force.

December 10th 1941 — (Pacific-Hawaii) American Carrier-based Aircraft detect and sink the Japanese Submarine I-170 off the coast of Hawaii. **(Pacific-Guam)** The Japanese swarm upon the sparsely garrisoned island of Guam. Over 5,000 Japs attached to the South Seas Detached Force land at two separate sites: Tumon Bay situated in the northern portion of the island, and at Talafofo Bay located on the eastern shore of the island. Another landing force of approximately 400 men, assigned to the 5th Defense Force stationed at Saipan, debark on Dungcas Beach. The overpowering strength of the enemy, forces Captain George McMillan U.S.N., the Governor of the island of Guam, to surrender his small Garrison. One of the Japanese, living on the island, is conspicuously smiling as the Japanese Planes are soaring overhead, bombing the island. Old Glory is ingloriously stripped from her staff by the Japanese troops. A few Americans refuse to surrender and take to the dense jungle. One of the American Sailors, Radioman George Tweed, harasses the Japs and evades capture for 31 months before being rescued by the U.S. Navy. Tweed virtually drives the Japs crazy as they search in vain on a daily basis, but the Chamorros (citizens of Guam), take great risks to shield him. Tweed is witness to some of their atrocities, which include the decapitation of children, one of which has his head severed and placed in gory fashion, between his shoulder and waist, about ten inches from the body. The boy's crime is looking up to the sky, as American Planes fly overhead during the campaign to retake Guam from the Japs, who boast it cannot be taken. When the U.S. Navy begins its return to bombard and capture Guam, a group of people seek shelter in a cave. Jap troops already in the cave decide to line the people up near some small craters, created by the bombs, after having accused them of being American spies. One person, a young girl, attempts to break away to safety and is quickly seized by the crazed Jap troopers, who proceed to restrain her. A Jap cuts off one of her breasts, leaving the young girl to bleed to death in front of their eyes. Another young girl is maliciously stabbed with a bayonet. The Soldier withdraws the bayonet, then pulls out her intestines. A couple of the victims are left for dead in their shallow graves, but miraculously, they recover from their wounds to be around when the Yanks hit the island. Tweed assists the Navy and ground troops, when they invade the island and not a minute too soon, before the Japs exterminate the entire populace. Can you imagine what they would do to Tweed? **(Pacific-Wake Island)** The Japanese continue to pound Wake Island. The Submarine U.S.S. *Triton* encounters an enemy Warship on the horizon, south of Wake. The Vessel's Captain, Lt. Commander W.A. Lent, attempting to obey orders "NOT TO ATTACK UNLESS ATTACKED," takes her down deep and prepares for a rough time. This unusual test, of wait to see if the Japanese can kill you, before you can fire at them, becomes nervewracking after a few hours of sweating it out on the bottom, so the *Triton* prepares to attack. Four tubes are emptied. Seconds pass and the vibrations felt throughout the Submarine, linked with the explosion heard, lets the men know they have struck oil, Japanese oil. The Vessel had not been sunk, but the action gives the *Triton* the honor of becoming the first Submarine in the Pacific Fleet to commence a torpedo attack during World War II. **(Pacific-Philippines)** Approximately 4,000 Japanese troops, which had departed Formosa in two separate Task Forces, strike northern Luzon, near Aparrí and Vigan. Inclement weather and unruly seas create some difficulty for the invaders, but two Companies of the Aparri Force are able to land at Aparri, with the remainder hitting shore about 20 miles further east, at Gonzaza. The Vigan Force sends a small contingent ashore at Pandan, with the balance striking shore a little under five miles further south. Camalaniugan Airstrip is quickly seized by the Aparri Force. In short order, Vigan falls without incident, allowing the Japanese to advance northward, to seize Laoag. The 11th Division (Philippine Army), which holds responsibility for this area (northern coast), offers no opposition. U.S. Planes attempt to forestall the Japanese, by assaulting the Japanese Naval Task Forces. Captain Colin Kelly, U.S.A., becomes America's first World War II hero during this confrontation, when his Plane attacks and sinks a Japanese Ship, which at first is thought to be a Battleship. Later, it is determined that no enemy Battleships participated in the engagement. Japanese Aircraft bomb Nichols and Nielson Airfields, both of which are close to Manila, while other enemy Aircraft inflict severe damages to Del Carmen Airfield, located in the vicinity of Clark Air Field. The American Naval base at Cavite suffers heavy damage also. Horizontal Bombers damage the Destroyer *Peary* (DD-226); Submarines *Seadragon* (SS-194) and *Sealion* (SS-195); Minesweeper *Bittern* (AM-36). In addition, U.S. Army Aircraft, based in the Philippines, sink two Japanese Minesweepers, Numbers 10 and 19. The fate of the *Sealion* is noteworthy. Because of extensive damage and the loss of the Cavite Navy Yard, the Vessel will be scuttled on the 25th. The U.S.S. *Seadragon* will be rescued by the U.S.S. *Pigeon* and towed to safety through flame and explosions to where she can get away on her own power. With the loss of the *Sealion*, comes the death of the first U.S. Submarine during World War Two and the death of the first Submariner, Ensign Sam H. Hunter to be killed by the Japanese. Four additional Seamen are killed in a subsequent explosion. The most devastating damage is suffered at Cavite, where over 1,000 die; an additional 400 pass away in the hospital. At Manila, damage is not severe. It becomes apparent, as the conflict wears on that only total and unequivocal defeat will end the Japanese plans for conquest. In addition, it becomes apparent that it is not a healthy idea for civilians or Soldiers to be captured by the Japanese. American POWs suffer about a 30% death rate. In the Atlantic Theater, the death rate of the American POW's is less than 3%. **(Pacific-Gilberts)** Tarawa and Makin Islands (Gilbert Islands) are seized by Japan. In a desperate move to save the contingent of the American Asiatic Fleet (still in the vicinity of the Philippines) from capture, orders are given to move out of Manila Bay and head south, to safer positions in the Makassar Strait (East Indies). The Fleet pulls out and eventually joins a Dutch Fleet in the East Indies. The combined Fleets will engage the Japanese in the Java Sea and will be badly defeated. **(China-Burma-India)** The British are receiving an equally tough time from the Japanese. The Japs have secured the skies over the northern portion of Malaya and are battering a British Fleet in the vicinity of Kauntan, destroying the H.M.S *Repulse* and the H.M.S. *Prince of Wales*. British Admiral Sir Thomas Phillips, Commander of the Eastern Fleet, is killed during the confrontation. The British Airfields in northern Malaya are also bombed heavily, forcing the R.A.F. to abandon Sungei Airfield and head for Butterworth. The Japanese keep the pressure on the British and a Bomber Squadron, operating out of Butterworth, is reduced to two Planes, mandating that they withdraw further to Taiping. A British Fighter Squadron, left with only six operational Planes, is compelled to move from Butterworth to Ipoh. At Penang Island, the Indian 9th Division sustains repeated heavy Air attacks, but holds its positions, just south of Kota Bharu. The Indian 11th Division is thinly stretched along the Thailand Frontier, in a desperate effort to slow the Japanese advance. **(Atlantic-North Africa)** In Libya, the British break the eight month long German siege of Tobruk. Polish troops manage to break out and join with additional British 8th Army troops at Acroma.

December 10th 1941 — Cavite Navy Yard, Philippines after Japanese air raid.

December 11th 1941 — (Pacific-Pearl Harbor) The Submarines *Gudgeon* and *Plunger* embark from Pearl Harbor, to harass the enemy in the Imperial waters of Japan, during an anticipated stay of about 50 days. The U.S.S. *Plunger* which takes the first radar set into battle will be compelled to make a quick return in three days for unexpected repairs. More Submarines will follow, with special thanks going to the Japanese, for not destroying their nest at Pearl Harbor. The *Pollack* departs for Tokyo Bay on the 13th, and the *Pompano*, speeds towards the Marshalls, with the *Dolphin* in close pursuit, leaving Pearl Harbor on Christmas Eve. Another Submarine, the *Tautog*, is also dispersed, to investigate unfamiliar Japanese waters. These Submariners are expected to not only seek and destroy enemy Shipping, but also are used for reconnaissance for future operations. **(Pacific-Wake Island)** — At dawn, a Japanese Squadron eases near the coast and begins to bombard the island. The Japanese then attempt to invade, but the Marine 1st Defense Battalion firing its shore guns, turns back the enemy Naval Squadron, while its 450 man Invasion Force is still embarked. To the dismay of their Squadron Commander, Admiral Kajioka, the Japanese are handily repulsed at both Wilkes and Wake Islands by the Marine Garrison, commanded by Major Devereux, numbering 15 Officers and 373 enlisted men. Old Glory will not be torn down on Wake, by the Japanese today. The Japs pay a heavy price as the remnants (five operational Planes left) of Fighter Squadron 211 bomb and strafe the withdrawing force, sinking two Destroyers. The *Hayete* is the first Japanese surface Ship to be sunk during World War II, and the honors go to Marine Shore Batteries. The other Japanese Destroyer sunk is the *Kisaragi*, by Marine Corps Pilots. **(Pacific-Philippines)** In the Philippines, resistance is crumbling and the Japanese seize northern Luzon. Japanese Planes continue to destroy what is left of the American Planes in the Philippines. The Japanese initiate murderous Air attacks against Burma and then put their troops on the offensive. **(Atlantic-France)** U.S. Ambassador Leahy confers with French Marshal Petain and French Admiral Darlan in Vichy. Ambassador Leahy is to request information for President Roosevelt, regarding French intentions for their Fleet based in North Africa. Leahy also informs the French about U.S., concerns relative to the French Naval Vessels in the Western Hemispheres. Both Petain and Darlan, express a desire to remain neutral. **(Atlantic-Europe)** Germany and Italy declare war on the United States. The United States reciprocates against both countries. Germany's decision to declare war against the United States forces Hitler into a two front war which he adamantly opposed. Hitler had been prodding Japan to declare war against Russia and apparently got caught by surprise when Pearl Harbor was attacked. His previous decision to destroy the Slavs rather than induce them to fight the Russians whom they despise and his declaration of war against the U.S. seals his eventual fate and is regarded by most historians as two of his worst mistakes.

December 1941 — U.S. Army troops at Honolulu, Hawaii subsequent to the Pearl Harbor attack.

December 12th 1941 — (United States) The U.S. Government begins seizing all French Ships in American ports. In other activity, the Naval Air Transport Service is established. **(Pacific)** The Carrier U.S.S. *Pensacola*, is assigned escort duty for an Allied Convoy which is departing Hawaii, heading for the Far East. The American troops, aboard the Transports, are organized as Task Force South Pacific and will be commanded by Brigadier General Julian F. Barnes, U.S.A. **(Pacific-Philippines)** In the Philippines, the Japanese land 2,500 men at South Luzon, who will seize the Airfield at Legaspi unopposed. A contingent of the Philippine 51st Division (Commanding Officer, General George M. Parker, Jr., U.S.A.) is moved up to delay the Japanese, but no contact is made for several days. The Japanese, who had landed previously at Aparri, seize the Airfield at Tuguegarao. In addition, Japanese Planes continue their destruction of the Airfields in Luzon, striking Iba and Clark Airfields. By the following day, the Japanese will have knocked out all Army and Navy Planes on the Philippines. **(Pacific-Burma)** The Japanese offensive through Burma begins as they strike the Airdrome in lower Burma at Tavoy. British General Sir Archibald Wavell, with approximately 30 Battalions, attempts to protect Burma. An American Fighter Squadron is rushed to assist the R.A.F., but the British Planes are obsolete and never become able to support land troops. **(Atlantic-Middle East)** In the Middle East, British General Auchinleck receives word that reinforcements heading toward him, are being diverted to Burma, to halt the Japanese advance in Indo-China. **(Atlantic-North Africa)** In Libya, the British 8th Army ascends upon the Egyptian — Libyan border and begins to destroy enemy Garrisons. **(Dutch East Indies)** In Malaya, the British order the withdrawal of the Indian 3rd Corps from Kelantan, because the Japanese already control the Airfields.

December 13th 1941 — (Pacific) Japanese Fighters and Bombers deliver the final blow to American Airfields in the Philippines. Del Carmen, Clark, and Nichols Fields sustain devastating attacks. Baguio, Batangas, Cabantuan and Tarlac are also struck. Enemy Aircraft leave behind a totally incapacitated American Air Force, the only exception being some B-17 bombers. The American Planes had been crammed close together, costing the U.S. over half of the Planes, during the first raids. The belief had been that Japanese Planes on Formosa could not reach them. Inquiries are held to ascertain the reason for this poor tactical placement of our Planes, but total blame is never pinpointed. The Heavy Bombers of General Brereton are spared, as they had been previously flown to Del Monte Airfield, in Mindanao. **(China-Burma-India)** In China, the Japanese keep advancing. As they press against the city of Hong Kong, the British abandon Kowloon, China. The British also evacuate Tenasserim, Burma (Victoria Point). **(Atlantic-North Africa)** The British 8th Army engages the forces of Rommel at the Gazalia Line, in Libya. Heavy casualties are sustained on both sides.

December 14th 1941 — (Pacific-Wake Island) Japanese Fighter Planes escalate the siege of Wake Island. Beleaguered Marines defiantly resist capitulation. At day's end, only one Airstrip remains operational. The U.S., in a desperate maneuver to reinforce Wake Island, dispatches Task Force 14, commanded by Rear Admiral F. J. Fletcher, from Hawaii. The Task

Force departs within 24 hours. **(Pacific-Philippines)** In the Philippines, American Admiral Thomas Hart removes the remaining Patrol Bombers, attached to Patrol Wing 10, Asiatic Fleet and three Tenders from the Philippines. On the following day, General MacArthur instructs General Brereton to transfer all remaining B-17's to Australia. This will leave a very meager amount of Fighters to defend the Philippines. There is some Naval activity northeast of Luzon, as the Submarine U.S.S. *Seawolf* encounters an enemy Destroyer and the opposing strategies begin, in terrible seas. After a day long seek and search, the *Seawolf* finally attacks on the 15th. Two torpedoes are fired, but no hits occur. Another torpedo is fired, and an unsubstantiated hit is believed to be scored. As these actions are taken in the Philippines, there is still hope by the defenders, that reinforcements are on the way. At a Staff meeting of the War Department, in Washington, D.C., the immediate destiny of the Philippine defenders is discussed. It is mentioned by General Eisenhower that reinforcements for MacArthur are further down the line and that the islands will fall before reinforcements arrive. General Marshall agrees with Eisenhower. **(China-Burma-India)** The Japanese press relentlessly in Burma. The British units continue to pull back. The Indian 11th Division withdraws to Gurun and takes new positions, but by nightfall the Japanese are ready to penetrate again. The Krohcol Force is split into other units and placed with the Indian 12th Brigade, and will be reassigned to the vicinity of Baling, approximately 9 miles west of Kroh. Small contingents of the 3 Corps are rushed to fill a gap on the undefended Grik Road. Over on the east coast, the Kelantan Force is also on the retreat, but does put up aggressive resistance as they withdraw.

December 15th 1941 — (Pacific-Hawaii) An attempt by the United States to reinforce Wake Island is initiated. Task Force 14, commanded by Rear Admiral Fletcher, departs Pearl Harbor. The reinforcements include contingents of the 4th Defense Battalion and Marine Fighter Squadron 211. In other activity, a Japanese Submarine commences firing against the island of Kahului, Maui. **(Pacific-Philippines)** The remaining Heavy Bombers of FEAF (Far East Air Force) are transferred to Darwin Australia. The American and Philippine defenders are now in even more desperate condition, with only a few Fighter Planes to protect them. The Japanese invaders are supported by a heavy Task Force, commanded by Vice Admiral Kondo. In other activity, the PT-33 becomes grounded, while operating in the Philippines and is destroyed by American Forces, to avoid its capture by enemy troops. **(Pacific)** American positions on Johnston Island are fired upon by two Japanese Warships. The enemy Vessels do not get any Planes or Ships; however, the bombardment nets them a 1,200 gallon oil tank. **(China-Burma-India)** In Malaya, the Japanese still advance with ease. The R.A.F. abandon the Butterworth Airfield, which prompts the defenders at the fortress on Penang Island, opposite Butterworth, to follow suit. On the west coast, the Indian 11th Division is forced to pull back from Gurun and head for the Muda River. **(U.S.S.R.)** Klin, located north of Moscow, is retaken by the Red Army.

December 16th 1941 — (United States) In the States, the Marine Corps establishes the 7th Defense Battalion, consisting of both Artillery and Infantry units. This force will subsequently depart San Diego for Samoa, to garrison the island. **(Pacific-Johnston Island)** Johnston Island is bombarded by a Japanese Submarine. **(China-Burma-India)** The Japanese

invade the northern coast of British Borneo. In Malaya, the Japanese continue pushing the Indian 11th Division back across the Muda River, but do not gain the south bank. The outnumbered Indian 3rd Division is forced to withdraw across the Krian River, against sustained Japanese pressure, the Indians having little Tank and Artillery support. During the night of the 16th, Penang Island is evacuated and on the 17th, British General Percival gives permission for the Indian 3 Corps to fall back further, if Japanese pressure continues. In other activity, the Submarine U.S.S. *Swordfish*, operating in the China Sea, destroys the Japanese Freighter *Atsutusan Maru*, in the vicinity of Hainan Island, giving the Freighter the distinction of being the first enemy Vessel sunk by an American Submarine. **(Atlantic)** In North Africa, a strenuous battle ensues between the British 8th Army and Axis troops. The Eighth Army pauses at battle's end to energize itself, then joins the other British troops in pursuit of the enemy Forces, which are withdrawing from the Gazalia Line in Libya.

U.S. Coast Guard Reservist Volunteer Port Security Bowsain Mate 1st Class Joseph J. Lynch on the left with another volunteer on duty at Girard Point of Philadelphia, part of ship security during WWII.

December 17th 1941 — (United States) The American Military sees a major change in Commanders. Rear Admiral Chester Nimitz is promoted to Admiral and replaces Admiral Husband E. Kimmel as Commander in Chief, Pacific Fleet. American Lieutenant General Walter C. Short, Commanding General, Hawaiian Department, is replaced by Lt. General Delos C. Emmons. Major General Frederick L. Martin, Commanding General of the Air Force, Hawaiian Department, is replaced by Brigadier General Clarence L. Tinker. The United States is on the move and now concentrates on winning the

Pacific campaign. The Japanese put intense pressure on British troops in Malaya, forcing the British to fall back further. In Borneo, Dutch Aircraft will initiate air strikes against Japanese Shipping, off the coast, but the Japanese are able to land troops at Miri, Sarawak, Borneo. **(Pacific-Wake Island)** Americans, cut off from the outside, still resist the relentless attack at Wake Island. This time, the enemy Warplanes strike a diesel oil tank and damage a unit, which the island depends on entirely for its water supply.

December 18th 1941 — (United States) The U.S. State Department makes public a decision with the French, an agreement on the neutral status of French Caribbean possessions. The negotiations have been handled for the United States by Rear Admiral F.J. Horne. The French High Commissioner is the negotiator for the French. In other activity, the U.S. Congress passes legislation which establishes the First War Powers Act. **(Pacific-Pearl Harbor)** The U.S.S. *Pompano*, commanded by Lt. Commander L.S. Parks, embarks from Pearl Harbor en route to Japanese controlled waters, to attack Japanese Shipping and gather information on the unfamiliar waters through photographs from a special periscope camera. In addition, the mission calls for the *Pompano* to place mines in enemy sea lanes. In other activity, Vice Admiral Dye (Kimmel's replacement) confers with Halsey and tells him that Task Force 11, which includes the *Lexington*, is to strike Wotje, while Task Force 14 heads for Wake Island to debark men and Planes on Wake Island. Halsey is told to take Task Force 8 toward Midway and protect the northern flank of the other two Forces. By the 20th, the orders are modified to the dismay of the disappointed Pilots on the *Saratoga* when ordered to abort the Wake operation. Task Force 8 and 14 are ordered to divert to Midway and Task Force 11 is called back to Pearl Harbor. Halsey makes Midway on the 21st and returns to Pearl Harbor on December 31st. **(Pacific-Wake Island)** The United States orders all Submarines (Task Force Seven), which are patrolling the area around Wake Island, to move South and await the Relief Force. Japanese Fighters swarm in again on the 19th, attempting to soften the defenses for a new assault. **(Pacific-Philippines)** Japanese troops (Legaspi detachment) move into Naga, Luzon. **(China-Burma-India)** Fierce fighting continues in Malaya. The British prepare to pull back further. Meanwhile, the Japanese invade Hong Kong. **(Pacific-Borneo)** The Japanese Destroyer *Shinonome*, hits a mine and is sunk in the vicinity of Miri, Borneo.

December 19th 1941 — (Pacific-Philippines) The Japanese slice the Philippines by seizing Sipoco, then move on Daet in Luzon. During the night, 5,000 more Japanese troops arrive off Davao. Bombing raids continue also, as Del Monte Airfield is hit again. **(Europe)** In the Atlantic Theater, German Field Marshal von Brauchitsch is fired by Hitler, who assumes personal command of the German Army.

December 20th 1941 — (United States) The Navy receives Admiral E.J. King as Commander in Chief, United States Fleet. He will maintain Headquarters in Washington, D.C. **(Pacific-Wake Island)** A U.S. Navy PBY lands at Wake Island, bringing physical contact with the outside world for the first time since the outbreak of war. The defiant defenders are informed of the Task Force which is rushing to their aid. It will be impossible to hold on much longer without help. **(Pacific-Philippines)** Another Japanese wave storms Mindanao. After

brushing aside 2,000 Filipino troops, the Japanese capture Davao and its Airfield. The Marines are ordered to evacuate Cavite. The 4th Marines are assigned to the command of General Douglas MacArthur. **(China-Burma-India)** In Malaya, British and Japanese troops still battle to a furious stalemate. In the China campaign, an American Air Unit, led by Colonel Claire Chennault, intercepts and defeats a contingent of Japanese Airplanes.

December 21st 1941 — (United States) The U.S. and Great Britain deliberate in Washington D.C. A result of the meeting, known as the Arcadia Conference, is in essence a detailed plan of attack against the Axis powers. The primary decision is to concentrate against Europe, while lending sufficient materials and men to support a gradual movement against the Empire of Japan. The hard-pressed defenders in the Philippines will be greatly affected by this decision. No reinforcements will be dispatched on their behalf. **(Pacific-Wake Island)** The U.S. Navy PBY, which had brought the news of reinforcements heading to Wake, departs, taking with it the last Americans who would leave the embattled island before its fall to the Japanese. American intelligence reports a strong build-up of Japanese Naval and Air forces in the vicinity of the Marshall Islands. This news suggests that the relief force which is heading for Wake might be detected by the enemy. Japanese Planes continue to pound the defenses on Wake as raids knock out the remaining Planes of Squadron 211. The Marine Planes on Wake have been eliminated, so the Pilots resort to the cardinal tradition that all Marines are Infantrymen first, and grab rifles to defend the beaches. **(Pacific-Philippines)** In the Philippines, additional Japanese troops (48th division), land at Lingayen Gulf and link with troops already there (Vigan-Aparri) for an offensive against Manila. In other activity, the Naval Defense forces under Rear Admiral F.W. Rockwell, transfer their headquarters to Corregidor.

December 22nd 1941 — (Pacific-Wake Island) The Japanese send two Patrol Boats directly toward the beach at Wake. Both of these old Destroyers, Nos. 32 and 33 are destroyed by Marine Corps gunfire. **(Pacific-Philippines)** In the Philippines, Japanese troops under General Homma that had landed the day before and those that continued storming ashore before dawn, begin to spread out from Lingayen heading for Baung, Aringay and Agoo. Baung falls after nominal opposition. San Fernando, La Union and Rosario follow suit, allowing the aggressors easier access to Manila. During the night, U.S. Submarines and Australian based B-17s, harass enemy ships off Davao. Four of these B-17s continue toward the Lingayen Gulf to strike the Jap Transports in that area. This would be the first action in the war by Australian based Planes. **(Pacific-Australia)** On this day, an American Convoy (Pensacola) arrives at Brisbane, Australia (originally heading for Philippines, but diverted). These troops, commanded by General Barnes, U.S.A., are the first American troops to arrive in Australia.

December 23rd 1941 — (Pacific-Wake Island) THE BATTLE OF WAKE ISLAND — Task Force 14 has not been able to reach the fatigued Marines at Wake. The Japs initiate a pre-dawn invasion of the positions, but the understrengthed defenders are braced for the final enemy assault. Fifteen hundred enemy Soldiers hit the beach at about 0100, assisted by Air support in an effort to exterminate the meager force of 85

Marines who dish out stiff opposition. At one location, three Marines crank out incessant machine gun fire, killing two hundred Japs. Captain Elrod, who previously had abandoned his useless Aircraft, takes command of his area and withstands ferocious attacks, until he falls, mortally wounded. Other Marines, manning a 5-inch gun, pour fire into the enemy Vessels offshore, sinking one Destroyer and damaging another. Lieutenant Arthur Poindexter, commanding a team of twenty men, counter-attacks and recaptures lost terrain. Commander W.S. Cunningham, U.S.N., the island Commander, appraises the situation and deems it necessary to order Major Devereux to capitulate. Devereux reluctantly complies with the order, stating: "I DON'T KNOW WHETHER THE MARINES HAVE EVER SURRENDERED BEFORE BUT THOSE ARE MY ORDERS AND THAT'S WHAT WE ARE GOING TO DO." The gallant 85 gave it their utmost, fighting on that island of death on this final day in the highest traditions of the United States. The Stars and Stripes had fallen, but the exploits of her proud defenders would live forever. Task Force 14, en-route to save the island, is diverted for other duty in the Pacific. It had sailed to within 425 miles of Wake. **(Pacific-Philippines)** In the Philippines, the Japanese press on against token resistance, pushing the Americans back further. MacArthur orders a retreat toward Bataan, in order to concentrate his forces. This strategy enables MacArthur to hold on for months in spite of no supplies. **(Pacific-Palmyra Island)** A Japanese Submarine, operating in the vicinity of Palmyra Island, moves close to shore and shells the island. **(China-Burma-India)** In Burma, the Japanese commence an Air War, which will rage until February of 1942, in an attempt to gain air supremacy over the British. **(Borneo)** The Japanese debark combat contingents at Sarawak, Borneo.

December 24th 1941 — (Pacific-Midway) The 4th Marine Defense Battalion arrives at Midway to bolster the Garrison. The U.S. Navy is taking precautions to preserve what is left of the Fleet, with emphasis being given to the tactical placement of the Carriers, in order to cut off any attempt by Japan to strike against the U.S. mainland. **(Pacific-Philippines)** In the Philippines, Fort Stotsenburg is evacuated. Major General Wainwright initiates the withdrawal from northern Luzon and heads for Bataan. Brigadier General Albert M. Jones departs South Luzon in an effort to join the other troops converging on Bataan. The 4th Marines are ordered to report to General MacArthur at Corregidor, where they are to position themselves at the beaches to meet the Japanese. A Japanese invasion force of about 7,000 men lands at Lamon, 70 miles Southeast of Manila. **(China-Burma-India)** In the China Theater, the Japanese close the net on the British Garrison in Hong Kong. **(Atlantic-North Africa)** In North Africa, British troops of the 7th Armored Division roll into Benghazi, Libya, but the enemy has already withdrawn.

December 25th 1941 — (Pacific-Philippines) Admiral T.C. Hart, departs the Philippines by Submarine, heading for Java, where new Headquarters are to be established for the Asiatic Fleet. All remaining Naval Forces in the Philippines are now under the command of Admiral Rockwell. **(Pacific-Midway)** The American defenders at Midway celebrate Christmas with the new arrivals from Marine Squadron 221, delivered by the U.S.S. *Saratoga* (diverted from Wake). **(China-Burma-India)** The British Garrison at Hong Kong falls to Japanese forces.

December 26th 1941 — (Pacific-Philippines) U.S. Naval Forces depart Manila, heading for Corregidor. Japanese

Fighters continue to assault American positions throughout the Philippines. By the 29th of the month, life on Corregidor would be spent underground for the most part, in an effort to survive the enemy carpet bombing. Japanese storm troops debark at Jolo, Philippine Islands and the U.S.S. *Sealion* (Submarine SS-195), previously damaged by the enemy on December 10th, is intentionally destroyed by U.S. troops.

Late-December 1941 — Japanese advancing on Manila.

December 27th 1941 — (Pacific Philippines) General MacArthur proclaims Manila an open city. The Japanese now anticipate a struggle with MacArthur's force outside of Manila, but MacArthur realizes his defenders are not sufficiently strong to make the stand. He orders a withdrawal toward the Bataan Peninsula, determining that if the troops move quickly, they can eliminate being encircled. At this time, MacArthur and the defenders still believe reinforcements are on the way. The 53rd Infantry is pushed back by Japanese troops at Candelaria, Philippines, and the town is seized by the Japanese. **(Atlantic-North Africa)** In Libya, British troops assault the forces of Rommel at Agedabia but are forced to retire, due to excessive mechanical failures with their Tanks. The Germans and British each suffer heavy casualties during this action.

December 28th 1941 — (United States) The U.S. Navy authorizes the establishment of the "Seabees," which are to be Armed Construction Battalions, formed to assist in the construction of Bases and Air strips. President Roosevelt dispatches this message to the Philippines. It is broadcasted: "NEWS OF YOUR GALLANT STRUGGLE AGAINST THE JAPANESE AGGRESSORS HAS ELICITED THE PROFOUND ADMIRATION OF EVERY AMERICAN. I GIVE TO THE PHILIPPINES MY SOLEMN PLEDGE THAT THEIR FREEDOM WILL BE REDEEMED AND THEIR INDEPENDENCE ESTABLISHED AND PROTECTED. THE ENTIRE RESOURCES IN MEN AND MATERIAL OF THE U.S. STAND BEHIND THAT PLEDGE. I GIVE YOU THIS MESSAGE FROM THE NAVY IN PART: THE U.S. NAVY IS FOLLOWING AN INTENSIVE AND WELL-PLANNED CAMPAIGN AGAINST JAPANESE FORCES WHICH WILL RESULT IN POSITIVE ASSISTANCE TO THE DEFENSE OF THE PHILIPPINE ISLANDS." On the following day, a headline in the New York Times: "ALL AID PROMISED (PHILIPPINES) PRESIDENT PLEDGES PROTECTION. NAVY SAYS OUR FLEET IS NOT DESTROYED AND WILL HELP DEFENSE."

December 29th 1941 — (Pacific-Philippines) The Japanese run into stiff opposition when they collide with the Philippine 91st Division, which repulses the Japanese at Cabanatuan; however, the Japanese do manage to cross the Pampanga River. In the Allied sector around Tarlac, Japanese troops advance near the positions of the 21st Philippine Division. The Japanese continue pressing the American Philippine defenders and the South Luzon Force begins to move to Bataan. The Japanese Air Force initiates raids over Corregidor, with Medium and Heavy Bombers. The enemy raid pounds the poorly constructed buildings, but the Military Fortifications sustain only nominal damage. The men manning the anti-aircraft guns within the Forts that guard Manila Bay shoot down several enemy Bombers. The Japanese, in turn, damage the Submarine Tender, *Canopus* (AS-91). **(China-Burma-India)** Chiang Kai-shek becomes the Commander of the Allies in the China Theater, which includes those portions of Indo-China and Thailand, not yet under Japanese. Allied advisers will assist Chiang Kai-shek. **(Burma)** In Burma, the British manage to halt a Japanese advance and push them from Bokpyin into Thailand.

December 30th 1941 — (United States) Admiral King assumes his duties today. Admiral R.E. Ingersoll will replace King as Commander in Chief, Atlantic Fleet and assume his new duties on the 1st of January. **(Pacific-Philippine Islands)** American and Filipino troops in the Philippines continue to converge on Bataan, where they expect to draw the final line of defense against the Japanese. The 91st Division moves through Gapan. Tank Battalions defend the Calumpit Bridge, which spans the strategic Pampanga River, and is the escape route for the South Luzon Force. The Tanks, soon reinforced by the 51st Infantry and a contingent of the 51st Field Artillery, assure a safe crossing from South Luzon by troops under General George M. Parker. During an enemy bombardment at Corregidor, Manuel Quezon is sworn in for his second term

as President of the Philippines, though in bad health with tuberculosis. **(Atlantic-Libya)** In Libya, the armored duel between Britain and Germany still rages. British troops pause to await reinforcements, as the Germans hang tough, continuing to control Agedabia. The British Tanks prove to be much less capable than the German Panzers. **(Atlantic-Russia)** Germans continue to give ground in Russia. Additional Russian troops close in from Kerch and Feodosia, forcing a German withdrawal from Moscow to meet this new threat.

December 31st 1941-January 1st 1942 — (Pacific-Hawaii) Admiral Nimitz takes command of the Pacific Fleet. In other activity, Japanese Submarines shell Hawaii, Kauai and Mauai. **(Pacific-Philippines)** All American and Filipino troops continue to head for Bataan, including the rear echelon American Headquarters, which departs Manila. General MacArthur accompanied by his wife, Jean Faircloth MacArthur and their four-year old son Arthur have already departed. MacArthur had decided to set up headquarters at Corregidor to fight the battle of Bataan. Japanese General Masaharu calculates MacArthur's intent and initiates a massive offensive to cut him off at the Calumpit Bridge. MacArthur, in turn, anticipates the Japanese strategy and places Artillery, men and Tanks in the path of the advancing Japanese. American Tank Units hold fast, meeting the enemy assault and throwing the Japanese back, giving the retreating forces a reprieve. All American Tanks which fight the rear action safely cross the Calumpit Bridge, by 2:30 A.M. on New Year's Day and enter Bataan. Infantry Squads jump into the remaining trucks as they speed for the bridge, dodging murderous enemy fire. Because a Platoon of Engineers is still operating on the endangered side of the Calumpit at 0500, General Wainwright's order to "BLOW THE BRIDGE" is temporarily halted. At 6 A.M., when the shrill sounds of small arms fire is heard and still no sign of the Engineers, the bridge is blown, as the Japanese come into view. The maneuver is a total success and prevents MacArthur's force from being trapped. General Pershing, MacArthur's Commander during World War I, when informed of the daring maneuver, would comment: "ONE OF THE GREATEST MOVES IN ALL MILITARY HISTORY. IT WAS A MASTERPIECE." General Albert M. Jones had assumed command of both the northern and southern Luzon troops, as they converged at the Calumpit Bridge. The Japanese offensive is relentlessly pressed by the Commander, but in the end, MacArthur had outwitted him and all the Japanese hold is Manila, instead of the Allied defenders. **(Pacific-Australia)** In Australia, American General Brett arrives to assume command of all American troops in that country. **(Pacific)** American Rear Admiral Nimitz assumes the position of Commander in Chief of the U.S. Pacific Fleet. In other activity, the Palmyra Atoll is greeted with the arrival of the Marine First Defense Battalion, which will take responsibility for defense of the area.

1942

Japanese troops strike the U.S. Colors on the Philippines.

Old Glory gives no ground on Midway.

General Williard A. Holbrook and his son Williard during the early days of the conflict at a Base in the U.S. Williard Holbrook III will follow in the tradition of the Holbrook family and retire from the U.S. Army as a Colonel during 1985.

U.S. Artillerymen at the point (El Guetar, Tunisia), relaying information back to the heavy 105's in the rear. Lt. Col. William C. Westmoreland using binoculars, Capt. Ed Carpenter (center) and Corporal Steve Hanzlik in photo. Photo courtesy General William C. Westmoreland.

January 1st 1942 — (United States) In Washington, D.C., twenty six nations sign the Declaration of the United Nations. **(Pacific-Philippines)** With American troops safely across the Calumpit Bridge, the South Luzon force is disbanded and its men continue on to Bataan. The Japanese advance to Calumpit, but cannot cross the Pampanga. Contingents of the 71st and 91st Philippine Divisions, which had afforded cover during the pull back now withdraw. The 11th and 21st Philippine Divisions continue to battle the Japanese as they head toward Porac-Guaga, arriving late on the 1st. **(China-Burma-India)** In Burma, Air Vice Marshal D.F. Stevenson assumes command of all Allied Air Forces in Burma.

January 2nd 1942 — (Pacific-Philippines) Manila is overrun by Japanese Soldiers. Cavite also falls. As American and Filipino troops continue their movement toward Bataan, they are hit by the Japanese on their west flank, in the vicinity of Porac, forcing the 21st Division to fall back. The Japanese also successfully cross the Pampanga river at Calumpit.

January 3rd 1942 — (Pacific-Philippines) The Japanese continue to pound the Americans in the vicinity of the Porac-Guaga line. The Philippine 21st Division successfully repulses the attack in the vicinity of Pio. **(China-Burma-India)** The well oiled Japanese machine roars through Borneo, taking Labuan Island in Brunei Bay without opposition. From there they would spring to the mainland.

January 4th 1942 — (Pacific-Philippines) The beleaguered Allied forces in the Philippines continue their desperate run to Bataan despite extensive punishment. As daylight disappears, the 21st Division covers the withdrawal of the 11th Division. Their planned escape route had been cut off by the Japanese. The pull-back continues throughout the night. **(China-Burma-India)** The Japanese continue to move forward in both Malaya and New Britain, but in China, their advance is halted by Chinese troops at Changsha (Hunan Province).

January 5th 1942 — (Pacific-Philippines) The Japanese are pummeling Corregidor from the Air, but the fortifications withstand the attacks, sustaining only slight damage. Other devastating Air Raids sting locations around Manila. American and Filipino troops begin to cross Layac Junction, which feeds all roads into Bataan. Contingents of the Philippine 71st Division, including the 31st Infantry (the singular completely U.S. Regiment in the Philippines), and the 26th Cavalry, deploy to delay the Japanese advance at what is known as the Layac line, allowing safer passage for the retreating troops. With supplies dwindling, it becomes necessary for rations to be cut in half for the Bataan Defense Force; the same orders are obeyed by the defenders of the Allied positions on the islands in Manila Bay. In other activity in the Philippines, American Brigadier General Richard J. Marshall establishes echelon headquarters on Bataan today. **(Atlantic-Russia)** On the Russian front, the Germans manage to withstand pressure from the Russians and retain their stranglehold on the naval base at Sevastopol.

January 6th 1942 — (Pacific-Philippines) The American retreat toward Bataan becomes increasingly difficult, without the assistance of Aircover to neutralize the menacing Japanese Planes. General MacArthur had received word from General Marshall that help in the form of Bombers might be coming. MacArthur had also been told that an invasion in the southern Philippines was possible. The Japanese easily take Dinalupihan. The American defense line waits for darkness before beginning a withdrawal from their delayed action positions at Layac Junction.

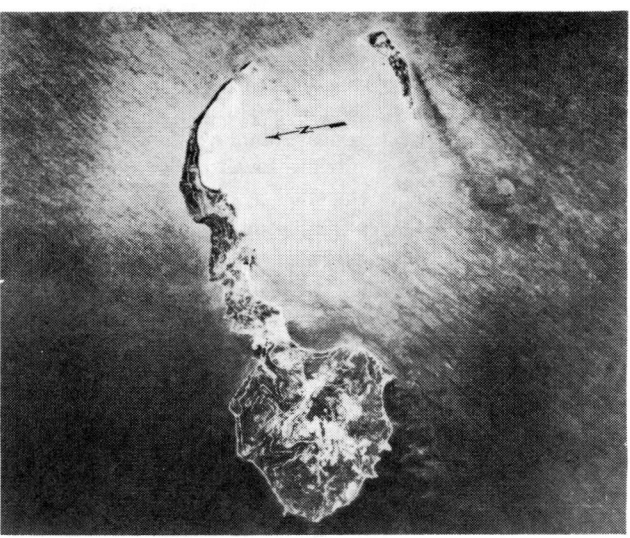

Map of Corregidor.

Officers, aboard a U.S. Carrier, briefing the men.

January 7th 1942 — (United States) The U.S. Navy is authorized to increase its Air strength from 15,000 to 27,500. **(Pacific-Philippines)** All American and Filipino troops have made it to Bataan. They begin to close ranks and prepare for the siege. The North Luzon Force becomes the I Philippine Corps consisting of 22,500 men of the 1st, 31st, 71st, 91st Divisions and Philippine Scouts. The II Philippine Corps (Bataan Force renamed), consists of 25,000 men of the 11th, 21st, 41st, 51st, Divisions and the 57th Philippine Scout Division. In addition, the Bataan defenses have some U.S. Air Corps personnel and a Battalion of Navy and Marine personnel. **(China-Burma-India)** The Japanese war machine rumbles through Malaya with its Tank-supported Infantry, leisurely reaching two miles south of Slim Village. The Japanese in this swift movement have immobilized the entire Indian 11th Division. The Japs also slice through Borneo, departing Sarawak and entering the frontier of Dutch West Borneo. **(Atlantic-North Africa)** In North Africa, the Germans withdraw from Benghazi, giving the British access to the mercurial port; stormy seas make full usage of this port extremely difficult.

January 8th 1942 — (Pacific-Philippines) The outnumbered Allies on Bataan prepare for the onslaught. The Stars and Stripes is in a precarious position, facing the Japs on all flanks and no Naval or Air support lingers in the sea to their backs.

January 9th 1942 — (Pacific-Philippines) At 3:00 P.M. the Japanese commence an assault on American positions in Bataan. Backed by Artillery, the Japs press against the East (II Corps) and West (I Corps) with some progress. One Japanese column moves into the area near Album without engagement. Another enemy column, moving toward Olongapo, will be delayed by Demolition Engineers.

January 10th 1942 — (Pacific-Philippines) Japanese Aircraft drop leaflets over American-Filipino positions on Bataan, demanding surrender. General MacArthur visits the ground forces on Bataan and informs them that they must hold until help arrives. MacArthur and his men erroneously believe that such help is on the way. This is the only day that MacArthur spends with the forces on Bataan during the entire campaign. He will return to his headquarters on Corregidor, from where he will command the operation, until he is ordered to depart for Australia. This causes resentment among the troops, who feel his presence is important for their morale. Meanwhile, Japanese Infantry roll into Olongapo unopposed. Other Japanese units tighten the noose on American positions on Bataan, by nudging themselves into the outpost lines. **(Dutch East Indies)** In Malaya, Japanese Planes continue their Air raids against the Airdromes at Singapore, boldly making daylight raids for the first time.

January 11th 1942 — (Pacific-Hawaii) A Japanese Submarine torpedoes, but does not sink the Carrier *Saratoga*, about 500 miles southwest of Oahu. **(Pacific-Philippines)** In the Philippines, the Japanese swarm down the East coast of Bataan, where they push the Allied defenders (57th Infantry) back. The tedious fighting continues through the night, with the American-Filipino forces initiating a counter-charge and recapturing lost ground. The 41st Division stops a Japanese advance to the West of where the 57th is fighting. On top of these crucial engagements, another Japanese column moves south, through central Bataan, to strike the positions of the 51st Division. As the American-Filipino pull-back to Bataan continues, casualties are remarkably light and now it is the Japanese who begin to have serious supply problems, as they expand their advances. **(Pacific-Dutch East Indies)** Japan declares war on the Netherlands East Indies and dispatches troops, supported by Air cover, to seize the sparsely garrisoned Dutch bases. Landings occur at Jesselton and Tarakan, Borneo, plus Menado and Kema in the Celebes. Tarakan and Menado, both captured by the Japanese, are quickly converted to Airbases. **(Pacific)** In other activity, an American, British, Dutch, Australian Command is established to monitor defensive measures in the western Pacific, enabling a co-ordinated effort to meet the Japanese threat from Burma, through the Philippines to New Guinea. **(Pacific-Samoa)** In Samoa, a Japanese Submarine fires on the U.S. Navy facility on Pago, Pago.

January 12th 1942 — (United States) The United States Navy is authorized to build its strength to 500,000 Enlisted men. **(Pacific-Philippines)** American positions on Bataan are further jeopardized as the Japs make progress against the 51st Division. Reinforcements are rushing to help stem the tide, but time is running out. The Japs press the 57th and the

21st Divisions, which are holding on the South bank of the Calaguiman River and the Japanese operating in the defense zone of the I Corps, seize the undefended island of Grande. In one action, 2nd Lieutenant Alexander Nininger, counter attacking with Company K, 57th Infantry, seeks and destroys snipers and enemy troops hidden in foxholes to greatly aid his unit in regaining ground. Although he had been wounded three times, this gallant Officer continues to use his rifle and hand grenades. When the position is finally recaptured, his body is recovered, surrounded by one dead enemy Officer and 2 dead Jap Soldiers. Nininger, would receive the Medal of Honor for his superlative efforts. **(Atlantic-Vichy France)** Henry P. Leveritch, 2nd Secretary to the U.S. Legation in Lisbon, arrives in Vichy with confidential instructions from President Roosevelt to be given orally to Ambassador Leahy. Leahy is instructed to inform Weygand that if he is willing to return to North Africa and assume command of the French troops there, he will receive full military and economic support from the United States. Weygand declines Roosevelt's suggestions, claiming that he is a private citizen who will remain loyal to Petain.

January 13th 1942 — (Pacific-Philippines) Japanese troops, preparing for a general assault against Allied positions on Bataan, are thwarted by a counter-attack initiated by the 21st Infantry, Philippine Scouts. The startling assault prevents the Japanese from commencing their offensive in the area west of the location of the 51st Infantry (Philippine Scouts). In other activity, the Japs penetrate the defense line of the 51st Division, and drive them toward the main line of defense at the Balantay River. Additional enemy troops push across central Bataan, but are not yet near enough to attack; another column, moving through central Bataan, delays moving up for attack, causing the American-Filipino force to receive more pressure from the Japanese, as the 51st Division is pushed across the river to support the efforts of the 41st. I Corps braces for the imminent approach of the enemy, by land and sea. A contingent of I Corps troops would be hurried by General Wainwright to meet the enemy at Moron. **(Pacific-Caroline Islands)** The U.S.S. *Searaven*, patrolling in the vicinity of Palau, notices some smoke in the distance to the southeast and begins to track down the enemy Convoy at 0900. On the 14th, slightly before 08:00, rising smoke is spotted about 15 miles distant. The *Searaven*, remaining submerged, revs the engines and steams toward the Convoy. At approximately 1130 hours, the *Searaven*, positioned perfectly for a kill, fires three torpedoes at the *Shiraha Maru*, a Cargo Vessel and another at a nearby Anti-Submarine Ship. Two strike the *Shiraha Maru*, and soon after, the results are heard through the Searaven's sound equipment which picks up the grinding noises and explosions. The Anti-Submarine Vessel, preoccupied with plucking survivors from the water does not attack. The *Searaven*, waits 45 minutes, then departs the area.

January 14th 1942 — (United States) The Arcadia Conference, between the U.S. and England concludes in Washington, D.C., with several top war priorities being established. The two countries agree that the defeat of Germany is paramount; and prepare for the occupation of French North Africa (preliminary code name, GYMNAST) and establishing the Combined Chiefs of Staff. President Roosevelt will soon recall the U.S. Ambassador to Vichy France, William Leahy, to become his Chief of Staff. In other activity, discussions take place in Washington concerning the war agenda. Lt. General

Hugh Drum had been interviewed by Secretary of War, Henry L. Stimson and General Marshall, concerning his ideas on how to run a campaign in China. The selection process eliminates him and General Stilwell, who is to be in charge of the North Africa campaign is informed by General Marshall, that he has twenty four hours to find another Commander for China or he (Stilwell) is to be the volunteer. Stilwell thus becomes the American Commander in the China Burma Theater (Chiang Kai-shek's Allied Chief of Staff). Discussions begin in Washington with T.V. Soong, Chiang's brother-in-law, concerning the China situation. It should be noted that Chiang Kai-shek has no Allied Staff; In addition, it is emphatically clear to General Stilwell, that the demands and conditions laid down by the China Lend-Lease staff are unrealistic, leading him to conclude that he will have no combat command in the China Theater. **(Pacific-Philippines)** The Japanese pressure the II Corps, driving the men guarding the outposts of the 41st Division across the Balantay River. The 51st Division reevaluates its positioning and withdraws to the south bank of the Balantay to reinforce the 41st, but the Japanese keep advancing. Enemy troops attempting to cut off and surround the Allies, move through central Bataan, short of the main Allied line of defense. In the I Corps area, the two-pronged Japanese assault nears Moron. The Sea Force debarks at a point between Olongapo and Moron, from where they advance on foot in conjunction with the Land Force which is speeding from Olongapo. General Wainright dispatches troops to Moron to meet the enemy threat. **(Pacific-Dutch East Indies)** The Japanese continue to over-run Allied positions in Malaya. The Indian 3 Corps has now completed its withdrawal into Johare and will be responsible for defending the southern section of the area. Fighting by this force, designated the East Force, will occur along the Malacca-Segamat Road. Additional heavy fighting takes place near Gemas, in the northwestern section of Johare, when the Japanese encounter an ambush set by the West Force. The Japanese suffer many casualties. In other activity, The Dutch dispatch native troops, commanded by European officers to Singapore, with instructions to begin guerrilla tactics against Japanese communications, in an effort to slow them down in the Labis area, N. Johore. **(Atlantic-Russia)** Medyn, situated northwest of Kaluga in the Soviet Union, is seized by the Red Army.

January 15th 1942 — **(U.S.-Alaska)** The Alaskan Air Force is established under the command of Lt. Colonel Everett S. Davis. Activation occurs at Elmendorf Field. **(Pacific-Philippines)** The Japanese strike harshly at the line defended by the 41st and 51st Divisions (II Corps) in Bataan. Reserves are thrust forward, but are unable to halt the superior forces. Additional reinforcements, including contingents of the 31st Division, I Corps, are rushed to the scene, buying additional time by prompting the enemy to halt the offensive and reevaluate their battle plans. In the meantime, the I Corps anticipates a strong assault from the enemy columns moving towards Moron. The defenders are totally without Air and Naval support, and unlike Dunkirk, there is no mass evacuation movement planned. **(Pacific-Samoa)** American General Henry L. Larsen is appointed the first Military Governor of American Samoa. **(Pacific-Malaya)** Advance elements of the Australian 27th Brigade (West Force) clash with Japanese troops in the vicinity of Gemas and once again inflict casu-

alties. After the successful engagement, the Australians withdraw to their main line of defense (Yong Peng). **(Pacific-Java)** Field Marshal Sir Archibald Wavell officially opens headquarters of ABDA (Australian-British-Dutch-American) Command at Batavia, Java. This new command for Wavell relieves him as Commander in Chief India. He will be replaced by British General Sir Alan Hartley. U.S. Admiral T.C. Hart becomes Commanding Officer of all Naval forces under Wavell. **(Atlantic-Middle East)** The U.S. War Department is informed that Iraq and Iran have been taken from the Indian Command and placed in the Middle East Command. The information is cabled to the appropriate American Military Missions in North Africa and Iran.

Jubilant Japanese troops on Bataan.

January 16th 1942 — **(Pacific-South America)** In Rio de Janeiro, Brazil, 21 American nations meet to draw up contingency plans to provide for mutual guidelines to be instituted for a united front against attack. **(Pacific-Philippines)** In the Philippines, desperate efforts are taken by the defenders on Bataan. The I Corps is attacked for the first time in the vicinity of Moron. The 1st Infantry and the 26th Cavalry hit the Japs hard, pushing them back to their starting point at the Batalan River. The Cavalry suffers heavy losses and is forced to withdraw after the battle. The Japanese, moving to encircle the II Corps, change direction and move eastward in an attempt to pass through the Abo-Abo River Valley. However; Contingents of the 23rd and 32nd Regiments merge with elements of the 41st and 51st Divisions to stem the tide. The U.S. 31st speeds to the left flank of the 41st Division in preparation for an offensive. The battle weary defenders would not submit to the Japanese. One man, Sergeant Jose Calugas, a mess Sergeant with the 88th Field Artillery, dashes 1,000 yards on his own to reactivate a gun which had been knocked out of commission, its entire crew killed. Calugas leads a new volunteer crew, which returns fire and holds the position. Japanese Artillery continues to ring the area with shells but does not silence the gun. (China-Burma-India) The Japanese spring from Thailand, invading Burma. They will be met by the 46th Brigade, Indian 17th Division, which manages to outflank the Imperial forces threatening Tavoy. (Pacific-Dutch East Indies-Malaya) In Singapore, British Airdromes are still struck by enemy Aircraft. The Allies fight back as best they can; the Australian 27th Brigade continues to inflict heavy casualties on the Japanese enemy around Gemas. In the vicinity of the Muar River, the enemy pushes the 45th Brigade back further. Additional enemy troops land near Muar-Batu Pahat, on the west coast, which surely threatens the Allied communications. The embattled R.A.F. is again jeopardized by the swift encroachment of the Japanese, forcing them to prepare to abandon another base. They will soon depart Singapore, heading for Sumatra. (Pacific-Australia) The U.S.S. *Seawolf* (SS-197), commanded by Lt. Commander Warder, becomes the first Submarine to receive a special mission in the Southwest Pacific. *Seawolf* departs Darwin, Australia, heading for the Philippines with ammunition. After unloading the precious cargo, the *Seawolf* departs with 25 Army and Navy Aviators and precious Submarine replacement parts aboard, breaking through the Japanese blockade and returning to Holland Pier in Soerabaja.

January 17th 1942 — (United States) General Brereton is appointed Commander of Tactical Forces in Australian-British-Dutch-American area (headquarters at Java). **(Pacific-Philippines)** Japanese Infantry and Artillery units maintain pressure on the I and II Corps defending Bataan. The II Corps counter-attacks, making slight progress on the Western defense line. The U.S. 31st Infantry heads north, toward the Balantay River, but it is unable to make further progress. Reserves are dispatched to strengthen the assault contingents. Japanese moving against the I Corps at Moron, succeed in pushing the defenders back to the ridges, located south and southeast of the town. **(Pacific-Dutch East Indies)** The Japanese debark at Sandakan, British North Borneo. The British Command surrenders two days later, giving the Japanese another easy conquest. In Malaya, the Allied East and West Forces attempt to quell the Japanese advances, but the odds are greatly against them. Allied Air support is enormously inadequate and the troops are overmatched. The Japanese roll forward, building their supply system as they advance. The Allies rush reinforcements into the Muar-Yong Peng sector to forestall defeat. **(Atlantic-North Africa)** In North Africa, the British 8th Army, 30th Corps, accepts the surrender of the Axis forces at Halfaya, after a two-month battle to culminate the first part of the Libyan campaign. The final few days have taken a heavy toll on the Axis defenders, who have been assaulted from the air, land and sea. With the cessation of enemy resistance in the Cyrenaica area, the British (13th Corps) now sets its sights on El Agheila, where the Germans and Italians are holding.

January 18th 1942 — (Pacific-Philippines) Intense fighting continues between the U.S. 31st Infantry and the entrenched enemy troops at the Balantay River. Reinforcements (45th Infantry Philippines Scouts) are sent in to assist, but Japanese troops halt their advance. The I Corps continues to give ground. **(Pacific-Dutch East Indies)** In Malaya, the Japanese utilizing Tanks, mount yet another attack in the Muar-Yong Peng area. The 45th Indian Brigade (reinforced) manages to repulse the enemy attack, but the Japanese who appear to have unending reserves, debark another large contingent of troops several miles north of Batu Pahat. The bolstered Japanese force the Allies to begin withdrawals again. The Australian 27th Brigade retreats behind the Segamar River and the Indian 9th Division is compelled to fall back across the Muar River. The endangered R.A.F. Bomber Group transfers to Sumatra. **(Atlantic)** In the Ukraine, Russian troops pierce German lines in the vicinity of Izyum. **(Atlantic-Germany)** Germany, Japan and Italy agree to a new military covenant, signing the agreement in Berlin.

January 19th 1942 — (Pacific-Philippines-Luzon) In the Philippines, the I and II Corps again attempt to throw back swarming Japanese. The 41st Infantry manages to reach the Balantay river to bolster the U.S. 31st and Philippine Army 41st Divisions. The 31st Division and contingents of the 21st Division counterattack Japanese positions, temporarily restoring lost ground, but the Japanese are able to regroup and force the Allies to withdraw. **(Pacific)** The Japanese accept the surrender of North Borneo. In Malaya, heavy fighting continues, with the Japanese besting contingents of the British 18th Brigade, which is attached to the Indian 11th Division in the vicinity of Yong Peng. The Allies are forced to retreat, leaving the defile and a bridge to the enemy. This deadly encounter causes the Indian 45th Brigade and two accompanying Australian Battalions (Muar Force) to be cut off from the main body. **(China-Burma-India)** Tavoy, along with its Airport, is seized by the Japanese. The Allied Garrison at Mergui not yet under attack, abandons its fortifications and departs by sea for Rangoon. In other activity, the remainder of the 6th Chinese Army's 93rd Division proceeds to Burma, to help meet the Japanese threat there. **(Atlantic-Middle East)** The situation in the Middle East sets the British strategy in motion, underscoring the importance of seizing Tripoli in Libya. The orders come down from British General Auchinleck, with instructions to back up the plan defensively, if the offensive stalls. **(Atlantic-Russia)** On the Russian front, heavy fighting continues as the Germans recapture Feodosia in the Crimea.

January 20th 1942 — (United States) Major General Thomas Holcomb, Commandant, becomes the first Lieutenant General in the Marine Corps (Act of Congress). **(Pacific-Philippines)** Intense fighting occurs on the west flank of the II Corps. Repeated attacks by the combined troops of U.S. 31st and 45th Philippine Scouts Regiments dislodge the Japanese foothold in the II Corps sector of Luzon. The Japanese withstand the assaults, then retire north of Guitol. The I Corps is struck in the vicinity of Mt. Silanganan; the Japanese coordinate the attacks with a series of encircling maneuvers. In two days, the Japanese will begin amphibious landings. By this time, the Japanese are befuddled by the stiff resistance they are receiving. Japanese General Masaharu had expected the island to fall quickly, having underestimated the resolve and number of defenders. In other activity, the U.S. loses a P.T.

Boat (31) in the Philippines, when it is grounded and subsequently sunk by friendly forces to prevent enemy seizure. **(Pacific-Australia)** Allied Vessels, operating off Australia, constantly seek enemy Vessels that might be approaching. Today, a Japanese Submarine (I-124) is detected by three Australian Corvettes and the Destroyer U.S.S. *Edsall* (DD-219) off the coast of Darwin, Australia. Shortly thereafter, the I-124 is sunk. **(Pacific-Bismarck Archipelago)** Rabaul, New Britain is hit heavy by a massive Air raid Assault Force, that exceeds 100 Carrier-Based Planes. A smaller scaled attack is launched against Allied positions at Kavieng, New Ireland. **(China-Burma-India)** In Burma, Japanese pour more troops into the Burma Thailand border area, where the Japanese commit land troops and Planes against the 16th Brigade, Indian 17th Division, which is deployed thinly on the Myawadi-Kawkareik Road. **(Atlantic-Russia)** Soviet forces capture Mozhaisk, 60 miles west of Moscow.

January 21st 1942 — (Pacific-Philippines-Luzon) In the II Corps area, the Allies are prevented from bolstering the west flank, as Japanese troops burst through the area in strength, in preparation for a major assault. Things are near equal in the I Corps area, as the Japanese maneuver on the east flank of the Allies, advancing within about four miles east of Mauban. This encircling movement succeeds in severing the West Road and blocking passage of the 1st Division, preventing access to the other Allied units stretched along the main line of resistance to the south. Reinforcements from other units are sent to destroy the Japanese blockade, but are unsuccessful. **(Pacific-Bismarcks)** Japanese Carriers unleash Warplanes, to bombard the fortifications at both Rabaul (New Britain) and Kavieng (New Ireland). **(Pacific-Malaya)** The Allied defenders, are still reeling against the Japanese onslaught. The cut-off Muar Force, has to be supplied by air. The Muar and Segamont Forces are both in the process of further withdrawal from the Yong Peng-Muar Road. The East force, however, is able to successfully ambush a Japanese contingent, which is moving along the trail to Mersing. **(Dutch East Indies)** The U.S. Navy experiences difficulties maneuvering in the waters in the East Indies. The U.S. Submarine S-36, run aground and damaged the previous day in the Makassar Strait, is destroyed by friendly fire. Before it is sunk, an S.O.S. had been received, and the U.S.S. *Sargo* and a PBY Plane arrive on the scene, but their efforts are in vain. A Dutch Vessel, the *Siberote* arrives around noontime and evacuates all crew members. In another Naval mishap, the U.S.S. *Boise*, a Light Cruiser (CL-47) runs aground in the Sape Strait. **(Pacific-New Guinea)** A Japanese Air Detachment, consisting of 50 Planes, attacks Allied positions at Lae Salamaua, New Guinea. **(China-Burma-India)** Generalissimo Chiang Kai-shek approves of General Stilwell as Allied Chief of Staff. U.S. Brigadier General John Magruder is presently in China as Chief of the China Mission, but is not a favorite of Chiang. General Stilwell will not remain in Kai-shek's favor for long. Stilwell has had long previous experience in China as a Military Attache and formally accepts the position on the 23rd. In other activity, the Chinese 49th Division (Chinese 6th Army) is authorized to move into Burma. **(Atlantic-North Africa)** In North Africa, the Germans under Rommel, with the support of formidable air strength, begin an offensive in western Cyrenaica, driving east and pushing the the British 8th Army back to Agedabia-El-Haseiat, Libya.

January 22nd 1942 — (Pacific-Philippines-Luzon) At Bataan, General MacArthur implements a plan which includes the withdrawal of troops from the entire Mauban-Abucay line and places the final defense stance to occur further south, at the rear of the Pilar-Bagac road. Troops are scheduled to withdraw from the Mauban-Abucay line for the next several days (23rd-26th). The Japanese initiate an offensive in the II Corps area, driving the Philippine Division back to where it had begun the offensive a week ago, in the area of Abucay Hacienda. In the I Corps sector, combined forces including units of the 91st Philippine Division, supported by Tanks and contingents of the 26th Cavalry, assault Japanese positions along the West Road. However, they are unable to break through the rigid enemy positions to reinforce the First Division, which is heavily engaged at the Northern portion of the main line of resistance in Bataan. Into the following morning, the Japanese 2nd Battalion, 20th Infantry, boards barges at Moron and embarks for Caibobo Point. The invaders get lost along the route and land at Quinauan Point and Longoskawayan Point, on the Southern tip of Bataan (night of 22nd-23rd). A U.S. Navy P.T. Boat intervenes and sinks two troop barges. U.S. Commander Francis J. Bridget will dispatch Naval and Marine personnel on the 23rd to meet the threat. **(Pacific-Malaya)** In Malaya, the Japanese are victorious again, at the six day battle for Muar. The Japanese devastate the Indian 45th Brigade, forcing them to destroy all vehicles and supplies, and abandon many wounded while escaping toward Yong Peng. Allied troops (East Force) at Yong Peng repulse an assault at the river near Mersing. Seven thousand Indian reinforcements pour into Singapore. In other activity, an enemy Convoy, passing through the Makassar Strait, is discovered and attacked by a U.S. Submarine. **(Atlantic)** In North Africa, the Axis offensive continues to sweep East as it seizes Agedabia, Libya.

January 23rd 1942 — (Pacific-Hawaii) A Japanese Submarine sinks the U.S.S. *Neches* (AO-5), an Oiler, off the Hawaiian coast. **(Pacific-Philippines-Luzon)** In Bataan. the I and II Corps persist in their struggle to stop the Japanese invaders, as their ammunition and supplies continue to diminish. In the II Corps sector, the withdrawal to the last line of resistance is initiated. To the South, Philippine Constabulatory troops are deployed at Quinaun Point, where many of the Japanese had debarked during the night. The Filipino troops make scant headway. Other Japanese, who had landed at Longoskawayan Point and occupied Pucot Hill, are engaged by Naval and Marine forces, committed by Commander Bridget, U.S.N. They accomplish the mission with the assistance of a Howitzer and a contingent of the 301st Chemical Co., but the enemy infiltrates during the night and reoccupies the position. **(Pacific-Samoa)** In American Samoa, the 7th Defense Battalion is greeted by the arrival of the 2nd Marine Brigade, to help to bolster the American position on Guam. **(Pacific-Bismarck Archipelago)** The Japanese 4th Fleet, advancing in the Pacific, strikes Rabaul, New Britain and shortly thereafter, seizes the sparsely garrisoned Australian Base. The advances bring the Japanese within striking distance of New Guinea. Rabaul becomes a tremendous thorn in the Allied side and acts as a primary junction for funneling Japanese troops and supplies in the Pacific. **(Pacific-New Guinea)** As the Japanese approach New Guinea, Allied troops based there prepare to evacuate. **(Pacific-Solomons)**

While elements of the Japanese Fourth Fleet keep busy at New Britain and New Ireland in the Bismarcks, other contingents of the Fleet strike the Solomon Islands, where they occupy Kieta, Bougainville Island, without resistance. **(Pacific-Dutch East Indies)** Japanese troops debark at Balikpapan, Borneo. In other activity, another Naval Task Force of the Imperial Japanese Navy, consisting of two Convoys, advances against additional objectives in the Pacific. One is arrogantly steaming across the Makassar Strait despite Dutch Air strikes to attack Balikpapan in Borneo, while the other assault Convoy sails through the Molucca Passage, heading for Kendari in the Celibes. The Japanese meet no resistance, at either target. At this time, there are still no U.S. Combat Divisions engaged against the Japanese in the Pacific, except those scattered across the beleaguered Philippines. Back in Washington, as reports, concerning China and Japanese war intentions, reach G2 Headquarters, one Officer responds to Stilwell at a briefing session: "YOU KNOW GENERAL STILWELL, WE'RE JUST GETTING AROUND TO STUDYING YOUR REPORTS ON CHINA. HOW RIGHT YOU WERE IN YOUR CONCLUSIONS." Stilwell, astonished by the remark, glances at Brigadier General Frank Dorn and quips: "MY GOD DORN, SOME OF THOSE REPORTS ARE SIX YEARS OLD. NO WONDER WE'RE IN THIS MESS NOW." In the Dutch East Indies, Japanese Planes attack Allied Airfields at Palembang, Sumatra. R.A.F. Planes, based in the Middle East arrive at Palembang, but the Planes, altered to cope with desert conditions in North Africa will be a detriment in the Pacific. Their ability to attain high altitude quickly, is prevented by filters, which had been applied while in North Africa, to protect the engines from desert dust, thus giving Japanese Pilots another advantage against the mostly obsolete R.A.F. Planes. **(Atlantic-North Africa)** In North Africa, the British 8th Army loses ground as the Axis troops seize Antelat and Saunna. **(Atlantic-Russia)** In Russia, the Red Army takes Cholm. Additional Russian troops are surrounding a German force in the vicinity of Rzhev.

January 24th 1942 — (Pacific) THE BATTLE OF MAKASSAR STRAIT — The A.B.D.A. Command is about to initiate the Java Sea campaign, which exposes the understrengthed Allied Fleets. Under darkened skies, an enemy Armada slips through the Makassar Strait, unaware that four U.S. Destroyers, commanded by Commander P.H. Talbot, lay in wait in the vicinity of Balikpapan. The escort enemy Destroyers pass without incident, taking no notice of the U.S. Warships, which choose to await the Troop Transports. Initially, the U.S. Fleet expects additional fighting power from the Cruisers *Boise* and *Marblehead*, but fate delivers an unexpected blow to the Americans. The U.S.S. *Boise*, strikes rocks as she slips through shallow water, ripping apart the hull, and ending her activity for the duration of the campaign. The U.S.S. *Marblehead* experiences some engine difficulty, which compels her to drop out of the battle zone. These unfortunate developments force the four Destroyers to act alone. As the enemy Troop Ships glide along, seemingly protected by their Warships, the U.S.S. *Parrott, Paul Jones, John T. Ford* and the *Pope*, pounces on the Convoys. The U.S. Destroyers pour fire upon the Japanese, seemingly from all directions, confusing the enemy about the size and type of the Assault Force. The gallant American Fleet runs the enemy Convoy line, dispersing deadly torpedoes, which strike their target, then make a

turn and begin another battle run, pounding the enemy Vessels again. The stunned Japanese, have not yet determined what is hitting them, as the Destroyers maneuver for a third run. Discovering they have exhausted their supply of torpedoes, Talbot's men improvise and open fire with their deck guns. The Japanese lose four enemy Transports and a Patrol Boat. Only one U.S. Destroyer, the *John T. Ford*, (DD-228) receives an incoming enemy shell. This is the first of the engagements during the campaigns of the Java Sea, and although it is a minor victory, morale is boosted. The Japanese Patrol Boat No. 37 is among the enemy Vessels sunk. **(Pacific-Philippines-Luzon)** In Bataan, the II Corps attempts to fight a rear action against the Japanese, while the combat troops continue the withdrawal. The Japanese maintain intense pressure on the retreating defenders. In the I Corps sector, along the main line of resistance, the Philippines Defense Force situation worsens as it is unable dislodge the Japanese along the West Road. The Japanese also repulse attempts to drive them from Longoskawayan and Quinauan Points. The Allies succeed, however, in forcing the Japanese from Pucot Hill. **(Pacific-New Guinea)** The Allies, faced with overwhelming odds against the Japanese, who are nearing their invasion date, evacuate Lae and Salamaua, New Guinea. **(Dutch East Indies)** U.S. P-40s, dispatched from Australia to operate against the Japanese in the Dutch East Indies, arrive. These are the first elements of the small allotment that will arrive at Java. In Malaya, the Japanese continue to push the Allies back, with heavy fighting occurring at Batu Pahat. **(Atlantic-Panama)** The U.S. Submarine S-26 operating in the Gulf of Panama with three other Submarines and the Submarine Chaser PC-460, move from Balboa to San Jose. During the movement, visual signals are given to proceed to designated positions, but only the S-21 recognizes the command and a collision occurs during the maneuver and the S-26 sinks. The Commander, Lt. Commander E.C. Hawk and three other men are on the bridge at the point of impact, allowing Hawk and two of the three men to survive. The remainder of the crew is lost.

January 25th 1942 — (Pacific-Philippines-Luzon) Japanese Infantry, supported by proficient Aircraft, continue to pummel the beleaguered retreating II Corps. The I Corps evacuates Mauban, with the Philippine 1st Division heading south, while other contingents of the I Corps attempt to distract the Japanese by attacking the West Road roadblock. Additional skirmishing occurs at Longoskawayan and Quinauan Points. **(Pacific-Midway)** American held Midway (Sand Island) is fired upon by a Japanese Submarine. **(Pacific-Malaya)** Japanese troops continue to punish the Allies in the Malaya campaign. British General Percival directs the evacuation of the total center line of defense in Central Johare, leaving the responsibility to the Indian 3 Corps. The Japanese compress the defenders at Batu Pahat. The defenders manage to fight a tough battle all day long but to no avail as the town is abandoned. Reinforcements attempt to assist, but are not able to reach the besieged defenders. The Japanese also mount pressure in the vicinity of Ayer-Hitam-Luang, but are driven off. **(Pacific-Celebes)** The U.S.S. *Swordfish*, encounters two Japanese Freighters and disregards the apparent possibility of enemy mines, choosing to close in fast, on the targets. Lt. Commander Chester Smith encroaches deep into the channel and orders two torpedoes fired at each Vessel. In a short time, the explosions are heard throughout the Ship. The *Swordfish* makes a safe escape and leaves the 4,000 ton *Myoken Maru*, heading for the bottom, while the crew of the *Swordfish* goes hunting for more Japs. Over the next few days, the Swordfish will make several attacks and report two more unconfirmed attacks and some missed opportunities. **(Pacific-Burma)** Rangoon is visited by British General Wavell. The Japanese move toward Moulwein, the objective, reaching the Salween River in the vicinity of Paan Moulmein. **(Thailand)** Thailand declares war against the United States. **(Atlantic-North Africa)** In Libya, the Axis troops seize Msus. The British 1st Armored Division (13 Corps) is ordered to pull back towards Mechili, leaving a contingent behind to cover the Indian 4th Division, presently retreating from Barce and Benghazi. The general order for retreat of the 13 Corps is rescinded by British General Ritchie. He takes command of the Indian 4th Division and orders it and the 1st Armored Division to initiate a counter-attack in the vicinity of Msus, to try to regain the lost terrain.

January 26th 1942 — U.S. Soldiers arriving in Northern Ireland.

January 26th 1942 — (Pacific-Philippines-Luzon) The Japanese tighten their grip on the Philippine Defense Forces after both Corps reach the temporary sanctuary of the final defense line, on Bataan. A continual line of defense is finally strung, stretching from the east, at Orion, to Bagac on the West. The U.S.A.F.F.E. command diverts the Philippine Division as its reserves, which permits gaps along the line in each sector. Contingents are maneuvered to replace the U.S. 31st Division and the 57th Philippine Scouts Regiment, which are both deployed in the II Corps sector. The 45th (Philippine Scouts) Infantry, positioned in the I Corps area. Responsibility for the defense of east Bataan, between the coast and the Pantangan River, belongs to the II Corps. Japanese Patrols, stretching along the eastern side of Mt. Samat, are in close proximity to the Allied line of defense, but are unaware of the vulnerable points. The I Corps takes responsibility of defending the area extending from the Pantangan River, to the west coast. The Japanese advance along West Road in a southern direction, heading for the Binuaangan River, but are detained by the 91st Division. The American-Filipino Force attempts to hit back by sending the 88th Field Artillery, from the II Corps sector to the west coast, where one Gun Battery is dispatched against Longoskawayan Point and another against Quinauan Point. **(Pacific-Malaya)** The Japanese approach Endau, to debark an Invasion Force and are struck by the R.A.F. as they approach. However; they make the landing successfully and advance immediately. The Royal Navy engages the Japanese Fleet soon after it drops anchor, but the confrontation costs the British the H.M.S. *Thanet.* As the Japanese begin to sweep across the peninsula, the British prepare another evacuation. The Batu Pahat Force is cut off and is struggling to withdraw, abandoning their wounded, as they disperse into the jungle to hopefully make it back to their lines. **(Atlantic)** A Naval Convoy brings the first United States troops to Europe, when the Expeditionary Force debarks at Northern Ireland. There are protests from the government of Northern Ireland.

January 27th 1942 — (Pacific-Hawaii) The U.S. Navy establishes another Naval Air Station, at Puunene, Maui. **(North Pacific-Alaska)** Two Submarines, the S-18, commanded by Lt. W. Millican and the S-23, commanded by Lt. J.R. Pierce, arrive at Dutch Harbor. which is better suited for Polar Bears. than Submarines. **(Pacific)** The Submarine U.S.S. *Gudgeon*, which had hunted unsuccessfully in Japanese waters for 50 days receives word from Headquarters that three enemy Submarines are in the area, one is reported on a direct collision course heading east to Midway. Grenfell confirms the information, then plans an ambush for the following morning. At about 09:00, the *Gudgeon* spots the enemy as it floats lazily floats atop the surface, its officers taking in the view, under the tropical rays of the sun, unaware of an imminent torpedo attack. Battle positions already taken, the orders are given and three torpedoes race across the water, culminating with tremendous explosions. The *Gudgeon* (SS-211) lays low, awaiting the possible arrival of the other enemy Submarines, but they are not in the area and neither is the I-173. Grenfell and his crew return to Pearl Harbor and are informed they have scored the first Submarine kill. **(Pacific-Philippines-Luzon)** The Japanese launch a violent attack against the main line of resistance in the afternoon at the II Corps sectors C and D. Sector C., which are being reinforced by the Philippine 41st Infantry. The Japanese drive back advance posts and cross the Pilar River. The Japanese also strike hard in the west, but the able 91st Division repulses the assault. Heavy resistance is put up by the defenders in the vicinity of Quinauan Point and Longoskawayan Point. The outnumbered defenders contain the enemy only temporarily by committing every operational gun at Longoskawayan Point. Contingents of the 4th Marine Regiment participate at this battle. The Japs repulse an assault against their position at Quinauan Beach. They then pause to bolster their defenses, with reinforcements by sea, before launching another major attack in the direction of Mariveles. In other activity in the Philippines, the U.S.S. *Seawolf*, a Submarine, successfully evades Japanese detection and brings more precious ammunition to the defenders. When the *Seawolf* (SS-197) departs Corregidor, it carries some additional crew members, Army and Naval Pilots. **(Pacific-Malaya)** British General Percival, having permission to withdraw to Singapore, departs on the night of the 30th-31st and moves through Johore Bahru to Singapore. The Malayan East Force is able to withdraw, without incident. Contingents of the 11th Indian Division (Batu Pahat Force) pull back to Benut, while others withdraw to the mouth of the Ponggor River, to be evacuated by Ship. In other activity, the West Force resigns itself to fighting skirmishes, as it pulls back along the main road. **(Dutch East Indies)** The Japanese attack the Singkawang II Airfield in Borneo, prompting the British to order its evacuation. **(Pacific-Australia)** U.S. General Barnes takes command of the Base facilities in Australia. **(Atlantic-North Africa)** In Libya, the British Eighth Army prepares to launch a counter-attack, against the Axis troops in the vicinity of Msus. The Germans and Italian Allies initiate another offensive; one force makes the primary thrust against Benghazi as the other moves against Mechili. **(Atlantic-Vichy France)** U.S. Ambassador Leahy confers with French General Petain, Admiral Darlan and a French Foreign Ministry Official, Charles Rochat, for the purpose of several war agendas, including a possible Allied invasion of North Africa.

January 28th 1942 — (United States) The Eighth Air Force is activated at Savannah, Georgia. Brigadier General Asa N. Duncan assumes command. The Alaskan Air Force, commanded by Lt. Colonel Everett S. Davis, had been activated less than two weeks ago at Elmendorf Field. **(South America)** The third meeting of the Foreign Ministers of the American Republics, which has been ongoing since the 15th of January in Rio de Janeiro, concludes. **(Pacific-Philippines-Luzon)** The situation in Bataan remains grave. The exhausted Defense Forces continue to take heavy casualties, as their diminishing supplies are further drawn down. The Japanese attack the II Corps sector and make some forays across the Tiawir River, but the defenders halt the attack (Sector C). The defenders also repulse another attack in the same sector. In the I Corps area, the Japanese ooze through a gap in the lines and get separated, causing them to span out into two pockets, dubbed Little Pocket and Big Pocket. Fierce fighting occurs in the vicinity of Longoskawayan Point, in the south sector. Mortars and Machine Guns of the 4th Marine Regiment are assigned to the 57th Philippine Scout Regiment, to aid in the relief of the Naval Battalion on Longoskawayan Point. The organized Japanese resistance ends in this sector. Other Allied elements develop a slow-developing, costly assault against Quinauan Point. The fighting continues until the 13th of February, when the last of the Japs, who had landed on the 22nd of January, are wiped out. Around Anyasan Bay, the American Filipino forces advance close to the coast, but after nightfall, they withdraw for fear of counter attack. **(Pacific-New Guinea)** The Island of Rossel, which lies off the coast of New Guinea, is invaded by Japanese troops. **(Pacific-Malaya)** The Japanese continue to pursue the British reaching Benut; while driving southward, right behind the Indian 11th Division. Complications develop as the Indian 9th Division withdraws toward Singapore, causing a gap between two Brigades; this causes the 22nd Brigade to become isolated from the

main body. In other activity, the East Force continues its withdrawal, without incident. **(Atlantic-North Africa)** In Libya, the British Eighth Army is fiercely engaged with the Axis troops, preventing them from sending any Armored Contingents to aid the beleaguered 4th Indian Division at Benghazi. The Indian 4th Division gains permission to withdraw, but finds its escape route cut off and drives punishingly without the help of British Armor, breaking out on its own, heading south to join the 8th Army.

January 29th 1942 — (United States) The Combined Chiefs of Staff establishes ANZAC Area, which is the ocean zone between Australia, New Zealand and New Caledonia. This command is under United States Naval authority. **(Pacific-Philippines)** The II Corps prevents another Japanese assault from penetrating the Main Defense Line while the I Corps courageously engages the enemy, at Little Pocket and Big Pocket against stiff resistance. In the south sector, Allied units experience success at Quinauan Point. At Longoskawayan Point, the Infantry is supported by gunfire from a U.S. Navy Minesweeper, which blasts the enemy positions in cadence with Field Artillery for a half hour. Afterward, the American Filipino Forces move forward and mop up the remainder of the enemy troops in the sector. **(Pacific-Malaya)** British troops continue their withdrawal toward Singapore. In related activity, a Squadron of Light Tanks arrives from India, but they are obsolete and prove to be of little value (only Tanks to reach Malaya). **(Pacific-Celebes)** Japanese troops continue to consume territory in the Pacific. Today, enemy landing parties debark at Badoeng and Mampawan, in the Celebes. **(Pacific-Dutch East Indies)** Pontianak, situated on the west coast of Borneo, is occupied by Japanese troops. **(Atlantic-Iran)** Iran signs a treaty of alliance with Great Britain and Russia, which provides for Iran remaining neutral and for both England and Russia to pull out all troops within six months after the cessation of hostilities with the Axis powers. This will provide Russia with use of the Persian Corridor to receive supplies from the Allies. Meanwhile, the men on Bataan are receiving meager supplies only through occasional visits by a U.S. Naval Submarine. **(Atlantic-Iceland)** German Submarines, paying little attention to the U.S. show of force in the Atlantic, sink a Coast Guard Cutter, the *Alexander Hamilton* (PG-34), off the coast of Iceland. The *Alexander Hamilton* becomes the first American Warship to sink, since the outbreak of war. **(Atlantic-North Africa)** The Germans and Italians continue to pursue the Indian 4th Division, British Eighth Army, in the vicinity of Msus, Libya, as it makes its way back to the main force at the Derna line. **(Russia)** The Russians claim the capture of Sukhinichi on the central front.

January 30th 1942 — (Pacific-Philippines) General MacArthur takes command of all Naval forces in the Philippines. In Luzon, intense fighting continues along the main line of resistance. The II Corps intensifies its efforts to root out the invaders in the vicinity of the Pilar River, but does not succeed. In the I Corps sector, heavy fighting ensues again in the effort to destroy resistance around Little Pocket and Big Pocket. In other activity, the quest to rid the enemy at Quinauan Point, is ongoing and continues until mid-February. **(Pacific-Malaya)** In Malaya, the British troops continue their withdrawal to Singapore, completing the operation on the following day. After all British troops are safely in Singapore, the causeway, used for the evacuation, is destroyed by explosives. The West Force delays its withdrawal, with feint hopes of reclaiming the long-isolated 22nd Brigade of the Indian 9th Division. separated some time ago. Some stragglers of the lost Brigade are eventually ferried to safety, across the Strait of Singapore. In other activity, the British decide to evacuate the Malaya Air Force to the Dutch East Indies, save for a single Squadron. **(China-Burma-India)** The Japanese initiate an offensive against Moulmein, Burma, while simultaneously sending another assault force, against the Naval Base at Ambon, Netherlands East Indies.

January 31st 1942 — (Pacific-Philippines-Luzon) The I and II Corps, Philippine Defense troops, manage to repulse Japanese attacks. In one sector, the 1st and 11th Divisions, which have been in constant battle with the enemy, now cut off Little and Big Pockets from their supply line. Neither side is able to make progress during ongoing engagements in the vicinity of Quinauan Point. The 192nd Tank Battalion (minus one Company) is dispatched to Quinauan Point to assist in the effort. **(Pacific-Dutch East Indies)** Japanese troops land on the island of Amboina. **(Pacific-Malaya)** By 8:30 A.M., the evacuation of British Malayan Defense force to Singapore is completed. The escape causeway is blown to hamper Japanese pursuit, and Singapore is divided into a three-sector defense zone, commanded by British Generals Heath, Keith Simmons and Bennett, north, south and west, respectively. The Japanese will begin Air raids over Singapore and exchange Artillery fire. Other activity is confined to Patrols, until the Japanese invade. British Antiaircraft units try to fend off the Air attacks, which are aimed primarily against the harbor and the Kalang Airdrome. Singapore Island's complement of troops include the Indian 3 Corps, commanded by Lt. General Sir Lewis M. Heath, and comprised of Corps troops, Indian 11th Division, British 18th Division (North sector); the Singapore Fortress troops, commanded by Major General F. Keith Simmons, comprised of fixed defense troops, 1st and 2nd Malayan Brigades and the Strait Settlements Volunteer Force (South Sector); and the Australian Indian Force, commanded by British Major General Gordon Bennett, comprised of Australian troops and the Indian 44th Brigade (West Sector). **(China-Burma-India)** The Japanese continue the strategy of attack, wearing the British down and forcing the Garrison at Moulmein to abandon its positions and withdraw across the Salween River, heading for Martaban. The Japanese take a temporary pause to prepare for a further thrust, but their Planes begin bombing Martaban, as their land forces commence another infiltration movement, crossing the Salween. **(Atlantic)** England acknowledges the independence of Ethiopia. In other activity, U.S. Major General John N. Greely, the Commander of the Military Mission to the U.S.S.R. arrives in Iraq. He will proceed to Tehran, Iran, where headquarters will be established in order to help the Russians on matters of the Lend-Lease program, which in essence, is the granting of Military supplies to the Russians.

February 1942 — (Atlantic-Panama) U.S. Captain Ralph W. Christie receives explicit orders to transfer Submarine Division 53 to Australia, which means the Vessels will be moving 12,000 miles, between Balboa and Brisbane. The Submarines are expected to shove off during early March. The Silent Armada will be led by the U.S.S. *Griffin*, commanded by Captain Christie and will include the S-42 (Lt. Kirk), S-43 (Lt. Hannon), S-44 (Lt. Moore), S-45 (Lt. Eddy), S-46 (Lt. R.C. Lynch), and the S-47, commanded by Lt. J. Davis. Two of

these older type Subs must come from Argentina and Newfoundland and be given quick overhauls for the long journey, which will see them make a stopover at Bora Bora in the Society Islands, giving the villagers a startling sensation, as the colossal Submarines burst unexpectedly, from beneath the water, crashing to the surface. The Vessels which have no airconditioning systems, complete the arduous journey, arriving without major mishap, at Brisbane on the 15th of April. Additional S-Boats, including the S-38, which is there to greet them upon arrival, will join the Task Force to play havoc with the enemy. These S-Boats of the Asiatic Fleet and their "Sugarboat" companions from Panama, become Task Force 42. To give you some idea of the glorious life of the Submariner on these illustrious S-Boats, the temperature, while submerged, is in the vicinity of 95 degrees F. with a humidity factor of 85%. In addition, they are not really suitable for long journeys and suffer frequently, from a combination of engine and electrical problems.

February 1st 1942 — Wotje, Marshall Islands, smoking under U.S. Planes.

February 1st 1942 — (Pacific) The United States takes a large forward step in the move to regain the Pacific. Two Carrier Task Forces, commanded by Vice Admiral William Halsey and Rear Admiral Frank Fletcher, and supported by a Naval Bombardment Group under Rear Admiral Spruance, spring a surprise attack on the Japanese in the Marshall and Gilbert Islands. This Task Force consists of two Carriers, five Cruisers and ten Destroyers. The U.S. Fleet heavily damages Air and Naval facilities at Kwajalein, Wotje, Maloelap, Jaluit and Mili, in the Marshalls, and batters enemy positions at Makin, in the Gilberts. This is the first large-scale attack by the U.S. Navy, since Pearl Harbor. During the Naval assaults, the U.S.S. *Enterprise* (CV — 6) is damaged after being struck by the first Kamikaze attack of the war. As the Plane heads for the Enterprise, an Aviation Mechanic, Bruno Peter Gaida races into a Plane on the rear of the Ship and begins firing its gun at the suicide Pilot. The Carrier swerves hard but the Plane crashes about three feet from Gaida. The Kamikaze rips the tail off Gaida's Plane and plows into the flight deck before skidding over the side. The Heavy Cruiser U.S.S. *Chester* (CA-27) is also damaged off Taroa, losing eight men killed, while assisting the Enterprise. On the day prior to the attack, a Japanese Patrol Plane nears the Task Forces but bad visibility prevents discovery. Admiral Halsey has a message translated into Japanese for the Japanese Commander and American Planes drop copies during the raid. It states: "IT IS A PLEASURE TO THANK YOU FOR HAVING YOUR PATROL

PLANE NOT SIGHT MY FORCE." At Roi, the Japanese receive about thirteen minutes warning and had been able to muster Anti-aircraft fire. Four Bombers are lost. The Japanese sustain the loss of three Fighters, seven Bombers, an ammunition dump, a couple of hangars and a fuel depot, plus the radio facility. Halsey's estimates of damages at Kwajalein "two Submarines sunk and a small Carrier and four Auxiliary Vessels badly damaged and possibly sunk, in addition to destroying two Patrol Planes on the ground." At Kwajalein all Planes return safely to their Carriers. Admiral Fletcher's Task Force loses seven Planes during the operation. As the Fleet is retiring, it is attacked by Japanese Planes; one is shot down by AA fire and the other makes a getaway. The Fleet loses the Japanese by changing course, then returns to Pearl Harbor. **(Pacific-Philippines)** In Luzon, Philippines, the I and II Corps still struggle against the Japanese. In C Sector, II Corps area, the Japanese withdraw from the bridgehead. In the I Corps area, futile efforts are initiated to eliminate the pockets, south of the Main Line of resistance. The Japanese hold tough. In the South sector, Japanese reinforcements heading for Quinauan Point, are spotted, during the night. Artillery and Infantry fire, originating from the Shore Batteries, assist Torpedo Squadron 3, which strikes from the sea, forcing the Japanese to abort the mission and land at Anyasan-Silaiim. Squadron 3, originally consisting of six Boats, is commanded by Lt. John Bulkeley, the Officer in charge of spiriting General MacArthur away from Corregidor and off to Australia, later in the conflict. There are four Boats remaining in the Squadron; the two which had been lost, had not been destroyed by enemy fire. These intrepid Motor Torpedo Boats are a most unusual type craft. They are 70′ long and 20′ wide, constructed of plywood, and carry no armor. Even the shield in front of the machine guns is made of wood, for protecting the gunner from water sprays, not enemy shells. Each boat is equipped with four torpedo tubes, supported by four 50 caliber machine guns, which fire in pairs, from each side of the boat.

February 1st 1942 — Jaluit, Marshall Islands aflame, subsequent to U.S. air attack.

(Atlantic-North Africa) In Libya, British General Ritchie, who had previously countermanded the order to retreat and ordered a counter-attack against the Germans in Libya, orders the British 8th Army, 13 Corps to retreat toward Gazala-Bir Hacheim, to evade being surrounded by the Axis troops.

February 2nd 1942 — (Pacific-Philippines-Luzon) Japanese are still relentless around the main line of defense at Bataan.

The II Corps meets heavy fire, as it attempts to clear a bridgehead, from which the enemy is retiring. Allied reinforcements are rushed to the area. The Japanese hold, but withdraw after dark. The I Corps fares no better, in an attempt to clean out Big Pocket. In the South sector, Infantry and Tanks are thrown against the Japanese entrenched on Quinauan, without success. The Japanese, who had figured on taking the Philippines in one month, are almost into their third. still meeting obstinate resistance. The bulk of the front line hardened troops consist of approximately 2,000 Americans and about 1,200 Filipino Scouts of equal fighting skills. About half of the Filipinos in the Army never even had a uniform until a few weeks before the start of the war. The defenders, justifiably pick up the nickname "THE BATTLING BASTARDS OF BATAAN."

In one of the more grueling incidents, and there are many, four Tanks are sent in front of Infantry, to meet an enemy force, which is landing near Batangas. The men are told the Japs have no machine guns and if they do, the Tanks will certainly knock them out quickly. The Tankers advance against hidden anti-tank weapons, which blow the lid off the first Tank and immediately disable the next two, with extremely accurate fire. The third and final Tank tries to maneuver around, but the roads are too small and it ends up on its side in a rice paddy. The Infantry, meanwhile, is being torn to pieces by enemy machine gun fire, and forced to retreat rapidly. The Infantry is without a single machine-gun. A surviving Soldier recounts this story, while recuperating in the hospital at Corregidor. The survivors of the lone Tank, who had played dead, under the eyes of the Japs, finally walked many miles back to the lines. In Naval activity, the U.S.S. *Seadragon* detects five enemy Vessels, transporting troops and equipment. The *Seadragon* fires five torpedoes and scores some damage to one Vessel. About an hour and a half later, just before 07:00, the Vessel *Tamagawa Maru* sinks. The *Seadragon* departs, taking with her 19 Naval (Radio Intelligence) Officers, two Naval Officers and a healthy supply of torpedoes, first breaking through the Japanese Naval defenses, then heading for Soerabaja. In other activity, the U.S.S. *Trout*, which had departed Pearl Harbor on the 12th and taken a circuitous route, arrives at Corregidor. During her brief stay, Japanese Planes attack, but the Vessel is unharmed. The U.S.S. *Trout* is in serious need of ballast and request bags of sand, to assist her in the voyage, when she departs. Instead, when the U.S.S. *Trout* departs at dawn on the 4th, she will be carrying two tons of gold bars, 18 tons of silver pesos, negotiable securities and U.S. mail. The *Trout* breaks through the blockade and on the ninth, manages to sink the Japanese Transport Freighter, *Chuwa Maru* and a Japanese Patrol Boat. Headquarters, deeply concerned, orders the Submarine to abort further offensive action and return to Pearl with her unusual cargo. **(Dutch East Indies)** The Japanese Minesweeper No. 9, strikes a mine and sinks. **(Atlantic-North Africa)** In North Africa, the British Eighth Army receives orders to hold Tobruk, which will be needed as a base of supply for future offensives. The British will draw the line here and prepare for siege.

February 3rd 1942 — (Pacific-Philippines-Luzon) In the II Corps area, the Japanese have retired from their bridgehead, allowing troops to advance. In the embattled Philippines I Corps area, the Japanese still hold Quinauan Point, in spite of repeated attempts by Infantry and the 192nd Tank Battalion to dislodge them. In other action, near Bagac, the 45th Infantry experiences bitter fighting. Lieutenant Willibald Bianchi takes charge of a Squad and assaults two enemy machine gun nests. Bianchi receives two bullets in his left hand, but moves forward, taking out a nest with a grenade, getting two bullets in his chest along the way. Lt. Bianchi, miraculously, climbs an American Tank and begins firing at the entrenched enemy positions, until he is hit for the third and final time by Japanese bullets, which kill him. **(Pacific-Dutch East Indies)** The Japanese initiate pre-invasion Air raids, against Allied positions, on Surabaya, Java, Netherlands East Indies. **(Pacific-New Guinea)** Japanese Planes assault Allied positions at Port Moresby, New Guinea, which maintains a small Australian Garrison. The Japanese expect to take New Guinea easily, but the Australians intend to hold. **(China-Burma-India)** Chiang Kai-shek agrees to permit the Chinese 5th Army to assume responsibility for the Toungoo Front. In addition, the remainder of the Chinese 6th Army is transferred to Burma.

February 4th 1942 — (Pacific-Philippines) There is very little activity in the II Corps area, however, Tanks supporting the Infantry combine to assault Japanese positions in the vicinity of the Big Pocket, but the Japanese repel the attack. Troops in the South sector strike Japanese positions at Quinauan, pushing the Japs toward the edge of the stronghold. In sporadic Naval activity, another U.S. Submarine, the *Seadragon* (SS-194), evacuates priority personnel, such as code-breakers from Corregidor. **(Pacific-Australia)** The Australian-New Zealand Naval Command is established to be commanded by Admiral H.F. Leary, U.S.N. **(Pacific-Madoera Strait)** BATTLE OF MADOERA STRAIT — An Allied Fleet, commanded by Rear Admiral Karel Doorman, Royal Netherlands Navy, steams through the Madoera Strait, en route to intercept and destroy the enemy, presently engaged in debarking troops at Balikpapan, Borneo. Japanese Aircraft are dispatched to engage the oncoming Fleet and succeed in forcing the Allies to abort the mission. This Naval Task Force, comprised of four Cruisers and seven Destroyers, suffers damage to three Vessels. Two of the damaged Vessels are the U.S.S. *Houston* and *Marblehead*. The U.S.S. *Marblehead*, is a story in herself during the fierce action. As the Japanese continue dropping bombs, in an attempt to destroy the *Marblehead*, a Light Cruiser, one of the bombs damage the rudder, crippling the steering. The Vessel, able only to move in a circular motion, is plagued with an Air assault for over three hours and begins to list and burn. Complicated maneuvering by the Captain, Arthur Robinson, keeps the Ship afloat, and capably avoids a killing blow. The disabled *Marblehead* manages to limp to port at Tjilatjap, before moving to South Africa, to be drydocked. The U.S.S. *Houston*, also taking bad hits, sustains a bomb strike that ignites a flash fire, and takes 60 lives, but she survives the ordeal and remains in the campaign for the duration. The Japanese sustain one Destroyer damaged, during the confrontation. **(Pacific)** The U.S. Asiatic Fleet, commanded by Admiral Hart, is informally abolished, its Vessels becoming the Southwest Pacific Force, commanded by Vice Admiral W.A. Glassford. Admiral Glassford will establish his Headquarters at Tjilatjap, Java on the 7th. **(Pacific-Dutch East Indies)** In the Dutch Indies, the small Australian Garrison at Ambon, Island, falls to the Japanese. These gallant men, numbering Battalion size, had held out since the 30th of January against overwhelming odds. **(Atlan-**tic-North Africa)** In North Africa, the fighting slows, as the British Eighth Army begins to strengthen its positions at Gazala-Bir Hacheim. This sector of Libya will see no more than slight skirmishes until after Spring, when both opponents have rejuvenated their troops and are prepared to initiate new offensives. While the British hold their positions, the Axis troops fortify Tmimi-Mechili. **(Atlantic-France)** British Airplanes make passes over France to drop leaflets. The message:

"MESSAGE FROM AMERICA TO THE PEOPLE OF FRANCE

TO THE COUNTRY THAT GAVE US THE STATUE OF LIBERTY

WE WILL GIVE LIBERTY"

One side of the leaflet has a picture of the American Flag and the other side shows a picture of the Statue of Liberty.

February 5th 1942 — (Pacific) The Japanese, entrenched at Quinauan Point, come under heavy attack by American-Filipino troops in the Southern Defense zone. The Japs are driven to the cliff's brink, their back to the beaches below. In other activity, the U.S.S. *Sargo* is deeply involved with getting supplies delivered to the embattled defenders on the Philippines. Between this day and February 24th, the *Sargo* delivers one million rounds of 30 caliber ammunition to the Philippines and evacuates 24 specialized Army troops. **(Pacific-Singapore)** Japanese Fighters continue to harass Ships in port. A Convoy approaching with reinforcements (final elements of British 18th Division and Indian contingents) is attacked and one of the Vessels, the *Empress of Asia*, sinks with great loss of life. The Air raids, against the harbor, hinder other Vessels from unloading at the docks. **(Atlantic-North Ireland)** Londonderry becomes the newest Naval Operating Base for the United States Navy.

February 6th 1942 — (United States) The Naval Coastal Frontiers receive new names and will now be known as Sea Frontiers: Caribbean; Eastern; Gulf; Hawaiian; Northwest; Panama; Philippine and Western. In addition, the United States and Great Britain establish the Combined Chiefs of Staff. **(Pacific-Philippines-Luzon)** Embattled defenders of Bataan continue to withstand the Japanese assaults. Heavy fighting occurs in the I Corps area, with Japanese troops forging ahead, in an attempt to relieve other units which are receiving heavy resistance in the pockets. They strike against the 1st and 11th Divisions. The 11th stops the attackers a mere 1,000 yards from their comrades. Other Japanese units begin to place Artillery in strategic locations, enabling them to fire into Fort Drum and Fort Frank on a daily basis, intending to break the morale, while damaging the fortifications. In addition more Japanese land at Lingayen Gulf. **(Pacific-Dutch East Indies)** The Japanese now control Samarinda, situated on the east coast of Dutch Borneo.

February 7th 1942 — (Pacific) The American-Filipino forces initiate an offensive against Japanese positions in Bataan. The drive in sector one, I Corps defense perimeter, manages to partially surround the enemy pockets. In the southern sector, the American and Filipino troops strike at a Japanese relief force which is attempting to evacuate troops from Quinauan Point; enemy boats are forced to return to Olongapo. Lt. Commander John D. Bulkeley, commanding a Torpedo Squadron during the siege, valiantly leads his P.T. Boats against these landings. His skilled attack plans and brilliant tactics did much to allow the Americans to hold out for four months and eight days against the overwhelming enemy forces. **(Pacific)** The Allied ANZAC Force is placed under the command of Vice Admiral Herbert F. Leary.

February 8th 1942 — (Pacific-Philippines) The Japanese forces under General Homma, having endured unexpected resistance from American Filipino defenders of Bataan, are forced to pull back and await reinforcements, before making another assault. In the southern sector, at Quinauan Point, the Japanese are routed, but a relief force arrives and safely evacuates 34 men from the southwest coast. In other activity, Bulkeley's Motor Torpedo Boats are patrolling along the west coast of Bataan when they come upon a Japanese Cruiser in Bagac Bay. The seagoing jackrabbits dash in and out of the blinding lights of the enemy Cruiser. As the Japs begin firing their six inch guns, the Navy shoots the works, sending their torpedoes against the Cruiser. The bold attack interrupts the landing of reinforcements. Later, reports filter into Bulkeley's headquarters indicating the Japanese had beached the Cruiser, about 75 miles away. **(Pacific-Midway)** The American island of Midway is once again fired upon by a Japanese Submarine which damages the radio towers. **(Pacific-New Britain)** In New Britain, the Japanese capture Gasmata. **(Pacific-Dutch East Indies)** The U.S. Submarine *S-37*, commanded by Lt. James Dempsey, operating in the Makassar Strait, encounters an Enemy Invasion Fleet, including five Destroyers. The *S-37* launches torpedoes, that sink the *Natsushi*, the 1st Destroyer sunk by Submarines in the Pacific War. Three days later, the *S-37* will attack another enemy Destroyer in the Strait of Makassar. **(Pacific-Singapore)** Allied forces are unable to halt the Japanese landing force although it is much smaller in size than the defending force. Elements of the 5th and 18th Divisions, in addition to contingents of the Imperial Guards, make the landing in the northwest portion of the island and begin pushing the Australians back, as they advance toward the Airport at Tengah. **(Pacific-Tifore Island)** The U.S.S. *Shark* (SS-174), had reported being damaged on the previous day by enemy depth charges. Today, the U.S.S. *Shark* does not respond to orders, directing her to head towards Menado. No further communication with the Submarine occurs and the cause of her loss is officialy undetermined. The U.S.S. *Shark* is officially reported missing and presumed lost, on March 7th 1942. Subsequent checking of enemy records note several attacks against an unidentified Submarine, east of Menado on the 11th and additional attacks against another unidentified Submarine, in the vicinity of Kendari on the 17th and 21st (February). If the *Shark* had been lost on the 8th or 11th, she would be the first Submarine sunk by an enemy Surface Ship; otherwise, the U.S.S. *Perch*, damaged by depth charges and scuttled on March 3rd in the Java Sea remains the first Submarine sunk by enemy Surface Vessels. The *Shark*, had been commanded by Lt. Commander Lewis Shane, Jr.

February 9th 1942 — (United States) The U.S.S. *Lafayette* (AP-53), a Troop Transport is destroyed by fire while docked at a New York pier. The *Lafayette*, prior to her short career as a Transport, was a French Liner. **(Pacific-Philippines)** On Bataan, the defenders in the I Corps area search for and destroy Japanese troops, in the vicinity of Little Pocket, and close off resistance there. The First Division, after securing the area, joins other troops to rid the Big Pocket of Japanese. Some action also develops in the south sector, which allows the American-Filipino troops to gain ground in the Anyasan-Sil-

aiim vicinity. However, supplies continue to run out and no reinforcements are en route to assist. **(Pacific-Malaya)** The Japanese driving through British resistance and approach Tengah Airfield. Later, during the night, additional enemy reinforcements are debarked at Singapore Island, sealing the fate of Singapore. General Percival directs his troops to defend the southern portion of the island, where reservoirs, supply centers and the Airfield are located. Enemy Aircraft bomb Batavia, Malang and Surabaya, Malaya. On the following day, British General Wavell comes to Singapore and orders the troops to hold the island. He also orders all operational R.A.F. Planes to move to the Dutch East Indies. In Singapore, the Far East War Council meets for the final time and then General Wavell departs. **(Atlantic-England)** Representatives of Great Britain, Australia, New Zealand and the Netherlands East Indies, meet in London and establish the Pacific War Council.

Japanese POWs on Bataan.

February 10th 1942 — (Pacific-Philippines) In Luzon, Japanese forces under General Homma are pushed further away from Big Pocket. The Japs begin to concentrate around Anyasan-Silaiim while awaiting reinforcements. Although the Japanese timetable has been badly hampered by resistance in the Philippines, they continue to take giant strides in Burma, Singapore and Borneo. **(Pacific-Midway)** American-held Midway Island is subjected to another shelling from a Japanese Submarine, but the enemy Vessel manages to get off only two rounds before being chased by Fighters from Marine Squadron 221.

February 11th 1942 — (Pacific-Philippines) The I Corps drives the Japanese back from Big Pocket, but the enemy manages to break out. In the south sector, the Japanese are pushed back to Silaiim Point. The hard pressed American-Philippine forces continue doing a masterful job, and now it is the Japanese who are becoming concerned about supply problems and lack of reinforcements. **(Dutch West Indies)** The United States deploys troops in Aruba and Curacao in the West Indies.

February 12th 1942 — (United States) The United States 10th Air Force is activated at Patterson Field, Ohio. General Stilwell receives the command. **(Pacific-Philippines)** In the Philippines, the Japanese are again struck hard, forcing them to withdraw closer to the sea at Silaiim Point.

February 13th 1942 — (Pacific-Philippines) The Japanese continue to get thrashed in Luzon. Troops from the I Corps search the entire area around the Big Pocket and find no live

Japanese. In the South sector (Silaiim), the remainder of the survivors from the Longoskawayan and Quinauan Point invaders are exterminated. However, the Japanese score more successes in Singapore, and Southeast Borneo. **(Pacific-Singapore)** The British order all remaining Vessels at Singapore to sea, to prevent capture.

February 14th 1942 — (Pacific-Philippines) The U.S. Submarine Service is still squirming its way through Japanese defenses in the Philippines when possible. Today, the U.S.S. *Sargo* (SS-188) unloads some ammunition at Polloc Harbor in Mindanao and embarks with additional personnel. **(Pacific-Duch East Indies)** The British are hit heavily in Singapore. Japanese Naval and Air forces pummel the British Flotilla, as it attempts to escape through the Bangka Strait. One boat, which carries high ranking Officers, is forced to beach at a small deserted island, where the survivors subsequently perish. In Sumatra, Dutch East Indies, Japanese Paratroopers strike Palembang and drive the small Garrison westward to the coast. Land-based Allied Planes which had departed to attack a Japanese Naval Force in the Bangka Strait, are unable to be diverted in time to meet the invasion force which is now controlling Palembang. **(Pacific)** Netherlands Vice Admiral C.E.L. Helfrich replaces U.S. Admiral T.C. Hart as Commander in Chief, Allied Naval Forces in the Southwest Pacific.

February 15th 1942 — (Pacific-Dutch East Indies) The Japanese achieve another success as British General Percival surrenders in excess of 64,000 troops to the Japanese, under General Yamashita, at Singapore. The unconditional surrender is effective at nightfall. The Japanese who have held Naval superiority and are seizing Allied territory rapidly, are now becoming more confident. In other activity, a Japanese Naval Flotilla debarks an invasion force in the vicinity of Palembang, to augment the Paratroop drop of the previous day despite heavy resistance from Air raids by both Dutch and R.A.F. Planes. Allied troops continue moving to the West Coast for evacuation.

February 16th 1942 — (Pacific-Philippines) In the Philippines, I Corps continues to compress the Japanese lines at their salient. In the southern sector, mop up operations continue as remnants of the Japs, who had escaped Silaiim Point are discovered approximately seven miles away. After a two day battle, the Japanese in this area are destroyed. The outnumbered American-Filipino forces are still maintaining their own, but supplies are still depleting rapidly. **(Atlantic-Caribbean)** German Submarines penetrate Western Hemisphere waters and bombard Aruba, an island off the coast of Venezuela, South America.

February 17th 1942 — (Pacific-Philippines) In the Philippines, the Japanese pull back, allowing the I Corps to reinstate the complete main line of resistance at Bataan. **(Pacific-Society Islands)** United States troops begin to arrive in Bora Bora, as the 1st Naval Construction Battalion (Seabees) arrives.

February 18th 1942 — (Pacific-Dutch East Indies) In the Netherlands East Indies, the Japanese launch another invasion, debarking troops at Bali, off the coast of Java. **(China-Burma-India)** The Japanese gain more ground in Burma in the vicinity of Bilin. Allied troops attempt to draw a line of protection to save Pegu and the sea approaches to Syriam. **(Atlantic-Newfoundland)** A tremendous storm passes the

area and in its aftermath, lies two destroyed U.S. Vessels, the Destroyer *Truxton* (DD-229) and the Supply Ship *Pollux* (AKS-2), both sunk in the Bay of Placentia.

February 19th 1942 — (Pacific-Dutch East Indies) THE BATTLE OF BADOENG STRAIT — The Allies send a Naval Task Force at night against the Japanese Imperial Navy in the Badoeng Strait. The battle lasts into the following morning. The Japanese Fleet retires sustaining damage to one Destroyer, but heavy damage is suffered by the Allied Fleet under Rear Admiral Doorman (Netherlands Royal Navy) loses one Netherlands Destroyer, while two Netherlands Cruisers and one U.S. Destroyer, the U.S.S. *Stewart* (DD-224) are damaged. **(Pacific-Australia)** In Australia, the Allies suffer another humiliating blow from Japanese Aircraft, which swoop down furiously at Darwin. The U.S.S. *Peary* (DD-226) is destroyed, along with every Plane on the Airfield. The compact location of the poorly defended Aircraft provide the jubilant Japanese with their largest victory since Pearl Harbor. **(Pacific-Dutch East Indies)** Japanese troops occupy Bali in the Netherlands East Indies. **(China-Burma-India)** Japanese Fighter Planes attack Allied positions in Mandalay, Burma.

February 20th 1942 — (United States) The United States authorizes a $1 billion dollar loan to Russia. **(Pacific-Philippines)** In the Philippines, the Japanese accelerate their bombardment of the fortified positions on the islands in an all out attempt to squash the resistance of the I and II Corps. The defenders, however; take it in stride. In other activity, Philippine President Manuel Quezon and his family depart Corregidor on the Submarine U.S.S. *Swordfish* (SS-193), which transports them to the Visayan Islands, some 160 miles distant. Two days later, High Commissioner Sayer and his family depart for Australia. **(Pacific-Netherlands East Indies)** The Japanese invade Timor and advance on the Penfoie Airport, which is defended by Australian troops. **(South Pacific)** The U.S.S. *Lexington*, escorted by Cruisers and Destroyers while heading to Rabaul, New Britain, to attack Japanese positions, is assaulted by Japanese Fighter Planes. The U.S. Task Force fends off the attack, inflicting heavy losses on the Japanese Planes, but aborts the mission. Lieutenant Edward Henry O'Hare, Fighter Squadron 3, intercepts nine approaching enemy Bombers and with his guns blazing, he descends directly into the enemy formation. O'Hare whizzes around and through the disorganized Jap formation, singlehandedly destroying five of the enemy Bombers and severely damaging a sixth, before the stunned enemy can unleash their bombs on his Carrier. This most extraordinary feat saves the *Lexington* from serious damage and simultaneously curtails the Japanese offensive plans against Allied positions at New Britain because of their Aircraft losses. O'Hare receives the Medal of Honor (O'Hare Airport in Chicago is named in his honor.)

February 21st 1942 — (United States) After much discussion concerning the embattled troops in the Philippines, the U.S. decides to get General MacArthur out of the islands. MacArthur will be informed on the following day that he is to transfer himself to Australia. **(Pacific-Philippines)** An austere calm overtakes the battle perimeter on Bataan with both sides fortifying their defenses in preparation for the next engagement. **(Atlantic-Europe-Vichy France)** U.S. Ambassador Leahy is informed by the Under Secretary of State Welles, that a German Submarine had entered the Port of Martinique. Washington instructs Leahy to "demand that the French government forbid any Axis Vessels or Planes to enter French ports or territories in the Western Hemisphere." On the 23rd, Admiral Darlan gives assurances it will not be permitted. In return, the U.S. promises to resume economic aid to North Africa. Ambassador Leahy remains in France until the end of May, when he is recalled to the United States to become President Roosevelt's Chief of Staff.

February 1942 — U.S. Fighter Plane above Wake Island, prior to a U.S. air strike.

February 22nd 1942 — (Pacific-Philippines) President Roosevelt orders General MacArthur to leave Corregidor and report to Australia. **(Atlantic-England)** The VIII U.S. Army Bomber Command led by General Ira C. Eaker will establish headquarters in Great Britain.

February 23rd 1942 — (United States) The Japanese Imperial Navy boldly places a Submarine off the coast of California in the vicinity of Santa Barbara. The enemy Submarine fires on the Bankline Oil refinery, initiating the first of infrequent raids against the American mainland. **(Pacific-Philippines)** General MacArthur receives the message from President Roosevelt, which directs him to depart the Philippines. The message: "The PRESIDENT DIRECTS THAT YOU MAKE ARRANGEMENTS TO LEAVE FORT MILLS (Corregidor) AND PROCEED TO MINDANAO." "FROM MINDANAO YOU WILL PROCEED TO AUSTRALIA WHERE YOU WILL ASSUME COMMAND OF ALL U.S. TROOPS." MacArthur places the Visayan Islands under the command of Major General Bradford Chynoweth, taking it away from Major General Sharp, who retains the Mindanao Defense Command. Corregidor and the harbor defenses remain under the command of Major General George Moore. All troops on Luzon come under the command of General Jonathan Wainwright. These command changes take place during March after the departure of MacArthur. **(Pacific-Dutch East Indies)** In the Netherlands East Indies, the Japanese announce the seizure of Ambon. **(Pacific-Bismarcks)** In the Bismarck Archipelago, the U.S. Fifth Air Force, based in Australia, dispatches six B-17s to strike Japanese positions at Rabaul. The mission is completed, but no assessment of damages is available. **(China-Burma-India)** Intense fighting still rages in Burma in the vicinity of the Sittang River Bridge. The Indian 17th Division destroys the bridge to hamper the enemy advance, but in so doing strands portions of the 17th on the East side, forcing them to either dash for small boats, or swim to safety. **(Atlantic-Middle East)** In the Middle East, British General Sir Claude Auchinleck changes his defense plans for the Northern Front

and directs the 9th and 10th British Armies to take appropriate measures to delay an anticipated enemy advance.

February 24th 1942 — (Pacific) The U.S. Navy strikes back. Admiral Halsey's Task Force 16, including the Carrier *Enterprise*, moves toward Japanese held Wake Island. Halsey has the luxury of aerial photographs of Wake, compliments of a Marine Pilot from Midway. Task Force 16 (previously Task Force 8) is split into two Groups for the assault; TG 16.7, comprising the Heavy Cruisers *Northampton* and *Salt Lake City* and the Destroyers *Balch* and *Maury*, strikes from the west while TG 16.7 comprising the *Enterprise* and the Destroyers *Blue, Dunlap, Craven* and *Ralph Talbot* swoop down from the north. Treacherous weather hampers the operation, causing the launching of Planes to be delayed for about 15 minutes. Upon launching, at about 05:44, one Plane is lost due to the severity of the storm. In the meantime, Task Group 16.7, deployed within fifteen miles of Wake, is effected by the delay, and with radio silence a must, the situation becomes critical. The Planes are overhead at 0800 and the belated bombardment ensues. The Japanese on the island have insufficient numbers of Aircraft available and do not cause any damage to the Cruisers and Destroyers nearby, but the Yanks have a good day, blasting the hangars and shore batteries. In addition the U.S. Aircraft and Surface Vessel fire strike and destroy 3 four-engine Flying Boats and several small Vessels plus fuel supplies and ammunition depots. The mission cost three Planes lost, one to enemy Antiaircraft fire and two to the inclement weather. Halsey departs heading northeastward to pull in the fuel Ship the *Sabine* and the Destroyer *McCall* and rendezvous with TG 16.7 for the cruise back to Pearl Harbor. **(Pacific-Dutch East Indies)** In the Netherlands East Indies, Japanese advances in Java force the continuation of the Allied evacuation. American General Brereton evacuates the area and heads for India. The defense of the island is left to the Dutch, who await aid from Australian, British and American units. **(Atlantic)** On the Russian Front, the Germans are being cut off and surrounded in the vicinity of Staraya. Other German troops are faring better against the Russians, while attempting to break through the central front to reach Smolensk.

February 24th 1942 — A U.S. Cruiser bombarding Wake Island.

February 25th 1942 — (United States) Responsibility for the security of U.S. ports comes under the U.S. Coast Guard. **(Pacific-Philippines)** In the Philippines, General MacArthur reluctantly makes preparations to depart for Australia. MacArthur had considered the option of resigning his commission and joining the troops as a volunteer, but chooses to go to Australia to raise another Army, in hopes of a triumphant return to the island. MacArthur, although he has visited Bataan only once since the siege began, has shown no reluctance to battle, often standing in the open, without as much as a helmet, as Japanese Planes bombed overhead. His reasons for remaining on Corregidor have never been explained. **(Pacific)** A dispatch from Admiral Nimitz at Pearl Harbor is received by Adiral Halsey. The message: "DESIRABLE TO STRIKE MARCUS IF YOU THINK IT FEASIBLE." Conversation aboard the American Vessels is curiously funny considering the danger of the mission. Marcus lies just under 1,000 miles from Tokyo and is within striking distance of the Japanese Planes on Iwo Jima. One of Halsey's Officers quips: "WHY DO WE ALWAYS SEEM TO RETIRE WESTWARDLY?" The attack is launched on the 4th of March.

February 25th-March 3rd 1942 — (Pacific-Dutch East Indies) The Submarine U.S.S. *Perch*, operating northeast of Kangean Island in conjunction with the vigil against enemy Convoys heading for Java, is attacked by enemy Vessels and sustains some damage to the conning tower. On the 28th, the *Perch* is directed to attack an Armada, which is approaching Soerabaja, but falls prey to additional bad luck. After spotting two enemy Destroyers, and diving deep, the Vessel strikes bottom at less than 150'. The Destroyers attempt to destroy the *Perch*, but the Submarine is able to free herself and resume her mission. At approximately 04:00 on the 2nd, the disabled Submarine detects two more enemy Destroyers and is again forced to dive and brace for attack. Enemy depth charges rattle the Vessel and cause irreversible damage. At 21:00 hours, the Destroyers relent and withdraw, giving the Submariners an opportunity to surface and receive some fresh air, but the disabled Vessel is unable to submerge. Soon after, three more enemy Destroyers close rapidly against the defenseless Submarine. Hoping to avoid a massacre, the commanding Officer, Lt. Commander Hart, orders the Ship abandoned, leaving the fate of the Yanks to the mercy of the Japanese. Japanese pick up all survivors and transport them to Ofuna, Japan, where they are enslaved to work in mines. Nine of these gallant Sailors die while in captivity. Lieutenant Commander Hart and 52 others survive the inhumane treatment and are reunited with the U.S. and the Stars and Stripes, after the Japs are finally defeated.

February 26th 1942 — (Pacific-Philippines) In Luzon, the Japanese initiate an offensive by dispatching an amphibious force from Olongapo to strike at Mindoro. **(Pacific-Australia)** An American Task Force, en route to New Caledonia, reaches Australia. **(Pacific-Dutch East Indies)** The Submarine *S-38* is directed to draw a line between Soerabaja and Bawean Island, investigate a possible enemy landing and destroy a suspected radio station on Bawean. At about 06:00, the *S-37* begins a surface attack and sprays the beach area from one end to the other in the first Submarine bombardment of the war. The radio station is not located, but enemy shore fire is silenced. **(China-Burma-India)** In Burma, the Japanese move forward pushing the Allies back. The Japanese are still experiencing heavy resistance as they push towards the Sittang River. **(Indian Ocean)** The U.S.S. *Langley* (AV-3), a Seaplane Tender en route to Java is sunk by Japanese Planes in the Indian Ocean.

The *Langley*, transporting 32 Planes is able to remain afloat and two days later, the H.M.S. *Seawitch* arrives to assist. After the Ship is abandoned, it is destroyed by the U.S.S. *Whipple.* **(Atlantic)** The British 13th and 30th Corps continue to build up their defenses in the vicinity of Gazala, Bir Hacheim and Giarabub in Libya.

February 27th 1942 — (Pacific-Philippines) The Amphibious Invasion Force, launched by the Japanese from Olongapo the previous day, reaches Mindoro, where it lands and secures the Airfield and town. The Japanese hold their positions, making no moves to seize the balance of the island. This significant landing pulls the knot tighter on the dwindling Allied Forces. General MacArthur and his Staff are still at Corregidor. **(Pacific-South China Sea)** A contingent of British and Australian troops, marooned on a small island named Chebia in the South China Sea, send out desperate SOS signals. The *S-39*, commanded by Lt. Commander Coe, is instructed to attempt evacuation before the Japanese get the stranded men. The Submarine creeps in slowly and after dark attempts contact without results. On the following night the Commanding Officer and volunteers search the island, finding some human footsteps at the edge of the water, where signs of a recently departed boat are visible. Unfortunately, the Japs had captured the British Australian force. Although the Submarine could not save the men, some revenge is attained later when a return trip to the area nets the *S-39* a 6,500 ton Tanker.

February 27th-March 3rd 1942 — BATTLE OF THE JAVA SEA — As the Japanese propel themselves deeper into the contest for control of the Dutch East Indies, another Armada steams toward Java, intending to lengthen its malignant grip in the Pacific. In the Java Sea, an Allied Task force (ABDA), commanded by Dutch Admiral Doorman and consisting of five Cruisers and nine Destroyers, spots the Japanese invasion force and prepares to attack. Unfortunately, the show is to go off with poor communications between the Vessels.

The Allied Force consists of American, Australian, British and Dutch vessels and there is no common language or signal flags, spelling disastrous results; some Vessels are not even equipped with translation books. The Japanese move their Troop Transports with Heavy Escorts, including Destroyers and Heavy Cruisers. At mid-afternoon, the Japanese open up their guns at a range of 30,000 yards. Admiral Doorman, not speaking fluent English, orders the attack, but closing the range without quick communications prevents a strong battle plan, giving the superior enemy Forces an advantage. As the furious slugfest rages, the Dutch Cruisers *Java* and *Ruyter* suffer hits. The U.S.S. *Houston* is hit by a dud that crashes into the Ship's engine room. The Japanese effortlessly pummel the Allied Force throughout the afternoon, scorching the water with burning wreckage and carnage. Before the sea duel slows down, later in the day, the Dutch Destroyer *Kortenaer* and the British Destroyer *Electra* are sunk, the *Electra* while rushing to assist the H.M.S. *Exeter*, which had been severely damaged. Dutch Admiral Doorman, staggered by the tremendous whipping, attempts to make a run for Soerabaja with the remnants of his Task Force. The American Destroyers had already expended all their torpedoes before departing the area. The Allied Vessels withdraw westwardly, anticipating darkness to assist in the retreat, but the Japanese do not relent.

The darkness only brings more misery and casualties. An enemy Vessel takes out the H.M.S. *Jupiter* as she heads for safety, with the Japanese Destroyers in close pursuit. The Allied Vessels, although much outgunned, clash with the closing enemy Destroyers and two of the four attackers are destroyed by Cruiser fire. The Japs maintain the pressure and move against the beleaguered column of battered Allied Ships, reinitiating the battle shortly before midnight, further devastating Doorman's Task Force. The skies become brightly illuminated after a massive skyburst of enemy starshells, spotlighting the Allied vessels for the deadly guns of the Japanese Armada. In quick succession, two more Allied Warships, the *Java* and Admiral Doorman's Flagship, the *DeRuyter* explode into flames, taking both of them to the bottom. With the exception of the American Destroyers, which had withdrawn earlier, when their ammunition became expended, the Task Force of Doorman, now consists of the U.S.S. *Houston* and the Australian Light Cruiser, *Perth*. The two surviving Vessels attempt to outrun the inevitable along the coast of Java, with the Japs in hot pursuit. As they enter the Sundra Strait, toward the later part of the night, they are greeted by another enemy Invasion Force, which includes 11 Destroyers, five Cruisers and additional Warships. The Japanese seemingly synchronize their guns and commence a lightning attack. The congestion of tracer shells, bullets and torpedoes, rakes the ill-fated Allied Ships. The *Houston* remains afloat under the curtain of fire, but the *Perth*, ravaged by enemy salvos, slumps badly. The enemy shelling continues, sending the valiant *Perch* to the bottom, leaving the embattled *Houston* to fight it out alone. For nearly an hour, the unyielding Vessel pours fire into the enemy Warships. As the ammunition is near expended, so is the life of the mighty *Houston* (CA-30), which goes down in glorious fashion, against insurmountable odds, taking about half of her crew with her. Another lopsided defeat for the Allies. With this victory, the Japanese command control of the Malay Barrier and the Java Sea.

By the following morning, the Australian, British Dutch American Fleet is abolished and the remaining American Destroyers are ordered to Australia. The Japanese land at the beaches west of Soerabaja on the following day, claiming the only damage sustained during the entire battle are the two Destroyers which had been eliminated by the Cruisers during the latter part of the battle. Captain Albert H. Rooks, Commanding Officer, of the *Houston*, posthumously receives the Medal of Honor for gallantry because of his actions during this and others February 4th-27th. During another brutal engagement a few weeks prior, Captain Rooks had repelled four attacks against his Ship, but a fifth inflicts heavy damage. Captain Rooks, by his excellent leadership, has his Ship seaworthy in a matter of days.

February 28th 1942 — (Pacific-Philippines) The U.S.S. *Permit* (SS-178) makes a dangerous run through the Japanese Naval defenses ringing the Philippines and discreetly enters the waters of Corregidor, delivering another pittance of ammunition to the beleaguered Yanks. This silent sentinel takes on priority personnel, and departs. **(Pacific-Dutch East Indies)** The Japanese launch an invasion force (16th Japanese Army) against Java, Netherlands East Indies. Their Air Forces will pummel the area, prior to landing, continuing their flights through the night, followed by Japanese troops hitting the

beaches in the vicinity of Batavia. The battle rages ferociously on land, while Naval Vessels pulverize each other in the waters offshore. On the following day, the Allied Ships are forced to break away and make a run for Australia. In related activity, the *S-38* encounters wreckage and survivors in the water. The survivors are 54 British Sailors, from the H.M.S. *Electra*. The *S-37*, commanded by Lt. Commander Dempsey, also discovers survivors. The *S-37* picks up a couple of American Sailors and gives supplies to Dutch Sailors.

February 28th-March 3rd 1942 — THE BATTLE OF THE SUNDA STRAIT — See Battle Of The Java Sea —

March 1st 1942 — (Pacific-Philippines) In Luzon, the I and II Corps take stock of a courageous stand against the Jap invaders. Since January 6th, they have inflicted nearly 7,000 casualties, 2,700 killed and more than 4,000 wounded. Japanese General Homma has been troubled by the fact that this outnumbered band of insolent defenders still holds on. The Japanese continue to close the stranglehold on the island, while General MacArthur is still preparing to depart. A U.S. Submarine will be designated to carry MacArthur and his Staff to Australia, but MacArthur will insist on leaving with the tiny fleet of PT Boats. **(Pacific-Dutch East Indies)** In the Netherlands East Indies, the situation is grave. The Japanese control the air and sea. Their land forces are about to take command on the ground as the Allied forces desperately make final evacuation plans. The Allied Naval Forces are splintered in an effort to make it to Australia. The U.S. Destroyers *Edsall* (DD-219) and *Pillsbury* (DD-227), and the Patrol Gunboat *Ashville* (PG-21) are sunk on the 3rd, south of Java. The Destroyer U.S.S. *Pope* (DD-225) is sunk after being struck by Naval Bombardment, combined with fire from an enemy Plane. The Oiler *Pecos* (AO-6) is also lost, when enemy Naval fire destroys her south of Christmas Island. and the Cruiser *Houston* (CA-30), fails to make her escape. Of the original Allied Task Force under Admiral Doorman, (10 Destroyers and 5 Cruisers), only four U.S. Destroyers survive the voyage to Australia. In other activity, the Submarine U.S.S. *Grampus*, which had missed out on several earlier attempts during late February to sink an enemy Warship, sinks the *Kaijo Maru* Number 2, a Tanker off Borneo with two torpedoes. **(Atlantic-Newfoundland)** Land-based U.S. Naval Aircraft detect and sink a German Submarine (U-656) south of Newfoundland. **(Atlantic-Russia)** Despite the horrendous Russian winter, vicious fighting continues between the Germans and Soviets. The Russian advance is halted, but the Germans cannot reach its beleaguered Sixteenth Army which is cut off, southeast of Staraya.

March 2nd 1942 — (United States) The U.S. Military is mobilizing as fast as possible, in an effort to initiate the long awaited push to recapture the ground they have lost in the Pacific. Marine and Naval forces are working at a furious pace to fortify what they control, while simultaneously endeavoring to outguess the Japanese. By this time most Code-breakers, previously stationed in the Philippines, have been evacuated and quickly reassigned. The Americans anticipate an attack at Midway as a Japanese stepping stone for an attack on the United States. In other activity, the United States Navy establishes the Anti-submarine Warfare Unit, Atlantic Fleet at Boston, Massachusetts. **(Pacific-Philippines)** Japanese ground troops land at Zamboanga (Mindanao), Philippines. **(Pacific-Dutch East Indies)** The momentum still lies with the Japanese, as they maintain their advances throughout the Netherlands East Indies, prompting further evacuation of Allied Ships from Java. **(Pacific-New Guinea)** The situation in New Guinea worsens as the Japanese accelerate their pre-invasion Air strikes to soften resistance. **(China-Burma-India)** The Japanese continue to pressure Allied troops in Burma, cutting a wedge further west, toward Rangoon.

March 3rd 1942 — (Pacific-Java Sea) The U.S.S. *Perch* (SS-176), a Submarine which had been struck by enemy fire and depth charges, is scuttled by its crew. In addition, the Japanese encounter and sink the U.S.S. *Asheville* (PG-21) south of Java.

March 4th 1942 — (Pacific-Hawaii) In Hawaii, Japanese Seaplanes swing over Oahu, dropping four bombs, however, the nuisance raid inflicts no damage to the facilities. **(Pacific-Australia)** The *U.S.S. Sargo*, moving toward Freemantle, Australia, is spotted by an R.A.F. Plane. The Pilot, mistaking the U.S. Submarine for an enemy Vessel, attacks, but no damage is sustained and the *Sargo* arrives safely on the following day. **(Pacific-Japan)** The Submarine service is beginning to have more luck in the Pacific. The U.S.S. *Tuna*, prowling in Japanese waters, nets itself a 4,000 ton can of Jap cargo after watching its fired torpedoes send the unnamed Cargo Ship to the bottom. Not to be outdone by the *Tuna*, the U.S.S. *Narwhal*, sinks the Cargo Vessel *Taki Maru*. **(Pacific-Philippines)** Zero Hour approaches for the departure of General MacArthur from Corregidor. Before leaving in one week, MacArthur will place General Wainwright in command (Bataan and Corregidor), with General Sharp commanding the forces on Mindanao. The Visayan forces will be led by General Chynoweth. MacArthur also anticipates two additional commands, in an effort to hold on until he can return with another Army. General Marshall will subsequently change this order of command. **(Pacific-Marcus Island)** Admiral Halsey's Task Force remains active in the Pacific. Planes from the U.S.S. *Enterprise* strike enemy positions at Marcus Island. At 0447, 32 Bombers and six Fighters take off from a point 125 miles northeast of the objective. The radio station blares a warning, but a well placed bomb silences it. The raid, intended to fray the nerves of the Japanese is apparently successful. Although no enemy Planes intercept the raiders, a Plane from Iwo Jima appears and sends word to Tokyo, prompting an alert and a black out. The *Enterprise* loses one Plane to Anti-aircraft fire. **(China-Burma-India)** Headquarters for American Forces, China, Burma, and India are established at Chungking. American General Stilwell completes his 23 day journey, reaching Chungking and assuming command.

March 4th-September 4th 1942 — The *S-17*, a U.S. Submarine, attempts to ram a German U-Boat which is spotted near the Virgin Islands. Lt. Thomas Burton Klakring retains his tenacity against the enemy and after he receives another Submarine, the U.S.S. *Guardfish*, he is off toward Japan to hunt Japanese Vessels. Cruising submerged near Honshu, the Submarine, which departed Pearl Harbor during early August, makes its first encounter with the enemy on August 19th, but the brushes with two enemy Vessels accounts for no recorded hits. Several other sightings of enemy Vessels over the next couple of weeks, keep the *Guardfish* busy and she is credited with the sinking of a Merchant Vessel near Kinkasan Harbor on the 24th of August. A few more harrowing encounters with

the enemy occur and give the *Guardfish* some shivers, but no damage from the enemy pursuers. On the 2nd of September, the *Guardfish*, operating on the surface, spots a conspicuous target less than ten thousand yards away and closes for the attack. From a perfect vantage point, the submerged raider prepares to fire. The orders are given. Fire one! Fire Two! Fire Three! Two of the three fish hit the mark, but the insolent Vessel stays afloat, prompting the crew to fire another torpedo. Astonishingly, there is no sighting of the torpedo's route; not only are the waters not parted, but there is no explosion. Shortly after the final phantom fish is fired or misfired as torpedoes are prone to early in the war, the crew of the *Teiku* is soon abandoning Ship as it splits in half. Now that's a Sailor story! The fish that missed sank a Ship.

The U.S.S. Enterprise (CV-6).

Admiral Chester W. Nimitz, U.S.N.

The *Guardfish* has a pretty good day on the 4th of September, when several enemy Freighters waddle by the periscope at about 1300. The *Guardfish* intuitively selects one of the three Vessels and fires one torpedo, which damages the Vessel. The *Guardfish*, lingers in these Japanese waters and before 1700 the periscope whirls and spots a couple of Freighters in the distance. About 45 minutes after sighting the enticing targets, torpedoes speed to the mark, traveling about 500 yards, and another Freighter is struck. The explosion occurs within seconds. Two additional torpedoes speed toward the second Vessel, with equally successful results; the *Tenyu Maru* follows the *Chita Maru* to the bottom. The periscope becomes popular and the crew is enjoying the sight. Lt. Commander Klakring's hunting expedition continues as two more Freighters are sighted. The Submarine takes a shot from long distance and another enemy Ship is taken off the rolls, after an explosion of great magnitude blows the Vessel apart as it sets anchored off Minato. The *Guardfish*, which has just fired one of the longest "bulls eye" of the war, from well over 6,000 yards is still not satisfied. Yet another enemy Ship, the *Keimei Maru*, traveling from the southeast is torpedoed and sent to the bottom. Furiously, the Japanese Patrol Vessels criss-cross the area, in search of the Submarine, but the *Guardfish* has departed the scene. Enemy Patrols chase futilely. The *Guardfish*, which is awarded one of her two Presidential citations for the astonishing accomplishment, during this Patrol, reaches Midway on the 15th of September. Klakring's Raiders have more than a few tales to tell and for evidence the crew had taken pictures from the periscope to substantiate what they had seen, including close up photographs of a Japanese horse race.

March 5th 1942 — (Pacific) The Battle for Java is becoming even more lopsided, with Dutch resistance insufficient to repulse the Japs. Most primary installations have been destroyed to prevent capture. **(China-Burma-India)** American General Brereton assumes command of the 10th Air Force, with his Headquarters being in New Delhi. In Burma, Lt. General Sir Harold Alexander arrives at Rangoon to assume command of the British Army. He immediately initiates an offensive to tighten the space between the 1st and 17th Indian Divisions. The Japanese, meanwhile, successfully assault Pegu and gain access to the town. **(Atlantic)** The Russians score additional successes against the Germans, by recapturing the town of Yukhnov (Central Front).

March 6th 1942 — (Pacific-Australia) In Australia, a U.S. Task Force embarks southwest for New Caledonia. **(China-Burma-India)** The British under Alexander evacuate Rangoon, Burma. In China, General Stilwell meets with Chiang Kai-Shek in Chungking to discuss strategy. At dinner with Chiang Kai-shek, the Generalissimo discusses his Military strategy with General Stilwell. Stilwell later shares the information with his aides, one of whom quips: "I HOPE THE OLD BOY NEVER TEACHES AT OUR WAR COLLEGE;" one of Kai-shek's strategies: "NEVER GROUP DIVISIONS TOGETHER, TO PREVENT SEVERAL DIVISIONS FROM BEING DEFEATED AT ONCE AND CREATING A MORALE PROBLEM." Another: "ALWAYS WAIT CAUTIOUSLY FOR ABOUT A MONTH TO SEE WHAT THE ENEMY WILL DO FIRST, IF NO ATTACK COMES, THEN POSSIBLY ATTACK."

March 7th 1942 — (United States) The United States lists the

Submarine U.S.S. *Shark* (SS-174) as missing in the Pacific and presumed lost. **(Pacific-Dutch East Indies)** The Japanese, unhampered by Allied resistance in the Netherlands East Indies presses Java to the brink of capitulation. Allied Aircraft have been annihilated, the troops battle weary and their supplies nearly diminished. **(Pacific-New Guinea)** In New Guinea, a Japanese Convoy that had departed New Britain on the 5th reaches the Huon Gulf and debarks assault troops, under cover of Naval guns, at Lae and Salamaua. **(China-Burma India)** The crisis in Burma is worsening. Allied troops evacuate Rangoon, but hit a Japanese force at Taukkyan, which severely impedes their escape. With the loss of Rangoon and its port, the Allies can only be supplied by air.

March 8th 1942 — (Atlantic) The First Marine Brigade (Provisional), which has been stationed in Iceland to defend against a possible German invasion, is replaced by U.S. Army troops. **(China-Burma-India)** In Burma, Allied troops receive supplies and reinforcements, which are brought in by Heavy Bombers attached to the American 10th Air Force. These missions, originating in India, will continue flying to Magwe, Burma, for the next five days.

March 9th 1942 — (United States) There is a major reorganization within the United States Army. General Headquarters is abolished, with the establishment of three commands (Army Ground Forces, Army Air Forces, and Services of Supply, to be later named Army Service Forces), which will come under the Chief of Staff, General Marshall. Army Field Forces will remain under the control of the General Staff, War Department. In addition, Admiral King is appointed Chief of Naval Operations in place of Admiral Stark, who is given command of all Naval Forces operating in European seas. In other activity, the United States Navy establishes the Naval Air Transport Squadron (VR-1). It is activated at Norfolk, Virginia and will operate in the Atlantic. **(Pacific-Philippines)** General Homma is replaced by General Yamashita as Commander in Chief of all Japanese troops in the Philippines. **(Pacific-Dutch East Indies-Java)** The Japanese conquer Java and set their sights on Australia. **(Pacific-New Guinea)** In New Guinea, the Japanese continue to use their aircraft to strike Allied positions. Allied Planes manage to assault a Japanese Convoy in the Huon Gulf, but the results of the raid are unknown.

Lt. General Joseph W. (Vinegar Joe) Stilwell, U.S.A., and Generalissimo Chiang Kai-shek and Madame Chiang.

March 10th 1942 — **(Pacific-Midway)** A Squadron of Marine Fighters intercepts and destroys a Japanese Kawanishi 97 Flying Boat. The Squadron initiates the first action between Marine Pilots and enemy Aircraft at Midway. The appearance of the enemy Flying Boat is one more indication of Japan's intent to make another strike at Hawaii. **(Pacific-Philippines)** In the Philippines, General Wainwright is informed by MacArthur that he will assume command of all Luzon troops. **(Pacific-New Guinea)** In New Guinea, the Japanese send another Invasion Force ashore at Finschhafen. U.S. Planes, based on the Carriers, *Lexington* (CV-2) and *Yorktown* (CV-5), strike Japanese Shipping and positions at Lae and Salamaua, causing severe damage. Australian Land Based B-17s will subsequently deliver another blow to the same area.

March 11th 1942 — **(Pacific-Japan)** The U.S.S. *Pollack*, another of the U.S. Submarines operating in Japanese waters, encounters a Japanese Cargo Vessel, the *Fukushu Maru* and destroys it with torpedoes. **(Pacific-Philippines)** General MacArthur and his staff depart Corregidor. Lt. Commander John D. Bulkeley pulls out of port with MacArthur and family in the PT-41. The Staff makes it to Mindanao, after some hazardous experiences on the 14th, but difficulties with the Aircraft make it necessary for MacArthur to remain at Mindanao until the 17th. Lt. Commander Bulkeley's PT Boats return to Corregidor to harass the Japanese for another month. In April, MacArthur orders the remaining crew members of the PT Boats to be flown to Australia.

A U.S. PT Boat on Patrol.

March 12th 1942 — **(United States)** President Roosevelt, by Executive Order, combines the positions of Chief of Naval Operations and Commander in Chief, United States Fleet, effective March 26th. **(Pacific-New Caledonia)** An American Task Force descends upon Noumea, New Caledonia. A combined American Force, consisting of 17,500 men begins fortifying the area, while simultaneously constructing a major Air Base in the vicinity of Tontouta.

March 13th 1942 — **(Pacific-Philippines)** Friday the 13th proves to be an unlucky day for the PT-32. The Americans scuttle her today. **(Pacific)** Powerful Japanese Naval Forces now replace Infantry in the area around Lae-Salamaua. The Imperial Japanese 4th Fleet departs Rabaul, New Britain, heading for Buka, which is situated in the Solomons. Back around Japan, American Submarines continue to stab at supply lines of the sea. The U.S.S. *Gar*, commanded by Lt. Commander Don McGregor, detects the *Chichibu Maru*, a small Cargo Vessel, as it is moving along the coast of China. The

Gar, fires four torpedoes and three of them hit the mark, costing the enemy another Cargo Vessel. Four days later, another enemy Vessel, the 1,520 ton *Ishikari Maru*, is sunk by the U.S.S. *Grayback*, during a daylight submerged assault.

March 14th 1942 — **(United States)** The United States Navy establishes the Amphibious Force, Atlantic Fleet, to be commanded by Rear Admiral R.M. Brainard. **(Pacific-Philippines)** General MacArthur and his Staff arrive at Mindanao, although Aircraft expected to take them to Australia is unavailable. MacArthur is forced to wait until the Navy sends alternate B-17s to pick them up. The wait is harrowing and causes friction between MacArthur and the Navy. Some American Code-breakers stationed on the Philippines have been sent to Australia by the Submarine U.S.S. *Permit*. Thirty-eight code-breakers board the *Permit*, but eight men of the crew must be left at Corregidor to make room, later to become prisoners of war and be subjected to the same fate as the rest of the Garrison.

March 15th 1942 — **(Pacific-Philippines)** Japanese Artillery continues to pound Forts Drum and Frank on fortified islands being held by the Americans. The Forts sustain heavy damage, but hold on. **(Caribbean)** German U-Boats strike in waters near Haiti; the Coast Guard Vessel *Acacia* (AGL-200), a Tender, is sunk by a torpedo. **(Atlantic)** American Land Based Aircraft track and detect a German Submarine, the *U-503*, and sink it in the North Atlantic.

March 17th 1942 — **(United States)** The United States Navy establishes, Naval Forces Europe. Admiral Stark will assume command on April 30th. In other activity, the United States agrees to bear responsibility for the daunting task of defending the entire Pacific Ocean. **(Pacific)** General MacArthur and his party depart Del Monte Airfield, located at Mindanao, miraculously in American hands. Upon arrival at Australia and during the trip from Darwin to Melbourne, MacArthur issues a statement to the press: "THE PRESIDENT OF THE UNITED STATES ORDERED ME TO BREAK THROUGH THE JAPANESE LINES AND PROCEED FROM CORREGIDOR TO AUSTRALIA FOR THE PURPOSE OF, AS I UNDERSTAND IT, OF ORGANIZING THE AMERICA OFFENSIVE AGAINST JAPAN A PRIMARY OBJECT OF WHICH IS THE RELIEF OF THE PHILIPPINES. I CAME THROUGH AND I SHALL RETURN." President Roosevelt would bestow the Medal of Honor on MacArthur-many times unsuccessfully nominated before; for his courage during the siege and the hazardous trip from the Philippines. In doing so, Roosevelt would increase the stature of MacArthur and raise the hopes of the American people, who can use some positive reassurance. General Douglas MacArthur and his father General Arthur MacArthur are the only father-son combination in history to receive the Medal of Honor.

March 18th 1942 — **(United States)** A Naval Task Force, commanded by Rear Admiral J.W. Wilcox, receives orders to head for England, where it will participate with the British Home Fleet. The U.S. Task Force includes one Carrier, two Battleships, two Cruisers and eight Destroyers. **(Southwest Pacific)** America is still initiating defensive measures throughout the Pacific Theater, while building her resources to go on the offensive against the Japanese invaders. Two companies of U.S. Army Engineers arrive at New Hebrides and will begin construction of an Air Base.

March 20th 1942 — (United States) Another mighty Battleship, the U.S.S. *South Dakota* (BB-57) is commissioned at New York. **(Pacific)** In the Philippines, General Wainwright is informed that he has been promoted to the rank of Lt. General and that he is to assume command of all American troops in the Philippines. **(Atlantic-North Africa)** The British 8th Army initiates an offensive against Axis positions around Benghazi and Derna, Libya.

March 21st 1942 — (Pacific) General Marshall, previously informed by General MacArthur of command changes he had made when departing the Philippines, revises them. Meanwhile, beleaguered troops in the Philippines continue to withstand capitulation and infuriate the Japanese. General Wainwright sets up headquarters on Corregidor and selects General Beebe as his Chief of Staff. Major General Edward P. King Jr. is appointed Commander of the Luzon force. In Australia, Lt. General George Brett U.S.A., assumes command of the combined Air Forces in Australia. **(China-Burma-India)** In Burma, American General Stilwell arrives at the front to direct the Chinese forces to help defend the lines around Toungoo-Prome. The Chinese Temporary 55th Division, is ordered to reinforce the 200th Chinese Division. The 200th is to replace the Burma 1st Division on the Toungoo front, and the 55th is to transfer to Pyawbwe. In addition, the Chinese 96th Division is ordered to Mandalay. The Japanese press further, taxing Allied efforts to halt their advance. Japanese Air attacks continue to inflict heavy damage to Allied positions, further depleting the few Allied Planes in Burma.

March 22nd 1942 — (United States) President Roosevelt informs General MacArthur of the intent to keep General Wainwright in command of all forces in the Philippines. MacArthur offers no opposition to the directive. **(China-Burma-India)** American General Stilwell, still in Burma, initiates plans to commence a counterattack to supply needed assistance to the Chinese 200th Division, at Toungoo. British and American Planes, based at Magwe Airdrome, receive another hit from Japanese Aircraft, prompting all remaining Planes to be moved to Akyab and Loiwing (on Chinese frontier) respectively, eliminating support for ground troops.

March 23rd 1942 — (Pacific) The Andaman Islands, located southwest of Burma and situated in the Bay of Bengal, (east of India and part of the Indian Ocean), are invaded by the Japanese against no opposition.

American troops defending Bataan (note the man on left has no weapon).

March 24th 1942 — (Pacific-Philippines) In Luzon, the determined Japanese raise the stakes. The severity of attacks intensifies from both Artillery and concentrated Aircraft assaults, in one more deliberate attempt to crumble the defenders. Bataan and Corregidor receive non-stop incoming shells. These raids will be commenced during the night to supplement the usual day bombardments. The besieged are still doing a remarkable job, but medicine and supplies are nearly exhausted. Japan is in complete control of the air and sea, in this area and have cut off attempts to bring in more supplies by Ship. During the siege, very little supplies manage to reach the defenders. American Submarines venture through the Japanese blockade as frequently as possible, on these dangerous missions, without losses, but the amount of supplies is only a trickle. **(China-Burma-India)** In Burma, the unstoppable Japanese counter-attack and encircle a portion of the Chinese Division at Toungoo. Both the Chinese and the Burma Army are forced to withdraw to safer positions. The Chinese 55th Division arrives, while the Chinese 200th and the Burma 1st are under siege, but does not attack. The Japanese seize the Airdrome at Kyungon. In other activity, British General Alexander is in Chungking, discussing strategy with Chiang Kai-shek. General Stilwell is informed by Madame Chiang of the developments. Chiang had stated as a matter of fact, in the past: "NO BRITISHER WOULD EVER COMMAND HIS TROOPS IN BURMA." After the meeting, Chiang has the title Commmander of British Empire and British General Alexander becomes Supreme Commander of all Chinese Troops in Burma.

March 25th 1942 — (Pacific) United States Army troops, 162nd Infantry, 41st Division, arrive at Bora Bora, in the Society Islands. **(China-Burma-India)** The Allied troops besieged at Toungoo, Burma, are further pressed by the Japanese, with their precarious positions becoming further endangered. The Chinese 55th Division, positioned north of Toungoo, still does not attack.

March 26th 1942 — (United States) Admiral H.A. Stark is replaced by Admiral E.J. King, as Chief of Naval Operations. Admiral King is also the Commander in Chief of the United States Fleet. Two of his principal aides will be Vice Admiral R. Wilson, Chief of Staff, and Vice Admiral F.J. Horne, Vice Chief of Naval Operations. In other activity, Army Air Corps contingents are transferred to Naval Control of the Eastern Sea Frontier, to supplement their Antisubmarine Patrols, in the Atlantic Ocean. The United States lists the U.S.S. *Atik*, an Auxiliary Vessel, as sunk by an enemy torpedo. **(Pacific)** A Japanese Carrier Force departs Kendari, (Celebes) and moves toward the Indian Ocean. **(China-Burma-India)** The Japanese continue to pound the Chinese 200th Division and the Burma First Division in Toungoo. The Chinese 55th Division still does not attack. The Chinese 22nd Division arrives on the scene, but takes the same posture as the 55th.

March 27th 1942 — (United States) In the United States, the Government authorizes free mail privileges for all U.S. Servicemen. **(Atlantic)** A British Naval Force moves near St. Nazaire, France. The Destroyer H.M.S. *Campbeltown* crashes the main lock gate and succeeds in landing demolition experts. **(Chinese-Burma-India)** U.S. General Stilwell is infuriated with the lack of combat spirit by the Chinese. The Fighting 200th and the Burma 1st are still holding tight, against tremendous odds, but with the nearby 22nd and 35th

Divisions failing to attack, General Tai An-Lin's 200th Division, has to withdraw to the walls of the city of Toungoo. Fierce fighting continues all day, with the Japanese seizing ground and then being thrown back; They retain the Airfield, however. In other activity in Burma, the R.A.F. is not having a good day either. Allied Planes that had only recently arrived from Magwe Field, are struck by another devastating Japanese Air raid. Eighty enemy Planes pummel Allied Aircraft that are crammed close together on the ground, destroying more than half of the R.A.F. Aircraft and those of The U.S. Volunteer Squadrons, including General Chennault's units. All British R.A.F. units and U.S. Volunteer Squadrons abandon Akyab after this humiliating attack and head for India. U.S. General Stilwell can't leave even if he wanted to, as there are no more Planes. Stilwell, directing a lopsided campaign in a Theater without any U.S. Combat Soldiers to hold the hordes of invaders, now loses his Aircover. Fortunately, the General retains his acid sense of humor. Not too long after this episode, General Stilwell receives a detailed directive from the newly appointed Commander of the British Empire, Chiang Kai-shek, who states: "BURMA IS A HOT PLACE. WATERMELONS ARE GOOD FOR THE MORALE OF THIRSTY TROOPS." The directive states that Stilwell will "PROVIDE ONE WATERMELON FOR EVERY FOUR CHINESE TROOPS." The decoded message further states: "ALL CHINESE SHOULD BE BURIED WITH THEIR ANCESTORS. THEREFORE, THE BODIES OF ALL MEN WHO ARE KILLED OR DIE IN BURMA WILL BE SHIPPED BACK TO CHINA IN PINE-BOARD COFFINS." U.S. General Frank Dorn, irresistibly snaps to General Stilwell: "AND WHERE DO WE FIND PINES IN BURMA. HAVE YOU SEEN ANY, SIR?" General Stilwell, keeping things in perspective, snarls jokingly at General Dorn, stating: "DON'T ARGUE DORN. HIS NIBS HAS SPOKEN."

March 28th 1942 — (Pacific) The U.S. Marine 7th Defense Battalion arrives at Samoa to establish a new Garrison. **(China-Burma-India)** Additional troops are to arrive later to further strengthen the defenses. British General Alexander heeds General Stilwell's request and orders an attack against the Japanese on the Irrawaddy Front. Stilwell hopes to aid the beleaguered 200th Division, still resisting tenaciously, against the Japanese. The assault commences on the following day. In other activity, contingents of the Burma I Corps, clash with the enemy at Paungde.

March 29th 1942 — (Pacific-New Hebrides) The U.S. Marine, 4th Defense Battalion, supplemented by Marine Fighter Squadron 221, is ordered to redeploy at Port Vila, Efate, New Hebrides. **(China-Burma-India)** The Burma I Corps attacks and seizes Japanese positions at Paungde. This does not alter the situation in Burma. The Japanese merely fortify their positions several miles to the north at Padignon. Stilwell, the American Commander without troops, notes while driving into Pyinmana during an enemy Air raid: "WHAT A HELL OF A WAY TO FIGHT A WAR! THIS IS PROBABLY THE FIRST TIME AN AMERICAN GENERAL HAS GONE INTO COMBAT WITHOUT A SINGLE AMERICAN COMBAT SOLDIER. HOW DO YOU WIN A WAR WITHOUT TROOPS?"

March 30th 1942 — (United States) The Pacific War Council is established in Washington, D.C. The Joint Chiefs of Staff decide to divide the Pacific Ocean into two Commands; the Pacific, under Admiral Nimitz and the Southwest Pacific area under General MacArthur. In other activity, the Inter-American Defense Board meets for the first time in Washington, D.C. and the Pacific War Council, comprised of representatives from Australia, Canada, China, England, Netherlands, New Zealand and the United States, is established. They meet for the first time on April 1st in Washington, to prepare strategy for victory in the Pacific. Also during March, American Japanese are being moved to camps which ostracize them for the duration of the war, in an attempt to keep them from collaborating with the enemy. Many of these Japanese are 2nd and third generation Americans and attempt to prove their patriotism, as Americans, but to no avail. Most Japanese businessmen lose everything. **(Pacific-Dutch East Indies)** The U.S.S. *Seawolf*, patrolling near Christmas Island during the early morning darkened hours, and aware that the Japs are on their way, moves cautiously along the surface through the night, submerging toward dawn to await the Japanese Fleet. At 0730 contact is made as the periscope spots four Cruisers, moving toward Flying Cove. The *Seawolf* fires two torpedoes, and a couple of insurance shots; to the jubilation of the crew, several of the Japanese, peering leisurely atop the bridge are quickly aroused as two of the torpedoes strike the mark. The Vessel becomes damaged, but not destroyed and continues its course, only with determined speed. The *Seawolf*, commanded by Lt. Commander Warder, crash dives, to await the Oriental depth charges and hopes for the best. Luck is on the side of *Seawolf* and she evades destruction, although the daylong barrage shakes the Vessel to its limit. The elusive Submarine successfully outwits the enemy and remains securely positioned, approximately 15 miles offshore, awaiting the appropriate time to strike again. The moon retains a spectacular glow, compelling the *Seawolf* to remain submerged. At about 02:00 on the 1st, the lone Submarine is able to surface and is again matched against the enemy Armada. The cautious approach toward Flying Cove continues, as the *Seawolf*, gliding through the sea at about 04:00, encounters another Cruiser, approximately 11 miles from Christmas Island. *Seawolf* immediately begins to dive and prepares to attack, maneuvering nearer and nearer, until 05:13, when the three torpedoes zip through the water toward the Cruiser, dead ahead. Within minutes, the sound of explosions are heard, followed by the familiar noises that filter through the sound equipment, when a Vessel has been severely hit. As the periscope rises and scans the area, there is neither a Cruiser, nor wreckage; however, two Jap Destroyers are moving to the area at high speed, prompting the *Seawolf* not to press her luck. This insolent Yankee interruption has the Japs infuriated and they scour the entire area to eliminate the nuisance. The *Seawolf*, crouches perilously on the bottom, under the most austere conditions. Nerves are stretched to the breaking point by the crashing bombs and the lack of oxygen. Any disturbance, even the slightest bubble from the inoperable latrines, could mean sudden death for the men of the *Seawolf*. The crew waits in anguish, until gasps for air and the nearly dead batteries force a trip to the surface. Upon arrival, they are greeted, not with the fresh air they require, but a patient Destroyer, waiting like a fox for the chicken. Fortunately, the Vessel is the *Seawolf* and not a chicken. Warder, bellows what might be the final order. "TAKE HER DOWN." The overstressed Submarine dives, followed closely by exploding depth charges, further shattering the nerves of the crew, but they withstand the terrible conditions and maneuver toward safety in deep water. It finally reclaims the surface after midnight, and heads for Australia. It should be noted that official Japanese records make no mention of any Cruisers being sunk off Christmas Island at this time. (Atlantic) Ascension Island, situated approximately halfway between South America and Africa, receives the first contingents of U.S. troops, who will proceed to construct an Air Field. (China-Burma-India) The Chinese 200th Division which has fought a most valiant fight against overwhelming odds, abandons Toungoo. During the ongoing fighting at Paungde, the Japanese push back the Task Force attached to the Burma I Corps, driving them to Prome. Losing discipline along the route, the troops leave their vehicles behind for the enemy at Shwedaung. After dark, the Japanese assault Allied positions at Prome, penetrating the defenses.

March 31st 1942 — (Pacific) Commander of All Forces Aruba and Curacao, Netherlands, East Indies, is established. U.S. Rear Admiral J.B. Oldendorf is the Commanding Officer. **(China-Burma-India)** The Chinese 200th Division leaves the area around Toungoo, heading north. Along the withdrawal route, they encounter the Chinese 22nd Division, still sitting where it had been since the 26th of March, without attempting to attack. The 200th moves north of Pyinmana as a Reserve Division. The pull out of the 200th Division causes the loss of Toungoo, and a considerable length of road leading to Mawchi is now defenseless. The Japanese keep their steamroller moving, taking a thinly manned Chinese Garrison at Mawchi, then drive east, advancing toward Prome. Contingents of the Chinese Temporary 55th Division, which also did not aid the 200th after its arrival on the scene on March 25th, are inconvenienced and forced to retreat back to Bawlake.

April 1st 1942 — (Pacific-United States) The Pacific War Council meets for the first time, holding a conference in Washington, D.C. In other activity, sixteen B-25s (Doolittle's Raid) land at Alameda Air Base situated close to San Francisco. The Planes are taxied to the dock area and placed aboard the Hornet (The Hornet's Planes are placed in the hangar decks to make room) and transported to rendezvous with Halsey's Fleet for the strike against Tokyo. **(Pacific-New Guinea)** Japanese assault troops, which had departed the Dutch East Indies, storm various points along the coast of New Guinea. This initial landing is only the first of many that occur between Hollandia and Sorong, both nestled on the northwest edge of the island, until the 20th of April. These landings are uncontested, allowing the Japanese to entrench themselves dangerously close to Australia. **(Pacific-Solomons)** The island of Buka, in the Solomons is occupied by Japanese troops. **(China-Burma-India)** In Burma, the Japanese swing furiously through the jungle, prompting the Burma I Corps to reel back. The Japanese drive the Burma Corps out of Prome. They retreat under enormous pressure to Allanmyo, to the north of Prome. Burma is ready to fall to the enemy. General Stilwell, still attempting to change the situation, directs two Chinese Divisions, the 22nd and the 96th, to ready a stand against the onrushing Japanese at Pyinmana. **(Atlantic-Western Europe)** German Lt. Colonel Gehlen is attached to "Foreign Armies East." By the following month he assumes control and begins to establish his own Intelligence section, unlike the other Intelligence organizations (Abwehr) under Baun (Walli I), and Heinz Schmalschlager (Walli III). Gehlen places Captain Gerhard Wessel in charge of Group 1, and Major Heinz D. Herre takes

responsibility for Group 2, both concerning Russia. The remaining four Groups deal with matters other than Russia, and are left alone. **(Atlantic-Russia)** The German II Corps, Sixteenth Army, is besieged in the area southeast of Staraya Russia. Although the zones of battle all along the line are at a stalemate, contingents of German Army Group Nine concentrate on rescuing the II Corps.

April 2nd 1942 — (Pacific-Samoa) The advance unit of Marine Aircraft Group 13, arrives in Samoa to bolster American troops. **(China-Burma-India)** The U.S. 10th Air Force, based in India, initiates its first combat flight by attacking enemy Vessels in the vicinity of the Andaman Islands. Soon after, their combat missions will take them over Burma to strike enemy positions.

U.S. P-40 Aircraft one of the types used in China.

April 3rd-8th 1942 — (Pacific-Philippines) BATAAN, THE FINAL DAYS — The lack of supplies and reinforcements has taken a deadly toll on the beleaguered defenders on Bataan, now near total collapse. The Japanese deliver more brutal Air and Artillery attacks, prior to an all-out Infantry Assault. At 10:00, the mighty guns open fire, hurling unending amounts of shells into the positions of the overtired defenders. The shrill sounds of thundering cannon are amplified as enemy Planes roar overhead, pounding the fortifications below. The heat of battle is as near to hell as anyone can imagine. The overwhelming strength of the enemy bombardment leaves little time to tend the scattered casualties. The catastrophic barrage finally culminates at 15:00, followed by Japanese Infantry charging furiously against the Allied lines. The majority of the thrust is against the west flank of the II Corps positions, defended by the 21st and 41st Philippine Divisions, neither of which is strong enough to withstand the attack. The 41st Division, holding the west flank, collapses and only one Regiment is able to withdraw with any discipline, ending the Division's effectiveness as a fighting unit. The Japanese simultaneously pound the 21st Division and succeed in driving back one Regiment. As darkness falls, the Allies attempt to regain the positions lost by the 41st, but the effort is unsuccessful. The Japanese also strike the I Corps sector, in equally tenacious fashion, reaching the main line of resistance, but the line holds firmly. On the following day, the Japanese repeat their assault, beginning with more horrid Air and Artillery bombardments. When the bombardment ceases, the Jap Infantry begins another charge, screaming as they forge ahead, against these tired and grossly undernourished defenders. The 41st retreats again and the 21st attempts to hold, but is compelled to pull back from the main defense line to a point near Mt. Samat, where they regroup. The Japanese pause to reform for an assault against Mt. Samat. Reinforcements are dispatched from the Luzon Force to help hold off the attackers. The U.S. 31st and the 45th Philippine Scout Regiments, both fierce fighting outfits, rush to the scene, but it is too little too late. The Japanese hold the upper hand, as the sun goes down at Bataan on the 4th of April.

The sun rises on the fifth and the Philippine defenders are soon greeted with another powerful bombardment that rocks their positions. After cessation, the Japanese move out again, taking Mt. Samat. The admirable 21st Division is nearly demolished, both physically and mentally. The Allies try to regroup and initiate a major counterattack on the 6th, but the match is outclassed. The Japanese, fully supplied with men and equipment, go against a battle-weary, understrengthed, underfed, dwindling Philippine Defense force, no longer able to be sustained by fighting spirit alone.

Dawn sparks another blood filled day on Bataan. Enemy Artillery and Planes give the defenders an all-day dose of incoming shells. Meanwhile, enemy Infantry moves out to meet the advancing counterattack of the II Corps and once again, pushes the defenders back. The U.S. 31st Infantry and the Philippine 21st Division unsuccessfully attempt to drive north, in the area east of Mt. Samat, but fierce enemy resistance prevents them from reaching the line of departure.

In the center, circumstances are worse. The Japanese strike the Philippine 33rd, 42nd and 43rd Infantry, in the area between Catmon and Mt. Samat, with devastating results. The 33rd is surrounded and cut off, and the two other Regiments following close behind are thoroughly routed. Troops on the west flank are now cut off from the remainder of II Corps.

On the west flank, the Philippine 41st and 45th Infantry make some progress, but with the advance, the 41st gets too far out front, leaving the 45th unable to close the distance. The 41st is now isolated. The U.S. 31st Infantry and the 57th Philippine Scouts are ordered to move to sector C, to join these forces, which are ordered to withdraw to the San Vincente River.

On the 7th of April, the Japanese begin to put the finishing touches on the destruction of the Bataan defenders. The II Corps sectors are bludgeoned, with another lopsided assault. The enemy Planes roar overhead, pouring bombs and machine gun fire into the now ragged troops. This is followed by more attacking Infantrymen, supported by Artillery. Wave after wave of onrushing Banzai Japs force the entire line to disintegrate. The entire Corps withdraws to the Mamala River, but the Japanese force this line to fold. The defenders withdraw further, to the Alangan River. Bataan had become expendable, and neither the Generals or their men can hold much longer without help from the states.

On the 8th of April, General MacArthur sends another of his desperate pleas to the U.S. for help. He informs General Marshall that the Japanese had overrun the main line of defense on Bataan and "HAD DRIVEN A WEDGE BETWEEN THE I AND II CORPS AND IS STILL ADVANCING." MacArthur further informs Marshall that a disaster on the Philippines is "imminent." The message is hardly received before the defense of Bataan ends. Light of day on the 8th is of no great consequence to the beleaguered American Filipino forces on Bataan. The incessant clobbering of Allied positions by both Air and land forces, simply overwhelms the defenders; inno-

vative steps are taken to fill the gaps to no avail. Before day's end, General E.P. King decides to surrender the Luzon force. The little remaining operational equipment is destroyed through the night, to prevent use by the enemy. At 0330, Allied troops moving toward the Japanese lines under a white flag of truce, approach Japanese Officers to offer surrender. General King surrenders the entire Luzon Force, consisting of approximately 78,000 men, both Philippine and American. About 2,000 men are able to escape to Corregidor, saving them temporarily from the Japs, who have overrun Bataan like a plague. Japanese troops are unmerciful, as they drive the captives like cattle toward a slaughterhouse. Many will die along the 80-mile death march in the tropical heat. Some die a quicker death along the roads as enemy bayonets plunge into fallen troops. Others are brutally beaten and tortured. Those that die along the way, are left to rot. The remaining forces reform under General Wainwright on Corregidor.

April 3rd 1942 — (Pacific) Admiral C.W. Nimitz assumes the position of Commander in Chief, Pacific Ocean Areas (CINCPOA). He simultaneously retains his position as Commander in Chief, Pacific Fleet (CINCPAC). **(China-Burma-India)** In Burma, Allied Chinese troops are being prepared by General Stilwell to make a stand against the advancing Japanese at Pyinmana, in the Sittang Valley. In other activity, Japanese Planes assault Mandalay.

April 4th 1942 — (Pacific-Philippines) The situation in Luzon (Bataan) goes from bad to worse, as more enemy Artillery and Air attacks pummel the besieged defenders. **(China-Burma-India)** In the Indian Ocean, a Japanese Naval Force engages and sinks two British Cruisers, the H.M.S. *Dorsetshire* and *Cornwall*, in the vicinity of Columbo, Ceylon. On the following day, Carrier-based Japanese Fighters will attack Colombo.

April 5th 1942 — (Pacific-Philippines) The Japanese continue to bludgeon the II Corps area of Bataan, with heavy bombardments. Afterward, the Infantry takes over the job of punishing the Allied forces in the II Corps area. In addition, an enemy Invasion Force, of nearly 5,000 men, embarks at the Lingayen Gulf, heading toward Cebu in the Visayan Islands. The enemy Vessels are seen by the island defenders as they approach on the 9th of April. Cebu, garrisoned by approximately 6,000 men, commanded by Colonel Irwin C. Scudder, attempts to halt the invaders at both Cebu City on the east coast and Toledo, but the onslaught is only delayed. Additional mounted pressure forces the troops to withdraw from both locations. Under instructions from General Chynoweth, reinforcements are rushed to halt the enemy advance at Cantabaco. The Japanese move viciously and swiftly, seizing the cross-island highway. The surviving troops of the Visayan Islands move to the mountains in northern Cebu, where General Chynoweth can organize the remaining troops to stage Guerrilla warfare. With Bataan and the Visayans under their control, the Japanese now concentrate on humbling Corregidor. Life on the rock is, for the most part, spent underground because of incessant bombing raids. During the darkened hours, the Submarine U.S.S. *Snapper* (SS-194) is able to deliver supplies to Corregidor and evacuate some additional personnel. **(Pacific-Admiralties)** Japanese troops dispatched from Truk, occupy Manus Island, debarking at Lorengau.

April 6th 1942 — (Pacific-Philippines) II Corps futilely counterattacks the Japanese at Bataan, with parts of some outfits isolated, while the remaining defenders are forced to pull back to the San Vincente River. In other activity, the U.S.S. *Seadragon* arrives at Corregidor and is able to partially unload supplies, before being ordered out of port because of Japanese attacks. The *Seadragon* waits offshore for about 48 hours, but the situation only deteriorates and the Vessel is ordered to depart, taking with her another sparse amount of personnel (18 enlisted men, an Army Colonel and 30 Communications Officers), for the voyage to Australia. The U.S.S. *Snapper* will pull silently, into Corregidor on the 9th of April, deliver some food to the U.S.S. *Pigeon,* then make a quick departure with a contingent of 27 men. **(Pacific-Australia)** American Field Artillery and other contingents of the 41st U.S. Division arrive at Melbourne, Australia. **(China-Burma-India)** In Burma, the Japanese continue to land additional troops at Rangoon. Chinese troops will assist the Burma I Corps with the defense of Pyinman.

April 7th 1942 — The U.S. Navy, determined to bolster its forces in the South Pacific sends Patrol Aircraft to Natal, Brazil, from where they can operate in the South Atlantic.

April 8th 1942 — (Pacific-Philippines) General MacArthur dispatches an urgent message to General Marshall, stating that Japanese forces had "driven a wedge between the First and Second Corps and are still advancing." MacArthur further informs General Marshall that disaster is imminent on the Philippines. The Japanese terminate organized resistance on Bataan, as they culminate a crushing offensive, which had begun on the 3rd of April. During the night of the 8th, the defenders request surrender terms and destroy what little usable equipment they have, to insure no use by the Japanese. The Luzon Force, composed of 78,000 men, will capitulate on the following day, with the exception of approximately 2,000 men, who successfully escape to Corregidor. There is an attempt made to cut the Filipino forces, under General Sharp, away from Wainright, but time is too short. Some of these forces make it to the southern islands. On Corregidor, the Silent Service makes another successful run to evacuate additional Military specialists. The U.S.S. *Seadragon* (SS-194) unloads some food supplies before she departs. In other activity on the Philippines, the U.S. scuttles the U.S.S. *Bittern* (AM-36), which had been badly damaged by the Japanese on the 10th of December at Cavite. Another U.S. Vessel, the Tug *Napa* (AT-32), is also sunk by the Americans. **(Atlantic-England)** U.S. General Marshall and Harry Hopkins meet with British representatives, to discuss preliminary objectives of Operation Bolero (U.S. build-up of men and equipment in Great Britain for intended cross channel invasion).

April 9th 1942 — (Pacific-Philippines) The Japanese accept the surrender of Bataan at 12:30 P.M. The exhausted warriors, who had reluctantly approached the Japanese with a white flag, are in for a torturous, humiliating forced march from Balanga to San Fernando, 85 miles away. The Anti-aircraft gunners from Mariveles, including Marine Battery C, escape to Corregidor, being among the two thousand of the luckier troops; the other 76,000 make the infamous Death March. The Japanese brutalize their captives, driving them in torrid heat for six days. Thousands die from thirst, exhaustion, untended wounds, and relentless beatings. In other activity, PT-Boat 34, one of the very few Naval Vessels remaining in the Philippines, is attacked and damaged by Japanese Bombers, causing it to be subsequently beached and abandoned. **(China-Burma-India)** THE FALL OF BURMA — The coveted Allied oil fields, near the Minhla-Taung Line, are on the agenda for the ever advancing Japanese. The worthy Burma I Corps, which has been doing extremely well against the enemy under the circumstances, is given responsibility of defending the line. The Chinese 38th Division, assigned to help defend the 40 mile front, does not assist, because of confusing orders from superior Officers. On the following day, advance Scouts of the Burma I Corps detect the Japanese, who are moving discreetly toward the Minhla-Taungdwingyi on the Irrawaddy Front, to seize the oil fields there. On the following day, the Japanese commence an offensive that carries them toward the Center Defense Line. The Chinese 38th Division, 66th Army, scheduled originally to help defend Mandalay, is hastily ordered to support the Burma Corps. The enemy advance gives them possession of Migyaungye during the night of the 12-13th, where they now threaten the west flank of the Burma I Corps. On the 13th, the Japanese shatter the resistance along the line, pushing the British back toward Magwe. In a desperate effort to keep the Japs from confiscating the oil fields, they are blown up during the night of the 14th-15th. The Japanese press against the Burma I Corps and the 7th Armored Brigade (minus the 7th Hussars), which had been dispatched to the area south of Magwe, to bolster the Burma Corps. The Japanese span out, bypassing the Chinese Temporary 55th Division, in the vicinity of Mawchi-Loikaw, while they drive north, evading the Burma 1st Division. General Stilwell prepares to make a stand at Pyinmana, but the Japanese keep pounding the defenders along the Irrawaddy Front. The Burma 1st Division receives the brunt of the punishment and reinforcements are sent to help. The Japanese also pounce the defenders to the south, meeting reinforcements, which had been diverted to aid the besieged 1st Division.

On the 18th of April, in the vicinity of Yenangyaung, the Burma 1st Corps, engages the enemy doggedly, driving to Twingon. The Chinese 38th Division makes progress against the enemy at Pin Chaung, but the situation on the Sittang Front is not helped when the Chinese 200th Division, ordered to move to Meiktila, refuses to advance. Concentrated pressure by the Japanese against the Temporary Chinese 55th Division in the vicinity of Loikaw, takes them out of action in a flash. The strategic Burma Road is now endangered. Before the end of the month, the defenders will continue to take many casualties, in addition to losing enormous amounts of terrain and being forced to prepare abandonment of Burma.

As the Allies are being thoroughly thrashed, Stilwell again attempts to bolster the defenders. The Chinese 6th Army is involved heavily against Japanese troops in the vicinity of Taunggyi. The 200th Chinese Division is ordered to the scene in an effort to strengthen the resistance. In a follow-up order, General Stilwell requests that the Chinese supply 150 trucks, in order to expedite the troop transfer; 22 arrive. Over 300 trucks had already been dispatched to Mandalay and other towns, to load contraband. After loading the stolen cargo, the trucks speed to China, where the goods can be sold. If that isn't enough frustration for Stilwell, on the same day, the Chinese 28th Division receives orders to move to Loilem, but stays put. Meanwhile, the Chinese 22nd Division, supported by the 17th Indian Division and the 7th Armored Brigade fortify Thazi and Meiktila. This is followed by the fall of Loilem on the 23rd and on the same day, the flight of the Chinese 6th Army to China. General Stilwell, still trying to fight "the forgotten war," attends an Allied Staff meeting at Kyaukse, about 20 miles south of Mandalay on the 25th. British General Alexander appraises the situation, based on the reports and on the following day, makes a decision to concede Burma to the Japanese and concentrate on the defense of India, by retreating north. Buddhist Monks inform the Japanese of the Allied meeting and it is greeted by Japanese Planes, which bombard the town.

By the 29th of April, it is apparent to even the most optimistic person in the Burma Theater, that the fight is over. Chiang Kai-shek orders Mandalay to be held, but on the 30th, he countermands his order, issuing new instructions to evacuate. The Japanese seize Lashio, the beginning of the Burma road, ceasing any possibility of Allied use of the serpentine land route to China and completing the blockade of China. The British begin the evacuation of Burma, making their way across the Irrawaddy River, by way of the Ava Bridge on the 30th. The bridge has two spans and demolition troops set the explosives after all have crossed safely, but only one of the two spans collapses, allowing the Japanese access and guaranteeing they can continue the rout. To make the situation even more confusing, the roads are all clogged with massive traffic jams, and Burmese "fifth columnists" are on the rampage.

By May 1st, most of Stilwell's staff have departed the area on a C-53, but the remaining 12 men on his staff are to accompany him to Myitkyina by train for his next duty station. Stilwell's trying tour of duty now takes him on a seven hour escapade to Shwebo, where the staff will catch the train. This trip is interrupted, because Chinese General Lo-Cho Ling has stolen the last train by gunpoint and is fleeing with his staff, on the single-track railroad, heading north. The hijacked train is stopped when it plows head on into another train heading south.

The Japanese now control Burma and the Allies are scattering. General Stilwell is unable to reach Myitkyina, forced instead to walk out of the jungle into India, where he vows to come back.

General Stilwell's command marches through the roughest of jungle terrain and encounters unspeakable difficulties, but his dauntless entourage of approximately 80 civilians and Soldiers make it to India successfully on the 20th of May, without the loss of a man. The only casualty is Captain George Hambleton, who had remained behind with the Chinese. General Stilwell begins immediately to convince the U.S. to go back to Burma. At a news conference on May 24th, General Stilwell, making the Burma situation very clear states: "I CLAIM WE GOT A HELL OF A BEATING. WE GOT RUN OUT OF BURMA AND IT IS HUMILIATING AS HELL. I THINK WE OUGHT TO FIND OUT WHAT CAUSED IT, GO BACK AND RETAKE IT." **(Indian Ocean-Ceylon)** Carrier-based Japanese Fighters swarm over Allied positions in Ceylon at Trincomalee, sinking a British Aircraft Carrier, the H.M.S. *Hermes*. **(Atlantic-Labrador)** U.S. troops arrive in Labrador, a peninsula located in northeast Canada, situated between the Atlantic Ocean, the Gulf of St. Lawrence and the Hudson Bay.

(Atlantic-Russia) The Germans and Russians clash in the vicinity of Kerch, in the Crimea. The Red Army also drives against the Germans along the central front, without substantial gains. On the northern front, the Germans make further attempts to reach three contingents surrounded near Cholm and Staraya, Russia; making slight progress against heavy resistance.

U.S. Prisoners of War on Bataan.

April 10th 1942 — (Pacific-Philippines) The Japanese mobilize to exterminate the resistance on the Visayan Islands in the Philippines. American Colonel Irwin Scudder and his 6,500 defenders engage the Japs, when they land at Cebu and Toledo. The defenders fight a sound delaying action before retreating inland. General Chynoweth dispatches the 3rd Battalion, 83rd Infantry, to defend Cantabaco, but the invaders still move effortlessly to the east. In other activity, in the Philippines, Japanese Planes destroy the U.S.S. *Finch* (AM-9), a Minesweeper The heavily damaged U.S.S. *Canopus* (AS-9), a Submarine Tender is later scuttled and two days later, the U.S. will scuttle another Vessel, PT-39. **(Pacific)** The U.S. Navy makes additional command adjustments in its Pacific Theater, specifying the command structure of specific groups. Vice Admiral William F. Halsey will Command the Carriers; Rear Admiral W.S. Anderson, the Battleships; Rear Admiral Fletcher, the Cruisers, and the Destroyers are Commanded by Rear Admiral R.A. Theobald. In addition, Rear Admiral T. Withers will command the Submarine Force and Rear Admiral J.S. McCain is to command the Patrol Wings. However, all Groups are in need of Supplemental Vessels and this, the

Service Force, is to be commanded by Vice Admiral W. L. Calhoun. **(Pacific-Japan)** The U.S.S. *Thresher*, operating off Japan, launches several torpedoes and sinks the *Sado*, a Japanese Freighter. **(China-Burma-India)** Advance elements of the Burma I Corps detect enemy forces advancing towards the Minhla-Taungdwingyi Line. The Japanese mount tough attacks, against the center of the defense line on the following day. **(Atlantic-Germany)** British Airplanes strike the town of Essen. During this bombing mission, the British drop their first two ton bomb.

April 11th 1942 — (Dutch East Indies) The U.S.S. *Searaven* is dispatched to Timor Island, in an attempt to locate shipwrecked Australians troops. The rescuers are under the able and agile Lt. Commander Hiram Cassedy. The sleek *Searaven* creeps into the cove, without enemy detection and remains offshore for two days, without any contact with the Australians. On the following day, a daring volunteer, Ensign George C. Cook attempts to take a small boat to shore, but the waters are too rough and he is forced to swim. Undaunted, Cook continues his adventure, which could be a story line for a Tarzan movie, as he encounters everything except the Australians, including a considerable group of men who vanish from sight, at point of visual contact. Ensign Cook makes his way back through the unfamiliar jungle to the beach, and swims back to the *Searaven*, where it is determined that the Australians are on the other side of the island. Ensign Cook is lucky he didn't get Cooked. The *Searaven* repositions itself and Ensign Cook, who had not learned the lesson of never volunteering, again offers to make the unusual trek to find the Aussies, and again, the unruly seas force him to abandon the boat and swim through the breakers, where he successfully, but not uneventfully, locates the Australians, who are most eager to greet the soggy Ensign. Cook, fortunately, a glutton for punishment, swims back to the *Searaven*, with a badly wounded Australian, strapped on his back. This fearless Sailor, had mingled with either a band of Cannibals or a Squad of Japs, neither worse than the other, but ultimately rescues the 33 ragged Aussies. Ensign Cook does not receive the Medal of Honor, but most certainly makes a good candidate.

April 12th 1942 — (United States) General Marshall, receives plans for the establishment of the Eighth Air Force, to be based in England, from Chief of Army Air Forces, General Arnold, while attending the Bolero Conference in London. **(Pacific-Philippines)** Japanese Artillery continues to pound the defenders on Corregidor. These guns, based on Bataan and Cavite, are supplemented by enemy Air strikes. The survivors of the Cebu Garrison retreat to the mountains and are organized under General Chynoweth to operate as Guerrillas.

April 13th 1942 — (Pacific-Dutch East Indies) The U.S.S. *Sturgeon*, operating in the Makassar Strait, encounters a Japanese Destroyer and fires three torpedoes, which destroy the enemy Vessel. The kill, however, is not verified. **(Pacific-Japan)** In another Submarine encounter with the enemy, the U.S.S. *Grayling*, operating on her second Patrol tour in Japanese waters, spots and sinks the *Ryujin Maru*, a 6,000 ton Vessel, off the coast of Kyushu.

April 14th 1942 — (United States) The British government and the U.S. Chiefs of Staff accept the Bolero Plan, which is proposed by American General Marshall and contains the objectives of an offensive thrust against Germany. In Naval activity, a German Vessel, the *U-85* is detected off the coast of Virginia. It is then destroyed by the U.S.S. *Roper* (DD-147), a Destroyer. **(China-Burma-India)** In Burma, the Japanese still advance at will. The Allied oil fields at Yenangyaung are ordered destroyed to prevent enemy use. (This operation lasts for the next 48 hours). By the 17th, the Japanese form a north-south roadblock at Pin Chaung. The Chinese 38th Division is dispatched from Kyaukpadaung, beginning a night march to assist the 1st Burma Division. Diversionary forces are also committed to draw attention, but without success. The Japanese maintain extreme pressure against the 1st Burma. In the meantime, the Japanese keep storming toward the north.

April 15th 1942 — (United States) The United States Navy establishes Submarine Bases in Alaska, at Kodiak and Dutch Harbor. These Bases eventually will become vital when the Japanese attempt to invade Alaska, during May of 1942. **(Pacific-Philippines)** The U.S. loses another PT-Boat when the PT-41 is scuttled by American forces. **(Pacific-Hawaii)** Another U.S. Naval Air Station is established, this one at Barber's Point in Oahu, Hawaii.

April 16th 1942 — (Pacific-Philippines) General Wainwright instructs General Sharp to prepare his Visayan-Mindanao Force to defend the line at Mindanao (Cebu is considered lost to the Japanese). A 7,000 man Force (Panay Force), under Colonel Albert F. Christie, retreats to the mountains, to begin concentrated Guerrilla actions, against the Japanese, but in doing so, over 4,000 Japanese troops land at Panay, without opposition.

April 17th 1942 — (United States) President Roosevelt recalls Admiral William D. Leahy (U.S. Ambassador to France) to Washington for consultation. Admiral Leahy subsequently becomes Chief of Staff to President Roosevelt. **(China-Burma-India)** The Japanese continue to batter the 1st Burma Division in the vicinity of Magwe, as reinforcements unsuccessfully attempt to relieve the pressure. The Japanese also hold commanding positions in the vicinity of Yenangyaung, in the Irrawaddy Valley. As they continue to suppress resistance, the Japanese maintain their forward thrust against Chinese positions at Mauchi and other Allied positions in the Sittang Valley. By the 18th, the Chinese are evacuating positions at Mauchi and the Sittang Valley.

A B-25 taking off from the deck of the U.S.S. Hornet (CV-8), en route to strike Japan (Doolittle Raid).

April 18th 1942 — **(Pacific-Australia))** General MacArthur, based in Australia, assumes command of all troops in the Southwest Pacific. **(Pacific-Japan)** Admiral Halsey's Force which had refueled on the previous day and left the Tanker and Destroyers behind, approach the departure point for Colonel Doolittle's B-25s on their mission to Tokyo. At 0300 enemy contact is made through radar screens but the Fleet avoids detection. Shortly thereafter at 0745 another Vessel is encountered 12,000 yards away. The *Nashville* is ordered to destroy it, but a signal is thought to have warned Tokyo before the Vessel is sunk. At 0800, Halsey, orders Admiral Mitscher to launch the Bombers. The launch is six hours ahead of schedule and the seas are rough. Doolittle's Plane leads the formation off the heaving deck of the U.S.S. *Hornet* (CV-8). Japan finally feels the sting of battle, as Lt. Colonel James Doolittle leads 16 B-25s on a 650 mile flight, to deliver strikes against Tokyo, Yokohama, Nagoya and Kobe. Fighter Planes from the U.S.S. *Lexington*, fly as escorts on this successful mission, which informs Japan, that it is now vulnerable to U.S. attacks. The Bombers, after the precedent setting mission, which mainly serves to boost U.S. morale, attempt to reach China after the attack, but bad weather causes the returning crews to either crash land or abandon their Planes. Two of the Planes are forced to land in enemy territory and are captured. The Japanese will execute some of the crewmen on October 15 1942. One of the Planes lands in "friendly" Vladivostok, where the crew is interned by the Russians, who prefer American ammunition, Tanks and dollars to distressed Yankee Pilots. The Naval Task Force, under Admiral Halsey, which consists of two Carriers, four Cruisers, eight Destroyers and two Oilers, pulls back without harm. Three hours after launch, Halsey's Planes attack 16 enemy Vessels, one of which is a Submarine. The U.S.S. *Nashville* picks up 4 prisoners, one telling an amusing story. He relates how he tried to wake his Captain early in the morning to see the Planes. A little later, the Captain is asked to look again, saying: "TWO OF OUR BEAUTIFUL CARRIERS AHEAD, SIR!" The Officer checks out the approaching Vessel and counters, "THEY'RE BEAUTIFUL, BUT THEY'RE NOT OURS." The prisoner further states that the Captain, upon spotting the American Carriers goes below deck and shoots himself in the head. This mission, the first to use Medium Bombers against an enemy's shores, does much to raise America's morale. While Doolittle's Planes are over Japan, the Japanese radio is broadcasting that Japan is "FREE FROM ENEMY ATTACK." The announcement is heard aboard Ship and, in fact, Halsey is aware the Planes are over Tokyo because the Air Raid alarms also come over the Ships' radios. Halsey evades the massive enemy pursuit and returns safely to Pearl Harbor on April 26th. President Roosevelt will proclaim that the Planes had originated from Shangri-La; Halsey and the men who participate hope to deceive the Japanese into thinking the B-25s had the capability of flying over 3,500 miles nonstop. Japanese newspapers proclaim that nine American Planes have been shot down, however, in addition to the accurate figures above, the American Ambassador notes that the only Plane shot down over Tokyo did not appear to be a Bomber and the impression is that Japanese gunners had shot down one of their own pursuit Planes. **(Pacific-Philippines)** In the Philippines, the Japanese maintain that Cebu is now under their control. By the following day, all of the Visayan Islands are in Japanese hands. The only resistance comes from units operating from the mountains as guerrillas. **(China-Burma-India)** More staggering losses are sustained by the weary Allies, as the Chinese Temporary 55th Division is reeling in retreat from Mauchi, and struck by the enemy in the area around Loikaw. The 55th disintegrates and flees into the hills. The entire Division, comprising over 7,000 troops, scatters. General Stilwell futilely requests that the Commanding General, Ch'en Mien-Wu, be executed for "cowardice." The Japanese advance unopposed to Loilem. The Chinese 93rd Division moves to aid the 55th, but to no avail.

April 19th 1942 — **(Southwest Pacific)** General Headquarters Staff, Southwest Pacific, is appointed by General MacArthur. The Chief of Staff is Major General Richard K. Sutherland, followed by Deputy Chief of Staff General Richard Marshall. Some of the additional members of the Staff include; Colonel Charles P. Stivers, (G1); Colonel Charles A. Willoughby, (G2); Brigadier General Stephen J. Chamberlain (G3) and Colonel Lester J. Whitlock, (G4). The future situation in the Pacific is constantly burdened by an acute shortage of all necessities of war, for an enormous period. The predetermined strategy of defeating Germany first, puts every American Serviceman in the Pacific Theater at great risk. Case in point: Convoys are transporting supplies to the Russians, while American fighting men are unequipped and undernourished on Bataan and Corregidor. The Pacific is to be won by American Commanders making the most out of the least; in essence, the distinct leadership qualities of the American Commanders. There will be marked differences between Commanders and their subordinates; however, these differences do not prevent maximum productivity on the fields of battle. When the United States does initiate its first offensive, it will be in the Pacific, but not until August of 1942, when Guadalcanal is stormed by one solitary Marine Division. **(Pacific-Philippines)** The Japanese claim the conquest of Cebu Island, in the Visayans. **(China-Burma-India)** The Chinese 113th Regiment, 38th Division, engages the Japanese at Yenangyaung. The fighting is fierce and successful gains are made by the 113th, who manage to eliminate three of five enemy strongholds. In other activity, the 1st Division, Burma Corps, makes slight gains against the Japanese in the vicinity of Twingon, but receive orders to pull out, because of heavy casualties. The Japanese, meanwhile, gnaw their way toward Loikaw, threatening the terminus of the Burma Road, which controls the fate of the Burma Campaign.

April 20th 1942 — **(Pacific-Philippines)** The fall of the Visayan Islands is complete, with the Japanese in total control of Cebu and Panay. There will be subsequent resistance from Guerrillas, operating from the mountains, but smaller contingents of Guerrillas, dispersed in the hills of Bohol, Leyte, Negros and Samar, are not nearly strong enough to impede the unchecked progress of the Japanese. **(Atlantic-Mediterranean Sea)** The U.S.S. *Wasp* (CV-7), having successfully transported British Spitfires for use against the Axis in the Mediterranean, launches the Spitfires, which land in Malta. **(China-Burma-India)** The Burma 1st Division withdraws towards Mt. Popa, while the Chinese 38th Division positions itself to cover the withdrawal. The Taunggyi-Meiktila Road, completely undefended, allows speedy progress for the enemy, which intercepts the Chinese 6th Army at Hopong, forcing it to withdraw to China by the 23rd. On the 22nd, General Stilwell orders trucks to speed the 200th Chinese Division to reinforce the 6th Army, but as usual, complications impede the operation and sufficient numbers of Vehicles are unavailable.

April 21st 1942 — (Pacific-Australia) The *S-47*, an American Submarine departs Brisbane on patrol, becoming the first S-Boat to initiate War Patrols, out of Australia. The remaining S-Boats will all be in service by the middle of May.

April 22nd 1942 — (China-Burma-India) Reinforcements attached to the Chinese 200th Division are ordered from Meiktila, to reinforce the battered Chinese 6th Army at Taunggyi. British contingents (17th Indian Division and 7th Armored Brigade), are utilized to support the Chinese 22nd Division, now holding responsibility for newly created gaps, left at Meiktila and Thazi, due to the transfer of the 200th Division to assist the 6th Army at Taunggyi. In addition, the Chinese 28th Division receives orders to march to Loilem, but declines the order. On the following day, Loilem falls to the Japanese.

April 23rd 1942 — (China-Burma-India) Japanese troops continue to blaze through Burma, seizing Loilem. Japanese Air superiority insures the enemy's domination. In other activity in the vicinity of Taunggyi, the 200th Division engages the enemy and in yet other Military activity, the Chinese 6th Army retreats into China. In Naval activity, the Submarine U.S.S. *Triton*, on the prowl in the East China Sea, knocks out an enemy Trawler. The *Triton* is considerably active in succeeding weeks, wrecking a couple of Sampans by employing its energetic deck guns and sinking several Freighters with torpedoes. The *Triton* culminates the operation, by destroying the enemy Submarine I-64 on the 17th of May. **(Atlantic-England)** German Luftwaffe Planes begin striking English towns during the night of the 23rd, continuing into the early morning hours. These raids against various historical towns are in retribution, for earlier bombing missions of the R.A.F., against German towns. These German Air assaults continue for some time, striking such historical places as Exeter, Norwich, York and Bath.

April 24th 1942 — (Atlantic-Great Britain) The Luftwaffe initiates raids against Exeter. Additional raids against other English historical towns follow, in retaliation for earlier raids by the R.A.F. against Lubeck, Germany.

A German Stuka Bomber.

April 25th 1942 — (China-Burma-India) The Japanese drive towards Lashio, Burma. In other activity, American General Stilwell meets with British and Chinese Commanders, to formulate defense plans for Lashio. The meeting, which includes Major General Franklin (Stilwell's Deputy), British General Alexander, British General T.J. Winterton (Alexander's Chief

of Staff), British General William Slim, Chinese Generals Lo Cho-ying, Tu Ming-ling (who dies 10 years later in a Red Chinese P.O.W. camp) and Sun Li-jen, meet at Kyaukse to appraise the severity of the situation. The meetings are repeatedly interrupted by Japanese Aircraft, prowling the area. The Japanese have prior notice of the meeting, having been informed by Buddhist monks. British General Alexander orders the troops along the Meiktila-Kyaukpadaung Line to await the fall of darkness, then withdraw to the north bank of the Irrawaddy River. At present, the 22nd Division is surrounded by the Japanese at Meiktila. In yet other activity in the waning hours of the Burma campaign, the Chinese 200th Division, supported by elements of the reformed Chinese 55th Division (previously fleeing to the hills), engage the Japanese at Taunggyi, inflicting some casualties.

April 26th 1942 — (United States) The U.S.S. *Sturtevant* (DD-240), a Destroyer operating in the Atlantic, strikes a mine off the coast of Florida and is sunk. **(Pacific-Philippines)** Enormous pressure continues to be exerted by the Japanese against the American-Philippine forces on Mindanao. As the Digos Force attempts to forestall capitulation, additional enemy forces are en route from Cebu Island. **(Fanning Island)** A contingent of American Soldiers arrives at Fanning Island. **(China-Burma-India)** British General Alexander hands down his decision to make India the priority and begins to prepare for a total withdrawal, conceding Burma to the Japanese. The Japanese press ahead, vanquishing Burma by the 20th of May. Some Chinese units make it back to China. Troops under General Stilwell will find their route to Myitkyina, the new duty station, blocked and divert to India. Stilwell, shortly after arriving in India on May 14th, will propose to organize a Chinese Force in India, for the sole purpose of retaking Burma.

April 27th 1942 — (United States) The U.S. Army Air Services is established. Major General Rush B. Lincoln assumes command and will take responsibility for Air Service from U.S. Army Forces in Australia. **(Pacific-Marshalls)** The U.S.S. *Tautog*, patrolling in the vicinity of the Marshall Islands, spots an enemy Submarine. Lt. Commander Willingham's crew opens fire, sinking the RO-30. An American Plane, operating in the vicinity, confirms the destruction of the Submarine. **(China-Burma-India)** General Stilwell, aware that the Burma campaign is lost, presents a proposal to Chiang Kai-shek, which calls for the organizing and training of a Chinese Force in India. The Generalissimo agrees, at least in principle, however, proper implementation of the plan will be stalled.

April 28th 1942 — (Pacific-Philippines) The Digos Force receives continuous tenacious assaults by the Japanese on Mindanao. On the following day, 5,000 more Japanese land, uncontested by the U.S. Navy, which has been ordered out of the area. The Philippine defenders are in bad shape, because of the lack of supplies and ammunition. Before it is over, the only reinforcements will be a few Sailors, who must come off a Submarine, to make way for some Code-breakers on a cramped Submarine. They will arrive just in time to become prisoners. **(Atlantic)** A U.S. Naval Force, commanded by Rear Admiral R.C. Giffen, embarks from Scapa Flow, Scotland, for duty in the Atlantic, protecting Convoys assigned to deliver supplies to the Russians. **(China-Burma-India)** The Chinese 28th Division, 6th Army, is ordered to move north from Mandalay, toward Lashio, which like everywhere else in Burma, is in jeopardy. Orders stemming from the meeting on the 25th had called for retreat to the north from Mandalay. Lashio falls on the following day, negating any possibility of holding the Burma Road. General Stilwell, ordered to build the Burma Road but not given the troops or supplies to complete the job, is now going to be run out of the country as the goat of the Burma fiasco. It is fitting that as the General marches out of Burma in rigid Military fashion, he has a pet goat to accompany him.

April 29th 1942 — (Pacific) Japanese press against beleaguered Mindanao. A Landing Force, consisting of just under 5,000 men, puts ashore at Cotabato and Barang and fends off elements of 1st and 101st Philippine Divisions; both towns are captured. **(Pacific-Command)** In other activity, Admiral Earnest J. King, Commander South Pacific, establishes the South Pacific Amphibious Force, which is composed primarily of the 1st Marine Division. **(China-Burma-India)** In Burma, the Japanese cut off the Burma Road, impeding the escape route to China at Lashio. British General Alexander orders withdrawal of Allied troops to Kalewa-Kkatha-Bhamo-Hsenwi, where a stand will be made against the Japanese.

April 30th 1942 — (United States) The U.S.S. *Indiana* (BB-58), a Battleship, is commissioned at Newport News, Virginia. **(Pacific)** A couple of U.S. Naval Patrol Planes successfully evacuate some civilians and Military personnel from Corregidor. **(Dutch East Indies)** The Japanese, having captured many Allied prisoners during their advances through Burma, show their colors. At one camp, a half-crazed Japanese guard continues to brutally beat an American Naval Officer. Lieutenant Richard Antrim, steps forward and informs his captors that he would take the balance of the punishment due the now unconscious Officer. As tensions mount, the 2,700 Allied prisoners begin closing in toward Antrim. The Japanese are thrown completely off guard by this amazing act of courage. The Allied prisoners roar their approval and the stunned Japs relent. Antrim's actions save the life of the beaten man and subsequently, life in this Japanese prison camp begins to improve immediately. **(Atlantic-Europe)** U.S. Admiral Stark assumes command of United States Naval Forces in Europe. He had been appointed to the post during March. **(China-Burma-India)** Central Burma falls to the Japanese. Pressure will continue to be applied to the remaining defenders to eliminate further resistance. British troops retreat across the Ava Bridge, which spans the Irrawaddy River and then destroy it to impede the Japanese pursuit. Further Allied plans are drawn to retreat towards Imphal, India if the defense at Kalewa-Katha-Bhamo-Hsenwi falters.

May 1st 1942 — (United States) The United States Navy establishes additional bases today, one in the Bahamas and another in Grand Cayman, British West Indies. In other activity, Admiral Leahy relinquishes his position as Ambassador to France. **(Pacific-Philippines)** The Japanese knock down resistance as they head north along highway 1, controlling the road as far north as Lake Lanao, while simultaneously eliminating the Philippine 61st Infantry. In other activity, Japanese troops move leisurely to the east, toward Sayre Highway, where it intersects at Kabacan. Other Japanese forces push through east Mindanao, but the resistance against it is stiff. In other activity, the Japanese prepare for the final thrust against Corregidor, increasing Artillery and Air bombard-

ments. **(China-Burma-India)** Just when it appears that things can't get any worse in Burma, the Japanese occupy Monywa. Chiang Kai-shek had ordered Mandalay held on the 29th of April. On the following day, the order had been countermanded and a retreat was called. Now Chinese Resolve deteriorates further, as some Regiments refuse orders entirely. The Burmese "fifth columnists" are on the rampage. Under the most trying of circumstances, General Stilwell keeps things in perspective. Most of his staff has been evacuated, having departed on a C-53. More are awaiting another Plane and 12 men are to remain with the General, to accompany him to Myitkyina, but bad weather cancels the flight. **(India)** Headquarters for the U.S. 10th Air Force is to be located in New Delhi. The 10th Air Force is activated today and Brigadier General Elmer E. Adler assumes command.

American Planes in China: North American Mitchell Medium B-25 Bomber.

May 2nd 1942 — (United States) The U.S. terminates the United States Mission in the U.S.S.R. (Russia), because the Russians refuse to allow the U.S. Mission diplomatic clearance. The United States, does not however, terminate supplies to the Russians, through Allied Convoys at great risk. Ironically, today, the H.M.S. *Edinburgh* (Cruiser) is sunk by enemy Warships, while she is escorting an Allied Convoy back from Russia. During the following month, another Allied Convoy, attempting to get to Russia, will nearly be annihilated along the way by German War ships. **(Pacific-Philippines)** The situation in the Philippines is coming to the end. Promised supplies have never been delivered. Reinforcements have not arrived. The equipment, which has been used against the unending hordes of Japanese invaders, is in most cases, inferior. Corregidor, the "Rock," will follow in the steps of the defenders of Bataan and capitulate within a week. **(Pacific)** The American High Command still anticipates another Japanese strike against Hawaii. U.S. Air searches are being conducted on a continual basis, to prevent another Pearl Harbor. The U.S. Navy is now better prepared to meet the Japanese threat, and the American people are hungry for a victory, to offset their anxieties. U.S. Land Forces are beginning to swell in the Pacific, readying for the long struggle ahead. Midway is on full alert, as Admiral Nimitz inspects the island's defenses. **(Pacific-Solomons)** In the Solomons, the Royal Australian Air Force, aware of a Japanese Invasion Force nearing Tulagi, which lies to the south of Florida Island, begins to abandon the installation. This is part of an Allied strategy, conceived to make the Japanese think their intended offensive against New Guinea will come off without a hitch. This enemy Task Force is to be the first step, in an attempt to encircle the Coral Sea.

The Royal Australian Air Force begins to demolish its Garrison and just prior to the approaching Armada, withdraws its sparse contingent to New Hebrides. **(Pacific-Japan)** The U.S.S. *Drum* (SS-228), operating in Japanese waters off the coast of Honshu, encounters and sinks the Japanese Seaplane Carrier *Mizuho* during a night surface assault. The *Drum* also attacks, but does not damage an enemy Destroyer. On the ninth, she sinks an unnamed Freighter. This is followed by two more sinkings before the end of the month: the *Shonan* (13th) and the *Kitakata* (25th). Another U.S. Submarine, the U.S.S. *Trout*, which had suffered from bad aim during April (possibly because of malfunctioning torpedoes), is greeted with some good luck, also. The Vessel hits the mark and takes out the Merchant Ship, *Uzan Maru*. This kill is followed by the destruction of the *Kongosan* two days later. **(China-Burma-India)** Contingents of the Burma I Corps (1st, 13th, and 63rd Brigades), continue the futile struggle against the Japanese, striking them at Monywa, allowing other contingents to evade the town and head towards Ye-U. Afterward, the engagement ceases and the 1st and 2nd Brigades pull back while other contingents of the Burma Army withdraw to Shwegyin.

May 3rd 1942 — (Pacific-Philippines) Japanese troops land at Mindanao, at Cagayan and at the mouth of the Tagoloan River. The 102nd Philippine Division unsuccessfully opposes the invaders and is forced to withdraw under intense enemy fire. Additional Japanese troops push the 73rd Infantry into the hills around Lake Lanao. The preinvasion bombardments have greatly aided the Japanese by further compressing the defenders on Corregidor. In the midst of these crucial Japanese advances, an American Submarine, the U.S.S. *Spearfish* (SS-190), sneaks into Corregidor and evacuates 25 people from the beleaguered fortification. The intrepid *Spearfish*, having evacuated 12 Officers, 11 Army Nurses, 1 Navy Nurse and a civilian woman, is the last Submarine to enter Corregidor and evacuate personnel. The Nurses are spared imprisonment and possible Japanese atrocities. **(Pacific-Solomons)** In the Solomons, the Japanese seize Tulagi Island. American Admiral Frank J. Fletcher, immediately sets Tulagi as the objective for his Task Force. The U.S. realizes they must win control of the Coral Sea.

May 4th 1942 — (Pacific-Philippines) Allied ground forces open fire on the U.S.S. *Tanager*, a Minesweeper, to scuttle the Vessel.

U.S. Marines on duty in Puerto, Rico during the war. Photo courtesy of Bill Ellis.

May 4th-8th 1942 — (Pacific) — THE BATTLE OF THE CORAL SEA — The Japanese have enjoyed considerable success since their sneak attack against Pearl Harbor, knocking off island after island and thinking nothing of literally severing the head of a P.O.W. with a sword, as they hack their way across the Pacific. In one instance, while transporting American P.O.W.s, captured on Wake Island, one of the captives is beheaded, with the swift conscienceless swing of a Samurai sword on the 20th of January, 1942. Four more merciless executions follow immediately, resulting in the ruthless decapitation of five Americans in an instant, while the other captives are held, down in the inhumane hull of the Japanese Vessel *Nitta Maru*, which is transporting the prisoners from Yokohama, Japan, to Shanghai.

The Japs seem to believe they can commit any atrocities, without threat of retaliation by the American "paper tiger." They have yet to meet any considerable opposition of great magnitude in the air, on the ground, or the sea, and do not contemplate any tenacious opposition, during their quest for command of the Coral Sea. They assume the remaining Allied bastions in the Southeastern Pacific will fold under the unyielding power of their Imperial Navy. They are convinced the balance of Allied resistance in the Southeastern Pacific is unwilling to withstand their next major thrust, for an extended period of time. Now that the Solomons have been annexed, they crash through the waves toward the next victim: Eastern New Guinea and its strategic harbor at Port Moresby. As some Ships of the Imperial Japanese Navy rest confidently at Tulagi in the Solomons, troops unload supplies to bolster this new seizure, which is to be a Seaplane Base. The Japanese at this time are completely unaware that American Code-breakers have uncovered their intentions. Based on the intelligence gathered by the decoded Japanese messages, the diminutive Australian Garrison at Tulagi had been intentionally abandoned, further inflating Japanese confidence.

The U.S. has been preparing for this upcoming episode in the ongoing duel for command of the Pacific area and is looking for a knockout punch. Two days prior, Admiral Nimitz had inspected the defenses of Midway and the readiness of its troops to fend off any attack. In the Coral Sea area, Task Force 17, commanded by Rear Admiral Fletcher, and supported by two additional Attack Groups, one of which contains two formidable U.S. Carriers, glides along the waves at a furious pace to intercept and destroy the Japanese Invasion Fleet, before it can reach Port Moresby.

On the fourth of May, the U.S.S. *Yorktown* moves out in advance of the Task Force, positioning itself within air striking distance of Tulagi. The massive Carrier begins to function furiously, amidst the anxieties of the crew, who are hurriedly readying the Planes for takeoff. Meanwhile, the skies are constantly checked for approaching enemy Aircraft as the engines roar in deafening fashion. The signal flags motion precise signals to the tense Pilots and in cadence with the wind and the sea, the launch commences. As the *Yorktown* rolls steady with the waves, her first wave of intrepid Chariots of the sky zoom from the decks and ascend to strike the unsuspecting enemy at Tulagi. As the Planes depart, the remaining crewmen maintain a concerned vigil, with wrenched stomachs and twisted feelings of pride and fear, hoping their contribution to the operation had been flawless to insure a better chance of all Planes returning safely.

The Planes storm from beyond the mountains of Guadalcanal and close on Tulagi, but Japanese Admiral Goto's Escort Ships have withdrawn. The Japanese are unloading equipment at the docks, when the first wave of Dive Bombers, consisting of just under 30 Planes, begins to sweep down on the port. At an altitude of approximately 7,000 feet, warm air masses stifle the dive, by fogging the windshields, causing the bombs to miss the mark. Two additional attacks commence. A combination of Dive Bombers and Torpedo Bombers, followed by another Dive Bomber contingent are committed, with each descending upon the Shipping, striking with deadly force, during these early morning hours. One of the courageous Pilots, Lt. John Powers, Bombing Squadron 5, recklessly swoops down, near tree top level and scores a direct hit on a Gunboat. He regains altitude and repeatedly comes back in low, and damages an Aircraft Tender and Transport Vessel. Lt. Powell, not quite finished with the Japanese, begins a furious straffing run, flying directly through heavy Antiaircraft fire, expending the balance of his ammunition against another enemy Gunboat, which is subsequently spotted discharging a heavy oil slick in its wake prior to beaching on a nearby island. After the successful mission, the Planes regain altitude and head for the *Yorktown*, knowing they have sunk or damaged several Vessels, leaving a battered harbor and spiraling clouds of black smoke in their wake. The Allied Task Force had also dispatched a small contingent of Wildcat Fighters against the enemy Shipping, prior to the third strike and damage a Destroyer.

The *Yorktown* then rejoins the main body of the Task Force. On the 5th, Fletcher's men set to refuel the Armada and recheck all equipment of the Fleet, while preparing the Planes for the next mission; to intercept and destroy the Japanese Escort Armada, commanded by Japanese Admiral Tagaki, and moving from Truk toward Port Moresby. The Japanese Fleet is still not aware of the presence of U.S. Carriers in the Coral Sea.

Fletcher's Command includes a British Task Force and is entrusted with the responsibility of holding the Coral Sea and preventing the enemy Assault Force from landing at Port Moresby. The combined Armada comprises several Attack Groups, namely: Rear Admiral Kinkaid's five Cruisers and Five Destroyers; Rear Admiral Fitch's Carriers, the *Yorktown* and *Lexington*, complemented by four Destroyers and British Rear Admiral J.G. Grace's Support Group 44, consisting of two Australian Cruisers, one U.S. Cruiser and two U.S. Destroyers. These Warships are further complemented by a Fueling Group, commanded by Captain J.S. Phillips, comprising two Destroyers, two Oilers (Tankers) and a Seaplane Tender.

On the 6th, Carriers *Yorktown* and *Lexington*, bolstered by the Escort Ships, continue the search for Japanese Admiral Shigeyoshi Inouye's 4th Japanese Fleet, (including Takagi's Strike Force) comprising three Carriers the *Shokaku*, *Shoho* and the *Zuikaku* supported by eight Cruisers 17 Destroyers seven Submarines, and a Seaplane Transport. These are augmented by several Gunboats and one Minelayer, in addition to support Vessels, including two Tankers and Supply Transports. Their mission is to insure a victorious landing at Port Moresby and reinforce the new Japanese installations at Tulagi.

As the ocean going game of seek and destroy continues in the Coral Sea on the Sixth, the enemy is moving against Port Moresby from three different directions, the Japanese Strike Force under Admiral Takagi, which includes the Carriers *Shokaku* and *Zuikaku* has passed the southeastern tip of the Solomons and is maneuvering to protect the left flank of the Port Moresby Invasion Force, which had departed Rabaul. Another Japanese Attack Group, attached to the 4th Fleet and commanded by Admiral Goto, had departed Tulagi and has moved beyond New Georgia and past the tip of Bougainville, enroute to join the Invasion Force. The Allied Task Forces, under Fletcher, set a course for the area northwest of their own positions, where the enemy is expected to be. On the 7th, Fletcher begins heading north, seeking a confrontation. Scout Planes search the vast sea lanes, hoping to detect the Invasion Force before the Japanese discover the Carriers.

Admiral Fletcher's Force moves toward the Louisiade Archipelago. The Destroyer *Sims* is to stand by the Tanker *Neosho*, but without the added protection of the Fleet, several things go wrong. While the American Planes are hammering the enemy Fleet in the Coral Sea, Army B-26 Bombers mistakenly identify the two isolated U.S. Vessels as part of the enemy Invasion Force and attack. In addition, enemy Planes stumble onto their positions and attack with full strength, believing a Patrol Plane's report that the Vessels are a Carrier and a Cruiser. The enemy Carriers launch over 75 Planes, including Dive Bombers, Torpedo Planes and Fighters, which devastate both Vessels. The *Sims* receives several hits that cause her to sink quickly and the *Neosho*, which lingers on for several days, despite taking repeated hits, including a Kamikaze.

British Admiral Grace's Task Force 44, dispatched by Fletcher to engage the enemy Transports, is about to be attacked by Land based Planes. The staunch Air assault, carried out by over 40 Planes, including Bombers and Fighters from Rabaul, inflict little damage, but the bombs and torpedoes do cost the lives of a couple of Sailors and wound several more. Soon after the enemy Air assault, Grace's Armada is mistakenly struck by Allied Planes, which had been dispatched out of Australia. The Air Corps Bombardiers miss the targets completely, prompting the British Admiral to later remark that the Fleet had been lucky because of the Air Corps' bad marksmanship.

Meanwhile, Aircraft from both the *Lexington* and *Yorktown*, converge on the Japanese Support Group Fleet, under Admiral Goto. The Airborne vanguard of the Fleet looks simultaneously for approaching enemy Fighters and targets. The enemy Fleet is spotted first. The startled enemy Escort Ships begin firing incessantly at the diving Planes, which have only one mission: to destroy the enemy Carrier.

There is no lull in the battle, as the Planes continue to pound the enemy. The Planes criss-cross through the flight paths of enemy shells, releasing more devastation upon the Fleet. One of the Planes, flown by Lt. Powers, swoops down, reaching a perilous altitude, before releasing his bomb. Powers scores a direct hit, creating an uproarious explosion that ignites a fire, transforming the enemy Carrier into a floating inferno. The chatter on the radio becomes more pointed, as the view from the cockpits centers on the enemy flightdeck, now consumed in flames. "SCRATCH ONE FLATTOP" is the joyous announcement. The unrestrained attack also eliminates a Destroyer. The *Shoho* had launched her last Plane and is preparing to settle on the bottom of the Coral Sea.

The American Planes depart, having suffered the loss of one Dive Bomber, before they return to the *Lexington* and *Yorktown*. Upon knowledge of the loss of the *Shoho*, Admiral Inouye prematurely orders the Transports to return to Rabaul, to await the outcome of the Carrier engagement. The Japanese dispatch Planes in the late afternoon, to locate Fletcher's Task Forces. Radar, which the Japanese Fleets do not possess, picks up the approaching enemy Planes, and Wildcats are dispatched to intercept at long range. Then additional Fighters are sent aloft to reinforce the Group. The dog fights begin at high altitude, when the Japanese are surprised by the American Fighters. Within about a half hour of murderous aerial combat, the Japanese are forced to scatter in all directions, a few of them actually approaching the Yorktown, thinking it their Carrier. To their surprise, their landing gear goes down and at the last seconds, realize the flight deck is that of the *Yorktown*. Unable to strike, having already exhausted their bomb loads, they divert to the Japanese Carrier. Soon after, additional Japanese Planes attempt to land on the *Lexington* in error and are greeted by Fighters and Anti-aircraft fire. A total of 27 enemy Planes had been sent on this night raid, but only six return. The remainder are ditched in the sea or shot down. The day closes without any contact between the opposing Naval Forces.

On the final day of this fiercely contested battle, the 8th of May, the major confrontation erupts. At approximately six o'clock in the morning, Patrol Planes from the opposing Carriers probe for contact. The Japanese include Land based Planes from Rabaul, to assist in the operation. The weather in the battle area favors the Japanese, as their Fleet receives added protection from cloud cover, while the American Carriers are exposed under blue skies. Down in the briefing room of the U.S. Carriers, the Pilots receive their final instructions. The loudspeakers blare; "AIRCRAFT UP AND READY." The Pilots bounce to their feet and sprint to the Aircraft. Torpedo Planes dart from the edge of the flight deck, their tails dipping slightly, with a few brushing precariously close to the sea, before surging upward toward the enemy Fleet, which American Scout Planes had located previously. Dive Bombers from the *Yorktown* are first to brave the intense Antiaircraft fire, to ignite the engagement. Planes from the *Lexington* soon enter the aerial combat. Lt. Powers, prior to takeoff, gives his Section the following message: "REMEMBER, THE FOLKS BACK HOME ARE COUNTING ON US. I AM GOING TO GET A HIT IF I HAVE TO LAY IT ON THEIR FLIGHT DECK."

Right in the thick of the battle, Lt. Powers' contingent of Douglas Dauntless Dive Bombers begins to dive from an altitude of 18,000 feet directly into the enemy's incessant Antiaircraft fire. Powers ignores the danger, dashing through the shellfire and flak, with his Plane's nose pointing directly at the *Shokaku*. Just as the Plane moves in close enough to guarantee a hit, Powers unleashes the bomb, which strikes a savage blow, in concert with his attempt to pull out of the dive. In that instant, murderous explosions occur, shattering parts of the Vessel, filling the area above and around the stricken Ship with deadly debris, including shell fragments and blinding smoke, which clutters Powers' escape path, greatly impeding a safe maneuver. Powers is spotted for the last time, at an altitude of about 200 feet, struggling to rejoin his Section. The other Japanese Carrier on the scene, the *Zuikaku*, manages to avoid damage by taking cover under the clouds of a rain squall. Powers is posthumously awarded the Medal of Honor for his extraordinary courage. The Air Mission is escorted by several Wildcat Fighters, which contain the Jap Fighters and successfully utilize their potent 50 caliber, wing-mounted machine guns to inflict severe damages to the enemy Fleet. This adds greatly to the mission, because many of the Torpedoes and Bombs had missed their targets entirely.

The battle turns to the American Fleet, which has confirmed by the use of its radar an approaching hostile Aircraft. Fighters are dispatched to intercept: the enemy Aircraft is finally tracked and shot down, but not before the location of the American Carriers had been radioed to the Japanese Command. Fighters are launched to defend the Fleet, against enemy Torpedo Planes. The radios become increasingly active. "Bandits" "Bandits!" Roaring 50 caliber machine guns begin pumping steel into the enemy Planes. Simultaneously the American Warships commence firing. Blistering fire sends many enemy Planes into the sea, but the Torpedo Planes score successes, damaging the *Lexington*. After Dive Bombers make a deadly run to inflict more damage, explosions ignite raging fires, that swarm across the deck. Dogfights continue to be active above the Fleet, while the Antiaircraft guns fire streams of tracers toward the enemy Planes. As the opposing Pilots trade bullets in the sky, some disabled Planes plummet to the sea, leaving large trails of smoke following, until the final burst of blazing fire, as they crash into the water. The once tranquil Coral Sea is interrupted with resounding firebolts, as Planes explode upon impact, cremating the downed Pilots.

Meanwhile, the men on board the *Lexington*, fight desperately against the fires, which have scorched the decks. In addition, bomb craters have blown open the deck. Valiant attempts are made to swing the fire hoses and damaged Planes are tossed overboard instinctively, to try to salvage the *Lexington*. As the engagement winds down, the Planes withdraw, heading for their respective Carriers, both sides having suffered losses.

Shortly after noon, fumes leaking from damaged fuel tanks seep up from below deck and trigger a horrifying explosion; walls shatter and chambers begin to flood. The dying Vessel, its flight deck now a steaming griddle, clearly must be abandoned. Toward the latter part of the day, the final blow is struck by torpedoes from the U.S.S. *Phelps* against the Lexington to eliminate any possibility of the Japanese seizing the "Grand Lady of the Coral Sea."

The *Yorktown*, also under severe attack, had possessed much greater maneuvering ability than the *Lexington* and had been able to avoid fatal damage. The total amount of American operational Planes had been diminished greatly, with the loss of the *Lexington*, causing the Americans to pull back to Pearl Harbor, but their mission to repel the invasion force is successful. The Japanese, although still in possession of two Carriers, opt to retire. With the strategic victory of the Coral Sea behind them, the Allied offensive is beginning to get underway. Admiral Fletcher's battered Task Force retires to Pearl Harbor with Old Glory intact.

During this most unusual Naval battle, a new precedent is set. The entire confrontation between Fleets is fought entirely by Planes. The Surface Vessels, although at one time coming to within a hundred miles of each other in the darkness, never make visual or physical contact. Sixty-six American Planes are lost in this vicious struggle, but the Japanese lose more than a hundred. The American Navy and its Pilots distinguish themselves, during this battle in these first months of the war and pride themselves, that thanks to their efforts, Australia is now considered to be temporarily out of harm's way. Two additional U.S. Navy men become recipients of the Medal of Honor, during this enduring test of America's resolve, Lt. William E. Hall (Pilot) and Lt. Milton Ricketts (Engineering Repair Officer, *Yorktown*). The Japanese lose the Destroyer *Kikuzuki* (4th); Carrier *Shoho* (7th). The Japanese Carrier *Shokaku* is damaged. The United States loses the Destroyer *Sims* (DD-409) on the 7th (loses, 176 crewmen); Oiler *Neosho* (AO-23), also on the 7th, and of course, the U.S.S. *Lexington* (CV-2), with the loss of over 200 crewmen. The Carrier *Yorktown* (CV-5), badly damaged on the 8th, survives.

May 5th 1942 — (Pacific-Philippines) In the Philippines, the Japanese preinvasion bombardment continues against Corregidor. Enemy troops pour ashore at North Point Corregidor during the night, continuing ashore until the early hours of the 6th. The U.S.S. *Pigeon* (ASR-9), a Submarine Rescue Vessel and the U.S.S. *Mindanao* (PR-8), a River Gunboat, are both destroyed by Japanese Aircraft. **(Pacific-Japan)** As the battle for control of the Coral Sea progresses, the Japanese Imperial Headquarters in Japan instructs the Combined Fleet to support the intended Army invasion of the Aleutians and Midway. **(China-Burma-India)** General Stilwell encounters a British merchant at Indaw and declines an offer to have Stilwell take several hundred elephants with him on the trek across the Himalayas to India. Instead, Stilwell will confiscate a mule track train and hire men to guide them on the balance of the trip. General Merrill and Colonel Holcombe both become ill along the route, but Stilwell, at 59 years old, manifests few signs of stress or fatigue. Several British Officers join Stilwell's group and move with him from Indaw.

May 6th-10th 1942 — (Pacific-Philippines) The courageous stand of the "Battling Bastards of Bataan" expires as American General Wainwright unconditionally surrenders all Allied forces throughout the Philippines. The surrender talks commence at 1030 and last until midnight, when the papers are signed. Colonel Samuel L. Howard, senior Marine Corps officer on the island, orders the Regimental and National Colors (4th Marines), to be burned, to prevent capture and desecration by the enemy. Colonel Howard, after hearing General Wainwright's plea to surrender, turns to Colonel Donald Curtiss and states: "MY GOD, I HAD TO BE THE FIRST MARINE EVER TO SURRENDER A REGIMENT." A number of individual units continue to resist. On the 7th, General Wainwright spreads the terms of surrender to the units still refusing to capitulate. Japanese Planes relentlessly pound the defenders in Mindanao, although organized Infantry activity ceases. A small amount of resistance continues on Luzon and Palawan for awhile. General Sharp instructs the Visayan-Mindanao defense forces to surrender on the 10th, but their obstinate reluctance keeps particular units resisting in the Philippines. America, still receiving very little good news concerning her fighting men, waits impatiently for retaliation.

May 6th 1942 — (Pacific-Philippines) General Wainright, by use of Japanese controlled airwaves, broadcasts surrender terms to his Forces. In other activity, enemy Aircraft and Artillery continue to maintain pressure against Allied resistance on Mindanao, even though Japanese ground forces are

inactive. The U.S.S. *Oahu* (PR-6) and the *Luzon* (PR-7), both River Gunboats are scuttled by the Americans. In addition, the U.S.S. *Quail* (AM-15), a Minesweeper is destroyed by the Americans, to prevent its capture. The coastal Bay Forts at both Corregidor and Manila, capitulate to the Japanese. **(Pacific-Hawaii)** The U.S. Navy establishes an Auxiliary Air Facility at Nawiliwili, Kauai.

May 7th 1942 — (Pacific-Coral Sea) The U.S.S. *Sims* (Destroyer) and U.S.S. *Neosho* (Tanker) are both destroyed in the Coral Sea by Japanese Planes. The *Sims* sinks quickly, but the Tanker *Neosho* survives for several days. In addition, U.S. Planes discover and sink the Japanese Light Carrier *Shoho* and an escort Destroyer. The main confrontation occurs on the following day. **(Atlantic-Malta)** Two Carriers, the U.S.S. *Wasp* and the H.M.S. *Eagle*, are in the vicinity of Malta to deliver Spitfires, which will bolster Planes on the island.

Dauntless Dive Bombers operating during the Battle of the Coral Sea.

May 8th 1942 — (Pacific-Philippines) The American and Philippine Officers who have not yet surrendered their commands to the Japanese receive messages from General Wainright, urging them to cease resistance and surrender. On Mindanao, the Japanese await darkness and re-initiate their attack, which presses throughout the night into early morning. The Philippine 62nd Infantry pulls back to Dalirig, with the Japanese in hot pursuit. **(Pacific-Command)** General MacArthur states his opinion, that an offensive should be initiated against the Japanese in the Pacific, but not until U.S. Naval, Ground and Air forces are built to a proper state of readiness and strength. **(Pacific-Coral Sea)** The main confrontation between Japanese and Allied Naval forces occurs today. The Task Forces of Fletcher engage the Japanese Fleet, consisting of two Carriers, four Cruisers and several Destroyers, the vanguard of the Japanese Invasion Force, heading for Port Moresby, New Guinea. In this first Naval-Air engagement, the confrontation is vicious. The enemy Carrier *Shokaku* is severely damaged. Both U.S. Carriers, the *Yorktown* and the *Lexington* are both damaged, the latter being sunk late in the day by an American Destroyer (*Phelps*) to prevent the enemy from seizing it. The U.S. loses 66 Planes and the Japanese over 100. Although the U.S. loses more Vessels during the five day confrontation, the battle is considered a strategic victory, because the enemy Invasion Force is turned back from Port Moresby, gaining valuable time for the Allies. This Sea battle terminates the defensive posture of the Allies in the Pacific. They now prepare to turn to the attack. The Americans take their battered Fleet back to Pearl Harbor to prepare for the next engagement. Code-breakers will again

Battle of the Coral Sea.

play a vital part in this war on the seas, when they verify Midway as the next objective of the Japanese. The *Yorktown*, which the Japanese thought had been sunk, will receive an extraordinary overhaul in time to meet the threat at Midway. **(China-Burma-India)** Myitkyina, a strategic town with its coveted Airfield, is easily overtaken by the Japanese. The recapture by Allied forces, later in the war, is a brutalizing campaign, which includes participation by American Volunteers, commanded by General Merrill, presently on his way to India, with General Stilwell, after being driven out of Burma by the Japanese. **(Atlantic-Russia)** The Germans are preparing to open a major summer offensive to seize the rich oil fields of the Caucasus. They initiate several preliminary actions, engineered to reposition their lines. In the Crimea, the German 11th Army (Army Group South), advances toward Kerch.

May 9th 1942 — (United States) The Coast Guard Cutter *Icarus*, operating off the coast of South Carolina, encounters and sinks a German Submarine (U-352). **(Pacific-Philippines)** In Mindanao, the Japanese take control. The defenders at Dalirig are thoroughly thrashed and routed. Allied positions in the Puntian area become indefensible ensuring Japanese domination. **(Pacific-New Guinea)** The defenders at Port Moresby rest easier, knowing the Invasion Force had been turned back. In other activity, the Japanese Imperial General Headquarters temporarily aborts the orders to attack Port Moresby. **(Tonga Islands)** A contingent of U.S. troops arrives at Tongatabu. **(Galapagos Islands)** U.S. troops embark at the Galapagos Islands, which are located off the west coast of South America.

The U.S.S. Lexington (CV-2) ablaze in the Coral Sea; her crew jumping into the sea.

A U.S. Vindicator Bomber taking off to engage a Japanese Fleet.

112

May 10th 1942 — (Pacific-Philippines) Allied defenders, not yet listed as capitulants, are reluctant to surrender, even though ordered to do so by American General Sharp. The troops comply in piecemeal fashion, taking until the 9th of June. In addition to the Visayan-Mindanao forces, additional fragmented groups, attempting to hold out on Luzon and Palawan, also surrender. **(Pacific-Japan)** The U.S.S. *Silversides* traveling cautiously at the tail end of a typhoon, about 600 miles from Japan and experiencing unruly seas, encounters a Jap Patrol Boat. The Japanese roar into action, commencing a wicked burst of fire that whips across the bridge of the *Silversides*. Return fire from the American Submarine scorches the enemy Vessel. The enemy fire had snuffed out the life of Second Loader, Mike Harbin and the crew becomes angry. As the burning enemy boat is pummeled, the Yanks then part company with the barbecued Vessel and prepare to give Harbin a proper sea burial. At sunset, the emotions of the crew run high as the eloquent cover of death, Old Glory is reverently placed upon the flag draped corpse of another American, who has died at the hands of the Japanese. Lt. Commander Burlingame, already hurt by the tragic loss, will remark: "THE FIRST FISH (Torpedo) WE FIRE WILL HAVE HARBIN'S NAME ON IT." Three days later, Harbin's torpedo is launched against an enemy Submarine and subsequent explosions are heard by the Yanks, but the hit is not confirmed. Still in search of Japs, the *Silversides* continues its Patrol and encounters a Merchant Vessel on the 17th, quickly eradicating it from the rolls of Jap Shipping. This is followed by the *Silversides* becoming involved with a most curious passenger, hanging on the periscope: a Japanese fishing net, often used as a flag. The *Silversides* attempts to make a deep dive to lose the advertisement, but not before the Japanese spot the Submarine and report it to Patrol Boats, which eagerly rush to the scene. The eager *Silversides*, undaunted by the Jap flag, fires her torpedoes, with two out of three striking the mark instantaneously, creating a tremendous explosion; the unfortunate vanishing Patrol Boat was carrying a cargo of ammunition. Not satisfied, the *Silversides*, still transporting the Jap banner, charges at the other Patrol Boat, unleashing more torpedoes at the Vessel, but the damage is not verified. Lt. Commander Davenport remarks later: "SILVERSIDES WAS PROBABLY THE ONLY AMERICAN SUBMARINE TO MAKE AN APPROACH WHILE FLYING THE JAPANESE FLAG." **(China-Burma-India)** The Japanese assault British contingents, operating as rear guards, in the vicinity of Shwegyin. The Japanese drive across the Salween River by the 12th, furthering their almost uncontested movements in Burma.

May 11th 1942 — (Pacific) A U.S. Submarine (S-42), operating in the vicinity of the Solomon Islands, spots a Japanese Minelayer, the *Okinoshima*, off the coast of New Ireland and ends its career. The *S-42* launches four torpedoes (Mark 10's, not the defective Mark 14's) and sinks the Vessel, which becomes the first victim of Task Force 42. The Submarine Service is getting adapted to the unfamiliar waters in the Pacific and becomes involved in many facets of operations, in addition to demolishing Japanese ships. For instance, the U.S.S. *Porpoise*, operating around New Guinea, is ordered to Ju Island to attempt rescue of some downed Army crewmen. This quaint little island slumbers between New Guinea and Haimahera and is inhabited by Cannibals and Head Hunters, who would like to invite the stranded Airmen for dinner. The innovative crew of the *Porpoise* takes this unorthodox mission in

early May and successfully rescues the Airmen, heads included and delivers them safely to Darwin, Australia. **(Atlantic)** In the Mediterranean, British Destroyers attack an Axis Convoy, without success. Three of the four attacking British Vessels are sunk by enemy Aircraft. **(China-Burma-India)** The Japanese, embarrassed by the Doolittle raids, seek reprisals and launch an offensive in Chekiang Province, China.

May 12th 1942 — (United States) The U.S.S. *Massachusetts*, a Battleship (BB-29), is commissioned at Boston. **(China-Burma-India)** The Salween River is breached by the Japanese. They storm further, driving toward Kengtung. **(Atlantic-Great Britain)** The U.S. Eighth Air Force arrives in strength, landing a strong contingent at England to initiate offensive movements. **(Atlantic-Russia)** Skirmishing continues between the Germans and the Russians. The Germans progress against Kerch in the Crimean, while the Red Army commences a two-legged assault against Kharkov, moving northward from Izium and southwest along the upper Donets.

May 13th 1942 — (Pacific) New Zealand troops holding the Fiji Islands, in the South Pacific, are relieved by American troops, who will now bear responsibility for the defense of the islands. **(Pacific-Australia)** A contingent of the U.S. 41st Division (Rear Echelon), arrives in Australia. On the following day, American forces will be further bolstered by the arrival of the U.S. 32nd Division. **(Atlantic-West Indies)** Three French Warships at Martinique are to be immobilized by the French, after reaching an agreement with the Allies.

May 14th 1942 — (United States) The Women's Army Auxiliary Corps (WAAC) is established by Congressional legislation. **(Pacific-Pearl Harbor)** Twenty five Submarines of the Pacific Fleet receive orders to report to Midway, which is expected to be the next target of the Japanese. During May, Admiral Withers, will be ordered back to the States, to assume command of the Portsmouth Navy Yard. The Pacific Submarine Fleet will come under the command of Admiral R.H. English. Of the entire contingent of 29 Submarines deployed around Midway, only four will participate. The assignment of getting to Midway is not all that easy for the Submarines. *Argonaut* and *Thresher* are receiving maintenance, the *Silversides* is ordered to remain in Japanese waters in the vicinity of Kiisuido and the *Triton* is racing from her deployment point in the China Sea, but is returning short of both ammunition and fuel. In addition, eight of the Submarines have been back from Patrol and are receiving needed repairs, while six others are deployed well out of range and are also forced to speed to the battle zone. The seagoing checker game will continue for several weeks. Six of the Submarines are ready, while not yet battle-tested. Another five Submarines have just recently been deployed on Patrol. In any event, the Navy will be ready during early June, when the attack comes. **(Atlantic)** A German U-Boat in the vicinity of St. John's, Newfoundland, lays a minefield to impede Allied shipping. **(China-Burma-India)** British troops, still on the retreat out of Burma, reach Tamu, Assam.

May 15th 1942 — (Pacific-Australia) The Japanese invasion force, intended for the capture of Port Moresby, had withdrawn from the area over one week ago. This allows Australian troops the luxury of safely embarking for Port Moresby to strengthen Allied fortifications on New Guinea. The units are the Australian 14th Brigade Group, plus 700 Australian Anti-aircraft troops, attached to strengthen their force. **(China-Burma-India)** British General Alexander moves into headquarters in the vicinity of Imphal. American General Stilwell has safely avoided capture by the Japanese and makes it from Burma to India. Stilwell's jungle weary troops had made the last leg of their journey with the assistance of Allied Planes, which had located their positions and dropped supplies from the sky. During the initial Airdrop, natives had alarmingly jumped from the brush and confiscated many of the supplies. Stilwell, taking mental notes at the time, had remarked about their queer signals, which sounded like animals, stating that they (Americans) should remember the sounds for when they come back. Upon arrival of General Stilwell's command, the Assam Rifles assemble for salute. Stilwell and the balance of the command are somewhat thinner from their unexpected expedition and there is no starch in their uniforms, but their spirit and determination is rigid. General Stilwell's command has come back without any losses, except that of Captain George Hambleton, who had remained in Burma with Chinese troops (22nd Division). He later dies in the Hukawng Valley. Stilwell, immediately gets his plans underway for retaking Burma and continuing the struggle, stating: "BURMA MAY BE LOST, BUT THATS NOT THE END BY A LONGSHOT." General Stilwell is determined to regroup and get the remainder of the Chinese troops out of the Hukawng Valley and safely to India. He further intends to receive permission from Chiang Kai-shek to commence a later offensive, from Yunnan into Burma. General Stilwell remarks: "GETTING HIS (Chiang Kai-shek) PERMISSION WILL BE A REAL JOB, BUT I'LL DO IT COME HELL OR HIGH WATER," adding, "AND GETTING THE BRITISH OFF THEIR CANS TO LAND A FORCE ON THE ARAKAN COAST WILL BE A BITCH OF A JOB, TOO." Chiang agrees with Stilwell's suggestions, after much deliberation, during 1943. **(Atlantic-Libya)** In Libya, the British continue their plans for a major offensive against Rommel's forces. Rommel beats the British to the punch by striking first, initiating his offensive on the 27th.

May 16th 1942 — (Pacific) The U.S.S. *Tautog*, damages, but fails to sink an enemy Freighter Vessel while out on her second Patrol. Later in the day, the Submarine *Tautog* attacks an enemy Submarine, however, there is no confirmation of a hit. On the 17th, it sinks another Vessel and before closing her second Patrol, will attack another enemy Vessel, the *Shoka Maru*, a 4,467 ton vessel, on May 25. **(China-Burma-India)** Elements of Service of Supply Troops arrive in India. The first contingents are the 393rd Quartermaster Port Battalion and the 159th Station Hospital detachments begin to file into Karachi.

May 17th 1942 — (Pacific-Caroline Islands) The U.S.S. *Tautog* (SS-199), a Submarine, destroys a Japanese Submarine (I-28) near the Caroline Islands. **(Japan)** The U.S.S. *Triton*, operating near Kyushu, Japan, discovers and destroys a Japanese Submarine (I-164). **(Atlantic)** The Russians and Germans are fighting viciously in the area of Kharkov. The Germans counter attack from their positions at Izyum advancing to a position east of Kharkov, stymying the Russian advance.

May 18th 1942 — (United States) The Office of Naval Inspector General is established by the U.S. Navy. The post will be filled by Rear Admiral C.P. Snyder. **(Pacific)** Midway is on full alert, in anticipation of an enemy attack. The U.S. 7th Air Force (Pacific Ocean Areas) is also on alert, bracing for possible attack on either Hawaii or Midway. Additional reinforcements are dispatched to Midway and the Aleutian Islands within a few days. U.S. Code-breakers on Midway are convinced that Midway is the primary objective. Early on, there is much speculation that Midway might be a diversion, with the Alaskan Aleutians being the main objective. Additional intelligence-gathering, by intentionally sending false uncoded messages that the fresh water supply on Midway is unoperational, soon ends speculation. The Japanese take the bait, sending their own cryptic messages, with a code name for Midway, tipping their hand and proving the accuracy of the American deciphering team on Midway, to the jubilation of the American Command. **(China-Burma-India)** Chiang Kai-shek directs the 5th Army, basically consisting of the Chinese 22nd and 96th Divisions, to man positions between Fort Hertz and Myitkyina. The 96th Division finally makes its way to China, by way of Fort Hertz, while the survivors of the Chinese 22nd Division straggle into Ledo, during July and August.

May 19th 1942 — (Atlantic-England) American General Ira C. Eaker, Commander U.S. Eighth Air Force assumes command of all U.S. Army Air organizations in the British Isles.

May 20th 1942 — (Pacific) The Allies are tirelessly at work to complete the construction of a secret Air Base in the Aleutians on Umnak Island. American Rear Admiral John S. McCain, assumes command of all Air Forces, South Pacific (Air Force South Pacific). American strategy is moving diligently to outmaneuver the Japanese Midway Invasion Force, convinced it will deliver another deadly surprise attack against the Americans. **(China-Burma-India)** With Burma now under complete control of the Japanese, they begin to take defensive measures, deploying contingents of the 15th Army; the 15th, 18th, 33rd, 55th and 56th Divisions bear this responsibility. In other activity, the Burma I Corps rear guard elements reach India. The I Corps now comes under the command of the Burma 4 Corps.

May 21st 1942 — (North Pacific-Aleutians) All American Army and Naval forces, plus all Canadian forces in the area of Alaska (North Pacific Force), come under the command of U.S. Rear Admiral Robert A. Theobold, who is the Commanding Officer of Task Force 8. **(Atlantic)** Adolph Hitler changes his strategy and postpones an imminent attack on Malta (Operation HERCULES) and concentrates on the capture of Egypt. The Germans are simultaneously concentrating on the Russians in the vicinity of Kharkov.

May 22nd 1942 — (Pacific) The 21st Troop Carrier Squadron begins moving three hundred men to bolster the Australian Garrison at Wau, New Guinea (Kanga Force). This Australian Garrison, consisting primarily of New Guinea Volunteer Reserves, is to defend the Bulolo Valley. **(Atlantic-Mexico)** Mexico joins the Allies, declaring war against Germany, Japan and Italy.

May 23rd 1942 — (North Pacific-Aleutians) The newly constructed Allied Airbase at Umnak Island, situated in the Aleutians becomes operational and receives the first contingents of U.S. Fighters. The Planes arrive and land safely without incident. **(Atlantic-Russia)** The Germans maintain their counterattack in the vicinity of Kharkov and cut off the Red Army troops deployed in the Izyum salient located west of the Donets.

May 25th 1942 — (Pacific-Midway) The U.S.S. *St. Louis* delivers Companies C and D, 2nd Raider Battalion and the 37mm battery, 3rd Defense Battalion, U.S.M.C., to assist the other Marines already on the island. **(Atlantic-West Indies)** An enemy Submarine stalks and sinks the Destroyer, U.S.S. *Blakely* in waters near Martinique. **(China-Burma-India)** The Chinese 38th Division escapes the Japanese and reaches Burma. The 113th Regiment, acting as a rear guard, has not yet arrived, as it is still overseeing the Chinese withdrawal and will filter in later. In the China Sea, the U.S.S. *Salmon* (SS-182), destroys the 11,000 ton Japanese repair Ship, the *Asahi*, slumbering in the China Sea. Lt. Commander McKinney, sees his Submariners take out another enemy Vessel, the *Ganges Maru*, on the 28th. In other Submarine activity, the U.S.S. *Pompano* (SS-181), commanded by Lt. Commander Parks, encounters and sinks a small Tanker, the *Tokyo Maru*, and follows this with another kill on the 30th, the 8,000 ton Transport, the *Atsuta Maru*; both Japanese losses are in the vicinity of Nansei Shoto.

May 26th 1942 — (Pacific Hawaii-Midway) The U.S. Navy is busy today as a Task Force, including the Carriers *Hornet* and *Enterprise*, under Rear Admiral Halsey, arrives at Pearl Harbor from the South Pacific, to resupply and prepare to move back to sea for another major confrontation, with the Japanese. Halsey's Fleet had been about 600 miles from Tulagi (Guadalcanal), preparing to occupy the Samoa-Fijis-New Caledonia Line when ordered back to Pearl Harbor. Upon his return, Halsey is diagnosed by doctors as having "general dermatitas" (incessant itching) preventing him from participating in the operation for which he was recalled to Pearl Harbor. Halsey convinces Nimitz to give Ray Spruance his command for the big fight. The Yorktown Force, under Admiral Fletcher, arrives on the following day. The U.S.S. *Kittyhawk* arrives at Midway, bringing with it, both ground and air reinforcements. Sixteen SBD-2s and seven F4F-3s also arrive, in addition to an Anti-aircraft Group and a light Tank Platoon (3rd Marine Defense Battalion).

May 26th 1942 — (Pacific-New Guinea) More reinforcements are flown in to bolster New Guinea: the Australian 5th Independent Company. **(Atlantic-Libya)** German General Rommel awaits nightfall before deploying Armor southeast of Bir Hacheim to threaten the southern flank of the British positions defended by the British 13 Corps to the north and the British 30 Corps to the south. The repositioning of the German Armor units is the preliminary strategy before Rommel reignites his offensive. **(Atlantic-Great Britain)** London is the site of an Anglo-American Air Conference, designed to consider an allocation policy. U.S. Rear Admiral John H. Towers, General Henry H. Arnold and British Chief of Air Staff Sir Charles Portal, are among those in attendance. In other activity, the Russians are greeted with a windfall, as a 20 year Anglo-Soviet mutual aid agreement is signed in London.

May 26th-30th 1942 — (Pacific-Midway) Japan prepares to strike Midway as Vice Admiral Nagumo sails from the homeland with his Carrier Strike Force. Japanese Troop Transports depart Saipan, while Cruisers and Destroyers embark from Guam to form a massive assault group, which intends to destroy American-held island. The principal part of the Task Force leaves Japan under the command of Admiral Yamamoto. Another Task Force, which is to be used to fool the Americans, steams from Japan on the 30th, moving to-

ward the Aleutians, feigning a major attack. The U.S., fully convinced of Japan's interest in Midway, does not buy the bait and further prepares to destroy the approaching Japanese Armada. American Admiral Spruance, his Task Force resupplied since arriving at Pearl on May 26th, embarks and returns expeditiously to the vicinity of Midway. American Admiral Fletcher departs Pearl Harbor with the miraculously reborn *Yorktown* and its Strike Force, two days later, to assist in the defense.

May 27th 1942 — (Pacific-Hawaii) Admiral Fletcher's Task Force 17, including the badly bruised Carrier *Yorktown* arrives at Pearl Harbor for resupply and repairs. Although the *Yorktown* is expected to last a long time in dry dock, Admiral Nimitz demands and receives a truly remarkable achievement from his men. They have the *Yorktown* battle-ready when she departs for Midway on the 30th. **(Pacific-Japan)** Japanese Vice Admiral Nagumo, commanding the Carrier Strike Force intended to attack Midway, departs Japan. Escort Destroyers and Cruisers embark simultaneously from Guam and the enemy Transports depart Saipan, with all three Forces rendezvousing for the assault against Midway. **(Pacific-New Caledonia)** The Americal Division is activated and will be commanded by General Alexander M. Patch, U.S.A. **(Pacific-Wallis Island)** A contingent of Seabees and Marines occupy Wallis Island in the South Pacific. **(China-Burma-India)** The United States continues to strengthen its support units. Base Section 1 (U.S.A.F.C.B.I.) is established at Karachi, India. Another Base will be established later at Calcutta, also in India. **(Atlantic-Libya)** Rommel, who had awaited darkness to deploy his Armor against the British right flank, now uses the first light of day to spring his offensive. German and Italian Tanks, situated south of Bir Hacheim, strike hard against the Gazala-Bir Hacheim line, from the south and initiate additional actions to the north. Rommel dispatches the Armored Divisions toward Acroma and El Adem. They will be engaged by the Indian 3rd Motor Brigade several miles east of Bir Hacheim. The Free French Brigade repulses an attack, initiated by the Italian Ariete Division at Bir Hacheim and the British 2nd Armored Brigade and the 1st Army Tank Brigade, successfully hold fast against the 15th and 21st Panzer Divisions, stymying Rommel's effort against the right flank. The German attackers lose Tanks and fuel steadily, which the Germans need desperately. The heavy fighting continues, but by the following day, the British have successfully contained the Axis threat and handily prevent the enemy from breaking through to the coast. **(Atlantic-Newfoundland)** Two American Ships, the U.S.S. *Prairie* (AD-15), a Destroyer Tender and the U.S.S. *Spry* (PG-64), a Gunboat, are both damaged by fire in the vicinity of Argentia, Newfoundland.

May 28th 1942 — (United States) The people at home still cling to their hopes of an offensive to halt the advancing Japanese threat in the Pacific. Americans appreciate that our Navy is not sufficiently strong enough to absorb another Pearl Harbor. If Midway and Hawaii fall to the Japanese, the West Coast of the United States will be virtually defenseless. Japanese Submarines have already shelled the California coast, causing little damage, however, the harassing raids cause much concern among the populace. **(Pacific)** Admiral Spruance, commanding a Carrier Task Force, departs Pearl Harbor, steaming toward Midway. In other related activity concerning Midway, the principle body of the Japanese Naval Force, commanded by Admiral Yamamoto, embarks from

Japan, following close behind the Carrier Force which had departed the previous day. **(Pacific-New Hebrides)** The Americans dispatch troops to Espiritu Santo, New Hebrides, for the purpose of constructing an Airbase (Bomber strip), from which Planes can be sent to assist with the imminent offensive to be launched against Japanese-held Solomon Islands. Allied Actions against Japanese ground forces up to this point have been largely lopsided. **(China-Burma-India)** The Japanese take more giant strides in Burma, capturing Kengtung, while other Japanese troops operating in China, press the Chinese to withdraw from Kinhwa, in Chekiang Province. In the vicinity of French Indo China, the U.S.S. *Seal*, cruising along the surface under a luminous moon, encounters a target in the distance. The *Seal* dives under the surface and after two attacks, wounds, but does not sink the Vessel. As the irritated Submarine closes further, to finish off the *Tatsufuku*, they are stunned by the after effects of a thunderous explosion, but they had not yet unleashed their final attack. In the past previous moments, as the *Seal* had been preparing the assault, another American Submarine, unaware of the presence of the *Seal*, had finished the job. Fortunately for the *Seal*, the Japanese Vessel had intercepted the torpedoes, launched by the U.S.S. *Swordfish* or the *Seal* might well have gone down in the history books, as the first U.S. Submarine to be sunk during the war by a U.S. Submarine.

Moving supplies in India, via truck and Camels.

May 29th 1942 — (Atlantic-Libya) Fierce fighting between Rommel's Forces and the British continues. German Armor pierces the British mine fields, pushing through newly created gaps against heavy British fire. The severity of the British fire and an organized counterattack, mounted by British 30 Corps Armored units, compel Rommel to pull back and take a temporary defensive stance, while the Germans ponder a way to open a supply route.

May 30th 1942 — (Pacific-Pearl Harbor) Admiral Fletcher's Task Force 17, including the rejuvenated *Yorktown*, departs Pearl Harbor, en route to join Admiral Spruance's Task Force 16, for the combined assault against the enemy's Midway Invasion Force. In related activity, the enemy Task Force, including two Transports, two Carriers, two Cruisers and three Destroyers, departs Japan and heads for the Aleutians, to initiate a diversionary assault. **(China-Burma-India)** The Chinese 113th Regiment, involved with covering the retreat of the Chinese 5th Army and the 38th Division, from Burma, fords the Chindwin River, heading for India. **(Atlantic)** Over 1,000 British Warplanes take off from England to assault German targets. During the evening and continuing into the early morning hours of the following day, the British Planes deposit in excess of 2,000 tons of bombs on the German city of Cologne, located on the picturesque Rhine River, in the western part of the country. **(Atlantic Libya)** In Libya, the British 8th Army continues to battle Rommel and prepares to counterattack but holds up for 24 hours. On the following day, the assault begins, achieving little success.

May 31st 1942 — (Pacific) The U.S. Task Forces of Admirals Spruance and Fletcher are about to converge on the 2nd of June, 325 miles northeast of Midway. **(Pacific-Australia)** The Japanese dispatch Midget Submarines into the harbor of Sydney; after the brief raid, they escape without harm. **(Atlantic-Libya)** Fierce fighting continues to rage as the Germans regain the momentum, driving against Sidi Muftah, defended by the 150th Brigade, 50th British Division, 13 Corps. The British mount a counterattack, but the Germans hold, forfeiting only nominal gains.

June 1st 1942 — (Pacific Australia) The harbor at Sydney, Australia is again struck by Japanese Midget Submarines, which penetrate the harbor defenses undetected, and destroy an Australian Vessel. **(Atlantic-Libya)** German pressure drives viciously against the British defenders at Sidi Muftah. The British 150th Brigade is demolished, along with the Armor unit (1st Army Tank Brigade) that had been rushed to lend its support. The Germans begin to fortify their line, while the British Eighth Army begins to plan for a counterattack.

June 1st 1942-August 15th 1943 — (North Pacific-Alaska) The Japanese Diversionary Force, intended to distract the U.S. from the primary Invasion Force, nears the Aleutians. Enemy Scout Planes have been observed at Cold Bay, Kiska and Kodiak. In addition, Japanese Seaplanes are spotted at Dutch Harbor and at Seattle. The total of American Submarines at Dutch Harbor numbers six; the *S-18, S-23, S-27, S-28, S-34,* and the *S-35*. In addition, the Aleutian Force has a contingent of 169 Planes, 11 Destroyers, five Cruisers and smaller Ships. The Japanese threat is a force of two Carriers, the *Ryuju* and the *Hayataka* accompanied by three Destroyers, two Heavy Cruisers and Auxiliary Vessels, with two Invasion Forces in their wake. The Armada maintains its course and hopes to draw the American Carriers into the net, leaving Midway with insufficient Aircover, but the Carriers of Spruance and Fletcher stay put, within reach of Midway and praying the Code-breakers are right in their assessment that the Japs will concentrate their full power against the Pacific bastion.

As the hours pass on the first of June, the tension continues to build, not only in the Pacific, at Midway, among the Commanders, but in the Aleutians and the American mainland as well. The suspense begins to unfold on the following day, when U.S. Scout Planes locate the enemy Task Force, closing fast behind a violent storm, against the Aleutians. The Land-based Planes are restrained from taking off on the 2nd, as the enemy sails within 150 miles of Unalaska, where a couple of Squadrons of Japanese Planes ascend from the Carriers, on a mission intended to harass the Americans and inflict some damage to the facilities. The enemy Pilots receive a new lesson about flying in Alaska, when they bump into intense fog, prompting many of the Planes to return to the Carriers, but others make the trip and strike Dutch Harbor installations. In addition, the Japanese Planes attack Fort Mears before returning. U.S. Guns are able to knock out one of the attacking Planes and inflict severe damage to another.

The Japanese receive some Allied offense on the following day, when the weather clears, allowing American and Canadian Planes to assault the enemy Carriers simultaneously, as the Japs make another strike at Dutch Harbor and Fort Glenn. The Japanese Carriers avoid noticeable damage and fade into the night air, moving steadily toward Kiska and Attu. Four of the Japanese Planes are shot down. Dutch Harbor, the furthest northern outpost of the U.S. co-incidentally the closest to Japan, had incurred damage. Although the invasion forces had been turned back, the troops are diverted to Attu and Kiska in the Aleutian chain, where they land unopposed on the 6th and 7th, posturing themselves as a visible threat against the United States West Coast.

However; the stunning American victory at Midway lessens the severity of the landing in the Aleutians. Japanese Carrier Forces are cut down to the two that had been in the North Pacific for this invasion. Prompt action by the U.S. Navy and Land-based Planes, will quickly neutralize the presence of the Japanese and make their stay temporary, but uncomfortable. Agile American Destroyers set up their lines to hold the horizon against any further intruders. These formidable Vessels, will be augmented by the intrepid PT-Boats, diminutive, but lethal. These Pt-Boats are a breed of their own, and proud of their unique contributions to the defeat of the Japanese. In yet another step to control the enemy, the Silent Service continues to build its complement of spirited Submarines to thwart the Japs. Dutch Harbor, situated at about an equal distance from both Pearl Harbor and Washington state, can use both points for supply and reinforcement. The siege has commenced, but the one solitary and most oppressive factor is the weather, which will constantly impede the eviction of the Japanese.

The U.S. makes fast use of obscure Military bases in Alaska. Although the Americans are not presently in an attack position, strong measures will be taken to ensure that the enemy is held in check with Planes, Surface Vessels and Submarines,

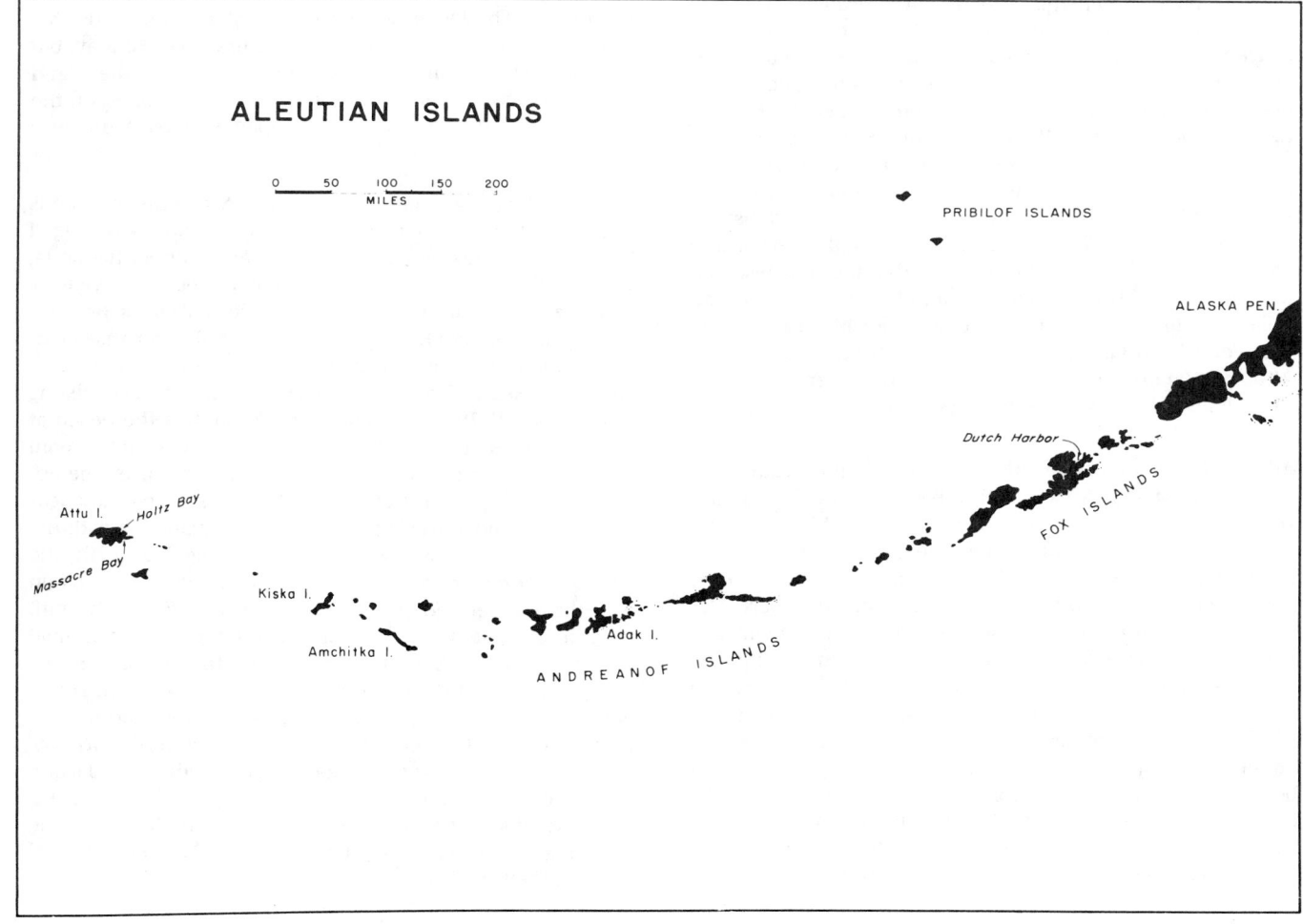

ALEUTIAN ISLANDS

until the Army is strengthened enough to reclaim the islands.

These Forces will be bolstered as Summer comes and the complement of Subs will then include the U.S.S. *Growler*, arriving during late June, followed during early July, by the *Finback, Triton, Trigger, Grunion* and *Gato*. In addition, the *Tuna* and *Halibut* arrive a little later. More S-Submarines will also arrive during July and August, when the *S-31, S-3, S-33* and last but not least, the *S-30*, moving in during August to augment the Land Forces. The initial Air Assaults do not strike Attu, which for the time being is out of range for the available Planes. The Navy plans to begin bombardments of the enemy positions, during July, but the usual terrible weather conditions postpones the initial attack until August 7th, the same day the Marines storm Guadalcanal. When Task Force 8 strikes, there is no confirmation of damage, because of the poor visibility. The U.S. selects Adak, in the Aleutians, as the designated location for an Airfield, from which to strike Kiska and troops will land there on August 30th, without incident. The Japanese on Kiska receive their first major attack on the 14th of September, when 28 Fighters and 12 Heavy Bombers drop quite a few tons of bombs on their positions, to keep them awake. The Japanese troops, which had landed on Attu, begin to move and join the Invasion force at Kiska and will complete the transfer, by the middle of September. Toward the end of October, the Japanese move back to Attu.

Before the end of the month (September), the Japanese will pull off a couple of small raids against Adak, but are preoccupied with the threat of Airraids. They are still unaware that there is no imminent plan, for the Americans to take the ground back. During December, on the 18th, a Reconnaissance Squad lands on Amchitka to determine if the terrain is suitable for a landing. The intelligence leads to a subsequent landing in mid-January, by troops commanded by General Lloyd E. Jones, who hit the beach unopposed. The Japanese soon initiate Air Raids against the Americans, but they are not a genuine threat. In the interim, the Yanks begin construction of another Airstrip to be quickly utilized against the Japanese on Kiska. Fighter Planes will land at the new facility on the 16th of February and from that day, the Japanese halt their Air raids. Two days later, Admiral McMorris, who had relieved Admiral W. Smith as Commander of Strike Group, Task Force 8, on January 4th, moves his Strike Group close to Attu, to open fire on the Japanese. They had been unscathed, since June of last year. Bad weather prevents the Navy from determining results of their raid.

Admiral Kinkaid recommends and receives authorization for an invasion of Attu. Kinkaid's Task Force 16 (previously Task Force 8), will transport the Invasion Force, which is designated to be the U.S. 7th Division. The fighting 7th is trained hard for assault. However, all its training was for the torrid conditions of mechanized war in a North African desert. The invasion is set for May 7th. The 7th Division begins embarking to their Alaska operation and will come in as different contingents, at Dutch Harbor and Adak. In the interim, the Navy helps the Air Force keep things warm for the Infantry. The Navy Surface Vessels give the Japanese a second greeting on the 26th of April when Holtz Bay and Chichagof Harbor are bombarded. As the Assault Convoy arrives at Cold Harbor on the 30th of April, allowing one week before jump off. The weather in Alaska has not cooperated with the Yanks, since the coming of the Japs and now is no exception.

The U.S. troops, waiting impatiently on Adak, are anxious to get the operation over with too. They are stationed on an island which provides nothing but water; everything else must be shipped into the base. The Engineers have constructed the Airfields out of the most forbidding of terrain. The Airstrips are actually placed in a once-shallow lagoon, with its water channeled into the sea. The Planes will land on a steel Airstrip, compliments of the U.S. Infantry, who have been given the task of putting it in place, after the Engineers have graded the lagoon. The Planes fly through all types of weather and must become familiar with landing in water, that is sometimes more than a foot deep. At times the Planes resemble speed boats moving through a channel and at other times resemble a disoriented bird making its first landing. The Pilots can't tell what the weather will be like, from one hour to the next, but missions must be flown on a twenty-four hour basis, to keep the enemy in check. Many Pilots lose their lives to enemy fire, during the endless flights. Each mission, in addition to bombarding enemy positions, is used to gather intelligence information with cameras. These observation Aircraft locate hangars, underground rail systems and the Bombers and Fighters harass the enemy on a daily basis. The Flights to harass the enemy will be ceasing soon and other flights will be covering the ground troops as they make their invasion.

The Invasion Force's departure, is delayed because of terrible weather and after the Force embarks, additional inclement weather and rough seas further impede the invasion of Attu. The lousy conditions force another postponement until the 11th of May. The Japanese on Attu, are informed of a possible invasion by the Americans during the first week of May, but they haven't seen any Yanks since they occupied the island and it appears to them, that none will be coming. So on the last days before the assault, the Japanese loosen up their defenses.

D-Day finally arrives on the 11th of May. Again, the weather is terrible, but the 7th Division, makes a successful two pronged landing, under restrained Naval guns, and without the assistance of Aircover. The Northern Force strikes in the vicinity of Holtz Bay, while the Southern Force makes its primary landing at Massacre Bay. By the afternoon, this surprise landing permits the Yanks to drive north, towards Jarmin, situated on Massacre Holtz Bay. A smaller contingent, consisting of a Platoon F, 7th Reconnaissance Troop, hits the beach at Alexai Point and moves without incident to join with the Main Force at Massacre Bay. Intense enemy fire repulses the advancing Southern Force at about 1700 hours, when they near the high ground, covering the valley. In conjunction with the Southern Force's drive, which has them moving north, the Northern Force grinds its way south, in an effort to hook up with the Southern Force. The drive pushes effortlessly, until the troops are less than a thousand yards from their original objective, Hill X. A contingent of the 7th Reconnaissance Troop and 1 Scout Company, attached to the Northern Force, had come ashore in the early morning hours, landing at a position designated Beach Scarlet, situated west of Holtz Bay. It advances inland, without opposition, heading for Jarmin Pass. The Commanding Officer, General Albert E. Brown, prepares an attack against the enemy holding the pass, for the following day; again, mother nature will play her part and paralyze the Vehicles.

On the 12th, Naval Guns burst the morning silence with a massive bombardment. In concert, are the throngs of American Planes, giving Air support to the ground forces of the 7th Infantry, advancing against Jarmin Pass. The Japanese, holding the high ground and the surrounding area, are in good position to punish the advancing Yanks. The two sided assault receives intense enemy resistance, at Hill X, but the undaunted 7th, claws its way forward, against vicious opposition and attains control of a portion of the crest of the hill. The Southern Force, assaulting in a direct frontal attack, is repelled at Jarmin Pass.

The night soon passes and on the 13th, the vicious fighting to take Jarmin Pass resumes, with incessant firing by both sides, and minimal gain. The most gruesome fighting occurs to the north, where the Japs attempt to repulse the attempt to seize Hill X; tenacity on the part of the 7th, gives them a solid piece of the hill by the time darkness arrives. Additional troops come ashore during the day to further fortify the Holtz Bay contingent, and although the weather is typically awful, the ground troops receive as much Naval and Air support as possible. The Americans are paying heavily, for their efforts to dislodge them. On the following day (14th), the ever-increasing intensity of battle continues to rage, but the Japanese retain possession of the pass.

The morning of the 15th has the 7th Division up and ready, to take another shot at the Japs holding Jarmin Pass. They awake to a day of heavy fog, which impedes their Air support. The 2nd Battalion, 32nd Infantry, advances against heavy resistance. Artillery supports the determined attack, but the assault is repulsed. The Holtz Bay Force, unable to move earlier because of the impenetrable fog, readies an attack at about 1100, just as the mysterious fog lifts. Not only has the fog lifted, but the enemy has abandoned its positions and pulled back. The Holtz Bay Force eagerly pursues close behind, until running into fierce enemy fire, pouring down from the heavily fortified heights. In addition, during the heavy day of combat, the ground troops get stung by an unsuspected source, when their Air support, intending to aid their quest, mistakes them for enemy troops and bombards their positions.

The Yanks, temporarily stymied on Attu, see their Commanding Officer, General Brown, replaced by General Eugene Landrum today. He is directed to make some fast progress. During the heated hours of ensuing combat, the Holtz Bay Force fights its way to the northern portion of the Holtz Valley Ridge, seizing a hold on the fringe, then taking the entire ridge. The Japanese, now facing assault from the rear, and a probable thrust from the front, take advantage of the cover of darkness and withdraw to Chichagof Harbor, where they have decided to make their final stand. By the following morning, the Massacre Bay Force finds no enemy opposition and occupies Jarmin Pass, in conjunction with the Holtz Bay Force, which finds no enemy troops around the Bay. The two Forces push further, with advance Patrols on the points, to hook the two forces together. By dawn of the 18th, contact is made, permitting a double strike against the bastion at Chichagof Harbor. Reinforcements have been coming in consistently and the control of Holtz Bay eases the supply problems. The Japs have withdrawn, but they have taken their tenacity with them. The fighting on the 19th, is fierce during the struggle to seize a strategic pass, standing between the Yanks and the Harbor. The coveted pass will subsequently be named

Clevesy Pass in honor of a Lieutenant attached to Company H, 32nd Infantry. The 2nd Battalion, 32nd Infantry, earns its pay, as the grinding battle to take the pass rages non-stop, falling to the Yanks by nightfall. Unfortunately, the Japanese still control the heights. As the contest spills blood at every turn, the Northern Force advances through intense enemy fire, fighting its way to secure the Holtz-Chichagof Pass, another enemy stronghold in the heights. The Americans push tenaciously against the entrenched resistance throughout the next several days, but the climb to take the high ground is brutalizing. Determined to maintain its progress, the Southern Force fights relentlessly, reaching the enemy positions which control Chichagof Valley, seizing the entrance, by the early morning hours of the 22nd. In the meantime, the Northern Force, which has been fighting non-stop for control of Fish Hook Ridge, remains where it is, to regroup. On the 23rd, the Southern Force attacks Fish Hook Ridge, but is pinned down by incessant fire, while the Northern Force is repelled at the Holtz-Sarana Pass. The Japanese positions have become compressed, but their fury has not been diminished. The 7th Division, fighting a literal uphill battle since the invasion, inches closer to the harbor. Communications between the two American forces is initiated today, giving them stronger coordination for the final drive to seize Chichagof Harbor. The struggle to seize Fish Hook Ridge continues for the next couple of days, against Japanese, entrenched in a vast tunnel chain, located just under the top of the ridge. The prolonged fight for Fish Hook Ridge culminates, on the 27th of May when the remnants of its defenders are mopped up by elements of the 7th Division. Other contingents close against the final stronghold of the Japanese Invasion Force, which had originally numbered about 2,500 men.

The Japanese, squeezed into Chichagof Harbor, make a valiant attempt to break out on the 29th, after having disregarded airdropped suggestions to surrender. The attempt is futile and now it is the newly entrenched American guns which pour fire from the high ground directly into the Japanese as they make their break. The resistance evaporates, as the enemy troops simply break off contact, fading away into smaller contingents. The Harbor is taken on the 30th, without opposition and in coordination with the operation, another Force of U.S. Army troops, commanded by Brigadier General John E. Copeland occupies Shemya Island without incident.

With Attu in possession, the Americans set their sights on Kiska. Troops are being specially trained in the states, in addition to others being readied in the Aleutians. The Air Force will pummel the area for a long period of time, before the actual invasion date, scheduled for August 15th. The weeks pass quickly and the Japanese, manage to evacuate Kiska without detection. When the Invasion Force, numbering over 34,000 troops, hits the beach, it finds no opposition. The elusive Japs had been retrieved and sent back to Japan. The Japanese that did occupy Kiska were so severely punished by the Air Force, that they spent most of their time hibernating in their underground lodgings.

June 2nd-6th 1942 — THE BATTLE OF MIDWAY — American intelligence reports prove correct. The Japanese Invasion Fleet is steaming towards Midway, unaware that two U.S. Task Forces 16 and 17, are rendezvousing northeast of Midway, before moving jointly to a point, about 200 miles from Midway to meet the enemy Armada. Japanese Fighters, dispatched from two Carriers, raid Fort Mears and Dutch Harbor,

Battle of Midway. Illustration, by Justin Crecescu.

Alaska, in an unsuccessful attempt to divert attention from the Japanese troops landing in the Aleutians. In addition to the U.S. Surface Vessels, the U.S. deploys 12 Submarines around Midway. The *Trigger, Narwhal* and *Plunger* deploy at a point where they can run interference between Oahu and Midway keeping a vigil to the east and north. Four other Submarines camp about 300 miles north of Oahu, while six additional Submarines are racing to the scene. The lone *Cuttlefish*, holds the point, about 700 miles out, to relay the signal at the first sign of the invaders. The U.S.S. *Saratoga*, a formidable Carrier, would be a welcome sight to the Yanks, but her voyage from the States, prevents her from reaching Midway in time. During the first rays of sunshine on the 4th, the *Cuttlefish* reports an enemy Tanker about 600 miles from Midway, then is forced to submerge, because of daylight and does not regain contact with the enemy. Shortly thereafter, Scout Planes detect the Invasion Force.

On the 4th, the Japanese strike Dutch Harbor again, causing slight damage. American Planes search in vain for the Carriers. Poor visibility works in favor of the Japanese, allowing them to escape southward without damage, but the Japanese ruse fails to rattle Nimitz. Search Planes based at Midway locate a genuine bonanza on the second of June, discovering two Japanese Carriers 400 miles south of Kiska.

Land-based Bombers, swarm above the approaching enemy Vessels on the 3rd, inflicting some damage, but not enough turn back the invaders. One hundred and thirty Japanese Planes are launched from four Carriers on the 4th, to destroy Midway and its defenders. The threat is met initially by U.S. Marine Corps Planes based on Midway. As the danger signals rattle the communication lines, every available Plane is sent

aloft. Approximately 50 Zeros, with superior maneuverability and speed, lead the parade, escorting an array of nearly 100 Dive Bombers and Torpedo Planes. The formation is interrupted, about 30 miles from their objective, when Marine Pilots pounce on the Bombers, before the Zeros can come to their aid. The badly outnumbered Marines, attached to Fighting Squadron 213, do a magnificent job, considering the odds. During the Air duel, the Jap Bombers penetrate and strike Midway. Fifteen of the 25 Marine Fighters are shot down and another seven are severely damaged, but they make their way back to Midway. The Japanese pay a high price for their Air attack, losing 34 Planes (damaged or shot down). The Marine Pilots return to base, passing over the smiling faces of the defenders who are waving excitedly in the shadow of Old Glory. They had intentionally avoided bombing the Airfields, that they might utilize the fields themselves in the near future. Instead, the Airfields remain useful to the Yanks.

Although the Marines, whacked the Japs as they encroached Midway, all hell is breaking out in the battle zones. Army Bombers, based on Midway and without Fighter cover stream through the skies, heading for the objective, as quickly as the coordinates of the enemy Strike Force are received through the radio system, zooming for the anticipated location of the enemy Carriers. The staunch aggressiveness of a PBY had made contact with the Strike Force, at a position about 150 miles from Midway and now the Eagles are close behind. While the Fortresses advance, the Submarines receive their orders; the *Cuttlefish*, and the *Flying Fish* and the *Cachalot*, are ordered to stand fast, while other Submarines are ordered to attack the Carriers. The unescorted Army B-26s and Navy Torpedo Planes dive without cover fire and are mangled by Antiaircraft fire and Jap Zeros. This heroic assault by six Torpedo Planes (Avengers) and four B-26s (Marauders) cost the U.S. seven Planes, as one TBF and two B-26s return alone. Additional Marine Squadrons follow the fury and are synchronized in the attack, with the Flying Fortresses. The Marine Dive Bombers penetrate the flying steel, again without cover fire. Out of 27 Dive Bombers who crash through the Zeros and ack-ack, eight are shot down and the remainder sustain severe damage. The Fortresses expend all bombs, but none strike the mark, invigorating the Japanese, who still contemplate the seizure of Midway. The unscathed Japanese Carriers have evaded destruction and receive reports detailing the location of the American Carriers, which are slightly beyond the horizon. At about 09:00, the Japanese alter their course to seek out the *Enterprise* and her counterparts, the *Hornet* and *Yorktown*.

Pilots from the *Hornet* and *Enterprise* desperately attempt to locate the Jap Flattops, but their fuel diminishes rapidly as the Japanese have changed course, making the Americans' task even tougher as they scour the clouds. The Flying Fighters from the *Hornet* are compelled to ditch at sea and the Bombers must head for Midway or suffer the same fate. The worries of the day become more serious for the Yanks at Midway, the most vulnerable of the objectives. Japanese Bombers from the *Enterprise* are skyward, but they see nothing, but wide open seas. Suddenly, a Squadron of Fighters from the *Enterprise* spots the enemy Carriers and roars the location to the Bombers. They immediately close the range in conjunction with testy Fighters from the *Yorktown*, whose memories of the Coral Sea are still vivid in their minds. As luck would have it, the Japanese on the *Kaga*, are caught reloading the Bombers as Planes from the *Yorktown* arrive. First, the Japs receive several reprieves. Torpedo Squadron 8, fresh off the *Hornet*, approaches, again without Fighter protection. The dauntless Pilots begin the attack, just prior to 09:30, fully realizing the expected odds and the entire Squadron, commanded by Lt. Commander John C. Waldron, of 15 is downed. The lone survivor is Ensign George H. Gay. The Pacific Theater is about to make a fibber out of Barnum, for it is Ensign Gay, who is about to have the front row seat, at the greatest show on earth, at least if you count the Pacific Theater. As Gay ponders his fate, while clinging to his life preserver, the clock nears 10:00 as friendly Yankee engines roar overhead, bound for the Carriers. A Torpedo Squadron from the Enterprise dives through the flying lead, followed closely by additional Skywarriors from the *Yorktown*. As an astonished Ensign Gay watches, a most magnificent roar trembles over the ocean. The initial explosion is soon followed by more, until the *Kaga* is consumed by fire and smoke. The battle rages, with more bombs striking, and more explosions, literally catapulting Japanese Sailors from the decks into the nearby inferno of the once unspoiled waters, which have instantly been transformed into a vision of carnage and wreckage. Both the *Akagi* and *Soryu* are ablaze. The American Planes return to their Carriers, although 10 Torpedo Bombers, from the *Yorktown* and a like number from the *Enterprise* are shot down. However, there are three less operational Carriers in the Japanese Navy.

Japanese Planes discover the location of the American Carriers at about 12:00 and close for the attack with 36 Planes, equally divided between Dive Bombers and Zeros. Twelve Fighters from the *Yorktown* are launched in quick succession, to meet the threat and they knock out half of the Bombers.

Several Japs break through the skywall, to be knocked down by gunners, but three bombs strike the Carrier, causing severe fires. The crew works feverishly to extinguish the inferno, but as they do, another group of Torpedo Bombers swoops down on the wounded Carrier. The Gunners knock out every Plane, but the Vessel is rocked with several additional torpedoes. Soon, Captain Elliot Buckmaster is forced to abandon his Carrier. The score is three to one, but the loss of the *Yorktown* is critical to the American cause. The key to victory depends on finding the 4th Jap Carrier, the *Hiryu*, which is retreating to the northeast, while the other three are burning, in what might be the biggest fish fry outside of Tokyo. The *Hiryu*, flanked by her escorts, is speeding out of the area, but Spotter Planes from the *Yorktown* locate the enemy Armada, which includes the lone Carrier, still operational and two Battleships, a few Destroyers and two Cruisers. Planes from the *Hornet* and the *Enterprise* are called out and combine to knock out the Carrier. Incessant enemy fire greets them, as they make the approach, from 10 Zeros but the *Hiryu* is hit and set ablaze. While the attackers from the *Enterprise* are pummeling the Hiryu, other Planes from the *Hornet* assault the escort Vessels.

Ensign Gay, remarkably floating alone in the middle of this gigantic graveyard in the sea, is unaware that he is not the only American in the area. Several fathoms below, lies the impetuous U.S.S. *Nautilus*, the only Submarine, out of a cast of 29, that will play a major part in the show. The crew of the *Nautilus* is a little aggravated with the day so far, as she has been assaulted at about 08:00, by a Jap Plane and a couple of aggressive Cruisers. A little later in the morning, the *Nautilus* spots a peculiar looking Vessel, a Battleship. The Warship now attacks the periscope of the Nautilus, while the crew is on its deck, scurrying around, anticipating a jubilant kill. The curious periscope scans the water and sees enemy Vessels at every point of revolution. Brockman, disgruntled by the irreverent treatment by his hosts, shakes loose of a barrage of depth charges, and rears forward to attack. The *Nautilus* fires torpedoes at a Cruiser, bringing even more depth charges. The Armada move ahead, leaving a lone Destroyer to catch *Nautilus*. The Destroyer searches in vain, but the Submarine skirts under the waves at a zesty pace, then impulsively, pokes her periscope atop the water, enabling the Vessel, to observe a sky full of bursting shells strewn in umbrella style, high above an enemy Carrier. Above the shellfire, is a more delightful view; soaring American Planes. Enemy escorts spot the protruding eye of the Submarine and initiate an attack. Taking corrective action, the *Nautilus* fires her torpedoes before diving for cover to the bottom. The enemy evades the incoming torpedoes and starts dropping depth charges wide of the *Nautilus*, which is beached nervously in sand. At about 10:00 it goes up for another look and finds all is clear, except for a few blazing Carriers, as reported over the radio. The *Nautilus* creeps near the burning, but operational Carrier *Soryu*, and fires a few poignant torpedoes. All three torpedoes hit the mark, triggering severe explosions and finally, a thunderous roar, that rocks the entire area after the Vessel is half way to the bottom. The final explosions are so terrifyingly violent, that the *Nautilus* momentarily thinks it is under attack. The periscope verifies no Ships, friend or foe, and the men of the *Nautilus* enjoy their dinner. Ensign Gay, holding the only front seat for the *Nautilus* performance, has enjoyed the show and will be later rescued to tell the tale.

The day is full of fury, heroics and glory. In another instance of American fortitude, Captain Richard Fleming's (U.S.M.C. Squadron 241) craft is struck by 179 hits during the day. His Plane dips to an altitude of 400 feet, to release its bombs, during the initial attack. He returns against the enemy again and after scoring a near miss from an altitude of 500 feet, is struck by additional enemy fire, that forces the courageous Pilot to crash in the sea. All in all, it has been a calamitous day for the Imperial Navy. The chastened Admiral Yamamoto has no choice, but to attempt to get back to Japan. He instructs a group of Cruisers, from his Occupation Force, to move close to Midway in a diversionary tactic, to lambaste the island, preventing Aircraft from pursuing him. However, the U.S. has this one figured out also. All the Submarines, which had been dispersed to search for the enemy, are hastily recalled to their original positions, to protect Midway in the event of an invasion and are deployed by the early morning of June 5th. The Japanese move cautiously, toward Midway, but are surprised to find the Submarines waiting in ambush. Contact is made, with unidentified Vessels, by the U.S.S. *Tambor*, at slightly after 02:00, but extreme caution is taken by Lt. Commander Murphy, in the event that they might be American Ships. Further probing by the Submarine verifies the Vessels as hostile Cruisers and unquestionably Japanese. The *Tambor*, dives as the enemy cruisers approach. When it comes up to periscope depth, the Tambor finds all four Cruisers had swung to the left, causing two to collide immediately after sighting the American Submarine. Yamamoto, finding more futility in the belated endeavor, orders the attack aborted well before the sun comes out. The four Cruisers retreat, with the *Mikuma* and the *Mogami*, both damaged, and lagging behind. Planes from Midway, following the trail of oil from the damaged *Mikuma*, deliver a brutalizing attack on the 6th of June. The Air assault incapacitates the *Mikuma* and staggers the *Mogami*. Admiral Spruance then dispatches Aircraft from the *Hornet* and *Enterprise* to finish the job. The Dive Bombers bury the *Mikuma* and take a severe toll on the *Mogami*. Amazingly, the Vessel is able to crawl back to Truk. Midway is saved, but again the cost is high. The gallant *Yorktown* is knocked out of action and while being towed to Pearl Harbor for repairs, one of three enemy Submarines, operating around Midway is able to get off four torpedoes, two of which strike the *Yorktown* and the other two hit the Destroyer *Hammann*. A tremendous explosion ignites the Vessel's ammunition, killing many of the crew and further damaging the nearby *Yorktown*, ensuring her demise. Other Warships in the area rush to get the Submarine *I-168*, culminating the battle. On the following morning, at 05:00, the *Yorktown* rolls over and sinks.

Admirals Nimitz, Spruance and Fletcher are the victors. Admiral Halsey, unable to oversee his Task Force, had made an admirable choice in Spruance. The U.S. Headquarters at Pearl is ecstatic as word had reached them about Yamamoto's retreat back to Japan. The U.S. Navy begins rescue operations, picking up surviving Pilots who had ditched in the Pacific. Aircraft losses on both sides are extremely heavy, costing the U.S. 150 Planes and the Japanese over 250. Surviving Japanese Pilots are rare, as few are issued parachutes. The Three American Carriers had turned the tide of battle and although the Yanks suffer the loss of the *Yorktown*, it has a successor, the *Saratoga* heading for the Pacific Theater. The principal body of Yamamoto's assault forces have escaped unscathed, but the Japanese have lost over 4,500 Sailors, and four Car-

riers during this confrontation. The Imperial Navy is down to only two Carriers and they have been preoccupied in the Aleutians, where U.S. and Canadian forces have stopped the Japanese thrust into Alaska. Yamamoto, devastated personally by the defeat, is prepared to call back the Aleutian force, but decides to instruct them to land at Attu and Kiska. In addition, the two consecutive losses at the Coral Sea and on Midway, has cost precious experienced Japanese Pilots. Both Air and Sea power in the Pacific now favor the United States. The U.S. Navy had won the decisive victory needed to raise morale and place the momentum on the side of the Allies.

June 3rd 1942 — (United States) The U.S.S. *Bunting* (AMc-7), a Minesweeper is involved in a collision in San Francisco Bay and sinks. **(Aleutians)** Japanese bomb Dutch Harbor Fort Mears and Unalaska Island.

U.S. Boeing B-26A Bombers.

U.S. Grumman Torpedo Bombers.

June 3rd 1942 — Dutch Harbor, Alaska under attack by Japanese Planes.

June 4th 1942 — **(Pacific-Midway)** The island of Midway is attacked by Carrier Based Japanese Aircraft. They are intercepted and defeated by Marine Corps and Army Aircraft operating out of Midway. The Japanese claim all Level Bombers and 36 Dive Bombers broke through Marine interceptors and struck targets. In addition, they claim one Dive Bomber shot down by AA fire and two Fighters do not return to their Ships (first wave). In the sea battle, the U.S.S. *Yorktown* is damaged by Japanese Aircraft. The Japanese Carrier *Kaga* is sunk by Carrier Based Planes and the Carrier *Soryu* is destroyed by the combined force of Carrier based Aircraft and the Submarine *Nautilus* (SS-168) (SEE June 2nd-6th 1942). The Japanese contend that the *Nautilus* had not sunk the *Soryu*, but rather had fired at the *Kaga*, without results. Japanese war records show no Submarine attacks against *Soryu*.

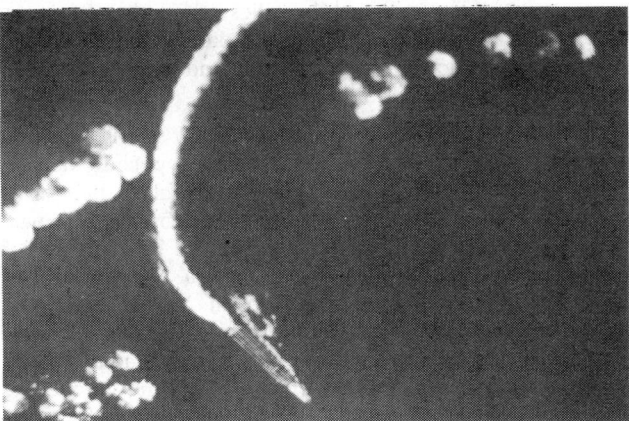

June 2nd-6th 1942 — A Japanese Carrier burning, during the Battle of Midway.

June 2nd-6th 1942 — The U.S.S. Yorktown (CV-5) under attack during the Battle of Midway.

June 5th 1942 — **(United States)** The U.S. Congress declares war on Bulgaria, Hungary, and Rumania. **(Pacific-Midway)** During the battle of Midway, the Japanese Carriers *Akagi* and *Hiryu*, both severely damaged by the American Planes, are self destroyed (SEE June 2nd-6th 1942).

June 7th 1942 — **(United States)** Several changes occur within the command structure of the U.S. Navy. The Atlantic and Pacific Fleets, Sea Frontiers and Special Task Forces all come under the command of Admiral E.J. King (Commander in Chief U.S. Fleet and Chief of Naval Operations). Other changes place the Local Defense Forces, Naval Transportation Services, Special Duty Ships and the Naval District Vessels come under the jurisdiction of Vice Admiral A. J. Horne, the Vice Chief of Naval Operations. **(Pacific-Midway)** The U.S.S. *Yorktown*, badly damaged during the fight at Midway, is sunk by a Submarine torpedo while she is withdrawing (SEE June 2nd-6th 1942). **(Atlantic-Bermuda)** The U.S.S. *Gannet* (AVP-8), a Submarine Tender, becomes the victim of an enemy Submarine off the coast of Bermuda. **(North Pacific-Aleutians)** A Japanese landing force, consisting of 1,800 men, debarks on Attu and Kiska unopposed. Weather conditions in the Aleutians are quite terrible at this time, making it difficult for the Allies to respond. Allied Commanders, upon knowledge of the enemy forces, subsequently dispatch Air strikes against Kiska. Attu, at the present time, is beyond the range of the Allied Planes. Allied Surface Ships commence firing on Japanese positions in the Aleutians for the first time, on August 7th, when a Task Force, commanded by Rear Admiral W.W. Smith (contingent of North Pacific Force under Admiral Theobald) commences a bombardment. U.S. troops land on the Aleutians (Adak), without resistance, on August 30th. Also on the 7th, American Brigadier General Howard C. Davison assumes Command of the Seventh Air Force, replacing Major General Clarence L. Tinker, who was killed at the battle of Midway.

June 8th 1942 — **(Pacific)** General MacArthur, enthusiastic since the American victory at Midway, recommends to General Marshall that a limited offensive should be initiated to regain positions in the Bismarck Archipelago. **(Pacific-New Guinea)** In New Guinea, a detachment of Australians and Americans flies from Port Moresby to Milne Bay to consider a site for an Air Base, needed to strengthen their defenses. **(Atlantic)** The U.S. Army establishes the European Theater of Operations, which will supersede U.S. Army forces in the British Isles. Major General James E. Chaney will command.

June 9th 1942 — **(Pacific)** Allied Resistance in the Philippines ceases. Japan is in complete control, with the exception of minor Guerrilla units, operating from the mountains. The organized force of 140,000 defenders is no longer operational, as a fighting unit (subject to Wainright's earlier surrender). **(North Pacific-Aleutians)** The U.S. Navy establishes an Operating Base at Kodiak, Alaska in the Aleutians.

June 10th 1942 — **(Atlantic)** The Germans occupy Bir Hacheim, Libya, after British General Ritchie orders evacuation. On the Russian Front, the Germans inch toward Sevastopol.

June 11th 1942 — **(United States)** The East Coast of the United States is again penetrated by enemy Submarines. German Submarines deploy mines in the vicinity of Delaware Bay and off the coast of Boston. On the following day, U-Boats place mines in Shipping lanes off the coast of Cape Henry, Va. **(Atlantic)** The Russians tap Uncle Sam for a bonus. The Russians convince the U.S. and Britain to allow them to repay lend-lease debts in kind, rather than in cash. In Libya, the Germans begin to move north, toward Tobruk from its base at Bir Hacheim.

June 12th 1942 — **(Atlantic)** The U.S. initiates Air raids on German positions at Ploesti, Rumania. The massive B-24s depart from Africa, in an attempt to destroy the rich oil fields. Some of the Bombers are forced to make emergency landings in Turkey and are interned.

June 13th 1942 — (United States) Four enemy agents are put ashore at Amagansett, Long Island, by a German Submarine. Four additional enemy agents will depart a German Submarine, at Ponte Vedra Beach, Florida, on the 17th. All eight enemy agents will be captured by June 27th. Much of the success of the seizure of the enemy agents is due to the Coast Guard, because one of their active beach patrols had discovered the landing in New York. Subsequently the F.B.I. quickly becomes involved. **(Atlantic-Cuba)** The U.S.S. *Thetis* (PC-115), a Cutter, encounters and sinks a German Submarine, the *U-157* near Cuba.

June 14th 1942 — (Pacific) The first contingent of the 1st Marine Division (5th Marines) arrives at Wellington, New Zealand. **(Atlantic-North Africa)** The British, under General Ritchie, in Libya, are pushed back further by superior German Tanks at El Adem. The Germans move toward Acroma and Tobruk, against heavy opposition. On the following day, British Major General Klopper receives orders to hold Tobruk at all costs. Superior enemy forces will take Tobruk on June 21st, pushing the British to Egypt.

June 17th 1942 — (United States) Another German Submarine enters U.S. waters in the vicinity of Jacksonville, Florida, at Ponte Vedra Beach. Local fisherman spot this unusual site and immediately report the landing of German spies to the F.B.I.

June 18th 1942 — (United States) British Prime Minister Winston Churchill arrives in the United States to confer with President Roosevelt. The two men will agree on a campaign to be launched against the Germans in Northwest Africa. **(Atlantic-Cuba)** The U.S. Navy establishes another Naval Air Facility at La Fe, Cuba. **(Atlantic-England)** In England, General Spaatz assumes command of the U.S. Eighth Air Force. On the following day, Admiral Ghormley takes Command of the South Pacific Force and South Pacific Area. **(Atlantic)** The Germans make further progress against the Russians, in the vicinity of Sevastopol.

June 19th 1942 — (North Pacific-Aleutians) The U.S. Submarine *S-27*, operating near Amchitka in the Aleutians, attempts a reconnaissance mission, however, the treacherous weather causes the Ship to be thrown to the rocks while it is attempting to regain its power. The Sub's crew, (40 men) using a three man boat, eventually succeed in reaching shore and are rescued about a week later and evacuated to Dutch Harbor.

June 20th 1942 — (International) The Arnold-Portal-Towers agreement is signed. The agreement concerns U.S. Air commitments and provides a strong Air Force for Operation Bolero. It will be approved by both the U.S. Joint Chiefs of Staff and the Combined Chiefs of Staff by July 2. **(Pacific-Australia)** The reliability of the M-14 Torpedo is coming under close scrutiny as far too many American Submarines miss the targets for no apparent reason. Admiral Lockwood orders testing, to be conducted at Albany, Australia. By the end of July, suspicions are confirmed. How many American fighting men are dead because of the defective torpedoes can never be determined. The problems concerning proper depth detonation have been solved, but the torpedo is still plagued with other ills. Admiral Lockwood, in Command for nine weeks, brings the problem out in the open to the great satisfaction of the Submariners.

June 21st 1942 — (United States) A Japanese Submarine surfaces near the shores of Oregon and commences firing on Fort Stevens. On the previous day, a Japanese Submarine had surfaced near Vancouver Island in British Columbia and bombarded Estevan Point. **(Atlantic-North Africa)** Tobruk, Libya is seized by the Germans.

June 22nd 1942 — (United States) Fort Stevens, Oregon, located near the mouth of the Columbia River is shelled by a Japanese Submarine, becoming the first Continental Military Fort to come under attack by foreign forces, since the War of 1812. No damage is sustained by the Fort. Fort Stevens is the only domestic U.S. Military Base to be attacked during World War II.

June 24th 1942 — (Atlantic) The Germans in North Africa, under Rommel, move against the Allies, who have withdrawn from Libya into Egypt. **(Atlantic-England)** Major General Dwight D. Eisenhower assumes command of the European Theater of Operations, U.S.A.

June 25th 1942 — (Pacific) American Admiral King and General Marshall U.S.A., meet to discuss the proposed offensive (Bismarck Archipelago). Santa Cruz Island, Tulagi, along with other islands in the area are to be seized by the Marines. After securing the Islands, the Marines will be replaced by U.S. Army troops, now based in Australia. **(Pacific-Japan)** The U.S.S. *Nautilus*, lurking near Honshu, Japan, detects the Japanese Destroyer *Yamakaze* by use of radar and sinks it. before the Japanese can use its depth charges. Radar on Submarines is not yet sophisticated, but that is about to change. Western Electric produces a type of Radar known as SJ and it becomes available during the summer. It will have greater capabilities, including the ability of the Submarines to scan beyond their range of normal visibility. SJ Radar can overcome surface haze as well as stormy seas and darkness. **(Atlantic)** British General Auchinleck relieves General Ritchie of command and takes personal control of the British 8th Army in Egypt-Libya and continues the British withdrawal to El 'Alamein.

June 26th 1942 — (United States) Major General Alexander Vandegrift, Commanding Officer 1st Marine Division, is informed of the impending assault on Guadalcanal-Tulagi. Total Marine Corps strength at the end of June will stand at 142,413; of which 7,138 are Officers. **(Atlantic-Cuba)** The U.S. establishes an Auxiliary Air Station at San Julian, Cuba. **(Atlantic-Germany)** Germany proclaims its intention to authorize its Submarines to operate along the East Coast of the United States without limitations.

June 27th 1942 — (United States) All eight of the enemy agents put ashore on Long Island and Florida have been captured. No sabotage has occurred. The eight are court martialled, with six executed. **(Pacific)** General MacArthur finishes his plans for the New Britain-New Ireland-Admiralty Island Offensive.

June 28th 1942 — (Atlantic-Russia) The Germans initiate their principal summer offensive, making additional progress against the Russians at Sevastopol. **(Atlantic-North Africa)** In Egypt, the Germans penetrate Allied positions at Fuka, forcing the 29th Brigade, Indian 5th Division, to retire toward El 'Alamein. In the Middle East, Lt. General Lewis H. Brereton assumes command of the newly established U.S. Army, Middle East Air Force.

June 29th 1942 — (Pacific-New Guinea) A contingent of the U.S. 46th Engineers arrives at Milne Bay in New Guinea, and begins constructing an Air Base.

Sailors embarking San Diego, California.

June 30th 1942 — (United States) The U.S. Army Headquarters Company for Army forces in the South Pacific Area is organized at Fort Ord, California. The total number of Navy, Coast Guard and Marine Personnel at this time is 843,096; Navy, 640,570; Coast Guard, 58,998; and Marines 143,528. In other activity, the U.S.S. *Hornbill* (AMC-13), a Minesweeper is involved in a collision in San Francisco Bay, and sinks. **(Pacific-New Guinea)** The Australian Kanga Force, presently guarding the Bulolo Valley, initiates its first offensive action, when it attacks enemy positions at Salamaua. This raid is followed by an attack against Lae within a few days. **(Atlantic-Egypt)** The Axis troops near El 'Alamein, unhampered by the efforts of the British Eighth Army. The British finish their planned withdrawal and take defensive positions, including the British 30 Corps, defending the north flank and the 13 Corps guarding the south flank. In addition, the 10 Corps staff is withdrawn to command the Delta Force, which has the responsibility of defending Alexandria and the Nile Delta. **Atlantic-Naval)** Naval Land Based Planes detect and sink the German U-Boat *U-701* in the Western Atlantic. **(Atlantic-Russia)** The Germans expand the offensive towards the Don River in the south sector. The 2nd Army and the 4th Panzers drive toward the river at Voronezh and the 6th Army pushes southeast of Belgorod. In the Crimea, the struggle for Sevastopol reaches its last stage. The German Army Group South finishes the reduction of the Russian fortress at Sevastopol on the following day.

July 1st 1942 — (United States) The 2nd Marines, reinforced 2nd Marine Division, embarks from California, being transported by five U.S. Ships and escorted by the U.S.S. *Wasp*. **(Egypt)** The Axis troops capture Deir el Shein, after overrunning the positions of the Indian 18th Brigade Group south of the British fortress at El 'Alamein.

July 2nd 1942 — (United States) The Joint Chiefs of Staff agree on the proposed plan to take the offensive in the Pacific. The target date is set for 1st August, but will be postponed until 7th August when U.S. Marines invade Guadalcanal in the first U.S. land offensive of the war.

July 2nd-20th 1942 — (Pacific-Australia) General MacArthur, has been contemplating his parting words to General Wainright, as he departed Corregidor, heading for Australia,

several months ago ("I'LL MAKE IT THROUGH AND I SHALL RETURN.") Now that command priorities have been clearly set, he can begin to keep his word. Upon his arrival in Australia, he had found the Aircraft in deplorable condition and the Army, mostly posted on paper rosters. Today, MacArthur prepares to turn the American initiative to the offense and prepares to halt the Japanese in New Guinea, before they can overrun Port Moresby. The key to his strategy is the Owen Stanley Mountains. MacArthur's profound spoken words after his arrival in Australia: "WE SHALL WIN OR WE SHALL DIE," soon sets the tone on New Guinea, a do-or-die campaign for the Australians and the Americans. General MacArthur establishes his advance headquarters at Port Moresby, and from here the Allies begin to repulse the Japanese under General Tomatore Horri.

July 4th 1942 — (North Pacific-Aleutians) The U.S.S. *Triton* (SS-201), commanded by Lt. Commander Kilpatrick, is cruising off the coast of Aggattu, in the Aleutians, where she encounters and sinks a Japanese Destroyer, the *Nenohi*, after stalking it for approximately 10 hours. Two torpedoes had been fired, with only one hitting the mark, but the Vessel rolls over while crewmembers are moving down the starboard side, walking directly into the water. On the following day, another Japanese Warship, the Destroyer, *Arare* will be sunk near Kiska, in the Aleutians, by the U.S.S. *Growler* (SS-215), a formidable Submarine. The *Growler* spots three Destroyers in the harbor and inches close to fire single shots at each of the first two targets and two torpedoes at the third. The raid not only sinks one Destroyer, but also creates enough damage to ensure the other two are pulled back to Tokyo for repairs. Lt. Commander Howard Gilmore and his Submariners will continue to venture beneath the sea and destroy a few more Jap Ships. **(Atlantic)** The United States begins to participate in the Air Campaign in Western Europe. Six American Aircraft join the R.A.F., in a raid against enemy positions in Holland. **(China-Burma-India)** The American Volunteer Group, which had been flying for China, against the Japanese, is now placed into the U.S. Tenth Air Force, after its contract with China is ended.

July 5th 1942 — (Atlantic-Russia) The Germans end organized Russian resistance in the Crimea today. Further North, the Germans are hitting stiff Russian resistance, as their 4th Panzer Army advances to the Don River at Voronezh. The Panzers press on and seize Voronezh on the following day.

July 7th 1942 — (United States) A German U-Boat, the *U-701*, encroaches near North Carolina and the U.S. Army dispatches Planes, which sink it. **(Pacific-Hawaii)** A U.S. Task Force, including the Carriers *Enterprise* and *Saratoga*, departs Pearl Harbor, for the South Pacific. The main body will remain at sea while a contingent of Vessels proceeds to New Caledonia and picks up the Marine 1st Raider Battalion. **(Atlantic-Iceland)** The U.S. Navy initiates another Naval Air Facility at Reykjavik, Iceland.

July 8th 1942 — (Pacific) Admiral Ghormley and General MacArthur agree to wait for further reinforcements before initiating the Solomon invasion, but the Joint Chiefs of Staff will direct the invasion to go as planned. Admiral Nimitz orders the South Pacific Force to seize Guadalcanal and Santa Cruz Island. **(China-Burma-India)** General Chennault assumes command of the Chinese Air Task Force. **(Russia)** The Germans force the evacuation of the Soviet Army from St. Oskol, southeast of Kursk.

Control Tower at Espiritu Santo, New Hebrides.

July 9th 1942 — (Pacific-Australia) Advance elements of the Australian 7th Brigade depart Townsville, Australia and head for Milne Bay in New Guinea. **(Atlantic-Russia)** The Germans split Army Group South into two sections. The objective for Group A (1st Panzers, 11th and 17th Armies) is the capture of Rostov and then drive through the Caucasus. Group B, consisting of the 4th Panzers, 2nd, Hungarian, 2nd and 6th Armies, is to capture Stalingrad, then move on Astrakhan.

July 10th 1942 — (Pacific-Philippines) Filipino resistance fighters continue their harassment raids against the Japanese. Today, radio messages are sent in an attempt to reach General MacArthur. The signals are picked up on the Japanese controlled island of Java, by an Allied sympathizer. The message in part, sent by Lieutenant Colonel Nakar: "DETACHMENTS OF FILIPINO-AMERICAN FORCES — WE HAVE NOT SURRENDERED — ARE ACTIVELY RAIDING BARRIOS AND TOWNS OF PANGASINAN, INCLUDING DAGUPAN." "YOUR VICTORIOUS RETURN IS THE NIGHTLY SUBJECT OF PRAYER IN EVERY FILIPINO HOME." LT. Colonel Nakar is caught and murdered by the Japanese. **(Pacific-New Guinea)** An Allied Reconnaissance Squad flies from Port Moresby to Buna to reconnoiter the area and determine whether the terrain is suitable for an Airfield site. **(Atlantic-North Africa-Egypt)** The Tel el Eisa mounds, east of El 'Alamein, are contingents of the 30 Corps, British Eighth Army. Counterattacks

to retake the ground are thrown back. **(Alantic-Russia)** The Russians announce the loss of Rossosh.

July 11th 1942 — (Pacific) The Japanese cancel their plans to seize Fiji, New Caledonia and Samoa. **(Pacific-New Zealand)** The rear echelon of the 1st Marine Division arrives at Wellington. **(Atlantic-Russia)** German Army Group A seizes Lisichensk, as it continues toward Rossosh.

July 12th 1942 — (Pacific-Australia) The U.S. 41st Division, undergoing training in the vicinity of Melbourne, departs for Rockhampton. **(Pacific-New Guinea)** Contingents of the Australian 39th Battalion, pushing overland from Port Moresby, advance to Kokoda.

July 13th 1942 — (Pacific) The U.S. 32nd Division departs Adelaide, heading to a camp in the vicinity of Brisbane Australia. In other activity, American Major General George C. Kenney, Commanding General 4th Air Force, is ordered to assume command of the Allied Air Force. Kenney replaces General Brett. **(Atlantic-British West Indies)** The United States, making good use of its agreement with the British to allow American Bases in their possessions, establishes a Naval Air Facility in Grand Cayman. **(Atlantic-Panama)** A German Submarine, the *U-153* is operating near Panama, when detected by the U.S. Forces. The German Submarine is damaged by a Submarine Chaser, the PC-458 and Army Planes, then sunk by the Destroyer U.S.S. *Lansdowne* (DD-486). **(Atlantic-Soviet Union)** The Soviet Military Council decides to withdraw its forces to positions behind the Volga, but to hold Stalingrad regardless of cost. This information leaks directly to German Intelligence (FHO) and within a few days the information is forwarded to Berlin. Lt. Colonel Gehlen, will conclude this as a first step in the anticipated Russian counter-offensive.

July 14th 1942 — (Pacific-Australia) Major General Millard F. Harmon is named Commander of U.S. Army Forces in the South Pacific area. The Solomon Islands invasion campaign is underway, as Task Force 44 departs Brisbane, Australia, heading for New Zealand. A Submarine Task Force (TF42) is dispatched to disrupt enemy Shipping in the vicinity of Rabaul, and the 7th Marines, 1st Marine Division is notified by Admiral Ghormley that it will leave Samoa for the Solomons in four days.

July 15th 1942 — (United States) The Navy establishes the Naval Air Transport Service Squadron (VR-3). It will be operational within the U.S. and its Headquarters will be Kansas City, Kansas. In other activity, another German Submarine, the *U-576*, encroaching on the coast of North Carolina, is sunk by Naval Planes (Land based VS-9) assisted by the Merchant Vessel *Unicoi*, exhibit no Southern hospitality and sink the intruder. **(Southwest Pacific)** The Allies prepare plans for the seizure of Buna, on the northern coast of New Guinea. The plan is coded "OPERATION PROVIDENCE." **(Pacific-New Hebrides)** Elements of the 4th Marine Defense Battalion arrive at Espiritu Santo, bringing heavy antiaircraft and automatic weapon batteries. **(Pacific-Midway)** A Submarine Base is established at Midway to bolster the U.S. strength in the area. **(North Pacific-Aleutians)** The U.S.S. *Grunion* (SS-216), protecting the waters around Kiska in the Aleutians, encounters two Japanese Submarine Chasers. The *Grunion*, fires three torpedoes, all which miss. The deadly encounter continues and later in the day, a scrambled type message arrives at headquarters, with the news that the *Grunion* had been in a pretty good fight. The garbled information declares the sinking of the Sub Chaser 25 and 27 and further notes the damaging of a third. The *Grunion* remains safe after the hostilities and continues her patrol uneventfully until the 28th, when another new encounter with the enemy occurs near Sirius Point. The *Grunion* fires a couple of torpedoes, none which strike, and the enemy reacts with a vociferous barrage that shakes and rattles, but does not eliminate the *Grunion*. Determined to maintain its surveillance of the Kiska region, the *Grunion* resumes Patrol, carrying a sparse supply of torpedoes. The saga continues on the 30th of July when reports filter into headquarters at Dutch Harbor, that the enemy has over-fortified its Naval screen in front of Kiska's Harbor. The *Grunion* also makes it clear that only ten torpedoes are aboard. The Command post at Dutch Harbor directs the *Grunion* to return to Kiska. The Submariners on the valiant *Grunion* do not respond to the order and as to what happened to their remaining ten torpedoes, no one knows. The Sub, commanded by Lt. Commander Mannert L. Abele, is never heard from again. **(Atlantic-Egypt)** An enemy Tank supported counterattack, recaptures some previously lost ground, in the vicinity of Ruweisat Ridge, but in so doing, the enemy is severely punished by British Artillery. **(Russia)** The Germans have taken Boguchar and Millerovo. The 1st and 4th Panzers, driving toward Rostov, advance to Kamensk on the Donets.

July 16th 1942 — (United States) Consular relations with Finland are broken by the United States, with August 1st as the effective date. General Harmon departs Washington, D.C., heading by air to the South Pacific, to assume his new command. **(Pacific)** American Admiral Ghormley issues plans (Operation Plan No. 1-42). The plan covers Task One of the projected American offensive. Task Force 61 (Solomons Expeditionary Force) will be commanded by Vice Admiral Frank J. Fletcher. An Amphibious Force, commanded by Rear Admiral Richmond K. Turner and Air Support Forces, commanded by Rear Admiral Leigh Noyes, come under Fletcher's command. Task Force 63, commanded by Admiral McCain and comprised of all Allied Land-based Aircraft in the South Pacific, will also be formed. **(Atlantic-England)** U.S. Rear Admiral A.C. Bennett is appointed Commanding Officer of Advanced Group, Amphibious Force, Atlantic Fleet. Its purpose is to begin amphibious training in Great Britain. **(Atlantic-Egypt)** The British 30 Corps expands its salient located west of El 'Alamein, by seizing an enemy held ridge in the vicinity of the railway station. In other activity, the British 13 Corps is engaged heavily along the enemy's south flank.

July 17th 1942 — (Pacific) Embarkation orders for the campaign to occupy Buna, New Guinea (Operation PROVIDENCE) are issued, directing the advance Contingents to depart Port Moresby on the 31st of July. D-Day is scheduled for 10-12 August. **(Atlantic-Great Britain)** Admiral King, General Marshall and Roosevelt's roving Ambassador, Harry Hopkins arrive in England to press for a limited cross channel invasion (Operation SLEDGEHAMMER) to be initiated during 1942.

July 18th 1942 — (Pacific) The U.S. establishes Amphibious Force, South Pacific, to be commanded by Rear Admiral R.K. Turner. Around New Britain, the Silent Service is engaged with another special mission. The *S-42*, commanded by Lt. O.G. Kirk, drops off an Intelligence Agent. Another S-Boat, the *S-43*, commanded by Lt. E. R. Hannon, debarks a British Officer off the coast of New Ireland (19th), however the Officer does not return to the rendezvous point. No communications develop and the *S-43* is forced to leave the area. **(Atlantic-Russia)** The Germans continue their drive, seizing Voroshilovgrad, a coal and coke center, in the Donets Basin. To the southeast, the Germans advance to the Don River at Tsimlyansk.

July 19th 1942 — (Southwest Pacific) A Japanese Invasion Force comprised of approximately 1,800 men departs Rabaul, heading for Buna, New Guinea.

July 20th 1942 — (United States) President Roosevelt accepts the resignation of Admiral Leahy, Ambassador to France and appoints him Chief of Staff, reactivating him to the Armed Forces. President Roosevelt makes the appointment public on July 21st. **(Pacific)** Major General Alexander A. Vandegrift, commanding General, 1st Marine Division, issues tactical orders relating to the invasion of the Solomon Islands. **(North Pacific)** The Navy expands its facilities in the Aleutians as a Naval Air Facility and a Naval Operating Base is established at Dutch Harbor.

July 21st 1942 — (Pacific-New Guinea) The Japanese invasion force, launched from Rabaul a few days earlier, lands at Buna in the vicinity of Gona, despite Allied Air attacks. This invasion causes the Allies, who were preparing to take the same ground to abort Operation PROVIDENCE. The enemy invasion is aided by a diversionary raid against Mubo and Komiatum. **(Atlantic-Egypt)** The British Eighth Army initiates an attack against the enemy's defenses near El 'Alamein. Infantry is used to clear mine fields, which are preventing the advance of British Armor.

July 22nd 1942 — (Pacific) The Allied offensive against the Solomons continues, as the 1st Marine Division embarks from Wellington, New Zealand. The Marine 3rd Defense Battalion sails from Pearl Harbor to join the 1st Marines. The U.S. invasion force reaches striking distance of the Solomons, completely undetected by the Japanese, on the 6th of August. **(Pacific-New Guinea)** The northern coast of New Guinea is attacked by Allied Planes which set a transport on fire. The Japanese who have landed send the Army forces toward Giruwa and the Navy forces toward Buna, approximately 150 miles, via the Owen Stanley Mountains, from Port Moresby. General MacArthur directs General Morris (Commander New Guinea Force) to reinforce the defenses at Kokoda immediately. **(Atlantic-Egypt)** The British Eighth Army continues the offensive against the enemy near El 'Alamein, but is prevented from breaking through the lines. The British 23rd Armored Brigade takes severe Tank losses and the New Zealand 6th Brigade, plus 1 Battalion of the Indian 161st Brigade are annihilated by fierce enemy counterattacks. **(Atlantic-England)** The British turn down the U.S. suggestion to launch an invasion against Europe via the channel during 1942 (Operation SLEDGEHAMMER). **(Atlantic-Russia)** The Germans (Army Group A) begin a major attack against Rostov.

July 23rd 1942 — (Pacific-New Caledonia) The 42nd Squadron of the 11th Heavy Bombardment Group arrives. **(New Guinea)** Japanese troops advancing along the Kokoda Trail encounter elements of the Australian Maroubra Force in the vicinity of Awala. Fierce fighting develops and the Aussies are forced to pull back towards Wairopi. Further pull-backs will cause Kokoda itself to be abandoned on the 26th.

July 24th 1942 — **(United States)** A German Submarine, again penetrates American waters, this time, laying mines off the Mississippi River passes. **(Pacific-Fiji Islands)** The 431st Squadron, 11th Heavy Bombardment Group, arrives in the Fiji Islands. **(Pacific-New Guinea)** Kokoda is in jeopardy, as the Japanese continue to advance against the small Allied defense force. The greatly outnumbered Maroubra Force retreats toward Kokoda, fighting as they retire. They cross the Kumusi River, then destroy the Wairopi bridge. **(Atlantic-Russia)** The German Army Group A takes Rostov.

July 25th 1942 — **(United States)** The Combined Chiefs of Staff agreement on the command structure for Operation Torch, the invasion of Northwest Africa (Operation GYMNAST renamed). **(Pacific-New Hebrides)** The 26th Squadron, 11th Heavy Bombardment Group, arrives at Efate, New Hebrides. **(Pacific-New Guinea)** The Japanese construct an improvised bridge over the Kumusi River and successfully outflank the Maroubra Force, causing it to fall back to within six miles of Kokoda (Oivi).

July 26th 1942 — **(Pacific)** American General Harmon assumes tactical command over all American Army forces in the South Pacific. General Harmon selects Suva, Fiji Islands as his Command Post. In other activity, Task Force 61 (Solomons Expeditionary Force), minus the elements which are transporting the 3rd Marine Defense Battalion over the Pacific, converge on a rendezvous point southeast of the Fiji Islands. **(Pacific-New Guinea)** The Japanese keep enormous pressure against the Allies. Thirty men attached to the New Guinea Force (Company D, Australian 39th Battalion), are flown to Kokoda to bolster the defenses. Fifteen of these reinforcements are rushed to Oiva in vain. Overpowering Japanese troops force the Allies to abandon Kokoda. The sparse defense contingent comprised of 1 Platoon of Company B and the 15 men from Company D, fight their way to Deniki. **(Atlantic-Egypt)** As darkness falls, the British 30 Corps, 8th Army, initiates an attack against enemy positions on its north flank.

July 27th 1942 — **(Pacific)** Task Force 61 embarks for the Fiji Islands, where they will begin practice invasions, in preparation for the assault against the Solomons. **(Pacific-New Guinea)** The Australian Oivi Force breaks out of the Japanese envelopment at Oivi, during the night and makes it to Deniki where it joins elements of the Maroubra Force. Reinforcements heading for Kokoda by air are recalled after learning of the abandonment of Kokoda. **(Atlantic-Egypt)** The British 30 Corps meets stiff enemy resistance as it continues its attack against the enemy lines. **(Atlantic-Russia)** The German 6th Army attacks a Soviet Bridgehead that crosses the Don river at Kalach, situated west of Stalingrad.

July 28th 1942 — **(Pacific)** General Harmon arrives at New Caledonia. General Kenney, the designate commander of Allied Air Forces arrives in Australia. In other activity, Admiral Fletcher gives Operation Order No. 1-42 to Task Force 61. **(Pacific-New Hebrides)** The Airfield at Espiritu Santo becomes operational. Planes attached to Marine Observation Squadron 251 begin arriving on the 2nd of August. **(Pacific-Japan)** The Japanese are ordered to initiate a major assault to secure New Guinea. The instructions from Tokyo include attacks against Port Moresby, from both overland routes and the sea, in addition to a major amphibious assault against Allied positions at Milne Bay. **(Pacific-New Guinea)** Kokoda is recaptured by the Maroubra Force after a strong counter-

attack but heavy Japanese reinforcements rushed to the scene from the beach threaten the newly won objective. **(Pacific-China)** The Japanese cease the ongoing offensive in Chekiang Province. The offensive was initiated, because of the U.S. Air raid against the Japanese mainland.

July 29th 1942 — **(Southwest Pacific)** General Harmon, (Commander U.S. Army Forces, S. Pacific) relocates his Headquarters from Suva in the Fiji Islands to Noumea, Caledonia. **(Pacific-New Guinea)** The unending struggle for Kokoda continues, as the Japanese recapture the village, forcing Allied defenders to withdraw to Deniki once again. The Japanese subsequently terminate the attack and begin to fortify their defenses. In other activity, the Japanese attempt to land troops from two Transports on the northern portion of the island with bad results. Allied Planes attack and turn one of the Vessels back, while sinking another. Some enemy troops do manage to reach shore at Giruwa by the use of small landing craft. **(China-Burma-India)** American General Stilwell calls for the recapture of Burma by Allied troops. The plan "Pacific Front" is to expand the offensive, using troops from Manipur and Yunnan.

July 30th 1942 — **(United States)** The U.S. Navy Women Reserve is established. The women will be known as WAVES. The initials stand for "Women Accepted for Volunteer Emergency Service." In other activity, the Joint Chiefs of Staff meet in Washington and give top priority to the proposed invasion of North Africa (Operation TORCH). In related activity, Axis Planes bombard Cairo, and Washington is inundated with emergency messages for Planes to be sent to Egypt. A decision is made to divert Planes, previously committed to General Stilwell in China. Stilwell is unhappy with the diversion, as it impedes his plans for retaking Burma. **(Pacific)** Admiral Turner issues Operation Plan No. A3-42 to the Solomons Amphibious Force. **(Pacific-Netherlands East Indies)** Aru, Kei, and Tanimbar Islands are invaded by Japanese troops. **(Atlantic-Egypt)** The British under General Auchinleck take defensive positions, rather than attack the enemy. Auchinleck chose to await reinforcements before resuming an offensive. **(Atlantic-Russia)** The Germans (Group A) establish a bridgehead across the Manych River, southwest of Proletarskaya. In the meantime, Group B is still intently involved with destroying the Soviet bridgehead across the Don River, west of Stalingrad. On the Central Front, the Soviets assault German positions in the vicinity of Rzhev.

July 31st 1942 — **(United States)** The waters near Charleston, South Carolina become the newest area for German mines, laid by a German Submarine. **(Pacific)** The U.S. Amphibious Force, commanded by Admiral Turner, escorted by Task Force 63 and the Air Support Force, commanded by Admiral Noyes, embark from the Fiji Islands, heading for the Japanese held Solomon Islands. B-17s from Task Force 63 are launched from New Hebrides for the purpose of assaulting Guadalcanal and Tulagi, to soften resistance for the imminent invasion. **(Pacific-New Guinea)** More Australian troops of the Maroubra Force reach Deniki.

August 1st 1942 — **(United States)** The U.S. establishes several more Naval facilities. A Naval Base is opened at Galapagos Islands; a Naval Station at Taboga Island, Canal Zone. The U.S. also establishes facilities at Salinas, Ecuador. In other activity, U.S. Coast Guard Planes, operating in the Gulf of Mexico, detect and sink the German *U-166*. **(Pacific-**

China) General Stilwell's proposal for an offensive, which was presented to Chiang Kai-shek on the 18th of July, is officially approved. **(Atlantic-Egypt)** The Germans and the British restrict their Military activity to the exchange of Artillery fire and Patrols, while each side regroups for renewing the offensive. **(Atlantic-Russia)** The Germans seize the rail junction at Salsk and in so doing, Group A severs the Novorossisk-Stalingrad Rail Road. The Germans (Army Group B) are involved with fierce fighting in the vicinity of the Don River, across from Stalingrad, as they attempt to further diminish the Soviet troops in the area. In other activity, the Russians maintain the offensive near Rzhev.

August 2nd 1942 — (Pacific) The U.S. Task Force scheduled to assault Guadalcanal finalizes preparations for the invasion. The attack against Guadalcanal is to be made by the 1st Marine Division (minus the 7th Marines).

August 3rd 1942 — (Atlantic-Egypt) Concerned with the lack of progress by the British Eighth Army in Egypt, Prime Minister Churchill and British General Brooke confer in Cairo to make Command changes. **(Atlantic-Russia)** German Army Group A drives further south, overrunning Voroshilovsk. In other activity, heavy fighting ensues opposite Stalingrad along the Don River. The Russians in the Central Front continue the assault against the Germans in the vicinity of Rzhev.

August 4th 1942 — (Pacific) American General Kenney succeeds General Brett as Commanding Officer of the Allied Air Forces in the Southwest Pacific Area. **(Pacific-New Hebrides)** The U.S.S. *Tucker* (DD-374), is destroyed when it inadvertently strikes a friendly mine in the Segond Channel, Espiritu Santo, New Hebrides.

August 5th 1942 — (Atlantic-Russia) German Army Group A establishes a bridgehead across the Kuban River, positioning it to take the Maikop oil fields. The German Group B Army also advances against the Soviets in the vicinity of a bend in the Don River, near Stalingrad.

August 6th 1942 — (Pacific) The Marine Amphibious Force nears the Solomon Islands. The U.S. Naval Task Force carrying the Marines moves without detection, by the Japanese. There is also some activity at Pearl Harbor. Two American Submarines, the *Nautilus* and the *Argonaut*, depart the harbor at 09:00, carrying a "few good men" who will be absent from the big show at Guadalcanal on the following day. The *Nautilus*, in addition to her normal crew, is accompanied by an additional seven Officers and 114 men, while her sister Ship, the *Argonaut* transports an additional 84 men and six Officers. The Submarines separate to avoid enemy detection, as they steam toward Makin Island in the Gilberts, maintaining surface speed for nearly the entire trip. Carlson's 2nd Raider Battalion, the recipients of this overcramped Navy hospitality, are embarking on a most perilous operation and all the extensive training and discipline will surely be appreciated when they hit the beach in Carlson's "Gung Ho!" style. The trip is uneventful for the ten days it takes to reach Makin.

The *Nautilus* arrives at 03:00 (16th), and begins to check out the landing sites. Contact is made with the *Argonaut* at 21:16, during a storm, as they move toward the designated jump off point. Plans are meticulously studied and equipment is checked. Meanwhile, last minute letters are hastily penned, and last, but not least, the weapons are checked in the closing moments. The clock passes the hour of midnight, as Marines

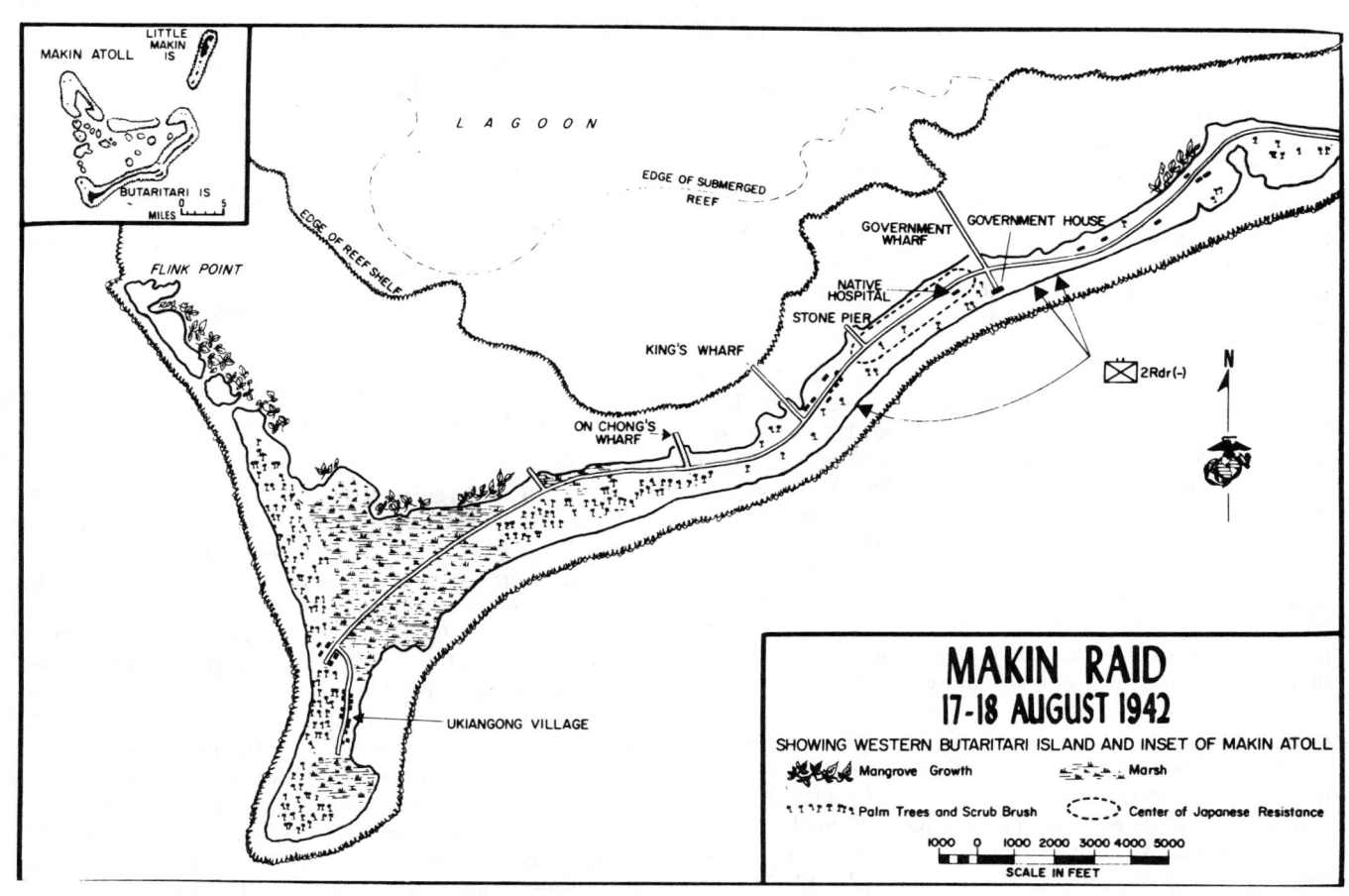

**MAKIN RAID
17-18 AUGUST 1942**

SHOWING WESTERN BUTARITARI ISLAND AND INSET OF MAKIN ATOLL

Mangrove Growth   Marsh

Palm Trees and Scrub Brush   Center of Japanese Resistance

1000 0 1000 2000 3000 4000 5000
SCALE IN FEET

scamper for the rubber boats. At 03:00 (17th), under trying conditions, the Raiders are fighting against the unruly surf, however, all are shorebound on schedule. Additional problems develop, prompting Carlson to order all boats to hit Landing Beach Z, opposite Government Wharf.

Fifteen of the eighteen landing rafts follow Carlson. Two wind up about a mile away, but are able to hook up with Carlson during the heated contest. The final boat comes ashore further south, behind Japanese lines. The Raiders land without incident, but one of the rifles is accidentally fired, alerting the enemy. Carlson sends a message to the waiting Submarines: "EVERYTHING LOUSY" Shortly thereafter, another Carlson quip: "SITUATION EXPECTED TO BE WELL IN HAND SHORTLY." Colonel Carlson orders Company A to cross the island and seize the Lagoon Road. Meanwhile, a contingent of Company A had already secured Government House unopposed. Its 1st Platoon, advancing down the Lagoon Road engages Japanese Infantry and support forces which include Flame throwers and machine guns. The Submarines fire salvos toward suspected enemy positions near Ukiangang Point. U.S. Reinforcements from Company B rush to the right flank of Company A and vicious combat ensues.

Sergeant Clyde Thomason, a Marine Corps Reservist, deploys his men and inspiringly leads them. Thomason, aware of a sniper, breaks down a door and eliminates him. Thomason continues to exhibit extraordinary courage and is killed leading an attack. The Marines break through by 11:30, however, Japanese Warships arrive in the lagoon, forcing the Submarines to take action. In effortless fashion, the Sailors redirect the Deck Guns and the two enemy Vessels are sunk. As the Raiders pressure the enemy, Jap Planes strafe. On a few occasions, the Submarines are forced to dive. Heavy skirmishing continues throughout the day. At 16:30 Japanese Planes strike suspected American positions, however, they bomb and strafe Japanese troops, which had occupied the positions.

At 19:30, the Submarines are waiting offshore to pick up the Marines, however, the surf prevents the troops from getting off the beach. Some have drowned in the attempt. At dawn, the Submarines submerge and await darkness. Early on the 18th, Carlson dispatches men to locate food and weapons. Much to their surprise, there is not an over abundance of Japs left on the island. The Patrols kill two enemy Soldiers, the only enemy encountered. Later in the day, the troops detonate a large supply of fuel and in addition, confiscate documents from the office of the Commanding Officer. During the day, Eighty three enemy dead are counted. The Marines recover 14 of their own dead. Total Marine losses hit a tragic note as 7 men drown in the surf and in the greatest of mistakes, and not known until after the close of hostilities, nine men had been left on the island. Explanations are unclear, but it is not a normal practice for Americans to abandon fellow fighting men. One theory presented by the Marines who live by the standard, "never leave a man behind," is that the men might have attempted to row back to the Submarines during the night of the 17th and were thrown back to the beach by the wild seas, but the possibility exists, that somehow, they could have inadvertently been left behind. Speculation aside, the fact remains that nine American Marines are later captured by the Japs and after a short time in captivity, the Japs execute these Marines. The Japanese disclaim these casualty figures. They claim in a letter to the History Branch G-3 Headquarters, U.S.M.C., Washington, D.C., that their records place 70 men on Makin at time of the raid and that 43 were killed, 3 missing and 27 survivors. **(Pacific-New Guinea)** All Australian and U.S. troops in Papua and Northeast New Guinea, are now under the Command of the New Guinea Force. **(Atlantic-Russia)** The Russians acknowledge the loss of Kotelnikov to the Germans. In addition, the Germans proclaim they have taken Tikhoretsk. Armavir also falls to the Germans. Heavy fighting continues along the Don River in the vicinity of Stalingrad, with the Germans gaining the upper hand in the battle.

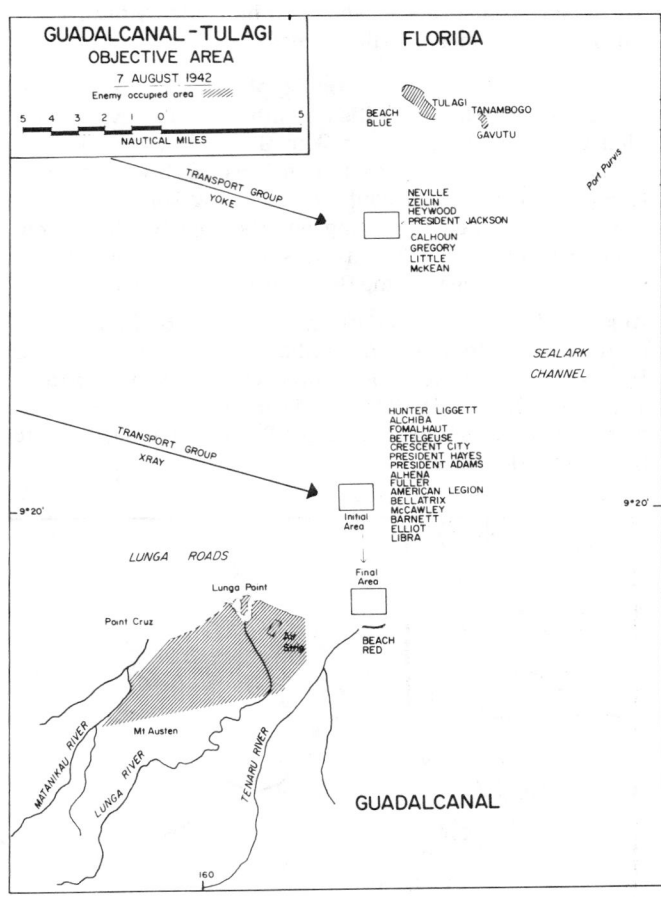

August 7th 1942 — Map of the invasion of Guadalcanal, Solomon Islands.

August 7th 1942-February 9th 1943 — (Pacific) THE BATTLE OF GUADALCANAL — The Japanese have, up to this point, knocked over and trampled over all Allied ground resistance in the Pacific and Asia. Because of a continual string of conquests, the Japanese are of course confident that any invasion mounted by the U.S. will be turned back. The Americans are coming, but not in force. Though it has been almost eight months since Pearl Harbor, the Americans are only attacking with one Division on their first offensive thrust of the war. But they are fortified with an extreme animosity against the Japanese. Stories are already legion about the Soldiers, Sailors and Marines, already slaughtered by the Japs during their carnivorous odyssey, that has already brought their terror to the gates of the U.S., in the Pacific. Stories of their rape and pillage, as they romped through their first inglorious trophies of conquest in Asia, have been added to the firsthand

August 7th 1942 — U.S. troops landing on Florida Island, Solomons.

stories of atrocities, against Americans. In addition, Jap propagandists have been giving the Yanks a steady broadside since the war has begun. The one-sided conflict on the ground is about to be strenuously tested.

The time has come for a reckoning with the Japanese and the Solomons have been selected as the first chain to be seized. The First Marine Division, commanded by General Alexander Vandegrift, are to do what they have been trained to do, kill Japs, seize the ground and kill more Japs. If these Oriental Supermen bleed, the Marines should be able to get the situation well in hand. Guadalcanal, in the southwest Pacific off New Guinea is the largest of the Solomon chain, and there is very little intelligence known by the U.S., concerning defenses or exact numerical strength. The island has no roads, however, it is inundated with enormous swamps and treacherous jungle, which surrounds the mountains. It must be taken.

Fresh in their minds as they ready for the assault, is the message just received from Colonel LeRoy Hunt (5th Marines): "OUR COUNTRY EXPECTS NOTHING BUT VICTORY FROM US AND IT SHALL HAVE JUST THAT. THE WORD FAILURE SHALL NOT EVEN BE CONSIDERED AS BEING IN OUR VOCABULARY. WE ARE MEETING A TOUGH AND WILY OPPONENT BUT HE IS NOT SUFFICIENTLY TOUGH OR WILY TO OVERCOME US BECAUSE WE ARE MARINES . . . WE'VE WORKED HARD AND TRAINED CAREFULLY FOR THIS ACTION. EACH OF US HAS HIS ASSIGNED TASK. LET EACH VOW TO PERFORM IT TO THE UTMOST OF HIS ABILITY, WITH

AN ADDED EFFORT FOR GOOD MEASURE. GOOD LUCK. GOD BLESS YOU AND TO HELL WITH THE JAPS."

The Armada, under Admiral Fletcher passes the enemy shoreline during the night of the sixth, under a moonless sky. The Navy maneuvers precariously between the neck of water, separating the Savo Islands and Guadalcanal, approaching the fringes of Tulagi Bay, without a solitary Japanese shell being fired. The enemy silence works in reverse and causes some concern among the members of the Strike Force, which is happy, yet bewildered by the non-action of the defenders on Guadalcanal. The Vessels crash their way through the waves, approaching jump off hour. Some of the assault troops are curiously peering through binoculars at their new residence, although vision is blurred by both the darkness and the constant interruption of passing Ships in the Convoy. The backdrops of this massive undertaking are huge darkly colored mountains, which stand out in great contrast to the lighter color of the near morning sky. Guadalcanal is gradually moving to the forefront, as the Ships move deeper into the Bay, passing Tulagi, situated to the east and the Florida Islands to the north, but still no enemy fire to induce a full throttle flow of adrenaline into the troops as they cruise southwardly.

U.S. Navy guns commence firing at 06:14. Darkness and anxiety is replaced by furious fire and impatient troops. The first volley originates from a Cruiser, followed by additional Cruisers. The rumbling of thunderous guns, spewing large fiery shells, including tracers, which arc toward the landing sites add an ominous note to the invasion. Navy Gunners are joined by Planes, which supplement the already multicolored skyline, giving the island an irridescent glow of death. One of the salvos hits a supply depot giving the exercise a magnificent finale.

By 06:19, part of the Armada (Admiral Turner), carrying General Rupertus' Force, which will invade Tulagi, tails off to the left toward the objective. By this time the balance of the Fleet has joined in the bombardment. The invasion timetable is pretty much on schedule. The Navy Guns are still plastering the island at 06:28, but a conspicuous raging fire to the front of the Convoy attracts the attention of the men. The towering smoke turns out to be a Japanese Vessel, which had gotten into the sights of the strafing Planes. The Schooner induces a mighty fire, as the cargo includes gasoline, and adds illumination to the American Vessels, nearing the debarkation point, for the sprint by the Marines to the beach. At this time there is still no return enemy fire, against the Armada, causing more intent thought, by the Commanders of the Invasion Force. The immense bombardment startled the Japanese, catching them offguard totally. The entire area had been pummeled, without any reciprocal fire from the enemy. Cruisers continue to pour fire upon selected areas.

Close Air support is afforded the 1st wave to hit the beaches, but the landing of the 5th Marines is completely unopposed at Guadalcanal (Beach Red). The First Marines, commanded by Colonel Cliftoon Cates, follow in Reserve. The Marines take full advantage of the lull and preparations are immediately taken to beat back an attack when it comes. Supplies pour ashore, including gasoline, ammunition and barbed wire. Within a couple of hours, the Marines have sent out extended Patrols to scout the jungle. Others begin fortifying the perimeter with the wire and other obstacles, such as machine gun positions and foxholes. Communication systems are strung and preparations are made to attack and seize Henderson Airfield, which they will accomplish, against nominal opposition on the following day. Later, Japanese Planes swarm in under a massive cloud cover several times and bomb the American Shipping in the bay. Two would be destroyed by American Planes and one other by Anti-aircraft fire. The Marines spend a jittery night, consumed by jungle silence occasionally penetrated by a shot or volley, but more often by disgruntled Macaws and dive-bombing aedes and anopheles Mosquitos.

The 7th Marines land on the Southern Solomons. During the day's operations, the Destroyer U.S.S. *Mugford.* is damaged by an enemy Dive Bomber. The 1st Raider Battalion, commanded by Colonel Merritt Edson, lands at Blue Beach, Tulagi, without incident and moves southeast, until heavy enemy resistance halts its progress at Hill 281 where the Japs have entrenched themselves firmly in caves. The Second Battalion, 5th Marines, which had not landed with the 5th Marines on Guadalcanal, comes in behind the 1st Raider Battalion on Blue Beach. In addition, the 1st Battalion, 2nd Marines, hit the beach at the Southern portion of Florida Island, without meeting any opposition. At noon, the 1st Paratroop Battalion invades Gavutu and Tanambogo, clearing the majority of the two islets. The Paratroopers, assisted by the 2nd Marines, secure both Gavutu and Tanambogo by the following day.

On the 8th, Japanese Planes attached to the Eighth Fleet, under Admiral Gunichi Mikawa, arrive from Rabaul and swarm over the American Transports at about noon and severely damage Allied Naval operations, in the vicinity of the Solomons. Suicide Bombers hit the *George F. Elliott* (Transport), inflicting enough damage that the U.S. scuttles the Vessel. The U.S.S. *Jarvis* (Destroyer) is also struck by a Suicide Bomber and damaged, and the Transport U.S.S. *Barnett* is struck by a torpedo. The U.S.S. *Jarvis* departs for Noumea, but it is never heard from again. During the night of the 8th, lasting into early morning of the 9th (Battle of Savo), the Japanese Eighth Fleet inflicts more punishment to the Fleet, sinking the U.S.S. *Astoria, Quincy* and *Vincennes* (Cruisers) and damaging other Allied Vessels, while losing none themselves. Seventeen thousand of the 19,000 men make it to shore, before the Support Ships are forced to withdraw on the 9th, taking approximately one half of the 60 day supply of food and equipment with them, however, the Japanese have exhibited their night Naval skills which becomes a costly lesson to the Yanks, who sustain over 1,200 men killed and over 700 wounded. Through some fortuitous luck, the U.S. Transports are not attacked. The Americans have grasped a foothold on the islands and are there for the duration. The Marines fortify their positions quickly as they prepare for a bitter campaign. These tenacious men will learn the ways of jungle warfare quickly, deciphering the sounds of an animal and of the impostoring enemy, the cries of a wounded comrade and the ruse of a Japanese ambush.

As September settles down in the Solomons, 17,000 Marines control a 4-by-7 mile strip of Guadalcanal. Japanese continue to assault their positions and the Allied Ships offshore, which are attempting to keep them resupplied, however The Marines intend to hold their mosquito, snake infested paradise at all costs. Four Japanese Carriers, with battle escorts, glide confidently through the sea, until they are confronted by two American Task Forces, commanded by the able Admiral

Kinkaid, in the vicinity of Santa Cruz Islands on October 26th. The Japanese lose two Destroyers sunk, in addition to having two Carriers and two Battleships damaged. The U.S.S. *Hornet* (Carrier) is damaged and subsequently sunk by Japanese Dive Bombers.

The 164th U.S. Infantry, the first Army troops to assist the Marines on Guadalcanal, arrive on October 13th and initiate their part in the campaign, which will soon see the balance of the Americal Division arrive to relieve the Marines. On November 13th, the Japanese make another attempt to retake Guadalcanal. The two opposing Fleets confront each other, in what is known as the Naval Battle of Guadalcanal. The engaging Vessels criss-cross each other at dangerously close distances, firing at point blank range. The U.S. loses two Cruisers sunk and two damaged. The Japanese lose one Battleship. On the 14th, Patrol Planes from the *Enterprise* spot another Japanese Fleet approaching and inform headquarters. Land-based American Bombers catapult from the Airstrips and deliver a decisive blow to the encroaching enemy, sinking seven Troop Transports and damaging the remaining four. The remnants of the enemy Fleet try to regroup and land on Guadalcanal, but yet another American Task Force, under Admiral Willis Lee, speeds across Iron Bottom Sound and crushes the Flotilla, sinking another Battleship and damaging two Cruisers. The invasion is halted and the disoriented Japanese retire.

As each day passes, the fighting becomes more gruesome, but once the threat of another Japanese Amphibious Invasion is over, the Americans move swiftly, through the dense jungle terrain, until every Jap sniper is plucked from the trees and each enemy nest is destroyed by grenades, rifles and when necessary, the Yank's second best friend; his silent and reliable bayonet. By early February, 1943, the Japanese evacuate approximately 12,000 troops from the northwestern tip of the island (Cape Esperance) as the triumphant U.S. secures the entire island by the ninth. The Americans, with Old Glory firmly entrenched, now share the island with monkeys, and mosquitoes. There are no live Japanese left to help celebrate the first American land victory and the first Japanese land defeat of the war.

August 7th 1942 — (North Pacific-Aleutian Islands) Allied Surface Vessels bombard Kiska for the first time, when Rear Admiral W.W. Smith's Task Force (attached to Admiral Theobald's North Pacific Force) comprised of Cruisers and Destroyers, opens fire. Results of the Naval bombardment are not observed. **(Pacific-Solomons)** With the Task Force of Admiral Fletcher at the door of the Solomons, Surface Vessels and Carrier Planes run interference for the Landing Force, which is about to land in the Pacific. Land-based Planes supplement the attacking force and also assist this the first offensive of the United States in the war. The Amphibious Vessels, commanded by Admiral Turner, speed to the beaches. The U.S. 1st Marine Division assaults the southern Solomons with Task Groups Yoke and X-Ray, landing in the vicinity of Tulagi and Guadalcanal. At 09:10 the 5th Marines, minus the 2nd Battalion, storm beach (Red) on the northern coast of Guadalcanal and quickly establish a beachhead between the Tenavatu and Tenaru Rivers. The landing force will be bolstered by reinforcements (1st Marines and support weaponry). Elements advance approximately one mile to the west and southwest before stopping for the night. At 08:00 the 1st

Raider Battalion with the 2nd Battalion, 5th Marines right behind them, storm the southern coast (Beach Blue), without opposition. The Japanese hidden in bunkers and caves on the southeastern end of the island put up a tremendous struggle and halt the advancing Raiders about 1,000 yards from the southern tip of the island. At noon, the 1st Paratroop Battalion assaults the islets of Gavutu and Tanambogo and secures them the following day, after reducing enemy resistance. During the day's action, the U.S.S. *Mugford* (DD-389) is struck and damaged by an enemy Dive Bomber. **(North Pacific)** A U.S. Naval Task Force, commanded by Rear Admiral W.W. Smith, bombards enemy positions in the Aleutians at Kiska. **(Atlantic-Egypt)** British Prime Minister Churchill tours the British Eighth Army Front.

A wounded Marine being transferred at sea to receive medical attention.

August 8th 1942 — (United States) A German Submarine penetrates U.S. waters and again deploys mines in the vicinity of Jacksonville, Florida near the mouth of the St. John's River. **(Pacific-Guadalcanal)** The Airfield and the village of Kukum, on Guadalcanal, are both abandoned hurriedly by the enemy and are secured by the 1st Battalion, 1st Marines and the 1st Battalion 5th Marines respectively. American Lieutenant Snell, an aide to Colonel Hunt, U.S.M.C. is brought into headquarters, suffering paralysis from heat stroke. Colonel Hunt, in an attempt to improve his (Snell) and others morale, would take a personal 8x12 inch American Flag out of the pocket, in which Snell had been carrying it since China and the Philippines, hoisting it up the barren Japanese flag pole, over the empty enemy headquarters. It was small,

but it was American and it flew proudly, bringing high spirits to those privileged to watch. On Tulagi, enemy resistance is cleared by the 1st Battalion, 5th Marines by 15:00. In other activity in the Solomons, the U.S.S. *George F. Elliott* (Transport AP-13) is damaged by enemy Planes and sunk by U.S. forces. The U.S.S. *Jarvis* (Destroyer DD-393) is damaged and attempts to sail for Noumea, but disappears from sight and is never seen again. In addition, the U.S.S. *Barnett*, a Transport (AP-11) is damaged. **(Atlantic)** President Roosevelt and Prime Minister Churchill, select General Eisenhower to be the Commander of Operation TORCH (Allied Invasion of Northwest Africa). **(Atlantic-Egypt)** General Alexander is flown to Cairo and is informed, that he will replace British General Auchinleck (Commander in Chief British Mediterranean Troops). Lt. General W.H. Gott, recently appointed to Commander British Eighth Army, is killed in a Plane crash. **(Atlantic-Germany)** Himmler discusses religion with his doctor, telling him that he believes "IN SOME HIGHER BEING, WHETHER YOU CALL IT GOD OR PROVIDENCE, OR ANYTHING ELSE YOU LIKE." He then explains that if "WE REFUSED TO BELIEVE, THAT WE SHOULD BE NO BETTER THAN THE MARXISTS." He further states that all his S.S. troops must believe in God. However, he makes it clear that he hates Catholicism, comparing the Church to: "A JOINT-STOCK COMPANY FROM WHICH THE CHIEF SHAREHOLDERS — SINCE ITS FOUNDATION AND FOR NEARLY 2,000 YEARS — DRAW A HUNDRED OR A THOUSAND PERCENT PROFIT AND GIVE NOTHING IN RETURN." **(Atlantic-Russia)** The Germans (Group B) seize Surovikino.

August 8th-9th 1942 — (Pacific Guadalcanal) BATTLE OF SAVO ISLAND — A Japanese Naval Task Force (Contingents of Japan's Eighth Fleet), consisting of Seven Cruisers and a Destroyer, moves undetected, west of Savo Island and thrashes the U.S. Fleet badly, severely hampering supply operations on Guadalcanal. The Japanese sink the Destroyers U.S.S. *Astoria* (CA-34), *Quincy* (CA-39) and *Vincennes* (CA-44). The Australian Vessel *Canberra*, a Destroyer (leads the Armada into Tulagi Bay) is also lost. The U.S.S. *Chicago* (Cruiser-CA-29), U.S.S. *Ralph Talbot* (DD-390), and the U.S.S. *Patterson* (DD-392), all Destroyers are damaged. After the sea duel, the Japanese retire to Rabaul, but the damage is done and the Marines onshore at Guadalcanal will be abandoned on the beach.

August 9th 1942 — (Pacific-Solomons) The American Task Force (61) departs Guadalcanal, after unloading about one half of the supplies destined for the Marines on shore. Task Force 61 heads for Noumea, with contingents (about 1,400 men) of the assault force still on board. Seventeen thousand Marines would be isolated, with neither air nor sea support, until the 20th of August. **(Atlantic-Russia)** The Germans (Group A) seize Krasnodar and Maikop.

August 10th 1942 — (Pacific) The *S-44*, a U.S. Submarine, sinks a Japanese Heavy Cruiser, the *Kako*, off New Ireland, in the vicinity of Kavieng.

August 11th 1942 — (Pacific-New Hebrides) Marine Observation Squadron 251 is operational at Espiritu Santo and is comprised of 16 F4F-3s (long range photographic Planes). **(New Guinea)** The Allies (Maroubra Force) evacuate the Kokoda Airfield, feeling that holding it is not possible. **(Mediterranean)** German U-Boats have been stalking and terrorizing Allied Convoys for some time. Today, the H.M.S. *Eagle*, an

Aircraft Carrier is sunk, while escorting a Convoy towards Malta. **(Atlantic-Russia)** The Germans (Group A) destroy a Russian bridgehead along the Don, in the vicinity of Kalach.

August 12th 1942 — (Pacific-Guadalcanal) Lieutenant Colonel Frank Goettge U.S.M.C., leads a 25 man Patrol on a reconnaissance mission in the vicinity of the Matanikau River. A Japanese ambush wipes out all but three men. In other activity, Admiral McCain (Task Force 63) receives instructions to transport ammunition, supplies and ground crews from Espiritu Santo to Guadalcanal, to assist the Marines already there. **(Atlantic-Egypt)** Lt. General Montgomery arrives in Egypt to command the British Eighth Army in place of British General Gott, who was recently killed in a Plane crash. **(Atlantic-Russia)** Churchill arrives in Russia for talks with Stalin, relating to a second front in Europe. In other activity, the Russians still battle the Germans in the vicinity of Rzhev, but the fighting peaks, without a clear victory for either.

August 13th 1942 — (Pacific-Guadalcanal) The Japanese order Lt. General Haruyoshi Hyakutake (Commander Japanese 17th Army) to take control of all ground action on Guadalcanal. **(Pacific-New Guinea)** Three thousand Japanese construction troops are on board a Transport Convoy, which reaches Basabua, situated close to Gona. In other activity, the Maroubra Force holding Deniki, is struck hard by the enemy, forcing them to pull back to Isurava, approximately five miles. The Japanese halt their movement after the victory and begin to reinforce their positions. **(Atlantic-Russia)** The Germans announce the capture of Elista, south of Stalingrad.

August 14th 1942 — (Atlantic) Orders are sent to General Eisenhower, concerning his appointment as Commander in Chief, of Operation Torch (Invasion of Northwest Africa). Eisenhower also holds the post of Commander in Chief of Allied Expeditionary Forces. The Allied Naval Commander, who is to serve under him, is British Admiral Sir Andrew Cunningham. **(Pacific-Louisiade Archipelago)** The *S-39*, an American Submarine is severely damaged by a reef. The Vessel cannot be salvaged and will be scuttled near Rossel Island on the 14th.

August 15th 1942 — (United States) The U.S. Navy establishes additional Naval facilities, to bolster its strength. Today, an Air Station is established at Whidbey Island, Washington. Another Auxiliary Air Facility is established in Jamaica. The Navy also commissions Patrol Wing 11, which is to operate in Puerto Rico. Keeping up with the Navy expansion, the Marines establish Marine Aircraft Wings, Pacific in San Diego, California. **(Pacific-Guadalcanal)** The first Ships with supplies and ground crews for the Planes, since the initial landing on August 7th, arrives at Guadalcanal today. The Marines have been using a Jap safe, as a griddle for their cooking, not necessarily to be construed as gourmet. There is one refrigerator in possession of the Yanks and it is run by a generator, but utilized for medicine, not to keep the captured Jap booze cold. Circumstances on the island force Marine rations to be cut in spite of the newly arrived supplies. **(Atlantic-Middle East)** British General Alexander assumes command of the Mediterranean Expeditionary Force, replacing British General Auchinleck. **(Atlantic-Egypt)** General Montgomery (Monty) is reorganizing and building the strength of the British Eighth Army for future action. **(Atlantic-Russia)** Georgievsk is said to be captured by the Germans.

August 16th 1942 — (United States) Portsmouth, Virginia is the location of the commissioning of the newest Battleship, the U.S.S. *Alabama* (BB-60). The Americans at home are working overtime to get the necessary war supplies to the troops as fast as possible. **(Pacific)** The U.S.S. *Grunion* (SS-216), which had sunk two enemy Submarine Chasers in the North Pacific on July 15, is reported as probably lost in the Pacific. **(Atlantic-North Africa)** U.S. Medium Bombers lend assistance to the British Eighth Army, by making their initial assault against enemy defenses along the Egyptian Front.

U.S. Brewster Buffalo Fighter Planes on Guadalcanal.

August 17th 1942 — (Pacific-Guadalcanal) Admiral Ghormley turns over responsibility for communications, with the troops on Guadalcanal, from Task Force 63, to Task Force 62, commanded by Admiral Turner. In other activity, the Japanese land reinforcements in the vicinity of both Kokumbona (500 troops of the 5th Japanese Special Landing Force) and Taivu Point (2nd Battalion 28th Japanese Infantry reinforced). American held Henderson Airfield (named for Major Loften Henderson, Marine Pilot killed at Midway) is declared operational. **(Atlantic-Europe)** The U.S. Eighth Air Force launches its first Air strike against enemy positions in Europe. A Squadron of B-24s, flying with British Spitfire escorts, strikes the enemy rail center, located at Rouen.

August 17th-18th 1942 — (Pacific-Gilberts) The Submarines *Argonaut* and *Nautilus*, skirt the waves, as the darkened shoreline of Makin is within rowing distance, for the Marines. The Subs surface in the eerie darkness and the 2nd Marine Raider Battalion, commanded by Lt. Colonel Evans F. Carlson, lands on the Gilberts. They receive some support fire from the *Nautilus*, while they are on the beach at Makin (Makin Atoll-Butaritari), The intention is to get intelligence and divert attention, from the Guadalcanal offensive. They succeed in damaging some Japanese installations, but lose 30 of 221 men, during the two day raid.

August 18th 1942 — (Pacific-Guadalcanal) The Japanese, committed to holding the Solomons, begin to reinforce the islands. Enemy troops brought in from Rabaul, arrive on Cruisers and Destroyers, to drive the Americans off the island. **(Pacific-New Guinea)** Japanese reinforcements arrive on three Transports, at Basabu and land without being detected. In other activity, Australian Major General Sydney F. Rowell takes command of the New Guinea Force, replacing Australian General Basil M. Morris. **(China-Burma-India)** American General Clayton L. Bissell is appointed Commander of the U.S. Tenth Air Force.

August 19th 1942 — (Pacific-Guadalcanal) A contingent of the 5th Marines raids the village of Matanikau, while another unit attacks Kokumbona to the west, in an effort to locate an enemy radio station and to cut off retreating Japanese. After clearing the coastal villages, the Marines return to Lunga Point. In other activity, Company A, 1st Marines, encounters an enemy force, consisting of 24, men in the vicinity of Taivu Point and totally destroys them. **(Pacific-New Britain)** Approximately 1,500 Japanese reinforcements depart Rabaul on four Transports, heading for Guadalcanal. The Ships are escorted by Japanese Destroyers. **(Pacific-New Guinea)** Allied reinforcements attached to the Australian 7th Division, arrive at Port Moresby, on their way to bolster the Maroubra Force, at Isurava. **(Atlantic-Egypt)** General Montgomery is ordered to hold at El 'Alamein and simultaneously prepare for a British offensive.

August 19th 1942 — (Atlantic-France) Operation JUBILEE: An operation is launched by the British to return to the shores of France and redeem the debacle at Dunkirk. A British Armada exceeding 270 Warships, transporting over 6,000 Canadian and British Assault troops, which had departed the British Isles two days previously, arrives off Dieppe France, expecting to surprise the Germans and gain a toehold on the continent by seizing control of the town and a nearby Airdrome. Sixty-nine Royal Air Force Squadrons join the Fleet to neutralize the Luftwaffe and give necessary support fire to the ground troops.

The Allies reach a point about seven miles from shore at about 03:45, and are unexpectedly intercepted by a German Naval force, igniting a fierce and premature exchange of fire, however, the Germans subsequently fail to determine the enormous size of the force and report it as a normal British Convoy. Despite, the absence of surprise, the Allies close for the beaches, anticipating victory.

At 03:45, preliminary flanking attacks begin to unfold at Puits and Berneval to the left of Dieppe, and Pourville and Varengeville on the right. One landing runs fifteen minutes late and the attackers are thrashed upon hitting the beach. Shortly after 05:00, the Royal Navy bombards the primary target, Dieppe, to soften resistance, however, the Germans are dug in and are unscathed; their machine guns and Artillery have the entire landing beach covered.

At 05:20, the first wave lands at Dieppe, against blistering fire. Within minutes, the casualties become catastrophic. The German enfilade ravages the Infantry, reducing Regiments to the size of Companies. Thirty Allied Tanks arrive within fifteen minutes, but to no avail. The unyielding slaughter continues to pulverize the 2,000 men pinned on the murderous beach. At 05:50, a second attack force lands at Pourville, as the Queen's Own Cameron Highlanders bolt from their Craft to receive their baptism under fire. The confident, but untested troops, push toward a farm outside of town from where they can strike the Airdrome, however, decimating fire bars any advance. Also, the Canadians at Pourville, lacking Tank support, and holding untenable positions, attempt to withdraw to the beach. Staunch rear-guard actions emerge in an attempt to forestall annihilation. However, another massacre is in process as German fire virtually cuts the men to pieces, at times scattering limbs in all directions during the unmerciful barrage.

While the German war machine is smashing the ground troops, a gigantic air battle is ensuing as the Royal Air Force attempts to destroy the intercepting Luftwaffe. Despite the glowing exploits of the British Pilots, in what becomes the greatest air battle since the Battle of Britain, German Planes break through and attack the Armada and the Allied ground forces, striking more grievous blows. The Germans sustain heavy losses in Planes, however, the vast overall enemy superiority simply overpowers the Allies.

The British Command speeds more reinforcements into Dieppe to turn the tide, however, as the troops hit the beach at 06:30, the carnage simply mounts as more withering Artillery and machine gun fire thrashes the troops as they debark the Landing Craft. In addition, menacing Tanks further butcher the Infantry. Undaunted, the Canadians and British continue to fight in vain. More reinforcements are plummeted into fruitless battle as the British commit the Reserve forces, which race to the beach under the umbrella of smoke and some Naval Surface Vessel fire, however, they too encounter an impregnable wall of tortuous fire and are being methodically annihilated.

British Command, realizing the futility of the invasion, orders a full withdrawal at 11:00, however, the Germans continue to ring the area with grid fire, slaughtering more of the invasion force. The thunderous enemy fire creates a gauntlet of death, making it nearly impossible to reach the precariously positioned evacuation Landing Craft. As the beleaguered Vessels dart toward the Fleet, German fire interdicts, scorching the surf and shattering many of the rescue Vessels. At about 1300, a Command Ship nears the shore to search for signs of additional survivors, however, there are no visible signs of life, merely a bloodstained beach, strewn with corpses. Shortly thereafter, a somber message is received aboard Ship: "OUR PEOPLE HERE HAVE SURRENDERED."

The grim statistics stun the Allies. About 2,000 Canadians, many of whom are severely wounded, are taken prisoner at Dieppe. The Allies sustain a total of about 4,600 men dead, wounded or captured, during the eight-hour ordeal; a staggering figure of 3,300 men of the Canadian 2nd Division are included in this figure. A U.S. contingent, comprising 50 Rangers, participate in the mission, and sustain the loss of six men wounded and seven missing. German losses; about 600 killed or wounded.

This exasperating British defeat is a sobering experience that quickly instills respect for the ability of the German fighting men and also compels the Allies to modify their war plans. The British will not return to France until June of 1944. However, the Germans are now predisposed with a new Allied threat and must alter their plans. Hitler will deplete his forces on the Russian front, weakening his positioning there to fortify the French coast.

135

August 20th 1942 —— (Pacific-Guadalcanal) The U.S.S. *Long Island* (Aircraft Escort Vessel) transports the first contingent of Marine Aircraft Group 23 to Guadalcanal. They arrive at Henderson Field, which is now fully operational. The mud Marines are glad to see the new arrivals. The first Army Aircraft (5 P-400s) arrive on the 22nd and 11 Navy Bombers arrive on the 24th, to further augment the Airwing. **(North Atlantic)** Land-based American Aircraft seek and destroy the German Submarine *U-464*.

U.S. Corsairs swarming in the Pacific.

August 21st 1942 —— (Pacific-Guadalcanal) The island experiences the first heavy combat of the campaign, which is initiated when the Japanese assault Marine positions at the mouth of the Ilu River. The Marines charge across the river circling the Japs. American Tanks roll forward and successfully end the attack. **(Pacific-New Guinea)** A Japanese Convoy successfully maneuvers from Rabaul to Basabua, where it debarks Japanese reinforcements, which will join in the overland attack against Port Moresby. **(Atlantic-Russia)** Krymskaya, situated on the east coast of the Black Sea, is taken by the Germans.

August 22nd 1942 —— (United States) During another Joint Chiefs of Staff meeting in Washington, D.C., Admiral Leahy states that the French will react in an unfavorable manner if British troops participate in the North Africa landing. Lt. Colonel William Eddy, U.S.M.C., recently back from Spanish Morocco, has similar feelings and is also of the opinion that the French will react in similar fashion to U.S. troops. British troops participate in the landing, but no announcement is made until the beaches are secure (invasion occurs November 8th, 1942). **(Pacific-Solomons)** Five P-40s attached to the 67th Fighter Squadron, arrive at Henderson Field, the first Army Aircraft to utilize the field. The Army Planes assist against the Japanese Planes, presently impeding the supply flow coming into Guadalcanal. In other activity, the U.S.S. *Blue*, a Destroyer (DD-420) is struck by a torpedo and severely damaged, causing the U.S. to destroy it on the following day. **(Pacific-New Guinea)** The Milne Force, of 7,429 Australians, 1,365. Americans and 664 men of the Australian Royal Air Force, receive a new Commanding Officer: Australian Major General Cyril A. Clowes. The Americans are mostly Engineers and Anti-aircraft personnel. In other activity, Japanese Major General Tomitaro Horii, departs to the front lines, to take personal charge of his troops, which number in excess of 11,000 men. **(Pacific-Hawaii)** The 4th Marine Aircraft Wing (4th Marine Base Defense Air Wing) is

commissioned at Ewa and will provide protection for the Bases in the Hawaii area. **(Atlantic-South America)** Brazil declares war on Germany and Italy. **(Atlantic-Panama)** U.S. Army Planes detect and destroy another German Submarine, the *U-654*, North of Panama. **(Atlantic-Nova Scotia)** The U.S.S. *Ingraham* (DD-444), collides with the Oiler *Chemung* (AO-30), off the coast of Nova Scotia and is sunk; the *Chemung* is only damaged. In other activity, the U.S.S. *Buck* (DD-420), another Destroyer, is damaged in a collision with a Merchant Vessel.

August 24th 1942 —— (Pacific-Guadalcanal) The Lunga perimeter is bombarded by Japanese Naval Vessels. Henderson Field is under constant attack by enemy Aircraft. **(Pacific-New Guinea)** An Allied coastwatcher spots Japanese landing barges, which are heading for Milne Bay. Japanese General Horii, had ordered a major offensive and nine Transports had departed from New Ireland and Buna.

August 24th-25th 1942 —— (Pacific) BATTLE OF THE EASTERN SOLOMONS —— The Japanese launch a Naval Task Force, consisting of three Carriers, eight Battleships, six Cruisers, and 21 Destroyers, escorting four Transports, in a concentrated effort to regain Guadalcanal and Tulagi, Solomon Islands. The enemy threat is met east of Guadalcanal by Planes dispatched from Rear Admiral Fletcher's Naval Task Force. The Carrier-based Aircraft, assisted by Land-based Planes from Henderson Field, punish the invaders, sinking the Carrier *Ryuju*, a Light Cruiser and one Destroyer. Other Japanese Vessels are damaged, before they withdraw. In the Air, the Japanese are also outfought. On the 25th, the U.S. Carriers launch Planes to chase the departing Japanese Fleet, but makes no contact. Land-based Planes (Marine-Army) strike the remaining enemy Transports, which are closing in on Guadalcanal, scoring many hits. One enemy Transport and a Destroyer, the *Muzuki*, are sunk. Army Aircraft destroys the Destroyer. One Japanese Cruiser is damaged and the combined destruction causes the mission to be aborted. On Guadalcanal enemy Planes are intercepted by Marine Fighters; the Japanese lose 21 Planes and the Marines lose three. During the battle offshore, the U.S.S. *Enterprise* (CV-6) is damaged by Japanese Planes and the U.S. loses 20 Planes to the enemy's 90.

August 25th 1942 —— (Pacific-New Guinea) The Japanese Transport Barges that departed Buna (24th) are stranded at Goodenough Island and D'Entrecasteaux Island and are assaulted by P-40s, based at Milne Bay. The U.S. Pilots sink all seven Barges. In other activity, the Milne Force engages a Japanese Invasion Force of about 1,000 men, successfully driving them back. Allied Aircraft from Australia and Milne Bay, intercept the enemy Convoy, but bad weather impedes the attack and the Convoy gets through. The enemy pours ashore, during the night of the 25th-26th, but withdraws to the landing point at dawn. Contingents of the Australian 61st Militia Battalion are rushing from Ahioma toward Milne Bay, but enemy fire sinks one of two troop laden-ketches. The Japanese evacuate the area by sea, during the night of the 4th-5th September.

August 26th 1942 —— (Pacific-Guadalcanal) The 5th Marines, 1st Marine Division, responsible for the western flank of the Lunga perimeter, ready for an offensive to eradicate enemy resistance in their sector. **(Pacific-New Guinea)** Heavy fighting continues between the Milne Force and the Japanese.

Allied Planes damage one of the enemy Transports and destroy the majority of supplies, which had been unloaded on the beach. During the night, the remainder of the Japanese force lands and subsequently makes another night attack, only to be pushed back again at dawn.

August 26th-28th 1942-March 1943 — (Pacific-New Guinea) The Allied Milne Force is assaulted by the Japs at the Milne Bay Airstrip, but the Australian 7th Brigade, supported by the 709th Airborne and 43rd U.S. Engineers, withstand the assault. Other Australians battle tenaciously as they withdraw across the Owen Stanley Mountains. The Japanese continue toward Port Moresby and reach within 30 miles by the middle of September. General MacArthur immediately bolsters the defenders with men, Planes and supplies, to repulse the Japanese. Informed by his staff, that it would be impossible to attempt such an Airlift, MacArthur asks General Kenney if he can do it. Kenney responds: " GIVE ME A FEW DAYS AND I'LL MOVE A WHOLE DAMNED DIVISION." Kenney's splendid Air Corps transports in excess of one million tons of ammunition and supplies, plus two Divisions, to meet the Jap threat. Kenney also entices civilian Pilots landing in Brisbane to help with the operation. The vicious battle ensues for nearly a year, but the Japanese will be driven back across the mountains. The Allies roll over the mountains in hot pursuit, seizing Buna, before pushing the Japs back to Rabaul. The Japanese advance had been totally stymied by MacArthur and now, the Japanese face the loss of Lae and Salamaua, their primary strongholds in New Guinea.

The Allied counter offensive progresses through the fall of 42, into the winter of 43. Japan, in a desperate move to save Rabaul from capitulation, speeds a 22-Vessel Task Force, toward Lae, hoping to land 7,000 reinforcements. As the Flotilla is en route, inclement weather appears to be aiding the enemy, keeping it from being detected until U.S. Patrol Planes luckily spot the Ships in the Bismarck Sea. Word of the Invasion Force's position is speedily transmitted to Headquarters and the U.S. Fifth Air Force, is brought to task. The Planes, based on Papua, soar through the sky and deliver an unmerciful blow to the Convoy. The combined Airpower of Major General Kenney's B-17s and B-25s, swoop over and destroy or damage the entire enemy Fleet. The Japanese lose the majority of their Landing Force to drowning. Very few survive the ordeal. In addition, the Japanese lose over 100 Aircraft. This severe loss, follows the Japanese defeat at Guadalcanal and further complicates their grand strategy. Now the Japanese will be forced to withdraw from the Indian border. The Japanese war machine, which had started in full motion, against the slumbering forces of the United States, is beginning to falter, as the Americans are thrusting into high gear. During this Allied victory in New Guinea, the Japanese lose approximately 418 Planes, 20 Warships, and about 90 Transports, in addition to the loss of about 150 Troop Transport Barges. Port Moresby has been saved by the enduring Air Corps and the unyielding American and Australian ground forces.

August 27th 1942 — (Pacific-Guadalcanal) Additional Marines (1st Bn., 5th Marines), land west of Kokumbona, and drive east along the shore, meeting stiff enemy resistance outside of Kokumbona. Another Marine unit (Company I, 3rd Battalion) drives west from Kukum, to head off retreating Japanese, that are moving inland. In other activity, additional Army P-40s land at Henderson. **(Pacific-New Guinea)** During the evening, the enemy mounts a Tank supported attack and presses the Allied defenders, at the K.B. Mission, to pull back. Meanwhile, the Japanese advance overland toward Port Moresby and continue to force the Australians to withdraw. **(Atlantic-Russia)** The Germans (Group A) seize Prokhladny and near Grozny, which is rich in oil supplies.

Douglas-A20s in action over New Guinea.

August 28th 1942 — (Pacific-Guadalcanal) Marines (1st Bn., 5th Marines) complete a successful flanking movement, without encountering enemy forces and return to the Kukum vicinity, with elements of the 3rd Battalion. In other activity near Guadalcanal, Marine Fighters depart Henderson Field and assault Japanese Vessels off the coast of Santa Isabel, in order to prevent them from debarking reinforcements. The Marines succeed in turning them back, but not before the Japanese lose the Destroyer *Asagiri* and have two others damaged. The Japanese also lose the Submarine *I-123*, after it engages the U.S.S. *Gamble* (DM-15), a Light Minesweeper, off the coast of Guadalcanal. On the following day, the U.S. Transport *William Ward Burrows* (AP-6), is run aground. **(Pacific-New Guinea)** The Japanese mount a strong attack, against Airstrip No. 3, but the Australians, supported by American troops, handily rebuff the attack. In other activity, the battle in the Owen Stanley Mountain Range, continues to rage, with the Japanese pushing hard to reach Port Moresby. **(Atlantic-Caribbean)** The H.M.S. *Oakville* and U.S. Naval Aircraft, operating in the Caribbean, encounter and destroy the German U-Boat *94*. **(Atlantic-Russia)** The Germans (Group A) initiate an attack against the Black Sea city of Novorossisk.

August 29th 1942 — (Pacific-New Guinea) A Japanese Naval Convoy is located, as it nears the Milne Bay area, however, about 775 enemy troops debark.

August 30th 1942 — (North Pacific) A U.S. Occupation Force, consisting of Army and Navy contingents, lands at Adak, Aleutian Islands without opposition. **(Pacific-Guadalcanal)** The U.S.S. *Colhoun* (Transport APD-2), is sunk by enemy Bombers. The rear echelon of Marine Group VMF-221 and 231 (18 Fighters and 12 Dive Bombers) arrives safely, at Henderson Field. **(Pacific-New Guinea)** In New Guinea, the Japanese are still prevented from capturing the Airstrip, at Milne Bay, losing many men in the futile effort. The momentum begins to swing to the Allies (Australian-American).

August 31st 1942 — (Pacific-Solomon Islands) The Carrier, U.S.S. *Saratoga* (CV-3), operating slightly over 250 miles southeast of Guadalcanal, is seriously damaged by a torpedo from an enemy Submarine and is forced to withdraw from the area, to seek repairs at Tongatabu; she subsequently returns to Pearl Harbor, where she stays until November. The loss of her Carrier support is something, that the U.S. can ill afford. A Japanese Force in excess of 6,000 men lands in the vicinity of Kokumbona, to threaten the Marine positions. Reinforcements (1st Raider Battalion and 1st Parachute Battalion) arrive to strengthen the perimeter defense against enemy attack. **(North Pacific-Aleutians)** The Destroyer U.S.S. *Reid*, coordinating with Naval Aircraft operating out of the Aleutians, destroys the Japanese Submarine *RO-61*.

September 1st 1942 — (Pacific-Guadalcanal) Two hundred Seabees arrive on the U.S.S. *Betelguese* (6th Naval Construction Bn.) to further develop the Airfield. These particular Seabees are the first contingent to serve in a war zone. Construction begins immediately, because it is imperative to increase the operational capacity, to accommodate more Fighter Aircraft to insure American control of the island. In other activity on Guadalcanal, the U.S. establishes the Air Force, Pacific Fleet, which is to be commanded by American Vice Admiral A.W. Fitch. **(Pacific-Japan)** Japanese Foreign Minister Shigenori Togo resigns. He is replaced by Hiddeki Tojo, who also holds the post of Prime Minister. **(Atlantic)** Heavy fighting continues between the Germans and Russians, in the vicinity of Stalingrad.

September 2nd 1942 — (Pacific-Samoa) Elements of the 5th Defense Battalion and the 7th Marines, depart Samoa, heading for New Hebrides. **(Pacific-New Guinea)** The Japanese maintain their progress along the overland route, driving the Australians back toward Port Moresby. During the night 2nd-3rd, about 1,000 Japanese reinforcements from Rabaul land at Basabua to support the overland drive. In other activity, the Milne Force continues its efforts to expel the enemy from the northern coast of Milne Bay.

September 3rd 1942 — (Southwest Pacific) American General Kenney disengages the U.S. Fifth Air Force from his Allied command (South West Pacific Area) and designates it a separate unit, for the purpose of attaining more efficiency. The Fifth Air Force receives responsibility for the northeast area and the Royal Australian Air Force is directed to defend Australia from enemy attacks.

September 4th 1942 — (Pacific-Solomons) The 1st Marine Raider Battalion scouts Savo Island and finding no enemy troops, returns to Guadalcanal. In other activity, enemy Warships prowling the Sealark Channel, in the vicinity of the Solomons after dark on the night 4th-5th, sink two U.S. Destroyer Transports, the *Little* (APD-3) and the *Gregory* (APD-4).

September 5th 1942 — (U.S.-England) The Allied decision to include landings at Algiers and Oran in Algeria and at Casablanca, Morocco as part of Operation Torch (Allied invasion of Northwest Africa), is finalized. **(Pacific-New Guinea)** The Japanese, under enormous pressure from the Milne Force, continue to evacuate the Milne Bay area. Approximately 1,300 of the original 1,900 troops depart by sea, under cover of darkness. The Australians seize the enemy supply depot at Waga.

September 6th 1942 — (Pacific-New Guinea) The Australians hold the line at Milne Bay, ending organized Japanese opposition. Mop up operations are initiated to destroy the remaining isolated pockets of enemy resistance in the area. This Australian victory ends the possibility of an enemy attack against Port Moresby from the Milne area, but the overland advance, across the Owen Stanley Mountain route, is still a serious threat. **(Pacific-Tonga Islands)** The U.S.S. *South Dakota* (BB-57), operating in the vicinity of the Tonga Islands, is damaged after striking a coral reef while maneuvering through the Lahai Passage.

September 7th 1942 — (United States) The U.S. and Cuba reach an agreement concerning Military and Naval cooperation between the two countries. **(Atlantic-Egypt)** British General Montgomery calls a premature end to the battle of 'Alam el Halfa, before the British can regain their original positions, allowing the enemy to retain possession of a large section of desert on the southern flank. The British Eighth Army, under "Monty," begins planning for an offensive to secure El Alamein. Montgomery's offensive commences on the 23rd of October.

September 8th 1942 — (Pacific-Guadalcanal) Marines (1st Raider Battalion and 1st Parachute Battalion minus parachutes) are transported by two Destroyers, east of Tasimboko, where they land and assault a Japanese installation from the rear. Planes based at Henderson Field, support the surprise attack, which culminates with the successful capture of the enemy supply base. The Japanese lose 27 killed. The Marines suffer eight casualties. **(Pacific-New Guinea)** Five Japanese reinforced Battalions, commanded by General Horii, assault the Australian 21st Brigade, 7th Division, at Efogi Spur. The outnumbered Aussies are driven from their positions and two Battalions are isolated.

Admiral William F. Halsey, Jr., U.S.N.

138

September 9th 1942 — (United States) A Japanese Plane launched from a Submarine releases a bomb over a mountain in the vicinity of Bookings, Oregon, causing slight fire damage. This is the solitary time an enemy Plane manages to bomb the Continental United States. In other activity, the U.S.S. *Muskeget* (AG-48), a Coast Guard Weather Ship, operating between the U.S. and Iceland, is lost at sea (circumstances unknown). **(Pacific-New Guinea)** Australian reinforcements are rushed to the Owen Stanley Mountain Range Front, to support the defenders against the enemy threat. In addition, elements of the Australian 6th Division are dispatched to Port Moresby. **(Atlantic-Madagascar)** British Troops (East Africa Command) commence a surprise attack against Majunga on the west coast and capture it, without opposition, during the night of the 9-10th. This prize greatly aids the British, who are attempting to control the air and sea routes of the Mozambique Channel. **(Atlantic-Germany)** The Royal Air Force (Bomber Command) releases its first two-ton incendiary bomb during an Air raid over Duesseldorf.

September 11th 1942 — (Pacific-Guadalcanal) Japanese Aircraft attack Henderson Field, continuing their efforts to maintain pressure against the Marine defenders. **(Pacific-New Guinea)** General MacArthur steps up the initiative to drive the Japanese from New Guinea by setting up specific plans for a major pincer movement, with the Australians striking in the vicinity of Port Moresby. MacArthur will supplement this operation by maneuvering the U.S. 33rd Division, behind enemy lines for a surprise attack at Wairopi. This calculated gamble turns into a test of endurance and the Allies, succeed by pressuring the Japanese to retreat desperately over the mountains, from which they came. In combat activity today, U.S. and British Aircraft catch a Japanese Destroyer, the *Yayoi*, as it is cruising in the vicinity of Normanby Island in the D'Entrecasteaux Islands, near New Guinea. The combined contingents destroy the enemy Submarine. **(North Pacific-Aleutians)** The American occupation force at Adak completes its Airstrip operation, paving the way for Air strikes to be launched against enemy positions on Kiska, which until this point had been out of range for the U.S. Aircraft.

September 12th-14th 1942 — THE BATTLE OF EDSON'S RIDGE (Guadalcanal) — Three Japanese Destroyers and a Light Cruiser, lurking in the Sealark Channel, commence a bombardment of Henderson Field. This Naval barrage is supplemented by a major enemy assault against Marine positions on Edson's Ridge, in the western sector south of Henderson. The Marines (800 men), commanded by Colonel Merritt Edson, are greatly outnumbered against the Japanese, who temporarily penetrate the Raider Parachute Battalion's positions on the 13th. Through the daylight hours, Japanese snipers ring the perimeter with shots, keeping all Marines on edge through the night. Major Kenneth Bailey, commanding Company C, on the right flank, leads his men in a fight of gruesome hand to hand combat for ten grueling hours, after the enemy penetrates the main line of defense, during the first assault soon after nightfall. Major Bailey, suffering gravely from a head wound, insists on maintaining command and leading his men. His troops, along with the other defenders, hang tough against no less than twelve brutalizing assaults throughout the night.

Old Glory is victorious over the Samauri Bandits. As the sun

rises on the 14th, exhausted, but enthusiastic Marines, their strength barely over two full Companies, have wrecked Kawaguchi's force, numbering over two full Battalions. As the remaining Japanese evacuate the slopes of what is now called "Bloody Ridge," heading toward Kokumbona, Aircraft blasts them with machine gun fire and bombs. Henderson Field remains in control of the Americans and 600 dead Japanese line the perimeter. The Marines sustain 143 casualties. Colonel Edson and Major Bailey both become recipients of the Medal of Honor for their valiant efforts. Bailey receives the Medal posthumously.

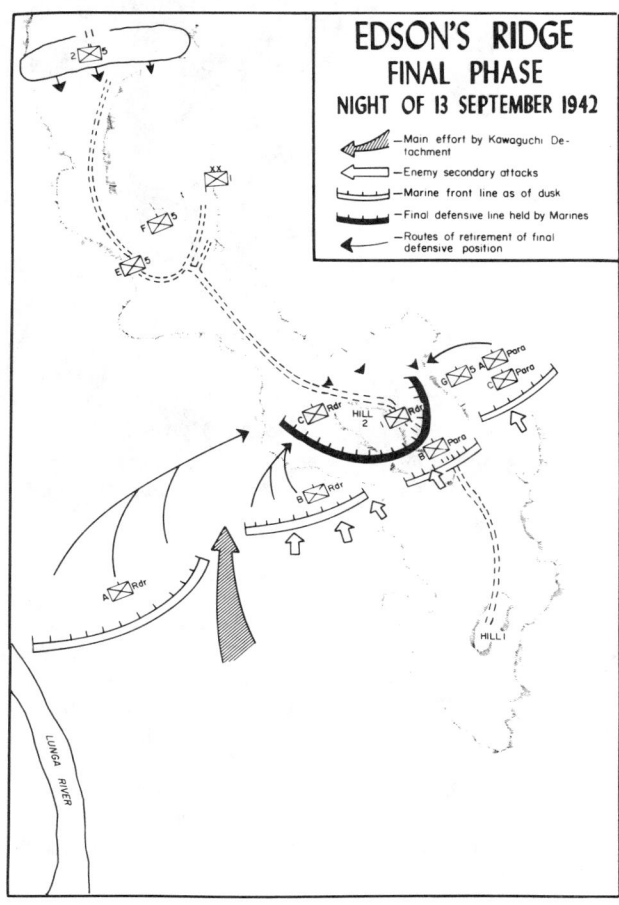

September 12th 1942 — (United States) The U.S. accepts operational command of the Brazilian Navy, which is to participate in the war against the Axis. **(Atlantic)** The Germans initiate a combined air-sea assault, lasting 10 days, against an Allied Convoy attempting to reach northern Russia with supplies. **(Atlantic-England)** General Eisenhower assumes command of the Allied Expeditionary Force, which will make the invasion of Northwest Africa (Operation TORCH). General Eisenhower will make his headquarters in London.

September 13th 1942 — (China) American General Stilwell proposes plans to Chiang Kai-shek, which will prioritize the defense of the ferry route, operating between India and China. **(Atlantic-Libya)** British troops, moving in small units, on both land and sea, assault German positions at Tobruk, but cause only minor damage.

Plane bombing Bloody Nose Ridge, Guadalcanal.

September 14th 1942 — (Pacific-New Guinea) The Japanese, pressing towards Port Moresby, drive the Australians further back, forcing them to regroup at Imita Ridge, a mere 32 miles from the Japanese objective. This is the final pullback of the Australians along this front. On the following day, U.S. troops are flown into Port Moresby, from Brisbane, Australia, initiating the first portion of MacArthur's counter-offensive. These contingents of Co. E, 126th Infantry, 33rd Division, are the first American Infantry units to arrive in New Guinea.

September 15th 1942 — (Pacific-Guadalcanal) An American Carrier Task Force, commanded by Rear Admiral Noyes, is attacked by two Japanese Submarines, while escorting Transport Vessels to the besieged American positions on Guadalcanal. The Carrier U.S.S. *Wasp* (CV-7), is struck and heavily damaged by an enemy torpedo, while still in the vicinity of New Hebrides. The concussion and fire, followed by explosions, costs the lives of approximately 200 men. The *Wasp* is subsequently destroyed by the U.S. Navy. The U.S.S. *North Carolina* (BB-55, Battleship), along with the Destroyer *O'Brien* (DD-415), suffer slight damage. The entire time lapsed during the assault is less than 10 minutes. In other activity, Japanese Battleships bombard Marine positions on Edson's Ridge. The Japanese maintain sporadic action, by firing upon the 3rd Battalion, 1st Marines, which is positioned along the southeastern portion of the Lunga perimeter. **(Pacific-New Guinea)** Advance contingents of the 126th U.S. Infantry, U.S. 32nd Division, arrive at Port Moresby. These

troops have been ordered in by Airlift by MacArthur, who is determined to whip the Japanese and deny them control of New Guinea. General Kenney's Air Corps begins a non-stop campaign to reinforce Allied positions. Planes, based in Australia, fly in and out of New Guinea around the clock transporting two Divisions and over a million tons of ammunition and supplies to the northern coast of New Guinea before the operation concludes.

September 15th 1942 — The U.S.S. Wasp (CV-7) after being struck by an Japanese torpedo.

September 16th 1942 — (United States) Navy Patrol Wing 12 is commissioned at Key West, Florida and will operate in the Gulf Sea Frontier. In other activity, U.S. Task Force 23, commanded by Vice Admiral J.H. Ingram, becomes the South Atlantic Force, Atlantic Fleet. **(Pacific-New Guinea)** The Japanese, short of both ammunition and reinforcements are thrown back at Iorabaiwa. The Australians, now fortified by the first elements of American Infantry, poise for a counter attack. The Japanese will evacuate Iorabaiwa Ridge on the 27th, retreating at full steam, with the Aussies in pursuit. **(North Pacific-Aleutians)** The Japanese complete the movement of their Garrison, from Attu to Kiska. The transfer had begun in late August. **(Atlantic-Russia)** The Germans move to the outskirts of Stalingrad.

September 17th 1942 — (Pacific-New Guinea) A reconnaissance team, led by Captain William F. Boice, departs Port Moresby heading for Kapa Kapa to scout inland toward Jaure. Another reconnaissance team moves towards Abau. The enemy suffers from massive supply problems and they are in a vulnerable position.

September 18th 1942 — (United States) A German Submarine squirms unnoticed through U.S. defenses and deploys mines in the vicinity of Charleston, South Carolina. **(Pacific Guadalcanal)** The Marines are put back on full rations. Most Marines were not compatible with the captured Japanese rations and are delighted to have their rations increased. In other activity, the remainder of the First Marine Division (7th Marines) arrives offshore on Task Force 65 and debarks at Kukum. The ammunition is the first to be brought ashore, since the request back on the 22nd of August. Badly needed aviation fuel also arrives on three different Vessels. After the successful unloading of troops and supplies, Task Force 65 embarks with the 1st Paratroop Battalion, some wounded and eight Japanese prisoners, heading for Espiritu Santo, New Hebrides. **(Pacific-New Guinea)** Japanese General Horii receives orders from Imperial Headquarters to retain the Buna-

Gona beachhead as the major defensive position and to hold his present positions as long as he can, however, a disciplined withdrawal is begun. **(Pacific-Australia)** The balance of the 126th Infantry (minus Artillery), 32nd Division, departs Brisbane Australia, heading for New Guinea, to bolster the American troops. **(Atlantic-Madagascar)** Elements of the British East African Command, land unopposed at Madagascar and move inland from the beachhead at Tamatave without incident.

September 19th 1942 — (Pacific-Guadalcanal) General Vandegrift, U.S.M.C., divides the Lunga area into 10 sectors. The Marines have held their positions and are now expanding their coveted terrain. Supplies are flowing in much more smoothly and they have adapted to jungle warfare. Marines who move around, do so with caution. Sometimes an alleged dead Jap, hanging from a tree, is merely fastened with wire, ready to kill an approaching Marine. They take precautions by ringing a few extra shots at the dead snipers.

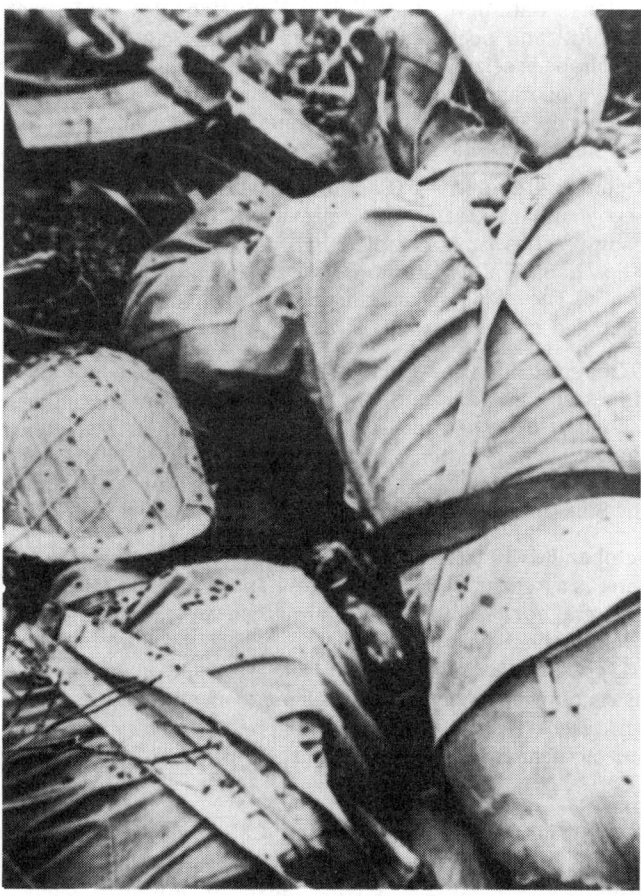

A deadly encounter between Japanese Snipers and Marine sharpshooters.

September 20th 1942 — (Atlantic-England) D-Day for the Allied invasion of North Africa is set for November 8. The code name for the operations is TORCH. **(Pacific-New Guinea)** The 127th Infantry, U.S. 32nd Division, receives orders to move to Port Moresby. **(Pacific-New Zealand)** The United States Navy establishes an Operating Base in New Zealand, a country located southeast of Australia. **(Atlantic-Russia)** The German Army Group A captures the town of Terek.

September 22nd 1942 — (United States) In Washington, the Combined Chiefs of Staff approve a plan, which gives the U.S. the responsibility of moving supplies to the Russians, via the Persian Corridor.

September 23rd 1942 — (Pacific-New Guinea) General Sir Thomas Blamey (Australian) arrives in Port Moresby and takes command of all New Guinea Forces. On this day, the 128th Infantry, U.S. 32nd Division, arrives at Port Moresby.

September 23rd-27th 1942 — (Pacific-Guadalcanal) Contingents of the 5th and 7th Marines, assisted by the 1st Raider Battalion, assault Japanese positions across the Matanikau River. Fierce fighting occurs in the vicinity of Mt. Austen and Matanikau village. The Marines are forced to withdraw on the 27th. Petty Officer Douglas Munro (U.S. Coast Guard) courageously leads 5 Higgins Boats to rescue the beleaguered Marines; 19 more follow. Munro is killed, but his dauntless courage and leadership saves the Marines. The Marines attack again on October 7th and after a brutalizing three-day battle, the Japanese lose 700 men. The Marines pull back to their positions suffering 65 men killed, 125 wounded. Artillery from the 11th Marines, assisted in the operation and greatly aided the attack across the river.

Marine Corps Artillery in action on Guadalcanal.

September 24th 1942 — (Pacific-Gilbert Islands) Japanese troops debark at Maiana, Gilbert Islands. Additional landings take place at Beru and Kuria on the 25th and 27th, respectively.

September 25th 1942 — **(Pacific-New Guinea)** The 25th Australian Brigade, 7th Division, mounts an intense counter-attack to push the Japanese back down the Port Moresby-Kokoda Trail, and give the Aussies an opportunity to seize Ioribaiwa. **(Atlantic-Madagascar)** The British secure control of central Madagascar.

September 26th 1942 — **(Pacific-Guadalcanal)** Heavy fighting continues between the Marines and Japanese in the vicinity of Matanikau village. Air and artillery support are called upon to assist the Marines.

September 27th 1942 — **(Pacific-Guadalcanal)** The Marines withdraw from Matanikau, unable to penetrate the solid Japanese defenses. **(Pacific-New Guinea)** Ioribaiwa Ridge is evacuated by the Japanese under strong pressure from the Australians. **(South Atlantic)** The U.S. Merchant Vessel *Stephen Hopkins* engages the German Vessel *Schiff.* The German Ship is damaged and subsequently sinks.

September 28th 1942 — **(Pacific-New Guinea)** The principal body of the U.S. 126th Infantry arrives at Port Moresby and will aid the Australians, during their advance to seize Wairopi. **(North Pacific)** U.S. Army Aircraft, based in the Aleutians, spot and destroy the Japanese Submarine *RO-65* in the vicinity of Kiska.

September 28th 1942 — U.S. Infantry troops crossing the Samboga River near Dobodura, New Guinea.

September 29th 1942 — **(Pacific-Solomon Islands)** A Japanese Submarine, stalking Shipping lanes near the Solomons, spots a U.S. Cargo Vessel, the *Albena* (AK-26) and sinks it with a torpedo. At the present time, the Garrison on Guadalcanal is composed of 19,261 men; Tulagi has 3,260 troops.

September 30th 1942 — **(Pacific-New Hebrides)** Two U.S. Vessels, the Destroyer *Breese* (DD-122) and the Heavy Cruiser *San Francisco* (CA-38) crash and become damaged, while cruising in the vicinity of New Hebrides.

October 1st 1942 — **(United States)** The U.S. Navy's Advanced Group, Amphibious Forces, Atlantic Fleet becomes Amphibious Forces, Europe and is part of the U.S. Naval Forces, Europe, under the command of Admiral H.R. Stark. **(Atlantic)** The Germans besieging Stalingrad, continue to pound the Russians with Air and Artillery bombardment. The Germans have extended their supply lines and will soon face the most terrifying enemy of all, winter. The Soviets try in vain to reinforce the defenders of Stalingrad. The other German offensive, driving toward the oil fields of Grozny, meets heavy opposition through October, however, subsequent to heavy fighting near the Black Sea, it tails off.

October 2nd 1942 — **(Pacific-Ellice Islands)** The Marine 5th Defense Battalion, stationed in New Hebrides, arrives at Funafuti and occupies the island. **(Atlantic-Madagascar)** Antsirabe is seized by the British. In other activity, U.S. Army Planes operating in the vicinity of French Guiana, located in the northeast section of South America, attack and sink the German Submarine *U-512*.

October 4th 1942 — **(Pacific-New Guinea)** The American reconnaissance team, which previously departed Port Moresby, reaches Jaure, completing its mission and finds that the Kapa Kapa Trail is laborious, but a crossing is feasible. **(Atlantic)** The island of Sark situated in the English Channel and occupied by the enemy is struck by a British Raiding party.

October 5th 1942 — **(Pacific-Guadalcanal)** Skirmishing continues on the island and off the coast, American Aircraft are launched from sea to assault enemy Vessels located near Bougainville. In other activity in the Solomons, U.S. Planes, operating from Carriers, assault enemy positions at Fais and the Buin-Tonolei areas, Bougainville.

October 6th 1942 — **(United States)** More aid to the Russians, is agreed upon, in Washington. The U.S. sends 3,300,000 tons via north Soviet ports and another 1,100,000 tons through the Persian Gulf. (Oct. 6th 1942 through July 1st 1943). **(Atlantic-Egypt)** British General Montgomery issues instructions pertinent to the El 'Alamein offensive in the western desert. **(Atlantic-Russia)** Malgobek, a city rich in oil, situated near Grozny, is seized by the Germans (Army Group A).

October 7th 1942 — **(Pacific-New Caledonia)** Task Force 64.2 (TF Sugar), commanded by Admiral Scott, departs Espiritu Santo escorting a Convoy transporting approximately 6,000 Soldiers (164th Infantry, Americal Division), the First Marine Aircraft Wing and some additional Marine units and supplies to bolster the Marines on Guadalcanal. The Task Force is composed of four Cruisers including Scott's Flagship, the *San Francisco*, and five Destroyers. Additional protection is situated west of Guadalcanal in the form of the *Hornet* Force; to the east, another Force which includes the Battleship *Washington*, stands guardian off Malaita. The Convoy reaches Guadalcanal on the 9th and remains off the southwest coast for two additional days. **(Pacific-Solomons-Guadalcanal)** The Marines open an offensive, dispatching elements of the 1st Division west in three columns from Henderson Field to expand their perimeter. The 5th Marines drive hard along the coast, heading for the mouth of the Matanikau, pushing the Japanese troops back toward the river. A large segment of the 7th Marines, trailed by the 3rd Battalion, 2nd Marines and a detachment of Snipers, commanded by Colonel William Whaling, drive to the southwest and surround Pt. Cruz. The 5th Marines bump into strong opposition, but the other two columns of Marines reach Hill 65 against minor resistance and make camp for the night. The 1st Raider Battalion joins the 5th Marines during the evening to bolster the coming offensive. Bad weather prevents the 5th Marines and the contingent of the 1st Raider Battalion from attacking across the Matanikau River during the morning of the 8th, but this doesn't prevent the Marines from making an improvised incision in the Japanese lines holding the east bank. In heavy fighting, the enemy beachhead is destroyed. General Vandegrift, informed of a probable enemy counterattack, diverts the troops intended for an assault against Kokumbona and Poha, against the enemy at Pt. Cruz in an all-out assault. The Yanks, consisting of Colonel Whaling's detachment and the 7th Marines, supplemented by the Artillery of the 11th Marines, attack vigorously, driving across the Matanikau charging toward the enemy to the north. Heavy fighting ensues in the vicinity of Matanikau Village and Pt. Cruz. After the brutalizing contest, the Marines withdraw eastwardly, crossing the Matanikau at its mouth under the cover fire of the 5th Marines, concluding the three day operation. The introductory engagement results in the loss of 700 Japanese troops. The Marines lose 65 men killed and 125 wounded. This operation prevents the Japanese 4th Infantry from crossing the Matanikau River and setting up Artillery units, which would threaten the American beachhead. **(Pacific-New Guinea)** A contingent of the U.S. 32nd Division, including Co. E, 126th Regiment, under Captain Alfred Medendorp, departs Kalikodobu, located 40 miles southeast of Port Moresby and moves towards Jaure for reconnaissance purposes. The arduous trek must be supplied primarily by air.

October 8th 1942 — (New Guinea) The Japanese continue to retreat from the Port Moresby area, but decide, to make a stand against the Allies at Templeton's Crossing. **(China-Burma-India)** General Chennault requests additional Planes, in order to destroy the Japanese Air Force in China. He also requests in his letter to the President permission to raid Japan, after the demise of the Japanese Airpower.

October 9th 1942 — (Atlantic) U.S. and R.A.F. Fighters, escort approximately 100 American Heavy Bombers as they deliver a blow to the industrial areas of Lille, France. The mission succeeds and the Germans suffer about 100 Planes, lost or damaged. **(Pacific)** The U.S. 164th Infantry aboard a Convoy, escorted by a U.S. Task Force under Admiral Scott departs Noumea, New Caledonia. Marine Fighter Squadron 121 and the last contingent of 2nd Marines, 2nd Marine Division, also departs. The Japanese who have been getting hammered by Marine Planes as they run Transports to reinforce their forces on Guadalcanal, speed troops (Tokyo Express) toward the contested island.

October 10th 1942 — (Pacific-Australia) General MacArthur is updated consistently, concerning the situation with the ongoing counter-offensive in New Guinea. The code-breaking unit, based in Melbourne, has continued its operation for months, with remarkable success, enabling MacArthur to use strategy based on his awareness of enemy plans. **(Pacific-Guadalcanal)** Marine defense positions, undergoing constant reinforcing to prepare for a Japanese counter-offensive, send out heavy Patrols to watch for enemy activity. Permanent defenses are being established at the mouth of the Matanikau. **(Pacific-New Guinea)** The Allied counter-offensive in New Guinea continues to relieve pressure at Port Moresby, preventing the Japanese from seizing it and holding a base within 300 miles from Australia. In other activity, the principal portion of the 2nd Battalion, 126th U.S. Infantry and its supporting contingents depart Kalikodobu, kicking off the strenuous march to Juare.

October 11th 1942 — (Pacific-Midway) The Submarine U.S.S. *Hancock*, equipped with SJ Radar, embarks from Midway on its second War Patrol and will spend its time navigating in the Yellow Sea near the China Mainland and Korea. **(Pacific-Solomons-Guadalcanal)** U.S. Scout Planes discover a Japanese Armada steaming down "the Slot" about 200 miles from Guadalcanal. Admiral Scott's Task Force moves to neutralize the threat and blockade the entrance to Savo Sound with his Cruisers and Destroyers. The enemy Force commanded by Admiral Aritomo Goto slips through, however, setting up a possible rerun of the battle off Savo (August 9 1942), but it doesn't occur. Trailing the bombardment Force are the Transports escorted by Seaplane Carriers and Destroyers.

October 11th-12th 1942 — (Pacific-Solomons) — BATTLE OF CAPE ESPERANCE — The Americans are holding precariously on Guadalcanal and the supply situation is critical. The 1st Marine Division has been heavily engaged since the initial landing on the island on August 7th without a lull. The mud Marines and their limited Air strength have withstood all enemy attempts to dislodge and destroy them, but it has been tremendously difficult. Between the 13th and 14th, enemy Planes heavily bombard American lines and this devastation is followed by 1,000 rounds of 14-inch shells from the Battleships *Kongo* and *Haruna*. As soon as the Navy attempts to bring in supplies, the Japanese Planes move in fast and force the Vessels to withdraw. In addition, malaria and dysentery have taken a high toll on the Marines. An American Task Force, commanded by Rear Admiral Scott is escorting a Convoy from Noumea to Guadalcanal to help alleviate the problem, but intelligence gathering by the code-breakers has been totally accurate, concerning a storm of enemy activity and as anticipated a large enemy Armada is converging on Guadalcanal. Scout Planes spot the enemy movement in the afternoon and report the enemy positions at about 210 miles distant. Scott's Force shifts to blockade the entrance to Savo Sound off Cape Esperance. At this point, the Americans do not control the seas and are outgunned, but unlike their last deadly encounter off Savo Island on the 8th-9th of August, the Americans will acquire more accurate information and be prepared. It is the Japanese who receive the unexpected surprise this night.

The Japanese have been consistently reinforcing their positions by navigating the "Slot" under cover of darkness with the "Tokyo Express" and have massed over 30,000 troops in the vicinity of Lunga Point by the beginning of October. The U.S. Navy intends to derail this floating train and bring it to a flaming halt before it can arrive and bolster General Kawaguchi. Admiral Goto, commanding the enemy Force is convinced the Imperial Navy cannot fail, but his thoughts of prostrating the Americans are premature. Scott's Force deploys under a lazily setting sun as the tranquil waters begin to stir while the two antagonists converge. The sweltering night air does little to relieve the pressure as midnight approaches.

The Japanese cruise forward under a slender moon with three swaggering Heavy Cruisers, all participating conquerors at the battle of Savo Island during August. With the Cruisers *Aoba, Furutaka* and the *Kinugasa* leading the pugnacious Armada, along with the Destroyers *Murakumo* and *Fubuki*, this vociferous vanguard expects to lambaste the Marines at Lunga Point and afford the trailing group of Warships the opportunity to debark the reinforcements and accompanying equipment, including Tanks.

At 23:30, a Pilot attached to the *San Francisco* sounds the alarm, signaling the presence of the Imperial Navy at the gateway to Guadalcanal. Admiral Scott reacts immediately, ordering a change in course that has the Task Force reversing its northeastward thrust for a sprint to block the pass between Cape Esperance and Savo Island. Three of the Destroyers get a late jump during the complicated maneuver and put on a burst of speed to overtake the Cruisers and become positioned between the American Cruisers and the enemy Armada.

At 23:46, unaware that American Destroyers might be in the direct line of fire, the *Helena* commences firing at a target sighted by radar. The *Boise* and the Heavy Cruisers *San Francisco* and *Salt Lake City* join in the shelling, broadsiding the surprised Japanese with deadly results before the call to battle stations. Unfortunately, the U.S. Destroyers *Duncan Laffey* and *Farenholt* are in harm's way.

The *Aoba, Furutaka* and *Murakumo* are splattered with shells during the encounter, but Admiral Scott, fearful for the safety of the U.S. Destroyers, orders a cease-fire until they can clear the fire zone. Admiral Goto attempts to reverse his course only to position his Armada back in line of fire from U.S. Ships, some of which have not received the order to cease fire. The turkey shoot resumes and additional deadly volleys crash into the beleaguered *Aoba*. The battered Ship survives the ordeal, but Admiral Goto falls mortally wounded. The U.S. Destroyers attempt to get on line with their guns and torpedoes firing as they move. The *Duncan* which is in the middle of the battle grid, while pursuing the enemy, becomes wedged between the enraged opponents and decides to break for the *Furutaka*. The pesty *Duncan* unloads her torpedoes, but is fatally hit herself, when an American salvo strikes a savage blow. The *Farenholt*, becomes the second American Vessel damaged at about the same time as the *Duncan*, probably by U.S. guns.

The sky is full of arcing tracers forming multi colored steams of fire during the semi-confusion with unremitting volleys. The origin of the shells is often undetectable as both sides suffer grievous losses due to firing on their own Ships. At a few strokes before midnight as the *Fubuki* stumbles through the darkness a stone's throw from the guns of the *San Francisco*, the U.S. Cruiser flips a switch and pins the Vessel in her searchlights. American Warships take a bead on the target and in unison commence firing, quickly extinguishing the lights of the *Fubuki* permanently. Possible enemy Warships

are tracked through the radar screen of the Cruiser *Boise*. In an attempt to verify identification, her searchlight beams in the general direction of the suspected target, resulting in an immediate response from two Japanese Warships. The *Boise* is riddled with fire and a subsequent explosion that illuminates the immediate area, exposing the location of the *Salt Lake City*. The spotlighted Vessel sustains several hits. Undaunted, the Yankee clippers continue to buzz forward giving chase to the westward bound *Kinugasa*, which had fired upon the *Boise*, lumbering volleys of shells upon the fleeing Vessel.

The contentious affair lasted only 34 minutes from inception to finale. By 00:20 on the 13th, the Fleets have totally disengaged. The enemy heads west and Admiral Scott instructs the Destroyer *McCalla* to circulate and lend aid to the disabled Vessels.

On the 12th, the Destroyers *Murakumo* and *Natsugumo*, trailing the retreating Fleet to pick up survivors, are blown from the water by Aircraft (Navy and Marine) based at Henderson Field. The Japanese have also lost the Cruiser *Furutaka* and the Destroyer *Fubuki*. The U.S. suffers damage to two cruisers, the U.S.S. *Salt Lake City* (CA-25) and the *Boise* (CL-47). In addition, the Destroyers *Duncan* (DD-485) and *Farenholt* (DD-491), are also damaged during the vicious confrontation, the *Duncan* to be sunk by enemy fire on the 12th. The Navy and Marines however, force the Japs to abort the planned invasion and return to Rabaul.

October 12th 1942 — (Pacific-Guadalcanal) Four Motor Torpedo Boats (Squadron 3), are brought in by tow to Tulagi, becoming the first Naval Vessels to be permanently based at Tulagi. **(China-Burma-India)** American General Joseph Stilwell requests that 30 additional Chinese Divisions be equipped for combat. The War Department grants approval of his request on the 19th of October.

A decimated Japanese Destroyer.

October 13th 1942 — (Pacific-Guadalcanal) Marine defenders continue to receive additional troops. The U.S.S. *McCawley* and *Zeilen* (Transports) deliver reinforcements from the 164th U.S. Infantry, Americal Division. In addition, over 200 men of the 1st Marine Air Wing, nearly 100 Marine casuals and weapons and ammunition are also on board. Sailors unload the Vessels during frequent Air attacks and successfully embark the 1st Raider Battalion, before departing for New Caledonia. Total troop strength of the 1st Marine Division stands at 23,088 men, excluding the forces on Tulagi. The Marines, anticipating a major assault by the Japs, split the perimeter into five sections, with their greatest strength placed to the west facing the Matanikau River where the Japanese would most probably strike. Henderson Field is struck again, by enemy Planes, causing damage including a hit which destroys 5,000 gallons of aviation fuel.

October 13th 1942 — U.S. Army troops arriving at Guadalcanal.

October 14th 1942 — (Pacific-Guadalcanal) Henderson Field sustains another hit by Japanese Planes, putting the Airstrip temporarily out of operation. The men work feverishly to repair the damage while ingenious improvisation is implemented, enabling Fighter Strip, located to the Southeast of Henderson to be used. The devastating enemy Air-raids have reduced operational Aircraft in the last two days from 90 to 42, and another Japanese Invasion Force is approaching the island. P-39s and SBDs (Torpedo Boats) are launched to attack the invaders, but they only manage to sink a Transport and damage another Ship. The Convoy, commanded by Admiral Tamaka, continues on course and debarks between 3,000-4,000 Japanese troops at Tassafaronga on the 15th. **(Pacific-New Guinea)** The 128th U.S. Infantry, 32nd Division and Australian contingents, are transported by the U.S. Fifth Air Force, from the coast to Wanigela. The Coastal Force is commanded by American Brigadier General Hanford MacNider. The Air movement, will be completed by October 18th.

October 15th 1942 — (United States) U.S. Naval Patrol Wing 14, is established at San Diego, California and will serve in the Western Sea Frontier. **(Pacific-Guadalcanal)** American Aircraft from Henderson Field and New Hebrides attack an enemy Convoy which had evaded destruction the previous day and is presently landing at Tassafaronga. The Japanese lose two Vessels, while others are damaged. The defenders on Guadalcanal receive desperately needed gasoline, via Army and Marine Transport Planes. In other activity, the U.S.S. *Meredith* (DD-434), a Destroyer, is attacked by enemy Planes and sunk by a torpedo, in the vicinity of San Cristobal. **(Pacific-Australia)** The U.S. Navy opens another Submarine Base to bolster its forces in the Pacific, in Fremantle-Perth.

October 16th 1942 — (Pacific-Guadalcanal) Japanese positions on Guadalcanal are struck from the sea by a Naval Task Force commanded by Rear Admiral G. Murray. Murray's Force also bombards enemy Seaplanes, based at Rekata, Solomon Islands. The Seaplane Tender U.S.S. *MacFarland* is caught in the Sealark Channel, by enemy Planes and is damaged. Although damaged, the *MacFarland's* crew is able to repair the Vessel. The *MacFarland* receives some assistance from Lt. Col. Harold Bauer, U.S.M.C. 212th Fighter Squadron, who spots the

troubled Vessel, as he is coming into Henderson for a landing, completing a mission of leading 26 Planes on a 600 mile trip. Bauer aborts his landing and intercepts the assault Planes, destroying four of them, before running out of fuel and being forced to ditch.

Japanese Transports afire in Solomons.

October 17th 1942 — (Atlantic-England) Allied Convoys prepare for Operation Torch, the strike against the Axis in North Africa. The Vessels converge on the Firth of Clyde.

October 18th 1942 — (Pacific) Admiral King orders Admiral William "Bull" Halsey, to assume command of the Solomons operation. He succeeds Admiral Ghormley as Commander, South Pacific Area. Admiral Halsey receives his orders upon landing at Noumea when he is handed a sealed envelope marked "SECRET." Admiral Halsey is not too overjoyed at replacing Admiral Robert Ghormley as they have been friends since Annapolis, both having played on the football team. The Joint Chiefs of Staff subsequently add additional Ships to the Pacific campaign, but most are committed to the conflict in Europe, leaving the Pacific shortchanged. The Pacific Commanders are perpetually in need of more Vessels. President Roosevelt will instruct Admiral Leahy to requisition 20 Ships and Leahy, will inform Admiral Emory Land (War Shipping Administration), on October 23rd.

October 19th 1942 — (United States) The U.S. 25th Division, in the Pacific, receives orders to bolster Guadalcanal. In the U.S., the War Department decides to equip 30 additional Chinese Divisions, in response to General Stilwell's previous request. In other activity, the U.S.S. *O'Brien*, a Destroyer, which had been damaged on September 15th near New Hebrides by an enemy torpedo, is destroyed near Samoa, after it splits in two, while attempting to reach the United States for repairs. **(China-Burma-India)** The Submarine U.S.S. *Gar* (SS-206), operating in the vicinity of the South China Sea, deploys mines in the Gulf of Siam, which is situated between the Malay and Indochinese peninsulas.

October 20th 1942 — (Pacific-New Caledonia) A meeting concerning the situation on Guadalcanal is held aboard Halsey's Flagship, the *Argonne*, moored in Noumea harbor. Major General Vandegrift, 1st Marine Division Commander, Major General Alexander M. Patch U.S.A., Major General Millard F. Harmon U.S.A. (Senior Army Officer in South Pacific), Lt. General Thomas Holcomb Commandant U.S.M.C., Major General Barney Vogel are among the Officers in attendance. The question, "ARE WE GOING TO EVACUATE OR HOLD?" is asked by Halsey. Vandegrift insists: "I CAN HOLD, BUT I'VE

GOT TO HAVE MORE ACTIVE SUPPORT THAN I'VE BEEN GETTING." Rear Admiral Kelly Turner indignantly proclaims the Navy is doing everything possible and further explains there are insufficient Warships in the area. The conversation continues to be heated. The situation is so bad that the Yanks are eating captured Japanese food and using captured gasoline for the Vehicles. Admiral Halsey agrees to send additional troops to Guadalcanal and he diverts the 147th Infantry (intended to strike Ndeni, Santa Cruz Islands), to bolster Vandegrift's force. Halsey informs Vandegrift: "ALL RIGHT, GO ON BACK. I'LL PROMISE YOU EVERYTHING I'VE GOT." In other activity, brief movements by the Japanese, in an attempt to cross the Matanikau River, cease after a concentration of fire from U.S. troops destroys one of the lead Tanks. **(Pacific-New Guinea)** Australian reinforcements; the 16th Brigade, 6th Division, replaces the 25th Brigade, 7th Australian Division, then advances steadily against the enemy positions at Eora Creek, immediately participating in the struggle to secure the Kokoda Trail. In other activity, elements of the U.S. 32nd Division, commanded by Capt. Medendorp, reach Juare, with the exception of those left behind at Laruni, to set up an Air dropping zone. Another unit, under Captain Boice, is presently at Juare and intent on locating strategic sectors, which can be turned into Airfields. **(Pacific)** The U.S.S. *Chester* (CA-27), a Heavy Cruiser is attacked and damaged by an enemy Submarine, while traveling between the Solomons and New Hebrides. **(Atlantic-Egypt)** Allied Planes increase their activity to insure Air superiority prior to the jumpoff of the British Offensive against El 'Alamein, scheduled to commence on the 23rd-24th. The Allied Pilots accomplish their mission by the 24th.

October 21st 1942 — (United States) Admiral King tells Admiral Nimitz about the Joint Chiefs of Staff's decision to strengthen the South Pacific Air Forces, by the First of January 1943. **(Pacific-Guadalcanal)** The Japanese, intent on crossing the Matanikau River, to reach the east bank, are again repulsed by the Marines, who are supported by Artillery and Tanks. American firepower destroys another Japanese Tank, prompting the enemy to pull back. **(Pacific)** The U.S.S. *Guardfish*, one of the nine Ships operating in enemy waters, spots a plump Japanese Convoy, consisting of seven Vessels and dives for an attack. She fires four torpedoes at about 10:45, sinking one of the leading Ships. The enemy reacts by rushing to the suspected position of the *Guardfish*, which in turn, maneuvers itself right in between the Convoy and is almost rammed. The *Guardfish* unleashes three more torpedoes from a distance of 1,000 yards and takes out another Ship, prior to diving deep to evade danger. Later in the day, a couple of enemy Bombers take a few pot shots at the *Guardfish*, without success. Inclement weather sets in and the *Guardfish* makes for home port, being attacked again on the 10th of November. The *Guardfish* returns to Midway for a refueling stop before heading back to Pearl Harbor. The *Guardfish* had exhibited so much "aggressiveness and tenacity" for this mission, that she receives a Presidential Citation, one of two which she receives during the war. **(Pacific-New Guinea)** A 50 man Patrol, (Cannon Co., U.S. 32nd Division) departs Juare, to set up defense lines in the Kumusi Valley. They hook up with Capt. Alfred Medendorp's main body and will be known as the Wairopi Patrol. These troops are supplied in part by Airdrops from friendly Aircraft.

October 22nd 1942 — (Pacific-Guadalcanal) The Japanese keep pressure on the Marine defenses with Artillery barrages, but due to the main enemy assault force not being on line, an intended attack against the Lunga perimeter is postponed. **(Pacific-New Guinea)** A Squadron of B-24s arrives in New Guinea, but they are forced to keep the Infantry company, as all Planes are damaged, having cracked nosewheel collars. The Allied offensive continues to move forward, in spite of the sparse assistance afforded by Washington; General MacArthur is unable to utilize Naval Vessels, because none are available. Replacement parts arrive in two weeks and the B-24s take to the skies. In other activity, Australian troops depart Milne Bay to expel a Japanese Force on Goodenough Island (stranded earlier during an intended attack against Milne Bay). The Aussies land after midnight and proceed to search and destroy enemy resistance. Approximately 60 of the 350 man enemy Force, had been evacuated by Submarines and an additional 200 would be saved by a Japanese Destroyer on the 24th. Japanese resistance on the island ends. **(Pacific-New Hebrides)** Two American Task Forces converge and combine, under the command of Admiral Kinkaid. This Naval Force including the Carriers *Enterprise* and *Hornet* meet on the 24th and speed towards the Santa Cruz, Islands, to engage a Japanese Naval Force, heading for Guadalcanal. **(North Pacific-Alaska-U.S. Territory)** The United States Navy chooses Otter Point, as its newest Naval Air Facility, establishing it today. **(Atlantic-England)** The Allied Invasion Force, known as Operation TORCH, is making final preparations for departure. The Supply Convoy, which is to support the invasion, embarks from England, heading for Africa. **(Atlantic-Algeria)** A British Submarine, which had arrived off Algeria the previous day, debarks U.S. General Mark Clark, Brigadier General Lemnitzer, Colonel Archelus L. Hamblen, Captain Jerauld Wright U.S.N., Colonel Julius Holmes and a few British Officers to confer secretly with Robert Murphy (U.S. diplomat) and a group of pro-Allied Frenchmen, concerning French co-operation with the Allies. General Clark is assured by French General Charles E. Mast that French co-operation will occur under the leadership of General Henri Giraud. Admiral Darlan, who is in North Africa visiting his son (ill with polio) is not invited. General Mast, unabashedly pro-American, gives the Americans deployment positions of French troops and gasoline depots. In addition, he tells Clark that his men control the Blida Airport at Algiers and the Airfield at Bone and would supply access to the Yanks on the first day of the invasion of North Africa. He also offers the best possible methods of invading North Africa. During the meeting, Police arrive and Clark and the other Allies hide in an empty wine cellar. The party has more trouble later with the surf. General Clark loses his pants on the way back to the Submarine. An inspection of the beach by Murphy on the following day to determine if any important papers had been left behind discover only Clark's pants. British Naval Lt. N.L.A. Jewell had taken his Submarine the *Seraph* and his passengers back to Gibraltar safely. **(Atlantic-Egypt)** A U.S. Advance Base Headquarters, becomes the Desert Air Task Force and will be commanded by General Brereton. In other activity, the British Eighth Army is deploying in assault positions, with the greatest amount of secrecy possible.

October 23rd 1942 — (United States) Operation TORCH is readied. The first contingent of American forces depart the U.S., heading for North Africa. This Western Naval Task Force, commanded by Admiral Henry K. Hewitt, departs Hampton Roads Virginia, with Old Glory flapping in the breeze. General George Patton departs Norfolk, on the following day on the U.S.S. *Augusta.* An Allied Cargo Convoy, had left England the previous day. **(Pacific-Guadalcanal)** A Japanese offensive, with Tanks supporting its advance Infantry, meets nasty resistance by the 3rd Battalion, 1st Marines. Rapid fire mauls the attackers and devastates their Tanks. The Japanese retire, badly bloodied, losing nearly 600 men and eight Tanks. The Marines suffer 25 killed and 14 wounded. The Main Body of the Japanese Force had not positioned itself properly for attack, forcing a postponement of the major assault until the following day. The Japanese primary force, is struggling along a primitive road, tramping through severe rains that greatly hamper progress and when it finally deploys for the attack against the Marines holding "Bloody Ridge" on the 24th, it is forced to assault without the assistance of Artillery, which is still bogged down along the jungle road. The fierce engagement commences late in the afternoon of the 24th and continues throughout the night. The Marines under Lt. Colonel "Chesty Puller" battle steadfastly killing as many Japs as possible. Holes develop along the Marine perimeter on Bloody Ridge, but the Japs do not penetrate. Army reinforcements arrive to stuff the holes and help to repulse the attack. At dawn on the 25th, Bloody Ridge still flies the Stars and Stripes, despite ill-controlled and undisciplined banzai attacks, which had cost the enemy heavy casualties. General Hyakutake had approximately 20,000 troops at his disposal against the Americans, but only about half had been committed during the offensive. Unsatisfied with the rebuttal by the Yanks, another unsuccessful assault is mounted on the 25th with the same dismal results; Old Glory reigns and the Japanese get thrashed. The Japanese Fleet, offshore, is informed of the lackluster showing by the Imperial troops and must modify its plans somewhat as the only ground troops now threatening the perimeter are dead. **(Atlantic-Egypt)** In Egypt, the British go on the offensive, opening up a thundering bombardment against enemy positions at El 'Alamein. As the 1,000 Allied guns cease their blistering attack, the British move against the Germans, with heavy fighting lasting into the next day. This concentrated effort of the British to break out leads to heavy casualties on both sides. The tremendous struggle, finally pays off for the British on the 4th of November when the Germans are in full retreat. Allied Planes assist the Ground Forces during the operation.

Dead Japanese on Guadalcanal.

October 24th 1942 — (United States) The U.S. Submarine Service is still plagued with mechanical problems. The torpedoes have major problems with detonation, causing much research to eliminate the problem. With no solution at present, the Japanese have no genuine threat from U.S. Submarines at the present time. These problems will be solved and the Submarines, after playing catch up in 1943, become a formidable Naval threat, for the balance of the conflict. **(Pacific-Guadalcanal)** The Japanese mount a strong attack, against the south flank of the Marine perimeter on Guadalcanal. The 1st Battalion, 7th Marines, assisted by cover fire of the 2nd Battalion, 164th Infantry, and reinforced by the 3rd Battalion, 164th Infantry, U.S.A., handily turns back the attacks, which last into the 25th. Sgt. John Basilone (U.S.M.C.), commanding two sections of heavy machine guns, holds firmly against the brutalizing attack. Enemy fire, including mortars and grenades knocks one section out of action, leaving the task of holding against a Regimental sized attack to two men, but Basilone moves another gun into position and then repairs another which he begins to fire until relieved. Basilone risks death again, going through enemy lines for desperately needed ammunition, required for the survival of his crew. Sergeant Basilone's extraordinary actions, hasten the destruction of an entire Japanese Regiment. The Japanese Fleet waits in vain for word that the Marines had been driven from Henderson. The Marines instead gain needed time for Rear Admiral Kinkaid's Task Force to arrive at New Hebrides. This gives Halsey two separate U.S. Carrier Forces, built upon the *Enterprise* and *Hornet,* which converge northeast of New Hebrides and are placed under the command of U.S. Admiral Kinkaid prior to departing for the Santa Cruz Islands. **(Pacific-New Guinea)** Organized Japanese resistance, on Goodenough Island, comes to an end. Two hundred fifty enemy troops are evacuated by sea and taken to Rabaul by Destroyer. In other activity, advance troops of the 2nd Battalion, 164th U.S. Infantry, make it to Jaure, from where they will be ordered to Buna. **(Atlantic-Egypt)** The British 30 Corps attacks with four Divisions and successfully clears two routes through dense enemy mine fields on the northern flank of the Eighth Army. The British 13 Corps successfully advances on the northern flank, when the 7th Armored and 44th Divisions clear an enemy minefield north of Himeimat and secure a bridgehead to the south during the night of the 24-25th. **(Atlantic-Italy)** Royal Air Force Lancasters are launched from England to strike Milan. This major attack, against a city that lies about 1,400 miles from England, is the first daylight attack made against Italy by home-based British Aircraft.

October 25th 1942 — (Atlantic) A Carrier Force departs Bermuda, heading for North Africa. **(Pacific-Guadalcanal)** Prior to daybreak, Japanese Warships, including a Heavy Cruiser and Destroyers, land reinforcements on Guadalcanal. The Warships bombard Henderson but the weather is so terrible that U.S. Planes cannot get off the ground to strike back until around noon. While the enemy Naval Guns pound the perimeter, two additional Japanese Naval Forces are detected moving toward Guadalcanal. The Army (six B-17s from Espiritu) and Marines combine with the Navy and bomb the Light Cruiser *Yura,* damaging it enough that the enemy destroys it. In addition some damage is inflicted upon two Destroyers. Admiral Halsey orders the *Enterprise* to dispatch Planes in search of the two approaching Naval Forces but no contact is made. Admiral Scott's Task Force is directed to search around

Savo Island during the night, but again no encounters with the enemy. Scott's Force, including two Cruisers three Destroyers and the Battleship *Washington* will not participate in the main battle of Santa Cruz except to fend off enemy Planes. Admiral Halsey, intuitively thinking the battle imminent had issued orders to his commands: "ATTACK REPEAT ATTACK." In other activity, the U.S.S. *Amberjack* surfaces near Tulagi and delivers Army personnel and supplies. U.S. Naval guns inadvertently fire upon and damage the U.S.S. *Hughes* (DD-410). Another American Vessel, the U.S.S. *Zane*, is damaged when it is encountered by enemy Warships in the Sealark Channel and the U.S.S. *Seminole* (AT-65), a Tug, is sunk by enemy fire. Marines repulse two attacks against their positions during night of 25th-26th. In one of the many acts of extraordinary courage, Sgt. Mitchell Paige directs the fire of his gunners until they are all killed or wounded, then singlehandedly barrages the advancing enemy with deadly fire until reinforcements arrive to give support fire. Paige, fearlessly grabs a rifle and leads a successful bayonet charge, driving the Japs away. The Marines hold the expensive ground. Paige receives the Medal of Honor. **(Pacific-Japan)** The Japanese mainland is intruded upon when the Submarine U.S.S. *Whale* (SS-239) creeps silently towards Honshu and discretely mines the waters near the mouth of the Inland Sea. **(Atlantic-Egypt)** British General Montgomery concentrates his efforts against the 30 Corps' northern flank, thus holding the 13 Corps strength in reserve. The Germans mount strong Tank supported counterattacks supported by Tanks, but the British repel the assaults. Both the British and Germans lose many Tanks during the encounter. German General Rommel had been in Germany when the battle for El 'Alamein erupted, but the sudden death of German Commander General Stumme causes Rommel to be rushed back to the front on the 25th. **(Atlantic-England)** General Clark telephones General Eisenhower to discuss the North Africa meeting. Ike is displeased with news that some changes have been made by Clark to a letter from Robert Murphy to French General Giraud. It is discussed further at Ike's house over dinner as he concerned about a premature placement of a French Officer in the Allied Command Organization.

October 26th 1942 — (Pacific-New Hebrides) The U.S.S. *President Coolidge* transports the 172nd Regiment, U.S. 43rd Division, to Espiritu Santo. After its arrival, the Ship is sunk off the coast by U.S. mines. **(Pacific-Guadalcanal)** Operational Aircraft are down to 29, but the Yanks have thoroughly shattered the Japanese on the ground, after they attempted unsuccessfully for three days to break through Marine lines. Army reinforcements rushed to help Colonel Puller's troops hold aptly named Bloody Ridge. **(Atlantic-Egypt)** The British and Axis troops battle feverishly for El 'Alamein, but the pace slackens, as General Montgomery decides to regroup for the break-out. Enemy Air action increases during the slow-down of the Allies' drive and leaders in Great Britain are concerned about the decision to regroup. **(Atlantic-Russia)** German Army Group A captures Nalchik, in the Caucasus. **(Atlantic-England)** The Convoy, transporting the Invasion Force to North Africa, departs England. In other activity, General Clark meets with Officers involved with Operation Torch to give them information from his meeting in North Africa. Word arrives that French General Giraud approves of the agreement reached between General Clark and French General

Mast and is prepared to depart for North Africa. The American have no Submarines in the Mediterranean and are fearful that Giraud will not board a British Submarine so the Americans work a deal with Churchill to place an American (Captain Wright U.S.N.) to take temporary command of the H.M.S. *Seraph* (commanded by British Lt. Jewell) to transport the French General.

October 26th 1942 — 172nd Regiment, U.S. 43rd Division, survivors of the Transport U.S.S. President Calvin Coolidge, which had struck a U.S. mine, coming ashore at Espiritu Santo, New Hebrides.

October 26th-27th 1942 — (Pacific) — BATTLE OF THE SANTA CRUZ ISLANDS — The Pacific is about to erupt with another raging slugfest as the Japanese attempt to eradicate the American hold on Guadalcanal. Admiral Kondo had been moving from Truk to bolster the Japanese ground operation on the canal by closing and destroying the American Naval Forces, isolating the Yanks and permitting General Hyakutake to eradicate the American beachhead. The Yanks, however, on the canal had withstood successive counterattacks on the ground by the 25th, foiling the master plan of the Japanese. Now it is up to Halsey's Carrier Groups to hold the line in the sea.

At just after 08:00, Scout Planes from the *Enterprise* spot the advancing enemy Forces moving steadily: 2 Battleships, followed by 5 Cruisers, 11 Destroyers, and a Carrier. To the rear is a Battleship Group: 2 Battleships, 3 Cruisers and 11 Destroyers and another Carrier Group consisting of three Carriers, a Heavy Cruiser and seven Destroyers. Deploying to intercept the threat are the combined forces of Admirals Kinkaid and Murray. These two groups include the *Enterprise* and *Hornet* in addition to 14 Destroyers, three Heavy and two Light Cruisers and the Battleship *South Dakota*. The Japanese, as usual, hold the edge in Naval power, but the U.S. Navy is unwilling to yield and allow a collapse of the beachhead.

The opposing Forces order up their Aircraft in the air at about the same time, guaranteeing a giant clash to protect their respective Fleets which stand about 250 miles apart. Bullets are traded in fierce dog-fights, while trails of ominous smoke pour from disabled Planes as they plummet to the sea. U.S. Pilots breakthrough and damage two enemy Carriers, two Destroyers and a Cruiser. Meanwhile the Japanese manage to savagely strike the *Hornet* with four bombs, two Kamikazes and two torpedoes, rendering the Carrier helpless. By a little after 11:00, an enemy Submarine strikes the Destroyer *Porter* causing it to be abandoned. In quick succession, the *Enter-*

prise is attacked by 24 Bombers, but the mighty *Enterprise* continues fighting and in fact retrieves orphaned Planes of the *Hornet*. The Japanese are paying a heavy price for their success, but they continue to press for victory, feeling confident that the *Enterprise* is doomed.

The Japanese mount three additional ferocious strikes against the American Fleet. A Kamikaze smashes into the Destroyer *Smith*. The *Enterprise* sustains more damage from a near miss and the Light Cruiser *San Juan* is struck. The Battleship *South Dakota* is also damaged. By evening, the *Hornet* is virtually destroyed, having fought off five major assaults during a six-hour period, including a mortal blow by a torpedo. Abandonment of the gallant Vessel is ordered at 17:27, and in essence, the battle subsides with the Americans receiving the worst of the exchange. However, they have repulsed the Japanese attempt to move to Guadalcanal and force them to retire with a crippled Force. The Yanks have inflicted enough damage to Kondo's Carrier Forces to ensure their unavailability for the upcoming seabattle of Guadalcanal.

The U.S.S. *Hornet* (Carrier CV-8)), damaged on the 26th, is lost to enemy torpedoes on the 27th. The Carrier *Enterprise* (CV-6) is damaged, after being struck by a torpedo from an enemy Plane. In addition, the Battleship *South Dakota* (BB-27) and the Light Cruiser, *San Juan* (CL-54) are struck and damaged, by Torpedo Bombers. The Destroyer *Porter* (DD-356) damaged by a Submarine's torpedo, sustains sufficient damage to force its destruction by the U.S. Navy. The Destroyer *Smith* (DD-378), struck by a Suicide Bomber, survives the ordeal. During the heated contest, the U.S.S. *Hughes* sustains damage, when it collides with another Vessel during the battle. On the 27th, the Battleship U.S.S. *South Dakota* (BB-57) damaged on the previous day, is involved in a collision, with the Destroyer *Mahan* (DD-364).

Twenty American Aircraft are lost to the Japanese in combat, but 54 other Planes are lost to other causes, such as running out of fuel or inability to locate their Carriers in the darkness. The Japanese lose 100 Aircraft in combat and an indeterminate number from other causes. Three Carriers and two Destroyers are damaged. The Japanese failures of their troops on the 'canal, coupled with their heavy damages incurred at sea, are enough to turn them back. The Japanese will no longer bring in Carriers for support during the remainder of the campaign to regain Guadalcanal. This virtually culminates the Japanese offensive initiative, on Guadalcanal, leaving the Marines holding the upper hand, although both sides have suffered extensively.

October 27th 1942 — (China-Burma-India) It is agreed between American General Stilwell and British General Wavell, that Stilwell will command the offensive in the Hukawng Valley (Northern Burma). The objective is to secure the Myitkyina-Bhamo area and hook up with the Chinese Yunnan Force. It is also understood, that the Americans are to establish a road to Myitkyina, which will subsequently link up to the Burma Road. **(Atlantic-Egypt)** The Germans under Rommel mount strong counterattacks, in the vicinity of Kidney Ridge, but are repulsed by the British.

October 28th 1942 — (Pacific) The U.S. 2nd Battalion, 126th Infantry, embarks from Jaure, taking a portable hospital with them, on the journey toward Bofu and Natunga, New Guinea. **(Atlantic-England)** A final meeting in London concerning the TORCH Operation is held. General Eisenhower states that 54

Officers are to go to Gibraltar to establish Allied Force Headquarters. In other activity, Eisenhower dispatches a message to General Marshall concerning the deployment of the U.S. Fifth Army in North Africa after it is fully formed. It is preparing itself in the U.S. at present. If Marshall consents, Mark Clark, a junior Major General, will receive the command. General Clark has had a good relationship with Marshall for many years and in fact, Mrs. Marshall had much to do with his appointment to West Point. The Marshall and Clark families have been close friends dating back to the early 1900's.

October 26th-27th 1942 — The U.S.S. Hornet (CV-8), under attack during the Battle of Santa Cruz (note Kamikaze at top of photograph diving for the Carrier's deck).

October 29th 1942 — (North Pacific-Aleutians) Japanese troops reoccupy Attu. **(Pacific-Guadalcanal)** The Japanese, aware that the reinforcements have been beaten back at sea and especially weary from their futile effort to take Guadalcanal from the Marines, start to withdraw toward Koli Point and Kokumbona. **(Pacific-New Guinea)** The Japanese, attempting to withdraw across the Kumusi River, receive additional reinforcements from their beachhead, which strengthens the positions at Oivi heights, during the pull back. **(China-Burma-India)** Although Tokyo Rose might not like it, the U.S.S. *Grenadier* (SS-210) is operating in the Tonkin Gulf, deploying mines. **(Atlantic-Egypt)** Australian troops repel fierce German assaults against their positions in the northern sector of the 30 Corps Front. British General Montgomery, aware of heavily numbered enemy troops in the area, improvises his breakout plans, attacking the Italians to the South, as opposed to assaulting the Germans, more staunchly positioned along the West coast.

October 30th 1942 — (Pacific-Guadalcanal) The Marines are preparing to launch an offensive, against the Japanese, who have been racked in recent days, sustaining heavy casualties. Cruisers and Destroyers bombard Japanese positions at Point Cruz on Guadalcanal. **(North Pacific-Aleutians)** The U.S. continues to build its forces for the attack to retake Attu. **(Atlantic-Egypt)** Allied Planes assist the Australian 9th Division, which is driving north to the sea. German Tanks are rushed to the vicinity of Thompson's Post, to help evacuate entrapped German troops, and the successful breakthrough from the West enables most of the enemy Soldiers to escape safely.

October 31st 1942 — (Pacific-Guadalcanal) The Marines finalize preparations for the offensive, which jumps off on the following day. Advance troops cross the Matanikau River and secure outposts on the west bank. Engineers construct three small bridges across the river to accommodate the Infantry.

November 1st 1942 — (United States) The Navy changes the name of its Patrol Wings to Fleet Air Wings. On the following day, Fleet Air Wing 6 will be established at Seattle, Washington. **(Pacific-Guadalcanal)** The 2nd Battalion, 7th Marines, moves east, near Koli Point toward the Metapona River. On the following day, the 2nd Marines support the 1st and 3rd Battalions, 5th Marines, as they begin to further isolate enemy resistance west of Point Cruz. **(Atlantic-England)** General Clark receives an urgent message from Robert Murphy concerning General Giraud's inability to depart France until November 20th; he also requests a delay in the invasion of North Africa, but receives a negative response. The message also informs Clark that the promised weapons had not been delivered to French General Mast (promised at meeting in North Africa). General Clark is angry, but the weapons never reach Mast. Subsequently (November 2nd) another message arrives from Murphy stating that General Giraud will make the engagement and meet the Submarine in the Gulf of Lyon. **(Atlantic-Russia)** The 62nd and 64th Soviet Armies stall the German 6th and 4th Panzers (Group B) in a fierce battle with heavy close-quartered combat. In other activity, German Group A succeeds in seizing Alagir.

November 2nd 1942 — (Pacific-Philippines) Guerrilla units active in the Philippines manage to get radio messages through to Australia. The Royal Australian Air Force intercepts a message from a Philippine Officer, Major Macario Peralta Jr., who states that an 8,000 man force (Fourth Philippine Corps) is conducting raids on Panay. His message expresses confidence that supplies can be successfully dropped from the air, providing the selected areas are at least 20 miles from the capitals. General MacArthur, informed of the information, advises Peralta to maintain the Force, but to hold off attacks, until notified. MacArthur states: "WE CAN NOT PREDICT THE DATE OF OUR RETURN TO THE PHILIPPINES, BUT WE ARE COMING." Upon receipt of MacArthur's instructions, Major Peralta responds with the following: "MISSION ASSIGNED TO US WILL BE ACCOMPLISHED. HUMBLEST SOLDIER HAS BLIND FAITH IN YOU." **(Pacific-Guadalcanal)** The addition of two 155 Howitzer Batteries (1, Army) gives more muscle to the American firepower in the Lunga area. These new weapons are the first to provide the effectiveness to match the long-range enemy guns. The 2nd Battalion, 7th Marines, still moving east from the march which had begun on the 1st, sets its defenses at Tetere village. Additional Marines, the 1st and 3rd Battalions, 5th Marines, and contingents of the 2nd Battalion, 5th Marines, press westward to apply more pressure. The Japanese land about 1,500 troops east of Koli Point in an attempt to supplement those already ashore. The Japanese then begin to construct an Airfield. **(Pacific-New Guinea)** The Allied Offensive is making progress as Kokoda Airfield is seized by the 25th Australian Brigade. General MacArthur is pleased with the progress of the pincer movement and sets the 15th of November as the probable date for an assault against the enemy positions at Buna-Gona. **(China-Burma-India)** U.S. Submarines prowl Japanese controlled waters in the vicinity of French Indo China. The U.S.S. Tambor (SS-198) lays mines in the Tonkin Gulf, while the Submarine Tautog (SS-199) drops mines south of Cape Padaran. **(Atlantic-Egypt)** The 30th Corps, British Eighth Army, begins Operation SUPERCHARGE, an offensive to break out at El 'Alamein. The Germans inflict heavy casualties on Montgom-

ery's 30 Corps. The 9th Armored Brigade suffers a 75 percent casualty rate from the 15th Panzers on the 2nd. The British, in spite of their losses, are able to push the Germans back on the 2nd, because Rommel's Tanks have also been taking a beating; his few remaining Tanks are dangerously low on ammunition and fuel.

November 3rd 1942 — (Pacific-Guadalcanal) The Marines continue to mop up enemy troops in the vicinity of Point Cruz. The 2nd Battalion encounters hardened resistance at the Nalimbiu River and is forced to withdraw to the west bank and await reinforcements. Headquarters, after being informed of the enemy reinforcements being landed, dispatches Planes and also directs Allied Naval Vessels to commence firing on enemy positions. The 1st Battalion, 7th Marines, embarks by barge heading for Koli Point. **(Pacific-China)** The U.S.S. Haddock, commanded by Commander A. H. Taylor, departed Midway on October 11th and is operating in the China Sea when it detects an enemy Vessel and unleashes three torpedoes at the Tekkai Maru, severing it. On the 8th of October, a Jap Patrol Plane spots the Haddock and delivers an unsuccessful attack. On the 11th, the Haddock, destroys a Japanese Freighter, the Venice Maru. **(Atlantic-Egypt)** British pressure forces Rommel to withdraw from El Alamein. Allied Planes strike German troops and Armored units, as they retreat along the coastal route. The British are delayed, somewhat stuck by German minefields.

A U.S. Convoy maneuvering along a muddy trail on Guadalcanal.

October 1942 — U.S. B17s attacking Gizo Island, Guadalcanal.

November 4th 1942 — (Pacific-Guadalcanal) The American area of responsibility is divided into two sectors. Brigadier General William Rupertus (assistant Commander, 1st Marine Division) will command the east sector; and Brigadier General Edmund B. Sebree, U.S.A., assumes command of the western sector with both under the command of General Vandegrift, Commanding Officer 1st Marine Division. In other activity, the 164th Infantry, U.S.A., departs the perimeter to assist the 7th Marines presently engaged at Koli Point. The 2nd Raider Battalion, commanded by Colonel Carlson, departs Aola Bay, heading for Koli Point to trap the Japanese who might attempt to flee east from the closing Marines and Soldiers. (See November 4th-December 4th 1942). **(Pacific-New Guinea)** The Japanese hold their positions at Oivi against the Australian 16th Brigade, which is concentrating its forces to clear the heights.

November 4th-December 4th 1942 — (Guadalcanal) CARLSON'S PATROL — A brilliant Patrol operation contributes tremendously to the success of the Guadalcanal campaign. It begins as an American Force debarks reinforcements at Aola Bay; the 8th Marines, supported by the 1st Battalion, 10th Marines (75mm pack howitzers) arrive. In addition, the 1st Battalion 147th Infantry, U.S.A., the 246th Field Artillery Provisional Battalion K, U.S.A., about 500 Seabees and Carlson's Raiders (contingents of the 2nd Raider Battalion), also land to supplement the American Force. The Seabees initiate the construction of an Airfield, but the plan is scuttled because the terrain is ill-suited for an Airfield. Subsequent to the landing, the Raiders drive west to intercept and destroy enemy supply bases. The Raiders are ambushed on the eighth by a small enemy unit, but advance and establish a base camp near Binu on the following day. Between the 11th and the 17th, the Raiders engage a strong force that had evaded encirclement by the 2nd Battalion, 7th Marines in the vicinity of Tetere. The Raiders pour heavy fire into their ranks, killing much of the force and scattering the remainder in the brush.

Carlson's command advances to the upper Tenaru on the 24th of November, splits his force into three groups; one operates from a base camp with two units in the field. Several supply paths and bivouac sectors are detected. On the 29th of November the Raiders destroy a large supply area, including Artillery pieces. On the following day, the Raiders surprise 100 Japs in a bivouac area, killing 75 of them. The Patrol returns to the 1st Marine Division lines on December 4th, having disrupted enemy supply lines and killed approximately 175 enemy troops while sustaining a loss of six Raiders during the operation.

The Patrol contributes immensely to the morale of the American efforts on the 'canal and the ultimate defeat of the Japanese. The timely hit and run attacks had unnerved the enemy, which had been operating behind the Marine positions near the Matanikau.

November 5th 1942 — (Pacific-New Guinea) The Australians and Japanese are still involved with a vicious fight, for control of the Oivi heights. **(Atlantic-Gibraltar)** General Eisenhower arrives by air in Gibraltar to establish a Headquarters Command Post for the Allied troops, which will be involved in the invasion of Northwest Africa (Operation TORCH). Eisenhower departs London, under the pretense of returning to Washington, but changes course for Gibraltar, escorted by five Flying Fortresses. An additional Fortress arriving on the following day, is attacked by four German Messerschmitts. Two of the enemy Planes are destroyed, but the American Co-Pilot is wounded. General Mark Clark also makes the journey and is to assume command if anything happens to General Eisenhower. The U.S.-British Staff is composed of British Admiral Sir Andrew Cunningham, Commander in Chief, Naval Forces; British Air Marshal Sir William Welsh, British Air Forces (Eastern Command) and General James H. Doolittle, American Air Forces. In addition, British Lt. General K.A.N. Anderson will command the British ground troops. The original strategy of displaying enormous strength, to convince the French to join forces with the Allies, is now ready for practical application. General Eisenhower and Prime Minister Winston Churchill had met frequently in London to co-ordinate the master plan, agreeing that no information concerning the invasion will be given to Charles DeGaulle, because his London-based group has been penetrated by German spies. In addition, it is believed that DeGaulle's staff, is aligned with the Communists. The Invasion Force, under the command of General Patton, will assault North Africa, on the 8th. **(Atlantic-Iceland)** U.S. Naval Aircraft (VP-84), based in Iceland, sink the German Submarine *U-408*, as it prowls, in search of Allied Vessels.

November 4th-December 4th — 1942 A U.S. Tank and a Marine at the Tenaru River on Guadalcanal.

November 6th 1942 — (Pacific-Guadalcanal) The 7th Marines continue attacking eastward, crossing the Nalimbiu River and driving across the coast, pushing the Japs before them. The Task Force, which debarked the reinforcements at Aola Bay, has completed its mission and now departs the area. In Air action, Japanese Dive Bombers damage the U.S.S. *Zeilin* (AP-9), a Transport, in the vicinity of the Solomon Islands. **(Pacific-New Guinea)** General MacArthur arrives at Port Moresby. **(Atlantic-Egypt)** The Axis troops continue to retreat, with the British 10 Corps in pursuit. The British 30 Corps is deployed, between El 'Alamein and Matruh, to reduce enemy remnants in the area. Severe rains bog down the Allied Vehicles.

November 7th 1942 — (United States) The organization of a Women's Reserve (U.S.M.C.), is approved by Major General Thomas Holcomb, Commandant. **(Atlantic)** The U.S.S. *Thomas Stone* (AP-59), a Troop Transport, heading for Africa, is attacked and damaged, in the western Mediterranean by an enemy Submarine about 150 miles out. Word of the disaster spreads among the Convoy, causing concern, but spirits rise when it is announced that the U-Boat had not sunk the Vessel. The Soldiers (Reinforced Battalion U.S.A.), are transferred to other Vessels, but are detained and will not reach Algiers until after its capitulation. The Sailors of the *Thomas Stone*, react quickly and make for smaller craft, to attempt to complete the mission, until severe weather conditions abort this endeavor and Escort Ships pick up the crew. In other activity, in conjunction with the imminent Allied invasion of North Africa, the U.S.S. *Barb*, move toward Safi, with a special contingent of advance personnel. As the *Barb* gets to within an anticipated two hour row to the beach, Lt. W. G. Duckworth leads four Army Scouts on what turns into a grueling, six hour marathon trek to the beach through most uncooperative waters. Their specific mission, to guide two Destroyers, the *Bernadou* and *Cole* through the tricky waters into Safi is beset by problems. The Volunteers arrive as the firing begins, too late to aid the invasion. They spend their first moments dodging enemy machine guns. **(Atlantic-France)** French General Giraud, is chosen over DeGaulle, to lead the Free French troops on North Africa, to weaken Vichy French resistance. He is secretly taken offshore, to a British Submarine, temporarily commanded by American Captain Jerauld Wright. The Sub then embarks with Giraud, transferring him to a Seaplane which will transport him to Gibraltar for a meeting with General Eisenhower. General Giraud is insulted when he is told that he will not command the Allied Expedition against the Axis on North Africa, but rather, will command only those French Troops who voluntarily come to his side. Giraud, emphatically declares that he "WOULD NOT ACCEPT ANY POSITION IN THE VENTURE, LOWER THEN THAT OF COMPLETE COMMAND." He further dictates: "GIRAUD WILL BE A SPECTATOR IN THIS AFFAIR" and goes to bed. American Generals Eisenhower and Clark follow Giraud's lead and also decide to get some sleep. As General Giraud awakes on the following morning, he decides to accept the proposed terms of Eisenhower, then attempts to convince Ike to abort the North Africa campaign and land in southern France. General Eisenhower quickly informs the French General that Allied troops are hitting the beaches, as they talk. **(Atlantic-North Africa)** In Egypt, the Germans and Italians continue to retreat, taking advantage of severe weather which is delaying British support Vehicles. The British have now captured 30,000 prisoners, including nine Generals. In other activity, an Italian Submarine, the *Antonio Sciesa*, operating in the vicinity of Libya, is attacked and sunk by U.S. Army Air Corps Planes.

November 8th 1942 — (Pacific-Guadalcanal) The 1st, and 2nd Battalions, 7th Marines and 164th Infantry, U.S.A., continue moving east to encircle the Japs at Koli Point. The Japanese have been landing reinforcements in the vicinity of Cape Esperance and Kokumbona, since late October. On the following day, the 164th Infantry and 7th Marines repel several Jap attempts to escape the net. In other activity, Admiral Halsey visits with the troops on Guadalcanal and confers with the Commanders. While staying in General Vandegrift's cramped quarters for the night he finds it hard to sleep and admittedly is scared when an enemy Destroyer commences a bombardment. American Artillery units return fire, but Halsey notes: "IT WASN'T THE NOISE THAT KEPT ME AWAKE; IT WAS FRIGHT. I CALLED MYSELF YELLOW-AND-WORSE AND TOLD MYSELF GO TO SLEEP YOU DAMNED COWARD!" He further states: "IT DIDN'T DO ANY GOOD; I COULDN'T OBEY ORDERS." During a press conference while on this trip he does issue his "recipe" for winning the war: "KILL JAPS, KILL JAPS AND KEEP ON KILLING JAPS." **(Atlantic)** Despite severe losses in Russia, Hitler re-emphasizes his resolve to take Stalingrad. Vichy France breaks diplomatic relations with the U.S. **(Atlantic-North Africa)** American Colonel William H. Wilbur volunteers to take a small unit, from the beach to Casablanca, to attempt an armistice with

the French. Colonel Wilbur's unit drives through the Vichy French territory under a white flag, but is still frequently fired upon. The French decline his offer to surrender. Along the route, back to American lines, Wilbur spots a French Battery firing upon American troops. Infuriated, Wilbur commandeers a Platoon of American Tanks and proceeds to capture the entire Battery. In a similar incident, Colonel Demas Craw, U.S.A.A.F., Major Piermont M. Hamilton U.S.A.A.F. and one additional Soldier, attempt to reach the French Commander in the vicinity of Port Lyautey, French Morocco. Enemy machine gun fire kills Colonel Craw at point blank range and Major Pierpont is captured, as they near Vichy Headquarters.

November 8th-11th 1942 — The Allied Fleet approaches North Africa.

November 8th-11th 1942 — (North Africa) THE INVASION OF NORTH AFRICA — The Allied invasion of Northwest Africa (Operation TORCH), under the Supreme Command of Lieutenant General Eisenhower, is launched. Allied Ships land men and supplies, on the beaches at Casablanca, Algiers and Oran, under the protection of Carrier-based Aircraft and Naval guns. (Western Naval Task Force) At approximately 07:15, six French Destroyers, including two already in flames, attempt to break for open seas, until intense shelling from Allied Naval Vessels turns them back to Casablanca. Enemy Aircraft swoop overhead, to strike Allied Transports and are met by Aircraft and Naval guns. Allied Ships, including the U.S.S. *Augusta*, pour fire into the French Ships as the morning passes. The Center Attack Group, commanded by Major General Jonathan Anderson U.S.A., loses 64 percent of its Landing Craft, while landing northeast of Fedala, but persistent troops seize the high ground and capture the surprised Garrison. The Northern Attack Group, commanded by Major General Lucian Truscott, hits the beaches in the vicinity of Mehdia and meets stiff opposition, while driving toward the Airport at Port-Lyautey. Major General Earnest N. Harmon secures his beachhead and captures Safi. Two American Destroyers enter Safi Harbor prior to the landings and silence the enemy Batteries, before sending a landing party ashore. The combined Army-Navy landing force seizes the harbor, without opposition, much to the liking of a selected group of volunteers, who had rowed to the beach from the Destroyers earlier. General Patton and his staff depart the U.S.S. *Augusta*, at approximately 12:45, to the loud cheers of the Sailors, who are leaning over the Ship. Casablanca surrenders on the 11th. (60th Infantry, 9th Division 1st Battalion. 66th Armored Battalion, 2nd Armored Division. under Truscott) (3rd Division, 1st Battalion, 67th Armored, 2nd Armored Division, under Anderson) (47th Infantry, 9th Division, 2nd & 3rd Battalions, 2nd Armored Division and special units under Harmon), all participate.

(Eastern Naval Task Force) The Eastern Assault Force begins landing at 01:00, with General Charles Ryder's command, hitting shore, East and West of Algiers, moving with little opposition, seizing Blida and Maison Blanche Airfields. Two British Destroyers carry troops into Algiers Harbor, to initiate a frontal attack. Intense enemy fire, forces one Vessel to pull out, but the other deploys assault troops, before withdrawal. The city surrenders by 19:00 (U.S. 9th Div., U.S. 34th Division and British Troops, commanded by Ryder, U.S.A.

(Center Naval Task Force) The U.S. II Corps, commanded by Major General Lloyd R. Fredendall U.S.A., storms the beaches, East and West of Oran, then proceeds to take Arzew, with the help of a combined U.S.-British Naval Force that seizes the harbor unopposed. The Allies then head for Oran, capturing an Airfield 15 miles outside of town. Regimental Combat Team 26 seize Bou Sfer and Ain et Turk, but is prevented from reaching Oran. The First Armored Division moves from Mersa Bou, against French opposition, but seizes LaSenia Airport on the 9th. (1st Division, 1st Ranger Battalion, Combat Command B, 1st Armored Division, 2nd Battalion 509th Paratroop Infantry and the Canadian-British troops).

Allied Ships and Planes pummel the French Navy into submission, after heavy fighting on the 8th and the 10th. French Shore Batteries inflict damage on the attacking Allies, but by the 10th, Oran and Algeria surrender. On the 11th, General Patton receives a French Officer at 04:30, who informs him that the French, at Rabat, are done fighting. Patton sends the French Officer back, with instructions to deliver a message to French Admiral Michelier "QUIT AT ONCE OR I AM GOING TO ATTACK." Patton then sends word, that if the French would quit, even at the last moment, he (Patton) would order a cease fire. At 06:40 with Bombers over their targets and Battleships positioned, the French hurriedly inform the Americans that they will surrender Casablanca. The U.S.S. *Massachusetts* (BB-59), Battleship; *Wichita* (CA-45) Heavy Cruiser; *Brooklyn* (CL-40) Light Cruiser; and two Destroyers the *Ludlow* (DD-438) and *Murphy* (DD-603) are damaged, during the operation. The U.S.S. *Leedstown*, a Destroyer Transport (AP-73), is damaged after an attack by a Torpedo Bomber on the eighth and will be sunk by a combined Submarine and Air attack on the 9th. The Minesweepers *Palmer* (DMS-5) and *Stansbury* (DMS-8) are also damaged, by coastal gunfire and a mine respectively, during the invasion operation. In addition, the H.M.S. *Walney* and *Hartman* are sunk. Other British Vessels suffer some damage. Operation TORCH consists of over 400 Fighting Ships, approximately 1,000 Planes and in excess of 100,000 men who easily meet the French resistance. France, after the capitulation, agrees to an armistice and throws their resources to the side of the Allies.

November 9th 1942 — (Paific-New Caledonia) Admiral Halsey returns from Guadalcanal and is immediately informed that U.S. Intelligence has intercepted information which points to a new Japanese offensive against the islands. The information seems to pinpoint an Air attack on the 11th, a Naval bombardment of Henderson Field on the evening of the 12th followed by a full scale Carrier attack on the 13th and culminated with an invasion by ground troops. The decoded information suggests a strong Force consisting of four Battleships, five Heavy Cruisers, two Carriers and approximately 30 Destroyers plus Cargo Vessels and Troops Transports. Halsey orders the Forces of Admirals Scott, Turner, Callaghan

and Kinkaid, composing four Heavy Cruisers, four Light Cruisers, 22 Destroyers and the Carrier Enterprise still under repair from damages suffered at Santa Cruz, and two Battleships the *Washington* and the *South Dakota*, itself under repair. To intercept the invasion force. **(Pacific-Solomons-Guadalcanal)** The 7th Marines, assisted by 164th Infantry, surrounds the enemy at Gavaga Creek and repulse several attempts to break out. In other activity, contingents of the 164th Infantry and units of the 8th Marines, withdraw from Koli Point and head for the Lunga perimeter, to participate in another attack on Kokumbona. **(Pacific-New Guinea)** The Allies reach Natunga with advance troops. **(Atlantic-North Africa)** Tunisia is seized by the Germans without French opposition. Advance contingents land at the Airport in El Aouina. **(Atlantic-Morocco)** Admiral Hewitt, U.S.N., transfers the command of all troops ashore to General George S. Patton. In other activity, U.S. General Clark and French General Giraud arrive in Algiers by Plane to confer with representatives of the Vichy Government, hoping to convince them to side with the Allies. Giraud is not well received by the French. French Admiral Darlan, presently in Algiers, is considered in the eyes of most Frenchmen to be the representative of Petain and they insist that it will take an order from Darlan, instructing them to cease fire and allow them their honor, based on their sworn personal allegiance to Petain.

November 10th 1942 — (United States) A German U-Boat deploys mines off the coast of New York, in the vicinity of Ambrose Light. **(Pacific-Solomon Islands)** The Minesweeper, U.S.S. *Southard* (DMS-10), encounters and destroys a Japanese Submarine, the *I-172*, off the Solomon Islands. **(Pacific-New Guinea)** The Allies (Australian 16th Brigade) continue their progress against the Japanese, driving them from the Oivi heights and pushing them further back. **(Atlantic-Honduras)** The U.S. Navy establishes a Naval Base at Puerto Castillo, in Honduras. **(Atlantic-North Africa)** The British Eighth Army in Egypt continues pressure against the retreating Axis forces. In Algiers, French Admiral Francois Darlan calls for all French Forces in North Africa to cease firing against the Americans. The order is the result of strenuous negotiations between General Clark and Admiral Darlan. The French under Darlan become infuriated with the actions of General Mast, who had acted independently of Vichy and cooperated with the Americans. Some French Officers suggest he be placed in protective American custody. The French had issued orders not to fire against the Americans and General Clark insisted that the words "or their Allies" be included as an insurance policy for the British. Oran capitulates at 12:30; Algiers also surrenders. By noon, Fighters from the 12th Air Force, stationed on the U.S.S. *Chenango*, begin landing on the Airport at Port-Lyautey. Morocco will surrender on the following day. Upon learning of Darlan's order, Petain becomes enraged, disavows the act and replaces Darlan with Admiral Nogues. On the following day, German troops invade southern France, giving Darlan good reason to align himself with the Allies, calling the invasion of France, a violation of the Armistice signed between France and Germany, during 1940.

November 11th 1942 — (Pacific-Guadalcanal) Three Cargo Vessels which departed Espiritu, escorted by Admiral Scott's Force arrives at Guadalcanal at 05:30 and begin to transfer cargo to the dock at Lunga Point. American Intelligence information had been correct and the enemy attack is right on time. Dive Bombers attack, inflicting damage to all three Cargo Vessels before they are shot down. Scott dispatches one Destroyer to escort a Cargo Ship back to Espiritu for repairs while the other Vessels continue unloading. Admiral Scott moves the remainder of his Force to the Indispensable Strait to hook up with Callaghan. Ships spread out and check the waters east and west of Savo Island for an invasion fleet, but no enemy presence is detected, permitting them to head toward Kukum Beach at dawn to add extra protection to the Cargo Vessels which Admiral Turner's Force had escorted from Espiritu. **(Atlantic-North Africa)** French resistance ends in North Africa, as Morocco capitulates moments before General Patton's assault begins. At 14:00, French Admiral Michelier and General Nogues, meet with Patton to discuss terms. Patton in his diary: "I HAD A GUARD OF HONOR (for the capitulating French). NO USE KICKING A MAN WHEN HE IS DOWN." "WE ARE IN CASABLANCA AND HAVE THE HARBOR AND AIRPORT . . . TO GOD BE THE PRAISE." Mrs. Patton, in a letter to the General: "That must have been a splendid birthday for you: Casablanca taken and an armistice over the whole of North Africa." Another meeting takes place between General Mark Clark (Ike's representative on North Africa) and Admirals Fenard and Darlan concerning the French Fleet. Clark suggests strongly that Darlan order the Fleet to North Africa and to order the French to fight the Axis powers who enter North Africa, but Darlan rejects the idea. Clark implies strongly that Darlan is not showing good faith toward the Allied cause and leaves the premises (Fenard's House) bidding the Admiral a sarcastic "Good Day." The French Admiral reverses his decision later in the day and both of Clark's pointed suggestions are carried out. Darlan will also accept the position of French Political Chief of North Africa and agree with Giraud being the Military Commander (French Forces). By the 12th, complications enter the picture. In other activity, the U.S.S. *Joseph Hewes* (AP-50), a Transport, is attacked and sunk, by an enemy Submarine, in the vicinity of Fedala Roads, North Africa. In addition, the U.S.S. *Hambleton* (DD-455), a Destroyer and the Oiler *Winooski* (AO-38), are both damaged by enemy Submarines in the same area. **(Atlantic-France)** The Germans react to the situation in North Africa by moving at the stroke of midnight into unoccupied France, reaching south to the Mediterranean Sea. The Italians land at Corsica and move into southeastern France.

November 12th 1942 — (Pacific-Guadalcanal) U.S. Scout Planes prove the decoders right again when they detect a formidable Japanese Armada closing fast on Guadalcanal. Transports from Espiritu speed up unloading as enemy Torpedo Planes swoop over and impede the operation for two hours while the Yanks fight them off. Admiral Turner subsequently escorts the Transports out of port under the protection of three Destroyers and several Minesweepers. **(Atlantic-North Africa)** The Transports U.S.S. *Hugh L. Scott* (AP-43), *Edward Rutledge* (AP-52) and the *Tasker H. Bliss* (AP-42), are destroyed off the coast of Morocco by enemy Submarines. **(North Africa-Algeria)** U.S. Paratroopers arrive at Duzerville Airdrome. This Paratroop Task Force is assigned under the operational control of the British First Army at Algiers. On the political side of this Military endeavor, General Clark is incensed with the French because the order to resist the Germans and Italians has been withdrawn. French

General Juin and Admiral Darlan are quickly called and instructed to report to Clark for clarification of the disintegrating situation. As it turns out, Clark has brought some of the grief upon himself by requesting Admiral Nogues to come to Algiers and for this reason the French had temporarily recalled the order to await his arrival later in the day. The confusion is finally cleared up by the following day when the French agree to reinitiate the order to fight the Germans. **(Atlantic-Caribbean)** The U.S.S. *Erie* (PG-50), a Gunboat, is sunk by an enemy Submarine in the Caribbean area.

November 12th-15th 1942 — (Pacific-Guadalcanal) — THE NAVAL BATTLE OF GUADALCANAL (Savo Island) — The Japanese, determined to drive the Americans from Guadalcanal, dispatch another Naval force and 10,000 troops to destroy Henderson Field and eradicate the American Naval presence off Guadalcanal. The American Task Forces, commanded by Admirals Callaghan and Scott, composing 13 Vessels are ordered to intercept the enemy and forestall their advance until Planes from the *Enterprise* can get from Noumea to the area on Friday the 13th.

Admiral Halsey pitches the *San Francisco* (Admiral Callaghan's Flagship), *Portland* (Heavy Cruisers), three Light Cruisers including the Atlanta (Admiral Scott's Flagship) and eight intrepid Destroyers against the overwhelming strength of the Japanese Force which includes two Battleships, a Light Cruiser and 15 Destroyers. Radar contact is made with three enemy columns at 01:24. Callaghan taking the odds into perspective initiates the attack, but the hazards of poor communications and the inability of precise radar tracking, due to the narrow sea passages causes grave complications for the U.S. Forces.

Immediately following the radar sighting, the U.S. begins to close on the enemy, almost 30,000 yards dead ahead; however the journey is leading them into the jaws of the enemy Warships which flank the advancing U.S. Force as it advances, its vision obscured by darkness. With a sudden flash of artificial illumination, the entrapped Warships are lit up by giant searchlights. The Yanks are caught in an avalanche of shells that threatens not only the pygmy Task Forces and the lives of thousands of U.S. Seamen, but the entire Solomon operation. Guadalcanal, the first American offensive of the war, and the lives of 20,000 Marines are at stake. Another striking force, including two Carriers and the main body of the Japanese 38th Division is closing aboard Transports escorted by additional Destroyers.

Callaghan and Scott instinctively strike back with heavy barrages of their own, attempting to escape the gauntlet and regain the momentum in time to bar Admiral Hiroaki Abe's passage. As exploding shells and tracer bullets electrify the sky, the opposing Ships criss-cross blindly exchanging blows in a relentless struggle. Communications between the American Vessels is practicaly cut off during the free-for-all; normal attack strategies are thrown to the wind and every Ship is on its own, often unable to distinguish friend from foe in a colossal circular stampede.

The blind shootout also has the Japanese strike force mesmerized as their own Ships fall out of position, with U.S. Destroyers and Cruisers in their place. In the end, the Japanese Admiral orders a retirement at 02:00, bewildered by the chaotic turn of events and totally unaware that only a few American Warships remain to hamper his advance. As the

Japanese head west, the *Kirishima* makes a wide swing and unleashes a few final volleys against the American Ships and then proceeds to speed westward. The *Hiei* is plagued by American fire as she retires and sustains hits from the guns of the *San Francisco*. The Destroyer *Yudachi* is left behind, fully ablaze. Additional exchanges continue for a few hours, but the main event terminates at approximately 02:25 after a whirlwind contest lasting less than an hour. By 02:30, the U.S. Fleet begins to retire.

Admiral Halsey had anticipated the *Enterprise* arriving on the scene, but the weather causes the Big "E" to run late. Admiral Halsey, sweating the battle out at Noumea, receives no word until after daylight and the first reports are staggering. It isn't until early afternoon that Halsey gets a clearer picture of the ongoing operation. The Destroyers *Barton* and *Laffey* have both been lost with catastrophic casualties; the former losing 90 percent of her crew subsequent to torpedo strikes. The latter is abandoned; however, the depth charges detonate without warning and the Ship plummets to the bottom, with the majority of its survivors caught in the vacuum and pulled through the boiling water.

The *Monssen* and the *Cushing* are also lost, the latter lingering until 17:00. The Cruisers *San Francisco*, *Atlanta*, *Portland* and *Juneau* and the Destroyers *Aaron Ward O'Bannon* and *Sterett* are also damaged. Only the Destroyer *Fletcher* and the Cruiser *Helena* remain unscathed. Both Admiral Scott and Callaghan are killed during the encounter, but their clearheaded decisions and heroic stance will have them remembered as the protagonists of Guadalcanal who had barred the Japanese from reaching the beachhead. One more somber incident occurs as the Light Cruiser *Juneau* attempts to make it back to safety. At about 11:00 the Japanese Submarine *I-26* unleashes a torpedo that virtually splits the Vessel into pieces. The nearby crippled Vessels cannot offer assistance, and later calls for help never reach Admiral Halsey. Slightly over 100 men reach the water, but only 10 will survive, pushing the loss of life to about 700.

The Japanese retreat with the knowledge that their ground forces have been whipped on the 'canal in conjunction with their own failure to penetrate. Planes from the *Enterprise* arrive in the afternoon and inflict additional punishment to the *Hiei*. The Vessel is struck by Marine Planes and by Planes from the Big "E." The riddled Warship is scuttled later in the day, giving the Japanese Imperial Navy their first Battleship loss since the war has begun.

By the 14th, the spunky but battered and exhausted remnants of the U.S. defending Force are unable to engage another enemy Fleet. Admiral Halsey anticipating this possibility, had during the afternoon of the 13th dispatched a message to Admiral kinkaid instructing him to speed two Battleships and four of his Destroyers, under the command of Rear Admiral W.A. Lee, toward Savo Sound (Iron Bottom) to lay ambush for the expected arrival of the next wave of enemy Ships. Kinkaid responds to Halsey that Lee is on his way, but will not arrive until 08:00 on the 14th. The Japanese begin closing within striking range of Henderson Field before dawn. General Vandegrift U.S.M.C., calls Halsey immediately, requesting aid as Henderson is under bombardment. The dispatch: "BEING HEAVILY SHELLED." While Halsey waits impatiently, he learns the uncontested enemy bombardment has subsided after a blistering hour and twenty five minutes without immediate

cause, with three Planes destroyed and seventeen more damaged during the attack. Halsey then learns that pesty PT Boats had impetuously raced out from Tulagi to engage the enemy Armada. Lt. Hugh M. Robinson, leading the Squadron, charges directly into the Force consisting of five Destroyers and six Cruisers. The menacing PTs display cavalier recklessness and force the enemy to expend their ammunition and withdraw, forestalling disaster and buying time for Halsey and Vandegrift.

Planes from Henderson and the U.S.S. *Enterprise* the only American Carrier afloat in the South Pacific, attack against the superior enemy force, dealing them devastating losses. The enemy Task Force loses seven of its 11 Troop Transports, one Heavy Cruiser; in addition, three other Warships are damaged. Four remaining but damaged Transports sputter toward Guadalcanal, beaching in the vicinity of Tassafaronga. The U.S. had committed every available Plane to destroy the enemy. They strike with vengeance between 10:00 and darkness, landing only to refuel and reload. A group of Marine Pilots share in a bonanza. A Japanese speedboat racing away from one of the wrecked Vessels and transporting what appears to be a lot of Oriental Brass is cut to pieces by the Marine Pilots.

The four remaining Transports, carrying approximately 4,000 of the original 10,000 Japanese reinforcements, manage to stumble toward Tassafaronga under cover of darkness and debark safely, but their sanctuary is temporary. On the following morning, the Transports are located and a combined Artillery, Naval and Air bombardment from New Hebrides and Henderson Field is poured upon them, wiping out half the Japanese force. The deluge of shells also ruins the supplies that had been unloaded on the beach.

Rear Admiral W. A. Lee prepares to engage the approaching enemy and culminate the pernicious conflagration which has transformed Leyte Gulf into a grotesque necropolis, its floor laden with castaway gray sepulchers. Lee's Force, comprising the Battleships *South Dakota* and *Washington* and the Destroyers *Walke*, *Benham*, *Gwin* and the *Preston* converge on Savo Sound to engage four Cruisers, the Battleship *Kirishima* and nine Destroyers. The confrontation erupts prior to midnight and continues raging into the 15th.

Sharknosed Fighters at Henderson Airfield, Guadalcanal.

Admiral Kondo, under the impression he is facing only Cruisers and Destroyers, divides his Task Force into four sections to grasp an advantage, but the move unbalances his total strength and allows the Yanks an opportunity to attack them piecemeal. The Japanese succeed in getting some of their Vessels behind Lee's Force, but the *Walke* flings several deadly volleys into the Sendai and accompanying Destroyers. The Japanese Warships react immediately, pounding away at the dauntless Destroyers. Meanwhile, the Battleships *South Dakota* and *Washington*, two self designated equalizers maneuver quietly into position.

The tone of the raging battle rises to a crescendo as the staggered Destroyers are fighting spreading fires. The Japanese become overconfident as the gallant Destroyers begin to totter under Kondo's missiles. At 23:36 the *Preston* is decimated at point blank range by the *Nagara* and ordered abandoned, costing the lives of four Officers and 112 enlisted men. The *Walke* is also abandoned, six minutes later, allegedly brought about by the guns of the *Nagara* and a subsequent torpedo. This costs the lives of 75 Seamen, many of whom succumb instantaneously when depth charges explode while they are alongside the incinerated Vessels. The *Benham* is also rocked with a devastating series of hits, but the Vessel shakes, quivers while capsizing, but recovers miraculously to roll back and survive the onslaught temporarily. Meanwhile the tempo of the enemy guns accelerate as the damaged *Gwin*, under the umbrella of the Battleships presses the attack. The disabled *Benham* struggles forward to rescue survivors of the *Preston* and *Walke* but the Japanese pour a continual fusillade, aborting the attempt.

The *Gwin*, damaged earlier by the *Nagara*, is hit again and unable to unleash her torpedoes. Meanwhile, the *South Dakota* steams forward, her turrets spewing shells upon the enemy. Her radar fails, however, and the knockout punch is delayed. Enemy searchlights expose her position and a flurry of enemy fire lambastes the Battleship, slaying about 40 men and demolishing one of her turrets. The *Washington* drives to crush Kondo's force from his flank. The *Washington* delivers a convincing barrage of five and 16 inch shells that silence the Kondo effectively. At 01:05, with the demise of a Destroyer and the imminent loss of the *Kirishima* which is running in circles like a punch drunk fighter, Admiral Nobutake Kondo heads his battered Fleet west for Tokyo.

The U.S. loses several Destroyers and the Japanese lose a Heavy Cruiser, the Battleship *Kirishima* and a Destroyer. Rear Admirals Daniel Callaghan and Norman Scott are killed during the initial stages of the bloody engagement, but the Japanese Navy has been repulsed at Guadalcanal for the last time on a large scale. Japan will not attempt to deploy a large Naval Force there again. The subsequent capture of enemy documents shows exactly where the Japanese intended to accept the surrender of General Vandegrift, but there will be no death march on Guadalcanal.

Although the Japanese continue to struggle fanatically against the Americans, this tumultuous victory at sea ultimately seals the fate of the island and preserves New Zealand and Australia in the process. Japan has been bragging on the radio that America is doomed, but their propagandists cannot suppress the facts and their animated editorials only achieve the furthering of American resolve.

After the fall of Guam in December of 1941, a Jap announcer had poured propaganda over the airwaves, profusely dishonoring America. Tokyo Rose is not the only endearing enemy voice that the Marines would like to quell. This particular lovable Nip, who speaks with a lisp had clamored after the fall of Guam: "GUAM NOW BELONG TO JAPAN FOREVER." "NEVER AGAIN WILL AMERICANS TOUCH ITS SOIL." After the 1st Marine Division landed on Guadalcanal, the same infamous announcer proclaims: "AT THIS RIDICULOUS RATE OF ADVANCE, AMERICA WON'T RECOVER ITS LOST TERRITORY FOR PERHAPS TWO HUNDRED YEARS." He subsequently states: "OUR AXIS ALLIES ARE PINNING AMERICA DOWN IN EUROPE. WE SHALL BE VERY MUCH STRONGER BEFORE AMERICA IS FREE TO MOVE IN THE PACIFIC." As if his big mouth isn't already making him unpopular with Americans, this "son of heaven" takes another shot at the Americans, stating: "WE ARE WILLING TO SELL YOU LAND AT 1,000 LIVES AN ACRE. FOR SUCH A PRICE WE WILL SELL YOU A MILLION SQUARE MILES IF YOU WISH." The Yanks are not intending to wait 200 years; they are on their way toward Guam and Tokyo.

In one of the saddest personal tragedies of the entire war, one mother and father back in the States are soon to be visited by a representative of the Navy Department. The Sullivan family, proud and patriotic, see their sons go to war immediately after the debacle at Pearl Harbor. Inspired by the disaster, they go together and are assigned to the same Ship, the Cruiser *Juneau*. The Fighting Sullivans' are busy during this battle against the Japanese. sticking together as they have since they were boys, until a Japanese torpedo crashes into the Vessel. All five Sullivans go down with the Ship. The Navy, which had allowed the Sullivans special permission to serve on the same Vessel, takes precautions that this type of tragedy can never happen again.

Naval Vessel casualties are as follows: November 12th: U.S.S. *San Francisco* (CA-38), a Heavy Cruiser, damaged by Air attack, the U.S.S. *Buchanan* (DD-484), a Destroyer, is accidentally damaged by U.S. Naval gunfire. November 13th: American Light Cruiser *Atlanta* (CL-51) and *Juneau* (CL-52), both sink, the *Atlanta* by Naval gunfire and the *Juneau* by an enemy torpedo; the Destroyers *Barton* (DD-599), *Cushing* (DD-376), *Laffey* (DD-459) and the *Monssen* (DD436) are also sunk. In addition, the following U.S. Vessels are damaged on the 13th: Heavy Cruiser *Portland* (CA-33), by enemy Surface Craft torpedo; Heavy Cruiser *San Francisco* (CA-38), by Naval gunfire; Light Cruiser *Helena* (CL-50), by Naval gunfire; Destroyers *Aaron Ward* (DD-483) and *Sterett* (DD-407), both by Naval gunfire and the Destroyer *O'Bannon* (DD-450), is damaged accidentally by U.S. guns.

The Japanese Navy sustains the loss of the Battleship *Hiei* and two Destroyers, the *Akatsuki* and the *Yudachi*. November 14th: the American Destroyers *Preston* (DD-379) and the *Walke* (DD-416) are both sunk. The Japanese lose the Heavy Cruiser *Kinugasa*. November 15th: The Destroyer U.S.S. *Benham* (DD-397) is sunk by U.S. Forces, after having been damaged by Japanese Surface Vessels. The U.S.S. *South Dakota* (BB-57), the Destroyer *Gwin* (DD-433), and the Cargo Ship *Almaak* (AK-27) are damaged. The Japanese lose the Battleship *Kirishima* and the Destroyer *Ayanami*.

Subsequent to the battle General Vandegrift sends the following message to Admiral Halsey: "TO SCOTT CALLAGHAN

AND THEIR MEN GOES OUR GREATEST HOMAGE & WITH MAGNIFICENT COURAGE AGAINST SEEMINGLY HOPELESS ODDS, THEY DROVE BACK THE FIRST HOSTILE STRIKE AND MADE SUCCESS POSSIBLE & TO THEM THE MEN OF GUADALCANAL LIFT THEIR BATTERED HELMETS IN DEEPEST ADMIRATION." Admiral Nimitz also rings praise upon the men who have defended Guadalcanal especially Admirals Callaghan and Scott. Referring to Admiral Halsey he states: "HE HAS THAT RARE COMBINATION OF INTELLECTUAL CAPACITY AND MILITARY AUDACITY AND CAN CALCULATE TO A CAT'S WHISKER THE RISK INVOLVED."

The U.S.S. Washington (BB-56).

November 13th 1942 — (Pacific-Solomons) Japanese troops are put ashore at Munda Point, New Georgia, with orders to begin construction of an Airstrip. On Guadalcanal Eight P-38s attached to the 339th Squadron, 347th Fighter Group, arrive from Milne Bay, at a Fighter Airstrip, situated east of Henderson Field. **(Pacific-New Guinea)** A Japanese rear guard contingent, attempting to fight a holding action at a Kumusi River crossing, is wiped out by the Australians. **(Atlantic-North Africa)** General Eisenhower arrives in Algiers to help to complete the armistice agreement with the French. Before departing Ike pins the third star on General Mark Clark, making him the youngest Lt. General in the U.S. Army. In Libya, the British Eighth Army seizes Tobruk and on the 15th, the British capture the Airfields at Martuba.

November 14th 1942 — (Pacific-Guadalcanal) (See November 12th-15th 1942.) **(Pacific-New Guinea)** The New Guinea Force issues instructions, for the operation, intended to destroy the enemy beachhead at Buna-Gona. In other activity, the U.S. Fifth Air Force makes passes over the Kokoda Trail near Wairopi and drops equipment for constructing bridges to assist the 25th Australian Brigade.

November 15th 1942 — (Pacific-Guadalcanal) Having lost the majority of their supplies and, coupled with the defeat offshore, the Japanese on Guadalcanal are nearly isolated. The struggle will continue, but everything now favors the Yanks.

November 16th 1942 — (United States) By this time, the agreement reached between General Clark and French Admiral Darlan is receiving mixed reviews in the U.S.; many are upset that the U.S. is negotiating with a known German collaborator. President Roosevelt now has to emphasize that the arrangement with Darlan is a temporary measure. **(Pacific-New Guinea)** The U.S. 32nd Division moves against Buna, while the Australian 7th Division presses toward Gona,

against entrenched Japanese. Enemy Aircraft destroy a small Allied Vessel while it is attempting to land supplies. On board, is Major General Edwin F. Harding, Commanding General, U.S. 32nd Division, who safely swims to shore. The well-fortified Japs are commanded by Colonel Yosuke Yokoyama (Forces west of Girua River and Captain Yoshitatsu Yasuda (forces east of river). Yokoyama replaced General Horii, who drowned during the Kokoda Trail battle. **(Pacific-New Britain)** The Japanese bolster their forces, establishing the Japanese Eighth Army Area. Lt. General Hitoshi Imamura, will command two Armies: the 17th, charged with the Solomons and the 18th, given the responsibility of destroying the Allies in New Guinea, before they can reach Rabaul. **(Atlantic-North Africa)** The British maintain their movement into Tunisia and mass a few thousand troops to establish a bridgehead in the vicinity of Bizerte-Tunis. In Tunisia, a French Battalion, involved for the first time in combat against the Germans, throws back a German Reconnaissance detachment. Off Casablanca, the German U-Boat *U-173* is sunk by three Destroyers, the *Woolsey* (DD-347), *Quick* (DD-490) and the *Swanson* (DD-443). **(Atlantic-Mediterranean)** An Allied Convoy departs Port Said, heading for Malta, under the protection of Martuba-based, Allied Aircraft.

A U.S. Submarine plows into a Japanese Vessel.

November 17th 1942 — (United States) The Navy establishes another Naval Air Station at DeLand, Florida. **(Pacific-New Guinea)** Australian and U.S. Forces converge on the enemy beachhead at Buna-Gona. Japanese reinforcements, being transported by Destroyer, arrive at Basabua, during the night, to bolster enemy troop strength. In addition, Japanese Planes knock two Allied Supply Luggers out of action, forcing the Warren Force to be resupplied by air, until replacements can be attained to supplement the one remaining Lugger. **(Atlantic-Tunisia)** The British 78th Division receives orders to prepare to advance on Tunis. Contact is made between elements of the 78th Division and the Germans, approximately 70 miles west of Tunis. In other activity, the 2nd Battalion, U.S. 509th Paratroop Regiment, seizes the Airstrip at Gafsa.

November 18th 1942 — (Pacific-Guadalcanal) The U.S. Forces (Western Sector), commanded by General Sebree, U.S.A., begin to advance to an offensive position. The 2nd Battalion, 182nd Infantry, with cover fire from the 8th Marines, crosses the Matanikau River, near its mouth and secures Hill 66. **(Pacific-New Guinea)** Task Force Warren (primarily 128th Infantry), is ordered to stay in place, because of desperate supply problems. The U.S. 126th Infantry, 32nd Division, moving toward Buna, receives orders to hook up with the Australians. **(Atlantic-Tunisia)** A German heavy assault is repelled by the British 36th Brigade, 78th Division, in the vicinity of Djebel Abiod.

November 18th-30th 1942 — (Pacific-Guadalcanal) U.S. Army and Marine Corps contingents continue skirmishing with the Japanese, as they gnaw toward the main Japanese Force, situated at Kokumbona and the Poha River. The Yanks clear the enemy from Point Cruz, but withdraw, during the end of November, to brace for an anticipated Japanese counter-offensive.

November 19th 1942 — (Pacific-New Guinea) The Allies (American-Australians) suffer heavy casualties along the coastal drive from hidden enemy guns. **(Atlantic-North Africa)** The French at Med-jez el Bab, Tunisia, reject a German demand for surrender. The Germans react, with an Infantry attack, supported by Tanks, Artillery and Air support, but they are repulsed by the French 19th Corps, assisted by U.S. Artillery and British troops. **(Atlantic-Russia)** The Red Army initiates its winter offensive, in an effort to trap the Germans at Stalingrad.

November 20th 1942 — (Pacific-Guadalcanal) The U.S. 1st Battalion, 182nd Infantry, is struck hard by a Japanese Force. After being driven back during the morning, the Yanks recapture the lost ground and move (assisted by Artillery and Air support) just outside of fortified Point Cruz. During the night, reinforcements (164th Infantry), move up to tighten the 182nd's defenses. **(Pacific-New Guinea)** Contingents of the Australian 25th Brigade penetrate Gona, but intense enemy fire drives them out after dark. In other activity, Task Force Warren still meets severe enemy resistance, along the coast, preventing movement toward Buna. **(Atlantic-Libya)** The British 10 Corps takes Benghazi. **(Atlantic-Tunisia)** French 19th Corps contingents, British units, and attached U.S. forces, withdraw from Medjez el Bal to join contingents of the Blade Force (British First Army) at Oued Zarga. **(Atlantic-Russia)** German positions at Stalingrad are breached south of the city by the Soviets, who assault in strength, with three Corps.

November 21st 1942 — (Pacific-Guadalcanal) The U.S. 182nd Infantry reduces enemy resistance in Point Cruz, but the enemy prevents any further advance. **(Pacific-New Guinea)** The Australian 16th Brigade, with the 126th U.S. Infantry, 32nd Division in support, encounters heavy Japanese resistance as it attempts to reach Sanananda: the Japanese also deals a punishing blow to the 2nd Battalion, 128th U.S. Infantry, as it attempts to reach the Buna Mission. Incessant enemy fire stalls the advance at the "Triangle," a junction of the Buna Mission and Buna village trails. The Japanese are protected by bunkers and flanked by swampy terrain on both sides of the trails, making it nearly impossible for the Yanks to advance without reinforcements which are on the way (2nd Bn. 126th Infantry). In other activity, the Warren Force, assisted by Planes and Artillery, jumps off late, and makes little progress. More guns are rushed in later to bolster the Yanks. **(Atlantic-Libya)** Tripoli Harbor is attacked by B-24s, attached to the IX Bomber Command. **(Atlantic-Tunisia)** The enemy withdraws across the river at Medjez, while the exhausted British 78th Division awaits reinforcements before resuming the chase.

November 24th 1942 — Tripoli under Air attack by U.S. Bombers.

November 22nd 1942 — (Pacific-Guadalcanal) The Japanese tenaciously resist U.S. attempts to dislodge them. The 164th and 182nd Regiments are stalled, as they drive west. The 8th Marines finalize preparations, to push through the 164th Infantry lines, in order to crash through the rigid Japanese defenses. On the following day, the Marines unsuccessfully attack the Japanese positions. The offensive will be halted on the 23rd, to await reinforcements. **(Pacific-New Guinea)** The battle for control of New Guinea rages, as the Americans drive against fierce enemy resistance blocking their route to Sanananda. The Australians simultaneously hit a strong roadblock as they attempt to reach Gona. **(Atlantic-North Africa)** In Algiers, the Formal agreement between the French and Allies (drafted in London) is signed. On the 24th, General Eisenhower and Admiral Darlan make some changes in the original agreement and both individuals initial the document. In Tunisia the Germans mount an unsuccessful attack against the British 36th Brigade, 78th Division, 1st Army, at Djebel Abiod. In other activity, Gafsa is reoccupied by U.S. and French forces. **(Atlantic-Russia)** The German 6th Army (Group B) becomes surrounded by Soviet troops at Stalingrad.

November 23rd 1942 — (United States) President Roosevelt signs the bill authorizing a Women's Reserve, for the U.S. Coast Guard. **(Pacific-Guadalcanal)** The combined amount of Army, Navy, Marine Corps and New Zealand Planes, operating on Guadalcanal, stands at 84. **(Pacific-New Guinea)** The

Japanese, holding Gona, offer tenacious resistance against the main body of the Australian 25th Brigade. The U.S. 3rd Battalion, 126th Infantry continues to advance under murderous fire as it moves against Sanananda; elements are virtually pinned down in some areas. Two Battalions of the 126th and 128th Regiments are to become the Urbana Force. In other activity, General MacNider, the Commanding General of the Warren Force, is wounded, while inspecting the front line and is replaced by Colonel J. Tracy Hale Jr. **(Atlantic-Libya)** The Axis troops depart Agedabia, to reform at El Agheila for a defensive stand. The move is prompted when the British 7th Armored Division outflanks their positions. **(Atlantic-Algiers)** Allied Headquarters is advanced from Gibraltar to Algiers. After General Eisenhower arrives, he finds the runway in a deteriorating position, because of excessive mud. A large tractor is required to drag a Flying Fortress from the Airstrip to allow other Planes to land. In other activity, Eisenhower is informed that reinforcements ordered to depart Oran and join with British General Anderson's 1st Army, which had departed on the 11th, advancing on Tunisia, have not moved. Eisenhower helps straighten out the communications problem and Brigadier General Lunsford E. Oliver, leading the Combat Command B, 1st U.S. Armored Division, commanded by Brigadier General Lunsford E. Oliver, embarks in half-tracs, on a 700 mile trek toward Souk-El-Arba to join the British First Army. They temporarily will come under the command of the British 1st Army on the 27th. **(Atlantic-Tunisia)** An agreement is reached whereby all Forces south of the Le Kef-Zaghouan Line will come under French Command, and those troops north of the line come under command of the British. **(Atlantic-Senegal)** The Allies seize Dakar, capital French West Africa, without opposition.

The Carrier Escort U.S.S. Bogue (CVE-9).

November 24th 1942 — (Pacific-New Guinea) The 3rd Battalion, U.S. 126th Infantry, drives toward Sanananda. The Urbana Force remains entwined in heavy skirmishing in the vicinity of the murderous "Triangle." An assault is initiated, but the Japanese repulse it. In the Warren Force sector along the coast, activity is extremely light. In activity offshore, the Japanese lose a Destroyer, the *Hasyashio*, after it is attacked by U.S. Army Planes off Lae. **(Atlantic-North Africa)** The U.S.S. *Thomas Stone* (AP-59), is damaged by enemy Horizontal Bombers as it travels in a Convoy heading to North Africa; it is beached and abandoned on the following day. **Libya** British General Montgomery finalizes plans for a British assault against El Agheila. Montgomery, in his typical manner of extraordinary preparation, awaits reinforcements before

attacking. In other activity, the son of French Admiral Darlan is seriously ill and both Admiral Leahy and President Roosevelt have expressed concern. Darlan sends a personal letter to Admiral Leahy, thanking the two of them. In addition, Admiral Darlan issues a policy statement. The policy in part: "IF WE (French) HAD NOT PROMISED TO DEFEND OUR TERRITORIES AGAINST ANYONE WHO CAME TO ATTACK THEM, THE AXIS PEOPLE WOULD HAVE OCCUPIED NORTH AFRICA A LONG TIME AGO. WE KEPT OUR WORD. WHEN I WAS IN AFRICA, I ORDERED THE FIGHTING STOPPED SO THAT A DITCH SHOULD NOT BE DUG TO SEPARATE AMERICA AND FRANCE." The letter arrives in Washington on the 24th.

November 25th 1942 — (Pacific-New Guinea) Heavy fighting continues at Gona and Sanananda, however, the Allies are unable to dislodge the Japanese. A short lull occurs, however, on the 29th, Allied Bombers intercept and turn back an enemy Destroyer Force, attempting to pass through the Vitiaz Strait with reinforcements for Gona.

U.S. troops firing 60-mm mortars toward Buna Mission (New Guinea).

November 26th 1942 — (Pacific-New Guinea) Elements of the U.S. 32nd Division's 126th Regiment assist the Australians to take the food depot on the Gona Front. The Urbana Force halts its attack on the Triangle to pivot and strike west of Entrance Creek. The Warren Force, supported by Air and Artillery attacks, however, the Japanese seek shelter in bunkers during the bombardment and are prepared for the Infantry. In other activity, the Japanese Planes sink a Supply Lugger, laden with ammunition for the Allies at Hariko. The 127th U.S.

Infantry, 32nd Division, arrives at Port Moresby, being transferred from Australia.

November 27th 1942 — (Pacific-New Guinea) American Colonel Mott arrives on the Urbana Front, to assume command of the troops. Preparations are made, to reinitiate the offensive. **(Atlantic-France)** French Admiral Jean de Laborde orders the destruction of the French Fleet, moored in the harbor of Toulon, France, to prevent it from being captured by the Germans. **(Atlantic-North Africa)** In Tunisia, the U.S. 1st Armored Division is detached from the U.S. 11 Corps in Oran and dispatched to operate under the British First Army.

November 28th 1942 — (Pacific-Guadalcanal) A Japanese Submarine sinks the Cargo Vessel, *Alchiba* (AK-23), off Lunga Point, Guadalcanal. With the loss of the *Alchiba*, only four U.S. Cargo Vessels remain in the entire South Pacific. **(Pacific-New Guinea)** Elements of the 32nd Division, led by Capt. Medendorp, arrive at the Sanananda Front, from Wairopi and deploy west of the Killerton Trail. **(Atlantic-French Somaliland)** Approximately 30 percent of the Vichy Garrison at Djibouti, moves into British Somaliland and sides with the Allies.

November 1942 — The Carrier Escort U.S.S. Santee (CVE-29) standing vigil off North Africa, her Stars and Stripes snapping briskly in the breeze.

November 29th 1942 — (United States) Approval is reached in Washington for the 25th Infantry Division U.S.A., to relieve the 1st Marine Division, on Guadalcanal. **(Pacific-Solomons)** On Guadalcanal, Aola Bay is rejected as a site for an Airfield, however, Carney Airfield is to be constructed at Koli Point. Contingents of the 147th Infantry Regiment, additional Sea-

bees, elements of the 9th Marine Defense Battalion, and units of the 246th Field Artillery Battalion arrive at Koli Point. **(Pacific-New Guinea)** Allied Bombers discover a Japanese Convoy transporting reinforcements through the Vitiaz Strait and turn the Destroyers back, depriving the Japanese at Gona supplies and reinforcements. In other activity, Lt. General Eichelberger is ordered from Australia by MacArthur to depart Australia and assist in the struggle for control of New Guinea. **(Atlantic-North Africa)** In Tunisia, the Germans convincingly stop the British First Army at Djedeida, however, heavy fighting continues between the 11th Brigade, 78th Division and the enemy. In other activity, U.S. Planes drop British Paratroopers over Depienne, to seize Oudna Airfield and to threaten Tunis from the south, however, again German resistance prevents the British from taking their objective. **(Atlantic-Soviet Union)** The Soviets continue to make progress at Stalingrad and enlarge their offensive to the Caucasus; attacks begin against the Terek bridgehead.

U.S. and Australian casualties waiting to be evacuated from Papua.

November 30th 1942 — (Pacific-Solomons-Guadalcanal) BATTLE OF TASSAFARONGA - During the night, an American Task Force, commanded by Rear Admiral C.H. Wright, holds firm at the entrance to Savo Sound and initiates a vicious sea battle with an approaching enemy amphibious Invasion Force, consisting of four Destroyers. The Americans sink the Destroyer *Takanami* and one additional Ship, once again preventing the debarkation of fresh troops on Guadalcanal. The U.S. Navy suffers damage to four of its Cruisers (*Minneapolis* (CA-36), *New Orleans* (CA-32), *Northampton* (CA-26) and *Pen-*

sacola (CA-24)), damaged by enemy torpedoes, launched by the Destroyers. The Northampton will be scuttled on December 1st. The Americans suffer about 400 killed during the engagement. The Japanese will wait in vain for the Tokyo Express. **(Pacific-New Guinea)** The Australian 21st Brigade relieves the Australian 25th Brigade and continues the fight on the Gona Front. Meanwhile, on the Sanananda Front, the U.S. 32nd Division continues pounding against the Japanese along the Soputa-Sanananda Trail: contingents of the 126th Regiment form a roadblock behind enemy lines, however, attacks by both the Urban and Warren Forces make only small gains. The Japanese at Buna Village repulse three attacks by the Urbana Force; contingents seize a crossing at Siwori Creek and establish an outpost. The Japanese also retain Coconut Grove, and prevent the force from advancing beyond the Triangle. In the Warren Force sector, the Japanese repulse an attack at Duropa Plantation, their main line of resistance. **(Atlantic-North Africa)** General Eisenhower informs General Mark Clark, that Washington has placed him in command of the 5th Army. This decision leaves General Patton with a Corps to command, instead of an Army, much to his dissatisfaction. General Clark has had little combat experience; during World War 1, but became wounded while leading three Rifle Companies and a Machine gun Company in France. Subsequently he becomes a Staff Officer. In Tunisia, the 11th Australian Brigade continues battling the Germans at Djedeida, however, still it is losing. Meanwhile, the British First Army prepares to attack Tunis. About 15,500 Axis troops defend Tunisia.

November 1942 — (United States) Captain George R. Jordan, having served as Lend-Lease expediter and Liaison Officer with the Russians is becoming increasingly concerned about the whole program and its ambiguity and clandestine operations under the guise of "DIPLOMATIC IMMUNITY." A series of unusual episodes at Newark Airport (New Jersey), starting during May of 1942, prompts him to maintain a detailed diary: A Commercial Pilot scrapes a U.S. Plane which is about to be given to the Russians, infuriating Russian Colonel Kotikov and his other troops. They imply the Pilot should be shot and American Airlines should be banished from the Field. Jordan explains that the U.S. doesn't operate that way. The Russian says he will take care of it himself; calls are made to the Russian Embassy and to Harry Hopkins (Head of Lend-Lease). American Airlines is astonishingly soon barred from the Airfield for the duration of the war. Also, during early June, a Russian dubbed Mr. Brown (Molotov) is in the U.S. and declines an offer to spend the night at the Blair House, pressing for a night at the White House; Molotov sleeps in the room across from Harry Hopkins. An interesting twist is that Molotov requests that one of the secretaries accompanying the delegation be allowed to come over and the request is granted. However, even more alarming is the fact that the U.S. Captain is quickly determining that the Russians are beginning to receive dangerous materials absolutely suited for building an atomic bomb. Among Jordan's records of items moving to Russia out of Newark during 1942: Graphite, over $800,000; aluminum tubes (used for cooking uranium into plutonium) $13 million; and a most secret ingredient, thorium (over 13,000 lbs.). In addition, the Russians, having received about 25 heavy Diesel engines costing about $17,500 each, request 25 more, however, Major General Deane, U.S.A., (Chief of Military Mission in Moscow) refuses to permit their shipment because of the dire need of them by MacArthur in the Pacific. The Russians appeal to Harry Hopkins and receive the engines. By the end of 1944, the Russians receive over 1,300 engines. As November closes, Captain Jordan is being transferred to Great Falls Montana the new Base for Lend-Lease for the Russians.

December 1st 1942 — (United States) The Navy commissions Fleet Air Wing 15 at Norfolk, Virginia; it will serve at Port Lyautey, French Morocco. **(Pacific-New Guinea)** General Eichelberger, U.S.A., meets with MacArthur and General R.K. Sutherland (MacArthur's Chief-of-Staff) throughout most of the night before taking command of the troops in the vicinity of Buna. MacArthur tells him: "TO MAKE COMMAND CHANGES INCLUDING PUTTING SERGEANTS IN CHARGE OF BATTALIONS AND CORPORALS IN CHARGE OF COMPANIES-ANYONE WHO WILL FIGHT." He further states: "TAKE BUNA." General Eichelberger inspires the men by conspicuously sporting his stars in full view of enemy snipers, and tops that by grasping a machine gun and eliminating several snipers. General MacArthur soon learns of an eighteen man detachment, led by Sergeant Herman Bottcher, which makes its way directly through enemy lines, under the noses of the Japs and reaches Buna Beach; Bottcher gains instant promotion to Captain and he receives the Distinguished Service Cross. Within six feverish weeks, the Japanese in Buna are thoroughly cracked and pushed further back, severing the enemy hold on New Guinea. The Australians will repel a Japanese attempt to land troops, by barge at Giruwa. They then seize Gona, forcing the Japs to evacuate to the Gona Mission, for a last stand. Other Allied troops are still struggling, in their attempt to capture Buna Village and Cape Endaiadere. **(China-Burma-India)** Airlift to China becomes part of Air Transport Command (India-China Wing, ATC), relieving General Stilwell of responsibility. In Burma, the rejuvenated Japanese resume the battle line Tengchung-Myitkyina-Kamaing-Kalewa-Akyab. **(Atlantic-Great Britain)** General Carl Spaatz is replaced by Lt. General Ira C. Eaker as Commanding Officer of the U.S. Eighth Air Force. Spaatz departs for Algeria to assume command of the Western Desert Air Force. **(Atlantic-North Africa)** In Tunisia, the Germans push toward Tebourba, inflicting heavy British Tank losses (Blade Force). C.C.B., U.S. 1st Armored Division, moves into position at Teboura, to bolster the British 78th Division. Heavy fighting continues, with the Germans seizing the town during the night of December 3-4, as the British 78th Division evacuates to safer positions. The Germans maintain superiority over Allied Tanks for the present, continuing to inflict severe damage. The losses alarm General Patton (still in Morocco), who subsequently flies to Algiers for a meeting with Eisenhower and Clark and to inspect the battlefields in person. During the meeting between Generals Eisenhower, Patton and Clark, a call comes in from Washington; General Marshal had selected Clark as commander of the 5th Army. Command of an Army usually demands three stars: Patton is a two star General; Clark had recently received his third star.

December 2nd 1942 — (United States) The Navy extends its Air capacity, establishing a Naval Air Station in Rio De Janeiro, Brazil. **(Pacific-New Guinea)** General Eichelberger relieves General Harding of command of the U.S. 32nd Division, placing Brigadier General Albert Waldron in the post. Approximately 800 Japanese reinforcements land 12 miles north of Gona and repel successive attacks to seize Buna village. Progress, for the Allies, is poor on two fronts (Urbana and Warren). An Allied offensive will commence on the fifth, but again, progress will be sluggish and casualties become high, as Buna Village is penetrated slightly by contingents of the Urbana force. The Warren Force suffers extremely high casualties. The 126th Infantry is under heavy attack from Japanese at Soputa-Sanananda Trail, from all sides and reinforcements are unable to reach them. **(Atlantic-North Africa)** In Tunisia, the Germans knock out about 40 British Tanks as they drive on Tebourba. American and French troops attack Faid Pass, situated six miles northeast of Gafsa and after incessant heavy fighting, the pass is captured on the following day.

General Mark Clark.

Douglas A-20s on a mission over Europe.

December 3rd 1942 — (Pacific-Solomons) U.S. Planes at Henderson Field spot enemy Destroyers attempting to reach Guadalcanal and damage one of them. The enemy Vessels drop off a few drums of supplies. These Destroyer hit-and-run missions continue until the 11th. In other activity on the 'Canal, the 18th Naval Construction Bn. and the balance of the 9th Defense Bn. join the Aola Force. On New Georgia, Allied Planes locate an enemy Airstrip under construction at Munda Point and initiate continual Airraids to destroy the facility. **(Pacific-New Guinea)** In New Guinea, the Allies are still battling viciously to drive the Japanese back, with elements of the 126th American Infantry, under heavy attack from the Japs, at Soputa-Sanananda Pass. General Eichelberger is promised Australian troops and Tanks to aid the beleaguered Americans. **(Atlantic-North Africa)** German forces pound Tebourba and occupy it during the night after the British 11th Brigade sustains heavy casualties and is forced to evacuate. Meanwhile, C.C.B., U.S. 2nd Armored Division battles the Germans southwest of Tebourba at El Guessa. Also, U.S. and French troops capture Faid Pass.

December 4th 1942 — (United States) Over two hundred Congressmen petition President Roosevelt for the establishment of a Jewish homeland in Palestine. **(Pacific-Guadalcanal)** The 2nd Marine Raider Battalion finishes its month-long journey from Aola Bay, reaching the Lunga perimeter; losses along the route amount to 17, against 400 enemy killed. The reports, turned into Major General A.A. Vandegrift, by Carlson, inform him of the enemy concentration of strength to the south. **(Atlantic-Italy)** Twenty B-24s, attached to the IX Bomber Command, initiate the first U.S. Airstrike, against Italy. The U.S. Planes strike the port and Shipping, at Naples.

December 5th 1942 — (United States) President Roosevelt places the Selective Service System under the Warpower Commission. **(South Pacific)** Army Air Force units in the South Pacific are to be designated Thirteenth Air Force, however, the Air Force has not yet been officially activated. **(Pacific-New Guinea)** The Allied Offensive (Urban and Warren Forces) begins, in an effort to capture Buna, but makes slow progress. General A.W. Waldron is wounded and replaced by Brigadier General Clovis E. Byers as commander of the 32nd Division. **(Pacific-FiJi Islands)** The U.S.S. *Grebe* (ATO-134), an Ocean Tug, becomes grounded, as it maneuvers south of the Fiji Islands. **(Atlantic-Tunisia)** General Eisenhower's plan to attack Axis Forces is approved by the Combined Chiefs of Staff, with the proposed operation to commence on the 9th. The British First Army is delayed by thin supply lines and lack of manpower to carry it through. Meanwhile, Allied Planes strike enemy-held ports.

December 6th 1942 — (Pacific-New Guinea) The U.S. 126th Regiment still holds the besieged roadblock along the Soputa-Sanananda trail, despite unavailability of supplies and ammunition. Meanwhile, the Urbana Force prepares to mount another attack against Buna Village and places first "time on target" fire of the campaign on the Buna Mission. The Warren Force, which has been taking severe casualties while making frontal attacks, pauses until Tanks arrive. **(Atlantic-North Africa)** Germans attack and penetrate U.S. positions on El Guessa heights.

December 7th 1942 — (Pacific-Guadalcanal) The Planes from Henderson successfully attack another Japanese Destroyer detachment attempting to bring in reinforcements to the 'Canal. The Henderson Skyhawks damage two of the enemy Vessels. On the following day, PT Boats move out and turn back Japanese Destroyers. **(Pacific-New Guinea)** Australian troops relieve the 126th U.S. Infantry at the front line, except those defending the Roadblock. The Australians press ahead immediately, but the Japanese holding Buna Village repulse their efforts. Japanese holding Buna Mission mount a feverish counterattack, but the Allies repel the charge successfully. The American-Australian Force is waiting for Tanks to support the drive to dislodge the Japanese from their stronghold.

December 8th 1942 — (United States) The Joint Chiefs of Staff propose a plan to recapture Burma to President Roosevelt (Operation ANAKIM). Roosevelt agrees that General Stilwell must receive everything necessary for his part of the operation (N Burma-Operation RAVENOUS). **(Pacific-New Guinea)** The situation, in New Guinea begins to improve for the Allies. A Japanese Destroyer Convoy attempting to land reinforcements is intercepted by Allied Planes and driven back to Rabaul. The Japanese take heavy casualties while withdrawing from Gona to Giruwa. The Urbana Force is still involved in bitter conflict for control of Buna Village and the Warren Force positions heavy guns to destroy enemy bunkers which are blocking their progress. The U.S. Navy again agrees to supply Vessels for transporting reinforcements to the Warren Front. **(Pacific-Guadalcanal)** The U.S. 3rd Infantry Regiment and the 132nd RCT, U.S.A., arrive in Guadalcanal to relieve the 1st Marine Division. On the following day, General A. A. Vandegrift, U.S.M.C., will be replaced by Major General Alexander M. Patch, U.S.A., as Commanding Officer of Guadalcanal. **(Atlantic-North Africa)** General Eisenhower grants permission for the British First Army to pull back to safer positions from which to prepare for the offensive.

December 9th 1942 — (Pacific-Solomon Islands) American Planes, based at Henderson Field, initiate daily raids against Japanese positions at Munda Point, New Georgia. In other activity, the Japanese Submarine I-3, operating near Cape Esperance, Guadalcanal, is sunk by a PT Boat. **(Pacific-New Guinea)** An Allied Air and Artillery bombardment commences against Jap positions in the Gona area. The Australian 26th Brigade then initiates its final assault against Gona, inflicting devastating casualties upon the Japanese and capturing the enemy positions after vicious hand to hand combat. The Allies continue to pound Japanese positions from the air and prepare to attack Buna village. The Allied defenders at the Roadblock (Sanananda Front) are threatened while short of supplies.

December 10th 1942 — (Pacific-New Guinea) Japanese still remaining on the coast northwest of Gona are ordered to dig in and await reinforcements. The U.S. 127th Infantry, 32nd Division, begins to relieve the exhausted 126th Infantry, which is badly understrengthed from heavy fighting on the Urbana Front; the defenders at Sanananda, greet the Supply Convoy while Soldiers on the Warren front observe that supporting Air Attacks continue to soften Japanese resistance. Meanwhile, the Japanese receive supplies by Airdrop. **(Atlantic)** U.S. Land-based Naval Aircraft (VP-84), operating in the Atlantic, sink a German U-Boat, the U-611. **(Atlantic-North Africa)** In Tunisia, German Infantry supported by Tanks are repelled at Medjez el Bab, despite their strong two pronged

assault. Subsequently, the 11th British Brigade, 78th Division and C.C.B., U.S. 1st Armored Division pull back to Bedja, the latter sustaining heavy equipment losses as it withdraws.

December 11th 1942 — (Pacific-Guadalcanal) The 164th and 182nd Infantries, U.S.A., positioned at Point Cruz, are relieved by the 8th Marines and the 132nd Infantry. This troop transfer continues through the middle of December. On the 17th, the 35th Infantry Regiment, U.S.A., 25th Division will arrive on Guadalcanal. **(Pacific-New Georgia)** U.S. Naval Aircraft, operating out of Henderson Field on Guadalcanal, attack an enemy Destroyer detachment off the coast. **(Atlantic-Middle East)** U.S. Military personnel begin to arrive in Iraq and Iran. **(Atlantic-North Africa)** In Libya, British General Montgomery directs an attack against enemy positions. In Tunisia, fighting continues to rage, but the German Tanks still remain superior to those of the Allies. General Patton had inspected the front lines the previous day and determined that tactical deployment was poor and that Light Tanks were unable to take heavy punishment by the powerful Panzers. Patton also determined that American 37-mm guns could not penetrate German armor. The medium Sherman Tank arrives soon and begins to neutralize the enemy Tanks. In Tunisia, again the Germans are repulsed at Medjez el Bab. C.C.B., U.S. First Armored Division is relieved by the 11th British Brigade, and reverts to 5 Corps Reserve. **(Atlantic-Soviet Union)** The Red Army keeps pressure on the Germans in the Caucasus and around Stalingrad.

December 12th 1942 — (Pacific-Solomons) U.S. PT Boats, operating off Guadalcanal, intercept several Japanese Destroyers. The PT-44 is sunk, as well as the Destroyer *Terutsuki*. On Guadalcanal, the 2nd Marine Division relieves the Americal Division west of Matanikau. During the night a Japanese contingent springs an attack against Fighter Strip No. 2. In other activity, the 2nd Marine Division's Signal Co. and the 18th Naval Construction Bn. arrive. **(Pacific-New Guinea)** Newly arrived Allied Tanks are transported by sea from Oro Bay to Hariko and then placed out of sight. Australian troops debark near Soena Plantation, but withdraw after being informed that the Japanese are sending another Naval Force to Buna. The Australians return on the following evening. **(Atlantic-North Africa)** In Tunisia, the British First Army disbands the Blade Force. Also, the British 6th Armored Division is skirmishing with the Axis forces outside of Medjez el Bab. **(Atlantic-Russsia)** The Germans mount a counterattack from Kotelnikov, trying to rescue the 6th Army which is trapped at Stalingrad.

December 13th 1942 — (Pacific-Solomons) Elements of the 182nd Infantry and Co. C, 2nd Engineering Bn. arrive on the 'Canal. **(Pacific-New Guinea)** A Japanese Destroyer Force manages to evade serious damage from attacking Planes and disembarks approximately 800 troops, including Major General Kensaka Oda (Gen. Horii's replacement) on the following day at the mouth of the Mambare River. **(Atlantic-North Africa)** The British push the Germans from El Agheila, Libya but the enemy quells pursuit with strong rear-guard actions, including several well placed mines. Allied Planes attached to the Western Desert Force join the pursuit. In Tunisia, the Allies make final preparations for an offensive against Tunis.

December 14th 1942 — (Pacific-Solomons) More units of the Americal Division arrive on Guadalcanal. **(Pacific-New Guinea)** Allied Reinforcements break through the enemy stranglehold to relieve isolated defenders at the Roadblock (Sanananda Front), while other troops attached to the 127th Infantry move into Buna Village, unopposed (Urbana Front). **(Pacific-Japan)** The U.S.S. *Sunfish* (SS-281), lays mines near Iseno. **(Pacific-New Caledonia)** The U.S. Navy establishes the Fleet Air Command, Noumea, New Caledonia, which will be commanded by Rear Admiral Marc A. Mitscher (Annapolis 1906, Midshipman No. 03620). **(Atlantic-North Africa)** In Libya, the British Eighth Army continues chasing the retreating Axis forces, and attempts to get the New Zealand 2nd Division behind the enemy.

December 15th 1942 — (Pacific-New Guinea) On the Urbana Front, the 2nd Battalion, 128th Infantry, 32nd Division surrounds the Coconut Grove, final enemy strong point west of Entrance Creek **(Atlantic-North Africa)** In Libya, the British Eighth Army's 7th Armored Division engages the enemy rear-guards. As the Germans retreat, the New Zealand 2nd Division races to the coast to cut off escape. The U.S. Ninth Air Force initiates its offensive against the Axis troops, by raiding the Tunisian port of Sfax. In other activity, French Admiral Darlan issues a public policy statement, acknowledging co-operation of the French Forces with the Allies, toward the defeat of Italy and Germany. The statement in part: "AMNESTY FOR ALL PERSONS PENALIZED FOR ALLIED SYMPATHY; END TO PERSECUTION OF JEWS AND CENSORSHIP OF RADIO AND PRESS BE LIMITED TO MILITARY NECESSITIES DETERMINED BY THE ALLIES." **(North Atlantic)** The U.S.S. *Ingham*, a Coast Guard Cutter (PG-35), destroys the German Submarine *U-626*, in the North Atlantic.

December 15th 1942 — The U.S. Ninth Air Force attacks Sfax.

December 16th 1942 — (Pacific-Solomons) The Americans on Guadalcanal continue skirmishing with enemy troops while preparing for a massive offensive to destroy the remaining Japanese resistance on the island. In other activity, the Japanese Submarine I-15, is destroyed by Land-based Planes. General Patch, U.S.A., orders elements of the 132nd Regiment, Americal Division to occupy Mt Austen which is the dominating position on the island. **(Pacific-New Guinea)** General Eichelberger takes command of the 32nd Division, after General Clovis Byers becomes wounded while overseeing the Urbana Front operations. The Japs are driven from their positions, at the Coconut Grove and the troops prepare to attack a strong enemy Force, holding the Triangle. **(China-Burma-India)** British Lt. General N.M.S. Irwin's Eastern Army of India Command commences an offensive to gain Akyab Island on the Mayu Peninsula. The attack move overland due to unavailability of amphibious Vessels; the Indian 123rd Bri-

gade occupies Maungdaw without incident. **(Atlantic-North Africa)** In Libya, Axis power troops retreat from El Aghelia, losing about 20 Tanks and about 500 prisoners. **(Atlantic-Soviet Union)** In Russia, the Red Army drives back the Italian 8th Army. By penetrating the Italian lines, the Russians are able to pressure the Germans into halting their drive to rescue the trapped 6th German Army, at Stalingrad. In other activity, the Germans abandon the Terek bridgehead.

December 17th 1942 — (Pacific-Solomons) Contingents of the 3rd Bn., 132nd Infantry advance up the northeast slopes of Mt Austen (Guadalcanal) against no opposition. Also, the 35th Infantry Regiment, 25th Division arrives. On New Georgia, the Japanese complete construction of an Airstrip at Munda. **(Pacific-New Guinea)** Allied Tanks are moved into position for the assault against the Japanese stronghold at Buna Mission. The Japanese, still unaware of the Tanks, move forward. In other action, Companies E and G, 128th Infantry, take heavy casualties, trying unsuccessfully to take the "Bloody Triangle." **(China-Burma-India)** The advancing 14th Indian Division takes Buthidaung without a fight. **(Pacific-Japan)** The U.S.S. *Sunfish*, is joined by the U.S.S. *Drum* while dropping off mines near Japan. **(Atlantic-Newfoundland)** A Coast Guard Vessel, the *Natsek*, a converted Trawler, sinks in the vicinity of Belle Isle Strait. **(Atlantic-North Africa)** In Tunisia, the 2nd Battalion, U.S. 509th Paratroop Regiment and the 3rd Battalion, RCT 26, U.S. 1st Division attack Maknassy, 30 miles outside Tebessa.

December 18th 1842 — (United States) The Joint Chiefs of Staff authorize the occupation of Amchitka, situated just under a hundred miles from Japanese-held Kiska, in the Aleutians. It will be used as an Airbase. **(North Pacific-Aleutians)** A Reconnaissance contingent surveys Amchitka and determines that the operation is achievable. **(Pacific-New Guinea)** The Australians, supported by American fire, plow through tough resistance on the Soputa-Sanananda Trail. Contingents of the 127th U.S. Infantry (Urbana Force), attempt to reach Musita Island, by use of a cable, but intense enemy fire turns them back. The Warren Force, aided by Tanks, makes great progress against Cape Endaiadere and New Strip. Three Tanks are lost in combat, but the concrete and steel fortifications are leveled in the process. In the Bismarck Sea, the U.S.S. *Albacore* (SS-218), torpedoes and sinks a Japanese Light Cruiser, the *Tenryu*. **(Atlantic-North Africa)** German rear-guards skirmish with contingents of the New Zealand 2nd Division (British Eighth Army) at Nofilia, however, subsequent to the fight, the chase is canceled due to administrative reasons.

December 19th 1942 — (Pacific-Guadalcanal) Fighting develops in the vicinity of Hill 35, as contingents of 132nd Infantry, Battalion U.S.A., skirmish Japanese troops, but make no progress in its attempt to advance against the Hill. The Commanding Officer, of the 3rd Battalion is killed during the battle. **(Pacific-New Guinea)** In New Guinea, heavy fighting continues, with the Allies repulsing an enemy attack in the vicinity of the Roadblock (Sanananda Front). The Urbana Force encounters an enemy cross-fire at the Bloody Triangle and suffers severe losses. In other activity, U.S. contingents land at Oro Bay to construct a road from there to Dobodura. **(Atlantic-Soviet Union)** Soviet troops advance to Kantemirovka.

December 20th 1942 — (Pacific-Solomons) On the 'Canal,

Japanese Riflemen fire upon the rear and the flanks of the 132nd Infantry on the slopes of Mt Austen. Meanwhile the 1st Battalion, 132nd Regiment searches unsuccessfully for the enemy's east flank. In other activity, U.S. Engineers complete a Vehicle road to Hill 35. **(Pacific-Bismarcks)** The Japanese Submarine I-4 is destroyed off New Britain by the U.S.S. *Seadragon*. **(Pacific-New Guinea)** More Japanese positions on the Sanananda Front are destroyed by the Australians, while consolidating their positions. Activity on the Urbana Front is fierce, in the vicinity of the Triangle. Enemy positions are bombarded and smoke screens are implemented, but the Japanese repulse the attacks; the Allies then decide to bypass the deadly Triangle. In other activity, General Eichelberger places Colonel Grose, in command of the Urbana Force. Meanwhile, the Warren Force attacks, subsequent to heavy Artillery fire and reduces enemy resistance east of Simemi Creek, except a small force at the mouth of the creek. **(Pacific-Japan)** More mines are laid by the U.S.S. *Trigger*.

A U.S. Tank near the Duropa Plantation.

December 21st 1942 — (United States) The Joint Chiefs of Staff direct that Amchitka be occupied on or about January 5th. **(North Pacific-Aleutians)** An enormous storm strikes Amchitka and bashes the S-35. Water gushes down the conning tower and the Crewmembers become helpless, as the engines fail and electrical problems develop. Smoke and fire then envelop the chambers and the steering is lost during the raging tempest off the Aleutians. The Submariners fight against the odds throughout the night, however, at about 07:00 more smoke erupts in the control room. Meanwhile,

terrible winds and frigid rains hammer the men. By late afternoon, the crew miraculously regains control and makes good use of one engine, forestalling disaster. The crippled Vessel creeps toward Dutch Harbor, and arrives there on Christmas Eve. **(Pacific-New Guinea)** Japanese Major General Kensaku Oda and his Staff arrive at Giruwa; on the following day he relieves Colonel Yokoyama of responsibility and personally takes over command of the Sanananda Front. Meanwhile, the Australians continue to bash the Japanese at the track junction. The Urbana Force kills many Japanese near the Triangle with Artillery fire. Elements of Company K, 127th Infantry, cross Entrance Creek and establish a bridgehead. Meanwhile, the Warren Force reduces final resistance east of Simemi Creek. **(Pacific-Solomons)** On Guadalcanal, Company C, 132nd Regiment drives 1,000 yards south upon orders to sever Maruyama Trail; no contact is made with the enemy, however, there is no sight of the trail. **(Atlantic-North Africa)** In Libya, elements of the British Eighth Army pursuing the retreating Germans encounter rear-guards at Sirte and become stalled.

Tripoli.

December 22nd 1942 — (Pacific-Solomons) The U.S.S. Submarine *Greenling*, sinks an enemy Patrol Boat (No. 35). **(Pacific-New Guinea)** Australian troops arrive from Gona and relieve the U.S. 126th Infantry contingents, which are holding the roadblock on the Soputa-Sanananda Trail. Fighting remains fierce on the entire front. On the Urbana front, the 127th Regiment strengthens its bridgehead at Entrance Creek, and also dispatches contingents to secure Musita Island. **(Atlantic-Tunisia)** The British First Army reinitiates its offensive to seize Tunis. During the earlier part of December, the Axis literally drive the Allies back from the edge of Tunis. During a pullback by the U.S. 1st Army's Combat Command B, huge amounts of ammunition are abandoned. In addition, the U.S. 18th Infantry takes heavy casualties and a British Regiment is nearly annihilated, prompting British General Anderson to concede Medjez-El-Bab, including its primary road junction, to the Axis. General Eisenhower emphatically denies permission to retreat. Elements of the British 1st Army (2nd Coldstream Guards) advance during the night (22nd), and seize a part of Djebel el Ahmera (Longstop Hill), situated northeast of Medjez el Bab. A severe rainstorm impedes the attack, immobilizing the troops in mud. **(Atlantic-Soviet Union)** In the Caucasus, the Soviets mount heavy assaults southeast of Nalchik; the Germans begin pulling back their vanguard in the region. Meanwhile, the Soviet offensive in the middle Don area and on the Stalingrad front gain more ground.

December 23rd 1942 — (Pacific-New Guinea) The Warren Force drives toward Old Strip, repairing a bridge along the route, while under strong enemy fire. The Urbana Force finishes seizing Musita Island and initiates firing on enemy posi tions at Buna Mission. In other activity, more Allied Tanks arrive today. **(Atlantic-North Africa)** In Tunisia, contingents of RCT 18, U.S. 1st Division are struck by a counterattack and compelled to pull back from their positions at Djebel el Ahmera.

December 24th 1942 — (Pacific-Guadalcanal) U.S. Land-based Bombers again depart Henderson Field and attack an enemy Airbase at Munda, New Georgia, around two hundred miles from Guadalcanal. Admiral Halsey reports 10 Planes destroyed on a runway and another 14 shot down in the air in dogfights or while taking off. All U.S. Planes return to Henderson safely. In addition a group of enemy troop barges are also destroyed. In other activity, the 3rd Battalion, 132nd Regiment attacks toward Hill 27, however, about 500 Japanese holding at Gifu between it and Hill 31 stop the advance. **(Pacific-New Guinea)** The U.S. 127th Infantry drives through the Governmental Gardens, running into well-fortified Japanese troops hidden in the high grass (kunai). One contingent, Company L, sweeps through a weak part of the line, but is surrounded and suffers severe casualties before escaping. During the bitter struggle to reach the beach (a distance of approximately 600 yards), Sgt. Kenneth Gruennert, attacks one of two enemy pillboxes, holding his Company back. Gruennert successfully destroys the nest, then forges ahead to take the second, although he had been seriously wounded. With no regard for his life, he tosses grenades into the enemy position, forcing them to abandon the fortification, and appear, where they could be shot by his Platoon. Before the Platoon gets to Gruennert, he is killed by a sniper. In other activity, (Urbana Force Front) heavy fighting erupts along the Sanananda Front: neither side gains an advantage, however, the Warren Force pays a tremendous price, to gain less than 500 yards. **(Atlantic-North Africa)** French Admiral Francois Darlan is assassinated, in Algiers, Algeria. The assassin, Fernand Eugene Bonnier de la Chapelle (carrying a valid passport with the name Morand) is tried on the 25th and executed (authorized by Giraud at midnight) by a firing squad at dawn on the 26th. On the first anniversary of his execution, about fifty people, many of whom hold official positions through the efforts of DeGaulle, appear at the grave and place a wreath and maintain a minute of silence. Subsequently, an Algerian Court of Appeals nullifies his crime and it is expunged from the record. Although the assassin claims he is the only person involved, twelve others are arrested, however, most are later raised to prestigious jobs such as: Prefect of Algiers, Prefect of Police, and Chief of Police of Algiers. Also, one of the alleged conspirators becomes a minister in DeGaulle's Cabinet and yet another becomes the Ambassador to Moscow. In Tunisia, General Eisenhower and General Sir K.A.N. Anderson agree to halt the Tunis offensive, until the rainy season ceases. The men and their equipment have been literally petrified by unending mud.

December 25th 1942 — (Pacific-Solomons) Japanese firmly entrenched at Gifu on Guadalcanal, stymie an attempt to secure Hill 27 by the 3rd Battalion 132rd Infantry. **(Pacific-New Guinea)** Christmas is just another blood filled day, as progress is slow on all fronts against strong Japanese resistance.

Supplies are brought ashore via Submarines to bolster the Japanese beachhead. The Urbana Force assaults with seven Companies to secure a route to the sea through the Government Gardens. In other activity, the Warren Force meets heavy resistance at the Old Strip. **(Atlantic)** In Libya, the British Eighth Army captures Sirte. In Tunisia, the Germans recapture Djebel el Ahmera.

General Eisenhower and French General Giraud in North Africa.

December 26th 1942 — (Pacific-Solomons) On New Georgia, U.S. Naval Planes attack Japanese Vessels at Wickham Anchorage. On Guadalcanal, Air and Artillery units bombard Japanese positions at Gifu prior to another attack by the 3rd Bn., 132nd Regiment; limited progress is made. In other activity, forward contingents of the 2nd Marine Air Wing arrive to relieve the 1st Marine Air Wing at Henderson Field. Brigadier General Francis P. Mulcahy of the latter, relieves Brigadier General L.E. Woods. **(Pacific-New Guinea)** The Warren Force manages to set up a continuous line at Old Strip and begins to expand to the northwest, destroying Japanese positions in its path. Japanese Planes based at Rabaul attack Dobodura, until Planes from the Fifth U.S. Air Force drive them away. The Allied success is slow, but steady and control of New Guinea is close at hand for the Allies. Additional reinforcements and Tanks arrive at Oro Bay, to quicken the end of the grueling contest. **(Atlantic-French Somaliland)** Contingents of Fighting French Force advance into French Somaliland and without incident, capture two railroad bridges, ensuring the rails from Djibouti to Addis Ababa.

December 27th 1942 — **(Pacific-New Guinea)** Japanese Major General Tsuyuo Yamagata, commanding at Napapo, is ordered to pull out and move his Force by sea, to Giruwa. The pressure on the Japanese at Old Strip continues, with the further reduction of remaining bunkers. More men and Tanks arrive at Oro Bay, and contingents of the U.S. 41st Division arrive at Port Moresby from Australia to bolster the operation. **(Pacific-Solomons)** Heavy fighting continues at Gifu on the 'Canal as the 132nd Infantry attempts to reduce resistance at Gifu strongpoint. **(China-Burma-India)** The Indian 14th Division still meets no opposition as it advances along the Mayu River toward Akyab. In the coastal region, the Indian 47th Brigade gets elements to Foul Point, at the end of the Mayu Peninsula. **(Atlantic-North Africa)** In Tunisia, the British 1st Army turns back a counterattack at Medjez el Bab.

December 28th 1942 — **(Pacific-New Guinea)** The Japanese Garrison at Buna, is ordered to Giruwa to join an assault against the U.S. left flank. Heavy fighting continues on the Urbana Front, with the Japanese preventing the Allies from establishing a bridgehead on the Mission side of Entrance Creek. In other activity, the Japanese evacuate the Triangle. On the Warren Front, Japanese resistance at the Old Strip ceases and the Warren Force begins to push north, to the coast. **(Pacific-Solomons)** On Guadalcanal, still the U.S. 132nd Regiment is unable to penetrate the Japanese lines at Gifu. **(China-Burma-India)** Chiang Kai-shek informs President Roosevelt that the Chinese forces in Yunnan will be prepared to take the offensive during spring of 1943, however, he also informs Roosevelt that the offensive requires more Naval forces in the Bay of Bengal before the Chinese can attack. **(Atlantic-East Africa)** French Somaliland joins the Fighting French. **(Atlantic-North Africa)** Patrols of the British Eighth Army continue to advance unopposed, and reach Wadi el Chebir.

December 29th 1942 — **(United States)** The French Mission in Washington strongly requests that the French Forces in North Africa receive top priority for supplies and also suggests that the French be equipped before U.S. troops. Admiral Leahy is not enthusiastic with their idea. **(North Pacific-Aleutians)** The U.S.S. *Wasmuth*, a Minesweeper (DMS-15), fighting terrible weather in the unpredictable North Pacific, is blown up when two of its own depth charges explode. **(Pacific-Solomons** On New Georgia, the Japanese complete an Airfield at Munda, despite relentless Air bombardments. On Guadalcanal, Staff discussions concentrate on the ongoing drive to seize control of Mt. Austen. **(Pacific-New Guinea)** In New Guinea, General Yamagata reaches Giruwa and will attempt to rescue the beleaguered Garrison from annihilation. Company B, 127th Regiment reaches the sea southeast of Buna Mission and cuts off the Japanese at Buna Mission from those at Giropa Point. Meanwhile, the Warren Force attacks northward toward the coast; Tanks lead the way between Simemi Creek and Giropa Point, however, resistance is fierce and the Infantry and Tank units are poorly coordinated. **(Atlantic-North Africa)** In Libya, forward contingents of the 4th Light Armored Brigade, (British Eighth Army) reach positions just west of the German positions at Buerat; the town and Bu Ngem are discovered abandoned by the enemy. The British Eighth Army halts to prepare to attack. **(Atlantic-Russia)** The Russians seize Kotelnikov, southwest of Stalingrad, squeezing the embattled Germans.

December 30th 1942 — **(Pacific-New Guinea)** The Urbana Force continues to press Buna Mission from the southeast, while simultaneously forming to attack from Buna Village and from Musita Island to invest it. **(Pacific-Solomons-Guadalcanal)** The 132nd Regiment prepares to reinitiate its attack against Hill 27. **(Pacific-Dutch East Indies)** The U.S.S. *Searaven* (SS-196) debarks Allied Agents at Ceram Island, in the Netherlands East Indies. **(Atlantic-North Africa-Morocco)** General Patton is quite dissatisfied with his present situation of being a Corps Commander, without action in battle and waits impatiently for orders to fight the Germans. In a letter to General Terry Allen in Oran, Patton quips "WHY IN THE HELL DON'T YOU GET INTO THE WAR! MAYBE IF YOU WOULD GET INTO TROUBLE, THEY WOULD LET ME GO UP TO GET YOU OUT."

A Japanese traitor directs U.S. Planes to enemy positions in the Solomons.

December 31st 1942 — **(United States)** The U.S. Navy Carrier Force is bolstered as the Carrier *Essex* (CV-9) is commissioned. **(Pacific-New Guinea)** Contact is made between the Urbana and Warren Forces, as both apply simultaneous pressure against the Japanese at Buna Mission. Meanwhile, additional Urban forces eliminate the final resistance in Government Gardens, however, the Germans retain control of positions in swamps to the north. **(North Atlantic)** An Allied Convoy heading for the Soviet Union is attacked by an enemy Naval Force, however, the enemy sustains damage to one Cruiser and several Destroyers.

Miscellaneous 1942 — U.S. General MacArthur is named father of the year for 1942. MacArthur responding to the honor states, in part: "BY PROFESSION I AM A SOLDIER AND TAKE PRIDE IN THAT FACT, BUT I AM PROUDER-INFINITELY PROUDER-TO BE A FATHER." "A SOLDIER DESTROYS IN ORDER TO BUILD, A FATHER ONLY BUILDS, NEVER DESTROYS." "IT IS MY HOPE THAT MY SON, WHEN I AM GONE, WILL REMEMBER ME NOT FROM THE BATTLE, BUT IN THE HOME, REPEATING WITH HIM OUR SIMPLE DAILY PRAYER, 'OUR FATHER WHO ART IN HEAVEN.'" ... In a note concerning the progress of the U.S. Navy: Since the devastation suffered by the Navy at Pearl Harbor, the U.S. has manufactured 37 new Submarines, while losing eight. The Japanese have lost 22 Submarines, excluding the Midgets at Pearl Harbor and their Sub Fleet has received 20 replacements. The loss of Major Combat Vessels on each side is equal, with each losing 37; the difference is that U.S. Shipyard workers have constructed 138 new Vessels, to 20 by the Japanese. The U.S. Submarine Force is ready for 1943, though short of functional torpedoes. During 1942, despite erratic Sub missiles, the Navy has destroyed just under 150 Vessels (in excess of 500 tons each). In the Aleutians, many changes have occurred. Construction of the Alcan Highway connecting Great Falls, Montana and Fairbanks, Alaska had been started during March. By October, 10,000 Americans and Canadians had finished over 1,600 miles of the road to connect Fairbanks with the mainland. By the end of 1943, the Army Corps of Engineers will be spending about one million dollars a day in Alaska to keep the supply lines expanding. Meanwhile, to fend off possible Japanese Submarine attacks against Allied Shipping, American and Canadian Planes fly constant Patrols over the Gulf of Alaska. Eight Airfields will be scattered along the route to be used as ferry Bases to get 8,000 U.S. Planes to the Russians; 31 Planes are lost during the operation. Russian Pilots will be stationed in Fairbanks for nearly two years and they receive excellent treatment while waiting to transport the Aircraft to the Soviet Union. U.S. Pilots transport the Planes to Fairbanks, however, as soon as the Aircraft are painted with the Red star, Soviet Pilots fly them to Siberia. In addition, the harbor at Cold Bay, Alaska, is used as an embarkation point to move American Lend-Lease goods including Ships, which also pour profusely to the Russians. This route had been much shorter than moving equipment by way of the Middle East and it is free of the Luftwaffe. Captain George Jordan, Liaison Officer with the Russians notes: "WE ACTUALLY BUILT BASES FOR THE RUSSIANS IN SIBERIA. COLONEL MAXWELL E. ERDOFY (ALCAN HIGHWAY PROJECT) AND CREWS ARE ORDERED TO RUSSIA AND KEPT IN ISOLATION UNDER SOVIET GUARD ... I FIND NO RECORD OF THIS WORK HAVING BEEN CHARGED TO LEND-LEASE. Excluding the Merchant Fleet, the U.S. provides the Russians 581 Naval Vessels, including 28 Frigates, three Ice Breakers, 105 Landing Craft, 77 Minesweepers, 202 Torpedo Boats, (chronic shortage on all U.S. invasions), and 103 Submarine Chasers, and the Light Cruiser *Milwaukee*." The Vessels are to be returned at the close of hostilities, however, only the *Milwaukee* and several other battered Vessels are returned.

A U.S. Coast Guard Cutter in the North Atlantic inundated with a coating of ice.

Rear Admiral Norman S. Scott, killed at the Naval Battle of Guadalcanal. (Nov. 1942).

1943

A U.S. medic during the Italian campaign — whew!

A Japanese antitank gun pit.

Medics on Butaritari, pausing while medium tanks pass: note stretchers on top of jeep.

Admiral Frank J. Fletcher (TF-17 Battle of Midway victor).

January 1st 1943 — (United States) A directive from Head-quarters Army Air Forces, Washington: The president has directed that "AIRPLANES BE DELIVERED IN ACCORDANCE WITH PROTOCOL SCHEDULES BY THE MOST EXPEDITIOUS MEANS. TO IMPLEMENT THESE DIRECTIVES, THE MODI-FICATIONS, EQUIPMENT AND MOVEMENT OF RUSSIAN PLANES HAVE BEEN GIVEN FIRST PRIORITY, EVEN OVER PLANES FOR U.S. ARMY AIR FORCES." One American Pilot lands and requests that a crew get his Aircraft ready for flight within a few hours, with clearance for Fairbanks and is in-formed he will be detained for four days due to Russian pri-ority. In utter disbelief, he presses the importance of an American Plane taking priority and is shown the Presidential order. **(North Pacific-Aleutians)** The U.S.S. *Rescuer* (ARS-18), a Salvage Vessel, sinks after becoming grounded. **(Pacific-Solomons)** The U.S.S. *Nautilus* (SS-168) evacuates 29 people, including three children and 14 nuns, from Teop Island and sails for Australia. Fresh troops arrive, the 2nd Marine Engi-neering Battalion and the 27th Regiment, 25th Division, U.S.A. **(Pacific-New Guinea)** The Japanese holding Buna Mission, contain an Allied assault during the day. As darkness falls, some Japanese resistance at the mission collapses. **(Pacific-CBI)** About 450 additional American P.O.W.s arrive at Than-byuzayat, having survived a harrowing cruise from Singapore and are thrown into Branch 5 for the building of the Burma-Thailand Railroad; the group consists of about 1,900 Yanks, Australians and Dutch prisoners. Also, Branch 3, another camp (Thailand) comprises about nine thousand Allied pris-oners. Most of the guards are Korean and their are no inter-preters, making the situation even worse. Branch 5 works south as Branch 3 moves north, the former being involved in the construction of a bridge made famous in the movies (Bridge on the River Kwai). The junction is made during Oc-tober and about 127 Americans die in the process. **(Atlantic-Northwest Africa)** General Eisenhower puts Major General Lloyd R. Fredendall in command of the U.S. II Corps which will embark on Operation SATIN for the capture of Sfax, a port town in Tunisia. This force, the 1st Armored Division with Infantry support, is deployed near the Eastern Dorsal Moun-tain Range and is part of a three sectioned Allied Front, that stretches well over 200 miles: the British 1st Army, com-manded by General Sir Kenneth A. Anderson, occupies the mountains overlooking Bizerte and Tunis; the third con-tingent is French which holds about 100 miles of the Eastern Dorsal, near Faid Pass. American Paratroopers, commanded by Colonel Edson D. Raff, continue to raid German lines near the French flank. By mid-January, the Allied plan to seize Sfax is aborted because the British Eighth Army is unable to join with the U.S. II Corps in time to bring a successful conclusion to the campaign. Eisenhower postpones the assault until spring, to allow the British time to reach the Mareth Line. Meanwhile, Allied supplies continue pouring into Tebessa. Also, the Rangers, under Colonel Darby, have remained at Azrew (Algeria), undergoing a vigorous non-stop training program since they landed and secured the area in early November 1942; Darby has been appointed temporary mayor. The U.S. Rangers, commissioned in Northern Ireland, during June of 1942 as an elite striking force are getting impatient for more action, but for two-months, they practice. **(Atlantic-U.S.S.R.)** The German Sixth Army is assaulted by six Soviet Armies. The Luftwaffe loses many Planes while attempting to resupply the beleaguered troops and evacuate the wounded. In addition, Soviet troops seize Velikie Lukie, a strategic rail center after overcoming fierce resistance. Elista, south of Sta-lingrad also falls.

January 1st-February 7th 1943 — (Pacific-Australia) The U.S.S. *Growler*, commanded by Lt. Commander Gilmore, de-parts Brisbane, heading toward the Western Solomons and Rabaul. The *Growler* destroys two enemy Transports and a Freighter by the end of January. On the 4th of February she tracks a Convoy near the Gazelle Channel and at 03:00 on the 5th, two enemy Vessels are sighted, however, terrible weather forces a surface attack. One enemy Vessel fires from long range, forcing *Growler* to dive deep. It sustains damage by a blistering attack, but survives. Subsequently, on the 7th of February, the *Growler* spots an enemy Warship about 2,000 yards distant, however, conditions again are terrible. Lt. Com-mander Gilmore and six other men are topside, as the enemy closes. Both Vessels smash together creating a thunderous roar, virtually locking the two Vessels together. The dazed crew of the *Growler* takes the collision in stride, as the Vessel rolls and swerves violently, while still under severe attack from the enemy's deck guns. Fifty caliber machine guns rake the bridge, killing one Sailor at his duty station and severely wounding Gilmore. Gilmore yells "CLEAR THE BRIDGE" and the wounded men are lowered through the hatch, but he remains topside. Gilmore then gives his final order: "TAKE HER DOWN." The crew waits, however, Gilmore remains at his post. The hatch is reluctantly slammed, and the Sub-marine dives and prepares for a depth charge attack. The *Growler*, under the command of Lt. Commander Schade, sur-faces after about one-half hour's wait to finish off the Patrol Boat, but as the men rally to the guns, there is no sign of the enemy Ship, which has probably perished.

January 2nd 1943 — (Pacific-New Guinea) The Urbana Force finally terminates Japanese resistance at Buna Mission at 1632. The two high ranking Japanese Officers, Colonel Hiroshi Yamamoto and Captain Yoshitatsu Yasuda, commit Hari Kari. Meanwhile, the Warren Force continues to seek Japanese in the vicinity of Giropa Point and to the east. The Japanese have lost at least 1,400 men at Buna. The U.S. 32nd Division and Australian 18th Brigade losses totaled 620 killed, 2,065 wounded and 132 missing. The victory is technically the first for the American Army over the Japanese, with total victory coming on the 22nd of January 1943, with the fall of the Sanananda Front (the next objective). **(Pacific-Solomons-Guadalcanal)** General Harmon activates XIV Corps, compris-ing the Americal (reinforced by 147th Regiment) and 25th Division; it is commanded by General A. Patch. General Sebree replaces Patch as Commander of the Americal Divi-sion. In addition, the 2nd Marine Division and other Marine units are attached to Corps. The 132nd Infantry moves against Gifu, and seizing the crest of Hill 27, then repulses several counterattacks. PT Boats attack an enemy Flotilla near Cape Esperance and damage one Destroyer. In addition, Naval and Army Planes attack an enemy Destroyer Convoy off Rendova, as they attempt to move supplies to the Solomons. The U.S.S. *Grayback* (SS-208) destroys the I-18, off the Solomons. **Atlan-tic-Soviet Union)** The German 1st Panzer Army begins to re-treat toward Rostov in order to prevent encirclement. German General Von Kleist hopes to prevent Army Group A from becoming totally isolated in the Caucasus.

January 3rd 1943 — (Pacific-Solomons-Guadalcanal) The 1st Battalion, 132nd Regiment drives against the eastern sec-tion of Gifu and makes contact with the 1st Battalion on the

Tanker burning as enemy Submarine observes.

left. **(Pacific-Japan)** Tokyo radios the text of the Japanese "Army-Navy Central Agreement on South Pacific" to Rabaul, describing strategy in the North and Central Solomons and in New Guinea, subsequent to the evacuation of Guadalcanal. **(Atlantic-North Africa)** In Tunisia, the Germans overpower contingents of the French 19th Corps at Fondouk. In the British First Army area, 5 Corps sector, the 36th Brigade, British 78th Division launches attacks at Djebel Ajred and Djebel Azag. **(Atlantic-Soviet Union)** Russian troops occupy Mozdok and Malgobek in the Caucasus, subsequent to German withdrawal.

January 4th 1943 — (North Pacific) Admiral Kinkaid replaces Admiral R.A. Theobald, as Commander Task Force 8. Admiral W.W. Smith, Commander of Strike Group is replaced by Rear Admiral Charles McMorris. **(Pacific-Solomons)** The Japanese holding Guadalcanal are ordered to pull out and head for New Georgia Island. Fighting on Mount Austen continues, with the 132nd Infantry stretched in a semicircle between Hills 27 and 31. The Army, fighting for about 20 days in this area, has killed between 400 and 500 enemy Soldiers, while suffering 383 total casualties themselves. Marine reinforcements (6th Marines) arrive, taking the 2nd Marine Division up to full strength for what becomes the last 36 days of battle on the island. Also, the 161st Regiment, 25th Division arrives on the 'Canal. In New Georgia, a U.S. Destroyer-Cruiser Task Force, commanded by Rear Admiral Ainsworth, shells the enemy Airport at Munda. **(Pacific-New Guinea)** The faltering Japanese still mount fierce resistance west of the Girua River. Japanese seize an outpost outside Tarakena; with Tarakena spit in their possession, they manage to rescue some of the beleaguered remnants of the Buna mission. **(Atlantic-North Africa)** A violent two-day storm strikes British positions in Libya, hindering operations of the British Eighth Army at the port of Benghazi, prompting General Montgomery to modify his attack scheduled for the 15th.

January 5th 1943 — (Pacific-Admiralties) The U.S. 5th Bomber Command strikes Rabaul. General Kenneth N Walker, Commander of the unit since January 5th, 1942, leads the mission through heavy anti-Aircraft fire despite the mission's success in sinking nine enemy Vessels, General Walker's Plane is shot down. **(Pacific-Solomons)** Rear Admiral W.L. Ainsworth's Group, comprising Cruisers and Destroyers, moves near Munda Airfield; long range guns again plaster the Airfield and other facilities again. **(Atlantic-North Africa)** The U.S. Fifth Army (I Armored and II Corps.), commanded by Lt. General Mark W. Clark is activated; its headquarters are

Vice Admiral Thomas C. Kinkaid.

located in Oujda, Morocco. In Tunisia, the British 5 Corps disengages at Djebel Ajred and also at Djebel Azag and pulls back to previous positions. **(Atlantic-Soviet Union)** The Soviets seize Nalchik in the Caucasus; contingents moving along the Don take Tsimlyansk.

January 6th 1943 — (Pacific-Solomons) An enemy Dive Bomber damages the Light Cruiser, U.S.S. *San Juan* (CL-54). On the 'Canal Brigadier General Alphonse De Carre, commanding the forward echelon of the 2nd Marine Division assumes responsibility for all Marine forces on the island (except Aviation). **(Pacific-New Guinea)** Allied Planes attack a Japanese Convoy as it moves from New Britain toward Lae, New Guinea. **(China-Burma-India)** The Indian 14th Division reinitiates its Arakan offensive and encounters fierce opposition; heavy combat ensues for weeks ending in stalemate. **(Atlantic)** Land-based American Naval Bombers, involved in sweeping the Atlantic clean of German Ships, sink the German Submarine U-164, off Brazil.

January 7th 1943 — (United States) President Roosevelt confers with the Joint Chiefs of Staff prior to going to Morocco for a major conference with the British Prime Minister and the Combined Chiefs of Staff. The agenda is to include the upcoming summer offensive plans and the setting of priorities. General Marshall believes that a cross-channel invasion is the only genuine way to thoroughly defeat the Germans, but he does agree with General Staff on the Sicily invasion, code named Operation HUSKY. General Marshall believes it to be: "AN UNAVOIDABLE CAMPAIGN OF CON-

TAINMENT;" he inquires! "IS SICILY TO BE A MEANS TO AN END — OR IS SICILY TO BE AN END IN ITSELF." At the conclusion of the conference, the question remains unanswered. **(Pacific-New Guinea)** Four thousand Japanese reinforcements arrive at Lae by Naval Vessels, despite being attacked by Allied Planes. Tarakena is threatened as units of the 127th Infantry move to within 500 yards of it. In other activity, the 18th Australian Brigade is now at Soputa and the 2nd Battalion, 163rd U.S. Infantry reaches the Sanananda Front. **(Pacific-Guadalcanal)** The XIV Corps continues to prepare for an offensive on the 10th. At present, about 50,000 Allied Air ground and Naval forces are in the 'Canal area. **(Atlantic-Iraq)** Americans take full jurisdiction over the port of Khorramshahr; U.S. troops have been at the port since December of 1942.

Generals Dwight D. Eisenhower and John Marshall.

January 8th 1943 — (Pacific-New Guinea) Allied Planes attack an enemy Convoy as it unloads 4,000 reinforcements at Lae. In other activity, Tarakena is captured by elements of the U.S. 127th Regiment. Elements of the 127th Regiment seize Tarakena. Meanwhile, the 163rd Regiment attacks to secure the road to Sananda, making limited progress. **(China-Burma-India)** Chiang Kai-shek informs President Roosevelt that he has rejected the planned offensive for an offensive in the spring of 44. **(Atlantic-Madagascar)** Lt. General Sir William Platt, CG British East African Command, relinquishes command of the island of Madagascar (off coast of East Africa), except for Diego Suarez region to General P. Legentilhomme, High Commissioner for French possessions in the Indian Ocean. **(Atlantic-Tunisia)** Combat Command B, U.S. 1st Armored Division is detached from British command and reassigned to the 1st Armored Division. **(Atlantic-Soviet Union)** German Field Marshal Paulus receives an ultimatum to surrender the German Sixth Army at Stalingrad from the Commanding General of the Soviet forces at the Don; the Germans do not respond. In other activity, Zimovniki falls to the Russians.

January 9th 1943 — (Pacific-New Guinea) The Japanese Convoy, which had landed reinforcements, departs Lae with Allied Planes in pursuit. The Air strikes have sunk two Transports and destroyed approximately 80 enemy Planes. Near Tarakena, fighting is heavy with the Japanese stopping the 127th Infantry from establishing a bridgehead across Konombi Creek. The worn-down 126th U.S. Infantry is relieved at the Sanananda Front. **(Pacific-Solomons)** On Guadalcanal, the XIV Corps makes final preparations before launching an attack on the following day. In other activity, the

147th Regimental Task Force, commanded by Captain Beach, lands at Beufort Bay and sets up beach defenses.

January 10th 1943 — (Pacific-Solomons-Guadalcanal) The U.S. 25th Division initiates its final drive to secure Guadalcanal immediately following an Artillery bombardment. The 27th Infantry jumps off and secures almost half of Galloping Horse. Elements of the 35th Infantry attack Sea Horse, without preparatory Artillery fire and capture a little hill south of Sea Horse. During the battle, Sergeant William Fournier's machine gun Squad is attacked by an overpowering enemy force which kills his gunner, wounds his assistant gunner and wipes out the adjacent crew. Fournier and a volunteer, Technician Fifth Grade, Lewis Hall, refuse to retire as ordered and advance together with another machine gun to stem the tide. Their effort inflicts many casualties, though both Soldiers lose their lives. The third objective; Gifu, is assaulted by the 2nd Battalion, but rigid opposition prevents any advance. **(Pacific-New Britain)** A five Vessel Japanese Convoy protected by three Destroyers moves southeast of New Britain. The U.S.S. Submarine *Argonaut* (APS-1), boldly disregards the odds and moves in to attack one of the Destroyers. Based on the observance of an Army Plane flying over the attack area, one Destroyer was damaged by a torpedo. The additional Destroyers dropped depth charges, which disable the Submarine. The Japs, seeing the bow of the Submarine hanging up in the waves, continue pounding the crippled Submarine until it sinks. The witnessing Plane had been out of bombs and unable to assist the *Argonaut*. Lt. Commander J.R. Pierce and all hands are lost. **(Pacific-New Guinea)** A bridgehead is established across Konombi Creek by elements of the 127th U.S. Infantry in the vicinity of Tarakena. In other activity, Japanese evacuate two of their entrenched positions between Kano and Musket. Kano is renamed Fisk, in honor of 1st Lt. Harold R. Fisk. **(Pacific-Japan)** The U.S.S. *Trigger* (SS-237) sinks the Destroyer *Okikaze*. **(Atlantic-Libya)** British General Montgomery speaks to the attack-troops of the British Eighth Army to reinforce the importance of the imminent drive (on 15th) from the Buerat Line, which must advance to Tripoli within 10 days after jump off. **(Atlantic-Soviet Union)** The Soviets initiate a strong attack to crush the besieged battle-weary German Sixth Army at Stalingrad, however, German General Paulus' force fights with enormous fervor to forestall capitulation and to gain time for Army Group A and the Don Army Group in the Caucasus.

January 11th 1943 — (United States) President Roosevelt and his staff advisers depart Miami, Florida discreetly, heading for Casablanca by way of Trinidad. The President reaches Casablanca on the 14th and remains there for conferences with Churchill and Military advisers until the 26th. **(Pacific-Guadalcanal)** The Americans initiate the final offensive to capture the island as the 25th Division, U.S.A., moves against Hills 43 (Sea Horse) and 44 (Galloping Sea Horse), and also strikes the Japanese stronghold at Gifu. The Japanese receive orders from Rabaul to evacuate the island by sea on the 11th, while the Americans are preparing to unleash a newly formed Army-Marine Division to attack along the coast starting on the 13th. In other related activity, Japanese are still attempting to bring in supplies to the Solomons and again are met by PT Boats which damage two Destroyers. The PT-112 is damaged and the PT-43 is forced to beach; it is abandoned. **(Pacific-New Guinea)** The Australian Kanga Force attacks

Mubo; the raids last three days and inflict severe damage to the Japanese. **(Atlantic-Soviet Union)** The Germans continue retreating from the Caucasus. Soviet troops occupy Georgievsk, Mineralnye Vody, and Pyatigorsk. Meanwhile, heavy fighting continues to ensue at Stalingrad.

U.S. Destroyer cutting through high seas in the North Atlantic.

January 12th 1943 — (North Pacific-Aleutians) U.S. troops, under the command of Brigadier General Lloyd E. Jones, land unopposed at Amchitka. In other activity, two U.S. Vessels are lost by grounding; the Destroyer *Worden* (DD-352) and the PT-28, at Amchitka and Dora Harbor, Alaska, respectively. **(Pacific-Australia)** The 1st Marine Division arrives at Melbourne from Guadalcanal. **(Pacific-Guadalcanal)** Japanese put up strong defense and repulse attempts to seize Galloping Horse, Sea Horse and Gifu. In one incident, overpowering Japanese machine gun fire halts elements of the 25th Division. Captain Charles W. Davis braves the danger and carries directions to the besieged Battalions. On the following day, he leads a gallant charge against more devastating fire and seizes the crest of the hill, permitting the Corps to seize the objective. Captain (later Major) Davis receives the Medal of Honor. In other activity, the 6th Marines and the Artillery of the 2nd Marine Division are attached to the Composite Army-Marine Division (Provisional) which also includes the 182nd and 147th Army Infantry Regiments and Artillery units of the Americal Division. **(Pacific-New Guinea)** A devastating Allied Artillery bombardment coupled with strong Infantry pressure supported by Tanks, forces the Japanese to pull out of the trail junction during the night. On the following day, General Eichelberger takes command of the Advanced New Guinea Force (Australian and American troops). **(Pacific-New Ireland)** The U.S.S. *Guardfish* (SS-217), sinks a Japanese Patrol Boat (No. 1). **(Atlantic-Soviet Union)** Russian troops from the Leningrad and Volkhov Fronts take the offensive, converging on Leningrad to lift the siege.

January 13th 1943 — (POA) Major General Millard F. Harmon activates the U.S. Thirteenth Air Force, commanded by Brigadier General F. Twining; Headquarters is located at Espiritu Santo, New Hebrides. **(Pacific-Guadalcanal)** The XVI Corps enlarges its offensive to secure the 'Canal. The 2nd Marine Division initiates its coastal assault moving from line Point Cruz-Hill 66 (to the right of the U.S. 25th Division.) Heavy enemy fire halts the advance of the 8th Marines as its attack expands from Hills 80 and 81. Meanwhile the 2nd Marines drives west from Hill 66 gaining about 800 yards. In conjunction, the 27th Regiment, 25th Division powers forward, reducing Hill 53 with its 2nd Battalion, completing the seizure

of Galloping Horse. Japanese resistance halts the advance of Company C, 35th Regiment; the 2nd Battalion drives against entrenched pillboxes at the Gifu strongpoint, making no genuine progress. **(Pacific-New Guinea)** General Robert L. Eichelberger assumes command of Advance New Guinea Force; he takes command of all Australian and U.S. Forces. Australian General Edmund F. Herring commands the New Guinea Force. **(Atlantic)** U.S. Naval Land-based planes (VP-83) sink the German Submarine U-507 off the coast of Brazil.

January 14th 1943 — (Pacific-Philippines) The U.S.S. *Gudgeon* moves near Negros and debarks specialized personnel and equipment in the vicinity of Catmon Point. **(Pacific-New Guinea)** The Allies begin pursuit of the Japanese who are retreating from the trail junction as the 167th U.S. Infantry moves South to cut them off and the Australian 18th Brigade mops up at the junction before meeting the 163rd on the Sanananda and Killerton Trails. **(Atlantic)** An Anglo-American conference begins in Anfa outside of Casablanca, Morocco, and lasts for ten days, concluding with plans for the invasion of Sicily and a subsequent invasion of Western Europe. Pacific strategy is also agreed upon: a drive through the Central and Southwest Pacific to the Philippines with the only terms to be offered to the enemy "unconditional surrender." President Roosevelt, Prime Minister Churchill and the Combined Chiefs of Staff are in attendance. By this time the gamble to land Americans in North Africa (Torch) to take pressure off the Russians on the Eastern Front had worked, however, it had also severed any chance of a cross-channel attack against the Germans during 1943 (ROUNDUP). President Roosevelt had previously continued to press "for any action, however, minor" to alleviate pressure on the Russian ground troops; the result had been TORCH. One American, Major General Thomas T. Handy (Operation Division) had previously offered his opinion concerning any operations in the Mediterranean subsequent to North Africa as "logistically unfeasible and strategically unsound." He recommended pressing on with (ROUNDUP) or throwing America's full strength against the Japanese. Lt. General Brehon B. Somervell, Commanding General, Services of Supply, had estimated that control of the Mediterranean would save the Allies an estimated 1,800,000 tons of Shipping in less than six months.

January 15th 1943 — (Pacific-New Guinea) Final preparations for a full scale offensive are made. Lt. Colonel Merle H. Howe assumes command of the Urban Force which will drive west along the coast. Meanwhile, on the Soputa-Sanananda road, the 1st Battalion, 163rd Regiment surrounds an enemy pocket between Fisk and Musket. **(Pacific-Solomons-Guadalcanal)** The Japanese entrenched at Gifu refuse a surrender demand and continue to defy American attempts to dislodge them, despite supporting Artillery, and flame-throwing Tanks. Also, the Japanese mount heavy resistance against the 2nd Marine Division which is advancing along the coast. In other activity, Planes from Henderson Field attack an enemy Convoy, damaging two of nine Destroyers. Also, the 2nd Marines depart for New Zealand. **(Atlantic)** The British Eighth Army advances further, while continuing to prepare for its attack against Tripoli and the Buerat line.

January 16th 1943 — (Pacific-Solomons) On Guadalcanal, the XIV Corps orders a new offensive to extend its positions westward to the Poha River. The Composite Army-Marine

Division (CAM), comprising the 6th Marines, 147th and 182nd Regiments, and the American and 2nd Marine Divisions' Artillery units advance on a 3,000 yard front in conjunction with the 25th Division attack against the Japanese south flank. (Pacific-New Guinea) Subsequent to Air and Artillery bombardments, the offensive to secure the Sanananda region commences. The Australian 18th Brigade sweeps the Killerton Trail clean, reaching the coast and secures a coastal path extending from Cape Killerton to the fringes of Sanananda, while elements of the 163rd Regiment reach a point about 1,000 yards behind enemy lines; other contingents hook up with the Australians. (Atlantic) Iraq declares war on Germany, Italy, and Japan. In Libya, the British Eighth Army continues rolling toward Tripoli, advancing beyond Buerat. In Germany, Berlin is struck by RAF bombers which use a target indicator bomb. (Atlantic-Soviet Union) Soviet troops continue to advance south of Voronezh and reach Rossosh; Italian forces are thrashed. Meanwhile, the German 6th Army continues to get pounded at Stalingrad.

January 17th 1943 — (Pacific-Guadalcanal) The Marines and Soldiers continue to attack along the coast with the 182nd Infantry on the left and the 6th Marines on the right. Meanwhile, the Japanese at Gifu have not responded to the earlier surrender request; a two and one-half hour Artillery barrage strikes the strongpoint to encourage reconsideration. A ground attack is aborted as darkness begins to settle. (Pacific-New Guinea) Heavy fighting continues as the Japanese lose Sanananda Point and Sanananda Village to the Allies, however, they maintain control of the terrain south and west of Sanananda. Still, the Japanese retain Giruwa. (Pacific-Australia) The U.S. Navy establishes a Naval Base and Air Station at Brisbane. (Atlantic-North Africa) In Libya, German obstacles such as mines and the desert terrain slow the advancing British Eighth Army. In Algeria, TF Satin (II Corps) is informed that the proposed drive on Sfax has been canceled. (Atlantic-U.S.S.R.) The Soviets take Millerovo along the Voronezh-Rostov Railroad.

January 18th 1943 — (Pacific-Guadalcanal) The Americans expand their defenses away from Hill 53 in a northward direction toward the coast. In other activity, the 2nd Battalion, 35th Infantry attacks Gifu. (Pacific-New Guinea) The Japanese continue to mount fanatical resistance on the Sanananda Front. (Atlantic-North Africa-Libya) The Germans, retreating toward Tripoli, evade the British. General Montgomery, after losing contact with the enemy, begins round-the-clock pursuit. (Atlantic-Tunisia) German General Jurgen von Arnim initiates an offensive to regain ground lost to the French during mid-January, and to gain the passes west of Kairouan. In the British First Army sector, German Mark VI "Tiger" Tanks are committed to support the main attack near Bou Arada; the Tanks push the French 19th Corps back from the north flank. (Atlantic-U.S.S.R.) The Soviet forces of Leningrad and Volkhov Fronts regain land communications with Leningrad, which has been cut off since fall of 1941. In the Caucasus, Divnoe and Cherkessk fall to the Soviets.

January 19th 1943 — (Pacific-Guadalcanal) Heavy fighting continues along the line. The 6th Marines and the 182nd Infantry attempt to close a gap between the two forces. The 182nd Infantry, operating on the left of the CAM Division advances a brutalizing 1,000 yards since beginning its push

on the 17th. Meanwhile, the Japanese are still under heavy attack at Gifu, by the 2nd Battalion, 35th Infantry ((25th Division). In other activity, the 147th Infantry is transferred to Point Cruz after being replaced at Koli Point by the American Reconnaissance Squadron. (Pacific-New Guinea) The Japanese battle with fanatical tenacity as they begin retreating from the Sanananda Front. General Yamagata departs by boat after issuing a general order for a retreat on the 20th. General Kensaku Oda and Colonel Kiyomi Yazawa are killed during the night while attempting to escape. The Allies squeeze the Japanese into pockets before the final kill. (Pacific-Burma) The Indian 47th Brigade continues to assault Donbaik, however, the Japs retain possession. (Atlantic-North Africa) The British reinitiate contact with the retreating Germans. In Tunisia, the Germans continue to advance; the French 19th Corps withdraws further toward Rebaa Oulad Yahia. British and U.S. reinforcements rush to the front to help the French, however, they come under French command. (Atlantic-Soviet Union) The Germans lose the rail junction of Valuiki, northeast of Kharkov. Kamensk also falls to the Soviets.

January 20th 1943 — (United States) The U.S.S. *Brennan* (DE-13), a Destroyer Escort is commissioned at Mare Island California; the first Vessel of this type to be commissioned. (Atlantic-Chile) Chile breaks relations with Germany, Italy, and Japan. (Pacific-Guadalcanal) At Mt Austen the Japanese at Gifu continue to take a pounding from the CAM Division and from Artillery. (Pacific-New Guinea) The Australian 18th Brigade continues to secure the region west of Sanananda and the area along the northern portion of Soputa-Sanananda road. Meanwhile, the 1127th Regiment, U.S.A., drives west along the coast to Giruwa. (Atlantic-North Africa) In Libya, the Germans slow the pace of the British Eighth Army in the Homs-Tarhuna area. In Tunisia, German Armor continues pouring down the Rebaa Valley, advancing to the Ousseltia Valley. The drive isolates much of the French 19 Corps in the mountains; C.C.B., 1st U.S. Armored, under French Command, is ordered to the Ousseltia Valley. (Atlantic-U.S.S.R.) Proletarskaya, along the Stalingrad-Novorossisk Railroad, falls to General Yeremenko's South Front (previously Stalingrad Front). Subsequent to its fall, contingents move to the Manych River, and others advance toward the River Donets. Meanwhile, the Germans under Von Kleist continue to fight rear-guard actions to forestall defeat.

January 20th-23rd 1943 — (Pacific-Guadalcanal) The combined forces of the 25th Army Division and the Army-Marine Division drive toward Kokumbona to finally crush the remaining Japanese force. By the 23rd, the 25th Division seizes the high ground south of the stronghold, giving it control of the coastal positions in the area, while the Army-Marine Division plows through enormous opposition and seizes the southeastern heights of Kokumbona on the 23rd, culminating all enemy resistance on Mount Austen; it then moves to cut the retreating Japanese off at Cape Esperance.

January 21st 1943 — (United States) Rear Admiral Robert H. English is killed in an air crash near Boonville, California. English, who had been the Commanding Officer of Submarines, Pacific Fleet, is replaced by Rear Admiral Charles Lockwood. (Pacific-New Guinea) Australian and U.S. troops establish contact on the Soputa-Sanananda road, east of Sanananda. Subsequently, Australian contingents attack Japanese positions west of Sanananda, eliminating all resistance except for one pocket. Meanwhile, the 2nd Battalion, 163rd Regiment eliminates two of three pockets on the Soputa-Sanananda road, killing more than 500 Japanese; the final pocket is encircled but refuses to capitulate. **(Pacific-Solomons)** The Japanese on Guadalcanal refuse to relent and continue mounting fierce opposition at their remaining strongholds. Meanwhile, the XIV Corps completes preparations for an offensive (22nd). **(Atlantic-North Africa-Libya)** British General Montgomery, informed of enemy strength at Tarhuna, decides to make his main thrust toward Tripoli by advancing along the coast. In Tunisia, General Eisenhower delegates authority of coordinating operations between British, French and U.S. Forces to British General K.A.N. Anderson. The U.S. 1st Armored Division, assisted by Air and Artillery support, drives the Axis troops back into the Ousseltia Valley; nightfall forces the attack to cease. Meanwhile, General Patton waits impatiently for orders to go into battle. **(Atlantic-Nicaragua)** Corrinto, Nicaragua becomes the site of the newest U.S. Naval Base. **(Atlantic-Nova Scotia)** The SC-709 sinks by grounding near Cape Breton. **(Atlantic-Soviet Union)** The Germans lose Voroshilovsk, east of Armavir.

January 22nd 1943 — Japanese Planes bomb U.S. positions on Guadalcanal.

January 22nd 1943 — (Pacific-New Guinea) The bloody six month struggle for New Guinea (Papua campaign) ends with a decisive defeat for the Japanese. Resistance on the Sanananda Front disintegrates. The costs for the Papua campaign are high for the Allies, but staggering for the Japanese. The American-Australian force buries 7,000 Japanese Soldiers. About 350 prisoners have been taken, the majority of them Chinese and Korean laborers. The Australian casualties total 5,700 and the American, 2,788. The exhausted conquerors are soon relieved and sent to New Zealand and Australia for rest and recuperation. **(Pacific-Solomons)** On Guadalcanal, at 06:30, the XIV Corps drives toward the Poha River. The drive is supported by Air, Naval gunfire and Artillery. The CAM Division advances west toward the high ground southeast of Kokumbona, while the 25th Infantry Division, operating on the south flank, attacks toward Hill 87. The 6th Marines hit heavy opposition near Hill 94; the 147th Regiment seizes Hill 95. By 17:00, elements of the 25th Division control Hills 90 and 98 east and south of Kokumbona respectively. Meanwhile, contingents of the 35th Regiment, 25th Division, bolstered by a Tank, drive a wedge into Gifu. **(Atlantic-North Africa)** In Libya, contingents of the British Eighth Army advance to within 20 miles of Tripoli as the Germans blow up port facilities and evacuate the city. In Tunisia, the Germans repel an Allied assault at the Ousseltia Valley. **(Atlantic-U.S.S.R.)** The Soviet South Front seizes Salsk. At Stalingrad the German 6th Army continues to come under heavy attack by the Russians.

January 21st 1943 — U.S. Patrol advancing along the beach toward the Sanananda Trail in New Guinea.

January 1943 — U.S. Infantry moves across a footbridge in Papua, New Guinea.

January 23rd 1943 — (Pacific-Bismarcks-New Ireland) The U.S.S. *Guardfish* (SS-217) sinks the *Hakazee*, a Japanese Destroyer. On the previous day, the *Guardfish* had sunk a 4,000-ton Cargo Vessel. **(Pacific-Solomons)** On Guadalcanal, the XIV Corps overpowers resistance at Kokumbona. Some resistance remains east of the Poha River near Hill 99. In addition, the 2nd Battalion, 35th Regiment seizes the Gifu, terminating all resistance on Mt Austen. **(Atlantic-North Africa)** The British Eighth Army, closing from the south and east enters Tripoli, Libya and captures the port. The Axis troops had destroyed the city before they withdrew. Although the British hold Tripoli, Rommel remains elusive and keeps his Army from being encircled and destroyed. In **Tunisia**, U.S. and British contingents help the French hold their general line Bou Arada-Djebel Bargou-Djebel Bou Dabouss. The U.S. 1st Armored Division's C.C.B., covers the isolated French forces as they come out of the hills east of the Ousseltia Valley. In **Casablanca**, President Roosevelt, Prime Minister Churchill and the Combined Chiefs of Staff, end the Casablanca Conference, which had convened on January 14th. The sessions which dealt with the war effort culminate with definitive decisions and agreement on the invasion of Sicily and a subsequent invasion of France, by way of the English Channel. However, all are still not in agreement, and a decision on what strategy to use after the fall of Sicily is unclear. It had been agreed that General Eisenhower (on the 18th) would be in command of the operation, but the Air Ground and Naval Forces will be under British command. The news infuriates Eisenhower, prompting him to state that he will fight the "INTRUSION OF THE BRITISH COMMITTEE SYSTEM" into the Allied Force Headquarters. **(Atlantic-Soviet Union)** Soviet troops break into Voronezh. The Germans also lose Armavir on the Baku-Rostov railroad.

January 1943 — President Roosevelt and Prime Minister Winston Churchill at Casablanca, surrounded by Allied Officers including General John Marshall.

January 23rd 1943 — (Pacific) The U.S.S. *Wahoo* penetrates enemy waters near Wewak Harbor, Mushu Island. Enemy Destroyers, alerted to the presence of the Yankee Submarine, rush to destroy it. From a range of 3,000 yards, the *Wahoo* fires four torpedoes, but all miss the mark. The Destroyer closes fast and two more torpedoes are fired; the second fish damages the enemy Warship and ends the attack. Several days later, the *Wahoo*, cruising about four-to-five hundred miles off New Guinea, spots billowing smoke in the distance and dives for an attack against a Transport and accompanying Freighter. The first Ship is rocked by two torpedoes and the other is struck by one torpedo. The latter charges the *Wahoo*, while a third enemy Warship arrives and attacks. The newest intruder is greeted by three torpedoes, followed by two more; delivered "down the throat" as the testy *Wahoo* dives deep. In less than ten minutes, the *Wahoo's* periscope scans the area. Of the three Japanese Vessels, one has sunk, another is limping badly and the third is a tempest of activity; the crew scrambles for safety as it sinks. Suddenly, the *Wahoo* encounters another enemy Vessel. The Yanks on board note seven torpedoes available; three stream toward the newly arrived Tanker and in a flash, the Tanker is struck with a grievous

blow, and a subsequent torpedo sinks it. The remaining crippled enemy Vessel charges, however, the *Wahoo* dives, forcing the Japanese to fire into the water. The *Wahoo*, commanded by Lt. Commander Dudley Morton surfaces and the enemy Ship retires toward a searchlight beam, but the Submarine fires two torpedoes sinking it. On the following morning, the *Wahoo*, spots another Convoy, however, she is out of torpedoes. Enemy Destroyers attack, however, the Submarine is unscathed. As the Ship heads for Hawaii, a report is dispatched to Headquarters: "ANOTHER RUNNING GUNFIGHT . . . DESTROYER GUNNING . . . *WAHOO* RUNNING."

January 23rd-24th 1943 — (Pacific-Solomon Islands) The beleaguered Japanese see no relief. They have been pummeled into defeat on New Guinea (Papua), are being driven to the sea on Guadalcanal and are now struck at their positions on Kolombangara, Solomon Islands, by two American Task Forces; a Carrier Destroyer Force, led by Rear Admiral Ainsworth and a Carrier Force led by the "Bull," Admiral Halsey. The Fleet pounds the Japanese at Vila-Stanmore.

January 24th 1943 — (United States) On Bases throughout the nation, the WAVEs and WAACs keep things running smoothly, and assuming responsibility for many jobs previously held by men. In addition to their exemplary actions in the medical field, many drive trucks, shuttle Aircraft, keep communications open, train male Pilots, and repair engines. During August of 1943, the Women's Auxiliary Corps becomes the Women's Army Corps. Also, women are doing the same things overseas, however, law forbids them from working near the battlefields. **(Aleutian Islands)** Japanese Planes initiate nuisance raids against Amchitka. **(Pacific-Solomons)** The Japanese are further compressed by the Yanks; the CAM Division advances to Hills 98 and 99 and establishes contact with the 25th Division. Meanwhile, the 25th drives toward the Poha. **(Atlantic-North Africa)** The U.S. II Corps is attached to the British First Army. The French 19th Corps awaits permission from General Giraud before attaching to the British First Army. Meanwhile, a major assault against Ousseltia Valley is aborted. The Germans prepare to attack Faid Pass. In other activity, the U.S. II Corps raids Sened Station then returns to Gafsa as planned.

January 25th 1943 — (Pacific-New Guinea) Major General Horace Fuller, CG, 41st Division, assumes command of all Allied troops in the Oro Bay region. **(Pacific-Solomons)** The 25th Division drives to the Poha River and secures Hills 105 and 106. **(Atlantic-Libya)** Still the Germans retreat with the British on their backs, as the Tommies move into Zavia. Benito Mussolini gives command of the German-Italian Panzer Army to General Giovanni Messe, replacing Field Marshal Rommel who has become sick; the transfer of command does not occur for awhile. **(Atlantic-Soviet Union)** The Red Army seizes Voronezh, further threatening German defenses at Stalingrad. German Field Marshal Erich von Manstein had asked Hitler to grant permission to General Paulus to surrender the 6th Army; however, Hitler denies the request, despite the fact the Army Group A is now able to get out of the Caucasus.

January 26th 1943 — (Pacific-Australia) The U.S.S. *Amberjack*, under the command of Lt. Commander Bole, embarks for the Buka Passage. Subsequently, the *Amberjack* attacks a Schooner, riddling the two-sailed Vessel with shells, and setting it afire. On the 4th of February, a robust Freighter is spotted. The Yanks prepare to fire torpedoes, however, the enemy Ship charges and opens fire, wounding an American Officer. Chief Pharmacist Mate Beman, darts to aid the wounded Officer, and is sliced by enemy bullets, killing him in gruesome fashion. The *Amberjack* destroys the Vessel which is an ammunition Ship, however, the Japanese disclaim the report. On the 14th of February, a report is dispatched to headquarters, notifying them that the waters are hot and that they have been attacked by two Destroyers and have rescued a Jap Pilot from the sea. The message is the final one; the Submarine and its entire crew is lost without a trace. **(Pacific-Solomons-Guadalcanal)** The 25th Division is pulled back to guard the Airfields against possible enemy attack to recapture the Lunga perimeter. **(Atlantic-North Africa)** In Tunisia, the French 19th Corps attacks in the Ousseltia Valley to recapture the Kairouan Pass.

January 27th 1943 — (Guadalcanal) The Army-Marine Division pushes further, advancing through the jungle to reach the Nueha River. **(Pacific-New Hebrides)** Headquarters 2nd Marine Aircraft Wing is established at Efate. **(Pacific-Burma)** The Royal Indian Navy sinks a Japanese troop-laden Launch on the Mayu River. **(Atlantic-Germany)** The U.S. Eighth Air Force makes its first air strike against Germany, bombing the port of Wilhelmshaven. **(Atlantic-North Africa)** In Libya, the Germans continue retreating toward Tunisia, however, it is a fighting withdrawal, giving the British 7th Armored Division a tough contest near Zuara.

A Boeing B-17 amidst a thunderclap of flak over Germany.

January 28th 1943 — (Pacific-Guadalcanal) The combined Army-Marine Force drives west from the Nueha River, eliminating resistance, however, Japanese Snipers remain active. **(Pacific-New Guinea)** The Japanese assault Allied positions at Wau in a last ditch effort to take Port Moresby by land. The Australians (Kanga Force) repel the assault and hold out until reinforcements arrive. By the 29th, the Australians number only about 200, but they mount rigid resistance, pouring fire into the enemy as they close on the Airfield. Wau, the outermost defense post of Port Moresby, holds by a thin line as the Japs nudge the edge of the Airstrip. Suddenly, U.S. Planes stream into the Airfield with reinforcements. The Australian 17th Brigade bolts from the Aircraft as they screech along the runway and race into the raging battle. Intense combat continues throughout the night of the 29th, with the Japanese being thrown back in total disarray. **(Atlantic-Tunisia)** The

French 19th Corps, assisted by American troops, fights vigorously at Ousseltia Valley and secures half of Kairouan Pass. Combat Command B, 1st Armored Division is detached from Corps and moved to Bou Chebka. RCT 26 (minus 1 Battalion), breaks off the engagement after being ordered to move to Sbeitla. Additional outfits, presently fighting alongside the French in the valley, are the 2nd Battalion, 126th Infantry; 1st and 3rd Battalions, 16th Infantry; 7th Field Artillery Battalion; a Battery of 33rd Field Artillery Battalion, and a Battalion of Engineers, in addition to a Tank Destroyer Company. Meanwhile, contingents of the 1st U.S. Division head toward the 19th Corps sector from Guelma, Algeria, and will be placed under French command upon arrival on the following day. **(Atlantic-Soviet Union)** Kasternoe, a rail junction between Kursk and Voronezh is lost by the Germans.

January 29th 1943 — (United States) Mrs. Ruth Cheney Streeter is commissioned Major in the U.S.M.C. Women's Reserve, and becomes its first director. **(Atlantic-North Africa-Tunisia)** The U.S. First Division (-) is placed under command of the French 19th Corps to support the defense of the Ousseltia Valley. C.C.B., 1st Armored Division reverts to the U.S. II Corps. **(Atlantic-Soviet Union)** Russian troops seize Kropotkin along the Baku-Rostov railroad line.

Allied Convoy pushing through the North Atlantic.

An oil-soaked survivor of a Convoy receives aid.

January 29th-30th 1943 — (United States) A U.S. Naval Task Force, commanded by Rear Admiral R.C. Giffen, escorting Transports to Guadalcanal is attacked by enemy Planes near Rennel Island. U.S. Land and Carrier-based Aircraft intercept the force. The U.S.S. *Chicago*, a Heavy Cruiser (CA-29), is damaged and taken under tow but before reaching Espiritu, it is struck by 12 additional Planes and sunk. The U.S.S. *LaVallette*, a Destroyer (DD-448) is damaged by enemy Aircraft.

January 30th 1943 — (Pacific-Alaska) Akutan Harbor, located at Fox Island, Alaska, becomes the newest Naval Station. **(Pacific-Guadalcanal)** The Japanese retreat toward Cape Esperance to escape by Ship. The U.S. 147th Infantry pursues westward, however, fierce enemy fire from the West bank of Bonegi River mouth stalls the 1st Battalion; the 3rd Battalion becomes stalled about 1,000 yards east of the river. **(Pacific-New Guinea)** The Japanese at Wau are handily defeated by the Australian Kanga Force, compelling them to withdraw. **(Pacific-Australia)** The 158th U.S. Infantry Regiment (Arizona National Guard until inducted into Federal Service), 40th Division arrives in Brisbane, Australia, via Panama. The Regiment, known as the "Bushmasters" embarks for Port Moresby (Papua) New Guinea on March 15th to join the Australian contingents. The unit, using its Indian members to good advantage, implements codes in the impenetrable Indian language, frustrating the Japanese and inciting a long lasting argument between them and the U.S. Marines as to whom was first to use Indian codes. Another advantage for the 158th and the Australians is that the natives on New Guinea who practice sorcery and cannibalism, side with the Allies against the Japanese. **(Atlantic-Tunisia)** The Germans seize Faid Pass (British First Army Sector), driving the French toward Sidi Bou Zid. Elements of the First U.S. Armored Division rush to support the operation, but arrive too late to assist. Other American units move hurriedly toward Maknassy and Tebessa. With control of Faid Pass, the Germans possess a route from which to strike Allied lines in the Eastern Dorsal. **(Atlantic-Germany)** Berlin celebrates the 10th anniversary of Hitler's rise to power as British Planes bomb the city. In other activity, Grand Admiral Karl Doenitz becomes Commander in Chief of the German Navy, replacing Grand Admiral Erich Raeder. **(Atlantic-Soviet Union)** The rail junction of Tikhoretsk is taken by the Russians, sealing the fate of the German Army Group A, by severing its final line of escape from the Novorossisk region. Meanwhile, Maikop falls to the Red Army. Also, Army Group Don has been rendered an ineffective Army, since separation from Army Group A, during the northward retreat.

January 31st 1943 — (Pacific-Solomons) U.S. Dive Bombers and Torpedo Planes receive orders to attack enemy Surface Vessels off Kolombangara Island. Elements of Marine Fighter Squadron 112, fly as escorts and intercept a huge contingent of enemy Zeros which are protecting the Fleet. 1st Lieutenant J. Joseph Deblanc, U.S.M.C., leads his greatly outnumbered section against the Zeros, protecting the Bombers which return to Base. DeBlanc remains in the area, destroying five Zeros before his Plane is damaged, forcing him to bail out at a dangerously low altitude over enemy positions. Captain DeBlanc is awarded the Medal of Honor. **(Atlantic-North Africa)** In Libya, the British Eighth Army completes the expulsion of Axis troops from the vicinity of Zuara, near the Tunisian border. On the *Tunisia* Front, the U.S. 1st Division

takes control of the Ousseltia Valley, as British First Army and French 19th Corps' troops withdraw for rest and recuperation. In the U.S. II Corps area, contingents of the 1st Armored Division (Combat Command A), launch an unsuccessful assault regain Faid Pass. Combat Command C, drives toward Eastern Dorsal to hook up with CCD, to seize Maknassy. The enemy mounts a stiff Air assault that disorganizes the assault before it can be initiated. **(Atlantic-Middle East)** General Lewis H. Brereton is appointed Commander of U.S. Air Forces in the Middle East. Brereton replaces General Andrew who becomes Commander of U.S. Forces, European Theater of Operations.

Sgt. Regina Weirauch, a W.A.C., stands near a Link Trainer at Marianna, Florida. She is one of the instructors responsible for teaching the troops to understand and use the basic instrument panels on Aircraft. The WACS often run the Control Towers.

January 1943 — (Pacific-Guadalcanal) Marine Fighter Squadron 121 has been in constant combat with the enemy since October. Captain Joseph J. Foss, between October 9 and 19 November, has singlehandedly destroyed 23 Japanese Planes, in addition to inflicting damage to many more while flying escort missions over the Solomons. On the 15th of January, 1943, three more enemy Planes are shot down by Foss. Subsequently, he leads eight Marine F4F fighters and four Army P-38s against an extremely large enemy force of Fighters and Bombers off Guadalcanal on the 25th of January. The smaller American force destroys four Japanese Fighters, and turns back the others before they can drop a solitary bomb.

February 1st 1943 — (United States) The Soviet Purchasing Committee (located in New York) contacts Hermann H. Rosenburg (Chematar Inc.) attempting to purchase 220 pounds of uranium oxide, 220 pounds of uranium nitrate, and 25 pounds of uranium metal. The purchase inquiry arrives six days subsequent to the War Production Board pulling in the rope on sales of such items, however, it only refers to domestic sales, giving the Russians an option. Rosenberg contacts S. W. Shattuck Chemicals in Denver and the Russians receive their merchandise. The U.S. project Oak Ridge (atom bomb) is being built, but will not be operational until next year. The War Production Board notifies the Manhattan Project about the clandestine sale, however, it is too late to stop it. General Groves, alert to the Russian conspiracy is able to stop all exports of the special chemicals by early April. Rosenberg gets the next shipment to the Russians by dealing with Companies in Canada. One of the major undetected problems throughout the war is the unchecked entry of Russians into the U.S. Although no Americans are permitted beyond Fairbanks Alaska, the Russians come to the U.S. in hordes, getting off Airplanes and vanishing into the countryside, realizing the U.S. has taken no precautions. **(Pacific-Guadalcanal)** The Japanese, with their backs to the sea, begin to evacuate Cape Esperance during the night of February 1st-2nd. The enemy Fleet, consisting of 20 Destroyers, is attacked by Planes from Henderson Field and by PT Boats. During the encounter, the U.S. sustains damage to three of its PT Boats; the 37, 111, and the 123. Enemy Aircraft damage the Destroyer *De Haven* (DD-469). The enemy sends in over twenty additional Destroyers and a Cruiser on the 4th; U.S. Planes again rush out to intercept and damage four Destroyers. The Japanese send in an additional 18 Destroyers on the 7th; two are destroyed. In related activity, the Destroyer *Makigumo,* is damaged on the 2nd after striking a mine near Doma Reef. **(China-Burma-India)** An Allied conference is held to formulate plans to be presented to Chiang Kai-Shek with reference to Operation ANAKIM, which will be launched during November 1943. The primary objective of the plan is to recapture Burma and to then attack Japan from China. **(Atlantic-North Africa-Tunisia)** A heavy Allied Artillery attack is followed by an assault by the Combat Command A, 1st Armored Division, which is experiencing difficulty penetrating enemy resistance in their assigned sector. C.C.D., assisted by contingents of the 168th Infantry, 34th Division, captures Sened Station, while CCC, moving through Maizila Pass, pulls out north of Maknassy and withdraws to Hadjeb el Aioun. **(Atlantic-Italy)** Mussolini fires Generale di Brigata Giuseppe Cavallero, replacing him with Generale d'Armata Vittorio Ambrosio, who detests the Germans. The relationship between the Germans and the Italians soon deteriorates as Mussolini attempts to get Hitler to seek peace with the Soviet Union or pull back from the east. However, Hitler discards the advice, choosing to crush the Bolsheviks. **(Atlantic-Soviet Union)** The Russians capture Svatovo, severing another rail line from the Germans; Kharkov to the Donets basin.

February 2nd 1943 — (Pacific-New Britain) The Submarine U.S.S. *Greenling* arrives off New Britain and lands a group of Allied agents. **(Atlantic-Tunisia)** The U.S. 1st Armored Division establishes headquarters in Sbeitla. Combat Command D, deploys firmly on a ridge East of Sened and turns back a counterattack. **(Atlantic-Russia)** Germany suffers a massive setback as the Red Army encircles the German 6th Army at Stalingrad; the Russian winter combined with an over-extended supply line, spells disaster. The Russians concentrate on driving the balance of the enemy forces as far west as possible before Spring arries.

General Eisenhower and President Roosevelt.

February 3rd 1943 — (Pacific-New Guinea) The ongoing Kanga Force drive continues to make rapid progress, pushing the Japanese toward Mubo. **(Pacific-Burma)** On the Arakan front, the Japanese repulse an attack by the Indian 123rd Brigade at Rathedaung. **(Atlantic-North Africa)** In Tunisia, fighting continues in the British First Army's U.S. II Corps sector, with no significant advantage going to either side. **(Atlantic-Soviet Union)** Soviet troops seize Kushchevkaya, a rail junction, while other troops slice the rails between Kursk and Orel.

February 4th 1943 — (Pacific-Guadalcanal) The Japanese continue to withdraw from Cape Esperance, as the Americans span out further to speed up the search. **(Pacific-New Guinea)** The Japanese continue their retreat from Wau, harassed along the way by Allied Planes and by hardened troops of the Kanga Force. **(Atlantic-North Africa)** In Tunisia, Rommel, faced with the approaching British Eighth Army, decides to make a stand at the Mareth Line. The British have seized Tripolitania, crossed into Tunisia and are now closing the gap between them and the elusive Rommel. In Algeria, Headquarters, North African Theater of Operations (NATOUSA) is established as a separate command under General Eisenhower at Algiers. Also, General Andrews becomes head of ETOUSA. **(Atlantic-U.S.S.R.)** Soviet Commandos land near Novorossisk on the Black Sea coast and are opposed by the nearly isolated German Army Group A. Meanwhile, the Soviets tighten the noose, closing on Kharkov, Kursk, and Rostov.

February 5th 1943 — (Pacific-Guadalcanal) American troops probe north of the Umasani River, but find no opposition. In other activity, an Army B-17 spots a enemy Naval Force consisting of two Carriers, six Heavy Cruisers, two Light Cruisers, 12 Destroyers and four Battleships. Halsey deploys his Force to intercept the enemy, but allows their advance Group free passage to snag the main body. The Japanese evacuate their forces from Guadalcanal on the 7th and the main body retires without attacking. **(Atlantic-Russia)** The Soviets and the Germans continue to engage in bitter battle in the vicinity of Novorossisk-Krasnodar. The Soviets seize St Oskol, southeast of Kursk, and Izyum, southeast of Kharkov also falls.

February 6th 1943 — (Pacific-New Guinea) Japanese Planes attack Wau Airdrome, but receive the worst of it, as Allied Planes intercept and destroy 24 enemy Planes, while losing no Aircraft. **(Pacific-Solomons-Guadalcanal)** The 25th Division continues pursuit of the retreating Japanese. **(Atlantic-Soviet Union)** On the southern front, Yeisk, on the Sea of Azov, falls to the Soviets and other troops close on Rostov, finalizing the isolation of German Army Group A. Also, Lisichansk (on the Donets) falls, as the Soviets advance deeper into the Ukraine below Kharkov.

O.S.S. Agents being dropped behind Japanese lines in China.

February 7th 1943 — (Pacific-Guadalcanal) Japanese Destroyers again move into Cape Esperance and evacuate the remaining troops. A plan to debark an Army unit west of Cape Esperance to sever the Japanese escape route does not succeed, as the remaining 13,000 troops safely board the Destroyers and escape to Buin and Rabaul during the night. **(Pacific-China)** Generalissimo Chiang Kai-shek expounds his version of the three demands in a letter to Roosevelt and agrees to participate in the Burma offensive. **(Atlantic-Tunisia)** The U.S. 1st Ranger Battalion is flown from Oran into Tebessa (Youks les Bains Airfield), the primary U.S. Base in Central Algeria. They immediately board buses for a grueling 120 mile drive to Gafsa, Tunisia to become part of the U.S. II Corps. As the final Vehicle is pulling away, enemy Aircraft swoop over and bomb the Airfield. Their mission is to mount quick-strike raids, cause severe enemy casualties and give the enemy the impression that II Corps strength in central

Tunisia is enormous. **(Atlantic-Soviet Union)** The Germans lose Azov, on the Sea of Azov and in the Ukraine, Kramatorsk is seized by Red Army forces. Also, the Russians sever the highway between Kursk and Orel.

February 8th 1943 — (Pacific-Guadalcanal) The 161st Regiment, 25th Division runs over light opposition at Tambalego and moves to Doma Cove. Meanwhile, elements of the Americal Division reach Kamimbo River. **(Pacific-Australia)** The 162nd Regiment, U.S. 41st Division embarks for New Guinea. **(Pacific-Burma)** The Chindits (Indian 77th Brigade), under British Brigadier General Charles Wingate, moves into Burma and initiates Guerrilla raids. **(Atlantic-North Africa)** In Tunisia, the Germans order an attack against Gafsa, but countermand the order when informed that the Americans are withdrawing. **(Atlantic-Soviet Union)** The Germans lose Kursk to the Soviets.

February 9th 1943 — (Pacific-Guadalcanal) Guadalcanal comes under total American control as the 1st Battalion, 161st Infantry, 25th Division encounters the 2nd Battalion, 132nd Regiment, Americal Division at Tenaro (1625). Major General Alexander M. Patch, (XIV Corps) U.S.A., announces the "TOTAL AND COMPLETE DEFEAT OF THE JAPANESE FORCES ON GUADALCANAL." The struggle which started on August 7th 1942 (first U.S. offensive of the war) had been a grueling contest, inflicting heavy casualties on both sides. Army troops had begun replacing the Marines during the latter part of 1942. The Japanese have been vanquished, giving them their first land defeat of the war. About 13,000 Japanese have escaped to Buin and Rabaul, 12,000 from the 17th Army and the balance, Naval personnel. **(Pacific-Shanghai)** At the Kiangwan P.O.W. Camp, Marines and civilian prisoners have been forced to construct what the Japanese claim is an Imperial Japanese Army recreation area, however, the project which the Americans have been working on for several weeks is actually a Rifle Range. Living conditions at Kiangwan are not too severe if compared with those in the Philippines, however, several men caught with extra items through a widespread "black market," receive a special treatment; the "water cure." Each man caught is tightly bound, while a Jap gushes water into his mouth causing choking and eventual unconsciousness if answers do not come quickly. Fortunately, all who undergo this ordeal survive, however, their memories of the Japanese remain indelible. **(Pacific-Australia)** The U.S.S. *Grampus* embarks from Brisbane, however, it is called back to port and reembarks on the 11th, for the Solomons. Communications from the U.S.S. *Grampus* cease on the 12th. **(Atlantic-North Africa)** The Germans change their attack plans after determining that the U.S. Forces are withdrawing from the area around Gafsa. Rommel prepares to assault Gafsa at a later time, and Sidi Bou Zid, is to be assaulted by von Arnim's troops. **(Atlantic-Soviet Union)** Belgorod is seized by the Soviets.

February 10th 1943 — (Alaska) A C-47 (without a heater) lands at Fairbanks to take personnel including Captain G. Jordan (Lend-Lease Liaison Officer) back to Great Falls. Jordan had been at Fairbanks for some time inspecting Lend-Lease. Ironically, Jordan has been (by Presidential order) designated a United Nations Officer, although at this time there is no United Nations. Jordan returns on the 17th with a scathing report which causes shock waves to roll through the Military. Some examples: thousands of crates of aircraft parts buried in the snow; over one hundred Pratt-Whitney motors ($25,000 each) perched precariously by the river which will soon flood; countless generators; complete Mobile Depot units; scores of other parts. Jordan's report is circulated and teams of inspectors are sent streaming to the area. Jordan is then informed by another U.S. Officer that he was now a "marked man." The supply system at Fairbanks is changed and so is the supple Officer; the Russian consignments are now separated to the Russians' delight. **(Pacific)** A downed Pilot is rescued from Rengi Island, by the U.S.S. *Grouper*, while the U.S.S. *Gudgeon*, is evacuating 28 people from the southeast coast of Timor. **(Atlantic-North Africa)** In Tunisia, British First Army area, U.S. II Corps sector, the U.S. 1st Armored Division is directed to contain the Axis forces at Faid. In the British Eighth Army area, the British operation to secure Ben Gardene, is postponed due to heavy rains, buying time for the main enemy outpost of the Mareth positions. **(Atlantic-Spain)** U.S. Army Land-based Planes sink a German Submarine, the U-519, off the coast of Spain. **(Atlantic-Soviet Union)** The Red Army seizes Chuguev and Volchansk as it closes on Kharkov.

February 11th 1943 — (Pacific-Coral Sea) An enemy Submarine, the RO-102, is sunk by the Light Cruiser *Helena* (CL-50), and the Destroyer *Fletcher*. **(Atlantic-North Africa)** In Tunisia, RCT 135, U.S. 34th Division (French 19th Corps) relieves the French troops in the Pichon-Maison des Eaux region. Also, General Fredendall, Commanding General II Corps issues his plan for the defense of Faid. **(Atlantic-Soviet Union)** Soviet troops drive the Germans from Lozovaya (railroad junction), south of Kharkov.

February 12th 1943 — (United States) Walter Winchell, a noted columnist and broadcaster, who had received a commission as a Lieutenant Commander, Naval Reserve, and continued taking broadsides at Senators and Congressmen such as Senators Taft and Wheeler who had been isolationists before the war (neglecting to note that after the start of hostilities they supported the cause) loses his commission. **(Pacific)** Now that Guadalcanal has fallen to the Yanks, plans are formulated for the next objectives; New Britain, New Guinea, and the New Ireland Area. The code name is ELKTON. **(Atlantic-North Africa)** Intelligence reports continue to flow into Allied Headquarters, warning of an anticipated major enemy assault against the rear positions of British General Anderson's 1st Army. General Eisenhower leaves Algiers at midnight for U.S. General Fredendall's II Corps sector at Tebessa, arriving at about noon and becomes annoyed at what he finds. The troops have not been properly deployed as ordered, rather; they are dispersed all along the line, with Infantry reserves manning dangerously situated djebels, unaware that a German offensive is imminent. In other activity, American General Omar Bradley celebrates his 50th birthday. **(Atlantic-Soviet Union)** Krasnodar, a rail center on the Kuban River is taken by the Soviets. Also, Shakhty, on the Rostov railroad line is seized.

February 13th 1943 — (Atlantic-North Africa) The Axis Commanders confer on strategy for their imminent assault against the Allies in Tunisia. In other activity, General Eisenhower, having arrived on the previous day, attempts to restructure the defense lines to prevent disaster. **(Tunisia)** Darby's Rangers, having completed a long trek through the hills after a previous stop at a French outpost near Sened, prepare to strike a contingent of the Italian Centauro Division (crack troops), holding ground directly in front of Rommel's

forces. At about 00:01, an enemy Patrol is detected. Four Scouts advance quietly; suddenly, several short muffled yelps are heard and the threat is over. The Rangers resume the march, reaching positions about fifty yards from the objective when an enemy Soldier begins firing blindly, followed by additional enemy fire, also inaccurate. The Rangers move forward, withhold their fire, then in a sudden and deadly burst, open up with everything in their arsenal. Grenades fly, exaggerated screams accompany rapid rifle fire and this is followed by a gruesome bayonet attack as the Rangers devour their prey. After about twenty minutes of horrendous close-quartered combat, only eleven troops of the 10th Bersaglieri (except those who have run) are dead. The Rangers lose one man, decapitated by a point-blank cannon shot and eighteen men wounded. German Tanks set out to catch the Rangers as they head for Sened, however, they halt and return to their lines. **(Atlantic-U.S.S.R.)** The Soviets secure the Rostov-Voronezh railroad in its entirety with the capture of Likhaya and Novocherkassk. In other activity, the Germans hold off Red Army attacks near Novorossisk, their last remaining stronghold in the Caucasus.

The U-Boats strike again. An ammunition Ship explodes in the North Atlantic.

February 14th 1943 — (Atlantic-Soviet Union) The Soviets occupy Rostov, a communication base for the German evacuation plans. Voroshilovgrad also falls. Meanwhile, the Germans regroup their forces. Army Group South, formerly Don assumes control of remaining troops of Army Groups Don and B. The 2nd Army transfers to Army Group Center and Army Group A retains the bridgehead at Kuban in Novorossisk region.

February 14th-21st 1943 — (Atlantic-North Africa-Tunisia) Rommel, preparing retaliation for the earlier Axis loss at El'Alamein, continues to bolster his defenses located near the Southern border of Tunisia in old French Fortifications, bracing for Montgomery's Eighth Army. German General Jurgen von Arnim's Force, numbering in excess of 100,000 men, stares West toward Eisenhower's Allied Force. At dawn, enemy Planes and Artillery break the silence. Spirited Tiger Tanks rumble forward, gaining clearer passage for the fast advancing Infantry. The Tanks crash through Faid Pass, compelling the Allies to pull back within a few hours; many Americans holding the djebels are surrounded. The astonishing attack also inflicts severe damage to the U.S. Tanks deployed in the II Corps area, forcing a withdrawal from Sidi Bou Zid. In conjunction, French and Americans, including contingents of the U.S. 1st Division and the 1st Ranger Battalion, withdraw from Gafsa during the night of the 14th-15th, moving to Feriana. Darby's Rangers are ordered to hold Gafsa for at least four hours to buy time. The order comes as a surprise to the Rangers, who had planned an attack against Djebel el Ank for the night of the 14th. As the tension mounts, the Rangers prepare to fire as the sounds of great movement begin to close on their positions, however, they are startled when their sights are pinned on an approaching herd of about several hundred stampeding Camels. The Rangers move to Feriana, choking with laughter. However, the Germans have penetrated without heavy losses; the assistance of the Stukas (German single engine Dive Bombers), handily repulse an Allied counterattack near Sbeitla. The isolated Yanks on Djebel Ksaira and Garet Hadid, repulse repeated counterattacks on the 16th, but while attempting to make it back to their lines, the Germans annihilate them. The U.S. has sustained heavy casualties during this encounter and some of the dead bodies are maliciously stripped by wandering Arabs. Now, the Germans command the terrain where the Faid Pass forks in two directions; Tebessa, 70 miles to the West, containing the American lifeline of supplies and to LeKef, and its massive British supply depot, about 80 miles to the north. U.S. General Fredendall had been ordered on the 15th, to retreat as soon as all possible precautions have been taken to rescue as many troops as possible, before retiring; he is trying to regroup and hold the Kasserine Pass.

On the 18th, again the Germans advance, forcing the British 1st Army to withdraw west in conjunction with the pullback of the U.S. II Corps, attempting to hold the passes at Sbiba, Abiod, Dernaia, and the Kasserine. Meanwhile German Artillery pounds the rear-guards (Rangers) at Feriana, however, no casualties are sustained. Subsequently, they are ordered to pull back to Dernaia; all transportation has gone, compelling the Rangers to walk twenty-four miles with the German Armor on their heels. During the furious attack, Thelepte Airbase falls to the enemy.

The U.S. Ninth Division commences a 700-mile march which includes passing over murderous frozen mountain roads to join British contingents to halt the juggernaut. Reinforcements are rushed to bolster the defenders. On the 19th, Rommel extends his Armor further, stretching out with a double stroke; one force grinding towards Sbiba, defended by the French; the other moving to maul the Americans at Kasserine Pass. Both attacks fail, however, new and powerful assaults on the 20th, gain critical ground at Kasserine Pass, inflicting heavy casualties and destroying many U.S. Tanks. Eisenhower, informed of the situation at the pass, rushes General Harmon to the front under orders to take personal battlefield command and drive the Germans back. Meanwhile, the U.S. Ninth Division arrives and joins with the British 6th Armored to break the German offensive on the 21st, at Thala near Tebessa-LeKef Road. Rommel, believing the Americans have been strongly reinforced, and under the impression that the British Eighth Army is approaching Mareth, begins to withdraw into the Pass on the 22nd; the Germans mine the area extensively as they pull back. General Harmon sees his beleaguered troops retake the Kasserine Pass by the 25th, culminating the vicious four-day battle.

February 15th 1943 — (Pacific-Guadalcanal) U.S. Rear Admiral C.P. Mason is appointed Commanding Officer, Joint Air Command Designated Aircraft, Solomon Islands, with Headquarters at Guadalcanal. **(Atlantic-North Africa)** British General Alexander, commander of Allied Forces in Tunisia,

arrives at Allied Headquarters in Algiers for a strategy conference. The situation in Tunisia worsens for the Allies. British General Anderson, Commanding General 1st British Army Area, orders the troops holding the high ground West of Faid to withdraw to Kasserine Pass to make a stand there. The troops in the U.S. II Corps counterattack to recapture Sidi Bou Zid and rescue the trapped troops; however, the attempt fails and the U.S. loses some Tanks. General Fredendall U.S.A., is ordered to withdraw the II Corps as soon as all isolated troops can be saved. Meanwhile, the Axis troops move into Gafsa without opposition.

The Coast Guard dealing with the ice and heavy seas off Greenland.

February 16th 1943 — (United States) The U.S. Navy establishes Fleet Wing 16; it is commissioned at Norfolk, Virginia. **(North Pacific-Aleutians)** The American Airstrip at Amchitka is complete, and receives its first Allied Plane. The Japanese make one final ineffective raid on the facility. **(Pacific-Guadalcanal)** Operation CLEANSLATE (invasion of Russell Islands) is implemented as the first elements of the 43rd Division Assault Force, commanded by Major General John H. Hester, arrive at Guadalcanal. **(Southwest Pacific)** The U.S. Sixth Army is established and comprises the 2nd Engineering Special Brigade, 503rd Paratroop Infantry Regiment supported by the 1st Marine Division, which is being attached. Lieutenant General Walter Krueger U.S.A., will command. **(Pacific-Australia)** The U.S.S. *Triton* leaves Brisbane for the area between Rabaul and the Shortland Basin. On the 6th of March, the *Triton* attacks a Convoy boasting a Destroyer and five other Vessels, sinking one Ship and damaging another. Several weeks later on March 11th, the *Triton* reports to Headquarters: "TWO GROUPS OF SMOKE, 5 OR MORE SHIPS EACH, PLUS ESCORTS . . . AM CHASING." Subsequent directions to report back to Base go unanswered; it had been the *Triton's* final message. The cause of loss is never determined, however, subsequent Japanese battle statistics report on the sinking of a Vessel at the appropriate time and place, and specifically mention that debris is sighted, labeled "MADE IN U.S.A." **(Atlantic-Tunisia)** Rommel rushes toward Sbeitla, thinking the Americans had been thrashed enough to evacuate without a fight, but his Armor meets stiff resistance. The 1st Armored Division suffers tremendous losses of both men and equipment, but rally with reinforcements from Combat Commands A, B, and C, which had come in from Maktar. The courage of these troops withstands the assault, allowing an orderly pull-back toward Western Dorsal. The enemy having been repulsed, breaks off action for the night, however, the Germans cut off the escape route of the trapped Americans on Djebel Ksaira and Garet Hadid; while attempting escape during the night of 16th, they are annihilated. In the British Eighth Army area, the British 7th Armored Division approaches the Mareth Line, reaching the enemy outpost of Ben Gardane, a Mareth line outpost. **(Atlantic-Soviet Union)** The Axis troops abandon Kharkov, heading for Poltava. Soviet troops occupy the town.

February 17th 1943 — (United States) A new U.S. Carrier is commissioned at Quincy, Massachusetts and its name is *Lexington* (CV-16), given in honor of the *Lexington* (CV-2), sunk during the battle of the Coral Sea during May of 1942. **(Pacific-Solomons)** An advance reconnaissance party (U.S. Officers) departs Guadalcanal under cover of darkness to scout Banika Island prior to the upcoming invasion and discovers that the Japanese have evacuated the islands. **(China-Burma-India)** General Cheng Chen is announced as Commander of the Chinese Expeditionary Force. In Burma, the Indian 55th Brigade makes another unsuccessful attack against the Japanese holding Donbaik, on the Arakan front. **(Atlantic-Mediterranean)** Mediterranean Air Command is activated by Allied Forces Headquarters, under Air Chief Marshal Sir Arthur W. Tedder, establishing unified command in the Middle East, Northwest Africa, and Malta. British Air Vice Marshal Sir Arthur Coningham receives command of Allied Air Support Command; British General Alexander becomes Deputy CinC of Allied Forces in North Africa, and Commander of the Group of Armies (18th Army Group; British First and Eighth Armies), effective February 20th. **(Atlantic-North Africa)** In Tunisia (British First Army area), the U.S. II Corps continues to withdraw toward Western Dorsal and begins to implement defense measures for the protection of the passes at Dernalia, El Ma el Aboid, Sbiba and Kasserine. The French 19th Corps withdraws toward Sbiba to co-ordinate with the Americans. The Germans take Feriana and seize Thelepte Airbase. In the British Eighth Army area, the British 7th Armored and 51st Divisions take Medenine and its Airfields. In other activity in North Africa, the Moroccan Sea Frontier (U.S. Navy), is established; Rear Admiral J.L. Hall becomes Commanding Officer.

February 18th 1943 — (United States) General Bradley, spending his first day at the Pentagon, is informed of the disaster at Faid Pass in North Africa. Bradley is subsequently dispatched to Algiers to help find a solution and bring about victory. **(Northern Pacific-Aleutians)** A Naval Task Force, commanded by Rear Admiral Charles H. McMorris, moves to Attu and shells the island, striking Holtz Bay and Chichagof Harbor. This is the first Naval bombardment launched against the island; inclement weather prevents damage results from being observed. Four Destroyers and two Cruisers participate in the attack. **(Pacific-Solomons)** The rear echelon of the Russell Island Assault Force (from 43rd Division) returns to Guadalcanal. Also, a Reconnaissance contingent returns to the 'Canal later after concluding that the Japanese have abandoned the islands. **(China-Burma-India)** In Burma, the Chindits (Indian 77th Indian Brigade) move across the Chindwin without opposition, inflicting damage to the Mandalay-Myitkyina rail system. In India, Lt. General Raymond A. Wheeler, receives orders to defend the Ledo Road; during December, he had been directed to construct the highway. **(Atlantic-Mediterranean)** The Mediterranean Air Command (U.S. Ninth and Twelfth Air Forces; R.A.F. E.A.C., M.E., Malta, Gibraltar) begins operations. Under M.A.C., Northwest African Air Forces, consisting of EAC and 12th Air Force is activated; General Spaatz commands. He also takes command of the Western Desert Air Force (21st). **(Atlantic-North Africa-Tunisia)** In the British 1st Army area, the Americans maintain a hectic but steady pace to fortify positions at the Central Tunisia passes to halt the relentless German advance. Enemy Armor stirs up activity during the night as the rumble of the Tanks signals the attack to the defenders guarding the eastern exit of the pass. Reinforcements, including the 1st Battalion, 39th Infantry, 9th Division, rush to Kasserine Pass to bolster the 1st Division. In other activity, the British seize Foum Tatahouine along their route to the Mareth Line. **(Atlantic-Russia)** The German II Corps, 16th Army, begins a retreat from the northern front.

February 19th 1943 — (Pacific) Units of the U.S. Navy in the Southwest Pacific area become the U.S. 7th Fleet. **(Pacific-Guadalcanal)** U.S. troops prepare to occupy the Russell Islands. **(Atlantic-Tunisia)** The Germans, under Rommel, launch two attacks; at Kasserine Pass against the Yanks and against the French at Sbiba Pass. Both assaults are repelled. Meanwhile, British General Alexander arrives at the front lines and takes command of the **18th Army Group** (British First and Eighth Armies, French 19 Corps and U.S. II Corps). **(Atlantic-Soviet Union)** The Soviets proclaim that the Germans have been driven from the Kharkov-Kursk Railroad and highway.

February 20th 1943 — (United States) The YMS-173, a Minesweeper sinks in Coos Bay, Oregon, after foundering. **(Pacific-Admiralties)** The U.S.S. *Albacore* (SS-218) sinks the Destroyer *Oshio* and a Patrol Boat near Manus. **(Pacific-Guadalcanal)** A U.S. Task Force, transporting assault troops of the 43rd Division, embarks for the Russell Islands "Operation CLEANSLATE." **(Atlantic-North Africa-Tunisia)** Rommel remains in Tunisia for several weeks, however, as Axis forces reorganize, his German-Italian Panzer Army is disbanded. General Messe assumes command of the Italian First Army. In other activity, enemy troops penetrate the British 1st Army area, U.S. II Corps sector, at the Kasserine Pass and drive north toward Thala and west toward Tebessa. Troops including the 26th Armored Brigade, British 6th Armored Division, commanded by General C.G.G. Nicholson are to intercept and drive the enemy back; C.C.B., 1st Armored Division and other contingents are to deploy at the passes in front of Tebessa. In addition, the Germans again attack French positions at Sbiba, however, they are repulsed. Meanwhile, preparations are made to counterattack on the following day. **(Atlantic-Soviet Union)** The Germans lose Krasnograd and Pavlograd.

February 21st 1943 — The German U-225 heads for the bottom after being attacked by the U.S.S. Spencer.

February 21st 1943 — (Pacific-Solomons-Russells) The Marine 3rd Raider Battalion, commanded by Colonel Harry B. (Harry the Horse) Liversedge, hits the beach at Pavuvu's Pepesala Point, without opposition and the U.S. 43rd Infantry Division, commanded by Major General John H. Hester, lands unopposed at Banika Island. By March 1st, about 9,000 men are ashore. The Marine 11th Defense Battalion dispatches Antiaircraft guns and crews to Banika. The Marines find themselves confined to Garrison duty as the Japanese have evacuated the island; after one month on the island, they depart to prepare for the invasion of Bougainville. **(China-Burma-India)** The Royal Indian Navy lands a contingent of men southeast of Akayab, Burma, at Nyebon; the force strikes enemy positions swiftly, then withdraws. **(Atlantic-North Africa) 18th Army Group** British General Alexander directs General Montgomery to attack the enemy's south flank to ease pressure on the British First Army. Montgomery, still unprepared for a large-scale operation against the Mareth Line, he sends small forces forward up the coast; in addition he commits the French forces (L-Force) under General LeClerc, sending them northward. In the British First Army area, Churchill Tanks arrive to bolster the French 19 Corps, helping them thwart another counterattack near Sbiba. In the U.S. II Corps sector, the Germans close on Thala, less than 50 miles from the supply Base at Tebessa. Reinforcements including Field Artillery Battalions of the 9th Division arrive, and after a bitter struggle, the Germans are repulsed. Meanwhile, C.C.B., 1st Armored Division, bolstered by contingents of RCT 16, 1st Division, repel a small secondary assault by the enemy. **(North Atlantic)** The U.S.S. *Spencer* (PG-36) sinks the German U-225 **(Atlantic-Soviet Union)** The German 6th Army, under Von Manstein, commences a counteroffensive, advancing from Stalino against Soviet forces near Kharkov.

February 22nd 1943 — (United States) The U.S.S. *Iowa* (BB-61) is christened at New York city. **(North Atlantic)** The Coast Guard Cutter U.S.S. *Campbell* (PG-32) amd the Polish Destroyer *Burza*, sink the German U-606. **(Atlantic-North Africa)** In the U.S. II Corps sector, the Germans continue to attack toward Le Kef. By afternoon, Rommel aborts the assault and orders his force to pull back into Kasserine Pass. Both sides suffer severe losses during the battle. **(Atlantic-Soviet Union)** The Red Army launches an offensive on the center front in the Orel-Bryansk region.

U.S. Infantry and Marines head for the beaches of the Russell Islands in rubber boats.

A. U.S. Coast Guard Cutter joins an attack.

February 23rd 1943 — (Pacific-New Georgia) A Japanese Naval Force, comprising nearly 2,000 men, lands at Kolombangara (Yokosuka 7th Special Naval Landing Force). **(Atlantic-Tunisia)** The Germans complete their movement back into the Kasserine Pass. The Allies pursue with caution. In related activity, Allied Planes engage the German Air Force throughout the day. Meanwhile, the U.S. 1st Armored Division prepares to recapture the pass. In other activity, Rommel is appointed Commander of the German Army Group, Africa. Included in the command are both the Fifth Panzer Army (General von Arnim) and the First Italian Army (General Messe). British General Alexander tells General Montgomery that the situation in Kasserine Pass is improving, then orders him not to take unnecessary risks. **(Atlantic-Soviet Union)** The Soviets seize Sumy in the Ukraine, northwest of Kharkov.

February 24th 1943 — (North Pacific-Alaska) The U.S. Navy establishes a Naval Air Facility at Amchitka. On the first of March, the Navy establishes a Naval Auxiliary Facility on Annette Island, Alaska. **(Atlantic-North Africa)** In Tunisia, in the British 1st Army area, U.S. II Corps sector, C.C.B., 1st U.S. Armored Division and the British 6th Armored Division pursue the retreating enemy. The 1st Armored Division is making final preparations to recover the Pass. In the British Eighth Army area, General Montgomery instructs the British 7th Armored and 51st Infantry Divisions to drive hard against the enemy along Gabes Road and also along the coast. In other activity, in North Africa, General Bradley arrives at Dakar on the French North African coast on a C-54, and soon heads for Algiers to help assess the situation, arriving on the following day. An armored car transports him across the mud drenched terrain to Eisenhower's Headquarters at the St. George's hotel.

February 25th 1943 — (Southwest Pacific) Operation RENO is unveiled; advance rough draft plans to seize the Philippines by way of the Bismarcks, along the northern coast of New Guinea and subsequently Mindanao, are complete. **(Pacific-Russell Islands)** The U.S. facility at Wernham Cove becomes an operational Torpedo Boat Base. **(Atlantic-England)** The Royal Air Force initiates round-the-clock Air assault against the Axis troops. **(Atlantic-Tunisia)** In the British First Army area, the U.S. II Corps overcomes mines and traps to recapture Kasserine Pass. The four-day battle has been brutalizing and many of the Americans are fresh troops, receiving their baptism under fire. Allied Armor is considered inferior to the Axis Armor, but the Allied troops hold on and fare well under the circumstances. In the British Eighth Army area, pressure is maintained against the Germans; however, Von Arnim succeeds in holding Montgomery at bay, while the Germans keep jabbing the Allied positions in the western sectors. In addition, the Germans continue to drive against Bedja and Medjez el Bab. Meanwhile, British General Alexander attempts to regroup the II Corps.

February 26th 1943 — (Southwest Pacific) All contingents of the U.S. Army in S.W.P.A. and all units of the Philippine Army which had been called into the service of the U.S. are assigned to U.S.A.F.F.E. (inactive since April 1942). **(Atlantic-Tunisia)** In the British Eighth Army area, plans are laid by General Montgomery for the attack against the Mareth Line, scheduled to commence on March 20th. The code name is PUGILIST. In the British First Army area, U.S. II Corps sector, RCT 16 comes under the direction of the 1st Division, which retains responsibility for the Kasserine Pass and is directed to continue to maintain communications with the U.S. 34th Division. The 1st Armored Division continues to regroup in front of Tebessa, which was spared when Rommel retired into the Kasserine Pass. The German 5th Panzers, commanded by von Arnim, move on Bedja and Medjez el Bab, defended by the British First Army's V Corps. The Panzers capture a British outpost at Sidi Nsir after a vicious contest and also make progress during their push for El Aroussa until halted short of the objective. Intense fighting occurs west of Jefna and at Medjez, with the British repulsing both attacks, gaining precious time for the British 46th Division to fortify the pass leading to Bedja.

February 27th 1943 — (Pacific-New Guinea) The U.S. 162nd Infantry, 41st Division advances to Milne Bay. **(Atlantic-Tunisia)** In the British First Army area, 5 Corps sector, heavy fighting still rages near Bedja but the Germans are contained.

February 28th 1943 — (Southwest Pacific) A Japanese Invasion Fleet departs Rabaul, heading for the northern coast of New Guinea to bolster the drive against Port Moresby. The Air Corps has begun to perfect a new type of bombing tactic and is anxious to test it on the enemy in the Bismarck Sea. In other activity, General Headquarters, Southwestern Pacific, revises the plans for the push to take Rabaul (Operation ELKTON). **(China-Burma-India)** The Ledo Road construction continues stretching across the Burmese border. In other activity, the Japanese advance two small contingents against a British outpost near Fort Hertz, and toward the Tanai River in Hukawng Valley. **(Atlantic-Tunisia)** The enemy evacuates Sbeitla and Feriana, moving to Eastern Dorsal. **(Atlantic-Soviet Union)** The Germans maintain their offensive and seize Kramatorsk and Lozovaya in upper Donets.

February 1943 — (Atlantic-Norway) A small group of Norwegians inflict severe damage to the Norse Hydroelectric plant where it is suspected that the Germans are experimenting with heavy water to create an atomic bomb. Previously, British Commandos had been air-dropped with a Norwegian advisor, Major Knut Haugland; Intelligence was gained, however, they were not able to reach the plant. During November, U.S. Bombers will totally eliminate the plant.

March 1st 1943 — (United States) The Marine Corps receives its first Medium-Bomber Squadron, as Marine Bomber Squadron 413 is commissioned at Cherry Point, N.C. **(China-**

Burma-India) Sumprabum is evacuated by British civilians, which is subsequently occupied by Japanese, but they do not advance toward Fort Hertz. **(Atlantic-North Africa)** General Spaatz assumes command of the Twelfth Air Force (had been on paper only since reorganization during February); it continues as administrative headquarters for U.S. Army units of North African Air Force. **(Atlantic-Soviet Union)** Moscow announces that Marshal Timoshenko's new offensive has regained Demyansk, Lichkova, and Zaluchie.

March 1st-4th 1943 — (Pacific-New Guinea) THE BATTLE OF THE BISMARCK SEA — Japan, feeling the heat from the advancing Australians and Americans on New Guinea, dispatches a Naval Convoy, commanded by Rear Admiral Masatomi Kimura, from Rabaul to the Huon Gulf to bolster its forces and eliminate the Allied pressure. The Convoy, consisting of eight Destroyers and eight Troop Transports speeds unsuspectingly, as a searching B-24 pinpoints the exact position of the enemy, quickly transmitting its position and its strength to Headquarters.

General Kenney's 43rd Bombardment Group and Australian Planes take off on the 2nd, and intercept the Armada and escorting Fighters. The dauntless Pilots, anxious to experiment with their newly developed low-level bombing techniques, descend and release their bombs which bounce across the water toward the bow of the Vessels, almost guaranteeing a hit. The combined killing power of the B-24s and Fighters is further augmented by PT Boats. The devastating raid rocks the Japanese. Some survivors of one sinking Transport are plucked from the water by an enemy Destroyer and deposited on the beach at Lae, during the night of the 2nd, however, the Convoy is overmatched and most do not survive. On the 3rd, PT Boats spot another crippled Transport and finish it off.

The Allies continue to clobber the Japanese on the fourth and final day of the one-sided battle which culminates in a humiliating defeat for the Japanese. The combined resources of the Planes and Torpedo Boats annihilate the Armada, sinking four Destroyers, all eight Transports and many escort Fighter Planes. Over 3,000 Japanese are lost to drowning in what becomes the final attempt by the Japanese to deliver a large Naval Force into the Huon Gulf for the remainder of the war. The Destroyers *Asashio, Tokitsukaze, Arashio* and *Shirayuki* are sunk.

March 2nd 1943 — (United States) The Submarine Chaser *SC-1024* sinks off the coast of North Carolina, after becoming involved in a collision. **(Atlantic-North Africa)** The U.S. II Corps in Tunisia receives orders to initiate an offensive no later than 15 March to take pressure off the British Eighth Army positions at the Mareth Line. The objective is to secure Airfields which will be used to support the Eighth Army offensive, and also to give the British an extra means of supply. In the British Eighth Army area, Montgomery makes quick use of the 2nd New Zealand Division, just in from Tripoli. **(Atlantic-Soviet Union)** Rzhez is evacuated by German Army Group Center.

March 3rd 1943 — (North Pacific-Aleutians) Admiral Kinkaid suggests a limited offensive be launched against Japanese held Attu. This operation will bypass the original objective; Kiska. **(Atlantic- North Africa-Tunisia)** The U.S. II Corps probes with Patrols without encountering any enemy resistance. Both Sidi Bou Zid and Hadjeb el Aioun have been evacuated by the enemy. The enemy is very active in the British 1st Army area, seizing Sedjenane, 12 miles outside of Jefna. The British 51st Division, 8th Army, repels an enemy assault in the vicinity of Mareth, inflicting heavy casualties upon the attacking troops. Meanwhile, the Africa Corps issues its plan to drive from the Mareth Line. **(Atlantic-Soviet Union)** The German 1st Panzer Army (Army Group South) captures Lisichansk and Slavyansk in the Donets, however, the Soviets seize Lgov and Dmitriev Lgovsky.

March 4th 1943 — (Atlantic-Tunisia) In the British First Army area, the 139th Brigade, British 46th Division, withstands enemy assaults along the Mateur-Tabarka road, however, the unit is forced to withdraw after dark to Tamera. In the British Eighth Army area, Axis troops (10th and 21st Panzers) are spotted moving west of Medenine. British reinforcements move up to counter the threat, giving the British an edge in both weapons and men. **(Atlantic-Soviet Union)** Sievsk, south of Bryansk, falls to the Red Army.

March 5th 1943 — (Pacific-Philippines) The U.S.S. Submarine *Tambor* surfaces in Pagadian Bay, near Mindanao and lands men, ammunition, and currency. **(Pacific-Solomons)** A U.S. Cruiser Destroyer Task Force, comprising three Cruisers and seven Destroyers, commanded by Rear Admiral A.S. Merrill, attacks Japanese positions at both Vila and Munda; two attacking enemy Destroyers, the *Mineguma* and the *Murasame*, are sunk during the confrontation, which lasts into the 6th. **(Atlantic)** The Escort Carrier *Bogue* (CVE-9) begins duty as Convoy Escort becoming the first Escort Carrier to be assigned Anti-Submarine duty as its primary responsibility. **(Atlantic-North Africa)** In Tunisia, the German threat to Tamera, prompts British reinforcements to be sent there. **(Atlantic-Soviet Union)** Soviet troops drive toward Staraya Russia.

A PBY-5A Catalina on Patrol in the Aleutians.

March 6th 1943 — (Pacific-Malay Archipelago) The Submarine U.S.S. *Tautog* lays mines near the southeast coast of Borneo. **(Pacific-Russell Islands)** Japanese Fighters and Bombers, aware of American presence on the Russell's, initiate Airraids against Marine positions (11th Defense Battalion). **(Atlantic-North Africa-Tunisia)** General George Patton replaces General Fredendall as Commander of the U.S. II Corps. General Eisenhower had made the decision the previous day, based on information received while in Tebessa (5th) conferring with advisors. Patton receives a message of instructions from Eisenhower: "REHABILITATE THE AMERICAN FORCES AND PREPARE THEM FOR THE ATTACK." Gen-

eral Patton commands four complete Divisions; Allen's 1st Infantry (Darby's Rangers are attached to 1st Division), Eddy's 9th Infantry, Ryder's 34th Infantry and Ward's 1st Armored, totaling approximately 90,000 troops. Meanwhile, Rommel's force strikes British positions at Medenine, but the Tanks have no support Infantry and all four attacks are handily repulsed. The Germans lose about 50 Tanks during this (Rommel's) final attack in Tunisia and withdraw after nightfall. The British who commit one Tank Squadron suffer no Tank losses. Rommel soon relinquishes his command and returns to Germany. **(Atlantic-Soviet Union)** The Soviets seize Gzhatsk, between Moscow and Smolensk.

Marine Dive Bombers in the Pacific.

March 7th 1943 — (Atlantic-Tunisia) General Patton inspects his troops and their positions, then begins to initiate changes (Djebel Kouif). General Omar Bradley is designated Deputy Corps Commander under Patton. Bradley had commanded a Division in the United States but at this time has no battle experience. Patton's mission is to support British General Montgomery by recapturing Gafsu, thereby pressuring the enemy at Gabes to transfer troops to engage the Americans, which should permit the British to move on the Mareth Line against weakened defenses. General Patton accepts his mission but would prefer to carry the fight, rather than be restrained in a support role. Patton had been stationed on the French Moroccan coast prior to this command. His purpose was to neutralize any attempt to close the Straits of Gibraltar and to exhibit American presence to deter the Germans from using Spain as a springboard to North Africa. In other activity, the Southeast Algerian Command (formed during late-January under French General Robert Boissau), which includes the French Camel Corps, occupies Redeyef, Tunisia and probes toward Tozeur, occupying it on the following day.

March 8th 1943 — (Alaska) Russian Colonel A.N. Kotikov, stationed in Fairbanks for Lend-Lease and other reasons, writes a letter to Lt. Colonel C.H. Gitzinger, U.S.A., requesting that Captain George Jordan be promoted to Major. The Russian is aware that a Major has more pull and it is in his best interests. However, although Jordan receives his promotion through circuitous intervention, he remains an absolute Patriot and continues to unravel the mysteries of the Lend-Lease. Synonymously with his promotion he detects many "black suitcases" passing through as "personal luggage." Their number stretches to lots of fifty at a crack weighing in at two tons. The Russians change the status of the suitcases to "diplomatic immunity," however, they are being sent to Moscow from the Soviet Government Purchasing Commission, Washington, D.C., not the Russian Embassy. A sampling of what is discovered when Jordan commandeers an American Plane preparing to take off for the Soviet Union: railroad mileage from point to point within the U.S.; documents concerning the Aberdeen Proving Grounds; naval and shipping intelligence; copies of secret reports filed by U.S. Diplomats in Moscow and sent back to the Washington; memo from the White House (Harry Hopkins) addressed to A. I. Mikoyan (No. 3 man under Stalin and Molotov) stating " — HAD A HELL OF A TIME GETTING THIS AWAY FROM GROVES," referring to documents acquired from the Oak Ridge Manhattan Engineering District (top secret operation involved with developing the atom bomb). Groves is Major General Leslie R. Groves, however, it is clear that the note means his organization as he strongly dislikes the Russians and does not trust them. Subsequently, Elizabeth Bentley gives testimony to Congress that while working with Jacob Golos (Soviet Spy in New York) during the spring of 1943, she was giving about forty rolls of 35mm film every several days to her contact in Washington D.C., Nathan G. Silvermaster and she also testifies that she would frequently help him and his wife develop the film in the basement of their home in D.C. The Office of Military Intelligence, considering him a security risk, attempted to have Silvermaster fired from the Board of Economic Warfare during 1942, however, a Presidential aide, Lauchlin Currie steps in and arranges for his transfer to the Farm Security Administration. Harry Dexter White, working in the Treasury Department, is also linked to the conspiracy with Silvermaster and Golos; it is White who ships U.S. engraving plates to the Russians as the American Occupation Force enters Germany, permitting the Russians to print currency at U.S. expense. Henry White subsequently dies of a suspicious heart attack during 1948 (between appearances in front of an Internal Security Committee). **(China-Burma-India)** In China, the Japanese force the Yangtze between Ichang and Yoyang, primarily to acquire rice and other food supplies. **(Atlantic-Dutch West Indies)** Allied Land-based Aircraft sink a German Submarine, the *U-156.* **(Atlantic-North Africa)** In Tunisia, **18th Army Group** assumes command of the U.S. II Corps, however, the French 19th Corps remains attached to British First Army. **(Atlantic-Russia)** The Germans lose Sychevka and withdraw toward Smolensk; German supply problems remain terrible. On the 10th, the Soviets take Byelyi.

March 8th-25th 1943 — (Pacific-New Guinea-Bougainville) The Japanese begin an offensive against Allied positions at Bougainville. The U.S.M.C. 3rd Defense Battalion's 155mm and 90mm Batteries are deployed as Field Artillery to bolster the firepower. The ferocious enemy attacks strike from the north, northwest, and east, but fail to succeed.

March 9th 1943 — (Pacific-New Guinea) The Japanese begin intense bombing missions over Allied positions in New Guinea, striking at Wau. Subsequent missions to destroy Allied defenses will be launched against Dobodura, Oro Bay, Porlock Harbor, Port Moresby and the Milne Bay area. **(Pacific-Solomons)** In the Solomons, the Japanese Kure 6th Special Naval Landing Force lands over 2,000 troops between Bairoko and Enogai and near Munda Airfield. Japanese Rear Admiral Minoru, commanding 8th Combined Special Landing Force, assumes responsibility for the New Georgia area. In

other activity, U.S. Naval Aircraft attack Japanese positions at Munda; Planes return on bombing missions regularly. **(China-Burma-India)** In Burma, the Chindits (Indian 77th Brigade) push further east, crossing the Irrawaddy River to harass the enemy. **(Atlantic-Tunisia)** Field Marshal Rommel exits North Africa and returns to Germany. German Field Marshal Kesselring assumes extended authority over all enemy forces in the Mediterranean Theater. German General von Arnim replaces Rommel as commander of Army Group Africa and General Gustav von Vaerst succeeds von Arnim as Commanding Officer of the Fifth Panzer Army. Hitler does not permit Rommel to return to Africa.

Major General Claire L. Chennault.

March 10th 1943 — (Atlantic-Tunisia) In the British First Army area, the Germans unsuccessfully assault the British 46th Division positions at Tamera. In the British Eighth Army area, General LeClerc's L-Force covering the British flank at Ksar Rhilane repulses an enemy assault.

March 11th 1943 — (Pacific-China) The U.S. 14th Air Force, commanded by Major General Claire L. Chennault, is activated. **(Atlantic-Russia)** The Germans drive to Kharkov and meet heavy Russian resistance. The battle continues to rage along the Russian Front, but time is running out for the Germans as their supplies are diminishing and reinforcements are lacking.

March 12th 1943 — (United States) The Pacific Military Conference convenes in Washington D.C. for the purpose of mapping strategy for the offensive against Japan, which will occur during 1943. General Sutherland, representing General MacArthur, presents the ELKTON Plan, which calls for the destruction of Rabaul by a two pronged attack; one from New Guinea to New Britain and the other by way of island hopping through the Solomons. The primary concern of the operation is the ability of sufficient transportation to carry men and supplies safely to their destination. The Pacific Theater is still the step-child of the war and an overabundance of Vessels and equipment is a most rare occurrence. **(Pacific-Solomons)** Marine Fighter Squadron 124 arrives on Guadalcanal from Espiritu Santo, introducing the F4U into combat. **(China-Burma-India)** General Stilwell, concerned with Japanese intrusion at Sumprabum, orders Chinese contingents to the Ledo area. On the Arakan front, the Japanese maneuver cunningly and begin encircling British Imperial troops after forcing them to break into small contingents. **(North Atlantic)** The German Submarine *U-130* is sunk by the U.S.S. *Champlin* (DD-601). **(Atlantic-North Africa-Tunisia)** Patton readies his troops for the offensive against Rommel's desert force, unaware that Rommel has departed the country, and expresses concern that the Germans might strike first. Patton is of the opinion that his troops are too defensive and must attack to gain confidence. Patton is informed that the radio has announced his promotion to Lieutenant General. **(Atlantic-Soviet Union)** The Soviets seize Vyazma. In addition, vicious street fighting ensues in Kharkov; the Germans claim capture on the following day.

March 13th 1943 — (Pacific-New Guinea) The Kanga Force advances beyond Guadagasel as its dogged attack slowly nudges the entrenched Japanese toward Mubo. **(Atlantic-North Africa-Tunisia)** The scheduled date for the American offensive is set for the 17th. American troops will begin forming, while Allied Aircraft initiate striking enemy Airfields prior to D-Day. Gafsa remains the primary objective of the offensive. Skirmishes develop during the day causing the Germans to lose the services of two Tanks while the Americans lose two Planes General Patton's orders to the 1st Division concerning the recapture of Gafsa and the thrust to El Guettar are short: "FIND THEM . . . ATTACK THEM . . . DESTROY THEM!"

Hitler and Mussolini in Sicily during one of Hitler's earlier trips.

March 14th 1943 — (United States) The Navy establishes Fleet Operational Training Command, commanded by Rear Admiral D.B. Beary. **(Pacific-Russells)** The advance echelon of Marine Aircraft Group 21 lands on Banika Island. **(Atlantic-North Africa)** French General Giraud reinstates representative government in French North Africa. **(Atlantic-Soviet Union)** The Germans claim the capture of Kharkov.

March 15th 1943 — (United States) Admiral E.J. King changes American Fleet designations. All Pacific Fleets receive odd numbers and all Atlantic fleets are given even numbers. **(Pacific-Hawaii)** At French Frigate Shoals, Territory of Hawaii, the Navy establishes a Naval Air Auxiliary Facility. In other activity in the Pacific, the 1st Marine Raider Regiment is organized for operations on Dragons Peninsula, New Georgia. **(Pacific-New Guinea)** Elements of the U.S. 41st Division occupy positions on the Mambare River without incident. **(Pacific-Solomons-Russell Islands)** In the Russell Islands, the Marine 10th Defense Battalion relieves the 11th Defense Battalion. **(Atlantic-Tunisia)** General Eisenhower arrives at U.S. II Corps Headquarters for the purpose of checking on the progress of the plans for the offensive.

March 16th 1943 — (Atlantic-North Africa) U.S. Rear Admiral H.K. Hewitt assumes command of Naval Forces, Northwest African Waters. The Command had been established on February 3rd 1943, **18th Army Group**. The U.S. II Corps deploys for the offensive, however, the 1st Armored Division is hindered by sloppy terrain as it moves to protect the 1st Infantry Division's flank. In the British Eighth Army area, a diversionary attack is launched during the night of the 16th-17th.

March 16th-17th 1943 — (Atlantic-North Africa) At 23:00 on the 16th, shrill sounds of shells bursting north of Gafsa, Tunisia, are heard by Patton. The offensive commences as the II Corps begins its expeditious drive toward Gafsa. After a horrid night march, Rangers find the town abandoned. The Americans move into Gafsa, taking the town against light opposition subsequent to German abandonment of the town. The same American troops which had fared badly at the Kasserine Pass, exhibit a true fighting spirit under "Blood and Guts Patton." American casualties are extremely light; Patton immediately prepares to mount another assault on the 18th, however, continuing rough weather immobilizes the American Armor.

March 17th 1943 — (Pacific-Johnston Island) Marine Scout Bomber Squadron 243 arrives on the island from Hawaii. **(Atlantic-North Africa)** Also See March 16th-17th. In the British First Army area, 5 Corps sector, Axis troops finally force the British from Tamera. In the British Eighth Army area, small scale attacks are mounted while General Montgomery continues preparing to attack the Mareth Line.

March 18th 1943 — (China-Burma-India) The 308th Bombardment Group (B-24s) arrives in India to bolster the U.S. Fourteenth Air Force. **(Atlantic-Tunisia)** The 1st Ranger Battalion supported by contingents of the U.S. 1st Infantry Division seize El Guettar, without opposition. Still, heavy rains impede progress of the U.S. 1st Armored Division, however, an Algerian command is able to move along the south flank of the II Corps and deploy south of Gafsa during the 19th. **(Atlantic-Germany)** Allied Planes bomb Vegesack, Germany. In one incident, the 359th Bomber Squadron, 303rd Bomber Group is struck by intense enemy Aircraft fire, damaging the lead Plane and mortally wounding the lead Bombardier, 1st Lt. Jack Mathis. Mathis, blown to the rear of the Plane and severely wounded, crawls back to his bomb sight, and hits the assigned target, permitting the balance of the Planes to score direct hits and complete the mission. Mathis receives the Medal of Honor posthumously. **(Atlantic-Russia)** Heavy

MEDITERRANEAN SEA

Gulf of Tunis

Bizerte

Djebel Abiod Mateur

Philippeville Bone La Calle Tabarka Djedeida TUNIS

St-Charles Jemmapes Mondovi Souk el Khemis Bedja

Souk el Arba Pont-du-Fahs

Constantine Souk Ahras Le Kef Enfidaville

Ouled Rahmoun

Telergma Maktar Sousse

WESTERN DORSAL DORSAL

Kalaa Djerda El Ala Pichon

Youks-les-Bains Thala Sbiba

Tebessa Fondouk el Aouareb

Bekkaria Kasserine Pass Sbeitla Hadjeb el Aioun

Bou Chebka Kasserine Faid

Thelepte EASTERN Faid Pass

Feriana

ALGERIA Maknassy Sfax

TUNISIA

Gafsa Sened

El Guettar Gulf of Gabes

Gabes

TUNISIA
1943

Mined area

0   30   60 Miles

0   30   60 Kilometers

fighting continues near Belgorod, north of Kharkov; the Germans gain the town.

March 20th 1943 — (Pacific-Solomons) Marine Torpedo Bomber Squadron 143, commanded by Major John Sapp, initiates the first aerial mine-laying operation in the South Pacific, deploying mines off the Solomons. **(Atlantic-North Africa-Tunisia)** In the U.S. II Corps sector, the weather clears sufficiently to permit the 1st Armored Division to renew its offensive, beginning the long trek through knee deep mud for Maknassy. Elements of RCT 60 and Combat Command C, capture Sened Station during the night of the 20th without opposition; with control of Sened, the U.S. mobilizes an eastward drive from El Guettar, utilizing the 1st Ranger Battalion and the 16th and 18th Regiments, 1st Division. Meanwhile, the British Eighth Army launches its attack against the Mareth Line, sending four Divisions against the enemy. In conjunction, the New Zealand Corps moves to strike the German flank and drive the enemy further up the Tunisian coast. In other activity, General Patton receives orders to transfer the U.S. Ninth Division to British General Anderson's command to protect the British left flank, during its attack against Bizerte; if the order is executed, the Americans play no active role in the final victory in Tunisia. Both Bradley and Patton protest this deliberate breakup of the U.S. II Corps to General Eisenhower who mandates that Anderson give the II Corps a specific sector, with explicit American command. Subsequently, Patton's II Corps seizes Bizerte.

German anti-personnel S-MINE. Upon detonation the canister springs up and rings a large circumference with steel pellets.

March 21st 1943 — (Pacific-New Georgia) An advance Marine detachment is landed by a PBY at Segi Plantation to check the feasibility of an amphibious invasion. After a careful study of the terrain, they return and inform Headquarters that the beach cannot sustain a large landing force. **(Atlantic-North Africa-Tunisia)** Sened village capitulates to U.S. RCT 60, enabling the U.S. 1st Armored Division to bypass the village and move within Artillery range of Maknassy. The weapons soon are deployed and Artillery barrages begin. The 1st Ranger Battalion maneuvers behind enemy lines by climbing a mountain near Djebel el Ank in conjunction with the 26th Infantry, which is pushing from the front. At 06:00, in a Ranger patterned attack, yelling starts in cadence with rapid small arms fire and exploding grenades, jolting the beleaguered Italian defenders, already in awe of the Rangers, dubbed the "Black Death" by them. Darby's troops charge down the opposite side of the mountain and up the El Guettar Heights, supported by some overtired Engineers, overrun-

ning about twelve machine gun nests and destroying a 88-mm battery. By 14:00, Rangers control the pass, clearing the way for the 1st Division to advance toward Sfax. The operation culminates with the capture of over 700 enemy prisoners. After questioning the captured Italians, it is determined that the Germans had pulled out two days prior. Meanwhile, the 18th U.S. Infantry seizes Hill 336, south of Gumtree Road, then pushes toward Djebel el Mcheltat. The British Eighth Army progresses slowly toward El Hamma and the British First Army meets powerful resistance in its sector. **(Atlantic-Soviet Union)** Durovo, 57 miles from Smolensk falls to the Red Army, however as the spring thaw sets in, the offensive begins to stall along the entire front.

March 22nd 1943 — (United States) Two American Submarines are officially reported as lost: the *Amberjack* (SS-219) and the *Grampus* (SS-207). **(Atlantic-Canary Islands)** The German U-Boat U-524, operating near the Canary Islands off the coast of North Africa is sunk by Army Aircraft. **(Pacific-Japan)** A new directive is issued by the Japanese Military laying out the importance of a defensive effort in New Guinea. **(Atlantic-North Africa-Tunisia)** The 1st Armored Division, commanded by General Ward occupies Maknassy without opposition, however, the enemy retains the nearby heights; General Patton sends General Hugh Gaffey to direct Ward to secure the heights (Djebel Naemia). The U.S. 1st Armored Division launches an unsuccessful night attack. The enemy continues to fortify their defenses. Meanwhile, the British Eighth Army's offensive against the Mareth Line is nearly totally stalled by severe rains. The enemy mounts a counterattack and advances through the rain and mud forcing the British 50th Division to pull back. British General Montgomery modifies his attack plans and concentrates on strengthening his western flank against the enemy threat.

March 23rd 1943 — (Atlantic-North Africa) The U.S. establishes a Naval Station and Naval Air Facility at Arzeu, Algeria. In other activity, Advanced Amphibious Training Bases are established at Beni Saf, NeMours, Tenes and Mostaganem in Algeria. A similar facility is established at Port Lyautey, Morocco. In Tunisia, U.S. II Corps sector, the U.S. 1st Infantry Division repulses two counterattacks at El Guettar, turning back both Italian and German Divisions. Both sides suffer heavy losses. The time of the attacks had been pinned to the minute by Intelligence. The enemy continues the futile offensive until the 27th. Also, the 1st Armored Division unsuccessfully makes repeated attempts to dislodge the Germans on Djebel Naemia.

March 24th 1943 — (United States) The Joint Chiefs of Staff approve the plan to occupy Attu (Aleutians). **(Atlantic-Tunisia)** The U.S. 1st Armored Division, commanded by General Ward, continues to pound but not dislodge the German positions at Djebel Naemia. Patton then orders another assault, to be launched at midnight, with no more success. Patton's Tanks move cautiously as this struggle to take El Guettar becomes a nasty fight against staunch defenses. The Germans have immersed the area with several types of mines including the infamous antipersonnel mines dubbed "Bouncing Betties," similar to a number 10 tin can, packed with steel pellets; when tripped by a wire, the mine soars three to four feet into the air before exploding, ravaging an area up to 50 feet around. The U.S. 1st and 9th Infantry Divisions (Benson Force), trailing right behind the Tanks, are a prime target. After attacking three straight days without success, Patton sends General Bradley to the front to get a first hand picture. Enemy Aircraft constantly assault the Americans during the advance. In other activity, British General Alexander calls for a broader offensive. The U.S. 1st Armored Division is instructed to break off the engagement at Maknassy and push for Gabes by moving southeast of El Guettar. General Ward is wounded during the assault. Subsequently, General Bradley is instructed by Patton to inform General Ward that he is to be replaced by General Ernest N. Harmon.

March 25th 1943 — (Pacific) Army and Naval Aircraft bomb Nauru Island, in the Western Pacific just south of the equator. **(Atlantic-North Africa-Tunisia) 18th Army Group**. The U.S. II Corps continues battling for Djebel Naemia, making some progress, however, the ground is not held. At Djebel Berda, the 18th Regiment, 1st Division, lacking reinforcements is forced to pull back. Also, the 1st and 9th Divisions are to clear passage for the 1st Armored Division to debouch southeast of El Guettar; the Rangers have been participating in the action, often being sent to break up enemy footholds. On the 27th, subsequent to six days of grueling battle, the Rangers are pulled-back for rest and recuperation; six Rangers of the 1st Battalion have been lost.

March 26th 1943 — (North Pacific) BATTLE OF KOMANDORSKI ISLAND — A U.S. Cruiser Destroyer Task Force (two Cruisers, four Destroyers) commanded by Rear Admiral C.H. McMorris, intercepts a superior Japanese Naval Force, under Vice Admiral Moshiro Hosogaya, moving toward Attu, transporting reinforcements and after a hard-hearted duel lasting three and one half hours, turns it back. After sustaining damage, the *Salt Lake City* conceals itself in the fog. Meanwhile, the Japanese become low on ammunition and Admiral Hosogaya anticipates being attacked by U.S. Land-based Bombers from Adak, prompting him to disengage and retire. However, terrible weather keeps all U.S. Planes grounded; it is so cold that the bombs are virtually frozen to the ground. This engagement, fought about 400 miles west of the Russian Komandorski Islands, proves to be the final sea battle fought without supporting Aircraft Carriers. The Heavy Cruiser, U.S.S. *Salt Lake City* (CA-25), and the Destroyer, U.S.S. *Bailey* (DD-492) are both damaged. The Japanese Cruiser *Nachi* is damaged; the Transports had retired at the opening of the engagement. The U.S. gains a strategic victory by barring entry of the reinforcements and in addition, the blockade of the Aleutians continues holding firm. All future supplies destined for the island are transported by Submarines. **(Atlantic-North Africa-Tunisia)** The British scrap "PUGILIST" (British assault against Mareth Line) and establish a modified attack plan coded "SUPERCHARGE." The British Eighth Army renews its attack against the Mareth Line during the afternoon, subsequent to over two hours of Air bombardment.

March 27th 1943 — (United States) The Coast Guard Cutter, No. 85006, explodes off Long Island, New York, and sinks. **(Atlantic-South America)** The U.S. Navy establishes several Naval Facilities in Brazil, including a Naval Air Facility at Natal. **(Atlantic-Tunisia)** In the U.S. II Corps area, the U.S. 34th Division (first operation as a Division), led by General Ryder, drives toward Fondouk Gap. The advance encounters violent resistance, halting their progress during the night. In the British Eighth Army sector, pressure applied by the Americans under Patton, weakens enemy resistance at the Mareth Line, enabling Montgomery's troops to strike vicious blows against the enemy, collapsing portions of the line,

however, the Germans retain control of El Hamma, allowing an escape route, which they use during the night of the 27th. Von Arnim, concerned about U.S. pressure at Maknassy, soon withdraws his Italian and German Infantry from the Mareth Line.

A German U-Boat under attack.

March 28th 1943 — (United States) The Joint Chiefs of Staff issue a new Pacific Directive, superseding the earlier plan of July 2nd, 1942. General MacArthur and Admiral Halsey receive authority to use their discretion for an offensive against Rabaul. The Plan calls for Air Bases to be constructed on Woodlark and Kiriwina islands (Trobiands), and for the subsequent capture of enemy installations on the Huon Peninsula. In addition the plan spells out the occupation of Southern Bougainville, Western New Britain, and New Georgia, Solomons. **(Pacific-New Guinea)** The MacKechnie Force is formed (primarily the 1st Battalion, 162nd Regiment, 41st Division) to seize Morobe harbor and the mouth of the Waria River. **(Atlantic-North Africa-Tunisia)** The U.S. II Corps begins a drive to seize Gabes. The U.S. 1st Division, supported by a major portion of the 9th Division on their right, attempts to open a gap for the 1st Armored Division to roll through, however, potent enemy fire stalls the attack. Some contingents become lost (because of bad maps), while attempting to locate Hill 369. In the British Eighth Army area, the Axis troops begin withdrawing from the Mareth Line during the night. The 15th and 21st Panzers have been hit hard suffering high casualties. In addition, the battered Italian troops have been thoroughly demoralized; they head for the Wadi area. Meanwhile, the British pursue the retreating Axis troops, but heavy rains continue for the next week; in addition, the routes to Gabes are inundated with land mines.

March 29th 1943 — (Pacific-Solomons) The Submarine U.S.S. *Gato* (SS-212) evacuates select Military and civilian personnel from Teop Island. **(Atlantic-Tunisia)** General Ward is ordered by Patton to be prepared to attack by dawn, but bad roads impede the operation and the 1st Armored Division is not in position until 07:00. Patton becomes annoyed with the poor pace of progress. Another attack commences on the following day with similar results. In the British Eighth Army sector, the enemy has successfully withdrawn from El Hamma.

March 30th 1943 — (Atlantic-Tunisia) The fighting between the Yanks and the Axis troops remains intense in the II Corps area. The 1st Infantry struggles against both bad weather and soggy roads in addition to a ferocious enemy burst which penetrates and secures portions of Djebel el Mcheltat. The

U.S. 9th Division makes gradual progress, but is forced to relinquish its hold in the vicinity of Djebel Lettouchi. The 1st Armored Division orders Task Force Benson to attack, but strong enemy fire and land mines impede their progress. In the British Eighth and First Army areas, fighting continues to rage in the vicinity of Wadi Akarit and near Sedjenane with the latter falling to the British 46th Division. In other activity in North Africa, the political situation among the French is turbulent. DeGaulle is upset because he is not the "top gun." The U.S. position is to not name a leader for the French, while the English are pro-DeGaulle for the time. DeGaulle's supporters have been conspicuously interfering with the war effort and have even attempted to convince French Seamen in U.S. ports to desert and flee to Canada. It has also been noted in the United States that reports coming in from England declare that DeGaulle is closely tied to the communists.

March 31st 1943 — (Pacific-New Guinea) The U.S. 41st Division's MacKechnie Force is transported by sea to the mouth of the Waria River and the Dona Airstrip. **(Pacific-Samoa)** The 2nd Marine Brigade is dissolved in Pago Pago. **(Atlantic-North Africa-Tunisia)** In the U.S. II Corps area, the 1st Armored Division rams through a path which has been cleared of mines and continues to secure the road to the foothills. The 1st Armored Division loses nine Tanks during the assault. Elements of the 751st and 813th Tank Battalions, supporting the 109th Combat Engineers, strike the enemy on the northwestern slopes of Djebel Touila to divert attention from the attacking 34th Infantry operating 5 miles north of Fondouk Gap. Brutal fighting continues until the U.S. 34th Division withdraws on the 2nd of April to conclude the battle at Fondouk Gap and establish defensive positions. In the British Eighth Army area, Montgomery is informed of the possibility of high casualties if he attempts to cross Wadi Akarit, without awaiting reinforcements; he awaits the additional manpower. In the British 1st Army area, all objectives are accomplished. The British move to seize the Bedja-Medjez road to alleviate pressure against the heavily engaged Allies at Medjez Road. In other activity, the French 19th Corps links with the U.S. 34th Division at El Ala, just West of Fondouk.

April 1st 1943 — (United States) The United States Navy establishes an Air Station at Patuxent River, Md. In other activity, Marine Aircraft Group 53, commanded by Lt. Colonel Frank H. Schwable, is commissioned at Cherry Point, N.C., becoming the Marine Corps' first Night Fighter Squadron. **(North Atlantic)** In Greenland, the U.S. Navy initiates a Naval Operating Facility at Grondal. **(North Pacific)** D-Day for the Allied invasion of Attu in the Aleutians is set for May 7th. Admiral Kinkaid's Task Force 16 leads the operation. The assault troops (7th Division U.S.A.) are commanded by Major General Albert E. Brown. The 7th has been trained for mechanized warfare in the desert. **(Pacific-Russell Islands)** Japanese Aircraft strike American positions in the Solomons diverting from their normal attack of hitting the Allied Bases in New Guinea for the past 30 days. **(Atlantic-Tunisia)** General Bradley and two additional Generals visit the command post to check the progress of the operation. While there, German Planes bomb the area sending everyone flying for the ditches. Captain Dick Jensen, Patton's aide, is killed instantly. General Bradley a mere 10 feet away from Jensen at time of impact is unhurt. Patton, distressed by the death of his friend, accompanies the body to the cemetery. There is considerable alarm in the American camp because the British who have

claimed Air superiority are not able to contain the enemy raids; the German Air Force is flying at will and bombing all American Command posts. An official report puts British General Coningham in an uncomfortable position. He responds, accusing the American report of containing falsehoods and that the Americans are using the British Air Force as an alibi for their lack of success on the ground. Coningham continues to blast the American II Corps by stating: "IF SITUATION REPORT IS IN EARNEST AND BALANCED AGAINST ... FACTS IT CAN ONLY BE ASSUMED THAT II CORPS PERSONNEL CONCERNED ARE NOT BATTLE WORTHY IN TERMS OF PRESENT OPERATIONS." He further states: "12 AIR COMMAND HAVE BEEN INSTRUCTED NOT TO ALLOW THEIR BRILLIANT AND CONSCIENTIOUS AIR SUPPORT OF II CORPS TO BE AFFECTED BY THIS FALSE CRY OF WOLF." This particular type of British brandishing does not sit well with the Americans, especially Patton. A meeting to try to repair the damage occurs on the 3rd of April. **(Atlantic-Iran)** The U.S. Army Air Force is given responsibility of assembling Airplanes for the Russians at Abadan Air Base. Previously, Douglas Aircraft Company had the responsibility.

April 2nd 1943 — (United States) Colonel William (Wild Bill) Donovan who has been in the war effort as head of O.S.S. (Office of Strategic Services) serving as a civilian without compensation, is made a Brigadier General. Donovan, a Medal of Honor recipient (New York 69th Division) during World War 1 has been deeply involved with the U.S. effort to win the war and has created a gigantic organization of civilians and Military personnel that is employed dangerously in every theater. President Roosevelt had attempted to promote him during 1941, and again during 1942, however, isolationist Congressmen had blocked the move. During 1944, he is promoted to Major General. The O.S.S. creates many ideas, some of which are eccentric such as: land-mines which resemble Camel dung; lumps of coal containing high explosives, however, the organization employs over 30,000 people by the end of the conflict. An example of the more serious operation: Donovan mounts a strong Guerrilla Force for deployment in Asia. He forms it (O.S.S. Detachment 101) at Nazira Assam during February 1943. The men train in an area congested with Tigers, Cobras and Vampire Bats and are led by Captain Carl Eifler, Captain John Coughlin (both 35th Regiment) and Captain Ray Peters, who succeeds Eifler. An allegiance is quickly formed with a Catholic Priest, Father James Stuart who becomes interpreter for the Kachins. The Kachins, who detest the Japanese guide the Chindits and also accompany Merrill's Marauders, inflicting heavy casualties against the Japanese. Subsequently, when the Kachins report to General Stilwell that they have killed 10,000 Japs, Stillwell in disbelief snaps back. And how do you record your kills? One of the Kachin leaders opens a Bamboo pole and slides out items which resemble "dried prunes." Stilwell asks what the items are and receives the response: "JAPANESE EARS. DIVIDE THEM BY TWO AND YOU KNOW HOW MANY JAPS HAVE BEEN KILLED. **(Atlantic-Tunisia)** The U.S. offensive is stalled by fierce enemy resistance, seriously impeding the advance of the 1st and 9th Divisions in the vicinity of Gabes and Gumtree Roads. In other activity, General Patton visits a field hospital where General Dunphie is recuperating. One Soldier in the hospital ward mentions in conversation with Patton that he had surrendered after he was shot. General Patton responds definitively: "NO SOLDIER OF MINE

EVER SURRENDERS," and walks out. Patton frequently visits hospitals to speak with the wounded. On one occasion, an Army Nurse named Molly Boundy arranges for Patton to observe an operation.

April 3rd 1943 — (Pacific-Japan) The U.S.S. *Pickerel* (SS-177) sinks the Imperial Navy's Sub Chaser *No. 13*. **(Pacific-New Guinea)** The Mackechnie Force (U.S. 41st Division contingents) arrives at Morobe Harbor and establishes defensive positions. **(Atlantic-Tunisia)** Heated conflict rages in the U.S. II Corps sector near the Gumtree-Gabes Roads junction. The 1st Division penetrates the enemy lines and captures Sakket, but the 9th Division is halted short of Hill 772. British General Alexander informs General Patton that he is to prepare to support the north flank of the British First Army as soon as the enemy defenses at Wadi Akarit are destroyed. The British prepare for an assault which will include 500 Tanks. In other activity, Patton still is infuriated with British General Coningham's mis-handling of Air support, and his disparaging comments about the Americans. Apologies had come from Coningham, after some prompting by Ike, but the tone and content is not satisfactory to the II Corps. During a meeting with British Air Chief Marshall Tedder, who is fast to reiterate the British belief of their Air supremacy, four German Focke-Wulf 190 Fighters attack Gafsa, strafing the streets unmolested and the very building of the conference. General Spaatz in a moment of sarcastic humor during the attack, asks Patton how he had managed to promote the attack. Patton quips: "I'LL BE DAMNED IF I KNOW, BUT IF I COULD FIND THE SONS OF BITCHES WHO FLEW THOSE PLANES, I'D MAIL THEM EACH A MEDAL."

April 4th 1943 — (Pacific-Russell Islands) The final contingents of Aircraft Group 21 arrive on Banika Island. **(Atlantic-North Africa-Tunisia)** **18th Army Group**, 9 Corps Reserve prepares to recapture Fondouk Gap. In the U.S. II Corps sector, vicious fighting continues for control of Gabes and Gumtree Roads, however, the Germans repulse all attacks. Meanwhile, the British Eighth Army continues to prepare for attack; nearly 500 Tanks are now deployed in the area.

April 5th 1943 — Pacific-Solomons) The U.S.S. *O'Bannon* (DD-450), a Destroyer, sinks the Japanese Submarine RO-34. **(China-Burma-India)** The Japanese secure the Mayu Peninsula in Burma, as far north as Indin. The 26th Indian Division replaces the Indian 14th Division at the Front. **(Atlantic-Tunisia)** The efforts of the 1st and 9th U.S. Divisions are in vain against the firmly entrenched enemy. The U.S. anticipates an enemy counterattack, but it doesn't materialize because the enemy is intending to withdraw. General Orlando Ward (1st Armored Division) is relieved of command and replaced by General Ernest Harmon.

April 6th 1943 — (United States) Charles DeGaulle, self-appointed leader of the French, designates M. Bertand the Governor of French Guiana. The U.S. refuses transportation for them on U.S. Vessels.

April 6th-7th 1943 — (Atlantic-Tunisia) U.S. Forces are involved in heavy combat throughout the day. As night settles over the area, the enemy breaks off the engagement. Under cover of darkness and an Artillery barrage, Axis troops begin to withdraw to the east. British General Alexander instructs Patton to attack down the Gabes Road on the flank of the Germans as they attempt to withdraw. Patton sends his Benson force with the orders: "GO LIKE HELL FOR THE MEDI-

TERRANEAN COAST." Before 17:00, Benson advances 20 miles through the Eighth Army boundary and is in position to join the British at the Gafsa-Gabes Road. The U.S. 9th Division pushes feverishly toward Bou Chebka during the night of the 7th-8th, then relinquishes its sector to the 1st Division, enabling the Big Red One to conduct mop-up operations. Meanwhile, the British Eighth Army assaults Wadi Akarit, driving the enemy into retreat during the night of the 6th. Heavy fighting occurs as the Germans mount savage counterattacks, which impede Allied progress. The British call in all available Aircraft on the 7th to support the pursuit of the enemy along the Wadi Akarit Line. In addition, the British prepare to assault Fondouk on the eighth to cut off escape.

April 7th 1943 — (Pacific-Solomons) An order is issued by Japanese Admiral Yamamoto, commencing a campaign to drive the Allies from the Solomons and from New Guinea. An enemy Fighter and Bomber Force, exceeding 185 Planes, assaults American positions at Guadalcanal. The enemy force is intercepted by Allied Planes and a vicious encounter follows. During the tenacious Air Battle, Marine Fighter Squadron 221 attacks vehemently. Lt. James Swett leads his four Plane Section into a wave of 15 enemy craft. Swett destroys three in mid-air before becoming separated from his Unit. Afterward, he singlehandedly attacks six enemy Bombers, destroying four. Out of ammunition, he feints off another enemy Plane, with his windshield useless after being smashed by enemy fire. Swett safely scuttles his Plane off Tulagi and is subsequently awarded the Medal of Honor. Only light damage is sustained by the Americans at Guadalcanal; however, the enemy sinks the Destroyer U.S.S. *Aaron Ward* (DD-483). The Oiler *Kanawha* (AO-1) is also sunk. The Oiler *Tappanannock* (AO-43) and the Cargo Vessel *Adhara* (AK-71) are both damaged. In addition, the New Zealand Corvette *Moa* is sunk. The Japanese suffer heavy Plane losses, while the Allies lose seven. The enemy Air threat against Guadalcanal is now neutralized, but Japanese reinforcements land at Kolombangara without opposition because of the enemy's expensive diversionary maneuver. **(Atlantic-North Africa)** **18th Army Group** Planes of the XII Air Support Command and the WDAF scour the skies and attack the enemy as they retire on all fronts. Meanwhile, the U.S. II Corps establishes contact with the British Eighth Army and contingents of the Southeast Algerian Command as it moves along the Gafsa-Gabes road. Also, the 1st Division assumes responsibility for the 9th Division sector as it move to Bou Chebka; the 1st Ranger Battalion returns to Oran. Colonel Darby will be ordered by General Eisenhower to establish four additional Battalions.

April 8th 1943 — (Atlantic-Tunisia) **18th Army Group** Heavy fighting erupts as the British 9 Corps assaults Fondouk prior to dawn. The U.S. 34th Division and elements of the British 46th Division spearhead the operation to open a gap for the British 6th Armored Division. Air assistance is nonexistent because of rugged weather. General Patton issues General Orders 25: in part; "AFTER 22 DAYS OF RELENTLESS COMBAT IN MOUNTAINS WHOSE RUGGEDNESS BEGGARS DESCRIPTION, YOU HAVE WON THE BATTLE OF EL GUETTAR."

April 9th 1943 — (United States) The U.S. Navy reintroduces the rank of Commodore. **(Pacific-Celebes)** The U.S.S. *Tautog* (SS-199), sinks the Japanese Destroyer *Isonami*. **(Atlantic-Tunisia)** The battle for control of North Africa is beginning to turn to the Allies, but enemy opposition remains heated. Al-

Admiral Isoroko Yamamoto.

lied planes have been confined to daylight flights, but German Aircraft operate at will, devastating unprotected Allied ground troops. The German Pilots have three years of war experience, giving them an added edge. **18th Army Group** In the 9 Corps Area, the U.S. 34th and British 46th Divisions press forward to destroy enemy resistance in the heights surrounding Fondouk Pass. In one of many heroic incidents, Pvt. Robert Booker transports a light machine gun and ammunition across 200 yards of open ground through a storm of enemy fire. Although wounded, Booker knocks out an enemy nest. Shortly after this fire fight, an enemy mortar wounds Booker mortally, but he continues firing until he succumbs. Pvt. Booker receives the Medal of Honor posthumously. The British 6th Armored Division succeeds in breaching the pass, but loses many Tanks. A successful night attack by the 1st Battalion, 133rd U.S. Infantry secures the crest of Djebel el Haouareb after an earlier failed assault. The British 1st Army secures Chaouach, located in the mountains four miles Northwest of Medjez. Meanwhile, the British 8th Army still pursues the retreating enemy along the Gabes Gulf.

April 10th 1943 — (United States) The United States announces that the U.S.S. *Triton* (SS-201) is officially presumed lost. **(Atlantic-Tunisia)** Operation "VULCAN," British General Alexander's plan for the final offensive to win North Africa, is officially approved. The British First Army is to make the primary attack on Tunis, while the British Eighth Army pressures the South to sever Cap Bon from Tunis. The Americans are to operate on the flank of the British First Army as it

drives toward Bizerte. General Patton has complained in his records and to aides that the British are exploiting the Americans and attempting to gain all the glory for themselves by keeping the Americans out of the primary objectives. The U.S. 9th and 34th Divisions and half of the 1st Armored Division begin moving to North Tunisia for the assault on Bizerte, the latter advancing toward Faid Pass. This American endeavor will transfer in excess of 30,000 Vehicles and more than 110,000 men across the British supply line. The Yanks virtually move the massive depot at Tebessa to Bedja, a maneuver totally unexpected by the Germans holding the northern front. Supply Convoys stretch the entire distance from Tebessa to the El Guettar Front as the II Corps starts to relieve the British units operating in the area. In the British Eighth Army area, Sfax is seized by 30 Corps. In the British First Army area, the French 19th Corps controls Djeloula Pass. **(Atlantic-Austria)** A three day meeting between Hitler and Mussolini concludes at Klessheim Castle near Salzburg. The Duce's last-ditch effort to persuade Hitler to seek a separate peace with the Russians fails. Hitler ignores pleas for added reinforcements and equipment for the Mediterranean Theater, however Mussolini is promised 36 Heavy German Tanks by Reichsfuehrer S.S. Heinrich Himmler to form a special contingent of Fascist militia to maintain order in Rome.

April 11th 1943 — (Pacific-New Guinea) Japanese Aircraft sink two Allied Merchant Ships during a bombing raid against Oro Bay. **(Atlantic-Tunisia)** General Patton's firm request that the U.S. II Corps remain under the control of **18th Army Group** instead of the British First Army is accepted by British General Alexander. **18th Army Group** The 9 Corps' 6th Armored Division occupies Kairouan without incident and makes contact with the British Eighth Army. In the U.S. II Corps sector, the U.S. 9th Division moves into the British 5 Corps zone.

April 12th 1943 — (Pacific-New Guinea) Port Moresby is struck by a heavy Japanese Air attack that results in slight damage. **(Atlantic-North Africa-Tunisia)** In the British Eighth Army area, Sousse is seized by 10 Corps as it drives north. In the British First Army area, 5 Corps sector, the U.S. 9th Division begins relieving the British 46th Division.

April 13th 1943 — (Atlantic-North Africa-Tunisia) 18th Army Group In the British Eighth Army area, 10 Corps reaches German outer defenses at Enfidaville. Later efforts to reduce the town before it can be further fortified are unsuccessful.

April 14th 1943 — (Pacific-New Guinea) The Japanese make their last in a series of large Air raids on Allied positions in New Guinea with a heavy attack on Milne Bay, delivering only minor damage. **(Atlantic-North Africa) 18th Army Group** The Allies meet at General Alexander's Headquarters at Haidra to finalize the last phase of winning the Tunisian campaign. Meanwhile, the Germans cling to a confined area. Alexander's Western Forces are to surge through Medjez El Bab toward Tunis, then split into two groups, one spinning to assist the II Corps against Bizerte and the other moving south to sever the enemy escape route that would otherwise allow them safe passage to Cape Bon.

April 15th 1943 — (United States) The Navy commissions the Carrier *Yorktown* (CV-10) at Newport News, Virginia, to replace the *Yorktown* (CV-5), lost at Midway. **(Pacific-Russell Islands)** The first of two operational Airfields is fully operational. **(North Pacific-Aleutians)** Forward contingents of the 7th Division embark for the Attu operation, sailing for Adak. Other contingents depart for Dutch Harbor to meet one Destroyer and two Submarines for transportation on the final steps of the trip. **(Atlantic-Brazil)** The Italian Submarine *Archimede*, is destroyed off the coast of Brazil by U.S. Land-based Aircraft. **(Atlantic-Tunisia)** General Patton has turned the American II Corps into a formidable force. The battle for North Africa continues until early May, however, the enemy is in full retreat. The U.S. VI Corps, commanded by Major General Ernest J. Dawley, had arrived in North Africa a short time ago and Dawley is to command the Attack Force in Patton's Army, but the VI Corps instead, will be assigned to Fifth Army. In the British First Army area, 5 Corps sector, the Germans recapture Djebel el Ang and Tanngouche, however, the British 78th Division counterattacks, regaining the former and part of the latter.

April 16th 1943 — (Pacific-China) The Japanese make preparations to secure the Upper Yangtze to control Shipping. **(Atlantic-Tunisia) 18th Army Group** The Allies prepare the final thrust toward Tunis and Bizerte. The U.S. II Corps transfers its Headquarters from Gafsa to positions outside Bedja. The U.S. 1st Armored Division moves into British 5 Corps zone. In the British Eighth Army area, General Montgomery aborts the ongoing bantam strikes against Enfidaville and makes preparations for a strong assault to be launched against it on the night of the 19th. In the British First Army area, the British 78th Division improves its positions greatly at Medjez el Bab, eliminating any German threat.

April 17th 1943 — (Atlantic) The Coast Guard Cutter *Spencer* (PG-36) sinks the German U-Boat 175.

April 18th 1943 — (Pacific-Australia) General MacArthur and Admiral Halsey who have been conferring at Brisbane, Australia on Pacific strategy, decide on May 15th as the tentative date for the planned invasion of New Georgia. D-Day is subsequently changed to June 30th. **(Pacific-Guadalcanal)** Japanese Admiral Yamamoto flies from Rabaul toward the Solomons to inspect the Japanese positions. However, 18 U.S. P-38s intercept his entourage of two Bettys and six Fighters, killing Admiral Yamamoto, one of Japan's chief Military Leaders. American code-breakers set the stage and the ambush is sprung over Buin, about 35 miles outside of Ballale Island. Captain Thomas G. Lanphier, 339th Fighter Squadron makes the kill. General MacArthur would subsequently remark: "ONE COULD ALMOST HEAR THE RISING CRESCENDO OF SOUND FROM THE THOUSANDS OF GLISTENING WHITE SKELETONS AT THE BOTTOM OF PEARL HARBOR." On the 19th, at a morning meeting, at Halsey's Quarters the daring episode brings much discussion. Admiral Kelly Turner begins applauding and Halsey interjects: "HOLD ON, KELLY! WHAT'S SO GOOD ABOUT IT?" "I'D HOPED TO LEAD THAT SCOUNDREL UP PENNSYLVANIA AVENUE IN CHAINS WITH THE REST OF YOU KICKING HIM WHERE IT WOULD DO THE MOST GOOD." Admiral Halsey notes that the story is suppressed because Captain Lanphier's brother is a P.O.W. with the Japanese and there is great fear for his life if the Japanese determine that it had been his brother that killed Yamamoto. Halsey relates a few acts of Japanese hospitality that cause his concern: "I HAVE IN MIND THE NUNS THEY CAUGHT ON GUADALCANAL AND RAPED FOR FORTY-EIGHT HOURS BEFORE CUTTING THEIR THROATS; AND THE TWO MARINES

WHOM THEY VIVISECTED; AND THE YOUNG GIRL ON NEW GUINEA WHOM THEY FORCED TO WATCH HER PARENTS BEING BEHEADED, BEFORE HER OWN TURN CAME; AND THE EXECUTION OF GENERAL DOOLITTLE'S PILOTS; AND THE MARINE PILOT IN A PARACHUTE, WHOSE FEET WERE CHOPPED OFF BY THE PROPELLER OF A ZEKE." **(Atlantic-Mediterranean)** Operation FLAX: Allied Planes conducting search operations score high, intercepting more than 100 enemy Transport Planes plus Fighter escorts. The German lose 16 escort Aircraft and between 50 and 70 Transports during the Air duel, devastating the Axis resupply operation between Italy and Sicily. The Allies lose six PBYs and one Spitfire. In other air activity, Allied Planes pummel enemy held Airfields in Tunisia during the night of April 18th further weakening German Air Power.

U.S. P-38s such as the ones used to shoot down Admiral Yamamoto off the Solomons.

April 19th 1943 — (Pacific-Japan) The U.S.S. *Scorpion* (SS-278), operating in the vicinity of Kashima Nada, Japan, lays mines.

April 19th-21st 1943 — (Atlantic-Tunisia) The Allies continue preparations for the final Tunisia offensive. Sharp fighting erupts as the British Eighth Army attacks Enfidaville; the enemy falls back on the 19th. The enemy makes a futile attempt to mount a counterattack, using Infantry and Tank units against British 1st Army positions during the night of the 20th-21st, and sustain extremely high casualties.

April 20th 1943 — (Pacific-Hong Kong) The U.S.S. *Runner* (SS-275) lays mines in the vicinity of Hong Kong. **(Pacific-Samoa)** U.S. Army Bombers, based on Funafuti, Samoa attack enemy positions at Tarawa in the Gilberts. **(Atlantic-North Africa-Tunisia)** Enfidaville falls to the British Eighth Army but the Germans check the British firmly at Djebel Garci preventing further advance. **(Atlantic-Western Europe)** Along the Eastern Front, the Germans make good use of a captured Russian, General Vlassov, who had turned to the German cause. OPERATION SILVER STREAK commences. Vlassov sends agents into Russia to infiltrate and work toward getting Russian troops to desert. There are plans to organize an Army under Vlassov, however, Hitler rejects the idea during June. The endeavor, engineered by Colonel Reinhard Gehlen is successful; by the middle of May, over 6,000 Soviets defect. Colonel (later General Gehlen) feels that hundreds of thousands of anti-Stalin Russians would have joined the fight under the leadership of Vlassov.

Hill 409 (Sicily).

April 21st 1943 — (North Pacific-Aleutian Islands) Admiral Kinkaid issues the plan for the recapture of Attu. **(Pacific)** Marine Aircraft South Pacific is tentatively established to coordinate the administrative and logistical duties of the 1st and 2nd Marine Aircraft Wings. **(Pacific-Dutch East Indies)** The U.S.S. *Grenadier* (SS-210), operating between the Malay Peninsula and Sumatra, encounters an enemy Convoy in the Malacca Strait, but does not get an opportunity to attack; instead, an enemy Plane attacks, severely damaging it. During the following morning, the Submarine is ordered abandoned by Lt. Commander J.A. Fitzgerald. The Japanese pick up the American crew and imprison them; four men perish while interned. However, the balance overcome the severe treatment and are freed after the close of hostilities. **(China-Burma-India)** The U.S.S. *Stingray* (SS-186) lays mines near Wenchow, China. In other activity, Japanese Admiral Mineichi Koga becomes Commander in Chief, Japanese Combined Fleet. **(Atlantic-Tunisia) 18th Army Group** Plans for the VULCAN operation are finalized. The U.S. 34th Division moves out during the night of the 21st-22nd to deploy in the newly designated U.S. II Corps zone. In the British Eighth Army area, General Montgomery is unable to overcome enemy resistance at Takrouna and decides to confine his activity around the coast, ordering 8th Army to regroup; the attack is not resumed. Word of Montgomery's decision to cancel the offensive reaches the American II Corps, which has British advisors. General Bradley jokingly says to General William Kean: "LETS RADIO MONTY AND ASK IF HE WANTS US TO SEND HIM A FEW AMERICAN ADVISORS TO SHOW HIM HOW TO GET THROUGH THOSE HILLS." In the British First Army area, strong enemy counterattacks are thrown back at Medjez el Bab, costing the Axis heavy casualties.

April 22nd 1943 — (Pacific-Ellice Islands) Japanese Aircraft strike American positions at Funafuti. **(Atlantic-Tunisia) 18th Army Group** The final Allied offensive to rid Tunisia of Axis forces commences. The British 5 Corps drives north and south of Medjez el Bab. The British 78th Division reduces remaining resistance at Djebel Tanngouche, then advances toward Djebel el Ahmera (Longstop) Ridge. Further south, the British 1st and 4th Divisions secure Grich el Oued and Goubellat, respectively. Meanwhile, the British 9 Corps drives between Medjez el Bab and Bou Arada on the Goubellat plain to support the 5 Corps and demolish the German Armor reserves. The British 46th Division hits vicious opposition north of Sebkret el Kourzia. In addition, the British 6th Armored Division passes through Infantry positions and is in-

tercepted by enemy Armor. Allied Convoys continue flowing into the jump-off point. Many accidents occur due to the dangerous night runs, undertaken on treacherous mountain roads without the use of headlights.

April 23rd 1943 — (Pacific-Formosa) The U.S.S. *Seawolf* (SS-197), sinks a Japanese Patrol Boat off the coast of Formosa. **(Atlantic-England)** The Combined Chiefs of Staff direct the establishment of an Anglo-American Staff to plan the invasion of Western Europe. British Lt. General Sir Frederick E. Morgan, Chief of Staff to the Supreme Allied Commander (designate) heads the staff. **(Atlantic-Tunisia)** The U.S. II Corps, commanded by General Omar Bradley, drives toward Bizerte. The north flank, comprising the U.S. 9th Division, with French support, pushes toward Jefna, making average progress on the flanks, but the center thrust meets obstinate resistance near Djebel Ainchouna. The south flank, composed of the U.S. 1st Division, supported by the 6th U.S. Armored Infantry, 1st Armored Division, pushes along the rim of Mousetrap Valley toward Djebel Sidi Meftah, encountering iron resistance. RCT 26 is stopped short of Kef el Goraa (Hill 575), and RCT 16 fights to a stalemate on Hill 400, however, to the south, RCT 18 is clearing the northern side of the Tine River. In the British First Army sector, the British reduce resistance at Djebel Tanngouche and on most slopes along Djebel el Ahmera Ridge. Enemy reinforcements rush to the Goubellat Plain during the ongoing violent Tank confrontation.

April 24th 1943 — (United States) The primary body of the American Force, which will invade Attu (Aleutians), embarks from San Francisco, steaming toward Cold Harbor, Alaska. **(Atlantic-Tunisia)** The U.S. 9th Division continues its drive toward Jefna. RCT 60, seizes Djebel Dardyss. During the heated struggle, Sergeant William L. Nelson deploys his Heavy Mortar Squad before he advances to a precarious observation position to direct the mortar fire. His bravery, while directing his Squad's accurate firing, halts a fierce counterattack, at the price of his life, when a German hand grenade mortally wounds him. Sgt. Nelson is posthumously awarded the Medal of Honor for extreme heroism under fire. In other activity, the Germans inflict heavy casualties on RCT 39 (center Thrust), as the struggle for Djebel Ainchouna rages. In the 1st Division sector, heavy Artillery barrages pound German positions on Hill 575 (Kef el Goraa), enabling Rct 16, to seize it and simultaneously prevent encirclement. Hill 407 falls to RCT 18, and the 6th Armored Infantry is tenaciously engaged at Hill 388. The Germans begin withdrawing from the 1st Division front during the night of the 24th. Meanwhile, Rct 168, 34th Division, assumes responsibility for the northern flank positions of the 1st Division. On the British First Army Front (Goubellat), fiercely contested Tank and Infantry battles continue relentlessly, but are inconclusive. The British 1st Armored Division enters the inferno and trails the British 6th Armored Division, which pushes east.

April 25th 1943 — (Atlantic-Tunisia) In the U.S. II Corps sector, U.S. RCT 39, 9th Division, secures Djebel Ainchouna. The enemy begins retreating during the night as other contingents of the II Corps pursue. Rct 26 seizes Hill 575 during the daylight hours and forges ahead to Djebel Touta. Meanwhile, the 6th Armored Infantry, drives on the south side of the Tine River, overrunning several hills. Forward contingents of RCT 18, advance to Djebel Sidi Meftah. In the British First Army's 5 Corps sector, the British 78th Division seizes Heidous. In the 9 Corps sector, feverish Tank battles continue, but still, no decisive victory. However, the enemy withdraws from its right salient. In addition, the Germans pull back from positions south of a key road, permitting the French 19th Corps to advance.

April 26th 1943 — (North Pacific) U.S. Naval Force composed of Six Destroyers and three Cruisers, commanded by Rear Admiral McMorris, bombards Chichagof Harbor and Holtz Bay in the Aleutians (second Naval attack against Attu). **(South Pacific)** General MacArthur issues the third plan for the capture of the New Britain, New Guinea, and New Ireland area (ELKTON III). The plan also calls for mutual supporting advances from the Pacific, against Rabaul. The entire operation code name is CARTWHEEL. **(Atlantic-North Africa)** In Tunisia, American troops battle arduously for every yard against crack defenders entrenched along the 9th Division Front. Artillery fire pounds the hills. RCT 39, seizes Hill 513, southeast of Djebel Ainchouna. Meanwhile, RCT 47 encounters heavy enemy forces at Hill 598, southwest of Djebel Ajred. The 1st Division seizes its initial objectives, allowing the 1st Armored Division to take over the Tine Valley sector and prepare to assault Mateur. In the British First Army's 5 Corps sector, Djebel el Ahmera is secured by the 78th Division, while the British 1st Division drives within four miles from Djebel el Ahmera, reaching Djebel Bou Aoukaz. In conjunction, the British 4th Division advances to positions less than ten miles from Medjez el Bab. In the 9 Corps sector, enemy Armor now numbering three Divisions, halts the British on the Goubellat Plain. The British 6th Armored reverts to reserve. In Morocco, a U.S. Naval Station is established at Mers el Kebir.

April 27th 1943 — (Atlantic-Aleutians) The German U-Boat, *U-174* is tracked and sunk in the North Atlantic by Land-based Bombers (VB-125). **(Atlantic-Tunisia)** The American II Corps grinds toward Jefna, pushing four Divisions against severe resistance. The attack force battles feverishly, however, constant counterattacks subject the advance to minimal progress until the 30th. A Contingent of the U.S. 39th Infantry, 9th Division, advances to Hill 382, northwest of Djebel Azag, but is stalled by steadfast defenses for a period of four days. The U.S. 34th Division pounds toward Hill 609: RCT 168 reaches Djebel el Hara; RCT 135 to the right drives west of Hill 609, and seizes positions near Hill 490, however, fierce resistance forces a withdrawal. Other II Corps contingents including the 1st Armored Division, which advances along the southern flank of the Corps, hits stiff resistance. In the British First Army area, the Germans check the advance of the British 5 Corps with repeated counterattacks. British General Sir Kenneth Anderson (Commanding Officer Allied Force Tunisia) directs U.S. General Kean to move faster toward the Chouigui Pass, stating: "NEVER MIND THE ENEMY OPPOSING YOU AT SIDI NSIR. I DON'T WANT YOU ONLY TO PUSH THE ENEMY BACK, BUT TO GET BEHIND HIM AND CAPTURE HIM BEFORE HE CAN ESTABLISH A BRIDGEHEAD AROUND BIZERTE." In essence Anderson is instructing the Americans to abort the siege to gain the Hills, moving instead, through the Valleys below. If Bradley consents to this plan, Kean's troops become an easier mark for the enemy guns which command the high ground and they will be annihilated. The U.S. Big Red One (First Division), is already taking severe casualties. Bradley holds his ground and convinces Anderson that Hill 609, must be gained to ensure

Generals George S. Patton, Omar Bradley and Matthew Ridgway making preparations for the invasion of Sicily.

success for the operation. On the 30th, Djebel Guermach and the heights north of Jefna fall to the U.S. 9th Division. The 1st Division makes some gains, but soon loses them to strong enemy counterattacks. The 34th Division drives to the summit of Hill 609, with the aid of Tanks, which absorbs some of the intense enemy fire. The 1st Armored Division attacks; C.C.A. drives from Hill 315, but is repulsed at Hills 299 and 315, northeast of Djebel el Ang. Other contingents are driven from Hill 312. This hard fought campaign for control of Tunisia, ensues relentlessly until the final capitulation of the enemy on the 13th of May.

April 28th 1943 — (Pacific) The U.S.S. *Gudgeon*, heading for home after a successful mission in enemy waters, encounters terrible weather, including unpredictable rain squalls while moving between Palawan and Negros. About midnight the storm worsens as streaks of lightning illuminate the sky and expose a robust Japanese Vessel hurrying southward. The *Gudgeon*, fires four torpedoes; three strike the unsuspecting *Kamakura Maru*, a converted 17,000 ton Passenger Ship, sinking it. The *Gudgeon* continues toward port, however, on May 12th, she encounters the Freighter *Sumatra Maru*, and sinks it. **(Atlantic-Tunisia)** In the U.S. II Corps sector, the 9th Division probes east, reaching Kraim Lerhmed on the north and Kef Sahan on the south. The hills north of Hill 382 are taken by Rct 39, but Hill 382 remains under German control. Also, the II Corps attacks Hill 609, which stalls the 1st and 34th Division's center thrust. Ryder's 34th Division clings precariously to the fringes of 609, stalled by entrenched crack German troops, who hold the high ground. Attempts are made to flank the hill from the rear. General Bradley, in an unorthodox move, offers the assistance of Sherman Tanks with their fierce 75s to take the hill. Shermans are like fish out of water in this terrain, but their powerful guns turn the tide and cut the severity of the American casualties, while barraging the Germans. They are thrown turrets first, directly into the battle on the following day. In addition, elements of the 1st Division, seize a slim hold on Hill 531, situated south of Hill 609. Meanwhile, RCT 18, drives south through heavy resistance and secures part of Djebel Sidi Meftah. On the southern flank, Combat Command A, 1st Armored Division, captures Hill 315, then drives against heavily defended Hill 299. During a heated struggle near Medjez el Bab, Company A, 6th Armored Infantry is pinned down by heavy fire. At risk to his life, Pvt. Nicholas Minue singlehandedly with fixed bayonet attacks the hostile nest, and kills ten enemy machine-gunners and riflemen, then assaults another obstacle, however, ripping fire mortally wounds him. Private Minue's actions inspire his Company to take the offensive and expel the enemy. In the British 5 Corps area, the British cannot advance due to heavy enemy counterattacks. The British 4th Division pulls back from Ksar Tyr.

April 29th 1943 — (Pacific-Solomons) The U.S.S. *Gato* (SS-212) lands Coastwatchers on Teop Island and embarks with a group of endangered missionaries. **(Atlantic-North Africa)** British General Alexander orders the British Eighth Army to provide reinforcements for the British First Army to assist with the final drive to seize Tunisia. In the U.S. II Corps area, Seventeen Sherman Tanks and the 34th Division secure a hold on the southern slopes of Hill 609. It is the 34th Division which has been receiving the wrath of the British, who declare it unworthy of battle and request its transfer. Subsequently, the 34th Division lands in Italy where it remains on the front lines for two years and sustains about 20,000 casualties. In other activity, the 1st Division (Big Red One) advances along the northern rim of Mousetrap Valley, as the enemy begins to recoil in the hills of Chouigui, where Von Arnim draws his final defense line directly in front of Tunis. The II Corps begins to move around the enemy's right flank, while the British mount a frontal attack. General Terry Allen's 1st Division starts down the edge of Mousetrap Valley and crosses Chouigui road in conjunction with General Harmon's 1st Armored Division, which is blistering through the southern section of the valley, making greater progress than British General Anderson had thought possible. Harmon quickly readies his troops for a breakthrough at Mateur. Meanwhile, General Manton Eddy's 9th Division closes on Bizerte, via the Sedjenane Valley and deploys Artillery which begins to pound Jefna on the following day, forcing the Germans to withdraw (May 2nd) to avoid being isolated. In the 1st Division sector, RCT 16 battles against fierce resistance on Hill 523, making slight progress. Meanwhile, the 1st Armored's CCA continues driving doggedly through tough opposition on Hill 299.

April 30th 1943 — (United States) The U.S. relinquishes responsibility of escorting Convoys between Halifax, Nova Scotia and Great Britain. Responsibility passes from the U.S. Atlantic Fleet to the combined British and Canadian Navies. **(North Pacific)** The Attu Invasion Force, which departed San Francisco on the 24th, arrives at Cold Harbor in the Aleutians; final assault plans are prepared. **(Pacific-Philippines)** The Submarine *Gudgeon* (SS-221) lands specialized personnel (Filipino troops which have been trained in the U.S.) and equipment near Panay. **(China-Burma-India)** The U.S.S. *Snook* (SS-279) operating near Saddle Island, China, deposits mines. **(Atlantic-North Africa)** General Montgomery releases his 7th Armored and Indian 4th Infantry Divisions, plus the 201st Guards Brigade, to the British 1st Division. In the U.S. II Corps sector, RCT 60, 9th Division, closes on Kef en Nsour, and seizes Djebel Guermach. RCT 39 seizes formidable Hill 382 and overruns the high ground north of the Jefna positions. Meanwhile, the 34th Division, supported by Tanks, surges to the crest of Hill 609 and is met by sheets of fire. In the 1st Armored Division sector, fighting continues to rage on Hill 299, however, it remains under control of the Yanks. Meanwhile, RCT 16, seizes two hills east of Hill 609, then loses both to counterattacks; the 1st Armored Division commits Tanks to assist the Infantry efforts.

Late-April 1943 — (United States) At Great Falls, Montana, the Russians have a dilemma. Despite the shortage of Planes in U.S. Theaters of war in the Atlantic and the Pacific, it seems as if there is an abundance of Planes waiting to be flown to Fairbanks for the Russians. About 200 Aircobras are cramped on the field because no Pilots are available. The Russian, Colonel Kotikov, unwilling to accept the Pilot shortage begins screaming: "NEVER, NEVER, DOES RUSSIA HAVE A SHORTAGE OF PILOTS!" He continues to rant and rave, claiming that "HE COULD ORDER 10,000 PILOTS TO GREAT FALLS IN A MATTER OF DAYS," then informs the Americans: "AND YOU'LL HAVE TO FEED THEM." The Russians pull strings quickly. Within two days, their phone calls to the White House have Pilots scrambling in from all over. Colonel d'Arce, Commander of Gore Field is reamed out for breaking the rules, which strictly forbid procuring Pilots except through Air Transport Command. D'Arce is saved; the Russian Kotikov steps in and takes the credit stating he had become tired of waiting and decided to call Harry Hopkins. Also, during one hectic morning at Great Falls, Kotikov requests space for a special shipment of 2,000 pounds and is informed by Jordan that there is no room. Shortly afterward, the Russian tells Jordan to take the phone; Harry Hopkins wished to speak to him. There is some question that it could be an American Russian spy, however, Jordan notes that Hopkins inquires: "DID YOU GET THOSE PILOTS I SENT YOU?" Jordan then relates that Hopkins instructs him to expedite the special shipment of chemicals: "I DON'T WANT YOU TO DISCUSS THIS WITH ANYONE . . . AND IT IS NOT TO GO ON THE RECORDS." That in itself is not unusual. The terms of Lend-Lease stipulate rigidly that all Lend-Lease goods must be confined to supplies for the war effort, however, Major Jordan reports that the Russians receive well over one and one half billion dollars for agriculture products and over $3 billion for domestic industrial products, which includes an Amusement Park for Moscow. Also, Jordan reports that Lend-Lease provides the Russians with lip stick, cigarette cases, perfume, household goods, Bank vaults, antiques, women's jewelry, dolls, and one of Jordan's favorite's; one pipe at a cost of ten dollars. Ironically, Jordan states that no U.S. Government publication lists the specific shipments to Russia, however, his close contacts give him access to the Russian records, which he uses in his diary.

May 1943 — (Pacific-Manchuria) As the bitter cold weather begins to thaw in Manchuria, the Japanese permit the Americans to bury 150 of their deceased buddies who have been lying in barracks due to the frozen ground which forbid digging graves. The Japanese Staff and American troops attend the ceremony and one U.S. Soldier, seemingly pulling a Bugle out of a hat, blows Taps. Many of the Americans held in this camp are pooled out to the Manchurian Machine Tool Company, which had been designed by several American Engineers.

May 1st 1943 — (Atlantic-Europe) Allied Planes returning from a bombing mission over Europe are subjected to enemy Aircraft and Antiaircraft fire. In one incident, a Plane attached to the 423rd Bombardment Squadron, 306th Bomber Group, is severely damaged and set afire. Sergeant Maynard H. Smith singlehandedly fights the fires and expels exploding ammunition canisters from the Plane. In addition, he commandeers a gun and drives off the hostile Planes. His reckless disregard for his own life saves the injured crew, and he is awarded the Medal of Honor. **(Atlantic-North Africa-Tunisia)** The Allies **(18th Army Group)** organizes for the final offensive to win Tunisia. In the U.S. II Corps sector, the faltering Germans begin abandoning positions after nightfall. Their attempts to recapture Hill 609 fail and the final enemy remnants on Hill 299 are eliminated. The 1st Armored prepares to attack Mateur. In the British First Army area, the French 19th Corps reorganizes for a final attack.

A U.S. Minebreaker used to clear the way for Infantry and Armor.

May 2nd 1943 — (United States) The U.S. Coast Guard Cutter, 58012, sustains an explosion off Manoet Point, Massachusetts and sinks. **(Pacific-Solomons)** The Japanese Command at Rabaul establishes the Southeast Detached Force for the defense of the central Solomons. **(Atlantic-North Africa)** In the U.S. II Corps sector, Kef en Nsour is occupied by RCT 60, 9th Division subsequent to the Germans abandoning it.

May 3rd 1943 — (United States) General Marshal informs General Stilwell that the President has decided to commit a major U.S. Air effort in China. Also, Stilwell is instructed to continue preparing a modified ANAKIM (recapture of Burma). **(Atlantic-Mediterranean)** Landing sites for the Allied invasion of Sicily are finalized. General Eisenhower stipulates that the American and British troops designated for the assault, land abreast on the southeast coast of Sicily. In Tunisia, the enemy is retreating out of Mateur, as the American 1st Armored Division approaches. The U.S. 34th Division

drives east without opposition toward Chouigui. American General Andrews, Commanding Officer European Theater of Operations, is killed in a Plane crash in Iceland. He is replaced by Lt. General Jacob Devers.

May 4th 1943 — (United States) Generals Stilwell and Chennault attend a Joint Chiefs of Staff meeting. Stilwell requests that the "limited Transports available" be shared by Air and Ground forces alike. **(North Pacific)** The U.S. Attu invasion force embarks from Cold Harbor heading for Attu. Inclement weather which has already stalled the operation, postpones D-Day until the 11th. **(Atlantic-Tunisia) 18th Army Group** In the U.S. II Corps area, German Planes raid American positions at newly won Mateur. Meanwhile, Corps deploys for the attack against Bizerte, scheduled for the 6th. In other activity, the British 1st Army prepares for yet another attack against Tunis. In support, General Spaatz's Airmen fly over 2,000 sorties, blasting a path between Medjez el Bab and Tunis. These airborne arsenals deposit enormous amounts of shells on the enemy. The attack, which is spearheaded by two Infantry Divisions, followed by two Armored Divisions, is further supplemented by over 1,000 guns. **(Atlantic-Italy)** Mussolini confers with Field Marshal Kesselring to decide strategy for dealing with the Allies subsequent to the Tunisia campaign. Kesselring offers the use of one German Division for the Italian mainland. On the 6th of May the offer is raised.

May 5th 1943 — (Southwest Pacific) General Headquarters issues a warning order to the New Britain Force for the occupation of western New Britain. **(Atlantic-Tunisia)** The U.S. II Corps' 1st Armored Division seizes Djebel Achkel, but firm opposition remains on the eastern slopes until the 11th. Meanwhile, RCT 47, 9th Division, secures ground northwest of Djebel Cheniti. In other activity, the 1st Division advances to the west bank of the Tine River, while the 34th Division pushes Patrols toward Eddekhila. In the British V Corps area, Djebel Bou Aoukaz is captured by the British 1st Division, which receives assistance from both Aircraft and Artillery.

May 6th 1943 — (Southwest Pacific) GHQ issues Warning Instructions for Operation CARTWHEEL, the drive on Rabaul. **(Atlantic-North Africa-Tunisia)** The Allies **(18th Army Group)** initiate the final assault (VULCAN) on Tunis, supported by the largest Air bombardment yet committed in North Africa. The British First Army (9 Corps) drives half way to Tunis, reaching Massicault with its 6th and 7th Armored Divisions. The U.S. II Corps hits stiff resistance, as it advances. Enemy fire stalls a Contingent of the 1st Infantry Division, at the West Bank of the Tine River. The U.S. 47th Infantry (9th Division), clears the hills North of Djebel Cheniti, while the 60th Regiment drives into the town and secures most of it. General Bradley orders General Manton Eddy to speed up his advance. General Eddy informs Bradley: "THE ROAD TO BIZERTE IS LOUSY WITH MINES, OMAR. WE CAN'T EVEN PUT A JEEP OVER IT, UNTIL THE ENGINEERS CLEAR IT." Bradley responds: "THEN GET OFF YOUR TRUCKS AND BEGIN WALKING, BUT GET THE HELL INTO BIZERTE." The U.S. First Division sends its 18th and 26th Regiments, reinforced by Company H, 1st Armored Regiment, across the Tine, but during the night of the 6th, they are driven back to the west bank, by elements of the German Barenthin Regiment, composed of Luftwaffe Volunteers from the Glider school at Posen and the Parachute school at Witsock. The vicious enemy counterattack keeps control of the

Chouigui Hills in the hands of the Germans. **(Atlantic-Italy)** German General der Infanterie Enno von Rintelen informs OKW that the Italian Armed Forces "HAVE NOT UP TO NOW FULFILLED THE MISSIONS ASSIGNED THEM IN THIS WAR AND HAVE ACTUALLY FAILED EVERYWHERE." He places blame on the poor training of Officers and lack of proper equipment and armament. He further emphasizes that only with German support could the Italians withstand an Allied invasion. In another meeting between Mussolini and Kesselring, Mussolini is informed that Hitler has authorized additional troops including many units (about three Divisions) which had been stranded in Italy, unable to assist in Tunisia because of lack of transportation. More support is offered on the 10th.

A 105-mm Howitzer Motor Carriage on maneuvers in England, preparing for the invasion of France.

May 7th 1943 — (Pacific-Solomons) U.S. Warships lay mines in the Kula Gulf near the Blackett Strait. **(Pacific-Burma)** Japanese pressure forces the Indian 26th Division to pull out of Buthidaung and retire northwest. **(Atlantic-Tunisia)** The American II Corps (9th Division) secures the hills as they push through the fragile northern front of the enemy. General Manton S. Eddy radios Headquarters: "BELIEVE ROAD TO BIZERTE WIDE OPEN. Request permission to proceed." The message is transmitted at 15:00 and confirmed. By 15:30, Tank Destroyers speed forward. Contingents of the 894th Tank Destroyer Battalion and the 751st Tank Battalion roll into Bizerte by 16:00, finding few enemy troops; however, the streets are permeated with mines and deadly booby traps. The 1st Ar-

mored Division charges through Ferryville and secures an important bridge at Oued ben Hassein. The 34th Division stalls near Chouigui Pass, however, resistance ceases when the enemy withdraws during the early morning of the 8th. The British First Army seizes St. Cyprien and Le Bardo, subsequently entering Tunis at 16:00. With capitulation of both Bizerte and Tunis, the last two German-held cities, General Harmon's 1st Armored Division roars out of Bizerte toward Ferryville to cut off the rear escape route of the enemy, which is now trapped between Tunis and Bizerte.

May 8th 1943 — (Pacific-Solomons) The Kula Gulf becomes a noisy place on this otherwise tranquil Saturday. Japanese Vessels are barraged by a combination of U.S. Aircraft and well placed mines as they travel through the gulf. The excursion costs the Japanese three Destroyers; the *Kagero*, *Oyashio*, and the *Kuroshio*. **(Atlantic-North Africa-Tunisia) 18th Army Group** In the U.S. II Corps area, the Corps Franc d'Afrique enters Bizerte (this Corps had flanked the Americans during the drive on Bizerte). U.S. troops move out of Bizerte to converge with the British, who are moving from Tunis. The advancing British First Army hits stiff resistance as it moves to hook up with the Americans. Intense enemy fire from rear guards stalls the British at Hamman Lif defile (a narrow pass). The British 5 Corps' 1st Division and the Indian 4th Division, move east alongside the French 19th Corps in the Zaghouan area. The Royal Navy, anticipating a major Axis evacuation by sea, dispatches all available Vessels in the Mediterranean to designated areas. The maneuver is dubbed "Operation RETRIBUTION," however, the Royal Navy only spots several smaller Vessels and Merchant Ships, which quickly come under fire. The Italian Navy, desperately needed to make evacuation successful, fails to venture from docks at Spezia and Taranto.

May 9th 1943 — (Pacific-China-Burma-India) General Wheeler, Commanding General S.O.S., is ordered to take charge of U.S. operations at Assam Airfield project. **(Atlantic-North Africa-Tunisia) 18th Army Group** In the U.S. II Corps area, General Harmon, speaking with General Bradley on the field phone, requests instructions from Bradley: "A COUPLE OF KRAUTS JUST DROVE IN UNDER A WHITE FLAG. THEY WANT TO TALK SURRENDER. WHAT DO YOU WANT ME TO TELL THEM? OR DO YOU WANT TO COME UP AND HANDLE THIS STUFF YOURSELF?" Bradley responds in part: "JUST TELL THEM WE HAVE NO TERMS. IT MUST BE UNCONDITIONAL SURRENDER." Bradley then directs Harmon: "HAVE ROSE (Colonel) MAKE CERTAIN THEY DON'T DESTROY THEIR WEAPONS," and further states: "IF WE CATCH THEM TRYING TO DESTROY THEIR STUFF, THE ARMISTICE IS OFF. WE'LL SHOOT THE HELL OUT OF THEM." At noon, the U.S. II Corps accepts unconditional surrender of all enemy troops in its sector. Six Generals, including German Generals Von Arnim, Fritz Krause and Gustav von Vaerst and Italian General d'Armata Giovanni Messe are among the thousands of prisoners. General Harmon informs Bradley, that when the Generals reported to Headquarters in the afternoon, they were in full dress uniform. Their dress code sparks Harmon to tell Bradley: "YOU WOULD HAVE THOUGHT THE BASTARDS WERE GOING TO A WEDDING." The U.S. 1st Armored Division rushes to the coast and makes contact with the British 7th Division. Still, the British First Army is stalled at Hamman Lif defile and unable to terminate enemy resistance within its sector. **(Atlantic-Mediterranean)** Preparations to seize Pantelleria (Operation CORKSCREW) prior to Operation HUSKY, the seizure of Sicily is begun.

May 10th 1943 — (North Pacific-Aleutians) Two U.S. Vessels, the Destroyer *MacDonough* (DD-351) and the *Sicard* ((DM-221), a Light Minesweeper, collide in the unpredictable ruthless waters near the Aleutians and are damaged. On the following day, American troops land on Attu. **(Pacific-Russells-Solomons area)** Japanese Planes based in Rabaul attempt to strike American positions in the Solomon and Russell Islands, but are intercepted by U.S. Planes, which drive them back to their Base. **(Atlantic-Tunisia)** The British First Army (6th Armored Division), breaks through at Hamman Lif Pass and moves quickly toward Hammamet and isolates the Cap Bon Peninsula; mop-up operations clear the remnant enemy forces. **(Atlantic-Italy)** Hitler offers Mussolini five full strengthed Mobile Divisions to defend Italy, however, Mussolini is uneasy about the Germans, and is convinced the Allies will land in France. After conferring with General Ambrosio, he decides to decline (12th) the offer, tilting the balance in the German-Italian relationship.

May 11th 1943 — (North Pacific-Alaska-Aleutians) During February, a decision had been made to bypass Kiska and to seize Attu, 200 miles west to further isolate the Japanese on Kiska. Both islands have been held by Japanese since June of 1942, unmolested by ground troops. However, they have been under constant air bombardment. During its initial air strikes, the 11th Air Force had few Planes to pound Kiska, but Colonel William O. Eareckson made their presence known to the Japs who became so familiar with his voice that they would radio him and say: "WE'LL GET YOU ERICK;" as he flew overhead singing the West Point Fight Song (using different lyrics). A Naval Task Force under Admiral Thomas Kinkaid prepares for invasion. The Armada comprises three Battleships, six Heavy Cruisers, one Light Carrier, and five overcrowded Transports laden with 11,000 men in addition to many support Vessels. About 2,600 Japanese defend the island. Despite bad weather, which hinders the Naval guns, and impenetrable fog, the U.S. 7th Division moves toward the beach subsequent to circling offshore for over seven hours. A Picket boat leads the Landing Craft toward shore, then halts and its Captain announces by megaphone: "the beach is 300 yards dead ahead," as the invasion force blindly inches forward. The Southern Landing Force hits the beaches (Blue and Yellow) at Massacre Bay, in the afternoon; the troops drive north toward Jarmin, but the Japanese holding high ground at Massacre Valley halt the advance by about 19:00 with impassable fire. Meanwhile, a Platoon of the 7th Reconnaissance Troop lands at Alexis Point and moves to the main body at Massacre Bay without incident. The Northern Landing Force strikes at Holtz Bay (Beach Red) and pushes toward Jarmin Pass from the south, advancing to about 800 yards from Hill X, its first objective without opposition. In addition, a Provisional Battalion lands on the north coast, west of Holtz Bay (Beach Scarlet) prior to dawn and it also advances inland toward the pass without incident. Disastrous road conditions, caused by knee-deep mud, immobilize the trucks, but General Albert E. Brown (CG 7th Division), sets the following day for the assault on Jarmin Pass. Some enemy small arms fire develops during the day, however, the Japanese make no attempt to engage the invasion force. As darkness sets in on the dreary island, a chilling rain does little to ease conditions for the men in the foxholes, which are only a few feet deep because the ground is frozen

solid. Lt. General John L. De Witt had requested that the 35th Division make the invasion because its Commanding General had been familiar with the Aleutians, however, the 7th Division, which had been trained for desert warfare has the job. In addition, Military strategists in California anticipate a short operation of about three days, despite warnings from General Bruckner and other Staff Officers that it would be a long process. Intense fighting continues to rage for weeks, as the Japanese retain the high ground and refuse to capitulate. The frozen terrain and frostbite take a bigger toll on the Yanks, than that suffered against the Japanese. The Northern and Southern Forces finally secure Attu on the 31st of May. The civilians on Attu, which had been captured previously by the Japanese, had at first been used mostly as fishermen to feed the troops, however, subsequently, they are taken to Japan and used as laborers for pay; they are not held as regular prisoners. Forty-four Attuans are taken to Japan; 24 will die of tuberculosis while there. Preparations for the invasion of Kiska are finalized after the capture of Attu. **(Pacific-China-Burma-India)** The monsoon rains arrive bringing a succinct halt to construction on the Ledo Road about forty miles from Ledo. **(Atlantic-North Africa)** In Tunisia, although the bulk of German forces have capitulated, a small pocket of Hermann Goering Division remnants remains at Djebel Achkel, and require special treatment. U.S. Colonel Benjamin A. Dickson instructs captured German General Gustav von Vaerst to order them to surrender. His orders are delivered under the protection of a white flag to this group of about 300 well-armed stragglers. Before surrendering, they require a certificate stating they are among the last to surrender. The Americans refuse the demand, but the Germans receive some extra persuasion from a U.S. Battalion Commander and they soon quit.

Old Glory on Attu.

May 12th 1943 — (United States) President Roosevelt and Winston Churchill meet in Washington with their Military advisors; the conference (Trident) convenes until the 25th. The British contingent had departed England on May 4th on the *Queen Mary* and upon arrival in New York, moved by train to Washington. Also, the U.S. Navy announces that the Submarine U.S.S. *Pickerel* (SS-177), is lost in the Central Pacific (1st Submarine lost in Central Pacific), cause unknown. The *Pickerel*, commanded by Lt. Commander A.. H. Alston departed Pearl Harbor on March 18th (7th War Patrol). She sinks the Sub Chaser 13, and the Freighter *Fukuei Maru*, on April 3rd and 7th, respectively, and receives orders to return to Pearl on May 1st. The Japanese report an attack against a

Submarine on April 13th near Honshu; the *Pickerel* is the only Submarine which could have reached the area near Shiramuka Lighthouse. **(North Pacific-Aleutians)** On Attu, heavy fighting continues as the 7th Division attacks toward Jarmin Pass from two directions. Frontal attacks from Massacre Bay make no headway. Meanwhile, contingents of the Northern Attack Force gain small hold on Hill X. **(Pacific-Japan)** The Submarine U.S.S. *Steelhead* (SS-280) lays mines off Erimo Saki, Japan. **(Pacific-Solomons)** Japanese held Vila and Munda are struck by an Allied Naval bombardment during the night and into the early morning of the 13th. **(Pacific-China-Burma-India)** The 26th Indian Division evacuates Maungdaw, ending the first Arakan campaign where it began. The Chinese had aborted their expected drive from Yunnan into Burma and necessary assistance from the 4 Corps in Assam had been insufficient, greatly contributing to the failure of the mission. **(Atlantic-North Africa-Tunisia)** The enemy is surrendering in large numbers in the 18 Corps' southern sector. German General von Arnim is among the capitulants. In other activity, the U.S. Navy establishes an Advanced Amphibious Training Base at Bizerte.

An M2A1 Howitzer bolsters the Holtz Beachhead.

May 13th 1943 — (Pacific) U.S. Rear Admiral W. L. Ainsworth's Destroyer-Cruiser Force is heavily engaged off the Solomons, pounding enemy positions at Munda and Vila. Other Vessels lay mines near the northwestern approaches to the Kula Gulf. In other activity, two U.S. Ships are damaged by accidental explosions; the Destroyer *Nicholas* (DD-449) and the Light Cruiser *Nashville* (CL-43). **(Atlantic-North Africa)** The North African Campaign officially ends. In Tunisia, Italian General Messe (Rommel's successor) surrenders. Messe is informed of his promotion to Marshal today. The Germans had been fighting fiercely for control of Africa and the Suez Canal but wind up with neither. In other activity, General Eisenhower asks General Bradley if he is ready to join Patton on the Sicilian invasion. Soon after, General Bradley's II Corps boards Ships and heads up the North African Coast. Bradley leaves Mateur and reaches Constantine, where General Spaatz dispatches an Aircraft to pick him up. **(Atlantic-Mediterranean)** U.S. Army Planes attack and sink an Italian Submarine, the *Mocenigo* at Cagliari, Sardinia.

May 14th 1943 — (United States) The Joint Chiefs of Staff confer in Washington with Roosevelt and Churchill in attendance. British Field Marshal Wavell expresses indifference to the Burma campaign. General Stilwell continues to emphasize

the "necessity of building up the Chinese Ground Forces." U.S. General Chennault sides with Chiang Kai-shek's philosophy of maximum Air support. **(North Pacific-Aleutians)** American Aircraft are again hindered by terrible weather while supporting ground troops which are attempting to seize Jarmin Pass (Attu). U.S. Naval Surface Ships keep pressure on the enemy by continuing the bombardment of enemy positions. **(Atlantic-Pantelleria Island)** The Mediterranean Air Command initiates an Air and Sea blockade of the island to prevent the Germans from discovering Allied intentions to invade Sicily. Within a few days, U.S. General Spaatz commences an Air assault, which continues until June 11th, when British troops storm the island. **(North Atlantic)** Naval Land-based Aircraft (VP-84), attack destroy the U-Boat *U-657*.

May 15th 1943 — (United States) The Combined Chiefs of Staff prioritize construction of Assam Airfields and set a goal of 7,000 tons per month to China, to be attained by July 1st. **(North Pacific-Aleutians)** The Americans continue attacking deeply entrenched enemy positions on Attu, making slow progress within the Southern sector (Massacre Bay). The Northern Force (Holtz Bay) is delayed by a thick fog, which delays the attack. When the fog lifts, it becomes obvious that the enemy has evacuated their entrenched positions and retreated to high ground on a nearby ridge. The U.S. troops pursue the enemy across the valley, meeting heavy fire from the heights. During the confrontation, Allied Planes, attempting to strike the enemy, mistakenly bomb the U.S. 7th Division. In other activity, the Navy establishes a Naval Air Station at Adak. **(Pacific-Solomons)** The U.S. Navy establishes an Advanced Naval Facility in the Solomons. In addition, a Naval Air Facility is established in the Russell Islands. **(Pacific-China)** Chiang Kai-shek orders General Chen to return to Ichang to defend the area because of intensified Japanese activity in central China. **(Atlantic)** U.S. Naval Planes attached to VS-62, combine with a Cuban Submarine Chaser (No.13) and sink the German Submarine *U-176*, off the coast of Cuba.

May 16th 1943 — (North Pacific-Aleutians) American General Albert E. Brown is replaced by Major General Eugene Landrum on Attu in an effort to accelerate completion of the operation. U.S. forces grind toward Holtz Valley Ridge. The Japanese withdraw during the night to make a final stand at Chichagof Harbor. Some Naval Vessels, under Admiral Rockwell, move further north to safer positions, with the remaining Vessels under the command of American Captain H.B. Knowles. **(Atlantic-Germany)** RAF Planes assault Moehne and Eder dams, flooding the Ruhr. German Antiaircraft fire downs about ten Planes. **(Atlantic)** The Destroyer *MacKenzie* (DD-614), patrolling off Morocco, near the Portuguese Madeira Islands, sinks a German Submarine, the U-182. On the following day, another German Submarine, the U-128, snooping off the coast of Brazil is sunk by Land-based Bombers (VP-74), along with two Destroyers, the *Jouett* (DD-396) and the *Moffett* (DD-362).

May 17th 1943 — (North Pacific-Aleutians) The Massacre Bay Force occupies Jarmin Pass and dispatches a Patrol to make contact with the Northern Force. On the following day, prior to dawn, the two forces link and prepare for a major assault against Japanese positions at Chichagof Harbor.

May 18th 1943 — (North Pacific-Aleutians) On Attu, a Patrol of the Massacre Bay front establishes contact with the Holtz

Bay Force prior to dawn. Holtz Bay is now used by the Americans, speeding up the supply lines of the Northern Attack Force. Meanwhile, contingents of the 32nd Regiment swoop through the entire Holtz Bay Valley, discovering no enemy troops. **(Atlantic-Mediterranean-Pantelleria)** Porto di Pantelleria and Marghana Airfields are hit by an intense Allied Air Raid, carried out in conjunction with the Naval blockade imposed upon Pantelleria. Heavy Air raids continue until early June and are concentrated against underground Airdromes. The Planes include R.A.F. Wellingtons and U.S. B-17s, the combined power of which will drop over 5,000 bombs prior to the invasion.

May 11th 1943 — At Holtz Bay in Attu, trucks and tractors are coming ashore.

May 19th 1943 — (North Pacific-Aleutians) The U.S. 2nd Battalion, 17th Infantry, supported by Company C, 32nd Infantry, meets heavy resistance, but it captures the pass leading to Sarana Valley. The enemy, however, retains two peaks which peer down on the pass (subsequently named Clevesy Pass). On the Northern Front, a Contingent of the 32nd Infantry, begins clearing the Holtz-Chichagof Pass and is met by heavy fire near Fish Hook Ridge. **(Pacific-Solomons)** Thirty TBFs attached to Marine Scout Bomber Squadron 143 and Navy Torpedo Squadron 11, escorted by six Heavy Bombers, mine Buin-Kahili off Bougainville.

May 20th 1943 — (United States) The U.S. Tenth Fleet is established under the jurisdiction of Admiral King, Commander in Chief, U.S. Fleet, and will oversee Anti-Submarine

efforts in the Atlantic Theater. In other activity, the Director of Aviation, U.S.M.C., also becomes Assistant Commandant (Air). **(North Pacific-Aleutians-Attu)** The Japanese realize their positions are untenable against the determined inch by inch advance of the Americans, but their guns still hold commanding positions. The Commanding Officer sends the following message to Japan: "THE ENEMY AIR FORCE BOMBED AND STRAFED, WHILE THE NAVAL GUNS SHELLED OUR TROOPS WHICH SUSTAINED HEAVY CASUALTIES. NONE OF THE OFFICERS AND MEN WERE AT ANY TIME DISCOURAGED OR DEMORALIZED. ON THE CONTRARY WE ARE FIRMLY DETERMINED TO DIE ON ATTU TO DEFEAT THE ENEMY. **(Pacific-Burma)** The Chindit Division announces the completion of its mission and returns to India. Over 30 percent of the original force is lost during the three month operation to disrupt the enemy behind the lines. British Brigadier General Orde C. Wingate's force had been supplied entirely by Air during the three-month operation, and is guided through the jungles by natives (Kachins) who work with the O.S.S. Also, British General Sir George Giffard replaces Lt. General N.M.S. Irwin as Commander of Eastern Army. **(Atlantic-North Africa)** The Allies stage a victory parade in Tunis. Ground rules for participation, clearly spell out token participation by all forces, however, as the parade passes the reviewing stand, it is clearly evident that the ranks are bulging with French Colonial troops. A Contingent of the U.S. 34th Division represents the United States. Neither General Patton or General Bradley are asked by Eisenhower to join the Allied Commanders on the reviewing stand. **(Atlantic-Austria)** German Generals including Keitel and Rommel confer with Hitler at his Headquarters concerning the situation in Italy. On the 22nd, OKW issues Plan ALARICH, to be instituted if Italy moves to the Allied side or if Fascism collapses. ALARICH specifies transferring forces from the Eastern Front to occupy northern Italy in synchronization with the withdrawal of Germans from the balance of the Italian boot. However, when the obvious threat lessens, Hitler chooses to launch an attack in the east, draining the necessary forces to bolster ALARICH; Rommel will have only about eight Divisions, rather than the anticipated thirteen or fourteen.

May 19th 1943 — U.S. Infantry moving through a pass toward Holtz Bay en route to hook up the two U.S. assault forces.

May 21st 1943 — (United States) During a Joint Chiefs of Staff meeting in Washington, a representative of Chiang Kai-shek (Dr. Soong), meets with Admiral Leahy and claims the Generalissimo will not commit anything to the Burma campaign, until the Allies attack the Japanese at Rangoon. **(Atlan-**

tic-North Africa) The Italian Navy loses another Submarine, the *Gorgo*, to the Destroyer U.S.S. *Nields* (DD-616) off Algeria. **(Pacific-China)** The Japanese open the final phase of their campaign in Central China.

May 22nd 1943 — (North Pacific-Aleutians) The Massacre Bay Force (Southern) secures the high ground leading to the entrance of Chichagof Valley and penetrates the valley. U.S. troops, with the capture of this terrain, now command an easy route to Chichagof. The Northern (Holtz Bay) Force holds in place, awaiting the assault against Fish Hook Ridge. The U.S. forces are plagued by improper clothing and inadequate boots which hinder the operation on the frigid terrain. **(Atlantic-North Africa)** The Navy establishes an advanced Amphibious Training Base in Tunisia. **(Pacific-India)** General Wheeler is instructed to speed up the construction project of the Assam Airfields. **(North Atlantic)** Planes (VC-9), attached to the Escort Carrier *Bogue* (CVE-9), sink the *U-569* Submarine in the North Atlantic. **(Atlantic-Italy)** Mussolini agrees to accept four German Divisions (15th and 90th Panzer Grenadier Divisions and the 16th, and Hermann Goering Divisions). Also, the Italians reluctantly accept General der Panzertruppen Hans Valentin Hube (XIV Panzer Corps) and his Staff to oversee training of the German units. **(Atlantic-Soviet Union)** The dissolving of Comintern is announced in Moscow.

May 23rd 1943 — (United States) Philadelphia, Pennsylvania; celebrates the commissioning of the newest Battleship, the *New Jersey* (BB-62). **(North Pacific-Aleutians)** The Northern Force (Holtz Bay) dispatches Patrols to puncture enemy defenses at Holtz-Sarana Pass, but the attempt is stalled by heavy enemy fire. Also, the Japanese halt elements of the Southern Force (Massacre Bay) at Fish Hook Ridge. Communications are finally linked between the two U.S. forces and preparations for a major assault are made. **(South Pacific)** Generals MacArthur and Sutherland inform General Whitney that because of his vast knowledge of the Philippine Islands and its people, he will take responsibility for overseeing the Filipino resistance movement and report directly to Sutherland and MacArthur. As the meeting takes place, Filipinos are already training in the United States. General MacArthur's Chief of Intelligence Officer is Major General Charles A. Willoughby and his planning staff is headed by Major General Stephen J. Chamberlain. **(Pacific-Solomons)** Japanese Bombers attack and sink the U.S.S. *Niagra* (AGP-1), a PT Boat Tender, in the vicinity of the Solomon Islands. **(Pacific-New Caledonia)** In New Caledonia, in the Southwest Pacific, west of Australia, a Japanese Submarine sinks two PT Boats, Nos. 165 and 173. **Pacific-Samoa)** The 22nd Marines are detached from the 3rd Marine Brigade and transferred to Tutuila to operate as a separate tactical unit; on the 27th it is organized as the Garrison Force, Defense Force, Samoan Group. **(Atlantic-North Africa-Tunisia)** The successfully completed North Africa campaign, allows the Allies to disband the **18th Army Group.**

May 24th 1943 — (United States) The Joint Chiefs of Staff authorize plans for the invasion of Kiska in the Aleutians, however, the Japanese decide on June 8th to evacuate the island. From 10th August until the 15th, the 11th Air Force drops 355 tons of bombs. **(North Pacific-Aleutians)** The fight for Fishhook Ridge continues to rage, however, severe resistance by the Japanese prevents much progress.

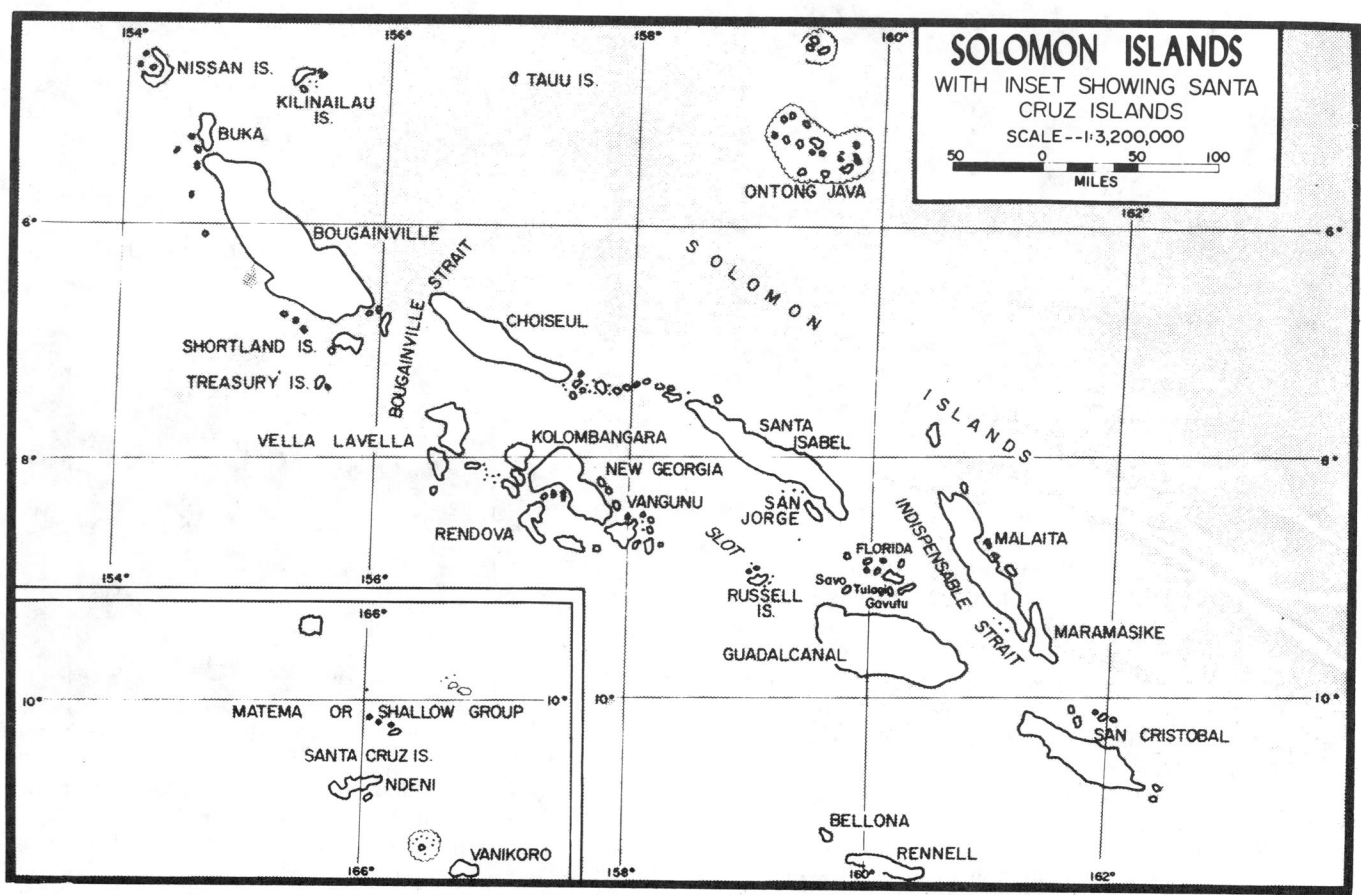

Martin B26s returing from a bombing mission (over Europe).

May 25th 1943 — (United States) The Trident Conference, in Washington D.C. concludes. This International meeting adjourns with specific plans for the defeat of Japan in the Pacific. The conference also sets May 1st 1944 as the tentative date for the large scale invasion of Northwestern Europe (Operation OVERLORD). However, intensive strategy by the British to convince the U.S. to mount a full scale attack against the Italian mainland had failed, to the dismay of Churchill, who now decides to fly to Algiers to speak with General Eisenhower to keep the flame alive. The meeting occurs on May 29th. In other activity, the *Bunker Hill* (CV-17), another formidable Carrier, is commissioned at Quincy, Massachusetts. **(North Pacific-Aleutians)** Heavy fighting continues near Fish Hook Ridge. The Southern Force discovers and gains entrance to an intricate enemy tunnel system, located under the crest of Fish Hook Ridge. Meanwhile, the Northern Force secures another enemy trench system, located in its sector of the Fish Hook. The Japanese still resist, but they are gradually driven into a small pocket at Chichagof Harbor. **(Atlantic-North Africa)** Combined Headquarters opens in Tunisia at Sousse in preparation of Operation CORKSCREW (seizure of Pantelleria).

May 26th 1943 — (United States) Winston Churchill and his staff return to England. U.S. General Marshal accompanies them on the trip, as Churchill wishes to stop at Algiers and speak with General Eisenhower in the presence of Marshall. **(North Pacific-Aleutians)** Elements of the 7th Infantry Division, engaged heavily on the slopes of the Holtz-Chichagof Pass, are stalled by tenacious machine gun fire. Private Joe P. Martinez, Company K, 32nd Infantry, infuriated by the enemy fire, confiscates a BAR (automatic rifle) along with hand grenades, and advances up the icy slopes, calling to his companions to follow. Some enemy nests are destroyed by Martinez, but his Battalion still is stalled, convincing Martinez to advance further. He leads the men to the pass, but while going from enemy trench to enemy trench, a bullet inflicts a mortal blow. His courage at the deadly pass and his decisive actions help bring about the ultimate conclusion of enemy resistance on the island, earning Private Martinez the Medal of Honor posthumously. **(Pacific-Philippines)** The Submariners are again off the coast. The U.S.S. *Trout* lands men, equipment, and currency at Bataan.

May 27th 1943 — (United States) Strategy sessions are held by Joint Staff Planners to decide specific target dates for the invasion of the Marshall Islands. In other activity, the U.S.

Navy establishes a Naval Air Station in the Panama Canal Zone at Coco Solo. **(North Pacific-Aleutians)** Japanese opposition on Fish Hook Ridge is eliminated. The U.S. begins construction of a Fighter Airstrip at Alexai Point. It will be used to strike Japanese positions on Kiska.

May 28th 1943 — (North Pacific-Aleutians) The Japanese are squeezed at Chichagof Harbor. Planes drop pamphlets which urge the remaining small groups of defenders to surrender, however, the Japanese ignore the request and prepare for a fight to the death.

May 29th 1943 — (Pacific-New Hebrides) The Japanese Submarine, the RO-107, is sunk by the Submarine Chaser *SC-669* off New Hebrides. **(Atlantic-North Africa)** General Eisenhower, based in Algiers, meets with Winston Churchill and Ten British Officers, plus several U.S. Officers to discuss strategy on the Sicilian and Italian campaigns. Also, it is decided that both the British and U.S. representatives would request permission from their respective governments to bomb Rome; it had been determined that it could now be accomplished without inflicting harm on the Vatican. While Churchill is en route between the U.S. and Great Britain, German agents have spotted what they believe to be Churchill; a German fighter Plane is dispatched and it knocks it out of the sky, however, Churchill is not aboard. Fourteen passengers are killed, including a noted British actor, Leslie Howard (Gone with the Wind).

May 29th-30th 1943 — (North Pacific-Aleutians) The U.S. Southern and Northern Forces have secured the area surrounding Chichagof Harbor. The Japanese Commanding Officer sends another and more desperate message to Japan: "MOST OF OUR POSITIONS HAVE BEEN CAPTURED BY THE ENEMY AND TODAY WE BARELY ARE ABLE TO HOLD THE REMAINING POSITIONS. THE WITHDRAWING FORCE WILL ATTACK THE ENEMY AND WILL DISPLAY THE TRUE GLORY OF THE IMPERIAL ARMY IN CARRYING OUT THE FINAL ATTACK. Colonel Yammazaki then orders the code-book and wireless destroyed and never receives the reply. Japanese Headquarters responds: WE RECEIVED REPORT OF YOUR RESOLUTE DETERMINATION AND FINE MORALE AND WERE FILLED WITH DEEP GRATITUDE. WE WISH YOU CALM SLEEP AS THE PILLAR OF THE NORTHERN DEFENSE." The Japanese attempt to break through a thin spot in the U.S. lines in the valley. The fanatical attack pushes toward Clevesy Pass during predawn hours, initially meeting success as it penetrates U.S. lines, however, an Engineering Battalion, commanded by Major James Bush holds commanding ground overlooking Massacre Valley and pummels the advancing Japanese, shredding the attackers before it can break through the valley to the beachhead to seize American ammunition and supplies. By dawn, the Japanese disperse into small units and slip into hiding. A disorganized weak attack is mounted on the 30th, ending resistance on the island. The Commanding Officer is killed while charging with his sword during the final charge. All except 29 of the 2,500 defenders are annihilated; the final remnants commit Hari Kari. Another futile attempt on the 30th, also is beaten back severely, ending resistance on the island. The U.S. 7th Division occupies Chichagof Harbor unopposed while another American Force, led by Brigadier General John E. Copeland, seizes Shemya Island without incident. The U.S. loses 549 dead and 1,148 wounded.

May 31st 1943 — (Pacific-Solomons) Japanese Major General Noboru Sasaki arrives at Kolombangara to command the Southwest Detachment, a combined Army-Navy defense force in New Georgia. **(Pacific)** The U.S.S. *Steelhead* (SS-280), unloads a substantial amount of mines near Erimo Saki, Japan.

June 1st 1943 — (United States-Aleutians) Fort Ord, California is the staging center for assault troops who undergo vigorous training in preparation for the invasion of Kiska, Aleutians. Upon completion of training they move to Attu. Meanwhile, Planes of the Eleventh Air Force continue to pound enemy positions at every opportunity. **(Atlantic)** Allied Planes continue to lambaste Pantelleria, located in the Mediterranean between Sicily and Tunisia. Some British Surface Vessels bolster the attacks. General Eisenhower had decided to seize the island subsequent to being informed by General Marshall that the eight requested Carriers to support the Sicilian invasion would not be available. Eisenhower will need the island for Air Bases, however, there is some concern about heavy casualties because the Italians might resist fiercely. Intelligence reports that five Italian Battalions defend the island supported by Militia units which maintain the AAA guns. The Allies are bolstered as the gunners have not been accurate against raiding Planes.

June 2nd 1943 — (United States) The U-Boat 521 is sunk by the Submarine Chaser PC-565 off Virginia.

June 3rd 1943 — (Pacific-Solomons) Admiral Halsey issues fundamental plans for the seizure of New Georgia. Rear Admiral Richard Turner will command the overall operation. The landing force, commanded by General Hester U.S.A. 43rd Division, comprises the 43rd Division U.S.A. and the 1st and 4th Marine Raider Battalions. **(Pacific-China)** The Japanese having reached their objectives in the Upper Yangtze region, initiate withdrawal. **(Atlantic-Algeria)** The French establish the French Committee of National Liberation, which becomes the French Empire's provisional government.

June 4th 1943 — The U.S.S. *Silversides* (SS-236) lays mines between New Ireland and New Hanover in the Steffan Strait. In other activity, the American Submarine Chaser *PC-496* is sunk after striking a mine (30-0 23' N., 09-0 52'W).

June 5th 1943 — (Atlantic) Planes (VC-9), attached to the Escort Carrier *Bogue* (CVE-9), operating in the mid-Atlantic, sink a German Submarine, the *U-217*. **(Atlantic-Mediterranean)** General Eisenhower orders the Commanding Officer of Force 141 (planning staff which subsequently becomes Headquarters 15th Army Group) to draw up plans for the invasion of Italy. In other activity, British General Alexander, who is to command 15th Army Group is given command of the British 5 and 10 Corps.

June 6th 1943 — (Atlantic-Mediterranean) Allied Air Raids against Pantelleria intensify and concentrate on enemy gun emplacements, as the second phase of the Air offensive begins. The island's installations have been pounded into ruins, however, the defenders have sustained few casualties.

June 7th 1943 — (Pacific-Guadalcanal) American Aircraft based on Guadalcanal intercept a Japanese Air Assault Force. Dog fights ensue and the enemy loses 23 Planes; the Americans lose nine.

June 8th 1943 — (North Pacific-Aleutians) The U.S. Naval blockade of Kiska is complete. U.S. Planes continue to strafe and bomb enemy positions, weather permitting, to soften resistance as the Japanese prepare to evacuate the island. While the Japs are readying the abandonment of their positions, the Navy establishes an Air Facility at Attu. **(Atlantic-Pantelleria)** British Naval Surface Vessels pound enemy positions on the island. Aircraft drop propaganda leaflets urging surrender, however, no response is forthcoming. The Italian Commander receives copies of the Allied surrender pamphlets: Supermarina proclaims the incident to Comando Supremo, boasting "PANTELLERIA WOULD RESIST TO THE UTMOST." On the following day, the lone operational radio on the island informs Rome that "DESPITE EVERYTHING, PANTELLERIA WILL CONTINUE TO RESIST." Although about twenty dispatches are sent during the night of the 10th, surrender is never mentioned.

June 10th 1943 — (United States) The Joint War Plans Committee proposes that the invasion of the Marshalls be commenced during late October and that Admiral Halsey and General MacArthur restrain their fighting to holding actions until the seizure of the Marshalls; the latter part of the proposal is scrapped due to lack of interest. In other activity, President Roosevelt, still concerned about the ongoing obstinateness and interference of DeGaulle, tells Churchill that Ike has been instructed to contact Giraud and DeGaulle to end the haggling. Roosevelt directs Ike to ensure that "NORTH AFRICA DOES NOT COME UNDER THE DOMINATION OF DEGAULLE." In his message to Churchill, Roosevelt states: "IF DEGAULLE SHOULD MOVE INTO FRENCH WEST AFRICA, I WOULD BE IMPELLED TO CONSIDER SENDING NAVAL AND GROUND FORCES TO DAKAR." Roosevelt further states: "GIRAUD MUST HAVE COMPLETE CONTROL OF THE FRENCH ARMY." In other activity, the Russians at Great Falls Montana have the Americans humming, as a special shipment of chemicals (uranium chemicals) is heading for a C-47, held up until the cargo arrives. Fifteen crates (guarded by a Russian Soldier) had arrived at the railroad yard, from Toronto. Colonel Kotivov instructs Major Jordan, AAF, to send a truck to pick up the cargo designated priority by Harry Hopkins about five weeks ago. Subsequently, it is determined that during 1942-44, three shipments of uranium chemicals (three quarters of a ton) and one shipment of uranium metal (2.2 pounds despite the fact that the U.S. stock amounts to only 4.5 pounds) moves to the Soviet Union. The Manhattan Project (formerly Oak Ridge, the Manhattan District) embargoes the export of uranium chemicals, however, pro-Soviets in Washington work around the problem to ensure Russia receives what it needs. Major Jordan, continues to alert authorities about the abuses in Lend-Lease to deaf ears. Subsequently (1949), Professor Harold C. Urey, deeply involved with the development of the atom bomb in the Manhattan Project, and aware that Colonel Jordan had discovered (by confiscating secret documents on the development of the atom bomb from Russia-bound Planes at Great Forks) states: "JORDAN SHOULD BE COURT-MARTIALED IF HE HAD REMOVED ANYTHING FROM PLANES BOUND FOR RUSSIA." **(North Pacific)** The Japanese Submarine *I-9*, is caught off the Aleutians and sunk by the Sub Chaser *PC-487*. **(Atlantic-North Africa)** General Omar Bradley is promoted to Lieutenant General (three stars). **(Atlantic-Europe)** The Combined Chiefs of Staff unveil Combined Bomber Offensive, subsequently coded Operation POINTBLANK, against Germany.)

June 11th 1943 — (North Pacific-Aleutians) During one of the usual deadly Arctic storms, the PT-22 is beached and lost near Adak. (Atlantic-Mediterranean) Enemy resistance on Pantelleria Island collapses subsequent to cessation of continuous air attacks which have dropped in excess of 6,000 tons of bombs since early May. While the Allied Fleet stands eight miles offshore, the Italian Island commander decides to surrender, however, poor visibility prevents it from being sighted. At 11:00, the clouds open and the Armada is spotted. Destroyers pound the shore, receiving no return fire. At 11:35, U.S. Flying Fortresses saturate the area with remarkable accuracy, and by 11:45, the British First Division lands without opposition and the island Garrison manned by over 10,000 Italian troops surrenders unconditionally. The Invasion Force suffers only one casualty and is met by a solitary white flag on Semaphore Hill. The injured British trooper had been bitten by an obstinate jackass. Allied Aircraft intensify their power against the next objective; Sicily (Operation HUSKY). Also, Allied Planes initiate attacks against Lampedusa, an eight square mile island between Malta and Tunisia. A British Naval Task Force escorting one Company of Coldstream Guards, joins in the bombardment, which continues into the early morning hours of the 12th. (Atlantic-Germany) Planes attached to the U.S. Eighth Air Force commence a daylight attack against Wilhelmshaven, however, still, no Fighters accompany the mission. German interceptor Planes arrive and hinder the mission's accuracy, but cause only minimal losses to the B-17s.

June 12th 1943 — (United States) The American Submarine *R-12*, sinks near Key West, Florida, reason unknown. (Pacific-Philippines) Specialized personnel and equipment are delivered to the Philippines, compliments of the U.S.S. *Trout*, which evades the Japanese Navy and debarks the contingent at Mindanao, after dark. (Pacific-Russells-Solomons) Another Japanese Air Assault attempts to breach Allied defenses and destroy American Fighters. Once again, the Americans outfight the enemy, dealing the Japanese heavy losses. Thirty-one of the Attack Force will be shot from the sky with the balance escaping back to Rabaul. The Americans lose six Aircraft. (Atlantic) Planes (VC-9), attached to the Escort Carrier *Bogue*, sink a German Submarine, the *U-118*, in the mid-Atlantic area. (Atlantic-Mediterranean) The Allies take Lampedusa as the Axis forces surrender unconditionally. The island Commander had informed Rome that although the island had been under incessant bombardment, it would not capitulate. He urgently requests Air support, however, none arrives. Rome sends the following message: "WE ARE CONVINCED THAT YOU WILL INFLICT THE GREATEST POSSIBLE DAMAGE ON THE ENEMY." The defenders, upon orders from their commander begin raising white flags and British Coldstream Guards occupy the island. On the following day, the British seize the unoccupied island of Linosa. (Atlantic-Germany) The Eighth Air Force launches dual attacks against the Submarine yards at Kiel and the installations at Bremen. German Planes intercept the attack force, causing the loss of 22 B-17s out of a force of the 60. In addition, the strength of the interception force prevents accurate bombing of the Submarine yards. The Eighth Air Force strikes again on the following day. Throughout the entire war, regardless of the sometimes overwhelming opposition, the Eighth Air Force is never turned back by the Germans. (Atlantic-Italy) Field Marshal Kesselring meets with Generale Ambrosio and informs him that Hitler intends to reinforce Sardinia and also Sicily. Ambrosio would prefer to keep Germans out of Italy, however, it is now apparent to him that Mussolini is not going to break from Hitler and that additional strength is required. By the end of June (43) five German Divisions will be in Italy and two additional ones are en route.

June 13th 1943 — (North Pacific) The Destroyer U.S.S. *Frazier* (DD-607), patrolling off the Aleutians, attacks and sinks an intruder, the Japanese Submarine *I-31*. (Atlantic-North Africa) During a conversation with the King of England, who is visiting Allied positions in Oran, General Patton is told by the King, that British General Alexander had told him, "THAT THE AMERICAN SOLDIERS WOULD SOON BE THE BEST SOLDIERS IN THE WORLD. Patton responds: "I DO NOT LIKE TO DISAGREE WITH GENERAL ALEXANDER, BUT AT PRESENT THE AMERICAN SOLDIERS ARE THE BEST SOLDIERS IN THE WORLD, AND WILL TAKE ON ANY SOLDIERS OF ANY COUNTRY AT ANY TIME." (Atlantic-Greenland) The U.S. Coast Guard Cutter *Escanaba* (PG-7), is sunk off Greenland, by torpedoes, launched by a German U-Boat. (Pacific-China) The Japanese expedition in central China terminates. (Atlantic-Germany) Superior German forces intercept the U.S. Eighth Air Force as it attacks the Kiel Submarine yards. Twenty-two of the 60 B-17s are lost during the air battle. However, the Eighth Air Force sends its main force of 102 B-17s against Bremen and receives only light resistance. On each mission, additional Squadrons are launched to feint attack and confuse the enemy, make them guess which is the designated target.

June 14th 1943 — (Pacific-New Guinea) The U.S. 41st Division combines the 2nd and 3rd Battalions, 162nd Infantry with contingents of the 215th and 218th Field Artillery Battalions (Coane Force). It is commanded by Brigadier General Ralph W. Coane. (Pacific-Solomons) Admiral J.H. Newton relieves Admiral Halsey as Commander Southern Pacific and the Solomons are annexed to the Southwest Pacific Area, terminating South Pacific's campaign against the Japanese. (China-Burma-India) In China, the advance echelon of the U.S. Fourteenth Air Force is established at Kweilin. (Atlantic-Mediterranean) The Allies now command all islands in the Sicily Strait, as a small British party lands at Lampione unopposed.

June 15th 1943 — (Atlantic-Mediterranean) General Eisenhower directs French General Giraud to select a ground forces commander and staff, to formulate plans for the invasion of Corsica (FIREBRAND). Giraud will suggest French General Juin as commander.

June 16th 1943 — (Pacific-Guadalcanal-Solomons) The faltering Japanese dispatch about 120 Planes, including Dive Bombers and Fighter escorts to strike Guadalcanal. The Japanese damage two Vessels, the LST 340, and a Cargo Vessel, the *Celeno* (AK-76). The enemy force is intercepted by 104 American Planes, which knock out nearly 100 Jap Planes. The American lose six Aircraft during the lopsided air duel. Meanwhile, an American Reconnaissance Bomber is attacked by about 20 Planes. The crew exemplifies extraordinary courage as it completes its mission; photographing the Buka vicinity. Several Aircraft are downed before the Yanks escape. Second Lt. Joseph R. Sarnowski loses his life attempting to save other crew members. Both he and Major Zeamer, the Pilot, receive the Medal of Honor for their great courage. In other activity, Major General John Hester, U.S.A., Commander, New Georgia

Occupation Force, sets June 30th as D-Day for the seizure of Munda.

June 17th 1943 — (United States) Again, President Roosevelt sends a message to General Eisenhower, relating his feelings concerning DeGaulle. The message in part: "THIS TIME WE ARE NOT GOING TO ALLOW DEGAULLE PERSONALLY OR THROUGH HIS PARTISANS TO CONTROL THE FRENCH ARMY IN AFRICA. YOU KNOW YOU ARE AUTHORIZED TO TAKE ANY ACTION YOU THINK BEST IN BEHALF OF THE U.S. GOVERNMENT." Washington is aware of British pressure on Ike to support DeGaulle. Eisenhower receives a similar message on the 19th. By the 23rd, Eisenhower reports back to Washington, indicating a compromise has been struck, giving French General Giraud command of the French forces in North and West Africa, and DeGaulle receives an equal command of French troops occupying other areas. In other activity, the Submarine Chaser SC-740, is lost due to grounding. Two LST's, Nos. 6, and 326, collide and are damaged off North Africa. **(Pacific-China)** General Stilwell meets with Chiang Kai-shek and gives him the TRIDENT proposals.

June 18th 1943 — (Pacific-Solomons) The 43rd Division prepares to move to New Georgia. **(Pacific-China)** General Chennault brings President Roosevelt up to date on the operations of the Fourteenth Air Force. Also, General Stilwell, commanding the Yoke-Force (all U.S. organizations coordinating with Y-Force) details to Colonel Dorn, his Chief of Staff, his duties in the operation. **(Atlantic-Sicily)** Preparations for Operation HUSKY continue. Messina and other strategic targets near Sicily are struck hard by Allied Planes. **(Atlantic-Great Britain)** Winston Churchill announces that General Wavell, Commander in Chief, India, is to become Viceroy of India and also announces General Auchinleck as his replacement.

June 20th 1943 — (Pacific-New Guinea) The U.S. 6th Army (ALAMO), commanded by General Krueger, establishes Headquarters at Milne Bay. Meanwhile, the Australians repulse several counterattacks near Mubo, during the next several days. **(Pacific-China-Burma-India)** British General Sir Claude J.E. Auchinleck succeeds British General Archibald Wavell as Commander in Chief, India. Wavell is appointed Viceroy of India. **(North Atlantic)** U.S. Naval Land-based Bombers destroy the German U-Boat *U-388*, in the North Atlantic. **(Atlantic-Germany)** R.A.F. Planes initiate their first shuttle-bombing raid between England and Africa, striking industrial targets at Friedrichshafen, Germany before landing in Africa. The Planes bomb the Axis Naval Base at Spezia, Italy during the night of the 22rd-24th on the return trip to the United Kingdom. **(Atlantic-Mediterranean)** The Airfield at Lampedusa become operational.

June 21st 1943 — (Pacific-Solomons) The 4th Marine Raider Battalion, acting upon the request of a coastwatcher who had been threatened by a Japanese advance from Viru Plantation, occupies Segi Point on the southern tip of New Georgia Island to prevent occupation of the southern tip of New Georgia by the Japanese. Contingents of the 103rd Infantry, 43rd Division, U.S.A. land on the following day to bolster the force. On Bougainville, the Third Defense Battalion, the final Marine Ground unit departs. **(North Pacific)** The Airfield on Shemya Island, Aleutians, becomes operational.

Summer 1943 — (United States) The Soviet Union's agents have been busily engaged in Washington, D.C., taking advantage of the lucrative information in the U.S. Patent Office. At Great Forks, Montana, Colonel Jordan Lend-Lease Liaison with the Soviets spots more alleged "diplomatic suitcases." A spot check discovers reprints of patents acquired with the able assistance of the Patent Office. The project had been initiated by Amtorg Trading Corporation (Russian Company) and subsequently taken over by the Four Continent Book Company. The United States finally halts the practice during 1949, however, in the meantime, the Russians waltz off with reprints of hundreds of thousands of U.S. patents, including such gems as helicopters, bombsights, ammunition, Vehicles, etc. The Soviets have ingeniously plundered the treasures of the U.S. during the war and the Lend-Lease program is noted by Colonel Jordan as: "THE GREATEST CATALOGUE IN HISTORY." The Soviets have also been stockpiling copper, another scarce U.S. commodity. Huge amounts of Lend-Lease copper are being stored in Westchester County, New York, for use in Russia after the close of hostilities. As early as 1942, when the Navy was suffering greatly because of the tragedy at Pearl Harbor, and in desperate need of copper, it fell under the Russian priority and was forced to borrow silver from the vaults at the Military Academy at West Point and use it. Strong attempts were made by Donald M. Nelson (War Production Board) to halt the shipments to the Russians, however, a personal plea from the President intercedes. Major Jordan notes that Roosevelt calls Nelson and states: "HE WOULD TAKE IT AS A PERSONAL FAVOR IF NELSON LET THE RUSSIANS HAVE ALL THE COPPER WIRE THEY REQUESTED." Lend-Lease will supply 642,503 tons of copper, brass and bronze ($283,610,000).

U.S. Warplane on Patrol.

June 22nd 1943 — (North Pacific) The U.S.S. *Monaghan*, operating near the Aleutians, sinks the Japanese Submarine, *I-7*. **(Pacific-Trobriand Islands)** Task Force Woodlark (112th Cavalry RCT, reinforced) deploys an advance party on Woodlark Island without opposition. This landing is a prelude to be followed by a second minor landing on the following night, both prior to the principle landing on the 30th. **(Atlantic-Germany)** The U.S. Eighth Air Force initiates its first large-scale daylight attack (daylight), striking a synthetic rubber plant at Huels, near the Ruhr. **(Naval Activity)** Two LSTs, Nos. 333, and 387, are damaged by enemy Submarine torpedoes off North Africa. Also, the Navy loses a Vessel today, when the Subchaser *SC-751* runs aground and is scuttled (21-0 56'S., 113-053'E).

June 23rd 1943 — (Pacific-Solomons) Two American Cargo Vessels, the *Aludra* (AK-72) and *Deimos* (AK-78) are sunk by enemy torpedoes, both in the vicinity of the Solomons.

June 23rd-24th 1943 — (Pacific-New Guinea) The Japanese begin to withdraw from the Mubo-Lababia Ridge area, lifting pressure from the Australian 17th Brigade, 3rd Division. (Pacific-Trobriand Islands) Advance U.S. Army units (Regimental Combat Team 158), land unopposed at Kiriwina Island after nightfall.

June 24th 1943 — (North Atlantic) U.S. Land-based Aircraft (VP-84), sink the German U-Boat *U-200*. (Atlantic-North Africa) The Tug YT-211 sinks during a violent storm.

June 25th 1943 — (Atlantic-Sicily) Allied Planes (Northwest African Air Force) again raid Messina, dropping over 300 tons of bombs on enemy positions. The Italian Battle Fleet is stationed at Spezia and the German Vessels are mainly Landing Craft. Comando Supremo had decided during May to withhold the Fleet except as a last resort, rather than face losing it in a surface fight. Meanwhile, the Italian Air Force, stocked with obsolete Planes, proves useless against the Allied Aircraft. Also, the severity of Allied Air raids against Sicily since the fall of Tunisia compels the Germans to transfer their Bombers to the mainland. The German Planes are also inferior to Allied Aircraft and between mid-May and early July, the Luftwaffe sustains heavy losses (twenty-one Air Battles).

June 26th 1943 — (Pacific-New Guinea) The Allies (MacKechnie Force) sail from Morobe to Mageri Point. After final preparations, the offensive against Nassau Bay is launched on the 30th. (Pacific-Japan) Tokyo orders the Air units deployed at Buin to defend the central Solomons to return to Rabaul. (Atlantic-England) Air Marshal Sir Trafford Leigh-Mallory, Air Officer Commanding in Chief, R.A.F. Fighter Command is selected to prepare Air plans for OVERLORD. (Atlantic-Mediterranean) The U.S. 33rd Fighter Group (P-40) is established on the island of Pantelleria.

June 27th 1943 — (Pacific-Solomons) Elements of 4th Marine Raider Battalion sail from Segi, New Georgia, to the Lambeti Plantation to initiate a forced march on enemy held Viru Harbor. They move out on the following day to seize the harbor intending to use it as a small craft Naval Base. (Atlantic) General Patton, in a speech to the 45th Division: "ALL MEN ARE AFRAID IN BATTLE. THE COWARD IS THE ONE WHO LETS HIS FEAR OVERCOME HIS SENSE OF DUTY . . ." In other activity, the U.S.S. *Redwing* (ARS-4), a Salvage Vessel is rocked by an underwater explosion of unknown origin and sinks off North Africa.

June 28th 1943 — (Pacific-New Georgia) The 4th Marine Raider Battalion begins to move toward Viru Harbor.

June 29th 1943 — (North Pacific) The Navy establishes an Auxiliary Facility at Shemya, Alaska. (Pacific-Solomons) U.S. Assault troops are in transit via Ship, heading to the Central Solomons. Surface Ships, commanded by Rear Admiral A. Stanton Merrill, bombard enemy positions at Munda, Vila, and the Shortlands during the night to soften enemy resistance. Meanwhile, Minelayers which lay their mines across the southern entrance to Shortland Harbor, Bougainville to deter access to the U.S. Forces on Munda are included in the Task Force. Planes from Kenney's Fifth Air Force are expected to cover the landing, however, inclement weather keeps the Planes grounded. (Pacific-Trobriands) The 158th Regimental

Combat Team, U.S.A. and the 46th Engineer Combat Company U.S.A., land on Kiriwina Island, without incident.

June 29th-30th 1943 — (Pacific) The Allied Offensive (Operation CARTWHEEL) to destroy Rabaul begins. The Allied thrust includes three Amphibious Landings; the Central Solomons, the Trobriands and New Guinea. Just before midnight, a U.S. Naval Task Force, comprising four Destroyers and four Cruisers, commanded by Rear Admiral Merrill, bombards Vila-Stanmore on Kolombangara and also attacks Buin-Shortland, Bougainville. In addition, the Navy plants mines in the area. The Third Fleet Amphibious Force, commanded by Rear Admiral Turner, and supported by Land-based Aircraft, lands the New Georgia Occupation Force. Other troops, traveling with Admiral Fitch's Task Force (Western Force), storm ashore at Rendova Harbor, against light resistance. Japanese Planes intercept the American Assault Force, but spirited Pilots from the Solomons, including Marine Fighter Squadrons 121, 122, and 213 are dispatched to quell this threat. The Japanese damage the Flagship *McCawley* (the *McCawley* will subsequently be sunk by friendly PT boats in error when its silhouette is mistaken for an enemy Ship). The Eastern Force lands elements of the 169th Infantry without opposition on Sasavele and Baraulu Islands. Outposts are established on Roviana Island. The Viru Occupation Force lands at Segi Point. In conjunction with the land movements, the Marine Raiders reach Viru Harbor by nightfall. The 2nd Battalion, 103rd Infantry and contingents of the 4th Marine Raider Battalion land unopposed at Vangunu and seize the objective. The Japanese begin to draw a rigid line of resistance to prevent American movement from Vangunu to Wickham Anchorage. In the Trobriand Islands, the U.S. 6th Army's Alamo Force, operating as a unit for the first time, lands unopposed on both Kiriwina and Woodlark Islands. In New Guinea, The MacKechnie Force (1st Bn. 162nd Infantry and additional U.S. and Australian Forces), lands unopposed at Nassau Bay, just after midnight 29th-30th. This combined American-Australian Force hits obstinate enemy opposition, as it begins its two-pronged drive north toward the Bitoi River and south toward the Tabali River.

June 30th 1943 — (United States) Navy records indicate total Naval strength at 1,741,750, Marines at 310,994, and Coast Guard at 154,976. In other activity, two U.S. Vessels, the Coast Guard Cutter *83421* and the Submarine Chaser *SC-1830*, collide as they move to Miami, Florida. The Coast Guard Cutter sinks. (Pacific-Solomons) The U.S.S. *Zane* (DMS-14), a Minesweeper becomes damaged by grounding. (Atlantic-Mediterranean) During preinvasion operations (period 18030 June), N.A.A.F. Aircraft fly 883 Bomber sorties and IX Bomber Command launches 107 sorties against Sicily and Italy, attempting to destroy supply depots, Shipping areas, and marshaling yards.

July 1st 1943 — (Pacific) Admiral Nimitz issues a tentative plan for the capture of the Marshall Islands. (Pacific-Solomons) The Americans (43rd Division) strengthen their beachhead at Rendova, while maintaining Patrols to detect enemy activity. Two Platoons of the 4th Marine Raider Battalion overrun a Japanese Garrison at Tombe Village, while the remainder of Company F, and Company Q, capture Tetemara, a village on the west side of Viru Harbor, giving the Marines control of Viru Harbor, New Georgia Island. Also, The 9th Defense Battalion U.S.M.C. arrives at Rendova, bringing welcome 90-mm and 155-mm Batteries. Meanwhile, the

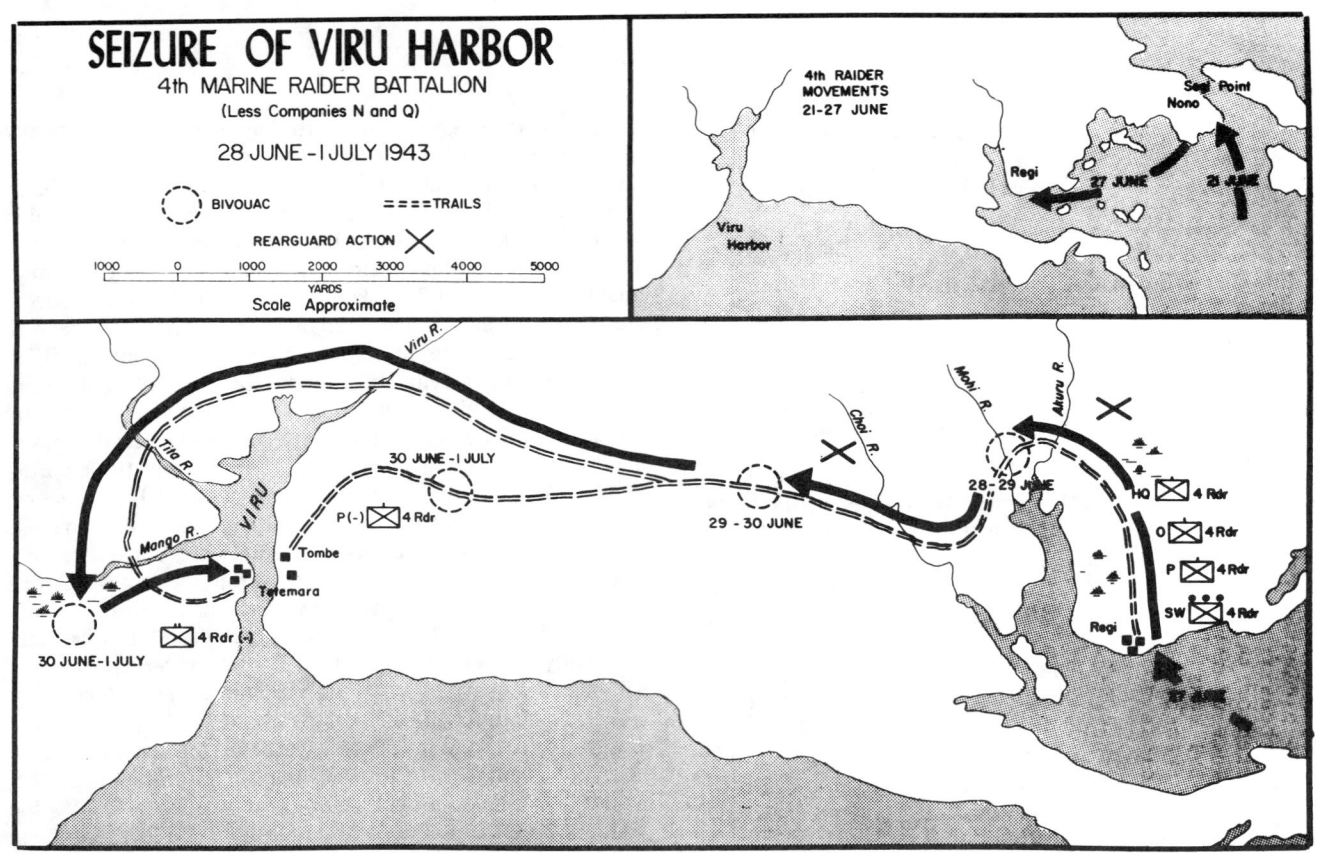

SEIZURE OF VIRU HARBOR
4th MARINE RAIDER BATTALION
(Less Companies N and Q)
28 JUNE-1 JULY 1943

- ⊙ BIVOUAC   ==== TRAILS
- REARGUARD ACTION ✕

1000 0 1000 2000 3000 4000 5000
YARDS
Scale Approximate

4th RAIDER MOVEMENTS 21-27 JUNE

Sege Point
Nono
27 JUNE
21 JUNE
Regi
Viru Harbor

Viru R.
Tita R.
Mango R.
VIRU
Tombe
Tetemara
30 JUNE-1 JULY
P(-) ✕ 4 Rdr
30 JUNE-1 JULY
4 Rdr (-)
Choi R.
Mohi R.
Anuru R.
29-30 JUNE
28-29 JUNE
✕
HQ ✕ 4 Rdr
O ✕ 4 Rdr
P ✕ 4 Rdr
SW ✕ 4 Rdr
Regi
27 JUNE

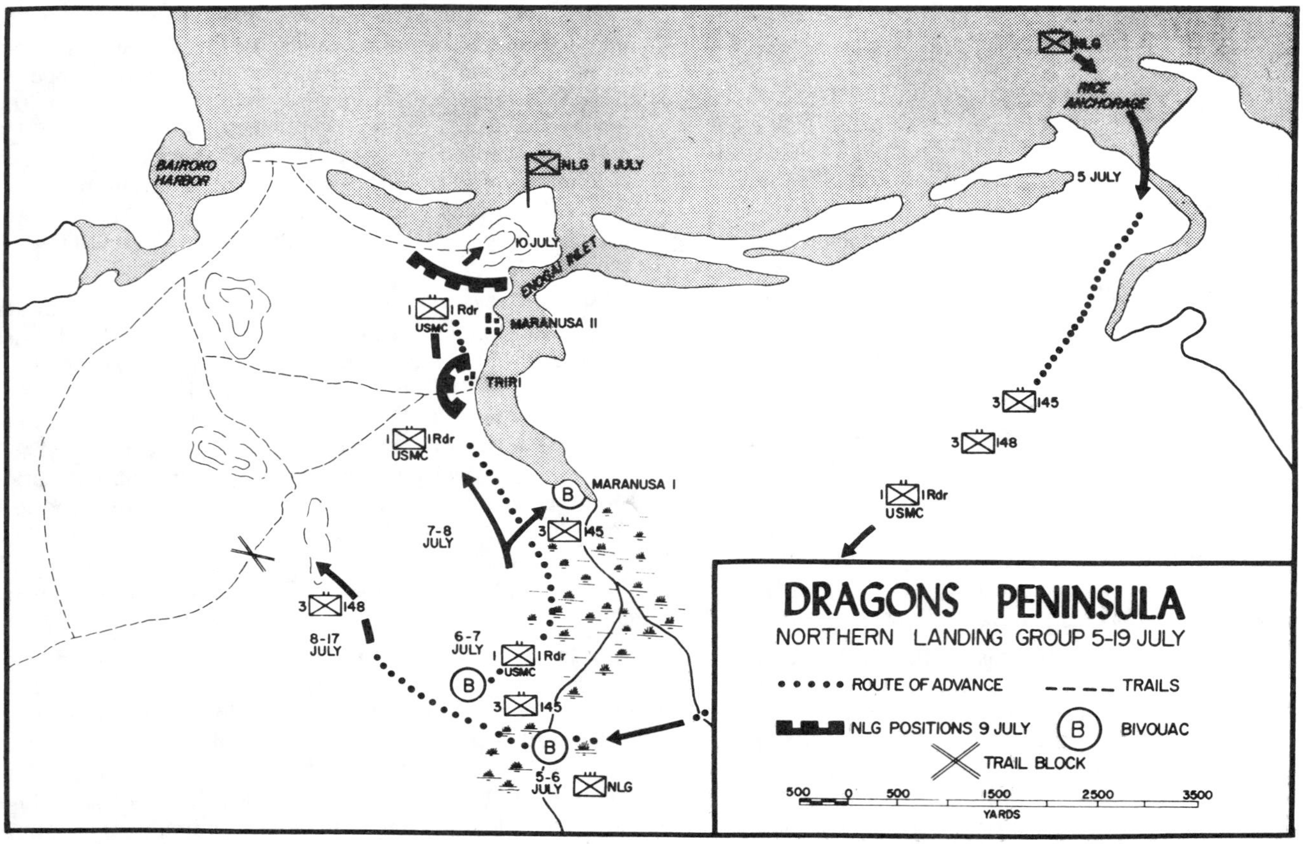

DRAGONS PENINSULA
NORTHERN LANDING GROUP 5-19 JULY

- ••••• ROUTE OF ADVANCE   ---- TRAILS
- ▙▟▙ NLG POSITIONS 9 JULY   Ⓑ BIVOUAC
- ✕ TRAIL BLOCK

500 0 500 1500 2500 3500
YARDS

BAIROKO HARBOR
RICE ANCHORAGE
✕ NLG
5 JULY
3 ✕ 145
3 ✕ 148
✕ NLG 11 JULY
10 JULY
ENOGAI INLET
1 ✕ 1 Rdr USMC
MARANUSA II
TAIRI
1 ✕ 1 Rdr USMC
MARANUSA I
Ⓑ
3 ✕ 145
7-8 JULY
3 ✕ 148
8-17 JULY
6-7 JULY
Ⓑ 1 ✕ 1 Rdr USMC
3 ✕ 145
Ⓑ
5-6 JULY
✕ NLG
1 ✕ 1 Rdr USMC
✕

Marine 4th Raider Battalion and Company F, 103rd Regiment, U.S.A., withdraw to Vura where raids are launched against the remaining Japanese at Cheke Point. The unit takes Kaeruka and overruns Cheke Point against slight opposition, completing the task by the 4th. In Naval activity, the Destroyer *Radford* (DD-446), circling the Solomons, spots and sinks the Japanese *RO-101*. **(Pacific-New Guinea)** The Allies consolidate their positions near the southern arm of the Bitoi River. **(Pacific-Dutch East Indies)** The U.S.S. *Gar* (SS-206), squirms into enemy waters near Timor and rescues some endangered people from Japanese capture. **(Pacific-China)** General Chennault instructs Fourteenth Air Force to concentrate on enemy Shipping and Port installations.

July 2nd 1943 — (Pacific-Solomons) The U.S. 41st Division prepares to take its next objective, Munda Airfield. Troops are transferred from Rendova to New Georgia. Japanese Aircraft launch an Air strike against Rendova, causing severe damage and inflicting heavy casualties. Further damage is incurred, when Japanese Naval Ships bombard Rendova during the night of the 2nd. In other activity, the PTs 153 and 158 are beached and abandoned. Also, Japanese Major General Noboiu takes command of all Japanese forces on New Georgia. **(Pacific-New Guinea)** The MacKechnie Force withstands the enemy attempts to dislodge it from its beachhead at Nassau Bay. Also, contingents establish contact with the Australian 3rd Division. **(Atlantic-Mediterranean)** Allied Planes continue a relentless bombardment of enemy positions in Italy and Sicily, with special emphasis given to Airfields and Planes. Operation HUSKY pre-invasion bombing is now in its final phase. NAAF Aircraft receive Fighter cover from Planes based on both Malta and Gozo. **(Atlantic-Great Britain)** Air Marshal Leigh-Mallory establishes Air Staff at Norfolk House.

July 3rd 1943 — (Pacific-Solomons) The Southern Landing Group, commanded by General Leonard Wing, dispatches the 1st Battalion, 172nd Infantry, to Zanana beach, about five miles east of Munda Airfield. It lands unopposed. Wickham Anchorage is taken by the Americans and is used as a staging area for Landing Craft.

July 4th 1943 — (Pacific-Solomons-New Georgia) A Japanese Destroyer Force attempts to land reinforcements at Kolombangara. However, it is intercepted and turned back. This is the final large scale daylight attempt to land reinforcements. Sixteen Jap Bombers break through the interceptor force; 12 are downed by the 9th Defense Battalion. The Northern Landing Group, commanded by Lt. Colonel Harry B. Liversedge awaits aboard Ships during the night of 4th-5th, while Warship escorts bombard Vila and Bairoko Harbor. In other activity, a 52 man contingent from the Marine 9th Defense Battalion's Special Weapons Group arrives to bolster the force against enemy Planes. **(Atlantic-North Africa)** The U.S.S. *Wilkes* (DD-441) becomes grounded in waters around North Africa and sustains some damage. **(Atlantic-Mediterranean)** British Commandos raid enemy Airfields on Crete during the night and successfully withdraw. Also, General Wladislaw Sikorski, Commander in Chief, Polish Forces, dies in a Plane crash near Gibraltar.

July 5th 1943 — (Pacific-Solomons) The majority of the New Georgia Occupation Force is ashore in the Central Solomons; the main body is deployed at Rendova. The Northern Landing Group, comprising the 1st Marine Raider Battalion, 1st Marine Regiment, reinforced by 3rd Battalions of the 145th

and 148th Regiments, 3rd Division, lands without opposition and sets up a beachhead perimeter on the northern coast at Rice Anchorage and is to subsequently occupy the Bairoko-Enogai area to ensure no enemy reinforcements reach Munda from Kolombangara. A Naval Force commanded by W. L. "Pug" Ainsworth comprising the Light Cruisers *Helena, Honolulu,* and *St. Louis* and the Destroyers *Chevalier, O'Bannon, Nicholas* and the *Strong* bombard both sides of the Kula Gulf. Enemy return fire is heavy, however, the only loss is that of the *Strong*, which is struck by a Submarine Torpedo and sinks. About 75 percent of the crew is rescued by the *Chevalier*, but many are lost to drowning and exploding depth charges. Contingents of the Southern Landing Force encounter entrenched resistance along the Munda Trail between Zanana and the Barike River. **(Atlantic-Russia)** The Germans launch the Kursk offensive. The 9th Army drives south from Orel in conjunction with Army Kempf and the 4th Panzer Army which drives north from Belgorod. The Soviets are also taking advantage of the spring thaw and their numbers far outweigh the German attackers: the offensive makes progress, but at heavy costs to the Tank units.

U.S. Landing craft moving under protection of Warships.

July 6th 1943 — (Pacific-Solomons) THE BATTLE OF THE KULA GULF — During the night of the 5th, ten enemy Destroyers attempt to deliver reinforcements to bolster the Forces at Kolombangara. Rear Admiral Ainsworth's Task Force, consisting of three Cruisers and four Destroyers races through darkness, and attacks the troop-laden Destroyers. The sky crackles as shells roar upward, streaming deadly tracer fire across the sky. The guns thunder throughout the merciless lightning fast battle, however, as the tempest subsides, two Japanese Destroyers, the *Niizuki* and *Nagatsuki* are lost (grounded and abandoned during the battle); the remainder retire. The enemy manages to land only about 850 troops. The U.S.S. Light Cruiser *Helena* (CL-50) is lost, but, more importantly, the enemy although superior in number, has again been turned back. **(Pacific-Solomons-Greenwich Island)** Lieutenant Commander Bruce A. Van Voorhis, Commander of Bombing Squadron 102, volunteers to fly a 700-mile mission to destroy enemy radio facilities on Greenwich Island. Pursued by many enemy Aircraft, he flies in at dangerously low altitudes, destroying Planes, Antiaircraft weapons and the radio station. Van Voorhis, destroys one enemy Fighter Plane in the air and three on the water, however, his Plane gets snared by one of his own bomb explosions, causing him to crash in the lagoon off the beach. He receives the Medal of Honor posthumously. **(Pacific-China)**

Fourteenth Air Force initiates anti Shipping operations off the West River estuary. **(Atlantic-Russia)** The Germans attempt to forestall total defeat by attacking the Soviet salient at Kursk. Both sides attempt to use the spring thaw to their advantage, but the exhausted German troops in Russia are far outnumbered and outsupplied by the Russians.

July 7th 1943 — (United States) French General Giraud arrives in Washington to discuss the Allies future plans concerning the invasion of Italy. **(Pacific-Solomons)** Still, the Southern Landing Group meets heavy resistance along the Munda Trail. The Southern Force runs into obstinate enemy resistance at Triri as they push toward Dragon's Inlet. **(Pacific-New Guinea)** The Allied ground troops receive Air support as they drive against the enemy near Mubo. The MacKechnie Force assaults Bitoi Ridge in the vicinity of Napier and the Australians capture Observation Hill, one mile west of Mubo. **(Atlantic)** Army Aircraft, on Patrol, spot and destroy the U-951, another German Submarine. On the following day, the German U-Boat U-232 is sunk off Portugal, by Army Land-based Planes. **(Atlantic-Soviet Union)** The Red Army counter-attacks, slowing progress of the German offensive north of Kursk. However, the Germans make some progress in the Belgorod area.

July 8th 1943 — (Pacific-Solomons-New Georgia) The U.S. 43rd Division dissolves an enemy roadblock along the Munda Trail. The Northern Force establishes a roadblock along the Munda-Bairoko Trail. The Marine 1st Raider Battalion turns Triri over to the 145th Infantry, then it moves toward Enogai against stiff opposition. In other activity, Naval Aircraft bombard enemy positions at Vila, Kolombangara. Also, Companies N and Q of the 4th Raider Battalion are dispatched to Gatukai Island to destroy 50-100 Japs reported to be on the island, however, the unit returns on the 10th after an uneventful search. **(Pacific-Wake Island)** American B-24s based on Midway strike the Japanese at Wake Island. This is the first time that Land-based Planes attack Wake Island, since it fell to the Japs in December of 1941. The Military personnel captured had been moved to Japanese prison camps and some were decapitated. The civilian construction workers had been imprisoned on Wake to work as slave laborers on the Jap defenses. When the U.S. begins heavy bombardment against the island later in the year (October), nearly 100 blindfolded civilians are set up like dominoes and executed by firing squad. **(Atlantic-North Africa)** The 82nd Airborne is making final preparations for the impending invasion of Sicily. There had been an ongoing spat between General Ridgway and British Lt. General Browning as to allocation of C-47s for the invasion, as Browning, attached to Supreme Headquarters, and known as the sage of Paratrooping, attempts to use his pull to get more Planes for the British. During the stay in North Africa, Browning, on several occasions, interferes with the 82nd. During one incident, he informs Ridgway that he is coming to see Ridgway's plan for the invasion of Sicily, however, Ridgway dispatches a curt message informing Browning that: "THERE IS NO PLAN FOR SICILY INVASION UNTIL SUCH TIME AS THEY ARE APPROVED BY GENERAL PATTON . . . UNTIL THEN THEY WOULD NOT BE AVAILABLE FOR INSPECTION BY ANYBODY, EXCEPT ON PATTON'S ORDERS." Soon after, General Smith reads the riot act to Ridgway, informing him that all U.S. Officers must implement the "UTMOST COOPERATION WITH THE BRITISH." He further states that "ANY U.S. OFFICER WHO IN THE SLIGHTEST WAY

TRANSGRESSES THAT RULE MIGHT AS WELL START PACKING UP FOR HE WAS GOING HOME. Fortunately, Ridgway had the permission of General Patton to send the note and he escapes the wrath of the British, retaining command of the 82nd Airborne.

July 9th 1943 — (United States) President Roosevelt sends a letter to Pope Pius XII, informing him that U.S. Planes will bomb Axis Rail depots in the vicinity of Rome. **(Pacific-Philippines)** The Submarine U.S.S. *Thresher* lands a contingent of men and some equipment at Negros. **(Pacific-Solomons)** Japanese rush reinforcements to the Central Solomons, moving about 3,700 troops from Kolombangara Island to Bairoko by the 12th. The Americans also are reinforcing their troops. Enemy resistance is heavy as the Americans drive toward Enogai from Triri and are halted at Enogai Point. However, Lt. Colonel Liversedge's Force clears the area on the following day, capturing Enogai. The U.S. 43rd Division makes very slow progress toward Munda, as it pushes through dense jungle terrain. In other activity, U.S. Destroyers move closer to shore and bombard enemy positions at Munda, New Georgia. **(Atlantic)** U.S. Naval Land-based Aircraft (VP-94) attack and sink the U-Boat U-590 near the mouth of the Amazon River in Brazil. **(Atlantic-Sicily)** The Axis Powers are still unsure of where the Allies will invade next. Operation MINCEMEAT had apparently been successful: plan to fool the Germans into thinking that Sicily would be a feint operation and that Sardinia and the Peloponnesus Islands are the objectives. On May 12th, The Germans had ordered Sardinia and the Peloponnesus reinforced, acknowledging they had bought the story. A phony dispatch (from the British War Office in London to General Alexander) had been previously sealed in an attache case and locked to the wrist of a of a deceased serviceman who had succumbed by pneumonia. A British Submarine discards the body (which contains two phony theater tickets for the night of April 22nd) off Spain and it is picked up by Axis sympathizers, and subsequently returned to British authorities. An inspection determines that the Germans had inspected the enclosed papers and resealed them. The corpse carried the fictitious name of Major Martin, Royal Marines and is known as the "man who never was." This is only one of many counterespionage operations carried out by the Allies. Today, Allied Planes launch a night attack, stinging Caltanissetta, Syracuse, Acreide, and Catania. **(Atlantic-Western Europe)** Hitler is informed that an Allied Fleet is near Sicily. He orders the German 1st Parachute Division to prepare to depart France for duty in Sicily.

July 9th-11th 1943 — (Atlantic-Sicily) THE INVASION OF SICILY — The Allied invasion force nearing Sicily is composed of over 3,000 Ships. Of these, nearly 2,000 participate. The massive American-British Armada is split into an East Force commanded by Vice Admiral Henry Hewitt, transporting the U.S. 7th Army under General Patton, and a West Force, commanded by British Admiral Sir Bertram Ramsay, which lands the British Eighth Army under General Montgomery. The British Mediterranean Ships split into two groups, with Force H feinting toward Greece then rendezvousing near the heel of Italy in the Ionian Sea to protect Montgomery's ground forces. A British Battleship Squadron, Force Z, diverts to block the Tyrrhenian Sea and subsequently cruises toward Western Sicily to draw attention away from the main objective. The U.S. Amphibious Task Force nears H-Hour when a smoke pot on one of the LST's (carrying high explosives) accidentally ignites. Ensign John Joseph Parle, fights through the heavy smoke and throws the exploding charges overboard. His bravery helps ensure the secrecy of the approaching Task Force, but he subsequently succumbs to the smoke and dies within a week.

The Stars and Stripes arrives on Sicily.

Messina becomes cloaked by smoke during one of the B-17 Bombing raids.

During the approach, the heavy winds and seas cause much concern for the success of the operation, prompting the Commands to cancel an important drop of Airborne troops prior to the main landing in the morning. One consolation is that although the Allies are experiencing extreme difficulty with the operation, the enemy is operating under the same weather conditions and can not search the skies. The weather is so terrible that the Germans are not expecting any type of amphibious attack. Sicily is defended by two German Divisions (15th Panzers, Generalmajor E. Rodt and Hermann Goering, Generalmajor Paul Conrath) which hold a combined Tank strength of about 85. In addition, Six Italian Divisions (under Generale Guzzoni who had replaced General Roatta) guard the coast, supported by four reserve Divisions scattered throughout the hills.

At about midnight, the wind speed decreases and the decision to go with the Airborne assault is given. The Paratroopers are aloft in a flying Convoy of 222 C-47s. Over 3,400 men of Ridgway's 82nd Airborne descend, expecting to land to the rear of Gela, and deploy to establish roadblocks to prevent enemy reinforcements from arriving, however, the inexperience of many of the Pilots, combined with the unpredictable wind currents and the difficulty of flying over water in darkness without guides, causes the Paratroopers to land along the entire 60 mile front, gaining only the advantage of having the enemy believe the troop strength is much more than its real number. The Paratroopers regroup in the enemy-infested hills, however, and begin to dislodge defenses, interrupt communications and blow as many bridges as possible. This is all in cadence with their objective of intercepting any enemy reinforcements rushing to engage the invasion force on the beaches. The scattered Paratroopers become plagued by some unexpected problems as they fight their way back to the Allied lines. The various British and the American units use several different pass-words, complicating the task of the 82nd, which uses the 1st Division's word. Patton later gives credit to the Paratroop landing for shortening his advance by at least 48 hours.

Things go no better for the 1,600 men of the British 1st Airborne who are struck with disaster as they attempt to land south of Syracuse and destroy a primary bridge over a canal at Ponte Grande. Of one hundred and forty-four Horsa and Waco Gliders (towed by 109 U.S. C-47s and 39 RAF Albermarles) which silently swing down toward the landing sites, several turn back, and 47 flop into the sea. An additional 74 Gliders land too far inland to be of any immediate help and the remainder face a herculean task. Eight British Officers and 65 enlisted men must hold the bridge until reinforcements arrive. The British are up against a reinforced Infantry Battalion, bolstered by Artillery.

Meanwhile, although the enemy still possesses no radar, piercing searchlights scan overhead, slashing their beams across the skyline, however, miraculously the Allied Task Force (Invasion Force) remains undetected. The Allies ponder the possibility of low tides and the consequences of having an inadequate number of proper Landing Craft (most are unsuitable for shallow water) as H-Hour approaches. Finally, the signal comes. Restless Naval guns preempt the Landing Force, and pound the beaches and suspected enemy positions with sheets of Artillery fire. Uncontested Allied Airpower shadows the Fleet and the Landing Force.

Patton's Seventh Army lands at three locations. The western contingent under Truscott, hits the beaches at Licata and quickly captures the town and its minute port. Two additional Task Forces under Bradley storm their objectives, the Rangers seizing Gela after a tough fight, and the U.S. 45th Division capturing Scoglitti and Vittoria, against scattered resistance. The Yanks drive inland to establish contact with the

Licata (steep cliffs in left foreground) and Beach Areas to the East toward Gela.

July 11th 1943 — U.S. Warships come under attack off Gela.

82nd Airborne. The 1st Division, which had stormed ashore at Gela with the Rangers, hooks up with the Parachutists and the town of Marina di Ragusa is then seized. Ernie Pyle, an astute correspondent relates how one Ranger, Sergeant Murel White explains an encounter with their first pillbox, manned by six men: "THREE OF THEM GOT AWAY, BUT THE OTHER THREE WENT TO HEAVEN." First Division reinforcements and the 2nd Armored Division come ashore to beef up the Seventh Army's beachhead, culminating a swift and startling landing, which had taken the Germans and Italians by complete surprise. In one instance, two Companies of Rangers under Captain James B. Lyle, seize an Italian coastal battery of three 77-mm guns which had not been fired. Advance Airborne troops using radios, do a magnificent job of directing traffic for the big Naval Guns, spotting precise locations of strategic targets. The toughest opposition is encountered by the Rangers who run into Italian Tanks at the Port of Gela; the Rangers still seize the objective. Skirmishing continues throughout the day, but lack of German Airpower hinders the enemy defense. The Destroyer *Maddox* (DD-622) is struck by torpedoes from a Dive bomber and sinks. In addition the LST 313 and the Minesweeper *Sentinel* are also hit by Dive Bombers and sink. Six other Vessels are damaged, but not from enemy fire.

Meanwhile, the British Eighth Army lands east of the Americans near Syracuse and Pozzallo, on the Pachino Peninsula, seizing Pachino, then driving toward the remnant British Paratroops at Syracuse, taking Avola along the way. The British had attempted to hold the bridge with a mere 73 men. When the 8th Army drives to the coveted bridge at about 15:30, only 15 Paratroopers are unwounded as their positions are overrun. Eight men withdraw, reaching the advancing British 5th Division, which attacks, crossing the bridge seizing it intact and also seizing Syracuse after a large fire fight that lasts through the night.

On the 11th, Bradley, comes ashore to prepare his force against counterattack. Meanwhile, the Hermann Goering Division readies a major attack against the American II Corps. The full fury of the enemy strikes heavily, just after 06:30, against advance positions of the 1st Division. Unfortunately, the Division's Antitank equipment and Artillery still is offshore. Improvisation becomes the order of the day. The 1st Division, which prides itself as being "BORN TO FIGHT ANYWHERE ANYTIME," realizes discretion is now the necessary ingredient required for success. The advance troops, unable to stop 20 Panzers, burrow under-ground and allow the Tanks to pass through. General Roosevelt grabs a field-phone and reports that the Panzers have penetrated and are closing against the main base of supplies at the beachhead. An additional 40 Mark IV's grind across the Big Red One's front. General Allen rushes all available guns to forestall the advance in front of Gela. The Yanks hold, exhibiting steadfast determination, repulsing the Germans and saving the beachhead. The Germans lose many Tanks and are forced to withdraw and regroup for another attack.

Reinforcements from the 45th Division race to the fight to reinforce the Big Red One. Later, the Panzers reinitiate their assault, however, the Yanks are prepared. The Tanks crash forward, roaring through heavy fire. Again the fighting becomes gruesome as the enemy nears the beachhead. Suddenly, the ground shakes as the U.S. Navy joins the melee and delivers a deluge upon the advancing enemy. Sheets of fire pass directly over the heads of the U.S. troops, striking a crushing blow to the encroaching enemy, which enables the Infantry to halt the attack 2,000 yards from the beach. The battered Germans withdraw to the hills and the Italians straggle into the II Corps perimeter to surrender. General Bradley, satisfied with the results of the troops, returns to Scoglitti to prepare for the upcoming missions of the II Corps in Sicily.

Meanwhile, in addition to assisting the 1st Division repulse the counterattack, the 43rd Division seizes the town of Comiso and its Airport and also captures Ragusa, and General Truscott's troops expand the Licata beachhead. Later during the night, additional reinforcements attached to the 82nd Airborne are dropped to further bolster the lines, however, again the drop is scattered and confusion develops as the Paratroopers come under fire by the Germans and by the Americans who mistake them for Germans. The 82nd incurs high casualties. Also, at Licata (11th), the LST 158 is struck by a Horizontal Bomber, causing it to be beached and abandoned. The U.S.S. *Barnett*, *Orizaba* and *Monrovia*, all Transports, are damaged (11th), while supporting the land activity.

July 13th 1943 — U.S. Paratroopers move through Vittoria with unusual transportation.

July 10th-August 17th 1943 — THE BATTLE OF SICILY — A few days earlier, aboard the *Monrovia*, General Patton overheard a few Soldiers talking outside of his room, one of whom remarked: "When we get ashore tomorrow, the papers will report that the Marines have landed in Sicily." The newly activated U.S. 7th Army under Patton goes quickly about its mission to conquer Sicily and receives full credit in the reviews at home. Assisted by the British, a relentless drive commences, driving the enemy out of the country. The Allies advance so quickly at times, that supplies have trouble keeping up with Patton. Thirty eight days after landing, the enemy is completely driven out of Sicily. The campaign to take Sicily, officially ends on August 17th when U.S. RCT 7, 3rd Division, roars into Messina at 10:00. The enemy offers little opposition as they complete their withdrawal into Italy. British troops enter Messina later in the day to join the Americans. With the capture of Sicily, the Mediterranean Sea is safely in Allied hands. Also, prior to the invasion of Sicily, there had been a great shortage of Transports for the Paratroopers, and some bickering as to priorities between the British and U.S. Airborne Divisions, however, the drop gets off. Despite the troops being scattered over a 100 square mile area, German General Karl Student, speaking while being held in a British P.O.W. camp during 1945, states: "THE ALLIED AIRBORNE OPERATION IN SICILY WAS DECISIVE . . . IT IS MY OPINION THAT IF IT HAD NOT BEEN FOR ALLIED AIRBORNE FORCES

BLOCKING THE HERMANN GOERING DIVISION FROM REACHING THE BEACHHEAD, THAT DIVISION WOULD HAVE DRIVEN THE INITIAL SEABORNE FORCES BACK INTO THE SEA."

U.S. Soldiers operating along the Munda Trail.

July 10th 1943 — **(Pacific-Kurile Islands)** U.S. B-25s, based on Attu, bombard Paramushiro, the point from where the Japanese Fleet embarked to attack Pearl Harbor; this is the first U.S. bombardment of the Kuriles. **(Pacific-Solomons)** The fighting on New Georgia remains fierce, however, the Americans have overcome much heavy resistance as they plow through the jungles and most of the area around Enogai has been secured by the troops under Liversedge, but not without cost, including difficult supply problems. Liversedge's command swings into a mop up operation by the following day. All incoming supplies must be delivered by parachute. Also, the Japs greatly hinder the timetable for construction of highways. Along the bloody Munda Trail, the 43rd Division, is forced to halt its drive when the enemy blocks passage of a trail which leads to the coast at Laiana. Orders are issued to Major General Oscar W. Griswold (Commander XIV Corps), directing him to report to New Georgia. In other activity, Companies O and P, 4th Raider Battalion return to Guadalcanal after being relieved. **(Pacific-New Guinea)** The Japanese holding at Mubo and at Salamaua lose communications between each other as the Americans and the Australians forge separate wedges between the two enemy bastions; the Yanks attacking from Nassau Bay, close the line and join with the Australians at Buigap Creek. **(Atlantic-Sicily)** The Allies invade Sicily. The Allied Commander is General Dwight D. Eisenhower. British Admiral Sir Andrew Cunningham commands the Naval Forces. The U.S. 7th Army, led by George S. Patton, is transported by the Western Task Force, commanded by Vice Admiral H.K. Hewitt, U.S.N.; the Eastern Task Force, commanded by Vice Admiral Sir Bertram Ramsay lands the British Eighth Army, which is led by British General Sir B.L. Montgomery. Naval casualties during landings of the 10th; Destroyer *Maddox* (DD-622), by enemy Dive Bomber attack; LST 313 by enemy Horizontal Bomber attack. Two Destroyers, the *Roe* (DD-418) and the *Swanson* (DD-443) are damaged when they collide with each other. The U.S.S. *William P. Biddle* (APA-8) collides with the LST-382 and the Submarine Chaser PC-621 collides with the LST-345. The invasion implements the use of several new types of Landing Craft on a large scale: LSTs, LCTs, LCIs, and LCVPs, and DUKWs. In other related activity, Colonel Darby, in charge of defending Gela with two Battalions of Rangers, personally

destroys an enemy Tank and displays great courage. He is offered the command of a Regiment and a promotion, but declines the offer, choosing to remain with the Rangers for the duration. The Rangers had been aboard the H.M.S. Prince Charles, and their U.S. built Landing Craft are manned by British Sailors. Also, General Albert Wedemeyer, requests a demotion to Colonel to permit him to take command of a Regiment. For Invasion coverage, see July 9th-11th, 1943.

July 11th 1943 — **(Pacific-Solomons)** General Vandegrift, Commanding Officer of 1st Marine Amphibious Corps is designated Commander of the land troops who are designated to invade Bougainville, the next step between the Americans and the major objective (Rabaul). Fighting continues on New Georgia Island and the Airfield at Segi Point is ready for light use by Fighter Planes. The 2nd Marine Raider Regiment receives special reinforcements, when the "1st Marine War Dog Platoon" arrives in the South Pacific to serve as messengers on Bougainville. Meanwhile, a U.S. Cruiser Destroyer Force, under Rear Admiral A.S. Merrill, bombards Munda and repeats the attack on the following day. **(Atlantic-Sicily)** The Allies strengthen their beachheads at Sicily, while other contingents advance. The 45th Division (which had sailed directly from the U.S. under General Troy Middleton) seizes Ragusa and Comiso, along with its Airfield and twenty five enemy Planes stranded on the ground. The 45th also lays claim to a few enemy spare parts, the remnants of many Aircraft, previously battered by Allied Artillery. The Yanks are startled when an unsuspecting German JU-88 lands at the newly won Airfield. The enraged Pilot, who had evaded AA fire jumps to the ground and begins yelling until he sees the new residents are Americans. Several more Germans unsuspectingly land later in the day and fall into the waiting hands of the Yanks. During one encounter with the enemy, troops attached to the U.S. 3rd Division are under extremely heavy enemy fire at Favoratta, Sicily. Three Officers attempt to destroy the hidden enemy machine gun nest and become wounded. A fourth Officer, 2nd Lt. Robert Craig, charges the nest, killing the crew with his rifle. Additional enemy fire halts the 15th Infantry again at a steep ridge. Craig orders his men to take cover, then draws concentrated fire from about 100 enemy Troops upon himself to save the command. Craig, with reckless courage, moves to within 25 yards of the enemy force, takes a kneeling position and commences firing, killing five and wounding three others before withering fire kills him. His inspired men regroup at the crest of the hill and drive the enemy off, inflicting heavy casualties upon them as they flee. In another tragic mistake of war, General Bradley is informed by General Kean, that reinforcements from the 82nd Airborne are to be dropped in the vicinity of Farello Airfield. The TWX specifically states location and time: "NOTIFY ALL UNITS, ESPECIALLY AA (Anti Aircraft Units) THAT PARACHUTISTS 82nd AIRBORNE WILL DROP ABOUT 23:30 TONIGHT JULY 11TH-12TH ON FARELLO LANDING FIELD." General Ridgway had urgently requested assurances of safe passage for the Planes, over Allied Vessels on June 22nd and also today. No promises are given because of Merchant Vessels in the area. Ridgway requests personal assistance from Patton and subsequently the Navy agrees to the request, alleviating fears of losing the troops to friendly fire. Two thousand Parachutists of the 82nd, depart Tunisia in 144 C-47s. As they approach the drop zone, Luftwaffe Planes appear in the darkened skies and begin firing at will, strafing Allied positions, then quickly disappear.

Despite the earlier notification of the 82nd's impending arrival, the jittery fingers of an Allied gunner opens fire at the U.S. Planes. Immediately, additional Antiaircraft guns commence firing, and tracer shells illuminate the sky, while racking the Aircraft. Simultaneously, the Parachutists are floating perilously to the ground, many of them being mistaken for Germans and shot as they hit the earth. The immense shelling by both enemy and friendly guns, inflicts 20 percent casualties on the troops. In addition, 23 Planes are lost. In other activity, the Navy also suffers casualties; LST-158, damaged by Horizontal Bomber and subsequently abandoned at Licata, Sicily; U.S.S. *Barnett* (APA-5), *Orizaba* (AP-24), both by Horizontal Bomber; U.S.S. *Monrovia* (AP-64), by Dive Bomber (All during Sicily Land ings). General Ridgeway had requested Fighter protection for the air drop, however, NATAF denies it stating that "other missions were of greater importance to the operation as a whole." Also, at 02:30, Paratroopers (under Colonel Gavin) establish first contact with U.S. ground forces (Company I, 179th Infantry) about five miles outside Vittoria. Gavin then advances west along Highway 115 and encounters additional Paratroopers and Infantry. Soon after, two Germans, an Officer and enlisted man turn a bend on a motorcycle and are captured without a fight. Meanwhile, two Ranger Companies under Lyle are standing west of Gela in the path of an advancing Italian Armor column. Colonel Darby orders them to engage them with every weapon available including the captured 77mms. Patton shows up and observes the Italian attack and tells Lyle as he is departing: "KILL EVERYONE OF THE goddam BASTARDS." Destroyer fire joins in the rout: enemy casualties are severe and bodies are seen hanging from trees, some "blown to bits." The Rangers capture about 400 befuddled survivors of the blistering 6-inch shell bombardment. The 82nd Airborne had trained in the states, however, during its buildup, a decision was made to form another Paratroop Division (101st), causing the Division to be splintered; interestingly, during training some Generals came to inspect the force and suggested that the Paratroopers land their Gliders in rougher terrain than the landing strips, prompting Ridgway to note that the Division had the use of only four Gliders for the training of his entire Division. In the **British Eighth Army** area, 30 Corps stretches its bridgehead to the Avola-Pozzallo road, taking Pazzallo. Meanwhile, the 13 Corps drives north toward Augusta. **(Atlantic-Soviet Union)** The 4th Panzer Army and Army Krempf combine their strength and drive toward Prochorovka.

A view to the South from the fortified town of Enna.

A young Coastguardsman makes the ultimate sacrifice in the Mediterranean.

July 12th 1943 — (Pacific-New Georgia) Supply problems plague the Americans as they press the advance. The 172nd Infantry runs out of food and water as they approach Laiana. The 169th Infantry driving toward Munda is held up near the outer defenses by well fortified Japanese. **(Pacific-Solomons)** BATTLE OF KOLOMBANGARA (Second battle of Kula Gulf-During the evening of the 12th into the 13th, a Japanese Task Force (1 Cruiser — 5 Destroyers), attempts to reinforce the central Solomons, but is intercepted by an Allied Fleet, commanded by Rear Admiral Walden Ainsworth. The Allied fleet, comprising three Cruisers and 10 Destroyers suffers major damage, losing the Destroyer U.S.S. *Gwin* (DD-443). The Light Cruisers *Honolulu* (CL-48) and *St. Louis* (CL-49) are damaged by torpedoes, fired by enemy Destroyers. In addition, the Destroyers *Woodworth* (DD-460) and *Buchanan* (DD-484) are damaged after they collide. Damage is also sustained by a New Zealand Cruiser. The Japanese lose one Cruiser, the *Jintsu*. Twelve hundred Japanese troops reach Kolombangara safely, however, this is the last time enemy Destroyers attempt to transport troops to New Georgia. In other activity, the Destroyer U.S.S. *Taylor* (DD-468) sinks the Japanese Submarine I-25. **(Pacific-New Guinea)** Japanese resistance is reduced greatly in the vicinity of Mubo. **(Pacific-China-Burma-India)** Chiang Kai-shek agrees to the Trident recommendations concerning the reopening of Ledo Road (SAUCY). **(Atlantic-Portugal)** Army Aircraft sink the German Submarine

U-506, off Portugal. **(Atlantic-Sicily)** The Allies continue strengthening their beachhead. Elements of the 1st Division seize the Airport at Ponte Olivo, then advance toward Niscemi. General Truscott's troops (Western Task Force) overrun Canicatti. The British 30th Corps captures Modica and Palazzolo but the British 13th Corps meets stiff resistance and is halted between Syracuse and Augusta. **(Atlantic-Russia)** The Germans and Soviets battle fiercely near Orel, as the Russians attack to destroy the Axis salient. The Soviet offensive follows the unsuccessful attempt by the Germans to take Kursk, which cost over 400 Tanks.

July 13th 1943 — (North Atlantic) The U.S.S. *Core* (CVE-13), an Escort Carrier, operating in the North Atlantic, launches Planes (VC-13), which sink the U-Boat U-487. **(Pacific-New Georgia)** Admiral Halsey, unsatisfied with the progress of the campaign, places General Harmon in command of the operation in New Georgia to speed up the offensive. Two days later, General John Hester U.S.A. is replaced by Major General Oscar Griswold, U.S.A., (CG XV Corps) as Commander of the New Georgia Occupation Force. Hester retains command of 43rd Division. In addition, Rear Admiral Theodore Wilkinson U.S.N., replaces Rear Admiral Richmond Turner as Commander, III Amphibious Force and TF 32; Turner departs for Hawaii. **(Pacific-New Guinea)** In New Guinea, enemy activity in the Mubo area ceases after a determined effort by the Australian 3rd Division, supported by American Artillery. **(Atlantic-Sicily) 15th Army Group** British General Alexander sets new boundaries between the British and American forces. The decision does not sit well with General Bradley whose troops are approaching the highway which is being taken away and given to the British Eighth Army. Enemy Airstrikes diminish, giving the Allies advantage. Seventh Army orders Canicatti held. The U.S. 7th Army presses forward. In the **II Corps** sector, elements of the 45th Division seize Licodia and Monterosso. In the **British Eighth Army** sector, heavy enemy fire detains the British 51st Division at Vizzini. The British 5th and 50th Divisions attack near Lentini and also receive fierce opposition. About 1,900 British Paratroopers (1st Parachute Brigade) are transported to jump at four landing sites to seize Primasole bridge (FUSTIAN) spanning the Simeto River, however, again heavy Antiaircraft fire creates problems: some Planes turn back. Others brave the incessant fire but at high costs because both friendly and enemy guns fire upon their Planes. Only about two hundred British Paratroopers and three Antitank guns reach the bridge. Of eighty-seven Pilots who run the gauntlet, only 39 deposit their troops within a mile of the drop zones: the balance except four Planes hit the mark within ten miles; the four stragglers hit Mount Etna, twenty miles away. Ironically, German Paratroopers had landed in the same area, north of the river and the main body of British Paratroops hit ground near the machine guns of the German 1st Parachute Division, inciting a wild fight, however, the small band of British troops hold throughout the day. Upon darkness, the Paratroops move back and take positions which prevent the Germans from crossing the bridge or blowing it. Meanwhile, British Commandos, dispatched from Ships, seize a nearby bridge (Lentini) and destroy the demolition charges, however, German fire drives them back. Also, Field Marshal Kesselring informs General Jodl that the situation in Sicily is critical because of Allied strength and the dismal performance of Italian coastal units. As word reaches Hitler in Germany, priorities again switch. Hitler cancels Operation ZITADELLE (campaign initiated on July 5th to retake Kursk on the Eastern Front) to get more troops into the Mediterranean Theater.

July 14th 1943 — (United States) The Marine Corps Glider Base at Edenton, North Carolina is designated a Marine Corps Air Station; the Marine Corps has previously discontinued Glider training. **(North Pacific-Aleutians)** The U.S. Navy establishes a Naval Operating Base at Adak. In other activity, U.S. Destroyers bombard suspected enemy positions on Kiska and on the following day, repeat the operation. **(Pacific-Solomons)** American reinforcements, including the 3rd Battalion, 103rd Regiment (43rd Division), and Engineers and Tank units (9th Defense Battalion), land at Laiana, to bolster the New Georgia operation. On Guadalcanal, RCT 116, U.S. 25th Division, receives orders to ship out to New Georgia Island. **(Pacific-Trobriand Islands)** The Airfield on Woodlark Island is prepared to handle C-47s. **(Atlantic-Sicily-Messina)** Over two hundred Allied, Heavy and Medium Bombers drop about 800 tons of bombs on Messina. Elements of the French North African Army land at Licata and are attached to the U.S. 3rd Division. Meanwhile, Infantry press the enemy on the ground. **15th Army Group** In the **II Corps** sector, the U.S. 45th Division seizes the Airfield at Biscari and inches close to Vizzini. The 1st Division seizes Mazzarino and Niscemi. In addition, a contingent of Rangers bolstered by Naval fire, seize Butera. In the **British Eighth Army's** 30 Corps sector, the British 51st Division, still receiving opposition at Vizzini, gets support from the U.S. 45th Division and the resistance is then eliminated. The main British force (13 Corps), stalled near Lentini, finally succeeds in taking the town, and gets troops toward Primasole bridge which is heavily defended by German Paratroops. The Germans hold the bridge throughout the day, however, during the night, the defenders withdraw to a nearby ridge. During the day, General Kesselring informs Italian Generals Ambrosio and Roatta that the existing line on Sicily is untenable without additional German forces. Kesselring also announces that General Hube is being transferred to Sicily to assume command of German forces. In other activity, General Bradley receives bad news during his Corps' trek to take the Vizzini-Caltagirone Road. A directive is received by Patton, instructing him to have Bradley relinquish the road to the British 8th Army, to allow the British easy access to flank Mount Etna and Catania. Bradley's troops are 1,000 yards from the road. Bradley remarks to Patton: "THIS WILL RAISE HELL WITH US. I HAD COUNTED HEAVILY ON THAT ROAD (Vizzini-Caltagirone)." Bradley, not impressed with the order, remarks to General Patton: "NOW, IF WE'VE GOT TO SHIFT OVER IT'LL SLOW UP OUR ENTIRE ADVANCE." In spite of the pleas, the order stands, but Bradley again requests permission to at least allow General Middleton's Force to access the road to prevent the complete redeployment of two Divisions. Patton informs Bradley that the transfer of the road is effective immediately. British General Alexander backs Montgomery, forcing Middleton's entire 45th Division to retreat all the way to the beachhead to get around General Allen's First Division. The redeployment wastes precious time and is finally completed by midnight on the 17th. Offshore, the U.S.S. *Brooklyn* (CL-40), sustains damage when it strikes a mine. **(Atlantic-Italy)** N.A.A.F. intensifies its efforts to interdict reinforcements and supplies heading for the Axis in Sicily; Naples becomes a primary target for the Aircraft.

U.S. Infantry takes a treacherous path heading east from Palermo.

July 15th 1943 — (Pacific-Kurile Islands) The *Narwhal* (SS-167), a U.S. Submarine, surfaces near the Japanese Air-base at Matsuwa and strafes it. **(Pacific-Solomons)** The Japanese attempt another daylight Air attack against American positions in the Central Solomons. About 75 Aircraft approach until intercepted by U.S. Planes. A furious Air duel ensues, and culminates after the Japs receive a devastating beating. During the lightning quick strike, the Yanks down 45 Planes, while losing three themselves in what becomes the final Japanese daylight attack against the Central Solomons. Also, General Griswold, CG, XIV Corps, assumes command of the New Georgia Occupation Force at midnight 15th-16th, relieving General Hester who retains command of the 43rd Division. In addition, Admiral Turner is relieved of posts of Commander South Pacific Amphibious Force (III Amphibious Force and TF 32) and Commander New Georgia Attack Force (TF 31); he embarks for Hawaii. **(Atlantic-Sicily) 15th Army Group** General Patton combines the 3rd Division, 3rd Ranger Battalion, 82nd Airborne Division, and elements of the 9th Division, plus other support troops to comprise the Provisional Corps (Major General Geoffrey Keyes). During the campaign, General Ridgway, Commanding Officer, 82nd Airborne, often moves with his troops who come under severe fire. In one instance, while advancing through a treacherous ravine, mortar fire kills some and wounds others. Ridgway, stops next to a man who has lost both eyes, but not his spirit. The trooper yells "WHO'S THAT" and receives the response: "GENERAL RIDGWAY," who is greeted with: "OH-GLAD TO SEE YOU." In the **British Eighth Army** area, the Canadian 1st Division seizes Grammichele and Caltagirone. In the British 13 Corps sector, ground troops hook up with the Paratroopers holding the recently occupied bridge over the Simeto River. In Naval activity, the Minesweeper U.S.S. *Staff* (AM-114), hits a mine and is damaged. **(Atlantic-Italy)** Mussolini meets in Rome with Kesselring, Rintelin, and Italian General Ambrosio to discuss the defense of Italy. Also, Field Marshal Kesselring assures Roatta that although General Hube is arriving in Sicily, the tactical command of German forces on Sicily would remain under Italian General Guzzoni. Essentially, Kesselring and Guzzoni believe that Sicily can be held, however, Hitler has already sent secret orders to abandon southern Sicily and prepare to defend the Italian and German homelands. The Italians are to be cut off from any future German planning once Hube assumes command. **(Atlantic)** The Germans lose the U-159, after it is attacked and sunk in the Caribbean by Navy Land-based Planes. In other Naval activity, Planes (VC-29) attached to the U.S.S. *Santee* CVE-29, Escort Carrier, sink the U-Boat U-509 west of Portugal, in the vicinity of the Azores.

July 16th 1943 — (United States) The Joint Chiefs of Staff decide to give shared command between Generals Stilwell and Chennault in the China Theater, hoping the compromise will be satisfactory to Chiang Kai-shek. It isn't. Chiang Kai-shek is not content until Stilwell is relived of command during October of 1944. **(Pacific-Solomons-New Georgia)** U.S. Army elements, assisted by Marine Tanks, begin expanding the Laiana Beachhead. They advance, seizing a hill, which is subsequently named Kelley Hill in honor 1st Lieutenant John R. Kelley (U.S.A.). **(Pacific-Philippines)** Commander Melvin H. McCoy, U.S.N., Major Steve Mellnick and Captain Ed Dyess are rescued by an American Submarine bound for Australia, however, other men in their group (seven) from Davao Penal Colony await a subsequent evacuation. **(Pacific-Trobriand Islands)** On Woodlark Island, the operational Airstrip receives the first Allied Plane to land on the island. **(Atlantic-Sicily)** Axis Aircraft terminate daylight raids, however, night attacks continue. **15th Army Group** The Axis forces are withdrawing toward the Messina Peninsula, which has the treacherous M. Etna at its base. In the U.S. Seventh Army area, Provisional Corps sector, the U.S. 3rd Ranger Battalion takes the Port at Agrigento, while the 3rd Division assaults the town. The 1st Division captures Barrafranca in II Corps area. Meanwhile, the 45th Division rolls along the left flank of the Corps. General Patton receives more distressing news from Army Corps, following the fiasco of redeploying Bradley's II Corps. Patton is informed that Montgomery's Eighth Army will move to take Messina and the U.S. 7th Army is to play second fiddle and seize Palermo in the western sector on the Tyrrhenian Sea. Also, just after midnight (16th), a contingent of Rangers under Major Herman W. Dammer encounters an Italian roadblock at the junction of Highways 118 and 12 outside of Porto Empedocle. A brief fire fight occurs and shortly thereafter Rangers take the position and 165 Italians surrender. After daylight, the Rangers move out and subsequently encounter another Italian force, composed of ten motorcycles and two troop-laden trucks. Suddenly, the first shots ring out and the Italians become instantly disorganized; heavy casualties are inflicted on the enemy and 40 additional prisoners are in custody as the Rangers move into Montaperto. Holding the high ground, Dammer's 60mm mortars ring down on Italian Artillery in the valley below. Some Italians escape, however, most raise their hands high and ascend the hill surrendering to the Rangers. In the British Eighth Army area, the British Canadian 1st Division seizes Piazza Armerina during the night of the 16th and the British 51st Division moves toward Paterno to relieve pressure against the British 13th Corps. In other activity, a bridgehead is established at the Simeto River by 13 Corps troops. On this day, President Roosevelt and Prime Minister Churchill both appeal to the Italian citizens to: "DECIDE WHETHER ITALIANS SHALL DIE FOR MUSSOLINI AND HITLER OR LIVE FOR ITALY AND FOR CIVILIZATION." In Naval activity in the Atlantic, the Escort Carrier *Core* (CVE-13), launches Planes (VC-13), which destroy the U-509, as it prowls in the mid-Atlantic. **(Atlantic-Soviet Union)** The Germans continue to face heavy pressure from Russian advances at the Kursk salient and at the Orel salient. In addition, Soviet troops mount additional assaults against the Germans' bridgehead at Kuban.

A. U.S. coastguardsman on duty in New York. The Woolworth Bldg. is among skyscrapers.

July 17th 1943 — (Pacific-New Guinea) The Coane Force and supporting units moves from Nassau Bay to join the Australian 3rd Division in the attack toward Salamaua to divert attention from the primary assault which is to secure the Huon Peninsula and Markham Valley, to gain control of the Dampier and Vitiaz Straits. **(Pacific-Solomons)** The 13th, and 229th Japanese Regiments mount an unsuccessful assault against American positions on New Georgia. The poorly organized assault is easily repulsed at the beachhead at Laiana and also at the northern positions of the just arrived

169th U.S. Infantry, and terminates Japanese initiative to regain the island. Meanwhile, Army and Naval Planes attack Japanese positions at Buin, Bougainville, damaging facilities, and sinking the Destroyer *Hatsuyuki*. **(Atlantic-Mediterranean)** General Eisenhower confers with his Commanders in Carthage. It is decided that the Italian mainland will be invaded subsequent to the seizure of Sicily, to squeeze Italy out of the war. **(Atlantic-Sicily)** General Patton is not in an especially good mood, because the 7th Army is still denied use of the four roads to Messina, which are exclusively for British progress. He requests permission for mutual use, stating that the roads can accommodate both Armies and he further presses his superiors by stating that "Monty" can not handle the job with his present strength. On the following day, Patton's observation is proved correct when Montgomery is unable to penetrate the enemy line at Catania, however, the British refuse to share the highways. Despite British arrogance, and denied access to the major roads, still the 7th Army pummels the enemy and advances. The 45th Division, which had reached its designated position at about midnight (16th-17th) jumps off at dawn, virtually without rest, after their rugged detour through the hills. The 45th ramrods forward, driving in leap frog motion, one Regiment charging ahead, with another close behind, racing right through their positions without a pause. During the advance, a letter taken from a deceased German Soldier, addressed to his brother serving on the eastern front in Russia, is given to General Bradley. The letter in part: "THESE ASTONISHING AMERICANS, THEY FIGHT ALL DAY, ATTACK ALL NIGHT AND SHOOT ALL THE TIME." The action packed day gains the Yanks Pietraperzia and a few Salso River crossings, south of Caltanissetta. In a coordinated effort with the 45th Division, the 1st Division gains ground and crossings east of Caltanissetta along the Salso River. In other activity, U.S. Navy guns pound Agrigento. This powerful blow combined with the firepower of the 3rd Division, virtually reduces the town. During the hellish fighting around Agrigento, darkness settles on the battlefield and a group of volunteers, led by Lt. David Waybur, 3rd Reconnaissance, 3rd Division, moves to locate an isolated Ranger contingent. The three Vehicle Squad crosses mine infested roads, which are defended by snipers, machine-gunners and road-blocks, but it advances until stalled at a demolished bridge. The Patrol soon finds itself cornered by four intimidating enemy Tanks. Lt. David Waybur and his Patrol disperse the Vehicles and begin pumping 30 and 50 caliber machine gun fire at the Tanks. As the lopsided battle rages, the Yanks exhaust their ammunition, but refuse to capitulate. Despite several men being wounded, and the situation grave, Waybur, himself wounded, grabs a 45 Thompson submachine-gun and defies death, moving directly in the path of fire, standing recklessly within 30 yards of the approaching Tank. He fires incessantly. The crew is killed and their Tank rolls uncontrollably onto the bridge and into the stream. The Yanks, quickly send a runner to get help, while the remainder of the Patrol holds off the remaining enemy; reinforcements arrive after day break. In the **British Eighth Army** 30 Corps area, the British 51st Division advances to within 10 miles of Paterno. During the night of the 17th, two British Brigades of the 50th Division probe toward Catania, however, the coast road is sealed by the enemy; the British are unable to penetrate the defenses of Colonel Wilhelm Schmalz. Meanwhile, the Hermann Goering Panzers stalk the Eighth Army and stand between the British and the Gerbini

Airfields. **(Atlantic-Soviet Union)** Moscow proclaims that all positions held prior to the German offensive in the Orel sector on July 5th, have been recaptured.

July 18th 1943 — (United States) An American Naval Airship, the K-74, is destroyed by a German Submarine in the Florida Straits; it is the only American Airship lost to enemy fire. **(Pacific-New Guinea)** The Coane Force secures the southern headland of Tambu Bay for use as a supply center. The 1st and 2nd Battalions, 148th Infantry, fight their way from Zanana to relieve the 169th Infantry, however, heavy enemy resistance halts the advance. **(Pacific-Solomons)** The Japanese holding positions at Buin-Kahile, Bougainville, are lambasted by another air assault, by Army and Naval Planes. **(Pacific-Solomons-New Georgia)** On New Georgia, XIV Corps prepares its final drive against Munda, however, Japanese mount several counterattacks; all are repelled. Meanwhile, contingents of 148th Regiment, 43rd Division, which have landed at Zanana, unsuccessfully attempt to relieve 169th Regiment, 43rd Division. In Naval activity, a Japanese Submarine sinks the LST-342. **(Pacific-Trobriand Islands)** The Airfield on Kiriwina Island becomes operational. **(Atlantic-Sicily) 15th Army Group** In the **U.S. Seventh Army** area, II Corps sector, The U.S. 3rd Division spearheads the Provisional Corps drive on Palermo. The enemy continues to retreat toward the northeastern part of the island with the 7th Army in pursuit. The II Corps closes on Palermo from the east; the U.S. 45th Division overruns Caltanissetta and drives to south Caterina. In the **British Eighth Army** area, General Montgomery co-ordinates a combined assault, utilizing Amphibious and Airborne troops to break the enemy line at the Catania Road, but the assault is repulsed. Subsequently, Montgomery diverts his effort and transfers his troops to the inland route being used by the Canadian 1st Division. Within two additional days, Patton receives a TWX from British General Alexander, ordering him to shift the 7th Army to the east and join Montgomery for a combined thrust to crush the enemy. In Naval activity, the Submarine Chaser *PC-562* strikes a mine and is damaged. Also, Patton describes the ongoing operations in his papers and mentions that the townspeople had been "unfriendly" during the first days of fighting; "BUT SINCE WE HAVE DEMONSTRATED THAT WE CAN DESTROY EITHER THE GERMANS OR ITALIANS, THEY HAVE BECOME AMERICANIZED AND SPEND THEIR TIME ASKING FOR CIGARETTES." Patton also notes that the Germans place mines to the rear of the Italians "SO THAT WHEN THE ITALIANS ATTEMPT TO RUN THEY GET BLOWN UP. THIS NATURALLY DOES NOT MAKE THE ITALIANS LOVE THE GERMANS."

July 19th 1943 — (Pacific-Aleutians) Admiral Kinkaid approves plans for the invasion of Kiska. **(Pacific-Solomons-New Georgia)** Additional U.S. Army troops reinforce the New Georgia Occupation Force during a lull in the fighting; more troops continue flowing into the area for the next few days. **(Atlantic-Brazil)** The U-513 is sunk by Naval Land-based Planes (VP-74). **(Atlantic-Italy)** Over 500 U.S. Bombers swarm over military objectives near Rome, including marshaling yards in Lorenzo, and Littoria and the Ciampino Airfields, dropping approximately 1,000 tons of bombs during the first large-scale Allied bombing attack on Rome. Meanwhile, Hitler and Mussolini are conferring at Feltre in northern Italy. While Hitler is speaking about strategy in Sicily (Feltre Conference), he is informed of the ongoing bombing raids. **(Atlantic-Sicily) 15th Army Group** Patton's 7th Army

rolls ahead feverishly, driving the enemy further back. The 3rd Division takes Casteltermini and Mussomeli and it has the 2nd Armored Division perched in the rear, awaiting the opportunity to bolt forward and crush the withdrawing enemy forces. Meanwhile, the British 13th Corps still meets obstinate resistance near Catania. The Canadian 1st Division drives toward Leonforte, however, it bypasses the fortified stronghold of Enna to reach positions north of Valguarnera; the maneuver exposes Bradley's (U.S. II Corps) supply depots.

U.S Soldiers debark a LCI (L) in New Georgia.

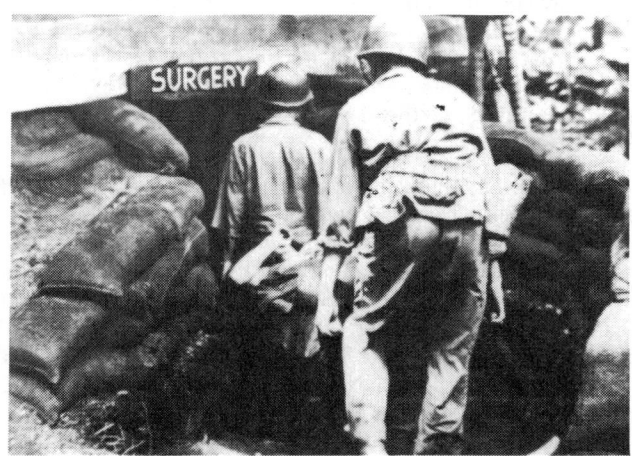

An Emergency Ward on the Solomons. Doctors tend the wounded in a modified operating room which is dug four foot in the ground and fortified with logs and sandbags.

July 20th 1943 — (United States) Admiral Nimitz receives orders from the Joint Chiefs of Staff to formulate plans to seize the Ellice and Gilbert Islands. In other activity, the U.S. announces that the U.S.S. *Runner* (SS-275) is presumed lost in the Pacific. The *Runner* had departed Pearl Harbor (3rd War Patrol) on May 28th for the Kuriles and was to patrol near Ominato and Hakodate, before departing for Midway on July 4th. The Submarine sinks the Freighter *Seinan Maru* off Ominato on June 11th and on the 26th sinks the *Shinryu Maru* off the Kuriles, however, no word is received by the Vessel. Japanese report no Submarine attacks in the area during the time period. **(Pacific-Solomons)** Marine Land-based Aircraft attack Japanese Vessels near Choiseul Island and sink two Destroyers, the *Kiyonami* and the *Yugure*. On New Georgia, the Liversedge Force, which includes the 4th Marine Raider Battalion, 1st Marine Raider Regiment and the 3rd Battalion, 148th Infantry, U.S.A., supported by Aircraft attacks Bairoko, however, it is forced to withdraw and return to Enogai. The U.S. 145th Infantry overcomes fierce resistance and relieves the 169th Infantry, which also is under heavy fire. Meanwhile, the U.S. 148th Regiment reduces enemy positions, which have been holding it up, and assists the 145th Regiment. A supply trail between Laiana and the Munda Trail is now clear. In Naval activity, the PT-166 is sunk by Japanese Planes. **(Pacific-New Guinea)** U.S. troops initiate the prolonged campaign to seize Roosevelt Ridge, Scout Ridge, and Mt Tambu, which command Dot Inlet and Tamby Bay. **(Pacific-China-Burma-India)** Brigadier General Howard C. Davidson assumes command of Tenth Air Force, replacing General Clayton L. Bissel who departs for Washington to become Assistant Chief of Staff, A-2. **(Atlantic-Sicily)** Patton's 7th Army is directed by British General Alexander to capture Palermo. The U.S. 82nd Airborne Division under Colonel Gavin, moving west along the south coast, captures Menfi and Sciacca and its abandoned Airfield. Lt. Colonel William Darby's (Darby's Rangers) Task Force X, is to secure Castelvetrano and the nearby Airfield west of it, then drive to Palermo. Italian rear guard elements engage the U.S. 45th Division near Vallulunga. General Montgomery directs the 1st Canadians to seize Enna, but stiff enemy resistance repulses the Canadians. General Leese then bypasses the fortified city with a right flanking movement. This maneuver inadvertently opens a wide gap leading directly to II Corps supply depots. Bradley, expressing concern, contacts General Leese, explains that he must have permission to use the British roads to attack Enna to ensure protection of the II Corps supplies. General Leese apologizes sincerely for not informing II Corps about the move and he grants permission to use all roads necessary, then adds a P.S. to the note, in the form of two bottles of Scotch.

Two belligerent Regiments of the First Division swing around and attack Enna from different directions. In ferocious fashion they thrash the defenders, who choose to withdraw, rather than face being cut off and captured. Old Glory is flying, compliments of the U.S. 1st Division by 09:00. Colonel Benjamin A. Dickson, after the seizure of Enna quips: "NOT BAD, NOT BAD AT ALL. IT TOOK THE SARACENS 20 YEARS IN THEIR SIEGE OF ENNA. OUR BOYS DID IT IN FIVE HOURS." Later, during the evening, British Radio stations proclaim that Enna had been seized by the British during their "spectacular drive to the north." In the British Eighth Army area, General Montgomery orders the 78th Division, presently stationed in Africa, to embark for Sicily. In the British 13 Corps area, the enemy has totally stalled the British advance

Hitler and Mussolini (photo taken at Brenner Pass).

at the Plain of Catania. **Atlantic-Bay of Biscay)** Army Planes, operating in the Bay of Biscay (north of Spain and west of France), sink the U-Boat, U-588. **(Atlantic-Mediterranean)** Operation BRIMSTONE (invasion of Sardinia) is canceled due to the progress of the Sicilian campaign. Planning now concentrates on Naples, Italy, strategically located near Rome and possessing a fine harbor. **(Atlantic-Russia)** The Soviets overrun Mitsensk and also advance against the German salient at Orel.

July 21st 1943 — (Pacific-Solomons-New Georgia) A small six man Patrol, composed of Army, Navy, and Marine Officers, lands near Barakoma on Vella Lavella during the night, scouting the area for the imminent invasion of the island and return to Guadalcanal, reporting on the 31st, that a landing in the Barakoma area is practical. **(Atlantic-Sicily)** Task Force X captures Castelvetrano and its Airport; it is seized by a Platoon which accepts the surrender of 400 Italian troops without a fight; the Platoon speeds to Alcamo, 27 miles from Palermo, where 800 Italians capitulate without incident. The 39th Regiment speeds to catch up with the Platoon. The 2nd Armored Division (under General Gaffey) awaits orders to pass through 3rd Division lines to drive the enemy to the sea. The 82nd Airborne overruns south Margherita, while the 3rd Division seizes Corleone and the 45th Division secures Valledolmo. Task Force X has captured about 4,000 Italians during its rapid advance today. In the British 30 Corps area, Leonforte falls to the British, but heavy enemy resistance near Gerbini, pushes the British 51st Division back. **(Atlantic-South America)** The U-662, navigating near the mouth of the Amazon River in Brazil, is sunk by Land-based Planes (VP-94).

July 22nd 1943 — (North Pacific-Aleutians) Unaware that the Japanese are evacuating the Aleutians, the U.S. commences a synchronized Air and Naval bombardment to soften resistance on Kiska. The combined firepower of two Task Forces, commanded by Admirals R.C. Giffen and R.M. Griffin, (nine Destroyers and five Cruisers, and two Battleships), pummels Japanese positions. **(Pacific-Solomons-New Georgia)** U.S. General Griswold issues orders to assault enemy positions at Munda (on 25th). In other activity, Naval Land-based Aircraft, destroy the Japanese Seaplane Carrier, *Nisshin*. **(Atlantic-Sicily)** The U.S. 7th Army terminates the second phase of its campaign as troops converge on Palermo, seizing it after reducing minor resistance. Enemy pockets in the western portion of the island are cleared, prior to initiat-

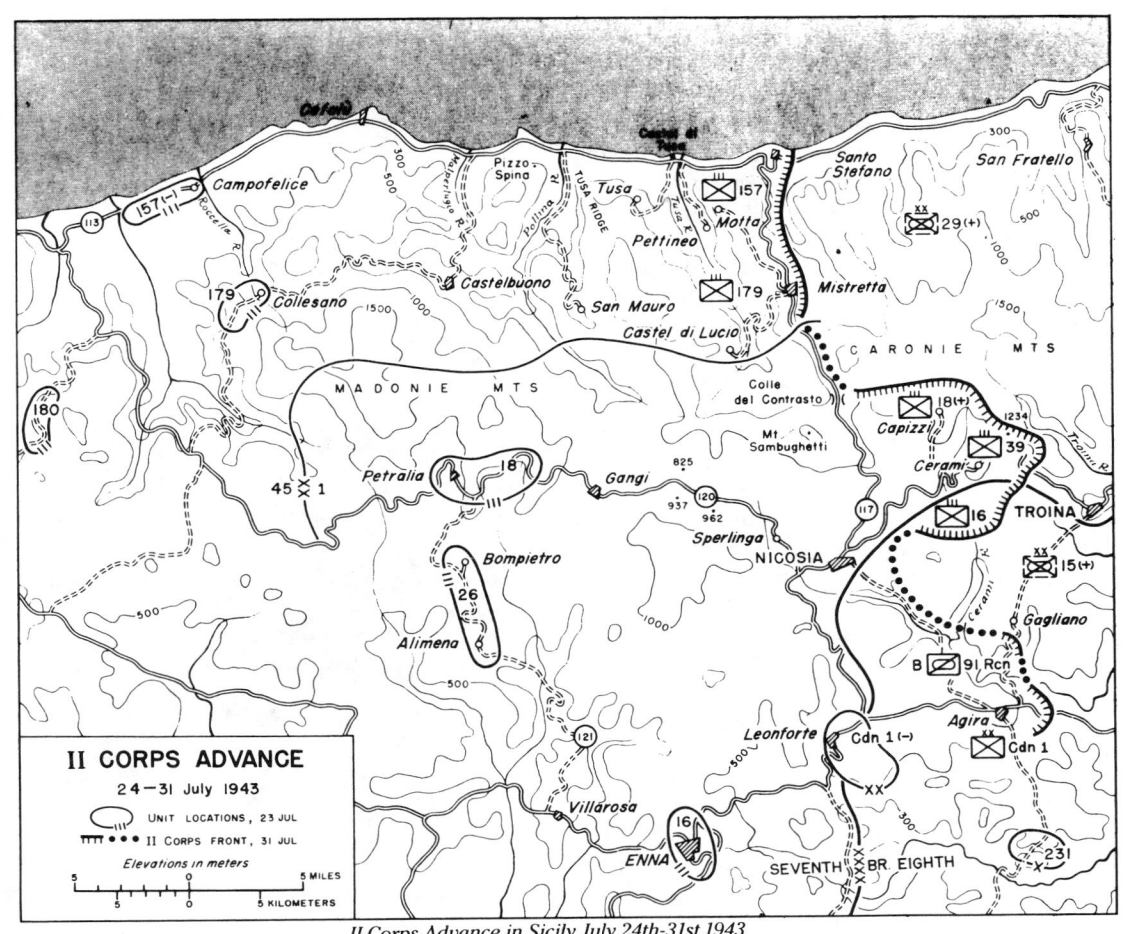

II CORPS ADVANCE
24–31 July 1943

UNIT LOCATIONS, 23 JUL
II CORPS FRONT, 31 JUL
Elevations in meters

5   0   5 MILES
5   0   5 KILOMETERS

II Corps Advance in Sicily July 24th–31st 1943.

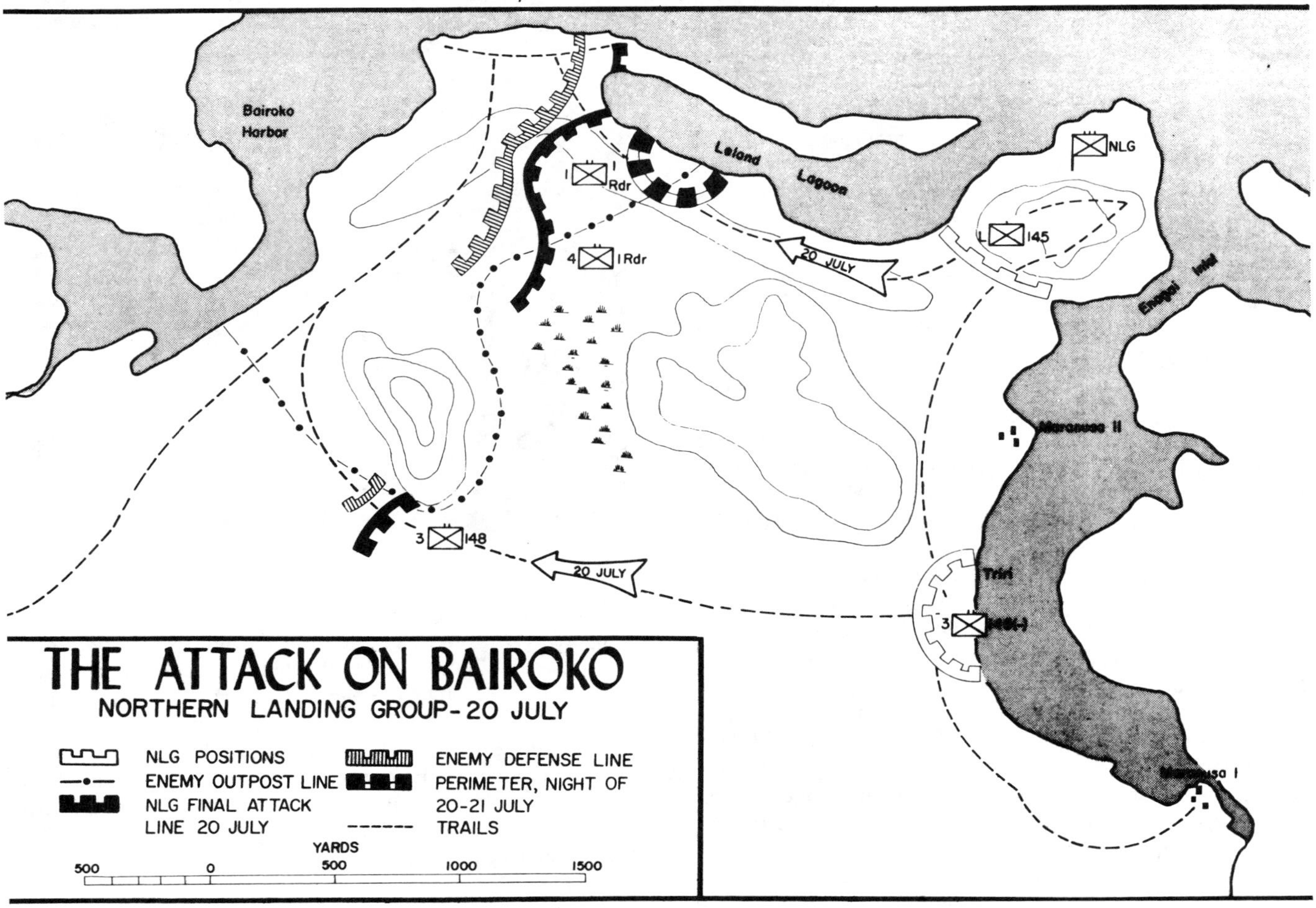

THE ATTACK ON BAIROKO
NORTHERN LANDING GROUP—20 JULY

NLG POSITIONS   ENEMY DEFENSE LINE
ENEMY OUTPOST LINE   PERIMETER, NIGHT OF
NLG FINAL ATTACK   20–21 JULY
LINE 20 JULY   TRAILS

500   0   500   1000   1500
YARDS

ing the final drive to the East. Task Force X, drives west along the coast guarding the rear and left flank. Meanwhile, the 2nd Armored Division bolts to the outskirts of Palermo in conjunction with the 3rd Division, which is moving to the southeastern edges of the city. The major assault planned to take the city is canceled, after it is known that resistance has totally ceased. Troops of the 3rd Division and the 2nd Armored Division flow into the city triumphantly without opposition, accepting the surrender of Palermo at 20:00 (8 P.M.). Actually, a contingent of civilians offer to surrender the city during the afternoon to Brigadier General Eagles (Asst. Commander 3rd Division), however, the offer is turned down as Eagles had received previous instructions that General Keyes was to accept the city's surrender. The 82nd Reconnaissance Battalion captures General Marciani, commander of the Italian defense forces and later in the day, a Patrol of CCA enters the city and returns with a prisoner; General Molinaro, Commander Port Defense "N", Palermo. In other activity, the U.S. 1st Division secures Bompietro. **(Atlantic-Soviet Union)** Bolkhov is taken by Soviet troops. Also, the Russians commence an offensive on the northern front near Lake Ladoga.

July 23rd 1943 — (Pacific-Trobriand Islands) The 67th Fighter Squadron arrives on Woodlark Island to initiate operations from the Airfield there. **(Atlantic-Azores)** Planes (VC-9) attached to the Escort Carrier *Bogue* (CVE-9) sink the U-Boat U-527 off the Azores. Her sister Ship, the U-613, is sunk by the Destroyer *Badger* (DD-126). **(Atlantic-Brazil)** Aircraft (VB-107) attack and sink the U-598 off the coast. **(Atlantic-Great Britain)** U.S. Navy Planes arrive to hunt Submarines. Squadron 63, is assigned responsibility for the Bay of Biscay and is based in Wales. **(Atlantic-Sicily) 15th Army Group** The Western Sicily campaign winds down, as 7th Army activity is confined to mopping up. Patton's Engineers immediately begin repairs on the damaged port of Palermo. Elements of the 3rd Division remain behind to hold Palermo, while the Main Force advances along highways 113 and 120, toward Messina. Army Group instructs Patton to step up the offensive: "THRUST EASTWARD ALONG THE COAST ROAD AND THE ROAD TO NICOSIA-TROINA-CESARA." The U.S. 7th Army takes many prisoners during pursuit. In the Provisional Corps sector, the 82nd Airborne Division (TF X attached) secures the Marsala-Trapani area of the west coast. As the Convoy rolls along, the Italians cheer and pass fruit, bread and chocolate (the latter confiscated from abandoned Italian Military depots. However, at 16:00, Italian Artillery rings down from the hills near Trapani in support of a roadblock along the road. Quick return fire and swift envelopment movements subdue the Artillery and demolish the roadblock. Soon after, Admiral Contrammiraglio Giuseppe Manfredi, Commander of the Trapani Naval District surrenders the city (5,000 troops) and his field glasses and sword to General Ridgway. Subsequently, Ridgway gives the field glasses to General Mark Clark, however, he later returns the sword to Manfredi. The trucks unload the 82nd contingents and return to pick up additional units. Trapani, on a high cliff overlooking the sea, contains a lighthouse which has been guiding mariners since before the time of Christ. The U.S. 45th Division severs the North Coast Road and drives to the Mediterranean Sea, despite minefields and blown bridges. In the British Eighth Army area, the enemy still gives fierce opposition to the British 30 Corps near Leonforte.

The Harbor and Airfield at Adak, in the Aleutians.

July 24th 1943 — The U.S. Eighth Air Force attacks Kjeller Norway.

July 24th 1943 — (Pacific-Solomons-New Georgia) U.S. Destroyers move toward Bairoko Harbor and heavily bombard it. Vicious fighting occurs as the Japanese prevent the 161st Infantry from reaching the Main Assault Force, which is forming for attack against Munda. **(Atlantic-Sicily)** The 540th Engineer Shore Regiment and the 20th Engineer Combat Regiment move into Palermo to open the port. The American 7th Army continues clearing enemy resistance in the western section of the island, again seizing many prisoners. The Provisional Corps (2nd Armored Division and 82nd Airborne) terminates its combat operations in Sicily. It had sustained 272 casualties (57 killed, 170 wounded, 45 missing), however, it had captured 53,000 enemy troops, primarily Italians and killed or wounded another 2,900. Also, it had seized 189 75mm guns, 359 Vehicles and 41 Tanks. In the II Corps sector, the U.S. 1st and 45th Divisions combined drives seize Cefalu, Castelbuono, and Gangi, the latter abandoned by Group Fullriede. RCT 26, 1st Division, secures the Bompietro road junction and sends its 1st Battalion toward Hills 825 (Monte Cannella) and 937 (Monte Caolina). The 3rd Battalion also closes on Hill 937, however, it is occupied by elements of the 2nd Battalion. At daybreak on the following day, the Germans counterattack to reclaim it. Meanwhile, the 45th Division continues to advance, despite strong resistance mounted by Group Ulich (29th Panzer Grenadier Division). However, the Germans blow a bridge over the Malpertugio and plant mines in the river bed, hindering the 157th Regiment temporarily. **(Atlantic-Italy)** The Fascist Grand Council convenes in Rome (called by Mussolini after his return from the Feltre Conference). However, during the meting a call for the King to resume command of the Armed Forces occurs in an attempt to dislodge Mussolini. At about 03:00 on the 25th after a prolonged debate the vote is 19-to-9 against Mussolini. The King informs Mussolini that he must resign. After the meeting, Mussolini cannot find his car and is escorted away in an ambulance, unaware that he is under arrest. **(Atlantic-England-Norway)** The U.S. Eighth Air Force launches a massive Air attack against Norway. Two hundred and eight Planes drop about 500 tons of bombs, hitting Heroya, an industrial center, and also, the Naval facilities at Trondheim. This is the furthest mission England's Land-based Planes have yet attempted; one Plane fails to safely return to base. U.S. Army Planes sink the U-622, a German Submarine, off Norway.

July 25th 1943 — (Pacific-Solomons) Major General Nathan F. Twining, U.S.A., replaces Rear Admiral Marc A. Mitscher, U.S.N., as Commander, Aircraft, Solomons. U.S. Airpower in the Solomons continues to build. Since early April, operational Planes have risen from 235 to 539. U.S. Fighter Pilots have destroyed 316 enemy Planes, while suffering the loss of 71, subsequent to the invasion of Rendova on the 30th of June. Also, U.S. Airpower has terminated enemy daylight Air assaults on Rendova. In New Georgia, the U.S. XIV Corps launches an offensive to capture the Airfield at Munda. Aircraft and Naval Surface Ships bombard entrenched enemy positions. Bitter enemy resistance faces the 37th and 45th Divisions as they plow slowly toward the objectives. Concentrated enemy fire, spewing from Bartley Ridge, stalls the advancing 37th Division. Its 161st Infantry must clear the ridge, however, Japanese defenders rip devastating fire upon the Americans and retain the Hill until the 31st of July. In addition, Jap pillboxes take their toll on the G.I's. Contingents of the 43rd Division fight vigorously and gain untenable ground near Terere; bad cover and exposure force withdrawal. These superbly fortified fanatical Japanese troops fight relentlessly. Jungle warfare rages from the end of July through August, however, the determined Americans secure Munda Airfield on August 1st. The treacherous fight for Bairoko Harbor ends victoriously for the Yanks on August 25th and the final drive to destroy the Japs in the central Solomons culminates on October 6th, when the Japanese evacuate Vella Lavella. **(Atlantic-Sicily)** Enemy troops mount a strong counterattack against the driving 1st Division in the vicinity of Gangi, but the Americans repulse it. During the night, the Germans re-

take Hill 937 as enemy Artillery pushes the troops from the crest. Infuriated, Colonel Bowen orders the 2nd Battalion to attack and seize the hill, which it does by early afternoon after a vicious fight with the reinforced Group Fullriede. Meanwhile, Brigadier General Clift Andrus (1st Division Artillery) turns six Artillery Battalions and two 155-mm gun Batteries loose in support of the 26th Regiment. Enemy fire is poured upon the 2nd Battalion on the crest of Hill 937, however, the Yanks hold firmly. In conjunction, the 3rd Battalion seizes Hill 962 (Monte Barnagiano) igniting a bloodbath on the 26th. Artillery plasters the crest throughout the 26th as the opposing sides battle for control in a see-saw fight between the Americans on the western and the Germans on the eastern slopes. Finally, after being bolstered by a Battalion of the 16th Regiment, the 3rd Battalion, 26th Regiment, wins control of the hill during the evening of the 26th. In the 45th Division zone, the 180th Regiment encounters a new German line in the heights near the Pollina River, where the Germans are dug in natural defensive positions which cling to the 3,000 foot high Pizza Spina. Fierce fighting ensues as Colonel Cochrane's troops attack doggedly. After a sustained battle begins to pause, Company E, suddenly burst forward tilting the battle as it overruns the German line and seizes positions near the crest of Pizza Spina, forcing the enemy to retreat down the eastern slopes. The Germans mount three strong counterattacks to regain the positions but are handily repulsed, despite withering German Artillery fire that scorches the crest of the objective. American Artillery and Mortars return fire ensuring the German attacks fail. Meanwhile, fourteen unidentified Warships appear offshore confusing both sides. General Bradley halts the 45th Division's advance, ordering Middleton to deploy to defend against a possible enemy landing and German General Hube, assuming the Vessels are American, alerts his forces to prepare for an Allied landing. By the following day, the Vessels are identified as U.S. Destroyers and Minesweepers. **(Atlantic-Italy)** Victor Emmanuel, the King of Italy (House of Savoy), announces the fall of Mussolini. Mussolini and his Cabinet members resign. Command of the Italian Army reverts to 71 year old, Marshal Pietro Badoglio. The Italian citizenry is elated; spontaneous parades commence and symbols of Fascism are torn down and Fascist offices are attacked by mobs.

July 26th 1943 — (United States) News concerning the resignation of Benito Mussolini reaches Washington. The Joint Chiefs of Staff meet at noon to discuss strategy regarding Italy. As a result of the meeting, General Eisenhower receives word from Washington to prepare plans for the invasion of Italy (Operation AVALANCHE). The invasion date is scheduled for September 8th, 1943 at Salerno). **(North Pacific-Aleutians)** Again, U.S. Planes launch a massive Air assault against enemy positions on Kiska to lighten resistance. The blockade of Kiska by U.S. and Canadian Warships is ongoing. Today, U.S. radar picks up suspected enemy activity, thought to be an enemy Convoy, however, darkness and dense fog prevents visual contact. Warships follow the beams and commence fire, pounding the area until their ammunition had been expended. On the following morning no wreckage or debris is discovered, leading the U.S. to conclude that the targets picked up on radar had actually been caused by terrible atmospheric conditions. Subsequently, the Vessels depart the area to refuel and pick up needed ammunition. Meanwhile, Japanese Destroyers had been hundreds of miles away. On the 29th, at about 08:00, the Japanese on Kiska receive word that evacuation Ships are on their way; the Destroyers, taking advantage of the absence of U.S. Warships move in under the cover of a thick fog and successfully evacuate the defenders of Kiska. **(Pacific-Solomons-New Georgia)** Admiral Halsey suggests to General MacArthur that the plans for invading South Bougainville mainland be scrapped and alternate plans for the invasion of the Shortlands and Ballale in the Bougainville Strait be implemented as planned. The modified attack plan will provide anchorages and Airfields. Macarthur subsequently approves. On New Georgia, the U.S. 103rd Infantry, 43rd Division captures Llangana and drives to the coast at Kia. Still, Japanese pillboxes and entrenched defenders hold Bartley Ridge. **(Atlantic-Germany-Italy)** In reaction to the fall of Mussolini, German Field Marshal von Ronstedt, O.B. West, is directed to divert two Divisions and deploy them at the Italian border; the 44th Infantry Division advances toward Brenner Pass and the 305th Infantry Division moves toward Nice. He is instructed to carry out two operations, which are essential to ALARICH: secure Mount Cenis Pass (KOPENHAGEN) and occupy the southern coast of France near the positions of the Italian Fourth Army (SIEGFRIED). Rommel is recalled from Salonika and will command Army Group B (Headquarters Munich), which will occupy northern Italy. In conjunction, von Ronstedt is to dispatch four additional Divisions from France and the II S.S. Panzer Corps is to be transferred from the Eastern Front to bolster Rommel. **(Atlantic-Sicily) 15th Army Group** The Germans hold firm on Hills 825 and 921 against the 1st Battalion, 26th Regiment, 1st Division. Also, two Battalions of the 16th Regiment bypass Hill 962 and drive to Sperlinga in conjunction with the 18th Regiment which is pivoting north of Highway 120 to seize the heights north of Sperlinga and sever Highway 117. In other activity, a German Horizontal Bomber damages the Destroyer *Mayrant* (DD-402), off Palermo, Sicily.

WACS attending retreat ceremony at Stewart Field, New York.

July 27th 1943 — (Pacific) The U.S.S. *Scamp* (SS-277), on patrol near the Admiralty Islands, sinks the I-24, a Japanese Submarine. The U.S.S. *Sawfish*, another U.S. Submarine, prowling off the coast of Japan, sinks the Minelayer *Hirashima* near Kyushu. **(Pacific-Solomons-New Georgia)** The U.S. 37th Division diverts its attention from Bartley Hill's devastating fire and concentrates on Horseshoe Hill. PFC Frank J. Petrarca, U.S. Army Medical Detachment, 147th Infantry, advancing with lead elements, reaches a badly wounded Soldier who is lying within 75 yards of the enemy, and too seriously

wounded to move. Petrarca defies withering fire and administers aid between burst of fire until Scott succumbs. Two other troops also are aided by the heroic medic. Two days later, the dauntless Petrarca rescues a buried Sergeant and on the 31st the gallant medic dispels strong urgings to be cautious and crawls to within 2 yards of a mortally wounded man (from direct mortar fire) and is himself struck and mortally wounded. Petrarca gets to his knees, taunts the enemy and struggles forward to reach the wounded man, but yields to the mortar wound and succumbs. He receives the Medal of Honor posthumously. **(Atlantic-Sicily) 15th Army Group** Elements of Patton's 7th Army (RCT 180, 45th Division) drive to Tusa, a few miles west of South Stefano, seizing it by 06:00 with its 3rd Battalion, however, nine hours later, the 3rd Battalion manages to advance a mere 300 yards to a deadly curve of the road overlooking the river. It is blocked by one of Colonel Max Ulich's reinforced Infantry Battalions. Some units cross the Tusa River, however, Artillery fire collapses the bridge, isolating the contingent. Coupled with heavy enemy fire and the impossibility of reinforcements reaching the opposing bank, the units holds precariously and upon darkness makes it back to the west bank. Also, RCT 179 drives to S. Mauro. Meanwhile, the 1st Division along Highway 120 toward Nicosia, flanked by the 4th Tabor of Goums and the 92nd Reconnaissance Squadron on its left and right respectively. General Allen commits thirty-two Tanks of the 70th Tank Battalion and a Platoon of medium Tanks from the 753rd Medium Tank Battalion to sweep through the area from Hill 825 to Hill 962 during the night boosting the morale of the Infantry, although the stinging attack costs three light Tanks and six casualties. The Germans have already decided to withdraw from the Nicosia Front during the night of the 27th, however, the Italians are not aware and expect to hold Nicosia. There had been some last minute discussions between General Guzzoni and German General Hube to halt the pullout of Group Fullriede, however, word is not received by either Fullriede or General Major Rodt. The Aosta Division joins the German withdrawal, virtually opening the floodgates on Highway 117, for the advancing Americans. Meanwhile, Admiral Hewitt establishes Task Force 88 (NTF-88), an improvised assortment of Vessels still in Sicilian waters, commanded by Rear Admiral Lyal A. Davidson. The Task Force is to support 7th Army operations and becomes known as "GENERAL PATTON'S NAVY." It is composed of fourteen Destroyers, 14 MTBs, 19 Landing Craft and some smaller craft.

July 28th 1943 — (United States) President Roosevelt announces his views on Italy and the war: "OUR TERMS FOR ITALY ARE STILL THE SAME AS OUR TERMS TO GERMANY AND JAPAN-UNCONDITIONAL SURRENDER." However, he changes his public stand and surrender terms are subsequently agreed upon. **(North Pacific-Aleutians)** The Japanese completely fool the Americans, by evacuating Kiska without detection. Allied invasion plans continue, including a Naval and Air bombardment on August 2nd, followed by another major bombardment initiated by five Cruisers and five Destroyers on August 12th. **(Pacific-Solomons)** A combined Reconnaissance Patrol, composed of Army, Navy, and Marine Corps Officers, returns to Guadalcanal with intelligence. The U.S. 37th Division maintains pressure against Horseshoe Hill. The struggling 161st Infantry secures evacuated positions on Bartley Ridge. In New Britain, two Japanese Destroyers, the *Ariake* and *Mikazuki* are sunk by Army Planes. **(Atlantic-**

Sicily) General Patton's Engineers open Palermo's harbor. Allied Ships begin unloading supplies and also debark General Manton Eddy's 9th Infantry Division, which reinforces the 1st Division, under General Allen, on the Troina Road. The U.S. 1st Division gets Patrols of the 3rd Battalion, 16th Regiment into Sperlinga by 08:30 and several hours later, into Nicosia, which is captured by the end of the day by the 16th Regiment; seven hundred Italians and a few Germans are captured. Meanwhile, the 45th Division inches closer to South Stefano. Also, the 727th Railway Operating Regiment is in place and the railroads in southern and central Sicily are back in service. The first train departs Palermo heading east on the 29th of July. Also, the 3rd Division begins advancing to relieve the 45th Division on the north coast road. The 157th Regiment drives to the Tusa River, despite a blown bridge at the Pollina River and mines, relieving the 180th Regiment, 45th Division with its first Battalion at 17:45. Soon after relief, the 157th attacks to secure Hill 335, seizing it from the 3rd Battalion, 15th Panzer Grenadiers. In the **British Eighth Army** area, Agira is secured by the 1st Canadian Division as Group Ens abandons it to join Group Fullriede. To forestall the American advance, General Hube orders the 29th Panzer Grenadier Division to fight a holding action in front of Santo Stefano di Camastra. (**Atlantic-Europe**) The 92nd Bomber Group moves toward Europe, and is intercepted by enemy Aircraft at the German coast, however, the Yanks drive them off. The U.S. suffers some casualties, but the mission is a success. In one Plane, the Pilot is seriously wounded and semi-conscious when 2nd Lt. John C. Morgan calmly takes control of the Aircraft and rejoins the formation to complete the mission. In Naval activity the German U-404 is sunk in the Bay of Biscay by combined efforts of U.S. Army and R.A.F. Planes. Another German Submarine, the U-359 is caught near the West Indies and it is destroyed by Naval Land-based Planes (VP-32).

July 29th 1943 — (Pacific-New Georgia) U.S. Tanks and flame throwers begin the systematic destruction of additional enemy obstacles near Munda Airfield. Major General John R. Hodge replaces General Hester as Commander of 43rd Division. The 145th Infantry grabs a foothold on the crest of Horseshoe Hill, but the terrain is untenable, forcing it to withdraw to safer ground. In an instance of extraordinary bravery, Lt. Robert Scott, 172nd Infantry, holds off a Japanese counterattack singlehandedly, subsequent to his Company's withdrawal. Although badly wounded, his accurate carbine fire and grenade tossing, turns the tenacious enemy back and he inspires the men to advance and capture the hill from which the attack to seize Munda is later launched. (**Atlantic-England**) The U.S. Navy establishes an Advanced Amphibious Training Base at Appledore, England. (**Atlantic-Sicily**) The U.S. 7th Army begins using the captured rails between Palermo and Cefalu. Enemy resistance in Western Sicily is almost non existent. The 82nd Airborne secures three minor islands, Favignana, Levango, and Marettimo, off the coast of Trapani. In the II Corps sector, the 2nd Battalion, 157th Regiment, 3rd Division hits fierce resistance as it drives toward Motta; the 1st Battalion rushes to assist, and Artillery is thrown into the fight. Fifteen hundred rounds catapulted by three Artillery Battalions crash to the immediate front of the beleaguered Battalions, but the going remains slow as Motta is 900 feet higher than Tusa Ridge line. As ordered, the 29th Panzer Grenadiers hold tight, refusing to abandon the line at the principal feature in front of Santo Stefano (objective of 45th Division) prior to the 30th. In the 1st Division zone, con-

tingents reach the fringes of Mistretta, prompting General Fries to order a counterattack to regain the Tusa Ridge (30th). The 45th Division must be prevented from advancing if Santo Stefano is to hold for an additional day. Group Ulich is reinforced by a Battalion from the 71st Panzer Regiment and two Artillery Battalions for the strike.

July 30th 1943 — (United States) The Chesapeake Bay is penetrated by a German Submarine, which plants mines there. (**Pacific-Solomons-New Georgia**) The Japanese mount an unsuccessful attack against the 145th Regiment, 37th Division at Horseshoe Ridge. Meanwhile, the 161st Regiment, supported by the 2nd Battalion, 145th Regiment works to secure Bartley Ridge. Contingents of the 148th Regiment establish contact with the 161st, however, the main body of the 148th Regiment remains isolated. (**Pacific-Manchuria**) Three Americans who had escaped from the P.O.W. Camp at Mukden during June, and subsequently recaptured by Chinese Mongolian police are executed by a firing squad. The Japanese charged that the two Marines and one Sailor had stolen something (item unknown) and also killed a policeman during the confrontation. Witnesses state that the Japanese returned the Americans (bound) to Mukden in the rear of a truck and that the men showed signs of a brutal beating. (**Atlantic-Sicily**) **15th Army Group** The U.S. 7th Army still pursues the retreating enemy. Elements of the 45th Division run into stiff opposition near South Stefano, however, by evening the enemy begins to withdraw. At 04:30, the Germans launch a startling surprise attack, gaining ground, but the U.S. 157th Infantry is bolstered by a furious fusillade of Artillery shells, which slashes the enemy attackers. By noon the Germans have sustained heavy casualties and the attack falters. By 13:00, subsequent to a thunderous fifteen minute barrage, the attack terminates. By darkness, Motta is seized effortlessly and the Germans remaining to hold at Santo Stefano number about one reinforced Battalion. The Germans also pull out of Reitano. Meanwhile the 1st Division moves toward Troina; Patrols advance to Cerami without incident. However, menacing resistance and incessant rains force termination of the 1st Division's pursuit of the 15th Panzer Grenadier Division. In the British Eighth Army area, 30 Corps sector, Catenanouva is seized by the British 78th Division. At Regalbuto, the enemy mounts heavy resistance against the British 231st Brigade. (**Atlantic-Italy**) The Germans are still inquiring as to where Mussolini is being held. On the previous day, Mussolini's birthday, Ambassador von Mackensen and Kesselring bring presents for him to Rome, the latter carrying a gift from Hitler, but they could not acquire accurate information about him. Also the Italian Minister of War had received information that German troops were massing in the German Tyrol with some contingents marching toward Brenner Pass. Today, the Italians still hold back information, but begin preparing to resist the Germans against a possible coup d'etat, giving the protection of Rome priority over defending the coast against the Allies. (**Atlantic-Naval**) The U-375 is destroyed by the Submarine Chaser *RPC-624*, near Tunisia and the U-43 is sunk by Planes (VC-29), attached to the Escort Carrier *Santee* (CVE-29), in the mid-Atlantic. A third enemy Submarine, the U-591, operating off Brazil is destroyed by Naval Land-based Bombers (VB-127). (**Atlantic-Soviet Union**) The Germans attempt to regain ground near Mius, however, the endeavor fails.

July 31st 1943 — (Pacific-Philippines) The U.S.S. *Grayling* (SS-209) penetrates the Japanese Naval defenses and lands

A German Soldier brandishing a band of ammo and a bayonet.

August 1943 — Salamaua is attacked by B-24s.

additional equipment and supplies at Pucio Point, Panay. **(Pacific-Solomons-New Georgia)** In New Georgia, the U.S. finally clears Bartley Ridge of the enemy, however, fierce resistance still is offered at Horseshoe Hill. In one instance, a Platoon of the 148th Infantry, halted from intense machine-gun fire, is ordered to fall back to assume safer positions for the night. Private Roger Young, already wounded, yells that he can see the enemy; he advances, and again becomes wounded, as he exchanges rifle fire against the rapid firing machine guns. Young then advances further and tosses grenades at the fortification, but another burst of fire slays him. Young's heroism saves his Platoon. He receives the Medal of Honor

posthumously. In other activity, the U.S.S. *Guardfish* (SS-217) nears the coast of Bougainville, and lands a contingent of surveyors. **(Atlantic-Sicily) 15th Army Group** In the **U.S. Seventh Army** area, General Patton, issues orders for an assault against Messina to commence on August 1st. II Corps composed of the 1st, 3rd, and 9th Divisions will make the primary attack driving down Highways 113 and 120. Santo Stefano falls to the 45th Division, concluding its offensive operations in Sicily, however, its 157th Regiment participates in the final thrust to seize Messina. The 45th had sustained 1,156 casualties during its impressive trek from Scoglitti to the north coast, seizing 10,977 prisoners as it advanced. The 3rd Division under Truscott replaces the 45th. Also, Colonel H.A. Flint's 39th Regiment, 1st Division drives toward Cerami at dawn; a Battalion enters the town at 09:00. In other activity, a 2nd Armored detachment composed of 10 men, led by Sergeant Gerry Kisters, advances to repair craters in the lone Vehicle route through Gagliano. Enemy fire (15th Panzers) rips into their positions. Sgt. Kisters is wounded five times during the firefight with the enemy, however, his actions succeed in the destruction or capture of the two enemy nests; the detachment supported by Artillery enters Gagliano on the following day. Kisters becomes the recipient of the Medal of Honor. **(Atlantic-Italy)** German troops attempt to enter Brenner Pass, however, the Italians have orders not to permit passage. Discussions continue at high levels and soon after a compromise is struck. By August 2nd, Army Group B's movement is back on track, including the arrival of contingents of the 2nd Parachute Battalion at Rome. Additional units which had not been agreed upon such as the German 65th and 94th Infantry Divisions also move into Italy. **(Atlantic-South America)** Brazilian Planes combine with a contingent of Naval Planes (VP-74), to attack and destroy the German Submarine U-199, off shores of Rio de Janeiro.

August 1st 1943 — (Pacific-Carolines) The U.S.S. *Mingo* (SS-261) surfaces close to shore and shells Sorol Island. **(North Pacific-Aleutians)** The U.S. Army initiates continual bombings of suspected enemy positions on Kiska, however, the Japanese have evacuated. **(Pacific-Solomons)** In New Georgia, U.S. troops approach Munda Airfield against slight resistance as the enemy has withdrawn. Also, the Japanese have evacuated their positions on Horseshoe Hill. The 148th Infantry finally slices through the concrete-like resistance and finally joins the Main Body. PT Boats are active around Rendova, attacking Japanese Destroyers and fending off enemy Planes. The PT-117 is sunk by a Dive Bomber and the PT-164 sinks after being attacked by an enemy Horizontal Bomber. **(Atlantic-Sicily)** Enemy troops give the advancing U.S. 1st Division tough resistance, however, the U.S. 9th Division (minus Regimental Combat Team 39) rolls into Palermo. Patton issues 7th Army General Orders 10: in part; "YOU HAVE, DURING 21 DAYS OF CEASELESS BATTLE AND UNREMITTING TOIL, KILLED AND CAPTURED MORE THAN 87,000 ENEMY SOLDIERS, YOU HAVE CAPTURED OR DESTROYED 371 CANNON, 172 TANKS, 982 TRUCKS AND 190 Cannon, 172 Tanks, 928 Trucks and 190 AIRPLANES-YOU ARE MAGNIFICENT SOLDIERS! THE END IS CERTAIN AND IS VERY NEAR. MESSINA IS OUR NEXT STOP!" Meanwhile, the 3rd Battalion, 39th Regiment, 9th Division is driving toward Troina, supposedly lightly defended, advancing to within four miles of the objective. The attack which had begun at 05:00 is bogged down by Artillery and mortar and small arms fire, forcing a withdrawal by mid-morning, however, the reversal

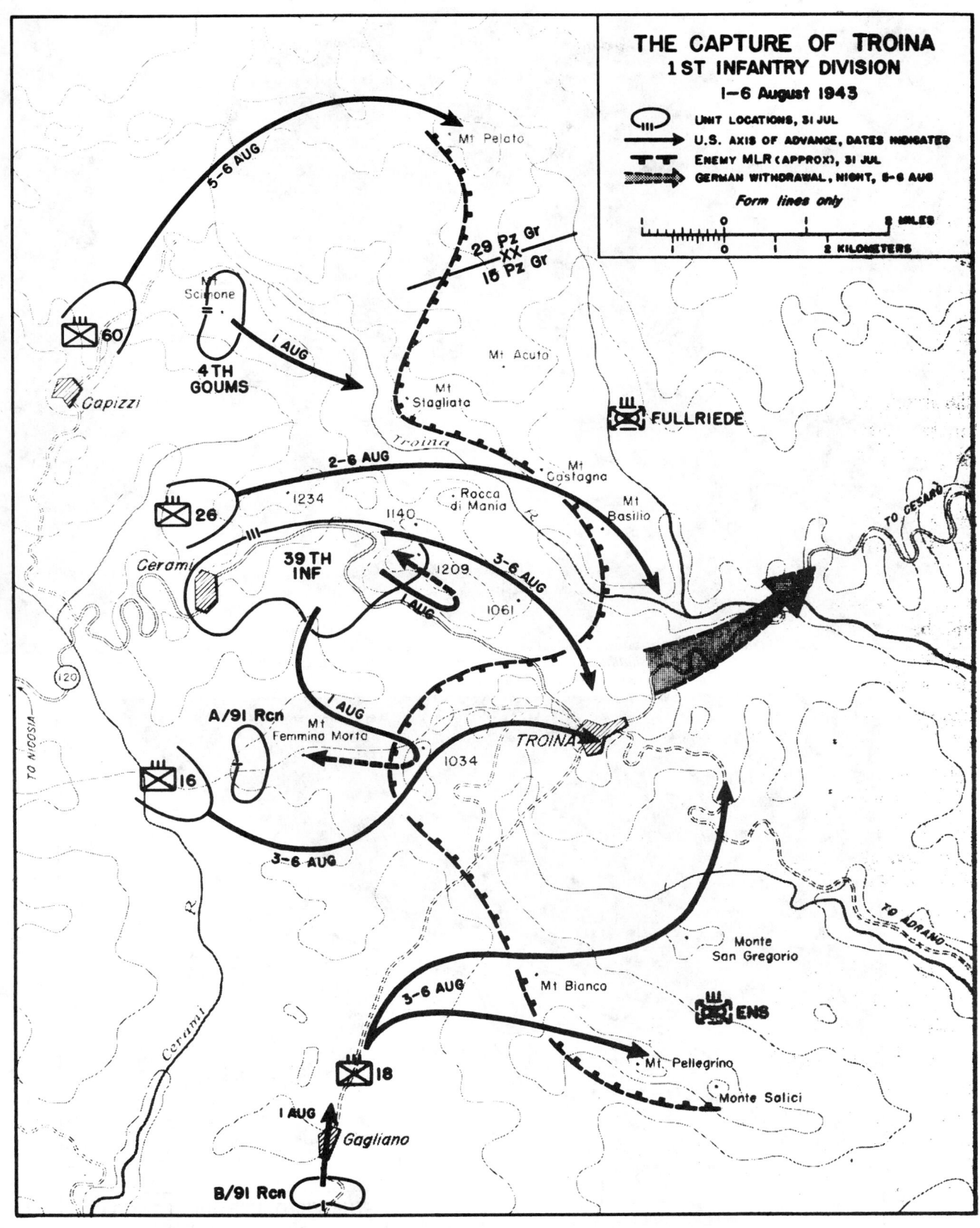

THE CAPTURE OF TROINA
1ST INFANTRY DIVISION
1-6 August 1943

UNIT LOCATIONS, 31 JUL
U.S. AXIS OF ADVANCE, DATES INDICATED
ENEMY MLR (APPROX), 31 JUL
GERMAN WITHDRAWAL, NIGHT, 5-6 AUG
Form lines only

MILES
KILOMETERS

Mt Pelato

5-6 AUG

29 Pz Gr
XX
15 Pz Gr

Mt Scimone

60

4TH
GOUMS

1 AUG

Capizzi

Mt Acuto

Mt Stagliata

Troina

FULLRIEDE

2-6 AUG

Mt Castagna

26

1234

Rocca
di Mania

Mt Basilio

TO CESARO

1140

Cerami

39TH
INF

1209

3-6 AUG

1 AUG

1061

120

A/91 Rcn

1 AUG

Mt
Femmina Morta

TROINA

1034

16

3-6 AUG

Cerami R.

Monte
San Gregorio

TO NICOSIA

3-6 AUG

Mt Bianca

ENS

TO ADRANO

Mt. Pellegrino

18

Monte Salici

1 AUG

Gagliano

B/91 Rcn

229

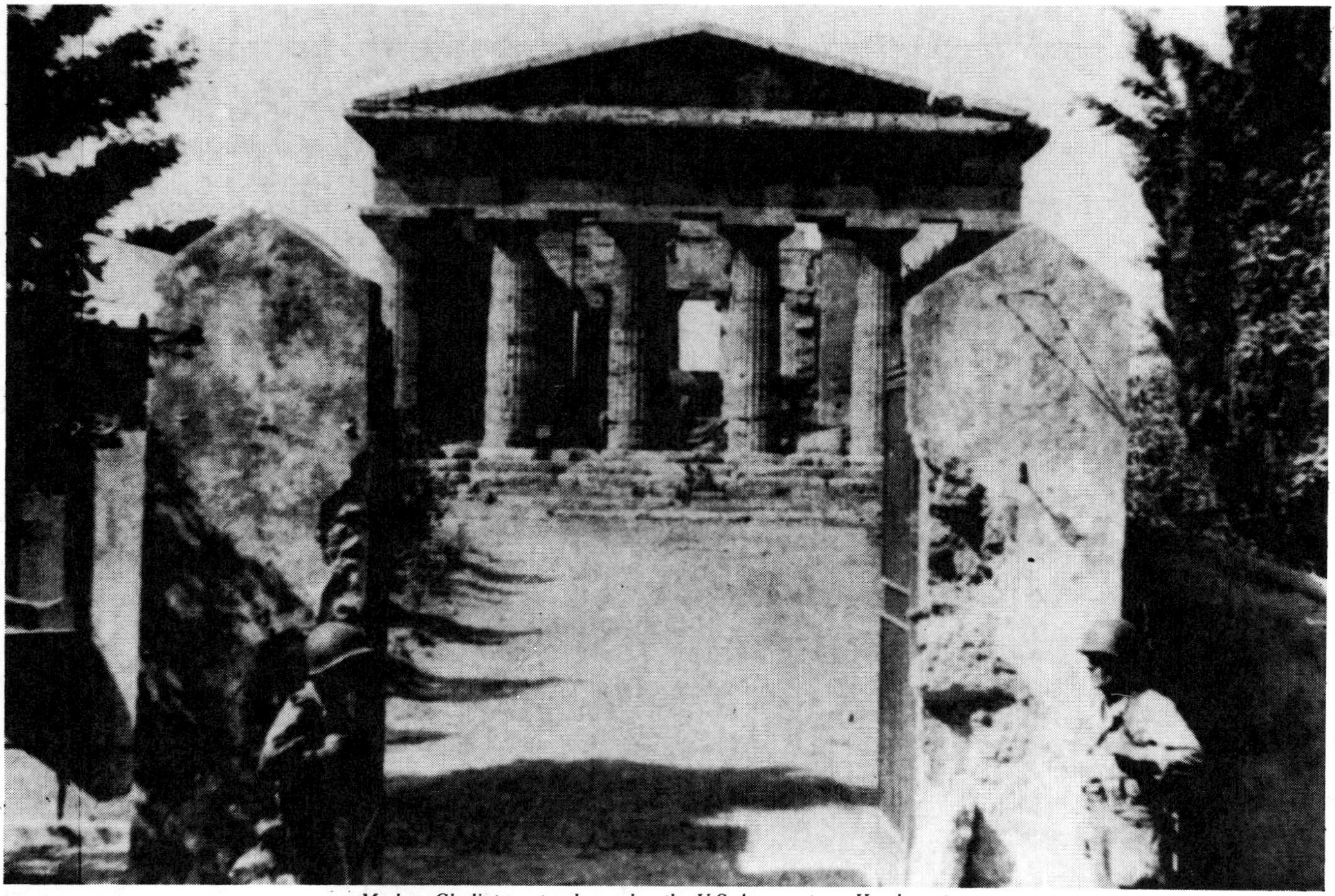

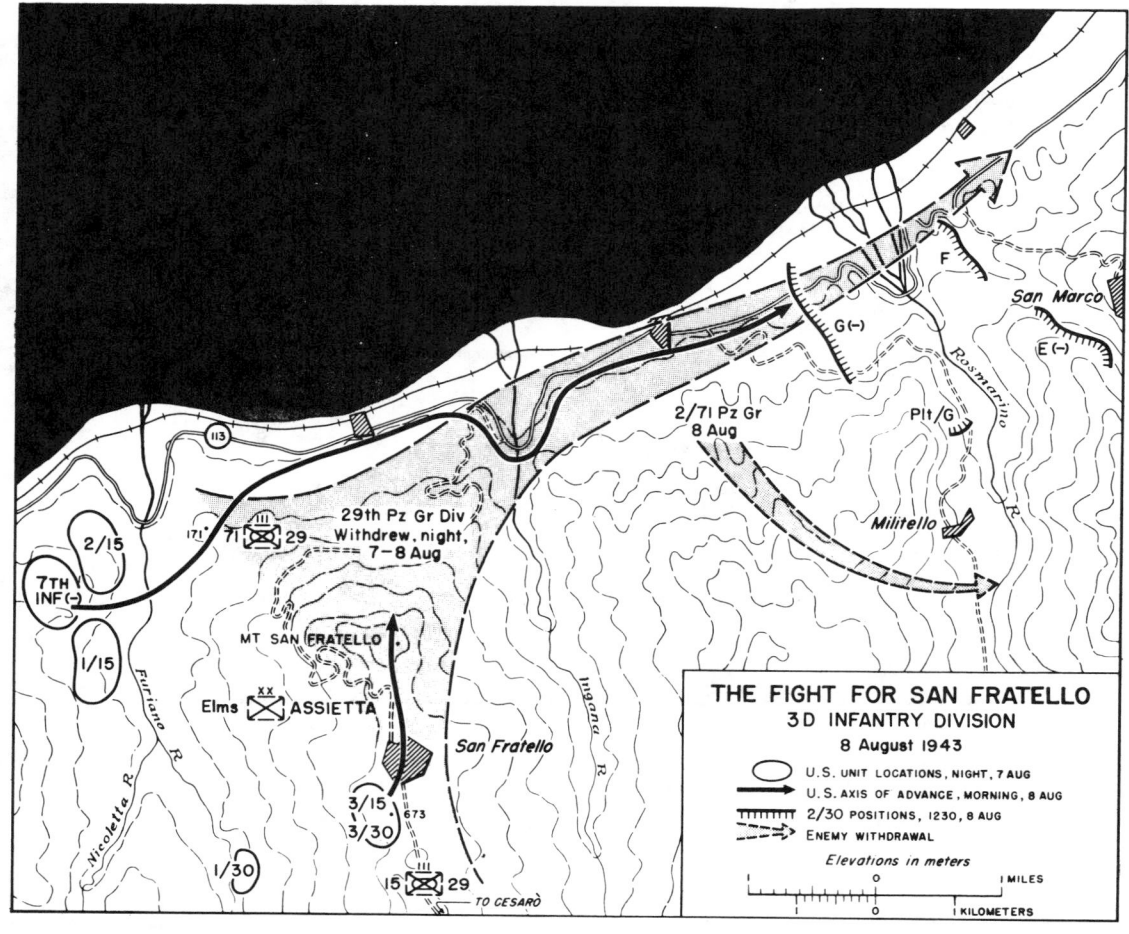

*Modern Gladiators stand guard as the U.S. Army sets up Headquarters
in the ancient Temple of Neptune, Paestum.*

THE FIGHT FOR SAN FRATELLO
3D INFANTRY DIVISION
8 August 1943

U.S. UNIT LOCATIONS, NIGHT, 7 AUG
U.S. AXIS OF ADVANCE, MORNING, 8 AUG
2/30 POSITIONS, 1230, 8 AUG
ENEMY WITHDRAWAL

Elevations in meters

0   1 MILES

0   1 KILOMETERS

allows Colonel Bond's 3rd Battalion to subsequently throw back a German counterattack before noon. The 39th's 1st Battalion, under Major P.C. Tinley, digs in on Hill 1034, west of Troina. In conjunction, the 26th Regiment, under Colonel Bowen, pivots and drives east toward a hill mass dominating the highway east of Troina. The attack is supported by Artillery and receives further strength by the 4th Tabor of Goums which seizes Capizzi. Meanwhile, during the afternoon, General Allen authorizes the 39th Regiment (1st Division) to send two Battalions to seize the heights north of Troina, however, strong enemy fire halts the advance. Later, Group Ens springs a night counterattack against the 1st Battalion, 39th Regiment holding Hill 1034; the Germans inflict heavy casualties on Companies A, and C, and push the beleaguered unit back, however, the Germans fail to take advantage and dig in on the seized ridge as opposed to continuing the attack. Also, the 3rd Division replaces the 45th Division on the line, to enable it to join Mark Clark's 5th Army as part of the Italian Invasion Force. The 3rd Division renews the advance along the North Coast Road. Enemy troops stymie the British advance near Centuripe. During the day's hostilities, the Minesweeper *Skill* (AM-115) is damaged by an enemy Bomber. **(Atlantic-Italy)** The Germans have anticipated the defection of Italy for some time and have a plan (ACHSE) ready for implementation if it occurs; if the code-word is issued, German troops are to seize the country with force. **(Atlantic-Rumania)** During the Trident Conference (May 12th-25th, 1943), it had been decided to destroy the Ploesti oil fields in Rumania (1,200 miles from Libya), which supply about one third of the German war machine. Previously, during June of 42, U.S. Planes based in Africa had attacked the installation, however, today is the first full scale low level assault against the installation. The attack force composed of U.S. Eighth Air Force Bombers, and others on loan from the U.S. Northwest African Air Force, all commanded by General Brereton. Prior to departure, the Pilots are briefed about the mission and informed that the area is basically protected by Rumanian Fighter Planes and also are told that the ground defenses are manned by Rumanian troops, not elite German forces. In addition, intelligence suggests that the Antiaircraft guns are deployed along the railroad tracks to defend against night attack coming from the south. The 177 Heavy Bombers must make the journey unassisted by long range Fighters, which are still unavailable. In addition, they fly at altitudes of 30 feet to avoid radar detection. The lead group makes a navigational error upon approach, turning prematurely at Floesti, and shattering the element of surprise. The miscalculation sends the 1st wave directly toward Bucharest, home of the German Defense Command which sounds the alarm. Radio silence is broken when the error is discovered, however, the 1st wave now encounters fierce resistance by both Antiaircraft batteries and German Fighters. The formations pass over the objective, moving through heavy flak followed by Fighters. Despite the overpowering resistance, the formations stay tight and drop their loads including time-delayed bombs, while simultaneously fighting off the Fighters. The second wave arrives, however, as it unleashes its bombs, others (time-delayed), belatedly dropped by the first wave, begin exploding right under them as they pass. Still, they resist and their gunners pour fire upon the interceptors during the vicious encounter. The Germans blow many Planes from the sky, however, the Bombers complete their perilous mission and head for Turkey, having destroyed much of Ploesti's cracking capacity.

Fifty-four Planes are lost; 41 in action. Although damaged, the installation continues to operate. Several Planes had been hit by enemy fire prior to reaching the target, but the Pilots ignore the glaring danger and fly directly into the inferno, knowing the results might be the loss of their lives. Participants in the raid include the 93rd Heavy Bombardment Group, 44th Bomber Group, 564th Bomber Squadron and 389th Bomber Group. Five men receive the Medal of Honor, the only single action of the war where it occurs. The tales of heroism are too numerous to mention all. In one instance, Major John L. Jerstad, leading an attack Group enters heavy fire and his Plane is hit and set afire three miles from the objective. Jerstad, declines a opportunity to land and continues the attack, releasing all bombs but the fire consumes the Aircraft and it crashes. Another Officer suffering similar circumstances and exhibiting extraordinary courage is Lt. Colonel Addison E. Baker, and yet another whose Aircraft is badly damaged and afire is Lt. Lloyd H. Hughes, whose Plane drops its bombs while flying through the raging fires with a leaking fuel tank which ignites and forces the Aircraft to crash. All three Officers (posthumously) are among those who become recipients of the Medal of Honor during this most hazardous mission. Eight missions had been planned, however, the costliness of the attack and the lack of Fighter protection cancels the operation (TIDALWAVE). Immediately, the Germans transport laborers to Ploesti and the facility is fully operational within six months. Subsequent raids are launched: from Italy (April 5th 1944); July 26th Fifteenth Air Force; August 6th 1944 Fifteenth Air Force. During June of 44 the raids become incessant to finish the refinery permanently. Well over 50,000 Airmen fly missions to strike Ploesti and drop about 27,000,000 pounds of bombs. The Russians walk into the facility after it is totally leveled by the Yanks during September 1944.

August 2nd 1943 — (North Pacific) Two U.S. Fleets (two Battleships, five Cruisers and nine Destroyers), commanded by Rear Admirals W.D. Baker, and H.F. Kingman, bombard Kiska in the first of ten Naval attacks against it between today and the 15th. **(Pacific-Solomons)** The PT 109, commanded by Lieutenant John Kennedy (future President U.S.) is devastated after being rammed by a Japanese Destroyer. The crew is subsequently rescued. On New Georgia, elements of the 43rd Division's 103rd and 169th Regiments reach Munda Airfield, against slight resistance as the main forces of the Japanese have evacuated. In the 37th Division zone, the Japanese abandon Horseshoe Hill. In conjunction, the isolated 148th Regiment breaks through and reaches the main body of the 37th. **(Pacific-New Guinea)** U.S. Army Aircraft sink two Japanese Torpedo Boats; Nos. 112, and 113. **(Atlantic-Sicily)** Enemy troops fight viciously around Troina as the Yanks begin to encircle it. The 26th Regiment (1st Division) moves out at 05:00 against fierce opposition from the onset; the attack gets forward units to Rocca di Mania, but because its flanks are totally exposed the advance is halted until the following day. Meanwhile, the 39th Regiment and the Goumiers are unable to make any progress. In other activity, General Patton, while visiting a hospital, becomes incensed when Pvt. Charles H. Kuhl, L Co. 26th Infantry, responds to a question telling Patton "I guess I can't take it." Patton curses, yells, and slaps the Private with a pair of gloves, then kicks the Soldier out of the tent. Later, Private Paul Bennett Battery C, 17th Field Artillery, responds to a question by Patton stating: "I can't stand the shelling anymore." Patton calls him a coward among other things, and slaps the man on his helmet, knocking it off his head. These two minor incidents, when measured against the full scale of the war, seem incidental, but they almost cost Patton his job. Patton pays heavily and sits out of the war for a long time, however, he survives the ordeal, much to the dismay of the Germans. Subsequently, thes incidents make world wide conversation. In the British sector, the British still struggle to clear the enemy from Centuripe without definite results. In other activity, in the Atlantic Theater, the U-706 is destroyed by Army Land-based Planes. **(Atlantic-North Africa)** General Doolittle's (N.A.S.A.F.) Heavy Bombers receive orders to abort further raids against the enemy in the Messina Strait area, to permit the over-taxed Airmen to receive some rest, however, the directive is soon rescinded (as the German evacuation of Sicily escalates) with the stipulation that Doolittle's forces would be restricted to night raids unless Doolittle decides otherwise and then only if a direct request comes from Air Vice Marshal Coningham. Between 5th and 9th August, Doolittle's Bombers fly three daylight missions against Messina and British Wellington Bombers strike the area nightly. **(Atlantic-Italy)** At Algiers, a warning to the citizens of Italy is broadcast, informing them of the upcoming invasion of the country.

Admiral R.R. Waesche, the head of the Coast Guard during World War II.

August 3rd 1943 — (Pacific-New Georgia) Heavy fighting continues as the Yanks take Bibolo Hill, just outside of Munda Field and close for the kill. Meanwhile, the Liversedge Force marches north to cut off escape routes. **(Atlantic-Dutch**

Messina, where the chase ends.

Guiana) Naval Land-based Aircraft, on Patrol north of Dutch Guiana, encounter and sink the U-572, further depleting the number of active German Submarines operating in the Atlantic. **(Atlantic-North Africa)** The Destroyer U.S.S. *Buck* (DD-420), sinks an Italian Submarine, the *Argento* off the coast of Tunisia. In other activity, Alberto Berio, former Counselor of the Embassy in Ankara is in Tangier to establish communication with the British, under the guise of replacing Badoglio's son as Consul General. The genuine purpose of the mission is to inform the British Consul that Italy wants to negotiate and is prepared to join the Allies to rid Italy of the Germans. Meanwhile, the Marchese Blasco Lanza D'Ajeta, Counselor of the Italian Embassy at the Holy See is sent to Portugal to contact the Allies and explain Italy's precarious position because of the Germans and the Communists. To prove good faith, D'Ajeta is to inform the Allies of the German order of battle in Italy. He meets with the British Ambassador on the following day. He also requests that the Allies continue to broadside the King and Badoglio in the media as a cover. The King and the government are laying plans to escape to Maddalena, an island off Sardinia. **(Atlantic-Sicily) 15th Army Group** In the **U.S. Seventh Army** area, II Corps sector, the U.S. 3rd Division pushes along the North Coast road, driving toward the Furiano River. Elements of the 2nd and 3rd Battalions, 15th Regiment, drive to the river and come under sever fire; in addition the river crossing sites are saturated with mines. About three miles away, the 3rd Battalion reaches the river outside of San Fratello, after an arduous trek over treacherous mountain trails and across deep gorges. Plans are made to establish a bridgehead which is imperative if the mines are to be cleared. In the 1st Division area, tenacious fighting continues at Troina. The 16th Regiment jumps off at 03:00; its 2nd and 3rd Battalions gaining positions on a ridge east of Troina, however, they become isolated. The Germans mount a fierce counterattack against the beleaguered units, prompting General Andrus to unleash the firepower of six Battalions of Artillery to forestall disaster; the Artillery and resolute fighting of the Infantry throws back the assault. Soon after the Germans attack again, reaching positions too close to permit additional Artillery, however, the weakened Battalions hold. General Allen attempts to renew the attack by outflanking Troina, then changes his mind after conferring with General Roosevelt. In conjunction, the 26th Regiment drives to Monte Basilio and the 39th Regiment reaches Monte San Silvestro. German Artillery, firing from the north slopes of Monte Acuto and Monte Castagna hammer the American positions at Monte Basilio, but R.A.F. Spitfires swoop in and pound the slopes quieting the guns somewhat. Colonel Flint (39th Regiment) requests an Airstrike to bomb suspected enemy positions, however, the request is denied because the 26th Regiment and the Goumiers are extremely close to the area, and the previous bombardment by the Spitfires had hit the Goumier area (no damage incurred). During the day, the Germans counterattack the 26th Regiment on Monte Basilio and are met by incessant machine gun fire, Riflemen and Artillery and thrown back despite the 26th's shortage of manpower because one Battalion loses its way and winds up on Monte Stagliata, separated from the besieged Battalions by two miles. With the retention of Monte Basilio, the U.S. is able to spot targets on Highway 120 for Artillery. In the **British Eighth Army's** 30 Corps area, the British 78th Division takes Centuripe. **(Atlantic-Russia)** The Soviets mount a large offensive to finish the Germans at Kharkov. In addition, the Soviets move on Orel from three directions.

August 4th 1943 — (North Pacific-Aleutians) The Eleventh Air Force offensive reaches its zenith as 134 sorties are flown, dropping 152 tons of bombs on Kiska. **(Pacific-Solomons-New Georgia)** Fierce Fighting continues as the Americans drive the Japanese out of Munda. The 43rd Division concentrates against the remaining resistance on Kokengolo Hill north of the runway at the Airfield. The 37th Division drives to the sea. **(Atlantic-Sicily) 15th Army Group** Strong enemy fire prevents the U.S. 15th Infantry, 3rd Division from fording the Furiano River. Naval fire is brought to bear upon the enemy positions on Monte San Fratello, but still, the crossing is prevented. Several hours later, Major F.J. Kobes Jr., pushes two Companies (2nd Battalion) against Hill 171 just across the river, however, sheets of machine gun fire forbid crossing; a few troops make it to the opposing bank and cling to it until darkness when they are recalled. No ground is gained, but the Regiment sustains 103 casualties. In the 1st Division sector, General Bradley, while at Cerami, witnesses a massive American Air and Artillery bombardment of enemy positions; eighteen Battalions unleash their guns with a thunderous roar, lofting innumerable shells into Troina. When the Artillery shelling subsides, 36 U.S. Bombers pass over the town and drop 500 pound bombs, reducing it to crumbled ruins and rising dust. Additional Airstrikes occur at 17:00, again by 36 P51s. In conjunction, General Allen calls for and receives an Air strike against Monte Acuto by eight A-36s, at 14:45. Subsequently, the U.S. 1st Division moves against Troina, however, a strong counterattack halts the advance on Highway 120. However, contingents of the 26th Regiment clears Rocca di Mania, two miles northwest of Troina, and the 39th Regiment gets two Battalions to the base of Monte San Mercurio. Offshore, the Destroyer *Shubrick* (DD-639) is damaged by a Dive Bomber. On the following day, again, U.S. Bombers enter the struggle, but they miss the target and in error, strike the Canadian positions at Cerami. The American thrust pounds the Germans; they evacuate Troina on the 6th.

August 5th 1943 — (Pacific-Solomons) American troops (XIV Corps) burst through Japanese resistance and seize Munda Airfield, New Georgia, culminating twelve brutalizing days of intense jungle warfare against fanatical Japanese troops. Old Glory is hoisted triumphantly over the installation. **(Pacific-New Guinea)** Lt. Colonel Malcolm A. Moore assumes command of recently formed Second Air Task Force at Tsili Tsili, in the Watut River Valley west of Lae; his mission is to expedite the operations against Lae. **(Pacific)** In Naval

activity in the Pacific, the U.S.S. *Plymouth*, (PG-57), a Gunboat is sunk by an enemy Submarine. In other activity, Admiral Spruance (formerly Chief of Staff, CinCPOA, becomes Commander Central Pacific, and also the Commander of the U.S. 5th Fleet. **(Atlantic-Sicily) 15th Army Group** In the Third Division area, General Truscott changes strategy and decides to move the Division through the mountains and strike San Fratello Ridge from the south as the frontal attack of the previous day had not succeeded. German General Fries has already decided to abandon San Fratello Ridge; his left flank becomes exposed as the 15th Panzer Grenadiers withdraw from Troina (1st Division zone). The withdrawal is in accordance with General Hube's plan to shorten the defense line. German rear-guard troops and a reinforced Italian Regiment (Assietta Division) will fight a delaying action to buy time for the enemy to move eastward, closer to Messina. In the 1st Division zone, enemy defenders at Troina continue to resist tenaciously during the day, preventing it from seizing the town, however, it captures positions in the nearby heights; this combined with the Air attacks prompts the enemy to evacuate Troina during the night of the 5th-6th. In one instance, a fierce firefight erupts when a mortar unit advances on Mt. Basilio to destroy enemy positions. Incessant enemy fire drives the Squad back. One man, Pvt. James Reese, 26th Infantry, crawls closer and fires his remaining three rounds of ammunition and scores a direct hit on the menacing enemy nest. Pvt. Reese is killed shortly thereafter, while advancing against the enemy. The attack is so violent that at its conclusion, Company I can account for only seventeen men. By mid-afternoon, the 2nd and 3rd Battalions, 26th Regiment, still isolated on Monte Basilio, are running out of ammunition and food. Attempts to drop supplies by Plane are insufficient for the need. The 39th Regiment makes gains, getting elements to positions about one mile north of Troina, however, the 16th and 18th Regiments encounter resolute resistance. Enemy rear-guards hold positions just outside of town, enabling the evacuation to proceed. Group Ens retains the key high ground, but General Rodt is aware that Troina is about to fall. He is concerned about the 26th Regiment which is close to slicing the remaining German escape route in addition to the ongoing envelopment by the 60th Regiment. In conjunction, the 60th Regiment (and attached Goumiers), 9th Division attacks enemy positions north and northwest of Cesaro. German General Hube concurs with a suggestion by Rodt and agrees to a fighting withdrawal from the Etna line. Italian General Guzzoni protests to no avail. Actually, the Hermann Goering Division had begun pulling back from Catania on August 4th, leaving only rear-guard troops to face the British, while the 29th Panzers received orders to stand and fight until pushed out. In the **British Eighth Army** area, the 30 Corps advances toward Adrano, while the 13 Corps captures Paterno, Misterbianco, and Catania. **(Atlantic-Russia)** The Russians have lost many casualties during the bitter struggle with the Germans on all fronts. The Germans also have suffered heavily, but cannot easily reinforce themselves. Orel and Belgorod fall to the Soviets, at the expense of the 2nd Panzer Army. The Germans now face serious consequences at their Kharkov salient.

August 6th 1943 — (Pacific-Solomons) BATTLE OF VELLA GULF — Just before midnight, a Japanese Destroyer Task Force, attempting to reach Vella Lavella with nearly 2,000 reinforcements, is intercepted by thunderous cannons of six American Destroyers, commanded by Commander Frederick

Moosbrugger. Tracer shells illuminate the skies exposing the accuracy of the bombardment. Three of the four enemy Destroyers plummet to the depths of the gulf. Japanese counterattack plans fall with the enemy Fleet, in the whirlwind battle that passes as quickly as a ruthless tornado. About 300 enemy troops reach shore at Vella Lavella. U.S. Vessels suffer no damage. The Destroyer *Kawakaze* sinks before midnight. The Destroyers *Arashi* and *Hagikaze* are destroyed in the opening moments of the 7th. **(Pacific-New Guinea)** The Japanese attempt to reinforce their positions by ordering Aircraft to Wewak. **(Atlantic-Sicily) 15th Army Group** In the **U.S. Seventh Army** area (II Corps), 3rd Division zone, smoke and Artillery fire precedes an attack by the 15th Regiment, which moves its 1st and 2nd Battalions out at 06:00. Menacing fire including accurate mortars bars progress and rolls up casualties throughout the day; thirty dead and 70 wounded. In conjunction, two Battalions of the 30th Regiment and attached 3rd Battalion, 15th Regiment attack the German flank in vain. Complications develop as units move out at 02:00 to attack San Fratello Ridge unaware of the nastiness of the unfamiliar terrain. The situation is harrowing throughout the day as enemy fire is incessant at the Furiano River. Elements of the 3rd Battalion (15th Regiment) get to Hill 673, to be joined later by Colonel Doleman's 3rd Battalion (30th Regiment); a Platoon of the former reaches the crest and is forced back down by fierce fire. At midnight, both Battalions cling precariously to the bottom slopes. Meanwhile, Colonel Sladen's 1st Battalion (30th Regiment) finally gets elements across the river at 15:30, but they are called back as resistance is resolute. In the 1st Division zone, Troina falls to the Americans without opposition. Planes bomb the highway east of Troina during the morning and General Allen holds his attack until noon, however, the enemy abandoned the town before dawn. The town is in ruins; 150 dead Italians, Germans and civilians, lay in the battered highway, streets and decimated houses. Ironically, a 200-pound unexploded aerial bomb is perched directly in the center of the church. During the afternoon, General Roosevelt turns the 1st Division over to General C.R. Huebner and Colonel W.G. Wyman. General Allen returns to the U.S. to command the 104th Division and General Roosevelt becomes Assistant Division Commander of the U.S. 4th Division: the "Big Red One" is now Huebner's. In the **British Eighth Army** area, 30 Corps sector, the Germans abandon Adrano, which the British 78th Division seizes. Also, the British 1st Division takes Biancavilla. In Naval activity, the LST No. 3 is sunk by an enemy Bomber. **(Atlantic-Italy)** The Tarvis Conference convenes: Italian and German foreign ministers and Chiefs of Staff exchange ideas, however, neither side is being truthful. The substance of the meeting concentrates on continuing the war, rather than searching for peace. While Italy is stalling for time, awaiting word from the Allies, the Germans are still searching for Mussolini's internment location. Hitler is determined to rescue him to startle the British and forestall invasion of the Italian mainland. Ribbentrop, Keitel, Guariglia and Ambrosio are in attendance. The conference does formalize German troops entering northern Italy. Also, OKW has decided not to seize Rome at this time. **(Atlantic-Caribbean)** The U-615, prowling in the Mediterranean, is attacked by three different Naval Air Squadrons, VB-130, VP-204, and VP-205, and by Army Planes. The German Submarine is sunk.

August 7th 1943 — (Pacific-Solomons-New Georgia) American held Munda Airfield is now operational for emergency use. **(Pacific-China-Burma-India)** General Stratemeyer arrives in India. In other activity, Colonel Dorn reports that General Chen refuses to return to Yunnan from Enshih to command the Y-Force until more troops and supplies are provided. Only two Chinese Armies are forming at this time. **(North Atlantic)** Planes (VC-1), launched from the Escort Carrier *Card* (CVE-11), sink the U-Boat U-117 and two days later, she again launches Planes and sinks the U-Boat U-525. **(Atlantic-Sicily) 15th Army Group** In the **U.S. Seventh Army** area, The U.S. 1st Division pushes against Randazzo, which also is struck by Allied Aircraft. Still, the enemy resists firmly at various locations, including South Fratello (3rd Division zone). The U.S. 9th Division drives east along Highway 120 and moves straight through Monte Pelato in pursuit of the retreating enemy. Patton orders a Battalion of Infantry to embark from Stefano and land at Sant'Agata. The mission, scrapped the night before due to enemy Aircraft activity, is again postponed: , however, the men land at 03:15 on the eighth: four Luftwaffe Planes had bombed and strafed the embarkation point, damaging one LST (LST-3), compelling Truscott to await another en route from Palermo. Two of the four attacking Planes are shot down. The operation commences at 19:40 on the 7th, landing near Sant'Agata at 03:15 on the eighth. This Amphibious landing places Patton's 7th Army within 75 miles from Messina. Montgomery's Eighth Army stands 52 miles outside of the town. Field Marshal Kesselring grants General Hube permission to evacuate.

Major General Curtis Lemay (right) standing with Brigadier General Haywood S. Hansell.

August 8th 1943 — (Pacific-New Guinea) One PT Boat, No. 113, becomes grounded in eastern New Guinea and is abandoned. **(Pacific-Solomons-New Georgia)** The Liversedge Force clearing the area East of Bairoko Harbor, while elements of the 27th Infantry, 25th Division, and RCT 161 purge the Western side of Bairoko. Also, Battery B, 9th Defense Battalion, U.S.M.C., deploys on Kindu Point to defend the seacoast of Munda. **(Atlantic-Sicily)** By the end of the day, Kesselring meets with General von Senger and is informed of the deteriorating crisis on Sicily; Kesselring then orders Hube to expedite the evacuation of German forces from Sicily without clearing the directive with Hitler. Hube issues the orders on the 10th to the dismay of the Italians. **15th Army Group** In the **U.S. 7th Army** area, a reinforced Infantry Battalion (Companies F and G, 30th Regiment, one Tank Platoon (first wave) and one Engineer Platoon (second wave), makes an amphibious landing about six miles behind San Fratello without opposition and coordinates with an overland attack by the 7th Infantry. However, soon after landing, German reaction is bitter. The amphibious Task Force, commanded by Lt. Col. Lyle Bernard, intended to land east of the Rosmarino River near Terranova and attack Monte Barbuzzo (one line southwest), however, the Navy lands his force west of the river outside Sant'Agata, forcing Bernard to improvise his attack. Almost simultaneously, the Germans mount a counterattack across the river, but some of the enemy Battalion gets trapped near Sant'Agata between the two closing forces, igniting a savage firefight. Bernard's troops open up with ravaging fire as Infantry and two Italian Renault Tanks and two German Mark IV's approach: both Italian and one of the German Tanks collapse suddenly; the remaining Tank escapes. The German Infantry retreats into Sant'Agata. The American Tanks and Artillery roll into a nearby lemon grove. The Germans send two convoys to find a circuitous route around Bernard's force; both come under murderous cross fire. One Convoy, composed of Motorcycles and Vehicles takes a curve and encounters rapid fire ending the excursion violently, as the hurricane of shells hits a truck transporting gasoline and the other Vehicles; all are destroyed, however; some troops escape the roadblock. Artillery joins the show and opens up forcing the other enemy column to withdraw toward Terranova. Meanwhile, the 7th Infantry is pressing San Fratello and the German-Italian force is evaporating quickly. The 2nd Battalion, 7th Infantry is in Sant'Agata by 11:30 and by 12:30, the two American forces link up. The remaining components of the 2nd Battalion, 71st Panzer Grenadier Regiment escape inland, however, the startling attack erases the Rosmarino River as a defensive line for the Germans. Also, one of Bernard's Rifle Companies (E) caught in the confusion of the landing zone and unaware of the improvised attack becomes separated and moves inland toward Monte Barbuzzo. One contingent passes through San Marco, seizing a ridge mistakenly thought to be Monte Barbuzzo and holds it until the Battalion arrives. The success of this operation prompts Patton to plan another amphibious attack on the 11th, to quicken the pace to Messina. In the **British Eighth Army** area, 30 Corps sector, Bronte is taken by the British 78th Division. The British 13 Corps is closing against the Hermann Goering Division on Highway 114. **(Atlantic-Italy)** OKW creates Tenth Army Headquarters. Within two weeks, it becomes operational under Generaloberst Heinrich von Vietinghoff geannt Scheel, who had commanded a Corps on the Eastern Front. He meets with Hitler on the 17th and is ordered to guarantee the withdrawal of German forces from southern Italy to Rome, subsequent to the anticipated Italian surrender.

August 9th 1943 — (Pacific-New Georgia-Solomons) The main force of the Japanese Southeast Detached Force has safely moved east from Munda to Kolombangara (8th-9th), with U.S. units in pursuit. The Northern and Southern Landing Groups establish contact when a Patrol (1st Battalion, 27th Regiment, 25th Division, U.S.A.) advances to a roadblock southwest of Triri, held by the 3rd Battalion, 148th Regiment, 37th Division. In other activity, the 37th Regiment, 25th Division receives orders to prepare to land on Vella Lavella. Also, a Light Antiaircraft Battery from the 11th Defense Battalion, U.S.M.C., arrives from Enogai. **(Atlantic-Sicily) 15th Army**

Group In the **U.S. Seventh Army** area, II Corps continues advancing east. In the coastal sector, contingents of the 3rd Division reach Torrenuovo forcing the Germans back to the Zappulla River. The 71st Panzer Grenadier Regiment retains a salient there under orders to hold as long as possible. The 15th Panzer Regiment is spread west of Highway 116, south of Naso; some remnant Italian forces are intermingled with the Germans, however, most of the 29th Panzer Division's Artillery units are deployed near the coast. Also, the 15th Panzer Grenadier Division is strung out along Highway 116 between Randazzo and Floresta; it is scheduled for transfer to the Italian mainland. In the 9th Division zone, the Germans retreat to the Simeto River line between Cesaro and Randazzo. In the **British Eighth Army** area, General Montgomery receives orders from General Alexander to seize a bridgehead on the Calabrian area, using his present forces. Meanwhile, the Germans continue to hinder the British advance via Randazzo toward Messina. Montgomery decides to change the attack and concentrate his force along the east coast. German General Rodt, senses the danger of the British and American forces converging on Randazzo and knows it must be held to permit safe evacuation of his forces and the Hermann Goering Division. In other activity, General Guzzoni is ordered by Comando Supremo to evacuate all Italian troops from Sicily and it also directs him to assume command of the defense of Calabria.

August 10th 1943 — (Pacific-Australia) Major Generals Courtney Whitney and Douglas MacArthur discuss various propaganda items, intended to be dropped over the Philippines to keep up the hopes of the captive citizens. The items include chewing gum, cigarettes, matches, candy and other nominal items. Photographs of the U.S. and Philippine flags in addition to MacArthur's signature will be printed on the items, with the slogan, " I SHALL RETURN." LARGE QUANTITIES ARE DROPPED ALL OVER THE PHILIPPINES AS A COUNTER PROPAGANDA MEASURE. **(Pacific-Solomons-New Georgia)** The 25th Army Division takes responsibility for control of the Northern Landing Group on New Georgia, allowing the 1st Marine Raider Regiment to return to Enogai. In other activity Admiral Halsey is informed that his son Bill is missing in action. They had visited together a few days before on Noumea. The Plane returning him to the Saratoga and two other Torpedo Planes are missing. Halsey is asked by members of his Staff if any "additional measures" should be taken and Halsey responds: "MY SON IS THE SAME AS EVERY OTHER SON IN THE COMBAT ZONE. LOOK FOR HIM JUST AS YOU'D LOOK FOR ANYBODY ELSE." On the night of the 12th, a Patrol Plane spots rafts on the island of Eromanga (situated between Efate and New Caledonia) and on Friday the 13th he and the other nine survivors are rescued. All three Planes had turned in the wrong direction and were compelled to ditch. **(Atlantic-Sicily)** German General Hube orders the evacuation of Sicily to commence on the night of the 11th and to continue every night until the 15th ((LEHRGANG). It is widely known that General Patton is hell bent on beating Montgomery to Messina, however, he is most certainly not alone. The British have been harsh on describing American participation in the war since Kasserine Pass and often take unfounded potshots. The British Broadcasting Company (main broadcasting company listened to by all troops in Sicily) has a propensity for outrageous one-sided editorials and battle descriptions that are purely wishful thinking on their part. Recently, the British propaganda has been stating that:

"THE GOING ON THE SEVENTH ARMY FRONT HAD BEEN SO EASY THAT THE TROOPS WERE EATING GRAPES AND SWIMMING WHILE THE EIGHTH ARMY IS FIGHTING HARD AGAINST GERMAN OPPOSITION." Today, the British Eighth Army is heavily bogged south of Maletto. **15th Army Group** In the **U.S. Seventh Army** area, during the night, elements of the U.S. Third Division outflanks enemy positions and lands amphibious troops just East of Capo d'Orlando, near Brolo, gaining surprise; the Yanks dig in effectively and repulse enemy attacks on the 11th. General Truscott leads a major night-attack, which drives the Germans back and in addition the advancing Yanks establish contact with other Americans, on a nearby hill. The U.S. 9th Division, pushing along Highway 120, nears Randazzo. Offshore, U.S. Naval fire inadvertently strikes the U.S.S. *Brant* (ARS-32), inflicting some damage.

August 11th 1943 — (Pacific-Solomons-New Georgia) The U.S. decides to bypass the strengthened Japanese positions at Vila on Kolombangara, choosing instead to strike Vella Lavella and capture its Naval facilities and Airstrips. Admiral Halsey orders Rear Admiral Theodore S. Wilkinson's Task Force 31 to handle the operation. The Amphibious Force, commanded by General Robert B. McClure, comprises RCT 35, 25th Division, and additional support troops. **(Central Pacific)** Lt. General Robert C. Richardson Jr., organizes a small Task Force (804th Aviation Engineering Battalion, Provisional AAA Battalion, Provisional Air Service Support Squadron, one Fighter Squadron and supporting units). Richardson is to develop Baker Island, near the equator, as a support Base to bolster the Central Pacific operations. **(Atlantic-Sicily) 15th Army Group** Patton's 7th Army moves rapidly in pursuit of the retreating enemy. The U.S. 3rd Division seizes Naso after overcoming light resistance. The 2nd Battalion, 30th Regiment makes a flanking amphibious movement in co-ordination with the main land attack, and hits the beach near Brolo behind enemy lines, temporarily stunning the Germans. An unexpected exchange of gunfire with an enemy Soldier sounds the alarm. First, a solitary enemy trooper on a motorcycle approaches Bernard's force; it freezes and permits the cyclist to proceed toward Naso without incident, however, soon after all hell breaks loose. Following is a German Half-trac which halts and glances to identify the troops. Rapid fire cuts him down, but within seconds a sedan appears on the scene, prompting the activation of a well placed Bazooka round which kills the Officer and wounds the driver. The Bazooka alerts every German on Monte Cipolla and just about everywhere else in the area. Suddenly, brilliant searchlights and flares beam the entire area and spot the Americans, whose Artillery still is on the beach. The beleaguered Battalion (under Colonel Bernard) is hit from two sides at Monte Creole, however, the men hold firmly, despite vicious firefights which continue incessantly. Some of Bernard's troops reach the crest of Monte Cipolla, subsequent to German Colonel Polack's hasty withdrawal down the far slopes reaching Brolo, where he calls General Fries to inform him of the crisis. Polack is ordered to commit the 1st Battalion, 71st Panzers, an Antiaircraft unit and available Tanks against the American beachhead. In conjunction, General Fries orders the 6th Company, 15th Panzers (reserves near Naso) to strike the beachhead from the east. Meanwhile, Companies F and G hold the crest of the hill, however, Artillery and Tanks are unable to deploy where they can assist the isolated Riflemen. Of the five Tanks, three belly near the railroad while attempt-

ing to cross ditches, and the remaining two become damaged trying to blow through stone walls. During the morning the Germans had been struck by Artillery fire and Naval Surface gun fire from the U.S.S. *Philadelphia*, greatly impeding their progress, but at 10:53, the *Philadelphia* heads for Palermo. At noon, the contingents on Monte Cipolla remain isolated and their ammunition is near exhausted. The Germans maintain pressure against the besieged Battalion, however, General Fries realizes he is on the ropes; most of the 15th Panzers have been pulled back beyond the Naso River and the 71st Panzers are clenched between the 7th Infantry (west) and Bernard's Battalion on the east. As the battle-clogged day continues, the Cruiser *Philadelphia* hits Palermo and immediately springs back to Brolo to bolster the attack; unleashing salvos into and around the town just after 14:00, pounding the beleaguered Germans. Simultaneously, twelve A-36 Bombers strike the town, followed by twelve additional A-36s one half hour later. Upon cessation of the strikes, the *Philadelphia* again returns to Palermo, only to receive yet another distress call to bring her heavy guns back. The Germans are closing on the beachhead. A sparse contingent of Yanks holds a bridge and drives off German Infantrymen, however, three unscathed Tanks from Brolo move up and commence firing in concert with heavy German Artillery which plaster Monte Cipolla. Soon after the Tanks bruise their way across the Brolo River, manhandling the U.S. Infantrymen who scatter. U.S. guns fire at the encroaching Tanks, however, to no avail. Company F, in a last ditch effort charges down Monte Cipolla under severe fire to aid Company E, which now finds its four remaining Artillery pieces inoperable. Colonel Bernard then directs all the troops to speed to the high ground to forestall disaster, however, some are stranded in the low country. As the Germans begin to bring down the curtain, the *Philadelphia* sweeps in for her third and most dramatic strike, however, again complications develop. In a communications mix-up, three DUKWs bringing in ammunition to the exhausted Yanks, begin moving back to sea. Meanwhile, the Naval Task Force begins blasting Brolo, Cape Orlando, and the highway east of the town. During the bombardment, eight German Planes arrive and another donnybrook emerges; after about thirty minutes, the U.S. Vessels which are supplemented by friendly Aircraft have destroyed all but one of the attacking Planes. After cessation of the contest with the Planes, the Cruiser and accompanying Warships return to Palermo. The situation remains critical at best for Bernard's troops, but by 19:00, the Germans control the highway to escape and decide to evacuate, ignoring the survivors of Company E, trapped on the flats. At 22:00, the Germans abandon the area, however, General Truscott believes the Battalion had been overrun. To the contrary, the valiant Battalion had held. In addition, two of Truscott's Regiments had seized the Nasa Ridge and are closing on Monte Cipolla. On the morning of the 12th, the bleary eyed survivors of Company E, spot the 1st Battalion, 30th Infantry and virtually bolt from their hiding places to cheer the reinforcements. Patrols leap up the slopes to contact Colonel Bernard. The gallant survivors under Colonel Bernard, minus 177 men killed, wounded or missing march down the hill with the Patrol of the 1st Battalion. The main body of the third Division including the recently attached 3rd Ranger Battalion arrives soon after. The amphibious part of the assault has been controversial since its inception; General Patton favored speed, however, General Bradley and General Truscott held the opinion that the amphibious landing should have commenced on the 12th to permit a quick hook up of the two Forces. In the 9th Division sector, although opposition is sporadic and extremely light, the area of advance toward Randazzo is inundated with mines; the 39th Regiment gains only three and one half miles. **British Eighth Army**: Meanwhile, the British 78th Division driving toward Maletto is also advancing slowly. Allied Planes continue saturating Randazzo with bombing and strafing, causing the Germans additional hardship; the road through the town is dubbed "death road." **(South Atlantic)** Naval Planes (VP-107 and VP-129), and the Destroyer *Moffett* (DD-362) damage the U-Boat, U-604; the damage forces the Germans to scuttle it. **(Atlantic-U.S.S.R.)** The Soviets close on Kharkov getting some elements to Akhtryka and others advance and sever the Kharkov-Poltava railroad.

August 11th-24th 1943 — (Atlantic-Canada) President Roosevelt, and Winston Churchill and their Military advisors confer in Quebec (QUADRANT); the meeting lasts until the 24th."

August 12th 1943 — (North Pacific-Aleutians) Five Cruisers and five Destroyers make one last run to bombard Kiska, pounding it with 60 tons of shells. **(Pacific-Solomons)** Advance U.S. Forces land at Barakoma on Vella Lavella, during the night of the 12th to make preliminary preparations for the Main Assault Force, scheduled to land on the 15th. The troops meet sporadic resistance from enemy stragglers. Elements of the 169th Infantry land at Baanga, hitting firm opposition, forcing them to pull out, stranding thirty-four men from Company L, on the beach. **(Atlantic-Sicily) 15th Army Group** In the **U.S. Seventh Army** area, II Corps sector, 9th Division zone, the Americans near Randazzo, prompting the enemy to withdraw from the town, during the night of the 12th to evade the Yanks who are closing from two sides, however, during the day, the German troops concentrate on Paddy Flint's 39th Regiment as the most serious threat to the town. Rodt required several hours of untiring effort to delay the Americans and his troops complete the task; Rodt also evacuates Floresta, threatened by DeRohan's 60th Regiment. In the 3rd Division sector, pursuit of the retreating Germans along the coast continues. In the **British Eighth Army** area, Maletto falls to the British 78th Division after several days of intense fighting. In other activity, the Submarine Chaser SC-526 becomes damaged after grounding. **(Atlantic-Soviet Union)** The Red Army takes Chuguev as it closes on Kharkov.

August 13th 1943 — (United States) Admiral Leahy, General Marshall, and Brigadier General J.R. Deane, depart Washington by Plane, en route to Canada, to attend the conferences between Roosevelt and Churchill. On the following day, during discussions between the Combined Chiefs of Staff, in a meeting presided over by British General Sir Alan Brooke, the British aggressively push for a Mediterranean campaign. U.S. General Marshall and Admiral King both disagree vehemently, the latter using some very choice words, insisting that not a single additional Vessel be committed to the Mediterranean, while the ongoing Pacific campaign is so desperately short of Naval Vessels. **(North Pacific-Aleutians)** The Kiska Invasion Force departs Adak for the objective. **(Pacific-Solomons)** Japan issues instructions (Navy Staff Directive No. 267), authorizing the evacuation of the Central Solomon Islands. A contingent of the U.S. 169th Infantry, 43rd Division, lands at Vela Cela, between Baanga and New

Georgia, without opposition. In other activity, Japanese Planes attack American positions on Guadalcanal and damage the U.S.S. *John Penn* (APA-23), a Transport. **(Pacific-Japan)** Japanese Imperial Headquarters issues Navy Staff Directive No. 267, authorizing the evacuation of the Central Solomons, subsequent to implementing delaying actions. **(Atlantic-Sicily) 15th Army Group** In the **U.S. Seventh Army** area, the Americans push further during the last phase of the Sicilian campaign. In the 3rd Division sector, the 30th Regiment closes on Patti, bypassing a nasty roadblock (blown tunnel and destroyed section of road at Capo Calava; the force separates, some continuing by foot and others being transported via water by DUKWs. In conjunction ingenious Engineers advance and place a near impossible "bridge in the sky," which transports General Truscott and his Jeep within eighteen hours after starting the project. Soon after, it is further shored up and heavy Vehicles begin moving across. By 04:00 on the 14th, Oliveri is entered by the 3rd Battalion, 15th Infantry. Meanwhile, RCT 15 and the 3rd Ranger Battalion destroy enemy pockets southwest of Patti. In the 9th Division sector, Randazzo falls to Regimental Combat Team 39. The enemy is retreating to Italy, but the number of enemy prisoners keeps rising. The British arrive at Randazzo subsequent to its seizure. General Rodt makes his escape easily without threat of Allied ground forces along the escape routes. Meanwhile, in the **British Eighth Army** area, although the progress of the U.S. 9th Division and the British 78th Division had been sluggish, it greatly outdistances Montgomery's Eighth Army, which is still inching along the eastern side of Mount Etna. Montgomery had declined several offers by Rear Admiral R.R. McGrigor, RN, to use his Inshore Squadron to speed the Eighth Army advance. In other activity, German General Conrath, pursued by Montgomery, retires at his own pace and commits portions of the Hermann Goering Division to delay the British, while effortlessly getting the bulk of his forces across the Messina Strait to the Italian mainland. **(Atlantic-Italy)** The U.S. 12th Air Force, again raids Military installations in the vicinity of Rome. Two hundred and seventy-four Bombers, escorted by Fighters, drop in excess of 500 tons of bombs, causing massive damage. The mission is completed with the loss of only two B-26s, despite heavy Fighter opposition. Sixty-six B-25s, 106 B-17s, and 102 B-26's participate. **(Atlantic-Soviet Union)** Spas Demensk is seized by contingents of the Red Army as the drive against Smolensk continues.

Marine Special Forces operating in a rowboat in the Pacific.

August 14th 1943 — (Pacific-Celebes) The U.S.S. *Finback* (SS-230) sinks the Japanese Submarine Chaser, No. 109 off the east coast of the Celebes. **(Pacific-Solomons)** Brigadier General Francis Mulcahy U.S.M.C. (COMAIR), transfers his New Georgia Air Command Post, from Rendova to Munda Point, enabling Marine Aircraft to begin using the Munda Airstrips for strikes against enemy positions. Also, Two Squadrons of Marine Aircraft (F4U) arrive. In addition, the 3rd Battalion, 169th Regiment, 43rd Division establishes a beachhead on Southeast Baanga with three Companies. Company L, attempts to rescue the force stranded there earlier, however, the Japanese encircle it, inflicting heavy casualties. Aircraft had attempted to locate the unit on the previous day. **(Central Pacific)** U.S. Army Forces in Central Pacific (USAFICPA) is activated; Lt. General Robert C. Richardson Jr., Commanding Officer, is to assume responsibility for the training of ground and air forces in the Central Pacific. **(Atlantic-Canada)** The Quadrant Conference opens in Quebec, attended by President Roosevelt, Prime Minister Churchill, and the Combined Chiefs of Staff. **(Atlantic-Sicily) 15th Army Group** The U.S. 7th Army rumbles along, with the 3rd Division pressing closer to Barcellona. Contingents of the roving Third Division meets elements of the U.S. 9th Division near Montalbano. While the Germans continue to evacuate Sicily, one reinforced Infantry Battalion is holding the front for the 29th Panzer Grenadier Division, with orders to maintain the line until darkness on the 15th. The Italians are also attempting to escape the clutches of the Allies, however, as usual their luck had not been too good. Their train ferry had caught fire on the night of the 12th, remaining out of action for 48 hours. Another inoperable train ferry is located with plans to tow heavy Artillery across the strait, but no towboats are found. Motor rafts are used to transport the troops. The Germans offer to help the Italians get across, but in the process confiscate some Italian equipment and in some cases press Italians into their service, giving them German uniforms and preventing them from returning to Italian units. In the **British Eighth Army** area, the British encounter no enemy forces. **(Atlantic-Mediterranean)** The Allies issue Naval Plan "Western Naval Task Force Operation Plan No.7-43" for Operation AVALANCHE (invasion of Italy at Salerno). Other forces will make a diversionary feint in the area near Naples. **(Atlantic-Italy)** The Italian Government announces "Open City" status for Rome. Fieldmarshal Albert Kesselring, aware that Hitler intends to replace him with Rommel, offer his resignation, however, it is refused by the Fuhrer.

ican and Canadian Assault Force, transported by nearly 100 Vessels, under the command of Vice Admiral T. Kinkaid, arrives off Kiska. Thirty Four thousand troops, led by Major General Charles H. Corlett, expecting heavy combat, find the island free of enemy troops. They had withdrawn earlier, without detection by U.S. and Canadian forces. During the landing, 21 men are killed and 121 are wounded by accidents and friendly fire; during the landing there are some cases of mistaken identity. The participating troops in the invasion: 17th Regiment; 7th Division; 184th Regiment, 7th Division; 53rd Regiment; 87th Regiment; 1st Special Service Force; Canadian 13th Brigade Group; Headquarter troops. Also, the 159th Regiment, 7th Division remain on Garrison duty on Attu. Upon landing, the troops discover the grave of an American Pilot, shot down during one of the many raids. The Japanese mark his grave in English with the following epitaph : "SLEEPING HERE, A BRAVE AIR HERO WHO LOST YOUTH AND HAPPINESS FOR HIS MOTHERLAND-July 25th, Nippon Army." **(Pacific-Solomons)** Admiral Wilkinson's Northern Landing Force successfully transports the McClure Landing Force (Regimental Combat Team 35) to Vella Lavella. This landing intentionally bypasses Kolombangara, another enemy strongpoint. The Invasion Force includes some Sailors and Marines. The Marine 4th Defense Battalion, receives responsibility for establishing the Antiaircraft beach defenses and will also be assigned a section of the beach. They debark near Barakoma. Japanese Planes harass the Naval Vessels, causing slight·damage, but the land forces hit no opposition from enemy troops, partially because of the actions of Marine Fighter Squadron 124, which intercepts a superior enemy force. First Lt. Kenneth A. Walsh intermingles with the enemy

August 13th 1943 — The Fleet stands off Adak.

August 15th 1943 — (North Pacific-Aleutians) The Amer-

August 13th 1943 — U.S. troops hit the beaches at Kiska and drive toward the hills. Note: *The Infantry, which debarks LCT(5)s, resemble little specks on the landscape.*

force, which outnumbers his section six to one. Lt. Walsh's Plane is hit several times, however, he singlehandedly shoots down two enemy Dive Bombers and one Fighter before returning to Base. **(Pacific-Solomons-New Georgia)** The U.S. 27th Infantry, 25th Division, captures Zieta, New Georgia. **(Pacific-New Guinea)** The recently completed Air Base at Tsili Tsili receives its first Japanese Air Attack. **(Pacific-Burma)** The construction project on the Ledo Road seemingly remains endless; since the end of March, the road has only progressed three additional miles. **(Atlantic-Mediterranean)** Italian General G. Castellano at the British Embassy in Madrid, Spain, initiates armistice negotiations. Also, U.S. Fifth Army issues its Outline Plan for the invasion of Italy (AVALANCHE). **(Atlantic-Sicily) 15th Army Group** The beleaguered enemy receives no rest. Patton's 7th Army pursues relentlessly, while Allied Planes pummel the retreating enemy 24 hours a day. The Germans continue to embark on ferries which cross the Straits of Messina and escape to the mainland of Italy. As the 7th Army races forward, it passes over huge amounts of deserted enemy supplies scattered along the coast road leading to Messina. General Patton, convinced that another amphibious landing will speed the capture of Messina and simultaneously cut casualties, orders another amphibious assault. Bradley and Truscott insist the landing is unnecessary, because the enemy is on the run, however it proceeds. As predicted by Bradley, Infantry greets the 45th Division's RCT 157 when it lands uneventfully before dawn on the 16th. In fact, it is the 7th Infantry which eliminates the rear-guards at Casazza crossroads and seizes the ridge line above Messina. Also, a Battery of 155-mm Howitzers is in place firing at the Italian mainland. In the **British Eighth Army** area, Field Marshal Montgomery finally agrees to make an amphibious landing on the following day to speed up his lagging Eighth Army. The British Eighth Army secures Linguaglossa and Taormina. British Commandos land at Ali, in an effort to catch the escaping enemy, but arrive too late, forcing them to alter their plans and move toward Messina. **(Atlantic-Soviet Union)** Fierce fighting continues near Kharkov. Also, Red Army contingents driving west along the Orel-Bryansk railroad, capture Karachev.

August 16th 1943 — (United States) The Carrier, U.S.S. *Intrepid* (CV-11) is commissioned at Newport News, Va. Also, the 4th Marine Division, commanded by Major General Harry Schmidt, is activated at Camp Pendleton, California and becomes the only Marine Division to be mounted and staged directly into battle directly from the Continental United States during World War II. **(Pacific-Solomons)** Enemy guns, on Baanga, shell American held Munda. The U.S. 43rd Division makes slow, but steady progress on Baanga. **(Mediterranean)** Allied Commanders confer in Carthage and finalize plans for the invasion of the Italian mainland. Elements of the British Eighth Army land at the Calabrian coast (Strait of Messina) between September 1st and September 4th (Operation BAYTOWN). This effort is followed within less than 48 hours by the major assault, launched by the U.S. 5th Army (Operation AVALANCHE), at Salerno. **(Atlantic-Sicily) 15th Army Group** In Sicily, the chase ends. Units of the U.S. 7th Army (Regimental Combat Team 7, 3rd Division), reach Divieto; an advance Patrol (Company L, 7th Infantry, commanded by 1st Lt. Ralph J. Yates enters Messina. At 05:30, German Generals Hube and Fries embark for Italy, the latter leaving less than 200 rear-guards at Acqualadrone and at the Casazza crossroads to engage the stampeding 7th Army.

Soon, Allied guns, dubbed Long Toms, are soon deployed to fire across the strait and strike Italy. In the **British Eighth Army** area, the amphibious force composed Tanks of the 4th Armored Brigade and a Commando unit (400 troops) lands on the east coast road and encounters remnants of the Hermann Goering Division rear-guard as it is heading for its embarkation point, however, the Germans stop to engage the British outside of Scaletta, keeping them pinned until dark; the Germans then head for Messina and the British resume the march toward Messina. The contingent moves through Tremestieri about two miles south of Messina at about daylight on the 17th, but a destroyed bridge over a deep gorge stops the advance.

August 17th 1943 — (North Pacific-Aleutians) The Japanese Main Camp is found abandoned, however, the search for Japanese continues. **(Pacific-Solomons)** The 2nd Echelon of the Northern Landing Force arrives at Vella Lavella and is struck by an enemy Airraid during debarkation. Contingents of the 43rd Division U.S.A., supported by Aircraft, unsuccessfully attack enemy positions on Baanga. Off the Solomons, two American Destroyers, the *Waller* (DD-466) and *Philip* (DD-498) collide damaging both Vessels. **(Pacific-New Guinea)** The U.S. 5th Air Force initiates intensive Air attacks against Japanese positions at Wewak and also strikes Boram, But, and Dagua. These raids are designed to give the Allies an edge, during the upcoming assault against Lae (September 4th). The raids inflict catastrophic damage to Japanese Planes and Pilots, neutralizing their striking power. **(Atlantic-Sicily) 15th Army Group** At 07:00, civilians from Messina approach General Truscott on the ridge above Messina, followed about one hour later by Colonel Michele Tomasello who offers to surrender the city, however, General Keyes has instructed Truscott not to enter the city without General Patton. Truscott dispatches his Assistant Division Commander, General Eagles to accompany Tomasello into the city. He advises him to oversee the American components already there and "TO SEE THAT THE BRITISH DID NOT CAPTURE THE CITY FROM US AFTER WE HAD TAKEN IT." U.S. Regimental Combat Team 7, 3rd Division, rolls into Messina at 10:00 with the Stars and Stripes flying, officially culminating the Sicilian campaign. Patton arrives at the ridge at 10:00, exclaiming: "WHAT IN HELL ARE YOU ALL STANDING AROUND FOR?," as he jumps in a lead car of a motorcade and races into the city, serenaded by enemy Artillery fire from the Italian mainland. Patton's 7th Army had done a magnificent job of crossing Sicily victoriously, in 38 days. The remaining German defenders had abandoned the city several hours earlier. Meanwhile, the British are still stalled at the gorge near Tremestieri: at 08:15, a Lt. Colonel, distant relative of Winston Churchill and in command of the Commando unit, decides to take a Jeep, circumvent the obstacle and beat the Americans into Messina. He had been unaware that the Americans had entered the city on the previous day. The British Armor reaches Messina and meets the British Commando Officer who has already been informed that the Yanks have taken the city. The British Armor moves through the city, stopping in a large park; the Senior British Officer greets Patton (just after the official surrender) with a hand shake and the words: " IT WAS A JOLLY GOOD RACE. I CONGRATULATE YOU." During the campaign, the Germans suffer about 10,000 casualties. The Italians sustain close to 100,000 (mostly prisoners). The combined Allied casualties mount to about 22,000 men. German troops, 70,000 Italian troops and massive amounts of supplies and Vehicles had been safely transported across the Messina Strait to Italy. Two islands north of Sicily, Lipari and Stromboli are greeted by American PT Boats and Destroyers. The Islands surrender to the Naval Forces. The Sicilian campaign proves to be a masterpiece, designed by General Patton. **(Atlantic-England)** Portugal permits England the use of Bases in the Azore Islands. **(Atlantic-Germany)** Over 300 Eighth Air Force Bombers are launched against Aircraft factories in both Regensburg and Schweinfurt. Enemy Aircraft intercept the Allied Planes, and a vicious battle erupts. The Eighth Air Force loses 60 bombers shot down, but the Germans lose many more Planes. Seven hundred and twenty four tons of bombs are dropped on enemy targets. Also, the R.A.F. initiates attacks against German Bases using V-weapons; nearly 600 Aircraft strike Peenemuende, on the Baltic coast during the night 17th-18th, depositing about 2,000 tons of bombs. In other activity, General Vietinghoff is summoned to Hitler's Headquarters and is told that Hitler has specific information confirming that Badoglio is negotiating an armistice with the Allies.

WACS preparing a map, (mounting it) for operations.

August 18th 1943 — (Atlantic-Canada-Quebec) Quadrant Conference: The Combined Chiefs of Staff instruct General Eisenhower to select representatives (Major General Walter B. Smith and Brigadier General Kenneth W.D. Strong) to travel to Lisbon, Portugal and negotiate an armistice with the Italians. During a recess of the intense strategy sessions, the Combined Chiefs visit the pre-Revolutionary War battleground on the Plains of Abraham, where the British, under General Wolfe, had defeated the French, commanded by General Montcalm, during 1759 (French and Indian War). Generals Wolfe and Montcalm had both been killed, during the battle. **(North Pacific)** The Destroyer *Abner Read* (DD-526) is damaged by a mine off the Aleutians. **(Pacific- Ellice Islands)** An advance reconnaissance party lands on Nanomea to determine a location for an Airfield from which to support the operation to seize the Marshalls. On the 22nd, a Marine detachment will land at Nukufetau, the selected site. **(Pacific-Solomons)** A U.S. Destroyer Force, commanded by Captain T.J. Ryan, engages an enemy Force, including four Destroyers, which is escorting Landing Barges north of Vella La Vella. Two enemy Submarine Chasers, Nos. 5 and 12, two Torpedo Boats and one Troop laden barge. Some barges evade destruction and land troops on the following day. Also, the LST 396 sinks

after sustaining an accidental explosion. **(Atlantic-England)** The U.S. Navy establishes an Advanced Amphibious Training Base at St. Mawes, Cornwall. Two days later, the Navy reinitiates a Naval Base at Roseneath, Scotland. **(Mediterranean)** The Air Plan, concerning Operation AVALANCHE is issued (Invasion of Salerno, Italy). In other activity, American Cruisers and Destroyers bombard the mainland of Italy, striking Gioia, Palmi and Taura. **(Atlantic-Soviet Union)** Zmiev falls to the Soviets, further pressing the Germans at Kharkov.

August 19th 1943 — (Atlantic-Canada) During the ongoing meetings (Quadrant) in Quebec, British Admiral Lord Mountbatten is approved for the position of Supreme Allied Commander, Southeast Asia Theater. He replaces Field Marshal Wavell. In addition, American General Stilwell is appointed Deputy Supreme Commander of Chinese troops in Burma. Also, he assumes command of American Ground and Air Forces in Southeast Asia. **(Pacific-Australia)** U.S. Naval Land-based Planes, attached to VS-57, combine with a New Zealand Ship and destroy the Japanese Submarine I-17 off the eastern shore of Australia. **(Pacific-Solomons)** In the Solomons, the U.S. 43rd Division, still embattled against tenacious Japanese troops on Baanga, makes slow progress, however, enemy guns which have been shelling Munda are seized. Also, Surviving Japanese Vessels from the attack on the previous day, put reinforcements ashore at Horaniu (Kokolope Bay), near northeast Vella Lavella. **(Pacific-New Guinea)** Allied pressure, continues to push the Japanese back, forcing them to evacuate Komiatum Ridge and Mount Tambu. The Japanese draw a final defense line at Salamaua.

August 20th 1943 — (Pacific-Solomons) The U.S. 43rd Division seals off the southern peninsula of Baanga Island. Resistance ceases, terminating the operation. Meanwhile, the Japanese evacuate South Baanga. American losses during the battle for Baanga: 52 dead, 110 wounded. On the following day, troops attached to the Northern Landing Force land at Vella Lavella, and are attacked by Planes, however, the Japanese inflict no serious damage. The operation was supported by Artillery components at Munda, New Georgia, including the 155-mm gun batteries of the 9th Defense Battalion, U.S.M.C. **(Pacific-New Guinea)** The New Guinea Force receives General Sir Thomas Blamey as its new Commander, in place of General Herring, who is transferred to Dobodura, to assume command of the Australian I Corps.

August 21st 1943 — (Pacific-Solomons) The third echelon of the Northern Landing Force is attacked by Japanese Planes as they near Vella Lavella, but again, the enemy causes very little damage.

August 22nd 1943 — (North Pacific-Aleutians) Allied troops continue to search without success for Japanese on Kiska. There are some casualties during the operation, but all are caused by mistaken identity. **(Pacific-Ellice Islands)** Forward elements of the 2nd Marine Airdrome Battalion lands at Nukufetau, the selected site of the newest Airbase to be used to seize the Marshalls. **(Pacific-New Guinea)** Japanese Airpower has been damaged sufficiently enough to allow four U.S. Destroyers, commanded by Captain Jesse H. Carter, to steam unhindered along the coast from Milne Bay to Finschhafen, and bombard enemy positions during the night of 22nd-23rd, then return without incident. **(Atlantic-Italy)** The German Tenth Army, commanded by General Vietinghoff is activated in southern Italy. On the 23rd, Vietinghoff meets with Italian General Arisio and it is agreed that the six German Divisions in southern Italy will come under German control. (Atlantic-Austria) Kesselring arrives at Hitler's Headquarters to suggest that Sardinia be reinforced, however, O.K.W., responds negatively and informs Kesselring that he should tell Ambrosio that Italian troops must defend Sardinia, while the Germans take responsibility for Corsica.

August 23rd 1943 — (United States) A U.S. Minesweeper, the *Crow*, running uncontrollably in Pugot Sound, Washington State, is destroyed by U.S. Aircraft. **(Pacific-Solomons)** The Americans press further during the final days of the campaign to seize New Georgia. Elements of the 25th Division culminate a blistering forced march through arduous swamp land and reach the Piru Plantation. **(Atlantic-Sicily)** Two American Submarine Chasers, the SC-694 and 696, are sunk by enemy Dive Bombers. In other activity, Pvt. Kuhl (previously slapped by Patton) comes to see General Patton. Patton explains his reason for slapping: "I DID IT, NAMELY TO MAKE YOU MAD AT ME SO YOU WOULD REGAIN YOUR MANHOOD." Kuhl, when asked to shake hands with Patton, does so. One day earlier, Patton had issued 7th Army General Orders 18: In part; "SOLDIERS OF THE 7TH ARMY; BORN AT SEA, BAPTIZED IN BLOOD, AND CROWNED IN VICTORY, IN THE COURSE OF 38 DAYS OF INCESSANT BATTLE AND UNCEASING LABOR, YOU HAVE ADDED A GLORIOUS CHAPTER TO THE HISTORY OF WAR. . .YOUR FAME SHALL NEVER DIE." **(Atlantic Russia)** Germans evacuate Kharkov after a long futile effort to win the area. The Soviets now press the Germans south of Izyum and also near Mius, severing the Taganrog-Stalino railroad.

August 24th 1943 — (Canada) The Quadrant Conference, which began in Quebec on the 14th, ends today. The Allies set a tentative date for the invasion of northwestern Europe (Operation OVERLORD) May 1st 1944. Operation POINTBLANK is agreed upon; combined Bomber offensive, to be initiated before execution of "Overlord." It is designed to totally reduce Germany's economic and Military strength. The conference also approves plans for the invasion of Italy and for the conquest of the Central Pacific, from Japan. **(Pacific)** The V Amphibious Force is established under Admiral Turner. **(Pacific-New Guinea)** In Salamaua, the Australian 5th Division relieves the Australian 3rd Division, then begins clearing the heights south of the Francisco River. Meanwhile, the 162nd Regiment, 41st Division continues sweeping the ridges in Dot Inlet. **(Pacific-Solomons-New Georgia)** Colonel William C. Brice, U.S.M.C., heading Fighter Command, transfers his Command Post to Munda Airfield, and takes command of Fighting Aircraft operating there, relieving Commander, Aircraft, New Georgia, of responsibility. **(Atlantic)** The Escort Carrier *Core*, operating in the Atlantic, launches Planes (VC-13) which sink two more German Submarines; the U-84 and U-185. **(Atlantic-Italy)** Italian Guerrillas attack a German supply train of the 24th Panzer Division near Lubliana.

August 25th 1943 — (United States) Amphibious Corps, Pacific Fleet based at Camp Pendleton, California is redesignated Amphibious Corps, however, Major General Holland M. Smith retains command. It is designated an administrative command with jurisdiction over Marine units in the central Pacific and also a tactical organization to direct amphibious assaults comprising Army and Marine forces. In conjunction, Troop Training Unit, Amphibious Training Command is activated simultaneously with V Amphibious Corps and will as-

sume responsibility for training troops on the west coast. **(Pacific-Solomons)** Enemy activity on New Georgia Island ends. The Americans control the entire island with the capture of Bairoko Harbor. The Stars and Stripes flies on one more island, as the Yanks move across the Pacific. Japanese stragglers withdraw to Kolombangara and Arundel. The 172nd U.S. Infantry works diligently to capture that portion of Arundel Island, which controls Diamond Narrows. In other activity, the U.S.S. *Montgomery* (DD-17) and the *Preble* (DD-20), both Minesweepers, collide causing damage to both Vessels. In other activity in the Pacific today, the U.S.S. *Patterson* (DD-392), a Destroyer, sinks the Japanese Submarine I-178 in the South Pacific. **(Pacific-Southeast Asia)** British Admiral Mountbatten is appointed Supreme Allied Commander, Southeast Asia. **(Atlantic-Mediterranean)** The U.S. Fifth Army issues Field Order No. 1, which relates to the invasion of Italy and encompasses the British portion of the campaign (Operation BAYTOWN) which is to secure the tip of Italy's heel. The U.S. 5th Army's Operation AVALANCHE is to seize the Naples area.

September 8th 1943 — Munda Airfield, New Georgia; the invasion occurred August 5th.

August 26th 1943 — (Atlantic-Mediterranean) U.S. and British Artillery, deployed on Sicily, is readied to support Operation BAYTOWN. In other activity, Operation AVALANCHE plans are altered changed to some extent, to adjust to the present situation. **(International)** The United States and several other Allied countries recognize the French Committee of National Liberation.

August 27th 1943 — (Pacific-Ellice Islands) U.S. Marines and Seabees arrive at Nukufetau, to join advance Forces. Defenses are established, while the Airbase is undergoing construction. **(Pacific-Solomons)** Elements of the U.S. 43rd Division cross Hathorn Sound and land unopposed on the southern edge of Nauro Peninsula (Arundel), secure a beachhead and dispatch a Force north, along the coast. These Patrols encounter no opposition, however, heavy enemy activity is reported in the Kokolope Bay area (Vella Lavella). American reinforcements continue to land until the 2nd of September. **(Pacific-New Guinea)** Allied Planes escalate their raids against enemy positions. The U.S. Fifth Air Force strikes furiously at Shipping, supply facilities, and Airfields in the New Britain-New Guinea areas. **(Atlantic-Italy)** A British Reconnaissance team lands at Bova Marina on the toe of Italy, against no opposition; the area is defenseless. **(Atlantic)** The U.S.S. *Card* (CVE-11), operating in the mid-Atlantic, launches Planes, attached to VC-1, which sink the German Submarine U-847. **(Atlantic-France)** The U.S Eighth Air Force launches

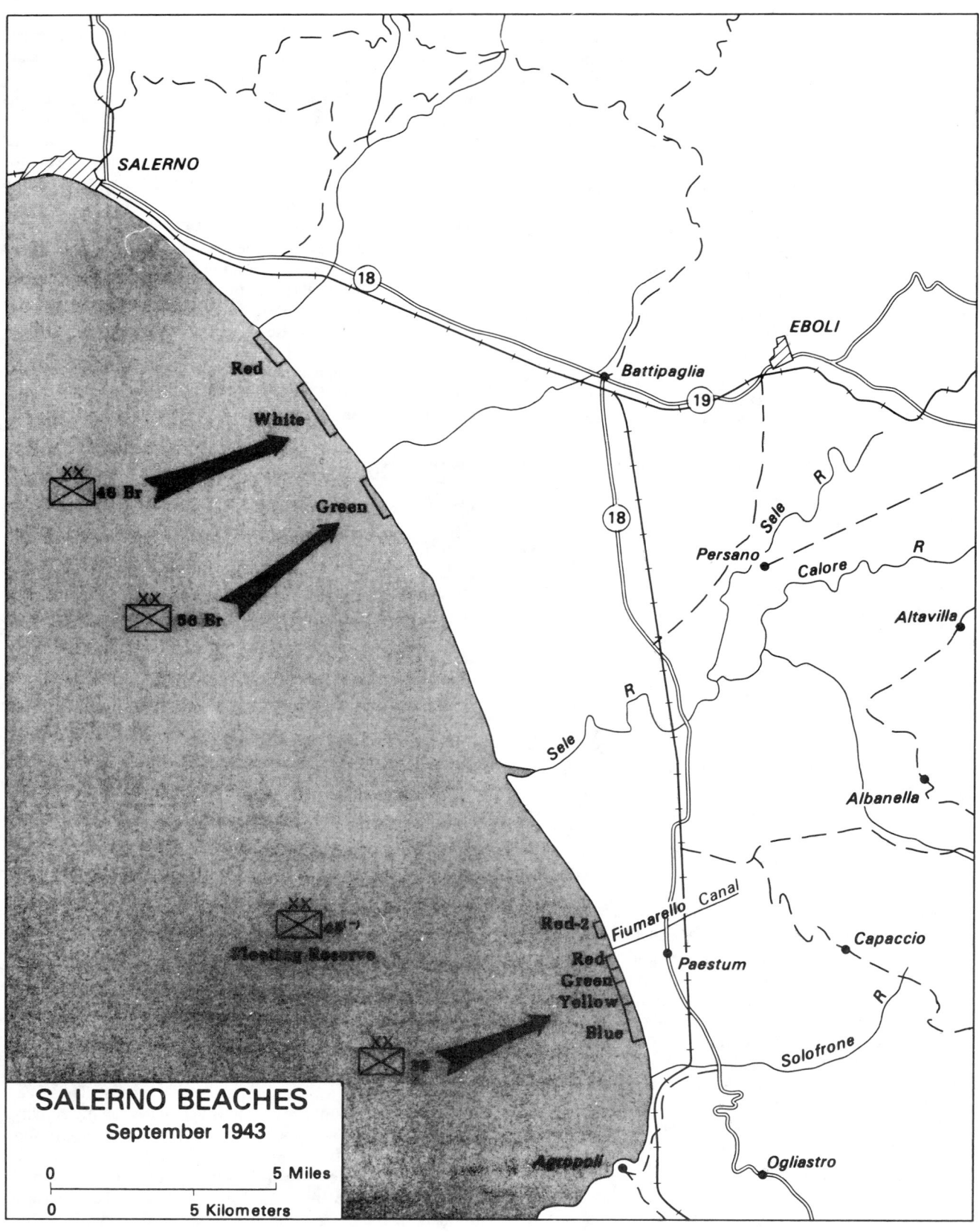

SALERNO BEACHES

September 1943

0 — 5 Miles

0 — 5 Kilometers

SALERNO

EBOLI

Battipaglia

Persano

Calore

Altavilla

Albanella

Capaccio

Paestum

Solofrone

Ogliastro

Agropoli

Sele R

Sele

Fiumarello Canal

Red

White

Green

46 Br

56 Br

Floating Reserve

Red-2
Red
Green
Yellow
Blue

18

19

18

its initial mission, relating to Operation CROSSBOW. One hundred Eighty-seven B-17s strike enemy facilities at Watten. **(Atlantic-Soviet Union)** The Red Army takes Sevsk, south of Bryansk.

August 28th 1943 — (Pacific-Ellice Islands) In the Ellice Islands, the Seabees, 16th Naval Construction Battalion and a contingent of the 7th Marine Defense Battalion, occupy Nukufetau Atoll. The Yanks prepare to move to the Gilberts. **(Pacific-Solomons-New Georgia)** The 1st Marine Raider Regiment, and the 4th Raider Battalion depart Enogai for Guadalcanal.

August 29th 1943 — (Pacific-Solomons-New Georgia) The U.S. 43rd Division dispatches contingents of the 172nd Infantry on a search and destroy mission, extending along the east and west coasts of Arundel. RCT 35, attached to the 25th Division, receives orders to move out and establish a radar site near Kokolope Bay. In other activity, Battery A, 9th Defense Battalion U.S.M.C., deployed at Viru Plantation near Munda Point bombards the Japanese positions on Kolombangara, with their 155-mm Batteries.

August 30th 1943 — (Pacific-Solomons) Marine Fighter Squadron 124 flies escort, during an important mission. First Lt. Ken Walsh encounters engine trouble and diverts to Munda to get another Aircraft. While proceeding toward Kahili to rejoin the Squadron, he is intercepted by approximately 50 Japanese Zeros. Undaunted by the number of enemy Planes, Walsh attacks and destroys four Planes before the insurmountable odds work against him. Walsh is shot down, however, his skill as a Pilot, enables him to safely crash land off Vella Lavella. Walsh becomes the recipient of the Medal of Honor. **(Atlantic-Soviet Union)** The Russians take Yelnya as contingents move against Smolensk. Meanwhile, the Soviets seize Gluchov, west of Kursk and yet other forces take Taganrog when the force reaches the Sea of Azov (Mius Front).

August 31st 1943 — (Pacific-Gilbert Islands) A U.S. Carrier Force, commanded by Rear Admiral C.A. Pownall, moves within striking range of Marcus Island and launches Planes which bombard enemy positions, stunning the Japanese. Within a week, Planes from Baker Island prepare to attack the Gilberts. Also, Aircraft from the *Essex*, *Yorktown*, and *Independence* participate, devastating about 70 percent of the installations. To prevent the Japanese from knowing F6fs are in use, wheels are painted on their wings to give the appearance of being F4fs (Wildcats). **(Pacific-Solomons)** There are brief firefights between the Americans and enemy troops on the eastern coast of Arundel. **(Pacific-Australia)** The 1st Marine Division receives word it is to prepare to move to an advanced staging area. **(Atlantic-Sicily)** Italian General Castellano arrives at Termini Imerse Airfield, outside of Palermo and is met by General Kenneth Strong. A U.S. Plane flies them to Fifteenth Army Headquarters at Cassibile for discussions on an armistice. The Italians demand that the Allies land north of Rome and comprise a force of at least fifteen Divisions. General Walter B. Smith refuses the proposal and counters with two alternatives: accept the conditions or refuse the armistice. The conference concludes without a definite result, however, the Italians will relent.

August 1943 — (Atlantic-Yugoslavia) Many of the U.S. Pilots and Airmen who had been shot down while on bombing mission over the Balkans attempt to parachute into the mountains to establish contact with Partisan (Communist Josef Broz "Tito") and Chetnik forces (General Draza Mihailovoch), two warring factions; O.S.S. agents under Walter Mansfield and Louis Huot are airdropped and operate in the respective areas. By November, Churchill, with the approval of President Roosevelt, terminates aid to Mihailovich, throwing all support to the Communists under Tito. Despite the ongoing infighting, over 100 downed Airmen are flown to safety from disguised Airstrips. The O.S.S. operates under British control until November.

August 27th 1943 — The 3rd Battalion, 172nd Regiment, 43rd Division lands on Arundel. Note: Rendova Island in the background.

September 1st 1943 — (United States) Orders are dispatched to Admiral Nimitz, concerning the operation in the Marshalls. Nimitz also is ordered to seize Wake, Eniewetok and Kusaie, after the completion of the Marshalls campaign. In other activity, the Navy takes complete responsibility for the U.S. Airborne Anti-Submarine operations in the Atlantic. Upon ordering the seizure of Wake Island, the U.S. still, has no knowledge that the Japs have retained the American Civilians on the island. The Navy bombards Wake Island heavily during early October and the Japs react by slaughtering the Americans on the island. **(Pacific-Hawaii)** The U.S. Navy establishes a Naval Air Station at Kahului, Hawaii. **(Pacific-Central Pacific-Baker Island)** The U.S. concentrates its efforts to seize the Gilberts. A U.S. Naval Force, commanded by Rear Admiral W.A. Lee, arrives at Baker Island and lands an Army Task Force to establish a base, from which assaults against the Japs in the Central Pacific can be mounted. Diligence pays off as an Airstrip becomes operational in one week's time. With the addition of Baker Island, situated near the equator, the Allies now control five Central Pacific Bases, which are capable of launching Bombers that can reach the Gilberts. **(Pacific-New Guinea)** The plans for the offensive against Lae intensify: Fifth Air Force Aircraft strike Airfields, Shipping and Supply depots in the New Guinea-New Britain area. **(Pacific-New Hebrides)** Aircraft Northern Solomons is established at Espiritu Santo, commanded by Brigadier General Field Harris, U.S.M.C., to assist with the northern Solomons seizure. **(Atlantic-Italy)** The Royal Navy participates with the ongoing bombardment of the Calabrian coastal area.

September 2nd 1943 — (United States) Marine Corps Air Depot, Miramar, California is established, commanded by Colonel Caleb Bailey. **(Pacific-Carolines)** The U.S.S. *Snapper*, operating near the Caroline Islands, sinks a Japanese Frigate, the *Matsure*. **(Pacific-Philippines)** Allied personnel wait patiently at Binuni Point, Mindanao, until the elusive U.S.S. *Bowfin* (SS-287) surfaces and evacuates personnel and delivers needed supplies. **(Pacific-Solomons)** The 3rd Battalion, 172nd Infantry, 43rd Division, lands at Nauro Peninsula, bringing the Regiment to full strength at Arundel. **(Atlantic-Italy)** The U.S. Army Air Corps continues to devastate enemy Airbases in southern Italy. American Bombers have flown nearly 3,000 sorties against these positions, since the 18th of August, putting every southern Airfield, except Foggia and its satellites, out of operation. Allied Planes begin to attack all enemy Airfields within striking distance of Salerno. The Air Attacks run round-the-clock as a preinvasion tactic. **(Atlantic-Russia)** Heavy fighting continues between the Soviets and the beleaguered Germans along a wide area. Sumy falls, and other contingents sever the Bryansk-Konotop railroad. The Russians tighten their advantage in two days, with the seizure of the rail junction at Merefa, virtually blocking the final rail exit from Kharkov.

A PT Boat laying a smoke screen.

September 3rd 1943 — (Pacific-Solomons) Elements of the 172nd Infantry advance to Bustling Point on the west coast of Arundel, without encountering any resistance. In Naval activity, the American beachhead at Vella Lavella is totally secure. In other activity in the Pacific, the Destroyer *Ellet* (DD-398), sinks the Japanese Submarine I-168 in the Pacific. **(Pacific-New Guinea)** The ongoing Allied Air Offensive against Lae continues to soften enemy resistance. Ships, transporting the assault troops, converge off Buna. **(Atlantic-Italy)** BAYTOWN Three years and one day since Britain's entry into the war, the British Eighth Army lands on the Mainland of Italy (transported by Ferry Boats) at the Calabrian coast, seizing Reggio, its Airdrome and Villa S. Giovanni at 04:30, taking them effortlessly from the Italians. Later, Commandos land at Bagnara to outflank the enemy and accelerate the advance. The mission is screened by Air, Naval and Artillery cover fire. The British 13 Corps is to march north. Meanwhile, the Germans on the peninsula initiate a slow and elusive withdrawal; the 26th Panzers are ordered to hold at Catanzaro, seventy-five miles from Reggio to buy time for the evacuation of heavy equipment. Also, the 29th Panzer Division is to move to Castrovillari, seventy five miles beyond Catanzaro. The movements occur with almost no interference from the Eighth Army, allowing ample time to lay cunning obstacles to impede the British. Much discussion develops among the Allies, questioning why Montgomery had not initiated the attack several days earlier to free Landing Craft for AVALANCHE. In other activity, Rudolf Rahn, the new German Ambassador to Italy, introduces himself to Badoglio, who promises the Ambassador an audience with the King on the

following day. **(Atlantic-Sicily)** Italian General Castellano, representing the Italian government of Marshal Badoglio, signs a short term armistice with the Allies at Cassibile, near Syracuse at 17:15. General Walter Smith signs on behalf of General Eisenhower, who had flown in to witness the ceremony. It becomes effective on September 8th. In other activity, the U.S. 82nd Airborne is to be dropped near Rome to assist the Italians against the Germans, however, the orders will be canceled. Also, the BBC is to signal the day of the invasion by broadcasting two special programs between the hours of 10:00 and 12:00, however, without explanation, the programs are never broadcasted.

September 4th 1943 — (Pacific) The V Amphibious Corps is established to train and control troops for amphibious landings in the Pacific. Major General Holland M. Smith, U.S.M.C. is the Commanding Officer. General Smith, born in Alabama, had been offered a seat at Annapolis, however, both his parents were, as he put it, Southerners who were still "unreconstructed and would not permit me to accept an offer, which in their minds, would be a surrender to Yankee ideology." Smith becomes a lawyer, however, not wanting to stay with his father's law firm he attempts to leave the Alabama National Guard and join the Army; no openings were available for 2nd Lieutenants (1904). He joined the Marines and ironically departs San Francisco for the Philippines on April 16th 1906, two days before the devastating earthquake which rocked the city. **(Pacific-Solomons)** Elements of the U.S. 172nd Infantry move freely, along the west coast of Arundel. The Americans have firmly secured the beachhead on Vella Lavella, however, they continue search and destroy missions to eradicate remaining Japanese resisters. The 1st Battalion, 172nd Infantry, closes on Wana Wana Lagoon. On the following day stiff resistance is raised by the Japs at the base of the Bomboe Peninsula. The Japanese also mount ferocious counterattacks on the Stima Peninsula. Intense combat ensues until the 18th of September, when the Japanese evacuate the island. **(Pacific-New Guinea)** The main thrust to secure Japanese held Lae commences, as a U.S. Task Force, commanded by Rear Admiral D.E. Barbey, lands Australian and American troops at the Huon Peninsula, less than 20 miles east of Lae. Seaman 1st Class Johnnie D. Hutchins, assigned to a Landing Ship, spots an enemy torpedo which is heading directly for the Ship. Hutchins takes evasive action. As he attempts to steer clear, a bomb strikes the Vessel, wounding him mortally, however, he expends his last moments evading the torpedo, succumbing right at the wheel, sacrificing his life to save the crew. Planes from the 5th Air Force intercept the Planes. The Allied drive continues; the Australians close from the East and the Americans drive from the West. The next objective of the New Guinea Force, upon orders from General MacArthur, will be the seizure of Dumpu and Kaiapit. In Naval activity, an enemy Bomber damages the Destroyer *Conyngham* (DD-371). The LST 471 and 473 are also damaged by enemy Planes during the engagement.

September 5th 1943 — (Pacific-Solomons) Heavy fire, originating from entrenched Japanese positions at the base of the Bomboe Peninsula on Arundel, hinders the assault of the 172nd Infantry. In other action, Americans continue to fortify their positions at the base of Stima Peninsula in the face of successive counterattacks by suicidal Banzai troops. **(Pacific-New Guinea)** The Australian 7th Division prepares to assault Lae. In order to support the operation, an Airstrip must be secured. MacArthur devises a plan to again utilize Kenney's flying eagles to accomplish the near impossible; a swift seizure of a Japanese Airfield. The Planes transport the U.S. 503rd Parachute Regiment on a complicated mission, requiring an accurate and aggressive drop. Along for a first hand view of this, the first principal Airdrop of the Pacific campaign, is the indefatigable MacArthur, who witnesses a precise and successful descent, which places the Parachutists near Nadzab, propped along the Markham River. The Airfield is seized in a blazing flash. Soon after, the formidable 7th Division lands according to schedule. In accordance with these actions, the amphibious troops transported by Rear Admiral Barbey, also land on schedule. The startled Japs give nominal opposition, as they spin to meet the new threats from the sea and are soon greeted by the timely arrival of another wave of Paratroopers, who drop behind Jap lines.

The Japanese prepare for a victorious Banzai attack, in conjunction with the anticipated arrival of Fighter Planes. However, over 100 Allied Planes play hide and seek in the clouds. These flying steel snipers loiter anxiously, awaiting the enemy. Suddenly, as the enemy Aircraft appear, the Yanks spring the ambush. Forty-one enemy Planes, boasting the rising sun insignia on the wings, are blown from the sky. None return to Rabaul. Lae falls to the Australian-American forces and MacArthur again has stunned the Japanese, moving his forces nearly two hundred miles in one spectacular jump. **(Atlantic-Italy)** The AVALANCHE Invasion Force begins moving from ports in North Africa to rendezvous for the invasion of the Italian mainland. **15th Army Group** In the **British Eighth Army** area, the 13 Corps advances north, having secured the Calabrian Peninsula up to Bova Marina on the east and Bagnara on the west, the British 5th Division encounters opposition north of the latter. **(Atlantic-Middle East)** General Brereton steps down as Commanding Officer of USAFIME.

September 6th 1943 — (Pacific-Solomons) On Arundel, Grant Island and the western sector of Bomboe Peninsula is secured by contingents (1st Battalion) of the 172nd Regiment, 43rd Division; the 2nd Battalion advances doggedly against the base of the peninsula and the 3rd Battalion holds the base of the Stima Peninsula. **(Pacific-New Guinea)** The 26th Brigade, 9th Australian Division, trailed by the 24th Brigade, engages the enemy for the first time as it reaches the Bunga River, driving toward Lae. Also, contingents of the U.S. 871st Airborne Engineering Battalion are transported by air to Nadzab. **(Pacific-China)** American General Stilwell, anticipating Japanese reaction to raids by the U.S. Fourteenth Air Force, proposes that all troops under Chiang Kai-shek (Communist and Nationalist) be employed in China, to meet any threat. **(Atlantic-Italy)** The Strait of Messina is open for Allied Shipping. In other activity. in the British Eighth Army area, the 13 Corps' 5th Division seizes Gioia. **(Atlantic-North Africa-Sicily)** AVALANCHE: Supply and Auxiliary Vessels, Twenty LSTs, and Admiral Hewitt's Flagship, *Ancon*, depart Tripoli for Italy and are joined by escort Warships which depart Algiers. Many other Vessels are embarking from points in Sicily. Later, about 180 Axis Planes bombard Bizerte, however, with the Fleet in motion, the strike fails to impede the operation. **(Atlantic-Germany)** Inclement weather hampers a U.S. Eighth Air Force raid over Germany. Four hundred and seven Heavy Bombers strike at enemy positions, but the toll is high; forty-five Allied Planes do not return to their base. **(Atlantic-Soviet Union)** The Germans lose Konotop.

Vice Admiral Henry K. Hewitt.

September 7th 1943 — (United States) The Joint Chiefs of Staff hold discussion on the possibility of using the Aleutians as a base for mounting an invasion of Paramushiro. **(Pacific-Ellice Islands)** The Americans complete another Airstrip in the Central Pacific. Nanomea, Ellice Islands, now has an operational 5,000 foot Airstrip, from which an American Squadron operates by the end of the month. The Japanese strike the Base, causing some damage. The PT-118 and the PT-172, become grounded and are subsequently destroyed by U.S. Naval fire. **(Pacific-New Guinea)** The Australian 7th Division begins moving to Nadzab, transported by C-47s. **(Atlantic-Italy)** The British, in an attempt to get in front of the retreating Germans spring a surprise landing near Pizzo (night of the 7th-8th) about fifty miles beyond Reggio; the unhindered German retreat has moved so swiftly that the Commandos and the 231st Brigade nearly miss the rear-guards of the 26th Panzer Division. In other activity, General Maxwell Taylor and Colonel Peter Gardiner depart Palermo on a clandestine operation via a British PT Boat through the Tyrrhenian Sea, debarking at Gaeta between Naples and Rome and proceeding by ambulance (posing as shot down Airmen P.O.W.s). They enter Rome at dusk and are taken to Palazzo Caprara to meet with Italian leaders. Subsequently, they meet with Marshal Badoglio. The conversation between Taylor and Badoglio is spoken in French. General Taylor determines that the Italians are ill-equipped, lacking both gasoline and ammunition. Also, he is informed that 12,000 German Paratroopers now circle

Rome, in addition to learning that the 3rd Panzer Panzer Division is up to a strength of 24,000 men, supported by 150 Heavy Tanks and 50 Light Tanks. He radios Algiers (Headquarters), recommending that the impending Airborne invasion of Rome (GIANT TWO) should be canceled. Both Americans are evacuated. **(Atlantic-Russia)** The Germans evacuate Stalino. Soviet forces occupy it on the following day, giving them control of the industrial area of the Donbas.

A U.S. Plane making a very low level attack against a Japanese Airfield.

September 8th 1943 — (Pacific-Baker Island) The Island's Airstrip goes into use for Fighter Planes. **(Pacific-Solomons)** Japanese reinforcements are transferred from Kolombangara to Arundel to bolster a counterattack to regain New Georgia. **(Pacific-New Guinea)** Four U.S. Destroyers move within striking range of Lae and commence a bombardment. Also, the 9th Australian Division closes on Lae, encountering Japs holding the west bank of the flooded Busu River and the Australian 5th Division advances to the Francisco River, near the Airfield as it closes on Salamaua. Meanwhile, the Japanese at Salamaua receive orders to abandon it and move to Lae. **(Atlantic-Italy)** The news of the Italian Armistice is announced publicly by General Eisenhower at 18:30. Marshal Badoglio, after a period of hesitation, makes the same information public shortly thereafter. Italy's Fleet and Airplanes are ordered to embark to designated locations, for their formal surrender to Allied Forces. Simultaneously, the Allied Assault Convoy closes on the Italian mainland; D-Day is now

only hours away. Complications develop, as word of the cancellation of the Airborne operation nearly fails to reach General Ridgway. The announcement of the armistice signals the Planes transporting the Paratroopers to take off. Meanwhile, another Plane, transporting General Lyman Lemnitzer and the orders to abort the Airborne operation arrive at Licata as the 62 Aircraft are preparing to take off. In conjunction, the news of the canceled airdrop reaches the supporting seaborne force of Lt. Colonel William Bertsch in time for it to divert and join the AVALANCHE Convoys. Meanwhile, German troops are rushing to Salerno. The Italian Generals in southern Italy are surprised and humiliated by the announcement of an armistice and many units give supplies and ammunition to the Germans and also give them their excellent coastal positions. An exception, the 9th (Pasubio) Division is decimated by the Germans as they race to Salerno. Also, General Gonzaga, refuses to obey a German order to disarm his unit (222nd Coastal Division) and he is executed. Also, British Lt. General Sir Brian G. Horrocks, 10 Corps Commanding Officer, had been wounded during an airraid on the 8th, and is replaced by Lt. General McCreery. At 22:00, the Allied Convoys detect beacon lights of advance Vessels in the Gulf of Salerno. Minesweepers contact a British Submarine which had been in the area since August 29th, locating mines, and begin to clear passage. Also, 16 PT Boats, commanded by Lt. Commander Stanley M. Barnes, guards the northern flank of the Fleet and moves into the Bay of Naples to create a diversion to coordinate with the other diversion, being carried out by Capt. Charles L. Andrews, Jr. in the Gulf of Gaeta. In other activity, Allied Planes pound Frascati, where Kesselring is headquartered. Kesselring crawls out of the wreckage uninjured.

September 9th 1943 — (Atlantic-Italy) THE INVASION OF ITALY — The massive invasion of Italy commences, as Lt. General Mark Clark's Fifth Army prepares to hit the beaches. At midnight of the eighth, a small detachment of the 82nd Airborne captures Venotene Island in the Gulf of Gaeta, neutralizing its radar station. At 00:01 on the 9th, the Convoy which has been off the coast and under radio silence since nightfall of the eighth, begins calling Boat Teams to their stations. Several hours later, the tedious task of forming in the rendezvous area is complete; the invasion force (each man donning wool uniforms) aboard Infantry Landing Craft sets out for the spearhead, trailed by DUKWs, transporting the Tanks, Artillery, Ammunition and Antitank weapons, and their crews. Meanwhile, at about 02:00 enemy shore guns commence firing at the Fleet transporting the Northern Attack Force (10 Corps). Return fire is aggressively returned. However, any thoughts of an unopposed landing, due to the armistice, vanish. Under the wings of Vice Admiral H. K. Hewitt's Western Naval Task Force, the U.S. VI Corps (Southern Assault Force, under General E. J. Dawley), hits the beaches south of the Sele River, 25 miles southeast of Naples near Paestum (beaches Red, Green, Yellow, and Blue, north to south) and the Northern Assault Force (British 10 Corps, under Lt. General Sir R. L. McCreery) lands north of the river (beaches Green, White and Red, south to north), making the major thrust of Fifth Army. In conjunction, a British Fleet slips into the harbor of Taranto, and lands one British Division at the docks in the arch of the Italian boot.

Prior to the main invasion, Rangers embark in Landing Craft just after midnight and move to about three miles from shore.

Colonel Darby, notes the uselessness of compasses, once the Landing Craft are laden with men and equipment, in locating the beach in darkness. However, Rangers and British Commandos hit the beaches at about 03:10, followed 20 minutes later by Infantry. Some units come under fire while approaching the beach and others hit stiff resistance at the beach. German Tanks and Artillery units crank out deadly fire to destroy the beachhead, which is defended by the 16th Panzer Division, under Generalmajor Rudolf Sickenius, composed of 36 Assault guns, 100 Tanks, and about 17,000 men. Sickenius requests XIV Panzer Corps, but Generalleutnant Hermann Balck, filling in for General Hube (on leave), plays it cautiously and does not release enough reinforcements to tilt the balance. Also, initially, the Italians raise fierce resistance, dispelling the idea that the Italians would happily greet the Americans. Subsequently, the Italians hear of the surrender and many abandon their positions; Germans take over their coastal guns. Despite the incessant fire, the Rangers advance to the heights near Sorrento Mountain mass. During the initial landings, under pitch black skies, tracer shells rake the beaches, and awesome Artillery and mortar fire ravage some of the landing craft, forcing the men to swim toward shore. In some instances Mortar and Artillery units hit the beaches, however, their ammunition is lost to the surf. Communication gear is also lost. As the troops struggle with the darkness and withering fire, scores of multicolored flares saturate the sky, giving the enemy a finer focus. The thunderclap is worst from Monte Soprano, the largest and most ominous of the monstrous features dominating the landing areas. Brigadier General John W. O'Daniel (Fifth Army) begins untangling the confusion (landing operations) on beaches Red and Green about 04:30, restoring discipline and order. Enemy fire keeps Yellow Beach closed all morning and equally devastating fire closes Blue Beach for the greater part of the afternoon. However, despite all the hardships, and the successive counterattacks to drive the Allies back into the sea, the beachhead holds and the exhausted ground forces take their objectives by nightfall.

The VI Corps' RCT 141, and 142, 36th Division (Major General Fred L. Walker), the vanguard of the force, repulse four counterattacks. The Rangers and British Commandos after landing on Sorrento Peninsula: the Commandos seize Vietri sul Mare and drive east toward Salerno, while the Rangers, landing without incident at Maiori advance north toward the passes leading to Naples. Meanwhile, the Infantry, armed with Bazookas and other weapons, virtually neutralizes the enemy Tanks during the initial hours of combat, saving the day. In one instance, Brigadier General Miles A. Cowles (Divisional Artillery Commander), joins a beleaguered gun crew of the 151st Field Artillery Battalion as a "Cannoneer." By mid-afternoon, the 751st Tank Battalion assumes central control of all Armored units ashore, many of which are employed in Antitank operations until the 601st and 645th Tank Destroyer Battalions get ashore later in the day to bolster the ground troops. Also, Air and Naval Surface Vessel fire supplements the landing throughout the day, bolstered by Major General Edwin J. House's U.S. XII Tactical Air Support Command. By nightfall, only 35 enemy Tanks remain in service. General Walker requests a Regiment of the 45th Division (Floating Reserve) to be landed and soon after, the 179th Regiment debarks on Red Beach. However, throughout the day, General Clark, still offshore aboard the *Ancon*, receives erroneous information from returning wounded troops who have exagge-

rated the fighting power of the enemy and painted a grim picture; Ship-to-shore communication is poor. By 20:45, General Mark Clark informs British General Alexander that the entire 36th U.S. Division is ashore.

Meanwhile, in the 10 Corps sector, the British secure their beachhead effortlessly by 04:45. The stiff resistance begins as the advance moves inland: the 56th Division (Maj. Gen. G.W.R. Templer) advances toward Montecorvino to seize its Airfield, but German counterattacks force it back; contingents reach Battipaglia, however, reinforcements arrive and it is retained by the enemy. The British 46th Division (Maj. Gen. J.L.T. Hawkesworth) thwarts several Tank supported counterattacks, partly encircles Montecorvino Airfield, then heads north along the coast toward Salerno, encountering vicious opposition. The Americans, also positioned precariously, hold firmly against fierce counterattacks mounted two successive days after the landings. The situation remains in serious doubt for several days; however, fresh reinforcements, including a Regiment of Paratroopers dropping on the beachhead, bolster the beachhead and the line is held. German General Vietinghoff, pulls back the 16th Panzer Division and pushes in additional reinforcements to protect the heights at the Salerno Plain, putting more pressure on the British. Meanwhile, Naval guns continue to pound the enemy. In conjunction, Aircraft attack without pause, and the Infantry fights relentlessly. Finally, on the 15th, the Germans begin to withdraw, pursued by the Allies. Naples, the first city on the Continent to be liberated, falls to the Yanks on October 1st, as the troops march past the ruins of ancient Pompei and take the city. The enduring campaign to seize Rome drags punishingly throughout the fall and the bitter winter, eventually concluding victoriously during June of 44. However, fighting continues in Italy, until the fall of Germany during 1945. The grievous campaign includes the siege of Cassino and the besieged beachhead at Anzio, both of which extract high costs from the Allies. The Germans hold both American and British Infantry, on the beachhead at Anzio, during January of 1944 until May of 44, when the Allies breakout at Cassino and subsequently at Anzio, and advance on Rome. Contingents of General Clark's 5th Army roll triumphantly into the Eternal City on June 4th 1944 to the jubilation of the Italian citizens. One young American reporter, Eric Sevareid, states distasteful things about Clark and when reporting on the seizure of Rome it appears that Sevareid editorializes when he claims that a conference held by Clark with the senior Commanders is: "A PHONY AND EMBARRASSING SCENE PLAYED FOR THE BENEFIT OF NEWSREEL CAMERAS."

September 9th 1943 — (Pacific-Philippines) The U.S.S. *Trout* (SS-202), operating in Philippine waters, sinks the Japanese Submarine I-182. **(Pacific-Solomons)** Admiral Halsey suggests that Treasury Island and Choiseul Bay be acquired for use as Bases, from which enemy positions on the south Bougainville-Shortlands can be attacked, however, General MacArthur disagrees with the proposed plan. In other activity, the U.S. 37th Division arrives at Guadalcanal, from New Georgia to receive additional training for the imminent Bougainville campaign. **(Atlantic-Italy)** The U.S. Fifth Army, comprised of U.S. VI Corps and the British 10 Corps, invades Italy south of Salerno at 03:30. The VI Corps, commanded by Major General Earnest Dawley, and spearheaded by RCTs 141, and 142, lands at Paestum, establishes a beachhead and repulses four major enemy Tank assaults. Regimental Combat Team 143 (Reserve) is deployed by midday in the center line.

Heroism abounds as the Americans establish their beachhead. In one instance, an irritated Sergeant, James M. Logan (36th Infantry), is with his Company at an irrigational canal when the Germans counterattack and threaten his command. Logan, surrounded by ringing bullets, advances against a stone wall and picks off three Germans, then dashes another 200 perilous yards and runs into a wall of fire coming from an obstinate machine-gun and kills two more Germans and commandeers their gun. With a quick swiveling maneuver, he turns it upon the fleeing enemy. Logan, then charges a house and within seconds after kicking in the door, eliminates a sniper at the bottom of the steps. His daring acts greatly contribute to securing the Salerno beachhead. The British 10 Corps lands just south of Salerno and receives heavy resistance. The British 46th, drives along the coast toward Salerno. Another landing is made in rough seas at the Sorrento Peninsula (British Commandos and American Rangers), with Vietri sul Mare falling to the Commandos and the Rangers landing unopposed at Maiori. In other activity, the Italian Fleet begins departing Genoa, Spezia and Taranto, sailing for Malta to surrender the Fleet to the Allies. The German Planes based on Sardinia sink the Battleship *Roma* (Ammiraglio Carlo Bergamini, the Commander and most of the crew is lost) and damage the Battleship *Italia*; the remaining Warships head for North Africa and are met on the following day by British Warships, which escort them to Bizerte. German troops reach La Spezia too late to seize the Fleet, however, they execute several Italian Officers who had not been able to get their Ships away and who scuttle them. Meanwhile, British Warships (SLAPSTICK), heading toward Taranto Harbor, pass the Italian Fleet and subsequently a British Minelayer, the *Adiel* hits a mine while waiting to debark elements of the British 1st Airborne and is lost along with over 200 Airborne troops. The British take the undefended city and advance unopposed, seizing Brindisi, again unopposed on the 11th. During the primary invasion, the Tug *Nauset* (AT-89) is sunk by an enemy Dive Bomber. In addition, four LST's are damaged by land batteries; LST 336; LST 375; LST 385; LST 389. The LST 386 becomes damaged, after it strikes a mine. In Rome, confusion permeates the city. No guards are stationed at the Quirinal Palace and at the Ministry of War, there are no high ranking officials. Unlike the Navy, the Italian ground forces near Rome begin capitulating to the Germans. Also, about 500,000 Italian troops in northern Italy and occupied France "vanish into thin air." Some Italian units of the 5th Pusteria Division raise resistance briefly at Mount Cenis and a group of men from the Fourth Army volunteer to fight with the Germans, however about 40,000 Italian troops are captured and sent to prison camps. **(Atlantic-North Africa)** General Eisenhower informs the Combined Chiefs of Staff of the AVALANCHE progress: "WE ARE IN FOR SOME VERY TOUGH FIGHTING . . . AVALANCHE WOULD BE A MATTER OF TOUCH AND GO FOR THE NEXT SEVERAL DAYS." . . ."OUR GREATEST ASSET NOW IS CONFUSION AND UNCERTAINTY WHICH WE MUST TAKE ADVANTAGE OF IN EVERY POSSIBLE WAY." Eisenhower expects no help from the Italian Army. **(Atlantic-Soviet Union)** Bakhmach, west of Konotop falls to the Red Army.

September 10th 1943 — (Pacific-New Guinea) Australian troops depart Nadzab, pushing east toward Lae. **(Pacific)** Headquarters V Amphibious Corps is made directly responsible to Commander Central Pacific. **(Middle East)** Major General Ralph Royce replaces General Brereton (stepped down on September 5th) as Commander of U.S. Air Forces in the Middle East. **(Atlantic-Italy)** The U.S. Fifth Army stabilizes its beachhead positions in preparation of enemy attacks. Elements of the U.S. 36th Division secure Albanella. In the British 10 Corps sector, a furious non-decisive battle ensues near Battipaglia and Montecorvino Airfield. The British 46th Division secures Salerno. In the British Eighth Army area, the German 29th and 26th Panzer Grenadier Divisions begin withdrawing from the Calabrian Peninsula, rushing them to the Salerno area to repulse the British. Also, Italian troops in the Balkans, Greece, and the Aegean areas are of no help to the Allies on the mainland and mount less than feeble resistance against the Germans. By the 15th, about 600,000 Italian troops straggle home. In addition, despite an overpowering four-to one advantage against the Germans on Corsica and Sardinia, the Italians are ineffective. Well over one German Division easily evacuates Sardinia and fights south of Rome. The Italian 184th (Nembo) Paratroop Division remains loyal to the German cause and fights with them. **(Atlantic-Soviet Union)** The Russians seize Mariupol on the Sea of Azov. Meanwhile, other Soviet forces establish a bridgehead across the Desna River near Novgorod.

September 11th 1943 — (United States) A German Submarine lays mines in the vicinity of Charleston, South Carolina. **(North Pacific)** The U.S. 11th Air Force sustains heavy losses during its air attack on enemy positions in the Kuriles. **(Pacific-New Hebrides)** The *Navajo*, a Tug (AT-64), sustains an explosion and sinks off New Hebrides. **(Pacific-Solomons)** The U.S. 27th Infantry, 25th Division, lands on the western portion of the Bomboe Peninsula and drives toward the base of the peninsula to support the 172nd Infantry in the attack to dislodge the enemy. The Army gets a new weapon, as 4.2-inch mortars are used in the South Pacific for the first time. In other activity in the South Pacific, the Japanese Minesweeper No. 16, is sunk by American Aircraft. **(Pacific-New Guinea)** The Japanese, feeling the pressure of the Allies (Australian 5th Division), evacuate Salamaua, withdrawing to Lae. **(Atlantic-Italy)** **15th Army Group** The British 1st Airborne Division seizes Brindisi. The Airborne troops maintain clearing operations in the heel of Italy, without incident. General Alexander's message prompting Montgomery to speed up his advance arrives. Montgomery, had halted "TO HAVE A SHORT PAUSE" near Catanzaro on the eighth because his Army had been "GETTING VERY STRUNG OUT." In the **U.S. Fifth Army** area, **VI Corps** sector, Regimental Combat Teams meet intense enemy resistance. RCT 142, 36th Division, captures Hill 424 and Altavilla. The enemy counterattacks and drives elements of the 45th Division's RCT 179 back from the slopes, which overlook Ponte Sele. Thunderous gunfire occurs all across the land, with Tanks grinding along supporting the Infantry against the German onslaught. Pressure forces the Germans to evacuate their positions at Persano during the night of the 11th-12th. However, they snap back quickly, infiltrating the area surrounding Hill 424, but the Americans hold on. In the British 10 Corps area, Montecorvino Airfield is seized, however, German troops hold the heights and the Airfield cannot be used. Also, enemy resistance at Battipaglia, on the right front, is savage. During the day, the Germans capture about 1,500 troops, mostly British. In the **British Eighth Army** area, the port of Crotone falls. Meanwhile, German Planes still pound the beaches, as 120 enemy Aircraft are counted. Efforts by Admiral Hewitt, U.S.N., and General Edwin J. House to maintain Allied Air support reach Tactical Air Force Headquarters: "SUFFERING LOSSES THAT CANNOT BE REPLACED." The response: "OUR INFORMATION FROM YOU INDICATES LIGHT ENEMY AIR ATTACK." Headquarters reluctantly sends in a Squadron of P38s for Patrol duty over Salerno. Another message is dispatched to Admiral Vian's Carrier Force: "AIR SITUATION HERE CRITICAL . . . COULD VIAN REMAIN ON STATION AND FURNISH EARLY MORNING COVER ON 12 SEPTEMBER?" The immediate response: "YES, CERTAINLY." The Destroyer *Rowan* (DD-405), is sunk by enemy Surface Ships. In addition, two Light Cruisers, the *Philadelphia* (CL-41) and the *Savannah* (CL-42), are both damaged by radio controlled bombs. **(Atlantic-Malta)** The Italian Navy surrenders to the Allies. While the Italian fleet is moving from Spezia toward Malta for the formal surrender to Sir Admiral Cunningham, the Germans sink the Battleship *Roma*. Also, Cunningham, acting on a request from Admiral Hewitt, sends the Cruisers H.M.S. *Aurora* and *Penelope* to bolster the Fleet off Salerno. He also sends three Cruisers to Tripoli to embark British replacements to speed them to Italy. **(Atlantic-Corsica)** The enemy Garrison at Sardinia evacuates, heading to Corsica.

Pvt. Paul Rizzo, standing with two children during the Italian Campaign. Pvt. Rizzo, U.S. Infantry gave his life on May 18, 1944 during an attack near Cassino (Italian front).

September 12th 1943 — (Pacific-New Guinea) The Japanese begin evacuating Lae in the face of the 7th and 9th Australian Divisions closing from separate directions. The Aussies already have secured Salamaua, its Airfield and the isthmus. In other activity, Japanese Planes damage the LST No. 455. **(Atlantic-Italy)** In the Fifth Army area, the Americans brace for an assault and aggressively repulse enemy efforts to destroy the beachhead: however, the enemy recaptures Hill 424 and Altavilla. The U.S. 179th Infantry occupies Persano and the 157th U.S. Infantry finally breaks the enemy hold at the Tobacco Factory, which had been halting its advance to the western side of the Sele River. In the British 10 Corps area, the enemy drives the British from their positions at Battipaglia, inflicting severe casualties. A U.S. Ranger contingent, deployed on the left flank of the British 10 Corps is also struck by successive assaults, but the Rangers hold firmly. In other activity, intent intelligence activity has finally unearthed the exact location where Mussolini, under arrest since 25 July, is being held. About ninety German Paratroops, transported by Gliders, land in Italy and rescue Mussolini from his captivity at Gran Sasso, a fortified mountain retreat. He is extricated and flown to Pratica di Mare, after a harrowing take off to rendezvous with three Heinkel 111 Planes which transport Mussolini to Munich to meet his wife. On the 14th, he meets with Hitler at Rastenburg (Wolf's Lair). The Italian guards offer no resistance and upon rescuing Mussolini, German Captain Otto Skorzeny demands surrender of the Garrison. An Italian Captain asks for time to consider the demand, then departs to ponder and returns shortly, flask of wine in hand, saluting the Germans.

September 12th 1943 — A decimated Salamaua, New Guinea.

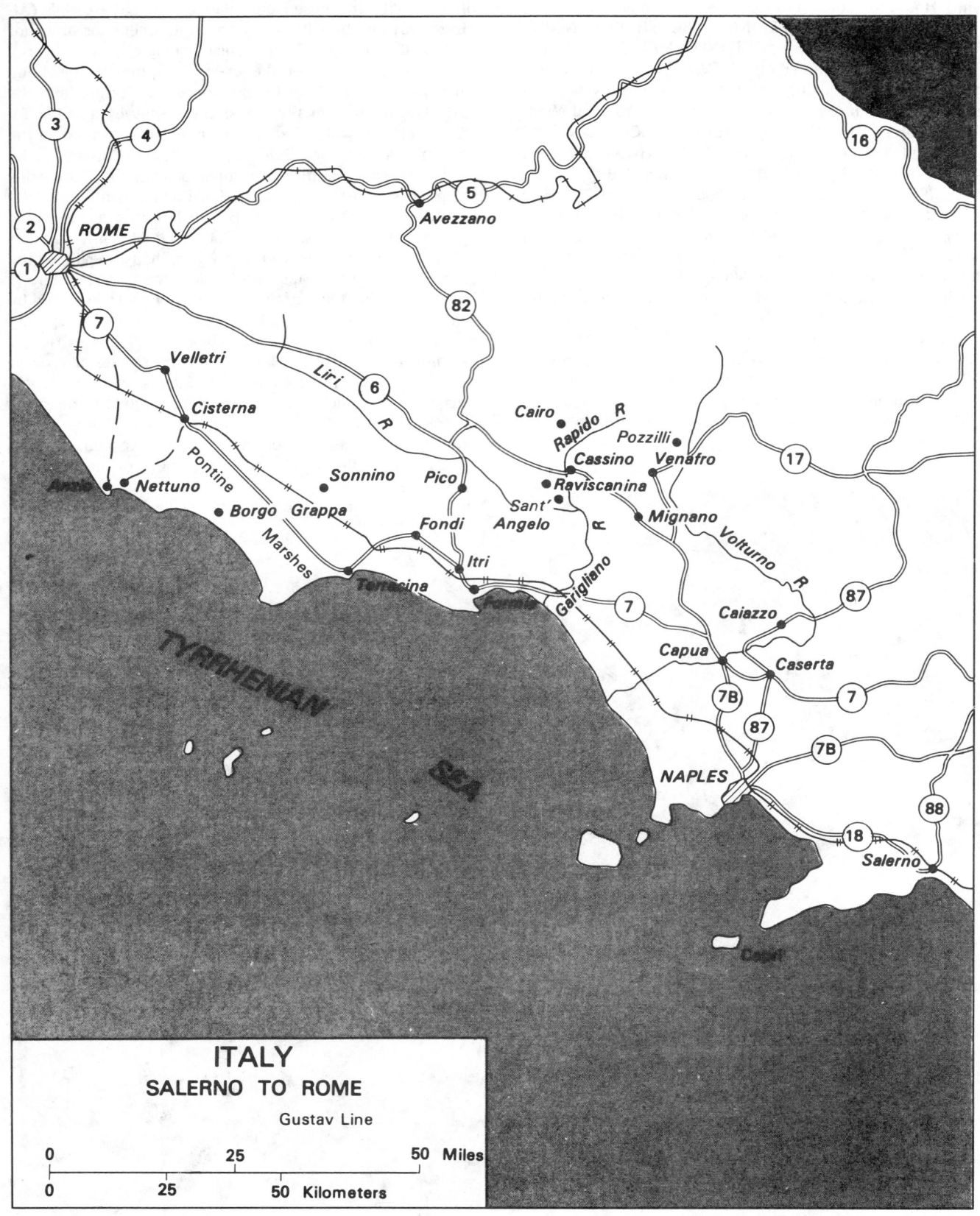

ITALY
SALERNO TO ROME
Gustav Line

Avezzano

ROME

Velletri

Liri

Cisterna

R

Cairo
Rapido R
Pozzilli
Cassino
Venafro
Raviscanina
Sonnino
Pico
Sant'
Angelo
Mignano
Nettuno
Borgo
Grappa
Fondi
R
Volturno
Marshes
Itri
R
Pontine
Terracina
Gaeta
Garigliano
Caiazzo
Capua
Caserta
Pontine

TYRRHENIAN

SEA

NAPLES

Capri

Salerno

| 0 | 25 | 50 Miles |
| 0 | 25 | 50 Kilometers |

B17s making bombing run over Rumania.

September 13th 1943 — **(Pacific-Solomons)** Contingents of the U.S. 169th Infantry establish outposts on islets west of Sagekarasa, while the 3rd Battalion, 27th Infantry, advances to seize Sagekarasa Island. The 2nd Battalion, 27th Infantry, previously ordered to reinforce the 172nd, makes radio contact with the 172nd Infantry on the Bomboe Peninsula. **(Atlantic-Italy)** The U.S. Fifth Army again is seriously threatened by elements of the 16th Panzers and 29th Panzer Grenadiers and the Americans (VI Corps) give ground in some areas. The 36th Division counterattacks to gain Altavilla, however, some units become isolated. The 1st Battalion, 142nd Regiment, nearly annihilated at Altavilla, is down to sixty troops. On the Corps north flank, the 2nd Battalion, 143rd Regiment is overrun at its positions in the Sele-Calore corridor and the 157th Regiment, 45th Division holds slightly west of the Sele. The beleaguered 2nd Battalion, poorly deployed, is told to remain covered while Artillery is called in; enemy Tanks and Artillery decimate their positions, costing more than 500 men killed or captured. Only nine Officers and 325 troops make it back to U.S. lines. General Clark dispatches a Plane, with a request for an immediate Paratroop drop directly on the beachhead, to General Ridgway in Sicily. Within hours, about 1,000 men of the 504th Paratroop Infantry, 82nd Airborne, touch down South of the Sele River, to bolster the perimeter. Meanwhile, General Clark departs the area in a PT Boat, moving to 10 Corps area to maintain what he calls "A CLAWHOLD" on the Italian mainland. However, Clark, despite

the strong protest General Dawley, had instructed Major General Alfred M. Gruenther (Chief of Staff) to "TAKE UP WITH THE NAVY," the task of evacuating the beachhead if it becomes necessary. Montgomery's Eighth Army is too far away to help. The Germans continue to close the net, however, fragments of the 158th and 189th Field Artillery Battalions, several Tank Destroyers, and the barest of troops, including cooks, clerks and truck drivers, forge a firing line on the south bank of the Calore to meet the onslaught and they hold the line. General Walker had split his Division into three sectors, each commanded by a Brigadier General. Generals Wilbur, O'Daniel, and Otto F. Lange, hold the left, center, and right respectively, with orders to hold at all costs. Naval Guns and Allied Aircraft also join the party and help turn back the enemy attack. On the following day, another 1,000 men are dropped, to face the Germans under General Heinrich von Vietinghoff (German 10th Army). Field Marshal Kesselring, the Commander in Chief (Italy) is deeply interested in the activities, as Hitler has ordered a retreat in Italy once the Italians surrender. However, the Germans still resist to get their troops out of the toe area, and are compelled to fight for retention of the road to Rome. The Allies have previously acquired Hitler's plans, prompting the invasion of Salerno to quicken the enemy's retreat. The Allies have also anticipated a quick demise of the Germans, but, the road to Rome is paved with blood. General Patton, who is sitting this one out, notes in his diary: "LAST NIGHT THEY FLEW IN A REGIMENTAL COMBAT TEAM OF THE 82nd AIRBORNE TO HELP OUT... "WHEN I ASKED SIMILAR ASSISTANCE LAST MONTH, I WAS TOLD THAT THE 82nd WAS TOO VALUABLE TO BE WASTED AS INFANTRY." "FORTUNATELY WE WON THE FIGHT WITHOUT THEM." During the German vicious combat near Altavilla, at Hill 424, enemy machine gun fire halts an attack. 1st Lt. Arnold Bjorklund (36th Infantry Division) ignores the intense fire and crawls forward with three grenades, destroying two enemy nests, allowing his men to advance to the crest of the hill. At that point, additional fire again pins down a Platoon. Private William Crawford (3rd Platoon, Company I) advances, destroying or capturing three enemy nests to open the way. In other action at Altavilla, Corporal Charles E. Kelly, Company L, 143rd Infantry, mans a machine gun at a storage house and comes under attack by the enemy. He fires incessantly until his weapon runs out of ammunition. Ingeniously, Kelly holds off the Germans by pulling the safety pins out of 60mm mortars, and throwing them as grenades. The balance of the detachment withdraws from the storage area, but Kelly remains to cover his unit. Kelly, improvises further and begins firing a rocket launcher at the enemy as they approach his position. Kelly holds them off and rejoins his outfit. Corporal Kelly is later awarded the Medal of Honor for his indisputable valor and fighting spirit. Offshore, the Submarine Chaser *SC-666*, is involved in a collision and sustains damage. General Clark is receiving better perception of the British Public Relations Officers in British General Alexander's Headquarters as they are up to their mischievousness as usual. The British tell the War Correspondents to "PLAY UP" Montgomery who is allegedly racing to Salerno where the Americans are having a difficult time. Montgomery is not racing. He is moving slowly, but the British, throughout the war, attempt to play up the British and merely mention the Americans in the newsreels. **Atlantic-Sicily)** General Patton receives word from General Alexander that Ships are en route to embark the U.S. 3rd Division to

Italy. General Truscott orders the troops to stage; about 2,000 men from the 1st and 9th Divisions are diverted to the 3rd Division, bringing it to full strength.

September 14th 1943 — (Pacific-Solomons) On Vella Lavella, elements of the 35th Infantry, 25th U.S. Division, move against Horaniu, but find it abandoned. In other activity, Japanese resistance at Sagekarasa prompts the sending of reinforcements to bolster the 3rd Battalion, 27th Infantry. **(Pacific-New Guinea)** Contingents of the Australian 7th Division seize Heath's Plantation as it drives toward Lae. **(Atlantic-Italy)** Tenth Army is ordered by Kesselring to make a gradual withdrawal toward Rome even if Fifth Army is dislodged. One hundred eighty-seven B-25s, 166 B-26s, and 170 B-17s run effective sorties over the Salerno Plain. **15th Army Group** In the **U.S. Fifth Army** area, several enemy counterattacks are halted by the combined strengths of the Infantry, Artillery and Air units of the U.S. Fifth Army. In the **VI Corps** area, RCT 505 (82nd Airborne), is dropped to further fortify the beachhead. During the first attack at 08:00, seven of eight enemy Tanks are immediately destroyed near the tobacco factory and the survivor is crippled; the Infantry (contingents of the 16th and 29th Panzer Grenadier Divisions) retires soon after. By day's end, the Germans lose about thirty Tanks in the VI Corps sector. In the British 10 Corps area, heavy fighting bogs the British down, however, they hold. Every unit of the 46th Division is thrown into the defense. And in the 56th Division zone, vicious combat ensues on wide open ground. Mark Clark has requested a priority airdrop. The mission had been postponed, however, it is now executed in a rush with poor intelligence on the drop zone. The U.S. 2nd Battalion, 509th Paratroop Infantry, comprising about 600 men under Lt. Colonel Doyle R. Yardley, is dropped behind enemy lines near Avellino to lend assistance to the British by destroying enemy communications, but the drop at 2,000 feet is scattered (as far as twenty-five miles from target) because of navigational errors and ineffective radar. Nearly all of its bazookas, mortars and other equipment is lost or strung up in tree tops. Unable to coordinate as a whole unit, the Paratroopers bolt to the hills in small units and mount Guerrilla raids against Convoys, outposts and supply trains. Initially, the Battalion is presumed lost, however, eventually about 400 men make it to Allied lines. General McCreery, noting the day's activity, reports: "NOTHING OF INTEREST TO REPORT DURING DAYLIGHT." General Alexander visits the battlefield and is impressed with the American defenses. Also, General Mark Clark has returned from 10 Corps sector and he roves the battlefield, making his presence conspicuous in the Sele-Calore zone. By nightfall it is obvious that the beachhead is permanent; evacuation plans are scuttled. Subsequently, according to General Truscott, General Clark is awarded the Distinguished Service Cross for conspicuous bravery during the operation. On the following day, he congratulates his fighting men and tells them: "... OUR BEACHHEAD IS SECURE. ...AND WE ARE HERE TO STAY. In the **British Eighth Army** area, the British 1st Airborne enters Bari. **(Atlantic-Aegean Area)** Leros, an island in the Aegean Sea is taken by a British contingent.

September 15th 1943 — (Pacific) The 2nd Marine Division is formally attached to the V Amphibious Corps in conjunction with the ongoing preparations for the imminent Central Pacific Offensive to seize the Tarawa Atoll. Also, General MacArthur orders the New Guinea Force to seize Dumpu and

Kalapit, with U.S. Planes flying support missions. In other activity, the U.S. Navy establishes Fleet Air Wing 17, commissioning it at Brisbane Australia. Also, Major General Charles Barrett relieves Lt. General A.A. Vandegrift as Commanding General, I Marine Amphibious Corps. The 2nd Marine Division is attached to V Amphibious Corps for the operation to capture the Tarawa Atoll. The Japanese Submarine RO-103, is destroyed off the Solomons by Planes attached to (VP-23), and the Destroyer U.S.S. *Saufley* (DD-465). **(Pacific-Solomons-New Georgia)** The Australian 9th Division seizes Malahang Airdrome and the Australian 7th Division secures Edward's Plantation. **(Atlantic-Italy)** The Allied beachhead at Salerno holds against counterattacks. Subsequently, the enemy begins to withdraw. Reinforcements (325th Glider Infantry, 82nd Airborne) arrive by sea to further bolster the beachhead. The U.S. Fifth Army receives orders to continue its offensive across the Volturno River. In the British Eighth Army area, advance contingents of the British 5th Division move to Sapri as it advances to establish contact with the U.S. VI Corps. The Public Relations Officer (British Eighth Army) and several British War correspondents encounter a U.S. Scout Vehicle about seven miles south of Ogliastro. The contingent had departed Eighth Army area at 10:30 on the 13th, using the coast road from Catanzaro about 150 miles south of Paestum. The small convoy encounters no Germans during the 48-hour trip. A small British Patrol arrives on the 16th and another on the 19th, however, on the 19th, Montgomery's main force is at Scalea, about 75 miles south of Paestum. According to a report from B.B.C., Montgomery is "DASHING UP THE ITALIAN BOOT TO RESCUE THE FIFTH ARMY, WHICH IS PREPARING TO EVACUATE THE BEACHHEAD."

September 15th 1943 — U.S Paratroopers, dropped by C-47s, land at Nadzab Airdrome about twenty miles northwest of Lae. One Battalion lands under cover of smoke and the other swoops down beyond the smoke landing behind a hill.

September 16th 1943 — (Pacific-New Guinea) The Australians move into Lae, which has been evacuated by the Japanese. **(Pacific-Solomons)** Reinforcements, including three U.S.M.C. Tank Platoons, arrive to reinforce U.S. Army troops on Arundel Island, New Georgia. **(Atlantic-Italy) 15th Army Group** The Germans launch their last attack to destroy the Allied beachhead and are easily repulsed, first by the British 56th Division, supported by the British 7th Armored Division and then by the U.S. 45th Division. Also, Patrols of the U.S. Fifth Army establish contact with a Patrol of the British Eighth Army near Vallo. In the VI Corps sector, the 504th Paratroop Regiment, 82nd Airborne Division attacks to regain Altavilla. Heavy enemy fire combs the approach routes, causing confusion and a breakdown in communications, however, the troops keep advancing, gaining a fragile hold, despite its Commanding Officer, Colonel Tucker being driven from his observation post by the artillery fire. On the following morning, the Germans surround his Command Post and the situation becomes desperate, however, by late afternoon, the Germans are retiring. The 504th Paratroop Infantry enters Altavilla unopposed on the following day. Meanwhile, Patrols discover Roccadaspide abandoned by the enemy. In the British Eighth Army 13 Corps sector, Reconnaissance contingent of the 1st Canadian Division encounters elements of the British 1st Airborne Division from the Taranto bridgehead. **(Atlantic-Mediterranean-Aegean)** Samos is occupied by a British contingent.

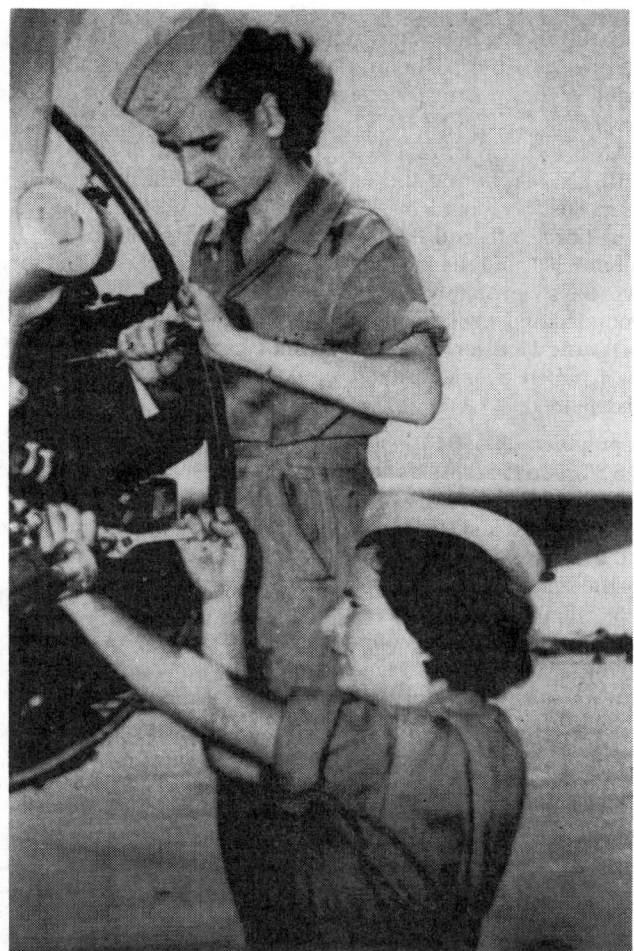

WACS working on an Aircraft Engine.

September 18th 1943 — (Pacific-Solomons) The New Zealand 3rd Division lands its 14th Brigade at Barakoma, relieving U.S. Army troops there. Major General H. E. Barrowclough, Commanding General New Zealand 3rd Division, replaces General McClure U.S.A., as Commander on Vella Lavella. Meanwhile, the Japanese still alive on the island, evacuate. Also, Admiral Halsey orders the Commanding General, V Amphibious Corps to establish a forward staging area on Vella Lavella. **(Pacific-Gilberts)** A U.S. Carrier Task Force, commanded by Rear Admiral C.A. Pownall approaches the Gilberts; its Planes, supplemented by U.S. Army Planes, swarm over the islands and bombard Abemama, Makin, and Tarawa. The Japanese have previously bragged that the islands will not yield. **(Atlantic-Italy)** The Germans have withdrawn from Altavilla, enabling the 5th Army (504th Regiment, 82nd A/B and components of the 191st Tank Battalion) to occupy it. Patrols dispatched to the North, seize Persano without opposition. The exhausted U.S. 36th Division, which has been battling incessantly, is relieved by the U.S. 3rd Division. The U.S. 45th Division occupies Persano without incident, and the Rangers under Colonel Darby, remain on the defensive on the Sorrento peninsula. In the British 10 Corps area, the British 7th Armored Division occupies Battipaglia without incident. Meanwhile, British 5 Corps Headquarters debarks at Taranto and assumes command of Taranto bridgehead forces. Also, Hitler promotes Vietinghoff to Generaloberst and gives him temporary command of Army

September 17th 1943 — New Zealander troops land at Vella LaVella to relieve U.S. forces.

September 17th 1943 — (Pacific-New Guinea) The U.S. 503rd Paratroop Infantry withdraws from the Nadzab area after successful completion of its mission. In other activity, the PT-136, is grounded and subsequently destroyed by U.S. Forces. **(Pacific-Solomons)** Major General Charles Barrett, U.S.M.C., is ordered by Admiral Halsey, ComSoPac, to establish a forward Marine Staging Base on Vella Lavella. **(Atlantic-Italy)** Enemy fire halts the 5th Army advance, short of Altavilla. However, during the night, the enemy abandons its positions.

Group B in northern Italy, replacing Rommel (incapacitated by appendicitis). General Hube assumes temporary command of Tenth Army. Vietinghoff, while praising his troops proclaims: "SUCCESS HAS BEEN OURS. ONCE AGAIN GERMAN SOLDIERS HAVE PROVED THEIR SUPERIORITY OVER THE ENEMY." During the fight for the beachhead, the Germans sustain about 3,500 casualties: Hermann Goering Division 1,000; 16th and 29th Panzer Grenadier Divisions, each about 1,300, and the 26th Panzers (one Regiment engaged for two days) probably slight. U.S. losses: 500 killed, 1,800 wounded and 1,200 missing. British losses total about 5,500. **(Atlantic-Mediterranean)** Sardinia capitulates without a fight, when a small Allied unit arrives and discovers it undefended.

September 19th 1943 — (Pacific-Australia) The Submarine, U.S.S. *Cisco* (SS-290) commanded by Lieutenant Commander J.W. Coe, departs Darwin heading for the China Sea and is subsequently lost without any communication. War records indicate that a Submarine, leaking fuel, had been destroyed by the Japanese on September 28th, in the Sulu Sea. No other U.S. Submarines had been assigned to that area. **(Pacific-Gilberts)** American reconnaissance of Tarawa is more complete. Army and Navy Planes equipped with cameras, attack Tarawa in conjunction with Carrier Task Force 15, commanded by Rear Admiral Charles A. Pownall. Planes are launched from the Carriers *Belleau Wood*, *Lexington* and the *Princeton*. The Army B-24s are supplied by the Seventh Air Force, and are dispatched from Canton and Funafuti. **(Pacific-New Guinea)** Bitter fighting ensues as the Australians seize Kaiapit, then dig in and repulse several counterattacks. **(Atlantic-Italy)** The U.S. Fifth Army VI Corps sector, advances steadily through vicious enemy resistance, gaining control of the Salerno Plain: the 36th Division seizes Serre and Ponte Sele; the 45th captures the heights above Eboli. British General Alexander is of the opinion the Rome will be entered during the beginning of November. In the British Eighth Army area, 13 Corps sector, the Canadian 1st Division occupies Potenza, while the British 5th Division occupies Auletta. The British will subsequently move toward Melfi and Spinazzola. **(Atlantic-Russia)** The Germans are driven from Dukhovshchina and Yartsevo. The Soviets seize German held terrain all along the front, to the East and Southeast of Kiev.

September 20th 1943 — (Pacific) The 4th Marine Division is attached to V Amphibious Corps for the upcoming operation to seize Tarawa Atoll. **(Pacific-Solomons)** Elements of the U.S. 27th Infantry on Sagekarasa search for Japanese without incident and conclude that the enemy has withdrawn from the island. The balance of the 27th Infantry, which is on Arundel, calls off its attack to locate its unaccounted for 122nd Infantry. On the following day, it is determined that the Japanese also have evacuated Arundel and other nearby islands. The Japanese leave about 600 dead on Arundel. **(Atlantic-Italy)** General Mark Clark receives a letter from General Montgomery, telling him to look for British troops near Potenza-Auletta during the evening. Clark dispatches a Piper Cub, transporting General Walker, however, he returns and reports no sign of the Eighth Army. **15th Army Group** General Mark Clark, relieves General Ernest J. Dawley. Major General John P. Lucas assumes command of VI Corps. Their have been differences of opinion between Dawley and Clark. The U.S. Fifth

Army grinds through mountainous terrain toward Naples, the largest city an American Army has ever attempted to conquer. The Germans mount tenacious resistance. The U.S. 3rd and 45th Divisions embattle enemy troops that steadfastly stall the Allied advance outside of both Acerno and Oliveto. American reinforcements (133rd Infantry, 34th Division) land at Paestum on the following day and bolster the VI Corps push on Avellino. British General Alexander confers with General Clark and expresses his wishes that the 5th Army should take Naples by the 7th of October and then it is to advance to the Volturno River to ensure the safety of the port (Naples). **(Atlantic-Russia)** The Germans lose more ground, as the Red Army captures Chernigov.

September 21st 1943 — (Pacific-Solomons) The 27th Regiment, 25th Division resumes the attack and discovers that the Japanese on Arundel have evacuated the mainland and the nearby islands; the Japanese have sustained about 600 dead on Arundel. Also, the Japanese by now have decided to abandon the Central Solomons completely and are making their way north. **(Pacific-New Guinea)** The Japanese are fleeing toward Dumpu. The Australians are launching a three pronged operation to catch them. The 20th Brigade Group (9th Division) embarks by sea for Finschhafen; the 21st and 25th Brigades (7th Division) depart Nadzab by Air transports for Kaiapit to drive through the Markham Valley, and the 22nd Brigade drives cross-country from Lae toward Langemak Bay. **(Atlantic-Italy)** British General Alexander outlines his plans for the Italian operation. In the U.S. Fifth Army area, VI Corps sector, the 3rd and 45th Divisions continue the trek over the mountains toward Highway 7. **(Atlantic-Soviet Union)** The Red Army seizes Chernigov.

September 22nd 1943 — (Pacific) Admiral Halsey, Commander South Pacific, orders the preparation of plans for an invasion of Empress Augusta Bay, and Treasury Island, Bougainville. Rear Admiral Wilkinson is appointed Commander of the operation. Allied General Headquarters, Southwest Pacific, issues orders for the invasion of Cape Gloucester, New Britain (Operation DEXTERITY). The scheduled jump off date is November 20th, but the assault will be postponed until the 26th of December. The Invasion Force (Alamo Force) uses the combined efforts of Airborne and Amphibious troops to take the island. **(Pacific-Solomons-New Georgia Group)** A U.S. Coastal Transport, the APc-35, becomes grounded off New Georgia and is abandoned. **(Pacific-New Guinea)** The Australians, transported by a Naval Task Force commanded by Rear Admiral Barbey, land at the mouth of the Song River. Enemy Aircraft appear overhead, but are intercepted and neutralized by Planes from the Fifth U.S. Air Force. The Yanks land against minor trouble, then move southward still protected by U.S. Planes toward Finschhafen. They overcome fanatical resistance on the following day and secure an Airfield near the Bumi River. **(Atlantic-Italy)** The British 10 Corps (U.S. Fifth Army) moves on Naples. The U.S. VI Corps is ordered to secure the Avellino-Teora line, then proceed to seize Benevento. The 3rd Division occupies Acerno and the 45th takes Oliveto. During the struggle for Oliveto, 2nd Lt. Ernest Childers, impaired by a fractured instep, leads his Squad up a hill to attack. Under cover fire by his Squad, Childers moves through a cornfield, and is fired upon by German Snipers holding a farmhouse. Childers kills both, then advances against two machine gun nests. He destroys the first, and nears the next. The Oklahoman improvises, by throwing a few rocks. When enemy heads pop up, he kills one and his Squad kills the other. One additional enemy Soldier who is stalking U.S. positions as a mortar observer is captured by Childers. In the **British Eighth Army** area, reinforcements (8th Indian Division) arrive from Africa. Also, in the 5 Corps sector, contingents of the British 78th Division and of the 4th Commando Brigade arrives at Bari and will attack toward Foggia. In other activity, General Clark's blood pressure soars after a censorship message arrives from British General Alexander's Headquarters: "PLAY UP EIGHTH ARMY PROGRESS. THE AMERICANS MAY BE MENTIONED."

September 23rd 1943 — (Pacific-Solomons) A combined Marine, Naval Officer and New Zealander Reconnaissance Patrol completes its second day of scouting the northern sector of Choiseul Island. They continue seeking intelligence until the 30th. Another scouting mission reconnoitering northern Bougainville near Kieta, determines the area unsuitable for a landing, and soon embarks on the Submarine, U.S.S. *Gato*. However, the Submarine U.S.S. *Guardfish* debarks another Patrol near the Laruma River in Northern Empress Bay, Bougainville, which determines that the area north of Cape Torokina is suitable for an Airfield and the defenses are not strong. **(Pacific-New Georgia)** The Americans complete repairs at Barakoma Airfield on Vella Lavella. Brigadier General Francis Mulcahy, U.S.M.C., is relieved by Brigadier General James T. Moore, who becomes a new task unit Commander under Aircraft, Solomons. **(Atlantic-Italy) 15th Army Group** In the U.S. Fifth Army area, British 10 Corps sector, the Germans raise opposition hindering progress of the British 46th and 56th Divisions as they advance toward Nocera-Pagani Pass and north along S. Severino Road respectively. In the VI Corps sector, German ingenuity for placing obstacles in the terrain impedes the American progress much more than the enemy itself. Heavy skirmishing continues in the vicinity of Oliveto. Enemy machine gun fire is taking a heavy toll on elements of the 157th Infantry. Corporal James Slayton, an advance Infantry Scout, crawls to an enemy nest and silently kills the machinegunner, then shoots another gunner. Intense enemy fire rings out from the left and Corporal Slayton again crawls under heavy fire and destroys the 2nd net with a grenade. Another machine gun opens up with more deadly fire, and Slayton, about 100 yards distant, kills both gunners. The two beleaguered Platoons retire and regroup, but, Corporal Slayton holds the advance position singlehandedly until ordered to withdraw at dusk, when enemy mortar fire zeros in on his location. In the **British Eighth Army** area, the Germans are driven out of Altamura. **(Atlantic-Russia)** The Soviets, well-supplied by the U.S., continue to battle the Germans, whose supply lines have evaporated. The Soviets take Poltava and move toward Kremenchug.

September 24th 1943 — (Pacific) Admiral Spruance suggests an invasion of Makin as an alternative to Nauru; Admiral Nimitz agreeswith the idea, and plans are laid. **(Pacific-Solomons)** The Airfield at Vella Lavella receives the first Allied Plane to land on the field. Offshore, the LST 167 is

damaged by an enemy Dive Bomber. **(Pacific-New Guinea)** The U.S. 41st Division, its mission complete, prepares to embark for Australia. Fighting is still fierce by the remaining hardened enemy troops, however, they are being pressed back continuously. Finschhafen falls to the Australians on the 2nd of October. Subsequently, the Amphibious troops link with the Australian 22nd Brigade, which had marched from Lae. Together, they mount an immediate drive against the Japs at Sattelberg and Wareo. **(Pacific-Bismarcks-New Britain)** Advance Scouts (Alamo Force) begin reconnaissance of New Gloucester, gathering intelligence for the invasion; it is the first party to go ashore on New Britain with Americans as Scouts. The search for a trail between Mt. Tange and Talawe is unsuccessful. **(Atlantic-Italy) 15th Army Group** General Montgomery meets with General Clark and receives a friendly reception. Clark tells him: "THE FIFTH ARMY IS JUST A YOUNG ARMY TRYING HARD TO GET ALONG, WHILE THE EIGHTH ARMY IS A BATTLE-TRIED VETERAN. WE WOULD APPRECIATE YOUR TEACHING US SOME OF YOUR TRICKS." During the meeting with his Commanders, Clark tells General Lucas that Generals Middleton (45th) and Truscott (3rd) must press at top speed to decisively influence the attack against Naples. However, supply problems and primitive roads impede progress and the 45th is further hampered because it must maintain contact with the Eighth Army on its right flank. Fifth Army is rounding up as many mules and other beasts of burden as possible and efforts are underway to requisition animals from the States. Within a month each Fifth Army Division wil have 300-500 animals to help facilitate movement of supplies. **(Atlantic-Russia)** The Germans withdraw further, evacuating Smolensk and Roslavl. The Germans fall back to the eastern bank of the Dnieper river. Meanwhile, the German 4th Army sets up positions west of Smolensk and prepares to hold.

September 25th 1943 — (Pacific-Solomons) Enemy Planes strike American positions at Vella LaVella. The LST 167 is damaged, by a Dive Bomber. On New Georgia, I Marine Amphibious Corps Forward Staging Area, Vella Lavella, lands on the east coast at the Junio River and Ruravai Beach, and further south on Barakoma, establishing an advance Marine Staging Base; the unit is replaced on October 8th by Vella Lavella Advance Base Command. **(Atlantic-Italy)** The U.S.S. *Skill* (AM-115), a Minesweeper is sunk by an enemy Submarine off the Italian coast. **15th Army Group** General Montgomery, intending to fortify his east flank begins to regroup the British Eighth Army. **(Atlantic-Soviet Union)** The Germans are forced to relinquish Smolensk to the Russians, however, the defending 4th Army deploys west of the city and holds. Meanwhile, the Soviets also take Roslavl and gain control of the east bank of the Dnieper River from Kremenchug to Dniepropetrovsk.

September 26th 1943 — (Pacific-New Guinea) Australians, firmly established on the beach near Finschhafen, turn back a concentrated Japanese assault. **(Dutch East Indies)** The U.S.S. *Bluefish*, patrolling off the East Indies, destroys the Japanese Vessel *Kasasagi*, a Motor Torpedo Boat. **(Atlantic-Brazil)** The U.S. Navy establishes a Naval Operating Facility at Natal, Brazil. **(Atlantic-Italy) 15th Army Group** The U.S. 82nd Airborne (General Ridgway) embarks to Maiori to reinforce positions on the west flank of the British 10 Corps and in addition, to take command of the U.S. Rangers and all units attached to them giving the 82nd a force comprising about

13,000 men, including 600 Rangers and 1,700 men of the British 23 Armored Brigade. In the British 10 Corps area, the Germans falter after consistent penetrating blows against their defenses on the Neapolitan Plain. In the VI Corps sector, the U.S. 45th Division secures Teora and knocks out resistance at the junction of Highways 7, and 91. In the **British Eighth Army** Patrols of the British 13 Corps advance to Canosa. **(Atlantic-Mediterranean-Ionian Islands)** A German contingent accepts the surrender of the island of Corfu, off the coast of Greece.

September 27th 1943 — (Pacific-Solomons) The 3rd Marine Division receives orders to seize Bougainville. Marine-Navy Patrols have been scouting the island for several days and have determined that Cape Torokina, Bougainville and the terrain stretching to the north is a satisfactory location for an Airfield. Also, Marine Planes land on Barokoma Airfield, Vella Lavella to begin operating there. **(Atlantic-Brazil)** A German U-Boat, the 161, is sunk by Naval Land-based Aircraft attached to Squadron P-74 off the coast of Brazil. **(Atlantic-Germany)** The U.S. Eighth Army launches 305 Planes to bomb strategic locations in Germany. This bombing raid is undertaken by Planes equipped with H2S, which act as Pathfinders, allowing the Aircraft to spot targets in the Emden port area despite overcast skies. In addition, this mission is escorted with P-47s, capable of protecting the Bombers during the entire mission for the first time. **(Atlantic-Italy)** The Italians have previously signed a shortened version of surrender with the Allies: today, Marshal Badoglio is given the complete version of the instrument of surrender. **15th Army Group** In the **U.S. Fifth Army** area, VI Corps sector, the U.S. Third Division crosses Highway 7, and closes on Avellino. In the 10 Corps sector, the 82nd Airborne advances through Chiunzi Pass against sporadic resistance, reaching the Naples plain by morning. The steady progress permits the British 46th Division to advance three miles, though it is still short of Nocera. In the **British Eighth Army** area, the Germans evacuate Foggia and its nearby Airfields. **(Atlantic-Soviet Union)** The Soviets seize Temryuk and deploy along the north bank of the Kuban River; the remaining German bridgehead on the Taman Peninsula becomes even smaller.

September 28th 1943 — (Pacific-Bismarcks) The U.S.S. *Grouper* (SS-214), lands men and supplies on the southern coast of New Britain. Also, the *Boko*, a Japanese Minelayer, is sunk by U.S. Aircraft off New Britain. **(Atlantic-Italy)** A U.S. Vessel, the U.S.S. *Brant* (ARS-32), a Salvage Vessel, is damaged by collision. **(Pacific-Solomons)** The Japanese on Kolombangara initiate evacuation plans at dusk and complete the operation by the 6th of October. Halsey's Forces have been sinking barges consistently, eliminating nine by Corsairs on the 9th of September, and five on the 14th, and PT Boats sink five more, and Destroyers decimate four more. During the next several days the number of sunken troop-laden barges soars. **(Atlantic-Italy) 15th Army Group** The U.S. Fifth Army is prepared to attack: the British 10 Corps drives toward Naples, shoving the Germans from the passes leading there; the 23rd Armored Brigade reaches Castellammare. Rangers seize Sala, and the British 131st Brigade, 7th Armored Division captures Nocera. Meanwhile, the VI Corps drives toward Avellino.

September 29th 1943 — (Pacific-Solomons) Two American Destroyers, the *Patterson* (DD-392) and *McCalla* (DD-488) collide and are both damaged. In other activity. the Japanese continue to evacuate Kolombangara losing three Barges to U.S. fire. On the following day the Yanks keep up the pressure and sink six more barges. **(Atlantic-Italy)** The formal surrender of Italy is complete as Marshal Pietro Badoglio and General Eisenhower sign an agreement on board the H.M.S. *Nelson*, off Malta. **15th Army Group** In the U.S. Fifth Army area, the British 10 Corps (British 7th Armored Division) captures a bridge intact at Scafati, the last bridge still spanning the Sarno River. In the VI Corps sector, the U.S. 3rd Division confidently opens a night attack against Avellino and seizes it on the following morning. During the night, Patrols composed of U.S. Paratroopers and the 23rd Armored Brigade move through the ruins of Pompei and enter Torre Annunziata.

September 30th 1943 — (United States) The U.S.S. *Grayling* is reported lost. She had departed Australia on July 30th, commanded of Lieutenant Commander R.M. Brinker. The *Grayling* on her eighth War Patrol, had reported sinking an enemy Vessel on August 19th and on the 20th, she reports sinking a small Tanker in the Sibitu Passage. However, when Headquarters attempts to reach the Submarine on the 12th of September, there was no response. Another American Vessel, the PT-219 had been lost (due to foundering) near the Aleutians during September. The Coast Guard Cutter *Wilcox* (YP-333) founders off Cape Hatteras, North Carolina and sinks. **(Pacific-New Guinea)** The PT-68 is damaged by grounding. **(Pacific-Philippines)** The U.S.S. *Bowfin* delivers supplies to Guerrillas at Siquijor Island, then takes on passengers and departs. **(Pacific-Solomons)** A U.S. LST, the 334 is damaged by an enemy Dive Bomber. In other activity, U.S. Surface Vessel fire, accidentally damages the PT-126. **(Atlantic-Italy)** The U.S. 3rd Division completes its operation with the seizure of Avellino, then moves rapidly to secure the Avellino-Montemarano-Teora line. With the fall of Avellino, comes the security of 10 Corps right flank, permitting British General McCreery to send the 56th Division north. In the British 10 Corps sector, M. Vesuvius is surrounded. **(Atlantic-Russia)** The Soviets continue driving toward Kiev, but the Germans refuse to capitulate and continue fighting viciously to prevent annihilation.

October 1st 1943 — (United States) The Naval Forces Europe Command, under Admiral H. R. Stark, becomes the Twelfth Fleet. **(Pacific-New Guinea)** The Australians commit another Battalion (making it three) to the attack on Finschhafen. **(Pacific-Solomons)** The decision to invade Bougainville is made. Admiral Halsey informs MacArthur that an Amphibious Force will assault Empress Augusta Bay on the 1st of November. Halsey is promised maximum Air support by General MacArthur. In Naval activity off the Solomons, the U.S.S. *Saufley* (DD-465), a Destroyer and the PT-448, are both damaged by enemy Horizontal Bombers. The Japanese Submarine I-20 is sunk by the U.S.S. *Eaton* (DD-510). In other activity, the Japanese take advantage of the moonless night and expedite their evacuation operation, but lose twenty Barges. On the following day, they lose another twenty, followed by the additional loss of sixteen on the 4th of October. Halsey's Forces have sunk about 598 Barges during the past three months and damaged almost 700 others. Halsey's Command estimates enemy troop losses to be between "three and four thousand." Admiral Halsey subsequently states: "IT WAS RICH, REWARDING, BEAUTIFUL SLAUGHTER." **(Atlantic-Brazil)** The U.S. Navy establishes a

Naval Air Facility at Recife, Brazil. **(Atlantic-Italy)** British troops (King's Dragoon Guards) enter Naples without opposition in the morning. American Rangers and Paratroopers are with them, however, a British Public Relations Officer (Alexander's Headquarters) requests that General Clark "TELL THE PRESS THAT THE BRITISH HAD ENTERED FIRST." The Allies begin repairs on the port, and have it operational quickly; it receives its first Allied Vessel on the 3rd of October. The Germans have virtually demolished the city before abandoning it, destroying military as well as civilian structures and even blowing up sewer mains and power plants. Allied bombing contributed to the destruction. In addition, the Germans place booby traps and bombs (with delaying action) to kill and mutilate unsuspecting Allied troops and to disrupt the rail lines. General Clark confers with French General Alphonse Juin to discuss the imminent arrival of French troops, which will fight alongside the Americans. Subsequently, Clark enters Naples and is astonished upon sight of the devastation. Clark sends a message to his wife, presently in the States, stating: "I GIVE YOU NAPLES FOR YOUR BIRTHDAY." In the **British Eighth Army** area, 13 Corps sector, contingents occupy the Airfields at Foggia. The Germans have abandoned Gargano Peninsula. **(Atlantic-Austria)** A combined Allied Bomber attack, which includes the XII British Bomber Command (Mediterranean) and three Planes from the U.S. Eighth Air Force, assault Wiener Neustadt, dropping 187 tons of bombs. Additional planned attacks against Augsburg, Bavaria are scuttled, because of overcast skies. The Planes seek alternate targets and drop their payloads in both Italy and Germany before returning to their Bases.

October 2nd 1943 — (Pacific) The U.S. 27th Division is informed that it will invade the Makin Atoll in the Gilberts. Previously, it had been planning for the invasion of Nauru. **(Pacific-Ellice Islands)** The LST 203 is damaged by grounding near Nanumea and sinks on the 5th. **(Pacific-Solomons)** As darkness falls, the beleaguered Japanese evacuate Kolombangara and complete the operation by the early morning hours of the 3rd. American Planes and Ships, attempt to intercept the rescue Vessels, without great success, enabling 9,400 Japs to escape safely on the elusive "Tokyo Express." **(Pacific-New Guinea)** Finschhafen falls to the Australians, but the Japanese still hold Sattelberg and Wareo, which must be taken to clear the total Finschhafen area of the enemy. The Japanese losses continue to mount, as they are forced to further compress their positions in the Pacific. **(Pacific-Dutch East Indies)** The U.S.S. *Kingfish* (SS-234), a Submarine operating off the East Indies, deploys mines near the southern Celebes, to impede enemy Convoys. **(Atlantic-Italy)** 15th **Army Group** In the U.S. 5th Army's British 10 Corps area, the U.S. 82nd Airborne Division moves into Naples for police duty, while the main body advances toward the Volturno River. In the VI Corps area, the U.S. 3rd Division drives toward the Volturno on the left flank, while the U.S. 34th and 45th Divisions drive separately against Benevento, a strategic road junction. In the British Eighth Army area, Commandos land during the night of the 2nd-3rd and seize the town and port of Termoli, along the Adriatic coast. They link with the British 78th Division, and the combined Force seizes a bridgehead across the Biferno River. Bitter, but indecisive fighting ensues for several days. German counterattacks puncture the perimeter of Termoli on the 5th, however, on the sixth, the British convincingly throw the tenacious Germans back and secure the bridgehead.

October 3rd 1943 — (Pacific-New Guinea) The Destroyer *Henley* (DD-391), is sunk by an enemy Submarine off the eastern coast of New Guinea. **(Atlantic-Aegean)** Axis troops invade Kos Island. **(Atlantic-Italy)** 15th **Army Group** In the **U.S. Fifth Army** area, VI Corps sector, Contingents of the U.S. 34th Division (133rd Infantry) occupy Benevento and establish a bridgehead across the Calore River. The U.S. 45th Division advances further, and relieves the 34th Division and expands the bridgehead. In the **British Eighth Army** area, reinforcements land during the night to bolster the Biferno bridgehead. Meanwhile, the British 78th Division is 15 miles outside of Vinchiaturo, hindered by the terrain.

October 4th 1943 — (Atlantic-Aegean) Kos Island, the solitary Allied Air Base in the Aegean, is captured by a German Soldiers, who had landed the previous night. The capitulation of Kos now threatens Leros and Samos. **(North Atlantic)** The U.S.S. *Card* (CVE-11), operating near the Azores, launches Planes (VC-9), which destroy two German Submarines, the U-422 and the U-436. In other activity in the North Atlantic, Naval Land-based Bombers, and a contingent of VB-128, sink the U-336. **(Atlantic-Corsica)** Axis troops evacuate Bastia under pressure by Allied troops, including the Battalion du Choc, Goums of the 4th Moroccan Mountain Division and a small U.S. unit (O.S.S.). **(Atlantic-Italy)** Hitler has decided to defend southern Italy instead of withdrawing to the north. He instructs Rommel (in northern Italy) to reinforce Field Marshal Albert Kesselring by dispatching some Artillery units and two Infantry Divisions. This change of strategy by Hitler makes the road to Rome a much more difficult task, especially with the approach of winter. Kesselring intends to stall the Allied advance, using his crack troops and the natural elements, establishing several lines of defense; the first at the Volturno, followed by equally stringent defenses at the Bernhard line in the mountains, and then, the most formidable of all established at Monte Cassino, the Gustav Line (Winter Line). **(Atlantic-Norway)** The U.S.S. *Ranger* (CV-4), one of the newer American Carriers, launches Planes which attack enemy Vessels along the coast of Normandy.

October 5th 1943 — (Pacific) Admiral Nimitz, Commander-in-Chief Pacific, issues operation plan 13-43. Admiral Spruance's orders are: "TO CAPTURE, OCCUPY, DEFEND AND DEVELOP MAKIN, TARAWA, AND APAMAMA AND VIGOROUSLY DENY NAURU..." D-Day for the Amphibious Assault is set for November 19th, but will subsequently be delayed one additional day. **(Pacific-Wake Island)** The island of Wake has been in the hands of the Japs since December 23rd 1941. Today, a mighty Allied Task Force, commanded by Rear Admiral A. E. Montgomery, comprising six Carriers, 24 Destroyers and seven Cruisers, strikes Japanese positions with a combined Naval Air bombardment that inflicts heavy damage; the Task Force duplicates the effort on the following day, forewarning the Japs that Americans are returning. After the island had been taken during 1941, the Military personnel had been moved to Japan and then on to Shanghai. Five Marines are decapitated (simultaneously) by the Japanese along the route. The attacking Yanks are also unaware that 96 civilian construction workers have been held on Wake to be used as slave labor on the Airfields. **(Atlantic-Italy)** 15th **Army Group** In the U.S. Fifth Army area, the British 10 Corps pushes forward elements to the Volturno. In the British Eighth Army area, heavy fighting continues at the Biferno bridgehead at Termoli continues; the Germans pierce British lines at Termoli.

257

October 6th 1943 — (Pacific-Wake Island) Again, Admiral A.E. Montgomery's Task Force bombards enemy held Wake Island. The Japanese retaliate and slaughter the American civilian prisoners on the island. The Japanese line the Yanks along the beach, tie their hands behind their backs and mandate that they kneel with their backs to the sea. Then the Japanese Firing Squad racks the American civilians, blowing their bodies to pieces, as they slump, bloodied and full of holes, at the water's edge. **(Pacific-Solomons)** Action in the Central Solomons ceases, as the U.S. Army lands unopposed at Kolombangara, New Georgia. U.S. casualties during the central Solomons campaign are 1,094 killed, 3,873 wounded. Enemy dead (counted), excluding those on Vella Lavella 2,483. During the campaign, the Allies secure four Airfields; Barakoma, Munda, Ondonga and Segi, all of which serve in the upcoming Bougainville campaign. **(BATTLE OF VELLA LAVELLA)** — During the night of the 6th-7th, three Destroyers, under the command of Captain F. R. Walker, intercept nine enemy Destroyers, which are evacuating troops from Vella Lavella. The Japanese rescue about 600 of their troops, terminating Japanese occupation of the Central Solomons, however, the Destroyer *Yugumo* is lost. The U.S.S. *Chevalier* (DD-451), an American Destroyer is damaged during the vicious confrontation, and subsequently sunk by U.S. Forces The other two U.S. Destroyers also sustain damage, the *O'Bannon*, by collision with the *Chevalier* and the *Selfridge* (DD-357), by an enemy Destroyer's torpedo. The Japanese ignore the U.S. cripples, and retire. **(Pacific-New Guinea)** Dumpu falls to the Australians; its Airfield is used as a staging area for Fighters. **(Pacific-New Britain)** Allied Scouts patrol on Gasmata to gather intelligence for invasion of the island. **(Atlantic-Italy)** The U.S. Fifth Army moves to the Volturno River and prepares for the next phase of the campaign; crossing the Volturno and driving across the mountains, heading directly for Rome. At Naples, a delayed-fuse bomb explodes in the Post Office, killing or wounding 35 Soldiers and about an equal number of civilians. In the **British Eighth Army** area, the 78th Division secures its position for the final time, securing the Biferno bridgehead. On the following day, the enemy withdraws across the Trigno River.

October 7th 1943 — (United States) Urgent requests from Churchill for U.S. Troops to reinforce the British at the Aegean Sea are received in Washington. British troops had unsuccessfully attempted to seize enemy positions in the Aegean Sea, by sending in General Maitland Wilson's force, however, they are defeated at the island of Kos. Churchill's request to divert troops and equipment, intended for Italy, is turned down. Admirals Leahy, and King, along with General Marshall, had discussed the subject with President Roosevelt, and it is denied because the Americans believe that any troop diversion would endanger the Italian campaign. **(Pacific-Kurile Islands)** The S-44, an American Submarine, had departed the Aleutians, under the command of Lieutenant Commander F.E. Brown, for a war patrol near the Kurile Islands, between the Kamchatka Peninsula and N. Hokkaido. These islands have belonged to Japan since the 1700s. Today, the S-44 spots what appears to be a Freighter and prepares to attack, however, the Ship is an enemy Destroyer. As the S-44, initiates its night surface attack, the Destroyer opens fire, seriously damaging the Submarine. The order to clear the deck and dive is given, but the badly injured Sub is unable to dive and becomes caught in a ring of enemy shells, which sets the

Sub afire. Additional shells pound the disabled S-44, and the order to abandon is given. Simultaneously, a white flag in the form of a pillow case is raised, however, the Japanese ignore it and continue to rip the battered Vessel. Two men survive the ordeal. Both are picked up and enslaved in the copper mines at Ashio, where they undergo brutalizing punishment until rescued after the fall of the Japanese Empire during 1945. **(Pacific-Solomons)** The evacuation of the Japanese from Vella LaVella is finished. Old Glory prevails. **(Atlantic-Italy)** D-Day for the offensive of the U.S. 5th Army's drive across the Volturno is set for the night 9th-10th, but subsequently is postponed two days. In the British Eighth Army sector, elements of the 78th British Division land in Italy and reinforce the bridgehead at Biferno. The enemy retires. **(Atlantic-Soviet Union)** Nevel, on the central front is seized by the Red Army, however, the German resistance is hardening and making the superior Soviet forces advances much more difficult.

October 8th 1943 — (Pacific) Major General A.A. Vandegrift, U.S.M.C., reassumes command of the 1st Marine Amphibious Corps, due to the sudden death of its Commander, Major General Charles D. Barrett (appointed on Sept. 15th). **(Pacific-New Guinea)** The Australia I Corps, commanded by Lt. General Sir Leslie Morshead, relieves the Australian I Corps. **(Atlantic-Italy) 15th Army Group** In the U.S. 5th Army sector, the 30th Infantry, 3rd Division, drives enemy stragglers across the Volturno River. The 34th Division relieves the 30th Infantry, 3rd Division, then joins the 3rd Division attack across the river, in pursuit of the enemy. **(Atlantic-Germany)** The U.S. Eighth Air Force uses a new instrument, named radio countermeasure (Carpet). The device intended to jam German radar is uninspiring on its first flight against Bremen and Vegesack. Despite the new technology, the force of 357 Aircraft still suffers the loss of 30 Aircraft. **(Atlantic-Panama)** Mines are laid by a German Submarine, near the Atlantic entrance to the Panama Canal.

October 9th 1943 — (United States) General Arnold suggests to the Joint Chiefs of Staff that Twelfth Air Force be split into two Air Forces to swell the power of the Combined Bomber Offensive. **(Pacific-Solomons-New Georgia)** Vella Lavella is declared secure by the 3rd New Zealand Division. **(Pacific-Ellice Islands)** The Airstrip at Nukufetau is now operational. **(Atlantic-Italy)** The Destroyer *Buck* (DD-420) is sunk by an enemy Submarine off the coast of Italy. **(Atlantic-Poland East Prussia)** The Eighth Air Force launches 378 Bombers to strike targets, including the Focke-Wulf assembly plant at Marienburg. On Sunday, the 10th, Hermann Goering is scheduled to dedicate the newly established runway; however, the occasion is postponed as the B-17s devastate the plant and the runway. Allied prisoners at nearby Marienburg prison camp are used to clear the wreckage. **(Atlantic-Russia)** The Germans holding out on Taman Peninsula finally crumble and remnants flee the area.

October 10th 1943 — (Atlantic-Panama) A German Submarine lays mines near the Panama Canal. **(Atlantic-Western Europe)** The U.S. Eighth Air Force attacks the German rail junction at Munster. German Fighters intercept and knock out thirty Fortresses; the Germans concentrate on the 100th Bombing Group and knock out twelve of thirteen Planes in the group; Lt. Robert Rosenthal's Plane, "Rosie's Riveters" is the sole Aircraft which returns to England. Some crewmen bail out and are imprisoned by the Germans.

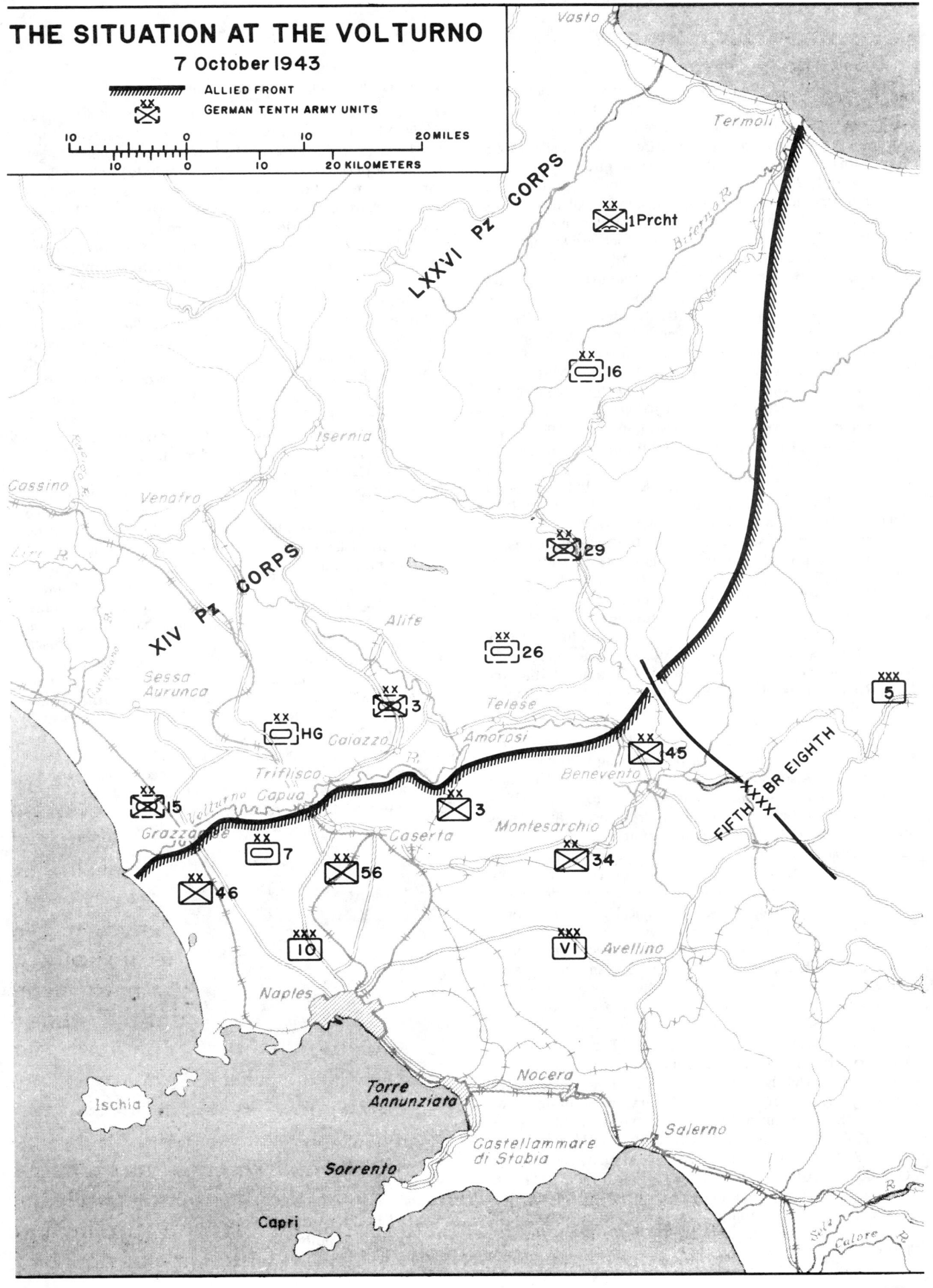

THE SITUATION AT THE VOLTURNO
7 October 1943

////////// ALLIED FRONT
⊠ GERMAN TENTH ARMY UNITS

10   0   10   20 MILES
10   0   10   20 KILOMETERS

LXXVI PZ CORPS

XIV PZ CORPS

Vasto

Termoli

1 Prcht

16

29

26

Alife

Isernia

Venafro

Cassino

Sessa Aurunca

3

HG

Calazzo

Telese

Amorosi

Benevento

45

FIFTH BR EIGHTH

5

Triflisco

Volturno   Capua

15

Grazzanise

3

Caserta

Montesarchio

34

7

56

46

10

VI

Avellino

Naples

Nocera

Torre Annunziata

Castellammare di Stabia

Salerno

Sorrento

Ischia

Capri

259

October 11th 1943 — **(Pacific-New Guinea)** A four Plane reconnaissance team, led by Colonel Neel Kearby (U.S.A.A.C.) flies over Wewak and reconnoiters four enemy Airbases, then encounters enemy Aircraft. This gallant four-Plane formation attacks the superior enemy Force (36 Fighters and 12 Bombers). Kearby, having a few moments earlier destroyed an enemy Fighter, knocks out three more enemy Planes before dashing to his comrades' aid, shooting down two additional enemy Fighters, which are about to destroy one of Kearby's section Planes. All American Planes return to their Base safely. **(Atlantic-England)** The U.S. Navy establishes an Advanced Amphibious Training Base at Falmouth, Cornwall, England. **(Atlantic-Sicily)** Still, General Patton waits impatiently for a Combat Command. He sits dutifully in Sicily, commanding less than 5,000 men. Patton, in a letter to his wife, remarks: "THINGS ARE PRETTY SLOW (in Italy) DUE TO RAIN AND SUPPLY DIFFICULTIES. PERHAPS MY LUCK STILL HELD WHEN I DID NOT GET THAT JOB (Command of 5th Army). Patton also notes that "HE DIDN'T THINK THAT THE NINE ALLIED DIVISIONS COULD ADVANCE AT ANY RATE OF SPEED, IF AT ALL, AGAINST THE EIGHT GERMAN DIVISIONS, BECAUSE THE ALLIES LACKED SUFFICIENT SUPERIORITY AND COULDN'T REST THEIR TROOPS." Patton Is aware that the mountainous terrain favors the Germans immensely, because of the natural defensive barriers they provide. He would also note: "THERE CAN WELL BE A DISASTER, BUT HARDLY AN ALLIED VICTORY. I DON'T GET THE PICTURE AT ALL. I FEEL THAT I AM LUCKY NOT TO BE IN CLARK'S PLACE." **(Atlantic-Italy)** In Naples, another German delayed fuse-bomb detonates in an Italian Army Barracks used by the 82nd Airborne. The unexpected blast kills 18 Paratroopers and wounds 56 more. **(Atlantic-U.S.S.R.)** Elements of the Red Army seize Novo Belitsa, a suburb of Gomel.

October 12th 1943 — **(Pacific)** Admiral Nimitz issues Operation Plan 16-43, the first formal plan dealing with capturing the Marshalls. Also, Admiral Halsey issues the standard plan for the invasion of the Northern Solomons. **(Pacific-Bismarcks-New Britain)** Three Hundred forty-nine Planes attached to the U.S. Fifth Air Force, launch a surprise attack against Rabaul. This attack is the largest yet mounted against Rabaul Airfield and Simpson Harbor and the cost is relatively low; four Planes fail to return to their Base. Severe damage is sustained by the Japanese (Shipping and Planes). **(Atlantic-Italy)** 15th Army Group The **U.S. Fifth Army** commences an offensive across the Volturno River. The American and British troops are stretched along a 40 mile front and meet heavy resistance as they drive across the Volturno river against the enemy's mountainous Winter Line. Terrible weather conditions plague the assault troops, but with the assistance of sustained Artillery fire, the river is forded. The British, under McCreery, are reluctant to attack and take issue with General Clark's orders. During a heated meeting between Clark and McCreery, prior to the assault, McCreery, not wanting to advance to the far bank of the Volturno, snaps at Clark: "WE ACCEPT YOUR ORDER OF COURSE, BUT I HAVE TO SAY THAT I AM EMBARRASSED WHEN A YOUNG AMERICAN COMMANDER GIVES BRITISH TROOPS ORDERS THAT WE DON'T LIKE." Subsequent enemy resistance at Mount Cassino proves invincible and prompts the Allies to plan an amphibious landing at Anzio (January 22nd 1944), which will place Clark's VI Corps, Fifth Army, 30 miles south of Rome and 60 miles behind the enemy's Winter Line.

October 13th 1943 — **(North Atlantic)** The Escort Carrier *Card* (CVE-11) launches Planes attached to VC-9, which sink the U-402. **(Pacific-Gilberts-Makin)** The U.S. succeeds in getting aerial photos of the atoll. **(Atlantic-Italy)** Italy declares war on Germany. Continuing bad weather restricts Air support for the troops at the Volturno River. The **U.S. Fifth Army**, meeting heavy opposition from the Germans, utilizes the special skills of its Engineers, giving them the job of fortifying the bridgehead on the northern bank of the Volturno by rebuilding bridge spans blown by the Germans as they withdrew. The British 10th Corps, positioned on the west flank of the Volturno, drives forward; its 46th Division spearheads near Cancello, assisted by the British 7th Armored in the center and the British 56th Division pushing on the right. The 46th Division makes a diversionary feint at Grazzanise and Capua. The drive nets a bridgehead by the 46th in the coastal sector and also gains the 7th Armored a slight grip on the north bank of the Volturno. However, the British 56th Division meets intense enemy resistance which halts its progress at Capua. The U.S. VI Corps crosses the river in two sections; the 3rd crosses east of Capua and the 34th jumps off to the right of the 3rd. The 3rd Division captures M. Majulo, M. Caruso and Piana di Caiazzo. Elements of the 15th Infantry, led by Captain Arlo Olson, spearhead the Regiment's drive across the Volturno and in 13 days push their way through 30 miles of enemy held mountainous territory. On the 13th, Captain Olson knocks out two enemy nests, which aids his Regiment's advance. This detachment sees constant battle as it plows ahead. On the 27th, Olson is mortally wounded, but refuses treatment until his men are all attended. The American 34th Division secures a bridgehead stretching from Piana di Caiazzo to the point where the Calore and Volturno Rivers meet. The American 45th Division (179th-180th Regiments) operating on the right flank of the VI Corps, concentrates on clearing enemy resistance on M. Acero. In the **British Eighth Army** area, the British 5th Division advances along route 87 as far as Casacalenda. In activity off the coast, an enemy Submarine sinks the Destroyer *Bristol* (DD-453).

A Douglas Dauntless Bomber soaring over Guam.

October 14th 1943 — **(Pacific)** Admiral Nimitz issues directives for the "capture, occupation and development of bases at Wotje, Maloelap, and Kwajalein." Target dates for invasions; January 1 1944 for Wotje and Maloelap, and Kwajalein on the following day. In other Allied Pacific strategy, General Headquarters approves a plan for the seizure of New Britain, calling for a landing by the 7th Marines (less one Battalion) to be known as Combat Team C, on the beaches along the northern shores of Cape Gloucester and Borgen Bay. The other Battalion will land in the vicinity of Taual. The 1st Marines (Combat Team B) are held in reserve. **(Atlantic-Brazil)** A U.S. Naval Air Facility is established at Igarape, Assu, Brazil. **(Atlantic-Italy) 15th Army Group** In the **U.S. Fifth Army** area, the U.S. 34th and 3rd Divisions are ordered to drive toward Dragoni, however, supply problems detain the 34th Division. The British 56th Division, halted by German resistance at their crossing point, receives permission to swing east and cross over a U.S. 3rd Division bridge which spans the Volturno within the Triflisco Gap. In the **British Eighth Army** area, the Canadian 1st Division seizes Campobasso. **(Atlantic-Germany)** The U.S. Eighth Air Force, still lacking Fighter support, suffers severe losses during another massive bombardment (Mission 115) of targets in Germany. The assault force, consisting of 291 B-17s, bombards targets in Schweinfurt (ball bearing plants), however, only 228 actually reach the objective because of poor weather, and drop 403 tons of bombs. The 1st and 3rd Air Divisions (B-17s) reach the objective, however, the 2nd composed of B-24s is unable to form over England: the 1st Division loses forty-five Fortresses: its 305th Group led by Curtiss E. LeMay, loses 13 of sixteen Planes before reaching the target; the 306th Group loses ten Planes during the mission. The U.S. loses 60 B-17s and additional Planes are damaged. In addition, about 600 crewmen are missing in action, about 300 of them shot down (30 Planes) five miles from target. The grave losses on this type of bombing mission prompt the U.S. to halt daylight attacks against targets deep in Germany. Many of the returning Planes are exposing colored flares to alert the Field of wounded aboard, to ensure priority landing. In conjunction, these Airmen fly at altitudes of 25,000 feet (five miles), discharging conspicuous vapor trails which make them billboards in the sky for the Luftwaffe, and the temperature at that altitude is 40 degrees below zero. One minute without oxygen causes unconsciousness and at twenty minutes, death occurs. During April of 1945, when the Rainbow Division captures Schweinfurt, it sends a captured German flag to England as a prize for the 8th Air Force with the inscription: TO THE EIGHTH AIR FORCE. THE RAINBOW DIVISION HAS REVENGED YOUR LOSSES AT SCHWEINFURT. **(Atlantic-Puerto Rico)** The U.S.S. *Dow*, a Coast Guard Cutter becomes grounded near Mayaguez and is subsequently abandoned. **(Atlantic-Soviet Union)** The Soviets take Zaporodzhe on the Dnieper bend in the Ukraine.

October 15th 1943 — (United States) The U.S.S. *Pompano* (SS-181), which had departed Midway Island on August 20th 1943, on her seventh War Patrol, is reported lost. The cause of the Ship's demise remains a mystery. **(Pacific-Northern Solomons-Bougainville)** The 1st Marine Amphibious Corps issues Order No. 1 directing the 3rd Marine Division to assault and secure Cape Torokina, Bougainville. Allied Airplanes initiate preinvasion bombardments to soften enemy resistance. Naval Task Force 31, commanded by Admiral Wilkinson, and General Vandegrift's 1st Marine Amphibious Corps seizes Bases on the Treasury Islands on October 27 as a preliminary step before the primary invasion of Bougainville, which commences on November 1. **(Atlantic-England)** U.S. General Brereton activates the U.S. Army Air Forces in the United Kingdom (USAAFUK), including the Eighth and Ninth Air

Forces. General Brereton will take command of the Ninth Air Force on the following day. The U.S. Navy is ashore at Fowey, Cornwall, England, establishing another Advanced Amphibious Training Base. **(Atlantic-Italy) 15th Army Group** In the **U.S. Fifth Army** area, VI Corps sector, the U.S. 3rd Division hits heavy opposition in the vicinity of Villa and Liberi but is successful in gaining Cisterna. The U.S. 2nd Battalion, 135th Infantry, 34th Division seizes Ruviano. In other activity, enemy troops near Titerno Creek are expelled by the U.S. 45th Division; contact is then established with the U.S. 34th Division on the opposite bank of the Volturno. At about this time, General Vietinghoff begins to pull his troops back further, according to Kesselring's plan to dig in deeper and forestall the Allied advance to Rome. In the British 10th Corps zone, the British 56th Division moves through former VI Corps sector and crosses the Volturno. In the **British Eighth Army** area, the 13 Corps halts, while the Canadian 1st Division seizes Vinchiaturo.

October 16th 1943 — (United States) The Joint Chiefs of Staff agree to split the 12th Air Force into two forces and suggest to Eisenhower that the Fifteenth Air Force be established from the XII Bomber Command. **(Pacific-Bismarcks-New Britain)** U.S. Army Planes sink the Japanese Auxiliary Submarie Chaser (No. 31) off the coast. **(Pacific-New Guinea)** Thanks to an important captured document, the Australian 9th Division has advance knowledge of an imminent enemy attack coming from Sattelberg and is able to handily repulse the first in a series of assaults. **(Pacific-Japan)** The U.S.S. *Tarpon*, on Patrol in Japanese waters, sinks a German Warship, the Schiff No 28, near Chichi Jima, Bonin Islands, in the Western Pacific south of Honshu. **(Pacific-China)** Admiral Mountbatten arrives in Chungking.

October 17th 1943 — (Pacific-Marianas-Solomons) Marine Fighter Squadron 214, commanded by Major Gregory (Pappy) Boyington, attacks enemy positions at Kahili in Swashbuckling fashion. The Marine Fighters swoop low, daring the Japanese to challenge. The Japs take off into trouble. There are 60 enemy Fighters on the ground. At the conclusion of the dog fight, Gregory "Pappy" Boyington's Squadron has shot down 20 Planes against no U.S. losses. Boyington has been in command of Marine Squadron 214 since September 12th and remains in this post until the 3rd of January 3rd 1944. Boyington personally shoots down 26 Planes during his tenure. **(Pacific-New Guinea)** Japanese troops from Sattelberg maintain attacks against Australian positions without success. Three more troop-laden barges attempt to reach shore near Finschhafen. One is destroyed by Allied fire; the others hit the beach near a machine gun manned by Private Junior Van Noy, U.S. Army Headquarters Company. The enemy wounds Van Noy's ammunition loader; however, Van Noy refuses to leave his post and remains to kill at least half of the 39 invaders before he is felled by enemy fire. His extraordinary heroism saves the lives of many men and makes it possible for the balance of his detachment to destroy the remainder of the enemy Force. **(Atlantic-Italy) 15th Army Group** In the **U.S. Fifth Army** area, VI Corps sector, The U.S. 3rd Division discovers the Germans have evacuated Liberi and Villa and it immediately secures them. Meanwhile, U.S. 34th Division contingents occupy Alvignano after Patrols find it abandoned. **(Atlantic-Russia)** Heavy fighting between the Soviets and Germans again ensues as the Red Army pushes through German defenses and seizes Loyev.

October 18th 1943 — (Pacific-Solomons) Allied Aircraft begin a heavy Air bombardment of enemy Airfields at Bougainville. **(Atlantic-Italy) 15th Army Group** In the **U.S. 5th Army** area, VI Corps sector, the 3rd and 34th Divisions continue their progress, moving through Roccaromana heading directly for Dragoni. The 34th Division, (133rd Infantry) maneuvers to cut off the escape route of Germans attempting to pull out of Dragoni, by initiating a second crossing of the Volturno River. They seize an important railway-highway bridge, closing that would otherwise be used as an escape route.

October 19th 1943 — (Atlantic-Russia) The British, Soviet, and U.S. Foreign Ministers begin a conference in Moscow. Uncle Sam gets tapped again, as the Third London Protocol is signed, assuring 2,700,000 tons of supplies for the U.S.S.R. via the Pacific and an additional 2,400,000 tons, to be transported through either the Persian Gulf or the northern Soviet Ports. **(Atlantic-Italy)** The Northwest African Air Force initiates air strikes for the next five days against bridges, compelling the Axis to modify strategy and begin heavier use of coastal Shipping and Motor Transport. **15th Army Group** In the **U.S. Fifth Army** area, VI Corps sector, the 167th Infantry, U.S. 3rd Division commences a predawn attack against Dragoni, but finds the enemy has withdrawn. Undaunted they continue to advance, moving northward against Mignano. The 133rd Infantry, which had crossed the Volturno northeast of Dragoni, drives against S. Angelo d' Alife, while and the 34th Division advances toward Capriati al Volturno.

October 20th 1943 — (Pacific-Japan) The Japanese order a Carrier Force to steam toward Rabaul, to bolster the Air Forces; it includes the *Hiyo, Junyo, Ryuho, Shokaku, Zuiho,* and the *Zuikaku.* **(Pacific-Gilberts)** Photographs of Tarawa defenses are procured by the Americans, who utilize cameras on their Planes. **(Pacific-New Guinea)** Reinforcements (Australian 26th Brigade) arrive by sea, to strengthen the Australian 9th Division which still is under attack by the Japanese. **(Atlantic-Italy)** In the 5th U.S. Army area, the U.S. 34th Division takes Alife, while the U.S. 45th Division seizes Piedmonte d'Alife. The 45th Division, its mission successfully concluded, reverts to reserve status. Meanwhile, the 3rd Division advances toward Mignano. In Naval activity, the U.S.S. *Core* (CVE-13), operating in the North Atlantic, launches Planes (VC-13), which sink the German U-378.

October 20th-24th-25th 1943 — (Pacific-Solomons) Allied Squadrons, composed of Bombers and Fighters, continue Air assaults against enemy positions at Rabaul and Simpson Harbor, inflicting serious damage. These missions intend to prevent the Japanese from mounting heavy opposition, against the upcoming invasion of Bougainville.

October 21st 1943 — (Southwest Pacific) The Alamo Force Headquarters transfers from Milne Bay to Goodenough Island. **(Atlantic-Italy)** German Planes begin bombing Naples. Despite the infrequency and lack of strength, the raids inflict casualties upon civilians and Soldiers. Between September 9th and October 1st, about 30,000 Vehicles and nearly 200,000 men have come ashore at Naples, however, the port is not yet able to receive Tankers until the end of the month when the necessary repairs are complete.

October 22nd 1943 — (United States) The Combined Chiefs of Staff agree to establish what becomes the Fifteenth Air Force, to take responsibility for the Mediterranean area. **(Pa-**

cific-Northern Solomons) The 1st Marine Amphibious Corps Commander, General Vandegrift, directs the 2nd Paratroop Battalion, 1st Marine Paratroop Regiment, to land at Voza (Choiseul Island) as a diversionary tactic and attempt to secure a permanent base in that area. The invasion commences during the night of the 27th, in advance of the main invasion at Bougainville. **(Atlantic-Italy)** In the U.S. Fifth Army area, VI Corps area, the U.S. 133rd Infantry meets heavy resistance during its assault against S. Angelo d'Alife and is stalled from taking the town, however, it is secured on the following day without opposition.

U.S. Aircraft strike Rabaul, depositing bombs by parachute.

October 24th 1943 — (United States) The U.S. announces that the U.S.S. *Dorado* (SS-248), commanded by Lt. Commander E.C. Schneider is unaccounted for and presumed sunk in the Atlantic. The recently commissioned *Dorado* had departed New London, Ct. on October 6th, however, she never reaches her destination at Panama. She becomes the second and final U.S. Submarine lost in the Atlantic; the exact cause is never determined. **(Pacific-New Britain)** U.S. Naval Land-based Aircraft sink the Japanese Destroyer *Mochizuki* off the east coast of New Britain. **(Atlantic-Italy)** The Germans evacuate Sant Angelo, enabling the U.S. 133rd Infantry to take the town and secure the strategic ground in the area.

October 25th 1943 — (Pacific Area) Admiral Spruance issues operational plans for the invasion of the Gilberts (Operation GALVANIC). **(Pacific-New Guinea)** The Australians see relief, as enemy troops begin withdrawing from Finschhafen and head toward Sattelberg. **(Atlantic-Italy)** Allied Comman-

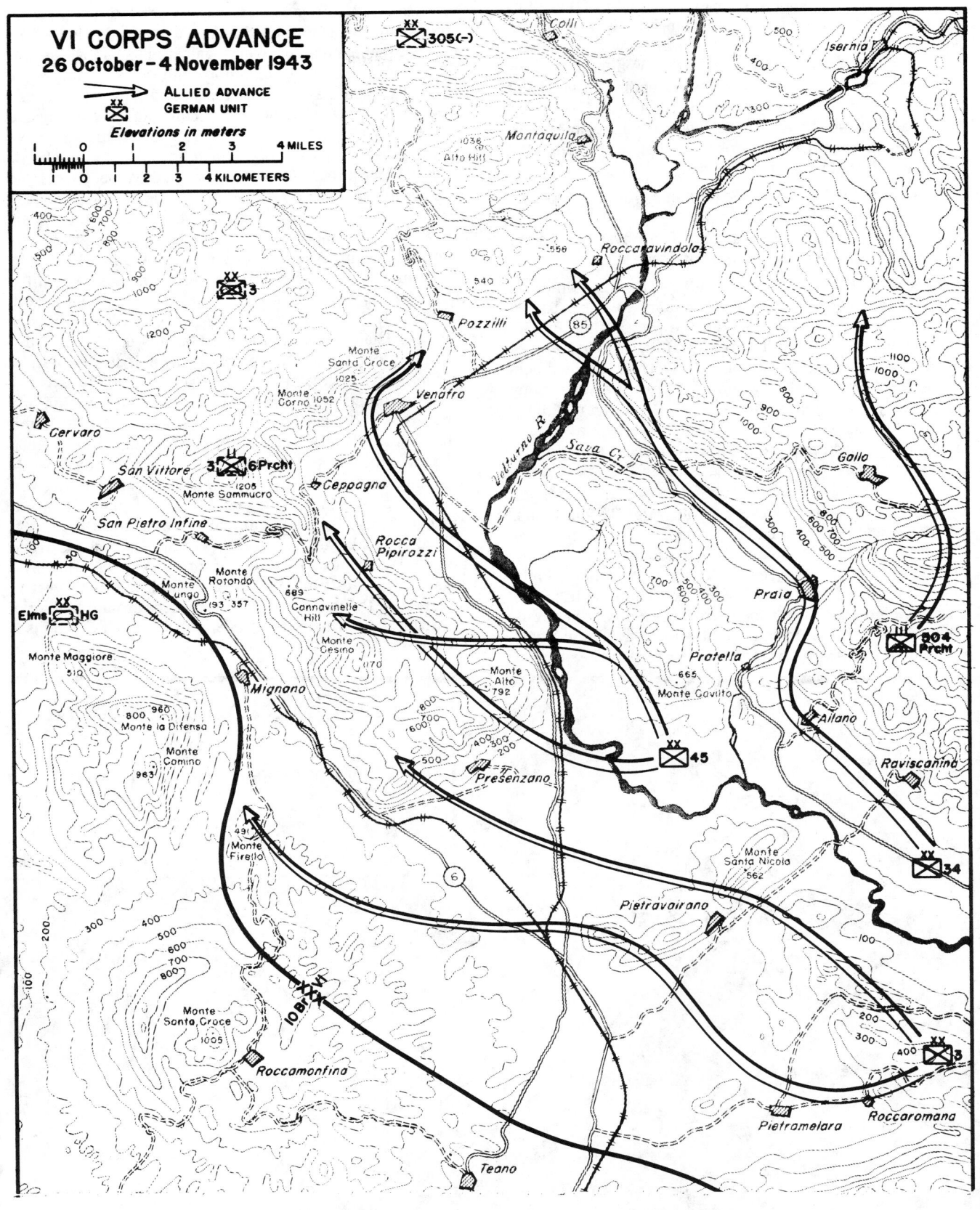

VI CORPS ADVANCE
26 October – 4 November 1943

ALLIED ADVANCE
GERMAN UNIT

Elevations in meters

4 MILES

4 KILOMETERS

ders decide that operations against the Germans in Italy must continue to prevent the enemy from mustering a counterattack prior to spring of 1944. The U.S. Fifth Army, its perimeter north of the Volturno well entrenched, prepares for the arduous drive through the mountains, extending from Mount Massico on the west coast to the Matese range. Fierce German delaying actions plague the slowly advancing Americans. The U.S. 135th Infantry (VI Corps area), begins pursuit of the enemy, which is moving toward Ailano.

October 26th 1943 — (Pacific-Solomons) An Allied Assault Force, commanded by Rear Admiral George H. Fort, U.S.N., steams toward the Treasury Islands. The Naval Vessels are attached to Task Force 31 (Admiral Wilkinson).

October 27th 1943 — (United States) The Joint Chiefs of Staff issue a directive authorizing autonomy for the O.S.S. on the Continent, taking it from under the wings of the British. The British agree reluctantly, however, they and General Donovan's O.S.S. work together congenially. Over 800 members of the O.S.S. receive decorations during the war, many posthumously. In one instance, fifteen American Italians (2677th Reconnaissance Battalion) volunteer for a mission calling for the destruction of a strategic coastal railroad tunnel running between Genoa and La Spezia. PT Boats arrive to evacuate them at a prearranged time, however, they unexpectedly are engaged by German E Boats; one PT Boat is lost. Additional attempts are made to rescue the men, however, despite Air Reconnaissance no trace is found. About a year later, a search party discovers their bodies (bullet hole in the back of their heads and their hands tied behind their backs). **(Pacific-Solomons)** An advance detachment of Marines lands north of the Karuma River near Atsinima Bay, Bougainville. Allied Planes, based on New Georgia swoop overhead as the

New Zealand 8th Brigade (seasoned at North Africa Crete and Greece) storms ashore on the Treasury Islands situated between Barakoma and Torokina, against mild opposition. Stirling is defenseless and at Mono, only sparse numbers of enemy troops are available to resist, and they retire quickly, pursued by the New Zealanders (commanded by Brigadier General R.A. Row). Control of the Treasury Islands is necessary to protect the flank of the main invasion and to afford a Fighter Airstrip Radar Station and a small-Vessel Base. In coordinated activity, the U.S.S. *Cony* (DD-508), a Destroyer, is damaged during the invasion and also two LST's, the 399 and 485 are both damaged by shore fire. In other activity, in the Solomons, enemy Aircraft attack Allied Shipping with negligible results. An assault is launched during the night of 27th-28th by the 2nd Marine Paratroop Battalion, commanded by Lt. Colonel Victor H Krulak, which lands on Choiseul Island, Solomons. The Marines use an old ploy, spreading out numerous Patrols to exhibit the impression that the Force is greater than it actually is. The Marines continue to feint strength during this diversionary mission until they are withdrawn, mission accomplished, on November 4th. **(Atlantic-Italy)** In the Fifth Army area, the U.S. 168th Infantry, 34th Division is instructed to begin an attack on the following day, to force progress. The enemy holding firm positions at Ailano, has the 135th Infantry pinned down at present. In the British Eighth Army area, the British 78th Division is unable to expand its bridgehead across the Trigno River. Heavy rains contribute immensely to the faltering progress. **(Atlantic-Russia)** The Germans still are getting thrashed by the incessant Soviet advances around Melitopol. However, the Germans regroup and fortify their positions in the areas of Nikopol and at Krivoi Rog.

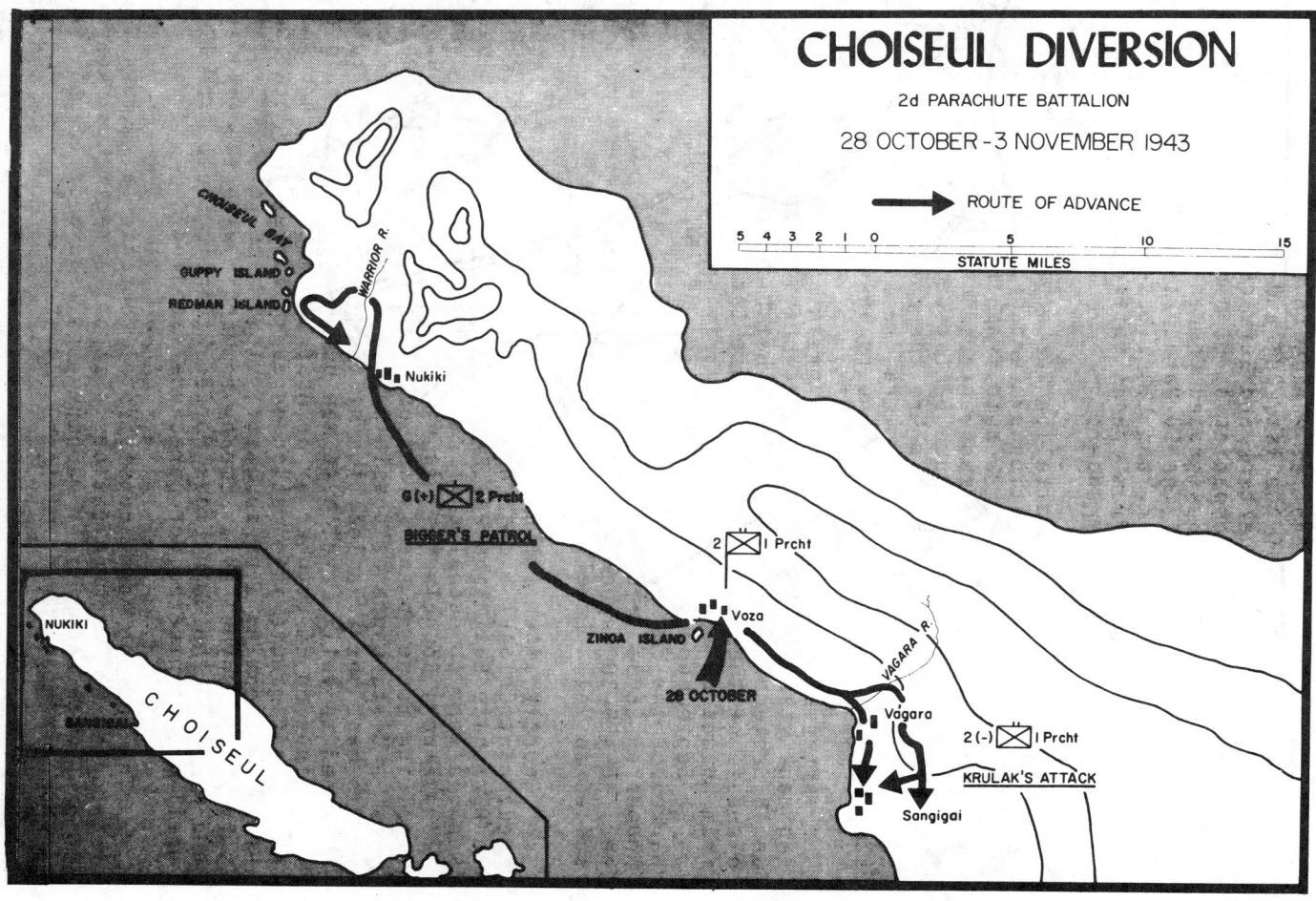

CHOISEUL DIVERSION

2d PARACHUTE BATTALION

28 OCTOBER - 3 NOVEMBER 1943

ROUTE OF ADVANCE

STATUTE MILES

October 28th 1943 — (Atlantic-Italy) In the Fifth Army, British 10th Corps area, the British 7th Armored and 46th Infantry, commences an assault against Mount Massico and Mount S. Croce. In the British Eighth Army area, an attack by Montgomery's Eighth Army (13 Corps) against the Axis Vinchidaturo-Isernia Line is postponed because of heavy rains. **(North Atlantic)** Planes (VC-1) from the U.S.S. *Block Island* (CVE-21), an Escort Carrier, operating in the North Atlantic, destroys a German Submarine, the U-220.

October 29th 1943 — (Atlantic-Italy) In the American Fifth Army area, the U.S. 135th Infantry, 34th Division, secures Pratella and Prata. The U.S. Third Division advances northward, west of the Volturno. The 504th Paratoop Infantry, 82nd Airborne, advances to Gallo. In the British Eighth Army area, the 13 Corps advances, under severe rains, during the night of the 29th, heading for Isernia.

October 30th 1943 — (Pacific) Final preparations are made for the Marine invasion of Bougainville. **(Atlantic-Russia)** The International Conferences end in Moscow. The representatives agree to demand the "unconditional surrender" of Germany. Britain, Russia and the U.S. participate in the major discussions; however, Chinese representatives participate in several discussions which concern their fate.

October 31st 1943 — (Pacific) U.S. Admiral Richmond K. Turner initiates practice maneuvers off the coast of Hawaii; his Task Force (52) is responsible for the seizure of the Gilberts (Operation GALVANIC). Another Fleet, Task Force 31, has its Vessels converging on points west of Guadalcanal, from where they will rendezvous and steam to Bougainville.

Allied Ships and Planes have destroyed enemy Airpower on the island, beyond the point of giving the American Task Force trouble. Also, the 22nd Marines are detached from Defense Force, Samoan Group and attached to V Amphibious Corps. **(Pacific-Bougainville)** The Allied Fleet (Task Forces 38 and 39) begins a preinvasion bombardment of Buka and Bonis Airfields, the Airstrip at Ballali and Faisi and additional targets, situated on smaller islands until the following day, November 1 (D-Day Bougainville). **(Atlantic-Italy)** In the U.S. Fifth Army area, the Italian 1st Motorized Group comes under the command of Fifth Army. In the British 10th Corps area, the British 7th Armored and British 46th Infantry Divisions maintain pressure against the enemy at both Mont Massico and Mont S. Croce, however, the enemy holds firmly. To the right, the British 56th Division seizes Teano. In the VI Corps area, contingents of the U.S. 34th Division occupy Ciorlano, on the slopes of La Croce Hill, while other units advance to Fontegreca. In the British Eighth Army area, the British 5th Division secures Cantalupo. **(North Atlantic)** The U.S.S. *Card* (CVE-11) launches Aircraft (VC-9), which sink the German Submarine U-584.

November 1st 1943 — (United States) Alaska is designated as a separate Theater of Operations. The Alaska Defense Command is detached from the Western Defense Command, renamed the Alaskan Department and comes under the direct control of the War Department. **(Pacific-Solomons)** The Destroyer *Fullam* (DD-474) becomes damaged by grounding. **(North Atlantic)** The U.S.S. *Borrie* (DD-215), a Destroyer, patrolling in the North Atlantic, sinks a German Submarine, the U-405.

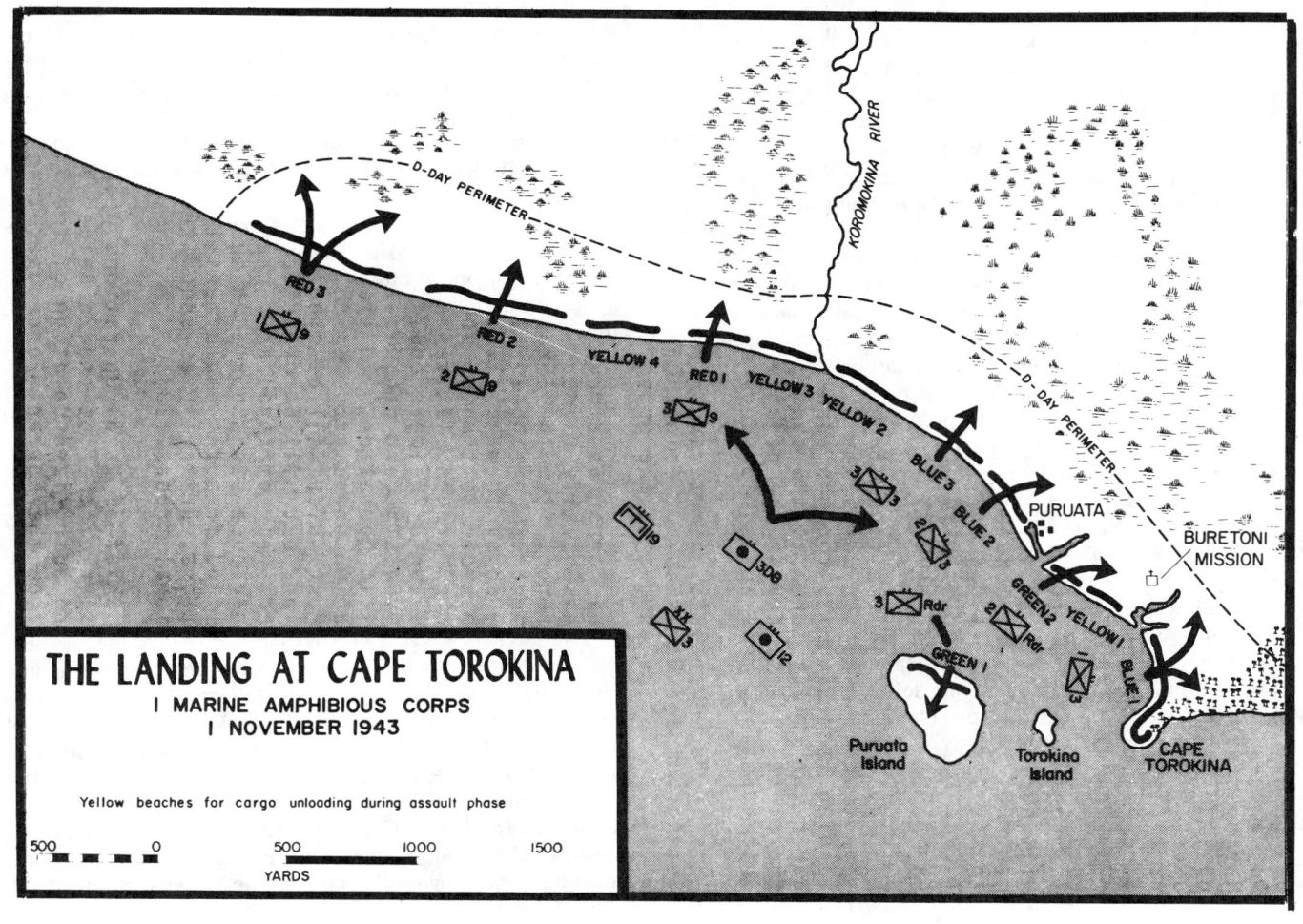

THE LANDING AT CAPE TOROKINA

I MARINE AMPHIBIOUS CORPS
I NOVEMBER 1943

Yellow beaches for cargo unloading during assault phase

500   0   500   1000   1500
YARDS

November 1st-2nd 1943 — (Pacific-Solomons) INVASION OF BOUGAINVILLE — An American Amphibious Force commanded by Rear Admiral T.S. Wilkinson arrives offshore and the First Marine Amphibious Corps, under Lt. General A.A. Vandegrift debark to seize the enemy strongpoint. Planes attached to Task Forces' 38 and 39 zoom overhead, shattering Japanese Airfields on the southern end of the island.

The Japanese commander, Lt. General Haroyoski Hyakutake, assumes the Air assaults are a prelude for the main assault. His conclusion allows the feint to prosper as the 3rd Marine Division, transported by Task Force 31, storms ashore at Empress Augusta Bay, Cape Torokina at 07:30, protected by Aircraft, including both Naval and Marine Squadrons and further supplemented by Surface Ship fire. The Invasion Force fortifies its positions against a small, yet defiant enemy force. While the troops are securing the beachhead and surrounding area, additional Warships, commanded by Rear Admirals A.S. Merrill and F.C. Sherman bombard the Airfields and Military fortifications in the Buka-Bonis area of the Solomons. This is followed by Admiral Merrill's Task Force, striking the Air facilities on Shortland Island. During the invasion, Sergeant Robert Allen Owens, and a four man Squad destroy a 75-mm regimental gun and its crew, enabling the troops to continue advancing.

In conjunction with the landing at Cape Torokina, another Force, the 2nd Marine Raider Regiment, seizes Puruata Island, off Cape Torokina by noon on the 22nd. On the heavily defended cape, site of the main invasion, the bulk of enemy strength is at the northern and southern tips, near the Airstrips. Fierce jungle and swamps separate the Japanese from the Marines and the Japanese Commander is not convinced that the invasion is the main assault. This indecision allows the Marines sufficient time to fortify, while engaging in the tedious work of wedging through dense jungle terrain, to clear the area of resistance and to expand their beachhead.

Word of the invasion reaches Rabaul and the Japanese react quickly, sending a powerful Armada including about 1,000 reinforcements, to break the spine of the U.S. Assault Force at Torokina. Planes from Rabaul are dispatched to supplement the operation. The enemy Task Force, commanded by Rear Admiral Sentaro Omori, steams toward the Yanks, however the Troop Transports fail to join the fast moving Armada at the proper time, causing the Commander to continue on course and order the Troop Transports to return to their base. The Japanese had spotted an American Submarine and conclude that the Troop Ships are too cumbersome and will shackle the balance of the Convoy. Pressing forward, the Japanese Fleet, consisting of six Destroyers and four Cruisers, nears the U.S. Naval Force slightly after midnight. The Armada burst through the waves under darkened skies, racing southward to an expected victory. Instead, the Japanese crash directly into a steel picket fence of waiting American Warships. As the Attack Force speeds forward, with the Heavy Cruisers Haguro and Myoko, spearheading, flanked by Light Cruisers and Destroyers, the Japanese are unexpectedly stunned at about 01:30, when a Yank Plane has some fortuitous luck and implants a bomb directly on the deck of the Haguro. The Japanese Convoy slows to accommodate the injured Vessel. Japanese Headquarters still holds the opinion that American Warships have departed the area to replenish supplies and ammunition, and have left the Troop Transports and ground Troops abandoned and susceptible to massacre.

Admiral Halsey, aware of enemy intentions, puts all gears in motion to intercept and foil the plot. Rear Admiral Merrill's Cruiser Destroyer Force is steaming from Vella Lavella to Empress Augusta Bay. Captain Arleigh (31 Knot) Burke's Destroyer Division 45, also is sprinting at top speed, after being informed of the upcoming crisis, while refueling his Destroyer Division, near the Kula Gulf. Meanwhile, Commander Austin's Destroyer Division 46 stands in place. The Warships rendezvous about 40 miles outside of Empress Augusta Bay; eight Destroyers and four Light Cruisers hold the line, in stark night air on the eerie shadowless waters, anxious to spring the attack. Two of Burke's Doctrine Points are: "IF IT WILL KILL JAPS, ITS IMPORTANT. IF IT WILL NOT KILL JAPS, IT IS NOT IMPORTANT."

American radar picks up the enemy Vessels as they move toward Torakina. Merrill's Force moves north, and separates at the predetermined point. Still, the Japanese cruise unsuspectingly toward Torakina to bludgeon the Yanks. Burke's Destroyers peel off and fire a steady stream of "iron fish". However, the Japanese have picked up the advancing Cruisers and are in the process of changing course, unwittingly avoiding the approaching torpedoes.

The U.S. Cruisers also enjoy a little luck themselves. The Japanese, spot the U.S. Vessels and spring a futile torpedo attack. The American Cruisers change course to engage the enemy, then commence a tumultuous bombardment, which inflicts grievous damage on the Light Cruiser Sendai, that ignites powerful explosions. The Vessel, although badly wounded and lying dead in the sea, still contains operational guns. Additional volleys by Merrill's men, casts more gloom on the Convoy. The Cruisers play tag in the dark throughout the night, however, neither side is able to knock out the other. Two Japanese Destroyers, the Samidare and the Shiratsuyu, smash into each other, and this prompts more erratic maneuvers, as the two Vessels retire. Commander Burke's Destroyers move back into the raging battle to assist other Destroyers engaged against the Sendai.

During the tumultuous sea battle, one of the torpedoes intended for the American Cruisers strikes the U.S.S. Foote just after 03:00 while it attempts to join Austin's Main Body. In addition, the Americans suffer damage when two Destroyers, the Thatcher and the Spence, collide while maneuvering at high speed. The Spence is subsequently struck by surface fire, by the Myoko at 03:20. Within minutes, the Myoko, and the Haguro, score several hits on the U.S.S. Denver, before she rejoins the formation to conclude the battle. During this exhibition, the U.S.S. Columbia, is struck by a large surface shell, but luckily, it is above the watermark and she remains operational. The Spence and the Destroyer Converse attack the crippled Cruiser Sendai, delivering a quick salvo of torpedoes, however, again the Sendai escapes the fatal blow, as all torpedoes miss the target. Burke's command finishes off the Sendai.

In the midst of this sea joust, the Myoko inadvertently rams into the Hatsukaze, amputating a section of the Hatsukaze's bow. The Japanese scatter with the Yanks in pursuit. Three of the U.S. Destroyers, the Thatcher, Spence and Converse close on the retreating enemy Destroyers and commence an unsuccessful attack. All torpedoes miss their mark, but the Japanese veer off balance, as they return fire and gain the same results; all torpedoes miss the American Destroyers. Commander Burke moves into action as the Spence is disengaging, due to diminishing ammunition and fuel. Commander Austin transfers command to Commander Lampman on the *Thatcher* and departs the area. The *Spence* comes under accidental fire from the guns of Burke's Force. Commander Austin snaps a message to Burke, after observing about a dozen shells falling near his Vessel: "WE'VE JUST HAD A BAD CLOSE MISS I HOPE YOU ARE NOT SHOOTING AT US." As Burke is speaking with Austin, he asks the question, "Are you hurt?" Austin yells, "NEGATIVE" and Burke follows with the following message: "SORRY BUT YOU'LL HAVE TO EXCUSE THE NEXT FOUR SALVOS THEY'RE ALREADY ON THEIR WAY." The *Spence* high tails it and runs right into the wounded *Hatsukaze*. Commander Austin attacks from a distance of about 4,000 yards, sending shells reeling into the Destroyer, stopping her dead in the water. Burke is directed to move in and complete the destruction.

At about 03:30, the Japanese retire toward Rabaul, scampering along the coast of Bougainville. The Cruisers, under Merrill, also disengage. Burke is also directed to halt pursuit and reform. The order is timely, as the Japanese Planes are moving to attack the Yanks.

At 08:00 "Colors" is attended by about 100 uninvited Japanese Pilots, swarming overhead. Fifteen Planes had intercepted, but the superior Force breaks through and bombards the disabled Destroyer *Foote*. A wall of Antiaircraft fire, by the *Foote* and her escorting Vessels foils the attack and she escapes injury. The enemy Planes then strike Merrill's Main Body. The sky fills with Antiaircraft fire and smoking Japanese Planes, which plummet to the sea. In a rare occurrence, several Jap Pilots are observed floating to the water in parachutes, nestling themselves right in the middle of Merrill's formation. The attack bellies out with about two dozen Planes shot down, and the balance making a run for their base with American Planes in pursuit. The Japanese damage the Cruiser *Montpelier*, but she and the rest of the Task Force, including the U.S.S. *Foote*, share in the momentous victory. Again, the savage power of the Japanese Imperial Navy had been halted. Old Glory flies high above the Fleet and just as proudly on Bougainville, where the struggle is really just beginning.

The Marines work feverishly to clear the hills, while simultaneously setting up defenses to protect against any possible Japanese counterattacks, as they prepare to take the entire island, yard by yard. Heavy fighting occurs on Bougainville for some time. As Christmas approaches, the Marines are concentrating on one obstinate pocket of resistance, known as, "Hellzapoppin Ridge" and in appropriate Marine fashion, thrash the enemy, securing the ridge on the 18th of December. Subsequently, U.S. Army troops (Americal Division), begin to replace the Marines.

The Marines would be relieved by the American Division U.S.A., in mid January. The Americans continue strengthening the island defenses, bracing for the Japanese counterattack, which occurs during March. The Army repulses the Japanese who close in from the northern and southern tips of the island, crossing swamps, hitting American mines and finally, withering Yankee fire. Japanese charge incessantly to overrun positions. The Japs penetrate American lines with some success, however, Infantry, supported by Tank counterattacks regain the lost terrain. After 17 days of bloody combat, the Japanese counterattacks finally cease on the 24th of March with heavy casualties. By the end of April, Bougainville

is secure and Airfields sprout up in the jungle clearings and begin launching American Planes to strike Rabaul. The Stars and Stripes flies proudly over Bougainville, bringing the Yanks and their Pilots one step closer to the heart of Japan.

November 1st 1943 — U.S. Marines assault Empress Agusta Bay at Bougainville.

November 1st 1943 — (Pacific-Solomons) During fierce fighting between the Americans and Japanese, Planes assist at Bougainville, intercepting an enemy force. One Pilot, Lt. Robert H. Murray, Marine Fighting Squadron 215, disperses six enemy Planes (Torpedo Bombers), shooting down one and driving the balance away, forcing them to drop their bombs prematurely near Augusta Bay. **(Atlantic-Italy)** In the U.S. Fifth Army area, the British 10th Corps still is occupied with the task of clearing resistance on Mont Sant Croce. Meanwhile, the 56th British Division captures Roccamonfina. In the VI Corps area, the U.S. 168th Infantry advances to Capriati al Vulturno.

November 2nd 1943 — (Pacific-Bougainville-Solomons) The 3rd Marines continue to fortify the beachhead. The 9th Marines switch positions with the 3rd Marines, which have been in bitter battle on the right flank since landing. The 3rd Marine Raider Battalion declares Puruata Island secure. The U.S. Naval Vessels damaged at the Battle of Empress Augusta Bay: Light Cruiser *Montpelier* (CL-57); Light Cruiser *Denver* (CL-58); Destroyer *Foote* (DD-511); Destroyer *Spence* (DD-512) and the Destroyer *Thatcher* (DD-514). Japanese Naval Vessels Sunk; Light Cruiser *Sendai* and Destroyer *Hatsukaze*. (See November 1st-2nd 1943). **(Pacific-Bismarcks-New Britain)** The

U.S. Fifth Air Force sends 75 B-25s escorted by P-38s against Japanese positions at Rabaul. The raid scores damage, after meeting its fiercest opposition since the war began. Major Raymond Wilkins, U.S.A. Air Corps, leads his Squadron against the enemy and his Plane is hit, but remains to attack. He takes the Aircraft into a low altitude dive, destroying a Destroyer and a Transport. Wilkins' Plane attempts to get away, but a Heavy Destroyer shoots his Plane down. Because of the courage of the entire crew, the remainder of his Squadron returns safely. **(China-Burma-India)** The Allies (Chinese 38th Division) engage in heavy combat with Japanese along the Tarung River. The Japanese withstand the assault and deal a heavy blow to the Allied Force inflicting severe casualties. **(Atlantic-Italy) 15th Army Group** In the **U.S. Fifth Army**, British 10th Corps sector, elements of the British 7th Armored and the British 46th Infantry advance to the Garigliano. In the VI Corps area, the U.S. 34th and 45th Divisions prepare to cross the Volturno. The 180th Infantry dispatches Company F across the river during the night 2nd-3rd in advance of the Main Body. They cross in the vicinity of Sesto Campano. In the **British Eighth Army** area, the enemy staunchly resists British 5 Corps' attempts to cross the Trigno River. Allied Artillery and Naval gunfire supports the troops attempting the crossing. **(Atlantic-Austria)** The U.S. Fifteenth Air Force assists an Allied bombing mission over Germany. One hundred twelve Heavy Bombers meet heavy Antiaircraft fire and enemy Fighters, while they bomb the Messerschmidt Aircraft factory at Wiener Neustadt. **(Atlantic)** The U.S.S. *Borie* (DD-215), a Destroyer, engages a German Submarine in the eastern Atlantic. During the heated battle, the *Borie* is struck by the U-405's deck guns and then the U-Boat rams the American Destroyer, sinking it.

U.S. Bombers attack the Ball Bearing Plants at Schweinfurt, Germany.

November 3rd 1943 — (POA) The Northern Attack Force (TF52) concludes its practice maneuvers for the seizure of the Gilberts (GALVANIC) at Hawaii. **(Pacific-Solomons)** The 3rd Marine Defense Battalion and the 12th Marines on Bougainville bombard enemy positions on Torokina Island. Afterward, a detachment of the 3rd Raider Battalion moves to Torokina, but finds no live Japanese. **(Atlantic-Italy) 15th Army Group** In the **U.S. Fifth Army** area, the U.S. 4th Ranger Battalion moves through the U.S. 45th Division sector in an effort to cross the Volturno and set up a roadblock northwest of Mignano. It meets opposition and is halted just short of the objective. Elements of the 2nd Battalion, 180th Infantry cross the Volturno southeast of Presenzano, then push west toward

Rocca Pipirozzi. In other activity, the U.S. 34th Division assisted by heavy Artillery, crosses the Volturno during the night of 3rd. The Allies are pushing against the Axis Winter Line, fighting hardened German troops and disastrous weather conditions. In the **British Eighth Army** area, the 5 Corps meets heavy opposition at S. Salvo Ridge. **(Atlantic-Germany)** The U.S. Eighth Air Force launches more than 500 Bombers, using Pathfinders to locate the targets. The Planes unload a massive barrage of bombs on Wilhelmshaven's North Sea port facilities, inflicting heavy damage. This is the largest daylight raid to date flown by the Eighth Air Force.

November 4th 1943 — (United States) The War Department Operations Division recommends that prior commitments to China be carried out. It is recommended that 30 Chinese Divisions be equipped and trained and also to provide equipment in reserve for an additional three Divisions, which will comprise the Zebra Force. **(Pacific-Bismarcks)** The Japanese Vessel *Tsukushi*, a Surveying Vessel, strikes a mine off New Ireland and sinks. **(Pacific-Caroline Islands)** The U.S.S. *Tautog* operating near the Carolines, east of Mindanao, Philippines, sinks the Japanese Auxiliary Submarine Chaser No. 30, near the Palau Islands. **(Pacific-Solomons)** The Marines (2nd Parachute Battalion) are withdrawn from Choiseul. These Marines under Lt. Colonel Krulak have spent 12 days conducting their raids and lose 12 men, while inflicting 143 casualties upon the enemy and diverting sufficient strength to prevent the Japanese from giving their full attention to Torokina. A Japanese Naval Force, dispatched earlier from Truk, enters the harbor at Rabaul, threatening the American beachhead at Bougainville. A Scout Plane spots eight Heavy Cruisers, two Light Cruisers and eight Destroyers. The U.S. assumption is that they will refuel and steam toward Torokina. This concerns Halsey who states: "THE MOST DESPERATE EMERGENCY THAT CONFRONTED ME IN MY ENTIRE TERM AS COMSOPAC." U.S. Task Force 38 (Admiral Ted Sherman) is directed to counter the threat by attacking Rabaul and drawing first blood. Allied Land-based Aircraft are ordered to fly cover escort for the Carriers, giving Sherman the opportunity to dispatch ninety-seven Planes from the *Saratoga* and *Princeton*. Admiral Merrill's Task Force is not within striking distance and Halsey is preoccupied with the thoughts of the Planes being wiped out and both Carriers being struck. Halsey ponders the order and then returns it for transit stating simply: "LET 'ER GO." **(China-Burma-India)** The 112th Regiment, Chinese 38th Division, which has had immense difficulty penetrating Japanese defenses in northern Burma is ordered to halt the murderous advance and dig in. The Japanese also have the 1st Chinese Battalion cut off near Yubang Ga. The 3rd Battalion is stalled at Ngajatzup. **(Atlantic-Italy) 15th Army Group** In the U.S. Fifth Army area, the British 10th Corps readies for an assault on Mont Camino. In the VI Corps area, the U.S. 180th Infantry (2nd Battalion) clears Rocca Pipirozzi and fortifies positions on a ridge to the northwest and contacts the 4th Ranger Battalion. The 179th Infantry, crosses the Volturno south of Venafro, and secures Venafro. The U.S. 133rd Infantry, 34th Division captures Sant Maria Oliveto and the 168th seizes Roccaravindola. The Allies press the enemy Winter Line, but the task remains difficult as supply problems are constant. In the **British Eighth Army** area, the enemy begins to pull, allowing the British 13th Corps to occupy Isernia without incident, while the British 5th Corps captures South Salvo Ridge. **(Atlantic-Russia)** The Soviets maintain pressure against the Germans and secure more terrain in the vicinity of the Dnieper river near Kherson. They then move to surround the Germans holding Kiev.

November 5th 1943 — (Pacific-Solomons-Bougainville) A bitter skirmish develops in the vicinity of the Mission Trail as the 3rd Ranger Battalion repulses a vicious Japanese attack. The Rangers then link with the 9th Marines and drive toward the Numa Numa Trail, one of two primary trails on Cape Torokina. In other activity in the Solomons, Enemy Aircraft damage the PT-167 off the Solomons. **(Pacific-New Britain)** American Carrier Task Force 38, commanded by Rear Admiral F.C. Sherman, dispatched a few days earlier, springs a surprise Air assault against the newly arrived Japanese Naval Force at Rabaul. About 100 Planes strike, inflicting heavy damage to five enemy Cruisers and two Destroyers. This is the first Carrier based raid unleashed against Rabaul. The Americans lose 10 Aircraft during the attack. Enemy Planes launched to destroy Task Force 38, search without success, while Planes attached to the U.S. Fifth Air Force, swoop overhead, delivering more damage to Rabaul. The enemy Naval Forces at Rabaul are immobilized and the threat against Bougainville is terminated. Halsey notes that the Japanese have Navy Pilots at Rabaul and that they had outfought enemy Pilots. The dogfights culminated with the loss of five U.S. Planes versus twenty-five lost enemy Aircraft. Halsey expresses dissatisfaction with some promised assistance in the form of a simultaneous attack by Planes of General Kenney's Eighth Air Force intended to "level Rabaul." Halsey's feelings: 'THE LAST THING OUR PILOTS SAW AS THEY DUCKED BACK INTO THE CLOUDS — THE SAME CLOUDS THAT HID OUR CARRIERS — WAS KENNEY'S BOMBERS, EIGHT OF THEM." It is interesting to note that Tokyo Radio covers the American raid against Rabaul, but their casualty figures are inaccurate as follows:" IN AN AIR RAID AGAINST RABAUL, THE MUCH VAUNTED REINFORCED ENEMY (American) AIR FORCE SUFFERED THE LOSS OF 200 PLANES OUT OF 230 . . . THE SHOOTING DOWN OF 90 PER CENT OF THE ENEMY TOTAL AIR STRENGTH REPRESENTS A NEW WORLD RECORD." Also Tokyo radio informs the Japanese people that a Japanese Torpedo Squadron had departed Rabaul during the night of November 5th and successfully destroyed four Cruisers and two Carriers. **(China-Burma-India)** General Stilwell presents updated plans of for the proposed attack by the Y Force against the Japanese. The report is given to Chiang Kai-shek. **(South Atlantic)** U.S. Army and Land-based Naval Planes (B-107), combine their strength and destroy the U-848, costing the Germans another of their dwindling supply of Submarines. **(Atlantic-Italy) 15th Army Group** In the **U.S. Fifth Army** area, an offensive is launched to secure the mountainous Winter Line of the enemy. It is a most gruesome task, plagued by supply problems and lack of reserves. The well-entrenched Germans vigorously withstand the assaults, inflicting heavy casualties on the Fifth Army. The assault will falter and cease for regrouping on the 15th without progress. In the VI Corps area, the U.S. Third Division moves against Mignano Gap and hits intense enemy resistance. The U.S. 7th Infantry drives directly against brutal enemy fortifications at Mont la Difensa. The battle hardened German defenders withstand the assault for ten days. Contingents of the 15th Infantry head northwardly over M. Cesima while the 30th Infantry inches toward Mont Rotondo. The American flanks are out but the Germans hold all the advantages and use them skillfully. In the British Eighth Army area, 5 Corps sec-

tor, the Germans withdraw northward with the British in pursuit. The Indian 8th Division captures Tufillo while the British 78th Division moves along the coast through Vasto.

November 6th 1943 — (United States) General Eisenhower's request to keep Landing Craft in the Mediterranean is accepted by the Combined Chiefs of Staff. They will be permitted to remain until the 15th of December and then another extension will be granted allowing them to remain until the middle of January. Twelve U.S. and 56 British LST'S are in question. **(Pacific-Ellice Islands)** The Seventh Air Force establishes advance Headquarters at Funafuto. **(Pacific-Solomons)** Reinforcements (1st Battalion, 21st Marines), arrive on Bougainville to bolster the beachhead of the 3rd Marines. Additional 3rd Marine Division troops land on Cape Torokina and Puruata Island. In other activity, the Japanese Submarine Chaser No. 11 is destroyed by American Planes. **(Pacific-Bismarcks-New Britain)** At present, there is one Cruiser and a few Destroyers in port at Rabaul; the other Vessels have departed for either Japan or Truk, giving Halsey and Sherman a well-deserved respite for themselves and the troops at Torokina. As the Japanese Navy continues to recoil, the Yanks become more numerous. Three Light Cruisers and a Carrier Force including the *Essex* and *Bunker Hill* and the *Independence* bolster Halsey and Admiral Merrill prior to the assault against Tarawa (November 21st). **(Pacific-India)** U.S. troops prepare to assist the operation of the Bengal and Assam railroad. **(Atlantic-Italy)** The Germans pour heavy fire into American assaults pinning down the 7th Regiment at Mont la Difensa, the 30th Infantry at Mont Rotondo, the 15th Infantry at Hill 253; also, the 34th and 45th Divisions are stalled in the hills and mountains to the East. **(Atlantic-North Africa)** An enemy Torpedo Bomber sinks the Destroyer *Beatty* (DD-640) off the coast of Northwest Africa. **(Atlantic-Russia)** The Soviets, maneuvering to surround the Germans at Kiev are foiled as the Germans anticipating defeat, withdraw.

November 7th 1943 — (Pacific-Solomons) The Japanese land just under 500 troops in the vicinity of the Laruma and Koromokina rivers, near Cape Torokina, Bougainville and attack the 3rd Marines, 3rd Marine Division positions at Koromokina lagoon, however, the Marines, using mortars and effective Artillery, hold firmly. During the heated battle, one Squad, led by Sgt. Herbert J. Thomas inches forward and destroys two menacing enemy nests. As the detachment nears another deadly machine gun nest, a grenade gets hung up in the dense jungle brush then suddenly bounces back upon the Squad. Sgt. Thomas covers the exploding grenade with his body to save his men. His incredible action inspires the remaining men to charge recklessly and destroy the enemy crew. The Japanese cut off a small Marine outpost, but these Marines are rescued by sea. The Marines counterattack on the eighth, terminating the enemy threat. **(POA)** The Southern Attack Force begins practice maneuvers for GALVANIC at Efate, New Hebrides. Also, another Carrier Fleet, commanded by Rear Admiral Alfred L. Montgomery, arrives in the South Pacific. **(China-Burma-India)** Intense fighting occurs between the Japanese and the Allies in the British Fourteenth Army, Four Corps area in the vicinity of Chin Hills. The Japanese seize Falam. **(Atlantic-Italy)** In the VI Corps sector, Major General Benjamin F. Caffey, commanding Task Force A, initiates a drive to seize Montaquila. **(Atlantic-Russia)** The Germans halt the advance of the Russians in the vicinity of Fastov.

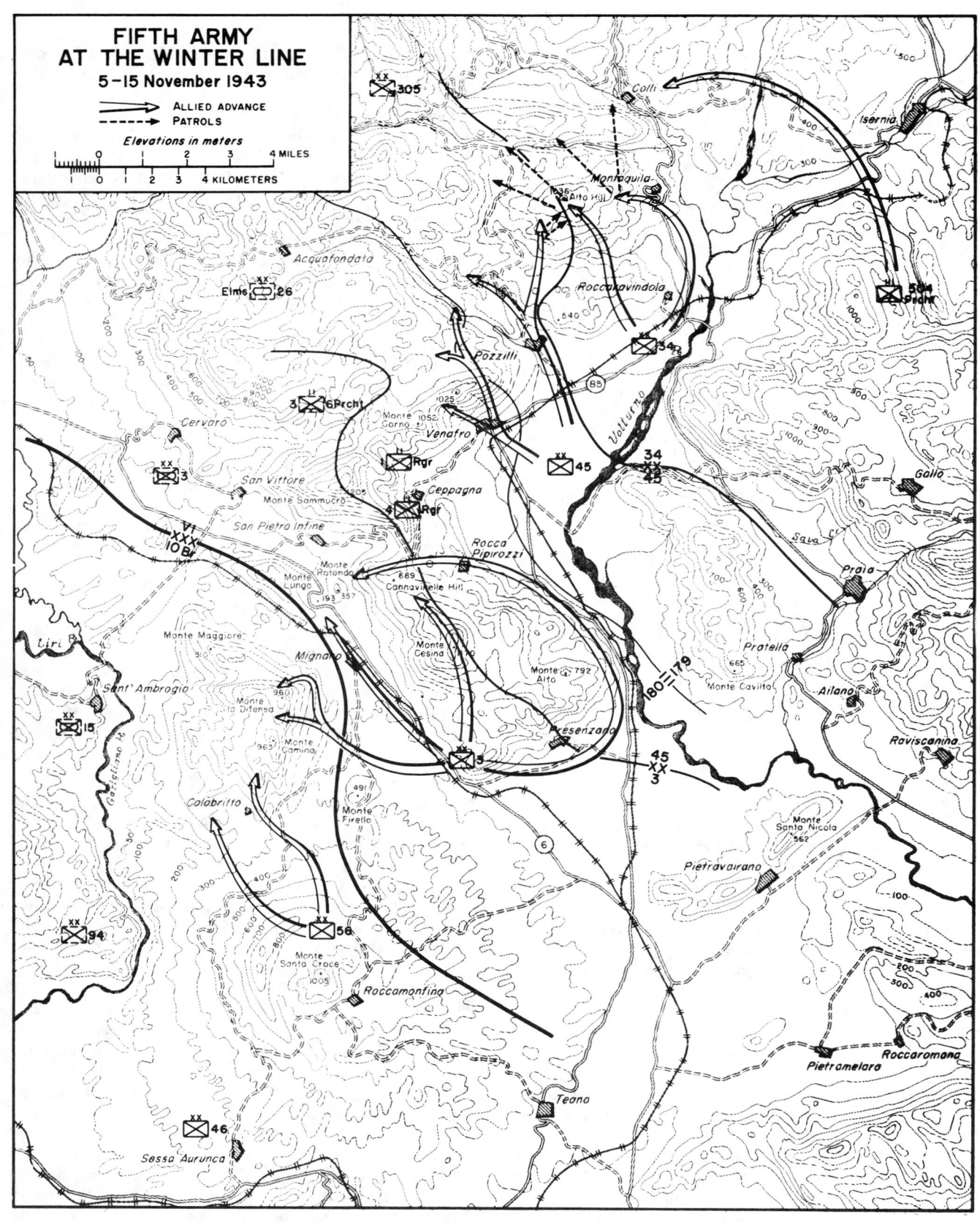

FIFTH ARMY
AT THE WINTER LINE
5-15 November 1943

ALLIED ADVANCE
PATROLS

Elevations in meters

0   1   2   3   4 MILES
1   0   1   2   3   4 KILOMETERS

Colli

Isernia

305

Acquafondata

Elms 26

Montaquila
Alto Hill

Roccaravindola

504
Sesto

Pozzilli

34

3 6Prcht

Cervaro

Monte
Corno
1052

Venafro

Volturno
(85)

45

34
XX
45

Gallo

3

San Vittore
Monte Sammucro
San Pietro Infine

Rgr

Ceppagna

Rgr

Rocca
Pipirozzi

Sava

VI
XXX
10 Br

Monte
Rotondo
Monte
Lungo
193 357

689
Cannavinelle Hill

Praia

180 179

Pratella

Monte Cavitto

Monte Maggiore
910

Mignano

Monte
Cesina

Monte
Alto

792

Presenzano

Ailano

Sant'Ambrogio

Liri R.

Monte
la Difensa

960

963
Monte
Camino

Monte Santa Nicola
562

Raviscanina

15

491

Monte
Firello

Calabritto

45
XX
3

(6)

Pietravairano

94

56

Monte
Santa Croce
1005

Roccamonfina

Pietramelara

Roccaromana

Teano

46

Sessa Aurunca

November 7th-10th 1943 — (Pacific-Bougainville) THE BATTLE OF PIVA TRAIL — A roadblock along the junction of the Piva-Numa Numa Trails (right flank of Marine perimeter) is assaulted by Japanese. An intense battle ensues, with the Marines pushing off on the 9th with a strong counterattack (2nd Raider Regiment, assisted by the 2nd Battalion 9th Marines), and driving the Japanese back in disarray. The 1st and 2nd Battalions, 9th Marines, move right through the trail junction, continuing beyond Piva Village and establish defensive positions along the Numa Numa Trail.

November 8th 1943 — (Pacific-Bougainville) The 1st Battalion, 21st Marines, assaults Japanese positions, followed by attacks from the 3rd, 9th, and 21st Marines, to defeat a Japanese landing force. The Japanese are heavily bombarded on the following day by Planes from Munda, which thoroughly devastate the enemy landing troops. In other activity, advance elements of the 37th U.S. Infantry Division arrive, to begin relief of the Marines. During the heated combat, the Light Cruiser *Birmingham* (CL-62), the Attack Transports *Fuller* (APA-18) and the *President Jackson* (APA-18) are damaged, by enemy Dive Bomber attacks. In other activity, the I Marine Amphibious Corps assumes responsibility for all forces ashore. **(Atlantic-Italy)** British General Alexander orders the U.S. Fifth Army to prepare for an amphibious landing on the west coast of Italy (Anzio), to outflank the Germans. In the Fifth Army, VI Corps area, strong enemy resistance keeps the U.S. 7th Infantry from seizing Mont la Difensa. The U.S. 3rd Battalion, 30th Regiment, makes the dangerous climb against enemy fire, and reaches the top of Mont Rotondo. In the mountains to the north of Venafro and Pozzilli, the Germans halt the U.S. 43rd Division advance. Montaquila relents, falling to the U.S. 34th Division, while the 179th Infantry initiates an assault against enemy positions on the hills between Polzzilli and Filignano. The Germans pull back and the 45th takes the hills in question on the 10th, without opposition.

November 9th 1943 — (United States) The U.S. *Wahoo* (SS-238) is reported lost. The gallant Vessel had departed Pearl Harbor on the eighth of August, heading back near Japan. The *Wahoo*, under the able command of Lt. Commander Morton, is on her sixth War Patrol, but has a surplus of bad torpedoes on board, causing severe problems. The *Wahoo* returns to Pearl for new torpedoes and sets a new course after departing Pearl on September 9th, but the Vessel is lost in action. The reason for the loss is attributed to enemy mines, but after the war, records seem to indicate that the *Wahoo* had been lost on October 11th in the Strait of La Perouse. **(Pacific-Bougainville)** American Aircraft, based at Munda, New Georgia, attack enemy positions between the Marine perimeter (Koromokina Lagoon) and the Laruma River, ending opposition from the remnants of the enemy Assault Force. The U.S. 148th Infantry Regiment, 37th Division, relieves the Marines on the left flank and takes responsibility for the area. The Army begins to replace the Marines on the island. In a heated firefight, a Platoon of the 3rd Marine Raider Battalion holds firm at a roadblock on Bougainville Island near Empress Augusta Bay. Marines pour steady fire upon the attacking Japanese. P.F.C. Henry Gourke, reacts instinctively when a lobbed grenade falls into his two-man foxhole. He pushes his sidekick away saving his life and falls on the grenade, permitting the other man to continue firing his automatic weapon. Gourke receives the Medal of Honor posthumously. In other activity, Major General Roy S.

Geiger replaces Major General Vandegrift, as Commanding General I Marine Amphibious Corps. Gen Vandegrift has been appointed Commandant of the Marine Corps.

November 2nd 1943 — A Japanese Transport at New Guinea attempting to hide from U.S. Planes.

November 3rd 1943 — U.S. Coast Guardsmen roping in a boat on Bougainville.

November 10th 1943 — (Pacific-Pearl Harbor) The Northern Attack Force, primary assault force for the invasion of the Gilbert Islands (Operation GALVANIC), departs Pearl Harbor. **(Pacific-Bougainville)** Admiral Halsey is told of a surprise inspection at a movie to ensure that all troops are wearing shoes and socks. One culprit is caught and it turns out that he is a Jap who had deserted his command and had been a regular at the movie for over a week before being caught. **(Pacific-New Britain)** The U.S. Fifth Air Force launches a strike against Japanese positions on Rabaul. **(Atlantic-Italy)** In the Fifth Army area, the U.S. 1st Ranger Battalion relieves contingents of the 45th Division, which are still pressing to seize control of Mont Corno. In the vicinity of Mignano, an enemy Force of about 100 men threatens a Company of the U.S. 3rd Division. The Germans attack fiercely, but Lt. Maurice Britt rallies his men, who disregard incoming hand grenades and machine gun fire to repulse the assault. Britt is wounded in several places, but he refuses medical aid, continuing leading his men in the battle. Britt personally wipes out an enemy machine gun nest and its crew, kills five enemy Soldiers and wounds several more. By the actions of Britt and his men, several captured Americans are able to escape from the Germans and the Americans capture several Germans, in addition to preventing the annihilation of their entire company. Lieutenant Britt becomes the recipient of the Medal of Honor for his heroism. **(Atlantic-Spain)** U.S. Naval Land-based Aircraft (VB-103 and VB-110), combine with Planes attached to the Czechoslovakian Air Force and sink the U-966 off the coast of Spain.

Pappy Boyington, U.S.M.C., (Medal of Honor Recipient) briefing his Pilots in the Pacific.

November 8th 1943 — U.S. troops firing a 105-mm Howitzer M2A2 against Japanese positions at Buretoni Mission on the Piva Trail.

November 11th 1943 — (Pacific-Bougainville) Marines hold the junction of the Mission and Numa Numa Trails after their successful drive, which kills about 550 Japs. The Marines (3rd Division) are ordered by General Geiger to drive in two directions, east and west, simultaneously to secure and hold an Airfield site. Also, additional contingents of the 21st Marines arrive. **(Pacific-New Britain)** The Japanese suffer more

damage to their ailing Fleet at Simpson Harbor, New Britain, as two American Task Forces, commanded by Rear Admirals A.E. Montgomery, and F.C. Sherman, destroy one Destroyer, the *Suzunami* and inflict heavy losses to the Japanese Eleventh Air Fleet (twenty four enemy Planes against a U.S. loss of seven Aircraft). Montgomery's Force strikes from the southwest and Sherman delivers his blows from the northeast, despite bad weather. Sherman's Force retires without detection. The Japanese locate Admiral Montgomery's Task Force and strike without consequence, although between sixty to seventy enemy Planes pursue. U.S. Land-based Planes from Barakoma intercept the Japanese Fighters and destroy over fifty of them. The U.S. loses three Planes. On the following morning no enemy Ships remain at Simpson Harbor. **(China-Burma-India)** General Chiang Kai-shek, after studying General Stilwell's proposal of November 5th, agrees to a combined British Chinese assault against Burma, with the Chinese being held in reserve until the British assault Kalewa. In the British Fourteenth Army area, the Japanese seize Haka. **(Atlantic-Italy-)** The struggle to gain the mountains blocking the Fifth Army's approach to Rome still is highly combustible. The U.S. 157th Infantry is assigned the task of taking Acquafondata, with orders to move out, wedging between the 179th and 180th Regimental positions. Meanwhile, the Germans still feel secure that they can hold the Winter Line. The 2nd Battalion, 509th Paratroop Infantry, clears a portion of Mount Croce. Every yard gained during this campaign for Rome costs the Allies heavily. German Soldiers do a masterful job of using the treacherous mountains to their advantage. They hold the high ground to observe all Allied movements. In a heated engagement involving elements of the U.S. 3rd Division, the Germans offer firm resistance near Mignano, then mount a counterattack. PFC Floyd K. Lindstrom's Platoon gives cover fire to a Rifle Company's advance when the enemy assault occurs, however, the German press ahead, forcing a withdrawal by the Americans, leaving Lindstrom's unit outnumbered about 5 to 1. Lindstrom advances with his machine gun, defying incessant fire and gains a position 10 yards from the enemy. Unable to score a kill, he intensifies his efforts and charges further over rocks and then kills two men with his pistol, confiscates their machine gun and returns to his own men. Still defying danger, he again returns to the enemy position and transports two boxes of ammunition back to his lines and begins firing his own machine gun in a fantastic display of dare that virtually breaks up the assault. **(Atlantic-Russia)** The Germans still hold firmly west of Kiev, but the Russians make progress. The Germans holding southwest of Kiev advance against the Russians.

November 12th 1943 — (Pacific-Treasury Islands) The Allies engage an enemy Garrison at Mono, killing over 200 Japanese defenders. The combined New Zealand-American force loses 52 men killed; 40 New Zealanders and 12 Americans. **(Pacific-New Britain)** The Japanese pull their Carrier Fleet Aircraft from Rabaul. This terminates any further threat from Rabaul to the Allied thrust in the Pacific. **(Atlantic-Italy)** The road to Cassino seems an endless journey. The weather remains terrible and the supply problems are ever present. In the British 10th Corps area, the Germans punish the attacking British 56th Division, forcing them to pull back from Mont Camino. In the VI Corps area, the American 157th Infantry makes a valiant attempt to reach Acquafondata, but defiant German defenders holding the high ground (Hills 640 and 769) stop the advance. The Allied advance is stymied across the whole front by stiff German resistance. In other activity in the Atlantic, Planes, attached to VB-103, which had participated in the destruction of the U-996, on the 10th, encounter the U-508 today, in the Bay of Biscay and sink it.

November 13th 1943 — (United States) Heeding the Naval superstition of not initiating a long mission on Friday, at 00:01 on the 14th, the *Iowa* glides through the Chesapeake Bay heading for Iran. The monstrous Battlewagon is accompanied by three Destroyers, as insurance, to protect their unusual cargo from enemy Submarines. On board, for the voyage, are President Roosevelt, Generals Marshall and Arnold, Admiral King and approximately 50 other Staff Officers, including Major General E.M. "Pa" Watson, and Admirals Wilson Brown and W. D. Leahy.

During a mock drill, an escort Destroyer inadvertently fires a torpedo at the *Iowa*. A message of great urgency is radioed to the *Iowa!* "THIS IS NOT A DRILL, THIS IS NOT A DRILL." The President sits atop the Iowa, watching the entire episode without flinching. As the runaway Torpedo continues on course, antiaircraft weapons begin to swirl and commence firing, scorching the water. Shot after shot is released until a round explodes the torpedo, just before it strikes the *Iowa*. The *Iowa's* Captain, John L. McCrea, along with the entire crew, gives a sigh of relief. The *Iowa* enters Mers-el-Kebir at 08:00 on the 20th. **(Pacific-Philippines)** The U.S.S. *Narwal* (SS-167) makes it to Mindoro, Philippines and lands men and supplies at Paluan Bay. Two days later, the *Narwal* surfaces, to drop off supplies at Nasipit and evacuates personnel. **(Pacific-Solomons-Bougainville)** More elements of the 37th Division, U.S.A., commanded by Major General Robert S. Beightler, arrive. Marines attached to the 2nd Battalion, 21st Marines, advance cautiously from their beachhead along the Numa Numa Trail, Bougainville to establish an outpost. A Coconut Grove about 200 yards from the junction of the East West Trail, erupts into a vicious battlefield, as cunning Japanese patiently await the advancing Yanks, then attack furiously. Reinforcements from Companies F and G, rush to bolster Company E and this combined force of Marines, and five Tanks send the Japs running. This action (13-14th), enables the Marines to expand their beachhead an additional 1,500 yards. Off shore, enemy Planes attack Rear Admiral Merrill's Task Force on Empress Augusta Bay, damaging the Light Cruiser U.S.S. *Denver* (CL-58). **(Pacific-New Britain)** The preinvasion bombardment of Tarawa-Makin commences, as the U.S. Fifth Air Force begins Air assaults against enemy positions on the Atoll. The Heavy Bombers receive Antiaircraft fire from land batteries but enemy Airpower is slight. **(Pacific-Gilberts-Marshalls)** U.S. Planes attached to Task Force 57, initiate raids on Japanese positions at various Bases in the Gilberts and Marshalls, on a daily basis, until the 19th. During the missions, complete photographic coverage of the bases is acquired by U.S. Planes. **(Atlantic-Italy)** In the U.S. Fifth Army area, the offensive is virtually stalled. Fierce enemy resistance drives the 157th Infantry from Hill 640, soon after they reach the peak. Acquafondata, the objective, cannot be secured until the enemy resistance on Hills 640 and 769 is eradicated.

November 14th 1943 — (Pacific-Bougainville) The fight for control of the junction of the Numa Numa- East-West trails ends with the 21st Marines the victors. **(China-Burma-India)** Allied Airfields in India, are about to receive B-29s. In an effort to prepare the fields for handling these large Planes, Engineers and dump truck Companies receive orders to proceed to India. **(Atlantic-Italy)** General Mark Clark's Fifth Army continues to meet murderous fire from the Germans, who still command the high ground on the route to Cassino. In the British 10th Corps area, the British 56th Division pulls back from Mont Camino, as previously planned. In the VI Corps area, the offensive comes to a halt. The Germans have held and the course of the battle is still in question, as the U.S. Fifth Army begins to temporarily abandon the offensive to regroup before making the next thrust toward the mystifying Monastery at the peak of Monte Cassino. **(Atlantic-Russia)** Battle-weary Germans, near the brink of disaster counterattack to regain Zhitomir from the Red Army.

November 15th 1943 — (United States) Certificate No. 366, signed by William C. Moore, Division for Soviet Supply, Office of Lend-Lease Administration authorizes the export of 1,000 grams of "heavy water" (deuterium oxide) needed for the developing of an atomic bomb. Hermann C. Rosenberg (Chematar Inc.) had acquired the chemicals from Stuart Oxygen Co. (San Francisco) which ship the order to Chematar in New York, from where it is reshipped to the Soviet Purchasing Commission in Washington, D.C. From D.C., it arrives in Montana on 29 November and is funneled through Lend-Lease (over 41 pounds at a cost of $80 an ounce) to the Soviet Union. During February 1945, Rosenberg receives another 100 grams of the "heavy water," again from Stuart Oxygen Company and delivers it to the Russians in Washington. The trail of this shipment terminates here. During August of 1945, Hermann Rosenberg becomes an American citizen by naturalization. Major Jordan notes that: "WITH COMMUNIST TENACITY AND ARDENT SUPPORT FROM THE WHITE HOUSE AND LEND-LEASE, THE SOVIET PURCHASING COMMISSION (based in Washington, D.C.) STROVE AGAIN AND AGAIN TO OBTAIN EIGHT AND ONE-HALF TONS EACH OF URANIUM OXIDE AND URANIUM NITRATE, PLUS 25 POUNDS OF URANIUM METAL (begins February 43) AND PERSISTED UNTIL THE RUSSIANS WERE SQUELCHED BY SECRETARY STIMSON DURING APRIL, 1944." **(Pacific)** Major General Holland "Howlin Mad" Smith, U.S.M.C., Commander V Amphibious Corps, issues Operation Plan 2-43, the original overall troops directive for the seizure of the Marshalls. The 2nd Marine Division, (designated Attack Force) is now aware of its objective. They had departed Wellington, New Zealand, expecting to participate in practice maneuvers at Hawkes Bay, then return to Base for liberty. Their neatly packed liberty clothes will not be used for some time. Their genuine destination is Efate, New Hebrides to rendezvous with Admiral Hill's Attack Force (Task Force 52). The ruse had been implemented to ensure secrecy of the upcoming invasion The U.S.S. *Nautilus* and U.S. Planes have been gathering intelligence for the operation (Galvanic) during September. An aerial photo of enemy latrines turns out to be invaluable. Enemy strength is estimated by the number of Officers' latrines; the figure is accurate. Meanwhile, Admiral Turner's Task Force is en route from Hawaii; the forces converge near the Marshalls on the 17th. In other activity in the Pacific Theater, the U.S. Navy establishes a Naval Auxiliary Air Facility and a Naval Air Base at Funafuti, in the Ellice Islands. **(China-Burma-India)** On the northern Burma Front, the Chinese 38th Division sends in reinforcements to bolster the 112th Regiment. The 114th Regiment arrives shortly and is followed by the 113th in the beginning of December. In the

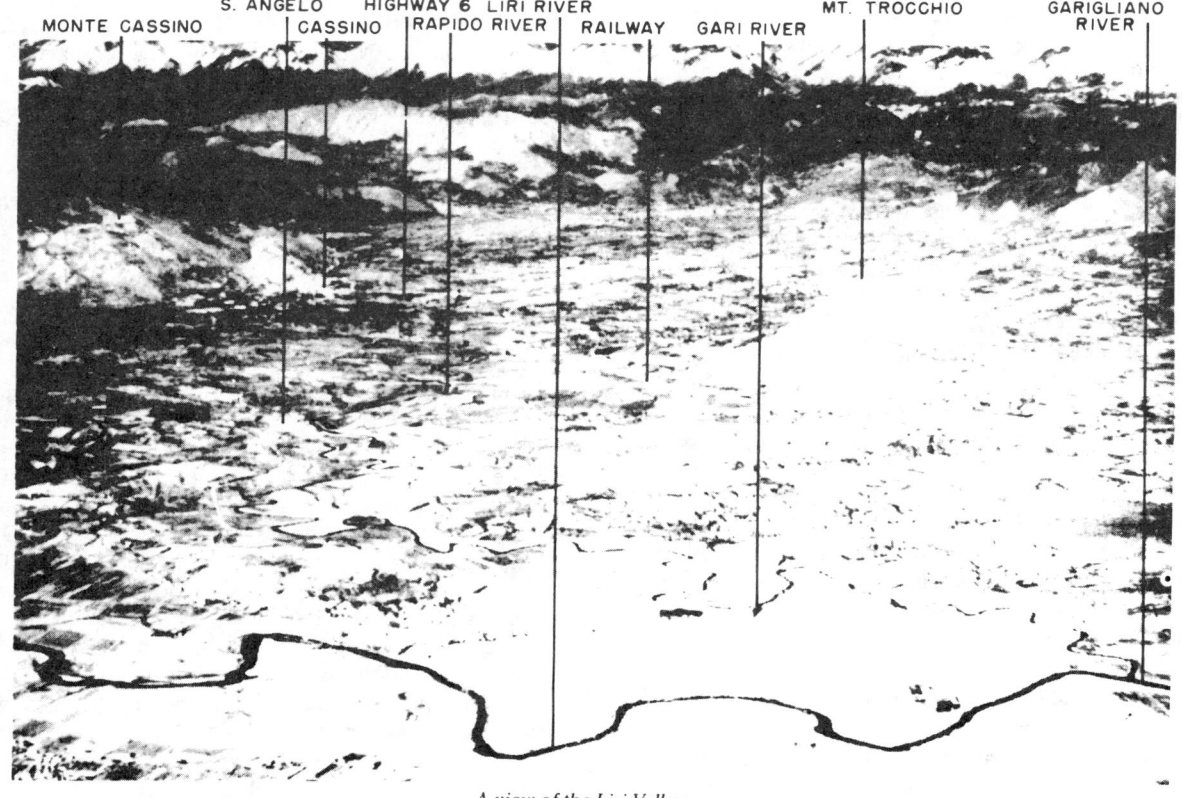

*Monte Cassino and its Benedictine Monastery standing high in the sky,
with a dominating view of the Liri Valley and the Rapido Valley.*

MONTE CASSINO · S. ANGELO · CASSINO · HIGHWAY 6 · RAPIDO RIVER · LIRI RIVER · RAILWAY · GARI RIVER · MT. TROCCHIO · GARIGLIANO RIVER

A view of the Liri Valley.

274

British Fourteenth Army sector, the Japanese drive the British from Fort White and occupy it. General Wheeler becomes principal Administrative Officer, SEAC, and is replaced as Commander SOS CBI, by Major General William E. R. Covell. British General Sir Alan Brooke receives a similar post with General Auchinleck's India Command. **(Atlantic-Italy)** In the U.S. Fifth Army area, the Allies halt their advance against the German Winter Line to regroup for another assault. The British 7th Armored Division withdraws from the left flank of the British 10th Corps area and returns to England. The British 46th Division fills in the gap on the left flank, replacing the 7th Armored. The American 82nd Airborne which has primarily been policing Naples, will also be returned to England. The U.S. 1st Armored Division begins arriving at Naples.

November 16th 1943 — (Pacific-Solomons-Bougainville) Supply problems are greatly alleviated as a supply road is completed from the Koromokina beachhead to the Piva River. **(Pacific-Marshalls)** An American Carrier Group from Espiritu Santo, attacks Nauru Island to immobilize the enemy Planes on the Airfield, eliminating them as a threat against the imminent invasion of the Gilberts. **(Pacific-Japan)** The Japanese Minelayer *Ukishima* is sunk by a torpedo off the coast of Japan. **(Atlantic-Mediterranean)** The Germans complete their occupation of Leros Island, off Greece. **(Atlantic Italy) 15th Army Group** In the U.S. Fifth Army area, the near exhausted 3rd Division is relieved by the 36th Division (Texas) in Mignano Gap. In the **British Eighth Army** sector, General Montgomery is ordered to commence an attack against the enemy line at Ortona-Laciano, but inclement weather prompts Montgomery to postpone the assault. The British 78th Division secures a bridgehead on the north bank of the Sangro River and begins to stretch it out.

November 17th 1943 — (Pacific-Australia) The U.S.S. *Capelin* (SS-289), commanded by Lt. Commander E.E. Marshall, departs Darwin. This is the last day there is any communication with the Ship. All hands soon will be lost without a trace. **(Pacific-Gilberts-Marshalls)** Up to this point, American Bombers (Seventh Air Force) have flown 141 sorties against enemy positions, dropping approximately 173 tons of bombs. These preinvasion bombardments continue for another two days. In addition, U.S. Destroyers bombard Buka and its Airfield. **(Pacific-Solomons)** The final detachments of the 21st Marines arrive in Bougainville, however, the U.S.S. *McKean* (APD-5), a Transport, is sunk by an enemy Plane, before it makes port. **(Pacific-New Guinea)** Contingents of the 9th Australian Division assault the well fortified positions of the Japanese at Sattelberg, which is protected by natural defenses as well as fanatical Japanese. The Australian Infantry is assisted by Aircraft, Artillery and Tanks. **(Atlantic-Russia)** The Soviets take Korosten in the Kiev area, but the Germans make progress near Zhitomir. Rechitsa is taken by the Soviets and Gomel is threatened.

November 18th 1943 — (Pacific-Celebes Sea) The U.S.S. *Bluefish* (SS-222) sinks the Japanese Vessel *Sanae*, one of Japan's older Destroyers. **(Pacific-Gilberts-Marshalls)** American Planes continue to raid enemy positions. The Army-Marine Strike Force heading for the Gilberts will meet extraordinary defensive positions at Betio. The Japanese Commander, Admiral Shibasaki has boasted: "THE AMERICANS COULDN'T TAKE BETIO WITH A MILLION MEN IN A HUNDRED YEARS." The Japanese have fortified Betio in such fashion that nearly every square inch of beach is under fire

from all flanks. The gun emplacements are buried deeply and bolstered by layers of thick concrete and palmetto logs. The pill boxes are constructed with steel. Before the Invasion Force encounters these obstacles, it must overcome a network of natural reefs that loiter anxiously to entrap Landing Craft. In addition, the enemy has strung out blankets of barbed wire, supplemented by mines and generous applications of concrete obstacles which resemble miniature pyramids that protrude from the reefs, ready to tear the bottom from unsuspecting Landing Craft. Today, the LSTs are spotted by an enemy Patrol Plane. Japanese Bombers are launched to attack the Armada, but Carrier-based Planes intercept and drive them away. On the 19th, the Convoy is approached by an enemy Bomber, but it is quickly destroyed and the Convoy maintains its course. **(Atlantic-Italy) 15th Army Group, U.S. Fifth Army** sector, General Keyes is given a zone of operation and assumes Command of the 3rd and 36th U.S. Divisions. The VI Corps contains the 34th and 45th Divisions. In other activity in the Atlantic, the PT-311 is sunk after striking a mine off Corsica.

U.S. Marines on Bougainville, sporting five enemy flags on their 40-mm Antiaircraft gun, pass the ammunition.

GIs lugging supplies through the mountains with a Mule Pack Train.

November 19th 1943 — (North Pacific-Aleutians) The Submarine Chaser SC-1067 is lost off the Aleutians in the vicinity of Attu, due to foundering. **(Pacific-Bismarcks)** The U.S. Fifth Air Force increases intensity of raids against enemy positions on New Britain. **(Pacific-Carolines)** Japanese Destroyers cripple the Submarine U.S.S. *Sculpin* off Truk Island. Additional depth charges strike a killing mortal blow. Captain John Philip Cromwell, aware of special Submarine tactics and strategy for the upcoming major offensive in the Pacific, orders his Vessel to surface and fight the Japanese Naval Force. Subsequently the crew is ordered to abandon the death Ship, however, Cromwell remains on board, sacrificing himself rather than be captured for the information, preventing the Japs from ascertaining American Submarine strategy, scheduled Fleet movements and specific attack plans. Captain Cromwell had been Commander of a Submarine Attack Group with his Flag aboard the *Sculpin*. His Group is the vanguard of the first large scale offensive in the Pacific. He has established a solid chain of Submarines extending to the primary enemy stronghold at Truk. For his extraordinary act of courage for his country, he is posthumously awarded the Medal of Honor. **(Pacific-Gilberts-Marshalls)** American Air raids against the Gilberts, Marshalls and Nauru, end with the assumption that the massive bombardment has devastated resistance on Makin and Tarawa Atolls. Meanwhile, the U.S. Invasion Force closes on the lagoon and anchors about six miles from the beaches. In other activity, the U.S.S. *Nautilus* (SS-168), a Submarine, is accidentally hit by U.S. Naval Fire off the Gilberts. **(Pacific-New Guinea)** The PT-147 becomes grounded off the eastern coast of New Guinea and is subsequently sunk by U.S. Forces. **(Atlantic-Italy) 15th Army Group** In the **British Eighth Army** Area, the enemy has completely withdrawn across the Sangro River in the Indian 8th Division sector. **(Atlantic-Soviet Union)** The Germans close on Zhitomir, forcing the Russians to withdraw to avoid encirclement

Strike Force at Makin and remain with General Ralph Smith for that campaign. For several days, relentless bombardments have delivered in excess of four million pounds of explosives against these Japanese positions. The Japanese have boasted that Tarawa could not be taken at any cost. A preinvasion message from Admiral Spruance is read to the men. The message points in the direction of success and co-operation, in part: "CLOSE CO-OPERATION BETWEEN ALL ARMS AND SERVICES, THE SPIRIT OF LOYALTY TO EACH OTHER, AND THE DETERMINATION TO SUCCEED DISPLAYED BY VETERAN AND UNTRIED PERSONNEL ALIKE." The message further states: "WE WILL NEVER STOP UNTIL WE HAVE ACHIEVED SUCCESS." General Smith also gives his words of encouragement to the 2nd Marine Division: "THE DIVISION HAD BEEN ESPECIALLY CHOSEN BY THE HIGH COMMAND FOR THE ASSAULT ON TARAWA BECAUSE OF ITS BATTLE EXPERIENCE AND COMBAT EFFICIENCY." ..."YOUR SUCCESS WILL ADD NEW LAURELS TO THE GLORIOUS TRADITION OF OUR CORPS. GOOD LUCK AND GOD BLESS YOU ALL."

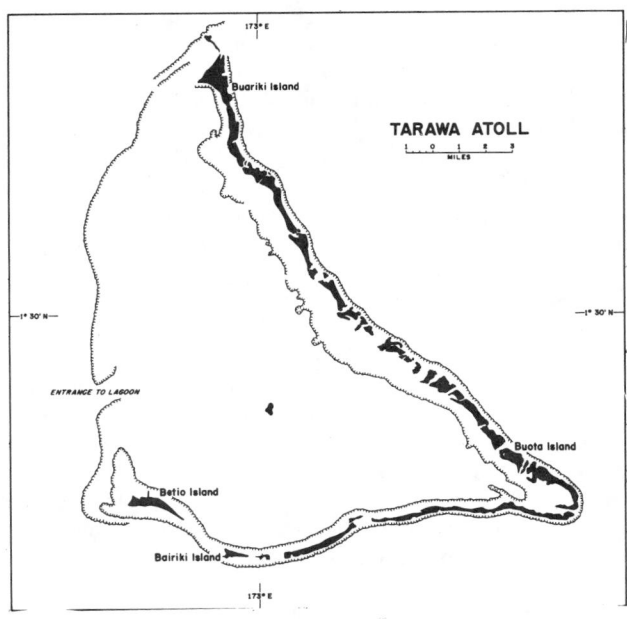

Map of Tarawa Atoll.

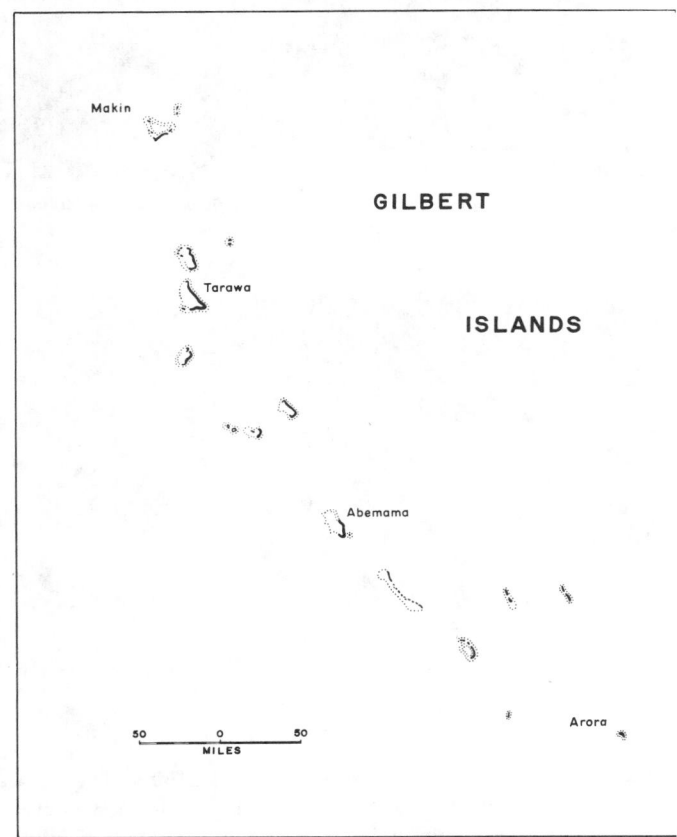

Map of the Gilbert Islands.

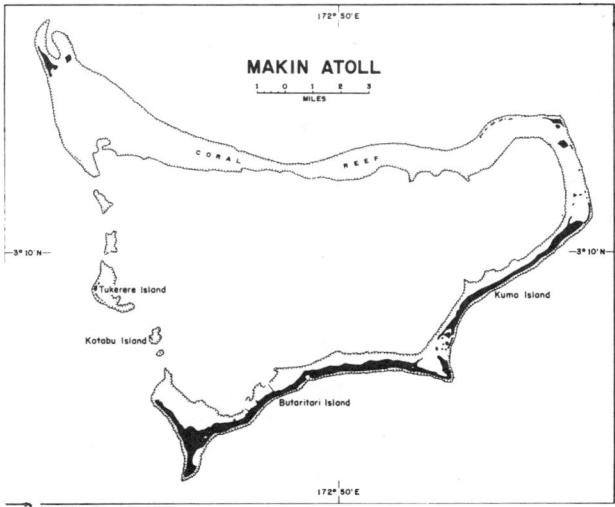

Makin Atoll Map.

November 20th-23rd 1943 — THE BATTLE OF TARAWA and MAKIN — The Army will storm Makin, and the Marines, will seize Tarawa and Betio, on the southwestern tip of the atoll. Major General Holland M. Smith, U.S.M.C., Commanding Officer of the Amphibious Force, chooses to land with the Army

November 20th 1943 — The U.S.S. Essex off the Gilberts during Operation Galvanic.

Before Dawn (03:55), assault troops board Landing Craft. At 05:07, surviving Japanese shore guns commence firing. U.S. Naval Guns track the origin of the incoming shells by searching for the location of gunfire flashes. Successive salvos hit the mark and create a huge explosion that temporarily quiets the guns. The Navy reinitiates its bombardment about 06:00 to allow safe passage for the Carrier Planes to resume their assault. Japanese defenses are pummeled. Smoke and debris cloaks the area including the lagoon, but there is still enemy firepower on shore and the Strike Force has no knowledge of how much has survived. Meanwhile, the two-pronged invasion is already running behind schedule.

The invasion of Makin goes off as scheduled at 08:30 and meets nominal opposition, allowing an Army Regimental Combat Team, attached to the 27th Division to move inland quickly and secure a beachhead perimeter and also to flush out light enemy resistance up to Ukiangong Point.

At Tarawa, things turn out much differently than anticipated. Prior to the assault, Marines are promised light resistance because of the relentless bombardments. Someone forgets to tell the Japanese. Three waves of Marines await the order to strike. A smoke screen is laid to obstruct the enemy's view of two Minesweepers, the *Pursuit* and *Requisite*, which are clearing the channel. Suddenly, enemy guns commence firing at the Minesweepers. Two Destroyers, shepherding the Minesweepers, the *Dashiel* and the *Ringgold*, unleash lethal dosages of shells themselves and eliminate the threatening shore guns, then proceed into the lagoon in the event their

guns are needed again. Soon after, other enemy guns fire upon the *Ringgold*, however, the hits fail to detonate. Again, the Destroyers strike paydirt, hitting a plump ammunition dump that quickly eradicates the threat and knocks out the guns. Some of the larger enemy shore guns have been captured from the British and transported to Tarawa.

The Assault Force approaches the channel pass at 07:15, however, the Landing Craft become blinded, as the incessant bombarding creates a wall of smoke and dust. The *Pursuit's* searchlight penetrates the haze and guides the Marines through safely, however, the operation is now one-half hour behind schedule.

The 2nd Scout Sniper Platoon, led by Lt. William Hawkins has the tedious task of knocking out a massive enemy stronghold at the edge of Long Pier in synchronization with the final wave of Planes that are strafing the beachhead at tree top level at 08:55. The Marines strike hard, quickly overcoming the defenders who are unable to repulse the Marines and their accompaniment of Flamethrowers. The emplacement is destroyed and along with it a portion of the pier. Mission accomplished, they depart in the LCVP, however, it gets hung up on the sinister reefs. Quick action on their part, transfers them to an LVT and they make it to shore.

Three waves of troops head for the beach objectives, designated Red 1, 2, and 3, against severe fire. Landing Craft become helplessly strung along the reefs, forcing the Marines to walk to the beach through a gauntlet of fire. The paralyzed Craft are trapped in a sea of horrors. Dead troops are slumped over the controls of Vehicles. The Marines have three beaches to take and at this time the Jap guns are confining many on the reefs. Those attempting to make it to Red Beach 2 are riddled with bullets from several directions. Suddenly, additional Japanese guns pound the Marines causing more casualties. Meanwhile, a Japanese Vessel strafes the Marines as they struggle to get to shore. U.S. Dive Bombers swoop down and pummel the Vessel, but each time the gunners are blown away, additional crews take their place. Finally, a Dive Bomber scores a direct hit. A blatant shortage of Amtracs magnifies the problem facing the invasion force. In addition, radio equipment has been lost to the surf and those which reach shore are unreliable. Two Platoons of Company E, 2nd Battalion, 2nd Marines make it to Beach Red 2. Other units divert to Beach Red 1, and advance over the seawall and eliminate a machine gun nest. Soon after, Marines take up residence in a vacant oversized bomb crater. Company F, 2nd Battalion, 2nd Marines also moves against Red Beach 2, under the same withering fire, taking grievous casualties, while forcing its way inland about fifty yards, where remnants of the Company Riflemen and Machinegunners fortify their tenuous positions. Later, Colonel Shoup arrives on Beach Red 2 and sets up his Command Post; three Sherman Tanks arrive to bolster the beachhead. Four other Tanks arrive at Beach Red 3 to bolster Colonel Crowe and one is lost to the surf. The boats that reach shore continue to come under murderous fire and the majority of men stranded on the reefs in the Higgins Boats (Landing Craft Vehicle and Personnel) are nearly annihilated. The enemy fire is so devastating that many of the Landing Craft land on the wrong beaches.

The situation of the 3rd Battalion, 2nd Marines on Red Beach 1, also remains grave. Company K, takes a severe thrashing and the survivors that reach the bloodied beach cramp low and tight under an iron cloud of enemy shellfire. To its rear, the sea is strewn with dead and wounded Marines, flanked by useless Vehicles, while others still operable struggle to aid survivors and ferry more men to shore. Company I, 3rd Battalion, 2nd Marines, also takes heavy casualties. Meanwhile, Company G comes under a furious fusillade, forcing one Platoon to land to the right of Beach Red 1.

Other landings by Companies E, and F, 3rd Battalion, 2nd Marines, receive similar fates. A fourth wave comprising Company L, 3rd Battalion, 2nd Marines, runs right into the Naval junkyard scattered along the reefs and maneuvers around the sunken Japanese Vessel and attempts to walk from the reefs. The stark reality is that it takes thirty-three percent casualties.

Marines pinned down on the beach at Betio.

The beachhead at Betio.

There is one glaring candle in this drama of death. The Destroyers *Ringgold* and *Dashiel* are in close proximity to the 2nd Battalion, 8th Marines, as it attempts to secure Beach Red 3, another of the ominous Japanese positions. The guns of the Destroyers, combined with the onrushing waves, being transported in proper Vehicles (LVTs) give the Yanks an ounce of success. The first wave strikes at 09:22, followed closely behind by two additional waves. The 2nd Battalion, 8th Marines penetrates a gap in the seawall and drives straight to the enemy landing strip, giving the Marines on Red 3, a hairpin line extending into the heart of the enemy positions. Thanks to the Navy, their casualty rate is nominal, but the fight is a long way from over. The skies remain clear.

Survivors amidst a line of Dead Marines at the water's edge at Betio.

Still, shrouds of dust and debris obscure vision, and the extreme temperature during mid-morning is already taking a toll on the bodies, creating a nauseous odor.

At 09:59, most of the 3rd Battalion, 2nd Marines, under Major Schoettel, remain stranded on the reefs. Schoettel using one of the few operating radios, calls Colonel Shoup, stating: "TROOPS HELD UP ON REEF ON RIGHT FLANK OF RED 1." "TROOPS RECEIVING HEAVY FIRE IN WATER." Shoup responds: "LAND RED 2 AND WORK WEST." Schoettel answers Shoup: "WE HAVE NOTHING LEFT TO LAND." Schoettel and the remnants of the 3rd Battalion, 2nd Marines, remain on the reefs unable to penetrate the enemy fire. During the afternoon, the Battalion receives another message from Shoup: "LAND AT ANY COST." The besieged Battalion reaches Beach Red 2 near evening instead of its initial objective (Beach Red 1).

The situation is grave. Never in the history of the Corps, have the Marines been positioned so badly and so close to being thrown back to the sea. To make the predicament worse, no Amphibious Vehicles are available for a rescue. More dead Marines line the beaches, some at the water's edge, their heads submerged in the sand, as insensitive waves roll over their corpses. Others, their bodies riddled with enemy bullets, are strewn about the bloodied beach. Still, about 1,500 Marines (many of whom are wounded), are cramped on the tiny beachhead, pinned down by murderous fire. Fanatical Japanese rush to the beaches tossing hand grenades into the Landing Crafts, but the agile Marines pump them right back and hold their ground.

Colonel Shoup and Colonel Carlson (observer) attempt to make it to the beach, but the Japanese compel them and their party to abandon the disabled Vehicle and walk to shore. A Reserve Battalion, 1st Marines, 2nd Battalion, reaches the reefs at 10:30, however, again, improper Vehicles hinder the landing and the Reserves are isolated, anxiously awaiting Amphibious Tractors (LVTs). Some arrive, but enemy guns commence firing and the Vehicles are abandoned, prompting more troops to race through the raging tempest.

Communications remain chaotic at best, but individual heroism and clear-thinking heads maintain discipline. One thing favoring the attackers is that despite an alarming casualty rate for Officers, their training has prepared them to assume positions of command when Officers are shot down. Colonel Shoup observes a wounded Marine (Red 2) that had lost an arm, become the recipient of a thrown enemy grenade. Wasting no time the ambidextrous Marine heaves it back upon the Japanese. At 11:03, the 3rd Battalion, 8th Marines is directed to land at Red Beach 3 to bolster the battered 2nd Battalion, 8th Marines, already there, however, again, no Vehicles (Tractors) are available. By noon, Tractors arrive and two waves sprint toward the beach, but enemy fire repulses the assault and these Marines, under Major Robert Ruad begin wading ashore initiating another walk of endurance. Unsuspecting deep waters clasp many of the Marines, transporting heavy packs, drowning them. Under one hundred men (first wave) make it to the beach. The second wave takes heavy casualties and the third wave is nearly annihilated. The fourth wave reaches the pier, but withdraws and comes ashore later.

At 12:30 (Day 1) Shoup requests that Carlson return to the U.S.S. *Maryland* to give a first hand report to the Commanders. He instructs Carlson to give this message: "TELL THE GENERAL AND THE ADMIRAL THAT WE ARE GOING TO STICK AND FIGHT IT OUT." Shoup, orders an advance at 14:00. General Holland Smith still has one Combat Battalion in Reserve, excluding the Sixth Marines which is being held back to support the Army on Makin. The Army, doing extremely well on Makin, permits the Sixth Marines to be reassigned to the 2nd Division and in addition, the 1st Battalion, 8th Marines is ordered to support the Tarawa invasion. Confusion abounds on the deployment of these men due to severe communication problems and they spend the day and night aboard Landing Crafts. Also, General Holland Smith orders Brigadier General Leo Hermie to go ashore and assume command, however, the directive is not forwarded and Shoup retains control of the ground operation.

During the course of the day's action, the majority of the Marines are confined to their precarious beachhead, but accurate return fire keeps Japanese maneuvering stymied. The balance of the bizarre afternoon continues to extract the strength of the beleaguered Marines. The Sherman Tanks (2nd and 3rd Platoons Company C, I Marine Amphibious Corps Tank Battalion), assigned to the 2nd Marine Division, share in the brutalizing struggle. The three Tanks that reach Shoup on Red 2, are dispatched to Red 1, however, enemy fire compels them to divert and lend their firepower to the troops trying to penetrate the west Taxistrip. One Tank participates, pumping shells into enemy emplacements. The other two are victimized by enemy fire and abandoned. The four Tanks on Red 3, sustain losses. A Japanese Plane destroys one and two others are hit by enemy fire and abandoned. Other Marines, under fire from the enemy stronghold at the Burns-Philp Pier are happy that the one remaining operational Tank is around to give assistance. Intense enemy fire pounds the Tank as it cranks along, but the successive hits fail to waste the Tank.

Colonel Crowe, still commanding the deepest inland positions, begins to regroup his scattered Forces with those of Ruad's 3rd Battalion, 8th Marines to bolster the tenuous hold in the Airfield Triangle. An extraordinary effort to knock out a large enemy emplacement proves costly. Flamethrowers and Demolition Teams move straight ahead. Another contingent of the 2nd Battalion, 8th Marines' attempts to flank the deadly bunker. The combined thrust fails to destroy the obstacle and the Infantry Platoon operating on the flank is nearly wiped out. The assault stalls, then aborted by Crowe. A unit of the 3rd Battalion, 8th Marines drives further inland and becomes threatened by enemy troops bolstered by a Tank. Quick redirection of several 37-mm guns repulses the attack which includes about 200 enemy troops.

The 1st Battalion, 2nd Marines, commanded by Major Kyle, had come ashore on Red Beach 2, bolstering the 2nd Battalion, 2nd Marines, commanded by Colonel Jordan who had assumed the position after the death of Lt. Colonel Herbert Amey, killed during the initial invasion). Meanwhile, the 2nd Marines continue to take more casualties as it advances within the Triangle; 57 men attached to Jordan's command hold the point.

Menacing enemy fire continues throughout the day on Beach Red 1, where Major Ryan is wedging his command forward. Six Sherman Tanks attempt to make it to Beach One to assist the besieged 3rd Battalion, 2nd Marines, but bodies of dead Marines obstruct their passage. Choosing not to move through the wounded and dead, the Tanks divert to Green Beach and four Tanks are lost to deep water in the process. Rather than face possible annihilation, Ryan, improvises his attack plans and decides to take Green Beach. The Tanks supplement the advance initially but one is knocked out and the other crippled. In addition to the obvious supply and communication problems, the asult is severely short of Flamethrower fuel and explosives. The Marines destroy the resistance that they can handle and avoid those too strong to attack without heavy weapons. The attack, initiated at 14:00, continues for about four hours and advances to within 300 yards of the southern shore, when Ryan withdraws to set up a night perimeter.

The Japanese spend the night infiltrating Marine lines and boarding some of the skeleton Vehicles lying dead in the water to ambush reinforcements heading toward the beach on the 21st. There is a conspicuous absence of mortars and there is no major counterattack. The Marines also get a bonus when Japanese Planes swarm over the island to blast American positions and mistakenly bomb Japanese positions, too. The Americans take advantage of the inactivity of the enemy and bring in additional men and Artillery including Lt. Colonel Presley Rixey's 1st Artillery Battalion, 10th Marines.

On this second day on Tarawa, the Marines will pay heavily again while attempting to expand their tiny beachhead. The 1st Battalion, 8th Marines, waiting in Landing Crafts since the previous day, receives its untangled orders to assault and is delegated to land on Red 2, then attack toward Red Beach 1, to bolster Ryan with his effort to seize Green Beach. The 1st Battalion's first wave scurries toward the reefs in LCVPs, passing the broken chain of green uniforms, blanketing the bodies of slain Marines which are being swished back and forth in the surf.

The 1st wave comes under riveting enemy fire, directed by Japanese deployed on the abandoned Vehicles. Three additional waves rush toward the reefs while the fifth wave is held back until the Navy can lend assistance. Marines, observing the spectacle from the beach, begin charging enemy pillboxes with audacious courage to divert fire. Rixey's Howitzers are redeployed and the barrels roar, opening up in cadence with Navy Hellcats which score damage with their machine guns, however, their bombs miss the mark. Rixey's Artillery picks up the slack and the Japs on the reefs in the two bunkers are silenced, permitting the 1st Battalion, under Major Lawrence Hays, to reach the beachhead. Although casualties are high, they attempt to drive toward Ryan's Force, but lacking Flamethrowers and Heavy Weapons, the palisade of piercing enemy fire prevents any advance.

Major Ryan is not deterred by the unavailability of reinforcements. In fact he has been heavily engaged for an hour before the attack of Hays' Battalion begins. Ryan's marauders are perched and ready for the attack at 11:00 hours. One Officer, Lt. Greene, spots targets for an American Destroyer, which commences firing on enemy pillboxes and is joined by another Warship. The Naval symphony continues pounding the enemy positions, gaining the Marines some running room. As the guns cease firing, the men of the 3rd Battalion, 2nd Marines advance and by 12:00, drive to the opposite end of Green Beach. The Marines drive speedily, assisted by two battered Sherman Tanks, one retrieved from the reefs and the other a crippled survivor of the initial fighting. The victors continue to drive inland behind the heat of the Demolition Teams and the Flamethrowers, to pay their respects to the landlords, still controlling stiff defenses to the north and south. Colonel Shoup is not yet aware of the progress on Green Beach.

As the hours pass, the tides change, and the Americans get more supplies and men ashore; however, the ferocity of the Japanese has not diminished. Contingents of the 2nd Battalion, 2nd Marines, drive to the positions of the 1st Battalion, 2nd Marine contingent, which is still holding a portion of the Airfield Triangle. In the meantime, the Japanese have closed the opening in their line at the Taxistrip, creating an impenetrable zone. The Marines within the Triangle are cut off. U.S. Planes strike Japanese positions near the Airfield, but the Japs are so closely intertwined that the raid further jeopardizes the stranded Marines and the attacks are aborted. Meanwhile, Shoup receives a message from General Holland Smith at 10:22 inquiring about his present needs: "DO YOU HAVE ENOUGH MEN TO TAKE THE ISLAND?" Shoup responds semi-ambiguously: "SITUATION DOES NOT LOOK GOOD." Smith requests more information and Shoup informs him that Colonel Carlson is delivering further details in person. Undaunted by the holdup at the Taxistrip, Shoup readies another attack, utilizing his Marines and their sparse amounts of ammunition to move swiftly across the Airfield runway. Heavy machine guns are deployed to disturb the enemy nests and distract their attention. At 13:00, Marines bolt from their positions and charge across a 200-foot open space through the Airstrip, sustaining light casualties, and push to the beach on the opposite shore. Subsequently, the Marines come under severe attack and the ensuing struggle extracts heavy casualties from both sides. The Marines, however, hold on and slice the island in half, further splitting the defenders communications. The Marines, holding tenuously on the south shore, tend their wounded and prepare to advance.

While contingents of the 1st and 2nd Battalions, 2nd Marines had been dashing to the beach, Kyle's Machinegunners continue to pound the Japanese in the vicinity of the Airfield (Green Beach) throughout the afternoon in a vicious engagement that culminates with another victory for the Marines who seize the Taxistrip. A subsequent assault, intended to hook up the 1st and 2nd Battalions with Crowe's Force, is abandoned after the available manpower maintaining the hold on the south shore is determined understrength. The protracted struggle extends into another bloodfilled night with the momentum tilting to the Yanks, especially after news of the success on Green Beach reaches Command. Kyle and Company C, eventually reach the south shore. Jordan, Commanding the 2nd Battalion, 2nd Marines since the death of Lt.

Colonel Herbert Amey, relinquishes command to Kyle.

At 16:00 on the 21st, Shoup brings Command up to date on the situation on Betio. In his report he states: "SOME TROOPS IN 232 (TARGET AREA DESIGNATION) DISHING OUT HELL AND CATCHING HELL. PACK HOWITZERS IN POSITION AND REGISTERED FOR SHOOTING ON TAIL. CASUALTIES: MANY. PERCENTAGE DEAD: UNKNOWN. COMBAT EFFICIENCY: WE ARE WINNING. SHOUP."

Colonel Edson comes ashore on the night of the 21st and takes command of the operation on Betio. A major thrust is prepared for the following day, but the Japanese are not finished yet. The Americans, unconcerned about Japanese intentions, are up and about bright and early on the 22nd for the purpose of finishing the operation. Men and equipment have been coming ashore throughout the night. Cruisers and Battleships standing offshore commence a strong bombardment at 07:00. Subsequent 20 minute salvos occur, with the final barrage banging the eastern portion of the island at 10:30. In synchronization with the Naval bombardment, the 3rd Battalion, 6th Marines, commanded by Lt. Colonel McCleod, is standing off Green Beach, waiting for orders to land. Spotters aboard Ship detect enemy troops attempting to swim to Bairiki and orders are changed to intercept and destroy the enemy on Bairoki. The 2nd Battalion, 6th Marines under Murray, get the assignment to wipe them out. Prior to the landing at 17:00, a Naval bombardment commences. Enemy machine guns open up against the troops and the U.S. counters with Planes, which strike the enemy positions and detonate a tank of gasoline. When the Battalion hits the beach there are no Japanese live or dead, except those who had been manning the machine guns.

In conjunction with the principal advance on the 22nd, the 1st Battalion, Sixth Marines lands on the south beach during mid-afternoon setting two precedents: they come in on rafts and they are the first contingent to arrive on Betio without being under fire. They sprint through the positions of the 3rd Battalion, 2nd Marines and drive down the south shore to join the 2nd Marines along the coast. The advance halts about 600 yards short of Jones' perimeter to establish sturdy night positions and act as a support group. The added firepower comes in handy as the night progresses. Meanwhile, infuriated Marines close on Japanese Headquarters, a bombproof blockhouse from which Japanese Admiral Meichi Shibasaki is directing the remnants of his 4,500 defenders. Marines blow up the blockhouse with grenades, gasoline and TNT, which is tossed down the air vents. The pocket is reduced by 10:00 and the two Battalions spread out further on a scavenger hunt across the Airfield giving the Japanese a heavy dosage of American firepower.

McCleod's Command, which had established night positions near Jones, is struck by a massive suicidal attack, however, this counterattack finally allows the Marines to see their elusive targets. Several assaults are mounted by the enemy and begin to further turn the tide toward the Americans. The Yanks deploy their Artillery and combine the firepower of the pieces available on Betio with those on Bairoki to direct protective fire directly in front of American positions. The first attack is beaten back with rifles and bayonets. Successive attacks are also greeted with Artillery and Naval gunfire.

The Japanese mount another counterattack at 23:00 when troops weasel out of the thick brush screaming Banzai and tossing grenades at the 6th Marines during what turns out to be a diversionary feint. The main assault starts with a bang at 03:00 when enemy machine guns pour fire into American positions, preceding an Infantry charge by hundreds of enemy troops. The Yanks return fire with every available piece including the Navy Long guns. Japs are everywhere, making it difficult for the Marines fire to miss. U.S. Artillery shells pour into a concentrated area about 75 yards in front of the Marine lines. The Japanese are being thumped and those that are able to pass the ring of fire and enter American lines are taken out by bayonets. Within about an hour, the assault terminates in failure. When the sun rises on the 23rd, the enemy's numbers are greatly reduced and those still resisting are about to be eliminated either by suicide or U.S. fire.

On the 23rd, at 07:00 the final bells begin to toll ending Japanese control of Tarawa. Carrier-based Planes strike the southeastern tip of Betio, ringing the remaining enemy positions with devastating fire. Still, the enemy holds about 2,000 yards of the beach, but their positions are becoming inundated with incoming shells and bombs from overhead, while being confronted by the Marines to their front and the sea to their backs. Positions are reversed. The Japanese are being vanquished by the Americans and it has not taken 100 years with a million men as the Japanese had bellowed through their propagandists, but rather, the task is handled by the 2nd Marine Division in slightly over three days. The attack carried out by Carrier-based Planes abets and at 07:30, a vigorous bombardment, lasting about fifteen minutes is commenced by Rixey's Artillerymen. In conjunction, the Navy launches another massive bombardment which lifts at 08:00, signaling the final advance to take control of the island. Its a grand march, spearheaded by the nine remaining Tanks. Flamethrowers and enthusiastic Demolition Squads accompany the Infantry as they advance 200 yards without incident, passing dead enemy troops at every step. Many of the remaining occupants of these monuments of Japanese engineering take their own lives as an alternative to surrendering and their powerful fortresses have been transformed into crypts of rubble, scattered between endless areas of jungle growth. McCleod's 3rd Battalion, 6th Marines effectively destroys everything in its path, while driving toward the final resistance still holding on the edge of the island. Additional Naval fire bolsters the effort and by 13:00, the objective is reached by frontal elements of the 6th Marines.

Remaining Japanese, squatting along the boundary line separating Red Beach 1 and Red Beach 2, are wiped out as elements of the 3rd Marines, commanded by Colonel Shoup, drive west. In addition, Company B, 2nd Tank Battalion, lands two Platoons, one grinding into Red 2 and the other reporting to Major Jones on Green Beach.The 2nd and 3rd Battalions, Eighth Marines, under Hays, storm toward Burns Philips Pier and eradicate the staunch enemy bunkers that had plagued the Marines for too long. Schoettel's 3rd Battalion, 2nd Marines, joins the Hays assault team. The force also is supplemented by Half-tracs and Flamethrowers. Within a few hours the remaining bunkers collapse and the attackers cross the Airfield and drive north toward the beach. All is going well for the Americans today. General Julian Smith informs headquarters that the situation has changed again. On the previous day, the Americans had been thinking it would take a longer time to take the island. Smith's dispatch brings pleasurable news to the Commanders offshore. The message in part: "DE-

CISIVE DEFEAT OF ENEMY COUNTERATTACK LAST NIGHT DESTROYED BULK OF HOSTILE RESISTANCE. EXPECT COMPLETE ANNIHILATION OF ENEMY ON BETIO THIS DATE." Coincidentally, this message is dispatched to Admiral Spruance on the *Indianapolis* and to General Holland Smith and Admiral Turner on the *Pennsylvania*, one of the Ships anchored in Pearl Harbor on December 7th 1941. By noon on the 23rd, the Marines control the entire island thanks to the combined efforts of the entire Strike Force. The Naval and Air Support units share in the victory and last but not least the often forgotten Seabees deserve great credit. Their Commanding Officer, Major Henry Drewes had been killed on the first day of the invasion. Undaunted, the Seabees cleared the land and paved the way for the arrival of Planes. One Plane lands today, before the island is declared secure. Some quick words are passed between the Pilot and ground troops and in a flash, the Plane receives minor adjustments and returns to the fight. The gallant Marines lose 1,081 dead (93 die of their wounds) and 2,233 wounded. In addition, 88 men are missing in action and presumed dead. Of over 4,500 Japanese who defended the island, only 17 survive, along with 129 Korean laborers to see the Stars and Stripes replace the Japanese colors. The Betio Island is declared secure at 13:30; however, mop up operations continue for several days on the remainder of the atoll. A defensive posture is taken by the Americans to prepare for any attempt by the enemy to retake the island. General Holland Smith subsequently remarks: "THE NAVAL GUNFIRE AND BOMBING WAS THE REASON FOR OUR SUCCESS. WITHOUT NAVAL GUNFIRE WE COULD NOT HAVE TAKEN THE ISLAND... THE REASON THIS BATTLE WAS WON WAS THAT THESE GREAT AMERICAN MEN WERE DETERMINED THAT THEIR NATION WOULD NOT GO DOWN IN DEFEAT." The Battleship *Mississippi* (BB-41) is damaged, by an accidental explosion; Light Carrier *Independence*, damaged by an Aircraft torpedo; the Destroyers *Ringgold* (DD-500) and *Dashiel* (DD-659) by coastal guns and enemy ground batteries, respectively.

November 20th 1943 — (Pacific-Gilberts-Makin) Task Force 52 lands the 165th Infantry U.S.A., reinforced by 3rd Battalion 105th Infantry, elements of the 193rd Tank Battalion and other support troops. The Invasion Force, commanded by Major General Ralph Smith U.S.A., meets only light resistance allowing them to establish a beachhead. As a diversionary move, troops also land on Kotabu and secure the island without incident. (SEE Nov. 20th-23rd) **(Gilberts-Tarawa-Betio)** The 2nd Marine Division (Bloody Division), hit the beaches, Red 1, Red 2, and Red 3, on the northern coast of Betio after passing savage resistance on the way through the reefs at 09:10, spearheaded by the 2nd Battalion, 8th marines, and the 2nd and 3rd Battalions, 2nd Marines in assault. The 1st Battalion 2nd Marines and the 3rd Battalion, 8th Marines are landed in reserve. Casualties are devastatingly high. In one instance, Sgt. William J. Bordelon 1st Battalion, 18th Marines, (attached to 2nd Marine Division) leading the four survivors of his Landing Craft, destroys 2 enemy pillboxes, then gives cover fire to other Marines attempting to scale the seawall. In addition, Bordelon, while wounded himself, rescues two wounded Marines before finally giving his life, while attacking a fourth machine gun nest. His incalculable heroism is in the finest traditions of the United States fighting man. The Invasion Force is under the overall command of Admiral Spruance. The U.S.S. *Mississippi* (Battleship), the U.S.S. *Inde-*

pendence (Light Carrier) and two Destroyers, the *Ringgold* and *Dashiell* are damaged. The *Independence* becomes the first C.V.L. to be seriously damaged during 1943 and the first of the Navy's newly-delivered Fleet of Carriers to sustain damage. The Independence, struck by three torpedoes (Jap Betty's double engine Bombers) makes it to the Ellice Islands (SEE Nov. 20th-23rd).

The Yanks attack a bomb proof strong point on Betio.

Wounded Marines being evacuated to offshore Ships for treatment.

November 20th 1943 — U.S. Light Tanks on Butaritari Island.

A Japanese Tank after an encounter with a U.S. Tank on Butaritari Island.

Its not a Witch Doctor, just a Marine with a sense of battlefield humor.

*November 20th 1943 — Marines on Betio advancing from behind a
beach barricade of logs.*

November 19th-20th 1943 — American positions on Bougainville, under bombardment by Japanese Aircraft.

A devastated Japanese Command Post on Betio and a destroyed enemy Tank after capture by the Marines.

November 21st 1943 — (Pacific-Gilberts-Makin) The 165th Infantry, quickly seizes an enemy position between the West and East Tank Barriers as it drives eastward toward Stone Pier. **(Pacific-Gilberts-Tarawa)** The 1st Battalion, 8th Marines land on Red Beach 2 to bolster forces already there. The 2nd Battalion 2nd Marines assisted by Companies A and B, 1st Battalion and the majority of the 2nd Battalion drive to the southern coast of the island to divide the enemy forces, while the 3rd Battalion, 2nd Marines, commanded by Major Ryan,

secures Green Beach. Elements of the 6th Marines land on the western tip of Bairoki Island late in the day, to cut off the Japanese attempting to escape the clutches of the Marines on Betio. While the Marines concentrate against the enemy on Betio, contingents of the 2nd Tank Battalion advance up the atoll in search of Japanese at Eita, but find none; another contingent locates an enemy pocket at Buota. During the struggle to secure Betio, many men die; in one instance of heroism, 1st Lt. Hawkins leads an assault against an impregnable enemy position, defended by 5 machine guns and destroys it. Although Lt. Hawkins becomes severely wounded, he refuses to withdraw and continues to lead his men against additional enemy pillboxes, knocking out three more before an machine gun fire kills him. Lt. Hawkins becomes the recipient of the Medal of Honor posthumously. On the Apamama Atoll, in the Gilberts, the V Amphibious Reconnaissance Company departs the Submarine U.S.S. *Nautilus* (SS-168) and lands on Joe Island. It encounters light resistance, and wipes it out, then advances to the next islet on the Atoll.

November 21st-25th 1943 — (Pacific-Solomons-Bougainville) The 3rd Marines expands its perimeter in the Piva Forks area, to eliminate any additional major enemy threats. During this operation, the 2nd and 3rd Battalions, 3rd Marines, defeat the Japanese 23rd Infantry in a vicious battle line that stretches 800 yards along the east fork of the Piva River on the 24th.

November 22nd 1943 — (Pacific-Gilberts-Makin) The U.S. 165th Infantry drives east toward Butaritari, advancing beyond East Tank Barrier, which has been evacuated by the Japanese. A Japanese counterattack during the night is repulsed; its fanatical Banzai assault force is wiped out. The Army pursues the fleeing remnants of the enemy by dispatching Company A, Boat Landing Team 1 to cut their escape route at the neck of the island and also sends another detachment to intercept the retreating enemy on Kuma Island. Admiral Turner declares the island secure, however, the Americans have yet to reconnoiter the eastern portion of the island. **(Pacific-Gilberts-Tarawa)** The U.S. again unleashes an intense bombardment of Japanese positions, using the combined guns of Naval Vessels, Planes and Field Artillery to assist the Marine ground forces. (SEE November 20th-23rd). In one incident concerning the innumerable acts of courage on Betio, 1st Lt. Alexander Bonnyman Jr., attached to the 2nd Battalion, 8th Marines, tires of being pinned down by enemy fire (20th) and leads his Squad off the Pier and onto the beach, then he proceeds to force a gap in the enemy lines by knocking out several enemy positions. Today, Bonnyman creeps out about 40 yards in front of U.S. positions and knocks out a large enemy bunker in his first step to eliminate the primary bunker containing several hundred enemy troops. Although under intense fire the entire time, he continues to advance. About 100 enemy troops are killed during a breakout attempt; the remainder are eliminated after they refuse to surrender. Bonnyman holds his ground against a severe attack, killing three more enemy troops before he becomes mortally wounded. Bonnyman receives the Medal of Honor posthumously for his actions. Colonel Shoup, (later General) is responsible for the entire land operation and although he himself has been seriously wounded, while coming ashore, his courageous action and distinctive leadership, masterminds the victory; he also is awarded the Medal of Honor. In other activity, in the Gilberts, the Destroyers *Frazier*

(DD-607), and *Meade* (DD-602), decide to play crunch the monkey and soon after, both Vessels ram the Japanese Submarine I-35. The *Frazier* receives some damage, but the I-35 folds like a can of fish and sinks. **(Pacific-New Guinea)** Heavy fighting continues in the vicinity of Sattelberg as the Australian 26th Brigade claws to the southern slopes. **(SWPA)** General MacArthur, already preparing to invade New Britain, adds Arawe as a second objective. **(Atlantic-Italy) 15th Army Group**; in the **British Eighth Army** area, five Battalions of the British 5 Corps reach the north bank of the Sangro River.

Admiral Halsey conferring with U.S. Officers in the Solomons.

Some Marines who are not coming home, at rest in a temporary cemetery on Tarawa.

November 24th 1943 — There she goes! The Stars and Stripes flies over Betio, Tarawa.

November 22nd-26th 1943 — (Atlantic-Egypt) (Sextant Conference) President Roosevelt, Prime Minister Churchill and Generalissimo Chiang Kai-shek meet in Cairo. On the 23rd, the Combined Chiefs confer with Roosevelt, Churchill, and Chiang Kai-shek and his wife on the situation in Burma. On the 25th, the British once again attempt to shift the priority to the Mediterranean, by calling for postponing the Normandy invasion and concentrating on the Aegean Sea and Turkey. The U.S. again disagrees and no agreement is reached.

November 23rd 1943 — (Pacific-Gilberts-Makin) Advance contingents of the 165th Infantry progress to the tip of Butaritari Island ending organized resistance on the island by 10:30. **(Pacific-Gilberts-Tarawa)** Enemy resistance on Betio ceases as the 3rd Battalion, 6th Marines drives through the 1st Battalion lines and clears the remaining area of enemy resistance, reaching the southeast tip of Betio by about 13:00. The 3rd Marines destroy the enemy pocket between Beaches Red 1 and 2. Major General Julian C. Smith, Commanding Officer 2nd Marine Division, declares the island secure at 13:30. **(Pacific-Solomons-Bougainville)** The 1st Marine Paratroop Battalion arrives to bolster the ongoing operation to wipe out enemy resistance. The U.S. Navy joins in, when Rear Admiral A. S. Merrill's Cruiser Destroyer Task Force bombards Buka-Bonis. **(Pacific-New Guinea)** The PT-322 becomes grounded off New Guinea and is later sunk by U.S. Forces. **(China-Burma-India)** The Japanese seize the Command Post of the 112th Regiment, Chinese 38th Division. In other activity, the U.S.S. *Gudgeon* (SS-211) sinks the Japanese Frigate *Wakamiya* in the East China Sea. **(Atlantic-Italy) 15th Army Group** In the **U.S. Fifth Army** Area, an elite group of American and Canadian troops, commanded by Colonel Robert T. Frederick arrives and is assigned to the 36th U.S. Division.

A short-circuited Japanese searchlight on Tarawa.

November 22nd 1943 — The U.S. Infantry on Makin during the seizure of the East Tank Barrier.

November 24th 1943 — (United States) The U.S. Navy is greeted with another Carrier, the U.S.S. *Wasp* (CV-18), christened in honor of the valiant *Wasp* (CV-7), which had been sunk on September 15th 1942. **(Pacific-Gilberts-Makin)** Regimental Combat Team 165, U.S.A., minus the 3rd Battalion, heads for Hawaii. Construction Forces and support troops remain on the island under the command of Colonel Clesen H. Tenney U.S.A. Army casualties during the Makin Operation; 58 killed, 160 wounded (eight men die of their wounds). Enemy dead; 550. Subsequent to the 24th, additional enemy troops die during mop up. **(Pacific-Gilberts-Tarawa)** The 2nd Defense Battalion arrives from Samoa to replace the 2nd and 8th Marines which departs for Kamuela, Hawaii. Major General Julian Smith, 2nd Marine Division Commander, instructs Brigadier General Leo Hermle to assault and occupy the Apamama Atoll (3rd Battalion, 6th Marines). The 2nd Battalion, 6th Marines, supported by Scouts of the 2nd Tank Battalion, begin their long trek through the jungles of the islands stretching up the eastern side of the atoll to eliminate any remaining the Japanese. In other activity, elements of the 3rd Battalion, 10th Marines, moves north to scout the area around Ida Island. Also in the Gilberts, the U.S.S. *Liscome Bay* (CVE-56), an Escort Carrier, is sunk by an enemy torpedo, costing the lives of 644 men. A young colored Sailor, Dorie Miller, is among the dead on the *Liscome Bay*. He had been a Messman aboard the *West Virginia* during the attack at Pearl Harbor when he became a hero by aiding his mortally wounded Captain, and then throwing his Cook's hat away to man a machine gun. He gets credit for knocking out enemy Planes and is decorated by Admiral Nimitz. The *Liscome Bay* is the second primary American Warship sunk by a Japanese Submarine since the opening of hostilities; it follows the loss of the Cruiser *Juneau* (lost during November of 1942). **(Atlantic-Italy) 15th Army Group** In the **U.S. Fifth Army** Area, plans are finalized for the offensive on December 2nd. The assault is comprised of three phases following the capture of Calabritto by the British 10th Corps on 1st December. 1st Phase, secure the Mt. Camino — Mt.la Difensa — Mt. Maggiore areas; 2nd phase, the capture of Mt. Sammucro on the drive west along the Colli-Atina road, and finally the assault through the Liri Valley. In the **British Eighth Army** area, the British 13th Corps seizes Castel Alfedena.

November 25th 1943 — (Pacific-Gilberts-Tarawa) The 2nd Battalion, 6th Marines continue their march up the Apamama atoll reaching Buariki, the final large island in the northwest portion of the atoll without incident. Meanwhile, Company D, 2nd Tank Battalion halts its advance about half way across the eastern side of the atoll and returns to Eita. The Third Battalion, 6th Marines, is en route to Apamama Atoll. Also, the 1st and 3rd Platoons, V Amphibious Corps Reconnaissance Company reports no resistance on Otto. In other activity, the Japanese Submarine I-19 is sunk by the U.S. Destroyer *Radford* (DD-446), north of the Gilberts. **(Pacific-Bismarcks-New Ireland)** THE BATTLE OF CAPE ST. GEORGE — On the previous day, Commander Burke had received orders to quickly depart Hathorn Sound on a northward course, however, he receives no instructions concerning an immediate destination or particular target. Burke's Destroyer Force is short-handed because the U.S.S. *Foote* and *Thatcher* are heading for Pearl Harbor before embarking to the States for a primary overhaul and the *Spence*, is being repaired alongside the U.S.S. *Whitney*. Some modification of Navy orders by Burke has the *Spence* later joining the operation. The Destroyers *Charles Ausburne*, *Dyson*, *Claxton*, *Converse* and the *Spence* round Vella La Vella shortly after 17:00 and are on their way. Subsequently, Burke receives the following orders: "GET ATHWART THE BUKA-RABAUL EVACUATION LINE ABOUT 35 MILES WEST OF BUKA. IF NO ENEMY CONTACT BY 03:00 LOVE (LOCAL TIME) 25TH COME SOUTH TO REFUEL SAME PLACE. IF ENEMY CONTACT, YOU KNOW WHAT TO DO!" Another message is dispatched from Headquarters (Halsey's) FOR COM TASK FORCE 33: "GET THIS WORD TO YOUR B-24s AND BLACK CATS. ADD A NIGHT FIGHTER FOR BURKE FROM 03:00 TO SUNRISE AND GIVE HIM AIR COVER."

Commander Burke is subsequently informed that his mission is to intercept a Task Force of about equal strength. The Japanese Force, commanded by Captain Kiyoto Kagawa, had debarked 1,000 troops on Buka and departed with about 700 troops attached to the Air Force which are no longer needed on the island. The Japanese are still unaware of American intelligence breaking their code and sail without knowledge of the American Task Force that has boldly entered deeply into enemy waters to ambush the enemy Convoy.

Rain squalls remain sporadic throughout the night and the moon is obscured by the dreary clouds, giving the Yanks perfect conditions for bushwacking the Japs. The Yanks are anticipating victory and plan a dual celebration on the 26th, Thanksgiving Day! One Officer aboard the U.S.S. *Claxton*, Rear Admiral Herald F. Stout, thinking out loud, mentions his immediate thoughts: "WONDERFUL! JUST WONDERFUL! IF THE BASTARDS JUST SHOW UP WE'LL TAKE EM." Everyone is excited about encountering the Japs too soon. One of the cooks is busily preparing turkeys and he is aware of the after effects of a Naval confrontation, having already experienced the frustration of his oven doors blowing open after every salvo.

Burke's blockade stands steadfastly north of Buka. At 01:41, the *Dyson*, commanded by Roy Gano spreads the news: "PLEASE CHECK BEARING ZERO-EIGHT-FIVE, DISTANCE 22,000 YARDS. WE HAVE A TARGET." At about the same time, Admiral Stout proclaims "WE HAVE TWO APPLEGADGETS (ENEMY SHIPS) AT ZERO-SEVEN-FIVE, DISTANCE 22,000 YARDS." . . . "HANG ONTO YOUR HATS BOYS! HERE WE GO!" The contest between Burke's "Boys" and the "sons of heaven" commences. Two Destroyers, the *Onami* and *Makanami* unknowingly approach Burke's Force, which closes the range to 4,500 yards and fires torpedoes. The *Onami* takes a direct hit and explodes, sending flames soaring into the sky. Within minutes, the flames are out and the Ship with its entire crew is lost to the sea, including the Commander of the Force, Kiyoto Kagawa. The trailing Destroyer *Makanami* also receives successive blows, however, the Vessel lingers. Vice Admiral Bernard L. Austin, quips to Burke: "I'M COMING NORTH TO FINISH OFF WHAT YOU DIDN'T FINISH." Burke fires back with the following: "KEEP YOUR TRANSMISSION SHORT PLEASE." The other three enemy Vessels spot the tempest and retire toward Rabaul with the Americans in pursuit.

A short game of cat and mouse begins, however, Burke refuses to take the bait by breaking his battle lines and engaging the enemy Vessels individually so deep in enemy waters. Meanwhile, Japanese find the range and fire salvos at the Americans, however, Burke anticipates the action and adjusts his course as the torpedoes whiz by, barely missing their

mark. The U.S.S. *Dyson* is ordered to attack the *Uzuki*. The *Claxton* and *Ausburne* strike against the *Yugiri*, but both Ships continue their escape with the Destroyers in pursuit. Meanwhile, the *Spence* and the *Converse* have taken out the disabled *Makanami*, but the survivors are sucking the Americans even deeper into enemy territory. Finally the Destroyer shelling takes its toll on the *Yugiri* and at 02:56, the *Ausburne* stands about 8,800 yards from the crippled Vessel. By 03:07 orders are given to the *Dyson* to finish off the Vessel, however, it suddenly turns to its side and capsizes. Torpedoes are fired to finish the job, but the *Yugiri* vanishes before the launched torpedoes arrive. Burke's Force then pulls out of the area under an umbrella of Aircover. This is Burke's last mission on a Destroyer. He is subsequently promoted and given command of the Carrier *Lexington*. The Japanese Destroyers *Makinami*, *Onami* and the *Yugiri* are lost and one additional Vessel is damaged. The U.S. Destroyers sustain no damage in what becomes the final night engagement of the Solomons campaign. **(Pacific-New Guinea)** After a tough campaign, Sattelberg finally falls to the Australian 9th Division. **(China-Burma-India)** The U.S. Fourteenth Air Force launches its first raid against Formosa and destroys 42 Japanese Planes at Shinchiku Airdrome. In Burma, U.S. and British Aircraft attack enemy positions near Rangoon, despite inclement weather. **(Atlantic-Italy)** The U.S. Fifth Army plan for the invasion of Anzio (Operation SHINGLE) is approved. The assault troops land on January 22nd. **(Atlantic)** U.S. Naval Land-based Aircraft attached to B-107, sink the German Submarine U-849, in the South Atlantic.

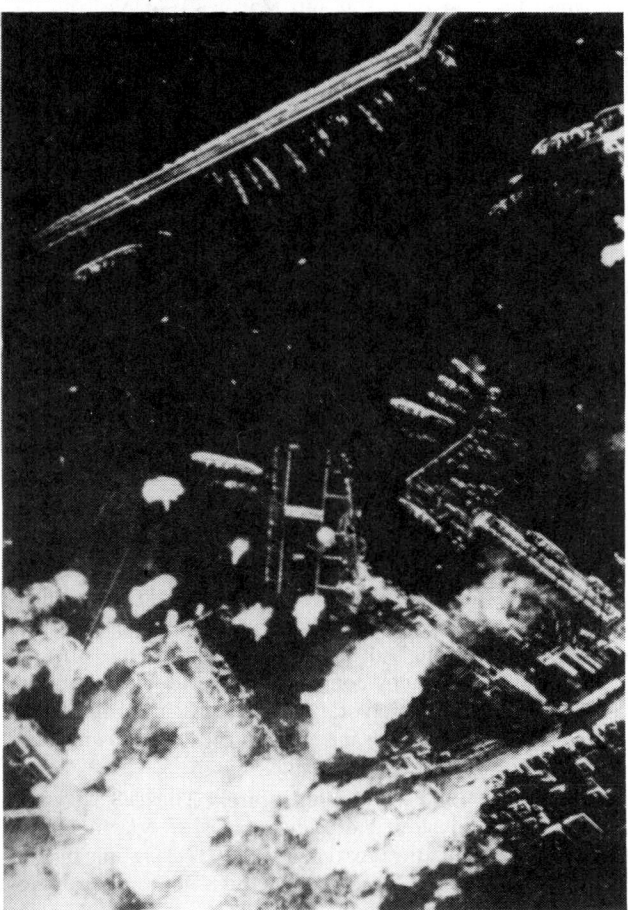

Naples Harbor.

November 26th 1943 — (Pacific-Gilberts-Tarawa) During closing mop up operations, the 2nd Battalion, 6th Marines, converges on the southern tip of Buariki, the last major island in the northwestern section of the atoll. Company E clashes with a Japanese Patrol. All resistance on Buariki ceases by the following day. **(Pacific-Gilberts-Apamama)** The Marines land troops at both John, and Steve Islands, initiating a defensive build-up. **(Pacific-Solomons-Bougainville)** Marines take over abandoned Japanese positions on Grenade Hill. **(Atlantic-Egypt)** The first phase of the Cairo Meeting adjourns with no definite plans for the Normandy invasion (Operation OVERLORD) reached. President Roosevelt and Prime Minister Churchill depart Cairo to attend a meeting in Teheran with Stalin. These meetings convene from November 27th until December 2nd. **(Atlantic-Brazil)** The U.S. Navy establishes several additional Naval Facilities in Brazil today. **(Atlantic-Russia)** The Germans evacuate Gomel, which has been a major position against the Soviets. **(Atlantic-Germany)** Six hundred thirty-three Bombers of the U.S. 8th Bomber Command are launched against Bremen. Heavy overcast skies prevent observation of any possible damage.

November 27th 1943 — (Pacific-Gilberts-Tarawa) The 2nd Battalion, 6th Marines terminate resistance on Buariki. **(Atlantic-Italy) 15th Army Group** The British 5 Corps (British Eighth Army area) prepares an attack on the Adriatic coastal area and begins moving Tanks across the Sangro River.

November 28th 1943 — (Pacific-Gilberts-Tarawa) Major General Julian C. Smith, U.S.M.C. declares the entire atoll secure when the 2nd Battalion, 6th Marines returns from the Naa Islet after locating no Japanese. Marine casualties on Tarawa total 3,301 killed or wounded. Japanese losses; about 4,690 killed, 17 captured. **(Atlantic-Italy) 15th Army Group** In the **U.S. Fifth Army** area, the U.S. 45th Division advances to clear the area north of Filignano-South Elia Road. The 178th Infantry meets heavy German resistance which prevents seizure of Hill 855, however, the 157th Infantry fights its way through enemy fire and captures Hill 460. Meanwhile, the 34th Division advances toward the Colli-Atina Road; its 1st Battalion, 168th Infantry moves against Mont Pantano. The 133rd Infantry is ordered to seize the hills between Castelnuovo and Cerasuolo. The assault against the German Winter Line will rage through the frozen mountainous terrain until it is secured. Hitler has ordered the crack troops to hold to the death. In the **British Eighth Army** area, the British 5 Corps opens the battle for the Sangro River during the late night hours. The Indian Eighth Division seizes Mozzagrogna. On the following day, the 4th British Armored Brigade begins to clear the Sangro Ridge. **(Atlantic-Teheran)** President Roosevelt is informed by the Russians that an attempt might be made against his life. The President, Admiral Leahy, Harry Hopkins and a Secret Service agent, commandeer a private car and speed through the narrow streets to the Russian Legation ahead of a decoy convoy. The President, unharmed, attends the meeting which starts at 17:00 with Churchill and Stalin in attendance. They meet again on the following day, with Stalin doing most of the talking.

November 29th 1943 — (United States) The U.S.S. *Hornet* (CV-12), is commissioned at Newport News Virginia. It is named in honor of the Carrier *Hornet* (CV-8), sunk by the Japanese on October 27th, 1942. **(Pacific-Solomons-Bougainville)** U.S. Construction troops begin to establish an Airstrip near the Piva River. Also, the 1st Parachute Battalion, with Company M, 3rd Raider Battalion, and an observer contingent from the 12th Marines land at a Japanese supply depot on Koiari beach to destroy communication and supplies, however, the unit is forced to evacuate. **(Pacific-New Guinea)** The Australians drive north, seizing Bonga and Gusika on the Huon Peninsula. In Naval activity, the U.S.S. *Perkins*, a Destroyer (DD-377), sinks after it collides with an Australian Ship. **(Atlantic-Azores)** The U.S.S. *Bogue* (CVE-9), launches Planes (VC-19), which sink the German Submarine U-86. **(Atlantic-Italy) 15th Army Group** In the **U.S. Fifth Army** area, the VI Corps initiates diversionary operations to distract attention from the main attack which is pending against Mont Camino. The U.S. 45th Division pushes toward the area north of Filignano-South Elia Road while elements of the 178th Infantry push toward La Bandita (Hill 855) where they meet heavy resistance and are prevented from capturing the objective. However, the 157th Infantry seizes Hill 460. In conjunction with the operation, the U.S. 45th Infantry attacks the enemy holding the high ground above the Colli-Atina road, gaining hard earned ground on Mont Pantano. In the **British Eighth Army** area, Allied Planes lend valuable assistance to a drive by the British 5 Corps allowing them to puncture a hole in the Winter Line near Mozzagrogna with elements battling to clear the heights on Sangro Ridge. **(Atlantic-Iran-Teheran)** Military advisers of the U.S., England, and Russia, meet in Teheran and discuss future priorities. The British maintain their position of taking the Mediterranean. The Russians press for an invasion through Southern France which will assist them by putting pressure on the Germans who are still in Russia. The U.S. maintains its position of invading France from across the Channel as the only way to solidly defeat the Germans. On the following day, Winston Churchill celebrates his 69th birthday and during the meeting, an agreement is reached concerning "OVERLORD," the impending invasion of France.

November 30th 1943 — (Pacific-Gilberts) Contingents of Company D, 2nd Tank Battalion, complete their search of Abaiang and Makakei Atolls north of Tarawa, but find only five Japanese troops. On the following day, additional Marine Scouts (Company D, 2nd Tank Battalion) land on the Maiana Atoll near Bickerel village, but depart after finding no Japanese. **(Pacfic-Solomons)** The U.S. Navy moves some Destroyers within firing range of Japanese positions at Empress Augusta Bay, Bougainville and commence a bombardment. **(SWPA)** General Krueger establishes Task Force Director (Brigadier General Julian W. Cunningham) for the invasion of Arawe. The landing will occur on December 15th. **(China-Burma-India)** Chiang Kai-shek inspects Chinese troops at Ramgarh. While in Ramgahr, Chiang Kai-shek again agrees to "Operation CHAMPION", the offensive to begin in Burma. **(Atlantic-Italy) 15th Army Group** The **U.S. Fifth Army** initiates a series of attacks against the German lines to divert attention from the main thrust, which will be launched toward Mount Camino. The U.S. 3rd Ranger Battalion springs toward S. Pietro, while the U.S. 23rd Armored feints toward Garigliano. In the VI Corps area, the 1st Battalion, 179th U.S. Infantry meets fierce German opposition and is prevented from taking La Bandita. The U.S. 34th Division holds firm at its recently won positions on Mount Pantano and fiercely drives a German counterattack back. Additional U.S. outfits move out; elements of the 1st Battalion, 133rd Infantry occupy Castelnuovo and the 3rd Battalion drives to Mount la Rocca. Croce Hill is overtaken by a contingent of the 100th Infantry.

In the **British Eighth Army** area, the ridge above the Sangro River is cleared of enemy resistance by the British 5 Corps. The British 4th Armored Brigade, supporting the British 78th Division, seizes Fossacesia. The New Zealanders operating to the west, forge the Sangro river against heavy resistance and link up with their Bridgehead Force. **(Atlantic-Russia)** German progress in the vicinity of Korosten forces the Soviets to evacuate. **(Atlantic-Iran)** The conference in Teheran between President Roosevelt, Prime Minister Churchill and Stalin concludes. Stalin, pushing for a priority for the Normandy Invasion and "Anvil" the invasion of Southern France, gets his way. Also, Stalin agrees to commit Russian troops against the Japanese after the defeat of Germany, however, the German High Command will surrender all land, air and sea troops to the Allies on 7 May 1945, yet Stalin makes no move to assist in the Pacific. On August 6th 1945, the U.S. Air Corps drops an atomic bomb on Hiroshima Japan. Two days later, Russia declares war on Japan, effective 9 August, ironically the same day the U.S. drops another atomic bomb on Japan.

December 1st 1943 — (United States) The U.S. Navy announces it has established a Naval Air Ferry Command. Also, the first Marine Corps air-transportable air warning Squadron is commissioned at Cherry Point, North Carolina. **(Atlantic-Italy) 15th Army Group** In the **U.S. Fifth Army** sector, Allied Air Assaults against enemy positions are stepped up in preparation of the offensive against the heart of the German Winter Line. Fierce German resistance halts the U.S. 179th Infantry at La Bandita and the 2nd Battalion is prevented from securing the crest and reverse slope of Hill 769 to the south. In the 34th Division sector, tenacious enemy fire keeps the 1st Battalion, 168th Infantry pinned on the first knob of Mont Pantano and separated from the main body. The 133rd Infantry also receives vicious enemy resistance which holds up its advance. In other activity, British Air Marshal Sir Arthur Coningham (Commander British Air Force in support of British 8th Army states: "I WOULD CONSIDER IT A PERSONAL AFFRONT AND INSULT IF THE LUFTWAFFE SHOULD ATTEMPT ANY SIGNIFICANT ACTION IN THIS AREA." On the following day, enemy Planes strike Bari, inflicting severe damage to the Vessels in port, one of which contains mustard gas.

December 2nd 1943 — (Pacific-Philippines) The U.S.S. *Narwhal* (SS-167), moves off Mindanao and unloads supplies and evacuates personnel. **(Atlantic-Italy)** The Allies, already suffering massive supply problems, are delivered another stunning blow when about 30 German Planes launch a night raid against the Shipping at Bari, inflicting massive damage. Two ammunition-laden Ships receive direct hits igniting a horrendous explosion that rocks the area and spreads the flames across the water, costing the Allies an additional 17 Vessels. The port suffers heavy damage and will take weeks of intensive work to repair. One of the seriously damaged Vessels, is the U.S.S *Aroostook* (AOG-14), a Gasoline Tanker. **15th Army Group** In the **U.S. Fifth Army** area, Allied Planes continue to bombard enemy positions to soften resistance for the assault against the staunchly entrenched enemy on Mount Camino (Operation RAINCOAT). The British 10th Corps attacks toward Calabritto, but the Germans guarding the approach route hold on, stalling the British advance. The British 56th Division assaulting the hill mass at Mont Camino drives feverishly against the Germans, seizing the objective on the 3rd. In the VI Corps sector, again the U.S. 45th Division presses for control of La Bandita and Hill 769 without success. The 34th

U.S. Division sends in reinforcements and after an intense battle advances to the second knob of Mont Pantano. In other action, the U.S. 133rd Infantry seizes Hill 1180, on the southern slope of Mont Marrone when Company L, successfully attacks the enemy during the night of the 2nd. Subsequently, the Germans form tightly, preventing any further advances by the Regiment. In the **British Eighth Army** area, the New Zealanders capture Castelfrentano. **(Atlantic-Russia)** The Germans are forced to relinquish more ground as the Soviets penetrate the Ingulets River, reaching within six miles of Znamenka.

December 3rd 1943 — (Pacific-Bismarcks) Invasion dates for amphibious assaults against New Britain are finalized. Arawe is to be attacked on (Z Day) December 15th and Cape Gloucester (D-Day, main invasion) on the day after Christmas, December 26. **(Pacific-Solomons-Bougainville)** The 1st Marine Parachute Battalion, dispatched from Vella Lavella, arrives and begins to expand its perimeter. **(Atlantic-Brazil)** The U.S. Navy establishes a Naval Air Facility at Sao Luiz, Brazil. **(Atlantic-Italy) 15th Army Group** In the **U.S. Fifth Army**, British 10th Corps area, Mount Camino falls to the British 56th Division, which then penetrates enemy positions on Hill 963 (Monastery Hill), but a vicious attack by the Germans drives it back. In the II Corps area, the Texas 36th Division seizes Mount Maggiore. In the VI Corps area, the U.S. 45th Division still meets stiff German resistance and is unable to make progress. The fighting in the vicinity of Mont Pagano remains violent; German defenders drive the advancing 3rd Battalion, 168th Infantry from its fragile hold on the third knob of the slopes. In the **British Eighth Army** area, the Indian Seventh and Eighth Divisions advance to the Moro River and capture Lanciano and South Vito. **(Atlantic-Egypt)** British and U.S. representatives, reopen the SEXTANT talks at Cairo, subsequent to returning from Teheran. **(Atlantic-Soviet Union)** The Red Army captures Dovsk.

December 4th 1943 — Gunners aboard the U.S.S. Yorktown dispose of a Japanese "Kate" Torpedo Bomber.

December 4th 1943 — (Pacific-Gilberts) Captain Jackson R. Tate, U.S.N., replaces Major General Julian C. Smith as Commanding Officer, Advanced Base Tarawa. A concentrated effort begins to establish Air Bases in the Gilberts to enhance the ongoing Allied successes in the Pacific. **(Pacific-Marshalls)** A large Task Force, commanded by Rear Admiral C.A. Pownall, which includes six Carriers, catapults a massive amount of Aircraft against enemy positions at Kwajalein and Wotje, concentrating on Nauru and Mille. The Task Force suffers some damage to the Carrier *Lexington* (CV-16), Light Cruiser *Mobile* (CL-63) (accidental explosion) and the Destroyer *Taylor* (DD-468), by accidental friendly fire. **(Pacific-Japan)** The Submarine U.S.S. *Sailfish* sinks the Japanese Escort Carrier *Chuyo* off Honshu, Japan. **(China-Burma-India)** In China, the Japanese 11th Army overruns Chang-te (Tungting Lake vicinity), completing its mission, then begins to withdraw. **(Atlantic-Italy) 15th Army Group** In the **U.S. Fifth Army** area, the British 56th Division still is prevented by heavy enemy fire from securing Monastery Hill, however, Hills 615, and 683, are seized. In the II Corps area, U.S. Special Service troops are struck by a strong counterattack which drives the Americans from their hold on Mont la Remetanea back to Mont la Difensa. The 1st and 2nd Regiments coordinate and clear the Mont la Remetanea-Mont la Difensa Ridge. In the VI Corps area, the 135th Infantry, U.S. 34th Division relieves the 168th Infantry which has been badly battered by the Germans holding commanding positions in the heights at M. Pantano. In the **British Eighth Army** area, 5 Corps moves toward Ortona; its Indian 8th Division crosses the Moro River.

December 5th 1943 — (United States) The President agrees with the British suggestion to cancel Operation BUCCANEER (amphibious landing in the Andaman Islands). **(Pacific-Solomons)** U.S. Destroyers bombard enemy positions at Choiseul Bay. **(China-Burma-India)** Japanese Planes attack Calcutta, striking the dock area. **(Atlantic-Italy) 15th Army Group** In the **U.S. Fifth Army** area, the Germans abandon Monastery Hill (963) in the path of the approaching British 56th Infantry Division. In the II Corps area, the American units hold their ground, though plagued by terrible supply problems. Also, the Troops in the VI Corps area hold, while consolidating positions and sending out Patrols. American casualties during the campaign have been high. In the **British Eighth Army** sector, the V Corps moves toward Ortona, which will be utilized as a Supply Base because of its harbor. The 8th Indian Division initiates its crossing of the Moro river. **(China-Burma-India)** Calcutta, India is attacked by Japanese Aircraft which inflict damage to the port facilities. **(Atlantic)** In the European Theater of Operations, the U.S. Ninth Air Force begins to assist with Operation CROSSBOW (search and destroy German secret weapon sites) by launching its P-51s as escorts for the strategic bombers of the U.S. Eighth Air Force.

December 6th 1943 — (United States) Based on British Admiral Mountbatten's statement to the Combined Chiefs of Staff that if BUCCANEER is aborted, there can be no major amphibious operations, the President tells Chiang Kai-shek that there will be no simultaneous amphibious landing with TARZAN (India based part of Burma offensive). **(Atlantic-Italy) 15th Army Group** In the **U.S. Fifth Army** area, the British 10th Corps occupies M Camino, which has been evacuated by the Germans. The British then advance to clear the western slopes toward the Garigliano River. In the VI Corps area, the U.S. 179th Infantry takes the crest of Hill 769, after bitter fighting, however, the enemy holds firm on the reverse slope. In the **British Eighth Army** area, the Canadian 1st Division crosses the Moro River.

December 8th-16th 1943 — THE BATTLE OF SAN PIETRO — The entire battle for the liberation of Italy is one massive bloodbath. The enemy stranglehold on the Liri Valley exemplifies the extraordinary will of the Yanks. The U.S. Fifth Army has the mission of taking the valley, but first it must eliminate the formidable entanglements that blanket the mountain ranges overlooking San Pietro, the gateway to Rome.

San Pietro lays in the middle of Italy flanked by four ranges of mountains and is approximately 40 miles west of Rome and 60 miles northwest of Naples. The peaceful village which contains a quaint church which had been constructed during the year 1438 is the connecting point for the two roads that lead to the valley, one a narrow pass that descends from the high ground and the other just as small that extends across the lowlands. Heavy bombardments have been striking the village since the end of October to drive the Germans out and the shelling has taken a toll on the civilian population, many of whom have taken refuge in nearby caves to escape the terror.

The Allied offensive to seize the coveted village commences and the battle is vicious from the onset, setting near impossible demands on those chosen to seize it. The weather conditions have not been favorable since the Americans have landed in Italy and the natural obstacles are just as fierce as those concocted by the Germans. The Rivers flow in unruly fashion, giving the impression that there are several tributaries within each one. The mud and the cold multiply the misery. Pieces of equipment are stranded on little rises amidst the free flowing currents. Beyond the natural obstructions lie the deadly entrapments of the enemy, which include treacherous barbed wire, unending irregular rows of personnel mines set to cause severe injury, especially below the waistline of unsuspecting advancing troops. The Germans have masterminded a superb system of near-invisible intertwining entrenchments that contain a chain of machine gun nests that can blanket all approaches in an instant. Mortars hold the range of any Yanks that venture in their line of fire. It is to be a death-defying advance, every peak must be taken inch-by-inch. The GIs control the high ground northeast of the objective extending eastward and south of San Pietro. Mt. Maggiore, the last enemy stronghold to fall had been seized by the Texas 36th Division on the 3rd. An Italian contingent had attempted and failed to take Mt. Lungo, sustaining such alarming casualties that the attack had been canceled. The bastion proves to be the key to the German success and it is up to the U.S. Army to annihilate it.

Four sturdy enemy Battalions man the trenches. They extend from the lower edge of Mt. Lungo to the fringes of Mt. Sammucro. Additional enemy troops at Battalion strength control the high ground to the northwest of San Pietro. The GIs mount the assault, following the earlier advances gained by certain elements the previous night. By the major jump-off on the 15th, the efforts of the 1st Battalion, 143rd Infantry during the previous night have gained Hill 1205 (Mt. Sammucro) and the 3rd Battalion, Rangers are making slow, but steady progress against Hill 950, about a mile north of Sammucro. As the contest progresses, pounding rains drench the troops throughout the night.

As the signal to assault is given, the 2nd Battalion, 143rd Infantry advances forward, directly into withering fire, with the 3rd Battalion in support just to their rear. The enemy fire honing down from Mt. Lungo creates a death trap. Daring Yanks attempt to breech the barbed wire only to have their bodies shredded by enemy bullets. Others attempt to advance only to receive the same fate. The 2nd Battalion is entrapped in a deadly whirlwind of steel. The 3rd Battalion is committed to the struggle but more shelling is concentrated into the attack zone and progress is halted. A lot of Yanks are slain and the attack nets only about 600 bloody yards.

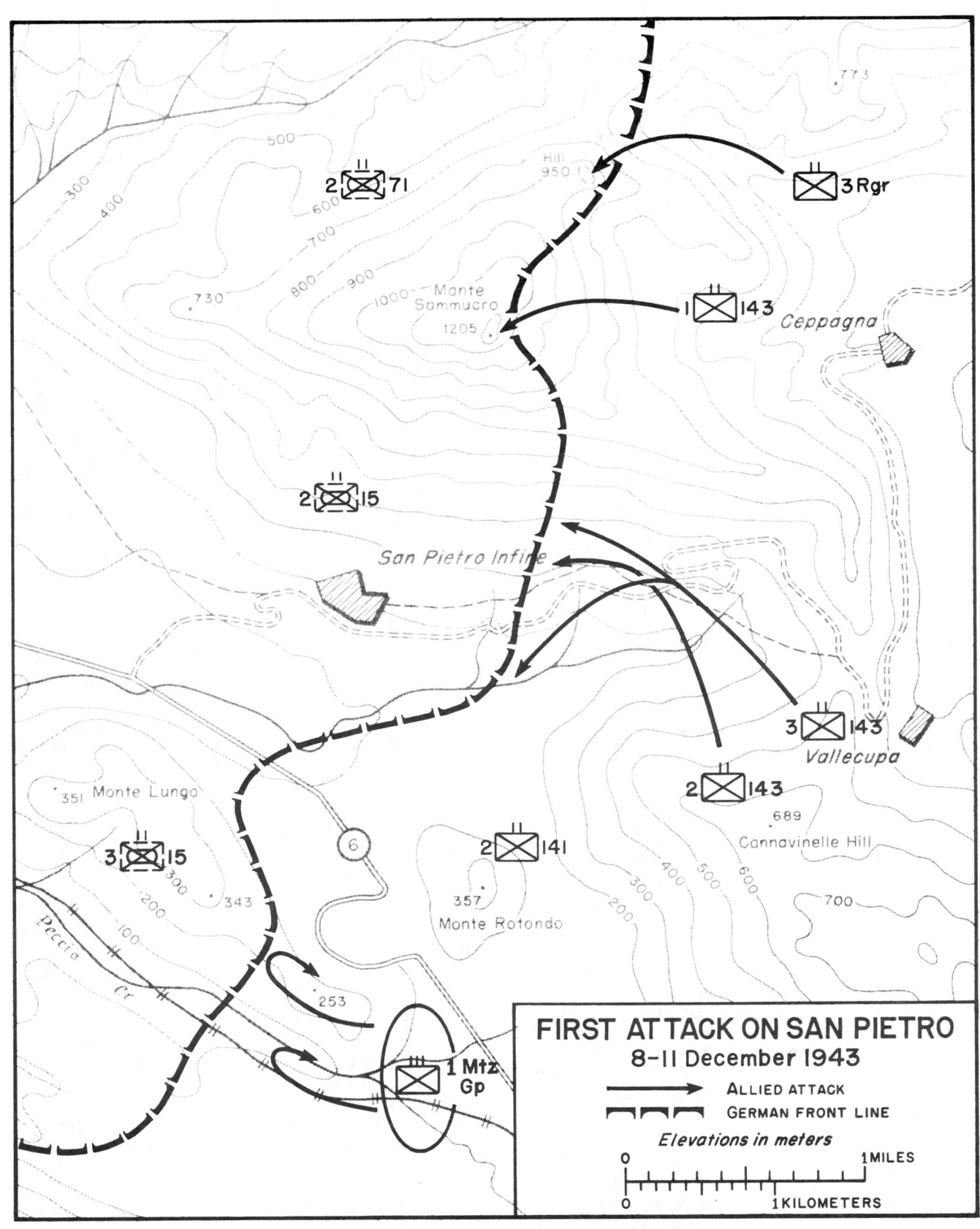

2 ⊠ 71

3 Rgr

1 ⊠ 143   Ceppagna

Monte
Sammucro
1205

2 ⊠ 15

San Pietro Infine

3 ⊠ 143
Vallecupa

2 ⊠ 143

Monte Lungo

Cannavinelle Hill

3 ⊠ 15

2 ⊠ 141

Monte Rotondo

Pecara Cr

1 Mtz Gp

FIRST ATTACK ON SAN PIETRO
8–11 December 1943

ALLIED ATTACK
GERMAN FRONT LINE

Elevations in meters

0   1 MILES

0   1 KILOMETERS

In the meantime the Germans have not forsaken their lost ground on Hill 1205 and the encroaching Rangers on 950. Gruesome fighting ensues at both places as the enemy mounts heavy counterattacks, but the Yanks hold on. The Germans lose Hill 950 to the Rangers on the tenth, after several heavy contests. The First Battalion, 143rd Infantry is relieved on the 12th by a Paratroop Battalion which takes over responsibility for Hills 1205 and 950 permitting the First Battalion to eradicate enemy resistance on a ridge sitting to the west of their positions. The 143rd has sustained so many casualties that there is serious doubt concerning their remaining strength being sufficient to finish the operation, however, the Regiment remains in the fight.

A brutalizing struggle in the valley continues. Volunteers offer to form Patrols to advance and eliminate the strongpoints that have crippled the drive, while pounding the positions and rolling up the casualties. Not a single man returns alive from the Patrols. Throughout the ordeal, enemy Planes have penetrated Allied Air Defenses and their thrusts have also hurt the Americans, whom are still halted by a wall of enemy fire. Headquarters decides on a Tank supported Divisional attack to permit a breakout.

On the 15th, the 2nd and 3rd Battalions continue their frontal assault against the defenses of San Pietro. In conjunction with the ongoing attack, the 1st Battalion, 141st Infantry advances through the valley, while the 142nd Infantry assaults the Germans holding Mt. Lungo. Every available gun roaring, their shells are creating huge pillars of swirling smoke and dust. The 2nd and 3rd Battalions, 143rd Infantry burst forth into another firewall. The 141st Infantry is stalled by vicious fire after it grinds about 400 yards. The 2nd ad 3rd Battalions reach eyeball contact with the defenders holding the trenches, but the enemy immobilizes both Battalions, holding them tight to the quivering ground.

Meanwhile, American Tanks move from the east along the mountain pass against San Pietro. The Tanks move down the pass the only way they can; in single file, coming directly under the sights of the German gunners. The Tankers advance 16 strong. Only three complete the mission by reaching the edge of San Pietro. Of the three that make it to the doorsteps of the town, two are destroyed and the other is unaccounted for.

After dark, the Germans refuse to relent and the battle-weary American attackers press forward. Two Companies of the 143rd Infantry successfully penetrate the enemy positions, but shortly thereafter intense fire drives them back. Company E is down to eight Riflemen and Company L sustains similar losses. The 1st Battalion, 143rd Infantry drives punishingly against enemy positions on a contested ridge, situated west of Mt. Sammuco; high casualties and utter exhaustion aborts any further attempt to advance.

The 142nd Infantry attacks on Mt. Lungo fare better. They blast through the fierce resistance and snap the latch key for the village of San Pietro and the Liri Valley. After a tedious battle that had been initiated at 12:00 hours on the 15th, the enemy is finally driven from their commanding positions before noon on the 16th. The 142nd Infantry, U.S.A., seizes Mt. Lungo by 10:00, compelling an enemy withdrawal all along the front. Severe enemy counterattacks cover the retreat of the Germans for five hours. In some instances, so many Officers are killed that enlisted men take charge. U.S. Artillery floats over the heads of the Yanks to land within 100 yards of their tenuous hold, interrupting the advancing enemy in the nick of time. The Yanks take San Pietro and splintered remnants of the 2nd and 3rd Battalions, now numbering less than a full Rifle Company, enter the town. The 143rd will be awarded 100 decorations for Valor, but it will take 1,100 replacements to bring it up to strength to enable the 143rd to carry the struggle westward to seize the balance of Italy from the Germans.

December 8th 1943 — (Pacific) A U.S. Task Force, commanded by Rear Admiral W. A. Lee moves near Nauru Island, in the Western Pacific, south of the equator and bombards enemy positions. During the Naval bombardment, the Destroyer *Boyd* (DD-554) is hit by land batteries. **(Pacific-New Guinea)** The Australian 9th Division seizes Wareo and will prepare to drive toward the next Japanese bastion, Sio. **(China-Burma-India)** Fifty Japanese Fighters, escorting 18 Bombers, strike Tinsukia Airfield in Assam. **(Atlantic-Italy)** The grueling task to break through the German Winter Line remains a grim task and makes no true genuine progress. The U.S. 143rd Infantry advancing toward the enemy is halted by severe enemy fire. The 1st Battalion, 143rd Infantry braces and repulses a bitter German counterattack in the vicinity of Mont Sammucro. The enemy is cleared from Mont la Remetanea (Hill 907) by the 1st Special Service Force. In the VI Corps area, the 2nd Moroccan Infantry Division begins to relieve the U.S. 34th Division. (European Theater) General Spaatz is informed that he will command the U.S. Strategic Air Force in Europe.

December 9th 1943 — (Pacific-Bougainville) The Allied Airstrip at Torokina is declared operational. Fighting will erupt as the U.S. 3rd Marines begin to secure the hills in the vicinity of their beachhead. The Marines track the Japanese doggishly until the end of the month. **(China-Burma-India)** Chiang Kai-shek requests air support and financial assistance from the United States. **(Atlantic-Italy)** In the Fifth Army, British 10th Corps area, enemy resistance on the Mont Camino Hill area collapses as Rocca d'Evandro falls to the British. Ferocious fire fights rage are raging in the II Corps area as enemy guns prevent the advance of the 2nd and 3rd Battalions, 143rd Infantry in the vicinity of southern Pietro. Another German counterattack against the defenders on Mont Sammucro is convincingly repelled. In the VI Corps area, the Germans lose Hill 769 but still command the terrain at Lagone and La Bandita (La Bandita will not fall until 15 Dec.). **(Atlantic-Russia)** A rail junction at Znamenka is seized by the Red Army.

December 10th 1943 — (Pacific-Solomons) Torokina Airstrip, Bougainville, slightly over two hundred miles from Rabaul, receives Marine Fighter Squadron 216. The Squadron flies its first Ground-Air Close Combat Support Mission on the 13th and directs its fire on "Hellzapoppin Ridge." In Naval activity in the Solomons, the U.S.S. *Sigourney* (DD-643) is damaged after becoming grounded. **(Atlantic-Italy)** The Allied Offensive crawls forward paying high costs for each frozen yard gained. Allied Aircraft accelerate the bombing raids, hoping to soften enemy resistance against the next phase of the Offensive which is to commence on the 15th. The U.S. 142nd Infantry, 36th Division, holding Mont la Difensa, is relieved by the British 10th Corps. In the II Corps area, the 3rd Ranger Battalion seizes Hill 950 on the northern flank of the II Corps. In the British Eighth Army area, Adriatic section, the Canadian 1st and Indian 8th Divisions, assisted by Allied

Air and Naval support, drive toward Ortona.

December 11th 1943 — (China-Burma-India) British Admiral Mountbatten orders the combining of the U.S. 10th Air Force and R.A.F. Bengal Command to form the Eastern Air Command and be placed under the command of British Air Chief Marshal Sir Richard Peirse. Quite often during World War II, American commands are placed under British Command to the dismay of many American Commanders. General Patton has frequently complained of such practices and mentions that he wished General Pershing of World War I fame were twins. Pershing prided himself that Americans would serve only under American Commanders, although on occasion Pershing did lend contingents to the Allies. **(Atlantic-Italy)** The American Fifth Army, still plagued by miserable weather, terrible supply problems and relentless opposition, is holding tough, amidst enemy counterattacks as they are regrouping for the next phase of the offensive. The new mountain routes will become more treacherous as the Fifth Army climbs from hill to hill against entrenched German Soldiers.

December 12th 1943 — (Pacific) The Commander in Chief Pacific Area and the Commander of the Central Pacific Area formulate a plan to capture Kwajalein and Majura Atolls, situated in the Western Pacific in the Marshalls. **(Atlantic-Italy)** In the U.S. Fifth Army area, the British 10th Corps expands its perimeter further east, completing relief of the U.S. VI Corps troops at Mont Maggiore. In the II Corps area, the 142nd Infantry seizes south Giacomo Hill situated between Maggiore and the main objective Mont Lungo. When darkness falls, the 142nd drives further, capturing Hills 72 and 141. **(Mid-Atlantic)** The German Submarine U-72 runs into an American Carrier and four Destroyers. Planes (VC-19), from the Escort Carrier *Bogue* (CVE-9) are launched and combined with the Destroyers, the U-72 is sunk. The Destroyers *Badger* (DD-126), *Dupont* (DD-52), *Clemson* (DD-186) and the *Ingraham* (DD-694), all participate in the attack.

December 13th 1943 — (Pacific) The Task Force which will strike the enemy at Arawe, New Britain, departs Goodenough Island and will stop at Buna before heading to the invasion rendezvous point off the New Britain coast. **(China-Burma-India)** The Submarine *Pompon* (SS-267), patrolling along the west coast of China deploys mines near Cochin. **(Atlantic-Germany)** The U.S. Air Corps continues its daring raids over Germany. These 710 Bombers, attached to the U.S. Eighth Air Force, have better odds for a return trip. They are protected by P-51 Fighters which fly escort for the entire mission as the Bombers drop their payloads on Kiel. The Bombers use radar to locate their targets and the raid is deemed successful. **(Atlantic-Mediterranean)** The Destroyer *General Wainwright* (U-593), named for relatives the U.S. General held by Japanese in the Philippines, and some British Vessels sink the U-593 in the Mediterranean today.

December 14th 1943 — (Pacific-Solomons) The PT-239 is damaged after being struck accidentally by friendly fire. **(Atlantic-Brazil)** A U.S. Naval Air Facility is established at Maceio, Brazil. **(Atlantic-Italy)** The U.S. Fifth Army finalizes preparations for the next offensive, expected to push them over the mountains toward Rome. During the night of the 14th-15th, the II and VI Corps move out to penetrate the German Winter Line, which to date, has held against tremendous Allied pressure. **(Atlantic-Russia)** The first phase of the Russian Winter Offensive commences as the Red Army moves toward the town of Vitebsk. Cherkassy, on the second Ukrainian Front, is captured by the Soviets and the Germans recapture Radomyshl, south of Malin.

December 15th 1943 — (Pacific-Bougainville) General Griswold, XIV Corps Commanding General, relieves General Geiger, Marine Amphibious Corps Commanding Officer, of responsibility for the defense of Bougainville beachhead. The beach is secure except for minor mop-up operations, while the 21st Marines, 3rd Marine Division, operating in the nearby heights, clears enemy remnants in the vicinity. **(Solomons-Treasury Islands)** The U.S. Navy establishes a Naval Operating Base on the Treasury Islands. **(Pacific-Bismarcks-New Britain)** THE BATTLE FOR THE ARAWE PENINSULA — During the early morning hours of the 15th, Naval guns and Aircraft bombard enemy positions on Arawe's west coast to soften resistance for Task Force Director which would be storming the beaches. In advance of the main invasion, troops make a futile attempt to assault Umtingalu on the mainland and the islet of Pilelo. The Japanese are quickly dispersed by the 112th Cavalry which bolts to the beach and quickly seizes the island. The main assault gets off at 07:00 and the 112th Cavalry troops, Commanded by Brigadier General Julian Cunningham, rapidly eradicate sporadic opposition. Enemy Aircraft attack the troops and also raid the Allied Vessels offshore during the assault for several days, but do not deter the movement of the Americans. The peninsula is captured for use as a Light Naval Base, but it does not come to fruition. The seized objective will be used as an Airfield. The Stars and Stripes is firmly emplaced on Arawe and is expected to be visiting the Japanese on Cape Gloucester soon. **(China-Burma-India)** The Chinese 38th Division is heavily embattled with the Japanese in Burma. The 1st Battalion, 114th Infantry struggles to reach the beleaguered 112th Infantry, but the Japanese repulse the attempt. After the Chinese assault subsides, the Japanese withdraw to their original positions and fortify them for any new attacks which could materialize. **(Atlantic-Italy)** The U.S. Fifth Army embarks on the next phase of the offensive to puncture the murderous Winter Line, advancing in full force against a dug-in German defense. The Germans withdraw slightly, but not far enough for the offensive to make much progress. In the II Corps area, the 142nd Infantry, 36th Division approaches Mont Lungo from the south, having begun the advance at dusk on the previous night. The 143rd Infantry charges from the slopes of Mont Sammucro, assaulting enemy positions at south Pietro while the 141st Infantry closes from another direction. Progress is extremely slow and casualties mount. The Germans hold firm on Hill 687, inflicting high casualties on the 2nd Battalion, 504th Paratroopers, and the 1st Battalion, 143rd Infantry, assaulting in the same general area, is totally pinned down near Hill 730. Things are not much better in the VI Corps area. The U.S. 45th Division, attacking in two directions makes slight progress as the 157th Infantry secures positions on Hills 470 and 640 to the north of La Rava Creek. The 179th Infantry is halted by heavy enemy fire outside of Lagone, and contingents of the 1st Battalion, 179th Infantry are finally able to dislodge the stubborn Germans from La Bandita. The 179th units take it without opposition after dark. In other action, the 8th Rifle Regiment, 2nd Moroccan Division, maneuvering on the north flank of the VI Corps, seizes Castelnuovo and south Michele Pass.

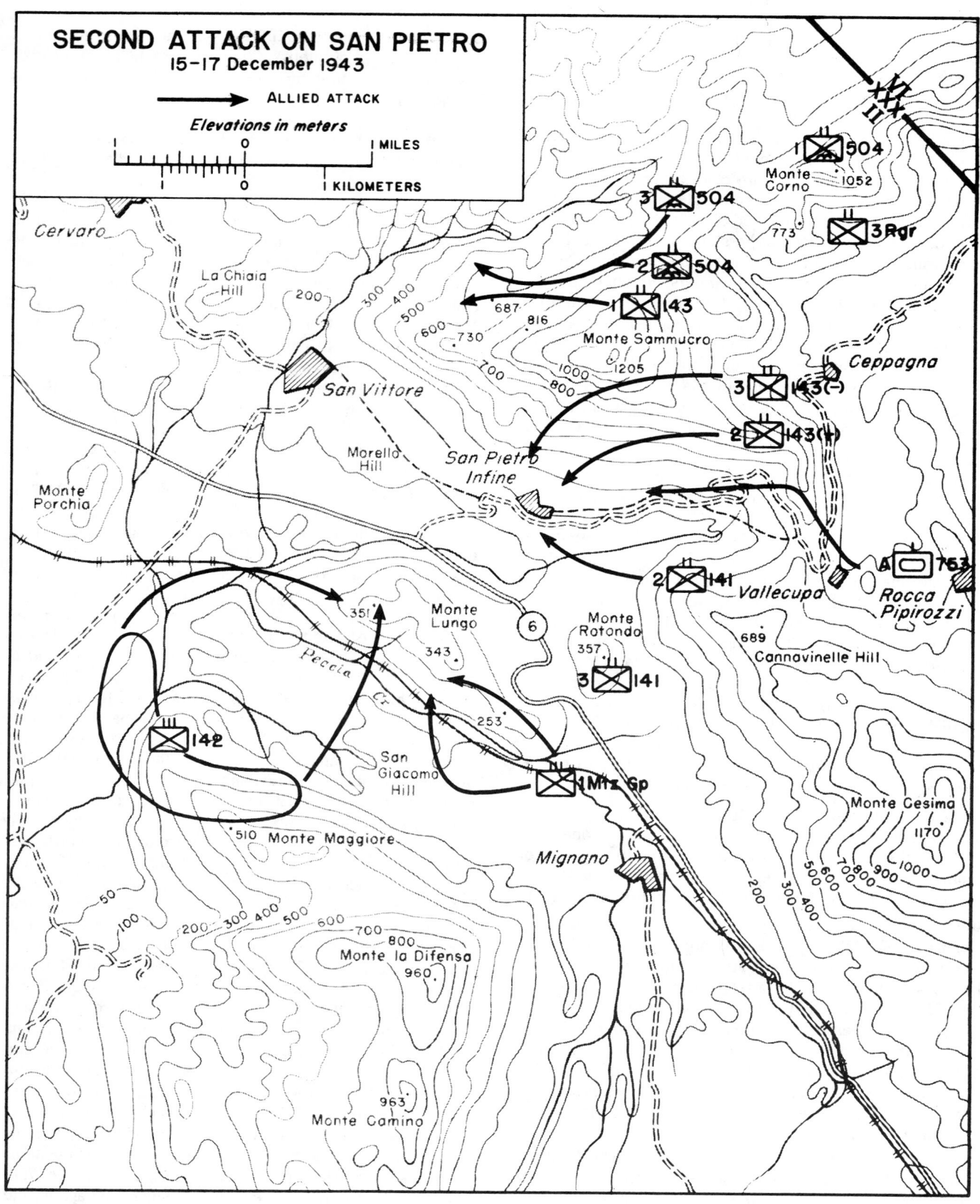

SECOND ATTACK ON SAN PIETRO
15-17 December 1943

ALLIED ATTACK

Elevations in meters

1 MILES

1 KILOMETERS

Cervaro

La Chiaia
Hill

200

300 400 500 600 700 730 800 1000 1205

San Vittore

Morello
Hill

Monte
Porchia

San Pietro
Infine

Monte Sammucro

687 816

Ceppagna

3 ⊠ 504
2 ⊠ 504
1 ⊠ 143
3 ⊠ 143(-)
2 ⊠ 143(+)

1 ⊠ 504
Monte
Corno 1052

773

3 Rgr

2 ⊠ 141

Vallecupa

A ☐ 753

Rocca
Pipirozzi

351

Monte
Lungo
343

253

Peccia Cr.

San
Giacomo
Hill

6

Monte
Rotondo
357

3 ⊠ 141

689

Cannavinelle Hill

Monte Cesima

1170

⊠ 142

510 Monte Maggiore

1 Mtz Gp

Mignano

50 100 200 300 400 500 600 700 800
Monte la Difensa
960

900 1000 800 700 600 500 400 300 200

963
Monte Camino

294

December 16th 1943 — (Pacific-Bismarcks-New Britain) Naval Land Based Aircraft attached to VP-52, destroy the Japanese Submarine I-179. **(Atlantic)** In Italy, the U.S. Fifth Army area, Mont Lungo is cleared of enemy opposition by 10:00 by the 142nd Infantry, 36th Division. The Italian 1st Motorized Group (fighting with the Allies) captures Hills 253 and 343 during the afternoon. The Germans hold firm at south Pietro until after the fall of Mont Lungo, which jeopardizes their position at Pietro, forcing them to withdraw. The Germans pull back fighting by mounting a counterattack against the 143rd Infantry to cover the withdrawal. The assault is repelled by the 1st Battalion on the western slopes of Mont Sammucro during the night of 16-17 after hours of tenacious fighting. In the VI Corps area, advance patrols of the 179th Infantry move into Lagone without incident. French troops secure the second knob of Mont Patano and a hill to the north of Lagone. The offensive moves slowly toward Monte Cassino, the colossal obstacle standing between the persistent American Fifth Army and Rome. In other activity in the Atlantic, the Destroyers *Trippe* (DD-403) and *Woolsey* (DD-437), patrolling off Oran, destroy the German Submarine U-73.

U.S. Paratroopers close on San Pietro, passing destroyed German equipment which is scattered around the abandoned town.

Army Medics enter bombed-out San Pietro.

December 17th 1943 — (Pacific-Bismarcks) In New Britain, an enemy Dive Bomber sinks a U.S. Coastal Transport, the APc-21. Enemy Planes also damage the Motor Minesweeper YMS-50 in the same vicinity. In New Georgia, Allied Fighters, including Marine Fighter Squadron 214, from Airfields in New Georgia, attack Japanese Planes that are attempting take off at

Lakunai Airfields in Rabaul. This attack is the first Fighter assault launched against Rabaul. **(Pacific-Solomons-Bougainville)** Torokina Airstrip is put into use as a Staging Base for Fighter Planes which are to attack the Japanese stronghold of Rabaul. **(China-Burma-India)** Generalissimo Chiang Kai-shek sends another request to President Roosevelt, asking for more Air strength to assist the Chinese Divisions and additional financial aid. **(Atlantic-Italy) 15th Army Group** In the **U.S. Fifth Army** area, II Corps sector, the 36th Division is in pursuit of the Germans who are withdrawing from South Pietro. In the VI Corps area, the Germans are pushed back along the center of the front and by dark, the 180th Infantry, U.S. 45th Division occupies Mont la Posta without incident. German rear guards are deployed to cover the withdrawal of their forces from Mont Pantano.

December 18th 1943 — (Pacific-Solomons-Bougainville) The 1st and 3rd Battalions, 21st Marines mop up opposition on the heights above the beachhead after culminating the operation which had begun on the 27th of November. Hellzapoppin Ridge, the most obstinate of the Japanese-infested hills falls to the Marines. **(Pacific-Bismarcks-New Britain)** A Japanese force lands at Omoi and marches toward Army positions at Arawe. **(China-Burma-India)** Japanese aircraft attack Kunming, China attempting to soften Allied resistance prior to the impending invasion. In other activity, Generalissimo Chiang Kai-shek delegates total command of the Chinese troops in India and the Hukawng Valley to U.S. General Joseph Stilwell. In Naval activity, the Submarine *Cabrilla* (SS-288), lays mines off the coast of Cambodia in Indochina. **(Atlantic-Italy) 15th Army Group** In the **U.S. Army Fifth Army** area, German resistance on the western slopes of Mont Sammucro continues (II Corps area). In the VI Corps area, the enemy pulls back as elements of the Fifth Army advance along the south Elia Road. Mont Pantano is totally occupied by the French troops who had previously secured part of the hill mass on the 16th.

December 19th 1943 — (Pacific-New Britain) The U.S. Fifth Air Force strikes targets in the Cape Gloucester area. **(Pacific-Ryukyu Islands)** The U.S.S. *Grayback* (SS-208), while patrolling near this island chain, laying between Taiwan and Kyushu, sinks the Japanese Destroyer *Numakaze*. The Japanese will be using this chain as their last line of defense toward the end of the war. The principal island is Okinawa, where one of the most savage battles of the entire war takes place. **(Pacific-China-Burma-India)** Japanese Aircraft strike Kunming, China. In other activity, Chiang Kai-shek gives General Stilwell full command of the Chinese forces in India and in the Hukawng Valley in Burma. On the following day, Chiang denies Admiral Mountbatten's proposal for a major attack. **(Atlantic-Italy)** General Mark Clark's Fifth Army is heavily engaged with German defenders who are holding firmly, preventing the 141st and 143 Regiments, 36th Division from breaking through the southern and western slopes of Mont Sammucro. The enemy's staunch defense is barring American access to Highway 6 and Mignano Gap.

December 20th 1943 — (United States) The U.S. Navy establishes a Naval Air Training Command, at Pensacola, Florida. **(Pacific)** Admiral Nimitz, Commander in Chief, Pacific, issues final plans for the invasion of the Marshalls. The priorities: bombing Maloelap, Mille, and Wotje to neutralize their effectiveness; the destruction of Eniwetok Kusaie by Air; and the capture of Kwajalein Atoll. **(Pacific-New Guinea)** Allied plans for the further isolation of Rabaul now include the assault of Green Island as the next step toward total isolation. This decision is made at a meeting held at Port Moresby. In other activity, the 2nd Battalion, 158th Regiment, commanded by Lt. Colonel Fred Stofft is deployed in Finschhafen, guarding Headquarters, however, Company G is dispatched to Arawe to bolster the attack. A group of Americans (U.S.O.) had been visiting the troops and one man, Marion Morrison, requests permission to go to the front lines, however, Colonel Stofft, informs his old High School classmate that the answer is no! He notes: "HE DIDN'T KNOW IF HE WAS GOING TO MAKE A CAREER OF THE ARMY . . . BUT HE WAS DAMNED IF HE WOULD SEE IT SHOT DOWN BY BEING THE MAN WHO SENT JOHN WAYNE TO HIS DEATH." **(Pacific-Philippines)** The Submarine *Puffer*, (SS-268), patrolling near the Philippines, destroys the Japanese Destroyer *Fuyo*. **(Pacific-Solomons-Treasury Islands)** Army Aircraft are flown from New Caledonia to Stirling Island from where they begin to operate against the enemy on Cape Gloucester. Additional Bombers are transferred from New Caledonia to the Russell Islands for the same purpose. **(Pacific-Bismarcks-New Britain)** The Japanese troops which have landed previously at Omoi on the 18th advance closer to American positions at Arawe. They are in the vicinity of the Pulie river, east of the Arawe beachhead. **(Solomons-Bougainville)** U.S. Destroyers bomb Japanese installations near the northeastern coast of Bougainville. **(China-Burma-India)** The continuing messages between President Roosevelt and Chiang Kai-shek are not yet in agreement. President Roosevelt urges China to keep its commitment to assist in the fight to seize Burma. Roosevelt also informs the Chinese leader that his request for more financial aid is under consideration. Chiang Kai-shek replies that the Allied capture of the Andaman Islands, Moulmein or Rangoon is mandatory before the Y-Force will be committed. Kai-shek also states that the Chinese troops will march into Burma without an amphibious operation if Lashio or Mandalay can be resecured from the Japanese first. **(Atlantic-Mediterranean)** Air Chief of the Mediterranean Allied Air Forces (newly created by Combined Chiefs of Staff on 5 December). American General Spaatz is appointed as his operational deputy. General Spaatz also assumes responsibility as Commanding General U.S.A.A.F./North African Theater. **(Atlantic-Germany)** The U.S. 358th Bomber Squadron, 303rd Bomber Group makes another raid against Bremen, Germany. Heavy enemy resistance meets the Allied Strike Force. In one instance, murderous fire rips into one of the Planes. Technical Sgt. Forrest Vosler was called upon to continue firing his weapon at the attacking enemy Planes while the Pilot attempts to ditch the damaged Aircraft. Vosler, although seriously wounded in the face and chest and only capable of seeing blurred images, soars above the call of duty and contributes greatly to the rescue of the crew. **(Atlantic-Italy)** The Fifth Army advances slowly against the solid German Winter Line. The inability of the Army to make sufficient progress causes the impending invasion of Italy's western coast (Anzio) by the Fifth Army to be canceled. Another problem contributing to the delay is the severe shortage of Landing Craft. **15th Army Group** In the **U.S. Fifth Army** area, elements of the 36th Division continue to clear the western slopes of Mont Sammucro and then push forward toward south Vittore. A night attack is to be launched against enemy-held Hill 730 and Morello Hill, but the Germans repulse the

attempt. In the **British Eighth Army** area, the Canadian 1st Division is engaged heavily with the Germans in the vicinity of Ortona. The Canadians finally secure the town on the 28th of December. **(mid-Atlantic)** The Escort Carrier *Bogue* (CVE-9), launches Planes (VC19) which sinks the German U-Boat U-850.

December 21st 1943 — (North Pacific) Naval Aircraft, based in the Aleutians, on Attu, bomb enemy positions in the Kurile Islands, in the vicinity of Paramushiro-Shimushu. **(Pacific-Bismarcks-New Britain)** Two Marine Patrols scout the beach areas, in the vicinity of Tauali prior to the landing. In Naval activity, the U.S. Coastal Transport APc-2, is attacked and damaged by an enemy Dive Bomber. **(Pacific-New Guinea)** Major General William H. Rupertus, U.S.M.C., runs his troops (Task Force Backhander), through the final rehearsal prior to the invasion of Cape Gloucester, New Britain. **(China-Burma-India)** General Stilwell arrives at Ledo and takes personal command of the troops (North Burma campaign). **(Atlantic-Panama)** The Coast Guard Cutter *Bodega*, (YP-342), grounded on the previous day near Margarita Point in the Canal zone is abandoned today. **(Atlantic-Soviet Union)** The Germans place pressure upon the Soviet salient near Zhlobin.

December 22nd 1943 — (China-Burma-India) Japanese Planes raid Kunming, China again, prior to their planned offensive against India. **(Mediterranean and European Theaters)** General Spaatz receives instructions to assume command of U.S. Strategic Air Forces in Europe. General Eaker, presently in the European Theater of Operations, will confer with Generals Spaatz and Doolittle before transferring to the Mediterranean Theater in the middle of January to command the Allied Air Forces in that Theater. **(Atlantic-Italy)** **15th Army Group** In the British Eighth Army's 13th Corps sector, the Indian 8th Division captures Villa Grandi. Bitter fighting between the Canadians and Germans ensues for control of Ortona.

December 23rd 1943 — (United States) The U.S.S. *Corvina* (SS-226) is presumed lost in the Pacific. The Submarine under Commander R.S. Rooney had departed Pearl Harbor on November 4th for duty off Truk. The *Corvina* stop sat Johnston Island, however when the operations in the Gilberts had completed, she fails to respond to orders on the 30th. Subsequently, Japanese records show the kill of a Submarine off Truk on November 16th, and the *Corvina* on her first War Patrol loses all hands, becoming the only U.S. Submarine lost to a Japanese Submarine. **(Pacific-Marshalls)** Six SBDs, attached to Marine Scout-Bomber Squadron 331 participate in a U.S. attack against Jaluit Atoll. **(Pacific-Solomons)** The U.S.S. *Griswold* (DE-7), a Destroyer Escort, sinks the Japanese Submarine I-39. Also, American Aircraft sink a Japanese Gunboat, the *Nanyo* at an unknown location. On New Georgia, U.S. Army Bombers initiate operations from Munda airfield against the Japanese. **(Pacific-New Britain)** Marine Fighter Squadron 214 assaults Rabaul. Enemy planes are launched to intercept the American Planes, prompting a duel in the sky over Cape St. George. The Marines Pilots inflict heavy losses on the Japanese interceptors. **(China-Burma-India)** Elements of the Chinese 114th Regiment, Chinese 38th Division, engage a contingent of Japanese about nine miles outside of Kantau, Burma in the Hukawng Valley. The Chinese fight their way to aid the beleaguered 1st Battalion, 112th Infantry still isolated by the Japanese. **(Atlantic)** General Eisenhower in a letter to General Marshall, concerning the American participation in

Europe offers his choice for the Commander. The letter in part: " MY PREFERENCE FOR AMERICAN ARMY GROUP COMMANDER, WHEN MORE THAN ONE AMERICAN ARMY IS OPERATING IN OVERLORD, IS GENERAL BRADLEY. ONE OF HIS ARMY COMMANDERS SHOULD PROBABLY BE PATTON." **(Atlantic-Italy) 15th Army Group** In the British Eighth Army area, the British 5th Division takes Arielli.

December 24th 1943 — (United States) Information concerning the assassination of French Admiral Darlan arrives in Washington. **(Pacific-Solomons-Bougainville)** The entire beachhead is now secure. The Marines have exterminated enemy resistance on all the heights in the surrounding area. On the following day, advance elements of the Americal Division, U.S.A., arrive to begin relieving the Marines, 3rd Division and take responsibility for the island. The Marines will be totally evacuated by the 16th of January. In other activity in the Solomons, Rear Admiral Merrill's Task Force, which includes four Destroyers and three Cruisers, bombards enemy positions in the vicinity of Buka-Bonis. **(Pacific-New Britain)** Allied Planes continue delivering intense Air bombardments against enemy positions, flying 280 sorties. **(China-Burma-India)** The 1st Battalion, 114th Regiment, assisted by Artillery, fights its way to the battle-weary trapped Chinese Battalion, successfully rescuing it. The Japanese still control the area at Yupbang Ga, Burma, preventing the Chinese from fording the river. **(Atlantic)** President Roosevelt and Prime Minister Winston Churchill publicize the appointment of General Eisenhower to the post of Supreme Allied Commander of the Allied Expeditionary Force. General Eisenhower will head Operation Overlord (invasion of Normandy). British General Sir Henry Maitland Wilson assumes command as Supreme Allied Commander, Mediterranean Theater. Churchill also announces that General Montgomery will succeed General Sir Bernard Paget as commander of 21st Army Group. General Montgomery will be succeeded by General Sir Oliver Leese who assumes the position Commander Eighth Army. **(Atlantic-Italy) 15th Army Group** In the British Eighth Army area, the New Zealand 2nd Division drives hard and advances to the heights overlooking German held Orsogna. In Naval activity in the Atlantic, an enemy Submarine attacks and destroys the Destroyer *Leary* (DD-158). In other Naval activity, the U.S.S. *Schenck* (DD-159), a Destroyer, attacks and sinks the U-645 in the North Atlantic. **(Atlantic-Middle East)** U.S. Brigadier General Donald H. Connolly is relieved as Commanding General, Persian Gulf Command by Brigadier General Donald P. Booth. **(Atlantic-Europe)** The U.S. Eighth Air Force launches 1,300 airplanes, including 722 heavy bombers, to attack suspected secret German weapon sites (Operation CROSSBOW). **(Atlantic-Russia)** The German defenses at Gorodok falter and the Russians, attacking from two directions, successfully secure the town. The Soviets then begin another offensive drive, before dawn on Christmas Day and regain ground they had previously lost to the German counter-offensive.

December 25th 1943 — (Pacific-Bougainville) RCT 164, American Division arrives to relieve the 3rd Marine Division. **(Pacific-Treasury Island)** A Fighter Airstrip is completed by the Seabees on Stirling. **(Pacific-New Ireland)** Kavieng Harbor is attacked by Planes attached to Admiral Frederick Sherman's Task Force; a Naval Surface bombardment of Buka had preceded the Air strike. **(Pacific-New Britain)** Japanese at-

tack the Arawe beachhead pushing the troops at the observation posts to withdraw. Meanwhile, Task Force Backhander departs New Guinea sailing toward Cape Gloucester. **(China-Burma-India)** Chittagong, India is attacked by Japanese Planes. **(Atlantic-North Africa) 15th Army Group** Plans for an amphibious landing below Rome are brought back on the table at a meeting in Tunis; the tentative assault will include Paratroopers in support of Infantry and Armor and is to commence about 20th January in conjunction with the Fifth Army drive from the south. **(Atlantic-Italy)** In the **Fifth Army** area. **II Corps** sector, Hill 730 is captured by the 1st Regiment of the 1st Special Service Force. Several additional hills to the north are seized by the 504th Paratroop Infantry. **(Atlantic-Soviet Union)** The Vitebsk-Polotsk highway is severed by Soviet troops.

December 26th 1943 — An overloaded Vessel, crammed with loaded trucks and troops during the Invasion of Cape Gloucester, New Britain.

December 26th 1943-January 16th 1944 — (Pacific-New Britain) THE BATTLE OF CAPE GLOUCESTER — General MacArthur is determined to take the Pacific and this skillfully planned invasion is part of his master plan. In a diversionary action, elements of the U.S. 6th Army debark at Arawe, New Britain, initiating the first landing of troops on the island which contains Rabaul. As the Japanese react to this U.S. ploy, MacArthur springs the main assault, sending the Marines (1st Division) into Cape Gloucester. The U.S. Naval Task Force, commanded by Rear Admiral D.E. Barbey moves up close and the Long Guns commence a thunderous bombardment. Shells from the Surface Vessels arc toward the enemy positions with deadly accuracy. U.S. Aircraft, including Squadrons from the Fifth Air Force and various Marine Fighter Squadrons, strafe and bomb relentlessly. The volume of exploding shells has the enemy observation post on Target Hill obscured by huge masses of smoke. This Japanese bastion, defended by 10,000 troops, braces for the onslaught of U.S. Marines who storm the beaches just after 07:00. The Japanese offer only minor resistance as the 7th Marines, 1st Division charge ashore, secure the beachhead and capture Target Hill. Secondary assault forces land on Tauali, southwest of the enemy Airdrome and Lons Island. The Marines fortify their positions and handily repulse successive Japanese counterattacks throughout the night. Enemy Planes dispatched from Rabaul sink one Destroyer and damage other Vessels, but the punishment doled out by the U.S. against the enemy Planes takes such a high toll that the Japanese are unable to mount any further strong daylight attacks against the Yanks. This landing at Cape Gloucester, on the western fringes of New Britain, has the Yanks pressing the Japs from all sides, convincing the enemy that they must prepare for the inevitable, the attack against Rabaul. MacArthur, after the capture of Cape Gloucester, chooses to isolate Rabaul, rather than take unnecessary casualties and strikes against Emirau and the Green Islands, on Rabaul's flanks.

Although the enemy had been blown from the skies, it still takes the Marines three brutalizing weeks to totally secure the island from the ferocious fanatical defenders. Japanese Major General Iwao Matsuda, commanding all forces on New Guinea, rushes his Reserves into the struggle and is also ordered to dispatch two other Regiments to Cape Gloucester. On the 31st of December, the Airfields and Airdrome on Cape Gloucester are declared secure, as Major General W. H. Rupertus raises Old Glory on this Pacific island as a New Year's Eve present for the folks back home.

The Marines begin driving south on the 2nd of January and abruptly run into heavy enemy fire, which prevents them from crossing so-called "Suicide Creek." The 7th Marines call in Engineers who promptly lay a temporary bridge, allowing Sherman Tanks to speed across it, in support of the Marines, who eradicate the resistance. The drive continues to the next objective held by well-hidden Japanese at Aogiri Ridge. These battle-hardened, exhausted mud Marines reach the deadly Japanese stronghold on the 11th and are tested severely. Enemy fire commences along with the shouts of Banzai! Aided by Artillery, the 3rd Battalion, 5th Marines charge the defensive positions held by the 2nd Battalion, 53rd and 141st Japanese Infantry Regiments and successfully capture the ridge. The Yanks turn back repeated counterattacks with vigor, strongly maintaining their grip on the ridge.

After these major unsuccessful enemy attacks, the Marines are struck by a final, all-out attempt to dislodge them on the 16th, but it is futile and culminates the enemy effort to destroy the American hold on Cape Gloucester. The Marines lose just over 300 killed and almost 1,100 wounded in this three-week campaign, but Cape Gloucester is in the hands of the Stars and Stripes. The 112th Cavalry at Arawe, having beaten back the major Japanese assault against their perimeter during late December, is in the process of mopping up after their extremely successful operation. Patrols are dispatched to regain isolated portions of the island to eradicate any remnants.

December 26th 1943 — (Pacific-New Britain) The 1st Marine Division invades Cape Gloucester, New Britain at 07:46. The 7th Marines secure the beach and General Rupertus establishes a Command Post on shore. The 1st Marines move through the 7th Marines area, searching the dense, swamp filled jungle for the enemy, discovering more than enough. During the night, fierce raids take a toll on the 7th Marines but the enemy suffers extremely high casualties and the attacks falter. Japanese Air attacks sink the U.S.S. *Brownson* (DD-518). Also, American Army positions at Arawe are threatened by the Japanese. Additional landings in the area are made with the 1st Marines landing at Tauali southwest of the enemy Airdrome and the 592nd Engineer Boat and Shore Regiment lands at Long Island, 80 miles west of Cape Gloucester, where they will set up a long range Australian radar station. In addition to the loss of the *Brownson*, the Destroyers *Lamson* (DD-367), *Shaw* (DD-373) and the *Mugford* (DD-389) are all damaged by enemy Dive Bombers. A Horizontal Bomber damages the LST 66. **(Atlantic-Italy) 15th Army Group** In the **U.S. Fifth Army** area, units of the 36th Division capture Morello Hill, while others clear Hill 730. The enemy holding Mont Sammucro are finally driven off. In the VI Corps area, the 8th Rifle Regiment, 2nd Moroccan Division, makes an unsuccessful assault against the enemy on Mainarde Ridge, north of Atina road.

December 26th 1943 — Marines, holding their rifles high, move through some crashing waves during the invasion of Cape Gloucester.

December 27th 1943 — **(Pacific)** Admiral Nimitz, Commander in Chief Pacific Area, publishes preliminary plans for the Central Pacific campaigns for 1944. The schedule for the Pacific Ocean Areas and Southwest Pacific Areas are as follows: Kwajalein, January 31st 1944; Kavieng and Truk (air assaults) March 20th 1944; Manus, April 20th 1944; Eniwetok, May 1st 1944; Mortlock July 1st 1944; Truk, August 15th 1944; and Tinian, Saipan and Guam, November 15th 1944. **(Pacific-Admiralties-New Britain)** Marine Combat Team C (7th Marines) repulses continuous savage attacks by the Japanese 2nd Battalion, 53rd Infantry, which had been seriously attempting to overrun their positions. The gallant 7th takes high casualties, but keep the center of the perimeter from being penetrated by the fanatical attackers. Marine Combat Team B (First Marines) captures Hell's Point, a Japanese stronghold guarding the Airdrome at Cape Gloucester. The Marines reach the Airdrome and proceed to reduce the enemy resistance at Hell's Point, during the 27th-28th. The Army at Arawe receives reinforcements (Company G 158th Infantry U.S.A.) in response to a request from General Cunningham. The Japanese will attempt to assault the perimeter on the 28th and 29th, being repulsed handily both times by the American Army at Arawe. In other activity, the U.S. Coastal Transport APc-15 is sunk by an enemy Dive Bomber off New Guinea. **(Pacific-Solomons)** Rear Admiral Ainsworth's Task Force, comprising four Destroyers and three Cruisers, bombards the enemy facilities at Kieta, Bougainville. Also, the Americal Division, U.S.A., begins relieving the 3rd Marine Division, assuming responsibility for the eastern sector of the beahhead, held by the 9th Marines. **(China-Burma-India)** The Chinese 65th Regiment is ordered to clear the enemy from the Taro Plain in Burma and then drive back to the Hukawng Valley, toward the flank of the enemy. **(Atlantic-Italy)** **15th Army Group** In the U.S. Fifth Army area, the French seize ground on the slopes of Mainarde ridge. **(Atlantic-Soviet Union)** Heavy fighting continues in the vicinity of Vitebsk. The Red Army severs the rail lines.

Corporal Robert Corbett and Sergeant Joseph Polya, Company A, 17th Battalion, pose with Polya's pet dog "Constance" at Camp Reynolds, Pa., a staging area for troops preparing to embark for overseas.

December 28th 1943 — **(Pacific-Hawaii)** The Navy establishes an Amphibious Training Base in Hawaii, at Kamaole, Maui. **(Pacific-Bougainville)** The Americal Division, U.S.A., completes the relief of the Third Marine Division positions along the perimeter. **(Pacific-Admiralties-Bougainville)** General Krueger, U.S.A., releases the 5th Marines (reinforced) to

General Rupertus, U.S.M.C. Also, the Japanese unsuccessfully attack the Arawe beachhead. **(China-Burma-India)** Contingents of the Chinese 38th Division clear areas of resistance along the Tarung river. **(Atlantic-Italy)** **15th Army Group** In the **U.S. Fifth Army** area, VI Corps sector, the French continue to advance, seizing Hill 1190 situated on the Mainarde Ridge. In the **British Eighth Army** sector, the Germans have finally been ousted from Ortona. **(Atlantic-Russia)** The Red Army attacks the German positions east of Zhitomir and captures Korostyshev.

December 29th 1943 — **(Pacific-Admiralties-New Britain)** Marines defending the Tauali beachhead devastate the 1st Battalion, 53rd Japanese Infantry, which makes repeated suicidal assaults against the perimeter during December 29th-30th. The 2nd Battalion, 5th Marines (Combat Team A) and the 1st Battalion, 1st Marines (Combat Team B) reach Airfields 1 and 2 and the Airport is declared secure on the 31st. **(Pacific-New Guinea)** Task Force Michaelmas issues formal plans for the invasion of Saidor. D-Day is set for January 2nd. **(China-Burma-India)** The Chinese 38th Division attacks relentlessly, attempting to clear more of the enemy from the Tarung River Line in Burma. The initiative pays off, as a Japanese strongpoint is broken up. **(Atlantic-North Africa)** The U.S. 7th Army planners are informed of the major objectives of (Operation Anvil), the proposed invasion of Southern France. **(Atlantic-Italy)** **15th Army Group** In the **U.S. Fifth Army** area, II Corps sector, Patrols of the 36th Division advance to south Vittore, but heavy enemy activity forces them back out. In the eastern portion of Mont Monna Casale, I Corps sector, French Forces capture several hills and begin to fortify their positions. **(Atlantic-Russia)** The Soviets clear Germans out of Korosten.

General Jopseph Stilwell eating K-ration dinner (Christmas Day 1943).

December 30th 1943 — **(Pacific-Gilberts-Tarawa)** The Forward Echelon of Headquarters Squadron, 4th Marine Base Defense Aircraft Wing, commanded by Brigadier General Lewis G. Merritt arrives on the atoll. **(Pacific-Solomons-Bougainville)** The Bomber Airfield at Piva is operational. American Patrols advance along the Numa Numa Trail, and set up outposts at Ibu village near the coast. Clearings will be cut out of the jungle for the construction of an Airstrip, which will accommodate Piper Cubs. **(Pacific-New Guinea)** U.S. Brigadier General Clarence A. Martin is informed that D-Day for the assault against Saidor is January 2nd. **(Atlantic-Italy)** In the U.S. Fifth Army area, II Corps sector, the exhausted battle-weary 36th Division gets well-deserved relief from the 34th Division. In the VI Corps area, the 180th Infantry, 45th

Division, fights tirelessly against strong opposition, in the hills east of Acquafondata and manages to get a grasp on Mont Rotondo. The weather is still terrible and the mountainous terrain, even when won, is difficult to retain, because of the Germans' grip on the high ground. **(Atlantic-Russia)** The Red offensive grabs another town, as German resistance crumbles at Kazatin.

December 31st 1943 — (United States) Lieutenant General Thomas Holcomb, Commandant of the Marine Corps, retires with the rank of General. **(North Pacific)** U.S. Naval Planes, stationed in the Aleutians at Attu, strike the Kurile Islands as they had on the 21st (Paramushiro-Shimushu area). **(Pacific-New Guinea)** Task Force Michaelmas, assigned the duty of attacking Saidor, departs Goodenough Island bound for the objective. **(Atlantic-Italy) 15th Army Group** In the **U.S. Fifth Army**, area, II Corps sector, the 6th Armored Infantry, 1st Armored Division, relieves the 15th Infantry, 3rd Division, on Mont Lungo. In the VI Corps area, heavy fighting brings in the New Year, as the 180th Infantry attempts unsuccessfully to clear the hills that lie east of Acquafondata. **(Atlantic-Russia)** The Germans abandon the garrison at Zhitomir. The Germans are under heavy fire and nearly surrounded at Vitebsk, but hold on.

The U.S. Fleet under attack at Cape Gloucester. Gunners aboard this Coast Guard Vessel are firing while one of their team points to another approaching enemy Plane.

Eugenia Kielar, one of the many Army Nurses who accompanied the GIs during the fighting in North Africa and on the Continent.

U.S. B-24 approaching landing strip on Midway — flight pattern being observed by goonie birds.

1944

General Mark Clark and Secretary of the Navy, James Forrestal review Nisei (U.S. Japanese) Troops.

Stars & Stripes fills the skyline over Kwatalein.

General Eisenhower speaks with U.S. Airborne Troops just prior to the departure for Normandy.

The Yanks return to the Philippines.

January 1st 1944 — (Pacific-Hawaii) The U.S. Navy establishes a Naval Air Facility at Honolulu, Oahu. **(Pacific-Solomon Islands)** The 182nd Infantry, U.S.A., Americal Division, relieves (1st-2nd) the 21st Marines on Bougainville. In other activity, the LST 446 sustains damage by accidental explosion. **(Pacific-Wake Island)** U.S. Planes begin a series of 996 sorties against Wake Island, one of the first islands to be seized by the Japanese that lasts through May. **(Pacific-Bismarcks-New Ireland)** A Carrier Task Force, commanded by Admiral Frederick C. Sherman, launches Planes to assault Shipping in Kavieng Harbor. The enemy Convoy, nearing New Ireland, is escorted by Destroyers and Cruisers. **(Pacific-New Guinea)** Allied Planes bombard enemy positions near Saidor. Simultaneously, U.S. Ships transporting the Assault troops, converge on Oro Bay to meet their Destroyer Escort Ships. In Naval activity, the Destroyers U.S.S. *Smith* (DD-378) and the U.S.S. *Hutchings* (DD-476) are damaged by collision. **(Pacific-Philippines)** General MacArthur broadcasts a message, to the Philippine people: in part: "TO MY COMMANDERS IN THE PHILIPPINES." "WITH THE DAWN OF A NEW YEAR, PLEASE CONVEY TO YOUR OFFICERS AND MEN AND TO THE CIVILIANS WHO ARE GIVING YOU THEIR LOYAL SUPPORT, MY WARM PERSONAL GREETINGS AND GRATEFUL ACKNOWLEDGMENT OF RESOLUTE PAST SERVICE." "TELL THEM I CONFIDENTLY LOOK TO THE COMING YEAR AS A PERIOD IN WHICH EVERY MONTH WILL SEE SIGNIFICANT AND DECISIVE GAINS TOWARD THE FINAL AND COMPLETE DESTRUCTION OF JAPANESE MILITARY POWER; AND THAT IN THIS PERIOD, I REQUIRE THAT EVERY MAN SHALL ADHERE TO THE PATH OF DUTY WITH THAT SAME COURAGE AND INVINCIBLE DETERMINATION THAT HAS CHARACTERIZED THE SPIRIT OF PHILIPPINE RESISTANCE DURING THE DIFFICULT AND TRYING PAST." **(Pacific-China-Burma-India)** General Stilwell forms an operations staff for Force Zebra. **(Atlantic-North Africa)** General George Patton is ordered to relinquish command of his 7th Army to General Mark Clark, who will also retain command of the Fifth Army. General Clark is to plan for Operation ANVIL (early plan for invasion of southern France). Patton notes in his diary: "I SUPPOSE I AM GOING TO ENGLAND TO COMMAND ANOTHER ARMY, BUT IF I AM SENT THERE TO SIMPLY TRAIN TROOPS WHICH I AM NOT TO COMMAND (on the battlefield) I SHALL RESIGN." .."I CAN THINK OF NOTHING MORE STUPID THAN TO CHANGE STAFF ON A GENERAL, NOR CAN I CONCEIVE OF ANYTHING MORE INCONSIDERATE THAN NOT TO NOTIFY HIM WHERE HE IS GOING." In other activity, AAF units are reorganized: USAAF/NATO becomes Army Air Forces, Mediterranean Theater of Operations (AAF/MTO); XII Air Force Service Command becomes Army Air Forces Service Command, MTO (AAFSC/MTO); II Air Service Area Command becomes XV Air Force Service Command; III Air Service Area Command becomes XII Air Force Service Command; XII Air Force Engineer Command (Prov) becomes AAFEC/MTO.

January 2nd 1944 — (Pacific-New Britain-Cape Gloucester) Brigadier General Lemuel C. Shepherd, Asst. Division Commander, orders the 2nd and 3rd Battalions, 7th Marines, to attack. The assault overcomes the enemy and presses forward, toward Borgen Bay. **(Pacific-New Guinea)** American Destroyers and Cruisers, under the command of Rear Admiral D.E. Barbey, commence a massive preinvasion bombardment of Saidor. Inclement weather prevents an air-

January 2nd 1944 — Navy LSTs at Saidor, New Guinea.

strike, but the skies subsequently clear for the Carrier Planes to fly cover support for the Assault troops. 126, 32nd Division, takes full advantage of the surprise landing, moves rapidly and secures the harbor and Airfield. Meanwhile, the Australian troops drive from Finschhafen toward Sialium, closing the gap between themselves and the Americans, to about 60 miles, when they advance to Kelanoa on the 5th. During the struggle for control of the Huon Peninsula, the U.S. Sixth Army lends superlative support and the Japanese, caught between the Americans at Saidor and the closing Australians, begin withdrawing after the Australians seize Shaggy Ridge in the Ramu Valley on the 23rd. The Allies now have virtual control of the Huon Peninsula. The retreating Japanese are under consistent pressure from Allied Planes, which strafe the escape routes. **(Pacific-China-Burma-India)** Major General Daniel I. Sultan arrives at New Guinea, becoming General Stilwell's Deputy. **(Atlantic-Italy) 15th Army Group** British General Alexander orders the U.S. Fifth Army to set up an Amphibious operation and to prepare for a landing at Anzio below Rome (Operation SHINGLE). In addition, the British Eighth Army is delegated the responsibility of maintaining pressure on the enemy troops in its sector, as a diversionary tactic. In Naples, civilians continue to cut communications wires to confiscate the copper wiring for sale on the black market. The problem reaches epidemic proportions. Thieves also steal manhole covers, causing serious problems on the roads. During February, Field Security Headquarters, Italy, at Castellammare is burglarized by civilians. Despite guards and thirty foot high walls, the barrier is breached and all Vehicles within the compound lose their wheels within a few minutes to the second story men.

January 3rd 1944 — (United States) Admiral King meets in San Francisco with Admirals Nimitz and Halsey; King emphasizes that the Marianas are the key to the Pacific. Subsequently, on the 27th, representatives of Nimitz, Halsey, and MacArthur will meet in Pearl Harbor for further discussions. Also, the Destroyer U.S.S. *Turner* (DD-648), sinks in the Ambrose Channel, New York Harbor, after sustaining an explosion. **(Pacific Area)** Rear Admiral Turner U.S.N., (Task Force 51) issues Operation Plan A6-43, which identifies the components and objectives of the Joint Expeditionary Force's assignment to seize the Marshall Islands. **(Pacific-New Britain)** The 1st Battalion, 7th Marines, repulses a Japanese counterattack mounted against its positions on Target Hill. Elements of the 7th Marines are stalled by heavy enemy resistance at "Suicide Creek." The Marines, unable to get their Tanks across by ordinary methods, improvise; by the following day, the Tanks roar across a modified version of a bridge to destroy the resistance. In other activity, Marine Fighter Squadron 214 has been in constant battle with enemy Planes, since the 12th of September 1943. During this time period, Major "Pappy" Boyington has been credited with the destruction of 26 enemy Planes. Major Boyington's aggressive leadership has molded an elite outfit, which has helped to accomplished many brave feats, leading to the disintegration of enemy Airpower in this strategic area of the Solomons. **(Pacific-Dutch East Indies)** The Submarine *Bluefish*, (SS-222) operating off the Malayan coast, deploys mines. **(Atlantic-Italy) 15th Army Group** In the **U.S. Fifth Army** area, the Allies make final preparations for the last phase of the campaign to take the Winter Line. The offensive commences on the fifth. Preliminary assaults begin during the night of the 3rd-4th, against the ridge southeast of enemy controlled Mont Majo. French General Juin, commanding the French Expeditionary Corps, takes command of the northern flank of the Fifth Army, replacing the VI Corps, which is being pulled back from the line for assignment with the amphibious assault against Anzio. The Algerian 3rd Division relieves the U.S. 45th Division. **(Atlantic-Russia)** Olevsk, situated northwest of Kiev, falls to the Russians. The Soviet Army penetrates the prewar frontier of Poland for the first time. In addition, the Novograd Volyinsk area falls to the Russians, adding another rail system from Korosten for the Red Army.

January 4th 1944 — (Pacific-New Britain) Contingents of the 3rd Battalions, 5th and 7th Marines, defeat the 2nd Battalion, 53rd Japanese Infantry, at "Suicide Creek," Cape Gloucester. The triumphant Marines move toward Aogiri Ridge, without opposition. **(Pacific-New Ireland)** American Carrier-based Planes, attached to Rear Admiral F.C. Sherman's Force, attack Kavieng, but no enemy Vessels are in port. **(Pacific-New Guinea)** American Patrols search for the enemy in the Saidor vicinity, without success. Australian contingents reach Cape Iris, west of Saidor. In Naval Activity, the PT-145 becomes grounded and is subsequently sunk by U.S. Forces. **(China-Burma-India)** The Submarine U.S.S. *Rasher* (SS-269), operating in waters near China, deploys mines near Cochin. **(Atlantic-Italy) 15th Army Group** In the **U.S. Fifth Army**

area, heavy enemy opposition meets elements of the British 10 Corps at its bridgehead across the Peccia River. In the **U.S. II Corps** area, the 1st Special Service Force, after securing positions on a ridge southeast of Mont Majo, secures Hill 775 and Mont Arcalone. **(Western Europe)** U.S. Aircraft initiate the flying of supplies to various patriot forces (Underground) scattered throughout Europe. The Operation is coded, "CARPETBAGGER." The Planes, based in England, continue the mission until September of 1944. **(Atlantic-Russia)** The Soviets take Belaya Tserkov in the Ukraine, southwest of Kiev and move toward Uman.

January 5th 1944 — (Pacific-New Guinea) Americans patrolling west of Saidor meet enemy opposition at Cape Iris. Also, the Australians advance to Kelanoa, narrowing the existing gap between U.S. and Australian forces. **(China-Burma-India)** The Chinese 38th Infantry meets heavy opposition as it attempts to destroy the last remaining obstacle between it and the Tarung River in Burma. The Japanese repulse the attack. **(Atlantic-England)** The Headquarters of U.S. Strategic Air Forces in Europe is established in England, commanded by General Spaatz, who will coordinate operations of the Eighth and Fifteenth Air Forces. **(Atlantic-Italy) 15th Army Group** The **U.S. Fifth Army** initiates final phase of the offensive to reduce the enemy Winter Line. The 10 Corps Tanks are unable to cross the Peccia River, prompting the British to withdraw the bridgehead. In the **U.S. II Corps** area, the 6th Armored Infantry, reinforced (Task Force A), 1st Armored Division, drives toward Mont Porchia; after relentless fighting, it finally falls on the 7th. The 3rd Battalion, 135th Infantry, attacks enemy positions near South Vittore and also secures more ground. The 1st Battalion, 135th Infantry, drives toward La Chiaia, northwest of south Vittore, but enemy resistance is fierce, halting the advance as it approaches south Giusta. The 168th Infantry, in coordination with the assault being made by the 135th, outflanks La Chiaia and secures enemy held Hill 425. **(Atlantic-Russia)** The Soviets seize Berdichev (another rail junction) southwest of Kiev.

January 6th 1944 — (United States) Major Jordan (Lendlease Liaison Officer) arrives at Washington from Great Falls, Montana in an attempt to blow out the flagrant abuse of the Lend-lease program, which scandalously is shipping illegal goods into Russia; he also is attempting to warn the State Department about the alarming rate of Russians which are stampeding into the country without even passing through any custom checks. Russians move into the country on unchecked flights and simply disperse into the towns and cities all across the nation. The State Department ignores his pleas; his warnings are placed under the rug. Major Jordan states that: "HIS CAREER IS THREATENED BY JOHN NEWBOLD HAZARD, A LOWER MEMBER OF THE LEND-LEASE LIAISON OFFICE." Jordan informs the State Department that "PLANE LOADS OF SUITCASES, FILLED WITH CONFIDENTIAL DATA, WERE PASSING EVERY THREE WEEKS WITHOUT INSPECTION, UNDER THE GUISE OF DIPLOMATIC IMMUNITY." The Russians continue to flaunt the U.S. without hindrance, despite the warnings. Subsequently, on the 6th of July, Charles E. Bohlen, of the State Department confers with several organizations including the F.B.I. and Military Intelligence people; the conference results in a decision to crack down on the Russians by enforcing censorship regulations; this too is ignored. Also, the Gunboat U.S.S. *St Augustine* (PG-54) sinks after being involved in a collision off the coast of North Carolina. **(Pacific)** The Operation Plan (No. Cen I-44) for the invasion of the Marshall Islands is issued. It specifies the landing forces to be used and includes a Northern Landing Force, Southern Landing Force, and the Majuro Landing Force. In addition, the plan designates possible landing beaches situated in the Kwajalein Islands, on Namur and Roi. In other activity, Major General Hubert R. Harmon assumes Command of the U.S. Thirteenth Air Force. **(Pacific-New Britain)** A concentration of enemy troops is discovered in the vicinity of the Arawe beachhead. **(Pacific-New Guinea)** The U.S. 808th Aviation Engineering Battalion arrives at Saidor. **(China-Burma-India)** British Admiral Mountbatten cancels the planned limited offensive against the Japanese on the south Mayu Peninsula, bypassing Burma, until after the defeat of Germany. Subsequent to the German defeat, a large and powerful offensive, beginning with the invasion of Sumatra will occur. The decision in made partly because all available Landing Craft are being transferred to the Mediterranean. American General Stilwell (Chief of Staff, China Theater) is informed of the decision to cancel (Operation PIGSTICK) and he sends representatives to Washington to present his views against the cancellation. In other activity, the Chinese concentrate on expelling the Japanese from the Tarung River area, but are unsuccessful as heavy fighting continues. **(Atlantic-Italy)** 15th Army Group In the **U.S. Fifth Army** area, Task Force A, 1st Armored Division, fights to the northern crest of Mont Porchia, where the Germans mount an unsuccessful counterattack. South Vittore, secured by the 135th Infantry, by 17:00 renews its advance toward La Chiaia. Other elements advance, but hit stiff resistance along the route to M. Majo. **(Atlantic-European Theater of Operations)** Major General Frederick L. Anderson and Brigadier General Hugh J. Knerr are appointed as Deputy Commanders for operations and administration respectively. (General Order No. I of U.S.S.A.F.E.).

Lt. General Jacob L. Devers.

January 7th 1944 — (China-Burma-India) The Japanese Southern Army receives instructions to deploy troops in the vicinity of Imphal India and fortify positions there as soon as the plan is deemed feasible. Also, British Admiral Mountbatten cancels Operation CUDGEL, a scaled opertion in the Arakan sector of Burma. **(Atlantic-Italy)** 15th Army Group In the **U.S. Fifty Army** area, Task Force B, 1st Special Service Force, takes Mont Majo during the early part of the day and, holds the ground against reeated enemy counterattacks. Task Force A, U.S. 1st Armored Division, seizes enemy held Mont Porchia and in so doing, puts the Germans holding Cedro Hill in jeopardy. During the struggle for Mount Porchia, Sergeant Joe Specker, 48th Engineer Combat Battalion, spots an enemy nest and advances singlehandedly with a machine gun. Specker is mortally wounded but drags himself to a strategic location and begins a withering fire, which destroys the nest and also forces the enemy snipers to withdraw. Specker is found dead near his gun when the main body advances; he receives the Medal of Honor posthumously. In other action, the U.S. 135th Infantry takes Mont La Chiaia, with the assistance of the 168th Infantry, which is pressing the Germans on a ridge northeast of the objective. The 135th Regiment, heads west, driving the enemy from Cicerelli Hill and from Hill 224. **(Atlantic-Russia)** The Soviets proclaim a breakthrough along the 60-mile front in the Kirovograd area, which in effect has the Germans almost totally enveloped in that area.

January 8th 1944 — (United States) The War Department decides that Airpower in the China-Burma-India zones must be made stronger to reinforce the primary offensive, which will be waged against the Japanese Empire in the Pacific. **(Pacific-Solomons)** U.S. Naval Vessels, under the command of Rear Admiral W. L. Ainsworth, open fire on the Shortland Islands. The bombardment ignites massive fires within the enemy positions, including damage at Faisi and Poporang, Solomons. **(Atlantic-Italy)** 15th Army Group In the **U.S. Fifth Army's** British 10 Corps area, Mont Cedro falls to the British 46th Division without opposition. In the **U.S. II Corps** area, Task Force B, seizes Hill 1109. The Germans have now withdrawn as far as the hills above Cervaro to form a line and hold the gateway to the Liri Valley. **(Atlantic-Mediterranean)** U.S. General Eisenhower relinquishes command of the Allied troops in the Mediterranean Theater to British General Sir Henry Maitland Wilson. American General Devers assumes command of the U.S. troops in the North Africa Theater of Operations. **(Atlantic-Russia)** The Germans indicate the initiation of an offensive in the Zhlobin sector. In other action, the Soviets capture the rail center at Dnieper bend.

January 9th 1944 — (Pacific-Solomons) At Bougainville, the 3rd Marine Division still is being replaced by the Americal Division U.S.A. In other activity, another Airfield, Piva Yoke, is complete. **(Pacific-New Britain)** The Japanese lose a portion of Aogiri Ridge, west of Hill 150. The Japanese, who have been ordered to hold at all costs, lose the contested ridge that controls a primary enemy supply route to the 3rd Battalion, 5th Marines, on the 11th. **(Pacific-China-Burma-India)** The Chinese 38th Division closes on Taihpa Ga, in the Hukawng Valley. **11th Army Group** In the **British Fourteenth Army** area, 15th Corps seizes Maungdaw. **(Atlantic-Italy)** In the **U.S. Fifth Army** area, the U.S. II Corps calls for an attack to commence on the 10th against Cervaro and Mont Trocchio, the two remaining obstacles of the Winter Line objectives. In other activity, remaining units of the U.S. 45th Division are replaced by troops of the 3rd Algerian Division, French Expeditionary Corps. In activity off the coast, U.S. Army Aircraft sink a German Submarine, the U-81, near Pola Italy.

January 10th 1944 — (North Pacific-Aleutians) A U.S. Minesweeper, the YMS-127, operating in waters around the Aleutians, sinks, after becoming grounded. **(Pacific-New Britain)** The Marines, who have maintained control of a portion of Aogiri Ridge since the previous day, repulse a series of counterattacks, then advance to attack enemy positions on Hill 660. **(Pacific-New Guinea)** General C.A. Martin, U.S.A., anticipating an enemy assault against Allied positions at Saidor, requests Teams 1 and 3 (Regimental Combat Team 128), to augment his present Force. His request for additional strength is granted by General Krueger. **(Atlantic-Italy)** In the **U.S. Fifth Army** area, **U.S. II Corps** area, the 168th Infantry, 34th Division, U.S.A., drives toward Cervaro, pushing through the hills north of South Vittore-Cervaro Road, in conjunction with the 2nd Battalion, 135th Infantry, striking from the south. In addition, Task Force B moves on the right flank, heading toward Capraro Hill, to break the fierce German resistance. The drive ends with the capture of Cervaro on the 12th and the defeat of the enemy at Mont Trocchio on the 15th. **(Atlantic-Russia)** The Red Army destroys a German pocket of resistance north of Kirovograd.

January 11th 1944 — (Pacific-Marshalls) Naval Planes under the command of Rear Admiral J. H. Hoover, based at both the Gilbert and Ellice Islands, combine to bombard enemy positions including Shipping and Military installations on Kwajalein. **(Pacific-New Britain)** U.S. Marines, assisted by Artillery, secure Aogiri Ridge from entrenched Japanese. **(Pacific-New Guinea)** The Airfield at Saidor is now handling C-47s. **(Atlantic-Italy)** The U.S. Fifth Army, U.S. II Corps, continues its advance against Cervaro. **(Atlantic-Germany)** The advance tactical movements (Operation POINTBLANK), taken in preparation for the invasion of Normandy (Operation OVERLAND), begin with the initiation of intensified Air raids in Germany. Six hundred sixty-three Heavy Bombers, attached to the U.S. Eighth Air Force, attack plants in Brunswick, Halberstadt and the Oschersleben areas. The damage inflicted by the Allied Bombers is heavy, at a cost of 60 Planes. During the raid over Oschersleben, a group of escort P-51s, commanded by Lt. Colonel James H. Howard, intercepts enemy Aircraft and engages them in a furious battle. Colonel Howard, who loses contact with his Squadron, rejoins the Bombers, then singlehandedly destroys three of the 30 attacking enemy Fighters and damages several others.

January 12th 1944 — (United States) The U.S. Third Army prepares to embark for the European Theater of Operations. Advance units depart Fort Sam Houston, Texas. Also, the planners in the War Department decide on clearing a land route to China, choosing to reject Operation CULVERIN (assault on Sumatra) **(Pacific-New Britain)** Company B, 1st Tank

Battalion, 1st Marine Division and Company F, 158th Infantry, U.S.A., arrive at Arawe to further bolster the perimeter. **(Pacific-Solomons)** The Americal Division movement to Bougainville is complete. **(Atlantic-Italy)** British General Alexander orders the U.S. Fifth Army to attack the enemy south of Rome and to sweep aside resistance in Rome. British General Alexander also emphasizes the importance of speed. American General Lucas receives orders to land his VI Corps at Anzio, on D-Day, January 22, 1944, and to move against Colli Laziali. **15th Army Group** In the **U.S. Fifth Army** area, **II Corps** sector, Cervaro falls to elements of the 168th Infantry, U.S. 34th Division, while other units of the Division secure the nearby hills. Task Force B, operating on the right flank of the II Corps and assisted by the 3rd Algerian Division and the 2nd Moroccan Division, pushes toward south Elia and makes consistent progress against the enemy. **(Atlantic-North Africa)** The U.S. Navy establishes a Naval Air Station at Port Lyautey, French Morocco. Also, Brigadier General Garrison H. Davidson moves his Headquarters (Force 163; Seventh Army planning group for ANVIL) from Sicily to Algiers to plan for the invasion of Southern France. **(Atlantic-Russia)** The Germans holding Sarny are surrounded; the Soviets move in force from the rear and secure the town. In other action, the Germans counterattack in the area of Vinnitsa, southwest of Kiev.

U.S. troops crossing a river near Saidor.

January 13th 1944 — (United States) General Eisenhower departs the United States heading back for England. His meetings with the President are the last time the two men see each other. Upon Ike's return to England, he transfers his Headquarters (Supreme Headquarters, Allied Expeditionary Force) from London to the countryside. **(Pacific)** The plan (GRANITE) for the seizure of the Central Pacific is issued and it sets up the following timetable: A Carrier Task Force Raid on Truk in support of the invasion of the Admiralties and Kavieng about the 24th of March; the capture of Eniwetok and Ujeland Atolls in the Marshalls (CATCHPOLE) on the first of May; the seizure of Mortlock and Truk, in the Carolines on the 1st of August. In addition, the plan calls for the invasion and capture of Saipan and Tinian (FORAGER) on November 1st, followed by the seizure of Guam on the 15th of December. If Truk can be bypassed, the plan proposes that the Palaus Islands be invaded on August 1st. **(Pacific-New Britain)** Heavy fighting is still raging near Hill 660. The Marines call in Artillery and Air support, but are prevented from capturing their objective until the following day. The U.S. 864th Engineering Aviation Battalion arrives at Cape Gloucester to help speed up repairs of the Airdrome. **(Pacific-Solomons)** The Americal

Division (Artillery units) is in the process of relieving the Artillery units of the 3rd Marine Division on Bougainville. **(China-Burma-India)** The Chinese 38th Division finally roots out the last enemy resistance in the vicinity of the Tarung River Line, when the 114th Regiment eliminates the last Japanese stronghold, lingering in the Yubang Ga area in Burma. Other Chinese units make substantial progress in the area lying between the Sanip and Tarung rivers. **(Atlantic-Italy) 15th Army Group** In the **U.S. Fifth Army** area, the U.S. 168th Infantry, 34th Division, secures the heights overlooking Le Pastinelle and drives the enemy from the Rapido Plain. Task Force B, consisting of the 1st Special Service Force, U.S.A., and the 133rd Infantry, U.S.A., is disbanded, after its mission has been accomplished. In the U.S. II Corps area, troops prepare for an assault against the remaining hill, which is barring them from moving against Mont Trocchio.

January 14th 1944 — (United States) President Roosevelt dispatches a message to Chiang Kai-shek and requests that the Yunnan Force commit to the Burma campaign in conjunction with the operations in India. The message also conveys a hint that the lend-lease agreement with China might be canceled if the needed troops (Chinese) are not committed. **(Pacific)** The U.S. Navy sustains the loss of a self propelled Fuel Barge in the Pacific after it is damaged by an enemy torpedo and subsequently destroyed by U.S. Forces. Also, the U.S.S. *Albacore* (SS-218), a Submarine, operating in the Central Pacific, sinks the Japanese Destroyer *Sazanami*. **(Pacific-New Britain)** The 3rd Battalion, 7th Marines, drives to the top of Hill 660 (final objective of the A.D.C. Group), ending the Japanese resistance in the Cape Gloucester-Borgen Bay area; the A.D.C. Group relief begins on the following day. **(Atlantic-Russia)** The Soviets overtake Mozyr and Kalinkovichi.

January 15th 1944 — (United States) The War Department dissolves the Central Defense Command, transferring its responsibilities to the Eastern Defense Command. **(Pacific-New Guinea)** Contingents of the 9th Australian Division reach abandoned Sio, located on the northern coast of the Huon Peninsula. **(China-Burma-India)** The U.S.S. *Crevalle* (SS-291), patrolling in waters near French Indo China, lays mines east of Saigon. **(Atlantic-ETO)** COSSAC is renamed Supreme Headquarters, Allied Expeditionary Force (SHAEF). **(Atlantic-Italy) 15th Army Group** In the **U.S. Fifth Army** area, the struggle for the German Winter Line ceases, as the II corps (135th Infantry, 34th Division), captures Mont Trocchio without incident. The Germans had previously pulled back across the Rapido River. Now the U.S. Fifth Army faces the Gustav Line, which stretches across more rugged mountains and along the Gari, Garigliano, and Rapido Rivers extending to Monte Cassino and to the British Eighth Army area in the hills above Cassino. U.S. General Mark Clark, would remark in later years about Cassino: "I FOUGHT IN THREE WARS, (WW1, WWII, AND KOREA) AND IT SEEMS TO ME, THEY ALWAYS SAVED THE MOUNTAINS FOR ME TO FIGHT IN AND I'VE LOOKED AT MANY A MOUNTAIN BUT NEVER HAVE I SEEN ONE MORE DEADLY OR FIERCE LOOKING THAN MONTE CASSINO AS IT STARED DOWN OUR THROATS." In other activity, the Germans evacuate south Elia, which is the objective of the French Expeditionary troops. **(Atlantic-Russia)** The Soviets assault the Germans in Leningrad. Novgorod is also under Soviet siege.

January 16th 1944 — (Pacific-Solomons) The final contingents of the U.S. 3rd Marine Division departs Bougainville.

(Pacific-Bismarcks-New Britain) The 3rd Battalion, 7th Marines, finish the Japanese on Hill 660 after what would be the last Japanese counterattack in Western New Britain, culminating the fighting in the Cape Gloucester-Borgen Bay area. At Arawe, the 2nd Battalion, 158th Infantry, attacks vigorously, supported by B Company, 1st Tank Battalion, U.S.M.C., driving against the Japanese who are attempting to penetrate the perimeter. The Tanks assist the troops to gain 1,500 tough yards and on the following day, enemy resistance in the area near Arawe will extinguished, while pursuit against the Japanese who have withdrawn toward Lupin continues. **(China-Burma-India)** Chiang Kai-shek implies to President Roosevelt, that if he does not receive the previously requested billion dollar loan or unless the United States finances the Cheng-tu project at an exchange rate of 20 to one, he might cut off the food supply and housing for U.S. troops based in China, effective March 4th. President Roosevelt sends a representative to China and states that as of March, 1944, U.S. expenditures will be limited to $25,000,000 a day. In other activity, British Admiral Mountbatten writes to U.S. General Marshall and offers to place British troops in charge of the Chinese Army in India, but American General Stilwell retains control (Operation GALAHAD). Meanwhile, the Chinese 38th Division (3rd Battalion, 114th Infantry) meets heavy resistance after they cross the Sanip River and are prevented from moving beyond the junction of the Tanai and Tarung Rivers. Other elements of the 38th, seize Gum Ga and then drive toward Warang. **(Atlantic-Italy) 15th Army Group** In the **U.S. Fifth Army** area, II Corps, receives orders to drive toward Anzio. **(European Theater)** General Eisenhower assumes the role of Supreme Commander, Allied Expeditionary Force. In the Atlantic, the U.S.S. *Guadalcanal* (CVE-60), an Aircraft Carrier, launches Planes (VC-13), which destroy the German Submarine U-544, in mid-Atlantic waters.

January 17th 1944 — (Pacific-New Britain) The Japanese remnants in the Arawe area are mopped up. **(Pacific-Burma)** The Chinese 38th Division's 113th Regiment bypasses Brangbrain Stream, heading for Taihpa Ga prudently; a contingent remains behind to neutralize the enemy at the stream. **(Atlantic-Italy) 15th Army Group** The U.S. Fifth Army, VI Corps, commanded by Major General John Lucas, practices an invasion landing on the beaches south of Salerno. The Operation (WEBFOOT) ends on the 19th. The practice is in preparation for Anzio (OPERATION SHINGLE). In the British 10th Corps area, Operation PANTHER, the attack across the Garigliano, commences at 21:00. Stiff opposition pins the British down and forces them to pull back some distance, on the 23rd. **(European Theater)** The ETOUSA S.O.S. is reorganized, forming a single Headquarters.

January 18th 1944 — (Atlantic) General Eisenhower delegates administrative responsibility for all U.S. Army Air Forces in the United Kingdom to Headquarters U.S. Strategic Air Forces, Europe. **(Atlantic-Italy)** Final preparations for the invasion of Anzio and for the assault against Monte Cassino continue. There is a large shortage of proper equipment. During a practice landing for the Anzio Operation, approximately 40 Amphibious Trucks (DUKWs) had been lost to the surf in the vicinity of Naples. The Texas 36th Division requires them to ford the Rapido, but none are available, because both British Lt. General Sir Richard McCreery and U.S. General Keyes had dispatched their supply to General Lucas at Naples.

January 19th 1944 — (North Pacific) Naval Land-based

Planes attack the Kurile Islands. The strikes are repeated for the next three nights, hitting targets in the Paramushiro-Shimushu area. **(Pacific-Bismarcks-New Britain)** The U.S. Army sends out Patrols in Western New Britain in search of fast retreating Japanese. The U.S. continues to expand its dominance across the western part of the island. **(Pacific-New Guinea)** The beachhead at Saidor is greatly strengthened by the majority of the 128th Regiment. **(Atlantic-Italy)** Fifteenth Army Group Headquarters is renamed; Headquarters, Allied Central Mediterranean Force (ACMF). In the **U.S. Fifth Army** area, British 10th Corps sector, the British 5th Division takes Minturno, while the 56th Division nears Castelforte. **(Atlantic)** General George S. Patton still awaits news on possible command. Meanwhile, General Eisenhower has already privately included General Patton in his plans for Operation OVERLORD. In a letter to his wife Beatrice, Patton would state: "IF I DID NOT BELIEVE IN FATE. . .I WOULD TELL THEM ALL TO GO TO HELL AND PUT THE WHEN AND IF IN COMMISSION AND SAIL." **(Atlantic-Russia)** The Soviet Red Army seizes Novgorod.

Major General John P. Lucas.

January 20th 1944 — (Pacific-Dutch East Indies) The U.S.S. *Tinosa* (SS-283), operating near Malay Archipelago, southwest of the Philippines, lands men and supplies at the northeast section of Borneo. **(Atlantic-England)** American General Spaatz assumes Command of all U.S. Army Air Forces in the United Kingdom. **(Atlantic)** General Patton notes his concerns about Anzio in his diary. "IF THE THING IS A SUCCESS, CLARK (General Mark Clark) WILL GET THE CREDIT. IF IT FAILS, LUCAS (Major General John P. Lucas) WILL GET THE

BLAME." "IT SEEMS INCONCEIVABLE THAT THE BOCHE WILL NOT GUESS THAT WE ARE COMING (invasion of Anzio) BUT HE HAS MADE SO MANY FOOLISH MISTAKES THAT WE MAY GET ASHORE UNOPPOSED AFTER ALL." Patton guesses correctly. The invasion is virtually unopposed. In Naval activity, in the Atlantic Theater, the LST 228 becomes grounded and is sunk in the vicinity of the Azores. **(Atlantic-Soviet Union)** Advancing Soviet troops (driving from Pulkovo and Oranienbaum) surround German troops and cut off their route to the Gulf of Finland.

January 20th-May 18th 1944 — (Atlantic-Italy) THE BATTLE FOR MONTE CASSINO — In the **U.S. II Corps** area, the attack begins with the U.S. 36th Division receiving close Air and Artillery support while crossing the freezing Rapido River, almost 10 feet deep and about 60 feet wide. The 36th has just undergone a taxing campaign against the Germans at San Pietro and many of the replacement troops are green. The effort to displace the enemy is nearly in vain. From their commanding positions, the Germans have been able to spot all troop movements for the last several days, prompting them to take immediate precautions against the attack. The German Commander quickly orders crack troops to sneak down and man forward camouflaged positions. These excellent defenses catch the Texas troops completely off guard. The 36th Division must carry their boats for some distance in terrible weather to reach the river and when the boats finally make it into the icy Rapido, the Texans become sitting targets for the Germans. While the Germans shell the Americans, confusion develops and units become separated in minefields. Nearly ten thousand men move forward in the dark under severe enemy fire and bitting cold. A few troops make it to the opposite shore. During the next two days, while attempting to establish a bridgehead, the Texans suffer 1,680 losses to enemy fire. A subsequent assault on the following day by General Walker to rescue his trapped contingents is also unsuccessful. The losses are so terrible that the 36th is forced to abandon the bridgehead on the 23rd. The U.S. 34th Division, commanded by General Ryder and operating in conjunction with the 36th, begins to move in a diversionary drive toward Cassino. While the vicious battle rages, American VI Corps moves by sea to Anzio.

The Commanding Officer at Anzio, General Lucas, orders his men to dig in and secure a beachhead before driving to Rome. His caution allows Field Marshal Kesselring the needed time to rush all available troops to the area. They speed from such places as Genoa, Leghorn and other points in northern Italy and arrive in time to pin the Allies on the beach for months. While the American VI Corps, which includes a British Division is stymied on the beach at Anzio, the Germans still hold the Winter Line at Monte Cassino, an impregnable strongpoint. The Allies push hard against the entrenched enemy positions high up on Cassino, but they are forced to transport supplies on foot and by mules because the difficult terrain cannot accommodate Vehicles. As the Allies press forward they are under constant surveillance by the enemy, which sprays fire on their positions. The tedious and deadly climb brings the advance troops to murderous Snakes Head Ridge, about 1,000 yards from the monastery, where the U.S. 34th Division is stopped cold and strung out on the barren ridge.

New Zealanders and Indian troops move up to relieve the 34th, only to meet the same fate. The Germans hold firmly, despite heavy losses. After realizing that the monastery cannot be taken by Infantry, the Allies level the hilltop sanctuary by an Air attack. Hundreds of Allied Planes strike the Monastery on the 15th of February 1944, but the Germans are not displaced. The Germans immediately jam crack Riflemen behind the rocks and in the crevices left in the rubble and wait, in ambush, for the next group of Assault Troops. A third attack against the stronghold is, first, by sending in another massive Air assault to level the entire town, followed by a massive Infantry charge. The town is destroyed by the bombs inflicting so much damage that the Allied Tanks, expected to support the Infantry, cannot clear the wreckage. The Germans, who have hidden their Tanks during the overpowering Allied bombardment, await the cessation of the attack then rush them out of the bunkers to cut down the Allied Infantrymen (Indian and New Zealanders). The Allies, carrying only their rifles and grenades, are pitted against the German Tanks and the entrenched ground troops.

The attack fails and the gruesome task of taking Cassino goes on through the balance of the bitter Winter into Spring. The Allies finally break through in May, when the French Expeditionary troops, under the control of the U.S. Fifth Army, scale the mountain and unhinge the German defenses forcing a German withdrawal from Cassino. The U.S. Fifth Army and the French and British Commonwealth reinforcements had begun the massive offensive on the 11th of May, pressing to break through to Rome. The German Line finally collapses. On May 18th, Polish troops enter Cassino culminating the struggle which had started on January 20th. The Allies advance steadily from Cassino, driving toward Rome. Troops at the beachhead at Anzio also break out during May. Men of the U.S. Third Division (Anzio) are the first Allied soldiers to enter Rome on June 4th.

January 21st 1944 — (Pacific-New Britain) Japanese General Hitoshi Imamura, Commander of the Eighth Area Army at Rabaul, directs the Japanese defenders in western New Britain to pull out and head for Iboki to concentrate their Forces and then withdraw to Talasea. **(Pacific-Marshalls)** The 25th Marines and the Special Weapons Battalion, 4th Marine Division, deploy organic weapons along the Northern shore of Ennugarret, zeroing in on Namur, to support the attack by the 24th Marines. **(China-Burma-India)** In Burma, General Stilwell makes the decision to assault Walawbum. The attack is spearheaded by Armor units, driving down the Kamaing Road, with Infantry following close behind. In other activity, the 113th Regiment, Chinese 38th Division, advances to Ningru Ga, which lies within a mile from Taihpa Ga. **(Atlantic-Italy)** 15th Army Group ACMF In the **U.S. Fifth Army** area, the Invasion Force (VI Corps), which is to land at Anzio on the 22nd, departs Naples. The U.S. Navy will begin a Naval bombardment of Civitavecchia as a diversionary tactic. In the British 10th Corps area, the Germans rush in reinforcements and counterattack to drive the British from their bridgehead at the Garigliano. In the **II Corps** area, the U.S. 36th Division remains under heavy fire from the Germans. The 1st Battalion, 141st Infantry, manages to hold a bridgehead, but becomes totally isolated from the main body, which had pulled back across the Rapido. In addition, the 1st Battalion, 143rd Infantry, which had made it across the river during the night of the 20-21st, is taking heavy casualties and forced to withdraw. Other elements of the 36th begin another attempt to assault across the river at 16:00, followed later by the 2nd

Battalion, 143rd Infantry, however, again, enemy fire devastates the American attackers. In other activity, Peter Tompkins, the leader of OSS in Naples, is smuggled into Rome to establish contact with Radio Vittorio and await orders to institute sabotage to coincide with the Allied invasion. In conjunction, OSS Radio continues to broadcast enemy troop locations to the Allies. During March, a radio technician betrays the OSS, going over to the Germans; an agent named Cervo is captured, but Tompkins and Vittorio are not captured. **(Atlantic-England)** General Eisenhower confers for the first time with his Commanders. The conference held at Norfolk House in London centers around Operation OVERLORD, the invasion of Normandy. **(Atlantic-Western Europe)** German Intelligence (FHO), under Gehlen, continues its updating of Russian Intelligence. The Third German Panzer Army reports that the Russian Tank Commanders receive 1,000 rubles for each Tiger Tank destroyed; each crew member receives 500 rubles. The FHO keeps meticulous records on the Russians and is even aware of daily morale within the various units. Some laughter erupts at Headquarters when they are informed that Russian Officers must now receive permission to marry and will receive it only if the bride has completed 10th grade education. The F.H.O. compiles about 10,000 orders issued by the Soviet Defense Ministry. By the end of year, Gehlen's compilations are the finest ever accomplished by anyone. After the end of the war, both the Allies and the Russians seek out this invaluable information. **(Atlantic-Soviet Union)** Soviet forces seize Mga, outside of Leningrad.

January 22nd 1944 — The United States Fleet off Anzio.

January 22nd-May 11th 1944 — (Atlantic-Italy) THE SIEGE OF ANZIO — A U.S. Naval Task Force, commanded by Rear Admiral F.J. Lowry, carrying the U.S. VI Corps (including. one British. Div.) arrives off of Anzio-Nettuno and launches rocket salvos just prior to the invasion. The assault troops, commanded by Major General J. P. Lucas, land at three different locations, gaining complete surprise. General William (Wild Bill) Donovan, Head of OSS goes in on an LST with the 1st wave of troops. The German defenders are not numerically strong enough to prevent the VI Corps from moving freely and establishing a beachhead. Major General Lucas's Force moves inland at a leisurely pace, questioning the whereabouts of the enemy as they advance a few miles before setting up the perimeter, against minimal opposition. Major General Lucas, under orders to establish a beachhead before any advance, fails to take advantage of the lax defenses, choosing to anchor his supply lines and secure the beachhead. The decision comes back to haunt the General who had initially caught the Germans off guard, but the fault is not entirely his. Neither British General Alexander nor General Clark give any specific instructions. Both men visit Lucas at Anzio on the 22nd and share his amazement concerning no opposition, but depart without stating whether he should hold the ports or to drive into the Alban hills toward Rome. However, he had previous instructions to secure his supply lines and beachhead before advancing. This 10 day endeavor, prompted by extra caution, allows the ill-prepared enemy to rush in reinforcements and trap the Americans on the beach for over three months, and pressures the other 5th Army troops attempting to take Cassino. The Germans initiate a massive counterattack combining Planes, Tanks, Artillery and troops to destroy the Yankee beachhead. Unperturbed, the Americans, aided by the U.S. Naval Vessels offshore, stand their ground, halting the powerful attack, which very nearly destroys the entire beachhead. German Artillery pummels the landing area from commanding positions, which overlook the American perimeter from the nearby hills for the duration of the siege. A stalemate settles in as the Yanks cannot break out and the Germans are unable to destroy the beachhead. On one occasion, a Patrol returning to camp decides to try to get a good night's sleep in a small house. One of the men, Bill O'Hara (3rd, Division, Roslyn, Pa.), suggests: "THE GERMANS HAVENT BOMBED THAT PLACE SINCE WE'VE BEEN HERE, LET'S SLEEP IN THERE." Within a short time, a bomb comes crashing through the house. Fortunately, it is a dud, but the Patrol jumps from the second floor without missing a step and flies to their damp, wet foxholes, their pale faces coated from the flying plaster dust.

The German Luftwaffe carries out many raids against the immobilized VI Corps (56 Air raids in the first seven days), who have been forced to bulldoze large craters for safer storage and to protect the Vehicles from damage. In addition to all the normal hazards of war, the isolated troops are barraged by "Sally and George", two German radio propagandists, who attempt to intimidate the Allies with repeated threats of their entire force being thrown back to the sea. This embattled beachhead spends a most miserable winter ducking shells and trying to find a way to sever the stranglehold, but to no avail. Finally, after over 100 days on the beach at Anzio, the VI Corps, now commanded by General Lucian Truscott, synchronizes with the major assault against Cassino and get an opportunity to break out and make a run for Rome. After the harsh winter, Allied Planes begin massive Air raids against German General Kesselring's troops all along the formidable Gustav Line. On May 11th, the Allies swarm across the Garigliano and Rapido Rivers, forcing the German lines to collapse. Truscott's VI Corps subsequently captures Cisterna during late May, then rolls triumphantly into Rome on the 4th of June, 1944, to cheering citizens. The Yanks can not find a Fascist in the entire city! For the first time in the history of the Eternal City, a conquering Army marches into Rome from the south. The U.S. Naval Task Force, commanded by Rear Admiral F.J. Lowry, that had transported the VI Corps to Anzio, remains offshore during the entire three month struggle to assist the beleaguered troops with Naval gunfire.

January 22nd 1944 — (Pacific) Operation GALVANIC gets underway, as the largest U.S. Amphibious Force yet assembled embarks for the Marshalls. Japanese Planes cease to be a major problem over Kwajalein as Land-based American

The WACs keep things in working order.

Planes operate at will. On the following day, the Attack Force Reserve (Galvanic) and the Majuro Attack Group embark for the objective. In other Naval activity in the Pacific, the U.S.S. *Buchanan* (DD-484) sinks the RO-37, a Japanese Submarine. The U.S.S. *Cache* (AO-67), an Oiler Vessel is attacked by an enemy Submarine and damaged. **(Pacific-Admiralty Islands)** Allied Planes begin pre-invasion Air strikes, bombing enemy Vessels off the coast. Planes with cameras accompany the B-25s and secure photographs of Lorengau and Momote. Army Aircraft sink the Japanese Submarine Chaser No. 40. **(Atlantic-Italy-Anzio) AMCF:** The U.S. Army VI Corps invades Anzio at 02:00. Enemy resistance is minimal, allowing troops to easily secure a beachhead seven miles inland. The 3rd Division lands on X-Ray beaches, east of Nettuno and secures the Mussolini Canal. By nightfall, German reinforcements rush and resecure the bridges. Three Battalions of Rangers, the 509th Paratroop Battalion and the 83rd Chemical Battalion land in the center, easily capturing Nettuno and the port at Anzio. The British 1st Division lands on the left at Peter Beach with the responsibility of blocking the primary road from Anzio to Albano. Allied Planes control the skies during the landing, offering much Close Air Support, while enemy Planes make some half hearted attacks which do little damage. During the invasion of Anzio, the U.S.S. *Portent* (AM-106), a Minesweeper, strikes a mine and sinks. **(Italy-Cassino)** In the **II Corps** area, the U.S. 36th Division continues its futile attempt to secure the Rapido beachhead, but casualties mount to an alarming level. The 36th withdraws across the freezing Rapido. During this deadly encounter, Company F, 143rd Infantry, crosses the river near San Angelo and meets intrepid resistance. Sergeant Thomas McCall and his machinegun squad cross an iced bridge and begin a tremendous burst of fire to expel the enemy. Return fire kills or wounds his entire crew. Sgt. McCall advances cowboy style with his machine gun on his hip, as shells pour in from all directions. Undaunted, McCall destroys one nest, then continues through the fire and takes out a second. McCall then dashes forward, with his machine gun still blazing from his hip, into point-blank fire of a third enemy machine gun crew and gives his life to save his companions. Sergeant McCall becomes the recipient of the Medal of Honor. In the British 10 Corps area, heavy fighting rages with the British losing Mont. Natale to the untiring Germans. Vicious combat also occurs near the northern outskirts of Tufo. **(Atlantic)** General Patton receives a crucial cable, ordering him to report to England. **(Atlantic-Russia)** The Germans at Vitebsk are nearly surrounded by the Red Army.

U.S. troops moving ashore at Anzio.

The Mussolini Canal being seized by a contingent of the 504th Paratroop Infantry, 82nd Airborne.

January 23rd 1944 — (Pacific-New Guinea) Allied Planes, lending Air assistance to the Australian 18th brigade, 7th Division, pay dividends. The Australians seize Shaggy Hill, located in the Ramu Valley about six miles north of Dumpu. This victory, coupled with the conquest at Saidor, puts the Huon Peninsula under total control of the Australians. The stunned Japanese withdraw toward Madang with Allied Planes in pursuit. **(Atlantic-Italy)** In the **U.S. Fifth Army** area, the **VI Corps** expands its beachhead with minor resistance from the enemy. The U.S. 3rd Division still concentrates on securing bridges across the Mussolini Canal. Enemy resistance is confined to German planes strafing the beachhead. In the British 10 Corps area, enemy attempts to destroy the British beachhead at the Garigliano are repulsed. The British pull back slightly in the vicinity of Minturno. In the **U.S. II Corps** area, the U.S. 34th Division prepares to mount another attack across the icy Rapido. French Expeditionary troops fight through heavy enemy resistance and recapture Mont San Croce, then move toward Terelle and Piedimonte to attack Monte Cassino from the north. These French troops (French Colonial Mountain troops), commanded by General Juin, speed through the mountainous terrain. **(Atlantic-England)** General Eisenhower suggests to the combined Chiefs of Staff that the Normandy Invasion (OVERLORD) comprise a larger area than originally planned and that the tentative D-Day be

postponed 1 month because of an acute shortage of Landing Crafts. Because of the shortage, Eisenhower recommends the use of only one Division for the invasion of Southern France (OPERATION ANVIL). On the following day, the planners preparing for Operation ANVIL are notified that only one Division will make the assault. **(Atlantic-Russia)** Severe rainfall bogs down the Soviet Red Army offensive near Vitebsk.

January 24th 1944 — (Pacific-Solomons) Japanese Fighters intercept American Bombers near Simpson Harbor in the Solomons. One Plane from Marine Fighter Squadron 215, piloted by Lt. Robert M. Hanson, destroys four Jap Zeros and probably a fifth, before he is shot down. From November 1st through today, Lt. Hanson has shot down 25 enemy Planes. **(Atlantic-North Africa)** Force 163 (ANVIL planners) are informed that the invasion of Southern France will comprise only one U.S. Division. **(Atlantic-Italy-Anzio)** The VI Corps, U.S. Fifth Army, under General Lucas, expands its beachhead slightly, but does not drive toward Rome. Enemy Aircraft continue intense raids over the entire perimeter and, in the meantime, German reinforcements rush in to strengthen the defenses. The 2nd Brigade, 1st British Division, advances to the Moletta River on the left flank and the U.S. 504th Paratroop Infantry takes control of the remaining bridges along the main Mussolini Canal. In conjunction with the operation, the balance of the 3rd Division deploys along the western section of the canal, poised for an operation to seize Campoleone and Cisterna. Enemy Bombers strike the U.S.S. *Plunkett* (DD-431) and the *Mayo* (DD-422), both Destroyers. In addition, the Minesweeper *Prevail* (AM-107), is also damaged. **(Italy-Cassino)** In the British 10 Corps area, the fighting is vicious as the Germans counterattack the Garigliano bridgehead, suffering heavy casualties, while recapturing Mont Rotondo (Hill 342), Castleforte and the northern slopes of Hill 413. After seizing the Allied positions, the Germans dig in to resume a defensive stance. In the **U.S. II Corps** area, the U.S. 133rd Infantry 34 Division makes another valiant but unsuccessful attempt to cross the Rapido north of Cassino, during the night of the 24th. Enemy fire is relentless. Some units reach the river, but the Germans allow none to cross. **(Atlantic-Germany)** Berlin publicizes a new Soviet offensive in the area near Kirovograd near Dnieper bend.

Army Air Corps Officer James Stewart, (Jimmy Stewart) being decorated for having completed ten successful missions.

The Yanks take casualties at the Rapido River.

January 25th 1944 — (United States) The U.S. Fourth Army relieves the U.S. Third Army at Fort Sam Houston, Texas at midnight on the 25th. **(Pacific-Burma)** The 65th Regiment, Chinese 22nd Division, had surrounded an enemy pocket in the vicinity of the Taro Plain during the night of the 23rd-24th, devastating them. As the troops move toward the Hukawng Valley, they count 323 enemy dead in the gorge where the Tanai flows into the Taro Plane. **(Atlantic-Italy-Anzio)** In the **U.S. Fifth Army, U.S. II Corps** area, the U.S. 504th Paratroop Infantry, in support of the main assault by the 3rd Division, attacks across the Mussolini Canal toward Littoria, then withdraws after nightfall. The British 1st Division pushes toward Aprilia (the Factory), north of Carroceto and clears it of the enemy. The main thrust by the Third U.S. Division consists of the 1st Battalion, 30th Infantry, driving along the Campomorto-Cisterna Road and the 2nd Battalion, 15th Infantry, battling their way along the Conca-Cisterna road; both encounter withering enemy fire which stops the advance. In other activity, a Minesweeper (YMS-30) is damaged after striking a mine offshore. **(Italy-Cassino)** In the **U.S. II Corps** area, the U.S. 133rd Infantry crosses the Rapido against heavy enemy fire and continues to strengthen the bridgehead along the west bank north of Cassino. The 4th Tunisian Infantry, French Expeditionary Corps, goes around Mont Cifalco and secures Le Propaia, but the Germans counterattack and regain a portion of the position. **(Atlantic-Soviet Union)** The Germans lose Krasnogvardeisk, southwest of Leningrad.

January 26th 1944 — (Pacific) The U.S. V Amphibious Corps Staff discusses tentative plans for the capture of Eniwetok Atoll, located in the Marshall Islands. Previous plans suggested a two Division invasion on March 19th, but the date is changed to May 1st. **(South America)** Argentina breaks relations with Germany and Japan. **(Pacific-Caroline Islands)** The U.S.S. *Skipjack* (SS-184), patrolling off the Carolines, sinks the Japanese Destroyer *Suzukaze.* **(Pacific-Marshall Islands)** American B-25s, escorted by Fighter Planes, destroy the majority of enemy Planes based on Maloelap. **(Pacific-New Guinea)** Two American PT Boats, the PT-110 and the PT-114, sink after a collision. **(Central Pacific)** U.S. Naval Land-based Planes sink the Japanese Submarine Chaser No. 14. **(China-Burma-India)** American General Chennault, in a letter to President Roosevelt, requests permission to use B-29s under the control of the Fourteenth Air Force to strike the industrial areas of Japan, subsequent to the destruction of Japanese Shipping in the area and the establish-

ment of American Air supremacy in China. General Chennault then suggests the Planes be used for Air strikes against Japanese Army bases in China, Formosa, and Hainan. In China, the Chinese 65th Regiment, Chinese 22nd Division, the Ahawk Stream close to the Ahawk Trail, the shortest route leading from Taro to the Hukawng Valley. **(Atlantic-Italy-Anzio)** In the **U.S. Fifth Army** area, the U.S. 3rd Division advances near Ponte Rotto and destroys an enemy strongpoint. The Germans mount a powerful counterattack against the British 1st Division at the Factory, but they are repelled. **(Italy-Cassino)** In the **U.S. II Corps** area, the Americans advance to Hill 213, but ferocious enemy fire drives them back by nightfall. Another unit of the 3rd Division, the 135th Infantry, reaches the edge of Cassino and joins with contingents of the 133rd Infantry to take a hill, but the attack fails; the Germans still hold the high grounds. In other activity, the French Expeditionary Corps (4th Tunisian Infantry) seizes Abate and Belvedere Hills and the 3rd Algerian Infantry pushes the enemy from Le Propaia. On the following day, the Germans mount a large counterattack and recapture Abate Hill and Hill 700 to the southeast, but the Algerian Infantry pushes the enemy from Le Propaia, and repulses an attempt to regain Belvedere Hill. **(Atlantic-United Kingdom)** General George S. Patton arrives in London where he confers with Eisenhower and is informed that he will command the Third Army.

January 27th 1944 — (Pacific-Hawaii) A conference is held in Pearl Harbor by members of Admirals Nimitz and Halsey and General MacArthur's staffs to formulate strategy to resecure the Philippines in the quickest fashion. The meeting concludes with concurrence that all resources should be thrown into the Southwest Pacific area. Admiral King, who is back in the States gets a copy of the minutes of the meeting and becomes infuriated because of his desire to seize the Marianas; Nimitz wants to secure Truk and King wants to bypass it. Despite King's strong feelings about the Marianas, many of his Staff disagree, realizing that the Marianas are not capable of handling large Fleet anchorages. In conjunction, General Sutherland sends word to MacArthur that Admiral Nimitz has agreed to support MacArthur's thrust toward the Philippines. **(Atlantic-Yugoslavia)** Allied Commandos raid enemy positions at Hvar during the night of the 27-28th. **(Atlantic-Italy-Anzio)** In the **U.S. Fifth Army, VI Corps** area, the U.S. 3rd Division again is repulsed at Cisterna. The fierce German resistance forces the Yanks to call off the assault and regroup. The Germans continue to resist the British 1st Division's attempt to secure the Factory. General Mark Clark embarks on an unexpected risky venture to confer with General Lucas on Anzio. Clark boards a PT Boat (one of two) and heads for Anzio, but along the way experiences difficulty; the first set of Allied Vessels accept their identification by acknowledging the flares, but subsequently, the flares are not enough and Allied Vessels begin shelling, mistaking them for attacking German Vessels. Clark's PT Boats evade further damage by running away at high speed, eventually pulling alongside Allied Minesweepers to transfer the wounded before moving on to Anzio where he instructs Lucas to attack boldly toward Cisterna. **(Atlantic-Italy-Cassino)** Heavy fighting rages throughout the area as the Germans continue to dominate the high ground firmly resist the British attempt to stretch its beachhead (British 10th Corps area). In the **II Corps** area, Allied Artillery pound enemy positions for one hour before elements of the 34th U.S. Division drive through the bridgehead of the 133rd Infantry. After vicious fighting, a few tanks followed by elements of the 168th and 756th Infantry reach enemy held Hills 56 and 213. As darkness falls, the 3rd Battalion makes a flanking movement. **(Atlantic-Russia)** The Red Army captures more territory near Leningrad. The Soviets also secure Tosno and the rail lines between Lyuban and Tosno. On the following day, the Soviet troops seize Lyuban and advance toward Chudovo.

January 28th 1944 — (European Theater of Operations) Lt. General Omar N. Bradley who had served under General George Patton during the North Africa and Sicilian campaigns, assumes command of the U.S. First Army. Bradley replaces Lt. General George Grunert. **(Atlantic-Italy-Anzio)** In the **U.S. Fifth Army VI Corps** area, the British 1st Division advances beyond the Factory about one and one half miles, then hesitates to prepare for an assault against Campoleone. In the vicinity of Isola Bella, a detachment of the 3rd Infantry Division, led by Technician Fifth Grade, Eric G. Gibson (Company Cook), attacks enemy positions, knocking four out of action and capturing two Germans. This squad continues to advance against withering fire and destroys several more enemy positions along the Fossa Femminamorta (a large stream) before Gibson is killed while reconnoitering around a bend, in advance of his unit. He received the Medal of Honor posthumously. **(Atlantic-Italy-Cassino)** In the **U.S. II Corps** area, German fire pushes the U.S. 168th Infantry, 34th Division from their newly acquired positions on Hill 213. The 3rd Battalion establishes a small bridgehead across the Rapido near Cairo. In other activity, the 3rd Algerian Division engages in heavy battle with the Germans between Belvedere Hill and Le Propaia, repulsing concentrated counterattacks. **(North Atlantic)** U.S. Land-based Planes attached to Squadron VB-103, operating in the North Atlantic, destroy a German Submarine, the U-271.

January 29th 1944 — (United States) General Marshall, dissatisfied with the line of communications (under British control) between Calcutta and Assam gets President Roosevelt to urge Winston Churchill to place it under joint U.S.-British control. **(Pacific-Marshall Islands)** The U.S. Task Force transporting the Assault Force, nears the Marshalls. A Carrier Task Force (58), commanded by Admiral Mitscher, dispatches Planes to strike enemy Airfields and installations on the Kwajalein Atoll. The devastating raids virtually paralyze enemy Airpower at Taroa Airfield on Maloecap Atoll. Additional successive raids are sent against Wotje Airfield. The Air strikes are supported by the Naval guns of Surface Vessels attached to Task Force 58. The Japanese also are pounded by Land-based Planes from the Gilberts and Ellice Islands, which strike various locations, including Roi-Namur and the Kwajalein Islands in the Kwajalein Atoll, to soften resistance. The Task Force maintains these Air attacks until the 6th of February. **(Pacific-New Guinea)** The U.S. 863rd Aviation Engineering Battalion arrives at Saidor. **(Pacific-Malay Peninsula-Borneo)** The U.S.S. *Bowfin* (SS-287), lays mines southeast of Borneo. **(China-Burma-India)** In Burma, General Stilwell expects to hold the road from Kamaing to Japanese lines along the Tanai, with the Chinese 38th Division, but when the 1st Battalion, 114th Regiment arrives, its commanding General diverts it to secure the river bank; the 3rd Battalion moves to the rear for rest. **(Atlantic-Italy-Anzio)** The U.S. VI Corps prepares for a major assault against the Germans at Campoleone and Cisterna, which must be taken prior to Colli Laziali. German Aircraft sink the H.M.S. *Spartan* in addition to a Liberty Ship. The German defenders have had ample time

to reinforce the area and the formidable 14th German Army, commanded by General von Mackensen, constitutes a major obstacle. In Naval activity, the American Tug ATR-1, is damaged by a Horizontal Bomber. **(Atlantic-Italy-Cassino)** The struggle for Cassino continues with the British slowly advancing toward Mont Jugo. German held Hill 413 is unsuccessfully assaulted by elements of the British 56th Division. In the **U.S. II Corps** area, under Artillery cover, Tanks assisted by Engineers bolt across the Rapido with the 168th Infantry, 34th Division trailing closely behind. The troops drive all night and capture Hills 56 and 213, by dawn. In other activity, the 2nd Battalion, 142nd Infantry, fights its way to Belvedere Hill, situated in the French Expeditionary Corps sector. **(Atlantic-Germany)** The U.S. Eighth Air Force musters 800 Heavy Bombers which use radar to guide their strike against strategic targets in Frankfurt am Main. This is the biggest Air attack yet mounted by the Americans. **(Atlantic-Yugoslavia)** The Allies establish a Base for coastal craft at Vis which is now being used to supply the Communists under Tito; many downed American Pilots are forced to drop into the country. **(Atlantic-Russia)** The Germans publicize their withdrawal from Smela, in the Dnieper bend. The Soviet Red Army First and Second Ukrainian Fronts assault the salient held by the German Eighth Army in the Ukraine. Chudovo falls to the Soviets during the heavy fighting on the Leningrad Front.

A Russian Pilot receives one of the thousands of U.S. Planes given to the Soviets through Lend-Lease.

January 29th 1944 — (United States) It has been decided that there will be a need for a uniform currency in Germany subsequent to Allied occupation. Uncle Sam gets tapped again! Averell Harriman, the U.S. Ambassador to Russia, informs the State Department that "GREAT IMPORTANCE IS ATTACHED BY THE BRITISH GOVERNMENT TO THE RUSSIAN GOVERNMENT'S PARTICIPATION IN THIS ARRANGEMENT." Soon after, on February 8th, Secretary of State, Cordell Hull, informs Harriman in Russia that: "THE U.S. WOULD BE GLAD TO PRINT THE MONEY FOR RUSSIA." However, on February 15th, the Russians respond that they prefer to print their own money; during March, Hull tells Harriman: "IT IS NOT EXPECTED THAT THE COMBINED CHIEFS OF STAFF WILL FAVOR THE DELIVERY OF PLATES (printing) TO THE RUSSIANS." Personnel in the State Department attempt to block the shipment of the engraving plates, but Henry Dexter White, the Assistant Secretary of the Treasury incessantly pushes the Russian cause. By April 14th, Henry Morgenthau informs Mr. James Clement Dunn (Treasury Department) that the Russians will indeed receive duplicate plates; Morganthau then informs Russian Ambassador Gromyko. As the race to help the Russians continues, the 1st shipment of plates for the manufacturing of M-Marks in Russian occupied territory, departs Washington Airport during May; the Aircraft is scheduled to depart on the 23rd; however, the Plane is held up until the 24th to await the arrival of some non-scheduled Russian personnel. Incredibly, on the 1st of June, the Russian Ambassador, Gromyko contacts the State Department and tells the story that the Plane had crashed and that the Russians need another Plane and new plates and the accompanying items required to duplicate the Allied currency; without questioning the site or circumstances of the crash or requesting any details, Secretary Morganthau tells the Russians on June 7th, that the U.S. will supply another "MONEY PLANE." Major Jordan, the American Officer who has meticulously detailed the shipments of Lend- lease and non-Lend-lease equipment, moving to the Russians, will arrive back at Great Falls, Montana on June 13th; it is his final stop there as an Army Officer; he is replaced by another Army Officer. Upon Jordan's return, the Russian, Colonel Kotikov (head of Soviet Mission at Great Falls, Montana) tells him of the "MONEY PLANE" which had allegedly crashed in Siberia; the Russian then explains that the shipment included: "PLATES, COLORS, INKS, VARNISH, TINT BLOCKS, AND SAMPLE PAPER." According to Major Jordan: "THE U.S. LOSSES AMOUNT TO $250 MILLION DOLLARS."

The Russians continue printing the currency without restriction (for 18 months) until 1946, with the permission of the State Department. The funds are drained from the U.S. Treasury to cover the Russian printed money. The Russians are handed the opportunity to learn the precise method of how the U.S. manufactures its money, and had smoothly bilked the U.S. taxpayers; the Russians then add insult to injury as the U.S. sends the Russians a bill for $18,102.84 to cover the costs of the materials and the engraving plates, which had been delivered to them to permit them to forge the Allied currency. The Russians use the currency to pay their soldiers (in Berlin) a two year bonus, then the Soviet Embassy refuses to acknowledge the bill and it remains unpaid.

During early 1946, a meeting is held at the White House in the office of Harry Hopkins; the Secretary of State (Cordell Hull), Secretary of War (Henry L. Stimson) and the Secretary of the Treasury (Henry Morganthau, Jr.) are in attendance; Henry Dexter White, Assistant to the Secretary of the Treasury details the "Morganthau Plan," which details how Germany's industry is to be gutted after the war. Stimson and Hull are appalled by the information and upon later information that President Roosevelt and Winston Churchill had agreed to the plan during the Quebec Conference, Hull becomes more aggravated. Henry Dexter White is subsequently promoted to Assistant Secretary of the Treasury and during 1946, he becomes the International Director of the International Monetary Fund; his salary is tax exempt.

During December, 1946, the U.S. Military Government discovers the tremendous loss of revenue; it becomes apparent that the cause is the Russians. Belatedly, the Senate opens hearings and decides to call Morganthau and White to the stand; this never occurs. During June 1947, Henry Dexter White resigns from his position at the International Monetary Fund. During 1948, White is called to testify and he swears under oath that he had never been a Communist and that he had committed no act of disloyalty to the United States. White's funeral is held two weeks later at Temple Israel; he

succumbs to a sudden heart attack. Major Jordan continues to wrest with the dilemma of the Lend-lease fiasco and his name comes up again at hearings during 1952, when Vice President Richard Nixon begins questioning witnesses to unravel the mystery. Jordan notes in his book, "Major Jordan's Diary," that during November 1952, Mr. Whittaker Chambers produces incriminating evidence concerning White: "CHAMBERS PRODUCED FIVE ROLLS OF MICROFILMED DOCUMENTS. AMONG THEM WERE EIGHT PAGES OF SCRIPT DIVULGING U.S. MILITARY SECRETS. FOUND IN THE POSSESSION OF A KNOWN COMMUNIST COURIER, THE HANDWRITING WAS IDENTIFIED AS THAT OF HENRY DEXTER WHITE." Note: The F.B.I. scrutinizes Major Jordan's stories and that is what causes the Congressional hearings. Many other Patriotic Americans offer collaborating testimony. One Army Officer, Colonel d'Arce (former Commandant of Gore Field), comments during an interview (subsequent to the close of hostilities): "THE RUSSIANS COULD HAVE SHIPPED THE CAPITOL DOME TO MOSCOW WITHOUT OUR KNOWING WHAT WAS IN THE BOXES." Another American Officer, Lt. Colonel J.D. McFarland (Alaskan Wing of the Air Transport Command), relates the following: "I WAS IN GREAT FALLS EVERY COUPLE OF WEEKS...THE RUSSIANS WANTED NO RESTRICTIONS FROM THE U.S. ARMY. EVERY TIME THE ISSUE GOT HOT, THEY WOULD TELEPHONE WASHINGTON, AND THEY ALWAYS GOT THEIR WAY."

JAPANESE BOMBPROOF SHELTER *of reinforced concrete and steel. Note steel door visible in the lower part of the entrance.*

January 30th 1944 — (Pacific-Solomons) Heavy fighting erupts on Bougainville between the enemy and the Americal Division. Under intense enemy fire, Staff Sergeant Jesse Drowley leaves his position to aid the wounded. During the rescue attempt, Drowley discovers a hidden enemy gun emplacement which is directing murderous fire upon the advancing Company. Drowley mounts the top of a Tank and proceeds to direct their path by firing tracer bullets at the hidden bunker. As they get closer, enemy fire rips into Drowley's chest, but he refuses medical aid and continues firing at the still unlocated deadly bunker. The Tankers finally destroy the bunker, but another enemy bullet strikes Sgt. Drowley, costing him his left eye. After the destruction of the bunker, Sgt. Drowley returns to his lines unaided for medical help; he receives the Medal of Honor for his extraordinary courage. **(Pacific-Marshalls)** American Planes, attached to Carrier Task Force 58 continue to neutralize enemy Airfields and Military installations, destroying 19 Planes on the ground at Eniewetok Atoll. They also inflict damage to targets located on

Kwajalein, Wotje, and Maloelap Atolls. The Americans display more massive power against the immediate objectives of Kwajalein Atoll, Roi-Namur and the Kwajalein Islands when the U.S. Navy orders its Surface Ships to commence a ferocious four hour bombardment. In addition, American Planes fly 400 sorties against the Japanese. Meanwhile, the U.S. Assault Force arrives offshore after dark. Troops of the Majuro Attack Group (T.G. 51.2), commanded by Rear Admiral Harry W. Hill, debark at the Majuro Atoll during the night of the 30-31st. In addition, other units land unopposed at Calalin and Dadap Islands in the atoll. During the action, the U.S.S. *Anderson* (DD-411), a Destroyer, is damaged by enemy shore fire. Planes and Surface Vessels combine to sink four Japanese Submarine Chasers, the 18, 19, 21 and 28, in addition to the Auxiliary Submarine Chaser No. 25. **(Pacific-New Britain)** The Airfield on Cape Gloucester is declared operational. **(China-Burma-India)** The 65th Regiment, Chinese 22nd Division, captures Taro, securing the Taro Plain. **(Atlantic-Italy)** The U.S. Fifteenth Air Force raids German positions in the Po Valley, reducing enemy strategic Air bombing missions and decreasing opposition to Allied daylight sorties. **(Atlantic-Italy-Anzio)** In the **U.S. Fifth Army** area, the **VI Corps** initiates an offensive to break the siege by driving toward Cisterna. The British 1st and 1st Armored Divisions, moving on the left flank, push toward the Albano Road and encounter stiff opposition, but elements of the 1st Division manage to capture the heights to the south of Campoleone overpass. The British 1st Armored Division advances to the left of Albano Road toward Colli Laziali. The U.S. Rangers are ambushed while attempting to spearhead the drive for the Third Division. At dawn, the 1st and 3rd Ranger Battalions are pinned by firing machine guns and camouflaged Tanks that virtually annihilate the two Battalions within a few hundred yards of Cisterna. Another Battalion, the 4th Rangers and elements of the 3rd Division attempt a rescue mission, but it comes too late. In the vicinity of Carano, the enemy mounts a vicious counterattack. In one heroic encounter, two wounded men lie within 30 yards of the enemy which is pumping out withering machine gun fire. One medic has already been wounded and two Riflemen turned back, when PFC Lloyd C. Hawks advances through a wall of bullets and flying debris. A bullet pierces his helmet knocking it off, and in a flash, bursts of fire ringing six inches from his body plug his helmet with 13 bullet holes. Hawks, however, continues advancing until a volley of machine gun fire shatters his right hip and immediately thereafter, another burst splits his left forearm. He advances and bandages the wounded, then drags a second man to cover. Hawks then drags the other man to cover and crawls 75 yards under fire to rejoin his Company and the wounded medic. He lives to receive his Medal of Honor. In the British 10th Corps area, Mont Natale is secured by the British 17th Brigade, 5th Division. **(Atlantic-Italy-Cassino)** The Germans attack U.S. positions west of the Rapido, but the 168th Infantry repels the assault. In other activity, the 2nd Battalion, 142nd Infantry, U.S. 36th Division, drives against Manna Farm.

January 31st-February 8th 1944 — (Pacific-Marshalls) THE BATTLE OF KWAJALEIN — An Amphibious Assault Force, under the command of Vice Admiral Spruance, springs upon the Japanese in the Marshalls. Two Task Forces, commanded by Rear Admirals Conolly and Turner, deliver Amphibious Troops to assigned beachheads. In addition, Landing Forces are supplemented by a Reserve Force and the Majuro Attack

Group, commanded by Rear Admiral H. W. Hill. Additional Naval Firepower comes from Rear Admiral Marc Mitscher's Carrier-based Planes, and Land-based Aircraft under Rear Admiral J. H. Hoover. Rear Admiral Sherman's Carriers are simultaneously launching Planes against Engebi Island, on the Eniwetok Atoll.

Task Force 51, commanded by Admiral Turner, initiates a Naval and Air bombardment of Kwajalein Atoll, just prior to the landing. As the guns silence, the coordinated Army-Marine Assault Force, commanded by Major General Holland M. Smith U.S.M.C., attacks. The (Northern Force) 25th Marines charges ashore against light opposition, taking Mellu (Ivan) and Ennuebing (Jacob) Islands, permitting it to move rapidly, seizing Ennubirr (Allen), Ovella, Ennumennet (Albert) and Ennugarret (Abraham) Islands in the Kwajalein Atoll. Regimental Combat Team 17, 7th Division U.S.A., storms ashore seizing Cecil and Carter, both islets that control the Ninni Pass on Kwajalein Atoll. Elements of Company B and Reconnaissance units, land on Chauncey (Gehh) in error, then after leaving Infantrymen to clear the enemy, the units jump to Cecil, seizing it without opposition by about 12:30 hours. Carter falls to elements of the 7th Division after a three hour battle at 09:30. Troops from the V Amphibious Corps secure Majuro Atoll without opposition.

Communications between Shore Forces and the Navy are excellent and the Air support substantial. On the following day, the 23rd Marines land at a lagoon across the south beaches of Roi Island and seize NAT Circle, the last Japanese pocket of resistance, after a brief encounter with the enemy defenders, then declare the island secure. An enemy Force of approximately 100 men attempts to infiltrate Marine lines, but is decisively repulsed during the night after intense hand-to-hand combat. The Marines drive north and seize the remaining islands in that portion of the Atoll. Eight islands are secured on the 2nd of February without opposition; the Army also seizes minor islands without opposition in the southern area of the Atoll. Combat Team 24 (U.S.M.C.), drives toward Namur from two directions converging on the point and securing Namur, the primary objective of the campaign for the 4th Marines. After securing Roi and Namur on the 2nd, activity remains brisk, with the Marines searching for enemy resistance. Between the 2nd and the 4th of February, the 1st Battalion, 23rd Marines, secures Boggerlap, Boggerik, and Hollis Islands without opposition. Landing Team 3 (3rd, Battalion, 25th Marines) replaces Landing Team 1 (1st Battalion, 25th Marines and proceeds to secure the remaining islands in the northern portion of the Kwajalein Atoll. From the 4th through the 7th, Landing Team 3, supported by Battery C, 14th Marines, supplemented by strong Naval support, secures 39 islands without opposition, culminating the mission of the Northern Landing Force. By the sixth of February, the Army (Southern Landing Force) had seized Ennugenliggelap Island, finishing their mission. By the eighth of February, Kwajalein Atoll is secure and the majority of the Northern Landing Force (Marines) departs the Atoll to prepare for the next objective. The U.S. Army remains on the island with responsibility for its security.

January 31st 1944 — (Central Pacific) The Submarine *Trigger* sinks the Japanese Minelayer *Nasami*. Meanwhile, the Japanese Auxiliary Submarine Chaser No. 33 is sunk by Aircraft. **(Pacific-Bismarcks)** The Destroyers *Guest* (DD-472) and *Hudson* (DD-475) combine their firepower and sink the

Japanese Submarine I-171. **(Pacific-Marshalls)** See January 31st, Invasion of Kwajalein. U.S. Naval Vessels damaged: Heavy Cruiser *Louisville* (CA-28), during invasion by Naval gunfire; Destroyer *Colohan* (DD-658) by becoming grounded during invasion. **(Pacific-Solomons)** The U.S.S. *Enceladus* (AK-80), a Cargo Ship, is damaged during a tropical storm in the Solomons. **(Atlantic-Italy-Anzio)** In the **U.S. Fifth Army** area, **VI Corps** sector, elements of the 3rd Division battle a German counterattack in response to a 16-hour assault against positions near Cisterna di Littoria on the previous night. During the night assault on the 30th, about half of Company B, 7th Infantry, 3rd Division had become casualties. Sergeant Truman Olson, realizing his Company nears annihilation, moves forward with his machine gun crew to halt the Germans. With the only remaining machine gun in the detachment, Olson and his Squad take the point. Over 24 hours, the only obstacle between the Germans and the survivors of Company B is Sgt. Olson. Olson is attacked by 200 enemy Soldiers, supported by mortars and machine guns, but he holds defiantly for one-half hour before being mortally wounded. Olson still refuses to budge and fires his gun relentlessly for another hour and a half until a second wound kills him. His gallantry manages to stall and push back the Germans, saving the lives of the remainder of his outfit; he receives the Medal of Honor posthumously. In the British 10th Corps sector, contingents of the British 46th Division reach M. Purgatorio. In the **II Corps** area, the 168th Regiment, U.S. 34th Division. captures Cairo village and repulses successive counterattacks. In the FEC sector, contingents of the 142nd Regiment, U.S. 36th Division overpower resistance at Manna Farm. Also, French troops seize Abate Hill.

January 31st 1944 — A 37-mm Antitank gun firing against an enemy pillbox on Kwajalein.

February 1st 1944 — U.S. Tanks on Kwajalein.

February 1st 1944 — (United States) The Combined Chiefs of Staff decide to postpone the invasion of France (OVERLORD), for approximately one month. The tentative date for the Normandy invasion is now set for early June, with the weather conditions at the time specifying the exact date. **(Pacific-Carolines)** The U.S.S. *Guardfish* (SS-217) sinks the Japanese Destroyer *Umikaze*. **(Pacific-Pearl Harbor)** Vice Admiral R.K. Turner, Commander of the Fifth Amphibious Force, receives new responsibility; the Navy establishes Amphibious Forces, Pacific and designates this responsibility to Turner as an additional Command. Headquarters will be located at Pearl Harbor. **(Pacific-Kwajalein Atoll-Marshalls)** Combined U.S. Army and Marine units land on the Kwajalein Atoll under cover of concentrated Naval and Air bombardment. By the end of the day, the 7th Division, commanded by General Corlet, U.S.A. (Southern Landing Force) controls approximately one-third of the Kwajalein Island including a portion of the enemy-held Airfield. The Marines hit the beaches at the southern shores of Roi and Namur at about noon, quickly seizing control of the Airfield from the unorganized and surprised Japanese. The Marines (RCT 23) drive to the edge of the northern coast, expelling enemy resistance with the exception of a pocket in the middle of the Airfield. The Marines (Regimental Combat Team 24) encounter dense jungle terrain and fortified buildings that had withstood the murderous bombardment but take the objective. During the operation, an ammunition dump explodes causing the Marines as many casualties as they would incur from battle. An enemy counterattack at dawn proves expensive for the Japanese, as the Marines devastate the attackers. During the day, one Marine, P.F.C. Richard B. Anderson, in a foxhole with two other Marines, pulls the pin on a grenade, but it slips from his grasp endangering everyone. Anderson, in an effort to save the others, throws himself over the explosion, saving the others. He receives the Medal of Honor posthumously. In another of the unending acts of undaunted heroism, 1st Lt. John V. Power (4th Division U.S.M.C.) is setting charges at an enemy pillbox and is struck viciously in the stomach. Unwilling to yield, he presses one hand against the bleeding wound and fires his weapon with his right hand then charges another pillbox, expending his ammunition into the pillbox, then re-loads to finish the job. Another round of fatal enemy fire rips into his stomach and head as he slumps to the earth. Mean-while, Private Richard K. Sorenson, stuffed in a shell crater with five other Marines, covers a grenade which falls among them. Miraculously, he survives after taking the full explo-sion. Both Sorenson and Power receive the Medal of Honor; Power's receives his posthumously. Also, a contingent of the V Amphibious Corps Reconnaissance Company seizes Arno Atoll. The Navy Vessel *Anderson* (DD-411) and the *Haggard* (DD-555) sustain damage by grounding and an internal explo-sion. The U.S.S. *Walker* (DD-517) destroys the Japanese Sub-marine RO-39. **(China-Burma-India)** The Allies begin to construct a major permanent road through the Hukawng Val-ley to support the Chinese troops operating against the Jap-anese in this area of Burma. In other activity, the 3rd Battalion, 113th Regiment, Chinese 38th Division, advances through Taihpa, Ga, on its way to assault a nearby Japanese stronghold. **(Atlantic-Italy-Anzio)** In the **U.S. Fifth Army** area, the 3rd U.S. Division again is repulsed at Cisterna. The Americans dig in to prepare for a counterattack. During the battle, PFC Alton Knappenberger, 3rd Division, wipes out an enemy nest by killing two men and wounding the other gun-ner. Knappenberger then destroys another enemy nest and holds off an enemy attack of Platoon strength for more than two hours; he receives the Medal of Honor. The American beachhead becomes strengthened with the completion of the arrival of the 4th and 1st Armored Divisions, U.S.A. **(Atlantic-Italy-Cassino)** In the **U.S. II Corps** area, vicious resistance meets the charging 135th U.S. Infantry, which is driving to secure Castellone and Majola Hill. Support fire from the 168th Infantry, spread across Hill 56 and 213 to punish and pin down the enemy, lends enormous help and the 135th cap-tures both objectives. In other activity, the Germans mount heavy counterattacks against Allied positions in the area ranging from Manna Farm to Hill 706. **(Europe)** (Antagonism and separate thrusts for control of German Intelligence oper-ations have been ongoing for years, especially since the death of Heydrich during May, 1942, which ignited a struggle be-tween the Abwehr, the Gestapo and the Sicherheitsdienst-Security Service. Hitler, had become suspicious of the Ab-wehr and its Commander, Admiral Wilhelm Canaris. The Fuhrer had issued orders during January to establish a single Intelligence unit under control of the Reichsfuhrer SS (Major General Walter Schellenberg).) During February, five mem-bers of the Abwehr Staff, Germany's intelligence network, de-fect to the Allies in Istanbul, bringing a wealth of information about German Intelligence operations; the defection gives the SS an opportunity to seize power, but Colonel Gehlen's For-eign Army East is undisturbed by the SS. Subsequent to the end of hostilities, it is Gehlen who evades the Russians and brings all his secret documents to the West. **(Atlantic-Russia)** The Soviets capture Kingisepp, situated within a mile of Es-tonia, giving them control of the last rail station on the route to Narva.

February 2nd 1944 — (Pacific-Marshalls-Kwajalein) The U.S. 7th Division meets stiff enemy resistance. Air, Artillery, and Naval guns are called in for support. The 2nd Battalion, 184th Infantry, drives across the lagoon side of the island, while the 2nd Battalion, 32nd Infantry, assaults enemy positions along the ocean. Meanwhile, the 3rd Battalion, 32nd Infantry, de-stroys an enemy pocket known as Corn. Advance elements

stretch farther than the Nora Road, but the main body organizes its line short of the road. In other activity within the sector of the Southern Landing Force, elements of the 7th Division land on Chauncey and engage in a severe fire fight. The Japanese lose 125 dead. In the Northern Landing Force area, the Marines mop up enemy resistance on Roi, then move to capture Namur; organized resistance on Namur is terminated by the Marines at 1215, ending the battle for the southern end of the Kwajalein atoll, except for mop-up opera-tions. Lieutenant Colonel Dyess, 1st Battalion, 24th Marines, directs his men against the last enemy position remaining on Namur, but a volley of enemy fire takes his life. His tremen-dous leadership during this attack contributes greatly to the success of the operation. Major General Henry Schmidt, com-manding the Northern Force, dispatches Combat Team 25, and Company A, 10th Amphibian Tractor Battalion and Land-ing Team 2, to secure the remaining islands in the northern section of the Kwajalein Atoll. They secure eight islands with-out opposition. Between the 2nd and the 4th, landing Team 1 secures Boggerlapp, Boggerik and Hollis Island, without op-position. In Naval activity offshore, the U.S.S. *Washington* (BB-56) and the U.S.S. *Indiana* (BB-58), both Battleships, be-come damaged after a collision. **(Pacific-Southwest)** The Headquarters for the U.S. Sixth Army is transferred from Aus-tralia to Cape Cretin, New Guinea. **(Atlantic-Italy-Anzio)** General Mark Clark, directs General Lucas to consolidate the beachhead and prepare his troops for a counterattack. **(At-lantic-Italy-Cassino)** In the British 10th Corps area, the Brit-ish 2nd Special Service Brigade assaults Mont Faito, but is driven back. In the **II Corps** area, the 135th Infantry, U.S. 34th Division, keeps driving toward Highway 6, with its 2nd Bat-talion crossing Hill 445 grinding ahead toward Hill 593. A strong German counterattack causes the 3rd Battalion, 168th Infantry to rush to their aid. The 1st Battalion successfully drives the Germans from Hill 324. The 1st Battalion, 142nd Infantry, 36th Division, takes control of Mont Castellone. The U.S. 133rd Infantry completes clearing the Barracks area to the north of Cassino, then advances, assisted by Tanks, to the northern end of the town of Cassino. The 133rd awaits darkness, then pulls back about 1,000 yards to safer positions. **(Atlantic-Russia)** The Soviets assault German 6th Army posi-tions, over a 60-mile front, west of the Dnieper. Also, the first Estonian village falls to the Red Army. Stalin agrees to provide six Bases for U.S. Planes in the U.S.S.R.

The results of saturation bombardment by the U.S. Navy on Kwajalein.

February 3rd 1944 — **(Pacific-Marshalls)** Troops of the U.S. 7th Division continue to clear the enemy from Kwajalein Island. Enemy blockhouses and concrete pillboxes are destroyed during the operation. The 184th Infantry, attacking on the lagoon side, meets staunch enemy resistance which pins down Company B. The frontal attacks prove costly to the Americans and the plan of attack is rapidly changed; the 1st Battalion, 184th Infantry moves to attack from the left as the 2nd Battalion charges through the right flank directly for Nathan Road. This action is coordinated with the 1st and 3rd Battalions, 32nd Infantry, which also drive toward Nathan Road. The units, involved with the advance, bypass several enemy strongholds along their route, then secure their positions and successfully repulse several counterattacks throughout the night. In other activity, the 1st Battalion, 17th Infantry, 7th Division, assisted by Destroyer and Cruiser Naval Fire and Air support that has virtually eliminated enemy opposition, lands on Burton at 09:35. The two Companies advance and encounter enemy resistance after about an hour's march inland. After the firefights, the troops advance to Bailey Pier. The drive is also supported by Amphibian Tractors and Tanks. Heavy support guns prevent the enemy from mounting counterattacks. Two islets, dubbed Buster and Byron, are secured by Amphibious Tank units without opposition. A meeting (Marshalls-Conference) is held between Major General Holland M. Smith, Brigadier General Thomas Watson, Rear Admiral Harry Hill and Rear Admiral Turner, concerning the invasion of Eniwetok. Admiral Hill is assigned overall Amphibious Command and General Watson's Tactical Group 1 receives responsibility for the landing. The date had been set for February 12th then changed to the 17th. In other activity, the Minesweeper U.S.S. *Chief* sinks after grounding. **(Pacific-Solomons)** Enemy coastal guns damage the U.S.S. *Claxton*, (DD-571), a Destroyer. **(Atlantic-Italy-Cassino)** The newly formed New Zealand Corps, comprised of the N.Z. 2nd Division, and the 4th Indian Division, is placed under the command of U.S. Fifth Army. In the **U.S. II Corps** area, elements of the 34th Division drive to within a mile and a half from Highway 6, while other units continue to clear the enemy from Hill 324. The 133rd Infantry, supported by Tanks, attacks toward Cassino against heavy enemy opposition and is forced to pull back. They renew the attack during the afternoon and inch to the northern fringes of town where they dig in securely before advancing against Hill 175. Second Lt. Paul Riordan leading an assault group, risks his life when enemy machine gun fire stalls his command. Riordan kneels in full view of the enemy and throws a grenade about 45 yards, onto the machine gun, kills one Soldier and wounds two others. As the advance continues, another Soldier goes after the pillboxes commanding the hill. P.F.C. Leo Powers claws to within 15 yards of it and lobs the grenade into a small opening in the roof, killing two men and chasing away the rest. Unperturbed by other enemy fire, Powers continues his advance and destroys the nest. The indomitable PFC advances to a third enemy pillbox, expending the balance of his ammunition, killing two men and capturing the remaining four. His undaunted ferocity cracks the resistance and his Regiment enters the city of Cassino; Powers receives the Medal of Honor. Meanwhile, the Germans press the Americans in the area between Manna Farm and Hill 706, but the persistence of the 135th Infantry pays off; the Regiment wins the hill. **(Atlantic-Russia)** Two Corps of the German Eighth Army, defending positions near Korosun, become totally surrounded by the

Soviets. The Germans halt their ongoing offensive operation and make a vigorous attempt to rescue the beleaguered troops.

February 4th 1944 — **(Pacific-Kurile Islands)** A U.S. Task Force, commanded by Rear Admiral W. D. Baker bombards Japanese positions on Paramushio. **(Pacific-Marshalls)** Vice Admiral Raymond Spruance declares the Majuro Atoll secure. Captain Edgar Cruise, U.S.N., receives responsibility for the area. **(Pacific-Marshalls-Kwajalein Atoll)** Elements of the U.S. 7th Division U.S.A., advance to Nathan Road after a difficult day of clearing enemy resistance. The operation takes a toll on the troops, causing them to arrive in a state of disarray. Additional units move to Nero Point on the tip of the island at about 17:00. Enemy resistance holds out until almost 21:30, however, the island is declared secure by General Corlett at 16:10. The Army has gathered many prisoners during the day, including both Japanese and their Korean laborers. The 1st Battalion, 17th Infantry, continues its northern attack against Burton, meeting stiff opposition, however, the troops secure the island by early afternoon. Units of the 2nd Battalion, 17th Infantry, capture Burnet and Loi north of Burton. Additional Japanese and Koreans (about 20) are captured on Blakenship. Landing Team 3, U.S.M.C., continues north and for the next three days, sweeps through 39 islands, capturing all without opposition. In other activity, two Planes attached to Marine Photographic Squadron 954 initiate the first photo reconnaissance of Truk Atoll. **(China-Burma-India)** In Burma, the Chinese 38th Infantry advances to Kaduja Ga. The Japanese, who have resisted fiercely in the Taihpa area, withdraw. In the **British Fourteenth Army** area, the Japanese mount an offensive against the 15th Corps on the Arakan Front. The Japanese overrun Taung Bazar then drive south and west. **(Atlantic-Italy-Anzio)** The murderous siege at Anzio continues with the Germans mounting a massive assault against Allied lines. The Germans break through British 1st Division lines, inflicting heavy casualties before the British withdraw from Compoleone to an area north of Carroceto and the Factory. In the **U.S. II Corps** area, the enemy holding Hill San Angelo repulses an assault by the 34th Division and drives the 3rd Battalion, 135th Infantry, back to Hill 706. The Germans holding Hill 593 contain an advance by the 2nd Battalion, preventing it from approaching closer than 500 yards of the objective. Elements of the 1st Battalion gain a slight hold on Point 445. While the 133rd Infantry and supporting Tanks regroup on the fringes of Cassino, the 1st Battalion punctures the northern corner of the town until withering German fire drives it back. **(Atlantic-Russia)** The Soviets secure the coast of the Gulf of Finland as far as the Narva River estuary. They also proclaim control of the rails from Leningrad to Novogrod.

February 5th 1944 — **(Pacific)** Admiral Nimitz, aware of the tremendous progress in the Marshalls and the fact that less troops will now be needed to secure the island chain, approves the final plan for the invasion of Eniwetok. **(Pacific-Kwajalein-Marshalls)** Mop-up operations ensue throughout Kwajalein Island. Scouting Parties reconnoiter various islands in the southern portion of the atoll. The 3rd Battalion, 17th Infantry, locates some Japanese on south Gugegwe (Beverly) and the 1st Battalion expels about 200 Japanese from north Gugegwe. Additional units, assisted by Tanks, secure Benson Island. Another force, including the 3rd Battalion, 184th Infantry, captures Bigei (Bennett) after a fierce firefight with the

Japanese. Ninety-four Japanese are killed during the operation. The Eastern Force of the 7th Division moves south from the southeastern tip of the atoll, closing toward Gugegwe, seizing five islands without incident. The Western Force marches north from Carlos and captures four islands, three of which fall without a fight. In Naval activity, two American Warships, the Destroyer Escort *Fair* (DE-35) and the Destroyer *Charrette* (DD-581), sink the I-21, a Japanese Submarine. **(Pacific-Philippines)** The U.S.S. *Narwhal* delivers more supplies to Philippine Guerrillas off Libertad, Panay, then evacuates personnel. **(China-Burma-India)** British General Wingate's Special Force is ordered to divert the enemy from the Myitkyina area and to inlict heavy casualties on the enemy in North Burma; it departs Ledo, advancing south supported by the U.S. 5318th Air Unit, commanded by Colonel Philip G. Cochran, whose responsibility is to resupply, transport, and evacuate Wingate's columns if necessary. **(Atlantic-Italy-Anzio)** In the **U.S. Fifth Army** area, the Germans continue to reinforce their positions while preparing a massive counter-offensive. The Germans continue to launch effective Air raids against American positions, forcing the Americans to evacuate the Airstrip at Nettuno. The German land troops jab at the American perimeter, probing for a weak link in the defenses near Cisterna. **(Atlantic-Italy-Cassino)** Heavy fighting rages in the **II Corps** area, but the Germans still hold firm. A detachment of the 1st Battalion, 135th Infantry, 34th Division, fights to the base of the towering walls which protect the abbey, then withdraws. This advance is the furthest climb made by the 34th Division during the struggle for Cassino. The brutalizing contest costs both sides heavily. The U.S. 36th Division is instructed to skirt the positions of the 34th and mount an assault from the northeast to capture Piedimonte.

A Grumman TBF Avenger being transferred to a Carrier.

February 6th 1944 — (Pacific-Kwajalein) In the Southern Landing Force area, elements of the 7th Division occupy Ennugenliggelap (Cohen), the first island north of Eller (Clifton), without incident, terminating the operation in the southern part of the atoll. The U.S. Southern Landing Force suffers 142 killed, 8,845 wounded and two missing. The estimated Japanese losses are 4,938 killed and captured. **(Pacific-Admiralty Islands)** The enemy Airbases at Momote and Lorengau are put out of operation by the U.S. Fifth Air Force. **(China-Burma-India)** In Burma, the Japanese assault the positions of the Indian 7th Division, capturing its Headquarters, and isolating it from the Indian 5th Division. The Indians regroup and reestablish a new Headquarters at Sinzweya.

(Atlantic-Italy-Anzio) In the **U.S. Fifth Army** area, the Germans assault Allied positions along the Moletta River as a diversion and are engaged by the 2nd Battalion, 157th Infantry, in vicious firefights throughout the night. **(Atlantic-Cassino)** The **U.S. II Corps** prepares for another thrust to destroy the German Line of defense on the final frozen ridge between it and Route 6. The New Zealand Corps replaces contingents of the II Corps south of Highway 6, enabling these II Corps troops to be thrown into the battle for Cassino. The Allied casualties have been continually mounting during this drive and Lt. General von Freyburg and British General Alexander now ponder whether or not to level the monastery by an Air attack. U.S. General Mark Clark is against such a tactic, but eventually relents and the raid is ordered to be carried out on the 15th of February. **(South Atlantic)** U.S. Naval Land-based Planes (VB-107) sink a German Submarine, the U-177. **(Atlantic-Russia)** The Third Ukrainian Front overrun enemy positions northeast of Krivoi Rog, and Nikopol. The Russians also trap a contingent of German troops in the vicinity of the Dnieper River near Nikopol.

February 7th 1944 — (Pacific-Marshalls-Kwajalein) The Northern Landing Force, 24th Marines, finishes its search of the islands in the northern Kwajalein Atoll. During this action which started on January 31st, the Marines suffer 963 total casualties; the explosion of an ammunition dump is responsible for about half of the deaths suffered by the Marines. The Japanese losses are reported as 3,472 killed and 91 captured. **(Pacific-Philippines)** The U.S.S. *Narwhal*, evacuates personnel from Balatong Point, Negros. **(Atlantic-Italy-Anzio)** The Germans initiate an offensive to destroy the Allied beachhead at Anzio in a night attack, hitting the British 1st Division and driving them from Buonriposo Ridge before dawn. The British 10th Corps attacks unsuccessfully near Mont Faito during the night of the 7th. In the **II Corps** sector, the U.S. 36th Division takes over the Castellone-Manna Farm area.

February 8th 1944 — (Pacific-Marshalls-Kwajalein) The vast majority of the Southern Landing Force (14th Marines, 23rd Marines, and the 2nd Battalion, 24th Marines), departs a secured Kwajalein. Combat Team 25 remains behind to garrison the atoll. **(China-Burma-India)** General Stilwell's representatives tell Washington that intelligence reports in Burma indicate a large Japanese offensive is expected. **(Atlantic-Italy-Anzio)** In the **U.S. Fifth Army** area, **VI Corps** sector, the British 1st Division remain embattled near the Factory; reinforcements rush in and help quell the enemy advance. In the vicinity of Carano, a six man Patrol attached to the 509th Paratroop Battalion encounters heavy enemy fire. Corporal Paul Huff advances through a minefield toward the German machine guns and destroys one nest. Huff returns to his Squad and goes back out in strength (Platoon) and routs the enemy; during the firefight, 27 Germans are killed and 21 are captured; Huff receives the Medal of Honor. The U.S. Patrol loses three men. In Naval activity off Italy, the Destroyer *Ludlow* (DD-438) is damaged by enemy shore-gun fire. **(Atlantic-Italy-Cassino)** In the British 10th Corps area, the bridgehead of the 46th British Division stretches further along the Garigliano, reaching about six miles northeast of Castelforte. A planned assault up the Ausonia Valley is aborted because the British 56th Division is diverted to Anzio to reinforce the beachhead; the British 10th Corps assumes defensive positions. In the **II Corps** area, the battle rages; the 133rd Infantry, 34th U.S. Division, inches to break the German hold at Cassino. In conjunction, the 168th Infantry charges Monastery Hill but is halted by withering enemy fire, despite heavy support fire pouring into the enemy positions from the 135th Infantry on the right flank. The enemy gives no ground and the assault troops suffer severe casualties. Additional elements hurriedly hook up with the 133rd Infantry and penetrate the perimeter after a grueling drive. Meanwhile, an unsuccessful assault is launched against the fortified city jailhouse; the Germans hold up an entire Platoon; Lieutenant Riordan (a hero several days earlier at Hill 175) attempts to take the jailhouse singlehandedly, but the overpowering enemy fire cuts him down at the steps of the building; he receives the Medal of Honor posthumously. **(Atlantic-Russia)** The Red Army seizes Nikopol in the Ukraine.

February 9th 1944 — (Atlantic-Italy-Anzio) The Germans concentrate on Allied positions at Anzio. The Germans overrun the factory and subsequently repel an Allied counterattack which is supported by Naval and Air sorties. The British 1st Division again takes heavy casualties, forcing more reinforcements to rush to the perimeter during the night of the ninth. **(Atlantic-Cassino)** The Allied situation at Cassino is no better than at Anzio, as casualties escalate. The Germans, also suffering staggering casualties, have seen their positions erode, but retain control over Highway Six and Cassino.

February 10th 1944 — (Pacific-Marshalls) Rear Admiral S.P. Ginder's Carrier Task Force bombards enemy positions on Eniwetok Atoll. Planes launch two successive assaults, bombing the Japanese again on the 11th and 12th. **(Pacific-New Guinea)** The Commanding General of the U.S. Sixth Army declares the end of Operation DEXTERITY, the Huon Peninsula campaign. The Michaelmas Task Force and the 5th Australian Division, converge on a point about four miles southeast of Saidor, culminating the campaign to expel enemy resistance on the peninsula. A Japanese Bomber damages the LST 170 off New Guinea. **(Pacific-New Britain)** The 1st Marine Division and RCT 112, U.S.A., link up, culminating the campaign in Western New Britain. **(China-Burma-India)** In the British Fourteenth Army area, the Japanese cut off the Ngakyedauk Pass and trap the Indian 7th Division in Sinzweya, forcing them to be resupplied by air. Off Formosa, the U.S.S. *Pogy* (SS-266) destroys the Japanese Destroyer *Minekaze*. **(Atlantic-Italy-Anzio)** The Germans keep pressuring the British 1st Division and seize the railroad station at Carroceto, despite Allied Air support and Artillery. **(Atlantic-Italy-Cassino)** The Allies ponder options to seize Cassino, while regrouping for the next attempt. **(European Theater)** The Combined Chiefs of Staff instruct the Mediterranean Commanders that all unnecessary LST's be dispatched to England. The date for the invasion of Normandy again is postponed about three weeks.

February 11th 1944 — (Pacific-Marshall Islands) The first U.S. Plane lands on the Airfield at Roi. **(Pacific-Solomons)** Two PT Boats, Nos. 279 and 282, collide off the Solomons; the PT-279 sinks. **(Atlantic-Italy-Anzio)** In the **U.S. Fifth Army** area, the U.S. 179th Infantry, 45th Division, assisted by the 191st Tank Battalion, assaults the factory but is repelled by vicious enemy firepower. **(Atlantic-Italy-Cassino)** In the **II Corps** area, German resistance remains staunch; yet another attack by the U.S. 34th Division is repulsed during a terrible storm. Severe casualties are inflicted upon the 34th Division at Albaneta Farm. Another assault mounted by the 168th Infantry, 34th Division, is repulsed at Monastery Hill. British General Alexander orders the Indian 4th Division to assault the heights west of Cassino. **(Atlantic-Russia)** The Soviets take Shepetovka, a rail center west of Kiev.

February 12th 1944 — (Pacific-Bismarcks) A contingent of the 1st Marines, 1st Marine Division, based on Cape Gloucester, lands on Rooke Island to search for Japanese; it remains until the 20th without encountering any enemy troops. **(Pacific-Marshalls)** U.S. Naval Task Force 58 departs Majuro, speeding toward Truk, while another Allied Assault Force sails toward Green Island. Japanese attack American positions on Roi Island and damage a supply depot. **(Pacific)** The U.S.S. *Macaw* (ASR-11), a Submarine Rescue Vessel, becomes grounded near the entrance to the Midway Channel and sinks. **(Atlantic-Italy-Anzio)** In the **U.S. Fifth Army** area, **VI Corps** sector, the U.S. 45th Division assaults the factory and again is thrown back by overwhelming fire. **(Atlantic-Italy-Cassino)** In the **II Corps** area, the U.S. 36th Division is struck by an intense German counterattack, bringing its advance to a halt; the enemy holds absolute control of the high ground and they are able to observe all Allied movements.

Also, the Allies are curtailed by the inability to use Vehicles for resupply on the treacherous mountainous terrain. Lt. General von Freyberg orders his New Zealand Corps to relieve the beleaguered II Corps of the responsibility to secure Cassino. **(European Theater)** The Combined Chiefs of Staff inform General Eisenhower of his duties as Supreme Allied Commander of the Allied Expeditionary Force. The tentative D-Day to invade Normandy is set for May of 1944. Eisenhower establishes Headquarters on the 14th. **(Atlantic-Soviet Union)** Contingents of the Red Army take Batetskaya and also push to the outskirts of Lugo.

February 13th 1944 — (Pacific) General MacArthur issues his directives concerning the capture of Manus in the Admiralty Islands and of Kavieng at New Ireland. D-Day is fixed for April 1st to gain control of the Bismarck Archipelago and to isolate Rabaul, which has been bypassed during the island hopping campaigns in the Pacific. **(Pacific-New Britain)** The 35th Fighter Squadron, U.S.A., moves to Airfield No. 2. **(Atlantic-Italy-Cassino)** In the **II Corps** area, the Indian 4th Division, New Zealand Corps, relieves the battle-weary 168th Infantry, U.S. 34th Division. The U.S. 133rd Infantry remains on line; however, a temporary lull occurs as preparations continue to level the monastery from the air. **(Atlantic-European Theater)** The Combined Chiefs of Staff direct a Bomber offensive to destroy the German "Military, Industrial, and Economic systems and also to demolish the communications systems and Airpower". **(Atlantic-Soviet Union)** Soviet troops secure the eastern shore of Lake Peipus.

February 14th 1944 — (Pacific-Bismarcks) The Light Cruiser U.S.S. *St. Louis* (CL-49) is damaged by a Japanese Bomber. **(China-Burma-India)** British Admiral Mountbatten informs the British Chiefs of Staff that intelligence indicates a strong Japanese offensive will be launched against the 4 Corps soon after the ongoing Arakan Operation is concluded.

February 15th 1944 — (Central Pacific) A new Naval Command, Central Pacific Forward Area, is established and is commanded by Rear Admiral J. H. Hoover. In other activity, the Submarine U.S.S. *Aspro* (SS-309) sinks the Japanese Submarine I-43. **(Pacific-Bismarcks-Green Islands)** Admiral Wilkinson's Task Force (Third Amphibious Force) lands contingents of the New Zealand 3rd Division, and American support units, including the U.S. 976th AAA Gun Battalion at Nissan Island, in the Green Islands. Japanese fighters are quickly driven off by Anti-aircraft Fire and Allied Planes. Construction units begin work on an advanced Naval Base. On the 16th, an enemy contingent is located and firefights rage until the 20th, when the estimated enemy force of about 70 Soldiers is eliminated. Three Americans and 10 New Zealanders are killed during the operation. During an Air strike against Kavieng Harbor in New Ireland, several Planes of the U.S. Fifth Army are shot down. Lieutenant Nathan Gordon, on alert near the Vitu Islands, rescues nine men by making three successive landings. After learning of another group of men down within 600 yards of the Japanese positions. He flies his overloaded Plane through intense enemy fire and rescues six additional American Airmen; Gordon receives the Medal of Honor. **(Pacific-Marshalls)** U.S. Task Force 51.11, commanded by Admiral Hill, departs Kwajalein steaming toward Eniwetok. The U.S.S. *Phelps* (DD-360) and the Minesweeper *Sage* (AM-111) destroy the Japanese Submarine RO-40. **(Pacific-Wake Island)** U.S. Naval Planes based on Apamama in the Gilberts, bombard the enemy defenses. **(China-Burma-India)** General Stratemeyer is relieved of command of the XX Bomber Command; however, he receives responsibility for logistics and for controlling administration for XX Command in India. **(Atlantic-Germany)** The Royal Air Force commences a strong night attack against Berlin. **(Atlantic-Italy-Cassino)** Allied concerns about the Germans having fortified the Benedictine Monastery at Cassino have caused much debate; the Americans cannot substantiate German occupation. The New Zealander, General Freyberg and British General Alexander hold the position that Germans have been detected within the monastery. General Mark Clark reluctantly agrees to bomb Cassino and Allied Artillery and American Bombers coordinate the attack, turning the monastery into a massive pile of rubble. Notices of the impending attack had been previously placed in shells and fired into the monastery, warning religious leaders and civilians inside, to evacuate. Later, the Allies find the Germans had not infiltrated the abbey; subsequent to its leveling, General von Senger deploys his troops in the ruins.

During the night of the 15th, the 4th Indian Brigade charges the heights west of Cassino, but again, the assault fails to penetrate Hill 593. Out of the ashes and ruins of the abbey, the Germans receive a tremendous piece of propaganda; the situation is neatly exploited by Hitler. Using a statement attributed to the Abbot, the Germans proclaim that no Germans had occupied the abbey. Actually, the Germans had removed the priceless art treasures and many original ancient manuscripts, safely transporting them to the Vatican. Miraculously, the tomb of St Benedict, founder of the abbey during 529 A.D., and the tomb of his sister St. Scolastica remain unscathed. General Von Senger, the German Commander at Cassino is a lay member of the Benedictine Order and German Lt. Colonel Schlegel, dispatched to the abbey to inform the monks about the imminent danger of the priceless collection, is an Austrian Catholic. The Yank ground troops stand in awe of the bombing of the monastery. One Soldier, Jerry Tague (Observation Battalion), attached to the 36th Division's Artillery: "IT WAS A BEAUTIFUL PLACE. I SAW EVERY DAMN BOMB THAT HIT THAT PLACE. IT WAS AN ASTONISHING AND DISTURBING SGHT AND I HAD HOPED THAT IT WOULD NOT BE RAISED BY BOMBING, BUT I UNDERSTOOD THAT IT WAS A TOUGH DECISION TO MAKE."

In Naval activity, the U.S.S. *Herbert C. Jones* (DE-137) is damaged near Anzio by the detonation of a radio controlled explosive.

February 15th 1944 — U.S. and New Zealander combat troops land on the Green Islands.

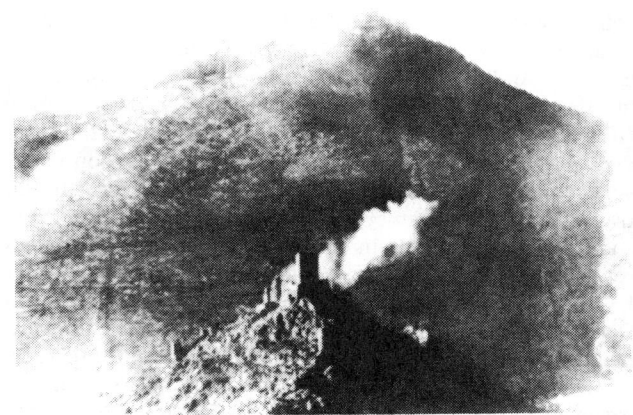

The Allies attack Cassino.

A decimated Cassino.

February 16th 1944 — (Pacific-Marshalls) U.S. Planes bomb Eniwetok Atoll to soften resistance prior to the main invasion. About 14 enemy Planes are destroyed on the ground at Engebi Airfield, and the facility is knocked out of service. The Pilots return with aerial photos of the atoll. **(Central Pacific)** The U.S.S. *Skate* (SS-305) sinks the Japanese Light Cruiser

Agano. **(Pacific-Bismarcks-New Ireland)** U.S. Army Aircraft destroy two Japanese Submarine Chasers, Nos. 16, and 39, north of New Ireland. **(Pacific-Bismarcks-New Britain)** U.S. Army Patrols dispatched from Arawe and Marine Patrols emerging from Cape Gloucester converge on Gilnit near the Itni River secure western New Britain and the Itni Valley.

February 16th-20th 1944 — (Atlantic-Italy-Anzio) The Germans attack in strength against Allied positions at Anzio. Enemy Artillery commences at 06:00, followed within one-half hour by assaults against the beachhead, with the main thrust against the left flank. Simultaneously, the Germans press the British 56th Division (British General Templer) positions and the U.S. Third Division at Cisterna. Over 170 sorties are flown by the German Air Force, and the Allies divert Aircraft to assist the besieged Anzio beachhead. Meanwhile, the U.S. 3rd Division repulses continuous enemy counterattacks. However, the Germans penetrate other Allied defenses, costing huge numbers of Tanks and heavy casualties. At about midnight on the 16th, the Germans renew the offensive, drive down the Albano Road toward the defenses of the exhausted U.S. 45th Division. Backed by Naval guns and Aircraft, the 45th is able to halt the Germans before a total collapse of the line occurs. The British 1st Division speeds to the aid of the 45th and is given the responsibility of holding the Albano Road (final beachhead line of defense). The murderous confrontation carries on for days. The British 56th Division beats a path against the crack enemy troops and regains lost ground. The Germans renew the attack on the 18th and force the U.S. 179th Infantry to withdraw to the final beachhead line. Allied Air support is absent because of the terrible weather. This penetration by the Germans is the deepest yet, but, still, the Allies cling to the beachhead.

Before dawn on the 18th, the Germans mount yet another formidable attack, and make slight progress, before the desperate Allies, threatened with annihilation, mount a fierce counterattack. On the 19th, a Task Force commanded by General Harmon, U.S. Fifth Army, jumps off with stunning effect, driving forward to gain 2,000 yards. Meanwhile, the British 169th Brigade, 56th Division, lands and awaits orders to join the assault. Harmon's Force halts the German advance, which includes recently committed enemy reserves. This stand strangles the German thrust, turning the momentum to the Allied cause. The enemy is thoroughly thrashed on the 20th by the VI Corps, terminating the German offensive.

February 17th-18th — Truk, Carolines, under attack by Task Force 58.

February 17th 1944 — (Pacific-Caroline Islands) Elements of U.S. Task Force 58 begin a two-day bombardment of Truk, inflicting heavy damage. The powerful Task Force commanded by Admiral Spruance, includes nine Carriers and six Battleships. During the Air attack, 70 Japanese Planes are blown out of the sky. In addition, the Japanese lose 40 more on the ground. The Carrier U.S.S. *Intrepid* (CV-11) is damaged by a Bomber during the two day operation. The Japanese lose the Light Cruiser *Naka*, the *Katori*, a training Cruiser, and three Destroyers: the *Maikaze, Oite,* and *Tachikaze.* In addition, Submarine Chaser No. 24 is sunk by the Destroyer *Burns* (DD-588). This formidable strike compels Japan to withdraw its Combat Aircraft from Rabaul. It also reinforces the American decision to bypass the atoll. On the 18th, the Japanese Destroyer *Fumizuki* and the Submarine Chaser No. 29 are destroyed by American Carrier-based Aircraft. **(Pacific-Marshalls)** A powerful U.S. Navy Task Force Group (51.11), commanded by Admiral Hill, bombards Engebi, Parry, Japan and Eniwetok Islands on the Eniwetok Atoll, while Planes attached to Task Force 58.4 simultaneously strike the landing zones. U.S. Marines (Tactical Group 1) land nd secure Aitsu (Camellia) and Rujiyoru (Canna) Islands without opposition. U.S. Army Artillery is deployed on the islands to position guns facing Engebi Island. The Marines (Co. D, 4th Tank Battalion) move toward Zinnia (Bogon), but initially land two islands short, because of confusion in the darkness, before moving rapidly to Bogon without incident. The Americans have taken their first day's objective without casualties. The newly established Artillery Detachment is ordered to commence firing against Engebi to supplement the Naval preinvasion bombardment. In a coordinated operation, Underwater Demolition Teams reconnoiter the beach areas. The Japanese Submarine I-11 is sunk by the U.S.S. *Nicholas* (DD-449). **(Pacific-Green Islands)** The New Zealanders slice through the islands. In other activity, a PT Boat Base is established. **(Pacific-Bismarcks-New Britain)** Allied Aircraft sink the Japanese Minesweeper No. 26 off Rabaul. **(Atlantic-Italy-Anzio)** In the **U.S. Fifth Army** area, the Germans mount a counterattack, ripping through the center of the U.S. 45th Division. Allied Planes drop more than 1,000 tons of bombs on the advancing Germans, who are also struck by salvos from the Naval Ships, halting the breakthrough. The British 1st Division is thrown in the contest to bolster the final beachhead line in an effort to take some pressure off the depleted 45th Division. In other activity, American General Truscott, 3rd Division Commanding Officer, is promoted to Deputy Commander VI Corps. Brigadier General John W. O'Daniel succeeds Truscott as Commanding Officer of the 3rd Division. **(Atlantic-Italy-Cassino)** The Allies make another futile drive against Cassino. Troops of the 4th Indian Division plow through frozen terrain against a wall of enemy fire coming from Hill 593. Again, the Infantry must attack without Air support as it has been diverted to Anzio to aid the beleaguered Allied beachhead. The courage of the Indian troops is commendable but the withering German fire chases them from the crest of the hill. Some of the Indian troops (2nd Gurkas) advance to the monastery and begin using their kukri knives in close combat, but the vast majority of the unit is killed or wounded; of those captured, none are ever seen again. Allied reinforcements manage to secure the heights between points 445 and 450. In other activity, the British 78th Division finally gets through a horrendous blizzard and takes positions in the New Zealand sector. **(Atlantic-Russia)** Contingents of the Second Ukrainian Front overrun German positions west of Cherkassy, dealing the Germans a devastating blow. The Germans lose about 100,000 killed or captured.

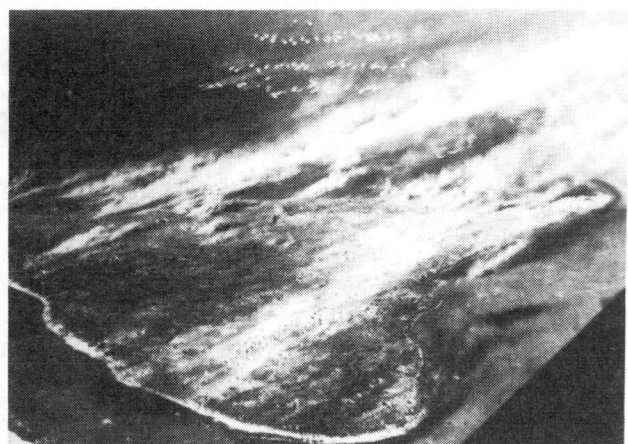

February 18th 1944 — The invasion of Eniwetok.

A Japanese soldier in a pillbox on Engebi Island, Eniwetok Atoll.

February 18th 1944 — (Pacific-Eniwetok-Marshalls) The U.S. Navy bombards Engebi to soften resistance; Carrier-based Planes, attached to Rear Admiral H.W. Hill's Task Force, also strike enemy positions. Meanwhile, the 22nd Marines, supported by a contingent of a U.S. Army Cannon Company, land on the beaches and quickly declare Engebi secure, except for an isolated pocket at the southern tip of the island. Elements of the Landing Force join the landing at Eniewetok with the 106th Infantry Regiment, U.S.A. In other activity, Marine Company D, 4th Tank Battalion, arrives on Bogon Island, situated west of Engebi, and establish positions to cut off Japanese escape routes. On the following day, Army and Marine Troops combine to assault Eniwetok Island. **(Pacific-Caroline Islands)** Japanese facilities and Vessels at Truk, including the Destroyer *Fumizuki*, are damaged by air attacks. Most of the Japanese Fleet had previously left port, and those remaining are struck severely. **(Pacific-Bismarck Archipelago)** Allied Ships bombard Rabaul in New Britain and also strike Kavieng, New Ireland. **(China-Burma-India)** General Stilwell, concerned about the whereabouts of the 66th Chinese Division, makes a personal search. He locates it and additional units in the vicinity of the Command Post; the troops had taken a wrong road and cleared the enemy from an area believed to be Yawngbang a couple of days earlier. The Chinese have located a primary Japanese trail, but the elusive enemy has escaped the trap. **(Atlantic-Italy-Anzio)** The Germans pressure the U.S. 45th Division, making some progress, but the line holds at the beachhead. In Naval activity, the U.S.S. *Pilot* (AM-104) is damaged, after a collision. A Tug, the YT-198, sinks after striking a mine. **(Atlantic-Italy-Cassino)** In the New Zealand sector, the Indian 4th Division assaults Monastery Hill, but makes only minor progress. During the night of the 17th, elements of the New Zealand 2nd Division seize Cassino Station only to be driven back out by the afternoon of the 18th. Both the Allies and the Germans begin to slow down operations during late February and early March to reorganize.

February 19th 1944 — (Pacific-Bismarcks) Japanese positions are bombarded by Army, Navy, and Marine Aircraft. This is the final opposed raid against Rabaul; the attacks force the enemy to withdraw all its Air Defense Units stationed there. Marine Corps Aircraft stationed on the Solomons initiate round-the-clock ombing which continues until the 15th of May, turning Rabaul into rubble. In New Ireland, U.S. Army Aircraft sink the Submarine Chasers Nos. 22, 34 and 40. **(Pacific-Marshall Islands)** U.S. Naval Vessels and Carrier-based Planes attached to Rear Admiral Hill's Task Force again bombard enemy positions on Eniwetok Atoll. Following cessation of the bombardment, elements of RCT 106, 27th Division, storm the beaches on the lagoon side, then drive past the outpost positions and push toward the ocean. The 1st Battalion pivots right, moving against enemy Artillery fortifications on the southern end of the island. Enemy resistance slows the progress of the march. The 3rd Battalion, 22nd Marines (Reserve Force), is committed during the afternoon to assist the drive and is given orders to move to the northern end of the island to meet the ongoing enemy counterattack. During the night of the 19th, the Japs creep close to Marine positions and toss a grenade into a foxhole containing three Marines. Corporal Anthony P. Damato (Shenandoah, Pa.), instinctively smothers the grenade with his body, absorbing the entire concussion and saving the lives of the others; he receives the Medal of Honor posthumously. **(Atlantic-Italy-Anzio)** The German onslaught is halted along the Albano Road. U.S. General Harmon awaits the cessation of Allied Artillery and Air strikes, then counterattacks. Navy Cruiser and Destroyer fire joins the fight and rattles the enemy counterattack with some well-placed volleys that shatter enemy positions. The Assault Force (minus the British 169th Brigade unready to assist) gains 2,000 yards. The British expel an enemy pocket that had built up during the early hours. In one instance, about 80 Germans assault Company G, 180th Infantry, near Padiglione on the 17th. P.F.C. William J. Johnston halts the advance with his machinegun, killing about 25 enemy troops and sending the remainder in retreat. Johnston, under extreme duress from enemy Artillery, Mortar and Sniper fire, maintains his calm for the balance of the day and throughout the night. On the 18th, Johnston continues to hold off the attacking Germans while his outfit pulls back; he is reported killed in action, after receiving a serious chest wound. However, on the 19th, he makes it back to U.S. lines to become a recipient of the Medal of Honor. **(Atlantic-Elba)** U.S. PT Boats attack a German Convoy as it passes southeast of Elba in the Tyrrhenian Sea, between Italy and Corsica Island is remembered as the final home of the exiled Napoleon during 1814-1815.

February 1944 — Some U.S. troops grabbing a breather amidst a tough contest on the Marshalls.

February 20th 1944 — (Pacific-Bismarcks) The Japanese evacuate Air fields in the vicinity of Blanche Bay. U.S. Army Aircraft sink the Japanese Submarine Chaser No. 48 off New Ireland. **(Pacific-Marshalls-Eniwetok)** The combined Army and Marine force wipes out resistance on Eniwetok. An Army contingent (3rd Battalion 106th Infantry) moves north against the enemy while the 3rd Battalion, 22nd Marines, assisted by the 1st Battalion, 106th Infantry, wipes out opposition in the southern end of the island. The assault against Parry, the last of the larger islands on the Atoll, is being prepared as Artillery based at Eniwetok Island, bombards enemy positions. Additonal Artillery stationed on Japan Island also rains on the island. In other activity, Allied Carrier-based Planes attached to Rear Admiral J.W. Reeves' Task Group, strike Jaluit Atoll. Company D, 4th Tank Battalion U.S.M.C., lands on the southern group of the western chain of islands, capturing Rigili Island after destroying minor resistance, then moves across the remaining seven islands in the chain without incident. **(Pacific-Green Islands)** The Assault Force of New Zealanders and American support troops that arrived on the 15th complete the destruction of the Japanese Garrison on the island. The operation costs the New Zealanders 10 killed; the Americans lose three men. **(Atlantic-Italy-Anzio)** In the **U.S. Fifth Army** area, the **VI Corps** wins a decisive victory over the Germans, by hitting the salient, ending the enemy attempt to break through. However, the Germans continue exerting great pressure against the flanks, while regrouping for another attack. In Naval activity, the LST 348 is sunk by an enemy torpedo off the coast of Italy. **(Atlantic-Germany)** The United States Strategic Air Force initiates heavy bombing raids for a week, sending over 1,000 Planes to hit installations in the Brunswick-Leipzig area. One Plane, attached to the 510th Bomber Squadron, receives direct hits, which knock out the Pilot and kills the Co-pilot. After all men are ordered to bail out, Sergeant Archibald Mathies and 2nd Lt. Walter Truemper refuse to leave the wounded Pilot and attempt to land the Plane themselves. The third attempt is unsuccessful and all three men are killed when the Plane crashes into a field next to the Airstrip; each man becomes a recipient of The Medal of Honor. In one other incident of superb heroism, about 20 enemy Fighters attack and damage a Plane of the 364th Bomber Squadron. Lt. William R. Lawley refuses to bail out because of his wounded crewmen. With his co-pilot dead, the instrument panel and windshield both splattered with blood, and an engine on fire, Lawley maintains control of the

February 1944 — U.S. Infantry, bolstered by Tanks during the campaign to seize the Marshalls.

Aircraft until slipping into unconsciousness. The Bombardier revives him, as another engine goes on fire. Miraculously, Lt. Lawley successfully crash lands the Plane at a Fighter Base, saving the crew; he receives the Medal of Honor.

February 21st 1944 — (United States) The Joint Chiefs of Staff meet with President Roosevelt to discuss the British pressure to abort Operation ANVIL; Roosevelt concurs with the Joint Chiefs-he had promised the Russians an invasion of Southern France; he notes: "THE RUSSIANS WOULD NOT BE HAPPY, EVEN IF WE TOLD THEM IT WOULD MEAN TWO MORE DIVISIONS FOR OVERLORD." **(Pacific-Bismarcks-New Britain)** The 5th Marines drive across the northern coast of the island toward Iboki Plantation, a Japanese stronghold. In other activity, the 3rd Battalion, 5th Marines, seizes Karai-ai near Cape Raoult with a two pronged assault, striking from the sea and on the ground to seize the Japanese Supply Base. **(Pacific-Marshalls-Eniwetok)** The combined troops of the Army and Marine Corps secure Eniwetok. The 3rd Battalion, 106th Infantry mops up, while the 3rd Battalion, 22nd Marines, pulls out to prepare for the invasion of Parry, which is presently under attack from the air and the sea as part of the preinvasion plan, which is finalized today. **(Atlantic-Italy-Anzio)** In the **VI Corps** area, the exhausted U.S. 45th Division is sent to bivouac. The replacements hit intense fire as they move up. **(Atlantic-Italy-Cassino)** New Zealand General Freyberg issues a plan for a new assault to seize Monte Cassino. **(Atlantic-Russia)** The Soviets advance to Krivoi Rog.

February 22nd 1944 — (United States) A PT Boat, maneuvering off Long Island, strikes an unknown object and sinks. **(Pacific-Bismarcks-New Ireland)** American Destroyers patrolling off New Ireland sink the Japanese Minelayer *Natsushima* and the Tug *Nagaura*. **(Pacific-Marianas)** U.S. Task Force 58, commanded by Admiral Mitscher, is attacked by enemy Planes as it steams toward the Marianas. However, Carrier-based Planes and Surface Vessel fire devastate the Japanese Force. **(Pacific-Marshalls-Eniwetok Atoll)** The 22nd Marines, Landing Teams 1 and 2, assault the northern portion of Parry Island. The 2nd Battalion, supported by the 3rd Battalion, moves south, forcing the capitulation of enemy resistance on the southern portion of the island by 19:00, successfully concluding the Eniwetok Operation. **(China-Burma-India)** General Merrill of Merrill's Marauders receives instructions on a plan to trap the Japanese. In other activity, a U.S. Submarine, the *Ray*, patrolling near Saigon, deploys mines. Also, the Japanese River Boat, *Francis Garnier*, strikes a mine and sinks. **(Atlantic-Germany)** The U.S. Strategic Air Force hits the Germans with another massive strike. Eighth Air Force Planes bomb Aircraft factories at Bernburg, Aschersleben, and Halberstadt. Fifteenth Air Force Planes, stationed in Italy, strike enemy facilities at Regensburg. **(Atlantic-Italy)** The Germans mount heavy resistance in the vicinity of Padiglione. First Lieutenant Jack C. Montgomery, 45th U.S. Infantry, advances in front of his Rifle Platoon prior to daylight. His daring exploits and dangerous close-quartered combat accounts for his singlehanded capture of 32 enemy prisoners, plus killing 11 enemy Soldiers and wounding several others. His actions also destroy several enemy strongholds; Lt. Montgomery receives the Medal of Honor. **(Atlantic-Russia)** The Soviets capture Krivoi Rog, in the Ukraine.

February 23rd 1944 — (Pacific-Marianas) U.S. Task Force 58 launches Planes striking Guam, Saipan, Tinian and Rota in the Marianas inflicting severe damage to enemy Vessels. **(Pacific-**

Admiralties) U.S. Planes survey ground activity in the Admiralties. **(China-Burma-India)** The Chinese occupy Yawnbang, Burma, but their arrival is too late to cut off the retreating Japanese. **(Atlantic-Italy-Anzio)** The British 56th Division, which has replaced the beleaguered U.S. 45th Division along the bloody Albano road, is struck by a devastating blow; the Germans, limiting themselves to smaller and more selective type offensives, annihilate the replacements that arrive at the front. In other activity, the VI Corps is placed under the command of General Lucius Truscott, who replaces General Lucas.

February 24th 1944 — (Pacific) General MacArthur, informed that the aerial reconnaissance flights over the Admiralties received no enemy reply, orders a landing Force to reconnoiter the island. MacArthur designates the 5th Cavalry Regiment (reinforced) to take the assignment. During strategy meetings, some Officers question the feasibility of the attack and also offer other opinions on why the assault should not be made. One Officer mentions that the 5th Cavalry has no battle experience, prompting MacArthur to relate a story from his youth. He tells his staff that when he was a young boy of four, living at Fort Selden, New Mexico, there was a danger of being attacked by Geronimo. He said: "A TROOP OF THE 5TH CAVALRY RODE THROUGH TO HELP US." "THEY'D FIGHT THEN AND THEY'LL FIGHT NOW. DON'T WORRY ABOUT THEM." The attack takes place on the 28th of February. **(Pacific-Bismarcks)** Two U.S. Destroyers, the *Buchanan* (DD-484) and the *Farenholt* (DD-491), are both damaged near the coast of New Ireland by enemy shore batteries. **(Pacific-New Guinea)** U.S. Patrols on Saidor advance to Biliau at Cape Iris. **(China-Burma-India)** The U.S. 5307th Provisional Unit (Merrill's Marauders) departs Ningbyen (Burma), moving toward the Hukawng Valley to initiate Guerrilla attacks against the Japanese as they advance toward their main objective, Myitkyina Airfield. Several men remain behind to keep the campfires burning and confuse the Japanese. The Marauders advance for seventeen straight hours. A Platoon led by Lt. Sam Wilson (1st Battalion) takes the lead. The Marauders are guided by some unsung heroes, Katchin natives (descendants of the hill people of the Himalayas who inhabit the area near the Irrawaddy and Myitkyina area). These Kathins (attached to Donovan's O.S.S.) have an unusual and fascinating interpreter; he is a Catholic priest who has been working among the Katchins for about nine years and has mastered their language; Father James Stuart carries a pistol strapped to his waist; he translates for the Allies. During one intriguing incident, the priest encounters a contingent of advancing Japanese; he inquires to an Officer: "CHINESE?" The indignant Officer spits, then bellows: "NO, JAPANESE!" He then stares fiercely at the priest , then snarls: "ENGLISH?" Father Stuart pauses, spits, then responds: "NO, IRISH." The Japanese Officer laughs and the lopsided encounter concludes; the priest is allowed to continue his journey. **(Atlantic-Germany-Austria)** Schweinfurt is again barraged by massive Air raids; first by the U.S. Eighth Air Force during the day, followed by another attack by the Royal Air Force during the night. In addition, the U.S. Fifteenth Air Force strikes enemy facilities at Gotha. Enemy Aircraft intercept all missions and heavy Air battles ensue. **(Atlantic-Gibraltar)** A German U-Boat, the U-761, is cornered off the coast of Gibraltar, a peninsula at the southern end of Spain and is sunk by a combination of U.S. Land-based Naval Planes (VP-63 and VB-127), British Planes and Warships. **(Atlantic-**

Russia) Units of the Second Baltic Front, in conjunction with troops of the Leningrad Front, take Dno. The Soviets also make progress against the German bridgehead on the left bank of the Dnieper River, south of Vitebsk. In addition, the Germans lose Rogachev, north of Zhlobin.

February 25th 194 — (Pacific-Bismarcks-New Britain) Marine Patrols reach Iboke Plantation to find it evacuated. According to reports the last solid Japanese force had gone through the village on the 16th. Also, the 1st Battalion, 141st Japanese Infantry, withdraws from the Lupin area, heading north. In other activity, U.S. Destroyers bombard Kavieng and Rabaul. **(China-Burma-India)** Marauders: Lt. Logan Weston's Platoon (3rd Battalion) and Lt. Grissom's Platoon (2nd Battalion) turn south and encounter Japanese. Wilson's contingent hears the firefights to the rear but it continues toward Tanja Ga, literally "sniffing for the mysterious odor emitted from Japanese Patrols." The Marauders find the village empty; Wilson and another man, riding horseback, speed 22 miles to the rear to inform General Merrill. As Lt. Wilson is crossing a creek, his saddle slips and he slides off the horse, but his foot gets caught in the stirrup. Suddenly he is threatened as two ferocious cats (probably Tigers), prepare to attack. Wilson begins to scream at the cats with his boisterous tone and the cats turn and vanish into the jungle. The two riders gallop to Merrill and then return to the village safely. The main body reaches Tanja Ga on the 28th. Meanwhile, Weston's Platoon closes on Nzang Ga; the pointmen encounter Japanese posing as Chinese, but the ruse doesn't work; the Platoon suffers one man wounded, but it safely pulls back to the main trail. Meanwhile, a contingent of Grissom's Platoon reaches Lanem Ga, finding it abandoned, but the Japs hold the heights; the lead Scout, Pvt. Robert W. Landis (first Marauder to die) is killed; his body is not recovered until the following day. **(Atlantic-Italy-Anzio)** The badly battered British 1st Division receives replacements as its 18th Brigade arrives. **(Atlantic-Germany)** The combined U.S. Eighth and Fifteenth Air Forces again strike Regensburg. In addition, Augsburg, Fuerth, and Stuttgart are attacked by the Eighth Air Force. German Planes intercept, concentrating on the Fifteenth Air Force, which loses 20 percent of its force. **(Atlantic-England)** Prime Minister Churchill reassures President Roosevelt that no amphibious operation including Operation CULVER (invasion of Sumatra) will cause the upper Burma campaign to be scaled down.

February 26th 1944 — (United States) The Combined Chiefs of Staff table a decision on Operation ANVIL (invasion of southern France) until it can be restudied. The bogged-down Italian campaign is given top piority in the Mediterranean. **(Southwest Pacific)** A modified Operation BREWER, the invasion of the Admiralties, is approved. The invasion force, composed of the 1st Cavalry Division U.S.A., is commanded by Major General Innis P. Swift. The initial objective upon landing is to reconnoiter the area around the Momote Airfield and to occupy and secure it if feasible. **(Pacific-Solomons)** Enemy coastal guns sink the PT-251. **(Atlantic-Italy)** The LST 349 becomes grounded and sinks. **(Atlantic-Russia)** The Soviets proclaim that the rail line in the vicinity of Dno-Novosokolniki is free of German troops. In other activity, Porkhov falls to the Red Army.

February 27th-March 11th 1944 — (Pacific-Admiralties) THE BATTLE OF LOS NEGROS — U.S. Planes pummel enemy positions at Momote and Lorengau. American Planes also strike Wewak and Hansa Bay in New Guinea. On the 27th, elements of the Alamo Force land on the southeast coast of Los Negros and discover a Japanese bivouac area which had not been detected by aerial Reconnaissance flights. The Scouting Force is withdrawn on the 28th in conjunction with the preinvasion Air strikes. The weather on D-Day, the 29th is overcast, affecting Air support; upon cessation of the Naval bombardment, troops of the 1st Cavalry hit the beaches around 08:00 against feeble resistance, securing Momote Airfield by 09:50. The Landing Force, considered insufficient to hold the perimeter, is ordered to pull back from the captured Airfield and reform on the Jamandilai Peninsula to prepare for a Japanese counterattack.

The Japanese launch a disorganized night attack, and the outnumbered Americans repulse it handily. The Japanese are again thrown back on March 1st. The 1st Cavalry holds resolutely and on the 2nd is reinforced by contingents of the 5th Cavalry. The 1st and 2nd Squadrons, 5th Cavalry, then attack Momote, seizing it easily; strong defensive positions are established. After dark on the 3rd, the sounds of enemy troop movements are heard. Suddenly, the Japanese boldly attack. Yank gunsights spot the moving targets as they scream" Banzai" while charging toward the defenses. Machineguns open up, mowing down the attackers. Grenades and Rifles further rake the area, killing more of the enemy and terminating the assault, costing the Japanese heavy casualties. The enemy dead remains on the field as the Japanese flee. No further full scale attacks are mounted against the Cavalry.

Fresh U.S. troops begin arriving to bolster the effort to capture the island chain. On the 5th, contingents of the 5th Cavalry seize Papitalai, while the 12th Cavalry secures the eastern shore of Seeadler Harbor. In rapid succession, Papitalai Mission and Lombrum Plantation fall to the Americans, while the Japanese are in fast retreat. With the occupation of Lombrum Plantation on the 8th, the occupation of Los Negros is complete. The island is secure and U.S. Naval Supply Vessels move into Seeadler Harbor without opposition. The Brewer Force sets its sights on the remaining islands in the Admiralty chain.

February 1944 — Innovative Yanks on the Admiralties, blasting Japanese positions with a captured Japanese gun.

February 27th 1944 — (Pacific-Admiralties) American Rear Admiral William M. Fechteler's attack group, presently at Oro Bay, New Guinea, begins loading reconnaissance troops attached to Brewer Task Force. In addition, a Navy PBY debarks a small detachment of the Alamo force on the southeast coast of Los Negros for reconnaissance.

February 29th 1944 — Momote Airfield, Admiralties.

February 28th 1944 — (Pacific-Admiralties) Allied Planes step up preinvasion Air raids against Japanese positions on the Admiralties and in New Guinea. The Brewer Task Force begins its voyage from Oro Bay to Los Negros. **(Pacific-New Guinea)** The U.S.S. *Abner Read* (DD-526) becomes damaged by grounding. **(China-Burma-India)** The main body of the Marauders, guided by Kachin natives arrive at Tanja Ga. The Kachins dislike the Japanese, however, their feeling for the Chinese are similar. The 3rd Battalion takes the point and advances toward Walawbum and the 2nd Battalion drives west through Wesu Ga across the Numpyek to cut the road about three miles beyond Walawbum. Meanwhile, the 1st Battalion moves down the access trails. The 3rd Battalion, under Weston, fights through Lagang Ga; a deep fog sets in at night as they cross the Numpyek on the 2nd of March. **(Atlantic-North Africa-Algeria)** British General Wilson informs General Mark Clark that he is relieved of responsibility for Operation ANVIL (invasion of southern France). Brigadier General Garrison H. Davidson will continue to lead the planning group until a new Army Commander is assigned. Clark remains with the 5th Army. The original decision for Clark to head Operation ANVIL had been based on the assumption that the drive to Rome would terminate and leave sufficient time for him to command the invasion of southern France. **(Atlantic-Italy)** Allied Commanders confer in Caserta for the purpose of planning the drive on Rome. **(Atlantic-Italy-Anzio)** The Germans still concentrate on destroying the beachhead at Anzio, again striking against the British 1st and 56th Divisions along the Albano Road in the morning. In addition, the Germans prepare an assault against the U.S. 3rd Division holding the right flank, first by putting out smokescreens and then, after dark, with an Artillery bombardment. Allied bickering continues as Churchill tells General Alexander to rename the troops at Anzio, and when referring to them in press reports, to call them the "Allied Bridgehead Force." Clark counters by suggesting that Alexander call them the "Fifth Army Allied Bridge Force." **(Atlantic-Italy-Cassino)** In the **II Corps** area, the U.S. 36th Division is relieved at Mont Castellone by contingents of the 88th U.S. Division and troops from the French Expeditionary Corps, leaving only one U.S. Battalion on line along the southern front.

February 29th 1944 — (Pacific-Admiralty Islands-Los Negros) ALSO SEE FEBRUARY 27TH-MARCH 11TH 1945. Los Negros is invaded by U.S. troops. Lieutenant Marvin J. Henshaw, the first Soldier to hit the beach is awarded the Distinguished Service Cross by General MacArthur. MacArthur and Admiral Kinkaid land on the beach and after inspecting it, they order the island defenses held at all hazards. MacArthur's words to the land Commander, General Chase: "HOLD WHAT YOU HAVE TAKEN, NO MATTER AGAINST WHAT ODDS." ... "YOU HAVE YOUR TEETH IN HIM NOW, DON'T LET GO." **(Pacific-Bismarcks-New Britain)** Enemy installations and Shipping at Rabaul come under attack by U.S. Destroyers, inflicting damage. **(China-Burma-India)** In Burma, **British Fourteenth Army** area, the 15th Corps engages the enemy in fierce and heavy fighting, expelling the Japanese and reopening the Ngakyedauk Pass. **(Atlantic-Italy-Anzio)** The weather at Anzio remains terrible, but it does not deter the Germans from mounting another assault against VI Corps positions. The U.S. Third Division is submitted to a heavy Artillery attack, followed by an Infantry assault intended to drive the Americans back to the Mussolini Canal, however, it is repulsed.

March 1st 1944 — (North Atlantic) The Destroyer Escort *Bronstein* (DE-189) sinks the U-603. Two other Destroyer Escorts, the *Bostwick* and the *Thomas*, join the *Bronstein* and sink the U-709. **(North Pacific-Alaska)** A U.S. Naval Auxiliary Air Facility is established at Tanaga, Alaska. **(Pacific-Admiralty Islands)** The Brewer Force concentrates on eliminating Japanese who have secretly infiltrated the perimeter. The Japanese are beaten off during another unsuccessful night Banzai attack. **(Pacific-New Guinea)** The U.S. Navy establishes a Naval Base at Milne Bay. **(Atlantic-Italy-Anzio)** The Germans are again repulsed from the beachhead at the 3rd Division's lines at Ponte Rotto. The American-English force at Anzio stem the tide, but are unable to penetrate German lines.

March 2nd 1944 — (Pacific-Admiralty Islands) The 1st Squadron, 5th Cavalry, commanded by Colonel Hugh T. Hoffman, lands at Los Negros; in coordination with the 2nd Squadron, Momote Airdrome is seized with considerable ease. **(Pacific-Philippines)** The U.S.S. *Narwhal* (SS-167) delivers ammunition to Guerrilla agents at Butuan Bay, Asipit, Mindanao, and evacuates personnel; on the following day, it sinks the Japanese Gunboat *Karatsu*. The *Narwhal* surfaces near Tawi Tawi on the 5th to deliver supplies to the Guerrillas, then evacuates additional personnel. **(China-Burma-India)** In Burma, **British Fourteenth Army** area, elements of the British Special Force cross the Chindwin River on rafts and dinghies (dropped from Planes), and push south from Ledo. In other activity, the U.S. 5307th Provisional Unit (Merrill's Marauders) organizes and assembles across the Tanai River as it continues to move against the Japanese. In the **British Fourteenth Army** area, the 81st West African Division takes Apaukwa. Later, a strong enemy counterattack forces it to withdraw to Kyauktaw. **(Atlantic-Mediterranean)** Lt. General Alexander M. Patch is appointed Commander of the U.S. 7th Army, which has the responsibility for Operation ANVIL (invasion of southern France). **(Atlantic-Italy-Anzio)** In the **U.S. Fifth Army** area, the **VI Corps** sector, the 509th Paratroop Infantry Battalion is relieved by the 30th Infantry, 3rd Division. In addition, British Royal Marine Commandos arrive to bolster the hard hit British 56th Division. In other activity, Allied Planes, including 351 Heavy Bombers and many additional Light, Medium, and Heavy-fighter Bombers strike enemy positions to alleviate pressure on the ground forces.

March 3rd 1944 — (United States) President Roosevelt proclaims that the Italian Fleet (previously surrendered to the

Allies before Italy joins the Allied cause) is to be divided among the Americans, British, and the Russians. (**Pacific-Southwest**) The Allies prepare to seize Hollandia, New Guinea; a meeting convenes at Brisbane, Australia to decide strategy. Land-based Planes are not within striking distance, making it imperative to recruit Carrier assistance to neutralize enemy resistance and to intercept Japanese Aircraft originating from Wake Island-Sarmi at Dutch New Guinea about 125 miles from Hollandia. (**Pacific-Admiralties**) The Japanese mount a savage but fruitless night attack against the U.S. Cavalry troops, costing the enemy many casualties. (**China-Burma-India**) In Burma, the Japanese begin moving to Walawbum to strike the Americans. Meanwhile, the U.S. 5307th Provincial Unit (Merrill's Marauders) advances feverishly to block the road on either side of Walawbum to thwart the Japanese. The 3rd Battalion (5307th) secures Lagang Ga, establishes a drop field for purposes of resupply, and turns back several counterattacks. In the Ngam Ga area, the 1st Provisional Tank Group (Chinese-American) arrives with elements of the Chinese 22nd Division in time to repulse a heavy Japanese assault during the night. (**Atlantic-Italy-Anzio**) In the **U.S. Fifth Army** area, the 3rd U.S. Division again withstands another enemy attempt to dislodge them at Ponte Rotto. The 3rd Division counterattacks during the afternoon gaining previously lost ground. This steadfast stand prompts the Germans to make this their major assault to reduce the beachhead.

March 4th 1944 — (Pacific-Admiralties) Allied Surface Vessels, commanded by British Rear Admiral V.A.C. Crutchley, including four American Destroyers and two U.S. Cruisers, bombard Japanese installations on Hauwei and Norilo, and repeat the performance on both the 6th and 7th of March. On Los Negros, during the early part of the morning, an eight man Squad (Troop G, 5th Cavalry) receives the bulk of an enemy attack launched by a 200 man force which is virtually intoxicated. The raid kills six of the eight defenders. Sgt. McGill orders the other man to withdraw, while he singlehandedly holds off the enemy until his weapon ceases to function. He continues to resist, with the butt of his rifle until the insurmountable odds overcome him. When reinforcements reach the area at dawn, they find his body with 105 dead Japanese sprawled around the gallant trooper's position; McGill receives the Medal of Honor posthumously. In other activity, the 2nd Squadron, 7th Cavalry, and the 82nd Field Artillery Battalion arrive at Los Negros to strengthen the beachhead. (**Pacific-Green Islands**) The Americans complete a Fighter Airfield in the Green Islands; this is followed by the construction of a Bomber Airfield which will be operational before the end of the month, adding more punch to the American Pacific Air campaign. (**Pacific-Marshalls**) The 4th Marine Defense Air Wing's campaign against the Japanese entrenched on the eastern Marshalls commences with the bombing of Wotje, Jaluit, Maloelap and Mille Atolls. These attacks continue until the final surrender of the Japanese. Also, Marine Scout-Bomber Squadron 331 assaults Jaluit. (**Pacific-Solomons**) U.S. Land-based Aircraft (Army and Navy) attack enemy positions on Choiseul Island. (**Atlantic-Italy-Anzio**) The opposing forces at Anzio each regroup. The Germans receive orders to hold their positions and take defensive postures. A period of calm overtakes the battlefield until the Allied Spring offensive commences during mid-May. Meanwhile, the struggle to capture Cassino continues to rage. (**Atlantic-Germany**) The U.S. Eighth Air Force launches a

Bomber strike against Berlin, the first American Bomber mission to be directed against the capital. German Fighter Planes and Antiaircraft guns take a high toll on the U.S. Planes, shooting down 75.

A WAC in conversation with a Pilot.

March 4th-9th 1944 — (Pacific-Burma) THE BATTLE OF WALAWBUM — In Northern Burma, the 2nd Battalion, (Merrill's Marauders) sets up roadblocks along Kamaing Road in coordination with the 3rd Battalion which fires from commanding positions on the heights overlooking Walawbum; the I and R Platoon becomes isolated. The Japanese attack from the south on the sixth against the Yanks who have their backs to the river. A Nisei interpreter, Henry Gosho hears the Japanese voices and relays the Japanese intentions, giving the Marauders time to set up. Three Yanks are wounded and their ammunition nears exhaustion. Frantic calls for assistance go back to the main body; Lt. Woomer (Woomer the Boomer) rushes into position with his mortars and opens up. Suddenly, cries of anguish are heard in the distance and the Marauder operator bellows: "Good, the last one blew two Japs clear up into the air forty yards out front." A Banzai attack then ensues, but withdraws under sever fire. Another Marauder, Sioux Chief Norman E. Janis, detects a Jap machine gun, knocks it out and eliminates six additional enemy troops. The Marauders throw back six assaults. In conjunction, the Japanese futilely attempt to cross the river and outflank the Americans; but the 2nd Battalion cuts them down. Heavy fighting continues against the U.S. roadblock north of the town until the 5th. On the sixth, hellish fighting continues, several Japanese bullets pierce the water jacket of a machine gun; the Marauders keep a steady flow of canteen water gushing into the crippled gun. One excited gunner yells: "Come on and get some more of it you sons-of-bitches;" four thousand rounds pump through the barrels, in unison with the constant noise of the Marauders' theme song: "Get those bastards." Subsequently, the 3rd Battalion pulls back to Wesu Ga, having sustained seven wounded, but miraculously, sustain no fatalities. The Japanese lose 350 men killed. The 2nd Battalion is ordered to pull out and get resupplied, then join the 3rd Battalion below Walawbum. During the contest to wrest Walawbum from the enemy, the Marauders have suffered eight fatalities and 37 wounded; 19 additional men are evacuated with malaria.

Chinese reinforcements arrive in the vicinity of Walawbum on the 6th in addition to the 1st Provisional Tank Group, compelling the Japanese to withdraw. The Americans and Chinese squeeze the surrounded Japanese; however, poor communications between the units allow the Japanese to evade the trap. Walawbum is secured on the ninth when contingents of the Chinese 22nd and 38th Divisions and the 1st Provisional Tank Group enter the village, placing most of the Hukawng Valley under Chinese control. The Japanese sustain about 850 killed. General Merrill, during a Staff meeting notes: "BETWEEN US AND THE CHINESE WE HAVE FORCED THE JAPS TO WITHDRAW FARTHER IN THE LAST THREE DAYS THAN THEY HAVE IN THE LAST THREE MONTHS OF FIGHTING." The Marauder force which had departed Margherita during early February numbered 2,600 men; about 2,300 continue the campaign. The Marauders begin to drive through the valley on the 12th.

March 5th 1944 — (Pacific-Southwest Area) General MacArthur suggests to the joint Chiefs of Staff that Hollandia be invaded during April in lieu of seizing Hansa Bay on the merits that this will further isolate the Japanese in New Guinea. MacArthur also recommends that Kavieng, New Ireland, be assaulted according to the original plan on April 1st. **(Pacific-New Guinea)** The U.S. 126th Infantry, 32nd Division, lands without incident at the Yalau Plantation, 30 miles west of Saidor. In other activity, the Australians drive through the Ramu Valley, as the Japanese retreat toward Madang. **(Pacific-Admiralties)** American General Innis P. Swift assumes command of Task Force Brewer. **(China-Burma-India)** In the **British Fourteenth Army** area, elements of the Indian 3rd Division, comprised basically from Brigades of the British 70th Division, are dropped from Planes in central Burma. Included with these Paratroopers are U.S. Engineers who are the first to jump. Number 1, Air Commando Group, commanded by Colonel Cochran, flies the 3rd Indian Division to their destination, an Airstrip dubbed Broadway, located about 50 miles northeast of Indaw and has them bail out. The Indian 3rd Division virtually has its own Air Force (No. 1 Air Commando) and is known as the "Chindits."

March 6th-9th 1944 — (Pacific-New Britain) Combat Team A, 5th Marines, 1st Marine Division lands at the Volupai Plantation on the Willaumez Peninsula to prepare for the assault against Talasea. Inclement weather prevents Air support, but the Marines fight through swampy terrain against fierce opposition and extend the beachhead 2,000 yards, then prepare to attack toward the Airdrome. The Fifth Marines meet little opposition on the following two days. On the 9th, the Marines pounce on Mount Scheleuther and the Waru VIllages in the Willaumez Peninsula only to find the Japanese had fled south. Subsequently, the Marines declare Talasea and its Airdrome secure. Three Infantry Battalions of the 5th Marines patrol the area to the north, south, and southeast of Bitokara, expelling Japanese stragglers from western New Britain; the mop-up operation lasts until the 25th of April.

March 6th 1944 — (United States) The U.S.S. *Scorpion* (SS-278) is unaccounted for and presumed lost. The *Scorpion* had departed Pearl Harbor on December 29th 1943, commencing its fourth War Patrol. No hints of her demise are available. Her final communication with another Vessel had occurred during early January, and Japanese war records cite no kills in *Scorpion's* area. **(Pacific-Admiralties)** The U.S. 12th Cavalry arrives at Los Negros and is immediately pressed into action to pursue the retreating enemy. Meanwhile, the U.S. bridgehead is expanded to include Porlaka and Salami. **(Pacific-Bismarcks)** Enemy coastal guns damage the U.S.S.

Nicholson (DD-442). **(Pacific-Solomons-Bougainville)** A tremendous number of enemy Soldiers are discovered by U.S. Army troops (XIV Corps) at Hill 700, the highest ground within the Empress Bay beachhead. **(China-Burma-India)** Generalissimo Chiang Kai-shek, concerned with the Japanese offensive on the Arakan Front (Burma), orders General Stilwell to halt the Chinese offensive. In other activity, Merrill's Marauders overwhelmingly defeats a large enemy force, killing about 400 enemy Soldiers, while repelling the attack in the Hukawng Valley at Walawbum.

March 7th 1944 — (Pacific-Admiralties) On Los Negros, Papitalai falls to units of the 5th Cavalry. The newly arrived 12th Cavalry secures the eastern shore of Seeadler Harbor, while other contingents control a beachhead at the Papitalai Mission. In other activity, Momote Field unexpectedly receives a B-25, which successfully makes an emergency landing. **(Pacific-Marshalls)** The First Reconnaissance Group, including two reinforced Companies from the 22nd Marines, leaves the Kwajalein Atoll to secure the Wotho Atoll. **(Pacific-New Guinea)** The PT-337 is sunk by enemy coastal guns. **(China-Burma-India)** During the campaign to retake Burma, Brigadier General Frank D. Merrill withdraws his Galahad Force south to establish a roadblock at the Kamaing Road. The Chinese 113th Regiment, 38th Division, takes up positions evacuated by the Marauders. The 1st provisional Tank Group tries to talk the 113th Chinese Regiment into assisting it with a frontal attack against Walawbum; subsequently, the 64th Chinese Regiment, 22nd Division, joins the operation. The combined force establishes two roadblocks just west of the Nambyu Stream. Some enemy resistance is encountered, but Tanks disperse the enemy.

March 8th 1944 — (Pacific) The U.S. 41st Division embarks from Australia, for Cape Cretin, New Guinea to prepare for the assault on Hollandia. **(Pacific-Admiralties)** The 2nd Squadron, 7th Cavalry, captures Lombrum Plantation ending the Los Negros campaign. **(Pacific-Bismarcks-New Britain)** The 5th Marines moves toward Talasea against only light resistance. Patrols have discovered Talasea unoccupied by the enemy. **(Pacific-Marshalls)** Japanese Planes attack U.S. positions on the Eniwetok Atoll.

March 8th-24th 1944 — (Pacific-Solomons-Bougainville) The U.S. Army, holding Bougainville since the withdrawal of the 3rd Marine Division on January 16th, comes under ferocious attack by the Japanese now reinforced from other parts of the island. The 37th Division receives an intense Artillery barrage which destroys one B-24, and three Fighters and damages 19 Planes. U.S. Naval Vessels open fire, in coordination with the Air support and ground Artillery, driving the Japanese back but the attack forces the withdrawal of Allied Bombers to safer ground at New Georgia. Meanwhile, the ground troops diligently destroy the attackers. A sustained enemy assault during the night 8-9th against Hill 700 breaks through the defenses of the 145th Infantry. The 145th Regiment counterattacks, but the Japanese hold their small gains. The struggle for Bougainville again erupts in furor on the 10th, when Japanese assault American positions on Hill 260 in the Americal Division sector, seizing South Knob from the 182nd Infantry; and hold against an American countercharge.

Vicious, but indecisive fighting continues for control of the area until the 11th as the Americans try to resecure Hills 260 and 700. The U.S. 145th Infantry regains part of Hill 700. Also, the Japanese push toward the Piva Airfields, meeting firm resistance by the 129th Infantry. A hefty counterattack shoves the Japanese back and protects the Airfields. On the 13th, the 129th Infantry, assisted by Tanks, rumbles through fierce Japanese resistance, recapturing all previously lost ground in its sector. The Japanese are driven from Hill 700, but staunchly hold Hill 260, turning back elements of the 132nd Infantry. For the next few days the pattern continues with the Japanese penetrating slightly, only to be driven back by Tanks and Infantry.

March 9th 1944 — (Pacific-Admiralties) Advance elements of an Allied Fighter Garrison arrive at Momote Airfield. The 2nd Cavalry Brigade lands at the Salami Plantation. **(Pacific-Bismarcks-New Britain)** Talasea falls to the 5th Marines. The 2nd Battalion seizes Mt. Scheleuther and the Waru villages on the Willaumez Peninsula. As the Japanese retreat south. Mop-up operations begin with the Infantry scouring the peninsula to rid the area of Japanese stragglers. The search and destroy operation lasts until April 25th. **(Pacific-Solomons-Bougainville)** Enemy Artillery fires on the Torokina Airstrip. The Japanese make minor gains against the 145th Infantry, 37th Division which is holding Hill 700. **(China-Burma-India)** In Burma, contingents of the Chinese 22nd and 38th Divisions and the 1st Provisional Tank Group (Americans and Chinese) enter Walawbum. This seizure secures the entire Hukawng Valley. **(Atlantic-Iceland)** The U.S.S. *Leopold* a Destroyer Escort (DE-319) is sunk by an enemy Submarine off the coast of Iceland. **(Atlantic-South America-Brazil)** The U.S. Navy establishes a Naval Air Facility (Lighter than Air) at Cruz, Brazil. **(Atlantic-Russia)** The Red Army moves into Tarnopol and heavy fighting begins. On the 23rd, troops of the First Ukrainian Front break through from the east, tightening the circle on the besieged Germans.

March 10th 1944 — (United States) The scheduled dates for the invasions of Hollandia (April 15th); Marianas (June 15th); Palaus (September 15th); Mindanao (November 15th); and Formosa February 15th 1945, are fixed. **(Pacific-Admiralty Islands)** Allied Aircraft strike enemy positions on Manus Island. **(Pacific-Solomons-Bougainville)** The enemy attacks the Americal Division's positions on Hill 260, capturing South Knob from the 182nd Infantry. The 182nd mounts a counterattack but cannot dislodge the Japanese. In other activity, heavy fighting ensues on Hill 700 with the 145th Infantry, 37th Division denting the enemy salient on the saddle of Hill 700. In other activity, the Submarine Chaser SC-700 is sunk by enemy fire near Vella LaVella, Solomons. **(China-Burma-India)** In the **British Fourteenth Army** area, the Japanese counter the landing of the Chindits (Indian 3rd Division) in Central Burma by launching Planes to assault Chowringhee Airfield. **(Atlantic-Italy)** The Allied Central Mediterranean Force has its name changed to Headquarters, Allied Armies in Italy (AAI). **(Atlantic-Western Europe)** The U.S. Ninth Air Force is ordered to consolidate its efforts on preinvasion operations. Up to this point, the unit has been assigned to support the Strategic Air Force on its bombing missions.

March 11th 1944 — (Pacific-Admiralty Islands) U.S. Patrols dispatched to reconnoiter Manus Island, in preparation for the main invasion, land at Bear Point without incident and determine that the location is unsuitable for the placement of Artillery. They head for Butjo, Luo, north of the Manus Islands. Another landing occurs at Hauwei Island, also north of Manus. The Japanese ambush the unsuspecting Patrol, initiat-

March 9th 1944 — U.S. Army contingents, supported by Armor, seizing a hill on Bougainville.

ing a fierce firefight. The trapped Patrol fights its way out safely. **(Pacific-Marshalls)** Elements of the 1st Battalion, 22nd Marines, secure Lib Island, south of the Kwajalein Atoll. **(Pacific-Solomons-Bougainville)** Vehement fighting rages as Japanese troops attack to seize the Piva Airfields from the 129th Infantry, 37th Division, making some minor gains. In other action, the 148th Infantry secures some ground on Hill 700, but the 182nd Infantry is repulsed in its attempt to recapture the South Knob of Hill 260. **(China-Burma-India)** In the **British Fourteenth Army** area, the remainder of the 77th and 111th Brigades are air-dropped over Central Burma, completing the landing of the Chindits (Indian 3rd Division). In other activity, the Indian 7th Division secures Buthidaung. **(Atlantic-France)** Off Toulon, the German Submarines U-380 and the U-410 are sunk by U.S. Army Planes. **(Atlantic-Italy-Anzio)** The VI Corps issues plans for the resumption of the offensive to break through the German obstacles at the Albano Road sector. **(Italy-Cassino)** In the British sector, the British 5th Division finishes replacing the battle weary British 56th Division. The lull in the fighting continues. **(Atlantic-Russia)** Soviet troops seize Berislav, along the Dneiper River.

March 12th 1944 — (United States-Pacific) The Joint Chiefs of Staff direct General MacArthur and Admiral Nimitz to make preparations to seize Luzon and Formosa by February 1945. The order calls for the invasion of Emirau, St. Matthias Island, instead of Kavieng in New Ireland. It also calls for the invasion of Hollandia, New Guinea in place of Hansa Bay. Kavieng and Rabaul, two Japanese strongpoints, are to be bypassed. In addition, MacArthur requires less men to handle the operation. **(Pacific-Solomons-Bougainville)** The 129th Infantry holds firm against a strong counterattack. Heavy fighting also ensues as the 182nd Infantry engages the enemy on Hill 260. Despite some progress, fierce enemy fire forces the troops to withdraw from the South Knob. **(Pacific-Admiralty Islands)** Elements of the 7th Cavalry land on Hauwei and meet fierce resistance. The 2nd Squadron fights inland and establishes a small beachhead. On the following day, the troops assisted by Tanks eliminate enemy resistance, securing the island so Artillery can be brought in to shell Manus Island. **(China-Burma-India)** Merrill's Marauders renew their campaign to surround the Japanese 18th Division, instituting roadblocks behind the enemy lines near the Hukawng and Mogaung Valley junction. They advance 20 miles today, however, it takes about two weeks to advance the next thirty miles. The Marauders are unaware that O.S.S. 101 detachment is operating in their vicinity. As the Marauders drive through the jungles they are pestered by savage leeches, which bite the men and their mules; the dried blood becomes even more of an annoyance. Within several additional days, the Marauders engage the Japanese at Tingkrung Hka as they advance. **(Atlantic-Italy-Cassino)** Razabil falls to the 5th Indian Division.

March 13th 1944 — (United States) The U.S. 3rd Army (principal portion of Headquarters section) embarks from New York for England. **(North Atlantic)** The German Submarine U-575 is sunk in the North Atlantic. The attacking Force consists of Squadron VC-95 attached to the U.S.S. *Bogue* (CVE-9), the Destroyer *Hobson* (DD-464), Destroyer Escort *Haverfield* (DE-393) and is supplemented by a Canadian Warship and British Planes. **(Pacific-Japan)** The U.S.S. *Sandlance* (SS-381), sinks the Light Cruiser *Tatsuta* near Honshu, Japan. **(Pacific-Solomons-Bougainville)** The U.S. 129th Infantry, 37th Division, supported by Tanks, regains all lost ground in its area. The Japanese are driven from Hill 700, but put up violent resistance in the vicinity of South Knob on Hill 260. **(China-Burma-India)** The 1st Battalion, U.S. 5307th Unit (Marauders) advances to Makuy Bum. In other activity, British Admiral Mountbatten orders reinforcements (5th Indian Division) flown in to bolster the British Fourteenth Army which is having difficulty restraining the advancing enemy in Central Burma. In yet other action, the Japanese bomb and strafe the Chindit's (Indian 3rd Division) Airstrip. **(Atlantic-Russia)** Kherson, along the Dnieper is taken by the 3rd Ukrainian Front.

March 14th 1944 — (Pacific-Marshalls) Marine Reconnaissance Teams, attached to the 1st Battalion (2 Companies), arrive at Kwajalein Atoll after seizing the islands and atoll in the western chain of the Marshall Group. In other activity in the Pacific, Admiral Nimitz offers to send Carriers against Hollandia and Wakde-Sarmi prior to the invasion. Nimitz also commits Air support during and after the invasion to bolster the ground forces. American Admiral Wilkinson receives the responsibility for directing the campaign to capture Emirau in the St. Matthias Islands. **(Pacific-Solomons-Bougainville)** The U.S. 129th Infantry, 37th Division, takes advantage of a lull in the hostilities and fortifies its positions; the Regiment aborts direct attacks against Hill 260, turning to prodding and tormenting the enemy with harassment tactics.

Seabees constructing an Airbase on Eniwetok.

March 15th 1944 — (Pacific-Solomons-Bougainville) Bolstered by Tanks, the Americans repulse another Japanese assault. **(Pacific-Admiralty Islands)** U.S. Naval Vessels and Aircraft bombard Manus Island to soften resistance. Afterward, the 2nd Brigade, 8th Cavalry, 1st Cavalry Division hits the beach on the north coast and attacks Lugos Mission. The 1st Squadron overruns the mission, then speeds east along coastal road No. 3, toward Lorengau to seize its Airdrome. Meanwhile, the 2nd Squadron drives south to road No. 1, which is the island route to the objective. As the assault troops advance, the 7th Cavalry comes ashore and establishes perimeter defenses. In other activity, on Los Negros, the U.S. 5th Cavalry drives west toward Hill 260 (similar Hill No. 260 at Bougainville). **(Atlantic-Italy)** The town of Cassino is leveled by Allied Planes; 1,200 tons of explosives transform the town into huge piles of rubble. The Allies assume that securing the town will be an easy task, but the Germans turn disaster into an asset. Their Tanks, hidden in bunkers, roll out to face the Allied ground troops. Additional Germans fill the gaps between the rocks, forming a perfect de fense which they could not have established themselves. Allied Tanks are immobilized by the rubble, forcing the Infantry to advance alone. At noon, the Allies assault the town, under protective Artillery fire. The New Zealanders sweep the north and eastern sections and the Indian 4th Division drives toward Monastery Hill against fierce resistance. A driving rainstorm causes the struggling Allies additional grief. American Generals Jacob Devers, Mark Clark and Ira Eaker, along with British General Alexander and New Zealand General Freyberg, are within a few miles of the Monastery, observing the bombing mission.

March 16th 1944 — (Pacific-Admiralty Islands) The 8th Cavalry, 1st Cavalry Division, approaches the Lorengau Airdrome (Manus Island) from two directions: the 1st Squadron drives half-way through the Airstrip against fierce enemy fire and is soon relieved by the 1st Squadron, 7th Cavalry. The 2nd Squadron pushes feverishly along road No. 1, to join the fight. A night-long Artillery barrage ensues and on the 17th the Airdrome is seized. The Lorengau Airdrome is found unsuitable for a Base and the Mokerang Plantation becomes the site of the Airstrip. **(China-Burma-India)** In the vicinity of Mawlu, Burma, the 77th Brigade, Special Force (Chindits) encounters a Japanese Force and drives them off. The contingent begins to destroy enemy communication lines leading to north Burma and establishes an Airbase. **(Atlantic-Italy-Cassino)** The New Zealanders press strenuously against the enemy lines at Cassino, but progress is slow as the Germans still command the high ground. **(Atlantic-Cape Verde Islands)** The German U-801, operating near the Cape Verde Islands off the coast of French West Africa, is sunk by Planes (Squadron VC-6), attached to the Carrier *Block Island*, and the Destroyer *Corry* (DD-463) and Destroyer Escort *Bronstein* (DE-189). **(Atlantic-Mediterranean)** British Warships and U.S. Naval Land-based Aircraft (VP-63) sink the German Submarine U-392.

March 17th 1944 — (Pacific-Solomons-Bougainville) The Japanese mount another unsuccessful attack to crush the 129th Infantry. In Naval activity, the PT-283 is damaged by enemy coastal guns. **(Pacific-Admiralty Islands)** The 1st Squadron, 5th Cavalry, captures Hill 260, on Los Negros, counting almost 50 enemy dead. **(China-Burma-India)** British Admiral Mountbatten asks the assistance of President

Roosevelt and Prime Minister Churchill to convince Chiang Kai-shek to commit another Chinese Division for the Burma campaign. In Northern Burma, a contingent of Tanks attached to the 1st Provisional Tank Group and fragments of the Chinese 22nd Division occupy the summit of Jambu Bum. **(Atlantic-Italy-Cassino)** The railroad station at Cassino falls to the New Zealanders after a vicious battle; the Germans extract a huge price before relinquishing the tracks. **(Atlantic-Finland)** Soviet peace terms are formally turned down by Finland.

March 18th 1944 — (Pacific-Bismarcks) An American Assault Force departs Guadalcanal, heading for Emirau in the St. Matthias Islands. The 4th Marines, transported by a Naval Force commanded by Commodore Lawrence F. Reifsnider, will arrive at the objective on the 20th and land without the support of a preinvasion bombardment. The Marines find the island undefended. It becomes a Light Naval and Air base to assist the island hopping campaigns. **(Pacific-Bismarcks-New Britain)** Contingents of the 5th Marines (Patrols) advance to Numundo Plantation at the eastern base of the Willaumez Feninsula. **(Pacific-Admiralty Islands)** The 2nd Squadron, 8th Cavalry seizes Lorengau village, then advances along road No. 2 toward Rossum. In other activity, the 12th Cavalry runs into fierce opposition near Hill 260. Enemy fire becomes sharp when Patrols advance toward the Papitalai Mission perimeter. **(Pacific-Marshall Islands)** A U.S. Naval Task Force including one Carrier, two Battleships and additional Destroyers, under the command of Rear Admiral W.A. Lee, bombards Mili Island in the Marshalls. During the assault, the Battleship U.S.S. *Iowa* is damaged by enemy coastal guns. **(Pacific-New Guinea)** Enemy positions on Wewak are bombarded by U.S. Destroyers, which return for a second strike on the following day. **(China-Burma-India)** General Stilwell orders Merrill's Marauders to establish roadblocks to prevent enemy pasage into the Tanai Valley (Burma) from the south. **(Atlantic-Italy-Cassino)** The New Zealanders still are embroiled in a costly battle for control of Cassino against crack German troops. **(Atlantic-Russia)** Zhmerinka is taken by the First Ukrainian Front after a very difficult struggle **(Atlantic-Germany)** British Royal Air Force Bombers assault Frankfurt, dropping more than 3,000 tons of bombs during the night attack which continues into the 19th. This is the biggest raid launched against Germany since the outbreak of war.

March 19th 1944 — (Pacific-Admiralty Islands) The U.S. 1st Cavalry Division dispatches its 8th Cavalry to the east and keeps its 7th Cavalry concentrating on the enemy positions scattered along Rossum Road. **(Pacific-New Guinea)** U.S. Planes attached to the Fifth Air Force destroy a Japanese Supply Convoy moving to Hollandia, after it dropped off supplies at Wewak the previous day. **(Pacific-Marshall Islands)** Two Assault Forces of Marines (3rd Battalion, 22nd Marines) embark from Kwajalein Atoll to secure the southern group of the chain. **(China-Burma-India)** In the **British Fourteenth Army** area, the Indian 5th Division is rushed by rail and by air from the Arakan sector to the central front to bolster the line. **(Atlantic-Italy)** Operation STRANGLE goes into effect. This Air operation is pointed to the interruption and destruction of enemy supply movements throughout Italy, with emphasis on rail lines, ports and distribution depots. In addition, Bombers continue to strike enemy communication lines which crisscross Italy. **(Atlantic-Italy-Cassino)** In the **U.S. Fifth Army** area, obstinate German opposition stifles the New Zealander advance on Cassino, forcing the assault force

to halt during the night of the 19th to reform. In other activity, Mount Vesuvius erupts, spewing lava. There is much concern at Naples, for the areas near Portico, San Sebastiano and Torre del Greco, but within a few days the tenacious volcano loses much of its punch. **(Atlantic)** The Carrier *Block Island* launches Planes (VC-6) which destroy the German Submarine U-1059. **(Atlantic-Russia)** Mogilev-Podolski, held by the Germans, is assaulted from two sides. The resistance collapses and the town is overtaken by the Soviets. The Germans also lose Kremenets to the Red Army.

March 20th 1944 — (Pacific-Bismarcks-St. Matthias Islands) The 4th Marines, commanded by Brigadier General Alfred H. Noble, U.S.M.C., land at Emirau Island, finding it undefended; it is transformed into a Light Naval and Air Base. This landing culminates a series of Operation CARTWHEEL offensives against Rabaul. In other activity, Rear Admiral R.M. Griffin's Task Force, consisting of Destroyers, four Battleships and two Escort Carriers, bombards New Ireland. **(Pacific-New Guinea)** U.S. Army Planes sink Japanese Auxiliary Submarine Chasers, Numbers 47 and 49 north of New Guinea. **(Pacific-Philippines)** The U.S.S. *Angler* (SS-240) surfaces near Panay to rendezvous with Allied Guerrillas; it evacuates 58 people, including women and children. **(China-Burma-India)** The 1st Battalion, Merrill's Marauders reach Nprawa Ga; the lead Platoon is ambushed by a Japanese machinegun crew, costing the contingent one man killed and two wounded. Mortars are quickly in action and the gun and its crew is eliminated; the Battalion continues moving toward Shaduzup. During the advance, they spot fresh enemy tracks and stumble upon a bivouac area; the troops move fast and clear the camp as they break through to the road. **(Atlantic-Italy-Cassino)** Vicious fighting continues at Cassino as the New Zealanders attack. German snipers take high tolls on the advancing troops; even Tanks are pummeled as they advance. German casualties also are high and their Commander, von Senger, is doubtful that his elite 1st Parachute Division (Green Devils) can continue to hold.

This horrendous battle rages until the 23rd. Enemy bazookas wipe out nearly twenty-five Tanks (American and Indian), which in turn blocks passage of the trailing Tanks. On the 23rd, Freyberg realizes his New Zealand Corps is both overextended and exhausted. British General Alexander orders the assault to cease. Allied troops holding precariously on Hangman's Hill receive orders to descend from the heights, beginning on the evening of the 25th, thus concluding the third major battle for control of Cassino. As the deafening sounds of battle become mute, an ivory blizzard blankets the blood splattered mountain and its frozen death-laden paths like a huge cloak of pure innocence. However, the illusion is fleeting and the falling snow is agonizing. Its chilling bite grips the already beleaguered troops with carnivorous horror, casting the dead as deformed sculptures seemingly carved by a demented artist in macabre style during medieval times. **(Atlantic-Hungary)** German troops occupy Hungary.

March 21st 1944 — (Pacific-Admiralty Islands) The 5th and 12th Cavalry scour Los Negros in pursuit of the withdrawing enemy. **(Pacific-Marshalls)** Two contingents of the 3rd Battalion, 22nd Marines, land at Ailinglapalap Island, Southern Group. The landing teams eradicate enemy resistance and secure the island; subsequently, one detachment embarks for Ebon located on the southern tip of the atoll. **(Pacific-New Guinea)** Patrols attached to the U.S. 32nd Division encounter patrols from the Australian 7th Division about eight miles from the Yalau Plantation. **(Atlantic-Mediterranean)** British Sir General Wilson, suggests that Operation ANVIL (invasion of southern France) be terminated for the purpose of concentrating strengths on the Italian campaign. On the following day, the British Chiefs of Staff also recommend that Anvil be dropped but the Americans hold firm on the necessity of Anvil. **(Atlantic-Italy)** The U.S. 34th Division lands at Anzio.

March 22nd 1944 — **(Pacific-Burma)** Merrill's Marauders, pushing through the dense jungle encounter Japanese roadblocks across the trails, forcing them to pivot and cut a new trail. In other activity, additional contingents of British General Orde Charles Wingate's Special Force is transported by air to assist in central Burma. **(Atlantic-Russia)** Soviet troops take Pervomaisk.

March 23rd 1944 — **(Pacific-Bismarcks)** A U.S. Flotilla of Destroyers bombards enemy positions on Eloaue Island, Massau Islands (St. Matthias Group) Islands; U.S. Patrols had discovered a small Seaplane Base there. **(Pacific-New Guinea)** General Eichelberger's I Corps has responsibility for securing Hollandia. The Corps is named Task Force Reckless and comprises the 24th and 41st Divisions (minus one RCT, 41st Div.). In addition, Task Force Persecution, commanded by Brigadier General Jens A. Doe (41st Division), receives responsibility for constructing an Air Base at Aitape. **(Pacific-Palau Islands)** The Submarine U.S.S. *Tunny* sinks the Japanese Submarine I-32 east of Mindanao off the coast of the Palau Islands. **(Pacific-Solomons-Bougainville)** Enemy night-counterattacks are mounted against the 129th Infantry, U.S. 37th Division without success. Minor inroads are made before American Artillery and Infantry units stiffen. **(China-Burma-India)** Merrill's Marauders advance to Kamaing Road near enemy held Inkangahtawng and establish roadblocks. **(Atlantic-England)** The town of Dunkeswell becomes the site of the newest U.S. Naval Air Facility. **(Atlantic-Italy-Cassino)** General von Freyberg calls off the assault against Cassino. The Germans are pressed into the western portion of the town and hold the monastery. In Rome, Partisans detonate a bomb which kills 32 German M.P.s on Via Rasella Street; the Germans announce that 320 civilians will be executed in retaliation. In conjunction, a captured O.S.S. agent, Cervo is severely beaten and subsequently killed. **(Russia)** Tarnopol is now nearly totally surrounded by the Soviets.

March 24th 1944 — **(Pacific-Admiralties)** Elements of the 5th and 12th Cavalry, supported by Artillery, capture Hill 260, terminating most heavy action on Los Negros. Sporadic fighting, however, continues during the mop-up operation. **(Pacific-Marshalls)** Contingents of the 3rd Battalion, 22nd Marines, accept surrender of the Japanese on Namu Atoll. Subsequently, the Marines depart for Kwajalein Atoll, arriving there on the following day. Other Atolls in the southern Group also fall to the Marines (3rd Battalion, 22nd Marines). In an operation initiated on the 23rd, the Marines seize Ebon Atoll, then jump to Namorik Atoll and Kili Island, seizing them without opposition. In other activity, the U.S.S. *Manlove* (DE-36), a Destroyer Escort, and the Submarine Chaser PC-1135 destroy the Japanese Submarine I-32. **(Pacific-Solomons-Bougainville)** The U.S. XIV Corps decisively blunts the final offensive by the Japanese on Bougainville, driving them back in fast retreat. The successful defense of the Cape Torokina beachhead allows the Americans to expand the perimeter as the Japanese begin evacuating the Empress Au-

gusta Bay area. This action is the final enemy offensive in the Solomons. Detachments of the U.S. 93rd Division arrive on the 28th to bolster the defenses. **(China-Burma-India)** Merrill's Marauders attempt to encircle Inkangahtawng, but they encounter a superior force, compelling them to postpone the operation. General Merrill, upon halting the advance, instructs his men not to relinquish any ground beyond Nhpum Ga. Two Battalions are compelled to reach the trail stretching between Nhpum Ga and Auche before the Japs. On the following day, Lt. McGee's 2nd Battalion is forced to pull back to the opposite bank of the Mogaung River and dig in about 300 yards from the Kamaing Road; they hold their fire until the enemy is almost on top of them. Sixteen enemy attacks are thwarted and many enemy troops are killed; during one of the assaults, a Japanese Lieutenant, whose body has almost been totally cut in half, keeps charging, while waving his sword; he falls at the top of the foxhole. The Marauders capture a map which details the movement of two enemy Battalions, which are driving to cut off the Americans. About 07:00 the 2nd Battalion and about half of the 3rd Battalion move out. Lt. Weston's Platoon is ordered to hold the trail leading from Poakim and Lt. Warren R. Smith's Rifle Platoon is to guard the trail at Tatbum; the two Platoons, composed of 90 men, battle any enemy force of more than 800 men and must hold the two trails for at least 48 hours until Merrill's main force can arrive. Weston's ambush is sprung about 14:00, when about 25 Japanese approach; 12 enemy troops die; the Marauders lose several animals but suffer no casualties. In the **II Army Group** area, British Brigadier General O.C. Wingate, Commander of the Special Force (Indian 3rd Division), is killed in a Plane crash while moving between Imphal and Laleghat. He is replaced by British Major General W.D.A. Lentaigne. **(Mediterranean and European Theater)** A decision is made to insure that Operations ANVIL and OVERLORD are not executed simultaneously. OVERLORD (invasion of Normandy) will commence during early June; ANVIL is tentatively scheduled for the 10th of July, then postponed until the 15th of August.

March 25th 1944 — **(Pacific-Admiralty Islands)** The U.S. 2nd Cavalry fights viciously to clear Road No. 2, which leads to Rossum, committing Tanks, Bazookas, and Flame Throwers to expel the enemy. In addition, Air support and Field Artillery further bolster the attack. This massive battle terminates organized resistance on Manus Island, but isolated Japanese groups still are being sought by American troops. **(Pacific-Bismarcks)** A Battalion of the 25th Naval Construction Regiment (Seabees) arrives at Emirau Island. Three additional Battalions arrive within a week and construction of the Air Base and Light Naval Base begins. **(Pacific-Japan-Bonin Islands)** The Submarine U.S.S. *Pollack* sinks the Japanese Submarine Chaser No. 54 north of the Bonins. **(Pacific-New Guinea)** The Japanese evacuate their Air Headquarters at Wewak, transferring it to Hollandia. **(Atlantic-Russia)** Proskurov is captured by elements of the First Ukrainian Front.

March 26th 1944 — **(Pacific-Carolines)** The U.S.S. *Tullibee* (SS-284) is sunk north of the Palau Islands, possibly, according to the U.S. Navy, by one of its own torpedoes making a circular run. **(Pacific-New Britain)** An Allied PT base is established at Talasea. **(China-Burma-India)** Intense combat ensues between the 5307th Provisional Unit (Marauders) and Japanese troops between Manpin and Nhpum Ga. A strong Japanese Patrol is ambushed on the Poakum Trail at about

10:20; Weston's force eliminates 28 (known dead). Within about five minutes, another enemy Patrol, comprising about 100 men, strolls into the waiting guns of the Marauders along the Tatbum ambush; 18 Japs are known dead. The Marauders have held for two days without sustaining any casualties. Also, Allied planes harass the enemy as they flee north from Kamaing. **(Atlantic-Italy)** The Allies are reforming boundaries of responsibilities. The British 10th Corps area remains under the jurisdiction of the U.S. Fifth Army. The area guarded by the French Expeditionary Corps and the New Zealand Corps becomes the responsibility of the British Eighth Army. The 13th Corps encumbers the units of the disbanded New Zealand Corps and now comprises the 2nd N.Z., 4th Indian, 3rd Algerian, British 4th, and the British 78th Divisions. The Polish 2 Corps assumes responsibility for the perimeter previously held by the 2nd Moroccan Division. The area between the Adriatic coast and Palena becomes the responsibility of 5th Corps.

Merrill's Marauders on the advance.

March 27th 1944 — (Pacific-Bismarcks) Two PT Boats, Nos. 121 and 153, are sunk by friendly fire originating from a Bomber. **(Pacific-Marshalls)** Troops attached to the 2nd Battalion, 22nd Marines, begin clearing the North and Northeast Groups of the chain. Ailinginae, Bikar and Rongerik Atolls are bypassed. **(Pacific-Solomons-Bougainville)** The Japanese evacuate the Empress Bay area. **(China-Burma-India)** The two point Platoons of the Marauders are struck by the Japanese, but despite the superior forces, the Yanks hold the attackers off and are able to pull-back and combine their forces before noon. The Japanese are unable to take the ad-

vantage; no attack is launched against the battle-weary Marauders; they withdraw further, reaching Auche by nightfall. The 2nd Battalion establishes a perimeter and the 3rd Battalion contingents spread out along the trail to Nhpum Ga. **(Atlantic-Italy)** Naval gunfire damages the PT-207. **(Atlantic-Russia)** Kamenets-Podolsk in the southern Ukraine falls to the Soviets.

March 28th 1944 — (Pacific-Admiralties) Loniu village, Los Negros is occupied by the 1st Squadron 5th Cavalry. Combat Patrols extend in all directions on both Los Negros and Manus in search of enemy pockets, but the Patrols encounter only minor resistance. **(Pacific-Bismarcks)** Allied Destroyers bombard enemy positions on the Kapingamarangi Atoll, north of New Ireland. **(Pacific-Marshalls)** Elements of the 3rd Battalion, 22nd Marines arrive back at Kwajalein Atoll after their successful mission to secure the islands and atolls in the southern group. A reinforced Battalion of the 22nd Marines unfurls Old Glory on Bikini Island while securing the island. **(Pacific-Solomons-Bougainville)** Stubborn Hill 260 is abandoned by the Japanese. RCT 25 and the 1st Battalion, 24th Infantry, U.S. 93rd Division, arrive at Empress Bay. **(China-Burma-India)** The main body of Merrill's Marauders (5307th Provisional Unit) arrive to fortify the defensive positions around Nhpum Ga; the Marauders have been moving through the mountains for seven weeks; the 2nd Battalion has moved across countless rivers and advanced seventy miles in the past five days. Also, the 1st Battalion strikes before dawn, surprising the enemy on the opposite side of the river and then sets up roadblocks along the Kamaing Road near Shaduzup. Soon after, the Americans repulse an enemy attempt to destroy their roadblock. The Chinese 113th Regiment moves in to replace the Yanks stationed at the roadblock, trapping the Japanese between the Chinese 22nd and 38th Divisions. The Japanese mount five unsuccessful counterattacks to attempt a breakout through the Chinese 22nd Division's positions. **(Atlantic-Italy-Anzio)** In the U.S. Fifth Army area, the U.S. 34th Division lands at Anzio, replacing the 3rd Division deployed near Cisterna. **(Atlantic-Russia)** Nikolaev is taken by the Third Ukrainian Front.

March 29th 1944 — (Pacific-Burma) General Stilwell and Chiang Kai-shek meet on the 28th and 29th. Stilwell requests reinforcements to bolster the campaigns against the Japanese. Kai-shek promises the 50th Chinese Division and in a few days offers to commit the Chinese 14th Division. In the NCAC area, contingents of the Chinese 22nd Division enter Shaduzup. Also, the Marauders continue battling feverishly against the Japanese. The 2nd Battalion is embattled at Nhpum Ga and the 3rd Battalion is holding Hsamsingyang and its Airfield; Patrols run between the two contingents twice a day until the 2nd Battalion becomes isolated. In the 11 Corps Group area, **British Fourteenth Army** 4th Corps sector, the Japanese sever the Imphal-Kohima road outside Kohima. Meanwhile, the 161st Brigade, 5th Indian Division arrives to bolster the Kohima garrison.

March 29th-April 9th 1944 — (Pacific-Burma) In the Northern Area Combat Command area, the 2nd Battalion, U.S. 5207th Provisional Unit (Marauders) at Nhpum Ga, is threatened by a superior Japanese force. The Yanks, however, repulse the attack; the isolated unit's slim perimeter (400 yards long by 100-250 foot wide) holds firm. During the siege, General Merrill is taken ill; he is flown out on the 2nd of April when it becomes clear that evacuation by ground will be difficult; he is not told that the 2nd Battalion has been cut off. On the 1st, Merrill had requested two Howitzers to bolster the 3rd Battalion. They arrive on the 2nd. Orange Combat Team, counterattacks, but is unable to penetrate enemy lines. The beleaguered 2nd Battalion is attacked repeatedly while awaiting reinforcements; they watch the Howitzers as they are dropped. The Japanese sever the trail to Hsamsingyang and secure the 2nd Battalion's water hole. The grueling contest also slaughters many animals within the Marauders' perimeter. It becomes a stalemate; the Japanese can't retrieve their dead and the exhausted Marauders are unable to bury their dead animals, creating a horrible stench. The Third Battalion makes another attempt to break the siege on the 3rd, but intense enemy fire halts its advance; the Artillery floats over the heads of the 2nd Battalion, dropping plenty of the Japanese. Air and Artillery units support an attack initiated by the 3rd Battalion on the 4th, helping it to advance to within 1,000 yards of the objective, but the final thrust is hurled back by a wall of fire.

The 2nd Battalion, still under an incessant barrage, withstands further vicious assaults, preventing the Japanese from overrunning the perimeter during a fanatical Banzai charge on the fifth. Meanwhile, the Japanese ferociously hold the line against hard-driving rescue Battalions. Subsequently, the 1st Battalion, arrives after an arduous march through enemy riddled jungles and quickly assists the 3rd Battalion. The combined Force storms the enemy lines from two directions, but the entrenched Japanese still hold firm on the 8th. As the Yanks prepare to strike on the 9th, they find the Japanese have withdrawn from the area. During operations at both Inkanghatawng and Nhpum Ga, the 5307th (Marauders) has suffered 59 men killed and 314 wounded. During the gruesome siege, the Marauders had been assisted by Sergeant Roy Matsumoto ((Nisei); during one Japanese attack, the Marauders pull back after placing booby-traps throughout their positions. The Japanese attack viciously, yelling Banzai! When the enemy closes to within fifteen yards, the Marauders blast them; a second wave charges, but the onslaught of fire halts their advance. The Japanese jump for cover, seeking refuge in the Marauders vacant foxholes, detonating all the booby-traps. Pandemonium sets in followed by new orders in Japanese; Matsumoto, the Marauder orders the enemy to attack, screaming in Japanese: "Attack! Attack! The Japs, thinking it is one of their leaders jump up and charge; many more die to the blistering fire of the Marauders.

March 30th 1944 — (United States) Admiral Leahy is informed by British Field Marshal Dill about the death of British General Wingate. In other activity, the U.S. announces the disappearance of the U.S.S. *Grayback* (SS-208). The *Grayback* had a successful War Patrol (10th) when ordered to report back to Pearl Harbor on February 2. Under the Command of Captain John A. Moore, she had sunk her last enemy Vessel, the *Ceylon Maru*, with her two remaining torpedoes (27th); then apparently continued on Patrol. The Japanese later report the sinking of a Submarine on the 26th (instead of 27th). **(Pacific-Admiralty Islands)** Mop-up operations go well on Los Negros and Manus, allowing troops to secure the other islands. Pityilu, about three miles north of Lugos Mission is struck by a thunderous bombardment, followed by the landing of elements of the 7th Cavalry which destroy the small enemy Garrison. **(Pacific-Bismarcks-New Britain)** A small Marine Corps Patrol destroys the rear guard of the retreating

17th Japanese Division in the vicinity of Linga Linga. **(Pacific-New Guinea)** The U.S. Fifth Air Force, escorted by long range Fighters, makes its first daylight attack against Hollandia. **(Pacific-Solomons-Bougainville)** The U.S. 93rd Division troops, based on the island, are attached to the Americal Division, which gradually feeds them into the lines to receive battle experience. **(Atlantic-Germany)** The Royal Air Force launches about 800 Heavy Bombers against Nuremburg at night. Enemy fire destroys about 100 of the Planes, compelling the Allies to temporarily discontinue the heavy night penetration raids. **(Atlantic-Russia)** The Soviets take Cernauti (Bessarabia) from the Germans.

March 30th-April 1st 1944 — (Pacific-Carolines) U.S. Task Force 58, commanded by Admiral R. A. Spruance, attacks enemy positions on the Carolines. Carrier-based Planes pummel the Airfields, Vessels in port, and other facilities at locations on Palau, Yap, Ulithi, and Woleai; this three day bombardment delivers heavy damage to the enemy Fleet and installations. The Planes deposit many mines throughout the channels and the approaches to the Palau Islands. The Japanese lose about 150 Planes, both in the Air and on the ground. The enemy also loses the Repair Ship *Akashi*, the Submarine Chasers Nos. 6 and 26; the Auxiliary Submarine Chasers Nos. 22 and 53; the Oilers *Ose, Sata* and *Iro* and the Patrol Boat No. 31. Many additional Vessels are damaged. The enemy loses about 104,000 tons of Shipping. This devastating blow eliminates any possible future interference by Japanese Warships, intercepting the Task Force Convoy which will be heading to seize Hollandia. The U.S. loses 20 Planes during the action. Aerial photographs of the objectives are taken during the raids. The Submarine U.S.S. *Tunny* (SS-282) is accidentally damaged by friendly Aircraft fire off of Palau Islands (30th).

March 31st 1944 — (Pacific-Admiralties) The mop-up operation of the 7th Cavalry (1st Squadron) at Pityilu is complete. **(Pacific-Carolines)** U.S. Carrier-based Planes sink the Japanese Destroyer *Wakatake* near Palau. **(Pacific-New Guinea)** The U.S. Fifth Air Force again strikes Hollandia and inflicts heavy damage. **(China-Burma-India)** In the **British Fourteenth Army** area, after reducing fierce resistance, British troops seize an intricate Japanese tunnel system along Maungdaw-Buthidaung Road. The Japanese, however, retain parts of the road. **(Atlantic-Italy)** The U.S. Fifth Army releases the British 10th Corps, but holds the British 1st and 5th Divisions at Anzio.

March 16th 1944 — U.S. troops in the Solomons.

The U.S. Fifth Army advancing in Italy. Note: deceased German Soldier in foreground.

April 1st 1944 — **(Pacific-Carolines)** Task Force 58 completes its bombardment of the Carolines, again inflicting heavy losses. **(Pacific-Admiralty Islands)** U.S. Naval Vessels begin shelling suspected enemy positions on Koruniat Island. Afterward, elements of the U.S. 12th Cavalry embark in canoes from Mokerang Point to secure the small islands in the vicinity. Koruniat and Ndrilo are both taken without opposition. **(Pacific-Marshalls)** A contingent of the 3rd Battalion, 22nd Marines, seizes Ailuk Atoll in the Northeast Group. **(Pacific-Japan)** The Imperial 32nd Japanese Army is activated with Headquarters on Okinawa and is given the responsibility of defending the Nansei Shoto Chain. **(China-Burma-India)** Orange Combat Team, U.S. 5307th Unit charges enemy positions which block the Hsamshingyang-Nhpum Road but it is prevented from reaching the isolated 2nd Battalion. Colonel McGee (2nd Battalion) gets some information from Colonel Hunter concerning the 1st Battalion: "THE NIPS ARE RUNNING LIKE HELL FROM SHADUZUP ... TOO MANY BODIES TO COUNT." McGee also learns of General Me:..ll's illness. General Stilwell, realizing the situation in Burma requires more men, requests that Chiang Kai-shek commit the 14th and 50th Chinese Divisions and have them airlifted to Burma.

April 2nd 1944 — **(Pacific-Marshalls)** Mejit Island (Northeast Group) is taken by elements of the 3rd Battalion, 2nd Marines. **(Pacific-New Guinea)** Bombers attached to the U.S. Fifth Air Force strike enemy positions at Hansa Bay. Inclement weather prevents them from hitting Hollandia, the initial target. **(China-Burma-India)** The 2nd Battalion, Merrill's Marauders are still under heavy assault from the Japanese, but holds its positions. Also, the 3rd Battalion attempts to break through the Japanese lines and rescue the 2nd Battalion, however, it too is unsuccessful. Some Artillery is dropped from the Air to aid the beleaguered troops holding the Airstrip at Hsamshingyang.

April 3rd 1944 — **(United States)** The Joint Chiefs of Staff emphasize the necessity of securing the Airfield at Myitkyina in Burma. The responsibility remains with Merrill's Marauders, who are basically the only U.S. Infantry troops between the Japanese and India. **(Pacific-Admiralty Islands)** The U.S. 12th Cavalry rushes ashore at Rambutyo, subsequent to cessation of a preliminary Naval bombardment, and encounters no opposition. Patrols immediately begin searching for remnant Japanese forces. **(Pacific-Marshalls)** Elements of the 3rd Battalion, 22nd Marines, capture Likiep Atoll, Northeast Group. **(Pacific-New Guinea)** The U.S. Fifth Air Force

hits Hollandia with another powerful strike. These continuing American raids, initiated on the 30th of March, have destroyed more than 300 Planes, mostly on the ground. Enemy air power in the area is nearly totally halted. **(China-Burma-India)** The 2nd and 3rd Battalions attempt to break through the Japanese positions and yet again are repulsed. Meanwhile, the 1st Battalion of Merrill's Marauders, is ordered to move as rapidly as possible toward Hsamshingyang to aid their embattled comrades.

Merrill's Marauders making good use of a footbridge.

April 4th 1944 — **(Pacific-Marshalls)** The 3rd Battalion (contingent of the 22nd Marines) is wrapping up its campaign to secure the Northeast Group of the Marshalls. In other activity, the Destroyer U.S.S. *Hall* (DD-583) is damaged by enemy coastal guns. **(Pacific-Burma-India)** Allied Artillery and Air support is implemented to assist the 5307th's 3rd Battalion's attack to reach Nhpum Ga, but the Japanese repel the attempt. The isolated 2nd Battalion repulses a fierce Japanese attempt to wipe them out. Chinese troops arrive by rail near Hsamshingyang. Troops from the 22nd Chinese Division attempt to surround the enemy's left flank, while other units fight a fierce holding action near Shaduzup. In the **British Fourteenth Army** area, 4 Corps sector, the Japanese mount a large attack against Kohima. The 161st Infantry, 5th Indian Division which had been ordered to Dimapur to strengthen the defenses there, are diverted back to Kohima.

April 5th 1944 — **(Pacific-Bismarcks)** Units of Marine Aircraft Group 12 arrive on Emirau, St. Matthias Islands. **(Pacific-Carolines)** U.S. Carrier-based Aircraft sink the Japanese Auxiliary Submarine Chaser No. 46. **(Pacific-Marshalls)** Contingents of the 2nd Battalion, 22nd Marines eradicate light enemy resistance at Utirik Atoll and secure the island; the unit subsequently returns to Kwajalein. **(Pacific-Burma-India)** Contingents of the British 33rd Corps converge on Dimapur. Advance elements of the 2nd British Division arrive. **(Atlantic-Rumania)** The U.S. Fifteenth Air Force strikes rail facilities near Ploesti, Rumania. This raid is the beginning of an Allied offensive to level the oil producing city of Ploesti. The U.S. Eighth Air Force participates in these raids beginning on the 12th of May.

April 6th 1944 — **(Pacific-New Guinea)** Operational Japanese Aircraft at Hollandia are reduced to 25 after raids by the U.S. Fifth Air Force. **(Pacific-Burma-India)** The Orange Combat Team, 3rd Battalion, (Merrill's Marauders) drives hard against Japanese positions at Nhpum Ga, advancing 200 yards, but still cannot reach the beleaguered 2nd Battalion. In the **British Fourteenth Army** area, Planes begin transporting the Indian 7th Division from the Arakan Front to Dimapur. Some units of the Indian 5th Division reach Kohima, but Japanese resistance prevents most of the 161st Brigade from breaking through to the town.

April 7th 1944 — (North Atlantic) The Destroyer U.S.S. *Champlin* (DD-601) and the Destroyer Escort U.S.S. *Huse* (DE-145) sink the German U-856. The U.S.S. *Champlin* becomes damaged after sustaining enemy fire and intentionally ramming the U-856. **(Pacific-Bismarcks-New Ireland)** The Destroyer U.S.S. *Saufley* (DD-465) sinks the Japanese Submarine I-2 north of New Ireland. **(China-Burma-India)** With the 2nd Battalion (Merrill's Marauders) still cut off by Japanese, the 1st Battalion completes its forced march and reaches Hsamshingyang and prepares to join the attack to take Nhpum Ga, and relieve the besieged Marauders. In the **British Fourteenth Army** area, 33rd Corps sector, the Japanese seize the principal water supply facilities at Kohima. In the **IV Corps** area, the Indian 17th Division, supported by elements of the Chinese 23rd Division, advances to Imphal and digs in north of the town.

April 8th 1944 — (Pacific-Admiralty Islands) The advance echelon of the XIII Bomber Command is transferred to Los Negros. **(Pacific-New Guinea)** The U.S. 24th and 41st Divisions practice invasion tactics for the upcoming assault against Hollandia at Taupota Bay (24th) and Lae (41st). **(Pacific-Burma-India)** Additional attempts fail to rescue the isolated 2nd Battalion. **(Atlantic-Russia)** A new offensive is opened in the Crimea by the Red Army.

April 9th 1944 — (Pacific-Admiralty Islands) The U.S. 12th Cavalry lands at Pak Island unopposed and begins to hunt down remnant enemy forces. This action culminates the objectives of the 1st Brigade's Combat Team. The 2nd Brigade still is involved with search-and-destroy missions on Manus Island. The U.S. Army at Los Negros establishes a radio station and a message center on the grounds of the Salami Plantation. **(Pacific-New Hebrides)** The American Submarine Chaser SC-984, operating in the Southwestern Pacific west of the Fiji Islands, is sunk by grounding near New Hebrides. **(China-Burma-India)** An attack to break the Japanese defenses at Nhpum and rescue the 2nd Battalion becomes unnecessary as the Japanese withdraw from the area. The Marauders do not pursue the retreating enemy as it is deemed unnecessary to advance further than Nhpum. The unit, commanded by General Frank Merrill until his evacuation due to illness, has suffered 59 men killed and 324 wounded; a total of 379 men are evacuated because of sickness or wounds. **(Atlantic)** Charles DeGaulle, now in control of the French Committee of Liberation, fires General Henri Giraud. In addition, DeGaulle demands (unsuccessfully) that France receive a share of surrendered Italian Ships, both war and merchant. In other activity in the Atlantic Theater, the German Submarine U-515, operating near Madeira Island off the west coast of Morocco is sunk by the Carrier *Guadalcanal* (CVE-60) and four Destroyer Escorts: the *Chatelain* (DE-149), *Pope* (DE-134) *Flaherty*, (DE-135) and the *Pillsbury* (DE-133). On the following day, Planes (VC-58) attached to the *Guadalcanal* destroy the Submarine U-68.

April 10th 1944 — (Pacific-New Guinea) Rehearsals for the invasion of Hollandia are complete. Task Force Reckless (assault team) loads its equipment and prepares to embark. **(Atlantic-Italy-Anzio)** The U.S. 85th Infantry begins filtering into

Allied lines west of Minturno. A planned assault by the Germans against the Anzio Beachhead is canceled. **(Atlantic-Russia)** Troops from the Third Ukrainian Front capture Odessa, a primary Black Sea port.

A. U.S. Headquarters Company at work during the Italian Campaign.

April 11th 1944 — (Pacific-Admiralty Islands) American General Kenney establishes the Thirteenth Air Task Force, commanded by Major General St. Clair Street; it comes under the control of Advon Fifth Air Force until its own Headquarters can be established on the Admiralties. **(Pacific-Bismarcks)** The 4th Marines, holding Emirau Island in the St Matthias Islands are relieved by the U.S. 147th Infantry, initiating Army responsibility for the island. Major General James T. Moore, U.S.M.C., takes command of all ground troops on Emirau Island. **(Pacific-Celebes Sea)** The U.S.S. *Redfin* (SS-272), operating in the Celebes Sea, north of Celebes (Indonesian Island north of Borneo and south of the Philippines) sinks the Japanese Destroyer *Akigumo*. **(Atlantic-England)** An Allied bombing mission is launched against enemy positions in Europe. In one instance, enemy Fighters ignore the Fighter cover and attack and seriously damage a B-17; the Pilot, 1st Lieutenant Edward S. Michael (364th Bomber Squadron), refuses to abandon the Plane although it has been ripped open with bullet holes and a fire is erupting in the cockpit. In addition, the Co-pilot is knocked unconscious. As enemy Planes pursue the crippled Aircraft, Lt. Michael, himself wounded, orders the crew to bail out. The Bombardier's parachute is riddled with bullet holes, prompting Michael to evade the enemy and attempt an emergency landing. He loses the enemy in a large cloudburst and heads for England; however, it is a harrowing flight. Lt. Michael, swinging in and out of consciousness because of his wound, has severe problems handling the craft. The altimeter is shot out, the bombay doors jammed open and his Plane is susceptible to an explosion at any moment due to the raging fire. Despite the problems, he successfully lands the Plane at an R.A.F. fighter field. Lt. Michael is awarded the Medal of Honor for this extraordinary heroism. **(Atlantic-Mediterranean)** A German Submarine damages the Destroyer Escort *Holder* (DE-401).

April 12th 1944 — (Pacific-Admiralty Islands) The Japanese are eliminated from Pak Island. Meanwhile, mop-up operations continue on Manus Island. **(Pacific-Bismarcks)** The PT-135 grounded and damaged, is destroyed by U.S. Forces. **(Atlantic-Azores)** The American Rescue Tug ATR-98 sinks after becoming involved in a collision.

April 13th 1944 — (Central Pacific) The U.S.S. *Harder* (SS-257) operating in the Central Pacific sinks the Japanese Destroyer *Ikazuchi*. **(Pacific-New Guinea)** Contingents of the Australian 15th Brigade seize Bogadjim without opposition. **(Pacific-New Britain)** A 16-man Marine Patrol lands on Cape Hoskins and advances inland 5,000 yards under the noses of enemy troops, gathering intelligence on the Japanese Airfields. **(Atlantic-Western Europe)** The U.S. Ninth Air Force and the British 2nd Air Force initiate a strong offensive against enemy batteries along the Normandy coast as part of the continuing campaign to bombard the enemy's defenses along the entire coast.

April 14th 1944 — (China-Burma-India) British Admiral Mountbatten suggests to the British Chiefs of Staff that the Northern Burma campaign be confined to the capture of Myitkyina and its Airfield. The troops operating in this area are American and Chinese. **(Atlantic-Europe)** General Eisenhower is given operational control of both U.S. and British Strategic Air Forces. Up to this point, this responsibility had come under the Combined Chiefs of Staff.

April 15th 1944 — (United States) The Carrier *Hancock* (CV-19) is commissioned at Fore River Massachusetts. **(United States-Alaska Territory)** The U.S. Navy establishes the Alaskan Sea Frontier, commanded by Vice Admiral F.J. Fletcher, with Headquarters at Adak in the Aleutians. In addition, the Seventh Naval District is established and is commanded by Rear Admiral F.E.M. Whiting. His Headquarters will be temporarily placed in Adak and subsequently moved to Kodiak, Alaska. **(Pacific-Gilberts)** A U.S. Naval Base is established at Abemama Island. **(China-Burma-India)** American General Stilwell is strongly urged by Chiang Kai-shek to move with caution toward the Mogaung Valley (Burma). General Chennault has forewarned the Generalissimo that a massive Japanese Air attack against China is anticipated. British Admiral Mountbatten's Headquarters is transferred from New Delhi, India to Kandy, Ceylon as a precaution against Japanese penetration. The Chinese 50th Division's airlift to Maingkwan is nearly complete. **(Atlantic-Italy)** The British Eighth Army concentrates its efforts on preparing a renewed offensive, scheduled to begin in the spring. In other activity, the British 10th Corps replaces the Polish 2nd Corps in the northern sector near the Gustav Line. **(Atlantic-Europe)** The Allied Expeditionary Air Force Headquarters issues overall plans

for Operation NEPTUNE. As of September 1943, all papers dealing with Operation OVERLORD's targets and dates use code name Neptune. **(Atlantic-Poland)** Tarnopol is taken by troops of the First Ukrainian Front.

Field Marshal Albert Kesselring.

April 16th 1944 — (United States) The U.S.S. *Wisconsin* (BB — 64) a Battleship, is commissioned at Philadelphia. **(North Atlantic)** The Destroyer Escorts *Joyce* (DE-317), *Gandy* (DE-764) and *Peterson* (DE-152) sink the German Submarine U-550; the *Gandy* becomes damaged after intentionally ramming the U-550. **(Pacific-New Guinea)** The assault troops (Task Force Reckless) embark for Hollandia by way of the Admiralty Islands. They are joined en route by Task Force Persecution on the 18th. **(Atlantic-Russia)** Yalta, located in the Crimea, falls to the Soviets (Independent Maritime Army).

April 17th 1944 — (United States) The U.S.S. *Trout*, which had departed Pearl Harbor on February 8th on her 11th War Patrol, is listed as lost; suspected date of loss, February 29th, while engaging enemy Convoy. A Japanese Vessel, the *Sakito Maru* is reported sunk and the only American Submarine in area had been the *Trout*. The battle report is acquired from the Japanese after the war. The *Trout* had not reported the attack or the counterattack. **(North Atlantic)** The U.S. Minesweeper *Swift* and the Submarine Chaser PC-619 sink the German Submarine U-986. **(Pacific-Admiralties)** The 2nd Squadron, 7th Cavalry departs Manus Island for Hauwei, subsequent to completing mop-up operations. **(Pacific-Marshalls)** Contingents of the 1st Defense Battalion, U.S.M.C., land on Erikub and Aur Atolls finding no enemy troops. Some troops return to Majuro, but contingents remain to keep a vigil for straggler enemy troops. **(China-Burma-India)** American General Chennault receives instructions from General Stilwell to hold the B-29 Bases at Cheng-tu against all hazards. The Japanese cross the Yellow River in Horan Province after dark and begin to regroup for an attack. This assault will be the last major offensive against China. In Burma, the Chinese make fair progress as they drive through the Mogaung Valley and find the Japanese have abandoned Warazup. In the **British Fourteenth Army** area, the 4 Corps launches an offensive against the Japanese positions near Imphal. **(Atlantic-Europe)** General Eisenhower orders all Strategic Air Forces to concentrate on the German Air Force, giving priority to oil refineries. The purpose is to get the German Planes in the air where they can be destroyed and also to eliminate the enemy oil supplies.

April 18th 1944 — (Pacific-Carolines) The U.S. Thirteenth Air Force launches B-24s, assigned to the 5th Bombardment Group, from Momote Airfield, Los Negros against enemy positions on Woleai to soften resistance. **(Pacific-New Guinea)** Task Force Persecution, moving from Finschhafen, joins Task Force Reckless to strike Hollandia on the 22nd. **(Atlantic-Russia)** The Red Army takes Balaklava.

April 19th 1944 — (Pacific-Dutch East Indies) An Allied Task Force, commanded by British Admiral J.F. Somerville, which includes the Carrier U.S.S. *Saratoga* and three U.S. Destroyers bombards enemy fortifications at Sabang, Netherlands, East Indies. **(Atlantic-Mediterranean)** The Combined Chiefs of Staff direct British General Sir Henry M. Wilson to launch an offensive in Italy to support Operation OVERLORD in France.

April 20th 1944 — (Pacific-Admiralty Islands) The U.S. Task Forces, steaming toward Hollandia, New Guinea, rendezvous off the Admiralties. In other activity, a special Squadron capable of launching night attacks (attached to the Thirteenth Air Force) arrives at Momote Airfield. **(Pacific-Marianas)** The Submarine U.S.S. *Seahorse* (SS-304) sinks the Japanese Submarine RO-45. **(China-Burma-India)** Burma: The Chinese 38th Infantry advances against violent opposition through the Mogaung Valley, pushing toward Kamaing and overrunning Hill 1725 along the route. The tenacious Japanese fight vehemently against the advance to buy time for their main body, which is retreating toward the Wala-Malakawng line. **India:** In the British Fourteenth Army area, the British 2nd Division fights off staunch Japanese resistance to reach the besieged Garrison at Kohima. Still, the Japanese maintain control of the town of Kohima and of the roadblock, preventing the Allies from reaching Imphal. **(Atlantic-Italy)** The French 1st Motorized Division arrives at Naples; additional French troops land during May. **(Atlantic-Mediterraneaan)** The Destroyer *Lansdale* (DD-426) is struck by a torpedo and sinks.

April 21st 1944 — (Pacific-Admiralty Islands) An Airstrip is completed at the Mokerang Plantation on Manus Island. This is another achievement for the Aviation Engineers and for the Seabees who are constantly carving Airfields and Bases out of the dense jungles to assist with the speedy capture of the Pacific. **(Pacific-New Guinea)** Planes, attached to Task Force 58, assist Allied Land-based Planes which devastate enemy Airfields to eliminate interference with the Hollandia Assault Force. The targeted enemy Bases: Hollandia, Sarmi, Sawar and Wakde also are bombarded by U.S. Surface Vessels.

(China-Burma-India) The American Force has been severely depleted during the agonizing campaign to secure Nhpum Ga. Three Combat Teams are established, linking Chinese troops with Merrill's Marauders. The three Battalions of the 3507th are linked with Chinese Regiments forming Teams K, H, and M; surgical Units accompany them. **(Atlantic-Germany)** Terrible weather forces the Eighth Air Force to abort its bombing mission over Germany.

April 22nd 1944 — U.S. troops landing at Hollandia.

April 22nd 1944 — (Pacific-New Guinea) THE BATTLE OF HOLLANDIA — The Japanese again are caught offguard, as MacArthur's strategy has them confused about the Allied objectives. Wewak, which had sustained saturation bombing during the end of March, is the anticipated target, but it is spared. Instead, the Australian-American force invades Hollandia, 450 miles up the New Guinea coast. MacArthur is pleased with this operation before it starts; for the first time, he has the cushion of a well supplied Naval Task Force to assist the invasion.

The Assault Operation is under the command of Rear Admiral D.E. Barbey and is supplemented by the massive guns and Planes of Vice Admiral Marc Mitscher's Carrier Task Force. Allied Surface Vessels pummel enemy positions prior to the landing. When it ceases, the first waves of 60,000 combat troops storm ashore on the northern coast of Hollandia, meeting no opposition. In addition, a Diversionary Force makes a simultaneous landing at Aitape. Japanese Officer, Vice Admiral Yoskikazu Endo, transported by Submarine from Wewok to Hollandia to escape the assault is in a state of utter disbelief. He soon strolls into the jungle and commits hari-kari.

Task Force Reckless lands at Humboldt and at Tanahmerah Bay to establish a beachhead, as contingents of the 24th Division secure two landing sites, Red Beach 1 and Red Beach 2 (Depapre Bay). The main thrust of the inland drive is to spring from Beach 2, but its terrain is swampy and dangerously narrow. In addition, no trails or roads connect the two beaches, forcing all supplies to be transferred from Beach 2 to the secondary choice. The 21st Infantry, 24th Division begins moving overland to Beach Red 1, while the 19th Infantry remains behind to defend Beach Red 2. Subsequently, the 1st Battalion, 21st Infantry moves inward from Red Beach 1, advancing about eight miles to Jangkena, before pulling back to Kantome for the night. The enemy makes strong but unsuccessful attempts to sever the trail. Meanwhile, the U.S. 41st Division lands at Humboldt Bay, its 162nd Infantry hitting the beaches at the north sandspit between Humbo!dt and Jautefa

Bays on Beaches White 1 and 2. The 2nd and 3rd Battalions drive inland toward Hollandia. A reinforced Rifle Platoon of Company A pushes south and captures Cape Pie, allowing elements of the 186th Infantry to land without incident. The Japanese pull back most contingents to concentrate their resistance at the coveted Airfields. Leimok Hill, Pim, and Suikerbrood Hill are secured by contingents of the 186th Infantry. Company I, 186th Infantry, which had landed at Beach White 3, seizes Tjeweri at the northern tip of the island and begins pressing toward Hollekang.

Task Force Persecution, landing in conjunction with TF Reckless, crashes ashore at Wapil, Aitape, east of Hollandia. RCT 163, 41st Division, quickly secures a beachhead which includes the Airfields at Tadji. The objective of this diversionary strike is to secure Aitape as a Base. During the course of the capture of Hollandia, more than 100 Nuns and Missionaries are saved. Within three weeks, Wake Island is enveloped by MacArthur. By the 20th, the Japanese lose an important coral Airstrip and about 800 dead. The U.S. suffers 40 killed. The isolated Japs on Wewak are no longer able to be supplied; as time passes, they revert to cannibalism. (Company A, 1st Tank Battalion, 1st Marine Division assisted the assault forces at Tanahmerah Bay during the Hollandia Operation).

April 22nd 1944 — (Pacific-Malay Peninsula-Borneo) The U.S.S. *Redfin* (SS-272) operating southwest of the Philippines near the Malay Archipelago lays mines near Sarawak.

April 23rd 1944 — (Pacific-Dutch East Indies) The Japanese Destroyer, *Amagiri* hits a mine while moving through the Makassar Strait and sinks. **(Pacific-New Britain)** Advance elements of the 40th U.S. Infantry Division, U.S.A., arrive at Cape Gloucester and begin replacing the 1st Marine Division. **(Pacific-New Guinea)** Hollandia (Humboldt area) is occupied by the 2nd and 3rd Battalions, 162nd Infantry, 41st Division without incident. In addition, they seize the heights overlooking the town. Elements of the 186th Infantry encounter strong enemy resistance near Pim-Lake Sentani. The U.S. 21st Infantry advances through Sabron and meets defiant organized resistance at a small stream, forcing a pullback to Sabron. U.S. troops that landed at Aitape, Tanahmerah Bay, drive west toward Hollandia. The 1st Battalion, 163rd Regiment overruns the uncompleted Tadji West Airstrip, while the 2nd Battalion, using the coastal route, advances to the Raihu River. RCT 127 lands on Seleo and Tumleo Islands, securing both with little effort. **(China-Burma-India)** In Burma, elements of the Chinese 38th Division move to Manpin to relieve the End Run Force (survivors of the Galahad Force (Merrill's Marauders) at the fringes of Manpin. The Chinese are to make the final attack against the town. **(Atlantic-Italy)** A contingent of the U.S. 30th Infantry, 3rd Division, is engulfed in a heavy firefight near Spaccasassi Creek near Padiglione. During this action, most of the noncommissioned Officers become casualties, compelling PFC John Squires to lead the men forward. The enemy counterattacks three times during the night but are repulsed. Squires, at one point, advances with his machinegun and captures 21 enemy Soldiers. In addition, he captures 13 enemy machineguns; he receives the Medal of Honor for his outstanding heroism. An enemy counterattack on the following night is handily repulsed.

April 24th 1944 — (Pacific-New Britain) The 1st Marines, 1st Marine Division, and some supporting contingents are withdrawn from Cape Gloucester. **(Pacific-New Guinea)** The U.S.

31st Division arrives at Oro Bay. The Australians occupy Madang subsequent to Japanese evacuation. Markham-Ramu trough and the Huon Peninsula are now secure. In the Hollandia Bay area, Task Force Reckless is bogged down with serious supply problems, restricting it to sending out Patrols and moving supplies forward. Additional supplies are to be dropped from Planes, inclement weather forces cancellation of the flights. In the Humboldt Bay area, the 186th Infantry moves to Lake Sentani and seizes the jetty. In other activity, the 163rd Infantry secures Aitape and Robin Point. Australian Engineers complete the Airstrip at Tadji; 25 R.A.F. P-40s land on the Fighter Strip. **(China-Burma-India)** The 1st and 3rd Marauder Battalions, having been relieved by Chinese troops at Manpin, force march to Naubum to assault Myitkyina and secure its Airstrips. Meanwhile, the 2nd Battalion continues patrolling north of Hsamshingyang.

A supply convoy advancing along the beach on Hollandia.

U.S. Tanks driving inland on Hollandia.

April 25th 1944 — (Pacific-New Britain) The First Marine Division turns the island of New Britain over to the 40th Infantry Division, U.S.A. **(Pacific-New Guinea)** In the Hollandia area, the U.S. 21st Infantry, still plagued by terrible supply conditions, halts its drive toward Hollandia. The 186th Infantry advances from Humboldt to Nefaar, by two routes. Some units march across the overland trail while other elements cross Lake Sentani. In the Aitape area, Task Force Persecution is heavily engaged; some Patrols scan the coastlines, while others penetrate inland. Ali Island is occupied by Company G, 127th Infantry.

April 26th 1944 — (North Pacific) The Destroyer Escort *Gilmore* (DE-18) sinks the Japanese Submarine I-180. **(Atlan-**

tic) In Naval activity in the mid Atlantic, four American Destroyer Escorts, the *Barber* (DE-161), *Frost* (DE-144), *Huse* DE-145) and *Snowden* (DE-246), sink the German Submarine U-488.

April 27th 1944 — **(Pacific-Carolines)** The U.S.S. *Bluegill* (SS-242) sinks the Japanese Light Cruiser *Yubari* southwest of the Palau Islands. **(Pacific-Japan)** The U.S.S. *Halibut* (SS-232), lurking near the Ryukyu Islands, sinks the Japanese Minelayer *Kamone*. **(Pacific-New Guinea)** General MacArthur sets the invasion of Biak for early June. In the Humboldt Bay area, Cape Soeadja, situated at the northwest tip, is captured by the 162nd Infantry. In Naval activity, the American Cargo Vessel *Etamin* is sunk by an enemy Torpedo Bomber off the coast of Western New Guinea. **(China-Burma-India)** In Burma, the final push to take Myitkyina is being prepared. General Merrill, recovered from his illness and back with his troops, will lead the Marauders. In other activity, Generalissimo Chiang Kai-shek plans for an assault across the Salween River in China by Chinese troops (Divisions attached to the Yunnan Force), which have been trained by the Americans. In the **British Fourteenth Army** area, the Japanese make a determined effort to break through British defenses to reach Imphal; they secure six miles of trail between Imphal and Silchar, but the British hang on, awaiting the monsoon rains to arrive and immobilize the advancing enemy. **(Atlantic-Italy-Cassino)** In the **British Eighth Army** area, the Polish 2nd Corps takes responsibility for the Monte Cassino sector, relieving the 13th Corps. **(Atlantic-France)** The U.S. Eighth Air Force participates in an Allied Air Offensive against Blainville and Chalons-sur-Marne.

April 24th 1944 — The Southeast slope of Bloody Ridge (Bougainville).

April 28th 1944 — **(United States)** Navy Secretary Frank Knox dies from a heart attack. He is replaced by James Forrestal. **(Pacific-Japan)** The Japanese Submarine I-183 is destroyed off Kyushu by the Submarine U.S.S. *Pogy* (SS-266). **(Pacific-New Guinea)** The 3rd Battalion, 163rd Infantry, encounters the first organized enemy resistance on Aitape in the vicinity of Kamti village where about 200 enemy Soldiers are discovered. Company C, 127th Infantry, and supporting units of Company D, are transported by boat to Nyaparake village, about 17 miles east of the Nigia River to cut off Japanese reinforcements, rushing from Wewak toward Hollandia. The Americans debark at the mouth of the Dandriwad river (8 miles from Nyaparake) and begin patrolling. **(China-Burma-India)** In China, the Japanese intensify their offensive in

Honan. The Allies dispatch Planes from the U.S. Fourteenth Air Force to destroy bridges that span the Yellow River and to neutralize the rail yards at Cheng-hsien and Kaifeng. American and Chinese troops tighten their defenses around the Air Bases at Cheng-tu to ensure the safety of B-29s based there. In Burma, the End Run Force (Marauders and Chinese) moves on Myitkyina by way of Ritpong. The Chinese 38th Division advances toward Wala, driving the Japanese back as it moves. **(Atlantic-Off Portsmouth England)** During the preparation for the invasion of Normandy, practice maneuvers are commonplace. During the early morning hours of the 28th, German U-Boats attack a group of six LSTs (Exercise TIGER) in the 'Channel. Two British Corvettes are assigned as Escort, however, the LSTs are alone when attacked. The British Warships arrive too late to assist. Also, earlier, the R.A.F. detects the E-Boat pack, but the information is never given to the Commander of the LST force. The unexpected attack costs the lives of nearly 1,000 Soldiers and Sailors; many more are wounded. The LSTs 507 and the 53, are sunk. Word of the attack and casualties are suppressed to keep the invasion preparations from the enemy. Petty Officer Walter Domanski (LST-496), a survivor of the ordeal, subsequently states that many of the men lost their lives due to drowning because they had not been instructed on how to activate their life belts. It will take more than forty years before the U.S. Government acknowledges this incident.

U.S. troops advancing past an enemy fuel depot which had been destroyed by U.S. Aircraft.

April 29th 1944 — **(Pacific-Bismarcks)** Two U.S. PT Boats, the 346, and the 347, are both sunk by friendly Aircraft fire. **(Pacific-Caroline Islands)** The Fast Carrier Task Force, commanded by Vice Admiral Marc Mitscher, attacks Truk. For two days, the Aircraft fly continuous sorties against Shipping, Aircraft installations, oil facilities and an ammunition depot. This mighty blow by the U.S. Navy cripples another Japanese Base, costing the Japanese about 120 Planes, half destroyed on the ground. Truk is no longer considered a major threat to the New Guinea campaign. Two Destroyers, the *MacDonough* (DD-351) and the *Stephen Potter* (DD-538), join forces with a detachment of Planes that had been launched from the Carrier *Monterey* (CVL-26) and destroy the Japanese Submarine I-174. **(Pacific-South China Sea)** The U.S.S. *Flasher* (SS-249) sinks the Japanese Gunboat *Tahure* in the South China Sea. **(Pacific-New Guinea)** The Alamo Force orders RCT 163 to begin staging for the campaign to take Wakde-Sarmi as soon as it is relieved at Aitape. **(China-Burma-India)** In Burma, Brigadier General Frank Dorn sets up Field Headquarters for the Yunnan Force, which is to accompany Chinese General Wei Li-huang's Headquarters (Commander Yunnan Forces). **(Atlantic-France)** U.S. Army Planes destroy the German Submarine U-421.

April 30th 1944 — (Pacific-Carolines) Satawan Island, situated in the Namoi Group, Caroline Islands, is bombarded by a U.S. Naval Force commanded by Rear Admiral Oldendorf. **(Pacific-New Guinea)** The 163rd U.S. Infantry pulls back from its outpost position at Kamti village. **(China-Burma-India)** The Marauder H Force, Task Force End Run, moves out following the Marauder K Force toward Myitkyina. In the **II Army Group**, 4 Corps sector of the British Army, the Indian 5th and 23rd Divisions overrun enemy resistance and advance toward Ukhrul. In the vicinity of Palel, elements of the Indian 30th Division contain their progress.

May 1944 — (Atlantic-Yugoslavia) O.S.S. units have been operating in Yugoslavia; U.S. Captain George Musulin, the son of Yugoslav immigrants, commands the A.F.R.U. Mission operating with the Chetniks (a non-Communist Partisan group); Musulin is ordered to evacuate his entire compliment of men and to bring out the 40 Airmen that are under the care of the Chetniks; he pleads for time to get and evacuate an additional 12 Airmen, but the request is denied. In conjunction, another group of Partisans led by the Communist, Tito has been telling Washington and London that Mihailovich, the leader of the Chetniks is working in collusion with the Germans. Musulin returns to Bari to persuade the U.S. that the Chetniks are on the Allied side, but to no avail; Tito's suggestion to mandate that all Pilots land in Communist controlled areas to prevent their being turned over to the Germans is believed by the U.S. Subsequently, during the latter part of June, Mihailovich informs the U.S. that his forces have 250 Airmen, many of whom are sick and wounded. Captain Musulin returns (Halyard Mission), dropping into Chetnik territory; he meets with Partisans about 50 miles outside of Belgrade and a tentative date of July 31st is scheduled for bringing in Planes to evacuate the Airmen. Bad weather hinders the operation until August. The O.S.S. Team lands in the mountains about 12 miles from a German force of 4,500 men; the opposite slope is manned by about 250 Germans. The Chetniks clear an Airstrip for the evacuation by August 9th, but the landing attempts are unsuccessful due to a shortness of the landing strip. On the following morning, six C-47s, protected by P51 Fighters zoom in to the area and at five minute intervals the rescue mission is on. The 60th Troop Carrier Command's second wave arrives at 09:00; 25 P-51s and six additional C-47s zip in and out. The operation extricates 241 U.S. Airmen, six British, four French, nine Italians; the U.S. Pilots also take out 12 Russians. Despite the lies of Tito, and the lack of confidence by the U.S., the Chetniks under Draza Mihailovich rescue more Americans. Subsequently, on the 26th-27th August, U.S. Planes arrive and evacuate another 58 American Airmen. Ironically, the evacuation terminate only when the Communists under Tito drive the Chetniks from the Airstrip as they are preparing to evacuate more Americans. Later, when the Russians finally arrive in Belgrade, they show their gratitude by expelling the American OSS units out of the country. The Chetniks are forced from their native land and General Mihailovich, the man responsible for saving the lives of hundreds of American Airmen is accused of war crimes by Tito; Mihailovich is executed.

May 1st 1944 — (Pacific-Carolines) A U.S. Naval Force of Battleships and Cruisers, commanded by Vice Admiral W.A. Lee, bombards Ponape Island, striking the harbor and Seaplane Base. The heavy attack is bolstered by Aircraft. **(Pacific-New Guinea)** The Japanese withdraw from Kamti village, allowing the 163rd Infantry to occupy it without incident. **(China-Burma-India)** The Allied ground troops supply problems begin to diminish with the appointment of Air Marshall Sir John Baldwin as coordinator of the Troop Carrier Command and the 3rd Tactical Air Force. **(Atlantic-Italy)** The Allies, stalled for the better part of the winter by stubborn German resistance at the Winter Line, finalize plans for the next offensive to take Rome. A meeting is held at Caserta to work out the details of a massive assault against Cassino, followed by a breakout at Anzio.

May 2nd 1944 — (United States) The Destroyer *Parrot II* (DD-218) is damaged after a collision near Norfolk, Va. **(Pacific-Admiralty Islands)** The U.S. 8th Cavalry prepares to depart Hauwei Island; participation in the Admiralty campaign has cost four killed and seven wounded, against 285 enemy dead. **(Pacific-Bismarcks)** Marine Fighter Squadron 115, the first Squadron from Marine Air Group 12 to arrive at Emirau Island, St. Matthias Islands, flies its first Air Combat Patrol.

May 3rd 1944 — (North Atlantic) The U.S.S. *Donnel* (DE-56), a Destroyer Escort, is damaged by an enemy Submarine. **(Pacific-New Britain)** Remnants of the First Marine Division prepare to pull out of Cape Gloucester. The withdrawal will be completed on the 4th of May, with the exception of the 12th Marine Defense Battalion, which remains to assist the Army. **(Atlantic-Mediterranean)** An enemy Submarine damages the U.S.S. *Menges* (DE-320) in the western Mediterranean.

May 4th 1944 — (Pacific-Marshalls) The United States Navy establishes an Air Facility on the Majuro Atoll. **(Pacific-New Guinea)** RCT 126, 32nd Division and other troops arrive at Blue Beach. The Commanding Officer of the 32nd Division assumes command of Task Force Persecution. The campaign for Aitape thus far has been one-sided, with the Japanese losing 525 killed and 25 captured since the 22nd of April. The Americans have suffered 19 killed and 40 wounded. American Admiral Barbey suggests that the invasion of Wakde-Sarmi be delayed until the 21st of May when tides will be more favorable to the operation. **(Pacific-China-Burma-India)** The Chinese 22nd Division, which is becoming more aggressive since receiving orders from Chiang Kai-shek, overruns Inkangahtawng, on the route to Kamaing. The Chinese receive assistance from Planes, Artillery and Armored units to take the town. After securing the village, the Chinese remain in the area for a long time. **(Atlantic-Mediterranean)** The U.S.S. *Pride* (DE-323) and another Destroyer Escort, the *Joseph E. Campbell* (DE-70), and some French and British Warships combine to sink the German Submarine U-371.

May 5th 1944 — (Pacific-Admiralty Islands) The U.S. 8th Cavalry starts clearing enemy stragglers from Manus Island. **(Pacific-Japan)** Japanese Admiral S. Toyoda is appointed Japanese Commander in Chief of the Combined Fleet, succeeding Admiral Koga who died on March 31st in a Plane crash. **(Pacific-Solomons)** The PT-247, patrolling near the Solomons is sunk by enemy coastal guns. **(China-Burma-India)** Merrill's Marauders and the Chinese drive closer to Myitkyina. As the troops reach the trail junction north of the

Ritpong River, Patrols are dispatched to cut a new trail and work behind the enemy. **(Atlantic-Italy)** British General Alexander initiates the drive against the German Gustav Line to take Rome and push the Germans from Italy. On the following day, Alexander sets the 11th of May as D-Day for the offensive. **(Atlantic-Mediterranean)** The U.S.S. *Fechteler* (DE-157) is sunk in the western Mediterranean by an enemy Submarine.

May 6th 1944 — (United States) Admiral William D. Leahy, Chief of Staff, celebrates his 69th birthday. **(Pacific-New Guinea)** Admiral Barbey's suggestion for the postponement of the invasion of Wakde-Sarmi is agreed upon by Military leaders. The date is sometime between the 16th and the 21st. General Krueger informs General MacArthur of the decision and MacArthur in turn modifies the assault plans by canceling the attack against Sarmi because its terrain cannot sustain a Heavy Bomber operation. The assault against Wakde will go as planned in order to get Aircraft operating from there to strike against Biak. **(China-Burma-India)** The 88th Chinese Regiment assaults Ritpong, but heavy enemy fire repulses the attempt. Despite the heavy losses, the Chinese kill many of the defenders. Meanwhile, Marauder Patrols work behind enemy lines and set up roadblocks south of the village to prevent the Japanese from escaping. **(Atlantic)** The U.S.S. *Buckley* (DE-51) and Planes dispatched from the U.S.S. *Block Island,* (CVE-21) destroy the German U-66 in the mid-Atlantic. The *Buckley,* a Destroyer Escort is damaged by ramming the German Submarine.

May 7th 1944 — (Pacific-New Guinea) The abandoned Airdrome at Cape Hoskins is seized by units of the U.S. 40th Division, without opposition. **(China-Burma-India)** The Japanese unsuccessfully attempt to break out of Ritpong during the night of the 7th. On the following day, the Chinese attack again but cannot take the village. **(European Theater)** General Eisenhower sets June 5th as D-Day for the invasion of Normandy. Inclement weather, which plagues the Allies prior to the invasion, causes the commencement to be set back to the 6th.

May 8th 1944 — (United States) Newport News, Virginia is the site for the christening of America's newest Carrier, the *Ticonderoga* (CV-14). **(Pacific-New Guinea)** The Americans at Aitape fortify their defenses. The 163rd Infantry is relieved by the 126th Infantry in the western sector of the perimeter. **(China-Burma-India)** The Japanese repulse a strong attempt by the Chinese to take Ritpong. The 114th Regiment, Chinese 38th Division, drives toward enemy-held Kamaing; its 112th Regiment makes final preparations to assault the Japanese at Warong.

May 9th 1944 — (Pacific-New Guinea) The Japanese begin to withdraw to make a stand at Sorong-Halmahera. **(China-Burma-India)** Chinese troops, assisted by the Merrill's Marauders, push the Japanese from Ritpong. The mop-up operation is handled by the Chinese, while the Marauders move toward Lazu to block the enemy retreat. The Chinese 114th Regiment, 38th Division, takes Hlagyi and East Wala as it advances toward the outposts of the 112th Regiment, just north of Manpin. **(Atlantic-France-Belgium)** The U.S. Eighth Air force launches attacks against enemy Airfields at Laon, Florennes, Thionville, St. Dizier, Juvincourt, Avord, Bourges and Orleans. The Allied Air Forces commence heavy Air raids against enemy positions almost a month before the invasion of Normandy to deal another devastating blow to the Germans. **(Atlantic-Italy)** Norman Lewis, a British Intelligence

Officer stationed in Naples, concerned about the black market, notes in his records: "FOR MONTHS NOW, OFFICIAL SOURCES HAVE ASSURED US THAT THE EQUIVALENT OF THE CARGO OF ONE ALLIED SHIP IN THREE UNLOADED IN THE PORT OF NAPLES IS STOLEN. Note: According to Lewis, the Army is suffering from lack of many items that are freely available on the black market. **(Atlantic)** The Submarine Chaser PC-558 is sunk by an enemy Submarine at 38o41'N., 13o43'E. **(Atlantic-Soviet Union)** The Red Army takes Sevastopol.

May 10th 1944 — (United States) James V. Forrestal becomes the Secretary of the Navy, replacing Frank Knox who passed away on the 28th of April. Some friction develops between Forrestal and Admiral King; Forrestal becomes annoyed because of not being kept informed by King of ongoing Naval Operations. **(Pacific-Marshalls)** The U.S. Navy establishes a Naval Base at Eniwetok. **(Pacific-New Guinea)** Australian Aircraft strikes Babiang prior to a ground assault by troops from the Nyaparake Force moving in steadily from the east. The assault troops take the village without opposition. **(Pacific-Philippines)** The Submarine U.S.S. *Cod* (SS-224) sinks an aging Japanese Destroyer, the *Karukaya.* **(Atlantic-Italy)** The Allies make final preparations to crush the Gustav Line. The U.S. Fifth Army is deployed from the Tyrrhenian Sea to the confluence of the Gari and Liri Rivers, with the II Corps positioned on the left and the French Expeditionary Corps on the right. The Texas 36th Division is held in reserve. The British Eighth Army is deployed with the 13th Corps on the left and the Polish 2nd and the 10th Corps on the right, with the 5th Corps in the Adriatic coastal sector. The Canadian 1st Corps and the South African 6th Armored Division are held in reserve.

May 11th 1944 — (Pacific-Philippines) Another U.S. Submarine, the *Crevalle* (SS-291) penetrates enemy controlled waters and evacuates 28 women and children from Negros, Philippines. **(China-Burma-India)** Team K, Marauder Force, begins its drive to reach Ngao Ga. In other activity, the Yunnan Force moves under darkness to cross the Salween River. **(Atlantic-England)** The U.S. Navy establishes an Advanced Amphibious Base at Southhampton, England. **(Atlantic-France)** The U.S. Ninth Air Force launches strikes against strategic targets within range of Caen, the Airfields at Beaumont-le-Roger and Cormeillesen-Vexin. **(Atlantic-Italy)** The Allies mount the final offensive to take Cassino and Rome. (See May 11th-18th 1944) During the attack, 1st Lieutenant Robert T. Waugh, 339th Infantry, 85th Division, advances against an enemy-held hill near Tremensucli. The Platoon opens up with cover fire as Waugh assaults and destroys six enemy bunkers, capturing or killing all defenders.

May 11th-18th 1944 — (Atlantic-Italy-Cassino) At precisely 23:00, the Allies launch the final thrust to crush the Gustav Line. U.S. and British Artillery units begin a massive bombardment prior to the Infantry assault. The thunderous roar of the guns breaks the silence while the monstrous shells pound the mountain. Huge clusters of fire spiral skyward and then lurk ominously overhead. The stunned enemy, while caught off-guard by this tremendous attack, storms forward with a dogged four-pronged counterattack.

The U.S. 2nd Corps drives along the coast toward the beachhead at Anzio. The U.S. 85th and 88th Divisions, accompanied by elements of the French Expeditionary Force, overcome heavy opposition southwest of Castelforte and capture several hills. The British 13th Corps moves out across the Rapido, stumbling across the wreckage left from the Texas 36th Division's futile attempt to take Cassino during January. The British fight throughout the night of the 11th-12th and gain control of a small bridgehead by dawn. At 01:00 on the 12th, the Polish II Corps advances against Cassino with a frontal attack, and after a bloody fight, takes Phantom Ridge, only to be thrown back. Casualties soar during the 12th as the attack is met by counterattacks all along the line. During the bloodbath, Company F, U.S. 88th Division becomes isolated and is virtually wiped out during the savage lunge to seize St. Maria Infante. The 350th Regiment hits heavy resistance near Mount Damiano; three machine gun nests open up with blistering fire, halting its advance while inflicting catastrophic casualties. 2nd Lt. Charles Shea, Company F, singlehandedly advances and destroys the emplacements, killing or capturing all defenders; Shea receives the Medal of Honor.

Major General Troy H. Middleton.

Also, Castelforte falls to elements of the French Corps on the 12th. The French 1st Motorized Division becomes engulfed in furious battle near San Andrea, but cannot dislodge the German defenders. On the 13th, the Americans seize several hills near San Martino Hill, then clear Mont Rotondo. The turning point in the battle occurs when French troops crash through the Gustav Line, taking Mont Girofano, Mont Feuci, and Mont Majo, after another agonizing struggle. The French continue to drive steadily ahead. On the 14th, the Americans pressure the Germans to pull back further as they advance ag-

gressively, toward Formia, seizing Santa Maria Infante. Along the Rapido, the British remain busy fortifying their bridgehead against German opposition. The battle intensifies on the 15th when the Americans push into evacuated Spigno. From there, they jump to Itri, bringing them closer to the besieged defenders at Anzio.

The Germans maintain a well disciplined rear guard action on the Allies, yet Scauri and Mont Scauri fall to the 339th Infantry, 85th Division. The 337th Infantry makes good progress until overpowering enemy fire halts it in the valley below Mont Campese. The 4th and 8th Indian Divisions, which have been battling for days, sees the British 78th Division move through their positions and break through the final defenses of the Gustav Line. On the 17th, the French scale treacherous Mont Oro, thought impossible by the Germans, snapping the main link in the German chain and sealing the fate of Cassino. Meanwhile, the Americans continue driving toward Anzio while the British, Indians, and the Poles close for the kill at Cassino, seizing it on the 18th when the Proud 3rd Carpathian Division takes the monastery. The remnants of the Gustav Line are totally reduced by British Eighth Army troops when they secure the ruins of Cassino.

May 12th 1944 — (Pacific-New Guinea) Bitter fighting continues between the Americans and Japanese at Aitape and Hollandia. The Allied Outpost at Charov is abandoned to pool the troops with those at Nyparake. **(China-Burma-India)** Brisk fighting ensues near Tingkrukawng between the Marauder K Force (Kinnison's 3rd Battalion and the Chinese 88th Regiment) and a superior enemy group. The Japanese, in this area, have a British led contingent of Kachins and Gurkhas stalled. Kinnison's Marauders, have lost many men to heat prostration during their trip through the mountains and become pinned down; two days of combat ensue and the Marauders sustain 8 killed and 21 wounded. As their ammunition nears exhaustion, Kinnison orders a pull-back. Meanwhile, Hunter's 1st Battalion (Marauders) and the Chinese 150th Division are closing on Myitkyina. Also, the depleted 2nd Battalion, under Colonel McGee and its accompanying Kachins are moving through the Kumon Mountains. The 113th Chinese Infantry, 38th Division nears West Wala and Maran. In other activity on the Salween Front, enemy outposts stationed at the end of the Tatangtzu Pass are surrounded by elements of the Chinese 36th Division, 53rd Army; the enemy mounts a night counterattack and drives the Chinese back to the Salween. Other heavy firefights develop as the 198th Regiment begins to clear the enemy from Mamien Pass. **(Atlantic-Germany)** U.S. and Royal Air Force Fighters fly escort to protect the Heavy Bombers of the U.S. Eighth Air Force, which deliver a menacing blow against strategic targets in Germany. Nearly 2,000 tons of bombs strike the oil plants at Boehlen, Bruex, Leutzkendorf, Merseburg-Leuna, and Zwickau. Despite the success of the raids, costs are high on Allied Planes and Pilots. Forty-six Bombers and ten Fighters are lost. The German losses are much higher, reportedly 200 Aircraft. **(Atlantic-Italy-Cassino)** Vicious fighting continues throughout the day. The Germans unsuccessfully assault the positions of the 339th Infantry, 85th Division, on San Martino Hill. The 1st Battalion, 337th Infantry, speeds through positions of the 339th, and secures the objective. The U.S. 351st Infantry takes Solacciano, near San Maria Ridge, after a bitter fight. Murderous fire isolates Company F of the 351st Infantry in the vicinity of San Maria Infante; the unit is nearly wiped out during the operation before it is finally rescued. The 350th Infantry seizes Ventosa and halts its advance to await the French who are fighting alongside the

American II Corps. In the French Expeditionary Corps area, the 4th Moroccan Mountain Division, supported by a Regiment of the 3rd Algerian Division, Tanks and Tank Destroyers, takes Castelforte. The French 1st Motorized Division and the 4th Motorized Brigade are stalled by stiff resistance near San Andrea. In the **British Eighth Army** 13 Corps area, the British 4th Division meets heavy enemy fire, preventing the expansion of its sparse bridgehead on the west bank of the Rapido. The 8th Indian Division, also struggling against heavy German fire, forces the Rapido, placing two bridges across the river. The Germans, however, despite the shock of the previous night's bombardment, resist vigorously. The monastery, defended primarily by the German 1st Paratroop Division, is attacked by the Polish II Corps which succeeds in taking Phantom Ridge. Enemy Paratroopers counterattack and push the Poles back to their point of origin, where they stay for the next several days.

May 13th 1944 — (Pacific-New Guinea) American Major General William H. Gill, realizing the positions at Marubian are untenable, orders the area evacuated. On the following day, Company C, 127th Infantry, attempts to withdraw, however, it is cut off by the enemy. Company A, positioned at the Ulau Mission, also is threatened, forcing both outfits to be evacuated. **(China-Burma-India)** The Marauder K Force launches a heavy attack against Tingkrukawng, striking from the flanks and also with a direct frontal assault, but the enemy holds on; the K Force bypasses the village and moves toward Myitkyina. On the Salween Front, Chinese reinforcements speed to the Mamien Pass, reaching it in time to save a Chinese Battalion from being annihilated. The survivors of the beleaguered Chinese Battalion and the reinforcements counterattack, driving the Japanese off, ending enemy resistance in the area. Elements of the Chinese 53rd Army move across the Salween river and strike enemy positions, recapturing previously lost positions in the Tatangtzu Pass. **(Pacific-Marshalls)** Japanese positions on Jaluit Atoll are struck hard by Land-based Army and Naval Planes, and repeat the attack on the following day. **(Atlantic-Italy-Cassino)** The Germans hold the line against the Allied drive to take Cassino throughout the day. During the night of the 13th, they make a gradual and disciplined withdrawal to their next line of resistance. In the **II Corps** area, the surrounded Company F, 339th Infantry makes a desperate but unsuccessful attempt to break out of their encircled positions at San Maria Infante. In the vicinity of San Martino Hill, Hill 60 and Cave d'Argilla are cleared of the enemy by the 2nd Battalion, 338th Infantry. Mont Rotondo is captured by the 1st Battalion, 350th Infantry 88th Division, which is closing fast. The French Expeditionary Corps, commanded by General Juin, working in coordination with the Americans, bolts through the near impregnable Gustav line and takes Mont Giorfano with the 2nd Moroccan Division. The tenacious Moroccans seize Mont Feuci and Mont Majo, situated in the center of the Corps zone. The Fourth Moroccan Mountain Division successfully charges Mont Ceschito, ridding the area of enemy resistance, while taking about 1,000 prisoners with the swift enveloping assault. The Mountain Corps deploys three Assault Groups, two moving west toward Spigno, while the third drives north toward Ausonia during the night of the 13th. In the **British Eighth Army** area, the 13th Corps extends its beachhead and gets a bridge placed across the Rapido in the British 4th Division sector. **(Atlantic)** A German Submarine, the U-1224, which had been transferred to the Japanese and renamed; under the

Flag of the Imperial Navy it is known as the RO-501 when it is sunk by the U.S.S. *Francis M. Robinson*, a Destroyer Escort.

May 14th 1944 — (Pacific) The U.S.S. *Bonefish*, operating south of the Philippines in the Celebes Sea, sinks the Japanese Destroyer *Inasuma*. **(Atlantic-Italy-Cassino)** The Germans continue stiff resistance, but their commanding positions finally are being breached by the Allies, forcing them to continue their withdrawal to regroup. In the French Corps area, elements of the Mountain Corps advance closer to Ausonia until fierce enemy fire forces it to halt. Meanwhile, the 4th Mountain Division and the Third Algerian Division mop up enemy resistance west of Mont Majo, along the left flank of the sector. In the center area, the 2nd Moroccan Division advances to Castellone and Cantalupo Hills, while other units drive toward Castelnuovo. In the **II Corps** area, the U.S. 338th Infantry seizes Hill 131 and advances to set up outposts on the Formia-Ausonia Road. The U.S. 2nd Battalion, 337th Infantry, 85th Division, pushes toward Castellonorato. In another action, the 339th Infantry, 85th Division is embroiled in a heated battle for a knoll near Tremensuoli; First Lt. Robert Waugh, who a few days earlier, had singlehandedly destroyed six enemy bunkers to aid his embattled Company, destroys two additional enemy pillboxes. Lt. Waugh's daring exploits allow penetration of the Gustav Line in this area. His actions are responsible for the death of 30 enemy Soldiers and the capture of 25 others. Lt. Waugh is subsequently killed in action at Itri, Italy, while leading his men in an attack; he receives the Medal of Honor posthumously. The 351st Infantry, 88th Division, captures Hill 126, and Santa Maria Infante village then advances with three Regiments to assault Spigno. In the **British Eighth Army** area, the 13th Corps steadily expands its bridgehead back at the Rapido in the event the Germans mount an attack. Also, the British prepare to attack Cassino in conjunction with the Polish II Corps on the following day; the operation must be postponed because the British 78th Division is delayed while attempting to cross the Rapido.

May 15th 1944 — (Pacific-Marshall Islands) The U.S. Navy establishes Air Bases at Ebeye and Roi-Namur on the Kwajalein Atoll. **(Pacific-New Guinea)** U.S. troops which are threatened by an enemy attack at both Ulau and Marubian are evacuated by sea and transported to Nyaparake. **(China-Burma)** The Chinese-American Marauder H Force advances to the Namkwi River, placing it about 15 miles from the Airfields at Myitkyina. Progress is halted when a poisonous snake bites the Kachin guide; about 02:30 on the 16th, the advance is renewed; the Kachin guide rides on Colonel Hunter's horse. They reach Namkwi about four miles from Myitkyina. **(Atlantic-Italy-Cassino)** In the **II Corps** area, the Yanks drive hard toward Anzio. The 337th Infantry, 85th Division, captures Castellonorato. Operating to the left of the 337th, the 3rd Battalion, 338th Infantry fights to the junction of Ausonia Road and Highway 7. The Germans evacuate Spigno prior to the approach of the charging 88th U.S. Division, allowing it to push through the ruins of the town and head for Itri. In the French Expeditionary Corps area, elements of the Mountain Corps push the Germans from Ausonia before noon; after the 2nd Moroccan Division secured Castelnuovo earlier in the day. However, the Germans succeed in halting the advance of the French 1st Motorized Division near San Giorgio. In the **British Eighth Army** area, the 13th Corps keeps slicing further into the Gustav Line. The British 78th Division completes its crossing of the Rapido and moves through the lines of the 4th and 8th Indian Divisions, advancing to the positions of the Polish II Corps, which has been stalled since its assault against Phantom Ridge on the 12th; both units will now combine and assault Cassino. In other activity, the Canadian I Corps begins to relieve the Indian 8th Division. **(Atlantic-Mediterranean)** The German U-731 is sunk in the Western Mediterranean by Land-based Naval Planes (VP-63) and British Warships.

May 16th 1944 — (Pacific-New Guinea) Task Force Tornado embarks from Hollandia with the Wakde Assault Force. **(Pacific-Solomons)** The Destroyers U.S.S. *Franks* (DD-554) and *Haggard* (DD-555), sink the I-176, a Japanese Submarine, north of the Solomons. **(China-Burma-India)** The Marauder H Force isolates and confines the villagers of Namkwi to ensure secrecy, then fords the Namkwi River. On the Salween Front, the Chinese 76th and 88th Divisions seize 13 villages as they close on Pingka. **(Atlantic-Italy Cassino-Anzio)** In the **U.S. Fifth Army** area, the German 94th Division is in full retreat, with the II Corps (85th and 88th U.S. Divisions) in hot pursuit. In the French Expeditionary sector, elements of the Mountain Corps advance rapidly to positions just south of Esperia, while another contingent meets only faint resistance as it moves toward Mont Revole. The junction of Sant Georgio-Esperia Roads is taken by contingents of the 3rd Algerian Division, which is subsequently struck by an unsuccessful German counterattack. In the **British Eighth Army** area, 13th Corps sector, the British 78th Division moves to the front and takes a primary role in the assault with the Poles to isolate and capture Cassino. The Polish II Corps, which had been driven from Phantom Ridge after a bloody confrontation, receives new orders to attack.

May 17th 1944 — (Pacific-Dutch East Indies) An Allied Task Force (British Eastern Fleet) commanded by British Admiral J.F Somerville, which includes the Carrier U.S.S. *Saratoga* (CV-3), attacks the Japanese Naval Base at Soerabaja (Surabaya). This assault is followed by another strike, carried out by the Southwest Pacific Area Force. **(Pacific-Marshalls)** Enemy positions on Eniben Island on the Maloelap Atoll are bombarded by Destroyers operating in the area. **(Pacific-New Guinea)** An Allied Naval Force consisting of Cruisers and Destroyers and commanded by U.S. Rear Admiral Russell S. Berkey, initiates a preliminary bombardment of suspected enemy positions on New Guinea. Subsequently, the U.S. 163rd Infantry lands near Arare on the mainland of Dutch New Guinea against no opposition; Artillery is deployed to face Wakde Island on the opposite shore. Other contingents land at Insoemanai Island and also find no enemy troops. **(China-Burma-India)** The Marauder H Force (Hunter's 1st Battalion) launches a surprise strike and seizes Myitkyina Airstrip. As the 150th Chinese Regiment is taking the Airstrip, the 1st Marauder Battalion seizes the Irrawaddy Ferry and Pamati; no Japanese reinforcements arrive from Myitkyina. The Marauders had isolated the villagers at Pamati to ensure secrecy as the Burmese have been giving assistance to the Japanese. Colonel Hunter sends requests to Kinnison (3rd Battalion) and McGee (2nd Battalion) for support; they begin rushing to the area. Meanwhile, elements of the Chinese 89th Regiment move by air to further bolster the assault, but the desperately needed supplies are not brought in to Hunter. In other activity, Strategic Air Force Bombers are committed to replace a Squadron of American Dakotas, which have been ordered to move from Troop Carrier Command and assist the Fourteenth Air Force with supplying the Yunnan Force. In yet other activity on the Yunnan Front, a fierce

battle ensues as the Chinese secure Hongmoshu village, 24 air miles from Teng-chung, only to lose it to a Japanese counterattack. **(Atlantic-Mediterranean)** The German Submarine U-616 is sunk when attacked by eight U.S. Destroyers and British Aircraft: the Destroyers *Ellyson* (DD-454), *Emmons* (DD-457), *Gleaves* (DD-423), *Hambledon* (DD-455), *Hilary P. Jones* (DD-427), *Macomb* (DD-458), *Nields* (DD-616) and the *Rodman* (DD-456) participate. **(Atlantic-Italy-Cassino-Anzio)** In the **U.S. Fifth Army**, II Corps area, the U.S. 85th Division chases the retreating enemy through the Formia corridor. Heavy enemy resistance meets the 338th Infantry as it enters Formia. The 337th Infantry pushes vigorously toward Maranola. Meanwhile, the 351st Infantry runs into stiff opposition including Tanks, near Mont Grande. Other elements of the 88th, Division drive in two Convoys toward Trivio. The 350th Infantry passes through Maranola and sets up positions just south of the 351st Regiment. In the French Expeditionary Corps area, the 3rd Algerian Division rushes into abandoned Esperia. It then drives toward Sant Olivia, hitting rigid rearguard resistance. Although the opposition is fierce, Mont Oro, a strategic position overlooking the Hitler Line, is reached by French troops; they begin to scale the treacherous heights and punch a hole in the German defenses, opening the way for the Allies to break through the Gustav Line. The French are not allowed to come down from the heights because General Alexander has reserved the Liri corridor for British troops. Meanwhile, other French Forces drive along the south bank of the Liri river where they are stalled by intense enemy fire, pouring down on them from Mont Oro. In the **British Eighth Army** area, the British launch a general offensive against Cassino with Canadian, Polish and British 13th Corps troops. The Polish II Corps recaptures Phantom Ridge and Colle Sant Angelo. The 13th Corps manages to sever Highway 6. As pressure against the German lines increases, the enemy is forced to withdraw from Cassino.

May 18th 1944 — (Pacific-Admiralty Islands) The operation to secure the Admiralty Islands is officially terminated by the Commanding General of the U.S. Sixth Army. The island had been invaded on the 29th of February. U.S. casualties during the campaign are 326 killed, 1,189 wounded and four men missing. The Japanese suffer 3,280 killed and 75 captured. Air and Naval Bases (Manus Island) which have been established greatly assist the ongoing Pacific thrust. **(Pacific-New Guinea)** Subsequent to a preinvasion naval bombardment, elements of the U.S. 163rd Infantry storm the beaches at Insoemoar, the primary island of the Wakde group. Severe enemy fire from bunkers and pillboxes slow the Yanks' advance; the Regiment fights from the beachhead to secure a good part of the Airfield and drive the Japanese to the island's northern tip. The Japanese mount an unsuccessful counterattack during the night of the 18th-19th. In other activity, the U.S. 3rd Battalion, 163rd Infantry, pushes across the mainland and secures a bridgehead after crossing the Tor River. **(China-Burma-India)** Merrill's Marauders attack Myitkyina, surrounding the Japanese 89th Regiment, 30th Division, which is holding the Airstrip. The 1st Battalion seizes Zigyun, just south of the town, while the 150th Regiment, Chinese 50th Division, assaulting from the north, drive against the railroad station. The Chinese become confused during the attack and begin firing at each other. On the following day, two Chinese Battalions attack and again they mistake each other for Japanese and begin blasting each other, sustaining severe casualties. The situation deteriorates further as each contingent drives the other back into the waiting guns of the 3rd Chinese

Battalion, which opens up on both retreating Chinese contingents, mistaking them for the enemy. Two days later, the Chinese attack and reach the railroad station, however, the Japanese open fire and the Chinese retreat. Colonel Hunter holds a weakened 1st Battalion under Colonel Osborne and the remnants of the Chinese Regiment. **(Atlantic-Italy-Cassino-Anzio)** In the **U.S. Fifth Army** area, the U.S. 36th Division begins its forced march toward the Anzio beachhead. In the **II Corps** area, the 85th Division advances toward Anzio along two routes, the 338th Infantry wiping out enemy stragglers at Formia then moving north and west to Mont Di Mola and Mont Conca. The 337th sweeps southwest to Highway 7 between Formia and Itri to cover the 338th's flank, followed by the 339th during the night. The Germans concentrate considerable firepower in the area defended by the U.S. 88th Division and temporarily halts progress of the 351st Infantry; Artillery is rushed to its aid and the obstacle is reduced. The Germans also offer fierce opposition against the French near Pico. The French inch to the heights of S. Oliva. The Germans also are driven from Mont Oro and Monticello. In the **British Eighth Army** area, Polish II Corps sector, the 3rd Carpathian Division captures the Monastery at Cassino. The total collapse of the Gustav Line is accomplished with the capture of the town of Cassino (13 Corps area), taken by the British 4th Division. Elements of the British 78th Division advance to the outskirts of Acquino, a German stronghold along the Hitler Line. The Canadian 1st Corps keeps its drive moving toward the Hitler Line at Pontecorvo.

May 19th 1944 — (Pacific-Marcus Island) U.S. Planes attached to Rear Admiral A. E. Montgomery's Carrier Task Group begin a two day attack on Marcus Island. **(Pacific-New Guinea)** U.S. troops rapidly terminate enemy resistance on Insoemoar Island and begin repairing the Airfield. Enemy stragglers flee to the northeastern tip of the island. The American contingent on Isoemanai is disbanded because of no further need and the components embark for Wakde. In other activity, the islands of Liki and Niroemoar are occupied by elements of the American Force without incident, allowing the U.S. Fifth Air Force to place radar detachments on the islands. In the Aitape area, Brigadier General Clarence A. Martin (Assistant Divisional Commander 32nd Division) assumes command of the East sector, in place of Colonel Howe. **(Pacific-Solomons)** The U.S.S. *England* (DE-635), a Destroyer Escort, sinks the I-16, a Japanese Submarine. **(China-Burma-India)** Merrill's Marauders (1st Battalion) set up south of Nankwi along the Nankwi River after first turning over responsibility for the Pamati Ferry to Chinese troops; the K Force (2nd Battalion, Marauders) closing from the north, seizes Charpate with slight opposition and the M Force (3rd Battalion, Marauders), advancing to Namkwi, squeezes the enemy Garrison at Myitkyina. Dysentery has taken a high toll on the Marauders; one Platoon is plagued so badly that the men have been compelled to cut out the seat of their pants, to lessen the handicap while under attack. The 1st Battalion has been cut down to about 600 men as the other Marauders rush to their aid. Also, General Merrill suffers another heart attack; he is evacuated on the following day. The command passes to Colonel John Easton McCammon; the Marauders question why Colonel Hunter does not get the command. Colonel McCammon, who is also sick, succumbs within ten days. In the **British Fourteenth Army** area, American General Stilwell is recommended by the British Fourteenth Army Commander to be given Command of all operations to facilitate opening the land route to China. **(Atlantic-Italy-Anzio)** The U.S. 509th

Paratroop Infantry Battalion is ordered to make a jump near Galla di Mont Orso, north of Mont Romano to accelerate the advance of the II Corps to Anzio. The operation is canceled as the 36th Division reaches the beachhead on the 22nd. In the **II Corps** area, the town of Gaeta is abandoned by the Germans, allowing the 338th Infantry, 85th Division, to seize it without incident. Units of the 339th keep advancing toward the 88th Division, which is battling at Itri. Other elements of the 339th Infantry, 85th Division steadily reduce enemy resistance on the hills south of Highway 7. In the 88th Division area, Mont Grande falls easily to the 351st Infantry. The Germans, now facing a confident and well-supplied Allied Force, abandon positions south of the Liri and east of the Pico, heading toward the Pico-Pontecorvo Line. In the French Expeditionary Corps area, Campodimele is seized by a contingent of the Mountain Corps, which severs Highway 82 near Mont Vele. In the **British Eighth Army** area, the Germans mount fierce resistance at the Hitler Line, repulsing an assault by the Canadian 1st Corps and by the British 13th Corps near Pontecorvo and Aquino. British General Alexander expects General Mark Clark to send General Truscott against Valmontone to relieve pressure from the British. Meanwhile, the French advance far ahead of the British (20 miles); upon Clark's suggestion, they attack and relieve pressure off the British. Alexander approves of the idea which will allow the British to advance through the Liri Valley. The French also relieve pressure off Clark, permitting him to dispatch a reserve Division to Valmontone if needed. **(Atlantic-Mediterranean)** The American Destroyers *Niblack* (DD-424) and *Ludlow* (DD-438), joined by British Aircraft, sink the German Submarine U-960.

U.S. Tanks and Infantry advancing on Aitape, New Guinea.

May 20th 1944 — (Pacific-Marcus Islands) Planes attached to the U.S. 5th Fleet bomb positions on the Marcus Islands. **(Pacific-New Guinea)** Subsequent to mopping up enemy stragglers on Insoemoar Island, Task Force Tornado returns to the mainland, leaving the island to the Army Air Force. The U.S. casualty list during the campaign to secure Wakde is 43 killed and 139 wounded. The Japanese suffer 759 killed on Insoemoar Island and an additional 50 dead on the mainland. American Forces controlling the Tor River crossing repulse a Japanese counterattack. In other activity, Persecution Task Force receives a warning from the Alamo Force to be prepared for a massive Japanese attack against the beachhead at Toem-Arare. **(China-Burma-India)** U.S. General Stilwell informs British Admiral Mountbatten that the Cairo agreement stipulates the release of Stilwell's troops after Kamaing is taken. In other activity, Warong is seized by the 112th Regiment, Chinese 38th Division. **(Atlantic-Italy-Cassino-Anzio)** Rome falls within reach of the Allies, as the Germans continue to withdraw following the collapse of the Gustav Line. Fondi falls to the 349th Infantry, U.S. 88th Division (II Corps) as it presses toward Monte Passignano. Meanwhile, the French Corps nears Pico and in the British Eighth Army area, the Polish II Corps attacks German positions at Piedimonte, where a heated contest ensues outside the town, raging for several days without a decision. The British have been sustaining severe casualties for some time and replacements are few; the British strip their present Divisions for replacements. In other activity, General Mark Clark calls for the U.S. Fifth and British Eighth Armies to mount a combined assault to reach the beleaguered Anzio beachhead; the British are unable to attack for about three days because of casualties. General Alexander visits Clark and asks if the Fifth Army can "attack and outflank" the Germans in order that the British could conserve casualties. General Clark explains that to avoid casualties in the British sector would only cause more in the American sector. Clarke, while sympathetic, recalls that Alexander had said at the onset of the Anzio Operation: "THE AMERICANS AND THE BRITISH WERE THE SENIOR PARTNERS IN THE ITALIAN ENTERPRISE AND THEY HAD TO SHARE THE RISKS AND THE GAINS AND THE LOSSES."

May 21st 1944 — (Pacific-Marshalls) Army and Naval Land-based Planes land a powerful blow against enemy positions on the Wotje Atoll. Destroyers bombard the island on the following day. **(Pacific-New Guinea)** The Airstrip on Wakde becomes operational. In other activity, RCT 158, Alamo Force Reserve unit arrives at Toem to supplement the Forces. **(Pacific-Pearl Harbor)** The U.S. Navy sustains damage after an accidental explosion; five LSTs are damaged; the 43, 69, 179, 353 and the 480. **(China-Burma-India)** Intense fighting breaks out between the 3rd Marauder Battalion and Japanese contingents in the vicinity of the Mogaung Road. The Marauders, halted at Radhapur, repulse an enemy attack. **(Atlantic-Italy-Cassino-Anzio)** In the **U.S. Fifth Army** area, **II Corps** sector, elements of the 338th Infantry land at Sperlonga without incident and advance inland toward Terracina. In conjunction, the 337th Infantry, 85th Division, rolls overland, also closing on Terracina and seizes Mont Sant Biagio. Monte Calvo and Cima del Monte falls prey to the 88th Division. In the French Expeditionary Corps area, vicious fighting occurs between the Mountain Corps and the Germans near the Itri-Pico Road. Heavy fighting erupts near Pico, where the 3rd Algerian Corps seizes a small hold, but the German pressure forces it to withdraw during the night. The Germans also hold up well against the 1st Motorized Division in the vicinity of Monte Leucio and Monte Morrone. **(Atlantic-France-Germany)** The Allies borrow from Glenn Miller and code name an operation to destroy enemy train movements "Chattanooga Choo-Choo." The Allied Expeditionary Air Force initiates Fighter missions to disrupt enemy supply movements.

May 22nd 1944 — (Pacific-Bismarcks) The U.S.S. *England* (DE-635), a Destroyer Escort, patrolling north of the Bismarcks, sinks the Japanese Submarine RO-106. **(Pacific-Japan)** The Japanese Submarine *Asanagi* is sunk by the U.S.S. *Pollack* (SS-180) southeast of Japan. **(Pacific-New Guinea)** Task Force Tornado having secured the Wakde Airdrome and the designated strip of the mainland, pushes west toward

Sarmi, about 16 miles west of the Tor River. Sporadic enemy resistance continues around the Wakde Airdrome, prompting elements of the 163rd Infantry to be dispatched to Insoemoar Island to terminate the stragglers. In the Aitape area, Nyaparake Force Patrols meet fierce resistance, forcing them to retire toward the beach at Parakovio. **(China-Burma-India)** In Burma, the 3rd Marauder Battalion pulls back from the Mogaung Road and regroups at Charpate. **(Atlantic-Italy-Cassino-Anzio)** German General Kesselring begins a disciplined retreat out of the Liri Valley, ordering the troops to fall back and concentrate their defenses at Cisterna and Valmontone. The U.S. II Corps inches closer to the VI Corps, which is poised at Anzio waiting for orders to break out. The U.S. 36th Division closes in on Anzio, permitting a previous order to drop the 509th Paratroop Infantry Battalion at the Pontine Marshes to be canceled. In other activity, the U.S. 337th Infantry, 85th Division seizes a portion of Monte San Croce, while under vicious enemy fire coming from Terracina. The 350th Infantry, 88th Division, fights its way toward Roccasecca, while the 351st sprints toward Monte Chiavino. In addition, the 349th Infantry captures Monte Monsicardi. In the French Expeditionary Corps area, the Hitler Line is thoroughly breached. Lenola falls to contingents of the Mountain Corps, linking its left flank with the U.S. II Corps. The 3rd Algerian Division, secures Pico. In the **British Eighth Army** area, the Canadian 1st Division, 1st Corps, unsuccessfully assaults German positions in advance of the main offensive.

Polish troops at Cassino.

General Eisenhower, Admiral G. Kirk and Admiral L. Deyo.

347

May 23rd 1944 — **(Pacific-Bismarcks)** The U.S.S. *England* sinks another Japanese Submarine, the RO-104. On the following day, sinks the Submarine RO-116. In addition, the *England* destroys the Submarine RO-108 on the 25th. **(Pacific-Bougainville-Solomons)** U.S. Navy and Marine T.B.F.s mine the Buin-Kahili waters. **(Pacific-New Guinea)** Elements of the 163rd Infantry, positioned at the mouth of the Tor River, are relieved by RCT 158, which then pushes west toward Sarmi. Enemy resistance pins down the Third Battalion about 400 yards east of Maffin No. 1, and darkness swoops down before the 1st Battalion can reach it. In the Aitape sector, the Nyaparake Force continues to withdraw; forward units reach Tadji. In other activity, Task Force Hurricane practices for the invasion of Biak. **(Pacific-Wake Island)** U.S. Rear Admiral A.E. Montgomery's Carrier Task Group launches Aircraft to bombard the island. The Task Group (U.S. Fifth Fleet) is unaware that American civilians are still held on the island. **(China-Burma-India)** The Japanese mount a fierce assault against the Marauders at Charpate, but the attack is vigorously repulsed by the battle-weary Yanks. On the Salween Front, the Chinese are pushed from hill positions on the southern flank by the Japanese. **(Atlantic-Italy-Anzio Cassino)** At 06:30, U.S. Artillery bombards enemy positions; Air strikes join the operation and the breakout begins. The 45th Division fights a holding action on the left flank, while the principal body of the VI Corps drives toward Cisterna, spearheaded by the 3rd Division which overcomes solid resistance and advances about half-way to Cisterna. The 1st Armored Division advances on the left flank beyond the railroad, and the 1st Special Service Force, supported by contingents of the 133rd Infantry, drives on the right along the Mussolini Canal moving toward the railroad. The 133rd hits fierce German opposition and is forced to pull back to Highway 7 when struck by a powerful counterattack. About 1,500 German prisoners are captured during the vicious fighting. In an example of the combat, 2nd Lt. Ernest Dervishian, 34th Infantry Division; 2nd Lt. Van T. Barfoot 45th Division; 2nd Lt. Thomas Fowler, 1st Armored Division; Sgt. George J. Hall, 34th Division; Privates John Dutko, Henry Schauer, Patrick Kessler, James H. Mills; and Sergeant Sylvester Antolak, all of the Third Infantry Division, receive the Medal of Honor for extraordinary heroism.

The II Corps drives close to the beachhead as the U.S. 85th Division's 337th Infantry reaching the outer limits of Terracina, while the 338th closes on Mont Lenano. In other activity, the 339th Infantry takes Sonnino. The U.S. 88th Division's 350th Infantry advances to Roccasecca. In conjunction with the breakout at Anzio, the French attack, but cannot penetrate German positions in the Liri Valley (II Corps area); the Germans hold the line to ensure the safe withdrawal of their troops from the besieged Hitler Line. The Mountain Corps succeeds in relieving the U.S. 88th Division on Mont Chiavino, then advances to seize Mont Pizzuto. Meanwhile, the 2nd Moroccan and the 3rd Algerian Divisions drive toward Pastena and Ceprano respectively, while the right flank along the Liri is guarded by the 1st Motorized French Division. Although the Allied effort is extraordinary, the Germans retain control of Cisterna. In the **British Eighth Army** area, the 1st Canadian Division strikes toward the Aquino-Pontecorvo road, slicing a hole in the enemy defenses; the Infantry, supported by the Canadian 5th Armored Division, is ordered to shoot through the gap. Meanwhile, General Clark, at a forward observation post with General Truscott, is con-

cerned about a press release on the operation. Clark insists that the wording be appropriate and specify that it is "primarily a Fifth Army matter." Generals Alexander and Clark make simultaneous statements on the following day, several hours after the actual hook up between the II Corps of Keyes and Truscott's VI Corps, with Alexander calling it a "SPECTACULAR FIFTH ARMY ADVANCE COVERING MORE THAN 60 MILES IN FOURTEEN DAYS." In Naval activity, off the coast of Italy, the Light Cruiser *Philadelphia* (CL-41) and the U.S.S. *Laub* (DD-613), a Destroyer, collide and sustain damage.

Silent U.S. Artillery, awaiting transportation from England to the coast of Normandy.

May 23rd-24th 1944 — **(Atlantic-Italy)** A FEW HEROES IN A WAR OF HEROICS (Medal of Honor recipients) — At Cisterna, entrenched Germans in firmly established dugouts, pour incessant fire upon advancing American contingents. Infuriated by the intense fire, Tech Sergeant Ernest Dervishian (34th Infantry) charges a stumbling block near a railroad embankment and using his Carbine Rifle, he captures 10 enemy troops. He advances further with his men alongside and 15 additional enemy troops are captured. Nine Germans are noticed fleeing and the rifles roar, wounding three; Dervishian pursues the balance, singlehandedly capturing all on a nearby ridge. He continues moving, taking four reinforcements, and meets a wall of machine gun fire in a vineyard, trapping the Yanks. Dervishian pretends to be dead and later lunges forward and captures the objective. The detachment is ordered back, Dervishian commandeers the captured machine gun and seizes three additional nests, returning to his lines with the prisoners. P.F.C. Henry Schauer (3rd Division) also provides his unit with an extraordinary burst of heroism at Cisterna, when he walks perfectly erect into the fire of four snipers, killing all with his BAR. Continuing forward, he advances against a machine gun nest that is ringing bullets all around him. Again he opens fire and eliminates the threat. Without losing a step, he wipes out another nest about 500 yards away. Schauer survives this ordeal and on the following morning he engages another machine gun nest and a Mark VI Tank. He again stands up and kills the four German defenders of the nest. Pvt. James Mills, Company F, 15th Infantry 3rd Division, fearlessly acting as point man heading down a draw, encounters enemy machine gunners standing five yards away. Mills fires a solitary shot, killing the gunner and capturing his assistant. Mills also captures a German about to throw a grenade. In an instant, another camouflaged Soldier attempts to throw a grenade, but a single shot from Mills M1 kills him; soon after, he moves into the direct line of fire originating from a machine gun, three Riflemen and two machine pistols some 50 feet away. Mills advances and captures all six enemy troops. He advances a few additional yards and again comes under fire from another machine gun, but he kills the gunner with one shot. Mills then volunteers to draw enemy fire to allow his Platoon to move unnoticed toward a stronghold. He advances and again stands to draw the enemy fire, repeating the feat four times without harm. Meanwhile, his Platoon surrounds and overpowers the enemy, capturing 22 enemy troops without loss. Lt. Thomas Fowler, a Tank Officer encounters a stalled Infantry unit in the midst of a minefield and immediately takes over, walking through the minefield clearing a 75 yard path. Then he returns and moves the Infantry through a Squad at a time. He follows this by again returning to lead the Tanks through; the objective is seized. The enemy mounts a vicious counterattack and one of Fowler's Tanks is seriously hit. The Americans are forced to retire, but Fowler remains behind and sprints through Tank fire to aid the wounded. Fowler subsequently sacrifices his life. During the counterattack, Tech Sergeant Van T. Barfoot (157th Infantry 45th Division), confiscates a Bazooka and stands steadfastly, firing at approaching Tanks. His first shot cripples the lead Tank and kills three of the crew. As two other Tanks change direction, Barfoot advances with a Tommy gun and some demolitions, destroying a German Field Artillery gun and then helping two seriously wounded men reach safety some 1,700 yards distance, while under heavy fire. Also, P.F.C. Patrick Kessler, Company K, 30th Infantry, (3rd Division), sees five of his fellow troops slain and his Company stalled by a wall of enemy fire. Without orders, he charges vehemently against automatic fire, jumping into a nest, killing two defenders, and capturing a third; he wounds the fourth defender who escapes. Returning with his prisoner, two more of his Company are slain. prompting Kessler to take a BAR and advance 75 yards under incessant fire through a minefield toward two machine guns. He stands, firing his BAR from his hip and seizes both objectives, by killing the gunners and capturing 13 other troops. Kessler, while returning with his captives, is fired upon by two Snipers, giving his prisoners an opportunity to escape; they choose not to test his aim. He retains the prisoners and captures the two Snipers. P.F.C. John W. Dutko, 3rd Division, is also under a wall of fire at Ponte Rotto by three machine guns. Dutko charges recklessly, taking the first, then advances through exploding Artillery shells and ringing machine gun bullets. As he nears the position, he becomes wounded. Undaunted, he keeps moving and destroys the second nest, then he drives toward the third. Again he is wounded, but refuses to relent. Despite the serious wounds, he singlehandedly charges the third nest. His riddled body is later retrieved from atop the dead enemy crew. Also on the endless list of bravery is Staff Sergeant George J. Hall, 135th Infantry, 34th Division, who singlehandedly attacks three machine guns and several sharpshooting Snipers which have stalled his Company. He unleashes grenades and seizes the position, its gun battered, its gunners dead. His ammunition exhausted, he confiscates grenades from the dead defenders and charges the second nest, seizing five prisoners and five corpses. The unperturbable Hall advances to the final obstacle, but a burst of artillery fire shatters his right leg; his invaluable efforts allow his Company to advance and eliminate the final nest.

May 24th 1944 — (Pacific-Bismarcks) The U.S.S. *England* sinks the Japanese Submarine RO-116 off the Bismarcks. **(Pacific-Dutch Indies)** The U.S.S. *Raton* (SS-270) destroys the Japanese Frigate *Iki.* **(Pacific-New Guinea)** The U.S. 158th

Infantry (Task Force Tornado) moves along the coast toward the Tirfoam River, supported by Tanks and Flame Throwers. In the Aitape sector, the Nyaparake Force still is being hard pressed by the enemy and prepares to withdraw to defensive positions about 3,000 yards west of Yakamul, near the mouth of a creek. **(Pacific-Philippines)** The U.S.S. *Narwhal* (SS-167) lands men and supplies on Samar. **(China-Burma-India)** The Japanese resist staunchly at Myitkyina and launch a vigorous counterattack against the battle-weary Marauder 3rd Battalion at Charpate, driving the under-supplied troops from the town and recovering the northern approach to Myitkyina. On the Salween Front, the Japanese repulse successive Chinese attempts to dislodge them at the southeast end of the Pingka Valley. **(Atlantic-Italy-Cassino-Anzio)** The **U.S. Fifth Army** assumes command of the 36th Engineering Combat Regiment and directs it to rush south through Littoria to join the II Corps, which is pressing to reach the Anzio force. The **VI Corps** assault to break through Cisterna continues. The 1st Armored Division, supported by an Artillery barrage, leaps far beyond Highway 7. Combat Command B, racing toward Cori, meets light resistance, while C.C.A. is hit by rigid opposition as it drives toward Velletri. The U.S. 7th and 30th Regiments, 3rd Division, pierce the center, to approach fortified Cisterna, while the 133rd Infantry, 34th Division on the right flank, drives doggedly toward Monte Arrestino. Meanwhile, Company B, 15th Infantry, 3rd Division, advancing toward Cisterna, is stalled by intense enemy fire. Sergeant Sylvester Antolak, well in advance of his Squad, is cut down by vicious enemy fire, his right arm shattered and his shoulder badly wounded and bleeding heavily. Despite his wounds, he continues his advance, using his good arm to fire; he kills two and captures ten others. Antolak singlehandedly drives toward the next objective, about 100 yards away; he is riddled by a hail of bullets less than 30 yards from the objective, his extraordinary courage inspires his men, who charge and seize the objective; Antolak receives the Medal of Honor posthumously. In the **II Corps** area, Terracina falls the 85th Division (337th Infantry), culminating the completion of the II Corps mission. Also, Engineers and skilled Reconnaissance troops are forcing the opening of the road to Anzio to shatter the siege. In addition, fighting in the French sector also remains heavy. The U.S. 88th Division assists the Mountain Corps to recapture the crest of Mont Pizzuto. Meanwhile, the Germans offer vicious resistance against the 2nd Moroccan Division near Pastena, and they also hinder progress of the 3rd Algerian Division. In the **British Eighth Army** area, the Canadian 1st Corps seizes the town of Pontecorvo and then advances to Aquino. The II and VI Corps establish contact at about 10:00 at Borgo Grappa, culminating the tedious three-month operation to join the two forces. General Clark is present at the link-up. Determined to take Rome as soon as possible, Clark orders General Truscott to dispatch two Divisions, plus additional units, toward Valmontone and to send three additional Divisions to the Alban hills to cover the flank of the Valmontone Force. Clark, still suspicious of the British motives, is preoccupied with the Fifth Army getting to Rome first. The British have been attempting to dominate the news releases since North Africa, and Clark intends to get the Americans their share of the limelight.

May 25th 1944 — (Pacific-New Guinea) U.S. Brigadier General Edwin D. Patrick assumes command of Task Force Tornado (Wakde-Sarmi), replacing Major General J.A. Doe (Assistant Divisional Commander 41st Division), who will command troops which will assault Biak. Task Force Hurricane departs Humboldt Bay during the night, heading for Biak. As it advances west, Maffin No. 1, falls to the 1st Battalion, 158th Infantry with little resistance, but the 2nd and 3rd Battalions driving toward Lone Tree Hill face vicious fanatical opposition. **(China-Burma-India)** General Stilwell becomes alarmed when the Chinese decide to abandon positions along and the Bhamo-Myitkyina Trail, including the roadblock of the railway at Namkwin. Stilwell is at Myitkyina and during a conference with Colonel Hunter, he is informed of Hunter's dissatisfaction with Headquarters: "GALAHAD (Marauder Force) TREATED UNFAIRLY." Hunter tells Stilwell that the Marauders had been deprived of Colors, insignia, and various other Military emblems, and in addition he states that it had been unfair to tell the Officers that no promotions would be forthcoming until the conclusion of the operation; his frustration goes further as he tells Stilwell that his men had not received any awards or citations except the Purple Heart; last but not least, the Marauders had felt betrayed because they had been promised evacuation as soon as the Airstrip had been taken. By the end of May, only 200 of the original Marauder Force are able to remain at Myitkyina; the ordeal had drained their strength. Subsequent to the end of the war it is determined that the Marauders had faced about 4,600 Japs at Myitkyina (as many as 3,500 at one time). In other activity, contingents of the Chinese 38th Division maneuver around Japanese positions and block the Kamaing Road at Seton. On the Salween Front, the Chinese 2nd Army receives responsibility for all operations near Pingka-Hsiangta-Mangshih, replacing the Chinese 88th Division, which joins the assault against Lung-ling. The Japanese are forced by the Chinese to abandon their positions in the Tatangtzu Pass and withdraw nearly 10 miles to form another defensive line. **(Italy-Anzio-Cassino)** The U.S. Fifth Army's VI Corps and the II Corps converge near Borgo Grappa, linking the Brett Force (1st Battalion 36th Engineers, Tank Destroyers and Reconnaissance units of the British 1st Division) and the II Corps' 91st Cavalry Squadron which has advanced along the Tyrrhenian coast; the siege of Anzio is considered lifted and Highway 7 becomes a motorized conveyor belt, churning supplies north toward the Eternal City. The breakout is complete as the stranded VI Corps sprints forward, seizing Monte Arrestino with the 3rd Regiment, 1st Special Service Force, and overrunning Cisterna, and Cori, with the 3rd Division. The massive Allied assault, supplemented by Aircraft, takes heavy tolls on the retreating German Vehicles. By 12:00, the Americans take over 2,500 prisoners. However, the Germans mount stiff resistance against the 1st U.S. Armored Division near Velletri. In other activity, the U.S. 34th Division minus the 133rd Infantry, establishes positions behind the 1st Armored units. Troops of the II Corps hold their positions, awaiting relief by the French Expeditionary Corps (VI Corps). The French seize San Giovanni Incarico with the 3rd Algerian Division and capture Vallecorsa with their Mountain Corps. During the German withdrawal, the British Eighth Army quickly expands its Melfa River bridgehead. The British 13th Corps occupies Aquino without opposition. Also, the Germans abandon Piedimonte allowing the Polish II Corps to take it without incident. **(Atlantic-France)** The U.S. Eighth Air Force participates in the Allied Air Offensive against enemy coastal batteries at Fecamp and St. Valery.

May 26th 1944 — (Pacific-Bismarcks) The U.S.S. *England* sinks the Japanese Submarine RO-108. **(Pacific-Marshalls)** A U.S. Naval Destroyer Force bombards Japanese positions on the Mili Atoll. **(Pacific-New Guinea)** The Japanese take advantage of an ill-timed Allied Naval bombardment and retake previously abandoned positions. The U.S. 1st Battalion, 158th Infantry, inches toward enemy-held Lone Tree Hill. The Japanese also heavily deploy in strategic areas which guard the approaches to the Maffin Airstrip. **(China-Burma-India)** The Marauders, holding precarious positions in the Myitkyina area, are rocked by a massive Japanese assault, which reclaims Namkwi from the 2nd Battalion; the Marauders retreat toward the Airstrip. On the Salween Front, the Yunnan Force's supplies are dwindling. The 27th Troop Carrier Squadron arrives to bolster Yun-nan-i. Airdrops are initiated within two days, speeding the replenishing of badly needed ammunition, medicine and food. **(Atlantic-Italy-Cassino-Anzio)** In the **U.S. Fifth Army** area, the British receive responsibility for the security of the Factory. The **U.S. VI Corps**, jumps off at 11:00 revitalizing the drive to Rome. The 34th, and 45th Divisions charge against intense opposition, gaining about 1½ miles on the route to Campoleone Station-Lanuvio Line. Impossible terrain bogs down the U.S. 1st Armored Division's penetration toward Velletri. Fast-closing darkness enables it to transfer the sector to the 36th Texas Infantry Division. Elements of the 36th shoot through the gap separating the 3rd and 34th Divisions, and sprint toward Velletri. Task Force Howze (contingent of 1st Armored Division) flanks the 3rd Division on the left, and the elite 1st Special Service Force takes the right flank, adding needed punch for the 3rd Division's center thrust toward Artena. The Howze Task Force severs the Velletri-Valmontone Road and rolls toward Highway 6. During the heated battle, 1st Lt. Beryl Newman, 133rd Infantry, 34th Division, singlehandedly silences three enemy machine guns, wounds two enemy Soldiers and kills two others, in addition to capturing 11 prisoners; he receives the Medal of Honor for his tremendous courage. In the **II Corps** area, the U.S. 88th Division catapults the 349th and 350th Regiments through the Amaseno Valley. In the French Expeditionary sector, the 2nd Moroccan Division takes Pastena and speeds to the hills east of Castro dei Volsci. In other activity, Falvaterra is seized by the 3rd Algerian Division. In the **British Eighth Army** area, with the Germans retreating, the British regroup while they continue pursuit. The 1st Canadian Corps advances to the Liri River, but is hindered by destroyed bridges. The Germans abandon their hold on Ceprano, allowing Patrols to enter without incident. In the 13th Corps sector, the Germans pound the advancing British 6th Armored Division, halting it at the Providero Defile, delaying the advance to Arce. In other activity, Roccasecca is seized by the Indian 8th Division.

May 24th 1944 — A supply column moving along a primary road on Arawe, New Guinea.

May 27th 1944 — U.S. troops, backed by Armor, advance on Biak.

May 27th 1944 — (Pacific-New Guinea) THE INVASION OF BIAK — U.S. Navy Surface Vessels bombard enemy shore positions to soften resistance. The bombardment is supplemented by Steel Eagles from the Carriers which swarm overhead, bombing and strafing the Japanese. Some Japanese Aircraft intercept the Task Force, but the effort is ineffective. After the pre-invasion barrage of Admiral Fechteler's Surface Vessels, Task Force Hurricane, commanded by Major General Horace Fuller and composed primarily of the 41st U.S. Division (minus RCT 163), lands near Bosnek on Biak Island, which is defended by more than 10,000 crack troops. The 186th Infantry meets minimal resistance and quickly secures a beachhead, then clears the trail leading over the ridges to the inland plateau north of Bosnek. The U.S. 162nd Infantry drives west to secure the Airfields. The Japanese are entrenched in multi-layered caves at the Parai Defile. The Yanks begin torching the caves with drums of gasoline to destroy the defenders. An enemy counterattack is mounted, but Task Force Hurricane thwarts it then seizes Parai. Meanwhile, the invasion force makes quick progress, while the elusive Japanese withdraw into the dense jungles, rather than divulge their full strength at the beach. On the Wakde-Sarmi front, the U.S. 158th Infantry fights viciously, gaining a hold on Lone Tree Hill. The Japanese mount several counterattacks to reduce the beachhead at Toem during the night of the 27th. In other activity, the PT-339 becomes grounded and is destroyed by U.S. Forces. In addition, the Submarine Chaser SC-699, operating off western New Guinea, is damaged by a Kamikaze. **(China-Burma-India)** Japanese assault the ex-

hausted 2nd Marauder and 209th Engineering Combat Battalions and attached Kachins, near Charpate, inflicting heavy losses against them as they attempt to reach Radhapur; the Japanese opposition is not too tough, but the Marauders are drained of strength; several men fall asleep during the heat of battle. Colonel McGee loses consciousness three times during the struggle; the situation in Burma is so drastic that a man must carry a fever of at least 102 for three consecutive days before he is eligible for evacuation. On the Salween Front, Monsoon rains hamper activities of both the Allies and the Japanese. A Chinese Force advances to within five miles of Hong-moshu, securing the Huei-jen Bridge. In China, the Japanese begin to phase in the 2nd part of Operation ICHIGO, sending two Divisions to the region east of the Hsiang River. The Japanese code-name this Operation "TOGO". **(Atlantic-Italy-Cassino-Anzio)** In the **U.S. VI Corps** area, the 34th and 45th Divisions advance along the left flank. The 1st Armored Division awaits orders to burst through the German line. Elements of the 36th Division, deployed behind the 1st Armored, prepare to bolt forward when the breakthrough occurs. The right flank of the VI Corps is vigorously engaged with the enemy. The 3rd Division's 15th Infantry takes Artena, but Task Force Howze encounters firm resistance in front of Highway 6, north of Artena. Despite the setback, the 15th Regiment secures positions which dominate Highway 6. The Germans mount an unsuccessful Infantry-Tank counterattack against the 3rd Division at Artena. In other activity, II Corps relinquishes its sector and troops to the IV Corps during the night of the 27th, except the U.S. 85th Division and some Organic Units. The U.S. 85th Division secures Sezze and the hills south of Roccagorga, while the 350th Regiment, U.S. 88th Division takes Roccagorga. In the French Expeditionary Corp area, Amaseno, Mont Siserno, and Castro dei Volsci, are seized by the French. In the **British Eighth Army** area, the 1st Canadian Corps, using Assault Boats, crosses the Liri River against heavy resistance, and occupies Ceprano, then awaits arrival of the British 78th Division (13th Corps). In other activity, the Indian 8th Division, combined with the British 6th Armored Division, continues to battle for Arce, seizing it on the following day. In the 10th Corps area, the Italian Corps of Liberation defeats a German rear-guard unit and captures Mont Cavallo.

Merrill's Marauders firing a machine gun near Myitkyina.

May 28th 1944 — (Pacific-New Guinea) The U.S. extends its beachhead on Biak Island, while some contingents drive toward the Airfield. The Japanese halt the 162nd Infantry's 3rd Battalion 200 yards from Mokmer Airfield. A fierce counterattack, later splits the 3rd Battalion, forcing it to pull back. Meanwhile, Japanese holding the caves overlooking Mokmer village pour ferocious fire upon the 1st and 2nd Battalions, preventing them from reducing the enemy resistance behind the 3rd Battalion. The furious battle continues throughout the night; the Yanks are compelled to transport ammunition and supplies to the isolated 3rd Battalion by small craft. In conjunction, Tanks are rushed along the coastal roads to reduce the threat. General Fuller, realizing the positions are untenable, orders the 3rd Battalion to withdraw until reinforcements can be committed to bolster the operation. In the Wakde-Sarmi area, the U.S. 158th Infantry, using Artillery cover, attempts to advance, however, strong enemy fire forces the Regiment to pull back to the Snaky River. In addition, General Patrick insists that RCT 163, scheduled to embark for Biak, be retained in the Wakde area until reinforcements from the 6th Division can be brought to the beachhead. MacArthur makes some observations: "THE CAPTURE OF THIS STRONGHOLD WILL GIVE US COMMAND DOMINATION OF DUTCH NEW GUINEA EXCEPT FOR THE ISOLATED POSITIONS. FOR STRATEGIC PURPOSES, THIS MARKS THE PRACTICAL END OF THE NEW GUINEA CAMPAIGN." ... He further mentions: "FROM THE FORWARD POINT REACHED BY THE JAPANESE, WE HAVE ADVANCED OUR FRONT APPROXIMATELY 1,800 STATUTE MILES WESTWARD AND APPROXIMATELY 700 MILES TO THE NORTH." Off Biak, in the Schouten Islands, the U.S.S. *Stockton* is damaged by coastal fire. During May of 1943, MacArthur and Admiral Halsey had conferred and the congenial meetings form a firm bond between the two men. At that time, it had been decided that MacArthur's Army would advance against Rabaul, while Halsey's forces envelop the Solomons. MacArthur, now closing on the Philippines, did not have any Amphibious troops during the entire New Guinea Papuan campaign, which closed successfully during February 1943. **(China-Burma-India)** Chinese General Li-huang commits the Chinese 71st Army to the campaign against Lungling. The 71st Army (minus the 88th Division already across the river) prepares to ferry troops across the swollen Salween, about eight miles below the Hwei-tung Bridge, while another Force assaults Sung Shan. **(Atlantic-Italy-Anzio-Cassino)** In the **U.S. Fifth Army** area, the Germans strengthen the force which is banging against the left flank of the Americans, while vicious fighting occurs along the front. The 157th and 180th Regiments, 45th Division, meet resolute resistance west of Albano road. The Germans counterattack, forcing the 157th Regiment to pull back. Also, the 3rd, and 34th Divisions are heavily engaged, the former on the right flank of the Corps and the latter, near Lanuvio. Meanwhile, the 1st Special Service Force repels a German counterattack along the Valmontone Road. French forces continue reducing resistance in the Lepini Mountains. In other activity, Norman Lewis, British Intelligence Officer notes in his records: "THE FRENCH COLONIAL TROOPS ARE ON THE RAMPAGE AGAIN. WHENEVER THEY TAKE A TOWN OR VILLAGE, A WHOLSALE RAPE OF THE POPULATION TAKES PLACE. RECENTLY, ALL FEMALES IN THE VILLAGES OF PATRICIA, POFI, ISOLETTA, SUPINO, AND MOROLO." Lewis then relates how at another village, Lenola, which had fallen the previous week, about fifty women were violated, but that the number was insuffient; children and old men are then violated, according to Lewis. The British construct a security camp at Ceccano to protect the women from the Moors. Subsequently, on June 4th, some Italians seek revenge. Five Moor Soldiers are lured to a house in Cancello on the pretense of having a good time with girls and wine. The party begins with the five Soldiers being served poisoned wine and ends when the troops are castrated and decapitated. In the **British Eighth Army** area, Arce is abandoned by the Germans during the night.

The Yanks prepare to move from England to France.

May 29th 1944 — (Pacific-New Guinea) The Japanese attack the 2nd Battalion, 162nd Regiment, west of Parai. Enemy Tanks leading the assault are intercepted by U.S. Tanks, initiating the first Tank battle in the Pacific. A U.S. counterattack drives the Japanese back. Enemy opposition is overwhelming, prompting General Krueger to have the 162nd Infantry withdrawn. The 2nd and 3rd Battalions deploy at Bosnek and Mandom; the remainder of Combat Team 162 moves to bolster a small defense perimeter near Ibdi. The Japanese retake the Parai Defile at a cost of over 500 men killed. Also, the Japanese threaten the beachhead at Toem-Arare on the mainland, but General Krueger orders two Battalions of the 163rd Infantry to embark for Biak. **(Canary Islands)** The U.S.S. *Block Island*, (CVE-21) an Escort Carrier Commanded by Captain F.M. Hughes, dubbed the U.S.S. *FBI (Fighting Block Island)* and several Destroyers operating near Monaco Deep, off the Canary Islands, detect an enemy Submarine (U-549) just after midnight on the 28th. Pursuit continues into the following day, terminating at 20:15. The enemy Submarine fires the first shots, damaging the *Block Island*. The Destroyers scan the area; however, again the *Block Island* is struck, igniting raging fires across her deck. The Submarine finally exposes its location and the Destroyer *Eugene E. Elmore* (DE-686) attacks unsuccessfully. The U.S.S. *Ahrens* (DE-575) and the *Robert I. Paine* close, but the U-549 again evades damage, then waylays the charging U.S.S. *Barr*, stopping her dead in the water by a torpedo that strikes her stern.

The hunters have been bushwhacked, and seemingly become the prey, however, the Destroyers are resolute and launch another deluge of torpedoes. Meanwhile, the Germans launch more torpedoes, but quick reaction by the Destroyer Escort *Elmore* prevents harm. As the contest mounts feverishly, massive rescue operations ensue to save the crew of the ill-fated *Block Island*. Miraculously, despite sustaining three lethal hits, the entire crew of the *Block Island* except six men killed by the initial explosion are picked up by the *Paine* and the *Ahrens*. Nine hundred and fifty one men are rescued from the sinking Ship, and live to tell the tale.

Another Vessel, the *Elmore*, avoids being struck by a torpedo by use of its sound detectors. Lt. Commander G.L. Conkey, Captain of the *Elmore*, orders continuous salvos which inundate the sea. Suddenly, small geysers permeate the water, followed by a tumultuous roar as the string of depth charges scores a direct hit. In an instant, the U-549 explodes and heads to the depths. The battle lasted about one hour. **(China-Burma-India)** The Japanese pressure mounts in East China, causing General Chennault to emphasize the desperate need for more adequate supplies. He requests the supplies be dropped by the Fourteenth Air Force as soon as possible. On the Salween Front, the supply situation also is terrible. The Chinese conduct makeshift repairs on a footbridge in the vicinity of the Mamien Pass, to open a thin supply route, but Air Drops become necessary to rectify the problem. **(Italy-Anzio-Cassino)** In the **U.S. Fifth Army** area, **VI Corps** sector, Armor-led Combat Teams A and B, wedge through the 45th Division positions and clear the enemy from Campoleone Station before 12:00. The Germans put up firm resistance and bog down the advance, inflicting severe losses on the Tanks. The U.S. 34th Division encounters fierce enemy resistance and sustains heavy casualties as it grinds forward toward Lanuvio. During the heated battle near Villa Crocetta, Captain William W. Galt commandeers a Tank Destroyer and traps 40 enemy Soldiers. After the enemy declines to surrender, Capt. Galt cuts them down. Soon after, an enemy 88 shell scores a direct hit on his Vehicle, killing him instantly; he receives the Medal of Honor posthumously. Bitter combat ensues for several additional days. The 34th takes the town on the 3rd of June. In other action, the 45th U.S. Division drives north with its 180th Infantry close behind Combat Team B, and its 179th Infantry, which is pushing north in the sector east of the Albano Road. The U.S. 36th Division is still locked up with the Germans outside Velletri. The II Corps assumes command of the 3rd Division and takes positions east of Frascati, filling a gap between the VI Corps and the British Eighth Army. In other **VI Corps** activity, the U.S. 85th Division zeros in on Rocca Massima-Giulianello. After being relieved by French troops, the 349th Infantry U.S. 88th Division, heads for Anzio. In the **British Eighth Army** area, Pofi is taken by the Canadians. The British 13th Corps moves toward abandoned Arce and establishes a bridgehead across the upper Liri. The Polish II Corps relieves the British 10th Corps in the Adriatic coastal sector; the British take responsibility for the inactive Polish II Corps area.

May 30th 1944 — (Pacific-New Guinea) On Biak, 186th Infantry Patrols probe eastward from Parai Defile, encountering only nominal activity. Patrols of the 162nd Infantry hit fierce opposition on a ridge northwest of Ibdi. In the Wakde-Sarmi area, the 1st and 3rd Battalions, 163rd U.S. Infantry, embark for Biak Island. The Americans set up new defenses along the Tirfoam River. In other activity, the Japanese strike American positions on the mainland at Arawe during the night. **(China-Burma-India)** American Brigadier General Haydon L. Boatner assumes Command of the Myitkyina Task Force, replacing Colonel John E. McCammon. **(Atlantic-Italy-Cassino-Anzio)** In the **U.S. Fifth Army** area, **VI Corps** sector, the outnumbered Germans mount fierce opposition in a last-ditch effort to halt the swarming Allies. Fighting near Albano, Lanuvio, and Velletri, is grueling but the stubborn German lines do not crack. The 157th Infantry quickly rushes to Campoleone Creek to supplement the 1st Armored's Combat Command B. The U.S. 34th Division's 135th Infantry reduces a small enemy pocket of resistance outside of Lanuvio, while

the 36th Division battles tenaciously below Velletri. Subsequently, the 36th mounts a night assault against Mont Artemisio. In the French sector, contingents of the 3rd Moroccan Division begin moving into the Palombara Pass. In the **British Eighth Army** area, the Canadians keep advancing toward Frosinone and hook up with French troops. Meanwhile, the British refuse to allow their designated roads to be used by French troops. General Clark remains concerned about the French Forces who have done an outstanding job in the rugged mountains and he feels they also should march into Rome. Clark has offered to send the French to take Ferentino (located in British Eighth Army area) if the British allow use of Highway 6. General Alexander is eager for the seizure of the town, but states that the French must subsequently leave the British zone. The move puzzles Clark because when the French take Ferentino the closest British troops would be at least 30 miles to the rear. Clark cancels the Ferentino Operation and keeps the French in the mountains, running atop Highway 6 on a solitary road. The situation continues to annoy Clark and he intends to hold a press conference on the following day to neutralize the possibility of a negative reaction by General Alexander. Clark states: "I FEEL THERE IS SOME INCLINATION ON THE PART OF ALEXANDER TO COMMENCE ALIBIING FOR HIS EIGHTH ARMY ... ALEXANDER IS WORRIED THAT I HAVE SABOTAGED HIS DIRECTIVE TO ATTACK VALMONTONE. I HAVE NOT DONE SO." Clark, also states: "FIRST, THE BRITISH HAVE THEIR EYES ON ROME, NOT WITHSTANDING ALEXANDER'S CONSTANT ASSURANCES TO ME THAT ROME IS IN THE SECTOR OF THE FIFTH ARMY...THE EIGHTH ARMY HAS DONE LITTLE FIGHTING. IT HAS LACKED AGGRESSIVENESS AND FAILED IN ITS PART OF THIS COMBINED ALLIED EFFORT." **(Atlantic-England)** Allied assault troops begin boarding Transports in preparation for Operation OVERLORD.

May 31st 1944 — (North Pacific) The U.S.S. *Herring* (SS-233) sinks the *Ishigaki* a Japanese Frigate. **(Pacific-Bismarcks)** The Japanese Submarine RO-105 runs into Yankee interference as it moves near the Bismarcks. The Destroyer Escort *England* (DE-635), accompanied by the *George* (DE-697) and *Raby* (DE-698), in addition to two Destroyers, the *Hazelwood* (DD531) and the *McCord* (DD-534) intend to destroy it. The U.S.S. *England* is masterfully yet unknowingly altering Japanese strategy in the Pacific as she continues her game of Oriental Eightball. The Japanese had placed six Submarines in waters extending from west of Manus to the seas south of Truk to act as spotters and protect the entrance to the Pelew Islands. Japanese Admiral Toyoda assumes the Submarine Scouts could keep him informed of American intentions in the Pacific as to whether the next thrust would be against the Carolines or the Marianas. Five of Toyoda's recently deployed Submarines have been eliminated by the *England* in one week and the lone survivor (RO-105) is now in the midst of being knocked in the corner pocket and annihilated. During the early morning hours of the 30th, the RO-105 is detected by the U.S.S. *Hazelwood* which attacks. Subsequent attacks by the *Raby* and *George* also show strong signs of damage, but the Submarine remains operational. The Commanders of the Destroyer Escorts *Spangler* and *England*, race to the scene to assist. On the 31st, the *Spangler* catapults a massive amount of depth charges at about 05:00, all of which miss the mark. At about 07:30, despite warnings from Admiral Halsey to seek safer waters, the *England* takes the opportunity to clear the table, and unleashes its salvos which strike a devastating blow, igniting explosions that stir the sea and shatter the

RO-105, culminating a short lived Japanese Scouting operation. The Japanese are unaware that the massive catastrophic damage to their Submarines had been inflicted by one U.S. Submarine. They believe that the area has been inundated by American Warships in preparation of an invasion of Palaut and they take precautions to defend that area more heavily. Actually, the Yanks are staging for a primary assault to seize the Marianas within a couple of weeks and owe a great debt to the "merry ole *England*" (DE-635). **(Pacific-New Guinea)** Task Force Hurricane continues to regroup on Biak, as preparations are finalized for the next offensive. The ground forces are bolstered with the arrival of the 1st and 3rd Battalions, 163rd U.S. Infantry. In the Wakde-Sarmi area, the defense perimeter of Task Force Tornado is decreased; the main body is deployed between the Tementoe and the Tor Rivers in addition to maintaining the strategic bridgehead across the Tor. In the Hollandia-Aitape area, the Nyaparake Force is relieved by Company G, 127th Infantry. The U.S. 1st Battalion, 126th Infantry, pushes out from the east to hammer the Japanese between it and the Drindarai and meets light opposition, allowing advancement to Parakovio. Meanwhile, the Japanese cross the Driniumor and attack elements of the 127th Infantry holding the opposite bank. **(China-Burma-India)** The U.S. 27th Troop Carrier Squadron increases the flow of badly needed supplies to the Chinese 53rd Army. **(Atlantic-Italy-Anzio-Cassino)** General Clark holds a press conference and says privately that the U.S. VI Corps with five Divisions is advancing toward Rome. He also mentions that well over two Divisions are attacking toward Valmontone to cut off the Germans by severing Highway 6. In the **U.S. Fifth Army** area, a major offensive is ordered to seize German-held Colli Laziali, to be made with the combined forces of both the VI and II Corps. Bitter fighting continues all along the line, as the Germans offer obstinate opposition against the U.S. 34th Division below Lanuvio. The situation is similar at Albano, where the U.S. 45th Division and other units are engaged in vicious battle. During the struggle for Lanuvio, a German force of 80 men strikes the positions of the 135th Infantry. Private Furman L. Smith, far out in advance of his unit, attempts to check the counterattack. He holds the point and assists the wounded, instead of withdrawing, however, his valiant effort is in vain. The Germans take heavy casualties, but overpower the position and Smith dies, rifle in hand; Private Smith receives the Medal of Honor posthumously. The 1st Armored Division is recalled and placed in reserve. The U.S. 36th Division makes great strides on the right flank as the Germans use cover of darkness to thin their ranks between Lanuvio and Velletri. The 142nd Infantry (36th) takes Machio d'Ariano and the enemy positions which had commanded the Velletri-Nemi Road. The 143rd lunges forward toward Mont Artemisio and the 141st claws its way yard by yard toward Velletri. The progress of the 36th opens a road leading from Valmontone to Rome. In the **II Corps** area, the entire Corps drives toward the point of departure for the main thrust. In other activity in the II Corps area, the U.S. 85th Division captures Lariano and secures positions on Mont Artemisio, in addition to penetrating across the Velletri-Arena road. In the **British Eighth Army** area, the Canadians enter unoccupied Frosinone as the British 10th Corps takes Sora.

June-August 1944 — (Atlantic-France) Special O.S.S. teams, composed of three men each, will be dropped in France subsequent to the invasion of Normandy to coordinate the French resistance fighters; 240 volunteers, comprising U.S., British, French, Belgian and Dutch troops participate and all

wear full uniforms. By the time General Patton breaks out during August, all the agents (Jedburghs) have arrived in France or the low countries. Eighty-two Yanks join the force. By August, some forward units are emplaced in Paris. Some of the people working with the O.S.S. are women and they are offered no quarter if captured. One woman, Virginia Hall, is the first civilian to receive the Distinguished Service Cross during World War II; she parachutes into France, despite being known by the SS and participates in attacks against the Germans including one ambush, which kills about 150 enemy troops, destroys a bridge and captures about 500 Germans. Virginia Hall had required special permission from both Donovan and President Roosevelt to make the jump; she jumps from the Aircraft with her wooden leg tucked under her arm to help ensure it does not get broken upon landing. Additional groups of O.S.S. units, considered "super secret" also drop into France during August to perfect the Allies counter-espionage operations; these contingents are code-named "X-2." Also, another woman, Gertrude Legendre, the 1st U.S. woman captured by the Germans, is wearing a WAC uniform; she is transported from prison to prison, but outwits the Germans and escapes; while her train is making a switching maneuver at the Swiss border, it rolls slightly into Switzerland and she bolts from the train to safety.

June 1st 1944 — (Pacific-New Guinea) The U.S. 186th Infantry, supported by Artillery and Tanks, advances from the beachhead perimeter on Biak toward the enemy Airstrip on the inland plateau, despite vicious enemy resistance. The Japanese counterattack from both the north and south, but the Yanks repulse the efforts. The 163rd Infantry is ordered to hold the beachhead, while the 2nd Battalion, 162nd Infantry drives north to join the 186th Infantry. The Japanese block a main coastal road and capture a water hole in the coastal sector. In the Hollandia-Aitape area, the Japanese push the 1st Battalion, 163rd Infantry back to Yakamul. The Yanks maintain their probes of the Harech Rail Road from this facility. **(Pacific-Philippines)** The U.S.S. Submarine *Narwhal* (SS-167) lands personnel and equipment at Mindanao. **(China-Burma-India)** The situation in the Myitkyina area begins to improve as American reinforcements are rushing to the scene. General Stilwell had previously considered requesting the British 36th Division, but he decided against it. The Reinforcements consist of two Engineering Battalions (they haven't had to use their weapons since basic training) which had been working on Ledo Road; 2,600 additional men (fresh green troops recently arrived in Bombay will also arrive. The Force is formed into three Battalions under Colonel Hunter and will also include the remnant Marauders. Presently, they have only the basic Food supplies for both the Americans and Chinese causing for grave concern; only two days rations remain. In addition to supply problems, monsoon rains hamper progress of the campaign. From the 26th of May until June 1st, elements of the Galahad Force are Airlifted to the area. In the vicinity of Kamaing, Moguang Valley, the Kamaing Road southeast of Nanyaseik is severed by troops of the Chinese 22nd Division. This, coupled with the ongoing operation of the Chinese 38th Division, which controls a major block at Seton, below Kamaing, threatens the Japanese Garrison at Kamaing. On the Salween Front, the Japanese transport reinforcements from the upper Shweli Valley to bolster Lung-ling. **(Atlantic-Italy-Anzio-Cassino)** The U.S. Fifth Army attacks to destroy the German Fourteenth Army and to seize Rome. German resistance against the Americans near Albano is heated, preventing the Yanks from advancing. British 1st Division attacks on the left are also stymied. The advancing U.S. 34th Division penetrates slightly and the Texas 36th engages in a violent struggle before taking Velletri. The II Corps plunges forward for Highway 6 and Cave Road, with elements of the 85th Division's 337th and 338th Infantry units clawing through stiff enemy resistance, toward Mont Ceraso. Contingents of the 88th Division plow forward on the right, advancing to the heights north of the railroad. The U.S. 3rd Division, operating on the north flank, pushes vigorously against resolute opposition near Valmontone. The U.S. 1st Special Force seizes the high ground southeast of Valmontone, a prize that British General Alexander has wanted Clark's command to seize for a long time. At 16:00, the IV Corps is pulled back from the line. In the **British Eighth Army** area, the Canadian 1st Corps advances up Route 6 and reaches Ferentino. With Valmontone secure, Fifth Army troops are scattered all around Highway 6 at the tip of the Liri Valley, clogging the British road. A British Officer is sent from the Eighth Army with a message from General Leese, inquiring if the Americans needed the Eighth Army to seize Rome and if no assistance is necessary, the British would head for Tivoli. Subsequently, General Alexander and his Chief of Staff, General Harding, confer with Clark on the 2nd of June and offer their assistance, telling him that if any help is needed the entire Eighth Army could be thrown into the fight. The topic ends with Clark's reassurance that the Fifth Army could handle the task. Clark insists that: "FIFTH ARMY TROOPS, NOT ALLIED TROOPS" will enter the city. On June 4th, Lt. Colonel Henry E. Gardiner leads his Tank Battalion (1st Armored Division) with some special passengers; contingents of the First Special Service Force comprising American and Canadian troops, roll toward the city.

June 2nd 1944 — (Pacific-Formosa) The Submarine U.S.S. *Guitarro*, (SS-363) sinks the Japanese Frigate *Awaji*. **(Pacific-New Guinea)** On Biak Island, the U.S. 186th Infantry pushes through the inland plateau, for the Airfields. Enemy resistance is sporadic. In the coastal sector, the enemy-held water hole is retaken by the 162nd Infantry, which then reduces an enemy roadblock and establishes another, preventing the enemy from utilizing the route leading inland. Elements of the 163rd Infantry occupy Owi and Mios Woendi Islands. In the Hollandia area, Task Force Persecution is divided into two contingents; the Herrick Force, ordered to maintain control of Yakamul, and the Bailey Force, which is given responsibility of probing with Patrols stretching south from Yakamul along the Harech rail line. **(China-Burma-India)** The final attack for Myitkyina commences. The Chinese start to tunnel underground toward the enemy positions. On the Salween Front, the Chinese 36th Division takes the village of Kaitou in the Sheweli Valley, and encircles the Japanese Garrison at Chiaotou. In China, the Japanese terminate the successful Honan offensive. **(Atlantic-Italy-Cassino-Anzio)** The Allies continue to battle tenacious resistance along the route to Rome, but the Germans begin to pull back faster than in previous encounters. The rear-guard troops mount defiant opposition. Villa Crocetta falls to the 34th U.S. Division. The 36th Division takes the hills east of Mt. Cavo and Tano Hill with its 142nd and 143rd Infantry. The 36th's 141st Infantry sprints to Highway 7 before the sun rises and moves west until the U.S. 45th Division's 157th Infantry comes in from the left flank of the VI Corps to take over the operation. Also, the enemy retreats in the II Corps area. The U.S. 85th Division charges with three Infantry Regiments at full stride. Mont Fiore falls to the 339th Regiment, attacking on the left. The 337th hammers up the center to secure Mont Ceraso, from where it advances

to within sight of Highway 6, while the 1st Battalion, 338th Infantry, pounds from the right, reaching Highway 6 at Sant Cesareo. Meanwhile, the 351st Infantry, 88th Division, seizes Sant Cesareo, severing Highway 6, while Gardella Hill falls to the 349th Infantry. The pressure continues to mount on the Germans who are forced to fall back from Valmontone as the 30th Regiment, 3rd Division closes. Heavy combat rages all along the route to Rome. The 1st Special Service Force charges down Highway 6 and links with the French near Colle Ferro before 16:00. Other French contingents mop up on the Lepini Mountains. In other activity, the U.S. Fifteenth Air Force begins "shuttle bombing", between Italy and Russia. The Operation is coded "FRANTIC." A total of 130 Bombers and 70 Fighters assault rail targets in the vicinity of Debrecen, Hungary, before flying into the U.S.S.R. to land at Morgorod, Piryatin, or Poltava, three temporary American Air Bases in the Soviet Union. In the **British Eighth Army** area, the 13th Corps takes Alatri.

June 3rd 1944 — (Pacific) A new schedule for the campaign to seize additional Japanese-held islands is released. It calls for the assault against Guam, Saipan and Tinian (Marianas), to commence on the 15th of June 1944; the seizure of Palau on the 8th of September; and the assault against Mindanao, Philippines on the 15th of November, 1944. In addition, the plans call for the capture of southern Formosa and either Amor or Luzon, Philippines, on the 15th of February, 1945. **(Pacific-New Guinea)** Various problems befall Task Force Hurricane on Biak Island. Supply routes are bogged down because of the terrain, and water must be transported inland from the seacoast for the advancing troops. The Japanese do not oppose the progress of the U.S. 186th Infantry, which moves slowly west in an effort to deploy north of Parai, but a decision is made to reduce the enemy resistance in the Ibdi Pocket before renewing the westward attacks. Heavy activity by the enemy in the Hollandia-Aitape area continues as the Japanese maintain their pressure within the Task Force Persecution zone in the vicinity of Yakamul as they maneuver around the Herrick Force to establish positions west of the village. In other activity, enemy Planes attack and damage the U.S.S. *Reid* (DD-369) off western New Guinea. **(China-Burma-India)** Chinese troops assault Japanese positions at Myitkyina, after some 300 casualties, the assault is canceled to allow time to train the fresh U.S. troops. **(Atlantic-Italy-Anzio-Cassino)** In the **U.S. Fifth Army** area, **VI Corps** sector, the 34th and 45th U.S. Divisions drive toward Albano, against heavy resistance. The advance is supported by the 1st Armored Division. Progress is steady as the 168th Infantry, 34th Division seizes Lanuvio. The 100th Battalion (Japanese Americans) meets rigid opposition from a German rear guard unit in the vicinity of Mont du Torri and battles to secure the objective by 01:00 on the 4th. The 133rd Infantry, 34th Division, engages the enemy in furious fighting near Genzano, ending the contest by overrunning the enemy positions prior to dawn on the fourth. The 157th U.S. Infantry, temporarily assigned to the 34th Division, rushes into the 34th sector, bypasses the area being maintained by the Japanese-American Battalion and seizes a key road junction on the Albano Road north of the railroad. The U.S. 36th Division also makes steady progress and captures Nemi and the road junction east of Lake Albano. The 143rd Infantry reduces an enemy strongpoint on Tano Hill. The 36th, led by General Walker, and anxious to distinguish their reputations with the rest of the 5th Army since the Rapido incident, succeed. Included with the capture of Nemi is "Anzio Annie," a massive cannon, which was emplaced on a railway car. The gun weighs more than 450,000 pounds and has a range exceeding 35 miles. The Yanks head for Rome as the Germans withdraw along the entire front in face of the overwhelming Allied strength. The II Corps pours on the pressure with the U.S. 3rd Division and the French plowing along Highway 6, against a staunch enemy rear-guard action. The Germans receive word from Hitler to evacuate Rome and to resist fiercely south of the city, while the 14th German Army and other troops evacuate the city. During the heated struggle for Rome, an American Patrol is under severe fire from the Germans near Valmontone. Private Herbert F. Christian, 15th Infantry, 3rd Division, sacrifices his life to save the remaining 12 men in his Squad. He draws fire from 60 enemy Riflemen, three machine guns and three Tanks. Enemy fire tears his right leg off, but he staggers on his left leg and continues firing his submachine gun. Pvt. Christian makes it to within ten yards of the enemy and continues firing his submachine gun until all his ammunition is expended. Subsequently, enemy fire kills him, however, his sacrifice helps his Squad to escape; he receives the Medal of Honor posthumously. Another remarkable endeavor during this Patrol is that of Private Elden Johnson, also of the 15th Infantry, attacks within five yards of the enemy; he singlehandedly destroys one machine gun crew, but is slain by machine gun fire; he also receives the Medal of Honor posthumously. Elements of the U.S. 88th Division zip through Colonna and reach Tor Spaienza by 04:00 on the fourth, then await orders to move on Rome. Task Force Howze, temporarily attached to the 1st Special Service Force (commanded by General Robert T. Frederick), meets heavy enemy resistance as it pushes up Highway 6, seizing Osteria Finocchio. In addition, the 2nd Moroccan Division deploys just outside of Paliano and Genazzano to protect the right rear of the French troops. In the **British Eighth Army** area, the Canadian 1st Corps seizes the town of Anagni. **(Atlantic-England)** Operation OVERLORD is imminent. The loading of the troops which will assault the beaches at Normandy is complete. The anxious moments begin for the thousands of Allied Soldiers cramped on Vessels in the English Channel. D-Day is scheduled for the 5th of June.

June 4th 1944 — (Southwest Pacific) Plans are being drawn up by General Headquarters for the capture of Noemfoor Island, between Biak and Manokwari. The island is crucial because of its three Airfields. **(Pacific-New Guinea)** There is little activity between the enemy and the Hurricane Force, which is driving west when intelligence states that an enemy attack is probable. The 186th Infantry, attached to the Hurricane Force maintains its Patrols. In the Ibdi area, the 162nd Infantry extends along an island trail making gradual progress. In the Hollandia, the Japanese initiate an Artillery Barrage prior to an unsuccessful assault against the Herrick Force near Yakamul. The Bailey force is ordered to relieve the Herrick Force and works around the enemy, evading a roadblock on the trail to Yakamul. In Naval activity, the U.S.S. *Nashville* (CL-43) and the U.S.S. *Phoenix* (CL-46), both Light Cruisers, are damaged after being attacked by enemy Dive Bombers off western New Guinea. **(China-Burma-India)** On the Salween Front, the Japanese guns in the heights near Huei-jen Bridge are put out of action by the Chinese. In additional activity, the Chinese 87th Division drives along the Burma Road, while the 88th advances from Pingka, closing on Lung-ling. The New Chinese 28th Division seizes Lameng and fights a containing action at Sung Shan. **(Atlantic-Italy-Anzio-Rome)** Elements of the U.S. 5th Army enter Rome to the jubilation of the Italian citizens. The Yanks, under the command of General Mark Clark, are the first victorious troops

ever to enter Rome from the south. It is a contingent of the 88th Reconnaissance Troop that first enters the city. In the **VI Corps** area, the 1st Armored Division, commanded by General Harmon, seizes Albano then rumbles along Highway 7 into Rome. In other VI Corps activity, the 34th and 45th U.S. Divisions secure crossing sites south of Rome, while the 36th Division pushes into the eastern outskirts of the city. In the **II Corps** area, the 1st Special Service Force and the U.S. 88th Division get snagged west of Centocelle for almost nine hours but eventually advance to the city. The 1st Special Service Force spreads out and secures the bridges that span the Tiber to the north of Ponte Margherita, as the 88th has elements take Ponte Milvio and Pinte del Duca d'Aosta. Ponte Cavour falls to a contingent of the 85th Division, while others sever Highway 7. A Battalion of Tanks from the First Armored is with the Special Service Force when it reaches the city limits, but Antitank guns hold up the advance. Generals Clark and Keyes arrive at the scene and are informed that the lead Tank has been knocked out and that a flanking movement is necessary to get into Rome. By late afternoon all enemy resistance is halted and the Americans along with French and British contingents, flow into the city, finding all bridges intact. At 01:30 on the 5th, Old Glory and the British Union Jack are raised simultaneously on two vacant flag poles at the monument to King Victor Emmanuel II. In other activity, the French relieve the U.S. Third Division and take responsibility for the right flank of the II Corps. In the **British Eighth Army** area, the British regroup add two fresh Armored Divisions to pursue the retreating Germans. **(Atlantic-England)** A conference is held at 04:00 at Portsmouth to determine feasibility of invading France on the 5th; advance elements are already at sea. If the invasion is aborted, the tides will not be adequate for several weeks, causing severe problems, including a prolonged period of time for keeping troops on board Ships. The alternative is to put the troops back on shore and perhaps alert the Germans. Another meeting is held at 21:00 and all matters are considered. British Sir Admiral Ramsay feels a landing can be made, but that adjusting Naval Gunfire will be difficult because of foul weather. British General Montgomery feels that the invasion should go off on time, fearing delay will make things worse. General Eisenhower, the Supreme Allied Commander of Operation OVERLORD, aware of the terrible weather between England and Normandy, makes the final decision and delays the scheduled invasion for one day, to June 6, stating: "I'M QUITE POSITIVE WE MUST GIVE THE ORDER ... I DON'T LIKE IT, BUT THERE IT IS...I DON'T SEE HOW WE CAN POSSIBLY DO ANYTHING ELSE." Fast Destroyers are sped to catch the advance Vessels in the westernmost sector and turn them back. **(Atlantic-French West Africa)** A German Submarine, the U-505 is captured off the coast of North Africa. This is the first time an American Force has captured an enemy Warship since the War of 1812! The effort results from strict planning over months. The Task Force, including the Carrier Escort *Guadalcanal* (CVE-60), commanded by Captain Dan V. Gallery, assisted by its Aircraft and five Destroyers, pull off the dangerous operation. The Destroyer *Chatelain* (DE-149) radios possible hostile sound contact at 11:10. The *Guadalcanal*, having a thin frame, veers off to safer waters, leaving the hunt to her Planes and the Destroyers. Two Fighter Planes commence the attack; it is followed by a Destroyer assault. The Submarine reverses engines to evade disaster and for a time believes she is out of sight, but the Planes overhead have a bead on it and stream bullets toward the Ship's position to guide the trailing Destroyers. At 11:01, the *Chatelain* discharges a massive amount of depth charges. Within a minute and a half the German Submarine surfaces and small arms fire criss-crosses the conning tower. The hatch opens and the Germans, who have set the crippled Submarine to flooding, make for their life rafts. During the unusual encounter, the guns have been ordered to cease fire as the Germans are abandoning Ship. Simultaneously, specially trained men are heading for the Submarine to board. One man is a photography specialist, detailed to photograph the inside of the Submarine in the event it can't be salvaged. Others are to prevent it from sinking and keep the engines running. The Submarine is circling like a runaway bull, its rudders jammed, causing a circular cruise to the right. The Sub is boarded and although large streams of water are flooding it, the Navy plugs the leak, and the Submarine is taken intact. The Captain had been thrown from the Vessel by the exploding gunfire, but he is captured too. Only one German is found dead on the deck. After a strenuous round up, which causes the Submarine to rip a hole in the U.S.S. *Pillsbury*, the *Guadalcanal* moves back into the area and tows the Submarine (dubbed Junior) until a Tug can be brought to take over. The enemy Sailors are transferred to the *Guadalcanal* and given food and cigarettes as they ponder their fate, in awe of the capture of their Vessel. The Nazi ensign is lowered and the Stars and Stripes is flying on board the captured prize, with the limp Nazi ensign humbly underneath as the U-505 is taken on a 2,500 mile jaunt to Bermuda, reaching there on the 19th of June. The boarding party had been led by Lt. Albert Leroy David (becomes recipient of Medal of Honor for his actions).

June 4th 1944 — The German Submarine U-505 after capture by U.S. Naval forces.

June 4th 1944 — Rome, subsequent to its capture by the U.S. Fifth Army.

June 5th 1944 — (Southwest Pacific) General Krueger is informed by General MacArthur that the Noemfoor assault will be directed by the Alamo Force. **(Pacific-New Guinea)** Task Force Hurricane is directed to speed up the operation to take the enemy Airfields at Biak. The U.S. 186th Infantry renews its westward advance without opposition and reaches a primary ridge, northeast of Mokmer Airfield. The ridge is cautiously scaled by the 3rd Battalion. On the following day, the 186th will descend the heights, but the assault is postponed because of supply problems, until the 7th. The 162nd Infantry beats inland to the vicinity of Ibdi and hooks up with elements of the 186th, but the enemy holding Parai Defile withstands the American attempts to dislodge them despite Naval gun support. In the Hollandia-Aitape area, advance elements of the 6th Division arrive at Toem and relieve the 158th Infantry (Task Force Tornado). The Herrick Force (Task Force Persecution) returns to the beachhead from Yakamul, while the Bailey Force completes its overland march to about two miles west of Yakamul and drives along the coast to Driniumor. During the fighting near Yakamul, the 1st Battalion, 126th Infantry, has killed between 200 and 250 Japanese while suffering 18 killed, eight missing and 75 wounded. In other activity, the Japanese abandon a ridge north of Afua, as the 127th Infantry mounts a strong effort to take it after failing for several days. **(Pacific-Philippines)** The U.S.S. *Nautilus* (SS-168) surfaces near Tucuran, Mindanao and delivers war supplies to the Guerrillas. **(China-Burma-India)** General Stilwell considers a request from Chiang Kai-shek, that additional B-29s be committed to the eastern Chinese arena. Stilwell states that if the situation deteriorates further, he will request additional Planes. On the Salween Front, 20,000 Chinese troops of the 71st Army cross the Salween River. The offensive to take Lung-ling is progressing. In the **11th Army Group** area, the **British Fourteenth Army** successfully concludes the battle for Kohima as the British 2nd Division reduces the enemy on Aradura Spur lying south of the town. Additional British units drive against the enemy on the Kohima-Imphal Road. In Thailand, the U.S. XX Bomber Command, flying its first combat mission, launches a large force of B-29s against Bangkok. **(Atlantic-Italy)** The **U.S. Fifth Army** pursues retreating Germans in the vicinity of Rome. The VI Corps thrusts along Highway 1, while the II Corps drives along Highway 2. The U.S. 3rd Division is assigned to garrison Rome and to protect the Vatican. Many U.S. troops receive the opportunity to meet with the Pope (Pius XII) and some are given specially blessed Rosary beads. General Clark and thousands of troops attend a subsequent mass of thanksgiving celebrated by the Fifth Army Chaplain in the Church of Santa Maria Degli Angeli at Piazza Esedra. In the **VI Corps** area, the British 1st and 5th Divisions, moving in the coastal area, reach the lower Tiber where the construction of bridges begins. U.S. Combat Teams A, and B, spearhead the advance of the 1st Armored and 36th U.S. Divisions as they burst across the Tiber, while retreating Germans escape down Highway 1. The II Corps hammers north with the 85th speeding on the left and the 88th racing on the right, supported by the 91st and 117th Reconnaissance Squadrons on the flanks. The French move quickly to the Tiber and halt until the South African 6th Armored Division can advance and pass its front. In the **British Eighth Army**, area, the South African 6th Armored moves east of Rome in pursuit of the Germans who are retreating north along Route 3. In other activity, the British 6th Armored Division, driving along Route 4, encounters enemy positions north of Rome; the bridges leading to and from

Rome have been spared. An agreement had been approved in Berlin to spare Rome because of its historical and cultural value. German troops had control of Rome, but the Vatican, although encircled had been unscathed. The glory of seizing Rome is soon overshadowed by the invasion of Normandy on the following day and from that point forward, differences of opinion remain within the Allied ranks. General Clark would like to drive north with his full force and be in southern France prior to launching Operation ANVIL. He and Churchill and Alexander are of the same mind, desiring a quick victory in northern Italy followed by a rapid thrust eastward toward the Balkans to meet the Russians as far to the east as possible. On the other hand, General Marshall and President Roosevelt want a quick defeat of Hitler's forces prior to finishing off Japan. The final disposition is that the Fifth Army is to lose troops to the operation in France under Eisenhower. Clark loses seven Divisions and the Canadian American Special Service Force in addition to the Paratroop units and many of the Artillery and special units such as Engineers and Signal Corps, seriously gutting the Fifth Army. With such significant depletion of resources, it will be up to the British Eighth Army to bear the heavy burden of responsibility in Italy. The 92nd Division, comprised of colored Soldiers and mostly white Officers, will be coming from the States to bolster Clark's Fifth Army. **(Atlantic-France)** Terrible weather continues to pound the coast of France and the English Channel, forcing the Germans to cancel Air Patrols and to leave Minelayer Vessels in port. The Germans feel there is no chance of any type assault in this weather, which includes winds of hurricane strength. In England, the Allies are again up early, holding another meeting to determine the status of the invasion of Normandy. The meteorologists predict a break in the weather on the 6th, while mighty winds whack their positions. At 04:15, Ike orders the attack. Within 24 hours, the English Channel bursts with thousands of Ships and men en route to strike the Germans in France. Many at the Staff meeting request permission to go aboard the attack Vessels, but Eisenhower refuses because of the possibility of major losses. The most vociferous is Winston Churchill, who after being refused permission by Ike, adamantly tells him that although he has been given command of the operation by both Britain and the United States, he (Ike) is not in Command of British Administration. Churchill then states: "SINCE THIS IS TRUE, IT IS NOT PART OF YOUR RESPONSIBILITY, MY DEAR GENERAL, TO DETERMINE THE EXACT COMPOSITION OF ANY SHIP'S COMPANY IN HIS MAJESTY'S' FLEET." ... "THIS BEING TRUE; BY SHIPPING MYSELF AS A BONA FIDE MEMBER OF A SHIP'S COMPLEMENT, IT WOULD BE BEYOND YOUR AUTHORITY TO PREVENT MY GOING." Ike, however, receives some unexpected assistance. The King of England receives rumors about the anticipated exploits of the Prime Minister and speeds a message: "IF THE PRIME MINISTER FEELS IT NECESSARY TO GO ON THE EXPEDITION, HE FEELS IT TO BE EQUALLY HIS DUTY AND PRIVILEGE TO PARTICIPATE AT THE HEAD OF HIS TROOPS." The matter is closed. Churchill does not go with the Invasion Force. General Eisenhower remains with the 101st Airborne until the last of the Planes are in the air, then takes a two hour drive back to his Headquarters. In other activity, Allied Planes strike enemy positions in Wimereaux, France. The 489th Bomber Group participates in the raid. Enemy fire severely damages the Plane of Lt. Colonel Leon R. Vance. Although badly wounded, he manages to get the Plane back to the English coast where he orders the men to bail out. Lt. Colonel Vance ditches his Craft in the English Channel; his body is secured within an hour by rescue teams; he is awarded the Medal of Honor posthumously. In Naval activity, the U.S.S. *Osprey* (AM-56), a Minesweeper is sunk after striking a mine off the coast of Normandy and the LST 981 is damaged after striking a mine.

June 6th-27th 1944 — (The INVASION of NORMANDY) — The momentous decision to land at Normandy and begin to liberate the Continent has been long in coming. The most opportune time, based on complex calculations, was to be early June when the moon and tides would be best for this tremendous amphibious gamble. General Eisenhower, after assuming command of Operation "OVERLORD" during January of 1944 would proclaim; "AN AROUSED DEMOCRACY IS THE MOST FORMIDABLE FIGHTING MACHINE THAT CAN BE DEVISED." The stage has been set with the world as the anxious audience.

Prior to this invasion, thousands of aerial photographs have been taken of the shoreline defenses. German General Rommel received orders from Hitler on the 15th of January, directing him to insure that the coast of France be impregnable against Allied invasion. Rommel masterminded a complex and extremely formidable defense system to thwart the Allied attack. The primary concentration is at Calais, the narrowest route across the English Channel. The Allies produced these thoughts by increasing air activity over the area and planting false intelligence that General Patton would lead the assault. Hitler insisted that his Tanks be kept far from the water so they could be diverted wherever necessary. While the Germans pondered the point of attack. The British Isles were transformed into a giant arsenal. The Germans were simultaneously turning the coastline of France into a death trap. Submarine mines lurk offshore for Vessels nearing the beaches. Millions of additional land mines, many plastic and undetectable by normal methods, lay hidden under the beaches. Steel barriers resembling huge pitch forks are scattered throughout the minefields. Machine guns guard the cliffs, while elite Riflemen are poised in every direction, supplemented by mortars and Field Artillery.

The huge German war machine has also constructed Infantry and Tank traps. In addition, artificial canals which can be easily flooded are constructed to trap approaching ground troops or Paratroops who miss their drop point. Hedgerows and fields have been converted to independent fortresses with interconnecting tunnels. Also, the Germans have established rail tracks to mobilize gargantuan guns with a range of more than 35 miles, enough to reach Allied Battleships offshore.

More than 5,000 overloaded Warships, Troop Transports, carrying more than 150,000 men and Landing Craft steam toward the coast of France, halting a little over 10 miles from land, close enough for the massive Battleships to pound the coast. Meanwhile, Planes based in England commence an enormous Air strike, pummeling positions all along the French coast. The Aircraft also strike enemy Vessels in the canals and rolling trains of boxcars. However, the vast majority of enemy guns, which had been deeply embedded in bunkers, withstand the barrage and remain fully operational. Three Divisions of British and American Paratroopers are dropped behind enemy lines at 02:00, prior to the main invasion, to cut off enemy reinforcements attempting to reach the beachhead. In addition the Paratroopers are to secure breakout routes for the Amphibious troops. Four hundred thirty-two Troop Transport Planes carry 6,600 men of General Taylor's 101st Airborne into action, attempting to drop them along the Cotentin coast; anti-aircraft fire and foul weather causes about 60 Planes to miss the mark, some by as much as 20 miles.

In a swift synchronized movement, coinciding with a tolerable tide and the slowly rising sun, the U.S. Infantry storm ashore in Normandy at 06:30, following cessation of the bombardment, achieving the element of surprise. The U.S. Fourth Division (V Corps), secures Utah Beach with relative ease, but the scene at Omaha is gruesome as the Amphibious troops are forced to battle ferocious elements, with wild seas crashing against the Landing Craft, spooning them toward the beach defended by the elite 352nd German Division, which commands the heights. Elements of the U.S. 1st and 29th Divisions are pummeled, virtually trapped on the sparse beach; 27 of their 32 Tanks remain offshore. The Yanks inch forward through a wall of fire. In conjunction with the invasion, British Planes plaster the area with 13,000 bombs; ascending clouds of smoke and dust, impair the Pilots' vision. While taking precautions against striking Allied positions in error, the majority of the bombs strike harmlessly three miles inland, giving little aid to the men on Omaha. The Yanks fight viciously. Fortunately, it is the battle hardened 1st Division, rather than a fresh Division that is trapped behind the seawall. By 12:00, only a scant portion of the first waves of 34,000 men and 3,400 Vehicles have made it to the beach and only six of 16 bulldozers are on the beachhead, creating a "critical situation." A secondary Force of 25,000 additional troops is due at 12:00. Despite all the unexpected setbacks on Omaha, the Yanks tend their wounded, cover their dead and hold on tight. Finally, toward the end of the day, the Yanks drive a wedge in the enemy's defenses, advancing far enough to forestall annihilation. By day's end, over 50,000 Yanks hold the beaches, ensuring the landing's tactical success. Meanwhile. The British and the Canadians who land a few hours after the Americans, quickly secure Gold, Juno, and Sword beachheads against nominal opposition. The combined casualties for the Allies is a little over 10,000 men, considerably lower than anticipated.

The Germans, stunned by the magnitude and location of the invasion, attempt to react, but this time they are thoroughly foiled; Old Glory is implanted for the duration. Giant Allied Naval guns pound the inland area, making it difficult for enemy reinforcements to rush to the scene. In addition, the Airdrop of the three Paratroop Divisions has placed the elite troops behind enemy lines; they secure the bulk of their objectives and concentrate on halting any advancing German reinforcements. Also, German Sea Power is not in evidence during the landing and enemy Planes are insufficient to deter or affect the invasion. An enemy counterattack is mounted against the British sector, but the beachhead perimeter contains a firm foundation, allowing the British to handily repulse the one solitary major assault mounted against the Allied Invasion Force for the duration of the struggle for the peninsula. Meanwhile, German General von Ronstedt directs the German 7th Army to destroy the beachhead by nightfall. Orders stream in to Normandy from General Alfred Jodl at Berlin, clamoring for all Reserve units to move against the attackers. One exception is the German Fifteenth Army, standing at the Channel near Pas de Calais, awaiting the arrival of another Allied Fleet. For several days, there are exaggerated fears on the beachhead that if the enemy mounts a major counterattack, the toehold will be jeopardized. One advantage held by the Allies is that British code-breakers have been able to decipher German messages since the very early days of the war and continue to intercept valuable intelligence on German intentions.

This heated vehemently fought contest for control of France manifests the pinnacle of endurance. The Germans, ordered by Hitler to fight where they stand; the Allies are instructed by Eisenhower to attack and conquer. As the Infantry perseveres along the beaches, British Commandos and U.S. Rangers scale dangerous sea cliffs to dislodge enemy strongpoints and drive the defenders back. The American Rangers, commanded by Lt. Colonel James E. Rudder, struggle to seize the enemy coastal guns at Pointe du Hoe. The crack German troops are not as hard on the Rangers as the elements; they are scaling 2,000 foot ragged cliffs, impeded by dangerously wet slippery rocks. Their hands have difficulty grasping a hold on the wet ropes and in addition, the Germans are tossing hand grenades down the slopes. The Rangers force their way to the top. Suddenly, the Rangers get some unexpected help; the U.S. Navy moves in a Destroyer which pays its respects to the Krauts on the high ground, terminating the tossing of grenades. The Germans take off while the Navy's oversized long range grenades are popping all over the area. The enemy and the coastal guns are soon spotted, hidden in an apple orchard about 1,200 yards from the Rangers. Soon after, the unfired guns are captured and the remaining enemy defending force is eliminated. The Germans mount counterattacks to recapture the guns, but the formidable Provisional Ranger Battalion holds out for two days, until reinforcements arrive.

As daylight disappears on the 6th, all five beachheads are secure. In the weeks to follow, man-made harbors are constructed off shore, enabling a steady stream of Vehicles and equipment to be shipped inland, further threatening the German hold on France. In a strange course of events, nature paralyzes the Allied offensive on the 19th, an accomplishment the enemy could not achieve. A violent storm suddenly erupts and the seas swell and churn great waves, crushing Ships against the rocks. Portions of the British harbor are severely damaged and the American harbor sector is totally demolished, sweeping both men and machines into the unyielding sea, and severing the lifeline of the desperately needed supplies. Mud and torrential rains hinder the men on both sides. Over 800 Allied Vessels are thrown from side to side until some are finally flung helplessly to the beach. The terrible three-day storm is the worst to strike France in nearly fifty years; it takes an astonishing toll and continues to worsen, however, the storm vanishes as quickly as it appeared, ending the threat as the skies clear mysteriously on the 22nd.

It takes three additional days to alleviate the supply problems and reorganize the offensive. The British and Canadians are ordered to attack Caen. On the 25th, three U.S. Divisions sweep the peninsula, moving abreast toward the strategic port at Cherbourg against heavy opposition. The virtually unopposed Allied bombing missions to level Cherbourg have been extremely successful. However, the German ground troops remain undaunted, as the American Divisions press forward. The treacherous hedgerow warfare is a stunning experience for the Yanks, but their flexibility enables them to learn quickly. The Tanks are stymied by the hedgerows, which prevent passage until Sgt. Culin, an innovative Yank, invents a new tool for the Tanks by confiscating abandoned enemy steel and applying two improvised steel blades to each Tank, allowing the blades to act as scythes and permit passage. By the 26th of June, the enemy is surrounded at Cherbourg. Remnant defenders hold out at a Naval Arsenal refusing to capitulate until finally convinced on the 27th that their effort is courageous but futile; they too surrender.

Twenty-one horrifying days of incessant battle have passed since landing at Normandy, but Cherbourg is liberated and returned to the local government. The port, thought to be totally destroyed by the Germans, is rapidly repaired in un-der three weeks by the superb efforts of the American Engineers, guaranteeing ground access to the remainder of the Allied Forces offshore. By the end of June, one million Allied troops are ashore. Cherbourg is secure and the ongoing influx of men and supplies doom the German Armies in France. The U.S. 1st Army, commanded by General Omar Bradley, is composed of four Corps, comprising two Armored Divisions and 11 Infantry Divisions. The strength of the British-Canadian force is about the same. They begin to advance toward Paris.

June 6th 1944 — Admiral Kirk, General Bradley and Admiral Strubble, peering toward the Normandy Beachheads.

U.S. Combat troops hitting the beaches at Normandy.

Yank reinforcements off Normandy.

The Quarry near Omaha Beach.

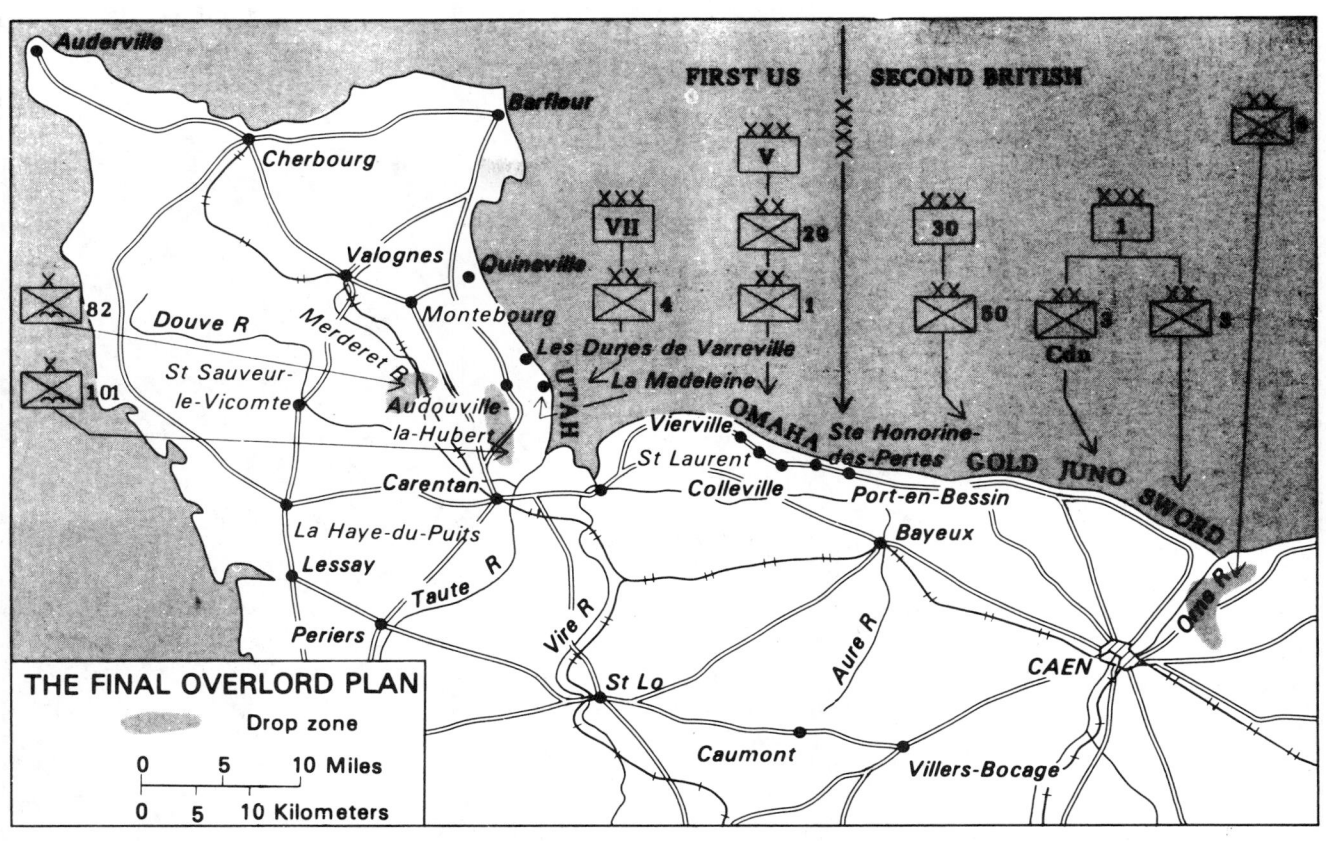

THE FINAL OVERLORD PLAN

FIRST US   SECOND BRITISH

Drop zone

0   5   10 Miles

0   5   10 Kilometers

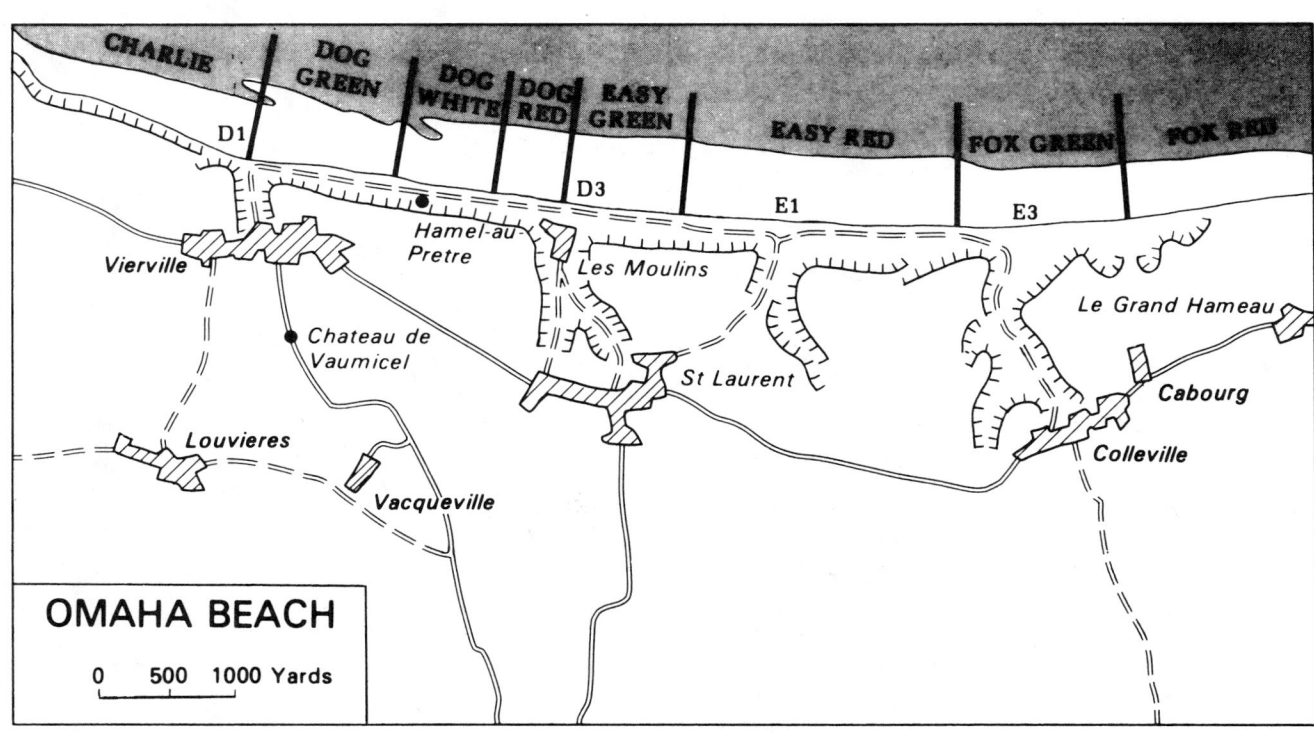

OMAHA BEACH

0   500   1000 Yards

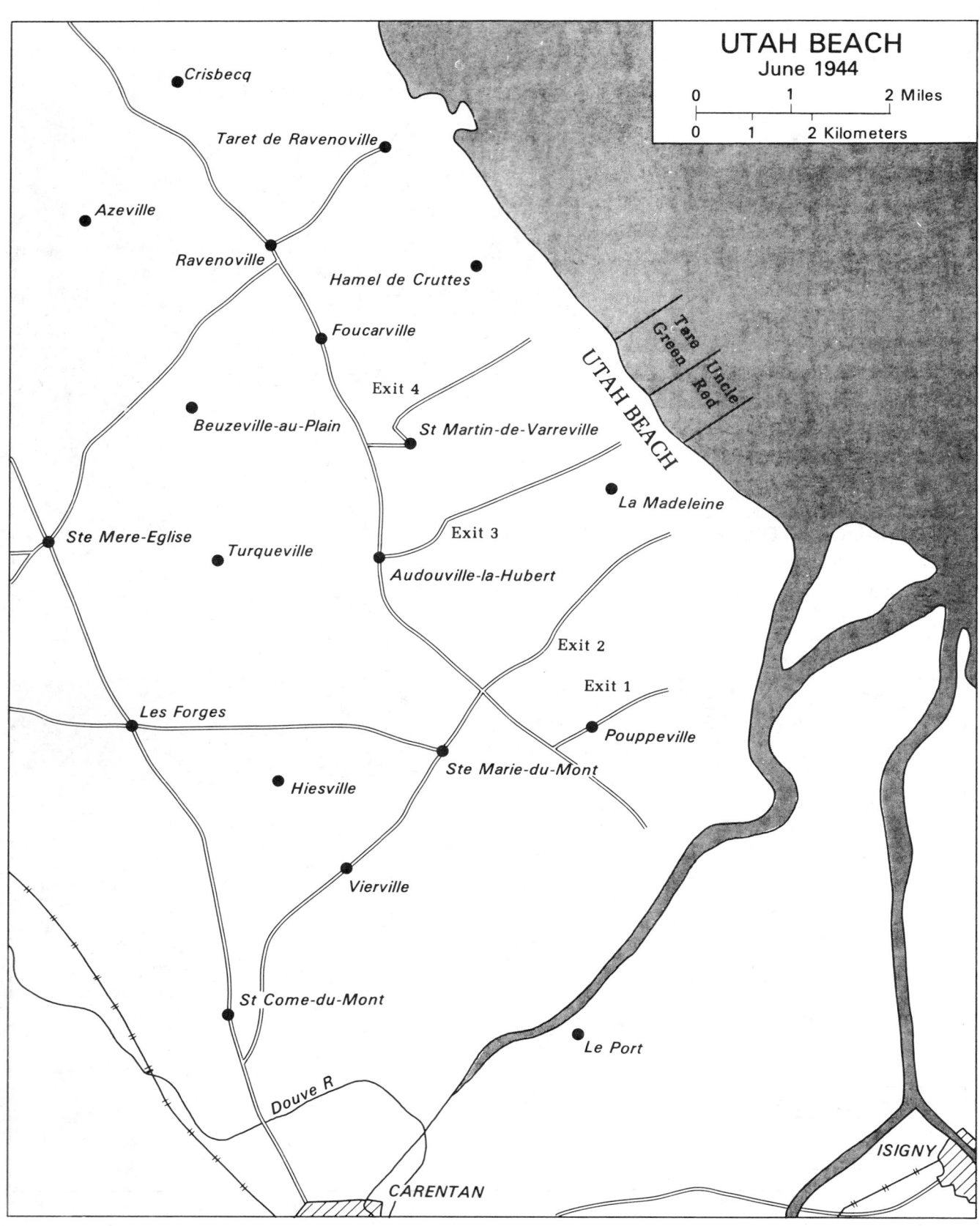

UTAH BEACH
June 1944

0		1		2 Miles

0	1		2 Kilometers

Crisbecq

Taret de Ravenoville

Azeville

Ravenoville

Hamel de Cruttes

Foucarville

Exit 4

Beuzeville-au-Plain

St Martin-de-Varreville

Tare
Green
Uncle
Red

UTAH BEACH

La Madeleine

Ste Mere-Eglise

Turqueville

Exit 3

Audouville-la-Hubert

Exit 2

Exit 1

Les Forges

Pouppeville

Ste Marie-du-Mont

Hiesville

Vierville

St Come-du-Mont

Le Port

Douve R

CARENTAN

ISIGNY

U.S. troops at a seawall on the Normandy Beachhead.

Old Glory, escorting U.S. Naval Landing Craft at Normandy.

June 6th 1944 — (United States) The Joint War Planning Committee issues the study "Operations Against Japan." The plans call for the seizure of the Bonins and the Ryukyus, plus additional attacks against the coast of China April 1st-30th, followed by a period of consolidation prior to the inva sion of the home islands of Japan starting with Kyushu on October 1st 1945 and Honshu on December 31st. In other activity, John Eisenhower, son of General Ike Eisenhower, graduates from West Point (Cadet No. 14,098). General Marshall permits him to take his leave in Europe to spend some time with his dad. They travel together until John is ordered to report back to the States by July 1st. **(Pacific-Celebes)** While passing through the Strait of Makassar carrying out its mission of spying on the Japanese Navy in its sector, the Submarine U.S.S. *Harder* is detected by a Japanese Patrol Boat. The *Harder* holds the enemy Vessel in abeyance, then retires, rather than risking a confrontation. It moves toward the Sibutu Passage, and discovers an enemy Convoy heading south, traveling at about 15 knots. As the Submarine selects its target, enemy Destroyers begin closing to 1,150 yards. Commander, Sam D. Dealey orders a dive and then attacks; two of the "fish" destroy the *Minatsuki*. **(Pacific-Marshalls)** U.S. Task Force 58, commanded by Vice Admiral Mitscher, embarks from the Marshalls for the Marianas to initiate the invasions of Guam, Saipan and Tinian. Japan expects the attack against the Palaus, not the Marianas and rushes 80 Planes there. **(Pacific-New Guinea)** The 186th Infantry (Task Force Hurricane) prepares to assault Mokmer Airfield (Biak), but postpones the assault until the 7th, to ensure proper amounts of supplies are on hand. The assault team is to take the Airfield then immediately push south to the coast. In other activity, the 162nd Infantry still is engaged in brisk fighting in the coastal area. **(Pacific-Philippines)** On Mindanao, the Japanese move over 1,200 P.O.W.s by truck to Davao harbor, from where they are moved to Manila; the men are bound to each other by rope and blindfolded. Between the harbor and Manila, two men escape by jumping overboard and safely reach Guerrilla forces. The Japanese soon transport more P.O.W.s as they begin retreating north, before an American onslaught. **(Pacific-South China Sea)** The U.S.S. *Raton* (SS-270) sinks the Japanese Coastal Defense Vessel No. 15. **(China-Burma-India)** American General Stilwell increases the amount of tonnage to be delivered across the Hump to offset the Japanese offensive in China. He brings the total supplies of the Fourteenth Air Force to 10,000 tons, the amount previously requested by General Chennault. **(Atlantic-France)** Western

Europe is invaded by the Allied Expeditionary Force. The English Channel is consumed with an armada of over 5,000 Warships (packed with countless numbers of combat and support troops) and unchallenged Allied air cover. Pre-invasion minesweeping operations are coordinated with a massive Naval and Air bombardment. Maximum Naval gunfire efforts are contributed by support groups commanded by Rear Admirals C.F. Bryant and M.L. Deyo. The cover fire extends well inland and with its spectacular accuracy is able to hinder the advancement of enemy reinforcements. Operation OVERLORD, the invasion of Normandy is under the Supreme Command of American General Eisenhower. British General Montgomery is placed in command of all land troops. British Air Chief Marshall Leigh-Mallory commands the Air Forces and the Allied Naval Forces are commanded by British Admiral Ramsay. The Invasion Force is split into two Task Forces; the Western (American) Task Force, commanded by Rear Admiral A.G. Kirk, U.S.N. It is sub-dived into two Assault Forces; "O" commanded by Rear Admiral J. L. Hall, U.S.N., and "U" under the command of Rear Admiral D.P. Moon, U.S.N. They land the 1st United States Army, commanded by Lt. General Omar N. Bradley, U.S.A., on "Omaha" and "Utah" beaches. The other Task Force, Eastern (British) lands the British 2nd Army, commanded by British Lt. General Myles C. Dempsey on Gold, Juno, and Sword beaches, situated to the left of the Americans.

During this operation, German General Rommel is back in Germany celebrating his wife's birthday and has to rush back to the front to deal with the threat. In the **U.S. First Army** area at 06:30, the **VII Corps**, commanded by Major General J. Lawton Collins, assaults Utah Beach, which lies west of Vire Estuary. The objective of the Corps is to secure the beachhead and charge toward Cherbourg to seize it as soon as possible. A few hours prior to the landing, the 82nd and 101st U.S. Airborne Divisions bail out behind enemy lines between Carentan and Ste Mere-Eglise where they successfully secure routes in the vicinity of the St. Martin-de-Varreville-Pouppeville region to be used by the land troops pushing out from the American beachheads. Contact is made between the Airborne troops and the Seaborne 1st Battalion, 325th Glider Infantry Regiment (82nd Airborne). Heavy fighting ensues between the Paratroopers and the enemy in the vicinity of Foucarville, which falls to the Americans during the night of the 6th. Enemy resistance is also fierce in the vicinity of Carentan. Ste Mere-Eglise is seized by the 82nd Airborne, but the enemy resistance prevents them from securing the crossings at the Douve and Merderet Rivers. As could be expected with an invasion of this magnitude, many things go wrong including mixups on the drop, but the Paratroopers excel in spite of the difficulties and manage to hook up and accomplish most of their mission. They concentrate on disrupting enemy movements and communications, in addition to seizing bridges and other objectives. At H Hour minus 2, the 4th Cavalry Group detachment lands at Iles St. Marcouf without opposition. The U.S. 4th Division reinforced by the 359th Infantry, 90th Division hits the beach and secures it against nominal opposition. The U.S. 8th Infantry which had spearheaded the assault advances some units to the Les Forges crossroads, while other elements of the 8th Infantry drive to the vicinity of Turqueville, where they detect enemy forces between them and the 82nd Airborne, holding Ste Mere-Eglise. A Tank Infantry Task Force (325th Glider Infantry 82nd Airborne and 746th Tank Battalion) is rushed in to Les Forges, but its efforts to penetrate the enemy salient and reach the 82nd Airborne are repulsed. In other activity at Utah Beach, the U.S. 12th Infantry drives to the vicinity of the Beuzeville-au-Plain region to the left of the positions of the 101st Airborne and the 82nd Infantry moves along the coast reaching Hamel-de-Cruttes-St. German-de Varreville.

In the **V Corps** sector, 1st Division reinforced by the 116th Infantry, 29th Division, commanded by Major General Leonard T. Gerow, debarks east of the VII Corps landing on Omaha Beach where enemy resistance is bitter. In addition to the precarious positions on the beachhead, the Landing Force is struck by the wild surf which takes a heavy toll on men and equipment. The Germans dispatch 15 E-Boats from Cherbourg to engage the Armada. When Bradley is informed at 05:47 of the impending sea duel, he and Major General Kean are talking aboard the *Augusta*. General Kean glances at Ike and smiles. By 06:15, General Bradley, aboard the Augusta offshore is informed that the first wave is ashore. Twenty seven of the Destroyer Tanks become stuck offshore by the heavy seas. This mishap, combined with many of the Paratroopers missing their mark, compounds the problems on Omaha. The invasion is spearheaded by the 116th Infantry, 29th Division, and the 16th Infantry, 1st Division, and a subsequent landing by the balance of the 1st Division later in the day. The 2nd and 15th Ranger Battalions (attached to 116th Infantry) are ordered to capture Pointe de Hoe. Elements of the 2nd Battalion successfully ascend the heights and secure the objective and its coastal battery. The Rangers withstand vicious enemy counterattacks for two days. Additional Rangers and 116th Infantry units land in the vicinity of Les Moulins, capturing it. In other activity, the 3rd Battalion 16th Infantry seizes Le Grand Hameau. Offshore, Naval Support Group Surface Vessels, commanded by U.S. Rear Admirals M.L. Deyo and C.F. Bryant, consistently bombard inland areas, giving welcome assistance to the Assault troops as they advance. Simultaneously the Navy pounds the ground where the enemy might attempt to rush in reinforcements. During the course of the days brutalizing activity, the U.S. Navy sustains some losses. The Destroyer *Cory* (DD-463) and the Submarine Chaser PC-1261 both strike mines and sink. In another incident, the LST 375 becomes damaged after becoming involved in a collision. In other activity, 1,300 R.A.F. Planes strike enemy positions along the French coast from Cherbourg to the Seine.

In the British sector, the British 2nd Army, commanded by Lt. General M. C. Dempsey, lands on three beaches, Gold, Sword, and Juno, between Le Hamel and Ouistreham and begins moving inland towards Bayeux and Caen. In the British 30th Corps area, elements of the 50th British Division, reinforced by Armor units of the 79th Armored and the 47th Royal Marine Commandos, land near Le Hamel-La Riviere (Gold) sector and encounter heavy resistance at Le Hamel as they advance toward Bayeux and make contact with the Canadian 3rd Division. The combined units mount a morning assault against Bayeux. The 1st Corps hits the beaches at Juno and Sword, from where it launches a drive toward Caen in an effort to hook up with the British Paratroopers who had landed during the early morning hours and are holding strategic bridges over the Orne River and the Caen Canal near Benouville. The German 22nd Panzers put up stiff resistance and withstand a British attempt to seize Caen. The Germans mount a counterattack to shoot the gap between the British 3rd Division and the Canadians near Caen but are repulsed. Brigadier General Theodore Roosevelt Jr. receives the Medal of Honor for his extraordinary leadership during the initial landings. Private Carlton W. Barrett, 18th Infantry 1st Infantry Division; Technician Fifth Grade John J. Pinder, Jr., 16th Infantry, 1st Division; and First Lieutenant Jimmie W. Monteith Jr., 16th Infantry, 1st Division, are also awarded the Medal of Honor for bravery during the invasion. **(Atlantic-Rumania)** U.S. Fifteenth Air Force Planes based in Russia, launch a strike against the enemy Airfield at Galati, Rumania. The Assault Force comprises 104 B-17s and 42 P-51s. **(Atlantic-Italy)** In the **U.S. Fifth Army** area, elements of the 1st Armored Division, VI Corps, sprint to within 25 miles from Rome; the U.S. 168th Infantry, 34th Division, glides through its positions prior to midnight and keeps moving. In the **British Eighth Army** area, the South African 6th Armored Division advances to Civita Castellana. The British 6th Armored Division pushes to Monterotondo.

June 7th 1944 — (United States) General Marshall denies General Stilwell's request for additional B-29s for the Fourteenth Air Force. Also, the success of the Normandy invasion is considered a tremendous success for Admiral King; he is also greatly responsible for the successes at Saipan later in the month. In other activity, the U.S.S. *Gudgeon* (SS-211) is reported as missing and presumed lost in the Pacific. **(Pacific-Celebes Sea)** The U.S.S. *Harder* (SS-257) sinks the Destroyer *Hayanami*. **(Pacific-New Guinea)** Heavy fighting continues on Biak as the U.S. 186th Infantry, using Air and Artillery cover fire, drives unopposed across Mokmer Airfield reaching the beach without incident, but the Japanese quickly bombard the beachhead. Subsequently, the 186th is forced to receive its supplies by sea and the Craft must move under severe enemy fire. In other activity, the 162nd Infantry deployed in the coastal sector begins to move to the Mokmer Airdrome by sea for the purpose of reducing the enemy at the Parai Defile. American fire power is also intensified against the caves slightly east of Mokmer Airfield and against enemy held positions near Ibdi. In the Hollandia-Aitape area, the Americans (1st and 2nd Battalions 158th Infantry, Task Force Tornado) extend their Patrols toward Maffin No. 1, meeting no opposition. In the sector governed by Task Force Persecution, fire fights develop between the Americans and the Japanese within 1,300 yards west of Afua along the Afua-Palauru supply line route. The U.S. Navy establishes an Advanced Base at Hollandia. **(China-Burma-India)** U.S. General Boatner is informed by Chinese Commanders that the present strength of Chinese units in the Myitkyina area is dangerously low. Offensive activity by the Allies is kept to a minimum to prepare for a general offensive on the 10th. **Atlantic-England-**

France) General Eisenhower departs England, for Omaha Beach in Normandy, to visit the 1st and 29th U.S. Divisions, which have broken through from the beachhead. The Destroyer transporting Eisenhower, runs aground during the day, forcing him to change to another Vessel, but he eventually meets with Bradley and stops at every beach sector. In the **U.S. First Army Corps** area, Eisenhower orders the V and VII Corps to seize Carentan and Isigny. The 101st Airborne gets the VII Corps assignment to take Carentan and the 29th Division is assigned responsibility for the successful seizure of Isigny. In other D-Day plus 1 activity, elements (12th and 22nd Infantries) of the U.S. 4th Division push north and meet substantial enemy resistance near Azeville and Crisbecq, where the Germans retain fortified bunkers. In the vicinity of Ste Mere-Eglise the U.S. 8th Infantry advances steadily, joining the 82nd Airborne to intercept and repulse a strong German counterattack that swoops in from the north. The Americans are aided by the presence of the advancing 70th and 746th Tank Battalions. The Germans isolate elements of the 82nd Airborne near La Fiere Bridge on the west bank of the Merderet. Rescue attempts by other elements of the 82nd clear enemy resistance on the east bank, but fail to cross to the west bank. The U.S. 325th Glider Infantry arrives by air and by sea to bolster the Allied drive. The 1st Battalion, rushed by sea, advances with the 8th Infantry, 4th Division, while the remainder of the 325th thrusts toward La Fiere to assist the 82nd and 8th Divisions, fighting north of Ste Mere-Eglise. Action in the southern sector is also intense, with the 101st Airborne accepting the surrender of enemy units in the vicinity of Le Port and La Barquette. Meanwhile, elements of the 506th Paratroop Infantry run into vicious enemy opposition near St. Come-du-mont. In the **V Corps** sector, contingents of the 29th Division hook up with the Rangers at Pointe du Hoe. The 175th Infantry secures La Cambe prior to dawn on the 8th. Huppain falls to the 16th Infantry, but heavy enemy resistance prevents the 26th Regiment from advancing to Formigny. Before the close of the 7th, U.S. and British troops have secured a large area along the Drome River to its junction with the Aure River, leaving the enemy holding a slim corridor between the Allied bridgeheads. In the **British Second Army**, 30th Corps area, Bayeux falls to the British 50th Division; after its capture, two Regiments advance south of the Bayeux-Caen Road. In other activity, the 47th Royal Commandos assault Port-en-Bessin. In the **I Corps** area, the Canadians drive south of the Bayeux-Caen Road. **(Atlantic-Italy)** In the **U.S. Fifth Army** area, the 168th Infantry, 34th U.S. Division drives without rest, and captures Civitavecchia, 40 miles northwest of Rome on the following day. The port facilities are quickly repaired to beef up the Allied supply line. The British advance toward Orvieto, east of the Tiber River and also drive toward Terni. In other activity, the U.S.S. *Tide* (AM-125) and the Transport *Susan Anthony* (AP-72) both strike mines and sink. In addition the Destroyer *Harding* (DD-625) becomes damaged by grounding; the PT-505 is damaged by striking a mine, and the U.S.S. *Pheasant* (AM-61) a Minesweeper is damaged by collision.

June 8th 1944 — (Pacific-North Borneo) The U.S.S. *Harder* (SS-257) evacuates a group of coast watchers. **(Pacific-New Guinea)** The Americans, with the islets south of Biak firmly in their possession, begin using the new PT Base on Mios Woendi. On Biak, the U.S. 186th Infantry fortifies Mokmer Airdrome. The 2nd Battalion, 162nd Infantry meets stiff Japanese resistance as it advances toward the caves east of Mokmer, preventing a hook up with the main body of the Regiment. The Japanese also offer violent resistance in the Parai Defile, holding off attacks from the west and from the east by contingents of the 162nd, 163rd, and 186th Regiments. Off Biak, Army Aircraft sink the Japanese Destroyer *Harusame*. In the Hollandia-Aitape area, the 1st and 2nd Battalions, 158th Infantry, bolstered by Artillery and Tanks scratch through vicious enemy resistance reaching positions about 1,500 yards of the Tirfoam River; the Yanks fight through the day and reach the river on the following day. In other activity, an Allied Naval Task Force that includes two U.S. Light Cruisers and additional Destroyers, commanded by British Admiral V.A.C. Crutchley, intercepts an enemy Destroyer Force near midnight, preventing Japanese reinforcements from reaching Biak. This engagement, fought off the Schouten Islands, proves to be one more staggering blow to the faltering Japanese Imperial Navy. **(Pacific-Philippines)** The U.S.S. *Hake* (SS-256) sinks the Japanese Destroyer *Kazagumo* near Mindanao. **(China-Burma-India)** Action is fierce on the Salween Front as the Chinese 88th Division, 71st Army, advances into the outer defenses of Lung-ling. Meanwhile, the Chinese 87th Division drives to the North Gate of the city, establishing a blockade at the Manio Bridge which severs the Japanese supply route along the Teng-chung-Lung-ling Road. **(Atlantic-France-Normandy)** The Americans continue driving toward Cherbourg as the British attack toward Caen. The U.S. 1st Army makes contact with the British Second Army near Port-en-Bessin. In the **U.S. 1st Army** area, the VII Corps launches an aggressive drive, sending four Regiments against Cherbourg. The 505th Paratroop Infantry, 82nd Airborne, advances west with the 8th Infantry, 4th Division, while the east flank is covered by the 12th and 22nd Regiments, 4th Division, pushing along the east flank. German resistance is resolute. The 22nd Infantry is hit by heavy enemy resistance at Azeville-Crisbecq where the Germans still hold massive fortified bunkers. The U.S. effort at Edmondeville by the 12th Infantry meets equally fierce opposition. Meanwhile, the 82nd Airborne, moving on the west side, advances to the Merderet via Magneville, and is engaged by the German 243rd Division at the river. In the **VII Corps** southern flank sector, the 101st Airborne begins its drive to seize Carentan to facilitate the hook up with V Corps. The reinforced 506th Paratroop Infantry plows the enemy from St. Come-du-Mont, then regroups near the Douve river before crossing near Brevands. In the **V Corps** sector, all D-Day objectives have been achieved. In addition, the 2nd Ranger Battalion holding Pointe de Hoe has been relieved by other Ranger units and by the U.S. 116th Infantry. During the fighting, Technical Sergeant Frank D. Peregory, 116th Infantry, watches as his outfit is stalled. He singlehandedly attacks an enemy machine gun nest near Grandcamp, killing eight Germans and capturing three. Peregory then speeds through the trench and captures 32 additional enemy Riflemen and the Machine gunners. The U.S. 175th Infantry secures Isigny during the night of the 8th-9th. Formigny is secured by contingents of the 18th Infantry, while units of the 26th Infantry, executing the main effort to cut off the enemy and squeeze them between it and the British bridgehead takes Tour-en-Bessin, and during the night of the 8-9th, the 26th seizes Ste Anne. In addition, the 16th Infantry concentrates on cutting the enemy escape route from Port-en-Bessin. The outnumbered and outgunned Germans slip out of the trap controlling an escape route, withdrawing most of their Forces during the night of the 8th. In the **British Second Army** 30th Corps area, the 47th Royal Marines capture Port-en-Bessin during the early portion of the day. The British 50th Division further reduces the escape route of the Germans, coordinating with the American

V Corps, seizing Sully and Chateau, at Fosse Soucy. Meanwhile, the Germans take the initiative and pressure the British 50th Division to pull back. In Naval activity, the Destroyer Escort U.S.S. *Rich* (DE-695) and the LST 499, both sink after striking mines. The Destroyers *Glennon* (DD-620) and *Meredith* (DD-726) both become damaged after striking mines. **(Atlantic-Italy)** The Germans, facing enormous Allied pressure, are forced to withdraw from the Adriatic sector along the coast, permitting the British 5 Corps to advance speedily. In the **U.S. 5th Army** area, the U.S. 133rd Infantry, spearheading the American pursuit of the Germans along Highway 1, moves aggressively until hitting stiff enemy rear-guard action near Tarquina. In the **II Corps** sector, Task Forces Howze and Ellis, take the point and race toward Viterbo, followed closely by the 85th and 88th U.S. Divisions. The Americans sprint to within six miles of the objective and are forced to halt to yield the right of way to the South African 6th Armored Division which is heading for Orvieto. In the **XIII Corps** area, while the South Africans are driving on the left flank towards Orvieto, the British 6th Armored Division meets heavy resistance, extending west from Monte Maggiore; it is halted at Passo Corese, forcing the Armor units to place Infantry at the point to dislodge the enemy during the night of the 8th.

June 9th 1944 — (Pacific-Bismarcks) Enemy Naval repair facilities on New Ireland at Fangelawa Bay are attacked by a Destroyer Force. **(Pacific-Bonin Islands)** The U.S.S. *Swordfish* (SS-193), operating in the Western Pacific, sinks the Japanese Destroyer *Matsukaze*. **(Pacific-Celebes Sea)** The U.S. Submarine *Harder* (SS-257) sinks the Japanese Destroyer *Tanikaze*. **(Pacific-New Guinea)** Intense enemy fire continues to hinder progress of the 162nd Infantry as it advances near the East Caves trying to make contact with the beleaguered 2nd Battalion. In the Hollandia-Aitape area, the 1st and 2nd Battalions, 158th Infantry (Task Force Tornado) reach the Tirfoam River after overpowering enemy obstacles along the route. The 158th Infantry is halted at the Tirfoam to prepare for an attack on Noemfoor Island. The 158th Infantry is to be relieved by another Regimental Combat Team of the 6th Division. In the Task Force Persecution zone, the Japanese pull out of their positions along the Afua-Palauru trail. In other activity, a Squadron of British Beaufighters, attached to Wing 71, arrives on Tadji to bolster the 110th Reconnaissance Squadron of the Fifth U.S. Air Force, the only unit at the Airbase since the 25th of May. **(China-Burma-India)** British General Sir George Giffard receives orders from Admiral Mountbatten to have the Dimapur-Kohima-Imphal Road cleared by mid-July and to be prepared to attack in force across the Chindwin near Yuwa-Tamanthi after the cessation of the monsoon (torrential rains). On the Salween Front, the Chinese 71st Infantry charges enemy positions on two hills at Lung-ling. The Chinese 9th Division, 2nd Army establishes roadblocks which paralyze the Burma Road about four miles south of Mang-shih, because of internal arguments between Army Commanders and Group Army Commanders. After settling the dispute, the blockade is lifted and the Chinese 9th Division returns to patrolling the area. **(Atlantic-Great Britain)** The Joint Chiefs of Staff arrive in London. **(Atlantic-Normandy)** In the **U.S. Fifth Army VII Corps** area, the U.S. 4th Division grinds closer to the port of Cherbourg. The 22nd Infantry seizes the German fortifications at Azeville, including the surrender of the Garrison. The 90th U.S. Division, commanded by General Jay W. MacKelvie, an inexperienced battle commander, is to co-ordinate with the 4th Division, but its progress is poor. Within three days, MacKelvie is replaced, but in fairness to him, his staff is not strong. The new Com-

manding Officer, General Gene Landrum, fares no better and the unit continues to hold up progress. General Bradley has not lost faith in the men, just the Officers. The next commander, General Raymond S. McClain, replaces 16 Officers and by Thanksgiving, the 90th is a fighting Division. After the successful operation, Task Force Barber is established to make a lightning thrust toward Quineville sending the 12th Infantry northward; it captures Joganville after a bitter struggle. In addition, the 8th Infantry drives through Magneville toward Ecausseville, forcing the Germans to evacuate under cover of darkness. Elements of the 82nd Airborne hammer away near La Fiere at the Merderet, driving to seize the Cotentin at its neck. Contingents of the 325th Glider Infantry and the 508th Paratroop Infantry crash through enemy positions and secure a bridgehead across the Merderet large enough to encompass all units including those previously isolated on the west bank. During this hotly contested battle, P.F.C. Charles N. DeGlopper, reacts boldly when his unit becomes isolated at dawn. He volunteers to draw fire to save the remainder of the Platoon. The dauntless Paratrooper, armed with his automatic rifle, taunts the enemy by strutting onto the road while firing incessantly. Return fire wounds him, but he continues firing, forcing the Germans to concentrate on him. More enemy fire again strikes him; he falls to the ground, mortally wounded and bleeding profusely, but amazingly he leans on one knee streaming shells into the enemy until he succumbs. Meanwhile, his unit makes it to the hedgerow, seizing this the first bridgehead at the Merderet. In other activity, damages to a bridge cause the delay of an attack by the 101st Airborne against Carentan. The V Corps initiates a three-pronged assault against Foret de Cerisy, with the 2nd Division squeezed between the 1st and 29th Divisions. The 29th pushes south from Isigny with some elements reaching La Fotelaie, and others including Tanks, crossing the Aure River, south of Auville-sur-le Vey. In addition, the 115th Infantry strikes across the Aure south of Canchy, extending to Bricqueville, La Folie, and Le Carrefour. In the **V Corps** area, the 38th U.S. Infantry, 2nd Division, penetrates enemy-held Trevieres and begins to clean out the enemy pockets. The U.S. 9th Division, driving east, reaches Rubercy and the equally hard driving 1st Division sees its 18th Infantry hitting from the right, while the 26th, hammering from the left, seizes Agy and Dodigny, the initial objectives on the left flank. With most of the pressure on the Germans and the air space over Normandy controlled by the Allies, it becomes easier for men and supplies to be brought ashore. The U.S. 2nd Armored Division lands to bolster the U.S. In the **British Second Army** area, the British 2nd Division drives toward Tilly-sur-Seulles (30th Corps zone) and against Caen in the 1st Corps sector, meeting violent opposition at each point. In Naval activity, the Destroyer *Meredith*, (DD-726) already damaged by a mine on the previous day, is sunk by an enemy Horizontal Bomber. In addition, the LST 314, is sunk by an enemy torpedo from a Surface Craft and the LST-376 is also struck and damaged; the LST 376 is subsequently sunk by U.S. Forces. Enemy Coastal Guns score some damage when they strike the Motor Minesweeper YMS-305. **(Atlantic-Italy)** In the **U.S. Fifth Army VI Corps** area, the 134th Infantry, 34th Division seizes Tarquinia, while the 361st Infantry, 91st Division moves on line and takes coastal positions under the direction of the Texas 36th Division. In other activity, Combat Command A, 1st Armored Division, takes Viterbo without opposition during the first part of the day. The French Expeditionary Corps begins to relieve the **II Corps**. In the **British Eighth Army** area, new boundaries are established between the 10th Corps and the 13th Corps along the Tiber River with elements of the 13th Corps (British 6th Armored and 4th Infantry) coming under command of the 10th Corps. In the 13th Corps area, contact is made between the **U.S. Fifth Army** holding Viterbo and elements of the South African 6th Armored Division who continue toward Orvieto. The British 6th Armored Division keeps moving toward Terni and the Indian 8th Division advances to Arsoli. **(U.S.S.R.-Finland)** Soviet troops attached to the Leningrad Front are diverted to the Karelian Isthmus, between Lake Ladoga and the Gulf of Finland, to eliminate a Finnish threat.

Winston Churchill and British General Sir Alan Brooke observing the Normandy operation.

June 10th 1944 — (United States) The U.S. Eighth Army is activated at Memphis, Tennessee. **(Pacific-Marshalls)** The RO-42, a Japanese Submarine caught near the Marshalls, is sunk by the U.S.S. *Bangust* (DE-739), a Destroyer Escort. **(Pacific-New Guinea)** General Fuller receives further instructions from General Krueger emphasizing the importance of a speedy seizure of the Airfields on Biak Island. The Japanese repulse U.S. attempts to seize Parai Defile. A strong contingent of the 162nd Infantry (Task Force Hurricane) heads west. A lull in the heavy fighting on the ridges along the trail leading inland occurs as the Americans are pulled back, after trying unsuccessfully since the 7th to secure the area. In the Hollandia-Aitape sector, Task Force Persecution begins to strengthen its perimeter along the Driniumor. Preliminary defenses are deployed at X Ray R-Koronal Creek and back-up defenses are established at the Nigia River. In addition, the Airfield is to be held. Japanese Patrols increase around the Niumen Creek reaching within 3,000 yards east of the Driniumor. **(Atlantic-France-Normandy)** In the **U.S. First Army VII Corps** area, the German Main Line of Resistance prevents Task Force Barber from advancing through Azeville to reach Quineville Ridge. The 12th Infantry, well in front of the balance of the U.S. 4th Division, advances and secures positions close to the Montebourg-Quineville Highway east of Montebourg, while the 8th Infantry takes objectives near the Le-Ham-Montebourg Highway. The Germans are driven from Montebourg Station by the 505th Paratroop Infantry, 82nd Airborne but are able to stop the Yanks short of Le Ham. The 90th Division, excluding the 359th Infantry, which has been attached to the 4th Division, meets stiff resistance as it drives west toward the Douve. In other activity, the 101st Airborne begins to surround the German strongpoint at Carentan (held by the 17th Armored Division). The 327th Glider Infantry advances from the northeast to seal off the eastern exits of the city, while other elements drive from the west and northwest. The Germans at Carentan mount heavy resistance. U.S. Artillery supports the action. Contact is made between the

401st Glider Infantry (101st Airborne) and troops from the V Corps at Auville-sur-le-Vey. The U.S. 9th Division also begins to come ashore to bolster the Allied Ground Forces. In the **V Corps** area, the Germans are driven from Caumont, creating a wide gap in their defenses, allowing the 115th Infantry, 29th Division, to reach the Elle River line, while the 9th and 38th Regiments, 2nd Division race through Foret de Cerisy. Meanwhile, the 18th Infantry, 1st U.S. Division, advances to the St. Lo-Bayeux highway. Near Goville, France, Staff Sergeant Walter Ehlers ravages the enemy with his Squad. In addition, he singlehandedly knocks out numerous strongpoints, eliminating two mortar sections and several machine gun crews. In addition, despite severe wounds, he covers the withdrawal of his Squad and successfully escapes encirclement, carrying a wounded Rifleman with him. His courage and unwavering leadership during the two day struggle greatly aids his Regiment (18th). Staff Sergeant Arthur DeFranzo, also of the 1st Division, becomes wounded repeatedly while attacking machine guns, fearlessly knocking them out one by one. He tosses several grenades, demolishing another gun which had stalled his unit, before being killed. In the British Second Army area, the Germans mount fierce resistance at Tilly-sur-Seulles, prompting the British to commit the British 7th Armored Division. The British 1st Corps is still embattled heavily near Caen. In Naval activity, the U.S.S. *Glennon* (DD-620) is sunk by enemy coastal guns.

German Artillery on Normandy, designated scrap, compliments of the U.S. Navy.

June 11th 1944 — (United States) The Battleship *Missouri* (BB-63) is commissioned at New York. The "Mighty Mo" will see its decks utilized to accommodate the Japanese when they sign the "UNCONDITIONAL SURRENDER" in Tokyo Bay during September of 1945. **(North Atlantic)** The German U-490 is sunk by a Squadron of Aircraft (VC-95) attached to the Carrier Escort *Croatan* (CVE-25) and the Destroyer Escorts *Frost* (DE-144), *Huse* (DE-145) and *Inch* (DE-146). **(Pacific-Bismarcks)** The Japanese Submarine RO-111 is sunk north of the Bismarcks by the Destroyer *Taylor* (DD-468). **(Pacific-New Guinea)** Heavy firefights erupt near Mokmer Airfield on Biak. Two Regiments from Task Force Hurricane drive north and west to rid the area of Japanese. The 186th Regiment moving along the coast, advances about 1,350 yards past the runway, while the 162nd Infantry drives to the first phase line of departure. The Americans are informed by Japanese laborers that the West Caves about 1,000 yards from the 162nd's 3rd Battalion are heavily fortified. Other elements of Task Force Hurricane, operating near the East Caves, are recalled to the Mokmer Airdrome. In the vicinity of Parai Defile, the Americans finally force the Japanese to give ground. In other activity, Major General Franklin C. Sibert, Commanding General 6th Division, arrives at Toem with his Headquarters and additional units, including the 20th Infantry. In Naval activity, the U.S. Navy establishes a Naval Base on Biak in the Schouten Islands. **(Pacific-Marianas)** U.S. Admiral Mitscher's Task Force 58, which has a complement of 15 Fast Carriers, departs a rendezvous point off the Marshalls and steams for the Marianas. Planes are launched from the Carriers to strike at Saipan and other islands such as Guam to soften enemy resistance. The Japanese intercept the American Planes, but suffer heavy losses. During the battle for supremacy of the skies, the Americans lose twelve Planes, while destroying an estimated 147 to 215 enemy Planes in the air and on the ground. The bombardment continues until the 14th when Task Forces 52 and 53 hook up with the Armada and supplement the bombing of Saipan and Tinian. Guam, Rota and the Pagan Islands also are attacked. Meanwhile, two Japanese Convoys are attacked. **(Pacific-China)** The Japanese mount a heavy attack, driving across the Liuyang River against nominal resistance by Chinese of the IX War area. **(Atlantic-France)** In the **U.S. First Army VII Corps** area, the Germans mount heavy resistance, keeping Task Force Barber from penetrating the Azeville Gap and breaking through to Quineville Ridge in the coastal sector. The Germans also prevent the American 8th Infantry from advancing beyond the Le Ham-Montebourg Road, blocking it from securing the railroad. The 505th Paratroop Infantry combines with the 325th Glider Infantry (both 82nd Airborne) and assaults Le Ham, against severe enemy fire, but upon entering the town, find it abandoned. The U.S. 101st Airborne keeps a steady, but grueling pace at Carentan. The Americans increase Artillery fire and other weaponry against the town, while elements of the 101st storm the bastion. Naval Battleships 10 miles offshore, bombard Carentan; the tremendous volume of fire forces the Germans to retire during the night of the 11th-12th. In the **V Corps** area, the 3rd Battalion, 41st Armored Infantry arrives to reinforce the bridgehead at Auville-sur-le-Vey because the 101st Airborne Division is fully engaged at Carentan. Other action in the V Corps area is units of the 2nd U.S. Division which are eliminating an enemy force at Haute-Littee Crossroads. In the **British 2nd Army's** 30th Corps area, the German defenses at Tilly-sur-Seull are broken by the British 7th Armored Division, but quick enemy reaction mounts a counterattack and drives the British back out of town. In Naval activity, enemy torpedoes sink the Ocean Tug *Partridge* (ATO-138) and the LST 496 sinks after striking a mine. In addition, enemy torpedoes damage the Destroyer *Nelson* (DD-623) and the LST 538. **(Atlantic-U.S.S.R.-Finland)** The Soviets keep the offensive moving and push hard against the Mannerheim Road, slicing a wedge 15 miles deep, along a 30-mile front. **(Atlantic-Rumania)** The U.S. Fifteenth Air Force launches a bombing raid against Focsani Airfield, while returning to Italy from its initial shuttle bombing mission between there and the U.S.S.R. **(Atlantic-Italy)** In the **U.S. Fifth Army** area, American General Crittenberger assumes command of the **VI Corps** sector and of the U.S. 36th Division. The VI Corps has handily advanced almost 65 miles north of Rome, but intelligence reports indicate that the Germans are bolstering their rear guard units in that area. The VI Corps is assigned to Operation ANVIL and will be attached to the **U.S. 7th Army**. In the French sector, the First French Motorized Division secures Montefiascone and the 3rd Algerian Division seizes Valentano. In the **British Eighth Army** 13th Corps area, the Germans hold the line below Bagnoregio and pin down the South African 6th Armored Division. In the 10th Corps area, the Germans withdraw from their positions along the Galantina River, permitting the British 6th Armored Division to cross easily and secure Cantalupo.

June 10th-11th 1944 — U.S. Artillery bombards Carentan.

June 12th 1944 — (Pacific-Marianas) U.S. Naval Bombardment continues. During the attack, the Japanese Torpedo Boat *Otori* is sunk by Carrier-based Aircraft. **(Pacific-New Guinea)** Japanese resistance is fierce on Biak as the Americans work to secure the island and make repairs on Mokmer Airdrome. In the Wakde-Sarmi area, General Sibert assumes command of Task Force Tornado. The transition changes the 6th Division Headquarters to Task Force Tornado Headquarters, which replaces Headquarters RCT 158. In Naval activity, the U.S.S. *Kalk* (DD-611) a Destroyer is damaged by a Horizontal Bomber. **(China-Burma-India)** The Chinese 115th Infantry engages the Japanese near the Huei-jen Bridge and regains Hongmoshu after a fierce struggle. **(Atlantic-France)** U.S. forces at Normandy still have not been attacked by the Germans; the only major counterattack occurred on the first day against the entrenched British. Sixteen Allied Divisions are ashore, nine American and seven British, each having more than one Division of Tanks. General Marshall, Admiral King and General Arnold inspect the beaches. In the **U.S. First Army, VII Corps** area, pressure from the 39th Infantry, U.S. 9th Division, forces the Germans to pull out of Crisbecq; it also drives the Germans from Dangueville and Fontenay-sur-Mer, pushing them back to Quineville Ridge, their Main Line of Resistance. Progress is gradual for the Yanks, but they are moving toward the main objective; Cherbourg. The Germans resist viciously near Montebourg, repelling the 8th Infantry, which finds the town too strongly fortified. U.S. Naval Vessels enter the fray as long range guns jolt the defenders holding the town of Ozeville. Following the Naval barrage, the surging 22nd Infantry Regiment secures the town. The U.S. 90th Division, operating west of the Merderet, is heavily engaged with the enemy and sends the 359th Infantry (recently reassigned back to the 90th from the 4th Division) forward. It moves through the middle of the 357th and 358th Infantries, but progress is slow. The 358th Infantry darts under cover of darkness during the night of the 12th-13th and takes Pont l'Abbe, already leveled by Allied Air and Artillery attacks. In other activity, the 508th Paratroop Infantry, 82nd Airborne, is reinforced and organized as a Task Force; it crosses the Douve after dark near Beuzeville-la-Bastile to join the 101st Airborne at Baupte. Meanwhile, the 101st Airborne closes on Carentan and by 06:00 several units overrun the enemy defenses, giving the U.S. a main road between Omaha and Utah beaches. The combined beachhead stretches 40 miles. The final assault to take the objective had been led by Brigadier General Anthony McAuliffe. The 101st Airborne's 501st and 506th Regiments speed toward Periers and Baupte to seize the approaches to Carentan, but heavy enemy resistance halts its advance. German resistance is also fierce in the **V**

Corps area, hindering progress of a Task Force consisting of two Companies of the 29th Division, stopping it well short of the objective, the bridges spanning the Vire-Taute Canal. In other activity, the Americans attempt to bolster a weak link in the defense line between the V and VII Corps. Colonel Benjamin Dickson informs Bradley that the Germans will launch a counterattack to regain Carentan and sever the newly won link between Omaha and Utah beaches. To rectify the situation, the 2nd Armored Division, under General Maurice Rose, deploys near Montmartinen-Graignes to bolster General Max Taylor's 101st Airborne. The V Corps attacks to secure St. Lo, immediately hitting strong opposition on the right flank. The Germans prevent the 115th Infantry 29th U.S. Division from crossing the Elle River, with the exception of the 3rd Battalion, which makes it across; however, enemy fire forces a withdrawal. The 116th Infantry pushes through the lines of the bruised 115th and gets across. The 23rd Infantry, 2nd Division, attacking St. Lo from the northeast is also halted at the Elle River before it can secure Hill 192, which controls the north and eastern approaches to St. Lo. However, the U.S. 9th Infantry, 2nd Division, coordinating with the U.S. 1st Division, punches a hole in the German defenses and against lighter opposition takes Litteau Ridge. In additional activity, the 1st Division plunging ahead with the 18th Infantry on the right and the 26th on the left, boasting the Big Red 1 insignias, drives to the fringes of Caumont. In the **British Second Army** 30th Corps area, the British 50th Division continues to attack the Germans in the vicinity of Tilly-sur-Seulles, while the British 7th Armored Division drives through Livry and deploys east of Caumont. **(Atlantic-Italy)** In the **U.S. Fifth Army** area, the Germans continue retreating north, with the IV Corps (36th Division reinforced by 361st Infantry, 91st Division, Tank and Tank Destroyer units) in hot pursuit. However, enemy rear actions (elements of the German 14th Army) intensify and begin to slow up the Yanks. Task Force Ramey, consisting of the 91st Cavalry Reconnaissance Squadron, the 141st Infantry, 36th Division and supporting units are ordered to cover the IV Corps' right flank and retain contact with the French Corps. Task Force Ramey is commanded by Brigadier General Rufus S. Ramey. The enemy concentrates heavily near Orbetello. **(Atlantic-Germany)** Germany initiates its pilotless V1 Rocket attacks against England. By August, the Germans begin launching the V2, a high altitude Rocket. Allied Planes attempt to detect the manufacturing locations, bombing Peenemuende, Germany and Trondheim, Norway. Ironically, the new weapon comes as no surprise to some in the U.S., as the first pilotless buzz bomb, had been developed in the U.S. by Charles F. Kettering (inventor-engineer), for the U.S. Army Signal Corps during 1917. Cessation of hostilities during 1918, canceled its use. Orville Wright and a famous race car driver, Ralph DePalma were among those involved with the secret project. Henry Ford built the engine at a cost of $40; total cost of the "Bug" was $400. Initial flights, which occurred over Dayton, Ohio, caused much excitement. A replica of the pilotless bomb was subsequently placed in the museum at Wright-Patterson Air Force Base.

June 13th 1944 — (United States) The Joint Chiefs of Staff request the opinions of Admiral Nimitz and General MacArthur on several proposals which follow: 1) advance target date so that the invasion of Formosa, tentatively planned for 15th February 1945, can be advanced; 2) bypass certain objectives including the Southern Philippines which will also hasten the invasion of Formosa; 3) bypass certain targets including the Southern Philippines and Formosa in order to advance directly to Japan. Admiral Nimitz and General Mac-

Arthur both express disapproval of the modified plans. **(Pacific-Dutch East Indies)** Enemy Oil Facilities on Bula, Cerami Island are bombarded by the deck guns of the visiting U.S.S. *Narwhal*, (SS-167). **(Pacific-Kurile Islands)** Rear Admiral E.G. Small's Cruiser Destroyer Task Force bombards Japanese positions on Matsuwa Island. **(Pacific-Marianas)** American Intelligence reports that Saipan is defended by 15,000 to 17,600 Japanese Soldiers and that Tinian is defended by 10,150 to 10,750 troops. Task Force 58 continues its campaign to reduce the enemy fortifications on these and other islands in the chain. U.S. Surface Vessels join the bombardment. A Task Force comprising seven Battleships and 11 Destroyers, commanded by Vice Admiral W.A. Lee, strikes the western coasts of Saipan and Tinian from long distance, placing doubt on the results. U.S. Planes destroy a Transport and several other Vessels off Saipan. In other Naval activity, the U.S.S. *Melvin* sinks the Japanese Submarine RO-36. The American Pilots are not challenged by any enemy Aircraft during the strike over Saipan. **(Pacific-New Guinea)** American General Krueger places the 34th Infantry, 24th Division on alert for transfer to Biak Island on the 18th. On Biak, brisk fire fights continue throughout the day. American firepower has effectively reduced enemy fire from the East Caves, allowing American Vehicles to begin using the coastal road. In other activity, Mokmer Airfield has been satisfactorily repaired and is now operational for Fighter Planes. **(Pacific-Burma)** Company K, New Galahad Force, repulses a heavy counterattack near Myitkyina. **(Atlantic-France)** The U.S. VII Corps concentrates its efforts on taking Cherbourg by first severing the Cotentin Peninsula. The XIX Corps, commanded by General Cortlett, will be operational soon and is given the task of pushing deeply into the Carentan-Isigny area to open a large corridor between the V and VII Corps positions. In the **VII Corps** area, the enemy is contained at Montebourg by elements of the 4th U.S. Division. Other elements of the 4th Division advance against heavy enemy strongholds, posted along the coast south of Quineville. The 22nd Infantry, 4th Division prepares to strike Quineville from a nearby ridge in conjunction with the 12th Infantry, 4th Division, presently holding firm at the western end of Quineville Ridge. The Germans have held against the 90th U.S. Division in the vicinity of Gourbesville-Pont l'Abbe, allowing only minimal advancement. The 82nd Airborne drives toward Baupte, with the 508th Paratroop Infantry reaching it by 08:00 as the Germans evacuate. In other activity, the 101st Airborne, holding Carentan, is hit by a strong German counterattack spearheaded by the 17th Armored Panzer Division. The hard driving enemy Assault Force reaches the city limits, within 500 yards of the Americans. The 101st is short of Tanks, but pitches small arms against the enemy Armor. The Panzers are held off and by 07:30, reinforcements from the 2nd Armored Division arrive, ending the threat. Subsequent to the unsuccessful enemy attack, the 101st, attacking with its 502nd Regiment, reaches the road that spans between Baupte and the Carentan-Periers highway. Meanwhile, the U.S. 327th Glider Infantry anticipates an enemy assault, but none occurs, allowing it to pull back and set up defenses along the northern side of the Railroad between Carentan and the Vire. In the **V Corps** area, the 116th Infantry, 29th Division, seizes Couvains and St. Clair-sur-Elle. The 38th Infantry, 2nd Division, supported by Heavy Artillery drives about two miles beyond the Elle River. In addition, Caumont falls to the 1st Division. The V Corps offensive against St. Lo is temporarily halted at the end of the day, but the V and VII Corps are now closely linked together with the V Corps awaiting the fall of Cherbourg. In the **British Second Army** 30th Corps area, the British 7th Armored Division advances to an important German communications center at Villers-Bocage, but a strong enemy counterattack by the German 2nd Armored Division forces the British to pull back and pivot north to link up with the American V Corps. In other activity in the British sector, the Germans still give the British 50th Division fierce resistance, containing it at Tilly-sur-Seulles. (Atlantic-Italy) In the British 30th Corps sector, the South African 6th Armored Division plows through enemy obstacles at Bagnoregio and drives toward Orvieto. In the 10th Corps area, the Germans destroy a bridge at Termi as the British 6th Armored Division approaches.

German prisoners on Normandy being herded toward U.S. Warships offshore for interrogation; Old Glory beams nearby.

June 14th 1944 — (Pacific-New Guinea) General Krueger replaces General Fuller (Commander Task Force Hurricane) with General Eichelberger, the Commanding General of the U.S. I Corps and Task Force Reckless. Eichelberger proceeds to Biak to assume his additional command. Fighting continues heavily on Biak as the Americans move closer to the enemy strongholds in the West Caves outside of Mokmer. During the night, the Japanese mount a counterattack to dislodge elements of the 162nd Infantry but the Americans repulse the assault during the early morning hours of the 15th. In the Wakde-Sarmi area, the remainder of the U.S. 6th Division debarks at Toem to reinforce the troops. (Pacific-Marianas) Two Task Groups, comprising Battleships, Cruisers and Destroyers move near Saipan and Tinian and join in the bombardment of the islands by Carrier Planes. This Naval Force comprises seven older Battleships, 11 Cruisers and 26 Destroyers in addition to several fast Troop Carriers and Mine Sweepers. The U.S.S. Battleship *California* (BB-44) and the Destroyer *Braine* (DD-630) are damaged by enemy shore guns during the bombardment. In additional activity, Admiral Hill's Western Landing Group, transporting the 2nd and 4th Marine Divisions, approaches Saipan. (China-Burma-India) The Japanese resist bitterly at Myitkyina and are able to isolate small Allied units. Task Force Morris is ordered to assault Myitkyina from east of the Irrawaddy, but Brigadier General Morris informs General Boatner that the area is flooded. The Japanese are holding all approach routes; and in addition, his men are exhausted from battle. In the Mogaung Valley, the Chinese close the net on Kamaing, continuing to encircle the objective. On the Salween Front, the Japanese continue to fortify positions at Lung-ling while mounting counterattacks against the Chinese. The Japanese drive the Chinese from the Manio Bridge and seize Liu-yang, threatening against Changsha. (Atlantic-France) 21st Army Group In the U.S. First Army area, VII Corps sector, the 4th Division advances.

The 39th Infantry (attached to the 4th) destroys heavy resistance in Quineville then moves southward along the coast and seizes Fort St. Marcouf. In related movement, the heights west of Quineville are secured by the 22nd Infantry. The 9th Infantry and 82nd Airborne Divisions relieve the U.S. 90th Division and drive west to the Douve River. The 90th moves to cover the left flank of the 9th Infantry Division. The 357th Infantry, 90th Division is engulfed with heavy firefights in Gourbesville, while the 358th Regiment, driving west of Pont l'Abbe, is relieved by the 82nd Airborne. The 507th Paratroop and 325th Glider Regiments, 82nd Airborne push further, advancing about one mile along the Pont l'Abbe-St. Sauveur-le-Vicomte Road. In other activity, the U.S. 79th Division comes ashore on Utah Beach. The XIX Corps becomes operational and is composed of the 29th Division (transferred from V Corps) and the 30th Division, which is engaged between Taute and the Vire River. In the V Corps sector, the assault toward St Lo remains in low gear, but skirmishes occur. In the 9th Division zone, a bitter skirmish develops at a road junction between the Germans and a contingent of Company F, 2nd Battalion, 60th Regiment. Captain Matt Urban, confiscates a Bazooka and some volunteers and two German Tanks are destroyed. Urban becomes wounded, but refuses evacuation. On the following day, Urban leads another attack and again becomes wounded; he is evacuated to England. While in the hospital, Captain Urban is informed that his outfit is moving out to attack St. Lo. Ignoring his condition, he flees from the hospital, hops a ride back to France and attempts to rejoin his outfit. He arrives at the Battalion Command Post at 11:25 on the 25th of July, only to discover that his Battalion had jumped off at 11:00. Undeterred, he races to the front and with his 45 pistol waving, he shouts for his men to "FOLLOW HIM INTO THE RIGHT FLANK." Subsequently, some of Urban's force get snagged and he rushes up to assist. Urban is struck with another wound (seventh time he has been wounded in action), but he gets off his two grenades. A member of the Battalion later relates that Urban "HAD GOTTEN US OFF OUR FEET AND RESTORED OUR CONFIDENCE AND ACTUALLY SAVED OUR LIVES." Captain Urban's neck wound is gushing blood, but he refuses evacuation until the strongpoint is taken. A Medic moves in and simply sticks his finger in to Urban's neck to stop the bleeding. Urban becomes a recipient of the Medal of Honor for his heroism, but it takes some time for it to come to fruition. His courageous actions get lost in the shuffle for over forty years. Captain (later Lt. Colonel) Urban, of Holland, Michigan is presented his Medal of Honor by President Carter during July 1980. In the British Second Army 30th Corps area, the Germans mount heavy pressure from the south, forcing the British 7th Armored Division to withdraw further north to Parfouru-l'Eclin. American artillery assists the British during their trek. In Naval activity, the LST 280 is damaged by a Submarine torpedo. (Atlantic-Italy) British General Alexander is informed that the American VI Corps will be immediately withdrawn for ANVIL (invasion of southern France); the 3rd Division departs on the 17th and the 36th leaves on the 27th of June. In the U.S. Fifth Army area, the Port of Civitavecchia is open for Liberty ships. The IV Corps presses north and northwest; elements seize Magliano. In the British Eighth Army area, the South African 6th Armored Division seizes Orvieto without incident. The British 78th Division, operating to the east, inflicts heavy casualties on German rear guard troops.

June 15th-July 7th 1944 — (Pacific-Marianas) The BATTLE OF SAIPAN (Operation FORAGER) — Admiral Nimitz has placed all troops under the command of Admiral Spruance,

Marines land on Saipan.

who has designated Admiral Turner to command the Joint Expeditionary Force to seize the Marianas. Marine General Holland M. Smith will command all forces once ashore. Turner's Northern Landing Force winds down its three-day bombardment of Saipan, which is defended by about 25,000 Soldiers (31st Japanese Army) and more than 3,000 Naval troops, all under Admiral Chuichi Nagumo. Surface Vessels and Planes pummel the landing areas to soften resistance, however, the buried Japanese shore guns remain potent. The 2nd Marine Division storms ashore at 08:40 near Charan Kanoa, north of Afetna Point on the west coast of the island, while the 4th Marine Division's Regimental Combat Teams 23, and 25, land south of Afetna Point. In addition, a diversionary operation executed by elements of the 2nd Marines, 24th Marines, and 29th Marines land unopposed near Tanapag Harbor. The primary landing forces advance speedily against intense fire. Despite vicious opposition which inflicts about 2,000 casualties, the Marines expand the beachhead to about 10,000 yards wide by 1,500 yards deep by nightfall; about 20,000 troops have landed.

During the night of the 15th-16th, the Japanese mount a surprise attack to drive the Americans back to the sea. However, U.S. Surface Vessels re-enter the fight and catapult star shells which expose attacking enemy troops and allowing Marine sharpshooters to mow them down under the brilliant illumination. On the 16th, the 4th Marine Division drives inland, while the 2nd Marine Division's 8th Marines seizes Afetna Point, and Charan Kanoa pier, establishing contact with the 4th Marine Division. After dark, the Japs again spring a foiled Tank attack against the 4th Marine Division's positions. Meanwhile, XXIV Corps Artillery and units of the U.S. 27th Division, arrive to bolster the beachhead. In addition, the Japanese are rushing reinforcements (Operation A-GO) to Saipan. Japanese Admiral Toyoda dispatches Admiral Ozawa's First Mobile Fleet, which will be joined en route by Warships of the Combined Fleet. Forewarned by U.S. Submarines, that the Japanese Armada is steaming toward Saipan from the southern Philippines, Spruance orders his Fast Carrier Task Forces under Mitscher, and some of Turner's Warships to sail west and intercept, while Turner takes his Transports out of harms way. The antagonists collide in the Philippine Sea on the 19th. At battle's end on the 20th, the Stars and Stripes prevails, vanquishing the enemy Fleet, demolishing the Carrier Planes and inflicting heavy casualties upon the Japanese in what is known as "The Great Turkey Shoot." The victory also prevents enemy reinforcements from reaching the besieged island.

Marines blasting through Saipan with flamethrowers.

On the 18th, the 165th Regiment, 27th Division U.S.A., seizes Aslito Airfield and two nearby ridges. In addition Japanese attempt to land near Flores Point, however, the 4th Battalion, 10th Marines batters the reinforcements, turning them back. On the following day, Marine and Army units continue driving: the 27th Division advances toward Nafutan Point, while the 1st Marine Division seizes Hill 790. Marine General Holland Smith orders the 2nd and 4th Marine Divisions to drive north to eradicate the main body of enemy resistance; two Regiments of the 27th Division U.S.A., will bolster the force. Hill 500 falls to the 3rd Battalion, 25th Marines. By the 22nd, the 2nd Battalion, 23rd Marines, storms the summit of Mt Tipo Pale, seizing it, and on the following day, the 2nd Battalion overruns Hill 600. Meanwhile, the 4th and 2nd Marine Divisions drive north to seize Mt. Tapotchau, on the east and west flanks respectively; U.S. Army elements are driving up the middle. Japanese resistance remains fanatical and fierce. Heavy resistance from caves hinders the advance of the 27th Division as it attempts to move through Death Valley between Mt. Tapotchau and Purple Heart Ridge, to relieve contingents of the 4th Marine Division, prompting General Holland Smith, U.S.M.C., to relieve General Ralph Smith, Commanding Officer of the 27th Division on the 24th.

On the 25th, the 4th Marine Division plunges east, driving through Kagman Peninsula. Meanwhile, the 6th Marines, 2nd Marine Division, continues to encounter fierce resistance north of Mt. Tipo Pale. After a bitter fight, the 8th Marines seizes Mt Tapotchau, Saipan's principal terrain feature. In addition, the 27th Division, under General Sanderford, makes some progress. The 165th Regiment hits withering fire at "Purple Heart Ridge" and is unable to climb the slopes, however, other elements pound the Japs on Hill 300, in southern Saipan, demolishing the enemy's main line of resistance, clearing the way to seize Nafutan Point and ensuring the demise of the enemy on Saipan.

Furious combat continues across the island on the 27th. The northern slopes of Mt. Tapotchau are engulfed with heavy skirmishing as the 2nd Battalion, 25th Marines, begins to eliminate the resistance. Meanwhile, contingents of the 106th and 165th Regiments battle fiercely at Hells Pocket and Purple Heart Ridge respectively, while additional contingents of the 106th advance across Death Valley under strong enemy fire. Meanwhile, the 2nd Battalion, 105th Regiment, secures Nafutan Point; 550 enemy bodies are counted and estimates of total force number over 1,000, rather than the original estimates of about 350 defenders. On the following day, Hells Pocket is vanquished by the 27th Division, but the iron resistance in Death Valley and on Purple Heart Ridge, continues to inflict severe casualties. Contingents of the 4th Marine Division reach the 0-6 line and give support fire to the 27th Division in the valley. On the 30th, Death Valley and Purple Heart Ridge fall to the determined 27th Division, while the 2nd Marine Division continues driving along horrendous terrain above Mt Tapotchau and Tipo Pale; contact is made between the Army units and the Marines, concluding the struggle for central Saipan.

As the Yanks close the noose, the Japanese begin retreating northward. On July 1st, the Yanks are close to victory, as the V Amphibious Corps drives to line 0-7, extending across the northern neck of the island. Garapan, leveled earlier by bombing, is seized effortlessly by the 2nd Marines, 2nd Marine Division. In addition, contingents of the 4th Marine Division push forward about 1,500 yards against feeble resistance. Meanwhile, the 27th Division advances on its left and right flanks, however, fierce resistance stalls the center assault of the 3rd Battalion, 105th Regiment. On the 3rd, the 23rd Marines, 4th Marine Division are driving hard against Hills 721, and 767; both are seized by the following day. Meanwhile, the 27th Division making the principal thrust, pivots north driving toward Tanapag Harbor, seizing the Seaplane Base at Flores Point on the 4th with its 1st Battalion, 105th Regiment.

On the 6th, the 4th Marine Division begins to pinch out the 27th Division and drive to Marpi Point. Meanwhile, the 27th Division is to eliminate resistance in the Tanapag-Makunsha-Narakiri Gulch area and simultaneously block the northern escape route of the Japanese. Elements of the 25th Marines overrun nominal resistance, reaching the slopes of Mt Petoskara; 700-800 civilians enter the lines to surrender. Meanwhile, the Japanese mount a fanatical Banzai attack on the night of the 6th-7th, hitting the 105th Regiment, 27th Division, deployed in the heights overlooking Harikiri Gulch, and the 3rd Battalion, 10th Marines, just southwest of Tanapag village, with the brunt of the assault. The Japanese overpower the positions of the 105th on the left flank and also the guns of the 10th Marines, however, the attack is repulsed at the Regimental Command Post where Japanese dead are piled high. The 4th Marine Division drives to Marpi Point, the northeast tip of the island, on the 9th of July, terminating organized resistance on Saipan. The Japanese Garrison of about 30,000 men is annihilated. Some choose suicide, rather than capture by the Yanks. Many Japanese including women and children, jump to their deaths from the cliffs at Marpi Point. The Commanding Officer of the defenders, Chiuchi Nagumo (Japanese

Carrier Commander at both Pearl Harbor and Midway), kills himself with his pistol. The Japanese Army Commander, Lt. General Yoshitsuga Saito, stabs himself in the stomach and is finished off by an aide who shoots him in the head. The Americans suffer 14,111 casualties: Army 3,674; Marines 10,437. Saipan, now flying the Stars and Stripes, allows the Americans to prepare for the next objective; Tinian. Saipan is transformed into a Base from which B-29s will strike Japan.

June 18th 1944 — Aslito Airfield, captured by the 165th Regiment, U.S.A.

The deadly results of refusing surrender when under siege by flamethrowers.

June 15th 1944 — **(South Pacific)** Admiral William Halsey, Commander of the South Pacific, relinquishes his command, becoming Commander of the U.S. Third Fleet; he is replaced by Vice Admiral J.H. Newton. **(Southwest Pacific)** Plans are issued for RENO V, the last of the string of plans calling for Airbases to be established: Between July and October, on Vogelkop Peninsula and on Moratai, the latter being synchronized with the Palaus invasion; invasion of Philippines at Mindanao on the 25th of October to bolster the mid-November operations against northern Philippine objectives; invasion of Luzon during early 1945. **(Pacific-New Guinea)** Japanese Tanks advance from the West Caves on Biak and hinder the progress of Task Force Hurricane, commanded by General Eichelberger. In addition, strong Japanese resistance also prevents Allied Aircraft on Biak from striking Japanese positions in the Marianas. **(Pacific-Marianas)** U.S. Surface Ships and Planes pummel enemy positions on Saipan prior to the landing of the Marines (reinforced by U.S. Army Teams). The U.S. lands a diversionary force at Tanapag Harbor while the main body storms ashore near Charan Kanoa at 08:40. The 2nd Division, deploys the 26th Marines to the north and the 8th Marines to the south after embarking north of heavily fortified Afetna Point. The 4th Marine Division, flanked by RCT 23 on the left and RCT 25, on the right lands south of Afetna Point. The Marines (4th Division) drive inland against Japanese opposition including Tanks and seizes Charan Kanoa. Although progress is made, the Japanese retain control of Afetna and still hold commanding positions as the bulk of their weaponry escaped damage during the preinvasion bombardments. In other activity, the U.S.S. *Tennessee* is damaged by enemy coastal guns. **(Pacific-Bonin-Volcano Islands)** Aircraft from two U.S. Naval Task Forces commanded by Rear Admirals J.J. Clark, and W.K. Harrill, strike Japanese installations (specifically Airfields, barracks and fuel storage areas) at Iwo Jima, Volcano Islands and Chichi Jima and Haha Jima in the Bonin Islands. The air strike against Iwo Jima will be repeated on the 16th. **(China-Burma-India)** Heavy but indecisive fighting ensures around Myitkyina. On the Salween Front, the Chinese mount an attack that gains control of the southeast corner of Sung Shan, a hill mass that extends along a 36 mile strip of the Burma Road (Salween Valley). The Japanese thwart Chinese attempts to seize the southwest corner of Sung Shan. **(Pacific-Japan)** American B-29s based in China and attached to Bomber Command XX launch their initial air attack against the mainland of Japan, dropping 221 tons of bombs on the Imperial Iron and Steel Works (Yawata facility) on Kyushu Island. **(Atlantic-France) 21st Army Group** In the **U.S. First Army** area, **VII Corps** sector, General Collins concentrates Corps actions on severing the Cotentin Peninsula. The 357th Infantry seizes Gourbesville, but the balance of the 90th Division is stalled by heavy German resistance. In the 9th Division sector, the Germans mount a strong counterattack, forcing the 47th Infantry to give ground east of the Douve. The Yanks then launch a counterattack of their own, regaining most of the lost terrain. In other activity, the 82nd Airborne's 505th Paratroop Infantry advances to positions south of Reigneville; the 325th Glider Infantry drives to within 1,000 yards of fortified St. Sauveur-le-Vicomte. The **VIII Corps**, commanded by Major General Troy H. Middleton, becomes operational; it assumes defensive positions extending from Carentan across Cotentin Peninsula, and will guard the southwest flank of the VII Corps. The U.S. **XIX Corps** fortifies its positions, but continues launching probing attacks to bolster the defenses. Montmartin-en-Graignes falls to the 120th Regiment, 30th Division, which attacks before the entire Division gets ashore. **(Atlantic-Italy)** In the **U.S. Fifth Army** area, the VI Corps is assigned to Seventh Army for Operation ANVIL. In the V Corps area, troops advance to the Ombrone River and send Patrols to probe enemy activity in Grosseto. The IV Corps begins fording the river after dark. In the **British Eighth Army** area, the 13th Corps reduces rear-guard resistance at Allerona and Ficulle. The 10th Corps continues pursuit of the enemy subsequent to a bridge being laid at Todi.

Generals Eisenhower, Bradley and J. Lawton Collins.

June 16th 1944 — **(Pacific-New Guinea)** Allied Commanders meet to discuss the invasion of Noemfoor; the tentative D-Day date is scheduled for June 30th. On Biak Island, the 2nd Battalion, 186th Infantry, heavily engages the enemy near the West Caves, but pulls back late in the day. **(Pacific-Marianas)** The 2nd Marine Division continues to strengthen its beachhead on Saipan, spreading the 8th Marines to the right and the 2nd Marines to the left, resulting with the clearing of Afetna Point and the Charan Kanoa Pier. In addition, the 2nd Division links up with the 4th Marine Division, which is regrouping prior to renewing its offensive. The 4th Marines commit their reserves (24th Marines) to the operation at 12:30. Also, the 4th Division meets stiff resistance on the right flank where the terrain is a formidable opponent. During the night, the Japanese unsuccessfully throw Tanks against the 4th Marine Division positions. Though heavy enemy fire isolates one Marine Tank, Gunnery Sergeant Robert H. McCard, Company A, 4th Tank Battalion, continues the fight. As superior enemy fire bears down, McCard orders the crew to evacuate while he remains and begins throwing grenades at the encroaching Japs. Upon expending his supply, he then rips a machine gun from the Tank to afford more time for his crew to reach safer positions. Sixteen Japs fall to his fire before he is overrun. McCard receives the Medal of Honor posthumously. During the night of the 16th-17th, the 165th Infantry 27th Division U.S.A., lands to bolster the beachhead. Artillery units attached to the XXIV Corps U.S.A. have arrived earlier in the day. In other activity, Admiral Spruance, Commander of Task Force 58 is informed of heavy enemy Fleet movements near the Philippines. This intelligence causes him to postpone the invasion of Guam to deal with the Japanese threat. Despite the decision to cancel the Guam assault scheduled for June 18th, U.S. Surface Vessels under the command of Admiral Ainsworth bombard the island which has been held by Japan since December 10th 1941. Meanwhile, Admiral Spruance directs his Fleet to prepare for the Battle of the Philippine Sea occurring on June 19th-20th. **(Atlantic-France) 21st Army Group** In the **U.S. First Army** area, the VII Corps establishes a bridgehead across the Douve River after clearing the area east of the river. The Yanks continue moving fast against the retreating Germans. Four Regiments of the 9th Division push through Ste Colombe; the 60th Infantry establishes a bridgehead near Nehou. The 82nd Airborne's 325th Glider and 505th Paratroop Regiments speed to St. Sauveur-le-Vicomte, reaching it before 12:00 and are joined by the 508th Paratroop Regiment; a 2,000-3,000 yard bridgehead is established. In the **XIX Corps** area, the strategic heights controlling the Vire-Taute Canal are taken by the 120th Infantry, 30th U.S. Division; it remains in the area to defend the Canal line. In conjunction, the 29th Division in co-ordination with the V Corps' 2nd Division, plows toward St. Lo against fierce enemy opposition, which stops the advance well short of the objective. **(Atlantic-Italy)** In the **British Eighth Army** area, the Germans mount heavy resistance and impede progress of the 13th Corps near Citta della Pieve. In the 10th Corps area, Bevagna and Foligno are overtaken by the 8th Indian Division. **(China-Burma-India)** Kamaing is finally overrun by elements of the 50th Chinese Division (149th Regiment), attached to the 22nd Division. On the Salween Front, the Japanese drive the Chinese 87th Division from Lung-ling, forcing it to withdraw three miles. Meanwhile, the Chinese 36th Division and 2nd Reserve Division seize Chiaotou. Fighting also is heavy in China, around Changsha where the Japanese are attacking the Garrison at Paoching.

June 17th 1944 — (Pacific-New Guinea) On Biak Island, enemy strongholds at the West Caves finally are overrun; the 1st Battalions of the 162nd and 186th Regiments storm the heights and secure the objective. In other activity, P-38s strike enemy positions on Sorong, but they are unable to reach Wakde Island. They are diverted to Owi, which is not yet fully operational, and land successfully. A serious threat against Aitape is anticipated. General MacArthur offers the service of a Regiment from the 31st Division U.S.A., to assist General Krueger's troops. **Pacific-Marianas-Saipan)** Marine General Holland "Howlin Mad" Smith and Brigadier General Arthur M. Harper U.S.A. (XXIV Corps Commander), establish a Command Post ashore. An intense bombardment is commenced by the Americans just prior to the jump off, by the Marines who make substantial gains against the enemy with the exception of the center of the assault which meets heavy enemy fire pouring from a large gap that exists between the 2nd and 4th Marine positions near Lake Susupe. The 2nd and 6th Marines, 2nd Marine Division, drive northeast, while the 8th Marines supported by elements of the 29th Marines drive

eastward toward entrenched Japanese in a coconut grove. In the 4th Marine Division sector, the Japanese halt progress of the 23rd Marines' left flank, creating a gap between the attacking Battalions, however it is filled in later by the 3rd Battalion, 24th Marines. Naval guns and Field Artillery are called in to bolster the Marines to capture Aslito airfield. Carrier-based Planes from Task Force 58 are recalled from their support duties to search for the enemy Fleet and to neutralize Guam and Rota. **(China-Burma-India)** On the Imphal Plain, British Fourteenth Army area, the British have lost nearly 10,000 wounded and 2,669 killed from the 4th of March to date. The Japanese have lost approximately 30,000 men according to Allied estimates. On the Salween Front, the Chinese 87th and 88th Divisions are directed to pull back from the Lung-ling area. **(Atlantic-France) 21st Army Group** In the **U.S. First Army VII Corps** area, German resistance continues to collapse on the Cotentin Peninsula. The U.S. 9th Division speeds full throttle, penetrating disorganized enemy defenses, advancing to the west coast where it seals off the peninsula, cutting the road at Barneville-sur-Mer along the coast and at Grande Huanville. The U.S. 90th Division pushes to Golleville-Urville. The 82nd Airborne is ordered to establish a bridgehead across the Douve at Pont l'Abbe. In the **XIX Corps** area, the Germans have become firmly entrenched between the U.S. 116th and 175th Regiments near Villiers-Fossard, halting progress of the 29th Division. The 115th Infantry unsuccessfully attacks the center to reduce the salient. **(Atlantic-Italy)** In the **U.S. Fifth Army** area, RCT 517 (Paratroop) is deployed along Highway 1, to gain battle experience prior to joining the Seventh Army for Operation ANVIL (invasion of southern France). In the **British Eighth Army** area, torrential rains fall in the 10th Corps area, bogging down British movements. In other activity, a French Task Force comprising the 9th Colonial Infantry Division is put ashore at Elba Island (Operation BRASSARD); it begins disrupting enemy seaborne traffic and also assists the ensuing offensive on the mainland.

June 18th 1944 — (Pacific-New Guinea) The Japanese still hold strategic locations, giving them the ability to fire on Mokmer Airfield. Task Force Hurricane is preparing for what is to be the final assault against all enemy pockets near the Airfield on Biak. The 34th Infantry, 24th Division, arrives from Hollandia and assumes the positions of the 186th Infantry, west of the Airfield. General Krueger directs General Sibert to initiate an offensive in the Wakde-Sarmi area. Sibert commences the attack on the 20th, committing the 20th Infantry which drives west from the Tirfoam River. In other activity, General Fuller is replaced by General Doe, who assumes command of the 41st Division. General Fuller departs to take a new position in the Southeast Asia Command. General Krueger tells General MacArthur that he prefers to use RCT 112, to bolster Aitape, rather than splintering the 31st Division. **(Pacific-Marianas)** On Saipan, the Japanese unsuccessfully attempt to transport reinforcements from Tanapag Harbor to the front lines; they are intercepted by LCIs (infantry landing craft) and Marine Corps Artillery which forces abortment of the mission. A lull develops in the 2nd Marine sector, with the exception of enemy pockets in the coconut grove which is cleared by the 8th Marines. The 4th Marine Division drives across the island, severing it in two by reaching Magicienne Bay on the east coast. The 165th Infantry, 27th Division U.S.A., seizes Aslito Airfield against light opposition during the morning. The Japanese had fallen back to Nafutan Point. The captured Airfield is named Conroy Field in honor of Colonel Gardiner J. Conroy, Commander of 165th Infantry, who had been killed at Makin. However, it is subsequently renamed Isley Field (misspelled) for a Naval Aviator, Commander Robert H. Isely who is killed over Saipan. The Army commences its main attack later in the day; RCT 165, advances close to Magicienne Bay, unopposed. However, RCT 105 encounters much difficulty because of the terrible terrain. **(China-Burma-India)** Task Force Myitkyina decreases its activity, limiting it to Patrols and skirmishes. In China, the Japanese seize the town of Changsha without opposition, as the Chinese have withdrawn from the area. **(Atlantic-France) 21st Army Group** British General Montgomery, Commanding General of 21 Army Group, issues his first written directive since the Normandy Invasion, calling for the speed up of operations to take Caen and Cherbourg. In the U.S. First Army area, the Yanks (First Army) finalize plans for the next jump to capture Cherbourg; it has previously split the German forces in half by advancing to the west coast of the peninsula. Now, the 9th is inflicting heavy casualties, while cutting off enemy escape routes to the south, infuriating the Germans. In the **XIX Corps** area, the Germans still offer fierce resistance in the vicinity of St. Lo. **(U.S.S.R.-Finland)** The Soviets penetrate the Finnish Mannerheim Line on the Karelian Isthmus. **(Atlantic-Italy)** The Germans mount rear-action resistance against the British who are approaching Perugia. The town of Citta della Pieve, situated in the British 13th Corps area, is abandoned by the Germans during the night of the 18th-19th.

June 19th 1944 — (Pacific-New Guinea) Heavy fighting continues as Task Force Hurricane initiates a synchronized assault to secure the Airfields on Biak. Artillery bombardments preceed the assault. Enemy opposition is scattered, making it easier for the Yanks who deploy the 186th Infantry, north and west of the West Caves, to sever the road leading south. It also permits units to get behind the enemy positions. The 186th concentrates on clearing the area northwest of the caves; the 162nd Infantry takes responsibility for reducing enemy resistance in the West Caves. In addition, the enemy held Airdromes at Borokoe and Sorido are captured by the 34th Infantry, 24th Division. **(Pacific-Marianas)** On Saipan, the 4th Marine Division speeds around the 2nd Marine Division, to secure the northern sector of the island. In the 2nd Marine Division sector, the 1st Battalion, 6th Marines captures Hill 790. The U.S. 27th Division is given the task of clearing Nafutan Point and the south coast, a mission which is expected to be no more than a mop-up operation; however, preliminary enemy troop strength estimates are off by about 60 percent. The 165th Infantry advances to the south coast of Magicienne Bay without incident and the 3rd Battalion, 105th Infantry slices unopposed through rough terrain, however, the 1st Battalion, 105th Regiment launches a frontal assault against enemy positions on a ridge at Nafutan and is repulsed, prompting the unit to attempt to outflank the enemy. During the day, a hole occurs in the lines of the 105th Infantry. The 1st Battalion, 165th Infantry rushes to the Airfield to fill the void. **(Atlantic-France) 21st Army Group** British General Montgomery directs his British Second Army to initiate an offensive on the 22nd-23rd of June; however, severe rains lasting until the 22nd, impede the build-up of both men and supplies. Montgomery subsequently decides to postpone the offensive until the 25th of June because of the delayed arrival of the British VIII Corps. In the **U.S. First Army** area, three American Divisions advance against Cherbourg. The 9th Division plows forward on the left in co-ordination with the 79th Division, driving up the center and the 4th Division pushing against fierce opposition on the right; the latter penetrating deepest, reaching staunch defenses of Cherbourg. In other activity, the 82nd Airborne and the 90th Divisions are trans-

ferred from the VII Corps to the VIII Corps, the former establishing a bridgehead south of the Douve, at Pont l'Abbe. (Elba Island) The occupation of the island is completed by the French Expeditionary Corps. **(China-Burma-India)** On the Salween Front, the town of Ku-tung is seized by units of the Chinese 2nd Reserve Division as it continues driving south toward Teng-chung. In other activity, the Chinese 53rd Army prepares to assault Chiangtso.

June 19th-20th 1944 — Japanese Warships under attack off the Marianas.

June 19th-20th 1944 — (Pacific-Philippines) THE BATTLE OF THE PHILIPPINE SEA — Japanese Planes en route to destroy the U.S. Fifth Fleet, Commanded by Admiral Mitscher, are intercepted by U.S. Aircraft off the Marianas. Meanwhile, other Fleet Aircraft search for the Japanese Task Force. The Japs mount four separate attacks, but they do not expect the new Grumman Hellcat Fighters, nor the gargantuan Anti-aircraft batteries on the new Battlewagons. The first waves of more than 400 Planes are decimated. Some enemy Planes penetrate and attack the U.S. Task Force, which is supporting the Saipan Operation, and damage the Battleships U.S.S. *South Dakota* and the *Indiana*, and also the Carriers *Bunker Hill* and *Wasp*. In addition, the attack also damages the Heavy Cruiser *Minneapolis*. After the five-hour contest, the Japanese find they have paid an exorbitant price for their nominal success; none of the U.S. Vessels are heavily damaged. Meanwhile, U.S. Planes whack the enemy Air Force in a wild shootout that overwhelms the less-experienced Jap Pilots, blowing over 300 Aircraft from the skies, against 17 losses. While the enemy Planes plummet to the sea, U.S. Submarines lend murderous fire and pulverize the Carriers *Shokaku* and *Taiho*

(Ozawa's Flagship), instantly cutting Admiral Ozawa's Carriers from nine to seven, eradicating any chance of Japanese control of the skies over the Marianas. The Japanese withdraw after the humiliating loss.

On the 20th, Admiral Ozawa's Fleet is spotted during the afternoon. Mitscher launches more than 200 Planes to strike the finishing blow. The Yanks sink the Carrier *Hiyo*, and batter the remainder of the enemy Vessels. The bewildered Japanese have lost two Destroyers. Three Japanese Carriers, three Cruisers, one Destroyer and three Tankers are severely damaged. Japanese Plane losses climb to 395 Carrier Planes, 31 Float Planes, and about 50 Land-based Planes from Guam. The lopsided battle, unquestionably breaks the back of the Imperial Japanese Navy and is remembered as the "Great Marianas Turkey Shoot." The two-day slugfest costs the U.S. 130 Planes, and 76 Pilots; 33 Aircraft are shot down. Non-battle losses occur when some Pilots are unable to locate their Carriers in the darkness or when the Planes are ditched after running out of fuel.

The vanquished Japanese Fleet retires, taking with it the 35 remaining operational Carrier Planes and twelve Float Planes. Pursuit begins, but no contact is made with the enemy. Admirals Spruance and Mitscher have won a tumultuous victory, giving the Americans total domination of the skies over the Marianas.

U.S. Infantry on Saipan — 105-mm Howitzer Motor Carriage M-7, mounted on Medium Tank M-3 chassis, dubbed "priest."

June 20th 1944 — (Southwest Pacific) During a strategy meeting at General Krueger's Headquarters, it is decided to postpone the invasion of Noemfoor Island until the 2nd of July. **(Pacific-Marianas-Saipan)** Enemy held Hill 500, west of Tsutsuuran Village, falls to the 3rd Battalion, 25th Marines after the conclusion of a joint northern pivoting movement by the 2nd and 4th Marine Divisions. The 4th Division is now perched just below the Japanese Main Line of Resistance, extending across the island from Garapan to the northwest fringes of Magicienne Bay. In other activity, the U.S. 27th Division concentrates its power against Nafutan. At about 12:00, upon cessation of an Artillery bombardment, the assault teams drive from the north and west. The 165th Infantry, supported by elements of the 105th Infantry (1st Battalion), grind southward in a fiercely contested firefight, which gains about 1,000 yards. The 3rd Battalion, 105th Infantry, driving east along the southern coast, advances about 600 yards, close to the newly arrived 106th Infantry. The 2nd Battalion, 105th Infantry is attached to the U.S. 27th Infantry and the 106th is utilized as a Corps Reserve unit. Army Artillery is also used against enemy positions on nearby Tinian; Battery B, 531st Field Artillery Battalion (XXIV Corps), deploys its weapons and commences a bombardment of the island. In Naval activity, the U.S.S. *Phelps* (DD-360), a Destroyer becomes damaged after being struck by enemy coastal fire off the Marianas. **(Pacific-New Guinea)** Enemy resistance still holds the line at the West Caves, impeding the progress of the 1st Battalion, 163rd Infantry. The 163rd sets up an outpost on Hill 330. Things go faster for the 34th Infantry as it steamrolls over minimal resistance and seizes the Airdromes at Borokoe and Sorido, in addition to occupying the village of Sorido. Vicious fighting also occurs on the Aitape Front; the Japanese are able to force termination of 128th Infantry Patrols near Yakamul. The Japanese still hold formidable positions near the Tirfoam in the Wakde-Sarmi sector. The U.S. 6th Division drive westward to seize Lone Tree Hill. The 20th Infantry advances against nominal opposition along the coast, reaching the Snaky River, but is halted by intense enemy fire originating from entrenched positions stretching from a defile that extends from the eastern tip of Mt. Saksin to Lone Tree Hill. **(Pacific-Philippines)** The U.S.S. *Nautilus* (SS-168) and the *Narwhal* (SS-167) reach Panay and Negros and unload supplies and evacuate personnel. **(China-Burma-India)** General "Vinegar Joe" Stilwell, Commander of Northern Combat Area Command in Burma, and his Force are transferred from operational command of the Fourteenth Army and attached

The U.S. Fleet knocking out enemy Planes off the Marianas.

U.S. Engineers laying treadway bridge over the Vire River, France.

to the direct control of General Eisenhower, Supreme Allied Commander. The troops operating as part of the Galahad Operation still attempt to take Myitkyina, but their numbers have been thinned by malaria, fatigue and battle-exhaustion. The quest to seize the coveted Airfield is slowed considerably. In activity on the Salween Front, the Chinese 36th Division battles heavily in the Shweli Valley, capturing Watien. Meanwhile, U.S. Vice President Henry A. Wallace meets in Chungking, China with Chiang Kai-shek and General Chennault. **(Atlantic-France)** In the **U.S. First Army** area, General Bradley instructs General Collins to break out and advance toward the west coast of the Peninsula and seize it before advancing north against Cherbourg. Collins designates the feisty 82nd Airborne and the 9th Divisions to take the objective. In conjunction, the U.S. 4th and 90th Divisions are driving against Cherbourg. Brigadier General Jay W. MacKenzie is an inexperienced Battlefield Commander and within three days, his unsuccessful efforts to advance bring about his recall. In fairness to MacKenzie, his subordinate Commanders had not been perceived as battle toughened either. After the change of Commanders, the 90th Division is transformed into a tenacious fighting unit that will surpass expectations. The Germans hold rigidly at their defenses, about four to six miles outside of Cherbourg. The 60th Infantry, 9th Division speeds northward toward its objective Hill 170, breezing through Vasteville, then halting east of Haut Biville, trailed by the 47th Infantry, which pivots east and heads for Bois du Mont du Roc. The 79th Division advances to a point between Bois de Roudou and St. Martin-le-Greard in synchronization with the 4th Division, moving effortlessly from their positions at Le Thiel to the fringes of the main enemy strongpoint in their sector at Bois de Roudou. Near Cherbourg, a contingent of Company A, 207th Engineering Battalion is holding positions; the town's people begin waving the American Flag and offer the Yanks wine. Everyone who drinks the wine gets severely ill. Sergeant Joseph Polya, who had not had any wine, then issues orders known as Polya's Rules. "IF YOU SEE ANY FRENCHMEN, SHOOT THEM." The Yanks, subsequent to receiving what they believed to be poisoned wine, were no longer bothered by the Frenchmen. In other activity the 29th Division, operating in the **XIX Corps** area, encounters stiff resistance at Villiers-Fossard; Engineers and Tank units are brought in to assist, but the Germans hold. In the British 10th Corps sector, the British 6th Armored Division occupies Perugia without incident. The British 13th Corps, deployed in the center and on the right flank, runs into resistance at German advance outposts in the area stretching from west of Chiusi to

Lake Trasimeno. **(Atlantic-Finland)** The Russians seize Viipuri, opening the Gulf of Finland to the Russian Ships and also guarantees the safety of Leningrad. **(Atlantic-Italy)** The Germans have reformed their lines and prepare a delaying action across Italy below the Gothic Line, bringing about a temporary abatement to the swift advance of the Fifth Army. At present, the **U.S. Fifth Army** stands midway between the Arno and Tiber Rivers, after grinding through vicious rearguard actions for the past 10 days. The Polish 2nd Corps, deployed across the Aso River, captures Fermo and Pedaso. The IV Corps anchors a line running east from the intersection of Highways 1 and 73. Contingents of the French Expeditionary Corps advance to the Orcia River and halts movement. The 2nd Moroccan Division moves in to replace the 1st Motorized Division at midnight (20th-21st), enabling the latter to prepare to participate in Operation ANVIL.

June 21st 1944 — (Southwest Pacific) The formal organization of Task Force Cyclone (force to seize Noemfoor) is formalized. Brigadier General Edward D. Patrick establishes a temporary Command Post at Finschhafen, New Guinea. **(Pacific-Marianas-Saipan)** Marine Major General Holland M. Smith instructs the 27th Division, U.S.A. (minus one Infantry Battalion and one Light Tank Platoon) to form northwest of Aslito Airfield in the Northern Troops and Landing Force Reserve, while one Battalion maintains the mop-up operation on Nafutan Point. Subsequently, RCT 105, takes over the mop-up task, but a mix-up in communication of the orders prevents the Combat Team from taking over until the 22nd. During the action on Nafutan Point, the 2nd Battalion, 105th Infantry replaces the 2nd Battalion, 165th Infantry on the left side; gains for the day are nominal. The 3rd Battalion, 105th Infantry, drives east along the south coast and demolishes an enemy stronghold, nearing the troops which had been driving down from the north. In other activity, General Holland Smith directs the 27th Division to begin reconnaissance northward to join the Marines. General Ralph Smith, U.S.A., orders RCT 105, to relieve RCT 165 contingents before 06:30 on the 22nd; to regroup and reinitiate the offensive. The Artillery of the 27th Division is placed under the direction of the XXIV Corps Artillery. Intelligence places the remaining number of defending Japanese on Nafutan point at between 300 and 500 troops. **(Pacific-New Guinea)** The U.S. Fifth Air Force begins using Owi Airfield for its Fighters. In other activity, the Japanese holding the West Caves still hold. The ongoing attack of the 162nd Infantry's 1st Battalion is bolstered by Flame Throwers and Tanks. The Japanese stymie the assault and simultaneously attempt to withdraw and infiltrate the lines of the 186th Infantry, which is assaulting from the south and southwest. The 186th repulses the escape attempt. The 3rd Battalion, 163rd Infantry, attempts to strike the enemy Teardrop position, slightly northwest of Hill 320, in synchronization with the attack of the 186th Infantry, advancing from the south and southwest. The distance is too great, preventing it from reaching the objective. In the Wakde-Sarmi area, Japanese still hold Lone Tree Hill and repulse a strong attack mounted by the 3rd Battalion, 20th Infantry. compelling the Yanks to withdraw to the east bank of the Snaky River. The 3rd Battalion bombards Lone Tree Hill with mortar and Artillery fire throughout the night. **(Pacific-Solomons-Bougainville)** The 3rd Marine Defense Battalion is withdrawn to Guadalcanal. It is the last Fleet Marine Ground contingent in the active South Pacific area. **(Atlantic-England)** Operation FRANTIC commences. The U.S. Eighth Air Force begins to shuttle Planes between England and the Soviet Union, bombing enemy installations along the route. Allied Base in Italy will also be utilized. Today, 70 P-51s and 114 B-17s bombard enemy oil installations at Ruhland, south of Berlin, then land in Russia. The Germans locate the base at Poltava and send Planes during the night of the 21-22nd, inflicting heavy damage to the Planes and the installations; an ammo dump is blown. **(Atlantic-France)** In the **U.S. First Army VII Corps** area, the 9th and 79th U.S. Divisions continue preparing for the final assault against Cherbourg. Patrols are dispatched to gather intelligence and capture prisoners. Meanwhile, the 4th Division continues to press primary strongpoints of Cherbourg's defenses. A Battalion of the 22nd Infantry seizes Hill 158 and severs a connecting road between Cherbourg and St Pierre-Eglise. The Commanding General of the Germans, Major General Karl Wilhelm von Schlieben, receives an ultimatum from General Collins instructing the Germans to surrender by 09:00 on the 22nd. Von Schlieben does not respond, choosing instead to follow the orders of Hitler: "FIGHT TO THE DEATH." Also, Allied Planes drop leaflets over Cherbourg instructing the enemy to surrender. Knowing that all escape routes are severed, the Americans add a note to the message stating: "AND DON'T FORGET YOUR MESS KITS". Von Schlieben issues the following order: "I EMPOWER ALL LEADERS OF WHATEVER RANK TO SHOOT AT SIGHT ANYONE WHO LEAVES HIS POST BECAUSE OF COWARDICE." The American ammunition and other critical supplies are in short supply, but Cherbourg is postured for the kill. In Naval activity, the Coast Guard Cutters 83415 and 83471 are both sunk during a violent storm. The Destroyer *Davis* (DD-395) is damaged after striking a mine. **(Atlantic-Italy)** Contingents of the Polish 2nd Corps reach the Chienti River and begin to establish a bridgehead near the enemy's river line. In the **U.S. Fifth Army** area, the IV Corps deploys the 1st Armored Division, reinforced by the 361st Infantry, 91st Division, to fill a void left by the departure of Task Force Ramey on the right flank of the 36th Division, which is continuing its rough advance along Highway 1. In other activity, the French Expeditionary Corps is stalled by vicious enemy opposition at the Orcia River Line. In the **British Eighth Army** area, elements of the 13th Corps engage advance positions of the enemy Trasimeno Line. Sanfatuccio offers fierce resistance, but it falls to the British 78th Division. Vaiano, a nearby village is retained by the Germans. Although the South African Armored Division gains ground up to the heights near Chiusi, it is prevented from penetrating, prompting the 13th Corps to commit reinforcements. The British 4th Division and the Canadian 1st Armored Brigade are committed to the struggle; the 4th Division relieves the British 78th Division near Vaiano during the night of the 22nd-23rd, then subsequently relieves the balance of the 78th Division, permitting it to depart the theater by the end of June. **(Atlantic-Finland-Russia)** The Red Army (Karelian Front) initiates an attack on both sides of Lake Onega, Finland.

June 22nd 1944 — (Pacific-Marianas-Saipan) The 2nd and 4th Marine Divisions continue their attacks northward against the 0-5 line, which stretches from the west coast below Garapan to the Lalau Village on the Kagman Peninsula on the east coast. Contingents of the 6th Marines, 2nd Marine Division, reach the peak of Mount Tipo Pale, situated about 1,200 yards from Mt. Tapotchau, which dominates the entire island. The 8th Marines, operating on the right flank, drive across rough ground against Tipo Pale; the 2nd Marines, already positioned along the line, stay in place. During the synchronized assault, the 4th Marine Division, its 23rd Mari-

nes pulling the center, 24th driving on the right and the 25th advancing on the left, strike toward the objective. The 27th Division, minus the 105th Infantry, receives instructions to drive forward between the positions of the 2nd and 4th Marine Divisions to alleviate pressure on the left flank and simultaneously permit the 4th Division to swerve eastward to tackle the Kagman Peninsula. Meanwhile, the 27th Division begins to reform near the Nafutan positions. The difficult maneuver causes the left flank to lose some terrain as the 2nd Battalion, 105th Regiment, relieves the 3rd Battalion, 165th Infantry. The 3rd Battalion, 105th Regiment swings north to relieve the 1st Battalion on the right flank. The 165th Infantry activity is northwest of Aslito Airfield, which becomes operational. Planes of the 19th Army Fighter Squadron land and immediately begin Combat Air Patrols. Mop-up continues on Nafutan Point with the 2nd Battalion, 105th Infantry, getting word to keep the operation going; enemy troop estimates have been grossly underestimated. In Naval activity, enemy Aircraft damage the Battleship *Maryland* (BB-46); in addition, enemy coastal guns inflict damage to the LST 119. In other Naval activity, the Destroyer *Newcomb* (DD-586) and the Minesweeper *Chandler* (DMS-9) sink the Japanese Submarine I-185. **(Pacific-New Guinea)** The first large Transports arrive at Biak. Japanese resistance in the West Caves has not diminished during the early morning hours, but improvisation by the 1st Battalion, 162nd Infantry, soon changes the situation; additional Flame Throwers and TNT charges are implemented, staggering the defenders. The caves are reported secure just before 16:00. After dark, remnant groups of enemy units attempt to break out of their caverns but are quickly eliminated by the 1st Battalion, supplemented by the 186th Infantry, stationed to the north, which is still pounding against the Teardrop to destroy three enemy guns which have been moved to new positions northwest of U.S. lines and are ringing fire upon them; the attacks fail to silence the guns. In addition, Mokmer Airdrome initiates operations of the Fifth Air Force's P-40s. Later in the evening, Reconnaissance Teams are transported by PT Boats to Noemfoor to gather additional intelligence for the imminent invasion. In other activity, RCT 158 is being relieved to allow it time to prepare for the operation at Noemfoor; to date, it has sustained 70 killed, 257 wounded and 4 missing, against the Japanese losses of about 920 killed and 11 captured in the Wakde-Sarmi campaign. In the Wakde-Sarmi area, P-47s from Wakde combine with Artillery to blast enemy positions prior to the attack against Lone Tree Hill. Upon cessation of the Air-Artillery assault, the 20th Infantry advances with the 2nd and 3rd Battalions reaching the crest of the hill. Both units reach the crest, but a gap is created, threatening defensive positions during the night, when the Japanese mount a fierce counterattack. The 3rd Battalion and Company L, 2nd Battalion, becomes isolated, and at dawn on the 23rd, the enemy strikes tenaciously. The 2nd Battalion, 20th Infantry tries driving north to hook up with the 3rd Battalion to solidify their positions, but enemy resistance prevents the advance, forcing them back down the slopes; they retrace the route of the Third Battalion. Enemy resistance is evident throughout the entire area, but volunteers attached to Company L, 1st Infantry brave the fire and carry necessary supplies and ammunition to the beleaguered Battalion. The contest is viciously fought and casualties are rampant on both sides. The Japs attempt to annihilate the troops on Lone Tree Hill during the night of the 23rd-24th. Major General Franklin C. Sibert orders a counterattack flanking maneuver. On the 24th, Task Force Toronado bangs against the outer defenses of Lone Tree Hill. In conjunction,

Companies K and L, 1st Infantry, swing in from the sea, striking the beaches west of the hill where they fortify a beachhead and attempt to drive inland. Enemy fire contains the advance and no progress is made, granting the Japanese continued control of the west side of the hill. Meanwhile, the 2nd, and 3rd Battalions, 20th Infantry, grind forward directly into the enemy fire coming from the summit. The attack, supplemented by Company L, 1st Infantry, opens a supply route ensuring continuation of the rescue operation. Company M, 1st Infantry, dashes along the coast. Japanese who are bottled-up on the hill, continue to inflict many casualties, while also sustaining heavy losses. On the 25th, the 2nd and 3rd Battalions, 20th Infantry and their sidekick, the 3rd Battalion, 1st Infantry, charge to break the hold. The propulsion of the combined attack shatters the enemy line and the Japanese flee from the hill. Infantry units begin to clean up the surrounding area. By the 26th, the 3rd Battalion, 63rd Infantry moves to the crest of Lone Tree Hill, relieving the battered and exhausted 2nd and 3rd Battalions, 20th Infantry. Old Glory and the U.S. Army own Lone Tree Hill. Along the Aitape Front, the 3rd Battalion, 127th Infantry moves to Afua to relieve the 1st Battalion. **(China-Burma-India)** In the Northern Combat Area Command (Burma), the Chindits, 77th Brigade, Indian 3rd Division, supported by the 114th Regiment of the Chinese 38th Division, assault Mogaung. On the Salween Front, the Japanese begin to withdraw from Chiangtso. As they hasten toward Teng-chung, they are strafed by Allied Aircraft. The Japanese holding Teng-chung are also about to be struck. The Chinese XX Group Army is in firm control of the Shweli Valley and prepares to assault Teng-chung. In the **British Fourteenth Army** area (11 Army Group), the 4th and 33th Corps join together as the enemy offensive has failed. The Japanese are in fast retreat, pestered by the Allies and monsoon rains. **(Atlantic-France)** In the **U.S. First Army** area, the VII Corps attacks, prefaced by a massive Air Assault. The Royal Air Force joins the show as ten Squadrons of Mustangs and Typhoons strike the enemy bastion of Cherbourg. U.S. Air Power commits more than 560 Fighter Planes and nearly 400 Medium Bombers of the IX Bomber Command which sweep the area. The air power, however, does not inflict severe damage to the installations. The attack does take a toll on the U.S. troops, as portions of the 4th, and 9th Divisions, Barton's and Manton Eddy's respectively, are mistakenly struck by friendly fire. At 14:00, the ground troops move forward. Eddy's 9th Division poised on the left flank lunges northeastward, its 47th Regiment on the right and the 60th charging from the left. Acqueville tumbles easily to the 60th, but the advance stalls at the fringes of heavily defended Flottemanville. Meanwhile, enemy controlled Hill 171 is penetrated by the sprinting 47th; advance units cling to the slopes west of Bois du Mt. du Roc. In the middle of the thrust, three Regiments of the 79th Division advance strongly; the 313th drives straight ahead along the right flank, delivering the primary punch and toppling the resistance near La Mare a Canards as it rumbles down the Valognes-Cherbourg Highway. In coordination with the Divisional charge, its 314th Regiment pushes east of Tollevast and the 315th doggedly sweeps the Hardinvast sector. To apply some additional pressure against the Germans, who have decided to fight to the death, the 4th Division attacks from the right flank of the VII Corps, committing three Regiments. The 12th drives against Tourlaville and encounters stiff resistance that limits its progress and the enemy also fares well at La Glacerie, holding the 8th Infantry to small gains. The determined 22nd Infantry is stalled, then surrounded as it attempts to take Digosville. **(Atlantic-Italy)**

The recently established beachhead by the Polish 2nd Corps across the Chienti River is abandoned. Troop transfers are initiated along with moving supplies forward to prepare for a reinforced attack against the enemy in its sector of the Adriatric coast. In the **U.S. Fifth Army** area, the French Expeditionary Corps is directed to outflank the heavily fortified enemy positions along the Orcia River line. In other activity, the U.S. 1st Armored Division deploys Task Force Howze between Combat Command A, and Combat Command B. **(Atlantic-Russia)** U.S. Planes get airborne prior to a heavy Air attack against Mirgorod by the Luftwaffe which inflicts severe damage to the facility.

Marines advancing with a bulldozer on Saipan.

June 23rd 1944 — (Pacific-Marianas-Saipan) Planes attached to a Carrier Task Force commanded by Rear Admiral J.J. Clark, strike enemy Airfield facilities on Pagan Island. The 2nd and 4th Marine Divisions and the 27th U.S.A. Division continue their three-pronged assault. The 8th Marines, advancing on the Division's (2nd) right seizes a cliff that controls a primary route to the summit of Mt. Tapotchau. The 27th Division, attempting to relieve pressure on the left flank of the 4th Marine Division, becomes sluggish, delaying its attack through "Death Valley," situated in no-man's land saddled on the right by an ominous ridge dubbed "Purple Heart" and on the left by a portion of the hills of Mt. Tapotchau. The 4th Marine Division attacks on the right flank, committing the 23rd and 24th Marines, the former having a rough time because of the inability of the 165th Infantry to break through the defenses at the caves; the 23rd Marines seizes Hill 600 and the 24th Marines drives along Magicienne Bay, reaching 0-5 line east of Laulau. The Marines hold the heights. During the night of the 23rd-24th, the Japanese mount a strong, but unsuccessful Tank-supported assault against Hill 600. Also, the U.S. 2nd Battalion, 105th Infantry reorganizes, then attacks Nafutan; only one Platoon reaches the crest; the others make some gains, then return to their starting line. In other activity, the 73rd Army Fighter Squadron arrives at Aslito Airfield. **(Pacific-New Guinea)** See June 22nd **(China-Burma-India)** U.S. Vice President Wallace and Chiang Kai-shek confer in Chungking; a proposal is discussed to allow a U.S. Observer Team to go to northern China to gather intelligence and to assist Allied Pilots who are shot down in that area. The proposal is subsequently approved and the mission coded "Dixie Mission" will be carried out by 16 Officers and men and 2 civilians; the O.S.S. joins the operation. Subsequently, Roosevelt demands that the Communist Chinese acknowledge the Nationalist Government before the U.S. will supply the Communists with lend-lease equipment. Later, General

Wedemeyer meets with Mao Tse-tung and Chou En-lai in Chunkging. In conjunction with the bickering the DIXIE Mission is withdrawn. The State Department advisors in Chunkging urge that the U.S. abandon Chiang Kai-shek and arm the Communists in northern China, infuriating Ambassador Pat Hurley. Hurley demands that State Department employees. John Davies and John Service be recalled. After the close of hostilities the Amerasia Scandal breaks in the United States. Drew Pearson, a noted columnist, uses the air-waves to proclaim that "THE U.S.A. IS BACKING THE WRONG HORSE IN CHINA." The lack of U.S. intelligence in northern China hurts the U.S. cause, but helps the Russians. At Yalta, Stalin is able to bluff his way through, giving the impression that the Russians are holding off huge Japanese forces of the Japanese Kwuntung Army in Manchuria, a myth. **(Atlantic-France)** In the **U.S. First Army** area, the outer defenses of Cherbourg show signs of crumbling. On the left flank, the 60th Infantry, 9th Division secures Flottemanville, and Hill 171 falls to the 47th Infantry. Second Lt. John E. Butts, Company E, 60th Infantry, having been wounded on the 14th and 16th, shuns medical treatment and stays with his unit; today Butts is at the head of his Platoon and again becomes seriously wounded by machine gun fire. He refuses medical aid and continues to advance, drawing fire away from his Platoon. He is killed within ten yards of the strongpoint, but his command seizes the objective; Butts becomes a recipient of the Medal of Honor posthumously. In addition, the 39th Regiment steamrolls over resistance in the vicinity of Beaudienville. The enemy strongpoint at La Mare a Canards waivers slightly under the pressure of the 79th Division but it does not capitulate. In other activity, the fighting is vicious near Tourlaville; the 12th Infantry, 4th Division, supported by Tanks, bolts forward, but some contingents operating on the flanks are compelled to advance at a slow pace. In the **British Second Army** I Corps area, Ste Honorine, northeast of Caen and east of the Orne, falls to the British 51st Division. The Germans hold tough in the area north of Caen. **(Atlantic-Italy)** British General Alexander proposes that the Allied Armies in Italy move through the Ljubljana Gap and advance into southern Germany. In the **British Eighth Army** area, a feverish battle rages. Contingents of the 13th Corps crash into Chiusi, however, they become surrounded. In other activity, the British 4th Division, 13th Corps, takes responsibility for the area between Lake Chiusi and Vaiano, relieving part of the British 78th Division. In the **British 10th Corps** area, the enemy loses some ground when the British King's Dragoon Guards force a foothold on Mt. St. Croce. **(Atlantic-Rumania)** Planes attached to the 15th Air Force attack the enemy oil facilities at Ploesti. Antiaircraft fire damages Lt. Kingsley's Plane, prior to reaching the destination, but he chooses to make the run. German ME-109s attack, further damaging the Plane and inflicting casualties. Kingsley assists the wounded tail-gunner, but eight more enemy Planes assault the crippled Aircraft. The crew is ordered to bail out; Kingsley gives the wounded man more assistance and he also gives the gunner his parachute; Kingsley's body is subsequently recovered with the wrecked Plane; he receives the Medal of Honor posthumously. **(Atlantic-Russia)** The Red Army begins its summer offensive; it spans a 350 mile front. The First Baltic and three White Russian Fronts attack the German Minsk salient in White Russia. The Germans are running out of Reserves and supplies. Heavy assaults, supported by Planes, hit Vitebsk and Bobruisk.

Mulberry Harbor at Normandy (prior to storm)

June 24th 1944 — (Pacific-Marianas-Saipan) The 2nd Marines, 2nd Marine Division advances to the southern fringes of Garapan, but are forced to stall, awaiting the contingents operating on their right flank. Meanwhile, the 6th Marines, 2nd Marine Division are heavily engaged with Japanese near Mt. Tipo Pale, while the 8th Marines combine with the 29th Marines (1st Battalion) and drive toward the summit of Mt. Tapotchau. The 27th U.S. Division receives responsibility for more terrain, but its progress is minimal. The 106th Infantry attempts to push through Death Valley without any success and the 165th Infantry is advancing through the valley, lying east of Purple Heart Ridge, but the center thrust by the 27th Division falters. The other part of the assault, being waged by the 4th Marine Division, sees progress. The hold up of the 27th prompts the 4th Marine Division to strike eastward; the 23rd Marines skim around the 24th Marines, creating a gap between the Army and Marines. General Holland Smith strongly urges General Ralph Smith, U.S.A., to speed up his 27th Division. Later in the day, General Ralph Smith is replaced by Holland Smith because of the inability of the 27th to advance. The temporary Commander becomes Major General Sanderford Jarman, U.S.A., the island Commander. The 4th Marines seize Chacha and Laulau. In the southern portion of Saipan, the attempt to take Mt. Nafutan by the 27th Division fails; the troops are ordered to withdraw. In addition to the ongoing campaign to seize the Marianas from the Japanese, the U.S. Navy pays an unannounced visit to other Japanese strongholds in the island chain. Planes from the Carrier Task Groups of Rear Admirals J.J. Clark, and A.E. Montgomery, bombard enemy positions on the Volcano and Pagan Islands in the Marianas. Iwo Jima island is also attacked. **(Pacific-New Guinea)** See June 21st 1944. In other activity, the PT 193 becomes grounded and is destroyed by U.S. forces. **(Atlantic)** The U.S.S. *Bogue* (CVE-9), an Escort Carrier, launches Planes (VC-69) which sink the Japanese Submarine I-52. **(Atlantic-France)** In the **U.S. First Army** area, the noose around Cherbourg becomes tighter. The 60th Infantry, 9th Division, clears the northern flank; simultaneously, the 39th and 47th Infantry Regiments close on the city; the 39th drives toward Octeville and the 47th advances toward the strongpoints near Equeurdreville and Redoute des Fourches. La Mare a Canards is seized by the 314th Infantry, 79th Division, in conjunction with the 313th Regiment which captures Hameau Gringer. In addition, the 315th Infantry is operating in the rear, eliminating the remnant enemy forces around Hardinvast. General Barton's 4th Division attacks; the 12th Infantry (reinforced 1st Battalion 22nd Infantry), spearheads the thrust and grinds down fierce resistance near Digosville, then sprints forward, taking Tourlaville by nightfall without incident. The balance of the 4th Division is heavily involved east of La Glacerie to the left of the Division advance; the 22nd Infantry, less 1st Battalion, concentrates against the defenders at Maupertus, containing them. In other activity, 3rd Armored Division, XIX Corps, arrives in France. **(Atlantic-Italy)** In the **U.S. Fifth Army** area, the **IV Corps** maintains its northward attack, engaging rear-action troops. Along the coast, the 117th Cavalry Reinforced Squadron seizes Follonica. In the French Expeditionary Force sector, the Guillaume Group, supported with Light Armor units, advances across the Ombrone River, but maintains communication with the 1st Armored Division, IV Corps. In the **British Eighth Army** area, three Divisions of the 13th Corps attack north. The British 78th Division, operating on the right flank, establishes a bridgehead across the Pescia River, while the South African 6th Armored Division, maintaining the left flank, is fiercely engaged with the enemy at Chiusi. The center of the advance, paced by the British 4th Division, runs into resolute opposition at Vaiano; during the night, the Germans evacuate and the British occupy the town. In the British 10th Corps sector, the enemy gets additional aid from the landscape; the British drive through the Tiber Valley against a shortened enemy line, but the mountains impede progress.

June 26th 1944 — Dead Japanese defenders at Aslito Airfield, Saipan.

June 25th 1944 — (Pacific-Marianas-Saipan) The battle for Saipan continues to rage. Stiff enemy resistance on Mt. Tapotchau is leveled by the 8th Marines, reinforced with contingents of the 29th Marines (both 2nd Marine Division); the victors comfortably control the primary strongpoint of the island. Rigid resistance is mounted by the Japanese, north of Mt. Tipo Pale, holding up the 6th Marines. On the right flank, the Kagman Peninsula is seized by the 4th Marine Division. The 27th Division, U.S.A., is still heavily engaged in the center thrust to secure Death Valley and Purple Heart Ridge, but the Japanese refuse to relent; the 165th Infantry is receiving severe punishing blows from the entrenched Japanese. In the southern portion of Saipan, the 2nd Battalion, 105th Infantry, drives to Nafutan, striking a thunderous blow and rattling the Japs; the Main Line of Resistance on Nafutan collapses and the 105th pulverizes the defenders on Ridge 300, solidifying the American effort on Saipan. It is now inevitable, the Japs have lost the Ridge which controls the fate of Nafutan Point and they will revert to fanatical acts of desperation. During the night, a Japanese Soldier who had feigned death, drops a grenade into a foxhole containing several Marines including P.F.C. Harold Epperson (2nd Division). Epperson, throws

himself over the grenade and his body is shattered. His actions save the other Marines; Epperson becomes a recipient of the Medal of Honor posthumously. **(Pacific-New Guinea)** On Biak, the enemy guns that have been harassing the American lines are captured by Company L, 186th Infantry; the enemy stronghold, Teardrop, has been partially evacuated when the 1st and 2nd Battalions, 186th Infantry charge forward, trampling the resistance and killing 38 enemy troops. In the Wakde Sarmi area, Lone Tree Hill is abandoned by the Japanese, while under heavy attack by two Battalions of the 20th Infantry and the 3rd Battalion, 1st Infantry. **(China-Burma-India)** On the Salween Front, the Chinese inform representatives of the American Military that the Commander of the Chinese 87th Division had attempted suicide after learning that one of his Regiments (261st) had been thoroughly thrashed by the Japanese. The Chinese 8th Army is en route to aid the 87th Division, but its efforts are futile as the battle has ended at Lung-ling and the enemy force numbers around 1,500 men. The approximate number of Chinese troops in the region stands at about 10,000. Chiang Kai-shek orders the Chinese to make an all-out effort to seize Teng-chung and Sung Shan, to fortify their positions in order to retake Lungling. **(Atlantic-France)** The Germans holding Cherbourg receive a thunderous bombardment by Allied Artillery, supported by Planes and Rear Admiral Deyo's Naval Surface Force. German shore batteries return fire, damaging one Battleship and three Destroyers. The ground troops lunge forward, igniting another blood filled struggle; the 47th Infantry, 9th Division crashes into the western suburbs of Cherbourg, seizing the fort at Equeurdreville, Hameau de Tot and Redoute des Fourches. Additional contingents advance to the coast, but are recalled. Octeville, another enemy stronghold, repulses the 39th Infantry. In other bitter fighting, elements of the 79th Division hit heavy opposition; the 314th Infantry slugs through tough resistance, reaching the upper defenses of Fort du Roule, Headquarters of General von Schlieben. The fort contains an overpowering view of the area and its deadly guns peer toward all approach roads while other guns are directed to the sea lanes. These long-range weapons greatly outdistance the available U.S. Naval guns. During the heated battle, Corporal (later Tech Sergeant) John D. Kelly volunteers to take out machine gun nests. He charges, transporting a ten foot pole dangling 15 pounds of explosives, but the detonation fails to knock out the obstacle. Kelly again volunteers, taking a bigger charge which blows open the rear door; he tosses several grenades and the survivors surrender. Another member of the 314th, 1st Lt. Carlos Ogden, Company C, takes action when his Company becomes pinned down by an 88-mm gun and two machine guns; he advances and is grazed in the head by a bullet, but continues to move and singlehandedly eliminates all three objectives; both Lt. Ogden and Corporal Kelly receive the Medal of Honor for their heroism. In related activity, the 313th Infantry, 9th Division enters the fringes of Cherbourg. The 12th Infantry, 4th Division, attacking toward the coast, east of Cherbourg, seizes its objective and subsequently receives orders to pivot and join the main assault; the 12th Infantry sprints forward and seizes control of a segment of the eastern portion of the city. In addition, the 22nd Infantry, 4th Division moves against Maupertus Airfield. In the British 30th Corps area, the British Second Army initiates its offensive, spurned to gain the strategic ground in the vicinity of Rauray. Elements of the 8th Armored Brigade combine with the British 49th Division's assault toward Tilly-sur-Seulles. The advance hits intense opposition, but gains some ground. Fontenay is breached by other units. Additional contingents drive toward Tessel-Bretteville. During the day's action the Battleship *Texas* (BB-35) and the Destroyers *Barton* (DD-722), *Laffey* (DD-724), and *O'Brien* (DD-725) are damaged by enemy coastal gun fire. **(Atlantic-Italy)** Today is the final day of action in Italy for the Texas 36th Division, which has been heavily involved throughout the entire campaign. In other activity, the U.S. 39th Engineers take the port of Piombino without incident. In the French Expeditionary Corps sector, the French troops continue their advance, crossing the Orcia River against light opposition. In the **British Eighth Army** 13th Corps area, the enemy retains Chiusi, but abandons it under cover of darkness. In other activity, the British 4th Division outguns the rear guards at Vaiano and drives them out of their positions. Also, in the British sector, the 78th Division enlarges its bridgehead at Pescia. **(Atlantic-Russia)** The Germans attempt to hold Vitebsk with five Divisions, but find themselves surrounded by the Russians. In addition, the Russians sever the highway running between Minsk and Smolensk.

Harmless German guns at Normandy, compliments of U.S. Planes and Artillery.

June 26th 1944 — **(Pacific-Kurile Islands)** A Naval Force, composed of Destroyers and Cruisers, commanded by Rear Admiral E. G. Small, bombards enemy installations on Kurabu Zaki, Paramushiro. **(Pacific-Marianas-Saipan)** The Japanese have been attempting to bolster their beleaguered forces on Saipan by transporting reinforcements by barges from Tinian. American Destroyers and Infantry Landing Craft Boats have been successful in dispersing them. Today, eleven barges attempt to break through; none succeed. This is the final at-

tempt. On the ground in Saipan, the heavily entrenched resistance north of Mt. Tipo Pale is demolished by the 6th Marines, 2nd Marine Division. Meanwhile, the 8th Marines, 2nd Marine Division, holding Mt. Tapotchau, begins to fortify its positions against counterattack. As the 2nd Marine Division maintains its pace, the 4th Marine Division, supported by the 1st Battalion, 105th U.S. Infantry and the 165th Infantry (less the 2nd Battalion), clear the remnant opposition on the right flank. Later in the day, the 4th Marine Division (Designated Northern Troops and Landing Force reserve) receives notice that it is to return to the lines on the following day and assume responsibility for the right of the V Corps front; the 25th Marines, holding Hill 500, are available as additional reinforcements if required. In conjunction, the 27th U.S. Division continues to plow forward in the center of the thrust, meeting heavy opposition; intense enemy fire originating from a Japanese stronghold dubbed "Hell's Pocket" stalls the 1st Battalion, 106th Infantry at the southwestern end of Death Valley. In coordinated fighting, the 2nd Battalion, 165th Infantry, strikes Purple Heart Ridge from the east, synchronized with an attack by the 3rd Battalion, 106th Infantry driving from the west; the combined attacks force the enemy to begin faltering. The Commanding Officer of the 106th Infantry is replaced today. On the southern end of Saipan, the enemy is thoroughly compressed at Nafutan Point by the 2nd Battalion, 105th Infantry. The Japanese await darkness and attempt to escape. The 317th Japanese Independent Infantry breaks through the outposts of the 2nd Battalion, 105th Infantry, U.S.A., and assaults Aslito Airfield and Hill 500, where they strike a hornets' nest dubbed the "25th Marines." The Japanese also attempt to destroy the 14th Marine Artillery positions that are poised between Hill 500 and the Airport; there is little slack in the American lines and the Japanese are severely beaten, sustaining grievous losses. In other activity, the American Cargo Ship *Mercury* (AK-42) is damaged by an Aircraft torpedo. **(Pacific-New Guinea)** On Biak, the Americans begin mop-up operations. Company C, is bushwhacked by the enemy and prevented from joining the operation; the balance of the 1st Battalion, 34th Infantry scours the area, seizing abandoned enemy fortifications on a ridge on the northwest tip of Teardrop. In the Wakde-Sarmi area, the exhausted 2nd and 3rd Battalions, 20th Infantry, maintaining control of Lone Tree Hill, are relieved by the 3rd Battalion, 63rd Infantry. **(China-Burma-India)** Brigadier General Haydon Boatner U.S.A., Commander of the Myitkyina Task Force, is struck with Malaria and is replaced by Brigadier General Theodore Wessels, U.S.A. Elements of the Chinese 38th Division and the 77th Brigade, 3rd Indian Division, seize Mogaung. In short order, the Commander of the 77th takes his outfit out of action, declaring exhaustion in direct defiance of the orders of General Stilwell, who fears the action could allow the Japanese to reinforce Myitkyina; the collapse of the stronghold finally gives the Myitkyina Force their first contact with friendly forces since their arrival in Burma. **(Atlantic-France)** In the **U.S. First Army VII Corps** area, the U.S. Navy is asked for assistance. General Bradley speaks to Rear Admiral Kirk to enlist some Destroyers to help crack the resistance at Fort du Roule. Kirk realizes that his Warships will be under heavy fire because of the capacity of the enemy guns, but he takes the mission; as expected, the range of the enemy weapons forces a withdrawal. The U.S. 39th Division speeds through Octeville and Cherbourg, reaching the coast, capturing German General von Schlieben and an additional 800 troops, including the German Naval Commander, Rear Admiral Walther Hennecke at the fortress (St Sauveur-le-Vicomte); von Schlieben refuses all attempts for him to order the remainder of his command to surrender. The U.S. Ninth Division commits its 47th Infantry to eradicate the resistance on the northwestern side of Cherbourg, but the arsenal stronghold does not fall. The 79th Division completes the seizure of Fort du Roule, completing its original mission. Maupertus Airfield feels the sting of the 22nd Infantry, 4th U.S. Division, which commences a strong attack to dislodge the enemy; it falls on the following day. The U.S. beachhead is now solidified. Initially, evacuation of the wounded had been extremely dangerous and only the lightly wounded could be evacuated, but as of today, 15,000 casualties have been taken to England. In the **British Second Army** area, 30th Corps sector, the British 8th Armored Brigade darts forward in advance of the British 49th Division, driving toward Rauray. Meanwhile, the main assault begins in the 8th Corps area; the attack is three pronged, sending the British 11th Armored Division toward Mouen, while the 15th and 43rd British Infantry Divisions drive east to the right of the 30th Corps; some elements of the 15th Division move to Colleville. **(Atlantic-Italy)** In the **U.S. Fifth Army IV Corps** area, the 36th Division relinquishes its sector to the 34th Infantry and begins to prepare for Operation ANVIL (Invasion of Southern France). In addition, RCT 517 (Paratroop) is also relieved of duty and withdraws from the line. RCT 442 (Nisei) less the 1st Battalion and other contingents, including the 100th Battalion, 804th Tank Destroyer Battalion is also attached to the 34th Division. In the French sector, the crossing of the Orcia River is completed, but the Germans have extracted serious casualties upon them for their efforts. In the **British Eighth Army** area, 13th Corps sector, the 6th Armored (South African) Division occupies Chiusi; the 8th Indian Division seizes M. Pilonica. **(Atlantic-Russia)** Planes attached to the U.S. Eighth Air Force depart Russia and bomb an oil installation at Drohobycz, Poland as they fly to Italy to participate in Operation FRANTIC. The Planes, while in Italy, support the Fifteenth Air Force against enemy positions before they depart for England. In other activity, the Germans are experiencing difficulty in obeying Hitler's orders to hold designated key positions at all hazards. The Russians take Vitebsk and Zhlobin, the former being one of Hitler's listings.

U.S. Artillery fifing upon German positions in Cherbourg.

June 27th 1944 — (Pacific-Saipan) Enemy resistance continues to be heavy against the 6th Marines, 2nd Marine Division as it advances in the center on the left flank of the V Corps attack. Other elements of the 2nd Marine Division are fighting to secure the northern slope of Mt Tapotchau. The 4th Marine Division moves additional units to the line 0-6. On the southern portion of Saipan, Nafutan Point is declared secure at 18:40 after the successful conclusion of the mission of the 2nd Battalion, 105th Infantry. Nafutan point had been defended by approximately 1,000 troops, substantially more than previously thought by the Americans. The enemy body count is 550. **(Pacific-New Guinea)** On Biak, enemy resistance in the West Caves has been eliminated, allowing Patrols to venture deeply into the caverns. Contingents of both the 41st Counter Intelligence Detachment and 1st Battalion, 165th Infantry, make the uncomfortable trek, trying to ignore the overpowering stench; the rapid moving survey indicates at least 125 dead Japanese. Mokmer Airdrome is now safe from further jeopardy. On the Aitape Front, there is much regrouping and revision of organization, including Major General Charles P. Hall, Commanding General XI Corps, assuming command of Task Force Persecution, which is considered to be susceptible to an imminent enemy attack. In the Wakde-Sarmi area, the remnant enemy resistance, including several enemy machine gun nests, continues to harass the 3rd Battalion, 63rd Infantry; the clean out operation terminates all resistance by the 30th of June on Lone Tree Hill. **(China-Burma-India)** The Japanese infiltrate Chinese positions and manage to reinforce their troops at Sung Shan. Also on the Salween Front, the Chinese make some Divisional deployment changes, allowing the Japanese to take advantage and retake terrain that had been lost during June. **(Atlantic-France)** In the **U.S. First Army's VII Corps** area, the heavily defended Arsenal in Cherbourg finally relents. The Deputy Commanding Officer, Brigadier General Robert Sattler, responds to the U.S. ultimatum and surrenders to the 47th Infantry, 9th Division. Cherbourg will be garrisoned by the 4th Division; while it is taking responsibility, elements of its 22nd Infantry seize the Airfield (Maupertus), while other units eliminate enemy resistance at Cap Levy. In the **U.S. VIII Corps** area, the 101st Airborne Division is replaced by the recently arrived 83rd Division, which takes defensive responsibility for the left flank of the Corps. In the **British 2nd Army** 30th Corps area, Rauray is seized by the British 49th Division; subsequently, it repulses a heavy counterattack. **(Atlantic-Italy)** In the **U.S. Fifth Army** area, the IV Corps continues advancing toward Highway 68; the French Expeditionary troops run into heavy resistance. The Germans begin to retire after dark. In the **British Eighth Army** 13th Corps area, German rear-guards in the vicinity of Gioiella are beaten back and dispersed by the British 4th Division. In the British 10th Corps area, the Germans are also on the retreat. Elements of the British 6th Armored Division advance to M. Bagnolo and M. Pacciano, securing them without incident.

A temporary cemetery at Normandy.

A U.S. Soldier glances up at a once deadly piece of German Artillery outside of Cherbourg.

June 28th 1944 — (Pacific-Marianas-Saipan) The 2nd Marine Division still meets intense opposition as it eliminates the remaining defenders on the crest of Mt. Tapotchau. Tipo Pale falls to Company K, 6th Marines. The 27th Division U.S.A., receives its new Commander, Major General George W. Griner. The 27th meets fierce resistance which causes severe casualties as it continues to eradicate heavy enemy resistance on Purple Heart Ridge and also within Death Valley; the efforts are supplemented by support fire from contingents of the 4th Marine Division, which is simultaneously fortifying its positions on the right flank of the Corps. Enemy resistance at Hell's Pocket is totally reduced by elements of the 27th Division. **(Pacific-New Guinea)** On Biak, the Japanese again withdraw from their positions to prepare for guerrilla activity. The Japs, still holding positions in the East Caves, also begin to abandon them. At the Ibde Pocket, where strong resistance is continuing, the ground attack is aborted, but the Japanese remain under constant bombardment by Planes and Artillery. Major General Jens A. Doe receives command of Task Force Hurricane from General Eichelberger before he departs the island. In other activity on Biak, the 34th Infantry continues to clear enemy resistance; it will be assigned as Reserve to supplement Task Force Alamo during the next operation against the Japanese. **(Western Pacific)** The Japanese Coastal Defense Vessel No. 24 is destroyed by the Submarine *Archerfish* (SS-311). **(Atlantic-France)** In the **U.S. First Army** area, the 4th Division is in control of Cherbourg, allowing the 79th Division to move south to the **VIII Corps** sector. In the **British Second Army** area, the 30th Corps seizes Bret-

tevillette after a fierce struggle, only to lose it to a strong counterattack. In other activity, the British 8 Corps enlarges its bridgehead near Baron, while simultaneously seizing another outside of Gavrus. **(Atlantic-Italy)** In the **U.S. Fifth Army** sector, Piombino is occupied by specialists and the town's port facilities are quickly repaired and modified to accept Liberty Ships within a month. In the **IV Corps** area, the combined strength of the 1st Armored Division driving on the right and the 34th Division surging on the left, brings them closer to Highway 68. In the **British Eighth Army** sector, the 6th South African Armored Division advances against Chianciano, but finds no enemy there. In other activity, the British 4th Division penetrates enemy resistance at Casamaggiore-Frattevecchia Ridge. **(China-Burma-India)** U.S. Vice President Wallace is in China meeting with Chiang Kai-shek; the Vice President then informs President Roosevelt that Stilwell should be relieved or that General Stilwell should be given a representative of the President (political appointee) as his deputy. Wallace urges the changes to meet the Japanese threat in Eastern China. In the Northern Combat area of Burma, elements of the Chinese 14th Division attack enemy positions near Sitapur, to eliminate Japanese resistance north of Myitkyina. On the Salween Front, the Japanese defenders at Sung Shan are greeted for the first time by their Planes, which pass over and drop supplies. In other activity in the CBI Theater, the Japanese initiate a bold attack against Heng-Yang in eastern China against staunch resistance. **(Atlantic-Russia)** Mogilev falls to the Russians, applying more pressure against the Germans who are jeopardized at Minsk.

An American helmet on a cross, bearing an inscription by a Frenchman; "died for France."

June 29th 1944 — (United States) The U.S.S. *Valor* (AMC 108), a Coastal Minesweeper, is sunk after becoming involved in a collision off Newport Rhode Island. **(Pacific-Dutch East Indies)** The U.S.S. *Darter* (SS-227), operating off the East Indies, attacks and sinks the Japanese Minelayer *Tsugaru*. **(Pacific-Marianas-Saipan)** On Saipan, the 2nd Marine Division is still engulfed in heavy combat on the left flank of the Corps. The 4th Marine Division and its accompanying 165th Infantry, 27th U.S. Division continue to bolster the right flank; the 27th Division, operating in the middle; is slowly advancing through Death Valley, gaining about 1,000 yards; its 2nd Battalion, 165th Infantry encounters fierce resistance on the northern slope of Purple Heart Ridge. **(Pacific-New Guinea)** On Biak, American Engineers are fired upon from enemy troops still entrenched in the East Caves, prompting the commitment of Tanks and Mortars to more quickly eliminate the resistance. In other activity, elements of the U.S. 34th Division continue clearing the area north of the 186th Infantry's positions, against nominal opposition. On the Aitape Front, Major General C. P. Hall splits Task Force Persecution into three separate Commands, designated: Eastern Defense Area, General Gill; Western Defense Area, Brigadier General Alexander Stark and Eastern Defense Command, General Clarence Martin, with the latter delegated to holding the outer defense lines along the Driniumor River with contingents including the Cavalry RCT 112, the 3rd Battalion, 127th Infantry and the 128th Infantry (less the 3rd Battalion). **(China-Burma-India)** In Burma, Colonel Charles N. Hunter assumes command of all U.S. troops in the Myitkyina area; his term is short as he is abruptly relieved of command on August 3rd. In other activity, the 1st Battalion, 42nd Regiment, Chinese Division, advances rapidly through enemy terrain, but then becomes stalled by heavy fire; an American unit, Company F, New Galahad Force attempts to reinforce, but takes the wrong route and is ambushed, suffering heavily and being eliminated as a fighting unit; smiling Japanese, posing as Chinese, await the approaching green troops. Not having any hardened Marauders with them, they fall prey as the impostors tell them to lay down their arms, then open up with machine guns. A few men escape, but the Company is never reformed. **(Atlantic-France)** In the **First Army VII Corps** area, the enemy Harbor Forts in Cherbourg surrender. In other activity, the 9th Division assaults, advancing toward Cap de la Hague, until halted by enemy resistance southeast of Beaumont Hague. In the **VIII Corps** sector, the 101st Airborne is detached from Corps and diverted to Cherbourg. In the **XIX Corps** area, Combat Command A, 3rd Armored Division begins to eliminate enemy resistance at the Villiers-Fossard salient, initiating the 3rd Armored's entrance into combat; the objective is northeast of St Lo, near the 29th Division's Line. In the **British Second Army** area, 8th Corps sector, Corps continues to expand its bridgehead, but it is struck by heavy counterattacks which are augmented by Armored units; 8 Corps is ordered to abort the offensive and regroup to strengthen its lines. **(Atlantic-Italy)** In the **U.S. Fifth Army IV Corps** area, the 135th Infantry replaces the 142nd Infantry, which has just reduced enemy resistance in Belvedere and Sassetta, while another contingent of the 34th Division, the 133rd Infantry drives toward Cecina, along Highway 1, hitting fierce opposition. In the **British Eighth Army** area, the Polish 2 Corps is placed under the command of the Eighth Army. Meanwhile, the enemy is abandoning their positions in this sector (Adriatic Coastal region). In the British 13th Corps sector, Acquaviva and Montepulciano are both seized by the 6th South African Armored Division and the British 78th Division occupies Castiglione del Lago without opposition. **(Atlantic-Russia)** The Germans lose Bobruisk to the Russians.

German prisoners at Cherbourg, under guard by U.S. troops.

U.S. Infantrymen tramping over a Japanese cave on Biak.

June 30th 1944 — (United States) The United States Navy has 46,032 Vessels of all types on active service. Navy personnel stands at 2,981,365, Marine Corps at 32,788 Officers and 442,816 enlisted men, and the Coast Guard at 169,258. **(Pacific-Marianas-Saipan)** At a meeting on Saipan, it is decided that the invasion of Guam will commence on the 21st of July and that the invasion troops will be reinforced with the U.S. 77th Division, which will arrive from Hawaii. The 27th Division U.S.A. culminates its trek through Death Valley and Purple Heart Ridge, making contact with the Marines on both flanks, ending the fighting for control of Southern Saipan. The Kagman Peninsula is being fortified by the Marine 4th Division, which also dispatches probing Patrols deeper into enemy territory beyond the O-6 line. **(Pacific-New Guinea)** On Biak, mop-up operations continue in the 34th Infantry sector, culminating the major phase of combat on Biak, and permitting the Regiment to return to the beachhead; the 162nd and 186th Regiments take positions on the main and reserve lines. In the Wakde-Sarmi area, Task Force Tornado finishes its clearing operation on Lone Tree Hill and the surrounding terrain. In other activity on New Guinea, at 18:00, the main Attack Force departs Toem, heading for Noemfoor. **(Atlantic-France)** British General Montgomery, the Commanding General of 21st Army Group, orders the U.S. First Army to break out from its positions to overcome the German defenses which have been excellent. Meanwhile, the British Second Army is to maintain its operation to seize Caen and to neutralize the German forces deployed between Caen and Villers-Bocage. The U.S. 9th Division, attacking in the **VII Corps** area, drives tenaciously, overpowering the German resistance at

Cap de la Hague Peninsula; elements begin probing the edge of the peninsula by nightfall. In other VII Corps activity, the transfer of the 101st Airborne is complete; it is positioned in Cherbourg, poised to drive south to join the offensive. In the American **XIX Corps** area, the 3rd Armored Division's Combat Command A completes its mission in the area north of St. Lo and is relieved by the 115th Infantry, 29th U.S. Division. **(Atlantic-Italy)** In the **U.S. Fifth Army** area (Tyrrhenian Coast), the 34th Division (IV Corps) is still fiercely embattled with the enemy for control of Cecina, but the Germans hold; the 168th Infantry is brought up to the front after dark by trucks to support the operation; elements cross the Cecina River without incident. The 135th Infantry had earlier in the day established a bridgehead across the Cecina and successfully defended it against a counterattack, in conjunction the 133rd Infantry had applied pressure against the town. In the **British Eighth Army** 13th Corps sector, Petrignano is tenaciously defended by the Germans, but the British 4th Division seizes the town.

A Yank catches up on his reading, undisturbed by the dead Japanese soldier to his left.

July 1st 1944 — (United States) General Marshall has a discussion with General Stilwell concerning his thoughts about turning the China Burma Theater into two Theaters, with Lt. General Daniel Sultan commanding in Burma and Stilwell commanding the Chinese troops in China proper. General Marshall does not inform Stilwell that he is to be promoted, to prevent interference with his decision. General Marshall has withstood many political attempts to relieve Stilwell.

Chiang Kai-shek has been trying to replace him and so has British Admiral Mountbatten. Stilwell has had severe problems with Kai-shek and the British since his return to Burma. The Chinese still have no total command and have been pushed from side to side by the Japanese, at one point prompting President Roosevelt to "WONDER WHERE THE CHINESE ARMY WAS." In addition, there is concern that civil war might break out between Chiang Kai-shek's forces and the Communists in northern China. Stalin has assured U.S. Ambassador Harriman that the Chinese Communists are "NOT REALLY COMMUNISTS, BUT A MARGARINE' IMITATION OF THE REAL THING." However, Chiang states vehemently, that the Communists are seeking power in China and are "MORE COMMUNISTIC THAN THE RUSSIANS." General Marshall had been to London during June and was informed by British General Sir Alan Brooke that "STILWELL WOULD HAVE TO BE RELIEVED AS DEPUTY TO MOUNTBATTEN BECAUSE HE COULD NOT GET ON WITH THE THREE SERVICE CHIEFS," erupting the inner feelings of Marshall who bellowed pointedly to the British General: "BROOKE, YOU HAVE THREE COMMANDERS IN CHIEF IN INDIA; NONE OF THEM WILL FIGHT. WE HAVE ONE MAN WHO WILL FIGHT AND YOU WANT HIM TAKEN OUT." Brooke becomes incensed, but acknowledges that all three were being recalled at Mountbatten's request. General Stilwell, subsequently and reluctantly accepts the offer to command Chinese troops in China provided he has specific instructions forthcoming from Roosevelt to Chiang Kai-shek; they arrive on July 6th. Chiang does not agree and more political maneuvering occurs until finally on the 30th of July Stilwell departs Burma to the dismay of the British when they discover he accepts command of the Southeast Asia Command, while Chiang is in London.

July 1st 1944 — (Pacific-Marianas-Saipan) The V Corps, composed of the 2nd and 4th Marine Divisions, operating on the flanks and the 27th U.S. Division, driving up the center, continue the campaign to gain Saipan, advancing toward the northern neck of the island. Japanese have been observed withdrawing to the north. The 2nd Marine Division makes its largest gain since arriving on the island and secures Garapan by the following day. **(Pacific-New Guinea)** Task Force Cyclone steams toward Noemfoor Island, compliments of Admiral Fechteler's Task Force 77 (VII Amphibious Force U.S. 7th Fleet), accompanied by Australian Warships; the island is bombarded; in addition, Vogelkop is also pummeled by Allied Planes as D-Day approaches. Meanwhile, on Biak, the Japanese attempt to regroup to concentrate their efforts on Guerrilla actions. Task Force Hurricane spreads around to eradicate the threat before it can become organized. In the Wakde-Sarmi area, elements of Task Force Tornado are breaking up resistance between the Tor and Woske Rivers, while the 1st Infantry drives toward Woske, moving along the coast. **(Atlantic- France)** In the **U.S. First Army** area, the offensive, ordered by British General Montgomery, is modified and the attack is now to commence on July 3rd, with the American VIII Corps, operating on the west flank of the British Army. Additional units (V, VII, and XIX Corps) advance later. General Eisenhower arrives at the front to be present when General Middleton commences the attack. In the **VII Corps** area, the final resistance is eliminated on the Cherbourg Peninsula as the 9th Division clears the edge of Cap de la Hague. In the **V Corps** sector, contingents of the 38th Infantry, 2nd Division, make slight progress with a light attack. In the **British Second Army** area, strong enemy attacks are repulsed by the British, who commit Tanks to thwart the assault. The British continue driving toward Caen. General Montgmery had expressed optimism during mid-June, concerning his objectives: "IT IS CLEAR THAT WE MUST CAPTURE CAEN AND CHERBOURG"...He continues speaking and instructs the British Army: "THE IMMEDIATE TASK OF THIS ARMY WILL BE TO CAPTURE CAEN."..."I SHALL HOPE TO SEE BOTH CAEN AND CHERBOURG CAPTURED BY JUNE 24TH." Cherbourg has already fallen (June 27th). **(Atlantic-Italy)** In the **U.S. Fifth Army** area, the 133rd Infantry, 34th Division gets contingents across the Cecina River and captures the village of Cecina. Meanwhile, the Germans unsuccessfully attempt to demolish a diminutive bridgehead east of the Cecina River, established by the 135th Infantry. Other activity has the 3rd Battalion, 168th Infantry making it across the Cecina before dawn, while Combat Command A drives against Casole d'Elsa. In the **British Eighth Army** area, the 10th Corps makes unit changes, including the arrival of the 9th Armored Brigade. There is no contact with the Germans, permitting the contingents to switch positions effortlessly. **(Atlantic-Russia)** The Germans lose Borisov to a strong Russian assault.

U.S. troops holding improvised command post near Kamiri Airstrip.

U.S. Paratroopers — 503rd Paratroop Regiment (Separate), bringing in the silk at Kamiri Airstrip, Noemfoor Island, New Guinea.

July 2nd 1944 — (Pacific-Marianas-Saipan) The 2nd and 4th Marine Divisions continue to advance across the island. The 2nd Marines, 2nd Marine Division enter a leveled (by bombardment) Garapan. The 27th Division also moves forward in its sector. In other activity, General Saito, Commander of Japanese troops on Saipan, issues orders directing all defenders to abandon their positions along the Garapan-

Tapatchon-Kagman line and to prepare to defend at the Tanapag — Hill 221-Hill 112 line. **(Pacific-New Guinea)** The Japanese defending Noemfoor are aroused early again today; U.S. Naval Planes and Surface Vessel guns plaster the enemy positions. Eighty minutes later at 08:00, the landing boats hit the beach near Kamiri Airfield without any opposition. RCT 158 (reinforced), dubbed Task Force Cyclone, moves inland prudently, eliminating sporadic resistance and secures a beachhead extending 3,000 yards wide and 800 yards deep. The progress of the invasion permits quick unloading of Artillery. In addition, the captured Airdrome is immediately modified for U.S. Planes. Admiral Fechteler, subsequently inspects the Airfield and requests that the 503rd Paratroop Infantry be brought in as reserve; he relinquishes command of the Amphibious troops to Brigadier General Edwin D. Patrick. The natives on Noemfoor who have resisted the Japanese have been subjected to many atrocities, but the arrival of MacArthur's 23,000 Yanks will soon ensure that the atrocities are terminated. The Japanese suffer over 100 casualties during the initial day of the invasion; Task Force Cyclone sustains two men killed during the fighting and one lost to accidental death. At Aitape, Task Force Persecution is reinforced with RCT 124, 31st Division, which is assigned as a reserve unit. **(China-Burma-India)** In the Myitkyina sector of Burma, Brigadier General Theodore Wessels recalls the Chinese contingents that had been dispatched to Sitapur to bolster the northern flank, which is anticipating a heavy enemy assault. On the Salween Front, enemy held Teng-chung comes under attack by elements of the Chinese 53rd Army, which eliminates some enemy pillboxes that have previously escaped destruction by Allied Airraids. In other activity in the CBI Theater, Heng-yang, in east China, receives a reprieve as the Japanese stall their attack to await Artillery units. (Atlantic-Azores) Planes (VC-58) from the U.S.S. *Wake Island* (CVE-65), sink the German Submarine U-543, southeast of the Azores. (Atlantic-France) The U.S. First Army makes final preparations for its imminent offensive. The V, VII, VIII and XIX Corps will initiate the attack, with the 101st Airborne and the 3rd Armored Divisions being retained as reserves. In other activity, the American Minesweeper YMS-350 strikes a mine and sinks off the coast of Normandy. (Atlantic-Italy) In activity, concerning O.S.S., S.S. troops surprise agents at Spezia, while they are making contact with O.S.S. Radio at Caserta; one agent, Vera, a fragile Italian girl, responsible for securing Airdrops of supplies for the Partisans, throws a grenade, destroying the radio and killing two Germans. Vera and the radio operator escape, reinstituting contact with Caserta within a week. In the U.S. Fifth Army IV Corps area, the 34th Division is active; its 13th Infantry maintains the bridgehead, then advances west, squeezing past the 133rd Infantry, which has eliminated enemy resistance on the left flank of the Corps with the seizure of Cecina Marine at the mouth of the Cecina River. At Casole d'Elsa, the Germans inflict heavy losses against Combat Command A, 1st Armored Division, losses are also heavy with Tanks. In other activity, the French Expeditionary Forces seize Simignano then advance toward Siena. In the British Eighth Army area, Patrols of the British 13th Corps reach the intersection of Highways 71 and 75, without encountering any Germans. In other British activity, the 6th South African Armored Division moves through Sinalunga without incident; it has been abandoned by the Germans. Fojano, standing in the path of the British 4th Division is also seized without incident. In the British 10th Corps area, enemy contact is finally encountered during the night. (Atlantic-Russia) The Germans at Minsk are becoming surrounded by two White Russian Forces, one of which severs the Minsk-Baranovichi Railroad.

July 3rd 1944 — (Pacific-Marianas-Saipan) The combined Army-Marine Force, with the 27th Division, U.S.A., driving up the center, heads for Tanapag Harbor. The 27th Division gains strategic terrain that controls the area, but certain elements (106th Infantry) receive heavy fire as they advance to positions near the 2nd Marine Division perimeter. The 3rd Battalion, 2nd Marines captures the heights overlooking Tanapag Harbor; the 1st and 2nd Marines secure Garapan. The 4th Marine Division also bumps into heavy resistance at Hill 721; Artillery is brought to bear on the stubborn hill throughout the night. The 23rd Marines, 4th Marine Division seizes Hills 721 and 767 on the following day. (Pacific-New Guinea) On Biak, the Japanese 18th Army prepares to attack with strength, across the Driniumor River on the mainland on the night of the 10th-1th. In other activity on Biak, enemy resistance in the East Caves has lost its fury; U.S. contingents advance through the concealed fortifications easily. Patrols are maintained for several additional days by units, including 542nd Engineer Boat and Shore Regiment and the 163rd Infantry. At Aitape, additional reinforcements arrive today and the embarkation of RCT 124, 31st Division continues until the 6th. On Noemfoor, the 158th Infantry stretches its beachhead toward Kornasoren Airfield (1,800 yards). Planes bring in the 1st Battalion, 503rd Paratroop Infantry, but the drop at Kamiri Airfield suffers ten percent casualties despite being uncontested. In other activity, elements of the 158th Infantry patrols west of the Kamiri River. (China-Burma-India) General Stilwell responds to General Marshall's offer concerning opera-

tional changes, giving specific ideas on the feasible ways of attempting to win the campaign, while putting conditions on his acceptance of a command change. (Atlantic-France) In the U.S. First Army area, during a pouring rain, the offensive (Battle of the Hedgerows) begins. The weather prohibits Air cover, but the VIII Corps, commanded by General Middleton, operating on the west flank drives down the west coast of the Cotentin Peninsula, three Divisions strong, heading for La Haye-du-Puits. Stiff German opposition is encountered, but the 82nd Airborne Division seizes Hill 131. The Carentan Marshes prove to be a formidable obstacle to the advancing Americans. The Yanks continue to press their offensive until the 14th, when General Bradley calls it off, realizing that the German line (Coutances-St Lo) is too powerful to allow a breakout. In activity concerning the German Armies in France, Field Marshal von Rundstedt, the German Commander in Chief West, is relieved by Field Marshal Guenther von Kluge. (Atlantic-Italy) In the U.S. Fifth Army area, IV Corps sector, the 34th Division, initiates a three Regiment assault, spearheaded by the 442nd Infantry pushing up the center, flanked by the 168th on the right and the 135th on its left; the objective, Leghorn, mounts enormous resistance. Elements of the 135th Regiment reach the southern fringes of Rosignano, southeast of Leghorn. In conjunction, two Companies of the 361st Infantry (attached to 1st Armored Division C.C.A.), become stalled at the approach to Casole d' Elsa. In addition, Siena falls to the 3rd Algerian Division. In the British Eighth Army area, 13th Corps sector, Cortona is found to be unoccupied by the enemy when the British 78th Division approaches. (Atlantic) The U.S.S. *Frost* (DE-144) and the U.S.S. *Inch* (DE-146), companion Destroyer Escorts, operating near Madeira, off the coast of North Africa, destroy the German Submarine U-154. (Atlantic-Russia) The First and Third White Russian Fronts capture Minsk.

July 4th 1944 — (Pacific-Guam) American Planes celebrate the 4th of July by swarming over enemy positions on Guam. During the raid, one of the Planes is struck by enemy fire while it is over Agana; it plunges into the water exploding upon impact. Luckily, the Pilot ejects about 400 yards from shore. Jap machine guns open up with everything they have to kill the Pilot, but American Fighters soar into the area and strafe to keep the Pilot alive until a Seaplane arrives to rescue him. Despite having no room in the Plane, he is saved; the Pilot is pulled further out to sea and after his chute lines are cut, he wraps himself around the wing and the Plane takes off amidst a storm of enemy fire at a few feet above the sea. (Pacific-Marianas-Saipan) The 3rd Battalion, 2nd Marines, establishes a perimeter on Matthew Point near Garapan. In other activity, the 2nd Marines (less 2nd Battalion) and the 6th Marines, 2nd Marine Division are temporarily attached to the Northern Troops and Landing Force Reserve. In yet other activity, the 1st Battalion, 105th Infantry, U.S.A., seizes Flores Point (Seaplane Base). During the day, elements of the 27th Division U.S.A., relieve two Battalions of the 4th Marine Division's left flank. The enemy penetrates the perimeter, but the new residents, 165th Infantry U.S.A., react quickly and drive the attackers away with losses. In Naval activity, the Destroyer *David W. Taylor* (DD-551) and the Destroyer Escort *Riddle* (DE-185) sink the Japanese Submarine I-10. (Pacific-New Guinea) The fighting on the ground continues as reinforcements continue to arrive. C-47s fly overhead and drop the 3rd Battalion, 503rd Paratroop Infantry, but again the drop is plagued by casualties; this time it is eight percent, prompting the balance of the 503rd to be detained until Planes can land safely at Kamiri. In coordinated activity, the

3rd Battalion, 158th Infantry continues its drive along the coast, seizing Kornasoren Airfield after an uneventful trek; elements of the 1st Battalion capture Kamiri village effortlessly and advance to Hill 201, where it halts and establishes defensive positions. **(Pacific)** U.S. Navy Task Groups commanded by Rear Admirals J.J. Clark and R. E. Davison bombard enemy positions on Iwo Jima in the Volcano Islands and also strike Chichi Jima and Haha Jima in the Bonin Islands. During the raids, the Japanese Vessel Auxiliary Submarine Chaser No. 16, the Coastal Minelayer *Sarushima* and the Japanese Transport No. 103 are sunk at the Bonins by U.S. Carrier-based Planes. In addition, the Japanese Transport No. 103 is sunk at Iwo Jima. In other U.S. Naval activity today, the S-28, an American Submarine participating in exercises near Hawaii, sinks by unknown causes. **(Atlantic-France)** Its the 4th of July; at Normandy the Generals have a sense of humor and have included the Germans in their festivities. General Bradley mentions the Military tradition of firing a 48 gun salute at 12:00 on all Military installations and the consensus is that the tradition should go as scheduled. Bradley instructs General Gerow to modify the normal salute and point the guns at the Germans. General Gerow inquired at the time, a few days prior: "JUST 48 GUNS!" Bradley responded: "NO, HELL NO ... WE'LL FIRE EVERY GUN IN THE ARMY." General Charles E. Hart takes the directive in stride and at the appropriate time, 1,100 guns fire in unison, timed to strike the enemy lines at precisely 12:00. It is not known if the Germans realized that the Yanks were simply celebrating the 4th, as they were jumping for cover. In the **U.S. First Army** area, the VIII Corps grinds slowly ahead. The 82nd Airborne takes Hill 95, perched near La Haye-du Puits; from the newly gained positions, the troops watch the 79th and 90th Divisions march past their flanks. Adding more pressure to the offensive, the VII Corps initiates its assault, spearheaded by the 83rd Division, which is entering combat for the first time. Enemy resistance is intense and the 83rd is compelled to halt progress as it wedges through a thin passageway between the Taute River and the swamps of Prairies Marcageuses, stopping it short of Periers, the primary objective. In the **British Second Army** area, 1st Corps sector, the British still prepare for their major offensive to seize Caen. Carpiquet falls to the charging 3rd Canadian Division, but German resistance is staunch at its Airfield; the Canadians are prevented from seizing it. In other activity, the British 43rd Division (8 Corps area) attempts to alleviate pressure on the British I Corps by driving northeast along the Odon River. **(Atlantic-Italy)** In the **U.S. Fifth Army IV Corps** area, elements of the 34th Division (135th Infantry) break through enemy resistance at Rosignano, seizing one third of the town. On the right flank, the 168th Infantry overpowers enemy resistance at M. Vitalba (Hill 675), but cannot get to the staunchly defended town of Castellina. In related combat, the 363rd Infantry, pushing forward to the right of Hill 675, secures some heights east of the hill and the 442nd Infantry, operating in the center of the drive, makes slight gains. The 1st Armored Division advances with its attached 361st Infantry, toward Casole d'Elsa; after tenacious fighting, elements enter the town before dawn, subsequent to the evacuation of its defenders. Soon after, the 361st Infantry reverts to the 91st Division and the 1st Armored Division will be relieved. In related activity, the U.S. Seventh Army transfers to Naples to prepare for the invasion of southern France. In the French sector, the 4th Mountain Division replaces the 3rd Algerian Division, which is sent to Naples. In the **British Eighth Army** area, the 13th Corps initiates an assault; the 6th Armored South African Division takes

the left flank and the British 6th Armored drives on the right flank of the British 4th Division, each heading for Arezzo. Enemy resistance falters as the British approach Lignano Hill, below the objective. The drive then stretches through Castiglion Fiorentino, but it stiffens upon running into enemy demolitions. **(Atlantic-Russia)** Polotsk is seized by elements of the First Baltic Front.

Two immobilized German Tanks along the road to St Lo.

U.S. Artillery pummeling German positions.

GIs tackling the hedgerows.

389

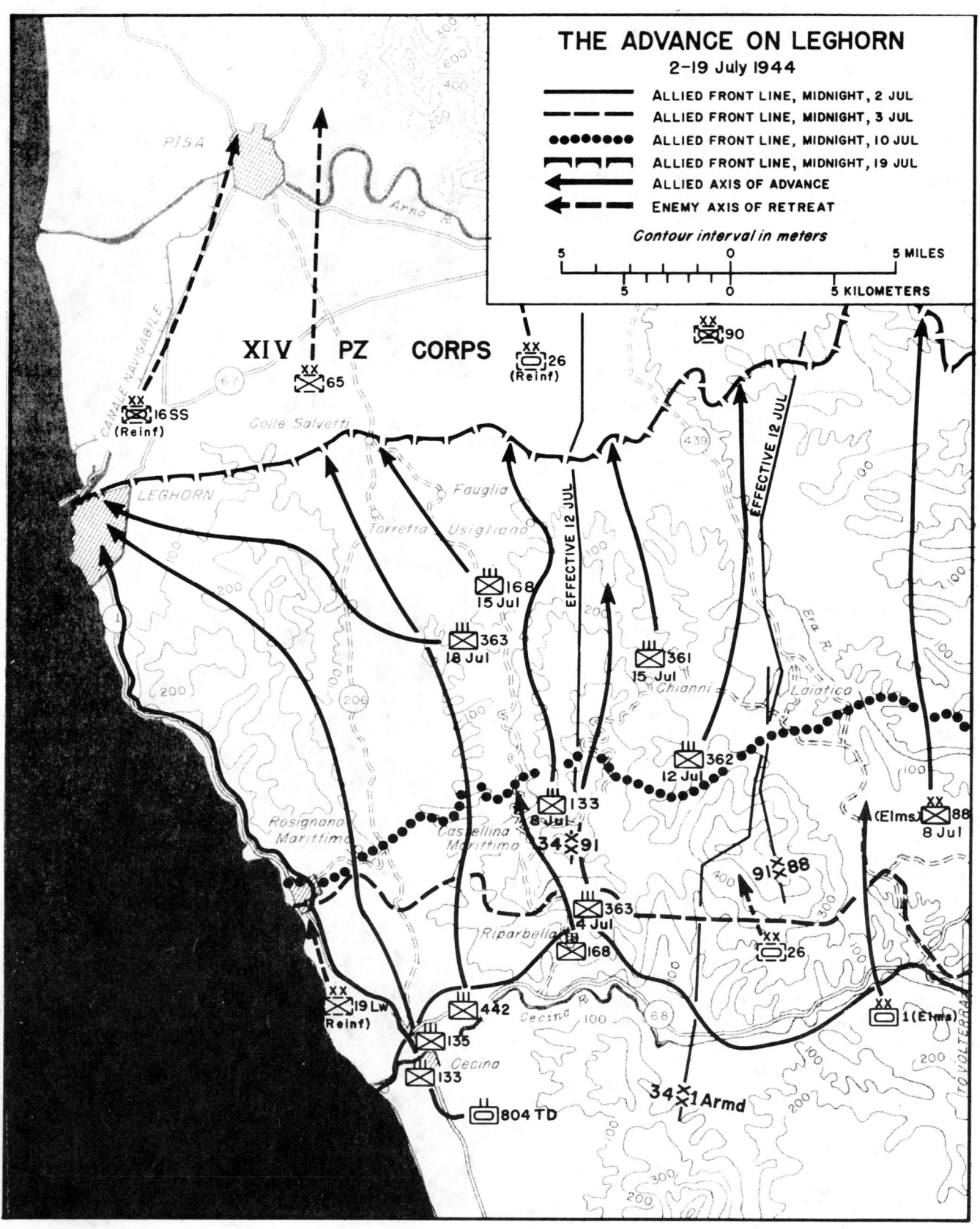

THE ADVANCE ON LEGHORN
2-19 July 1944

——————————— ALLIED FRONT LINE, MIDNIGHT, 2 JUL
— — — — — — — ALLIED FRONT LINE, MIDNIGHT, 3 JUL
● ● ● ● ● ● ● ● ALLIED FRONT LINE, MIDNIGHT, 10 JUL
⊔ ⊔ ⊔ ⊔ ⊔ ⊔ ALLIED FRONT LINE, MIDNIGHT, 19 JUL
←━━━━━ ALLIED AXIS OF ADVANCE
←- - - - ENEMY AXIS OF RETREAT

Contour interval in meters

5   0   5 MILES
5   0   5 KILOMETERS

July 5th 1944 — **(Pacific-Marianas-Saipan)** The operation to secure the island enters its final phase. The 4th Marines pushes on the V Corp's right, moving handily through unorganized opposition. The 27th Division, U.S.A., advances on the left; contingents reach an enemy strongpoint, Harakiri Gulch, but the Japanese bar entrance, despite the 65th Infantry's attacks. **(Pacific-New Guinea)** On Noemfoor Island, the Japanese counterattack to crush the elements holding Hill 201; about 350 to 400 Japanese assault to the sound of Banzai! Banzai! The 158th Infantry answers with rapid fire; the attack sizzles, its troops are annihilated, thus terminating the final major counterattack of the campaign during the Noemfoor Operation. In related activity, the Regiment's 2nd Battalion is readied for an Amphibious Landing at Namber Airdrome, on the southwest coast, the third enemy Airfield to be seized. In the Wakde-Sarmi area, enemy held Mt Saksin falls to contingents of the 63rd Infantry. **(China-Burma-India)** On the Salween Front, the Chinese mount a steady attack against Japanese positions during the day, but a counterattack regains the ground. **(North Atlantic)** The German Submarine U-233 is sunk by the Destroyer Escorts *Thomas* (DE-102) and *Baker* (DE190). **(Atlantic-France)** In the **U.S. First Army** area, **VIII Corps** sector, the attack continues; contingents seize the La Haye-du-Puits' Railroad facilities. Engineers continue mine-clearing operations; a large contingent of volunteers is stringing the mine pattern (plastic mines, unable to be detected by metal detectors) to blow them in unison. However, somehow the Germans are informed of the operation. Long range enemy Artillery opens up and the entire area becomes devastated; casualties are high. Sgt. Joseph Polya, 207th Engineering Battalion is wounded, but his mother receives a telegram that her son is dead. Polya, miraculously survives after a prolonged hospital stay. The 207th continues to move toward the Seine. The **VII Corps** advances against heavy opposition, which slows the operation down considerably. In Naval activity, U.S. Army Planes sink the Submarine U-586 off Toulon. **(Atlantic-Italy)** British General Sir Henry Maitland, in accordance with the decision to invade southern France, directs the AAI (Allied Armies in Italy) to proceed to the Venice-Padua-Verona-Brescia Line; he promises the arrival of reinforcements, including a Brazilian Division and the U.S. 93rd Division, expected to begin arriving by mid-September. In the **U.S. Fifth Army** area, the Germans continue to mount stiff resistance against the 135th Infantry at Rosignano, but the 135th with about a third of the town in its possession, keeps pounding forward, gaining control of half of the objective; other elements of the 34th Division secure a ridge outside of the town. In the **British Eighth Army** area, the Germans repulse an attempt to reach Highway 69, but the British 4th Division seizes Tuori. In the British 10th Corps area, the Germans are retreating, permitting the Indian 10th Division to easily approach Umbertide. In the Polish 2nd Corps area, the 3rd Carpathian Division takes Badia.

July 6th 1944 — **(United States** Charles De Gaulle arrives in the United States, remaining there for several days. **(Pacific-Celebes Sea)** The U.S.S. *Paddle* (SS-263), operating in the Celebes Sea, south of the Philippines, sinks the Destroyer *Hokaze*. **(Pacific-Marianas-Saipan)** At 09:00, battle orders are changed, directing the 4th Marine Division to drive forward, take the front and sweep the island north of Makunsha to Marpi Point; during the advance of the 25th Marines, approximately 800 civilians walk into the 1st Battalion's area to surrender. The 23rd Marines, attacking Paradise Valley from the west, hits tough resistance; the 24th Marines drives ahead about 1,800 yards. The 27th Division's zone is confined to the

General Holland M. Smith, U.S.M.C., on Saipan.

western coastal area, which includes Paradise Valley, south of Makunsha village and the obstinate Harakiri Gulch. The efforts of the 27th Division again are repulsed; the gulch remains in Japanese hands, preventing passage to the valley. During the night of the 6th-7th, the Japanese mount counterattacks along the Tanapag Front and against 4th Marine positions to the northeast. The 105th Infantry deployed in the heights above Harakiri Village and the 3rd Battalion, 10th Marines, holding outside Tanapag Village, receive the brunt of the attack. In other activity concerning the Marianas, Marine General Holland M. Smith, attaches the U.S. 77th Division to the III Amphibious Corps to strengthen the Assault Force for the invasion of Guam. In Naval activity, enemy positions on Guam and Rota, in the Marianas, receive premature signals that the Yanks are coming. Carrier-based Planes begin bombardments, hitting Airfields, supply depots and coastal guns. The Japanese, show no mercy to the islanders and continue committing atrocities. Radioman George Tweed U.S.N., still a fugitive on the island after 31 months of evading the enemy, witnesses them. He will be rescued on the 11th of July; through use of a mirror and Naval signals, he pinpoints enemy gun positions and notifies the Navy that all Pilots forced to bail out and land on Guam are immediately executed by the Japs, as they prefer murder to keeping prisoners of war. The island is now garrisoned by approximately 25,000 Japanese. **(Pacific-New Guinea)** At Noemfoor Island, off the western coast near Namber Airfield. Naval Surface Ships catapult a deluge of shells into suspected enemy positions. Upon cessation of the bombardment, the 2nd Battalion, 158th Infantry storms ashore, but the Navy guns had run off the Japs; the Airdrome is seized without incident. Subsequent Patrols discover that enemy forces on Noemfoor have dwindled to small numbers. In other activity, the Australians land a Squadron of P-40s at Kamiri Airfield. On Biak, the U.S. Army positions blaring speakers in the East Caves, to coach surrender, but the few defenders still alive had abandoned their positions. Also, Regimental Combat Team 124, 31st Division, embarks from Oro Bay to the Aitape front. **(Atlantic-France)** In **21st Army Group** area, the **U.S. Third Army**, commanded by General George S. Patton, establishes Headquarters at Nehou France. Its been a long time coming, but Patton will again, soon be in the thick of battle. The 3rd Army will consist of the **VIII Corps** (presently attached to the U.S. 1st Army), commanded by Major Troy H. Middleton, comprising the 6th Armored and the 8th and 83rd Infantry Divisions; the **XII Corps**, commanded by Major General Gilbert R. Cook (becomes extremely ill on August 19th) and subsequently commanded by Major General Manton S. Eddy, comprising the 4th Armored Division, and the 80th Infantry Division; the **XV Corps**, commanded by Major General Wade H. Haislip, comprising the 5th Armored and the 79th and 90th Infantry Divisions; Third Army is further bolstered by the French 2nd Armored Division; and the **XX Corps**, commanded by Major General Walton H. Walker, comprising the 5th and 7th Infantry Divisions and the 7th Armored Division. Patton's 3rd Army will also be augmented by the XIX Tactical Air Force, commanded by Brigadier General O.P. Weyland, assigned to provide Air support. In addition, specialized units including Engineers, Signal Corps, Tank Destroyers, Artillery and Medical contingents are attached. Mechanized Cavalry units are also utilized by the 3rd Army (2nd, 15th and 106th Mechanized Groups). General Patton slips inconspicuously across the channel with his advance command, landing in the Cotentin area while the Germans are staring blindly into the channel at Pas de Calais, convinced their Nemesis, Patton, would make the major attack there. Patton is readying to break out on August 1st. In the **U.S. First Army** area, elements of the **VIII Corps** are tightening the noose on La Haye-du-Puits, but the Germans still resist defiantly. In the **VII Corps** sector, German opposition is incessant near Periers, as the 83rd Division battles fiercely, supplemented by the 4th Division, which enters the battle west of the 83rd's positions. **(Atlantic-Italy)** In the **U.S. Fifth Army** area, **IV Corps** sector, Castellina falls to the 168th Infantry, 34th Division which then severs a major road that extends from there to Chianni. Mt Vase (Hill 634) is seized by the advancing 363rd Infantry; the 135th Infantry continues to reduce resistance at Rosignano, clearing it completely by the following day. In the **British Eighth Army** area, 13th Corps sector, the British 4th Division seizes Poggio all'Olmo, however, the enemy continues to impede progress of the Corps at Arezzo. In the British 10th Corps area, the Germans throw up a new and more rigid line that halts progress. In the Polish 2nd Corps area, Osima is seized by the advancing 3rd Carpathian Division. **(Atlantic-Russia)** The Germans have abandoned Kovel; it is quickly seized by the First White Russian Front.

July 7th 1944 — (Pacific) Admiral Nimitz issues a second warning order concerning the Palaus invasion and states that the operation will be undertaken in two phases. The southern Palaus Operation commences on September 15th against Angaur Peleliu and Ngesebus and the second phase against Yap and Ulithi, northeast of the Palaus, begins on the 5th of October. **(Pacific-Japan)** Kyushu Island is struck by American B-29s during the night 7-8th; this is the second time B-29s have ventured against Japan. In other activity in Japanese waters, the Submarine *Skate* (SS-305) sinks the Japanese Destroyer *Usugumo* off the Kurile Islands, and the Submarine *Mingo* (SS-261) destroys the Destroyer *Tamanami* in the South China Sea. **(Pacific-Marianas-Saipan)** In a last ditch effort to forestall defeat, about 3,000 Japanese push through the left flank of the 27th Division, against the 105th Infantry and the 3rd Battalion, 10th Marines, P.F.C. Harold C. Agerholm, 4th Battalion, 10th Marines, commandeers an ambulance and makes repeated trips under constant fire, rescuing 45 men. Agerholm then rushes to the aid of what he believes to be two wounded Marines, but is cut down by a sniper; he receives the Medal of Honor posthumously. The 106th Infantry, U.S.A., rushes to the scene and halts the attack, retaking most lost territory. In another instance of bravery, Private Thomas A. Baker (later Sergeant) during the period June 19th until today, grasps a Bazooka when incessant fire holds up his unit; he rushes forward to within one hundred yards of the enemy and eliminates the obstacle. His Company takes the ridge, then he deploys to the rear, to

guard against surprise attack and stumbles into enemy strongpoints that had been missed during the advance; he kills the defenders (two Officers and ten men). Shortly afterward, he discovers another concealed emplacement and destroys the six occupants (behind American lines). Later in the day, approximately 2,000 Japanese attack the American positions and Baker is severely wounded, but he refuses to be withdrawn, preferring his comrades save themselves from the onslaught closing from three sides. He requests a lone pistol and eight rounds of ammunition. Propped against a tree and prepared to die, he awaits the enemy. When his unit returns, he is still against the tree, his weapon empty and immediately to his front, lay eight dead Japs; he receives the Medal of Honor posthumously. In another brilliant example of extraordinary courage, Lt. Colonel William J. O'Brien, 1st Battalion, 105th Infantry, after sensing his Platoon's untenable positions because of intense enemy fire, orders three Tanks to assist. O'Brien mounts a Tank and in direct line of enemy fire leads the attack, demolishing one of the obstacles on the 23rd. On the 28th of June, he singlehandedly moves through 1,200 yards of enemy infested jungle brush to reach a halted Platoon and takes a four man detachment behind the enemy lines, then driving the enemy from the ridge and freeing his Battalion's advance. Today, the 7th of July, O'Brien, undaunted by the attacking throngs of Japanese, refuses to withdraw although his ammunition is running out. In General Custer style, he moves daringly up and down the line firing his pistols and inspiring his men. His ammunition becomes exhausted and he is badly wounded, but still, he clings to the front lines, trying to stem the tide. When last seen alive, he is standing in a jeep, pouring machine gun fire into the advancing enemy. When his body is recovered it is surrounded by dead enemy troops. O'Brien receives the Medal of Honor posthumously. In other activity, the 165th Infantry mops up nominal opposition in Harakiri Gulch, and advances to the plateau above the coastal plain. The 4th Marine Division, operating on the right flank, makes quick progress. The island will be totally secure within two days. **(Pacific-New Guinea)** On Biak, the Japanese are fortifying their emplacements and establishing additional ones in an attempt to retain Ibdi Pocket. Aerial bombardment is reinitiated. **(China-Burma-India)** The British 36th Division replaces a contingent of the Indian 3rd Division and it is put under the command of General Stilwell. On the Salween Front, the Chinese 246th Regiment, 82nd Division captures some heights, then loses them to a Japanese counterattack. **(Atlantic-France)** In the **U.S. First Army** area, **VIII Corps** sector, heavy fighting erupts in the vicinity of La Haye-du-Puits-Mont Castre Forest as the 79th and 90th Divisions attack and then successfully repulse heavy enemy counterattacks. Intense fighting also develops along the Carentan-Periers Road as the enemy resists fiercely in the **VII Corps** sector. In other activity, St. Jean-de-Day, in the **XIX Corps** area, falls to the 30th Division. Late in the day, Combat Command B, 3rd Armored Division moves across the Airel bridgehead, intending to stretch it toward St Gilles. **(Atlantic-Italy)** In the **U.S. Fifth Army** area, **IV Corps** sector, the Germans are pushed from Rosignano by the 135th Infantry, 34th Division, but the Germans maintain presence on the outskirts. In other activity, the 363rd Infantry, which had seized Hill 634 (M Vase) on the previous day, is struck by a heavy counterattack and forced to relinquish possession. In other activity, Colle di Val d'Elsa, southwest of Poggibonsi, is seized by the French 4th Mountain Division. In the **British Eighth Army** 13th Corps area, the Germans strike with force at M. Lignano, but are repulsed by the 6th South African Armored.

Marian Bomher, Radioman 1st Class, one of the many selfless Waves who served Old Glory selflessly during the conflict. Photo courtesy of Marian Bomher.

July 8th 1944 — (Pacific-Marianas-Guam) The enemy coastal emplacements of Guam come under heavy fire from Rear Admiral C.T. Joy's Cruiser Destroyer Force. Battleships arrive on the 14th to give added punch. **(Pacific-Marianas-Saipan)** The 2nd Marine Division sweeps through the 27th Division's perimeter to eliminate the remaining enemy opposition on Tanapag Plain. In conjunction, the 27th Division reverts to the Northern Troops and Landing Force reserve. During the drive, Sergeant Grant Timmerman, on board his Tank in front of the Infantry keeps a steady stream of fire pouring into the enemy until intense enemy fire halts the advance. Timmerman stands up to fire the 75mm, after first directing the Infantry to hit the deck. A Japanese grenade is tossed toward the open turret; Timmerman covers the hatch with his body, smothering the grenade with his chest, saving the balance of the crew by giving his life. The 4th Marine Division pushes through the Karaberra Pass; its 23rd Marines reaches the beach by 12:05. The 25th Marines advances unopposed up the east coast and the 24th Marines arrives at its assigned positions by early afternoon. In other activity, the 165th Infantry, 27th Division assaults from the heights above Harakiri Gulch and drives through Paradise Valley. **(Pacific-New Guinea)** General Krueger confers with his Commanders to discuss strategy for the pending operations in the Sansapor-Mor area of the Vogelkop. There is strong feeling about acquiring more information on the terrain before finalizing plans. In the Aitape area, General Hall is directed by General Krueger to dispatch strongly manned Patrols across the Driniumor River. In other activity, Task Force Persecution renames its commands: the Western Defense Area becomes Western Sector; the Eastern Defense Area is renamed the Eastern Sector and the Eastern Defense Command becomes the Persecution Covering Force. **(China-Burma-India)** The Generalissimo, Chiang Kai-shek, concurs with President Roosevelt's suggestion that Stilwell be granted Command of the Chinese Forces, but he also wants Roosevelt to send a personal representative (giving Kai-shek a direct link to Washington). In other activity in the theater, the Japanese holding Teng-chung are surrounded by five Chinese Divisions. **(Atlantic-France)** In the **21st Army Group**, **U.S. First Army** area, the **VIII Corps** rushes forward and takes La Haye-du Puits with its 79th Division. In the **VII Corps** area, vicious fighting ensues all along the Carentan-Periers Road. The **XIX Corps** is heavily involved with expanding its bridgehead; elements of the Corps (113th Cavalry Group) seize Goucherie and Le Mesnil-Veneron. During the day, final contingents of the 35th Division arrive and are assigned to the XIX Corps. In the **British Second Army** area, U.S. Heavy Bombers support a three-Division assault against Caen, with the Canadian 3rd Division and the British 3rd Division operating on the right and left flanks respectively and the British 59th Division advancing up the center; the city's defenses are pierced late in the day and the troops clasp a hold on the northeastern fringe of it. **(Atlantic-Italy)** In the **U.S. Fifth Army** area, the 34th Division (IV Corps) advances closer to Leghorn, while elements of the 88th Division seize the heights east and north of Volterra. The 349th Infantry, 88th Division seizes Roncalla. In the French sector, Hill 380, several miles north of Highway 68 is captured by the 4th Group of Tabors. **(Atlantic-Russia)** Baranovichi is seized by the Russians.

July 9th 1944 — (Pacific-Marianas-Saipan) Old Glory flies victoriously over Saipan, concluding another excruciating campaign. The Northern Troops Landing Force consisted of 71,034 men, against about 30,000 well entrenched Japanese. The Japanese have been totally eliminated, their troops destroyed. The Americans suffer about 20% casualties; 3,674 Army and 10,437 Marines, however, the Yanks close on Japan. B-29s will operate from Saipan to bomb the Japanese homeland. **(Pacific-New Guinea)** Planes of the Army Air Force supplement the bombardment of the remaining Japanese defenders in the Ibdi Pocket. In the Wakde-Sarmi area, the 1st Battalions of the 1st and 63rd Infantry Regiments reduce the final enemy stronghold in the Maffin Bay area, Hill 265. **(Pacific-Philippines)** The U.S.S. *Nautilus* (SS-168) maneuvers near Pandan Island, off Mindoro, Philippines and lands supplies and men without incident. **(Atlantic-France)** In the **U.S. First Army** area, the hedgerow defenses impede the advance of the **VIII Corps**. Horrendous fighting ensues across the entire front. The **VII Corps** sector is no exception. The 4th and 83rd Divisions grind their way through especially rough resistance, taking St Eny with the 83rd. In the **XIX Corps** sector, elements of the 113th Cavalry Group and CCA, 3rd Armored Division, controlling the right flank, stay in place while Combat Command B, and the 30th Division plow toward Hauts-Vent, rumbling into severe resistance near St. Lo; a counterattack is halted with the assistance of Artillery. During the course of the day's vicious contest, Combat Command B streaks through the lines of the 30th Division and advances to the fringes of Hauts-Vents, but the Germans hold the town. Also, Combat Command A, 3rd Armored Division (XIX Corps), is transferred to the VII Corps and the U.S. 5th Division arrives in France. In the **British Second Army** area, the coveted city of Caen falls to the Canadian 3rd Division, which enters from the west and the British 3rd Division, rushing in from the south. In addition, the Airfield at Carpiquet and Bretteville-sur-Odon falls to the 3rd Canadian Division. (Atlantic-Italy) In the U.S. Fifth Army area IV Corps sector, the 34th Division presses beyond the captured Rosignano against tenacious opposition. The 363rd Infantry resecures Hill 634 (M Vase) and the 168th seizes Casale, after bitter fighting, before dawn on the following day. Meanwhile, the Germans mount effective opposition on the right flank, against the advancing 88th Division. In addition, Task Force Ramey, comprised of Armored units, receives orders to protect the Corps' right flank; it advances along Highway 68, attempting to maintain contact with the French Expeditionary troops. In the French sector, the 4th Group of Tabors push against Hill 380; however, the contest ceases with the Germans retaining the hill. The 1st and 6th Moroccan Infantry units relieve the Tabors and after a long night of incessant battle, Hill 380 is retaken. In the British Eighth Army area, the 13th Corps prepares to attack Arezzo on the 15th, allowing the British to wait for the New Zealand 2nd Division (Canadian I Corps) to reinforce the assault. In the Polish II Corps area, the town of Filottrano, holding out for nearly a week, falls to Italian troops after a vehement struggle. In Naval activity, the Minesweeper U.S.S. *Swerve* (AM-121) strikes a mine and sinks. (Atlantic-Rumania) American Planes raid Ploesti. One of the Planes, piloted by 1st Lt. Donald Pucket is struck soon after it drops its bombs; the initial impact kills one crewmember and wounds six others. The Plane is unable to attain altitude and the bomb doors are jammed, causing gasses to permeate the Plane. Pucket orders the crew to abandon the Aircraft, but three members refuse to jump for reasons never to be explained. Pucket attempts to bring the Plane home, but it crashes into a mountain, causing Pucket to die while attempting to save his comrades; he receives the Medal Of Honor posthumously. (Atlantic-Russia) The Third White Russian Front captures Lida.

July 10th 1944 — (Pacific-Marianas Guam) Radioman Tweed, U.S.N., still uncaptured, observes U.S. Warships bombarding Japanese positions, taking note that two Destroyers remain offshore, about ten miles south. Enemy shore guns commence firing on the Destroyers, but return fire silences the guns. Tweed excitedly, uses the late afternoon sunlight to his advantage and manages to make contact with the Destroyers. Although the Navy is overly suspicious, they respond. Tweed hastily informs them through signal flags all his intelligence information, then he requests that the Navy pick him up. The Sailors are astonished at the possibility of an American being on Guam. No immediate answer is forthcoming to the dismay of Tweed. About 15 minutes later, a boat is lowered in the water and Tweed ecstatically runs a marathon down the mountain and is rescued. On Tinian, Marine Reconnaissance and Underwater Demolition Teams spend their second day gathering intelligence and clearing obstacles for the impending invasion. (Pacific-New Guinea) On Biak, the Ibdi Pocket is entered by two Companies of the 163rd Infantry Regiment, 41st Division. At Aitape, Patrols of Task Force Persecution probe deeper, east of the Driniumor, it encounters and chasing enemy forces. During the night, the Japanese mount a heavy counterattack across the river; it drives west and penetrates the 128th Infantry positions. (China-Burma-India) Heavy fighting continues in the vicinity of Sung Shan, on the Salween Front. In the 11th Army Group, British Fourteenth Army area, the resistance at Ukhrul is terminated. (Atlantic-France) British General Montgomery calls for an offensive, directing the U.S. First Army to attack south, supported by the British Second Army, which is ordered to drive south and east of Caen. In the VIII Corps area, the U.S. 90th Division

seizes Mont Castre Forest. In the VII Corps area, the 4th, 9th and 83rd Divisions advance near St Eny, Le Desert and Tribehou. The XIX Corps' Combat Command B, 3rd Armored Division advances, but is repulsed at the fringes of Hauts-Vents, while elements of 30th Division grind to the steps of Belle-Lande. In other activity, a new Command: United States Ports and Bases France, is established at Cherbourg, commanded by Rear Admiral J. Wilkes. In the British Second Army area, mop-up operations continue in Caen; other British troops (43rd Division) take Hill 112 and also seize Eterville. (Atlantic-Italy) The U.S. IV Corps, still battles toward Leghorn against vicious opposition. (Atlantic-Russia) The Germans are struggling against the odds. Field Marshal Walter Model requests permission to withdraw Army Group North to assist with the ongoing fighting on the Central Front; however, Hitler denies the request, making a bad situation worse, as the German 4th and 9th Armies have already been eliminated on the Central Front.

July 11th 1944 — (Pacific-New Guinea) On Noemfoor, mop-up operations are initiated. In the Aitape area, Persecution Task Force withdraws from the Driniumor River to establish a new defense line near the Koronal Creek, following its unsuccessful attempt to rout the enemy at the Anamo-Afua trail. General Krueger orders the River Line established. During the fierce contest along the trail, at least eight enemy machine guns hamper the movement of elements of the U.S. 32nd Division. Staff Sergeant Gerald Endl assumes command after his Platoon leader is wounded. A second Platoon is rushed to the scene, but by now, twelve members of Endl's Platoon are wounded and seven others are isolated by superior forces. Endl singlehandedly advances to assist the seven trapped men. In a vicious lopsided conflict he holds off the enemy, while others move up and evacuate the wounded. Four more men lay wounded; Endl continues to bring them back individually until a sudden burst of gunfire slays him while he is transporting the last man. His heroic actions save all but one man; the two besieged Platoons withdraw safely. Endl receives the Medal of Honor posthumously. (China-Burma-India) Air support is brought into the struggle at Heng-yang to assist the Chinese who raise rigid resistance against the newest Japanese attempt to take the town. (Atlantic-France) In the U.S. First Army area, the V Corps adds its punch to the offensive as the Americans attempt to break out. The Germans mount a heavy Tank supported counterattack that strikes the U.S. 9th Division on the left flank; quick reaction by Tank Destroyers, Artillery units and Aircraft, allows the Infantry to turn the attack back. Progress is costly all along the front, but persistent assaults by elements of the 2nd Division (23rd and 38th Regiments) seize Hill 192. In addition, the Germans holding St Georges-d'Elle and the surrounding terrain are overrun; the seizure of Hill 192 permits the severing of the Bayeux-St-Lo highway near La Calvaire. In the British Second Army area, the Germans mount an unsuccessful assault against the British 43rd Division at Hill 112. In the I Corps sector, the Germans repel the British 51st Division, east of the Orne, near Colombelles. (Atlantic-Italy) The Allies spring Operation MALLORY MAJOR designed to demolish the Po River bridges by sustained Air attacks. In the U.S. First Army area, fighting is heavy in all areas. Enemy resistance at Pastina halts the advancing 442nd Infantry, 34th Division just short of the city. The 133rd Infantry hits stiff opposition further east, at Hill 529; other contingents of the 34th Division drive against other tough resistance, making gradual progress. German resistance is also vicious at Laiatico, stalling the recently committed 351st Infantry, 88th Division.

July 12th 1944 — (Pacific-Marianas-Saipan) Major General Holland Smith assumes command of the Fleet Marine Forces Pacific and turns over command of the V Corps to Major General Harry Schmidt. **(Pacific-New Guinea)** On Biak, several hundred Japanese evade the 163rd Infantry and escape from Ibdi Pocket. On Aitape, General Clarence A. Martin is relieved by General Gill, who assumes command of Persecution Covering Force. Martin becomes the Commander of the Eastern sector. The Americans are preparing another assault at the Driniumor. In other activity, the Japanese mount a night-attack against the lines of the 2nd Battalion, 128th Infantry, but the Yanks repel the assault. **(China-Burma-India)** The enemy holding Myitkyina is struck by a strong attack that includes close Air support but they retain the position. The Myitkyina Task Force sustains additional casualties after they are struck by friendly bombs that inadvertently strike their positions. On the Salween Front, the Japanese retain control of Sung Shan. Afterward, the Chinese abort the assault and two weeks pass before the Chinese 8th Army reinitiates its attack. **(Atlantic-France)** German opposition evaporates in the vicinity of the Ay and Seves River, permitting the **VIII Corps** to advance south with considerable ease; Hill 92 falls to the 8th Division. Enemy resistance in the **VII Corps** sector remains violent; Corps encounters stiff opposition as it closes on St. Lo, but the advancing V Corps takes out its opposition at Hill 192 and secures a road between Berigny and La Calvaire. In other activity, the 101st Airborne is detached from the U.S. First Army and embarks for England. In the British area, the 2nd Army regroups for future action. **(Atlantic-Italy)** In the **U.S. Fifth Army** area, the battle to take Leghorn continues. Armored contingents sprint past Castiglioncello. The Germans halt the 442nd Infantry, 34th Division at Pastina; at Hill 529, the 133rd Infantry is repulsed. After dark, the Germans abandon the hill. At Laiatico, the enemy is in firm control; the newly committed 351st Infantry, 88th Division, stalled just short of its objective the previous day, adds mortars and artillery to its attack and seizes the town handily. In other activity, Operation MALLORY MAJOR commences; Tactical Air Force Medium Bombers strike the Po River Bridges. During action with the 91st Division, the 362nd Infantry is rebuffed as it advances toward the Arno. Sergeant Harmon, orders his Squad to hold in place as he attempts to eradicate devastating fire coming from modified haystacks containing at least three machine guns; Harmon charges singlehandedly, knocking out the first and continuing toward the next, using his submachine gun and a few grenades; he is wounded by enemy fire but he destroys the nest, then he advances against a third haystack and is again wounded; he presses ahead against a wall of fire, gets to his knees to toss a grenade and is yet again struck by enemy fire; he rises in great agony, only to be struck mortally; while falling dead to the ground, he unleashes a grenade and scores a big one, unaware that his final grenade destroys the enemy nest and saves the balance of his Platoon. Sergeant Harmon becomes the recipient of the Medal of Honor posthumously.

July 13th 1944 — (United States) President Roosevelt responds to a request from Chiang Kai-shek, agreeing to appoint a political representative for communication between Kai-shek and Washington. In addition, Roosevelt makes final preparations for his trip to Hawaii for conferences with MacArthur and Nimitz, concerning the next moves to secure the Pacific. In other activity, the U.S.S. *Herring* (SS-233) is officially reported missing. The *Herring* had departed Pearl Harbor on May 16th, on her eighth War Patrol. After the close of the war, Japanese records acknowledge the sinking of the *Herring* subsequent to the Submarine sinking two enemy Vessels in the Kurile Islands on the 1st of June. If the Japanese records are accurate, it is the only U.S. Submarine sunk by enemy coastal guns. **(Pacific-Marianas-Saipan)** The 3rd Battalion, 6th Marines, 2nd Marine Division capture Maniagassa Island in Tanapag Harbor, terminating Marine operations on Saipan. **(Pacific-New Guinea)** On Noemfoor Island, the main enemy forces remaining on Noemfoor are on Hill 670; the 1st Battalion, 503rd Paratroop Infantry is closing on them. The enemy abandons the hill on the 17th. In Aitape the assault against enemy positions near the Driniumor continues. A fierce contest develops near the coast between the Anamo and the Driniumor, where the 1st Battalion, 128th Infantry decisively defeats the enemy's Coastal Attack Force and demolishes its Artillery. In related activity, the 2nd Battalion, 128th Infantry resists several enemy attacks in the Tiber area, west of the Driniumor. **(Atlantic-France)** General Bradley approves the plan for Operation COBRA; the official breakout offensive by the First Army to commence on July 25th. Some alterations will be applied to the original plan. In other activity, there is some progress along the line, but enemy resistance is fierce. The VII Corps halts its attack. The XIX Corps maintains pressure against St. Lo, but still the Germans hold. In the **V Corps** area, the 1st Division is replaced by the 5th Division on the line to allow the 1st Division to withdraw for redeployment in the VII Corps sector. General Theodore Roosevelt (son of President Teddy Roosevelt) dies of natural causes, unaware that he is to become the Commanding Officer of the 90th Division. He had been second in command to Terry Allen with the 1st Division. In other activity, the 4th Armored Division comes ashore. In the **British Second Army** area, the Canadian 2nd Corps becomes operational; it consists of the 2nd and 3rd Canadian Divisions. In other activity, the British continue to regroup, assigning the 12th Corps to assume responsibility for the British 8 Corps sector. **(Atlantic-Italy)** In the **U.S. Fifth Army IV Corps** area, Pastina and Hill 529 fall to the 34th Division, while the 91st Division commits it 362nd and 363rd Infantry Regiments against extremely heavy opposition in front of Chianni. The Germans continue to mount iron opposition, but the Americans keep moving. The resistance on the right flank of the IV Corps falters and the 88th Division takes advantage, sprinting forward. In the French sector, South Gimignano is seized by the 4th Mountain Division. In related activity, the 2nd Moroccan Division charges to the fringes of Poggibonsi and to Castellina against fractured resistance. **(Atlantic-Russia)** The Third White Russian Front takes Vilna.

July 14th 1944 — (Pacific-Marianas) Special Underwater Demolition Squads initiate the treacherous mission of clearing enemy barriers that would otherwise impede the invasion of Guam. In addition, these teams continue reconnoitering the beaches; simultaneously, they scout possible landing sites on the west coast. In other activity in the Marianas, the Destroyer Escort *William C. Miller* (DE-259) destroys a Japanese Submarine, the I-4. **(Pacific-New Guinea)** Task Force Cyclone is directed by General MacArthur to ensure that they have the Airdrome at Kornasoren prepared to accept 50 P-38s, needed to support the invasion of the Vogelkop Peninsula, by the 25th of July. In other activity, Reconnaissance Squads are dispatched to the northern coast of the peninsula where a three day operation ensues to collect intelligence for the invasion. In the Aitape area, a gap that has developed over the past few days, between the North and South Forces, is being closed; the Northern Force encounters trouble in the sector of the 3rd Battalion, 124th Infantry, during the night of the

13th, but eradicates it quickly, destroying about 135 of the infiltrators. In the Wakde Sarmi area, the 6th Division, maintaining Makin Bay, is relieved by the 31st Division (minus RCT 124). **(China-Burma-India)** British Major General W.D. Lentaigne requests permission to withdraw the weakened Morris Force from Myitkyina; its strength is down to three Platoons; the response is denied as Myitkyina has to be taken. In other activity, the British 33th Corps, eliminates a strong enemy force near Ukhrul, securing the area. In the British 4th Corps area, the 5th and 17th Indian Divisions overpowering enemy resistance on the Tiddim Road. **(Atlantic-France)** The ongoing offensive is slowed, as the VIII Corps receives orders to hold its positions. In the **VII Corps** sector, Les Champs-de-Losque-Le Desert, a persistent strongpoint, is under severe assault by the U.S. 9th Division; it seizes a primary crossroad by the following day. In the **XIX Corps** area, the 119th Infantry, 30th Division, knocks out the enemy at Pont Hebert. In conjunction, the 35th Division fights through tough opposition, reaching the Pont Hebert-St. Lo Highway. Meanwhile, the 29th Division is poised east and northeast of St. Lo. In the **V Corps** area, the 5th Division is firmly deployed on the left of the Corps. In the British area, regrouping continues. **(Atlantic-Italy)** In the U.S. Fifth Army IV Corps area, the 34th Division closes the noose on Leghorn, but the rapid advance is hit with a counterattack on the following night. S Pieve di Luce falls to the 442nd Infantry, while the 133rd Infantry nears Usigliano. Chianni falls to the 363rd Infantry, 91st Division without any opposition and Patrols sent out by the 162nd discover Terricciola undefended. The **IV Corps** area is active; on its right flank, elements of the 88th Division storm Belvedere and Villamagna, seizing both. In the French sector, the enemy abandons positions all along the sector, giving the French possession of Poggibonsi, as they advance toward Certaldo. In the **British Eighth Army** 13th Corps sector, the New Zealanders are heavily engaged on the crest of M. Carmucino. In other activity in Italy, the Commander of Allied Armies in Italy directs the British Eighth Army to attack and seize Ancona and Florence. **(Atlantic-Russia)** Pinsk falls to the Russians.

July 15th 1944 — (Pacific-New Guinea) On Biak, enemy resistance continues at the Ibdi Pocket; more Artillery fire is brought in and U.S. ground forces return into the pocket. On Aitape, U.S. troops work to shrink the hole which stands at about 1,500 yards, and still jeopardizes the Persecution Covering Force. In Naval activity, the PT-133 is struck by enemy coastal gun fire and sinks. **(China-Burma-India)** The Japanese at Myitkyina still hold, but their casualties keep climbing, despite no major assaults against it by the Myitkyina Task Force for the last three days. **(Atlantic-France)** The U.S. First Army halts its offensive, it retains positions west of the Taute River and prepares for Operation COBRA. The **VIII Corps** holds along the Ay River, controlling the area with the exception of Lessay; it regroups its command, which includes 4th, 8th, 79th, 83rd and 90th Divisions. The **VII Corps** continues its attack in the Champs-de-Losque sector, overcoming tenacious resistance to secure a strategic crossroad with the 9th Division while simultaneously regrouping; later, the 30th Division and the 1st Infantry Division arrive. The sector of the 2nd and 3rd Armored Divisions expands east to the Vire River. In the **XIX Corps** area, the 117th and the 30th Regiments (prior to transferring to VII Corps) assaults the enemy positions at Le Mesnil-Durand. The 29th and 35th Divisions continue to press the enemy at St. Lo; contingents of the 35th Division (134th Infantry) grind toward the northern slopes of Hill 122, less than 2,000 yards from St. Lo, but the Germans resist

fiercely at Le Carillon-Pont Hebert, repelling the balance of the Division. During the heated exchange, the 2nd Battalion, 116th Infantry, 29th Division, advances to the Bayeux-St. Lo Highway, but to no avail as it becomes isolated from the main command, cut off near La Madeleine. In the 29th Division sector, the 115th Infantry attacks on the right flank against stiff resistance as it drives toward La Luzerne; the 175th Infantry maintains its perimeter on the left of the Division. The V Corps also regroups; its 2nd and 5th Divisions deploy facing the left flank of the Germans. The U.S. First Army holds the 4th Armored Division in reserve. In the **British Second Army** area, the 12th Corps attacks, after dark, led by the British 15th Division; it drives toward the Bougy-Evrecy-Maizet line. **(Atlantic-Italy)** The operation to demolish the enemy bridges scanning the Po River is successfully terminated; the operation expands to strike bridges throughout the entire Po Valley and some bridges west of the Piacenza. In the **U.S. Fifth Army IV Corps** area, the enemy stalls the advance of the U.S. 34th Division with a heavy counterattack that draws a solid line in front of Leghorn. The 34th brings in Artillery and begins to penetrate the rigid line, driving the Germans back. During the heated advance, the 133rd and 168th Regiments shove toward Pisa; the 133rd bypasses Lorenzana. In other related activity, the 363rd Infantry, 91st Division speeds into Bagni di Casciana unopposed; subsequently it withdraws to support the 34th Division's assault against Leghorn; Morrona falls to the 361st Infantry as it advances on the right flank of the 91st Division. The 88th Division advances along the Corps' right flank. In the French sector, enemy activity is also fierce. A stiff line is developing in the Certaldo-Tevernelle vicinity, but as the Allies approach, the town of Castellina falls to the 8th Moroccans. The 4th Moroccans continue to reduce remnant opposition east of Poggibonsi. In the British 13th Corps area, the British Eighth Army attacks Arezzo. The areas defenders include the 334th and 719th German Infantry Divisions, elements of the LXXVI Panzerkorps and units of the 15th Panzergrenadiere. Arezzo is also bolstered by the German 1st Parachute Division. The New Zealand 2nd Division and the British 6th Armored drive forward and by nightfall, the Germans are abandoning positions all across the front. In addition, the 2nd New Zealanders hold M. Lignano. **(Atlantic-Russia)** Opochka is seized by the Second Baltic Front.

A North American P-51 Mustang (detachable gasoline tanks).

July 16th 1944 — (Pacific-New Guinea) The Japanese abandon Hill 670 and disperse into the jungle; the 503rd Paratroop Infantry pursues them. In Aitape, elements of the 124th Infantry and the 112th Cavalry, continue tightening the gap between the North and South Forces; contingents of the closing forces encounter a Japanese force and kill about 40 of them.

Also, Japanese are spotted south of Afua crossing the Driniumor. Elements of Troops E, 112th Cavalry, are held down by a machine gun; Lt. Dale E. Christenson orders his men to keep low, while he advances about 15 yards from the objective and eliminates it with a hand grenade. In yet other activity, elements of the 127th Infantry mop-up the remainder of the enemy west of the Driniumor. **(Atlantic-France)** In the **U.S. First Army** area, the **VII Corps** presses south toward Periers; its 30th Division drives on the left and the 9th Division ahead on the right. The 30th Division expands its salient between the Terrette and Vire Rivers. In other activity, Combat Command B is detached from the 30th Division and attached to the 3rd Armored Division. The isolated 2nd Battalion, 116th Infantry is still unable to rejoin the other contingents of the 29th Division; other units of the 29th attempt unsuccessfully to rescue the trapped Battalion, but they succeed in turning back an Armor supported Infantry assault. On the following day, the 3rd Battalion, 116th Infantry fights to the beleaguered 116th, but it also becomes trapped. The bitter struggle of St. Lo culminates on the 18th. The battle weary 29th Division is reinforced with 29th Division Artillery and the 113th Cavalry Group. In the **British Second Army** area, the British 59th Division (30th Corps) pushes toward Noyers and surrounds most of the enemy held town. In the British 12th Corps area, the British 15th Division seizes Bougy, Esquay and Gavrus, all near Evercy. Meanwhile the British 53rd Division takes Cahier. **(Atlantic-Italy)** The U.S. Fifth Army attacks to eliminate the enemy at Leghorn; The IV Corps starts early, when the 135th Infantry, 34th Division, pours into enemy positions at 01:00, seizing M. Maggiore, consisting of Hills 413 and 449. In conjunction with this attack, Hill 232 also falls. The blazing advance gets the 168th Infantry to the fringes of Fauglia, taking Lorenzana along the way. Elements of the 133rd Infantry drive to a stone's throw from the Arno Valley, seizing Usigliano. The 91st Division nears the valley, after overcoming diminished resistance, but a counterattack is subsequently thrown at it; the 361st Infantry, throws back enemy Armor, while the 362nd sprints to the outskirts of Capannoli. The Germans falter against the mighty thrust and begin abandoning positions, allowing the U.S. 88th Division to speed north. In the French sector, the British prepare to relieve the French Expeditionary Forces to give them a rest. In the **British Eighth Army** 13th Corps area, Arezzo falls to the British 6th Armored Division after dousing effective rear-guard actions, to allow the Germans additional time to fortify their Gothic line; the 6th Armored bolsters its newly gained positions, and establishes a bridgehead while preparing to seize Florence. In the British 10th Corps area, the Germans feel extra pressure against Alpe di Poti because of the loss of Arezzo. In conjunction, the British can now concentrate on Bibbiena. **(Atlantic-Russia)** The Russians advance toward East Prussia. Elements of the 2nd and Third White Russian Fronts converge and overpower Grodno, a strategic railroad junction.

July 17th 1944 — (Pacific-Japan) The U.S.S. *Gabilan* (SS-252), operating near Honshu, sinks a Japanese Minesweeper, No. 25. **(Pacific-New Guinea)** The Japanese on Aitape attempt to widen the gap, which the Persecution Covering Force is trying to close; during the night, the enemy again penetrates. In addition, the Japanese reposition their forces near Afua for a strengthened attack. **(Atlantic-France)** An Allied Plane strafes Rommel's command car, causing it to overturn. Field Marshal Rommel sustains severe head injuries and is forced to return home to recuperate. This ends his active military service, because he is subsequently believed

involved with an unsuccessful plot to kill Hitler on the 20th. German General von Kluge, Commanding Officer of the Western Front, assumes command of Army Group B, in Rommel's absence, but also retains his normal responsibilities. In the **U.S. First Army** area, the 4th Armored Division (reserve), is attached to the VIII Corps. In the **VII Corps** area, the enemy Main Line of Resistance on the right flank of the Corps is penetrated violently; the charging U.S. 9th Division closes on the St. Lo Highway. In related action, the 30th Division pressures the left flank and stretches its salient to La Houcharderie. In the **XIX Corps** area, the fighting is also fierce. The 37th Division pierces enemy lines opposing the Corps' right flank; its drive forces the Germans from Le Carillon. The 29th Division encounters rigid opposition as it attacks to rescue its beleaguered 2nd Battalion, 116th Infantry, to no avail. In the **British Second Army** area, moderate progress is enjoyed by the 30th Corps; the British 53rd Division, which is involved in ferocious combat in the 12th Corps sector, secures the right flank north of Odon and relieves the British 15th Division, and continues the attack against Evrecy. **(Atlantic-Italy)** Fighting is vicious in the IV Corps area; the Germans maintain rigid opposition at Leghorn, stalling the advance of the 135th Infantry, 34th Division; U.S. Armored units bolster the right flank. The 133rd and 168th Infantry Regiments reach the southern section of the Arno Valley after a strenuous march; the 168th is forced to eliminate staunch resistance at Fauglia before it can reach the valley. Other Yank units are closing on the valley; the 91st Division's 361st Infantry rolls toward Pontedera knocking over Ponsacco; the 362nd Infantry pushes through Capannoli and crosses the Era River during its dash to the valley. Palaia falls to the 88th Division after a heated confrontation between the enemy and the 3rd Battalion, 349th Infantry. In related activity, Armored Task Force Ramey receives a Battalion of the 351st Infantry and takes Montaione. In the **British Eighth Army** area, British General Leese decides that the Gothic Line shall be attacked by two Corps driving up the axis Florence-Firenzuola and Florence-Bologna. Meanwhile, the British 13th Corps pursues the retreating Germans who are moving toward Florence. In the British 10th Corps area, Alpe di Poti is reached by the 4th Indian Division; it attacks to secure the hills. In other activity, the Polish 2nd Corps, supported by Planes, attacks Ancona.

U.S. Tanks nudge past German Armor, driving toward St Lo.

July 18th 1944 — (Pacific-Japan) A new government is formed in Japan under General Kuniaki Koiso immediately following the collapse of the Cabinet of Premier Tojo. In Naval activity, near Japan, the U.S.S. *Plaice* (SS-390) sinks the Submarine Chaser No. 50. **(Pacific-Bismarck Sea)** The U.S. Motor Gunboat PGM-7 sinks after becoming involved in a collision. **(Pacific-New Guinea)** There is still plenty of combat on New Guinea and the Americans have more to worry about than the enemy. This particular part of the word is inhabited by an assortment of despicable creatures, such as cannibal ants, mosquitoes, chiggers and poisonous spiders, to say nothing about the swamps that harbor crocodiles as well as Japs and giant bats. The Japanese have assembled some gruesome body snatching traps that defy penetration. In some instances during this horrid New Guinea campaign, Allied troops are ambushed and slaughtered by rings of fire as they trek through chest high muddied trails. Today, Major General John C. Persons, Commanding Officer of the 31st Division assumes command of Task Force Tornado, replacing Major General Franklin C. Sibert (Commanding Officer 6th Division); Sibert takes command of Task Force Typhoon (6th Division reinforced minus 20, attached to the 31st Division). In the Aitape area, the momentum to close the gap along the Driniumor continues; the 124th Infantry forces the Japanese to withdraw from the Driniumor heading east and west. The 127th Infantry mops up between the river and Koronal Creek. After dark, the Japanese spring an attack against the 1st Squadron, 112th Cavalry, making slight progress, but the resilient Cavalry retaliates firmly on the following day. **(Atlantic-France)** More Yanks arrive in France; the U.S. 6th Armored Division comes ashore at the permanent beachhead at Utah Beach. In the **U.S. First Army** area, the German stronghold at St. Lo collapses under incessant pressure by the XIX Corps. This strategic gain opens the keyhole to the big breakout and culminates the bloody struggle for the Hedgerows. Operation COBRA is being finely detailed. The 9th and 30th Divisions reach the Periers-St. Lo Road with advance elements (VII Corps area). Old Glory reigns at St. Lo; the Germans initiate Artillery bombardments on U.S. positions. Patrols are sent to probe the depth of the enemy's retreat. In the **British Second Army** area, the British attack to draw fire away from the U.S. First Army, which has been designated responsible for the major thrust. The British limited offensive receives the biggest and strongest Air support of any ground troops' action since the invasion of Normandy. Planes drop 7,700 tons of bombs. The British 8 Corps spearheads the effort and meets tenacious resistance as three Armored Divisions forge ahead; after a long bitter contest, they are able to advance through the I Corps and reach the Hubert-Folie-Tilly-la-Campagne-La Hogue-Frenouville-Cagny general line. In related activity, the Canadian 3rd Division seizes Colombelles and Giberville; the Canadian 2nd Division is fiercely engaged near Louvigny. The British I Corps is relegated to a support role, but does secure three villages in its sector. **(Atlantic-Italy)** In the **U.S. Fifth Army** area, **IV Corps** sector, Leghorn is standing on its last leg. The 135th Infantry, 34th Division with Task Force Williamson, RCT 363, 91st Division (attached to 34th) commences the final assault against Leghorn. The intense drive advances to the fringes of the town, but the elusive Germans get most of their forces out of the Garrison, leaving behind a massive death trap; they deploy over 25,000 booby traps before evacuating. Leghorn falls on the following day. In other activity, the 804th Tank Destroyer Battalion, operating along the coast, advances to Montenero and by 08:00 the Arno River is breached at Pontedera by contingents of the 361st Infantry, 91st Division; the Germans pull back along the entire front; the 362nd Infantry drives to the final ridge controlling the Arno. The 88th Division pushes to the sole remaining enemy controlled heights above the Arno at Palaia. With information that the German Front is collapsing, the French Expeditionary Corps intensifies its pursuit. In the **British Eighth Army** area, 13th Corps sector, the 6th South African Division overpowers Radda, in Chianti. The British 6th Armored and 4th Infantry Divisions drive against heavy resistance near Arezzo; the 4th Division seizes Montevarchi located on Highway 69. In the British 10th Corps area, preparations are made to pivot west and attack Bibbiena, while simultaneously engaging the enemy in other small scaled attacks. In other activity, the Polish 2nd Corps seizes Ancona, on the Adriatic coast. The Germans also mount fierce resistance near Citta di Castello, but they are driven from M. Arnato. **(Atlantic-Russia)** The Germans receive heavy pressure on the Russian Front and are unable to spare more men due to extraordinary pressure being applied by the Allies in both France and Italy. Some German Officers have previously requested permission to withdraw and consolidate their positions, but Hitler steadfastly refuses all requests. The Russians seize Brody and to the north, the Russians move west from Kowel. In addition, Pskov and Ostrov are threatened by the Russians. The Germans, however, are able to mount an attack which stalls the Russians at Augustow on the East Prussian border.

GIs approaching the ruins of St Lo.

July 19th 1944 — (Pacific-New Guinea) In the Aitape area, elements of the Persecution Covering Force regain ground near Afua, but the Japanese mount a late afternoon assault to surround and eliminate Troop A, 112th Cavalry; the Cavalry reacts boldly and the enemy is driven back about 600 yards from their starting point, giving the 112th extra breathing room along the Afua-Palauru Trail. Second Lt. Dale Christensen Troop E, 112th Cavalry, having saved his Platoon a few days earlier, is again called upon; heavy machine gun fire keeps the Platoon pinned down; he advances, but his rifle is shot from his hands. Undaunted, he continues moving forward, smashing the nest with grenades. Then he discovers the positions of four additional nests; soon after, the Cavalrymen attack, driving the Germans from their fortifications and capturing 10 machine guns and four mortars. Christensen is subsequently killed on the 4th of August while leading an attack against another enemy machine gun; he receives the Medal of Honor posthumously. **(Pacific-Naval)** The U.S.S. *Flasher* (SS-249) sinks a Japanese Light Cruiser, the *Oi*. The Destroyer Escort U.S.S. *Wyman* (DE-38), operating in the Central Pacific, sinks a Japanese Submarine, the RO-48. **(Atlantic-France)** In the **U.S. First Army** area, the **XIX Corps** controls St Lo and finishes securing the surrounding area; the Patrols dispatched the previous day, discover that the Germans have only retreated slightly and intend to offer serious resistance.

With St Lo secure, the 35th Division, reinforced by 29th Division Artillery and the 113th Cavalry Group, takes responsibility for the area, relieving the 29th Division. In the **British Second Army** area, Fleury and Ifs, both on the south bank of the Orne, and Louvigny on the opposite side, are seized by the 2nd Canadian Division; the 3rd Canadians take Faubourg de Vaucelles and Carmelles. In the 8th Corps sector, the Germans lose Cagny, but they resist steadfastly at Troarn in the I Corps sector. **(Atlantic-Italy)** In the **U.S. Fifth Army** area, **IV Corps** sector, Leghorn falls to the 34th U.S. Division. The Germans withdraw, but leave their mark; their specialist teams have ravaged the harbor area and a good deal of the town has been demolished; at 02:00, the 3rd Battalion, 135th Infantry advances into it, followed closely by the 363rd Regiment; Patrols dispatched toward the Arno meet fragile opposition. The 88th and 91st Divisions probe the center and right flanks of the Corps to ensure against counterattack. As **Fifth Army** claws forward against wavering resistance, the French Expeditionary Corps' 4th Mountain Division overruns Certaldo, and the 2nd Moroccan Division seizes south Donato, northwest of Castellina. In the **British Eighth Army** area, contingents of the British 6th Armored Division, secure another crossing at the Arno River near Laterina. The Germans stand firm and obstruct progress in most areas, including fierce resistance against the South African 6th Division in the hills at Chianti. **(Atlantic-Russia)** The Russians proclaim that their 1st Ukrainian Front has further damaged the Germans at Brody by surrounding five Divisions deployed west of the recently captured town.

July 20th 1944 — (United States) The Joint Chiefs of Staff reach a consensus that Japan should be bombed during late-January 1945; Admiral King states: "TOO LATE, WHY NOT HIT JAPAN BY THE END OF 1944? King then directs Nimitz: "DRAW UP PLANS FOR THE BOMBING OF THE JAPANESE HOMELAND." This action by King initiates a competitive race between the Carrier Forces and the Heavy Air Force Bomber contingents. **(Pacific-Marianas)** The U.S. Navy launches more Planes from Carriers to lambaste Guam in synchronization with Surface Vessel Gunfire. In other activity, Tinian, another bastion of the Japanese also receives a thundering preinvasion bombardment. **(Pacific-New Guinea)** In the Aitape area, the 1st and 2nd Battalions, 127th Infantry, manning positions at their newly established Patrol Base near the East Branch of Koronal Creek receive orders directing them to prepare to drive southeast toward Afua. In other activity, the first contingents of the U.S. 41st Division arrive on Aitape. On Biak, American Artillery maintains its celebrated bombardment of the Ibdi Pocket, while Task Force Hurricane terminates the remnant opposition in the East Caves. **(Atlantic-France)** The **U.S. First Army** fine tunes its plans for Operation COBRA (Breakout from St Lo to capture Countances). In the **XIX Corps** sector, the 134th Infantry, 35th Division relieves elements of the 29th Division in St Lo. In other First Army activity, the 4th Division is transferred from VIII Corps to VII Corps. In the **British Second Army** area, the Germans holding St Andre-sur-Orne resist boldly, but the town falls to the Canadian 2nd Division. In the British 8th Corps sector, the British 7th Armored Division seizes Bourguebus in coordination with the Guards Armored Division, which captures Frenouville, culminating the effort to stretch the Orne bridgehead and threaten Falaise. **(Atlantic-Germany)** A well thought out, but unsuccessful plot to assassinate Hitler fails today. The key player in the attempt is a Catholic German Officer, Colonel von Stauffenberg. He had made his decision

to assist with the elimination of Hitler soon after he had been wounded in Tunisia during April 1943. His motive is to save Germany, and if the attempt fails, that the world should be aware that an attempt had been made. Hitler has already escaped assassination several times in the past. Today, a meeting has been called at "The Wolf's Lair" (Wolfsschanze), Hitler's Headquarters nestled in a forest at Rastenburg, East Prussia.

Early in the morning, von Stauffenberg crosses Berlin by car, heading for the Airport. Tucked inside his briefcase is the bomb (using silent fuse). The flight takes three hours delivering von Stauffenberg to his destination at around 10:00. At 12:00, plans change because Hitler is expecting Mussolini and the meeting is moved up one half hour. The conference room is moved; the new location contains space and windows that lessen the power of the explosion. In addition, a German Officer inadvertently moves the bomb to the end of the table, adding to the failure of the mission. Von Stauffenberg departs the meeting less than 10 minutes before the explosion. Four Officers are killed, however Hitler survives, suffering loss of hearing in one ear and he becomes temporarily paralyzed; still he meets with Mussolini at 16:00. The bomb had detonated at 12:42 and von Stauffenberg, convinced that Hitler is dead, returns to Berlin with the misinformation at 16:30; the situation deteriorates rapidly. Before the ordeal is ended, over 5,000 people will be executed. Several of the leaders are executed today, including von Stauffenberg. In other activity, Himmler informs Doctor Kersten that the United States is having a lot of difficulty with the Russians, and that the problems would culminate with a "decisive effect on the war." **(Atlantic-Italy)** In the **U.S. Fifth Army** area, **IV Corps** sector, elements of the 34th Division set up advance outposts along Highway 67, southeast of Pisa, while the 91st Division extends its perimeter, taking responsibility for some of the western terrain previously held by the 34th. On the right of the IV Corps, the 88th Division, in conjunction with Task Force Ramey, secures the heights along the Orlo River, east of Palaia. In other activity the British prepare to relieve the French.

U.S. troops landing at Guam.

July 21st-August 11th 1944 — (Pacific-Marianas-Guam) The American III Corps awaits the cessation of the preinvasion bombardment of Guam. Army Land-based Planes join the Marine and Naval Carrier-based Squadrons' attack. In concert, Surface Vessels open up with incessant salvos that pound the island. That boastful Japanese prediction after the fall of Saipan, stipulating that Guam will not fall, is at risk: ..."NOT GUAM. GUAM IS SECURE...GUAM IS JAPANESE FOREVER." After the seizure of Guam, the Japanese had imple-

399

U.S. Marines, backed by Armor, advance on Guam.

mented plans to essentially enslave the approximate 21,000 Guamanian natives. Japan permitted colonization of their new possession and the colonists anticipated the Chamorros doing their bidding. As the Japanese fortify the island in preparation of the attack, they force the natives to do the work; those unable to withstand the task die. Some islanders had been lucky and been in the U.S. Armed Forces when the island was seized and a portion of them are now offshore. As one Guamanian aboard Ship had mentioned, they grew up with a strong desire to become Sailors and their heroes were the United States Marines as they watched them drill and practice in their perfectly fitted uniforms.

Offshore is the Task Force of Rear Admiral R.L. Conolly, which has transported the Army and Marine Forces, commanded by Major General R.S. Geiger U.S.M.C. As the storm of Yankee shells begin to simmer, Japanese Planes attempt to engage the Yanks, but they are no match for the American Pilots.

At approximately 08:30, the western coast of Guam receives three Regiments of the 3rd Marine Division, moving abreast in synchronization with the First Marine Provisional Brigade, landing to the south, with the 4th Marines, striking on the right. The 22nd Marines lands on the left between Agat Village and Bangai Point. The 3rd Marine Division is positioned between Adelup and Asan Points. The combined units drive inland against medium resistance, expanding the toehold of two beachheads to a distance two miles wide and 1 mile deep. Later, RCT 305, U.S.A., 77th Infantry Division, lands to reinforce the beachhead, taking positions about 400 yards inland at Gaan Point. During the night of the 21st, the Japanese assault the perimeter of the 1st Provisional Brigade with vociferous cries of Banzai! Banzai! The unperturbed Marines open up with everything available, including swinging rifle butts and savage bayonets, decimating the Japanese 38th Infantry (minus the 3rd Battalion). Morning exposes many dead attackers; the unit is eliminated as a fighting force.

On the 22nd, Regimental Combat Team 305 and the 1st Battalion, 4th Marines capture the crest of Mt. Alifan. Subsequently, the 1st Provisional Marine Brigade is ordered to take the Orote Peninsula as soon as the 77th Division U.S.A., relieves them. Meanwhile the 3rd Marine Division is concentrating on eliminating the heavy resistance in the hills commanding the northern beachhead. The Marines continue to scour the island yard by yard, compressing the Japanese as they advance. The 77th Division holds and expands the beachhead as the days pass. Patrols from the Army and the Marines probe jointly as the enemy is chased north.

U.S. Infantry at Agat Beach, Guam.

The Japanese launch futile attacks against the Marines on the 25th through the 27th. The 3rd Marine Division's beachhead at Asan is rammed with a tremendous blow, but the line is rock hard. The Japanese fare no better on Orote Point where their assault receives withering fire and steadfast determination, leaving the enemy battered and crunched. The combined force of the 58th Keibitai Regiment (reinforced) and the 218th Japanese Regiment, minus the 1st Battalion, suffer devastating losses.

On the 26th, the big Naval guns, in orchestra with the ground Artillery, supplement the 1st Provisional Marine Brigade during a three day operation to secure the Orote Peninsula. Orote Airfield is declared operational and will soon receive its first Fighters.

On the 27th the 77th Division, U.S.A., sends Patrols, attached to the Reconnaissance Troops, south to weigh the strength of the Japanese and extends north to assume responsibility for some terrain beyond Mt. Tenjo, captured by the 3rd Marine Division on the 25th. By the 29th, the combined thrust of the 77th Division and the 3rd Marine Division, secures the Force Beachhead Line and the commanding ground along Adelup-Aluton-Tenjo-Alifun-Futi Point, terminating enemy resistance in the center of the island, culminating Phase 1 of the operation.

The battle continues to rage; newly secured positions give the Yanks a commanding view of the northern portion of the island. Small arms fire is incessant. The 1st Marine Brigade assumes responsibility for the Force Line Beachhead Line, releasing the 77th Division, U.S.A. to drive north. On the following day, the III Amphibious Corps attacks to secure the northern part of the island; against fanatical resistance, Agana, the capital of Guam falls to the 3rd Marines, 3rd Division. On the following day, the 77th Division powers forward and secures the Agana-Pago Bay Road.

As the sun rises on the second of August the 9th Marines, 3rd Marine Division, secures Tiyan Airfield as they push north, firing at anything that moves; occasionally Japs stick their heads up from a burrow; often it is their last glimpse of sunlight as a sudden burst of gunfire riddles the opening. As the Yanks advance, one Marine notices a Jap playing possum and snaps viciously as his weapon empties: "DON'T PLAY DEAD WITH ME YOU BASTARD." Nearby, American wounded are being transported in stretchers, heading back to the Ships.

On the third of August the 1st Provisional Brigade and elements of the 4th Marines secure Toto, further diminishing the resistance in the north. The 77th Infantry seizes Barrigada and its water supply. On the following day the 77th Division bolts to the mountain north of town seizing it; in conjunction, the 3rd Marine Division secures the Finegayan defenses, cracking the outer defense of the Mt. Santa Rosa defense line. In quick succession, the 77th gnaws toward Mt. Santa Rosa, capturing Yigo and it by the eighth, eliminating all resistance in the Divisional area. On the 11th, the 306th Infantry, 77th Division U.S.A., seizes the enemy command post on Mt. Mataguac; the effort kills the highest ranking Japanese Officer on the island, Lt. General Obata. Organized resistance had ended on the 10th.

Throngs of mystified Japanese civilians come out of hiding, their visions of grandeur obscured by limitless rows of GIs and Marines. Even after the escape of Radioman Tweed, the arrogance of Japanese justice continues. Tweed is anxious to return to Guam to thank the people who saved him from capture and torture. Many of them, including children, had been tortured and beaten with unparalleled savagery. One young girl named Tonie, accused of harboring Tweed had been severely whipped with telephone wire until her legs and back bore continuous and crisscrossed bleeding stripes. Unsatisfied, the captors covered her head with a towel and gushed water into her mouth and face, leaving her near death and unconscious, the excess water cascading from her ears, nose and mouth. Tonie recovers, but not necessarily for the better.

While the American Navy is bombarding the island, Tonie is one of three young women who attempts to seek shelter in a cave, already containing Jap troops. Tonie is greeted by a staggering blow delivered with a bayonet. Still unsatisfied, the Japanese Soldier pulls out the bloodied bayonet and also her intestines; several minutes pass, then she slumps dead to the earth. Tweed's appraisal of Japanese "terrible butchery" and his fervent desire to return to Guam with the Invasion Force does not occur for two months. Tweed also states: "I KNOW THAT THESE PEOPLE (CHAMORROS) WERE AS BRAVE AND LOYAL AS ANY WHO EVER LIVED UNDER THE AMERICAN FLAG." The island cost the lives of 1,226 Americans. The Japanese sustain an actual body count of over 10,000. Many of the Jap stragglers take to the hills and the Americans initiate a system of weeding them out by establishing ambushes; the average catch is about 30 to 35 dead per night.

July 21st 1944 — (United States) President Roosevelt departs California aboard the U.S.S. *Baltimore* en route to Hawaii for conferences with Military Commanders. The Ves-

Marines on Guam salute the U.S. Coast Guard.

sel, commanded by Captain W.C. Calhoun is out at sea for two days when information reaches him that an enemy Task Force is 200 miles from Oahu. The President arrives without incident, but upon his departure, four Destroyers escort the *Baltimore* on the trip to Adak, Alaska. **(Pacific-Marianas)** (SEE ALSO JULY 21ST — AUGUST 11TH INVASION OF GUAM) In one incident of extreme bravery on Guam, P.F.C. Luther Skaggs, 3rd Battalion, 3rd Marines, assumes command of his section after its leader is wounded during the invasion by enemy mortar fire. Skaggs leads his men inland to a position from where they can better defend themselves; during the night, enemy infiltrators penetrate Marine positions and a grenade is thrown into Skaggs' foxhole severely wounding him. He places a tourniquet on his shattered leg and positions himself for a fight. He exchanges fire with the enemy for eight hours, then crawls to the rear to join the main battle; Skaggs receives the Medal of Honor for his extraordinary courage. On Tinian, the Naval and Air bombardment becomes more powerful. In Naval activity, the U.S. Submarine Chaser SC-1326 is damaged by an enemy coastal mortar. **(Pacific-New Guinea)** In the Aitape area, the Americans fortify their positions at the Driniumor. Meanwhile, the Japanese mount an attack that lasts through the night of the 21-22nd near Afua, against the 112th Cavalry. Troop C, having just replaced Troop A, becomes separated from the main command (South Force), but Troops from Company I, fight to the beleaguered outfit. During the battle, a Company of the 127th Infantry, 32nd Division attempts to pull back, but the enemy isolates one of its Platoons; Private Donald R. Lobaugh volunteers to knock out the enemy emplacement, including a machine gun, commanding the only escape route. Racing across open ground, he closes and throws a grenade, but becomes wounded; undaunted, he continues to advance firing his weapon as he runs. More enemy fire rips all around him, tearing the ground, then another burst of fire again wounds him. However, he advances further, bleeding more profusely and absorbing more bullets, but kills two more Germans before he dies. His most courageous actions inspire the unit to tear ahead and drive the enemy from their positions during these early hours of the 22nd; Pvt. Lobaugh receives the Medal of Honor posthumously. **(China-Burma-India)** In Burma, the battle-weary Morris Force of the Indian 3rd Division receives permission to withdraw from Myitkyina. **(Atlantic-France)** The U.S. First Army continues to prepare for Operation COBRA, while simultaneously maintaining its perimeter. **(Atlantic-Italy)** The U.S. Fifth Army issues instructional orders for the drive to the Gothic Line. The II Corps assumes responsibility for the Fifth Army Front to permit proper adjustments for the offensive. Upon reaching the Arno River, the 34th Division is to detach from the IV Corps and be assigned to Fifth Army control. Fifth Army is scheduled to cross the Arno between the 5th and 10th of August, to seize Lucca, M. Albano and Pistoia. In the **IV Corps** area, the 91st Division sweeps the south bank of the Arno but does not experience any heavy opposition. In other activity, **British Eighth Army** contingents are assigned responsibility of securing the heights north and northwest of Florence. **(Atlantic-Poland)** The Russians advance and take Ostrov with units of the Third Baltic Front. In other activity, the Russians move toward Brest, Litovsk and Lublin.

July 22nd 1944 — (Pacific-Marianas-Guam-Tinian) Elements of the First Provisional Marine Brigade (1st Battalion, 4th Marines), reinforced by 305th U.S.A., secure Mt. Alifan. In other activity, the Japanese spring an unexpected attack against elements of the 2nd Battalion, 3rd Marines, as it clears opposition in a ravine along the Asan-Adelup Beachhead. Two machine guns, firing from a distance of 15 yards, jeopardize the operation. P.F.C. Leonard F. Mason, acting instinctively, bolts from the gully and attempts to get behind the Japs. A deadly burst of fire from troops in the heights snaps into his shoulder and his arm, but he drives further and reaches the stronghold where another round of fire from a machine gun wounds him mortally. Mason, unwilling to succumb, perseveres, destroying five Japanese and wounding another. Mason, subsequently rejoins his Platoon and is evacuated for medical treatment; however, the savage wounds take his life; he receives the Medal of Honor posthumously. On Tinian, the massive Air and Surface bombardment continues to soften enemy resistance. **(Pacific-New Guinea)** In Aitape, the Japanese unsuccessfully attack the North Force to repossess a crossing of the Driniumor River. In the Afua area, Troop C, of the 112th Cavalry, still is isolated; although besieged, the gallant unit retains its composure and outlasts the enemy, which at times numbers 2,000 men. The heavy resistance forces the South Force to abandon its right flank, giving the enemy Afua, and leaving the trapped 112th to fend for itself as all attempts to relieve it are futile. On Biak, elements of the 163rd Infantry charge into the Ibdi Pocket, eliminating the remaining enemy resistance. **(China-Burma-India)** General Stilwell, known for his candid statements, radios his Chief of Staff General Hearn, and informs him of the establishment of a CBI policy on supporting the Chinese troops operating in eastern China. Stilwell mentions that General Chennault should inform Chiang Kai-shek that his (Chennault) working theory that the Japanese can be stopped by Air Power alone is a failure. Stilwell feels this will give Kai-shek an opportunity to consider revision in the tonnage allotment for the Hump (Air flights over the Himalayas). **(Atlantic-France)** In the **U.S. First Army VIII Corps** area, the German 7th Army holds firmly in the vicinity of St Germain-sur-Seves, compelling the U.S. 90th Division to withdraw upon reaching it. In the **British Second Army** 12th Corps sector, Maltot falls to the British 43rd Division. **(Atlantic-Europe)** The U.S. Fifteenth Air Force reactivates Operation FRANTIC after inactivity for about a month; 58 P-51s and 76 P-38s strike enemy Airfields in Rumania, while Heavy Bombers strike the Ploesti oil refineries. **(Atlantic-Italy)** In the **U.S. Fifth Army** area, the 91st Division continues clearing out resistance below the Arno, while the 34th Division ousts the enemy from terrain below the Arno on the left flank of the Corps. In the **British Eighth Army** area the British 13th Corps moves west to assume responsibility for the sector recently held by the French Expeditionary Corps. In the British 10th Corps area, the 10th Indian Division seizes Citta di Castello, then pushes further north. **(Atlantic-Russia-Finland)** The Russians advance to the Soviet Finnish border, as placed during 1940.

July 23rd 1944 — (United States) As President Roosevelt heads for Hawaii, a radio message from General MacArthur reaches Washington, describing his schedule of invasion targets in the Pacific: Morotai, September 15th; Talauds, October 15th and Mindanao November 15th. **(Pacific-Marianas-Guam-Tinian)** On Guam, the 77th Division, U.S.A. (minus 307th Infantry) lands in the southern section (Agat) and begins to relieve the 1st Provisional Marine Brigade. In other activity, the 3rd Marine Division extends its beachhead and finishes the occupation of Cabras Island, deploying Artillery to support subsequent island operations. On Tinian, the Japanese feel confident despite the usual Allied Naval and Air bombardment; the Japanese guns control the island approaches and expect to annihilate the Marines if they attempt to land. The opposite side of the island is undefended because of the alleged unscalable cliffs and two slim but deadly passages through the reefs. In Naval activity, the U.S.S. *Norman Scott* (DD-690) is damaged when struck by enemy coastal fire; the Minesweeper (High-speed) *Chandler* (DMS-9) sustains damage from a fire. **(Pacific-New Guinea)** In Aitape, the 1st Battalion, 127th Infantry relieves Troops A and B, 112th Cavalry, allowing the two units to drive toward trapped Troop C; during the punishing drive, the Japanese mount fierce resistance, pinning down an advancing Platoon. As 2nd Lt. George W. Boyce Jr. directs his command through a small passage, the enemy tosses grenades. Boyce, reacts immediately, and blankets the grenade closest to the troops with his own body ensuring their lives at the sacrifice of his own; Boyce receives the Medal of Honor posthumously. Afua is seized handily by the Cavalry and the 2nd Battalion, 127th Infantry, driving tenaciously from the southeast, reaches Troop C, but during the day, Japanese reinforcements numbering about 2,000 hold the rear and right flank of Afua, forbidding a breakout by either Troop C, or the 2nd Battalion. In related activity, elements of the 503rd Parachute Infantry meet intense opposition as it attempts to rescue the trapped Soldiers. Sergeant Ray Eubanks leads a detachment to eliminate killing fire from several different positions. Eubanks' Squad advances to within 30 yards of the objective; however, incessant fire halts its progress. Eubanks holds his Squad back and advances alone, reaching a point 15 yards from the enemy and commences firing; return fire wounds him and destroys his rifle. Eubanks, continues to advance despite being severely wounded and takes on the machine gunners with the butt of his rifle, smashing four of the defenders with his rifle butt before the other Japs ring him with additional fire, killing him; he receives the Medal of Honor posthumously for his heroic actions. The Northern Force unsuccessfully tries to secure a crossing of the Driniumor. **(China-Burma-India)** A message is sent from Kai-shek to President Roosevelt informing him that he agrees with the appointment of Stilwell to command Chinese Forces, but stipulates demands that the Chinese Communists must accept Chinese authority ahead of Stilwell; he also insists that General Stilwell's duties be clearly spelled out, and last but not least, Chiang insists that the Chinese have total authority on the lend lease distribution; however he doesn't clearly define how the lend lease equipment is going to be distributed, nor to whom. In other activity, British Admiral Mountbatten formulates preliminary plans for attack; one by way of crossing the Chindwin (CAPITAL) and another (DRACULA), a two pronged assault sending Amphibious and Airborne troops against Rangoon. On the Salween Front, the Japanese come under an Artillery supported attack by three Regiments of the Chinese 8th Army at Sung Shan. **(Atlantic-France)** The **U.S. First Army** checks last minute details for Operation COBRA, but the breakout intended to commence on the 24th will be canceled due to terrible weather conditions. **(Atlantic-Italy)** In the **U.S. Fifth Army IV Corps** area, the 34th Division completes the reduction of resistance in its sector up to the Arno, against slight opposition, By mid-afternoon, the 363rd Infantry stands at S Pisa, already having seized Marina di Pasa below the Arno; the Germans have demolished the bridges across the river and have deployed Artillery against both the port of Leghorn and S Pisa. In addition, the Germans mount formidable resistance along the Corps' right flank against the 88th Division. In the **British Eighth Army** area, Tavernelle is taken by New Zealanders and the summits of M. Domini and M. Fili are secured by the 6th South African Armored Division, while the British 4th Division advances to South Giovanni. **(Atlantic-Russia)** Pskov is taken by the Third Baltic Front.

July 24th 1944 — (Pacific-Marianas) On Guam, the Japanese are being squeezed on the Orote Peninsula. Also, the Southern Landing Force's beachhead is secure. In other activity, the 77th Division, U.S.A., assumes responsibility for most of the beachhead line. (ON TINIAN, SEE JULY 24TH-AUGUST 1ST 1944.) In Naval activity, the Battleship U.S.S. *Colorado* (BB-45) and the LST 481 become damaged by enemy coastal gun fire. **(Pacific-New Guinea)** In the Aitape area, the Japanese unsuccessfully attempt to secure positions at the Driniumor, being repelled during the night 24-25th in what becomes the final attempt to secure a crossing. In other activity, Japanese troops numbering more than 2,000 attack the right flank of the South Force (Persecution Covering Force) and also against the rear of Afua, virtually eliminating any possible breakout by Troop C, 112th Cavalry and the 2nd Battalion, 127th Infantry. In other activity, Task Force Typhoon departs Maffin Bay, heading for the Sansapor-Mar Operation. **(China-Burma-India)** In China, the beleaguered Garrison at Heng-yang continues to repulse Japanese attempts to destroy it; despite no Aircover, resistance is steadfast, compelling the Japanese to fall back and reorganize. In Burma, the struggle to seize Myitkyina is ongoing. The Chinese 50th Division makes some changes on the line after the arrival of the 149th Regiment, which relieves units of the 42nd and 150th Chinese Regiments. **(Atlantic-France)** Operation COBRA is postponed because of bad weather conditions. During the day's actions, Colonel Paddy Flint, a close personal friend of General Patton is advancing up a road when he encounters a Tank that isn't moving. Colonel Flint inquires and is told that the turret is jammed. Flint directs the Tank to advance with him as an "Infantry Colonel Bodyguard." Shortly thereafter, Flint boards the outside of the Tank to give directional instructions and enemy fire twice hits him, but he defies the danger and returns fire at close range. The radioman then gets hit. An Infantry Platoon rushes to the scene to help and finds Flint already giving its Sergeant instructions. During the conversation, an enemy bullet strikes Flint in the head, wounding him mortally. He dies on the following day and is buried on the 26th with honors. In other activity in France, the British 30th Corps dispatches the Scottish 15th Division to assume responsibility for a portion of the left flank of the U.S. V Corps area. In addition, the U.S. 28th Division arrives in France. **(Atlantic-Italy)** The **U.S. First Army** begins reforming along the Arno River, in addition to changing boundary lines separating the II and IV Corps, effective on or about the 25th of August.

Japanese Destroyer comes under low level attack.

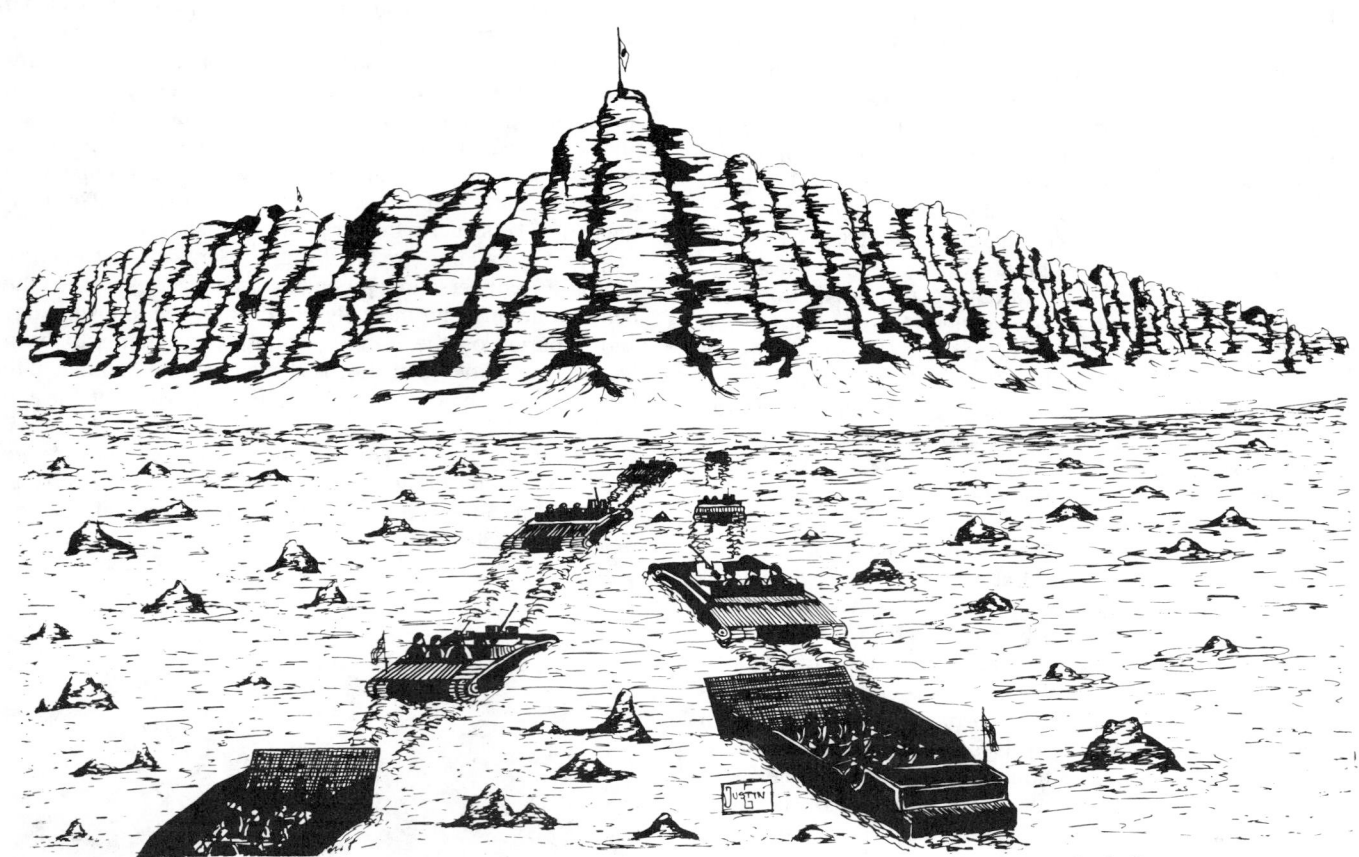

July 24th 1944 — Marines invade Tinian.   *Illustration by Justin Grecescu.*

July 24th-August 1st 1944 — THE INVASION OF TINIAN —
U.S. Rear Admiral H.W. Hill's Task Force prepares to take Tinian, a few miles south of newly won Saipan. Planes, based in
Saipan, lend their killing power to the operation, subsidizing
the Carrier-based Aircraft and Naval Surface Vessels. The island is to be taken by the 2nd and 4th Marine Divisions.
Serious lessons have been previously learned at Tarawa, and
will be applied at Tinian to lessen the severity of casualties.
Naval guns catapult shells toward the island with quivering
shock, pounding the island. More shelling and bombs are
committed by the Planes in dazzling fashion; the impact
pumps debris and fire and blinding smoke all across the
beach area. The Japanese peer defiantly as the Landing Craft
begin moving toward the shore heading directly into the
sights of the Japanese guns. The Japanese at Tinian Town, the
obvious choice of landing sites, prepare to fire, but become
momentarily bewildered when the 2nd Marine Division halts
the invasion just short of the range of the shore guns. The
Japs suspect the invasion is to be aborted for fear of the
Marines receiving similar resistance as that sustained by Marines at Tarawa slightly over six months ago. The Landing
Craft simply wallow in the water holding in place, to the
growing amazement of the confident defenders, now thoroughly convinced their shore guns have prevented invasion.

As the Japanese relish the apparent indecision of the 2nd
Marine Division, the 4th Marine Division is inconspicuously
closing at the reverse side of the island to attempt a most
remarkable maneuver, landing as if threading a needle, a mission that requires extraordinary skill to ensure success. The
Japanese maintain no vigil on the northwest tip of the island,
confident that the erratic reefs are nearly impenetrable and if
some craft penetrate, the rocky cliffs still forbid entrance. The

4th Marine Division defies the odds and the Leathernecks
squirm through the treacherous reefs.

In a startling burst of daring speed, the reefs are conquered
and the Landing Craft gates bolt open. Marines devour the
beachhead and scale the rugged cliffs grasping a solid
foothold on the island. While the Japanese man the southwest
sea walls and pound the water with shells to keep the 2nd
Marines at bay, 15,000 other Marines had come ashore. The
2nd Division, having served as bait, soon delivers its 1st Battalion 8th Marines to add more punch to the beachhead,
which stands at just under 3,000 yards at it widest point.
During the lightning assault, the 2nd Battalion, 24th Marines
advances to the fringes of Airfield No. 3 (Old Ushi Point Airfield), splicing the primary road that extends from Ushi Point
through the central portion of the island to its southern end.

The Japanese attempt to turn the tide and blow the Marines
away, but their reaction time is insufficient. The Japanese
regroup and mount a vicious assault during the early morning
hours of the 25th, but the Marines sleep lightly. The 135th
Japanese Infantry commences the attack, striking against the
center and both flanks of the Marine perimeter; it is violently
repulsed by devastating fire that decimates the enemy's 1st
Battalion. Subsequently, the 8th Marines attack against nominal resistance, seizing the remainder of the Airfield at Ushi
Point, while the 25th Marines secures Mt. Maga.

By the 26th, the 2nd Division is completely ashore and the
8th Marines revert back to its jurisdiction. Aware of the vantage point controlled by the Japanese on Mt. Lasso, Naval
Surface Vessel guns and Artillery are called into action by the
Marine Infantry as the 2nd and 4th Divisions race under the
iron umbrella, seizing the objective without opposition, denying the enemy the opportunity of bombarding the expanding

American beachhead with Artillery or Mortar fire.

The 27th brings more rapid advancement to the Marines who drive across the island and secure the northern portion of Tinian by 16:00. Marines supplemented by Tanks, scour the island advancing toward the final bastion, Tinian Town. Japanese resistance remains moderate to light for the duration. The Marines advance tenaciously taking Tinian Town and Airfield No. 4 on the 30th. On the following day, with the enemy stampeded and corralled on the southern tip of the island, the drive intensifies and the Yanks converge for the final surge, overpowering the resistance by August 1st. Enemy troops hold up in caves on the southern sector; Squads, equipped with Flame Throwers are brought to bear on those unwilling to surrender. On August 3rd, the Stars and Stripes is officially raised in victory. The invincible Japanese are again vanquished. The combined Marine losses including the 2nd and 4th Marine Divisions are slightly over 300 killed and approximately 1,550 wounded. The Japanese sustain over 5,000 killed.

July 25th 1944 — (Pacific-Bonins-Caroline Islands) Admiral Mitscher's Task Force 58 assaults enemy installations in the Western Carolines. Planes from six Carriers attack Fais, Ngulu, Palau, Sorol, Ulithi and Yap. The Air bombardment continues until the 28th. Today, the Japanese Minelayer *Sokuten* is sunk during the attack. **(Pacific-Dutch East Indies)** Sabang, off Sumatra's northern tip, is bombarded by British Naval Ships, damaging the Navy Yard. In conjunction, Carrier Planes raid the nearby Airdromes. **(Pacific-Marianas-Guam-Tinian)** On Guam, elements of the 77th Division, U.S.A., assume responsibility of the Force Line Beachhead and the 1st Provisional Marine Brigade receives orders to secure the Orote Peninsula. The 3rd Marine Division is ordered to take the heights above the Mt. Tenio Road. The Japanese mount successive futile assaults against the Marines' Asan beachhead and also against the 25th Marines' perimeter on the Orote Peninsula from today until the 27th and are decisively defeated sustaining tremendous losses. During ferocious fire fighting near Fonte Hill, the 2nd Battalion, 9th Marines, 3rd Marine Division pushes toward the heights against machine gun and rifle fire, but still advances 300 yards, and seizes the obstinate objective. Captain Louis H. Wilson Jr., Commanding Officer of a Rifle Company, takes command of the units in the area and directs deployment procedures for the night. Wounded three times during a five hour period, he still finishes the task before seeking medical aid and retiring to his Command Post. The Japanese commence a savage counterattack, prompting Wilson to forego his sleep and rejoin the troops on the line; he engages in hand-to-hand combat for a period of ten hours and at one point, goes out to retrieve a wounded Marine lying helplessly, within reach of the enemy. By the following morning, the attacks in his zone have been crumbled. Wilson still unable to properly tend his wounds or rest, takes a 17 man Squad to secure a strategic slope, ensuring permanent stability of his positions, losing 13 men to the casualty list as they plow through intensified machine gun and mortar fire, supplemented by rifle men. The Marines, undaunted by the odds, capture the objective guaranteeing success of the Regimental objective, and destroy about 350 Japs in the process; Wilson becomes a recipient of the Medal of Honor. On Tinian, the Japanese mount a heavy counterattack, but are repulsed by the 4th Marine Division. The Airfield at Ushi Point falls to the 8th Marines (2nd Division under jurisdiction of 4th Division) and the 25th Marines seize Mt. Maga. **(Pacific-New Guinea)** The 127th Infantry (Companies

B and E) finally penetrate the Japanese defenses and rescue Troop C, which has withstood enemy attempts to annihilate it for four days; the 127th then drives toward the Afua-Palauru Road to engage heavy Japanese forces. On Noemfoor, the Japanese abandon the Inasi region, ceasing contact with the 503rd Paratroop Infantry. In other activity, the Airfield at Kornasoren is partially operational and able to handle one Fighter Group. **(China-Burma-India)** The contest for Myitkyina still rages and the pressure is finally taking its toll; the Japanese show signs of relenting. To add additional pressure, elements of the Chinese 30th Division arrive. **(Atlantic-France)** With clearer skies and more reasonable weather, the Eighth and Ninth U.S. Air Forces commence Operation COBRA, launching a massive surprise raid against enemy positions with startling success, preceding the breakout. Unfortunately, of the 4,000 tons of bombs dropped, many mistakenly strike Americans deployed for jump off along the 9th and 30th Division lines, causing casualties, including the death of Lt. General Wesley J. McNair when a bomb scores a direct hit on an observation post from which he had been watching the assault. Ironically, Heavy Bombers had also struck American positions two days prior on Sunday the 23rd. By 11:00, the ground troops are on the move; the **VII Corps** is directed to dislodge the enemy lines near Marigny-St. Gilles. The 4th Division in the center, flanked by the 9th on the right and the 30th on the left flank, pushes across the Periers-St. Lo Road, moving swiftly, enabling it to drive the Germans back about two miles. In the **VIII Corps** area, units of the U.S. 6th Armored Division are attached to Corps. In the **British Second Army** area, a diversionary feint is initiated. The Canadian 2nd and 3rd Divisions drive forward at 03:30, meeting heavy resistance along the Falaise Road and after a short gain are forced to disengage. **(Atlantic-Italy)** In the **U.S. Fifth Army** area the 88th Division's attempt to clear the area below the Arno continues. In addition, the 88th Division releases Task Force Ramey. In the **British Eighth Army** area, the 13th Corps maintains its push against the next enemy delaying line, which stretches through the perimeters of the 6th South African and the 2nd New Zealand Divisions. **(Atlantic-Poland-Operation FRANTIC)** American Fighter Bombers (15th Air Force) which had taken off from bases in Russia, strike Mielec Airdrome, in the vicinity of Lwow. **(Atlantic-Eastern Europe)** Troops of the 2nd Baltic Front sever the Dvinsk-Riga Road in Latvia. Brest Litovsk, held by the Germans is jeopardized as Soviet Armored units are closing.

July 26th 1944 — (United States) The Submarine U.S.S. *Golet* (SS-273) is reported missing and lost. The *Golet*, commanded by Lt. Commander J.S. Clark, had departed Midway for the Honshu vicinity on May 28th; Headquarters never made contact with the Submarine which was on her second War Patrol. After the conclusion of the war, Japanese records indicate an attack against a Submarine on June 14th and the *Golet* had been the only Submarine in that area at that time. **(Pacific-Hawaii)** President Roosevelt confers with General MacArthur and Admiral Nimitz at Pearl Harbor. Admiral Leahy (Roosevelt's Chief of Staff) also is in attendance. The spirited discussions include Pacific strategy and the pros and cons of seizing or bypassing the Philippines and taking Formosa. Nimitz favors the latter and MacArthur is determined to invade the Philippines; ultimately the Philippines are invaded. **(Pacific-Guam)** Seven Battalions of Artillery open up against enemy positions on the Orote Peninsula. The 4th Marines and the 22nd Marines (1st Provisional Marine Brigade), operating on the left and right respectively, advance about

1,500 yards through heavy jungle entanglements across the neck of the peninsula; the peninsula which includes the Marine Barracks, will be secure by the 29th. The 22nd Marines (minus 3rd Battalion), subsequently transfers into the III Amphibious Corps Reserve, deploying south of Agat; the 3rd Battalion remains on the peninsula. The Orote Airfield is declared operational during the three day operation. The 3rd Marine Division handily repulses a strong enemy counterattack during the night 21st-22nd, thrashing the attackers. **(Pacific-Marianas-Tinian)** The 2nd Marine Division completes its landing and prepares for action after reclaiming the 8th Marines. Artillery and Air support are committed to a major attack, supporting the 2nd and 4th Divisions' drive across the northern portion of the island against light resistance; Mt. Lasso is seized without incident. **(Pacific-New Guinea)** The Allies prepare for a counterattack in the Aitape area, but none are forthcoming. **(Pacific-Philippines)** The U.S.S. *Sawfish* (SS-276) sinks the Japanese Submarine I-29 in the Luzon Strait. In other activity, the Submarine U.S.S. *Robalo* (SS-273) is lost off western Palawan, cause unknown. Subsequently, four Sailors who survive the sinking, swim to shore but are picked up and imprisoned by Japanese on Palawan Island; during August, 1945, the prisoners are moved by a Japanese Destroyer. Records do not show the Destroyers destination, but it probably never made it; the four Americans are never found. **(China-Burma-India)** On the Salween Front, the Japanese call in Air support to strike attacking Japanese in the vicinity of Sung Shan. The air raid effectively aborts the attack, by damaging the guns of the Chinese. In other activity, the Chinese successfully assault Teng-chung; the attack, supplemented by Artillery and Air support, nets Lai-feng, a fortified peak that controls entrances to the town. In a coordinated assault, the Chinese drive against the southeastern wall of the city, but are rebuffed. **(Atlantic-France)** In the **U.S. First Army** area, the **VIII Corps** is committed to the breakout assault (Operation COBRA), commencing its attack at 05:30 with three Divisions advancing and a fourth, the 79th Division jumping off later, following the route of the 8th Division, which severs the Lessay-Periers Road. A bridgehead is established at the Seves River by the 90th Division, pushing up the center. The 83rd Division also makes progress. In other activity, the **VII Corps** commits additional contingents to bolster its drive. The Big Red One (1st Division) moves through the 9th Division lines and secures Marigny. Combat Command B, 3rd Armored Division, advances and deploys west and southwest of Marigny. In conjunction, the U.S. 4th Division advances rapidly toward La Conviniere, while the 2nd Armored Division roars through the positions of the 30th Division, holding the left flank of the Corps, seizing Canisy and St. Gilles. The **XIX Corps** is reinforced as the 28th Division is attached to it. In the **V Corps** area, an Artillery bombardment directed by British and American guns, adds extra punch as the 2nd and 5th U.S. Divisions advance toward the Vidouville-Rouxeville Road, attacking east of St. Lo. **(Atlantic-Italy)** The **U.S. Fifth Army IV Corps** receives anticipated reinforcements; Task Force 45, consisting of 91st AAA Group, 107th AAA Group and the 2nd Armored Group is organized under the Headquarters of the 45th AAA Brigade and deploys on the west flank of the Corps; relieving the 34th Division. In a coordinated move, the 363rd Infantry reverts back to the 91st Division, being detached from the 34th Division. **(Atlantic-Rumania)** Operation FRANTIC — American Planes attached to the Fifteenth Air Force, again bombard Ploesti as they make another run between Russia and Italy. **(Atlantic-Russia)** Narva, Estonia falls to the Russian Leningrad Front.

A French woman passes destroyed German Armor, attempting to return to her house, subsequent to German withdrawal.

July 27th 1944 — (Pacific-Caroline Islands) Carrier-based Aircraft destroy the Japanese Transports Nos. 1 and 150, off the Palau Islands. **(Pacific-Marianas-Guam)** On Guam, Patrols of the 77th Division U.S.A. move south to gather information on enemy strength in that portion of the island, expanding their positions beyond Mt. Tenjo, taking responsibility for ground previously covered by 3rd Marine Division. On Tinian, the Ushi Point Airfield is declared operational. In other activity, the 2nd and 4th Marine Divisions continue the operation to eliminate enemy resistance on the island, securing the northern portion by 16:00. **(Pacific-New Guinea)** In the Aitape area, the 2nd Battalion, 127th Infantry (South Force) pushes south, crossing the Afua-Palauru trail, but an enemy threat emerges, threatening its communications, and forcing the troops to withdraw to their jump off point. In other activity, enemy troops also threaten the South Force supply depot, however, elements of the 112th Cavalry and the 1st Battalion, 127th Infantry sweep the heights nearby, eliminating the enemy. In the Wakde-Sarmi area, elements of the 6th Division depart to participate in the Vogelkop campaign. **(China-Burma-India)** The Myitkyina northern Airstrip is captured by the 3rd Battalion (New Galahad Force); its defense becomes the responsibility of 209th and 236th Engineering Battalions. On the Salween Front, the Chinese complete mopping up Mt. Lai-feng; their losses 1,200; the Japanese 400. **(Atlantic-France)** In the **U.S. First Army** area, delaying obstacles scattered along the western flank hinder the advance of the **VIII Corps**, but under the aggressive leadership of General Middleton, the Corps continues its thrust, plunging through mine (many plastic, undetectable by metal detectors) infested paths. The **VIII Corps** becomes part of Patton's Third Army, soon to become operational. The 8th Division drives south wedging between Lessay and Periers; the latter is simultaneously seized by the 79th Division. The 83rd Division, operating on the Corps left flank, pushes advance elements across the Taute River, while the 90th Division takes possession of Periers and drives across the Taute, east of the city. In other Corps activity, the heights near Le Bingard are secured by Troop A, 86th Cavalry Reconnaissance Squadron (6th Armored Division), which pinches through the perimeter of the 8th Division to reach the objective. The 8th Division is attached to the 4th Armored Division today. In the **VII Corps** area, elements drive south, while additional contingents enlarge the existing perimeter on the flanks of the salient. Combat Command B, 3rd Armored Division, in conjunction with the 1st Division, reach Camprond, as it closes on Coutances. Meanwhile, the 2nd Armored Division ramrods elements to Fervaches and Notre Dame de Cenilly. The **V Corps** expands its area west, incorporating the 35th Division, which is driving against St. Lo, capturing the high ground south and west of the objective in a coordinated attack with the advancing 2nd and 5th Divisions; the advance captures Notre Dame d'Elle. **(Atlantic-Italy)** In the **British Second Army** area, the New Zealand 2nd Division seizes S Casciano, threatening the German positions in the British 13th Corps area, compelling them to withdraw toward Florence. **(Atlantic-Eastern Europe)** Dvinsk, along the Dvina River falls to the Second Baltic Front. Bialystok, which has endured a week of vicious fighting, falls to the Second White Russian Front. In other activity, Lwow and Stanislawow are seized by contingents of the First Ukrainian Front.

July 28th 1944 — (Pacific-Guam) Tanks arrive (Army and Marine units) to supplement the 4th Marines and lead an afternoon drive that makes substantial progress, which links the 4th Marines with the 22nd Marines at the eastern end of the Airstrip. In other activity, the 77th Infantry and the 3rd Marines join the northern and southern beachheads, completing the final beachhead line. The 3rd Marine Division (3rd Battalion, 307th Infantry U.S.A. attached) secures Mt. Chachao and Mt. Tenjo, clearing travel on a road stretching from Mt. Tenjo to Adelup Point. On Tinian, the Japanese continue to withdraw, mounting slight opposition against advancing Marines who handily secure the Airfield at Gurguan Point. **(Pacific-New Guinea)** On Biak, enemy resistance at the Ibdi pocket is terminated, however, the overall mop-up operation continues. Japanese dead are estimated at 300 of the 800 defenders, but only 154 bodies are located (period July 22-28). In the Aitape area, the South Force withdraws from Afua to stabilize the security of its supply depot and to fortify its defensive posture. **(Pacific-Naval)** The Destroyer Escorts *Wyman* (DE-38) and the *Reynolds* (DE-42) combine and destroy the Japanese Submarine I-55 in the Central Pacific. Also, Carrier-based Planes sink a Japanese Submarine Chaser (no name determination). **(Atlantic-France)** In the **U.S. First Army**, area the Germans continue to withdraw. Orders are given to the Corps to take the advantage, intensify the breakout effort and accelerate pursuit of the enemy; Middleton's **VIII Corps** speeds its 4th and 6th Armored Divisions to the point to spearhead the Infantry. Combat Command A, 6th Armored, acting as the vanguard, drives south with the 79th Division trailing, heading toward the southwestern area of Coutances. In conjunction, Combat Command B, 4th Armored Division steamrolls forward seizing Coutances before 17:00, giving Operation COBRA a solid "mission accomplished."

This tremendous progress of the VIII Corps, combined with the exemplary actions of the **VII Corps** (1st Infantry and 3rd Armored Divisions) links the two Corps, entrapping an enormous amount of enemy troops, which otherwise could have escaped through the left flank of the VII Corps. During the day's fast paced activities, Combat Command B, 2nd Armored Division, advances to St. Denis-le-Gast. Combat Command A, 2nd Armored Division, drives south, straight through Villebaudon, reaching the fringes of Moyen in conjunction with the advancing 30th Division which is moving along the western bank of the Vire River, heading south toward Tessy-sur-Vire. The Germans also feel pressure along the east bank of the Vire, by the 35th Division which is grinding toward Ste Suzanne-sur-Vire. In addition, St. Jean-de-Baisants falls to the 2nd Division. **(Atlantic-Eastern Europe)** Brest-Litovsk is taken by troops of the First White Russian Front. Jaroslaw and Przemysl, on the west bank of the San River, fall to troops of the First Ukrainian Front.

July 29th 1944 — (Pacific-Marianas-Guam-Tinian) On Guam, the remaining enemy resistance on Orote Peninsula is eliminated by the Marine First Provisional Brigade, culminating the first phase of the operation by 17:00. The 77th Division U.S.A., and the 3rd Marine Division, dispatch numerous Patrols from the beachhead to prepare for the next level of operations to secure Guam. On Tinian, the Japanese mount strong resistance against the 4th Marine Division's drive to clear the heights to the east. The 2nd Marine Division sprints rapidly to the west; the combined attack toward the southern end of the island continues. In Naval activity, the LST 340 is damaged after becming grounded. **(Pacific-New Guinea)** In the Aitape area, General Hall orders a counterattack, utilizing the 124th Infantry supported by elements of the 169th Infantry (2nd Battalion). Near Afua, the South Force mounts an attack to strengthen its positions, but the Japanese resistance is rigid and the assault gains little ground. **(China-Burma-India)** British General Giffard, Commanding General 11th Army Group, instructs British General Slim (Commanding Officer British Fourteenth Army) to make detailed plans for the attack across the Chindwin River toward Mandalay (Opration CAPITAL). **(Atlantic-France)** In the **U.S. First Army** area, the **VII Corps** pivots, heading south, driving to the Cerences-Hambye-Percy line, while the **VIII Corps** drives toward Granville. Combat Command A, 6th Armored Division gains a crossing at the Sienne River on the west flank of the Corps near Pont de la Roche. Meanwhile, Combat Command A, 4th Armored Division, pushes toward Cerences. The pressure against the Germans heightens and in the **VII Corps** area, they are under severe Artillery and Air attack, hindering their line of retreat American Tanks enter the conflict; the retreating enemy Tanks sustain heavy casualties. During the vociferous contest a vehement engagement ensues near Grimesnil, where the 2nd Armored Division is in the thick of battle. A Platoon of the 41st Armored Infantry becomes scattered and the Platoon leader and Platoon Sergeant are both missing in action, forcing Sergeant Hulon Whittington to assume command and stabilize the troops to ensure the steadfastness of the roadblock, which is blocking about 100 Vehicles of a Panzer unit. Whittington, jumps onto an American Tank, disavowing the flying shells and while under intense fire, instructs the Tank Commander to fire at the challenging Mark V Tank, leading the counterattack. The Mark V is destroyed, forbidding passage of the remainder of the menacing column. As the enemy Tanks attempt to withdraw, the Yanks have a field day; the Germans are pummeled by Tank fire. The Infantry begins tossing volleys of grenades.

Bazookas shock the stranded German columns. Bold men begin attacking Armor, inspired by the indomitable and inspiring Sergeant who had only intended to slow down the column. Whittington leads a gallant and successful bayonet attack against the immobilized and bewildered Germans, inflicting severe casualties on the enemy in addition to totally destroying the Panzer unit numbering at least 100 vehicles. After his medic becomes wounded, Whittington administers first aid to his wounded Platoon members; he receives the Medal of Honor. In other activity, the VII Corps links up with the XIX Corps, as the 29th Division advances against Percy. In the **XIX Corps** sector, the Germans mount fierce resistance along the road to Tessy-sur-Vire, impeding the U.S. 30th Division's drive. In the **V Corps** sector, elements reach Torigny-sur-Vire. **(Atlantic-Germany)** Army Aircraft sink two German Submarines, the U-872 and the U-2323 at Bremen Germany. **(Atlantic-Italy)** In the **British Eighth Army** 13th Corps area, M. Scalari is seized by the British 4th Division.

July 30th 1944 — (Pacific-Marianas-Guam-Tinian) Operations continue to secure the island. On Tinian, Airfield No. 4 and Tinian Town are secured. During the day's combat, Private Joseph Ozbourn gives his life to save his Squad. While the 1st Battalion, 23rd Marines are cleaning out the Japanese from remaining ditches and pillboxes, Ozbourn and four other men are working a section when he readies a grenade to toss into a nearby entrenchment; a huge explosion originating at the entrance of the enemy position wounds all five members of the detachment. Ozbourn too badly wounded to throw the grenade and aware that his companions will be killed, instinctively covers the grenade with his body absorbing the explosion; he receives the Medal of Honor posthumously. **(Pacific-New Guinea)** A Naval Task Force, commanded by Rear Admiral W. M. Fechteler lands Task Force Typhoon (6th U.S. Division) on the Vogelkop Peninsula without the support of Aircover to gain the advantage of surprise. Troops land near Cape Opmarai in northwest New Guinea and on the nearby islands of Amsterdam and Middleburg, hitting shore at 07:01. The 1st Infantry lands without incident on the peninsula and immediately expands its beachhead. In synchronization, the 6th Cavalry (reinforced) lands at Middleburg at 07:30 without opposition, then jumps to Amsterdam finding it undefended also. General Sibert takes command on land before 10:30. In Aitape, Company G, 127th Infantry (South Force) is isolated and surrounded by the Japanese on a slope west of Afua, but it holds and joins the main body on the following day. In other activity, the North Force finalizes plans for a strong counterattack. **(China-Burma-India)** Myitkyina is about to fall. The Japanese receive orders to withdraw. It is the final order of the Japanese Commander before he commits Hari Kari. Also, General Stilwell, to the surprise of many, had accepted the offer from Chiang Kai-shek to temporarily take Kai-shek's place as Commander, while Kai-shek is in England. Stilwell is aware (information from Japanese prisoners) that the defenders at Myitkyina are on rations of less than one bowl of rice a day, giving him a personal feeling of satisfaction, knowing that he is leaving, but his determination to seize Myitkyina will be realized. **(Atlantic-France)** In the **U.S. First Army** area, Combat Command B, 4th Armored Division drives into Avranches; elements secure bridges that span the See River, while Combat Command B, 6th Armored Division zooms through Combat Command A, pushing about three miles beyond Brehal, closing fast on Granville, and keeping the **VIII Corps** pace at a high pitch. The **VII Corps** drive has the 1st Infantry and the 3rd Armored Divisions pumping south, holding the right

flank of the Corps. Combat Command B, 3rd Armored, advances rapidly to Villedieu-les-Poles, while Combat Command A, crosses the Sienne at Gavray and begins constructing a bridge. The **XIX Corps** throws back a heavy counterattack on its right flank near Percy. In the **V Corps** area, solid enemy resistance pops up all along the front, preventing rapid movement to the south, but the 5th Division overcomes it and fights viciously to cross the contested Torigny-sur-Vire-Caumont Road. In the **British Second Army** area, regrouping is complete, following its short burst a few days previous to draw attention from the American Offensive (COBRA). The British reinitiate their attack and are supplemented with another powerful show of Air Power. Planes, both American and British unload 2,227 tons of bombs against enemy positions to lighten the resistance as the British 8th and 30th Corps take the offensive. The British 11th Armored rolls parallel to the 15th British Division, heading east; combined, they drive through La Fouquerie and Les Loges. In conjunction, the British 43rd and 50th Divisions on the west and east respectively, attack on the left of the 8 Corps, however, German opposition slows the advance, especially that of the 50th Division. **(Atlantic-Italy)** In the **British Eighth Army** area, the New Zealand 2nd Division assaults Pian dei Cerri Ridge.

U.S. Armor advancing north, between Avranches and Granville, France.

July 31st 1944 — (Pacific-Hawaii) The U.S. 81st Division begins practice maneuvers for the campaign to seize the Palaus. **(Pacific-Marianas-Guam-Tinian)** The III Amphibious Corps (77th Division U.S.A. and 3rd Marine Division) attacks to secure the northern part of Guam; Agana, the capital, is seized by the 3rd Marines (3rd Division), extending the line from there to Yona to the east where the 77th Division meets slight resistance. On Tinian, the Navy launches Planes and also adds its Surface Vessel guns to the Marine Artillery to thump the Japanese as the Marines maintain their southward drive across stubborn and rugged ground against medium resistance. **(Pacific-New Guinea)** In the Vogelkop area, the 3rd Battalion, 1st Infantry, 6th Division, lands at Cape Sansapor at 08:44, without incident. The newly arrived troops snap up Sansapor Village and the Plantation, then implement immediate defensive measures to ensure control of the area. A quick check proves the harbor unsuited for use as a PT Boat Base, but the effort is not in vain; the facility will be used as a radar station to forewarn the U.S. of impending threats. MacArthur's policy of "HIT EM WHERE THEY AIN'T" still is being executed like a lucky charm. The seizure of Sansapor adds power and leverage to the American thrust. U.S. Engineers move in behind the Infantry and begin reconstructing the terrain, establishing major Airfields at Noemfoor and Sansapor, to act as major slingshots to catapult MacArthur's Bombers over Japanese positions in the Philippines. Soon, the Japanese deduce MacArthur's next strategic move, but he reverses the obvious, Oriental style and strikes where least expected. The Japanese prepare to defend Halmahera, but the attack strikes Morotai. Halmahera, unable to receive supplies or reinforcements becomes benign, unable to threaten the American thrust. In Aitape, the 124th Infantry reinforced by the 2nd Battalion, 169th Infantry, becomes the Ted Force. Colonel Edward M. Starr leads the contingent along the Driniumor, jumping off at 08:00 in the North Force sector. Progress is made by three of the four attacking Battalions, all advancing to the Niumen Creek; the other Battalion hits heavy resistance, overcomes it and joins the main unit on the following day. In the South Force sector, from the 13th of July until today, estimated Japanese killed stand at over 700. In turn, the South Force has sustained nearly 1,000 total casualties, 260 from the 112th Cavalry. **(Pacific-Naval-Formosa)** During the previous day, the U.S.S. *Steelhead* had been tracking a Japanese Convoy, but the Japanese Air Force prevented an attack. Captain, W. H. Welchel, transmits the information and probable course to the U.S.S. *Parche* at 20:15. At midnight, the *Steelhead* closes quietly. Meanwhile, the *Parche* streaks along the surface to join the hunt. At just after 03:30, the *Steelhead* fires six torpedoes toward a complacent Tanker and a non-cantankerous oversized Freighter; within moments there is a loud roar and water is surging upward amidst swirls of black smoke pronouncing the rupture and demolition of the Tanker. A Freighter is also struck by the volley. The *Steelhead* then fires six more torpedoes at another Freighter. The Japanese react and catapult signal flares into the air. The galloping *Parche* sees the alarm as clearly as the Japanese. Commander Lawson P. Ramage blares orders mandating full steam ahead. Ramage is about to give the Japs an expensive lesson about the U.S. Navy. With Japanese flares in abundance throughout the night sky, the *Parche* heads directly for the enemy, unleashing a mighty blow at a target less than 500 yards away. The *Parche* maneuvers to avoid the charging enemy Ship, causing its torpedoes to miss when the enemy takes evasive action, but the *Parche's* motion places her within killing range of two Freighters. Immediately, Commander "Red" Ramage attacks and the first Freighter is blown to oblivion. The *Parche*, retains her momentum and swerves toward the two Tankers. Unhesitatingly, the *Parche* closes and torpedoes are again fired, four heading for the lead Tanker and three for the trailer. The first blow destroys the lead Vessel, but the other three strike in rapid succession, causing the Tanker, now in sections to plummet to the bottom, leaving only burning oil to attest to its prior existence. The other Tanker is crippled by two hits, and slowly limps away, its crew yelping several unprintable quotes concerning the U.S. Navy. Meanwhile, Japanese Escort Vessels close in on the *Parche*, but the valiant Vessel reacts by firing more torpedoes, and another Transport Ship is struck. Ramage, in calculated calmness, orders his men below as enemy Escorts close tighter, but he remains on deck to continue this masterful attack. The *Parche* is firing torpedoes at the enemy like a lawman from the old West unloading his six shooters while riding horseback. The *Parche* maneuvers left and right, then right to left, testing the skill and the nerves of the crew, who are unrelenting, while maintaining their precision movements. Its a modernized version of a nineteenth century sea duel, with a outgunned and outnumbered Yankee Warship humiliating and whipping the enemy. The Japanese by this time, are understandably bewildered at the audacity of these Sailors aboard the *Parche*.

Admiral Lawson P. Ramage, Commanding Officer of the U.S.S. Parche.

The Warship, which caused Ramage to order his crew below deck, approaches to ram the Submarine, but Ramage again evades, avoiding a collision by about fifty feet, equivalent to a cat's hair, by any mariner's standards. Suddenly, the Submarine is surrounded by Japanese War Ships and a Tanker is dead ahead, moving toward the *Parche* with the determination of a seagoing Kamikaze. Unperturbed, Ramage orders three "DOWN THE THROAT" shots, halting the raging Tanker; he follows with another killing blow, succinctly terminating the futile voyage. Satisfied that there are no more targets of value in the near vicinity, the *Parche*, heads for calmer seas, its crew exhausted, but victorious and unharmed. The remnants of the beleaguered Convoy departs also, coincidentally heading toward the *Steelhead*, which pumps a few torpedoes into a Passenger Cargo Vessel and dispatches another volley toward a large Freighter. The Freighter sinks as a Japanese Plane comes over during the early morning dusk, prompting the *Steelhead* to dive deep prematurely, giving the remaining Passenger Cargo Vessel an extended life. The devastation sustained by the Japanese Shipping during this abrupt encounter, according to a post war inquest held by the Joint Army-Navy Assessment Committee: the *Parche* receives credit for sinking the *Koei Maru* (Tanker) and the *Manko Maru* (Passenger-Cargoman). The *Parche* receives shared credit with the *Steelhead* on the sinking of the *Yoshino Maru* (Transport) and the *Steelhead* is also credited with the destruction of the Freighter *Daku Maru* and the Transport *Fuso Maro*. Commander (later Vice Admiral) Lawson Patterson Ramage receives the Medal of Honor for his extraordinary leadership and courage in battle. Within 46 minutes, his Submarine had fired nineteen torpedoes and registered fourteen or fifteen hits, while rampaging through a virtual wall of severe enemy fire, and bringing the *Parche* through unscathed. Subsequently, when the author asked Rear Admiral Lawson where he got his extraordinary courage, he responded: " I DIDN'T NEED COURAGE. MY FAMILY WAS WITH ME IN PEARL HARBOR WHEN THE JAPANESE ATTACKED. I SIMPLY WAITED FOR THE OPPORTUNITY AND TOOK PROPER ACTION." **(China-Burma-India)** In **11 Army Group** area, **British Fourteenth Army** area, 4th Corps Headquarters is recalled to India and its contingents are transferred to the 33th Corps to supplement the effort to drive the Japanese back across the Chindwin River. At present, the enemy is in complete retreat, heading down the Tiddim Road. On the Arakan Front, the monsoon rains continue to deluge the area, but the British 15th Corps keeps its Patrols active. **(Atlantic-France)** General Bradley assumes command of the U.S. 12th Army Group; Patton commands 3rd Army and General Hodges commands the U.S. First Army. On the British Command, General Montgomery commands 21 Army Group; General Dempsey the 2nd Army and the Canadian First Army is commanded by General Henry Duncan Crerar. In the **U.S. First Army VIII Corps** area, Combat Command R, 6th Armored Division, seizes Granville; then the entire Division drives straight to Avranches where it relieves the 4th Armored Division; the 4th Armored heads south and secures a crossing of the Selune near Pontaubault. In related activity, the 1st Infantry Division and Combat Command A, 3rd Armored, move with great speed, advancing to Brecey, seizing a crossing at the See River in the VII Corps area. In other **VII Corps** activity, the 4th Division, supported by Combat Command B, 3rd Armored Division, penetrates Villedieu-les-Poeles and keeps moving, gaining more terrain. The **XIX Corps** still is engaged tenaciously with the enemy at Tessy; north of Tessy, Troisgots is overpowered by the 30th Division. The **V Corps** grinds south, heading for the Vire River. Torigny-sur-Vire is taken by the 35th Division along the way. In the **British Second Army**, 8th Corps area, the Guards Armored Division advances to Le Tourneur. In the 30th Corps sector, Cahagnes is seized and the town of Jurques is being approached. In other activity in the British area, the Canadian First Army takes command of the Canadian 2nd Corps. **(Atlantic-Eastern Europe)** Jelgava, Latvia, falls to the First Baltic Front, threatening German Army Group North. In other activity, advance elements of the Third White Russian Front reach Kaunas (Kovno), former capital of Lithuania. Elements of the Second White Russian Front advance toward Eastern Prussia. The First White Russian Front advances to Siedlce as it drives toward Poland.

U.S. Infantry at Mail-call in France.

August 1st 1944 — (Pacific) The U.S. Army Forces Pacific Ocean Area, commanded by Lt. General Robert C. Richardson Jr., supersedes U.S. Army Forces in the Central Pacific Area and those forces deployed in the South Pacific also. In addition, the Army Air Forces, Pacific Ocean Areas is activated and will be commanded by Lt. General Millard F. Harmon. In other activity, Admiral William Halsey issues a preliminary plan for the invasion of the Western Carolines. **(Pacific-Marianas)** On Guam, the Agana-Pago Bay Road is captured by the 307th Infantry, U.S.A. The seizure clears passage for equipment being sent to the northeastern portion of the island. On Tinian, organized Japanese opposition is terminated, but remnant troops refuse to relent and hold out in caves along the southern coast. Lt. General Harry Schmidt U.S.M.C., Commanding Officer North Force and Landing Force, declares Tinian secure. On August 3rd, the American Flag is officially raised. **(Pacific-New Guinea)** A PT Squadron begins operating from Amsterdam Island. In other activity, Engineers are being transported to Middleburg to establish an Airbase. On Biak, extensive alterations have been completed at the Borokoe Airdrome, stretching its Airstrip to 4,000 feet and at Mokmer Airfield, the Airstrip is extended to 7,000 feet. On Aitape, the final elements of the Ted Force arrive at Niumen Creek. The South Force prepares to commence some probing reconnaissance, but the Japanese mount a fierce counterattack. The 112th Cavalry's Troop C, still irritated from being entrapped some days before, receives a fanatical Banzai attack by two Companies; Troop C decimates them. The tenacity of Troop C has the Japs reeling and the effort allows Troop G, and contingents of the 127th Infantry to reconnoiter well south of the South Force's perimeter against scattered opposition. **(Pacific-International)** Philippine President Manuel Quezon dies of Tuberculosis; he is replaced by Vice President Sergio Osmena. **(China-Burma-India)** General Joseph Stilwell (promoted to Full General) arrives in Kandy, Ceylon. Ironically British Admiral Mountbatten, who has been anxious to see "Vinegar Joe" Stilwell out of Burma, departs Ceylon for England to confer on future strategy for the Burma Operations. Upon General Stilwell's arrival, Chiang Kai-shek's Black Cadillac, bedecked with flying Allied flags, is waiting to chauffeur Stilwell to Admiral Mountbatten's residence, the "King's Pavilion". Stilwell, conspicuously unimpressed, clamors: "GET ME A JEEP;" Stilwell climbs the mountain in the jeep, with the Cadillac leading the way, transporting Stilwell's baggage. Two days later, General Stilwell gets his wish; Myitkyina falls and on the following day in his own unique style, Stilwell notes: "OVER AT LAST."

U.S. troops in the Pacific, watching for enemy aircraft.

"THANK GOD. NOT A WORRY IN THE WORLD THIS a.m. FOR FIVE MINUTES ANYWAY." British General Brooke, in London, would subsequently state: "IT IS CLEAR, NOW THAT STILWELL HAS LED US DOWN TO MYITKYINA, WE SHALL HAVE TO GO ON FIGHTING IN BURMA." British strategy prior to Imphal and Myitkyina had been "global strategy," and would have precluded Burma. With Stilwell's surprising and unexpected achievements, everything changes. It is also notable that Stilwell is unimpressed with Mountbatten's residence and chooses to stay in an Officers' Barracks, rejecting the magnificent palace with its nine hole golf course, promenading peacocks and overpowering and breathtaking views, including waterfalls. With the promotion of General Stilwell, the Marauders (Merrill's 5307th) are convinced that promotions are in store because it has been their sweat and blood that has contributed to the success of the operation, but it does not occur. **(Atlantic-France)** There are now 35 Allied Divisions in Europe and back in England, there are two Reserve British and four Reserve U.S. Divisions. By the first of October, there will be 54 Allied Divisions in Europe, including the 6th Army Group moving through Southern France and an additional six Divisions will remain in England as Reserves. General Bradley assumes command of the **U.S. 12th Army Group** (operational today) which includes all U.S. Divisions in France; First Army, commanded by Lt. General Courtney H. Hodges and the Third Army commanded by George S. Patton. British General Montgomery still remains in command of all land forces throughout August (the American Commanders are not enthralled by this decision). The XIX Tactical Air Command becomes operational today to support the Third Army. The IX Tactical Air Command maintains its support of the First Army. By today, Bradley's forces have maneuvered through Avranches, reaching the bottom tip of the peninsula, positioned behind enemy lines. General Patton's Third Army is deployed on the right flank of the First Army (furthest right flank of Allied Forces) and its primary objective is Brittany and its coveted ports; however, elements of Third Army begin advancing toward Le Mans. The **U.S. First Army** sets its sights on Mortain. In the **First Army** area, the **V Corps** drives to the heights north of Vire, but the 5th Division is deployed in the rear as Reserve, being relieved by the British. The **VII Corps** expands it Brecey Beachhead, while elements drive toward St. Pois. The **XIX Corps** seizes Tessy and Percy with Combat Command A, 2nd Armored Division and the 28th Division respectively. In the **Third Army VIII Corps** area, elements including the 6th Armored Division cross La Selune River fanning out to the south, west and southwest. The 6th Armored pivots to Pontorson. Patton notes: "THE 6th LOST A BATTERY OF SELF PROPELLED GUNS DUE TO STUPIDITY...TOO FAR TO THE FRONT, TOO CLOSE TOGETHER, AND HAD NO SECURITY DETACHMENT." In the 4th Armored sector, there is a close call; reports of an approaching enemy column are received and Aircover is requested for assistance. The advancing column turns out to be the 4th Armored, moving rapidly toward Remmes. The Planes don't locate the column (near dusk), but do succeed in racking the resistance in front of the 4th Armored. Patton subsequently states: "IT WAS LOVE AT FIRST SIGHT BETWEEN THE XIX TACTICAL AIR COMMAND AND THE THIRD ARMY." The responsibility of the XV Corps, commanded by Major General Wade Haislip, is to intercept the enemy between the See and Selune Rivers, preventing their advance against Avranches. In the **British Second Army's** 8th Corps area, Le Beny-Bocage is seized by the British 11th Division. In the **Canadian First Army** area the 2nd Corps meets feverish resistance at Tilly-la-Campagne-La Hogue, below Caen, but the British I Corps' 49th Division secures the Sannerville-Troarn area. **(Atlantic-Mediterranean)** Allied Force Headquarters Mediterranean changes the code name for the invasion of Southern France from ANVIL to DRAGOON. In other activity, 6th Army Headquarters is established at Bastia, Corsica commanded by Lt. General Jacob L. Devers. Devers subsequently assumes command of all U.S. and French troops in southern France. **(Atlantic-Lithuania)** Kaunas, Lithuania is taken by the Third White Russian Front (Red Army). **(Atlantic-Poland)** Polish troops revolt against German occupation. The insurrections last for 63 days and during the period, 250,000 Polish troops fall in what is known as "General Bor's Uprising." These Polish troops are closely aligned with the exile government in London. Politically they contain factions, but are basically anti-communist and intend to have a government intact when the Russians complete their ongoing drive. The Russian drive reverts to neutral and ceases to advance, proclaiming subsequently that their July advance required a pause. The Russians procrastinate without discretion and the Americans and British requests to lend them assistance to support the Poles does not become a priority. Finally, after consistent negotiations, the Russians attempt to airdrop some supplies.

In China, Generals Henry Arnold, Claire L. Chennault, Joseph Stilwell, British Field Marshal Sir John Dill, and U.S. Brigadier General Clayton L. Bissell. (U.S. Tenth Air Force) (left to right).

August 2nd 1944 — (Pacific-Marianas) The 9th Marines, 3rd Marine Division, seizes Tiyan Airfield as it drives northwest. In other activity, elements of the U.S. 77th Division run into stiff resistance beyond Mt. Barrigada at the Barrigada village where the enemy is strongly entrenched in camouflaged positions, stalling them 2 miles from the O-3 line objective. **(Pacific-New Guinea)** On Biak, the 2nd Battalion, 163rd Infantry, lands at Korim Bay. In the Aitape area, the Japanese continue attacks against South Force and suffer more severe losses (approximately 300 killed). **(China-Burma-India)** The Japanese holding Teng-chung come under severe attack by the Chinese, supported by Aircraft. The Chinese penetrate the heavily thickened wall in five separate locations. **(North Atlantic)** The U.S.S. *Fiske* (DE-143), a Destroyer Escort, is sunk by an enemy torpedo delivered by a Submarine. **(Atlantic-France)** American General Eisenhower suggests strongly that British General Montgomery step up the attack. On the 4th, Montgomery will order the British Second Army to continue its eastward swing and to attack toward Falaise as soon as possible. In the **U.S. 12th Army Group, First Army area, VII Corps** sector, the 1st Division and contingents of the 3rd Armored Division, drive south toward St. Pois; the 9th Division heads north toward Villeudieu, cutting a road southeast of the town. The 2nd Armored Division is transferred to the XIX

A U.S. Carrier advances in the Pacific.

Corps, which is driving beyond Percy-Tessy, hitting resistance from rear guards of the retreating Germans. In the **V Corps** sector, the 2nd and 35th Divisions advance across the Vire and Souleuvre Rivers. In the **Third Army VIII Corps** area, the Brittany drive continues. The Germans establish heavy resistance to halt the Americans. Hitler orders a counterattack designed to entrap the Americans in Brittany, with his forces striking between Avranches and Mortain. Rennes becomes increasingly active as the 4th Armored Division secures more terrain; elements of the 8th Division advance to the area. In addition, Task Force A is established under the command of Brigadier General Herbert L. Earnest, and is assigned responsibility for eliminating previously bypassed resistance along the northern coast of the peninsula. In the **V Corps** area, the U.S. 90th Division, marching east from Avranches, has an extra Soldier walking its ranks; General Patton treks with the troops for a few hours. The 90th Division attacks; General Weaver Assistant Divisional Commander, leads a spirited attack over a German defended bridge. The Germans mount a heavy amount of Air raids which harass the troops on the peninsula. In one instance, German Planes bomb a prisoner compound holding a few thousand Germans. The Provost Marshal sets them free, rather than have them face death, and nearly all return to the compound more than a little aggravated with the German Air Force. In the **British 21st Army Group**, **British Second Army** area, 8 Corps sector, the Germans resist strongly above Vire, but the 11th Armored drives to the edge of the town. The Guards Armored Division encounters fierce resistance at Estry, being stalled outside the objective. In the 30th Corps area, the British 50th Division seizes Amaye-sur-Seulles. **(Atlantic-Italy)** In the **British Eighth Army** area, 13th Corps sector, the 2nd New Zealand Division continues to battle the enemy tenaciously on a ridge near Florence, forcing the Germans to begin to pull back behind the Arno. In other activity, Captain Roderick "Steve" Hall (New Hampshire) is the 1st O.S.S. leader to parachute into northern Italy. He works with a Swiss agent code-named "Tell," whose mission include running messages to another O.S.S. leader, Benucci. Subsequently, Captain Hall is betrayed to the S.S. (January 1945); he is captured in full uniform, then tortured and executed by hanging.

August 3rd 1944 — (United States) The U.S. Navy establishes the Office of General Counsel (formerly named Procurement Legal Division, Navy Department). **(Pacific-Guam)** The U.S. 77th Division seizes Barrigada and on the following day secures the mountain north of the town. The 3rd Marine Division captures Finegayan and continues its tenacious penetration, driving toward the outer defenses of Mt. Santa Rosa. During the fiercely contested fighting at Finegayan, P.F.C. Frank P. Witek, 9th Marines, 3rd Marine Division, is part of a Rifle Platoon that is bushwhacked by deviously concealed enemy positions. Witek reacts to the startling and devastating fire by charging; at point blank range he eliminates eight of the human moles, then remains with a wounded Marine, while the Platoon seeks better positions. He further endangers his life by covering the stretcher bearers as they take the casualty to safety. An enemy machine gun opens fire and Witek singlehandedly charges the position, killing another eight Japanese. He is then struck and killed by a Japanese Rifleman, but his Platoon takes the objective, due to his extraordinary courage and determination; he receives the Medal of Honor posthumously. **(Pacific-New Guinea)** The recently activated Ted Force still drives convincingly toward the Torricelli Mountains, determined to interrupt enemy trails and destroy the Japanese in its assigned

area. The Japanese resist tenaciously, rebuffing elements of the 124th and 169th Infantries as they advance south along the Niumen Creek. The 1st Battalion, 124th Infantry, evades the blockage and shifts its drive to the west. The South Force, operating near Afua, meets and defeats an enemy assault, transforming the resistance from heated to tepid. **(China-Burma-India)** Myitkyina, wavering in the past few weeks under enormous Allied pressure, is struck by another attack at dawn, which turns out to be the final thrust to capture the town. With the Chinese 50th Division leading the last assault, Myitkyina is seized by 15:45 and with it, 187 prisoners (primarily wounded and sick). The other defenders have either escaped or been killed during the enduring siege. Since the inception of the assault, 272 Americans and 972 Chinese have been killed; 955 Americans and 3,184 Chinese wounded. Myitkyina is a major Allied victory against the Japanese and greatly pleases Generals Stilwell and Merrill, whose troops have undergone a savage campaign, operating with near primitive circumstances and sweltering heat and the barest of medical supplies. However, the Marauders seem to get the short end of the stick; Colonel Hunter is abruptly relieved of duty as the objective is taken; he is then ordered back to the U.S. by Ship, rather than by Air. The Marauders are deactivated on August 10th, without any fanfare; there is no final muster, nor words of praise. On the On the Salween Front, the determined attacks against Teng-chung and Sung Shan are continued by the Chinese. **(Atlantic-France)** In the **U.S. First Army** area, Mortain falls to the **VIII Corps** handily, permitting elements of the 4th Division to sprint close to St. Pois in conjunction with the 9th Division's charge toward Foret de St. Sever. In the **V Corps** area, the Germans resist vehemently at the Vire, but the XIX Corps, driving southeast, is closing to assist. In the **U.S. Third Army VIII Corps** area, Loudeac is threatened, however, the closing 6th Armored is purposely halted and ordered to reverse direction and eliminate Dinan; these orders are also countermanded and the 6th Armored will be ordered to drive against Brest (August 4th). German resistance, lingering at St. Malo, is threatened by the approaching Task Force A, which arrives on the following day. In other **VIII Corps** activity, the 4th Armored assaults tightly held Rennes. In the **XV Corps** area, Fougeres is taken by the 79th Division. In the **21st Army Group**, British Second Army's 8 Corps area, German resistance is steadfast, denying good progress near Estry and Vire. The British 30th Corps encounters similar rigid opposition at Aunay, Mont Pincon and Villers-Bocage. In the British 12th Corps area, the 53rd Division seizes Missy and Noyers.

August 4th 1944 — (Pacific-Bonin Islands) Japanese Shipping in the Chichi Jima area are struck by two Naval Task Forces; Carriers of Rear Admiral J.J. Clark and the Destroyer Cruiser Force of Rear Admiral L. T. DuBose, crunch a Japanese Convoy and assault additional enemy Vessels as detected. In addition, another formidable Naval Task Force, commanded by Rear Admiral A. E. Montgomery, launches Planes to destroy facilities at Iwo Jima in the Volcano Islands. The Japanese Destroyer *Matsu*, Transport No. 4, and Transport No. 133, are sunk by Carrier-based Aircraft. On the following day, Saturday the fifth, the assault is repeated, with the combined power of the three Task Forces striking enemy facilities at Chichi Jima and Haha Jima. The Japanese Transport No. 2 is sunk. **(Pacific-Marianas-Guam-Tinian)** Planes attached to Marine Aircraft Group 21 land on Guam and are the first Marine Planes to serve on the island since 1931. In other activity, the Army and the Marines continue the operation to secure the island. On Tinian, during mop up operations, a

Squad is surprised by a hot grenade tossed into their path; P.F.C. Robert Lee Wilson, 2nd Battalion, 6th Marines, 2nd Marine Division, yells a warning and then covers the grenade with his body to save his comrades; he receives the Medal of Honor posthumously. **(Pacific-New Guinea)** In the Aitape area, the Japanese suffer another devastating defeat in what becomes their final fanatical attack, costing them over 200 dead. They pull back from Afua with the Yanks in pursuit. Elements of the Ted Force meet with the South Force, but the scheduled attack is halted until both main forces are enjoined at the Driniumor. **(China-Burma-India)** On the Salween Front, Chinese troops penetrate Teng-chung's defenses, igniting an intense long-lasting battle for control of the city, which finally falls to the Chinese on September 14th. **(Atlantic-France)** In the **U.S. First Army** area, the **VIII Corps** firms up its positions at Mortain and dispatches strong Patrols south toward Mayenne. Vicious, but indecisive combat ensues at St. Pois, and in the nearby hills. The Germans offer intense opposition at Foret de St. Sever, however, the U.S. 9th Division drives into the town. The **V Corps** advances to its objective above the Vire, but halts progress to allow the XIX Corps, which is encountering heavy resistance including a supersaturation of land mines, to penetrate and join with the 2nd Division in an assault against Vire. In the **U.S. Third Army** area, the 6th Armored drives toward Brest, reaching Carhaix. Contingents of the 83rd Division and Task Force A, reach the heavily fortified town of St. Malo and engage elements of the German XXV Corps (General Farmbacher). The German XXV Corps has withdrawn and deployed at St. Malo, Brest, Lorient and St. Maire, to deter an American breakthrough. In other activity, the 13th Infantry, 8th Division, seizes Rennes, while the 4th Armored rolls toward Vannes. In the **British 21st Army Group**, 30th Corps area, Hermilly is taken by the British 43rd Division, but the enemy raises fierce resistance to continue repelling British advances at Vire and Estry in the 8th Corps sector. **(Atlantic-Eastern Europe)** The Russians have requested U.S. assistance (first time) in raiding the Rumanian Airfields. Fighter Bombers attached to the Fifteenth Air Force respond and after the assault, head for a landing in Russia. **(Atlantic-Italy)** The 13th Corps, British Eighth Army, advances to Florence at the Arno, culminating its campaign objectives for the central Italy operation. Elements penetrate the town's limits, but the Germans as usual, have impaired progress by demolishing all bridges, except the Ponte Vecchio span. Tentative plans to assault the center of the German Gothic Line are modified and the new plan (OLIVE) will commit the British Eighth Army in an attack from the right flank. The British 13th Corps is temporarily attached to the **U.S. Fifth Army** to initiate a feint toward Bologna from Florence. The British begin elaborate regrouping preparations for the attack which will not occur until the 25th of August. **(Atlantic-Poland)** The Polish continue the struggle against the Germans, still anticipating a victory and a genuine Polish government when the advancing Russians arrive, but the Russians, aware of the ongoing struggle, slow their advance to a crawl.

August 5th 1944 — (Pacific) Fast Carrier Task Force is reorganized becoming the First Fast Carrier Task Force, Pacific Fleet, under Vice Admiral Mitscher, and the Second Fast Carrier Task Force, Pacific Fleet, commanded by Vice Admiral J. S. McCain. **(Pacific-Bonin Islands)** The Japanese Transport No. 2 is sunk by Aircraft during the heavy raids against the Bonins. **(Pacific-Marianas-Guam)** The U.S. 77th Division receives orders to capture Mt. Santa Rosa; the balance of the island resistance is to be a III Corps objective, with the 77th

assuming major responsibility. **(Pacific-New Guinea)** Japanese opposition is heightened east of Afua, impeding the progress of Task Force Ted in front of the primary east west trail, permitting the enemy to keep the Driniumor crossing point accessible. **(Atlantic-France)** In the **U.S. 12th Army Group, First Army** area, the assigned sectors of the U.S. and British forces are realigned. In the **American V Corps** area, the 2nd and 29th Divisions are to seize Vire, then push directly between St. Jean-du-Boise and Tinchebray. In the **VII Corps** area, the U.S. 1st Division continues to bolster its positions in the vicinity of Mortain. St. Pois is seized by the 4th Division and the 9th Division drives straight through Foret de St. Sever. In the **XIX Corps** area, the 29th Division closes against heavy opposition on Vire. In the **U.S. Third Army** area, Patton's troops are assaulting from four directions simultaneously (W, SW, S and E). The 6th Armored drives to Huelgoat, heading west to Brest. The 83rd Division is driving against the outer defenses of St. Malo, while the 4th Armored reaches Vannes, severing the Brittany Peninsula and Task Force A pushes west tenaciously along the northern coast of Brittany. In the **XV Corps** area, the 79th Division nears Laval, while elements of the 90th Division seize Mayenne. In the **British Second Army** area, enemy pockets of resistance are being eliminated by elements of the 8th Corps. In the 30th Corps sector, Aunay is seized by the British 7th Armored Division and in the 12th Corps area, troops are advancing along the Orne between Caen and Grimbosq. **((Atlantic-Italy)** In the **British Eighth Army** area, contingents of the 10th Corps secure the summit of M. il Castello.

U.S. Corpsmen and Infantry advance toward Brest.

August 6th 1944 — (United States) The Carrier U.S.S. *Bennington* is commissioned at New York. **(Pacific-Marianas-Guam-Tinian)** On Guam, the III Amphibious Corps drives forcefully to the O-4 line and by now has two thirds of the island secure. The 305th Infantry, 77th Division, U.S.A. suffers high casualties while turning back an early morning Banzai attack, which is supported by Tanks. On Tinian, the 2nd and 4th Marine Divisions depart (6th-7th); the 4th Marine Division heads for Hawaii and the 2nd Marine Division embarks for Saipan. Mop-up operations are maintained by the 8th Marines, 2nd Marine Division. **(Pacific-New Guinea)** In the Aitape area, the Ted Force is struck by a predawn assault that emerges into a heated and brutalizing contest, lasting into the afternoon. Elements of the Ted Force eventually outflank the enemy and compel them to pull back. **(Pacific-Philippine Islands)** U.S. Planes initiate night Air attacks against Japanese positions in Mindanao at Davao. **(China-Burma-India)** Sahmaw is taken by the British 36th Division (Northern Combat

Army Command Burma). In the **British Fourteenth Army** area, British General Slim orders the 33th Corps to pursue the withdrawing Japanese by driving to the Chindwin and crossing in the vicinity of Kalewa. **(Atlantic-France)** British General Montgomery issues orders for an attack leading to the Seine River. Offshore, U.S. Army Aircraft have a bonanza mission, sinking four German Submarines near Toulon; the U-471, U-642, U-952, and the U-969. In the **U.S. 12th Army Group, First Army** area, the advance is ongoing. The 30th Division, which has been fighting with little rest since the breakout, moves up to fill in for the 1st Division, but as soon as it is in place (following day), the full impact of the first major German offensive strikes its perimeter. In the **VII Corps** area, the 3rd Armored and the 1st Infantry Divisions push toward Ambrieres-le-Grand and to Mayenne, to flank the Germans at Mortain; contingents of the 90th Division, holding Mayenne, are relieved upon their arrival. In other activity, the Germans mount tenacious resistance against the advancing 9th Division, which is driving toward Sourdeval. In the **XIX Corps** sector, Vire falls to the 29th Division, giving the V Corps friendly troops to contact as the seizure of Vire eliminates the enemy temporarily. In the **U.S. Third Army** area, Patton receives an inaccurate report that Brest has been seized and passes the information to General Bradley. Actually, the Germans have decided to make a stand at Brest, while other detachments prepare for a similar stand at Lorient and St. Nazarie. Brest falls on September 19th, but the latter two positions hold out until the cessation of hostilities. In the **VIII Corps** area, the four directional drive continues with Combat Command B, overpowering enemy resistance on the right flank of the 6th Armored positions in the vicinity of Lesneven and Morlaix. The Germans impede the progress of Combat Command A, which is driving south, but the advance continues. The 83rd Division bangs relentlessly against the superior defended bastion at St. Malo and Task Force A grinds past St. Brieux, attacking fiercely as it drives west along the northern coast of Brittany. In yet other activity, the 4th Armored Division presses vehemently against Lorient. In the **XV Corps** area, Le Mans is in reach of driving advance elements of the Corps and Laval is overtaken by the 79th Division. Also, the **XX Corps**, commanded by Major General Walton H. Walker, is reinforced; the 35th Division arrives to bolster his 5th Division to safeguard the south flank of Third Army. In the **British Second Army's** 8th Corps area, the Germans attack British positions and supported by Armor, penetrate the perimeter. Subsequently, the British reclaim the lost ground. At Vestry, the Germans also mount ferocious resistance and repel a British attempt to overpower them. The British 3rd Division attacks south toward Vire. In the British 30th Corps sector, the 43rd Division gains slightly at Mont Pincon, while the British 7th Armored continues to drive toward Thury-Harcourt. In other activity, the British 59th Division (12 Corps), advancing near Grimbosq, crosses the Orne and establishes a slim bridgehead. **(Atlantic-Italy)** Orders come down from Allied Armies Italy, implementing particular operation objectives previous to the main offensive. **(Atlantic-Poland-Rumania)** Operation FRANTIC, an ongoing operation, has elements of the U.S. Fifteenth Army Air Force departing Airbases in Russia, then attacking strategic targets in Ploesti and Bucharest, Rumania, as they head for Bases in Italy. These raids continue to eliminate resistance for the Red Army; by the time they advance to the area, it is leveled, compliments of the U.S. Army Air Force. In other activity in Eastern Europe, elements of the U.S. Eighth Army Air Force attack an enemy Aircraft factory at Gdynia, Poland before landing in Russia.

August 7th 1944 — (Pacific-Japan) The Submarine U.S.S. *Croaker* (SS-246) destroys the Japanese Light Cruiser *Nagara* off Kyushu. **(Pacific-Marianas-Guam)** The III Amphibious Corps commences the final attack to secure the northern portion of Guam. The U.S. 77th Division secures Tigo and presses toward Mt. Santa Rosa. Marine Aircraft, attached to VMF-225, launch sorties from Orote Airfield to bolster the effort to end enemy resistance on the island. **(Pacific-New Guinea)** In the Aitape area, the South Force wastes no time in severing a new Japanese Trail which splits off the main path. Afterward, the Ted Force maintains its pace, driving toward the Driniumor to hook up with the South Force, which is dispatching probing Patrols while waiting for the Ted Force. At this time, the Japanese are apparently making a general and complete retreat from the vicinity. **(Pacific-Philippines)** The U.S.S. *Seawolf* (SS-197) successfully lands men and equipment at Tawi Tawi. While the *Seawolf* is evading the Japanese, another U.S. Submarine the *Guitarro* destroys the Japanese Frigate *Kusagaki* off the Philippines. **(Atlantic-France)** In the **U.S. First Army** area, the Germans counterattack to repulse the advancing Americans, while permitting them access to the sea and also dividing the U.S. Force. The primary thrust of the assault, spearheaded by Panzers and SS Divisions, diverted from the British Front, strikes between the VII and XIX Corps and penetrates the lines, driving into Mortain and steamrolling beyond to Le Mesnil-Tove and Juvigny. Planes are hurried to assist and the massive enemy counterattack is brought to a halt; a good deal of thanks is due to the recently clearing skies. Included in the Air support are R.A.F. rocket firing Typhoons. The German thrust lasts until the 12th of August. Due to the speed of the vicious enemy advance, elements of the VII Corps (2nd Battalion, 120th Infantry, 30th Division) are isolated at Mortain. This Battalion ignores the danger and refuses repeated surrender ultimatums, answering each with bursts of fire. By the following day, the beleaguered troops request urgently needed ammunition and medicine; the Planes miss the mark and most of the supplies fall into enemy hands. Artillery units of the 30th Division use GI ingenuity and load their shells with supplies, firing them right over the heads of the Germans into the center of the 2nd Battalion's tiny perimeter. When reinforcements finally reach them on the 12th, the 2nd Battalion guns are still firing and the area is amply covered with dead Germans. General Hobb's men had outfoxed the enemy. Additional troops rush to stem the tide of the massive enemy offensive; the 2nd Armored and the 4th Infantry Division head for the center of the line to neutralize the attack. The American command calculates the risk and decides to bolster the line with four additional Divisions. Patton's 35th Division bolts to fill a gap and thus ensure failure for von Kluge and his attempt to seize Avranches. In the **Third U.S. Army** area, the 6th Armored nears Brest, but not in sufficient strength to mount a serious assault, giving the enemy more time to fortify their positions. On the following day, the Germans ignore an ultimatum to surrender Brest. Task Force A closes on Morlaix and at St. Malo, the contest ensuing between the Germans and the U.S. 83rd Division is vicious. Meanwhile, the 4th Armored Division surrounds Lorient. In the **XV Corps** sector, the Corps nears Le Mans. In the **British 21st Army Group, British Second Army** area, 30th Corps sector, the seizure of Mont Pincon is complete, but the effort has been expensive; the British have inflicted severe casualties against the Germans but have also sustained heavy casualties, while defending against counterattacks. The British 12th Corps attacks south, driving toward Thury-Harcourt. In the Canadian First Army area, the British 2nd Corps awaits cessation of a Heavy Bomber attack, then assaults south toward Falaise. The Canadians are unaware of the German counterattack against the Americans. By 12:00 of the second day of the assault, the Germans stall the assault and Montgomery changes tactics to react to the German offensive. The British attack from the north to hook up with the Yanks attacking from the south. The British drive for five days, but the Germans permit only moderate gains; the British are half way to Falaise. **(Atlantic-Italy)** The **U.S. Fifth Army** temporarily postpones the impending assault scheduled for August 19th. **(Atlantic-Poland)** Polish fighters continue their futile struggle against the Germans. In other activity, U.S. Planes attached to Eighth Air Force attack the oil installations at Trzebinia, Poland. The Russian offensive, which has been moving rapidly seems to (according to the Russians) have overextended itself. **(Atlantic-Russia)** The Russian offensive has taken them to the Vistula River, a distance of 400 miles from the Dnieper.

Hengyang Airfield, China, a U.S. 14th Air Force Base, after ordered abandoned by General Chennault.

August 8th 1944 — (Pacific) Commander in Chief Pacific, Admiral Nimitz, orders certain changes when permissible: that Major General Roy Geiger and principal Staff members report to Guadalcanal to assume responsibility for the Palaus invasion troops; Major General Holland M. Smith is ordered back to Pearl Harbor where he will continue to be Commanding General, Fleet Marine Force, Pacific; in addition, Vice Admiral John N. Hoover, U.S.N., Commander Forward Area, Central Pacific, is to assume responsibility for the defense of the Marianas. **(Pacific-Marianas-Guam)** Old Glory reigns once again on Guam, dispelling once and for all, the Japanese proclamation that U.S. troops would never again touch its soil. The U.S. 77th Division seizes Mt. Santa Rosa, terminating sustained resistance, but will continue to eliminate remnant forces which have taken to the caves and jungles. **(Pacific-Marshalls)** U.S. Destroyers and Land-based Marine Bombers, stationed at Majuro in the Marshalls, bomb Japanese positions at Taroa on the Maloelap Atoll. **(Pacific-New Guinea)** In the Aitape area, the Ted Force has most of its units reach the Driniumor in the vicinity of Afua, joining with the South Force. **(China-Burma-India)** The Japanese secure a strategic objective when they capture Heng-yang; this Allied loss jeopardizes the U.S. Airfields in southeastern China. There is deep rooted dislike between Chiang Kai-shek (Nationalists) and the Communists who are in northern China. This loss raises concerns by both factions. In addition, the Chinese "war lords" intend to establish a new government in eastern China and will subsequently demand Chiang Kai-shek's resignation. Ultimately, Chiang will be ousted by the Communists

after the cessation of World War II. **(Atlantic-France)** British General Montgomery orders U.S. troops to attack north against Alencon to encircle the Germans in the vicinity of Falaise-Mortain in conjunction with the main drive to the Seine River, which is in progress. In the **U.S. First Army, VII Corps** sector, the German 2nd, and 116th Armored Divisions, unsuccessfully attempt to further penetrate through the lines; the isolated 30th Division, holding near Mortain, is unable to break out. In related activity, in the **XX Corps** area, contingents of the 2nd Armored, combined with the 35th Division (on loan from VII Corps), assault toward Mortain to alleviate the stress against the trapped 30th Division. In the **U.S. Third Army** area, **VIII Corps** sector, plans are readied for an attack against stubborn Brest, but German reinforcements pouring into the area from Plouvien force modification of the attack. At St. Malo, the struggle is agonizing; the advance against Dinard is also difficult. At St. Malo, the 83rd Division, commanded by General Macon, has up to this point sustained approximately 800 casualties, while capturing 1,300 prisoners. Today, Patton and Major General E. S. Hughes (Eisenhower's Staff), appear at the front lines of the 83rd to check out the situation. In the **XV Corps** sector, Le Mans is surrounded and seized, while elements drive further, crossing the Sarthe River. In the **XX Corps** sector, the 5th Division envelops Angers and Nantes, where the enemy has positioned contingents of the 708th German Infantry and the 9th Armored Division. The U.S. 8th Division takes responsibility for Le Mans. In yet other activity in the U.S. area, Secretary of the Treasury, Henry Morgenthau is at American Army Group Headquarters near Mortain. During his stay, Bradley informs him that the destruction of the German 7th Army appears imminent. In the **British Second Army** area, the 12th Corps maintains its bridgehead east of the Orne and attempts unsuccessfully to drive down the eastern bank; the Germans repel the attempt by mounting strong counterattacks. In the **Canadian First Army** area, another massive show of Air support is exhibited when the U.S. Eighth Air Force and the R.A.F. unload over 5,200 tons of bombs. At 13:55, the Polish 1st and the Canadian 4th Armored Divisions attack toward Falaise. Despite the Air power, the Germans mount fierce resistance and the drive toward Falaise is quickly intercepted by tenacious defense, originating at the enemy's Main Line of Resistance. **(Atlantic-Rumania)** Operation FRANTIC is ongoing. Eighth Air Force Planes en route to England from Russia, again bombard the Airfields in Rumania.

August 9th 1944 — (Pacific-Marianas-Guam) Remnant Japanese defenders express actions that they prefer to be killed rather than surrender; the Americans oblige and continue to eliminate those remaining alive. Effective resistance had been eliminated on the previous day; all organized resistance is terminated by the 10th. The 3rd Marine Division attacks to seize the remainder of the island. In other activity Brigadier General Lemuel Shepherd, Commander 1st Provisional Marine Brigade, announces that all enemy resistance in his Brigade's sector has been eliminated. In other activity, Admiral Nimitz and General Alexander A. Vandegrift (Commandant U.S.M.C.), land at Orote Airfield to make an assessment of Guam's future in the plans to defeat the remaining Japanese bastions in the Pacific. **(Pacific-New Guinea)** At Aitape, it is noted that Japanese resistance has disintegrated. **(Pacific-Philippines)** The U.S.S. *Seawolf* (SS-197), which has just delivered personnel to the Philippines two days prior, makes another successful mission, dropping off men and supplies at Palawan without incident. **(China-Burma-India)** On the Salween Front in Burma, Sung Shan is bombed by the Japanese, successfully striking the installations and supply depot of the Chinese 8th Army. In China, the Military Advisory Council at Chungking dispatches a message to the American Consulate (Kweilin) officially informing the U.S. of the war lords' intentions of forming a provisional government to halt the Japanese. The U.S. takes the message from Marshal Li Chi-shen, but takes no action. **(Atlantic-France)** The Americans launch 30 Medium B-26 Bombers to destroy a strategic enemy Railroad Bridge at L'Isle Adam, which spans the Seine; the Bombers are struck by anti-aircraft fire as they approach and the Commander's Plane is struck. Captain Darrell Lindsey continues the attack, aware that his Plane might explode momentarily with the bombs still on board. As the pass is made, the Plane receives more fire and Lindsey ensures that all crewmembers bail out safely, while he controls the flying inferno. The bombardier is the last one to bail out. Before Lindsey can exit, the Plane explodes; his heroism saves the lives of the rest of the crew; he receives the Medal of Honor posthumously. In the **U.S. First Army** area, the attackers pivot, heading northeast to enjoin the British who are grinding south toward Falaise to trap the Germans between both forces in the Vire-Mortain-Domfront-Ger area. A German counterattack in the VIII Corps sector loses strength, but individual bouts of fighting remain feverish at Avranches. In the **XIX Corps** area, the Germans hold up the 28th Division near Gathemo; the 29th is confined to slow progress as it advances below the Vire. In the **U.S. Third Army** area, **VIII Corps** sector, the 6th Armored Division swivels north to engage the German reinforcements which are attempting to crash through the rear of the Corps. The enemy attempt is intercepted and crushed by the 6th Armored near Plovien, demolishing almost an entire Division. The U.S. 83rd Division maintains intense pressure against the Germans at St. Malo where the bulk of the enemy has been compressed at the Citadel. In other VIII Corps activity, the 4th Division slams the enemy further at Lorient, keeping the momentum, then dispatching contingents toward Nantes. In the **XX Corps** sector, Angers is approached by the U.S. 5th Division. In the **XV Corps** area, the 5th U.S. Armored and the French 2nd Armored Divisions spearhead the march toward Alencon, trailed by Infantry. The 80th Division (temporary attachment VIII Corps) remains behind at Le Mans to continue the mop-up operation. In the **British 21st Army Group** area, the **Canadian First Army** sends its 2nd Corps south, straddling the Caen-Falaise road. The enemy resists strongly, but the Polish 1st Armored Division captures Cauvicourt and St. Sylvain, and the Canadian 4th Armored overcomes opposition and takes Bretteville-le-Rabet. **(Atlantic-England)** The PT-509 is sunk by Naval gunfire in the English Channel off the Isle of Jersey. **(Atlantic-Italy)** In the **British Eighth Army** area, 13th Corps sector, the area below the Arno, containing Florence is now secure.

August 10th 1944 — (Pacific-Marianas-Guam) The northern tip of the island is secured by the 3rd Marine Division, ending all organized opposition. Subsequently, a few hundred additional Japanese will be killed during mop-up operations. The island of Guam had been defended by a force estimated to be in excess of 18,000 men. The Americans count over 10,000 dead Japanese. On Tinian, the Capture and Occupational phase of the operation ends. The 8th Marines, 2nd Marine Division is assigned mop up operations. **(Pacific-New Guinea)** On Noemfoor, the 503rd Paratroop Infantry approaches Hill 380, outside of Inasi and reinitiates contact with the enemy; The 1st Battalion deploys to prevent escape, while Artillery and Planes supplement an operation of the 3rd Bat-

talion to destroy the Japanese on the hill. In Aitape, the Persecution Covering Force starts moving back to Blue Beach. **(China-Burma-India)** The name of Brigadier General Patrick Hurley, U.S.A., is mentioned to Chiang Kai-shek as President Roosevelt's personal representative. Also, Merrill's Marauders are disbanded. The 475th Infantry Regiment is formed; those few healthy Marauders of the 1st Battalion are attached, as well as the survivors of the New Galahad Force. During the final days of the battle for Myitkyina, the fresh troops (untrained for warfare) which had relieved the Marauders, had on occasion broken and run, leaving their wounded behind, but as Charlton Ogburn, an original Marauder had subsequently noted: "EVERY CASE OF PANIC COULD BE MATCHED BY ONE OF HEROISM." **(Atlantic-France)** In the **British 21st Army Group** area, the British and Canadians still are advancing toward Falaise. Vimont is reached by the British 49th Division and the Canadian 2 Corps. In the **U.S. Third Army** area, the enemy at Brest and Lorient are kept at bay by elements of the VIII Corps, while other contingents battle the Germans at Dinard and at the Citadel in St. Malo. In the **XV Corps** sector, Alencon is nearly reached as Armored columns push north toward both Alencon and Sees. Heavy fighting develops and the 2nd French Armored combines with the U.S. 5th Armored in a slugfest against the Germans. In the **XX Corps** area, Angers is seized by the 5th Division. **(Atlantic-Mediterranean)** The British Chiefs of Staff inform British General Wilson to continue with the plan for Operation DRAGOON (Invasion of Southern France) as described. Phase 1 of the operation ceases today. From the 28th of April to present, over 12,500 tons of bombs have been dropped on strategic enemy positions. With the commencing of Phase 2, Allied Planes will strike bridges that span the Rhine and in an effort to deceive the Germans of the actual invasion area, Planes will strike positions in Italy and at Beziers, near the border separating France and Spain. Meanwhile, other Aircraft concentrate on the real objectives, striking enemy facilities all along the coast of southern France.

U.S. Infantry, manning a Browning machine gun at St Malo.

August 11th 1944 — (Pacific-Marianas-Guam) The 306th Infantry, 77th Division, seizes the Japanese Command Post atop Mt. Mataguac, killing Japanese Lieutenant General Obata the highest ranking Japanese Officer on the island. **(Pacific-New Guinea)** In Aitape, elements of the Persecution Covering Force still deployed at the Driniumor, are relieved by the 103rd Infantry, 43rd Division. **(China-Burma-India)** In Burma, on the Salween Front, the Chinese have been unsuccessful in penetrating Japanese positions on the Sung Shan hills, prompting the Chinese to improvise and begin digging tunnels under the enemy positions and deploying mines. **(Atlantic-France)** In the **U.S. First Army** area, **VII Corps** sector, the day is filled with fury. The 30th Division battles exhaustively to drive the Germans back into Mortain, while the 35th Division is heavily engaged as it attempts to advance below Mortain. In other fierce activity, the Germans are repulsed by the 2nd Armored Division northwest of Barenton. The **V Corps** strengthens its positions at the Vire. In the **XIX Corps** sector, the 28th Division pushes southeast, away from Gathemo, while Combat Command A, 2nd Armored, combined with the 29th Division, attack the Germans holding ground in the hills near St. Sauveur-de-Chaulieu. In the **U.S. Third Army** area, things are heating up all across the front. The Germans refuse to relent at both St. Malo (Citadel) and Dinard, despite intense pressure from the U.S. 83rd Division. Nantes is reached by Combat Command A, 4th Armored Division, relieving contingents of the U.S. 5th Division (XX Corps), which has been containing the city. The **XV Corps** receives orders from General Patton to push beyond Falaise, even though the U.S. boundary is below there. The **XX Corps** is ordered to attack northeast toward the Carrouges-Sees Road, but a Regimental Combat Team of the 80th Division is to remain behind to control a bridgehead at Le Mans. A gap is created between the British, attacking south and the Americans attacking northward. In the **British 21st Army Group** area, 8th Corps sector, the British 3rd Division drives toward the Vire-Conde road, heading south toward Tinchebray; the 30th Corps is heading for Conde, driving southeast from Mt. Pincon. In the British 12th Corps sector, contingents of the 53rd and 59th British Divisions advance to the fringes of Thury-Harcourt, and encounter elements of the Canadian 2nd Corps. The Canadian First Army, driving to Falaise, meets German opposition. **(Atlantic-Italy)** An Allied Assault Force embarks from Naples toward southern France for the invasion.

August 12th 1944 — (United States) A Plan is submitted by the Joint War Planning Committee to the Joint Chiefs of Staff, noting that Iwo Jima is the only practical target in the Bonin Islands, because of its suitability for handling many Fighter Planes and because its terrain appears to be one which can be softened by preliminary bombardment. **(Pacific-Marianas-Guam)** Major General Roy Geiger, U.S.M.C., departs Guam for Guadalcanal. He is replaced by Major General Harry Schmidt, U.S.M.C. General Geiger, on the following day, replaces Major General Julian Smith, U.S.M.C., as Commander of Western Landing Forces (Task Group 36.1); Julian Smith continues in command of the higher echelon, designated Expeditionary Troops, Third Fleet. **(Pacific-New Guinea)** The Airstrip at Sorido, extending to 4,000 feet, is being utilized by Transport Planes, but it is subsequently abandoned. **(China-Burma-India)** The Generalissimo Chiang Kai-shek, agrees with Roosevelt's choice of General Hurley and he also agrees to Mr. Donald M. Nelson becoming President Roosevelt's representative to study China's economy. **(Atlantic-France)** In the **U.S. First Army** area, the German effort to break through to Avranches has been futile and they have been handily defeated; some German reinforcements are rushing from Mortain, hoping to collapse the left flank of the XV Corps (3rd Army). In the **U.S. Third Army** area, the Germans refuse to relent and maintain formidable opposition at St. Malo and Dinard. Advance elements of Combat Command A, 4th Armored Division, enter Nantes, while the **XV Corps** (Major General Haislip) drives beyond Alencon and Sees, pushing toward Argentan, reaching there after dark. Patton desires to advance from Argentan. The British as of yet, have not been

able to advance. In addition, U.S. Tank units are closing on Falaise, but General Haislip turns them around. Carrouges is reached by the French 2nd Armored Division. In other activity, the U.S. 5th Armored seizes Sees. General Patton and his staff realize that the XX Corps is hitting no resistance and orders it to make contact with the XV Corps at Alencon. General Patton's Third Army is making great progress and Patton would like to go right into Falaise and close the existing gap, but permission is denied by Bradley. Patton says: "WE WERE ORDERED NOT TO DO THIS (enter Falaise), ALLEGEDLY BECAUSE THE BRITISH HAD SOWN THE AREA WITH A LARGE NUMBER OF TIME BOMBS. THIS HALT WAS A GREAT MISTAKE AS I WAS CERTAIN THAT WE COULD HAVE ENTERED FALAISE AND I WAS NOT SURE THE BRITISH WOULD." Elements of the Third Army are reconnoitering the town when orders to pull back arrive. In the **British 21st Army Group**, the 8th Corps is fighting intensely about three miles southeast of Vire. The 12th Corps is engaging the enemy near Thury-Harcourt. In the **Canadian First Army** area, the 2nd Corps is still stalled along the highway to Falaise, but does join with the British 12th Corps at Barbery.

U.S. Artillery Outpost near Barentan, between Mortain and Domfront.

August 13th 1944 — (Pacific-North Borneo) The Submarine U.S.S. *Flier* (SS-250) sinks after sustaining an explosion while operating in the Balabac Strait off North Borneo. **(Pacific-Philippines)** The Submarine *Bluegill* (SS-242), operating off the Philippines, sinks the Japanese Submarine Chaser No. 112. **(China-Burma-India)** Planes attached to General Chennault's Fourteenth Air Force, fly reconnaissance missions over Manila and spur strong reaction from Generals Stilwell and MacArthur, the latter warning General Chennault not to consider bombing Manila. **(Atlantic-France)** A message dispatched from General Eisenhower to the Allied Command: "I REQUEST EVERY AIRMAN TO MAKE IT HIS DIRECT RESPONSIBILITY THAT THE ENEMY IS BLASTED UNCEASINGLY BY DAY AND NIGHT AND IS DENIED SAFETY EITHER IN FIGHT OR IN FLIGHT." "I REQUEST EVERY SAILOR TO MAKE SURE THAT NO PART OF THE HOSTILE FORCE CAN EITHER ESCAPE OR BE REINFORCED BY SEA." "I REQUEST OF EVERY SOLDIER TO GO FORWARD..."LET NO FOOT OF GROUND ONCE GAINED BE RELINQUISHED NOR A SINGLE GERMAN SOLDIER ESCAPE THROUGH A LINE ONCE ESTABLISHED." In the **U.S. Third Army VIII Corps** area, the 6th Armored continues to batter Brest, but the Germans refuse to capitulate. Also, the German defenders at St. Malo and at Dinard, offer strong resistance to the 83rd Division. The 4th Division enters Nantes without incident and pushes to St. Calais. In the **XV Corps** area, the advance moves rapidly, but General Bradley halts the XV Corps at Argentan. Subsequently, the Germans withdraw thousands of troops out of the Falaise-Argentan region, escaping a pending trap. The XII Corps (organized with the 4th Armored VIII Corps and 35th U.S. Infantry VII Corps) receives its first order to attack. Led by Major General Gilbert R. Cook; the XII Corps drives east, protecting the south flank of the Third Army, while pressing toward Orleans. In the **U.S. First Army** area, the VII Corps closes on Vire-Argentan Road to cut off the Germans and compress their forces. Troops of the V Corps head south toward Ger, with elements reaching La Francaisere. In other activity, the 2nd Division attacks toward Tinchebray, seizing Truttemer-le-Petit. **(Atlantic-Italy)** In the **U.S. Fifth Army** area, **IV Corps** sector, the 1st Armored Division replaces Task Force Ramey and assumes responsibility for the protection of the right flank of the Corps. In the **British Eighth Army** area, 13th Corps sector, contingents of the 8th Indian Division rush through Ponte Vecchio and stream into north Florence to assist the Italians, who are attempting to retain control of the city.

August 14th 1944 — (Pacific-Marianas-Guam) The V Amphibious Corps establishes a line extending from Naton Beach to Sassayan Point. The U.S. 77th Division and the 3rd Marine Division each deploy an Artillery and Infantry Regiment to continue mop-up operations above the line; other 77th Division elements occupy the heights east of Agat, while the balance of the 3rd Marine Division deploys between the Pago and Ylig Rivers, stretching down the east coast road. **(Pacific-New Guinea)** In Vogelkop, a damaged B-24 Bomber makes a safe landing on the Airstrip at Middleburg. **(Atlantic-France)** It is common knowledge (Allied Command) that although Montgomery has been designated Eisenhower's Deputy for the Normandy invasion, it is clear that the U.S. Army Group will essentially operate as a separate command and eventually become equal; today, an Associated Press reporter prematurely breaks a story claiming parity between the 12th U.S. Army Group and the British 21 Army Group. England's Press reacts indignantly, claiming it is a "DELIBERATE AFFRONT TO BRITAIN'S WAR HERO." General Montgomery is well aware of the full story, but makes no attempt to quell the misinformation. In the **U.S. First Army** area, **VII Corps** sector, the 3rd Armored whizzes through stiff enemy opposition and drives through Carroughes, reaching Ranes, with the 9th Division trailing close behind to seal German escape routes. In the **XIX Corps** sector, Combat Command A, 2nd Armored Division, continues driving east, overpowering Domfront, Ger

and Lonlay-l'Abbaye. In the **V Corps** sector, the 29th Division, also driving east, advances to St. Jean-du-Bois, but obstinate opposition halts the 2nd Division, Tinchebray. In the **U.S. Third Army** area, **VIII Corps** sector, units of the 6th Armored Division move to Vannes and Lorient to relieve the 4th Armored units, allowing them to join the XII Corps, which is moving against Orleans. At St. Malo and at Dinard, fighting continues with the 83rd Division pounding the area. St. Malo is seized, however, stiffened opposition at the Citadel holds out until the 17th. The **XV Corps** finishes mopping up in the Alencon-Sees-Argentan region. General Patton flies to Le Mans to confer with General McLain (90th Division), then heads for the XV Corps perimeter to see General Haislip; it is determined that Haislip feels confident that he can hold the Falaise Gap with two Divisions and move against Dreux with the other two. Patton's Plane ride brings with it some additional apprehension; he had been informed by his staff that it would be a dangerous ride. They mention: "IF THE GERMANS FAILED TO SHOOT ME FROM ABOVE, THE AMERICANS WOULD GET ME FROM BELOW, AS THEY WERE TRIGGER HAPPY DUE TO THE CONSIDERABLE BOMBING." Today is the first night that the Germans do not bomb the Americans. On the following morning, an American Plane makes up for the lapse by losing its way and inadvertently bombing the U.S. lines. By the end of the day, General Bradley concurs with the plan of attack. Patton's renewed plea, as he awaits Montgomery at Argentan, had succeeded in getting Bradley's ear. At 20:20, three Corps initiate the assault: the **XII Corps** moves against Orleans; the **XV Corps** strikes Dreux; and the **XX Corps** advances toward Chartres. In addition, Bradley permits Patton to take the 80th Division, which will be joined by the French 2nd Armored and U.S. 90th Divisions to form a Provisional Corps, commanded by Major General Hugh Gaffey. Patton subsequently notes: "AS OF AUGUST 14TH THE THIRD ARMY HAD ADVANCED FARTHER AND FASTER THAN ANY ARMY IN HISTORY." In the **British Second Army** area, the British 8 Corps continues closing on Tinchebray. In the 12th Corps area, the British 59th Division seizes Thury-Harcourt and maintains the momentum, driving toward Falaise. In the **Canadian First Army** area, the 2nd Corps initiates the main thrust against Falaise, striking from the north along the Caen-Falaise highway. With the assistance of the R.A.F., which drops over 3,700 tons of bombs, a bridgehead is secured at the Laize River; other elements advance to less than five miles from the objective. **(Atlantic-English Channel)** An enemy Submarine torpedo sinks the LST 921. **(Atlantic-Mediterranean)** The Invasion Force (Operation DRAGOON) moves from its rendezvous point off Corsica, steaming toward southern France. **(Pacific-Dutch East Indies)** The U.S.S. *Cod* (SS-224) sinks the Japanese Transport, No. 129. **(Atlantic-Poland)** The Polish continue the struggle against the Germans. British Planes drop supplies to support the effort in Warsaw.

August 14th-15th 1944 — INVASION OF SOUTHERN FRANCE — The Germans are being hit hard by the U.S. First and Third Armies in Normandy. The British are engaged heavily, trying to knock the Germans out of Falaise. Now another hammer is about to slam the Germans in France. The prelude to the invasion of southern France commences during the night of the 14th-15th. Vice Admiral H. K. Hewitt's U.S. Western Task Force (also Commander U.S. Eighth Fleet) is offshore making final preparations. The U.S. 7th Army prepares to hit the beaches; as the midnight hour strikes, the Sitka Force (U.S. Special Service Force) lands and secures Levant, and also jolts the defenders at Port Cros, seizing a good deal of it before the Germans can respond effectively. These swift moves contribute greatly to the success of the impending invasion. Meanwhile, French Commandos land east of Cap Negre on the mainland and expeditiously eliminate the coastal defenses in their sector, then establish roadblocks along the coastal road. To bolster the Allied positioning, a French Naval Force lands near Theoule-sur-Mer to cover the right flank of the main invasion beaches; however, this operation fails and the Germans inflict severe casualties against the French. As the early morning hours pass tediously, the Germans are startled when Planes pass overhead at 04:30 and the skies become dotted with legions of Parachutists from the 1st Airborne Task Force, which drops and sets up positions to intercept and repel any attempt to reinforce the coast defenders. The 1st Airborne accomplishes the primary mission; the Germans lose several villages in the Le Muy-Le Luc region, but retain Le Muy.

Paratroopers (1st Airborne Task Force) dropping in Southern France.

The Germans, having been caught offguard by the preliminary attacks, are struck by a furious bombardment by Surface Vessels and Aircraft. The relentless lambasting of enemy positions strips the Germans of the instant capability of offering steadfast resistance. The Naval Force continues blasting the enemy coastal defenses and lends support fire to the land troops. At 08:00, the coastline between Nice and Toulon receives the American VI Corps, commanded by General Truscott, when three Divisions pour ashore, driving inland abreast against feeble German resistance. The Third Division (Alpha Force) swings in two separate directions, heading north and west, overpowering Cavalaire and establishing contact with French Commandos (left flank) who had landed during the night. During this intrepid advance, a Platoon of the 7th Infantry attempts to penetrate resistance and mines. The enemy holds a commanding position that hinders the Divisional progress. Sergeant James P. Connor assumes command after his Lieutenant and Platoon Sgt. are both killed. Connor, himself wounded by the identical mine that kills the Lieutenant, leads his men forward through several thousand yards of mine infested terrain. Connor again becomes wounded, but he continues to advance, killing two enemy Snipers as they move forward, hampered by heavy mortar fire and machine guns. The gallantry is conspicuous as the Platoon moves. Connor takes a third wound and is unable to continue; he bellows orders from a prone position, while still ignoring medical aid. The Platoon, reduced to less than 12 men out of 36, drives more intently, inspired by Connor, capturing the three menacing machine guns, in addition to killing seven of the defenders and capturing 40 others; Connor receives the Medal of Honor. On the right flank, elements push

to St. Tropez joining the 1st Airborne and French contingents as they are reducing the final opposition there. The Third Division seizes Cogolin, Grimaud, La Croix and La Mole. The Delta Force (45th Division) driving up the center secures its beaches then forges ahead to Ste Maxime where the Germans hold out until mid-day. Subsequently, the 43rd Division races toward Frejus and Le Muy and hooks up with the 1st Airborne. The 36th Division (previous duty in Italy) lands on the right flank and seizes the coastal defenses near Agay and at Drammont, then pushes north toward St. Raphael. Before the end of the day, 86,000 men and 12,000 Vehicles are ashore. Additional French troops land on the following day and attack Marseille and Toulon to snatch the ports. Lt. General Alexander Patch's 7th Army continues driving north to hook up with Patton's Third Army. Within two days, the Germans defending southern France begin retreating. The U.S. Seventh and Third Armies make physical contact on September 17th. Meanwhile, the reeling Germans attempt to reach the German frontier. Paris will be liberated on the 25th of August.

A U.S. Medium Tank advancing in Dreux.

August 15th 1944 — (Pacific Area) The III Amphibious Corps is committed to the operation to seize the Palaus. In the Southwest Pacific area, the Alamo Force issues orders mandating the invasion of Morotai, in the northern Moluccas (south of Philippines-northwest of New Guinea). The assault group is the XI Corps Task Force Tradewind, composed of the 31st Division and Regimental Combat Team 126 (32nd Division U.S.A.), commanded by General Hall. **(Pacific-Marianas-Guam)** Major General Henry L. Larsen assumes command of the island. **(Pacific-New Guinea)** During the night 15th-16th, about 200 Japanese, comprising the main force holding Hill 380, withdraw, moving toward Pakriki on the southern central coast. On Biak, the remaining enemy remnants are further divided as the 162nd and 163rd Regiments hook up in the vicinity of Sorido-Korim Bay track. In the Aitape sector, the Persecution Covering Force is disbanded. Major General Leonard F. Wing, commander 43rd Division and the Tadji Defense and Perimeter Covering Force (43rd Division and Regimental Combat Team 112) assumes responsibility for the objectives of the Persecution Covering Force. **(Atlantic-France)** In the U.S. **First Army** area, the **VII Corps** makes rapid progress with the 3rd Armored Division seizing Ranes, then driving northwest toward Fromental and northeast toward Ecouche. In related activity, the 1st Division heads north toward the Vire-Argentan road. In the **V Corps** sector the heights south of Tinchebray are seized by the 29th Division and Tinchebray is captured by the 2nd Division, culminating the Corps objectives. In the U.S. **Third Army** area **VIII Corps** sector, the 6th Armored contains Brest and Lorient; the 83rd Division takes Dinard. At the Citadel in St. Malo, the Germans hold off the Americans for two more days. In the **XII Corps** sector, the 4th Armored Division closes on Orleans and the 35th Division presses against Chateaudun. In the **XV Corps** area, Dreux is threatened by both the 5th Armored and 79th Infantry Divisions, while additional Corps contingents engage a compressed pocket of German resistance in the Argentan-Falaise region. In other activity the Provisional Corps, commanded by Major General Hugh J. Gaffey is formed and consists of the 80th Infantry Division (less the 319th Infantry), the 90th Infantry Division and the French 2nd Armored Division. In the **XX Corps** area, fierce fighting erupts at the outskirts of Chartres. Subsequently, the command goes to General Gerow. The U.S. Submarine Chaser SC-1029 is damaged by an explosion. The LST 282 is struck by a radio controlled bomb; the Vessel is subsequently beached and abandoned. **(Atlantic-Italy)** The **British Eighth Army** prepares to attack the Gothic Line and shifts a large number of troops to the left flank of the Army's positions.

August 16th 1944 — (Pacific-New Guinea) There is some enemy activity in the Aitape area along the Driniumor where Patrols bump into resistance at the mouth of the Dandriwad. **(Atlantic-France)** In Northern France, U.S. **First Army** area, **VII Corps** sector, units attack north, meeting only slight opposition, the exception being the 3rd Armored Division, which encounters stiff resistance near Fromental. In the U.S. **Third Army VIII Corps** area, the obstinate resistance at the Citadel in St. Malo continues to take a pummeling from the 83rd Division, but it refuses to collapse. In other activity, the 8th Division advances to the vicinity of Brest. In the **XV Corps** area, Dreux is seized by the 5th Armored Division; other elements secure a bridgehead at the Eure River. In the **XII Corps** area, the combined efforts of Combat Command A, 4th Armored Division and the 135th Infantry, 35th Division, culminate with the seizure of Orleans. In other activity, contingents of the 35th Division approach Chateaudun. In the **XX Corps** area, a bridgehead is established at the Aunay River near Chartres. During the day's fighting near and in Chartres, Patton arrives and meets General Walker at the bridge, while it is still under fire; the bridge had been blown by a German Soldier causing some damage and killing several American Soldiers. Later, General Bradley calls Patton and informs him that General Gerow's V Corps had been pinched out and his Divisions have been transferred to the VIII Corps. Gerow assumes command of these troops (2nd French Armored Division, 80th and 90th Divisions) and takes over the assault against Trun in the Falaise Gap. Off Normandy, the LST 391 is damaged by a mine. In the **British 21st Army Group, British**

Second Army area, the British 3rd Division (8th Corps) takes Flers without opposition. In the 30th Corps sector, the British take Conde-sur-Noireau without opposition. In the **Canadian First Army** area, the 2nd Corps has encircled Falaise. The British 1st Corps moves east, heading toward the Seine River. In other activity, the 51st British Division seizes St. Pierre-sur-Dives and continues driving toward Lisieux. **(Southern France)** In the U.S. **7th Army** area, the Germans have been rattled, but not disoriented; resistance is fierce at Port Cros Island where the enemy remains entrenched at a fort on the western portion of the island. In other activity, the 1st Airborne demolishes the remaining opposition at Le Muy. In the **VI Corps** area, resistance is intense along the coast beyond Cap Negre, impeding progress of the 7th Infantry, 3rd Division, but the 30th Infantry, 3rd Division overpowers La Guarde Freinet, Les Mayon, Gonfaron and Collobrieres, solidly gaining positions along the Blue Line. The 36th Infantry Division, operating to the right of the 45th Division, seizes Frejus and Puget with its 142nd Regiment, while the 143rd Infantry takes St. Raphael. The 141st Infantry, 36th Division, in conjunction with the 142nd and 143rd, seizes Theoule and subsequently bolsters its positions near La Napoule. In yet other activity, **French Army B**, commanded by French General de Lattre de Tassigny (under command of U.S. 7th Army) comes ashore upon American VI Corps beaches and prepares to attack the ports of Marseille and Tulon. In Naval activity, the PT-202 and the PT-218 are sunk by mines; the Minesweeper YMS-24 is also sunk by a mine. **(Atlantic-Italy)** Allied Plans for a breakthrough of the German Gothic Line (discretely drawn up on the 4th) are presented as Operation Order No. 3. The British Eighth Army is to make the initial effort in the Adriatic sector; however, American General Mark Clark is unaware of the modification of plans and he is compelled to make some rapid adjustments in strategy. The Fifth Army, in an effort to bolster the 2 Corps, moves toward Bologna, then begins advancing toward Modena. **(Atlantic-Poland)** Fighting between the Polish resistance and the Germans continues to be a lopsided affair; the Russian offensive is still not moving toward the desperate Poles.

August 17th 1944 — (Pacific-New Guinea) On Noemfoor, the remaining organized enemy resistance is exterminated by the 503rd Paratroop Infantry. On Biak, elements of the 186th Infantry debark from LCMs, storming Wardo Bay against minimal opposition; the remaining enemy force on Biak scatters into small units, foregoing any possible future stands. In the Vogelkop area, the Airstrip at Middleburg Island is prepared to handle Fighters (one day ahead of schedule). **(Atlantic-France)** German General von Kluge is replaced as Commander of O.B. West by Field Marshal Model (ordered by Adolph Hitler). In the U.S. **First Army** area, **VII Corps** sector, the 3rd Armored Division spins through tough opposition and seizes Fromental. The **VII Corps** regroups prior to continuing the assault. The **V Corps** receives orders to close the Argentan-Falaise Gap, still existing between the Americans and the British, to facilitate the prevention of any more Germans escaping the entrapment. In other V Corps activity, the 90th Division attacks viciously below Chambois, engaging the Germans in a furious contest that culminates with the Yanks victorious at Le Bourg-St-Leonard. In the U.S. **Third Army** area, Patton's 83rd Division terminates the obstinate resistance at the Citadel, ending the vicious battle for St. Malo. In the **XX Corps** sector, the 5th Division deploys outside of Chartres, awaiting any Germans who might escape the clutches of the 7th Armored Division, which is completing mop-up within the town. In the **XII Corps** area, the enemy withdraws across the Loire River on the south flank. In other activity, General Gilbert R. Cook becomes extremely sick and incapacitated because of circulatory problems; reluctantly, General Patton abides by doctors' orders and relieves him of command (occurs on 19th). Patton makes it clear that he is a tremendous Soldier and his absence will be a great loss. In the **British 21st Army Group**, the 2nd Corps, **Canadian First Army** seizes Falaise, further compressing the German escape routes. **(Southern France)** In the **U.S. Seventh Army** area, the U.S. Special Service Force accepts the surrender of the German Garrison of Port Cros Island. In other activity, other units continue filing into place at the Blue Line, completing the initial phase of the southern France operation for Seventh Army. While the 3rd Division is clearing the left flank and heading for Toulon, elements of the 7th Infantry encounter enemy resistance near La Londe; Sergeant Stanley Bender jumps aboard a knocked out Tank amidst deadly volleys of machine gun fire. Bender, impetuously stands on the turret trying to discover the origin of the fire as bullets are zinging all around him. Spotting the gun at about 200 yards distant, Bender leads a detachment directly into the devil's lair, close enough to become recipients of grenades. Bender continues walking through the bullets which continue to bounce all around him. In a calm calculated fashion, he destroys the first nest with a quick solitary burst of fire, then with impunity and total disregard for his safety heads for the second nest. Unperturbed, despite the machine gun fire aimed directly at him, Bender keeps moving and eliminates the crew. Subsequently, the unabashed Yank orders his men to attack the Rifle pits, then he leads them against the remainder of the Germans manning the stronghold. His extraordinary actions under fire inspire the spellbound Squad; they charge, overpowering a roadblock, take out two antitank guns and charge into the town, capturing 26 Germans and killing 37 more. In addition, the assault Company captures three bridges that span the Maravenne River; Sgt Bender receives the Medal of Honor. **(Atlantic-Italy)** The U.S. **Fifth Army** orders an attack against Florence and Pontassieve (8 mile front) to commence upon 72 hours notice, subsequent to 00:01, 25th August. The **U.S. II Corps**, assigned the primary task, is to secure M. Calvana, M. Morello and M. Senario. In conjunction, the British 13th Corps is to seize M. Giovi. The Gothic Line is to be severed during the next phase of the operation. In other activity, **British Eighth Army** area, the Polish 2nd Corps is forced to abort a preplanned attack against the Germans on the opposite bank of the Cesano River until mine fields can be deactivated. **(Atlantic-Eastern Europe)** The Germans mount fierce counterattacks in the vicinity of Sialiai (Lithuania) in an effort to regain communications with its Baltic Forces. Forces of the Third White Russian Front advance to East Prussia at the Sesupe River.

August 18th 1944 — (United States) U.S. Major General Albert C. Wedemeyer confers with the Joint Chiefs of Staff to discuss a British request to delay Admiral Mountbatten's operations in Burma until additional forces can be mounted. The Joint Chiefs disagree and inform the British to press the attack against Mandalay and to seize the supply road to China. U.S. General Stilwell has been recently transferred out of Burma and is in Ceylon. Admiral Mountbatten soon departs England returning to Burma to continue the post Myitkyina objectives. **(Pacific-Philippines)** The U.S.S. *Rasber* (SS-269) sinks the Japanese Escort Carrier *Otaka*. In other Submarine activity in the vicinity of the Philippines, the U.S.S. *Hardhead* destroys the Japanese Light Cruiser *Natori* off east Samar. **(Atlantic-France)** In the **U.S. First Army** area, efforts

to further eliminate enemy pockets in the Argentan-Falaise vicinity continues The **VII Corps** mops up and prepares to reinitiate its offensive. In the **V Corps** area, a determined effort is made to close the gap still existing between the Americans and British. The U.S. 90th drives toward Foret de Goffern in conjunction with the 80th Division, driving through Bordeaux, heading for Argentan. The French 2nd Armored supports the advance, giving protection on the flank and by cover fire. In the **U.S. Third Army** area, the **XV Corps** drives toward the Seine. In the **VIII Corps** area, the 2nd Division, rushing from the First Army sector to Brest to relieve the 6th Armored Division, is attached to the VIII Corps. In the **XX Corps** area, the 7th Armored Division assumes responsibility for the bridgehead at Dreux. In the **XII Corps** sector, the 35th Division finalizes mop-up operations in Orleans, then advances to Janville, while the 4th Armored Division continues clearing the area near Orleans. The **British Second Army** is moving toward the south to eliminate an enemy pocket of resistance in the region consisting of Conde, Flers and Falaise. In the **Canadian First Army** area, the Canadian 2nd Division captures Falaise. In other activity, the Canadian 4th Armored presses toughly southward to hook up and assist the Polish 1st Armored Division, driving on the left. On the following day, the Canadian 2 Corps drives closer to the Americans and makes contact with contingents of the U.S. V Corps at Chambois. **(Southern France)** In the **U.S. 7th Army** area, the Germans are beginning to get a large dosage of U.S. firepower; the Yanks are overpowering the enemy coastal defenses in the **VI Corps** area. The 30th Infantry presses firmly against Brignoles; the engagement lasts through the night 18-19th. At Cabasse-Carces, the 3rd and 45th Divisions overpower the opposition. The 179th Infantry, 45th Division is fighting viciously against steadfast resistance at Barjols. In other activity, Task Force Butler, commanded by Brigadier General Frederick B. Butler, takes the point of the inland advance, driving northwest to Grenoble from Le Muy, while the 36th Division spins elements off toward Callian to rescue a contingent of trapped Paratroopers. On the following day, after long and inconclusive combat, the 147th Infantry clears Callian. In Naval activity, the Amphibious Force Flagship *Catoctin* (AGC-5) sustains damage by an enemy Horizontal Bomber off Southern France. **(Atlantic-Italy)** The **U.S. Fifth Army** takes command of the 13th Corps, British Eighth Army. In the **British Eighth Army** area, the Polish 2nd Corps attacks, crossing the Cesano River and driving toward the Gothic Line. The 3rd Carpathian Division takes the right flank, while the Italian Corps of Liberation (previously called Utili Div.) drives on the left and the 5th Kresowa in the center, presses the advance. **(Atlantic-Lithuania)** The Germans maintain their strengthened counterattack near Siauliai. **(Atlantic-Poland)** The First Ukrainian Front takes Sandomierz, in southern Poland along the western bank of the Vistula River.

August 19th 1944 — (Atlantic-France) The U.S. **7th Army** is driving up from Southern France to join with Patton's Third Army. Meanwhile, the Americans begin to close on Paris. In less than a week, Paris will be liberated. The Stars and Stripes will be flying up and down highways on Vehicles, in an encirclement of the French capital. Although the Yanks will have the city contained, the Americans hold in place and the French move into the city. Today German Field Marshal von Kluge commits suicide. The Germans ask for and receive an armistice lasting until the 23rd to permit time to withdraw from Paris. In other activity, the Canadians hook up with the American V Corps, closing the gap at Argentan-Falsise, but not before about seventy thousand Germans have escaped due to the British not being able to advance quickly enough. In the **British 21st Army Group** area, **British Second Army** sector, the 11th Armored (30th Corps) reaches Argentan-Bailleu. In the 12th Corps area, the British 51st Division nears Bailleu-Trun. In the **Canadian First Army** area, the Canadian 4th Armored Division seizes St. Lambert-sur-Dives and holds steadfastly against severe enemy counterattacks. The 2nd Corps' Polish 1st Armored gets a Patrol forward, which contacts elements of the U.S. V Corps; now that the Canadian First Army is linked to the Yanks, the German Fifth Panzer Army and the 7th German Army are trapped. In the **U.S. Third Army** area, activity is again, brisk and tenacious. The 79th Division Task Force roars into Mantes-Gassicourt, finding no Germans. The 7th Armored drives feverishly along the west bank of the Seine heading northward to catch the Germans before they can cross the river at Louviers. In the **XII Corps** area, Major General Gilbert R. Cook is relieved as Corps commander, being replaced by Major General Manton S. Eddy. In the **U.S. First Army** area, the 80th Division (V Corps) approaches Argentan. In addition, the 90th Division drives to Chambois and at 19:30, makes contact with a Polish Patrol. In the **XIX Corps** area, the 2nd Armored Division, in synchronization with the 30th Division, attacks north toward Evreux to sever the escape route of the Germans between Paris and Elbeuf, along the Seine River. **(Southern France)** In the **U.S. Seventh Army** area, the **VI Corps** is ordered to seize Aix-en-Provence, in conjunction with the French operation, to seize the ports of Marseille and Toulon. The **VI Corps** completes capture of Barjols (179th Infantry, 45th Division) and the 3rd Division secures Brignoles; the 3rd Division then speeds toward Aixen-Provence and the 179th Infantry keeps pace by finishing at Brignoles and jumping to Rians, thus opening a route to the lower Durance Valley. Meanwhile, Task Force Butler attacks toward Sisteron with contingents moving along the east bank of the Durance River to intercept the enemy, which is retreating south to Digne where they eventually surrender. The 141st Regiment, 36th Division seizes Callian after a day-long fight. In the French Sector, elements of the French 1st Division drive toward Hyeres-Toulon; however, stiff opposition halts its progress outside of the town, prompting the French to attempt to outflank the enemy. **(Atlantic-Italy)** In the **British Eighth Army** area, the 3rd Carpathian Division (Polish 2nd Corps) is halted, as it drives along the coast, by stiff opposition at south Constanzo.

U.S.S. Hardhead.

August 20th 1944 — (Pacific-New Guinea) General Krueger declares the Biak Operation complete; the Airfields will be of great value in the continuing quest to rid the Pacific of the Japanese. During the time period from the 27th of May to today, Task Force Hurricane has sustained approximately 400 killed, 2,000 wounded, 150 missing in action. In addition, five men are missing without explanation. The Japanese, during the identical time period have suffered about 4,700 dead and 22 captured. Mop-up operations continue for several months, with the U.S. 41st Division handling the chore. **(China-Burma-India)** On the Salween Front, subsequent to the detonation of explosives under Japanese positions at Sung Shan, Chinese troops charge with flame throwers and secure the objective; however, pockets of resistance pop up in the area. **(North Atlantic)** The U.S.S. *Bogue* (CVE-9), launches Planes which destroy the German Submarine U-1129. **(Atlantic-France) 21st Army Group** British General Montgomery, still commanding all land forces in France, orders the **British 21st Army Group** to destroy the enemy pocket at Falaise-Argentan before attacking toward the Seine. **12th Army Group** In the **U.S. Third Army** area, the **XII Corps** drives toward the Yonne River at Sens to establish a beachhead, spearheading the assault with its 4th Armored Division. In the **XV Corps** area, the 79th Division grabs a crossing of the Seine near Mantes-Gassicourt and establishes a bridgehead. In the **XX Corps** area, the 7th Armored is on the offensive, driving with the 5th Armored Division to seize crossings and establish bridgeheads along the Seine at Melun and at Montereau. As the 5th Armored clears Evreux, it is hit by German Armor units from the rear; the 7th Armored rushes to aid the 5th, and together they drive off the Germans who depart with ten fewer Tanks. In the **U.S. First Army** area, the **XIX Corps** driving north, crosses the Aure River between Nonancourt and Verneuil, while the 80th Division, V Corps, overcomes resistance at Argentan. The U.S. 90th Division is involved with the encirclement of the Germans in the vicinity of Chambois; a strong enemy attempt to break through the positions of the 359th Infantry prove foolhardy. Of course, the Germans have not yet been introduced to Sergeant John D. Hawk. Enemy Tanks and Infantry try forcing Hawk's positions, but his rip roaring accurate fire turns them back. During the exuberant exchange, Hawk becomes wounded and simultaneously, an artillery shell knocks his gun out of commission. Undeterred, Hawk instinctively takes a volunteer and using a Bazooka, impulsively attacks two Tanks, chasing them into the woods. A short time later, this Yank stands in full view of enemy fire, directing antitank fire against additional attacking Armor, while enemy shells are ringing all around him. Unable to properly communicate with the gun crews, he dashes through more intense fire and adjusts the distance, then returns to his conspicuous spot to redirect the Tank Destroyer fire, while standing amidst another storm of bullets. Two more Tanks are destroyed and a third races for cover. Still unsatisfied, Hawk, with indescribable presence of mind and cool calculating demeanor, despite his severe wounds, directs fire toward enemy positions in the woods. His spirited actions are greatly responsible for the repulse of two enemy attacks and for the 500 prisoners who are seized; he receives the Medal of Honor. In the **British 21st Army Group, Canadian First Army** area, the British 7th Armored Division seizes Livarot, while the Canadian 2 Corps rebuffs a final enemy attempt to escape the Falaise-Argentan Pocket. **(Southern France)** In the **U.S. Seventh Army** area, the 3rd Division (VI Corps) pushes to the outskirts of Aix-en-Provence. The U.S. 7th Division soon joins them. The 157th Infantry, 45th Division using extra prudence, crosses a damaged bridge spanning the Durance River, then speeds to overtake Mirabeau and Pertuis. Meyrargues and Peyrolles are overpowered by the 180th Infantry, 45th Division. In addition, Task Force Butler maintains effective roadblocks running south from Grenoble. In other related activity, the 1st Airborne Task Force assumes responsibility for the region between Fayence and La Napoule. In **French Army B's** area, elements move west toward Marseille. The Chapuis Group advances through the hills overlooking Toulon, while the Bonjour Group moves southeast toward Toulon. Hyeres is contained by the French 9th Colonial and 1st Infantry Divisions, but an attack by the 1st Division to penetrate the frontal defenses is thwarted. **(Atlantic-Italy)** The **U.S. Fifth Army** reforms for impending attack, with elements spread across a 55 mile front. **(Atlantic-Eastern Europe)** The Russians open an assault against the Germans in Rumania, driving toward Iasi and Kishinev. In Poland, the resistance fighters still battle the Germans, hoping for Allied aid, and remain convinced that the Russians are coming. In other activity, the Germans continue their counterattack to reinitiate contact with their Baltic Forces.

August 21st 1944 — (Pacific-Marianas-Guam) Rear Admiral L.F. Reifsnider, Senior Officer present in the area, turns his duties over to the Deputy Commander, Forward area, Central Pacific, and by so doing, Task Force 53 is formally disbanded. **(Pacific-New Guinea)** In the Wakde area, Regimental Combat Team 20 is returned to the command of the 6th Division, being detached by the 31st Division. **(Atlantic-France) 21st Army Group** In the **Canadian First Army** area, 2nd Corps sector, the Polish 1st Armored and the Canadian 3rd Divisions remain to eliminate the final resistance in Falaise-Argentan region, while the remainder of Corps drives east toward the Seine. In the **British Second Army** area, 30th Corps sector, the British 11th Armored Division, spearheading the Corps advance, bypasses Gace and speeds toward Laigle. **12th Army Group** In the **U.S. First Army** area, the British 30th Corps relieves the U.S. 80th Division (V Corps) and takes over its sector. On the following day, the U.S. 90th Division is relieved by the British 30th Corps; both American Divisions receive some rest, while awaiting new orders. The relaxation time is short; the V Corps is ordered to free Paris. In the **VII Corps** area, the 9th Division deploys defensively in the Mortagne area. In other activity, the 30th Division seizes Nonancourt and the 28th Division initiates action to secure Verneuil. In the **U.S. Third Army** area, Patton is pressing the Seine to the north and south of Paris; the Germans on the west bank are attempting to evade General Hodges' closing First Army. Supplies are having trouble reaching Patton. Two days prior, C-47s landed at Le Mans with about 50 tons of rations. Patton's supply line now extends back to Cherbourg, a distance of 250 miles. In the **XV Corps** sector, positions are strengthened at bridgeheads and in the **XX Corps** area, Etampes is trampled by the 5th Division. Meanwhile the 7th Armored Division is charging to the Arpajon-Rambouillet region. According to Third Army figures, as of the 21st of August, after three weeks of battle with the Germans, the casualties are: killed 1,713; wounded 7,928; missing 1,702; non-battle casualties 4,286; (total 15,629). The German casualties: 11,000 killed, P.O.W.s 49,000, wounded 108,000. Third Army equipment losses: 70 Light Tanks; 157 Medium Tanks and 64 Guns. The Germans: Medium Tanks 269, Tiger or Panzer Tanks 174 and 680 Guns. **(Southern France)** In the **U.S. Seventh Army** area, the 1st Airborne Task Force prepares for an attack against Cannes by securing the coastal sector around La Napoule. In the **VI Corps** sector, Aix-en-Provence, containing few Germans, falls to the 30th, Infantry, 3rd Division and contingents of French forces. In other activity, the 45th Division drives toward Apt, Avignon and Volonne. Task Force

Engineers of a U.S. Armored Division take a break in the Falaise-Argantan area.

Butler relinquishes its roadblocks to the Texas 36th Division, then drives straight through Die, and Crest, heading for the Rhone Valley. Along the route it encounters an enemy Vehicle Convoy near Livron and destroys it. The 36th Division, subsequent to relieving the Butler Force, receives orders to dispatch elements to assist it in the Rhone Valley. In the French sector, Hyeres falls to the 1st French Division. French Commandos seize Mt.Coudon, and elements of the 3rd Algerian Division contain Mt.Caumes, giving the Allies control of two hilltop strongholds north of Toulon; the noose closes tighter on the German held port. **(Atlantic-Italy)** The British are getting closer to launching their major offensive. The **U.S. Fifth Army** continues to fool the enemy by feigning major activity near Florence, drawing attention from the British. In the **U.S. II Corps** sector, the 88th Division dispatches the 350th Infantry to bolster the IV Corps efforts at Leghorn. In the British 13th Corps area, the Germans are retreating from the opposite side of the Arno and the British take the opportunity to initiate limited advances across the river. Also, the Germans are forced to withdraw (British Eighth Army area) and take positions behind the Metauro River, because of extreme pressure applied by the Polish II Corps during the night 21st-22nd. **(Atlantic-Eastern Europe)** The Germans maintain their counterattack and seize Tukums, 35 miles east of Riga.

August 22nd 1944 — (Pacific-Philippines) U.S. Submarines are again lurking in Philippine waters. The Japanese Frigate *Sado* is destroyed by the U.S.S. *Haddo* (SS-255) and the Frigates *Matsuwa* and *Hiburi* are sunk by the U.S.S. *Harder* (SS-257). **(China-Burma-India)** Admiral Mountbatten returns to Ceylon after his stay in London where Burma strategy had been discussed. On the Salween Front, the Japanese mount unsuccessful counterattacks in the vicinity of Sung Shan. **(Atlantic-France) 21st Army Group** In the **Canadian First Army's** British 1st Corps sector, Deauville is seized by the Belgium Brigade, which is under command of the British 6th Airborne Division; at Pont Eveque, elements of the 6th Airborne Division are heavily engaged against the enemy; the British 49th Division fords the Touques River near the contested town. Contingents of the 2 Corps also reach the Touques. Meanwhile, in the **British Second Army** area, 30th Corps sector, the 11th Armored Division advances rapidly to Laigle. **12th Army Group** In the **U.S. First Army** area, the 4th Division **(VII Corps)** is transferred to the V Corps, which gets the job of liberating Paris. The advance into Paris commences on the following day, after termination of a German requested Armistice (19th to 23rd) to allow them to withdraw from the city. In the **XIX Corps** area, Breteuil is seized by the 2nd

Armored Division as it steamrolls north. In coordinated action, the 30th Division races toward Evreaux and Verneuil is cleared by the 28th Division. In the **U.S. Third Army** area, the Germans initiate a strong counterattack against the **XV Corps**, but it is firmly repelled by the 79th Division. In other Corps activity, the Germans mount rigid lines of opposition between the Eure and Seine Rivers, however, the 5th Armored Division rolls confidently toward Louviers. In the **XX Corps** area, the 5th Division speeds toward Fontainebleau, and Melun is jeopardized by the advancing 7th Armored Division. The balance of the Third Army is also bristling with activity; Vehicles are running the 29th Division (VIII Corps) toward Brest and in the **XII Corps** sector, the 4th Armored, driving east, whacks through opposition and seizes Villeneuve, while the 35th Division drives to the fringes of Montargis. **(Southern France)** In the **U.S. Seventh Army** area, the 1st Airborne Task Force is reinforced by the 1st Special Service Force, which is immediately deployed in the center, replacing the British 2nd Paratroop Brigade. In the **VI Corps** area, the French (FFI) forces and contingents of the 157th Infantry secure, Apt. Grenoble falls to the 36th Division without resistance. In the French sector, elements of the 3rd Algerian Division seize Mt. Faron, signaling the demise of the final hilltop fortress north of Toulon; this prize opens a route to Toulon through the Dardennes ravine. The Germans also are driven from La Vallette by elements of the 9th French Colonial Division. **(Atlantic-Italy)** In the **British Eighth Army** area, the Polish 2 Corps secures the south bank of the Metauro River, giving it domination from the coast to south Ippolito. In other activity, the Italian Liberation Corps, advancing up the left flank, approaches Cagli. **(Atlantic-Rumania)** Iasi collapses under the thrust of the Second Ukrainian Front. On the following day, the King of Rumania capitulates, surrendering Rumania without conditions.

August 23rd 1944 — (Pacific-Marianas) Aguijan Island, Marianas, is bombarded by a Naval Task Force consisting of Destroyers and other Vessels; these attacks continue to strike the installations until the 26th. On Guam, Operational Command of the 3rd Marine Division is passed to Island Command and the 1st and 3rd Battalions, 306th Infantry, U.S.A., are assigned to the 3rd Marine Division. **(Pacific-New Guinea)** On Noemfoor, the 503rd Paratroop Infantry advances to clear the Kamiri Airdrome area, but leaves three Companies behind to patrol the southern portion of Noemfoor. **(Pacific-Palau Islands)** The U.S.S. *Batfish* (SS-310), patrolling off the Palau Islands, destroys the Japanese Minesweeper No. 22. **(Pacific-Philippines)** A U.S. Submarine, the *Haddo* (SS-255), sinks the Japanese Destroyer *Asakaze*. **(China-Burma-India)** General Stilwell is notified by the War Department that the land road (Ledo Road) to China is to be limited to a two way all-weather type surface to Myitkyina and from there, the opening of a trail to China. The restrictions are mandated to permit increased manpower for the other Pacific objectives. In other activity, Chiang Kai-shek receives a dispatch from President Roosevelt, which strongly requests that General Stilwell be quickly placed in command of the Chinese Troops. On the Salween Front, the Japanese at Lungling request reinforcements; on the following day, enemy troops depart Man-shih to bolster the Garrison. **(Atlantic-France)** General Eisenhower makes the decision for a solitary push; Field Marshal Montgomery will lead the primary thrust up the channel coast. Montgomery had previously requested that Patton be held idle at the Meuse, while he pushes alone to Berlin. General Bradley had requested a joint attack, but Montgomery has his way once again. The Third

Army is not immobilized, but Montgomery acquires the priority for supplies and the U.S. First Army for support. In the **U.S. XII Army** Group, the **XV Corps** and its 5th Armored and 79th Armored Infantry Divisions are attached to the First Army, effective 06:00 on the following day. In addition, boundary lines effecting the First and Third Armies are adjusted to complement the personnel changes. In the **First Army** area, **V Corps** sector, the French 2nd Armored, supported by Troop B, 102nd Cavalry, drives toward Paris to assist the French resistance, but iron fisted opposition halts their progress, then stalls the advance at Versailles-Bois de Meudon. In conjunction, the U.S. 102nd Cavalry (minus Troop B) and the U.S. 4th Division, advance closely behind the French Armored and reach Arpajon, south of Paris. In the **XIX Corps** area, the 2nd Armored, splintered into two columns, drives toward Le Neubourg and Elbeuf. The 28th Division secures Conches, allowing the 2nd Armored to bypass it. In other activity, the 30th Divi sion enters Evreux encountering no enemy troops; it contacts the U.S. 5th Armored Division on the right in the XV Corps sector. In the **U.S. Third Army** area, **XV Corps** sector, the 5th Armored is concentrating on ridding the area west of the Seine of German resistance; the 79th Division is maintains control of the bridgehead over the Seine at Mantes-Gassicourt. In the **XX Corps** area, Fontainebleau folds under the pressure of the 5th Division, which subsequently sweeps toward Montereau. The town of Melun is threatened by the U.S. 7th Armored Division; In the **XII Corps** area, Montargis is seized by the 35th Division. In the **VIII Corps** area, the 38th Infantry, 2nd Division, which had replaced the 6th Armored at Brest, is involved with the enemy at Plougastel, Brittany. Enemy machine gun fire keeps the Yanks pinned down; Sergeant Alvin P. Carey, disregarding his personal safety, grabs hand grenades and singlehandedly advances into the fierce fire moving about 200 yards up Hill 154, killing one enemy Soldier as he moves. He begins tossing grenades and is struck and badly wounded, but the pill box crew continues firing. Casey, despite his mortal wound, throws additional grenades, blowing the target; inspired by his heroism, his men overpower the remaining enemy in the area. Sergeant Casey becomes the recipient of the Medal of Honor posthumously. **British 21st Army Group** In the **Canadian First Army** area, the British I Corps is bogged down along the coast and at Orbec; the British 2nd Corps is also viciously engaged against firm resistance. In the British 30th Corps area, the British 50th Division advances to the Verneuil-Breteuil area and comes to a stop to allow the U.S. XIX Corps (First Army) to pass its front. The Yanks drive for two days to reach Elbeuf, overrunning it on the 25th, pushing right through to make contact with the British to the north. **(Southern France)** In the **U.S. Seventh Army** area, Engineers, acting upon information that the Germans have abandoned Cannes, are busily preparing to clear the entrance for the 1st Airborne Task Force. In the **VI Corps** area, intense and precise decisions are made to ensure sealing the Rhone Valley at Lyon to prevent the Germans from making an escape. In other activity, the Germans mount heavy resistance at Montelimar, repulsing repeated attacks, which include those by elements of the Butler Task Force and the 141st Infantry, 36th Division. The 3rd Division drives toward the Rhone, and discovers no enemy presence at Martigues. In **French Army B's** area, the 9th Colonial and the 1st Division penetrate the eastern sector of Toulon, then drive to the center of town. Also, the Germans holding a Battery on the eastern tip of the Giens Peninsula, surrender without opposition to French troops. At Marseille, contingents of the 3rd Algerian Division and elements of the 1st French Armored, crash into the outskirts from the east and west, but the Germans refuse to surrender the port. **(Atlantic-Rumania)** Rumania surrenders to the Russians.

August 24th 1944 — (Pacific) The Administrative Command Fleet, Marine Forces Pacific, is abolished by the redesignation of its Headquarters to Provisional Headquarters Fleet Marine Force, Pacific. **(Pacific-New Guinea)** In the Vogelkop area, Brigadier General Charles Hurdis replaces General Sibert (leaves to assume command of X Corps) as commander of the 6th Division and Task Force Typhoon. **(Pacific-Philippines)** The U.S.S. *Harder* (SS-257) is sunk by depth charges off the Philippines. **(Atlantic-France)** In the **U.S. First Army** area, the **XIX Corps** is closing toward Elbeuf. In the **XV Corps** area, the 5th Armored Division drives to Houdebouville. In the **V Corps** area the French 2nd Armored grinds toward Paris against stiff opposition. Units of the 102nd Cavalry, screening for the 4th Division, advance to the Seine south of Paris and are ordered by General Bradley to attack the city; the attack is mounted by the 4th Division and the 102nd Cavalry in conjunction with the French who are assaulting from the southwest. The 4th Division leaves one Regimental Combat Team behind to ensure a crossing of the Seine south of Paris. In the **U.S. Third Army** area the **XX Corps** sector, the 7th Armored secures a bridgehead across the Seine River at Melun; the 5th Division seizes one at Montereau. In the **XII Corps** area, the 35th Division pushes to Courtenay, while Combat Command B, 4th, Armored drives to St. Florentin and Combat Command A, advances toward Troyes. **(Southern France)** In the **U.S. Seventh Army** area, the 1st Airborne Task Force gets advance elements to Cannes. The 509th Paratroop Battalion, trailed by the 1st Battalion, 551st Paratroop Infantry, enter the city against no opposition and then to Antibes. In other activity, the 1st Special Service Force seizes Grasse effortlessly, then takes Valbonne, making contact with the Paratroopers extending themselves from Cannes. The 36th Division, operating on the left of the Airborne, seizes St. Vallier and establishes defenses along the Roubion River to keep the enemy from breaking through to the north. The 36th Division has established its main line of defense and at its weakest section, Bonlieu, contingents of the 111th Engineering Battalion deploy and are attacked on the following day. In other activity, advance units of the 3rd Division reach Arles at the Rhone River. In **French Army B's** area, organized resistance in the eastern part of Toulon ceases, However, the Germans still control the western section, including the dock area. In related action, the 3rd Algerian Division drives a wedge into Marseille. **(Atlantic-Italy)** The **British Eighth Army** completes preparations for the main assault against the Gothic Line. **(Atlantic-Eastern Europe)** Kishinev is occupied by the Russians.

August 25th 1944 — (Pacific-New Guinea) General Krueger proclaims the Aitape Operation terminated. During the operation, Allied losses stand at 440 killed, 2,550 wounded and 10 missing. The Japanese 18th Army defending the area suffers 8,821 killed and 98 captured, losing well over 2 Divisions, rendering them ineffective as a major threat in New Guinea. At Vogelkop, Task Force Typhoon's positions are struck by a Japanese Airraid, the first to be launched on the region. **(Pacific-Philippines)** The U.S.S. *Picuda* (SS-382), operating off the Philippines, sinks the Japanese Destroyer *Yunagi*. **(Atlantic-France)** Paris is virtually cut off by U.S. troops. For political and protocol reasons, the honor of accepting the surrender of the Germans, commanded by Lt. General Dietrich von Choltitz, is given to the French 2nd Armored Division, commanded by French Brigadier General Jacques Philippe Leclerc. The French Armored units evade strong resistance at Versailles and push advance elements from the southwest into the city at 07:00. They are followed by Americans who enter from the south at 07:30, spearheaded by Troop A, 38th Cavalry, trailed by the U.S. 4th Division. The Germans have been ordered by Hitler to destroy the cultural treasures of Paris, such as the museums and public buildings, but General von Choltitz ignores the directive. The city's bridges are also spared from Hitler's rage. As the morning progresses, bullets are clanging, bouncing off buildings and Armored Vehicles as civilians unleash their frustration, joining the fight. As the Germans race their equipment through the streets, swerving around abandoned burning trucks, hand grenades are lobbed from rooftops stirring the enemy; as the grenades explode some Germans are catapulted from the Vehicles, their bodies consumed in flames. Impassionate men and women rush out amidst scattered small arms fire and strip the enemy corpses of their weapons and ammunition, to further assist the struggle. As opposed to continuing a fruitless struggle, the Germans surrender at 17:15. The mood in Paris is jubilant; the citizens are enthralled with their return to freedom. The U.S. 4th Division comes in to aid the French and restore order. After the capture of Paris, General Eisenhower informs Charles De Gaulle that he should make his entrance before Eisenhower (the entire endeavor including the surrender being handled by the French, is to restore confidence in the French Army and government). Eisenhower and Bradley decide to make a formal call on De Gaulle on Sunday (27th) British General Montgomery declines an invitation to accompany Ike and Bradley, because of the situation on his front; the two American Generals arrive in Paris before 12:00 on Sunday and then return to Bradley's Headquarters at Chartres. The U.S. 4th Division establishes a bridgehead south of Paris at the Seine. There is a great deal of activity in the U.S. **V Corps** sector; the 1st and 9th Divisions converge south of Paris, while Combat Command B, 3rd Armored Division, bolts across the Seine at Tilly. In the **U.S. Third Army** area, the 80th and 90th Divisions (First Army) are attached to the Third Army, assigned to the XII and XX Corps respectively. In the **VIII Corps** area, a tumultuous hour-long Artillery bombardment sets the stage for a massive assault against Brest. The German XXV Corps is deeply entrenched and unwilling to give ground without a bitter struggle. At 13:00, Brest is struck from three sides by three American Divisions, the 2nd, 8th and 29th; resistance is vicious on the outskirts of the city, preventing rapid progress. Elements of the 29th Division (Task Force Sugar), commanded by Lt. Colonel Arthur T. Sheppe, 175th Infantry, fights toward Le Conquet Peninsula to knock out the Batterie Graf Spee, while Task Force B clears the peninsulas south of Brest. In the **XII Corps** area, Combat Command A, 4th Armored, strikes like a bolt of lightning at Troyes; the assault to seize Troyes begins with Combat Command A, perched about 3,000 yards from the town in a concealed gully. Colonel (later General) Bruce Clark leads a Tank Company, and two full Armored mounted Infantry Companies at a full charge with every gun blazing. The startling assault seizes the town without losing a man, but the lightly numbered force is unable to hold, causing a stronger assault to be launched to retake the town. In the **XX Corps** sector, the established bridgeheads at Melun and Montereau, which cross the Seine, are maintained, while the 5th Division speeds across the Yonne River at Missy; during this heated exchange, boats laden with wounded Soldiers are being rowed back to the friendly bank when enemy machine gun fire batters the craft. The wounded scramble to the water, but three men are unable to maneuver. Pvt. Harold A. Garman defies the incessant gunfire and dives into the water, bringing the three men to safety by singlehandedly towing the boat to shore; later, while General Patton is decorating him with the Medal of Honor, Patton asks him why he did it and receives the response: "WELL, SOMEONE HAD TO." In the **British Second Army** area, the British 15th Division prepares to cross the Seine at Louviers. In the British 30th Corps area, Artillery commences firing to assist the British 43rd Division establish a bridgehead across the Seine at Vernon. **(Southern France)** In the **U.S. Seventh Army** area, the Germans mount a strong counterattack, striking the weakest part of the line, driving against Bonlieu along the Roubion River, compelling the Engineers to pull back. The momentum of the enemy drives a nasty wedge between the 141st and 142nd Regiments, 36th Division. Elements of the 143rd Regiment pour into the area to plug the hole, but it takes until the 27th to restore the line. While the enemy assault continues, the 141st Regiment attempts to clear the hills north and northeast of Montelimar; other elements of the 141st attack with Task Force Butler in an unsuccessful attempt to block Highway 7 at La Coucourde. In related activity, the enemy continues to escape up the Rhone Valley, but Aircraft and Artillery assist the land troops stem the tide. In the **French Army B** area, heavy fighting ensues between the Germans and the French 2 Corps at Marseille and at Toulon. **(Atlantic-Rumania)** Rumania which has just surrendered to the Russians on the 23rd, declares war against Germany. Hitler has already exposed his feeling on the matter by ordering Air attacks against Rumania. **(Atlantic-Italy)** In the **U.S. Fifth Army** area, the **British Eighth Army** commences a primary assault against the Gothic Line. The plan to attack the Gothic Line had been modified on the 4th of August and it is specified that the main thrust would not be against the center of the enemy, but would be initiated by the Eighth Army from the right flank. The Germans, not expecting a British assault, are taken by complete surprise and can only commit nominal resistance. The offensive beginning during the night of the 25th-26th has the Canadian 1st, Polish 2nd and British 5th Corps, steamrolling ahead making tremendous progress.

August 26th 1944 — (Pacific-Carolines) The U.S. Submarine *Batfish*, (SS-310) patrolling off the Palau Islands, sinks the Japanese Destroyer *Samidare*. **(Pacific-Marianas-Guam)** The 1st and 3rd Battalions, 306th Infantry, U.S.A., are detached from the 3rd Marine Division and reattached to the 77th Division, U.S.A. **(Atlantic-France)** The British mount a major attack with the American First Army in support. The Canadian First Army is directed to secure Pas-de-Calais, while the British Second Army drives into Belgium. The **U.S. First Army** travels along the axis Paris-Brussels. The British First Army prepares to cross the Seine River south of Rouen. In the **U.S. Third Army** area, the recent gains of the extended 3rd Army necessitate Planes bringing in gasoline. The **VIII Corps** still is experiencing heavy opposition as it drives to Brest. In the **XX Corps** area, the 7th Armored Division is ordered to drive against Chateau-Thierry and the Marne. Patton is unhappy with the sloppy appearance of the 7th Division and so informs the commanding officer. Meanwhile, the 5th Division captures Nogent-sur-Seine. In the **XII Corps** sector, mop-up operations continue in Troyes. **(Southern France)** The 3rd Division pushes north in pursuit of the retreating Germans; the withdrawing enemy also is faced with aggressive Air and Artillery bombardments that assist the 3rd overcome rear-

guard resistance and seize Orange. In **French Army B's** area, the German organized resistance at Toulon is terminated, but the nearby San Mandrier Peninsula, south of Toulon, remains in German control. The resistance at Marseilles is wavering also, as the heights of Notre Dame de la Garde located within the city limits are captured. **(Atlantic-Eastern Europe)** The Danube River in Rumania is reached by the Third Ukrainian Front as it pushes toward Galati. In other activity, Bulgaria initiates surrender negotiations with the Allies. **(Atlantic-Italy)** In the British 13th Corps area, the positions north of the Arno River are consolidated; the South African 6th Armored Division relieves the U.S. 85th Division on the line. In other activity, the British Eighth Army secures bridgeheads across the Metauro.

155-mm Howitzer M1 Gun in-tow crossing the Seine River via a Bailey Bridge.

August 27th 1944 — (Pacific) Several weeks prior, the British decided to send troops to the Pacific with the intention of operating under British authority, outside of MacArthur's jurisdiction. MacArthur is informed of these intentions by Australian Prime Minister Curtain (who opposes these measures). MacArthur's unwavering rejection of the plan is reinforced and backed by Washington; he welcomes all British forces provided they are under his command "TO ENSURE THE SOUTH WEST PACIFIC AREA BE RETAINED UNTIL A SUCCESSFUL CONCLUSION OF THE CAMPAIGN HAS BEEN COMPLETED." During August of 1945, the set up is changed (subsequent to the successful campaign at Borneo and the Philippines). **(Pacific-New Guinea)** On Noemfoor, contingents of the 503rd Paratroop Infantry are relieved by the 1st Battalion, 158th Infantry. **(Pacific-Philippines)** The U.S.S. *Stingray* (SS-186) avoids Japanese detection and lands men and equipment in the Philippines on the northwest coast of Luzon. **(China-Burma-India)** In Burma, the British 36th Division continues moving down the Mogaung-Mandalay Railroad. **(Atlantic-France)** **21st Army Group** Contingents of the British 1st Corps advance to the Seine in the coastal region. In the British 4 Corps area, the Canadian 3rd Infantry and 4th Armored Divisions cross the Seine near Elbeuf, which had been captured by the U.S. First Army. In the **British Second Army** area, 12th Corps sector, the British 15th Division crosses the Seine near Louviers and establishes a bridgehead in the Muids-Porte-Joie vicinity; additional contingents of the 15th Division drive against heavy opposition about one mile further upstream, but are denied the bridgehead and forced to withdraw. In the British 30th Corps sector, the bridgehead at Vernon is firmed up and expanded. **12th Army Group** The U.S. First Army receives priority over the Third Army for supplies, which are in short supply all along the American lines. In the **U.S. First Army** area, the **XV Corps** extends its bridgehead at Mantes-Gassicourt with a solid attack by the 79th Division, striking from the left and by the 30th Division whipping forward from the right. In the **V Corps** area, French elements knock out heavy opposition and seize Le Bourget Airfield. In the **U.S. VII Corps** area, the 4th Cavalry Group spearheads a determined attack against Soissons, followed close behind by the 3rd Armored and 9th Divisions. They burst across the Marne, snatching Mimeux and continue pursuit of the Germans who are moving rapidly. In the **U.S. Third Army** area, the race for Rheims is on, full steam ahead; the leading 7th Armored advances to the Marne at Chateau-Thierry seizing it. Following close behind are the 5th and 90th Divisions. In the **VIII Corps** area, the Germans holding Brest are completely surrounded. In the **VII Corps** area, Combat Command A, 4th Armored Division, spearheads an attack toward Chalons-sur-Marne; the 80th Division, also in the Troyes area, trails right behind the Armor. In conjunction, the 35th Division, operating on the south flank of Army, protects the area stretching between Troyes and Orleans. **(Southern France)** In the **U.S. Seventh Army's VI Corps** area, the fighting is intense, but the momentum is with the Yanks; the 36th Division restrings the line at Roubion and the 3rd Division, charging from the south at a rapid pace, moves into position to launch an attack against Montelimar. The Germans are getting whacked, but still defiantly try to forestall the inevitable. In one instance, elements of the 143rd Infantry spearheading a drive, hit ferocious small arms fire; followed by many tossed grenades. Tech Sergeant (later 2nd Lt.) Stephen R. Gregg, light machine gun on his hip, charges with his gun blazing, allowing enough cover fire to rescue seven wounded. Gregg, after expending all his ammunition is surrounded by four Germans; instantly, his comrades spot his predicament and begin firing, prompting the Germans to hit the deck; Gregg grabs a machine pistol and escapes. The adventure continues with Gregg killing one of his captors and wounding another, fully confusing the enemy. On the following morning at about daybreak, a German Tank supported attack is mounted and Gregg is in the thick of the battle all day, directing about 600 rounds of mortar fire upon the enemy; later, he is informed that the Germans have captured his mortar sector; infuriated, the New Yorker takes two men to give him cover fire; Gregg advances, tosses a grenade that kills one German, wounds two, and takes the last two prisoners; Gregg receives the Medal of Honor. At Highway 7, Task Force Butler reaches La Coucorde; although unable to establish a roadblock, it receives help from Artillery. The big guns pour devastating fire upon the enemy Armor turning it into an instant pile of rubble; the German Armor becomes a U.S. roadblock. Also, enemy Armor columns moving near Montelimar-Livron are thumped by Aircraft and Artillery, inflicting huge amounts of casualties and massive losses of equipment. The 45th Division, driving from Grenoble toward Lyon, seizes Bourgoin with its 179th Infantry. The Germans also find a lot of Frenchmen on their tails; at Marseille, Fort St. Nicolas capitulates, but some sporadic opposition continues. At Toulon, the French still are clearing the town, but the end is at hand. A massive Artillery bombardment of the San Mandrier Peninsula ceases at 17:45, having served its purpose; convincing the Germans to surrender, effective on the 28th; during the evening hours, the Germans ask for a meeting to discuss surrender. Meanwhile, the Germans attempt to escape, but the Allies set traps to cut off the routes. **(Atlantic-Eastern Europe)** Galati, Rumania, the primary port city on the Danube is taken by the Third Ukrainian Front.

Focsani is seized by the Second Ukrainian Front as the Russians advance to Ploesti.

U.S. troops during the victory parade in Paris; note the U.S. troops are actually marching toward the next battle line.

August 28th 1944 — (United States) Admiral Leahy, Chairman of Joint Chiefs of Staff, is informed by the State Department that French General Giraud had been shot by an Arab assassin at Mazagan Morocco, but that the wound had not been fatal. Mr. Robert Murphy (Ike's chief civilian adviser in North Africa) reports that sources pin the attempt to "the war cabinet of the French committee of liberation," but the report is unconfirmed. **(Pacific-Japan-Kurile Islands)** U.S. Army Planes sink the Japanese Submarine Chaser No. 77 off the Kurile Islands. **(Atlantic-France)** In the **U.S. First Army** area, **V Corps** sector, American General Gerow informs the Military Governor of Paris by letter, that the French 2nd Armored is now in charge of Paris. The U.S. 4th Division continues its attack northeast of Paris. In other activity, the 5th Armored and 28th Infantry Divisions are attached to the V Corps. In the **XV Corps** sector, breakout preparations are made. The 2nd Armored, now attached to Corps, leads the attack after sliding through the 79th Division's positions. In the **U.S. Third Army** area the **VIII Corps** is relentlessly lambasting the defenders at Brest. In the **XII Corps** area, the 80th Division and Combat Command A, 4th Armored Division, drive toward the Marne at Chalons-sur-Marne and Vitry-le-Francois. Also, General Bradley meets with General Patton and there are some restrained conversations concerning Patton continuing the drive to the Meuse, but Bradley does consent. **(Southern France)** The **U.S. Seventh Army** prepares another trap to catch the Germans before they escape to the Belfort Gap. In other activity, the **VI Corps** drives north, to make contact with the Allies in northern France and cut the Germans off at the Rhine before they can reach Germany. In other **VI Corps** activity, heavy fighting ensues at Montelimar. The 36th Division captures hills to the north and northeast of the town while the 3rd Division reduces fierce rear-guard activity. The fighting is equally fierce at the Drone River in what is the final phase of the struggle for Montelimar. Livron, north of the Drome River is encircled by the 142nd Infantry, 36th Division, but the majority of the German Nineteenth Army escapes through the Montelimar trap, being chased relentlessly by Planes and bombarded by American Artillery fire which takes a high toll on the retreating enemy forces. In the **French Army B** sector, the enemy resistance at Toulon is totally reduced and with it comes the capitulation of the San Mandrier Peninsula to the 9th Colonial Division. In addition,

Marseille surrenders. The German Commanders at Toulon and Marseille are both captured. **(Atlantic-Italy)** In the **U.S. Fifth Army** area, British 13th Corps sector, elements of the 8th Indian Division initiate a night attack (28th-29th) and seize Tigliano. In the **British Eighth Army** area, the advance to the Gothic Line continues. The Polish 2nd Corps drives to the Arzilla River. **(Atlantic-Rumania)** Transylvania, Rumania is taken by the Second Ukrainian Front.

August 29th 1944 — (Pacific-Celebes) The U.S.S. *Jack* (SS-229) sinks the Japanese Minesweeper No. 28. **(Atlantic-France)** General Eisenhower orders the main effort of the assault to drive north. It is led by the British under Montgomery, with the U.S. First Army in support. The Third Army under Patton is not utilized to its greatest advantage. Montgomery gets priority on supplies and gasoline, then comes the First Army. Patton's Third Army does receive alleged air priority for gasoline delivery. According to General Patton, this is to become one of the critical days of the war. He is of the opinion that historians will write frequently about it in the years to come. He feels that there is no one to stop his advance if given the okay, stating " THERE WAS NO REAL THREAT AGAINST US AS LONG AS WE DID NOT ALLOW OURSELVES TO BE STOPPED BY IMAGINARY ENEMIES." Today, Patton is scheduled to receive 140,000 gallons of gasoline for his Army, but it does not arrive, due to plan changes by the high command; Patton attributes it to "being implemented by General Montgomery." In the **21st Army Group**, elements of the 12th Corps cross the Seine River and in the 30th Corps area, the 11th Armored and contingents of the 8th Armored Brigade spearhead the drive to the Somme. **12th Army Group** In the **U.S. First Army** area, the 2nd Armored Division drives to Magny en Vexin, while the 30th Division pushes to Wy-dit-Joli-Village-Saillancourt. The **V Corps** leaves Paris driving northeast. French General DeGaulle requests a demonstration of Allied Force in Paris. The U.S. mounts a parade and gets blasted by the British press. Unknown to the citizens and to the British press, the 28th Division marches to placate DeGaulle and keeps moving right through the city toward its next battle, regaining the offensive immediately. The British press doesn't often blast the Allies, but frequently the media including the newsreels are often prodded to "PLAY UP THE BRITISH AND MENTION THE AMERICANS." In the **U.S. Third Army** area, with the permission of Eisenhower, the attack against the Meuse is maintained. In the **XX Corps** sector, Reims is captured by the 5th Division. In the **XII Corps** area, Combat Command A, 4th Armored Division overpowers the enemy defenders at Chalons-sur-Marne and duplicates the performance at Vitry-le-Francois. At Vitry, the engagement is action packed, with the daring 4th Armored charging with all guns blazing; having advance information from a French civilian, it is aware of four 88's perched side by side at the far side of a bridge on the causeway approach. The Tanks drive ferociously; troops begin tossing grenades at the Germans in synchronization with the attacking Armor. In a flash of gunfire and roaring Tank fire, the bridge is taken and the 88s are knocked into the ditches. In the **VIII Corps** area, vicious fighting continues against the hardened resistance at Brest. During one brutalizing incident, Sergeant John J. McVeigh, 23rd Infantry, 2nd Division, becomes another heroic but dead American for the liberation of France; a sudden enemy counterattack strikes his Platoon just as it readies its defenses, prompting McVeigh to stand erect in absolute defiance of enemy fire, signaling to his men where to return fire until the enemy is just about on top

of him. McVeigh, armed with his trench knife attacks and kills one German and continues toward the next three, but is struck at point blank range; however, his gallant actions allow the remainder of his Squad to eliminate the remaining three enemy troops and in essence his Squad is basically responsible for turning back the assault. McVeigh receives the Medal of Honor posthumously. **(Southern France)** In the **U.S. Seventh Army** area, the 1st Airborne Task Force, deployed on the Mediterranean coast, starts moving across the Var River. In the **VI Corps** sector, the 3rd and 36th Divisions eliminate the resistance at Highway 7 in the vicinity of Livron and Loriol. Some rear guard actions still ensue. In other activity U.S. Marines attached to the U.S.S. *Augusta* and the *Philadelphia*, debark at the islands of Ifs and Ratonneau, in Marseille Harbor; they accept the surrender of all German troops on the islands and stay ashore to disarm the Garrisons. **(Atlantic-Italy)** In the **U.S. Fifth Army** area, British 13th Corps sector, the British 6th Armored Division advances to Consuma at Highway 70. In the **British Eighth Army** area, the Polish 2nd Corps is engaged at Pesaro on the Adriatic Coast. The Canadian 1st and British Fifth Corps drive to the Foglia River; the Germans attempt to rush in reinforcements to halt the advance. As the British 10th Corps advances, elements moving along Route 71 discover the enemy has withdrawn from Bibbiena. **(China-Burma-India)** The Japanese 11th Army departs Heng-yang, heading south by rail toward the U.S. Fourteenth Air Force Bases at Kweilin and Liuchow.

August 30th 1944 — (Southwest Pacific Area) The U.S. 81st Division initiates its final practice maneuvers for the Palaus invasion. The rehearsals take place in Guadalcanal. **(Pacific-Philippines)** Additional men and supplies are put ashore by the U.S.S. *Narwhal* at Luzon. **(Atlantic-France)** In the **21st Army Group**, the **Canadian First Army's** British 1st Corps starts to cross the Seine River. In the 2nd Corps area, the British 2nd Division crosses the Seine reaching the bridgehead, subsequent to clearing the west bank of enemy resistance. The British 3rd Division secures Rouen without incident. In the **British Second Army** area, the 12th Corps drives 25 miles, reaching Gournay with forward elements. **12th Army Group** In the **U.S. First Army** area, the **XIX Corps** drives against nominal resistance, having some elements advance to within 10 miles of Beauvis; the U.S. 2nd Armored spearheads this northeastward drive. In the **V Corps** area, the Germans are retreating north with Corps in pursuit; as it drives through the friendly positions of the French 2nd Armored, it pulls abreast of the U.S. 4th Division, then the 2nd U.S. Armored leads the attack toward Compiegne. In the **VII Corps** area, Laon falls to the Yanks. **12th Army Group** In the **U.S. Third Army** area, the remaining enemy resistance on the Daoulas Peninsula, south of Brest, is eliminated by Task Force B. In other activity, General Patton, greatly alarmed by lack of adequate gasoline supplies to ensure the safety of his men and allow a speedy advance, meets with Generals Bradley, H.R. Bull (Ike's G-3) and Allen (Bradley's Chief of Staff). Patton pleads for permission to drive east to sever the Siegfried Line before the Germans can set up a defense. His request bears neither fruit nor gasoline; it is heading north with the British and the U.S. First Army (in support of the British drive). Patton subsequently notes: "IT WAS MY OPINION THEN THAT THIS WAS THE MOMENTOUS ERROR OF THE WAR. SO FAR AS THE THIRD ARMY (U.S.), WE NOT ONLY FAILED TO GET THE BACK GAS DUE US, BUT GOT PRACTICALLY NO MORE, BECAUSE, IN CONSUANCE WITH THE DRIVE TO MOVE NORTH, IN WHICH TWO CORPS OF THE FIRST ARMY (U.S.) ALSO PARTICIPATED, ALL SUPPLIES-BOTH GASOLINE

AND AMMUNITION-HAD TO BE THROWN IN THAT DIRECTION." In addition, other necessary supplies required to sustain the Third Army by Air are being sent to Paris to feed the French. Patton is also informed that British 21st Army Group is to receive an Air drop. In yet other activity, General Eddy's Armor had expended its gasoline and requested and was granted permission to halt at St. Dizier. However, Patton directs him to advance his command until it runs out of gas and then to begin walking to ensure a crossing at the Meuse. **(Southern France)** In the **U.S. Seventh Army** area, the 1st Airborne Task Force operating on the Mediterranean coast, meets no opposition as it zooms through Nice, reaching Beaulieu. In the **VI Corps** area, the 1st Battalion, 143rd Infantry, 36th Division finishes eliminating opposition at Montelimar, reaching the junction of the Drome and Rhone Rivers. With the culmination of its mission, Task Force Butler is disbanded. The VI Corps sets its sights upon Lyon, which is also threatened by the U.S. 36th Division, driving up the east bank of the Rhone. French troops are also closing on Lyon, advancing along the west bank of the Rhone. French resistance fighters in Lyon await the Allies to assist them. Nimes and Montpellier are seized by elements of the French 2nd Armored. **(Atlantic-Rumania)** The oil fields of Ploesti have been virtually leveled by U.S. Planes. Today Russian troops occupy Ploesti.

August 31st 1944 — (United States) The Commandant of the U.S. Marine Corps orders the abolishment of the Administrative Command and orders the establishment of Fleet Marine Force Pacific. **(Pacific)** A U.S. Carrier Task Force, commanded by Rear Admiral R.E. Davison, begins a three day bombardment of Iwo Jima and the Bonin Islands. On the following day, continuing into the 2nd of September, Destroyers and Cruisers move into the area to bolster the Aircraft and add more punch to the assault. **(Pacific-New Guinea)** The campaign to seize Noemfoor is declared terminated by General Krueger. Task Force Cyclone has sustained 63 dead, 343 wounded and three missing. The Japanese have lost about 1,730 killed and 186 captured. The operation in Sansapor is also declared to be at an end, the results of which have cost Task Force Typhoon, 14 dead and 35 wounded, in addition to having nine injured. Japanese losses stand at approximately 385 dead and 215 captured (including Formosans). **(Pacific-Philippines)** The U.S.S. *Redfin* (SS-272) surfaces off Palawan Island, Philippines and evacuates personnel. In other Submarine activity, the *Sealion* (SS-315) sinks the Minelayer *Shirataka* in the Luzon Strait. **(Atlantic-France)** In the **21st Army Group**, **Canadian First Army** area, the British 1st Corps continues to cross the Seine River. The British 2nd Corps is driving eastward. Elements advance rapidly to Buchy and Forges. In the British Second Army area, 12th Corps sector, the British 7th Armored, followed closely by the British 4th Armored, drive speedily toward the Somme, advancing to the Poix-Aumale line. In the British 30th Corps area, the British 1st Armored drives into Amiens and seizes an undestroyed bridge across the Somme. In the **12th Army Group, U.S. First Army V Corps** area, the 5th Armored and 4th and 28th Divisions drive northeast with the 28th Division and Combat Command B, 5th Armored, advancing along the Oise River in the vicinity of Chantilly-Compiegne. Combat Command A, pushes to the Aisne River, west of Soissons and moves right through the U.S. 4th Division Lines; both move to Villers-Cotterets. In the **VII Corps** sector, the 1st Division (Big Red 1) strengthens its perimeter in both the Lyon and Soisson areas. In other VII Corps activity, the 9th Infantry and 3rd Armored Divisions continue to chase the retreating Germans, reaching the Montcornet-Rethel line. In the **XIX Corps** area the 2nd Armored Division pulls ahead of the 30th and 79th positions and takes positions northeast of Montdidier; the latter two Divisions deploy between Creil and Beauvais. In the **U.S. Third Army** area, intense enemy resistance at Brest prompts the **VIII Corps** to halt the assault and regroup momentarily, while awaiting more ammunition. In other activity, a strong bridgehead across the Meuse is established at Verdun. The 90th Division holds at Reims. The **XX Corps** is halted; its gasoline supplies have not arrived since the priority has shifted to the British drive, compelling it to await the next delivery. By the following day, the bulk of Patton's Third Army will be nearly out of gasoline. General Patton requests 400,000 gallons, but receives only 30,000 gallons when the delivery arrives. He says to Bradley: "BRAD, JUST GIVE ME 400,000 GALLONS OF GASOLINE AND I'LL PUT YOU INSIDE GERMANY IN TWO DAYS." The Planes scheduled to deliver the gasoline, are flying over Tournai, dropping Paratroopers. During the following week, the absence of Planes cost Patton's Third Army almost a million and a half gallons of gasoline. **(Southern France)** In the **U.S. Seventh Army** area, Task Force Bibo occupies Briancon without incident. **(Atlantic-Italy)** In the **U.S. Fifth Army** area, the Germans are retreating. General Clark orders the Fifth Army to pursue. In the **IV orps** area, small contingents cross the Arno River to prepare for the primary crossing. In the British 13th Corps area, elements seize M. Muscoli and another contingent takes M. il Pratone. In the **British Eighth Army** area, heavy fighting continues at Pesaro where the Polish 2nd Corps is battling to secure the town. In other activity, contingents of the Canadian 1st Corps and the British 5 Corps penetrate the Gothic Line. **(Atlantic-Rumania)** The Russians seize Bucharest, the capital of Rumania.

September 1st 1944 — (Pacific-Marianas) The U.S. Navy establishes a Naval Operating Base at Saipan. On Guam, Island Command assumes control of all forces remaining on the island. **(Pacific-New Guinea)** RCT 123 (attached 33rd Division) lands at Maffin Bay with orders to protect the 31st Division, which is staging for the invasion of Morotai Island. **(Pacific-Philippines)** The U.S. Submarine *Narwhal* (SS-167) lands personnel and equipment on the east coast of Luzon. **(Atlantic-England)** The British Chiefs of Staff suggest an Airborne and Amphibious attack against Rangoon; the operation is coded (DRACULA). **(Atlantic-France-Northern Group of Armies)** 21st Army Group (Northern Group of Armies), the British 1st Corps has elements driving toward Le Havre and other Corps contingents are pushing against St. Valery-en-Caux. In the 2nd Corps area, the British 2nd Division seizes Dieppe and within a week, its port becomes operational (The British had suffered a tremendous defeat at Dieppe on August 17th 1942). Other elements drive toward the Somme. In the **British Second Army** area, 12th Corps sector, the 7th Armored crosses the Somme near Airaines. In the 30th Corps area, Corps makes fast progress as contingents drive northeast. **(France-Central Group of Armies)** 12th Army Group no longer under the command of British General Montgomery, reverts to Supreme Headquarters Allied Expeditionary Force. In the **U.S. First Army** area, **V Corps** sector, contingents close on St. Quentin; elements reach Chauny. In the **VII Corps** sector, a pivoting maneuver is initiated as contingents driving northeast swing north. Combat Command B, 3rd Armored, sprints through Vervins, driving to La Capelle in synchronization with Combat Command A, and the 9th Division, which push into the vicinity of Etreaupont-Aubenton. Voyenne, on the left flank of the Corps is reached by the First Division. In the **XIX Corps** area, the 2nd Armored, supported by Infantry, advances to positions northwest of Cambrai. In the **U.S. Third Army** area, the Germans take advantage of Third Army immobilization and fortify their positions behind the West Wall. In the **VIII Corps** area, there is minor activity at Brest, including bombardment by Planes, however, a major thrust to dislodge the Germans is awaiting ammunition replenishment; the Third Army is at Verdun, about 300 miles from Cherbourg, but it has an innovative group of Corps Commanders. In the **XII Corps** sector the bridgehead at Commercy is expanded by Combat Command A, 4th Armored Division. Combat Command B crosses the Meuse south of Commercy. In the **XX Corps** sector, the 3rd Cavalry Group utilizes captured gasoline and probes toward the Moselle River. The 7th Armored advances on gasoline fumes, driving to Etain along the Verdun-Metz Highway and on the following day it feints to the north, running out of gas prior to reaching Sedan. Patton's 7th Armored is recalled on the 3rd, but stalls due to lack of gasoline. In the **British Second Army** area, 12th Corps sector, the 7th Armored crosses the Somme near Airaines. Elements of the British 30th Corps advance to St. Pol-Arras road. **(Southern France-Southern Group of Armies)** In the **U.S. Seventh Army** area, enemy-held Lyon is threatened; contingents of the 36th Division reach the heights commanding it; in conjunction, the 3rd Division and elements of the 45th Division are also closing. The 179th Infantry, 45th Division, remains behind to protect Meximieux. The Germans mount a fierce attack to annihilate the 179th Regiment, but to no avail. French resistance troops are dispatched to assist the isolated Yanks and by the following day, the 179th restores control, inflicting heavy casualties against the enemy. The Americans subsequently hold their positions, letting French troops enter Lyon. In the **French Army B** area, the 2nd Corps moves toward Lyon, seizing Serrieres and Firminy. In Naval activity, the American Minesweeper YMS-21 sinks after striking a mine off the coast of Southern France. **(Atlantic-Italy)** In the **U.S. Fifth Army** area, the enemy is retreating across the Arno with the **V Corps** in pursuit. The 1st Armored, spearheading the chase, gets Combat Command A, to M. Pisano, while Combat Command B drives toward Altopascio. Task Force 45 gets the 100th Battalion (Nisei-Japanese Americans) across the Arno east of Pisa. During the duration of the war, this Infantry Battalion comprised of Japanese Americans receives 7 Presidential citations, while participating in seven major European campaigns; it sustains 9,486 casualties and in addition, receives 18,143 individual decorations becoming the highest decorated outfit in the Army. In other **IV Corps** activity, the South African 6th Armored makes a mid-afternoon crossing of the Arno and drives toward M. Albano. In the **British Eighth Army** area, the Canadian 1st Corps and the British 5 Corps drive through the primary defenses of the Gothic Line, striking M. Gridolfo and Tomba di Pesaro, which controls the Foglia River Valley. In other activity the Germans raise staunch resistance on the eastern slopes of Pozzo Alto. **(Atlantic-Balkans)** German Army Group F begins to withdraw from Greece and also from the islands in the Agean and Ionian Seas, using the rails through Yugoslavia, but this route of escape becomes too dangerous, thanks to the Planes of the R.A.F. and the U.S. Fifteenth Air Force, which pummel the enemy. The Germans revert to the Airfields at Athens, but before the end of September, the Fifteenth Air Force lambastes and completely devastates its three Airfields.

September 2nd 1944 — (Pacific-New Guinea) General Krueger declares the Wakde-Sarmi operation over. Brigadier General Donald J. Meyers relieves General Persons as the Commanding Officer of Task Force Tornado. In other activity, a C-47 becomes the first Plane to land at the Mar Airdrome at Vogelkop. At Noemfoor, Construction troops complete another 7,000 foot Airstrip at Kornasoren. **(Pacific-Bonin Islands-Chi Chi Jima)** Aircraft, including VT-51, under Commander Doug Melvin, from U.S. Carriers again strike Japanese targets in the Bonins. Heavy enemy anti-aircraft fire is encountered by the attacking Planes. The Plane (dubbed *Barbara*, piloted by George Bush (later President of the U.S.), is hit by enemy fire as it attacks radio broadcast stations on Chi Chi Jima, but the mission is carried out. Bush instructs his crew to bail out over the water as they head back to the *U.S.S. San Jacinto* (CVL-30) (flies the Texas flag into battle); both other crew men, John Delaney and Ted White are lost. Japanese craft attempt to capture Bush, but friendly Aircraft drive them away; at about 12:00, circling Hellcat Fighters are relieved as the Submarine U.S.S. *Finback* surfaces and picks up George Bush who is happy that his 50th combat mission was not his last. The *Finback* picks up additional Pilots during the attacks and gets them back to Pearl Harbor on October 30th. Lt. Bush (20 years old) then heads for Admiral Halsey's Fleet and resumes his duties as a Fighter Pilot; he flies his last mission (59th) on November 29th 1944 over Luzon, Philippines. **(Atlantic-France-Belgium)** General Eisenhower details plans for the drive to the Siegfried Line, to commence as soon as supplies can be ascertained by Third Army; Eisenhower has been convinced by his thoughts of a great battle in Germany, during his discussions with Bradley, Hodges and Patton; Ike's final determination is to allow the Third Army to secure crossings at the Moselle. Patton informs Eisenhower that the Third Army is presently patrolling along the Moselle near Nancy and that contingents of the 3rd Cavalry had entered Metz. The V Corps, (First Army) will participate in the assault. In the **British 21st Army Group** area, elements of the Canadian First Army drive toward the port on the Le Havre Peninsula, reaching enemy outposts. St. Valery-en-Caux falls to the British 51st Division. In the **British Second Army**, 12th Corps area, the British 7th Armored drives northeast, advancing beyond St. Pol. In the 30th Corps area, the advance makes such progress that the anticipated Airdrop at Tournai becomes unnecessary. The British 11th Armored reaches the vicinity of Lille and the Guards Armored Division advances to Tournai. **12th Army Group** In the **U.S. First Army** area, the **VII Corps** commanded by General Collins rolls across the Belgium border driving toward Brussels through Mons. Upon its approach to Mons, the Yanks get an unexpected surprise and intercept 20 retreating German Divisions which are making a run for Germany; A spontaneous battle erupts with the fury of an active volcano. The swastika rams the Stars and Stripes in a fierce but futile contest; when the confrontation ceases, enormous and irretrievable losses are incurred by the German Seventh and Fifteenth Armies, preventing many of them from defending the Siegfried Line. The donnybrook drains the resolve of the Germans; Collins' Yanks seize 30,000 prisoners while killing 2,000. First Army is poised to roll straight into Aachen. Also, Tank contingents attached to 3rd Armored, are on the fringes of Tournai, but the town is in the British sector; General Hodges receives instructions to seize the city. General Bradley had previously informed Eisenhower that the Airdrop was unnecessary and that the Yanks would be on the scene to greet the Paratroops. Bad weather stalls the Airdrop, but does not deter British General

Montgomery's complaining to Bradley that U.S. troops are blocking the road intended for moving the British to Brussels. The **XIX Corps** pushes advance elements into Belgium; they move against Tournai. In the **U.S. Third Army** area, the assault against Brest continues, although literally out of gas. The 2nd Division charges on foot, seizing Hill 105, which commands the eastern approach to the city. The fighting is also vicious at Hills 80 and 103, which are under siege by the 8th and 29th Divisions respectively. Ile de Cezembre capitulates to units of the 83rd Division. In the **XII Corps** area, elements patrol to the Moselle River, using captured gas, but they have not captured sufficient quantities and will stall. **(Southern France)** In the **U.S. Seventh Army** area, the 1st Airborne Task Force, in pursuit of the elusive enemy, destroys a stronghold at La Turbia. In other activity the French 2nd Moroccan Division relieves Task Force Bibo at Briancon. The French are assigned to protect the right flank of the U.S. Seventh Army. In the **VI Corps** area, the U.S. 36th Division drives east and northeast of Lyon, then stands in place, dispatching Patrols that report the city clear. The French 2nd Armored moves up and takes Lyon. In the **French Army B** sector, Lt. General Aime de Goislard de Monsabert assumes command of the French 2nd Corps. **(Atlantic-Italy)** In the **U.S. Fifth Army** area, Task Force 45 (IV Corps) is on the advance; its 100th Battalion gets contingents across the Arno; they secure the northern part of Pisa, while other contingents reach the Serchio River. M. Pisano is besieged by Combat Command A, 1st Armored, which secures most of it. In other activity the South African 6th Armored Division secures the slopes of M. Albano. In the **II Corps** sector, RCT 442, 88th Division, encounters troops of the British 1st Division, 13th Corps at Sesto. The British 13th Corps is heavily engaged in the hills north of Florence against stiff enemy resistance. In the **British Eighth Army** area, the British are making great progress as the enemy is withdrawing from the area; elements race to the Conca River and secure a bridgehead. In addition, the Polish 2 Corps takes Pesaro and because of the enemy evacuation, the Corps stretches its positions along the coast to Castel di Mezzo. **(Atlantic-Mediterranean)** British General Sir Henry Maitland Wilson, Supreme Allied Commander Mediterranean, appoints British Lt. General R. M. Scobie, Commander Land Forces, Greece. It is known as Force 140 and comprises British and Greek forces, including local police. The Force is further fortified with Air and Naval contingents. The primary mission is to secure Athens and vicinity and restore law and order, setting the stage for returning the Greek Government. U.S. General Percy L. Sadler is Deputy Commander of Allied Military Liaison Headquarters, Greece and is responsible for relief items.

Generals Patton, Bradley and Hodges (right to left).

September 3rd 1944 — (Pacific-New Guinea) MacArthur's quest to retake the Philippines nears. The strategic plan for the invasion of Moratai Island, situated close to the Philippines is complete. In other activity in New Guinea, the Mar Airdrome at Vogelkop is operational for use by Bombers. **(Pacific-Wake Island)** A U.S. Naval Task Force, commanded by Rear Admiral A.E. Smith, comprising a Carrier, three Cruisers and three Destroyers, bombards enemy positions on Wake Island. **(Atlantic-France)** In the British **21st Army Group** area, General Montgomery directs the **British Second Army** to make an expeditious drive to the Rhine River and to secure a bridgehead crossing. He instructs the Canadian First Army to secure the coastal region in its sector of northern France. The British Second Army moves its 7th Armored (12th Corps) northeast to Lillers during the advance to Ghent, while the 30th Corps moves across the border into Belgium. The Guards Armored Division pushes to Brussels and sets up roadblocks to cut off escape from the city. The British 11th Armored, pressing against Antwerp, becomes engaged in a savage contest in the Lille-Tournai vicinity; it reaches positions east of Alost. In the **Canadian First Army** area, Le Havre is threatened as last minute details are completed for a major assault against the city and port. In the 2 Corps area the 4th Armored Division sets up a bridgehead across the Somme near Pont Remy. In the **U.S. 12th Army Group First Army** area, the **XIX Corps** maintains its positions at Tournai, keeping an enemy pocket of resistance southwest of Mons neutralized. The **V Corps** is directed to dash to the Meuse and the **VII Corps** is feverishly involved at Mons, Belgium, seizing the city with the 3rd Armored. The Big Red One is poised perfectly to squeeze an undisciplined, yet large enemy pocket in the Mons — Bavai-Foret de Mormal vicinity. In the **U.S. Third Army** area, Patton arrives at Ligny-en-Barrois (XII Corps); he confers with General Eddy and discovers that the XII Corps has captured 100,000 gallons of aviation gasoline and 600,000 pounds of meat. Patton also stops to see Colonel Bruce Clark, 4th Armored Commander in his sector to receive an update on his progress. In the **XX Corps** area, the Tanks that have advanced toward Sedan with captured gasoline are ordered to return, but they are out of gas and must stay in place until gas can be brought up to them. Patton notes that rumors have persisted that members of his Third Army had impersonated First Army personnel and been able to receive gasoline allotments from First Army Depots. Patton states that "OFFICIALLY I HOPED IT WAS UNTRUE." Patton also lists Third Army casualties (end of fourth week): 2,678 dead; 12,756 wounded; 2,474 missing and in addition 6,912 non-battle casualties for a total of 24,820. Patton's Third Army estimate of German casualties: 19,000 dead; 62,000 wounded; and 73,000 prisoners of war. Equipment casualties, Third Army: 94 Light Tanks; 223 Medium Tanks; 83 pieces of Artillery. Germans: 402 Medium Tanks; 247 Panzer and Tiger Tanks and 1,236 pieces of Artillery. **(Southern France)** In the **U.S. Seventh Army** area, the French conquest of Lyon terminates its original mission, but the **VI Corps** is directed to continue pursuing the retreating Germans to the Belfort Gap. The 36th Division drives toward Macon; the 117th Cavalry Reconnaissance Squadron drives to Bourg-en-Bresse and Montrevel and runs into the Germans who are attempting to escape from Meximieux. The Germans mount a strong armor-supported counterattack against the slim defenses of Montrevel. During the vicious confrontation to wrestle the town from the Yanks, Lieutenant Daniel W. Lee, Troop A, 117th Reconnaissance Squadron, organizes a Patrol to eliminate deadly mortar fire, which is pouring upon his troops. Lee singlehandedly advances to a position within 30 yards of the mortars and withering fire; despite being severely wounded and bleeding profusely, he refuses to stop, advancing further and killing five of seven enemy troops at the mortar positions before he is fired upon by an Armored Vehicle. Undaunted by the newest enemy threat, Lee confiscates an enemy Panzerfaust (rocket launcher) which equalizes the odds; the Germans retire. Assured the slope is clear, Lee returns to his lines and receives necessary medical attention; he receives the Medal of Honor. Both sides sustain heavy losses. In the **French Army B** area, the French 2nd Corps seizes Villefranche, north of Lyon. as it advances to hook up with the Allied Forces which had landed at Normandy. In Naval activity, the Submarine Chaser SC-535 is lost to a violent storm off the coast of Southern France. **(Atlantic-Italy)** In the **British Eighth Army** area, the 5th Corps secures a small bridgehead across the Conca River in the Morciano vicinity, while the Canadian I Corps keeps moving north, its 5th Armored secures Misano.

September 4th 1944 — (Pacific-New Guinea) Task Force Tradewind is at Aitape practicing for the Moratai invasion (dubbed INTERLUDE). **(China-Burma-India)** U.S. Major General Patrick Hurley and Mr. Donald Nelson arrive in India. General Hurley will subsequently recommend that General Stilwell be replaced as Commander of Chinese Army (on the 13th of October). In the **11th Army Group**, British General Slim, Commander British Fourteenth Army, informs the British 4th and 33rd Corps that a major offensive across the Chindwin will be launched by them during December. The British 15th Corps is to neutralize the enemy on the Arakan Front. In other activity, Sittaung is seized by the East African 11th Division without incident. **(Pacific-Solomons)** The Marine III Corps begins embarking from the Solomons, for the Palaus Islands, Carolines. Subsequently, other Vessels of the Convoy depart; the invasion takes place on the 15th of September. **(Atlantic-Western Europe)** General Eisenhower orders the 21st Army Group and the U.S. First Army to attack toward the Ruhr River and he orders the U.S. Third Army to head for the Saar. In other activity, Hitler reappoints von Runstedt as Commander in Chief West (O.B. West). In the **21st Army Group** area, **Canadian First Army** sector, elements of the 2nd Corps stay in place along the Somme near Pont Remy, while the Polish 1st Armored heads toward St. Omer. In the **British Second Army** area, the British 2nd Armored (12 Corps) bypasses the Germans in the vicinity of Bethune-Lille and continues to move against Ghent. The British 53rd Division and 4th Armored Brigade stays behind to mop up. In the **U.S. 12th Army Group**, **First U.S. Army** area, elements of the XIX Corps and the 1st Division (VII Corps) persist in eliminating the enemy pocket at Mons. During the heated exchange, the Germans mount a heavy and superior numbered attack against the 1st Division positions at Sars la Bruyere, Belgium; one Company of the 18th Infantry is driven back by the power of the enemy thrust; a machine gun position manned by 10 men feels the brunt of the assault as they attempt to cover the withdrawal. Withering fire penetrates the position killing the assistant gunner. The Germans overrun the position capturing nine Yanks, however, Private First Class Gino J. Merli lies prone, next to his dead friend and fools the Germans. They depart and the spirited Merli pours fire into the enemy. The enemy returns to the position, but finds the same two dead bodies and departs thinking they had run off the new intruders; the Germans leave the machine gun in operation. Merli, the magician, continues to pop shells into the enemy during the night and during the following morning when the Amer-

ican launch their counterattack, the Germans request a truce to surrender. When the Americans reach the seemingly lost machine gun position, Merli is still at his gun and on the battlefield are 52 enemy dead, 19 of whom are directly in front of Merli. P.F.C. Merli receives the Medal of Honor for his gallantry. In other **VII Corps** activity, the 79th Division is attached to Patton's Third Army; the 3rd Armored and 9th Infantry Divisions drive east to the Meuse, arriving in the vicinity of Namur-Dinant. In the **U.S. Third Army** area the **XII Corps** attacks to outflank the enemy at Nancy; the 317th Infantry, 80th Division, sends a fortified Reconnaissance Patrol; it hits the Moselle north of Nancy, near Pont a Mousson, where it discovers several crossing sites. Elements of Combat Command A, 4th Armored Division, drive toward Marbache; in addition, contingents of the 80th U.S. Division ford the Moselle and establish a bridgehead on the eastern bank near Toul. **(Southern France)** In the **U.S. Seventh Army** area, **V Corps** sector, the U.S. 45th Division encounters heavy opposition outside of Bourg-en-Bresse, but eliminates it and seizes the objective. The V Corps then drives toward the Doubs River to strike against the strengthened enemy stronghold at Besancon. **(Atlantic-Finland)** A truce is agreed upon by Finland and the Russians; Finland had previously stopped advancing against the Russians after retaking lost ground and refusing to continue beyond it with the Germans. This decision in essence abandons the Germans who are fighting the Russians on this front. **(Atlantic-Italy)** In the **U.S. Fifth Army** area, final attack orders are issued concerning the assault against the Gothic Line. The **II Corps** is ordered to secure hills Morello, Senario, Calvana and Giova, then it is to spring against the line at Il Giogo Pass (altering previous plans to attack Futa Pass) and bolt toward Firenzuola. In the **U.S. IV Corps** area, Combat Command A, 1st Armored Division, reaches the fringes of Lucca, while Combat Command B, encounters and thumps heavy opposition at Altopascio. The American II Corps is to attack by moving through a sector held by the British 13th Corps; it rolls in front of the British and deploys for the attack. However, the Germans pull out and the American assault becomes unnecessary. In the British 13th Corps area, orders are given to attack through Dicomano-Forli and through Borgo S. Lorenzo-Faenza. In the **British Eighth Army** area, 10th Corps sector, there is contact with the enemy's outer Gothic Line defenses. The British 5th Corps sector is active as the British 46th Division expands its Conca bridgehead against firm opposition near S. Clemente. The British 1st Armored deploys to take advantage quickly if the 46th manages to breakthrough. The British Armor initiates the battle to seize the southern portion of S. Savino-Coriano Ridge.

A Yank machinegunner. Illustration by Justin Grecescu.

433

September 5th 1944 — (Atlantic-Western Europe) 21st Army Group: In the **British Second Army** area, 12th Corps sector, Ghent is taken by the British 7th Armored. The Germans, although driven from the city, maintain strong positions on the outskirts, giving the British stiff opposition for a few more days. The British 30th Corps prepares to attack and will reorganize and consolidate its defensive positions. In the **Canadian First Army** 2nd Corps area, the 3rd Division, driving along the coast, reaches the vicinity of Calais after bypassing Boulogne. The Germans defend both of these objectives, each containing a port. In other activity, British General Montgomery arrives in Antwerp, but the clearing of the Scheldt to permit passage of Allied Ships does not occur for nine additional weeks. In the **U.S. 12th Army Group**, the **U.S. Ninth Army** becomes operational and assumes command of the sector and the troops of the VIII Corps, U.S. Third Army, positioned on the Brittany Peninsula. La Trinite, abandoned by the Germans, is occupied by the U.S. 29th Division. In the **U.S. First Army** area, the V Corps drives east, securing a crossing of the Meuse near Sedan by the 5th Armored. Combat Command R takes the crossing at Mohon while Combat Command A seizes the crossing at Bazeilles; both are closely followed by the 28th Division. In the **XIX Corps** area, the 2nd Armored, supplemented by the 113th Calvary Group, thrusts into Belgium, advancing to the Brussels-Gembloux line. In the **U.S. VII Corps** area, the Big Red 1 continues to weed out remaining German resistance in the Mons Pocket, simultaneously netting the 1st Division huge amounts of prisoners. The 9th Division roars across the Meuse, securing crossings to the north and south of Dinant, while the U.S. 3rd Armored prepares to drive against Liege. In the **U.S. Third Army** area, the XII Corps is ordered by Patton to seize Nancy and from there to be prepared to drive to the Rhine. The Germans mount heavy resistance and prevent the 317th Infantry, 80th Division from fording the Moselle at Pagny-sur-Moselle and at Blenod-Pont a Mousson. After dark, the 80th pushes out and after vicious fighting during the night of the 5th-6th, elements of the 317th Regiment cross at Pont a Mousson. In addition, the 318th Infantry, 80th Division assaults Hill 326 at Marbache. The 319th Infantry expands its Toul bridgehead and consumes Fort de Gondreville; however, the defenders at Fort de Villey-le-Sec hold. **(Southern France)** In the **U.S. Seventh Army** area, the **VI Corps** drives to Besancon, deploying near the city. The U.S. 36th Division is already positioned southwest of the objective. In other activity, the 45th Division drives northeast in concert with the 3rd Division which is moving due south to crush the Germans. **(Atlantic-Italy)** In the **U.S. Fifth Army** area, **IV Corps** sector, Lucca falls to the 1st Armored Division's Combat Command A. The South African 6th Armored secures a portion of M. Albano and is able to advance some contingents to Monsummano. The enormous amount of Allied pressure compels the Germans to evacuate their positions north of Florence. In the **British Eighth Army** area the Germans stiffen their resolve at the S. Savino-Coriano Ridge and halt the advance of the British 5 Corps and Canadian I Corps. Vicious fighting also stalls the Indian 4th Division at Pian di Castello, and the British 56th Division is receiving similar opposition at Croce-Gemmano. **(Atlantic-Russia)** The U.S.S.R. (Russia) declares war on Bulgaria.

September 6th 1944 — ((Pacific-Caroline Islands) Aircraft attached to Carriers (Third Fleet) assault enemy positions on the Palaus to soften resistance for the impending invasion (September 15th). The Volcano-Bonins and Yap and Ulithi are also struck. Previous Air assaults carried out by Land-based Bombers have greatly reduced enemy targets, but for three days the attack continues and will be supplemented by Naval bombardment by Cruisers and Destroyers of Admiral Mitscher's Fleet, which includes 16 Carriers. **(Pacific-New Guinea)** Practice maneuvers for the invasion of Moratai continue on the mainland east of Wakde Island. On Noemfoor, General McNider assumes command of Task Forces Cyclone and 158. **(China-Burma-India)** General Hurley and Mr. Donald Nelson arrive in Chungking, China. On the Salween Front, the Japanese Commander of Sung Shan dies. **(Atlantic-Western Europe) 21st Army Group** In the Canadian 2nd Corps **Canadian First Army** sector, the 2nd Division, moves through the Canadian 3rd Division in the vicinity of Calais. The Canadian 4th Armored drives toward the Ghent-Bruges Canal while the Polish 2nd Corps crosses the canal at St. Omer. **12th Army Group** In the **U.S. First Army XIX Corps** area, the 113th Cavalry Group and the U.S. 2nd Armored Division advance in strengthened Reconnaissance detachments to the Tirlemont-Namur line. In the **VII Corps** area, Huy is taken by the 3rd Armored Division as it plows forward along the Meuse. The 9th Infantry Division receives heavy resistance at its Meuse bridgeheads, but it fortifies its positions to repulse any further enemy threats. In other activity, the U.S. 1st Division drives east, but holds the 16th Infantry in place at Mons to eliminate final enemy resistance in the Mons pocket. The **V Corps** area is bristling with activity. The 4th Infantry drives on the left in conjunction with the 5th Armored Division which is lunging forward from the Meuse; the 4th Division reaches Bievre, and the 5th Armored overpowers the resistance at Sedan. In the **U.S. Third Army** area, at 03:00, the 7th Armored (XX Corps) commences the attack to force the Moselle. Four Armored columns drive to the river in search of crossings and to support the main assault force while simultaneously bolstering the 3rd Cavalry Group. The Germans mount intense resistance prior to the main attack which commences at 14:00. The 7th Armored elements grind forward to Ste Marie-aux-Chenes where Combat Command A is stalled by tough resistance; at Rezonville, Combat Command B encounters vicious opposition and is also stalled. Quick improvisation gets contingents to the canal between Arnaville and Noveant. In coordinated movement with the assaulting 7th Armored, the 90th Division forces the Meuse and deploys near Etain. In the **XII Corps** area, the Germans overpower the bridgehead held by the 3rd Battalion, 80th Division and in so doing compel the 317th Infantry to abort the attempt to cross the Moselle. In other activity, the 318th Infantry seizes Hill 326 at Marbache and also attacks the western portion of Foret de I' Avant Garde. The ensuing attack at Fort de Villey-le-Sec continues to crack the defenses, but the Germans do not relent and maintain control. The Germans in the vicinity of the Madon River line hit unexpected American fire as they attempt to escape. The 2nd Cavalry Group pounds the withdrawing enemy column, inflicting heavy losses. **(Southern France)** In the **U.S. Seventh Army** area, Chalon-sur-Saone falls to the French 2nd Corps. In the **VI Corps** area, the Germans mount stiff resistance that hinders the Corps' jump off. During the night of the 6th-7th, contingents of the 3rd Division seize Fort Fontain, cracking open a route to the outer defenses of Besancon. In other activity, the French 1st Corps becomes operational, commanded by General Emile Bethouart, with responsibility of operating on the right flank of the U.S. Seventh Army. **(Atlantic-Italy)** In the **U.S. Fifth Army** area, the **IV Corps** regroups, but simultaneously commits contingents that probe and grab extra terrain as the

Germans continue to retreat. The **II Corps** assumes responsibility for its new sector and takes temporary command of the British First Division and elements of the Indian 8th Division, British 13th Corps within its zone. In the **British Eighth Army** area, the British prepare a large attack against S. Savino-Coriano. Meanwhile the Canadian Corps dispatches Patrols to the Marano River.

September 7th 1944 — (United States) The Commandant of the United States Marines directs that his earlier letter of 31st August and attached chart be modified by the deletion of Fleet Marine Force, Air Pacific, and he states that the command status of the Air units will be forthcoming at a later date. **(Pacific Area Southwest)** General Eichelberger, Commanding Officer I Corps, assumes command of the U.S. Eighth Army. **(Pacific-New Guinea)** U.S. Naval Vessels arrive at the Schouten Islands, off the coast of New Guinea, and land U.S. Army troops at Soepiori Island. **(Pacific-Philippines)** The U.S.S. *Paddle* (SS-263), discovers a Convoy off Mindanao, and sinks the *Shinyo Maru*, a Cargo Vessel of over 2,000 tons; however, it is not known that the Ship contains U.S. P.O.W.s; about 500 Yanks are lost. Meanwhile, those able to get into the water are shot at by Japanese guards. As other enemy Vessels pick up Japanese survivors, the Americans are abandoned in the water. Over eighty Americans make it to shore, and with the assistance of Guerrillas, the U.S.S. *Narwhal* (SS-167) picks them up on the 22nd of September. **(China-Burma-India)** Chiang Kai-shek confers with Generals Stilwell and Hurley in Chungking. Kai-shek agrees to allow Stilwell to command all Chinese troops, but he requests a new Chinese Services of Supplies, staffed by Americans. Donald Nelson (Roosevelt's personal representative as requested by Kai-shek) is in attendance. On the Salween Front, the mop-up of Sung Shan is over, but the cost for this Burma Road strongpoint has been expensive. The Chinese have sustained 7,675 killed (majority of losses suffered by Chinese 8th Army) and the Japanese, numbered at approximately 2,000, have been annihilated. **(Atlantic-Bulgaria)** Bulgaria declares war against Germany. **(Atlantic-Western Europe) 21st Army Group** In the **British Second Army** area, unit changes take place, with the 12th Corps relieving contingents of the 30th Corps at Antwerp and Alost. The British 30th Corps moves to the Meuse-Escaut Canal. The Guards Armored Division departs Louvain, heading for Diest to secure a crossing over the Albert Canal, but the Germans have destroyed the bridges. The British 11th Armored Division scours the area north of Antwerp for a crossing, but finds none. On the following day, the British discover two crossings and ford the canal, but the Germans are deployed at both locations to offer stiff resistance. **12th Army Group** In the **U.S. First Army** area, **XIX Corps** sector, the 113th Cavalry Group advances to the Albert Canal en route to Holland. From Hasselt, near the canal, it advances on the following day to Maastricht, Holland. In the **VII Corps** area, the 3rd Armored Division pushes to Liege. At Dinant, the 9th Division completes mop-up operations and drives east. At Mons, mop-up is completed by the 1st Division. In the **V Corps** area, the lack of gasoline has the 5th Armored stalled, watching the 28th Division pass by as it moves to positions 15 miles east of Sedan. In the **U.S. Third Army** area, **XX Corps** sector, Combat Command A, 7th Armored Division, eliminates resistance at Ste Marie-aux-Chenes and at St. Privat, attacks toward Mondelange at the Moselle, and then drives south toward Hauconcort. In Combat Command B's sector, fierce enemy resistance drives some units back near Arnaville and Noveant. Additional elements

reach the river at Dornot, but the Germans bring fire upon them from both sides of the river. Combat Command R rushes to the scene to assist, but halts to allow passage of the 5th Division, which is attacking toward the Metz. The Germans mount opposition all along the front. Regimental Combat Team 2, 5th Division, is stopped near Amanvillers-Verneville; in other activity, RCT 11 drives to the heights west of the Moselle near Dornot. The 90th Division sees its 357th Infantry stalled at the fringes of Briey. In the **XII Corps** area, the 318th Infantry, 80th Division, seizes Hill 356 at Marbache and establishes outposts around the town during the night of the 7th, while the 319th Infantry pushes to the protective moat of Fort de Villey-le-Sec. A ring of enemy fire turns it back. In other activity, the 2nd Cavalry Group drives to the Madon River and seizes a bridge intact. **(Southern France)** In the **U.S. Seventh Army** area, **VI Corps** sector, the 3rd Division takes Besancon. During this heated battle, a German Platoon assaults a contingent of the 7th Infantry. Technician Fifth Grade Robert D. Maxwell and three other Soldiers, armed only with pistols, defend the Battalion observation post. With extreme calmness and gallant actions, Maxwell defies the enemy fire and inspires his detachment to continue the lopsided struggle. The Germans toss a grenade into their hole and Maxwell shields the other men by throwing his blanket and his body on the grenade, taking the full blast. He is permanently disabled; however, his extraordinary actions save the other men and allow the forward detachment to safely withdraw; Maxwell receives the Medal of Honor. In other activity, the 36th Division hits stiff resistance southwest of Besancon and is prevented from crossing the Doubs river; however, contingents of the 36th cross in the 3rd Division sector. In addition, the 45th Division bolts across the river near Baume-les-Dames. **(Atlantic-Italy)** In the **U.S. Fifth Army** area, the attack is imminent, but the enemy pulls out of its positions in the hills north and northeast of Florence and heads for the Gothic Line, abandoning Calvana, Giovi, Morello and Senario. In the **British Eighth Army** area, the British 4th Division, British 25th Tank Brigade and the Greek 3rd Mountain Brigade arrive to reinforce the area.

September 8th 1944 — (United States) The Joint Chiefs of Staff issue a directive to the Commander-in-Chief Southwest Pacific area and to the Commander-in-Chief Pacific, calling for the invasion of the Philippines. **(China-Burma-India)** General Hurley officially begins his new duties as President Roosevelt's representative to Chiang Kai-shek. General Stilwell reluctantly agrees to the War Department proposal to split CBI Theater Command, with Stilwell relinquishing lend-lease business (supplies coming in to the Chinese and being distributed thereof). Stilwell is to direct the Pacific Operations from China. Kai-shek suggests to Stilwell that the Chinese troops at Myitkyina be committed against the enemy at Lung-ling. On the Salween Front, reinforced Japanese units commence an attack against the Chinese positions to the north of Lung-ling. In China, the Japanese overrun Ling-ling, but the U.S. Fourteenth Air Force, anticipating the attack, has pulled out. The Japanese, attacking from the south, threaten Kweilin and Liuchow; the Japanese 23rd Army is driving north from Canton. **(Atlantic-England)** London is struck by the first of the newest line of Rockets in the German arsenal. These V-2s move swiftly and without warning; the R.A.F. cannot pursue and shoot them out of the sky. Allied bombing raids have stopped construction at the primary missile bases near Dunkirk, but the rockets are being launched from Dutch islands. The Germans also implement the V-2s against Antwerp until

April 5th 1945, with London remaining the primary target until March 27th 1945. **(Atlantic-Western Europe) 21st Army Group** In the **Canadian First Army** 2nd Corps sector, the 2nd Canadian Division attacks Dunkerque (Dunkirk), scene of the earlier massive British-French evacuation. Bruges is approached by the Canadian 4th Armored Division while Polish Armor drives to Thielt and to Dixmude. In the **British Second Army** area, the Germans resist viciously at the Albert Canal. The British 50th Division establishes a small bridgehead near Gheel. **12th Army Group** In the **U.S. First Army** area, the **XIX Corps** drives into Holland getting its 2nd Armored to the vicinity of Hasselt-St. Trond while the 30th Division is rumbling along on the right flank of the Corps. In the **VII Corps** area, 3rd Armored Division, reinforced by the 47th Regiment, 9th Division mops up in Liege while the remainder of the 9th Division continues driving eastward. The **V Corps** also attacks east, meeting opposition between Jemelle and Margut, where rear guard actions hit both the 4th and 28th Divisions. The Corps orders the capture of Koblentz, behind the West Wall. In the **U.S. Third Army** area, **XX Corps** sector, the 90th Division, deployed near Landres and Mairy, is struck by a German Armored assault. The 106th Panzer Brigade drives a wede between the 358th and 359th Infantry Regiments and threatens the Command Post, but the 90th Division meets the threat, giving the German Panzers a lot more than they expected. The assault becomes a lopsided engagement. The Germans are pounded and thumped, losing 30 Tanks, 60 Half-tracs, and about 100 other Vehicles, sending the survivors off in disarray. The Germans near the southern flank of the 90th Division at Briey, surrender to Combat Command A. The 7th Armored Division is heavily engaged near Talange. The 2nd Infantry, 5th Division (attached to 7th Armored) continues to press the defenders at Metz. Although the enemy opposition is fierce, the 2nd Infantry takes Verneville and drives to the fringes of Amanvillers. In the 5th Division sector, a fragile hold is grasped on the east bank of the Moselle near Dornot. Four Companies of the 11th Infantry and contingents of the 23rd Armored Infantry, 7th Armored Division (attached to 5th Division) drive across the river, but become pinned down on the small beachhead. This force repels several heavy counterattacks over the next couple of days but is unable to expand its ground. After determining that the position is untenable due to exhaustion and thinning numbers, it withdraws the night of the 10th. The 11th Infantry unsuccessfully drives against Fort Blaise; the 11th Infantry sustains high casualties. In the **XII Corps** area, the Germans counterattack and retake Marbache from the 80th Infantry. **(Southern France)** In the **U.S. Seventh Army** area, Menton, on the Mediterranean coast, is seized by contingents of the 1st Airborne Task Force; after securing it, the Airborne units drive to the Italian border. In the French 2nd Corps area, the 1st French Armored advances to Beaune. Autun is seized by the 1st French Division. In the **VI Corps** area, the 141st Infantry, 36th Division crosses the Doubs River behind the 143rd Infantry at Avanne; soon after, the highways west and northwest of Besancon are severed, threatening German escape routes. The Germans begin withdrawing from the vicinity of Baume-les-Dames. In the **U.S. Ninth Army** area, an assault against Brest commences at 10:00, subsequent to a massive bombardment. The 2nd, 8th, and 29th Divisions drive hard. During one of the innumerable heavy skirmishes, the Germans stall a contingent of the 13th Infantry, 8th Division, with mortars and machine gun fire outside in the vicinity of Les Coates in Brittany. The Germans also deploy excellent marksmen as snipers. P.F.C. Ernest Prussman impetuously leads his Squad across a hedgerow and personally takes two prisoners. Prussman leaps over another hedgerow, surprising a machine gun crew, destroying the gun, and seizing its crew and two Riflemen. He rushes ahead of his Squad toward the next objective, but a burst of enemy fire wounds him mortally. While dropping to the ground, he throws a grenade, taking out the German that shot him. His extraordinary heroism has gained the opening needed for the two Battalions to advance; Prussman receives the Medal of Honor posthumously. **(Atlantic-Italy)** In the **U.S. Fifth Army** area, **IV Corps** sector, a small contingent of the 435th AAA (Anti Aircraft Artillery) Battalion, Task Force 45, enters Vecchiano without incident. With the Arno River flooded, reinforcements for the 6th South African Armored cannot cross the river. The British 13th Corps advances as Germans retire. Elements occupy M. Morello and M. Senario while the Indian 8th Division takes over M. Calvana and M. Giovi. In the **British Eighth Army** area, British General Alexander comes to the front lines and postpones the British Eighth Army's assault against Rimini until S. Savino-Coriano is secure. British General Alexander also directs the U.S. Fifth Army to attack the very center of the staunchly-held Gothic Line. In the British 5th Corps area, the 56th Division akes slight progress against on Gemmano Ridge, which must be secured before the assault against S. Savino-Coriano.

September 9th 1944 — (Pacific-New Guinea) The repairs and modifications on Kamiri Airfield are finished. **(Pacific-Philippines)** From Aircraft Vice Admiral M.A. Mitscher's Fast Carrier Task Force bombs the Japanese installations at Mindanao. **(Atlantic-Western Europe) 21st Army Group** In the **Canadian First Army** 2nd Corps sector, the 4th Armored encounters heavy resistance as it crosses the Ghent-Bruges Canal southeast of Bruges. In other activity, Allied Patrols probing along the coast move into Ostend and Nieuport. In the **British Second Army** 30th Corps sector, the bridgehead at Beeringen gets reinforced by the Royal Netherlands Group and is then expanded despite severe opposition. The British bridgehead at Gheel is also being enlarged by the 50th Division. **12th Army Group** In the **U.S. First Army VII Corps** area, the 1st Division jumps across the Meuse at Liege, then pushes east. The 3rd Armored moves against Verviers while the 9th Division and Combat Command B, 3rd Armored, drive to Limbourg. In the **XIX Corps** area, the 113th Cavalry Group reaches Maastricht in the Holland panhandle while the balance of the Corps prepares for an offensive. In the **U.S. Third Army** area, **XII Corps** sector, the Commander orders an offensive to begin on the 11th. In other activity, the 80th Division continues to hold off a German counterattack. In the **XX Corps** area, advance contingents of the 90th Division drive to Fontoy and Neufchef, placing elements of the 90th less than 10 miles from Thionville. Also, the Command Post of the 90th Division comes under attack. General McClain is awakened and spots a German Tank within 20 feet of his Headquarters, but the Tank is disoriented and begins firing blindly, causing no harm. In other activity, the 2nd Infantry, bolstered by a Task Force, Combat Command A, 7th Armored advances west of the Metz River against steadfast resistance. Meanwhile, the fragile bridgehead at Dornot refuses to collapse under the pressure of enemy counterattacks, despite the thinning ranks. **(Southern France)** In the **U.S. Seventh Army** area, the French 2nd Corps drives toward Dijon. In the **VI Corps** sector, the 45th Division rips through opposition at Baume and closes on the Villersexel road junction. In other activity, the U.S. 36th and 3rd Divisions move across the Ognon River. In the **French First Army** sector, the Germans lose Seez, a strategic communication center, southwest of Little St. Bernard

Pass. **(Atlantic-Italy)** In the **U.S. Fifth Army** area, General Mark Clark orders the U.S. II Corps and the British 13th Corps to attack against the Gothic Line on the tenth. Boundaries are modified to give Highway 6521 to the British 13th Corps for the assault. In the **II Corps** area, the 91st Cavalry Reconnaissance Squadron reconnoiters north, reaching M. Maggiore without enemy contact. In the British 13th Corps area, the British 1st Division pivots and moves east after finishing its mission of screening for the II Corps. **(Atlantic-Russia)** The Russians cease hostilities against Bulgaria after agreeing to Bulgaria's request for an armistice.

September 10th 1944 — (Pacific-Palaus Islands) Task Force 38.4, attached to the U.S. Third Fleet, arrives in the vicinity of the Palaus Islands, subsequent to participating with the bombardment of Yap and Ulithi, several days prior. The Fleet bombards enemy installations on Peleliu and Angaur to destroy enemy shore guns and demolish beach defenses. **(Atlantic-Western Europe)** General Eisenhower meets in Brussels with his Commanders. Ike holds the conference on his Plane and for a time, strong differences of opinion are offered, prompting Eisenhower to remind General Montgomery who is the "Boss." Montgomery's exuberance concerning the British rushing to the Ruhr (with supply priorities) while Patton's Third Army stays in place, ignites the reprimand. Montgomery retains priority for the supplies, but Operation MARKET-GARDEN is to be completed before the push to open the port of Antwerp. The operation will entail Airborne troops employed in a grand scheme to seize bridges over the Rhine (General Montgomery had suggested use of Airborne). Eisenhower is excited about the possibility of isolating the German Fifteenth Army. In other activity, Patrols from Operation DRAGOON (Southern France) and OVERLORD encounter each other today, initiating the link-up of the two forces. **21st Army Group** In the **Canadian First Army** area, British 1st Corps sector, a staggering Air and Naval bombardment pounds the enemy at Le Havre. Allied Planes drop almost 5,000 tons of bombs, and Naval Surface Vessels pulverize the landing area. At 17:45 the British 49th and 51st Divisions attack, driving into the German defenses. By the following day, the heights that control the city are taken, and by the third day (12th), the German Garrison capitulates. In the British 30th Corps area, heavy fighting at the Albert Canal is ongoing, holding up a British advance, but the Guards' Armored Division moves to the Meuse-Escaut Canal and establishes a bridgehead. **U.S. 12th Army Group** General Bradley orders the seizure of the West Wall and also directs the seizure of bridgeheads across the Rhine. Allied pressure has forced the Germans to transfer some guns to other locations and, in addition, has drained many of the German reserves. First Army is to secure a crossing over the Rhine at Bonn, Cologne, and Koblentz. In addition, the Third Army is to drive to the Rhine and secure a crossing at Mannheim. The Operation is part of MARKET GARDEN and is in conjunction with the Airborne attack at the Arnhem River. This strategy also places British General Montgomery in position to speed to the Ruhr (General Montgomery has long awaited a march to the Ruhr), providing Eisenhower gives him the order to advance. In the **U.S. First Army** area, the **VII Corps** is racing feverishly toward the German Frontier, forcing its way through rear guard resistance. The 1st Division surges to Battice while the 3rd Armored rolls through Verviers. Activity in the **U.S. V Corps** area is also brisk. The 28th Division stampedes into Arlon, Longvilly, Selange, Wiltz, and Bastogne, and in conjunction, Combat Command A, 5th Armored, strolls effortlessly into Luxembourg. Then Contingents of 5th Ar-

mored bolt east toward Germany, reaching a point less than 10 miles from the border (Combat Command R). In the **XIX Corps** area, Fort Eben Emael slides easily into the control of the 30th Division. The 113th Cavalry Group moves across the Meuse at Liege and drives north. In the **U.S. Third Army** area, **XV Corps** sector, a Patrol encounters the welcome friendly troops of DRAGOON at Sombernon. In the **XX Corps** area, the Germans mount stiff resistance against the 90th Division, which is grinding toward Thionville. Aumetz falls to the 359th Infantry, and Hayange is seized by the 357th. Meanwhile, the 358th Infantry overpowers Algrange. The Germans resist fiercely west of the Metz River, giving the 2nd Infantry, 5th Division and elements of Combat Command A, 7th Armored, a vicious struggle. The 10th Infantry, 5th Division, assisted by smoke screens, crosses the Meuse between Arnaville and Noveant. This is the first time Third Army uses smoke on a big scale and the experiment is worth the effort as the troops thoroughly surprise the Germans; the assault which jumps off at 02:00 gives the 10th Infantry stunning victories at Hills 370 and 386. As a bonus, the Yanks also seize Bois de Gaumont. After regaining their composure, the Germans counterattack, but Aircraft attached to XIX Tactical Air Command rush overhead and simmer the heated attack. The Air Corps had diverted Planes from the Brest to bolster the operation. At Dornot, the defenders of the bridgehead (contingents of 5th Division) are recalled due to untenable positions and dwindling manpower; they pull back during the night of the 10th. After dusk, Engineers construct a bridge across the river under consistent enemy fire. In the **XII Corps** sector, the Germans abandon Fort de Villey-le-Sec and head for Nancy. New occupants, the 319th Infantry, 80th Division take over the fort. The 35th Division prepares to attack across the Moselle at Flavigny. The 2nd Battalion, 134th Infantry, moves across the bridge before it is destroyed by the Germans. The Infantry is pressed terribly when struck by a heavy counterattack. Some troops are able to swim back to the opposing west bank. In other activity, the U.S. Navy establishes Naval Forces France, commanded by Vice Admiral A.G. Kirk, with Headquarters in Paris. The U.S.S. *Seer* (AM-112), a Minesweeper, is damaged by a mine. **(Southern France)** In the **U.S. Seventh Army** area, the French 2nd Corps advances to Dijon and makes contact with Patrols of the OVERLORD Force. In other activity, the 3rd and 36th Divisions close against Vesoul in conjunction with the 45th Division, operating on the right and pushing toward Villersexel. **(Atlantic-Italy)** In the **U.S. Fifth Army**, **II Corps** sector, the attack commences as two Divisions, the 34th driving on the left and the 91st alongside, jump off at 05:30, moving against the Gothic Line with the 91st reaching the Seine during the night of the 10th. Meanwhile, the 34th Division advances beyond M. Maggiore. The British 13th Corps, three Divisions strong, attacks on the left in support of the II Corps. Its 1st Division drives to the Seine and secures a bridgehead at Borgo San Lorenzo. The Indian 8th Division holds its positions, having no access roads, and the 6th Armored, rumbling along Highway 67, seizes Dicomano. In the IV Corps area, additional elements of Task Force 45 cross the Serchio River at Vecchiano. Villa Basilica falls to the 6th Armored Infantry Battalion. In the **British Eighth Army** area, the 46th Division is sent to bolster the 56th Division to speed the clearing of Gemmano Ridge.

September 11th 1944 — (Southwest Pacific Area) Contingents of Task Force Tradewind from Aitape arrive at Maffin Bay and rendezvous with the Maffin Bay Group. **(Pacific-Japan)** The U.S.S. *Albacore* (SS-218) sinks the Japanese Submarine Chaser No. 165 off the coast of Kyushu, Japan. **(Pa-**

cific-Russell Islands) Marine Night Fighter Squadron 531st arrives in the Russells, becoming the first night Fighter Squadron to operate in the South Pacific Theater. (Atlantic-Western Europe) 21st Army Group In the Canadian First Army area, the British I Corps pushes into Le Havre and secures the heights that control the harbor. In the 2nd Corps area, contingents of the 2nd Division advance to Zeebrugge. In addition, the Corps contains the enemy holding the ports at Boulogne, Calais, and Dunkerque (Dunkirk). Also, the Germans have been eliminated from the Coast of Pas de Calais. In other activity, the Polish 1st Armored, meeting fierce opposition at the Ghent Canal, is diverted to Ghent to relieve the 7th Armored (12th Corps). In the British Second Army area, the 30th Corps fortifies its Meuse-Escaut Canal bridgehead and dispatches Patrols across the Dutch border. In other activity, the British 50th Division holds its bridgehead at Gheel, despite intense heavy opposition. 12th Army Group In the U.S. First Army area, the V and VII Corps are directed to probe in strength to drive a wedge in the West Wall. In the V Corps area, the 85th Reconnaissance Squadron, U.S. 5th Armored Division is the first Allied outfit to have a contingent enter Germany. The dismounted Patrol enters Hitler's domain by crossing over the frontier at 18:05 and moving to the fringes of Stalzenburg without encountering any enemy troops. In other activity, the 28th Division (minus RCT 112, attached to 5th Armored) secures a crossing at the Our River by seizing a bridge that has not been destroyed by the Germans (during night 11th-12th). In the U.S Third Army area, XII Corps sector, the ingenuity of the Engineers is severely tested by an assignment to build a bridge across the Moselle despite insufficient equipment. The 2nd and 3rd Battalions, 137th Infantry, 35th Division force their way across the Moselle southeast of Flavigny, but enemy fire pins them down. Subsequently, the 1st Battalion crosses at Neuviller-sur-Moselle and drives to Lorey. Elements of Combat Command B, 4th Armored Division, cross the Moselle at Bainville-aux-Miroirs. Also, at Bayon, the Germans are steadfast; a bypass of Bayon is implemented and a contingent seizes hills overlooking Bremoncourt. During the night (11th-12th), physical contact is made with the 137th Infantry. In other activity, the Germans decide to attack the fort at Pont St. Vincent, manned by the 134th Infantry. Two Companies charge; some troops penetrate by going over the walls; however, they are met with unyielding opposition. Reinforcements supplemented with Artillery are committed, terminating the threat. In the XV Corps area, a hole develops between Epinal and Charmes along the Moselle. An offensive is initiated to close the gap at 08:00. The 121st Cavalry Squadron, 106th Cavalry Group acts as pathfinder and screens the advance, followed by the 79th Division. (Southern France) In the U.S. Seventh Army area, VI Corps sector, the 3rd and 36th Divisions attack Vesoul to seize the last remaining German escape route to Belfort. During the day, contact is made between the French 2nd Corps and elements of the 36th Division near Pont-sur-Saone. In addition, the 45th Division maintains pressure against Villersexel, securing Rougemont as it closes. (Operation FRANTIC) The final shuttle bombing missions of the U.S. Eighth Air Force begin. Seventy Five B-17s and 64 P-51s launch a spirited attack against a munitions plant at Chemnitz, Germany, on the way to their temporary bases in the U.S.S.R. (Atlantic-Italy) In the U.S. Fifth Army area, the offensive against the Gothic Line continues. Aircraft bolster the attack, striking suspected enemy positions. In the IV Corps area, Task Force 45 gets elements to the fringes of Viareggio, on the Ligurian coast. Pistoia is seized without incident by units of the 6th South

African Armored. In the II Corps sector, the 168th Infantry, operating on the 36th's right flank, rolls through Cavallina and Barberino, moving toward M. Frassino, a strategic outpost of the Gothic Line.

September 12th 1944 — (United-States) The U.S. Minesweeper YMS-409 is lost by foundering off the Atlantic coast. (Atlantic-Canada) The Combined Chiefs of Staff meet in Quebec. President Roosevelt and Prime Minister Winston Churchill meet in Quebec (Octagon Conference) with their respective staffs to review strategy. Churchill had felt the conference necessary, however, the Joint Chiefs prefer not having it. Churchill, now anxious to get the British back into the Pacific where their Empire had vanished, mentions in his memoirs: "THE TIME HAD NOW COME FOR THE LIBERATION OF ASIA." Admiral King is of the opinion that the British had gotten their chance in Burma and muffed it and he is convinced that the British Navy is not "too active." The conference convenes until Saturday the 16th, and with the unrelenting pressure of Churchill, President Roosevelt agrees with the Prime Minister of England. There are no major changes in the general plan for victory in Europe and in the Pacific. Agreement is reached for the Burma Campaign, and it is also agreed that the British will participate in the final Pacific Operations under British command; King remains adamant, feeling that the British will be a liability because they are not used to being at sea for prolonged periods of time; British Task Force 57 (British Carriers under Vice Admiral Sir H.B. Rawlings) will join the U.S. Fleet and do a fine job. The British Carriers have steel decks on their Carriers, unlike the U.S. Carriers which have wooden decks and this proves valuable during the Kamikaze attacks during the battle for Okinawa; the British strike the Japanese Airfields at Sakishima, Gunto Islands about 250 miles southwest of Okinawa and they are also committed against Formosa. The target date for the end of the war with Japan is set for 18 months, subsequent to the defeat of Germany. (Pacific-Palaus Islands-Carolines) The Western Fire Support Group of Admiral Fort's Western Attack Force (TF 32) arrives at the Palaus and initiates a preinvasion bombardment to soften resistance. In addition, special teams clear demolitions and obstacles that impede the assault. Also, mine sweeping operations begin. During the activity off the Palaus, the High Speed Transport Noa (APD-24) sinks after a collision with the Destroyer Fullam (DD-474). The Fullam sustains damage. (Pacific-Philippines) Vice Admiral Mitscher's Fast Carrier Task Force commences a tumultuous bombardment against the Japanese positions in the Visayas. The Planes continue striking the Airfields and installations for three days. On the 14th, Vice Admiral J.S. McCain's Carrier Group shifts its Planes to strike Mindanao; the Japanese offer only nominal opposition from Leyte. Admiral Halsey is ecstatic about the statistics: over 1,400 sorties flown during the three-day period and losses are confined to ten men, eight Planes (combat), and one Plane due to operational problems, while destroying 173 enemy Planes in the Air and over 300 on the ground. In addition, 55 enemy Ships are sunk. Admiral Halsey sends the following message to all his Carriers: "BECAUSE OF THE BRILLIANT PERFORMANCE MY GROUP OF STARS HAS JUST GIVEN, I AM BOOKING YOU TO APPEAR BEFORE THE BEST AUDIENCE IN THE ASIATIC THEATER". Admiral Halsey is referring to Manila and the enormous amount of Japanese Planes based there. Admiral Halsey is convinced that the central Philippines is "the vulnerable belly of the Imperial Dragon." (Pacific-New Guinea) Task Force Tradewind embarks for Moratai. (Pacific-South China Sea) The U.S.S. Growler (SS-215) sinks the Japanese Destroyer

Shiinami and the Frigate *Hirato*. **(Atlantic-Western Europe) 21st Army Group** In the **Canadian First Army** British 1st Corps sector, the Garrison at Le Havre surrenders; about 12,000 German prisoners are taken. In the **British Second Army** area, the 12th Corps advances near Gheel-Diest-Malines-Antwerp. In the **U.S. 12th Army Group** area, **First Army** sector, the **XIX Corps** completes a bridge at the Albert Canal at midnight. Soon after, C.C.A., 2nd Armored bolts across before the Engineers get an opportunity to admire their work. The **VII Corps** pushes strong Reconnaissance Patrols to the West Wall. The 1st Division springs into the Aachen Municipal Forest and is met by an unsuccessful German counterattack. Aachen is evaded on orders of General Collins, who chooses to isolate the city in coordination with the XIX Corps. The V Corps also moves toward the West Wall, but on a smaller scale. The 4th Division runs over nominal resistance as it heads for St. Vith. Sevenig falls to contingents of the 109th Infantry, 28th Division, while units of the 110th Infantry speed across the German frontier, reaching positions west of Grosskampenberg. The 3rd Platoon fords the Our River effortlessly at Luxembourg in a dismal fog. The 2nd Platoon follows closely behind and when it reaches the bank, the Germans spring a line of withering fire ripping into the troops, killing both the Platoon Leader and Platoon Sergeant and paralyzing the advance on exposed terrain. Sergeant Francis J. Clark (Company K, 109th Infantry) crawls on his stomach to the pinned-down Platoon and gets many of the men to safety. Clark then takes a Squad and elements of the Second Platoon toward the enemy strongpoints. Clark dodges more bullets and singlehandedly charges nest after nest, exterminating an indeterminable number of enemy troops. His actions stagger several enemy Platoons and scatter a full Company of Germans whose automatc weapons had been no match for the particular Sergeant; Sgt. Clark receives the Medal of Honor. In the **U.S. Third Army XX Corps** area, the Germans destroy a primary bridge at Thionville, but the 90th Division racks up a pretty good score, eliminating the Krauts from most of the city, ridding the area west of the Moselle near Thionville of German presence. The Germans mount a strong counterattack against the bridgehead at Arnaville, but it is repelled. In other activity, Engineers complete a bridge across the Moselle, permitting quick access to elements of the 7th Armored which speed Tanks and Tank Destroyers into the bridgehead. In the **XII Corps** area, elements of the 80th Division attack across the Moselle near Dieulouard, finding the area weakly defended; the bridgehead is expanded to Bezaumont, La Cote Pelee, Loisy, and Ste Genevieve. In other activity, the bridgehead at Lorey is fortified with the arrival of Combat Command B, 4th Armored, and the 137th Infantry 35th Division, improving Corps positions south of Nancy. In the **XV Corps** area, the 106th Cavalry Group crosses the Moselle north of Charmes. The 314th Infantry, 79th Division secures Charmes. The 313th Infantry skirmishes heavily near Poussay while the 315th presses Neufchateau where the Germans are trapped. In addition, the French 2nd Armored Division seizes Vittel (Combat Command A) and Combat Command V secures Andelot. German reinforcements are rushing from Epinal to attempt rescue of the encircled Garrison at Vittel. **(Southern France)** In the **U.S. Seventh Army** area, contingents of the French 2nd Corps advance to Langres. In the **VI Corps** area, the 3rd and 36th Divisions scour their respective areas (Vesoul), clearing enemy resistance. In another example of Yankee intrepidity, 1st Lieutenant John Tominac, Company I, 15th Infantry, 3rd Division, singlehandedly charges across 50 yards of open territory and with a solitary burst of fire from his Tommygun, an enemy machine gun is destroyed and its three defenders killed. He then leads a Squad against another strongpoint, defended by mortars and machine guns. Soon after, the position is a crypt, holding about 30 German corpses. Immediately following this encounter, the dauntless Tominac moves out about 50 yards in front of his detachment and discovers another enemy strongpoint in the suburbs of a town that holds a deadly 77mm Self-Propelled gun and many Infantry troops. In Hollywood fashion, an American Tank supports Tominac against the menacing 77-mm gun until a direct hit splatters it. The crew abandons it as it rolls like a burning inferno toward the Germans. Tominac, badly wounded from metal fragments when the Tank was struck, shrugs off his disabling wounds and jumps aboard the runaway Tank, commandeers its operational machine gun, and pours fire into the enemy. The rolling time bomb, now totally engulfed in flames, still has a gunner, and the fire continues, driving the Germans from their positions. Miraculously, Tominac jumps from the Vehicle only seconds before it explodes. The gallantry of Lt. Tominac could have ended here, but not with this Yank. Astonished medics are able to hold him long enough to take several shell fragments from his battered body. However, almost instantly, he leads another attack against yet another position containing 32 Germans. Hand grenades flow like lava into the strongpoint, and the survivors surrender. Unquestionably the United States Army got a fair day's work from this Lieutenant. His extraordinary heroism plays a vital part in the capture of the city of Saulx de Vesoul, and Tominac is responsible for the death or capture of 60 enemy troops; he receives the Medal of Honor. In the 45th Division sector, the Germans counterattack against Villersexel, but it is thrown back. In other activity in France, two Tanks attached to the 756th Tank Battalion supplement an Infantry assault against Noroy le Bourg. German fire stalls the Tanks, and Lt. Raymond Zussman moves out alone to dislodge the obstacles and returns with captured prisoners. He then directs the fire of his two Tanks, frequently walking in front of them amidst heavy enemy fire. Zussman's actions culminate with the destruction of the enemy resistance and the capture of 92 Germans, plus 18 killed. Lt. Zussman is killed during subsequent action; he receives the Medal of Honor. **(Atlantic-Italy)** In the **U.S. Fifth Army** area, **IV Corps** sector, the South African 6th Armored Division applies more pressure against the Germans who are dashing to the Gothic Line. In the **II Corps** area, the Germans fortify their positions at the Gothic Line. Enemy-deployed mine fields obstruct movement of the 34th Division southwest of M. Frassino, but some units, operating on the right flank, seize the lower slopes. The 91st Division moves tenaciously, but hits similar opposition and is unable to overrun the enemy outposts at M. Calvi or Hills Altuzzo and Monticelli, which collectively control the strategic Giogo Pass. The attack is supplemented by Medium-bombers which strike Firenzuola. In the British 13th Corps sector, the British 1st Division encounters the outer defenses of the Gothic Line while the 21st Brigade, Indian 8th Division, gets across the Sieve and moves expeditiously toward M. Citerna. In the **British Eighth Army** area, a heavy Artillery barrage begins prior to the 5th Corps' and the Canadian 1st Corps' assault to capture S. Savino-Coriano Ridge. The troops attack at 17:00, supported throughout by Artillery fire. By the following day, the Canadian 5th Armored secures the northern spur of the ridge and Coriano while the British 1st Armored grabs a solid grip on the ridge. **(Atlantic-Rumania)** Rumania signs an armistice with the United States, Great Britain, and Russia. Rumania agrees to join in the war against Germany and Hungary. It also agrees to pay reparations. The agreement is drawn up in Moscow. The Russians agree to establish the border between themselves and Rumania by reverting to that boundary established by agreement of the 28th of June, 1940. Russia also says it will return Transylvania to Rumania.

September 13th 1944 — (Pacific-Moratai) Task Force Tradewind, en route to Morotai, joins the Covering Force and Escort Carriers. The Convoy maintains secrecy for the entire journey. **(Pacific-Philippine)** The Japanese Submarine Chaser No. 55 is sunk off the coast of the Philippines by Carrier-based Aircraft. Planes attached to the U.S.S. *Independence* strike enemy facilities in the Visayans at night and repeat the effort on the 14th. About 20 sorties are flown over a three-day period while simultaneously operating with the Fast Carrier Task Force during the day. **(China-Burma-India)** General Hurley draws up U.S. proposals for the appointment of General Stilwell to the post of Field Commander of the Ground and Air Forces of the Republic of China and another directive for Chiang Kai-shek to General Stilwell. Kai-shek receives them by the 16th of September. In other activity, representatives of the Chinese Communists meet with Stilwell before he departs for Kweilin to inspect the eastern China defenses. **(Atlantic-Western Europe)** General Eisenhower orders the seizure of two objectives: the option of taking Antwerp or Rotterdam and securing the Rhine. **21st Army Group** The **Canadian First Army's**, 2nd Corps dispatches thin forces of the 4th Armored across both the Canal de Derivation and the Leopold Canal in the vicinity of Bruges during the night of the 13th. In the **British Second Army** area, the British 15th Division relieves the 50th Division at the Gheel bridgehead, then advances to the Meusse-Escaut Canal. In other activity, the 53rd Division fights to expand its grasp of the dock area of Antwerp. **12th Army Group** In the **U.S. Ninth Army** area, **VIII Corps** sector, the Germans at Brest ignore ultimatum to surrender and refuse to capitulate. The 129th Infantry, 29th Division seizes Fort Keranroux. The balance of the Division and the 2nd Division squeeze Brest tighter. During this exchange of deadly fire, one German strongpoint has resisted defeat for three days and keeps the 2nd Battalion contained. Sgt. Sherwood H. Hallman singlehandedly jumps over a hedgerow and lands in a sunken road from where he astonishingly charges a machine gun position bolstered by 30 enemy Riflemen. Hallman defies all danger and advances with his gun smoking and his other arm tossing grenades. This impetuous charge wounds or kills four of the enemy. Hallman captures 12 Germans. This startling maneuver inspires the balance of his Company (F) to capture 75 nearby Germans; Hallman receives the Medal of Honor. In other activity, Combat Command A, 4th Armored, is relieved by the 94th Division, which takes over the job of seizing Lorient. Elements of the VIII Corps spot a fragile position along the Siegfried Line and advance 10 miles south of Aachen, putting Collins' Tanks into Germany. The charge stalls abruptly, as supplies have totally diminished. In the **U.S. First Army** area, **XIX Corps** sector, Combat Command A, 2nd Armored, drives hard toward the Meuse, throwing the Germans back several miles. Elements of the 30th Division are closing on the DeGeul River; units enter Wijk, a suburb of Maastricht, discovering the bridge leading to Maastricht (an island) has been destroyed by the enemy. In the **VII Corps** area, the fighting is terribly heavy. Combat Command B, 2nd Armored crashes through the West Wall between Roetgen and Rott, penetrating the defenses at two spots. In conjunctive action, Combat Command A, and

elements of the 1st Division, barge into Nutheim after reducing Antitank obstacles, opening a route to Kornelimuenster and beyond to the Stolberg corridor. In other VII Corps activity, the Germans mount a counterattack against the 16th Infantry, 1st Division in the Aachen Municipal Forest, but the effort is in vain. The 16th defeats the attackers and prepares to strike the West Wall at Ober Forstbach. In the **V Corps** area, the 28th Division assaults the West Wall; its 109th and 110th Regiments attack, the former drives toward Irsen Creek; the 110th pushes without incident through Grosskampenberg before bumping into stiff resistance that halts its progress about half the distance from the German line. In the **U.S. Third Army** area, **XX Corps** sector, the Germans take advantage of the American shortage of ammunition and gasoline, as full-throttled battle ensues in the vicinity of Thionville; the U.S. 90th Division is ordered to rush southwest to relieve the embattled units. At Fort Driant, incessant enemy fire wrecks a pontoon bridge, still under construction at Arnaville, and in addition, destroys a ferrying raft. Although nearly out of ammunition, the Yanks hold the tenuous bridgehead; Combat Command B rumbles across the river into the bridgehead and drives toward Mardigny, but intense enemy resistance at Arry halts its progress. In the **XII Corps** area, the Germans withdraw from Nancy in a calculated move to assemble a huge force to counterattack the bridgehead at Dieulouard. A vicious see-saw battle erupts when the enemy attacks at 01:00 with their all available troops. The lightning strike pours through the lines, and the Germans take Bezaumont, Loisy, and Ste Genevieve, bringing them dangerously close to the American held bridges; however, the onslaught is halted. American Armor drives across the bridges into the thick of the battle and supports a strong counterattack by the 80th Division. With the assistance of Combat Command A, all lost ground is retaken; Combat Command A then rushes through Ste Genevieve to Fresnes-en-Saulnois. Combat Command B and elements of the 35th Division attack toward the Meurthe, piercing through the recently created gap instituted by the rapid retreat of the Germans. In the **XV Corps** area, the 313th Infantry, 79th Division advances into Poussay, while the 315th Regiment seizes Neufchateau. At the 79th's bridgehead across from Charmes, the 314th keeps the situation in hand with the assistance of the 106th Cavalry Group. Meanwhile, the Germans attempt to spring another attack. Two enemy Armor columns inch toward Vittel until both are spotted by Combat Command L, 2nd French Armored which intercepts the approaching Vehicles at Dompaire and Ville-sur-Illon. The XIX Tactical Air Command lends a lethal hand, and combined with the French Armor, the Germans are thrashed from the air and on the ground, sustaining severe losses including losing 60 Tanks; Chaumont is taken by Combat Command D. **(Southern France)** In the **U.S. Seventh Army** area, the French 1st Armored captures Langres. In the **VI Corps** area, German-held Vesoul capitulates, sealing the final escape route to the Belfort gap in the U.S. area. In other activity, Villersexel and 1,300 prisoners fall to the U.S. 45th Division. During the early morning hours of the 13th, a Platoon attached to Company E, 157th Infantry attacks a well-fortified position in the hills near Grammont, advancing near a deadly machine gun nest. Lt. Almond E. Fisher bolts out alone and kills the entire crew, permitting the advance to restart. Within a few minutes more tenacious fire stalls the advance, and Lt. Fisher again inches his way toward the obstacle, eliminating it with a few grenades. Fisher seems inexhaustible and several other deadly encounters occur, including killing a German that jumps into his foxhole and attempts to grab another Soldier's weapon. Subsequent to these actions the Germans mount another attack, but by now, the American Platoon has seen its numbers greatly reduced. Yet again, the indomitable Fisher inspires his men to repulse a vicious attack which strikes both flanks and their front. Fisher, wounded twice during this latest engagement, refuses medical aid. Having lost the ability to walk due to his wounds, he crawls from man to man, bolstering their confidence and giving orders. After the attack is thwarted completely, he crawls 300 additional yards to receive belated medical attention; Fisher receives the Medal of Honor. **(Atlantic-Hungary)** U.S. Eighth Air Force Planes which had taken off from Russian Bases attack Diosgyoer, Hungary, as they head to their Bases in Italy. Operation FRANTIC shuttle bombing is now halted permanently. **(Atlantic-Italy)** In the **U.S. Fifth Army** area, the **IV Corps** is confined to patrolling its perimeter. The South African 6th Armored, attacking enemy-held hills north of Prato, seizes M. Acuto. In the **II Corps** area, an all-out assault is mounted to secure the Po Valley. Heavy opposition stalls the 338th Infantry, 85th Division at M. Altuzzo, and opposition at M. Monticelli stalls the advance of the 363rd Infantry, 91st Division. The 339th Infantry of the 85th halts after a tenacious but futile attempt to seize M. Veruca. In other activity, the 34th Division is engulfed in a raging contest on the left flank of the Corps at M. Frassino. In the British 13th Corps area, the British 1st Division attacks hills M. Guivigiana and Poggio Prefetto which collectively dominate Highway 6521. The Indian 8th Division captures M. Veruca and lunges almost to the crest of Alpe di Vitigliano. In the **British Eighth Army** area, the bitter fighting to take the obstinate S. Savino-Coriano Ridge is incessant, but the Germans don't relent. The British 5th Corps seizes a tight hold on the ridge, and the Canadian 5th Armored takes Coriano and the northern spur of the ridge. **(Atlantic-Poland)** The pleas for help from the Poles and the Allies are finally answered by the Russians, who drop some supplies to the Polish freedom fighters in Warsaw. The Russians also take Lomza, between East Prussia and Warsaw.

September 14th 1944 — (United States) A violent storm hits the area around Cape Hatteras, North Carolina. The Coast Guard Cutters *Bedloe* (P-128) and *Jackson* (P-142) both sink as a direct result of the hurricane. In addition, another Vessel, No. 73, a Lightship, is lost to a similar vicious storm off the coast of Vineyard Sound, Massachusetts. **(Pacific-Philippines)** Carrier-based Aircraft sink a Japanese Transport, No. 5, off the Philippines. **(Pacific-South China Sea)** The Submarine U.S.S. *Pargo* (SS-264) lays mines across enemy Shipping lanes in the South China Sea near Natunga Island. **(China-Burma-India)** General Stilwell is informed in Kweilin that Chiang Kai-shek has directed three Chinese Divisions to remain inside the city to ensure its defense. On the Salween Front, Teng-chung falls to the Chinese, culminating a 10-day struggle. This and other setbacks for the Japanese force them to terminate their counteroffensive. **(Atlantic-Canada)** During the ongoing conference at Quebec, the Combined Chiefs of Staff formulate new plans for British Admiral Mountbatten, including the retaking of Burma which is the main priority. In addition, the assault to seize Rangoon (Operation DRACULA) and the assault across the Chindwin River to initiate a land and Air route through Burma to China is also approved; the tentative target date is March 15th 1945. **(Atlantic-Western Europe) 21st Army Group** British General Montgomery prepares for another offensive which is to commence on the 17th. He directs the British Second Army to seize crossings across the Meuse and Rhine Rivers from which they can pre-

pare for a big assault on the Ruhr. He also directs the Canadians to open Antwerp's port and seize Boulogne and Calais. At this time, the British are unable to take any offensive action because they are in the process of regrouping and waiting for supplies. **12th Army Group**, Brigadier General Richard E. Nugent assumes command of the newly-activated XXIX Tactical Air Command (Provisional), with the responsibility of providing direct support to the U.S. Ninth Army's operations. This newest Command is attached temporarily to the IX Tactical Air Command. In the **U.S. First Army** area, **XIX Corps** sector, the Germans are pressed by the approaching 2nd Armored and the 30th Infantry Divisions and begin abandoning Maastricht Island. Elements of the 117th Infantry force the river and find the island undefended. Combat Command A, 2nd Armored, charges to the Maas River and crosses a canal without incident later in the day. The 119th Infantry crosses the DeGeul River near Gulpen without encountering any resistance, but other units crossing near Valkenburg barely manage to retain their slim grasp on the east bank, prompting the 36th Division to hold where it stands until bridges are constructed across the DeGeul. In the **VII Corps** area, Task Force Lovelady, commanded by Lt. Colonel William B. Lovelady of Combat Command B (3rd Armored Division), bursts forward to the Vicht River, crossing it southwest of Stolberg. Combat Command A advancs to the fringes of Eilendorf, a suburb of Aachen, and waits there for the 16th Infantry, 1st Division which is advancing along the left flank. On the right flank, elements of the 9th Division push into the Roetgen Forest, surrounding the villages of Vicht and Zweifall, while yet other units push along the Vicht River; the 60th Infantry charges across the German border and captures Kalterherberg. Other contingents of the 60th Infantry unsuccessfully attacks Hoefen-Alzen Ridge, allowing the Germans to forestall an attack against the West Wall from the Lammersdorf corridor. The 39th Infantry pushes from Roetgen to Lammersdorf from where it attacks northward against fortified defenders at the Scharnhorst Line until being halted by extremely heavy fire. In the **V Corps** area, the 4th Division pounds against the West Wall with its 12th Infantry, splicing a wedge through the Schnee Eifel Highway, then attacks and captures Hill 698. In conjunction, the 22nd Infantry advances to the crest of Schnee Eifel Ridge getting some units on the eastern slopes within sight of Hontheim. The West Wall feels the effects of the American attack at its center point, but the assault is repelled, foiling the 28th Division's effort to take Hill 553 and the Heckhuscheid-Uttfeld Highway. The 5th Armored penetrates effectively along the Corps right flank; Combat Command R storms across the Sauer River and seizes Wallendorf. In the **U.S. Third Army** area, General Patton had been given two days (on the 12th) to crack the Moselle River or to take a defensive posture. Patton reports that he has four Divisions across the river. However, both he and General Hodges (First Army) are stymied by lack of supplies. In the **XII Corps** area, the town of Nancy is surrounded, and the Germans at Luneville are poised for an anticipated assault. At Loisy and Ste Genevieve, the situation is grave. A strong counterattack by the Germans recaptures both places. The attack had been launched against the 80h Division's bridgehead at Dieulouard and unquestionably the Germans had made progress; however, the 80th mounts a counterattack, retakes the lost terrain, and stretches its bridgehead. The 317th Infantry encounters heavy resistance at Mt. Toulon. The 318th seizes Atton and continues driving north, gaining ground on the crest of Mousson Hill. A 20-man contingent of the 319th Infantry attacks an enemy strongpoint manned by approximately

200 German troops near Pompey. 1st Lt. Edgar Lloyd becomes incensed when the detachment is halted by incessant fire. He daringly jumps up and charges, plowing into an enemy nest. He knocks out the gunner with a sturdy punch and pulls the pin on a grenade, leaving it behind as he jumps out of the hole. Lloyd moves from one nest to another, singlehandedly demolishing five machine gun nests. The balance of the contingent overruns the remaining resistance and seizes the objective; Lt Lloyd receives the Medal of Honor. In other activity in the Third Army area, the 4th Armored moves quickly to sever the escape routes from Nancy. By the end of the day, the junction of C.C.A. and C.C.B. completes the task. Combat Command B advances through Foret de Vitrimont to the Marne River Canal near Dombasle, sealing escape routes heading west from Luneville, while CCA drives to Arracourt-Moncourt. During the advance, German 88s spring an ambush and score a direct hit on one of the leading Tanks as it nears Valhey. The enemy attack is sudden and startling as the 88s fire from a distance of 20 yards, causing disorientation in the ranks. Sergeant Joseph J. Sadowski's Tank, among those on the point, is totally consumed by fire and near the point of exploding. After ordering the crew to abandon it, he realizes that a wounded man is still inside the Tank, and he immediately jumps aboard to rescue him. A hail of enemy bullets rips Sergeant Sadowski apart as he tries to open the hatch, inspiring the command. The remaining Tanks roar forward, taking the town without suffering any further losses; Sgt Sadowski receives the Medal of Honor posthumously. While at Etain, General Patton receives word that Nancy has been seized and that the XV Corps, protecting the flank of the XII Corps, has destroyed German General Lieutenant Ernst Haeckel's 16th Army and 60 of its Tanks. The XV Corps has crossed the Moselle at Charmes to intercept this attack. **(Southern France)** In the **U.S. Seventh Army VI Corps** sector, the 3rd Division attacks toward Lure while the 36th Division heads for Luxeuil. Meanwhile, the 45th Division makes no progress as it attempts to press the l'Isle-sur-Doubs-Villersexel. **(Atlantic-Italy)** In the **U.S. Fifth Army** area, the **II Corps** throws everything it has at the Gothic Line, but the relentless pounding does not convince the enemy at Il Giogo Pass to capitulate. The 85th Division mounts a gallant effort to secure Mt. Altuzzo, but it is costly and gains only a fragile and temporary piece of a ridge west of the primary ridge. Fighting is vicious, but the II Corps does not penetrate. In one particular action, elements of the 85th advance to within 50 yards of their objective on the western ridge, driving into a storm of machine gun and mortar fire, supplemented by enemy snipers. The Germans initiate three successive counterattacks to dislodge the Yanks. All attacks fail, but Company B sustains severe losses, including all Officers and non-commissioned Officers (2nd and 3rd Platoons) falling to the casualty list. The two Platoons now number 20 men. Staff Sergeant George D. Keathley, guide of the 1st Platoon, crawls to the besieged Platoons, traveling from one man to another inspiring them, while confiscating ammunition from the dead to ensure the lives of the survivors. Meanwhile, the Germans prepare a fourth attack. Keathley instills exaggerated confidence by his actions. The Germans, two Companies strong, charge repeatedly, but the Yanks hold. Yet another unsuccessful assault begins, and a grenade strikes near the intrepid Sergeant Keathley, wounding him mortally. Still removing his hand from the wound to steady his aim, he raises himself to a standing position and pours fire upon the attackers. A rejuvenated burst of energy has the remnants of the two Platoons fighting in phenomenal fashion for a period of 15 minutes,

mowing down the assault troops. The blazing Yankee fire and their unyielding Sergeant then receive assistance; Artillery fire zooms in directly over their heads, demoralizing the attackers. Sergeant Keathley lives to see them saved; however, he succumbs about three minutes after the arrival of the Artillery; he receives the Medal of Honor posthumously. At Monte Frassino, the contest is agonizing. The Germans command treacherous positions that continue to stall the 34th Division. At one location, the enemy is deployed behind terraced stone walls that halt all advances. The 3rd Platoon's, Company K has been repulsed twice, losing all its Officers in the futile effort. Another Officer, 2nd Lt. Thomas Wigle, leads the next assault against a storm of fire. In a leap-frog, man-to-man over the wall jaunt, the detachment ascends the first terrace and then the second with Wigle in the forefront. All are soon up and over the third wall as Wigle attacks and clears a nearby house full of Germans. Repeating the feat, he drives the enemy from their newest roost and then pursues to the third, bursting through the door. Soon after, the balance of his command joins him, but the arrival is too late. Wigle is mortally wounded at the top of the cellar stairs, unable to get to the basement. His courageous actions lead to the capture of 36 enemy troops and the strongpoint; Lt Wigle is awarded the Medal of Honor posthumously. In the British 13th Corps zone, the British 1st Division is heavily engaged at Prefetto Hill, and the Indian 8th Division secures the crest of Alpe di Vitigliano. In the **British Eighth Army** area, the 10th Corps starts regrouping, enabling it to transfer some units to other British sectors. In other activity, the British 5 Corps and Canadian 1st Corps, consolidate their positions at the S. Savino-Coriano Ridge and begin crossing the Marano River. **(Atlantic-Poland)** The Russians get assistance from Polish forces, and together they seize Praga, a suburb of Warsaw. The Germans, although holding precarious positions, are prepared to fight and hold the line at the Narew and Vistula Rivers. **(Atlantic-Yugoslavia)** A contingent of British troops, accompanied by some hefty 25 pounders, arrives on the Peljesac Peninsula and bombards an enemy forming location at Trpanj to harass their withdrawal operation.

A camouflaged Howitzer during the siege of Brest.

Marines pinned down on the Peleliu beachhead.

Marines advancing up a steep hill on Peleliu.

September 15th 1944 — (Pacific-Palaus) — THE INVASION OF PELELIU — Just another island in an obscure chain within the western Carolines in the awesome Pacific Ocean is one way of describing this diminutive speck, barely visible while scanning a global map. That's what it had been until the outbreak of hostilities between the Japanese and the Americans, but now it is to become recognizable to future generations because of the role it plays in the overall plans to wipe the Japanese Armed Forces off the face of the map. There have been heated differences of opinion on whether or not to take the Palaus, but similar exchanges had transpired on whether or not to seize other Islands. In this instance, Peleliu is to be secured to insulate MacArthur's imminent move against the Philippines in opposition to the wishes of Admiral Halsey who prefers to simply isolate it and let the defenders wither and die. Admiral Nimitz makes the decision, and the Marines get the task of securing the islands to ensure that MacArthur's right flank remains safe.

Offshore, the powerful Fleet of Vice Admiral T.S. Wilkinson hosts the III Amphibious Corps, commanded by General Geiger, a battle-ready determined group of Americans that is anxiously awaiting the orders to hit the beaches. The scene is reminiscent of recently won campaigns. Final instructions are being bellowed as the Planes are pummeling enemy positions during these early morning hours. The booming guns of the Surface Vessels are overshadowing the interaction aboard Ship. Continuous puffs of friendly smoke permeate the sky directly over the Warships as the giant guns clear their throats, coughing out deadly strings of fire in seemingly con-

tinuous links that arc toward the beaches and burst in spectacular fashion, igniting multicolored fires, detonating massive explosions, and catapulting dust and debris that virtually creates a horrid wall of smoke, forbidding penetration by the human eye. Anyone watching the magnificent display might easily form the opinion that nothing alive could survive this thrashing. Last minute letters and portions thereof are left aboard Ship by Marines for their loved ones at home. Another check of their weapons, another prayer or two jammed into their litany of words that help to keep them calm, and off they go. In a matter of moments, some will be dead and others will have their bodies wrenched with pain, but they are on their way to deliver another promissory note to the Japanese. Meanwhile, the Navy attempts to draw attention from the main invasion by some diversionary maneuvers that feint a landing at Babelthuap by the Angaur Attack Group under Rear Admiral William H. P. Blandy.

The Japanese on Peleliu number over 10,000 and their positions are deeply entrenched, unscathed by the zealous bombardments of the Carrier Planes and Surface Vessels. The Japanese again are buried in interconnecting caves that are generously dispersed throughout the center of the island on the impartial slopes of the Umurbrogol Ridges. The skillful deployment of their weaponry has given them extraordinary advantages. The water approaches have been thoroughly saturated with underwater explosives to destroy approaching Landing Craft. Beyond these dangling instruments of death, the Marines must overcome innumerable personnel mines that mischievously conceal themselves on the beaches, lying in deadly ambush beneath the sand. After the Marines overcome these murderous inconveniences, they must conquer a terrifying gridlock as the Japanese have their guns placed in order to catch the Yanks in a crossfire as they attempt to overcome the Antitank obstacles.

It's 08:30 and the Marines are landing. General Rupertus' 1st Division strikes the southwest shore of Peleliu, unaware that the Japanese have changed their defensive tactics and will not defend the beaches with their usual tenacity, choosing to draw the Americans to their inland positions. The resistance is heavy, but the battle plan hopes to draw the 9,000 Marines into the spider's web. Absolute orders have been issued to the Japanese forbidding them from mounting suicidal attacks. General Sadao Inoue, commanding the Palaus, intends to destroy the invaders with his command, considered to be one of the Emperor's finest.

Opposition at beaches Orange and White is resolute, beginning nominally, then increasing with determination as the Marines push inland. The 5th Marines forces the center, flanked by the 7th Marines on the right and the 1st Marines driving on the left, with the iron-fisted thrust of the center penetrating unhesitatingly to the coveted Airfield where the 2nd Battalion, 5th Marines pivots during its eastward drive and races north, securing the southern portion of the Airfield. Meanwhile, Company L bolts across the island in buzz-saw fashion, chopping the island into two parts, inconveniencing the landlord and making Japanese excursions hazardous to their health. The 1st Marines hit rigid resistance along the northern perimeter of the beachhead. Enemy machine guns rake every square yard, inflicting severe casualties upon Chesty Puller's 1st Marines. The unending burst of fire originating from sinister pillboxes must be exterminated one by one before the perimeter collapses. Within a couple of hours, Company K has lost the majority of two Platoons to the casualty list, but the obstacles are taken, and the death trap known as the "Point" is demolished by intrepid troops by use of grenades being deposited through the tiny slits of the pill boxes. In addition, the Marines saturate the stronghold with fire from flamethrowers and generous dosages of killing power from other available weaponry.

The irritated Japanese mount a fierce counterattack, comprising Tanks and Infantry, to retake the Airfield near dinnertime, but the effort is futile and handily repulsed, resulting in a great number of Japanese being killed. The Yanks take quick advantage of the failed assault. Company L, 2nd Battalion, 5th Marines drills forward nearly to the center of the Airfield. Nearby, the 7th Marines advances south where the 1st Battalion rounds up scattered enemy troops in its sector. By day's end, the Yanks have secured a solid beachhead that professes permanency although in measurement it is only several hundred yards deep and 2,800 yards running north to south (slightly deeper within perimeter of center salient). Of course, the possibility of 10,000 Japanese relocating 9,000 U.S. Marines without their consent is unlikely. Old Glory is here to stay. During the actions taking place on the beach, heroism abounds, but many individual acts of courage will never be known. Two men of the 5th Marines receive the Medal of Honor for their sacrifices: Corporal Lewis Bausell and 2nd Lieutenant Carlton Rouh, each throwing their bodies on live grenades to save the lives of their fellow Marines, the latter giving his life.

On the 16th, the Marines turn on the pressure. The 5th Marines, supplemented by the 1st Marines, secure the northern sector of the Airfield. Elements of the 3rd Battalion sweep to the eastern shore and fortify the sector, while Company K, 3rd Battalion, pushes south toward the high peaks that extend into the water on the southeastern tip of the island. General Nakagawa, commanding the Japanese on Peleliu, orders the ridges in the northern portion of the island to be the main line of resistance. The enemy prepares to resist the 1st Marines under Puller, which launches its attack. The Japanese take horrendous casualties, but their determination to outlast the invaders does not subside. The Marines also take severe casualties as the task of driving the Japanese from the caves is an excruciating endeavor. On the 17th, the enemy is dislodged on the southern promontory by the 7th Marines (Company L, 3rd Battalion), while the 2nd Battalion, 1st Marines, secures Hill 200.

Peleliu has the scent of death and destruction as the sun rises on the 18th. The Japanese have already sustained over 2,500 dead. The Marines lose less than fifty, although they sustain slightly over 400 wounded. The torrid tropical heat also is taking a toll on the Marines. With the temperatures hovering uncomfortably, well over 100 degrees, heat exhaustion is prevalent. Despite the enduring temperatures, the drive continues, and Hill 210 falls to elements of the 1st and 7th Marines. In addition, the 1st Battalion, 1st Marines exterminates the resistance and seizes Hill 205, while the menacing southeast promontory resistance collapses under the duress of the 1st Battalion, 7th Marines, giving the 7th Marines control of the southern portion of the island.

The Marines gnaw forward, crossing the island, and many more Marines are wounded, their ranks thinning faster than anticipated. Today, the 19th, elements of the 1st Marines force their way to the Five Sisters, the southern front of the final enemy resistance, where the lingering pocket of resistance still stands defiantly. By the 21st, the 1st Marines under Chesty Puller have taken such casualties that they are rendered unable to continue as a Regimental Team and are compelled to pull back to the eastern defense zone to regroup and rest. By the 23rd, Regimental Combat Team 321, 81st Infantry, U.S.A. is brought into the battle. An invasion force usually outnumbers the defending force by at least four to one, but at Peleliu, the opposing forces are nearly equal in size. Army units have been available as reserves, but General Rupertus had expressed a vehement reluctance to have them participate on Peleliu. The grim casualties take preeminence, and the Army troops land on Orange Beach, receiving orders to invest the enemy resistance in the Umurbrogol Mountain in cooperation with the 7th Marines.

Now the Soldiers and Marines attack simultaneously, each having savage engagements as they ascend the mountain, stone by stone with fervent passion. On the 24th, Company E, 321st Infantry advances to the furthermost point of the ominous mountain and methodically eliminates the opposition, seizing Hill 100. On the following day, Neal Task Force, U.S.A., shredding the enemy resistance in the sector south of Hill 100, whips its way upon Hill B, trapping and isolating the remaining Japanese on the northern peninsula, while the 5th Marines assault enemy positions on the tip of the peninsula and set up a perimeter.

Non-stop activity is the order of the day on the 26th, as the 1st Battalion, 5th Marines drives toward another obstinate group of hills known as Amiangal "Mountain." The assault takes Hill 2 after a superlative effort by Company B. The 2nd

Battalion drives north, bypassing Hill 1, reaching the eastern shore of the northern peninsula. seizing Hill 80; its capture ensures the closure of the northern tip of the island. On the following day, the Japanese are further compressed as RCT 321 drives north to dissolve the Umurbrogol Pocket and eradicate the enemy still holding tenaciously in the central ridges that have been previously bypassed by the Marines. By today, it is apparent that the Yanks are to be the victors. Old Glory is raised at the 1st Marine Division Command Post to symbolize the quest, although the fighting continues for some time. The crushing jackhammer thrust of the combined Army-Marine force drives through the remaining resistance, inflicting enormous casualties on the enemy while taking heavy casualties themselves. The Japanese maintain discipline and avoid suicidal assaults. When getting behind U.S. lines, they revert to concealment in order to strike suddenly from within the American perimeter, but to no avail. By the 30th, northern Peleliu is declared secure. Mop-up operations, carried out by contingents of the 5th Marines and elements of Regimental Combat Team 321, U.S.A., culminate on the 2nd of October. The balance of the island still holds Jap strongpoints, but the effective use of flame throwers, grenades, and, of course the Infantry, eliminates them. The Marines eventually are completely relieved by the Army, allowing the 1st Marine Division to prepare for its next offensive. At the end of a month of brutalizing combat, including pulling the Japs out of the caves or blowing away those that refuse to capitulate, the Japanese lose most of their defenders; however, the 1,100 plus that still remain linger for another month and a half. The island is officially declared secure on November 27th. The Marines suffer 1,250 killed and 5,275 wounded. The U.S. 81st Division sustains 3,275 casualties, including 542 killed. Total Japanese losses, including action on the small islands off Peleliu and Angaur, amount to 13,600 killed and 400 captured.

September 15th 1944 — (United States) The Carrier U.S.S. *Shangri La* (CV-38) is commissioned at Norfolk, Va. In other activity, the Joint Chiefs of Staff make the decision to invade the central Philippines, altering the original plan which had been to assault the southern Philippines. By this action, the attacks against Mindanao, Talaud, and Yap are aborted. All attention now centers on Leyte. American progress in the Pacific permits a rapid step up to take the Philippines, and the target date is changed from December 20th to October 20th. **(Pacific Dutch East Indies)** THE INVASION OF MOROTAI — General MacArthur's strategy is working near perfectly from the standpoint of time and energy, as the quest for a return to the Philippines nears. Morotai is the objective, and since the beginning of September, precautionary bombardments have been carried out by Carrier and Land-based Planes against targets near the primary objective and include Halmahera, Batjan Island further south, and Celebes. The weather is intolerable today, but the invasion commences, following a two-hour Naval bombardment, compliments of the U.S. Navy. The Cruisers and Destroyers of Rear Admiral Berkey and the Planes attached to Rear Admiral Sprague's Escort Carriers bolster the confidence of the invasion troops who debark from Rear Admiral Barbey's Task Force (VII Amphibious Force Task Force 77). At 08:30, the southwest coast of Morotai is inundated by Task Force Tradewind, commanded by General Hall (Commanding General XI Corps, ALAMO). The enemy offers no opposition, and in a synchronized movement, two Regiments secure the landing area at the tip of the Gila Peninsula, while a third Regiment hits an adjacent beach, further south on the western side of

Invasion of Moratai, Dutch East Indies.

the peninsula. In short order, the Gila Peninsula and the towns of Pitoe and Drome are seized as the 155th, 167th, and 124th Regiments join to drive inland about 2,000 yards. A Command is established onshore by General Persons. Enemy resistance is sporadic throughout the day into the following morning. By the second day ashore, Regimental Combat Team 125, 32nd Division, lands on the Gila Peninsula to relieve the 124th Infantry. The beachhead is expanded to a distance of 3,000 yards long and approximately 2,000 yards deep, permitting solid positioning to swat the feeble opposition that is raised by the Japanese. By the 18th, the troops ascertain enough information to prompt them to seek another Airfield besides Pitoe, which is unable to handle large Bombers. The Yanks begin to establish a Bomber Base, capable of supporting the assault against the Philippines, at Gotalalamo Village on the southern coast. Inventive Soldiers dub Pitoe Field "THE CRASH STRIP" and the new Bomber Base as "WAMA DROME." Subsequently, construction begins on another field about 1,200 yards north of the latter and is called the "PITOE DROME." The Operation continues for some time, interrupted occasionally by the sparse amount of enemy troops still alive on the island. Offshore, the Carrier Escorts maintain an umbrella of protection for the island during its transformation. By the 25th, Task Force Tradewind is disbanded, and General Hall (Commanding General XI Corps) takes total responsibility for the island. On the 4th of October, General Krueger proclaims the Morotai Operation terminated as the Permanent Fighter detachment arrives and the Carriers depart the area. During the occupation, protective radar is established on an offshore island (Raoe). The

Americans suffer about 30 dead, 85 wounded, and 1 missing. The Japanese suffer 102 killed on the island and an additional 200 (approximate) killed on barges while moving between Morotai and Halmahera. In addition, 13 Japanese are captured. **(Pacific-Molucca Sea)** The Molucca Sea, Indonesia, between New Guinea and the Celebes has an underwater guest today. The U.S.S. *Stingray* (SS-186) moves through and lands men and equipment at Majoe Island, Molucca Islands. **(Pacific-Philippines)** The U.S.S. *Gauvina* (SS-362), on War Patrol, sinks a Japanese Transport, No. 3, off the Philippines. **(China-Burma-India)** General Stilwell meets in Chungking with Chiang Kai-shek and is informed by the Generalissimo that if the Chinese troops at Myitkyina do not attack toward Bhamo within a week, he (Kai-shek) will pull out the Salween Forces. This information is dispatched to General Marshall (attending Quebec Octagon Conference with President Roosevelt). There is still a great deal of turmoil in the China Burma Theater, much of it political. Stilwell had recently suggested the importance of getting arms to the Communists who had agreed to fight the Japanese, but Kai-shek insists they must fight under Chinese Command. The Communists have agreed to fight under Stilwell's command and had reinforced this position to Stilwell only two days prior. The animosity between Stilwell and Kai-shek is about to explode. General Marshall informs President Roosevelt of Kai-Shek's message and ignition occurs. A non-ambiguous directive comprising six hundred words is sent by Roosevelt to Chiang, explicitly mandating that Chiang Kai-shek press the attack in the Salween or assume personal responsibility for the possible catastrophic results of inaction. The letter (drawn up by men on Marshall's Staff) further scolds Kai-shek, informing him that the expeditious progress of the U.S. as it thrusts across the Pacific will not arrive in time to save China. General Stilwell delivers the message (Chinese translation) without any soft insulation and in fact takes great pleasure in the mission. The threat is in essence just that, a threat, and in the end, the Generalissimo gets his way, calling the President's bluff, subsequently refusing to give Stilwell command and simultaneously demanding he be replaced. Chiang also insists on Chinese being in charge of Lend-Lease. Toward the end of November, an American O.S.S. outfit will discover a bonanza of American arms stashed in more than 20 warehouses near Tushan (Province of Kweichow) including 50 tons of ammunition and weapons being hoarded for possible use against the Communist Chinese in east China. **(Atlantic-Western Europe)** The Germans are getting pushed back to the Fatherland. Attempts are made to stem the tide, but the overpowering waves of Allied troops become increasingly burdensome. German General Blaskowitz's Army Group G is setting up defenses between Epinal and Metz, deploying the 5th Armored under General Manteuffel and the 1st Army commanded by General Knobelsdorff. To the north, General Model's Army Group B sits uncomfortably in the path of the Yanks, who are securing vital links as they drive toward Germany. German Generals Zengen (15th Army), Brandenberger (7th Army), and General Student (1st Parachute Army) have responsibility of defending the terrain along the German border between the Ruhr and Saar Rivers. The Allies ignore the impending resistance and drive forcefully. **21st Army Group** Elements of the **Canadian 1st Army** secure a bridgehead across the Canal de Derivation. British General Montgomery is planning another attack. The target is Arnhem, and the approval of General Eisenhower has been given privately. Bradley does not receive the tidings kindly. An American Liaison Officer to the British 21 Army Group

informs Bradley of the upcoming assault. The news causes some mixed feelings of consternation and disbelief, in view of the fact that a recent mutual agreement reached between the two men had apparently been broken. Montgomery's proposed plans jeopardize Bradley's left flank by creating a dangerous gap, forcing Bradley to make drastic changes and direct Patton to divert an Armored Division to General Hodges to rectify the situation. The American Commanders protest vociferously, but to no avail. General Montgomery wins again. In the **12th Army Group** The **VIII Corps, U.S. Ninth Army** is still encountering firm resistance at Brest with both the 2nd and 29th Divisions making only gradual progress. In other activity, the 8th Division initiates an attack to capture the Crozon Peninsula. In the **U.S. First Army** area, mop-up operations at Maastricht Island are finished. At the De Geul River, the Germans offer heavy resistance, but Combat Command B successfully establishes a bridgehead near Meerssen. In the **VII Corps** area, elements of the 1st Division have Aachen almost totally surrounded. The 3rd Armored Division is heavily engaged with the enemy near the second defense line of the West Wall, known as the Schill Line. The Germans knock out six of Combat Command A's Tanks near Geisberg Hill; however, the 16th Regiment, 1st Division, eliminates many of the enemy strongholds. Combat Command B's Task Force Lovelady crosses the Vicht and moves rapidly against moderate opposition, crashing through the West Wall, driving toward Eschweiler. The enemy halts the advance and forces the Task Force to pull back. German Infantry and Tanks hold fast near Stolberg and compel Task Force Mills (commanded by Major Herbert N. Mills) to withdraw and reform behind Task Force Lovelady. Other fierce actions in the **XIX Corps** area include skirmishes at Hoefen-Alzen Ridge and Monschau, with the 60th Regiment hitting stiff resistance. At Lammersdorf, the 39th Regiment encounters extremely heavy resistance at the Scharnhorst Line. The Yanks are also busily engaged in the V Corps zone. The 8th Division hits enormous opposition. A serious gap exists between the 12th and 22nd Infantry Regiments when the 22nd is struck by a severe counterattack that prevents it from assaulting Brandscheid. Enemy resistance at Roscheid halts the 109th Infantry, 28th Division, which continues to attack unsuccessfully for three additional days. Hill 553 falls to the 110th Infantry and a contingent of Engineers. Yankee Armor is diligently engaged in the **V Corps** sector as Combat Command R, 5th Armored, punches a hole in the West Wall and advances to the fringes of Bettingen, while the 112th Infantry (attached to C.C.R.) secures Biesdorf and drives to Stockigt to guard the southeast flank. In the **U.S. Third Army** area, the **XX Corps** launches an assault against the Germans holding firm positions west of the Metz River. Elements deploy for an attack against Fort Amanvillers (Kellermann works). Combat Command B, 7th Armored Division enlarges its Arnaville bridgehead prior to the attack against Metz. Arry, Lorry, Mardigny, Vittonville, and Hill 396 are seized. In the **XII Corps** sector, Task Force Sebree, comprising elements of the 134th Infantry, 35th Division and the 319th Infantry, 80th Division enter Nancy without resistance. The Yanks, holding a bridgehead at Dieulouard, are struck by a severe bombardment, followed by a tenacious attack that penetrates American positions and gains control of Ste Genevieve and Atton. Contingents holding Mousson Hill become isolated, but they hold out until reinforcements reach them on the following day to drive the Germans back. Casualties on both sides are grave. The 35th Division, in conjunction with Combat Command B, 4th Armored, advances to the area southeast of Nancy and elements of the 320th Infantry cross the Marne-Rhine Canal while Combat Command B forces its way across the canal at Crevic and Maixe, the latter mounting the fiercest of the opposition. In the **XV Corps** area, the bridgehead is maintained at the Moselle across from Charmes by the 79th Division, and mop-up operations in the area west of the Moselle continue. Russian troops visit Patton's Headquarters, but he avoids them by going to the front. He subsequently states: "I RETALIATED FOR THEIR TREATMENT OF OUR OBSERVERS BY FIXING THEM A G-2 MAP WHICH SHOWED EXACTLY NOTHING." **Sixth Army Group** The U.S. **Sixth Army**, commanded by General Devers, becomes operational at 00:01 and immediately assumes control of Allied Force Headquarters (Mediterranean forces that are presently in France). French Army Group B, commanded by French General de Lattre de Tassigny, but previously under General Patch's command, receives autonomy, gaining parity with the U.S. Seventh Army. **(Atlantic-Italy)** In the U.S. **Fifth Army** area, **IV Corps** sector, Viareggio is occupied by Task Force 45. In other activity, a Brazilian unit, Regimental Combat Team 6, becomes the first Brazilian unit to join the fight in Europe. It relieves the 434th AAA Battalion which had been maintaining a 5-mile zone between the coastal plain and the Serchio Valley. Subsequently, the remainder of the 1st Brazilian Division will enter Europe. In other activity, M. Moscoso is seized by the South African 6th Armored Division. In the **II Corps** area, the vicious fight to control Altuzzo Ridge continues with the 338th Infantry, 85th Division battering the defenders who refuse to submit. At M. Veruca, tenacious resistance stalls the 339th Infantry, and the critical fighting at M. Monticelli gains very little ground as the enemy impedes the advance and forestalls entrance to Futa Pass. The contest is equally fierce at Torricella Hill with the 34th Division pressing, but not dislodging the enemy. Close by, elements seize M. Frassino. In the British 13th Corps area, Poggio Prefetto is taken by the 1st British Division, and in conjunctive action, the Indian 8th Division seizes M. Stelleto and Le Scalette while the British 6th Armored fights its way slightly up the slopes of M. Peschiena. In the **British Eighth Army** area, a rapid movement to the next delaying line occurs. It is named the Rimini Line and extends from S. Fortunato, which controls a good deal of Highway 16, down to Ceriano Ridge. During the day, disoriented and vicious combat erupts near S. Martino in M. L'Abate.

September 16th 1944 — (Atlantic-Canada) The Quebec Conference between the British and Americans (Roosevelt and Churchill) in session since the 11th ends today. Fundamental agreement is reached concerning the direction of the Pacific War, expected to culminate during 1945. Plans are initiated to invade Japan with an invasion of Kyushu in October followed by an assault against Tokyo Plain (Honshu) during December. These plans become unnecessary after the Atomic bomb is dropped upon Japan during August 1945. **(Pacific-Hawaii)** Marine Aircraft Wings, Pacific, is redesignated Aircraft, Fleet Marine Force, Pacific in accordance with an earlier directive (September 7th) from the Commandant. The Commander is Major General F.P. Mulcahy and Headquarters is at Ewa, Oahu, Territory of Hawaii. **(Pacific-Morotai)** During the Morotai Operation, Carrier Planes have been lending assistance. One Naval Pilot is forced to ditch his Aircraft, and in another spectacular display of heroism, Torpedo Boat Squadron 33 goes to the rescue. The downed Pilot is within two hundred yards of a heavily fortified Japanese position at Wasile Bay, Halmahera Island. The rescue craft travels 60 miles of dangerous waterways permeated with mines. Led by

Lt. Arthur Preston, the PT Boats encounter incessant fire from the shore guns at the mouth of the bay, twice repulsing the rescue attempt. Undaunted, Preston defies the fire, and with the assistance of smoke cover provided by Planes, he gets near the endangered Pilot only to be turned back again. The covering Aircraft expend their available fuel and are forced to abandon the effort. The PTs 489 and 463, led by Preston, race through the wall of fire and rescue the Pilot, then reverse and speed through the mine fields to safety; Lt. Preston receives the Medal of Honor. **(Pacific-Peleliu)** The 5th and 7th Marines secure most of the Airfield at Peleliu. In addition, Company I, 3rd Marine Battalion, 5th Marines, advances to the east shore and fortifies the beachhead there. Company K drives to the southeastern promontory. In other activity, the 1st Marine Division commences a strong assault against the well-entrenched enemy, deployed in the central ridges that permeate the axis of the northwest peninsula. In Naval activity, the U.S.S. *Wadleigh* (DD-689) becomes damaged after striking a mine off the Palau Islands. **(China-Burma-India)** General Stilwell informs the Joint Chiefs of Staff about the seriousness of the Japanese successes against the U.S. Fourteenth Air Force Bases and of the potential ramifications. It is conceivable that Air cover for the invasion of Formosa and the Philippines will not be supplied from China. This information has much to do with the strategy of invading Luzon as opposed to Formosa. **(Atlantic-Western Europe)** The Allies drive toward Germany, making tremendous progress. Hitler, in an attempt to forestall defeat, confers with his Commanders and details his plan for a major counteroffensive in the Ardennes. **21st Army Group** In the **Canadian First Army** area, the Canadian 4th Armored Division advances from the Balgerhoek toward the Ghent-Terneuzen Canal. In the **British Second Army** 12th Corps area, the British 53rd Division is relieved at Antwerp by the British 7th Armored Division. **12th Army Group** The U.S. **Ninth Army**, operating along the Loire, is deployed in perfect position to accept the surrender of 20,000 Germans (German Group Elster). The U.S. Third and Seventh Armies have joined together, forming a perfect trap that prevents escape and forces surrender. In the **VIII Corps** area, Fort Montbarey is seized by the 29th Division. The conquest secures a direct route from the west leading to Brest. The 175th Infantry, in unusual fashion, pushes into Brest by way of an underground tunnel positioned under a stone wall while the 116th Infantry nears Recouvrance, and the 117th closes upon the Submarine pens. In other activity, the 2nd Division maintains pressure against the Germans, continuing its advance from the north. In the **U.S. First Army** area, **XIX Corps** sector, an enormous gap stretching nine miles now exists between the British and American Armies due to the opposing direction of the assaults. The Yanks attempt to plug the gap and dispatch Task Force Stokes, comprising the 99th Infantry Battalion, a Tank Battalion, 2nd Armored, and other contingents across the Willems Vaart Canal, north of Maastricht. Activity is furious all across the XIX Corps sector. Combat Command B, 2nd Armored Division encounters vicious fire from the enemy at its Meerssen bridgehead. At Valkenburg, the situation of Combat Command A is similar as the enemy raises a tempest of opposition to prevent them from advancing into the 30th Division's bridgehead. The Yanks press relentlessly, reinitiating the strengthened assault toward the West Wall near Aachen. Elements force their way to within three miles of Germany. The Germans mount equally fierce resistance in the **VII Corps** area at the Stolberg Line. At Weissenberg Hill and in the northern suburbs of Stolberg, Combat Commands B and

A, respectively, are halted abruptly by intense fire and unflappable resistance. The vicious contests have created a four-mile gap between their lines. Task Force Hogan, commanded by Lt. Colonel Samuel Hogan, is established, comprising a Tank contingent and the 1st Battalion, 26th Infantry; it wastes no time overpowering Buesbach. Vicht and Schevenhuette are victimized by the 47th Infantry, 9th Division, while the ensuing combat at Lammersdorf sees the momentum side with the 39th Infantry. The obstinate strongpoint which has stalled the 39th is finally destroyed, allowing Hoefen, on the Hoefen-Alzen Ridge, to be seized by the 60th Infantry, supplemented by Tanks. In the V Corps sector, enemy opposition seriously hinders the progress of the 4th Division and retains the stumbling block for three additional days. The fighting is also incessant in the sector of the 28th Division, but persistent efforts gain some penetration through the West Wall and the drive seizes two strategic hills, Losenseifen and Spielmannsholz, placing the 28th well within reach of its primary objective: Uttfeld. The vehement enemy resistance inflicts heavy casualties against the attacking American units, prompting the Commanding Officer of the V Corps, General Gerow, to temporarily terminate the offensive after he determines that the costs are far too expensive for the gains received. The assault is canceled at 20:40. In the U.S. Third Army area, the Germans offer more steadfast resistance and repulse the attacks of the 90th Division west of the Metz, but they sustain high casualties. At Arnaville, Combat Command R, 7th Armored, attacks from its bridgehead, but is stopped shortly thereafter by withering enemy fire. Combat Command B rushes into the bridgehead during the early morning hours, participating in the advance at 14:00, gaining enough ground to begin closing on Marieulles. Soon after, it is relieved by the 2nd Infantry, allowing Combat Command B to pivot and drive to Vittonville. The Germans mount vicious opposition throughout the Corps sector. Hitler, in a reverse of his earlier strategy, decides to further reinforce his Metz salient in a determined effort to prevent investment of Metz. In the XII Corps area, the heated battle resembles an uncontrollable inferno as the unyielding Germans mount yet another heavy counterattack against the Dieulouard bridgehead in an attempt to crush it, but the 80th Division, with the expertise of Artillery men and skilled Pilots assisting its cause, inflicts a severe thrashing upon the Germans and once again turns them back. The Yanks chase the retreating enemy to Lesmenils. The 80th Division mops up the area and drives east to finish off the Germans. As the 1st Battalion, 318th Infantry moves back to the bridgehead, it startles the Germans holding Ste Genevieve and retakes the town. Meanwhile, the 319th Infantry heads back for the bridgehead and has its 1st Battalion regain Atton. In addition, the 1st Battalion rescues troops which had been trapped on Mousson Hill the previous night. In the vicinity of Nancy, the 35th Division is heavily engaged with the Germans. Elements seize Buissoncourt and at Luneville, the pressure forces the Germans to abandon their positions. In the V Corps sector, more contingents of the 106th Cavalry Group force the Moselle and initiate strong reconnaissance probes toward the Mortagne River. In other activity, the French 2nd Armored Division maintains a bridgehead at the Moselle near Chatel. The Germans attack boldly, using Armor against Combat Command V. Reinforcements are rushed in to successfully neutralize the attack, but the French choose to retreat rather than fight a major battle. During the day, Bradley calls Patton and tells him that Montgomery wants all American troops to halt, so that he can initiate "A DAGGER THRUST WITH THE 21ST

ARMY GROUP AT THE HEART OF GERMANY." Patton asks Bradley: "NOT TO CALL ME UNTIL AFTER DARK ON THE NINETEENTH." 6th Army Group The 36th Division seizes Luxeuil, and the 3rd Division jostles against nominal opposition before taking Lure. (Atlantic-Estonia-Latvia) The Russians begin an offensive, committing the Leningrad and Baltic Fronts in a drive toward the Baltic Sea. These two nations, liberated by the Russians, lose their independence and become part of the U.S.S.R. (Atlantic-Bulgaria) The Third Ukrainian Front (Russian) enters Sofia, the capital of Bulgaria, as it drives west to cut off the German escape from Yugoslavia. (Atlantic-Mediterranean-Greece) The British 9th Commandos land at Kithira Island off the south coast of Peloponnesus and find no opposition. Reconnaissance of the island is initiated to pave the way for Force 140, which lands soon after. Subsequently, an Advance Coastal Forces Base is established on the island. (Atlantic-Italy) In the U.S. Fifth Army area, IV Corps sector, U.S. Task Force 45 is regrouping, subsequent to being relieved by Brazilian Expeditionary Forces. The Brazilians (RCT 6) seize Massarosa and deploy north of Lake Massaciuccioli. The U.S. 1st Armored Division initiates strong Reconnaissance Patrols to impede the enemy's withdrawal, but all through the day, enemy resistance against the right flank of the Corps is bitter. Alto Hill and M. Pozzo del Bagno are taken by the 6th South African Armored. In the II Corps area, night activity keeps both sides from acquiring any rest. The 338th Infantry, 85th Division, presses toward the tip of M. Altuzzo during the night (16-17th), but halts the attack short of the crest due to heavy shelling originating from Allied Artillery. The 337th Infantry, advancing on the right, passes through elements of the British 13th Corps as it climbs up the slopes of M. Pratone. In other brutalizing incidents of incessant combat, the 361st and 363rd Regiments, 91st Division, encounter unbendable resistance at M. Monticelli, west of Il Giogo Pass, while the 362nd Infantry drives punishingly toward Futa Pass. In a war where there are virtually hundreds of thousands of individual heroes, there is never sufficient detail to inscribe all the names, but then and again, an unbelievable act of heroism is recorded for posterity. This is another of those grand unselfish episodes. During the struggle near Scarperia at Monticelli Ridge, Company B, 363rd Infantry is advancing until intense fire stops the assault. Sergeant Oscar Johnson, a Mortar Gunner without ammunition, trades in his Mortar for a Rifle and leads a seven man Squad to establish an outpost 50 yards out on the left flank. By afternoon, all his men are either wounded or dead. Johnson moves from man to man and confiscates all guns and ammunition, becoming a one-man Army amidst a storm of enemy fire. Johnson defies death and stands erect, inflicting serious casualties against the attacking enemy. Several of the enemy Troops who are able to get close to him are exterminated with grenades. During the night (16-17th), the enemy mounts a counterattack against Company B's positions, the brunt of the assault forcing against the lonely G.I. (Oscar). Johnson gives the Germans a resounding one-man show. His expertise with his weapons and grenades, in conjunction with his apparent nerves of steel, keeps him calm as he remains in place, bombs bursting in air and mortars crashing all about his hole, but when morning comes, Johnson is still there, standing close to about 20 dead Germans. Twenty-five additional Germans surrender to him, and the attack, launched by five Companies of a German Paratroop Regiment, has been humbled by the tenacity and spirit of the dauntless Sergeant Oscar G. Johnson, United States Army. In addition to his noted remarkable achievements under fire, Johnson also comes to the aid of two men who attempt to come to his aid on the 17th, until they are snagged by a brutalizing Mortar and Artillery assault which severely wounds both men and nearly buries them alive. He dashes forward and helps a Medic save their lives, then makes sure they get to the rear. He stays on line with his finger in the dike, until his Company gets some well-deserved relief. The Germans have met the Yank from Michigan who did a fine job of impersonating an Armored Regiment; Sgt. Johnson receives the Medal of Honor. The skirmishing is especially violent near Torricella Hill, where the 34th Division is unable to pierce the wall of opposition, yet on the right, elements are driving north from M. Frassino, making good progress. In the **British Eighth Army** area, orders are issued to launch an assault against the Rimini Line. The 5th Corps is instructed to drive against Bologna while the Canadian I Corps strikes toward Ferrara and Ravenna. However, the German opposition stands firm at Montescudo, preventing any advance by the British 46th Division. During the night of the 16th, the British 4th Division secures Cerasolo Ridge by using searchlights to good advantage. In other fighting, the Canadian 1st Division fails to eliminate the resistance from S. Martino on M. L'Abate.

September 17th 1944 — (Pacific-Palaus) INVASION OF ANGAUR — The defenders of Angaur are the recipients of an early reveille call, compliments of the U.S. Navy. Naval Surface Vessels and Aircraft swarm overhead bombarding enemy positions, completing some instant renovations of Japanese facilities in the immediate area. Upon cessation of the preinvasion exercises, the 321st and 322nd Infantry Regiments, 81st Division land on the east coast, against nominal opposition, while the 323rd Infantry approaches the west coast on the pretext of forcing a landing. The Japs respond to the invasion with half-hearted resistance. The sporadic small-arms fire and ineffective mortar barrages do not impede the landing. The 322nd pushes from the northern beachhead to the area north of Lake Aztec, while the 321st takes possession of the island from Rocky Point at the southern end of the island to Cape Ngariois to the north, the depth reaching about 350 yards inland. The Japanese plan and launch a lavish, but unsuccessful, night attack against the American positions.

On the following day, the Yanks drive toward the enemy phosphate plant in the center of the island on the western shore. These troops of the 322nd Regiment are inadvertently bombed by friendly Planes. In addition, other units driving along the northern coast become separated and are cut off. The Japanese mount stiff resistance against the 321st Infantry as it advances along the Southern Railroad toward Green Beach, preventing it from reaching the objective, about 600 yards below Rocky Point. By the 19th, elements of the 81st Division attack to eradicate the enemy in south Angaur. The drive attempts to divide the enemy forces as it moves to establish positions from south Angaur to Garangaoi Cove. The tenacity of the Japanese has been waning all across the Pacific, but individual detachments continue to mount fanatical opposition. The Yanks renounce the myth of Japanese superiority and continue to dismember their ranks. On the 20th, organized resistance on Angaur is declared at an end by General Mueller, U.S.A.

Fragments of the enemy units become compressed on the northwest sector of the island, but they intend to fight to the end. The 322nd Infantry begins a strong attack to annihilate the galvanized pocket that has formed near Lake Salome. The assault gnaws forward, following an Artillery bombardment

U.S. troops advancing on Angaur, Palau Islands. A dead enemy soldier lays along the tracks.

on the 21st, but the Japanese resist and their withering fire compels the 321st to abandon its positions. The attack is repeated on the following day, but again the defiant Japanese hold their pocket, and as darkness falls, the 321st again moves back. The Yanks change tactics, requesting the Japs to surrender their positions, but the offer nets only two enemy Soldiers, prompting the 321st to call in more Artillery. For the balance of the day and into the night (24th), an incessant pounding hits the Lake Salome pocket. Still, the Japs refuse to capitulate. Engineers are brought up to cut a road from the north to permit an attack from the opposite direction. By the 27th the enemy pocket is surrounded, and final elimination becomes inevitable. As the Japanese attempt to fortify their shrinking strongpoint, the Yanks press ahead, squeezing the enemy into an area less than 50 yards deep and 100 yards long by the 18th of October. By the 21st, all opposition, except stragglers, is reduced. The Japanese suffer 1,300 dead and 45 captured. The U.S. 81st Division sustains 264 killed and 1,355 wounded or injured. During the campaign to clear Angaur, elements of the 81st have been diverted to Peleliu to assist the Marines who continue to receive heated opposition on that island. On the 23rd, Antitank and Cannon Companies relieve the Infantry and resume the task of exterminating the few unyielding Japanese who prefer death to surrender.

September 17th 1944 — (United States) Upon authority from the Commandant of the Marine Corps (August 31st), the word Provisional is dropped, and Headquarters, Fleet Marine Force, Pacific, and Headquarters and Service Battalion, Fleet Marine Force Pacific are both officially established. **(Pacific-Palaus-Peleliu)** The 2nd Battalion, 1st Marines, captures Hill 200. In other activity, elements of the 3rd Battalion, 7th Marines, seize the southern promontory (ridges extending into the water). **(Pacific-Morotai)** The U.S. 126th Infantry begins setting up outposts on the islands off the west and southwestern coast of Morotai while on the main island, activity is restricted to probing Patrols which seek out the elusive small bands of remaining resistance. **(China-Burma-India)** In the British Fourteenth Army area, the Indian 5th Division seizes Tuitum. **(Atlantic-Western Europe) British 21st Army Group** The Canadian First Army's 3rd Division attacks Boulogne, which is heavily defended by the Germans. The assault, augmented by both Air and Artillery, makes slight progress against the entrenched fortifications. The British 1st Corps begins to open the Schelde Estuary, which is infested with Germans and holding up Allied use of the port of Antwerp. The Germans resist fiercely, greatly impeding the British. The first Allied Ship enters Antwerp during the latter part of November. In the **U.S. 12th Army Group**, the ambitious battle for Brest continues. Elements of the 9th Division secure the area up to the Penfeld River while 2nd Division units crash over the old city wall. In addition, the 8th Division whacks its way through the Crozon Peninsula, advancing to Crozon. In the **U.S. First Army** area, the enemy is pushed back from the vicinity of the Meerssen and Valkenburg bridgeheads as both American strongpoints are enlarged. The 30th Division whips into Heerlen, then bolts across the German border toward Simpelveld. In the **VII Corps** area, the Germans drive against the 16th Infantry, 1st Division and Combat Command A, 3rd Armored, subsequent to a massive enemy Artillery bombardment. The advancing Germans are pummeled, stopping the counterattack and sending them back reeling with severe losses. Combat Command B rushes through opposition to seize Weissenberg Hill, but a sustained counterattack pushes it back slightly, prompting reinforcements (Task Force Hogan) to rush to its aid. In another brisk action, the Germans prepare to jump off against the Yanks from their positions at Gressenich, but a 147th Infantry Patrol detects the Force and lies in ambush. As the unsuspecting Germans advance into open spaces, the U.S. opens fire, inflicting catastrophic losses upon the enemy. In the **V Corps** area, the Germans fare better. The fighting at Brandscheid hits a high pitch as the 4th Division presses to blow through the German defenses. The effort is expensive and unsuccessful, becoming stalled at the fringes of the Schnee Eifel Forest. The Divisional offensive is aborted and defensive positions are taken. At Wallendorf, the Germans unsuccessfully attempt to destroy elements of the 5th Armored Division's Combat Command R. In the **U.S. Third Army** area, **XX Corps** sector, tentative plans for a combined Air-ground offensive near Metz (Operation THUNDERBOLT) are issued by Major General Walton Walker. The 5th Division perimeter at Arnaville is struck by a powerful but futile counterattack that attempts to drive a wedge between the 10th and 11th Regiments. In the 90th Division sector, the Germans mount hefty resistance, causing high casualties which force an end to the attack. In the 7th Armored area, Marieulles is seized by Combat Command A, reinforced by units of Combat Command B. Afterward, Combat Commands B and R drive to the Seille River. In the **XII Corps** area, Task Force Sebree attacks the enemy on a plateau northeast of Nancy. Combat Command B, 4th Armored, drives toward Nomeny to join the 80th Division, but the resistance is potent, forcing the advance to stall. In other Corps activity the Germans infiltrate U.S. lines at Luneville, but the Yanks retain control. In the **6th Army Group** area, the **U.S. Seventh Army** advances toward the Moselle, encountering strong rear-guard action as it pushes to Remiremont. As the 30th Infantry, 3rd Division nears Radden, a sudden burst by the enemy overpowers a contingent of Company L. The Germans charge with guns blazing. U.S. Sergeant Harold Messerschmidt scampers between the hail of bullets, moving from man to man. During the wretched skirmish, all Messerschmidt's men are killed or wounded. He is also hit, suffering multiple wounds, but he refuses to lie down and die, choosing to stand erect and expend his ammunition against the attackers, finally using an empty submachine gun as a club. Nearby, one of the Germans is poised to shoot one of the wounded, but Messerschmidt kills him. Yank reinforcements rush to aid Messerschmidt who then initiates a charge; another burst of enemy fire takes his life; he receives the Medal of Honor posthumously. **(Atlantic-Italy)** In the **U.S. Fifth Army** area, **IV Corps** operating on the right flank of the Army, advances. The Germans mount nominal opposition against Task Force 45 as it plows along the coast. The 1st Armored Division drives north, CCA moving along the Serchio while CCB attacks toward M. Liguana. On the right flank of the Corps, the 6th South African Armored Division encounters stiff opposition that hinders its progress. In other Corps activity, Brazilian RCT 6 tries to maintain pace with Task Force 45. In the **II Corps** area, the staunch resistance at the Gothic Line is crumbling. Elements burst through the line at Il Giogo Pass. M. Altuzzo is taken by the 338th Infantry, 85th Division, while the 337th takes M. Pratone with equal tenacity. The combat is vicious throughout the day, but the determination of the assault forces an enemy withdrawal after dark. The 91st Division pushes to the crest of M. Monticelli. The Gothic Line is abandoned during the night of the 16th-17th, and the Yanks are plowing forward against a more sedate but still deadly enemy. In the British 13th Corps area, the Germans have abandoned M. Giuvigiana, and it is occupied by the British 1st Division. The British 6th Armored Division encounters tenacious opposition at M. Peschiena. In the **British Eighth Army** area, the Germans abandon their positions around Montescudo, and the British 46th Division assaults, cross ing the Marano River west of Vallecchia. The British 56th Division is unable to breakthrough the resistance at M. Oliva; however, elements make progress west of Cerasolo. In the Canadian 1st Corps sector, the British 4th Division advances toward S. Fortunato, which is soon to be struck by a massive Allied Air attack. In conjunctive activity, the Canadian 1st Division is heavily engaged with a strong German force at S. Martino in M. l'Abate; the Germans retain the strongpoint.

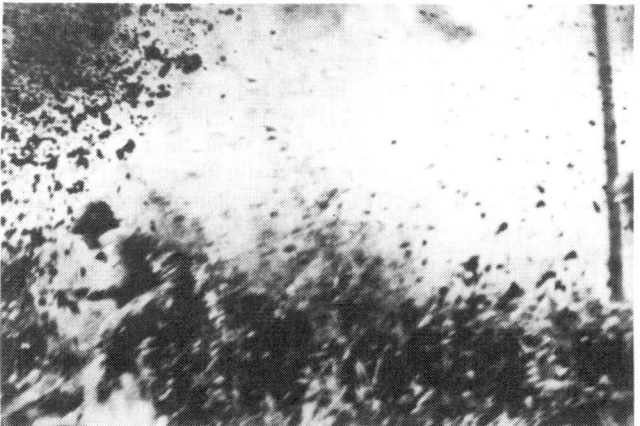

U.S. Paratroopers moving rapidly through a field of fire at Arnhem.

September 17th 1944 — (Atlantic-Western Europe) — OPERATION MARKET GARDEN: OBJECTIVE ARNHEM — British General Montgomery, straying far from his usual assault strategy, mounts a massive Airborne assault to outflank the enemy, committing both Airborne and Armor in a silk-and-iron attack. U.S. General Brereton's Allied Paratroopers are soaring high in the sky over Holland to secure the axis of advance toward Zuider Zee for the British Second Army. The daylight assault commences at 13:00, supported by heavy Air cover, and is so startling that in the early going, it achieves the edge of surprise, preventing quick response from the Germans.

As the chutes cascade toward earth, Gliders are swooping silently toward their landing spots, the combined force numbering 20,000 men, comprised of British and U.S. troops. The operation is a success from the standpoint of losses in Planes and Gliders, less than 3 percent. The British 1st Airborne

Division, including the Polish Paratroop Brigade, the U.S. 82nd under James Gavin and the 101st under Maxwell Taylor participate.

The British 1st Airborne is charged with responsibility of seizing three bridges over the lower Rhine (Neder Rijn) at Arnhem, but the premeditated drop point is eight miles from the objective, permitting the defending Panzers sufficient time to bolster the opposition. The Guards' Armored, moving in synchronization with the Paratroops, encounters the enemy Armor between the Waal and Arnhem. Meanwhile, less than a Battalion of the British Airborne reaches the northern end of a designated highway bridge; they become cut off and isolated. The two remaining targets are both destroyed by the Germans, denying use by the Allies. The magnificent assault is both daring and especially heroic, but ends in failure. Of the 9,000 British Paratroopers who make the jump, only 2,500 return to Allied lines. For five days, the British wage a relentless but futile battle to crush the resistance. Montgomery recalls his command. In conjunction, the Guards' Armored completes its punishing drive to the Nijmegen on September 19th, but the entire effort is abandoned on October 4th.

The American Paratroopers have been ordered to capture the bridges and surrounding terrain in the vicinity of Nijmegen-Grave. The 82nd, clamoring for an opportunity to kill Germans, drives hard, hitting and overcoming heavy opposition, thereby seizing the Maas Bridge at Grave; it also succeeds in capturing another strategic objective, the Maas-Waal Canal bridge at Heumen. The 82nd continues its string of successes, overpowering the resistance and securing the Nijmegen-Groesbeek Ridge. In full stride, the tired but undaunted 82nd bolts toward the highway bridge at Nijmegen, but German reinforcements arrive a pace before the Yanks and are able to prevent its capture. Meanwhile, the 101st Airborne drives toward its objective, seizing the bridge against light opposition at Veghel. However, the next objective, the bridge at Son, is destroyed by the enemy moments prior to the approach of the Airborne. The 101st Airborne improvises and makes ample use of a footbridge, crossing it and driving speedily toward Eindhoven.

General Ridgway had initially been "Bitterly disappointed" when General Brereton had given British General Browning command of Operation MARKETGARDEN. Two Airborne Divisions of Ridgway's XVIII Corps participate in the operation with the British Airborne Corps composed of one Division. Ridgway notes after the mission: "IT (stand at Arnhem) WAS A MONUMENT TO BRITISH VALOR, BUT A MONUMENT, TOO, TO HUMAN WEAKNESS, TO THE FAILURE TO STRIKE HARD AND BOLDLY."

September 18th 1944 — (Pacific-Peleliu) Hill 210 falls to the 2nd Battalions of both the 1st and 7th Marines. The 1st Battalion, 1st Marines' Company B, secures Hill 205 while the southern promontory is taken by the 1st Battalion, 7th Marines, the latter giving the Marines control of the southern sector of the island. During the fiercely contested conflict between the 7th Marines and the Japs, one small detachment of four men gets caught in an exposed position during a furious forward thrust. A pull-back is ordered from the untenable position, but extrication is extremely dangerous as they are exposed just under a fortified cave. A volley of Jap grenades descends upon them, one of which severely wounds P.F.C. Charles Roan. Immediately following this barrage, another grenade flies into their midst. Roan absorbs the full impact, giving his life to save the other four men in his detachment; he receives the Medal of Honor posthumously.

In another personal endeavor concerning extraordinary heroism, P.F.C. Arthur Jackson, 3rd Battalion, 7th Marines, becomes infuriated when his Platoon is halted by a well-fortified Jap strongpoint. Jackson darts forward, reaching the obstacle. He begins firing his automatic weapon through the slim openings of the position which contains about 35 enemy troops. Another Marine rushes up and throws white phosphorous grenades, eliminating the threat and killing all remaining occupants. Private Jackson continues his impetuous advance through incessant enemy fire, knocking out pillbox after pillbox, until a total of 12 nests have been singlehandedly destroyed by him; in addition, 50 Japanese defenders are killed; Pvt. Jackson receives the Medal of Honor. **(Atlantic-Western Europe) 21st Army Group** The Germans holding Arnhem react to the massive British Airdrop of the previous day and establish heavy resistance, including a counterattack. British reinforcements do not arrive in time to turn the tide, and all attempts to rescue isolated troops at the northern end of the Arnhem bridge fail. In the U.S. 82nd Airborne sector, a bridge at the Maas-Waal Canal near Honinghutie is seized, but subsequent efforts to take the Nijmegen bridge are unsuccessful; with the exception of an isolated unit, the 82nd pulls back. In other activity, the Germans unsuccessfully attack in force, attempting to batter their way through American lines between Groesbeek and the Reichswald. Meanwhile, the U.S. 101st Airborne, driving through Eindhoven, knocks over the opposition and advances far enough to encounter the British Guards' Armored, which is driving north. The Guards' Armored advances to capture a bridge southeast of Brest that spans the Wilhelmina Canal near Son, but the Germans destroy the bridge. In the British 8 Corps area, the British 3rd Division establishes a small bridgehead at Lille St. Hubert during the night 18th-19th. **U.S. 12th Army Group** The **U.S. Ninth Army** brings enemy-organized resistance in Brest to an end, but German Commander, General Hermann Bernhard Ramcke, eludes capture and makes it to the Crozon Peninsula; however, he is captured on the following day. During a brutalizing contest at the Wilhelmina Canal for control of a bridge, the Germans isolate a small detachment of the 502nd Parachute Infantry. P.F.C. Joe E. Mann, one of the encircled members, squirms to within striking distance of a menacing German 88 and destroys it and a nearby ammunition dump. The intrepid Private remains in his tenuous position and, in direct defiance of intense enemy fire, continues to pick off the enemy one by one, becoming wounded four times. He is eventually taken back for medical aid, but refuses to stay out of the fight and insists on standing guard during the night on the point. The Germans attack the position in the morning and heave grenades into his hole. Unable to raise his arms because they are taped to his body, he yells the alarm "Grenades" and throws his body upon it to save his fellow troopers; P.F.C. Mann receives the Medal of Honor posthumously. In the **U.S. First Army** area, **XIX Corps** sector, General Corlett orders an assault against the West Wall. The 2nd Armored bursts into Sittard. Elements of the 30th Division operating on the left flank make gradual progress; the 119th Infantry advances to the Wurm River. The **VII Corps** is holding a precarious perimeter, and the German threat hampers any genuine major progress for some time. The 3rd Armored is battling fiercely at Stolberg and Weissenberg Hill while elements of the 9th Division are holding off German counterattacks against its 47th Infantry near Schevenhuette. In the 39th Infantry sector, German resistance at Hill 554, southeast of Lammersdorf, resists all efforts to reduce it until the latter part of the month. The 60th Infantry seizes Hoefen-Alzen

Ridge southeast of Monschau. In the **V Corps** sector, General Gerow is ordered to Washington. Major General Edward H. Brooks assumes temporary command of the Corps. In the **U.S. Third Army** area, **XX Corps** sector, the 7th Armored and 5th Infantry Divisions head for the Seille River. Combat Command R, 7th Armored runs into stiff opposition at the fringes of Sillegny. Equally tenacious resistance faces Combat Command B, as it approaches Hill 223. In an unusual encounter for the Yanks of the 7th Armored, Patrols roll into Bouxieres-sous-Froidmont and discover it uninhabited by the Germans. In the **XII Corps** sector, the bridgehead at Dieulouard is under severe stress on the right flank and center, but the 80th Division maintains its steady but punishing operation to enlarge its grasp. Pain de Sucre falls to Task Force Sebree as it continues clearing the area northeast of Nancy. The Germans commence an offensive against the Third Army, with a sudden and heated thrust toward Luneville, overpowering advance outposts of the 2nd Cavalry Group, forcing it to retreat through the city. Rapid interdiction by CCR, 4th Armored, and units from CCA foil the attack. The aggressive stance of the U.S. Armored holds the line, diverting the Hun hordes, funneling them southward. By nightfall the Germans pull back to Parroy. In the **XXV Corps** area, instructions arrive, ordering an immediate crossing of the Moselle River for a drive north to the Mortagne River. **6th Army Group U.S. Seventh Army** area: The Army offensive is ordered to halt in place, 15 miles from the Moselle while it completes regrouping. **(Atlantic-Italy)** In the **U.S. Fifth Army** area, **IV Corps** sector, Task Force 45 closes fast against Pietrasanta on the coast. Castelvecchio and M. Liguana are consumed by Combat Command B, but fierce resistance at Ponte a Moriano hinders the advance of Combat Command A. Also, the Germans defending near Pistoia give the 6th South African Armored tough opposition. In the **II Corps** area, the collapse of the Gothic Line continues. Corps, having savored the victory at Il Giogo Pass, drives to the Santerno River Valley. The remnant opposition on Mt. Monticelli is eliminated by the 91st Division which presses to destroy the western defenses of the pass. The 362nd Infantry charges against Mt. Calvi in the Futa Pass region and reduces the enemy resistance, but hardened opposition near Mt. Morciano remains steadfast. In the vicinity of Torricella Hill and at Mt. Frassino, the 34th Division encounters horrid opposition. In the British 13th Corps sector, Femmina Morta falls to the Indian 8th Division, and at M. Peschiena a grueling battle ensues between the Germans and the British 6th Armored. In the **British Eighth Army** area, a major assault is begun. The British Armor is held in reserve for later pursuit, but the Infantry jumps off against the Rimini Line against entrenched opposition. The Germans counterattack to neutralize the British offensive at every point.

September 19th 1944 — (Pacific-Carolines-Peleliu) Contingents of the 2nd Battalion, 1st Marines advance to the final southern pocket of enemy resistance (Five Sisters). Elements cross Horseshoe Valley and seize the summit of Hill 100. A Patrol from Company K, 2nd Battalion, 5th Marines advances to Purple Beach on the east coast; Company G occupies the southern tip section of the beach and patrols northeastward. The 1st Battalion, 1st Marines, which had secured Hill 205 on the previous day, is struck during the night of the 18th, with intense resistance, as it attempts to ascend a steep sloped hill. Point blank Artillery fire causes heavy casualties and creates confusion within the ranks. Captain Everett P. Pope leads the remaining men of his detachment through a ring of fire and reaches the summit. He succeeds in holding the ground with 12 men and one wounded Officer. By the following morning, eight men still hold the crest, having turned back continuous attacks throughout the night. The ground becomes untenable, and they are ordered to withdraw; however, the Japs couldn't penetrate, and those who did met death with the bayonet and hand-to-hand combat. Captain Pope becomes the recipient of the Medal of Honor for his outstanding leadership. **(Pacific-Dutch East Indies)** U.S. Forces sink the PT-371 after it becomes grounded and damaged. **(Pacific-Japan)** The Japanese Frigate *Ioshima* is sunk by the U.S.S. *Shad* (SS-235) off Honshu. **(China-Burma-India)** The Postman rings twice. Chiang Kai-shek receives two messages today, one originating from President Roosevelt and Winston Churchill concerning decisions of the Octagon Conference, and the other is the one which informs Kai-shek in firm English that he must take the initiative in China. Chiang Kai-shek is not ecstatic over the news and begins to take measures to get his own way despite the President's pointed threats. **(Atlantic-Western Europe) 21st Army Group** In the **British Second Army** area, the inclement weather is bad news for the ground troops as Planes again have difficulty lending proper support. The Germans press tenaciously against the British 1st Airborne at Arnhem and by so doing, keep the isolated troops from breaking out or being rescued. To make a difficult situation worse, the Airdrop of food and equipment intended to resupply the troops is seized by the Germans. The British Guards' Armored Division, which has linked up with the U.S. 82nd Airborne at Grave, moves up with the Yanks to seize the bridges at Nijmegen to permit the British drive against Arnhem to continue. German resistance stalls the British drive just short of the objectives. The U.S. 101st Airborne holds its ground, deploying defensively at Eindhoven, Son, St. Oedenrode, and Veghel. The Germans try to push the 101st back, but the effort fails. A strong counterattack is repulsed at Son, and later, during the night, about 100 enemy Long-Range Bombers attack Eindhoven in what is the only heavy scaled Air attack mounted by the Germans in the west during Autumn 1944. The devastating assault inflicts severe casualties upon the civilians and also against British Soldiers in the town. The Americans deployed outside the town sustain no losses. In other related action, the German opposition outside of Best is overcome; however, the enemy retains the town. In the British 12th Corps area, the British 53rd Division advances to the Eindhoven-Turnhout bridge near Cuizel. Veldhoven is seized, and a subsequent link up with the British 53rd Division occurs at Mereveldhoven. In the British 8th Corps area, the 11th Armored pushes north to the British 3rd Division's bridgehead near Leende, from where it dispatches Patrols that probe to Heeze. **12th Army Group** In the **U.S. Ninth Army** area, the Britany campaign terminates successfully as the 8th Division completes its mission on the Crozon Peninsula. The Commanding Officer, General Ramcke, is captured and along with him, approximately 20,000 German troops. In the **U.S. First Army** area, **XIX Corps** sector, the 2nd Armored spearheads a drive that hammers a stiff wedge directly between two German Armies near Geilenkirchen, but a strong counterattack during the night reopens communications for the enemy. The XIX Corps is perched to assault the West Wall on the following day. In the **VII Corps** area, the fighting is brisk, but for the most part the Germans retain what they have. In the **V Corps** sector, the 1st Battalion, 12th Infantry, is driven back early in the day, but it regroups and retakes the lost ground, then pushes to seize additional terrain. At the Wallendorf bridgehead, the 5th Armored positions come under severe assault, but Planes rush to their aid and the enemy is driven off. A decision is reached to reduce the perimeter of the bridgehead. In the **U.S. Third Army** area, the bitter struggle for Sillegny appears to have ceased, as Combat Command R drives into the town without incident; the Germans who abandoned it are close by and heavy shelling combined with a strong counterattack compels the Americans to withdraw. Near Coin-sur-Seille, the Germans launch an attack and advance confidently until Artillery and Planes are quickly pushed into action. The German columns become stalled by the ring of fire. In the **XII Corps** area, the activity at the Dieulouard bridgehead is vigorous, yet all attempts to enlarge the bridgehead continue to receive heavy resistance. Task Force Sebree is bounced back by a strong counterattack at Pain de Sucre, but determined stances turn the situation around and the enemy is driven back beyond Agincourt. The Germans also stall the advance of the 137th Infantry, 35th Division at the Chateau-Salins-Nancy highway, preventing it from gaining control of Amance Hill. Meanwhile, the Germans storm the Yanks in the vicinity of Arracourt, spearheading the attack with Infantry and Tanks. Sparsely numbered Combat Command A units of the 4th Armored Division hold the line, sending the Germans off in retreat while inflicting heavy losses upon them, including the destruction of over 40 Tanks. In other activity, the Germans are thumped hard when they attempt to blow through the American defenses at Lezey and at Rethicourt-la-Petite. In the **XX Corps** area, units operating in advance of the Corps cross the Mortagne River. The 313th Infantry, 79th Division, bolts across near Xermamenil and eliminates the opposition. The Germans withdraw from Gerberville, subsequent to the 314th Infantry canceling its attack against the town. Combat Command D, French 2nd Armored Division, crosses the river near Vallois and captures Vathimenil. Germans, manning positions at the Meurthe River, are insufficiently numbered to hold for long and are ordered to withdraw during the night due to the penetration of the Mortagne Line. In the **U.S. Seventh Army** area, the U.S. 45th Division, which has been relieved by the French 1st Division, attacks toward the Moselle, striking Epinal. **(Atlantic-Finland)** Finland signs an Armistice with the Allies (at Moscow). The Soviet-Finnish border lines of 1940 are put back in place with exceptions. Finland leases the Porkkala headland (south of Helsinki) to the Russians as a Military Base, but relinquishes Petsamo. In addition, Russia gives up Hangoe to Finland. Finland must pay reparations to the Allies. Another condition of the Armistice: the Allies receive the use of Finnish Ships and Airfields. **(Atlantic-Estonia)** Valga, on the Latvia-Estonia border, is overtaken by troops of the Third Baltic Front. **(Atlantic-Italy)** In the **U.S. Fifth Army** area, **IV Corps** sector, elements of Task Force 45 drive to the coast, reaching Montrone and Pietrasanta. In the **II Corps** area, the 85th and 91st Divisions pursue the Germans toward the Santerno River, but on the left flank of the Corps, the Germans halt the 34th Division's advance. In the **British Eighth Army** area, 10th Corps sector, regrouping is finalized. The front line of the Corps is held by small contingents and is forced to contain its activity to Patrols. In the **V Corps** sector, the resistance at the Rimini Line is rough at Ceriano, but persistent efforts by the British 46th Division drive a wedge through it during the night of the 19th near Torraccia. In the Canadian 1st Corps area, Acqualina falls to the British 4th Division. Before daybreak on the 20th, S. Fortunato is encircled by the Canadian 1st Division.

September 20th 1944 — (Pacific-Carolines-Peleliu) In the 1st Marine Division sector, the 2nd Battalion, 7th Marines, drives east. Company F seizes the crest of Hill 260 in front of the Five Sisters. The northern tip of the island is secured by Company G, 2nd Battalion, 5th Marines. Marine Observation Squadron 3 initiates flights out of the captured Airfield. The excruciating struggle to eliminate the Japanese from their entrenchments is expensive. The Japs are holed up in near invulnerable caves, some of which have sliding steel doors. The casualties sustained by the 1st and 7th Marines keep climbing. The 321st Infantry, U.S.A., is informed that it will be needed on Peleliu; it assumes responsibility for the southern part of Angaur and for the obstinate pocket of resistance at the northeastern tip of the island. **(Pacific)** The 1st Marine Aircraft Wing is informed that its seven Dive-Bomber Squadrons are to participate in the Luzon campaign to retake the Philippines. **(China-Burma-India)** General Stilwell receives word that his plan, established to defend Kweilin, has met with the approval of Chiang Kai-shek. **(Atlantic-Western Europe)** In the **Canadian First Army** area, 2nd Corps sector, Polish Armor contingents seize Axel and Hulst. In the British Second Army area, the Germans have the British jammed badly at Arnhem, and the crucial situation nears catastrophic proportions as the shrinking British forces trying valiantly to hold the north end of the bridge are too weakened; 400 wounded men surrender to the Germans. Still, 140 troops of the 1st British Airborne hold. The Germans keep them isolated, while further compressing other remnant British Paratroopers at Oosterbeek and at Heaveadorp Ferry. The weather remains terrible and continues to stymie Air efforts to drop the Polish 1st Brigade. In the American sector, a determined effort is made to keep the British drive going. The British Armored Guards, operating directly with the U.S. 82nd Airborne, engage in a bold move that succeeds in capturing both bridges at Nijmegen. Other American troops, two Battalions of the 504th Paratroop Infantry, 82nd Airborne attempt to cross the unyieldy Waal River, using British assault boats. The attack is afforded Artillery support, but a protective smoke screen is unsuccessful. Undaunted, the Airborne troops dash across, drive to the northern end of a railroad bridge, and seize it, before bolting toward the highway bridge. In synchronization, contingents of the Guards Armored dart across the Highway bridge and hook up with the Paratroopers. With these two major conquests, the Yanks and the Guards Armored Division begin moving toward Arnhem. There is some heavy skirmishing at Wyler near the Nijmegen-Groesbeek ridge, but the Germans are turned back with the exception of small advances against outposts near Wyler. In the British 30th Corps area, the U.S. 101st Airborne comes under a counterattack; however, British Tanks give assistance and the attack is thwarted. In the British 12th Corps area, a gradual advance toward Best and Oirschot commences. **12th Army Group** In the **U.S. First Army** area, the **XIX Corps** is forced to cancel its planned assault against the West Wall due to the continuing terrible weather conditions. Lack of sufficient ammunition and supplies also is a big factor. The British northward drive receives priority, creating a severe shortage of necessary ammunition, especially Artillery ordnance; in addition, the left flank of the Corps is unprotected. In the **VII Corps** area, the Yanks get a reprieve as the Germans decide to abort their planned offensive and deploy defensively. The U.S. takes the offensive and attacks. The impudent resistance at Weissenberg Hill receives a surprise visit by Task Force Hogan which seizes it. At Muensterbusch, Combat Command A, 3rd Armored, clears its sector meticulously. Task Force Mills and Combat Command B, implementing smoke cover, forge ahead and secure a hold on the Donnerberg heights, which control the eastern entrance to Stolberg. When the smoke dissipates, the Germans launch a staunch counterattack. In the **V Corps** area, the IX Tactical Air Command is again called upon to assist Corps. In the **U.S. Third Army** area, the situation concerning lack of Artillery ammunition and inclement weather are identical to that in the First Army area: deplorable. General Patton continues to encourage his troops and insists on progress, unaware that in two days, Eisenhower will place additional restraints on Third Army's forward movement. Pournoy-la-Chetive is taken by the 2nd Battalion, 10th Infantry; Coin-sur-Seille is captured by the 1st Battalion, 2nd Infantry, both attached to the 5th Division. At the front steps of Sillegny, beleaguered Combat Command R is relieved by Combat Command A, and in conjunction with Combat Command B, the two units of the 7th Armored attack toward the Seille against heavy opposition, causing CCB to pull back after reaching the river. In the **XII Corps** area, the 80th Division gets advance contingents into Bois de la Rumont. All along the front, fighting is fierce. The Germans mount a counterattack that drives toward the 134th Infantry, 35th Division's perimeter at Agincourt, retaking the town. At Foret de Champenoux, the situation is appalling. The 137th Infantry attacks aggressively to reach the Amance plateau, but the effort fails subsequent to the exhaustion of Artillery ammunition. In another fierce encounter, Combat Command A, 4th Armored, drives toward Sarreguemines, but diverts to intercept an Armor counterattack that is threatening Arracourt. The attack is repulsed, and the Germans lose all eight Tanks which had been committed. Combat Command A whips through Ley and Moncourt, engaging in several small scale Tank battles. In the **XV Corps** area, the 313th Infantry, 79th Division speeds through Luneville, then pivots and heads southeast to outflank the German Meurthe River line. The 314th Infantry encounters heavy resistance as it advances to the Meurthe, south of Luneville. General Patton, while at General Bradley's Headquarters, inspects a map of the line of advance. Patton is further convinced that he should have two more Infantry Divisions and must also keep four Armored Divisions to ensure his progress. He believes (correctly) that the Germans have no depth to his front and decides to contain Metz as opposed to seizing it, utilizing the fewest amount of troops possible to permit a strong and immediate drive to the Rhine. **U.S. Sixth Army Group**: The Army's regrouping is complete. In the **U.S. Seventh Army** area, **VI Corps** sector, Corps is directed to cross the Moselle to capture the German town of Vosges, a strategic communication center. The 45th Division is ordered to seize Baccarat and Rambervillers, then shoot through the Saverne Gap. The 36th Division is ordered to cross the Moselle near Eloyes and seize St. Die outside the Saales Pass. In addition, the 3rd Division is moving to the Moselle. At the present time, the French 1st Army is maintaining the area to the right of the Seventh Army. **(Atlantic-Italy)** In the **U.S. Fifth Army** area, **IV Corps** sector, the U.S. 1st Armored Division regroups to allow for the transfer of Combat Command A to the II Corps. In other activity, the Brazilian Expeditionary Force (RCT 6) secures a portion of M. Prano, but the staunchly held crest remains in German hands. In the **II Corps** area, the 85th and 91st Divisions pursue the retreating Germans, advancing to the Santerno River. In the British 13th Corps area, the British 1st Division races through Casaglia Pass, subsequent to its abandonment by the Germans, and advances toward the Indian 8th Division positions. In the **British Eighth Army** area, the Germans withstand a strong British attempt to crush the Rimini Line throughout the day, but during the night 19th-20th, the Germans evacuate the area, taking new positions behind the Marecchia River. In the Canadian 1st Division sector, the Germans are unable to break out from their encircled positions at S. Fortunato.

September 21st 1944 — (Pacific-Carolines-Palaus) On Peleliu, the 1st Marines have sustained heavy casualties and are unable to continue as a Regimental Combat unit; they move to the rear for rest and rehabilitation (eastern defense zone). On Angaur, the 321st Infantry is ordered to relieve the 1st Marines on Peleliu. The 322nd Infantry U.S.A., drives vigorously into the Lake Salome bowl against strong resistance; however, the positions are untenable, forcing the unit to withdraw to safer positions during the night. In other activity, RCT 323, U.S.A., III Amphibious Corps (Reserve) embarks from the Palaus heading for Ulithi. **(Pacific-Philippines)** The Philippines are nearly in the view of MacArthur's binoculars. With a fervent desire and fiery disposition, he methodically lays out the final plans to return to the Philippines. With Morotai eliminated and the ongoing battle at Peleliu ensuring his flank's safety, the giant surgical scissors of the U.S. Navy is about to sever the enemy bloodlines by cutting another artery. Morotai had been the final step, prior to the first movement from the Halmahera-Philippine Line. Today, Vice Admiral M.A. Mitscher's 12 Aircraft Carriers strike Luzon. The Planes strike Airfields and enemy Ships relentlessly for two days, joined by Surface Vessels. The mission's success includes sinking the Destroyer *Satsuki* and the Oiler *Sunosaki* in Manila Bay. Other enemy Vessels sunk in the Philippine vicinity include the Auxiliary Submarine Chaser No. 39, Coast Defense Vessel No. 5, and a Minesweeper No. 7. One of the destroyed Vessels was transporting over 1,000 Allied POWs; less than 200 make it to shore. In addition, the Submarine U.S.S. *Haddo* destroys the Survey Vessel *Katsuriki.*. Admiral Halsey is concerned that the bad weather has shortened the amount of strikes, but Mitscher's Aircraft account for the loss of 405 enemy Planes destroyed or damaged and 103 Ships sunk or damaged. Clark and Nichols Airfields are both devastated. The U.S. Ships stand 40 miles from the east coast of Luzon, about 150 miles from Manila, but suffer no damage. The U.S. loses 15 Planes and 12 men. Meanwhile, American P.O.W.s at Cabanatuan become mesmerized as they watch the U.S. Planes attack the harbor. In other activity, General MacArthur informs the Chiefs of Staff (by radio) that the invasion of Luzon can commence (tentatively) on December 20th 1944, based on the modified date pushing up the invasion of Leyte. In addition, he informs them that an invasion of Formosa could prove unnecessary, subsequent to the occupation of Luzon. **(Atlantic-Western Europe)** 21st Army Group General Montgomery's master strategy to drive through to the Ruhr Basin with a solitary northward thrust under British Command is turning into a disaster. The massive Airdrop, intended to strike speedily and take Arnhem, fails. Although the Americans have been able to secure their objectives, the British have been miffed and torn apart by the granite resistance. The sparsely numbered remaining British Paratroops holding suicidal positions (without needed reinforcements at the northern end of the Arnhem bridge) are annihilated as they try to break out in small contingents. The weather conditions improve and 750 men of the Polish Brigade are Air-dropped, but too late to be of any genuine help. The surviving British Paratroopers holding near the Heaveadrop Ferry have been squeezed into a tiny pocket on the north bank of the Rhine, just west of Oosterbeck. Meanwhile, the Germans have retaken the northern end of the coveted ferry. The situation is equally critical in the British 30th Corps sector. The Guards' Armored departs the U.S. 82nd Airborne positions at Nijmegen advancing toward Arnhem; however, the Germans intercept the columns about three miles from point of departure and halt the advance. In one instance of horrid combat at the bridgehead, near Oosterhout (Holland), a force of about 100 enemy troops supplemented by two Tanks and a Half-trac form for a devastating attack that jeopardizes not only a large contingent of Yanks, but the entire Nijmegen bridgehead. Without orders, Pvt. John R, Towle (Company C, 504th Paratroop Infantry, 82nd Airborne) bolts from his foxhole, taking his Rocket Launcher as he moves 200 yards to the point, in full view of the enemy. Unperturbed, he fires and strikes both approaching Tanks. Neither is destroyed, but the damage is severe enough for them to withdraw. Towle then charges a house containing nine enemy Soldiers and kills all with one perfectly aimed round. He singlehandedly charges another 175 yards (after getting more ammunition) to take out the Half-trac, but a final hail of withering fire kills him as he prepares to fire. Pvt. Towle sacrifices his life, but the bridgehead is preserved; he receives the Medal of Honor posthumously. In the U.S. 101st Airborne sector, the Yanks move along the highway between St. Oedenrode and Veghel without incident; in conjunction, contingents eliminate remnant troops in the Glider landing zone, then divert to a secondary road and advance, occupying Schijndel during the night of the 21st. **12th Army Group** In the **U.S. First Army** area, more terrible weather mandates another cancellation of the planned offensive against the West Wall. In the **VII Corps** area, mop-up operations at Muensterbusch are terminated by C.C.A., 3rd Armored. Meanwhile, Task Force Mills advances to Donnerberg and grasps a fragile hold in this suburb of Stolberg. In other activity, the 60th Infantry, 9th Division, encounters unmovable opposition as it drives against Huertgen and against Germeter, gaining nominal progress there. In the **V Corps** sector, the Germans have destroyed the Wallendorf bridges. The American bridgehead is ordered to pull back by fording the river. The precarious operation receives tremendous help from the IX Tactical Air Command. In the **U.S. Third Army** area, **XX Corps** sector, the Germans holding the Seille River Line mount heavy resistance against the 7th Armored Division. The situation in the 5th Division sector is pathetic, as the ammunition is diminishing rapidly, forcing the Division to remain where it is and attempt to repel continual counterattacks at Pournoy-la-Chetive. In the **XII Corps** area, the struggle for Bois de la Rumont ensues with tenacity as the 80th Division grinds feverishly, but cannot reduce the resistance; two Battalions are isolated, making it necessary to supply them by Tanks. At Agincourt, the 134th Infantry recaptures the town, but the 137th Infantry fights tenaciously without dislodging the Germans at Foret de Champenoux. Combat Command A, 4th Armored Division, runs over Bures and Coincourt. In the **XV Corps** area, the 313th Regiment, 79th Infantry, departs Luneville, but leaves a Battalion behind to continue house-to-house fighting, while it advances and seizes Moncel before coming to a halt at the fringes of Foret de Mondon. In conjunction, elements of the 315th deploy defensively at Luneville while units of the 314th Regiment attempt to reach the Foret de Mondon by crossing the Meurthe River near Ste Clement and driving from there. Enemy guns hold commanding positions that forbid movement across the open terrain, forcing the 314th contingent to withdraw upon darkness. In other activity, General Patton is informed that the Sixth Army Group (General Devers) is to receive many troops from Third Army. Patton flies to Paris, but he is unable to convince Ike not to transfer his troops. On Saturday the 23rd, Patton forfeits the 6th Armored and assumes a defen-

sive position because his meager supplies are exhausted. He refers to the 23rd as "ONE OF THE BAD DAYS OF MY MILITARY CAREER." **Sixth Army Group** In the **U.S. Seventh Army** area, the **VI Corps** starts across the Moselle River. The 36th Division crosses first, near Eloyes. The 2nd Battalion, 147th Infantry clears the town to the river bank. The river is forded by the 1st and 3rd Battalions, followed by the 143rd Regiment which joins the clearing operation and helps expand the bridgehead, taking Hill 783 in the process. In other activity, the resistance at Remiremont is rugged, but the 142nd Infantry pierces the enemy defenses and secures a portion of the town. The Germans also give the advancing 3rd Division steady opposition as it drives toward the Moselle. **(Atlantic-Italy)** In the **U.S. Fifth Army** area, **IV Corps** sector, Task Force 45 stretches its perimeter deeper, reaching down the coast to Forte dei Marmi. In other activity, the Germans repel an attempt by the Brazilians to take M. Prano. In the **II Corps** sector, Firenzuola is captured by the 338th Infantry, 85th Division, while the 339th Regiment seizes M. Frena and M. Coloreta. In other activity, the Germans establish stiff resistance against the 362nd Infantry, 91st Division, at the approaches to S. Lucia and M. Gazzaro, but both objectives are seized. The Regiment enters Futa Pass, realizing that the Germans still control a strategic hill to the west. In another brutalizing contest, the ensuing struggle for Torricela Hill is terminated, and again the Yanks are the victors. The U.S. 85th Division begins to drive down the Santerno Valley heading for Imola. In the British 13th Corps area, the British 1st Division is about half the distance between Crespino and Marradi. In other activity, the British 6th Armored Division seizes M. Peschiena. In the **British Eighth Army** area, the Germans evacuate Ceriano Ridge. The British dispatch Patrols that reach the Marecchia River before dawn on the 22nd. The British 1st Armored and 56th Infantry Divisions are so understrengthed that further pursuit of the retreating enemy is canceled and the units are ordered to regroup. In the Canadian 1st Corps area, the Canadian 1st Division establishes a bridgehead across the Marecchia River near Rimini while mopping up at S. Fortunato. In other activity, the Greek 3rd Mountain Brigade (attached to the Canadian 1st Division) seizes an Airfield south of Rimini, then enters the city, discovering it abandoned.

Infantry catching a ride on 1st Army Armor.

September 22nd 1944 — (Pacific-Philippines) The U.S.S. *Narwhal* (SS-167) lands equipment and men at Mindanao on its west coast. Planes from the *Independence* bombard Clark Field at Manila. Commander Caldwell personally destroys six grounded Aircraft. Two days later, Planes strike enemy positions at Coron Bay. **(Pacific-Ulithi)** RCT 323, 81st Division, diverted from III Amphibious Corp Reserve on Peleliu, lands on Ulithi, finding no opposition. The Naval Task Group transporting the Army contingent is under the command of Vice Admiral W.H.B. Blandy. **(Atlantic-Western Europe)** General Eisenhower confers with his Staff Commanders at Versailles. A result of the conference is that a deep water port is required to ensure the final defeat of the Germans. Eisenhower directs that General Montgomery (not in attendance as is his usual practice) is to receive priority for logistical support for a British advance against the Ruhr. The 21st Army Group, supported by the U.S. First Army (12th Army Group) on its flank, is to undertake the mission to secure the Schelde approaches to Antwerp. In essence, this directive restrains activity of the U.S. Third Army. Eisenhower's intentions are easy to interpret: "THE REMAINDER OF THE 12TH ARMY GROUP TO TAKE NO MORE AGGRESSIVE ACTION THAN IS PERMITTED BY THE MAINTENANCE SITUATION AFTER THE FULL REQUIREMENTS OF THE MAIN EFFORT HAVE BEEN MET." The Boundary between the 12th and 21st Army Groups are modified effective September 25th, extending northeast from Hasselt through Bree, Weert, Deurne, and Venray (totally 12th Army Group) to the Maas at Maashees, stretching along the river to the original boundary north of Maastricht. The boundary adjustment gives the XIX Corps, U.S. First Army a wide area west of the Maas that comprises in excess of 500 square miles, including the huge Peel Marshes (swamps). The 7th Armored and 29th Infantry Divisions are transferred to the XIX Corps to assist with the massive endeavor. **21st Army Group** In the **Canadian First Army** area, 2 Corps area, Boulogne capitulates to the Canadian 3rd Division. The Canadian 4th Armored Division advances to the Schelde Estuary. In the **British Second Army** area, the Germans continue to isolate the British 1st Airborne Division in the vicinity of Arnhem; the besieged troops cannot receive supplies because the weather remains atrocious, keeping Planes grounded. The British 30th Corps attempts to lend assistance. Mechanized Equipment transports ammunition to Driel; however, heavy rains have created impassible regions of deep mud. A contingent of Polish troops unloads the DUKWs and transports the ammunition across the river on rafts during the night of the 22nd. The U.S. 82nd Airborne Division secures the south bank of the Waal River, three miles east of the highway bridge. In the 30th Corps area, the Germans resist the advancing British 43rd Division, halting its progress, but some elements reach Driel. The 101st U.S. Airborne holding at Veghel is struck by a strengthened German counterattack. Reinforcements rush to the scene and the enemy is repulsed; however, the Germans cut the highway between Veghel and Uden. **12th Army Group** The **U.S. First Army** goes on the defensive along most of its sector. At Schevenhuette, (VII Corps sector) the 47th Infantry, 9th Division repulses a massive German counterattack, inflicting heavy losses upon the enemy. The 60th Infantry aborts its assault against Huertgen village, enabling it to dispatch reinforcements to bolster the 47th Regiment. However, their assistance is not necessary. Heavy fighting continues in the Huertgen Forest where a solitary Battalion (60th Regiment) remains engaged in a brutalizing stalemate for three days. The remainder of the 60th Regiment swings back and attacks to relieve pressure on its besieged Battalion in the forest. In the **U.S. Third Army** area, the positioning of the XII and XX Corps compels the enemy at Cheminot to abandon the town. In the **XII Corps** area, Combat Command B, 4th Armored Division, overcomes heavy resistance and seizes Armaucourt as it

drives against Amance from the rear. The 134th Infantry, 35th Division attacks Bois de Faulx at 12:00, while the 137th, supplemented by Air and Artillery, charges through the balance of Foret de Champenoux; the combined pressure pushes the Germans out of the Amance plateau. In the vicinity of Moyenvic, the Germans advance with Tanks and Infantry, until intercepted by Combat Command A, 4th Armored Division at a point west of Juvelize. The Yanks provide a rigid stumbling block and the enemy sustains severe losses. In the **XV Corps** area, the Germans retake a portion of Luneville from the 315th Infantry, 79th Division; however, their success is short-lived as the 317th regains the ground. Also, the Germans mount a counterattack at Moncel, preventing the 313th Infantry from reaching Foret de Mondon. In other 79th Division activity, elements of the 314th Infantry ford the Meurthe River, but halt progress due to lack of Tank and Artillery support. In yet other XV Corps activity, the French 2nd Armored Division gets Patrols into the southern portion of Foret de Mondon after crossing the Meurthe, but German opposition pushes them out. **(Atlantic-Estonia)** Tallinn is seized by the Russians. **(Atlantic-Italy)** In the **U.S. II Corps** area, the actions against the Gothic Line are complete. Advance outposts are established across the Santerno River by elements of the 91st Division, while another contingent, the 362nd Infantry, terminates the remaining enemy resistance at the Futa Pass. The 135th Infantry, 34th Division seizes M. Citerna, while the 168th takes Hill 1134, east of Montepiano. In other activity, the Germans evacuate Vernio, allowing the 91st Cavalry Reconnaissance Squadron to occupy it without incident. In the vicinity of M. la Fine, the 85th Division drives in two directions to bolster the 91st Division's assault against Radicosa Pass while simultaneously assisting the 88th Division operating on the right. During a heated skirmish, 1st Lt. Orville Bloch, Company E., 338th Infantry, 85th Division, leads a three-man Squad against numerous enemy machine guns which are holding up the entire Company near Firenzuola. Lt. Bloch singlehandedly moves against and through several hostile buildings, while under intense fire. When the furious ordeal ends, Bloch has accounted for the destruction of five machine gun nests and the capture of 19 prisoners; he receives the Medal of Honor. In the **British 13th Corps** area, the Indian 8th Division finishes the occupation of Giogo di Villore against no opposition. In the **British Eighth Army** area, the 5th Corps attacks across the Mareccia River with three Divisions during the night of the 22nd in an attempt to secure the ridges to the north. In other activity, the British 56th Division is forced to retire from the line because of casualties.

September 23rd 1944 — (Pacific-Midway) The Submarines U.S.S. *Escolar* (SS-294), *Perch* (SS-313), and *Croaker* (SS-246) embark from Midway to patrol the Yellow Sea above the 30 degree parallel. The wolf-pack known as "Millican's Marauders" is led by Commander Millican (*Escolar*). **(Pacific-Carolines-Palaus)** RCT 321, 81st Infantry Division, U.S.A., lands on Orange Beach and receives responsibility for isolating enemy resistance on Umurbrogol Mountain in coordination with the 7th Marines; in addition, the 2nd and 3rd Battalions (RCT 321) relieve the 1st Marines. In other activity on Peleliu, Company G, 2nd Battalion 5th Marines, captures a tiny island north of Ngabad which concludes the Regiment's objectives. **(China-Burma-India)** On the Salween front, Japanese reinforcements head toward Pingka to rescue the Garrison. **(Atlantic-Western Europe) 21st Army Group** In the **British Second Army** area, the skies clear, permitting General Montgomery to have the remaining contingents of the U.S. 82nd and 101st Airborne brought into Holland. In addition, the balance of the Polish 1st Brigade joins the drop, landing at Graves to act as Reserves for the 82nd. The British 53rd Division, scheduled to be flown into Holland, is held back by British General Dempsey. In the British 1st Airborne Division sector at Hartestein, near Arnhem, Aircraft and Artillery lend assistance at the bridgehead. During the night, about 250 Polish Paratroopers cross the river and join the Airborne Forces. In the 30th Corps area, elements of the 43rd Division drive into Driel. The U.S. 506th Paratroop Infantry, 101st Airborne Division clears enemy resistance, reopens the Veghel-Uden Highway, and subsequently encounters units of British Armor moving southwest from Uden. The Germans maintain their attack toward Veghel, despite the closing British 8th Corps, which is pushing toward Helmond. **12th Army Group** In the **U.S. Third Army** area, **XX Corps** sector, Patton's Force is becoming thinner. The 7th Armored is forced to abort its planned assault across the Seille River because of its transfer to the U.S. First Army, which is to protect the flank of the British northern thrust. In the **XII Corps** area, the Germans pull back as the 80th Division advances, but they retain control of positions in the hills east of Serrieres and at Bois de Faulx. The 35th Division eliminates rear-guard resistance, capturing many Germans in the process. In other activity, the frequent and spirited Tank battles of the 4th Armored cease, allowing it to get a breather. In the **V Corps** area, Foret de Mondon is well-braced against a strong attack by the 3rd Battalion, 314th Infantry, 3rd Division; however, it falls to the Yanks who themselves suffer heavy casualties. At Domjevin, the Germans establish resistance along the La Vezouse River, but they are driven from the town by French contingents. **6th Army Group** The 179th Infantry, 45th Division seizes Mossoux while the 180th Infantry secures a portion of Epinal, west of the Moselle; it then bolts across the river at three different locations. The Germans, however, mount fierce resistance against the 157th Infantry and prevent it from enlarging the bridgehead toward Girmont. In the 36th Division sector, Remiremont is seized by the 142nd Infantry, prior to crossing the Moselle. In conjunctive activity, the 7th Infantry crosses the Moselle, entering Rupt by way of a bridge which has not yet been destroyed by the enemy. In the **French First Army** area, General de Lattre orders a limited offensive with elements of the French Armored assaulting on axis Melisey-Le Thillot, while Infantry commences diversionary attacks to draw attention away from the Armor. **(Atlantic-Italy)** In the **U.S. Fifth Army** area, **II Corps** sector, the 34th Division seizes Montepiano with its 133rd Infantry, penetrating the Gothic Line. In the British 13th Corps area, Poggio Cavalmagra and M. Villanova are seized by the British 1st Division and the Indian 8th Division respectively. **(Atlantic-Estonia)** The Russians advance to the Gulf of Riga at Paernu. **(Atlantic-Greece)** The British Special Boat Squadron, Mediterranean, is Air-dropped on Araxos, on the northwestern coast of the Peloponnesus; the purpose is to seize the Airfield and occupy Patras.

September 24th 1944 — (Pacific-Ulithi) RCT 323, 81st Division, secures the remainder of Ulithi without opposition; the island is transformed into a strategically powerful Base for the Pacific Fleet. **(Pacific-Palaus)** Hill 100 is seized by Company E, 321st Infantry, 81st Division, eliminating the main portion of the center of Japanese resistance on Umurbrogol Mountain. A Japanese counterattack pushes the 321st Regiment back slightly, but quick reaction regains the lost territory. A gap is created between the U.S. Infantry and the 7th Marines because the Marines must secure ground to the right rear that was bypassed by the 321st Regiment. Meanwhile,

the Japanese reinforce their Garrison by bringing in troops from another island to the north. In yet other activity, the first elements of Marine Night Fighter Squadron 541 arrive on the island. At Angaur, the Americans urge the Japanese to surrender. The suggestion is unheeded with the exception of two enemy Soldiers who surrender. Upon failure of the enemy surrendering, Artillery commences and the bombardment continues. In Naval activity, the Motor Minesweeper YMS-19 sinks after striking a mine. **(Pacific-Philippines)** The Naval Force of Admiral Mitscher strikes the Japanese positions in the Visayas. The Japanese Vessels *Hayabusa* (Torpedo Boat), *Akitsushima* (Seaplane Tender), *Yaeyama* (Minelayer), and the Submarine Chaser No. 32 are sunk by Carrier Aircraft. **(China-Burma-India)** The British 36th Division departs Namma heading south and discovers heavy enemy presence; it halts further movement until mid-October. **(Atlantic-Western Europe) 21st Army Group** The Canadian 2nd Division establishes a bridgehead near St. Leonard at the Antwerp-Turnhout Canal. In other activity in the British 13th Corps area, contingents of the British 49th Division advance to Turnhout. In the **British Second Army** area, 1st Airborne sector, elements of the 43rd Division cross the Neder Rijn in assault boats, but their effort to reach British lines at Hartestein are unsuccessful. Polish troops, perched on the south bank, cannot make the crossing due to unavailability of additional assault boats. British Lt. General B.G. Horrocks orders the 43rd Division to cross at Rekum, but within a few hours, he countermands the order. In the British 30th Corps area, the Germans still drive toward Veghel, severing a vital road northeast of Koevering. In other activity, units of the British 43rd Division are embattled heavily at both Bemmel and Elst. **12th Army Group** In the **U.S. First Army** area, 1st Division sector, the Germans attack to overpower the 2nd Platoon, Company I, 18th Infantry, which is defending a strategic crossroad. Two Companies of the enemy force advance during the early morning hours, and with an unexpected surge, push one Squad back and capture another. The remaining Squad, led by Sergeant Joe Schaeffer, moves under fire to stronger positions at a nearby house. Schaefer holds at the doorway and repulses the first attack, then with unrelenting defiance repels the next assault, which includes flamethrowers. The Germans mount a third attack striking against the front of the building and also from an angle coming out of a hedgerow, but the intrepid Sergeant takes out six enemy troops then unabashedly charges to the hedgerow, his rifle smoking the entire way, eliminating the threat. With a final thrust he combs the area and singlehandedly captures 10 enemy troops. Sergeant Schaeffer's gallant action under intense fire succeeds in killing between 15 and 20 Germans in addition to wounding at least an equal amount, and rescuing the captured Squad, while buying time for his Company to mount its attack. Thanks to Schaeffer, the enemy breakthrough is prevented; he receives the Medal of Honor. In the **U.S. Third Army** area, **XX Corps** sector, relief of the 7th Armored by the 5th Division begins. The Third Army has been ordered by Eisenhower to stop its rapidly advancing offensive and to maintain a defensive stance. In the **XII Corps** area, the Germans commence a strong counterattack committing Infantry and Tanks, which drive toward Chateau-Salins and Fresnes-en-Saulnois. Combat Command B, 4th Armored, supplemented by the firepower of P-47s, turns back the attack, pushing the enemy toward Foret de Chateau-Salins, costing the enemy about 300 killed and 11 Tanks. The Airpower had accomplished a spectacular rescue. The Planes fly under extremely dangerous weather conditions, with the use of radar at levels of 15 feet above ground. The two Squadrons ordered by General Wey land to fly the mission had also been aware that once off the ground, a subsequent safe landing might become impossible; however, the Planes penetrate the clouds deep in France and land safely. As of September 24th, Third Army losses: 4,541 killed, 22,718 wounded, and 4,548 missing, (total 31,807) plus 13,323 non-battle casualties (45,130 total); the Germans sustain 30,900 killed, 89,600 wounded, and 95,600 prisoners of war. (total 216,100). Tank losses: Third Army: 140 Light Tanks, 342 Medium Tanks. The Germans lose 708 Medium Tanks and a combination of 415 Panther or Tiger Tanks. In addition, Third Army loses 103 Guns to the German losses of 1,718 Guns. General Patton confers with Generals Eddy, Haislip, and Walker (Corps Commanders) at Nancy. There are strong feelings about General Haislip leaving the Third Army. Third Army prepares for selective crossing points of the Moselle in case its defensive stance is lifted. **6th Army Group** In the **U.S. Seventh Army** area, **VI Corps** sector, Girmont is seized by the 157th Infantry while the 180th Infantry, also of the 45th Division, is still engaged in securing Epinal. In the 36th Division sector, St. Ame, east of Remirement, is taken by the 141st Infantry. In the 3rd Division area, the bridgehead at Rupt is enlarged as La Roche and Maxonchamp are consumed, while ongoing clearing operations in Rupt eliminate the remaining snipers. **(Atlantic-Italy)** In the U.S. **Fifth Army** area, **IV Corps** sector, elements of the 1st Armored Division are transferred to assist the II Corps. In the **II Corps** sector, the 34th Division pounds toward M. Bastione, its 135th and 168th Regiments seizing the pinnacle of M. Coroncina and subsequently repelling a determined counterattack, then thrusting forward and overpowering Roncobilaccio. In another heated battle, the 91st Division commences a drive that powers them toward M. Oggioli; its 361st and 362nd Infantries topple resistance and advance to the line from Covigliano westward. Later during the night, the 362nd is relieved by the 363rd, which takes positions on the line. In the 88th Division sector, the Germans mount fierce resistance at M. Acuto and mount heavy counterattacks which hinder progress near Imola. In other activity, the 85th Division solidifies its perimeter at M. la Fine, while its 338th Regiment grinds punishingly toward M. Canda. In the British 13th Corps area, Marradi and Palazzuolo are seized, but the Germans retain control of M. Gamberaldi. In the **British Eighth Army** area, the 5th Corps gains the heights stretching from Montebello to Poggio Berni and beyond to S. Arcangelo. Meanwhile, the 46th Division, operating in the center of the Corps, establishes a bridgehead at the Uso River, seizing Camerano on the far bank. **(Atlantic-Greece)** Elements of the R.A.F. (transported by sea) arrive at Araxos from where they depart with Special Boat Squadron for Patras. In other activity, U.S. Army Aircraft sink the German Submarines U-565 and U-596, off Salamis, Greece.

September 25th 1944 — (Pacific-Palaus) On Peleliu, 321st Infantry, (U.S.A.) Patrols meet nominal resistance and advance toward the fifth phase line. Elements of the 321st on the right flank, assisted by the 5th Marines, continue to clear the northern portion of the island. In other activity, the 7th Marines continue to eliminate Japanese in its sector of the island. While a contingent of the 2nd Battalion is directing mortar fire upon enemy positions, a Japanese Soldier creeps out from a cave and throws a grenade into the Marines' position. Without hesitation, P.F.C. John Dury New blankets the grenade with his body to save the lives of two observers. P.F.C. New receives the Medal of Honor posthumously for his most courageous action. On Angaur, the 322nd Infantry, which has been prevented on all attempts from penetrating the Japanese defenses at the Lake Salome bowl, diverts its efforts to attack from the north. Having ended without success, the southern attacks prompt quick reaction by Engineers who are ordered to construct a road to permit an attack from the east-northeast. **(Pacific-Philippines)** The U.S.S. *Nautilus* (SS-168) lands supplies on Cebu in the Philippines. **(Pacific-Morotai)** Task Force Tradewind is disbanded. General Hall, Commanding General of the XI Corps, is responsible for future development of the Base. **(China-Burma-India)** Generalissimo Chiang Kai-shek refuses to permit General Stilwell to command the Chinese troops. **(Atlantic-Western Europe)** The new boundary between the 12th and 21st Army Group becomes effective today. **21st Army Group** In the **Canadian First Army** area, 2nd Corps sector, the 3rd Canadian Division, which has advanced into Calais, commences a major offensive subsequent to a heavy preparatory bombardment. In the **British Second Army** area, 1st Airborne sector, orders are issued to abandon the Arnhem bridgehead upon nightfall. The reluctant retreat forces the British to abandon their wounded. The remnant forces evacuate their positions at the Neder Rijn by ferry; some swim across the river. In other activity, the U.S. 101st Airborne, combining its strength with the British 50th Division, threatens the enemy roadblock in the vicinity of Koevering with encirclement, but the Germans abandon the stronghold at dusk. In other activity, German resistance at Bemmel and Elst is eliminated by the 30th Corps. In the 8th Corps sector, Helmond and Gemert are seized; subsequent Patrols make contact with the 30th Corps near St. Antonis. **12th Army Group** The U.S. First Army, supporting the British northern drive to the Ruhr, is assigned responsibility for capturing Aachen and protecting the right flank of the British. In the **U.S. First Army** area, the **XI Corps** assumes responsibility for the new area turned over to it by the British. The British have secured the area up to the Nederweert-Wessem Canal with the exception of a pocket near Wessem. The 7th Armored (transferred from Third Army) will coordinate with the U.S. 29th Division to secure the new objectives. In the **VII Corps** area, incessant combat has taken a serious toll on the 60th Infantry, 9th Division. The severe losses sustained while holding the south flank of the Corps hinder its ability to maintain the fight. In the **U.S. Third Army** area, Patton makes known his plans for limited attacks (discussed at Nancy on previous day with Corps Commanders), which will keep his Army ready for breakout. In the **XII Corps** area, the Germans take due advantage of Patton's unusual stillness and strike with a heavy blow in the vicinity of Marsal and Moyenvic. The swift movement of the German Fifth Panzer Army bursts through violently, overcoming the resistance of Combat Command A, 4th Armored, advancing to Vic-sur-Seille where it joins the German First Army. In addition, the German counterattack also seizes Moncourt by driving a wedge through other positions of C.C.A. Combat Command B quickly turns over its positions to the 35th Division and bolts from Chateau-Salins to reinforce CCA, deploying south between the canal and Rechicourt. **6th Army Group** In the **U.S. Seventh Army** area, Epinal is totally cleared of enemy resistance by the 45th Division. The 36th Division at St. Ame is relieved by the U.S. 3rd Division, enabling the 36th to attack toward Bruyeres and Tendon. In the **French 1st Army** area, the French 2nd Corps commences a limited offensive, but German aggressiveness hinders the progress of the French. In Naval activity, the American Minesweeper *Miantonomah* sinks off Normandy after striking a mine. **(Atlantic-Italy)** In the U.S. **Fifth Army** area, Task

Force 92, commanded by Brigadier General John S. Wood, assumes responsibility for the sector previously held by 1st Armored Division. In other activity, contingents of the 6th South African Armored Division relieve the 34th Reconnaissance Troop and assume responsibility for screening the left flank of the Corps. In the **II Corps** area, M. Beni falls to the 91st Division, but resilient resistance continues on the left where the Germans hold firmly at M. Bastione. The Germans also hold M. Canda, foiling an attempt by the 338th Infantry to outflank them and seize Torre Poggioli, further northeast. The 3rd Battalion, 339th Infantry attempts to bolster the attacking 338th Regiment, but stiff resistance halts its progress in front of Montarello. The British 13th Corps continues to press the hills commanding Marradi, Palazzuolo, and S. Benedetto. The Germans repulse successive attempts by the British 1st Division to take M. Gamberaldi. The Germans also mount tenacious resistance against the Indian 8th Division at M. di Castelnuovo. The British 6th Armored Division, which had received orders to report to the British Eighth Army, is now ordered to stay and protect the Corps' right flank. In the **British Eighth Army** area, 5th Corps sector, the Germans hold up the advance of the Indian 4th Division, but during the night 25th-26th, the Germans withdraw from Cornacchiara, permitting the 4th to cross the Uso. The British 46th Division enlarges its bridgehead from the Uso toward Canonica, while the British 1st Armored establishes a bridgehead across the Uso at S. Arcangelo by Highway 9 and is subsequently relieved by the British 56th Division. In other activity, the Canadian 5th Armored Division establishes a bridgehead across the Uso in the Canadian 1st Corps area.

September 26th 1944 — (Pacific-Palaus) Hill 2 is secured by Company B, 1st Battalion, 5th Marines, while Hill 80 is seized by the 2nd Battalion, 5th Marines, cementing the fate of the northern tip of the island. In other activity, Marine Fighter Squadron 114 arrives on the Airfield. In Naval activity, the U.S.S. *McCoy Reynolds* (DE-440) destroys the Japanese Submarine I-175 off the coast of the Palau islands. **(Pacific-Malay Archipelago)** The U.S.S. *Pargo* (SS-264) sinks the Japanese Submarine *Aotaka* off Borneo. **(Atlantic-Western Europe)** In Naval activity, the Minelayer U.S.S. *Miantonomah* (CM-10) is sunk by a mine off Normandy. **21st Army Group** In the **British Second Army** area, 1st Airborne Corps is forced to cancel its withdrawal because of daylight, while approximately 300 troops are still stranded on the northern bank of the Neder Rijn. Some escape to the south. Operation MARKET-GARDEN has not succeeded in reaching Montgomery's goals and in fact has cost many lives without collapsing the enemy's resistance. Fortunately, the objectives which have been seized during the operation prove valuable to the Allied cause, and the two U.S. Airborne Divisions that have fared well with their objectives are still well-entrenched and are needed to assist the British. General Montgomery changes his tactics after this endeavor and stops bickering constantly with General Eisenhower. **12th Army Group** In the **U.S. Ninth Army** area, the 2nd and 8th Divisions (VIII Corps) are transported to the rear of the First Army's V Corps. In the **U.S. First Army** area, efforts are made to fortify the beleaguered 60th Infantry Regiment in the Huertgen forest. A reserve Battalion and elements of the 39th Infantry are rushed to sever the Lammersdorf-Huertgen highway where it joins with a major road heading northwest to Zweifall. In the **U.S. Third Army** area, **XX Corps** sector, a restricted assault is planned against Fort Driant, and the directive issued by General Walker stipulates that it is to commence on the 27th; the date is irrevoca-

Major General Geoffrey Keyes.

ble. The Metz forts, also held by the Germans, come under daily attacks from Planes attached to the XIX TAC. The Third Army is under restraints, but the 90th Division commits elements to secure a stretch of highway between Gravelotte and St. Hubert's Farm to pave the way for a major attack. In the **XII Corps** sector, the Germans capitalize on a defensive move initiated by the 4th Armored by occupying Coincourt and Juvelize without incident, subsequent to the Armored scaling down its Main Line of Resistance on the Corps' right flank. At the Seille River, the Germans repulse an attempt by the 80th Division to penetrate the river line, stopping the 317th at Moivron and halting the 318th at Mt. St. Jean. In other heated action, the Germans pound against the 37th Division perimeter at Foret de Gremecey. The brutalizing contest, fought under darkened skies, rises to a pitch during the night with the Germans penetrating the outposts. It continues the following day when German columns advance to join the fight, only to be met by a more fervent resolve. **(Atlantic-Italy)** In the **U.S. Fifth Army** area, **II Corps** sector, the 34th Division is heavily engaged against the Germans near the Bruscoli-Gambellate Creek area. The 91st Division, subsequent to the seizure of M. Freddi, moves against M. Oggoli. The combat is vicious near Torre Poggioli as the 85th Division presses forward. Elements seize Montarello, but the iron resistance halts other contingents at Sambuco. The 88th Division grinds forward, taking favorable steps that topple the resistance at M. del Puntale and M. Pratolungo on its flanks; then it propels toward Castel del Rio. In the **British 13th Corps** area, the Germans keep firm control of M. Gamberaldi, thwarting all frontal attacks by the British 1st Division. After dark, the British try a flanking movement by pivoting toward M. Toncone. The 61st Brigade, British 6th Armored, advances along Route 67, meeting no resistance as it drives on the Corps' right flank toward Bucconi. In the **British Eighth Army** 5th Corps' area, the Indian 4th Division secures a bridgehead near Cornacchiara, but the Germans holding the heights near this portion of the Uso block all attempts to enlarge the perimeter. In other activity, Canonica falls to the British 46th Division. A conference is held at General Sir Henry M. Wilson's Headquarters at Caserta, and plans are formulated for a reoccupation of Greece. It is determined that British General Scobie will have responsibility for controlling all Guerrilla units in Greece.

September 27th 1944 — (Pacific-Palaus) On Peleliu, RCT 321, U.S.A. maneuvers to shrink the Umurbrogol pocket and spreads out in a northward drive to secure the central ridge system which has been bypassed by the 5th Marines. The Japanese meet the advance with incessant fire. The 1st Battalion sweeps north and secures Kamilianlul Mt. with surprising ease. The rapid seizure permits further movement to the intersection of the East and West roads where contact is made with the 5th Marines. The 1st Battalion, 5th Marines, secures Hill 1. In other activity, Old Glory is raised at the 1st Division Command Post to signify that the island is secure. **(Pacific-Philippines)** The Submarine *Narwhal* (SS-167) zips into Mindanao while the *Stingray* (SS-186) zooms to Luzon, both depositing supplies without incident. **(Pacific-East China Sea)** The Japanese Defense Vessel No. 10 is destroyed by a Submarine torpedo. **(Atlantic-Western Europe) 21st Army Group** Orders are issued to British General D.G. Crerar by General Montgomery to secure the Schelde as soon as possible. The operation takes some doing; the first Allied Ship to enter Antwerp does so during the latter part of November. **12th Army Group** In the **U.S. Third Army** area, **XX Corps** sector, the ongoing assault by the 359th Infantry, 90th Division to secure the highway to St. Hubert's Farm is aborted. The restrained attack against Fort Driant by the 5th Division commences following a low-level air bombardment that fails to inflict any serious damage to the enemy. The 2nd Battalion, 11th Infantry, jumps off at 14:15, but the Germans hold firmly, prompting the attackers to pull back to their starting point. In the **XII Corps** area, the Germans bolster their attack with additional Armor and advance boldly toward the 4th Armored perimeter, which they had penetrated the previous night. The Tanks make a wild rush against the south flank and seize Hill 318, gaining temporary control of the highway leading to Nancy. Lesser strengthened assaults mounted against Xanrey and Bezange-la-Petite are stalled and controlled. The Germans shoot toward the Foret de Gremecey salient to force a collapse of the lines held by the 35th Division, but reinforcements rush to the scene despite the enemy Armor; they advance toward Gramecey. The arrival of the 320th Infantry dilutes the threat and prevents the Germans from reaching their goal. The advance reverses itself at Pettoncourt and heads back to Chambrey. The enemy thrust also pierces the forest at its northeastern fringes, but the majority of lost terrain is reclaimed. Twelve Generals arrive at Third Army Headquarters, including Hughes and Spaatz. Patton is informed that he is to lose the XV Corps. The news is alarming as the shortage of troops is already acute, and he notes that the recently arrived Motor Transports of all Divisions must be used to carry supplies, in addition to committing 11th Infantry Battalions' use as stevedores. Patton refers to the manpower shortage (Third Army) as "scandalous." **(Atlantic-Italy)** In the **U.S. Fifth Army** area, **IV Corps** sector, Task

Force 92 drives through the Serchio Valley making superb progress. In the **II Corps** area, Aircraft and Artillery bolster an attack by the 91st Infantry against M. Oggioli, but the resistance is fierce and progress is nominal. In the 85th Division zone, Sambuco is secured while the 88th Division operating in its zone succeeds in seizing Castel del Rio, lying in its center path, M. Battaglia, a strategic strongpoint blocking the road to Imola, and a nearby hill on its left flank which commands Highway 937. The Germans mount a strong counterattack to retake M. Battaglia, but the 2nd Battalion, 350th Infantry holds its ground. The contest for M. Battaglia ensues viciously right into October. During the siege, the 2nd Battalion is forced to pull back at one point and is subsequently shoved almost totally off the hill, but reinforcements pour in to aid the beleaguered Battalion; it is then relieved by the British. The incessant battle is expensive with heavy casualties to both sides. In the British 13th Corps area, M. Toncone is seized by the British 1st Division, which also threatens M. Gamberaldi. In the **British Eighth Army** 5th Corps sector, the Germans are pitting everything they have available to stem the tide of the advancing British. Ridges on the left flank of the Corps are virtual bastions that prevent the Indian 4th Division from advancing. Meanwhile, the Germans, holding tenaciously on Castelvecchio Ridge, bar further advance by the British 56th Division, which is attempting to reach Savignano.

September 28th 1944 — (Pacific-Carolines-Palaus) Ngesebus, off Peleliu's northern coast, is seized by the 3rd Battalion, 5th Marines, and Company G, 2nd Battalion secures the northern portion of the northwest peninsula (28th and 29th). The 321st Infantry, U.S.A. completes the elimination of enemy resistance in the northern portion of the Umurbrogol Pocket up to its previously designated line. On Angaur, the 322nd Infantry is heavily involved against tough opposition in the ominous bowl. The unit sustains its highest one-day casualty tally, suffering about 80. **(Pacific-Marianas)** The Carrier *Independence* arrives at Saipan and pushes toward Ulithi, reaching there on the 1st of October to prepare to strike against Formosa. **(China-Burma-India)** In the **British Fourteenth Army** area (Burma), the 15th Corps receives orders to take the offensive on the Arakan front to secure Chittagong, Cox's Bazaar, and in addition, the Naaf River estuary. **(Atlantic-Western Europe) 21st Army Group** In the **Canadian First Army** area, 2nd Corps sector, Calais is penetrated by the Canadian 3rd Division; it captures the citadel. In the **British Second Army** area, the salient at Eindhoven-Arnhem is struck by a feverish, but unsuccessful German assault to seize the roadbridge at Nijmegen. **12th Army Group** In the **U.S. First Army** area, the **XIX Corps** receives orders from Major General Charles H. Corlett to initiate an assault to secure the Peel Marshes. In the **U.S. Third Army** area, the top priority is Metz. In the **XII Corps** area, the 4th Armored Division is engaged in a heavy battle with the Germans who have mounted a serious string of counterattacks. The combatants pound each other in a struggle that sways back and forth with no conclusive victor. The summit of Hill 318 falls to Combat Command B, but the Germans come back tough and regain it during the night of the 28th-29th. The steady plowing by the Germans pushes them to the fringes of Bois du Benamont, and in addition, they seize Hill 293. In yet other heavy scaled fighting, the Germans strike the entire perimeter of the 35th Division with the strongest surge hitting the northeastern fringes of the Foret de Gremecey, temporarily gaining ground, but a determined counterattack by the Yanks reclaims the ground. The Germans who assault the 35th's right flank are thwarted by accurate Artillery fire. Additional enemy troops rushing to Pettoncourt are also halted. In the **XV Corps** area, the 313th and 315th Regiments, 79th Division, await cessation of an Air attack, then bolt forward during the afternoon toward the Foret de Parroy, driving into the fringes of the forest. **(Atlantic-Italy)** In the U.S. **Fifth Army IV Corps** area, Task Force 92, driving parallel to Lima Creek, secures Highway 12 between Fornoli and S. Martello, capturing Lucchio as it moves. In the **II Corps** sector, Radicosa Pass, a formidable enemy strongpoint, is evacuated by the Germans. In other activity, M. Bastione is secured by the 135th Infantry, 34th Division, while the 338th Infantry , 85th Division seizes M. Canda. The 91st Division captures the summit of M. Oggoli with its 361st Infantry. On M. Battaglia, the besieged 2nd Battalion, 350th Infantry, 88th Division is struck by another counterattack; forward posts are forced to pull back. Reinforcements and ammunition are rushed forward. During the previous night as the Yanks repulse the sixth enemy counterattack, Captain Robert E. Roeder, Company G, takes hold after the enemy overruns an outpost and leads his men in close hand-to-hand combat, inflicting severe casualties on the enemy. His gallant actions continue throughout the night, and when the enemy mounts another strong assault on the morning of the 28th, he is wounded and knocked unconscious. He later regains consciousness and refuses medical aid, struggling to the door of the Command Post where he props himself up with his rifle to meet the onslaught, killing several of the charging Germans before he is killed by an exploding shell. The inspiration of Captain Roeder, who receives the Medal of Honor posthumously, injects a surge of power into his men, and the position is held. In the British 13th Corps area, the Germans evacuate M. Gamberaldi. In the **British Eighth Army** area, V Corps sector, the Indian 4th Division halts its offensive tactics and holds in place to await reinforcements. In the British 56th Division zone, progress is made at Castelvecchio Ridge during a night attack, but the Germans regain the ground on the following morning. At the Fiumicino River, the 1st Corps is struck by tragedy when a Company of the Canadian 5th Armored Division crosses the river only to be ambushed and annihilated. Also, the weather stymies further advance as torrential rains and accompanying floods hit the area.

September 29th 1944 — (Pacific-Carolines Palaus) The 1st Battalion, 7th Marines relieves RCT 321 and takes responsibility for eliminating the balance of enemy resistance in the Umurbrogol Pocket. The exchange of places permits the 3rd Battalion, 321st Regiment to drive northward to clear the resistance previously bypassed by the 1st Battalion, RCT 321. Different contingents of RCT 321 relieve the 5th Marines on Kongauru and Ngesebus islands, but the 5th Marines continue the operation to clear Amiangal. On Angaur, the 322nd Infantry secures the floor of the Lake Salome bowl, while pushing the Japanese to the northwestern edges of the island. In Naval activity, Task Force 32, commanded by Admiral Fort (Western Attack Force), takes over responsibility for the W. Carolines, giving Admiral Wilkinson's Task Force 31 the maneuverability to prepare for participation in the Philippine campaign. **(Pacific-Morotai)** The original Airstrip on Morotai, dubbed Pitoe Crash Strip, becomes operational for Fighters; however, the field is subsequently abandoned. **(Pacific-Philippines)** The U.S.S. *Nautilus* (SS-168) arrives off Mindanao and evacuates 81 American P.O.W.s (survivors from the previously torpedoed Japanese Vessel *Shinyo Maru*). **(China-Burma-India)** Construction of a trail between Myitkyina and

Kunming begins today. A huge amount of Chinese laborers assisted by a contingent of U.S. Engineers begin the task. **(Atlantic)** The German Submarine U-863 is sunk in the South Atlantic by Land-based Naval Aircraft (VP-107). **(Atlantic-Western Europe) 21st Army Group** In the **Canadian First Army** area, the pitched battle at Calais between the 2 Corps and the Germans is brought to a halt by a mutually agreed upon armistice to allow civilians to evacuate the area without risk. In the **British Second Army** area, the enemy damages the Nijmegen bridges by using swimmers to detonate charges, but the damage is repairable. **12th Army Group** In the **U.S. First Army** area, **XIX Corps** sector, the 7th Armored rolls through the British lines to deploy for an attack toward the Peel Marshes. In the **VII Corps** area, the inconclusive fighting ends; Hill 554 falls to the 39th Infantry, 9th Division, giving it positions within the West Wall, southeast of Lammersdorf. In the **U.S. Third Army** area, General Patton sanctions the **XX Corps'** plan to commence another assault against Fort Driant. In the Foret de Gremecey, donnybrook breaks out when the 35th Division counterattacks to retake the road to Fresnes-en-Saulnois and crashes into the Germans who are driving south from Fresnes. Both sides wallop the other, and the shivering sheets of deadly steel strike with a terrorizing thud that causes spontaneous disoriented combat by the opposing troops. The Germans retain the eastern section of the forest, but the 3rd Battalion, 320th Infantry bursts through the lines of the 134th and 137th Regiments, plowing to the northern portion of the woods. Meanwhile, the 134th Regiment barges into Han and overpowers the resistance. In other activity, the XV Corps transfers to the command of U.S. Seventh Army. **(Atlantic-Italy)** In the **U.S. Fifth Army** area, **IV Corps** sector, Stazzema is taken by contingents of RCT 6 (Brazilian). In the **II Corps** area, the 34th Division drives on the right advancing to Fornelli while simultaneously throwing back a severe counterattack on its left at Montefredente. The 91st Division commits two Regiments which pound their way forward about two miles north of Radicosa Pass. At M. Battaglia, the Germans relentlessly press against the beleaguered but unyielding 2nd Battalion, 350th Regiment (88th Division). The remainder of the Regiment rushes to the scene and turns over its right flank to Combat Command A, 1st Armored. In the British 13th Corps area, the Germans abandon M. di Castelnuovo. The Maradi-S. Benedetto Road is being opened by Engineers. In the **British Eighth Army** area, the severe flooding and the driving rain continue to obstruct any movement. During the night (29th-30th) the British 5th Corps occupies Castelvecchio and Savignano, taking swift advantage of the restrained German pullback in the area and receives no opposition.

September 30th 1944 — (Pacific-Carolines-Palaus) Admiral George H. Fort declares Peleliu, Ngesebus, Kongauru, and Angaur occupied. Organized resistance on northern Peleliu ceases. The 5th Marines report 1,170 enemy killed or captured although a recent estimate of enemy strength had been 500. Regimental Combat Team 321, U.S.A. relieves the Marines and mops up the remaining resistance. **(Pacific-Philippines)** The U.S.S. *Nautilus* (SS-168) moves to the vicinity of Libertad, Panay in the Philippines and lands supplies, then evacuates personnel. **(Atlantic)** The U.S.S. *Fessenden* (DE-142), a Destroyer Escort, sinks a German Submarine, the U-1062, in the mid-Atlantic. **(Atlantic-Western Europe) 21st Army Group** The brief armistice at Calais ends at 12:00, and the Canadian 3rd Division reinitiates its attack. The Canadians have the objective secure by dark, and the operation turns to mopping up the area. **12th Army Group** In the **U.S.**

First Army area, XIX Corps sector, an afternoon assault develops as the 7th Armored springs from its positions near Oploo and drives south through a corridor west of the Mass River, but the Germans intercept it and establish fervent resistance that prevents the armor from reaching Overloon and Vortum. In the U.S. Third Army area, the Germans mount an eventful but unsuccessful attack to retake the Foret de Gremecey. General Gaffey, at Nancy, summons Patton to ensure he has first hand knowledge of the criticalness of the situation. He arrives on the scene as the two German Divisions (15th and 539th) attack the 35th Division east of Nancy. Patton is distressed to discover that the 35th had been allowed to withdraw from the woods west of Chateau Salins and that the 6th Armored had not been committed to the fight. Thanks to General Gaffey, who summoned Patton to Nancy, the crucial situation comes under control. In line with his methods of improvisation, Patton uses a tactic which had worked perfectly during the Sicilian campaign. He looks at the situation, and being of the opinion that hesitation on the part of an attacking General might prove deadly, speaks to the Officer involved and subsequently relates the story: "I TOLD A GENERAL WHO WAS SOMEWHAT HESITANT TO ATTACK, THAT I HAD PERFECT CONFIDENCE IN HIM AND THAT TO SHOW IT, I WAS GOING HOME...IT WORKED AGAIN." The enemy strikes both flanks of the 35th's perimeter with such pressure that the Corps commander orders a pullback after dark. The 6th Armored is ordered by Patton to counterattack to relieve the pressure and retake the ground. Meanwhile, the 35th Division tightens its lines and holds firmly by committing its remaining reserves. During the vicious fighting, an enemy shell strikes within a couple of feet of three American Generals. The Generals escape harm, but two MPs are killed and three others are wounded. The 6th Armored attacks at dawn on the following day and recaptures the hill. 6th Army Group In the U.S. Seventh Army area, savage skirmishing breaks out in the iV Corps sector at Foret de Parroy, with both sides pounding each other relentlessly. The forest rings with the crackle of small arms fire and thundering Armor, determined to annihilate the opposition. The 79th Division, with the assistance of Tanks, blows through the resistance, but it does not secure the objective until the expensive battle ends on the 9th of October when the Germans are forced to withdraw. (Atlantic-Italy) In the U.S. Fifth Army area, IV Corps sector, Task Force 92 advances swiftly to La Lima. In other activity, the Brazilian Expeditionary Force (RCT 6) gets elements to Fornoli. In the II Corps sector, the 351st Infantry, 88th Division engages the enemy in a powerful contest at M. Cappello, and persistence finally topples the acrimonious resistance and secures the objective. In another furious battle, the exhausted elements of the 350th Infantry, 88th Division, clinging tenuously on M. Battaglia, are hit with another series of sledgehammer attacks that shove them back further, almost entirely off the hill. They are pressed, but undefeated, and on the following day, despite a fragile grasp, the 3439th Infantry attacks and protects the right flank of the 85th Division. In addition to the misery of combat, the Yanks are forced to endure more of the incessant rains that have plagued the Allies since their arrival in Italy. The Corps prepares to attack through the Po Valley. In the British 13th Corps area, the 3rd Brigade, British 1st Division, stays at M. Toncone, awaiting repairs on the Marradi-Palazzuolo Road. The 17th Brigade, Indian 8th Division, unhampered by the bad roads, advances to A. Adriano. In the British Eighth Army area, 5th Corps sector, the Indian 4th Division secures Tribola, while the British 46th Division seizes Montalbano and gets Patrols beyond

to the Fiumicino. A full scale assault by the Corps commences during the night of the 30th. Borghi and M. Reggiano both fall to the Indian 4th Division before the sun rises on October 1st, but the Germans prevent the British 56th and 46th Divisions operating on the right and center respectively, from crossing the Fiumicino. (Atlantic-Rumania-Yugoslavia) Elements of the Third Ukrainian Front, having seized the Iron Gate-Turnu-Severin-Orsova area, cross the Danube where it passes through the Transylvania Alps and drive toward Belgrade.

October 1st 1944 — (United States) The Office of Deputy Commander in Chief, United States Fleet, and Deputy Chief of Naval Operations (Vice Admiral R.S. Edwards) is established. (Pacific-Carolines-Palaus) Marine Fighter Squadron 122 and Marine Night Fighter Squadron 541 (final elements) arrive at Peleliu, bringing strength to total allotted for Group 11 Marine Aircraft on the island. In Naval activity, the Motor Minesweeper YMS-385 sinks after striking a mine off the western Carolines. The Destroyer Bailey (DD-492) is damaged by enemy Planes. In addition, the U.S.S. Forrest (DD-461) becomes damaged after being involved in a collision. (Pacific-Japan) The U.S.S. Snapper (SS-185), operating northwest of the Bonin Islands in the Western Pacific south of Honshu, sinks the Japanese Coastal Minelayer Ajiro. (Atlantic-Greece) Greek Naval Port parties land on Lemnos, Levita, and Mytilene. In other activity, British Commandos, having departed Kithira Island, debark at Poros Bay for purposes of reconnaissance. (Atlantic-Western Europe) 21st Army Group In the Canadian First Army area, 2nd Corps zone, the mop-up operation at Calais is terminated. In the British 1st Corps sector, the Canadian 2nd Division drives west, taking big strides across the Antwerp-Turnhout Canal. It moves through the northern suburbs of Antwerp toward the Beveland Peninsula. In the British Second Army area, the Germans are again prevented from reaching the Nijmegen bridges. 12th Army Group The XXIX TAC, U.S. Ninth Air Force is detached from the I Corps and becomes an independent unit. In the U.S. First Army area during October, First Army concentrates on surrounding and reducing Aachen and subsequently mounting a drive from there against Cologne. In the XX Corps area, the Germans continue to hold firmly in the Peel Marshes. The primary Corps offensive is halted because of poor weather that prohibits an attack against the West Wall between Aachen and Geilenkirchen. In the U.S. Third Army area, XX Corps sector, Company C, 329th Infantry, 83rd Division, advances to Grevenmacher on the north bank of the Moselle outside of Remich. In the XII Corps area, heavy skirmishing ensues in the Foret de Gremecey. Contingents of the 35th Division drive to the fringes of the forest at selected points. Combat Command R, 6th Armored Division secures Chambrey, while C.C.A., 6th Armored, swings around the western fringes of the forest and seizes Lemoncourt-Fresnes Ridge, then turns it over to the 134th Infantry. The gusty surge of the 6th Armored caps the struggle in Foret de Gremecey, giving another prize to the Yanks. General Baade, Commander 35th Division, is wounded today. The 80th Division, operating on the north flank of the Corps, initiates successive assaults against German-held terrain west of the Seille River. Elements of the 318th Infantry unsuccessfully attack an enemy stronghold on a farm that commands the Pont a Mousson-Nomeny Road. Perseverance prevails and the Yanks take it on the following day. 6th Army Group In the U.S. Seventh Army area, V Corps zone, heated combat still ensues between the 79th Division and the enemy, with the Americans making only nominal progress in the Foret de Parroy. (Atlantic-Italy) In the **U.S. Fifth Army** area, the Germans commence a strong counterattack that pushes the 6th South African Armored Division back from its positions on M. Catarelto. Task Force 45 and RCT 6 (Brazilian) are placed under operational command of Major General Enrice Gaspar Dutra (Brazilian Minister of War). In the **II Corps** sector, an offensive follows an Artillery bombardment that ends at 06:00; it drives toward Bologna. The 168th Infantry, 34th Division, slices forward, but encounters rigid resistance at Hill 789. The 133rd Infantry is stalled at the crest of M. del Galleto. The Germans also mount iron resistance against elements of the 91st Division which are pressing heavily toward Loiano. The advance is stymied near Monghidoro. In the 85th Division sector, La Martina, a stumbling block in front of M. Bibele, is seized by the 339th Infantry in conjunction with the seizure of the ridge on the right by the 337th Infantry, securing it as far as Spedaletto. In one instance of extraordinary courage, the enemy pins down Company L as it advances against Casoni di Remana, by extensive use of machine guns, mortars, machine pistols, and accurate rifle fire. Sergeant Chris Carr (previously Christos Karaberis) bolts ahead of his Squad, moving across barren rocky terrain, and captures eight enemy troops. He rushes beyond, using his submachine gun to kill four of five defenders at the next nest while capturing the lone survivor. He follows this by charging yet another nest in a burst of speed, bewildering the four defenders who also surrender. Carr sprints under fire to two additional menacing machine guns and eliminates four men of the first nest while capturing three; his performance is so convincing that the six men holding the nearby nest decide to surrender to him. His exploits net eight dead Germans and 22 POWs, but more importantly this one-man wrecking crew clears the ridge. He becomes the recipient of the Medal of Honor for his inspirational actions. In the British 13th Corps area, the British continue to repair the Palazzuolo-Marradi Road to expedite the movement of the 1st Brigade, 1st British Division. In other activity, the 19th Brigade, Indian 8th Division, attacks against M. Cavallara. In the **British Eighth Army** area, General Sir Oliver Leese, selected to lead the Allied Land Forces in Asia, is replaced as Commander of the British Eighth Army by General McCreery (former Commander 1st Corps). In the 5th Corps sector, heavy flooding still impedes progress, but advance elements of the 10th Indian Division seize Montecchio without opposition. This action encompasses Corps activity along the Fiumicino. In the Canadian 1st Corps area, the situation is also controlled by the weather, with the opponents locked in stalemate. There are sporadic plans to attack issued, but in each case they are canceled because of the elements.

October 2nd 1944 — (United States) At a meeting in San Francisco between the Commander-in-Chief POA and the Commander-in-Chief, the decision to invade Formosa is dropped in favor of the invasion of Okinawa. **(Pacific-Carolines-Palaus)** Contingents of RCT 321, bolstered by Company G, 2nd Battalion, 5th Marines, seize Radar Hill, terminating the mop-up operation on the northern peninsula of Peleliu. On Angaur, the 322nd Infantry, continues attacking the pocket on the northwestern portion of the island, but is forced to halt the operation and revert to close-in fire. A violent storm sweeping the area inflicts damage upon several Naval Vessels: the LST's 129, 278, and the 661. **(Pacific-Marianas)** The Submarines *Blackfish*, *Seadragon*, and *Shark* embark from Saipan, heading for Patrol half-way between Hainan and the western tip of the Bashi Channel. The *Shark* will be lost, presumably on the 24th. **(Southeast Asia Command)**

The British Chiefs-of-Staff and the British War Cabinet concur that the intended attack against Rangoon (DRACULA) cannot be implemented without further draining the primary objective, which is Europe where the British are driving north with the U.S. First Army in support. The decision is made to push the assault from March of 1945 to November of 1945, but British Admiral Mountbatten, responsible for planning DRACULA and CAPITAL (attack against Mandalay), responds to Churchill's request and issues orders to commence CAPITAL on a reduced scale immediately. **(China-Burma-India)** On the NCAC Front, gasoline is now being delivered to Myitkyina by pipeline. The NCAC participation in CAPITAL is to be aired out in two phases: securing the area reaching the Indaw-Kunchaung-Sikaw-Namhkam Line by the middle of December, and the successful advance to the Lashio-Mongmit-Thabeikkyin Line by mid-February 1945. The general responsibility of the NCAC is to keep the Air lanes to China open while simultaneously keeping overland communications clear, in addition to seizing the portions of upper Burma and Assam. **(Atlantic-Western Europe)** British General Montgomery's initiative to drive north has not succeeded. Today he changes the direction of the assault and orders the attack to drive southeast to the Ruhr. Now that the northern drive is terminated, General Eisenhower requests that Montgomery transfer the two American Airborne Divisions back to American command. **12th Army Group** In the **U.S. First Army** area, **I Corps** sector, Air and Artillery bombardments commence against enemy positions, but the Air assault is ineffective. Following the preliminary festivities, the 30th Division charges across the Wurm River at a shallow point between Aachen and Geilenkirchen. Pillboxes stand fiercely at Marienburg in the path of the 117th Infantry, but each obstacle is eliminated as the 117th rolls forward, seizing Palenberg. During the advance, one trooper, Private Harold Kiner, while pinned to the ground by a wall of fire, saves the lives of his comrades when a grenade is tossed in their midst. Kiner takes the brunt of the blast by covering the grenade with his body. He receives the Medal of Honor posthumously. The 119th Infantry pushes tenaciously against immovable resistance at Rimburg, but cannot pass the railroad embankment. Armor rushes to assist, but gets stuck on the east bank of the Wurm. The Germans attack at about midnight, but the effort fails miserably. Heavy resistance arises against a diversionary attack mounted by the 115th Infantry, 29th Division; however, the 115th overpowers it and bolts into Birgden, Hatterath, and Kreuzrath, in addition to piercing the enemy lines at Schierwaldenrath. In the ominous pocket west of the Maas, American and British Artillery supplement the movement of the U.S. 7th Armored. Vortum is seized by Combat Command B, but the Germans mount a counterattack preventing the seizure of Overloon. In other activity, the 113th Cavalry Group establishes a fragile bridgehead across the Saeffler Creek, but the Germans impede progress at Roermond. In the **V Corps** sector, orders are given to attack the West Wall on the 7th (tentative) and drive to Bonn. In the **U.S. Third Army** area, contingents of the 80th Division overcome resistance and secure the stronghold at the farm (attacked on previous day). The 318th Infantry, 80th Division, mounts an unsuccessful and expensive attack against Serrieres. Also units of the 317th Infantry prepare to assault Sivry. **6th Army Group** In the **U.S. Seventh Army** area, **XV Corps** sector, the fighting in the Foret de Parroy rages with unlimited fury. **(Atlantic-Italy)** The boundary between the U.S. Fifth Army and the British Eighth Army is moved approximately one mile east of Highway 67. In the **U.S. Fifth Army** area, **IV Corps** sector, elements of the 6th South African Division are halted at M. Catarelto; the attacks have proven to be costly. In the **II Corps** sector, the 34th Division seizes Cedrecchia, but the galvanized resistance at Hill 789 and at M. del Galletto cannot be overcome until the Germans abandon these objectives during the night 2nd-3rd. In the 91st Division area, Monghidoro is taken, eliminating opposition in the region. The 85th and 88th Divisions are battling to clear the Germans from the Idice Valley and the area east of the Sillaro respectively. In other activity, the Germans maintain their vicious posture at M. Battaglia, where the British 6th Armored Division is relieving the outnumbered and battle-weary 350th Infantry, U.S. 88th Division. In the **British Eighth Army** area, 5th Corps zone, elements of the Indian 4th Division maintain pressure against S. Martino. **(Atlantic-Poland)** The Polish insurrection in Warsaw ceases to exist and the losses are catastrophic, as the city has been demolished. The Poles lose over 250,000 killed in their attempt to have a government in place when the closing Russians arrive at the city. The Polish Leader, Tadeo Bor, signs the surrender. The Russians, whose offensive ironically stalls in synchronization with the rebellion, are still not in Warsaw, but they are very close.

October 3rd 1944 — (United States) The Joint Chiefs-of-Staff order General MacArthur to secure operating Bases on Luzon (December 20th 1944) for the purpose of supporting subsequent Pacific efforts. MacArthur is to receive wide cover support from Admiral Nimitz. Nimitz is also expected to seize Iwo Jima (January 20th 1945) and the Ryukyus (Okinawa) (March 1st 1945). **(Pacific-Carolines-Palaus)** The 7th Marines secure a firm hold on the ridges stretching along the east side of the Umurbrogol Pocket. The 2nd Battalion, 7th Marines, seizes Walt Ridge and Company K, 3rd Battalion, advances to the crest of Boyd Ridge. In Naval activity, the U.S.S. *Samuel S. Miles* (DE-183) sinks the Japanese Submarine I-364 off the Palau Islands. **(Pacific-Morotai)** The U.S.S. *Seawolf* had departed Brisbane on her fourteenth Patrol on September 21st 1944. Today she is traveling presumably in a safety free zone protected from attack. The Submarine is running a day behind schedule, but Headquarters is informed of the situation, including the high seas. She is spotted by the *Narwhal*, and everything is reported fine, except that later in the morning a Japanese Submarine attacks a Seventh Fleet Task Force and sinks the Destroyer Escort *Shelton* (DE-407) (vicinity Dutch East Indies); Planes are launched to kill the enemy Submarine. Planes launched from the *Midway*, one of the Carriers that had been attacked, sight a Submarine and bomb it as it is diving (Pilot sees no recognition signals and is unaware that the Submarine is in an attack free area). The U.S.S. *Rowell*, a Destroyer Escort, descends on the target and commences a continuous bombardment. Signals are received from the besieged Submarine, but the American Surface Vessel doesn't accept the information as any thing other than an enemy Submarine attempting to jam the sound gear. Soon after, following multiple underwater explosions, various parts of wreckage rise to the surface. Subsequent information will determine that the sunken Submarine is the U.S.S. *Seawolf*, sunk in error. Unfortunately the U.S. Antisubmarine forces had received no information informing them of the *Seawolf's* late arrival in the vicinity and as noted prior, the Pilot was also uninformed; this is a classic case of important information not being communicated to all concerned. The Japanese Submarine RO-41 had made the attack against the Fleet and was not attacked, permitting it to return unscathed to Japan. **(Atlantic-Western Europe)** Planes attached to the R.A.F. Bomber Command, numbering just under 250, strike the Westkapelle Dike at Walcheren, Holland, flooding the area. **12th Army Group** In the U.S. **First Army** area, **XI Corps** sector, brisk house-to-house fighting develops as the 117th Infantry, 30th Division, drives into Uebach. Combat Command B, 2nd Armored, joins the 117th as it enlarges the bridgehead from Marienberg. The traffic at Uebach is so thick that neither Infantry nor Armor is able to advance beyond Uebach. The 119th Infantry seizes Rimburg Woods and the castle, the former by the use of the combination of flanking and frontal assaults; determined resistance prevents the small bridgehead (800 yards deep) from being expanded further. In other activity, the 7th Armored Division maintains its attack against Overloon, but the investment is still not complete. In the U.S. **Third Army** area, **XX Corps** sector, elements of the 357th Infantry, 90th Division, reach a huge pile of slag on the northwestern part of town (Metz). At 12:00, the 5th Division reinitiates its assault against Fort Driant, supported by Artillery and smoke screen protection, in lieu of Air support, which bad weather has prevented. The effort is valiant but the cost is high. The Germans sit it out in caves and await darkness, then counterattack. The fighting remains vicious throughout the night, and on the following day, reinforcements are sent forward to aid the 11th Infantry. In the **II Corps** zone, the Corps line in the center and on the right flank is solidly reestablished as the 2nd Battalion, 317th Infantry has Sivry secure by 05:55. **6th Army Group** In the U.S. **Seventh Army** area, the 79th Division, augmented by Tanks, drives deeper into the Foret de Parroy, evading an enemy roadblock as it advances. **(Atlantic-Italy)** In the U.S. **Fifth Army** area, **IV Corps** sector, the Germans retreat from their positions on M. Catarelto, but they do not withdraw at M. Vigese and mount heavy resistance against the 11th Armored Brigade, 6th South Armored Division. In the **II Corps** sector, the U.S. 34th Division attacks, its 168th Infantry stomping through Campiano to the lower portion of Hill 747, while the aggressive pace of the 133rd Infantry carries it to victory on M. del Galletto. The 91st Division advances to about one mile outside of Loiano. In other activity, the U.S. 85th Division, driving against nominal resistance, seizes I Boschi and stands at the vestibule of Quinzano. The 337th Infantry sprints across the ridge straddled between the Idice and Sillaro Rivers, seizing Hill 628, and then throws back successive counterattacks at Hill 751. In the 88th Division sector, the 349th Infantry drives to Sassoleone while the 6th British Armored Division continues to relieve the 350th Infantry embattled on M. Battaglia. In the British 13th Corps area, a hotly contested battle for M. Ceco erupts as the 3rd Brigade, 1st British Division attacks with fervor. In the **British Eighth Army** area, the Indian 10th Division assumes responsibility for the Indian 4th Division's sector on the left flank of the Corps, permitting the British 4th Division to become Corps reserve. **(Atlantic-Estonia)** Elements of the Leningrad Front debark at Dagoe (Hiiumaa) off the coast of Estonia in the Gulf of Riga to secure the island.

October 4th 1944 — (Pacific-Carolines-Palaus) On Peleliu, the 7th Marines continue attacking the Umurbrogol Pocket, but the incessant fighting has taken a heavy toll on the unit, depleting its numbers sufficiently enough to render them too understrengthed to continue. On the following day, the 5th Marines relieves them. During a violent counterattack on the night of the 4th, a grenade is thrown into a foxhole, and Private Wesley Phelps instinctively yells a warning to his fellow Marine, then throws himself forward to take the full impact and save the other Marine; Phelps is awarded the Medal of Honor (posthumously). **(Pacific-Morotai)** General Krueger declares the Morotai Operation terminated, but mop-up operations continue. The Allies suffer 30 killed, 1 missing, and 85 wounded. The Japanese sustain 102 killed plus about 200 killed on barges. In other activity, Wama Airfield is operational and a permanent Fighter Garrison lands, permitting the Carriers to depart the area. **(China-Burma-India)** In the **British Fourteenth Army** area, the East African 11th Division seizes Yazagyo in the Kabaw Valley. In other 33rd Corps activity, the Indian 5th Division nears Tiddim. **(Atlantic-Western Europe)** The Royal Air Force strikes the Westkapelle Dam for a second time in two days and inflicts more grievous damage. **21st Army Group** The Canadian 2nd Division secures the Merxem-Eekeren vicinity as it drives toward Zuid Beveland. **12th Army Group** In the **U.S. First Army** area, **XIX Corps** sector, sparks are flying. A reinforced counterattack is mounted by the Germans against Uebach. The Yanks of the 117th Infantry, bolstered by Tanks and Artillery, repulse it. Combat Command B, 2nd Armored drives swiftly from Uebach. Its Task Force Hinds overpowers the resistance on the heights above Hoverhof, then pushes further, reaching the heights east of Zweibruggen. Task Force Disney, commanded by Colonel Paul A. Disney, sustains heavy casualties as it drives a punishing 800 yards toward Geilenkirchen-Aachen Highway, losing 11 Tanks and sustaining severe casualties. Task Force Cox, commanded by Lt. Colonel William Cox, moves north to surround an enemy force at Rimburg woods, which has halted the 119th Regiment. Meanwhile the 120th Regiment attacks toward Kerkrade, west of the Wurm.

The Germans continue their counterattack, but withdraw during the night. Breberin is seized by the 115th Infantry, 29th Division, but vicious fighting costs them Company K, in Schierwaldenrath; at Overloon, the 7th Armored is still embattled with a gruesome fight, but there is no clear victor. The 113th Cavalry Group terminates its attack south of the Peel Marshes due to severe losses. In the **V Corps** sector, the tentative date for the assault against the West Wall is rescheduled for October 10th. In the **U.S. Third Army** area, **XX Corps** sector, the 90th Division retains its positions on the top of the slag pile outside of Maizieres-les-Metz, perched to attack Metz. In other activity, the Germans, who still hold commanding positions within caves at Fort Driant, await nightfall and mount new counterattacks. The endeavor to clear them out is tedious and costly. In the **XII Corps** area, units of the 317th Infantry, 80th Division are struck before dawn by the brunt of a German assault and become cut off in Sivry. Company E rushes to assist, but cannot penetrate the German stranglehold. Survivors of the trapped contingents subsequently rejoin the main force. **6th Army Group** In the **U.S. Seventh Army** area, the Germans commence a strong counterattack that halts the advance of the 314th Infantry, 79th Division, but the 315th is able to force its way to the north-south road through the Foret de Parroy, reaching a point close to the junction of the east-west road. In the **VI Corps** area, the 7th Infantry, 3rd Division, assaults Vagney. In the **French 1st Army's** 2nd Corps area, the French 1st Armored Division advances to seize Le Thillot, but rugged resistance at Longegoutte and in the forest outside of Gehan stops the attack in its tracks. At Servance-Chateau Lambert, the string of resistance is equally fierce and the French Armor is unable to penetrate. **(Atlantic-Italy)** In the **U.S. Fifth Army** area, M. Venere is seized by the 133rd Infantry, 34th Division. The Germans also stymie the 91st Division at Loiano. Meanwhile, elements of the 85th Division (339th Infantry) overpower the resistance at Quinzano, then race to the slopes of M. Bibele. In addition, the 337th Infantry captures Hill 566,

but it ends up far in advance of the flanking forces. In the British 13th Corps area, the contest at M. Ceco still blazes; the Germans hold firmly, repulsing all attempts by the British 3rd Brigade, 1st Division to dislodge them. In the **British Eighth Army** area, 5th Corps sector, orders are given to commence an attack across the Fiumicino during the night 6th-7th. In other activity, the Indian 10th Division plows forward slowly against intense opposition in an attempt to reach the Uso river. Advance contingents cross the river and assault the heights at Sogliano al Rubicone-S. Martino Ridge.

October 5th 1944 — (Pacific-Carolines-Palaus) The 5th Marines initiate relief of the 7th Marines on Peleliu at the Umurbrogol Pocket. During the day's skirmishing, a four-man detachment, including P.F.C. Richard E. Kraus, 8th Amphibian Tractor Battalion, volunteers to extricate a wounded Marine. The contingent advances against withering enemy fire that forbids further progress. While attempting to make their way back, the men are approached by two men who appear to be Marines. The Squad yells for the password, but the impostors are Japs, and the response is a tossed grenade. Krause (Medal of Honor Recipient), in an effort to save the other Marines, flings his body upon the live grenade and absorbs the full impact, giving his life that the others might live. **(Pacific-Formosa)** General Wainwright and other U.S. P.O.W.s depart Muksaq in trucks for Taihoku and from there, they are moved by train to Heito on the southern tip of Formosa. The Yanks are then transferred by Plane to Manchuria, Sheng Tai Tun near the Gobi Desert. The Americans are forced to endure harsh treatment and lack even the most basic of supplies, including soap. The Japanese exhibit no compassion. Many of the Yanks lose their teeth from severe beatings. During December, after 31 months of confinement, 288 American Red Cross packages arrive; this is the second shipment that the Japanese have permitted to reach these P.O.W.s. During the winter, temperatures drop to 45 degrees below zero. During May of 45, the group is moved to Mukden. General Wainright is told during May of 1945 that "IF THEY OBEY ALL RULES IN THE NEXT TEN OR TWENTY YEARS TO COME, THEIR RELATIVES FROM AMERICA WOULD BE ALLOWED TO VISIT." The U.S. Officers refuse to obey Japanese orders to work despite the ill-treatment. **(Atlantic-Western Europe) 21st Army Group** Advance elements of the British 1st Corps push to Alphen. **12th Army Group** In the **XI Corps** sector, U.S. First Army area, Combat Command B, 2nd Armored Division, advances rapidly on the left flank toward Geilenkirchen, overpowering Frelenberg and Zweibruggen. The forward thrust of the drive severs the Geilenkirchen-Aachen Highway, but stalls short of its objective: Beggendorf. Combat Command A speeds to reinforce the defenders at Uebach; the 3rd Battalion, 116th Infantry, 29th Division, also races there. Task Force Cox continues its drive, advancing to a point east of Merkstein-Herbach, and knocks out all resistance on a ridge to the rear except one stubborn pillbox on the southern edge. At Overloon, the Germans are nearly surrounded, but they build more defiant resistance and prevent the 7th Armored from penetrating by concentrating Artillery fire on the advancing Armor. The Americans counter with almost 100 air missions, despite their dangerously depleting ammunition supplies. In other activity, the Germans send Planes against Palenberg, which inflict slight damage. In the **VII Corps** area, the nasty weather continues to plague the American attack plan, preventing any possible assault against Schmidt and the Schwammenauel Dam. In the **U.S. Third Army** area, the menacing struggle to eliminate Fort Driant and other nearby enemy forts ensues. The 5th Division has clawed through a

465

storm of enfilade fire from the surrounding forts, but clings to its fragile hold on Driant. A new Task Force, commanded by Brigadier General A.D. Warnock, is forming and will be committed to carry on the operation to destroy the fort. In other XX Corps activity, Grevenmacher, another enemy stronghold, receives the wrath of Fighter Planes and Artillery in support of attacking contingents of the 329th Infantry, 83rd Division. The combination works magnificently and the objective is secured after a bitter fight. In the **XII Corps** area, Artillery and Air bombardments of enemy positions commence and last for several days. The bombardments are intended to soften resistance for a 3-Divisional assault, which is to commence on the 8th. **6th Army Group** In the **U.S. Seventh Army's XV Corps** sector, the incessant and brutalizing contest in the Foret de Parroy continues to rage without victory. The Germans hold fast and tough at the primary road junction, intercepting the advancing 315th Infantry, 79th Division. The fierce exchange of fire proves extremely expensive, and elements of the 315th are cut off. Another contingent, the 314th, also undergoing a tenacious struggle, is unable to breakthrough the southern portion of the forest. Although the 79th has secured about one half of the forest, the remainder is still strongly fortified. The 79th Division takes a defensive posture to ensure keeping what it has gained; it regroups before attempting to seize the entire objective. In the **VI Corps** sector, the 7th Infantry, 3rd Division continues its attack against Vagney, but the town holds. The 15th Infantry concludes the furious battle for control of a quarry stronghold outside of Cleurie, seizing it. In the French 1st Army area, the French 2nd Corps drives against the Germans, holding the heights north of the Moselle in the Gehan forest and Longegoutte. The effort, spearheaded by the Algerian 3rd Division, forces the enemy to retire to the high ground in the Foret de Longegoutte. **(Atlantic-Italy)** In the **U.S. Fifth Army** area, there is some doubt as to whether or not the Germans have evacuated the Valle di Commachio-Apennines pocket as elements reach Highway 9. The unsettled conclusion forces modification of the assault plan. The IV Corps presses toward La Spezia, encountering a continual string of hills that must be reduced. An attempt is made to coordinate with the II Corps on the right flank. The maneuvering drains much of the IV Corps' strength, forcing it to abort any heavy forward thrust. Major General Edward M. Almond, commanding Task Force 92, which includes Tanks and Tank Destroyers, takes over the coastal sector previously defended by Task Force 42 and drives toward Massa to seize M. Cauala. In the **II Corps** area, the Germans retain control of Hill 747 to the rear of M. Venere, but the 168th Infantry, 34th Division reaches Hill 661 northwest of the objective. Meanwhile, the 133rd Infantry seizes Monzuno and completes the reduction of resistance in the M. Venere sector. M. Loiano and M. Bastia come under heavy bombardment, and upon cessation, the 361st Infantry, 91st Division seizes both. The 85th Division retains control of Hill 566 on its right and simultaneously captures M. Bibele. The Germans are fiercely defending Hill 587 and successfully repel an attempt by the 88th Division to seize it. In the **British 13th Corps** area, the British 1st Division prepares an attack against M. Ceco and will commit its 2nd Brigade to the left of its 3rd. The assault is to commence on the night of the 6th, following a heavy Artillery bombardment. In the **British Eighth Army** area, the Indian 10th Division pounds the enemy in a vicious round of fighting at Sogliano-S. Martino Ridge, gaining the ridge and pushing the defenders across the Fiumicino. **(Atlantic-Eastern Europe)** Strongly numbered contingents of the Third Baltic Front drive toward East Prus-

sia and the Baltic to encircle and isolate the German Army Group North. The advance frees the Second and Third Baltic Fronts to maintain the advance toward Riga. In other activity, the Second Ukrainian Forces, located far to the south, push from Arad, Rumania, driving into southeastern Hungary; they then pivot toward Vienna, driving northwest toward Budapest and Szeged.

October 6th 1944 — (Pacific-Carolines-Palaus On Angaur, the Japanese hold defiantly on the northwestern tip of the island, but a brisk Artillery barrage begins to shake their confidence. In conjunction, the 322nd Infantry feints an assault, and the ruse works perfectly as the Japanese take the bait and come out of their holes, taking exposed positions. **(China-Burma-India)** General Hurley visits Chiang Kai-shek and gives him Roosevelt's response which gives in to Kai-shek by agreeing to recall General Stilwell; however, he refuses to place another American Officer in command of Chinese troops. Stilwell is to command the Chinese troops in Burma and in the Yunnan Province; to the liking of Kai-shek, Stilwell is disassociated from Lend-Lease programs (distribution of American supplies). The responsibility for over-the-Hump supplies is given to General Sultan. In Naval activity, the Japanese lose the Gunboat *Saga* when it strikes a mine off Hong Kong, and the Coastal Defense Vessel No. 21 is sunk by the U.S.S. *Seahorse* (SS-304) in the South China Sea. **(Atlantic-Western Europe) 21st Army Group** In the Canadian First Army area, an assault against Breskens is launched by the 2 Corps. The Canadian 3rd Division forces the Leopold Canal north of Maldegem, overcomes the resistance, and establishes a small bridgehead. **12th Army Group** Major General Charles H. Corlett, aware that the XIX Corps bridgehead is solidly established, orders his troops to halt the advance until a link-up with VII Corps can be accomplished (issued latter part of the day). Combat Command B, 2nd Armored, pushes ahead seizing the towns of Beggendorf and Waurichen, but heavy resistance halts its progress less than a thousand yards in front of Geilenkirchen. Combat Command A, supports the 117th Infantry, bolstered by Air cover; they forge ahead and seize a primary crossroad intersection southeast of Uebach, half the distance to Alsdorf. Combat Command A swings around and drives east, reaching the vicinity of Baesweiler. In the zone protected by Task Force Cox (119th Infantry, 30th Division contingent), the Germans mount a tenacious counterattack that plows right through four of the defending pillboxes, but quick reaction by the Yanks regains the lost ground and resecures the area. More brutalizing combat ensues across the Corps territory. The 120th Infantry, 30th Division, charges daringly against the Rimburg woods where the Germans are supported by strong Artillery fire; however, the opposition loses steam after the day's contest. In another viciously contested battle, the 7th Armored, attempting to secure the Peel Marshes, calls off the assault because of the expensive costs. The endeavor, initiated after the area had been given to the Americans, has only gained about two miles and the 7th is still in British zoned terrain. In the **VII Corps** area, the Germans mount vehement resistance against the advancing 39th and 60th Regiments of the 9th Division as it drives through the Huertgen Forest toward Schmidt. The attack is supplemented by Artillery fire. In other activity, Lt. General Leonard T. Gerow assumes command of the V Corps. In the **U.S. Third Army** area, an attack against Maizieres-les-Metz; commences on the following day. Meanwhile, the Germans unsuccessfully attempt to drive the Americans from the slag pile outside of Metz. In addition, U.S. assaults against Fort Driant are planned to commence on the 7th. **6th Army**

Group In the **U.S. Seventh Army** area, **VI Corps** sector, the 3rd Division is still engulfed in brutal fighting at Vagney. The Germans resist bitterly, but the defenders, holding entrenched positions along the Tendon-Le Tholly Road, are driven out. In the French 1st Army's 2nd Corps area, the Germans counterattack and pound the French, halting their advance and preventing them from approaching the heights north of the Moselle. The Germans also trap forward French contingents. **(Atlantic-Italy)** In the **U.S. Fifth Army** area, M. Vigese falls to the South African 6th Armored Division after it springs a surprise attack under cover of a thick mist. In the **IV Corps** area, M. Cauala becomes the site of a long and heated battle as Task Force 92 attacks to seize it. The Germans, who have been holding fiercely on Hill 747, abandon their positions. The 168th Infantry, 34th Division completes its job of securing the left flank of the Corps and is placed in Corps reserve. In the 85th Division sector, the 337th Infantry advances in conjunction with the 338th Regiment, which is driving on the left flank, both pushing toward La Villa and Castelnuovo di Bisano. In the 88th Division sector, the fight to seize Hill 587 on the right flank of the Corps begins and continues for three days until the Yanks reach the crest and find it abandoned. In the **British 13th Corps** area, the 3rd Brigade, 1st British Division mounts a night attack and grasps a slim hold on the slopes of M. Ceco. In the **British Eighth Army** area, the impending attack by the 5th Corps is held up for 24 hours. In the meantime, the British send the 20th Brigade, Indian 10th Division to assault M. Farneto. The aggressiveness of the Brigade propels it through Strigara, securing the summit prior to dawn on the 7th.

October 7th 1944 — (Pacific) The Commander-in-Chief Pacific Area issues the Joint Chiefs-of-Staff study depicting the tentative plans for the invasion of Iwo Jima, Volcano Islands, in the Nanpo Shoto. **(Pacific-Carolines-Palaus)** The 3rd Battalion, 5th Marines, supported by Tanks, attempts to reduce the Umurbrogol Pocket, but the assault is unsuccessful and ground assaults are temporarily halted. **(Pacific-Morotai)** The Allied Bombers attacking the Philippines begin to receive added strength as the Fighters on Morotai start to cover the flights. **(China-Burma-India)** In the NCAC area (Burma), the Chinese 22nd Division, in training since the capture of Myitkyina, begins to advance to Kamaing. **(Atlantic-Western Europe) 21st Army Group** General Marshall arrives on the front today to get a first hand look at the troops and their equipment. Generals Marshall and Bradley, speak with Patton, Hodges, and other staff. General Marshall is anxious to stay and watch the offensive on the following day, but a previous commitment to visit with British General Montgomery prevents his remaining. In the Canadian First Army 2nd Corps sector, the Canadian 2nd Division encounters rigid resistance at Woensdrecht (the Division is transferred from the 1st Corps). The 2nd Corps gets the job of initiating the campaign to open Antwerp's port in addition to receiving responsibility for securing Zuid Beveland and the Breskens Pocket south of the Schelde. In other activity, the Germans establish a wall of resistance at the Leopold Canal. Reinforcements from the Canadian 3rd Division pour into the area, but the resistance is stiff and they are unable to cross. **12th Army Group** In the **U.S. First Army** area, the 30th Division, supported by C.C.A., 2nd Armored, makes rapid progress in the XIX Corps area and corrals about 1,000 prisoners as it drives forward, reaching a point about three miles from Wuerselen. In the **VII Corps** area, the 9th Division continues driving against the Germans in the Huertgen Forest as it closes upon Schmidt; elements reach a section of woods near Aermeter

Multiple Gun Motor Carriage M-16.

and Richelskaul, but the primary force is stalled in the rear. In the **V Corps** sector, the 4th and 28th Divisions move to the jump-off point, preparing to mount the offensive against the West Wall. In the **U.S. Third Army** area, **XX Corps** sector, Echternach is seized by the 3rd Battalion, 329th Infantry, 83rd Division, but it has taken a week of incessant battle to wrestle control from the enemy. Wormeldange is taken by the 331st Infantry, which also clears the area west of the Moselle in the area of Luxembourg. At Metz, the Germans bolt tenaciously against the 357th Infantry's Company F, at the slag pile, but the attention given it permits Companies E and G to evade the counterattack slip into the town, and secure the northern half, in addition to penetrating the factory area. At the strongpoint, Fort Driant, the struggle continues as Task Force Warnock commits its 1st Battalion, 10th Infantry, 5th Division. The unit makes expensive progress as two Platoons are isolated and then annihilated. Upon fall of darkness the 3rd Battalion, 2nd Infantry is committed. **6th Army Group** In the **U.S. Seventh Army** area, the obstinate stronghold of Vagney is seized by the 7th Infantry, 3rd Division. At one point, after the town is secure, two Platoons of enemy Infantry and a belligerent Tank make good use of the fog and penetrate American lines, attacking an Infantry outpost (21:00). Grenades are thrown as the attackers close, but the outpost gets big help when an M4 Tank, commanded by 2nd Lt. James Harris, roars to the scene. The enemy pulls back slightly, waiting in ambush. Harris jumps from his Tank and advances on foot to seek out the enemy, but through the mist comes a volley of machine gun fire that wounds him mortally. Lt. Harris crawls back to the Tank, but is wounded too severely to get inside. He issues firing orders as he lies dying between the two opposing Tanks. Ultimately, Harris' Tank is destroyed, but he contains the enemy until reinforcements can get to the area and drive them back. Harris is hit again during the menacing duel when a shell amputates his left leg at the hip, but he still refuses medical attention and insists that another man be tended. The wounded Yank is carried to safety, and the gallant Lt. Harris (Medal Of Honor Recipient) succumbs before he can receive medical aid. His extraordinary actions are an inspiration to the other men in the 756th Tank Battalion. **(Atlantic-Italy)** In the **U.S. Fifth Army** area, 2 Companies of the 6th South African Division (Frontier Force Rifles) gain the tip of M. Stanco, but they lose communication with the main force and are forced to return to Prada. In the **IV Corps** sector, the inclement weather and massive flooding prevents all attempts to reinforce the troops attacking M. Cauala. It is virtually impossible to get the Tanks and Tank Destroyers across the streams. In the **II Corps** area, the Germans repulse a strong counterattack by the 362nd Infantry, 91st Division, retaining M. Castellari. The 85th Division, charging toward La Villa, seizes Castelnuovo, but is halted short of the former. The 88th Division has its 349th Infantry assaulting Hill 587, continuing its thrust to capture it and seize a ridge below II Falchetto Hill; the 351st Infantry mounts its first strengthened assault on the right flank. In the **British 13th Corps** area, the fragile hold on M. Ceco is retained by the South African Armored. The 19th Brigade, Indian 8th Division secures M. Cavallara. In the **British Eighth Army** area, an attack is commenced. The British 56th Division feints an attack at Savignano while Planes pummel the real strike zone prior to the assault by the Indian 10th and British 46th Divisions, which drive across the Fiumicino. The 12th Brigade, 46th Division seizes Montilgallo, and the 25th Brigade, 10th Indian Division captures ground on a ridge between S. Lorenzo and Roncofreddo.

October 8th 1944 — (Pacific-Volcano Islands) Aircraft based on the Marianas step up the heat against Iwo Jima, striking with additional power and frequency. **(Atlantic-Western Europe)** The boundary between the 21st and 12th Army Groups reverts to previous positions, giving the British responsibility for the Peel Marshes, west of the Maas. **21st Army Group** In the **British Second Army** area, the 8th Corps assumes command of the U.S. 7th Armored Division and the Belgian 1st Brigade (including American contingents). The British 8th Corps directs these units to relieve the British units within their sector. **12th Army Group** In the **U.S. XIX Corps** area, the 30th Division is still anticipating joining forces with the VII Corps at Wuerselen, but the Germans hinder this action by posting firm resistance against the east flank. The 120th Infantry, recently relieved by the 29th Division, jumps off and secures two small villages; then it is struck by a huge counterattack as it nears a railroad west of Mariadorf. The German thrust reaches Alsdorf before it is stopped. The 117th Regiment withdraws to Alsdorf during the grueling exchange and is reinforced by units of the 120th Infantry. The devastating contest inflicts grievous casualties upon both sides. Combat Command A, 2nd Armored, bolts forward and takes Oidtweiler. In the **VII Corps** sector, the 1st Division, working in conjunction with the XIX Corps, attacks toward Aachen in an attempt to surround the defenders. The 16th Infantry holds in place deploying defensively while the 26th Regiment sets up to attack from the east and drive directly into the center of the city. Meanwhile, the 18th Division grinds northward through Verlautenheide. During the trek of the 18th Infantry, a hill called Crucifix stands ominously in its path. As Company C and a Ranger Platoon of the 1st Battalion drive against the hill, they are hit by an Artillery barrage and machine-gun fire. Fire from pillboxes blankets the hill and forces the Yanks to keep low. Captain Bobbie E. Brown advances 100 yards, as bullets whiz just over his head. He drags an explosive pole as he moves. Leaping to his feet, he dashes to the first pillbox and stuffs the explosive pole into the fortification, destroying it. After rejoining his outfit, he sets out alone and destroys a 2nd pillbox. Meanwhile, a third pillbox is keeping his Company pinned down. He returns to the unit and gets more explosives. Then Captain Brown annihilates the occupants, but he himself is wounded by a mortar shell. Undaunted, he returns to his command. Brown goes out again to reconnoiter the area to gather information and is wounded two additional times, but he still refuses medical treatment. His actions ensure the destruction by his command of several more guns and inspire them to throw back successive counterattacks. Brown, born in Dublin, Georgia,

receives the Medal of Honor. In other activity, Tanks and Tank Destroyers move into position by darkness, prepared to supplement the 9th Division's drive through the Huertgen Forest toward Schmidt. In the **V Corps** zone, the Germans' outer defenses at the West Wall are ready as the 28th Division nears. Lively firefights develop. In the **U.S. Third Army** area, furious and sometimes disoriented fighting erupts. At Fort Driant, the fighting is vicious as the opposing sides whack each other in fierce firefights that spread like wild fire; however, no victor evolves. At Maizieres-les-Metz, house-to-house fighting erupts as the 2nd Battalion, 357th Infantry, 90th Division, charges into the town. The struggle is tedious, consuming time and casualties. In the **XII Corps** area, a strong assault is launched at 06:15, subsequent to an hour of bombardment. As the Corps heads for the Seille River, spearheaded by the 6th Armored Division, Moivron is seized by the Armor and taken over by the 80th Division. The 6th Armored, in a synchronized movement with the 80th Division, then seizes Jeandelincourt and Bois de Chenicourt. However, Chenicourt is retained by the Germans. The Germans also take Arraye-et-Han. Manoncourt, on the left, is grabbed by the 318th Infantry, 80th Division; Lixieres, Sivry, and Mt. Toulon are secured by the 319th Regiment. In related activity, the 317th Infantry secures Mt. St. Jean. The U.S. 35th Division advances near the Seille on its left flank and quickly seizes Fossieux and Ajoncourt. The U.S. ground troops, attacking between Moivron and Jeandelincourt, are bolstered by P-47s which strike the enemy positions in the heights. **6th Army Group** In the **U.S. Seventh Army** area, the 7th Infantry, 3rd Division, moves out of Vagney, heading for Sapois. In the 3rd Algerian Division sector of the French 1st Army area, a three-day battle for Longegoutte ceases; the Algerians are victors. **(Atlantic-Italy)** In the **U.S. Fifth Army** area, **IV Corps** sector, Task Force 92 drives to the slopes of M. Cauala, but the bitter resistance originating from the entrenched positions of the defenders pushes the attackers back. In the **II Corps** area, C.C.A., 1st Armored is attached to the 34th Division, which is continuing its assault against Monterumici hill mass. The 91st Division pushes units to the summit of M. Castellari during the night of the 9th-10th. In other activity, the 85th Division overcomes heavy opposition, throwing the enemy back to M. delle Formiche. The Germans hold Hill 566, but are forced to abandon Hill 587. The 349th Infantry climbs Hill 587 and finds it unoccupied, while other elements seize Il Falchetto Hill. In the British 13th Corps area, elements of the British 1st Division seize the summit of M. Ceco. At Portico the British 6th Armored reaches the fringes of town, but opposition halts entrance. In the **British Eighth Army** area, **5th Corps** zone, the Germans controlling M. Farneto repulse an attempt by the 20th Brigade, 10th Indian Division, but at S. Lorenzo, the Indian 25th Brigade overpowers the opposition and continues rolling toward Roncofreddo. In Rome, General Kesselring has proclaimed October 8th through 14th as "anti-Partisan week," to emphasize getting rid of the resistance; as the Germans move north, Partisans poison their water, blow the railroad tracks and bridges; while Kesselring is informing his Commanders of the proclamation, his Headquarters suffer a blackout, compliments of the Guerrillas who detonate a bomb at a power plant. Kesselring, regarding O.S.S. agents, stipulates that: "ANY ALLIED AGENT CAUGHT WORKING WITH PARTISANS IN UNIFORM OR NOT, WOULD BE SHOT ON SIGHT." German retaliation against Partisans is agonizing; some are castrated and others have their eyes gouged; some others are strung on meat hooks and displayed in village squares; the hooks penetrate their jaw, but death for some is slow and agonizing, taking at times about 24 hours. **(Atlantic-Greece)** British troops, running reconnaissance missions along the northern coast of the Peloponnesus, reach Corinth and discover no enemy troops. British Commandos advance to Nauplia, south of Corinth.

October 9th 1944 — (United States) The U.S.S. *Randolf*, a Carrier (CV-15), is commissioned at Newport News, Va. **(Pacific)** A warning order for the invasion of Iwo Jima is given. Few men in the Pacific have heard about the island, which is to be assaulted during early 1945; subsequent to the invasion, few will forget its name. Admiral Spruance is designated Commander of the Operation (CTF 50). Vice Admiral Richmond Turner is to command the Joint Expeditionary Force (Task Force 51), and Major General H. M. Smith U.S.M.C. will command the Expeditionary Troops (Task Force 56). The necessary troops are to be assembled in Hawaii and in the Marianas. The tentative invasion date is scheduled for January 20th 1945. **(Pacific-Carolines-Palaus)** On Peleliu, the 5th Marines mount another attack against the entrenched Umurbrogol Pocket, but the stronghold defends fiercely and the assault makes only nominal progress. In other activity, contingents of Regimental Combat Team 321, U.S.A. secure Garakayo, the biggest island off the northern approach to Peleliu. **(Pacific-Marcus Islands)** The U.S. Third Fleet dispatches Surface Vessels (Cruisers and Destroyers) to striking distance of the Marcus Islands. The Task Group commanded by Rear Admiral A.E. Smith initiates a bombardment to strike enemy coastal gun emplacements. **(China-Burma-India)** U.S. General Hurley receives a memorandum from Chiang Kai-shek (delivered by T.V. Soong) that lambastes Allied strategy in southeast Asia. In it he blames General Stilwell for the loss of east China; however, a lot of his criticism indirectly blames President Roosevelt. The friction between Stilwell and Chiang Kai-shek, or as Stilwell refers to him "the Peanut", is nearly at an end as the General is about to be officially recalled. **(Atlantic-Western Europe) 21st Army Group** In the Canadian First Army area, the 2nd Corps continues to clear the Breskens Pocket. Elements of the 3rd Canadian Division land at the eastern end of the pocket, startling the Germans who are not expecting an amphibious assault. The Canadians establish a bridgehead, while additional contingents expand the territory north of the Leopold Canal near Maldegem. The Canadian 4th Armored Division drives against the eastern portion of the canal. At Woensdrecht, the Germans mount vigorous opposition at the Zuid Beveland causeway, hindering progress of the Canadian 2nd Division. In the **British Second Army** area, the 1st Airborne departs for England. The British Paratroop Division had participated in Operation MARKET-GARDEN. **12th Army Group** General Bradley orders the Ninth Army Headquarters transferred to the northern flank of the Army Group and directs it to assume command of the IX Corps of the First Army. He also orders the VIII Corps to retain its current positions as it is to be attached to the First Army effective October 22nd. In other activity, the 94th Division is detached from Ninth Army and attached to 12th Army Group. In the **First Army** area, elements of the 30th Division plow through Bardenberg and reach Wuerselen. The 117th Infantry secures Schaufenberg, but it is prevented from advancing to Mariadorf; subsequently it receives orders to take the defensive in the region near Alsdorf-Schaufenberg. After nightfall the Germans spring a quick and deadly attack that bolts to Bardenberg and drives a small contingent of the 119th Infantry into a hasty retreat, isolating the majority of the Regiment at north Wuerselen. Reinforcements rush to their aid, but become

stalled north of the city. In the **VII Corps** area, the 1st Division racks the enemy at Aachen; the Germans do not relent. In the Huertgen Forest, the 9th Division continues to attack, using supporting Tanks. Elements of the 39th Infantry break through to Wittscheidt, and a Battalion of the 60th Infantry breaks out at Richelskaul. In the **V Corps** area, the planned assault against the West Wall is again postponed until the 11th of October. In the **U.S. Third Army** area, the expensive and inconclusive struggle at Fort Driant is halted. At Maizieres-les-Metz the close house-to-house fighting continues with no victor. In the **XII Corps** area, C.C.A., 6th Armored, charges toward Letricourt, but stiff opposition repulses the assault. CCB sends reinforcements to the forward area. In conjunction, the 80th Division moves toward the Armor and assumes responsibility for the zone. The Corps Offensive to the Seille River ceases. In the 35th Division sector, the Germans retain Letricourt and initiate sporadic and ineffective attacks, but the area remains virtually peaceful until the early part of November. **6th Army Group** The Germans holding the Foret de Parroy are struck again by the 79th Division (XV Corps), which penetrates deeply, seizing a primary road intersection that makes the German positions untenable; they abandon the forest during the night. In the Third Division sector, the 15th Infantry encounters strong enemy presence near La Forge. 1st Lt. Victor Kandle has already captured five prisoners today when he is intercepted by a German Officer. Kandle engages in a personal duel and kills the German. With a pesky fog settling over the area, Kandle, in front of a 16-man Squad reinforced with a Light Machine gun detachment, scrambles across treacherous mountainous terrain to get behind a German strongpoint near the quarry and captures the stunned defenders. Shortly thereafter, he knocks out a nest, and then with the support of his detachment, another enemy nest is destroyed. Lt. Kandle bursts into a house containing two enemy Officers and 30 troops. Bewildered by the exploits of the Yank, all occupants capitulate; Kandle receives the Medal of Honor. In the French 1st Army 2nd Corps area, the 3rd Algerian Division crosses the Moselotte and captures Trougemont. **(Atlantic-Italy)** In the **U.S. Fifth Army** area, the boundary is modified between the U.S. II Corps and the British 13th Corps. Meanwhile, General Clark is becoming increasingly upset with the critical situation of the Seventh Army. Many of its troops have been diverted to southern France, and getting replacements for casualties is becoming increasingly difficult. Clark seems to think the Seventh is being treated as a reluctant step child; the Seventh Army is taking casualties at an approximate rate of 500 per day, and his Artillery units have been pillaged for use in other areas. Manpower concerns are critical and to get through the beastly mountains, the Seventh needs more men. Bologna, a coveted prize for Clark, is within reach, slightly less than two miles away, but it cannot be taken. Clark has frequently requested Air support, but his pleas have been unheeded. He states: "I COULD WRITE FOR HOURS ON THE LACK OF CO-OPERATION BY THE ROYAL NAVY IN SUPPORT OF MY GROUND EFFORTS...I HAVE ASKED FOR NAVAL GUNFIRE ON MY WEST COAST. IT HAS BEEN REFUSED REPEATEDLY, YET THE EIGHTH ARMY HAS IT ALL THE TIME." The weather has also been uncooperative. The streams are uncrossable, causing wounded Soldiers to be dangerously evacuated by sending them across wild streams by means of precariously positioned cables strung overhead. The same cables are utilized to transport supplies. The torrential rains are relentless, further jeopardizing the Seventh Army. In the **IV Corps** area, Task Force 92 propels to the pinnacle of M. Cauala without incident, but German pressure mounts later in the day and pushes the Task Force off, forcing it to spend the following two days preparing for another attack. In the **II Corps** area, the 91st Division stands firmly, repels a heavy counterattack that originates from Livergnano, then bounces back ready to knock out the Germans assembled there. A strong Patrol comprising Company K, 361st Infantry reaches the outskirts of Livergnano and becomes cut off from the Regiment. Companies G and E drive to a point above Bigallo, but heavy resistance keeps them pinned. In other Corps activity, the Germans continue to hamper the efforts of the 34th Division to seize Monterumici (a hill mass). In the 85th Division sector, plans are readied to assist the 91st Division in the assault against M. delle Formiche. In the British 13th Corps area, the British 78th Division (reinforced) assumes full responsibility for M. Cappello and M. Battaglia. In other activity, the Indian 8th Division deploys for an assault against M. Casalino. In the **British Eighth Army** area, elements of the 10th Corps are chasing the retreating Germans along Highway 71. Reconnaissance units discover M. Castello and Mercato Saraceno undefended. In the 5th Corps area, a vicious German counterattack is repulsed at S. Paola.

October 10th 1944 — (Pacific-Carolines-Palaus) Companies G and E, 2nd Battalion, 5th Marines, maintain pressure against the staunch resistance in the Umurbrogol Pocket. The effort gains Baldy Ridge after another bloody fight. **(Pacific-Ruykyus)** Okinawa, the point in the vast Pacific where the U.S. Navy is soon to be known as "THE FLEET THAT CAME TO STAY", receives a thundering letter of intent from Uncle Sam today. Seventeen bountiful Carriers, escorted by 14 Cruisers, 5 Battleships, and 58 Destroyers, commanded by Vice Admiral Mitscher, arrive off Okinawa and commence a bombardment. Squadrons of Flying Eagles in concert with the long guns of the Naval Surface Ships pound the island. The U.S. Aircraft rule the skies and pummel the shipping and facilities on Okinawa and other nearby islands. The Yanks have brought fireworks made in the U.S.A. and are testing them on the Japanese. The Planes return to their Carriers with a grand assortment of aerial photographs that prove valuable for the final invasion plans. The Japanese Submarine Tender *Jingei* and Transport No. 158 are both sunk. **(Atlantic-Western Europe) 12th Army Group** In a meeting which includes Generals Hodges, Patton, and Simpson at Army Group Headquarters, General Bradley recounts the thinking of Generals Eisenhower and British General Montgomery, concerning the Ruhr attack, relating that Montgomery believes the capture of the Ruhr is a "two Army job" and that Montgomery feels he should command. Bradley then explains that Ike agreed to it being a two Army endeavor, but that he (Eisenhower) thinks it should be two American Armies. After this discussion, the conversation turns to the critical supply situation, and as Patton has requested, an Officer (General R.C. Crawford) is being assigned to "UMPIRE" the supply situation. In the **U.S. First Army** area, **XIX Corps** sector, the 30th Division proclaims it has destroyed 20 German Tanks in skirmishing since the previous day. In other activity, the 30th transfers the 119th Infantry from its positions to permit Allied shelling of enemy strongpoints in its zone. In other activity, the 120th Infantry threatens Bardenberg, subsequent to the capture of Birk Crossroads. In the **VII Corps** area, the situation appears much more favorable than it is, prompting the 1st Division to demand the surrender of Aachen, which is nearly encircled. The ultimatum falls on deaf ears, but not silent weapons. The Germans establish fanatical resistance, and when their positions become untenable, they are di-

rected to fight to the death. In the Huertgen Forest, two Platoons of the 39th Infantry, 9th Division are overpowered at Wittscheidt, but powerful thrusts by the 39th retake the ground and propel the troops into Germeter without resistance. Meanwhile, contingents of the 60th Infantry drive back into the forest and take a road junction about a mile southwest of Richelskaul. In the **U.S. Third Army** area, the III Corps Headquarters (recently arrived on Continent) is attached to Third Army and is commanded by Major General John Millikin. In the **XII Corps** sector, the Germans are driven from Fossieux by the 35th Division. General Patton meets with General Marshall during breakfast and requests that Colonels Bruce Clarke and George W. Read both be promoted on Merit (the two Colonels are subsequently promoted to Brigadier General). After Patton departs the 35th Division area, the Germans commence firing, and a shell lands about three hundred feet away from his Vehicle. This is the 3rd time he has been fired upon while using this road. **(Atlantic-Italy)** In the **U.S. Fifth Army** area, the Germans on M. Stanco repulse all attempts by the S. African 6th Armored to dislodge them. In the **II Corps** zone, the next phase of the Bologna offensive commences. The 34th Division pivots to outflank the Monterumici hill mass, but the Germans prevent success of the maneuver. The 91st Division is heavily engaged at Livergnano. Beleaguered Company K is further shredded when rescue attempts fail to extricate the troops; most are captured. In the 85th Division area, Artillery and Air support is afforded the 2nd Battalion, 338th Infantry when it assaults M. delle Formiche. The aggressive charge batters its way close to the crest of the hill, but unyielding German return fire holds the high ground, repulsing the attack. In the 85th Division battle zone, the Germans resist strongly at Gesso Ridge, making the 351st Infantry work tirelessly for nominal gains. In the British 13th Corps area, the Indian 8th Division grasps a hold near the crest of M. Casalino. In the **British Eighth Army** area, there is an abundance of activity as British elements put on a good show. The Indian 10th Division overpowers Spaccato, and the prize nets a bonanza as the Germans' stiff resistance falls apart at the Fiumicino. Longiano is taken by the British 46th Division and La Crocetta is also seized. In other activity, British Reconnaissance elements attached to the British 1st Division move across the Fiumicino at Savignano di Romagna against no opposition. **(Atlantic-Eastern Europe)** The First Baltic Front has contingents reach the Baltic Sea near besieged Memel, Lithuania. Other Soviet elements advance to the Niemen River near the border of north eastern Prussia. Troops attached to the Third Ukrainian Front advancing through Yugoslavia sever the Nis-Belgrade Railroad at Velika Plana.

October 11th 1944 — (Pacific-Carolines-Palaus) Contingents of the 2nd Battalion, 5th Marines, seize Hill 140, an objective that is enormously strategic in nature, giving its occupants a perfect view of the Horseshoe and the draw between Boyd and Walt Ridges. **(Pacific-Japan)** The American Submarine *Trepang* (SS-412) sinks the Japanese Transport No. 105. **(Pacific-New Guinea)** The PT-368 becomes grounded off New Guinea and is subsequently destroyed by U.S. Forces. **(Pacific-Philippines)** Two Carrier Task Groups, commanded by Vice Admiral McCain and Rear Admiral R.E. Davison, arrive within striking distance of Luzon. Planes are launched to strike enemy installations and Airfields in the northern portion of Luzon. The two Task Groups and the Carrier Forces that struck Okinawa the previous day are attached to Admiral Halsey's Third Fleet. **(China-Burma-India)** Chiang Kai-shek requests that President Roosevelt recall

General Stilwell immediately. **(Atlantic-Western Europe)** **12th Army Group** In the **U.S. First Army** area, the town of Bardenberg is seized by a Reserve Battalion, 120th Infantry, 30th Division. The capture gives the 30th a route to northern Wuerselen. During the engagement to secure the objective, as Company I moves through town, a wall of incessant fire by a menacing machine gun halts progress. Staff Sergeant Jack Pendleton takes a Squad and advances toward the gun. Pendleton receives a severe wound, but elects to advance singlehandedly with a few grenades. The heroic trooper diverts attention from another contingent, which is moving against the gun. Pendleton reaches within ten yards of the machine gun and is riddled with bullets, killing him instantly. His intentional drawing of enemy fire allows the others to destroy the obstacle, and the Battalion advances. Sergeant Pendleton receives the Medal of Honor posthumously. In the **VII Corps** area, the Germans within Aachen have permitted the allotted time to respond to the surrender ultimatum of the previous day to expire without response. The omission ignites a walloping Artillery bombardment by the Yanks, but the Germans are not dislodged. In the Huertgen Forest, the Germans mount a heated, but unsuccessful, counterattack against a roadblock maintained by the 60th Infantry, 9th Division. The enemy then strikes at another roadblock along the route to Jaegerhaus, but it also fails. A section of No Man's Land causes problems when the 39th Infantry attempts to cross it against vicious enemy fire. In the **U.S. Third Army** area, ammunition supplies continues to dwindle. The guns in use against Fort Driant are severely restricted; the 155s are averaging approximately seven rounds per gun a day and about 15 rounds per day for the 105s. The assault against the fort is aborted. **6th Army Group** In the **U.S. Seventh Army** area, orders are issued specifying a drive to the Meurthe River and include the seizure of Brouvelieures and Bruyeres with a subsequent assault to be launched against St. Die. The Corps uses diversionary Artillery fire against Gerardmer to foil the enemy. In the French 1st Army area, the 2nd Corps is clearing the area south of the Moselotte River. **(Atlantic-Italy)** In the **U.S. Fifth Army** area, a night attack is launched against M. Cauala by Task Force 92. Barga is captured by Brazilian RCT 6. At Livergnano in the II Corps sector, the German positions on the slope come under a fierce attack by the 363rd Infantry and give up some ground at a harsh cost. The crest of M. delle Formiche is the scene of a furious exchange of fire as the 3rd Battalion, 338th Infantry, 85th Division, clears the eastern slopes and the 2nd Battalion seizes the summit. The 337th Infantry is slugging its way slowly but persistently toward Hill 578, in the Monterenzio hill mass. In the 88th Division sector, the 350th Infantry grasps a hold on M. delle Tombe while the 351st Infantry maintains its clearing operation on Gesso Ridge. In the British 13th Corps area, the Germans charge British positions on M. Battaglia, but to no avail. In the **British Eighth Army** area, 5th Corps sector, Montecodruzzo is seized as the Indian 10th and British 46th Divisions advance toward the Cesena and Savio Rivers. In the Canadian 1st Corps sector, the Canadian 1st Division enlarges its Fiumicino bridgehead by continuing to advance along Highway 9, closing upon the Rigossa. In other activity, the New Zealand 2nd Division supports two bridgeheads across the Fiumicino, north of Savignano without any enemy opposition, and it is able to seize Gatteo during the night of the 11th-12th. **(Atlantic-Eastern Europe)** At Hungary's second largest city, Szeged, Russian elements of the Second Ukrainian Front cross the Tisa (Tisza) River, closing against Budapest, while additional elements strike the Germans east of Budapest at Debrecen. In

other activity, the capital of Transylvania, Cluj, is taken by a combination of Russian and Rumanian forces.

October 12th 1944 — (Pacific-Carolines-Palaus) General Roy S. Geiger, U.S.M.C., declares the Peleliu assault and occupation phase terminated. The III Amphibious Corps Command Post is moved ashore. Command Functions are transferred from the Assault Forces to the Central Pacific administrative echelons, comprising the Forward Area, Vice Admiral J. H. Hoover U.S.N., the Western Carolines Submarine Area, Rear Admiral J.W. Reeves Jr. U.S.N., and the Island Command, Brigadier General H.D. Campbell. The 321st Infantry assumes responsibility for the eastern portion of the island and initiates relief of the Marines, but the Marines retain responsibility for the Umurbrogol Pocket, which is still resisting tenaciously. **(Pacific-Formosa-Philippines)** Admiral Halsey's Third Fleet launches Planes to attack Formosa and northern Luzon. The raids continue to hit the Japanese for the next five days, striking Airfields, Shipping, and factories. The Japanese launch Planes to intercept and destroy the American Invaders. On the following day a Kamikaze Pilot drives his Plane against a Carrier and scores damage. The Kamikazes emerge quickly and frequently in the near future and cause considerable damage and loss of life to the U.S. Forces. In a Naval mishap, the U.S.S. *Prichett* (DD-561) is accidentally damaged by U.S. Naval gunfire off Formosa. **(Pacific)** General MacArthur issues the orders for the invasion of Luzon, Philippines. The mission is to be carried out by the U.S. Sixth Army's I Corps, comprising the 6th and 43rd, Divisions reinforced and the XIV Corps which is comprised of the 37th and 43rd Divisions reinforced. The initial invasion force will have the 11th Airborne and 25th Infantry Divisions, RCT 158, 6th Ranger Battalion and the 13th Armored Group in addition to other units in reserve. Also, Marine Artillery Units and Air Squadrons participate. **(Atlantic-Western Europe)** **21st Army Group** In the **British Second Army** area, Overloon is secured by the British 3rd Division as it attacks to secure the Peel Marshes. In a deceptive maneuver, the U.S. 7th Armored launches a diversionary attack along the Deurne-Venray Road. **12th Army Group** In the **U.S. First Army** area, the Germans are reinforced to drive the U.S. Forces back. Successive counterattacks against the XIX Corps fail, thanks due partly to the interdiction of Artillery and Planes, which support the ground troops' initiative at Birk and at N. Wuerselen. Meanwhile, the Corps prepares to handle the influx of additional Panzer units. In the **VII Corps** area, the 3rd Battalion, 26th Infantry, 1st Division attacks the factory area between Aachen and Haaren in a preliminary move, prior to the major attack against Aachen. The assault succeeds and the area is secured. In the Huertgen Forest, the agonizing struggle continues. The Germans strike swiftly and cut a road leading into Germeter, severing the main supply route of the 39th Infanty, 9th Division. Reinforcements drive from the north to rectify the situation. Intense fighting ensues for several days but all lost ground will be retaken by the 39th Regiment. In the **U.S. Third Army** area, **XX Corps** sector, the exhausted 2nd Battalion, 357th Infantry is reinforced by the 3rd Battalion at Maizieres-les-Metz. On the previous day, General Patton had decided that the assault against Fort Driant should be terminated because of the critical shortage of ammunition. Today the remaining elements of the 5th Division are withdrawing from Fort Driant (completed during night 12th-13th). **(Atlantic-Italy)** In the **U.S. Fifth Army** area, Task Force 92 reaches the summit of M. Cauala, but enemy resistance is unyielding, and another pull back becomes necessary. In the area of Livergnano, the Germans hold firmly against new attempts by the 91st Division to overpower them. In the 85th Division zone, heated battles continue on M. delle Formiche where the 3rd Battalion, 338th Infantry, advances to the summit and the 337th Infantry drives punishingly against obstinate resistance atop Hill 578. In other activity, elements of the 88th Division attack M. delle Tombe, securing Gesso Ridge with its 337th Regiment. In the British 13th Corps area, the British transfer the Indian 8th Division southwest of M. Ceco to alleviate pressure against the British 1st Division. In the **British Eighth Army** area, orders are received directing the Army to release the Indian 4th Division and the Greek 3rd Mountain Brigade for service outside Italy. In the 5 Corps area, the British 46th Division assaults across the Rubicon River, capturing Casale. In other activity, heavy fighting erupts at Sorrivoli between the Germans and elements of the Indian 10th Division. **(Atlantic-Greece)** An advance contingent of the British 4th Paratroop Battalion and Royal Engineers is dropped near Megara with orders to seize and repair the Airfield. Kalamata and Piraeus are checked, and they are discovered free of the enemy. **(Atlantic-Corfu-Albania)** A contingent of British Commandos, attached to Land Forces Adriatic, land at Corfu and near Sarande, in S. Albania.

October 13th 1944 — (Pacific-Hawaii) Headquarters V Amphibious Corps is transferred to Pearl Harbor to ease conditions, while planning for the operation against Iwo Jima. On the following day, Major General Harry Schmidt, Commanding General V Amphibious Corps, will be designated Iwo Jima Landing Force Commander. **(Pacific-Carolines Palaus)** The 322nd Infantry starts its final drive to eradicate the remaining enemy resistance in the pocket on N. Angaur. **(Pacific-Formosa-Philippines)** Task Force 38s Carriers, which includes the *Independence*, launch Planes to strike the enemy targets on Formosa and Luzon. The Japanese mount opposition. The Carrier *Franklin* (CV-13) is damaged by a Kamikaze Plane, and the Heavy Cruiser *Canberra* (CA-70) is damaged by an enemy aircraft torpedo. **(China-Burma-India)** General Hurley suggests that President Roosevelt recall General Stilwell and that a new U.S. Officer be appointed to command the Chinese troops. **(Atlantic-Western Europe)** Antwerp is struck by V-bombs for the first time, and it follows right behind London on the German list of primary targets. **21st Army Group** The British Second Army's 3rd Division departs Overloon, attacking through heavy opposition toward Venray, lying 3 miles to the front. **12th Army Group** In the **U.S. First Army** area, **XIX Corps** sector, elements of the 29th Division, bolstered by Tanks of the 2nd Armored, attack to close the Aachen Gap. In one fierce skirmish, Company B, 66th Armored Regiment encounters vicious resistance on the outskirts of Aachen. Captain James M. Burt leads his Tank from the outside, advancing through pointblank fire. Burt is wounded twice, but Artillery fire pours into the area and the objective is taken; he becomes a recipient of the Medal of Honor. In the **VII Corps** area, all stops are pulled as the 1st Division assaults Aachen. The streets are consumed with fiercely contested fire fights as the Yanks scramble from house-to-house to clear the city. The 2nd Battalion, 26th Infantry handles the in-city struggle while the 3rd Battalion plows against Observatory Hill, one of three strategic hills that command the city from the north. General Collins' troops attempt to induce enemy capitulation by pitting 155s (Long Tom Rifles) against the buildings. On the 21st, Americans, using the 155s as Sniper weapons, convince the Germans to surrender. In the Huertgen Forest, the important road junction, 471, is seized by the 60th Infantry, 9th Division, while the 39th Division closes off the enemy penetration and reclaims all lost

U.S. Infantry driving through a French town.

ground. In the **U.S. Third Army XX Corps** sector, the proposed assault against Maizieres-les-Metz is aborted due to a Third Army order freezing all artillery ammunition over three inches. **6th Army Group** Embermenil is seized by the 79th Division. **(Atlantic-Italy)** In the **U.S. Fifth Army** area, M. Stanco is struck by an Air and Artillery bombardment, followed by a successful assault by the 12th Motorized Brigade, 6th S. African Armored Division, which seizes the objective. Bombiana, left of M. Stanco, also falls. In the **II Corps** area, the 91st Division assaults the Germans at Livergnano, fortified by Artillery and Aircraft, which staggers the enemy's confidence; the village of Casalino and Hill 603 are seized. In the 85th Division sector, Hill 578 is taken after a prolonged contest, and the enemy is driven from the Monterenzio hill mass during the night 13th-14th, giving the 337th Infantry little sleep; they are then relieved by the 339th Infantry. In the British 13th Corps area, an attack against M. la Pieve is begun by the British 78th Division. In the **British Eighth Army** area, Sorrivoli is seized by the Indian 10th Division, but the Germans stall the British advance in front of M. delle Vacche. In other activity in Italy, O.S.S. Mission Aztec, led by Captain Joe Benucci is executed; the team including Sergeants Nick Gangelosi (Elmont, N.Y.) and Sebastian Gionfriddo (Hartford, Ct.) are dropped into the lower Alps near Venice to establish contact with a large Partisan force. Their numbers have been shredded as the Germans had trapped and executed about 500 Partisans during the previous week; only 50 Partisans escaped the massacre. By November, the force rises to about 200 people; at that time the group ambushes a German Convoy and confiscates the payroll which was heading to the

Garrison at Belluno; the O.S.S. also helps the Partisans steals the supply of food supplies and cigarettes. Fifteen German Soldiers are killed; the Germans place a price of $5,000 on Benucci's head and subsequently double the ante to $10,000. Also, during November, the O.S.S. and their Partisans capture an Italian girl who had been intimate with a German Sergeant in addition to keeping the payroll records of the Germans' local spies. The list includes many members of the Aztec Group; thirty-three of these German sympathizers are caught and subsequently shot by the O.S.S. Alpine Group under Benucci. **(Atlantic-Greece)** A contingent of British Commandos and elements of the Greek Sacred Regiment land at Piraeus and seize the Airfield, at Kalamata in advance of the primary landing to commence on the 15th. Additional troops land at Megara and seize the Airfield then move to Kalamata and Athens without opposition. In other activity, the U.S. Troop Carrier Wing participates in the British occupation of southern Greece (Operation MANNA). The U.S. contingent transports personnel and equipment (October 13th-18th). **(Atlantic-Eastern Europe)** Russian forces seize Riga, the capital of Latvia, and in addition, secure a Naval Base in the Gulf of Riga. With this acquisition, a huge force of Germans is trapped beteen it and the Soviets who have driven to the Baltic, reaching Memel, Lithuania.

October 14th 1944 — (Pacific-Carolines-Palaus) Admiral Fort turns over control of operations in the Palaus to Rear Admiral John H. Hoover who heads Forward Area Central Pacific (TF57). On Angaur, a minor pocket of resistance remains on the northwestern tip; however, the occupation phase is terminated by the III Amphibious Corps. **(Pacific)** The III Amphibious Force and elements of the Leyte invasion force, which have arrived at Manus, debark for Leyte. **(Pacific-Philippines-Formosa)** Task Force 38 has accomplished its mission, taking Formosa out of the picture. The Japanese have sustained approximately 280 Aircraft destroyed since the raids began on the 12th. Japanese opposition causes the following damage near Formosa and Luzon: Carrier *Hancock* (CV-19), by a Horizontal Bomber; Light Cruiser *Houston* (CL-81), aircraft torpedo; Light Cruiser *Reno* (CL-96), Kamikaze Plane; Destroyer *Cassin Young* (DD-793), by strafing. Also, the Destroyer *Cowell* (DD-547) is damaged by a collision. **(China-Burma-India)** General Stilwell flies to eastern China. It is from here that a Chinese offensive is to commence. **(Atlantic-Western Europe) 21st Army Group** The 3rd Canadian Division secures an overland route from the east to Breskens at Isabella on the edge of Savojaards Plaat. **12th Army Group** In the **VII Corps** area, the Germans still offer formidable resistance at Aachen, impeding the progress of the 1st Division's 26th Infantry there and on Observatory Hill. In other activity, contingents of the 9th Division's 47th Infantry plunge forward to guarantee the safety of Road Junction 471 in the Huertgen Forest. **6th Army Group** The French 1st Army area is bristling with skirmishes. The 3rd Algerian Division culminates the struggle at the Foret de Gehan victoriously and also at Cornimont, but severe losses sustained prompt the offensive to halt. **(Atlantic-Italy)** General Clark confers with American and British Officers concerning the critical nature of the ongoing campaign in Italy. He displays figures which show American casualties "six times more" than British casualties, and he further states that the Americans have captured "fourteen times as many prisoners of war." In addition, he states that the Yanks have secured 45 of the 60 miles between Florence and Bologna, insisting that the struggle continue relentlessly (unfortunately the attacking

Contingents are too depleted to maintain the initiative). Clark also calls British General Alexander on the phone, inquiring why he has one Armored and four British Infantry Divisions held in reserve behind the Eighth Army while the Seventh Army is committing all its strength. The tensions are rising between the Allies, but although Alexander's response is unsatisfactory and ambiguous in Clark's mind, the Eighth Army has also been greatly reduced in strength. The Seventh Army continues driving forward, as Clark is resolute in reaching Bologna, but by the 30th of October, the offensive is canceled and the Seventh Army is stuck in the freezing cold mountains for the winter. In the **U.S. Fifth Army** area, Grizzana, abandoned by the Germans, is occupied by the S. African 6th Armored Division. In the **II Corps** sector, the 135th Infantry, 34th Division and Combat Command A, 1st Armored strike with jackhammer force against Monterumici, but the Germans refuse to yield. Meanwhile, the 91st Division bangs forward at Querceta, and its seizure helps strengthen positions near Livergnano. The pressure continues to mount and the Germans are compelled to withdraw from Livergnano Village. In other activity, the 2nd Battalion, 350th Infantry, 88th Division, sweeps forward and after bitter fighting secures Hill 373, north of Hill 339. The major gripe of the GIs seems to be that every road in Italy leads up. At Gesso Ridge, the 351st Infantry receives orders to halt the assault and regroup. In the British 13th Corps area, the British 78th Division maintains against M. la Pieve. In the **British Eighth Army** area, the Polish 2nd Corps receives responsibility for the British 10th Corps, and it is ordered to mount an attack from its left flank against Forli. In the 5th Corps sector, the British 46th Division captures M. dei Pini outside of Carpineta. In the Canadian 1st Corps area, the village of Bulgaria falls to the Canadian 1st Division. In other activity, contingents of the 2nd New Zealand Division secure S. Angelo during a brisk exchange on the night of the 14th-15th. **(Atlantic-Yugoslavia)** The Germans become surrounded at Belgrade as Soviet and Yugoslavian troops close on the city.

October 15th 1944 — (Pacific-Carolines-Palaus) The Airfield at Angaur receives its first Plane today. On Peleliu, the 81st Infantry Division, U.S.A. begins the permanent relief of the 1st Marine Division. The 2nd Battalion, 321st Infantry assumes responsibility for the northern end of the Umurbrogol Pocket, relieving the 3rd Battalion, 5th Marines. **(Pacific-Japan)** The U.S.S. *Besugo* (Commander T.L. Wogan) sights Admiral Ozawa's Carriers emerging from the Bungo Suido. Between 08:00 and 09:00 three Heavy Cruisers and a Light Cruiser are spotted heading southeast, traveling at 18 knots. At 11:15, two additional enemy Warships are detected. Another U.S. Submarine, the U.S.S. *Skate*, reports a hit against one of the Cruisers near Nansei Shoto. On the following day, two more Japanese Heavy Cruisers are noticed traveling in the same general direction. **(Pacific-Marianas-Saipan)** The Aslito Airfield at Saipan is now operational for B-29s. **(Pacific-Philippines-Formosa)** Rear Admiral R.E. Davison's Task Group (attached Task Force 38) launches Planes which strike Manila. The U.S. Fleet sustains more damge when a Japanese Horizontal Bomber hits the Carrier *Franklin* (CV-13) off the Philippines. **(Pacific)** The U.S. Navy establishes the Minecraft, Pacific Fleet Command, commanded by Rear Admiral A. Sharp. **(Southeast Asia Command)** British Admiral Mountbatten departs Ceylon for Cairo to confer with Winston Churchill. **(China-Burma-India)** Operation CAPITAL is sprung; it is the offensive to clear northern Burma and secure a supply route to China. The offensive drives from Myitkyina toward the Katha-Shwegu-Bhamo line, encountering nominal opposition. Included in the NCAC (Burma) command are the U.S. 475th Infantry (containing Galahad survivors) and the U.S. 124th Cavalry (Texas National Guard) which is to be attached to the 5332nd Brigade (Provisional), subsequently named Task Force Mars. **(Atlantic-Greenland)** The U.S. Coast Guard Cutter *Eastwind* (AG-279) seizes the German Trawler *Externsteine* while patrolling off the northeastern coast of Greenland. **(Atlantic-Western Europe) 21st Army Group** The U.S. 104th Division is detached from the Ninth Army and attached to the 21 Army Group to bolster the British 1st Corps and to participate in the battle to secure the port of Antwerp. **12th Army Group** In the **U.S. First Army** area, **XIX Corps** sector, the Germans continue to resist attempts to reduce Aachen. The ensuing assault by the 116th Infantry, including the support of Tanks, is able to gain a mere 1,000 yards. The frontal assault, proving expensive and unfruitful, prompts modifications which will enlist the support of the VII Corps. During the struggle to seize Aachen and eliminate the gap, the 2nd Armored is still heavily involved. One particular Officer, Captain James M. Burt, exhibits extraordinary courage, leading his Tank 300 yards into enemy held terrain, then jumping out and remaining exposed for about an hour to feed information to U.S. Gunners throughout the day. Captain Burke, during the effort to secure the gap, has two Tanks in which he is riding destroyed, but maintains his inspirational leadership. His command is greatly responsible for winning the battle for the gap; he receives the Medal of Honor. In the **VII Corps** area, a vicious see-saw battle ensues at Observatory Hill as elements of the 26th Infantry drive methodically and seize the majority of the objective, but the Germans, just as determined to retain the hill, mount a strong counterattack against the contingents of the 1st Division and reclaim the ground in the northern section. The perimeter of the 16th Regiment at Aachen becomes vulnerable from enormous pressure forcing the 1st Division to postpone its offensive. In other explosive confrontations, the Germans pitted against the 9th U.S. Division at Schmidt sustain severe casualties, but they inflict similar punishment against the Yanks, preventing them from penetrating the city. Meanwhile, the 39th Infantry retakes all its recently lost ground and maintains a solid grip on Germeter and Wittscheid. **6th Army Group** In the **U.S. Seventh Army's XV Corps** area, the Germans continue to hold firmly in the hill mass east of the Foret de Parroy, despite aggressive thrusts by the 313th Infantry, 79th Division. In the **VI Corps** sector, the 45th Division attacks through the woods north of Bruyeres to sever the highway leading to Brouvelieures; the 36th Division attacks from the west and south utilizing its 442nd Infantry (Nisei), including the 100th Battalion, just arrived from Italy, and its 143rd Infantry pushing from Fays. In other activity, the U.S. 3rd Division moves north quietly, without fanfare to ensure secrecy, while it deploys to make a swift strike against St. Die. **(Atlantic-Italy)** In the **U.S. Fifth Army** area, **II Corps** sector, the 1st Armored Division continues to outflank Monterumici. In other activity, the British 13th Corps receives orders to take over Gesso Ridge from the II Corps. The British 78th Division initiates relief of the U.S. 88th Division. In the **British Eighth Army** area, the 5th Corps seizes M. delle Vacche and M. Burratini without incident, but subsequent opposition hinders Corps progress in front of M. Reale and M. Romano. In the Canadian 1st Corps area, the New Zealand 2nd Division takes Gambettola without incident. **(Atlantic-Finland)** The port at Petsamo is taken by Russian troops (Karelian Front). **(Atlantic-Greece)** Force 140, commanded by British General Scobie, land at Piraeus. The Force,

comprised of the British 3rd Corps and Greek contingents, initiate pursuit of the retreating enemy.

October 16th 1944 — (Pacific-Carolines-Palaus) RCT 321, 81st Division, U.S.A. finalizes relief of the 5th Marines and assumes total responsibility for the operation in the Umurbrogol Pocket. The 5th Marines remains on Peleliu as Reserves, while the 7th Marines prepares to depart for the Russells. **(Pacific-Philippines)** Japanese Aircraft attack and damage the Light Cruiser *Houston* (CL-81) near Luzon. **(Pacific-East China Sea)** Army Aircraft sink the Japanese Torpedo Boat *Hato* in the East China Sea. **(Atlantic-Western Europe) 21st Army Group** British Field Marshal Montgomery calls off all offensive actions except those which concentrate on the opening of the port at Antwerp. In the **Canadian First Army** area, Woensdrecht in the 2nd Corps area is captured by the Canadian 2nd Division. The seizure locks the Zuid Beveland Isthmus. In the **British Second Army** area, Combat Command B, 7th U.S. Armored Division, establishes a bridgehead across a canal on the Deurne-Venray Road. In other activity, the British 3rd Division makes it to Venray. **12th Army Group** In the **U.S. First Army** area, Aachen Patrols of the XIX and VII Corps converge on Ravels Hill at 16:15, tightening the noose around the besieged Germans at Aachen. The Germans at Wuerselen also are being pounded by the 116th Infantry, 29th Division. In the **VII Corps** sector, the Germans forestall the closing of the Aachen gap by attacking a roadblock along the Aachen-Wuerselen highway during the night of the 16th. In other activity, the 16th Infantry, 1st Division firms up its perimeter in the vicinity of Eilendorf. **6th Army Group** In the **U.S. Seventh Army** area, the 36th and 45th Divisions drive doggedly through caustic opposition and close on Bruyeres. In the **French 1st Army** area, elements of the 3rd Algerian and 1st French Armored Divisions advance against tough opposition toward the hills east of Moselotte in an attempt to penetrate the Vosges (Winter Line). **(Atlantic-Italy)** At 23:30 a new boundary becomes effective between the British 13th Corps and the II Corps, passing between M. delle Tombe and M. Spadura and, in effect, compressing the sector of the U.S. 88th Division. In the **U.S. Fifth Army** area, the 6th South African Armored Division in cordination with the II Corps operating on the right, reinitiates its attack against the enemy holding the terrain to the north between the Reno and Setta Rivers. In the **II Corps** area, the operation to capture Bologna comes into its final phase. The 34th and 91st Divisions drive toward M. Belmonte and Lucca respectively. The trial use of artificial illumination by searchlights is implemented during this assault. The 85th Division, utilizing its 338th and 339th Regiments, drives toward M. Fano and Monterenzio. The 339th seizes Hill 622 in the vicinity of Monterenzio. In addition, the 88th Division, driving on the right flank of the Corps, encounters stiff opposition as it pushes toward M. Cuccoli-M. Grande ridge. The 349th Infantry overcomes resistance at M. delle Tombe and drives beyond to S. Clemente; however, the Germans halt the advance of the 350th at M. Cuccoli. In the **British Eighth Army** area, M. Romano and M. Reale fall to the 5th Corps during the night of the 16th. In other activity, elements of the 10th Indian Division establish a small bridgehead across the Savio river near the point where it flows into the Borello. In other activity, the New Zealand 2nd Division seizes Bulgaria without any opposition. **(Atlantic-Yugoslavia)** The Russians occupy Nish, subsequent to its abandonment by the Germans. In other activity, the Germans are resisting violently in Belgrade against the combined force of Russians and Yugoslavia troops.

October 16th-20th 1944 — (Pacific) General Courtney Whitney, recently back from Hollandia where he had been supervising Guerrilla Operations, joins General MacArthur on the Flagship Cruiser U.S.S. *Nashville* to participate in the Philippine campaign. General Whitney is not the first U.S. Soldier to touch down when the Yanks arrive at the Philippines; his son receives that honor while attached to a Submarine during secret operations to supply friendly forces; he becomes the first GI to return to the Philippines. The *Nashville* flaunts its escort Armada, which exceeds 650 Vessels, including Battleships, Cruisers, Destroyers, Troop Transports, and Landing Craft. The massive Task Force is further bolstered by Carriers. In other Naval activity, the Submarine *Escolar* sends a dispatch, which is picked up by the U.S.S. *Perch* (SS-313), stating that she is moving eastward. This is the last transmission from *Escolar*, which is scheduled to return to Midway about mid-November. She is officially reported missing and presumed lost on November 27th 1944. The Vessel had departed Pearl Harbor on September 18th on her maiden Patrol, stopping at Midway prior to this final mission.

October 17th 1944 — (Southwest Pacific) The Commander, Army Air Force issues specific instructions regarding the Luzon campaign and identifies the units which are to participate. The First Marine Aircraft Wing provides Seven Dive-Bomber Squadrons. (Pacific-Carolines-Palaus) The 3rd Battalion, 5th Marines, engages Japanese who infiltrate the area and reoccupy a group of caves south of the Umurbrogol Pocket. The skirmishing continues into the following day and is the final combat activity of the 1st Marine Division on Peleliu. In Naval activity, the U.S.S. *Montgomery* (DM-17) sinks after striking a mine east of the Palaus. (Pacific-Philippines) The tumultuous return of the Americans to the Philippines is three days away, but the preliminaries begin now. Visual contact is made as the Convoys of the III and VII Amphibious Forces converge on Leyte. The 6th Ranger Battalion, U.S.A., lands and quickly seizes Dinagat, Homonhon, and the Suluan Islands, all in Leyte Gulf. The quick success brings with it the conclusion of phase 1 of the Leyte campaign. Major General Ralph J. Mitchell U.S.M.C. and three additional Marine Officers participate in the landing as observers. Company B, 6th Ranger Battalion is temporarily prevented from landing on Homonhon when the rough seas become too unyielding. The turbulent waters hinder the minesweeping operations to a great degree; the storm costs the U.S. the Minesweeper YMS-70. In other activity, Carrier-based Aircraft continue to lambaste Japanese positions on Luzon, and the Submarine *Narwhal* (SS-167) struggles with the stormy seas and delivers necessary supplies to friendly forces on Tawi Tawi, Philippines. (Atlantic-Western Europe) 21st Army Group In the **British Second Army** area, 8th Corps sector, Venray is seized by the British 3rd Division. In other activity, the British 11th Armored Division moves through the U.S. Seventh Armored Division's bridgehead and attacks eastward. Subsequently, the 7th Armored drives south along the eastern bank of the canal. **6th Army Group** In the **U.S. Seventh Army** area, **XV Corps** zone, the 44th Division (fresh) is approaching Luneville. In the **VII Corps** area, the 36th and 45th Divisions encounter firm resistance, which hinders its progress against Bruyeres. In the **French 1st Army** area, the Germans establish rigid opposition; General de Lattre orders the French 1st Armored Division to halt its offensive, which has made nominal progress at high costs. (Atlantic-Italy) In the **U.S. Fifth Army** area, **IV Corps** sector, Task Force 92 drives to the summit of M. Cauala during the night of the 17th. In the **II Corps** area, the Germans retain control of the Monterumici hill mass, holding the combined attack of the 135th Infantry and Combat Command A, 1st Armored, to minor progress. The 91st Infantry and 1st Armored Divisions are instructed to improvise to ensure success of the offensive while taking precautionary measures to fend off any counterattacks. The enemy initiates a strong Artillery bombardment of the Livergnano region. In other activity, the 34th Division seizes the summit of M. della Vigna and is also fighting to secure the slopes of M. Belmonte. In the 85th and 88th Divisional zones, the ongoing assaults continue. In the British 13th Corps area, elements of the Indian 8th Division advance against M. Pianoreno. In other activity, contingents of the British 1st Division assault the area near M. Ceco. In the **British Eighth Army** area, elements of the Polish II Corps await the latter part of the evening, then jump off against Forli. (Atlantic-Greece) Military Liaison Headquarters Greece (until October 3rd designated Allied Military Headquarters, Greece) begins debarking at Athens to initiate the distribution of relief supplies.

October 18th 1944 — (United States) In Washington, the Joint War Plans Committee issues "Operations for the defeat of Japan." Iwo Jima is paramount in the master plan to end the war (the island is required to give the U.S. Planes a refueling stop upon return from bombing mission over the Japanese mainland) and to give the U.S. a primary stepping stone at the doorstep of Japan, which is ultimately to be invaded according to present war plans. (Pacific-Carolines-Palaus) The 321st Infantry, 81st Division, U.S.A., finalizes relief of the 1st Marine Division contingents at the Umurbrogol Pocket on Peleliu. The concentrated resistance now comprises about 400 yards east to west and stretches 850 yards north to south. This small pocket is responsible for a great many of the 6,526 casualties sustained by the Marines during this campaign. On Angaur, the enemy resistance is now condensed into an area comprising about 50 x 100 yards. (Pacific-Japan) The Japanese now recognize fully the impending Allied threat against the homeland, and in an attempt to turn the tide, the Government issues instructions to commence a major counterattack (Operation SHO-GO) the instant the U.S. Invasion Force moves against the Philippines. (Pacific-Philippines) The U.S. Navy sits near San Bernardino and Surigao Straits, serving notice on the enemy. Planes are launched from 13 of Admiral Halsey's Third Fleet Carriers; they attack the enemy Shipping in northern Luzon and in the vicinity of Manila. The Japanese on Leyte are bombarded by Rear Admiral J.B. Oldendorf's Cruiser Task Group. The U.S. Seventh Fleet also stands by confidently as the Leyte Assault Convoy nears, ensuring a solid ring of security, while simultaneously commencing a full-hearted preinvasion bombardment. In other Naval activity, enemy coastal guns strike a damaging blow against the U.S.S. *Goldsborough* (APD-32), a High Speed Transport, near Leyte Gulf. The Japanese Auxiliary Submarine Chaser No. 95 and the Transports Nos. 135 and 136 are sunk near Luzon by Carrier Aircraft. (China-Burma-India) President Roosevelt recalls General Stilwell and informs Chiang Kai-shek that although no other U.S. Officer will be directed to command Chinese troops, General Wedemeyer is authorized to act as his (Kai-shek) Chief of Staff. The Generalissimo accepts the President's proposal. In the **British Fourteenth Army** area, 13th Corps sector, Burma, the Indian 5th Division, culminating a difficult period of driving to Tiddim against fierce opposition, occupies the town without resistance. (Atlantic-Western Europe) 21st Army roup General Eisenhower holds a meeting at 21st Army Group Headquarters in Brussels to discuss and prepare for the Allied Offensive to be launched during November. British General Montgomery emphasizes a single pronged attack. The Americans, unwilling to play second fiddle to the British, again press for a two-pronged attack for more momentum and additional leverage. General Eisenhower discards Montgomery's strategy and concurs with General Bradley, permitting the Americans to play a full role. This decision permits the Third Army to attack. The plan stipulates that Montgomery's 21st Army Group is to open the port at Antwerp for Shipping. The British Second Army will attack southeastward between the Meuse and Rhine Rivers with the tentative jump-off date to be November 10th in support of the American offensive across the Rhine. The U.S. First Army is to ford the Rhine River at Cologne between the 1st and 5th of November. The U.S. Third Army is to protect the right flank of First Army, then hold in place until the necessary logistical support is available. The Ninth Army is to cover the northern flank of the 1st Army and subsequently will assist the First Army in securing the Ruhr. **12th Army Group** In the **First Army** area, **XIX Corps** sector, General Charles H. Corlett, the commanding General, who is suffering from ill health, is relieved by Major General Raymond S. McLain. In the **VII Corps** zone, Observatory Hill is taken by the 26th Infantry, 1st Division, while it simultaneously drives into the center of Aachen. The Germans do everything possible to shatter the encirclement, but the Yanks keep pressing. Task Force Hogan, 3rd Armored rushes to bolster the 26th Infantry. Other elements from the V Corps sector speed to the aid of the 26th to try to fill the existing gap between the city and the Engineers fighting to the south. The 18th Infantry, 1st Division, comes under counterattack near Haaren, Germany. Company K is struck by a Battalion sized force, supported by Tanks; the vicious lashing continues incessantly for about an hour; the 3rd Platoon's positions are overrun. Sergeant Max Thompson grabs an unattended machine gun and attempts to singlehandedly stem the rapid advance of the enemy. A Tank scores a solid blow that destroys the gun, but it only stuns and bewilders Thompson. Undaunted, he confiscates an automatic rifle and charges to the gap, firing unhesitatingly as the enemy closes. The threat, abated but not terminated, prompts Thompson to discard the automatic rifle (jammed) and utilize a nearby rocket gun to neutralize the Tanks. Moments later, a Light Tank is in flames, compliments of the unyielding Sergeant. Later in the day he again is out in front of his Squad, braving direct enemy fire to claw his way to one of the several remaining enemy pillboxes. Again he attacks, driving the enemy from the pillbox, despite being wounded twice as he advances. The Squad finishes the job, eliminating the remaining threat; Thompson receives the Medal of Honor. **6th Army Group** In the **U.S. Seventh Army** area, Bruyeres is penetrated by the 36th Division in a spring action that has them bolting quickly through the objective, securing most of it. **(Atlantic-Italy)** In the **U.S. Fifth Army** area, the Germans hold off elements of the 34th Division at M. Belmonte and at M. della Vigna. The 85th Division presses against stiff opposition, its 339th Infantry advancing to a position north of Monterenzio at the fork in the primary ridge straddled between the Idice and Sillaro Rivers. Meanwhile, the 88th Division is involved with bringing up reserves as it clears the approaches to the M. Cuccoli-M. Grande Ridge. In the British 13th Corps area, the 36th Brigade, 78th British Division discovers no opposition as it takes M. la Pieve. The Indian 8th Divisions' 21st Brigade (Eighth Army area, Polish 2nd Corps sector) and the 5th Kresowa Division seize Galeata

effortlessly as it is undefended. In the 5th Corps area, the Indian 10th Division seizes Acquarola while Celincordia is taken by the British 46th Division. In other activity, the Canadian 1st Division, operating in the Canadian 1st Corps sector, seizes Ponte della Pietra. Meanwhile, the Greek 3rd Mountain Brigade prepares to leave Italy. **(Atlantic-Czechoslovakia)** The Fourth Ukrainian Front advances through the Carpathian passes departing Poland and reaching eastern Czechoslovakia. **(Atlantic-Greece)** The Greek Government returns to the city of Athens. The British had been met by the cheers of Communist partisans (ELAS) when they invaded Greece; these partisans aid the British in ridding the Germans from Greece. Subsequently, trouble erupts between the Monarchs and the Communists and during December, 1944, civil war begins.

A B-29 enroute from Saipan to bomb Japan.

October 19th 1944 — (Pacific-Philippines) The Seventh Fleet is present as the Assault Convoy cruises leisurely to Leyte under its protection. Additional Naval Forces continue the preinvasion bombardment of the enemy facilities and the landing area. In related activity, special Underwater Demolition Teams finish their task of reconnoitering the assault areas. The U.S.S. *Narwhal* (SS-167) lands men and supplies on the southwest coast of Negros. The Japanese Air Force again attacks the U.S. Fleet and sustains heavy losses. The Escort Carrier *Sangamon* (CVE-26) is damaged by a Horizontal Bomber; the Destroyers *Ross* (DD-563) and *Aulick* (DD-569) are damaged by a mine and coastal gun respectively, and the Salvage Vessel *Preserver* (ARS-8) also is damaged by a Horizontal Bomber. **(China-Burma-India)** The Japanese evacuate their positions at Mohnyin, abandoning huge quantities of supplies and ammunition; the 29th Brigade, British 26th Division, occupies the town. **(Western Europe) 21st Army Group** In the **Canadian First Army** area, 2nd Corps sector, the recently arrived 52nd Division assumes responsibility for the Canadian 3rd Division's bridgehead north of the Leopold Canal and enters the fighting in the Breskens Pocket. **12th Army Group** In the **U.S. First Army's VII Corps** area, the outlook for the German Garrison at Aachen is bleak. Their efforts to cut through the encirclement have been futile, and further attempts cease. Orders are issued to continue the struggle to the end. Salvator Hill topples to the 26th Infantry, 1st Division as it continues to reduce the resistance within the city. In other activity, Task Force Hogan seizes Lousberg heights; the 3rd Armored contingent receives orders to sever the Aachen-Laurensberg highway. **6th Army Group** In the **U.S. Seventh Army** area, the 36th Division terminates the operation to secure Bruyeres. In other **VI Corps** activity, the 3rd Division (minus the 30th Infantry) deploys behind the 45th Division and waits for the signal to attack St. Die. The 30th Infantry holds at Le Tholy. **(Atlantic-Italy)** In the **U.S. Fifth Army** area, units of the 6th South African Armored Division secure a grasp on the slopes of M. Salvaro, but other contingents fighting to the southeast at M. Alcino are unable to overpower the resistance. In the **II Corps** sector, the 34th Division shifts the direction of its attack and drives toward M. Cerere and M. Grande, subsequent to its inability to penetrate enemy resistance directly in front of the Corps. The 34th halts its advance later in the day and regroups while deployed behind the 85th Division. The 88th Division attacks M. Cerere, subsequent to an Artillery and Air bombardment; it seizes the objective, then attacks M. Grande reaching the summit by dawn of the 20th, seizing it one day ahead of schedule. In other activity, the 85th Division lends a hand to the 88th Division and captures the lower portion of M. Fano. The positions of the 1st Armored and the 91st Divisions remain unchanged. In the British 13th Corps area, elements of the British 78th Division take M. dell'Acqua Saluta and also grasp a slim hold on M. Spadura. Mt. Pianoreno is secured by the Indian 8th Division's 21st Brigade. Another contingent, the 17th Brigade, fights to the summit of M. Casalino, but the Germans drive the Brigade back. In the **British Eighth Army** area, the Polish 2nd Corps' 5th Kresowa Division gains the abandoned Civitella di Romagna without a fight. In the 5 Corps area, elements of the British 46th Division rush into Cesena, but the surge to seize the bridge in the southern portion of the objective is repulsed. In other activity, elements of the Indian 10th Division cross the Savio during the night of the 19th, and together with elements of the 25th Brigade from Roversano, a small bridgehead is established near Falcino. There is much progress all along the front with the exception of the coastal area, where the Germans resist fiercely.

October 20th 1944 — INVASION OF THE PHILIPPINES — The Japanese cannot claim surprise as stealth-winged messengers have been proclaiming the arrival of Uncle Sam for some time. The Planes' engines, purring like pampered kittens, had alerted the citizenry and the POWs that the Americans had come to their rescue, admittedly late, but undoubtedly in garrison style. Schoolchildren as well as adults can distinguish the notable difference in the engine sounds before a bomb is dropped. Many Japanese Planes belch a sputtering gargling type sound that has gained them the dubious nickname "Washing machine Charlie." Japanese Aircraft have dominated the skies over the Philippines since December 1941, and it had been their devastating power that had bombarded the Philippines with impunity. They flaunted their superiority while returning to their bases, flying well above the range of the inadequate guns of the U.S. forces, whose volleys simply burst harmlessly beneath the departing attackers. It had been the Japanese Planes which pummeled the American facilities and strafed the retreating American-Filipino forces as they made their way to Bataan and to Corregidor, driven back because of insufficient equipment and understrengthed units; however, the Japanese paid dearly and the defenders earned their name: "THE BATTLING BASTARDS OF BATAAN."

The Japanese have been unremitting in their ruthlessness. There had been no dishonor on the part of the expendable defenders. They had resisted with glory and valor until their exhausted bodies and empty weapons could stand no more and then, they continued to resist, despite being ordered to surrender. Those who had made it to the hills by eluding the

General MacArthur and General Sutherland aboard the U.S.S. Nashville off the Philippines; Captain C.E. Coney, U.S.N., peers toward the beaches.

sadistic Japanese conquerors are returning from the bushes. The survivors of the "DEATH MARCH" and the other captives are about to be liberated. The time for MacArthur's redress is here.

Some of the Emperor's finest in Japan might have been startled as they held preliminary celebrations several days earlier upon eceiving news from the Belle of the South Pacific, Tokyo Rose, who had intentionally, but erroneously reported heavy losses to the Third Fleet. The darling of the airwaves poetically noted "ALL OF ADMIRAL MITSCHER'S CARRIERS HAVE BEEN SUNK TONIGHT." Subsequent to this exasperating bit of spectacular vernacular journalism, Admiral Halsey sends one of his classic notes to Admiral Nimitz: "ALL THIRD FLEET SHIPS REPORTED BY TOKYO RADIO AS SUNK HAVE NOW BEEN SALVAGED AND ARE RETIRING IN THE DIRECTION OF THE ENEMY."

At precisely 06:00 on the 20th, the long guns of the U.S. Navy begin to snarl in unison. The slender barrels, staring impassionedly and pokerfaced, begin to roar while huge man-made clouds of smoke hover over the turbulent sea, forming a non-transparent veil. The uproarious bombardment shivers the massive Warships, forcing them to sway back and forth with each resounding volley as another iron monsoon rain squall thunders through the sky, dropping its terrifying wrath upon the enemy positions. The powerful display relents at 08:50 to permit clear passage for the lightning strikes of the Carrier Planes which zoom overhead, then dive methodically upon Dulag, depositing more devastation to further ensure a softening of resistance for the invasion troops who are waiting for the order, "Attack".

Aircraft remain in the skies over the landing zones throughout the day, providing close air support. The seas are uncooperative, but the landing craft overcome the cumbersome voyage and deliver the cramped troops close enough to wade ashore. The U.S. Sixth Army, commanded by General Krueger, storms ashore on the eastern coast of Leyte at approximately 10:00. The X Corps strikes near Tacloban, the capital of Leyte, landing the 1st Cavalry (Major General Verne Mudge) and the 24th Infantry (Major General Frederick Irving) Divisions. The XXIV Corps drives ashore with its 7th and 96th Divisions, the latter fresh and not yet battle tested will receive the fiercest dosage of resistance.

One contigent of the 24th Division (21st Infantry) had gone ashore further south at 09:30, seizing the Panaon Strait without incident. Elements of the 1st Cavalry quickly capture San Jose, the Tacloban Airstrip, and the Cataisan Peninsula. The

Leyte Beach, Philippines.

U.S. Infantry on the Leyte Beachhead, moving inland.

24th Division encounters heavy opposition immediately following its first wave's arrival on the beach, but the 19th and 24th Regiments crunch toward the Leyte Valley, overpowering the resistance and seizing Hill 522, which dominates the northern approach to the valley. In addition, a steadfast bridgehead stretching about a mile in depth is established. The XXIV Corps lands in the vicinity of Dulag, the 7th Division to the south and the 96th to the north. General James Bradley's 96th Division plows through nasty terrain and intense enemy fire, making slow but steady progress. The first efforts under fire net the men of the 96th Hill 120 and additional ground near San Jose at the Labiranan River. The dogged determination pushes the 96th Division inland about 1,300 yards on the south and 2,500 yards on the north and an eventual hook up with the 7th Division. The 7th, Major General Archibald Arnold commanding, which had landed to the left of the 96th, springs elements across Highway 1. It secures Dulag and drives to the perimeter of the Airstrip. During the night of the 20th-21st, it repulses heavy counterattacks.

The situation on the two beachheads is good, but a gap of about 10 miles separates the two Corps by day's end. General MacArthur makes his well-rehearsed return, taking the microphone and stating: "I HAVE RETURNED." The advanced echelon of General Headquarters is established ashore by mid-day. By this time the Japanese reaction is too little, too late. The U.S.S. *Honolulu* (CL-48), a Light Cruiser, is damaged by an Aircraft Torpedo, and the H.M.S. *Australia* is hit by a

Kamikaze. The Japanese also score a damaging hit against the Destroyer *Bennion* (DD-662) and the LST 452, both by coastal gunfire. Japanese Admiral Toyoda directs the commencement of "Plan SHO-GO," sending Admiral Ozawa's Carriers toward the Philippines to draw the American Fleet to the north, thereby enabling Admiral Kuritas Second Fleet to strike a stunning and deadly blow against Leyte. The first clash between the steel Titans occurs on the 23rd, followed by a series of fatal encounters with casualties and loss of Warships sustained by both sides, but by the 26th it is apparent that the Japanese have been severely thrashed, and the utilization of the Kamikaze Pilots cannot neutralize the U.S. Navy.

The U.S. Submarines have been blowing the enemy fuel Convoys down in rapid succession, but their critical need for fuel eases slightly now as there are fewer Japanese Warships afloat. Admiral Ozawas Carriers (four), steaming from Japan, had previously lost most of their Planes and experienced Pilots, causing his Fleet to be committed as a decoy. His Pilots have been instructed to strike the U.S. Third Fleet and then land in Luzon, mandated because they had not been trained to land on Carriers. Admiral Kurita's Second Fleet had sped through the South China Sea heading north from Lingga near Singapore to Leyte. The Fleet had trained there because fuel shortages at home could not accommodate the Armada. Admiral Toyoda throws all the dice, but only snake eyes appear. Japanese Radio might proclaim another tumultuous victory over the U.S. Navy, but there are fewer Japanese Sailors around to listen.

MacArthur's troops drive against relentless resistance. The Sixth Army keeps advancing tree by tree when necessary to eliminate the wetched state of life presently endured by the Philippine people and the Allied captives. By December, the notorious weather subsides, giving the U.S. offensive more punch. The Japanese retain their tenacious and fanatical opposition. The Yanks reach Manila by the early part of February, but ferocious resistance holds the city until the 3rd of March, 1945. The Stars and Stripes, which had been desecrated and dishonored by the Japanese, is vindicated and the Philippine people have their liberty returned. The promise of the U.S. to give the Philippines their independence is kept. Thanks to the Yanks, and in particular to the determination of the Guerrillas in the hills and the zeal of General MacArthur, the Filipinos are extricated from Japanese domination (Independence granted by U.S. 1946).

October 20th 1944 — (Pacific-Carolines-Palaus) The 81st Division Commander, Major General Paul Mueller, assumes responsibility of ground operations on the Palaus, taking it from the III Amphibious Corps. In other activity, the island of Pulo Anna, between Palaus and Morotai, is seized by contingents of the 81st Division. **(Pacific-Philippines)** See October 20th Invasion of Philippines. **(Atlantic-Western Europe) 21st Army Group** In the **Canadian First Army** area, the British 1st Corps attacks toward the Bergen-op-Zoom-Tilburg Highway. **12th Army Group** In the **U.S. Seventh Army** area, VII Corps sector, the Germans are pushed to the western and southwestern suburbs of Aachen. In the **U.S. Third Army** area, the Germans commence a vicious bombardment of the XX Corps sector at Maizieres-les-Metz, striking the positions of the 90th Division. In the **XII Corps** area, P47s attack a dam, releasing water from the Etang de Lindre to delay subsequent flooding of the Seille River by the enemy. **6th Army Group** In the **U.S. Seventh Army VI Corps** area, the 179th Infantry, 45th Division attacks behind Artillery fire and gains the heights above Brouvelieures. The 3rd Division assaults St. Die, sending its 7th Infantry driving toward Vervezelle, northeast of Bruyeres. In other activity, two additional Divisions arrive at Marseille (100th and 103rd). **(Atlantic-Italy)** In the **U.S. Fifth Army** area, the Germans mount strong counterattacks against the 6th South African Division at M. Salvaro; the South Africans repulse them and in addition seize the slopes of M. Alcino. In the **II Corps** area, the 88th Division drives hard; its 350th Infantry seizes the crest of M. Cuccoli and takes Farneto. The 88th Division is bolstered by the arrival of the 337th Infantry, 85th Division. In other activity, Artillery and Planes concentrate on all approaches to the M. Grande hill mass, interdicting to prevent an enemy assault. In the British 13th Corps area, the enemy attacks the British 78th Division and retakes M. Spadura. In the **British Eighth Army** area, 5th Corps sector, the British 4th Division advances to a bridge at Cesano just as the Germans demolish it. Contingents cross in shallow water near the collapsed bridge. In other activity, elements of the Indian 10th Division seize S. Carlo. In the Canadian 1st Corps sector, the Canadian 1st Division (2 Companies) charges across the Savio River, but enemy resistance is fierce and they are unable to maintain the bridgehead. In other activity, the town of Cesenatico is evacuated by the Germans and occupied by the Canadians. **(Atlantic-Hungary)** The Germans evacuate Debrecen. **(Atlantic-Yugoslavia)** The Yugoslavians proclaim the capture of the Dalmatian port of Dubrovnik. In other activity, the Yugoslavian Army (under Marshal Tito) and the Third Ukrainian Front capture Belgrade. **(Atlantic-Egypt)** Prime Minister Winston Churchill meets with Admiral Mountbatten in Cairo to discuss the war strategy in Southeast Asia. Churchill arrived from Moscow.

October 21st 1944 — (United States) The Joint Chiefs of Staff order the invasion of Luzon to commence on December 20th. In addition, the invasion of Iwo Jima is scheduled for January 20th 1945, with the subsequent invasion of the Ryukyus (includes Okinawa). In other activity, Marine Carrier Groups, Aircraft, Fleet Marine Force is established today, headquartered at Santa Barbara, California. **(Pacific-Carolines-Palaus)** At Angaur, the opposition has been eliminated with the exception of a few stragglers. The U.S. has suffered 264 killed and 1,355 wounded or injured. The Japanese have sustained 45 captured and 1,300 killed to date. **(Pacific-Japan-Philippines)** The U.S.S. *Seadragon* spots a Japanese Carrier and two

Cruisers in addition to six Destroyers cruising along the southern edge of Formosa at 18 knots, passing through the South China Sea. The *Seadragon* launches torpedoes and scores damage against a Cruiser and a Carrier, then dives deep to avoid a depth charge attack. The U.S.S. *Shark II* keeps seven enemy Vessels under surveillance in the same vicinity; they are traveling on the same course, heading for the Philippines. The *Blackfish* spots a Carrier, two Cruisers, and six Destroyers steaming for the Philippines. The Palawan Passage is being watched diligently by the Submarines *Darter, Dace, Bergall,* and the *Rock.* In other related activity, the *Blackfin* is poised northwest of the Palawan Passage; the *Batfish* is an able sentry in the Sulu Sea east of Mindanao, and the *Gurnard* stands ready at Brunei Bay. Ironically, the Japanese had never considered the American Submarines a formidable foe, and it is the Submarines which have been plundering their Convoys, strangling their bloodline. There are other Submarines stalking the Japs also. The *Corbia* holds vigil at the Sibutu Passage, while the *Angler* and *Guitarro* guard the entrance to Manila. The Submarines are performing a task similar to that of the communications of the old west, only the Japs can't sever the wires, destroy the telegraph poles, or hinder the seagoing Pony Express. The nautical Western Union boys and submersible Pony Express riders get the mail through, and it all reads well! The Japs are coming. The list of participating Subs continues; the *Bream, Cero, Nautilus,* and *Cod* are positioned off Luzon. Last, but not least, is the legendary *Tang* which is a story in herself that staggers the imagination (October 23rd-24th). **(Pacific-Philippines)** Japanese positions on Cebu, Masbate, Panay, and Negros are struck by Carrier-based Aircraft attached to Rear Admiral G.F. Bogan's Task Group. In other Naval activity, the Transport *Warhawk* (AP-168) becomes damaged by collision. The LST's 269, 483, 486, and 704 all sustain damage by Japanese coastal guns. On the ground, Headquarters is quickly established ashore by General Krueger (Sixth Army Commander). In addition, General Sibert establishes Headquarters for the X Corps, and General Hodge sets up Headquarters for the XIV Corps. In combat activity, Tacloban (X Corps area) is captured by the 2nd Brigade, 7th Cavalry, 1st Cavalry Division. The 1st Brigade pushes west seizing Caibaan and Utap. During the early morning hours, the Japanese mount a tenacious assault in the vicinity of Pawing. The 34th Infantry, 24th Division holds the line until daylight when Carrier Aircraft and Artillery bolster their strength. The calculated risk on the part of the Japs turns badly and they are thrown back with heavy losses, including over 600 killed; almost 200 of the dead are attributed to one Soldier, Private Harold H. Moon, Jr., Company G. The gallant trooper holds his foxhole against insurmountable odds. The unperturbable Moon repulses successive counterattacks for a period of four hours and directs friendly guns which eliminate a machine gun that is ravaging the surviving remnants of his detachment. Subsequently he holds off a Platoon-sized bayonet assault by propping himself comfortably behind his weapon, killing his attackers. Shortly after rebuffing this assault, he stands to lob a grenade at an Enemy machine gun, and he is struck and killed instantly. Private Moon's body is recovered from a prone position; within a range of 100 yards are the corpses of just under 200 dead Japanese, compliments of Private Moon who receives the Medal of Honor posthumously for his extraordinary courage. In subsequent activity, the 2nd Battalion attempts unsuccessfully to seize a ridge to the west, but is repulsed. Palo is taken by the 19th Infantry. In the **XXIV Corps** area, the Japanese resist fiercely near Catmon Hill as the 96th Division presses forward. The 383rd Infantry's 1st Battalion seizes Labiranan Head. In turn, Japanese numerical strength forces the 1st Battalion to pull back to the river. The 2nd and 3rd Battalions attack Tigbao and the barrio respectively, while the 382nd Infantry assaults Tigbao, encountering heavy fire originating from pillboxes as it tramps through the swampy terrain. The 7th Division attacks Dulag and Burauen Airfields. The 184th Infantry seizes the Dulag facility by 09:00. **Offshore**: Reinforcements continue moving toward the Philippines. Some of the Sailors who had earlier departed San Francisco questioned their superiors upon debarkation. Al Lohr, a Ship's Cook had emphasized that he and the other men in his contingent had not received all their gear. An Officer determines that the missing gear is a weapon and tells Lohr that his contingent will be going in on the seventh wave to establish a Field Kitchen and that a weapon would not be necessary. Lohr, is unhappy with the decision, but has no options. Later, he and several other Sailors attempt to take a short trip in a weapons carrier, but Japanese snipers open fire. The unarmed Sailors make an abrupt u-turn and head for the Ship. Lohr had remarked that he was thrilled to cook for the Navy and that he had hoped that he would never have to sleep in a foxhole, eat C-rations or receive the Purple Heart; he wasn't about to face snipers with apple pie. **(Atlantic Western Europe) 12th Army Group** The Americans prepare to attack against the Rhine. General Bradley instructs the First and Ninth Armies to commence the offensive on November 5th. Patton's Third Army is to jump off on November 10th. In the **U.S. First Army** area, **VII Corps** sector, the prolonged contest for Aachen ceases as the German Garrison surrenders at 12:05. **6th Army Group** In the **U.S. Seventh Army** area, **XV Corps** sector, the Germans still hold commanding positions in the hills east of Foret de Parroy. The 79th Division attacks in strength, but the resistance is fierce, holding three Regiments to moderate gains. In the **VI Corps** area, the Germans have abandoned Brouvelieures, but rearguard contingents remain. They are engaged by the 179th Infantry, 45th Division, which enters the town and reduces the opposition. In conjunction, the 15th Infantry, 3rd Division attacks south of Brouvelieures, taking some pressure off the 45th Division. The 7th Infantry, 3rd Division maintains its attack toward St. Die, seizing Domfaing. **(Atlantic-Italy)** In the **U.S. Seventh Army** area, the 6th South African Armored Division seizes M. Alcino and makes an ostensive move to capture M. Salvaro by pouring additional troops into the struggle. In the **II Corps** area, the opposing forces battle to a stalemate. In the British 13th Corps area, the Germans hold M. Spadura against an aggressive attack by the 38th Brigade, (British) 78th Division. In the **British Eighth Army** sector, the Polish 2nd Corps' 5th Kresowa Division advances aggressively, taking the crest of M. Grosso and Strada S. Zeno in the Rabbi River Valley as it drives toward Forli. It may never rain in California, but that certainly isn't the case in Italy. In the 5th Corps sector, the deluge continues and the rivers continue to rise, causing great hardships on the troops employed to enlarge the three bridgeheads across the Savio. Cesena falls to the British 4th Division; contingents cross the Savio there. In the Canadian 1st Corps area, a bridgehead is secured across the Savio by the Canadian 1st Division when its 2nd Brigade, supported by fire delivered by its 3rd Brigade, charges across the river in a spirited night attack. **(Atlantic-Hungary)** Contingents of the Second Ukrainian Front advance from Szeged, reaching the Danube south of Budapest at Baja.

Old Glory returns to Leyte, Philippines.

October 22nd 1944 — (Pacific-Philippines) In the **U.S. Sixth Army** area, the 7th Cavalry, 2nd Brigade, 1st Cavalry Division completes the seizure of the hill southwest of Tacloban, in addition to mopping up the town. The 5th Cavalry's 1st Brigade struggles to overcome the rugged terrain west of Caibaan and is directed to abort the advance and remain where it stands. In other activity, the 4th Infantry (24th Division), supported by Artillery and Carrier Aircraft fire, takes the hill west of Pawing, which in effect secures the entire area. In the 19th Infantry sector, the Japanese mount a futile assault against Palo, losing 91 men in the process. In the **XXIV Corps** area, Contingents of the 383rd Infantry, 96th Division drive solidly along Highway 1 and seize San Roque, while the 1st Battalion attacks Labiranan Head, subsequent to a night-long bombardment, and retakes it. The 382nd Infantry plods ahead and takes Canmangui and Tigbao. In other Corps activity, the 7th Division runs into intermittent resistance as it drives toward Burauen. **(Atlantic-Western Europe) 21st Army Group** In the **Canadian First Army** area, the Canadian 3rd Division seizes Breskens, reducing the enemy pocket. In other activity, the Canadian 4th Armored Division advances to Esschen. In the **British Second Army** area, 12th Corps sector, an offensive to secure the area west of the Maas commences. The British 7th Armored and 53rd Divisions (trailed by the 51st Division) slug their way toward Hertogenbosch, while the British 15th Division drives toward Tilburg. **12th Army Group** Three American Armies step up the preparational phase of the impending offensive against the Rhine. The Ninth Army Headquarters, presently at Luxembourg, between the First and Third Armies, deploys on the left flank of the First Army. In the **U.S. Third Army** area, **XII Corps** sector, some nominal offensive probing takes place as the 28th Division sees its first combat mission as a whole unit, attacking east of Arracourt. Contingents of the 704th Tank Destroyer Battalion bolster the assault; the effort gains territory west of Moncourt. **6th Army Group** Activity in the **U.S. Seventh Army** area's **XV Corps** sector is heated. The high ground east of Foret de Parroy is secured by the 79th Division. In the **VI Corps** area, the 3rd Division leaps forward moving toward St. Die. The 179th Infantry, 45th Division, ceases its mop-up operation in Brouvelieures. The 180th Regiment, driving east of Fremifontaine, crosses the Mortagne River, but the enemy raises tough opposition which halts its progress and causes the Regiment to pull back. **(Atlantic-Finland)** Russian troops of the Karelian Front, driving from Petsamo, advance to the Norwegian Frontier. **(Atlantic-East Prussia)** The German defenses along the northeastern frontier of East Prussia are cracked by Soviet troops, but the Germans raise stiff resistance and halt the offensive in front of Insterburg. The heavy combat soon dissi pates, and the opposing forces retain their positions until January of 1945. **(Atlantic-Yugoslavia)** With the capitulation of Sombor, southwest of Subotica, the Germans have lost control of the majority of the east bank of the Danube River all the way up to Baja, Hungary. The Germans (Army Groups E and F, commanded by Generals Lohr and von Weichs) have been pushed back considerably by the Bulgarian 1st Army and partisans. **(Atlantic-Italy)** In the **U.S. Fifth Army** area, the South African 6th Armored, plagued by torrential type rains, keeps driving toward the summit of M. Salvaro. In the **II Corps** sector, the 85th and 88th Divisions commence a night attack (22nd-23rd) and thrust a mile beyond M. Grande before dawn. In the wake, Hills 459, 568, and M. Castellaro succumb to the onslaught of Yanks. In the British 13th Corps area, the elements are equally terrible as in the American areas. In Italy it seems to rain all day and rain all night with showers in between. Orders are issued calling for the capture of M. Spadura, and then the Corps is to initiate a northward drive between the Imola and Castel San Pietro roads. British guns commence firing upon German positions on M. Spadura. The 13th Corps takes advantage of the German withdrawal. As the Germans head east, elements of the Indian 8th Division occupy M. Romano without incident. In the **British Eighth Army** area, 5th Corps sector, intense fighting develops between the 20th Brigade, 10th Indian Division and the Germans controlling M. Cavallo. The Brigade forces its way to a point just under the crest of the objective. In the Canadian 1st Corps area, the agonizing rains continue to swell the Savio River, greatly hindering ongoing operations. The Canadian 1st Division is unable to transport needed heavy equipment across the bulging river into its bridgehead. Unhampered by the annoying rains, elements of the 5th Armored Division seize Cervia and Pisignano as they whip up the coast. **(Atlantic-Mediterranean)** Lt. General Joseph T. McNarney becomes head of North African Theater of Operations, U.S.A., replacing General Devers. Devers, General Clark's American boss in Italy, concentrates all his attention on his new command, the 6th Army Group in France.

October 23rd 1944 — (International) The United States, England, and Russia recognize the Committee of Liberation as the Provisional Government of France. **(Pacific-Carolines-Palaus)** Some enemy stragglers remain on Angaur; the Infantry is replaced by Antitank and Cannon contingents that eliminate the nuisance. **(Pacific-Philippines)** (Battle of Leyte

Gulf- SEE OCTOBER 23RD-26TH 1944) General MacArthur, at a ceremony in Tacloban, restores Civil Government under President Sergio Osmena. In the **X Corps** area, elements of the 1st Cavalry Division (8th Cavalry, 2nd Brigade) are ordered to secure the San Juanico Strait between Leyte and Samar in an effort to constrict Japanese movement. Reconnaissance detachments probe as far as Babatngon and scour the ferry termini connecting Leyte and Samar without encountering any sign of the enemy. Other contingents of the 8th Cavalry advance to the Diit River, seizing a bridge from where it will launch an attack against Santa Cruz on the Carigara Bay. The Japanese on Leyte are commanded by General Tomoyoku Yamashita whose forces comprise the 35th Army (16th, 26th, 30th, and 106th Divisions). Contingents of various U.S. 24th Division units assault several hills that command entrance to the Leyte Valley. The 1st Battalion, 34th Infantry drives against Hill C on the western fringes of Palo while the 2nd Battalion, 19th Infantry assaults what appears to be the summit of Hill B; the 1st Battalion, 19th Infantry is directed to seize Hill 85, south of Palo. In other **X Corps** activity, the Japanese strike against Palo during the night and are repulsed handily, losing approximately 60 dead. The Japanese had used Filipinos to fool the Americans, but the ruse is unsuccessful. In the **XXIV Corps** area, the arsenal of democracy has failed again. The progress of the 96th Division is hindered by lack of supplies, rather than by the enemy. The critical supply shortages curtail the 96th Division's progress. At 12:00, elements of the 383rd Infantry cross the Guinarona River and drive to a point west of Pikas; the 82nd Infantry limits its activity to patrols. In other activity, the 7th Division continues to drive toward the San Pablo Airfield. The 2nd Battalion, 184th Infantry, and contingents of the 17th Infantry, bolstered by Tanks (767th Tank Battalion), plow into Burauen causing the Japs to flee hurriedly. The 32nd and 184th Regiments follow behind the main thrust which burst upon the remaining obstacles. The drive rolls through Julita and San Pablo, culminating with seizure of the Airfield. In other activity, the U.S.S. *Nautilus* (SS-168) debarks men and equipment at Luzon on its east coast; the operation is repeated on the following two days. **(Atlantic-Western Europe) 21st Army Group** The U.S. 104th Division is yet untried in battle. It moves on line in the **Canadian First Army's** British 13th Corps sector, deploying along the Antwerp-Breda Highway between the British 49th and the Polish 1st Armored Divisions. **12th Army Group** There is no major activity on the front as readiness for the upcoming offensive continues to progress. **6th Army Group** General Devers receives a personal letter from General Eisenhower instructing him to prepare his 6th Army Group to defend the southern flank of the 12th Army Group during the offensive to secure the Rhine. In the **U.S. Seventh Army** area, **XV Corps** sector, the 71st Infantry, 44th Division relieves contingents of the 79th Division which have just recent ly secured the area east of Foret de Parroy after a bitter struggle. In the **VI Corps** area, the Germans mount stiffer resistance as the 3rd Division nears Les Rouges Eaux which must be held by the Germans to forestall the advance against St. Die. To the left of this bitter skirmishing, the 180th Infantry, 45th Division drives across the Mortagne River and establishes a bridgehead east of Fremifontaine. In the 36th Division sector to the right, the Germans contest fiercely as the 36th expands its real estate holdings east of Bruyeres by pushing to Biffontaine. During the vicious contest, the 1st Battalion, 141st Infantry gnaws across the heights north of La Houssiere, but the attempt to secure them is derailed by the enemy; the 141st becomes cut off in the Foret Domaniale de Champ. **(Atlantic-Italy)** In the **U.S. Fifth Army** area, the South African 6th Armored grinds to the crest of M. Salvaro. In the **IV Corps** sector, the Germans retain control of the region northeast of M. Cauala, compelling Task Force 92 to abort its advance and deploy defensively in its coastal perimeter. In the **II Corps** area, the 85th Division comes under a heavy counterattack on Hill 459 and is forced to relinquish it to the enemy. In other activity, the right flank of the Corps is volatile. The 2nd Battalion, 351st Infantry, 88th Division drives toward Vedriano; Company G seizes the town before dawn on the following day. The 133rd Infantry, 34th Division mounts a strong assault and captures M. Belmonte. In the British 13th Corps area, elements of the British 78th Division reinitiate the drive to capture M. Spadura. In other activity, M. Cornazzano is taken without incident by the British 1st Division which also seizes ground north of M. Ceco. The 21st Brigade, Indian Eighth Division takes M. Giro as it drives toward M. Colombo; the 17th Brigade captures M. Casalino. In the **British Eighth Army** area, 5th Corps sector, the Indian 10th Division climbs to the summit of M. Cavallo Ridge, a strategic strongpoint that controls Highway 9 north to Bertinoro. Pressure from the Indians forces the Germans to withdraw. In other activity, the weather begins to offer some compromises as the Savio becomes calm, allowing reinforcements to forge the river and bolster the bridgehead of the British 4th Division. In the Canadian 1st Corps area, the Canadian 1st Division maintains its bridgehead at the Savio, but it is unable to fortify it.

October 23rd-24th 1944 — The headlines mark the return of MacArthur to the Philippines and relate the ongoing major battle in Leyte Gulf, but there is another magnificent story unfolding in near obscurity in the Pacific near Formosa. This story actually begins on September 24th, when the U.S.S. *Tang*, commanded by Commander R.H. O'Kane, departs Pearl Harbor on its 5th and final War Patrol. The *Tang* has borne some responsibility for the lack of Japanese replacement parts for Planes and for intermittent replenishment of fuel as she has been one of the Submarines knocking out enemy Cargo Vessels with dashing dare. The proud Submarine stops at Midway on the 27th of September before proceeding to the Formosa Strait. Only the Japanese make contact with her after embarking from Midway. The 27th is the last day of communication by the *Tang* with any American forces.

The slender silent intruder makes her way down the East China Sea to blockade the Formosa Strait, choosing to make the journey alone, rather than join other Submarine Groups. On the 11th of October, the *Tang* electrifies the skies when her torpedoes rip into two enemy Freighters. The *Tang* gets a reprieve from action for the next 12 days as the patrol detects no activity in the sea lanes, but the lethargy ceases on the 23rd when the Submarine selects a course expected to place her in the middle of some plump Convoys. O'Kane's crew draws an X on the chart, shoots to the mark, and waits, but not too long. Three Cargo Vessels, a Tanker, and a Troop Transport escorted by Warships come prancing into the torpedo lanes of the *Tang*, and the engagement begins fast and furiously with an aggressive surface attack.

The *Tang* deletes the preliminary introduction and forges ahead like a howling winter wind, advancing swiftly toward the target. The enemy formation is penetrated dead center by the intrepid *Tang*, her deadly volleys preceding her grand entrance. The *Tang* finds herself among a staggered and disoriented force. Ships are afire and their guns are thundering angrily without restraint, or accuracy. The darkened skies,

illuminated by giant fires and the burst of shells, serve as guide to the Submarine, which is blasting her way through the smoke, taking evasive action to avoid a calamity as her heavy hand continues to bludgeon the enemy Convoy. The Troop Transport attempts to ram, but O'Kane's maneuvers take her from harm's way.

The structure-busting speed avoids a collision with the charging Transport; however, the *Tang* becomes nestled between several burning enemy Ships, fast approaching Destroyers, and other Warships, giving the Sailors little options other than the obvious: Attack. O'Kane, atop the bridge during this seagoing barnstorming ride, orders the remaining torpedoes sent special delivery to the enemy. They are immediately on their way, striking a Freighter and the Troop Transport without missing a beat. The *Tangs* available torpedoes are exhausted, but the enemy is unaware as this raging gray stallion of the sea stampedes with disciplined rage toward an approaching Destroyer. The gamble pays off; the Destroyer swings hard to avoid the invisible torpedoes as the *Tang* high tails it through the flurry of blistering fire and harmless depth charges that are lambasting the seawater. The *Tang* makes her getaway and finds suitable tranquil waters to submerge and await another tantalizing Convoy.

On the 24th, the persistent Japanese make another run for Leyte to reinforce their garrisons. The *Tang* is poised belligerently atop the water, preparing another surface attack. The overburdened Convoy, stacked with an abundance of Planes and equipment in addition to Troop Transports crammed with reinforcements for the Philippines, is cruising, unaware of the lurking danger.

The *Tang* is discovered prematurely, and enemy Warships make a rapid move to destroy the Submarine. Guns pound and shells roar, but the Submarine runs the gauntlet, firing six torpedoes as she weathers the enfilade. In an extemporaneous manner, the opaque sky is dappled with clusters of brilliant colors resembling a peerless fireworks display. Streams of radiant illumination ascend in swirling splendor while huge ominous puffs of bouncing smoke choke the air, creating eerie silhouettes as tracer shells pierce the skyline, further confusing the deadly encounter. Three enemy Vessels are afire. Two more obese targets are nearby and Destroyers are moving closer for the kill. The *Tang*, caught in another boxed sea canyon, attacks.

Torpedoes ready! Full speed ahead, and the contest renews. In short order, O'Kane's marauders release three menacing shots that score punishingly, demolishing the imminent threat. Like a buzz saw slicing chop sticks, the Tanker, a Transport, and a Destroyer are inoperable. By the light of the glimmering Tanker, now fully aglow and her crew befuddled, the inexhaustible *Tang* gallops through the beleaguered Vessels, reduced to floating scrap piles, outdistancing the Destroyer Escorts; the crewmen of the *Tang* load the remaining torpedoes to finish the mission.

Before midnight on the 24th, the *Tang* displays an awesome amount of stunning fire power. As the early morning hours of the 25th are upon her, the final two torpedoes are prepared for a grand finale. The bruised and burning Troop Ship is the selected prey. Fire one! Fire two! The fish are off and running, but destiny deals a horrid blow, as one of the torpedoes becomes erratic and makes a circular run heading straight for the *Tang*. All emergency measures are undertaken, but twenty seconds allow little reaction time, and the valiant Submarine, unscathed by the enemy, self destructs as the torpedo strikes a mortal blow. The Vessel plummets to the bottom, mutilating some of the crew and trapping the balance, except the nine men who are topside and virtually blown from the deck.

Desperate actions ensue as the crew attempts to escape the death trap; miraculously, some are successful. With a stern sense of duty, despite the predicament, all important documents are destroyed before the men head for the escape hatch. In the meantime, enemy Warships drop depth charges that blast the dying Vessel. Thirteen crewmen evade death and make it out of the hatch, amidst raging fires and chambers which are permeated with asphyxiating smoke, fueled by the flames that have wrecked the electrical apparatus. Eight men are alive when they reach the surface. Four of the original nine blown from the deck and five of the thirteen additional survivors are also alive when the Japanese pick them up in the morning. The nine survivors, including Commander O'Kane, are subjected to harsh treatment, including brutal beatings and malicious lickings, but they survive the ordeal and are eventually released from Japanese prison camps after the close of hostilities when Old Glory is flying over the remnants of the Japanese Empire. The *Tang* had fought gallantly, and before her demise, her five War Patrols had accounted for a total of 24 sunken Japanese Vessels. Commander O'Kane becomes a recipient of the Medal of Honor for his extraordinary leadership and courage. The inspirational actions of the entire crew of the U.S.S. *Tang* is in the splendid tradition of the U.S. Navy and its men who defend liberty regardless of the cost.

Japanese Planes attacking the U.S.S. Sangamon.

October 23rd-26th 1944 — BATTLE OF LEYTE GULF — It has been several days since the U.S. Sixth Army has landed in the Philippines, escorted by a most formidable Armada of Warships. The Philippines remain as one of the final hinges supporting the door to Japan. The Japanese, clinging precariously to their shrinking empire, have initiated a desperate set of maneuvers engineered to destroy the U.S. Fleet and hold the Philippines. The showdown gives no outward appearances of an indolent duel, but Nimitz and MacArthur are betting on Halsey and Kinkaid to hold the pass and clear the sea lanes to Tokyo.

The Japanese attack (SHO-GO) has been sprung. The battered Imperial Navy is in motion, under orders of Admiral Toyoda, who directs the assault from his headquarters in Japan. Admiral Kurita's Force is racing from the south, having departed Lingga (near Singapore) on the previous day. This Battleship Force, including the *Yamato* and *Musashi*, heads for Leyte Gulf with thirteen Cruisers and 18 Destroyers as escorts. In a coordinated movement, Admiral Ozawa's four Carriers are steaming from Japan to be used as bait to draw part of the American Force, while Kurita's Group splices into two groups intending to trap and annihilate the U.S. Warships remaining in the gulf. The plan is daring in design and impetuous in nature, but the bottom line is fulfillment and success depends on a perfect score. It is a natural comparison between theory and practicable application. The plans exhibit not so much a "Paper Tiger," but Paper Warships. Leyte Gulf contains genuine U.S. Vessels and skilled Pilots and Sailors anxious to exterminate the foe. As an added nemesis, U.S. Submarines are posted as pickets, deployed to bushwhack the Japs, sound the alarm, and drive the enemy directly into the tempest where Halsey and Kinkaid can reduce the Fleets to rubble.

Japanese Warships streak across the waters near Cape Calavite on an uneventful voyage, unaware of the U.S.S. *Bream*. Suddenly, at 03:24, the tranquil excursion is transformed into a colossal display of man-made thunder and lightning. The *Bream* strikes with precision, selecting the Heavy Cruiser *Aoba*, which is leading the three Vessel column. The surface attack is a prosperous venture. Six torpedoes are dispersed, and as Commander Chapple orders the dive, the skies become a kaleidoscope of brilliant colors. The Cruiser is aflame amidst the pounding sea and shattering sounds of explosions. The *Aoba* stays afloat, but the damage precludes its participation in the upcoming sea battle. The Yanks had struck first blood before dawn.

Radar detects another group of enemy Warships during the waning hours of the previous night. Just after midnight, by use of a megaphone, the *Darter* blares a directional message to the *Dace*: "WE HAVE CONTACT. LET'S GO." The Submarines pour their power to the limits, but their speed of 19 knots becomes a test of endurance, as the 11 Warships are steaming at about 22 knots. Nevertheless, the Flotilla is within striking distance by dawn as their cruising speed had reduced to about 15 knots. The parade of unsuspecting Vessels, promenading through the Palawan passage like Peacocks in the night, are about to have their plumes plucked; no zig-zag movements have been used. At the point are several Heavy Cruisers, trailed by what appears to be a Battleship. Less than 3,000 yards distant is the indomitable *Darter*. The quarry advances into the tempest at 05:32. Torpedoes away! The ferocious stingers part the waters, plowing into the target within one minute, inflicting damage and causing disorientation on the part of the startled crew, which takes evasive action and maneuvers into more dangerous positioning. Additional torpedoes wallop the beleaguered Cruiser, which is so near the *Darter* that only a portion of the Vessel is visible through the periscope. Huge banners of multicolored flames are twisting and spiraling. Ominous streams of choking black smoke intertwine, forming enormous iridescent clouds that hover with a sense of doom. Fires rage from stem to stern as the Vessel plummets to the bottom; the *Atago* had been the Flagship of Admiral Kurita, and the omen is not optimistic as he transfers his flag to the awesome *Yamamoto*.

Mclintock's crew also concentrates on a second enemy Cruiser, but enemy Destroyers are closing for the kill; the *Darter* dives deep. Soon after, McClintock hears the distinct sounds of a hit. At 05:32, the second Cruiser is struck. Four fish hit the mark. McClintock holds patiently while four enemy Destroyers dump depth charges from 05:39 until a little after 06:30 to no avail.

The *Dace* is close by; in stride with the *Darter*, Commander Claggett's men are eager to join the fight. The bewildered Japanese are scrambling to get a bearing on the Yankee intruders. After a time lapse of a few minutes, more torpedoes are on their way. At 05:42, the *Dace*, itching for a kill, peers through the somber skyline and spots eight Ships, two of which are burning. The selected target turns out to be one of two Heavy Cruisers. A self-confident statement is noted: "WILL LET THEM GO BY...THEY ARE ONLY HEAVY CRUISERS." At 05:52, the two Cruisers unwittingly pass by unmolested, but close behind is the prey, and at 05:54 another ocean tremble occurs. The *Dace* commences firing; six torpedoes whiz through the sea, followed by repetitive explosions. The battered Vessel begins breaking up, metal squealing against metal, as the mass of molten superstructure of the Heavy Cruiser *Maya* sinks. The *Dace* undergoes a subsequent depth charge attack for a period of about one half hour, but suffers no harm.

Although the Japanese have not inflicted any damage to the Yanks, the *Darter* gets trapped in heavy seas during the night and is abandoned and sunk. All important documents and equipment are destroyed, but the Submarine doesn't capitulate easily; it is boarded by enemy troops before her demise. The badly crippled *Takao* heads back for Brunei. Before the main event begins, four enemy Warships have been eliminated, and the communication network between Japanese Ships has been gutted due to massive loss of life.

The remaining Japanese Warships continue toward Leyte. Kurita drives northeastward, passing the southern portion of Mindanao. Ozawa's Carriers near Luzon and Nishimura's Armada is pushing through the Sulu Sea to merge with Shima's Group in the Mindanao Sea. The moves are secretly monitored by U.S. Submarines. Admiral Halsey, under the command of Nimitz, orders Rear Admiral Bogan to deploy near the entrance to the San Bernardino Strait, and he directs Rear Admiral R. E. Davison's Force to hold east of Leyte Gulf to bolster Admiral Kinkaid's Seventh Fleet at the Surigao Strait. In addition, another Task Force, commanded by Rear Admiral F.C. Sherman, is deployed to bar entrance to Luzon from the north. Rear Admiral McCain reverses course and prepares to refuel at sea to be positioned at the ready to aid Halsey if circumstances warrant. The mouse trap is set as the enemy closes, and by the morning of the 24th, the Japanese will be thoroughly aware of the steel gray curtain of submersible fortresses that stand resolute in their path.

The 24th brings some success to the enemy. Planes from Ozawa's Carriers and Land-based Bombers attack the U.S. Fleet and damage the Carrier *Princeton*. While Sherman's Group is under attack, about 120 enemy Planes are shot down. Rescue and salvage operations ensue, but the efforts are overcome by savage explosions that destroy the *Princeton* and damage several nearby Ships, including the Destroyer *Birmingham*, which sustains a staggering loss of 233 men, in addition to grievous injuries to over 200 men. Another 215 men suffer minor injuries, the sum total being greater than those suffered on the *Princeton*.

The *Princeton* is the first Fast Carrier to be lost by the Navy since the loss of the *Hornet* on October 26th 1942 at the Battle of Santa Cruz. Carrier-based Aircraft (Admirals Davison and Bogan) hammer Kurita's Fleet into submission with a steady bombardment. The 12:00 meal aboard the Japanese Vessels is anything but calm as the incessant pop of impacting bombs has the enemy scurrying for safety. The battle-weary Armada is whacked into a frenzy. By day's end, all Battleships in the group have sustained some damage, including the capsizing of the *Musashi* and the sledgehammer thrashing of the *Myoko*, which has been bludgeoned and forced to retire toward Singapore. In addition, the Destroyer *Wakaba* is victimized and it plops violently to the bottom. Kurita, who had been steaming east like a lion, is now heading west with his remnant force, but a signal arrives from Japan ordering him to continue the attack with words of inspiration: "ADVANCE COUNTING ON DIVINE ASSISTANCE."

Reluctantly, the Admiral complies and reverses course, heading back toward the Philippines. The journey has the beleaguered Fleet advancing toward Leyte; first impressions build some false confidence as Kurita breaks out of the strait on the 25th without incident, as Halsey, unaware that the Fleet is a decoy, had dispatched the Third Fleet to engage the approaching Carriers of Ozawa. The decision creates problems for Kinkaid who must hold Leyte Gulf with his Seventh Fleet, and possibly against three enemy Armadas: Shima's Task Group, closing from Formosa; Nishimura's Force, driving toward the Surigao Strait; and the remaining Warships of Kurita, which are closing toward Leyte. Fortunately, Admiral Olendorf's Force is available. Olendorf's foresight entices him to throw up an honor guard at the southern entrance to the Surigao Strait. Thirty PT Boats greet the Jap Vessels and deliver an array of surprise packages. The Admiral further ensures recognition of their presence by stringing a deadly line of Destroyers and Cruisers across Leyte Gulf's junction with the strait. Admiral Olendorf, aware of the Japanese interest in their ancestors and belief in Divine intervention, has one more surprise up his sleeve; six Battleships are also on line, most of which have been resurrected since Pearl Harbor. The U.S.S. *West Virginia, California, Maryland, Tennessee* and *Pennsylvania*, all present at the Pearl Harbor Massacre, are back from the dead, straddling alongside the *Mississippi* and poised to give retribution to the glorious sons of heaven who venture into the range of their guns.

During the latter part of the night (24th), while the Japanese Force under Nishimura moves north through the Surigao Strait, PT Boats dart toward the Flotilla, but the night bushwhacking does not stop the advance. The Japanese move deeper into the inferno. The night air adds to the trepidation as the enemy Ships advance, unaware of the dangers lurking ominously in the shadows. The steel gray fence comprises the combined firepower of 28 Destroyers, eight Cruisers, and six Carriers.

A U.S. Fleet on the advance.

At 03:00 the sparks begin to fly. Nishimura's Destroyers slip cautiously through the strait, converging on Captain Coward's Eastern Attack Group. In an instant, 27 torpedoes are flung. Quick reaction on the part of Coward has his force pulling back, leaving a trail of smoke as they retire in erratic fashion, zig-zagging to evade return fire. Japanese crewmen spin into action and click on their searchlights. Return fire is expeditiously returned, but the enemy marksmanship is less than poor. By 03:09, Kinkaid's Western Attack Force initiates action. The Destroyers *McDermutt* and *Monssenn* launch 20 torpedoes at the approaching enemy Vessels, then retire unscathed from the fading sounds of enemy guns. U.S. Gunners knock the Battleship *Fuso* out of commission, leaving it dead in the water. Another enemy Vessel, the Destroyer *Michishio*, is also destroyed.

The fatalistic encounter continues as Nishimura plods ahead moving into more devastating fire. By 03:30, the *Yamagumo* is reduced to scrap and sunk, followed within an hour by the mighty Battleship *Yamashiro*, which is blown into oblivion by a combination of 5" shells and successive torpedo strikes which tear out the steel spine of the Vessel. The Japanese lose four major Warships. Admiral Nishimura, attempting to continue compliance with his directive from Japan, issues orders to continue the attack. The order is issued just prior to the sinking of the *Yamashiro*, making it his final order. The surviving Vessels, including the Destroyers *Assagumo*, *Shigure* and the Cruiser *Mogami*, continue to advance into the next layer of Kinkaid's defenses.

Three more Destroyer Sections commence the attack. Two of the groups, comprising six Destroyers, fire their torpedoes at a three-minute interval beginning at 03:55, then make a fast and safe withdrawal, running through a gauntlet of enemy fire, while camouflaged by trailing smoke. Group 1, commanded by Captain Smoot, joins the battle committing his three Destroyers which race to the undesigned battle grid, consumed with furious combat. Smoke and fire screen the entire seascape, stretching across the narrow distance between Leyte and Dinagat Island. The skies, still inky black during these presunlight hours, cast a mystifying and chilling shadow on the gruesome duel. The Destroyers pierce the smothering pea soup, but detecting the enemy is difficult. The use of radar is seriously impaired because of the proximity of the shoreline. Sightings appear from every direction on the radar screens. Friend and foe are indistinguishable. Smoot's Destroyers surge ahead, following the sights and sounds of apparent enemy guns, then swerve to the west from where selected targets are fired upon. At 04:05 torpedoes are away. The predatory iron fish strike the Destroyer *Asagumo*. The Destroyers trip to safety is jeopardized by the elements. A decision is made to veer north to give the enemy guns a minimal target; the run is led by the U.S.S. *Newcomb* (Smoot's Flagship), followed by the other two Ships. Friendly guns inadvertently join the Japs' return fire, and the combined salvos whirl inbound as the Ships begin the turn, pummeling the U.S.S. *A.W. Grant* before the maneuver is completed. The *Grant*, which is the trailing Vessel, is the only U.S. casualty of the engagement, but the savage nature of the loss is spellbinding.

Unending screams of anguish bellow through the chambers of this Ship of horrors. Some men have had their legs torn off while others lose their arms. The Vessel, shot to pieces yet afloat, sustains hits from 7 Japanese shells and 11 American projectiles, causing rampant fires and huge explosions, trapping many men below deck, some with their bodies scorched.

The communications crew is nearly wiped out, the Doctor is dead, and all radios are inoperable. The radar is out of commission, and the steering mechanism is useless. Frantic, but disciplined calls for help are sent out by the blinker system as the dying Ship fights on courageously, awaiting aid. The scene is a nightmare as bodies are strewn wretchedly about the decks. There appears to be more flowing blood than water, but the Ship does not falter. The remaining crewmen, led by the intrepid Commander Nisewaner, refuse to capitulate, making spontaneous dangerous dashes through uncontrollable fires to attempt to save others.

The fighting spirit of the men is personified by the immortal words of the mortally wounded Radioman First Class W. M. Selleck: "THERE'S NOTHING YOU CAN DO FOR ME, FELLOWS. GO AHEAD AND DO SOMETHING FOR THE OTHERS." Selleck, both his legs blown off, speaks these words on the wardroom table as he is dying from massive loss of blood. His crewmates follow his inspiration; the *Grant* remains afloat, and by 06:30, the *Newcomb* is towing the valiant Vessel out of Surigao Strait. The *Grant* had been struck at 04:07; the cries for help had been heard and the big guns silenced by 04:10. The agonizing saga emblazoned on the minds of all surviving participants consumes a mere three minutes of ghastly war. Before they are out of the strait, a new brush with death descends upon them as yet another Japanese Naval Force under Admiral Shima arrives on the scene.

While Halsey is intercepting the Northern Force, all hell is breaking out near Leyte. Admiral Shima's Fifth Fleet approaches the southern end of the Surigao Strait and is received by Olendorf's PT Boats, which blow torpedoes into the *Abukuma*, leaving her dead in the water. The remaining enemy force moves into Kinkaid's Lair. The Japanese Vessel *Mogami*, which had collided with the *Grant* during the blind shoot out, is making its getaway while afire and nearly totally out of control. The *Shigure* is high tailing it under full power, the only Vessel from Nishimura's Force still able to do so. The rapidly withdrawing survivors pass Shima's approaching Fleet. Shima advances into the arena and stumbles upon the blazing *Mogami*. Shima orders an attack against the U.S. Warships; a torpedo barrage ensues without success. No American Vessels are struck, but the disoriented enemy makes more mistakes. The Cruiser *Mogami* collides with Shima's Flagship, the *Nachi*; he orders a retreat and speeds for the Mindanao Sea, pursued by avenging U.S. Aircraft. The Planes exhibit a dazzling performance and bludgeon the disabled Vessels *Mogami* and *Abukuma*, sending both to the bottom like sizzling comets. The non-dilatory retreat is anticlimactic. In an astonishing five hour marathon of death, ten Japanese Warships have been eliminated; the U.S. loses no Vessels. Even the death-ridden *Grant* remains afloat. The Japanese Fleet had been thrashed, but the victory is not complete. As the Yanks regroup, the alarm rings again. More Jap Ships have arrived and are attacking an Escort Carrier Force; Admiral Kurita's Fleet spots Sprague's Force off Samar, and another bitter battle begins (See Battle of Samar 10/25). In yet another vicious contest, the Forces of Halsey are engaging the Japanese Northern Force (See Battle of Cape Engano 10/25).

October 24th 1944 — (Pacific-Philippines-Leyte) In the **U.S. Sixth Army** area, elements of the 1st Cavalry Division are transported by Ship to Babatngon. Stiff defenses are to be established, and Patrols are to probe along the northern coast. In other activity, Japanese Planes bombard the harbor at Tacloban, impeding ongoing operations. After the interruption, Troop C, reinforcements of the 8th Cavalry, embark for Samar to establish a beachhead at La Paz and construct roadblocks along the route to Basey. The Japanese await nightfall before mounting a futile assault; the roadblock holds. The primary force of the 8th Cavalry treks north to Guintiguian by way of Highway 1 to control the Juanico Strait. In the vicinity of Palo Hill, Nan is taken by the 1st Battalion, 34th Infantry without incident. The 3rd Battalion seizes Hill Mike without opposition. At Hill B, the 2nd Battalion, 19th Infantry, is engaged in a fierce firefight to wrest control of the crest from the entrenched Japanese. The 19th Infantry's Company K drives south, attempting to establish contact with the XXIV Corps; it captures San Joaquin, on Highway 1. In the **XXIV Corps** area, the Yanks hold their positions due to chronic supply problems. The 383rd Infantry. 96th Division searches for supply routes. During the mission, it is determined that Tabontabon is stuffed with Japanese defenders. In other Divisional activity, Anibung and Hindang are seized by the 382nd Regiment. In the 7th Division sector, Burauen falls to the 17th Infantry, which then drives toward Dagami. The Buri Airstrip is assaulted by the 1st Battalion, 32nd Infantry, but the assault fails; the Battalion withdraws to San Pablo. U.S. losses BATTLE OF LEYTE GULF The following is a recap of U.S. Naval Vessels sunk: Light Carrier *Princeton* (CVL-23), damaged by Dive Bomber (Battle of Leyte Gulf) sunk by U.S. Forces; Ocean Tug *Sonoma* (ATO-12) (Battle of Leyte Gulf); U.S.S. *Darter* (SS-227), damaged by grounding Palawan Passage sunk by U.S. Forces; U.S.S. *Tang* (SS-306) by circular run of own torpedo. U.S. Naval Vessels damaged (Battle of Leyte Gulf): Light Cruiser *Birmingham* (CL-62), Destroyers *Gatling* (DD-671) and *Irwin* (DD-794), incurred while assisting *Princeton*, being alongside during explosions and catapulting debris; Destroyer *Leutze* (DD-481) by Horizontal Bomber; Destroyer *Albert W. Grant* (DD-649) by Naval fire friendly and enemy; Oiler *Ashtabula* (AO-51) by Aircraft Torpedo; the LSTs 552 and 695, Horizontal Bomber and underwater explosion respectively. Japanese Vessels sunk: Battleship *Musashi* by Carrier Based Aircraft Sibuyan Sea and Destroyer *Wakaba* Carrier Based Aircraft; Submarine I-362 by Destroyer Escort *Richard M. Rowell* (DE-403). **(Pacific)** The Submarine U.S.S. *Shark* (SS-314) dispatches a message that is picked up by the U.S.S. *Seadragon* (SS-194), stating that she had spotted an enemy Freighter and was moving in for an attack. The Japanese subsequently report the sinking of a P.O.W. Ship and a depth charge assault against an undetermined Submarine, which had probably been the *Shark*. Other U.S. Submarines had been attacked today, but none report sinking the Freighter. The *Shark* is officially listed as missing and presumed lost on the 27th of November. **(China-Burma-India)** The CBI Theater is divided into two theaters: the India Burma Theater (IBI) and the China Theater (CT); the former is to be commanded temporarily by General Chennault prior to General Wedemeyer assuming command. The India Burma Theater to be headed by Lt. General Daniel Sutherland (India) and Major General Albert Wedemeyer. **(Atlantic-Western Europe) 21st Army Group** In the **Canadian First Army** area, the Canadian 2nd Division attacks the Beveland Isthmus. The Canadians enter the neck of the isthmus, fighting in waist high water a good deal of the time as they drive west toward the German positions on South Beveland. The British 52nd Division makes an amphibious landing the night of the 25th-26th, to bolster the attack. By the 30th of October, the objective is seized. **12th Army Group** In the **U.S. Third Army** area, the 104th Infantry, 26th Division attacks a hill, capturing most of it; however, General Paul decides to commit another Regiment to make the next attack. Colonel D.T. Colley informs his lead Battalion that the honor of the Regiment will not allow turning over an "incomplete job" and that he will lead the attack himself. The 104th takes the objective; however, Colonel Colley is wounded in his right shoulder, "the bullet progressing through both lungs and emerging from the lower part of his left lung." He is decorated by Patton and recovers, returning to command another Regiment. **6th Army Group** In the **U.S. Seventh Army** area, **VI Corps** sector, the town of Mortagne is taken by the 179th Infantry, 45th Division which has crossed to the enemy-held bank of the Mortagne River. In other activity, the 3rd Division ups the ante, throwing its entire strength against St. Die; the 30th Infantry joins the fight, driving to St. Die on the right of the 7th Division. In the **French 1st Army** area, the Operation to capture Belfort (INDEPENDENCE) begins. French General de Lattre orders the 1st Corps to initiate a surprise attack against the Germans. **(Atlantic-Italy)** In the **U.S. Fifth Army** area, the South African 6th Armored Division seizes M. Termine. In the **II Corps** area, the Germans retake Vedriano. A large majority of Company G, 351st Infantry, 88th Division, is captured during the struggle. In other activity, a night attack is commenced by the 85th and 88th Divisions, but the assault which continues into the following morning is unable to dislodge the Germans. In the British 13th Corps area, the British 78th Division tightens its positions on M Spadura, and the 61st Brigade, British 6th Armored Division advances to Orsara as it closes on M. Taverna. In the **British Eighth Army** area, 5th Corps sector, the Canadian 1st Corps chases the Germans toward the Ronco River; the Indian 11th Division also advances toward the Ronco River on the right flank of the Corps. The British 4th Division pushes forward; elements reach the Madonna di Ceribano road junction on the left flank, while additional contingents driving on the right flank reach Castellaccio along Highway 9.

A Grumman Hellcat being prepped for action.

Vought Corsairs, dubbed "whistling death" ready for take off from their Carrier in the Pacific.

October 25th 1944 — (Pacific-Philippines-Leyte Gulf) — BATTLE OF SAMAR — The Naval confrontation in and around the Leyte Gulf to control the Philippines is awesome. Already, U.S. Submarines have dealt decisive killing blows to the enemy. Admiral Kurita's Fleet, which had taken a thrashing on the 24th and turned for home, is ordered to change course again and head for Leyte to destroy the U.S. Transports. With reluctant diligence, Admiral Kurita continues the attack. The Armada sprints along, unaware of many of the latest developments; he has no knowledge of the pending misfortunes of Admirals Nishimura and Shima, whose forces have undergone a tremendous thrashing in a wild and reckless sea joust that ensues through the night of the 24th into the morning of the 25th in the Surigao Strait. Admiral Kurita, based upon earlier information from Nishimura, anticipates a rendezvous with him off the coast of Leyte at approximately 09:00, from where they intend to launch a combined assault. In addition, the Japanese are counting on the scheme to lure the Yanks (Halsey's Carriers) toward the Northern Force (Ozawa's Naked Carriers) to drain American strength and permit a giant thrust against Leyte.

At a little after 19:00 (24th), Admiral Halsey, acting upon intelligence supplied by his Pilots that Kurita's Force had been severely damaged and unable to inflict a major assault, makes the decision to head north to destroy Ozowa's Carriers. A message is dispatched to Admiral Nimitz: "CENTRAL FORCE (KURITA) HEAVILY DAMAGED ACCORDING TO STRIKE REPORT. AM PROCEEDING NORTH TO STRIKE CARRIER FORCE AT DAWN." Confusion abounds. Kinkaid and Nimitz are under the impression that Task Force 34 has remained at the San Bernardino Strait; however, the latch is left open. All hands had begun steaming north.

Admiral Kurita's Main Force, including the Battleship *Yamamoto*, passes through the Pacific entrance to the Philippine Sea just after midnight on the 24th and continues without duress, thanks partially to the intentional yelping of Admiral Ozawa who had been trying everything except sending Admiral Halsey an embossed invitation to join him and share a bottle of Sake.

Admiral Sprague's Escort Carrier Force (TF-77.4.3) is inferior to the encroaching enemy Fleet, yet is the only available strength that Kinkaid has on hand for immediate combat. Sprague's Planes have been utilized to support the ground operations on Leyte and are not sufficiently supplied with Armor-piercing bombs or torpedoes, further constricting the operation against the enemy Battleships and Cruisers. If Kurita breaks through, the long barrels of his Battleships will demolish the Leyte beachhead and trap about 80,000 American fighting men.

Admiral Sprague is first to be informed of the imminent threat of Kurita's Warships; when the hurried message is blared from the voice of Ensign W. C. Brooks, just after 06:00 (25th), there is instant disbelief. Sprague insists upon verification, thinking the information is erroneous. However, they are enemy Ships, funneling into the waters off southern Samar, less than twenty miles from the U.S. Seventh Fleet, steaming on an irreversible collision course. Kurita, finding no opposition upon entering the gulf, excitedly sends a message to Admiral Toyoda at dawn: "BY HEAVEN-SENT OPPORTUNITY WE ARE DASHING TO ATTACK ENEMY CARRIERS." The startling revelation catches the Americans flatfooted. Kinkaid, informed by Pilots that the San Bernardino Strait is undefended, snaps off a pointed question at about 06:30 to Halsey: "IS TASK FORCE 34 GUARDING SAN BERNARDINO STRAIT?" The response: "NEGATIVE X. IT IS WITH OUR CARRIERS NOW ENGAGING ENEMY CARRIERS." Halsey is confident Kinkaid can hold the strait and maintain his attack against the Northern Force. Kinkaid's concern continues to deepen in the next strenuous hour.

Immediate assistance is unavailable for Sprague. Olendorf's Forces have expended their Armor-piercing ammunition at Surigao Strait; his fuel supply is nearly exhausted, and his force is deployed more than five hours running time from the scene. Sprague's only solace is found in the Escort Carrier Force of Admiral F. B. Stump, which stands slightly southeast of Sprague's Carrier Force (TF 77.4.2). Together they must stand like sparrow hawks against the onslaught of Kurita's buzzards to preserve the ongoing Leyte land operations.

The opponents have located each other at about the same time; battle is imminent. From a distance of about 17 miles, the massive guns of the Japanese Battleships commence firing. Admiral Sprague takes immediate evasive action and swings his Armada from its northward course, turning it southeast; his Carriers steam for cover underneath a rain squall. Generous smoke covers are laid to supplement his sparsely armored Force, while he simultaneously sends urgent requests for help and directs his Destroyers and Destroyer Escorts to converge on the closing enemy Fleet. The evasive action buys some time. Every available Plane is thrown against the enemy, which has broken from one Force into three separate fighting groups, spearheaded by the Herculean Battleships, which crash toward the center as vanguard; they are flanked by the Cruisers swarming in from the east and the Destroyers closing from the west to invest and destroy the flimsy U.S. Force standing in Leyte Gulf, clearing passage to Leyte and the U.S. 6th Army. The chore should be effortless, matching such overwhelming power and strength against three Destroyers and four Destroyer Escorts, the designated protectors of Sprague's Escort Carriers. The three-directional attack causes unrelenting problems for Spragues' Carriers. The instantaneous Fleet-preserving maneuvers position his Carriers badly, making it impossible to swing into the wind for launching.

At 07:20, the U.S.S. *Johnston* charges one of the Heavy Cruisers, unleashing her torpedoes. Enemy return fire is vicious and accurate, inflicting damage. Undaunted, the wounded Destroyer continues the slugfest, catapulting round after round without retiring, despite sustaining a wicked pounding. The Vessel is reluctantly abandoned at 09:45 after a valiant stand; its Commanding Officer, Commander Ernest E. Evans, receives the Medal of Honor for his extraordinary leadership during the battle. No less is the glory of the few other Ships attempting to stem the tide. For these desperate hours, the Destroyers *Hoel* and *Heermann*, enjoined by the Destroyer Escorts *Dennis*, *John C. Butler*, *Raymond*, and the *Samuel B. Roberts*, also trade devastating shots with the enemy in a legendary battle equivalent to any other in the annals of Naval Warfare. During the violent and unrelenting duel, the opposing crews sometimes become blinded from the blazing guns, terrifying explosions, and incessant smoke. The situation deteriorates further as punishing rains occur.

The *Hoels* guns have been working tirelessly since sustaining a hit just prior to 07:30; within two minutes thereafter, she dispenses torpedoes at an onrushing Battleship: the *Kongo*. Within another minute or so, heavy shells begin pummeling the *Hoel*. Undaunted, the gallant Ship launches more torpedoes at a Cruiser, but the incredible weather and battle conditions prevent identification. The *Hoel* exhausts her torpedoes, then tries to make a run for it, but the heavy guns are saturating the entire area; during the dangerous escape attempt, the Vessel sustains more hits, bringing the deadly total to 40. The Warship is nearly cannibalized by the blistering shellfire. Floating on pride and courage, the Sailors refuse to leave their battle stations. Scorched bodies are everywhere. Severely wounded men scramble to save others, while the operational guns continue to fire against the Jap hordes. Over 253 American men go down with the capsized Vessel, and of the few survivors, another 15 Sailors of the *Hoel* succumb subsequent to abandonment.

The *Roberts* lunges toward a Cruiser at about 08:00; in whirlwind motion she fires three torpedoes, one of which hits paydirt. Retribution is swift. Additional enemy Cruisers sweep close and unload round after round upon the *Roberts*, which tries to keep pace, matching her small barreled guns against the Cruiser for over two bloody hours of anguish-filled combat. At just after 09:30, the dying Vessel is abandoned after sustaining 20 hits. She goes down at 10:05, having fired over 600 rounds in the arena of death. Nearly 90 men are lost with the Ship, including its Captain, Lt. Commander Copeland. Meanwhile, the *Raymond* is blasting away, hitting one of the enemy Warships with successive strikes by shells and by torpedoes; she escapes injury during her fling with death. In similar fashion, the *Heermann* and the *Dennis* flaunt dangerously close to the claws of death, but survive the ordeal with damages and some loss of life.

The Japanese Warships keep advancing toward the Carriers, tightening the vise as they close. The powerful shelling continues raking the area. At around 08:30, Halsey receives another call for help from Kinkaid: "URGENTLY NEED FAST BBS (BATTLESHIPS) LEYTE GULF AT ONCE." Halsey is presently involved with devastating the Carriers up north and firmly believes it is necessary to protect the beachhead from Ozawa's Carriers. He is unhappy with the request, but orders Rear Admiral John S. McCain (refueling to the east) to move to Leyte with his five Carriers, his Cruisers, and accompanying Vessels to help deliver a mortal blow to the enemy.

The hell-raising inferno encompasses everything imaginable, leaving little to the imagination. The Destroyers have packed a lot of explosives in their tiny arsenal and have delayed, but not halted, the mighty Japanese Armada. The Japs have penetrated and inflicted damage to the Carriers. The Japanese employ colored dyes that spew forth from the burst of shells to help spot the American Vessels, but the colors, which include pink, red and green, are unable to force the Red, White, and Blue to falter. In turn, Planes from Stump's Force arrive to add more power to the Yankee punch. Meanwhile, Jap Planes from Luzon have been pounding Sprague's Forces, adding to the dilemma. As the grueling contest rages, the Japanese begin to waiver. At about 09:00, Kurita moves the *Yamamoto* behind the Fleet to gain sanctuary while he ponders his next move to secure victory. The big question for Kurita is, where is the other Fleet, under Nishiuma, expected at 09:00? It is the Fleet that cannot come, compliments of Admiral Olendorf's Force.

The incessant violence has plundered the sea and nearly obscured the sky as shells and bullets are traded. Bodies are scattered about the burning waters with appalling reality, and more carnage arrives with every volley. Instead of another enemy Fleet, Kurita is greeted by more U.S. Planes, which cause the vacillating enemy Commander grave concern.

The casualty list of Warships spirals. The sea is crimson with both sides bleeding more profusely. Sprague's "Boys" have elicited the consternation of Kurita and performed magnificently, exhibiting fearless tenacity while enduring brutal punishment, emulating "Preble's Boys" of old. The *Raymond* and *Butler* have been damaged. Savage hits from the Kamikaze Planes cripple the *Kalinin Bay*. The Flagship of Sprague, *Fanshaw Bay*, is also struck. The Escort Carrier *Gambier Bay* sustains vicious damage, too severe to save the Vessel. By this time, Halsey has disengaged and his Third Fleet is rushing to the scene with its Carrier Planes. Admiral Mitscher's Force remains to the north, continuing pursuit of the retreating Japanese Carriers.

The Escort Carrier *St. Lo*, damaged previously, is destroyed by a Suicide Plane. The mortally wounded Vessel explodes, creating total conflagration before it capsizes. Stump's Task Force has catapulted its Planes into the inferno. They shoot over the horizon placing additional pressure on Kurita's advance, confusing his strategy. Suicidal Japanese Pilots strike the U.S. Carriers, damaging the *Santee*, *Swannee*, and *Sangamon*, but the tortuous pain is endured stoically. A Jap Submarine also strikes the damaged *Santee*. The fragile hold is slipping fast as the Spartan stand by the diminutive force has been shattered, its Destroyers and Destroyer Escorts either sunk or damaged and the "Jeep" Carriers under a tumultuous barrage. The floodgates are about to open unless more help arrives. Fortuitously, Sprague's Bombers return from their missions over Mindanao and charge into the battle, in cadence with Stump's Planes and other 7th Fleet Aircraft, which have hastily refueled in Leyte and returned in time to help stave off an enemy breakthrough. Aircraft begin to sting Kurita's Cruisers, pummeling the *Suzuya*, *Chikuma* and *Chokai*.

Kurita, believing the newly arrived Planes are attached to the 3rd Fleet, decides that the Leyte Beachhead is no longer a high priority; he starts heading north, allegedly to engage Halsey, but his Battleships do not press further. Orders are issued by the Japanese Admiral to destroy his crippled Cruisers as he skidaddles north. The beachhead remains intact; the Navy has held the pass. The Admiral makes an elegant retreat by attacking north; along the route, Kurita aborts the attack against Halsey as he approaches the San Bernardino Strait. Suddenly, Kurita bolts into the strait, heading west. A U.S. Carrier Plane spots the quick moving Armada heading toward the Sibuyan Sea; Admiral Kurita has to concern himself with another problem: how to avoid being crushed by a raging "Bull" called Halsey (See Battle of Engano for further details 10-25).

Japanese "Kawasaki Hien."

U.S. Carriers.

The U.S. Navy at Leyte.

The Carrier Zuiho under attack by Planes from the Enterprise.

October 25th 1944 — THE BATTLE OF ENGANO — The bitter struggle to control Leyte Gulf has evolved into a nasty trilogy of Naval encounters beginning on the 23rd of October: the battles of Surigao Strait, Samar, and this, the grand finale which pits Halsey's Carriers against those of Admiral Ozawa. Actually the battle in the Surigao Strait is ensuing simultaneously with this engagement, but the Surigao Strait ends victoriously for the Americans by 12:00. The Great Carrier Chase actually begins on the 24th, during the evening, after Admiral Halsey has digested reports from his Pilots that imply Admiral Kurita's Battleship Force is heavily damaged (Sibuyan Sea — 24th) and unable to create a major problem in the Leyte Gulf. The information had not been totally accurate, but Kurita had been struck severely enough to begin retiring until Admiral Toyoda dispatches instructions from Japan to the somber Admiral, ordering him to return to Leyte; with expectations of "divine assistance," he is to attack and destroy the American Transports near the Leyte Beachhead.

Admiral Halsey is confronted with several options on the afternoon of the 24th with regards to the Japanese Northern Force; more specifically, he could hold the San Bernardino Strait with Task Force 34 and attack with his Carriers, hold the strait with the entire Force and wait for the enemy, or attack north with the entire Fleet. He chooses the latter, assuming that this is the safest way to ensure destruction of the Carriers and preserve the Leyte beachhead. Halsey, under the command of Nimitz, not MacArthur, is confident that Kinkaid's 18 Light Carriers can defend the Seventh Fleet, and he is convinced Kurita has been too severely damaged to cause great harm.

The Third Fleet concentrates on locating the enemy Carriers. During the afternoon of the 24th, neither the Submarines nor the Planes have detected the enemy Fleet, but the search continues to determine from where the Carriers would strike. Finally at 17:30, discovery is made. Admiral Sherman informs Halsey that an enemy Force comprising three Carriers, two Light Cruisers, and three Destroyers is about 200 miles east of Cape Engano off the north eastern tip of Luzon. At 19:50 on the 24th, dispatches are sent by Halsey, giving instructions to Admirals McCain, Davison, Sherman, and Bogan. Another message is dispatched to Admiral Kinkaid: "CENTRAL FORCE (JAPANESE) HEAVILY DAMAGED ACCORDING TO STRIKE REPORTS X AM PROCEEDING NORTH WITH 3 GROUPS TO ATTACK CARRIER FORCE AT DAWN". (McCain is ordered to remain to the southeast and refuel at sea while awaiting orders). The suspense builds as the Third Fleet begins the 300-mile journey to engage Ozawa's Northern Force. By 02:30 on the 25th, Halsey has a bead on the enemy, having located two groups of Warships, including Battleships. Subsequent identification determines Four Carriers, two Battleships, three Cruisers, and about eight Destroyers, indicating an imminent explosive encounter.

At 06:30, the decks are cleared as the Planes are launched. The Pilots, comprising the first wave, speed toward the enemy Carriers, anticipating interception by enemy fighters, but their path is unimpaired. While the Air assault is in progress, the crewmen of the Fleet prepare for an expected enemy attack. The waiting is excruciating; the guns peer skyward, radar screens are studied intently, and the radiomen await word from the birds. At almost the same time, the slugfest off

Samar is commencing between Sprague and Kurita, causing the airwaves to singe the dispatches between Kinkaid and Halsey, concerning the situation off Samar. At 06:48, Kinkaid inquires of Halsey alarmingly: "AM NOW ENGAGING ENEMY SURFACE VESSELS SURIGAO STRAIT X QUESTION IS TF 34 GUARDING SAN BERNARDINO STRAIT?" Admiral Halsey, aware that he had dispatched his intentions to Kinkaid on the previous night, and in another private dispatch had also informed his (Halsey's) boss, Admiral Nimitz, responds: "NEGATIVE X IT IS WITH OUR CARRIERS NOW ENGAGING ENEMY CARRIERS." The Third Fleet maintains its high speed hoping that Ozawa is cruising at 15 knots; if so, the deadly clash will occur at about 12:00. Meanwhile, the suspense heightens as the minutes keep a seemingly lethargic beat. The clock passes 08:00 without word from the first wave of Planes. Back on the Surface Vessels the guns are at the ready, but no attack comes. A message comes into the Battleship *New Jersey* from Kinkaid to Halsey at 08:02: "ENEMY VESSELS RETIRING SURIGAO STRAIT X OUR LIGHT FORCES IN PURSUIT." Halsey accepts the good tidings and keeps advancing, but at 08:22 Kinkaid rushes another message to Halsey informing him that enemy Vessels including Battleships and a Cruiser are firing upon Sprague's Task Force from a distance of 15 miles. The news is distressing to Halsey who now wonders how Kinkaid (informed previous night about movement of Third Fleet) had allowed Sprague to be put in such bad positioning. Halsey is still convinced that the 18 Carriers of Kinkaid can hold the line until Olendorf reaches the battle area; he continues pursuit to destroy the enemy Carriers.

At 08:30, Admiral Kinkaid sends another urgent dispatch to Halsey requesting Battleships to neutralize the long guns of the Japs. Halsey is still of the opinion that his task is to stay on the offensive and attack to ensure the safety of the combined Fleets, and he is still unaware that there are no Planes with Ozawa's Carriers. Halsey orders McCain to rush from his southeast positions to assist beleaguered Sprague. Much of the confusion has been brought about by joint command. Sprague's predicament is critical for a time, but the extraordinary efforts of his small intrepid Force holds the gate until reinforcements arrive to halt the advance and drive Kurita's Fleet into an expedient withdrawal before 12:00 on the 25th.

By 08:45, Halsey has received four dispatches from Kinkaid, but none from his own Third Fleet Aircraft. The Fleet is at battle stations; however, no attack appears imminent. The nervousness aboard Ship increases with each tick of the clock. Two hours and fifteen minutes since launch time, and no word has come back to the nest. Finally, the trepidation ends with a startling note. At 08:50 information arrives and brings with it a feeling of exhilaration. Halsey gets the word! "ONE CARRIER SUNK AFTER TREMENDOUS EXPLOSION X 2 CARRIERS, 1 CL (LIGHT CRUISER) HIT BADLY OTHER CARRIER UNTOUCHED X FORCE COURSE 150 SPEED 17." The quarry had been discovered. Halsey's Planes had delivered a sound strike and more Planes follow. Additional friendly complications develop within minutes after word of the First Wave's success reaches Halsey when another dispatch arrives from Admiral Kinkaid, again urgently requesting help: "OUR CVES (Escort Carriers) BEING ATTACKED BY 4 BBS (Battleships) 8 CRUISERS PLUS OTHERS X REQUEST LEE (Task Force 34 Commander) COVER LEYTE AT TOP SPEED X REQUEST FAST CARRIERS MAKE IMMEDIATE STRIKE.

This, the fifth dispatch from Kinkaid, makes Halsey furious.

He has the Japs right where he wants them, and he is not within striking distance of Kurita; Halsey has already dispatched McCain's Force. Before 09:30, yet another request for help is received by Halsey; this one mentions that Kinkaid's older Battleships had expended most of their ammunition. Halsey can't understand why he hasn't been notified of this situation in earlier dispatches. He then dispatches a message to Kinkaid explaining the situation and informing him that McCain is en route, but that distance prevents the Battleships from reaching him in time.

By 10:00, emotions are highly sensitive, and the next two dispatches that arrive in Halsey's hands do little to rectify anything. Kinkaid wants to know where Admiral Lee's Force is at present, and Nimitz inquires: "THE WHOLE WORLD WANTS TO KNOW WHERE IS TASK FORCE 34." When Nimitz's message is clarified, it is determined that an encoder should have deleted the first five words as gingerbread, but he had neglected to do so. In any event, Halsey reacts angrily, thinking that Nimitz had sent him the nasty message intentionally. At 11:15, Halsey turns his Fleet 180 degrees and shoots south, instructing Admiral Mitscher with Task Force 38 (Sherman and Davison) to maintain the attack against the bleeding enemy Carriers. Halsey sends the following message to Kinkaid: "TG 38.2 PLUS 6 FAST BBS (Battleships) PROCEEDING LEYTE BUT UNABLE ARRIVE BEFORE 08:00 TOMORROW."

With Halsey and his Battleships heading south and the Carriers under Mitscher moving north to tear out the remaining heart of Ozawa's floating firedragons, the Japs are in for a hot time. Mitscher's Planes strike again, inflicting more devastation, followed by the third wave arriving upon the scene. The one-sided seabattle inflicts enormous pain on the enemy. As they attempt to retire, more damage is sustained; their battered Fleet is pounded without mercy. To make matters worse for the Japs, U.S. Submarines wait in ambush. By the time the Yanks under Sherman and Davison (Mitscher's Task Force 38) and the Submarines finish their work, the Japanese lose four Carriers, one Light Cruiser, and two Destroyers. In addition, two Battleships, two Light Cruisers, and four Destroyers are damaged. In essence, the joint operations in Leyte Gulf have ravaged the Japanese Imperial Navy beyond recovery.

Mitscher's Eagles had sunk the *Zuikaku*, *Chiyoda*, and *Chitose Zuiho*, and most of the others are in rapid retreat. Several enemy Warships remain in the area to pick up survivors; however, hesitation gives the U.S. Submarines, strung between Japan and the Philippines, advantage; six of them rush from Saipan to participate in the donnybrook upon receiving word that Mitscher is in contact with Ozawa's Carriers. The *Halibut* is the first of the Silent Service to hit paydirt, demolishing a Vessel thought to be a Battleship. The encounter occurs as the sun is setting and identification is impossible, but the successive explosions are indisputable. When the *Halibut* comes up for air several minutes later, the enemy Warship is bottom up and going down, its exact name remains anonymous; the *Halibut* also receives credit for sinking the Destroyer *Akitsuki*. Other Submarines encounter a group of five Warships, but there is no engagement as the enemy outdistances the striking range of the Subs. Later, and further north, the Submarine *Jallao* sinks the Light Cruiser *Tama* (previously damaged by U.S. Planes).

While Mitscher is dismembering Ozawa's Force, Halsey continues racing to assist Sprague, reaching the battle area around midnight. Kurita's Center Force had retreated earlier in the day and made a dash up the San Bernardino Strait at about 22:00. One of Halsey's Destroyers is right on their tail and picks up one of the trailing Vessels slightly after midnight. The big guns of U.S. Cruisers open up against the enemy Ship, and subsequently a U.S. Destroyer plows torpedoes into it. Explosions occur, and then the big bang ignites the magazines. Admiral Halsey, 15 miles away on the *New Jersey*, is watching the battle from the bridge and notes that he "felt the explosion distinctly." The Yanks continue pursuit and at daybreak, the battle resumes.

The surviving Japanese Warships (Kurita's Central Force) are greeted at dawn on the 26th by Planes attached to Bogan and McCain's Groups. Their westward flight is hazardous. Meanwhile other American Ships are plucking American Airmen from the waters off eastern Samar. The operation spots no enemy Vessels, but there is an abundance of enemy troops swimming around, prompting an American Officer to run up to Halsey and exclaim: "MY GOD ALMIGHTY, ADMIRAL, THE LITTLE BASTARDS ARE ALL OVER THE PLACE! ARE WE GOING TO STOP AND PICK THEM UP?" Halsey responds: "NOT UNTIL WE'VE PICKED UP OUR OWN BOYS." Halsey proceeds to extricate the American survivors yet keeps the Japs' positions in mind and subsequently orders his Destroyers: "BRING IN THE COOPERATIVE JAP FLOTSAM FOR AN INTELLIGENCE SAMPLE. NONCOOPERATORS WOULD PROBABLY LIKE TO JOIN THEIR ANCESTORS AND SHOULD BE ACCOMMODATED. (Admiral Halsey states he didn't want to risk their getting ashore, where they could reinforce the Garrison);" the Destroyrmen bring in six enemy troops.

Meanwhile, Bogan and McCain ignore the inclement weather, continuing pursuit of Kurita's remnant Navy. The enemy Battlewagons race to avoid destruction, but Yank Planes reinitiate contact on the 26th, and the water begins boiling when the Aircraft resume their menacing attack. By day's end, reports arrive at Halsey's Command Station aboard the U.S.S. *New Jersey* stating that a Battleship is burning dead in the water off Mindoro; two other Battleships are damaged by a combination of bombs and rockets. A Light Cruiser is also reported struck, in addition to a Destroyer with its bow severed. The Yanks have also stopped a Heavy Cruiser, leaving it burning in the Tablas Strait, and have sunk a Seaplane Tender in the Guimaras Strait. Admirals Bogan and McCain state a loss of 11 Planes due primarily to AA fire, while knocking out 40 enemy Planes, thus culminating the three day battle for Leyte Gulf with a magnificent victory for the U.S. Navy, in fact much bigger than realized at first.

Admiral Halsey had dispatched a message to Admiral Nimitz on the 25th: "THE JAPANESE NAVY HAS BEEN BEATEN AND ROUTED AND BROKEN BY THE THIRD AND SEVENTH FLEETS." The message is received in Washington with a degree of cynicism. Admiral King informs Admiral Nimitz that there is no information to substantiate Halsey's claim, but by the 29th there is great joy in the Capital and in the Pacific as Admiral Halsey and Kinkaid are both told by Admiral King: "A LARGE PART OF THE ENEMY NAVY HAS BEEN EFFECTUALLY DISPOSED OF FOREVER AND THE REMAINDER FOR SOME TIME TO COME X ALL OFFICERS AND MEN OF YOUR FLEETS HAVE THE HEARTIEST ADMIRATION OF ALL HANDS X WELL DONE." Other congratulatory messages pour into Halsey and Kinkaid. From MacArthur: "WE HAVE COOPERATED WITH YOU SO LONG THAT WE EXPECT YOUR BRILLIANT SUCCESSES X EVERYONE HERE HAS A FEELING OF COMPLETE CONFIDENCE AND INSPIRATION WHEN YOU GO INTO ACTION IN OUR SUPPORT"; from General Marshall:

"A SPLENDID AND HISTORIC VICTORY X THE ARMY OWES YOU A DEBT OF THANKS." The three-ring Sea Circus had pummeled the enemy, costing them 26 Vessels sunk and 25 damaged as opposed to the Americans' loss of six Warships sunk and 11 damaged, enunciating another U.S. victory at sea. Admiral Halsey, in retrospect, has some important words of his own to add to the legendary battle. Halsey notes that although the dispatches from Kinkaid had "puzzled him," subsequent information had "filled in the gaps." Halsey further states: "I NOT ONLY APPRECIATE HIS PROBLEMS, BUT FRANKLY ADMIT THAT HAD I BEEN IN HIS SHOES, I MIGHT HAVE ACTED PRECISELY AS DID HE." Admiral Halsey agrees that the joint command could have caused disaster and attributes the conquest to: "WHAT BROUGHT US VICTORY INSTEAD WAS SIMPLY THIS: ALL HANDS THOUGHT ALIKE. AND THAT WE DID SO IS A TRIBUTE TO OUR INDOCTRINATION IN THE UNITED STATES NAVY."

Another battle had been won and more are approaching, but the Imperial Navy is no longer a serious factor. Now the U.S. Fleet will face the "divine winds" and the Kamikaze Pilots as they plot further victory alongside MacArthur during the advance toward Tokyo. The Third and Seventh Fleets are exhausted, but not susceptible to retiring. They stand at the ready having convincingly whipped the presumptuous Japanese Admiral Toyoda, cremating his grand scheme, concluding the struggle for control of Leyte Gulf and vanquishing the enemy in the trilogy of horror. The U.S. Navy stands alone off the Philippines with Old Glory beaming, her glorious Stars and Stripes gleaming in honor of her gallant sons who refuse to relent until they run her up over Tokyo. The dauntless Fleets continue the attack, while simultaneously working tirelessly to rest the weary Pilots and crewmen and bring more manpower and equipment to the scene. In turn, the enemy intensify their Kamikaze attacks, giving the Americans another perspective on warfare, Japanese style. This victory is considered to be the final nail in the coffin of the Emperor's Navy. It was Halsey's Carriers which rushed to the premature funeral of the U.S. Navy at Pearl Harbor, and it is fitting that Halsey and many of the men and Vessels thought destroyed on that fateful day at Pearl are here to observe the humbled Imperial Navy scatter haphazardly to avoid meeting their ancestors.

October 25th-26th 1944 — NAVAL LOSSES BATTLE OF LEYTE — U.S. Vessels sunk: Escort Carrier *St. Lo* (CVE-63), Naval gunfire; Escort Carrier *Gambier Bay* (CVE-73), Naval gunfire; Destroyers *Hoel* (DD-533) and *Johnston* (DD-557) and the Destroyer Escort *Samuel B. Roberts*, Naval gunfire; PT-493, enemy coastal defense guns. U.S. Vessels damaged: Escort Carriers *Kalinin Bay* (CVE-68), *Kitkun Bay* (CVE-71), *Sangamon* (CVE-26), and the *Suwannee* (CVE-27), Suicide Planes; *Santee* (CVE-29), Suicide Plane and enemy submarine torpedo; and *White Plains* (CVE-66), Suicide Planes and Naval gunfire; the *Fanshaw* (CVE-70) sustains its damage by Naval gunfire; the Destroyer *Heermann* (DD-523) by Naval gunfire, the Destroyer Escorts *Richard M. Rowell* and *Dennis* by strafing and Naval Gunfire respectively. Also, the PT-132 is sunk by a Dive Bomber. JAPANESE LOSSES: Carrier *Zuikaku*, Carrier Aircraft; Light Carriers *Chioda* and *Zuibo*, Carrier Aircraft; Light Carrier *Chitose*, Carrier Aircraft and Naval gunfire; Battleships *Fuso* and *Yamashiro*, Naval Surface Vessels; Heavy Cruisers *Chikuma*, *Chokai*, and *Suzuya*, Carrier Aircraft; Heavy Cruiser *Mogami*, Carrier Planes and Surface Vessels; Light Cruiser *Tama*, Carrier Planes and Submarine *Jallao* (SS-368); Destroyers *Asagumo*, *Hatsuzuki*, *Mihishio*, and

Yamagumo, Surface Vessels; and the Destroyer *Aizuki* by the Submarine *Halibut* (SS-232). BATTLE LOSSES ON THE 26TH: U.S. Vessels sunk: Escort Carrier *Suwannee* (CVE-27) (damaged previous day by Kamikaze), by Dive Bomber and Suicide Plane; PT-132 by Dive Bomber. JAPANESE VESSELS SUNK: Light Cruiser *Abukuma*, Surface Craft; Light Cruisers *Kinu* and *Noshiro*, Carrier Planes; Destroyers *Hayashimo* and *Uranami*, Carrier Planes: and the Destroyer *Nowaki* by Naval Surface Ships.

October 25th 1944 — (United States) Secretary of the Navy, Forrestal holds a press conference in Washington; Admiral King is in attendance. One of the newer Naval Officers is speaking and mentions that the Japanese Northern Decoy Fleet includes two old Battleships, the *Ise* and the *Hyuga*; King interrupts the dissertation, explaining that the man is new and unfamiliar with the enemy Fleet; King then states that the two Vessels are Carriers, but the Officer, William Smedberg, fends off the Admiral and restates that they are Battleships to the displeasure of Admiral King. Subsequently, King informs his subordinate that if he ever tries to contradict him again he better make absolutely sure he is right; on this occasion, he was. The Warships in question are Battleships and the Planes which take off from them can not return for a landing. **(United States-England)** The U.S. and Great Britain both reinitiate diplomatic relations with Italy. **(Pacific-Palaus)** The 323rd Infantry, 81st Division, which had arrived from Ulithi, begins to relieve the 321st Infantry on Peleliu. **(Pacific-Marianas-Tinian)** The 1st Battalion, 8th Marines takes responsibility for mop-up operations. Other contingents of the 8th Marines depart for Saipan. **(Pacific-Philippines)** On LEYTE, in the **U.S. Sixth Army** area, **X Corps** sector, Babatngon Harbor is attacked by Japanese Aircraft. In other activity, the 1st Cavalry Division dispatches its 1st Squadron to probe the area around Carigara Bay to determine enemy strength, but during the following several days, it encounters only nominal Japanese presence. The 8th Cavalry strengthens its positions at Juanico Strait; its 2nd Squadron is ordered to halt its advance toward Santa Cruz and stand in place near the Diit River until its supply problems can be resolved. In the vicinity of Palo, the 24th Division is also active. The 3rd Battalion, 34th Infantry secures Hill C, while Hill B is seized by the 2nd Battalion, 19th Infantry; the 1st Battalion, 19th Infantry captures Hill 85. The 24th Division gains secure access into the north Leyte Valley. The 3rd Battalion, 19th Infantry advances to Castilla, moving toward Pastrana. The X and XXIV Corps make contact in the early afternoon when Company K, 19th Infantry encounters a contingent of the 383rd Infantry, 96th Division at Tanauan. In the **XXIV Corps** area, the Japanese repulse an attack by Company K, 19th Infantry (reinforced) at Tabontabon; the 24th Division (X Corps) withdraws due to untenable positions. Aslom and Kanmonhag are both seized by the 382nd Infantry, 96th Division. In other activity, another assault supplemented by Tanks is mounted by the 2nd and 3rd Battalions, 32nd Infantry, 7th Division, objective Buri Airstrip. The Japanese offer heavy and determined resistance that prevents the 2nd Battalion from advancing to the Airstrip, but the 3rd Battalion drives to the fringes of the field. In other activity, the 17th Infantry, 32nd Division maintains its attack against Dagami. In Naval activity, the U.S.S. *Nautilus* (SS-168) lands men and delivers supplies on the east coast of Luzon. Planes from the *Independence* commence new night attacks against Luzon, repeating the effort on the 29th, 30th and 31st. **(Pacific-Burma)** The NCAC offensive continues. The British 29th Brigade, 36th Division has advanced nearly 25 miles against slight opposition, but it encounters brisk opposition at Mawpin. **(Atlantic-Western Europe) 21st Army Group** In the **Canadian First Army** area, 2nd Corps sector, the Canadian 2nd Division advances west along the Beveland Isthmus, making slow progress and reaching Rilland. In the British 1st Corps area, the U.S. 104th Division is pushing north with three Regiments toward Zundert, Holland, along the Antwerp-Breda Road just within the border of Holland. **12th Army Group** In the **U.S. First Army** area, the boundary separating the V and VII Corps is modified to give the V Corps responsibility for Schmidt. In other activity, the 9th Division, minus the 47th Infantry deployed at Schevenhuette, comes under the jurisdiction of the V Corps. The 28th Division initiates its relief of the exhausted 9th Division and will carry the attack against Schmidt. **6th Army Group** In the **U.S. Seventh Army XV Corps** area, elements of the German 19th Army mount a series of heavy attacks against the U.S. 44th Division lines, east of the Foret de Parroy, but each is repulsed. A contingent of the 141st Infantry, 36th Division becomes isolated near La Houssiere; the 36th unsuccessfully mounts a rescue, and another attempt extricates the troops on the following day. Also, German Infantry, supported by a Mark IV Tank, converge on a Battalion Command Post near Bruyeres. One lone Tank Destroyer intercepts the attack, but it is struck twice; Staff Sergeant Clyde L. Choate (601st Tank Destroyer Battalion) orders his crew to abandon it, but he returns to search for possible trapped men. Meanwhile, the enemy Tank and supporting Infantry are overrunning U.S. positions, prompting him to take a Bazooka and charge. He destroys the turret and kills two crewmen as they emerge from the demolished Tank, then he boards it and flushes a grenade down to finish it off. His extraordinary action turns back the assault and saves the position; he receives the Medal of Honor for his bravery. **(Atlantic-Italy)** In the **U.S. Fifth Army** area, contingents of the 6th South African Division ford Setta Creek and seize Hill 501. In the **II Corps** area, there is a determined effort to strengthen and enlarge the defenses at the M. Grande salient, but the night-long operation is costly and futile, prompting the U.S. to attach the 362nd Infantry, 91st Division to the 88th Division to bolster the next attempt. In the British 13th Corps area, contingents of the 61st Brigade, 6th Armored Division reach M. Taverna, but supplies are inadequate, forcing a pull-back. In the **British Eighth Army** area, the 5 Corps advances to the Ronco River. Elements of the British 4th Division seize Forlimpopoli without opposition. In other activity, the British attack across the Ronco during the night 25th-26th, using the newly established bridgeheads of the Indian 10th Division as a springboard. In the Canadian 1st Corps sector, the enemy is hotly pursued toward the Ronco. In other activity, Major General Edward H. Brooks assumes command of the VI Corps area, replacing General Lucian Truscott Jr. Truscott succeeds General Clark as Commander of the U.S. Fifth Army in Italy (December 16th). **(Atlantic-Norway)** The Karelian Front (Russians) pushes from Finland, entering Norway to seize Kirkenes on the Barents Sea.

October 26th 1944 — (Pacific-Palaus-Peleliu) The mission to reduce the Umurbrogol Pocket, now comprising an area approximately 600 yards from north to south and 350 to 475 yards from east to west, is assumed by RCT 323. Terrible weather conditions impede the operation, prompting the Combat Team to bolster its defenses. The Japanese have resigned themselves to a fight to the death and retain some positions in well-entrenched caves within the perimeter. The

321st Infantry, which had relieved the Marine contingents of the 1st Marine Division, has sustained 146 men killed and 469 wounded since initiating the operation to reduce the pocket. **(Pacific-Philippines-Leyte)** In the **U.S. Sixth Army X Corps** sector, the U.S. 24th Division begins its advance through the Leyte Valley. The 2nd Battalion, 34th Infantry pushes down highway 2, reaching Santa Fe. The 3rd Battalion, 19th Infantry drives to the fringes of Pastrana where it encounters a formidable fortress that guards entrance to the town. In the **XXIV Corps** area, the 382nd Infantry, 96th Division drives toward Tabontabon to capture the Japanese supply depot located there, but fierce enemy resistance originating from within the barrio forces it to withdraw to the Guinarona River. The 96th Division's Artillery contingents commence an artillery barrage against the barrio; it lasts throughout the night of the 26th-27th. Company E, 383rd Infantry probes in strength against San Vicente Hill and on the northern tip of Catmon Hill, but enemy resistance forces a withdrawal. The Japanese subsequently evacuate most of their troops from Catmon Hill. The 3rd Battalion, 381st Infantry commences its northward penetration, driving along Highway 1 toward Tanauan to seize the northern flank of the beachhead along the Tanauan-Dagami Road. In other activity, the fiercely contested struggle at Buri Airfield continues to rage. The 32nd Infantry, 7th Division gets its 1st and 2nd Battalions through the defenses; positions are established along the fringes of the Airfield. Elements of the 17th Infantry, 7th Division drive toward Dagami, advancing to the vicinity of Guinarona. Meanwhile, the Japanese land approximately 2,000 reinforcements at Ormoc. **(Pacific-South China Sea)** A single B-24, piloted by Major Horace S. Carswell Jr., 308th Bombardment Group, attacks an enemy Convoy comprising twelve Ships escorted by several Destroyers. The attack damages a Tanker; enemy flak during his second pass inflicts severe damage and wounds the Co-pilot. It is determined that one man's parachute is inoperable, prompting Carswell to remain with the man and order the balance of the crew to bail out while he attempts to reach a friendly Base. Suddenly, a third engine fails, and the Plane crashes into a mountain during an attempted crash landing. Carswell, who had saved the remainder of the crew, receives the Medal of Honor posthumously for his heroism. **(Pacific-Burma)** In the N.C.A.C. area, the Chinese 22nd Division completes its rugged trek over the hills, reaching the abandoned Airstrip previously held by the Chindits. The weary Division remains at the Airstrip known as Broadway for a few days to recuperate before pushing toward Shwegu. **(Atlantic-Western Europe) 21st Army Group** In the **Canadian First Army's** 2nd Corps sector, an amphibious assault is launched by elements of the British 52nd Division which embark Terneuzen and strike Beveland, storming ashore on the southern coast near Baarland to establish a beachhead. In other activity, the Canadian 2nd Division continues driving through the Beveland Isthmus, and the 3rd Canadian Division is engaged at the Breskens Pocket. In the British 1st Corps sector, the U.S. 104th Division deploys for an imminent assault against Zundert, Holland. In the **British Second Army** area, 12th Corps sector, Hertogenbosch is seized by the British 53rd Division. **12th Army Group** In the **U.S. Ninth Army** area, the U.S. 104th Division receives its baptism under fire, entering its first combat mission. The 405th Infantry is attached to the 2nd Armored Division, the 406th and 407th are attached to the 30th and 29th Divisions respectively. In the **U.S. First Army's V Corps** area, there is much activity with troop redeployment, including the 28th Division assuming responsibility for the area previously protected by elements

of the 9th Division and the transfer of the 5th Armored Division to the rear of the 4th Division. In the **U.S. Third Army** area, heavy fighting ensues in the **XX Corps** sector near the Hotel de Ville in Maizieres-les-Metz, which is held staunchly by the Germans. Company K, 357th Infantry, 90th Division drives to the hotel, but heavy enemy fire forces them to withdraw. **6th Army Group** In the **U.S. Seventh Army** area, heavy skirmishing develops in the VI Corps sector as the 3rd Division continues to plow ahead, despite intense enemy Artillery fire. The town of Les Rouges Eaux is seized by the 7th Infantry. The 45th Division, driving on the left flank of the Corps toward Raon-l'Etape, clears the Foret d'Housseras as it advances. Activity is just as brisk on the right flank; the 36th Division extricates its isolated 141st Infantry. The 141st then attacks west. **(Atlantic-Hungary)** The 1st German Armored and the First Hungarian First Army withdraw from the vicinity of Mukacevo. The Second and Fourth Ukrainian Fronts (Russian) converge upon Mukacevo and join forces. **(Atlantic-Italy)** In the **U.S. Fifth Army** area, the 6th South African Division breaks off the attempt to seize M. Sole and in so doing, the contingents operating on Hill 501 become isolated. In the **II Corps** area, the 362nd Infantry (91st Division attached to 88th Division) is prevented from fording the Sillaro River because of flash flooding caused by the unruly weather pattern that is blanketing the entire front, nearly paralyzing the U.S. efforts. The 85th and 88th Divisions are ordered to disengage their offensive and redeploy defensively in a more secure area. In the British 13th Corps area, the 17th Brigade, Indian 8th Division pushes elements to Lutirano and Tredozio. In other activity, the Germans mount an unsuccessful drive to dislodge the 61st Brigade, British 6th Armored Division from Orsara. British Armor mounts an unsuccessful attack against M. Taverna, then concentrates its efforts on Patrolling. In the **British Eighth Army** area, Polish 2nd Corps zone, the 5th Kresowa Division, subsequent to the successful capture of M. Mirabello-M. Colombo Ridge, dispatches contingents to seize Predappio Nuovo on the Rabbi River; heavy enemy resistance forces a withdrawal. In the 5th Corps area, the Indian 10th Division continues to bolster the Ronco River bridgeheads. In other activity, the British 4th Division is pitted against heavy opposition, unable to sustain the attack without Armor; the troops take severe casualties as they attempt to draw back from the southern bank of the swollen river which is flowing uncontrollably, immobilizing the British attack. In the Canadian 1st Corps sector, the situation is similar as the unmanageable river currents stymie activity.

October 27th 1944 — (Pacific-Philippines-Leyte) The U.S. Navy Carriers relinquish control of the air to the Army Air Force; the first P-38s reach Leyte. Control is handled from Tacloban Airfield. In the **U.S. Sixth Army, X Corps** sector, the 1st Battalion, 34th Infantry, 24th Division moves through its 2nd Battalion's positions, reaching the Mudburon River without incident. In other X Corps activity, Artillery bombards Pastrana throughout the night into the following morning, giving the 3rd Battalion, 19th Infantry easy access on the morning of the 28th; it combines with the 1st Battalion to mop up the remnant defenders. In the **XXIV Corps** area, Tabontabon is assaulted again by the 382nd Infantry, 96th Division; its 1st and 3rd Battalions penetrate the northwestern portion of the town, driving almost a mile outside and to the northwest. The 2nd Battalion encounters stiff resistance, hindering progress and forcing it to hold defensively in the middle of the town throughout the night; the attack resumes in the morning and advances toward Kiling. In Naval activity, the Carrier forces of Admirals Sherman and Davison launch Aircraft which strike the Japanese positions in the Visayans and in the northern Luzon area. The Japanese Destroyers *Fujinami* and *Shiranui* are both sunk. In addition, the Battleship U.S.S. *California* (BB-44) is damaged by a Japanese strafing attack; the Submarine Chaser PCER-848 is damaged by a Horizontal Bomber, and the PT-523 sustains damage by a Japanese Dive Bomber. Also, the U.S.S. *Nautilus* (SS-168) makes another trip to the eastern coast of Luzon and debarks more men and equipment. **(Pacific-Volcano Islands)** The U.S.S. *Kingfish* (SS-234) sinks the Japanese Transport No. 138 off the Volcano Islands. **(Pacific-China)** The U.S. Air Bases become jeopardized as the rejuvenated Japanese reinitiate their offensive to seize the Airfields in eastern China. Several enemy Divisions are driving toward Kweilin and Liuchow. **(Pacific-Burma)** In the N.C.A.C. area, the U.S. 124th Cavalry arrives to bolster the Allied forces. **(Atlantic-Western Europe) 21st Army Group** In the **Canadian First Army** area, II Corps sector, advance contingents of the Canadian 2nd Division push to the western tip of the Beveland Isthmus in the vicinity of the Beveland Canal. The elements ford the canal during the night of the 27th-28th. In other activity, the British 52nd Division enlarges its Baarland bridgehead, extending it to Oudelande. In the British 1st Corps sector, the Canadian 4th Armored Division seizes Bergen-op-Zoom. In other activity, there is a fiercely contested battle to secure Zundert, Holland. The U.S. 413th Infantry, 104th Division, British Tank units and Artillery contingents seize the town. In the **British Second Army** 8th Corps sector, German artillery bombards Allied positions then launch a synchronized Infantry-Tank assault toward Asten engaging the thinly defended lines of the U.S. 7th Armored Division which is deployed along the Canals de Deurne and du Nord. The enemy advance seizes Meijel and breaks through the American lines at Heitrak, along the Meijel-Deurne Highway; they also make progress near Nederweert, but an intense effort by CCA, 7th Armored repulses the attack, buying time. The British 11th Armored Division rushes in and relieves C.C.B., 7th Armored, allowing it to prepare for a counterattack. **12th Army Group** In the **U.S. Third Army** area, **XX Corps** sector, the 357th Infantry, 90th Division, continues its futile assault to capture the Hotel de Ville in Maizieres-les — Metz. **6th Army Group** In the **U.S. Seventh Army** area, **VI Corps** sector, the U.S. 3rd Division drives punishingly toward St. Die. In other activity, the 141st Infantry, 36th Division fails to break out; the attempt exhausts the unit. Attempts are made to drop supplies and ammunition by air, but they also fail. Subsequent attempts alleviate the problem until the Nisei troops rescue the beleaguered Battalion on the 30th when the Japanese American Regiment breaks the entrapment. The 141st Regiment has been embattled at Belmont sur Buttant near Hill 623 since the 24th. Tech Sergeant Charles H. Coolidge, leading a contingent of Company K, has thrown the enemy back repeatedly. Today, the Germans, supported by Tanks, begin to overwhelm the small U.S. contingent. Coolidge advances singlehandedly with a Bazooka and grenades to meet the newest threat, scoring much damage with his grenades; however, the superior force compels the Yanks to withdraw. Coolidge's leadership under fire had restrained the enemy for four days; he receives the Medal of Honor. In the **French 1st Army** area, French General de Lattre meets with General Devers and suggests a plan for an assault against Belfort; Devers is impressed with the idea and concurs. The French commence their attack on the 13th of November in concert with the general Allied Offensive.

(Atlantic-Hungary) Ungvar (Uzhorod) on the northern border is taken by contingents of the Fourth Ukrainian Front, concluding the Russian seizure of the Carpatho-Ukraine, which had been Ruthenia prior to March 1939. **(Atlantic-Italy)** In the **U.S. Fifth Army** area, British 13th Corps sector, the 26th Armored Brigade Group moves into Rocca S. Casciano subsequent to German abandonment of the positions. In the **British Eighth Army** area, Polish 2nd Corps sector, the town of Predappio Nuovo is retaken by contingents of the 5th Kresowa Division. In the 5th Corps area, additional contingents of the 10th Indian Division ford the Ronco River under cover of darkness during the night of the 27th-28th. In other activity, the attempt to relieve the Canadian 1st Division and the Canadian 5th Armored Division is canceled due to bad weather; forward contingents that are across the Bevano River are pulled back.

October 28th 1944 — (Pacific-Philippines-Leyte) In the **U.S. Sixth Army** area, **X Corps** sector, the 1st Battalion, 34th Infantry, 24th Division advances to the Mainit River, attacks Japanese defenders at the steel bridge, and secures the area. In other activity, the 2nd Cavalry Brigade is dispatched to Carigara where heavy fighting breaks out. Troop C, 7th Cavalry is transported by sea from Babatngon to Barugo; it then moves overland to Carigara. During the later part of the afternoon, the Yanks move back to Barugo. In the **XXIV Corps** sector, the 2nd Battalion, 382nd Infantry, 96th Division completes the seizure of Tabontabon, then drives to Kiling. At 12:00, the 381st Infantry attacks the eastern slopes of Catmon Hill, meeting intense fire. In other activity, the 17th Infantry, 7th Division drives toward Dagami, encountering heavy resistance as it advances. The 2nd Battalion, spearheading the drive, sustains severe casualties. P.F.C. Leonard C. Brostrom, Company F, and P.F.C. John F. Thorson, Company G, both receive the Medal of Honor posthumously for their heroism. Brostrom singlehandedly attacks a pillbox under a storm of fire; he tosses a grenade into the obstacle; however, six enemy troops bolt from a nearby trench and attack with their bayonets. He kills one man and drives the others off, but is mortally wounded. Thorson blankets a grenade with his body to save his nearby companions. **(Pacific-Burma)** In the N.C.A.C. area, the 113th Regiment, Chinese 38th Division moves toward the Mainit River and drives enemy Patrols away, permitting the Chinese to reach Myothit. **(Atlantic-Western Europe)** General Eisenhower readies the November Offensive, issuing the directive which orders the establishment of bridges across the Rhine River, followed by the thrust into Germany, while simultaneously destroying all enemy forces operating west of the Rhine. **21st Army Group** In the **British First Army** area, British 1st Corps sector, the U.S. 104th Division seizes Rijsbergen, then drives toward Roosendaal-Breda Highway. In the **British Second Army** area, 12th Corps sector, the British 15th Division seizes Tilburg. In the 8th Corps area, the U.S. 7th Armored Division attacks to retake Meijel, which had fallen to the Germans on the previous day; the enemy mounts heavy resistance, keeping the two-pronged drive to minimum progress. **12th Army Group** In the **U.S. Third Army's XX Corps** sector, elements of the 90th Division concentrate on eliminating the strongpoint at the Hotel-de-Ville in the center of Maizieres-les-Metz. Other contingents converge on the factory area to spring an attack, while yet another contingent mounts a diversionary strike north of the hotel. The 761st Tank Battalion (colored), commanded by Lt. Colonel P. T. Bates, arrives at Third Army, the first such Battalion (colored) to report. **6th Army Group** Orders are issued to seize Strasbourg and for the complete elimination of the enemy forces west of the Rhine. In the **U.S. Seventh Army** area, **XV Corps** sector, the Germans begin a partial withdrawal along the line, pulling back to the Leintrey-Blemerey Line. In the 3rd Division zone, the Germans pour fire upon a Company of the 30th Regiment as it moves through the Mortagne Forest near St. Die. Staff Sergeant Lucian Adams flings a BAR as he charges singlehandedly, killing nine enemy troops, capturing several more, and destroying three enemy machine guns, enabling his unit to reopen a supply route. Adams receives the Medal of Honor for his extraordinary bravery. **(Atlantic-Italy)** In the **U.S. Fifth Army** area, **IV Corps** sector, RCT 6 (BEF) outflanks Gallicano in the Serchio Valley. The II Corps has been sustaining heavy casualties for the past six weeks due to strenuous conditions and lack of reinforcements. Orders come through directing the Corps to establish a defensive perimeter and abort the attack. In the **British Eighth Army** 5th Corps area, the Indian 10th Division gets additional units across the Ronco River during the night 28th-29th; it commences an assault which springs from the Meldola area. In other activity, the Canadian 1st Corps is placed into reserve; the 12th Lancers (5th Corps) assumes responsibility for the left flank. The Porter Force (Eighth Army command) receives responsibility for the coastal sector, relieving the Canadian 5th Armored Division. **(Atlantic-Bulgaria)** The Allies sign an armistice with Bulgaria with the stipulation that Bulgaria agrees to relinquish those portions of Greece and Yugoslavia taken in 1941. Also, Bulgaria must agree to pay reparations (sum not yet determined) and agree to place their Armed Forces under the command of the Soviet High Command. **(Atlantic-Yugoslavia)** Partisan units capture Split, the capital of Dalmatia and Adriatic port.

October 29th 1944 — **(Pacific-Philippines-Leyte)** General MacArthur determines that the 77th Infantry is unneeded to complete the operations on Leyte and transfers it from the jurisdiction of General Krueger to Admiral Nimitz's command. In the **U.S. Sixth Army X Corps** sector, the 24th Division advances toward Jaro, spearheaded by the 3rd Battalion, which overruns the opposition and enters the town at 17:00. The 19th Infantry supports the southern flank of the Division; Company K establishes a roadblock at Ypad. In other activity, Troop C, 2nd Cavalry, 1st Cavalry Division, deployed at Barugo, is bolstered by additional elements of the 2nd Cavalry Brigade. In the **XXIV Corps** area, Catmon and Labir Hills are seized effortlessly by the 2nd Battalion, 381st Infantry, 96th Division. It is joined later by the 1st Battalion, which is subsequently relieved at Labiranan Head, reverting to Sixth Army reserve. At Dagami, the 1st and 3rd Battalions, 17th Infantry, 7th Division penetrate the southern defenses and enter the town. The weakened 2nd Battalion is placed in reserve. In other activity, elements of the 32nd Infantry, 7th Division, advance toward Abuyog, following the steps of the 7th Cavalry Reconnaissance Troop which is sprinting along Highway 1 near the coast toward Baybay. In Naval activity, Rear Admiral Bogan's Carrier Task Force strikes enemy Shipping at Manila and at the nearby Airfields. The U.S.S. *Intrepid* (CVE-11) is damaged by a Kamikaze Plane; the Vessel sustains slight damage, but six men are killed. In other activity, the Navy establishes a Naval Operating Base and a Naval Air Station at Leyte and Samar respectively. **(Pacific-India-Burma)** On the Salween Front, General Wei Li-huang's Chinese Expeditionary Force reinitiates its offensive against Lung-ling, spearheading the operation with its 200th Division. The offensive receives close Air support from the U.S. Fourteenth Air Force. In the NCAC area, the British 36th Division reinitiates its drive

through the RR corridor, after having recuperated at Mawpin. **(Pacific-Western Europe)** In the **Canadian First Army** area, the 2nd Corps is heavily involved with securing south Beveland and eliminating the Breskens Pocket. Goes falls to the 52nd Division, which makes contact with the Canadian 2nd Division on south Beveland. The Polish 1st Armored Division seizes Breda. In the **British Second Army** 8th Corps area, the Germans mount a fierce attack, driving from Meijel toward Asten and Liesel. The clash pushes Combat Command R units about half way back toward Asten and also shoves Combat Command B, 7th Armored out of Liesel. Reinforcements (15th Division and a Tank Brigade) are rushed in during the night to strengthen the Corps' positions and relieve the 7th Armored. **12th Army Group** In the **U.S. Third Army's XX Corps** area, the operation to eliminate the hotel fortress at Maizieres-les-Metz continues; elements of the 357th Infantry, 90th Division drive from the factory sector, reaching positions south of the objective. Meanwhile, two additional Companies strike from the north, and by nightfall, five Companies control the majority of the town. Colonel G. B. Barth, Regimental Commander, is wounded severely, but he recovers. **6th Army Group** In the **U.S. Seventh Army** area, **VI Corps** sector, Bru and Jeanmenil, both staunchly defended by the Germans for about a month, are abandoned, permitting the U.S. 45th Division to occupy them without a fight. In addition, to the right of this activity, the attack against Raon-l'Etape continues. At St. Die, the 3rd Division strengthens its positions, and in the 36th Division sector, the operation to extricate the isolated 141st Infantry from entrapment in the Foret Domaniale de Champ also continues. **(Atlantic-Italy)** In the **U.S. Fifth Army** area, the Indian 10th Division closes against the German Garrison at Meldola; the two-pronged attack strikes from the bridgeheads and from south of the town.

October 30th 1944 — **(Pacific-Palaus)** The 5th Marines reinforced, the final Marine contingent on the island, departs Peleliu. **(Pacific-Philippines)** General Kenney, Commander U.S. Far East Air Force (Fifth and Thirteenth Air Forces), receives orders from AAF SWPA to support the Mindoro Operation, committing the Fifth Air Force as the "Assault Air Force." The Thirteenth Air Force (Carrier Based Royal Australian Air Force) assigned to the U.S. Third and Seventh Fleets, Land-based Aircraft of the Seventh Fleet and B-29s of the U.S. Twentieth Air Force also support the operation. On LEYTE, in the **U.S. Sixth Army** area, **X Corps** sector, the 3rd Battalion, 34th Infantry, 24th Division, moves from Jaro toward Carigara, but Japanese resistance is fierce and progress is immediately stopped. The 1st and 2nd Battalions offer support to the 3rd Battalion when it reinitiates the attack, but the enemy again repels it. At Rizal, a skirmish develops between Company C, 19th Infantry, and the Japanese; Company K advances to Lopdak and meets elements of the XXIV Corps. In the **XXIV Corps** area, the 2nd and 3rd Battalions, 383rd Infantry, 96th Division, drive from Guinarona to San Vicente and discover the hill and barrio unoccupied by the enemy. At Dagami, the 17th Infantry, 7th Division completes the seizure and mops-up in the afternoon. During the day, the 17th completes its mission when contact is made with the X Corps elements north of the Binahaan River and with the 96th Division. The 7th Division receives instructions to transport contingents from Abuyog to Baybay, then awaits new orders to move to the west coast. In Naval activity, suicide Planes damage the Carriers *Franklin* (CV-13) and *Belleau Wood* (CVL-24); both Vessels retire for repairs; the combined losses include 158 men killed and 45 Planes destroyed. **(Atlantic-Western Europe)** **21st Army Group** In the **Canadian First Army** area,

2nd Corps sector, the Canadian 2nd Division terminates its drive through S Beveland, advancing to the eastern end of Walcheren causeway. In the sector covering the Breskens Pocket, the Canadian 3rd Division is still involved with reducing the remaining enemy resistance. In the British 1st Corps sector, the 415th Infantry, U.S. 104th Division, drives to the Mark River to secure the bridge at Standdaarbuiten, but the Germans demolish it. In the **British Second Army** area, The 7th Armored Division pushes west toward Oosterhout where it encounters the Polish 1st Armored Division. In the 8 Corps area, the Germans mount a large attack to push through the Peel Marshes, but are repulsed handily; it is the final attempt. **12th Army Group** In the **U.S. First Army** area, **V Corps** sector, the 28th Division continues attacking to secure the Vossenack-Schmidt line. In the **U.S. Third Army** area, **XX Corps** sector, the 357th Infantry, 90th Division secures Maizieres-les-Metz, gaining an access route to Metz from the north. **6th Army Group** In the **U.S. Seventh Army** area, **VI Corps** sector, St. Benoit, on the Rambervillers-Raon-l'Etape Road, is seized by contingents of the 45th Division. In the 3rd Division zone, the Germans pound the 350th Regiment near St. Jacques; Company G has lost 55 out of its 88 men attacking to dislodge an elite group of German mountain troops. Private Wilburn Ross, about ten yards in advance of his unit, holds off a strong counterattack; the enemy reaches within four yards of his light machine gun emplacement. Ross expends all his ammunition and is ordered to pull back. Eight remaining supporting Riflemen fix bayonets to make a last-ditch effort; however, desperately needed ammunition arrives. Ross opens fire as the enemy is about to devour the contingent, repulsing the attack. He is personally responsible for the killing or wounding of 58 of the attackers during the horrendous five-hour ordeal. He remains at his post for a total of thirty-six hours and is also responsible for saving the survivors of his Company from annihilation; he receives the Medal of Honor for his heroism. In the 36th Division zone, the isolated 1st Battalion, 141st Infantry is reached and rescued by the 442nd Infantry. **(Atlantic-Italy)** In the **U.S. Fifth Army** area, the South African 6th Armored Division withstands incessant German counterattacks in the vicinity of Palazzo for several days. In the **IV Corps** area, RCT 6 (Brazilians) captures Lama hill mass, north of Barga. In the **British Eighth Army** area, Polish 2nd Corps sector, the Germans abandon their positions in the vicinity of Caminata. In the 5th Corps area, the Indian 10th Division takes Meldola without incident, then drives toward the Rabbi River where it encounters fierce opposition. In other activity, the Germans repulse 5th Corps Patrols at the Ronco River along the northern flank, preventing any crossings.

October 31st 1944 — (Pacific-Japan) The U.S.S. *Gabilan* (SS-252) sinks the Japanese District Craft *Kaiyo* No. 6 near Shikoku. **(Pacific-Philippines-Leyte)** In the **U.S. Sixth Army** area, **X Corps** sector, the 3rd Battalion, 34th Infantry, 24th Division is clearing a hill near Jaro; the 2nd Battalion sprints toward Tunga, and the 19th Infantry deploys along the southern flank to ensure the enemy escape routes are capped. In the **XXIV Corps** area, mop-up operations continue throughout the Catmon hill area. **(Pacific-China)** General Wedemeyer replaces General Stilwell and assumes command of the U.S. Forces, China Theater. His major responsibility is to maintain the Air operations from China with consistent logistical support from India Burma Theater. **(Pacific-India-Burma)** **11th Army Group** In the **British Fourteenth Army** area, 4th Corps Headquarters transfers from India and establishes new quarters near Imphal. In the N.C.A.C. area (Burma), the British 36th Division overcomes heavy opposition and drives to Mawlu. **(Southeast Asia Command)** British Admiral Mountbatten, subsequent to his conference with Churchill in Cairo, tells the Combined Chiefs of Staff that Phases 1 and 2 of Operation CAPITAL are to be completed; Arakan and Akyab will be secured (Operations ROMULUS and TALON respectively) in order to release main body of the 15th Corps for duty for other operations; forward Base must be seized on the Kra Isthmus during March 1945; the capture of Rangoon must take place subsequent to the 1945 monsoon and the invasion of Malaya. **(Atlantic-Western Europe) 21st Army Group** In the Breskens Pocket, resistance is confined to small groups which have been compressed into the coastal area. In the British 1st Corps sector, the U.S. 104th Division crosses the Mark River near Standdaarbuiten, encountering heavy enemy resistance, which compels a withdrawal after dark to break its surrounded positions. German resistance is fierce throughout the area, forcing the Polish 1st Armored Division to pull back and hold firmly on the south bank near Zevenbergen. In the **British Second Army** area, the 12th Corps takes Raamsdonk. In the 8th Corps zone, U.S. Major General Robert W. Hasbrouck assumes command of the U.S. 7th Armored Division, relieving Major General Lindsay McD. Silvester. In other activity, Liesel is secured by the British 15th Division. **6th Army Group** In the **U.S. Seventh Army** area, elements of the French 2nd Armored spring a surprise attack, seizing Merviller, the northern portion of Baccarat, and Montigny. Additional units reduce Menarmont and Nossoncourt. **(Atlantic-Hungary)** Contingents of the Second Ukrainian Front cross the Tisza River and enter Kecskemet, encountering stiff resistance resulting in heavy street fighting. **(Atlantic-Italy)** In the **British Eighth Army** area, the Germans are abandoning their positions near the Rabbi River; the Indian 10th Division gives heated pursuit. In other activity, the British 4th Division establishes two bridgeheads across the Ronco, between Selbagnone and Highway 9.

October-November 1944 — (Atlantic-Germany) The O.S.S. infiltrates Germany; over 200 agents are dropped to fine tune espionage and sabotage operations; many of these agents implement use of special communications devices (dubbed Joan-Eleanor) which enable them to maintain contact with specially equipped Allied Aircraft as they pass over at altitudes of 30,000 feet; the J-E devices weigh four pounds. During November, 14 J-E teams drop near Berlin, Munich, Regensburg, Stuttgart and also some parachute into the low countries.

November 1st 1944 — (Pacific-Philippines-Leyte) In the **U.S. Sixth Army X Corps** area, the Japanese evacuate their positions at Tuba to avoid encirclement by the 34th Infantry, 24th Division; elements of the 34th advance to the edges of Sagkanan. An assault against Carigara is readied, but the Japanese pull out and take for the hills near Limon. In the **XXIV Corps** area, the 96th Division culminates mop-up operations in the Catmon Hill area. In other activity, the U.S.S. *Ray* (SS-271) debarks men and supplies on the west coast of Mindoro. The Japanese land reinforcements at Oroc, Leyte. In other activity, Japanese Planes attack the U.S. Naval Force off Leyte; the Destroyer *Abner Read* (DD-526) is sunk by a Suicide Plane; the Destroyers *Bush* (DD-529) and *Killen* (DD-593) are damaged by Horizontal Bombers; the Destroyers *Ammen* (DD-527), *Anderson* (DD-411), and the *Claxton* (DD-571) are damaged by Suicide Planes. **(Atlantic-Western Europe) 21st Army Group** In the **Canadian First Army** area, the 2 Corps commences a full scale assault against Walcheren. Air support is thin because of bad weather in Great Britain, but the offensive is bolstered by Ships which lend close support, trading shells with German land batteries. In addition the Support Vessels encounter mines and sustain heavy damage. The Canadian 2nd Division advances about three hundred yards up the S. Beveland causeway against heavy fire, but the Germans force it back. Elements of the 4th Special Service Brigade, supported by the 155th Brigade, 52nd Division, cross the estuary to the southern coast and begin to secure Flushing. Westkapelle is seized by combined forces of the 41st, 47th, and 48th Commandos, 4th Special Service Brigade, and a contingent of Dutch Commandos. Resistance will be terminated by the ninth. About 10,000 prisoners are captured. Allied losses: almost totally British and Canadian, 27,633. In other activity, the British 1st Corps prepares for an assault against the Mark River. In the **British Second Army** area, 12th Corps sector, the German resistance is confined to a small area between the Afwaterins Canal and the Maas River; the sector is being reduced. In the 8 Corps sector, the British 53rd Division deploys on the right flank of the Corps and is reinforced by the Belgian 1st Brigade and the British 4th Separate Armored Brigade (attached to 53rd). In other activity, the U.S. 7th Armored Division readies an attack to secure the northwest bank of the Canal du Nord. **12th Army Group** In the **U.S. Third Army** area, General Patton and his Staff prepare for the Third Army offensive which is to follow the offensive of the First Army by one day. On the 2nd, Ike requests that Third Army attack alone as the First Army is unable to get off on time. In the **XX Corps** area, the Arnaville bridgehead is taken over by the 96th Division, which returns and relieves the 95th Division. In the **XII Corps** sector, Letricourt and Abaucourt are both captured by the 319th Infantry, 80th Division. **6th Army Group** In the **U.S. Seventh Army** area, **XV Corps** sector, the French 2nd Armored Division culminates the battle for Baccarat victoriously, then drives to the Blette River to assist the 117th Cavalry, Reconnaissance Troop (VI Corps) to seize Bertrichamps. In the **VI Corps** area, La Bourgonce, in the valley northwest of St. Die, is seized by the 15th Infantry, 3rd Division. **(Atlantic-Mediterranean)** The North African Theater (NATOUSA) is redesignated Mediterranean Theater of Operations (MTOUSA). **(Atlantic-Greece)** Since the withdrawal of the Germans from Florina and Salonika, the only resistance remaining south of the Yugoslavian border is rear guard troops. **(Atlantic-Hungary)** The Germans are forced to evacuate their communications center stronghold at Kecskemet, southeast of Budapest. **(Atlantic-Italy)** In the **British Eighth Army** area, 5th Corps sector, the Indian 10th Division advances to the Rabbi River at Collina and at Grisignano; however, the Germans are able to prevent the British 4th Division from reaching the Forli Airfield.

November 2nd 1944 — (Pacific-Palaus) The 323rd Infantry, 81st Division attacks to eliminate the final resistance of the Umurbrogol Pocket; the Japanese hold steadfastly on Peleliu preventing genuine progress. **(Pacific-Philippines)** The U.S. Sixth Army has concluded its second phase of the Leyte campaign with the control of the Leyte Valley. In the **X Corps** area, the 1st Cavalry and the 24th Infantry Divisions converge on Carigara, which has been evacuated by the Japanese. The hook-up places them near the northern entrance to the Ormoc Valley. In the **XXIV Corps** area, there is some skirmishing between the Japanese and elements of the 382nd Infantry, 96th Division in the vicinity of Dagami. **(Pacific-Burma)** **11th Army Group** In the **British Fourteenth Army** area, 33rd Corps sector, the Indian 5th Division, assisted by Air and Artillery support, captures an enemy stronghold dubbed "Vital Corner" near Tiddim. **(Atlantic-Western Europe)** **21st Army Group** Field Marshal Montgomery directs massive regrouping subsequent to securing southwestern Holland and the Schelde Estuary in preparation for the British Second Army's planned offensive to annihilate the German bridgehead west of the Mass; this objective is preeminent prior to the conquest of the Rhineland. In the **Canadian First Army's** 2nd Corps sector, the Germans mount rigid resistance against the Canadian 2nd Division along the Walcheren causeway. During the night, reinforcements attached to the 156th Brigade ford the Slooe Channel about two miles south of the causeway. The Germans are driven from Flushing. In other activity, heavy Artillery bombardments precede the 1st Corps' attack across the Mark River. The British 49th and U.S. 104th Divisions establish bridgeheads, the latter at Standdaarbuiten and the 49th a little to the west. At Standdaarbuiten, the 413th, 415th, and 104th Regiments overcome the resistance and seize the town. During the struggle under moonlit skies, 1st Lt. Cecil Bolton, Company C, 413th Infantry, attempts to knock out two machine guns. He becomes wounded in both legs and then gets knocked unconscious by a German shell; after regaining consciousness, he leads two Bazooka Teams through high water to the first nest and singlehandedly takes out its two gunners. The other team eliminates the next nest. They continue forward and knock out an 88-mm gun which is menacing the U.S. positions. Bolton refuses aid until getting back to his lines; he receives the Medal of Honor. In the **British Second Army** area, 8th Corps sector, skirmishing develops when Combat Command A, U.S. 7th Armored Division attacks to secure the Canal du Nord. In other activity, Patrols from the British 53rd Division meet up with troops from the U.S. XIX Corps in the vicinity of Maeseyck. **12th Army Group** The U.S. 28th Division, following a substantial Artillery assault, attacks Schmidt. Vossenack Ridge is seized by the 2nd Battalion, 112th Infantry with the assistance of Tanks, but the Germans mount rock hard resistance, bringing an abrupt halt to the progress of the main assault and preventing access to Kommerscheidt and Schmidt. In the **U.S. Third Army** area, General Bradley informs General Patton that the First Army is unable to attack until the British release two U.S. attached Divisions; he then inquires if Third Army can initiate the offensive alone. Patton tells Bradley that Third Army is prepared to attack upon 24-hour notice. It is agreed that Patton will attack as soon as the weather cooperates enough to allow softening of the enemy resistance, but if the inclement weather continues, the XII Corps assault will commence on November 8th. In the **XX Corps** sector, the 10th Armored arrives on line in the Fort Driant zone. **6th Army Group** In the **U.S. Seventh Army** area, **XV Corps** sector, contingents of the VI Corps begin to assume responsibility of the southeastern perimeter of the XV Corps sector, relieving the French 2nd Armored. In the **VI Corps** sector, the 45th Division is relieved by the 100th Division. In other activity, Nompatelize falls without a fight to the 15th Infantry, 3rd Division; the Germans retain a tight hold on La Salle further south. In the **French 1st Army** area, General de Lattre receives responsibility for the French offensive toward Belfort, France (Operation INDEPENDENCE). **(Atlantic-Germany-Air Corps)** During a bombing mission over Merseburg, enemy flak damages one of the Planes of the 711th Bombing Squadron, 447th Bomber Group. The Navigator, 2nd Lt. Robert E. Foymoyer, is hit three times, but refuses morphine to ensure his ability to read his charts and instruments enabling the damaged Plane to return to England. After a grueling two and a half hour flight, the Plane arrives over the English

Channel; Foymoyer permits the injection. Shortly after, the Plane lands, Foymoyer dies; he receives the Medal of Honor posthumously. **(Atlantic-Italy)** In the **U.S. Fifth Army** area, written instructions supersede and confirm the verbal orders given on October 30th regarding the future operations during the present winter lull. They stipulate the consolidation of positions at the Bologna salient, while permitting limited action on its flanks. In the British 13th Corps area, the Polish 2nd Corps assumes responsibility for the area along Highway 67, relieving the British 26th Armored Brigade. The Indian 8th Division sector is enlarged, giving it the area encompassing M. delle Valle, which had been held by the British 1st Division. In the **British Eighth Army** area, the 5th Corps is experiencing communication difficulties and is ordered to remain in place. In other activity, the Indian 10th Division reverts to reserve, being replaced by the 128th Brigade, British 46th Division. **(Atlantic-Yugoslavia)** The Dalmatian port of Zara is captured by Partisans.

November 3rd 1944 — (Pacific-Guam) The U.S. 77th Infantry, U.S.A., embarks from Guam, heading for New Caledonia, but it will be diverted to Leyte while en route (10th). **(Pacific-Marianas)** Japanese Aircraft repeatedly attack U.S. Airfields on Saipan and Tinian. These Bases are utilized to launch Heavy Bombers against the Japanese mainland. **(Pacific-Philippines-Leyte)** In the Ormoc Valley, U.S. Planes swoop overhead, attacking columns of enemy reinforcements, inflicting casualties, and impeding progress. Japanese Planes bomb and strafe Tacloban Airstrip on Leyte. The Airstrip is bombed again on the following day. In the **U.S. Sixth Army** area, the X and XXIV Corps receive orders to commence a joint attack against Ormoc. In the **X Corps** area, the 34th Infantry, 24th Division seizes Capoocan and pushes against Pinamopoan until enemy resistance brings the advance to a halt. In the **XXIV Corps** sector, the 1st Battalion, 382nd Infantry, 96th Division, assaults a formidable ridge, later dubbed "Bloody Ridge," west of Dagami; it treks through rice paddies against entrenched opposition and withdraws after nightfall. In Naval activity, the U.S.S. *Cero* (SS-225) lands men and supplies on the east coast of Luzon. In other activity, the Light Cruiser *Reno* (CL-96) is damaged by a Japanese Submarine torpedo off Leyte. **(Pacific-South China Sea)** The Japanese Destroyer *Akikaze* is sunk by the U.S.S. *Pintado* (SS-387). **(Pacific-India-Burma)** On the Salween Front, the Chinese Hon 1st Division retakes Lung-ling after several months of heavy fighting. In the N.C.A.C. area, the Chinese 22nd Division advances to the Irrawaddy River, near Shwegu, without incident. **(Atlantic-Western Europe) 21st Army Group** In the **Canadian First Army's** 2nd Corps area, the enemy resistance in the Breskens Pocket has ended; the Canadian 3rd Division mop-up operations are terminated. About 12,500 prisoners have been taken since the operation began. On Walcheren Island, the British 52nd Division, reinforced by the 4th Special Brigade, keeps its advance moving. Additional assault forces from Westkapelle meet with those from Flushing. The eastern Walcheren positions are now extended. In the British 1st Corps area, the Germans abandon some positions along the Mark River in response to the expanding bridgeheads of the British 49th and U.S. 104th Divisions' bridgeheads, but several formidable strongholds remain. In other activity, the Polish 1st Armored Division establishes a bridgehead on the right flank of the Corps near Zevenbergen. In the **British Second Army's** 8th Corps sector, C.C.A., U.S. 7th Armored Division overpowers resistance, seizing the villages of Horik and Ospel while continuing the clearing operation on the northwest bank of the

Canal du Nord. **12th Army Group** In the **U.S. First Army's V Corps** sector, Kommerscheidt and Schmidt are seized by the 112th Infantry, 28th Division; the seizure of Schmidt, along a prime supply route, further curtails the enemy logistics in the area (Lammersdorf Corridor). In conjunction with the 112th Regiment, the 109th and 110th operate on the flanks against immovable enemy opposition, making nominal progress. In the **U.S. Third Army** area, the XII and XX Corps receive orders to attack; the former is to seize Faulquemont, secure a Rhine bridgehead between Mannheim and Oppenheim, and prepare for a possible assault toward the Darmstadt region; the latter is to eradicate the Metz Garrison, secure a crossing point at the Sarre River, and await orders to drive northeast. In other activity, a nuisance enemy pocket remains west of the Moselle at Berg-sur-Moselle; the 3rd Cavalry Group advances after nightfall and attacks it on the following day, but enemy pressure forces it back; on the 5th, following Artillery support, it seizes Berg and a hill to the north. **6th Army Group** In the **French 1st Army**, 2nd Corps sector, the 3rd Algerian Division attacks the entrenched enemy near Gerardmer and meets stiff opposition. **(Atlantic-Italy)** The U.S. Fifth Army is scheduled to receive reinforcements-the 366th Infantry, but the Regiment does not arrive at Leghorn until the 21st. In the **British Eighth Army** area, the British 4th Division attacks, but the German resistance is fierce, prompting 5 Corps to abort the limited assault and await better weather to launch a heavier offensive.

November 4th 1944 — (United States) President Roosevelt, running for reelection, speaks to an audience of about 40,000 people in Boston. The engagement opens with Frank Sinatra singing a popular song, "America." **(Pacific)** Marine Carrier Groups, Fleet Marine Force Pacific, is redesignated Marine Air Support Groups, Fleet Marine Force, comprising four Carrier Air Groups. **(Pacific-Philippines-Leyte)** In the **U.S. Sixth Army** area, concern about a possible amphibious assault by the Japanese near Carigara prompts X Corps to deploy defensively and send out reconnaissance Patrols to find strategic points to locate Artillery pieces for a bombardment of Ormoc. The Patrols of the 34th Infantry, 24th Division advance beyond Colasian and Pinamopoan to a ridge subsequently named Breakneck Ridge. The Patrols discover that the Japanese have begun to withdraw. During one incident, a burst of enemy fire kills the leader of a Squad which is crossing a stream; Sergeant Charles Mower assumes command and leads the men across. More enemy fire wounds him, but he refuses to take shelter and continues to direct fire. The Japanese recognize his efforts, which knock out two machine gun nests, and pour their remaining fire on his position, killing him; Sgt. Mower receives the Medal of Honor posthumously. In the **XXIV Corps** area, the 1st Battalion, 382nd Infantry, 96th Division advances about 1,000 yards against nominal opposition toward Bloody Ridge, followed by elements of the 2nd Battalion which take over mop-up operations. The Japanese commence an attack during the night of the 4th-5th and are met by unexpected Artillery fire; they make a hasty retreat, leaving 254 dead on the field. **(Pacific-Burma)** In the **British Fourteenth Army** area, 33 Corps sector, the Indian 5th Division secures Kennedy Peak, south of Tiddim. **(Atlantic-Western Europe) 21st Army Group** At Antwerp, in the **Canadian First Army** area, the first Minesweeping Vessels arrive. In the 2nd Corps area, enemy resistance at Walcheren is being reduced systematically by the British 52nd Division and Commandos from the 4th Special Service Brigade. In conjunction, the troops which have crossed the Slooe Channel join with those at the causeway. The pressure assures clearance of the enemy from the northern coast. In the British 1st Corps area, the British 49th and U.S. 104th Divisions, driving north from the center of the Corps, close on the Maas. On the right flank, the Polish 1st Armored Division seizes Geertruidenberg; Steenbergen, on the left, is invested. The U.S. 104th Division receive orders to advance to Aachen upon release from its current operation to rejoin the VII Corps, U.S. First Army. In the 8th Corps area, the reduction of enemy resistance at the Canal du Nord continues by the U.S. 7th Armored Division. On the following day, the 7th Armored closes on Meijel from the north; on the 6th, the 7th Armored will be detached from the British and rejoin the 12th Army Group for the U.S. offensive. **12th Army Group** In the **U.S. First Army** area, **V Corps** sector, the Germans mount strong attacks to retake Schmidt and Kommerscheidt; the enemy seizes Schmidt, but Tanks support the defenders at Kommerscheidt and the enemy is driven back. To the north, the enemy is repulsed by the 109th Infantry, 28th Division, and to the south, the Germans lose Simonskall to the 110th Infantry Regiment. **6th Army Group** In the **U.S. Seventh Army**, **VI Corps** area, the Foret de Mortagne is being cleared by the 3rd Division, which is also reducing enemy resistance in the open ground to the north of St. Die. In other activity, the 36th Division is exterminating the enemy in the Foret Domaniale de Champ and simultaneously driving toward Corcieux on the south flank of the Corps. **(Atlantic-Italy)** In the **U.S. Fifth Army** area, the IV Corps assumes responsibility for the 6th South African sector and the U.S. troops attached to the Division (Combat Command B, 1st Armored Division). The IV Corps also releases the 92nd Division to the control of the Fifth Army to protect the coastal area on the left flank of the Corps and to control the Serchio Valley. In the British 13th Corps area, contingents of the British 6th Armored Division relieve the British 1st Division, which then relieves the U.S. 88th Division and contingents of the U.S. 85th Division (II Corps) stationed to the west. **(Atlantic-Hungary)** The Second Ukrainian Front takes Cegled and Szolnok, between Debrecen and the capital, Budapest. The fierce resistance by the Germans and Hungarians, combined with terrible rains, forestalls the approach of the Red Army. **(Atlantic-Yugoslavia)** Sibenik, another city on the Dalmatian coast, falls to Partisans.

Brigadier General Benjamin O. Davis, Sr. speaking with Sgt. Joe Louis (Heavyweight Champion of the World).

November 5th 1944 — (United States) Admiral Leahy, accompanying President Roosevelt back to Washington, receives a telegram with the news that Sir John Dill, Chief of British Military Mission, has succumbed at Walter Reed hospital after a prolonged illness. He is replaced by Sir Henry Maitland Wilson. **(Pacific-Philippines)** Planes attached to Vice Admiral J.S. McCain's Carrier Task Force commence a two-day bombardment of Japanese facilities and Shipping at Luzon. In other Naval activity, the Carrier *Lexington* (CV-16) is damaged off Luzon, and the PT-320 sustains damage off Leyte, by a Suicide Plane and Horizontal Bomber respectively. The Japanese lose the Heavy Cruiser *Nachi* and the Patrol Boat No. 107 (Manila Bay) by Carrier Plane attack; the Seaplane Tender *Notoro* is sunk off Singapore by Army Aircraft. In the **U.S. Sixth Army** area on LEYTE, the **X Corps** sends Patrols into the central mountains. In other activity, the 34th Infantry is relieved by the 21st Infantry at Breakneck Ridge. In the **XXIV Corps** area, Artillery bombards the enemy positions on Bloody Ridge and is followed by another strike by the 382nd Infantry, 96th Division, supported by Tanks. U.S. Planes attack enemy troops advancing along Highway 2. On the following day, the X Corps is ordered to drive down Highway 2 and secure Ormoc expeditiously. **(Atlantic-Western Europe) 21st Army Group** In the **Canadian First Army** area, the 2nd Corps maintains its quick pace on Walcheren Island. Meanwhile the 1st Corps gets advance contingents to the Maas River. The U.S. 104th Division (minus contingents of 414th Infantry assigned to assist Polish 1st Armored Div.) seizes Moerdijk and prepares to depart for Aachen. In the **British Second Army** 12th Corps area, the enemy is driven from the south bank of the Maas by the British 51st Division. In the 8th Corps area, the British 15th and the U.S. 7th Armored Divisions close on Meijel from the north and south respectively. **12th Army Group** In the **U.S. First Army V Corps** area, the Germans unsuccessfully storm Kommerscheidt; the 28th Division holds firmly. The Germans continue to press and by the 7th, the Kall bridgehead is abandoned, then taken by the enemy. The Yanks at Vossenack come under heavy attack; their positions are becoming untenable. In other activity, Task Force R (Col. Ripple, CO of 707th Tank Battalion) is formed to assist the 112th Infantry assault Schmidt on the following day. The Task Force comprises a Tank Battalion and Tank Destroyers. In the **VII Corps** area, inclement weather stalls the planned offensive. In the **Third Army XX Corps** sector, Berg falls to the 3rd Cavalry Group. In the **XII Corps** area, sporadic rainstorms occur as Corps awaits orders from General Patton to open the offensive. **6th Army Group** Orders from Seventh Army direct the capture of Strasbourg and the eradication of enemy resistance west of the Rhine; the offensive is to commence on November 13th. The **XV Corps** is scheduled to jump off on D Day, secure Sarrebourg, and shoot the Saverne Gap; the **VI Corps** is to attack no later than D plus 2, bolting through the Vosges passes to secure Strasbourg. In other activity, the 36th Division continues to skirmish in the Foret Domaniale de Champ while the 3rd Division is clearing the area west of the Meurthe, north of St. Die. In the **French 1st Army** 2nd Corps area, the 3rd Algerian Division seizes Rochesson, Menaurupt, and the hills in the vicinity. **(Atlantic-Italy)** In the **U.S. Fifth Army** area, **IV Corps** sector, the 1st Division (Brazilian) assumes command of C.C.B., U.S. 1st Armored Division in place. Additional units operating in the Corps sector are the 107th AAA Group and the 6th South African Armored Division. In the **British Eighth Army** area, more favorable weather permits Allied sorties to be launched to soften resistance prior to the 5th Corps assault against Forli.

November 6th 1944 — (Pacific-Malay Archipelago) The U.S.S. *Gurnard* (SS-254), operating in waters southwest of the

Philippines, lays mines off Borneo. (Pacific-Philippines) On LEYTE, in the U.S. Sixth Army area, X Corps sector, the Japanese mount rigid resistance and turn back the 3rd Battalion, 21st Infantry, 24th Division as it attempts penetration of Breakneck Ridge; the 1st Battalion makes a futile attempt to deploy at positions to support the attack against the ridge, but enemy fire is too heavy. In the XXIV Corps area, the 382nd Infantry plows ahead, dislodging entrenched defenders on Bloody Ridge and eradicating most resistance, except a few scattered pockets. (Pacific-China) The Japanese have Kunming invested, causing grave concern at China Theater Headquarters. (Pacific-India-Burma) In the N.C.A.C. area, elements of the Chinese 22nd Division force the Irrawaddy, seizing Shwegugale after overpowering nominal resistance. (Atlantic-Western Europe) 21st Army Group In the Canadian First Army area, Middleburg (Walcheren Island) is seized by elements of the II Corps by a surprise attack that nets the Corps the enemy Garrison and its Commanding Officer, General Daser; prisoners total in excess of 2,000. In the British 1st Corps Sector, the principal part of the U.S. 104th Division debarks for Aachen; contingents of its 415th Regiment jump off with the Polish 1st Armored Division against Moerdijk to sever the enemy escape routes there. 12th Army Group In the U.S. First Army area, V Corps sector, the Germans mount another furious attack to dislodge the 28th Division. The 28th gives no ground at Kommerscheidt; however, it is compelled to pull back from the eastern portion of Vossenack. Near Kommerscheidt, the 893rd Tank Destroyer Battalion has been engaged for three days. First Lt. Turney Leonard has consistently led his men in battle and has frequently been way out in front of his men, becoming wounded twice, the latter hit shattering his arm. His intrepid leadership under fire greatly assisted the effort to hold the town, and he is personally responsible for the destruction of at least six enemy Tanks. Leonard is last seen receiving aid at a medical station which is overrun by the enemy; he receives the Medal of Honor posthumously. In other activity, 28th Division unit transfers are behind schedule as the 109th Infantry is unable to relieve the 12th Infantry, causing postponement of Task Force R's assault against Schmidt. (Atlantic-Italy) In the U.S. Fifth Army area, IV Corps sector, Task Force 45 takes command of the coastal sector held by the 107th AAA Group. In the British 13th Corps sector, M. Monsignano is seized by the Indian 8th Division without incident. In the British Eighth Army area, the Polish 2nd Corps advances, subsequent to the Germans pulling back portions of their lines. M. Chioda is seized, along with M. Pratello, by the 3rd Carpathian Division, which is operating west of Highway 67. The 5th Kresowa Division, advancing east of the highway, captures M. Testa, east of Dovadola.

November 7th 1944 — (United States) President Roosevelt is elected to a fourth term. Up late, keeping an eye on the election, Roosevelt hears Dewey concede at 3:45 a.m. As the President goes to his room, he quips to Admiral Leahy: "WELL, AT LAST DEWEY KNOWS HE HAS LOST THE ELECTION." (Pacific-New Guinea) The PT-301 suffers damage subsequent to sustaining an accidental explosion off the coast of Western New Guinea. (Pacific-Philippines) In the U.S. Sixth Army area on LEYTE, the X Corps initiates its drive toward Ormoc, heading south along Highway 2. Enemy fire is intense against the advancing 21st Infantry, 24th Division and its support group, the 3rd Battalion, 19th Infantry. A huge concentration of U.S. fire is directed at an enemy strongpoint on a ridge about 400 yards ahead, but the Japanese hold, forcing the Yanks to deploy at the beginning of Breakneck Ridge to await daybreak. Company G, 19th Infantry assaults in conjunction with the 21st Infantry, pushing toward Hill 1525 southeast of Limon, but enemy resistance halts its progress well short of the ridge. In the XXIV Corps area, the battle for complete control of Bloody Ridge continues to rage. All three Battalions of the 382nd Infantry, 96th Division thrust forward against the remaining resistance; the effort gains the objective, decimating the defenders who lose about 474 dead. (Pacific-Solomons) Dive Bomber Squadrons of the 1st Marine Aircraft Wing and Headquarters and Services Squadrons of Marine Aircraft Groups 24th and 32nd are assigned to the U.S. Fifth Air Force (308th Bombardment Wing H), for operational control during the Lingayen Gulf, Luzon occupation campaign. Marine Scout-Bomber Squadron 133rd, 142nd, 236th, 241st, 243rd, 244th, and 341st, 1st Marine Air Wing are instructed to provide close Air support for ground operations in the Lingayen region and in Central Luzon. Marine Aircraft Groups 24 and 32 are to establish base and servicing facilities for the Marine Scout-Bomber Squadrons. (Pacific-India-Burma) In the N.C.A.C. area, the Chinese 22nd Division seizes Shwegu, then jumps off to attack Man-tha, leaving the 64th Regiment in place to man the Garrison; the 65th and 66th Regiments head for the objective. (Atlantic-Western Europe) 21st Army Group The Canadian First Army assumes responsibility for the remaining mop-up operations on Walcheren Island. In the British 1st Corps area, the Germans control Moerdijk, but the majority of terrain in the sector is free of the enemy. The contingents of the 104th Division (414th Infantry), relieved by the British in the Moerdijk region, rejoin the Division. In the British Second Army 8th Corps area, the U.S. 7th Armored Division is transferred back to U.S. control, returning to 12th Army Group. In other activity, the final assault against Meijel is postponed temporarily to coordinate with the British 12th Corps' drive from the southwest. 12th Army Group In the U.S. First Army area, successive German counterattacks against the 28th Division at Kommerscheidt and vicinity have battered the defenders. A decision is reached to abandon the bridgehead at the Kall River; the enemy takes Kommerscheidt and drives the 28th Division into the woods on the fringes of the town. It holds the line there and resists further attempts to push it back. In other activity, a contingent of Tanks and Engineers drive into the eastern section of Vossenack and secure it, quickly turning over its defense to the 2nd Battalion, 109th Infantry. At Germeter, the 109th Regiment, holding north of the town along the Corps north flank, is relieved by the 12th Infantry, 4th Division. In the U.S. Third Army area, General Patton disregards the ongoing heavy rains and flooded streams; he orders the attack to commence on the 8th. At 19:00, Generals Eddy and Gerow confer with Patton and attempt to have him postpone the assault. Patton asks them: "WHOM THEY WISHED TO NAME AS THEIR SUCCESSORS BECAUSE THE ATTACK WAS GOING OFF AS SCHEDULED." Patton notes: "THEY IMMEDIATELY ASSENTED AND, AS USUAL, DID GREAT WORK." The casualty report, Third Army, as of November 7th: Killed, 5,7343; Wounded, 28,273; Missing, 5,421; Total 39,428. Non-battle casualties 24,386, Grand Total 63,814. Total casualties for period September 24th to November 7th inclusive, 18,684. Patton notes: CONCERNING LATTER CASUALTIES: "THE NECESSITY OF HALTING ON THE MOSELLE RESULTED IN THE ABOVE LOSS, WHICH, HAD WE BEEN ABLE TO CONTINUE OUR ADVANCE ON THE 24TH, MIGHT NOT HAVE OCCURRED AND CERTAINLY NOT IN SUCH NUMBERS." Enemy losses (against Third Army): Killed, 42,500; Wounded, 117,000; Prisoners of War, 103,000; Total

262,500. Equipment losses Third Army Light Tanks 157; Medium Tanks 374; Guns 109. Enemy equipment losses: Medium Tanks 834; Panther or Tiger Tanks 445; Guns 1,173. **6th Army Group** In the **French 1st Army** area, contingents make their way to jump off points that lie south, to form for the 1st Corps attack against Belfort. The French receive some unexpected assistance as their movement is somewhat muffled by roaring guns firing in the 2nd Corps area, repulsing an enemy counterattack at Gerardmer. **(Atlantic-Italy)** In the **British Eighth Army** area, a hefty Artillery barrage precedes the 5th Corps offensive, which begins to roll forward toward Forli at 22:50; the 46th Division pushing on the left jumps from Grisignano, streaming toward S. Martino in Strada in synchronization with the British 4th Division, which is driving toward the Airfield at Forli.

November 8th 1944 — (Pacific-Philippines-Leyte) In the **U.S. Sixth Army** area, a violent typhoon tears through the area, but its fury does not abort the 21st Infantry's assault against Breakneck Ridge. The 2nd Battalion, 19th Infantry drives toward Hill 1525, seizing a less formidable hill along the way, but the Japanese halt its progress before it can advance to the main objective. Some contingents pivot west and advance about 1,000 yards to secure a nearby ridge; the 1st Battalion, 21st Infantry drives to Hill 1525. In the **XXIV Corps** sector, the 382nd Infantry dispatches Patrols that discover an enemy contingent deployed outside of Patok. In other activity, the Japanese debark an additional Division at Ormoc and promptly dispatch the troops to the mountains in central Leyte. In Naval activity, the U.S.S. *Growler* (SS-215), scheduled to join with the U.S.S. *Bream*, is sunk; cause unknown. En route to join the *Bream*, the *Growler* detects an enemy Convoy and radios its position to the *Hardhead*, directing it to attack. About an hour later, an explosion of unknown origin is heard by the *Hake*, another of the Subs in the area. Simultaneously, a crashing sound is heard by the *Hardhead*, which is preparing to torpedo the enemy Convoy. The enemy Tanker *Manei Maru* is sunk, and the *Hake* and *Hardhead* are soon deluged with depth charges, but they escape. The *Growler* is not heard from again. The Japanese list the sinking of the *Manei Maru*, but make no mention of a torpedo attack against a Submarine. In other activity, the Japanese Torpedo Boat *Sagi* is sunk by the U.S.S. *Gunnel* (SS-253). **(Pacific-Burma)** British Admiral Mountbatten issues the directive (Operation ROMULUS) to seize and secure the coastal sector of Arakan. **11 Army Group** In the **British Fourteenth Army** area, the Indian 5th Division occupies Fort White, an abandoned Japanese stronghold, without incident, thus concluding the operation to secure the area south of Tiddim. **(Atlantic-Western Europe) 21st Army Group** British Field Marshal Montgomery initiates a large regrouping of the 21st Army Group to deploy the British Second Army along the Meuse River facing east. In the **Canadian First Army** area, the Canadians have scooped up about 8,000 prisoners, while securing Walcheren Island; today, mop-up details are terminated ceasing the operation to forge openings to Antwerp. The British 1st Corps moves further east, encompassing the sector previously held by the British Second Army 12th Corps; it also assumes command of the U.S. 7th Armored and attached contingents. **12th Army Group** In the **U.S. Ninth Army** area, the **XII Corps**, commanded by Major General Alvan C. Gillem Jr., moves on line, wedging into the extreme left of the Group, tightly straddled between the XIX Corps and the British 30th Corps sectors. In the **U.S. First Army** area, the bridgehead at the Kall is withdrawn. The 1st Division is relieved by the 104th Division, recently released by the British. In the **U.S. Third Army** area, the offen-

sive against the Sarre begins as about 220,000 men drive toward the Siegfried Line. At 06:00, following a tumultuous Artillery barrage, the XII Corps bolts the Seille River, its 35th Division at the center, seizing Jallaucourt and Malaucourt; the 137th and 320th Regiments attack toward Morhange Plateau in conjunction with the 26th Division. The Germans stop this drive in front of Bois d'Amelecourt on the right and at Fresnes-en-Saulnois on the left. The 104th Infantry, 26th Division, bolstered by two Task Forces, captures Vic-sur-Seille and its bridges; the 101st Regiment seizes Moyenvic and its bridge, while the 328th Infantry overpowers the resistance at Moncourt and Bezauge-le-Petite; at the latter, Technician Alfred Wilson, Medical Detachment, 26th Infantry, is wounded while tending the casualties and refuses to receive medical aid, despite his serious condition. Wilson moves from man to man until unable to walk, then he begins crawling from patient to patient. He continues until the massive loss of blood immobilizes him completely. Determined to continue aiding the wounded, Wilson still refuses medical aid; he speaks barely above a whisper instructing others to tend the wounds until he drops into unconsciousness and dies. Corporal Wilson saves the lives of ten Soldiers and receives the Medal of Honor posthumously. In addition, the 80th Division, driving on the northern flank, crosses the Seille River and takes Aulnois-sur-Seille, Eply, and Nomeny. The **XX Corps** prepares to attack across the Seille River, push through the Maginot Line, and seize Koenigsmacker to invest the heavily defended Metz region. By dawn, the 90th Division has moved to the Foret de Cattenom without detection and is poised for assault. The 10th Armored Division is redeploying to the north to assault in conjunction with the 90th. At 21:00, the 95th Division commences Operation CASANOVA, a diversionary attack, driving toward and across the Moselle. Company C, 337th Infantry fords the river in assault boats south of Uckange, meeting nominal resistance, while Company C penetrates about 400 yards inland against stiff resistance, which prevents establishment of a bridgehead. Meanwhile, in synchronization with the crossings, the 2nd and 3rd Battalions, 377th Infantry engage an enemy force in a pocket west of the Moselle near Maizieres-les-Metz. By nightfall, every unit reaches its objective. **6th Army Group** In the **U.S. Seventh Army** area, the **XV Corps** sets November 13th as the day to launch the offensive. Infantry contingents of the 44th and 79th Divisions are to drive through enemy defenses, followed by the French 2nd Armored shooting through the gap. **(Atlantic-Italy)** In the **British Eighth Army** area, Polish 2nd Corps sector, the 3rd Carpathian Division is securing the hills between Dovadola and Modigliana, seizing the former as it moves. The 5th Kresowa Division takes M. della Birra without incident. In the 5nd Corps area, the Germans resist strongly at Forli, impeding Corps' progress. The British 46th Division attacks across the Rabbi River after dark. **(Atlantic-Greece)** The Indian 4th Division debarks at Salonika; contingents traverse to Thrace to ward off the threat of civil war between the controlling forces of the EAM and the nationalist guerrillas.

November 9th 1944 — (Pacific-Java Sea) The U.S.S. *Flounder* (SS-251), operating between Borneo and Java, sinks a German Submarine, the U-537. **(Pacific-Philippines)** The Japanese debark more reinforcements at Ormoc, but the operation is interrupted by U.S. Planes, forcing the Vessels to evacuate the area before unloading the supplies and ammunition. The Vessels are destroyed by U.S. Aircraft as they retire. In the **U.S. Sixth Army** area on LEYTE, **X Corps** sector, the 24th Division prepares to attack Breakneck Ridge on the 10th with a full

503

scale assault. The 21st Infantry is heavily engaged, gnawing forward with minimum progress; in conjunction, the 34th Infantry strikes the enemy positions from the rear. At Hill 1525, the Germans mount strong counterattacks against Company A, 1st Battalion, 21st Infantry. The balance of the Regiment, which is attacking near the Ormoc road south of Limon, races back to aid the beleaguered Company. The 2nd Battalion, 19th Infantry is advancing to the hill to relieve the 1st Battalion, which gets pushed back to Pinamopoan. In the **XXIV Corps** area, the 382nd Infantry, 96th Division cancels an assault against enemy positions west of Patok because of severe rains. **(Pacific-Burma)** In the N.C.A.C. area, the British 36th Division reinitiates its march. **(Pacific-China)** U.S. General Wedemeyer's urging to have Chiang Kai-shek direct the Y Force to pursue the Japanese who are retreating from Lung-Ling, is agreed upon; the Generalissimo directs the XII Army Group to attack; the 2nd, 52nd and 71st Armies move toward Man-shih. **(Atlantic-Western Europe) 21st Army Group** In the **Canadian First Army** area, the British 1st Corps concludes the operation to secure the region south of the Mass. The 2nd Corps assumes control of the Nijmegen sector, relieving the 30th Corps, and takes command of the U.S. 82nd and 101st Airborne Divisions in addition to assuming command of the Guards Armored, 43rd and 50th Infantry Divisions, and the 8th Separate Armored Brigade. In the **British Second Army** area, the 12th Corps assumes control of the British 51st and 53rd Divisions and the Belgian 1st and 8th Separate Armored Brigades in place, to the right of the 8th Corps along the Meuse. The British announce the Schelde is open, clearing the way for Allied Ships. The U.S. Navy clears the mines in the estuary by the 26th, permitting the first Vessel to arrive and unload cargo. **12th Army Group** The U.S. 7th Armored Division arrives at U.S. Ninth Army's XIII Corps area (subsequent to release from British Second Army sector). In the **U.S. Third Army** area, 1,476 Planes from the U.S. Ninth and Tenth Air Forces bombard enemy positions in the Metz-Thionville region, preceding an Infantry assault; at 03:30, the 358th and 359th Regiments pour across the unruly Moselle at Cattenom and Malling, taking the enemy by surprise. The swift fording of the river nets the Infantry a bridgehead, but enemy fire combined with the unmanageable currents prevents the building of bridges or the infusion of heavy support weapons. The 358th Infantry seizes Basse and Hamm and secures a portion of Fort Koenigsmacker, followed later by elements of the 357th Infantry capturing Koenigsmacker. To the north, Petite-Hettange, Hunting, Kerling, Malling, and Metrich are overrun by the 359th Infantry. At Uckange, the 95th Division's bridgehead is enlarged, bypassing Bertrange. The woods north of Semecourt, slag pile near Maizieres-les-Metz, and Chateau Brieux are seized by the 377th Infantry, 95th Division. The 5th Division, driving across the Seille River south of Metz with the use of assault boats and a footbridge, establishes a bridgehead; it seizes Cheminot with its 2nd Infantry and Hautonnerie with the 10th Infantry, the former without a fight. Every bridge on the Moselle River except one at Pont-a-Mousson is out, and the Seille River has expanded from two hundred to five hundred feet. By nightfall, the operable bridges are also out. The **XII Corps** offensive continues with full fury, seizing the majority of Delme Ridge with its 80th Division, supported by Planes and additional U.S. troops advancing on its flanks. At Nomeny, mop-up operations by the 80th Division continue, and the 35th Division's Combat Command B, 4th Armored Division, followed by the 137th Infantry, drives toward Fonteny and Hannocourt in two columns, reaching the latter, but the advance is halted in front of Fonteny by stiff resistance. Delme village is seized by the 137th Infantry, 35th Division in conjunction with the 80th's assault against Delme Ridge. The 320th Infantry drives into the forest at Bois d'Amelecourt, encountering heavy resistance; the 134th Infantry is clearing the eastern section of the Foret de Chateau-Salins. In addition, the 104th Regiment, 26th Division captures Chateau-Salins while an attached Task Force seizes Morville-les-Vic. The 101st Infantry maneuvers to outflank Hill 310 and takes Salival. **6th Army Group** In the **U.S. Seventh Army** area, the 100th Division finalizes relief of the 45th Division and takes over responsibility for securing Raon-l'Etape and protection of the northern flank of the VI Corps. **Air Activity** During an Air raid against Saarbrucken, Lt. Gott's Plane, attached to the 729th Bomber Squadron 452nd Bombardment Group, is severely damaged, and three of its four engines are on fire; flames are spurting back to the tail section. Gott manages to release the bombs over the target and return the seriously disabled Plane to Allied territory, despite the fires and wounding of several of his crewmen; upon reaching friendly lines he orders all men to bail out; the Co-pilot, 2nd Lt. William E. Metzger Jr., and Gott remain on board with a wounded man, attempting to land safely. The Aircraft explodes 100 feet from the ground, then crashes and explodes again, instantly killing all as the Plane disintegrates; Gott and Metzger receive the ility for the II Corps area, presently protected by the U.S. 88th Division and contingents of the 85th Division. In other activity, the Indian 8th Division presses north in hot pursuit of the Germans, who are making partial withdrawals; it takes M. Budriatto. In the **British Eighth Army** area, the British 4th Division eliminates the remnant defenders at Forli. In the 46th Division area, the Germans raise fierce fire, preventing the British from crossing the Montone River. A Platoon fords it later, but the Germans isolate it at Terra del Sole and annihilate the unit.

November 10th 1944 — **(Pacific-Philippines-Leyte)** In the **U.S. Sixth Army** area, **X Corps** sector, the 1st Cavalry Division dispatches its first Patrols into the central mountains. At Breakneck Ridge outside Carigara, the 24th Division initiates a full scale assault to reduce the remaining resistance. Elements of the 19th and 34th Regiments drive forward against entrenched resistance south of Limon; the 21st Regiment plows straight ahead. Additional contingents of the 34th Infantry are transported seven miles down Carigara Bay by LVTs from where they drive toward Belen to attack a nearby ridge. In he **XXIV Corps** sector, the 1st and 3rd Battalions, 382nd Infantry, 96th Division seize Bloody Ridge without incident. **(Pacific)** The 4th Marine Base Defense Air Wing is redesignated the 4th Marine Aircraft Wing, commanded by Major General Louis E. Woods. **(Pacific-Burma)** In the N.C.A.C. area, the British 36th Division advances through the railroad corridor and encounters strong resistance near Pinwe along the mainline of resistance. The Chinese 38th Division outflanks the enemy's forward outpost along the Taping River and reaches the Bhamo plain. **(Pacific-China)** The garrison towns of Kweilin and Liuchow are easily seized from the Chinese by the Japanese who continue pressing toward Kweiyang, a primary road junction south of Chungking. **(Atlantic-Western Europe) 12th Army Group** In the **U.S. First Army** area, the boundary separating the V and VII Corps is adjusted, giving V Corps responsibility for Huertgen. In the **VII Corps** sector, the 12th Infantry, 4th Division (detached by

28th Division) is struck by a fierce German counterattack and driven back from its positions on a plateau southwest of Huertgen. Two Companies are invested, prevented from withdrawing; Combat Command R, 5th Armored Division is attached to Corps for added strength. In other activity, relief of the 1st Division by the 104th Division is complete. In the **V Corps** area, contingents of the 28th Division attack toward the woods near Huertgen, making nominal progress. In the **U.S. Third Army** area, **XX Corps** sector, the Germans mount a Tank-Infantry drive that storms into Kerling at about 03:00; Artillery fire and a concentrated effort by the 359th Infantry break up the assault. The 357th Infantry attacks the fortifications at Metrich, southeast of Koenigsmacker, making progress while some contingents of the 358th Regiment continue to batter Fort Koenigsmacker; others drive to Bois d'Elzange ridge. At the Uckange bridgehead, the 1st Battalion, 377th Infantry is holding firmly, but supplies must arrive by Air; west of the Moselle its units abort the effort to reduce the enemy salient due to flooding conditions at Hauconcourt; contingents of the 338th Infantry build a bridge across the Moselle near Malling by midnight, advancing it closer to Thionville. Pagny-les-Goin, Silly-en-Saulnois, and a roadway junction outside of the latter are seized by Combat Command B, 6th Armored. In the **XII Corps** sector, the 80th Infantry and 6th Armored Divisions drive swiftly along the northern flank of the Corps, disregarding the mines and the congested mud-saturated highways; Combat Command A drives to Luppy, while Combat Command B streaks to Buch and Vigny in stride with the 5th Division (XX Corps). Combat Command B, 4th Armored Division dispatches units to Fonteny, but the Germans impede passage at Viviers; hard fighting ensues when the 137th Infantry, 35th Division moves in to dislodge the enemy. Subsequently the stalled Armor and the 137th Regiment drive through Laneuvevlle-en-Saulnois, reaching the vicinity of Fonteny. The 30th Regiment pumps into Foret de Chateau-Salins in synchronization with the attack of the 134th Infantry, which is driving against Gerbecourt. In addition, Combat Command A, 4th Armored drives to Hampont while the 101st Infantry pounds the flanks of Hill 310, seizing a ridge northeast of the hill and some additional enemy positions in Bois St. Martin. At slightly after 17:10, General Bradley calls Patton and instructs him not to commit the 83rd Division. Patton becomes annoyed and considers the order a mistake claiming: "HAD TWO COMBAT TEAMS OF THE 83rd BEEN USED TO ATTACK SAARBURG, THAT TOWN WOULD HAVE FALLEN ON THE 12TH OR THIRTEENTH, AND WE WOULD PROBABLY HAVE CAPTURED TRIER." Patton is convinced that the fall of Trier would have prevented Von Rundstedt's break-through. **6th Army Group** In the **U.S. Seventh Army** area, the Germans holding west of the Meurthe are faltering conspicuously. The defenses at Vanemont and La Houssiere are abandoned, permitting the 142nd Infantry, 36th Division to take them without a fight as it drives through the Foret Domaniale de Champ, heading southeast. Etival is seized by the 15th Infantry, 3rd Division. **(Atlantic-Italy)** In the **U.S. Fifth Army** area, British 13th Corps sector, the Indian 8th Division discovers M. Ponpegno free of the enemy and continues toward M. Bassana. In the **British Eighth Army** area, the Germans mount fierce opposition against the British 4th Division, which is attacking from Forli; heavy skirmishing continues throughout the day and on the following day, the British overcome the resistance and advance toward Montone.

A U.S. Infantryman pauses to check out a destroyed German Rocket launcher.

November 11th 1944 — (International) It is the 26th anniversary of the end of World War I. **(Pacific-Palaus)** The 81st Cavalry Reconnaissance Troop, U.S.A. captures Gorokoltan Island. **(Pacific-Philippines-Leyte)** In the **U.S. Sixth Army** area, **X Corps** sector, U.S. Artillery bombards enemy positions on Breakneck Ridge, preceding another attack by the 21st Infantry, 24th Division; the 1st Battalion shoots forward taking a ridge, but aborts the attack short of the crest. The 1st Battalion, 34th Division is forced to move to Agahang northwest of Limon, to secure food from the Filipinos there. In Naval activity, Planes from three Carrier Groups, under Rear Admiral F.C. Sherman, strike a Japanese Convoy off Leyte in Ormoc Bay, sinking four Destroyers and a Minesweeper: *Hamanami, Naganami, Shimakaze,* and *Wakatsuki* and the Minesweeper No. 30. **(Pacific-Volcano Islands)** A Cruiser and Destroyer Task Group, commanded by Rear Admiral A.E. Smith and attached to Admiral Halsey's Third Fleet and Land-based Bombers, attack the Airfields and installations on Iwo Jima, commencing the assault before midnight and continuing the pounding on the 12th. **(Pacific-Burma)** In the N.C.A.C. area, the Japanese repulse an outflanking attack by the British 36th Division at Pinwe. **(Pacific-China)** The Japanese Airfield at Heng-yang receives a savage blow from Planes of the U.S. Fourteenth Air Force that staggers the enemy and prevents them from utilizing the Base for operations, except those which are considered Army cooperation flights. **(Atlantic-Western Europe)** 21st Army Group The **British Second Army** regrouping continues to allow it to support the U.S. Ninth Army's offensive in the Roer Valley northeast of Aachen. **12th Army Group** In the **U.S. Ninth Army** area, the VIII Corps assumes command of the 83rd Division, detached from the XX Corps. In the **U.S. Third Army** area, **XX Corps** sector, the bridgehead of the 90th Division is greatly expanded; the 359th Infantry fends off several counterattacks and drives forward to some ridges, establishing outposts at Kerling and forging roadblocks southeast of Rettel; however, it cannot dislodge the enemy at Oudrenne along the southern flank. At Metrich, contingents of the 357th Infantry continue to reduce the remnant defenders, while the balance of the Regiment attacks toward the high ground near Breistroff-la-Petit, sprinting far ahead of the Regiments which are advancing on the south flank against Fort Koenigsmacker, which capitulates. Hill 254, situated on Bois d'Elzange ridge, is captured by the 358th Infantry. The 2nd Battalion, 378th Infantry, 95th Division and Engineers take advantage of the subsiding waters of the Moselle and establish a bridgehead across the river at Thionville; it then assaults Fort Yutz. In conjunction, the 377th Infantry maintains its small bridgehead near Bertrange, while the 2nd Infantry, 5th Division roars ahead, reaching Aube and Dain-en-Saulnois along the southern flank by the Nied Francaise River. In the **XII Corps** area, the 6th Armored Division, in concert with the 80th Division, establishes bridgeheads across the Nied Francaise at Sanry-sur-Nied, Remilly, and then places a treadway bridge at Baudrecourt. The Germans begin abandoning their positions in the Foret de Chateau-Salins; the 314th and 315th Regiments are in pursuit. Combat Command A, 4th Armored Division and the 104th Infantry, 26th Division, attack along the southern flank of the Corps; Rodalbe is seized by the latter. The 101st Regiment, 26th Division takes Hill 310 and establishes firm positions on Koecking ridge. **6th Army Group** In the **French 1st Army** area, the 1st Corps Commander's request to temporarily postpone Operation INDEPENDENCE from the 13th to the 14th is granted, permitting further preparations to continue. **(Atlantic-Italy)** In the **U.S. Fifth Army** area, British 13th Corps sector, the Indian 8th Division launches a small assault, jumping off from M. S. Bartolo; the enemy repulses it handily. In the **British Eighth Army** area, the British 4th Division penetrates the enemy entrenched positions outside of Forli and sprints toward the Montone River.

November 12th 1944 — (Pacific-Philippines-Leyte) In the **U.S. Sixth Army** area, **X Corps** sector, Breakneck Ridge and its crest fall to the 21st Infantry, 24th Division, but Japanese resistance along Highway 2 prevents it from pressing the advantage and driving south toward Ormoc. The 1st Battalion, 34h Infantry receives supplies from an Airdrop, and it is able to move to Cabiranan from Consuegra. South of Limon, Highway 2 is defended by the 2nd Battalion, 19th Infantry, and although it comes under severe enemy pressure, the roadblock holds until the 23rd. In Naval activity, Japanese Suicide Planes damage the U.S. Repair Ships *Egeria* (ARL-8) and *Achilles* (ARL-41). In other activity, the Japanese Submarine I-37 is sunk south of Yap Island by the Destroyer *Nicholas* (DD-449). Carrier-based Planes sink the Japanese Transport No. 39 in Manila Bay. **(Pacific-Borneo-Philippines)** Between the 10th of October and today, Major Richard I. Bong, U.S. Air Corps, a Gunnery instructor, volunteers to fly combat missions over Balikpapan, Borneo, and in Leyte. During these missions, he personally shoots down eight enemy Aircraft; Major Bong receives the Medal of Honor. **(Southeast Asia Command)** Allied Land Forces South East Asia (ALFSEA) is activated under Lt. General Sir Oliver Leese, and he assumes command of British troops in N.C.A.C. (Burma) and CAI

(China and India), and Chinese troops operating in SEAC. The post of Deputy Supreme Allied Commander, SEAC, formerly held by General "Vinegar Joe" Stilwell, is assumed by Lt. General Raymond A. Wheeler, U.S.A. **(Pacific-China)** The first elements of the East China Air Task Force, established by General Chennault to support the Chinese effort to defend the Airfields in eastern China, arrive at Suichwan and will be committed against the enemy within a week. **(Atlantic-Western Europe) 21st Army Group** In the **British Second Army** area, the 30th Corps assumes responsibility for the U.S. Ninth Army's northern flank, stretching south to the Wurm River. **12th Army Group** In the **U.S. First Army** area, **VII Corps** sector, the beleaguered contingent of the 12th Infantry, 4th Division, trapped on the plateau southwest of Huertgen, is reached by two Companies, but the Germans also surround them. The isolated troops hold until the 15th when they are rescued. In the **U.S. Third Army** area, the 359th Infantry, 90th Division, has no Tanks or Tank Destroyers at its disposal, and the bridge to the rear is out; it is struck by a strengthened counterattack by elements of the German 1st Army at Kerling, to clear a path to the Moselle at Malling. Enemy Tanks and Infantry units rumble forward, dislodging outposts at Kerling and threatening Petite-Hettange; however, a sturdy defense thwarts the assault and drives the Regimental sized Infantry force back with heavy losses, due in part to the support of 30th Artillery Battalions, which pours in a thunderclap of fire.

During the heated battle and before dawn, Technical Sergeant Forrest Everhart attempts to singlehandedly equalize the enemy and protect the left flank's remaining machine gun. He races 400 yards through enemy fire, then unleashes the gun's fury. As the enemy closes, he charges, pouring hand grenades upon them. Within 15 minutes, 30 enemy Soldiers lay dead. Everhart then dashes to the right flank and engages in another hand grenade duel that lasts a half hour; he kills another 20 Germans in addition to turning the attack back and saving the position; Everhart receives the Medal of Honor. Enemy Artillery subsequently destroys the Malling bridge. Meanwhile, the 357th and 358th Regiments continue to attack, the former driving through Breistroff-la-Petit toward Inglange and the latter seizing the villages of Elzange and Valmsestroff. P.F.C. Foster J. Sayers, Company L, 357th Infantry, while carrying his machine gun, charges up a hill at Thionville and from a distance of 20 yards from the enemy, dashes to distract the enemy to allow his Company to seize the crest. At point blank range, he kills 12 dug-in Germans, but he is killed; the objective is taken; P.F.C. Foster receives the Medal of Honor posthumously. At Cattenom, a bridge to span the Moselle is started. The 2nd Infantry, 5th Division, operating on the southern flank of the Corps, moves into the 6th Armored bridgehead at Sanry-sur-Nied (XII Corps sector); shortly thereafter it is struck by an enemy counterattack that lasts into the following morning before being repulsed. The 5th Division prepares for its drive against the Metz; the 11th Infantry pushes its right flank to the Seille River. In the **XII Corps** area, a contingent of Combat Command A, 6th Armored, overpowers heavy resistance at Herny, then advances toward Faulquemont; another detachment rolls across the Nied Francaise at Baudrecourt. These penetrations by the 6th Armored Division fortify the positions of the 80th Division, which the Germans had hoped to entrap between Rotte Creek and the Nied Francaise. With the threat terminated, the 6th Armored Division heads south of Faulquemont to seize the high ground. Faxe capitulates to the 137th Infantry, 35th Division; the seizure reinstates communications between columns of the 4th Armored Division's Combat Command B, which chases the enemy to Oron and takes a bridge intact. The 137th Infantry continues to drive east; the 320th Regiment finishes reducing the enemy in the Foret de Chateau-Salins, then reverts to reserve. The 134th Infantry reaches Bellange and is ordered to halt. The Germans dig in deep and commit Armor Reserves which stop the attack of the 26th Division and Combat Command A, 4th Armored, on the south flank of the Corps. The Germans strike C.C.A., pushing it from the vicinity of Bermering back to Bois de Conthil where it is forced to wait for replacement Tanks. The 3rd Battalion, 104th Infantry, holding Rodalbe, is annihilated when an enemy counterattack retakes the town. Another unit of Combat Command A, driving on the right flank, seizes Hill 337 near Lidrezing, and contingents recapture Conthil, reopening the main supply line. In other activity, the 328th Regiment, reinforced by the 101st Regiment, drives through the forest on Koecking Ridge, advancing to Berange Farm where it convincingly reduces a formidable enemy stronghold. At St. Medard, the Germans repulse an attack by the 101st Infantry. **6th Army Group** In the **U.S. Seventh Army** area, **VI Corps** sector, the 100th Division initiates a flanking attack at Raon-l'Etape, committing its 397th and 399th Regiments which ford the Meurthe at Baccarat to sever the enemy escape route and assault it from the rear. **(Atlantic-Italy)** In the **British Eighth Army** area, the Polish 2nd Corps drives toward the Castrocaro-Converselle-St. Lucia line to coordinate with the 5th Corps. In the 5 Corps area, the British 4th Division's forward progress is frozen by fierce resistance, north of Highway 9, at S. Tome outside of Montone. In other activity, the 138th Brigade, British 46th Division drives across the Montone River southwest of Forli, reaching M. Poggiolo on the following day. **(Atlantic-Norway)** British Lancaster Bombers sink the German Battleship *Tirpitz* in the Tromso Fjord. In other activity, Warships of the Royal Navy attack a German coastal Convoy. **(Atlantic-Yugoslavia)** Kumanovo, on the Skoplje-Nis rail line, is taken by elements of the Bulgarian 1st Army.

November 13th 1944 — (Pacific-Philippines-Leyte) In the **U.S. Sixth Army** area, **X Corps** sector, the 21st Infantry, 24th Division gnaws forward on Breakneck Ridge, gaining about 500 tough yards, further reducing the resistance there; the 1st Battalion, 34th Infantry drives to Kilay Ridge without opposition, taking the strategic objective which lies about 700 yards west of the roadblock held by the 2nd Battalion, 19th Infantry along Highway 2. In Naval activity, Planes of three Carrier Task Groups, commanded by Rear Admiral Sherman, commence a two-day assault against enemy Shipping and installations in central Luzon and in Manila. The Japanese lose the Light Cruiser *Kisa*; the Destroyers *Akebono, Akishimo, Hatsuharu,* and *Okinami*; and the Auxiliary Submarine Chaser No. 116. **(Eastern Pacific)** The U.S.S. *Rockford* (PF-48), a Coast Guard Cutter, and the Minelayer *Ardent* sink the Japanese Submarine I-38. **(Pacific-Burma)** ALFSEA: In the **British Fourteenth Army** area, 33rd Corps sector, Patrols from the Indian 5th Division and the East African 11th Division converge near Kalemyo. **(Atlantic-Western Europe) 21st Army Group** In the **Canadian First Army** area, 2nd Corps sector, the U.S. 82nd Airborne reverts to the First Allied Airborne Army; its sector is taken over by the Canadian 3rd Division. **12th Army Group** In the **U.S. Third Army** area, **XX Corps** sector, Kerling is recaptured by the 359th Infantry, 90th Division; it sets out to join the 357th Regiment near Oudrenne, while the 358th Regiment maintains its pressure against the enemy at Bois d'Elzange Ridge; both Regiments are severely

hampered by mines. At Cattenom, the bridge is open for traffic; it receives incessant use as legions of Vehicles and support weapons pour across. The enemy bastions at Fort Yutz and Basse Yutz are seized by the 2nd Battalion, 378th Infantry, 95th Division. The 377th Regiment gets its final contingents across the bridgehead at Uckange; it captures Bertrange and Imeldange without heavy effort, then it repels a German counterattack. The U.S. 5th Division heads west for Metz, its 11th Infantry seizing territory near Fey, Pournoy-la-Chevite, and Coin-les-Cuvry. Forts Aisne and Yser are seized by the 10th Regiment. In conjunction, Ancerville is seized by contingents of the 2nd Infantry and with the support of Engineers, a bridge is built and held; the troops repel a heavy enemy counterattack during the night, keeping the Regiment from being shoved back across the Nied River. In the **XII Corps** sector, the Germans mount a tenacious drive that pushes back the forward outposts of the 6th Armored Division at the Sanry bridgehead, but Combat Command B's main line of defense holds firm. The 5th Division relieves the 6th Armored Division which then moves southeast and assumes responsibility for the bridgehead. The 370th Infantry, 80th Division, and a contingent of Combat Command A, 6th Armored, drive toward Faulquemont. Arraincourt is seized by another contingent of C.C.A. Morhange, a German communication center, is the objective of C.C.B., 4th Armored and the 35th Division. Spearheaded by the Armor, the advance gains Villers-sur-Nied and a strategic ridge near Achain by the 137th Regiment; the 134th Infantry takes Achain on its left and pushes to Rougemont on the right. During the fighting at Achain, Staff Sergeant Junior J. Spurrier, Company G, 134th Infantry, a Kentuckian, flanks the village on his own and attacks from the west with his BAR and an M1 Rifle, killing 3 Germans. His exploits continue throughout the day against an assortment of enemy troops and weapons, resulting in the singlehanded killing of one Officer and 24 enlisted men, plus the capturing of two Officers and two enlisted men. His extraordinary actions are in the highest traditions of the U.S. Army, and he is awarded the Medal of Honor. Meanwhile the 328th Infantry, 26th Division encounters severe enemy fire as it maneuvers through the woods on Koecking Ridge. At St. Medard in the rear, the Germans battle to stalemate with the 101st Regiment; at Haraucourt the right flank of the 328th Infantry is endangered due to frail defenses. During the day, General Bradley visits Patton at Chateau-Salins, and then he visits the 4th Armored Division positions, seeing firsthand the terrible conditions; Tanks that move off the muddy roads actualy "belly down." **6th Army Group** In the **U.S. Seventh Army** area, the **XV Corps** commences a drive against Sarrebourg; its 44th Division jumps off from Leintrey toward Avricourt, encountering tenacious enemy fire; the 79th Division presses punishingly, advancing to the fringes of Ancerviller. In the **VI Corps** area, the northern flank, defended by the 100th Division, is struck by a German counterattack; with the assistance of Artillery, the assault is repulsed, but the encounter delays the imminent attack of the 100th Division. At St. Die, the Germans set the town ablaze prior to abandoning their positions. In the **French 1st Army** area, Winston Churchill and French General DeGaulle meet with General de Lattre at Besancon. In the 1st Corps area, both sides are immobilized by a hefty blizzard. **(Atlantic-Greece)** With the liberation of Greece complete, the Anglo-Greek covenant of March 9th is modified and places all Greek forces under British High Command. **(Atlantic-Italy)** In the **U.S. Fifth Army** area, M.S. Bartolo falls to the Indian 8th Division, following a bitterly contested fight. In the **British Eighth Army** area, 5th Corps sector, the 138th Brigade, British 46th Division, stretches its Montone bridgehead to the M. Poggiolo vicinity; its 128th Brigade seizes S. Varano. The replacement problem is grievous, causing the British to fill gaps with under-strengthed units; the weakened 167th Brigade, 56th Division is deployed along Highway 9, between the 4th and 46th Divisions.

November 14th 1944 — (Pacific-Philippines-Leyte) In the **U.S. Sixth Army** area, **X Corps** sector, General Krueger directs General Sibert to utilize the 32nd Division by sending it to relieve elements of the 24th Division. The Japanese have been displaced from Breakneck Ridge with the exception of some nearby spurs. The 1st Battalion, 34th Infantry patrols on Kilay Ridge, relying on Filipinos to keep them supplied. In other activity, RCT 112 debarks on Leyte and is placed under Corps control. In the **XXIV Corps** sector, the 32nd Infantry, 7th Division is ordered to march north to the Damulaan-Caridad area and await orders to strike toward Ormoc. **(Pacific-SEAC)** Sir Trafford Leigh Mallory, en route to assume the position of Air Commander in Chief SEAC, is killed in a Plane crash; the position is subsequently filled by Sir Guy Garrod. **(Pacific-Burma)** In the N.C.A.C. area, the Chinese 22nd Division seizes Man-tha effortlessly, then advances toward Si-u. Elements of the Chinese 38th Division approach Bhamo, the 113th Regiment crosses the Taping River at Myothit and advances west along the southern bank, and the 113th, also converging on Bhamo, encounters stiff resistance near Momauk, eight miles east of the objective. **(Pacific-China Sea)** The Japanese Auxiliary Vessel *Kurasaki* and the Coast Defense Vessel No. 7 are sunk by the Submarines *Raton* (SS-270) and *Ray* (SS-271) respectively. **(Atlantic-Western Europe) 21st Army Group** In the **British Second Army** area, the 12th Corps attacks across the Nord and Wessem Canals, its 51st and 53rd Divisions driving toward the German bridgehead west of the Maas in the Roermond-Venlo region. **12th Army Group** In the **U.S. First Army** area, **V Corps** sector, the exhausted 28th Division begins transferring to the VIII Corps area. The 112th Regiment departs after relief by the 109th Infantry (28th Div.) which is reinforced by the 2nd Ranger Battalion. In the **U.S. Third Army** area, **XX Corps** sector, the 359th Infantry, 90th Division seizes Oudrenne while the 358th takes Distroff and severs the Inglange-Distroff road. The 90th's crossing of the Moselle is tedious; subsequent to the successful crossing of two Battalions, the bridge goes out, forcing the balance to use assault boats. At Thionville, a Bailey bridge is complete, and the 10th Armored's Combat Command B rolls across the Moselle in the afternoon. In conjunction, Combat Command A, 10th Armored Division and the 3rd Cavalry Group ford the river at Malling. The 379th Infantry, 95th Division attacks west of the Metz; its 1st Battalion charges toward an enemy stronghold known as Seven Dwarfs, capturing three of the northern redoubts, but it is repulsed at the fourth, Fort Bois la Dame; its 2nd Battalion, outflanking Fort Jeanne d'Arc to assault it from the rear, beats back a strong German counterattack. The penetration places the Regiment too deep to be resupplied, except by air. The 2nd Battalion, 378th Infantry, 95th Division seizes Haute-Yutz, then attacks Fort d'Illange. The Germans holding Bertrange and Imeldange come under heavy attack by the 1st Battalion, 377th Regiment. The 5th Division maintains its pressure against Metz. The 11th Infantry overruns Prayelle Farm and clears the woods southwest of Verdun, while the 10th Infantry secures about half of Bois de l'Hopital. In the **XII Corps** sector, Combat Command A, 6th Armored Division seizes

Brulange, Suisse, and Landroff, the latter coming under a tenacious counterattack at dusk that breaks into the town. Combat Command B, 4th Armored Division, and the 137th Infantry, 35th Division engage the Germans fiercely at Destry and at Baronville, seizing both as they close on Morhange. In addition, Combat Command A, 4th Armored, punches its way through Bois de Kerpeche; contingents advance northeast from Koecking Ridge, reaching Guebling, while the 328th Infantry, 26th Division drives through the Koecking Forest, reducing its resistance. The Germans await darkness and begin to abandon their positions throughout the night 14th-15th. In other activity, Patton, along with General Van Fleet, visits the scene of the battle on the twelfth; Patton remarks: "I HAVE NEVER SEEN SO MANY DEAD GERMANS IN MY LIFE. THEY EXTENDED FOR ABOUT A MILE, PRACTICALLY SHOULDER TO SHOULDER." It should be noted that many of the dead resulted from heavy concentrations of Artillery fire and that many bodies had been relocated to the roadside by the Graves Registration Service. **6th Army Group** In the **U.S. Seventh Army** area, **XV Corps** sector, the 79th Division seizes Ste Pole and Ancerviller after hard fighting. The 44th Division is heavily engaged with the Germans at Leintrey; by the following day it continues its drive toward Avricourt. In the **French 1st Army** area, the 1st Corps begins its drive to the Belfort Gap at 12:00, driving along the Doubs River, catching the enemy offguard by its swiftness. The 9th Colonial Division drives on the right, while the French 5th Armored and the 2nd Moroccan Divisions plow ahead on the left. **(Atlantic-Norway)** The Norway government (in exile) proclaims that Colonel Arne Dahl has landed in Norway with Norwegian troops which will fight alongside the Soviet Karelian forces against the Germans on the Arctic front. **(Atlantic-Italy)** In the **British Eighth Army** area, 5th Corps sector, the British 4th Division advances to the Montone River north of Highway No. 9. In other activity, the British 46th Division continues heading for the Samoggia River. **(Atlantic-Yugoslavia)** Yugoslavian troops occupy Skoplje, eliminating the main staging point used by the Germans during their retreat from Greece. It had been abandoned by the Germans on the previous day.

November 15th 1944 — (Pacific-Philippines-Leyte) In the **U.S. Sixth Army** area, **X Corps** sector, the 112th Cavalry is attached to the 1st Cavalry Division. In other activity, the 128th Infantry, 32nd Division receives orders to pass through the lines of the 21st Regiment, 24th Division and drive south toward Ormoc; the 1st Battalion, 34th Infantry unsuccessfully sends Patrols toward Ormoc to make contact with the 2nd Battalion, 19th Infantry. **(Pacific-New Guinea-Asia Islands)** The **U.S. Eighth Army** commences its first offensive action. Contingents of the 31st Division, supported by U.S. and British Warships under the command of Admiral Lord Ashbourne, Royal Navy, support the amphibious invasion of Mapia Island, about 160 miles northeast of Sansapor. The invasion encounters nominal resistance by the Japanese. **(Pacific-Marianas-Saipan)** The 3rd 155mm Howitzer Battalion arrives from Peleliu. **(Pacific-Palaus)** The 81st Cavalry Reconnaissance Troop, U.S.A., captures Ngeregong Island. **(Pacific-Burma)** In the N.C.A.C. area, the U.S. 475th Infantry departs Camp Landis to aid the Chinese 22nd Division at Si-u. The Chinese 38th Division maintains effective roadblocks near Bhamo. In the **British Fourteenth Army** area, 33rd Corps sector, the British part in Phase 1 of Operation CAPITAL nears its conclusion as Kalemyo is taken without opposition. The 15th Corps passes to the direct command of ALFSEA. **(Atlan-**

tic-Western Europe) **12th Army Group** In the **U.S. First Army's VII Corps** area, the four surrounded Companies of the 4th Division are rescued by the 12th Infantry, but the Regiment now controls only a small portion of the southern edge of the plateau outside of Huertgen. In the **U.S. Third Army** area, **XX Corps** sector, the Germans initiate a large counterattack and drive to Distroff before being repulsed by the 358th Infantry, 90th Division. Meanwhile, the 359th Regiment reverts to the reserves. The 357th Regiment assaults the enemy between Budling and Buding, encountering incessant enemy fire at the Hackenberg works that halts its progress. The 10th Armored Division begins its attack; Combat Command A seizes Lemestroff; Combat Command B encounters great difficulty from obstacles including mines that slow its drive toward Bouzonville. In other activity, troops of the 95th Division, deployed east of the Moselle, become Task Force Bacon (Colonel Robert Bacon), which is to attack Metz. The 2nd Battalion, 378th Regiment seizes the Illange Forts, terminating enemy opposition in the northern sector of the 95th Divisional zone, and the 1st Battalion, 377th Regiment finishes mopping up at Bertrange and Imeldange before joining the Task Force. West of the Metz, the 95th Division deepens its offensive effort; Fort de Feves is seized by the 378th; it also seizes the heights southwest of and Bois de Woippy; the 377th secures La Maxe, then assaults against Woippy, establishing contact with the 378th after dark. The 5th Division reforms for its final drive against Metz. The 11th Infantry seizes Augny and drives to the fringes of the Frescaty Airport, while the 10th Regiment drives into Marly against vicious resistance. In conjunction, the 2nd Regiment clears Mecleuves and holds the Sanry bridge, withstanding strong enemy attempts to take it. In the **XII Corps** area, contingents of the 319th Infantry, 80th Division, and the 6th Armored Division storm into Landroff, securing it. Cote de Suisse falls to an Armored Task Force. The Metz-Sarrebourg railroad is reached by Combat Command A, 4th Armored, but due to exposure on its right flank and its movement being confined to roads, the unit is halted. The Germans have evacuated Morhange, permitting the 35th Infantry to breeze through and advance to the Metz-Sarrebourg railroad. In the Koecking woods, the 26th Division makes progress in the eastern section, its 101st Regiment and the 2nd Cavalry Group running up the heels of the retreating Germans who are heading for Dieuze. At Guebling, Combat Command A, 4th Armored, which had seized the town after an expensive battle, is forced to withdraw; it has been unable to dislodge the entrenched Germans who control the nearby terrain, which commands the town. **6th Army Group** In the **U.S. Seventh Army** area, **XV Corps** sector, the 44th Division drives toward Avricourt. The 79th Division advances toward the Vezouse River, seizing Halloville. In the **VI Corps** area, the 100th Infantry Division crashes through enemy lines north of Raon-l'Etape. In other activity, the 103rd Division prepares to enter offensive warfare by attacking entrenched positions on a hill mass outside of St. Die. In the **French 1st Army** area, the 3rd Algerian Division advances to Le Tholy. In the 2nd Corps area, the 2nd Moroccan Division, supported by the 5th Armored Division, drives through Arcey, heading toward Hericourt, while the 9th Colonial Division seizes Colombier-Fontaine, Ecot, and Ecurcey, a route to Herimoncourt. **(Atlantic-Hungary)** Soviet troops take Jaszbereny as they advance toward Budapest. **(Atlantic-Italy)** In the **U.S. Fifth Army** area, British 13th Corps sector, elements of the Indian 8th Division move into Modigliana, establishing contact with the Polish 2nd Corps.

A U.S. Soldier and his Guard Dog, on duty in the Philippines.

November 16th 1944 — (Pacific-Philippines-Leyte) In the **U.S Sixth Army** area, **X Corps** sector, the 1st and 3rd Battalions, 128th Infantry, 32nd Division, attack toward Ormoc, funneling through the lines of the 24th Division on Breakneck Ridge; the 3rd Battalion advances 300 yards without incident; the 1st Battalion is stopped shortly after jump off. In other activity, Patrols of the 1st Battalion, 34th Infantry are still unable to make contact with the 2nd Battalion, 19th Infantry. The 24th Division has responsibility for defending the Jaro-Ormoc trail. **(Pacific-Burma)** In the N.C.A.C. area, the British 36th Division is still encountering heavy enemy opposition, which holds up its advance in the railroad corridor near Pinwe; the two isolated Companies which had been snagged at an enemy roadblock withdraw. **(Atlantic-Western Europe) 21st Army Group** In the **British Second Army** 8th Corps area, the 15th Division enters Meijel, discovering it abandoned by the enemy. In the 12th Corps sector, Patrols penetrate as far as the Zig Canal, southeast of Meijel. **12th Army Group** The U.S. First and Ninth Armies open up a joint offensive to secure the Roer Plain (Operation QUEEN) and drive to the Rhine (northern). The operation receives massive Air support, encompassing 1,204 U.S. Bombers and 1,188 British Bombers, the largest close air support to date by the Allies. Coordination between the air and ground is excellent, and the bombardment, exceeding 10,000 tons, spares the friendly lines with the exception of one minuscule incident concerning a malfunctioning bomb. At 12:45, the offensive commences. In the **U.S. Ninth Army** area, C.C.B., 2nd Armored Division rolls forward seizing Floverich, Immendorf, and Puffendorf, the latter on the fringes of the outer defenses of Juelich. At Apweiler, the Germans repulse attempts by elements of the Armor to reduce it; another contingent grinds forward and takes a hill about 700 yards outside of Puffendorf. The 29th Division attacks from Bettendorf and Siersdorf toward Juelich, but the Germans halt the advance soon after jump off. Elements of the 30th Division, bolstered by contingents of the 84th Division, seize Mariadorf and Euchen, but the enemy holds firmly at Wuerselen. During one vicious skirmish, Company K, 119th Infantry, 30th Division is stopped by intense fire on bare ground 100 yards from the objective. Staff Sergeant Horner lunges forward with his submachine gun, answering a burst of fire with a devastating response that eliminates one gun. He then charges the other two, prompting the gunners to abandon their positions and seek shelter in the basement. Horner tosses a couple of grenades down the basement and requests surrender; four of the enemy oblige; Sgt. Horner receives the Medal of Honor. The First Army, synchronized with the Ninth, also jumps off at 12:45, heading

509

toward the Roer; its 104th Infantry bolts toward the Donnerberg (Hill 287) and the Eschweiler woods, encountering vicious resistance from the high ground at Donnerberg, impeding progress; some contingents grasp a shallow hold on Birkengang outside of Stolberg. Combat Command B, 3rd Armored Division drives toward four villages near the western base of Hamich Ridge. Task Force Mills attacks Hastenrath and Scherpenseel, encountering iron resistance, losing 15 Tanks, and failing to gain the objectives. Kottenich and Werth are both seized by Task Force Lovelady. The 1st Division, bolstered by the 47th Infantry, 9th Division, initiating the primary thrust of the Corps, drives through the Huertgen Forest toward Langerwehe and Juengersdorf; one Battalion enters Gressenich. The 16th Infantry, missing Tank support, grinds its way on the right against stiff resistance; the 26th Regiment forces its way to the woods near Hamich. A heavy counterattack strikes the 16th Regiment. Tech Sergeant Jake Lindsey, at the point 10 yards in front of his Platoon, destroys two machine gun nests and turns back two Tanks. The intrepid Lindsey, although wounded severely, spots the enemy setting up additional machine gun positions and engages them in hand-to-hand combat, resulting in the death of three men, the capture of three more, and the withdrawal of the remaining two. Lindsey holds his Platoon's position, and for his bravery he is awarded the Medal of Honor. Meanwhile, the 4th Division, bolstered by the 5th Armored, swings through the forest between Huertgen and Schevenhuette to support the efforts of the 1st Division, but the Germans hold masterful positions and dole out heavy fire, reducing the progress of the 8th and 22nd Regiments; on the plateau south of Huertgen enemy fire has the 12th Infantry nearly paralyzed. In the **U.S. Third Army** area, the 357th Infantry seizes a ridge beyond Hackenberg, subsequent to knocking the guns out of commission; the 358th Regiment grabs Inglange and Metzervisse for the sequel. In addition, Task Forces are drilling forward: Ste Marguerite falls to Combat Command A's T.F. Standish, while T.F. Chamberlain, also of the 10th Armored, drives beyond Laumesfeld. Tremery is approached by T.F. Bacon, 95th Division. West of the Moselle, the Germans begin to pull back speedily from Woippy under the heated pursuit of the 377th and 378th Regiments, while St. Hubert Farm and Moscou Farm fall prey to the 379th Infantry, 95th Division. During one of the firefights at Woippy, Staff Sergeant Andrew Miller's Rifle Squad becomes trapped in a crossfire. Miller advances singlehandedly and barges into a building capturing its machine gun crew by bayonet. He then advances and singlehandedly knocks out the 2nd nest, killing two men, wounding three, and capturing two additional Soldiers. On the following day he singlehandedly wipes out another machine gun nest that endangers his Company; he receives the Medal of Honor. The 5th Division also presses toward Metz, investing the Verdun Forts; it drives doggedly against the Frescaty Airfield with its 11th Regiment, while the 10th Infantry secures Marly, then bolts toward Magny; vicious combat also ensues between the 2nd Regiment and the Germans at the Nied Francaise River.

During the confrontation, a Battalion breaks through, moving toward Frontigny. In the **XII Corps** sector, heavy U.S. Guns at Cote de Suisse pummel the area near Faulquemont, giving extra punch to a large scale assault by Combat Command A, 6th Armored, and the 318th and 319th Regiments. The formidable force overruns five towns, dispersing the enemy and penetrating the high ground south of the town, sequestering 1,200 prisoners. **6th Army Group** In the **U.S. Seventh Army** area, **XV Corps** sector, the 79th Division seizes Barbas, then drives beyond, gaining ground closer to Vezouse. Elements of

Combat Command R, French 2nd Armored secure Nonhigny. In the **VI Corps** sector, the 103rd Division secures part of a hill mass southwest of St. Die. In the **French 1st Army** area, the 1st Corps drives through Ste Marie, then presses toward Montbeliard on its left; to the right, it strikes Roches-les-Blamont. **(Atlantic- Italy)** In the **U.S. Fifth Army** area, the British 13th Corps halts its advance to implement troop rotation. In the **British Eighth Army** area, the 5th Corps stops along the line of the Montone and Cosina Rivers for regrouping, including withdrawal of the 56th Division from the line.

November 17th 1944 — (United States) The Combined Chiefs of Staff approve British Admiral Mountbatten's plan (offered during October) to secure the Arakan coast; however, they disapprove his proposal for the Kra Isthmus operation and in addition, they request a specific strategy to utilize the Cocos Islands as a staging Base. **(Pacific-Philippines-Leyte)** In the **U.S. Sixth Army** area, **X Corps** sector, elements of the 128th Infantry, 32nd Division, fight to less than a thousand yards from Limon, but the enemy contains the 1st Battalion on Corkscrew Hill. In Naval activity, the Attack Transport *Alpine F-3* (APA-92) is damaged by a Kamikaze Plane (Philippine Sea). The Japanese Submarine I-26 is sunk by the Destroyer Escort *Lawrence C. Taylor* and Planes (VC-82) from the Carrier Escort *Anzio* (Philippine Sea). In other activity, the U.S. 77th Division departs Manus Island, heading for Leyte. **(Pacific-China)** In an attempt to secure a route to Kunming, the Hump terminus, and Chungking, the Japanese initiate an attack, driving from the Kweilin-Liuchow area to seize Kweiyang. **(Pacific-South China Sea)** The Japanese Torpedo Boat *Hiyodori* is sunk by the U.S.S. *Gunnel* (SS-253). **(Pacific-Yellow Sea)** The U.S.S. *Spadefish* (SS-411) sinks the Japanese Escort Carrier *Jinyo*. **(Atlantic-Western Europe) 21st Army Group** In the **British Second Army** area, the 12th Corps advances contingents to the Maas River; they seize Wessem, across from Roermond. **12th Army Group** In the **U.S. Ninth Army** area, **XIX Corps** area, C.C.B., 2nd Armored Division is struck by severe counterattacks at Immendorf and Puffendorf, losing a hill near the latter, but otherwise turning back the assault. C.C.A., 2nd Armored Division attacks through Puffendorf; the enemy halts progress, preventing it from getting out of the town. Elements of the 29th Division make an unsuccessful attempt to overrun Setterich, urgently needed to support the 2nd Armored Division. Further south, the Germans retain control of Bettendorf and Siersdorf. The 30th Division, sweeping along the south flank of the Corps, seizes Heengen, overpowers Broichweiden, and reduces the balance of Wuerselen. In the **U.S. First Army** area, **VII Corps** sector, the 104th Division is viciously engaged at the Donnerburg River, but it secures the majority of Birkengang. The sluggish advance of the 104th Division complicates matters for Task Force Mills (C.C.B., 3rd Armored) which is holding precariously on the southern edges of Hastenrath and Scherpenseel, positioning it within range of the guns of Eschweiler woods and from other Artillery along the Donnerberg; half its complement is destroyed by dark. The 47th Infantry, 1st Division eliminates the rear guard at Gressenich; its 16th Regiment, supported by Tanks, closes on Hamich, while the 26th Infantry fights for a few hundred tough yards on the right flank. The Huertgen Forest remains a bloodbath as the 4th Division pounds futilely under heavy rains and extreme cold, against rigid resistance. In the **U.S. Third Army** area, **XX Corps** sector, the 10th Armored, using close Air support to good advantage, flexes its strength, stretching wide in pursuit of the retreating enemy, which is bolting toward the Saare. Hackenberg is vacuumed by the 357th Infantry, subsequent to its reduction by pointed heavy fire, then it secures Klang; the 358th Regiment overruns Metzeresche, prompting the enemy to await nightfall and abandon their positions. Task Force Bacon, 95th Division grinds intently toward the Metz, pausing within sight of Fort St. Julien. West of the Moselle, the 95th Division is also closing on the Metz; the 377th Regiment drives to the entrance of Sansonnet. The 5th Division attacks in strength toward the Metz, encountering nominal resistance as its 10th Infantry advances until halted at Fort Queuleu; its 11th Regiment secures the majority of Frescaty Airfield before being stopped by heavy fire from Fort St. Privat. In the **XII Corps** sector, the Germans initiate a general withdrawal during the night 17th-18th. Combat Command B, 4th Armored, rejoins the Division as the Corps readies its final drive to the Sarre. In other activity, prisoners inform the Americans that Falkenberg is saturated with time-delayed bombs, some with as many as 21 days delayed action. About 15 will subsequently explode. **6th Army Group** In the **U.S. Seventh Army** area, **XV Corps** sector, the 44th Division seizes Avricourt. The French 2nd Armored Division takes Badonviller, then jumps to Bremenil. In the **VI Corps** area, Raon is targeted by the 100th Division; its 398th Regiment crosses the Meurthe at Baccarat, preparing to strike a deadly blow from the north. The 103rd Division completes its clearing operation in the hills southwest of St. Die; after dark, it dispatches Patrols into St. Die, discovering the enemy is abandoning the town. In other activity, the 36th Division dispatches Patrols into Corcieux, guided by the lights of burning buildings set ablaze by the Germans. In the **French 1st Army** area, Western French Forces sector, Forces Francaise de l'Quest (FFO) is organized by General de Larminat to defend the coast of the Bay of Biscay, extending its line from the island of de Re and La Rochelle on the north to Pointe de Grave and Royan in the south. The 1st Corps plows through the enemy defenses at Belfort near the Lisaine and Gland Rivers and seizes Hericourt, Montbeliard, and Herimoncourt. During one ruthless firefight near Schevenhutte, Company F, 8th Regiment, 4th Division, is halted by concertina-type wire; its ranks are belted by mortars, machine gun fire, and Artillery in addition to facing small-arms fire and being stuck in the midst of a minefield. First Lt. Bernard Ray, against the opinions of his men, stuffs his pockets with explosive caps, confiscates a few bangalore torpedoes, and wraps his body with highly explosive primer cord, then races through direct enemy fire, dodging enemy mortar shells. Lt. Ray keeps moving and is struck by a mortar shell. He throws his body on the detonator, blasting through the wire by giving his life. His extraordinary sacrifice ultimately allows his Company to gain the approaches to the Cologne Plain; he receives the Medal of Honor posthumously. **(Atlantic-Italy)** In the **British Eighth Army** area, the Polish 2nd Corps engages the enemy in bitter fighting at M. Fortino, taking it from the Germans only to relinquish it to a severe counterattack. **(Atlantic-Albania)** German resistance at Tirana ceases.

November 18th 1944 — (Pacific-Philippines-Leyte) In the **U.S. Sixth Army** area, **X Corps** sector, the 3rd Battalion, 128th Infantry, 32nd Division drives to positions outside Limon and halts to await the arrival of the 1st Battalion, which is still engaged on Corkscrew Ridge. On Kilay Ridge, the Germans commence a heavy bombardment that jeopardizes the 1st Battalion, 34th Infantry; Company B, taking the brunt of the Artillery barrage, is relieved from the forward positions by Company C. **(Pacific-Yellow Sea)** The U.S.S. *Spadefish* (SS-411) sinks the Submarine Chaser No. 156. **(Atlantic-West-**

ern Europe) 21st Army Group In the **British Second Army** area, the 30th Corps commences its offensive to seize the Geilenkirchen salient (Operation CLIPPER). The U.S. 84th Division, reinforced by the British Drewforce, comprising Flail Tanks and a Searchlight Battery on the right, attacks in coordination with the British 43rd Division, driving on the left; the former (334th Infantry) seizes Prummern while the 43rd takes Tripsrath and secures most of Bauchem. The assault against Prummern ensues throughout the night due to the implementation of the searchlights, and it gains strategic positions near Sueggerath. Mahogany Hill, controlled by the Germans, does not capitulate; however, Geilenkirchen is cut off on three sides. **12th Army Group** In the **U.S. Ninth Army** area, **XIX Corps** sector, C.C.B., 2nd Armored, throws back an enemy counterattack of limited nature at Immendorf, then launches an attack, seizing Apweiler. The 29th Division reduces Setterich; bolstered with Tanks and Artillery fire, it forges ahead taking large strides; the 116th Infantry tightens the screws at Setterich while other contingents barge into Bettendorf and Siersdorf, battering the forward defenses of Juelich. At Broichweiden, the 30th Division mops up while other contingents take Warden during the third assault. In the **U.S. First Army** area, **VII Corps** sector, the majority of the Donnerberg is secured by the 104th Division, which also drives into Eschweiler woods, against wobbly opposition. Task Force Mills Commander Lt. Colonel Herbert N Mills is killed during the attacks against Hastenrath and Scherpenseel. He is replaced by Colonel John Welborn. The 26th Infantry, 1st Division meets stiff resistance as it advances toward its first objective, Laufenburg Castle, but the 16th Infantry propels to the top of Hill 232, gaining a strategic position there while gaining most of Hamich; it throws back enemy counterattacks at both points. Meanwhile, the 4th Division drives full blast into the Huertgen Forest, its 8th Infantry closing against Dueren and the 22nd Regiment advancing toward Grosshau; the fast pace movement creates a gap between the Regiments. In the **U.S. Third Army** area, **XX Corps** sector, C.C.B., 10th Armored, drives into Launstroff and Schwerdorff, while elements of C.C.A. advance to the Nied River across from Bouzonville and come upon a damaged bridge; they move across it prudently in hot pursuit of the retreating Germans. The 90th Division is deploying to sever the southern escape route. The 90th Reconnaissance Troop takes Avancy. Metz is entered by Task Force Bacon, 95th Division, which penetrates and overpowers Forts Bellacroix and St. Julien. The 95th Division contingents, operating west of Metz, drive expeditiously to the Moselle, but the retreating Germans have destroyed all bridges except one. An island between the Hafen Canal and the Moselle is secured by the 377th Regiment, while elements of its 378th start across the bridge, aborting the attempt suddenly when the Germans blow it. Other contingents invest Fort Plappeville. The 379th Regiment pushes to the Moselle, but is halted due to a blown bridge. Fort St. Privat is maintained by elements of the 11th Infantry, but the remainder of the Regiment drives into Metz from the south, in conjunction with contingents of the 10th Infantry which have driven from Fort Queuleu into the city, trampling through Ars-Laquenexy and Courcelles-sur-Nied en route finalizing the isolation of Metz by establishing contact with the 90th Division. In the **XII Corps** sector, the 26th and 35th Divisions, supported by Artillery fire, thrust forward elements of the latter seize Bistroff and gain terrain east of Vallerange while units of the 26th Division, bolstered by Tanks and Tank Destroyers, recapture Guebling after overrunning Bois de Benestroff. In a subsequent drive to Bourgaltroff,

Company F, 104th Infantry, is cut off and annihilated. **6th Army Group** In the **U.S. Seventh Army** area, **XV Corps** sector, Fremonville is attacked by the 79th Infantry. In the **VI Corps** sector, the 100th Division strikes Raon-l'Etape; the 398th Regiment penetrates the town while the 397th begins to ford the Plaine River. Gerardmer is approached by the 36th Division which deploys overlooking the objective. In the **French 1st Army** area, 1st Corps sector, the French 5th Armored, in conjunction with the 2nd Moroccan Division, places the clamps on Belfort, converging from the northern flank of the Corps. The 9th Colonial and 1st Armored Divisions shoot through the Belfort Gap straddling the Swiss border and the Rhine-Rhone Canal, sprinting to Delle and dispatching units toward the Rhine, swallowing Courtelevant, Faverois, Joncherey and Suarce during this swift eastward drive. In Naval activity, the LST 6 sinks on the Seine River after striking a mine. **(Atlantic-Estonia)** The Russians reinitiate their effort to dismantle the formidably entrenched German Garrison on Oesel Island's southern tip to ensure domination of the Gulf of Riga. **(Atlantic-Italy)** In the **British Eighth Army** area, the Polish 2nd Corps and the British 5th Corps receive orders to commence attack against Faenza on the 20th. **(Atlantic-Mediterranean)** The PT-311 is sunk by a mine in the Mediterranean.

November 19th 1944 — (Pacific-Palaus Islands) The Destroyer Escorts *Conklin* (DE-439) and *McCoy Reynolds* (DE-440) sink the Japanese Submarine I-177. **(Pacific-Philippines-Leyte)** One thousand three hundred troops of the 77th Division are to be detached and diverted upon debarkation at Leyte for participation in a special operation against Mindoro. In the **U.S. Sixth Army** area, **X Corps** sector, the 1st Battalion, 128th Infantry, 32nd Division, continues pounding the determined enemy on Corkscrew Ridge; the 1st Battalion, 34th Infantry is still under heavy fire on Kilay Ridge. In Naval activity, Planes attached to Vice Admiral J.S. McCain's Fast Carrier Task Force attack enemy Aircraft and Shipping in the vicinity of Luzon. **(Pacific-Asia Islands)** In the **U.S. Eighth Army** area, contingents of the 31st Division make an amphibious invasion of the Asia Islands, about 1,000 nautical miles northwest of Sansapor. **(Pacific-Burma)** In the **British Fourteenth Army** area, 4th Corps sector, the Indian 19th Division, poised at Sittaung, crosses the Chindwin. **(Atlantic-Western Europe) 21st Army Group** In the **British Second Army** area, 30th Corps sector, the Germans repulse the 334th Infantry, 84th U.S. Division at Mahogany Hill, a stubborn stronghold; however, the Regiment's clearing operation at Prummern continues effectively and the 333rd Regiment drives forward, seizing Geilenkirchen and Sueggerath. In other Divisional activity, the 405th Infantry, U.S. 102nd Division is attached to the 84th Division on the condition it be committed only as a last resort. In the 12 Corps area, the British 51st Division captures Helden and Panningen. **12th Army Group** In the **U.S. Ninth Army** area, **XIX Corps** sector, the Germans strike tenaciously at Apweiler, but they are handily repelled by C.C.B., 2nd Armored Division; Combat Command A drives between Ederen and Freialdenhoven, sprinting in two columns toward the high ground. Resistance in Setterich is terminated, and an Antitank obstacle outside the village is overrun by the 29th Division, which then advances and seizes Duerboslar and Schleiden. At Kinzweiler, heavy Artillery barrages support the 117th Infantry, 30th Division's assault, giving it a quick victory there and at St. Joeris. In the **U.S. First Army** area, **VII Corps** sector, mop-up operations wind down,

allowing the 104th Division to throw its full strength toward the enemy industrial complexes northeast of the Inde River, while the 47th Infantry, 9th Division, sweeping near the north flank of the 1st Division, advances from Hill 232 against Hill 187; the 1st Division's 16th Infantry plows toward Bovenberger Wald, after having secured Hamlich; the 18th Regiment (reserve) drives toward Langerwehe, advancing to Wenau, permitting the 26th to assault Merode and Juengersdorf; it drives to positions just outside Laufenburg Castle. The Germans mount a fierce counterattack against the 26th Regiment's positions. P.F.C. Francis X. McGraw, Company H, holds tough and pours machine gun fire upon the advancing enemy, driving them back. The Germans bring in a machine gun, but McGraw plops his gun atop a log and stands defiantly, pouring more fire and eliminating the gun. The Germans launch a rocket that dislodges his gun, but he reclaims it and pulverizes the advancing enemy, destroying yet another machine gun before making trips to get more ammunition. The Irish Philadelphian, now badly wounded, is annoyed when he returns to find his gun blanketed with mud as the enemy encroaches. Undaunted, he patiently cleans his weapon amidst falling mortars, then turns back another attack, again expending his ammunition. P.F.C. McGraw, desiring to finish the fight, grabs a Carbine, killing one advancing German and wounding another before a third arrives and kills him with a burst from a machine-pistol; he receives the Medal of Honor posthumously. An existing gap between the 8th and 22nd Regiments forces the 4th Division to halt its advance and reform. In the **V Corps** sector, the 8th Division assumes responsibility for the Vossenack — Schmidt region, relieving the 28th Division and deploys to strike against Huertgen and Kleinhau; its 121st Infantry advances to the Huertgen Forest. Plans have been laid for a full-scale Corps attack to commence subsequent to the VII Corps crashing through the enemy defenses west of the Roer, but General Hodges directs the assault to take place on the 21st. In the **U.S. Third Army** area, the **XX Corps** has Metz squeezed tautly, totally surrounded by the 5th, 95th, and 90th U.S. Divisions, elements of the latter establishing a rigid line to sever the escape route through Les Etangs. Task Force Bacon, 95th Division, whips into Metz, engaging in bitter street fighting throughout the northeastern section, while the 377th and 378th Regiments ford the Moselle and crash into the town from the northwest. During the heated contest for Metz, Sergeant Miller leads an unusual attack against an enemy Barracks. With cover fire, he sneaks through a window and captures six Riflemen in the room, and he is soon followed by the entire Company; the building is secured along with 75 prisoners. Miller repeats the feat at another building and is faced by four Gestapo agents and a machine-pistol, but they surrender. On the following morning, the Sergeant climbs toward a roof to eliminate a machine gun nest, which is holding up his Company. A grenade greets him, but the concussion is no deterrent; he fires his Bazooka, scoring a direct hit, prompting the enemy in the area to begin surrendering in large numbers; he receives the Medal of Honor. In conjunction, the 5th Division is fighting viciously in the southern section of Metztown; the 2nd Regiment makes contact with contingents of the 90th Division north of Retonfey, and the 10th Infantry encounters elements of the 95th Division near Vallieres. In other activity, Combat Command A abandons its Nied bridgehead to expedite the 10th Armored assault against the Sarre River, demolishing the bridges as it departs; C.C.B., driving against Merzig and the Sarre, encounters heavy fire which hinders its progress. Tenacious enemy resistance along the Orscholz Switch line halts the 3rd Cavalry Group as it drives toward the ground between the Sarre and the Moselle. In the **XII Corps** sector, C.C.B., 6th Armored Division, in conjunction with the 137th Regiment, 35th Division, seizes Bertring and Gros-Tenquin, while the 320th Regiment, assisted by elements of the 4th Armored Division, overruns Virming. The Germans, initiating a major withdrawal during the night, garnish plenty of strength to cover the pull-out, engaging the 26th Division along the Di-euze-Benestroff line in ferocious combat. The Germans hold Marimont and Marimont Hill (Hill 334), withstanding assaults by the 101st and 104th Regiments throughout the day, but they abandon the positions upon darkness. The 4th Armored Division lends an iron hand to the 328th Infantry; jointly, they gnaw toward Dieuze, hook up with the 2nd Cavalry Group, and enter the town, seizing a bridge intact due to the hasty withdrawal of the enemy. C.C.A., 4th Armored Division recaptures Rodalbe, located in the 26th Division sector. **6th Army Group** In the **U.S. Seventh Army** area, **XV Corps** sector, Ibigny and St. George is seized by the 44th Division as it drives against Sarrebourg. Fremonville is consumed by the 77th Division, while elements of the French 2nd Armored take Cirey, applying such pressure that the enemy line in the Bla-mont-Cirey area along the Vezouse folds and permits a massive breakthrough. C.C.L., 2nd French Armored shoots into the Severne Gap, forcing an opening to speed the advance on Strasbourg; it is bolstered on its southern flank by the U.S. 77th Division. In the **VI Corps** sector, C.C.A., 14th Armored Division is attached to the Corps. The 100th Division continues to close the net on Raon; its 398th Regiment swoops south across the Plaine to gain control of the highway southeast of town, in conjunction with the 397th Regiment, which storms a well-fortified quarry lying on the fringes of Raon. In conjunction, the Division Reconnaissance Troop and the 117th Reconnaissance Squadron take Badonviller without incident. In the **French 1st Army** area, 1st Corps sector, the 5th Armored and 2nd Moroccan Divisions converge on Belfort, advancing to the suburb of Chalonvillars. The Germans repulse the French 1st Armored's attempt to secure an opening to Dannemarie, impeding the progress of the French 5th Armored's drive toward Cernay; additional elements driving on the right flank advance to Rosenau on the Rhine, seizing Seppois, the first town in Alsace to be recovered by the French. This drive to the Rhine gives the French the distinction of being the first Allied troops to reach the Rhine. **(Atlantic-Greece)** Land Forces Greece and Military Liaison Greece are consolidated under General Scobie and renamed Headquarters Land Forces and Military Liaison Greece.

November 20th 1944 — (Pacific) A Japanese Submarine sinks the Oiler U.S.S. *Mississinewa* (AO-59) off the Marianas. In other activity, the U.S.S. *Atule* (SS-403) sinks the Japanese Minesweeper No. 38 in the South China Sea. **(Pacific-Philippines)** LEYTE: In the **U.S. Sixth Army** area, **X Corps** sector, the fighting on Corkscrew Ridge rages; the Japanese continue to stymie the 1st Battalion, 128th Infantry, 32nd Division. At Kilay Ridge, the 1st Battalion, 34th Infantry pulls Company C back from its forward positions, and Company B is repulsed in its attempt to recapture a knoll lost to the enemy on the 19th. In other activity, the U.S.S. *Gar* lands supplies on the north coast of Mindoro. **(Pacific-Asia Islands)** The U.S. Eighth Army concludes its operations successfully and establishes radar stations on the islands. **(Pacific-India-Burma)** Elements of the Chinese XI Group drive through Mangshih on the Salween Front and prepare to use its Airfield to land sup-

plies. **(Atlantic-Western Europe) 21st Army Group** In the **British Second Army** area, the XII Corps' 49th Division, bolstered by contingents of the 51st Division and units of the 4th Separate Armored Brigade, drives forward and discovers the villages along the Maas River southwest of Venlo unoccupied by the Germans. In the 30th Corps sector, the 334th Regiment, U.S. 84th Division, supported by British Tanks (flame throwers), reduces the enemy resistance at Prummern, but the Germans resist tenaciously along the Corps front and retain control of the hills northeast of Prummern. **12th Army Group** In the **U.S. Ninth Army's XIX Corps** area, the 2nd Armored and British Tanks (attached) rumble forward during a torrential rainstorm, spooning three Task Forces of C.C.B. into Gereonsweiler and securing it, while C.C.A. Task Forces seize Ederen and Freialdenhoven. The 29th Division, having secured Niedermerz, uncorks a two-pronged assault, seizing Aldenhoven within the defensive works of Juelich. In the **U.S. First Army** area, **VII Corps** sector, the Rohe-Hehlrath-Duerwiss area is consumed with bitter combat, pitting the 104th Division against the Germans; at Hill 187 on Hamich Ridge in the 1st Division sector, the fighting is equally grueling with the enemy repulsing attempts by the 47th Infantry to reduce it. Elements of the 18th Infantry, 1st Division secure Wenau, then bolt across the Wehe Creek pushing toward Langerwehe; additional contingents advance into Heistern and take half of the town. The Laufenburg Castle is overrun by the 26th Infantry as it closes against Merode. In other Corps action, the dogged contest for the Huertgen Forest continues, costing the 4th Division severe casualties for the four-day battle that nets it a mere one and a half mile advancement, due partially to a critical supply shortage. During one savage encounter, the 2nd Battalion, 8th Regiment, 4th Division is paralyzed by enemy fire and a minefield. Lt. Colonel George Mabry moves out front with some Scouts and blasts through a booby-trapped section of reinforced concertina-wire, then quickly captures three Soldiers by bayonet persuasion. Mabry charges forward through an abandoned bunker into another and engages nine enemy Soldiers with his bayonet and the butt of his Rifle, holding his own until the Scouts rush in to subdue the remaining enemy defenders. Mabry assaults a third bunker, and six of the enemy surrender at the point of his bayonet; he then advances further, leading his Battalion through a ring of deadly fire to seize high ground and threaten both enemy flanks; he receives the Medal of Honor. During another brutalizing encounter, German Artillery rains on the slopes near Scherpenseel, knocking out a lead Vehicle of the attacking 899th Tank Destroyer Battalion. Staff Sergeant Herschel Briles bolts forward and pulls the wounded men from their burning Vehicle. On the following day, Briles spots enemy movement and pours deadly fire their way, inflicting severe casualties, while enticing 55 Germans to surrender, clearing passage for units which had been halted for two days. In addition, the dauntless Sergeant Briles rescues additional men from burning Vehicles amidst exploding ammunition, exhibiting extraordinary courage in the face of the enemy; he receives the Medal of Honor. In the **U.S. Third Army** area, **XX Corps** sector, the 5th and 95th Divisions continue to systematically destroy the enemy rear guard resistance remaining within Metz and simultaneously neutralize the forts scattered throughout the city; it also makes preparations for the final sprint to the Sarre, which Third Army will cross on December 2nd. By this time, the Yanks are shelling the forts with German ammunition. At Merzig, enemy resistance forces C.C.B., 10th Armored, which has advanced to Hill 378, to pull back to Hill 383. In the **XII**

Corps area, elements of the 80th Division capture a bridge intact at Faulquemont and control a bridgehead north of the Nied Allemande River. The 137th Infantry, 37th Division, advancing behind Combat Command A, 6th Armored, is struck by a sudden enemy counterattack as it exits Bois de Freybouse, and it is routed in disarray. Combat Command A, 4th Armored, spearheading for the 320th Infantry, tramples the resistance at Francaltroff. The 26th Division continues pursuit of the Germans who are retreating in its sector. C.C.A., 4th Armored departs for Conthil for regrouping after its victory at Francaltroff; C.C.B. is directed to pass through the 26th Division perimeter at Mittersheim, and C.C.A., 6th Armored receives orders to forge toward the Sarre River in the 35th Division sector to secure crossing sites. **6th Army Group** In the **U.S. Seventh Army** area, **XV Corps** sector, the French 2nd Armored Division dispatches Combat Command D to outflank the Saverne Gap from the north, in conjunction with C.C.L., which is driving from the south to surround the enemy in the gap. Combat Command V is thrown into the battle alongside C.C.L., which is encountering fierce resistance near Wolfsberg Pass slightly southwest of Saverne. In addition, Combat Command D fords the Sarre north of Sarrebourg and slings two columns eastward; one heads toward La Petite Pierre situated north and the other toward Phalsbourg, sitting at the western entrance of the gap. In the **VI Corps** area, the 7th and 30th Regiments, 3rd Division, make an early morning crossing of the Meurthe to be on line as vanguard for a major assault against Strasbourg commencing at 06:45. The enemy is rattled prior to the assault by the combined strength of Artillery and intent Air cover by the XII Tactical Air Command. The surging 3rd Division swallows Hurbache, Le Paire, and La Voivre against disorganized opposition which is further threatened by the pounding it is receiving from the 100th Division, driving from the left flank of the Corps at Raon-l'Etape. The Germans are also under severe pressure by the 103rd Division, which spreads its 409th and 410th Regiments across the Meurthe through the friendly lines of the 3rd Division, positioning them for the drive to St. Die. On the southern flank of the Corps, a strategic ridge controlling Anould and Clefcy is overrun by the 143rd Infantry, 36th Division. In the **French 1st Army** area, Combat Command 6, French 5th Armored Division and the 2nd Moroccan Division penetrate Belfort; heavy skirmishing ensues lasting several days. In the 2nd Corps sector, Gerardmer falls to the 3rd Algerian Division without a fight, and Champagney and Plancher-les-Mines are seized by the 1st Division. In the 1st Corps sector, the 5th Armored Division drives toward Cernay and Fontaine against resolute resistance along the Rhine-Rhone Canal below Fontaine. **(Atlantic-Italy)** In the **British Eighth Army** area, 5th Corps sector, Allied Planes strike hard against German fortifications. In other activity, the British 46th Division seizes Castiglione and starts clearing Cosina loop to the north while waiting to commence the main attack which is postponed until the 21st.

November 21st 1944 — (Pacific-Formosa) The U.S.S. *Sealion* (SS-315) sinks the Japanese Battleship *Kongo* and the Destroyer *Urakaze*. **(Pacific-Kurile Islands)** Rear Admiral J. L. McCrea's Task Force bombards enemy Naval Air Facilities on Matsuwa Island. **(Pacific-Philippines-Leyte)** In the **U.S. Sixth Army** area, **X Corps** sector, the 1st Battalion, 128th Infantry remains in the area to neutralize opposition on Corkscrew Ridge, while the balance of the Regiment moves to secure a crossing of a Leyte River tributary to the south and to capture

Limon. At Kilay Ridge, activity is confined to Patrols and sporadic firefights. In the **XXIV Corps** area, the 3rd Battalion, 32nd Infantry, 7th Division departs Baybay and deploys south of the 2nd Battalion. **(Pacific-Burma)** General George E. Stratemeyer deactivates the Third Tactical Air Force to allow the 221st Group's availability to provide close Air support for the British Fourteenth Army and the 224th Group, supporting the Arakan offensive. **(Pacific-China)** General Wedemeyer presents his Alpha Plan to Chiang Kai-shek. His strategy calls for concentrating the Chinese Forces at Kunming immediately. General Cheng Chen, considered to be the best available Chinese General, is recommended as the Commanding Officer. Kai-shek prefers General Ho Ying-chin. The Chinese Army will receive American assistance in the form of maximum Air support and a contingent of Liaison Officers. **(Western Europe) 21st Army Group** In the **British Second Army** area, 12th Corps sector, the British 49th and 51st Divisions drive toward Venlo. Meanwhile, at 19:30, the 53rd Division assaults to secure the Roermond bridgehead. In the 30th Corps area, a combination of fierce resistance and an incessant rainstorm greatly stalls progress. The U.S. 84th Division unsuccessfully attempts to advance to the villages of Beeck, Muellendorf, and Wurm. In addition, permission to deploy the U.S. 104th Division to defend the southeast flank of the 30th Corps is received. **12th Army Group** In the **U.S. Ninth Army** area, the **XIX Corps** initiates its final phase in the drive to the Roer. North of Gereonsweiler, the Germans counterattack C.C.B., 2nd Armored, which has just secured the heights within view of the Roer. In addition, C.C.A. advances to the fringes of Ederen and Freialdenhoven. Englesdorf is seized by the 116th Regiment, 29th Division; its 3rd Battalion subsequently attacks toward Koslar. In conjunction, the 2nd Battalion, 175th Infantry occupies Bourheim after the German Garrison withdraws because of lack of a relief force; German reinforcements arrive later, and during the night they retake the town. In other activity, the 120th Infantry, 30th Division, supported by the 743rd Tank Battalion, drives to within a few miles of the Roer, advancing to Fronhoven. In the **U.S. First Army** area, Hehlrath and Rohe are secured by the 104th Division, and at Duerwiss a vicious battle erupts. Resolute resistance at Hamich Ridge prompts improvisation: twenty Battalions of Artillery firepower are massed against Hill 187 by the 47th Infantry, 1st Division to reduce the opposition; the steady rain of lead continues throughout the night into the following morning. The 18th Infantry throws back a counterattack at Heistern, then secures the town. The Germans, holding Hills 203 and 207, repulse attacks by the 3rd Battalion, 18th Regiment. In the **V Corps** area, German positions are bombarded prior to an attack by the 8th Division's 121st Infantry, which encounters heavy enemy fire as it advances. One Battalion is stalled within a minefield. Staff Sergeant Minick, Company I, defying the enemy Artillery and mortars, leads a four-man detachment through the barbed wire and other obstacles, traveling about 300 yards until halted by a machine gun nest. The intrepid Sergeant advances, storms the position, kills two crewmen, and captures another three, then dashes ahead, stumbling into an entire Company, taking them on alone. His impetuous stint forces a showdown which costs the enemy twenty dead and twenty prisoners, paving the way for his Platoon to seize the remainder of the enemy. Acting as a one-man vanguard, Minick charges and knocks out another machine gun nest, permitting his Battalion to advance. Undaunted, the indefatigable Minick encounters yet another minefield and advances amidst incessant enemy fire until he strikes a mine and is killed instantly. His superb actions greatly aid his Regiment in taking the objective; he receives the Medal of Honor posthumously. In the **VII Corps** sector, the intimidating natural obstacles of the Huertgen Forest continue to hamper Corps progress. In the **U.S. Third Army** area, **XX Corps** sector, C.C.A., 10th Armored, drives toward Saarburg, its Task Forces Chamberlain and Standish driving on the right and left respectively, encountering difficulty with obstacles at the Orscholz Switch Line that stops progress. West of Merzig, the German pressure forces C.C.B., 10th Armored from its defensive posture, pushing it back slightly, but the sector then remains relatively quiet for several days. In addition, the in-town fighting at Metz continues to rage; however, final preparations for the major assault against the Sarre continue. In the **XII Corps** zone, the Nied bridgehead is expanded by the 80th Division which makes contact with the XX Corps. Combat Command A, 6th Armored Division, in conjunction with the 137th Infantry, 37th Division, seizes Fremestroff and Hellimer while the 37th's 320th Regiment grinds toward Grening. Albestroff and Montdidier are captured by the 104th Regiment, 26th Division, giving the Yanks an important road junction at the latter, but at high cost; the contingents at Albestroff become cut off and are wiped out. **6th Army Group** The VI Corps hits stiffening opposition, impeding its progress; the Seventh Army gives permission to either the VI or XV Corps to seize Strasbourg, the latter making much better progress. Both prepare to bolt the Rhine. In the **XV Corps** area, elements of the French 2nd Armored Division advance through La Petite Pierre, reaching Alsatian Plain; another Task Force of C.C.D. is halted at Phalsbourg. Sarrebourg is outflanked and seized by the U.S. 44th Division. In the **VI Corps** area, Moyenmoutier capitulates to the 100th Division without a fight, but a feverish battle ensues in the high ground overlooking the city. Elements of the 398th Regiment jump off at dawn to secure the heights before assaulting the city. They approach the woods near St. Pravel by 12:00. Scouts spot an enemy sentry guarding a house, then suddenly a burst of machine gun fire, followed by other automatic weapon fire, freezes a Squad. Lt. Edward A. Silk, Company E, returns fire for a sizzling 15 minutes without results; Silk then singlehandedly races 100 yards, catapults a wall, and runs an additional 50 yards under severe fire, reaching the enemy's building. After a pause, he plops a grenade through a window in the building, eliminating the machine gun and two gunners. Without hesitation, he dashes through a second storm of bullets, silencing another machine gun and killing its two gunners. Out of ammunition, but not ingenuity, the Lieutenant begins throwing rocks through a farmhouse window, demanding surrender. Astonished by this indomitable one-man task force and his eccentric methods, 12 disoriented Germans capitulate to Lt. Silk. His intrepid actions lead to the seizure of his Regiment's objective; Lt. Silk receives the Medal of Honor. In other activity, the 3rd Division enlarges its Meurthe bridgehead, seizing St. Jean d'Ormont. At St. Die, the Germans are jeopardized when the 103rd Division gains the heights round the town. In conjunctive action, Combat Command A, 14th Armored Division, plows toward Schirmeck to sever the enemy's northeast escape routes. In the **French 1st Army** area, the 1st Corps is struck by a fierce German counterattack that pushes the French 5th Armored from Lepuix and Suarce cuts the Delle-Basle road outside of Courtelevant. In the Alps sector, the U.S. 44th AAA Brigade assumes responsibility for the right flank, replacing a U.S. 1st Airborne Task Force along the Franco-Italian border. **(Atlantic-Italy)** In the **British Eighth Army** area, Polish 2nd Corps zone, the 3rd Carpathian Division seizes M. Fortino. In the 5th Corps area,

close Air support is afforded a general Corps offensive which drives toward Faenza. The Indian 10th Division encounters strong opposition west of Villafranca at the Montone. The British 46th Division, driving on the south flank, is still engaged in clearing the menacing enemy resistance at the Cosina River loop north of Castiglione, while the 4th Division, advancing in the center, gets contingents across the Montone west of Villafranca.

November 22nd 1944 — (Pacific-Caroline Islands) Rear Admiral R. E. Davison's Carrier Task Force attacks enemy positions on Yap Island. **(Pacific-Philippines)** LEYTE: In the **U.S. Sixth Army** area, **X Corps** sector, Limon falls to elements of the 128th Regiment, 32nd Division, essentially terminating the sege of Breakneck Ridge. Some resistance remains in isolated bypassed pockets; they will be eliminated by mid-December. In other Corps activity, the Japanese squeeze the 1st Battalion, 34th Infantry on Kilay Ridge, but the unit closes ranks to forestall being encircled. In the **XXIV Corps** area, the 7th Division, minus the 17th Infantry, is ordered to secure the eastern shore of Ormoc Bay, prompting the commitment of the 11th Airborne Division, not originally scheduled to operate on Leyte. **(Pacific-South China Sea)** The U.S.S. *Besugo* (SS-231) torpedoes and sinks the Japanese Transport No. 151. **(Western Europe) 21st Army Group** In the **British Second Army** area, 8th Corps sector, the 15th Division occupies Horst and Sevenum, northwest of Venlo. In the 12th Corps sector, the 53rd Division advances to the Maas River across from Roermond while the British 49th and 51st Divisions approach Venlo. In the 30th Corps area, the 334th Regiment, U.S. 84th Division, launches a swift surprise assault, seizing Mahogany Hill, northeast of Prummern. The 333rd Infantry attacks toward Muellendorf; assisted by Tanks, the Regiment advances to within 500 yards of the objective. A forward Platoon that reaches the village is annihilated. At Beeck, the Germans contain the advance of the U.S. 102nd Division. **12th Army Group** In the **U.S. Ninth Army** area, **XIX Corps** sector, the Germans reverse the obvious and stuff reinforcements into the area, rather than withdraw as anticipated, thereby establishing rigid resistance in front of the Roer. At Merzenhausen, C.C.A., 2nd Armored, drives into the town, but intense opposition throws it back to the southwest fringes. The Germans also stifle the advance of the 175th Infantry, 29th Division at Bourheim, driving it from the town before sunlight and blocking reentry; at Koslar, the enemy repulses the 116th Regiment. In other ferocious fighting, Erberich is seized by the 120th Regiment, although attacking elements are repelled at Lohn. In the **U.S. First Army** area, **VII Corps** sector, the 104th Division has a long night, overpowering resistance at Nothberg, then sweeping through Eschweiler after sunlight; it then secures Duerwiss before driving toward Puetzlohn. The tremendous success gets the Regiment a bonus; instead of halting at the Inde River as planned, it is ordered to maintain the attack and drive to the Rhine. The First Division sector is in high gear. The Germans holding Hills 207 and 203 pour fire upon the 18th Infantry, halting it in the Wehe Creek Valley; the 126th Regiment is ordered to assist the 18th and curtail its attacks. Meanwhile, the 47th Infantry completes clearing Hamich Ridge without incident. The 4th Division grinds forward; its weakened 12th Regiment attacks slowly to secure the right flank of the 22nd Regiment while the 8th and 22nd Regiments feint east and simultaneously get elements around the enemy. Advance contingents of the 8th Regiment reach the first objective, the heights at Gut Schwarzenbroich; contingents of the 22nd bolt to positions within 700 yards west of Grosshau.

In the **V Corps** sector, the Germans continue to frustrate the 121st Infantry, 8th Division, barring any progress in the Huertgen Forest. In the **U.S. Third Army** area, **XX Corps** sector, resistance in Metz is terminated; mop-up operations cease. Enemy Forts in the vicinity (Verdun, Driant, Jeanne d'Arc, Plappeville, St. Privat, and St. Quentin) have been neutralized and isolated, preventing any major threat against ongoing operations. A full-scale offensive directed against the Sarre is ordered by Corps, to commence on the 25th. The Germans repulse U.S. attempts to break through the Orscholz Switch Line; Task Force Standish, C.C.A. 10th Armored drives to Nennig and Tettingen, but the Germans halt its progress at both towns and drive the force back. Task Force Chamberlain makes some progress through dragon's teeth on the right. In the **XII Corps** sector, Leyviller and St. Jean-Rohrbach topple to the 137th Infantry, 35th Division, while the 320th Regiment takes Grening. The Germans abandon Albestroff after dark as the weakened 104th Regiment, 26th Division begins to encircle the town. In conjunction, the 328th Infantry rushes to aid the 104th, taking Munster as it advances through flooded terrain; its progress is further hindered by mines and other obstacles. In other activity, C.C.B., 4th Armored Division forges ahead, pushing through Mittersheim. **6th Army Group** In the **U.S. Seventh Army** area, **XV Corps** sector, units of the French 2nd Armored Division approach Saverne. In the **VI Corps** sector, the Germans continue to withdraw with the Yanks giving chase. The pursuit, led by Armor, nets the 100th Division Senones. St. Die falls to the 409th Regiment, 103rd Division without opposition, and the 3rd Division charges to positions near Saales and St. Blaise. In addition, a bridgehead is established near Saulcy. The Germans menace the bridgehead on the southern flank of the 36th Division, driving the 141st Regiment back to positions west of the River, but they fail to budge the 143rd Infantry which holds the eastern side. In the **French 1st Army** area, 2nd Corps sector, Giromagny is seized by the French 1st Division, severing the German line along the Savoureuse. In addition, the 1st Corps pushes into Mulhouse, regaining lost terrain in the process. **(Atlanic-Finland)** Finnish troops advance to the Norwegian border, in accord with the terms of the armistice, subsequent to the enemy withdrawal. **(Atlantic-Italy)** In the **U.S. Fifth Army** area, **II Corps** sector, the 88th Division moves back on line and takes responsibility for the zone previously occupied by the 85th Division. In addition, the 34th Division and the 1st Armored Division relieve the 91st Division. The British 13th Corps' regrouping is complete and deployed left to right are 1st Division, 78th Division, 6th Armored Division, and the Indian 8th Division.

The U.S.S. McDermutt.

November 23rd 1944 — (Pacific-Philippines-Leyte) In the **U.S. Sixth Army** area, **XXIV Corps** sector, the Japanese open the battle for Shoestring Ridge, attacking the overextended 32nd Infantry, 7th Division at the Palanas River, pushing it back slightly. In the **X Corps** sector, the 128th Regiment, 32nd Division begins to regroup south of Limon and initiates Patrols. The 112th Cavalry, operating at Mt. Minoro, is ordered to move southwest to release pressure from the 32nd Division. In Naval activity, the Attack Transport *James O'Hara* (APA-90) is damaged by a Kamikaze. The U.S.S. *Gar* debarks men and supplies on the west coast of Luzon. **(Atlantic-Western Europe) 21st Army Group** In the **British Second Army** area, attempts by the U.S. 102nd Division unsuccessfully attack Beeck. In other activity, the British 30th Corps takes a defensive stance and releases the U.S. 84th Division to the U.S. Ninth Army's XIII Corps. **12th Army Group** In the **U.S. Ninth Army** area, **XIX Corps** sector, C.C.A., 2nd Armored Division, halts to regroup after securing half of Merzenhausen. Bourheim erupts with tumultuous fighting; it falls to the 175th Infantry, 29th Division. For the next several days, the German 7th Army counterattacks. Lohn is seized by the 120th Regiment, 30th Division and holds it against fierce German assaults. Pattern is seized by the 119th Regiment with the support of concentrated fire from Erberich. Subsequently, the 30th Division halts its attack until Kirchberg and Inden capitulate. In the **VII Corps** sector, the Germans mount tenacious resistance at Puetzlohn and at Weisweiler; the 104th Division penetrates both. The Germans also raise tenacious opposition at Huecheln, halting the 47th Infantry, 1st Division. In related combat, Rosslershof Castle, southeast of Wilhelmshoehe, collapses under the pressure of the 16th Regiment; the 18th Regiment overpowers Hill 207. In the Huertgen Forest, an inferno emerges as the 8th Infantry, 4th Division drives northeast; additional contingents pound the enemy at Gut Schwarzenbroch. At Grosshau, the 22nd Infantry pauses without mounting an attack. In the **V Corps** sector, the 121st Regiment, 8th Division, supported by Light Tanks, drives southwest of Huertgen, hitting iron resistance. Nevertheless, the German counterattack fails to penetrate U.S. lines. In the **U.S. Third Army** area, **XX Corps** sector, C.C.A., 10th Armored is relieved by the 358th Infantry, which resumes the attack toward Muenzingen and Sinz; friendly fire falls short, hitting positions of the 2nd Battalion, but the 3rd Battalion clears the woods east of Tettingen. In the **XII Corps** sector, contingents of the 137th Infantry, 35th Division pierce Hilsprich and secure it as a springboard for Armor; however, the Germans drive them back. At Albestroff, the 104th Infantry, 26th Division retakes the objective, although it is unprepared to continue the attack. Units of C.C.B., 4th Armored Division drive to Fenetrange, reaching the west bank of the Sarre. In other activity, the 25th Cavalry Reconnaissance Squadron makes contact with elements of the 44th Division (XV Corps) after crossing the Sarre at Bettborn. Contingents of the 130th Panzer Lehr Division, commanded by General Lieutenant Fritz Bayerlein, moving between the XII and XV Corps are struck a heavy blow by the 4th Armored. In other Third Army activity, Patton accommodates Generals Eddy and Walker with a guard of honor and the playing of "Ruffles and Flourishes" for their respective victories at Nancy and Metz. **6th Army Group** In the **U.S. Seventh Army** area, **XV Corps** sector, the French 2nd Armored Division secures Strasbourg, but the Germans retain control of the Kehl bridge. Phalsbourg, at the western end of Saverne Gap, is abandoned by the enemy. U.S. troops, funneling through the gap, are struck by a German counterattack near Sarrebourg. In the **VI**

Corps sector, Saales and Saulxures are captured by the 3rd Division. The 100th Division seizes St. Blaise. Near St. Marie, the Germans come under heavy assault by detachments of the 103rd and 36th Divisions. Fraize is threatened by the 141st and 143rd Regiments, 36th Division; Mandray is crushed by the 143rd in the process. In the **French 1st Army** area, Chateau-Lambert is seized by the 2nd Corps; however, the Germans neutralize progress in the remaining areas. In the 1st Corps sector, near Seppois, the Germans again sever the route to the Rhine River. **(Atlantic-Estonia)** The Soviets gain control of the entrance to the Gulf of Riga as they reduce the remaining pocket of resistance on south Oesel Island. **(Atlantic-Hungary)** The Rail junction at Cop (Csap), which has been engulfed in furious battle for several weeks, is taken by the Red Army. **(Atlantic-Italy)** In the **British Eighth Army** area, M. Ricci is overrun by the Polish 2nd Corps. In the 5th Corps sector, the bridgeheads at the Cosina River are consolidated. The Germans begin pulling back to the Lamone, another water barrier, yet they mount rigid resistance on the right flank of the 5th Corps and slug it out violently along the Montone River north of Highway 9, against the Indian 10th Division.

November 24th 1944 — (Pacific-Japan) Tokyo is bombed by 111 Superfortresses (B-29s) originating from Bases on Saipan and Tinian the Marianas, the first of many such raids. Jubilant Allied P.O.W.s watch the massive demonstration of unprecedented U.S. force over Tokyo. **(Pacific-Philippines-Leyte)** In the **U.S. Sixth Army** area, **X Corps** sector, the Germans mount an unsuccessful counterattack against the 1st Battalion, 34th Infantry, 24th Division at Kilay Ridge. In the **XXIV Corps** area, the 32nd Regiment seizes some previously lost ground on Shoestring Ridge, then repels a nasty counterattack during the night of the 24th-25th. In Naval activity, the Submarine Chaser PC-1114 is damaged by a Dive Bomber off Leyte. The Japanese Submarine Chaser No. 46 and the Transports Nos. 111, 141, and 160 are sunk off Masbate Island in Cataingan Bay by Army Planes. **(Pacific-China)** Nanning is seized by Japanese troops as they drive to hook up with their forces in Indo-china. **(Atlantic-Western Europe) 21st Army Group** In the **U.S. First Army** area, **VII Corps** sector, the 104th Division drives to Puetzlohn and Weisweiler, taking the former without incident; at Weisweiler the struggle erupts into house-to-house fighting. Task Force Richardson (Lt. Colonel Walter B. Richardson), consisting of contingents of the 3rd Armored Division and one Battalion of the 47th Infantry, 9th Division, is formed and given orders to attack Frenzerburg Castle, Wilhelmshoehe, and Huecheln; the latter is seized subsequent to a methodical clearing of a protective minefield. The 18th Regiment drives toward Langerwehe with some contingents advancing to Schoenthal, but the Regiment cannot dislodge the Germans on Hill 203. In the **V Corps** sector, the Germans resist vehemently near Huertgen and have thus far inflicted 600 casualties against the attacking 121st Infantry, 8th Division which is gnawing its way through the Weisser Weh Valley; C.C.R., 5th Armored joins the attack on the following day and pushes along the Germeter-Huertgen highway despite its lack of cover. In the **U.S. Third Army** area, **XX Corps** sector, the enemy Orscholz line comes under further attack. The 3rd Battalion, 358th Regiment, 90th Division, repulses a counterattack, then bolts toward Butzdorf and Tettingen elements advance into the former and become cut off. The 2nd Battalion, reinforced by the 1st Battalion, drives into Oberleuken; however, the Germans are not dislodged. In the **XII Corps** sector, Hilsprich falls to the 1st Battalion, 134th

Infantry, 35th Division which is supported by Artillery and Tanks. German rear-guard actions are vicious at the Vittersbourg-Altwiller line; the stronghold at Bois de Bonnefontaine inflicts heavy punishment upon the 101st Regiment, 26th Division. In other activity, C.C.B., 4th Armored Division jumps the Sarre at Gosselming and Romelfing, then drives northeast, taking Kirrberg and Baerendorf, the latter after horrendous house-to-house fighting. **6th Army Group** The German line along the Vosges is pierced. General Eisenhower inspects the front lines and meets with the Commanders; a decision is made to secure the area west of the Rhine before attacking across it. The U.S. Seventh Army is to drive north to assist the Third Army, and the French 1st Army is to eliminate the German bridgehead (Colmar Pocket) west of the Rhine. In the **U.S. Seventh Army** area, **XV Corps** sector, German pressure threatens the French Armor in Strasbourg. On the following day, contingents of the 106th Cavalry Group and the 44th Division repulse an enemy column at Schalbach. On the 27th, contingents of the 3rd Division relieve the French 2nd Armored. In the **VI Corps** sector, units of the 3rd Division advance to Rothau. Meanwhile, the 103rd Division secures Lubine as it continues to outflank Steige. The 36th Division attacks east; its 142nd spearheading the drive, it advances to Ban-de-Laveline and La Croix-aux-Mines. In the **French 1st Army** area, the 1st and 2nd Corps rush to Alsace to trap the enemy. Grosmagny and Petit-Magny are seized by the 2nd Corps as it advances. The 1st Corps is forced to concentrate on keeping routes to the Rhine clear, despite stiffening enemy opposition near Mulhouse. **(Atlantic-Italy)** General Clark receives a message from Winston Churchill: "IT GIVES ME THE GREATEST PLEASURE TO TELL YOU THAT THE PRESIDENT AND HIS MILITARY ADVISORS REGARD IT AS A COMPLIMENT THAT HIS MAJESTY'S GOVERNMENT SHOULD WISH TO HAVE YOU COMMAND THE 15TH GROUP OF ARMIES." Clark is to succeed British General Sir Harold R. L. G. Alexander who is promoted to Field Marshal and will go to Washington to replace Sir John Dill, the British Chief of Staff representative there. In conjunction, General Lucian Truscott takes command of Fifth Army. In the **U.S. Fifth Army** area, **IV Corps** sector, M. Belvedere is taken by Task Force 45, only to lose it back. In the **British Eighth Army** area, Polish 2nd Corps sector, German discipline is collapsing as the Corps drives toward the Marzeno River. In the 5 Corps sector, the British 4th Division moves toward the Lamone River; the British 46th Division fords the Marzeno on the south flank of the Corps. In conjunction, the Indian 10th Division holds its positions on the northern flank, east of the Montone.

November 25th 1944 — (Pacific Ocean Areas) Admiral Nimitz (CINCPOA) issues Operation Plan 11-44, directing the invasion of Iwo Jima. The Commander of the Fifth Fleet is to secure Iwo and establish Airbases. The tentative date for the invasion is February 3rd 1945. **(Pacific-Philippines-Leyte)** In the **U.S. Sixth Army** area, General Krueger orders work on the Airfields stopped. In the **X Corps** sector, the Japanese mount a strong counterattack at Kilay Ridge during the night of the 25th-26th, but the attempt is squashed by Company A, 1st Battalion, 34th Infantry, 24th Division, preventing the Japs from penetrating the forward positions. In the **XXIV Corps** sector, the Japanese are also repulsed as the 32nd Infantry, 7th Division turns back another night-assault. In other activity, the 511th Paratroop Regiment, 11th Airborne Division initiates an arduous ten-mile march over the mountains, driving from Burauen toward Mahonag to ease the strain against other Corps contingents driving against Ormoc. In Naval activity, Japanese suicide Planes attack the U.S. Carriers, severely damaging the *Essex* (CV-9) and costing 14 dead. The *Intrepid* (CV-11) is struck by two Kamikazes and becomes engulfed in flames; 69 men are killed or missing and 17 Planes are lost, forcing the Vessel to return to Pearl Harbor. An attacking Kamikaze misses the *Hancock* (CV-19), but a piece of its wing lands on the Vessel, igniting a fire. In addition, the Light Carrier *Cabot* (CVL-28) is heavily damaged by a Suicide Plane, 34 men are killed. The Light Carrier *Independence* (CVL-22) sustains damage when a friendly Plane crash lands. Aircraft attached to Rear Admirals G.F. Bogan and F.C. Sherman strike Japanese Shipping and Aircraft facilities in central Luzon. The raid sinks the Japanese Heavy Cruiser *Kumano*, the Cruiser *Yasoshima*, and the Transports Nos. 6 and 10 (Marinduque Island). The Destroyer *Shimotsuki* is sunk by the Submarine *Cavalla* (SS-244) off Borneo; the Submarine *Hardhead* (SS-365) sinks the Coastal Defense Vessel No. 38; the Submarine *Atule* (SS-403) sinks Patrol Boat NO. 38. Today marks the last day that Admiral's Halsey's Warships strike in support of the Leyte operation; since the 5th of November, his Planes have destroyed 756 Japanese Aircraft in addition to devastating enemy Convoys and Airfields. Halsey had reminded MacArthur of an underused Marine Air Group and it had been quickly brought in to cover Admiral Kinkaid's request for more Aircover; Halsey subsequently notes: "WITHIN 24 HOURS AFTER THE MARINE PLANES ARRIVE, THEY HAD JUSTIFIED MY RECOMMENDATION. THANKS TO THEM AND TO OUR STRIKE ON LUZON, KINKAID'S DAILY REPORT BEGAN TO READ, NO BOGEYS." **(Pacific-Burma)** In the N.C.A.C. area, the Japanese forces defending the Pinwe region of the R.R. corridor are ordered to withdraw toward central Burma. **(Atlantic-Western Europe) 12th Army Group** In the **U.S. Ninth Army** area, **XIX Corps** sector, the 29th Division holds firmly against strong German drives at Bourheim; contingents of the 116th Infantry drive to Koslar; the troops become isolated and must be supplied by Air. On the following day, the Germans pour incessant Artillery fire upon Bourheim, in support of the powerful counterattack, despite their diminishing ammunition supplies. U.S. Reserves and Planes are committed to support the 29th Division, which repulses the assault. In the **U.S. First Army** area, **VII Corps** sector, the 104th Division plows ahead from Weisler, securing the Inde River Valley. Wilhelmshoehe is seized by Task Force Richardson, at high cost; it sustains grievous losses driving across the exposed Roer Plain to envelop Frenzerburg Castle. In other Corps activity, the 16th Infantry, 1st Division drives toward the Weisweiler-Langerewehe highway, but cannot penetrate the resistance. A Platoon of the 18th Infantry, supported by two Tanks, attacks toward the crest of Hill 203 and is stopped just short of the objective. The 4th Division strengthens its attack; the 8th Regiment grinds forward to positions about one mile from the Huertgen Forest alongside C.C.R., 5th Armored Division; the 22nd Infantry assaults toward Grosshau meeting fierce opposition. In the **V Corps** sector, enemy mines and an enormous crater force C.C.R., 5th Armored, from continuing an attack with the 121st Infantry, 8th Division. In the **U.S. Third Army** area, the **XX Corps** commences its drive to the Sarre. In the 10th Armored sector, the 358th Regiment keeps hammering the Orscholz line; Tettingen is taken by the 3rd Battalion with the assistance of Tanks and Planes. In addition, the isolated contingents at Butzdorf are rescued; the 1st and 2nd Battalions are heavily engaged at and around Oberleuken; the 2nd drives to the crest of Hill 388, taking severe casualties. A decision is reached to relieve the exhausted 358th Regiment. The 90th

Division advances to Oberesch, four miles from the Sarre, while the 95th Division, bolstered by Artillery of the 5th Division and the V Corps, speeds across the Nied River, penetrating the Maginot Line and discovering the enemy has evacuated their defenses; Boulay, Hallering, Momerstroff, and Narbefontaine are quickly seized. In the **XII Corps** sector, the Germans manning the northern flank of the Corps are overpowered by three Regiments of the 80th Division, bolstered by Artillery and the 42nd Cavalry Squadron, which screens its northern flank. The 6th Armored Division, reinforced by contingents of the 134th Infantry, 35th Division, drives toward Maderbach Creek against fierce opposition, deep mud, minefields, and other obstacles. C.C.B. reaches the creek at Remering; Valette falls to Combat Command A, which receives Air support. Meanwhile, the 328th Regiment, 26th Division breaks through enemy defenses and seizes Vittersbourg, at Bois de Bonnefontaine, the enemy stronghold is reduced by Company G, 101st Regiment. However, the Germans repulse Company K and retain control of the northern edge of the woods. At Baerendorf, C.C.B., 4th Armored Division repulses a hefty enemy counterattack, awaits reinforcements, then resumes its assault. In other activity, General Patton visits the 95th Division, then he drives through Metz, noting how "pleasant" it was to pass through a city which had not been seized for thirteen hundred years. Third Army receives replacement Captains. It is Patton's policy to place them under Lieutenants until they become experienced, although the practice is not authorized by Army policy. Ambassador Averell Harriman visits Third Army; Patton takes him on a tour of the 4th Armored positions to show him: "THE RUSSIANS ARE NOT THE ONLY PEOPLE WHO HAD TO CONTEND AGAINST MUD." **6th Army Group** In the **U.S. Seventh Army** area, **XV Corps** sector, C.C.A. 14th Armored Division encounters the 3rd Division VI Corps around Schirmeck and reverts back to the Corps. In the **VI Corps** area, the 100th Division fights to Grandfontaine, and the 36th Division seizes Ste Marie, giving the Yanks control of the routes to Ribeauville and Selestat. In the **French 1st Army** area, the Germans abandon positions all along the 2 Corps front to avoid being surrounded, yet the Germans continue mounting stiff resistance, which interrupts the progress of the 1st Corps' drive toward Burnhaupt. In the Alps zone, the U.S. 1st Airborne Task Force is ordered to proceed to Lyon, Mourmelon, and Soissons, immediately. **(Atlantic-Hungary)** Red Army troops operating in the vicinity of the Danube secure Csepel Island, south of Budapest. **(Atlantic-Italy)** In the **British Eighth Army** area, contingents of the Polish 2nd Corps cross the Marzeno River. In the 5th Corps sector, the British 4th Division advances to the Lamone River, east of Faenza; this advance permits the Indian 10th Division to push units across the Montone to drive north toward the enemy switch line stretching between Casa Bettini on the Montone to the area north of Scaldino on the Lamone. In other activity, the British 46th Division holds its bridgehead across the Marzeno, but the Germans prevent it from breaking out.

November 26th 1944 — (United States) The Carrier *Bonhomme Richard* (CV-31) is commissioned at New York, New York. **(Pacific-Philippines-Leyte)** In the **U.S. Sixth Army** area, contingents of the 1st Battalion, 34th Infantry, 24th Division hold threatened positions on Kilay Ridge and must still rely on Artillery to retain control. Company C is relieved by Company A on the highly contested ridge. In the **XXIV Corps** sector, Shoestring Ridge is assaulted again; the nighttime raid penetrates the U.S. perimeter, and about 200 Japs infiltrate a dense bamboo thicket; however, when the guns silence during the early morning hours of the 27th, 400 enemy bodies are counted. **(Pacific-Andaman Sea)** U.S. Army Planes sink the Japanese Transport No. 161 in the Andaman Sea, which is part of the Indian Ocean, west of the Malay Peninsula. **(Pacific-Burma)** In the N.C.A.C. area, the British 36th Division substitutes the 29th Brigade for the 72nd Brigade at Pinwe, and Patrols are instituted. **(Pacific-South China Sea)** U.S. Army Planes destroy the Japanese Minesweeper No. 18 in the South China Sea which is part of the western Pacific. **(Atlantic-Western Europe) 12th Army Group** In the **U.S. Ninth Army** area, XXIX Corps sector, the 29th Division neutralizes a strong counterattack at Bourheim. Major General Raymond S. McLain, Corps Commander, mandates the offensive toward the Roer be maintained along the entire front. In the **U.S.First Army** area, VI Corps sector, Frenz is taken by the 104th Division, subsequent to driving through Weisweiler. The Germans at Frenzerburg Castle are besieged by elements of Task Force Richardson, but the formidable Fortress, constructed during medieval times, withstands the Infantry and its accompanying long range Artillery. During the assault, Company K captures two buildings in the courtyard of the castle; however, the fighting strength of the unit is reduced to 35 men in the process. P.F.C. Carl Sheridan, garnished with a fresh supply of bazooka ammunition, rejoins his unit while it is engaged in a vicious fight with enemy Paratroopers who are holding the gate house on the opposing side of a 20 foot moat. Sheridan scurries through heavy enemy fire, positioning himself at the drawbridge; then he fires three direct hits, blows the doors open, turns to the others, and yells: "COME ON, LETS GET THEM." Despite being out of bazooka ammunition, he advances with his 45, drawn and blazing, into a hail of enemy bullets, giving his life. The subsequent charge to secure the castle is through the doors Sheridan had blown open; he receives the Medal of Honor posthumously. The 4th Division regroups in the Huertgen Forest, its 12th Infantry deploys north and west of Huertgen to defend the south flank of the 22nd Regiment. In the V Corps sector, the Germans abandon the woods in front of Huertgen, permitting the advancing 121st Regiment, 8th Division to accelerate their pace, but the enemy rebuffs the Regiment between the woods and the town. In the **U.S. Third Army** sector, the 358th Infantry reverts to the 90th Division and deploys defensively upon relief by C.C.A., 10th Armored Division. Meanwhile, C.C.B. extends its northern wing eastward against little opposition and closes on the Sarre. In conjunction, the 90th and 95th Divisions sustain their corkscrew drives against the Maginot Line, the latter lunging south, consuming the area containing Bois de Kerfent. In the 5th Division sector, the Verdun Forts capitulate, surrendering to the Yanks. In the XII Corps zone, the Germans mount fierce resistance through rear-guard actions at St. Avold, engaging the advancing 80th Division. In addition, strong resistance emerges against C.C.A., 6th Armored, after it pushes through Foret de Puttelange; the fire is so fierce it compels C.C.A. to withdraw into the woods. Simultaneously, C.C.B. mops up near the Maderbach, encountering difficulty with the soggy mud-permeated terrain which forbids movement of Armor, leaving the job for the Infantry. At Honskirch, more tenacious opposition builds as German rear-guards halt the progress of the driving 328th Infantry, 26th Division. In addition, 4th Armored begins churning toward the next line of resistance, attacking in unison with the two Task Forces of C.C.B., driving east of the Sarre toward Wolfskirchen-Eywiller-Durstel Road and encountering severely flooded streams; C.C.A. fords the river and moves east

through the rear of C.C.B. **6th Army Group** In the **U.S. Seventh Army** area, German attacks from the north continue to jeopardize the XV Corps. The 100th Division, driving toward the XV Corps front, receives orders to halt. In other activity, the 3rd Division bursts from the Vosges upon the Alsatian Plain, and the 103rd Division consumes Steige and Ville, two strategic strongpoints on the Giessen River. In the **French 1st Army** sector, the 1st and 2nd Corps enjoin at Burnhaupt, attempting to clamp down the German escape routes, but resolute enemy resistance hampers its progress. In addition, the Germans again sever the communications line to the Rhine in the 1st Corps sector, the third occurrence. **(Atlantic-Hungary)** Hatvan is taken by Soviet troops, and Budapest is now poised for seizure. **(Atlantic-Italy)** In the **British Eighth Army** area, 5th Corps sector, although the British 46th Division advances to the Lamone on the southern flank of the Corps, the Germans retain control of the switch lines between Lamone and the Montone rivers. Inclement weather again becomes a factor as rainstorms drench the area, terminating the offensive. **(Atlantic-Yugoslavia)** Some British Naval and Air Force units are authorized by Marshal Tito to have access to certain Airfields and Ports on a temporary basis.

GI medics tend a wounded German Soldier.

November 27th 1944 — Two U.S. Submarines, the *Escolar* (SS-294), commanded by Commander W. J. Millican (SS-294), and the *Shark* (SS-314), commanded by Commander E.N. Blakely, are officially reported missing and presumed lost. There is no trace of the *Escolar* which had departed Pearl Harbor on its first mission on September 18th; its last transmission was on October 17th, while operating in the Yellow Sea, and it was expected at Midway during mid-November. For information on the *Shark*, see October 24th 1944. **(Pacific-New Guinea)** The Australian 5th Division relieves the U.S. 40th Division. **(Pacific-Carolines-Palaus)** RCT 323, U.S.A., reduces the Umurbrogol Pocket; its Commander reports that the Peleliu operation is terminated. The Japanese lose approximately 13,600 killed on Angaur, Peleliu, and the tiny islands off Peleliu. In addition, about 400 prisoners are taken. The U.S. 81st Division and attached units sustain over 3,275 casualties, including 542 killed. The First Marine Division, reinforced, sustains about 1,250 killed and 5,275 wounded. **(Pacific-Marianas)** Japanese Planes bomb Airfields on Saipan, damaging Aircraft dispersed on the ground. **(Pacific-Philippines)** LEYTE: One Battalion of the 306th Infantry, 77th Division departs Leyte to participate in the Mindoro operation. In the **U.S. Sixth Army** area, X Corps sector, word spreads among the 1st Battalion, 34th Infantry, 24th Division that reinforcements are on the way, but the beleaguered troops on Kilay Ridge are struck by a huge counterattack from the east that severs their supply line to Consuegra. In the **XXIV Corps** sector, elements of the 1st Battalion, 184th Regiment, rush from Caridad to Damulaan to bolster the 32nd Infantry, 7th Division. The reinforcements drive steadily, penetrating dense bamboo woods and throwing back Japanese infiltrators who had pierced the perimeter of the 32nd Regiment's area. The Yanks count 109 dead enemy troops and reinforce their defense perimeter, withstanding several nominal infiltration assaults during the night. The Japanese move to recapture the Airfields. U.S. intelligence is informed, and precautions are taken at Burauen. In Naval activity, Japanese positions at Ormoc Bay are bombarded by U.S. Destroyers which duplicate the effort on the following day. Enemy Kamikaze Planes attack the U.S. Fleet in Leyte Gulf, damaging the Battleship *Colorado* (BB-45) and the Destroyers *St. Louis* (CL-49) and the *Montpelier* (CL-57). In addition, the Submarine Chaser SC-744 is sunk. **(Pacific-China)** Generalissimo Chiang Kai-shek turns down a proposal by General Wedemeyer to arm the Chinese Communists to assist against the Japanese. **(Atlantic-Western Europe) 21st Army Group** The U.S. 101st Airborne Division is relieved in the Canadian 2nd Corps sector. **12th Army Group** In the **U.S. Ninth Army** area, **XIX Corps** sector, Merzenhausen and the nearby hills are totally secured by C.C.A., 2nd Armored Division. The 29th Division sweeps its sector clear to the Roer, except two persistent strongholds in Juelich; the 115th Regiment startles the Germans at Kirchberg and overpowers them, while contingents of the 116th Regiment break through to the isolated troops in Koslar. Near Altkirch, the Germans establish fierce opposition, halting the 120th Infantry reinforced with one Battalion of the 119th. In the **U.S. First Army** area, **VII Corps** sector, the Weisweiler-Frenz zone is mopped up by the 104th Division. The Germans retain control of Frenzerburg Castle, but their counterattack against TF Richardson fails. In the Huertgen Forest, the 4th Division continues to consolidate its positions; near Grosshau, two enemy machine gun nests pin down Company B, 22nd Infantry. Artillery and mortar fire interdict, making the situation more grave. Private Marcario Garcia singlehandedly attacks, becoming wounded; he refuses evacuation and crawls forward tossing several grenades, eliminating the gun. He then picks off three escaping Germans with his rifle before rejoining his beleaguered unit. Garcia attacks, killing three additional Germans, captures four, and silences another menacing gun. Garcia is awarded the Medal of Honor for his intrepid heroism. At Hill 203, the enemy loses the crest to the 18th Infantry, 1st Division, but maintains control of the rear slopes. In the **V Corps** sector, the 8th Division, supplemented with Artillery, powers its way to the northeast and the western fringes of Huertgen. In the **U.S. Third Army** area, **XX Corps** sector, the 10th Armored Division eliminates German infiltrators from Tettingen and throws back a vicious counterattack at Borg, before disengaging the attack toward Saarburg. General Walker orders the 3rd Cavalry Group to protect the northern flank of the Corps, subsequent to relieving C.C.A.; he instructs the 10th Armored to deploy facing east. The 90th Division, well in advance of the flanking units, halts to prepare for the short sprint to the Sarre River. The 95th Division forges ahead, its 378th Regiment seizing Dalem and Falck; its 377th Infantry bolts to within a mile of the German border. In the **XII Corps** sector, the 80th Division occupies St. Avold, subsequent to German abandonment; the pressurized attack has forced a general enemy retreat across the Maderbach. Honskirch and Altweiler are entered without incident by the 328th and 101st Regiments, 26th Division respectively. C.C.A. and C.C.B., 4th

Armored Division roll ahead, overpowering Eywiller, Gungwiller, and Wolfskirchen, but the Germans resist tenaciously at Durstel, halting C.C.A. **6th Army Group** General Eisenhower orders Seventh Army to attack to assist Third Army in securing the Saar Basin. In the **XII Corps** sector, German pressure diminishes; however, the positions on the northern flank are still questionable. In the **VI Corps** sector, the French 2nd Armored Division at Strasbourg is relieved by units of the 3rd U.S. Division, enabling the French to prepare to advance south along the Rhine. The drive is to be complemented by C.C.A., 14th Armored, which is to advance toward Baar and Erstein, thus severing enemy escape routes from the Vosges. In other activity, the 36th Division drives east toward Ste Marie. The 103rd Division seizes Le Hohwald as it dashes toward the Baar-Selestat Road. **(Atlantic-Italy)** In the **U.S. Fifth Army** area, the British 13th Corps is ordered to initiate an offensive as soon as the inclement weather ceases. In other activity, the Indian 8th Division loses contact with the enemy. In the **British Eighth Army** area, orders are issued for a full scale winter Army offensive, scheduled to commence during early December. In the Polish 2nd Corps sector, enemy resistance south of Faenza and east of the Lamone terminates. In the 5th Corps sector, contingents of the Indian 10th Division, deployed on the right flank, are relieved by units of the Canadian 1st Corps, permitting the Indian units to assault the strategic bridge at Casa Bettini, required desperately in order to funnel the Canadian 1st Corps to the Adriatic sector. In the 10th Corps sector, elements of the Cremona Group begin arriving.

Another B-29 en route to bombard Japan.

November 28th 1944 — (Pacific-Japan) The Submarine *Scabbardfish* (SS-397) receives notice that a Japanese Submarine will be passing through its zone. During the latter part of the afternoon, the enemy Ship is spotted at 15,000 yards distant. Soon after, three torpedoes are fired, and the I-365 is sunk off Honshu. Two survivors are spotted in the water, and an attempt to bring them aboard prompts one to drown himself intentionally, rather than be captured. The other chooses to swim to the Submarine and is brought aboard. Upon learning that he will not be shot or have his throat cut, the prisoner called Sasaki relaxes. The Submarine, known as "Scabby" to the crew, had sunk a Cargo Vessel, the *Kisaragi Maru*, on the 16th; the Vessel is also responsible for saving several downed American Airmen. Legend has it that when the Ship's cook, Nick Christodolou, arrived on board during late 1943, he was greeted by the Captain, Lt. Commander Frederick A. Gunn, known as "Pop Gunn," who instructed him: "I EXPECT MY MEN TO BE THE BEST FED CREW ON ANY

Nick Christodoulou, Jr., Cook aboard the U.S.S. Scabbardfish. Photo courtesy of Nick Christodoulou.

BOAT IN THIS WHOLE DAMN NAVY, YOU GOT THAT COOKIE?" Soon after, while the cook was engaged in learning how to play poker while simultaneously trying to bake a cake, several other crewmen sneak five pounds of baking powder into the ingredients. Suddenly, the Submarine is forced to surface as the Vessel is consumed in smoke; from that point, the Captain and the cook remain on a first name basis! **(Pacific-Philippines)** On LEYTE: in the **Sixth Army** area, **X Corps** sector, the Japanese mount a snarling attack to take Kilay Ridge during the night; the effort isolates Company C, 134th Infantry which is deployed on the southwestern end; on the following day, amidst continuing enemy attacks, the 1st Battalion drives forward and relieves its stranded contingent. Additional reinforcements are requested, and the 2nd Battalion, 128th Infantry, 32nd Division moves out; Company G spearheads the drive. In the **XXIV Corps** sector, the exhausted 32nd Infantry, 7th Division is assigned to reserve; the 17th and 184th Regiments continue to engage the enemy on Shoestring Ridge; the 1st Battalion, 184th Regiment withdraws slightly under pressure of a heated counterattack at the bamboo thicket and the 2nd Battalion, 184th Regiment relieves the 2nd Battalion, 32nd Infantry (7th Division) at Damulaan. The 11th Airborne Division completes its march over the mountains and enters the Leyte Valley to relieve the 7th Division (minus the 17th Regiment); it deploys to defend the Bayug and Buri Airfields. In other activity in the Philippines, the Commander of Task Force 77 issues the operation plan for the invasion of Mindoro. Responsibility for the amphibious phase is given to Rear Admiral Arthur D. Struble, Commander, TG 78.3 (Mindoro Attack Group), U.S. Seventh Fleet.

(Pacific-Carolines-Palaus) Contingents of the 81st Division begin clearing Kayangel Atoll, north of Kossol Passage. **(Pacific-China)** U.S. General McClure becomes Chief of Staff to General Wedemeyer. The Japanese 11th Army, disregarding orders, advances from Nanning and moves across the Kwangsi-Kweichow border. **(China-Burma)** In the N.C.A.C. area, the Chinese 38th Division's 114th Regiment continues to close on the primary Japanese defenses along the northern perimeter of Bhamo; the 113th Regiment, which has the task of breaking into the city, has not been able to penetrate. **(Atlantic-Western Europe)** Antwerp's port is open to traffic. **12th Army Group** In the **U.S. Ninth Army** area, **XIX Corps** completes clearing its sector to the Roer; Barmen is seized by C.C.A., 2nd Armored Division, which then advances to the Roer near it. In the 29th Division zone, the two enemy strongholds in Juelich linger, but the enemy abandons Koslar. Elements of the 30th Division secure Altkirch, but a small triangular strongpoint remains between the Roer and Inde Rivers. The offensive is temporarily suspended. In the **U.S. First Army** area, **VII Corps** sector, the 104th Division surges into Lammersdorf and Inden, seizing a bridge intact at the latter. Task Force Richardson takes Frenzerburg Castle, subsequent to abandonment by the enemy. The 1st Division captures Juengersdorf and Langerwehe. In the **V Corps** sector, the elusive Huertgen falls to a three-directional assault by the 8th Division. Major General Donald A. Stroh, Divisional Commanding General, is replaced by Brigadier General William G. Weaver. In other activity, General Hodges orders the Corps to continue the offensive. Kleinhau, the next Corps objective, is bombarded by Artillery and Aircraft. In the **U.S. Third Army** area, **XX Corps** sector, the 378th Regiment, 95th Division encounters rough resistance near Falck that hampers progress; the 377th Infantry drives into Germany. In the **XII Corps** sector, the 317th Regiment, 26th Division plows into Farebersviller, capturing part of it; then it repulses a Tank-Infantry assault consisting of about 2,000 German troops. In other activity, the 4th Armored Division is heavily involved clearing towns and villages east of Drulingen-Sarre-Union highway; Berg falls to Combat Command B. **6th Army Group** In the **U.S. Seventh Army** area, **VI Corps** sector, elements of the 2nd French Armored Division advance to Erstein against strong resistance. The German opposition against Combat Command A, 14th Armored is equally tenacious at both Barr and Erstein. The 36th Division discovers Koenigsbourg, Chateau, and Liepvre abandoned by the enemy. In the **French 1st Army** area, the Germans at Alsace become compressed and encircled as the 1st and 2nd Corps converge at Burnhaupt during the afternoon. In the Alps sector, the 100th Battalion, RCT 442 relieves the 1st Special Service Force on the Franco-Italian frontier. **(Atlantic-Italy)** In the **U.S. Fifth Army** area, Casola, M. Taverna, and Valsenio, abandoned by the enemy, are seized. In the **British Eighth Army** area, 5th Corps sector, the Indian 10th Division cancels its operation to seize the Casa Bettini bridge due to inclement weather. In other activity, the Canadian 1st Corps prepares to attack along the Adriatic coast.

November 29th 1944 — **(Pacific)** Admiral Nimitz suggests the postponement of the invasion of Mindoro and Luzon, preferring that a build-up of Air strength on Leyte be accomplished first. **(Pacific-Japan)** The U.S.S. *Archerfish* (SS-311) sinks the Carrier *Shinano* south of Honshu. **(Pacific-Philippines)** LEYTE: In the **U.S. Sixth Army** area, **X Corps** sector, enemy counterattacks continue, but reinforcements arrive to help stem the tide. In the **XXIV Corps** sector, the 184th Regiment, 7th Division retakes some terrain in the bamboo thicket, but the enemy is not totally dislodged; the Regiment subsequently throws back three severe counterattacks. In Naval activity, Suicide Planes attack the U.S. Fleet in Leyte Gulf, damaging the Battleship *Maryland* (BB-46) and the Destroyers *Saufley* (DD-465) and *Aulick* (DD-569). The Japanese lose Patrol Boat No. 105 by U.S. Surface Vessel fire and the Submarine Chaser No. 45 to Army Aircraft. **(Atlantic-Western Europe) 12th Army Group** In the **U.S. Ninth Army** area, the **XIII Corps'** offensive commences prior to dawn. Without preliminary Artillery fire, the Divisions jump off; the 84th drives on the left flank toward the Roer, striking against Lindern and the high ground northeast of Beeck; the 102nd Division streaks down the Lindern-Linnich highway, parallel to the 84th Division on its left, gaining sufficient ground to regroup for the next assault. Meanwhile, the 84th Division's 335th Infantry pushes a contingent of about 100 men of the 3rd Battalion to Lindern; they hold the town from daybreak until reinforcements including Tanks arrive later; a German counterattack to regain the town fails. The 2nd Battalion, pressing Beeck, encounters heavy resistance at the heights outside of town; the 335th Regiment in conjunction with the 113th Cavalry supplements the 335th with fire support and attacks Beeck. In addition, the Corps retains the 7th Armored Division in reserve. In the **U.S. First Army** area, **VII Corps** sector, the Germans unsuccessfully counterattack Inden and Lammersdorf; the bridge at the latter is blown by the enemy. At Merode, elements of the 26th Infantry, 1st Division drive into the town, but become cut off and nearly annihilated during a brutal counterattack. The Huertgen Forest again erupts into a blazing battle as the 4th Division reignites its offensive against a much strengthened enemy which has fortified its positions during the pause. The 12th Infantry pours into the gap between the 8th and 22nd Regiments, sealing it; the 22nd bolstered by Armor lunges toward Grosshau, seizing it and cutting the road to Gey. In the **V Corps** sector, Kleinhau is secured by a Task Force of Combat Command R, 5th Armored; the unit, commanded by Lt. Colonel William A. Hamberg, is subsequently relieved by the 1st Battalion, 13th Regimental Combat Team. Complications develop during the night when the relief force abandons two strategic roadblocks in the high ground, making the imminent VI Corps assault against Grosshau more difficult. Huertgen and Kleinhau are considered imperative locations from which to gain Brandenberg-Bergstein Ridge. In the **U.S. Third Army** area, **XX Corps** sector, a synchronized assault toward the Sarre is mounted by the 90th and 95th Divisions, the former getting a Patrol to the river in effortless motion. German resistance against the latter in the heights near Saarlautern is iron-fisted; the 95th is struck by ten counterattacks, yet it still secures the general line Kerpich-Hemmersdorf-St. Barbara-Merten. During the day's gruesome fighting, Company G, 377th Infantry is pinned down by heavy enemy fire. Staff Sergeant Andrew Miller, who has already acted above and beyond the call of duty frequently since the 16th, is at it again, jumping from his position to lead his detachment forward. Several Platoons follow, and the enemy is beaten back; however, the gallant Miller is finally felled. Because of his superlative heroism over the past weeks, he is awarded the Medal of Honor posthumously. The entire Third Army front is consumed with incessant hellish combat. Near Metz, the 5th Division seizes Fort St. Privat, and in the **XII Corps** sector, the Germans bang hard against the 317th Infantry, 80th Division, retaking Farebersviller, despite Tanks and Tank Destroyers sent forward in support. The 317th is relieved by the 318th Regiment. In additional activity,

the 4th Division's C.C.A. takes Durstel with one of its Task Forces. **6th Army Group** In the **U.S. Seventh Army** area, **XV Corps** sector, Tiefenbach falls to the 114th Regiment, 44th Division. The 45th Division bolsters its positions along the northern bank of the Moder River near Rothbach-Mertzwiller. In addition, the 314th Infantry, 79th Division, secures Niederschaeffolsheim. In the **VI Corps** sector, the 411th Regiment, 103rd Divsion, seizes Andlau and Barr. The French 2nd Armored Division takes Erstein. Meanwhile, C.C.A., 14th Armored Division spins through Barr, driving south along the eastern fringes of the Vosges. The 36th Division discovers Le Bonhomme abandoned; the 36th is also mopping up around Liepvre. Patton moves from Chateau Salins to St. Avold, crossing the Maginot Line stating that he: "WAS IMPRESSED BY ITS LACK OF IMPRESSIVENESS," and noting that contingents of the 80th Division slugged their way through that part of the line without realizing it was the famous Maginot Line. At the present time, Third Army replacement shortages amount to 9,000 men, prompting Patton to drain five percent of the Corps and Headquarters troops, transforming them into Infantry. **(Atlantic-Hungary)** Elements of the Third Ukrainian Front enjoin the offensive and cross the Danube south of Budapest, advancing toward Lake Balaton north of the Drava River. Mohacs and Pecs have been abandoned by the Germans. **(Atlantic-Italy)** In the **U.S. Fifth Army** area, the British 13th Corps seizes Fontanelice without incident. The Germans regain M. Castellaro, wresting it from the British 1st Division. In the British 5th Corps sector, the British 7th Armored Brigade departs Recanati for the 5th Corps area to participate in the December offensive.

A U.S. Army Bulldozer Tank and additional Armor.

November 30th 1944 — (Pacific-Philippines) LEYTE: In the **U.S. Sixth Army** area, **X Corps** sector, the 112th Cavalry continues its southern drive toward Limon to support the 32nd Division; however, heavy enemy resistance is encountered, forcing the Cavalry to stop and dig in at a ridge about 5,000 yards southeast of Limon to repulse enemy Patrols. In the **XII Corps** sector, contingents of the 184th Regiment, 7th Division, secure the remainder of the bamboo thicket and establish a night perimeter, successfully concluding the enduring battle for Shoestring Ridge. In other activity, General MacArthur postpones the Mindoro invasion for a period of ten days. Final target dates for the invasions of Mindoro and Luzon are 15th, December 1944 and 9th, January 1945 respectively. **(Pacific)** Allied Air Forces direct that four F4U Squadrons of the 1st Marine Aircraft Wing be attached to the operational control of the Fifth Air Force on Leyte, Philippines to allow the Third Carrier Fleet to concentrate its efforts on the attack against Japan. **(Pacific-Burma)** In the N.C.A.C. area, the British 36th Division discovers Pinwe abandoned by the Japs. **(Pacific-China)** General Wedemeyer informs the Joint Chiefs of Staff and Admiral Mountbatten that Chiang Kai-shek has decided to transfer the Chinese 22nd and 38th Divisions from Burma to defend Kunming, and that he is committed to provide 270,000 replacements for ALPHA (Plan to defend Chungking and Kunming) by the 1st of April; he also states that the Generalissimo flatly rejects the request to supply arms to the Chinese troops in the IX War Area (communists). **(Atlantic-Western Europe) 21st Army Group** In the **British Second Army** area, the 8th and 12th Corps pummel the German bridgehead west of the Maas, inflicting high casualties and compressing the remaining enemy Paratroops into a pocket at Blerick. In other activity, Field Marshal Montgomery writes Eisenhower and requests a meeting at Maastricht with Ike and Bradley with their Chiefs of Staff "WHO MUST NOT SPEAK." Ike becomes annoyed, but calls the meeting for the 7th of December. **12th Army Group** In the **U.S. Ninth Army** area, **XIII Corps** sector, the 102nd Division becomes the vanguard of the attack; the 405th Regiment battles determinedly along the Lindern-Linnich road; the 406th rams against the edge of Linnich; in conjunction, the 407th drive closes on the Roer, seizing Welz. Also, the Germans are driven from Beeck by the 335th Regiment, 84th Division, but they retain possession of the high ground northeast of town. In the **U.S. First Army** area, **VII Corps** sector, Lammersdorf and the northern sector of Inden are totally cleared by the 104th Division. Relentless German opposition in the Huertgen Forest inflicts severe casualties upon the 8th Infantry, 4th Division. At Gey, the 12th Regiment drives doggedly, advancing over 1,000 yards through the nearby woods against treacherous resistance. The beleaguered Regiment is unable to mount an assault; the 22nd Regiment, supported by Armor attacks to clear the area between Gey and Grosshau, encounters intense opposition and sustains high casualties, but a few contingents reach the fringes of Gey and take cover in nearby woods, which attribute fewer losses. In the **U.S. Third Army** area, **XX Corps** sector, contingents of the 10th Armored close against the Sarre; C.C.B. advances to the river across from Merzig, but the Germans have blown the bridges. The 359th Infantry, 90th Division rolls into Fremersdorf on the western bank of the Sarre without incident. The 1st Battalion, 357th Infantry fords the Nied River in assault boats near Niedaltdorf, then bolts to Bueren, encountering firm opposition. Elements of the 95th Division seize the heights which control Saarlautern; its 377th Regiment mops up Ste Barbara, then drives to Felsberg, while the 378th Regiment overpowers the enemy on a nearby hill. Task Force Bell, comprising elements of 10th Regiment, 5th Division, the 5th Reconnaissance Troop, and additional support units, is organized to defend the left flank of the 95th Division; it is commanded by Colonel Robert P. Bell and attached to the 95th. In the **XII Corps** sector, the 4th Armored Division seizes the high ground at Mackwiller, then deploys to assault Sarre-Union. **6th Army Group** In the **U.S. Seventh Army** area, **VI Corps** sector, C.C.A., 14th Armored Division secures St. Pierre, then drives south, followed by the 103rd Division, which is moving toward Selestat. The 36th Division forms to strike west of Selestat and seize Chatenois. **(Atlantic-Hungary)** Elements of the Second Ukrainian Front capture Eger, northeast of Budapest, and approaches Miskolc. **(Atlantic-Italy)** In the **U.S. Fifth Army** area, British 13th Corps sector, the British 1st Division loses Casa Nuovo to the Germans. In the **British Eighth Army** area, 5th Corps sector, the weather clears sufficiently for the Indian 10th Division to re-

initiate its attack to seize the Casa Bettini bridge, taking Albereto as it penetrates the switch-line positions.

December 1st 1944 — (Pacific-Carolines-Palaus) The occupation of Kayangel Atoll is completed by contingents of the U.S. 81st Division. **(Pacific-Marshall Islands)** A U.S. Naval Operating Base is established at Kwajalein. **(Pacific-New Guinea)** U.S. troops on Aitape are relieved by Australian contingents. **(Pacific-Philippines)** On LEYTE, in the **U.S. Sixth Army** area, **X Corps** sector, Artillery pounds enemy positions on the knolls at the southeastern part of Kilay Ridge prior to an attack by Company E, 128th Regiment, 32nd Division, which moves through the positions of Company C, 34th Infantry and seizes the first one. The 1st Battalion, 34th Infantry is ordered to withdraw from the ridge, but is unable to pull back for several days. In the area southeast of Limon, the Japanese repel attempts by the 112th Cavalry Group to push them from a ridge. In the **XXIV Corps** sector, word is received that the attack against Ormoc is imminent. In other activity on Leyte, the Japanese have consumed their food supplies. **(Pacific-Burma)** Lt. General George E. Stratemeyer reorganizes the Eastern Air Command, effective December 4th. On the N.C.A.C. front, the Chinese 30th, spearheaded by the 90th Regiment, advances across harsh land as it drives from Bhamo toward Namhkam. **(Pacific-China)** General Wedemeyer instructs General Chennault to concentrate the Fourteenth Air Force on protecting both the Air line to China and Service of Supply. Chennault is also directed to continue providing logistical support of U.S. Military priorities and to support particular Chinese troops in the China Theater. On the Salween front, Che-fang falls to the Chinese. **(Atlantic-Western Europe) 12th Army Group** In the **U.S. Ninth Army** area, **XIII Corps** sector, the 406th Regiment, takes Linnich, while the 405th Regiment seizes heights along the Lindern-Linnich highway by implementing a double envelopment. In the **XIX Corps** sector, the 116th Infantry, 29th Division assaults two enemy strongholds west of the Roer, across from Juelich. Enemy resistance is fierce as the troops charge across exposed terrain, halting their progress before they can reach either the section of buildings known as Hasenfeld Gut or the athletic complex, the Juelich sporplatz. In the **U.S. First Army** area, **VII Corps** sector, the 104th Division makes nominal progress in the southern portion of Inden. In the Huertgen Forest, the contest continues to ensue in the 4th Division zone; the 8th Regiment is prevented from emerging, and it has gained only about one thousand yards during three brutalizing days. In conjunction, the 22nd Regiment, by committing its reserves, breaks out near Gey. The assault is halted by orders of Major General J. Lawton Collins. In the past sixteen days, the 4th Division has sustained heavy casualties and gained slightly more than three miles against the entrenched German defenders in the forest. In the **V Corps** sector, contingents of the 28th and 121st Regiments, 8th Division secure part of the Tiefen Creek bottom land and Brandenberger Wald on the right and left flanks respectively, creating a fairly secure path for the Armor to drive down the Kleinhau-Brandenberg highway which shadows the ridge line. In the **U.S. Third Army** area, **XX Corps** sector, preparations for the assault across the Sarre continue. At Merzig, nominal opposition is overpowered by the 10th Armored Division; the 90th Division sweeps its sector south of the town with relative ease. The 95th Division is supported by a preliminary Air strike as it begins to ford the Sarre. Medium Bombers strike Ensdorf, Fraulautern, and Saarlautern while Fighter Bombers paralyze enemy movement east of the Sarre, but the Germans mount intense resistance against the 95th's attack. Only four of the eight Bombing Groups had struck the target, making the 95th's Division task tougher than anticipated. On the following day, ten groups of Medium Bombers strike Saarlautern, destroying the electric plant; this prevents the Germans from detonating the Bridges, and they are taken intact. The 379th Regiment spearheads the assault, attacking through the positions of the 377th, driving toward Saarlautern; the 377th overruns Felsberg and storms into Ste Barbara where heavy fighting develops; the 378th Regiment takes a hill near Berus, then it encounters heavy resistance which halts its progress short of Bisten. In other activity, Task Force Bell is to be relieved by Task Force Fickett, commanded by Colonel E. M. Fickett (6th Cavalry Group and 5th Ranger Battalion); the newly formed Task Force assumes responsibility for protecting the southern flank of the Corps. In the **XII Corps** sector, C.C.B., 4th Armored Division and the 101st Regiment, 26th Division, encounter spirited opposition at Sarre-Union, but the 3rd Battalion takes it; inability to seize a fortified hill north of the town compels the 3rd Battalion to pull back until morning. In conjunction, the 1st Battalion secures Bannholtz woods, and Hill 318 is seized by In other activity, the 6th Armored Division and the 35th Division and 80th Infantry Divisions receive orders to commence an attack on the 4th, to straighten the center and left of the Corps line. **6th Army Group** In the **U.S. Seventh Army** area, **XV Corps** sector, the German 19th Army, commanded by German General Wiese, mounts fierce resistance against the 44th Division at Tieffenbach and near Zinswiller-Meitesheim; the enemy exhibits similar tenacity against the 45th Division. Schweighausen is secured by the 79th Division, reinforced by the 94th Cavalry Reconnaissance Squadron, 14th Armored Division. In the **VI Corps** sector, the French 2nd Armored Division continues its southward attack along the Rhine, and the U.S. 36th and 103rd Divisions approach Selestat. In other activity, C.C.A., 14th Armored Division reverts to Corps reserve. **(Eastern Europe)** In eastern Czechoslovakia, Soviet forces cross the Ondava River near Humenne and Trebisov; the Germans hold firm against elements of the Second Ukrainian Front at Miskolc, northeast of Budapest, Hungary. In related activity, the Third Ukrainian Front drives from southwest of Budapest toward Pecs. **(Atlantic-Italy)** In the **U.S. Fifth Army** area, the British 13th Corps' attack plans are modified because of German withdrawals; the first phase specifies the British 6th Armored Division seizure of M. Penzola. In the **British Eighth Army** area, preparations for an attack continues. In the British 5th Corps sector, the Indian Division seizes the Casa Bettini bridge over the Montone. The Canadian 1st Corps, which takes responsibility for the 5th Corps right flank, crosses the Montone using the captured bridge at Casa Bettini.

December 2nd 1944 — (Pacific-Philippines) LEYTE: In the **U.S. Sixth Army** area, **X Corps** sector, elements of the 128th Regiment, 32nd Division spread to the south on Kilay Ridge, encountering firm resistance as they advance. Also, the 112th Cavalry Group's operation to secure the ridge southeast of Limon continues. In other activity, enemy positions at Palompon and northern Ormoc Bay, Leyte, are struck by four Destroyers. Another group of Destroyers, under Commander J.C. Zahm, engages enemy Destroyers, Aircraft, and shore batteries during the night and into the early morning hours of the 3rd. The *Allen M. Sumner*, *Moale*, and *Cooper*, searching for enemy Vessels suspected of debarking troops, enter a hornet's nest and are savagely attacked. The slugfest costs the Japanese the Destroyer *Kuwa* and several Marus; however,

the Destroyer U.S.S. *Cooper* (DD-695) is blown up by an undetermined underwater explosion; the Destroyers *Sumner* (DD-692) and *Morate* (DD-693) sustain minor injuries, the latter losing two men and suffering 22 wounded. **(Pacific-Burma)** In the **British Fourteenth Army** area, 33rd Corps sector, the East African 11th Division arrives at Kalewa on the Chindwin River. **(Pacific-China)** General Wedemeyer proposes another plan, offered by Colonel David D. Barrett (U.S. Observer Group in Yennan), which calls for establishing three Communist Regiments to be equipped by the U.S.; they are to serve in Yennan under the command of a U.S. Officer; the idea is rejected by Kai-shek. A subsequent proposal by General McClure to commit U.S. Airborne contingents of Technicians in Communist China will be casually offered to the Nationalists and Communists later in the month. In other activity, Japanese elements reach Tu-shan as they advance on Kweiyang. **(Atlatic-Western Europe) 21st Army Group** In the **Canadian First Army** area, 2nd Corps sector, the Germans penetrate the dyke area along the Neder Rijn and intentionally flood the area southwest of Arnhem, compelling the Corps to compress its Waal River bridgehead; it pulls back to the rail line extending west from Elst. **12th Army Group** In the **U.S. Ninth Army** area, **XIII Corps** sector, the high ground northeast of Lindern and the town of Leiffarth are both seized by the 334th Regiment, 84th Division. The 407th Regiment, 102nd Division attacks Flossdorf and Roerdorf simultaneously, capturing the latter. In the **XIX Corps** sector, the Germans offer stiff resistance at both strongholds in Juelich, engaging the 116th Regiment, 29th Division ferociously. In the **U.S. First Army** area, **VII Corps** sector, Inden is cleared by the 104th Division along with the rest of its zone west of the Inde, subsequent to a major surprise assault which is launched at 23:00, resulting in a swift surge across the Inde by the 414th and 415th Regiments, each afforded cover fire by the 413th. On the following day, the Germans recover from the shock and counterattack viciously. In the 1st Division sector, the Germans have been extremely formidable against the hard driving Big Red One, hampering its progress to less than four miles during 15 days of grueling battle. At Gey, Artillery assists the 22nd Regiment, 4th Division which halts an enemy counterattack. In the **V Corps** sector, Task Force Hamberg, C.C.R., 5th Armored Division rolls down the Kleinhau-Brandenberg highway under a hail of enemy shells originating from Kommerscheidt Ridge until it is temporarily stopped by a menacing minefield, which is cleared during the night under the protection of interdictory fire. In the **U.S. Third Army** area, **XX Corps** sector, 10th Armored caps off securing its zone west of the Sarre with the reduction of Dreisbach; then it deploys C.C.A. 10th Army elements as outposts on the west bank of the river between the 3rd Cavalry Group and the 90th Division; C.C.B. 10th Army reverts to reserve. House-to-house fighing erupts in Saarlautern, subsequent to an Air-supported night assault by the 95th Division which is seeking a crossing of the Sarre; the 2nd Battalion, 379th Regiment, penetrates the western end of town while the 377th seizes St. Barbara and attempts to capture an intact bridge leading to Saarlautern. In conjunction, the 378th Regiment evicts the enemy at Pikard. In addition, the 3rd Battalion, 11th Regiment, 5th Division, combined with the 10th Infantry, drives through the southwest portion of Foret de la House. In the **XII Corps** sector, the 101st Regiment, 26th Division discovers that Germans have reoccupied Sarre-Union and begin to clear it once again. Contingents of the 104th Regiment advance to strengthen their hold on the town. The German eastward escape routes from Sarre-Union leading to Domfessel and Voellerdingen are severed by the 4th

Armored Division and supporting Aircraft. General Patton orders the 4th Armored to withdraw as soon as the XV Corps relieves it. General John Shirley Wood, Commanding Officer, 4th Armored is relieved by General Gaffey (presently Army Chief of Staff) in order that General Wood can receive some needed rest. General Hugh J. Gaffey assumes command on the 4th. **6th Army Group** General Devers, Group Commander, directs te U.S. Seventh Army to prepare for the northward assault. Reduction of the Colmar Pocket will be the responsibility of French forces. In the **U.S. Seventh Army** area, **XV Corps** sector, Waldhambach is seized by the 44th Division while the 45th Division clears Meitesheim, then advances into Engwiller. In the **VI Corps** sector, the French 2nd Armored Division halts in the Kogenheim-Freisenheim area and reverts to the French 1st Army. The U.S. 36th and 103rd Divisions engage the Germans in malicious house-to-house fighting at Selestat. In addition, the 36th Division reinforces the French 1st Army. General de Lattre orders attacks against the Colmar Pocket from the north and south concurrently to converge near the Rhine at Neuf-Brisach. **(Eastern Europe)** The Soviets continue to advance toward Budapest. Elements of Fourth Ukrainian Front enlarge the bridgehead at the Ondava River in Czechoslovakia; the Second Ukrainian Front assaults German positions in the Miskolc region in Hungary. Also, the Third Ukrainian Front, operating in southwest Hungary, advances north and northwest between the Danube and Drava Rivers. **(Atlantic-Italy)** In the **British Eighth Army** area, preparations for the primary assault continue as the British make limited advances. The Canadian 1st Corps starts reducing the enemy resistance at the switch lines, between the Lamone and the Montone Rivers.

December 3rd 1944 — (Pacific-Philippines) LEYTE: In the **U.S. Sixth Army** area, **X Corps** sector, Troops G, 112th Cavalry attacks vigorously attempting to take a ridge southeast of Limon; the attempt to scale the slopes is unfruitful as the Germans retain control. In the **XXIV Corps** sector, Major General Archibald V. Arnold directs the 7th Division to prepare an attack to commence on the 5th; it is to secure the area south of the Talisayan River and includes Hills 380, 606, and 918. In other activity, Marine Night Fighter Squadron 541 (2nd Marine Aircraft Wing, Peleliu) and Marine Aircraft Wing 12 (VMF-115, 211, 218, and 313, Solomons) land at Tacloban and are attached to the 308th Bombardment Wing, Fifth Air Force. **(Pacific-South China Sea)** The Submarine *Pipefish* (SS-388) sinks the Japanese Coastal Defense Vessel No 64. **(Pacific- SEAC)** British Admiral Mountbatten concurs with Generalissimo Kai-shek's decision to transfer the Chinese 22nd and 38th Divisions from Burma to China; subsequently, the Chinese 14th Division replaces the 38th. **(Pacific-Burma)** In the **British Fourteenth Army** area, 33rd Corps sector, the 11th East African Division gets a bridgehead across the Chindwin at Kalewa, despite heavy Japanese fire; the Indian 20th Division secures a crossing further north near Mawlaik, and a Brigade of the 20th crosses there; however, the balance of the Division crosses at Kalewa. **(Pacific-China)** The Japanese 11th Army, which had crossed into Kweichow Province without orders, is forced to halt due to exhaustion of supplies. **(Atlantic-Western Europe) 21st Army Group** In the **British Second Army** area, Blerick is seized by the 12th Corps, totally clearing its sector west of the Maas. **12th Army Group** In the **U.S. Ninth Army** area, the **XIII Corps** advances to the Roer. The 407th Regiment, 102nd Division, seizes Flossdorf. In the **XIX Corps** sector, the Commander of the 116th Infantry, 26th Division is relieved due to the unsuccessful progress against

the two enemy strongholds at Juelich. In the **U.S. First Army VII Corps** sector, the Inde bridgehead is expanded east, reaching beyond Lucherberg. The 16th Regiment, 1st Division, supplemented with Tanks and Tank Destroyers, takes Luchem. One enemy strongpoint containing five enemy machine guns is attacked by Private Robert T. Henry; he is mortally wounded within ten yards of the fortification, but gets off hand grenades which force the enemy from their positions, allowing others to overrun them; seventy prisoners are taken; Pvt. Henry receives the Medal of Honor posthumously. In the **V Corps** sector, the 8th Division stiffens its attack to secure the flanks of the primary assault force in Brandenberger Wald and the Tiefen Creek vicinity. In coordinated activity, the 5th Armored Division's Task Force Hamberg, bolstered by Air support, resumes its advance, steaming down the Kleinhau-Brandenberg highway, overpowering Brandenberg; however, the enemy retains control of the nearby terrain and no U.S. reinforcements are available, causing some concern. The German Air Force makes an unusual appearance; about sixty ME-109s strike in the afternoon, causing little harm, and the Germans lose about nineteen Planes for the effort. Task Force Boyer, commanded by Lt. Colonel H.E. Boyer, C.C.R., 5th Armored Division is securing an enemy strongpoint at Vossenack and takes it on the following day. In the **U.S. Third Army** area, **XX Corps** sector, the 1st Battalion, 379th Regiment, 95th Division, seizes a bridge to Saarlautern-Roden road, but the Germans have damaged it by fire, preventing immediate use; the 2nd and 3rd Battalions take the majority of Saarlautern, while other contingents of the 95th Division advance to the river line. Near Lauterbach, the 6th Cavalry Group, combined with the 2nd Ranger Battalion, repulse a heavy counterattack, and at Creutzwald, the 10th Regiment, 5th Division overcomes tenacious resistance, seizing it. In the **XII Corps** sector, the Germans spring a strong, but unsuccessful, counterattack from Oermingen, against the 26th Division at Sarre-Union. **6th Army Group** Heavy fighting continues at Ratzwiller where the Germans hinder progress of the 44th Division. Zinswiller is taken by the 45th Division, and the 100th Division drives toward Bitche, its 398th Infantry moving through the 44th Division lines. In the **VI Corps** sector, the 36th and 103rd Divisions continue reducing Selestat. Company F, 142nd Infantry, 36th Division engages the Germans in gruesome street fighting at St. Hippolyte; Sergeant Ellis R. Weicht singlehandedly advances against a machine gun emplacement, killing two gunners; then he advances further against two 20-mm guns which are drilling his Company. Weicht drives off the enemy, while killing two troops, then he leads his Squad toward a roadblock; he moves to a nearby building and begins firing, killing several of the defenders and wounding several others; however, he becomes a conspicuous target and is killed by a direct hit by an Anti-tank gun; Weicht receives the Medal of Honor posthumously. **(Eastern Europe)** Soviet troops take Miskolc, northeast of Budapest, Hungary, a war supply center and strategic German defense line. **(Atlantic-Italy)** In the **British Eighth Army** area, the offensive against Bologna commences at 23:00 when the Polish 2nd Corps attacks the foothills to the left of the 5th Corps; the 5th Corps advances down Highway 9, toward the Santerno River. The Canadian 1st Corps continues its drive in the Adriatic sector, its 1st Division seizing Russi, while the Canadian 5th Armored Division takes Godo during the night of the 3rd-4th as the Canadians close on the Ravenna and Santerno.

December 3rd 1944-July 1945 — (Atlantic-Greece) The friction between the Monarchs and Communists ignites civil strife; Police open fire on civilian demonstrators, upon instigation by Communists; civil war erupts in Athens and Piraeus and the British are compelled to quell the fighting and eliminate the Communist threat. In conjunction, the British have been attempting to bring the U.S. into the dispute, but Admiral King has remained steadfast on committing U.S. Vessels. The media enters the arena and begins proclaiming that the British are: "USING LEND-LEASE WEAPONS THAT ARE KILLING GREEK PATRIOTS (Communists); this is in conjunction with protests that are springing up across the United States. Admiral King had informed Admiral Hewitt that: "U.S. LSTs ARE NOT TO BE USED FOR FERRYING TROOPS AND MILITARY EQUIPMENT TO GREECE." The British had protested to no avail; Churchill calls Harry Hopkins and soon after, Hopkins speaks with Admiral Leahy; Admiral King, subsequent to speaking with Leahy, changes his orders and U.S. LSTs are brought into the area, flying the British flag. The British attack the Communist rebels, quickly ending the fighting; the Communists put down their arms and agree to free elections. Churchill arrives at Athens on Christmas Day and within several additional days it is announced that a Regency will be formed (occurs on the 31st). By July of 1945, the Monarchists who control the country have arrested about 20,000 Greeks. There is British concern about the right wing elements; however, their priority remains the Communist threat.

A U.S. B-25 comes into focus as it launches a low level attack against a Japanese Destroyer.

December 4th 1944 — (Pacific-Philippines) LEYTE: The U.S. Seventh Air Force raises the stakes, initiating night raids against the Luzon Airfields. General Krueger, Commanding

General Sixth Army, orders an attack to secure the Ormoc area, commencing on the following day; the X Corps is to drive south along Highway 2, to support the XXIV Corps, which will strike from the sea with its 77th Division and by land with its 7th Division. In the **X Corps** sector, the 1st Battalion, 34th Regiment, 24th Division withdraws from Kilay Ridge, toward Pinamopoan. The 112th Cavalry Group is still unable to dislodge the entrenched enemy from the ridge south of Limon. In conjunction with the assault against Ormoc, Patrols of the 184th Regiment, 7th Division, advance north to Balogo, and the 776th Amphibious Tank Battalion advances under cover of darkness to waters about a mile west of it. In Naval activity, the Destroyer *Drayton* (DD-366) is damaged near Leyte by a Horizontal Bomber. **(Pacific-South China Sea)** The Submarine U.S.S. *Flasher* (SS-249) sinks the Japanese Destroyers *Iwanami* and *Kishinami*. **(Pacific-China)** Chiang Kai-shek appoints T.V. Soong premier as well as foreign minister in an attempt to make the government more progressive and efficient; Soong is Kai-shek's brother-in-law. In other activity, General Wedemeyer requests that B-29s, which are a strain on hump tonnage, be moved from China. **(Atlantic-Western Europe) 12th Army Group** In the U.S. **Ninth Army** area, the **XII Corps** halts its offensive until the 18th, having secured its sector west of the Roer, with the exception of Muellendorf and Wurm. In the **U.S. First Army** area, **VII Corps** sector, the 104th Division bolsters its bridgehead at the Inde river by crossing additional support weaponry. In the **V Corps** sector, the Germans are repulsed at Bergstein by the 8th Division which stops the Armor, despite lack of reinforcements; Infantry contingents continue securing the flanks of the Brandenberg-Bergstein Ridge. In the **U.S. Third Army** area, **XX Corps** sector, the 95th Division takes advantage of the seizure of the Saarlautern bridge, dispatching its 3rd Battalion 379th Infantry toward Fraulautern, reaching its suburbs and igniting a fierce struggle for control of the town, situated within the West Wall; the Germans mount strong Tank supported counterattacks which are repulsed by the 1st and 3rd Battalions; the 378th Regiment overruns Lisdorf, south of Saarlautern on the Sare River. On the southern flank of the Corps, the 10th Infantry, 5th Division withstands a severe counterattack; the 3rd Battalion, 11th Regiment deploys to the right and attacks to secure the area between the Roselle and the Sarre Rivers. The XII Corps begins its final attack to reach the Sarre and the West Wall; artillery precedes a successful drive by the 318th Regiment, 80th Division which takes Farebersviller; the 318th also seizes the hills to the northeast of the town. The 35th Division attacks before dawn; it drives across the Maderbach, taking the startled enemy by complete surprise, gaining Puttelange with its 134th Infantry, but the Germans halt the advancing 320th Regiment with concentrated fire as it drives on the right. In conjunction, the 6th Armored Division presses toward Mont de Cadenbronn while elements of the 104th Regiment, 26th Division reduce the remaining resistance at Sarre-Union. Upon knowledge of the German withdrawal, the 4th Armored Division begins the chase; C.C.B. units race across Eichel Creek near Voellerdingen. German fire hampers C.C.A., 4th Armored at Domfessel. **6th Army Group** In the U.S. **Seventh Army** area, **VI Corps** sector, Selestat is totally secure, permitting the 36th to remain there; the 103rd is released for other duty. **(Atlantic-Eastern Europe)** Soviet and Yugoslav troops secure the area between the Danube and Sava Rivers in Yugoslavia and take Mitrovica. In Hungary, the Germans continue to fight hard in the area around Budapest. **(Atlantic-Italy)** In the U.S. **Fifth Army** area, British 13th Corps sector, the British 6th Armored Division captures the bulk of M. Penzola during a successful night attack. In the **British Eighth Army** area, Montecchio falls to the Polish 2nd Corps. In the 5th Corps sector, the British 46th Division drives toward Pideura Ridge, against mean resistance. Also, the Canadian 1st Corps seizes Ravenna, then bolts to the Lamone River where it severs Highway 16. After dark, the British 1st Division attacks across the Lamone.

December 5th 1944 — (Pacific-Marianas) A U.S. Naval Base is established at Tinian. **(Pacific-Philippines)** LEYTE: The **U.S. Sixth Army** commences its offensive against Ormoc. In the **X Corps** sector, elements of the 32nd Division are struck by a counterattack as they prepare to drive down Highway 2. P.F.C. William A. McWhorter, Company M, 126th Regiment, holding his machine gun position with one other man, continues to dole out rapid fire to stop the advance until a hand grenade is tossed into the foxhole; McWhorter intentionally takes the full brunt of the blast, killing himself to save his comrade; the assault is turned back; McWhorter receives the Medal of Honor posthumously. The 776th Tank Battalion lands beyond Balogo near Tabgas and initiates a strong concentration of fire to support the 7th Division, which is attacking with its 17th Regiment on the right and the 184th on the left, the latter seizing a line extending 300 yards from the beach, about 300 yards south of Balago to the heights southeast of the Palanas River on the right. The 776th Tank Battalion advances by sea to reconnoiter the Calingatngan area. The 3rd Battalion, 184th Regiment, fords the Palanas and climbs the heights of the first ridge on Hill 380; Company K, 32nd Infantry, 7th Division, fills the gap existing between the 17th and 184th Regiments; the 17th seizes a ridge west of Hill 918. In other activity, the 77th Division at Tarragona beach prepares for an amphibious landing below Ormoc. The recently arrived Marine Air units (3rd), covering the Naval forces, encounter Japanese Planes for the first time. In Naval activity, the Submarine *Hake* (SS-256) lands supplies on Panay. In other Naval activity, the U.S.S. *Drayton* (DD-366), which had been struck by a Bomber on the previous day, is damaged by a Kamikaze. The Destroyer *Mugford* (DD-389) is also damaged by a Suicide Plane. **(Pacific-SEAC)** The U.S. Tenth Air Force initiates the Airlift of the Chinese 14th Division from Burma to China; the Chinese 22nd Division is instructed to ready for transfer to China. **(Pacific-Burma)** In the N.C.A.C. area, a Japanese Task Force, composed of about 3,000 men, rushes toward Bhamo to support the besieged Garrison as it withdraws; it departs Namhkam, moving north during the night. The Chinese 30th Division advances south toward Namhkam, encountering enemy fire originating in the hills. **(Atlantic-Western Europe) 12th Army Group** In the **U.S. First Army** area, **VII Corps** sector, the Germans are repulsed at Lucherberg by the 104th Division. In the **V Corps** sector, Task Force Boyer of C.C.R., 5th Armored resumes its attack against Bergstein, successfully spinning three columns into the village; Germans, holding Castle Hill to the east, threaten the newly won prize. In the **U.S. Third Army** area, **XX Corps** sector, the 1st and 3rd Battalions, 379th Infantry, 95th Division strengthen their attack toward Fraulautern and Saarlautern; however, progress is held to a minimum. The Germans mount a determined counterattack, but the 2nd Battalion, which passes through the lines of the 1st Battalion, repels the assault at the fringes of Saarlautern-Roden. Meanwhile, the 3rd Battalion drives into the southern portion of Fraulautern, and two Battalions of the 378th Regiment drive across the Saare at Lisdorf and advance to the steps of En-

sdorf. The 5th Division takes Lauterbach without incident. In the **XII Corps** sector, Patrols from the 35th Division reach the Sarre. The 2nd Battalion, 134th Regiment reaches the suburbs of Sarreguemines. The 2nd Cavalry Group, operating along the Roselle River on the left flank of the Corps, dispatches Patrols into the German frontier in the vicinity of St. Nicolas. C.C.A., 6th Armored, gets elements to the Sarre north of Sarreguemines. Meanwhile, C.C.A., 4th Armored, fords the creek at Domfessel and drives north toward the communication center at Rohrbach; heavy resistance inflicts severe casualties upon it, halting progress in front of Bining; C.C.B. pushes to Schmittviller. The 26th Infantry Division is moving behind the 4th Armored. **6th Army Group** The U.S. Seventh Army commences a major attack, driving north toward the Maginot Line and against the West Wall. In the **XV Corps** sector, Ratzwiller falls to the 44th Division; Wimmenau and Wingen are being seized by the 100th Division. The VI Corps, consisting of four Infantry Divisions and one Armored Division, attacks with its 45th and 79th Divisions, the former encountering stiff resistance at Mertzwiller. In the **French 1st Army** area, the French receive full responsibility for the reduction of the German bridgehead west of the Rhine in the Colmar area; the U.S. 36th Division and the French 2nd Armored Division bolster the French. **(Atlantic-Eastern Europe)** The Third Ukrainian Front advances quickly, reaching Lake Balaton; elements take Szigetvar. Berlin reports the Soviet crossing of the Danube near Vukovar. **(Atlantic-Italy)** In the **British Eighth Army** area, the Polish 2nd Corps seizes M. Rinaldo and also secures the left flank of the Eighth Army before halting to await the 5th Corps' reduction of resistance on Pideura Ridge where the British 46th Division is experiencing difficulty against entrenched Germans. In the Canadian 1st Corps sector, the Canadian 1st Division withdraws from its bridgehead across the Lamone because of enemy pressure. East of the Lamone River, mopping-up operations last for several days, while bridging is underway.

December 6th 1944 — (United States) President Roosevelt receives a telegraph from Winston Churchill that reflects disappointment because the Allies have not yet reached the Rhine; Roosevelt responds on the 9th, informing Churchill that he has full confidence in the Commanders and that a conference of the Joint Chiefs of Staff is unnecessary. **(Pacific-Philippines)** LEYTE: In the **U.S. Sixth Army** area, **X Corps** sector, consistent attacks to dislodge the Japanese from the hills south of Limon fail. In the **XXIV Corps** sector, the 7th Division continues attacking toward Ormoc, seizing Balogo, Kang Dagit, and Hill 918; contingents reach a ridge on Hill 380, while additional troops advance to the Palanas River. The 77th Division embarks from Deposito, sailing with Destroyer escorts and umbrella coverage by Fifth Air Force Planes toward Ormoc Bay. In other activity, about 150 Japanese troops spring a surprise attack on Buri Airstrip, penetrating woods north of the Airstrip. **(Pacific-Burma)** In the N.C.A.C. area, the U.S. 475th Regiment receives orders to relieve the Chinese 22nd Division, north of Tonk-wa in the Mohlaing area. In other activity, Japanese forces cross the Shweli, moving toward Tonk-wa. **(Atlantic-Western Europe) 12th Army Group** In the **U.S. First Army** area, **V Corps** sector, the Germans drive into Bergstein, but they are thrown back. Permission is granted to use the 2nd Ranger Battalion to reinforce the sparse defending force at Bergstein. In the **U.S. Third Army** area, **XX Corps** sector, the 90th Division's attack across the Sarre commences at 04:15; using assault boats, the drive strikes between Rehlingen and Wallerfangen;

a bridgehead is established near Pachten-Dillingen. German opposition soon halts progress of the 357th Regiment; however, the 358th penetrates to the perimeters of Dillingen and Pachten. The 95th Division continues to encounter fierce opposition as it attacks toward the West Wall. The 5th Division, working to complete securing its sector to the Sarre, accepts the surrender of Germans at St. Quentin Works. In the **XII Corps** sector, the west bank of the Sarre from Grosbliederstroff to Wittring is secured by the 6th Armored and 35th Infantry Divisions. The 35th, supported by Tanks of the 6th Armored, pushes into Sarreguemines, securing the western section, while the 6th Armored, its mission fulfilled, pivots to defend the northern flank of the Corps. The 26th Division sprints toward the Sarre while the 4th Armored grabs a solid clasp on Singling and overpowers the resistance at Bining before receiving orders to halt and await relief by the XV Corps' 12th Armored. After dinner, Generals Doolittle, Spaatz, and Vandenberg meet with Patton, and plans are made for a massive Air attack against the Siegfried Line subsequently, it is bombarded for three successive days, implementing 1,000 Heavy Bombers each day. **6th Army Group** In the **U.S. Seventh Army** area, **XV Corps** sector, Montbronn and Meisenthal fall to the 44th and 100th Divisions respectively; the latter then envelops Mouterhouse. In other activity, the Germans mount a strong counterattack against the 45th Division that regains the northern part of Mertzwiller. In the **French 1st Army** sector, the Germans resist tenaciously at Guemar and at Ostheim the persistence of the U.S. 36th Division gains Guemar. **(Eastern Europe)** The Russians exploit the success north of Budapest and expand the front. In Hungary, Rumanian troops assist the Russians to secure the northeast section, and Yugoslav forces seize the rail and road center of Sid. **(Atlantic-Italy)** In the **U.S. Fifth Army** area, British 13th Corps sector, the 19th Brigade, Indian 8th Division transfers to the west flank of the Corps and operates under the British 1st Division. In Naval activity, the Tug ATR-1 is damaged by a collision.

December 7th 1944 — (Pacific-Philippines) LEYTE: In the **U.S. Sixth Army** area, **X Corps** sector, the Japanese still hold the ridge southeast of Limon, preventing any advances by the 2nd Squadron, 112th Cavalry; the 1st Squadron drives to the Leyte River and makes contact with Troop A and the 126th Infantry 32nd Division. On the following day, the 1st Squadron begins to sever the supply line feeding the ridge. In the **XXIV Corps** sector, Rear Admiral A. D. Struble's Task Group commences a carpet bombardment against enemy positions prior to the 77th Division's unopposed landing at Deposito around 07:00; the Division drives inland; Ipil falls to the 307th, and the 305th bolts to the Bagonbon River. The 7th Division continues grinding toward Ormoc, its 17th Regiment seizes Hill 380, culminating the battle of the ridges, although sporadic fighting continues for a few days until the Division reaches its objective, the Talisayan River. In conjunction, the 184th Regiment advances to the Tabgas River. In other activity, Japanese Planes launch 16 attacks against Allied Shipping in Ormoc Bay. The Destroyer *Mahan* (DD-364) is sunk by a Kamikaze; the High Speed Transport U.S.S. *Ward* (APD-16) is severely damaged by another suicide Plane and is subsequently sunk by U.S. Forces. In addition, the Destroyer *Lamson* (DD-367) and the Transport *Liddle* (APD-60) are both damaged by Kamikaze Planes. The Japanese Transport No. 11 is sunk by Army Aircraft. Marine Aircraft attack a Japanese Convoy transporting reinforcements to Ormoc. Planes from Marine Fighter Squadron 211 damage a Japanese Destroyer

which is retiring from Leyte. Also, Planes attached to Marine Fighter Squadrons 218 and 313 combine with Army P40s, sinking a Transport and damaging two Destroyers of the Convoy. The entire Convoy, comprising six Transports and seven Escort Vessels, is thought to be destroyed. **(Pacific-Manchuria)** Nearly 100 U.S. Bombers strike an Aircraft factory and a nearby arsenal at Mukden; weather conditions are terrible, and several stray bombs strike the P.O.W. Camp; the P.O.W.s are lying on the parade ground, having been forbidden from digging foxholes; over fifty men are killed or wounded. **(Atlantic-Western Europe)** A conference is held at Maastricht by Eisenhower: Generals Bradley, Bedell Smith, British Field Marshal Montgomery, and General Tedder attend. Subsequent to the meeting, Montgomery, who is unhappy because he does not get control of all land troops, tells General Brooke: "I CAN DO NO MORE MYSELF...IF WE WANT THE WAR TO END WITHIN ANY REASONABLE PERIOD, YOU HAVE TO GET EISENHOWER'S HAND OFF THE LAND BATTLE. I REGRET TO SAY THAT IN MY OPINION HE JUST DOESN'T KNOW WHAT HE IS DOING." **21 Army Group** The British, under Montgomery, are still preparing for an offensive to be launched in January 1945. **12th Army Group** In the **U.S. Ninth Army** area, **XIX Corps** sector, the German strongpoints at Juelich continue to resist relentlessly, inflicting severe casualties upon the 116th Infantry, 29th Division, compelling its Commander to report the Regiment unfit to continue the attack; the 116th is relieved by the 115th Regiment which takes over the mission; the Regiment enlists assault guns and smoke cover, seizing the objectives on the 8th. In the **U.S. First Army** area, **V Corps** sector, the 2nd Ranger Battalion drives to the summit of Castle Hill while under severe enemy fire, then repulses two counterattacks; a Platoon races to assist and the enemy withdraws. C.C.R., 5th Armored Division pulls back from Bergenstein. In conjunction, the 8th Division's 28th Regiment, driving from the south, approaches the village. In the **U.S. Third Army** area, **XX Corps** sector, the Germans continue banging against the 90th Division's bridgehead in the Pachten-Dillingen area; the 357th Regiment, holding the northern flank, thwarts a heavy counterattack, but the West Wall remains an obstacle between it and the 358th Regiment. Intense enemy fire pevents construction of a Vehicle bridge; improvisation occurs, and a footbridge is modified to handle rolling traffic. The 95th Division is heavily engaged at the West Wall in its Saarlautern bridgehead; its 378th Regiment stalls near Ensdorf; its 2nd Battalion is not yet across the Sarre; at Saarlautern-Roden, the 379th drives doggedly, earning its modest progress, and the 377th Regiment takes over the battle for Fraulautern. In the 5th Division sector, Fort Plappeville capitulates to the 2nd Infantry. In the **XII Corps** sector, regrouping occurs for an assault against the West Wall between Saarbruecken and Zweibruecken by the 26th and 35th Divisions, the latter presently engaged at Sarreguemines; the former advances close to the Forts at Achen and at Wittring along the Maginot Line. The 6th Armored Division and the 2nd Cavalry Group relieves the 80th Division which then pulls back to the rear. The 4th Armored Division, pausing at Bining, is relieved by the 12th Armored Division, XV Corps. **6th Army Group** In the **U.S. Seventh Army** area, **XV Corps** sector, the Germans mount spirited opposition at Enchenberg against the 44th Division. The 100th Division drives convincingly, seizing Mouterhouse. In the **VI Corps** sector, Gambsheim is besieged by the 94th Cavalry Squadron and contingents of the 19th Armored Infantry Battalion (attached to the 79th Division). The 103rd Division is committed between the 45th and 79th

Divisions. In the **French 1st Army** area, activity is bristling; the 2nd Corps, which includes the U.S. 36th Division, holds steadfast against counterattacks at Guemar, Mittelwihr, and Ostheim. Meanwhile, the 1st Corps launches attacks against Cernay and Thann, its 2nd Moroccan Division seizes Bischwiller and establishes a solid bridgehead at Pont d'Aspach. **(Eastern Europe)** Adony, south of Budapest, and Enying, about twenty miles outside of Sekesfehervar, are taken by contingents of the Third Ukrainian Front; additional elements, operating in the center of the thrust, proclaim the south bank of Lake Balaton clear; Barcs is seized by troops securing the area between Lake Balaton and the Drava River. An announcement from Moscow states that the Germans are transferring reinforcements from the Western Front and Italy to fortify the defense of Budapest. Yugoslavia reports several crossings of the Danube near Vukovar in Slovenia by Yugoslav and Soviet contingents. Berlin states that the German withdrawal from western Montenegro and western Serbia "progressed according to plan." **(Atlantic-Italy)** In the **British Eighth Army** area, 5th Corps sector, Piedura capitulates to the British 46th Division; however, the nearby ridges are retained by the Germans.

December 8th 1944 — **(Pacific-Philippines)** LEYTE: in the **U.S. Sixth Army** area, **XXIV Corps** sector, strong columns, consisting of the 307th Regiment, 77th Division, reinforced by the 2nd Battalion, 306th Regiment Company A, 776th Tank Battalion, and Co. A, 88th Chemical Weapons Battalion, drive north from Ipil, alongside Highway 2, advancing to less than one mile from Ormoc; artillery fire supports the drive. The 350th Infantry covers the Division's south flank. In conjunction, one Platoon, of Company A, 776th Tank Battalion, transported by sea, encounters enemy resistance as it reconnoiters the Camp Downes area. In the 11th Airborne sector, elements of the 511th Parachute Infantry unsuccessfully attack enemy positions to eliminate deadly mortars and automatic weapons which are hindering their progress. Private Elmer E. Fryar attempts to hold off an entire enemy Platoon and successfully drives it off inflicting at least 27 dead. The action saves his Company from being outflanked; subsequently, as he attempts to assist some wounded men, an enemy sniper attempts to kill the Platoon leader. Fryar jumps and takes the full impact of the burst, saving his Platoon leader's life; as he falls mortally wounded, he throws a grenade and kills the sniper. His actions allow the safe withdrawal of his Battalion and the capturing of the objective; Pvt. Fryar receives the Medal of Honor posthumously. At Buri Airfield, before dawn, heavy machine gun and mortar fire keeps elements of the 382nd Infantry, 96th Division pinned down. Mortar fire is laid upon the enemy positions, but it doesn't take them out completely. Private Ova A. Kelley, Company A attacks singlehandedly and dislodges the enemy with grenades. He follows this action by grabbing an M1 rifle and firing it at the retreating Japs, killing three; his ammunition expended, he takes a carbine and knocks out three more. Additional men follow him, and the Japanese force of two Officers and 34 enlisted men are quickly annihilated. As the attack lunges forward to an Airstrip, enemy fire mortally wounds Kelley; he receives the Medal of Honor posthumously. As the day progresses, the U.S. consolidates its positions. **(Pacific-Volcano Islands)** A U.S. Task Group comprising Cruisers and Destroyers, commanded by Rear Admiral A. E. Smith, bombards shore batteries and Air facili-

ties on Iwo Jima; B-24s and B-29s join the assault. **(Pacific-Burma)** In the N.C.A.C. area, Tonkwa, garrisoned by the Chinese, is overpowered by a superior Japanese force. In the **British Fourteenth Army** area, 4th Corps Headquarters transfers from Imphal to Tamu and comes under the command of Lt. General Frank Walter Messervy, successor to Lt. General Sir Geoffrey Scoones. The Corps is to traverse secretly through the Gangaw Valley and seize a bridgehead near Pakokku on the Irrawaddy to provide a springboard to Meiktila and Thazi. **(Atlantic-Western Europe)** In Germany, Hitler has ordered that all American and British Officers (prisoners) be shot; General Berger receives the information from Himmler, but refuses to carry out the order, stating that he would first shoot himself. Himmler is asked to release 5,000 Dutch prisoners (women, children and civilians). He tells Doctor Felix Kersten that the Dutch are almost as bad as the Jews, and that they are "traitors to the Germanic ideals." He releases 1,000 Dutch women and some Danish and Norwegian women and children, plus students and policemen. In addition, Himmler agrees to send 1,700 French, Belgian, and Polish women to Switzerland. Between two and three thousand Jews are also sent to Switzerland because of Himmler's efforts. **12th Army Group** In the U.S. **Ninth Army** area, **XIX Corps** sector, Hasenfeld Gut and the sportplatz are taken by the 115th Infantry, 29th Division, culminating a grueling siege. In the **U.S. First Army** area, **XX Corps** sector, the Germans mount another determined counterattack against the 357th Regiment's lines at the 90th Division's Dillingen bridgehead; ferocious hand-to-hand combat tips the scales to the Yanks, and the assault is repulsed. The 357th Regiment is also struck by counterattacks which compel the Regiment to retain a defensive posture, but some contingents push across the railroad tracks, capturing Dillingen Station. Later, during the night, the 359th (held in reserve) moves into the bridgehead. The 95th Division is heavily engaged at the Saarlautern bridgehead in a brutal struggle, encompassing vicious house-to-house fire-fights and the methodical yard-by-yard elimination of pillboxes. Subsequent to the capitulation of Fort Driant, the 2nd Infantry, 5th Division turns its Metz sector over to the III Corps' 87th Division, which takes responsibility for reducing Fort Jeanne d'Arc. In the **XII Corps** sector, the 35th Division drives across the Sarre, its 320th Regiment using assault boats, while the 134th sprints across a bridge south of Sarreguemines. The 3rd Battalion, 320th Regiment is not able to cross, but it establishes a bridgehead before the enemy counterattacks; Artillery and Fighter Bombers support the beleaguered Battalion, and the enemy is thrown back. Also, the 134th storms Sarreinsming, seizing it, then drives northeast under heavy fire from the guns at Sarreguemines. Subsequent to an Artillery and Air bombardment, the 26th Division lunges toward the Maginot Line in its sector. The 104th Regiment, operating on the right, seizes four forts near Achen with little effort; the 328th Regiment assaults Forts Wittring and Grand Bois in battles that last throughout the night, seizing the former before dawn. Shortly after, it discovers Fort Grand Bois evacuated. In other activity, General Patton reports that since Third Army began its attack to capture Metz and the Saar on November 8th 1944, it had liberated 873 towns and about 1,600 square miles of French ground; he also reports capturing 30,000 prisoners, while killing or capturing about 88,000 additional Germans. It had also relieved the German Army of 137 Tanks and 400 Guns while sustaining 23,000 men killed, wounded or missing; an additional 18,000 non-battle casualties are sustained by Third Army during the time period. **6th Army Group** In the **U.S.**

Seventh Army area, **XV Corps** sector, the 44th and 100th Divisions drive into Encherberg and Lemberg respectively, each encountering strong opposition. In the **VI Corps** sector, a diversionary operation is initiated to convince the Germans that a major attack is going to drive across the Rhine near Bischwiller or Strasbourg. The 45th Division assaults Niederbronn. In the 79th Division area, Gambsheim is secured by the 94th Cavalry Reconnaissance Squadron. In the **French 1st Army** area, the Germans continue to counterattack. Contingents of the U.S. 36th Division drive toward Kayserberg. Also, the 1st Corps penetrates Thann. **(Atlantic-Eastern Europe)** Berlin confirms that the Soviets have "widened their breach," north of Budapest. Contingents of the Third Ukrainian Front are less than ten miles from Szekesfehervar. German resistance between Lake Balaton and the Danube is fierce; Soviet attempts to break through are repelled. **(Atlantic-Italy)** In the **U.S. Fifth Army** area, British 13th Corps sector, the enemy abandons M. Penzola. In the **British Eighth Army** area, 5th Corps sector, the Indian 10th Division relieves the British 46th Division.

December 8th 1944-February 19th 1945 — (Pacific-Volcano-Bonin Islands) B-24s stationed in the Marianas attack the islands, softening the defenses for the upcoming invasion. PBJs from Marine Bomber Squadron 612th participate in these Seventh Air Force attacks from early December until the end of January.

December 9th 1944 — (Pacific-Philippines) LEYTE: The final Japanese reinforcements arrive on Leyte, debarking at Palompon. In the **U.S. Sixth Army** area, **XXIV Corps** sector, the final contingents of the 306th Regiment, 77th Division arrive on a Convoy which is also transporting supplies; the 307th Regiment seizes Camp Downes while the 306th's 3rd Battalion deploys to protect the east and center of the beachhead; the 305th Regiment secures the area northeast of the camp. At Buri Airfield, the 1st Battalion, 149th Infantry, pushes north across the Airstrip, but intense enemy fire turns it back. In conjunction, the 1st Battalion, 382nd Regiment reconnoiters to discover the enemy positions, and subsequently, a night counterattack against its perimeter is repulsed. In Naval activity, the Attack Transport *Cavalier* (APA-37) is damaged by a Submarine torpedo. **(Pacific-Burma)** In the N.C.A.C. area, Japanese troops, which had departed Tonk-wa, reach Mo-hlaing, threatening the Chinese 22nd Command Post; however, the 475th Regiment arrives to counterattack with the Chinese and regain the positions. The 114th Regiment, Chinese 38th Division, having absorbed the U.S. suggestion to exploit full use of available Artillery and support Aircraft, is driving ahead in the northern defenses south of Bhamo; the 113th Regiment is repulsed outside of Bhamo, and contingents of the 90th Regiment, Chinese 30th Division become cut off during a Japanese counterattack. **(Pacific-China)** General Wedemeyer protests strongly to Chiang Kai-shek, after two Chinese Armies, the 5th and 6th, fail to concentrate on the defense of Kunming, thus jeopardizing the success of· Alpha plan. The Generalissimo responds that he is keeping the 5th Army back to defend Kunming. **(Atlantic-Western Europe)** 12th Army Group In the **U.S. Ninth Army** area, the 30th Division receives orders to secure the area between the Inde and Roer Rivers within its sector. In the **U.S. Third Army** area, **XX Corps** sector, heavy fighting continues at the Dillingen bridgehead. The 90th Divisions' 357th Regiment repels repetitious counterattacks that cost both sides high casualties. The 358th is engaged at the railroad tracks in Dillingen; the 359th Regiment sweeps through the area between the 357th and 358th Regiments. The logistics problems continue, and the 357th and 359th Regiments must rely on assault boats, Planes, and carrying parties for their equipment and reinforcements. The 95th Division experiences similar supply problems, and the situation is compounded by the rise of the Sarre River, frustrating efforts to enlarge the Saarlautern bridgehead. In the **XII Corps** sector, despite severe enemy fire, the 35th Division completes building two Class 40 bridges across the Sarre by midnight. **6th Army Group** Singling falls to C.C.A., 12th Armored Division. In addition, Enchenberg and Lemberg are seized by the 44th and 100th Divisions respectively. In the **VI Corps** sector, Niederbronn is secured by the 45th Division. Bischwiller is stormed and seized by the 79th Division, which then drives to the fringes of Haguenau. In the **French 1st Army** sector, Mittelwihr is cleared by the 2nd Corps. The 1st Corps' Mountain Division encounters strong resistance at Lautterbach. **(Atlantic-Eastern Europe)** Contingents of the Second Ukrainian Front reach the bend of the Danube at Vac. Additional elements cross the Danube south of Budapest, further jeopardizing the German-held city. Sofia proclaims that the Germans have been driven out of Serbia and from Macedonia in the past few days. **(Atlantic-Italy)** In the **U.S. Fifth Army** area, British 13th Corps sector, the 78th British Division moves to M. dell'Acqua Saluta-M. del Verro, while the British 6th Armored Division prepares to renew the offensive. In the **British Eighth Army** area, the 5th Corps becomes exhausted after mounting consistent counterattacks and must postpone its offensive, unable to take advantage of its success.

U.S. Infantry blazing a path in the Philippines.

December 10th 1944 — (Pacific-Marianas) The Marine 8th 155mm Gun Battalion arrives at Saipan from Peleliu. **(Pacific-Philippines)** LEYTE: in the **U.S. Sixth Army** area, **XXIV Corps** sector, Ormoc is seized. Company A, 776th Amphibious Tank Battalion moves into the town at 09:00 and begins pounding the buildings prior to an attack by the 77th Division. Supported by Artillery and Naval Surface Vessel fire, the 77th takes the objective with its 306th and 307th Regiments. The 7th Division continues its drive to enjoin the 77th at Ormoc. A heavy skirmish erupts near Burauen when Japanese troops, who had come over the mountains from Ormoc Bay, attack the 11th Airborne positions, but are thrown back. At 19:30, the Japanese commence their final major assault against Burauen Airfields, pushing the Fifth Air Force troops back; a determined counterattack quickly restores the lost ground and drives the Japanese away. In Naval activity off Leyte, Kamikazes damage the PT-323; it is subsequently beached and abandoned. In addition, the Destroyer *Hughes* (DD-410) is also damaged by a Kamikaze. **(Pacific-Burma)** In the N.C.A.C. area, elements of the British 36th Division enter Indaw and Katha, ending its part of Phase 1 CAPITAL. The Division subsequently drives toward Kyaukme. The Japanese penetrate the perimeter of the Chinese 38th Division south of Bhamo; however, a tenacious counterattack drives the enemy back, preventing them from reaching the beleaguered Garrison at Bhamo and compelling them to revert to defensive tactics. In other activity, the U.S. 475th Infantry, minus the 1st Battalion, initiates a holding action at Mo-hlaing-Tonk-wa region, while the Chinese 22nd Division is transported by Air to China. **(Pacific-China)** The Chinese offensive is at a halt since the seizure of Che-fang on the 1st. Chiang Kai-shek is urged by General Wedemeyer to order the Y-Force to seize Wanting (Salween Front) at the northeast exit of the Shweli Valley at the proposed junction of the Ledo and Old Burma Roads. The Japanese French-Indo-Chinese Garrison Army is joined by Japanese from south China; this link-up, in addition to the drive into Kweichow which culminated on the 3rd, marks the high water mark of the Japanese invasion of Asia. **(Atlantic-Western Europe)** In Germany, Himmler, during a previous discussion with his physician, mentioned that England should still join Germany against the Russians and that he is perplexed that England's ruling class doesn't realize that a Russian victory will seal the fate of England. Today, he states that it is "UNHAPPILY EVIDENT THAT THIS BATTLE BETWEEN BROTHERS HAD TO BE FOUGHT BETWEEN BROTHERS TO THE BITTER END. THE JEWS IN ENGLAND HAD TRIUMPHED." Himmler believes, as does Hitler, that Germany is simply the vanguard against Bolshevism, and he is perplexed that England and America cannot understand this viewpoint. **12th Army Group** In the **U.S. First Army** area, **VII Corps** sector, the 9th, 83rd, and 104th Infantry Divisions and the 3rd Armored Division, attack simultaneously to secure the city of Dueren and the west bank of the Roer. Contingents of the 414th Regiment, 104th Division pierce the enemy defenses of Pier, but strong resistance pushes them out. Units of the 3rd Armored in conjunction with the 60th Infantry, 9th Division, gain positions in Echtz and also capture Obergeich, from where contingents of the 39th Regiment drive toward Merode and Schlicht. In conjunction, the 83rd Division overruns Gey and Strass, committing its 330th and 331st Regiments; its 329th Infantry sweeps the left flank. In the **U.S. Third Army** area, **XX Corps** sector, the 90th Division mounts resolute opposition along its entire line, repulsing a full scale counterattack that preserves the Dillingen bridgehead, but it is unable to advance. In the 95th Division sector, strong counterattacks prevent any forward movement by the 378th and 379th Regiments, but the 377th drives deeper into Fraulautern. In the **XII Corps** sector, the 137th Regiment, 35th Division, sprints across the Sarre, charging into the eastern section of Sarreguemines where heavy skirmishing develops into brutal house-to-house fighting. In addition, the 134th and 320th Regiments close on the Blies River, and the 104th Regiment, 26th Division seizes Gros Rederching. **6th Army Group** In the **U.S. Seventh Army** area, Task Force Harris and Task Force Linden, formed by the newly arrived 63rd and 47th Regiments respectively, are attached to 6th Army. In the **XV Corps** sector, Rohrbach-les-Bitche is overrun by Combat Command A, 12th Armored, while the 44th Division takes the crossroads outside of Petit Rederching. In the **VI Corps** sector, Gundershoffen and Reichshoffen fall to the 45th Division, and the 79th Division takes Kaltenhouse and Marienthal; however, the Germans repulse the 79th Division at Haguenau. In the 103rd Division sector, the northern portion of Mertzwiller is cleared. In the **French 1st Army** area, Thann is secured by the 2nd Moroccan Division, and the final enemy bridgeheads west of the Rhine, between Kembs and the Swiss border, are seized by the 9th Colonial Division. **(Atlantic-Italy)** In the **British Eighth Army** area, the Canadian 1st Corps commences a late afternoon assault across the Lamone River. By the following day, the British 1st Division and 5th Armored Division establish bridgeheads and drive to the Fosso Vecchio Canal. **(Eastern Europe)** The Second Ukrainian Front closes on Pest, a section of Budapest, east of the Danube; German resistance near Miskolc and southwest of Budapest repels Soviet attempts to advance. In northern Yugoslavia, the Yugoslavs and Soviets enter Vukovar, according to Yugoslav reports. **(Atlantic-Russia)** France and the U.S.S.R. sign a treaty of alliance in Moscow.

December 10th-25th 1944 — (Pacific Philippines) Planes attached to Marine Aircraft Group 12 attack enemy positions in support of ground troops fighting on Leyte.

December 11th 1944 — (Pacific-Philippines) LEYTE: Planes of the Fifth Air Force begin striking enemy positions on Mindoro to soften defenses. In the **U.S. Sixth Army** area, **X Corps** sector, an effective Artillery barrage pounds the Mt. Cabungaan area prior to an assault by the 1st Squadron, 12th Cavalry, which succeeds in reducing an enemy stronghold. Another Artillery bombardment precedes an attack by the 2nd Squadron, 7th Cavalry against a ridge southeast of Limon; the attack coming from the flank and the front, halts at the base of the slopes. In the **XXIV Corps** sector, Ormoc comes under Corps control as advance contingents of the 7th Division roll ahead of the 77th Division at Ipil, splitting the enemy forces on Leyte and isolating the troops in Limon. The 77th Division's 306th and 307th Regiments drive from Ormoc, encountering firm resistance. Japanese reinforcements arrive at Ormoc Bay during the night of the 11th-12th, but few succeed in landing and those that do fail to participate in the contest for the Ormoc corridor; twelve F4Us attached to Marine Aircraft Group 12th and P-40s intercept the Convoy near the northeast tip of Panay and then strike it again off Palompon, sinking four of the ten Vessels. In other activity, the Destroyer U.S.S. *Reid* (DD-369) is sunk off Leyte by a Kamikaze. The Submarine U.S.S. *Gar* (SS-256) delivers supplies to friendly forces on Luzon. **(Pacific-Ulithi)** The U.S. Third Fleet's Fast Carrier Groups depart for Luzon to support the Mindoro invasion; his Task Force retires on the 16th, having destroyed 270 Japanese Planes and sunk 33 enemy Ships. Halsey will note: "NOT A SINGLE BOGEY HAD BEEN ABLE TO PENETRATE

CLOSER TO OUR FORMATION THAN 20 MILES." On the 17th, Halsey's Task Force will encounter a deadly storm. **(Pacific-Burma)** In the British Fourteenth Army area, 4th Corps sector, contingents of the 268th Brigade advance to Indaw. **(Pacific-China)** Directives proposed by General Wedemeyer, concerning ALPHA, are finalized; Chiang Kai-shek will approve them. General Ho is to command ALPHA Forces, but General Chennault is to command the Air Forces in the area; Ho's tasks are to complete concentration in Kweiyang region and to defend Kunming and Kweiyang, while simultaneously training reserves. **(Atlantic-Bahama Islands)** The Submarine Chaser SK-1050 sinks after grounding. **(Atlantic-Western Europe) 12th Army Group** In the **U.S. First Army** area, **VII Corps** sector, Merken and Vilvenich are seized by the 415th Regiment, 104th Division; other contingents are unable to wrest Pier and Schophoven from the Germans. Geich is overpowered by the combined thrust of the 60th Regiment, 90th Division and elements of the 3rd Armored Division. The Germans hold Hoven, repulsing C.C.R., 3rd Armored and one Battalion of the 60th Infantry, inflicting heavy casualties on the U.S. troops. In the **U.S. Third Army** area, **XX Corps** sector, the 90th Division compresses its Dillingen bridgehead slightly as the 357th Regiment pulls back to tighten its front and secure the supply line. A strong German counterattack overruns three pillboxes of the 359th Regiment as it is attempting to hook up with the 358th Regiment. The 95th Division ignites a heavy fight to enlarge its Saarlautern bridgehead; the 378th Regiment secures five city blocks in Ensdorf after fierce skirmishing, while the 377th drives into the center of Fraulautern; the 379th Regiment pounds enemy defenses at Saarlautern-Roden without making progress. In the **XII Corps** area, the 35th Division drives toward the Blies River; Sarreguemines has been secured by its 137th Regiment, which remains there to eliminate the few remaining snipers and several blocks of resistance at Frauenberg; the 35th readies for an assault across the Blies on the 12th. The 328th Regiment, 26th Division advances closer toward the German frontier. **6th Army Group** In the **U.S. Seventh Army** area, **XV Corps** sector, Petit Rederching falls to the 44th Division; contingents advance to Siersthal. Meanwhile, Haguenau is seized by the 79th Division. **(Atlantic-Italy)** In the **U.S. Fifth Army** area, British 13th Corps sector, the British 6th Armored Division receives instructions to mount an assault against Tossignano on the night of the 12th. In the **British Eighth Army** area, Canadian 1st Corps sector, the Canadian 1st Infantry and 5th Armored Divisions establish bridgeheads across the Lamone and jump to the Fosso Vecchio Canal; the Tanks are unable to cross into the bridgehead.

A U.S. Armor contingent driving through a French village.

December 12th 1944 — (Pacific-Philippines) On LEYTE: U.S. Sixth Army area, X Corps sector, the 32nd Division's Artillery bombards Japanese positions along Highway 2; the shelling penetrates as far south as Lonoy. In the **XXIV Corps** sector, an enemy Vessel is spotted off Linao about dawn, but is quickly turned back by heavy guns. At Leyte Gulf, Task Groups 77.3 and 78.3 embark for Mindoro, sailing with Task Group 77.12, which has come from Kossol Roads; the Warships enter the Mindanao Sea after emerging from Surigao Strait during the night of the 12th-13th. On Luzon, at the Bilibad P.O.W. Camp, over 1,000 Allies are readied for transfer to Japan; they are shoved into cramped quarters, and many are thumped by Jap Rifle butts as they are shoved down the ladder into the filthy hull where they wait in anchor until the 14th, suffering under temperatures of well over one hundred degrees and a critical lack of water. Some succumb from suffocation; others dive into comas, and yet others become mentally unstable; by time of departures, thirty men are dead. Soon after the *Oryoku* embarks, it is attacked by U.S. Planes which are unaware of the Americans on board; the Vessel is struck twice, inflicting heavy damage. The Vessel debarks its Japanese wounded at Subic Bay, then reembarks on the following day; U.S. Planes reappear and sink it. In other activity, Kamikazes strike again, sinking the Destroyer *Caldwell* (DD-605). Marine Aircraft from Group 12 and P40s sink a Japanese Destroyer escorting a Troop Convoy, and a Tank Landing Ship is set ablaze off Panay in what turns out to be the last major attempt to reinforce the beleaguered Leyte Garrison. U.S. Surface Craft sink the Destroyer *Uzuki*. **(Pacific-Burma)** In the ALFSEA area, the 15th Corps initiates its offensive (ROMULUS) to secure the Arakan coastal region and seize Air and Naval Bases, which are required to ensure success of subsequent operations. A three-pronged assault thrusts the Indian 25th Division through the Mayu Peninsula toward Akyab, while the West African 81st and 82nd Divisions drive through the Kaladan and Kalapanzin Valleys respectively. **(Atlantic-England)** During a meeting in London, Eisenhower proposes his plan of attack to Churchill and the British Chiefs of Staff. British General Brooke dissents, claiming the Allies are unable to mount two attacks across the Rhine. On the following day, Ike informs General Marshall that his primary goal is to reach the Rhine from Bonn northward, and a secondary goal is to prepare Forces to assault Frankfurt. **(Atlantic-Western Europe) 12th Army Group** 12th Army G-2's assessment of German resistance: "IT IS NOW CERTAIN THAT ATTRITION IS STEADILY SAPPING THE STRENGTH OF GERMAN FORCES ON THE WESTERN FRONT AND THAT THE CRUST OF DEFENSES IS THINNER, MORE BRITTLE AND MORE VULNERABLE THAN IT APPEARS ON OUR G-2 MAPS OR TO THE TROOPS IN THE LINE." In the **U.S. First Army** area, **VII Corps** sector, the 104th Division overpowers the Germans at Pier, striking from two directions and driving them out of town and across the Roer. Contingents of the 60th Regiment, 90th Division, pour into Mariaweiler. Meanwhile, Hoven is swept clean; C.C.R., 3rd Armored, in conjunction with the 60th Regiment, eliminates enemy resistance west of the Roer, northwest and west of Dueren by day's end. The 39th Regiment, 9th Division, drives into Derichsweiler. In the **U.S. Third Army** area, General Patton visits the Command Posts of the 4th Armored, the 26th, and the 87th Divisions, and also the 35th Division. In the **XX Corps** sector, the Dillingen bridgehead is firmed up by the 90th Division; its 357th Regiment eradicates previously bypassed resistance in its sector; the 358th and 359th Regiments finally break through the enemy wedge and join forces. Tanks and Tank Destroyers rush forward to support the endeavor by use of an effective smoke screen that permits safe movement across a Vehicle ferry. The 95th Division continues battling heavily to fortify its Saarlautern bridgehead, making some progress; however, it is suffering with the same problems as the 90th Division: sheer exhaustion due to lack of reinforcements. In the **XII Corps** sector, the 35th Division commences an early morning attack; the 134th Regiment gets the 1st Battalion across the Blies into Habkirchen, against strong opposition to secure a fragile hold. A Tank-supported attack by the 320th Regiment secures Bliesbruck prior to crossing the river. The 26th Division pushes forward contingents of its 328th Infantry across the German border, and later, during the night, the 87th Division begins relieving it. **6th Army Group** In the **U.S. Seventh Army** area, **XV Corps** sector, German resistance near Hottviller-Bitche along the Maginot Line is impenetrable, totally halting progress, but C.C.A., 12th Armored advances to its objective, Bettviller. In the **VI Corps** sector, the Germans abandon Soufflenheim, heading for the West Wall as the 79th Division approaches; the 79th then moves to secure Seltz. In the **French 1st Army** area, General de Lattre changes the attack plan to secure Cernay and Colmar, and he postpones the attack against Brisach on the Rhine unless the situation becomes more favorable. The 2nd Corps is ordered to make the primary effort through Colmar to Rouffach, where contact is to be made with the 1st Corps, which is advancing from Cernay; however, the 1st Corps is too weakened to continue and halts its offensive until the fifteenth. **(Atlantic-Italy)** In the **U.S. Fifth Army** area, British 13th Corps sector, the 19th Indian Brigade, defending M. Cerere, is hit by a counterattack and is temporarily driven back. The British 6th Armored Division initiates the second phase of its offensive; the 61st Brigade plows into Tossignano and comes under severe enemy fire. In the **British Eighth Army** area, Canadian 1st Corps sector, the Canadian 1st Infantry and 5th Armored Divisions advance to the Naviglio Canal, mounting a night assault across it. The 1st Division secures a bridgehead north of Bagnacavallo. Also, the Germans drive the 5th Armored back to its departure point at Fosso Vecchio.

December 13th 1944 — (Pacific-Philippines) The U.S. Seventh Fleet's Task Groups travel through the Mindanao Sea toward Mindoro, escorted by Carrier Aircraft. Japanese Aircraft, including Kamikazes, attack the Warships, damaging the Destroyer *Haraden* (DD-585) and Admiral Struble's Flagship, the Light Cruiser *Nashville* (CL-43), forcing both Vessels to turn back. LEYTE: In the **U.S Sixth Army** area, **X Corps** sector, the 32nd Division continues pushing south; its forward contingents penetrate far ahead of the pack and become isolated without food. A Japanese counterattack, during the night 13th-14th, crashes through the 126th Regiment's Command Post, but the Regiment hurls the assault back before sunrise. In other activity, the Japanese on the ridge southeast of Limon repulse another attempt to dislodge them. In the **XXIV Corps** sector, an enemy strongpoint fortified by a blockhouse holds Highway 2 north of Ormoc near the Antilao River and is hampering progress of the 305th Regiment, 77th Division in the region near Cogon; a Task Force comprising Companies E and L, under Colonel Paul L. Freeman, unsuccessfully attack the blockhouse. The 306th Regiment gives cover fire to the 305th, while the 307th Regiment, operating on the left flank, springs to Linao and seizes it. **(Pacific-South China Sea)** The Submarine U.S.S. *Pintado* (SS-387) sinks the Japanese Transports Nos. 12 and 104. **(Pacific-Burma)** In the

N.C.A.C. area, the 114th Regiment, Chinese 38th Division drives through the northern end of Bhamo, fighting forward to the center of town. At Tonk-wa, the 475th Infantry is struck by an enemy counterattack and disperses it easily. **(Atlantic-Western Europe) 21st Army Group** The British Second Army initiates regrouping for an offensive to secure the area between the Maas and Rhine Rivers. **12th Army Group** In the **U.S. Ninth Army** area, **XIX Corps** sector, the 30th Division attacks and eliminates most of the resistance between the Inde and Roer Rivers. In the **U.S. First Army** area, **VII Corps** sector, the 104th Division advances to the Roer River, while the 39th Regiment, 9th Division completes its clearance of Derichsweiler, culminating the Corps' objectives. In the **V Corps** sector, attacks are mounted by the 2nd, 78th, and 99th Divisions, which drive against the Roer and Urft dams, exposing the 78th to its first taste of combat. The 99th drives into the Monschau Forest taking its objectives; the 2nd Division, driving in the center of the Corps, moves slowly, but overcomes heavy enemy fire and obstacles. The fresh 78th Division encounters fierce resistance which stalls its advance near Kesternich. In the **U.S. Third Army** area, **III Corps** sector, the remaining fort in Metz, Jeanne d'Arc, capitulates. In other activity, the 90th Division concentrates its efforts on thoroughly reducing the remaining resistance in Dillingen, securing it on the 15th. The 95th Division improves its Saarlautern bridgehead. In the **XII Corps** sector, the Germans mount an attack against the 1st Battalion, 134th Infantry, 35th Division, at Habkirchen during the morning, pushing it back toward the Blies River; the 3rd Battalion rushes to assist. Meanwhile, one Battalion of the 320th Regiment fords the Blies at Bliesbruck and seizes Hill 321, while another smaller force attached to the 137th Regiment crosses the river north of Habkirchen where it encounters heavy fire and is unable to move. **6th Army Group** In the **U.S. Seventh Army** area, **XV Corps** sector, enemy-held Fort Simershof hinders U.S. progress near Hottviller. The 44th Division initiates a siege to reduce it, but the enemy holds firmly until the 19th when the pressure forces abandonment. Another stumbling block, Fort Schiesseck, comes under siege on the following day by the 100th Division; it resists ferociously until the 20th. In the **VI Corps** sector, C.C.A., 14th Armored Division rolls between the 79th and 103rd Divisions and storms Soultz-sous-Forets, while the 79th reduces final resistance at Seltz and overpowers Niederroedern. **(Eastern Europe)** Advance contingents of the Second Ukrainian Front advance to about eight miles east and six miles northeast of Budapest. **(Atlantic-Italy)** In the **U.S. Fifth Army** area, British 13th Corps sector, additional contingents of the 61st Brigade, British 6th Armored Division drive into Tossignano. Later, during the night, the 36th Brigade, 78th Division attacks Parocchia di M. Maggiore; the Germans repel the assault under the crest, and the Brigade pulls back at dawn. In the **British Eighth Army** area, the Germans mount a vicious but unsuccessful counterattack against the Canadian 1st Division's bridgehead at the Naviglio Canal.

December 14th 1944 — (United States) The Navy establishes the rank of Fleet Admiral. **(Pacific-Philippines)** Planes attached to the Third Fleet are launched against Japanese Airfields in Luzon. Japanese send more Kamikazes against the Fleet. Meanwhile, a U.S. Fleet is spotted near Palawan by the Japanese. A Japanese Airfield on Palawan Island (built by Allied P.O.W.s) is on alert for attack; orders come down to prevent the U.S. from getting the prisoners. The P.O.W.s are returned to Camp; however, upon their return, Japanese begin shooting some prisoners, while others pour gasoline into their shelters and ignite them. Other Japs bayonet the survivors, and although some men escape to the cliffs and jump for the water, the Japs continue firing at them. Eleven Americans out of 150 escape the butchery and subsequently locate Guerrillas who have them flown out by a Navy Plane; the Fleet heads to Mindoro, sparing Palawan for several months. On LEYTE, in the **U. S. Sixth Army's X Corps** sector, the 126th and 127th Regiments continue to gnaw along Highway 2, encountering even more fierce resistance at the main line of defense which controls the route from two menacing ridges. The 12th Cavalry is directed to embark from Mt. Cabungaan, drive toward the highway south of the 32nd Division's positions, and hold it, while attacking north toward the 126th and 127th Regiments. The 2nd Squadron, 7th Cavalry, 1st Cavalry Division eliminates the stubborn ridge southeast of Limon, culminating a brutalizing fifteen-day struggle. In the **XXIV Corps** sector, the 305th Regiment, 77th Division eliminates the opposition in the Cogon region, the blockhouse and road junction seized by Task Force Freeman. Lieutenant Robert P. Nett, Company E, 305th Regiment, is wounded three times during the attack to reduce the blockhouse and kills seven Japanese in hand-to-hand combat. Subsequent to the seizure of the objective, Nett walks back to the rear and receives medical treatment; he becomes the recipient of the Medal of Honor for his extraordinary courage. In Naval activity, Carrier-based Aircraft sink the Japanese Transport No. 109. The Submarine U.S.S. *Blenny* (SS-324) sinks the Coast Defense Vessel No. 28. **(Pacific-Burma)** In the N.C.A.C. area, preparations for abandoning Bhamo are made by the Japanese Garrison. In other activity, at Tonk-wa, the 475th Regiment repulses another Japanese counterattack, then confine their efforts to Patrols, one of which encounters the British 36th Division when it approaches Katha. **(Pacific-China)** General Wedemeyer begins a field inspection trip. **(Atlantic-Western Europe) 12th Army Group** In the **U.S. Ninth Army** area, **XIX Corps** sector, enemy resistance between the Inde and Roer Rivers is terminated by the 30th Division. In the **U.S. First Army** area, **VII Corps** sector, the Germans are eliminated at the factory between Dueren and Mariaweiler. Near Birgel, an enemy Tank, twenty Infantry troops counterattack elements of the 329th Regiment, 83rd Division. Sergeant Ralph G. Neppel holds his machine gun fire until the enemy is about 100 yards distant, then pours fire upon them, killing a few; the cantankerous Tank closes fast and unleashes a vicious round that wounds the entire American crew and blows Neppel out of his position, severing one leg at the knee and inflicting other serious wounds. Undaunted, Neppel crawls on his elbows, reclaims his machine gun, and kills the remaining enemy Infantry; the Tank retreats; Neppel receives the Medal of Honor. In the **U.S. Third Army** area, **XX Corps** sector, German guns destroy the recently fabricated Vehicular ferry in the 90th Division zone. In the **XII Corps** sector, elements of the 35th Division maintain pressure against Habkirchen; later during the night of the 14th, a Bailey Bridge is assembled and strung across the Blies. Also, Rimling is taken by the 87th Division. **6th Army Group** In the **U.S. Seventh Army** area, **XV Corps** sector, contingents of the 100th Division are pinned down by a storm of enemy fire coming from Fort Schiesseck, outside of Bitche. In the **VI Corps** sector, the 45th Division overruns Lembach. In related activity, the 79th Division pushes advance elements to the fringes of Lauterbourg. **(Atlantic-Italy)** In the **U.S. Fifth Army** area, British 13th Corps sector, contingents of the British 6th Armored Division, which are stranded in Tossignano, lose communication with

the main body, which mounts a firm but vain assault to take the town; no further action is mounted against the stronghold. In the **British Eighth Army** area, the Polish 2nd Corps restarts its offensive late in the night and by the following day is fording the Sintria River, driving toward the Senio River. In the **V Corps** sector, another night attack is initiated; the 2nd New Zealand Division, driving on the right, and the Indian 10th Division pushing on the left, charge toward Pergola. In the Canadian 1st Corps sector, the Canadian 5th Armored Division fights across the Naviglio Canal and establishes a bridgehead to the right of the 1st Division.

December 15th 1944 — (United States) Congress creates the rank of General of the Army, a rank equivalent to that of Marshal in Armies other than the U.S.: Henry (Hap) Arnold, Dwight D. Eisenhower, Douglas MacArthur, and George C. Marshall receive the rank. **(Pacific-Philippines)** THE INVASION OF MINDORO — U.S. Naval Warships, under Rear Admiral A. D. Struble, and Planes attached to a Carrier Task Force under Vice Admiral McCain support the invasion. Surface Vessels and Aircraft strike a preliminary blow, followed by a three-pronged assault commencing at 07:30, which lands the 19th Regiment, 24th Division between San Agustin and Caminawit Point; elements of the 503rd Paratroop Infantry land at the former, and Company C, 503rd hits the beach at the mouth of the river across from San Agustin; the 3rd Battalion, 503rd pushes inland expeditiously, seizing the Airstrip, a sugar plant, and the village of San Jose without incident. Meanwhile, the 19th Regiment moves inward, reaching the final beachhead line, encountering some enemy opposition at Caminawit Point. An Airdrome is put under construction about two miles northwest of White Beach. No casualties are incurred by the Western Visayan Task Force; its Commander, General William C. Dunckel, is given command of the land operation by Admiral Struble. The Navy unloads supplies quickly and departs ahead of schedule as enemy Kamikazes arrive and damage two LSTs, the 472nd and 738th, causing them to be sunk by U.S. Forces. In addition, the Escort Carrier *Marcus Island* (CVE-77), the Destroyers *Paul Hamilton* (DD-590) and *Howorth* (DD-592), and the PT-223 are damaged by suicide Planes. The Submarine U.S.S. *Hawkbill* (SS-366) sinks the Japanese Destroyer *Momo*, and Carrier Aircraft sink the Coastal Defense Vessel No. 54 and the Transport No. 106. U.S. Planes also sink the *Oryoku* which had been recently damaged while transporting over 1,600 P.O.W.s; about 1,300 men make it to the beach but are recaptured. In conjunction, two men escape and are subsequently embarked; one on a U.S. Submarine and the other by Destroyer. **Leyte:** In the **U.S. Sixth Army** area, **X Corps** sector, elements of the 1st Squadron, 12th Cavalry, move toward a banana plantation east of Lonoy to await an Airdrop of the balance of the Regiment, which is scheduled to arrive by the 17th. In the 32nd Division zone, Sergeant Leroy Johnson, Company K, leads a reconnaissance Patrol which encounters an enemy machine gun nest. An attempt is made to knockout the gun; however, enemy grenades are snapped into the American positions; Sergeant Johnson flings himself on the two loose grenades to save the other three men; Johnson receives the Medal of Honor posthumously. In another incident, Jap Tanks strike a roadblock manned by elements of the 126th Regiment; P.F.C. Dirk J. Vlug bolts from his cover, taking his rocket launcher and ammunition; he fires one round and knocks out the first Tank and its crew. Enemy troops begin to dismount the second Tank, then Vlug kills one with his pistol, prompting the others to return to the Tank which Vlug immediately destroys with a solid shot. Undaunted by the approach of three more Tanks, Vlug advances singlehandedly and destroys two additional Tanks; the remaining one keeps advancing against the intrepid P.F.C., who uses his lone remaining shell to strike the Tank and force it to career down a hill; P.F.C. Vlug receives the Medal of Honor. In the **XXIV Corps** sector, Ormoc's port is wrapped tight, permitting the 77th Division to consolidate and catch their breath. In other activity, Company G, 511th Airborne, which has been isolated from its main body for four days, makes contact with the 32nd Regiment, 7th Division. The 2nd Battalion, 32nd Infantry moves east to reach the main body of the 511th Paratroop Regiment, while the 1st and 3rd Battalions strangle a pocket near Ormoc. **(Pacific-Burma)** In the N.C.A.C. area, the besieged Japanese Garrison at Bhamo escapes through Chinese lines during the early part of the morning, permitting the enemy relief columns deployed south of the village to begin breaking off the contest. The Chinese 38th Division occupies Bhamo; the 112th Regiment, which had been withdrawn earlier from the battle, attacks Namhkam. The U.S. 475th Regiment's elements at Mohlaing embark for Tonk-wa. **(Atlantic-Western Europe) 12th Army Group** In the **U.S. First Army** area, **V Corps** sector, enemy opposition stiffens; the Corps advances, but the pace is slow. Although Kesternich is reduced, the Germans infiltrate and initiate vicious firefights, isolating some contingents. In the **U.S. Third Army** area, **XX Corps** sector, the 90th Division attacks, implementing smoke screens to support the effort to complete the seizure of Dillingen and the nearby Prims River bridge on the Dillingen-Saarlautern Road. The 358th and 359th Regiments penetrate enemy defenses, advancing deep into the town; a pause in the contest occurs, and the attack is postponed. At the Saarlautern bridgehead, the Germans continue to mount fierce opposition, preventing sustaining progress by the 95th Division. At Breiterwald, vicious enemy fire and a determined counterattack push the 137th Regiment from the town, inflicting severe casualties on the Regiment; to the right, Habkirchen falls to the 134th Regiment which is bolstered by Tank support. The combat is equally fierce at Obergailbach, where the 347th Regiment, 87th Division, overcomes the resistance and takes the town. **6th Army Group** In the **U.S. Seventh Army** area, **VI Corps** sector, C.C.A., 14th Armored, overruns Riedseltz, while Salmbach and Schlerthal fall to Combat Command B. Meanwhile, elements of the 79th Division secure Lauterbourg, and another contingent drives to Schiebenhardt on the Lauter River. In the **French 1st Army** sector, the attack to clear the German resistance west of the Rhine in the Colmar region begins; 2nd Corps, spearheading the assault, reaches Orbey and pierces the enemy defenses. **(Atlantic-Eastern Europe)** Soviet troops advance across the Ipely (Ipel) River north of Budapest and establish a bridgehead in Czechoslovakia at Sahy. **(Atlantic-Italy)** The Germans, defending at Faenza in the **British Eighth Army** area, 5th Corps sector, are nearly totally surrounded; however, a surge develops, and the New Zealanders are soon neutralized near Colle. The Indian 10th Division, hit with equal tenacity, is completely stopped outside of Pergola, buying time for the Germans to abandon their positions during the night.

December 16th-26th 1944 — THE BATTLE OF THE ARDENNES (BULGE) — This enormous and surprising enemy counterattack has been engineered by Hitler, based on his opinion that the Americans had no genuine desire to fight the Germans and that a major defeat would thoroughly demor-

alize them. His master plan had been shared with a selective group of confidants at the Wolf's Lair on September 16th; however, Generals Model and Rundstedt are not informed of the impending offensive until the latter part of October, and other Officers learn of the assault on 8th, December with stringent restrictions placed upon them, including being forbidden to fly west of the Rhine for fear of capture. The go-for-broke strategy is shared with key Commanders on the 11th when the Fuhrer meets with them; however, the assault troops remain uninformed until 05:30 today.

Operation WACHT AM RHINE, originally scheduled to commence on November 10th, has been postponed three times due to the brutal fighting against the Allies at Alsace Lorraine, which is seriously draining their strength and because of a critical shortage of fuel. German Infantry Divisions and Panzer units are secretly funneled from the Roer across treacherous icy routes, between the 13th and 14th. A combination of Artillery fire, Aircraft and the wrapping of Vehicle tracks with straw, conceals the depth of the movement, convincing the Americans that the activity is most probably normal relief maneuvers. Hitler had also directed Paratroops to be dropped near Aachen, to secure a key highway, but thanks to some fortuitous luck on the part of the Americans, the drop is delayed until the Seventeenth, and the operation fails. One large contingent lands behind German lines and the others are spread far and wide, with most being captured. Some English speaking infiltrators, donning American uniforms and driving American Vehicles, have penetrated U.S. lines and will cause some disruption; however, their primary mission to seize the Meuse bridges fails, as they are soon discovered. The primary ruse works perfectly, transforming the seemingly tranquil woods near Schnee Eifel into a gargantuan springboard from which to catapult the Fifth and Sixth Panzer Armies' legions of rolling Armor and accompanying Infantry comprising a total of twenty-four Divisions, plus support troops toward Antwerp and Brussels.

The Allies have been advancing steadily, pressing feverishly toward Germany, despite massive supply problems and catastrophic shortages of replacement Infantry troops. At this time, the Americans are greatly disadvantaged with both Tanks and troops and are totally unprepared for the Hun hordes in the Ardennes. The recent campaigns have diminished their ranks by about 20,000 Riflemen and U.S. Tanks, which will face a newer more heavily Armored German Tank, number about half the enemy's. U.S. Intelligence has given no indication of the German buildup, although unintentional signals have been sent. In one instance, a German document is captured, its contents spelling out an urgent request for troops which speak American. Other alarms that go by unnoticed are: aerial discovery of major movement east and west of the Rhine, and information from a civilian who walks into the U.S. 28th Division sector, telling of the woods near Bitburg being consumed with German equipment. The civilian is taken to First Army Headquarters on the 16th. Other incidents occur, but only one is reported to 12th Army Group.

The Americans have announced their dilemma to the enemy by careless use of communications, essentially informing the Germans that no reinforcements are coming, while speaking freely on commercial telephones and in uncoded terminology on their radios. The Germans also take advantage of the bad weather, realizing Allied Air cover will be unavailable. As the enemy offensive is launched, General Ridgway (XVII Corps A/B) is in England and is forced to rush to the scene; also, General Maxwell Taylor, Commanding Officer of the 101st Airborne, has been sent by Ridgway to the U.S. for a conference; Taylor also rushes back to Europe.

Under a light cover of fog and the thunderclap of 2,000 guns, the startling juggernaut commences during the early morning hours of the 16th, bashing into U.S. lines along a wide front which is defended lightly. General Sepp Dietrich's Sixth Panzer Army makes the primary thrust, in conjunction with General Manteuffel's Fifth Panzer Army; they burst from their concealed positions, the former on the north and the latter on the south, rumbling forward with flashing gunbarrels which devastate the flimsy forward positions of the Americans; the Fifth Panzers are to protect against an Allied counterattack. Accompanying Infantry Divisions (Brandenberger's Seventh Army), primed with confidence, plow through the snow in cadence with the Armor toward the Meuse, 60 miles distant; the 6th Panzers press toward the Albert Canal in the Maastricht area, while the 5th Panzers steamroll toward Brussels-Antwerp area.

The U.S. 99th Division (Major General Walter E. Lauer) holds a twenty-mile front (V Corps U.S. First Army) between Hofen and Monschau, through which the 2nd Division is attacking toward the Roer Dams. To the south in the VII Corps zone, the 14th Cavalry Group is screening the Losheim Gap with its Light Tank Force and the newly arrived 106th Division is deployed alongside it in the Snow Eifel. In addition, the battle-weary 28th Division, exhausted by the excruciating Huertgen Forest campaign, is deployed in the center, while the right flank of the VIII Corps is jointly defended by the seasoned 4th Infantry and the inexperienced 9th Armored, the former having sustained 5,000 battle and 2,500 non-battle casualties in the Huertgen struggle.

Advance contingents of the 6th Panzers pound against resolute contingents of the 99th Division, but are hurled back with fury, stunning the enemy, forcing them to commit Tanks early, a delaying movement the enemy had not anticipated. The gallant stand of the 99th surrenders no strategic ground. Intelligence had reported only two horse-drawn Artillery pieces near a U.S. Battalion; upon cessation of an enemy Artillery bombardment lasting more than one hour, a Battalion Officer remarks: "THEY SURE WORKED THOSE HORSES TO DEATH." Meanwhile, the 2nd Division is continuing its assault without knowledge of the ongoing massive enemy offensive. The 2nd takes its objective before being recalled at 07:30 on the following day by General Gerow (Corps Commander) to deploy on Elsenborn Ridge to stem the tide. If Elsenborn Ridge doesn't falter, the Germans will be denied penetration of the VIII Corps perimeter, while simultaneously securing the V Corps front and preserving the 99th Division.

General Robertson, commanding the 2nd Division, takes command of the 99th Division and in resplendent fashion, exhibits enormous skill and leadership over the next few days, deploying elements of the 99th to cover the recall of the two attacking Regiments of the 2nd Division, which subsequently maintain key positions to permit the 3rd Regiment and the less experienced 99th Division to pull back. By the 19th, the 2nd Division is entrenched on Elsenborn Ridge and reinforced by the 1st and 9th Divisions, commanded by Generals Clift Andrus and Louis Craig respectively; their combined strength repels the counteroffensive and holds the northern shoulder, thus compelling General Model on the following day to transfer responsibility for the main thrust to the Fifth Panzer Army to the south.

Abandoned German equipment.

German troops advancing

In the south sector, one Regiment of the 28th Division, an Armored Infantry Battalion of the 9th Armored Division and a Regiment of the 4th Division are struck viciously by the German Seventh Army, which commits the LXXX and LXXXV Corps, each containing two Volks Grenadier Divisions. The Yanks hold strategic strongpoints; however, the overwhelming enemy force crosses the Our River to the north and pits its snarling Tanks against a Regiment of the 28th, which puts up a magnificent fight that forbids advance for two days before it withdraws to the southwest. On the 17th, a Combat Command from 10th Armored, Third Army arrives near Luxembourg and reinforces the beleaguered 4th Division which has barred the enemy south of Orweiler and Dickweiler and isolated several of its own units in the process. By the 18th, the southern shoulder is firmed up and holds, causing the enemy to lose valuable time. In addition, Luxembourg city, sitting twelve miles from German lines and housing the advance outposts of 12th Army Group and U.S. Ninth Air Force, is no longer in imminent peril.

The remaining two Regiments of the 28th Division, deployed slightly south of Schnee Eifel, and the fresh 106th Division which has two Regiments positioned in an alleged tranquil sector of the Schnee Eifel are straddled between the northern and southern shoulders, with the Command Post of the latter being at St. Vith. The full weight of the 5th Panzers presses against the exhausted Regiments of the 28th, which are overextended defending a ten mile front with two Battalions of the 110th Regiment. Two Panzer Corps of the 5th Panzer Army smash against the Regiment attempting to reach Wiltz. The 112th Regiment, under Colonel Gustin Nelson, speeds north to St. Vith, while Colonel Hurley Fuller's 110th Infantry establishes roadblocks to thwart the Panzers. The delaying action is costly; however, the enemy is held up until the night of the 17th. General Gota, Divisional Commander, holding at Wiltz finds his positions untenable by the end of the 18th and is forced to abandon Headquarters and retreat southwest, early on the nineteenth, his beleaguered Division totally disorganized by the powerful display of the Panzers. The battering of the Pennsylvania 28th ultimately proves valuable as the valiant effort seriously delays the timetable of the XLVII Panzer Corps. Many of the men who remain unaccounted for are discovered when the Spring thaw occurs and the corpses appear.

The situation of the 106th Division is grave. Contingents of both Panzer Armies slash ferociously, their clanking Armor converging upon two Squadrons of the 14th Cavalry manning the Losheim Gap, overrunning the positions and swiveling toward the southwest to bludgeon the supporting Artillery. German Colonel Joachim Peiper, 1st S.S. Panzers, after forcing American prisoners to fill the Tanks with gasoline, reinitiates his attack. Later in the morning, Peiper's command spots a Convoy, transporting Battery B, 285th Field Artillery. The results of the attack are appalling. The Artillerymen are corralled, placed in a field and shot; those screaming in anguish are finished with a bullet to the head. About 86 die, while so few escape the massacre. The SS troops under his command have also killed close to seventy other unarmed prisoners at two separate locations today, his savage ruthlessness taking the lives of about 350 U.S. P.O.W.s and nearly 100 unarmed civilians by the 20th. The swift movement of the enemy, combined with confusion in communications, jeopardizes two Regiments of the 106th. Based on the assumption that the 7th Armored is rushing to their aid, General Alan Jones does not recall the Regiments, one of which contains his son. The untried Regiments subsequently attempt to break out and many become lost, ultimately becoming killed or captured. The 106th, comprising 16,000 men, is nearly annihilated within a week; General Jones is relieved of command.

The 7th Armored (commanded by General Hasbrouck), hampered by icy conditions and standing 60 miles distant, does not reach the area until late on the 17th, although General Bruce Clarke (7th Armored) arrives earlier in the day. At one point, he and General Jones are atop a roof peering for the Armor, neither General having any genuine numbers of troops at their disposal; Clarke assumes responsibility for the defense of the town, but is forced to postpone a counterattack until the following day. Another reason for the delay is the retreating remnants of the 106th and the 14th Cavalry Group, which are abandoning equipment as they run and are clogging the access roads; it takes General Hasbrouck five hours to navigate the clogged roads between Vielsalm and St. Vith. The 7th Armored arrives late in the day and General Clarke establishes a defense at St. Vith, holding against heavy odds until the 21st. The Germans had expected St. Vith to capitulate in two days.

The 5th Panzers pause outside of Stavelot, 20 miles southeast of Liege (30th Division zone), curiously observing constant traffic of Convoys which appear to be shuffling troops; however, the trucks are actually transporting gasoline from a nearby depot. The delay permits the defending force, an Engineering contingent, to receive some reinforcements which prevent the Germans from clearing the town until the latter part of the morning of the 18th. Meanwhile, one detachment

U.S. Airborne troops manning a 75-mm Howitzer at the Bulge.

U.S. Airborne troops manning a machine gun at the Bulge.

scurries to the fuel depot and ingeniously flushes nearly 125,000 gallons of gasoline into a gaping hole along the Panzers' route at a point where the enemy Tanks cannot maneuver freely, compelling the enemy to pivot and push westward without the fuel. Additional U.S. units mount tenacious delaying actions which result in the destruction of most of Peiper's force. Of the 2,000 attackers, only about 800 return to enemy lines.

The grueling contest for Bastogne simmers down by the end of the 17th, and Bradley and his Commanders are confident that the German onslaught will culminate in failure. During the early part of the 17th, General Middleton's Headquarters is at Bastogne; however, few troops are there. He informs Bradley of his predicament, but emphasizes the town must be held, even if surrounded. Before fall of night on the 17th, about 60,000 men including the 82nd and 101st Airborne Divisions are moving to short circuit the German surge, the former diverted to the left flank to control the area between Malmedy and St. Vith; the 101st races recklessly toward Bastogne, unaware that German General von Luttwitz has intercepted the message and is sending his XLVII Panzer Corps to beat the Yanks to Bastogne. Fortunately, the 101st wins the race, arriving about midnight on the 18th, following elements of the 10th Armored which arrive at dusk, forcing the Germans to fight for a city they could have taken easily a day before. General Ridgway arrives on the 18th and remains at Middleton's Headquarters overnight. With communications out, Middleton is unaware of exactly where the Germans are deployed and is unable to determine from where the attack will come. Ridgway leaves to locate the 3rd Armored Division and locates a few troops at Thieux Belgium; General Rose had been out in front of his Armor and encountered an enemy Tank column; he is killed after being captured.

The defenders of Bastogne receive another stroke of luck on the 19th, when contingents of the LVIII Panzer Corps seize Houffalize and turn northwest rather than surround the city. Meanwhile, Eisenhower had called for a meeting in Verdun earlier in the day to confront the threat in the bulge. General Patton is prepared to attack within 48 hours; however, skepticism abounds. No other Army is able to commit, including the British who are in attendance. Patton tells Bradley he is unhappy about canceling his Saar attack, but notes: 'WHAT THE HELL, WE'LL STILL BE KILLING KRAUTS.' Within two days, Patton's Third Army, the sole remaining Army under Bradley, is moving toward Bastogne, spearheaded by an Armored and an Infantry Division, followed by four additional Divisions and over 133,000 Vehicles and yet another Division is diverted to the shoulder.

Although the American Field Commanders are positive the situation is under control, everyone is not in agreement. On the 19th, an annoying message is received by Bradley's Headquarters: "MAKE CERTAIN THAT NO BRIDGE OVER THE MEUSE FELL INTO THE ENEMY'S HAND." General Lew Allen snaps to Bradley: "WHAT THE DEVIL DO THEY THINK WE'RE DOING, STARTING FOR THE BEACHES?" Subsequently, Bradley receives a call from General Bedell Smith stating: "IKE THINKS IT MAY BE A GOOD IDEA TO TURN OVER TO MONTY YOUR TWO ARMIES ON THE NORTH (Hodges 1st and Simpson 9th) AND LET HIM RUN THAT SIDE OF THE BULGE FROM 21ST GROUP...IT MAY SAVE US A GREAT DEAL OF TROUBLE IF YOUR COMMUNICATIONS WITH HODGES AND SIMPSON GO OUT." Bradley agrees reluctantly; the change occurs on the 20th. Montgomery places four British Divisions on the flank of the U.S. First Army (in reserve); however, he only provides the equivalent of a Brigade throughout the ordeal as he regroups for an attack to be launched from Nijmegen during January 1945.

By the 22nd, the Germans hold St. Vith and have Bastogne surrounded, but the stands at St. Vith and at Elsenborn Ridge have paid grand dividends, forcing General Rundstedt to shift two of Dietrich's Panzer Divisions to Manteuffel's force due to

General Matthew Ridgway and a trooper at Born, Belgium.

U.S. troops in snow clothing, moving through the Ardennes.

monstrous traffic congestion, blended by massive U.S. Artillery interdiction. In addition, the Germans have intercepted messages concerning the advance of Third Army and are establishing delaying tactics to impede progress. The 7th Armored, under General Hasbrouck and contingents of the 9th Armored Division, plus scattered remnants of the 106th Division fight steadfastly near St. Vith; Ridgway and 3rd Armored establish contact with Hasbrouck, telling him they will extricate his command from the German trap; the mission is successful and all are rescued without losses of men or equipment on the 21st. Also, the defenders at Bastogne are besieged but not forlorn. The Germans demand surrender and receive an unusual response as General Anthony McAuliffe sends back his legendary message: "NUTS."

On the 23rd, Bradley pleads with Eisenhower to have Montgomery attack; however, Monty is continuing to work on his frontal defenses. Montgomery does request the 82nd Airborne, under Gavin, to pull back further; however, the American Commanders, whom Montgomery has already restrained, react vehemently. Bradley to General Hodges: "ALTHOUGH YOU ARE NO LONGER IN MY COMMAND, I WOULD VIEW WITH SERIOUS MISGIVINGS THE SURRENDER OF ANY MORE GROUND." Consequently, Montgomery retracts his order to retreat. Meanwhile, Fighter Bombers and Medium Bombers, numbering about 2,800, exploit a flimsy break in the weather and strike enemy columns while over 250 Transports drop supplies over Bastogne; however, the Aircraft do not deter the assaulting 2nd and 116th Panzer Divisions which continue to pound Bastogne. The U.S. 2nd Armored (General Harman) engages the 2nd Panzers slightly after dawn on the 25th. Supported by U.S. Fighters and some British Armor, the Panzers are turned back near Celles, less than five miles from the Meuse, having lost 82 Tanks, 405 Trucks, and 81 Artillery pieces, in addition to losing 2,500 killed or wounded and 1,200 captured. Meanwhile, the 3rd Armored Division, deployed further east, shatters the 2nd SS Panzer attack short of Namur on Christmas Day.

On the ground at Bastogne, on Christmas morning, there are few visions of sugar plums. At 03:00, it is the Germans who are trying to come down the chimney. A fresh Panzer Grenadier Division attacks from the northwest subsequent to two bombings, penetrating the defenses of Bastogne, but it is only temporary; all eighteen Tanks are destroyed and the holes sealed. On the following day, the Panzers mount another assault, but Bastogne holds magnificently throughout the day, and at dusk an advance column of the 4th Armored, 3rd Army, commanded by Captain William Dwight, rolls into Bastogne, lifting the siege and being greeted by General McAuliffe with the words: "I AM MIGHTY GLAD TO SEE YOU."

December 16th 1944 — (Pacific-Philippines) MINDORO: The assault troops limit activity to bolstering their defenses around the Airfield and dispatching Patrols. The Japanese continue to attack U.S. Shipping. The U.S. Seventh Fleet Warships return to Leyte; Task Groups 77.3, 78.3 and 77.12 arrive safely on the following day. On LEYTE, the Airfield at Tanauan is operational. In the **U.S. Sixth Army** area, **XXIV Corps** sector, the 305th Regiment, 77th Division seizes Cogon and reduces opposition in the area, while the 307th advances to San Jose, followed by the 306th Regiment as they drive toward Valencia. **(Pacific-Burma)** In the N.C.A.C. area, the U.S. 124th Cavalry pushes out from Myitkyina, advancing toward Bhamo to join the fight. In the **British Fourteenth Army** area, 4th Corps sector, the Indian 19th Division seizes Banmauk and Pinlebu, then dispatches a Patrol which reaches Indaw and meets the British 36th Division (N.C.A.C.). **(Pacific-China)** General McClure complains to Chiang Kai-shek, upon learning from General Frank Dorn that the Chinese 57th Army will not move to defend Kunming. Subsequently, some of the Army is flown to the threatened city. In other activity, the ongoing negotiations between the Nationalist and Communist Chinese cease, being terminated by Chou En-lai, the Communist leader. **(Atlantic-Western Europe) 21st Army Group** In the **British Second Army** area, the **30th Corps** begins preparing for its drive against Krefeld, scheduled to commence on 12th, January 1945; it begins concentrating in the Nijmegen area. **12th Army Group** The Germans commence a full scale assault in the Ardennes. General Bradley meets with Eisenhower to discuss critical shortage of Infantrymen. During the meeting they are informed of German penetration of General Middleton's VIII Corps lines in front, and to the right of General Gerow's V Corps. The Germans had launched a similar offensive during 1940. It too was led by Rundstedt and its success took France out of the war and flung England out of Europe. British Air Chief Marshal Tedder is in attendance. For more information, see December 16th-26th. In the **U.S. Ninth Army** area (Lt. General H. Simpson), **XIII Corps** sector, in conjunction with the German counteroffensive, the 84th Division lines at Leiffarth are pierced; however, the holes are sealed quickly. In the **U.S. First Army** area (Lt. General Courtney H. Hodges), **VII Corps** sector, the German thrusts toward Guerzenich and Mariaweiler are neutralized; in the **V Corps** (Major General L. T. Gerow) sector, the 99th Division, under Major General Walter E. Lauer, mounts rigid resistance

at Hofen; however, enemy advances are gained near Buellingen. Field Marshal Model, intending to spare Monschau, has forbidden the use of Artillery against it; he orders the 326th Volks Grenadier Division to drive north of it and secure Mutzenich and to join the 246th Volks Grenadier Division to seize Hofen and Kalterherberg. U.S. strength at Hofen-Monschau comprises one Reconnaissance Squadron and the 3rd Battalion, 395th Regiment under Lt. Colonel McClernand Butler at Hofen and the 38th Cavalry Reconnaissance Squadron, under Lt. Col. Robert E. O'Brien near Monschau. The Infantry is bolstered by recently arrived Company A, 612th Tank Destroyer Battalion and other Artillery units. The heavy thrust of the attack is met head-on; despite being understrengthed, the men of the 3rd Battalion, hold their fire until they see the whites of their eyes, then mow the Germans down. About thirty or forty troops penetrate, but they are captured. At Monschau, the Cavalry turns back several attacks by the 1st Battalion, 752nd Regiment. At day's end, the Germans have not hooked up. Meanwhile, the 78th Division repulses the Germans at Rollesbroich, but the 78th's attempt to seize Kesternich is unsuccessful.

The 2nd Division is assaulting toward the Roer Dams through the positions of the 99th and will be recalled due to the turn of events. During the 1st S.S. Panzer Corps' attack against the 99th positions, a small contingent led by Tech Sergeant Vernon McGarity holds back a massive German attack against Krinkelt through the night. By morning, McGarity's indomitable leadership and good marksmanship thwart the Germans. He pops the lead Tank with a bazooka shell and destroys it. Support fire from his Squad drives the Infantry back and the remaining Tanks withdraw. The Germans attempt to outflank the beleaguered Squad; however, McGarity singlehandedly destroys the newly emplaced machine gun that blocks the only escape route. McGarity and his men hold until their ammunition is totally expended, then make a disciplined withdrawal, having successfully held up the German advance; McGarity receives the Medal of Honor. During the first attack, all but one Platoon of Company K, 3rd Battalion, 393rd Regiment is killed or captured. By darkness, the German 989th Regiment reaches Jansbach Creek, but the advance which carries them half way through the forest is expensive; the 3rd Battalion, under Lt. Col. Jack G. Allen, seizes many prisoners. Nearby, the 1st Battalion, commanded by Major Matthew L. Legler, stalls the German 990th Regiment. Both U.S. Battalions sustain heavy losses, but their resistance is staunch. In conjunction, reinforcements from the 2nd Division arrive during the day to bolster the defenders.

In the **VIII Corps** area, the bulk of the assault hits the recently arrived 106th Division, which is deployed in the Snow Eifel; it does not surrender too much ground on the first day. Within a week, the Division will be struck hard. It had been rushed through training in the States and many of its prime candidates for higher rank had been sapped prior to departure and placed in other units as replacements. In addition, its leaders are not battle tested. The Division is in a semi rest zone and expected to have a quiet Christmas before joining in the fight to rout the German forces. The 106th (newest Division on the front) will sustain 16,000 men dead or captured, many without firing their weapons, by the 22nd of December. A serious gap is soon created as the 14th Cavalry Group, under Colonel Mark Devine, receives a strong attack against their positions adjacent to the 99th Division. The swiftness of the enemy drive places them in position to overrun St. Vith and they have Echternach surrounded, entrapping two Regiments of the 106th. The 7th and 9th Armored will be committed to defend St. Vith.

The 14th Cavalry Group is spread north of the Schnee Eifel and near the northeastern entrance to the Losheim Gap; it is capable only of fighting a delaying action if struck by a fierce attack; a counterattack is not considered feasible to lack of maneuvering ability. Heavy skirmishing occurs at Krewinkel; the enemy pushes into the town but is shoved back out. The situation at other towns including Berterath, Merlscheid, Manderfeld and Lanzerath is grave. It is also serious at Roth and Kobscheid. Early in the day, Colonel Devine requests that the 106th Division to commence a counterattack, but he is informed by General Jones that it is not possible; the 106th Division is preparing to counterattack on the following day, anticipating reinforcements. At 16:00, the 14th Cavalry Group requests permission to withdraw to line Andler-Holzheim near the Our River.

Meanwhile, the 28th Division (Major General Norman D. Cota), the 9th Armored Division and contingents of the 4th Division (holding the North flank) are also forced to give ground to the charging Germans. In the 9th Armored's (no prior battle experience) zone, the equivalent of a Combat Command is available as most of the Division is to the west in reserve. Beaufort and Haller come under heavy bombardment by the LXXX Corps, which is supporting the 212th and 276th Volks Grenadier Divisions; the 986th Regiment makes the largest crossing at the confluence of the Sauer and Our Rivers near Wallendorf; its attempt to capture Hill 402 near Bigelbach succeeds in annihilating a contingent of Armored Infantry (60th Armored Infantry Bn.), but guns of the nearby 109th Regiment interdict and halt the advance. The German 986th Regiment closes on unoccupied Bigelbach while the 988th Regiment drives toward Beaufort and Haller. The Germans continue the attacks throughout the night. In the 4th Division zone (Major General Raymond O. Barton), the 12th Regiment fights hard, but it stands alone and without communications against the onslaught of the 212th Volks Grenadier Division; five Companies hold the towns of Bergdorf, Dickweiler, Echternach, Lauterborn, and Osweiler, where the crucial battles are to be fought. At Bergdorf, the German hordes overrun three of Company F's advance Outposts, but Outpost No. 2 escapes the surprise attack; 22 men and two Artillery Observers of the 2nd Platoon hold Birklet Farm for four days against heavy odds. At Bergdorf, 1st Lt. John L. Leake and his force of 60 men, one 50 caliber machine gun and one BAR turn the Parc Hotel into a citadel; the hotel circled by open terrain gives the enemy a royal welcome, ensuring future attacks are feint-hearted. At Lauterborn, the 7th Company, 423rd Regiment drives to sever the Echternach-Luxembourg road; Company G's outposts are isolated, but the remainder of the Company fights tenaciously, despite being surrounded at a mill just outside of town. Meanwhile, Company E gets surprised at Echternach, however, many of the troops posted at the outposts pull back to a hat factory on the fringes of the town; it becomes a strongpoint. In conjunction, Company I, stands tough at Dickweiler, turning back two enemy Companies before 12:00. At 12:00, the one observation Plane of the Regiment has clarified the battle situation, but still the poor communications hinders the defense. The 1st Battalion, under Lt. Col Oma R. Bates, is brought out of reserve and eighteen Tanks of the 70th Tank Battalion (Lt. Col. Henry E. Davidson) arrive but the area is mud-bound, restricting the Tanks to the roads. General Barton requests

added reinforcements and is informed by General Middleton that he can use the 159th Engineer Combat Battalion if they can be located. Meanwhile, Company A, moves on Light Tanks to beat back opposition southwest of Lauterborn; it leaves a Platoon to hold Hill 313, then drives to the village and rescues twenty-five men that had been captured during the morning fighting. Also, Company B, moving on ten Tanks, advances to establish contact with Company F; German opposition halts the advance outside of Berdorf; the Tanks return to Consdorf to refuel and the Infantry digs in facing the 1st Battalion, 423rd Regiment. In the 3rd Battalion zone (Major Herman R. Rice, Jr.), the Germans are repelled at Dickweiler, but more enemy troops are forming to launch another attack; three Tanks of Company B, 70th Tank Battalion rolls to extricate a 3rd Battalion Rifle Squad at their outpost in Herborn, then secure the road to Osweiler. When the slim detachment is notified that Dickweiler is again threatened, it pivots and drives toward it; as the Tanks encroach the village, they encounter the flank of the 2nd Battalion, 320th Regiment as it forms for attack. Quick and decisive action stuns the Germans hitting their flank and rear, inflicting heavy casualties; 35 men and one Company Commander surrenders to the Yanks. Although, the Germans have been stalled, the 3rd Battalion is in trouble; as the day's fighting quells, Company L and I remain surrounded. The reserve 2nd Battalion, 22nd Infantry is ordered to move early on the 17th and bolster the 12th Regiment's Command Post at Junglinster; it will be beefed up with two Tank Platoons and a contingent of the 9th Armored Division. Also, three Battalions of 155s and two Batteries of 105s move to bolster the 12th's 15 supporting Howitzers. In conjunction, the 4th Engineer Combat Battalion and the 4th Cavalry Reconnaissance Troop deploy to the rear of the Regiment. The besieged 4th Division receives more good news! A strong 10th Armored contingent is en route to help hold the line and neutralize the German Armor. In the 28th Division zone, the 110th Regiment (Col. Hurley E. Fuller) faces three German Divisions; the 1st Battalion's (Lt. Col. Donald Paul) Company B and one Platoon of the 630th Tank Destroyer Bn. defends at Marnach on the Skyline Drive and along the Dasburg-Bastogne Road; Company C and the Regimental Cannon Company defends at Munshausen and guards the side road running from Marnach to Drauffelt; Company A is at Heinerscheid and Company D is holding Grindhausen. The 3rd Battalion (Major Harold F. Milton) is deployed to the right; Company K and Company B, 103rd Engineering Bn. is spread above the Our River along the Skyline Drive at Hosingen; Company I is stretched along the ridge line at Weiler-les-Putscheid, supported by the 110th Antitank Company at Hoscheid and west of the ridge is Company L, at Holzthum. Also, Headquarters Company and Company M are based at Consthum, protecting the approaches to the Clerf River at Wilwerwiltz. General Cota holds the 2nd Battalion (Lt. Col. Ross C. Henbest at Donnage, west of the Regimental Command Post, in reserve.

At Consthum, the defenders repulse five German attacks before 12:00; a subsequent attack takes the town, but a counterattack drives them out. In conjunction, the Germans attempt to sever the highway between Holzthum and Consthum in the 3rd Battalion's (110th Regiment) zone, but twenty men under Captain Norman G. Maurer drive the attackers back convincingly. Also, the 109th Field Artillery's Battery C is struck hard, but stands like a rock, then is bolstered by Tanks of the 707th Tank Bn. However, the Germans drive into Hosingen, engaging in house-to-house fighting with the 103rd Engineer Battalion's Companies B and D. Four Tanks arrive at Hosingen at 22:00, but they bring no rifle ammunition. Along the Wahlhausen road, the 1st Platoon, Company I, 3rd Battalion holds tenuously with its supporting Artillery; at Weiler, the remainder of Company I, supported by mortars and Antitank units, repels successive attacks; as the ammunition of the mortarmen and Antitank components is expended, the men form ranks with the Infantry. Germans approach with a white flag offering the Yanks an opportunity to surrender, but the offer is ignored; they fight until their ammunition is near exhausted, then despite being surrounded, fight their way west to join friendly forces. During the blistering attack, Armor begins to overrun the Observation Post of Company I; the detachment calls for Artillery fire on its positions; one man survives.

In the 1st Battalion, 110th Regiment zone, German troops of the 2nd Panzers reach Marnach and are pounded with fire from the guns of the 630th Tank Battalion and Company B. The 707th Tank Battalion rushes reinforcements to the town but the Infantry is driven from the road; some Tanks make it. At dusk, things deteriorate as German Half-tracks begin closing; communications cease but there is hope that the Yanks can hold through the night. Meanwhile, the 112th Regiment holds its positions east of the Our; the German 560th Volks Grenadier Division sustains about 1,000 casualties, including its attached Fusilier Company which gets lost in the forest; the 116th Panzer Division incurs moderate losses.

In the 109th Regiment's zone, the troops under Lt. Colonel James E. Rudder are deployed at the Our and Sauer Rivers; the 3rd Battalion (Lt. Col. Jim H. McCoy) holds a 3,000 yard line overlooking the valley road leading west to Ettelbruck; the 2nd Battalion (Major William J. Maroney) controls a fragile sector further north, comprising a width of five miles; the 1st Battalion (Lt. Colonel H. R. Williams) and the 107th and 108th Field Artillery Battalions are at Diekirch as reserve. The German 352nd Volks Grenadier Division under Col. Erich Schmidt and the 5th Parachute Division opposes the 109th. The German Artillery bombardment pounds Bastendorf, Diekirch and the ridge road extending north from Ettelbruck. Walsdorf is seized without a struggle, giving the enemy a crossroads village, but the Germans fail to take advantage. Longsdorf and Tandel also fall to the Germans; a counterattack pushes the Yanks to the fringes of Longsdorf and also gains them the heights between there and Tandel.

By day's end, the Germans have driven to positions near Auw and Roth-Kobscheid; they stall to await heavy weapons. The 26th Volks Grenadier Division hooks up with the German 5th Parachute Division toward the latter part of the day, however, they are running behind schedule; they do not reach the Clerf River crossings. Also, the reconnaissance Battalion of the Panzer Lehr Division is struggling to advance from the Gemund bridge. The Americans regroup and General Middleton instructs his beleaguered VIII Corps to hold as long as possible.

In the **U.S. Third Army** area, **VIII Corps** sector, the 95th Division is heavily engaged, attempting to expand its Saarlautern bridgehead. In the **XII Corps** sector, word of the enemy offensive reaches Corps; consequently, the assault against the West Wall is aborted. **6th Army Group** In the **U.S. Seventh Army** area, some contingents of all VI Corps assault Divisions reach the German border. Combat Command A, 14th Armored, occupies Wissembourg after the 103rd Division

bypasses it; C.C.B., 14th Armored, and the 79th Division encounter tenacious resistance at Bien Wald. Bobenthal and Nothweiler fall to the 45th Division. Near Kaysersberg, 1st Lt. Charles P. Murray, Jr., Company C, 30th Regiment, 3rd Division, leads his reconnaissance Platoon into enemy terrain and detects a large force numbering about 200 men which is pounding an American Battalion on the crest of a ridge from positions which are not visible from below. Lt. Murray chooses not to attack because of the overwhelming numbers, but crawls to a dangerous position and calls for Artillery which pummels but does not dislodge the enemy. His radio goes dead and he decides to attack singlehandedly, using a rifle to launch grenades. He soon returns to his positions and confiscates more ammunition and an automatic weapon with which he kills about twenty of the enemy and disorients the remainder. As they attempt retreat, he knocks out a truck which is transporting three mortars. Meanwhile, an American mortar is brought up and Murray utilizes it to inflict more casualties. With his Patrol, he advances and takes a bridge and establishes a roadblock in addition to taking ten prisoners. Another nearby German feigns surrender, but throws a grenade that blasts Murray to the ground. Undaunted although bleeding terribly, he deploys his detachment before seeking medical assistance; Murray receives the Medal of Honor for his extraordinary leadership and courage. **(Atlantic-Italy)** Field Marshal Sir Henry Maitland Wilson is appointed head of British Joint Staff Mission in Washington, succeeding Field Marshal Dill (deceased). British Field Marshal Sir Harold R.L.G. Alexander replaces Wilson as Supreme Allied Commander, Mediterranean Theater (AFHQ). General Mark Clark becomes Commander of all Allied Armies in Italy and Lt. General Lucian K. Truscott, Jr. succeeds him as Commander of the U.S. Fifth Army. In the **British Eighth Army** area, 5th Corps sector, the Indian 43rd Brigade in conjunction with the New Zealand Division eliminates remaining opposition in Faenza effortlessly. The New Zealand 2nd Division advances to the Senio and the Indian 10th Division seizes Pergola.

December 17th 1944 — (Pacific-Philippines) On LEYTE: **U.S. Sixth Army** area, **X Corps** sector, the enemy is still mounting serious opposition against the 32nd Division south of Limon. In the **XXIV Corps** sector, an Air and Artillery attack precedes an attack by the 307th Regiment, 77th Division, which jumps off at 14:15, and drives to the tip of the Airfield at Valencia, while the 305th Regiment secures Tambuco and deploys along the Tambuco-Dolores Road. Meanwhile, the 306th, also driving toward Valencia, halts about 500 yards outside of Cabulihan, awaiting daylight. MINDORO: Operations to bolster defenses continue. In other activity, the PT-44 is sunk by a Kamikaze. Admiral Halsey's Third Fleet gets snagged in a terrible storm, about 500 miles east of Luzon; attempts are made to refuel, but the cross-swell and the winds which vary from 20 to 30 knots make it too dangerous; the operation is postponed at 13:10; another attempt is made on the following day. **(Pacific-China)** Hump Tonnage Allocation and Control Office is established in Rear Echelon, China Theater Headquarters. **(Atlantic-Western Europe) 12th Army Group** The 82nd and 101st Airborne Divisions are rushed to the Ardennes to defend strategic road centers. In the **U.S. First Army** area, **VII Corps** sector, precautions are taken to thwart a possible Paratroop attack, while simultaneously edging its right flank toward the Roer. Roelsdorf and Lendersdorf are captured by the 83rd Division and the 9th Division is simultaneously encountering tenacious opposition as it advances doggedly west of Dueren. In the **V**

Corps area, the Germans assault is visibly overwhelming as the Panzers press toward Malmedy; the U.S. 1st and 30th Divisions react and prepare to counterattack; the 1st Division had moved out to support the V Corps at midnight 16th-17th for Camp Elsenborn; the 30th Division, under Major General Leland S. Hobbs, will intercept Colonel Peiper's 1st S.S. Panzers. The 30th Division had just concluded vicious fighting in the Roer River area. A resolute stand by the 99th Division on the previous day at Losheimergraben delayed the Panzer Tanks arrival to the Bullingen-Malmedy road, but the Armor has made great strides against the 14th Cavalry Group. As Colonel Peiper's Panzers moves toward Malmedy, an American Convoy runs into the advance elements; the advance enemy troops pulverize the Convoy and continue the advance leaving the Yanks of Battery B, 285th Field Artillery for the trailing troops; about 83 men are executed; some feign death and escape, but others are heard groaning and are shot in the head; Peiper has already massacred 19 unarmed Yanks at Honsfeld and another 50 have been murdered earlier in the day at Bullingen. News of the hellish acts of the 1st S.S. Panzer Division spreads rapidly throughout the U.S. lines as survivors reach safety; at about 14:30, a passing contingent of the 291st Engineering Bn. picks up several survivors. German pressure against Losheimergraben forces a withdrawal, but not before some heroic fighting; at one point, about fifty defenders, many armed only with pistols stall the Armor; ammunition is rushed to the point in the Chaplain's Jeep, but by dusk, the town is lost; the battered contingents of the 99th's 394th Regiment fight their way to friendly lines and assemble at Murringen. About midnight (17th-18th) the Germans enter Buchholz; most of the Platoons of Company K had departed to bolster Losheimergraben, the few defenders are overwhelmed; one man escapes capture, hiding in the basement of an abandoned Command Post; he smuggles out hourly radio reports on German movements, including tracking the main body of the 1st S.S. Panzers, which move through at 05:00; he counts 30 Tanks, 28 Half-tracks and endless columns of Infantry. In the **VIII Corps** area, the 14th Cavalry Group, struck by the 3rd Parachute Division, is falling back rapidly, collapsing the right flank of the Corps; the objective of the enemy remains ten miles to the northwest (Schoppen-Eibertingen line); Armored Infantry trail (1st and 12th Panzers). The remnants of the two Cavalry Squadrons receive orders to make their way back to Recht; three Reconnaissance Teams get there, but the two Squadrons wind up on the St. Vith-Poteau highway; subsequent orders go out about midnight instructing the Cavalry to reoccupy Born. Peiper's 1st S.S. Panzers speed toward Malmedy, but it encounters a force from C.C.B., 9th Armored which delays it; a lead Panzer and several Armored Vehicles are destroyed by the roving Shermans as they move to defend St. Vith; Peiper's Panzers advance to positions near Stavelot in the Ambleve Valley, but no attack is launched, de spite the fact that the town is lightly defended by only one Squad of the 291st Engineer Battalion which had been dispatched from Malmedy to establish a roadblock; three Panzers attack across the solitary bridge spanning the Ambleve River, but some unexpected U.S. mines end the threat; two Tanks reverse direction and Peiper is stalled at the Stavelot bridge about 42 miles from the Meuse. The situation deteriorates further as two Regiments of the 106th (Golden Eagle) Division become isolated as the enemy exploits the disorganized retreat of the 14th Cavalry and the inexperience of the 106th, rolling over Heuem and driving confidently toward St. Vith where the 7th and 9th Armored Divisions are to hold. C.C.R., 7th Armored Division establishes Headquarters

at Reicht during the afternoon, the 17th Tank Battalion is nearby, however, its Armored Infantry Battalion has been diverted to St. Vith. C.C.R. (Colonel John L. Ryan Jr.) is informed of German presence and Lt. Colonel Fred M. Warren, acting Commandng Officer, orders Lt. Colonel John P. Wemple to dispatch a Company of his 17th Bn. Tanks to Recht, Warren and Wemple. Colonel Church M. Matthews's entourage had encountered a huge enemy Tank column earlier in the day; his driver had reported the incident and informs Headquarters that Colonel Matthews is missing; his body is discovered during January 1945. During the arduous day, it is difficult getting reinforcements to the crucial points as withdrawing troops are abandoning equipment and creating horrendous traffic jams. By darkness, about nine thousand Yanks are effectively neutralized west of the Schnee Eifel; in addition to the two Regiments of the 106th, the units include all or components of the 589th Field Artillery Bn., 590th Field Artillery Bn., Company B, 81st Engineer Bn., Company C, 820th Tank Destroyer Bn., Company B, 331st Medical Bn., 106th Reconnaissance Troop and Troop B, 18th Cavalry Reconnaissance Squadron. Meanwhile, the Germans pierce the 9th Armored sector in several spots to endanger the 60th Armored Infantry Battalion; three Companies become isolated; a counterattack secures the heights above Beaufort, but the enemy remains deeply rooted in the woods to the rear of the isolated Companies. Also, an unsuccessful counterattack is launched to retake Muller; Troop B, 89th Cavalry Reconnaissance Squadron and contingents of the 811th Tank Destroyer Battalion pull back to the hills flanking the exit of the Waldbillig-Mullerthal defile. The Germans take Beaufort before day's end, however, the rear-guard actions hold long enough for the troops to evacuate for Savelbor; Troop A, 89th Cavalry, under Captain Victor C. Leiker, departs the town at 20:30 and the men fight their way south to Waldbillig; the unit loses 16 Jeeps, seven of its 12 Armored Cars and also sustains 43 casualties. The German 276th Volks Grenadier Division had advanced but not sufficiently; orders come down to replace the Commanding Officer, however, General Moehring is cut down by machine gun fire as he travels between Beaufort and Mullerthal and is not available to meet his successor. The Yanks plan a counterattack to reestablish contact with the isolated Companies.

Elements of the 28th Division are also struck hard. They have been recuperating after a difficult campaign, which has drained their manpower and strength, and the Germans drive almost to Wiltz. By 12:00, the 2nd Battalion, 110th Regiment is clogged along the ridge extending from Urspelt to the Clerf road; Company B had been badgered at Marnach; they attempt to reach Clerf, but the road is held by the 2nd Panzers; the Artillery to its left had been overrun and half of the Howitzers at Buchholz are destroyed before the Battery can evacuate. In conjunction, the 707th Tank Battalion commits Light Tanks; concealed heavy velocity guns shred them as they depart Heinerscheid. During the ten minute battle, eight Tanks are destroyed, three are lost to Bazooka fire and the two surviving Tanks return to their point of departure only to be destroyed later in the day. Five additional Tanks make it to Urspelt. At Clerf, the 707th's Company A rolls out to engage approaching German Armor; four enemy Tanks are destroyed and the Yanks lose two. Meanwhile, C.C.R., 9th Armored Division is extracted from reserve and rushed to establish a roadblock along the Bastogne-Trois Vierges road to bolster the center position of the 28th. In addition, Company B, 2nd Tank Battalion speeds to Clerf to support the 110th Regiment; nineteen Tanks arrive; they are dispersed to Reuler to aid the 2nd Battalion and to Heinerscheid where they quiet the German Armor, avenging the loss of the Light Tanks there earlier in the day. The other contingent presses to expel the Germans from the south end of Clerf. At 18:25, Colonel Fuller reports that his 110th Regimental Command Post is under attack at Clerf; he is subsequently captured while attempting to evacuate he area. Heinerscheid had been lost during the afternoon and the defenders at Reuler, the Germans had overrun the 1st Battalion. Despite the setbacks, a small contingent of 102 men hold the south bridge at the chateau in Clerf, amidst the roving German Armor; they make their final contact with the 28th Division at 05:28 on the 18th; these magnificent stands at the Clerf crossings delays the German onslaught, buying valuable time at Bastogne. In the 112th Regiment's zone (Colonel Gustin M. Nelson), things are getting tighter; four self propelled Tank Destroyers (811th Tank Destroyer Bn.) arrive to bolster Trois Vierges and in addition, Antitank and Cannon Companies arrive to protect the bridges at Ouren. The Germans strike hard along the line; the 1st Battalion positions feel the brunt of the attack. The 229th Field Artillery Battalion is also struck hard. Mark IV Tanks race down the ridge toward Ouren in synchronization with the 1130th and 156th Regiments which are driving hard to annihilate the advance positions. Company A, takes severe casualties. Company D, ambushes an enemy Infantry Company as it becomes blinded by the glare of its own headlights, but soon after, more German troops overrun the positions. Nearby, the Germans lose to within one thousand yards of the Regimental Command Post at Ouren; Cannon fire is brought to bear and four of the attacking Tanks are destroyed. In conjunction, about fifty men from Headquarters and from Ouren take positions and neutralize the advancing German Infantry on a ridge to the east. However, the giant thrust of the Armor penetrate the center of the 1st Battalion perimeter, forcing contingents of Company A, C, and D to withdraw toward Welchenhausen; at 10:00, Battery C, 229th Field Artillery Battalion joins with Company C, 447th Antiaircraft Artillery Battalion; advancing enemy Tanks are blasted at near point blank range by the Howitzers, while the machine guns of the Antiaircraft unit shred the trailing Infantry. This is followed by a counterattack by the 2nd Battalion; it jumps off at 12:00 and relieves the pressure. Meanwhile, the 229th Field Artillery Battalion bombards Lutzkampen in concert with a limited air attack, but the strength is limited. Heavy fighting continues throughout the afternoon, but by 14:00, the Artillery is compelled to move behind the river. Meanwhile the 1st Battalion remains trapped. The 3rd Battalion resists fiercely, using its pillbox line effectively; a second counterattack by the 2nd Battalion gives it added life. In the meantime, the German Tanks are swooping all over the area, preventing the components from extricating the 1st Battalion. By dusk the positions become untenable and the 112th is forced to withdraw; Ouren is abandoned as the Germans enter. A 3rd Battalion Patrol, dispatched to tell the 1st Battalion to fight its way back, never returns, but a subsequent order, transmitted by radio around midnight reaches the besieged Battalion; about 235 men head for German-held Ouren; the Yanks spot a small contingent of Germans guarding the bridge and immediately form in German style. A bilingual Officer bellows orders in German and the impostors march smartly across the bridge under the noses of the enemy. Other troops eventually reach safety, however, the valiant contingent of Headquarters Company which had held the ridge, never establishes contact; they are totally surrounded and on the following morning, while attempting to break out, most are captured. The 112th had inflicted heavy casualties on the Germans before yielding the ground. The Germans seize a bridgehead at the Our, but in the two days of vicious fighting, they lose about 45 Tanks and sustain between 400-600 killed or wounded and 186 prisoners are taken by the 112th. The 112th Regiment forms a new line stretching through Beiler, Lieler, and Lausdorn, but receives subsequent orders to fight a delaying action as it moves to the defense of Bastogne. Meanwhile, in the 109th Regiment's zone, three German Regiments plow into the defenses at Fuhren, which had been bypassed on the previous day; the Germans need to secure this to ensure junction of their scattered units; Fuhren holds, but attempts to relieve the beleaguered defenders are fruitless. On the following morning, a detachment reaches the town but no sign of U.S. troops is visible and the Command Post is afire. Throughout the night, attempts are made to resupply the 109th Companies. In the 4th Division zone, the troops, deployed south of Osweiler and Dickweiler, repulse the enemy's advance; however, some units become isolated; Company B, 70th Tank Battalion and ten Tanks attack Berdorf to reach Company F. Mistakenly, the Tanks begin firing on American occupied Hotel Parc; luckily, a Yank from Company F finds an American Flag and hoists it conspicuously on the roof, ending the friendly fire; the attack resumes, but the heavily defended Germans halt progress; in conjunction, another relief force unsuccessfully attempts to drive to Echternach to reach Company E, 12th Regiment which controls two-blocks, barring enemy passage through the town. Also, Company A, 12th Regiment has pulled back from Hill 313, but its desperate call for help at Scheidgen is too late; they are overrun, leaving only one Antitank Company, composed of sixty men, holding the ground between the advancing Germans and the 2nd Battalion Command Post at Consdorf. Another unit, Company C, drives toward Osweiler to bolster the two Companies there; one Platoon is decimated by the 2nd Battalion, 320th Regiment as it hits the Germans head on; all troops are either killed or capture. However, the other two Platoons moving on the right are unscathed; they drive forward; Company F, 2nd Battalion, 22nd Regiment (just arrived) moves out on Tanks of the 19th Tank Battalion, 9th Armored Division; it drives to Osweiler, encountering Germans along the way; after a flash firefight, the force rescues some of the captured men of Company C. As the defense line forms around Osweiler, the remaining contingents of the 22nd Regiment advance toward Osweiler; they are intercepted by a German force and the fighting continues until dark; the Yanks dig in for a long winter night and the Germans move toward Scheidgen where they control the crossroads. Dickweiler and Osweiler remain in U.S. hands. The 10th Armored Division arrives at Luxembourg city and deploys to meet the threat; one Combat Command is ordered to Bastogne, but the remainder bolsters the 4th Division; Major General William H. H. Morris, Jr. moves out ahead of his command and arrives at Bastogne to confer with General Middleton. Although the 4th Division is outmanned, the Armor is superior to the Germans, and cuts the odds. The German 423rd Regiment had advanced on the previous day to the Berdorf Plateau, annihilating an Infantry Squad and one 57-mm Antitank-Gun, but 4th Division reserves arrive on the 17th with sufficient time to dig in and guard the gorge and prevent an enemy rout. At 09:36, the Yanks spot five enemy Companies of the reserve 987th Regiment, 276th Volks Grenadier Division, advancing in the 9th Armored's zone. Eight Tanks of Company C, 70th Tank Battalion speed to Breitweil er to assist; additional units form in Colbet to meet the threat;

these contingents become Task Force Luckett (Col. James S. Luckett). Meanwhile, a German force plows through opposition and reaches Mullerthal, creating a threat to the 2nd Battalion Command Post at Consdorf; one Tank, the cooks, some straggler troops and some MPs deploy to hold the line, but the German 987th Regiment fails to attack. In the 2nd Division sector, tenacious fighting erupts at Krinkelter Wald, Belgium, and at Rocherath. P.F.C. William A. Soderman, Company K, 9th Regiment, 2nd Division knocks out a lead Tank and withstands a night Artillery bombardment, then at daybreak engages another column of Tanks, disabling the first and forcing the other four to turn. Orders come down to withdraw from the untenable positions; however, additional Tanks arrive before the men can fully evacuate. Soderman again singlehandedly attacks and disables the lead Tank, forcing the others to abort the attack. Soderman is grievously wounded during this last attempt, but he crawls back to his lines near Rocherath and survives to receive the Medal of Honor. At Krinkelt, German Infantry and Tanks attempt to envelop elements of the 23rd Regiment, 2nd Division. Splendid resistance and intrepid actions by individuals hold the line against superior numbers. Six waves are repulsed, but a seventh supported by Tanks kills or wounds all but three of Pvt. Cowan's (Company M) section. About 20 Riflemen of Company I are able to lend support fire and he maintains his position. He kills about 40 of eighty attackers during the next charge; Cowan receives the Medal of Honor. Nearby, Sergeant Jose Lopez, Company K, kills ten Germans with his machine gun as they advance alongside a Tank. About twenty-five more are killed when they attempt to outflank Lopez and then as he swings his eyes, another attack is coming at him. Lopez's quick thinking saves him. Realizing he can't hold much longer, he swings the machine gun over his shoulders and heads toward the rear; however, as the Huns begin to swarm, Lopez, blown over by a shell concussion, snaps up and sets up his gun to cover the withdrawal and singlehandedly stops the counterattack. Lopez, the galloping machinegunner, plops the gun back on his shoulders and starts to run to catch the Company, but he hesitates to assist another small detachment of Yanks, firing until his ammunition is exhausted. His actions eliminate at least 100 enemy troops and successfully allow his Company to retire; Lopez receives the Medal of Honor. In the **U.S. Third Army** area, **XX Corps** sector, relief of the 95th Division by the 5th Division is ongoing. In other activity, Engineers finish constructing a bridge near Ensdorf. **6th Army Group** In the **U.S. Seventh Army** area, the **XV Corps** is unable to make any headway at Forts Schiesseck and Simershof, and the Germans have also halted the VI Corps as it attempts to take the West Wall. In the **French 1st Army** area, Keintzheim is taken by the 2 Corps. **(Atlantic-Eastern Europe)** The Second Ukrainian Front is encroaching upon Budapest, less than 5 miles distant. **(Atlantic-Italy) 15th Army Group** In the **British Eighth Army** area, **5th Corps** sector, the Indian 10th Division establishes small bridgeheads across the Senio; however, they cannot be enlarged until their critical supply situation improves and the area around Faenza becomes more stable. Presently, the Indian 43rd Brigade is stymied by opposition and is unable to advance from the town.

December 18th 1944 — (Pacific-Philippines) LEYTE: In the **U.S. Sixth Army** area, **X Corps** sector, the 126th Regiment, 32nd Division slowly overcomes opposition south of Limon; however, the determined effort seals the existing gap between it and the 127th Infantry. In the **XXIV Corps** sector, the

307th Regiment, 77th Division occupies Valencia without incident and gains its Airfield without a fight. Meanwhile, the 305th Regiment establishes a roadblock on the road to Dolores. Now the Ormoc Valley between Ormoc and Valencia is secure. In Naval activity, a vicious typhoon rolls through the islands inflicting severe damage to the Third Fleet. On the previous day, Admiral Halsey's Aerologist had described the storm as a "tropical disturbance;" it is now a "killer typhoon." The refueling operation can not get underway; Halsey changes course, speeding south to get the Fleet out of harm's way; some Vessels don't make the run. The Destroyers *Hull* (DD-350) is lost; 44 men survive; the *Monaghan* (DD-354) sinks; only six men survive, and 24 men survive on the *Spence* (DD-512) which is also lost. U.S. The Destroyer Escort *Tabberer* is thought lost, however, it survives and is responsible for saving several men of the *Hull*, according to Halsey who remarks : "THANKS TO THE BRILLIANT MANEUVERING IN THE SEA-BY LT. COMMANDER HENRY L. PLAGE OF ATLANTA." This is Plage's second time at sea and Halsey remarks: "HOW COULD ANY ENEMY EVER DEFEAT A COUNTRY THAT CAN PULL BOYS LIKE THAT OUT OF ITS HAT." Vessels damaged: The Light Carriers *Cowpens* (CVL-25), *Monterey* (CVL-26), *Cabot* (CVL-28), and the *San Jacinto* (CVL-30); Escort Carriers *Altamaha* (CVE-18), *Nebenta Bay* (CVE-74), *Cape Esperance* (CVE-88), and the *Kwajalein* (CVE-98); Light Cruiser *Miami* (CL-89); Destroyers *Dewey* (DD-349), *Aylwin* (DD-355), *Buchanan* (DD-484), *Dyson* (DD-572), *Hickox* (DD-673), *Maddox* (DD-731), and the *Benham* (DD-796); Destroyer Escorts *Melvin R. Nawman* (DE-416), *Tabbereer* (DE-418); and the *Waterman* (DE-740). In addition, the storm also ravages the Oiler *Nantahala* (AO-60) and the Fleet Tug *Jicarilla* (ATF-104). The Fleet returns to Ulithi for repairs. **(Pacific-China)** The U.S. Fourteenth Air Force and the XX Bomber Command (latter, previously utilized against Industrial targets in Japan) strike Hankow, Japan, devastating the supply depot and industrial center. Seventy-seven B29s and 200 Fourteenth Air Force Aircraft participate. **(Atlantic-Western Europe) 21st Army Group** In the **British Second Army** area, the 8th Corps enlarges its perimeter southward to the Meeuwen-Maeseyck line. **12th Army Group** In the **U.S. Ninth Army** area, **XIII Corps** sector, the 84th Division seizes Muellendorf and Wurm against light opposition. In the **U.S. First Army** area, the sectors of the 9th and 83rd Divisions are secured; the **VII Corps** is now able to move quickly to cover part of V Corps zone to meet enemy counterattack. In the **V Corps** area, Corps is ordered to maintain the Monschau-Butgenbach-Malmedy-Stavelot line. The 78th Division, reinforced by the 2nd Ranger Battalion and the 102nd Cavalry Group is assigned the task of retaining control of the road center north of Konzen and Paustenbach knoll. The Germans break through the Losheim Gap south of Butgenbach. RCT 26 is attached to 1st Division and deploys near Malmedy. The Germans enter Honsfeld and Beullingen and drive to Stavelot; however, the 30th Division subsequently retakes most of the lost terrain at Stavelot and holds firm at Habiemont and Stoumont. Peiper commits his Infantry against Stoumont on the 19th at first light. After the stunned Yanks lose Stavelot, Major Paul J. Solis orders his contingent to take to the hill above the town; some units retire to the road to Malmedy during the confusion, but Solis' detachment takes gasoline from the Francorchamps and makes Colonel's Peiper's day! Peiper's Panzers advance but the free-flowing gasoline zips into a deep cut in the road, followed by the zap of ignition and the Tanks begin to feel the heat of the gasoline they so desperately need. The Tanks are compelled to return to Stavelot, minus the 124,000 gallons that are stinging their tails; some of Peiper's 1st S.S. Panzers drive to seize the bridge at Trois Ponts to secure the gasoline stores there and then frolic to the Meuse, but standing in his way is an American 57-mm Antitankgun and its recently found crew (passing through with a contingent of the 7th Armored Division) which had been lost in the confusion during the movement of the 526th Armored Infantry Battalion; Major Robert T. Yates procures nets the crew and the gun is deployed on the Stavelot Road to greet any advancing enemy Armor. The 140 men, 10 machine guns and eight Bazookas of Yates' Company C, 51st Engineer Battalion are close behind guarding the two approach bridges. Just before 12:00, the Panzers approach; suddenly the lead Tank is crippled by a blast from the 57-mm, stalling the other Tanks long enough for the other troops to blow the bridges and withdraw into the town; a short duel destroys the gun and kills four of the crew; the Engineers and remainder of the crew retreat, but the Panzers watch the Ambleve and Salm bridges disintegrate and are forced to return to Stavelot. Again, Peiper is stalled and his Panzers have no easy way out of the Ambleve Valley. Later, his columns turn north, heading toward La Gleize under heavy skies and discover an intact bridge over the Ambleve at Cheneux; the 1st S.S. Panzers speed up until the skies clear and several U.S. Fighter Bombers stalk the Armor, destroying three Tanks and seven Half-Tracks, jamming the tiny path. Eventually the columns reach a point about three miles from Werbomont, the latchkey to Bastogne and Liege. Soon after, Peiper's men receive a surprise from Company A, 291st Engineer Battalion who blow the bridge at Lienne Creek; other nearby bridges are unable to carry the Tiger Tanks. Undaunted, Peiper's force continues to advance and reaches Chevron, only to be greeted by an ambush by the 30th Division which had been dispatched to sniff out Peiper; few Germans are alive to retreat as the contingent is decimated. By dark, the Armor of the 1st S.S. Panzers is over-extended along the roadways and has been under attack by the U.S. Ninth Air Force. Also, the 82nd Airborne is closing and the balance of the 30th Division is racing north from the Ninth Army area to cut off and exterminate the 1st S.S. Panzers. Meanwhile, the pre-dawn entry into Honsfeld is executed effortlessly; the German columns simply merged into the steady flow of U.S. traffic heading into the city and spread out; some units resist, but others flee the area, abandoning their equipment; the 3rd Battalion 254th Engineering Battalion repulses two attacks, but is forced to withdraw; it deploys northwest and is joined by units of the 99th Division; a Platoon of the 644th Tank Battalion arrives to intercept the Tanks, but they are over whelmed; most are captured or killed. Meanwhile, outside Hofen, the 3rd Battalion, 395th Regiment engages the 326th Volks Grenadier Division; assisted by Artillery and the 612th Tank Destroyer Battalion, the line is held, except for some Tanks which break through. Colonel Butler calls Artillery upon his own positions; it arrives along with his Reserves, one Platoon of I Company. A counterattack is launched and the Germans retire; the Yanks terminate the Sixth Panzer Army's attempt to reach Eupen; the Germans lose 554 known dead at Hofen, and 54 captured; the 3rd Battalion, under Colonel Butler sustains five killed and seven wounded. The defeat prevents the Germans from moving against Monschau; two Squadrons of the 366th Fighter Group lend some assistance, but it is doubtful that their strikes caused the Germans to halt the attack. During the night of the 17th-18th, the German 989th Regiment, supported by Tanks, launches a poorly coordinated attack to

seize Krinkelt and Rocherath from the 2nd Division; more than a Battalion of the 9th Regiment, several Platoons of the 23rd Regiment and the majority of the 38th Regiment under Colonel Francis H. Boos is deployed near the villages; the forces are bolstered by contingents of the 741st Tank Battalion and the weaponry of the 612th and 644th Tank Destroyer Battalions; at Elsenborn Ridge, the Artillery of the 2nd and 99th Divisions and additional Corps Artillery Battalions stand ready to help the Infantry meet the threat. As daylight peeks over the horizon, German Tanks and Infantry advance from the east to crush the American positions; the 1st Battalion, 9th U.S. Infantry, laying in the dense fog, receives the first pounding; it permits the enemy Armor to pass, then attacks it with Bazookas; others swivel and engage the enemy Infantry along the foxhole line. In concert, the guns of Eisenhorn pulverize the roads; the first assault is beaten back. At about 08:30, the fog lifts and another attack is underway; Company A is stormed; Lt. Stephen Truppner calls in U.S. Artillery on their positions; 12 men escape the barrage. Meanwhile, Company K is overrun; Captain Jack J. Garvey refuses to pull out because his Company is trapped; one Officer and ten men escape. Nearby, Companies B and C, operating on the left, hold their ground. Suddenly, Sherman Tanks arrive and the remnants of the 1st Battalion make it back to Krinkelt; about 240 men of the original Battalion and its attached units survive the six hours of non-stop fighting. However, the valiant stand buys time for the 38th Regiment meet the German onslaught; the 2nd Battalion under Lt. Colonel Jack K. Norris, holds the line and despite penetrating Rocherath, the Germans are driven back out. In conjunction, the Germans are also closing on Krinkelt; the German Tankers pause to confer with their Infantry, but the darkness is soon shattered as Company L, 23rd Infantry opens up, trimming the German force by forty men; the Tanks quickly disperse. At about 08:30, the Germans begin to make a serious move; Artillery interdicts and the attacks are broken; several Tanks penetrate to the south road to Wirtzfeld, but U.S. guns and bazookas decimate them also. In the **VIII Corps** sector, the 422nd and 423rd Regiments, 106th Division are cut off; an attempt to break out toward Schonberg is futile and the 7th Armored, which is preparing to attack to rescue them becomes furiously engaged at St. Vith, unable to assist the drive; north east of St. Vith, two Troops of the 87th Cavalry Reconnaissance Squadron and several Anti-aircraft Half-tracks must hold the line. German pressure pushes the delaying force back, however, reinforcements rush to the scene. C.C.B., 9th Armored Division dispatches two Companies of the 14th Tank Battalion and one Company of the 811th Tank Battalion, which roar into action and pick up the fight, joined by the 31st Tank Battalion, 7th Armored. Shermans rake the Panzers near Wallerode and the Tank Destroyers pound the enemy columns on the Hunnage road; the Yanks sustain light casualties and the Germans are thwarted; by day's end the Hunningen position is secure. Recht is taken by the Germans who also sever the St. Vith-Vielsalm Road at Poteau; Combat Command A, 7th Armored attacks and retakes the town. In conjunction, German forces move forward east of St. Vith, hitting the troops of the 38th Armored Infantry Battalion, led by Lt. Col. H.G. Fuller and support troops including the 168th Engineers and B Troop, 87th Cavalry; the German 294th Infantry makes inroads, but by dark all 1st ground is recaptured. Another fierce engagement is fought at Gouvy, southwest of Beho; the Headquarters Battery, 440th Antiaircraft Battalion, under Lt. Col. Robert O. Stone and a Light Tank Platoon approaches the town's railroad station to establish an Outpost, however, three German Tanks arrive at about the same time; the enemy expends all its ammunition, scoring some damage that damages an air compressor truck which blocks the road, causing the Tanks to retire. Stone's contingent discovers a huge supply of stores (afire) and 350 German P.O.W.s in a cage compound; the Yanks douse the flames quickly and set up a defense of the area. In the meantime, other 14th Cavalry Group elements had retreated to Petit Thier and are transferred from 106th Division control to that of 7th Armored. On the previous day, Colonel Devine had departed Poteau to reach the 106th Division Command Post, but the contingent is ambushed near Recht; Colonel Devine and two Officers escape. A fragmented group of the 18th and 32nd Squadrons are rounded up and joined with the one Platoon of the 820th Tank Destroyer Battalion; under Major J.L. Mayes, the improvised Task Force attacks toward Recht, but after moving only two hundred yards, enemy Bazooka fire shreds the lead Tank and an Armored Car. Suddenly, enemy Infantry bolts forward pushing the unit back into the village of Poteau; the Germans increase pressure and soon after the town is abandoned; many of the defenders make it to Vielsalm on foot. The Germans plow ahead, overrunning many of the 28th Division positions. The 5th Parachute Division gets contingents into the Kautenbach bridgehead. The 109th Regiment is forced to withdraw haphazardly after becoming disorganized; about 500 men and Officers have been lost during the three days of battle and the majority of its guns have been lost. However, the 109th had stalled the Germans short of the Ettelbruck crossing. The attacking 352nd Volks Grenadier Division is unable to reform until the 19th and is unable to launch a concentrated attack until the 20th. The 110th Regiment has been decimated; some survivors head west to link up with the 9th Armored, (Major General John W. Leonard) and others move south toward the Divisional Headquarters; a line of defense is established along the road to Bastogne. The defenders at Hosingen had continued to fight despite being out of ammunition, until forced to capitulate on the morning of the 18th; the 3rd Battalion defenders at Consthum raise the final resistance in the 28th Division zone. By 13:00, another heavy fog rolls over Consthum, cloaking the advancing German Tanks. A fierce Tank battle ensues, buying time for the Infantry, which exits the town and digs in to defend a battery of the 687th Field Artillery and subsequently makes a disciplined withdrawal to Nocher. The Germans advance near Bastogne and Houffalize, crashing through roadblocks of C.C.R., 9th Armored Division, along the Bastogne-St. Vith Road. Also, a counterattack is launched by two Task Forces of the 9th Armored Division to extricate the three isolated Companies. Intelligence had assessed German strength as light, however, on the previous night, just prior to his demise, General Moehring had transferred troops for an attack against Medernach; the concealed Germans pour withering fire on the advancing Americans; the rescue attempts are canceled and orders are forwarded for the troops of the battered 60th Reconnaissance Bn. to fight their way out; after a grueling three additional days, about 60 percent of the troops are guided to safety by volunteers; the unit sustains 231 casualties. C.C.B., 9th Armored Division and the 424th Regiment, 106th Division hold the bend of the Our River near Steinebruck; the German LXVI Corps has seized two of three bridges (previous day) on their list and move to seize the Steinebruck bridge; nearby, is the Troop D, 89th Cavalry Reconnaissance Squadron, bolstered by a Light Tank Platoon and an Assault Gun Platoon; they are dispersed between Steinebruck and Weppler. German pressure brings the Tanks into Steinebruck, but this exposes the left flank; the 423rd Regiment is stuck in Schnee Eifel and is unable to move. Engineers speed to the scene and blow the bridge. The Cavalry yells for aid and U.S. guns open up, but the Germans drive forward entering unoccupied Weppler, then decimating a Platoon on a nearby hill; five men escape. The Germans also take Steinebruck; calls for Tanks by Troop D are denied. C.C.B., 10th Armored and remnants of C.C.R., 9th Armored stays with VIII Corps to defend Bastogne. At Wiltz, the survivors of the 707th Tank Battalion composed of six disabled Tanks and five assault guns joins the recently arrived 44th Engineer Combat Battalion (Lt. Col. Clarion J. Kjeldseth) and the several scattered Tanks and Guns bolster the defenders; this force is composed of Bandsmen, Paymasters, Telephone Linesmen and Engineers. The perimeter is bolstered by elements of the 630th Tank Destroyer Battalion, 447th Antiaircraft Battalion, and some Armored Vehicles of the 28th Reconnaissance Battalion. The lopsided struggle ensues incessantly, but the overwhelming enemy Armor presses relentlessly, squeezing the beleaguered Yanks toward Weidingen. The defenders are ordered to blow the bridge at Weidingen, then retreat to more tenable positions behind the Wiltz River; without explanation, the bridge is not detonated, but the Americans get a break; the Panzer Lehr Reconnaissance Battalion reverses the direction of its attack and moves toward Bastogne, leaving Infantry of the 26th Volks Grenadier Division to carry the assault. On the following day, the 5th Parachute Division stumbles into a fight for Wiltz. Meanwhile, in the 4th Division zone, T.F. Chamberlain (Lt. Col. Thomas C. Chamberlain) dispatches a unit into the narrow Schwarz Erntz gorge to seize Mullerthal; it drives from Breitweiler, but must move its Tanks in single file; the Infantry remains under fire and only the lead Tank is positioned to fire. Upon reaching the T in the gorge road just outside of the town, the advance stops; in conjunction, T.F. Luckett is ordered to bypass the town and secure the wooded heights just north of Mullerthal; the remaining T.F. under Lt. Col. Miles L. Standish drives punishingly toward Berdorf, getting strafed by Aircraft fire as it moves. Contingents break into Berdorf and establish contact with the Tankers and the two Companies already in the town, but fierce German fire commences and a three-hour duel ensues. The battered Hotel Parc receives more punishing blows and its walls have been somewhat shattered; incredibly, the 60 defenders have sustained only one casualty and morale remains high as they have a cook who is preparing genuine meals in the cellar and delivering a primitive version of "meals on wheels" to the men at their firing positions. Another contingent of TF Standish unsuccessfully attempts to seize Hill 329; 40 men are wounded after the detachment is caught in a crossfire about half the distance to its objective. The third Task Force under Lt. Col. J. R. Riley seizes Scheidgen without opposition during the early afternoon. Soon after, the Task Force locates the Engineers that General Middleton had offered; a surprise attack is launched against Hill 313, but a heavy fog blankets the area before the objective can be taken; other units of TF Riley drive to Company G's Command Post at Lauterborn and two Tanks and a detachment of Riflemen advance to the hat factory at Echternach, establishing contact with Company E, 12th Regiment. Elements of the 4th Division eradicates infiltrators around Osweiler and Dickweiler, then with the assistance of Tanks and Cannoneers of the 176th Field Artillery Battalion, a strong enemy assault is repulsed. However, the 2nd Battalion, 22nd Infantry comes under fire by friendly Tanks as it approaches Osweiler; the Tankers believe the troops are German; after a serious exchange of fire for several hours, a contingent of the 2nd Battalion approaches under a white flag and the situation is rectified. Heated skirmishes also develop at Maisons Lelligen and Geyershof. In the **U.S. Third Army** area, **XX Corps** sector, Dillingen is secured except for isolated pockets by the 90th Division. The 5th Division takes over the Saarlautern bridgehead and springs forward, seizing ground. Meanwhile, the 95th Division, minus 378th Infantry, is taken out of combat; the 378th remains to hold Ensdorf. In the **XII Corps** sector, Nieder Gailbach is seized after a vicious fight by the 2nd Battalion, 320th Regiment, 35th Division. The 87th Division receives orders to break off its attack. **6th Army Group** In the **U.S. Seventh Army** area, **VI Corps** sector, contingents of the 45th Division become isolated subsequent to an attack against Budenthal. In the **French 1st Army** area, Ammerschwihr is seized by the 2nd Corps. In the 36th U.S. Division sector, near Mittelwihr, Sergeant Bernard Bell, 142nd Infantry, leads an eight man Squad against an enemy held school house. Bell startles and overpowers two guards without firing any shots, then captures 26 other troops in the cellar. On the following morning, an enemy Tank and Infantry troops attempt to retake the structure. Bell climbs to the second floor which is being pummeled by Tank fire and calls in Artillery forcing the Tank to retire. As the enemy troops are advancing, he redirects mortar fire and the hordes are repulsed with heavy casualties. With some assistance from a friendly Tank, Bell stands exposed and directs their fire toward enemy positions behind a wall. By the time the guns cease, the Germans lose 87 men killed and 32 captured, with Sergeant Bell singlehandedly accounting for about 20 killed and 33 captured; he receives the Medal of Honor for his heroism. **(Atlantic-England)** General Ridgway, who splits his time between England with the 17th Airborne (in training) and France, with the 82nd and 101st Airborne Divisions, receives word about the German offensive. Ridgway rounds up all available personnel and heads for France, instructing General Bud Miley to move out as soon as possible; fifty-five C-47s take off as a heavy fog sets in and all reach Reims safely after some harrowing landings in a similar fog. Ridgway, bolts from the Airfield in a Vehicle, heading for General Middleton's Command Post; as the Vehicle slows, Ridgway asks the driver if he is having trouble seeing and receives the response: "NOT TOO GOOD, I CAN'T SIR;" the General takes over the wheel and somehow reaches the destination safely. **(Atlantic-Eastern Europe)** Soviet Forces advance to the Hungarian Czechoslovakian border and cross along a large front.

December 19th 1944 — (Pacific-Philippines) LEYTE: The Japanese 35th Army becomes aware that no reinforcements or supplies are coming. In the **U.S. Sixth Army** area, **X Corps** sector, the area south of Limon is still embroiled in heavy skirmishing between the 127th Regiment, 32nd Division and the Japanese. The 1st Squadron, 12th Cavalry drives toward Lonoy on Highway 2 and takes a barrio. Meanwhile, in the **XXIV Corps** sector, the 307th Regiment, 77th Division drives toward Libongao and gains about three miles after tough fighting. Meanwhile, the 306th Regiment to the west gets elements to Palompon road. In addition, the 305th continues to defend Valencia. On LUZON, the Japanese receive a reprieve when unfavorable weather forces a postponement of the Third Fleet's planned Air strike. On MINDORO, the Western Visayan Task Force, bolstered by guerrillas, initiates a group of recon Patrols, which probe the south and west shores in addition to some nearby small islands. MINDORO : Patrols of the Western Visayan Task Force, guided by Guerrillas, reconnoiter the south, northwest and westrn shores of Mindoro and dispatch detachments to the offshore islands. **(Pacific-Burma)** In the **British Fourteenth Army** area, 4th Corps sector, Wunthe is seized by the Indian 19th Division. In the 33rd Corps sector, the British 2nd Division, which has moved from Kohima, fords the Chindwin at Kalewa and begins relieving the East African 11th Division. **(Pacific-East China Sea)** The U.S.S. *Redfish* (SS-395) sinks the Japanese Carrier *Unryu*. **(Atlantic-Western Europe)** General Eisenhower calls a conference at Verdun and requests improvisation to meet the German offensive. Patton's Third Army is the only Army in position to act immediately; it moves within 48 hours to relieve Bastogne and thwart the counterattack, then bolts to Houffalize. Soon after, Ike becomes concerned (subsequent to conversations with British Major General Sir John F. M. Whiteley) and confers with Bedell Smith; Smith in turn calls Bradley and informs him that Ike wants the 1st and Ninth Armies turned over to Montgomery, in case communications cease, feeling that Montgomery is in better position to command. Bradley reluctantly agrees; accompanying U.S. Air Commands transfer to British 2nd Tactical Air Force jurisdiction. It becomes official on the following day. **21st Army Group** Field Marshal Montgomery reacts to the German counter-offensive, aborting his plan to deploy the 30th Corps at Nijmegen, choosing to have them move to Louvain-St. Trond-Hasselt to defend the Meuse River line. **12th Army Group** The U.S. Ninth Army receives orders to take a defensive posture. In the **U.S. First Army** area, **V Corps** sector, the enemy is repelled at Krinkelt-Rocherath by the 2nd and 99th Divisions, which then pull back to defend Elsenborn Ridge; the 2nd Battalion possesses less than one Battalion of Sherman Tanks, proven inferior to the Panzers and Tigers of the Germans, but the veteran battle-tested 741st Tank Battalion has used the defensive terrain to good advantage. The 741st Tankers have knocked out about 27 enemy Tanks, striking when possible from the flank or the rear to bypass the heavy frontal armor plating; the 741st has lost 11 Shermans. Also, Infantry troops are always near the Tanks and they have an abundance of Bazookas to help stem the tide; the 801st Tank Destroyer Battalion (towed unit) had also been instructed to move to Elsenborn Ridge; its utilization has been tough; the mud has slowed it down considerably, frequently placing in the direct line of enemy fire. The 1st Division stays put east of Malmedy, holding firm. The bridge across the Amblève at Stavelot is destroyed by Engineers; the town is held by the 30th Division. German Infantry supported by Armor strikes at Stoumont; the guns of the 823rd Tank Destroyer Battalion are immobilized and the visibility is less than fifty yards preventing the troops from distinguishing the enemy. Desperate calls for flares are in vain; all eight guns are captured. Suddenly, ten promised Tanks of the 743rd Tank Battalion arrive on scene to assist, but the enemy power is overwhelming. In addition, there is no available Artillery support. After several hours of bitter fighting the town is abandoned; a Rifle Company to the south is isolated and the Company within Stoumont is decimated. The third Company 3rd Battalion is evacuated under cover of smoke. The 3rd Battalion commanded by Lt. Col. Roy D. Fitzgerald loses nearly all its equipment and 267 Officers and men; the Tank contingent under Lt. Walter D. Machts escapes unscathed, transporting many wounded Soldiers. The German Armor presses forward and the only Armor standing between the

119th Regimental Command Post and Liege is ten hastily assembled Sherman Tanks of the 743rd Tank Battalion, whose ammunition is nearly expended. As the Americans retire, Tanks are called in but they are equipped with unfamiliar British radios and few of these First Army's Shermans are battle ready. Lt. Col. Robert Herlong, 1st Battalion Commander, decides to make his stand at a narrow curve beyond Targnon and Stoumont Station; the Germans are delayed, but not stopped. However, again the lack of fuel holds up the enemy. In conjunction, the 2nd Battalion is releasing its zone to the 82nd Airborne and will rush to assist the 1st Battalion, 119th Regiment. Peiper's Tanks pull back to Stoumont. The **XVIII Airborne Corps** assumes positions south of the Amblève and deploys near Houffalize, a primary road center linking Bastogne and St. Vith. Roads are the key to the battle of the Bulge because the terrible weather and dense forests mandate Armor remain on the highways. The 82nd relieves the 30th Division elements at Werbomont. By midnight, the 505th places a Battalion in the villages of Basse-Bodeux and Haute-Bodeux, which bolsters the Yank force at Trois Ponts; in conjunction, the 504th Paratroop Regiment moves two Battalions into Rahier. By dawn of the 20th the 82nd Airborne has an effective screen running north, south, east and west of Werbomont, but the enemy is still elusive to the Airborne. In the **VIII Corps** sector, the beleaguered 422nd and 423rd Regiments, 106th Division find their situation deteriorating badly in the Schnee Eifel. Meanwhile, east of St. Vith, contingents of the 7th and 9th Armored Divisions fight tenaciously, withstanding the enemy advance. Reconnaissance contingents of the 2nd and 116th Panzer Divisions advance through a small opening between Houffalize and Noville; they are trailed by two Corps of the Fifth Panzer Army. Elements of the 7th Armored stand resolute; heavy fighting ensues near Noville, the German 2nd Panzer Division is unable to breach the Houffalize-Bastogne road until the night of the 20th. In conjunction, the 116th Panzer Division contingents drive toward the Ourthe bridge near Bertogne; the Yanks blow the bridge, stalling the enemy. Scouts discover a Bailey Bridge at Ortheuville, but General Krueger (Fifth Panzer Corps Commander) orders the 116th to halt at Salle, three miles from the bridge; subsequently, Krueger shifts his LVIII Panzer Corps ordering it to attack north. Also, the Germans have been sustaining heavy losses as they press the 9th Armored; the new Commanding Officer of the 276th Volks Grenadier Division, General Dempwolff, awaits an assault gun Company, before continuing the attack; he is informed that the train which is transporting the unit has derailed; the attack is postponed until the 20th. On the 20th, the overwhelming strength of the Germans takes Waldbillig from the exhausted Yanks. In the 28th Division zone, the Regimental Band boldly attempts to withstand a severe attack, but the Germans drive the Bandsmen from the high ground; the action exposes the precarious positions of the 44th Engineers. As the Germans close against the Engineers, they sustain heavy casualties, but the Yanks take high losses and lack replacements; the beleaguered Assault Gunners have fought nearly non-stop for four days and now their ammunition is almost exhausted; the Engineers pound the attackers. By dusk, the Engineers and the assault gunners pull back into Wiltz, still expecting the arrival of a 10th Armored Combat Team; their losses stand at four Officers and 150 men; the vicious contest at the Erpeldange crossroads has been won and lost four times. In conjunction with the withdrawal, the bridge is finally blown. The three surviving assault guns are positioned to guard the

blown bridge, however, the fate of these men is never determined. The battered 28th Division is ordered to pull out of Wiltz and make it back to friendly positions; its 112th Regiment is attached to the beleaguered 106th Division; Headquarters evacuates the town during the morning, moving to Sibret, southwest of Bastogne. The withdrawal is harrowing; the troops encounter mines and roadblocks as well as tremendous pockets of enemy fire; the collapse of Wiltz terminates the 28th Division's delaying action in front of Bastogne. Casualties are high for both side, but the Germans lose more precious time and devour more of their dwindling fuel supplies. Also, the 101st Airborne completes its harrowing journey, reaching besieged Bastogne, which is nearly totally cut off; C.C.B., 10th Armored (Col. William Roberts) and elements of C.C.R., 9th Armored are on the scene also. The 101st raced from Camp Mourmelon through rain and snow for 107 miles; an attached unit, the 7055th Tank Destroyer Battalion (Lt. Col. Clifford Templeton) is equipped with new 76-mm self propelled guns. Also, the 755th Armored Field Artillery Bn. (Lt. Col. William F. Hartman) and the 969th Field Artillery Bn. bolsters the defenses of Bastogne. Germans dressed in American garb overrun the 101st Airborne Division Service area at Mande-St. Etienne; many of the Quartermaster and Ordnance troops escape to the VIII Corps sector, however, nearly all of the Division's Medical Company is captured or annihilated; eight Officers and 44 men survive, leaving the besieged defenders with the barest of medical help. Fortunately, more than one hundred trucks including those of C.C.B. escape destruction, but few return with supplies as the knot is tightened on the 101st; by the 21st, C.C.B., 10th Armored and C.C.R., 9th Armored will have a combined strength of about 40 Medium Tanks, supported by Cavalry Assault Guns, Antiaircraft weapons, Light Tanks and the able 705th Tank Destroyer Battalion; General McAuliffe commands the Bastogne defenses; the 502nd Paratroop Infantry deploys to the north near Longchamps and Sonne-Fontaine and the 506th stretches in the southern sector from Foy to points along the Bourcy-Bastogne rail line; the 501st Paratroop Regiment digs in facing east, along the rail line and south of Neffe; in conjunction, the 2nd Battalion, 327th Glider Infantry Regiment prepares to hold the area around Marvie near the Bastogne-Arlon highway; the 326th Glider Infantry Battalion extends west from the Neufchateau road. In Bastogne, the situation is deteriorating as the roads are clogged; General Middleton gives permission for General Cota to withdraw his beleaguered remnants of 28th Division from the town. By the following day, General Cota advises the 4th Armored to keep its Vehicles out of the grid-locked town. In the 2nd Division sector, at Rocherat, Technician 4th Grade Truman Kimbro, scouting for a Squad which is to mine a strategic crossroad, spots heavy enemy presence, including a Tank at the location. Kimbro makes two attempts to lead the Squad forward; however, withering fire halts it. He goes on alone, carrying the mines, receiving a grievous wound as he crawls, but forcing himself to advance and lay the mines. More intense fire saturates the area and his body is virtually riddled with rifle and machine gun shells. His actions delay the German Armor at the cost of his life; he receives the Medal of Honor posthumously. In the 4th Division zone, T.F. Luckett advances to secure the heights above Mullerthal; heavy casualties cause the attack to be aborted; the Task Force moves to guard the road way to south of the town. In conjunction, T.F. Chamberlain advances to Consdorf. Meanwhile, Task Forces Riley and Standish reinitiate their attacks in the vicinity of Berdorf and Echternach;

tedious house-to-house fighting erupts at Berdorf and Tanks are committed to blow the enemy out; the Germans hold tight and reinforcements are rushing to their aid. German held Hill 329 comes under another attack; severe casualties are sustained by the Americans and the assault is halted to initiate evacuation of the wounded. The lengthy Convoy receives word that the Germans control the road to Consdorf, forcing a detour to Berdorf. Heavy fighting develops as Tanks engage the 2nd Battalion, 423rd Regiment in a night-long battle to preserve Consdorf. At Echternach, Company E, unaware that permission had been given for them to evacuate, gets trapped; two volunteers brave the heavy fire and speed to Lauterborn to get Tanks, but they are told that Tanks can not be risked in the dark; the volunteers are the last men to leave the besieged town. Company E is told to fight its way out, but Germans overrun Echternach. Also, Engineers depart Scheidgen and secure Hill 313 without incident. The German LXXX Corps Commander, General Franz der Infanterie Beyer concludes that his forces are too weakened to continue the attack; the Corps takes a defensive stance, but on the following day he orders his 212th and 276th Volks Grenadier Divisions to annihilate all U.S. troops behind their line, while simultaneously commencing small attacks. The enemy supplies are also running low and the gap between it and the LXXXV Corps is becoming deeper. In **U.S. Third Army** area, a Provisional Corps is established by extracting former First Army contingents south of the Ardennes (4th and 10th Armored Divisions, less C.C.B.); its task, to check the German thrust on the southern flank and simultaneously seal a large gap existing between it and contingents of the 9th and 28th Divisions deployed near Ettelbruck. In accord with orders from Eisenhower, Patton's Saar offensive had been halted to allow Third Army to swing toward Bastogne; the **XX Corps** pulls back from its positions east of the Saare; however, the 5th Division retains terrain east of the Saare at Saarlautern. The 378th Infantry, 95th Division is directed to withdraw from Ensdorf. **III Corps** receives orders to advance toward the southern flank of the Germans at the Bulge. In the **XII Corps** sector, the 35th Division halts to receive relief. Meanwhile, the 4th Armored and 80th Divisions revert to III Corps. **6th Army Group** The U.S. Seventh Army Group is ordered to take a defensive posture. In the **XV Corps** sector, Fort Simershof is abandoned by the Germans, along with the town of Hottviller; however, the 44th Division still receives opposition from Fort Schiesseck. In the 79th Divisional sector, elements attack enemy positions near Berg along the outer defenses of the Siegfried Line. During the heavy skirmishing, Sergeant Robert E. Gerstung, Company H, 313th Regiment, stays in position with his supporting machine gun for eight hours despite all other members of his crew being wounded from the intense fire. After expending his ammunition, Gerstung scurries through open terrain under fire to secure more ammunition and resumes battle. His machine gun jams, but he improvises and crawls fifty yards to confiscate another machine gun, which is lying silent since its crew had been killed. The Germans send a Tank after him, but although it rips a glove from his hand with an armor piercing shell, he doesn't budge. As the attack is ordered to cease, Gerstung stays behind to offer cover fire then withdraws with the dependable machine gun tucked in his arm and a belt of ammunition around his neck. He is finally struck by a mortar shell, but continues to crawl to safety; he becomes the recipient of the Medal of Honor. **(Atlantic-Italy)** In the **British Eighth Army** area, the 5th Corps reignites its offensive during the night; it secures the area around Faenza, where the 56th Division will be able to

deploy. The Canadian 1st Division attacks after dark, pushing out of the Naviglio Canal bridgehead; by the night of the 20th, the Germans are driven back across the Senio River by the Canadian 1st and 5th Armored Divisions.

U.S. prisoners at St Vith.

December 20th 1944 — Pacific-Philippines) On LEYTE, **U.S. Sixth Army** area, **X Corps** sector, the 12th Cavalry, 1st Cavalry Division drives toward Kananga. The 127th Regiment, 32nd Division eliminates final enemy resistance in its sector, south of Limon. In **XXIV Corps** sector, the 307th Infantry, 77th Division takes Libongao; later during the night, the 77th's Artillery commences its heaviest bombardment since landing. Meanwhile, strong enemy fire holds up the 2nd Battalion, 32nd Infantry, 7th Division, preventing it from joining with 511th Paratroop Infantry, 11th Airborne. MINDORO: U.S. Planes initiate operations from Hill Airdrome. In other activity, about 50 Guerrillas, supported by a small contingent of the 503rd Paratroop Infantry, embark Agustin to Pasugi-Pianag by boat, encountering no enemy. On LUZON, the Japanese maintain their attempt to get the P.O.W.s out of the Philippines; trucks roll out of Olongapo, transporting P.O.W.s to San Fernando, with more following on December 21st. **(Pacific-Burma)** In the **British Fourteenth Army** area, 4th Corps sector, Kawlin is taken by the Indian 19th Division. **(Pacific-China)** General Wedemeyer strongly suggests that Y-Force resume its attack toward Wanting; however, this effort to attack and enjoin the CAI Force on the Salween Front does not begin until the end of December. General Wedemeyer meets with leaders of India Burma Theater and the China Theater in Kunming to explain his proposal to defend Chungking and Kunming (ALPHA). **(Atlantic-Western Europe) 21st Army Group** The U.S. First and Ninth U.S. Armies come under British Field Marshal Montgomery's control. Montgomery appears at General Hodges' 1st Army Headquarters before 13:00. He declines an offer by Hodges to join him for lunch, having brought his own food in a lunch pail. Montgomery chooses to eat alone. Montgomery also declines use of the large detailed First Army maps, preferring to use his own British map, which he carries crumpled in his pocket. Montgomery makes his visits to First Army Headquarters almost every day. Field Marshall Montgomery prepares to "tidy up" his front before initiating his counterattack. General Collins' VII Corps is preparing to attack from the north; however, he deploys his Corps (under Montgomery) along a retaining wall. In the **U.S. First Army** area, **VII Corps** sector, 5th Armored Division re-initiates its attack against the Roer, driving into Untermaubach and establishing a roadblock on the Winden-

Untermaubach Road. In **V Corps** sector, the 2nd and 99th Divisions withdraw to Elsenborn Ridge area. There is some penetration by the enemy near Wirtzfeld, where elements of the 99th isolate and then annihilate them. The 1st Division repels an attack in the Butgenbach-Faymonville region and it also secures the area south of Eupen. At one point, enemy Tanks penetrate the line. Corporal Henry F. Warner, 2nd Battalion, Antitank Company, destroys the first Tank with a scoring shot and then takes out the second with another round. While still under direct fire, a third Tank approaches to within five yards of his position. His gun jams and he is forced to tangle with the Tank with only a pistol. He jumps from his hole and engages the Tank Commander who is standing in the turret, killing him; the Tank retires. On the following morning, another Tank, a Mark IV, is driving directly toward Warner who fires another round and sets the Tank afire. While attempting to reload and get off another round, a burst of fire takes him down, killing him. His courageous actions in the face of enemy fire greatly aided in repulsing the attacks; Warner receives the Medal of Honor posthumously. In the **XVIII Corps (Airborne)** sector, the 30th Division and attached C.C.B., 3rd Armored Division assault the enemy at Stoumont and La Gleize, encountering heavy opposition. Other contingents of the 30th stand tough at Malmedy and Stavelot. C.C.B. is separated into three Task Forces, Lovelady, McGeorge and Jordan. Task Force Lovelady sets up roadblocks between La Gleize and Trois Ponts; Task Force McGeorge and the 117th Regiment's Company K move against German positions at La Gleize; Task Force Jordan drives from the north along the Spa road, but German fire halts its progress in front of Stoumont. In conjunction, Company B, 1st Battalion, 119th Regiment and Tanks from the 740th Tank Battalion ramrod through five minefields and reach the western fringes of Stoumont by darkness; a heavy fog settles over the area and Colonel Herlong digs in for the night; two Tanks have been lost, however, one is turned over and used as an obstacle; in conjunction, Companies B and C are moving against a sanatorium, located near the town. Just before midnight, the Germans attack and a vicious battle ensues; the Germans secure the sanatorium and about 30 men from Company B are captured. The heavy fighting continues throughout the night; U.S. Tank reinforcements arrive to bolster the 1st Battalion; about half of Companies B and C are lost, however, the Germans are further strangled. Peiper is constricted, the roadblocks hold and Task Force Lovelady and the Yanks in Stavelot have severed the German line of supply. Meanwhile, C.C.A., 3rd Armored strings out defensively near Eupen and the remainder of the Division prepares to attack to secure the Bastogne-Liege highway between Manhay and Houffalize; three Task Groups or more appropriately, Reconnaissance Teams under Lt. Col Prentice E. Yeomans, composed of a Reconnaissance Troop, a Battery of Armored Field Artillery and a Platoon of Light Tanks gets the Task. Also, Colonel Robert L. Howze has a reserve force composed of an Armored Infantry Battalion, tow Companies of Light Tanks and one Medium Tank Company, supported by a Company of Engineers. A contingent of Tanks under Lt. Denniston Averill (7th Armored Division) is knocked out at Samree and the town is taken by the Germans; they quickly use the gasoline stores to refuel their Armor. Task Force Kane advances to Manhay and pushes elements to Malempre. Orders come down to retake Samree. The 82nd Airborne is rushing forward to assist friendly forces at Vielsalm-St. Vith; contingents are tightening the noose around Peiper's neck by encircling most

of the Germans at their Cheneux, southeast of Stoumont. General Gavin eventually gets a clearer picture of the confusing operations he dispatches the 504th to Cheneux and orders the 505th to move to Trois Ponts. The 1st Battalion sends Companies against Cheneux at 19:30; blistering fire from the 2nd S.S. Panzer Grenadier Regiment scorches their ranks, pushing the troops back on two successive attacks as they attempt to charge up naked terrain. Meanwhile, in the **VIII Corps** sector, the Germans relentlessly pound the defenders (7th Armored Division, 106th Division, C.C.B., 9th Armored, and the 112th Infantry, 28th Division) at St. Vith. At Bastogne, contingents of the 10th Armored Division, 101st A/B Division and the 705th Tank Destroyer Battalion crash through an encirclement and deploy defensively to halt the enemy advance. The 501st and 506th Paratroop Regiments are struck hard at the Bourcy-Bastogne railway by the 26th Volks Grenadier Division. A Patrol of the 506th discovers a German contingent to the rear of their right flank; soon after, Companies D and F attack to close the gap at the rails in concert with the Artillery of the 501st's guns which forbid movement on the side; the nasty contest ensues for about three hours and concludes with the Germans heading into the guns of the 501st; about 50 enemy troops are killed and 85 are captured. The Germans seize Noville during the afternoon and by midnight, they move into Ortheuville; contingents of the 158th Engineer Combat Bn. damage the bridge with Howitzer fire as they retire toward St. Hubert, but the enemy Armor speeds across heading toward Tenneville. German Rear-guards face Bastogne to defend against a U.S. counterattack. Colonel Sink's (Commander 506th Parachute Infantry) 1st Battalion, under Lt. Col James L. LaPrade, is hard hit at Noville, but contingents of this force aid the defenders at the rail lines. The Germans stay in place on the 21st waiting for fuel. At Marvie, a strenuous Tank battle erupts and the town falls to the Americans. A deep freeze blankets the area on the 21st, giving some aid to the defenders. About 25 miles southeast of Bastogne, the Germans are advancing against the 109th Regiment, 28th Division's positions at Ermsdorf where it is supporting C.C.A., 9th Armored and at Ettelbruck-Oberfeulen. The 28th Division's Headquarters personnel and stragglers of its 110th Regiment attempt to hold the Neufchateau-Bastogne highway, but the enemy stampede forces abandonment by early the following morning. Engineers obstruct the highways and destroy the bridges as far west as St. Hubert. In the 4th Division zone, the Germans press at Berdorf and Waldbillig; at Berdorf, the scant defending force of Company F, 12th Regiment still retains the Parc hotel, but the Germans continue to halt progress of Task Force Standish with fierce house-to-house fighting; a subsequent counterattack gains the German 1st Battalion, 423rd Regiment all lost terrain. Berdorf is evacuated, but the 4th Division contingents fight hard to get away; the Germans have the road to Consdorf blocked. Task Force Riley send elements forward to Echternach to rescue Company E, but the advance is fruitless; it is believed that the trapped defenders surrender late in the day; German Generalmajor Franz Sensfuss (C.O. 212th Volks Grenadier Division), infuriated by the defiant defenders leads the 212th Fusilier Battalion in the attack, getting slightly wounded; Company E, composed of 111 men and Officers and 21 men attached to Company H are taken. Also, the Company F outpost at Birkelt, surrenders after holding firm since the 16th of December. The German thrust through Waldbillig is stopped. Dickweiler and Bech also hold; in conjunction the 10th Armored's C.C.A. retains control of Eisenborn. The German attack is stalling badly and the Americans are forming new and stronger lines of defense to meet the threat; in this sector, the 212th and 276th Volks Grenadier Divisions are running well behind schedule. **12th Army Group** In the **U.S. Third Army** area, the **III Corps** transfers its Headquarters from Metz to Arlon, Belgium. At Bastogne, contingents of C.C.B., 4th Armored Division force their way toward Bastogne, contacting units of the 10th Armored and 101st Airborne Divisions. Meanwhile, the 80th Division deploys in the heights north and northeast of Mersch, taking reserve defensive positions. In the newly formed Provisional Corps sector, Patton attaches the 5th Division, C.C.A., 9th Armored Division and RCT 109th of the 28th Division to infuse additional strength. At Echternach, Tanks are committed to assist the 4th Division in its rescue attempt to extricate isolated units; the endeavor is futile. In the **XX Corps** sector, the 378th Regiment, 95th Division concludes its pull-back from Ensdorf, taking new positions west of the Sarre. **6th Army Group** In the **U.S. Seventh Army** area, the fresh 77th Division is organized as Task Force Herron. In the XX Corps sector, the 100th Division seizes Fort Schiesseck; the Corps then moves toward St. Avold where it will release the XII Corps to support the fighting in the Ardennes. **(Eastern Atlantic)** The LST 359 is sunk by an enemy Submarine. In addition, the Destroyer Escort *Fogg* (DE-57) is damaged by an enemy Submarine torpedo. **(Atlantic-Italy)** **15th Army Group** In the **British Eighth Army** area, 5th Corps sector, the British 56th Division moves north from Faenza to clear the region between the Lamone River and the Naviglio Canal. In the Canadian 1st Corps sector, the Canadian 1st Division and 5th Armored Division mount a night assault and drive the Germans back behind the Senio River.

Patton's Third Army moving to lift the siege of Bastogne.

December 21st 1944 — (Pacific-Philippines) LEYTE: In the **U.S. Sixth Army** area, the Ormoc Valley comes under control of the U.S. as the X and XXIV Corps converge at 16:45, south of Kananga; Highway 2 is clear from Ormoc to Pinamopoan. Kananga, in the X Corps sector, falls to the 12th Cavalry, which subsequently sends Patrols which encounter the 77th Division further south. In the **XXIV Corps** sector, elements of the 306th Regiment, 77th Division seize a ridge above the Togbong River; however, the enemy forces a withdrawal. During the heated combat, P.F.C. George Benjamin Jr., Company A, is trailing behind his Company when a Rifle Platoon, supporting a Light Tank, stops moving, due to ferocious enemy fire which is detaining an entire Battalion. Benjamin bolts to the Tank, shouting for his Platoon to follow. He charges singlehandedly, armed only with his Rifle, killing one enemy soldier and advancing to a machine gun nest where he anni-

hilates the crew. He advances further, still carrying his radio upon his back, and kills two more enemy troops, but a burst of enemy fire wounds him mortally. Lying on his death bed, he continues worrying about his Platoon and calls for the Operations Officer to give him all the details of enemy positions which he had discovered prior to being struck. P.F.C. Benjamin receives the Medal of Honor posthumously for his extraordinary heroism. On MINDORO, the Japanese attack a supply Convoy, destroying the LSTs 460 and 749, by Suicide Planes. In addition, a Kamikaze damages the Destroyer *Foote* (DD-511). On Luzon, the Japanese holding the P.O.W.s at Olongapo are instructed to murder all American prisoners not well enough to be moved to Japan. Subsequently, fifteen men are brought to a mass grave site; seven unsuspecting wounded Americans are bound and decapitated; bayonets massacre the other eight; all are dumped into the unmarked grave. **(Pacific)** The U.S.S. *Albacore* (SS-218) and the *Scamp* (SS-277), both Submarines, are officially reported missing and presumed lost. **(Pacific-Burma)** In the N.C.A.C. area, the Chinese 114th Regiment, 38th Division continues to advance, nearing the U.S. 5332nd Brigade. In the ALFSEA area, the British 15th Corps gains ground as it advances on the Arakan front. Admiral Mountbatten calls a meeting of Commanders to take advantage of the situation. **(Atlantic-Western Europe)** **21st Army Group** The British 51st Division reinforces the U.S. Ninth Army, which enlarges its sector. In the **U.S. First Army** sector, C.C.A., and C.C.B., 5th Armored Division, secure about half of Schneidhausen and Untermaubach respectively. In the **V Corps** sector, at Monschau, contingents of both the 9th Division and 102nd Cavalry Group capture most enemy troops still operating in the area. The enemy in the 99th Division zone is struck by heavy Artillery fire that disorients its formations. At Elsenborn Ridge, the enemy is again repelled by the 1st Division. In the **XVIII Corps (A/B)** sector, defenses are fortified in front of Neufchateau and Arlon. Also, lines are strengthened at St. Hubert, Libramont, Sibret and Martelange. Middleton orders his troops to dig in and hold the positions at Arlon and Neufchateau for at least 40 hours to buy time for the advancing reinforcements and to protect the Corps right flank. Martelange is held until dusk; Company B, 299th Engineer Combat Bn. blows two bridges and withdraws, while under attack by Tanks and Infantry. Contingents of the 28th Division, 333rd Field Artillery Bn. and the 630th Tank Destroyer Bn. (using rifles) defend at Sibret; elements of the nearby 771st Field Artillery Bn. pour fire upon the enemy also. Premature reports give the town to the Germans, but the Yanks hang tough, delaying the Germans several hours before being compelled to withdraw to Vaux-lez-Rosieres. C.C.B., 7th Armored Division, pulls out of St. Vith, while C.C.A. engages and stops the Germans near Poteau; C.C.R. clears the Vielsalm-Poteau Road. The 35th Engineer Combat Bn. holds the line between Bastogne and St. Hubert; other units move to hold Libramont, including the 158th Engineer Combat Bn. and the 724th Engineer Base Depot Co. arrive to bolster the perimeter, delaying the Germans there; the Panzer Lehr Division makes slow progress. Meanwhile, the 82nd Airborne's 504th Paratroop Infantry throws the Germans out of Cheneux and Monceau, driving them back across the Ambleve River; the 505th fortifies its lines at the Salm River and the 508th reinforced by the 325th Glider Infantry deploys along the Vielsalm-Hebronval-Regne line without encountering the enemy. Meanwhile, elements of the 82nd Airborne Division make contact with other U.S. troops near St. Vith. The 30th Division, which holds resolutely at Malmedy and Stavelot, is not able to dislodge the Germans at Stoumont and La Gleize.

German Armor advance to positions of the 120th Regiment near Malmedy, forcing elements to retire toward a nearby factory. Sergeant Francis S. Currey takes a Bazooka and destroys one Tank, then darts toward a house containing three Germans, killing or wounding all. Soon after he observes five Yanks who are immobilized by enemy fire originating from three Tanks. Currey dashes to an abandoned Vehicle, grabs antitank grenades and bombards the Tanks he then commandeers a Half-trac and attacks the house where the Tanker has taken refuge. The beleaguered Yanks are able to withdraw under his cover fire and Currey is able to safely withdraw; he receives the Medal of Honor. The Germans are repulsed by the 99th Regiment (dubbed the Norwegians) west of Malmedy. Lt. Col. Harold D. Hansen's 99th tears the enemy up with mortars, machine guns and Artillery. In other activity, the 3rd Armored Division neutralizes the enemy advance at Hotton and maintains its operation to gain the Manhay-Houffalize road. About 200 men of the Divisional service detachments and C.C.R. are stationed in buildings east of the Ourthe in the middle of Hotton; a Platoon of the 51st Engineer Battalion, supported by Antitank Guns and a Sherman Tank are deployed on the west bank and in the middle is a non-vehicular class 70 bridge; slightly south, a detachment of Engineers guards a footbridge at Hampteau. Enemy Tanks approach and knock out several Tanks, then enemy Infantry advances taking some buildings until small arms fire and bazookas check their progress. Germans, wearing U.S. uniforms overpower the unsuspecting troops at the footbridge. Heavy skirmishing continues , but the stunned Americans regroup and a subsequent counterattack by Colonel Howze helps get the town back. The Germans abandon their positions. Later, the Commander of the 116th Panzers pays great tribute to the Engineers who defend at Hotton. In conjunction, the attacks by the three Task Forces on the previous day which had taken a toll on the 116th Panzers is due credit and also, Howze's grand charge which catches Kampfgruppe Bayer's flank by surprise. **12th Army Group** In the **U.S. Third Army** area, **VIII Corps** sector, Bastogne is under total siege by the Germans, who are beginning to cross the Neufchateau-Bastogne road, driving westward. The defenders are holding with the barest of necessities and weather conditions impede rescue attempts. The German 77th Regiment under Generalmajor Heinz Kokott and the 902nd Panzer Grenadier Regiment slash at the 501st's 3rd Battalion positions throughout the day, but an anticipated second and heavier thrust does not come to fruition; the 902nd is ordered to move west to join the Panzer Lehr. Meanwhile, the 2nd Battalion 327th Glider Regiment at Marvie experiences some sporadic activity from enemy Infantry and Tanks, but nothing serious; the Germans claim that they had executed some "miscarried operations" in the area; it is presumed that the Tanks of C.C.B., strung along the Arlon road is responsible for the misfortune of the German 901st failures; in conjunction, a contingent of the 327th, dispatched to attempt rescue of survivors of the Divisional Medical units comes under attack and becomes isolated, but the troops fight their way back to the Battalion. The 2nd Battalion C.C.A., 10th Armored Division attacks Waldbillig; however, the Germans repel the assault and hold the town. Further west, Kampfgruppe Kunkel drives toward Senonchamps where Lt. Colonel Barry D. Browne's 420th Field Artillery Battalion, is plastering German positions north and east of Bastogne; the U.S. 755th and 969th Field Artillery Battalions man a roadblock near Villeroux about 2,500 yards south of Senochamps.

As the Germans advance north from Sibret, they encounter

the 771st Field Artillery Battalion, but it doesn't fight, choosing to abandon its weapons and run. Fortunately, Team Pyle, a patched up group formed by remnants of C.C.R. and straggler Infantry, approaches the Neufchateau road; a fierce fight erupts as Kunkel's Krauts run into the ragged Yanks and their 14 Tanks; the Americans are pushed back toward Senonchamps, but again valuable time is bought. The 755th and 969th Howitzer Battalions get a reprieve and make a disciplined pull back to Senonchamps. Visibility becomes less than poor and fortuitously, Company A, 755th and the Headquarters Battery of the 969th pours out a thunderous belt of machine gun fire that momentarily stuns the attacking Germans and buys a few more precious moments. At about the same time, two straggler U.S. Tanks stumble into the battle, lay down fire and move on; this saves the rear-guard; only one Howitzer has been lost (due to a mortar) during the pullback to Senonchamps. As the Germans close for the kill at Senonchamps, they encounter Team Pyle, which has drawn a line in front of the Artillery. The Germans form for assault, but the U.S. fire power deters movement and the attack is postponed until the following day. At Tillet, Colonel Paton's 58th Armored Field Artillery Battalion becomes surrounded and he requests help; General Middleton refers the S.O.S. to Bastogne, but Colonel Browne (Team Browne), under attack also, is unable to reach Paton; a small contingent, Team Yantis moves out to give assistance; on the night of the 22nd, Lt. Yanis' detachment is sent to get more ammunition and is ambushed at Pinsamont, forcing the contingent to abandon its Vehicles. In conjunction, a Platoon of thirty stragglers, formed by an Air Corps Officer, holds positions several hundred yards n front of the guns at Senonchamps and thwarts the German advances for 48 hours ending the valiant stand after all men are killed or captured. Colonel Browne uses the Shermans (brought in by Teams Pyle and Van Kleef) to their greatest advantage; nine Tanks point their barrels toward the woods west of the Batteries; four pound enemy positions to the south and the other four deploy on the Villereux road. Successive enemy attacks are turned back and Team Van Kleef reports the death of 18 enemy Tanks. As the day progresses the weather becomes more foul and visibility gets worse. Colonel Browne informs General McAuliffe that his forces are taking severe casualties; Company C, 327th Glider Infantry and Team Watts, composed of about 100 men are dispatched to bolster the dwindling force. Near Osweiler and Consdorf, the Germans are thrown back by the 4th Division; however, elements of the 4th, holding at Echternach, have lost communications with the main body. C.C.A., 9th Armored and C.C.R., 10th Armored Division are combined, establishing C.C.X., 10th Armored. During the heavy fighting near Gruffingen, Corporal Horace M. Thorne, Troop D, 89th Cavalry Reconnaissance Squadron, leads a Patrol to dislodge Germans from nearby woods when the Patrol encounters a Mark III Tank. American Tanks disable the enemy Tank and Thorne reacts quickly, shooting two of the enemy as they attempt to jump from the Tank. He begins crawling forward amidst fierce enemy machine gun fire, getting close enough to lob two grenades into the open turret, killing the other two Tankers. Improvising, he returns to his Patrol to get a machine gun and then mounts it atop the rear of the Tank and drives two enemy machine gun crewmen from their positions; his gun jams and a subsequent burst of enemy fire kills him instantly. Meanwhile, the 35th Division is totally relieved in the 10th Corps sector; the Corps establishes a forward Command Post in Luxembourg. **(Atlantic-Eastern Europe)** Troops of the Third Ukrainian Front continue to advance southwest of Budapest between the Danube and Lake Balaton. The Germans continue pulling out of the Balkans. Berlin confirms the heavy fighting in this region. General Patton reports Third Army casualties for the period of Nov. 8th-Dec. 21st. at 53,904. In addition, material losses stand at Light Tanks 198; Medium Tanks 507; Guns 116. German losses: Medium Tanks 946; Panther or Tiger Tanks 485; Guns 2,216. **(Atlantic-Italy) 15th Army Group** In the **U.S. Fifth Army** area, British 13th Corps sector, the British 6th Armored assumes command of M. dell'Acqua Saluta-M. del Verro, relieving the British 78th Division. In the **British Eighth Army** area, Polish 2nd Corps sector, the 5th Kresowa Division mops up east of the Senio. The 5th Corps continues to advance north, parallel to the Naviglio Canal, clearing enemy resistance as it moves. The Canadian 1 Corps secures Bagnacavallo and advances to the Senio River, but the Germans hold commanding positions near the river on both flanks.

December 22nd 1944 — (Pacific-(Hawaii) A Honolulu newspaper prints two photographs (released by Air Corps) showing U.S. Bombers over an island in the Pacific. Admiral Nimitz becomes infuriated as the island designated "K" conspicuously exposes Mt Suribachi on Iwo Jima. Subsequently, Tokyo Rose broadcasts the exact units which are to land there, and a later discovery of a dead Japanese Soldier's diary (taken on Iwo) indicates that the 4th Marine Division will invade Iwo Jima by February 19th 1945. **(Pacific-Philippines)** LEYTE: In the **U.S. Sixth Army** area, **X Corps** sector, the 127th Regiment, 32nd Division drives into Lonoy, while elements of the 34th Infantry, 24th Division, supported by a newly arrived Mortar Platoon, secure Tuktuk. In the **XXIV Corps** sector, Engineers trail closely behind contingents of the 305th Infantry, 77th Division to repair the bridges between Valencia and Palompon on the coast. MINDORO: The U.S.S. *Bryant* (DD-665), a Destroyer, sustains damage by a Kamikaze. **(Pacific-Burma)** In the N.C.A.C. area, the Japanese withdraw from Tigyaing prior to advancing Patrols of the 29th Brigade, British 36th Division, which is heading toward Mongmit by crossing the Irrawaddy; the main body of the Division drives toward Mongmit from the north. **(Pacific-Clipperton Island)** The LST 563 sinks subsequent to grounding. **(Pacific-Japan)** The Submarine U.S.S. *Tilefish* (SS-307) sinks the Torpedo Boat *Chidori* off Honshu. **(Atlantic-Western Europe) 21st Army Group** In the **U.S. Ninth Army** area, **XIX Corps** sector, Schneidhausen and Untermaubach are secured by the 5th Armored Division; it is subsequently relieved by the 83rd and 8th Divisions, the latter launching an unsuccessful assault against Obermaubach. In the **U.S. First Army** area, **V Corps** sector, the Germans penetrate 1st Division lines at Butgenbach and the perimeter of the 9th Division in the Monschau Forest; however, the advance is stopped in time to prevent a major breakthrough. Near Kalterherberg, the Germans open a heavy mortar and Artillery barrage, then mount a fierce early morning assault to secure a road junction, held by elements of the 39th Regiment, 9th Division. As the enemy threatens to overpower the position, Sergeant Peter Dalessondro, Company E, begins to encourage his troops to hold the line. He then advances forward and begins lobbing mortar rounds into the enemy attackers, while simultaneously firing his Rifle and attempting to rally his men. The attack is repulsed. Later in the day, another assault is mounted and again Dalessondro continues to rally the troops and carry the brunt of the battle. He expends his ammunition, then crawls to get a machine gun, returns and

maintains his position, firing at point blank range. He uses his last burst to kill several Germans about to murder an aid-man and two wounded Soldiers in a nearby foxhole. The Germans close on Dalassondro, and he continues lobbing grenades and yelling for mortar fire, while he gives cover fire to his Platoon as it withdraws. As the Germans close for the kill, he is last heard calling for a direct mortar hit on his position: "OK, MORTARS, LET ME HAVE IT-RIGHT IN THIS POSITION;" Dalessondro receives the Medal of Honor posthumously. In the **XVIII Airborne Corps** sector, the 82nd Airborne holds, while other delaying forces begin moving through their lines, pulling back from St. Vith. Colonel Otto Remer Fuehrer Begleit Brigade seizes Rodt, severing the St. Vith-Vielsalm road, but declines an attack against C.C.A., 7th Armored to the west or C.C.B. to the south. Meanwhile, the withdrawal continues; at Hinderhausen Task Force Boylan deploys to defend against attack from Rodt. Task Force Lohse deploys near Hinderhausen, but by 12:00, most of T.F. Lohse gets across the Salm at Vielsalm. The German 1st S.S. Panzer Division fails to gain a bridge across the Salm; some troops make the crossing, but the 505th Parachute Infantry exterminates them effortlessly. Two Companies attempt to seize the bridge at Grand Halleux, but as the span is consumed with the lead elements, the bridge is blown. Meanwhile, Stoumont is taken by a contingent of the 30th Division, and the 3rd Armored Division continues to hold its roadblocks, while simultaneously attacking to secure Hotton. Task Force Orr encounters the German 1128th Regiment at Dochamps; despite being down to a strength of about seven hundred men, it is the strongest contingent remaining in the 560th Volks Grenadier Division. Subsequent to brisk fire fights lasting until around noon, Colonel Orr withdraws to the starting point at Amonines; it had discovered troops of the 1129th German Regiment moving toward Beffe to relieve the 116th Panzer Division; the Germans do not follow in force. In conjunction, Task Force Kane keeps the Germans at bay outside of Amonines. Throughout the action, the U.S. Tanks seemingly prove too much for the German Infantry; it is thought that about one Battalion of the 1128th Regiment had been lost during the German advance toward Orr. At Marcouray, Task Force Hogan becomes isolated; it had been thrown into battle with near empty gas tanks and shortages of supplies. Orders come through for Hogan to drive northeast; a Task Force from C.C.A. is dispatched to help. German pressure against Malmedy is light, raised by elements of the 3rd Parachute Division. The German Command apparently believes that Germans continue to hold the town; Luftwaffe Planes drop gasoline supplies for Peiper's Tanks, however, they fall into the arms of waiting Americans. The 1st S.S. Panzer Corps Commander's plan to have Peiper break out and head east is foiled and Mohnke's attempts to break through to Peiper is postponed due to lack of strength. In the **VII Corps** sector, the 75th and 84th Divisions and the 2nd Armored Division are ordered to take defensive positions in the Durbuy-Marche region of Belgium. **12th Army Group** In the **U.S. Third Army** area, **VIII Corps** sector, Bastogne is inundated with Artillery Fire and repeated attacks, yet the besieged defenders do not relent. The combatants pound each other across a wide front between Villereux and Mande-St. Etienne, slightly north of the Marche highway. German shelling prompts the 501st to attempt to evacuate its baggage train which has lost 15 trucks and nearly all of its bed rolls, while the Kampfgruppe has plowed toward Villereux. A German contingent, composed of four Soldiers approaches the positions of the 2nd Battalion, 327th Glider Infantry Battalion, under a white flag and demands surrender, rather than face "annihilation". General Anthony McAuliffe, seemingly unperturbed by the dire circumstances, responds with Airborne bravado: "NUTS." The Germans are perplexed with the response and are not quite sure of the translation; but it soon sinks in. Although the weather continues to forbid air supply and impedes rescue, Bastogne holds, despite their dwindling ammunition. Morale remains high and the word that 4th Armored and 7th Armored units are supposedly on their way gives the exhausted Yanks some extra adrenaline. In the meantime, German General Brandenberger, Commander of the Seventh Army, had visited Luettwitz (XLVII Panzer Corps) on the previous night to emphasize the necessity of crushing Bastogne, but without the use of Panzer Lehr. The Germans strike the exhausted 28th Division southwest of Bastogne, compelling the troops to withdraw to Neufchateau; 28th Division Headquarters had informed VIII Corps that their supply of Bazookas has dwindled to five but that they could match the Tiger Tanks. West of Bastogne, the 58th Armored Field Artillery Battalion which had supported the 101st Airborne Division at Longvilly; the 58th's Commanding Officer, Lt. Col. Walter J. Paton had circled his guns and carved a giant foxhole around them; by afternoon, the Germans surround the unit; at midnight, the Bn. is ordered to break out, but fierce enemy fire forbids an easy exit; the troops return to their positions and await daylight to escape through the snow in small detachments. Meanwhile, General George S. Patton's III Corps is initiating its drive to lift the siege, tramping over icy roads strewn with obstacles; Patton is inspired by the response of McAuliffe. On the west, the 4th Armored Division has contingents reach Burnon and Martelange, and to their right, the 26th Division drives over 15 miles and engages the Germans at Rambrouch-Grosbous. Meanwhile, the 80th Division encounters tenacious resistance at Merzig and Ettelbruck, securing most of the latter. In the **XII Corps** sector, elements of the 4th Division attack from their positions, encountering brutal resistance near Echternach which confines progress to minor gains. In the **XX Corps** sector, the 90th Division's bridgehead at Dillingen is totally abandoned.

December 23rd 1944 — (Pacific) The Commanding General V Amphibious Corps Landing Force issues plans for the invasion of Iwo Jima, VACLANDFOR Operation Plan 3-44, directing the 4th and 5th Marine Divisions to assault the southeastern shores of Iwo Jima, landing abreast on D-Day; the tentative date is scheduled for 19th, February. The 3rd Marine Division is to be held in floating reserve until released to Corps. **(Pacific-Philippines)** LEYTE: In the **U.S. Sixth Army** area, the **X Corps** bolts from Highway 2, driving west to the coast, its 1st Cavalry Division acting as vanguard; it encounters terrible terrain, but moves without incident. The 32nd Division dispatches the 127th and 128th on reconnaissance prior to its main drive. In the **XXIV Corps** sector, 77th Division Artillery and Aircraft bombard Palompon to soften resistance for the impending amphibious assault by the 1st Battalion, 305th Regiment (reinforced). In conjunction, the balance of the Regiment is driving through Matagob against tenacious resistance, taking the overland route to the objective. During the night, Japanese assault U.S. lines, but are thrown back. MINDORO: Ellmore Airfield, recently constructed near the south bank of the Bugsanga River, is operational for limited use. **(Pacific-Burma)** In the **British Fourteenth Army** area, **33rd Corps** sector, Kokoggon is seized by the Indian 19th Division. **(Atlantic-Western Europe) 21st Army Group** In the **U.S. Ninth Army's XIX Corps**

Beleaguered Yanks at Bastogne.

U.S. Infantry pressing toward Bastogne.

sector, a down-scaled assault is launched by the 83rd Division, which drives to the fringes of Winden. In the **U.S. First Army** area, **V Corps** sector, the 1st and 9th Divisions restore the lines at Butgenbach and the Monschau Forest respectively. In the **XVIII (Airborne) Corps** sector, scattered remnants of the 106th Division, RCT 112, 28th Division, C.C.B., 9th Armored and the 7th Armored Division pull back from St. Vith, moving through the lines of the 82nd Airborne; the withdrawal is according to schedule; the majority of the LXVI Corps is crammed in St. Vith and nearby roads, but two Regiments of the 62nd Volks Grenadier Division are poised for attack. C.C.A., 7th Armored is struck at Crombach; by daybreak it is difficult to determine whom holds the town; Neubrueck also falls; the 164th Grenadier Regiment also penetrates General Hoge's center, overpowering a Tank Platoon in Grufflange. In conjunction an enemy attack is launched against Thommen at dawn; a contingent of Cavalry is driven out and when they are ordered to reenter the town, they find it jammed with enemy Infantry. The Fuehrer Begleit Brigade engage T.F. Boylan at Hinderhausen; T.F. Loshe pulls back, followed by T.F. Boylan, which has inflicted damage upon the attackers; the Yanks move to Commanster, chased by several Tanks and some Infantry. TF Lindsey pulls back to Salmchateau, picking up additional units as it moves. Task Force Jones is directed to cover the withdrawal of the remaining elements holding the southernmost positions of the St. Vith salient; the German onslaught had been derailed at St. Vith, despite the setbacks sustained by the Yanks. In other Corps activity, the 30th Division is repulsed at La Gleize. At Petit-

Coo, heavy skirmishing develops between Company I, 120th Regiment, 30th Division and the Germans. Staff Sergeant Paul L Bolden takes spectacular action while his Company is pinned down by heavy fire. He attacks a stronghold with one other Soldier. Bolden tosses a phosphorous grenade and a fragmentation grenade into the building while under cover fire from his comrade across the street. The Germans kill the other trooper, but Bolden bursts through the door firing at the 35 enemy troops, killing twenty. Bolden is severely wounded in the exchange and gets out of the building to await the enemy's surrender. Bolden daringly goes back into the building and eliminates the additional fifteen who chose not to surrender. His extraordinary heroism, despite his severe wounds, clears the way for his Company to take the objective; Bolden receives the Medal of Honor. Another man, Tech Sergeant Russell N. Snoad, is killed while assisting Bolden; he receives the Distinguished Service Cross for his heroism. The Germans have been driven into the cellars because of the use of the new POZIT fuses being used by the 113th Field Artillery Battalion, but the Germans continue blasting the U.S. Armor as it approaches. The forces under Peiper are compressed more as the night encroaches and by the following day, most of his forces are retreating through the woods to the south of La Gleize. In the **VII Corps** sector, the enemy prevents the 3rd Armored from taking Hotton-Soy road. Task Force Kane attacks to seize Dochamps, but is repulsed; it launches another unsuccessful assault later in the day, despite being low on ammunition and men. The Germans sustain high casualties at Freyneux and Lamormenil, but are unable to seize the road. After dark, the Germans hit a scant force of Yanks at the crossroads sector of Baraque de Fraiture (Belgian Ardennes), southeast of Manhay; the 2nd S.S. Panzer Division's units get a heavy dose of heated fire from the sparse force, composed of five Tanks and a detachment of Riflemen; the Yanks withdraw when they are nearly totally surrounded, after receiving orders. Task Force Kane is holding a small corridor protecting both flanks and the rear of the Armor; Task Force Orr holds Amonines, but the German 560th Volks Grenadier Division make no genuine move to attack it; Task Force Hogan is out of fuel, but the Germans do not apply extra pressure and the Yanks hold; a surrender demand is given to Hogan, but it is ignored. Subsequently, Artillery shells shoot in supplies, but they become damaged upon impact; soon after an Airdrop is initiated, but that too is a failure. Major Olin F. Brewster's force holds the line in the woods several thousand yards north of the crossroads; reinforcements pour in through the night and at first light, the Americans still control the ground between Manhay and the 2nd S.S. Panzers. The enemy also make penetrations through the lines of the 84th Division, between Hargimont and Rochefort. The Germans have Hotton surrounded. In an attempt to relieve the pressure, an attack is mounted by elements of the 517th Parachute Infantry Regiment. P.F.C. Melvin E. Biddle, acting as lead Scout during the assault, instinctively dashes around the area for twenty hours, knocking out machine gun nests and eliminating snipers. At one point he tosses his last grenade into one of the nests and then charges with his rifle blazing. At daybreak on the 24th he is still at it, harassing the enemy, knocking out another nest which is holding up his entire unit. He also feeds information to Armor which eradicates two enemy Tanks. His actions completely disorganize the enemy and Hotton is taken with a minimum amount of casualties due to Biddle's extraordinary courage; he receives the Medal of Honor. **12th Army Group** In the **U.S. Third Army** area, the skies begin to clear and the Air Corps is over Bastogne, delivering desper-

ately needed supplies and ammunition to the beleaguered defenders. At about 09:00, a Pathfinder Team parachutes into the perimeter and establishes drop zones; soon after, a string of 241 C-47s zoom overhead, dropping supplies (primarily Artillery ammunition) to extend the bloodline; on the following day, 160 Aircraft make the drop. Fighter Aircraft accompany the missions and take time to pound enemy positions. In the **VIII Corps** sector, the Germans close tighter against Bastogne; however, General McAuliffe continues to maintain constant communications with General Middleton. The 26th Volks Grenadier Division and an attached Regiment of the Panzer Lehr continues the attack against Senonchamps; it also strikes the 327th Glider Regiment at Marvie and Flamierge. The German 5th Parachute Division, over-extended along an 18 mile front is of no genuine value to Kokott at Bastogne; Kokott bleeds his force to fill the gap created by the 5th Parachute Division between Clochimont and Hompre. The battleground becomes increasingly cold and white as fresh blizzards hit the area; the Germans advance with their newly painted white Tanks, wearing white snow capes; the Americans improvise and engage the enemy in their newest attire, whitewashed Tanks and recently confiscated Belgian bed linens. At Flamierge, some Germans penetrate, but the Yanks push them out with a counterattack; Company C, at Marche highway; it is reported prematurely that the Americans had been lost; Artillery, including pieces at Senonchamps, beats back the attack and the 3rd Battalion withdraws to positions near Bastogne; additional Infantry is rushed to Senonchamps and at 18:00 McAuliffe sends Team Cherry to bolster the force under Colonel Browne, however, the available Tanks and Tanks Destroyers have been doing an admirable job, permitting the Cannoneers to catapult an abundance of their shells upon the enemy near Marche highway. In conjunction, wandering U.S. Fighter Bomber Squadrons seemingly induce the 901st Panzers to abort its daylight attack against the Yanks holding positions between Marvie and the Arlon road, however, Artillery shells rock the positions of the 2nd Battalion, 327th Glider Infantry Regiment. After dark, the German 901st Panzers move against the 2nd Battalion and Team O'Hara which has Tanks; a Platoon of enemy Paratroopers reaches a hill to the rear of the Yanks positions, but they are isolated and annihilated; at about the same time, a detachment of Tanks and a Half-trac move into Marvie, encountering a quick reaction including a well-placed round that cripples the Half-trac and blocks passage of the Tanks. Another contingent of Tanks drives against the right flank of the 2nd Battalion, but Company F, bolstered by Team O'Hara and the 609th Tank Destroyer Battalion repulses them. At midnight, the Germans throw another attack against Marvie; by dawn, the battle subsides, but Germans and Americans share the town. In the **III Corps** sector, C.C.A., 4th Armored Division takes Martelange and C.C.B. seizes Chaumont; however, the Germans counterattack and retake the latter. Meanwhile, C.C.R. pushes toward Bigonville (Luxembourg). The 101st at Bastogne has requested that 4th Armored accelerate their pace to relieve some pressure. In the 26th Division zone, the 104th Regiment overruns Grosbous, then darts to Dellen and Buschrodt, while its 328th Regiment seizes Wahl. Meanwhile, the town of Heiderscheid is taken by the 80th Division, which holds firmly, throwing back successive counterattacks; it simultaneously completes the clearing of Merzig, the seizure of Kehmen despite being heavily engaged at Ettelbruck. In **XII Corps** sector, the Germans resist strongly, hampering progress at Echternach. **6th Army Group** Near Bennwihr, elements of the 15th Infantry, 3rd Division, engage the enemy and vicious fire fights develop. Staff Sergeant Gus Kefurt vaults over a wall into the midst of fifteen Germans. He opens fire, kills ten and captures the remainder. As darkness settles over the town, he retains a three man outpost in the center of town which repulses repeated enemy Patrols. On the following morning he leads his detachment in tough hand-to-hand fighting until a Tank blocks progress. Undaunted, he launches rifle grenades and accepts surrender of the Tank crew, then leads the Platoon into more house-to-house fighting, which lasts throughout the day. He becomes grievously wounded, but refuses medical aid and dies; however, his personal leadership and extraordinary courage saves the position from being captured; Kefurt receives the Medal of Honor posthumously. **(Atlantic-Eastern Europe)** German-held Budapest is about seventy-five percent surrounded by the Russians. **(Atlantic-Italy) 15th Army Group** In the **U.S. Fifth Army** area, British 13th Corps sector, M. Tondo and M. della Volpe are seized with small effort by the Indian 8th Division.

December 23rd-24th 1944 — (Atlantic-English Channel)
The Allies attempt to speed reinforcements to the Ardennes; the operation begins haphazardly. About 2,000 Paratroopers (17th Airborne) board the Belgian Vessel *Leopoldville* on the night of the 23rd, only to be ordered off when it is determined that they had boarded the wrong Ship; they are replaced by the 262nd and 264th Regiments (green troops) of the 66th U.S. Division; the 263rd is scheduled to depart on the following day. About 5,000 men arrive at Pier 38 and an additional 1,000, including support troops and Artillery units are diverted to other piers. Confusion abounds aboard the transformed Liner *Leopoldville*; it can never be determined exactly how many troops board the ill-fated Vessel. Complaints are heard immediately as the tired Vessel has been evading enemy torpedoes since 1941, while transporting 120,000 troops and covering about 220,000 miles.

At 09:00, on the 24th, the *Leopoldville*, trailed by the *Cheshire* heads for Cherbourg and is joined later by several protective Warships including the H.M.S. *Brilliant*, H.M.S. *Anthony*, H.M.S. *Hotham* and the French Frigate *Croix de Lorraine*. A Submarine alert is blared at 14:30 and by 14:45, the Escort Warships spread out and unleash barrages of depth charges, but no contact is made; within fifteen minutes another Submarine warning is given. Nearby is the U-486, commanded by Oberleutnant Gerhard Meyer; it continues to stalk the Convoy, but harnesses its torpedoes until just before 18:00. Some of the troops are ignoring the chilling winds and their seasickness by singing Christmas Carols on the deck. Suddenly, when the *Leopoldville* is about one hour from its destination, the improvised Christmas spirit is shattered as a torpedo plows into the aft side of the Vessel, striking compartment number four. The troops remain disciplined, but most do not realize the devastation that has struck them; about 300-350 men are killed by the initial blast.

The distressed Vessel sends out S.O.S. signals, but the radio frequency is hooked to Portsmouth, which is eight hours away; Cherbourg is on a different frequency and remains unaware of the impending disaster. The rumor mill pours out false information and the troops are anticipating the quick arrival of Tug Boats. Meanwhile, the few troops on duty at Fort L'Quest in Cherbourg are becoming incensed as the Convoy has stopped within sight of the dock, and they are anxious to join the Christmas parties. The duty personnel send out messages by blinker, but receive no response from the

Convoy, increasing their frustration. Soon after, the men on shore determine that the *Leopoldville* is drifting west toward the minefields; more messages are sent, but again no response. About 100 Vessels, including PT Boats are at Cherbourg and could be committed to rescue operations, but the lack of communications causes the situation to deteriorate further. New messages are dispatched to the *Leopoldville* at 18:25; they too go unnoticed; the Ship's loudspeakers still blare information that Tugs are en route and that the Ship is seaworthy and in no danger of sinking. Ironically, no one ever admits making the announcements.

The Belgian crew is preoccupied with its own safety, and to the amazement of the Yanks, the crew is making for lifeboats, carrying items such as suitcases, radios and pets. The Americans stand aside as the word is passed: "MAKE WAY FOR THE CREW." One Yank, P.F.C. Rolland Carichner notes about the crew: "THE MOST SCARED RATS I EVER SAW IN MY LIFE." However, the British Gunners assigned to the Vessel are impressive; they have rushed to man the guns and remain at their posts. In conjunction, the Convoy's leader, Commander Pringle (British Royal Navy), is not aware that the Vessel is endangered; therefore, he does not order it towed by the H.M.S. *Brilliant*.

Meanwhile, the men at Fort L'Quest realize that a tragedy has occurred; they contact Joint Operations Center, but the word is not passed to higher ranking Officers. In conjunction, over an hour has passed since the attack and Portsmouth has not forwarded the information to Cherbourg through emergency channels and in addition, the Army Control tower at Cherbourg has no knowledge of the dilemma.

As the crisis worsens, the seas become more unyielding. Nonetheless, the H.M.S. *Brilliant* moves in close to transfer the troops; many refuse to jump; one man is crushed from the waist down as the *Brilliant* nudges against the *Leopoldville*, but he survives. Back at Fort L'Quest, Lt. Colonel Tom McConnel and Ensign Natt Divoll become incensed with orders that forbid communication with the disabled Ship and mandate "radio silence." They improvise and turn on the fort's searchlights, but new orders arrive: "TURN OFF YOUR LIGHTS." McConnel's vocabulary burns the telephone wires, attempting to penetrate Headquarters; he finally reaches General Aurand at 18:45. In the meantime, Ensign Divoll has struck out with his attempts to contact Navy brass; undaunted, and without authorization, he orders Coast Guard and Navy Vessels to speed out of the harbor to commence rescue operations. In conjunction, Lt. Commander Richard Davis (Port Defense Officer) rips the red tape; he screams and bludgeons his desk with his fists as he demands that Ships move out. Within several minutes, two PT Boats are racing to sea; another PT Boat is close behind. Soon after, all of the command at Cherbourg is cognizant of the disaster.

Although the Yanks had become enraged when the crew abandoned Ship, taking personal items and pets instead of people, a deserted Parrot gets a reprieve when two Yanks go below deck to rescue it; its salty language makes it a perfect mascot and the smiling Yanks present it to the crewmen of the *Brilliant* who are instantly broadsided with some choice words. Other Yanks had risked their lives to save trapped men below decks, some losing their own lives in the process. At 19:30, subsequent to about fifty harrowing minutes, the *Brilliant* pushes away from the *Leopoldville*; many had refused to jump to safety, believing the Vessel safe; their confidence is bolstered by the sight of approaching U.S. Vessels.

By 19:45, the last of the wounded are being transferred to U.S. Ships, but the operation is primitive; the stormy seas become worse; nevertheless, a Launch continues to hug the *Leopoldville* precariously for about 15 minutes, rescuing most of the wounded. Several of the remaining Yanks greet an approaching Vessel with Season's Greetings, yelling: "MERRY CHRISTMAS NAVY." The crew is not impressed and yells back: "WE AIN'T NAVY YOU DUMB SONS-OF-BITCHES! WE'RE COAST GUARD." Additional Navy and Coast Guard Vessels arrive to assist; one PT Boat crew becomes infuriated as some crew members jump in with their luggage; the Sailors throw the bags into the water, but stop shot of tossing the crew overboard. As the clock strikes 20:00, about 1,200 men remain aboard the stricken Vessel; of 195 Belgians and Congolese, about 24 remain. In French, the Captain states: "GENTLEMEN, THE MOMENT HAS COME. WE MUST NOW LEAVE THE SHIP. GENTLEMEN, BOARD THIS BOAT."

Moments before the Captain's final order is given, a Navy Tug (ATR-3) had arrived, but a lifeboat had been lowered in its path, slowing its mission; finally it moves close and shoots a line, but no one secures it; additional frantic efforts to shoot a line are started during the Ship's final moments and a Soldier grabs one and fastens it, but by now the Vessel is beginning to sustain explosions. At 20:05, the Vessel dips to a near vertical position; the men just walk into the water. Of the more than two thousand Soldiers who boarded the Vessel on the 23rd, more than 800 are lost; many are lost in the water due to panic, however, even more tragically, some are shredded by the propellers of rescue Vessels, which are working in rough seas in the dark.

Captain Limbor (Belgian) is the only Ship's Officer to lose his life; also, three Congolese and one white crewman lose their lives. Before midnight, the crew is being settled in a hotel at Cherbourg; the survivors are also billeted there. On Christmas Day, General Aurand orders Turkey dinners for the survivors. The 66th Division gets little rest; it goes into action during early 1945. Between Christmas Day and the termination of the war, the 66th Division (Black Leopard on its uniforms) loses 43 men killed in combat.

During April 1945, the U-486, which had sunk the *Leopoldville*, experiences engine trouble and is forced to surface; a lurking British Submarine, the *Tapir* sinks it.

Wounded U.S. troops being evacuated from the Bulge.

December 24th 1944 — (Pacific-Philippines) LEYTE: In the **U.S. Sixth Army** area, **X Corps** sector, the 1st Cavalry Division continues its westward drive, encountering light resis-

tance. In conjunction, the 32nd Division initiates its westward drive toward the coast, hitting nominal resistance, but its path is hampered by terrible terrain. In the **XXIV Corps** sector, the 1st Battalion (reinforced), 305th Regiment, 77th Division, departs Ormoc at 20:00, heading by sea toward Palompon, under the protection of PT Boats; the balance of the Regiment continues moving overland toward the objective. **(Pacific-Volcano Islands)** A Cruiser Destroyer Force, commanded by Rear Admiral R. E. Smith, bombards Airfields and Japanese installations on Iwo Jima. The Japanese Transports NO. 8 and No. 157 are sunk. The raids continue through the 27th. **(Pacific-Burma)** The British 2nd and Indian 20th Divisions, subsequent to fierce fighting, eliminate Japanese resistance in the Pyingaing area. **(Atlantic-Western Europe) 21st Army Group** In the **British Second Army** area, **30th Corps** sector, the British 29th Armored Brigade engages the spearhead of an enemy advance between Ciney and Dinant. In the **U.S. Ninth Army** area, **XIX Corps** sector, Winden is almost totally secured by the 83rd Division, while the 8th Division fortifies its positions near Obermaubach and will assault it on the 25th. The 8th Division also secures Winden on the 25th. In the **U.S. First Army** area, **V Corps** sector, the Germans attack Butgenbach; however, once again, the 1st Division repulses the assault. In the **XVIII (Airborne) Corps** sector, La Gleize falls to the dogged 30th Division; Peiper's remnants numbering about 800 men including wounded begins crossing the Salm after dark; rear-guards had remained behind to destroy the Vehicles and guns; the troops rejoin the 1st S.S. Panzer Division at Stavelot on Christmas Day. About 170 U.S. P.O.W.s, captured at Stoumont on the 19th, are liberated at La Glaize. The 117th and 120th Regiments sweep the woods between the Salm and the Ambleve to round up stragglers of the 1st Panzer Regiment; about 50 Germans who had not received the word to retreat attempt to fight it out north of La Gleize and die suddenly. U.S. Planes inadvertently strike the positions of the 120th Regiment at Malmedy on the 24th and 25th, inflicting casualties and setting the twon on fire. By the 26th of December, the entire area around the north bank of the Ambleve is free of enemy troops who have been killed, captured or dispersed. Meanwhile, the enemy forces the 82nd Airborne from Manhay. Also, the 7th Armored Division is committed to help hold the balance of the Manhay region and the 17th Airborne Division is en route to France from England to bolster the VIII Corps. In the **VII Corps** sector, heavy fighting erupts all across the area. The 3rd Armored Division loses its roadblock on the road to Manhay at Belle Haie; in other heavy skirmishing, C.C.R. sends columns which attack from the east and west, securing the Hotton-Soy Road. The 77th Division receives its battle initiation: RCT's 289 and 290 are attached to C.C.A. and C.C.R., 3rd Armored Division respectively. Meanwhile, in the 84th Division sector, the enemy plows into Verdenne, overwhelming the 2nd Platoon of Company I, 334th Regiment subsequent to heated house-to-house fighting; a follow up attack drives into the balance of Company I and Company K, driving them to the critical Marche-Hotton road; at Rochefort, the 333rd Regiment's Companies I and K, withstand a thunderstorm of fire against their positions at a hotel; General Bolling orders them to withdraw and under another hail of fire, they escape to the Meuse; fifteen wounded men and a medic remain in the battered town and another 25 have been captured or killed. The German Commander of the Panzer Lehr Division subsequently states, that the courage of the defenders of Rochefort compared with the defenders of Bastogne. C.C.A., 2nd Armored Division pushes to Buissonville; the swiftness of the attack envelops the town and also intercepts an enemy column approaching from the opposite side; Yankee Artillery interdicts and the Germans take a thrashing, losing 38 Vehicles, four Antitank guns, 6 Artillery pieces; the Germans also sustain severe losses of dead and 106 prisoners are seized. The 4th Cavalry Group, attached to the 2nd Armored Division, makes contact with British troops at Sorinne; Troop A enters Humain with after eradicating light opposition. General Harman orders an attack to seize Ciney, where there is a large concentration of German force; earlier in the day, a British Light Armored Cavalry Patrol had been pushed back from there toward Dinant and two U.S. P51s flew over to the tumultuous greeting of heavy flak; Harman finally gets permission and the town is taken by the 25th. Meanwhile, Field Marshal Montgomery orders the British 51st Division to move across the Meuse and deploy behind the U.S. First Army to bolster the rear; Montgomery directs other British troops to move to Givet and Namur to fortify the British 29th Armored Brigade, which is guarding bridges at both sites, in case the Germans break for the river. **12th Army Group** In the **U.S. Third Army** area, the Germans pound Bastogne, Planes reducing most buildings to rubble; during a night raid, one Belgian Nurse and many wounded Paratroopers are killed. Nevertheless, the Yanks refuse to relent and Patton's III Corps is rushing to the rescue. Combat Engineers are deployed along the Meuse River and protect the approaches to the bridges. Team O'Hara and a Platoon of the 705th Tank Destroyer Battalion are attached to the 501st Parachute Regiment; in conjunction, the 502nd receives two Platoons of the 705th and Team Anderson (comprise two Cavalry Assault Guns, one Tank Destroyer and two Jeeps); the 506th also receives two Platoons of the 705th, but no Tanks. In conjunction, the 326th Airborne Engineer Battalion, two Platoons of the 9th Armored Engineer Battalion, four Platoons of the 705th Tank Destroyer Battalion and Team Roberts (comprising the conglomerate of troops with Colonel Browne's force) are attached to the 327th Glider Infantry; Colonel Browne is wounded during the fighting today and he succumbs on the 25th. McAuliffe's reserves are thin, comprising Col. William Roberts' C.C.B. (Teams Arnsdorf and Cherry), remnants of C.C.R., 9th Armored (Team SNAFU), and some stragglers. U.S. P51s bombard the enemy which encroach on the 101st at Bastogne, but their cargo drops so close to the Airborne that the raids are called off by concerned Paratroopers; the 512th, 513th and 514th Squadrons, XIX Tactical Air Command suspends their raids. In the meantime, the promised (by Model to Luettwitz) 115th Kampfgruppe, 15th Panzer Grenadier Division arrives to strengthen Kokott's attack against Bastogne. The Yanks have pulled back from their roadblock at Mande-St. Etienne and have reeled in the 3rd Battalion, 327th Glider Infantry and Team Roberts. While the Americans await rescue, the Germans spend Christmas Eve preparing to crush Bastogne on Christmas Day. General Patton sends his regards to the defenders at Bastogne: "XMAS EVE PRESENT COMING UP. HOLD ON." In the **III Corps** area, C.C.A. and C.C.B., 4th Armored are heavily engaged at Warnock and Chaumont respectively; C.C.R. overruns Bigonville. Koetschette and Rambrouch are captured by the 26th Division; however, the enemy halts its progress at Arsdorf at Hierheck. Meanwhile, strong counterattacks are thwarted by the 80th Division. In the **XII Corps** sector, the 5th Division makes nominal progress against heated opposition as it drives toward Haller and Waldbillig. At the Moselle, Task Force Reed relieves elements of the 4th Division which are deployed on the right flank of the Corps. C.C.A., 10th Armored storms into Gilsdorf and Mostroff at the Sauer River, seizing both. **6th Army Group** Information concerning an imminent enemy offensive is passed to all units. In the **French 1st Army's 2nd Corps** sector, Bennwihr is taken by the U.S. 3rd Division, culminating Divisional operations in the Colmar region. **(Atlantic-Eastern Europe)** The Germans at Budapest are confined to an escape route that is less than 20 miles wide. The Third Ukrainian Front has advanced rapidly for the past several days, overrunning over 150 towns and villages, including Biske and Szekesfehervar. The onslaught has sealed western escape routes entirely, and in addition, other units are closing from the southwest against Budapest.

Destroyed Third Army Tanks along the road to Bastogne.

December 25th 1944 — (Pacific-Philippines) LEYTE: The U.S. Eighth Army relieves the U.S. Sixth Army and assumes responsibility for Leyte-Samar area, allowing the Sixth Army to concentrate on the Luzon operation. The ongoing work at the Dulag, Tacloban and Tanauan Airfields proceeds with marked progress. A Naval Air Station is established at Samar. In the **U.S. Sixth Army** area, **X Corps** sector, Aircraft resupply the advancing 32nd Infantry Division as it moves toward the coast in conjunction with the 1st Cavalry Division. A force of about 300-400 Japs is encountered and driven off by the 1st Battalion, 127th Regiment. In the **XXIV Corps** sector, preparatory fire is laid to assist the 1st Battalion, 305th Regiment, 77th Division which lands without incident north of Palompon and quickly con sumes barrios of Buaya and Look, then Palompon. Heavy enemy resistance is met by contingents of the 305th Regiment, which is driving along the road to Palompon. LUZON: The Allies accelerate the Air bombardment of enemy positions to soften resistance against the imminent invasion. During the bombardment, Major Thomas B. McGuire leads his Squadron of fifteen P-38s against Mabalacat Airbase, where they are intercepted by twenty Japanese Fighters. McGuire personally shoots down three Zeros and after his guns jam, he remains heavily involved, forcing an enemy Plane into his Wingman's line of fire. On the following day, McGuire leads a mission against Clark Field and shoots down several more Planes, giving him a total of 38 victories in aerial combat. He will fly another mission over Los Negros and attempt to save a downed flyer; however the low altitude maneuver causes him to crash and subsequently be reported missing in action. He receives the Medal of Honor for his unselfish actions and tremendous bravery during the attacks on 25-26 December. **(Atlantic-Western Europe) 21st Army Group** In the **British Second Army** area, the 30th Corps is deployed along the west bank of the Meuse between Givet and Liege. In the **U.S. Ninth Army** area, the British 51st Division reverts from reserve and is shifted to U.S. First Army reserve. In the **U.S. First Army** area, Patrols from the V Corps encounter some German troops and skirmishes develop. In the **XVIII (Airborne) Corps** sector, the 82nd Airborne withdraws from its Vielsalm salient, as ordered, and redeploys at Trois Ponts-Basse-Bodeux-Bra-Manhay to firm up and hold the line. Meanwhile, the 30th Division secures the area between Stavelot and Trois, north of the Ambleve River. The 7th Armored Division, bolstered by RCT 424, 106th Division attacks Manhay in vain. In the **VII Corps** area, orders come down instructing the Corps to take a defensive posture; instead, it launches a small assault to strengthen First Army's right flank. At Grandmenil, recently taken by the Germans, the 3rd Armored advances to the tip of the objective, while establishing defensive positions in the Werpin-Amonines region. Task Force Hogan, still isolated at Marcouray, begins to advance through enemy occupied Soy to break out. In the 84th Division zone, the town of Verdenne is recaptured by the 84th Division; however, some resistance remains in isolated pockets between it and Bourdon. In related activity, C.C.A. 2nd Armored takes Havrenne and C.C.B. overruns Celles, the latter prize severing the German westward path to Dinant.

12th Army Group In the **U.S. Third Army** area, the Germans press solidly against Bastogne from all sides, but the determined defenders do not relent; using the recently arrived ammunition and supplies, McAuliffe's ragged troops hold resolutely, frustrating the Germans. At 03:00, the Luftwaffe bombards Rolle, the Regimental Command Post of the 502nd Parachute Infantry; this is followed by streams of Artillery and mortar shells ringing Company A's positions near Champs. About 50 Grenadiers of the 77th Regiment burst into Champs at 04:00, but by around 05:15 an entire German Battalion enters the fight. Nonetheless, the Yanks hold and the Germans become stalled. In conjunction, the 15th Panzers drive against the beleaguered lines of the 3rd Battalion, 327th. shortly thereafter, a jubilant message is relayed to the German Command Post exclaiming the arrival of German Tanks and Infantry at the fringe of Bastogne; the ecstasy is temporary as the primary information proclaiming the Tanks have entered the town is not forthcoming; eighteen Mark IVs, crammed with riding Infantry, jackhammer through the lines of Companies A and B, 327th and some pierce the lines of the 7545th Field Artillery. Slightly west of Hemroulle, about half of the Tanks pivot left and advance toward the road extending between Champs and Bastogne, driving toward the advancing B and C Companies of the 502nd Parachute Infantry; two advance Tank Destroyers of Co. B, 705th Tank Destroyer Bn. are destroyed at the initial eruption of combat, but Colonel Chappuis deploys his two Companies and soon after, the German Infantrymen aboard the Tanks are inundated with bullets as they drop off into the snow; the Tanks again pivot and move toward Champs only to run into the guns of the trailing Tank Destroyers which are bolstering Company C; five Panzers are gutted. As the other contingent keeps rolling toward Hemroulle, it meets its fate at the hands of four Tank Destroyers, the Tanks of Team Roberts, Bazookas of the Glider Infantry and the 463rd Field Artillery Bn.; Colonel S. L. A. Marshall remarks after the contest: "THE GERMAN TANKS WERE FIRED UPON FROM SO MANY DIRECTIONS AND WITH SUCH A MIXTURE OF FIRE THAT IT WAS NOT POSSIBLE TO SEE OR SAY HOW EACH TANK MET ITS DOOM." The accompanying Infantry which avoids destruction is isolated; by 12:00, contingents of the 755th capture about 50 enemy troops as they attempt to conceal themselves in a stream bed. German General Kokott lists the 1st Battalion, 115th and its accompanying Infantry as lost, but the German Command is

unsure of how its demise came about. The 2nd Battalion, 115th, however, advances west of Hemroulle, without incident, until dawn, but at about first light, all hell breaks loose as the guns of Company C, 3rd Battalion reserve are unleashed pounding the Panzer Grenadiers; desperate attempts to dig in are fruitless on the frozen terrain, leaving the Germans no alternative but to absorb their climbing losses. German Colonel Maucke, attempts to reform his badgered forces; the 1st Battalion survivors withdraw to a hill near Flamizoulle, but find no solace as Allied Fighter Bombers pulverize their positions and at Champs where the German thrust began, the Germans in an attempt to surround the village is short-circuited by sheets of fire as the enemy attacks up the slopes toward Hemroulle; another attack is scheduled to commence after dark, but it doesn't get off the ground. Bastogne is intact, its defenders sensing rescue. Now it is the Germans who are suffering from lack of supplies and the offensive is faltering. Meanwhile, the **III Corps** is driving tirelessly to lift the siege. The 4th Armored springs a surprise attack which secures the road from Vauxles-Rosieres to Chaumont; C.C.A. and C.C.B. overpower Chaumont, Hollange and Tintage. At Eschdorf, the 26th Division commits a Task Force to seize the town. A fragile grasp is gained, and additional units secure Arsdorf. In conjunctive activity, the 319th Regiment, 80th Division, eradicates enemy resistance in its sector to the Sauer River and makes contact with contingents of the 26th Division. Subsequent counterattacks are thrown back by the 319th, reinforced by the 317th Regiment; the drive advances to the area near Kehmen. The 318th Regiment, 80th Division is engaged at Chaumont, Belgium. German machine gun fire is holding up the advance of an entire Platoon, stranding it in open ground upon ice and snow, prompting Staff Sergeant Paul J. Wiedorfer to singlehandedly charge through a hail of enemy fire, slipping and sliding as he moves, until reaching a position where he lobs a grenade and then lunges forward with his rifle to kill the remaining crewmen of the first nest. He immediately pivots and attacks the second nest, wounding one enemy Soldier and capturing the remaining six. Sergeant Weidorfer receives the Medal of Honor for his actions. The Germans abandon Ettelbruck. In the **XII Corps** sector, Haller and Waldbillig are seized by the 5th Division. **6th Army Group** In the **U.S. Seventh Army** area, Major General Frank W. Milburn arrives with advance contingents of XXI Corps. **(Atlantic-Eastern Europe)** Contingents of the Third Ukrainian Front eliminate the final western rail exits leading from Budapest; the escape route is now about nine miles wide. **(Atlantic-Italy) 15th Army Group** In the **U.S. Fifth Army** area, there is activity in the Serchio Valley during the night of the 25th-26th, as German Patrols begin probing the IV Corps sector.

December 26th 1944 — (Pacific-Philippines) Leyte is declared secure; however, the newly arrived 8th Army will still be involved in heavy fighting and the last of the resistance is not terminated until 8th, May 1945. In the **U.S. Eighth Army** area, **X Corps** sector, the 1st Cavalry and 32nd Infantry Divisions plow through tough terrain as they drive west. Meanwhile, the 24th Division readies its assault to secure the northwest portion of Leyte Peninsula. At 23:00, Companies F and G embark, being transported by sea through the Biliran Strait toward Gigantangan Island where they bivouac for the night. On the following morning, the unit sails to Taglawigan. In the **XXIV Corps** sector, the 77th Division pauses in the area around Palompon. MINDORO: Japanese Warships survive an Air assault and arrive off the coast, commencing a bombardment against the beachhead about an hour before midnight. The Japanese Destroyer *Kiyoshimo* sinks after being attacked by Naval Surface Ships and Army Aircraft. **(Pacific-Burma)** In the **British Fourteenth Army** area, 15th Corps sector, the Japanese evacuate Akyab. The Indian 25th Division, running well ahead of schedule, advances to the tip of Mayu Peninsula, reaching Foul Point. **(Pacific-China)** General Wedemeyer meets with Ambassador Hurley, T.V. Soong and Chiang-Kai-shek. He suggests that there is room for improvement in wages and food and clothing for Chinese troops. He also informs the Generalissimo that Operation BETA, the offensive against Canton, Kweilin and Liuchow, is being readied. **(Atlantic-Western Europe) 21st Army Group** In the **British Second Army** area, the 30th Corps takes command of the British 6th Airborne Division and releases the 43rd Division to the 12th Corps. In the **U.S. Ninth Army** area, the German thrust is stopped short of the Meuse River and the situation for the enemy deteriorates wildly as their dwindling supplies have caused much of the Armor to stall. Allied Planes capitalize and initiate ravaging strikes that pummel enemy positions unmercifully. In the **XVIII Corps** sector, the Germans futilely attack the Airborne positions in front of the Meuse. In the **VII Corps** zone, the 7th Armored captures Grandmenil and secures the heights south of Soy-Hotton road, however, the 3rd Armored operating to its right is busily fortifying its front and awaiting contact with the 7th to ensure its left flank. The 84th Division eliminates the nuisance pocket between Bourdon and Verdenne in addition to repulsing a counterattack in front of Menil. The Germans drive heatedly against Frandeux and Havrenne, being handily repelled at both locations and sustaining severe casualties. **12th Army Group** In the **U.S. Third Army** area, Generalmajor Heinz Kokott throws his last stones against Bastogne; a compact assault force squeezes through the lines between the positions the two Companies of the 327th, which are manning the right flank; the fast paced advance is unexpectedly interrupted by the Howitzers posted west of Bastogne; as the enemy troops become exposed on open terrain, the guns open up, shredding their ranks; four Tank Destroyers make a break for Hemroulle, but they inadvertently get swallowed by a huge ditch; U.S. Artillery and Tank Destroyer fire blows them to oblivion from close range. If Kokott believes he is having a bad day, he soon finds out that things are getting worse; he is informed that the 5th Parachute Division, which had been given responsibility to neutralize Patton's Armor in the south, has been sent reeling and that the 39th Regiment is under attack near Assenois and that Patton's Armor has rolled through. Kokott is in no position to offer much help and his Tanks are held in harness until dark because of the prowling U.S. Fighter Bombers. As the night closes, Field Marshal Model will order the 26th Volks Grenadier Division to keep the defenders in Bastogne holed up until the Fuehrer Begleit Brigade can arrive to seal the narrow gap that the 4th Armored had created. In the 4th Armored Division zone, C.C.R. closes fast on Bastogne. Along the way, near Assenois, Belgium, two German 88s and some small arms fire impede progress; Private James R. Hendrix, Company C, 53rd Armored Infantry, jumps from his half-trac and attacks. Using only his rifle, he succeeds in taking both crews prisoner. Shortly afterward, he rushes to the aid of two wounded U.S. Servicemen, under fire from two enemy machine gun crews, and eliminates both, allowing the wounded to be evacuated. In addition, Hendrix rushes to the aid of another wounded Soldier trapped in a burning half-trac and with extraordinary courage while braving enemy fire and mines, extricates the wounded trooper and saves his life; Hendrix receives the Medal of Honor. Bastogne is reached and the siege is lifted at 16:45; however, the wedge is small and will have to be expanded to allow for massive resupply. The 101st Airborne Division sustains casualties that total 105 Officers and 1,536 men; C.C.B., 10th Armored casualties amount to 25 Officers and 478 men; there is no accurate account killed, wounded or missing of the various unrecorded Tankers, Gunners, Infantry, and others who helped to defend Bastogne; and no casualty compilation is available from those units which fought east of Bastogne, prior to December 19th, to buy time for the 101st at Bastogne. The 26th Division takes Eschdorf, then bolts across the Sauer River. The 80th Division secures Scheidel. In the **XII Corps** sector, Berdorf falls to the 5th Division, which also fortifies its positions at Echternach. The 6th Armored Division arrives at Luxembourg and begins relieving the 10th Armored. **6th Army Group** In the **U.S. Seventh Army** area, regrouping is complete. The **XV Corps** is deployed from St. Avold to Bitche and consists of the 106th Cavalry Group and the 44th, 100th and 103rd Divisions. The **VI Corps** is deployed between Bitche and the Rhine and is composed of the 45th and 79th Divisions and Task Force Hudelson. In the U.S. 3rd Division sector, enemy Artillery near Sigolsheim, France, is pinning down one Company of the 1st Battalion, 15th Regiment. Lt. Colonel Keith L. Ware advances alone about 150 yards in front of the most advanced positions to reconnoiter the enemy and draw fire to expose their positions. Lt. Col. Ware returns and grabs eleven men and one Tank. The detachment knocks out four enemy machine guns and the hill is taken, thanks to the tremendous heroism and leadership of Ware; he becomes the recipient of the Medal of Honor. **(Atlantic-Eastern Europe)** The Third Ukrainian Front takes the fortress city of Esztergom; the capture seals the fate of the Germans in Budapest, which is totally encircled. **(Atlantic-Italy) 15th Army Group** In the **U.S. Fifth Army** area, the 1st Armored Division (reserve) is ordered to Lucca. In other activity, the Germans attack the left flank positions of the 92nd Division near Leghorn. Some colored Soldiers abandon their positions and flee to the rear. General Mark Clark had shifted a veteran Division to back up the less experienced units and the lost ground is recaptured. Clark had previously informed the War Department that the "92ND DIVISION WILL NOT ACHIEVE A SATISFACTORY LEVEL OF COMBAT PERFORMANCE." Subsequently, after the close of hostilities, Clark would remark: "THE NEGRO SOLDIER NEEDED GREATER INCENTIVE AND A FEELING THAT HE WAS FIGHTING FOR HIS HOME AND COUNTRY AND THAT HE WAS FIGHTING AS AN EQUAL. THE FAILURE OF THE 92ND DIVISION WAS NO REFLECTION ON THE COURAGE OF BLACK SOLDIERS, BUT RATHER ON THE SOCIETY THAT DENIED THEM EQUALITY." In other activity in Italy, Captain Howard Chappell (O.S.S. agent from East Cleveland, Ohio), Corporal Silsby and Tech Sergeant Fabrega are dropped into northern Italy to join the Aztec operation; they land near Belluno and soon meet with O.S.S. agent, Captain Benucci; Bennucci remains with the 7th Alpinei (Partisans) and takes command of the Val Cordovale Brigade. Chappell assumes command of the Mazzini and Tollot Brigades (called Nanette Division) which are Communists forces; one Brigade buries their guns when fighting with the Germans begins; the Communists are unconcerned with the liberation of Italy, and preoccupied with the political situation in post-war Italy. The Partisans under Chappell's unit rescues 21 U.S. Pilots who are shot down.

December 27th 1944 — (Pacific-Philippines) LEYTE: In the **U.S. Eighth Army** area, **X Corps** sector, Companies F and G, 34th Regiment, 24th Division embark Gigangtangan Island and assault Taglawigan, landing against no opposition; the units then embark by sea and by overland routes, securing Daha. Company G, reinforced, moves by sea hitting shore south of San Isidro, while its 1st Battalion drives from Calumbian by land and advances to the heights overlooking the objective, which falls on the following day to the 1st and 2nd Battalions. In the **XXIV Corps** sector, the 77th Division encounters heavy resistance as it advances against superbly entrenched enemy troops along the Palompon road; the 3rd Battalion, 305th Regiment seizes some heights as it moves. Meanwhile, the 2nd Battalion awaits transportation by sea from Ormoc to Palompon. Japanese Planes attack Shipping and shore positions at Mindoro. The Air strikes are repeated on the 28th, 29th and 31st of December. **(Pacific-Volcano Islands)** Naval Surface Ship fire destroys the Japanese Transports Numbers 7 and 132 off Iwo Jima. **(Pacific-Burma)** In the N.C.A.C. area, the U.S. 124th Cavalry culminates its march to Momauk and initiates reorganizing for combat. **(Atlantic-Western Europe)** During the morning, General Bradley confers with Ike and Montgomery; he is attempting to regain the First and Ninth Armies, but he is not successful. Both Bradley and Patton are of the opinion that Montgomery will not attack. **21st Army Group** In the **U.S. First Army** area, **XVIII (Airborne) Corps** sector, the 30th Division continues to regroup. The 508th Paratroop Infantry, 82nd Airborne drives forward outside of Bra. In other activity, Manhay is retaken by the 7th Armored. RCT 112, 28th Division bolsters the 9th Armored Division. In the **VII Corps** sector, C.C.A., 3rd Armored Division zone, RCT 289 slashes at German infiltrators which pierce its lines attempting to reach Sadzot. The Germans take the objective on the following day; however, they are pushed back out. At Verdenne, an enemy pocket is eradicated by the 84th Division. The enemy is mounting stiff resistance at Humain, but 2nd Armored units surround the town and terminate the opposition. In other activity, the 83rd Division begins relieving the 2nd Armored Division. **12th Army Group** In the **U.S. Third Army** area, **III Corps** sector, C.C.R., 4th Armored Division has blown the roadway open, allowing Ambulances and other Vehicles, which had been detained, to pour into Bastogne. Reinforcements from the 9th Armored and 80th Divisions bolster the 4th Armored, and combined they spread wide to expand the corridor to Bastogne and secure the Arlon-Bastogne highway. The 35th Division streaks north advancing through the lines of the 4th Armored and 26th Divisions; its 320th Regiment seizes Boulaide and Boschleiden, while the 137th grabs Surre. The 26th Division funnels through the 101st Division lines and takes Kaundorf and Mecher-Dunkrodt. In the **VIII Corps** sector, the Meuse River sector is taken over by the 17th Airborne Division. In the **XII Corps** area, the 80th Division establishes roadblocks north and northeast of Ettelbruck and also repels a counterattack near Ringel. The 6th Armored Division assumes responsibility for the area south of the Sauer between Ettelbruck and Mostroff. Meanwhile, the 5th Division's 11th Regiment seizes Waldbillig and Patrols of the 4th Division discover Echternach abandoned. In the **XX Corps** sector, strengthened Patrols are dispatched by the 90th Division to keep the Germans pinned down. **6th Army Group** In the **U.S. Seventh Army** area, **XXI Corps** sector, the 12th Armored and 36th Infantry Divisions arrive. In the **VI Corps** sector, Task Forces Harris (63rd Division), Herren (70th Division) and Linden (42nd Division) reinforce the Corps. In the **French Army** area, 2nd Corps area, the U.S.

Third Division is engaged at Sigolsheim, France. Ferocious house-to-house fighting ensues as elements of the 15th Regiment attempt to take the fortress town. 1st Lt. Eli Whiteley leads his Platoon and is struck with a terrible blow; however, he charges into the house and kills its two defenders. Ignoring his shoulder and arm wounds, he charges the next house and kills two additional men and captures eleven of its defenders. Undaunted, although his left arm is now useless, he commandeers a bazooka and blasts out a wall, then bursts through the opening with his good arm wielding a blazing submachine gun, killing five men and capturing twelve. Whiteley continues to attack and charges yet another stronghold, only to be hit in the eye with a shell fragment. Still refusing to quit, despite his savage wounds and impaired eye, he continues leading his Platoon until taken out by force. His actions kill nine Germans and capture 23 additional men, plus opening the way for the command to seize the objective; Whiteley receives the Medal of Honor. **(Atlantic-Eastern Europe)** Fierce fighting erupts in the eastern and western suburbs of Budapest as the Germans struggle to forestall capitulation. The Second Ukrainian Front has secured an island north of the city on the Danube and initiated contact with the Third Ukrainian Front, totally enveloping the beleaguered defenders within the city. **(Atlantic-Italy) 15th Army Group** In the **U.S. Fifth Army** area, advance elements of the 10th Mountain Division arrive. In the **IV Corps** sector, the 92nd Division is forced to withdraw under pressure; contingents of the Indian 8th Division move through the 92nd's positions and make Patrol contact with the enemy.

German prisoners at Bastogne.

December 28th 1944 — (Pacific-Caroline Islands) Marine Fighter Squadrons VMF-124 and 213 embark from Ulithi aboard the U.S.S. *Essex*, becoming the first Marine Fighter Squadrons to board a big Carrier. The Carrier will strike Formosa and Luzon during early January. **(Pacific-Philippines)** LEYTE: In the **U.S. Eighth Army** area, **X Corps** sector, the 1st and 2nd Battalions, 34th Regiments, 34th Division pounce light opposition and seize San Isidro. The 5th and 12th Cavalry Regiments arrive at Tibur barrio on the west coast. In the **XXIV Corps** sector, elements of the 305th Infantry, 77th Division move by sea from Ormoc to Palompon, while the 3rd Battalion continues driving overland encountering resistance, which holds progress to about 1,000 yards. MINDORO: Ellmore Airfield becomes fully operational. In Naval activity, the LST 750 is sunk by U.S Forces, subsequent to being damaged by an enemy Aircraft torpedo off Negros. **(Atlantic-Western Europe)** General Eisenhower travels by train to meet with Field Marshal Montgomery at Hasselt, Belgium, to plan an offensive. Montgomery tells Ike that recent attacks have struck his northern line. He also informs Ike about his plans to attack Houffalize and about intelligence that anticipates a strong enemy assault. Eisenhower agrees with Montgomery; however, if no attack comes, Montgomery is to commence an assault on 3rd, January 1945. **21st Army Group** In the **U.S. Ninth Army** area, **XIX Corps** sector the pocket south of Obermaubach is reduced by the 8th Division. In the **U.S. First Army** area, **V Corps** sector the Germans make a futile effort to dislodge the 1st Division at Elsenborn. In the XVIII Corps (Airborne) sector, activity is relatively tranquil. Reinforcements advance to bolster the 3rd Armored and 75th Divisions. In the **VII Corps** sector, the 75th Division, minus RCTs 289 and 290, is attached to XVIII Corps. At Sadzot, German infiltrators pierce the 3rd Armored perimeter and take the town, but they are thrown back out. Elements of 83rd Division drive into Rochefort. **12th Army Group** In the **U.S. Third Army** area, **VIII Corps** sector the 11th Armored Division (SHAEF reserve) is attached to Corps. The **III Corps** engages rear guards in the area between the Sauer and Wiltz Rivers, making gradual progress. Meanwhile, the 26th Division is also driving toward Wiltz and the 35th Division is encountering heavy resistance as it drives against the south flank of the enemy salient southwest of Villers-la-Bonne-Eau. In the **XII Corps** sector, the 80th Division holds Ringel against a counterattack. **(Atlantic-Italy) 15th Army Group** In the **U.S. Fifth Army** area, the offensive against Bologna is postponed, due mainly to the setbacks sustained in the Serchio Valley. Meanwhile, the Germans initiate a withdrawal in the Serchio Valley (IV Corps sector).

Germans passing burning equipment.

December 29th 1944 — (Pacific-Philippines) LEYTE: In the **U.S. Eighth Army** area, **X Corps** sector, Villaba, on the west coast, falls to the 1st Cavalry. In addition, the 32nd Division takes its designated objectives on the west coast to the north of the 1st Cavalry; 127th Infantry seizes the heights con trolling Antipolo Point, while the 128th Infantry takes the high ground above Campopo and Tabango Bays. Additional enemy contingents, operating along the coast, are being eradicated by contingents of the 34th Regiment, 24th Division. In the **XXIV Corps** sector, the 3rd Battalion, 305th Regiment, 77th Division grinds forward another 750 yards through intense resistance, inching closer to Palompon; however, the enemy

fire pins it down. In other activity, the Provisional Mountain Force deploys to jump off and drive east toward Palompon Road. **(Pacific-Marianas-Tinian)** B29s land on the Airfield. **(Pacific-Burma)** Patrols of the British 36th Division make contact with the Indian 19th Division; the encounter joins the N.C.A.C. and Fourteenth Army fronts. On the Arakan front, the towns of Kudaung and Rathedaung are now controlled by the 15th Corps. **(Atlantic-Western Europe) 21st Army Group** In the **British Second Army** area, the 30th Corps initiates relief of the U.S. 2nd Armored Division which is holding the western flank of the U.S. VII Corps. In the **U.S. Ninth Army** area, **V Corps** sector, the German and U.S. troops have taken defensive postures. The XVIII (Airborne) Corps sector remains unchanged. In the **VII Corps** sector, remnant infiltrators are being eliminated. Patrols are dispatched. In other activity, elements of the 83rd Division assault toward Rochefort. **12th Army Group** In the **U.S. Third Army** area, **VIII Corps** sector, preparations are made for an attack against Houffalize. In the **III Corps** sector, the Arlon-Bastogne highway is blasted open by C.C.A., 4th Armored Division. Meanwhile, the Villers-la-Bonne-Eau-Lutrebois area is being cleared by the 35th Division. The attack has some forward units advancing to Marvie, southeast of Bastogne, where they encounter troops of the 101st Airborne. In other activity, the 26th Division maintains its grueling advance toward Wiltz against heavy opposition. **(Atlantic-Eastern Europe)** Soviet forces penetrate the beleaguered defenses of the Germans at Budapest and street fighting erupts. The Germans forestall capitulation, holding their untenable positions against overwhelming odds until the 13th of February.

December 30th 1944 — (Pacific-Philippines) LEYTE: In the **U.S. Eighth Army** area, **X Corps** sector, the 1st Cavalry Division establishes contact with the 32nd Division outside of Villaba. In the **XXIV Corps** sector, the 77th Division attacks to clear the Palompon Road, closing from two directions. Meanwhile, the 3rd Battalion, 305th Regiment, maintains its drive, advancing to about 1,000 yards from Tipolo. The Provisional Mountain Force is halted by fierce opposition about four miles east of the Palompon River; however, the Japanese begin to pull out after dark. Abijao, north of Palompon, is set afire by elements of the 305th Infantry, which advance further north and establish radio contact with the 1st Cavalry. MINDORO: A second Supply Convoy arrives with reinforcements (3rd Battalion, 21st Regiment), but it is attacked; Kamikazes damage the Auxiliary Vessel *Porcupine* (IX-126 subsequently sunk by U.S. Forces) and damage the Destroyers *Pringle* (DD-477) and *Gansevoort* (DD-608). The PT-Boat Tender *Orestres* (AGP-10) is also damaged. In addition, several Merchant Vessels are lost, along with three LSTs and two LCMs. **(Pacific-Burma)** Kaduma falls to the British 33 Corps. **(Atlantic-Western Europe) 21st Army Group** In the **U.S. First Army** area, **XVIII Corps (Airborne)** sector, RCT 424 is released by 7th Armored to the 106th Division. In the **VII Corps** sector, the Germans abandon Rochefort. In other activity, the Corps gives the region southwest of line Marche-Namur to the British. **12th Army Group** In the **U.S. Third Army** area, **VIII Corps** sector, an assault against Houffalize commences; the Germans mount rigid resistance and inflict heavy damage to the 11th Armored Division, holding it to small progress. In related activity, Moircy is taken by the 87th Division and then lost to a counterattack. In the **III Corps** sector, the enemy mounts another attack to sever the Arlon-Bastogne highway and re-isolate Bastogne. The drive reaches Lutrebois and envelops two Companies of the 137th Regiment, 35th Division, at Villers-la-Bonne-Eau. Subsequent futile attempts are made to rescue the beleaguered troops. The German counterattack forces against the 11th Armored and 87th Divisions include the 130th Panzer Lehr and the 26th Volksgrenadier Divisions; the 1st S.S., (Brigadier E. Wisch, S.S. Oberst Mohmke) and the 167th Regulars, commanded by General Lt. Hocher, strike the 26th and 35th U.S. Divisions. On the following day, the Germans mount 35 counterattacks; however, all are thrown back. In other activity, one group of four German troops donning U.S. uniforms are discovered and killed. In another instance, seventeen more are spotted; the 37th Division states: "ONE SENTINEL, REINFORCED, SAW SEVENTEEN GERMANS IN AMERICAN UNIFORMS. FIFTEEN WERE KILLED AND TWO DIED SUDDENLY." **6th Army Group** Army again warns of a possible enemy assault. **(Atlantic-Eastern Europe)** The Germans continue to struggle against the Third Ukrainian Front in western Budapest. Mean while, elements of the Second Ukrainian Front penetrate German defenses and enter the eastern portion of the city.

82nd Airborne attending Mass at the Bulge.

December 31st 1944 — (Pacific-Philippines) LEYTE: In the **U.S. Eighth Army** area, **X Corps** sector, the 1st Cavalry Division, which is being relieved by the 77th Division, repulses repeated counterattacks at Villaba. In the **XXIV Corps** sector, enemy resistance is terminated along the remainder of Palompon Road by the 305th Regiment, 77th Division. Subsequently, elements of the 3rd Battalion establish contact with the Provisional Mountain Force outside of San Miguel. The 77th Division reports about 5,779 Japanese have been killed during the operation 21st-31st, December, and losses within the Division stand at 17 dead. MINDORO: Japanese Suicide Planes continue to strike U.S. Shipping. Also, Admiral Halsey's Fleet departs to join MAcArthur's forces and will support the Lingayen Gulf invasion. **(Pacific)** The Commander, 5th Fleet, issues Operation Plan 13-44, which directs a Joint Expeditionary Force to seize Iwo Jima for use as a Base, establish Military Government, and prepare to withdraw the invasion force as the conclusion of the capture and occupation phase. D-Day is confirmed; 19th, February 1945. **(Pacific-Burma)** In N.C.A.C. area, the U.S. 475th Infantry initiates a march toward Mong Wi subsequent to being relieved by the Chinese 50th Division at Tonk-wa. In the **British Fourteenth Army's** 33rd Corps sector, the British 2nd Division seizes Kabo. **(Atlantic-Western Europe) 21st Army Group** In the **U.S. First Army** area, **VII Corps** sector, the 83rd Division is reinforced by RCT 290, 75th Division and assumes responsibility for 3rd Armored's sector. **12th Army Group** In the **U.S. Third Army** area, **VIII Corps** sector, the town of Remagen is captured by the 87th Division; it closes against Moircy. Meanwhile, C.C.R., 11th Armored Division seizes Acul and Pinsamont; C.C.B. seizes Chenogne. In the **III Corps** sector, elements of 6th Armored take the high ground near Wardin while another column drives to the fringes of Rechrival. The Germans hold Lutrebois, and the isolated contingents of the 137th Regiment fail to be rescued at Villers-la-Bonne-Eau and are considered lost. Corps Artillery places TOT's (time on target) on Wiltz. **(Atlantic-Italy) 15th Army Group** Positions for the U.S. Fifth Army in the Serchio Valley are now about where they were at the end of October, since the retrieval of ground lost by the IV Corps. In the **British Eighth Army** area, the British have advanced to positions along the Naviglio Canal between the Lamone and Senio Rivers, but they cannot take Granarole. Plans are formulated to commence limited assaults to get the entire Eighth Army to the Senio.

U.S. Tanker takes time out to make a few stitches with a sewing machine.

1945

President Roosevelt's funeral procession (April 1945).

U.S. Coast Guard Plane escorting some Yanks back to the U.S.A.

The "Enola Gay" returning to Tinian, subsequent to dropping the atomic bomb on Hiroshima, Japan.

563A

Marines on the beach at Iwo Jima.

Infantry & Tanks moving through a minefield on Okinawa.

An American Officer pulls back his hand as a Japanese Officer extends his hand on the Philippines.

General Wainwright (Liberated) returns to Philippines in time for Japanese surrender. He is also on the U.S.S. Missouri in Toyko Bay, to witness Japan's capitulation.

A scuttled Japanese Carrier in Tokyo bay adding a Touch of somber finality to the demise of the once undefeated Japanese Imperial Navy.

January 1st 1945 — (United States) The Southern Defense Command is absorbed into the Eastern Defense Command. (Pacific-Caroline Islands) Contingents of the 321st Infantry, U.S. 81st Division debark on Fais Island, southeast of Ulithi, to destroy a Japanese radio station. The units depart on the 4th of January. (Pacific-Marianas) The 1st Battalion, 8th Marines, departs Tinian for Saipan, subsequent to five months Garrison duty on the island. (Pacific-Philippines) The U.S. initiates operations in Mindoro to clear the northeastern portion of the island, and subsequently commences similar missions in south Luzon to deceive the Japanese about Allied intentions in Luzon. On Leyte, the U.S. Eighth Army begins mopping up; the operation concludes May 8th. The Submarine U.S.S. *Stingray* (SS-186) lands supplies at Tawi Tawi. (Pacific-Burma) The **British Fourteenth Army** transfers its Headquarters from Imphal to Kalemyo; joint Army-Air Headquarters are established to ensure tight co-operation. (Pacific-China) General Wedemeyer informs the War Department that he plans to use U.S. Officers to advise the Chinese Alpha Force from Group Army Headquarters down to Regimental level. (Atlantic-Western Europe) German Planes numbering about 800 bombard Airfields in Belgium, France and Holland; the Operation, dubbed "BODENPLATTE" (Ground Plate). The Germans dispatch Reserve Aircraft and lose about 150 Planes and their crews to destroy about 800 Allied Planes on the ground. **12th Army Group** General Kramer, Commanding General, 66th Division, assumes the task of neutralizing German resistance in region containing Lorient and St. Nazaire (France), taking responsibility from the 94th Division. In the **U.S. Third Army** area, the III and VIII Corps step up the counteroffensive. In the **VIII Corps** sector, Jenneville and Moircy fall to the 87th Division, while elements of the 11th Armored Division secure Chenogne and woods to the north. C.C.A., 9th Armored Division pounds its way toward Senonchamps. Meanwhile, the 101st Airborne at Bastogne lends fire support to the 11th Armored's drive to the left and to the 6th Armored Division which is advancing on its right in the III Corps sector, seizing Bizery, Neffe and Mageret, then losing the latter. In the **III Corps** sector, a German salient southeast of Bastogne is neutralized. The 4th Armored Division maintains a corridor into Bastogne and simultaneously uses its guns to support the 35th Division, which is driving through Lutrebois, securing part of it. Elements of the 35th advance to strategic crossroads southeast of Marvie; however, no progress is made at Villers-la-Bonne-Eau, Belgium or Harlange, Luxembourg. **6th Army Group** Operation NORWIND is launched by the Germans against the U.S. Seventh Army. German General Balck commits ten (understrengthed) Divisions at Alsace, forcing the 44th and 100th Divisions and the 106th Cavalry Group to surrender ground. The 6th Army Group is to withdraw from Alsace and form a new line to the west along the Maginot Line on the crest of the Vosges and to occupy a line on its left at Bitche — Strasbourg. In the **XV Corps** sector, Germans pierce the 44th Division perimeter at Rimling; however, the infiltrators are driven out. During the vicious contest, Sgt. Charles MacGillivary, Co. I, 71st Regiment, while leading his Squad in the darkness through the snow, encounters units of the 17th Panzer Grenadier Division. The Germans open fire and halt the American advance. The intrepid Sergeant singlehandedly kills several enemy troops and destroys four machine guns in addition to buying time for other units to move in and exterminate the threat. MacGillivary is seriously wounded as he advances; however, he recovers and becomes a recipient of the Medal of Honor. The 100th Division is strapped between the two attack forces and its right

flank is exposed due to the withdrawal of Task Force Hudelson (VI Corps), which is forced to pull back to Lemberg-Mouterhouse. RCT 141, 36th Division speeds to fill the gap between the XV and VI Corps. In the **VI Corps** sector, the Germans drive a wedge into the left flank of the Corps south of Bitche. The enemy strikes the 45th Division lines at Philippsbourg-Neuhoffen-Obersteinbach, but is unable to advance. At Dambach, the 45th clears out infiltrators. The 79th Division and Task Force Herren (70th Division) rush to bolster the 45th Division and C.C.B., 4th Armored moves to guard the Vosges exits. (Atlantic-Eastern Europe) The Germans and Russians battle heavily in and around Budapest. (Atlantic-Italy) There is little activity along the entire front as each side prepares for a renewal of fighting. German Army Group C, under Vietinghoff, composed of the Tenth and Fourteenth Armies of Generals Herr and Lemelson respectively, use the pause to strengthen their defenses. The British Eighth Army, under General McCreery, is deployed along the Senio, and the Fifth Army, under Truscott, is still about ten miles from Bologna.

January 2nd 1945 — (Pacific) The V Amphibious Landing Force Operation Plan 3-44, regarding the invasion of Iwo Jima, is approved. (Pacific-Philippines) Leyte Gulf is buzzing with activity as the assault Convoys are assembling for the attack against Luzon. Advance Warships including Minesweepers and Hydrographic Group (TG-77.6) embark for Luzon and are soon attacked by enemy Planes including Kamikazes. The Oiler *Cowanesque* (AO-79) is damaged by a Suicide Plane. U.S. Army Aircraft sink the Japanese Coastal Defense Vessel No. 138. On **Mindoro**, construction is begun on one Heavy Bomber Field; a second field is to be started later. After dark, Japanese Planes bomb Airfields and destroy twenty-two Aircraft. (Pacific-Burma) In N.C.A.C. area, the U.S. 475th Infantry crosses the Shweli by way of an improvised bridge, laid previously by elements of the Chinese 50th Division during December 1944. (Atlantic-Western Europe) **21 Army Group** In the **British Second Army's 30th Corps** sector, the British 53rd Division takes responsibility for the Marche-Hotton sector in Belgium, relieving the U.S. 84th Division. **12th Army Group** In the **U.S. Third Army's VIII Corps** sector, the 87th Division takes Gerimont, and Senonchamps is seized by the combined efforts of C.C.A., 9th Armored and C.C.B., 10th Armored. Meanwhile, the 11th Armored Division overruns Mande St. Etienne. In an effort to assist the III Corps clear the woods in the vicinity of Lutrebois, the 4th Armored commits elements while it simultaneously widens the southern corridor into Bastogne. In the **III Corps** sector, C.C.B., 6th Armored pushes elements into Michamps. Additional contingents push into Oubourcy, but are forced back out; yet other contingents drive unsuccessfully against Arloncourt. Meanwhile, C.C.A. seizes Wardin. **6th Army Group** In the **U.S. Seventh Army** area, the Command Post at Saverne transfers to Luneville. In the **XV Corps** sector, German advances force the 100th Division to withdraw its right flank further, and the right flank of the 44th Division is compelled to draw back beyond Gros Rederching. In the **VI Corps** sector, the west flank of the 45th Division, despite being reinforced, comes under severe pressure from the enemy. There is heavy fighting at several sectors along the Bitche salient. The Center and right flank contingents of the Corps initiate withdrawal to prepared positions at the Maginot Line. (Atlantic-Eastern Europe) The Germans mount heavy counterattacks northwest of Budapest to attempt to crack the encirclement of the city. (Atlantic-Italy)

15th Army Group The British Eighth Army initiates a series of limited attacks to terminate resistance on the eastern bank of the Senio River. In the Canadian 1st Corps sector, Conventelle is seized as the Corps drives toward the sea.

January 2nd-12th 1945 — (Pacific-Philippines) Marine Aircraft Group 14 (VMC-212, 222, and 223) land at Guiuam, Samar, and will operate under command of the Fifth Air Force.

January 3rd 1945 — (Pacific-Formosa-Ryukyus-Pescadores) In preparation for the invasion of Luzon, Carriers, under Vice Admiral J.S. McCain (U.S Third Fleet), launch Planes against enemy Aircraft and Shipping, with the primary thrust being against Formosa and secondary strikes against the Ryukyus and Pescadores. The assaults are hindered because of bad weather. Marine Corps Planes (Fighter Squadrons 124 and 213) attached to the U.S.S. *Essex* participate; this is the first time Marine Fighter Squadrons attack land installations from a Carrier. **(Pacific-Philippines)** Task Group 77.2 en route to Luzon shoots down a Kamikaze. On Mindoro, a Guerrilla force of about seventy men unsuccessfully attacks the Japanese at Pinamalayan. In other activity, Company K, 21st Infantry embarks for Marinduque Island to assist Guerrillas in eliminating the remaining enemy resistance concentrated in the northeastern portion of the island at Boac. In Naval activity, the Escort Carrier *Sergeant Bay* (CVE-83) and the Destroyer Escort *Robert F. Keller* (DE-419) are damaged by a collision. In addition, the Minesweeper *Monadnock* (CM-9) is damaged by collision off Luzon. The Japanese Submarine Chaser No. 10 is sunk by Army Aircraft. **(Pacific-Burma)** In ALFSEA area, the British 15th Corps invades Akyab without any Artillery cover fire as no opposition is anticipated. The 3rd Commando Brigade debarks landing craft in the Naaf River, followed by contingents of the Indian 25th Division. In the **British Fourteenth Army** area, **33 Corps** sector, Ye-u is occupied by the British 2nd Division. **(Atlantic-Western Europe)** General Eisenhower confers with General De Gaulle. By coincidence, Winston Churchill is in attendance. De Gaulle prefers to hold Strasbourg "WITH THE WHOLE FRENCH ARMY IF NECESSARY," rather than abandon it without a fight. De Gaulle further informs Eisenhower in writing that he will act independently if Ike doesn't authorize the initiative. Ike responds by telling De Gaulle: "THE FRENCH ARMY WILL RECEIVE NO AMMUNITION, FOOD OR SUPPLIES UNLESS IT OBEYS MY ORDERS," and emphasizes the fact that if the French had cleared the pocket around Colmar, the conversation would not have occurred. **21st Army Group** The **U.S. First Army** initiates its counteroffensive to eradicate the German Ardennes salient from the north. The **VII Corps** assaults southeast against Houffalize, taking Trinal, Magoster, Floret and Malempre. In addition, positions are gained in Bois de Tave, Freineux and Le Batty, in addition to gaining ground near Belle Haie. The 2nd and 3rd Armored Divisions and the 83rd and 84th Divisions participate. In the **XVIII Corps (Airborne)** sector, the 82nd Airborne drives southeast to improve its positions. **12th Army Group** In the **U.S. Third Army** area, **VIII Corps** sector, the Germans surround contingents of the 87th Division east of St. Hubert. The 17th Airborne Division mounts a drive that positions it about five miles northwest of Bastogne. C.C.A., 4th Armored maintains its protective wing, defending the corridor into Bastogne, and Task Force Higgins, composed of contingents of the 101st Airborne and C.C.A., 10th Armored, is formed to stop any possible enemy attack into Bastogne. Meanwhile, elements of the 101st Airborne and the 501st Paratroop Infantry are clearing Bois Jacques. In the **III Corps** sector, the 6th Armored Division unleashes heavy Artillery bombardments upon Arloncourt, Bourcy, and Michamps, while repulsing enemy attacks west of the latter and seizing a road junction south of Wardin. Meanwhile, the 35th Division secures about two thirds of Lutrebois and seizes crossroads west of Villers-la-Bonne-Eau, Belgium; however, the Germans repel the Yanks at Harlange (Luxembourg). East of Harlange, the 26th Division battles heavily to secure the area north of Mecher-Dunkrodt and Kaundorf. **6th Army Group** Army Group receives responsibility to defend Strasbourg. In the **U.S. Seventh Army** area, **XV Corps** sector, the Germans pierce the defenses at Aachen, but they are pushed out. At Gros Rederching, elements of the French 2nd Armored Division enter the town; however, German resistance prevents it from clearing it and the U.S. 44th Division tries unsuccessfully to relieve the French 2nd Armored. In the **VI Corps** sector, the enemy enlarges its Bitche salient taking Wingen and Philippsbourg; they are repulsed at Reipertsweiler and at Sar reinsberg-Meisanthal by the U.S. 45th Division. In the 14th Armored zone near Philippsbourg, P.F.C. George B. Turner is isolated from his unit (Battery C, 499th FA Battalion) by the charging enemy when he spots a friendly contingent of troops. He immediately confiscates a Rocket Launcher and advances singlehandedly on foot to duel two approaching Tanks. Standing amidst ringing cannon and small arms fire, he hits the bull's eye, destroying the first Tank and scores a direct hit that disables the second. With uncompromising tenacity, he jumps aboard a Half-trac commandeers its machine gun and again stands conspicuously in the line of enemy fire, rattling off incessant rounds against the approaching Infantry and disorganizing their attack. A counterattack is mounted by the Americans and the Germans quickly disable two Vehicles. Turner brandishes a light machine gun and begins giving cover fire, enabling the troops to evacuate their burning Vehicles. One Soldier, unable to extricate himself, is spotted by Turner. He rushes to rescue the man, but the Tank's ammunition explodes, seriously wounding him. Turner refuses evacuation and on the following day participates in action which drives off an enemy Patrol. Meanwhile, the center and right flanks of the Corps complete the withdrawal to the Maginot Line. **(Atlantic-Italy) 15th Army Group** In the **British Eighth Army** area, the Canadian 5th Armored Division advances to Canale di Bonifica Destra del Reno as it drives north. The Canadian 1st Division attacks to clear the enemy between it and the British 5th Corps near Cotignola. Elements of the 5th Corps push out from Felisio, clearing the bank of the Senio as far north as Severo.

The crew of the B-29 Waddy's Wagon take a moment for some fun.

Medics lugging supplies in Luxembourg.

January 4th 1945 — (Pacific-Formosa-Ryukyus) Admiral McCain's Task Force (under Halsey) continues to bombard enemy facilities under terrible weather conditions; nevertheless, despite the curtailed raids, the U.S. Aircraft destroy 110 Planes during the two day attack, sink twelve enemy Vessels, including the Submarine Chaser No. 210, and damage 28 others. Task Force 38 loses eighteen Planes during the raids. A few days earlier, Admiral Halsey, speaking to his Task Forces via the TBS (Ship broadcasting system) as they move to support the Lingayen Gulf invasion: "THIS IS BLACKJACK HIMSELF. YOUR WORK SO FAR HAS BEEN SUPERB. I EXPECT EVEN MORE. KEEP THE BASTARDS DYING." **(Pacific-Philippines)** Task Forces 77.6 and 77.2 are attacked by enemy Planes as they cruise toward Lingayen Gulf. The Carrier Escort *Ommaney Bay* (CVE-79) is damaged by a Kamikaze and subsequently sunk by U.S. Forces. Other U.S. Vessels damaged by Japanese Planes today are the Destroyer *Bell* (DD-587) and the Oiler *Pecos* (AO-65). U.S. Aircraft sink the Japanese Submarine Chaser No. 210 in the Formosa Strait. In other activity, Admiral Halsey directs Task Force 38 to broaden its coverage of Luzon by extending south. After nightfall the Main body of the Luzon Task Force departs Leyte Gulf. In the **U.S. Eighth Army** area, **X Corps** sector, offensive operations cease on Leyte. At Mindoro, Japanese Planes strike and destroy an ammunition Ship. **(Pacific-Burma)** In ALFSEA area, the 15th Corps completes its occupation of Akyab and now controls its strategic port and Airfield (Ara-

kan Front). In N.C.A.C. area, the U.S. 475th Infantry completes its crossing of the Shweli and awaits supplies by Airdrop. **(Atlantic-Western Europe) 21st Army Group** In the **British Second Army** area, the 30th Corps launches an offensive west of the Ourthe River to the right of the U.S. First Army. The British 53rd Division drives south abreast of the U.S. VII Corps. The British 6th Airborne encounters strong opposition outside of Rochefort. In the **U.S. First Army** area, **VII Corps** sector, Beffe and Lamormenil fall to the 2nd Armored Division, which also repulses repeated counterattacks at Devantave and shoves units to the outskirts of Odeigne. Meanwhile, 3rd Armored storms into Baneux, Jevigne and Lansival in addition to establishing a bridgehead at Groumont Creek. In the **XVIII Corps (Airborne)** sector, the 82nd Airborne ramrods forward, consuming Heirlot, Bergeval, Mont de Fosse and Odrimont, in addition to seizing the wooded heights north and northeast of Abrefontaine and simultaneously getting other elements to the Salm River. **12th Army Group** In the **U.S. Third Army** area, **VIII Corps** sector, the Germans mount fierce resistance, repelling the 87th Division at Pironpre and resisting tenaciously against the 17th Airborne Division in the Pinsamont-Rechrival-Hubermont region. During one enemy attack, Staff Sergeant Isodore Jachman, 513th Paratroop Infantry, attempts to aid his Company which is immobilized by Artillery, Small Arms and Mortar fire: he grabs a Bazooka and dashes through; he singlehandedly intercepts two Tanks, disabling one and forcing the other to reverse direction, before he succumbs to mortal wounds. His unwavering courage contributes greatly to the failure of the attack. Sergeant Jachman receives the Medal of Honor posthumously. In addition, the Germans launch an attack against the 101st Airborne Division positions; however, the Paratroopers hold the line. In the **III Corps** sector, German pressure from successive assaults compels the 6th Armored to compress its line east of Bastogne near Mageret-Wardin. Furious fighting continues at Harlange, with the Germans holding tough against the 35th Division, but, it is able to seize Lutrebois. In the 26th Division sector, vicious combat ensues with the Germans surrendering only a few hundred yards. **6th Army Group** In the **U.S. Seventh Army** area, **XV Corps** sector, the Germans retain Frauenberg and Gros Rederching, following futile attacks by the 44th Division. Some ground is seized by the 36th Division after a hard fight on a hill between Goetzenbruck and Lemberg. In the **VI Corps** sector, the 45th Division pounds its way to the edge of Wingen as it continues to eliminate the enemy salient at Bitche. Elements of the 45th Division drive northeast across Wingen-Wimmenau road to lift pressure off Reipertsweiler, while additional units overpower resistance at Saegmuhl as they drive to clear the Reipertsweiler-Wildenguth road. The advance establishes contact with isolated contingents at Wildenguth and secures nearly half of Philippsbourg.

January 5th 1945 — (Pacific-Kurile Islands) Rear Admiral J.L. McCrea's Cruiser and Destroyer Task Force strikes Japanese facilities on Surabachi Wan, Paramushiro. **(Pacific-Volcano-Bonins)** A Cruiser Destroyer Task Force under Rear Admiral A.E. Smith bombards Chichi Jima, Haji Jima, and Iwo Jima, Bonin Islands, while Army Aircraft (Seventh Air Force) attack the same installations. The Destroyer *David W. Taylor* (DD-551) becomes damaged after striking a mine. **(Pacific-Philippines)** About thirty enemy Planes attack Task Groups 77.2 and 77.6. Most Planes are shot down, yet Kamikazes again inflict terrible damage: the Escort Carriers *Manila Bay* (CVE-61), *Savo Island* (CVE-78; the Heavy Cruiser *Louisville*

(CA-28); the Destroyers *Helm* (DD-388), *David W. Taylor* (DD-551) and the Destroyer Escort *Strafford* (DE-411) sustain damages. In addition, a small Seaplane Tender, the *Orca* (AVP-49) and the Ocean Tug *Apache* (ATF-67), are also struck by Suicide Planes. The Destroyer Escorts *Edwin A. Howard* (DE-346) and the *Leland E. Thomas* (DE-420) become damaged off the Philippines after colliding. Aircraft from U.S. Carriers intercept and damage two Japanese Destroyers. **(Pacific-Burma)** In N.C.A.C. area, contingents of the 90th Regiment, Chinese 30th Division begin fording the Shweli River. **(Pacific-China)** The 22nd Division, Chinese New Sixth Army, completes its move to China. **(Atlantic-England)** During early January, British Press had presented an illusion that Field Marshal Montgomery had saved the American Armies at the Bulge. This propaganda does little to heal the festering difficulties between the two Allies. General Bradley protested bitterly to Eisenhower about the distortions. Today, SHEAF issues clarification concerning American and British participation at the Bulge; however, the message is still not clear. In two days, Montgomery issues his statement concerning his views about the Bulge; his words infuriate the American Commanders, particularly because Montgomery never mentions that his Command is temporary. In addition, he fails to state that the enemy offensive had already been stabilized when he received command. **(Atlantic-Western Europe) 21st Army Group** In the **U.S. First Army** area, **VII Corps** sector, contingents of the 2nd Armored Division secure part of Odeigne, while others drive toward Dochamps; the main attack hits heavy opposition and is unable to make much progress toward Consy. The 3rd Armored Division takes Lavaux and enters Lierneux, but the German rear action at Bois de Groumont is tenacious. In the **XVIII Corps** sector, enemy counterattacks are thrown back along the line and the U.S. Paratroopers advance all along the line. **12th Army Group** In the **Third Army** area, **VIII Corps** sector, the 87th Division encounters stiff resistance as it advances west of Bastogne near Bonnerue and Pironpre, (The remainder of Corps is in a defensive posture). In the **III Corps sector**, the 35th Division is engaged in a stalemate battle. **6th Army Group** The French First Army is to relieve U.S. contingents and assume responsibility for Strasbourg, but the transfer is delayed due to an enemy assault. In the **U.S. Seventh Army** area, **XV Corps** sector, the Germans are pushed from Frauenberg and Gros Rederching. In the **VI Corps** sector, the enemy mounts fierce resistance at the Bitche salient against the 45th Division. The majority of Wingen is secured and enemy resistance is totally reduced at Philippsbourg. On the right flank of the Corps, the Germans take Offendorf, Herrlisheim and Rohrweiler, subsequent to establishing a bridgehead across the Rhine at Gambsheim. Task Force Linden is struck as it attempts to relieve elements; it reacts by mounting a two-pronged attack against Gambsheim. Meanwhile, Task Force A drives from Weyersheim, advancing to the west bank of the Landgraben Canal, and Task Force B, which is pushing from Kilstett, encounters rigid opposition immediately upon attacking north and is halted. **(Atlantic-Italy)** The U.S. Fifth Army orders regrouping. In the **British Eighth Army** area, **5 Corps** sector, the Canadian 1st and 5th Corps link up along the Senio River, having completed their limited attacks to fortify the Winter Line positions.

January 6th 1945 — (Pacific-Philippines) Two American Task Forces reach Lingayen Gulf and bombard enemy positions, while minesweeping operations ensue to clear way for following invasion forces. Japanese Suicide Planes intercept and inflict more damage; however, the original 150 Aircraft which had been deployed by the Japanese on Luzon on January 1st are now down to about thirty five; enemy Air activity diminishes greatly subsequent to today's raids. During the Suicide attacks, the U.S.S. *Walke* is attacked by four enemy Planes. Commander George D. Fleming positions himself on the unprotected wings of the bridge and directs fire, which destroys the first two Planes, and he remains steadfast as the third closes and explodes on the bridge. Commander Fleming is mortally wounded; still, he witnesses the fourth Plane being shot from the sky. Within a few hours he succumbs to his wounds. He receives the Medal of Honor. On Mindoro, fresh enemy troops from Luzon reoccupy recently abandoned Pinamalayan. Soon after their arrival, Guerrillas and Company I, 21st Infantry assault and drive the Japs back toward Calapan. U.S. Naval damages Kamikazes; Battleships *New Mexico* (BB-40) and *California* (BB-44); Heavy Cruisers *Louisville* (CA-28) and *Minneapolis* (CA-36); Light Cruiser *Columbia* (CL-56); Destroyers *Richard P. Leary* (DD-664), *Allen M. Sumner* (DD-692), *Walke* (DD-723), and *O'Brien* (DD-725), and the *Newcomb* (DD-586), the latter also sustaining accidental damage by U.S. Planes. The High Speed Minesweeper *Southard* (DMS-10) and the High Speed Transport *Brooks* (APD-10) are also damaged by Suicide Planes. The Destroyer *Lowry* (DD-770) is accidentally damaged by U.S. Planes. In addition, the High Speed Minesweeper *Hovey* (DMS-11) is sunk by an Aircraft Torpedo and the High Speed Minesweeper *Long* (DMS-12) is sunk by a Suicide Plane. **(Pacific-Tinian)** General Hansell is relieved of command of the Twenty-first Bomber Command. There has been dissatisfaction with the way the air attacks over Japan have been going, prompting General Arnold to send a representative to to inform Hansell. On the following day, General Curtis LeMay arrives to assume command. LeMay concentrates on heavy saturation bombing missions which carry high explosives and incendiary bombs. The Japanese find they have no effective defense against the attacks and many cities are raised. **(Pacific-Burma)** In N.C.A.C. area, monsoon rains begin as the U.S. 475th Infantry intiates bivouac around Mong Wi. The Chinese 38th Division becomes the first CAI outfit to return to Chinese territory; its 112th Regiment advances to Loiwing and dispatches Patrols across the Shweli River. **(Atlantic-Western Europe) 21st Army Group** In the **U.S. First Army** area, **VII Corps** sector, the 84th Infantry and 2nd Armored Divisions drive toward Consy, each deploying outside the town; elements of the 2nd Armored Division eliminate opposition at Odeigne, securing it totally; they also get contingents ahead to make contact with the 3rd Armored at the Manhay-Houffalize road, seizing Fraiture, La Falise and Lierneux as they move. Meanwhile, Bois Houby is secured by the 83rd Armored Reconnaissance Battalion. In the **XVIII Corps** sector, the 82nd Airborne consolidates its positions, while the 30th Division maneuvers to protect its left flank, driving south toward Spineux and Wanne; RCT 112, 28th Division participates in the assault. **12th Army Group** The **U.S. Fifteenth Army** commanded by Major General Ray E. Porter becomes operational. In the **U.S. Third Army** area, **VIII Corps** sector, German Tanks burst into Bonnerue, striking the thinly held lines of the 87th Division, which is attacking toward Tillet with scaled down thrusts. In the **III Corps** sector, the 6th Armored Division repulses several counterattacks. In the **XII Corps** sector, Dahl and Goesdorf are seized by the 319th Regiment, 80th Division. The 90th Division advances for battle as General Patton drives toward III Corps Headquarters. Moving in the opposite direction is a long line of ambulances transporting wounded Yanks back to receive medical aid. When the men of the 90th spot General Patton, there is a roar of applause for the General who is again at the front. **6th Army Group** In the **U.S. Seventh Army** area, **XV Corps** sector, the attack to restore the Main Line of Resistance on the right flank of the 45th Division ceases on the line extending along the southern edge of Bois de Blies Brucken to the region north of Gros Rederching. In the **VI Corps** sector, the 45th Division encounters fierce resistance at the Bitche salient against the center and left positions; however, it succeeds in neutralizing strong counterattacks against Philippsbourg. Meanwhile, the Germans continue to fortify their positions west of the Rhine on the east flank of the Corps. At Stattmatten, the isolated elements of Task Force Linden are relieved by the 79th Division, which clears the town; Rohrweiler and Sessenheim are also seized as it drives to the outskirts of Drusenheim. Task Force Linden reinitiates its effort to take Gambsheim, but it fails. **(Atlantic-Italy) 15th Army Group** The U.S. Fifth Army continues regrouping.

January 7th-9th 1945 — (Atlantic-Western Europe) Field Marshal Montgomery refers to the German offensive at the Bulge in part: "HE OBTAINED TACTICAL SURPRISE. HE DROVE A DEEP WEDGE INTO THE CENTER OF FIRST U.S. ARMY AND SPLIT THE AMERICAN FORCES IN TWO. THE SITUATION LOOKED AS IF IT MIGHT BECOME AWKWARD; THE GERMANS HAD BROKEN RIGHT THROUGH A WEAK SPOT AND WERE HEADING FOR THE MEUSE." "AS SOON AS I SAW WHAT WAS HAPPENING I TOOK CERTAIN STEPS TO ENSURE THAT IF THE GERMANS GOT TO THE MEUSE THEY WOULD CERTAINLY NOT GET OVER THAT RIVER. AND I CARRIED OUT CERTAIN MOVEMENTS SO AS TO PROVIDE BALANCED DISPOSITIONS TO MEET THE THREATENED DANGER; THESE WERE AT THE TIME, MERELY PRECAUTIONS i.e. I WAS THINKING AHEAD."

"THEN THE SITUATION BEGAN TO DETERIORATE. BUT THE WHOLE ALLIED TEAM RALLIED TO MEET THE DANGER; NATIONAL CONSIDERATIONS WERE THROWN OVERBOARD; GENERAL EISENHOWER PLACED ME IN COMMAND OF THE WHOLE NORTHERN FRONT. I EMPLOYED THE WHOLE AVAILABLE POWER OF THE BRITISH GROUP OF ARMIES; THIS POWER WAS BROUGHT INTO PLAY VERY GRADUALLY AND IN SUCH A WAY THAT IT WOULD NOT INTERFERE WITH THE AMERICAN LINES OF COMUNICATION. FINALLY IT WAS PUT INTO BATTLE (January 3rd) WITH A BANG AND TODAY BRITISH DIVISIONS ARE FIGHTING HARD ON THE RIGHT FLANK OF THE FIRST U.S. ARMY." "YOU THUS HAVE THE PICTURE OF BRITISH TROOPS FIGHTING ON BOTH SIDES OF AMERICAN FORCES WHO HAVE SUFFERED A HARD BLOW." ... "THE BATTLE HAS BEEN MOST INTERESTING; I THINK POSSIBLY ONE OF THE MOST INTERESTING AND TRICKY BATTLES I HAVE EVER HANDLED, WITH GREAT ISSUES AT STAKE." Word of Montgomery's press conference reaches American command on the following day, incensing U.S. Commanders. General Bradley releases a statement in an attempt to straighten the record and "RETRIEVE THE INTEGRITY OF U.S. COMMANDERS." On the ninth, General Bradley speaks with General Eisenhower: "YOU MUST KNOW, AFTER WHAT HAS HAPPENED I CANNOT SERVE UNDER MONTGOMERY. IF HE IS TO BE PUT IN COMMAND OF ALL GROUND FORCES, YOU MUST SEND ME HOME, FOR IF MONTGOMERY GOES IN OVER ME, I WILL HAVE LOST THE CONFIDENCE OF MY COMMAND." Eisenhower, who had earlier brushed off lightly the comments of Bradley referring to General Marshall's as-

surances of "AMERICANS NEVER COMING UNDER BRITISH COMMAND," responds to Bradley: "I THOUGHT YOU WERE THE ONE PERSON I COULD COUNT ON FOR DOING ANYTHING I ASKED YOU TO." Bradley, determined to hold his ground and integrity as a loyal General retorts. "YOU CAN IKE, I'VE ENJOYED EVERY BIT OF MY SERVICE WITH YOU, BUT THIS IS ONE THING I CANNOT TAKE." In addition, General Patton, aware of Bradley's sentiments, tells Bradley: "IF YOU QUIT, BRAD, THEN I'LL BE QUITTING WITH YOU."

Generals Bradley and Eisenhower with Air Chief Marshal Sir Arthur W. Tedder and Field Marshall Montgomery during an earlier meeting at Maastricht.

Generals Eisenhower and Patton.

January 7th 1945 — (Pacific-Philippines) Vice Admiral J.B. Oldendorf's Task Force, which includes Battleships, Cruisers and Destroyers, commence a two day bombardment of Luzon in the Lingayen Gulf area in concert with Carrier Planes attached to Rear Admiral C.T. Durgin's Escort Carrier Group, to soften resistance. Meanwhile, underwater demolition teams are clearing obstacles. The U.S.S. *Palmer* (DMS-5), a High Speed Minesweeper, is sunk by a Horizontal Bomber and the LST 912 and the Attack Transport *Callaway* (APA-35) are both damaged by Kamikazes. On Mindoro, the diminishing Japanese Air Force makes no appearance over the San Jose area for the first time. **(Pacific-Burma)** In the **British Fourteenth Army** area, **33 Corps** sector, the British 2nd Division and the Indian 19th Divisions approach Shwebo. **(Pacific-China)** The Submarine U.S.S. *Barb*, operating in the East China Sea on her second war patrol with the Submarines *Picuda* and *Queenfish* spots a Convoy in the Formosa Strait (Nankuan Chiang Mamkwan Harbor). The *Barb*, commanded by Eugene B. Fluckey, sinks an ammunition Ship in addition to other tonnage (*Shinyo Maru, Amnyo Maru*). The Freighter *Hiroshima*

Maru is sunk by the actions of the Wolf Pack. **(Atlantic-Western Europe) 21st Army Group** In the **British Second Army** area, **30th Corps** sector, Grimbiermont falls to the British 53rd Division. In the **U.S. First Army** area, **VII Corps** sector, the U.S. 84th Infantry and the 2nd Armored Divisions continue to progress as they drive toward Houffalize, seizing Dochamps and Marcouray, in addition, only rear action enemy troops remain near Consy. The 3rd Armored Division plows forward, overrunning Grand Sart, Regne, Verleumont and Sart. In the **XVIII Corps (Airborne)** area, the 82nd Airborne continues to sprint forward, taking Goronne, Farniers, Mont and Rochelinval; other contingents secure positions on a ridge just outside of Comte. In conjunction, RCT 112 seizes Spineux, Wanne and Wanneranval. **12th Army Group** In the **U.S. Third Army** area, **VIII Corps** sector, the Germans mount some resistance near Bonnerue against elements of the 87th Division, which is also attacking against Tillet, Belgium. In one deadly exchange, enemy machine guns jeopardize Company I, 346th Regiment and threaten to wipe out a contingent which is exposed on frozen open terrain. Staff Sergeant Curtis F. Shoup disregards the danger and advances with his Automatic Rifle being struck by enemy rounds several times as he moves. Undaunted, he keeps moving until close enough to toss a grenade which takes out the menacing machine gun and assures the safety of his Company, while sacrificing his own life. The 17th Airborne Division seizes Flamierge, Rechrival and Millomont and drives to the fringes of Flamizoulle. In the **III Corps** sector, the 6th Armored Division remains under heavy attack east of Bastogne. In the **XX Corps** sector, the Commanding General of the 94th Division assumes command of the area previously held by the 90th Division. **6th Army Group** The boundary between the U.S. Seventh Army and the French 1st Army is adjusted, giving the French responsibility for Strasbourg. In the **U.S. Seventh Army** area, **VI Corps** sector, the remaining resistance in Wingen is reduced by the 45th Division, which also gains positions on the heights at Althorn. Near Wissembourg, the Maginot Line is threatened by the enemy, prompting the Corps to fortify its left flank; the 79th Division forms Task Force Wahl, composed of the 827th Tank Destroyer Battalion, C.C.A., 14th Armored Division and contingents of the 222nd, 313th and 315th Regiments. Meanwhile, the Germans attack against Aschbach and Stundweiler, pushing back outposts at each; at the Gambsheim bridgehead, the enemy is successful in repelling the 314th Infantry, 79th Division at Drusenheim. It is relieved by the French 3rd Algerian Division, which resumes the attack, driving toward Gambsheim from Kilstett. **(Atlantic-Eastern Europe)** The Germans continue determined efforts to rescue the beleaguered Budapest Garrison, seizing Esztergom, northwest of the city. **(Atlantic-Italy) 15th Army Group** In the **British Eighth Army** area, the Polish 2nd Corps retires from the line; its sector and the 5th Kresowa Division is turned over to the 5th Corps.

January 8th 1945 — **(Pacific)** Commanding General V Amphibious Corps Landing Force issues an alternative plan for the invasion of Iwo Jima (No. 4-44), which suggests invading the western beaches; however, the original plan is implemented on D-Day. **(Pacific-Philippines)** The Minesweeping operations off Luzon is completed. The Naval and Air preinvasion bombardment of enemy positions in the Lingayen Gulf area continues. Suicide Planes damage the Escort Carriers *Kitkun Bay* (CVE-71) and *Kadashan Bay* (CVE-76). **(Pacific-Burma)** In the N.C.A.C. area, the U.S. 475th Infantry deployed at Mong Wi is directed to advance for combat. **(Pacific-**

China) The Chinese Training and Combat Command is split. Chinese Training Center is to operate a Command and General Staff School and Service schools. Chinese Combat Command is to control the operations of the Alpha Force and to provide liaison sections for each major Chinese command under General Ho. **(Atlantic-Western Europe) 21st Army Group** In the **U.S. First Army VII Corps** area, the 4th Cavalry Group and the 84th Division battle the retreating enemy near Cielle and Marcourt and also at Manhay. Meanwhile, the 2nd Armored Division attacks against Samree. The 3rd Armored Division takes Hebronval, Joubieval, Ottre, Joubieval, and Provedroux. **12th Army Group** The VIII Corps, Third Army is hit heavily by the Germans, losing Bonnerue. At Flamierge, contingents of the 17th Airborne Division are pushed from the town; other elements gain, then lose the high ground outside of Laval. In the **III Corps** sector, the Germans are driven from their recently captured positions at Neffe-Wardin by the 6th Armored Division. In the 80th Division sector, the Germans mount a fierce assault supported by Artillery, Mortar and Rocket fire against contingents of the 319th Regiment at Dahl, Luxembourg. Sergeant Day G. Turner, Company B, commanding a nine-man Squad is besieged by Infantry and Tanks; however, he orders the men into a house and subsequently repulses successive attacks. A Tank finally crashes through. Although five men are wounded and one killed, Turner refuses to relent, choosing to fight room to room. He lobs a can of burning oil on the attackers, then exchanges hand grenades prior to nasty hand-to-hand combat. He ultimately holds the house and bayonets two Germans with their own weapons. Sergeant Turner's heroism nets the capture of twenty-five prisoners. In addition, eleven Germans are killed. Turner receives the Medal of Honor. **6th Army Group** In the **U.S. Seventh Army** area, **XV Corps** sector, the Germans take Rimling and repulse attacks against their Gambsheim bridgehead. During one fierce exchange, about 200 Infantry and twelve Tanks charge the positions of the 379th Regiment, 100th Division at Rimling, costing the unit its guns. Sergeant Charles F. Carey Jr. rounds up stray troops and rescues two threatened Squads. He evacuates the wounded, then singlehandedly attacks a German-held house, under cover fire from his detachment, and returns with sixteen prisoners and sufficient information for the other U.S. troops to capture an additional 41 enemy troops. Leading another Patrol, Carey inches toward an enemy Tank and damages it from close range with a rocket. As the Tankers abandon it, Carey kills three and wounds a fourth. On the following day, Sgt. Carey is killed by Sniper fire. He receives the Medal of Honor posthumously. In addition, the enemy also holds firmly at Drusenheim. In the **French 1st Army** area, elements of the 3rd U.S. Division commence an attack against Hill 616, near Keyserberg, France. Tech Sergeant Russell E. Dunham dons a white robe to blend in with the snow-covered terrain and singlehandedly attacks three machine gun nests, advancing under incessant fire, which rips a 15 inch wound across his back and spins him down the hill in great pain. He recovers and reinitiates his attack, still transporting a dozen hand grenades and twelve carbine magazines. A grenade is tossed, but he instinctively kicks it aside, kills the machine gunner and his assistant gunner, then tugs the remaining Soldier out by his collar. Still bleeding extensively, the intrepid Sergeant drives ahead through another storm of fire, destroying the second machine gun before unleashing his carbine against the Infantry in the nearby emplacements. The dauntless Dunham destroys a third machine gun with grenades. His tremendous courage inspires his Platoon and ensures a successful diversionary assault; Sgt. Dunham receives the Medal of Honor.

January 9th 1945 — (Pacific) While the U.S. Sixth Army, under General Krueger, is invading Luzon, other heavy support strikes occur. The Airfields and other targets, including Shipping at Formosa, Pescadores, and Ryukas, are struck by Carrier Planes attached to Task Force 38, while the Armada slips into the South China Sea without incident, although it passes near Luzon and Formosa. Meanwhile, XX Bomber Command's B-29s fly in concert with the Carrier Planes pounding Formosa, while XXI Bomber Command B-29s strike Japan's mainland to level the Musashino Aircraft factory in Tokyo. The Seventh Air Force attacks Iwo Jima and the Volcano Islands. **(Pacific-Philippines)** The **U.S. Sixth Army**, under General Krueger, initiates the invasion of Luzon at 09:30, subsequent to a Naval and Air bombardment by Admiral Kinkaid's Task Force 77. The I and XIV Corps land abreast, receiving no opposition; however, as they push inland, the I Corps encounters heavy resistance as it establishes its beachhead. Meanwhile, the XIV Corps drives inland about four miles by the end of the day. Also, American P.O.W.s aboard the *Enoura* suffer greatly when it is struck by American bombs. The Japanese begin removing the dead from the hold two days later, and on the 13th, the remainder of 300 bodies are taken to a mass grave. The survivors are transferred to the *Brazil Maru*, and the prisoners continue to die at a rate of about 25 a day due to no medical help and despicable inhumane conditions. Of the approximate 1,600 men who started the voyage of death lasting 48 days, only 500 reach Moji, Japan, on the 29th of January, and many are in such poor health that another 100 men succumb within the next several weeks. In Naval activity, U.S. Vessels damaged: Battleship *Colorado* (BB-45), accidentally by U.S. fire; Battleship *Mississippi* (BB-41), Kamikaze; Light Cruiser *Colombia* (CL-56), Kamikaze; Destroyer Escort *Hodges* (DE-231), Kamikaze; Transport *Warhawk* (AP-168), Suicide Boat; Oiler *Guadalupe* (AO-32), by collision; and the LSTs 925 and 1028, by depth charges. Japanese Vessels sunk: Submarine Chaser No. 61, Carrier Based Aircraft; Submarine Chaser No. 96, Carrier Based Aircraft; Coast Defense Vessel No. 3, Carrier Based Aircraft. **(Atlantic-Western Europe) 21st Army Group** In the **U.S. First Army** area, **VII Corps** sector, elements of the 84th Division seize the high ground at Harze and secure positions in the woods southeast of Manhay. **12th Army Group** In the **U.S. Third Army** area, **VIII Corps** sector, the 87th Division is engaged heavily near Tillet and Haies-de-Tillet Woods. In other activity, Recogne is seized by the 501st Paratroop Infantry. In the **III Corps** area, an attack is commenced to surround and eliminate the enemy in a pocket southeast of Bastogne; Berle falls to the 26th Division. **6th Army Group** In the **U.S. Seventh Army** area, **XV Corps** sector, the Germans place pressure on the 100th Division near Risling, forcing the troops to pull back and join the 44th Division at Guising. In the **VI Corps** sector, Obermuhlthal is seized by Task Force Herren; however, the Germans strike the northeast flank, pushing the 242nd Infantry's (42nd Division), Task Force Linden from Hatten. The Tank-supported enemy assault also presses Rittershoffen, but the Yanks counterattack and drive the enemy back to Hatten, regaining a portion of the town. During the brutalizing struggle at Hatten, Master Sergeant Vito R. Bertoldo, Company A, 242nd Regiment, attempts to hold the German hordes singlehandedly after they overrun the main line of defense. He positions a machine gun in the street and holds off the attackers for twelve hours, before pulling back to

the Command Post to reinitiate his one-man defense, dueling with Tanks less than 75 yards distant. Bertoldo covers the withdrawal and remains all night, being thrown across the room by a shell burst. Undaunted, on the following day in another Command Post, he continues to battle the approaching Germans and interrupts another attack which includes a Tank and 15 Infantrymen. Reinforcements and a Bazooka appear on scene and destroy the enemy guns. The decision to evacuate the Command Post is given, but more German pressure prevents an immediate pull out. Again, enemy fire wounds Bertoldo as he is again blown across the room (by Tank fire), but he refuses to abandon the position, choosing to remain and cover the withdrawal. He receives the Medal of Honor. Also, the Germans hold tough at Drusenheim and near Rohrweiler, hindering progress of the 79th Division. **(Atlantic-Italy) 15th Army Group** In the **U.S. Fifth Army** area, the decision to halt the offensive is announced. The Allies set April 1st as the tentative date for renewing the offensive and will use the pause to regain troop strength and accumulate large amounts of ammunition and supplies.

U.S. Invasion Fleet off Luzon in the Lingayen Gulf — PBY Catalina Flying Boats zoom overhead.

January 10th 1945 — (Pacific-Philippines) In the **U.S. Sixth Army** area, **XIV Corps** sector, Labrador falls to the 185th Infantry, 40th Division. In conjunction, the 160th Infantry reaches Umanday as it drives toward Aguilar. Meanwhile, contingents of the 108th Regiment deploy around Polong. In the **I Corps** sector, the 103rd Regiment, 43rd Division, takes San Jacinto without incident, then moves out toward Hill 200 and Manoag. Meanwhile the 43rd's 169th and 172nd Regiments encounter fierce opposition, but the 169th takes Hill 470 and presses against Hills 318 and 351, while the 172nd Infantry secures Hill 385, then moves against heavily defended Hill 351. U.S. Naval Vessels damaged: Destroyer *Wickes* (DD-578), Horizontal Bomber; Destroyer Escort *Leray Wilson* (DE-414), Kamikaze; High Speed Transport *Clemson* (APD-31), by collision; Attack Transport *Dupage* (APA-41), Kamikaze; Attack Transport *Latimer* (APA-152), by collision; LST 567, by collision; LST 610, by Suicide Boat. Japanese Vessels sunk: Coast Defense Vessel No. 45, by Submarine *Puffer* (SS-268) off Ryukyu Islands. **(Pacific-Burma)** In the **British Fourteenth Army** area, **33 Corps** sector, Shwebo falls after a combined attack by the British 2nd and the Indian 197th Divisions. In addition, Budalin is seized by the Indian 20th Division. In the 4th Corps sector, the East African 28th Brigade and the Lushai Brigade, bolstered by heavy Air strikes, attack the heavily fortified enemy positions near Gangaw. **(Pacific-China)** Japanese troops begin to advance toward the Canton-Hankow Railroad to reopen the Canton-Hengyang section. **(Atlantic-Western Europe) 21st Army Group** In the **British Second Army** area, **30th Corps** sector, the British 51st Division advances to Laroche. In the **U.S. Ninth Army** area, **XIX Corps** sector, the U.S. 78th Division advances to the hills which overlook the Kall River. In the **U.S. First Army** area, **VII Corps** sector, the majority of the Laroche-Salmchateau Road is now clear of enemy. Meanwhile, the 2nd Armored Division seizes the section of the Laroche-Salmchateau Road in its sector and simultaneously seizes Samree. Bihain falls to the 83rd Division. In the **XVIII Corps (A/B)** sector, contingents of the 82nd Airborne Division secure a bridgehead at the Salm River outside of Grand Halleux. **12th Army Group** In the **U.S. Third Army's VIII Corps** sector, Tillet falls to the 87th Division, while elements of the 101st Airborne begin clearing Bois Jacques. Villers-la-Bonne-Eau and its high ground to the northeast are taken by contingents of the 35th Division. Meanwhile, elements of the 6th Cavalry Squadron seize Betlange in conjunction with the 28th Cavalry which captures Harlange. In other activity, contingents of the 90th Division fight the Germans to a stalemate at Trentelhof. **6th Army Group** In the **U.S. Seventh Army** area, **VI Corps** sector, units of the 45th Division move into Althorn, but German resistance at the Bitche Salient repels attempts to reduce it. Some indecisive fighting ensues between the 79th Division and the enemy at Hatten, and further south, elements of C.C.B., 12th Armored Division are encircled at Herrlisheim until Tanks rush to the scene and burst through to reinforce the beleaguered Infantry. On the following day, the Armor pulls out and redeploys west of the Zorn River.

January 11th 1945 — (United States) The Motor Minesweeper YMS-14 sinks in Boston Harbor, after a collision. **(Southwest Pacific Area)** The U.S. 11th Airborne, Eighth Army, receives orders to prepare to land at Nasughu and Tayabas Bays (Luzon) toward the latter part of January. Meanwhile, the landing at Vigan by the XII Corps is canceled. **(Pacific-Philippines-Luzon)** In the **U.S. Sixth Army** area, Regimental Combat Team 158 attacks toward Rabon and relieves contingents of the 172nd Regiment, 43rd Division. In the **XIV Corps** sector, the 40th Division advances to Aguilar and encounters Filipino Guerrillas who have liberated the town. In the **I Corps** area, the 6th Division moves toward Santa Barbara and it too is occupied by Filipino Guerrillas. Meanwhile, the 103rd Regiment, 43rd Division takes Manoag without incident, then fights for positions on a hill mass under Hill 200. Fighting is fierce at Hill 318; still, the enemy holds its positions against the attacks of the 169th Regiment, 43rd Division;

contingents manage to secure a fragile hold on Hill 560. The Japanese mount stiff resistance against the advancing 172nd Regiment, 43rd Division, halting its progress. Although resistance is rising, the Corps widens its front which now spreads 30 miles south to north. Marinduque Island is secure. In Naval activity, the LSTs 270 and 918 are sunk by coastal gunfire; the LST 700 sinks due to accidental U.S. Naval gunfire. In other activity, Marine Aircraft Groups, Dagupan, commanded by Colonel Clayton C. Jerome, are organized. Advance elements of Marine Aircraft Group 24 arrive in Lingayen Gulf. The units fly close air support missions to assist U.S. Army ground troops. In Air activity over Luzon, two U.S. Fighter Planes are flying a reconnaissance mission toward enemy Airfields when twelve enemy Fighters and a Twin Engine Bomber are discovered. Major William A. Shomo, 82nd Tactical Recon Squadron, leading the Air detachment, attacks the 13 Planes. Before the action ceases, the Japs lose seven Planes including the Bomber to Major Shomo and three more to his Wingman. Major Shomo receives the Medal of Honor for his extraordinary action. **(Pacific-Formosa)** B24s, attached to the Fifth Air Force, initiate night attacks against the Japanese stronghold. **(Pacific-Burma)** In the **British Fourteenth Army** area, **4 Corps** sector, Gangaw falls to East African troops; this allows the Corps to advance toward the Irrawaddy to prepare for an attack against Meiktila. **(Atlantic-Western Europe) 21st Army Group** In the **British Second Army's 30th Corps** sector, Patrols from the British 6th Airborne Division advance to St. Hubert and encounter contingents of the U.S. VIII Corps. In the **U.S. Ninth Army** area, **XIX Corps** sector, enemy resistance in the hills above the Kall River is eliminated. In the **U.S. First Army** area, **VII Corps** sector, Laroche falls to elements of the 84th Division. Meanwhile, Langlir and Petite Langlir come under attack by the 83rd Division. **12th Army Group** In the **U.S. Third Army** area, **VIII Corps** sector, the 347th Regiment plows through and secures the woods at Haies-de-Tillet, then occupies Bonnerue, Pironpre, St. Hubert, and Vesqueville after they are abandoned by the enemy. In the 17th Airborne Division sector, the Germans are also retreating, evacuating Flamierge, Flamizoulle, Mande St. Etienne, and Heropont. At Bastogne, in the **III Corps** sector, the Yanks have driven the Germans from their positions southeast of the town. Meanwhile, many units are converging on Bras. Elements of the 6th Armored Division storm the woods near Wardin, while the 35th Division secures high ground near Lutrebois-Lutremange. Near Bastogne, a Platoon from Company A, 9th Armored Infantry Battalion (6th Armored) is halted by heavy machine gun fire, supporting Infantry and a Tiger Tank. Instinctively, Sgt. Archer T. Gammon advances about 30 yards through deep snow and annihilates the crew of a machine gun nest, saving his unit from destruction. He then attacks toward the Tank, taking out an automatic weapon crew of four men, killing three and wounding the fourth. As he closes on the Tank, two enemy Infantrymen are killed by his fire and the Tank starts to turn around. Suddenly a burst of fire kills him instantly; the Tank retreats allowing the unit to advance. Gammon receives the Medal of Honor for his extraordinary bravery. In addition, Task Forces Fickett and Scott are driving forward, the latter taking the forest near Harlange as Task Force Fickett takes Wantrange and assaults Tarchamps. Subsequently, the Task Forces combine and take the heights southwest of Sonlez. The 90th Division severs the Bastogne-Wiltz Road at Doncols. In the **XII Corps** sector, Bockholz-sur-Sure is seized by the 80th Division, which also takes the high ground outside of Burden. At Machtum, the Germans are victimized by the 2nd Cavalry Group, costing them their last stronghold west of the Moselle. **6th Army Group** In the **U.S. Seventh Army** area, **VI Corps** sector, Althorn is seized by the 45th Division; however, German resistance at Wildenguth-Saegmuhl-Reipertsweiler compels it to pull back. In addition, the Germans assault the 79th Division's positions along the Maginot Line near Wissembourg, placing more pressure on the 315th Regiment, which is surrounded. The assault gains over half of Rittershoffen, which is defended by the 3rd Battalion, 315th Infantry. The 14th Armored Division dispatches C.C.A., but German pressure halts the advance outside of Rittershoffen.

January 12th 1945 — **(Pacific Area)** Task Force 51 (minus contingents in the Marianas) initiates rehearsals in Hawaii for the Iwo Jima invasion scheduled for February 1945. **(Pacific-Philippines)** Luzon Port Sual, the western terminus of Army Beachhead Line, is seized without incident by the 185th Regiment, 40th Division. Meanwhile, contingents of the 37th Division take Bayambang and Urbizondo without opposition. In the **I Corps** area, the 43rd Division is bitterly engaged at Hill 560 for the second day; however, it is seized; elements then attack Hills 200 and 318. In addition, Regimental Combat Teams 158 (assigned to 43rd for added strength) and RCT 63 attack to secure the Damortis-Rosario road. During the heavy fighting, Staff Sergeant Robert E. Law, Company G (43rd) attacks enemy positions, covered by his Squad. Law is wounded by enemy fire, but keeps inching closer and destroys a pillbox with grenades. He leads his Squad up a hill and is again wounded (both arms, both legs, about the body and in the head), yet maintains the attack. Three Japanese charge the wounded Soldier. He calmly empties the magazine of his machine pistol and two Japanese die suddenly; the third attempts to get Law. The Yank grabs the Jap's rifle and a struggle ensues as the two antagonists tumble about 60 feet down a hill in a cloud of dust. Only one man gets up; its the Yank and he is seen walking back up the hill with a large cut in his head. The gallant Sergeant receives the Medal of Honor. **Mindoro** The Japanese stronghold at Calapan becomes the target of the 21st Infantry, 24th Division; it assembles at Pinamalayan to prepare. In other activity, Guerrillas advance to the northern coast and enter Wawa, near Abra de Ilog. U.S. Naval damages: Destroyer Escorts *Richard W. Suesens* (DE-342), and *Gilligan* (DE-508), the Attack Transport *Zeilin* (APA-3), and the LST 700, by Kamikaze Planes; the LSTs 710 and 778 are accidentally damaged by U.S. Naval gunfire. **(Pacific-Burma)** In ALFSEA's 15th Corps area, the 3rd Commando Brigade lands at Myebon on the Arakan coast, subsequent to an Air and Naval bombardment. A sturdy beachhead is established, which repulses later enemy counterattacks. In N.C.A.C. area, a U.S.-Chinese Convoy departs Ledo, India. **(Pacific-South China Sea)** Task Force 38 (Vice Admiral J.S. McCain) launches Planes which strike French Indo China. The Aircraft blast Airfields and other installations in the area extending north from Saigon to Tourane, while simultaneously bombing Japanese Shipping off the coast; the surprise raids cost the Japanese about 40 Ships sunk and others damaged. Major Japanese losses due to Carrier Based Aircraft: Training Cruiser *Kashii*, Frigate *Chiburi*, Submarine Chaser No. 31, Submarine Chaser No. 43, Minesweeper No. 101, Transport No. 140, Patrol Boat No. 103, Coast Defense Vessels, Nos. 17, 19, 23, 35, 43, and 51. Halsey had dispatched the force to intercept enemy Warships which reportedly would attempt to break out of Camranh Bay, but no Warships are discovered there; the Yanks inflicted the damage after

spotting a Convoy off Cap St. Jacques. French reports indicate 41 Ships sunk and 28 damaged. Subsequent to the U.S. Forces moving out of the area, a typhoon moves in, causing more damage to enemy Vessels. **(Atlantic-Western Europe) 21st Army Group** In the **U.S. First Army VII Corps** sector, Chabrehez falls to C.C.A., 2nd Armored Division and C.C.B. seizes Les Tailles and Petite Tailles. Combat Command R overruns Bois de Cedrogne. Meanwhile, Task Force Hogan advances to Bihain, then sweeps the high ground southwest of the town. The 83rd Division reduces opposition at Langlir and Petite Langlir, while establishing a bridgehead south of Langlir-Ronce. In the **XVIII Corps** zone, a bridgehead is established across the Ambleve River, south of Stavelot (106th Division sector). **12th Army Group** The Germans continue to pull back all across the Corps sector. Amberloup, Tonny, Fosset, Lavacherie, and Orreux are taken by the 87th Division, which also seizes a road junction outside of Sprimont. The 17th Airborne retakes Flamierge; however, the enemy has inundated Flamizoulle with mines. In addition, the German rear guards hold Hubermont and Renuamont. In the **III Corps** sector, Wardin falls to C.C.A., 6th Armored, as it drives toward Bras's doorstep. Meanwhile, the 357th Regiment, 90th Division mops up Sonlez; the 359th Regiment, holding the crossroads northeast of Doncal, repulses a counterattack. **6th Army Group** In the **U.S. Seventh Army VI Corps** sector, the enemy salient at Bitche halts its attack and begins to formulate a stiff defense. The 45th Division is engaged heavily at Wildenguth area, attempting to regain previously lost ground (11th), but the fighting nets small gains. The 315th Regiment, 79th Division is under heavy pressure at Hatten and Rittershoffen; 14th Armored attacks to relieve the beleaguered Regiment. Its C.C.A. secures part of Rittershoffen. Meanwhile, the situation at the Gambsheim bridgehead remains the same. **(Atlantic-Eastern Europe)** The Soviets initiate a strong winter offensive, which is bolstered by heavy Artillery bombardments. The First Ukrainian Front drives across the Vistula River in southern Poland. Meanwhile, the bitter fighting for Budapest continues; the Russians drive deeper into the city, but the Germans hang tough.

Japanese positions in the Philippines come under attack by U.S. Planes (P38s).

January 13th 1945 — **(Pacific-Philippines)** In Luzon, the Japanese commence some sporadic Air attacks against Lingayen Gulf, but this is the final enemy air raid against the Luzon Attack Force. In the **U.S. Sixth Army** area, General Krueger assumes command of all ground forces. In the **XIV Corps** sector, contingents of the 185th Regiment, 40th Division advance to Calbalitan Bay, finding the area already occupied by Allied Naval forces, which secured it without opposition. The 37th Division commits units, which take Wawa. In the **I Corps** sector, the 6th Division takes its holding line, Malisiqui-Cataliban-Torres. In the 43rd Division sector, RCT 158 takes Damortis effortlessly. The 63rd Regiment bolts from Alacan, driving toward Hill 363. The 169th and 172nd take Hills 318 and 580 respectively, although some minor resistance remains. In Naval activity, the Escort Carrier *Salamua* (CVE-96) is damaged by a Kamikaze. **(Atlantic-Western Europe) 21st Army Group** The 51st Division, 30th Corps, British Second Army advances to the Ourthe River, near Laroche, culminating the Corps Ardennes operation. In the **U.S. First Army** area, **VII Corps** closes on Houffalize, while the 84th Division breezes through several small towns and villages. The Sommerain-Cherain road is severed at the junction road leading to Mont le Ban, permitting it to neutralize the town. Meanwhile, Lomre falls to C.C.B., 3rd Armored Division. In other activity, the **XVIII Corps (Airborne)** starts an offensive, driving southeast; the 517th Paratroop Infantry and elements of the 106th and 30th Divisions plow toward La Neuville-Coulee-Logbierme-Houvegnez line, reaching the Henumont area. Additional units reach Hedomont. **12th Army Group** In the **U.S. Third Army** area, contingents of the 87th Division drive to the Ourthe River and encounter British troops. Salle falls to the U.S. 17th Airborne, without opposition. Bertogne is encircled by contingents of the 11th Armored Division. Foy collapses to the 501st Paratroop Infantry, 101st Airborne, while the 327th Glider Infantry eases through the Paratroop lines at Bois Jacques, then bolts toward Bourcy. In the **III Corps** sector, C.C.B., 6th Armored Division storms into Mageret, seizing part of the town. At Bras, the 90th Division seizes Hill 530 and simultaneously overruns Bras. The weather all across the front is freezing cold and the troops which are killed are soon frozen solid. One dead German machine gunner is discovered by Patton, "half-sitting, his arms extended holding a loaded belt of ammunition." **6th Army Group** In the **U.S. Seventh Army** area, the **XXI Corps** becomes operational; it is headed by Major General Frank W. Milburn. In the **VI Corps** sector, heavy fighting continues at the Bitche salient and at Rittershoffen. Meanwhile, C.C.R., 14th Armored Division drives into Hatten, securing part of it. German resistance repulses C.C.B.'s attempt to sever the roads north and northeast of the objective.

January 14th 1945 — (Pacific-Philippines) In Naval activity, the PT 73 is lost due to grounding. **(Leyte)** In the **U.S. Eighth Army** area, **XXIV Corps** sector, the 96th Division relieves the 11th Airborne of tactical responsibility on Leyte and dispatches two Battalions to Samar Island to relieve the 8th Cavalry, 1st Cavalry Division at Catbalogan and take over garrisoning the area. In other activity, a Task Force of the 7th Division, composed of the 776th Tank Battalion, contingents of the 536th and 718th Amtrac Battalions and the 3rd Battalion, 184th Infantry, debark to secure Camotes Island. **Luzon** In the **U.S. Sixth Army** area, a Reconnaissance Troop of the 41st Division advances to Alaminos; its 160th Infantry reaches Mangatarem, while the 129th Regiment, 37th Division seizes Bautista. Meanwhile, Camiling, which is free of enemy troops, is taken by the 37th Division's Reconnaissance Troop. In the **I Corps** sector, Japanese resistance at Amlang forces the attacking 158th Regimental Combat Team, 43rd Division, to pull back almost to its starting point, preventing it from reaching Rosario, the primary objective; Hill 581, previously bypassed, is taken by the 172nd Infantry, then Hills 565 and 585 are secured. In conjunction, Hill 580 is mopped up. The 169th Regiment mops up Hill 318 and deploys to assault Hill 355. Meanwhile, the 103rd Infantry establishes an outpost slightly southeast of Pozorrubio. **(Pacific-Dutch East Indies)** The Submarine U.S.S. *Cobia* (SS-245) sinks the Minelayer *Yurishima* off Sumatra. **(China-Burma)** In the **British Fourteenth Army** area, **33 Corps** sector, the 19th Indian Division seizes a bridgehead across the Irrawaddy at Thabeikkyin; however, the Japanese, mistaking the Division for a Corps, initiate strong attempts to reduce it, sacrificing strength in other areas. The bridgehead sustains repeated attacks for about a month, but does not fold. **(Atlantic-Western Europe) 21st Army Group** In the **U.S. First Army** area, **VII Corps** sector, Filly, Grande Mormont, Nadrin, and Petite Mormont fall to the 84th Division, which culminates its final objectives with the captures. Dinez, Cheveoumont, Wibrin, and Wilogne are seized by a 2nd Armored Patrol, while the 3rd Armored Division takes Baclain and Mont le Ban. In conjunction, the Yanks of the 83rd Division overrun Honvelez, while securing the high ground near Bovigny. In addition, Patrols of 4th Cavalry Group encounter a Patrol of the Third Army, as the Yanks begin to claim ground in expeditious fashion. In the **XVIII (Airborne) Corps** area, the 106th Division sector, the 517th Paratroop Infantry secures Henumont, then pounces upon Coule and Logbierme as it drives south. Meanwhile, contingents of the 30th Division are battling their way toward Hedomont, seizing it before dawn on the 15th; it takes Ligneuville and Villers. **12th Army Group** In the **U.S. Third Army** area, **VII Corps** sector, the 17th Airborne's 517th Paratroop Regiment takes abandoned Bertogne, while the 194th Glider Infantry overruns Givroulle; both Regiments continue driving toward the Ourthe River. The 11th Armored Division commits a Task Force of C.C.A., which secures the Falaise Woods, then continues driving until heavy fire halts its progress on the Longchamps-Compogne highway. The Germans counterattack and push the 101st Airborne from Foy and Recogne, but the Airborne strikes back viciously and regains the towns. The Germans are also tossed from Cobru. At Noville, intense fighting erupts as Infantry and a Tank Task Force of C.C.B., 11th Armored drive into the town and encounter tenacious resistance, which forces a pull back. In the **III Corps** sector, Benonchamps is taken by the 6th Armored Division's C.C.A., which also secures the woods east of Wardin; Combat Command B eliminates remnant resistance at Mageret. Contingents of the 90th Division advance toward Niederwampach. In conjunction, the 26th Division dispatches Patrols toward German positions at the Wiltz River. In the **XX Corps** sector, controlled attacks are launched by the 94th Division to bolster the defensive position in the Saar-Moselle triangle south of Wasserbillig; its 376th Regiment seizes Butzdorf and Tettingen. **6th Army Group** In the **U.S. Seventh Army** area, **XXI Corps** sector, Task Force Herren relieves the 103rd Division, prompting the 36th Division's RCT 142 to swing into the 103rd's area to protect the changes. In the **VI Corps** zone, the Germans continue to resist tenaciously at the Bitche salient. The 45th Division grinds its way forward making only nominal gains. The 14th Armored Division is furiously engaged at Hatten and Rittershoffen. **(Atlantic-Eastern Europe)** Berlin announces a new Soviet offensive has begun in Schlossberg (Pillkallen) area of northeastern East Prussia. Meanwhile, the Soviet offensive in Poland spreads; the First and Second White Russian Fronts attack, the former across the Vistula River, near Warsaw, and the latter across the Narew River north of the city. In the southern portion of Poland, the First Ukrainian Front severs the Kielce-Cracow Railroad. Meanwhile, the Germans continue to resist feverishly at Budapest;

however, their resources are getting slimmer and the over-powering numbers of Russians are inflicting severe punishment, forcing the beleaguered Germans to give ground. The Germans initiate a general withdrawal from Yugoslavia. **(Atlantic-Italy)** The **U.S. Fifth Army** establishes a new Regiment, subsequent to dissolving the 45th AAA Brigade. It contains personnel which had previously been AAA contingents of Task Force 45.

U.S. Infantry on the advance in Luzon.

Philippine Guerrillas waiting to strike the enemy.

January 15th 1945 — (Pacific-Philippines) In Naval activity, the U.S.S. *Hoggart Bay* (CVE-75), a Carrier, is damaged subsequent to an accidental explosion. **Luzon** In the **U.S.**

Sixth Army area, **XIV Corps** sector, sporadic fire-fights develop on the Dasol Bay-Balinao Peninsula as the 40th Division initiates probing operations. San Clemente is seized by the 2nd Battalion, 160th Regiment. The Japanese retire toward Camiling, and contingents of the 129th Regiment and the 37th Reconnaissance Troop, 37th Division intercept the enemy troops near Camiling, routing them. In the **I Corps** sector, Patrols of the 6th Division discover Japanese troops controlling the Cabaruan Hills and Urdaneta. In the 43rd Division zone, an enemy defile at Amlang, along the road to Rosario, is pounded by Aircraft, Artillery, and Naval gunfire in conjunction with an assault by the 158th Regimental Combat Team. Meanwhile, the 63rd Infantry grinds north to hook up with the 158th, stopping south of Amlang for the night. In addition, the 172nd Infantry seizes Hill 665 and advances to within about a mile from Rosario, while the 103rd Regiment seizes most of Hill 200. Hill 355 repulses an attack by the 169th Regiment. **Camotes** The 7th Division, under umbrella coverage by PT Boats and Aircraft of the Fifth Air Force, debarks on the northern and southern tips of Ponson Island without incident. **Mindoro** The 503rd Paratroop Infantry, which had been bolstering Guerrilla units, culminates its operations on Mindoro. In other activity, the Japanese mount stiff opposition against the 2nd Battalion, 21st Infantry, 24th Division. **South China Sea** Admiral McCain's Task Force 38 launches Planes, despite deplorable weather, striking Japanese Shipping and installations at Formosa and along the China coast between Amoy and Hong Kong. The inclement weather greatly hinders the operation, forcing some Planes to divert to Mako Ko in the Pescadores, while others are compelled to head for Prates Reef. Japanese Vessels sunk by Carrier-based Planes: Destroyer *Hatakarze*, Destroyer (Old) *Tsuga*, and the Transport No. 14. **(Pacific-Burma)** During a meeting in Myitkyina, Generals Wedemeyer (Stilwell's replacement), Stratemeyer, and Sultan concur that an American Air Force Headquarters must be established in China to command the U.S. Tenth and Fourteenth Air Forces. In the N.C.A.C. area, the Convoy which had departed Ledo, India, on the 12th, arrives at Myitkyina, then pauses to await the reduction of Japanese troops which are further ahead. In other activity, Namhkam falls to the Chinese 30th Division; the easy conquest give the 38th control of the lower end of the Shweli Valley. **(Atlantic-Western Europe) 21st Army Group** In the **British Second Army** area, **12th Corps** sector, preparations are made for Operation BLACKCOCK (intended to seize a triangular enemy salient between the Meuse and the Roer-Wurm Rivers from Roermond southward). Bakenhoven, Holland, on the left flank of the Corps, falls to the British 7th Armored Division; it will be used as the jump off point for the 7th's main assault. In the **U.S. First Army** area, **VII Corps** sector, Achouffe, Tavernaux and Mont are taken by the 2nd Armored Division; Patrols move to the Ourthe River and to the abandoned town of Houffalize. Meanwhile, the 3rd Armored Division's C.C.R. takes Vaux. Bovigny is attacked by a Battalion of the 83rd Division, but German resistance holds it. In the **XVIII Corps (A/B)** sector, Bech and Salmchateau are assaulted by the 75th Division; both towns are overrun before dawn. Ennal is seized by the 106th Division, while the 30th Division reduces resistance at Beaumont, Francheville, Houegnez and Pont, while simultaneously clearing the northern part of Thirimont and improving its positions south of Ligneuville. In the **V Corps** sector, an offensive is commenced to bolster the left flank of the XVIII Corps, seizing the terrain between Ambleve and Buellingen. At Butgenbach, the Germans halt progress; however, Remonval, Steinbach, and a large portion of Faymonville are seized by contingents of the 1st Division and RCT 23 (2nd Division). **12th Army Group** In the **U.S. Third Army's VIII Corps** sector, Compogne and Rastadt fall to C.C.A., 11th Armored Division, which advances to Vellereux. A German counterattack in the Rau de Vaux defile forces C.C.A. to withdraw and deploy west of Vaux. Meanwhile, C.C.B. bypasses Neville and seizes the woods to the east of the town; it is occupied by the 506th Paratroop Infantry, 101st Airborne. In the **III Corps** area, violent house-to-house fighting in Oubourcy ceases through the combined efforts of the 6th Armored Division and the 320th Regiment, 35th Division. In conjunction, C.C.B. overruns Arloncourt and C.C.A. secures the hills southwest of Longvilly. During the fighting at Arloncourt, Belgium, Corporal Arthur O. Beyer, Company C, 603rd Tank Destroyer Battalion, fires upon a machine gun position and scores a direct hit, killing one man and eliminating the gun. He then dismounts his Vehicle and singlehandedly seizes the two remaining crewmen while under fire by antitank, machine gun fire, and riflemen. Undaunted, Beyer races through a thunderstorm of fire toward another machine gun, 250 yards distant, destroying the gun with a grenade. The one man Regiment keeps advancing, using his Carbine and grenades to demolish inhabitants of foxholes. He kills eight of the enemy, captures eighteen, including two Bazooka teams, and destroys two machine gun positions. Corporal Beyer becomes the recipient of the Medal of Honor. The Germans offer tenacious resistance in the 90th Division zone; nevertheless, the 1st Battalion, 358th Regiment, supported by Artillery (14th Field Artillery contingents), takes Niederwampach. In conjunction, the 357th Regiment storms German positions around the Wiltz River Valley to force the enemy from the entrenched strongpoints in the railroad tunnels. In the **XX Corps** sector, the Germans mount fierce counterattacks against Butzdorf and Tettingen; however, the 1st Battalion, 376th Regiment, repulses both assaults. Meanwhile, the 3rd Battalion fights its way into Berg, Nennig, and Wies, seizing all three. **6th Army Group** Army Group issues tentative instructions to the French First Army, concerning the planned assault against the Colmar Pocket. In the **U.S. Seventh Army** area, **VI Corps** sector, brisk fire-fights occur at the Bitche salient. At Rittershoffen and Hatten, the Germans still maintain tenacious resistance against the 14th Armored Division. **(Atlantic-Italy) 15th Army Group** In the **U.S. Fifth Army** area, the South African 6th Division comes under the control of the II Corps, being transferred from Army jurisdiction. **(Atlantic-Eastern Europe)** The Fourth Ukrainian Front widens its offensive, attacking from Sanok, southwest of Crakow, in the Carpathian Mountains, while the First Ukrainian Front seizes Kielce.

January 16th 1945 — (Pacific-South China Sea) Task Force 38 again launches Aircraft to strike enemy positions along the China coast, concentrating its efforts against Hong Kong, while also striking the area extending from Swatow to Luichow Peninsula and Hainan Island. The Planes do not score well against the enemy Shipping, yet the strikes against ground installations inflict heavy damage. **(Pacific-Philippines)** Luzon The Airstrip in Lingayen Gulf becomes operational. In the **U.S. Sixth Army** area, **XIV Corps** sector, preparations are made to construct bridges across the Agno to handle heavy equipment. In **I Corps** area, the 43rd Division attacks Rosario; however, it is met by furious enemy resistance there and at the road junction of routes No. 3 and No. 11, giving the effort small gains. Meanwhile, Hill 200 and the

immediate vicinity are secured by the 103rd Regiment and its supporting Tank units; Pozorrubio is occupied. The Japs await darkness and mount several counterattacks which cost them severe casualties in the futile attempts to regain the terrain. **Mindoro** The 19th Regiment, 24th Division establishes an Outpost at Bulalaco and soon discovers the entire area is swarming with Japs. **(Pacific-Burma)** In the N.C.A.C. area, the U.S. 5332nd Brigade is poised for its drive down the Burma Road to secure the region between Hsenwi and Wanting, in the Namhkam-Namhpakka area. Meanwhile, the Chinese 38th Division, maintaining its pace along the Namhpakka trail, reaches Ta-kawn. **(Pacific-China)** China Theater is informed that B-29s are to be transferred to the Marianas. **(North Atlantic)** The Destroyer Escorts *Otter* (DE-210), *Hubbard* (DE-211), *Hayter* (DE-212), and *Varian* (DE-798) combine their killing power and destroy another of Hitler's U-Boats, the U-248. **(Atlantic-Western Europe) 21st Army Group** In the **British Second Army** area, the 12th Corps commences Operation BLACKCOCK (campaign to secure enemy salient between Meuse and Ruhr-Wurm Rivers south of Roermond). The 7th Armored attacks northeast and captures Dieteren, Holland. In the **U.S. First Army** area, **VII Corps** sector, contact is made between Corps troops and Third Army outside of Houffalize, north of the Ourthe River; the sector is occupied by the 2nd Armored Division. The 3rd Armored takes Cherain, Sommerain, and Sterpigny, but fierce enemy resistance prevents the fall of Brisy. In conjunction, Tanks, attempting to reach Rettigny from Cherain, are halted by enemy fire. In the **XVIII Corps (Airborne)** sector, the Germans mount heavy resistance east of the Salm River, impeding progress of the 77th Division. The 106th Division mops up in its area including the heights northwest of Petit Their. Meanwhile, the 30th Division reduces the remaining resistance in Thirimont and south toward an enemy strongpoint on the Malmedy-St. Vith Road. In the **V Corps** sector, the Germans resist tenaciously in the woods south of Butgenbach; however, the determined 1st Division does topple Ondenval and crushes the remaining resistance in Faymonville. **12th Army Group** In the **U.S. Third Army** area, **VIII Corps** sector, C.C.A., 11th Armored Division rumbles into Velleroux and drives forward pursuing the Germans through Mabompre, while C.C.B. moves through Wicourt and seizes the heights south of Houffalize. The 502nd Paratroop Infantry, 101st Airborne is stopped near Bourcy; on the other hand, the 506th Paratroop Infantry seizes Rachamps and Vaux. In the **III Corps** sector, the 6th Armored Division powers forward, its 320th Regiment overpowering Michamps, while TF Lagrew (C.C.A.) moves through Longvilly. In conjunction, the 90th Division takes the high ground east of Longvilly and captures Oberwampach and Shimpach. In other activity, Lt. General Gerow assumes command of the Fifteenth Army. **6th Army Group** The U.S. 28th Division is attached to Seventh Army, but it is to operate under the jurisdiction of the French 1st Army. In the **U.S. Seventh Army** area, **VI Corps** sector, the 45th Division holds firmly against an onslaught of German pressure in the vicinity of Obermuhlthal. In the 14th Armored zone, the Germans halt the advance of C.C.A. in Rittershoffen and push C.C.R. back in the town of Hatten. In the 79th Division sector, contingents of the 232nd Regiment intercept a strong force of Germans at Dengolsheim and, after a brisk fight, turn the enemy back toward Dahlhunden. In the 12th Armored Division zone, the Germans retain their Gambsheim bridgehead; contingents of C.C.B. (Infantry) attack but are forced back into Rohrweiler. C.C.A. gains some ground as it drives against Offendorf, but the Germans prevent it from reaching its objective. **(Atlantic-**

Eastern Europe) The First White Russian Front captures Radom, Poland. In other activity, the First Ukrainian Front is advancing against Cracow and Czestochowa.

Infantry advancing through the Santa Fe Mtns., Philippines.

January 17th 1945 — (Pacific-Philippines) In Naval activity, the Escort Carrier *Nehenta Bay* (CVE-74) is damaged during a severe storm. In **Luzon, U.S. Sixth Army** area, General Krueger receives instructions from MacArthur to accelerate the drive toward Clark Field and Manila. In the **I Corps** sector, the 1st and 20th Regiments, 6th Division attack Urdaneta and the Cabaruan Hills respectively. In conjunction, the 27th and 161st Regiments, 25th Division drive forward, the latter reaching Binalonan, which is heavily defended by the Japs, and the former driving to the Binalonan-Urdaneta Road. Meanwhile, Pozorrubio is seized by the 103rd Regiment, 43rd Division against remnant defenders. In conjunction, its 158th Infantry (RCT 158) overruns a ridge slightly northeast of Damortis, while the 63rd Regiment joins the 158th to help secure the hills which control the Damortis-Rosario Road in the Amlang-Cataguintingan area. **(Pacific-Burma)** In the N.C.A.C. area, the U.S. 5332nd Brigade knocks out a Japanese outpost in the hamlet of Namhkam, a few miles off the Burma Road, then pushes into the nearby hills to eliminate the resistance there. Elements of the Chinese 38th Division advance toward Wanting. **(Pacific-Japan)** The Submarine *Tautog* (SS-199), patrolling off Kyushu, Japan, sinks the Japanese Transport No. 15. **(Atlantic-Western Europe) 21st Army Group** At midnight, 17th-18th, General Montgomery relinquishes control of the U.S. First Army. It reverts back to U.S. control (12th Army Group); Montgomery still does not release the U.S. Ninth Army, because he needs it to assist with his offensive (Rhine). U.S. Generals Bradley and Simpson are both dissatisfied with Eisenhower's decision to allow the Ninth Army to remain under Montgomery. Bradley notes: "I BEGGED EISENHOWER TO RETURN THE NINTH TO ME IF ONLY FOR 24 HOURS, THAT WE MIGHT COMPLETE THE CYCLE AND RECLAIM OUR COMMAND NOW THAT THE BULGE HAD BEEN FLATTENED. BUT IKE REPLIED THAT HE WAS ALREADY EXHAUSTED IN HIS STRUGGLE TO BLOCK THE BRITISH ON A SUPER GROUND COMMAND FOR MONTY." In the **British Second Army** area, **12th Corps** sector, Echt and Susteren are seized by contingents of the British 7th Armored Division. In the **U.S. First Army** area, **VII Corps** sector, mop-up operations are carried out by the 3rd Armored Division, while elements simultaneously shore up their defenses at Cherain and Sterpigny. The area around Courtil is being swept by the 331st Regiment, 83rd Division. In the **XVIII (Airborne) Corps** sector, Petit Their and Vielsalm are taken by the 75th Division. The Germans holding the junction of the Recht-Born and Malmedy-St. Vith Roads continue to repel attempts by the 30th Division to oust them. In the **V Corps** sector, spirited fighting develops between the 1st Division and the enemy at a stronghold south of Ondenval. Meanwhile, the 23rd Regiment, 2nd Division, assaults enemy positions outside of Iveldingen and advance across the high ground, pressing the Germans into a pocket in the northern sector of the Wolfsbusch. The Regiment moves cautiously through the Rohrbusch. U.S. G2 estimates that German casualties (Bulge fighting) are about 250,000 including 36,000 prisoners. **12th Army Group** In the **U.S. Third Army** area, **VIII Corps** sector, a defensive posture is taken subsequent to securing the area between Bastogne and the Ourthe River; the 101st Airborne seizes Bourcy and Hardigny. In the **III Corps** sector, the Germans mount heavy resistance along the Bourcy-Longvilly Road, slowing the advance of the 6th Armored Division, and other enemy contingents unsuccessfully attempt to regain Oberwampach. In the **XII Corps** sector, preparations for the attack are complete; it commences early on the following morning. **6th Army Group** In the **U.S. Seventh Army** area, **XXI Corps** sector, heavy fighting is ongoing at Rittershoffen, between C.C.A., 14th Armored, and the enemy; the 1st Battalion, 315th Regiment (79th Division), attached to the 14th Armored, drives toward the embattled C.C.A.; however, resistance prevents it from reaching the town. The Germans pound C.C.R., 14th Armored, at Hatten, but the Germans are driven back. Enemy troops are able to take Dengolsheim, Roeschwoog, and Stattmatten, as well as a section of Sessenheim, all in the 79th Division area. A strong counterattack regains Sessenheim. At the Gambsheim bridgehead, the Germans still offer vicious resistance, against the 12th Armored, stopping C.C.B. outside of Rohrweiler and hindering C.C.A., which has taken a slight hold at Herrlisheim with its 17th Armored Infantry Battalion. During the heated struggle, the 43rd Tank Battalion becomes isolated outside of the town and is annihilated. **(Atlantic-Eastern Europe)** The Germans finally lose Warsaw to the Soviets. The capital falls to the First White Russian Front. To the north, Ciechanow is controlled by the Second White Front, and the First Ukrainian Front advances to Czestochowa. **(Atlantic-Italy) 15th Army Group** In the **U.S. Fifth Army** area, **II Corps** sector, the U.S. 85th Division assumes responsibility for the British 1st Division sector. The British 1st Division comes under jurisdiction of Allied Force Headquarters Mediterranean and is subsequently deployed in the Middle East.

January 18th 1945 — (Central Pacific) The U.S.S. *Fleming* (DE-32), a Destroyer Escort sinks the Japanese Submarine RO-47. **(Pacific-Philippines)** In Naval activity, the LSTs 710 and 752 are damaged due to separate collisions, and the LST 219 is damaged by grounding. On Luzon, Sixth Army directs the XIV Corps to advance from its general line and push south beyond the Agno. In the I Corps sector, Urdaneta is seized by the 1st Regiment, 6th Division, while the 20th Infantry pushes deeper into the Cabaruan Hills, against slight enemy opposition. At Binalonan, enemy opposition is eliminated by the 161st Regiment, 25th Division. During the fighting, Technician 4th Grade Laverne Parrish, a Medical Aid man, is constantly under fire as he comforts the wounded. Between today and the 24th, he rescues three wounded men and brings them to cover, and in addition, he treats almost all of the 37 casualties suffered by his Company. Ultimately, a mortar round mortally wounds him as he gives his life to save the others. He becomes a recipient of the Medal of Honor for his intrepid courage under fire. The 63rd and 158th Regiments, 43rd Division meet heavy resistance when they assault Blue Ridge, outside Amlang. **Camotes** A 7th Division Task Force, composed of the 3rd Battalion, 184th Regiment, reinforced, embarks for Poro Island and establishes a bridgehead. **(Pacific-Palau Islands)** A Japanese landing party debarks at Peleliu and attempts to demolish parked Aircraft and destroy ammunition dumps; however, U.S. Army troops annihilate them before any damage can be inflicted. **(Pacific-Burma)** In the N.C.A.C. area, the U.S. 5322nd Brigade seizes part of Loi-kang ridge and immediately deploys Artillery to fire upon Burma Road. Meanwhile, Japanese reinforcements are transported to Namhpakka. **(Atlantic-Western Europe) 21st Army Group** In the **British Second Army** area, **12th Corps** sector, the British 7th Armored Division takes Schilberg, giving it a route from the left flank of the Corps to Sittard and to Heide, northeast of Susteren. In conjunction, the 52nd British Division commences its offensive, darting up the center and seizing a few German towns and villages along the German-Dutch frontier. **12th Army Group** In the **U.S. First Army** area, **VXIII Corps** sector, activity is brisk. The 75th Division secures part of Burtonville and will vanquish the town on the 19th, while the 30th Division overruns Poteau and spreads out to encircle the obstinate roadblock at the Recht-Born and Malmedy-St. Vith Roads; it will be knocked out on the following day. The **V Corps** sector is another hornets' nest. The Germans attack aggressively, but the Big Red One turns it back after heavy fighting in the Rohrbusch; the 1st Division also drives through the Wolfsbusch, reduces an enemy strongpoint south of the Ambleve River and continues to gnaw its way through rigid opposition in the woods south of Butgenbach. In the **U.S. Third Army** area, **III Corps** sector, the Germans are repulsed at Oberwampach; subsequently, the 90th Division, which holds it, comes under increasingly heavier Artillery bombardment. In the **XII Corps** sector, the 4th and 5th Divisions jump off at 03:00, driving across the Sauer River between Ettelbruck and Reisdorf, hitting the enemy by surprise. The 4th Division gets some prodding by General Eddy who insists that the Divisional Commander get across the river to personally see what is happening. RCT 8, attacking with the 4th Division, speeds to the area between Hosdorf and Longsdorf, securing the hills that command a portion of the Our River. Meanwhile, Regimental Combat Teams 2 and 10, storming forward with the 5th Division, seize Erpeldange and Ingledorf in addition to securing the heights along the northern bank of the Sauer River. Heavy fighting also erupts for control of Bettendorf and Diekirch, and the Yanks secure part of the

GIs moving the tube and recoil mechanism of an 8' gun.

latter. Both fall to the Americans on the following day. The 80th Division seizes Nocher, but cannot dislodge the entrenched Germans in the heights near Masseler. In the **XX Corps** sector, the Germans strike swiftly and seize Butzdorf from the 94th Division; however, the 91st repels the enemy at Tettingen. **6th Army Group** The French 1st Army is ordered to initiate an assault to eliminate the Colmar Pocket; it is to attack on the 20th and complete a double envelopment of the objective. In the **U.S. Seventh Army** area, **VI Corps** sector, the Germans penetrate the U.S. lines at the Bitche salient and cut off the 3rd Battalion, 157th Regiment, 45th Division. Tough fighting erupts as rescue attempts continue for a couple of days; some of the trapped troops make it back to the main body. In addition, the Germans pound against U.S. positions at Bois de Sessenheim and Sessenheim, taking both from Task Force Linden. At the Gambsheim bridgehead, which is now further fortified, the enemy continues to frustrate the 12th Armored Division. C.C.A. aborts its positions at Herrlisheim and attempts to rescue the Infantry, which is isolated in the town, but the attack doesn't succeed. In the **French 1st Army** 2nd Corps sector, the U.S. 28th Division starts to relieve the U.S. Third Division. **(Atlantic-Italy) 15th Army Group** The British 13th Corps, composed of the British 6th Armored and 78th Divisions is detached from the U.S. Fifth Army and reassigned to the British Eighth Army.

January 16th 1945 — First and Third Armies converging on Houffalize as they prod deeper into Germany.

January 19th 1945 — (Pacific-Philippines) Luzon In the **U.S. Sixth Army** area, the **XVI Corps** drives toward Clark Field, plowing forward at rapid speed, reaching the Camiling-Paniqui-Anao line 24 hours ahead of schedule. Contingents of the 129th Regiment, 37th Division roar into Carmen and moves beyond to San Manuel without encountering opposition; another column drives into Moncada, overrunning the enemy. In addition, another contingent takes Paniqui. Meanwhile, the 160th Regiment, 40th Division rushes into Nambalan on Route 13, while the 148th Regiment, 37th Division deploys along the Camiling-Paniqui Road. In the I Corps sector, 43rd Division zone, fierce fighting erupts at the 169th Regiment's roadblock outside of Sison; reinforcements are sped to the 2nd Battalion, but the Japanese retake the position. The 103rd Regiment, also of the 43rd Division, commits two Battalions against Hill 600, off Pozorrubio Road. **Camotes** The 7th Division contingent on Poro Island continues sweeping the island, yet there is only sporadic contact with the enemy. **(Pacific-Burma)** In ALFSEA's 15th Corps area, the 25th Indian Division, operating on the Myebon Peninsula, seizes Kantha. In the N.C.A.C. area, the Artillery of the U.S. 5322nd Brigade saturates the Burma Road with shells, scoring it with irregular holes, while the troops continue to scour the hills above it, eliminating the enemy. In other activity, the elements of the Chinese 38th Division sever the Namhkam-Namhpakka Road. **(Atlantic-Western Europe) 21st Army Group** In the **British Second Army** area, **12th Corps** sector, the British 7th Armored Division reduces the enemy resistance in Stevensweerd. Breberen, Broichhoven, Isenbruch, and Saeffelen are seized by the British 52nd Division; some contingents move across the Dutch border and capture Koningsbosch. **12th Army Group** The weather is so severe that mobile equipment is virtually paralyzed. Some Divisions are bogged down by the impenetrable ice and sleet. In the **U.S. First Army** area, the 3rd Armored Division seizes Brisy, Renglez, and Rettigny, then sweeps its area south to the Ourthe River, culminating its task. The 83rd Division reduces remnant resistance in the woods in its sector, then sends units into Courtil and Bovigny. In the **XVIII Corps (Airborne)** sector, the 75th Division repulses a German assault outside of Burtonville, but although heavily engaged at Grand Bois, it cannot take the town. The 30th Division takes Recht and proceeds to overrun the heights southeast of Poteau at Bois d'Emmels. In the **V Corps** sector, the 1st Division attacks and clears a corridor into St. Vith; the 7th Armored flows forward, overrunning Eibertingen, Iveldingen, Montenau, and Schop-

pen. In the **U.S. Third Army** area, the 4th Division, operating northeast of Bettindorf, captures the heights above the Our River, while the 5th Division seizes the town however, contingents of the 5th are unable to oust the German stronghold near Reisdorf. Meanwhile, the XX Corps sector is another hotbed; the 94th Division acts as a ramrod and blows through previously bypassed fortifications to gain a clear path for C.C.A., 8th Armored Division, which is forming for attack outside of Koenigsmacker. **6th Army Group** In the **U.S. Seventh Army** area, the Germans at the Bitche salient commence a tenacious, but unsuccessful, counterattack against the 157th Regiment, 45th Division, which is simultaneously attempting to rescue its trapped 3rd Battalion. Heavy enemy attacks also occur south of Hatten, against the 14th Armored Division lines. The 25th Tank Battalion speeds to Hochfelden to bolster the defenses, and at Sessenheim, the 79th Division, reinforced by units of the 103rd Division, breaks into the town, but iron resistance forces a withdrawal. The 12th Armored begins pulling back in order to get relieved; the Germans strike at the point of transfer and get thrown back. Meanwhile, enemy troops isolate the 2nd Battalion, 314th Infantry, 79th Division in Drusenheim, but some manage to escape to U.S. lines. **(Atlantic-Eastern Europe)** The German report of a new Soviet offensive in the East Prussian area is confirmed by Moscow. The Third White Russian Front secures Schlossberg (Pillkallen), and the First White Russian Front seizes Lodz. Cracow and Tarnow are taken by the First Ukrainian Front, and the Fourth Ukrainian Front converges on Gorlice.

U.S. troops on the attack in First Army zone, pushing from Butgenbach-Malmedy.

Morotai I.

HALMAHERA I.

Biak I.

Noemfoor I.

Sansapor

VOGELKOP

Wakde I.

Tanahmerah Bay

Humboldt Bay

Arare

Hollandia

NEW GUINEA

Karas I.

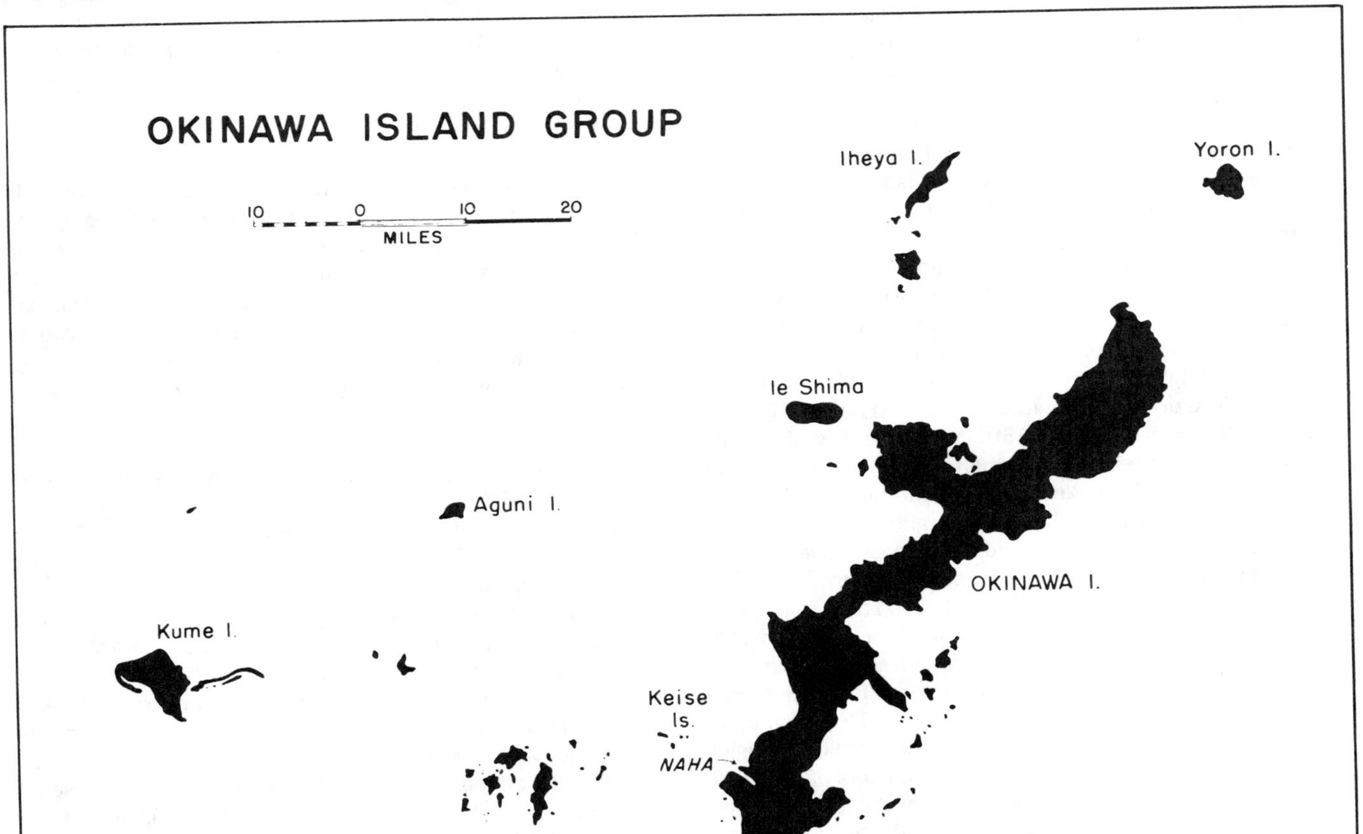

OKINAWA ISLAND GROUP

10   0   10   20
MILES

Iheya I.

Yoron I.

Ie Shima

Aguni I.

OKINAWA I.

Kume I.

Keise Is.

NAHA

Kerama Is.

January 20th 1945 — (Pacific-Philippines) In Naval activity, the U.S.S. *Tautog* lands supplies on the south coast of Mindanao. **Luzon** In the **U.S. Sixth Army** area, General Krueger informs the Allied Air Forces that the bridges south of the Agno River will be required to secure Manila, and he requests that they be spared destruction. In the **XIV Corps** sector, the 160th Regiment, 40th Division, followed by the 108th Infantry, closes on Tarlac, while abandoned Victoria is taken by advance contingents of the 37th Division. In the **I Corps** sector, the 25th Division commences its attack against Asingan and San Manuel, committing the 27th and 161st Regiments. Meanwhile, the 169th Regiment (less 2nd Battalion), 43rd Division drives toward Mt. Alava, getting units to the crest; the 103rd Regiment is heavily engaged on Hill 600, seizing a hold on the southern slopes. **Camotes** Contingents of the 7th Division Task Force reconnoiters Pacijan Island, but does not encounter any resistance. **Mindoro** A large contingent of the 2nd Battalion, 19th Infantry, 24th Division is dispatched to Bulalacao to eliminate the Japs. **Southwest Pacific** In an effort to concentrate Air and Naval support, without endangering the troops involved in the landing on Luzon, General Eichelberger suggests to General MacArthur that the 11th Airborne should land at Nasugbu Bay and eliminate the second site which is to be either Balayan or Tayabas Bay. MacArthur accepts the suggestion; the landing occurs on January 31st. Also, Admiral Halsey's Fleet maneuvers through the Balintang Channel, en route to photograph Okinawa, encountering unyielding seas north of Luzon between Luzon and Formosa; 15 enemy Planes close fast, but all are shot down. **(Pacific-Burma)** The official Allied Convoy is still stalled at Myitkyina, while enemy forces are being eliminated along the Burma Road; however, a secondary Convoy, commanded by Lt. Hugh A. Pock, an Oklahoman, reaches Kunming, China via the Teng-chung cutoff, culminating a sixteen-day trip from Myitkyina; however, this rugged route has no genuine value. In other activity, Wanting is discovered abandoned by the enemy. The U.S. 5332nd Brigade continues to fortify its perimeter along the Burma Road. **(Atlantic-Europe)** In Naval activity, Naval Technical Mission in Europe is established, to be commanded by Commodore H. A. Schade; Headquarters is established in Paris. **21st Army Group** In the **British Second Army** area, **12th Corps** sector, the British 52nd Infantry takes Bocket and Waldfeucht in Germany, and in addition overruns Echterbosch, Holland. Meanwhile, the British 7th Armored advances to St. Joost. The British 43rd Division, operating in Germany on the right flank of the Corps, seizes Langfroich and has contingents relieve units of the 52nd Division at Breberen. **12th Army Group** In the **U.S. First Army's XVIII (Airborne) Corps** sector, the 75th and 30th Divisions are reducing remnant resistance in their zones, the latter closing on St. Vith. The U.S. 7th Armored rolls through the Ondenval defile; C.C.A. plows through Deidenberg; however, C.C.B. encounters innumerable mines hidden beneath heavy snowbound terrain, which prevents it from taking Born. In the **U.S. Third Army** area, **VIII Corps** sector, C.C.R. 11th Armored advances through abandoned enemy positions and spreads across Boeur, Bois aux Chenes, and Wandesbourcy. The 17th Airborne moves beyond Tavigny. In the **III Corps** sector, Moinet and Hill 510 fall to C.C.A., 6th Armored. German resistance forces contingents of the 358th Regiment, 90th Division to halt at Derenbach and pull back; contingents of the 359th Infantry take Allerborn and Chifontaine. In the **XII Corps** sector, Regimental Combat Teams 8 and 12, 4th Division, occupy Tandel. The 5th Division seizes Brandenburg and Kippenhof. In addition, Burden is taken without opposition by the 318th

Regiment, 80th Division. In the **XX Corps** sector, German resistance at Orscholz holds off the 1st Battalion, 301st Regiment, 94th Division; however, the 302nd Regiment secures enemy positions in its sector and repels attempts to regain them. At the Saarlautern bridgehead, the Germans are convincingly repulsed by the 95th Division; German Artillery aids the Yanks, as the Germans attack prematurely and the 400 troops get struck by their own shells as well as those of the Yanks. Only forty prisoners are captured. **6th Army Group** In the **U.S. Seventh Army** area, after nightfall, the **VI Corps** initiates a scheduled withdrawal to deploy along a new defensive position at the Rothbach Rau-Moder River line. Continuing efforts by the 45th Division to rescue the surrounded troops at the Bitche salient are futile; some escape to the main force. In addition, trapped troops of the 2nd Battalion, 314th Regiment at Drusenheim are pounded; some manage to escape, but the balance are reported missing in action. In the **French First Army** sector, the weather is inclement; nevertheless, the offensive to reduce the Colmar Pocket commences on schedule. The 1st Corps attacks with two Divisions (4th Moroccan Mtn. and 2nd Moroccan Infantry), but Ensisheim, the primary objective is not reached until the 3rd of February. In the 2nd Corps sector, the U.S. 28th Division assumes responsibility for the area extending southwest from Sigolsheim to Le Valtin, now that its relief of the 3rd Division is complete. **(Atlantic-Eastern Europe)** The Second and Third White Russian Fronts saturate East Prussia. Tilsit is taken by the latter. The First White Russian Front drives across Poland toward Berlin, while the Second Ukrainian Front, also storming across Poland, drives toward Silesia. In other activity, Nowy Sacz, Poland, in the Carpathians, falls to the Fourth Ukrainian Front, while it also seizes Bardejov, Kosice (Kassa), and Presov in Czechoslovakia. The beleaguered Germans are faltering badly, but they still do not capitulate easily. Ferocious fighting develops southwest of Budapest, Hungary, as the Germans try to penetrate Soviet positions to reach the Danube.

January 21st 1945 — (Pacific-Philippines) Task Force 38 strikes another mighty blow against Japanese Shipping and Military targets at Formosa, Sakishima Gunto, Okinawa, and the Pescadores, sinking about eight Oilers and two Transports, in addition to damaging other Vessels. The attack also demolishes more than 100 Planes caught on the ground; however, the Japs strike back, sending four Kamikazes against the Fleet. The Carrier *Ticonderoga* (CV-14) receives heavy damage by two Suicide Planes and also loses 140 men; the Carrier *Hancock* (CV19) is damaged by an accidental explosion on the flight deck, killing 48 men; the Light Carrier *Langley* (CVL-27) sustains slight damage by a Kamikaze costing one Sailor's life; and the Destroyer *Maddox* (DD-731), is damaged by a Kamikaze, losing four men. This is the final Japanese air attack which causes damage to Task Force 38 (except a Kamikaze which strikes the Destroyer *Borie* one week before the surrender of Japan) while Admiral Halsey commands the Third Fleet. The Japanese Transports No. 101 and No. 102 are sunk by Carrier Planes. **Luzon** In the **U.S. Sixth Army** area, the **XIV Corps** moves aggressively, passing its objective. It receives orders to continue driving toward Clark Field, although it means leaving its left flank defenseless for a stretch of almost twenty miles. Tarlac is seized without a fight by the 160th Regiment, 40th Division. The 37th Division pushes advance units to La Paz. Meanwhile, the 103rd Regiment, 40th Division, battles fiercely and secures the crest of

Hill 600, while RCT 158 and the 163rd Regiment eliminate the remnant enemy forces on Blue Ridge. Subsequently, the 163rd is placed in Corps Reserve. In addition, the 172nd Regiment is bolstered by the Philippine 2nd Battalion, 121st Infantry, while it is fighting to secure the hills around Rosario. **(Pacific-Burma)** In ALFSEA's 15th Corps area, Air and Naval bombardments precede the landing of a contingent of the Indian 26th Division on the northern coast of Ramree Island which seizes Kyaukpyu. **21st Army Group** In the **British Second Army** area, 12th Corps sector, Hontem and Selsent are taken by the British 52nd Division; subsequent to the seizing of these two villages, the 52nd occupies undefended Braunsrath. Meanwhile, the British 43rd Division advances to Schierwaldenrath against no opposition. **12th Army Group** In the **U.S. First Army** area, **VII Corps** sector, the 84th Division assumes responsibility for the previous 83rd Infantry and 3rd Armored Divisions' zones and readies an attack against the Gouvy-Beho area between St. Vith and Houffalize. In the **XVIII Corps (Airborne)** sector, the remaining resistance in Grand Bois is reduced by the 75th Division. At Born, vicious house-to-house fighting ceases as the 7th Armored eliminates the resistance. In the **V Corps** sector, the enemy offers heavy resistance northeast of Schoppen as the 1st Division works on bolstering its positions. In the **U.S. Third Army** area, General Patton becomes annoyed when coming upon contingents of the 17th Airborne which are stuck in the ice; after prodding by Patton, the Officers have the men dismount and push the Vehicles, ending the dilemma. In addition, Patton discovers that the nasty weather has disarmed both the American and German mines as the ice has seeped under the "spiders" and no amount of weight would cause detonation. The 17th Airborne Division (VIII Corps) maintains its drive northeast of Tavigny. Buret is reached by contingents of C.C.A., 11th Armored Division. Crendal, Baraques de Troine, Hachiville, Lullange, Hoffelt, and Troine are captured by the 6th Armored Division. Derenbach capitulates to the 358th Regiment, 90th Division, which also seizes Boevange-les-Clervaux and Hill 480; Hamiville, Wincrange and Hill 520 fall to the 359th Regiment. Meanwhile, contingents of the 26th Division take Bruhl and Winseler after driving across the Wiltz River, while other contingents coordinate with the 6th Cavalry Group and eliminate the remaining resistance at Wiltz in Luxembourg. In the **XII Corps** sector, the Germans retain Fuhren by repelling the elements of the 4th Division; still other contingents overrun Longsdorf. Landscheid and Lipperscheid are taken by the 5th Division and the 318th Regiment, 80th Division seizes Bourscheid and Welscheid, then probes through the surrounding woods as far as the Sauer River. In addition, the 317th Regiment, 80th Division takes Kehmen. In the **XX Corps** sector, the Germans mount rigid resistance at Orscholz prompting the 94th Division to postpone its attack due to heavy casualties sustained by the 1st Battalion, 301st Regiment; the German pressure is equally tenacious against the 302nd Regiment, but it is able to repulse the attacks and hold Nennig and Tettingen. **6th Army Group** In the **U.S. Seventh Army** area, **XV Corps** sector, C.C.B., 10th Armored Division converges on the area northeast of Fenetrange. In the **VI Corps** sector, the Corps' withdrawal to the new line of resistance is complete. It is spread along the line Althorn-Rothbach-Niedermodern-Haguenau-Bischwiller. In other activity, the Germans pressure the 79th Division's Outpost Line in Camp d'OBerhoffen, and it is forced to pull back. **(Atlantic-Eastern Europe)** The Third White Russian Front takes Gumbinnen. The Second White Russian Front takes Tannenberg, both in East Prussia. The First White Russian Front in conjunction with the First Ukrainian Front maintains its pace across Poland and moves into Silesia, Germany, near Czestochowa, and overruns several towns.

January 22nd 1945 — (Pacific-Philippines) Luzon The **U.S. Eighth Army** receives orders from General MacArthur to commit a Regimental Combat Team of the 11th Airborne for a landing at Nasugbu, Luzon, to initiate forced reconnaissance of the area. The landing date is set for January 31st and will determine the operation of the entire Division. Allied Planes commence a preinvasion bombardment of Corregidor. In addition, the Airstrip at Mangaldan becomes operational. In the **U.S. Sixth Army** area, **XIV Corps** sector, advance contingents of the 40th Division reach Capas, while units of the 37th Division seize La Paz. In the **I Corps** sector, the 27th Infantry, 25th Division sprints toward Asingan against nominal opposition; the 161st Regiment overruns a hill outside of San Manuel as it encroaches the town. The Japanese repel a strong attack by the 2nd Battalion, 169th Infantry, 43rd Division (supported by Artillery and Tanks) against Hill 355. **Mindoro** the 3rd Battalion, 21st Regiment, 24th Division embarks to the north coast of Estrella. **(Pacific-Ryukyu Islands)** Admiral McCain's Fast Carrier Task Force 38 launches Aircraft, which attack enemy installations on the islands including Okinawa. The Planes collect photographic intelligence while carrying out the mission. Subsequent to this operation, Task Force 38 embarks for Ulithi, arriving there on the 25th. **(Pacific-Formosa)** Land-based Heavy Bombers of the Fifth Air Force depart their Base in the Philippines and strike enemy positions at Heito Air Base. **(Pacific-Burma)** In ALFSEA area, 15th Corps sector, the 3rd Commando Brigade debarks at Kangaw on the Arakan Front, subsequent to an Artillery bombardment. The landing sparks the Japanese who take countermeasures and begin to cut off Allied forces along the southern coast. In the **British Fourteenth Army** area, 33rd Corps sector, Monya, the final Japanese-held port on the Chindwin River, is seized by the Indian 20th Division, which also overpowers Japanese resistance at Myinmu on the Irrawaddy. In the 4th Corps sector, Tilin falls to the East African 28th Brigade. In the N.C.A.C. area, Chiang Kai-shek directs the Chinese Expeditionary Force to assemble north of the Sino-Burmese border and delegates C.A.I. (Chinese Army in India) to complete the clearing of the Burma Road. General Sultan, later in the night, announces that the Burma Road is open. The U.S. 5332nd Brigade has a Patrol advance to a ridge across the Burma Road; however, it receives directions to confine its activity to Patrols and interdicting traffic on the road. **(Pacific-China)** The Japanese, during the past few days, have set up positions at strategic bridges and tunnels along the Canton-Hankow Railroad. **(Atlantic-Western Europe) 21st Army Group** In the **British Second Army** area, 12th Corps sector, vicious but indecisive fighting occurs at Montfort where the British 7th Armored Division is battling for control. Waldenrath falls to the 43rd Division and the 52nd Division takes Laffeld and Obspringen. **12th Army Group** In the **U.S. First Army** area, **VII Corps** sector, Beho and Gouvy are seized by the 84th Division and attached 3rd Armored units. In the **XVIII Corps (Airborne)** sector, Commanster and the woods to its northeast are secured by the 75th Division. The 30th Division rolls forward, seizing Hinderhausen, Ober Emmels, Nieder Emmels, and Sart-lez-St. Vith. Meanwhile, Hunningen is taken by C.C.A., 7th Armored Division, bolstered by Tanks attached to C.C.B. In addition, elements of 38th Armored Infantry Battalion encounter stiff resistance at a roadblock outside of St. Vith, preventing it from advancing into the town. In the **U.S. Third Army** area, General Patton calls General Bradley to

579

urge that all U.S. Armies attack, regardless of fatigue or casualties, due to the Russian advance toward Berlin (at present 165 miles outside). Later in the day, General Weyland calls Patton and reports that an immense amount of German Armor is traveling in several different directions north of Diekirch and that they are being intercepted by U.S. units. In the **VIII Corps** sector, contingents of C.C.A., 11th Armored Division occupy Bois de Rouvroy and cross the Luxembourg border against no opposition. Steinbach and Limerle are taken without incident by the 17th Airborne. In the **III Corps** sector, Basbellain is entered by C.C.B., 6th Armored Division, while C.C.A. takes Asselborn and Weiler. The 359th Regiment, 90th Division seizes Deiffelt, Donnange, Rumlange and Stockem, while the 357th Regiment advances to Boxhorn and Sassel. The Third Army continues to acquire German-held real estate as the 6th Cavalry Group and the 26th Division eliminate the final resistance at Wiltz, while also seizing Eschweiler, Kleinhoscheid and Knaphoscheid. In addition, the 28th Cavalry Squadron eases effortlessly through Weicherdange. In the **XII Corps** sector, the 4th Division continues to advance along the west bank of the Our River, seizing Walsdorf; however, the Germans hang tough at Fuhren, preventing the Yanks from seizing it. The 10th and 11th Regiments, 5th Division, surge forward, seizing Gralingen sprinting to the high ground east of Nachtmanderscheid, and securing it. Meanwhile, the 80th Division sends contingents through previously secured ground (by 6th Cavalry Group) into the area around Wiltz. In the **XX Corps** sector, a German counterattack strikes swiftly against the 302nd Regiment, 94th Division and retakes about half of Nennig. **6th Army Group** In the U.S. **Seventh Army** area, **XV Corps** sector, the 101st Airborne converges on the Drulingen-Sarraltroff region. In the **VI Corps** sector, defenses are improved to neutralize enemy aggressiveness; the outposts of the 79th and 103rd Divisions are pulled back to the Moder River line. In the **French 1st Army** area, the 2nd Corps advances toward Colmar, striking against the area between Ostheim and Selestat to support the assault of the I Corps, which is driving north in an effort to seal off and reduce the Colmar Pocket. The attacking Divisions are the U.S. 3rd and 5th Armored Divisions plus the 1st Moroccan Infantry, bolstered by the French 2nd Armored which is maintaining the Rhine Plain, affording protection to the assault troops. Meanwhile, the U.S. 28th Division, operating further west, initiates night raids against enemy positions. **(Atlantic-Eastern Europe)** In East Prussia, the Third White Russian Front takes Insterberg, and the Second White Russian Front captures Allenstein and Deutsch-Eylau. In Poland, Inowroclaw falls to the First White Russian Front as it drives toward Posen. Gross Strehlitz and Konstradt in Silesia fall to the First Ukrainian Front, subsequent to heavy fighting along the Polish-Silesian border. **(Atlantic-Italy) 15th Army Group** The U.S. Fifth Army begins preparations for a spring offensive.

January 23rd 1945 — (Pacific-Carolines) The Destroyer Escorts *Corbesier* (DE-438), *Conklin* (DE-439), and the *Raby* (DE-698) sink the Japanese Submarine I-48 off Yap Island. **(Pacific-Philippines)** The Submarine *Nautilus* lands supplies on Mindanao's east coast. **Luzon** In the U.S. **Sixth Army** area, **XIV Corps** sector, the 160th Regiment, 40th Division pounds steadily against fierce resistance at Bamban and eliminates it, seizing the town and its Airfield, plus a strategic river crossing. Concepcion falls to the 108th Regiment. In the **I Corps** sector, Hill 355 remains a tight-fisted battle as the 2nd Battalion, 169th Regiment, 43rd Division, continues to hammer

the enemy, which refuses to relent. In conjunction, the 172nd Regiment seizes a ridge at the Pugo Valley. **Camotes Islands** The 7th Division Task Force encounters intense opposition at Hill 854 as it continues to secure Poro Island. **(Pacific-Burma)** In the N.C.A.C. area, the Convoy, still stalled at Myitkyina, departs for China. **(Pacific-China)** The U.S.S. *Barb* (SS-220), under Commander Eugene B. Fluckey, creeps into Namkwan harbor challenging uncharted five fathom waters and discovers about 30 enemy Vessels. Torpedoes launched from a distance of 3,000 yards while running, strike eight direct hits on six Auxiliary Vessels and an ammunition Vessel, igniting a voluminous display of bursting shells. Under a brilliant sky, the *Barb*, disregarding the shallow water and ragged rocks, tears away at high speed; four days later the *Barb* destroys a Transport. This action coupled with the Barb's two-hour sea duel on January 8th which culminated with the sinking of another ammunition Vessel and additional Shipping gives the *Barb* a spectacular Patrol; Commander Fluckey receives the Medal of Honor. **(Atlantic-Western Europe) 21st Army Group** In the **British Second Army** area, 12th Corps sector, heavy but indecisive fighting ensues at Montfort, as the British 7th Armored Division continues to secure the area. Meanwhile, the British 52nd Division takes Aphove against feeble opposition, while the British 43rd Division captures Scheifendahl and Straeten in quick time. **12th Army Group** In the U.S. **First Army's VII Corps** sector, Ourthe is overrun by the 84th Division, which follows the gain by sweeping the high ground between there and the Beho River. In the **XVIII (Airborne) Corps** sector, the U.S. 7th Armored whips into St. Vith, seizing it; in conjunction, the 75th Division seizes Braunlauf and Maldingen, while the 30th Division roars into Crombach, Neundorf, and Weisten. In the U.S. **Third Army** area, **VIII Corps** sector, contact is made between the 11th Armored Division and the 17th Airborne as Patrols continue to probe around Bois de Rouvroy. In the **III Corps** sector, Biwisch and Trois Vierges fall to C.C.A., 6th Armored. Basbellain is occupied by Combat Team Miltonberger (RCT 134, 35th Division attached). The Bischent woods are secured by the 359th Regiment, 90th Division; the 357th bolts across the Clerf River and captures the hills on the sides of a draw outside of Hupperdange and its 1st Battalion takes Binsfeld. Eselborn is taken by the 28th Cavalry Squadron, which also becomes heavily involved at Clerf and Drauffelt. Later, during the night, Task Force Fickett attacks Clerf and Mecher, seizing the latter. In the **XII Corps** sector, the 4th Division takes Fuhren, while the 5th Division advances against heavy opposition to Hoscheid and Nachtmanderscheid; however, both remain under German control. Merkols is seized by the 317th Regiment, 80th Division. Wasserbillig, where the Sauer and Moselle Rivers meet, is taken by the 346th Regiment, 87th Division. In the **XX Corps** sector, Berg is regained from the 94th Division, following a strong German counterattack; however, determined fighting on the part of the 302nd Regiment, supported by a Battalion (attached) of the 376th Regiment and contingents of C.C.A., 8th Armored, retake Nennig. Meanwhile, the 3rd Battalion, 302nd Regiment repulses the enemy and retains Wies, while simultaneously shortening the gap between there and Nennig. During the heated combat near Tettington, Master Sergeant Nicholas Oresko, Company C, 302nd Regiment, takes swift action after his unit is pinned down by intense enemy fire. He drives forward, closing on a bunker which contains a machine gun, and tosses a grenade directly into the position; he immediately follows with a brisk surge that swivels him atop the bunker from which spot he kills all who survived the blast. A nearby machine gun commences fire and wounds him; however, he refuses evacuation and goes to the front of the Platoon and leads the attack until the advance is halted by a tremendous storm of fire. Advancing singlehandedly, he rushes the second bunker, despite his badly wounded hip, and annihilates the defenders with a grenade that eliminates the gun and his rifle that exterminates the remaining resistance. Sergeant Oresko again refuses medical aid until he is certain the attack is successful. It is his actions alone that account for 12 enemy dead. The 94th Division reports 40 men killed or wounded and 400 men missing in action. Patton immediately directs General Walker to investigate. In other activity, the 35th Division, which has been in combat since the 6th of July with the exception of five days, is transferred to the Sixth Army Group; despite efforts by both Bradley and Patton, SHAEF insists on the move to help the French reduce the Colmar Pocket. The American Commanders express great determination in continuing the Twelve Army Group until a successful conclusion otherwise, General Bradley might be compelled to give 12 Divisions to British General Montgomery. **6th Army Group** In the **U.S. Seventh Army** area, the Germans mount a strengthened counterattack, penetrate the left flank of the 103rd Division (VI Corps sector) and drive it back beyond Rothbach. In the **French 1st Army** area, 2nd Corps sector, the 1st Moroccans ford the Ill River, north of the U.S. crossing area. The U.S. 3rd Division is driving south toward the Canal de Colmar; its 7th Regiment secures Ostheim, and the 30th crosses the Ill and drives to the fringes of Holtzwihr, where it is forced to retire to the river line at Maison Rouge because the supporting Armor is unable to get across. **(Atlantic-Eastern Europe)** In the northeastern part of East Prussia, the Third White Russian Front takes Wehlau, while the Second White Russian Front seizes Ortelsburg as it advances toward Elbing in northern Poland, taking Brodnica and Lipno as it moves. The First White Russian Front captures Bromberg and Kalisz. The weakening German forces are struggling to break through to the Danube, driving the Russians from Szekesfehervar. In addition, another Russian offensive begins as the Second Ukrainian Front attacks the Germans north of Miskolc, joining with the Fourth Rumanian Army, and captures several Czechoslovakian towns and villages.

January 24th 1945 — (Pacific Formosa) U.S. Land-based Planes, launched from the Philippines, bombard enemy installations and Shipping at Keelung. **(Pacific-Philippine Sea-China Sea)** The Salvage Vessel *Extractor* (ARS-15) is accidentally sunk by a U.S. Submarine. The Japanese Destroyer *Shigure* is sunk by the Submarine *Blackfin* (SS-322) in the Gulf of Siam. **(Pacific-Philippines)** The U.S. Landing Ship Dock *Shadwell* (LSD-15) is damaged by an Aircraft torpedo. **Luzon** In the **U.S. Sixth Army** area, **XIV Corps** sector, the 160th Regiment, 40th Division encounters the Japanese outpost lines in the hills west of Bamban, overrunning one of the hills. The 145th Regiment 37th Division secures the line extending from Concepcion to the Bamban River. In the **I Corps** sector, the 161st Infantry attacks and secures a small hold at San Manuel barrio. The Stark Force (103rd and 169th Regiments, 43rd Division and the 3rd Battalion, 63rd Regiment, 6th Division) is formed. In addition, the Yon Force, composed of the 63rd Regiment minus the 3rd Battalion, is established; RCT 158 and the 172nd Infantry, 43rd Division are designated the MacNider Force. **Mindoro** The 2nd Battalion, 21st Regiment, 24th Division advances into Calapan. **(Pacific-Volcano Islands)** Task Group 94.9, commanded by Rear Admiral O. C.

B-29s on the attack.

Badger, bombards Iwo Jima despite terrible weather. In addition, B29s and B24s of the XXI Bomber Command and Seventh Air Force, respectively, pound enemy Shipping and installations, meeting no aerial interference. **(Pacific-Burma-China)** U.S. Brigadier General Robert M. Cannon receives word from the Chinese New First Army Commander that the Burma Road will be operable by the 27th. The Salween campaign closes as the Chinese Expeditionary Force halts to await relief by C.A.I. In other activity, the Chinese Nationalists and Chinese Communists reinitiate their negotiations; talks had stopped during mid-December (16th). **(Atlantic-Western Europe) 21st Army Group** In the **British Second Army** area, 12th Corps sector, the British 7th Armored Division thumps the enemy and seizes Aandenberg, Montfort, and Weerd. Meanwhile, the British 52nd Division reduces the final resistance at Heinsberg and occupies Haaren without incident. In addition, the British 43rd Division secures Schleiden and Uetterath. **12th Army Group** While going over the prisoners' credentials today, it is noticed that out of one contingent numbering 100 men captured by the 5th Division, five different German Divisions are represented and in a sampling of 6th Armored prisoners numbering 150 men, ten German Divisions are represented. Generals Bradley, Hodges and Patton join for lunch to discuss items including boundaries. General Bradley, according to Patton, becomes incensed when British General Whitely (SHEAF G-3) calls Bradley and tells him that he wants to take a Corps Headquarters from Twelve Army Group and place it in Sixth Army Group. Bradley states to

Whitely: "IF HE WANTS TO DESTROY THE WHOLE OPERA- TION HE COULD DO SO AND BE DAMNED, AND TAKE NOT ONLY ONE CORPS HEADQUARTERS BUT ALL THE CORPS AND DIVISIONS." Bradley then repeats the message to General Bull, Whitely's assistant. The Yank Generals tell Bradley they are happy with his attitude, and in addition, all agree that the effort to reduce the Colmar Pocket is a "foolish" venture and a waste of troops. In the **U.S. First Army** area, the **VII Corps** is squeezed out as the 84th Division finishes securing its zone. In the **XVIII Corps (Airborne)** sector, Aldringen is taken by the 75th Division, ending its Salm River operation. In the **V Corps** sector, the 1st Division drives forward, its 16th Regiment securing the Bambusch woods against nominal opposition, while the 18th Regiment seizes Moderscheid. Meanwhile, the 26th overpowers the roadblock at the Buellingen-Butgenbach-St. Vith junction near Richelsbusch. In the **U.S. Third Army** area, contingents of the 17th Airborne drive toward Landscheid and Thommen. Other Corps contingents advance toward St. Vith. In the **III Corps** sector, the Corps shifts the direction of its attack, pivoting from northeast to east; its C.C.A., 6th Armored secures the triangular region composed of Trois Vierges-Wilwerdange-Binsfield, securing Breidfeld and Holler. The 90th Division is struck by a stiff counterattack near Binsfield before dawn however, the enemy is thrown back. In the **XII Corps** sector, the 5th Division seizes Hoscheid and Nachtmanderscheid. The 80th Division knocks out the remaining resistance at Alscheid, Enscherange, and Kautenbach. In the **XX Corps** sector, the Germans maintain control of Berg, despite a heavy 8th Armored Artillery-supported attack by the 94th Division. A scheduled assault by C.C.A., 8th Armored is temporarily suspended because of the failure to take the town. **6th Army Group** In the **U.S. Seventh Army** area, the 45th Division's outpost is forced to withdraw from Saegmuhl, due to heavy enemy pressure; however, the 103rd Division is able to thwart a fierce German counterattack at its main line of resistance at Bischoltz and Muhlhausen. In the 79th Division sector, the Germans strike after dark against the 222nd Infantry's positions across the Moder between Neubourg and Schweighausen, seizing the western part of the latter. In the **French 1st Army** area, 2nd Corps sector, U.S. and French forces encounter fierce resistance as they attempt to enlarge their bridgehead at the Ill River. Well-camouflaged Tanks peer from the woods near Elsenheim, and upon the approach of the French, the Tanks initiate an incessant barrage which halts the advance. Meanwhile, the U.S. 3rd Division plows toward the Canal de Colmar, the 7th Regiment heads south toward Houssen, and the 15th Regiment takes over for the beleaguered 30th Regiment and drives to the fringes of Riedwihr. **(Atlantic-Eastern Europe)** Berlin announces a Soviet offensive has commenced in Latvia. In other activity, the First Ukrainian Front operating in Silesia takes Oppeln on the Oder River and Gleiwitz, outside of Breslau. In addition, other contingents take Trachenberg and drive across the Polish border. **(Atlantic-Italy) 15th Army Group** In the **U.S. Fifth Army** area, the 91st Division is relieved by the 88th Division, which has just returned from a short period of rest.

January 25th 1945 — (United States) General Joseph Stilwell is appointed Commander of Army Ground Forces, replacing Lt. General Ben Lear who becomes Deputy Commander to General Eisenhower. **(Pacific- Philippines)** Luzon In the **U.S. Sixth Army** area, **XIV Corps** sector, the Japanese still offer fierce opposition in the hills outside of Bamban; however, the 160th Regiment, 40th Division continues its

General Stilwell and General Merrill during the campaign to seize Myitkyina.

gnawing pace to eliminate the defenders. Meanwhile, the 145th Regiment, 37th Division seizes Mabalcat Airfield and probes beyond to Mabalcat. In the **I Corps** sector, the 103rd Regiment, 43rd Division bypasses Hill 700 and seizes Hills 600 and 800, while the 169th Regiment captures Hill 500; the 172nd Regiment reduces the resistance on Hill 900, gaining the high ground over Highway 11, which runs into Baguio. The 2nd Battalion, 63rd Regiment, 6th Division overpowers Bench Mark Hill. **(Pacific-Burma)** In ALFSEA area, British General Sir Oliver Leese instructs the 15th Corps to establish Air Bases at Akyab and Kyaukpyu. He also directs that the Taungup-Prome Road be opened to facilitate progress, and in addition, orders are issued to secure the balance of the Arakan coast. The West African 82nd Division occupies Myohaung. In the N.C.A.C. area, the Chinese 113th Regiment, 38th Division advances to complete clearing the Burma Road. **(Pacific-China)** General Wedemeyer sends General McClure to Kunming to lead the Chinese Combat Command. **(Pacific-Japan)** Tokyo instructs its China Expeditionary Forces to put its primary efforts into the seacoast area and in the northern part of China, as opposed to advancing into the interior. **(Atlantic-Western Europe)** Generals Eisenhower and Marshall, during an unscheduled meeting at Marseille, discuss strategy for the Allied campaign to the Rhine. General Marshall concurs with Ike's master plan, but the British disagree. Eisenhower intends to utilize a double force to extend the area of attack, but the British expect a single thrust, with British General Montgomery in command. General Marshall suggests that General W. Bedell Smith come to Malta to bolster support for Ike's plan. **21st Army Group** In the **British Second Army** area, 12th Corps sector, the British 7th Armored Division takes Linne and Putbroek. The British 52nd Division seizes Kirchhoven without opposition, then sends Patrols toward the Wurm River. Meanwhile, the British 43rd Division advances to the Wurm; its Patrols discover Horst and Randerath abandoned by the enemy. **12th Army Group** In the **U.S. First Army** area, **XVIII Corps (Airborne)** sector, Medel and Wallerode fall to RCT 424 and C.C.A., 7th Armored Division, respectively. In **V Corps** sector, Ambleve and Mirfeld capitulate to the 16th Regiment, 1st Division. In the **U.S. Third Army** area, **III Corps** sector, the majority of the Corps is across the Clerf River and pushing hard toward the Luxembourg-St. Vith Road (Skyline Drive), running above the Our River. Heinerscheid and Lausdorn fall to the 357th Regiment, 90th Division; Grindhausen and Hupperdange are taken by the 359th Regiment. Clerf is taken by elements of the 6th Cavalry Group and the 101st Regiment, 26th Division. Meanwhile, Reuler and Urspelt fall to the 328th Infantry. In **XII Corps** sector, Berg falls to an advancing 8th Armored Division Task Force. **6th Army Group** In the **U.S. Seventh Army** area, **XV Corps** assumes control of XXI Corps sector and its troops, composed of the 106th Cavalry Group and the 275th and 276th Regiments of Task Force Herren. It also receives the 10th Armored Division, minus C.C.B. In the **VI Corps** sector, strong German pressure forces the 103rd Division to withdraw its outpost from Kindwiller; the enemy attack also penetrates Nieffern and Schillersdorf; however, the 103rd battles determinedly and restores its main line of resistance between Muhlhausen and Schillersdorf. The 79th Division perimeter, also penetrated, reacts by reforming Task Force Wahl 222nd, 232nd Regiments (42nd Division) and the 314th Regiment (79th Division), and C.C.B., 14th Armored Division; in addition, it contains a Recon Troop and contingents of the 781st Tank Battalion. The Task Force secures Schweighausen and clears a portion of Bois de Ohlungen. Meanwhile, the 242nd Infantry, 42nd Division repulses a heavy counterattack between Haguenau and Kaltenhouse, throwing the Germans back across the Moder. In the **French 1st Army** area, the **U.S. XXI Corps** Headquarters is attached to Army. In the 2nd Corps sector, the German Tank contingents stymie French progress in the Elsenheim woods, stopping French Armor. The U.S. 7th Regiment, 3rd Division, bolstered by Armor, pierces Houssen, while the 15th Regiment strikes against Riedwihr and has contingents enter the town late in the day. During the day's fierce fighting, P.F.C. Jose F. Valdez, 7th Infantry, greatly aids his unit when the enemy approaches an Outpost manned by him and five other Soldiers. The detachment is in the direct path of the intruding German advance. Valdez spots a Tank, bolts from his position, and attacks it, forcing it to withdraw; he then daringly attacks and kills three enemy Infantry men approaching his position. The Germans become increasingly infuriated with the insolent Private and attack with two Companies, compelling Valdez to order his small band to pullback while he remains to cover the withdrawal. As the Yanks dash for safety, three of them are wounded, and Valdez sustains a vicious blow to the stomach, but refusing to relent, he maintains his cover fire until all others are behind U.S. lines. Valdez still refuses to pull back, choosing to call in Artillery and mortar fire and directing it until it is about 50 yards from his own position which is unable to be moved because of the 200 attacking enemy troops which are the recipients of the Yankee fire. Following cessation of the attack, Valdez crawls back to his lines, succumbing later. His extraordinary courage and heroism are directly responsible for repulsing the enemy. He becomes a recipient of the Medal of Honor. The 254th Regiment, deployed along the Weiss River, is relieved by the 84th Division, allowing it to drive toward Jebsheim. **(Atlantic-Eastern Europe)** The Second and Third White Russian Fronts are squeezing the German pocket in East Prussia. The First Ukrainian Front seizes Ostrow in Poland and Oels in German Silesia.

January 26th 1945 — (Pacific-Philippines) Luzon In the **U.S. Sixth Army** area, General Krueger issues orders to expedite the drive to Manila; the **XIV Corps** is to cross the Pampanga at Calumpit, subsequent to seizing Clark Airfield, and send Reconnaissance Patrols south and southeast to the Hagonoy-Malolos-Plaridel line. Meanwhile, the **I Corps** is to maintain its thrust toward Cabanatuan. The **XIV Corps** drives persistently; its 160th Regiment clears Hills 600 and 636. Hill 5 is assaulted by the 108th Regiment. The 37th Division is also hammering the Japs, seizing Clark Field Runway Number 1

and securing Magalang. In the **I Corps** sector, the stubborn ridge outside of Cataguintingan is toppled by the 158th Regiment, 43rd Division. Contingents of the 172nd Regiment, 43rd Division seize Rosario. **Mindoro** Camina Air Drome is declared operational for Heavy Bombers. Japanese resistance in the Bulalacao region terminates. **(Pacific Ocean Area)** Operation Plan CINCPOA 11-44 (Iwo Jima) becomes effective. The Commander Fifth Fleet assumes control of all forces assigned to Central Pacific Task Forces which will participate in the invasion of Iwo Jima. Also, Admiral Halsey notes the recent record of the Third Fleet: "IN OUR FIVE MONTHS AT SEA, WE HAD DESTROYED 7,315 ENEMY PLANES AND HAD SUNK 90 WARSHIPS AND 573 MERCHANT VESSELS TOTALING MORE THAN 1,000,000 TONS." (JUNE 15TH 1944-JANUARY 25TH 1943). **(Pacific-Burma)** In ALFSEA area, 15th Corps sector, Cheduba Island is invaded by Royal Marines attached to the East Indies Fleet. **(Atlantic-Western Europe) 21st Army Group** In the **British Second Army** area, the 12th Corps concludes its Operation BLACKCOCK; however, a small German bridgehead still exists at Vlodrop, and the Corps will not list it as a priority. In the **U.S. Ninth Army** area, **XIII Corps** sector, the Brachelen-Himmerich-Randerath triangle is cleared by U.S. troops, including the 11th Cavalry Group and the 106th Division; the Yanks encounter feeble resistance as the Germans are on the run. **12th Army Group** In the **U.S. First Army** area, **XVIII (Airborne) Corps** sector, Meyerode is secured by RCT 424. At St. Vith, the U.S. 7th Armored Division bolsters its perimeter. In the **U.S. Third Army** area, **VIII Corps** sector, the Germans continue to withdraw behind the West Wall with Third Army troops on its tail. The 90th Division (III Corps) occupies Lieler. In the **III Corps** sector, Weiswampach is swept clean by C.C.B., 6th Armored, while Fischbach is taken by the 328th Regiment, 26th Division. Marnach and the nearby high ground east of Clerf and Drauffelt are jack-hammered thoroughly by the hard-hatted 101st Regiment, which plants the Stars and Stripes in the area. In the **XII Corps** sector, Hoscheiderdickt falls to the 5th Division's RCT 11, while its 5th Cavalry Reconnaissance Troop reduces Schlindermanderscheid, a town easier taken than pronounced. Meanwhile, the 80th Division sprints forward continuing Third Army's domino thrust, capturing Lellingen and Siebenaler while advancing to the edges of Bockholz, in conjunction with contingents of the 79th Division which push forward and assume the zone previously defended by the 87th Division. In the **XX Corps** sector, resistance in Butzdorf is knocked over by contingents of the 94th Division and attached units of the 8th Armored Division as they roll toward Sinz. **6th Army Group** In the **U.S. Seventh Army** area, **VI Corps** sector, the enemy has scattered out of harm's way, and the 45th Division is essentially roaming freely without encountering the Germans in any type of strength in both the 79th and 103rd Division areas. The final enemy resistance is eliminated at Schillersdorf by the 103rd Division, which also reinstates the MLR. In conjunction, the 79th Division restores its MLR. Meanwhile, Hochfelden is ready to fall as the 101st Airborne drives quickly toward it. In the French 1st Army's 2nd Corps sector, heavy fighting ensues along the Illhaeusern-Jebsheim road, as the 1st Moroccans battle tenaciously to win it. Meanwhile, the French 5th Armored begins to prepare an attack against Brisach. The U.S. 3rd Division, operating in the French area, attacks, seizing Houssen and Rosenkranz with its 7th Regiment, while its 254th surges straight ahead, pushing forward contingents into Jebsheim; in conjunction, the aggressiveness of the 15th Regiment bowls over the resistance in Riedwihr. Near Holtzwihr, the Germans assault with a large contingent of Infantry, supported by six Tanks, forcing Company B, 7th Regiment to retreat upon orders by its Commanding Officer, 2nd Lt. Audie Murphy (Murphy becomes a Hollywood Star subsequent to the war and plays himself in the movie about his endeavor in France). Lt. Murphy remains at the Command Post and directs Artillery fire by telephone. During the blazing exchange, an American Tank Destroyer to his rear is struck by a direct hit, but the crew escapes to the woods. The U.S. fire is taking a toll on the enemy, still they keep closing, forcing Murphy to board the burning Tank Destroyer and man its guns, exchanging fire with the enemy on three sides as the Vehicle is nearly engulfed in flames and on the verge of exploding at any second. Murphy does not flinch as he kills many of the attackers, including one entire Squad which had crept discretely to within ten yards of his conspicuous position. Subsequent to about an hour of futile attempts to annihilate Murphy, the enemy Infantry begins to falter, which in turn prompts the Tanks to retire. The intrepid Murphy, a Texan, kills or wounds about fifty of the enemy and despite a leg wound, dismounts after expending his ammunition and rallies his men to a successful counterattack. Murphy becomes the recipient of the Medal of Honor. **(Atlantic-Eastern Europe)** In East Prussia, Soviet Forces continue to badger the beleaguered Germans who are greatly under-equipped and still improperly clothed. Repeated requests by German Generals to withdraw, had been ignored by Hitler, who had appointed the unqualified S.S. leader, Himmler (24th), to command a new Army Group (Vistula) to halt the Russian hordes, despite what the move meant to German morale at the front. Meanwhile, the Second White Russian Front takes Marienberg and advances to the Danzig near Elbing. The Third White Russian Front converges on Koenigsberg. In Poland, the Germans mount some resistance, but time is running out; Posen and Thorn are nearly totally surrounded by the Red Army. In Silesia, Hindenburg is taken by the First Ukrainian Front. **(Atlantic-Italy) 15th Army Group** The **U.S. Seventh Army** concentrates on keeping the enemy guessing as the dreary winter continues; it takes precautions to keep the Germans from attempting to mount any type of offensive.

U.S. Armor driving deeper into Germany.

January 27th 1945 — (Pacific-Hawaii) The Joint Expeditionary Force (minus) embarks Hawaii for the Marianas, completing the transfer by February 5th. **(Pacific-Java Sea)** The Submarine U.S.S. *Bergall* (SS-320) sinks the Japanese Minesweeper No. 102. **(Pacific-Philippines) Leyte** Prepara-

tions for the invasion of Nasugbu, Luzon, are commenced as the 11th Airborne (less RCT 511), U.S. 8th Army, stages a scaled down rehearsal and then Task Group 78.2, commanded by Admiral Fechteler, embarks for the debarkation point. **Luzon** Additional Yanks arrive at Lingayen Gulf to bolster the U.S. Sixth Army's campaign; the 1st Cavalry Division and the 32nd Infantry Division debark as well as a Regimental Combat Team of the 112th Cavalry. In the **XIV Corps** sector, the Japanese controlled Manila Railroad gets derailed, as the 40th Division secures it from Bamban south to Mantitang; Route 3, which parallels it, also comes under the control of the Stars and Stripes. The Japs are continuing to withdraw, getting pounced as they move. The 37th Division roars over Culayo and Dau and then surges to Angeles, finding it abandoned. In the **I Corps** sector, vicious fighting ensues at San Manuel as the 161st Regiment attempts to destroy the resistance; in conjunction, the 27th Regiment, 25th Division advances against nimble resistance reaching Asingan, while the 43rd Division's 172nd Regiment and Regimental Combat Team 158 converge at Cataguintingan and clear the Damortis-Rosario Road there. **(Pacific-Burma)** In the N.C.A.C. area, the Japanese blockade of China ceases, as a powerful Artillery barrage supplements the attacking Chinese 38th Division and its supporting Tanks, which drive forward and hook up with the Y-Force on the Burma Road securing the land route to China, a luxury lost during the early days of the war when the Japs ran the British and U.S. General Stilwell out of Burma. In other activity, the Chinese 30th Division pushes contingents to a point about three miles north of the U.S. 5322nd Brigade; however, this advance permits the Japanese a path to flee encirclement. In the British Fourteenth Army's 4th Corps sector, Pauk falls to the 7th Indian Division. **(Pacific-China)** General Wedemeyer informs General Marshall that his command has been instructed that no negotiations are to transpire between the Americans and the Communist Chinese without express approval by Chiang Kaishek; Wedemeyer informs Officers of the China Theater on the 30th that they are forbidden to conduct negotiations with the Communists. **(Atlantic-Western Europe) 21st Army Group** In the **U.S. Ninth Army** area, **XIX Corps** sector, the boundary change between the First and Ninth Armies stretches the 78th Division zone further south to Gemund. **12th Army Group** In the **U.S. First Army** area, **XVIII Corps (Airborne)** sector, the 7th Armored's C.C.B. continues the tedious task of eradicating stiff resistance in Bois de St. Vith. In the **U.S. Third Army** area, the 87th Division drives hard, overrunning several towns south of St. Vith. The 90th Division, sweeping on the right flank of the Our River, sends its 358th Regiment north; it attacks across the border of Luxembourg, seizing Lascheid, Belgium. In the **III Corps** area, contingents of the 26th Division continue securing Munshausen, but the balance of the Division is withdrawn from the line. In the **XII Corps** sector, Weiler and Wahlhausen are seized by RCT 11, 5th Division; in conjunction, the 5th Reconnaissance Troop overruns Consthum and Holzthum. Also, a Task Force, composed basically of the 317th Regiment, 80th Division, secures the heights west of Honsingen; it also seizes Bockholz, Dorscheid, Marburg, and Neidhausen, culminating the Division's offensive. In the **XX Corps** sector, the 94th Division drives punishingly to the fringes of Sinz; heavy casualties force it to withdraw. **6th Army Group** In the **U.S. Seventh Army** area, **VI Corps** sector, the Germans mount light and sporadic resistance. The 101st Airborne takes responsibility for the Moder River area between Schweighausen and the boundary of the 103rd Division. Meanwhile, T.F. Linden (minus 242nd Regiment) approaches the Chateau Salins region and reverts to reserve. In the **French First Army** area, 2nd Corps sector, Elsenheim Road and Elsenheim Forest are secured by the French forces who then advance toward Jebsheim. Holtzwihr and Wickerswihr are seized by the U.S. 30th Division; its 254th Regiment is battling in Jebsheim and secures most of it. **(Atlantic-Eastern Europe)** The Masurian Lake area of East Prussia falls to White Russian forces; the Russians also continue to tighten the rope on the besieged Germans at Kosenigberg. In Poland, the Soviets complete the investment of Posen and Thorn, and in Upper Silesia, the First Ukrainian Front advances deeper into the industrial sector. In Central Czechoslovakia, Dobsina falls to the Fourth Rumanian Army.

January 28th 1945 — (United States) The Carrier *Antietam* (CV-36), is commissioned in Philadelphia, Pa. **(Pacific-Philippines) Luzon** In the **U.S. Sixth Army** area, **XIV Corps** sector, two more Clark Field Runways are seized, as the 129th Regiment, 37th Division grinds forward, tumbling the Japanese Outpost line of resistance, driving to the southeast corner of Fort Stotsenburg in an effort to retake the Fort, which had been abandoned by the Americans on Christmas Eve, 1941. The Yanks press further; contingents of the 148th Regiment, bolstered by the 37th Reconnaissance Troop, advance to San Fernando. The 160th Regiment, 40th Division, driving north of the Bamban River, seizes Hill 600 and bolts an additional 1,200 yards, where it encounters the Japanese Main Line of Resistance, which is delivering incessant fire. In the **I Corps** sector, remnant enemy presence at San Manuel is eradicated by the 161st Regiment, 25th Division, which remains in the town while the balance of the Division maintains its attack. The PT 338 becomes grounded off Luzon and is sunk by U.S. forces. **Mindoro** The 19th Regiment, 24th Division deploys around San Jose now that its task on Mindoro has culminated successfully. **(Pacific-Burma)** In the N.C.A.C. area, the original Convoy, which had departed Ledo, reinitiates its advance, rolling across the China border on course for Kunming. Chiang Kai-shek, subsequent to celebrations at Muse, renames the Ledo Road, calling it "Stilwell Road." Unfortunately, General Stilwell is not there for the ribbon cutting ceremony; the Generalissimo had him recalled (October 18th 1944) to Washington for political reasons. **(Pacific-Yellow Sea)** The Submarine *Spadefish* (SS-411) sinks the Japanese Frigate *Kume*. **(Atlantic-Western Europe) 12th Army Group** The U.S. First Army initiates another of the Yanks' countless drives, steaming toward Euskirchen and the famed West Wall. Supplemented by U.S. Artillery, Armor, and Air power, the troops jump off prior to dawn. The XVIII Corps' 1st Division and 82nd Airborne bolt from the north and south respectively. The 16th Regiment, 1st Division seizes Valender, while the 18th overruns Hepsheid and Heppenbach and the 26th Regiment plows through Richelbusch. The 82nd Airborne, its 325th Glider Infantry to the north and its 504th Paratroop Infantry to the south, streaks through the 75th Armored positions and sweeps the woods clean as far as Wereth, while capturing Herresbach. Meanwhile, the 7th Armored eliminates the resistance at obstinate enemy positions in the high ground at Bois de St. Vith, thus concluding its St. Vith operation. In the **U.S Third Army** area, the majority of the VIII Corps has advanced to the Our River. The St. Vith sector is taken over by the 87th Division. The 4th Division occupies the Burg Reuland-Maspelt area, deploying between the 87th and 90th Divisions to the north and south respectively. The 358th Regiment, 90th Division secures Weweler and

Stoubach, and the 357th eliminates the enemy in its sector, except for the towns along the river. In the **III Corps** sector, German resistance at Kalborn is resolute and halts the advance of contingents of the 6th Armored Division. Meanwhile, in the **XII Corps** sector, the 5th Division seizes Putscheid and continues to eradicate the enemy on the western bank of the Our River. The 94th Division (XX Corps) mounts a scaled-down attack to strengthen its positions. **6th Army Group** In the **French 1st Army** area, the **U.S. XX Corps** takes control of area between the French 1st and 2nd Corps and is directed to assist the French with the operation to reduce the Colmar Pocket by driving toward Brisach to enjoin the French 1st Corps. The French 2nd Corps had been assigned the task. The U.S. 3rd Division continues its clearing operation north of the Canal de Colmar in its sector. Meanwhile, the 254th Regiment, 63rd Division (attached to 3rd Division) is struggling to dislodge the Germans in the southern part of Jebsheim. **(Atlantic-Italy)** In the **U.S. Fifth Army** area, the 10th Mountain Division is attached to Task Force 45 for the purpose of giving it combat experience. **(Atlantic-Eastern Europe)** The First Baltic Front takes Memel, giving the Soviets Lithuania in its entirety. In East Prussia, the Soviets take Bischofsburg and Sensburg; however, the Germans resist tenaciously at Elbing and attack strongly outside of Allenstein. In addition, the Polish border cities of Czarnkow, Leszno, and Sepolno fall to the Red Army. Guhrau in Silesia also falls. The First Ukrainian Front, operating in Silesia and along the southern Polish border, seizes Beuthen in the former and Katowice in Poland. In the Carpathians, the Fourth Ukrainian Front advances to Poprad, Czechoslovakia.

A contingent of the 6th Ranger Battalion moving to liberate an Allied P.O.W. camp behind enemy lines in the Philippines.

January 28th-30th 1945 — (Pacific-Philippines) With Alamo Scouts out in advance, Lt. Colonel Henry Mucci, Bn. Commander and Company C, 6th Rangers (Captain Robert W. Prince) jump off at 05:00 to extricate Allied P.O.W.s at Cabanatuan. The contingent is bolstered by Company F, 6th Rangers (Lt. John P. Murphy). By 14:00, they encounter about eighty Guerrillas that fatten their striking power. The troops press forward, reaching Balangkare at 06:00 on the 29th and meet an additional 250 Guerrillas, 90 of whom are armed. Soon after, Scouts report heavy concentration of Japanese, forcing a 24-hour delay on the rescue attempt. At 17:00, the raiders cross the Pampanga River then split their forces; the Filipinos, under Platero advance south toward Cabanatuan, while other Guerrillas, under Pajota move north to Cebu bridge. In the meantime, the Rangers belly through the rice paddies, virtually crawling two miles, reaching a point about two miles from the P.O.W. camp without hesitation, two Platoons of Rangers encroach upon the north front gate; in conjunction, Murphy's Platoon is poised at the south end of the camp, waiting for the fireworks to begin. At 19:45, Lt. Murphy's men clear the barrels of their weapons creating a wild stir in the Jap camp. The communication wires at both ends of the camp are severed in synchronization with the gunfire, creating more confusion for the stunned enemy. Murphy's force crashes through the barbed wire mesmerizing the Japs who become pinned down. In concert, O'Connell's Platoon charges through the front gate, killing the guards as the weapons blaze incessantly, cutting down all Japanese in sight and probably a few unseen. Bullets and grenades are flying all over the area as the Rangers stampede through the camp, annihilating its defenders; most of the 200 Japs are killed or wounded. The P.O.W.s, nearly oblivious to the savage but lopsided fight are soon greeted by Lt. Melville H. Schmidt's Platoon who splash into the melee with a bigger bang, thoroughly disorienting the enemy. The charging Rangers under Melville waste no time in getting the P.O.W.s to safety. At the south end of the camp, Lt. Raymond Bliss a straggler P.O.W. discovers the huts empty, but fortunately runs into a Ranger and he too is taken to safety. The full moon, which is greatly aiding the Rangers, seemingly brings taboo to the Japanese. By 19:15, Captain Prince races through the camp twice to ensure no one is left behind, then he high-tails it, after firing a flare signaling the Rangers to withdraw from the killing ground. As the Rangers successfully devastate the P.O.W. camp, the Guerrillas achieve surprise at the Cebu bridge, blowing it, while simultaneously wiping out the Japanese on the opposite bank. At 20:15, Captain Prince fires another flare, signaling the Guerrillas to retire; a contingent under Captain Pajota remain near the bridge to cover the Ranger withdrawal. During the startling raid which last about one and a half hours, the Rangers lose two men, the Bn. Surgeon, Captain James Fisher (mortally wounded) and Corporal Roy Sweezy, killed during the withdrawal. The Philippine Guerrillas sustain no casualties. The Rangers reach Sibul by 08:00 on the 31st. Within four hours, emergency Rescue Ambulances arrive to evacuate the wounded taking them to the 92nd Evacuation Hospital.

January 29th 1945 — (Pacific-Philippines) Luzon A Naval Attack Group, under Rear Admiral A.D. Struble, lands Army contingents near San Antonio, northwest of Subic Bay. **(Mindoro-Marinduque)** The Western Visayan Task Force is disbanded. The islands are now under the protection of the X Corps. Major General Frederick Irving, Commanding General, 24th Division arrives on southwestern Mindoro and assumes control of all Army forces attached to Corps. In other activity, the Fifth Air Force transfers its Headquarters to Mindoro. Off the Philippines, the Transport *Cavalier* (APA-37) and the Repair Ship *Amycus* (ARL-2) are damaged by a submarine torpedo and Horizontal Bomber respectively. **(Pacific-Solomons)** The Cargo Vessel *Serpens* (AK-97) suffers an explosion and sinks off Guadalcanal. **(Pacific-Burma)** In the N.C.A.C. area, the Japanese are retreating from the Burma Road; however, they mount a severe attack against the Chinese 114th Regiment, 38th Division and inflict heavy casualties. In one incident, a solitary Chinese Company, attempting to hold against the pressure about 80 miles outside of Lashio, is nearly wiped out. The tragedy prompts the Chinese to terminate activity to block the road. Meanwhile, the U.S. 5332nd Brigade endeavors to bolster its positions on the western side of the Burma Road, despite heavy enemy

shelling. **(Pacific-China)** General Ho, Commander of the ALPHA Forces, introduces a similar plan to that of General Wedemeyer's, which calls for a 36-Division attack force, to be divided into six different commands to be deployed around Kunming; the force will expand into a 39-Division command, subsequent to the return of the New First Army during June. In other activity, the U.S. Fourteenth Air Force Base at Suichwan is occupied by Japanese. **(Atlantic-Western Europe) 12th Army Group** In the **U.S. First Army** area, **XVIII Corps (Airborne)** sector, Buellingen is seized by the Big Red One (1st Division), while the 82nd Airborne's 325th Glider Infantry swoops into Wereth, seizing it. Simultaneously, the 82nd's 508th Paratroop Regiment moves through the 325th's lines and takes the high ground near Eimerscheid and also seizes Holzheim and Medendorf. The Americans have marched 15 miles through a blizzard prior to the attack. At Holzheim, Belgium, Sergeant Leonard Funk, Company C, 508th Regiment assumes command of the Company after the Commanding Officer becomes a casualty. He initiates an attack on the right flank to terminate menacing Artillery fire. Sgt. Funk advances with a Platoon of quickly assembled Headquarters personnel, secures fifteen houses, and captures thirty prisoners without sustaining any casualties. Company C seizes Holzheim and captures eighty prisoners; however, few extra men are available and the prisoners must be guarded by only four Soldiers. The cunning Germans take advantage of the understrengthed detachment and attack, rescuing the prisoners, while preparing to retake the town. An unsuspecting Sergeant Funk turns a corner and finds a German pistol sticking in his gut, pointed by a German Officer who demands surrender. Sergeant Funk, not belonging to the Paratroop Infantry because of timidity, begins to comply sheepishly by cautiously removing his submachine gun from his shoulder; with sudden and uncompromising speed he swivels the deadly muzzle, irrigates the German Officer, and begins yelling to the Yanks to overpower the enemy and take their weapons as he continues to pour fire into their ranks. When the tussle ceases, 21 Germans lie dead, many others are wounded, and the balance captured, by the direct actions of the 82nd Airborne Sergeant. He receives the Medal of Honor. In the **U.S. Third Army** area, an assault against the West Wall commences; its purpose is to fortify the right flank of Army, in addition to destroying the resistance. In the **VIII Corps** sector, the 4th, 87th and 90th Divisions burst from the high ground west of the Our River, charging forward abreast of each other. Contingents of the 345th Regiment, 87th Division take Schlierbach and Setz, as the 347th converges upon Breitfeld and Neidingen. At Lommersweiler, the Germans mount fierce resistance, stalling the 8th Regiment, 4th Division; however, its 12th Regiment avoids Hemmeres and plows across the Our River, driving into Elcherath. The 90th Division, delegated to defend the right flank of the Corps on the eastern side of the Our River, bolts across the river and the German border; its 357th Regiment overruns Welchenhausen, while the 358th, which fords the river at Stupbach, enters and seizes it. In the **III Corps** sector, the Corps is in control of its objective, the N-S ridge and highway which controls the Clerf River and the Our Valley. Probing Patrols in strength sweep the left flank; Combat Team Miltonberger seizes Kalborn. In the **XX Corps** sector, the 26th Division relieves the 95th Division at the Saarlautern bridgehead and assumes responsibility for it. Third Army reports its casualties as of January 29th: killed, 14879; wounded, 71,009; missing, 14,054; non-battle casualties, 73,011; total, 172,953. German losses: killed, 96,500; wounded, 269,000; P.O.W.s, 163,000; total, 528,500.

Third Army material: Light Tanks, 270; Medium Tanks, 771; Guns, 144. German equipment losses: Medium Tanks, 1,268; Panther and Tiger Tanks, 711; Guns, 2,526. Patton notes about the Bulge: "DURING THIS OPERATION, THE THIRD ARMY MOVED FURTHER AND FASTER AND ENGAGED MORE DIVISIONS IN LESS TIME THAN ANY OTHER ARMY IN THE HISTORY OF THE UNITED STATES-POSSIBLY IN THE HISTORY OF THE WORLD. THE RESULTS WERE MADE POSSIBLE ONLY BY THE SUPERLATIVE QUALITY OF AMERICAN OFFICERS, AMERICAN MEN, AND AMERICAN EQUIPMENT. NO COUNTRY CAN STAND AGAINST SUCH AN ARMY." **Sixth Army Group** In the **French 1st Army** area, **U.S. XXI Corps** sector, the 3rd Division surges across the Canal de Colmar, its 7th Regiment driving to Bischwihr, while the 15th pushes to the outskirts of Muntzenheim. Meanwhile, the 254th Regiment reduces the enemy resistance to the canal south of Jebsheim, then sprints toward the Rhone-Rhine Canal; still stubborn German contingents refuse to capitulate at Jebsheim. **(Atlantic-Malta)** Admiral King arrives at Malta to attend the conference with the President and the Allies. **(Atlantic-Eastern Europe)** In East Prussia, the defiant Germans, understrengthed and badly badgered by superior forces, continue to fight resolutely at Elbing and Koenigsberg. The First White Russian Front moves into Pomerania and seizes the German villages of Schoenlanke and Woldenberg. Meanwhile, in the Carpathian sector, Nowy Targ, along the southern border of Poland, falls to the Fourth Ukrainian Front.

General Williard Holbrook, C.C.B., 11th Armored Division, escorting a captured Hungarian General.

January 30th 1945 — (Pacific-Philippines) Leyte-Samar In the **U.S. Eighth Army** area, the Americal Division starts to relieve the X Corps on Leyte; in conjunction, the 1st Battalion, 182nd Regiment is dispatched to Catbalogan, Samar, to relieve the 3rd Battalion, 381st Regiment, 96th Division. **Luzon** In the **U.S. Sixth Army** area, General Krueger issues specific orders for the continuation of the drive to Manila. The **XIV Corps** is to push south with its 37th and 1st Cavalry Divisions to line Malolos-Plaridel-Cabanatuan, while the I Corps, reinforced by the 32nd Division, is to confine itself to advancing down Route 7 as it crosses the Bataan Peninsula to hook up with the XIV Corps at Dinalupihan-Hermosa region. In the **XIV Corps** sector, Ft. Stotsenburg is seized by the 129th Regiment, 37th Division, which also captures Sapangbato and the high ground near Dolores. In conjunction, contingents of the 37th Division advance Patrols to within a mile from Calumpit. At the Japanese Main Line of Resistance north of the Bamban River, the 160th Regiment, 40th Division encounters iron resistance; it gnaws forward, while the Japs inflict heavy casualties for the yards gained. Meanwhile, the 108th Regiment, 40th Division wedges forward taking Hill 5 and Thrall Hill, exterminating the resistance in the section. In the **I Corps** sector, the 1st Infantry, 6th Division seizes Talavera with ease however, the 20th Regiment encounters incessant fire which pins it down about 1,000 yards outside of Munoz. In other activity, the XI Corps is transferred from Eighth Army to Sixth Army, and simultaneously, command passes from Admiral Struble to General Hall; the Corps has secured all of its initial objectives. Regimental Combat Team 34, 24th Division spearheads the attack, piercing and capturing Subic as it drives to the Kalaklan River and plows into the Japanese defenses at the Route 7 bridge. The Yanks scatter the enemy then ford the river and vanquish Olongapo. To complete the security of Subic Bay, the 2nd Battalion, 151st Regiment, 38th Division seizes Grande Island without opposition. **(Pacific-Burma)** In the ALFSEA area, 15th Corps sector, the enemy counterattacks against the 25th Indian Division's bridgehead at Kangaw have been thwarted. The 25th attacks and seizes Kangaw village. Meanwhile, the West African 82nd Division is advancing toward Kangaw, driving south from Myohaung. In the N.C.A.C. area, the majority of the Chinese 38th Division is at the junction of the Burma and Ledo Roads, poised to advance to Lashio. Plans are set for a combined assault by the U.S. 5332nd Provisional Brigade and the Chinese 30th Division, to be launched against the hills around Hpa-pen to seal the fate of the Japanese still on the Burma Road; however, the Chinese request that the assault be postponed until February 2nd, and later request that it be postponed until the 3rd. The objective will be taken by the Yanks on the 2nd, as the Chinese Division gives only token performance. **(Atlantic-Malta-Yalta)** Preliminary talks take place in Malta between the British and the Americans prior to the main session at Yalta with Stalin. This segment of ARGONAUT (Anglo-American) is coded CRICKET. Admiral King had arrived at Malta on the 29th. During the sometimes heated meetings, the British accuse Eisenhower of "NOT BEING BOLD AND AGGRESSIVE DURING THE LATTER MONTHS OF 1944." The British emphasize that Ike's plan is too conservative and too cautious, then push to execute Montgomery's plan which calls for a single thrust into Berlin. Admiral King and General Marshall become incensed upon hearing the no-confidence vote on Ike. President Roosevelt had departed the U.S. at Newport News, Va., on the U.S.S. *Quincy*, a Cruiser, on January 23rd, with three Destroyers in escort, en route to Bermuda to hook up with the U.S.S. *Springfield*, a Light Cruiser. Air cover is afforded the

Convoy as it approaches the Azores. The entire trip is under radio blackout; when necessary, a Destroyer drops out of formation and relays appropriate messages, then rejoins the Convoy; the President arrives on February 2nd. Also, subsequent to the conference, the Russians approach Admiral King and attempt to con him by greeting him in his room with gifts, including caviar, vodka and fresh fruit. The Russians attempt to give King a long list of U.S. Naval equipment that they expect to be given to them. The Russians continue to prod King to sign the list; he declines and finally boards a train to Saki. **(Atlantic-Western Europe) 21st Army Group** In the **U.S. Ninth Army** area, **XIX Corps** sector, the 78th Division advances south toward the Roer River; its 310th Regiment seizes Konzen while its 311th takes Huppenbroisch and secures most of Kesternich. At Kesternich, Staff Sergeant Jonah E. Kelley, leading Company E against the enemy during the early hours, drives relentlessly from house-to-house being wounded twice as he directs the advance. Compelled to fire his Rifle with one hand and pull the grenade pins with his teeth, he disregards all danger and keeps driving, eliminating the enemy as he moves, killing five of the enemy, including a Sniper. Upon darkness he instructs his men to pause, but he refuses to receive medical aid. On the following morning, he resumes the attack until intense fire stalls its advance. Kelley advances and finds the needle in the haystack, virtually killing the gunner who had burrowed in the hay. He follows this by singlehandedly attacking a machine gun position, advancing to within 25 yards of it when a flurry of bullets bring him to the ground. Refusing to relent, he forges ahead with mortal wounds and empties his weapon, eliminating the enemy gun just before he dies. Staff Sergeant Kelley's extraordinary heroism is in the highest tradition of the U.S. Army; he becomes the recipient of the Medal of Honor posthumously. Eicherscheid is vanquished by C.C.A., 5th Armored (attached to 78th Division). **12th Army Group** In the **U.S. First Army** area, the **V Corps** joins the operation to crush the West Wall defenses; its 9th Division seizes Rohren as it pushes to the fringes of the Monschau Forest outside of Alzen. Krinkelt and Wirtzfeld are seized by the 38th Regiment, 2nd Division, which then has contingents forge ahead to Rocherath. Meanwhile, the 9th Regiment overcomes resistance and secures a hill stronghold between Muerringen and Wirtzfield. In the **XVIII Corps (Airborne)** sector, the 1st Division overruns several enemy-held towns west of the German frontier, including Honsfield, Hunningen, seized by the 18th Regiment, and Muerringen, captured by the 26th Regiment. The 82nd Airborne maintains its quick pace as its 508th Paratroop Regiment and the 325th Glider Infantry sweep to the Honsfield-Losheim Railroad line, securing Eimerscheid and Lanzerath. In the **U.S. Third Army** area, **VIII Corps** sector, RCT 346, 87th Division drives toward Andler and Schonberg, while the 345th overruns Rodgen and moves against Heuem. Hemmeres and Lommersweiler are secured by the 4th Division; however, its progress is limited. Auel is overtaken by the 359th Regiment, 90th Division, which also enters Steffeshausen; Stein-Kopf is captured by the 358th, and in the 357th sector, Tanks move across a ford constructed by Engineers at Welchenhausen. In the **III Corps** sector, contingents advance against nominal resistance to reduce the remaining resistance along the west bank of the Our River, except in the area further south where the 17th Airborne Division's 193rd Glider Battalion and the 28th Cavalry Squadron (attached TF Fickett) are attacking to establish an Outpost Line. **6th Army Group** In the **French 1st Army** area, **U.S. XXI Corps** sector, the 3rd Division's 7th Regiment, bolstered by French Armor,

seizes Bischwihr and Wihr-en-Plaine. In conjunction, the 15th Regiment overpowers Fortschwihr, Muntzenheim, and Urschenheim. Meanwhile, the lingering resistance at Jebsheim is terminated by the 254th Regiment, which is unable to complete its drive to the terminus of the Colmar and Rhone-Rhine Canals. In the 2nd Corps sector, the French 1st Moroccan Division secures the woods east of Illhaeusern. **(Atlantic-Eastern Europe)** In East Prussia, the Soviets take Marienwerder and close the knot tighter at Koenigsberg. Russian troops are now streaming across the Polish border, closing on Berlin; Stolzenburg, about seventy miles outside of Berlin, is seized.

Hitler taking a first hand look at the devastation delivered by Allied Bombers.

January 31st 1945 — (Pacific-Formosa) Army Planes sink the Japanese Destroyer *Ume*. **(Pacific-Philippines)** A Japanese Suicide Boat sinks the Submarine Chaser PC-1129. **Luzon** The **U.S. Sixth Army** commences the final thrust to capture Manila. In the **XIV Corps** sector, the 129th Regiment, 37th Division moves against a hill just outside of Ft. Stotsenburg, dubbed Top of The World; it gains positions about half way from the crest. Toward the latter part of the day, the 358th Regiment, 90th Division secures river crossings over the Pampanga at Calumpit. In conjunction with the offensive, the Provincial Reconnaissance Squadron acts as vanguard for the 1st Cavalry Division; it fords the Pampanga and takes Santa Rosa without incident, while the 5th and 8th Cavalry Regiments follow closely behind. Meanwhile, the 40th Division sweeps the mountains west of Ft. Stotsenburg and Clark Field. The **I Corps** is heavily involved at Munoz, but its efforts fail to gain the objective. The Japanese are also deeply entrenched at Umingan and are prepared to give formidable opposition to the approaching 25th Division. The 28th Division is held in reserve; however, the Japanese launch a strong counterattack against a small contingent of the 126th Regiment. P.F.C. William R. Shockley instructs the detachment to pull back while he affords cover stating that he will "remain to the end." One attack is repulsed by the lone defender; however, the Japanese close on the left flank, killing him. Shockley's actions save the remainder of the Squad, and he becomes a recipient of the Medal of Honor posthumously. The XI Corps is moving doggedly toward Manila; its 38th Division has elements driving across the base of the Bataan Peninsula, advancing to enemy held Zig Zag Pass, about three miles northeast of Olongapo. In the **U.S. Eighth Army** area, Rear Admiral W. M. Fechteler's Attack Group, supported by Carrier-based Aircraft (Rear Admiral W. D. Sample), lands troops at the south end of Manila Bay. A Naval Bombardment precedes the landing of the 188th Glider Infantry, 11th Airborne Division at Nasugbu; it quickly seizes Lian, Nasugbu, and Wawa, then moves effortlessly toward Tagaytay Ridge without opposition. The 187th Glider Infantry is able to come ashore sooner than expected, due to the rapid progress of the invasion. In addition, General Eichelberger requests that the Fifth Air Force drop the 511th Paratroop Infantry on February 2nd, a day ahead of schedule. **Camotes** The 7th Division Task Force prepares to return to Leyte, now that enemy resistance on Poro Island is completely eliminated. **Mindoro** Contingents of the 21st Regiment, 24th Division departs Pinamalayan-Calapan area of northeastern Mindoro; about 135 Japanese troops have been killed here. The units move to San Jose. Company D, 21st Regiment debarks for Mindoro, but a Platoon remains on Marinduque. **(Pacific-Burma)** In the N.C.A.C. area, the British 36th Division advances toward Mongmit; elements reach the Shweli River and dispatch Patrols across it. **(Atlantic-Western Europe) 21st Army Group** In the **U.S. Ninth Army** area, **XIX Corps** sector, the U.S. 78th Division seizes its objectives and encounters the 9th Division, U.S. First Army at Widdau. **12th Army** In the **U.S. First Army** area, **V Corps** sector, the 9th Division jumps from Widdau and pushes through the Monschau Forest, advancing to the Monschau-Schleiden Road. Resistance at Rocherath is totally reduced; it falls to the 2nd Division. In the **XVIII Corps** sector, elements of Corps cross the German border as it drives through the Buchholz Forest; the 1st Division approaches Neuhof. The 82nd Airborne, sweeping further south in the forest, advances to the Neuhof-Losheim-Manderfeld line. In the **U.S. Third Army** area, **VIII Corps** sector, 87th Division zone, RCT 346 takes Andler and Schonberg, while Amelscheid is overrun by RCT 345, which also seizes Alzerath and Heuem. Meanwhile, RCT 347 occupies Laudesfeld. In addition, Elcherath and Weppeler are taken by the 4th Division. The U.S. 90th Division continues to forge ahead, driving to secure the road running between Pronsfeld and Winterspelt at Gros Langenfeld; the 359th Regiment rips through Auel and Bei Auel and encounters German resistance at Winterspelt and Wallmerath, but evades the opposition to ensure reaching the road. Meanwhile, the 358th Regiment seizes Heckhalenfeld. **6th Army Group** In the **U.S. Seventh Army** area, **VI Corps** sector, the 36th Division initiates an attack against Oberhoffen-Drusenheim to secure the area west of the Rhine to the south. In the **French 1st Army's U.S. XXI Corps** sector, French Armor units continue to support Yank Infantry of the 3rd Division; its 7th Regiment drives to the vicinity of Colmar and seizes Horbourg after a bitter confrontation. Meanwhile, the 15th Regiment smacks into heavy resistance at Durrentzen and is prevented from taking the objective. In other activity, a scheduled assault by the 75th Division is postponed until the following day. **(Atlantic-Eastern Europe)** In East Prussia, the Red Army takes Friedland and Heilsberg. Other Soviet forces advance to Jestrow in Pomerania and to Brandenburg, seizing Landsberg, Meseritz, Schwiebus, and Zullichau. At Budapest, the Germans maintain formidable resistance in the western part of the city against insurmountable odds.

February 1st 1945 — (Pacific-Philippines) The PT-77 and the PT-79 are accidentally sunk by U.S. Naval gunfire. Army Aircraft sink the Japanese Transport No. 115. The Destroyers *Jenkins* (DD-447), *Obannon* (DD-450), and *Bell* (DD-587) and the Destroyer Escort *Ulvert M. Moore* (DE-442) sink the Japanese Submarine RO-115. **Luzon** In the **U.S. Sixth Army** area, **XIV Corps** sector, the Provincial Reconnaissance Squadron, 1st Cavalry Division continues its mission as vanguard, driv-

ing to Manila; contingents of the 5th and 8th Cavalry Regiments reduce most of the opposition in Cabanatuan, with Motorized units of the latter driving to Santa Rosa. In conjunction, the 148th Regiment, 37th Division sprints toward Plaridel; however, the Japanese intercept forward contingents at the town's Airfield, and heavy fighting ensues. Close by, Hagonoy falls to the 145th Regiment. Meanwhile, the P.O.W.s at Bilibid prison camp pick up the pleasant sounds of Tanks and machine gun fire. A succinct firefight at the University frees about 700 U.S. and other Allied civilians. On the following morning, the Japanese make an announcement as the 1st Cavalry closes its hammer; "THE JAPANESE ARMY IS NOW GOING TO RELEASE ALL THE PRISONERS-OF-WAR AND INTERNEES HERE ON ITS OWN ACCORD." The P.O.W.s remain apprehensive. In the **I Corps** sector, the 1st and 3rd Battalions, 20th Infantry continue to pound Munoz, but German resistance prevents the 6th Division's unit from capturing it. Additional heavy skirmishing ensues near Umingan, where the 27th Regiment, 25th Division, supplemented by fire power of the 35th Regiment, wedge forward contingents into the barrio. Meanwhile, the 32nd Division maintains its knuckle hold at the Cagayan Valley, preventing a southern escape route by the Japanese. Further north, the 43rd Division firms up the Corps' flank with the assistance of RCT 158. In the **XI Corps** sector, the 38th Division's 152nd Regiment advances slowly against overzealous fire originating from Zig Zag Pass; the Regiment gains about 1,000 expensive yards. In the **U.S. 8th Army** area, the deeply entrenched Japanese deployed between Mt. Batulao and Mt. Cariliao near Tagaytay Ridge fight solidly, impeding the progress of the 188th Regiment, 11th Airborne, compelling the drop of the 511th Paratroop Battalion to be held off until the 3rd. The Fifth Air Force launches Planes from Mindoro to quicken the eradication of the enemy. **Morotai** Eighty-two enemy Air raids have struck Moratai from the 12th of September until today. **(Pacific-Burma)** The British 36th Division encounters enemy fire as it begins to ford the Shweli River near Myitson. **(Atlantic-Western Europe) 21st Army Group** The **U.S. Ninth Army**, still attached to Montgomery's command, makes final preparations for Operation GRENADE, a full scale assault across the Roer. In its **XIII Corps** sector, the U.S. 78th Division's mop up operations are ongoing in the Imgenbroich-Kesternich area. **12th Army Group** In the **U.S. First Army** area, **V Corps** sector, the 2nd, 9th, and 99th Divisions maintain their drive against the Roer and Urft River dams. The 9th Division drives east through the Monschau Forest, seizing the Hofen-Harperscheid road junction, about the half-way mark of the woods. The 99th is placed in reserve, subsequent to taking its objectives, while the 2nd Division drives across the German border where it meets the 9th Division. In the **XVIII (Airborne) Corps** sector, the 26th Division is rumbling through the Buchholz Forest, reducing sporadic resistance. Meanwhile, the 82nd Airborne tightens its positions while receiving the 517th Paratroop Infantry; Patrols are dispatched to reconnoiter the West Wall. In the **U.S. Third Army** area, **VIII Corps** sector, the German positions at Schnee Eifel along the West Wall come under severe attack by the Corps; the 87th Division overruns Manderfeld, Belgium and Auw in Germany. The 4th Division driving up the center closes on Bleialf about four miles into Germany, its 8th Regiment seizing Urb and Muetzenich, while the 12th Regiment captures Ihlren, Schweiler, and Winterscheid. The 90th Division, assigned to intercept an enemy advance against the south flank, has its 359th Regiment seize Gros Langenfeld; its 358th Regiment seizes Heckhuscheid; Company B advances across open ground during the attack and becomes pinned down, sustaining casualties. Corporal Edward A. Bennett inches forward, his nose to the ground, toward the origin of fire, completing the trek and surprising a rear guard with a silent stroke of his bayonet. He moves into the darkened house containing seven German Soldiers, three of whom die succinctly by rifle fire, one succumbs to a powerful blow by his rifle butt, and the remaining three are eliminated by his .45 pistol. Corporal Bennett's actions lead to the seizure of the town. In addition, the **III Corps** continues to fortify its positions in Luxembourg, bolstering its perimeter which is strewn along a ridge between the Our and Clerf Rivers. In the **XX Corps** sector, the 94th Division mounts a scaled down assault; however, the balance of the Division front is relatively quiet. Contingents of the 1st Battalion, 302nd Regiment, attacking southeast of Tettingen, reduce the resistance in about half of the Campholz woods. **6th Army Group** In the **U.S. Seventh Army** area, XV Corps sector, Task Force Harris (63rd Division) is disbanded. In the **VI Corps** sector, the 36th Division continues to encroach on the Rhine. Elements of RCT 142 ford the Moder and enter Oberhoffen against stiff resistance. During the intense combat, Sergeant Emile Deleau Jr. attacks one house and eliminates a machine gun by lobbing grenades. He is then fired upon from another house and he immediately moves against it, crashing through the door and capturing ten German Soldiers. At dawn on the following day, the fearless Sergeant encounters more rapid fire just after he eliminates two Snipers, prompting him to charge against the house and toss more grenades that terminate the gun and kill the gunners. Deleau moves to the front of the building to destroy the other machine gun, but the Germans kill him instantly with a burst from the gun before he can throw his grenade. Sergeant Deleau receives the Medal of Honor for his selfless courage and extraordinary actions. C.C.B., 14th Armored Division engages enemy contingents east of the town, but pulls back at nightfall. Meanwhile, the 117th Cavalry Squadron (attached to the 36th Division) reduces the resistance in the Stainwald woods outside of Gambsheim. The Corps front remains static for the remainder of February with activity confined to defensive postures and intermittent attacks across the Moder. In the **French 1st Army** area, U.S. XXI Corps sector, the 3rd Division's 15th and 30th Regiments keep pushing along the Rhine-Rhone Canal and reach positions just outside of Neuf-Brisach. In conjunction, the U.S. 75th Division has two Regiments closing on Andolsheim. The 28th Division attacks toward Colmar at 21:00. The Germans retain the towns of Cernay and Ensisheim, however, the 1st Corps' operation to secure the area between the two towns south of the Thur River continues. **(Eastern Europe)** In East Prussia, the Germans continue to receive a heavy pounding by the Soviets. The situation is similar in Poland as the Germans are invested at Posen and in addition lose a communication center with the capitulation of Torun. The beleaguered Garrison in Budapest (Hungary) offers stiff resistance, but the fall of the city is inevitable; in Germany, the Soviet Armies close on Berlin surrounding Schneidemuehl as the drive toward the Oder continues.

February 2nd 1945 — (Pacific-Philippines) Luzon In the **U.S. Sixth Army** area, **XIV Corps** sector contingents of the 1st Cavalry Division advance to the Sabang-Baliuag vicinity; elements of its 5th Cavalry encounter the 6th and 37th Divisions outside of Cabanatuan and Plaridel respectively, the latter being seized by the 148th Infantry. Meanwhile, the forward contingents of the Corps reach the general line. In addition, the 129th Regiment, 37th Division culminates its task at Ft.

Stotsenburg and assembles to head for Manila. In the **I Corps** sector, deployment is complete, ensuring the eastern flank of the XIV Corps against counterattacks from the east. The Japanese at Munoz maintain their grip on the town, offering steady resistance against the 20th Regiment, 6th Division, and at San Jose, the Japanese brace for an attack by other contingents of the Division. The 25th Division drives toward Lupao, seizing Umingan as it advances. Meanwhile, in the **XI Corps** sector, the Japanese still command Zig Zag Pass, making it impossible for the 152nd Infantry, 38th Division to advance. In the U.S. Eighth Army area, Tagaytag Ridge is jeopardized as the 11th Airborne closes against it. **Leyte** In the **XXIV Corps** sector, the Americal Division is to relieve the 77th Division which has terminated its combat duties on the island; upon relief it will prepare to participate in the invasion of Okinawa. In other activity, the 7th Division Task Force leaves the 2nd Battalion, 94th Regiment (Philippine Army) to garrison Pacijan and Poro, and embarks the Camotes for Leyte. **(Pacific-Burma)** In the N.C.A.C. area, the recently established British bridgehead at the Shweli River is abandoned due to Japanese pressure. In other activity, a vicious battle erupts between the enemy and the 124th Cavalry, U.S. 5332nd Brigade in the high ground around Hpa-pen, culminating with a victory for the Yanks. First Lt. Jack L. Knight leads an assault which overruns the enemy position; however, while deploying defensively, Knight discovers active pillboxes and foxholes, which jeopardize the 124th Cavalry's right front. Taking immediate action, he jumps in front of his attacking force; destroys two pillboxes, and kills the Japs defending several of the foxholes. He continues his singlehanded attack and approaches a third pillbox; an enemy grenade blinds him, Lt. Knight totally disregards his handicap, rallies his men, and continues to participate in the assault by his troops against the remaining pillboxes. He falls mortally wounded, while his inspired men exterminate most of the remaining Jap positions. **(Pacific-French Indo China)** Information that the Japanese have insisted that French forces in Indo China lay down their arms and leave the area is forwarded to Washington by General Wedemeyer. The French request help from the U.S.; Aircraft of the U.S. Fourteenth Air Force give some assistance; however, there is some confusion as to boundaries and it is thought that Indo China comes under the China Theater (Chiang Kai-shek). **(Pacific-Malay Peninsula)** The Submarine *Besugo* (SS-321) operating in waters between Singapore and the Isthmus of Kra, sinks the Japanese Coast Defense Vessel No. 144. **(Atlantic-Western Europe) 21 Army Group** In the **U.S. Ninth Army** area, XXI Corps sector the U.S. 78th Division reverts to V Corps, First Army (in place). **12th Army Group** In the **U.S. First Army V Corps** sector, the 2nd and 9th Divisions exit the Monschau Forest, the former driving toward Schleiden and the latter toward Dreiborn. The 9th Regiment, 2nd Division takes Harperscheid and Schoneseiffen. In the **XVIII (Airborne) Corps** sector, at 04:00, the 1st and 82nd Airborne Divisions charge the West Wall, ignoring machine guns, pillboxes, dragons' teeth, and other deadly obstacles; the 1st Airborne bursts from Buchholz Forest close to Ramscheid, swivels through the 82nd positions where it penetrates the West Wall, and vanquishes Neuhof and Udenbreth. In other activity, the 30th and 84th Divisions are detached from Corps. In the **U.S. Third Army** area, General Patton drives to Spa, Belgium to attend a meeting and is informed that Eisenhower has been ordered by the Joint Chiefs of Staff, to assign the U.S. Ninth Army to British 21st Army Group; Patton notes: "COULD THIS BE AN ATTEMPT ON THE PART OF GENERAL MARSHALL TO SE-

CURE THE SERVICES OF THE FOURTEEN BRITISH DIVISIONS WHICH HAD BEEN DOING VERY LITTLE FOR SOME TIME?" In the **VIII Corps** sector, the 347th Regiment, 87th Division secures Loscheim after a night attack; the 346th gains Krewinkel prior to dawn (3rd). In **XII Corps** sector, Hosdorf on the Our River is reduced by Task Force Oboe, composed of 4th Armored Division units. Meanwhile, contingents of the 302nd Regiment, 94th Division mount additional scaled down assaults to exterminate the remaining resistance in Campholz woods. **6th Army Group** In the U.S. **Seventh Army** area, **VI Corps** sector, the 36th Division attacks toward Rohrweiler while still engaged at Oberhoffen; RCT 142, bolstered by Tanks and Tank Destroyers, takes the southern part of Oberhoffen. Reinforcements from the 14th Armored Division (C.C.B.) rush to assist RCT 142, but enemy fire stalls the advance. Meanwhile, RCT's 142 and 143 cross the Moder and capture Rohrweiler with a synchronized assault. Further south, progress of RCT 141 is stifled by floods. In the **French 1st Army's U.S. XXI Corps** sector, the 3rd Division's 7th Regiment, supported by Tanks, pushes through Artzenheim and heads toward Biesheim. In conjunction, the 75th Division plows through Andolsheim as it advances against Neuf-Brisach. Meanwhile, the U.S. 28th Division drives to the entrance to Colmar and halts to permit French 5th Armored Tanks to be the first to enter; the city falls, but some mop up operations ensue. **(Atlantic-Yalta)** President Roosevelt arrives on the U.S.S. *Quincy* for the conference.

President Roosevelt, flanked by Winston Churchill and Stalin on his left and right respectively, at the Yalta Conference.

February 3rd 1945 — (Pacific-Philippines) Luzon In the U.S. **Sixth Army** area, orders come down from General MacArthur calling for the reopening of Manila Bay, which mandates the securing of the southern coast of Ternate and the simultaneous mission of seizing Bataan and Corregidor. In the **XIV Corps** sector, the 1st Cavalry Division has its forward contingents reach Manila, and it is given permission to send the units into the city, the first Yanks to return to Manila since its fall; General MacArthur had ordered the city abandoned on December 23rd 1941. The 37th Division is also closing on the capital. In the **XI Corps** sector, the fighting at Zig Zag Pass is still non-stop; however, the Japanese refuse to relent. **(Pacific-Burma)** British Admiral Mountbatten receives instructions from the Combined Chiefs of Staff stipulating the liberation of Burma as his primary objective, followed by the seizure of Malaya; he is informed that the job must be accomplished with the present complement of troops. However, there is a possibility that troops from the European Theater

might eventually arrive as reinforcements. In the N.C.A.C. area, the 475th Regiment, U.S. 5332nd Brigade takes great strides during its attack to secure the remaining resistance on Loi-Kang ridge. The British 36th Division's 29th Brigade continues advancing east toward Mongmit, but the enemy which had been near Twinnge, vanishes. **(Pacific-China)** Namyung capitulates to the Japanese. **(Atlantic-Western Europe) 21st Army Group** In the U.S. **Ninth Army** area, the 2nd Armored Division and the 30th, 83rd, 84th and 95th Divisions are attached to Army. In the **XVI Corps** sector, the 35th Division completes its assembly at positions outside of Maastricht, Holland. **12th Army Group** In the U.S. **First Army's V Corps** sector, under winter conditions, the 1st Battalion, 311th Regiment, 78th Division crosses the Roer by swimming and seizes Dedenborn. The 60th Regiment, 9th Division captures Dreiborn subsequent to brisk house-to-house fighting and jumps to Herhahn, capturing it also. In conjunction, the 47th Regiment eliminates resistance at Einruhr. Meanwhile, the 2nd Division advances doggedly and seizes Berescheid and Ettelscheid with its 9th Regiment, while overrunning Bronsfeld with its 23rd Regiment. In the **XVIII (Airborne) Corps** sector, the 1st Division continues to whack the West Wall; contingents discover Ramscheid abandoned. In other activity, the Germans strike heavily against the 82nd Airborne's positions; however, the attacks fail. In the **U.S. Third Army** area, **VIII Corps** sector, orders to attack toward the Pruem are received. Elements of the 87th Division occupy Roth. The 4th Division's 8th Regiment seizes Buchet and victimizes Halenfeld, while the 2nd Battalion, 12th Regiment reduces final resistance at Bleialf. **6th Army Group** In the U.S. **Seventh Army** area, **XV Corps** sector, the 70th Division receives components of Task Force Herron, which is disbanded; the Division is attached to Corps. In the **V Corps** sector, the battle for Oberhoffen continues to heighten as RCT 142, 36th Division maintains its efforts to eradicate the enemy until relieved by the 14th Armored's C.C.B. Meanwhile, RCT 143 secures the Drusenheim woods; however, German reaction prevents them from holding most of the section lying south of the Moder; it is compelled to relinquish two captured bridges and a road junction. At Herrlisheim, a stiff counterattack pushes RCT 141 back, forcing it to withdraw across flooded ground. In the **French 1st Army** area, **U.S. XXI Corps** sector, Neuf-Brisach is threatened by the converging forces of the 3rd and 77th Divisions, the former seizing Biesheim after a violent confrontation. During the night, the Germans ambush a contingent of thirty-five 3rd Division Infantrymen near Biesheim, slinging incessant artillery mortar, machine gun, and small arms fire upon them; as the stunned GIs break for cover in a nearby ditch, they discover it is inhabited by the enemy and vicious hand-to-hand combat ensues. Disregarding the tremendous fire, Technician 5th Grade Forrest E. Peden rushes to give assistance to two wounded Soldiers. Peden, realizing the radio is out of order, dashes 800 yards to the Command Post to prevent annihilation of the detachment and secures two Light Tanks. Although seriously wounded, he jumps aboard one of the Tanks to guide it to the besieged troops. Peden, completely exposed on the outside of the Tank, gets back to the jeopardized contingent; upon reaching it, a direct hit strikes the Tank and it is instantly consumed in spiraling flames, killing him instantly. The burning Tank is spotted from all directions, and reinforcements arrive by dawn to rescue the beleaguered survivors and drive off the enemy. Peden, attached to Battery C, 10th Field Artillery Battalion, 3rd Division, receives the Medal of Honor posthumously for his extraordinary heroism. German resistance in the Foret Domaniale impedes progress of the 77th Division. The 12th Armored Division, committed to the Corps to shorten the southern drive, pushes through the positions of the 28th Division; C.C.B. takes a bridgehead at both Sundhoffen and Ste Croix en Plaine granting crossings at the Ill River. The 28th, subsequent to culminating its mop up details at Colmar, assists French Armor with blocking deployment along the Vosges Rivers south and west of the city. Meanwhile, the 1st Corps secures the south bank of the Thur River between Cernay and Ensisheim, seizing towns including Pulversheim and Wittelsheim. The Corps then regroups to bolt the river and hook up with the U.S. XXI Corps. In the **U.S. Eighth Army** area, Aircraft drop the 511th Paratroop Infantry along Tagaytay Ridge; however, the formation is widely scattered. The Paratroops receive no opposition and advance to take a road junction at the eastern extension of the ridge.

February 4th 1945 — (Pacific-Philippines) Luzon In the **U.S. Sixth Army** area, **XIV Corps** sector, the Japanese retain control of the Quezon bridge at the Pasig River in Manila, despite concentrated efforts of advance contingents of the 1st Cavalry. Two Battalions of the 37th Division enter the city and hook up with the Cavalry units in the northern part of the city. In the **I Corps** sector, Planes support the attack of the 6th Division's 1st Infantry which seizes San Jose-Highway 5, gaining entrance to the Cagayan Valley; the Regiment deploys to defend the approaches against counterattack. Meanwhile, the Japanese raise resolute resistance at Munoz, frustrating the efforts of the 20th Regiment's attempt to overrun it; the Japanese also mount stiff opposition against the 63rd Regiment, preventing it from penetrating and advancing to San Jose. The boundary separating north and south Luzon is reached by elements of the 35th Regiment, 25th Division as it drives to Lupao, a Jap stronghold, and in conjunction, the 161st Regiment drives to San Isidro; the progress virtually cuts off contact between the enemy forces in north and south Luzon. At Zig Zag Pass, in the **XI Corps** sector, the 34th Regiment is again unable to dislodge the entrenched enemy; the Regiment is absorbed by the 38th Division which will mount its attack on the 5th. The U.S. Eighth Army commences its attack against Manila, advancing from the south to Paranaque, about 4 miles south of Manila; it encounters heavy opposition as the primary southern defenses are established there. **(Pacific-Burma)** Brigadier General Lewis A. Pick leads the first Convoy from Ledo into Kunming and receives a tumultuous welcome. In the N.C.A.C. area, the 475th Infantry, U.S. 5332nd Brigade reduces the remnant resistance on Loi-kang ridge. The Japanese have abandoned the area; U.S. participation is now limited to Patrols and Artillery exchanges. **(Atlantic-Yalta)** The U.S.-British-Soviet conference (Magneto) begins. Political and military issues are discussed. The conference is the second part of ARGONAUT. The meetings adjourn on the 9th, concluding with an agreement on the plan to invade Japan subsequent to the defeat of Germany. **(Atlantic-Western Europe) 21st Army Group** In the **U.S Ninth Army** area, **XVI Corps** sector, the U.S. 35th Division relieves the British 52nd Division. In the **XIII Corps** sector, the 29th Division is transferred to the XIX Corps. **12th Army Group** The **U.S. First Army** is ordered to attack in conjunction with the U.S. First Army; it is to drive from Dueren to Euskirchen. In the **V Corps** sector, the 311th Regiment, 78th Division seizes Ruhrberg and the surrounding heights. In the 9th Division zone, the 47th Regiment takes Wollsiefen and advances to Urft Lake and captures Dam 5. On the right, the 39th Regiment repulses a counterattack at Herhahn and seizes Mor-

sbach as it moves toward Gemund. In the **XVIII Corps (Airborne)** area, the 1st Division continues its attack against the West Wall. The 26th Regiment seizes Hollerath as the 395th drives to the high ground southwest of Hellenthal. The 82nd Airborne is relieved by the 99th Division. Para RCT 517 is detached from 82nd and attached to 78th Division V Corps. In the **U.S. Third Army** area, the boundary changes and a new Corps mission causes Army to regroup. In the **VIII Corps** sector, the 8th and 22nd Regiments, 4th Division, break through the outer defenses of the West Wall along the Schnee Eifel ridge northeast of Brandscheid. Along the south flank of Corps, contingents of 6th and 11th Armored Divisions relieve the 90th Division, east and west of the Our River respectively. The 90th is to attack with the 4th Division against Brandscheid. In the **XII Corps** zone, regrouping also occurs for an assault across the Our and Sauer Rivers through the West Wall. **6th Army Group** In the **French 1st Army** area, C.C.A., 12th U.S. Armored takes Hattstatt; C.C.B. protects the bridgeheads across the Ill River until relieved by 109th Regiment, 28th Division; however, C.C.R. hits heavy opposition driving northeast of Colmar-Rouffach road and halts. The 4th Moroccan Mountain Division, French 1st Army takes Guebwiller and drives to the southern fringes of Rouffach by night. Cernay, along the Thur River, is abandoned by the Germans and will be used for an assault against Ensisheim. **(Atlantic-Italy) 15th Army Group** In the **U.S. Fifth Army** area, IV Corps sector, the 92nd Division's 365th and 366th Regiments attack east and west of the Serchio River respectively, taking Albiano, Castelvecchio, and Gallicano against slight opposition.

February 5th 1945 — (Pacific-Philippines) S.W.P.A. Headquarters assigns Sixth Army's XI Corps with reopening Manila Bay. Planes increase their bombing runs over Corregidor. In the **U.S. Sixth Army** area, General MacArthur directs that Manila be the primary objective, and he states that the Japanese in northern Luzon are to be contained. In the **XIV Corps** sector, contingents of the 1st Cavalry and the 37th Infantry Division enter Manila to clear the northern section. Both units drive south toward the Pasig River line as the Japanese ignite demolition charges firing the area. During the advance of the 37th, enemy pillboxes halt Company K, 148th Regiment. 2nd Lt. Robert M. Viale leads a detachment of two other men toward the enemy. He destroys the first obstacle singlehandedly; one of the other men and a Bazooka Team knocks out a second. The team advances and gets trapped by encircling flames and an enemy machine gun, prompting Viale, who is now wounded, to move against the machine gun. He enters a room filled with civilians while trying to knock out the gun. As he climbs a ladder to hurl a grenade, his disabled arm fails him and the live grenade drops to the floor. To save the civilians and others in the room, he grasps it and smothers it between himself and the wall, dying within a few minutes. He receives the Medal of Honor posthumously. In the I Corps sector, the 20th Regiment, 6th Division meets fierce resistance at Munoz; Company E is pinned down, prompting 2nd Lt. Donald E. Rudolph to take action. He creeps to a culvert and eliminates three Japanese before dashing across open ground to attack pillboxes. Rudolph takes out the first with a grenade, a second with a grenade and Rifle fire, then finishes the job by sealing the exit. He continues darting from pillbox to pillbox, destroying six more; later in the day, he again singlehandedly attacks a Tank which is holding up his Platoon by jumping aboard and dropping a grenade down the turret. Lt. Rudolph receives the

Medal of Honor. Rizal is seized by the 1st Regiment. The 35th Regiment, 25th Division drives against Lupao. The 32nd Division's 2nd Battalion, 127th Regiment starts moving up the Villa Verde Trail; it has been sending Patrols from Santa Maria at the entrance to the mountains since the end of January. In the **XI Corps** sector, bitter fighting continues at Zig Zag Pass as the 38th Division attempts to dislodge the entrenched Japanese. In the **U.S. Eighth Army** area, the 511th Regiment, 11th Airborne Division attacks against heavy resistance, driving north toward Manila along Highway 1. **(Atlantic-Western Europe) 21st Army Group** In the **U.S. Ninth Army** area, the boundary between the First and Ninth Armies shifts north to general line Liege-Aachen-Cologne. In the **XIX Corps** sector, responsibility for Corps zones passes to VII Corps, First Army, which assumes command of 8th and 104th Divisions in place. **12th Army Group** In the **U.S. First Army** area, the **VII Corps** moves from Belgium to the Roer River line in Germany. In the **V Corps** sector, at 03:00, the 78th Division drives toward the Schwammenauel Dam; C.C.R., 7th Armored (attached) attacks later in the morning and secures Strauch and Steckenborn. The 9th Division's 39th Regiment mops up toward Gemund and the Olef River. In the 2nd Division sector, the 38th Regiment gains a fragile hold on Hellenthal, and the 9th Regiment pushes Company A into Scheuren. In the **XVIII (Airborne) Corps** area, the 1st Division sweeps toward the Olef and Prether Rivers until nightfall when it is relieved by the 99th Division. The 99th Division assumes responsibility for entire Corps zone. In the **U.S. Third Army** area, **VIII Corps** sector, the 4th Division's 22nd Regiment eliminates an obstinate road intersection northeast of Brandscheid, then pushes contingents into the city, overrunning heavy resistance. Another column takes the high ground above Sellerich. Meanwhile, the 8th Regiment seizes the crossroads in Schlausen Bacher Wald. Southeast of Kobscheid, contingents of the 87th Division seize a crossroad junction and others drive down the Losheim-Pruem road. In support of the 4th Division drive against Brandscheid, the 90th Division strikes Habscheid and Hollnich. **6th Army Group** In the **U.S. Seventh Army** area, **VI Corps** continues toward the Rhine. The 36th Infantry and 101st Airborne Divisions relieve the 79th Division. The 117th Cavalry Reconnaissance Squadron relieves RCT 141 of its Zorn Canal outposts; it finds Offendorf free of enemy. In the **French 1st Army** area, the U.S. XXI Corps and the French I Corps make contact, splitting the Colmar pocket in half. The remaining resistance west of the Ill River is isolated, capable only of putting up minor resistance. In the **U.S. XXI Corps** sector, C.C.A., 12th Armored drives into Rouffach at 05:12, establishing contact with the 4th Moroccan Mountain Division which had arrived earlier. C.C.R. takes Herrlisheim-pres-Colmar and is relieved there by the 28th Division. Meanwhile, the 75th Division seizes Appenwihr, Hettenschlag, and Wolfgantzen. The French 9th Colonial Division drives into Ensisheim at 22:30. **(Atlantic-Eastern Europe)** Soviet troops advance to the middle Oder in Prussia on a wide front about 30 miles outside of Berlin. The fortified cities of Frankfurt and Kuestrin are outflanked. Berlin acknowledges the Red Army has crossed the upper Oder below Breslau, north and south of Brieg. Meanwhile, bitter fighting ensues at Posen and Budapest. **(Atlantic-Italy) 15th Army Group** In the **U. S. Fifth Army** area, **IV Corps** sector, the 92nd Division seizes Calomini easily with its 366th Regiment, but the Germans hold firm on the slopes of M. Faeto. The 365th Regiment, working the other side of the Serchio, drives to the slopes of Lama di Sotto, but the Germans hold the slopes which control Castelnuovo, despite heavy attacks; the fighting remains fierce for several days.

February 6th 1945 — (Pacific-Philippines) The Japanese continue to pull back in northern Manila beyond the Pasig River as the area falls under American control (1st Cavalry Division); the 160th Regiment, 40th Division, supplemented with Tanks and Air support, drives forward securing positions at McSevney Point on the western side of Storm King Mountain. In the **U.S. Sixth Army** area, **I Corps** sector, Artillery fire is poured into Japanese positions at Munoz in an effort to annihilate the defenders, but the Japs refuse to capitulate; their escape routes from the town are sealed. In the XI Corps sector, the Japanese holding Zig Zag Pass receive a thunderous ovation from Yankee Artillery and Planes stationed at San Marcelino Airstrip. The pounding supplements the attack of the 149th Regiment, 38th Division, which is driving toward the pass from the west, in conjunction with the 152nd Regiment, attacking from the east; the 152nd pierces the enemy's perimeter during the later part of the day. In the **U.S. Eighth Army** area, orders arrive from GHQSWPA directing Army to establish operational plans to seize Palawan (Victor III) and the Sulu Archipelago (Victor IV). The 511th Paratroop Infantry, 11th Airborne is heavily involved as it fights hard to gain 500 yards. **(SEAC)** British Admiral Mountbatten calls for plans to recapture Rangoon and Singapore. **(Atlantic-Western Europe) 21st Army Group** In the **U.S. Ninth Army** area (still under British control), the **XVI Corps** is operational and assumes responsibility for the British 12th Corps sector (British Second Army). The British 7th Armored is attached for operations only. The U.S. 35th Division finalizes its relief of the British 52nd Division and assumes responsibility for its sector. In the **XIII Corps** sector, C.C.B., U.S. 5th Armored is attached to the 102nd Division for commitment during Operation GRENADE. **12th Army Group** In the **U.S. First Army** area, **V Corps** sector, the 310th Regiment, 78th Division, reinforced by a Battalion of the 309th Regiment, drives toward Schmidt-Harscheid-Kommerscheidt area, but the Germans mount fierce resistance and keep the advance under a thousand yards, despite Tank support. At Steckenborn, mop-up operations ensue, and at Bergstein, Paratroop RCT 517 commences an attack at midnight (5th-6th), but cannot advance easily as it stumbles upon a minefield. In the **XVIII (Airborne) Corps** sector, the Corps begins advancing toward the Huertgen area. In the **U.S. Third Army** area, **VIII Corps** sector, the 87th Division overruns a road junction along the Losheim-Pruem road; however, the Germans still offer fierce resistance in the vicinity and the 87th is halted short of taking crossroads east of Kobscheid in the Schnee Eifel. Meanwhile, the 4th Division's 8th Regiment, in concert with the 87th's southern flank contingents, continues to sweep the enemy from Schnee Eifel ridge. At Brandscheid, the 1st Battalion, 358th Regiment, 90th Division attempts to relieve the 3rd Battalion, 22nd Regiment, 4th Division, but the Germans mount a ferocious counterattack which causes incessant combat for several hours resulting in a victory for the Yanks. Other units of the 22nd Infantry attack at 12:00 and take Herscheid, Hontheim, and Sellerich. Meanwhile, the 90th Infantry and 11th Armored Divisions synchronize their attacks and drive through the West Wall defenses, surprising the Germans before dawn: the 359th Regiment, 90th Division takes Habscheid, but become held up outside of town. C.C.R., 11th Armored seizes Hill 568 and gets elements into Grosskampenberg, Lutzkampen, and Berg, but it is only able to stay in Berg. In the **III Corps** sector, an assault across the Our is begun by contingents of the 6th Armored and 17th Airborne Divisions at 19:00: by midnight, elements of the former reach the west bank near Dahnen and Kalborn; the 507th Paratroop

Infantry, 17th Airborne crosses north of Dasburg. **6th Army Group** In the **U.S. Seventh Army** area, **VI Corps** sector, the 68th Armored Infantry Battalion continues determined fighting in Oberhoffen; however, German resistance remains steadfast. Herrlisheim is occupied by RCT 143 without incident; like Offendorf, it is saturated with mines. In the French 1st Army area, the final step to seize the Colmar Pocket begins. The U.S. XXI Corps pivots east and moves toward the Rhine. The 3rd Division seizes Neuf-Brisach with its 30th Regiment, which is led into the fortress city by civilians to eliminate the scattered resistance. The French 2nd Armored Division takes Oberaasheim and is relieved by contingents of the U.S. 75th Division. Meanwhile, the 12th Armored Division blocks exit from the Vosges and gives the 28th Division fire support. Contingents of the French 5th Armored Division assists 12th Armored in reducing the Vosges pockets. In the French 1st Corps sector, the 2nd Moroccan Mountain Division drives across the Ill River beyond the Rhine-Rhone Canal and seizes Hirtzfelden, while the French 9th Colonial Division eliminates the final resistance in Ensisheim before dawn. On the west flank of Corps, the 4th Moroccan Division blocks exit from the Vosges. Organized resistance in the Vosges ceases. **(Atlantic-Eastern Europe)** Troops of the First Ukrainian Front secure bridgeheads north and south of Brieg and subsequently attack and seize the city. Grottkau, Lowen, and Ohlau also fall to the Russians. In addition, heavy fighting continues in Budapest and Posen as the Red Army continues to reduce the German pockets.

February 7th 1945 — (Pacific-Philippines) The Japanese Submarine RO-55 is sunk by the Destroyer Escort *Thomason* (DE-203). **Luzon** In the **U.S. Sixth Army** area, XIV Corps sector, the 37th Division spreads wide, taking responsibility for the majority of Manila, north of the Pasig, thereby permitting the 5th and 85th Cavalry Regiments to attack and secure the city's eastern outlying areas as far south as the Pasig. Meanwhile, orders to attack are received by the 37th, prompting it to delegate part of its sector to a Provisional Security Force; its 2nd and 3rd Battalions, 148th Regiment ford the river in assault boats. Meanwhile, the 185th Regiment, 40th Division drives west of Storm King Mountain, attacking toward Snake Hill North. In the **I Corps** sector, the bloody fight for Munoz concludes, gaining another Jap stronghold for the Stars and Stripes, planted by the 20th Regiment, 6th Division. Columns of the Jap defenders attempting to flee are caught in a thunderous roar of U.S. fire and all are killed. The Japanese at Lupao continue to control the town against the repeated efforts of the 35th Regiment, 25th Division; Two Companies of Company G are pinned by five Japanese Tanks, ten machine guns and a Platoon of Riflemen. Master Sgt. Charles McGaha runs a gauntlet of fire to rescue a wounded man and carries him 75 yards to safety. Although wounded, he returns to the firing line and then darts to assist a litter team which is under heavy fire, and he is wounded again. A shell explodes, killing two of the party, but despite becoming wounded again, McGaha carries the third to safety, then he intentionally draws enemy fire to permit the detachment to withdraw. He receives the Medal of Honor. At the Villa Verde Trail, the 2nd Battalion, 127th Regiment, 32nd Division reinitiates its advance along the trail; however, its positioning becomes precarious as the area is completely exposed to enemy fire. In the **XI Corps** sector, the enemy strongholds dispersed along Highway 7 are being wiped out one by one as the 151st and

152nd Regiments drive westward along the road; the 149th Regiment, also advancing westward, reaches a point near Balsic. In the **U.S. Eighth Army** area, Nichols Field, outside of Manila, is approached by the 11th Airborne Division; the Airfield had been destroyed by Jap Planes during the first days of the war. Japanese resistance is fierce, especially near Cut-Cut Creek, where the 188th Infantry cannot cut through the withering fire. **(Pacific-China)** Kanchow, a U.S. Fourteenth Air Force Base, is seized by the Japanese. The U.S.S. *Bergall* (SS-320), a Submarine operating in the South China Sea, sinks the Japanese Coast Vessel No. 53. **(Atlantic-Western Europe) 21st Army Group** In the **U.S. Ninth Army** area, **XII Corps** sector, the 84th Division takes responsibility for the Linnich-Himmerich area, relieving the 102nd Division. In the **XIX Corps** sector, the U.S. 30th Division assumes responsibility for defending the west bank of the Roer River between Kirchberg and Merken. **12th Army Group** In the **U.S. First Army** area, **V Corps** sector, the 78th Division, supported by a half-hour Artillery barrage, again attacks; its 309th Regiment seizes Kommerscheidt, despite obstacles such as mines and heavy machine gun fire, while the 310th Regiment takes the high ground outside of Schmidt. Meanwhile, the 311th, driving on the right, alongside the 310th, secures the western portion of Schmidt and has elements reach the southwest sector of Harscheid. At Bergstein, the advancing elements of Paratroop RCT 517 encounter innumerable mines which saturate the terrain southeast of the city and forbid movement. In the **U.S. Third Army** area, **VIII Corps** sector, German defenses at the West Wall increase tenacity, but the U.S. continues to push forward. Crossroads east of Habscheid fall to the 345th and 346th Regiments, 87th Division; the Regiments then bolt from the Schnee Eifel and drive north along the Losheim-Pruem Road. The 4th Division pushes southeast toward Pruem, seizing Wascheid and Ober Mehlen, with its 8th Regiment; the 8th also overruns the heights above Steinmehlen. The 90th Division forges ahead through murderous fire as it hammers the primary West Wall defenses at Habscheid and begins eradicating pillboxes one by one. The 359th Infantry seizes Hollnich; however, enemy resistance is thorough and progress is tedious, causing complications for the 11th Armored Division, whose C.C.R. is viciously engaged at Hill 568 and cannot move beyond the hills as its northern flank is partially exposed without the protection of the 90th. Tanks and Tank Destroyers are sped to the hill area to bolster the Infantry. In the **III Corps** sector, the attacking contingents of the 6th Armored and 17th Airborne Divisions are across the Our River and Germany's border before mid-day; nevertheless, the Germans intensify their resistance after adjusting to the initial shock of the assault. In the **XII Corps** sector, the assault troops drive across the Our and Sauer Rivers during the early morning hours. The 5th and 80th Divisions ford the rivers with difficulty, despite Artillery fire as the unruly currents between Echternach and Vianden, combined with the thunderclap of German Artillery fire, greatly hinder the operation and restrict the amount of troops which make it across the rivers. Small bridgeheads are established by the 80th Division's 318th and 319th Regiments, the latter capturing Wallendorf after dark. In the **XX Corps** sector, the 94th Division's 301st Regiment seizes the town of Sinz, but the enemy is not dislodged from one house; it is exterminated on the following day. The three attacking Battalions also attack to secure the high ground northwest of the town. In conjunction, the 302nd Regiment drives into the formidable entrenchments of the enemy in the Campholz woods and Tettingen and knocks out four pillboxes. Meanwhile, the 26th Division launches quick hit-and-run raids in the vicinity of Fraulautern and other targets around the Saarlautern-Roden bridgehead sector. **6th Army Group** In the **U.S. Seventh Army** area, **VI Corps** sector, the 1st Battalion, 142nd Infantry relieves the 68th Armored Infantry Battalion at Oberhoffen in the 36th Division zone and continues the attack against the resistance, which is holding tough in the northwestern portion of the city. In the **French 1st Army** area, **U.S. XXI Corps** sector, the Corps tightens its grip along the Rhine from Balgau heading north. The French 2nd Armored Division advancing south takes Balgau and Heiteren as it drives toward Fessenheim; contingents of the U.S. 75th Division swing into Heiteren and relieve the French.

February 1945 — U.S. Planes pummel Japanese positions west of Bambing, Philippines.

February 8th 1945 — (Pacific-Philippines) Luzon In the **U.S. Sixth Army** area, **XIV Corps** sector, the eastern suburbs of Manila are being secured by the 1st Cavalry Division. Meanwhile, the bridgehead of the 37th Division near the Pasig is further fortified. The 185th Regiment, 40th Division intensifies its attack against Snake Hill North, while the 160th penetrates deeper and secures most of McSevney Point, then repulses successive counterattacks. In addition, the 108th Regiment moves from Top of The Hill and lunges west, driving against a group of nearby hills numbered 3, 4, 5 and 6, from north to south; Hill 5 capitulates. In the **I Corps** sector, the 25th Division's 35th Regiment eliminates the final resistance at Lupao, permitting the Corps to complete clearing the central plain. At Zig Zag Pass, Japanese resistance remains feverish, preventing its fall to the determined efforts of an ongoing two-pronged assault by the 37th Division. In the **U.S. Eighth Army** area, at Nichols Field, the Japanese are resisting tenaciously; however, the 188th and 511th Regiments, 11th Airborne converge at the southwestern corner of the coveted Airfield. On the 10th, the 11th Airborne is transferred to Sixth Army's XIV Corps, but it retains responsibility for the field, which finally falls to the Yanks on the 13th. **(Pacific-Burma)** The 26th Brigade, British 36th Division, operating in the N.C.A.C. area, establishes a bridgehead outside of Myitson on the Shweli. **(Atlantic-Western Europe) 21st Army Group** Operation VERITABLE commences. The Canadian First Army attacks at 10:30, subsequent to a huge Artillery bombardment to secure the area between the Rhine and Maas Rivers. The British Corps, composed of the Canadian 2nd and the British 15th, 53rd, and 51st Divisions (left to right), encounters only mild resistance as it drives from the Nijmegen-Mook line; some strong resistance is encountered on the right, and in addition, the flooded roads and menacing mines impede the advance. The Canadian 2nd Division seizes Wyler after a heavy fire-fight, while Kranburg falls to the British 15th Division. In conjunction, the 51st and 53rd British Divisions secure the southwest and northwest heights southwest of the Reichswald respectively. Meanwhile, at 18:00, the Canadian 3rd Division commences an amphibious assault over flooded terrain taking Zandpol and Zyfflich effortlessly, despite the poor weather which costs the operation most of its Air support. General Simpson's U.S. Ninth Army, attached to the 21st Army Group, is halted at the river, awaiting recession of the flood waters; it attacks on February 23rd. General Montgomery prefers that General Bradley halt the attacks of his First and Third Armies, saving them for future use in the northern region, but General Eisenhower does not agree. **12th Army Group** In The **U.S. First Army** area, **V Corps** sector, heavy fighting breaks out in Schmidt before dawn, when the 3rd Battalion, 310th Regiment, 78th Division secures the eastern sector of the town. In conjunction, the 1st Battalion drives against the high ground outside of Harscheid and secures it. The 3rd Battalion, 311th Regiment captures Harscheid, while the remainder of the Regiment secures the terrain between Urft Lake and Schmidt. In the **XVIII Corps** sector, the 82nd Airborne, minus the contingents fighting with the V Corps, moves from Salmchateau, Belgium, to positions near Rott, Germany. In the **U.S. Third Army** area, **VIII Corps** sector, Olzheim and the nearby heights to the south and east are seized by the 345th Regiment, 87th Division. The advancing 4th Division encounters heavy resistance as it encroaches Pruem; its 8th Regiment seizes most of Gondenbrett, while the 22nd Regiment battles to victory at Ober Mehlen. Meanwhile, the 90th Division maintains its battering ram status and continues to press its clamps against the primary defenses of the West Wall; its 358th Regiment does not succeed in dislodging the Germans on Hill 519 however, it does secure most of the area south of Brandscheid and encounters contingents of the 359th Regiment outside of Habscheid. A vicious confrontation develops at Hill 511, slightly southeast of the town, culminating late in the day with victory for the 357th Regiment, which retains firm control of the terrain. Meanwhile, the 359th continues to move prudently as it demolishes additional pillboxes to the rear of the Division's perimeter. In the **III Corps** sector, C.C.R., 6th Armored Division enlarges its northern bridgehead. The 44th Division secures two bridge crossings over the Our, outside of Kalborn. The 9th Armored Infantry Battalion crosses the river, too, but it completes the endeavor too late to enlarge its bridgehead; in addition, the 17th Airborne deployed north of Dasburg holds its bridgehead, but cannot expand it. In the **XII Corps** sector, the

5th and 80th Divisions fortify and enlarge their bridgeheads. In the area around the 5th Division positions, much activity is concentrated on mopping up remnant resistance including the elimination of enemy-held houses within Weiterbach. In the **XX Corps** sector, the final resistance in Sinz is crushed by the 301st Regiment, 94th Division, which then dispatches units to reduce menacing pillboxes southeast of the town. In conjunction, the 302nd Regiment eradicates the last two pillboxes standing between Tettingen and the Campholz woods. Meanwhile, the 104th Regiment, 26th Division pushes contingents into Fraulautern, which engage in a bitter contest that gains it one city block. **6th Army Group** In the **U.S. Seventh Army** area, **XV Corps** sector, German pressure forces the withdrawal of the O.P.L.R. of the 276th Regiment, 70th Division to pull back. In the **VI Corps** sector, battle rages at Oberhoffen as RCT 142, 36th Division pounds against the resolute defenders holding the northwestern sector of the city. In conjunction, RCT 143 drives eastward through Bois de Drusenheim. In the **French 1st Army** area, **U.S. XXI Corps** sector, the French 2nd Armored Division advances to Fessenheim and encounters the French 1st Corps' 1st Armored Division, culminating the Corps offensive. Subsequent to its capture of Fessenheim, the 1st French Armored Division advances southward along the Rhine and seizes Blodelsheim. The German-held terrain is being greatly compressed; additional Corps units secure the Harth Forest and advance to the Rhine near Homburg, confining the remaining German bridgehead west of the Rhine to four villages — Bantzenheim, Chalampe, Ottmarsheim, and Rumersheim. **(Atlantic-Italy) 15th Army Group** In the **U.S. Fifth Army** area, **IV Corps** sector, the Germans strike hard against the beleaguered 92nd Division, forcing it to relinquish terrain east of the Serchio, while it battles tenaciously in an undecided struggle for the heights on both sides of the river. Despite the dilemma, the 92nd launches an attack across the Cinquale Canal (TF 1) and drives inland, its 370th Regiment advancing a tough mile, while the 371st beats a track a mere 800 yards against blistering resistance.

A U.S. Plane flying a mission over the Hump (Himalaya Mtns.).

February 9th 1945 — (Pacific-Philippines) The Submarine *Batfish* (SS-310) sinks the Japanese Submarine I-41, and two days later, destroys the RO-112; the *Batfish* continues the hunt and kills her third Japanese Submarine, the RO-113, on the 12th. **Luzon** The **U.S. Sixth Army** releases the 112th Cavalry RCT to the 1st Cavalry Division. In the **XIV Corps** sector, the 37th Division units fighting south of the Pasig in Manila are encountering heavy resistance, unable to make much prog-

ress. Near the Manila Gas Works, the 148th Regiment is locked in battle. As casualties soar, P.F.C. Joseph Cicchetti improvises and forms a litter team which dashes back and forth along a four-hundred yard fire zone, dodging mortars, machine guns and heavy artillery for about four hours, rescuing 14 men. At one point, Cicchetti takes on a machine gun and eliminates it with his Rifle. Later, he is struck in the head with a shell fragment, but continues carrying a wounded man for fifty yards to safety before collapsing and dying. Meanwhile, Company B, 148th Regiment drives against heavily fortified Paco Railroad, defended by 300 troops. P.F.C. John N. Reese Jr. and P.F.C. Cleto Rodriguez head out together and begin a two-man battle. For about two hours, the two Soldiers kill over 82 enemy troops, prevent reinforcement of machine gun nests, and thoroughly disorganize the defenders. As the two intrepid Infantrymen attempt to get back to their lines, Reese is killed while attempting to reload his Rifle. Their extraordinary courage directly leads to the subsequent capture of the objective. Both men receive the Medal of Honor, Reese posthumously. Meanwhile, The 1st Cavalry Division finishes clearing the eastern suburbs and crosses the Pasig. Meanwhile, the 40th Division's sector is also caustic; the 108th Regiment seizes Hills 3 and 4, then attacks toward Hill 6. The 160th continues to retain McSevney Point, and the 185th Regiment deploys to strike Snake Hill north. In the **I Corps** sector, the Japanese launch an unsuccessful counterattack against the 127th Regiment, 32nd Division, which then moves to secure the Villa Verde Trail until enemy fire compels it to halt. Meanwhile, at Zig Zag Pass, the battle continues to rage as the 38th Division advances doggedly to eradicate the resistance. **(Pacific-Burma)** In the ALFSEA area, the British 15th Corps concludes its operation to seize Ramree Island. **(Pacific-China)** The Chinese establish Chinese Services of Supply. **(Atlantic-Western Europe) 21st Army Group** In the **Canadian First Army** area, British 30th Corps sector, Keeken, Mehr, Milligen, and Niel are seized by the Canadian 3rd Division. The British 15th Division penetrates the West Wall defenses at Nuetterden and drives to the heights near Materborn. The 43rd Division initiates its drive toward Goch. Meanwhile, the British 53rd Division secures Stuppelburg feature and the heights southwest of Materborn. The British 51st Division advances through the southern portion of the Reichswald, seizes a road center, and severs the Mook-Gennep road as it closes on Hekkens. **12th Army Group** In the **U.S. First Army** area, the 9th Division initiates its final drive toward the Schwammenauel Dam. In conjunction, the 78th Division's 310th Regiment, reinforced by one Battalion of the 311th Regiment, secures the region north of Schmidt-Hasenfelde Road and, in addition, sets up roadblocks along the Harscheid-Nideggen Road in an effort to defend the 9th Division's northern flank. Meanwhile, the 9th Division's 60th Regiment secures the majority of Hasenfelde as it secures its sector to the Roer. In conjunction, the 311th Regiment secures the north bank of the Urft Lake and advances to within several hundred yards of the Schwammenauel Dam; contingents of the 309th Regiment capture the control house at the northern section of the dam. In the **U.S. Third Army** area, **VIII Corps** sector, the 3rd Battalion, 345th Regiment, 87th Division seizes Neuendorf, while the 4th Division's 8th Regiment terminates resistance at Gondenbrett, secures Hermespand, and pushes contingents across the Pruem; the 22nd Regiment overruns Nieder-Mehlen and the 12th Infantry is heavily involved at Steinmehlen where it gains solid positioning against rigid resistance. As the 90th Division streams through the West Wall defenses in its northern sector, the

Germans are falling back quickly. The 358th Regiment seizes Hill 519 and drives an additional 2,000 yards. The German pull-back has not diminished their aggressiveness, as they still mount fierce opposition that prevents the 90th Division and its collaborating 11th Armored Division from completely closing the hook; however, despite the resistance, the two Divisions are able to make contact with each other. In the **III Corps** sector, C.C.R., 6th Armored fortifies its bridgehead at the Our, establishing contact with the 17th Airborne to the south, while transporting Armor across the recently laid Bailey Bridge; the 6th is about to relieve the 17th Airborne. In the **XII Corps** sector, the bridgeheads of both the 5th and 80th Divisions are fortified and enlarged. In the **XX Corps** sector, heavy fighting erupts in the Bannholz woods, but the efforts of the 301st Regiment, 94th Division fall short, as the Germans holding these positions east of Sinz repulse the attack. In other activity, the 104th Regiment, 26th Division engages the Germans in brutal house-to-house fighting in the Saarlautern bridgehead and reduces the enemy in several of the houses. **6th Army Group** In the **U.S. Seventh Army** area, **VI Corps** sector, the area is fairly quiet as enemy encounters are few except at Oberhoffen where tenacious combat ensues as RCT 142, 36th Division is engaged in house-to-house fighting. In the **French 1st Army** area, the Colmar Pocket is thoroughly destroyed, including the defending 19th German Army which is no longer rendered a fighting unit. The successful conclusion of this operation is due in great part to the U.S. XII Tactical Air Command and its supporting French 1st Air Corps, which have been pounding the enemy since the inception of the operation. The Germans destroy the bridge at Chalampe as the French 1st Corps is eliminating the small bridgehead in the vicinity, thus concluding the campaign on the Alsatian plain of France.

Japanese machinegunners.

February 10th 1945 — (Pacific-Philippines) New boundaries are established between the U.S. Sixth and U.S. Eighth Armies, giving the former responsibility for Luzon and the latter receiving the area south of Luzon which amounts to about two-thirds of the ground area of the Philippines. In other activity, the Samar Task Force is established under Brigadier General L. H. Slocum, Commanding General, Americal Division; the unit is primarily composed of the 1st Battalion, 182nd Infantry, Americal Division and Guerrilla forces. **Luzon** The U.S. 33rd Division arrives from Morotai. In the **U.S. Sixth Army** area, **XIV Corps** sector, the Japanese continue to resist vigorously in southern Manila, making the 37th Division's efforts expensive; the casualties are soaring, compelling the

U.S. to saturate the enemy positions with even heavier Artillery bombardments. Meanwhile, the 1st Cavalry Division continues to enlarge its perimeter south of the Pasig and makes contact with elements of the 37th Division outside of Paco Station. The 40th Division drives toward Object Hill, its final objective after discovering McSevney Point abandoned by the enemy; contingents seize positions on Scattered Tree Ridge and Snake Hill West. In the **I Corps** sector, the 2nd Battalion, 127th Regiment, 32nd Division is relieved by the 3rd Battalion on the hotly contested Villa Verde Trail; however, the 3rd Battalion meets identical resistance. It attacks persistently on the following day, but the commanding positions of the Japanese push it back to its starting point. In the **U.S. Eighth Army** area, the 11th Airborne continues to press the enemy at Nichols Field; assigned to Sixth Army, it is ordered to maintain pressure and also to determine the locations of enemy positions at Cavite. **Leyte** The X Corps assumes command of tactical operation on both Leyte and Samar. The 92nd Division, Philippine Army is attached to the Americal Division and ordered to assist with mop-up operations. **(Pacific-Burma)** In N.C.A.C. area, Myitson is seized by the British 36th Division. In the British Fourteenth Army area, 4th Corps sector, Seikpyu is captured by the East African 28th Brigade. **(Atlantic-Western Europe) 21st Army Group** In the **Canadian First Army** area, British 30th Corps sector, the Germans mount resistance; this, compounded by flooded roads and near grid lock congestion, causes Corps severe difficulties as it attempts to advance. The Canadian 3rd Division closes against the Cleve-Rhine Canal, but the British 43rd Division is halted at Cleve and Materborn. In conjunction, the British 15th Division is busily engaged in Cleve, battling heavy opposition as it secures part of the town. Meanwhile, the British 51st Division encroaches Hekkens and pushes contingents across the flooded Niers River during late night at positions north of Gennep. The Canadian 2nd Division is detached from Corps. In the **U.S. Ninth Army** area, the Germans destroy Roer dams which cause immediate impenetrable flooded roads and bring the Army plans to ford the Roer to a stop. Meanwhile Ninth Army continues finalizing its plans to initiate Operation GRENADE (Large attack of 21st Army Group from the Roer to the Rhine). **12th Army Group** In the **U.S. First Army** area, **V Corps** sector, the 9th Division mop-up details at Hasenfelde conclude before dawn. The 60th Regiment crosses the river there. In conjunction, the 309th Regiment, positioned at the north end of the Schwammenauel Dam, sends Patrols across; however, the Germans have blown the bridge, preventing a strong crossing. Before end of day, the entire Corps sector (west of the Roer) is free of enemy resistance. C.C.R., 7th Armored Division is detached from the 78th Division and reverts back to parent unit. Meanwhile, the advancing 82nd Airborne cracks through resistance as it drives eastward and has its 505th and 508th Paratroop Regiment reach and seize the heights above the Roer River east and southeast of Bergstein; the 517th Paratroop Regiment is detached from Division. In the **U.S. Third Army** area, **VIII Corps** sector, Corps begins to initiate a defensive posture; the 87th deploys defensively now. The 8th Regiment, 4th Division tightens its bridgehead east of the Pruem, while the 22nd Regiment wedges ahead, closing on Pruem. In conjunction, the 12th Regiment over runs Steinmehlen and gets contingents to the river line across from Nieder Pruem. The 90th Division is also reaching the Pruem, its 359th Regiment crushing the three final pillboxes on the Divisional right flank, while the 358th dashes to positions above the Pruem River. Meanwhile, C.C.R., 11th Armored reinitiates its attack, demolishing bunkers and pillboxes obstructing progress south and southeast of Hill 568. In the **III Corps** sector, C.C.A., 6th Armored Division relieves the 17th Airborne. Meanwhile, C.C.B. relieves C.C.R. at the bridgehead east of the Our River and subsequently establishes contact with elements of 11th Armored (VIII Corps). III Corps is assigned to U.S. First Army and begins transferring troops to XVIII (Airborne) Corps sector. Command of Corps sector and of the 6th Cavalry Group and 6th Armored Division (in place) passes to VIII Corps at 24:00. In **XII Corps** sector, elements of the 80th Division continue to enlarge the bridgehead at Wallendorf-Dillingen; its 318th Regiment secures Biesdorf after dark. The 5th Division expands its Weiterbach-Echternach bridgehead into the West Wall subsequent to the crossing of its 10th and 11th Regiments. At Echternach, Engineers construct the first two foot bridges in Corps sector. In the **XV Corps** sector, the 10th Armored (released by Seventh Army) starts for Metz as part of Third Army attached to XX Corps. In the **XX Corps** area, the 2nd Battalion, 376th Regiment attacks into Bannholz Woods upon cessation of a forceful Artillery bombardment; however, enemy fire compels a withdrawal. Meanwhile, the 26th Division's 2nd and 3rd Battalions, 104th Regiment drive forward enlarging the bridgehead at Saarlautern. **6th Army Group** In the U.S. Seventh Army area, **VI Corps** sector, the struggle for Oberhoffen is ongoing; steel-fisted resistance by the Germans holds off two Battalions of RCT 142, 36th Division; Regimental Combat Team 143 drives against Drusenheim, hitting brick resistance which forces a pull back. **(Atlantic-Eastern Europe)** In East Prussia, the Soviet advance continues pounding the weakened German forces, toppling Elbing with its Second White Russian Front and taking Preussisch Eylau, a strategic communications center, with its Third White Russian Front. The beleaguered German Armies are jeopardized on all fronts; however, most refuse any type of surrender terms offered by the Russians. **(Atlantic-Italy) 15th Army Group** In the British Eighth Army area, the Canadian 1st Division assumes command of the Canadian 1st Corps.

An Artillery spotter at work in Germany.

February 11th 1945 — (International) The U.S., Great Britain, and the Soviets issue the Yalta Declaration, underscoring the conclusions reached at the ARGONAUT Conference. The conference ends, after having been in session since the 4th of February. **(Pacific-Marianas-Tinian)** The Joint Expeditionary Force commences its final rehearsals for the invasion of Iwo Jima. **(Pacific Philippines)** The LST 577 is damaged by a

Submarine torpedo, east of the Philippines, and is subsequently destroyed by U.S. forces. The Ocean Tug *Takelma* (ATF-113) is damaged by collision. **Luzon** In the **U.S. Sixth Army** area, **XIV Corps** sector, the Japanese falter as overpowering and unending streams of U.S. forces continue to pound them from the Air and on the ground, in a determined effort to secure Manila; the 11th Airborne takes Pasay and eradicates more of the enemy defenders at Nichols Field and also establishes contact with an outpost of the 8th Division. The 37th Infantry and 1st Cavalry Divisions, clearing the resistance in the northern part of Manila, continue to make nominal progress against what is considered to be the more aggressive defenses. In the **I Corps** sector, the 161st Regiment, 25th Division departs San Isidro and drives to Puncan; its 1st Battalion moves toward Balaho to establish observation posts along Highway 5. Meanwhile, the 3rd Battalion, 127th Regiment, 32nd Division is futilely involved with securing the Villa Verde Pass; both the Yanks and the Japs confine activity after today to probing each other's defenses. In the **XI Corps** sector, the 151st Regiment, 38th Division is released from Corps, due to the increasing progress against the entrenched enemy at Zig Zag Pass. **(Atlantic-Western Europe) 21st Army Group** In the Canadian First Army area, the British 30th Corps maintains its progress despite the flooding conditions and fervent enemy resistance. The 15th British Division eliminates final resistance at Cleve, in conjunction with the British 43rd Division, which seizes Materborn and Hau, while firming its positions southwest of Cleve. Meanwhile, the Canadian 3rd Division drives to the Cleve-Rhine Canal and the 53rd British Division captures Gennep and Hekkens, two strategic road centers. The 53rd Division maintains its operation to reduce the Reichswald. **12th Army Group** The U.S. First Army, acting in accordance with instructions concerning the imminent attack across the Roer, begins to regroup. In the U.S. Third Army area, the **VIII Corps** goes on the defensive. At Pruem, the 3rd Battalion, 22nd Regiment, 4th Division whips into Pruem to exterminate remnant enemy defenders. The 4th Division deploys to protect the Pruem River line, extending from Olzheim to Watzerath, the latter establishing brief tenacious resistance; Company I, 358th Infantry attempts to take the town before dawn and is repulsed; however, three Battalions strike a second lethal blow, toppling it and Weinsfeld. After this successful venture, the 90th Division regroups. During the night, the 17th Airborne Division (relieved by 6th Armored) moves to Chalons-sur-Marne (France) where it is attached to SHAEF. In the **XII Corps** sector, the German defenses at the West Wall, in the Wallendorf bridgehead, continue to crumble at the hands of the 80th Division; its 319th Regiment (minus 3rd Battalion) mops up in Dillingen and seizes the heights above Bollendorf. The 5th Division is also grinding along, commencing an attack within its northern zone against Bollendorf, while simultaneously seizing the heights along the Sauer River within its sector. Meanwhile, the 417th Regiment detached; however, it complies with orders for the 76th Division to secure the southern sector of the Corps bridgehead. It drives forward, overrunning Echternacherbruck. **6th Army Group** In the U.S. Seventh Army area, **XV Corps** sector, the 101st Cavalry Group finishes its relief of the 106th Cavalry Group and takes responsibility for the sector. The 12th Armored Division is attached to Corps and initiates screening missions, which had been handled by the departing 10th Armored's C.C.B. In the **VI Corps** sector, the heated battle for Oberhoffen continues to ensue. Sergeant Edward C. Dahlgren, RCT 142, spots a besieged unit which is surrounded. He races to a barn house and fires upon several enemy troops about one hundred yards away, killing six with his sub-machinegun, scattering the contingent. His Platoon advances and rescues the trapped unit. Dahlgren races to an enemy-held house and tosses a grenade, which persuades all eight occupants to surrender. Just ahead, another machine gun rattles Dahlgren's advance. He tosses more grenades and captures five more Germans. Soon after, his exploits gain him the capture of ten additional Germans. Dahlgren drives into another house and sweeps a cellar stairway with bullets, instantly convincing 16 Germans to climb the steps with their hands high. His tremendous courage contributes greatly to turning back a counterattack and saving a Platoon. In the **French 1st Army's U.S. XXI Corps** sector, the U.S. 75th Division is detached from Corps, reverting to Army control. **(Atlantic-Eastern Europe)** Moscow confirms the fighting northwest of Breslau, German Silesia, proclaiming the offensive commenced four days prior. It reports that the First Ukrainian Front forded the Oder, penetrated German defenses and seized Haynau, Kanth, Liegnitz, Lueben, and Neumarkt, in synchronization with its attack southeast of Breslau, threatening the Silesian capital as well as jeopardizing Dresden, Germany, 80 miles distant (west). In northeast Germany, the Russians take Deutsch Krone; additional contingents take the German Garrisons at Schneidemuehl and Posen. The Russians also proclaim capture of 45 city blocks in Budapest. **(Atlantic-Italy) 15th Army Group** In the **U.S. Fifth Army** area, **IV Corps** sector, the 92nd Division halts its attacks in the Cinquale Canal area; the bridgehead is withdrawn, and it also ceases the assault in the Serchio Valley.

U.S. troops on the advance in the Philippines.

February 12th 1945 — (Pacific-Philippines) In the **U.S. Sixth Army** area, **XIV Corps** sector, the 5th and 12th Cavalry Regiments converge on the western shores of Manila Bay, trampling the resistance at Nielson Field and isolating the remaining Japanese troops in Manila. The 188th Regiment and contingents of the 187th Regiment, 11th Airborne Division storm Nichols Field, eliminating the Japanese resistance there. Meanwhile, the 40th Division tramps forward, seizing Hill 6 and Snake Hill north with its 106th and 185th Regiments respectively. However, enemy resistance intercepting the center thrust of the Division is vicious and progress is tedious. In the **I Corps** sector At Highway 5, the 27th Regiment, 25th Division, which has relieved the 1st Infantry, 6th Division, begins to fortify its positions along the highway near San Jose. Meanwhile 6th Division forces deploy along the eastern coast, dividing the enemy units on the island. In the **XI Corps** sector, RCT I, 6th Division departs Dinalupihan heading for Bataan. **(Visayan Passage)** General Eichelberger issues plans covering Eighth Army participation in the seizure of Visayan Passage. **(Pacific-Burma)** In the **British Fourteenth Army** area, 33 Corps sector, the Indian 20th Division encounters feeble opposition as it fords the Irrawaddy, west of Mandalay, near Myinmu-Allagappa. **(Atlantic-Western Europe) 21st Army Group** In the **Canadian First Army** area, British 30th Corps sector, Kellen and Warbeyen fall to the Canadian 3rd Division; it subsequently assumes responsibility for Cleve, relieving the British 15th Division of that responsibility. The 15th encounters heavy resistance as it advances toward Calcar. The British 43rd Division overruns Bedburg as it advances toward Goch; however, soon after, the forward thrust is stopped when strong resistance develops along the Hau-Goch Road. At the Reichswald, the Germans attack the British 53rd Division on its eastern perimeter; however, the assault is repulsed and the Division continues to eliminate the resistance within its sector. Meanwhile, the 51st British Division advances through the southern part of the Reichswald and takes Heien, south of Gennep. **12th Army Group** In the **U.S. First Army** area, the Advance Headquarters of the **III Corps** transfers to Zweifall, Germany, where it assumes responsibility for the XVIII (Airborne) Corps zone; the XVIII Corps then takes over the 82nd Airborne Division's sector. In **V Corps** sector, regrouping occurs. In the **U.S. Third Army** area, **VIII Corps** sector, enemy resistance in Pruem ceases totally, culminating the 4th Division efforts successfully. The 41st Cavalry Reconnaissance Squadron (attached 6th Armored) closes against Knapschoscheid. The 6th Cavalry Group sweeps into Vianden, seizing the portion of town west of the Our River. In the **XII Corps** sector, the 5th and 80th Divisions establish contact at Bollendorf. Tanks and Tank Destroyer outfits roll into the 5th Division bridgehead and supplement the 10th Infantry, which seizes Bollendorf. **6th Army Group** In the **U.S. Seventh Army** area, **XV Corps** sector, the French 2nd Armored Division is attached to Corps. In the **VI Corps** sector, the Railroad station and factory at Oberhoffen, the last strongholds against the 36th Division, are set ablaze. **(Atlantic-Italy) 15th Army Group** In the **British Eighth Army's** 13th Corps sector, the Indian 10th Division takes over the British 78th Division sector. In Northern Italy, an O.S.S. detachment and Partisans under the American Officer Benucci and Sgt. Gangelosi, having transported explosives from their mountain hideaway attack a bridge which spans the Piave River at San Felice. The 300 foot 4 span structure standing midway between Belluno and San Felice is a primary German supply route. At 00:30, the Guards at the northern and southern approaches are eliminated. The Partisans then rush the bridge, set the charges and vanish as the bridge blows. The Germans send about 500 troops to capture the saboteurs. Benucci and another U.S. Officer, Chappell, meet at San Antonio, Italy, but Italian traitors expose their positions and the Germans close on them. Several escape but Chappell and two of his men are captured; they escape but are recaptured. Undaunted, Chappell breaks the neck of his guard and gets away, spending his time in hiding at San Antonio with another O.S.S. agent, Sgt. Eric Buckhardt (a medic-dropped later). Meanwhile, Benucci and two of his Sergeants are hibernating in the belfry of a Catholic church in the village of Mel, perched atop the noses of the German 20th Division; they remain in seclusion until the 31st of March when the Germans are ordered to depart Mel, and head for the Adriatic sector to reform with the 26th Panzer Grenadiers. As the Germans depart, Partisans and O.S.S. agents come out of hiding, killing many and blowing the enemy ammunition dumps in the area. One German Officer, Lt. Carl, an S.S. torturer is killed while attempting to escape. Subsequent to the close of hostilities, General Donovan decorates Sgt. Gionfriddo (Legion of Merit), Sgt. Nick Gangelosi (Bronze Star), Capt. Chappell (Silver Star), Corporal Silsby and Tech Sgt. Fabrega (released from German prison camps) are also decorated. In addition, Captain Hall receives the Legion of Merit posthumously.

February 13th 1945 — **(Pacific-Marianas-Tinian)** The final rehearsals for the invasion of Iwo Jima conclude. **(Pacific-Philippines) Luzon** In the **U.S. Sixth Army** area, **XIV Corps** sector, the remaining Japanese strongholds along the approaches to the Intramuros in Manila are being eliminated by the combined efforts of the 37th Infantry and 1st Cavalry Divisions. At Nichols Field, remnant enemy resistance is eliminated by the 11th Airborne. In other activity, Hill No. 7 is seized by the 108th Regiment, 40th Division; however, a counterattack regains it. In the **I Corps** sector, regrouping continues. In the **XI Corps** sector, the U.S. Navy initiates minesweeping operations off Corregidor in concert with a Naval gunfire bombardment to soften resistance against the imminent invasion. In other activity, the formidable Zig Zag Pass is secured by the 38th Division, except for one lingering position strung between the 149th and 152nd Regiments; it is totally reduced by the 15th. During the night, Motor Torpedo Boats probe Manila Bay, becoming the first U.S. Naval Vessels to enter the bay since May 1942. **(Pacific-Burma)** In the N.C.A.C. area, the 26th Brigade, 36th British Division continues to retain control of its Shweli bridgehead, despite mounting enemy pressure. In the **British Fourteenth Army** area, the Indian 20th Division enlarges its Irrawaddy bridgehead. In other activity, the Indian 7th Division fords the river near Nyaungu with the support of the East African 28th Brigade, which feints toward the Yenangyaung to divert attention. **(Atlantic-Western Europe) 21st Army Group** In the **Canadian First Army** area, British 30th Corps sector, the British 15th Division seizes Hasselt, while the British 43rd Division captures a heavily defended hill in the vicinity of Cleve Forest. Meanwhile, the British 53rd Division eliminates the final opposition in the Reichswald and meets contingents of the British 51st Division. The U.S. Ninth Army turns the 95th Division over to the operational control of the British 8th Corps. **12th Army Group** General Patton arrives at Bastogne. He and General Middleton depart for Bastogne, passing the remaining devastation of the initial Tank battle when the German Armor moved into the Ardennes. Patton counts more than 100 Vehicles and orders that every one of them be inspected

thoroughly to determine which type of armament had destroyed it and how it had been hit. The information is to be compiled to help the U.S. manufacture stronger Tanks. St. Vith has been so completely devastated that it is impassable; VIII Corps constructs a road to bypass it. In the **U.S. First Army** area, **III Corps** assumes responsibility of the XVIII Corps (Airborne) sector and with it operational control of the 82nd Airborne and the 1st and 78th Infantry Divisions in place. In addition, the 14th Cavalry Group is detached from the 1st Division and attached to III Corps. In other activity, contingents of the 78th Division occupy Blens. Meanwhile, Corps prepares for the attack across the Roer. The **XVIII Corps** (Airborne) Command Post ceases at Zweifall, Germany, and reopens at Epernay, France, where it begins to plan for Operation Varsity (Airborne drop east of the Rhine). In the **V Corps** sector, the 99th Division closes its assembly area in Belgium, as it is relieved by the 69th Division. In the **U.S. Third Army** area, the **VIII Corps** is involved with defensive operations along the Our and Pruem Rivers, which continue until February 18th. In the **XII Corps** sector, Ameldingen is taken by the 319th Regiment, 80th Division. Ferschweiler falls to the 10th Infantry, 5th Division, while the 11th Regiment drives to the entrance to Ernzen. In the **XX Corps** sector, activity is relatively tranquil; however, protective Patrols sweep the area. **6th Army Group** In the **U.S. Seventh Army** area, **VI Corps** sector, the bulging Moder and Rhine Rivers burst, inundating the area with flood waters, immobilizing the advance of the 36th Division; nevertheless, at Oberhoffen, RCT 142, 36th Division continues to retain possession. **(Eastern Europe)** The Soviet Forces take Budapest where the battered German defenders have kept them at Bay for about a month and a half. In German Silesia, the Red Army takes Glogau and Beuthen, as it closes the ring on Breslau. **(Italy) 15th Army Group** The **U.S. Fifth Army** releases the Indian 8th Division (Army Reserve) to the British Eighth Army.

U.S.S. Hornet's Pilots off Iwo Jima.

February 14th 1945 — **(Pacific Area)** Task Force 54 (Gunfire and Covering Force), commanded by Rear Admiral B.J. Rodgers, and Rear Admiral W.H.B. Blandy's Task Force 52 (Support Carrier Group of Amphibious Support Force) embark Saipan, heading toward Iwo Jima to launch pre-D-Day operations. The Iron-scribes of the Navy begin to implant autographs on the target; however, the Japanese ground forces, which number over 60,000, have been virtually living underground in caves, unscathed by the previous bombardments and those that are to come. They will have to be eliminated by ground forces of the 4th and 5th Marine Divisions, tunnel by tunnel and yard by yard. The volcanic island is considered an arm of Tokyo and its troops are ordered to defend to the death. **(Pacific-Java Sea)** The Submarine *Hawkbill* (SS-366) sinks two Japanese Submarine Chasers: Nos. 4 and 114. **(Pacific-Philippines)** The U.S. Motor Minesweeper YMS-48 is sunk and the Destroyers *Fletcher* (DD-445) and *Hopewell* (DD-681) are damaged by enemy coastal defense guns. In addition, the Destroyers *Radford* (DD-446) and *LaVallette* (DD-448) are damaged by mines. The damaging blows against the *Fletcher* send fragments directly into the No. 1 gun magazine. Watertender 1st Class Elmer C. Bigelow, with utter disregard for his life, dashes into the inferno without protective gear and begins to extinguish the flames before the entire Ship is aflame. The gallant Seaman succeeds in preventing further damage; however, he succumbs on the following day from breathing "acrid, burning powder smoke, which seared his lungs." Bigelow receives the Medal of Honor posthumously for his actions. **Luzon** In the **U.S. Sixth Army** area, **XIV Corps** sector, Japanese strongpoints in Manila refuse to capitulate. In the **I Corps** sector, elements of the 25th Division prepare to assault Balete Pass. In the **XI Corps** sector, the final confrontation is winding down in Zig Zag Pass as the 38th Division is eradicating the remnant defenders; it is totally secured on the following day. Meanwhile, Corps makes preparations to secure the Bataan Peninsula, a needed prize to ensure the reopening of Manila Bay. The East Force (RCT I. 6th Division) moves south along the eastern coast of the peninsula, advancing to Pilar, while the South Force (RCT 151, 38th Division) departs Subic Bay for Mariveles. **Leyte** In the **U.S. Eighth Army** area, **X Corps** sector, a Provisional Task Force, composed of contingents of the 1st Philippine Infantry and the 1st Battalion, 182nd Infantry, reinforced, is formed to secure the northwest coast of Samar and the islands in the San Bernardino Strait. **(Pacific-Yellow Sea)** The Submarine *Gato* (SS-212) destroys the Japanese Coast Defense Vessel No. 9. **(Atlantic-Western Europe) 21st Army Group** The 3rd Canadian Division seizes a village on the Rhine, across from Emmerich. The 51st Division takes Kessel during a night attack and is subsequently reinforced by the 32nd Guards Brigade, Guards Armored Division, which seizes Hommersum. Meanwhile, the British 43rd Division is heavily engaged near Cleve Forest, and north of Asperberg, and the Germans are mounting resistance against the 53rd Division in the heights. **12th Army Group** In the **U.S. Third Army** area, The Air Corps drops 103 Plane loads of supplies to the 4th and 87th Divisions. In the **XII Corps** fortifies its solid bridgehead, plowing through the West Wall and deploying to bolt to the Pruem River. The 317th Regiment, 80th Division is driving the Germans from the Bollendorf area, while the 5th Division's 11th Regiment seizes Ernzen; its efforts are supported by contingents of the 417th Regiment, 76th Division, which has been methodically eradicating pillboxes and seizing nearby hill positions. **6th Army Group** In the French 1st Army area, the **U. S. XXI Corps** sector detaches the 28th Division which is then attached to the Seventh Army. **(Eastern Europe)** In East Prussia, Schneidemuehl is seized by Soviet troops, and in German Silesia, the Red Army takes more ground around Liegnitz. **(Italy) 15th Army Group** In the **British Eighth Army** area, the Canadian 1st Corps British 6th Armored Division prepares to embark to the E.T.O.; it is replaced by the Cremona Group, an Italian contingent, which deploys on the right flank of the Corps.

February 15th 1945 — (Pacific-Philippines) Luzon In Manila, incessant fighting continues. The 40th Division is battling tenaciously in the hills, systematically eliminating the Japanese; the 185th Regiment takes Hill 1500, its final objective, while the 160th Regiment pounds against stiff resistance in the center of the Divisional thrust. Meanwhile, the 108th Regiment continues attacking to regain Hill 7. The **I Corps** takes over part of the XIV Corps sector (around Tarlac). The 126th Regiment, 32nd Division occupies San Manuel-Asingan-San Nicolas triangle, which frees the 127th Regiment to advance up the Villa Verde Trail. In the **XI Corps** sector, Admiral Struble's Task Force lands the South Force on the Mariveles harbor area without incident at 10:00. Admiral Struble relinquishes command to General Chase, subsequent to the landing. The Japanese launch what is their final organized attack on the east coast during the night; it fails. The Motor Minesweeper YMS-46 is damaged by enemy coastal gunfire. **(Pacific)** The U.S.S. *Swordfish* (SS-193), the Submarine which sank the *Atsutasan Maru* (Cargo Ship — Dec. 16th 1941), the first Japanese Vessel to be sunk by a U.S. Submarine, is reported lost. She had responded to orders on January 9th, but does not return to Saipan as expected. The Submarine, commanded by Commander K. E. Montross, may have been lost on January 12th, near Okinawa. **(Pacific-Burma)** In the **British Fourteenth Army** area, 33 Corps sector, the Japanese raise fierce opposition against the Indian 20th Division's attempts to enlarge its Irrawaddy bridgehead. Meanwhile, the 4th Corps' Indian 4th Division widens its bridgehead across the Irrawaddy, extending it to Pagan, while other contingents, still on the west bank of the river, overrun Pakokku. **(Atlantic-North Africa)** President Roosevelt, en route to the States from the conference in Yalta, arrives at Alexandria, Egypt; the President confers with Prime Minister Churchill, then departs on the U.S.S. *Quincy* for a stop in Algiers before returning to Washington. This is the last meeting between Churchill and Roosevelt. **(Atlantic-Western Europe) 21st Army Group** The **Canadian First Army** commits another Corps (2) to Operation VERITABLE. The 2nd Corps assumes responsibility for the left sector of the British 30th Corps front. The Canadian 3rd Division (attached to Corps) seizes Huisberden. The Corps will conduct limited attacks toward Calcar, its primary objective, (February 15th-25th) and then regroup to participate in a general assault. In the British 30th Corps sector, the Germans continue to mount resistance at Goch, Asperberg, and Asperden. **12th Army Group** In the **U.S. Third Army** area, **XII Corps** sector, the 80th Division continues to regroup. In the 5th Division zone, Patrols reach the Pruem River; other contingents close against Schankweiler. The 76th Division is still reducing pillboxes and securing the heights north of Minden. In the **XX Corps** sector, the 2nd Battalion, 302nd Regiment, 94th Division knocks out a few more pillboxes and entrenchments east of Campholz Woods; however, the enemy counterattacks during the night and regains them. **6th Army Group** The U.S. **Seventh Army's XV Corps** launches attacks to reduce enemy salients at Gros Rederching and at Wilferding in the 44th and 63rd Divisional zones, respectively; the action is intended to simultaneously tighten its front line. Rimling falls to the 71st Regiment, 40th Division, while the 114th Regiment overcomes stiff opposition at Bellevue Farm, then surges forward, seizing its objective lying beyond Bois de Blies Brucken, which is attacked by the 63rd Division's 255th Regiment. Meanwhile, to the left of the 44th Division, the U.S. 100th Division commences convincing diversionary strikes. In the **French 1st Army** area, the U.S. 3rd Division is attached to the

French 2nd Corps, being detached from the U.S. XXI Corps. **(Atlantic-Eastern Europe)** The First Ukrainian Front takes Gruenberg in northern Silesia and also moves into Brandenburg.

February 16th 1945 — (Pacific-Marianas) Joint Expeditionary Force (TF 51) embarks Saipan for Iwo Jima. **(Pacific-Iwo Jima)** Task Forces 52 and 54 appear off Iwo Jima. U.S. Naval Surface Vessels lambaste suspected enemy positions; however, Carriers are unable to launch a major attack because of inclement weather; only eight Planes are launched. Forty-two Land-based B-24 Liberator Bombers from the Marianas arrive and circle at 10,000 feet for one half hour, but poor visibility prevents attack; the Planes return to Base. Task Force 58 (Fast Carrier Force), operating under azure skies and good weather, bombards Japan with a cogent attack that destroys 37 buildings of the Nakajima Aircraft Company, less than fifty miles outside of Tokyo, in addition to knocking down 117 interceptor Planes. The Destroyers *Ingraham* (DD-694) and *Barton* (DD-722) are damaged by collision. In addition, other Naval Vessels begin sweeping the invasion lanes to clear mines. A Cruiser and Destroyer Task Force, commanded by Rear Admiral J. L. McCrea, bombards Japanese positions at Kurabu Zaki, Paramushiro, Kurile Islands. **(Pacific-Philippines)** The Submarine U *Barbel* (SS-316), commanded by Commander C.L. Raguet, is reported lost. On the 3rd, the *Barbel* informs the Submarine *Tuna* that she had survived three attacks by Japanese Planes, which had dropped depth charges and that she will update her condition on the following day, but the Ship is not heard from again. Later information shows that it is sunk on the 4th off Palawan. **Luzon** In the **U.S. Sixth Army** area, **XIV Corps** sector, Hill 7 is recaptured by the 108th Regiment, 40th Division. In the **XI Corps** sector, a thunderous Air and naval bombardment rocks Corregidor to soften resistance for the invasion. Upon cessation of the shelling, the Rock Force (503rd Regimental Combat Team and the 3rd Battalion, 34th Regiment, 24th Division, reinforced), launches the invasion; the 503rd Paratroop Regiment is dropped by Aircraft of the Fifth Air Force and floats to the ground at about 08:30 without difficulty, as the bombardment had thoroughly stunned the defenders. The 34th Infantry contingent makes an amphibious landing at about 10:30, and a beachhead is quickly established. Communication and contact between the Paratroopers and the Infantry is near effortless as the enemy has still not recovered from the shock. Japanese coastal defense guns sink the Submarine Chaser PC-1119. **(Pacific-Burma)** In the ALFSEA area, 15th Corps sector, with the assistance of Planes and Artillery which had been secretly deployed on a nearby island, the Indian 25th Division lands near Ru-ywa on the Arakan coast and will coordinate its efforts with the West African 82nd Division to seal off enemy escape routes from Pruem. In the **British Fourteenth Army's** 33rd Corps sector, the Japanese increase the pressure against the Indian 20th Division's bridge head at the Irrawaddy, and vicious fighting ensues for several days. **(Pacific-Japan)** The Submarine U.S.S. *Sennet* (SS-408) sinks the Minelayer *Nariu* off Shikoku. **(Atlantic-Western Europe) 21st Army Group** In the **Canadian First Army** area, British 30th Corps sector, the British 43rd Division advances toward the steep slopes above Goch; the British 53rd Division reaches Asperberg and finds the German calling card: a blown bridge. In conjunction, the British 51st Division seizes Asperden, and Afferden is taken during the night by the British 52nd Division. **12th Army Group** In the **U.S. Third Army** area, **XII Corps** sector, the 5th, 76th

and 80th Divisions each mount limited actions to strengthen their bridgehead perimeters. In the **XX Corps** sector, the 328th Regiment, 26th Division maintains its short distanced actions to fortify its bridgehead at Saarlautern. Meanwhile, the 94th Division regroups for an offensive. **6th Army Group** In the **U.S. Seventh Army** area, the 44th Division repulses successive counterattacks in its sector. The 63rd Division's ongoing attack ceases upon seizure of its objective and the successful straightening of the Gros Rederching line. In the **VI Corps** sector, the XXI Corps is detached from the French 1st Army and reverts back to Seventh Army. **(Atlantic-Eastern Europe)** German-held Breslau in Silesia is completely surrounded by Soviet forces. **(Atlantic-Italy) 15th Army Group** The **U.S. Fifth Army** orders its IV Corps to commence an attack on February 20th to strengthen its positions west of Highway 64. In the British Eighth Army area, British the 5th Corps assumes command of the Canadian 1st Division in place.

February 17th 1945 — (Pacific-Hawaii) Divers become trapped while working under a previously sunken LST (40 feet of water and 20 feet of mud) when steel wreckage collapses. Instinctively, Owen Francis Patrick Hammerberg dives into the blackened waters and works tirelessly for several hours, freeing the first man. Exhausted, but determined, he continues to work to free the other Seaman until another cave-in occurs and traps him. The full impact of the wreckage is upon Hammerberg, which saves the other man; Hammerberg remains trapped for eighteen hours before succumbing, but the other man is saved. Hammerberg receives the Medal of Honor posthumously. **(Pacific-Japan-Formosa)** Carrier Planes attached to Task Force 58 again bombards Tokyo in support of the Iwo Jima invasion operation. Army Planes sink the Japanese Transport No. 114, off Formosa. Meanwhile, the Submarine *Bowfin* (SS-287) sinks the Japanese Coast Defense Vessel No. 56, off Honshu, Japan. **(Pacific-Iwo Jima)** At 08:40, the Battleships *Nevada*, *Tennessee*, and *Idaho* launch a carpet bombardment of Chidori Airfield and its escarpments, while the Heavy Cruiser *Pensacola*, standing about 750 yards offshore, sizzles the slopes of Mt. Suribachi. Meanwhile, twelve wooden hulled Minesweepers, equipped with rockets, race back and forth scooping up anything which might impede the invasion. In conjunction, twelve Gunboats and three Destroyers close in on the beach and deliver an acrimonious shelling which scorches the landing areas and further pockets the desolate landscape. Iwo Jima's Commanding Officer, General Kuribayashi, peers ambivalently at the massive show of force and focuses on the approaching Gunboats which are merely transporting the Navy and Marine Frogmen, who are to clear the landing areas of demolitions. Each Vessel carries about fifty-man crews and about 100 Frogmen. Kuribayashi decides it is the long anticipated invasion and orders his force to open fire as the Gunboats reach positions about 250 yards from shore, breaking his abstinence of fire. The Japanese retaliation tears the area asunder. Enemy fire rips into the Gunboats as the underwater teams swim through the frigid waters toward the beach, oblivious to the raging battle: the 457 is sinking; 471's engine is knocked out; 459 and 467 are ablaze, but get towed to safety; and 473 is afire, having sustained 200 hits. In addition, the Jap guns have severed the bow gun of the 438. Also, the 449 takes grievous casualties; its Commanding Officer, Commander Rufus H. Herring, receives the Medal of Honor for his actions during the battle. The Vessels receive smoke cover and withdraw; the ordeal costs 43 crewmen killed and 153 wounded. Meanwhile, the Frogmen come up for air and are greeted by a cyclone of machine gun fire. Undaunted, they dodge the gunfire and attend to their tasks, including placing a bumptious sign on the beach which reads: "WELCOME TO IWO JIMA."

The U.S.S. *Pensacola* attempts retrieval of Frogmen and receives six hits within three minutes of blistering fire which kills the Commanding Officer Austin C. Behan and seventeen other men. An additional 127 men are killed aboard the *Kingfisher* when ammunition explodes. Admiral Blandy's Armada had joined the ongoing fight, and Aircraft from the *Wake Island*, *Lunga Point*, and *Bismarck Sea* rush to the area and unleash a doughty low level attack to enunciate the intent of the Fleet. In addition, the island is struck by B-24 Liberators from the Marianas. The U.S. Fleet moves over the horizon at 18:21, culminating the day's action. Upon checking reconnaissance photographs of the island, it is determined that seventeen of the 20 blockhouses still stand on the beachhead and that almost all pillboxes on the beach remain unscathed. The photographs also disclose that the dug-in Artillery and Naval guns on the slopes of Suribachi remain operational.

General Kuribayashi radios Tokyo, informing it that his forces had repulsed the invaders, but cautions that they will return. He is unaware that the invaders had been Frogmen, clad in swimming trunks and sneaks and had only been armed with small knives. Tokyo broadcasts that the Garrison on Iwo Jima had intercepted the troops on the beach and "REPELLED THEM INTO THE SEA." There had been no mention of the humorous sign installed on the beachhead. The Battleship *Tennessee* (BB-43), the Heavy Cruiser *Pensacola* (CA-24), and the Destroyer *Leutze* (DD-481) sustain damage. In addition, the Destroyer *Dortch* (DD-670) is damaged by strafing; the Destroyer *Waldron* sustains damage by intentionally ramming a Japanese picket Boat. **(Pacific-Philippines) Luzon** In the **U.S. Sixth Army** area, the **XIV Corps** commences a concentrated fire upon enemy positions in Manila. The 6th Division (less RCT I) is attached to the XIV Corps and ordered to participate in an attack to secure the ground east of Manila to guarantee the safety of the capital. In the **I Corps** sector, RCT 169 receives responsibility for defending the western part of the Central Plain north of the Tarlac-Palauig line and west of the Agno River. In the **XI Corps** sector, the East Force, reinforced, drives west along the Pilar-Bagac Road, crossing Bataan without incident. Meanwhile, the South Force is driving north, while the Rock Force is systematically reducing opposition on Corregidor. The Tug *Hidatsa* (ATF-102) is damaged by mines. **Mindoro** The U.S. Eighth Army activates the Palawan Task Force (186th Regiment, 41st Division, reinforced), commanded by Brigadier General Harold Haney; its mission is to assault Palawan (Operation Victor III) on February 28th. In addition, the 41st Division is also instructed to secure the Zamboanga Peninsula on Mindoro and to commence that assault on March 10th. **(Pacific-Burma)** In the ALFSEA area, 15th Corps sector, the Indian 25th Division extends its bridgehead on the Arakan coast to Ru-ywa village. In the N.C.A.C. area, the Japanese continue to strike against the bridgehead, held by the British 36th Division on the Shweli River; however, although the defenders can only be resupplied by air, the bridgehead holds. **(Pacific-China)** General Wedemeyer informs Chiang Kai-shek that the Japanese might attempt to seize the Airfields at Chihchiang, Hsian, and Laohokon. The only Airfield in east China still held by the U.S. Fourteenth Air Force is Changting. **(Atlantic-Western Europe) 21st Army Group** In the **Canadian First Army** area, the British 30th Corps, utilizing its British 43rd, 51st and 53rd Divisions, converges on Goch. In conjunction, contingents of

the Guards' Armored Division secure Hassum to the west. In other activity, the U.S. 79th Divisions attached to the U.S. Ninth Army and placed under the operational command of the British Second Army. **12th Army Group** In the **U.S. Third Army** area, the XII Corps initiates limited actions to increase and consolidate the Our-Sauer bridgehead. In the **XX Corps** sector, the 328th Regiment, 26th Division, engages the Japanese at the Saarlautern bridge head. **6th Army Group** In the **U.S. Seventh Army** area, the **XV Corps** continues to straighten and shorten its line; the 276th Regiment, 70th Division encounters fierce resistance and is unable to seize Oeting, but it secures the heights which command the town. Behren and Kerbach are overpowered by the 274th Regiment, and the 275th is driving toward Grosbliederstroff and Lixing. The 63rd Division advances northward toward the woods beyond Auersmacher; its 253rd Regiment gains fragile hold in the town. In the 44th Division sector, counterattacks are thrown back. In addition, the 100th Division ignites diversionary raids, while protecting the right flank of the Corps.

U.S. Carrier Planes ready for take off during high seas off Iwo Jima.

February 18th 1945 — (Pacific-Iwo Jima) The U.S. pre-invasion bombardment of the island continues and special emphasis is given to the landing beach area when the guns of the Battleships *Tennessee, Idaho, Nevada* and *New York* bellow at 07:45, and continue for five hours. Cruisers and Destroyers also bombard the island and are joined by Aircraft however, heavy rain squalls impede the Air raid, confining it to 28 sorties; the napalm fails to explode. B-24s from the Marianas have difficulty locating the islands because of severe cloud cover and return without releasing any bombs. When the cease fire terminates at 18:21, the Fleet has ample ammunition for additional strikes, but Admiral Blandy informs Admiral Turner that the invasion should go as ordered. Marine Lt. Colonel Donald M. Weller suggests a 24-hour delay, but to no avail. The island absorbs tremendous shock; however, the primary forces are entrenched well into caves and tunnels and sustain no substantial losses. Major General Holland (Howlin) H. M. Smith had requested ten days bombardment for his Marines and gets three. Admiral Turner tells the press that Iwo " IS AS WELL-DEFENDED A FIXED POSITION, PARTICULARLY AN ISLAND POSITION, AS EXISTS IN THE WORLD TODAY. WE EXPECT LOSSES OF SHIPS AND MEN... HOWEVER, WE EXPECT TO TAKE THE POSITION." General Smith, V Corps Commander, simply nods in agreement, aware that victory is a congenital trait of the Marines. In addition, Secretary of the Navy James Forrestal, aboard to see the invasion first hand, adds: "MY HAT IS OFF TO THE MARINES." The Light Minesweeper *Gamble* (DM-15) and the High Speed Transport *Blessman* (APD-48) are damaged by Horizontal Bombers. The *Blessman* is one of the Vessels boarding Frogmen and upon being struck, two Frogmen are killed and twenty injured. Eleven crewmen also sustain injuries. The Plane had been shot from the sky, but its bomb struck. **(Pacific-Japan)** Task Force 58, operating off Japan, encounters inclement weather which forces abandonment of its Air attacks; it embarks for Iwo Jima to supplement the invasion forces. Admiral Nimitz, accompanying the Fifth Fleet, reports on the past several days' progress that 332 enemy Planes had been shot down and 117 were destroyed on the ground. He also states that the raids inflicted damages to many buildings and small Merchant Ships as well as leaving a small Carrier burning. The U.S. loses 49 Planes and saves nine Pilots. **(Pacific-Philippines) Luzon** In the **U.S. Sixth Army** area, **XIV Corps** sector, Artillery continues to pound the Intramuros in Manila, while simultaneous activity is wedging forward clearing the approaches for an assault. In the **I Corps** sector, the 35th Regiment discovers Pantanbangan abandoned. In other activity, the South Force encounters the East Force at Limay on Bataan. Meanwhile, the Rock Force is still involved with its clearing operation on Corregidor. Pvt. Lloyd G. McCarter, 503rd Parachute Infantry Battalion, singlehandedly wipes out six snipers. Later in the day, he takes the point and singlehandedly repulses counterattacks throughout the night, although by 02:00 all the men nearby have been wounded. McCarter is forced to return to U.S. lines for more ammunition several times, and after his Submachine gun becomes inoperable, he confiscates an automatic rifle; however it overheats and he is compelled to use a rifle. At dawn, another counterattack is launched; McCarter, although seriously wounded, stands and continues firing against the attackers until the Americans attack. His actions kill more than 30 of the enemy and contribute tremendously to the capture of Corregidor. **(Atlantic-Western Europe) 21st Army Group** Goch comes under attack by the British 30th Corps; the British 51st penetrates the northwestern part of the town, while the 15th British 15th Division advances to the northern fringes of it, and the 43rd Division advances toward it from the east. **12th Army Group** The 82nd Airborne, relieved by the 9th Division, prepares to depart its positions near Walheim, Germany and head for Reims, France. In the **U.S. Third Army** area, **VIII Corps** passes through the XII Corps lines and strikes the West Wall defenses near Pruem, hitting the Germans by surprise by attacking during early morning without Artillery fire sending an alarm; contingents of the 11th Armored and 90th Divisions stampede over numerous obstacles including pillboxes. The 358th Regiment, 90th Division takes a strategic hill near Pronsfeld, while Kesfeld falls to the 359th. Meanwhile, C.C.R., 11th Armored seizes Leidenborn and Grosskampenberg. The 4th Division mounts several diversionary strikes to assist the attack of the 90th Division. In other Corps activity, the 6th Cavalry Group scoops up a small bridgehead on the Our River, between Biewels and Gemund. In the **XII Corps** sector, the Germans can mount only sporadic resistance as Corps advances toward the Pruem; the 318th Regiment, 80th Division tramples Cruchten and attacks toward Hommerdingen. The 317th Infantry captures Stockigt and streams toward Nusbaum. The 319th Regiment anchors the 80th Division at the West Wall defenses where it keeps the Germans positioned there in check. In the 5th Division sector, troops ford the Enz River and advance to the west bank of the Pruem; Schankweiler capitulates to the 2nd Regiment, while

the 11th Regiment concentrates on reducing resistance on the west bank of the river. In the XX Corps sector, the 26th Division's 328th Regiment continues to tighten its lines; however, it is obliged to repulse several counterattacks against its positions at the Saarlautern bridgehead. **6th Army Group** In the **U.S. Seventh Army** area, **XV Corps** sector, Oeting, Etzling, Grosbliederstroff and Lixing fall to the advancing 70th Division. The Germans, however, mount a successful counterattack against the 63rd Division's 253rd Regiment and recapture Auersmacher. In other activity, the **XXI Corps** finalizes its movement to the Morhange area, and in the **VI Corps** sector, the 45th Division reverts to Army reserve. **(Atlantic-Italy) 15th Army Group** In the **U.S. Fifth Army** area, the 1st Battalion, 86th Regiment, 10th Mountain Division initiates preattack activities and begins to scale the treacherous Sarasiccia-Campania cliff to secure more formidable positions west of Highway 64, to ease the pressure on the primary assault against M. Belvedere and M. Castello; the raid commences at 19:30 and gains immediate surprise, seizing its objectives during the night. Meanwhile, the primary attack force moves with discretion to a Base at Belvedere-Gorgolesco.

Canine Patrol in the Pacific; the Army and Marines use the dogs for messengers as well as guard-attack dogs.

February 19th 1945 — (Pacific) THE INVASION OF IWO JIMA — At 03:00, reveille sounds "wake up" throughout the restless Transports. Groggy-eyed Marines are rousted from their improvised bunks in a flurry, and they instinctively are ready for the landing. The seas, unruly at midnight, become calm as the Armada maneuvers for the operation commencement. Warships deploy for pre-invasion and cover-fire positions while the Carriers prepare to launch Aircraft. Landing Craft personnel finalize last minute details, while Marines are treated to the customary pre-invasion meal: steak. The 3rd, 4th, and 5th Marine Divisions have been delegated to seize this annex of hell, and it is the Marines which must attack into the eyes of the volcanic devil. The island's eastern beach sectors, from south to north, are designated Green, Red 1, and Red 2, assigned to the 5th Division, and Yellow 1, Yellow 2, Blue 1, and Blue 2, which will be invaded by the 4th Division. The landing zones stretch about 3,000 yards, not nearly large enough to consume three Divisions; the 3rd awaits offshore.

The Japanese have been steadily reinforcing Iwo Jima for over twenty years; however, it has become a high priority since the fall of Saipan during July 1944. The endeavor has transformed the once obscure eight-square mile volcanic island into a near invincible fortress under command of the adept Lt. General Kuribayashi, known as a "tiger hearted" leader. He has trained as a Cavalry Officer in the U.S. at Fort Bliss, Texas, and speaks fluent English. The island, a mere 700 miles from Tokyo, contains no harbors or fresh water sources; however, its two operational Airfields and a third under construction mandate its seizure to afford the U.S. a Base from which Fighters can fly escort missions to safeguard Bombers which attack Japan. In addition, it is imperative to gain the Bombers a refueling stop on the return flights from Japan.

Iwo Jima, about two miles wide and five miles long, stands as a bulwark and contains the ominous Mt. Suribachi to the south which extends well over five hundred feet above the beaches; to the north is the treacherous Motoyama Plateau, guarded on both sides by ridges which plummet abruptly to the sea. The island is inundated with intertwining caves and tunnels, which conceal the majority of the 23,000 defenders, who, to the man, have sworn "to fight to the death." In addition, the island citadel has its awesome guns well hidden and deeply entrenched. The Tanks are stationary, buried right up to their turrets, which protrude just above the ground, and the big Naval Guns also are capably concealed. Innumerable machine guns and mortars further bolster the defenses. Layers of lethal firepower mirror the island and are capable of strafing every square yard of it. Solid blockhouses and pillboxes adorn the dismal island, guaranteeing a gruesome struggle.

General Kuribayashi realizes that the Americans control the Air and the Sea, ensuring no reinforcements will arrive, and he has concluded that his troops can fare better by retaining their commanding positions and refraining from Banzai attacks. The landing will be unopposed by Infantry. The Yanks are to be drawn slightly inland to isolate the beachhead, while Artillery destroys all incoming Craft and annihilates the invasion force. The Japanese are prepared; however, the primary question remains: Will the invasion force strike the east or west beaches?

The Invasion of Iwo Jima.

General Holland M. Smith, U.S.M.C. and Secretary of the Navy James V. Forrestal observing the invasion of Iwo Jima.

Iwo Jima.

IWO JIMA

Contour interval 100 feet

1000   0   1000
YARDS

At 06:30, Admiral Turner gives the cue: "LAND THE LANDING FORCE." Within minutes, Heavy Guns of over 70 Capital Ships fire in unison, delivering another deluge upon the already scarred landscape. Roaring 16-inch shells of the Battlewagons pound the slopes of Suribachi, quivering the ground. Nine Gunboats move to within 250 yards of the beachhead and unleash nearly nine thousand scorching rockets within one half hour. Troops offshore wonder aloud how anyone could survive such a copious bombardment; however, the enemy is so deeply entrenched in caves that they are unscathed, except for being stunned.

At 08:05, the awesome Armada of floating thunderclap relents, subsequent to delivering a more powerful fusillade than that which was expended at Normandy during June of 1944. One Sailor aboard the Heavy Cruiser *Salt Lake City*, Francis Early, of Glenside Pa., related that the tracer fire was so intense and bright that anyone on deck "could easily read a newspaper at anytime during the night-bombardments." Upon cessation of the Naval guns, about 120 Navy Corsairs and Hellcats soar overhead and unleash murderous fire upon the landing area and nearby terraces, then swerve toward the northern hills and back over Suribachi, delivering more killing fire, exhibiting a dazzling display of Airpower. As the Naval Pilots turn toward their Carriers, 48 Marine Corsairs, circling at 5,000 feet, dive against the landing zones under orders to "scrape the beach with their bellies." The Pilots oblige, flying at tree-top level to saturate the beachhead with more shells. In addition, fifteen B-24s from the Marianas arrive over the island; however, cloud cover obscures their target and only thirty-six bombs are dropped. By 08:25, all Planes have vanished and again the Navy commences firing, plastering the island with another earth-shaking bombardment.

At 09:00, over 65 Amtracs initiate the 4,000 yard dash to the beach, transporting three machine gun crews and one 75 m.m. Howitzer crew each. Their mission is to seize the beachhead and hold it for the 8,000 Infantry troops, which are trailing close behind in six waves, at five-minute intervals. Higgins Boats dove-tail and transport additional troops, designated for holding and expanding the beachhead. The Landing Craft close upon the beaches with the words of V Corps Commander Schmidt ringing in their ears: "HERETOFORE IT HAS ALWAYS BEEN OUR POLICY TO GRAB THE MONKEY BY THE TAIL AND HANG ON. NOW WE'RE CUTTING THE MONKEY'S TAIL OFF."

Japanese peer intently, but their heavy guns remain silent, waiting to spring the ambush, while the advance waves strike the beach against light opposition at about 09:05 and begin a nightmarish advance. As they move forward, their feet sink deeply into the sand. The black ash envelops Vehicles, bogging them down and creating an instant quagmire, which surely invites slaughter. Suddenly, the ongoing crackle of machine gun fire is joined by incoming mortars and an onslaught of heavy Artillery fire, which consumes the entire exposed beachhead in an attempt to exterminate the invasion force. Attempts to dig fox holes are futile, as the sand simply caves in. Stranded Landing Craft attempt to break for the water, from where their guns can aid the Marines, while Higgins Boats simultaneously attempt to land. Withering fire sinks several Craft, with their cargoes of Tanks and Trucks, further congesting the landing approaches. Burning Vessels create a traffic jam in the water. The sting of death hovers above the din of battle; however, there is no disillusionment on the beach. The besieged Marines, noted for their ability to

improvise and endure, stare in stark horror as their ranks are unmercifully decimated, but there is no despair. Instead, the aroma of victory permeates the stench of death and forges a more galvanized beachhead.

Marines landing on Iwo Jima.

Enemy fire pins Marines on the Iwo Jima beachhead.

Marine flamethrowers on Iwo Jima.

Surprisingly, the Japanese still withhold the counterattack, affording the Yanks one hour to land about 6,000 men, a few Tanks, Artillery units and some Seabees with their bulldozers, a luxury that the Japanese would soon regret. Although the situation is grave, a bulldog posture evolves spontaneously as the legendary Esprit de Corps asserts itself and the irreversible course is set; advance! Amidst whizzing bullets, whining mortars, and crashing Artillery shells, the Marines attempt to drive inland. Walls of fire, originating from an invisible enemy, slice further into their ranks. Cries of anguish are everywhere, including some garbled ones, coming from beneath the ash, as men are buried under the crushing blows of the devastating fire. Others bleed to death slowly, as menacing grid-fire prevents any aid from reaching them.

Undaunted, despite the incessant fire, other Marines daringly inch forward through deadly minefields. The carnage is horrendous. Some men collapse, minus arms or legs, others have portions of their faces ripped off and yet others are blown to oblivion; however, the breakout attempt continues to gnaw toward Suribachi and Airfield No. 1. By 10:45, the 25th Marines, operating on Blue beaches 1 and 2, are tightly pinned down about 200 yards from the Quarry, and the 23rd Marines are sprawled nakedly on the terraces in front of Airport No. 1, pinned by a blistering enfilade. In the southern portion of the crammed beachhead, the 27th Marines are halted by an avalanche of impregnable fire and in desperate need of Tanks to alleviate the monstrous pressure. Meanwhile, the 28th Marines slug their way across most of the island's neck toward Suribachi; however, this too, is abruptly halted by a hurricane of fire. Its 1st Battalion continues to press forward, but is stopped by 12:00; during this struggle, Corporal Tony Stein, 1st Battalion, singlehandedly assaults enemy pillboxes, taking out twenty enemy troops. He also makes eight trips back to the beach for additional ammunition and tends many of the wounded. Stein becomes a recipient of the Medal of Honor for his extraordinary courage.

Admiral Turner orders the beaches closed for several hours at 13:00 and moves up Warships to blast pinpointed enemy strongholds from point blank range. By 15:00, six Tanks, attached to the 5th Division, and the 1st Battalion, 26th Marines come ashore: two Tanks are lost and the Infantry takes high casualties. Still, the enemy remains mysteriously concealed; however, fire seems to emanate from behind every rock and from within every rancid hole as if the earth has become Satan's nefarious apprentice. The Marines react extemporaneously with countless individual acts of courage, which become the hallmark of the campaign on this island of gore. Casualty lists spiral and include an exorbitant amount of dead and seriously wounded Officers and NCOs, as the day's fury winds down. At 17:00, General Hermlie, assistant Commander, 5th Marine Division orders the troops to consolidate and brace for the usual frenzied night counterattack. Sunset arrives at 18:45 and the temperatures begin to dip toward 40 degrees, a far cry from the tropical temperatures of the Solomons.

Droll humor, always evident on a battlefield, is abundant throughout the day's struggles and continues for the duration. There is the story about the Marines who goad some Japs in a strongpoint, prompting one to come out and angrily set up a gun, while a Marine quips that the Jap has no sense of humor, as yet another Marine peels off a few rounds and ends his frustration with a killing blow. In another of the unending stories, a Marine requests permission from a frugal Officer to have a Flamethrower wipe out a Jap in a nearby pillbox. The Officer, aware of the acute shortages of ammunition and supplies, wants confirmation of the threat and asks: "HOW DO YOU KNOW THERE IS A JAP IN THERE," and receives the response: "BECAUSE I THREW IN A GRENADE AND HE THREW IT BACK OUT." Another Marine quips to a buddy: "ARE YOU STILL AN ATHEIST? and receives the response: "I'M GOING TO START PRAYING IN THE MORNING." Last, but not least, is the entrepreneur's beachhead sign which boasts, "Lots for Sale," emphasizing their ocean view and nightly

fireworks displays. With a note of sardonic wit, the advertisement closes with "Available for U.S. Army personnel soon," with the addendum (We Hope).

On Iwo Jima, a near-buried Marine catches a drag on a cigarette.

Morning arrives, but the counterattack remains dormant, like the nearby towering volcano. Marines reinitiate the grueling advance, blowing pillboxes and blockhouses and sealing cave entrances. Tanks and vulnerable Flame-throwers work tirelessly. Elements of the 4th Division overrun Airfield No. 1, and the 5th Division, bolstered by Naval Surface fire and flame-throwing Tanks, presses its dogged advance against Suribachi. At the Airfield, the Marines spot some Japs who snap off a few rounds, then disappear mysteriously. Soon after, they reappear on the other side of the Airfield by dashing through storm pipes, which run under the field. The scheme is discovered and the pests are eliminated. Meanwhile, the Seabees, which had landed with the 4th Division, immediately begin to bulldoze the rubble of the skeleton Jap Planes and renovate the cratered surface to provide access for U.S. Aircraft. The gallant Seabees, much older than the average Fighting man on the island, achieve a rating of excellence on this their first invasion, despite sustaining heavy casualties. Their resolve and dedication is outstanding.

On the 21st, elements of the 4th Division attack toward Airfield No. 2, and the 5th Division continues to assault the Japs around Suribachi; however, the ferocious resistance limits both the northern and southern assaults to slow and costly progress. Meanwhile, a few Kamikazes penetrate the Air defenses, sink the Escort Carrier *Bismarck Sea*, and damage the

Escort Carrier *Lunga Point* and the Carrier *Saratoga*. In addition, the Suicide Planes damage several LSTs and a Cargo Vessel. During the night of the 21st, the Japanese mount several disciplined counterattacks; however, all are thwarted.

On the 22nd, the northern assault receives heavy support from Naval Surface guns and Artillery to bolster its attack against Airfield No. 2, but the heights between it and Airfield No. 1 are staunchly defended and pour incessant fire, halting its progress; RCT 21, 3rd Marine Division continues to press, but it is forced to pull back. Meanwhile, in the southern portion of the embattled island, the 3rd Battalion, 28th Marines surges forward and has Suribachi nearly surrounded. Subsequently, it is encircled when the 27th and 28th Marines establish contact. Heavy fighting continues throughout the day and during the night, the Japanese mount counterattacks, which again are repelled by the Marines.

The quest to vanquish Mt. Suribachi begins early on the 23rd. Just after sunrise, Patrols are dispatched to search for the enemy. Around 08:00, 2nd Lt. G. Greeley Wells, at the command post, is able to empty his map case, in which he has been carrying a Flag since the departure from Guam, one which he received from the Transport *Missoula*. A forty-man Patrol, under Lt. Harold G. Schrier, Co. E., is ordered by Lt. Col. Chandler W. Johnson to conspicuously place the Colors on the crest of Mt. Suribachi. The "word" spreads among the troops on the ground and throughout the Fleet offshore. Eyes strain with every cautious step, during the ascent. Nearby Ships use binoculars and the rear guard is kept informed by signals. Some caves and abandoned weapons are discovered; however, there is no sign of the Japs as the Patrol climbs. Another detachment composed of four men, approaching from the opposite side, also advances without incident. The Patrol takes its last strides and holds the summit, while anxious hearts pound excitedly across the island. The troops fan out and secure a section of Japanese pipe which is used as a staff for the Stars and Stripes, and she is prepared for her next appointment with destiny.

At 10:31, the Marines below shout: "THERE GOES THE FLAG," as the improvised staff, with Old Glory affixed, is lunged into the ground by three Marines. The stirring activity spontaneously causes epidemic chills to spread through the spines of the Marines and the Sailors offshore. Lumps gather in throats when the Stars and Stripes springs briskly into the sky, atop the newest outpost in the Western Pacific and crackles commandingly in the breeze. The balance of the Patrol scours the crest for the elusive enemy. Suddenly, two men, one with grenades and the other brandishing a sword, bolt from a cave. The sharpshooters quickly riddle them with shells. A brief and lopsided firefight erupts, as two Marines secure the Stars and Stripes, while the others charge the cave and eliminate any further threat. Sure-handed Flamethrowing troops join in and scorch the caves in response to tossed grenades, incinerating the entrances. Coincidentally, Secretary of the Navy James Forrestal and Major General Holland Smith had observed the spectacular Flag raising from the beach. During the unfurling, which was the first of two such occasions on the volcano this morning, Tech. Sgt. Louis R. Lowery had caught the action on film; however, when the Japs darted from their cave, he had rolled to avoid a grenade and slid about 50' down the slope, culminating the fall with a broken camera: the film was saved. Subsequently, a twelve-man Patrol, led by Sgt. Ernest L. Thomas, probes a cave and discovers about 150 dead Japs, most having died by clenching a grenade next to their stomachs; it is permanently sealed.

Mt. Suribachi — There She Goes!

The first raising of Old Glory on Mt. Suribachi: Sgt. H.O. Hansen, Sgt. E.I. Thomas and 1st Lt. H.B. Shrier support the staff while PFC J.R. Michaels is at the ready with his Carbine. Cpl. C.W. Lindberg stands to the right.

Lt. Col. Johnson, concerned that his Battalion will lose its ceremonial Flag, moves to get it back. Another, much larger Flag is taken up as a replacement. The giant Flag is hoisted as Lt. Well's historic banner is simultaneously brought down. Two Marine photographers, Sgt. William Genaust, using color movie film, and Pvt. Robert Campbell, equipped with black and white still film, are along for the 2nd raising, as well as Joe Rosenthal, a civilian war photographer for Associated Press. Genaust is killed within a few days and never sees his footage, which is shown across the world without giving him credit. Both Lowery and Campbell receive little attention for their shots, as the fortuitous photograph taken by Rosenthal receives worldwide publicity and goes on to become one of the most famous shots ever taken of Old Glory. The 28th Regiment, oblivious to its new found fame, resumes the war, initiating the mop up of Suribachi. Since D-Day, it has sustained almost 900 casualties.

By the end of the 25th, the 3rd and 4th Divisions control most of Airfield No. 2, and the remainder of it is overrun by RCT 9, 3rd Division on the following day. The Combat Team also secures the nearby heights. The 3rd Division reduces Motoyama village on the 28th, after another bloody contest. Hill 326A, a superbly fortified cross-island defense base, and the obstinate Hill 882 fall by March 2nd. The 3rd Division grinds forward and seizes Airfield No. 3, on March 3rd. Meanwhile, vicious fighting continues east of the Motoyama Plateau, where determined attacks force the collapse of resistance on Hills 357 and 362B.

On March 4th, the situation brightens even more, despite the gruesome fighting, when the 1st crippled B-29 arrives on the island. The drudgery of eliminating the strongpoints one by one does not deter the Yanks, who prepare to batter and demolish the last Japanese line of defense. On the 6th, contingents of the 3rd, 4th, and 5th Divisions drive east and northeast to accomplish the mission. Tanks, Bazookas, and Flamethrowers accompany the Infantry in a yard-by-yard advance. One by one the tenacious obstacles fall, but the price of the real estate remains high. A fierce counterattack is mounted against the 4th Division's positions on the 8th-9th; however, it is convincingly thrown back. The rigid resistance continues unrelenting; however, by the ninth, Patrols of the 3rd Marine Division grind to the northeast coast.

On the 10th, the 3rd Division uproots and destroys the resistance in its sector, except for one pocket remaining in the 9th Marines' zone and some sporadic opposition in the nearby cliffs. Meanwhile, the heavily defended Amphitheater (Turkey Knob) gets roasted by the 4th Division. By the following day, the full thrust of the Marines is committed to open the final phase of the campaign; the 5th Division drives north in conjunction with the 3rd and 4th Divisions, which press toward the east coast.

By the 14th, the conclusion of the campaign is inevitable. The Colors are officially raised, synchronized with the striking of the Colors on Suribachi, proclaiming control of the Volcano Islands. Marine Lt. General Holland M. Smith departs for Guam. The Japs are being systematically eliminated, but those still alive have not lost their fervor. Cushman's Pocket, another stronghold, is eradicated on the 16th by the 9th Marines, 3rd Division, further diminishing the Japanese forces. The indefatigable 3rd Division presses toward Kitano's Point. Meanwhile, RCT 25, 4th Marine Division streaks to the east coast. The powerful juggernaut terminates resistance in both the 3rd and 4th Division sectors; the bloodied island is declared secure. The 147th Infantry Regiment, U.S.A., arrives on the 20th to assume responsibility for the island: it is attached to the 3rd Marine Division, which remains behind to assist the Army forces, while the 4th and 5th Marine Divisions reembark.

On the 20th, in a last futile effort, between 200-300 Bandana-attired Japs mount a Banzai attack against the Army and Marine bivouac areas, but the assault troops are quickly intercepted and destroyed by the VII Fighter Command, U.S.A., and the 5th Pioneer Battalion. The frustrated Japanese die a swift death for their Emperor. Meanwhile, General Chaney, U.S.A., assumes command of the island.

The 23,000 defenders had been nearly annihilated, but the U.S. also sustains heavy casualties. Two hundred and seventy-five Officers are killed, 60 dying of their wounds, and 6,610 Enlisted men die, 1,271 succumbing to wounds. Eight hundred and twenty-six Officers and 16,466 Enlisted men are wounded. In addition, three Officers and 43 Enlisted men are missing in action and presumed dead. The figures do not include the many Navy casualties. For their efforts, about 2,400 crippled Planes will touch down on Iwo Jima and about 25,000 Airmen will be saved. In addition, more will be saved by the ability of Fighters to fly escort missions. History will debate the cost and necessity for centuries; however, the men who took the island did it because they were ordered to seize it. Admiral Nimitz sums up the battle and its young warriors by stating: "UNCOMMON VALOR WAS A COMMON VIRTUE."

Dead and wounded Marines on Iwo Jima.

Dead Japanese on Iwo Jima.

A 5th Marine Cemetery on Iwo Jima.

609

February 19th 1945 — (Pacific-Iwo Jima) ALSO SEE FEBRUARY 19TH 1945, INVASION OF IWO JIMA. In one instance during the savage fighting, menacing Japanese fire holds up a section of Company B, 1st Battalion, 23rd Marines, 4th Marine Division. Sergeant Darrell S. Cole leads his Squad toward Airfield No. 1, against a wall of fire. Cole eliminates two enemy positions with hand grenades and advances further, encountering three enemy pillboxes. He deploys his one remaining machine gun and knocks out the first obstacle; however, the gun jams and his unit is again pinned down. Cole, armed with his pistol and one grenade, advances, singlehandedly attacks and then returns for more ammunition. He then makes a third assault, taking out the obstacle; however, as he returns to his lines, an enemy grenade kills him. Sergeant Cole's actions eliminated the obstacles allowing his Company to seize the objective; he receives the Medal of Honor posthumously. Cpl. Tony Stein, 28th Marines, also receives the Medal of Honor posthumously; he singlehandly kills 20 enemy troops. The Heavy Cruiser *Chester* (CA-27) is damaged by collision with the Amphibious Force Flagship *Estes* (AGC-12) The Destroyer *Bradford* (DD-545) and Destroyer Escort *Finnegan* (DE-307) are damaged by separate collisions, and the Destroyer *John W. Weeks* (DD-701) is damaged by enemy coastal guns. **(Pacific-Philippines) Luzon** In the U.S. Sixth Army XIV Corps area, the thunderclap of Artillery continues to pound enemy positions in Manila. In conjunction, the 40th Division's 160th Regiment, 40th Division overruns Object Hill, concluding its operations on the Corps' right flank. In the I Corps area, the 33rd Division attacks toward Bench Mark and Question Mark Hills, northeast of Sison, while the 25th Division, supported by Aircraft and Artillery, drives toward Japanese positions northwest of Lumboy, toppling the first four hills in their path. In the **XI Corps** sector, the East Force pauses during its drive across the Bataan Peninsula to permit the 149th Regiment to locate enemy positions. Meanwhile, the Rock Force thwarts a counterattack on Corregidor. **Southern Philippines** In the U.S. Eighth Army area, X Corps commences attacks to secure Shipping lanes to Manila, via the San Bernardino Strait; Marine Aircraft cover the landing of the Provisional Task Force (American Division) contingents on the northwestern tip of Samar at Allen, and the landing of the 1st Battalion, 182nd Regiment on Capul Island at the western entrance of the strait. **Leyte** American Division contingents are reducing an enemy pocket of resistance near Villaba. **(Pacific-Burma)** In the ALFSEA area, 15th Corps sector, the Indian 25th Division sustains heavy counterattacks at its Ruywa bridgehead. In the N.C.A.C. area, Hsenwi is taken by the 30th Division, Chinese New First Army. **(Atlantic-Western Europe) 21st Army Group** Heavy fighting ensues at Goch as the British 30th Corps is engaged in vicious house-to-house fighting. **12th Army Group** In the U.S. First Army area, **V Corps** sector, the 99th Division reverts to First Army control from Corps attachment. In the U.S. Third Army area, General Patton writes to General Bradley, requesting additional Divisions, but Bradley is not available. General Bull calls Patton and informs him that Third Army can use the 10th Armored, but Bull specifies that it is only for one operation (break through the Saar Triangle). General Patton, reflecting his felling on the matter: "IT ALWAYS MADE ME MAD TO HAVE TO BEG FOR OPPORTUNITIES TO WIN BATTLES." **VIII Corps** sector, Masthorn and a hill outside of Pronsfeld are overrun by the 358th Regiment, 90th Division, while the 359th Regiment seizes Ober and Nieder Uttfeld. Task Force Gassman (90th Reconnaissance Troop supported by Tanks) advances toward Binscheid, as it affords protection to the right flank of

the 357th Regiment. Herzfeld capitulates to the 11th Armored's C.C.R., which also mops up in Leidenborn. In **XII Corps** sector, Freidlingerhohe, Hommerdingen, and Nusbaum fall to elements of the 317th and 318th Regiments, 80th Division. Meanwhile, the 319th condenses the enemy positions remaining at the West Wall; contingents take Niedergegen. Stockem is secured by units of the 5th Division's 2nd Battalion, 2nd Regiment. On the southern flank of Corps, a night raid across the Moder by a 2nd Cavalry Task Force captures Wincheringen, an important road center. In the **XX Corps** sector, an attack, supplemented by Air and Artillery bombardment, to secure the Saar-Moselle triangle commences; contingents of the 94th Division overrun Faha, Keblingen, Munzingen, and Oberleuken. **6th Army Group** In the U.S. Seventh Army area, XV Corps sector, Forbach is penetrated by the 276th Regiment, 70th Division; fierce fire-fights ensue. The 253rd Regiment, 63rd Division retakes Auersmacher and seizes Kleinblittersdorf in the process. In the **VI Corps** sector, the right flank contingents of the 103rd Division are relieved by units of the 14th Armored Division. **(Atlantic-Eastern Europe)** In Prussia, the besieged Germans at Koenigsberg on the Samland Peninsula attempt to break out to the west; vicious fighting occurs. In northwestern Poland, Grudziadz is totally enveloped by Soviet troops as they advance toward Danzig. Meanwhile, the Soviets continue to hammer the German Garrison at Breslau in Silesia as well as the surrounding region. **(Atlantic-Italy)** In the U.S. Fifth Army area, IV Corps sector, the 10th Mountain Division repulses counterattacks against its positions on Sarassiccia-Campania Ridge, prior to commencing its main assault (23:00) against the Belvedere-Gorgolesco hill mass; the attack gains good progress against nominal opposition.

February 20th 1945 — (Pacific-Iwo Jima) Heavy fighting ensues throughout the day. The 4th Marine Division seizes Airfield No. 1. Meanwhile, the 5th Marine Division drives toward Mt Suribachi. Captain Robert Hugo Dunlap, Commanding Officer, Company C, 1st Battalion, 26th Marines, 5th Marine Division receives the Medal of Honor for his extraordinary leadership. Dunlap advances with his men against impregnable caves, then moves out singlehandedly, remaining in an exposed position for two days directing accurate fire against the enemy positions. Also, P.F.C. Jacklyn H. Lucas, 1st Battalion, 26th Marines absorbs the blasts of two grenades to save his detachment as it is moving through a ravine and hits an ambush. He saves the Patrol which then routs the Japanese Patrol; Lucas receives the Medal of Honor. Casualties continue to climb; Tank losses are also heavy. Offshore, the Light Cruiser *Biloxi* (CL-80) and the Hospital Ship *Samaritan* are accidentally damaged by U.S. Naval gunfire. The Attack Transports *Napa* (APO-157) and *Logan* (APA-196) are damaged by collision. In addition, the Attack Cargo Ship *Starr* (AKA-67) is damaged by collision, and the LST 779 sustains damage by coastal mortar fire. **(Pacific-Philippines) Luzon** In the U.S. Sixth Army area, **XIV Corps** sector, the 7th Cavalry captures crossing of the Mariquina River in the Ugong-Rosario area. Meanwhile Corps prepares to assault the Intramuros in Manila. In the **I Corps** sector, elements of the 25th Division assault four hills northwest of Lumboy; three of the four are gained by the 161st Regiment. **(Southern Philippines)** In the U.S. Eighth Army area, **X Corps** sector, elements of the Provisional Task Force dispatches land and sea Patrols to Lavezares on the northwestern coast of Samar. Contingents, protected by Marine Aircraft, land without opposition on Macarite Island, from where they cross the channel and establish a beachhead on Biri Island, on the eastern entrance to the San Bernardino Strait. (**Pacific-South China Sea**) The Submarine *Pargo* (SS-264) sinks the Japanese Destroyer *Nokaze*. (**Atlantic-Western Europe**) SHEAF opens forward Headquarters at Reims. In addition, the 20th Armored Division debarks on the Continent. **21st Army Group** In the **Canadian First Army** area, British 30th Corps sector, the Bailey Bridge laid over the Meuse at Gennep begins accepting traffic. At Goch, the Germans continue to raise vigorous resistance. **12th Army Group** In the **U.S. First Army** area, **VII Corps** sector, the 99th Division (less 394th Regiment) is attached to Corps and moves to deploy at Aubel and Clermont. In the **V Corps** sector, the 28th Division relieves the 2nd Division subsequent to being attached to Corps. In the **U.S. Third Army** area, **VIII Corps** sector, the Germans at Lichtenborn seemingly mount the most tenacious resistance in the Corps' 90th Division sector, as incessant fire is pouring into U.S. positions as the enemy attempts to break out. The 359th Regiment crashes through the woods east of Ober and Nieder Uttfeld, while the 2nd Battalion, 357th Regiment charges and captures Houf and a nearby hill; however, the opposition at Binscheid holds off TF Gassman and Company A. Meanwhile, C.C.R., 11th Armored seizes Sengerich, then rolls into the nearby heights, clearing them. Combat is bitter along the Our River as 6th Armored restarts its attack; C.C.B. drives over the West Wall defenses within its sector and gains two miles north of Dahnen, thanks in part to diversionary actions by C.C.A. In the **XII Corps** sector, the 317th Regiment, 80th Division secures the heights north of Nusbaum, then bolts across the Enz River to capture Enzen, while the 318th maneuvers to positions near Mettendorf, and the 319th continues to eliminate the resistance at the West Wall. The 5th Division mops up in its sector along the west bank of the Pruem; contingents of the 2nd Regiment seize Halsdorf. Also, Generals Patton and Eddy arrive at the XII Corps front at the Sauer and are greeted by a sign: "GENERAL PATTON'S BRIDGE-BUILT BY THE MIGHTY MIDGETS. It was constructed by Company F, 1303rd General Service Engineer Regiment, after having earlier heard Patton pass a remark NEAR THE SITE: "I HAVE NEVER SEEN SO MANY LITTLE MEN DOING SUCH A BIG JOB." In the **XX Corps** sector, the 10th Armored Division, reinforced by RCT 376, joins the fight for the Saar-Moselle triangle; RCT 376 seizes Kreuzweiler and Thorn, while C.C.R. crushes the opposition at Dilmar, Helfant, Palzem, Rommelfangen, Sudlingen and Wehr. C.C.A., surging forward on the right, overruns Dittlingen, Fisch, Kelsen, Kirf, Korrig, and Meurich. In addition, the 94th Division is closing against the Saar; its 301st Regiment seizes Freudenberg and Kollesleuken, while its 302nd overruns Weiten and Orscholz. **6th Army Group** In the **U.S. Seventh Army** area, **XV Corps** sector, the house-to-house fighting in Forbach continues to rage as the 276th Regiment, 70th Division attempts to secure the town. Meanwhile, the 70th's 275th Regiment overpowers the villages of Alsting, Hesseling, and Zinzing. (**Atlantic-Italy**) **15th Army Group** In the **U.S. Fifth Army** area, the 10th Mountain Division surges to the crests of Belvedere and Mt. Gorgolesco, tucking both under the fold of Old Glory during the early morning hours, before dashing toward the ridge leading to Mt. Torraccia.

February 21st 1945 — (Pacific-Caroline Islands) Truk is attacked by Naval land-based and Army Aircraft. (**Pacific-Iwo Jima**) Marines continue attacking north toward Airfield No. 2 and south against Mt Suribachi. Japanese resistance remains fierce and again Marine casualties are high. RCT 21, 3rd Marine Division (Corps reserve) lands on Beach Yellow and is attached to 4th Marine Division. During the heavy fighting on Iwo, P.F.C. Donald Jack Ruhl, Company E, 28th Marines, 5th Marine Division, intentionally takes the impact of a grenade, saving the life of his buddy. Prior to being killed by the grenade, Ruhl had singlehandedly attacked eight Japanese, killing two as they were escaping and also braved heavy fire to assist a wounded Marine. Ruhl receives the Medal of Honor posthumously for his extraordinary bravery as his unit moves to secure Mt Suribachi. During the attack against Motoyama Airfield No. 2, Captain Joseph Jeremiah McCarthy, 2nd Battalion, 24th Marines, 4th Marine Division, leads a spectacular charge against an enemy pillbox, destroying it with his small force of Riflemen and accompanying Flamethrowers. McCarthy kills several of the enemy, then jumps into the ruins of the obstacle, taking out several more. McCarthy continues the attack securing the ridge; he becomes a recipient of the Medal of Honor. Near Airfield No. 1, Sergeant Ross Franklin Gray, Company A, 25th Marines, orders his detachment to withdraw from within range of enemy grenade range as they come under severe fire. He advances alone, discovering a large minefield, and subsequently clears a path through it. He then, under cover fire by three Marines, advances, taking out six enemy positions and killing about twenty-five enemy troops. Gray receives the Medal of Honor. The Escort Carrier *Bismarck Sea* (CVE-95) is sunk by a Kamikaze. The Carrier *Saratoga* (CV-3) and the Escort Carrier *Lunga Point* (CVE-94) are both damaged by Suicide Planes. The Net Cargo Ship *Keokuk* (AKN-4) and the LSTs 477 and 809 also sustain damage by Kamikazes. In addition, the Destroyer *Williamson* (DD-244) and the LST 390 sustain damage by collisions. (**Pacific-Philippines**) Luzon In the **U.S. Sixth Army** area, XI Corps sector, the East and West Forces converge south of Bagac, concluding the Bataan Peninsula campaign. The U.S. sustains about 50 killed or missing. The Japanese suffer about 200 dead. An insignificant numbered force of Japanese is scattered around the Mt Natib region; however, it is subsequently annihilated. The Corps assumes command of the 40th Division, which pauses while Air units initiate sorties to destroy enemy positions in their area. The Destroyer U.S.S. *Renshaw* (DD-499) is damaged by a Submarine torpedo. (**Pacific-Burma**) In the British Fourteenth Army area, 4th Corps sector, the Indian 17th Division departs the Nyaungu bridgehead, attacking toward Meiktila. (**Atlantic-Western Europe**) **21st Army Group** Goch falls to the British 51st Division, culminating a drive which originated on February 9th. In the **U.S. Third Army** area, **VIII Corps** sector, Euscheid and Strickscheid are seized by the 359th Regiment, 90th Division, while the 357th Regiment, bolstered by the firepower of Planes, seizes the high ground over Lichtenborn, seizes Stalbach and has contingents assist TF Gassman with its seizure of Binscheid. Meanwhile, the 358th Regiment clears a gully stretched between Halenbach and Hickeshausen and overruns both towns. C.C.R., 11th Armored enlarges its breach in the West Wall and seizes Roscheid. Dahnen and Dasburg are seized by the 9th Armored Infantry Regiment, while the 50th Armored Infantry Battalion secures Daleiden and Reipeldingen. In the **XII Corps** sector, the heights south of Mettendorf are secured by the 318th Regiment, 80th Division, while the 319th Regiment, supplemented by contingents of the 53rd Armored Infantry Battalion, 4th Armored, seizes Roth and reduces the resistance at the West Wall between the Our and Gay Rivers; the towns of Lahr and Korperich also fall. In the **XX Corps** sector, the 10th Armored advances against unorganized resistance toward the Kanzem and Wiltingen bridges; its C.C.R. takes

611

Fellerich, Nittel, Rehlingen, and Temmels, all in the Saar-Moselle triangle. Meanwhile, C.C.A. overruns Wawern as it drives toward the Saar, reducing the opposition as it advances. RCT 376, 94th Division engages in mop-up operations to the Saar in the area around Ockfen. **6th Army Group** In the **U.S. Seventh Army** area, **XV Corps** sector, heavy combat continues at Forbach; however, the 276th Regiment, 70th Division controls about one-third of the objective. Meanwhile, the 274th and contingents of the 275th Regiments seize Spicheren and advance beyond Saarbruecken and Stiring Wendel, securing the heights, and subsequently turn back several enemy attempts to regain them. **(Atlantic-Italy) 15th Army Group** In the **U.S. Fifth Army** area, **IV Corps** sector, the 10th Mountain Division maintains its advance against the crest of Mt. Torraccia, plowing through heavy resistance. In other activity, the Brazilian 1st Division assaults toward Mt. Castello; its 1st and 11th Regiments seize the objective and also take Abetaia.

February 22nd 1945 — (Pacific-Iwo Jima) V Amphibious Corps maintains northward attack toward phase line O-2 (Tachiiwi Point on east coast to Motoyama village in center to west coast south of Hiraiwa Bay); however, grid fire from pill boxes on high ground between Airfields 1 and 2 hinder the advance. To the south, RCT 28 continues surrounding Mt Suribachi. In other activity, the Destroyer Escort *Melvin R. Nawman* (DE-416) is damaged by collision with the LST 807. **(Pacific-Philippines) Luzon** In the **U.S. Sixth Army** area, the **XIV Corps** continues plans for the final thrust against the center of Manila. East of the capital, the 6th Division and the 1st Cavalry Division commence an assault across the Mariquina toward the Taytay-Antipolo-Montalban line. Contingents of Cavalry advance through Taytay. In the **I Corps** sector, a drive to secure Balete Pass is mounted. Contingents of the 25th Division drive along a primitive trail toward the Pampanga River Valley; its 2nd Battalion, 161st Regiment is directed to seize Bryant Hill northwest of Puncan. Meanwhile, the fierce fighting at the Villa Verde Trail continues as the 127th Regiment, 32nd Division reinitiates its attack and makes progress. In other activity, Bench Mark and Question Mark Hills crumble under four successive days of attacking by the 33rd Division. **(Pacific-Burma)** In the **British Fourteenth Army** area, two mechanized Brigades of the Indian 17th Division and the 255th Tank Brigade embark from Nyaungu toward Meiktila. **(Pacific-China)** General Chennault is informed that Chinese forces commanded by General Hsueh Yueh (Eastern China) have finally received arms from Chungking, subsequent to the fall of Suichwan. Chiang Kai-shek has been in no hurry to arm the Communists in eastern China. **(Atlantic-Western Europe)** German General von Ronstedt has been requesting permission to withdraw the 1st Paratroop Army, which is defending the east bank of the Rhine, but Hitler always responds with "No." In this instance he reiterates that "GERMANY MUST BE DEFENDED TO THE LAST MAN." **21st Army Group** The Canadian 2nd Division (Canadian 2nd Corps area) seizes Moyland. **12th Army Group** In the **U.S. First Army** area, **III Corps** sector, the 82nd Airborne secures the area. In the **V Corps** sector, the 2nd Ranger Battalion is attached to the 102nd Cavalry Group. In the **U.S. Third Army** area, General Patton decorates some Army Nurses with the Bronze Star. He also decorates Lt. James H. Fields with the Medal of Honor. Subsequently, Patton tells General Gerow not to send Fields to the front again, stating: "IT HAS BEEN MY UNFORTUNATE OBSERVATION THAT WHENEVER A MAN GETS THE MEDAL OF HONOR OR EVEN THE DISTINGUISHED SERVICE CROSS, HE USUALLY ATTEMPTS TO OUTDO HIMSELF AND GETS KILLED." In the **VIII Corps** sector, German opposition throughout the Corps sector vanishes. Lichtenborn is taken effortlessly by the 357th Regiment, 90th Division; the 358th reinforced (Task Force Spiess) takes Arzfeld, Holzchen, and the heights southwest of Heckeshausen to southeast of Neurath. C.C.R., 11th Armored takes Eschfeld and Reiff. Irrhausen and Olmscheid fall to C.C.B., 6th Armored. C.C.A., 6th Armored fords the Our and seizes Affler and Preischeid, subsequent to relieving C.C.B. at Dasburg. The 15th Tank Battalion overruns Ober Eisenbach, which eradicates the final enemy position along the West Wall within its sector. In the **XII Corps** sector, regrouping occurs. In the **XX Corps** sector, the 10th Armored Division reduces the final resistance in the Saar-Moselle triangle and attempts to establish a bridgehead across the Saar River outside of Ockfen. A shortage of assault boats prevents a crossing by RCT 376, 94th Division; boats are procured; however, the inclement weather halts the operation until late in the night. Further south, the 301st and 302nd Regiments, 94th Division ford the river and penetrate Serrig, securing part of the town. Task Force Polk and its attached 5th Ranger Battalion are busily engaged, securing their border sector. **(Atlantic-Italy) 15th Army Group** In the **U.S. Fifth Army** area, **IV Corps** sector, the 10th Mountain Division has all its objectives to the left secured; however, relentless opposition remains on the crest of M. Torraccia. Meanwhile, the Brazilian 1st Division consolidates its positions on M. Castello.

U.S. 3rd Armored Division at Dragons Teeth, West Wall.

February 23rd 1945 — (Pacific-Iwo Jima) Old Glory is raised on Mt Suribachi by contingents of Company E, RCT 28. The 3rd Marine Division (minus RCT's 3 and 21) are detached from Expeditionary Troops reserve and attached to V Amphibious Corps. Meanwhile, the 2nd Marine Division reverts to area reserve. Offshore, Task Force 58.5 continues to support the land operation and provides night Fighter protection, while Task Force 58 moves out to launch air strikes against Tokyo. The Submarine Chaser PC 877 is damaged by collision. The LSTs 684 and 792 sustain damage by enemy coastal guns, and the LST 716 is damaged by grounding. In the Third Marine Division area, enemy fire holds up Tank movements. Corporal Hershel W. Williams, working under cover fire of four other Marines, advances singlehandedly to take out enemy positions and in one instance actually places the muzzle of a flamethrower into the air vent of a pillbox, incinerating the occupants. Soon after, a detachment of enemy troops charge toward him and encounter instant death as his flamethrower unleashes deadly accurate bursts of fire. Williams' Company reaches its objective; he becomes the recipient of the Medal of Honor. **(Pacific-Philippines) Luzon** In the **U.S. Sixth Army** area, the Intramuros, an aged and walled sector of the capital, is assaulted by the 37th Division, subsequent to another massive Artillery bombardment; the 3rd Battalion, 129th Regiment crosses the Pasig River in assault boats and traverses through the Mint building in conjunction with the 145th Regiment, which storms the Parian and Queon Gates, catching the Japs offguard momentarily; however, their resistance quickly stiffens and the fighting rages furiously. Activity is brisk east of the city where 1st Cavalry contingents and the 6th Division are advancing. Strong Japanese fire originating from the Customs Building strikes Troop E, 5th Cavalry as it advances, wounding the commanding Officer. P.F.C. William Grabiarz attempts to rescue him, but he is wounded. Unable to move the Officer, he shields him from further danger by covering him with his own body, giving his life to save the Officer. Meanwhile, contingents of the 11th Airborne, implementing a land assault, combine with Airborne and Amphibious troops to liberate the internment camp at Los Banos. In the **I Corps** sector, the Japanese defenses in the bowl of the Villa Verde Trail are thoroughly eliminated by the 127th Regiment, 32nd Division. In the **XI Corps** sector, the western section of Corregidor is now under the control of Rock Force. In addition, the 108th and 185th Regiments, 40th Division reinitiate their assault to secure the Zambales Mountains in Luzon. **Southern Philippines** In the **U.S. Eighth Army** area, the Americans at Biri give control to the 1st Philippine Infantry and depart for Samar. The U.S. loses three men during the operation, while the Japanese sustain 72 killed. The Verde Island Attack Force (reinforced Rifle Company, 1st Battalion, 19th Infantry) departs Mindoro for Verde Island. **(Pacific)** The Submarine *Hammerhead* (SS-364) sinks the Japanese Frigate *Yaku* off Indo China. The Japanese Submarine Chaser No. 35 is sunk in the South China Sea by Army Aircraft. **(Pacific-SEAC)** A meeting of Commanders is held in Calcutta, resulting in a decision to withhold an amphibious assault against Rangoon, Burma, until after the monsoon, and to initiate an overland move toward the city. **(Atlantic-Western Europe) 21st Army Group** Army Group, commanded by British General Montgomery, initiates Operation GRENADE. In the **U.S. Ninth Army** area, Operation GRENADE commences at 03:30, following a forty-five minute Artillery barrage that shatters the early morning silence. The U.S. Ninth Army's XIII and XIX Corps attack, while a third American Corps, the XVI, strikes diversionary blows at jump-off time to confuse the Germans. Yanks begin bolting across the swollen Roer, while Engineers are desperately stringing bridges, despite severe currents and intermittent enemy shelling and Air attacks, gaining the element of surprise over the enemy. The XIII Corps' 84th and 102nd Divisions, commanded by Generals Alexander Bolling and Frank Keating respectively, dash forward, the former seizing Baal, Koerrenzig, and Rurich, while the 102nd seizes Boslar, Gevenich, and Glimbach. Synchronized with the XIII Corps surge, the XIX Corps streams forward with its 29th and 30th Divisions, commanded by Generals Charles Gerhardt and Leland Hobbs, respectively. The 29th Division overruns Broich and its nearby heights, and also seizes a good part of Juelich, despite enormous difficulties with bridging; it also establishes a roadblock on the Mersch-Pattern road. The 30th Division takes Altenburg, Daubenrath, and Selgersdorf, and the villages of Krauthausen and Selhausen, prior to initiating an assault against Hambach at 23:00. Meanwhile, the **U.S. First Army** (12th Army Group)

VII Corps is also attacking; its 8th and 104th Divisions cross the Roer at 03:30 upon cessation of the pre-assault bombardment and drive forward. Contingents of Terry Allen's 104th seize Huchem, Birkesdorf, Stammeln, and the sector of Dueren north of the Railroad, while the 8th Division cuts into Dueren from the south and is simultaneously pressing against Stockheim. The unyielding river currents are creating more difficulties for the troops than that which the Germans can mount. In the **U.S. Third Army** area, **VIII Corps** sector, the 90th Division's 357th Regiment roars into Kopscheid and advances to Manderscheid and Waxweiler; the Germans blow the bridge at the latter. The 358th, reinforced with Task Force Spiess, secures Berkoth, Heilbach, Krautscheid, and Upperhausen, in addition to clearing the Lauperath area. The 6th Armored Division's C.C.A., sweeping to the south, overruns Jucken and its surrounding heights and Olmscheid, the last of its objectives. In conjunction, C.C.A. mops up its sector east of the Our River, while the 15th Tank Battalion fords the river and secures the area southward between the Our and Irsen Rivers. In the **XII Corps** sector, the Germans are being battered and bruised as the Yanks advance against a faltering and disorganized foe. At Ober Geckler, mop-up details are carried out by contingents of the 80th Division. Nieder Geckler is seized by C.C.B., 4th Armored, which then jumps to Sinspelt, gaining it before the bridge can be blown. In the **XX Corps** sector, RCT, 10th Armored takes its objectives east of the Saar and seizes Ockfen. The 94th Division encounters difficulty getting across the Saar; however, with an extraordinary effort it takes Serrig on the west bank, while the 94th Reconnaissance Troop overruns Krutweiler. **6th Army Group** In the **U.S. Seventh Army** area, **XV Corps** sector, the 276th Regiment, 70th Division clears remnant resistance in Forbach, while the balance of the Division bolsters its perimeter below Saarbruecken. In the **VI Corps** sector, the U.S. 36th Division starts to relieve the 82nd Airborne. **(Atlantic-Eastern Europe)** Moscow proclaims the capitulation of Arnswalde in Pomerania and Posen in Poland. In Silesia, heavy fighting continues in and around Breslau as Soviet troops penetrate the city's southern perimeter. **(Atlantic-Italy) 15th Army Group** The contest for control of M. Torraccia continues; the 10th Mountain Division is still unable to dislodge the enemy from the crest. The Brazilian 1st Division seizes Bella Vista and M. della Casselina.

First Army approaches the Rhine River.

February 24th 1945 — (Pacific-Iwo Jima) The remainder of the 3rd Marine Division lands on Beach Black. The V Amphibious Corps attacks toward line O-A, which splits the island about 800 yards north of Airfield No. 2; the assault disintegrates resistance in the center. The 2nd and 3rd Battalions, 24th Marines overcome strong resistance on Charlie-Dog Ridge near the east-west runway of Airfield No. 2. In other activity, the 2nd Separate Engineers complete repairs on the north-south runway of Airfield No. 1, and in addition, a Seaplane Base is established. Offshore, the LST 792 is damaged by enemy coastal defense guns. A violent storm wreaks severe damage upon others: the Heavy Cruiser *San Francisco* (CA-38) and the Destroyers *Colahan* (DD-658) and the *Moale* (DD-693) feel its wrath. In addition, the Destroyers *Heywood L. Edwards* (DD-663) and the *Bryant* (DD-665) and the Submarine Chaser PC-578 incur damage by collision. **(Pacific-Philippines) Luzon** In the **U.S. Sixth Army** area, **XIV Corps** sector, the 37th Division eradicates the organized resistance at the Intramuros, reducing the enemy strongpoints to three: the Agriculture, Finance, and Legislative Buildings, all of which have heavy fire poured upon them. In other activity, the contingents of the 6th Division seize Montalban, San Isidro, and seize the heights south of Mataba, while the 1st Cavalry Division's 2nd Cavalry Brigade drives toward Antipolo. In the **I Corps** sector, enemy machine guns pin down a Platoon of Company B, 27th Regiment, 25th Division. Staff Sergeant Raymond H. Cooley singlehandedly attacks, tossing a grenade which is thrown back at him. Undaunted, he lobs a second grenade which eradicates the gun and its crew instantly. Cooley then advances against the next obstacle, tossing grenades into enemy foxholes as he runs; however, troops follow and upon approaching the second objective, six Japs confront him. Unable to throw his live grenade without causing harm to other Americans which are now involved in close hand-to-hand combat, Cooley covers the grenade with his body. He is badly wounded, but lives and receives the Medal of Honor. In the **XI sector**, the Rock Force has eliminated all resistance on Corregidor, except a small pocket which is compressed in a 3,000 yard pocket perched precariously at the eastern tip of the island. In other activity, the 160th Regiment is thrown into the campaign to clear the Japanese from the Zambales Mountains of Luzon, as the 40th Division attempts to conclude the operation. **Southern Philippines** In the **U.S. Eighth Army** area, Major General Frederick A. Irving releases X Corps of its responsibility for the final mop-up details on Leyte, Samar, and the Camotes. The Americal Division, under jurisdiction of the new command, maintains its operations on Leyte in Villaba, while simultaneously carrying out missions to secure the San Bernardino Strait. Meanwhile, the Verde Island Attack Force debarks on the northeast tip of Verde Island without incident. **(Pacific-Burma)** In the **British Fourteenth Army** area, 33 Corps sector, the British 2nd Division starts to ford the Irrawaddy west of Mandalay at Ngazun; however, the Japanese are waiting and raise heavy opposition. In the IV Corps sector, Taungtha, a Japanese supply center, falls to the Indian 17th Division as it drives toward Meiktila. **(Pacific-Japan)** The Submarine *Lagarto* (SS-371) sinks the Japanese Submarine RO-49 off Kyushu. **(Atlantic-Western Europe)** Army Planes sink the German U-Boat U-3007 off Bremen, Germany. **21st Army Group** In the **Canadian First Army's** British 30th Corps sector, the British 53rd Division, spearheading the Corps drive from Goch, approaches Weeze sluggishly. In the **U.S. Ninth Army** area **XIII Corps** sector, the Germans are repulsed when they attempt to regain Rurich. Doveren falls to the 1st Battalion, 335th Regiment, 84th Division (assisted by recently arrived Armor). German counterattacks against the 102nd Division are thrown back prior to the Division's advance, which overruns Din-

gbuchhof, Hompesch, Hottorf, and Kofferen. In the **XIX Corps** sector, the final resistance in Juelich is eliminated by the 175th Regiment, 29th Division, including the pulverization of the Citadel by the use of Flame-throwing Tanks; other contingents of the 29th seize Stetternich and establish contact with the 30th Division. The 30th Division overruns Hambach by 01:30, seizes Niederzier by 06:30, and fights doggedly for the balance of the day, taking Grosse Forst and Lindenberger Wald sections of Staats Forst Hambach by 21:30. Meanwhile, its 117th Regiment fords the Roer at 16:30, driving toward Steinstrass; however, intentionally felled trees and mine blanketed roads halt the advance of Armor; Infantry Troops dismount the Tanks and grind forward reaching a point about 1,000 yards from the objective. **12th Army Group** In the **U.S. First Army** area, **VII Corps** sector, the 104th Division secures Oberzier and over half of Arnoldsweiler and at midnight (24th-25th) it mounts an attack against Ellen. The 8th Division's 13th Regiment clears south Dueren and the outlying suburbs, while the 28th seizes Krauthausen and Niederau, but it is compelled to give some ground northwest of Stockheim. In the **U.S. Third Army** area, **VIII Corps** sector, Bellscheid, Nieder Pierscheid, Ober, and Ringhuscheid fall to the 90th Division, which is due to be relieved. The 6th Armored clamps its final objectives; C.C.B. seizes Leimbach, Muxerath, and Neuerburg and continues driving south to establish contact with the 80th Division (XII Corps); a combat Patrol of C.C.A. captures Sevenig. In concert with the 6th Armored Division, the 6th Cavalry Group seizes Karlshausen, then overruns Bauler, Berscheid, Herbstmuhle, Koxhausen, and Rodershausen. In the **XII Corps** sector, the 4th Armored's C.C.B. advances to Outscheid and Brimingen encountering only moderate resistance as the Germans continue to fall back. Late in the day, the 5th and 76th Divisions begin to cross the Pruem River. In the **XX Corps** sector, the 10th Armored Division expands the Ockfen bridgehead toward Schoden and Beurig, while the 94th Division's 301st and 302nd Regiments pour into the bridgehead at Serrig-Taben, despite intense enemy fire; the final Battalion west of the river moves into it; the 5th Ranger Battalion, operating behind enemy lines, becomes isolated near the Irsch-Zerf road. The Rangers hold out against attempts to annihilate them; the pressure will be relieved in a few days. **6th Army Group** In the **U.S.Fifth Army** area, the 10th Mountain Division seizes the summit of Mt. Torraccia before 12:00. La Serra is taken by the Brazilian 1st Division. **(Atlantic-Turkey)** Turkey declares war against the Axis Powers; the declaration is timely, as it affords Turkey membership at the U.N.

The U.S. Ninth Army at the Roer River.

614

February 25th 1945 — (Pacific-Carolines) The Motor Minesweeper YMS-275 is damaged by a mine. (Pacific-Iwo Jima) Marines continue advancing toward O-2 line, making progress at Airfield No. 2. The 3rd Marine Division takes responsibility for securing the central part of the Motoyama Plateau; the terrain includes Motoyama village and Airfields No. 1 and No. 2. In other activity, the 12th Marines begin landing. The Attack Cargo Vessel *Muliphen* (AKA-61), the Attack Transport *Fayette* (APA-43), and the LST 928 suffer damage by collision. The Seaplane Tender *Hamlin* (AV-15) is damaged accidentally by U.S. Naval gunfire. (Pacific-Japan) The XXI Bomber Command's B29s' use of incendiary bombs over Tokyo has proven successful, although the weapon is still experimental. The U.S. changes its strategy, halting the daylight raids against Tokyo's industrial area, and concentrates on night raids against the urban areas; the raids are especially deadly because of the flimsy construction of Japanese houses and buildings. In other activity, Task Force 58 strikes Tokyo and repeats the raid on the following day. The Destroyer *Harrison* (DD-573) is damaged off Honshu by a storm. (Pacific-Philippines) Luzon In the **U.S. Sixth Army** area, the **XIV Corps** makes final preparations for the attack to disintegrate the three remaining Japanese obstacles in Manila. At Antipolo, the Japs continue to raise fierce resistance against the 2nd Cavalry Brigade, 1st Cavalry Division. The 6th Division is also experiencing obstinate resistance as it advances; Patrols of the 63rd Regiment probe toward Mt. Pacawagan, while mop-up details continue in its sector. In conjunction, elements of the 20th Regiment reach positions about a mile from Mt. Mataba peak, while the 1st Infantry advances toward Wawa and Wawa Dam. In the **I Corps** sector, elements of the 35th Regiment, 25th Division repulse a Japanese counterattack subsequent to their effortless trek to the area around Carranglan; the 1st Battalion nears Pantabangan. The 27th Regiment is involved with vicious fire-fight at a commanding hill at Highway 5 in Lumboy, while the 161st takes Bryant Hill northwest of Puncan. In the **XI Corps** sector, the Japanese are further compressed as their fragile hold on Corregidor is reduced to 2,000 yards, facing the Yanks. However, the sea is to their backs. On Luzon, the 185th Regiment, 40th Division captures Hill 1700, culminating its mission; the 160th Regiment secures the majority of its zone. (Pacific-Burma) In the British Fourteenth Army 4th Corps sector, the Indian 17th Division seizes Mahlaing. (Atlantic-Western Europe) **21st Army Group** In the **Canadian First Army** area, British 30th Corps sector, the British 53rd Division advances to about a mile from Weeze; however, it receives orders to stop; the town is secured on the 3rd of March. The British 15th Division is relieved by the Canadian 3rd Division, which assumes responsibility for the left flank of the Corps with the Guards Armored Division. In the **U.S. Ninth Army** area, the 35th Division crosses the Roer to participate in the offensive. In the **XIII Corps** sector, the advance is driving north toward Erkelenz. Granterath and Hetzerath fall to the 334th Regiment, 84th Division, and Houverath is seized by the 335th. Ralshoven is captured by the 3rd Battalion, 405th Infantry, 102nd Division; Katzem and Lovenich are seized by the 406th and 407th Regiments respectively. In the **XIX Corps** sector, Mersch, Muentz, and Pattern are overrun by RCT 130, 29th Division, and Welldorf falls to the 116th Regiment, which then drives to Guesten and dispatches units which move north and take Serrest. The 30th Division keeps advancing; its 119th Regiment seizes Hollen and Rodingen, and the 117th Regiment overruns Steinstrass and subsequently mounts an attack against Lich. **12th Army Group** Generals Patton, Middleton, Walker, and Gaffey (Acting XII Corps Commander while General Eddy is sick) meet to discuss strategy and are joined by Generals Bradley and Allen. Patton gets permission from Bradley to retain the 10th Armored Division until the 27th, contingent upon Ike permitting Patton to list the 90th Division as reserve. Patton's objective is Trier. Patton notes: "HAD WE BEEN REFUSED PERMISSION TO CONTINUE THE ATTACK, THE WHOLE HISTORY OF THE WAR MIGHT HAVE CHANGED, BECAUSE THE CAPTURE OF TRIER WAS ONE OF THE TURNING POINTS." In the **U.S. First Army** area, **VII Corps** area, Dueren is totally secure; Corps advances to bridgehead line. The 104th Division's 415th Regiment seizes Ellen and reduces the balance of Arnoldsweiler, while its 413th captures the hills northeast of the latter, and at 21:00 thrusts toward Morschenich. Meanwhile, its 414th Regiment mounts an early morning attack (03:00) seizing Merzenich by 12:00, and at 21:00 it launches an attack against Golzheim. In other Corps activity, the 8th Division has elements seize Binsfeld and Rommelsheim in addition to securing portions of Stockheim and Girbelsrath. In the **III Corps** sector, an attack is launched by the 1st Division; elements of the 16th Regiment capture Drove and Kreuzau; however, its 3rd Battalion encounters heavy resistance outside of Stockheim and is unable to pass. In the **U.S. Third Army** area, **VIII Corps** sector, the 6th Cavalry Group engages the Germans at Scheuren and whips them thoroughly. In the **XII Corps** sector, Mettendorf is completely cleared by contingents of the 80th Division. The Germans are continually pulling back with the Yanks on their heels. As the 4th Armored regroups, it remains on the offensive; C.C.B. roars east steamrolling over unsteady resistance to the Pruem at Hermesdorf. It bolts across the Pruem and advances to Rittersdorf at the Nims River and establishes a bridgehead. The 5th Division's Combat Teams ford the Pruem; RCT 2 seizes Wettlingen, Bettingen, and Olsdorf, while RCT 10 takes Peffingen and Ingendorf. In conjunction, the 76th Division crosses the Pruem through positions of the 5th Division and seizes Holsthum. In the **XX Corps** sector, the Germans maintain stiff opposition at the Saar, preventing bridging by the 10th Armored, forcing C.C.B. to ford the river at Taben and drive from there toward Zerf; C.C.A. and C.C.R. make preparations to cross. Meanwhile, the 5th Ranger Battalion receives assistance from Artillery units and holds off strenuous enemy attempts to annihilate them at their isolated positions south of the Irsch-Zerf Road. (Atlantic-Italy) 15th Army Group In the **U.S. Fifth Army** area, **IV Corps** sector, organized enemy resistance ceases on Mt. Torraccia and simultaneously folds in La Serra, culminating the first phase of Corps limited offensive west of Highway 64. In the **British Eighth Army** area, 5th Corps sector, the Canadian participation in the Italian campaign culminates; the 1st Canadian Division gives it sector responsibility to the Indian 8th Division and prepares to embark for the E.T.O.; it will be on the battle line by the middle of March.

February 26th 1945 — (Pacific-Volcano Islands-Iwo Jima) On the ground, enemy resistance remains fierce. Artillery plasters the heights at Airfield 2 in support of the advancing RCT 9, 3rd Division. Meanwhile, the 4th Division drives against heavy resistance; contingents reach the southern slopes of Hill 382. P.F.C. Douglas T. Jacobson (3rd Battalion, 23rd Marines) takes over a Bazooka, subsequent to the death of its handler, then advances toward Hill 382 against withering fire which has his Platoon pinned down. Jacobson eliminates two machine gun positions, then knocks out a blockhouse before moving against a second pillbox. He continues driving forward, knocking out six enemy positions, and then volunteers to assist another Company. He advances, knocking out a pillbox and a Tank which is pouring fire into American positions. His individual actions take out 16 enemy positions and kill about seventy-five Japs. Jacobson becomes the recipient of the Medal of Honor. In addition, the 5th Marine Division advances northward. In other activity, two Planes attached to Marine Observation Squadron 4 fly in from the Escort Carrier *Wasp*, becoming the first U.S. Aircraft to land on the island; the Planes spot for Artillery units. Anti-aircraft Artillery begins bombarding Kangoku and Kama Rocks off the west coast. Off Iwo Jima, the LST 121 becomes damaged after a collision and subsequent grounding; the LSTs 760 and 884 are damaged by enemy coastal defense guns. Japanese Submarines, operating near the Volcano Islands, are struck heavily by U.S. forces: Planes (VC-82) from the Escort Carrier *Anzio* (CVE-57) sink the Japanese Submarines I-368 and the RO-43. The Destroyer Escort *Finnegan* (DE-307) destroys Japanese Submarine the I-370. **(Pacific-Philippines) Luzon** The Minesweeper *Saunter* (AM-295) is damaged by a mine. In the **U.S. Sixth Army** area, **XIV Corps** sector, the operation to eliminate the remaining three enemy-held buildings starts. The fiercely contested battle swings into the 28th before the Legislative Building is secure; the Agriculture Building is secured on the 1st of March; and the last stronghold is overcome on March 3rd, placing the entire city under the control of the American and Philippine forces. At Mt. Pacawagan, the 63rd Regiment, 6th Division climbs to the summit; however, enemy Artillery forces it to pull back after midnight. Meanwhile, the Japanese repulse the 1st Regiment at Mt. Mataba, but the 20th Regiment is advancing up the southernmost slopes. The Japanese continue to repel all attempts and by the 27th, U.S. positions become untenable and a withdrawal is ordered; the stronghold finally folds on April 17th. The Japanese mount ferocious resistance against elements of the 25th Division at Carranglan: the 2nd Battalion, 35th Regiment reaches there, but the Japs cut the supply line; on the following day it moves toward Puncan, its supply route protected by the 1st Battalion. In the **XI Corps** sector, the 108th Regiment, 40th Division seizes Hill 12 in the Zambales Mountains, culminating the present mission of the Division. By 16:00, Rock Force terminates its operations on Corregidor; still, some mop-up details are required. **Southern Philippines** The U.S. Eighth Army receives instructions to formulate plans for the seizure of Panay and northern Negros. In other activity, two Task Groups, TG 78.2 and TG 42.2, commanded by Rear Admirals W. M. Fechteler and R. S. Riggs, respectively, embark from Mindoro toward Palawan, under the umbrella coverage of units of the Fifth and Thirteenth Air Forces, while a simultaneous Air bombardment of Puerto Princess, Palawan, ensues. On Leyte, the Japanese entrenched along the northwest coast are encircled by the Americal Division; its Provisional Task Force has concluded, reducing the enemy presence from northwest Samar to Balicuatro Island and west to Capul and Naranjo on the southern part of the San Bernardino Strait. **(Pacific-Burma)** In the **British Fourteenth Army** area, 33rd Corps sector, the Indian 19th Division initiates a vigorous drive toward Mandalay. In the 4 Corps sector, the Indian 17th Division overruns the Airstrip at Thabutkon. **(Pacific-Japan)** The Light Cruiser *Pasadena* (CL-65) and the Destroyer *Porterfield* (DD-682) are damaged by enemy Naval fire south of Honshu. **(Pacific-South China Sea)** The Submarine *Hoe* (SS-258) sinks the Japanese Frigate *Shonan*. **(Atlantic-Western Europe) 21st Army Group** In the **Canadian First Army** area, the Canadian 2nd Corps launches

an offensive (BLOCKBUSTER) at 04:30, spearheaded by Canadian Infantry and Armor, to seize Calcar, Udem, and the region between there and Xanten. The Corps assault forces comprise the Canadian 4th and the British 11th Armored Divisions, plus the Canadian 2nd Armored Brigade in addition to the Canadian 2nd and 3rd and the British 43rd Infantry Divisions. The first day's progress has contingents at the steep slopes south of Calcar, Keppeln, and also secures positions close to Udem. In the **U.S. Ninth Army** area, **XVI Corps** sector, the 35th Division advances; its 137th Regiment moves through Bruck, driving toward Hueckelhoven, while its 134th takes a bridge at Hilfarth and speeds across the Roer, bulldozing its way about a mile forward. In the **XIII Corps** area, elements of the 84th Division seize Golkrath and Matzerath. The 102nd Division overruns Bellinghoven, Kueckhoven, Tenholt and Wockerath; it then launches an assault and overruns Erkelenz. Meanwhile, the advancing 5th Armored rolls over Hauthausen, Mennekrath, and Terheeg, with its C.C.B. In the **XIX Corps** sector, the 29th Division swallows Gevelsdorf, Hasselsweiler (330th), Guesten (116th), Ameln, Speil, and Titz (115th). In the 30th Division sector, Kirch, Oberembt, and Troisdorf fall to the 117th Regiment, while Kalrath is seized by the 120th. **12th Army Group** In the **U.S. First Army** area, **VII Corps** sector, heavy skirmishing develops between the enemy and the 24th Squadron of the 4th Cavalry Group along the northeastern edge of the Hambach Forest. The 3rd Armored, reinforced by the 13th Regiment, 8th Division drives northeastward. Spearheaded by the Armor, the advance makes good progress; C.C.B.'s Task Forces Lovelady and Welborn reach positions near Berrendorf, Elsdorf, and Wuellenrath, on the left, while C.C.A.'s Task Forces Doan and Kane race into Blatzheim and Buir, toppling both. In conjunction, the 83rd Armored Reconnaissance Battalion (reinforced) squeezes between the two Combat Teams and seizes Manheim with the assistance of Task Force Kane. The 104th Division seizes Morschenich and Golzheim with its 413th and 414th Regiments respectively. The 8th Division forges ahead, overrunning Eschweiler and Girbelsrath, then it drives north without encountering the enemy. The remaining resistance at Stockheim is reduced by the 28th Division; Frauwullesheim is captured in addition to villages near Rommelsheim. In the **III Corps** sector, the 1st Division takes Soller (16th Regiment), Leversbach, Rath, and Udingen (26th Regiment). Meanwhile, the 18th Regiment relieves the 8th Division (VII Corps) of responsibility for Stockheim and seizes Jakobwuellesheim. In the **U.S. Third Army** area, the 87th Division commences an attack against Hallschlag and Ormont at 17:00, and is intercepted by heavy resistance, as well as the varying degrees of German-laid obstacles that plague the attacking troops throughout the night. In the **XII Corps** sector, Mauel and Phillipsweiler are seized by the 319th Regiment, 80th Division. The Germans are able to retain Erdorf against C.C.B., 4th Armored; however, it seizes the high ground north of Bitburg. The 5th Division seizes Birtlingen, Stahl, Dockendorf, and Messerich. In the **XX Corps** sector, the German 2nd Mountain Division, commanded by Generalmajor Degen launches attacks east of Saar and north of Clerf. The 94th Infantry and 10th Armored Divisions enlarge and connect the Ockfen and Serrig bridgeheads, then combine their strengths to secure the area around Beurig, from where a heavy-duty pontoon bridge sprouts at the Saar. C.C.B., 10th Armored Division speeds down the Irsch-Zerf road, alleviating the pressure on the stranded 5th Ranger Battalion; C.C.A. drives to Irsch.

February 27th 1945 — (Pacific-Iwo Jima) The 1st and 2nd Battalions, 9th Marines, 3rd Marine Division reduce final resistance at Airfield No. 2. Meanwhile, the 1st Battalion, 9th Marines seize Hill Peter and the summit of 199 OBOE. During the fighting in the Third Marine Division sector (during 26th-27th), heavy enemy fire holds up the 2nd Battalion, 9th Marines. Private Wilson D. Watson, using his BAR, advances singlehandedly and charges a pillbox, keeping it neutralized until he gets close enough to throw a grenade. Subsequently, he and his assistant BAR man charge up the crest of the hill, receiving severe fire from the reverse slopes. Watson holds the hill until his Platoon joins him, despite heavy opposition, and kills sixty Japs in the process. He receives the Medal of Honor for his extraordinary courage. In the 4th Marine Division sector, RCT 23 drives to the summit of Hill 382, but it pulls back for the night. In the Fifth Marine Division sector, heavy enemy machine-gun fire holds up the advance of Company G, 3rd Battalion, 27th Marines as it attempts to secure Hill 362. Gunnery Sergeant William G. Walsh leads an attack and is thrown back by withering fire. Undaunted, Walsh leads a second charge up the ridge, and again his unit takes high casualties; nevertheless, the ridge is gained. Soon after, an enemy grenade is thrown into the midst of the surviving men of his detachment; instinctively, Walsh throws his body on the grenade, saving the other men. His courageous actions allow his Company to seize the hill. Walsh receives the Medal of Honor posthumously. In other activity, Marine Observation Squadron 5 begins operations from Airfield No. 1. Major General James E. Chaney, Commanding General, Army Forces and Island Commander, lands with his Headquarters and a contingent of the 147th Infantry Regiment, U.S.A. Also, advance contingents of VII Fighter Command, U.S.A. arrive on the island. The following Vessels sustain damage by collision: Light Carrier *San Jacinto* (CVL-30); Destroyer *Colhoun* (DD-801); Oiler *Merrimack* (AO-37); Attack Transports *President Adams* (APA-19) and *Knox* (APA-46); Attack Cargo Ship *Tolland* (AKA-64); LST 779, by collision and grounding, and the LST 809. **(Pacific-Philippines) Luzon** In the **U.S. Sixth Army** area, the Japanese charge American positions; however, the 63rd Regiment, 6th Division repulses it and retains Mt. Pacawagan. Meanwhile, the Japs suffer the loss of some paperwork, as a contingent of the 27th Regiment, 25th Division captures the Japanese plan for the defense of Balete Pass. **Southern Philippines** In the **U.S. Eighth Army** area, a contingent of the 19th Regiment, 24th Division is transferred to Verde Island to establish a roadblock; the unit sent is an 81-mm. Mortar section. **(Pacific-Burma)** In the **British Fourteenth Army** area, 33rd Corps sector, the Indian 20th Division's bridgehead at the Irrawaddy appears solvent, as enemy resistance dissipates. In the 4th Corps sector, Air Transports move a Brigade of the Indian 17th Division from Palel to Thabutkon to coincide with the balance of the Division, reaching the fringes of Meiktila. **(Atlantic-Western Europe)** U.S. Naval Land-based Aircraft and British Surface Ships sink the German U-Boat U-327 in the English Channel. **21st Army Group** In the **Canadian First Army** area, Canadian 2nd Corps sector, the British 43rd Division tramples Calcar, then bursts into Grieth on the Rhine, giving the Germans the heave-ho. The Canadian 2nd Infantry and 4th Armored Divisions drive into Hochwald Forest, seizing ground between it and the Balberger Forest to the south. Near Rechicourt, 1st Lt. James H. Fields, U.S. 10th Armored Infantry leads a counterattack against enemy positions, which are supported by Tanks. He becomes seriously wounded and is unable to speak, but continues to lead his men, using hand signals. Fields grabs a light machine gun from a crew which had been wiped out and charges, firing from the hip, and silences two enemy machine

guns, which have his Company pinned down. Lt. Fields receives the Medal of Honor. Udem, sitting east of the Hochwald Forest, is seized by the Canadian 3rd Division. The British 11th Armored moves from the town toward Kervenheim. In the British 30th Corps sector, pressure is lightened by the Canadian offensive, permitting the British 52nd Division to advance east from Afferden and assume responsibility for the British 51st Division zone. The British 3rd Division slices the Udem-Weeze Road. In the **U.S. Ninth Army** area, the German 15th Army, under General Zangen, is struggling to keep ranks and is unable to offer forceful opposition. In the **XVI Corps** sector, the 35th Division, pressing the area east of the Roer, snatches Altmyhl, Gerderath, Gerderhahn, and Myhl with its 137th Regiment, while the 134th Regiment wraps up Luchtenberg, Millich, Orsbeck, Ratheim, and Schauffenberg, in addition to Wassenburg and a couple of smaller towns. Meanwhile, C.C.A., 8th Armored fords the Roer and drives toward Wegberg. In the **XIII Corps** sector, Task Force Church is organized by the 84th Division to mount a motorized assault against the apparent disorganized enemy; it speeds forward, spearheaded by Co. B, 771st Tank Battalion, gaining ten miles and overrunning Beeck, Rickelrath, and Wegberg, plus many villages, despite encountering stiff opposition at a road junction southeast of Waldniel. On the right flank, C.C.B., 5th Armored is trudging through thick mud, but persists and advances as far as Guenhoven and Rheindahlen before being inundated and unable to penetrate the mud. Meanwhile, the 102nd Division Infantry shimmy through the stalled Armor and take Rheindahlen. In the **XIX Corps** sector, the Germans are capable only of mounting superficial resistance against the advancing 29th Division, which seizes Borschemich, Holzweiler, Keyenberg, and Kuckum with its 175th Regiment, while the 116th Infantry overruns Immerath, Pesch, and Otzenrath, and the 115th Regiment captures Jackerath and Opherten. Meanwhile, the 30th Division seizes Koenigshoven and Garzweiler with its 119th and 120th Regiments respectively. **12th Army Group** In the **U.S. First Army** area, also defended by General Zangen's forces, resistance is stiffer than in First Army area; however, the Yanks keep advancing. In the **VII Corps** sector, the troops push forward, tramping heavily across the flatlands of the Cologne Plain, grinding over fierce opposition in front of Cologne. Esch and Tollhausen are seized by the 4th Cavalry Group. Two bridgeheads are gained by the 3rd Armored's C.C.R. at the Erft River, while Task Forces Hogan and Task Force Richardson make good use of the prizes, the former using a bridge at Glesch and the latter wading across at Paffendorf. The 83rd Armored Reconnaissance Battalion is not quite so lucky; it seizes Grouven and Zieverich, but not before the occupants had destroyed the bridge at the Erft. C.C.B. Task Forces (3rd Armored) claim Berrendorf, Elsdorf, Giesendorf, and Wuellendorf. C.C.A's Task Force Kane seizes Heppendorf, and Sindorf in concert with Task Force Doan, which secures Bergerhausen and part of Kerpen with assistance from contingents of the 8th Division. Both the 3rd and 102nd Divisions are right on the heels of the 3rd Armored Division, vacuuming the captured towns. In the **III Corps** sector, Frangenheim and Vettweiss fall to the 16th Regiment, 1st Division as it drives toward the Neffel River, while the 18th Regiment advances to Irresheim and Kelz. The 9th Division plows forward, taking Nideggen and Thum on its way toward Berg. In the **IV Corps** sector, scaled-down attacks are launched by the 69th Division toward a ridge east of the Prether River, needed to guarantee the safety of the Hellenthal-Hollerath Highway which is to be utilized as a primary supply route; Dickerscheid and Giescheid are seized by the 271st and 273rd Regiments respectively. In the **U.S. Third Army** area, **VIII Corps** sector, Ormont and Hallschlag come under attack by the 87th Division; however, the Germans raise vicious opposition, setting the tempo early. C.C.A., 6th Armored Division gets a small bridgehead across the Pruem; the 9th Armored Infantry Battalion crosses near Manderscheid, capturing Heilhausen, but contingents of C.C.B., attempting a crossing further north, encounter intense enemy fire and pull back. In the **XII Corps** sector, the 80th Division's 317th Regiment overpowers Wissmannsdorf, while C.C.B., 4th Armored is overrunning Fliessem and Nattenheim and C.C.A. is diligently seizing Matzen. The advance also continues in the 5th Division sector, as RCT's 10 and 11 sever the Bitburg-Trier highway; RCT 10 secures Esslingen and Moetsch is taken by RCT 11. In conjunction, the 76th Division seizes Gilzem and Meckel with its 304th Regiment. Meanwhile, its 417th surges toward Idesheim and Welschbilig, taking Irrel and Niederweis with elements of its 385th Regiment. Near Prumzurley, a contingent of the 301st Engineer Tank Battalion (76th Division) is clearing mines from a roadway. P.F.C. Herman C. Wallace inadvertently steps on an S-type antipersonnel mine, activating it. Rather than diving for the ground and possibly risking injury or death to his comrades, he intentionally uses his other foot to detonate it. Wallace becomes a recipient of the Medal of Honor posthumously for his selfless courage. In the **XX Corps** sector, C.C.A., 10th Armored Division rolls over Baldringen. In other activity, the Ockfen-Serrig bridgehead is expanded to the north and northeast.

A Medic tending a wounded GI in Germany.

U.S. Marines on Iwo Jima, display captured enemy flags.

February 28th 1945 — (Pacific-Iwo Jima) The 3rd Battalion, 21st Marines, 3rd Marine Division secure Motoyama Village and the heights above Airfield No. 3. In the 4th Marine Division sector, RCT 23 still meets heavy opposition at Hill 382; RCT 25 seizes more ground, but the Japanese still retain a pocket near Minami. In the 5th Marine Division sector, RCT 27 takes the forward slopes of Hill 362 south of Nishi. During the violent confrontation, many Marines are badly wounded. Pharmacist's Mate First Class John H. Willis, U.S.N., becomes wounded while tending disabled Marines and is sent back to the aid-station. However, he moves back to the front without being released, reaching the front lines in the midst of heavy close-in fighting. He is administering plasma to an injured Marine when he comes under a grenade attack. Continuing to give the aid, he picks up the enemy grenade and tosses it back, then throws seven of his own grenades in rapid succession while simultaneously continuing to give the wounded Marine the transfusion. The next grenade goes off in his hand, killing him instantly. His inspirational actions greatly affect his outnumbered unit to take the objective and repulse a subsequent counterattack. Willis receives the Medal of Honor posthumously. The Destroyer *Bennett* (DD-473) is damaged by an Aircraft bomb and the Destroyer *Terry* (DD-513) becomes damaged by coastal defense gunfire. In addition, the Submarine Chaser PCS-1461, the Attack Cargo Vessel *Whitley* (AKA-91), and the LSTs 641 and 787 incur damage by collision. **(Pacific-Philippines) Luzon** In the **U.S. Sixth Army** area, the **XIV Corps** is ordered by General Krueger to open the Balayan and Batangas Bays, southwest Luzon. In the 6th Division sector, the summit of Mt. Pacawagan is reached by Company C, 63rd Regiment. In the XI Corps sector, the 188th Regiment (minus 2nd Battalion) reinforced, 11th Airborne Division deploys for an assault against the Ternate region on the southern coast of Manila Bay. **Southern Philippines** In the **U.S. Eighth Army** area, Task Force Victor IV, commanded by Major General Jens A. Doe, is formed on Mindoro to secure the area around Zamboanga on Mindoro; it is also directed to secure parts of the Sulu Archipelago. In other activity, Attack Group Victor III (TG78.2) arrives off Puerto Princesa, Palawan, at dawn and embarks RCT 186, which lands and secures its Airfields without encountering any opposition; radar facilities are quickly placed. At Samar, the 1st Battalion, 182nd Regiment, American Division, and the 1st Philippine Infantry move to secure the Mauo area. **(Pacific-Burma)** In the **British Fourteenth Army** area, 4 Corps sector, the Indian 17th Division attacks Meiktila, encountering stiff opposition. **(Atlantic-Western Europe) 21st Army Group** In the **Canadian First Army** area, Canadian 2 Corps sector, the Canadian 2nd Infantry and Canadian 4th Armored Divisions continue their explosive advance through the Hochwald Forest and across the terrain between there and the Balberger Forest, which is entered while the British 43rd Division, moving on the left flank of Corps, continues to move southeast along the Rhine. In the **U.S. Ninth Army** area, **XVI Corps** sector, the 35th Division seizes Rogden, Station Vlodrop, and Wildenrath (137th Regiment), Birgelen, Effeld, Rosenthal, and Steinkirchen (134th Regiment). Meanwhile, the 320th Regimental Task Force (TF Byrne) makes final preparations for its northward motorized trek against Venlo, Holland, 200 miles distant. The Eighth Armored Division, driving north beyond Wegberg, seizes Arsbeck, Merbeck, and Tetelrath. In the **XIII Corps** sector, the 84th Division encounters strong resistance; still, it gains about two miles, seizing Hardt, Hehn, and Voerst in addition to securing part of Waldniel. In other activity, the **XIX Corps**, pressing feverishly, its 29th Division in a near gallop, reaches positions near Munchen-Gladbach, while its 2nd Armored Division drives about eight miles; the Rhine lies 6 miles distant. In the **U.S. First Army** area, **VII Corps** sector, the 3rd Armored rebuffs a concentrated Tank Infantry assault at the Paffendorf bridgehead. In the 8th Division sector, elements of the 121st Regiment mop up in Kerpen, while the balance of the Regiment attack toward Moedrath. In the **III Corps** sector, the 1st Division seizes Gladach and Luxheim, while the 9th Division seizes Berg and the heights between there and Thum, in addition to overrunning Abenden and eliminating the remaining resistance on the east bank of the Corps within its zone. In the **V Corps** sector, the 69th Division seizes the balance of its objectives in the heights east of the Prether River, extending between Honningen and Rescheid. In the **U.S. Third Army** area, **VIII Corps** sector, skirmishing is ferocious in the 85th Division area; however, Neuenstein falls to the 345th Regiment. Meanwhile, the Corps commences a predawn assault which topples Kleinlangenfeld and Dausfeld with the 4th Division, while the 6th Armored's C.C.B. takes Lierfeld, Lunebach, and Merlscheid, and the 44th Armored Infantry Battalion seizes Dachscheid and Eilscheid. In addition, the 6th Cavalry Group fords the Pruem and overruns Waxweiler. In the **XII Corps** sector, the Germans are establishing sporadic resistance, engaging the 317th Regiment, 80th Division at Liessem and Niederweiler, losing both towns to the Yanks; the balance of the Division encounters no enemy forces. The Germans mount tenacious resistance in front of Malbergweich and Sefferweich, halting the advance of C.C.B., 4th Armored in the woods near Nattenheim; C.C.A. makes contact with contingents of the 5th Division, which is securing its zone to the west bank of the Kyll River, knocking over Bitburg, Irsch, Roel, Scharfbillig, Suelm, Dahlem, Idenheim, and Trimport. In conjunction, the 76th Division moves speedily, taking Eisenach, Helenberg, Hofweiler, Idesheim, and Ittelkyll. In the **XX Corps** sector, the northern drive toward Trier continues to progress. C.C.A., 10th Armored, trailed by C.C.B., plows through a menacing mine field and captures Obersehr and Paschel. Regimental Combat Team 376 (attached 10th Armored), supported by its parent 94th Division's 301st and 302nd Regiments, maintains its expansion of the Ockfen-Serrig bridgehead and responsibility of guarding the 10th Armored's flank, and demolishes obstructive pillboxes. **(Atlantic-Eastern Europe)** Moscow proclaims the capture of Neustettin and Prechlau, both important German communication centers in Pomerania; it also announces additional progress in Silesia. Meanwhile, the Germans are refusing to relent and are garnishing additional troops to launch a counterattack in Hungary; troops are being drained from the western front to support the action. **(Atlantic-Italy) 15th Army Group** In the **U.S. Fifth Army** area, the 10th Mountain Division and the Brazilian 1st Division conclude their regrouping and deploy for their second phase of securing the heights west of Highway 64. **(Atlantic-North Africa)** The Destroyer Escort *Fowler* (DE-222) and a French Warship sink the German U-Boat 869 off Morocco.

February 1945 — (United States-Soviet Union) The Russians begin to expose their lack of appreciation for the assistance handed them by the Allies. Reports about Russian mistreatment of American P.O.W.s, previously interned by the Germans, is most disturbing to the U.S., which immediately requests that Stalin clarify the reports. Stalin replies: "A Soviet Committee has been formed to take care of Foreign prisoners of war." In addition, he explains that the large numbers of U.S. prisoners (Poland) are on their way home by way of Odessa, while some unable to travel are hospitalized. The U.S. requests permission to allow U.S. Planes to land in Poland to assist its P.O.W.s; the request is refused by Stalin, despite the fact that at Yalta the Russian leader promised cooperation in the liberated areas.

A. U.S. Plane being shot down.

March 1st 1945 — (United States) President Roosevelt, exhausted from the long trip, addresses Congress regarding Yalta, from his wheelchair. **(Pacific-Iwo Jima)** RCT 21 seizes the western part of Airfield No. 3. In the 4th Marine Division sector, heavy fighting ensues at Hill 382; it falls to the 2nd Battalion, RCT 24 on the following day. Meanwhile, the 5th Marine Division's RCT 28 relieves RCT 27 and seizes Hill 362. Off Okinawa, the Destroyers *Terry* (DD-513) and *Colhoun* (DD-801) become damaged by enemy coastal guns. In addition, the Attack Transport *Berrien* (APA-62) is damaged by collision. **(Pacific-Philippine) Luzon** In the **U.S. Sixth Army** area, **XIV Corps** sector, east of Manila, the 6th Division regroups to assault the Shimbu Line which spreads from Antipolo to Mt. Oro. In the **I Corps** sector, Philippine Guerrilla forces, commanded by Lt. Colonel Russell W. Volckmann, and contingents of the 33rd Division are converging on Baguio from the north and south respectively. Meanwhile, the 25th and 32nd Divisions press along Highway 5 and the Villa Verde Trail respectively, closing against Balete Pass via the Cagayan Valley. Japanese entrenchments including pillboxes hinder progress of the 2nd Battalion, 127th Regiment, 32nd Division as it advances to Salacsac Pass along the Villa Verde Trail at the Cabalisian River. Meanwhile, the 25th Division has columns converging on Digdig and Puncan. **Southern Philippines** In the **U.S. Eighth Army** area, the Zamboanga area (Mindanao) and selected islands of Panay are carpet bombed to soften resistance for the invasion forces; subsequent to the bombardment, the 1st Battalion, 21st Regiment, 24th Division debarks at Lubang Island on the western tip of Verde Island where it secures Tilic and sweeps the balance of the island, securing most of it within a few days. Contingents of Company E, 21st Regiment embark Mindoro for Verde Island. On Palawan, Puerto Princess Harbor is seized by RCT 146, 41st Division, giving the Yanks guaranteed control of the island. **(Pacific-Ryukyu Islands)** U.S. Naval Surface Warships of Task Force 58 bombard enemy positions throughout the island chain, including Okino Daito, about 450 miles from Kyushu, Japan, while Aircraft attached to Vice Admiral Mitscher's Fast Carrier Task Force strike Air facilities, ground installations, and Shipping in Okinawa; the Torpedo Boat *Manazuru* is sunk. The Japanese Minelayer *Tsubame* is sunk off Formosa by Carrier-based Planes. In conjunction with the strike against Okinawa, Planes photograph enemy positions. **(Atlantic-Western Europe) 21st Army Group** In the **Canadian First Army** area, the Canadian 3rd Division seizes Kervenheim. However, the 2nd Corps hits heavy resistance while it moves toward Sonsbeck. In the **British Second Army** area, the U.S. 75th Division (minus RCT 289) reverts to the U.S. Ninth Army's XVI Corps. In the **U.S. Ninth Army** area, Task Force Byrne, 35th Division sprints 20 miles from positions near Wildenrath, overrunning Venlo, Holland; the rapid pace of the advance startles the enemy and gives the Yanks control of about 20 towns and villages as it moves. RCT's 134 and 137 zig-zag through the dismembered enemy positions, securing the remaining pockets bypassed by the dynamic thrust of Task Force Byrne, further exasperating the Germans. In the **XIII Corps** sector, a predawn assault is launched simultaneously by the U.S. 84th and 102nd Divisions in another record-paced advance; TF Church, 84th Division takes Boisheim before being disbanded; the 333rd Regiment pounces upon Duelken then advances to Oedt, reaching the Niers Canal, as the 11th Cavalry Group (attached 84th Division) expands its screen to Boisheim and snatches Viersen and also pounds a bridgehead across the Niers Canal. In conjunction, C.C.A., 5th Armored bolts the canal and gains control of Anrath prior to dawn on the 2nd. In the **XIX Corps** sector, the 29th Division seizes Munchen-Gladbach after subduing moderate resistance; 2nd Armored Division zooms forward, taking Kleinenbroich and its intact bridges. It then bolts to line Willich-Osterath with its C.C.A., while C.C.B. drives for Uerdingen and its Adolf Hitler Bridge. Meanwhile, C.C.R. trails C.C.A. and eliminates remaining resistance. The 83rd Division keeps pace during these deep penetrations; its 331st Regiment secures its sector to the Erft southwest of Neuss, taking Grevenbroich and Holzheim. **12th Army Group** In the **U.S. First Army** area, the **VII Corps** maintains its pressurized drive toward the Rhine and Cologne. The 3rd Armored and RCT 395 (99th Division) take Bergheim, Kenten, and the nearby eastern woods; the 4th Cavalry Group further ensures the protection of the Corps' left flank by seizing the heights northeast of Glesch, and it is then attached to the 99th Division. Contingents of the 104th Division burst across the Erft Canal and seize Horrem, Ichendorf, and Quadrath, while the 8th Division badgers the enemy holding Moedrath and the nearby heights. In the **III Corps** sector, the advance to the Rhine continues to make progress. The 1st Division seizes Dorweiler, Pingsheim, Rath, and Wissersheim with its 18th Regiment, while the 16th Regiment overruns Eggersheim be-

fore driving across the Neffel River. The 9th Armored Division advances, crumbling resistance at Disternich, Mueddersheim, and Sievernich with its C.C.B., which then gives responsibility for its prizes to the 39th Regiment, 9th Division, and attacks toward the Roth River. In conjunction, C.C.A. closes on Drove and transfers to Berg, from where it drives toward Wollersheim and encounters tenacious resistance, which halts its progress. Subsequently, both Combat Teams, reinforced by Infantry contingents of the 78th Division, sweep south along the east bank of the Roer, gaining bridgeheads as well as securing the area between Abenden and Blens, destroying the opposition at Heimbach and reaching positions slightly north of Heimbach. Later in the day, the 309th Regiment, 78th Division fords the Roer at Blens. Meanwhile, the 69th Division continues to battle for control of the heights east of the Prether River; its 271st and 273rd Regiments commit contingents, which seize Herscheid and the high ground outside Schnorrenberg. In the **U.S. Third Army** area, **VIII Corps** sector, the Germans are resisting the eastward advance with everything available; however, the 87th, which receives the brunt, is still able to eliminate the pillboxes and seize Ormont. The 4th Infantry and 6th Armored Divisions also make headway, the former pushing its 12th Regiment into the Pruem River bridgehead, while the latter enlarges its bridgehead at the Pruem, seizing Matzerath with C.C.B. Meanwhile, the 6th Cavalry Group bounces across its recently completed Bailey Bridge over the Pruem at Waxweiler and seizes Gremelscheid, Hargarten, and Lambertsberg. In the **XII Corps** sector, the 80th Division continues sweeping north between the Nims and Pruem Rivers, seizing Oberweiler and Schleid. Close by, the 4th Armored, supported with tight Air and Artillery support, overruns Malbergweich and Sefferweich as it clears the area between the Pruem and Kyll Rivers. Meanwhile, the 76th Division, operating to the south, takes Mohn, Newel, and Olk, as it drives to the Kyll River. In the **XX Corps** sector, the 10th Armored Division, reinforced by RCT 376 (94th Division) penetrates Trier, seizing the Moselle Bridge and initiating action to secure the German communication center. The bridge is seized intact because of the bravery of Lt. Colonel J.J. Richardson (10th Armored), who bolts from the lead Vehicle and races across the bridge to the far end, slicing the wires before it can be blown. Lt. Col. Richardson gives his life in the process. RCT 376 crushes the resistance of about thirty pillboxes as it maneuvers east of the Saar and overruns Wiltingen. In an attempt to cut off a German escape route from Trier, the 94th Division, reinforced by the 3rd Cavalry Group's Task Force Polk, and the 5th Ranger Battalion, spread its Saarburg bridgehead wide, moving northeast to Hentern, Lampaden, Obersehr, and Schomerich. German opposition on the right is resolute, preventing the 301st Regiment from making great strides. **6th Army Group** establishes DA ALPS (d'Armee des Alppes), giving it responsibility for the Alpine region, which stretches from the convergence of France, Switzerland, and Italy, down the Franco-Italian border to the Mediterranean Sea. The new command, led by French General Doyen, comprises U.S. and French troops. In other activity, the French Forces of the West (sometimes referred to as Western French Forces) is designated DA ATL (d'Armee de l'Atlantique). The U.S. Seventh Army deploys its XXI, XV, and VI Corps to form a rigid defensive line along the Saar, Rothbach, and Moder Rivers extending from Emmersweiler, Germany, and Oberhoffen, France. Meanwhile, the French First Army retains a defensive posture along the Rhine, guarding the right flank of the U.S. Seventh Army and the 6th

Army Group. **(Atlantic-Italy) 15th Army Group** Inclement weather forces cancellation of the planned offensive by IV Corps; it is rescheduled for March 3rd. **(Atlantic-Middle East)** USAFIME assumes responsibility for Northwest Africa, relieving MTOUSA; it is redesignated Africa Middle East Theater (AMET). **(Eastern Europe)** Soviet forces are whipping through Pomerania. One woman, a survivor and the wife of Doctor Mackow, subsequently relates what happens to her village: "THE RUSSIANS CAME TO OUR VILLAGE ON MARCH 1ST...EVERY HOUSE WAS RANSACKED, AND EVERY WOMAN FROM THE OLDEST TO THE GIRLS OF TWELVE WAS RAPED. ALL OF US WITHOUT EXCEPTION, RECEIVED THE SAME. SOME WOMEN CHOOSE TO HANG THEMSELVES. Meanwhile, the Germans holding Kolberg, hang on.

Marines spraying dead Marines with disinfectant.

March 2nd 1945 — (Pacific-Iwo Jima) Elements of the 5th Marine Division drive against the western anchor of the Japanese cross-island defenses and secure Hill 362A. The 3rd Marine Division moves into Airfield No. 3; however, enemy fire pounds the area. Meanwhile, the 4th Marine Division, operating on the right flank of the Corps, advances against the entrenched enemy in caves and fortified pillboxes. In other activity, Airfield No. 1 becomes operational for Transport Aircraft. The following U.S. Vessels sustain damage by collision off Iwo Jima: the Attack Cargo Ship *Stokes* (AKA-68); LSTs 224, 247, and the 634. The LST 042 is damaged by grounding. **(Pacific-Philippines)** Destroyers bombard Japanese positions on Parece Vela Reef in the Philippine Sea. **Luzon** In the **U.S. Sixth Army** area, the **XIV Corps** reduces final resistance in Manila; the progress prompts orders to come down directing the I Corps to continue and accelerate its northward attack. In other Corps activity, contingents of the 32nd Division trample the obstinate stronghold barring its progress and bolts further down the Villa Verde trail, as contingents of the 25th Division takes Puncan. Meanwhile, other units assault Digdig. In the **XI Corps** sector, the Rock Force eliminates final resistance on Corregidor, paving a smooth return for General Douglas MacArthur. The Japanese have sustained 4,500 killed and twenty captured; in addition, about 500 have been sealed in tunnels and caves, and another 200 are killed while attempting escape. The Americans lose slightly over 1,000 killed, wounded, or missing. Old Glory reigns over Corregidor once again; Paratroop Regimental Combat Team 503 remains on the "Rock, assuming Garrison duty." **Southern Philippines** In the **U.S. Eighth Army** area, the 1st Battalion, 132nd Regiment, American Division departs

Leyte to conduct amphibious operations against Burias and Ticao Islands. Meanwhile, on Samar, elements of the Americal Division drive to Mauo, where they meet additional contingents who report Mt. Bermodo abandoned. On Palawan, the 186th Regiment, 41st Division locates enemy presence at Hill 1125; heavy fighting erupts and does not culminate until the 4th of March. **(Pacific-Ryukyu Islands)** Rear Admiral F. E. M. Whiting's Task Group, composed of Cruisers and Destroyers, bombards Okino Daito, Jima. **(Pacific-Burma)** In the **British Fourteenth Army** area, 33rd Corps sector, the Indian 20th and the British 2nd Divisions enjoin their Irrawaddy bridgeheads west of Mandalay. **(Atlantic-Western Europe) 21st Army Group** In the **Canadian First Army** area, British 30th Corps sector, the British 3rd Division takes Winnekendonk, and Weeze falls to the British 53rd Division. In the **U.S. Ninth Army** area, **XVI Corps** sector, the 35th Division's Task Force Bryne drives into Germany from Venlo, seizing Sevelen, while the 15th Cavalry closes at Venlo to screen the 35th and establish contact with the Canadian First Army. The 8th Armored Division is racing north, plowing through Lobberich to Wachtendonk with its C.C.A., while C.C.B. passes C.C.A. at Wachtendonk and encounters a downed bridge; it retires to Wankum. In the **XIII Corps** sector, contingents of the 84th Division initiate an assault against Krefeld, after passing through St. Tonis; in conjunction, the 405th and 406th Regiments, 102nd Division assault Krefeld from the southeast. Meanwhile, C.C.A., 5th Armored pauses during its assault against Fischeln to permit safe passage of the 102nd Division, then resumes the pitch, seizes the town, and relinquishes it to units of the XIX Corps. In the **XIX Corps** sector, the pinched-out 29th Division consolidates at Munchen-Gladbach. Nearby, C.C.R., 2nd Armored repulses a heavy counterattack at Schiefbahn. At Neuss, the 329th Regiment, 83rd Division overruns Neuss prior to dawn and clears the approaches to the bridge over the Rhine; however, the Germans blow the bridge. In addition, the 83rd is struck on its right flank by a tremendous Tank-Infantry counterattack, but it holds. **12th Army Group** In the **U.S. First Army** area, **VII Corps** sector, contingents of the 99th Division ford the Erft River near Glesch to shore up the north flank of the Corps and sweep to the Rhine: the 4th Cavalry Group seizes Bedburg, Broich, Buchholz, and Frimmersdorf, then assists the 393rd Regiment, which takes Neurath. The Germans raise fierce resistance against the 3rd Armored as it attempts to increase its bridgehead by stretching northeast; Task Force Hogan (Combat Command Howze) badgers its way through Garsdorf and Wiedenfeld, reaching Auenheim, while Task Force Richardson secures Niederaussem. In addition, RCT 395 secures the Fortuna factory area east of Bergheim, and this is followed by Task Forces Doan and Kane (Combat Command Hickey) taking Oberaussem. In other Corps activity, the 104th Division defends its bridgehead east of the Erft, while it regroups, and in the 8th Division sector, heavy fighting continues at Moedrath, where the 28th and 121st Regiments make solid progress. Meanwhile, a column of the 28th Regiment seizes Habbelrath. In the **III Corps** sector, the 1st Division's drive to the Rhine secures Erp, Gymnich, Lechenich and Poll. The 9th Armored's C.C.B. operating in the 9th Divisional sector drives to the Roth River and establishes a bridgehead at Friesheim, while getting contingents to Muelheim and Wichterich; C.C.A., operating in the 78th Division sector, secures Langendorf and Wollersheim. The 39th Infantry, 9th Division, supported by a column of C.C.B., seizes Niederberg. The 9th Division seizes Bessenich, Embken, Fuessenich, Geich, Juntersdorf, and Roevenich. Activity is also brisk in the 78th Division zone; its final combat units have crossed the Roer into a stabilized bridgehead where bridging is ongoing to further expand the operation; Heimbach, Hausen, Eppenich, Buervenich, and Vlatten are captured. In the **V Corps** sector, consolidation operations continue. In the **U.S. Third Army** area, **VIII Corps** sector, the beleaguered Germans continue to resist, but the Yanks keep coming, tramping the entrenched obstacles; the 87th Division reduces sixty pillboxes as it fortifies its positions around Ormont. However, the Germans stymie the advance of the 4th Division as it drives east of the Pruem, making slight gains only. The 6th Armored Division overruns nimble resistance and punches forward contingents to the Nims River. Its 44th Armored Infantry Battalion (C.C.A.) takes Heisdorf on the rebound, after first bypassing it. Again greeted by a sunken bridge, the Infantry dismounts the Vehicles and fords the river, reaching the east bank. C.C.B. seizes Dingdorf, Nieder Lauch, Ober, and Winringen, while the 6th Cavalry's 28th Squadron seizes Pluetscheid and the high ground to the south. Meanwhile, the 6th Squadron encounters fierce resistance as it drives on the left; however, contingents pound their way to the Nims River and push into Reuland. In the **XII Corps** sector, an attack to gain a bridgehead between Erdorf and Philippsheim on the Kyll River commences at midnight (2nd-3rd), while the 4th Armored provides diversionary fire. The 5th Division spearheads the attack. The 80th Division, manning the north flank of the Corps, stays in place, except for its 80th Reconnaissance Battalion, which seizes Heilenbach. Meanwhile, the 76th Division, on the Corps right flank, reduces most of the resistance in its zone north of the Moselle and west of the Kyll, taking Aach, Besslich, Butzweiler, Kordel, and Lorich with its 417th Regiment (supported by a Battalion, 318th Regiment, 80th Division); the 385th Regiment secures the area west of Trier, and the 2nd Cavalry Group runs a screen, bolting across the Sauer, and positions its troops to guard the right flank, which is running along the east bank of the Sauer and the north bank of the Moselle. In the **XX Corps** sector, the 10th Armored culminates the battle for Trier. Combat Command B keeps driving north and reaches another blown bridge at the Kyll, near Ehrang. In conjunction, C.C.A. seizes Konz Karthaus, and Regimental Combat Team 376, 94th Division secures the Filzen peninsula and Kommlingen. Meanwhile, the 94th Division's Saarburg bridgehead is enlarged, reaching six to eight miles deep, while simultaneously repulsing counterattacks. **(Atlantic-Italy) 15th Army Group** In the **British Eighth Army** area, V Corps sector, an attack against Comacchio Spit, lying between the Adriatic and Lake Comacchio, is launched by the Cremona Group (supported by the 28th Garibaldi Brigade).

March 3rd 1945 — (Pacific-Iwo Jima) The 3rd Marine Division secures Airfield No. 3; its 2nd Battalion, 21st Marines overruns Hills 357 and 362B, east of Motoyama Plateau, virtually terminating resistance between it and the eastern coast of the island. In the 5th Marine Division sector, Japanese infiltrators penetrate the lines of the 1st Battalion, 28th Marines. Sergeant William G. Harrell kills two of the attackers as they come out of a ravine and continues to fire, despite falling grenades. He continues holding his post, but is struck severely, losing his left hand and suffering a fractured thigh. While he attempts to reload his weapon, another Soldier arrives with another weapon. However, the Japanese keep rushing and one wounds him again with the slash of a sword. Undaunted, Harrell kills the Jap and orders his wounded comrade to withdraw as two additional Japs advance into his foxhole. Ignoring the agonizing pain, he kills one with his pistol and takes the grenade which is very near his head and tosses it to the other Jap, killing him. Finally, at daylight, reinforcements arrive to evacuate Harrell, discovering twelve dead Japanese nearby, at least five of whom had been eliminated by Harrell. Sergeant Harrell receives the Medal of Honor for his unyielding courage and heroism. Also, Pharmacist's Mate Second Class, George E. Wahlen, U.S.N., distinguishes himself while assisting the 2nd Battalion, 26th Marines, 5th Marine Division. He had been severely wounded on 26th February, but remained on the battleground to continue giving aid to wounded Marines and was again wounded badly on March 2nd; however, he continued to treat about fourteen wounded men while under fierce mortar and small arms fire. His courageous actions under fire continue today as he moves across the battlefield, becoming wounded for the third time. Unable to walk, he crawls 50 yards through a wall of fire to give aid to a downed Marine. Wahlen receives the Medal of Honor for his extraordinary courage. Corporal Charles Joseph Berry, 1st Battalion, 26th Marines receives the Medal of Honor posthumously, after diving on a grenade to save the life of his buddies during the Japanese surprise attack against their positions. P.F.C. William R. Caddy, Company I, 3rd Battalion, 26th Marines attempts to knock out an enemy obstacle as his Platoon is advancing. Fierce Sniper-fire pins them down and a burst of hand grenades is exchanged by the opposing forces. An enemy grenade falls into the foxhole and Caddy blankets it with his body to protect the other Marines. He receives the Medal of Honor posthumously. In addition, Pharmacist's Mate Third Class Jack Williams, serving with the 3rd Battalion, 28th Marines, becomes wounded three times while giving aid to the Marines. He continues exposing himself to enemy fire to assist the troops, ignoring his own wounds. Subsequent to giving aid, he dresses his wounds and attempts to make it back to safety. A Sniper's bullet cuts him down with a mortal wound; Williams receives the Medal of Honor for his extraordinary courage. In other activity, the Attack Transport Vessel *Bolivar* (APA-34) is damaged by a Japanese coastal defense gun. **(Pacific-Philippines)** Luzon In the **U.S. Sixth Army** area, **XIV Corps** sector, Manila capitulates at the hands of the 37th Division, which eradicates the final resistance. In conjunction, the 11th Airborne Division concludes its operation, reducing the final resistance at Ternate and its surrounding area, securing Manila Bay. In the **I Corps** sector, the 35th Regiment, 25th Division seizes Digdig and is eliminating final resistance around Puncan. **Southern Philippines** In the **U.S. Eighth Army** area, contingents of the Americal Division, bolstered by Naval Surface fire and Marine Aircraft, land on Masbate, Burias, and Ticao Islands against no opposition, finding Ticao vacant; a sweep of Burias is initiated; however, no enemy forces are encountered until the 6th. Philippine Guerrillas take over the islands on the 11th, permitting the 1st Battalion, 132nd Regiment to return to Leyte. **(Pacific-Borneo)** The Submarine *Tuna* lands men and supplies on the northeast coast. **(Pacific-French Indo China)** The Japanese Oiler *Hario* is sunk by a mine. **(Atlantic-Western Europe) 21st Army Group** The 1st Commando Brigade, attached to the British 52nd Division and the 15th Cavalry Group, (U.S. XVI Corps, Ninth Army General Simpson) establish contact at Walbeck, southwest of Geldern. In the **U.S. Ninth Army's XVI Corps** sector, TF Byrne, 35th Division hits tenacious resistance outside of Sevelen and is held to minor gains. The 8th Armored is pinched out by the 35th Division and the XIII Corps; however, its C.C.B. seizes Aldekerk prior to it reverting to reserve. In the **XIII Corps** sector, RCT 334 encounters its first heavy resistance at Rath, eliminates it, and heads toward Homberg. In addition, other 84th Division contingents make progress; the 333rd continues driving along the left flank, while the 335th reduces the final opposition at northeast Kerfeld and bolts toward the Rhine. Meanwhile, the 102nd Division secures southeast Kerfeld. In the **XIX Corps** sector, the 29th Division reverts to reserve, but remains deployed at Munchen-Gladbach. The 2nd Armored Division, reinforced, continues rolling over the Cologne Plain; C.C.A. roars through Viertelscheide; C.C.R., attached to C.C.A., drives toward Kaldenhausen, halting short of the objective upon orders, and C.C.B. is viciously engaged at the wobbly Uerdingen bridge, damaged, but not totally blown. The 3rd Battalion, 330th Regiment, 83rd Division advances to the bridge at Oberkassel, finding it partially submerged. In other activity, the 95th Division attacks toward the Rhine on the following day. **12th Army Group** In the **U.S. First Army** area, **VII Corps** sector, Grevenbroich and Wevelinghoven fall to contingents of the 99th Division (24th Squadron, 4th Cavalry Group); the 393rd drives from Neurath to Muchhausen, while the 394th reaches Rommerskirchen. In other activity, the 395th Regiment is detached from 3rd Armored, reverting back to 99th Division; it then seizes Sinsteden. The 4th Cavalry Group is detached from the 99th Division and attached to 3rd Armored. The 3rd Armored gets an early morning start and springs its C.C. Howze and C.C. Hickey, on the left and right respectively, against Stommeln and Pulheim, each being struck by two Task Forces and Air support. In conjunction, Combat Command Boudinot (C.C.B.) drives between the Howze and Hickey positions, supporting the Howze forces, and takes Stommeln (TF Lovelady). Meanwhile, Task Force Welborn takes Sinnersdorf effortlessly. The 104th Division drives toward Cologne, seizing Dansweiler, Glessen, and the heights east of Horrem, then initiates an assault against Koenigsdorf. The 8th Division's 28th Regiment takes Bottenbroich and Grerath with predawn attacks and by 19:30 is driving toward Frechen. In the **III Corps** sector, elements of the 1st Division seize Blessem, Dirmerzheim, and Liblar; it drives to the Erft. The 9th Division has contingents advance to Lommersum and establish a bridgehead; its 47th Regiment takes Ober Elvenich and Ober Wichterich, while the 60th Regiment overruns opposition at Zulpich. C.C.A., 9th Armored Division seizes Merzenich; the Division receives orders to secure a crossing of the Erft at Euskirchen. Meanwhile, the 78th Division's 311th Regiment defends its bridgehead at Heimbach, while the remaining resistance in Buervenich is eradicated by the 309th Regiment, which also supports the 9th Armored Division, and topples Sinzenich and seizes Linzenich and Loevenich. In the **V Corps** sector, the 102nd Cavalry Group drives to the heights south of Heimbach; Task Force S, 2nd Division fords the Roer there and pushes south toward Gemund. Meanwhile, the 23rd Regiment fortifies its positions west of Gemund and occupies Malsbenden. In the **U.S. Third Army** area, **VIII Corps** sector, the Germans mount vehement resistance, dragging the progress of the 87th Division, including its Tank and Tank Destroyer support, to a crawl, both in the area north of Ormont and near Reuth. In the 4th Division's line of advance, the Germans also intercept with iron resistance near Gondelsheim; however, its progress on the right flank is favorable; the 22nd Regiment seizes Weinsheim and the enemy entrenchments west of Fleringen, while the 12th Regiment takes Rommerscheim against feeble resistance. In conjunction, C.C.B., 11th Armored secures Fleringen as it drives to the Kyll. The 6th Armored Division advances to the Nims; a contingent of C.C.B. secures Giesdorf;

a unit of C.C.A. seizes Schoenecken and Wetteldorf. Meanwhile, the 6th Cavalry Group reduces the resistance at Reuland. In the **XII Corps** sector, the 5th Division establishes a bridgehead east of the Kyll and seizes Metterich, Gondorf, and Huettingen. In the **XX Corps** sector, C.C.R., 10th Armored Division maintains its drive toward Sweich until it reaches a blown bridge at the Ruwer River outside of Eitelsbach. RCT 376 is detached from 10th Armored and reverts to the 94th Division. **6th Army Group** In the **U.S. Seventh Army** area, scaled down attacks are launched in the 63rd and 70th Division zones to bolster its positions, the latter utilizing C.C.A., 112th Armored Division. The French Lorraine Division drives beyond Forbach-Saarbruecken road, and its 276th Regiment takes Forbach, establishing a roadblock in front of Stiring Wendel. Meanwhile, the 274th Regiment penetrates Stiring Wendel. The 253rd Regiment, 63rd Division drives toward the Hahnbusch and nearby heights; its Company C is halted short of the woods by a rain of enemy fire. **(Atlantic-Italy) 15th Army Group** In the **U.S. Fifth Army** area, reinforcements continue to flow in to the sector in preparation of the upcoming spring offensive. An abundance of Artillery also arrives. The IV Corps launches an offensive (second phase) to secure the ridges northeast of Mt. Torraccia and Mt. Castello. The 10th Mountain Division secures Mt. Terminale and Mt. della Vedetta and establishes a roadblock along the road to Pietra Colora. The Brazilian Expeditionary Force's 1st Division works the right flank during the assault, coordinating with the 10th Mountain Division. In the **British Eighth Army** area, the British 56th Division seizes a solid position on the east bank of the Senio, near south Severo, while the ongoing Cremona Group attack against Comacchio Spit continues.

General Lucian Truscott.

U.S. B-29s passing Mt. Fujiama during a bombing mission over Japan.

March 4th 1945 — **(Pacific-Iwo Jima)** The island receives its first crippled B-29 Bomber. **(Pacific-Japan)** The XXI Bomber Command commits 192 B-29s against the Musashino Aircraft factory in Tokyo. This is the final precision bombardment phase of XXI BC operations against Japan's Aircraft factories. **(Pacific-Philippines) Luzon** In the **U.S. Sixth Army** area, **XIV Corps** sector, the drive against the Shimbu line continues; the 11th Airborne is directed to secure Balayan and Batangas Bays in southern Luzon. In the **XI Corps** sector, contact is established between the 38th and 43rd Divisions at Tiaong. Subsequently, the 43rd drives into the ragged Zambales Mountains west of Clark Field. In other activity, Air Warning Squadron 4 arrives in Leyte Gulf from the Admiralties. **Southern Philippines** In the **U.S. Eighth Army** area, Hill 1125 on Palawan capitulates to the 186th Regiment's Company B, which uses the flame-thrower for added incentive. Meanwhile, a methodical search is ongoing on Samar in the Mauo area for signs of enemy presence. **(Pacific-Burma)** In the British Fourteenth Army area, 4 Corps sector, Meiktila is virtually secured by the Indian 17th Division. **(Atlantic-Western Europe) 21st Army Group** In the **Canadian First Army** area, German resistance begins to subside; the 2 Corps takes advantage and plows forward, making substantial gains as the British 43rd Division seizes Appeldorn and Vynen as it continues to clear the west bank of the Rhine; the Canadian 2nd and 3rd Divisions take Hochwald and secure the Balberger Forest. Meanwhile, the British 11th Armored maintains its perimeter south of the forest, and the Canadian 4th Armored assembles in it to await further orders to advance. In the British 30th Corps sector, the British 53rd Division secures Geldern and Issum, making contact with the U.S. 35th Division at the former. In the **U.S. Ninth Army** area, **XVI Corps** sector, the 35th Division is encountering strong resistance as it drives northeast toward the Rhine. Reinforcements arrive to bolster the assault against Lintfort. In the **XIII Corps** sector, the brutalizing house-to-house fighting in Repelin ceases; after its victory, C.C.R., 5th Armored Division bolts southeast to sever the enemy's escape route by gaining control of the Rheinberg-Moers Road. The 84th Division's 335th Regiment drives to the Rhine, seizing Baerl and Moers, encountering stiff resistance at the intact Rheinhausen Railroad bridge (at the former), while the 334th Regiment pushes toward the Admiral Scheer Highway Bridge that spans between Duisburg and Homberg. In the **XIX Corps** sector, the 95th Division drives toward the Rhine on the northern flank of the Corps, bolstered by its RCT 379 recently returned from the 2nd Armored Division; contingents secure part of north Uerdingen;

however, German resistance at the pocket near Adolf Hitler bridge is resolute. Meanwhile, the 2nd Armored Division winds down its Cologne Plain operations, seizing Kaldenhausen, Viertelsheide, and the surrounding areas. **12th Army Group** In the **U.S. First Army** area, **VII Corps** sector, the 99th Division drives rampantly along the Erft River, seizing over thirty towns and villages. A Battalion of the 83rd Armored Reconnaissance Battalion, Third Armored overruns Hackhousen and gets Patrols to the Rhine outside of Worringen; it had bypassed a well-fortified Roggendorf, which is soon taken with the support of Task Force Lovelady. The combined thrust also seizes Worringen, and the U.S. repulses major counterattacks. The 4th Cavalry Group overruns Delhoven, Hackenbroich, and Shaberg. Meanwhile, the 4th Division launches an attack at midnight (3rd-4th) seizing Brauweiler, Buschbell, Freimersdorf, Koenigsdorf, Loevenich, Weiden, and Widersdorf with its 414th and 415th Regiments. In addition, the 28th Regiment, 8th Division takes Frechen. In the **III Corps** sector, the 1st Division's 16th Regiment secures Bliesheim and Obler Liblar, and establishes a bridgehead across the Erft, while its 16th Regiment mops up Weilerswist. East of the Erft, the 9th Division seizes Derikum, Frauenberg, and Hausweiler; C.C.B., 9th Armored, attached to the 9th Division, seizes a bridgehead at the Erft and takes Gross Buellesheim and Wuescheim. Meanwhile, the 9th Armored drives east at 14:00; C.C.R. advances to the Erft River line north of Euskirchen, while C.C.A. seizes Euskirchen. In the 78th Divisional zone, Duerscheven, Enzen, and Uelpenich fall to the 311th Regiment. In the **V Corps** sector, the 102nd Cavalry Group, operating on the north flank, secures the Vlatten-Hergarten-Duttling line southwest to the 2nd Division area outside of Gemond. Contingents of the 2nd Division reduce some obstinate pillboxes along the northern bank of the Urft and seize Gemund. Meanwhile, the 28th Division reduces Schleiden and simultaneously begins relieving contingents of the 2nd Division, which are deployed south of Gemund. The 69th Division also relieves contingents of the 28th Division, as it moves north. In the **U.S. Third Army** area, **VIII Corps** sector, German pillboxes jeopardize the north flank of the Corps, until the 87th Division tramples over 110 of them, reducing them to rubble; the 346th and 347th overrun Hallschlag, Kronenburgerhuette, Kerschenbach, and Scheid as they reach the Kyll River. In conjunction, the towns of Reuth and Schoenfeld are taken by the 345th Regiment. Activity is robust in the 4th Division zone; it stampedes eastward, seizing Gondelscheim and Schwirzheim, while simultaneously eradicating resistance at Buedesheim and Wallersheim, which had been bypassed by the 11th Armored Division. In addition, the 90th Division makes great strides, overrunning light opposition to seize Nieder, Ober Hersdorf, Seiwerath, and Neustrassburg. Meanwhile, the 6th Cavalry Group overruns its area east of the Nims, reducing the remaining resistance in Lasel, Wawern, Huscheid, Barbach, Balesfeld, and Neuheilenbach, and establishing contact with the XII Corps on its right. In the **XII Corps** sector, the 5th Division enlarges its bridgehead at the Kyll River, capturing Badem, Dudeldorf, Erdorf, and Ordorf, while contingents of the 76th Division ford the Kyll and secure Auw, Hosten, Orenhofen, Preist, and Speicher. In other activity, the imminent assault of the 4th Armored Division is suspended until the 5th Division bridgehead is further expanded. **6th Army Group** In the **U.S. Seventh Army** area, **XXI Corps** sector, the 276th Regiment, 70th Division drives into the Forbach Forest; the 274th Regiment is still heavily engaged at Stiring Wendel where the brutalizing house-to-house fighting continues to rage. Meanwhile, the 253rd Regiment, 63rd Division secures part of the Hahnbusch and seizes nearby Birnberg Hill. **(Atlantic-Eastern Europe)** Soviet forces wedge through the German lines in Pomerania, delivering a key blow which separates the forces, cuts the communications between Danzig and Stettin, and drives to the Baltic coast. The Second White Russian Front has contingents penetrate the coastal sector at Koeslin, and the First White Russian Front strikes near Kolberg. In conjunction, other forces of the latter advance to the Oder, southwest of Stargard, and overpower the resistance at Pyritz. **(Atlantic-Italy) 15th Army Group** In the **U.S. Fifth Army** area, **IV Corps** sector, the 10th Mountain Division continues to advance steadily, its 87th Regiment seizing Mt. Acidola, Madonna di Brasa, and Mt. della Croce, while the 86th Regiment takes Mt. Grande d'Aiano. The Brazilian Expeditionary Force's 1st Division assumes responsibility for the 10th Mountain Division's sector, east of the Pietra Colora. In the British Eighth Army area, 5th Corps sector, the Cremona Group seizes Torre di Primaro, a commanding feature needed to launch operations against Comacchio Spit.

March 5th 1945 — (Pacific-Iwo Jima) V.A.C. regroups for an offensive which commences on the following day. In other activity, the 3rd Marines, Expeditionary Troops Reserve embarks for Guam. The LST 642 is damaged by collision. **(Pacific-Philippines) Luzon** The U.S. 37th Division is attached to Sixth Army and assigned Garrison duty in Manila; in conjunction, RCT 158 reverts to XIV Corps. In the **XIV Corps** sector, the 11th Airborne, reinforced by RCT 158, launches its assault to secure the Balayan and Batangas Bays; however, the Japanese raise vociferous resistance and halt RCT 158, near Langanan in southern Luzon. In the **I Corps** sector, the Japanese still retain control of the area from Vigan, extending south to the San Fernando Valley, but the Guerrilla Force, N. Luzon controls the remainder of the west coast and also controls the northern coast of the island west of the Cagayan River mouth. The 33rd Division, driving through the Villa Verde Pass, is fiercely engaged at the Salacsac Pass, and the 32nd Division is closing against Baguio and San Fernando to hook up with the Guerrillas and squeeze the remaining Japanese tightly between the two converging forces. Meanwhile, the 25th Division eliminates the final resistance in Puncan and concentrates on keeping Highway 5 clear between Digdig and San Jose, as it concludes its initial phase of the Cagayan Valley drive. **Southern Philippines** The 19th Infantry, 24th Division receives orders to secure Romblon Island. On Palawan, the 2nd Battalion, 186th Regiment advances to positions outside of Iratag and prepares to attack the heavily entrenched Japanese defenses there. The Hill resists bitterly, repulsing several determined attacks including those which are supported by Artillery, mortars, and Aircraft, until finally capitulating on the 8th. **(Pacific-Dutch East Indies)** Army Aircraft sink the Japanese Submarine Chaser No. 110. **(Pacific-Ryukyu Islands)** The Submarine *Tilefish* (SS-307) sinks the Japanese Minesweeper No. 15. **(Pacific-Burma)** In the ALFSEA area, 15 Corps sector, Tamandu, on the Arakan coast, is seized by the 25th Indian Division; an advance Supply Base is established for use in Operation DRACULA, prior to the Division embarking for Akyab. In the British Fourteenth Army area, 33rd Corps sector, the Indian 19th Division fords the Chaungmagyi in the Madaya region, nearing Mandalay. **(Atlantic-Western Europe) 21st Army Group** In the **Canadian First Army** area, the British 43rd Division and Canadian 2nd Division close against Xanten, converging cautiously on the Germans' final stronghold west of the Rhine. In conjunction,

the Canadian 3rd Division drives fiercely against entrenched German positions in the heights north of Sonsbeck. Meanwhile, the British 43rd Division continues to advance toward Alpen. In the **U.S. Ninth Army** area, TF Byrne (35th Division) secures Camp and Camperbruch, while RCT 137, supported by C.C.B., 8th Armored, seizes Lintford and Rheinberg; subsequently, the force is redesignated TF Murray and it assaults Wesel. In the **XIII Corps** area, C.C.R., 5th Armored storms to the Rhine at Orsoy, seizing it and Rheinkamp before hurling its power against enemy columns which are in free flight from the area. In the 84th Division sector, the Germans detonate the Rheinhausen Bridge, inflicting damage, but not total destruction; the 334th Regiment overruns spirited resistance and secures Homberg, then makes a sprint to the Admiral Scheer Bridge, arriving a few steps too late; the Germans have blown it. In the **XIX Corps** sector, 95th Division zone, the 379th Regiment vanquishes the pocket near the Adolf Hitler Bridge in south Uerdingen, while the 377th and 378th Regiments drive to the area near the blown bridges at Rheinhausen; remnant resistance west of the Rhine in the 95th Division zone is eradicated, concluding the Corps' participation in Operation GRENADE. **12th Army Group** In the **U.S. First Army** area, **VII Corps** sector, the 99th Division is charging toward the Rhine, seizing Delrath and Nievenheim in addition to many smaller towns and villages. The 3rd Armored Division overruns resistance at the I.G. Farben factory and brick plant and also seizes Dormagen and Horrem. In addition, contingents of 3rd Armored and the 104th Division converge on Cologne during the early morning hours; units of 3rd Armored penetrate quickly. Contingents of the 104th swing against it from the east, overrunning Junkersdorf before piercing the defenses and advancing about 4,000 yards into the city. Meanwhile, the 8th Division mounts tremendous pressure as the 121st Regiment moves swiftly; by dawn on the 6th it controls Alstadten, Bachem, Burbach, Gleul, and Stotzheim and is closing on Huerth; the 28th Regiment reinitiates its attack at midnight (5th-6th) and notches its belt with Berrenrath and Knapsack before dawn. In the **III Corps** sector, subsequent to a boundary adjustment between it and the VII Corps, the 1st Division smashes into the pocket lying between the two Corps; the 26th Regiment bolts to the heights southwest of Dorf Pingsdorf and to Walberberg, while the 16th Regiment drives aggressively to Roesberg, Merten, and Metternich, seizing the latter. The Yanks continue their sleepless nights as they continue to pound the enemy at every turn, and the 9th Division is no exception. Its 47th Regiment secures Gross, Mueggenhausen, Neukirchen, Schwarzmaar, and Vernich, while the 39th overruns Schneppenheim and Strassfeld. The 9th Armored Division rolls across the Erft, streaking toward Rheinbach and Stadt Meckenheim; C.C.B. seizes Esch, Klein Buellesheim, and Ludendorf, while the trek of C.C.A. overruns Cuchenheim, Odendorf, Roitzheim, and Weidesheim. The 79th Division whacks everything in its path; the 311th Regiment topples Antweiler, Billig, Firmenich, Rheder, Satzvey, and Stotzheim, while the 309th, subsequent to pausing to allow the 311th to pass through its lines, bashes its way into Elsig, Euenheim, and Weiskirchen, seizing all three. In the **V Corps** sector, the Germans are pressed hard and forced to withdraw with expedience toward the Rhine. The 102nd Cavalry Group slashes through Gehn, Irnich, Kommern, Ober Gartzem, Schaven, and Schwerfen. The 2nd Division's 23rd Regiment drives south, knocking over Berg, Eicks, and Floisdorf; meanwhile, T.F.S. is disbanded and the 3rd Battalion, 38th Regiment maintains the pressure south of Gemund and seizes the heights near Nierfeld, prior to being relieved by the 28th Division. In other activity, the 69th and 106th Divisions make preparations for an attack, the latter stretching its 424th Regiment widely to establish contact with the 69th to the north and the Third Army to the south. In the **U.S. Third Army** area, **VII Corps** sector, the 345th Regiment, 87th Division secures the heights east of Reuth, concluding the Division's immediate mission. The 4th Division seizes Duppach and Oos as it advances east, then it knocks out opposition on two hills to the north, assisting the 11th Armored Division's advance. The 90th Division overruns Birresborn, Hinterhausen, and Lissingen with its 357th Regiment. In the **XII Corps** sector, the 318th Regiment, 80th Division, takes Malberg and Neidenbach, disintegrating the resistance in its zone west of the Kyll, except a tiny pocket in the Usch-St. Thomas sector. The 4th Armored Division secures Kyllburgweiler, Seinsfeld, and Steinborn (25th Cavalry Reconnaissance Squadron), Meisburg, Salm, Wallenborn, and Weidenbach (C.C.B.), and C.C.A. overcomes treacherous roads to seize Gindorf and Oberkail. Meanwhile, the 5th Division expands its bridgehead to include Orsfeld, Philippsheim, and Pickliessem, while the 304th Regiment, 76th Division cleans out the remnant resistance within its bridgehead, which had been previously bypassed. In the **XX Corps** sector, the 10th Armored bridgehead at the Rower River is enlarged about 1,500 yards to the northeast. The Germans, although badly badgered, are still capable of mounting deadly resistance. The 94th Division, which had taken Ollmuth without opposition during the night of the 5th, is struck by a fierce counterattack, which breaks through the perimeter of the 302nd Regiment. In other activity, the 65th Division receives its baptism under fire; its first combat mission is to relieve the 28th Division at the Saarlautern bridgehead. **6th Army Group** In the **U.S. Seventh Army** area, XXI Corps sector, there is heavy skirmishing in the Forbach Forest and the woods northwest of Marienau as the 276th Regiment maintains its pressure at both points. Meanwhile, the 274th Regiment reduces the final resistance in Stiring Wendel. The 63rd Division finishes its operation to secure the Hahnbusch, seizing the woods and the nearby peak. **(Atlantic-Eastern Europe)** Stargard, a once solid German stronghold, folds under pressure of the First White Russian Front, clearing the Soviet path to Stettin. **(Atlantic-Italy) 15th Army Group** In the **U.S. Fifth Army** area, the IV Corps completes its second phase of its limited attacks. The 85th Division repulses counterattacks at its positions on Mt. della Spe during the night of the 5th. The Brazilian 1st Division seizes positions above Vergato after bypassing Castelnuovo.

March 6th 1945 — (United States) The U.S.S. *Gilbert Islands* (2nd commissioned Marine Escort Carrier) embarks the Marine Carrier Group 2 (VMF-512, VMTB-143, and CASD-2) at San Diego, California, and sails for the Pacific during April 1945. **(Pacific-Iwo Jima)** The 3rd, 4th, and 5th Marine Divisions mount a full scale attack driving northeast and east to eliminate the remaining resistance on the island. In other activity, Brigadier General Ernest C. Moore, U.S.A., Commanding General Fighter Command, arrives at Airfield No. 1 with Planes of the 47th Fighter and 548th Night Fighter Squadrons. **(Pacific-Philippines)** Luzon In the **U.S. Sixth Army** area, **XIV Corps** sector, Planes and Artillery lay barrages upon enemy positions to soften resistance for the next assault. In the 11th Airborne sector, the 158th Infantry advances to Lemery, across the Lemery River. In the **I Corps** sector, General Krueger insists upon a speed up of the operation to secure Balete Pass-Santa Fe-Imugan area. On the Villa Verde Trail, the 1st Battalion, 127th Regiment, 32nd Division,

fords the Cabalisian River, closing on Salacsac Pass No. 2, while the 25th Division parallels Highway 5 as it drives north toward Putlan; the 3rd Battalion begins to push reconnaissance units up the Old Spanish Trail toward Salazar. **(Southern Philippines)** In the **U.S. Eighth Army** area, Patrols of the 21st Regiment discover two additional islands of the Lubang Group defenseless. On Palawan, the Japanese holding Hill 1445 repel attempts by the 2nd Battalion, 186th Regiment, 41st Division to dislodge them, and on Burias, the 1st Battalion, 132nd Regiment, Americal Division, makes its first contact with the Japanese. **(Atlantic-Western Europe) 21st Army Group** In the **Canadian First Army** area, the Canadian 2nd and British 43rd Divisions sustain a hefty bombardment and continue to bolster their positions at Xanten, while simultaneously preparing to launch an attack. The Canadian 3rd Division advances into Sonsbeck and establishes contact with the British 30th Corps, concluding its operation. Also, the Canadian 4th Armored Division drives from Sonsbeck toward Veen. In the British 30th Corps sector, the British 53rd Division moves prudently along the road to Wesel, closing on Alpen. In the **U.S. Ninth Army** area, Operation GRENADE ends successfully as the drive from the Roer to the Rhine has been attained. In the **XVI Corps** sector, the 35th Division mops up in Rheinberg, and the 30th Division is detached from XIX Corps and attached to XVI Corps. **12th Army Group** In the **U.S. First Army** area, **VII Corps** sector, the 395th Regiment, 99th Division seizes the four remaining enemy-held towns on the Corps' northern flank, including Udesheim and a zinc factory. In the 3rd Armored's zone, the lone remaining resistance stands in the northeastern section of Cologne along the Rhine; C.C. Boudinot, supported by C.C. Howze's Task Force Hogan, overruns Feldkassel, Merkenich, Merheim, and Niehl, while C.C. Hickey, bolstered by TF's Doan and Kane, plow through Cologne reaching the Rhine, securing the city except for the lone pocket in the northeast portion of the town. Most of the southern sector of the city is secured by the 104th Division. The 8th Division maintains 24 hour-a-day attacks toward the Rhine; by dawn on the 7th, its 121st Regiment secures Huerth, Hermulheim, and Kendenich, and its 28th Regiment controls Kalscheuren and Meschenich. In the **III Corps** sector, Badorf, Dorf Pingsdorf, Eckdorf, Schwadorf, and Walberburg are taken by the 26th Regiment, 1st Division, while the 16th Regiment secures Dersdorf, Hemmerich, Merten, Roesberg, Tripelsdorf, Ullekoven, and Waldorf. In the 9th Division sector, the Erft bridgehead is enlarged; Buschoven, Dunstekoven, Heimerzheim, and Ollheim are secured. The 9th Armored Division drives toward the confluence of the Ahr and Rhine Rivers; Flerzheim, Miel, Morenhoven, and Stadt Meckenheim are secured by C.C.B., while C.C.A. clears Altendorf, Bettlehoven, Bollingen, Gelsdorf, Lantershofen, Ober Drees, Rheinbach, and Wormersdorf. In the 78th Division sector, Flamersheim, Loch, Merzbach, Nieder Kastenholz, Queckenberg, Schlebach, and Schweinheim are secured. In the **V Corps** sector, the 102nd Cavalry Group takes Antweiler, Arloff, Kalkar, Kirspenich, and Wachendorf. The 2nd Division crams Tanks and Tank Destroyers with Infantry troops and drives through 25 towns, reaching the general line Iversheim-Noethen-Pesch. The 28th Division is driving southeast toward the Ahr, taking a road junction outside Eichen, Golbach, and Rinnen with its RCT 112, while RCT 110 drives to Kall and Soetenich, and other contingents reach Zingsheim. Meanwhile, the 69th Division drives east, three Regiments abreast in pursuit of the Germans; the advance moves through Blumenthal, Ober Wolfert, Oberhausen, Reifferscheid, Wildenburg, and Zingsheid. In the **U.S. Third**

Army area, VIII Corps sector, the 87th Division seizes Birgel, Glaadt, Goennersdorf, Juenkerath, Krimm, Lissendorf, Niederkyll Schueller, Stadtkyll, and Staffeln, while the 4th Division overruns Roth, and secures the heights north of Oos. The 90th Division seizes Gerolstein, Michelbach, Niederbach, and Buescheich; elements also drive northeast to secure Gee and the heights outside of Gerolstein; the 1st Battalion, 359th Regiment fords the Kyll to secure the balance of Muerlenbach and occupy Densborn. In the XII Corps sector, the 318th Regiment reduces the final pocket of resistance in the 80th Divisional zone, as the 4th Armored pushes to the Rhine: C.C.B. races through Darscheid, Daun, Puetzborn, Ober Stadtfeld, and Schoenbach, and establishes outposts at Ulmen, while C.C.A. encounters terrible roads and pivots to follow behind C.C.B., advancing to Salm-Wallenborn-Uedersdorf region. During the impressive drive, the German 53rd Army Corps is overrun and General K. von Rothkirch and General Lieutenant Botsch are among the captured; Third Army has been averaging about 1,000 prisoners per day for the last month. The 5th Division's 2nd Regiment penetrates Schwartzenborn; however, fierce resistance forces it to withdraw; the 11th Regiment sweeps northward seizing Etteldorf and Wilsecker, and Task Force Onaway, 76th Division drives to Herforst. In the XX Corps sector, C.C.B., 10th Armored Division encounters tenacious opposition at its Kyll River bridgehead, which prevents it from getting a bridge laid. At the Ruwer River bridgehead, RCT 417 (minus) expands its area taking Kenn, Ruwer, and Mertzdorf into its sector. 6th Army Group In the U.S. Seventh Army area, XXI Corps sector, heavy skirmishing continues at Forbach woods, where the 70th Division continues to secure the area. (Atlantic-Eastern Europe) Forces of the Second White Russian Front finish reducing the German resistance at Grudziadz, a strategic defense system on the lower Vistula in Poland. The force continues toward Danzig, eliminating surrounded German troops holding southwest of Koeslin in German Pomerania. The First White Russian Front continues to make big strides in northern Pomerania where Belgard and other German strongpoints are cleared. (Atlantic-Italy) In the U.S. Fifth Army area, IV Corps sector, the 81st Cavalry Reconnaissance Squadron is detached from 1st Armored Division (II Corps) and attached to IV Corps to relieve contingents of the Brazilian Expeditionary force. In the II Corps sector, the 34th Division relieves the 88th Division which is deployed along Highway 5.

Marine flamethrower on Iwo Jima.

March 7th 1945 — (Pacific-Iwo Jima) Company K, 3rd Battalion, 9th Marines, 3rd Marine Division seizes Hill 362C in the northeastern part of the island. During the heavy fighting, several contingents become isolated. Second Lt. John H. Leims advances 400 yards singlehandedly and lays telephone lines. Orders come in to withdraw his Platoon; however, several wounded men are still on the abandoned ridge. Leims defies heavy enemy fire and returns to rescue one wounded Marine; despite apparent exhaustion, he returns for a third time and carries out another wounded man. Leims becomes a recipient of the Medal of Honor for his heroism. In the 5th Marine Division sector, Hill 215 is overrun. In other activity, General James Chaney, U.S.A., takes responsibility for operation of the Airfields, including air defenses. Brigadier General Ernest C. Moore, U.S.A., becomes Commander, Air, Iwo Jima. **(Pacific-Philippines)** Luzon Headquarters U.S. Armed Forces Far East closes on Leyte and establishes its Headquarters in Manila. In the **U.S. Sixth Army** area, preparations by the 6th Infantry and 1st Cavalry Divisions continue to unwind for the imminent combined attack against the Shimbu line. Enemy positions are bombarded effectively by both Artillery and Air craft. In the 11th Airborne sector, the 158th Regiment takes undefended Taal and moves beyond, gaining several miles to both the east and south; the 187th Infantry jumps into the fight, its 1st Battalion pushing north of Lake Taal against nominal resistance, gaining much terrain. In the **I Corps** sector, Aringay and its bridge are seized by the 33rd Division without interference; it begins probing toward Mt. Magabang. Mean-

Cologne, Germany.

while, the 32nd Division elements (1st Battalion, 1217th Regiment), working the Villa Verde Trail, encounter impenetrable opposition, prompting the 3rd Battalion to drive from Santa Maria to outflank the obstinate resistance. In addition, the 25th Division continues to press forward, its 27th and 161st Regiments advancing alongside Highway 5; the 1st Battalion, 35th Regiment seizes the high ground northeast of Putlan, effortlessly. **(South Philippines)** In the **U.S. Eighth Army** area, the Americal Division is directed to secure Cebu, Bohol, and Negros Oriental in addition to the smaller adjacent islands. On Palawan, Hill 1445 continues to resist capitulation. **(Pacific-Burma)** In the N.C.A.C. area, Lashio is occupied by contingents of the Chinese 38th Division; this concluded the second phase of Operation CAPITAL. In the **British Fourteenth Army** area, the Japanese counterattack to resecure Meiktila and seize Taugtha, which virtually isolates the Indian 17th Division at Meiktila. **(Atlantic-Western Europe)** 21st Army Group In the **Canadian First Army** area, the Germans retain control of Veen, despite a concentrated effort by the Canadian 4th Armored. The 2nd Corps, meanwhile, continues its plans for the attack against Xanen. In the **U.S. Ninth Army** area, things are relatively tranquil across the front, except near Wesel, where the action is brisk between the Germans and Task Force Murray, which is stopped outside of Ossenberg. However, activity to strengthen its positions continues, especially with Patrols on the east and west bank of the Rhine. Preparations for the imminent assault across the Rhine are ongoing. **12th Army Group** In the **U.S. First Army** area, **VII Corps** sector, the 3rd Armored and 104th Infantry Divisions capture Cologne, the third largest city in Germany; organized resistance ceases before 12:00, and the city is declared secure by 16:00. Contingents of the 8th Division clear Fischenich and mop up Kendenich. In addition, they secure Godorf and a section of Rodenkirchen, leaving only a small pocket of resistance in the Corps zone at Rodenkirchen-Weiss-Surth, and that is totally cut off. In the **III Corps** sector, the unexpected happens as the 9th Armored, under General John Leonard, bursts through the Kothen Forest, reaching the confluence of the Rhine and Ahr Rivers, establishing bridgeheads at both and acquiring one of the finest prizes of the war when a column of General William Hoge's C.C.B. reaches the Ludendorf Railroad bridge (Remagen Bridge) and finds it intact, although damaged. General Courtney Hodges calls Bradley and proclaims: "WE'VE GOTTEN A BRIDGE. LEONARD NABBED THE ONE AT REMAGEN BEFORE THEY BLEW IT UP." Bradley calls General Harold Roe Ball to inform him of the prize and receives his response: SURE YOU'VE GOT A BRIDGE BRAD, BUT WHAT GOOD IS IT GOING TO DO YOU. YOU'RE NOT GOING ANYWHERE DOWN THERE AT REMAGEN. IT JUST DOESN'T FIT INTO THE PLAN (General Montgomery has priority for his single thrust, with 3rd Army making secondary assault). Bradley retorts: WHAT IN THE HELL DO YOU WANT US TO DO, PULL BACK AND BLOW IT UP?" General Eisenhower receives a call at his Headquarters in Rheims from Bradley and gives him permission to use the captured bridge. The tremendous significance is not yet realized; however, its seizure leads to the capture of more German troops than all those captured on the eastern front by the Russians: it is the lone bridge across the Rhine which is not destroyed by the Germans. Crossing begins immediately as Infantry moves cautiously, followed by prudent Armor advances by C.C.B., and finally as if the flood gates have opened, the Yanks are pouring across, while Engineers work tirelessly to repair it and neutralize the remaining explosive charges. The Germans become frustrated as they

had substituted a less powerful explosive on the bridge and in addition, a fortuitous shot by an American Tank severed a demolition cable; Hitler orders court-martials for all troops that he considers responsible for losing the bridge and all but one man are convicted and executed. 9th Armored soon hoists a sign over the span: "CROSS THIS BRIDGE WITH DRY FEET, COMPLIMENTS OF THE 9TH ARMORED DIVISION." Meanwhile, the other C.C.B. column has seized Sinzig and a crossing at the Ahr. Further south, C.C.A., 9th Armored roars to the Ahr, reaching it at Bad Neuenahr and Heimersheim, seizing both with their bridges intact. The 1st Division seizes Berzdorf, Fruhl, and Sechtem, with its 26th Regiment, while the 16th seizes Alfter, Bornheim, Botzdorf, Brenig, and Roister; the Division is now perched on the fringes of Bonn, where it deploys to attack the city. In the 9th Division zone, the 60th Regiment seizes Rottgen, Volmershoven, and Witterschlick, and pushes to about 2,000 yards from Duisdorf. The 78th Division, advancing southeast, captures 3 Railroad and 2 Vehicle bridges intact at the Ahr River near Dernau and at Ahrweiler. In the **V Corps** sector, the 2nd Division advances about ten miles on its left and about five miles on its right, seizing a bridge intact at the Ahr when the 23rd Regiment reaches Kreuzberg. Blasnkenheim is seized by the 28th Division as it streaks to the Ahr, while the 69th Division, also moving rapidly, clears Dahlem, Hecken, Kreuzberg, and Schmidttheim. In other activity, the 7th Armored is detached from the Corps. In the **U.S. Third Army** area, General Patton and other Officers attend a photo session where a P.O.W. gets his picture taken with a sign attached claiming him as the 200,000th P.O.W., however, 12th Army Public Relations Officers decline the photo, stating that it is degrading to the prisoner and is against the Geneva Convention. **VIII Corps** sector, the 87th Division clears Esch, Feusdorf, Allendorf, Ripsdorf, Mirbach, and Wiesbaum, as it spreads northeastward closing on the Ahr. Gigantic gains continue all across the area. The 4th Division captures Bewingen, Bolsdorf, Dohm, and Hillesheim, while the 11th Armored seizes Boxberg, Dreis, Dockweiler, and Kelberg. In addition, the 90th Division advances quickly, pushing its 358th Regiment to Dreis and Ober Ehe to extend its northern flank; in conjunction, the 359th Regiment clears Hinterweiler, Kirchweiler, and Waldkenigen, and the 90th Reconnaissance Troop secures Salm Wald. In the **XII Corps** sector, the 4th Armored Division roars forward, its C.C.B. using the Tanks and Infantry to full effectiveness, punches with its Armor, then stings with its Infantry, leap-frogging over the resistance to the high ground above the Rhine south of Andernach. The 5th Division races with its motorized 11th Infantry following Armor, occupying Darscheid, Daun, Puetzborn, and Salm, while the 2nd Regiment recaptures Schwarzenborn, seizes Gransdorf, and secures Eisenschmitt; the 10th Regiment takes Spang, Dahlem. and Spangdalem, prior to dawn. In the 76th Division zone, TF Onaway clears Binfield and Niederkail, while Beilingen and Arrenrath (night attack) fall to the 304th Regiment. Meanwhile, the 42nd Cavalry Squadron takes Schleidweiler and Zemmer. In the **XX Corps** sector, one contingent of the 10th Armored attacks toward Wittlich and others close on Sweich: C.C.A. reaches Orenhofen and C.C.B. secures Ehrang and Quint. Meanwhile, German infiltrators, which have penetrated the 94th Division's bridgehead at Saarburg, are being eliminated. **6th Army Group** In the **U.S. Seventh Army** area, the **XXI Corps** suspends its limited attacks, pending intelligence from ongoing reconnaissance. **(Atlantic-Italy)** 15th Army Group In the **British Eighth Army** area, the boundary between the Polish 2nd Corps and the British 5th Corps is modified in order to shrink the British 5th Corps zone prior to the spring offensive. The Indian 8th Division (5th Corps), reinforced by a Jewish Brigade (during March), begins river-crossing exercises over the Montone.

Dead Japanese on Iwo Jima.

March 8th 1945 — (Atlantic-Mexico) The Inter-American conference, which convened in Mexico city on February 21st 1945, ends today. **(Pacific-Formosa)** The Japanese Transport Ship No. 143 is sunk by Army Planes. **(Pacific-Iwo Jima)** Strong Naval and Artillery bombardments precede an assault by the VAC. Some ground is gained against heavy opposition. A counterattack (8th-9th) is repulsed by the 4th Marine Division; the Japanese suffer heavy losses. In the 5th Marine Division sector, 27th Marines zone, Japanese sneak up and throw a grenade into a foxhole manned by three Marines. P.F.C. James D. La Belle shouts a warning, then throws his body on the grenade to shield the others, giving his life that they might live. He receives the Medal of Honor posthumously for his tremendous sacrifice. During another heated skirmish in the 5th Marine Division sector, enemy fire, which has been incessant for two days, continues to hinder operations. As the 2nd Battalion advances, intense fire halts it. First Lt. Jack Lummus advances to knock out the objective and is stunned by an exploding grenade; however, he recovers and destroys the pillbox, then moves against a second. He encounters more fierce fire and another grenade throws him to the ground, but he advances and destroys the obstacle. Soon after, he destroys a third pillbox singlehandedly and continues to attack until subsequently being mortally wounded after stepping on a land mine. His command continues the

drive, inspired by his heroism; Lummus receives the Medal of Honor posthumously. In other activity, Army Planes (15th Fighter Group) assume combat air patrol duties and fly close support missions until March 10th. Advance echelon units of Marine Torpedo-Bomber Squadron 242 arrives from Tinian to fly antisubmarine patrols. **(Pacific-Philippines) Luzon** In the **U.S. Sixth Army** area, the XIV Corps attacks the Shimbu line: the 6th Division encounters slight resistance and gains its immediate objectives; the 1st Cavalry Division seizes Bench Mark Hill No. 11, as it drives against several features near Antipolo. In the 11th Airborne Division zone, the 158th Infantry Regiment is mopping up its area, while columns of the 187th Regiment converge on Talaga and push beyond to Hill 660, where they encounter fierce resistance that halts progress. In the **I Corps** sector, Mt. Magabang is seized by the 130th Regiment, 33rd Division, while the 1st Battalion, 35th Regiment, 25th Division secures Putlan on Highway 5; however, the Japanese demolish the Putlan bridge. **(Southern Philippines)** In the **U.S. Eighth Army** area, the 41st Infantry Division contingents on Leyte depart for Zamboanga, Mindanao. On Palawan, Company G, 186th Infantry, 41st Division, drives to the summit of Hill 1445, without opposition, terminating organized resistance on Palawan; Patrols search for enemy stragglers. Subsequently, the Palawan Force secures Busuanga Island, off the southern tip of Palawan, and also the Balabac and Pandanan Islands. **(Atlantic-Western Europe) 21st Army Group** In the **Canadian First Army** area, Xanten is secured by the Canadian 2nd Division and the British 43rd Division. In the **U.S. Ninth Army** area, **XVI Corps** sector, TF Byrne (35th Division) seizes Huck and Millingen, southeast of Alpen; however, at Ossenberg, Task Force Murray encounters stiff resistance as it drives persistently, securing the factory area. **12th** In the **U.S. First Army** area, **VII Corps** sector, the 28th Regiment, 8th Division reduces the remaining resistance west of the Rhine in its zone and the VII Corps sector; Corps sector is expanded to encompass Bonn. The 1st Division, reinforced with Combat Command Howze, 3rd Armored Division, attacks toward the Rhine from Bonn and is attached to Corps; RCT 16 secures the northern part of Bonn, while RCT 18, operating on the right, drives northeast and seizes Duisdorf, Endenich, Lengsdorf, Lesse ninch, Odekoven, and Messdorf; it also drives into Bonn where it establishes contact with RCT 16. In the **III Corps** sector, the Germans mount Air and Artillery attacks to destroy the Remagen Bridge, but it survives, and the Engineers maintain their extraordinary efforts to repair it while under severe fire. The congestion of U.S. Vehicles proves more of a handicap than the enemy fire, but the ongoing expansion of the bridgehead continues to progress. In the 9th Division sector, the 7th Armored moves in and assumes responsibility for the zone, taking over the ongoing attack of the 9th Division; RCT 39 occupies Bad Godesberg and is attached to 7th Armored (minus 1st Battalion). The 7th Armored finds no opposition as it sweeps its area west of the Rhine. In the **V Corps** sector, the 102nd Cavalry Group, 2nd Division, and the 2nd Division secure their respective zones north of the Ahr, while the 272nd Regiment, 69th Division eradicates the remaining resistance in the Divisional sector as it advances to Hungersdorf and Waldorf Ripsdorf south of the Ahr. In the **U.S. Third Army** area, **VIII Corps**, rapid progress is achieved as Corps sprints to the Rhine. The 87th Division drives forward to Hungersdorf and Ahrhutte and seizes an intact bridge at Ahrhutte, giving it access to the other bank of the Ahr before 12:00. Meanwhile, the 11th Armored closes on the Rhine; Mayen is seized by C.C.A.; C.C.B. bolts the Kyll at Lissingen and seizes Mannebach, where it encounters heavy resistance from a German pocket wedged between the First and Third Armies. The 90th Division continues to Patrol within its sector; however, no enemy presence is sighted. In the **XII Corps** sector, the 4th Armored mops up west of the Rhine while simultaneously attempting to locate crossing sites. C.C.B., 4th Armored secures Saffig-Ketting and the surrounding area, while C.C.A. seizes Bassenheim, Kaerlich, Muelheim, Rubenach, and Wolken, demoralizing the enemy in the area. The 4th Armored, commanding the heights above the Anderenach-Koblenz Highway, splatter an array of shells into fleeing German Convoys, further depleting their numbers. In the 76th Division zone, elements of the 385th Regiment seize Lanscheid, while contingents of the 304th Regiment seize Greverath and Niersbach, making contact with the 42nd Cavalry at the former; the 42nd seizes Gladbach. In the **XX Corps** sector, the 10th Armored's C.C.A. drives east toward the Salm River, plowing through Dierscheid, Erlenbach, Heidweiler, and Naurath as it advances. Meanwhile, the 94th Division rids the Saarburg Bridge of remaining enemy presence, driving them from the area, then deploys to attack, reversing earlier plans to retire to the rear. **6th Army Group** The **U.S. Seventh Army** continues to build its strength for a mid-March attack to reduce the West Wall. **(Atlantic-Italy) 15th Army Group** In the **U.S. Fifth Army** area, **II Corps** sector, the 1st Armored Division mounts an attack to fortify its left flank perimeter; it seizes Carviano.

The Ludendorff R.R. Bridge at Remagen.

March 9th 1945 — (Pacific-Iwo Jima) Elements of the 3rd Marine Division drive to the northeast coast, severing the remaining Japanese on the island. In the Fifth Marine Division sector, Japanese fire halts the advance of a Platoon of the 1st Battalion, 27th Marines. Sergeant Joseph R. Julian orders his men to deploy their guns while he advances and knocks out a pillbox, killing its occupants. Sergeant Julian gets more ammunition and advances further, eliminating two more cave positions. He continues the one-man attack moving against the final obstacle, but a devastating burst of enemy fire wounds him mortally just as he destroys it. Sergeant Joseph Julian receives the Medal of Honor posthumously. Admiral Turner's Carrier Force departs for Guam, subsequent to turning over command to Admiral Hill (redesignated Senior Officer Present Afloat Iwo Jima). **(Pacific-Japan)** The U.S. concentrates on reducing the Japanese resolve to continue the war by commencing five tumultuous Air raids against the mainland. The XXI Bomber Command unleashes unprecedented awesome night raids against Japanese cities, reversing its previous tactics of bombing industrial targets. The raids are extremely effective, due in great part to the poor construction of the wooden buildings, allowing the flames to spread rapidly. Carrier Planes will join the attacks later. **(Pacific-Philippines)** In the **U.S. Sixth Army** area, **XIV Corps** sector, the 1st Cavalry Division and the 6th Infantry Division maintain their eastward attacks. The 12th Cavalry, 1st Cavalry Division drives to the slopes of Hill Bench Mark 9. Meanwhile, contingents of the 11th Airborne Division's 187th Regiment attack Hill 660 and encounter resolute resistance. In the **I Corps** sector, the 33rd Division maintains Patrols in its sector. The 127th Regiment, 32n Division culminates its move to the Vill Verde Trail to eradicate the resistance still blocking progress on the route. In other activity, the Japanese concentrate heavy fire upon the 1st Battalion, 35th Regiment, 25th Division at the Putlan Bridge; elements of the 161st Regiment push through Anabat, advancing to about 1,000 yards from Putlan. **(South Philippines)** U.S. Planes and Naval Warships bombard Zamboanga, Mindanao to soften resistance for the imminent offensive. On Samar, the remaining contingents of the Americal Division depart, leaving responsibility for eliminating final resistance to the 1st Philippine Infantry Regiment. On Lubang, progress continues to climb. By the middle of March, the Americans sustain eight killed, against Japanese dead mounting to 250. By the end of the month, the island is turned over to Guerrilla forces. **(Pacific-Burma)** The Indian 19th Division crashes into Mandalay, and vicious fighting ensues for several days. Meanwhile, the Indian 20th Division is closing from the southwest. **(Pacific-Nansei Shotos)** The Submarine U.S.S. *Kete*, on its second War Patrol, attacks a Japanese Convoy, sinking three Cargo Vessels, the *Keizan Maru*, *Sanka Maru*, and the *Dokan Maru*. Several days later, the Submarine, commanded by Lt. Commander Edward Ackerman, attacks another Japanese Vessel, but a sinking is not reported. The Warship, having only three torpedoes remaining, is ordered to depart her area on the 20th and return to Pearl Harbor; however, the *Kete*, which dispatches a weather report to Headquarters on the 20th, is never heard from again and is reported officially lost on April 16th. **(Atlantic-Western Europe) 21st Army Group** British Field Marshal Montgomery issues his instructions for a crossing of the Rhine, north of the Rohr River. The Germans destroy the last remaining bridge across the Rhine at Wesel and evacuate the bridgehead during the night. In the **Canadian First Army** area, the remaining enemy resistance around Xanten is eradicated by contingents of the Canadian 2nd and British 43rd Divisions. In other activity, the British 52nd Division closes slowly toward the Rhine, while the Canadian 4th Armored Division advances cautiously through minefields and seizes Veen. In the **U.S. Ninth Army** area, **XVI Corps** sector, TF Byrne (35th Division) fights toward Drupt, making slow progress, while TF Murray finalizes the seizure of Ossenberg and drives north beyond Borth and Wallach. **12th Army Group** Bonn falls to RCT's 16 and 18 (1st Division) by 16:00, terminating German resistance west of the Rhine. In the **III Corps** sector, the 9th Division assumes responsibility for the Remagen bridgehead; contingents initiate expansion of the perimeter to include Bruchhausen, Rheinbreitbach, Scheuren, the balance of Linz, and about half of Honnef, encountering tenacious local resistance despite the absence of full scale concentrated opposition against the bridgehead. A counterattack strikes the center of the bridgehead, forcing the surrender of some ground. German Artillery strikes the Remagen Bridge and on the 11th, it receives another barrage. In the **U.S. Third Army** area, **VIII Corps** sector, the advance to the Rhine is complete. C.C.A., 11th Armored clears a large portion of Andernach, at the Rhine, while C.C.B. takes the heights above the river near Brohl. Meanwhile, the 4th Division's Task Force Rhine swallows Adenau, Honerath, and Reifferscheid, culminating the Divisional mission; the 6th Cavalry Group then zooms through the lines of the 4th and 87th Divisions (both out of contact with enemy), driving east without incident and establishing contact with the 11th Armored. In the **XII Corps** sector, the 4th Armored has units including C.C.B., and advances to Treis only to discover a demolished bridge across the Moselle; C.C.A. and C.C.R. take the towns along the Rhine between Andernach and Koblenz. The 5th Division tramples its intruding resistance, taking Bettenfeld, Bleckhaus en, Manderscheid, and Pantenburg; in addition, contingents are transported to embarkation points for a southeastward drive. Meanwhile, the 76th Division operating on the Corps south flank takes Grosslittgen and Musweiler with its 385th and 304th Regiments; the 42nd Cavalry Group bolts the Salm River driving toward Dreis and Bergweiler, and Task Force Onaway is dissolved. In the **XX Corps** sector, C.C.A., 10th Armored Division secures Hotzerath, Rievenich, and Sehlem, then pivots north to a crossing site near Dorbach, where a bridge is placed across the Salm by Engineers; Bekond and Foren fall to C.C.B., while C.C.R. sweeps strategic ground east of Sweich. In other activity, contingents of RCT 417 repulse a counterattack against the bridgehead northeast of the Ruwer River. The Saarlautern bridgehead comes under severe pressure; however, the 65th Division, which had just completed relieving the 28th Division, repels the assault. **6th Army Group** In the **U.S. Seventh Army** area, the 71st Division is attached to XV Corps. **(Atlantic-Italy) 15th Army Group** In the **U.S. Fifth Army** area, M. Belvedere and M. Valbura fall without opposition to contingents of the 10th Mountain Division, giving the Division strengthened positions north of Castelnuovo. In other activity, British Field Marshal Alexander receives word from the O.S.S. in Italy that German General Karl Wolf (Senior S.S. Officer in Italy) is interested in arranging a meeting in Switzerland to work out details for the surrender of all German forces in Italy. On the 11th, the Russians demand participation and are informed that if a surrender occurs, they will be invited to Italy; however, their presence at Switzerland is not required. Ambassador Harriman, referring to the Russian demands: "BRINGS OUT IN THE OPEN A DOMINEERING ATTITUDE TOWARD THE UNITED STATES, WHICH WE HAVE BEFORE ONLY SUSPECTED". U.S. General John R. Deane states: "APPROVING THE RUSSIAN REQUEST (having three Russian Officers at the meeting) WILL BE AN ACT OF APPEASEMENT WHICH WILL REACT AGAINST US IN FUTURE NEGOTIATIONS". The meeting convenes on the 19th.

March 9th 1945 — (Atlantic-Eastern Europe) The Russians pound Kolberg with Artillery "Stalin's Organs." The town is defended by German Colonel Fullriede's 3,300 troops, eight Tanks, eight Artillery pieces and 15 Anti-aircraft guns. The heavy fighting takes a big toll on the civilian population; when the Russian Tanks penetrate the perimeter, they fire from house-to-house, igniting a huge inferno. By the 17th, about 30,000 people escape. About 2,200 Soldiers remain on the beach with orders to hold, but they retire. By mid-March, some of the scattered German forces make it across the Oder and head west, but those remaining never escape.

March 10th 1945 — (Pacific) Marine Fighter Squadrons begin returning to the United States. By the 13th, Squadrons 112, 123, 124, 212, 213, 216, 217, and 451 are detached from Task Force 58 for the return trip. U.S. Marine ground crews remain behind to accommodate Navy F4u's. **(Pacific-Iwo Jima)** The 3rd Marine Division sector is cleared of resistance except for a Japanese pocket in the 9th Marines' area and some sporadic resistance in the cliffs overlooking the beach. Meanwhile, the 4th Marine Division terminates resistance at the Amphitheater Turkey Knob. **(Pacific-Philippines)** In the **U.S. Sixth Army** area, fierce fighting occurs near Bench Mark Hill B, as the 1st Regiment, 6th Division battles forward about 300 bloody yards to seize a small ridge. Meanwhile, the Japanese plan to mount a full-scale attack against the 6th Division; however, carpet bombing and Artillery barrages are launched east of Manila against the Shimbu line during the 10th and 11th, inflicting heavy losses on the Japanese troops as they group for attack. The 1st Cavalry advances to the crest of Hill Bench Mark 9, while the 11th Airborne's 1st Battalion, 187th Regiment advances doggedly and seizes most of Hill 660; meanwhile, columns of the 511th Regiment drive south and east toward Santa Anastasia and along Laguna de Bay respectively, against no opposition. In the **I Corps** sector, contingents of the 25th Division converge in the Putlan sector of Highway 5; the 35th Regiment swivels its concentration to probing activity up the Old Spanish Trail. In the 32nd Division zone, at 03:00, about two Companies of Japanese attack the positions of Company A, 127th Regiment striking a three man outpost, killing two of the Yanks. P.F.C. Thomas E. Atkins, despite severe wounds, continues to hold the ground. By 07:00, he has used three rifles and expends 400 rounds, directly to his front lay 11 dead Japs. He takes advantage of a pause in the attack and withdraws to get an operational weapon and more ammunition, but is restrained for medical treatment. While he is being treated, a Jap infiltrates the area, but Atkins confiscates a rifle and kills him. Shortly thereafter, Atkins spots more Japs moving in behind the Platoon's lines and begins rapid firing his weapon, driving them off. Atkins receives the Medal of Honor for his extraordinary actions. In the **XI Corps** sector, the 43rd Division has breached the final enemy positions; the 38th Division takes over its sector and releases RCT 169 to the 38th. **(Southern Philippines)** On Mindanao, subsequent to a massive Air and Naval bombardment, Rear Admiral F. B. Royal's Naval Attack Group lands contingents of the 41st Division unopposed on the Zamboanga Peninsula; the troops seize the Airfield at Wolfe, the hamlet of San Roque, and then drive toward Mindanao city. General Doe assumes command ashore, and General Eichelberger comes ashore to inspect the beachhead. Meanwhile, Guerrillas, supported by two Companies of the 21st Regiment, 24th Division seize Dipolog and its Airfield. **(Pacific-Burma)** In N.C.A.C. area, the British 36th Division seizes Mongmit. **(Pacific-Indo-China)** The Japanese suffer trepidation, based on their perception of a possible American invasion of French Indo-China and the possibility of French troops joining with the Yanks; the Japs begin expelling the French from key Garrisons and strip the French of their authority over the Colony. Japanese methods of brutality are increased, prompting more fervent resistance from the natives. **(Atlantic-Western Europe) 21st Army Group** In the **Canadian First Army** area, 2nd Corps sector, the battle of the Rhineland is successfully concluded, terminating Operations BLOCKBUSTER AND VERITABLE. The Canadian 2nd Corps moves to the Rhine against scattered light resistance along the Xanten-Rheinberg road. The British 52nd Division reaches the Rhine, encountering Canadian and American forces. In the **U.S. Ninth Army** area, **XVI Corps** sector, RCT 134 (35th Division) seizes Buederich. Task Force Byrne is disbanded and the 320th Regiment moves to Sevelen, reverting to reserve. Meanwhile, RCT's 289 and 291 are returned to the 75th Division from the British 8th Corps and U.S. 35th Division respectively. The 75th establishes a Command Post in Germany near the 84th Division. **12th Army Group** In the **U.S. First Army** area, the **VII Corps** maintains its defensive positions along the Rhine. In the **III Corps** sector, the Germans continue to lambaste the Remagen bridgehead; however, the 9th Division repulses their efforts, while the Engineers continue to repair the damaged bridge. Contingents of the 7th Armored Division occupy two small islands in the Rhine, west of Honnef. In the **V Corps** sector, units of the 23rd Regiment, 2nd Division pound the Germans in Nieder Breisig, seizing about half of it. Meanwhile, the 102nd Cavalry Group, driving south of the Ahr, revs the engines and advances to Dedenbach, Gonnersdorf, Nieder Zissen, and Waldorf. In the **U.S. Third Army** area, **VIII Corps** sector, the 11th Armored maintains the Rhine River line and systematically sweeps its sector west of the Rhine, between the First and Third Armies, seizing several towns: C.C.B.'s surge draws the curtain on a substantial force of Germans caught between the two Armies as it links with the V Corps and draws the cord, encircling the enemy; C.C.A. and C.C.R. engage in effective mop-up operations. The 90th Division terminates mop-up details in its sector. In other activity, the 4th Division is detached from Corps and attached to Seventh Army. In the **XII Corps** sector, the 4th Armored Division maintains its mop-up operations west of the Rhine (Andernach to Koblenz), and north of the Moselle from Cochem to Koblenz. In the 5th Division sector, the 1st Battalion, 2nd Regiment seizes Gillenfeld, Immerath, Nieder, Ober Winkel, Strohn, Strotzbusch, and Udler, while the 42nd Cavalry Squadron clears Bergweiler and Dreis, then has units sprint to Dorf and Flussbach. In the **XX Corps** sector, preparations for a breakout from the Saarburg bridgehead (to commence on 13th) are being made. The assault will be reinforced by the 80th Division, returned to XX Corps from XII Corps. In the 10th Armored sector, Bombogen and Wittlich fall effortlessly to C.C.A., which also secures the heights between the two objectives, while C.C.B. establishes a bridgehead across the Salm and seizes Clausen, Esch, and Karmes. The Yanks are not permitting the Germans to catch their breath, pounding them at every opportunity as they have completed their mission in the Wittlich region and have begun closing on the Moselle; C.C.R. secures Kirsch, Longuich, and the high ground near Mertesdorf. The 3rd Cavalry Group moves into Kasel and Riol, where it initiates relief of RCT 417, which is deployed at the Ruwer bridgehead. **6th Army Group** The French 1st Army is directed to maintain its defensive posture along the Rhine; however, it is to initiate probing operations east of the Rhine and it is also directed to release the 3rd Algerian Infantry Division to the U.S. VI Corps, effective March 13th. **(Atlantic-Italy) 15th Army Group** In the **British Eighth Army** area, 13th Corps sector, the Indian 10th Division starts to relieve the U.S. 85th Division on M. Grande.

March 11th 1945 — (Pacific-Caroline Islands) A Kamikaze Plane damages the Carrier *Randolf* (CV-15) off Ulithi. **(Pacific-Iwo Jima)** The V.A.C. commences the final phase to secure the island; the 3rd and 4th Marine Divisions push to the east coast, while the 5th Division drives north. Enemy resistance is terminated in the 4th Division sector, except one obstinate pocket to the right. **(Pacific-Philippines)** Luzon The fundamental plan of the U.S. Sixth Army's participation in the seizure of the Bicol Peninsula and the Visayan Passage is issued

by Army. It specifies that RCT 158 will make an amphibious landing at Legaspi, in the Bicol Peninsula, and that the 511th Paratroop Infantry Regiment (less 1st Battalion), 11th Armored Division, is delegated as a Reserve unit for the operation. The 6th Division presses forward. Bench Mark Hill B is totally reduced by the 3rd Battalion, 1st Regiment. During the night, the Japanese mount attacks against all Divisional Regiments, but the 6th holds firmly. In the 11th Airborne sector, the 2nd Battalion, 158th Regiment secures Batangas and its surrounding area, while the balance of the Regiment is eradicating resistance to the west and northwest. The 1st Battalion, 187th Regiment secures Hill 660; however, the Japs holding Mt. Bijang pour incessant fire upon the 3rd Battalion, 511th Infantry, pinning it down. In the **I Corps** sector, the Japanese continue to raise impenetrable resistance at Salacsac Pass on the Villa Verde Trail, preventing any advance by the 127th Regiment, 32nd Division. Meanwhile, the 25th Division's 3rd Battalion, 35th Regiment drives along the Old Spanish Trail, capturing Salazar. **(Southern Philippines)** In the **U.S. Eighth Army** area, Zamboanga City, Mindanao, and its Airfield fall to the 163rd Regiment, 41st Division, while the 162nd Regiment stretches its positions toward Calder Point. The East entrance of Visayan Passage is now secure, and Philippine Guerrillas assume responsibility of Burias and Ticao Islands, permitting U.S. troops to return to Leyte. Later, at about midnight, elements of the 19th Regiment, 24th Division land at Romblon without incident. **(Pacific-Burma)** In the **British Fourteenth Army** area, the Indian 19th Division fights strenuously to secure Mandalay and seizes a strategic hill in the northeastern sector of the city. **(Pacific-SEAC)** British Admiral Mountbatten announces that a Regiment of the U.S. 5332nd Brigade is to immediately debark for China, to be followed by the remainder of the Brigade on April 1st. **(Atlantic-Western Europe)** U.S. Naval Land-based Planes (VPB-103) sink the German U-Boat U-681 off western France. In other Air activity, Army Aircraft sink two additional German Submarines, the U-2515 and the U-2530 near Hamburg, Germany. **21st Army Group** In the **U.S. Ninth Army** area, **XVI Corps** sector, the 35th Division concludes its drive toward Wesel, as Patrols of the 134th Regiment seize Fort Blucher. **12th Army Group** In the **U.S. First Army** area, **III Corps** sector, the 78th Division assumes responsibility for the north flank of the Remagen bridgehead and begins driving toward the Cologne-Frankfurt-Autobahn with its 39th and 309th Regiment; both encounter fierce resistance. The 9th Division makes some progress near Hartgarten and Hill 448. On the southern flank, the 99th Division grinds ahead, and its 393rd Regiment manages to advance only several hundred yards. The 394th drives about 3,000 yards south along the east bank of the Rhine and secures Ariendorf and Leubsdorf. In the **V Corps** sector, the 2nd Division continues to bolster its positions at the Rhine. Its 23rd Regiment finishes clearing Nieder-Breisig, while the 9th Regiment clears Ober Breisig and Rheineck and establishes contact with the 23rd Regiment. In the **U.S. Third Army** area, **VIII Corps** sector, mop-up operations west of the Rhine continue. The 90th Division is attached to the XII Corps, which is also mopping up along the Moselle and Rhine, while it prepares to drive across the Moselle. In the 76th Division sector, the 42nd Cavalry Squadron advances to Bausendorf and Hasborn, while the 304th Regiment and the 2nd Cavalry Squadron close south and southeast racing toward the Moselle River line, the latter securing the Sweich-Piesport region. In the **XX Corps** sector, C.C.A., 10th Armored, reinforced by the 2nd Battalion, 417th Regiment drives from Bullay toward the Moselle; however, it halts at Alf where the bridge has been destroyed by the Germans. Meanwhile, the 1st Battalion, Regimental Combat Team 417 sustains a stiff counterattack and is driven from a hill near Mertesdorf. In other activity, the Corps is preparing for the imminent offensive. Navy Landing Craft ferry Army troops across the Rhine River at the Remagen bridgehead in Germany; the operation continues until the end of March. **(Atlantic-Eastern Europe)** Soviet troops are investing the Baltic ports of Danzig and Gdynia. In other activity, the Soviets expand the Oeder bridgehead, piercing German lines in the vicinity of Kuestrin; Berlin acknowledges the penetrations. **(Atlantic-Italy) 15th Army Group** In the **British Eighth Army** area, 5th Corps sector, the British 78th Division assumes responsibility for positions of British 56th Division, allowing the 56th to prepare for offensive.

March 12th 1945 — (Pacific-Iwo Jima) The 1st and 3rd Battalions, 9th Marines, 3rd Marine Division, drive west toward "Cushman's Pocket, the last remaining stronghold on the island; it is permeated with interconnecting caves and pillboxes. Despite the destruction of many obstacles, only slight gains are made. In other activity, the island's Airfields are renamed South, Center, and North Airfields. **(Pacific-Philippines) Luzon** In the **U.S. Sixth Army** area, **XIV Corps** sector, the 20th Regiment, 6th Division attacks the Shimbu line. Some down-scaled counterattacks are repulsed by contingents of the 6th Division. Patrols of the 43rd Division's 103rd Regiment advance and discover Antipolo destroyed and abandoned. In the 11th Airborne zone, the 3rd Battalion, 158th Regiment is halted near Minaga, preventing it from continuing to Mabini, its objective at the mouth of the Calumpan Peninsula. In other activity, effective Air and Artillery bombardment of Japanese positions on Mt. Bijag keeps the enemy at bay. In the **I Corps** sector, the 3rd Battalion, 35th Regiment, 25th Division maintains its roadblock on Old Spanish Trail slightly north of Salazar; however, plans to advance further are aborted as the idea is deemed unfeasible. **(South Philippines)** In the **U.S. Eighth Army** area, the 162nd Regiment, 41st Division, reaches Recodo on Caldera Point on Mindanao, finding it evacuated by the Japanese; however, near San Roque, the 3rd Battalion encounters vicious opposition in a small village. At Simara, a Naval and Artillery bombardment precedes a post-dawn assault landing by Company B, 19th Regiment. The unit debarks without opposition. **(Atlantic-Western Europe) 21st Army Group** In the **U.S. Ninth Army** area, **XVI Corps** sector, the 35th Division is relieved by elements of the 75th Division, which assumes responsibility for its sector along the Rhine. **12th Army Group** The Americans continue to capture many prisoners. A German General, inadvertently spots a large contingent of idle German troops. He moves into their midst to determine why they have stopped fighting, but before he receives a response he is tapped on the shoulder and given the reason; an American MP invites him to join the huge group of P.O.W.s. In the **U.S. First Army** area, **III Corps** sector, the 78th Division, deployed along the northern part of the Remagen bridgehead, repulses several counterattacks against Honnef. In the 9th Division sector, the Germans maintain tenacious resistance at Hartgarden and Kalenborn; however, contingents drive into Hartgarden during the latter part of the day. Meanwhile, the 99th Division is making substantial gains around the southern part of the bridgehead. In the **U.S. Third Army** area, the **VIII Corps** terminates its mop-up operations west of the Rhine. The **XII Corps** is in the final stages of mop-up in its sector, permitting it to prepare for the assault across the Moselle. The 89th Division receives its baptism under fire as it begins to drive toward the Rhine at the Cochem-Alf region. In conjunction, the 76th Division is also sweeping toward the Moselle, and the 90th Division moves contingents up to the Moselle, which they can combine with the 5th Division in the cross-river attack. In the **XX Corps** sector, Bausendorf is cleared, and a bridge near Olkenbach is seized by Infantry troops, while C.C.A., 10th Armored reaches the high ground above the Moselle across from Bullay and is relieved by the 76th Division (XII Corps). Meanwhile, the 1st Battalion, 417th Regiment springs a surprise attack prior to dawn and regains the hill outside of Mertesdorf. Third Army casualties as of March 12th 1945: 18,529 killed; 87,566 wounded; 15,328 missing; non-battle casualties 93,801. Casualty total up to January 29th, 172,953 — cost of the Eifel campaign 42,217. German casualties versus Third Army: 116,000 killed; 321,800 wounded; 216,500 P.O.W.s. Third Army equipment losses: Light Tanks 284; Medium Tanks 837; Guns 158. German equipment losses: Medium Tanks 1,369; Panzer and Tiger 805; Guns 2,811. **6th Army Group** The U.S. Seventh Army prepares to launch a full blast assault against the West Wall. **(Atlantic-Eastern Europe)** The First White Russian Front seizes German-held Kuestrin as it closes against Berlin from the east, and it also makes gains against the bridgehead east of Stettin. Meanwhile, the Second White Russian Front drives to the Gulf of Danzig north of Danzig, closing the knot on the Germans at Danzig and Gdynia.

U.S. Tanks in Wesel.

Engineers' pontoon bridge across the Rhine River.

March 13th 1945 — (Pacific-Iwo Jima) The 3rd and 4th Marine Division continue mop-up operations. Meanwhile, the 5th Marine Division, supported by Flamethrowers, Tanks, and Artillery, continues its attack against the remaining resistance and advances steadily; Air support is absent due to the terrain. In other activity, Co. B, Amphibious Reconnaissance Battalion lands on Kangoku and Kama Rocks Islands off the west coast of Iwo and seizes both without incident. **(Pacific-Philippines)** Luzon The U.S. Sixth Army suspends its Legaspi operation for a week. In the **XIV Corps** sector, the Japanese mount a few counterattacks against the 6th Division; however, the 6th shreds the enemy with near effortless fashion. Also, contingents of the 103rd Regiment, 43rd Division advance to the western base of Bench Mark No. 7. In the 11th Airborne Division sector, the 3rd Battalion, 158th Regiment unsuccessfully attempts to outflank the Japanese at a strongpoint north of Mainaga and becomes cut off, as Japanese troops launch an amphibious operation which seals a road to their rear at the Baliti River. The Japanese holding Mt. Bijang give some ground to a contingent of the 11th Airborne (511th Regiment), but then mount enough fire power to drive it off. Planes and Artillery increase their attacks against the strongpoint for several days to loosen resistance. In the **I Corps** sector, elements of the 25th Division are ordered to assault Norton's Knob on Highway 5, southwest of Kapintalan. **(Southern Philippines)** In the U.S. Eighth Army area, the Japanese increase their resistance in the area north of San Roque and south of Pasananca on Mindanao. **(Pacific-Burma)** In ALFSEA area, 15th Corps sector, contingents of the Indian 26th Division make an amphibious landing near Letpadan on the Arakan coast and advance to cut the Ru-ywa-Tangup Road. **(Pacific-South China Sea)** Army Planes sink the Japanese Defense Coast Vessel No. 66. **(Atlantic-Western Europe) 12th Army Group** In the U.S. First Army area, **III Corps** sector, the 78th Division hits heavy resistance as it advances to enlarge its bridgehead northeastward; the 311th Regiment, bolstered by the attachment of the 60th Armored Infantry Battalion (9th Armored), and the 78th Reconnaissance Troop occupy Rhine Island, slightly west of Honnef and simultaneously mop up in Honnef. Meanwhile, the 309th and 39th Regiments combine and gain the high ground west of Kalenborn. The 9th Division completes its seizure of Hargarten, then advances against heavy opposition in the Kalenborn-Notscheid-Hargarten area. On the Corps south flank, the 99th Division repels successive counterattacks while bolstering its perimeter. In the U.S. Third Army area, **VIII Corps** sector, the 4th and 11th Armored Divisions are relieved by the 6th Cavalry Group which assumes responsibility for the Rhine extending south from Andernach. In the **XII Corps** sector, preparations for an attack across the Rhine are complete. The 76th and 89th Divisions have cleared the majority of the terrain in their respective sectors along the Moselle between Cochem and Sweich. In the **XX Corps** sector, a heavy artillery barrage precedes a Corps attack against the West Wall. At 03:00, the 94th Division drives from the Saarburg bridgehead across the Ruwer River and seizes Bergheid Bonerath, Holzerath, and Schondorf. The 80th Division cracks the enemy defenses and seizes the solitary good road through the Wadern Forest, blocking it in the middle of the forest with the 318th Regiment while its 317th Infantry takes Greimerath. Second Lt. Harry J. Michael, Company L, 318th Regiment, is leading his Rifle Platoon up a ridge when he hears the deadly click of an enemy machine gun. Instinctively, he orders his men to quietly take cover; however, he ventures forward alone, discovering two enemy machine

gun nests. He takes both crews by surprise and captures them. Later, at daybreak, Lt. Michael detects enemy voices in the woods and carries out a flanking movement. Subsequent to a fierce struggle, twenty-five Germans attached to a mountain Division are captured, in addition to three Artillery pieces and twenty horses. Soon after, Michael scouts the area and kills two men, wounds four additional troops, and captures thirteen. During the afternoon, Michael leads another assault against German pillboxes, capturing thirty men and killing ten. On the following morning, Lt. Michael is killed by sniper fire; he receives the Medal of Honor posthumously. In conjunction, the 26th Division encounters fierce resistance at roadblocks along the Zerf-Britten Road. Meanwhile, the 65th Division drives against the enemy on the left flank of the Corps to divert attention from the main thrust. On the left flank, the Germans pound the positions of the 3rd Cavalry Group. The 19th Squadron, 16th Cavalry Group secures Morscheid and Sommerau and the Morscheid-Sommerau ridge. **6th Army Group** In the U.S. Seventh Army area, preparations for the offensive are ongoing; there is some activity, as contingents of the 70th Division discover Germans abandoning their positions; the Yanks begin to pursue the enemy toward the Sarre River. In the 36th Division zone, action to enlarge the bridgehead across the Moder River continues. One detachment, led by Tech Sergeant Morris E. Crain, is attacking with Crain as the pointman. He singlehandedly kills ten enemy soldiers and captures 12 additional troops. German Artillery fire blasts the newly won positions throughout the day. Another Platoon rushes to assist, but German strength, including a Tank, close in and house-to-house fighting develops. German troops enter the final line of defense and Crain orders the other men in the Platoon to retreat, while he holds the position. Meanwhile, a Tank is firing point blank into the house, despite German troops being in the adjoining room. Crain kills several more Germans; however, the house is destroyed and Crain is killed. His men regroup and inspired by his courageous actions, hold off the counterattack and keep the bridgehead; Crain receives the Medal of Honor posthumously. **(Atlantic-Italy) 15th Army Group** The Indian 10th Division, British 13th Corps, relieves the U.S. 85th Division of responsibility for the M. Grande hill mass.

It's not Holiday Inn, but this Marine is catching some rest in his foxhole.

March 14th 1945 — **(Pacific-Dutch East Indies)** The Submarine *Rock* (SS-274) lands men and supplies on Lombok Island. **(Pacific-Japan)** Marine Fighter Squadrons 214 and

452 stationed aboard the USS *Franklin* join the Fifth Fleet and participate in raids against the Inland Sea, the Kobe, and the Kobe and Kure harbors (19th). **(Pacific-Iwo Jima)** The Stars and Stripes is officially raised on Iwo Jima at V Amphibious Corps Headquarters (09:30), proclaiming U.S. Naval Military government of the island. Subsequent to the celebration, Lt. General Holland M. Smith, Commander Expeditionary Troops, departs for Guam. Meanwhile, the 3rd and 4th Marine Division continue mop-up operations in their respective sectors. The 5th Marine Division's 1st and 2nd Battalions, 9th Marines, drive about 600 yards against heavy resistance. The attack is supported by P51s and becomes the final Air support of the campaign. During this fighting, the Japs have continued to infiltrate American lines. In one instance, an enemy grenade is tossed into a foxhole while the troops are trying to get some sleep after another bitter night-long fight. Private George Phillips, 2nd Battalion, 28th Marines, the only man aware of the deadly intruder, shouts a warning, then dives onto the grenade taking its full concussion, giving his life to save the other Marines; he receives the Medal of Honor posthumously. Also, Private Franklin E. Sigler, 2nd Battalion, 26th Marines, leads a Rifle Squad and singlehandedly wipes out a nest which had been hindering his Company's progress for several days. Suddenly, more Jap guns begin firing at Sigler. He dashes up the cliffs to get to the caves, startling the enemy with his one-man assault. Despite being badly wounded, he crawls back to his Squad and continues to direct their fire. Meanwhile, he carries several wounded Marines back behind the lines and returns to continue the fight. Private Sigler becomes a recipient of the Medal of Honor. **(Pacific-Philippines)** Luzon In the **U.S. Sixth Army** area, **XIV Corps** sector, the Japanese mount unsuccessful counterattacks against the 6th Division; the Japanese sustain heavy casualties. Contingents of the 20th Regiment seize positions on Mt. Mataba. Meanwhile, the 43rd Division (minus 169th Regiment) initiates an attack against the Shimbu line. It drives toward the heights north and east of the Morong River Valley, encountering heavy resistance at the forward defenses of Sugar Loaf Mountain. **(Southern Philippines)** In the **U.S. Eighth Army** area, the 162nd Regiment, 41st Division closes on Mt. Capisan, Mindanao; contingents secure San Roque and also a road junction about 500 yards outside of Masilay. In conjunction, the 163rd Regiment takes Pasananca. **(Pacific-Burma)** In the N.C.A.C. area, the transfer of the U.S. 5332nd Brigade (T. F. MARS) from Burma to China is begun by Air. In the **British Fourteenth Army** area, the Indian 19th Division secures the city of Mandalay; however, the Japanese maintain control of Fort Dufferin, which comes under tremendous Air and Artillery bombardment for the next several days The enemy holds tenaciously, but when the fort is penetrated on the 20th, it is found abandoned. **(Western Europe) 12th Army Group** In the **U.S. First Army** area, **VII Corps** sector, the Corps continues to regroup for the attack east of the Rhine. In the **III Corps** sector, the 78th Division advances cautiously north and northeast toward Konigswinter and the Aotobahn respectively, gaining objectives near Aegidienberg, Kalenborn, and Rottbitz. The 9th Division drives forward from the center of the bridgehead pushing contingents into Lorscheid, while the 395 Regiment, 99 Division makes some progress on the southern flank of the bridgehead. In other activity, the 7th Division lays a cable across the Rhine. Meanwhile, the Germans maintain frequent Air attacks against the Rhine bridges and commit many Jet Planes; however, they swing most of their Artillery fire and direct it against the U.S. troops. U.S. Anti-aircraft fire downs 80 of the

372 Planes which have attacked the bridges since the 7th of March. In the **U.S. Third Army** area, **VIII Corps** sector, the 11th Armored Division (Corps Reserve) deploys to defend the Corps northern flank; it maintains contact with the First Army. The 87th Division deploys in its new zone along the Moselle and initiates defenses around Koblenz-Lehmen; Patrols are sent across the river. At 02:00, the XII Corps jumps from its positions along the Moselle and drives toward the Rhine. The 90th Division, committing its 357th and 359th Regiments, seizes Alken, Brodenbach, Herschwiesen, Noerdersausen, and Udenhausen with the former and Burgen and portions of Macken and Morshausen with the latter; the Germans retain pos session of Pfaffenbach against determined attempts by the 357th. Meanwhile, the 358th crosses at Hatzenport as reserve and assembles in Brodenbach. The 5th Division overruns Eveshausen, Lutz, and Tries in addition to securing the high ground near these objectives. Bridges are established by Engineers. To the west and north of the Moselle, almost all remaining resistance is terminated by the combined efforts of the 76th and 89th Divisions. In other activity, the 2nd Cavalry Group is detached from the 76th Division. In the **XX Corps** sector, Hoddert is secured by the 94th Division, which also improves its positions advancing about 1,500 yards and gaining terrain within Hoch Wald and Osburger. The 2nd Battalion, 318th Regiment, 80th Division becomes cut off at Weiskirchen, while it is participating in the Division's mop-up operation; the balance of the Regiment moves to rescue the 2nd Battalion on the following day. The 104th and 328th Regiments, 26th Division advance slowly southeast, working to the right of the 80th Division. Meanwhile, the 65th Division maintains its activity at the Saarlautern bridgehead. The 316th Provisional Cavalry Brigade is operating on the northern flank of the Corps; the 16th Squadron, 16th Cavalry Squadron drives toward Waldrach and encounters fierce opposition which bogs it down at the steps of the town; however, the 3rd Squadron, 3rd Cavalry Group overruns Fell and Nieder Fell. **6th Army Group** The **U.S. Seventh Army** moves its assault troops to the embarkation line as it prepares to commence its West Wall offensive. In the **XXI Corps** sector, the 101st Cavalry Group joins the hunt as it drives along the left flank of the Corps to assist the 70th Division in the pursuit of the retreating Germans. Both units penetrate into Germany and dispatch Patrols to the south bank of the Sarre River.

March 15th 1945 — (United States) President Roosevelt nominates Generals Mark Clark, Devers, Bradley, McNarney and five others to full four star Generals. The promotion means same pay, but increased allowance of $2,200 per year. **(Pacific-Iwo Jima)** The 3rd and 4th Marine Divisions continue to eradicate remaining enemy resistance. The 5th Marine Division advances another 400 yards on the right and 200 yards in the center against heavy opposition. In the 4th Marine Division zone, the Japanese pound the positions of contingents of the 2nd Battalion, 24th Marines. Pharmacist's Mate First Class Francis J. Pierce, seeing two of eight stretcher bearers wounded while transporting wounded Marines, takes charge. He carries the two recently wounded men to safety, then directs the evacuation of three other wounded men. He stands exposed, trading shots with the enemy to distract attention from the evacuation. He begins to give aid to another wounded man, but a nearby Jap begins firing from close range. Pierce again stands to draw fire, bringing the Jap from his cave and killing him before throwing the wounded Marine over his shoulders and transporting him about 200 yards through heavy fire to safety. On the following morning,

Pierce leads a Combat Patrol to the Sniper's hideout, and while he is giving aid to yet another wounded Marine, he becomes severely wounded himself; he declines medical treatment for himself and continues laying cover fire for the attacking Marines. **(Pacific-Philippines) Luzon** In the **U.S. Sixth Army** area, **I Corps** sector, the Japanese continue to offer fierce opposition along the Villa Verde Trail; the 127th Regiment, 32nd Division drives to Imugan; however, it is stopped abruptly just short of it. On Norton's Knob above Highway 5, the Japanese repulse an attack by the 1st Battalion, 127th Regiment, 25th Division and retain control until the 27th, despite repeated attempts to exterminate them. The XI Corps assumes responsibility for the XIV sector, east and northeast of Manila, subsequent to receiving orders to make a ful scale assault against the Shimbu line. Meanwhile, the XIV Corps penetrates enemy positions in the Montalban-Antipolo region, while contingents of the 43rd Division squeeze the enemy tightly on Bench Mark 7, and at Sugar Loaf, the Japanese continue to mount fierce opposition against the 172nd Regiment. Further west, the 38th Division is battling tenaciously to reach Mt. Pinatubo. The XIV Corps, bolstered with the 11th Airborne and 1st Cavalry Divisions, concentrates on securing south Luzon. The 11th Airborne's Company C, 158th Regiment, captures Mabini on the Calumpan Peninsula; however, its 3rd Battalion encounters fierce resistance as it drives south toward the town and is halted about a mile outside of the town. **(Southern Philippines)** In the **U.S. Eighth Army** area, the Third and Fifth Air Forces provide umbrella coverage for the Convoy, as the Panay invasion force embarks Luzon. On Mindanao, the heights north and east of the Pasananca Reservoir are swept clean by the 1st Battalion, 163rd Regiment, 41st Division in short order, while the 2nd Battalion drives about 1,000 yards beyond the Santa Maria River and establishes a firm line north to the Pasananca Road junction. In other activity, the Yanks have the San Roque Airfield in operational condition. On Romblon, Company C, 19th Regiment, 24th Division completes its trek to the far side of the island by use of shore-to-shore and land movements; it is determined that only about seventy Japanese troops are still alive in the southwestern portion of Romblon. **(Pacific-Burma)** In the **British Fourteenth Army** area, 4 Corps sector, the besieged Indian 17th Division holds resolutely at Meiktila, despite its isolation and dependency upon Planes to deliver supplies; the 9th Brigade, Indian 5th Division is being rushed by air to bolster the defenders. In other activity, two Mechanized Brigades of the Indian 5th Division are racing from Jorhat to shore up the Indian 7th Division along the western flank of the Corps. **(Pacific-Kurile Islands)** A Cruiser and Destroyer Task Force, commanded by Rear Admiral J. L. McCrea, bombards Japanese shore installations on Matsuwa. **(Atlantic-Western Europe) 21st Army Group** In the **Canadian First Army** area, the Canadian I Corps (previously fighting in Italy) is now deployed in northwestern Europe. **12th Army Group** The German Planes relent slightly, as the attacks against the Rhine bridges decrease; 16 of 21 attacking Aircraft are shot down. The Germans resort to additional attacks against the bridge; a new Jet Aircraft makes an attack and in addition, the Germans launch Rockets, but the V-Rockets hit the bridgehead and spare the bridge. However, the span is enduring overbearing stress as the Yanks continue crossing in strength, while the tireless Engineers work incessantly to bolster it. In the **U.S. First Army** area, **VII Corps** sector, RCT 26, 1st Division (first unit of the VII Corps to cross the Rhine) crosses into the III Corps sector and deploys for an assault through the 78th Division lines; at present, the 76th

Division is inching closer to the Autobahn, its 39th Regiment securing Schweifeld, while the 311th Regiment drives forward about 2,000 yards. The 9th Division seizes Notscheid and reduces the remaining resistance in Lorscheid. Meanwhile, the 99th Division attacks east and southeast to enlarge its beachhead and gains about 2,500 yards. In the **V Corps** sector, the 102nd Cavalry Group (minus) is detached from Corps and attached to the VI Corps, Seventh Army. In the **U.S. Third Army** area, **VIII Corps** sector, the 87th Division deploys to attack across the Moselle to capture Koblenz, then drive south to secure the area between the Moselle and Rhine Rivers. In the **XII Corps** sector, contingents of the 2nd Cavalry Group move in and relieve the left flank units of the 90th Division, which is committing units that advance and seize Dieler, Halsenbach, Kratzenburg, and Ney; in addition, the 359th Regiment finalizes the capture of Morshausen, as well as seizing Beulich, Gondershausen, Mermuth, Nieder, and Ober. In the 5th Division sector, Dommershausen, Dorweiler, and Lieg fall as the bridgehead is expanded northeastward, and in the 4th Armored Division zone, C.C.A. overruns Liesenwald and Schwall, while C.C.B. secures Beltheim, Goedenroth, Laubach, and Simmern in addition to seizing a bridge that spans the Simer River. Meanwhile, the battered Germans are retreating expeditiously and in bad order under the guns of the Yanks, which inflict severe casualties and heavy loss of equipment; while the Infantry pursues, Tanks roar forward and Artillery shells and U.S. Planes permeate the skies, pounding the enemy columns unmercifully. In the **XX Corps** sector, the German resistance is wavering also; Waldrach is secured by contingents of the 16th Cavalry Group, while the 94th Division advances steadily, gaining about 10,000 yards, taking Hill 708 and Reinsfeld with its 302nd Regiment, and seizing Gusenburg, Kell and Schillingen with its 301st. In the 80th Division area, mop-up details continue in the 318th Regimental zone while it prepares to attack toward Weiskirchen to rescue its isolated 2nd Battalion; the 317th Regiment takes Waldholzbach and Scheiden while advancing to the area around Mitlesheim; Bergen is seized by the 319th, which advances toward Britten and Loesheim. Meanwhile, the 26th Division closes against Saarholzbach. **6th Army Group** The **U.S. Seventh Army** commences Operation UNDERTONE. It attacks with three Corps abreast, driving to crash through the West Wall and hook up with Third Army to the north to secure the Saar-Palatinate triangle between the Moselle, Rhine, and Lauter-Sarre Rivers: the XXI Corps' 63rd Division driving on the right flank seizes Ensheim, Eschringen, and Fechingen. On the left flank of the Corps, the 70th Division has contingents attack toward Saarbruecken; however, stiff opposition forces the assault to halt; other contingents and the 101st Cavalry Group mop up south of the Sarre. In the **XV Corps** sector, the 3rd and 45th Divisions push northward into Germany, while the 100th Division races forward toward Bitche, overrunning two Maginot forts and Schorbach as it advances to the high ground near Reyersviller. Meanwhile, the **VI Corps** drives across the Moder and Rothbach Rivers with four Infantry Divisions supported by Armor. The 36th Division secures Bitschhoffen and cracks the German lines at the Moder, while the 42nd Division severs the Baerenthal-Mouterhouse Road and advances to commanding ground at Baerenthal. In the 36th Division zone, German machine gun fire halts the advance of a Platoon of Company E, 142nd Regiment. P.F.C. Silvestre S. Herrera attacks singlehandedly, capturing eight enemy troops; however, as the Platoon begins to advance, more enemy fire originating beyond a minefield again stops its progress, prompting Herrera to advance. He steps on a mine, losing both feet; nevertheless, despite the horrendous pain and great loss of blood, he begins firing and holds the enemy in check until another Squad outflanks the position and secures it. Herrera becomes a recipient of the Medal of Honor because of his magnificent courage. Meanwhile, the 103rd Division advances toward Zinsweiler. The 3rd Algerian Division, bolstered by contingents of the French 5th Armored Division, drives from Oberhoffen toward Lauterbourg; the Germans mount ferocious resistance which halts the advance. **(Atlantic-Eastern Europe)** Forces of the Third White Russian Front advance to the East Prussian coast, striking it southwest of Konigsberg; the advance drives through a fortified German pocket. Russian Artillery pounds Gdynia as the Sixty-fifth and Seventieth Russian Armies close. Warships of the Admiral Baltic Sea East begin evacuating civilians and troops. **(Atlantic-Italy) 15th Army Group** In the **U.S. Fifth Army** area, **II Corps** sector, the Germans pour heavy fire into advancing contingents of the 1st Armored Division, frustrating attempts to establish an outpost on the left flank of the Corps at Salvaro.

U.S. Artillery shelling Bingen, Germany.

March 16th 1945 — (Pacific-Iwo Jima) The remaining Japanese at Cushman's Point on the northern coast are decimated by the 1st and 2nd Battalions, RCT 21 (reinforced), 3rd Marine Division, ending all resistance in its sector. Also, all enemy resistance in the 4th Marine Division area ceases as RCT 25 drives to the beach road on the east coast of the island. Iwo Jima is declared secure, but some resistance remains at Kitano Point and the draw to the southwest. The Japanese defenders had not been reinforced or resupplied. In addition, their water supplies had become exhausted; enemy troops would sneak out of their caves after dark and search for empty food cans (discarded by the Yanks) hoping to find them full of rain water. In other activity, the LST 928 is damaged by grounding. **(Pacific-Philippines) Luzon** In the **U.S. Sixth Army** area, **I Corps** sector, the 3rd Battalion, 35th Regiment, 25th Division stays behind to maintain the roadblock on Old Spanish Trail; the balance of the Regiment departs to relieve the 1st Battalion, 27th Regiment, which is heavily embattled further up the trail. In the **XI Corps** sector, the 6th Division prepares to reinitiate the offensive to secure the Shimbu line. The 172nd Regiment, 43rd Division continues to futilely pound the defenders on Sugar Loaf Hill. Bench Mark 20, slightly northeast of Teresa is seized by the 103rd Regiment, which also drives to the summit of Bench Mark 7, the final Japanese stronghold west of the Morong River Valley. In the **XIV Corps** sector, the 3rd Battalion, 158th Regiment drives to Mabini, culminating the seizure of the

Calumpan Peninsula. **(Southern Philippines)** In the **U.S. Eighth Army** area, Artillery Cub Planes are flown into the northern portion of the island; they land on an Airstrip built by Guerrillas, and they can be utilized from here to assist the 40th Division with its landing on Panay. On Mindanao, Company F, 162nd Regiment, 41st Division embarks from Zamboanga to Basilan Island, Sulu Archipelago; subsequent to a bombardment by a Destroyer, the Regiment (reinforced) lands against no opposition. **(Pacific-Burma)** In the N.C.A.C. area, CAI forces reach Hsipaw, northeast of Kyaukme. **(Pacific-South China Sea)** Army Aircraft sink the Japanese Coast Defense Vessel No. 69. **(Atlantic-Western Europe) 12th Army Group** In the **U.S. First Army** area, responsibility for the northern flank of the Remagen bridgehead is assumed by the VII Corps. The 78th Division, attached in place, maintains its northward thrust to enlarge the bridgehead, taking Aegidienberg and Hovel with its 309th Regiment. This also severs the Cologne-Frankfurt Autobahn, while the 311th Regiment, reinforced with contingents of the 310th, secures the greater part of Konigswinter. Meanwhile, the 39th Regiment and the 60th Armored Infantry Battalion, detached from the 78th Division, revert to the 9th and 9th Armored Divisions respectively. In conjunction, RCT 310, less the 1st and 2nd Battalions, revert to the 78th Division, and RCT 18, 1st Division deploys east of the Rhine and the 4th Cavalry Group and the 104th Division relieve the 3rd Armored Division during the night. In the **III Corps** sector, Kalenborn falls to the 39th Regiment, 9th Division, while the 60th Regiment seizes Strodt, and the 47th Regiment drives doggedly toward Vettleschoss. The 99th Division continues plowing east and south through Honningen Wald, overrunning several towns and villages; the 394th Regiment penetrates Honningen, only to battle the Germans to stalemate. In other activity, the Air attacks against the Rhine bridges cease. In the **U.S. Third Army** area, **VIII Corps** sector, elements of the 87th Division jump off early, bolting across the Moselle against slight resistance near Winningen-Kolberg; the 347th Regiment, driving southwest along the eastern bank of the Moselle, takes Dieblich, Dieblicherberg, and Nieder Fell in addition to seizing ground near Waldesch; the 345th advances through Lay heading northeast, reaching the fringes of Koblenz. In other activity, the Corps receives the 28th Division from the V Corps and releases the 11th Armored Division to XII Corps. In the XII Corps, sector, heavy skirmishing ensues around Pfaffenheck as the Germans resist tenaciously against the 90th Division's 357th Regiment; the 3rd Battalion, 358th Infantry seizes Ehr, then pivots to bolster the 357th. Task Force Spiess (90th Reconnaissance Troop reinforced) speeds across the Moselle, knocking off Hirzenach, Holzfeld, Hungeroth, Karbach, Rheinbay, Werlau, and Weiler as they advance to the Rhine. The 4th Armored Division races southeast to the Nahe River and seizes a bridgehead near Bad Kreuznach. The 5th Division continues to drive southeast, encountering nominal resistance. At 03:30, the 89th Division's 353rd and 354th Regiments, by use of boats, cross the Moselle and establish a small bridgehead as they drive toward Grenderich and Hill 409 respectively, while other contingents, sweeping west of the river, seize Alf and Ernst. In the XX Corps sector, the 26th Division advances speedily and seizes Mettlach and Saarholzbach; its Task Force D crosses the Seffers River and pushes toward Rimlingen. Meanwhile, the 10th Armored Division's C.C.B., supported by the 94th Division, advances to the line Hermeskeil-Nonweiler in conjunction with C.C.B., bolstered by the 80th Division, which advances to the Ober Morscholz-Noswendel-Nieder

Losheim-Wahlen line. **6th Army Group** In the **U.S. Seventh Army** area, **XXI Corps** sector, the 63rd Division continues its attack against the West Wall positions facing the right flank of the Corps. In the **XV Corps** sector, the 100th Division completes the capture of Bitche and the surrounding area, and the 3rd and 45th Divisions maintain their pounding of the outer defenses of the West Wall. In the **VI Corps** sector the 42nd Division drives through enemy defenses near Baerenthal, and the 103rd Division pushes forward, clearing Oberbronn and Zinsweiler as it drives to the fringes of Reichshoffen. In other activity, the 142nd Regiment, 36th Division crosses the Zintzel River and seizes Mertzweiler, while the 141st Regiment drives deeper into the Haguenau Forest. A motorized column of the 143rd Regiment advances toward Soultz, where it encounters fierce opposition and is halted near Eberbach. In the 3rd Algerian sector on the right flank of the Corps, the Germans abandon their positions, permitting the Division to advance quickly. **(Atlantic-Eastern Europe)** The Soviets initiate an assault against Vienna, as they initiate the drive from positions near Szekesfehervar, Hungary.

March 17th 1945 — (Pacific-Formosa) The Submarine *Spot* (SS-413) is damaged by Japanese Naval gunfire. **(Pacific-Iwo Jima)** Contingents of 5th Marine Division drive north to destroy the remaining resistance at Kitano Point. **(Pacific-Philippines)** Luzon In the **U.S. Sixth Army** area, **I Corps** sector, the 27th Regiment, 25th Division drives toward Mt. Myoko on Balete Ridge, lying about 5,500 yards from Balete Pass. In the **XI Corps** sector, the 6th Division drives east against the Shimbu line, making good progress. At Sugar Loaf Hill, the 43rd Division continues to encounter iron resistance as the Japanese bar any progress. **(Southern Philippines)** In the **U.S. Eighth Army** area, the 162nd Regiment, 41st Division seizes a hill near San Roque to fortify their positions, and the 163rd Regiment is advancing northwest of Pasananca; the Japanese are heavily entrenched at both Pasananca and Masilay. On Palawan, the 1st Battalion, RCT 186 departs for Zamboanga, Mindanao, to join the 41st Division. **(Pacific-Burma)** In the **British Fourteenth Army** area, 33rd Corps sector, the Japanese continue to control Fort Dufferin; however, Fort Ava, near the bend in the Irrawaddy south of Mandalay, is captured by the British 2nd Division. **(Atlantic-Western Europe)** **12th Army Group** In the **U.S. First Army** area, **VII Corps** sector, The 1st Division initiates an attack, pushing its Regiments toward the Sieg River, assisted by cover fire provided by the 78th Division. In the **III Corps** sector, Major General James A. Van Fleet assumes command of the Corps, relieving General Milleken. In other activity, the bridge at Remagen suddenly collapses just before 15:00, while Engineers are still working to reinforce it. The Remagen Bridge which permitted the Yanks to overcome the final natural barrier in Germany has greatly shortened the war before its demise; at one point, over 8,000 men transgressed it during a 24-hour period. But many undaunted Engineers make the ultimate sacrifice when the structure slips into the Rhine; at the conclusion of desperate rescue operation, 28 men are lost and another 63 have become injured. Fortunately, additional bridges have been strung across the Rhine, and small Naval Craft are also operating. As the saying goes in this area, "JOIN THE NAVY AND SEE GERMANY." In the meantime, the Allies continue to pour across the Rhine in great numbers. The advancing 9th Division slices the Autobahn at Windhagen and seizes Vettelschoss in addition to sweeping the high ground east of Strodt, along the Wied River. In conjunction, the 99th Division advances steadily; its 393rd Infantry seizes Hausen and Solscheid, while the 394th Regiment eliminates heavy opposi-

tion at Honningen. In the **U.S. Third Army** area, **VIII Corps** sector, Moselweiss on the Moselle is secured by the 3rd Battalion, 345th Regiment, 87th Division, and the 2nd and 3rd Battalions combine to push through Koblenz, securing about a third of the city subsequent to severe house-to-house fighting; the 347th Regiment seizes Waldesch and enters Rhens. Meanwhile, bridges are placed across the river at Kobern and Winningen. In the **XII Corps** sector, the 90th Division, advancing against a faltering enemy, seizes Boppard with its 358th Infantry and St. Goarer Stadwald with contingents of the 358th, while TF Spiess sweeps along the Rhine between Boppard and St. Goar, accepting the surrender of the latter. In the 4th Armored zone, C.C.A. crosses the Nahe and overpowers the resistance at Biebelsheim, Ippesheim, and Zotzenheim; C.C.B. expands the Nahe bridgehead, then after dark, attacks toward Bad Kreuznach. In the 5th Division area, contingents of Task Force Breckenridge advance to Waldboeckelheim; however, the remainder of the column halts at Tiefenbach; the 11th Regiment reaches Argenthal, Ellern, and Riesweiler. In the 80th Division sector, the Bullay bridgehead expansion continues; contingents of the 11th Armored pass through and initiate an attack toward the Rhine from Worms at 12:00; the 41st Cavalry Squadron seizes Loetzbeuren and Wahlenau, while C.C.A. advances through Kappel, driving toward Kirchberg. Meanwhile, C.C.B. advances to the area around Buechenbeuren. In the **XX Corps** sector, the 10th Armored's C.C.B. crosses the Nahe outside of Turkismuhle, while C.C.A. drives to the west bank of the Prims River. In conjunction, the 80th and 94th Infantry Divisions are driving forward, making substantial gains beside the Armor, the former establishing a bridgehead across the Prims River near Krettnich-Nunkirchen. In the 26th Division sector, Brotdorf, Dueppenweiler, and Honzrath fall to the 101st Regiment, and the 104th Infantry captures a bridge across the Prims River at Huettersdorf. In addition, the 328th Regiment overruns Haustadt and Merzig. In the 65th Division sector, final preparations are made for the breakout from the Saarlautern bridgehead; the 261st Regiment fords the Saar near Menningen and secures the heights south of Merzig to gain a jump-off spot for the attack against Dillingen, and on the northern flank, the 316th Provisional Brigade completes its task of securing the remainder of the Trier-Hermeskeil Road, the main supply route. In other activity, the 12th Armored Division is attached to Corps to take advantage of the 94th Division's breakthrough at Birkenfled. **6th Army Group** Generals Eisenhower and Patton meet at Seventh Army Headquarters in Luneville to discuss cooperation between the Third and Seventh Armies during the upcoming offensive scheduled to commence during the latter part of March. In the **U.S. Seventh Army** area, **XXI Corps** sector, the 63rd Division maintains its pressure against the West Wall; the 12th Armored Division, which had been deployed to pass through the 63rd, is transferred to the XX Corps, Third Army. In the **XV Corp** sector, the 3rd and 45th Divisions both drive to the West Wall fortifications at Zweibruecken. In the **VI Corps** sector, the Germans are unable to mount any stiff resistance, permitting large gains for the 42nd Division, which is advancing on the left flank of the Corps. During the six-mile advance, Baerenthal, Bannstein, Dambach, Neunhoffen, Niedersteinbach, Philippsbourg, and Sturzelbronn collapse under U.S. pressure; in conjunction, the 117th Cavalry Reconnaissance Squadron captures Mouterhouse. In addition, the 103rd Division, facing similar opposition in its sector, topples a sizable number of towns and hamlets, including Niederbronn, Reichshoffen, and Woerth. In other activity, the 143rd Regiment, 36th Division, maintains its pursuit of the retreating Germans, until it reaches the Bieberbach River near Gunstett and encounters another sunken bridge. Meanwhile, the 141st Regiment continues to drive through the Haguenau Forest.

The Remagen Bridge, subsequent to collapse.

March 18th 1945 — (Pacific-Iwo Jima) Contingents of the 3rd Marine Division Patrol and also complete mop-up operations until relieved by Garrison troops. **(Pacific-Japan)** Task Force 58 launches Planes which strike Kyushu on the mainland; the raid is extremely effective and scores heavily, damaging the Airfields, facilities, and large numbers of grounded Planes; however, the Carrier *Intrepid* (CV-11) is damaged by a Suicide Plane and by accidental firing by U.S. forces. In addition, the Carriers *Enterprise* (CV-6) and *Yorktown* (CV-10) are damaged by Horizontal Bombers. The raids are intended to neutralize enemy Air activity against the imminent Operation ICEBERG (invasion of the Ryukyus). **(Pacific-Philippines)** The LST 635 is damaged by grounding. **Luzon** In the **U.S. Sixth Army** area, the Japanese are ordered to begin a withdrawal from San Fernando on the 20th, due to the extreme pressure exerted by the U.S. driving from the south and from the Guerrillas closing from the north. Outside of Putlan, the 25th Division finally dislodges the obstinate resistance which had been suspending their advance for several days; the Division begins to drive north along Highway 5, toward Kapintalan, the next objective. In the **XI Corps** sector, some ground previously lost in a counterattack is retaken by the 1st Regiment, 6th Division. In other activity, contingents of the 103rd Regiment, 43rd Division drive to the southern end of Bench Mark 23, while the 3rd Battalion drives to the slopes of Mt. Tanauan. In the **XIV Corps** sector, the 158th Regiment transfers responsibility for Calumpan Peninsula to an Antitank Company. **Southern Philippines** In the **U.S. Eighth Army** area, Task Group 78.3 (Victor I Attack Group) debarks the 185th Regiment, 40th Division on southern Panay subsequent to a quick but furious bombardment of the landing beaches near Tigbauan that helps diminish any opposition; the landing force speeds inland toward Iloilo, with knowledge that the 2nd Battalion, 160th Regiment is moving ashore to protect the northwestern portion of the bridgehead. Ashore, the Commanding General, 40th Division, assumes command of the troops. On Mindanao, Company F, 162nd Regiment, 41st Division, moves from Basilan Island to Malamaui Island; however, the search for the enemy is fruitless. **(Atlantic-Western Europe) 12th Army Group** In the **U.S. First Army** area, **VII Corps** sector, the 78th Division secures Nieder and Ober Dollendorf and seizes the high ground which controls the Konigswinter Bridge site. In the 1st Division zone, Brungsberg, Orscheid, Stockhausen,

Wullscheid, and nearby Hill 363 fall to the advancing Yanks. In the **III Corps** sector, the 9th Division topples Ober Windhagen, Windhagen and the heights along the Wied River near Strodt, while the 99th Division continues to mop up in its sector along the Wied and searches for crossing sites. In the **U.S. Third Army** area, **VIII Corps** sector, German-held Fort Constantine sustains heavy shelling as the 87th Division presses to conquer the strongpoint. In conjunction, the 345th Regiment's operation is ongoing with the balance of Koblenz now under the Stars and Stripes; the 347th continues to drive south under the heated breath of German Artillery entrenched on the opposite side of the Rhine; the push nets the 347th Brey and Niederspay, as well as gaining it the balance of Rhens. In the **XII Corps** area, orders are issued to attack toward the Mainz-Worms area of the Rhine: specifically, the 90th Division is to capture Mainz, but new orders direct it to seize Worms. In the 90th Division zone, TF Spiess sweeps from Oberwesel to Nieder Heimbach, conducting methodical mop-up details, while the 358th Regiment clears the sector extending between Nieder Heimbach to Bingerbruch; at 24:00, the 359th Regiment reverts to the 90th Division. The 4th Armored Division's C.C.B. secures the portion of Bad Kreuznach east of the Nahe and has elements penetrate and secure part of Volxheim; C.C.A. seizes Sprendlingen, St. Johann, Wolfsheim, and Gau Bickelheim. In the 5th Division sector, progress is rapid also, as Task Force Brechenridge reaches the Gemuenden-Mengerscheid-Sargenroth vicinity. The 2nd and 11th Regiments plow through the woods, advancing to Weitersborn, Seesbach, Pferdsfeld, Begroth, Argenshwang, Dalberg, Winterbach, and Ippenscheid. In the 11th Armored sector, Air cover supports the advance and simultaneously pummels the retreating German forces; contingents of the 11th Armored drive to the Nahe River finding submerged bridges. Ignoring the dilemma, the troops improvise and get units across to continue pursuit. In the 89th Division area, the perimeter is expanded east of the Moselle and establishes contact with the 5th Division, while the 76th Division is establishing a bridgehead across the Moselle near Wittlich; its 304th Regiment overruns Muelheim, Filzen, Wintrich, Reinsport, Mustert, and Nieder Emmel. As the 304th Regiment debarks its assault boats in darkness, the enemy had been retreating; however, the area is saturated with mines. Two of the attackers are severely wounded and bleeding profusely. Private William D. McGee (Army Medical Detachment) moves into the minefield and successfully evacuates one man, then returns to get the other; however, he steps on a mine and is seriously wounded. McGee then yells to others who might venture in to the minefield and tells them to stay put and not attempt to reach him; he succumbs to his wounds. He receives the Medal of Honor for his bravery. In the **XX Corps** sector, the Germans are retreating in disarray toward Baumholder, with the 94th Division close behind. Meanwhile, contingents of the 12th Armored pass through the 94th in a gallop, reaching the Rhine at Worms, while the 10th Armored Division storms toward St. Wendel and Thalichtenberg with C.C.A. and C.C.B., followed by the 80th Division which is being transported by motorized Vehicles as well as the Infantry's chief method of transportation; G.I. Boots. In the 26th Division sector, rapid progress is being made as well; its 104th Regiment seizes Aschbach, Dirmingen, and Thalexweiler, while the 101st Infantry overruns Bubach, Kalmesweiler, and Lebach; in addition, the 328th Regiment assembles at Haustadt. In the 65th Division sector, the breakout begins with the 261st Regiment jumping from the Saarlautern bridgehead to seize Dillingen; the 259th and

260th Regiments bolster their bridgehead positions but are unable to make the break. During the heated fighting, P.F.C. Frederick Murphy (Medical Corps), 259th Regiment, becomes seriously wounded soon after the attack begins; however, he refuses to withdraw for medical aid. Murphy moves through heavy Artillery and mortar fire, attempting to aid the wounded in a minefield, and walks on a mine, losing one of his feet. He again refuses evacuation, continuing to give aid to other wounded Soldiers; however, in the process of crawling to assist another wounded man, he hits another mine which kills him. P.F.C. Murphy becomes a recipient of the Medal of Honor for his extraordinary bravery. **6th Army Group** In the **U.S. Seventh Army** area, plans are being readied for an attack across the Rhine. In the **XXI Corps** sector, Engineers supporting the 63rd Division blow through a gap in the Dragon's Teeth of the West Wall north of Ensheim and Ommersheim. In the **XV Corps** area, the 3rd and 45th Divisions attack against the Dragon's Teeth and surrounding pillboxes of the West Wall, while the 100th Division begins pulling back from Bitche upon relief by the 71st Division. In the 45th Division zone, activity is heated near Nieder-Wurzbach. German fire has Company F, 180th Regiment pinned down at the base of a hill. Eight men sent to eliminate one of the interlocking obstacles get strung out on an exposed slope and become casualties. Captain Jack L. Treadwell advances singlehandedly, taking 18 prisoners including the Commanding Officer of the hill's defenses and knocking out six pillboxes. His heroism sparks the balance of Company F, which rushes forward to finish the job, overrunning the enemy on the hill and penetrating the Siegfried Line. Also, Company C, 150th Regiment, 45th Division comes under thundering fire. Corporal Edward G. Wilkin ignores the intense rifle and machine gun fire, advancing against one obstacle after another, destroying the pillboxes and killing enemy troops as he moves. He is halted by barbed wire, but undaunted, he uses bangalore torpedoes to blast his way through. Racing toward additional pillboxes, he disregards the burst of shellfire and thrown grenades, trading shots with the Germans who are behind thick fortifications. Wilkin winds up about 200 yards in advance of the closest U.S. unit. He refuses to rest and works tirelessly throughout the night, giving out rations and helping to evacuate wounded. By the 20th, Wilkin has personally killed about nine Germans, captured 13 and assisted with the capture of 14 more, and wounded 13 others. Corporal Wilkin becomes the recipient of the Medal of Honor; however, he is killed during April of 1945 while fighting deep in Germany and receives it posthumously. In the **VI Corps** sector, the 42nd Division breaches Germany's border, crashing into the West Wall on the left flank of the Corps. In conjunction, the 103rd Division speeds north across Germany's border, seizing Bobenthal and its bridges, which span the Lauter River; still German resistance stiffens and halts progress near Niederschlettenbach. In the 36th Division sector, contingents seize Dieffenbach, and other units take Surbourg; close behind, the 14th Armored rolls forward to take advantage of the 36th Division gains. In other activity, the 3rd Algerian Division's transfer to the French 1st Army is suspended to permit the Division to continue its advance to the Erlen River in pursuit of the retreating Germans; the Algerians reach within one mile of the German border. **(Atlantic-Eastern Europe)** Kolberg (Pomerania) falls to contingents of the First White Russian Front, costing the beleaguered Germans their final pocket on the Baltic coast between the Polish corridor and Stettin Bay. **(Atlantic-Italy) 15th Army Group** In the **U.S. Fifth Army** area, the Italian Legnano Group is

attached to II Corps and comes under jurisdiction of U.S. 91st Division. In other activity, the 85th Division reverts to Army reserve.

March 19th 1945 — Kobe, Japan under attack by U.S. Planes.

U.S. Carrier Planes attacking Kure Harbor, Honshu, Japan.

March 19th 1945 — (United States) The U.S.S. *Block Island* (first Marine Escort Carrier commissioned) embarks Marine Carrier Group 1 (VMF-511, VMTB-233, and CASD-1) at San Diego, heading for Pearl Harbor to deploy with the Fleet. **(Pacific-Iwo Jima)** The 4th Marine Division embarks for Hawaii. Contingents of the 5th Marine Division continue to drive against Kitano Point. **(Pacific-Japan)** Carrier Planes from Task Force 58 again strike the Japanese mainland, devouring at least sixteen Warships and several other Vessels in the vicinity of Kure-Kobe, despite incessant antiaircraft fire. The Japanese retaliate with Aircraft and damage the U.S.S. *Franklin* (CV-13), causing a lingering fire; during the afternoon, the Fleet retires escorting the disabled *Franklin*, while delivering Fighter Plane attacks over Kyushu Airfields. During the harrowing experience aboard the *Franklin*, nearly 300 men are trapped in a smoke-filled compartment, and additional men are caught in other compartments. Lieutenant Junior Grade Donald A. Gary and Commander Joseph Timothy O'Callahan (Chaplain) both receive the Medal of Honor for their conspicuous bravery during the ordeal. Gary gets the three hundred men to safety by making three successive trips through the smoke-filled inferno after miraculously finding an escape route. Chaplain O'Callahan tends to his spiritual duties comforting men of all faiths; however, he also moves about the burning Ship amidst the burst of bombs and other ammunition. He organizes and leads fire-fighting teams and directs teams to get rid of live ammunition, to flood the magazine. The Carriers *Wasp* (CV-18) and *Essex* (CV-9) are damaged off Shikoku, the former by Dive Bombers and the latter by accidental U.S. fire. **(Pacific-Philippines) Luzon** In the **U.S. Sixth Army** area, Bauang and its bridge are seized effortlessly by the 33rd Division. In the **XI Corps** sector, elements of the 6th Division advance to about 1,200 yards west of Mt. Baytangan before lunch, while other elements move to Mt. Caymayuman to combine with the 172nd Regiment, 43rd Division, for a two-pronged assault against Sugar Loaf Hill, which refuses to relent. At Mt. Tanauan, the Japanese resist fiercely, but the dogged determination of the 3rd Battalion, 103rd Regiment, 43rd Division, keeps pressing forward. Meanwhile, a contingent of the 151st Regiment, 38th Division (from Corregidor) lands unopposed on the eastern tip of Caballo Island, and drives inland; a concentrated bombardment of discovered enemy positions is initiated, lasting one week. In the **XIV Corps** area, Mt. Bijang is taken without incident by elements of the 11th Airborne's 511th Infantry and accompanying Guerrillas. In other activity, RCT 158 drives against three enemy-held hills, toppling two with little stress; however, the final holdout, Mt. Macolod, resists rigidly; the intense fire halts progress in front of Cuenca. **Southern Philippines** In the **U.S. Eighth Army** area, the Thirteenth Air Force commences a furious bombardment of Cebu to soften resistance for the assault troops. On Mindanao, the 1st Battalion, 186th Regiment, 41st Division arrives at Zamboanga; the American forces already there are continually gaining more control. Meanwhile, on Panay, Japanese resistance becomes vicious at Molo, halting the progress of a column of the 185th Regiment. Another Regimental column bolts through intense opposition near Molo and seizes a bridge which spans the Iloilo before the Japanese can blow it. In conjunction, a third column drives into Mandurriao, seizing it and its Airfield without encountering any opposition. The besieged Japanese await darkness, then break through Guerrilla lines at Jaro, escaping to the mountains. **(Pacific-Burma)** In the **British Fourteenth Army** area, 33rd Corps sector, the Indian 19th Division continues to unsuccessfully pound Fort Dufferin. Meanwhile, Planes score decisively, blowing holes in the walls of the fort. In other activity, a contingent of the Indian 20th Division departs Pyinzi moving toward Pindale, south of Mandalay. **(Pacific-China)** The Japanese River Boat **Suma** sinks after striking an Army mine, off Shanghai. **(Atlantic-Western Europe) 12th Army Group** In the **U.S. First Army** area, **VII Corps** sector, Obercassel and Romlinghoven fall to the 311th Regiment, 78th Division, while the 310th Regiment seizes Bennert, Busch, and Heisterbacherrott. In the 1st Divi-

sion sector, the Germans stiffen their resistance as the Big Red One attempts to advance from the Rhine; its 18th Regiment overruns Eudenbach, while the 26th Regiment charges to Gratzfeld before dawn and drives east toward the Airfield. In other activity, the 7th Armored Division is attached to Corps, and the first "Class 40" bridge to span the Rhine is complete. In the **III Corps** sector, the 9th Division maintains its eastward thrust and establishes a bridgehead line by dawn of the 20th. In the **V Corps** sector, contingents of the 9th Regiment, 2nd Division, clears Rhine Island near Namedy. In the **U.S. Third Army** area, **VIII Corps** sector, the zone west of the Rhine is cleared by the 87th Division. Resistance at Koblenz is terminated by the 345th Regiment, while the 347th seizes Oberspay. In the **XII Corps** sector, the 90th Division attacks toward Mainz on the Rhine. The 4th Armored Division races through fractured resistance, seizing Eckelsheim, Gumbsheim, Siefersheim, Wendlesheim, Wollstein, and Wonsheim, with C.C.B.; C.C.A. overruns Rommersheim, Schimsheim, Sulzheim, Wallertheim, and Vendersheim. The 11th Armored is also actively engaged as it drives against a demoralized and retreating German Army, which is streaming east toward the Rhine. The 41st Cavalry Squadron pushes to Medard and Odenbach, where it establishes contact with the 12th Armored (XX Corps on right); C.C.B. hammers the enemy defenses south of the Nahe, then bolts to Meisenheinm and seizes the Glan River bridge before continuing to Rockenhausen where it secures a bridge across the Alsenz River. Meanwhile, rear contingents of C.C.A. weed out remnant resistance within an enemy pocket near Rohrbach, while the remainder of the Combat Team crosses the Nahe and pounds the German positions, overpowering the Main Line of Resistance at Merxheim and thrusting further to Meisenheinm. Also, an enemy rocket disables a Tank of Company C, 41st Tank Battalion (11th Armored), wounding the Platoon Sergeant and compelling the crew to abandon it. Staff Sergeant Herbert H. Burr (Tank's bow gunner), deafened but otherwise unharmed, jams into the driver's seat and continues into Dorrmoschel (Germany) to reconnoiter the roads; however, as he turns a corner, a German 88mm antitank gun prepares to fire from pointblank range. Handling the Tank alone without a gunner leaves him little choice. He puts the Tank to full speed and charges the startled enemy, crushing the gun and sending the crew running, then disorganizing the area by plowing into some enemy equipment before returning to his lines. In other activity, Task Force Breckenridge, 5th Division, is dissolved; RCT 10 is attached to the 4th Armored Division. The advance is so swift that countless prisoners are taken. In the 76th Division sector, a bridge is laid across the Moselle at Muelheim by the 304th Regiment, giving quick access to the XX Corps; Andel, Bernkastel, Gornhausen, Graanch, Longkamp, and Monzefeld topple with little effort to enlarge the bridgehead. Meanwhile, the XX Corps maintains its pace to the Rhine. The 94th Division lunges 22 miles in the 302nd Regiment's area and advances about 12 miles in the zone of the 376th Regiment. The 12th and 10th Armored Divisions advance rapidly, the former driving to positions beyond Winnweiler, and the latter to positions near Kaisewrlautern, securing St. Wendel (assisted by 80th Division). Kusel is secured by the 80th Division, while the 65th Division consumes more ground to enlarge its bridgehead at the Saarlautern; Bilsdorf, Nalbach, Piesbach, and Saarwellingen are seized by the 261st Regiment; the 260th secures Saarlautern and Saarlautern-Roden, and is subsequently pinched out; Ensdorf and Fraulautern are overrun by the 259th. **6th Army Group** In the **U.S. Seventh Army** area, **XXI Corps** sector, the 63rd

Division pumps the adrenaline and crashes into more menacing pillboxes as it continues to crack the West Wall, while the 70th Division reinitiates its assault to gain Saarbruecken and some Saar River crossing sites. Meanwhile, C.C.A., 6th Armored is attached to the 63rd Division to help exploit the anticipated breakthrough. In the **XV Corps** sector, the 3rd and 45th Divisions drive relentlessly against the West Wall, demolishing pillboxes and bunkers as they advance; the former drives to positions east of Zweibruecken, and the latter overruns Alschbach, Blieskastel, and Webenheim. In the **VI Corps** sector, the 42nd Division drives on the Corps' left flank encountering ferocious resistance as it moves sluggishly but persistently against the West Wall. The 103rd Division is equally hard-pressed by stiff resistance as it drives against vicious opposition near Nieder Schlettenbach and Reisdorf. In the 36th Division sector, the Germans raise spirited resistance; however, the 36th drives through the Wissembourg Gap, secures Wissembourg, and rushes across the German border, advancing to Ober Otterbach. Meanwhile, the 14th Armored fords the Lauter River northeast of Schleithal. In the French sector, Groupement Monsabert is established using troops of the 3rd Algerian Division and attached contingents of the 5th French Armored Division; it moves across the Lauter River and seizes Lauterbourg and Scheibenhard. **(Atlantic-Switzerland)** Allied Representatives (no Russians) meet with German General Wolff at Locarno to discuss surrender of all German troops in northern Italy; however, the meeting concludes without results. Wolff informs the Allies that he will head for Germany to confer with General Kesselring, whom Hitler has placed in control of the entire Western Front; General Heinrich Vietinghoff has been given command of the Italian front.

The U.S.S. Franklin, afire.

March 20th 1945 — (Pacific-Dutch East Indies-Borneo) The Submarine *Perch* (SS-313) lands men on the east coast of Borneo. **(Pacific-Iwo Jima)** The 147th Infantry, U.S.A., arrives from New Caledonia to assume responsibility for defense of the island; it is attached to the 3rd Marine Division. In other activity, the Submarine *Devilfish* (SS-292) is damaged by a Kamikaze off the Volcano Islands. The Cargo Ship *Hercules* (AK-41) sustains damage by collision. **(Pacific-Philippines)** In the **U.S. Sixth Army** area, **I Corps** sector, a 33rd Division Task Force departs Bauang for San Fernando to join Guerrilla forces operating in northern Luzon. After dark, the Japanese abandon San Fernando. At Norton's Knob, the Japanese continue to repulse the attacking contingent of the 161st Regiment, 25th Division; however, Co. C., 1st Battalion, overpowers the defenders on a ridge west of the knob. At the

Villa Verde Trail the 32nd Division continues hitting heavy resistance. A vicious fire-fight erupts as a detachment of Company F clashes with Japs entrenched in caves and connecting foxholes. Staff Sergeant Ysmael R. Villegas maneuvers from man to man to keep morale and discipline amidst the burning machine gun fire and burst of grenades. Villegas singlehandedly destroys the defenders in five foxholes and bolts toward a sixth; however, all enemy guns concentrate on him and he is killed just in front of it. Villegas' men, inspired by the valiant Sergeant, attack and thrash the enemy, pushing them from the area; Villegas receives the Medal of Honor posthumously. In the **XI Corps** sector, the 6th Division advances a few hundred yards and seizes the high ground above the Bosoboso River. At Mt. Caymayuman, the 172nd Regiment, 43rd Division is struck by a powerful counterattack after dark, but the Japanese are thrown back. Meanwhile, Artillery is concentrated upon Mt. Tanauan to soften resistance; the 3rd Battalion, 103rd Regiment cancels its attack to await the cessation of the shelling. In the **XIV Corps** sector, contingents of the 158th Regiment drive toward Cuenca and Mt. Macolod and discover the former is abandoned by the enemy. **Southern Philippines** In the **U.S. Eighth Army** area, X Corps is dubbed Victor V Task Force and is directed to capture the Malabang-Parang-Cotabato region of Mindanao in addition to seizing the area east of Zamboanga Peninsula. The 24th and 31st Divisions revert to the X Corps, allowing the 41st Division and Paratroop RCT 505 to be placed in Eighth Army reserve. On Mindanao, Company F (-) departs Basilin Island for Zamboanga; however, one Platoon remains behind with Cos. K and L and a Guerrilla detachment to ensure control of the island. On Panay, the 185th Regiment sweeps the area between Molo and Iloilo, securing it effortlessly, culminating organized resistance on the island; as Japanese attempt to make it to the mountains, they are intercepted by the 3rd Battalion and the 40th Reconnaissance Troop. Planes arrive to add to the trepidation of the fleeing troops. Meanwhile, the search for additional enemy forces on the island continues. **(Pacific-Burma)** In the **British Fourteenth Army** area, the Indian 19th Division penetrates Fort Dufferin and discovers it abandoned. **(Pacific-Japan)** The Carrier *Enterprise* (CV-6) is accidentally damaged by U.S. fire. The Destroyer *Halsey Powell* (DD-686) is damaged by a Suicide Plane. **(Atlantic-Western Europe) 12th Army Group** In the **U.S. First Army** area, the **VII Corps** advances easily and with great speed, trampling Bennerscheid, Berghausen, and Oberpleis, while contingents sever the Eudenbach-Bucholz Road seizing positions near its Airfield. In the **U.S. Third Army** area, **XII Corps** sector, the 76th Division continues its relief of the 2nd Cavalry Group along the Rhine and also withdraws its Moselle bridgehead on the southern flank of the Corps. The speeding 90th Division advances to Ebersheim, Klein Wintenheim, Mommenheim, Ober Olmer Wald, and Selzen. The 5th Division, pushing from the Nahe, advances and seizes the Gau Odernheim-Spiesheim-Woerrstadt area. Meanwhile, the 4th Armored Division catapults its forward contingents to the Rhine; they strike at Worms and establish roadblocks to tighten the noose around the city; the 11th Armored Division drives to within four miles of the city, followed by the 80th Division which exterminates bypassed resistance. In the **XX Corps** sector, the 94th Division advances rapidly, some of its units driving as far as 23 miles. At Ottweiler, the 26th Division conducts mop-up operations, and in the 65th Division zone, the 3rd Cavalry Group moves the southern flank of the Corps where it is attached to Corps and directed to defend Saarlautern. Contact is established with the Seventh Army to the right. **6th Army Group** The activity is furious in the XV and XXI Corps sectors as the West Wall is badly punctured by both Corps. The 70th Division (XXI Corps) roars into Saarbruecken against no opposition and establishes contact with the XX Corps, Third Army, while the 63rd Division, hammering on the right, drives to Ober Wurzach and into Hassel and St. Ingbert; C.C.A., 6th Armored Division speeds through the 63rd's lines, encountering slight opposition, and stops at Homberg. In the **XV Corps** sector, the 3rd and 45th Divisions splatter the West Wall defenses in their zones, the former driving into Zweibruecken, capturing the bridges intact and the latter seizing Homberg. In the **VI Corps** sector, the Germans resist with vigor, mounting tenacious fire that halts the 42nd Division as it attempts to advance on the left flank. Close by, the 103rd Division encounters similar resistance, but penetrates the wall of fire, seizing Nieder Schlettenbach. Meanwhile, the 14th Armored Division shoots the Wissembourg Gap and reaches the main defenses of the West Wall at Steinfeld. Meanwhile, the French Groupement Monsabert is engaged at Bien Wald and makes sluggish progress against the enemy. In other activity, the 4th Division is attached to the Corps. **(Atlantic-Eastern Europe)** Alt Damm (Pomerania) is seized by units of the First White Russian Front; the troops also eliminate the last bridge across the Oder, across from Stettin. In East Prussia, contingents of the Third White Russian Front seize Braunsberg. Meanwhile, pressure against the Baltic ports of Danzig and Gdynia is increased by Soviet troops.

General Alexander A. Vandegrift, U.S.M.C.

March 21st 1945 — (United States) Commandant General Alexander A. Vandegrift becomes the first four-star General in the Marine Corps on active duty. **(Pacific-Philippines) Luzon** In the **U.S. Sixth Army** area, **I Corps** sector, the 33rd Division's 130th Regiment encounters Guerrilla troops of the U.S. Army Forces of the Philippines near San Fernando; contingents of the 130th discover Naguilian and its Airfield abandoned. The West coast of Luzon is now secure. However, the Japanese are not finished. As contingents of the 161st Regiment, 25th Division, advance toward Crump Hill, about 1,000 yards west of Kapintalan, the Japanese send a wall of fire against the Yanks. The entrenched enemy keeps the attackers restrained until the 8th of April. Meanwhile, the 27th Regiment, 25th Division is struck by a thunderous, but unsuccessful counterattack on a ridge near Mt. Myoko. In the **XI Corps** sector, Planes and Artillery precede the Infantry attack of the 1st Regiment, 6th Division, which then powers forward about 600-800 yards where it cuts a trail extending between Antipolo and Wawa. Documents are confiscated which contain information about Japanese plans to reinforce the region. In the 43rd Division sector, the Yanks have banged the enemy relentlessly, forcing a thorough breakdown of resistance; the 172nd Regiment crushes the remaining resistance on Sugar Loaf Hill, Mt. Caymayuman, and Mt. Yabang, all falling to the Stars and Stripes with ease. In addition, the 3rd Battalion, 103rd Regiment drives to the summit of Mt. Tanauan, and Company B, supported by Guerrillas, races two miles north of Bench Mark 23 and crosses the New Bosoboso River near New Bosoboso barrio. In the **XIV Corps** sector, the 158th Regiment sweeps east from Cuenca to the hills of Mt. Macolod without incident. **South Philippines** In the **U.S. Eighth Army** area, Company B, 19th Regiment, 24th Division, concludes its mission of clearing Simara and returns to Romblon where it joins Company C. The operation costs the U.S. ten killed, against Japanese losses of 118. In other activity, the 2nd Battalion, 160th Regiment, 40th Division lands on Guimaras Island and begins a fruitless search for the enemy. **(Pacific-Burma)** In the **British Fourteenth Army** area, organized resistance ceases on Mandalay. In other activity, the British 2nd Division opens the highway between Avba and Mandalay, while the Indian 20th Division moves to Wundwin. **(Pacific-China)** At darkness, the Japanese drive toward the Airfield at Laohokow. **(Pacific-Japan)** Japanese Aircraft initiate first use of piloted bombs during an unsuccessful attack against Admiral Mitscher's Fast Carrier Task Force, but the attempt fails. **(Pacific-South China Sea)** Army Aircraft sink the Submarine Chaser No 33 and the cable layer *Tateishi*. **(Atlantic-Western Europe) 12th Army Group** In the **U.S. First Army** area, the 78th Division drives to the Sieg; the 310th Regiment seizes Hangeler, Menden, Muelldorf, and Niederpleis; its 311th Regiment reaches it at Meindorf. The 4th Squadron, 4th Cavalry Group, and C.C. Howze, 3rd Armored Division, are attached to the 78th Division; the latter drives north along the Sieg and secures part of Buisdorf. In the 1st Division zone, the 16th Regiment secures Bucholz, Pleiserhorn, Rott, Soven, Uthweiler, and Westerhausen, while the 18th Regiment secures Eisbach, Ruebhausen, and Kurtscheid. In conjunction, the 26th Regiment overruns Germscheid. Meanwhile, the III Corps prepares for a breakout assault and the V Corps commences an offensive at 04:00. In the **U.S. Third Army** area, **VIII Corps** sector, the 76th Division concludes its relief of the 2nd Cavalry Group (XII Corps), taking responsibility for the area along the Rhine from Boppard to Bingen. The 90th Division converges on Mainz, while securing most of its sector west of the Rhine, and makes contact with the 42nd Squadron of the 2nd Cavalry Group, which has taken Bingen and expanded its lines to Frei

Weinheim. In the 4th Armored sector, C.C.B. and C.C.A. secure the terrain on the west bank of the Rhine between Worms and Oppenheim; in conjunction, C.C.R. deploys in Stein Bockenheim to establish roadblocks on the Corps' south flank. Meanwhile, the 11th Armored Division finalizes its second drive to the Rhine as C.C.B. overruns the Airport south of Worms; then it enters Worms, a city of rubble. In addition, C.C.A., 12th Armored Division, drives to the fringes of Ludwigshafen and is joined there by the 94th Division, which will support the assault against the city; the 94th relieves C.C.B. and C.C.R., 12th Armored at the Rhine. The 10th Armored advances southward quickly toward Speyer; C.C.R. secures Annweiler, Rinnthal, and Queichhambach, while C.C.A. drives to Dannstadt and Neustadt, and C.C.B. reaches Densieders. As the Armor tramples forward, the 26th and 65th Divisions maintain their eastward thrust until orders arrive to halt. Third Army casualtes as of March 21st 1945: 19,281 killed, 91,081 wounded; 15,556 missing; non-battle casualties 96,593; casualties incurred during Palatinate campaign, 6,405. Enemy casualties against Third Army: 123,800 killed; 337,300 wounded; P.O.W.s 282,900. On the following day, Patton issues General Order No. 70 (January 29th-March 22nd 1945): "YOU HAVE WRESTED 6,484 SQUARE MILES FROM ENEMY...3,072 CITIES, TOWNS, VILLAGES...CAPTURED 140,112 ENEMY TROOPS...KILLED OR WOUNDED 99,000, THEREBY ELIMINATING PRACTICALLY ALL OF THE GERMAN 7TH AND 1ST ARMIES." 6th Army Group The U.S. Seventh Army Command Post transfers from Luneville to Sarreguemines. In the XXI Corps sector, organized resistance ceases. In the XV Corps sector, the 6th Armored rolls to the Rhine and establishes contact with Third Army at Worms. In the VI Corps sector, Air and Artillery again precede an attack by the 42nd Division, which commences its assault against the West Wall at 19:00, charging into empty pillboxes. A Task Force of the 103rd Division drives into Reisdorf. In the 36th Division sector, German strongholds are overrun, but resistance is fierce at Steinfeld, where the 14th Armored Division is grinding through the town. At Bien Wald, the Groupement Monsabert is heavily engaged with the enemy. In the French 1st Army area, the Detachment d'Armee de l'Atlantique concludes its relief of U.S. forces, within scope of Alpine Front Command. (Atlantic-Russia) The Russians are informed by U.S. Ambassador Harriman that the meeting with the Germans in Switzerland had produced no results. Two days later on the 23rd, Molotov sends a letter to the U.S., which states in part: "DURING THE LAST TWO WEEKS...BEHIND THE BACKS OF THE SOVIET GOVERNMENT, WHICH HAS BEEN CARRYING ON THE MAIN BURDEN OF THE WAR AGAINST GERMANY, REPRESENTATIVES OF THE AMERICAN AND BRITISH COMMAND ON THE ONE PART AND REPRESENTATIVES OF THE GERMAN MILITARY COMMAND ON THE OTHER ARE CARRYING ON NEGOTIATIONS. THE GOVERNMENT OF THE U.S.S.R. CONSIDERS THAT THIS IS INADMISSIBLE. Subsequently, words are exchanged between President Roosevelt and Stalin; however, Stalin's accusations are untrue. Admiral Leahy, writing later about the incident, states: "IT WAS A CLEAR DEMONSTRATION OF THE DANGEROUS UNDESIRABILITY OF HAVING UNNECESSARY ALLIES IN WAR, AND IT REINFORCED MY CONVICTION THAT WE WERE MAKING A MISTAKE TO EMBRACE THE SOVIET UNION AS A CO-PARTNER IN THE FINAL STAGES OF THE WAR ON JAPAN."

March 22nd 1945 — (P.O.A.) Task Force 58 enjoins Logistic Support Group south of Okinawa and takes on supplies and ammunition for upcoming operations. The Task Force has devastated many ground installations of the enemy, in addition to destroying 528 Planes and sinking 126 Vessels as a prelude to the invasion, since the 18th of March. (Pacific-Iwo Jima) Elements of the 5th Marine Division, assisted by flame-throwing Tanks, continue advancing against the final opposition at Kitano Point. The Japanese continue to resist fiercely. The LST 727 becomes damaged by grounding. (Pacific-Philippines) Luzon In the U.S. Sixth Army area, fighting on the Villa Verde Trail continues to flourish. The 128th Regiment, 32nd Division receives orders to relieve the 127th Regiment. Along the Balete Pass in the Putlan Valley region, entrenched Japanese resistance paralyzes the advance of the 35th Regiment, 25th Division. In the XI Corps sector, Mt. Balidbiran is seized by Company B, 103rd Regiment, 43rd Division as it pounds forward through the Bosoboso River Valley. The 3rd Battalion, 103rd Regiment mops up Mt. Tanauan. Southern Philippines In the U.S. Eighth Army area, the Americal Division (minus RCT 164) initiates rehearsals in Leyte Gulf for the amphibious landing at Cebu, prior to embarking for the objective. On Panay, Co. G, 185th Regiment debarks at Inampulugan Island and initiates operations which demolishes a mine-control depot and conducts reconnaissance details. (Dutch East Indies) Japanese Aircraft strike their last blow against Morotai, culminating a long stretch of such attacks. (Pacific ALFSEA) During a conference of Commanders in Monywa, it is determined that CAI be transported from Burma immediately to lessen the supply problems of the British Fourteenth Army; the crisis is not easily solved, as Admiral Mountbatten declines the use of transports from SEAC for this purpose. (Atlantic-West Germany) 12th Army Group In the U.S. First Army area, C.C. Howze, subsequent to aiding the clearing of the 78th Division area, reverts to 3rd Armored Division. The III Corps commences measured night-attacks across the Wied River, startling the already beleaguered Germans. The 9th and 99th Divisions jump off at 22:00 and 24:00 respectively. The 7th Armored Division, relieved of the necessity of protecting the west bank of the Rhine, deploys to attack across the river. RCT 38, with the support of the 99th Division, secures Datzeroth, Rodenbach, and Segendorf. The V Corps secures the area stretching between the Wied and Rhine Rivers and establishes a bridgehead across the former, through the actions of RCT 38, 2nd Division and C.C.B., 9th Armored Division. C.C.B., 9th Armored Division, reduces resistance in Neuwied; its Commander, General William Hoge, is selected to command the 4th Armored Division, prompting C.C.A. Headquarters to cross the Rhine and assume command of the assault. Another Class 40 bridge is constructed and laid across the Rhine (Hommingen). Meanwhile, the 28th Division reverts to Corps control in response to interarmy boundary adjustments. In the U.S. Third Army area, the XII Corps, having completed its drive to the Rhine, commences an assault across the river: contingents of the 358th and 359th Regiments seize Mainz with little perspiration, while the 357th deploys defensively, yet finds time to capture Weisenau; Task Force Spiess is relieved by the 5th Division and is then disbanded. At 22:00, units of the 5th Division jump across the Rhine, encountering feeble resistance. In other activity, the 11th Armored Division completes mop-up in its sector and pauses, while awaiting relief by the 80th Division. In the XX Corps sector, Task Force Cheadle is formed (RCT 336 and C.C.A., 12th Armored Division) by the 90th Division, for an assault against Ludwigshafen; it drives into Friesenheim, Mundenheim, and Rheingonheim. In the 12th Armored sector, attacks are launched to secure a bridge crossing at either Germersheim or Speyer: C.C.B., reinforced by the 92nd Reconnaissance Squadron, drives to Mutterstadt, then pivots to assault Speyer, while C.C.R. seizes Boehl, Hafsloch, and Iggel heim. Meanwhile, the 10th Armored consumes Landau. **6th Army Group** In the **U.S. Seventh Army** area, the XXI Corps assumes control of the 71st and 100th Divisions in the vicinity of Bitche and takes responsibility for the XV Corps' right flank. In the **VI Corps** sector, the Germans evacuate their West Wall positions, permitting easy access to Dahn. Elements of the 103rd Division make contact with the U.S. Third Army, and other contingents secure Silz. Meanwhile, the 36th Division advances, crunching many pillboxes as it converges upon Bergzabern, and the 14th Armored is reducing the remnant defenders in Steinfeld. In addition, the retreating Germans come under heavy attack by Aircraft and Artillery as the columns become stalled on blocked roads. **(Atlantic-Eastern Europe)** The German pocket in East Prussia comes under more severe pressure by superior Soviet forces of the Third White Russian Front; however, at Danzig and Gdynia, the Germans mount stiff resistance that greatly impedes the progress of the Second White Russian Front. Some Russian forces break through to the gulf between Danzig and Gydnia, splitting the German Second Army. It is announced in Russia that the First Ukrainian Front has penetrated German positions south and west of Oppeln, in Silesia, and Berlin indicates heavy Soviet breakthrough attacks between the Danube and Lake Balaton.

March 23rd 1945 — (P.O.A.) A British Carrier Task Force (TF 57), commanded by Vice Admiral Sir Bernard Rawlings, is assigned to the U.S. Fifth Fleet and is directed to operate from Ulithi to neutralize Japanese Air operations at Sakishima Island in the Ryukus chain. **(Pacific-Iwo Jima)** The Ocean Tug *Zuni* (ATF-95) is damaged by grounding. **(Pacific-Philippines)** The Destroyer *Haggard* (DD-555) becomes damaged after intentionally ramming and sinking the Japanese Submarine I-371 in the Philippine Sea. **Luzon** In the **U.S. Sixth Army** area, the Fifth Air Force commences a chain of assaults against Legaspi and the surrounding area to soften resistance for the imminent invasion. In the **I Corps** sector, General Krueger attaches RCT 127, 37th Division to Corps in an effort to accelerate the drive to Baguio. On the Villa Verde Trail, the 128th Regiment, 32nd Division starts to relieve the embattled 127th Regiment. In the **XI Corps** sector, orders are given, calling for the capture of Caballo, Carabao, and El Fraile Islands, and for the elimination of the Japanese deployed in the Antipolo-Montalban region to conclude the campaign to open Manila Bay. The directive further states that contact with the XIV Corps is to be established east of Laguna de Bay to seal the gap between the Corps. On Mt. Tanauan, the 2nd Battalion, 103rd Regiment, 43rd Division, relieves the 3rd Battalion, then drives toward New Bosoboso. In the **XV Corps** sector, the 187th Regiment, 11th Airborne Division, receives responsibility for the seizure of Mt. Macolod, and the 511th Paratroop Battalion is to participate in the Legaspi operation. **Southern Philippines** In the **U.S. Eighth Army** area, Company G, 185th Regiment, 40th Division arrives at Panay from Inampulugan. On Leyte, RCT 108, 40th Division concludes its relief of the Americal Division's 164th Regiment. **(Pacific-Ryukyu Islands)** Admiral Mitscher's Carriers launch Planes against Okinawa. The raids continue daily. In other Naval activity, the Submarine *Seahorse* (SS-304) is damaged by a Horizontal Bomber. **(Pacific-Burma)** In the **British Fourteenth Army** area, 33rd Corps sector, an Indian 20th Division column drives north from Wundwin to Kume. In the 4th Corps sector, the Indian 7th Division, supported by contingents of the Indian 5th Division, seizes Myingan. Mean-

while, the besieged Indian 17th Division continues to hold at Meiktila. **(Atlantic-Western Europe) 21st Army Group** The British, under General Montgomery, await cessation of a thunderous Air and Artillery bombardment, then attack across the Rhine north of the Ruhr at 21:00, committing the British Second Army. The Canadian First Army stays in place, holding the left flank. The British 51st Division bolts the Rhine and attacks toward Rees, while the 1st Commando Brigade crosses northwest of Wesel at 24:00 and drives against the city. **12th Army Group** In the **U.S. First Army** area, **VII Corps** sector, the 1st Division launches an attack at 20:00; the town of Wellesburg is seized prior to midnight. The 104th Division attacks at 21:00; contingents advance as much as 1,000 yards, and the Airfield east of Eudenbach is captured. In other activity, forward contingents of the 86th Division arrive on the continent. Meanwhile, the 3rd Armored crosses the Rhine. In the **III Corps** sector, the 9th and 99th Divisions continue to pounce upon the opposition; the 60th Regiment, 9th Division takes Neschen, Rahm, Strauscheid, and Weisenfeld, while the 99th Division drives through Breitscheid, Kurtscheid, Nieder Breitbach, Rossbach, and Waldbreitbach. In the **V Corps** sector, the bridgehead is extended, as RCT 38, 2nd Division secures Altwied, Ehlscheid, Melsbach, Rengsdorf, and Wolfenacker. In other activity, the Rhine area becomes inundated with Yanks, as the 69th Division concludes its trek to the River and relieves the 2nd Division; RCT 23, 2nd Division, fords the Rhine. In the **U.S. Third Army** area, **VIII Corps** sector, the 6th Cavalry Group relieves the 87th Division and assumes responsibility for the Koblenz-Boppard region. In other activity, the 89th Division (XII Corps) is transferred to Corps. In the **XII Corps** sector, the 5th Division pushes four Regiments and their supporting weapons across the Rhine; a bridgehead extending five miles deep and about eight miles wide is established: RCT 11, driving up the center, takes Geinsheim, Trebur, and Wallerstaedten in conjunction with RCT 10, which drives on the right and seizes Erfelden and Leeheim as it advances toward Dornheim. RCT 357 (90th Division) is temporarily attached to the 5th Division and is dispatched to the area near Erfelden to relieve RCT 10. On the left, RCT 2 overruns Astheim. Meanwhile, the Engineers have completed another Class 40 bridge. The 4th Armored and 90th Divisions prepare to cross the Rhine. The 26th Division is attached to Corps and moves to the Mainz-Nackenheim region to take responsibility and release the 90th for the crossing; the 90th Division turns over the 2nd Cavalry Group to the 26th Division. In conjunction, the 11th Armored Division relieves the 4th Armored to free it. In the **XX Corps** sector, a huge Artillery bombardment greets the defenders of Ludwigshafen; upon cessation, Task Force Cheadle attacks, securing the suburbs and entering the city during the latter part of the day. Meanwhile, the Germans mount stiff resistance against C.C.R., 12th Armored Division; however, with the assistance of the Air Force, it drives into Speyer. In other activity, the 10th Armored Division drives south toward Lauterbourg and establishes contact with contingents of the Seventh Army, which are pushing north; it is attached to Seventh Army (XXI Corps). **6th Army Group** In the **U.S. Seventh Army** area,, the XV Corps releases the 6th Armored Division to Third Army. In the **VI Corps** sector, the 36th and 103rd Divisions continue to mop up in the area west of the Rhine. The 36th moves through Bergzabern. In the 14th Armored zone, Schaidt falls to C.C.A., and contingents of C.C.B. reach Herxheim and Germersheim. In the French zone, the Germans dole out severe fire and inflict heavy casualties on the attacking forces of the Groupement Monsabert as they drive against the West Wall. **(Atlantic-Eastern Europe)** The

Germans holding Danzig and Gdynia receive a heavy blow as the Second White Russian Front drives a wedge between them and advances to the Gulf of Danzig, seriously jeopardizing their positions at both port cities. In other activity, the Soviets maintain great pressure against the German pocket in East Prussia; in Upper Silesia, the Red Army continues making progress. **(Atlantic-Italy)** General Heinrich von Vietinghoff replaces Field Marshal Kesselring as Supreme Commander of Axis forces in Italy.

March 24th 1945 — (United States) President Roosevelt sends a personal message to Stalin, attempting to politely explain that the talks between the Allies and the Germans in Switzerland, concerning the surrender of German forces would not be abandoned because a "SURRENDER WOULD SAVE AMERICAN LIVES." Stalin responds on the 3rd of April, dispatching a nasty letter containing sarcastic lies. **(Pacific-Iwo Jima)** RCT 28, 5th Marine Division is given the task of eliminating the final Japanese pocket on the island. The pocket is about 50 square yards along the coast. It is thought that General Kuribayashi is alive and holding out in a concealed cave, but he is never discovered. **(Pacific-Philippines)** Luzon Headquarters Fifth Air Force is established at Fort Stotsenburg. In the **U.S. Sixth Army** area, **XI Corps** sector, the 6th Division continues to battle furiously near the Bosoboso River; the Japanese contain the 1st Battalion, 20th Regiment at a hotly contested ridge; however, the 1st Regiment secures its zone overlooking the river. The 103rd Regiment, 43rd Division, suspends its advance against the river as friendly Artillery pummels the area to its front. In the **XIV Corps** sector, the 1st Cavalry and 11th Airborne Divisions begin converging on Lipa, the former overrunning Santo Tomas effortlessly. Meanwhile, the 187th Regiment, 11th Airborne commences an attack against Mt. Macolod and encounters tough resistance. **Southern Philippines** In the **U.S. Eighth Army** area, a Cruiser-Destroyer Covering Force, commanded by Rear Admiral R.S. Berkey, embarks Subic Bay for Cebu. It will rendezvous with the Cebu Attack Group, commanded by Captain Albert T. Sprague, off Cebu on the following day. On Mindanao, the 162nd Regiment, 41st Division, reinforced, captures Mt. Capisan. Mop-up operations ensue subsequently, as organized resistance in the region of the Sinonog River has ceased. **(Pacific-Ryukyu Islands)** Admiral Mitscher's Carriers continue to lambaste Okinawa. The Japanese also come under attack by the heavy guns of Admiral W. A. Lee's Battleships. The Navy begins mine-clearing operations under the protection of Naval and Air protection. **(Pacific-South China Sea)** The Japanese Coast Defense Vessel No. 68 and the Torpedo Boat *Tomazuru* are sunk by Carrier-based Planes. **(Pacific-Japan)** The Submarine U.S.S. *Tirante* sinks a Japanese Tanker off Kagoshimo; on the 28th, continuing her string of luck during her first War Patrol, she dunks a Freighter off Nagasaki on the 28th. The *Tirante* swings into the Yellow Sea and will find new prey on 9th April. **(Atlantic-Western Europe) 21st Army Group** In the **British Second Army** area, 33rd Corps sector, German Paratroopers holding Rees perplex the British 51st Division's attempt to seize the objective. In the **XII Corps** sector, the British 1st Commando Brigade emerge the victors following brutalizing house-to-house fighting in Wesel, as the British seize a large part of the city. Meanwhile, the British 15th Division, commences its attack across the Rhine at 02:00 and seizes Haffen and Mehr. General Patton notes that British Broadcasting Company delivers a speech by Winston Churchill, congratulating Field Marshal Montgomery "for executing the first

assault crossing of the Rhine in modern history." Patton explains that BBC had made a mistake, considering that Third Army (5th Division at 22:30, March 22nd.) had crossed the Rhine about 36 hours prior to the British. The **XVIII (Airborne) Corps**, attached to the First Allied Airborne Army (controlled by the British Second Army), unleashes seventeen hundred Planes and thirteen hundred Gliders, transporting two Divisions (14,000 men). The British 6th (General Bols) and the U.S. 17th Airborne (General Bud Miley) Divisions drop east of the Rhine outside of Wesel at 10:00, but they are right on top of German Artillery positions, costing casualties. Nonetheless, the Paratroopers advance and quickly take their objectives as they advance to the Issel River and establish contact with each other. However, the fourteen days of preparations allow the Germans ample time to adjust defenses and 55 Planes fail to return to base. Colonel Coutts' 513th Paratroop Infantry (transported in 72 twin-engine C-46s) encounter fierce fire, losing 22 Aircraft to ground fire; 14 set on fire in the air; the Paratroops bail out, but many of the crews remain in the crippled Planes too long and are lost. General Ridgway calls the C-46s "firetraps." Trailing B-24s, transporting supplies, also take heavy losses. The Germans mount determined, but unsuccessful counterattacks north of Wesel during the night. During the drop, one detachment of the 507th Paratroop Regiment lands about 75 yards from an overactive machine gun crew, which severs them from their equipment. Private George J. Peters, singlehandedly and without orders, charges the menacing gun to draw attention from the other ten men, being severely wounded as he closes. Undaunted, he gets up and continues toward the nest, and is mortally wounded; still, he advances, tossing grenades, destroying the obstacle, and saving the others. Peters receives the Medal of Honor posthumously for his indomitable courage. In conjunction, P.F.C. Stuart S. Stryker, Company E, 503th Parachute Infantry, bolts to the front of his Platoon, which is pinned by murderous enemy fire. He advances, yelling to the others to follow toward the menacing German Headquarters building near Wesel. Enemy fire kills P.F.C. Stuart about twenty-five yards from the objective; nevertheless, his courage inspires the attack to continue and the Yanks capture about 200 German Soldiers, in addition to gaining the freedom of three American Airmen who had been held there by the enemy; Stuart also receives the Medal of Honor. General Ridgway crosses the Rhine in an amphibious vehicle to locate the 17th Airborne, catching up with General Miley. At about 23:00, he locates General Bols' Command Post. After midnight, Ridgway departs and is ambushed by a German Patrol. A bitter firefight develops and Ridgway is nearly killed when a grenade lands several feet from him. He is spared when the wheel of the Jeep takes the brunt of the explosion, but he receives a shoulder wound. About 4,000 Germans are captured during the day's fighting. By the sixth day, Corps Headquarters pulls out, leaving the two Airborne Divisions to continue advancing. General Ridgway notes that it is "A SMALL OPERATION, BUT OPENS THE WAY FOR BRITISH SECOND ARMY'S DRIVE ACROSS THE RHINE, A MOMENTUM THAT WAS TO CARRY IT, PRACTICALLY WITHOUT PAUSE, TO THE BALTIC AND THE JOIN-UP WITH THE RUSSIANS AND THE END OF THE WAR IN WESTERN EUROPE." In the **U.S. Ninth Army** area, **XVI Corps** sector, the assault across the Rhine commences at 02:00, following a one-hour bombardment, when the 30th Division attacks; a subsequent assault is undertaken by the 79th Division at 03:00. Many towns and villages, including Friedrichsfeld, Lohnen, Mehrum, Moellen, Ork, Spellen, Stockum, and Worde, are seized by the 30th Division, while the advancing 79th secures Dinslaken, Stapp, Overbruch, Vier Linden, and Walsum. Meanwhile, the 75th Division gets contingents of the 290th Regiment across the Rhine, and they successfully defend the bridges and establish a bridgehead. **12th Army Group** In the **U.S. First Army** area, the **VI Corps** expands its bridgehead and prepares for breakout. The 1st Division pounds forward, but it is a bloody advance as the Germans resist with great fervor; Geisnach, Heuchel, Lichtenberg, and Ukerath are secured. The 104th Division takes the heights northeast of Eudenbach and a road junction near the Airfield. Meanwhile, the 78th Division, driving on the north flank, overcomes a tenacious stronghold northwest of Menden. In the **III Corps** sector, the 9th Division secures Borscheid, as it enlarges its bridgehead east of the Wied and commits its 39th and 47th Regiments in the area west of the Wied. In addition, the 99th Division commences an eastward drive against the Autobahn with its 395th Regiment at 22:00. The V Corps' RCT 38, 2nd Division, extends its Wied bridgehead, taking Gladbach and Ober Bieber. In the **U.S. Third Army** area, Patton calls Bradley: ""BRAD, DON'T TELL ANYONE, BUT I'M ACROSS." Bradley to Patton: "WELL I'LL BE DAMNED-YOU MEAN ACROSS THE RHINE?" Patton: "SURE AM, I SNEAKED ACROSS LAST NIGHT, BUT THERE ARE SO FEW GERMANS AROUND THERE, THEY DON'T KNOW IT YET." "BRAD, TELL THE WORLD WE'RE ACROSS. WE KNOCKED DOWN 33 KRAUTS TODAY WHEN THEY CAME AFTER OUR PONTOON BRIDGES. I WANT THE WORLD TO KNOW THIRD ARMY MADE IT BEFORE MONTY STARTS ACROSS." The **VIII Corps** concludes its preparations for an attack across the Rhine. The **XII Corps** fortifies its breakout force with Armor as the Rhine bridgehead is bolstered and expanded; it drives toward the Main against a strong enemy reaction, including a fruitless Air assault to destroy the bridges. In the **V Corps** sector, Bauschheim, Dornberg, Dornheim, Gross Gerau, and Nauheim are swallowed into the bridgehead. The 4th Division advances toward the Main, while the 90th Division relieves the 10th Regiment, 5th Division at Erfelden and Dornheim. The 4th Armored secures Stockstadt, Hahn, and Hahnlein with C.C.B.; C.C.A. drives to the outskirts of Ober Ramstadt. In other activity, the 26th Division (less 104th Regiment) readies its attack across the Rhine, and the 6th Armored (attached to Corps) deploys to drive against the Main. In the **XX Corps** sector, contact is established west of the Rhine with Seventh Army. The 94th Division battle for Ludwigshafen continues throughout the night; however, the attack troops converging from the north and south each drive to the middle of the city during the morning. Meanwhile, Speyer falls to the 14th Armored's C.C.B. in the morning, and Germersheim is taken during the night by C.C.R. The Germans destroy a bridge at Germerscheim. **6th Army Group** The **U.S. Seventh Army** aborts its plan to Airdrop troops east of the Rhine. The XV Corps finalizes its preparations for the assault across the Rhine, and upon darkness, begins to assemble the troops along the River. In the **VI Corps** sector, the 36th Division concludes its drive to the Rhine, seizing Leimerscheim along the way. Meanwhile, the French forces advance to the Erlen River, seizing Kandel, Neupfotz, and Rheinzabern. In the **XXI Corps** sector, the 12th Armored is attached to Corps. **(Atlantic-Eastern Europe)** The Russians announce from Moscow that the Third Ukrainian Front, driving southwest of Budapest, has advanced about 44 miles, seizing many towns including Enying, Mor, Szekesfehervar, Veszprem, and Zirc. **(Atlantic-Italy) 15th Army Group** A Spring offensive is imminent. Orders call for the British Eighth Army to initiate some

activity on April 10th; however, the main thrust is to be carried by the U.S. Fifth Army. The attack date is subsequently changed to April 9th.

Third Army Jeeps and Tanks crossing the Rhine near Boppard, Germany.

March 25th 1945 — **(Pacific-Iwo Jima)** RCT 28 reduces the remaining pocket of resistance in the western half of Kitano Point. **(Pacific-Philippines)** In the **U.S. Sixth Army** area, **I Corps** sector, relief of the 127th Regiment, along the Villa Verde Trail is completed by the 128th Regiment, 32nd Division, which continues the assault toward Salacsac Pass and Santa Fe. Meanwhile, the 3rd Battalion, 35th Regiment, 25th Division gives responsibility for the roadblock on Old Spanish Trail to Guerrilla forces, culminating U.S. operations on the primitive trail. In other activity, the 27th Regiment, 25th Division drives about 4,000 yards, reaching entrenched forward positions of Mt. Myoko. In the **XI Corps** sector, the 6th Division pours fire into enemy positions near the Bosoboso River, while the 2nd Battalion, 103rd Regiment, 43rd Division, overruns the barrio of New Bosoboso and the nearby ridges, essentially funneling the escaping Japanese into a single file, running northwest. Steps are quickly taken to seal this path of flight as the 1st Battalion charges Hill 1200. In the **XIV Corps** sector, contingents of the 1st Cavalry Division stroll into Los Banos, while another column drives toward Tanuan. **Southern Philippines** In the **U.S. Eighth Army** area, **X Corps** issues orders for the upcoming operations on Mindanao, specifying that the 24th Division will debark at Malabang on April 7th, to be followed five days later by the 31st Division's landing in the Parang region. **(Pacific-China)** The U.S. Fourteenth Air Force destroys its installations at Laohokow before abandoning the Base which is the final one to be seized by the Japanese. Subsequent attempts to overrun the Airbases at Ankang and Sian are thwarted by the Chinese. **(Pacific-Ryukyu)** The Navy steps up its preinvasion bombardment as Battleships, Cruisers, and Destroyers, under Rear Admiral M. L. Deyo, bombard Keramah Retto and the southeast coast of Okinawa. The ongoing minesweeping operations impede the Warships ability to get close for more effective firing against Okinawa. In addition, special Underwater Demolition Teams work tirelessly to clear the invasion area of explosives and obstacles. Meanwhile, the Japanese strike back with Kamikazes. The Destroyer *Kimberly* (DD-521), the Light Minesweeper *Robert H. Smith* (DM-23), and the High Speed Transport *Gilmer* ((APD-11) are damaged by Suicide Planes. In addition, the Destroyer Escort *Sederstromm* (DE-31) and the High Speed Transport *Knudsen* (APD-101) are damaged by collisions. **(Atlantic-Western Europe) 21st Army Group** In the **British Second Army** area, the Germans retain only a minor pocket in Rees, as the British 51st Division has secured most of the town. The British 15th Division takes Bislich. In the **U.S. XVIII (Airborne) Corps** area, the British 1st Commando Brigade is attached to the U.S. 17th Airborne. At 15:00, the 17th Airborne attacks across the Issel Canal, advancing to positions known as Phase Line London, about 3,000 yards east of Wesel. In the **U.S. Ninth Army** area, **XVI Corps** sector drives forward throughout the night (25-26) and seizes Hunxe in addition to making contact with the British 1st Commando Brigade during its 4 mile advance. In other activity, the 79th Division, reinforced, crosses the Rhine east of Rheinberg. The Germans hold steadfastly. **12th Army Group** In the **U.S. First Army** area, **VII Corps** sector, a strong attack is mounted, with the 3rd Armored Division, reinforced (414th Regiment, 104th Division) acting as vanguard, gaining about nine miles, and reaching the half-way mark to the initial objective: Altenkirchen. To the left, TF Welborn drives through Kircheib and Uckerath while advancing toward Hasselbach, and to the right, TF Kane reaches All Creekand TF Doan pushes to Flammersfeld. Following behind the Armor, the 1st and 104th Divisions mop up. In the **III Corps** sector, the Corps enjoins First Army's offensive; its 9th Division drives rapidly, while the 99th Division knocks out several towns and severs the Autobahn outside of Willroth. In other activity, the 7th Armored deploys east of the Rhine and will spearhead the Corps drive across the Rhine. In the **V Corps** sector, C.C.A., 9th Armored Division, keeps rolling southeast along the Rhine and captures Bendorf and Vallendar, while the parent Division pushes east to Grenzhausen. In **U.S. Third Army** area, the **VII Corps** commences an attack across the Rhine. At midnight, the 87th Division speeds across and gains a substantial bridgehead against feverish opposition in the Braubach-Boppard region. The 6th Armored Division jumps the Rhine at Oppenheim and drives toward Frankfurt and the Main River. C.C.A. reaches the Main near Raunheim while C.C.B. drives to the vicinity of Walldorf, the former encountering fierce fire from Frankfurt. Meanwhile, the 4th Armored Division pushes ahead, cracking the German defenses, driving to the Main River in the area around Aschaffenburg and Hanau, and establishing bridgeheads. C.C.A. seizes a bridge at Klein Auheim, while C.C.B. captures a highway and rail bridge near Schweinheim and C.C.R. rushes to Dieburg, where it sets up blocking positions. In addition, C.C.R. send elements to Darmstadt, which is essentially undefended; as it enters the town from the west, a Reconnaissance Troop of the 90th Division is entering from the opposite direction. The 5th Division seizes Hassloch and Koenigstaedten, while the 90th Division

gets contingents to Langen, as it severs the Autobahn. **6th Army Group** The **U.S. Seventh Army** regroups to cross the Rhine, subsequent to having captured the Saar Palatinate in conjunction with 3rd Army. In other activity, the 71st and 100th Divisions are released from XXI Corps and attached to the VI Corps, which in turn releases the 4th and 42nd Divisions to the XXI Corps. In the **XXI Corps** sector, an attack across the Rhine is mounted. French Armor destroys an enemy bridgehead at Maximiliansau. **(Atlantic-Eastern Europe)** Heiligenbeil in East Prussia is taken by the forces of the Third White Russian Front, while Oliva is seized by contingents of the Second White Russian Front. In Hungary, the Second Ukrainian Front continues to advance toward Austria, seizing Esztergom, Felsoegall, and Tata. **(Atlantic-Italy) 15th Army Group** In the **British Eighth Army** area, the 10th Corps assumes command of the Jewish Brigade (detached from 5th Corps). In other activity, the new 13th Corps Commander, Lt. General Sir John Harding, arrives.

March 26th 1945 — (Pacific-Iwo Jima) The Japanese initiate their final attack as 200 or more troops attempt to infiltrate U.S. lines; 196 die suddenly. During the violent contest, 1st Lt. Harry Linn Martin, 5th Pioneer Battalion, groups the Marines near his foxhole to form a line of fire to halt the intruders; however, the Japs keep rushing. Martin spots several of his men who are isolated and attempts to rescue them, braving heavy fire from a captured Marine machine gun to reach them. He then guides them to safety, blasting several Japs as he moves. Soon after, he singlehandedly destroys four more Japs who had seized an overrun foxhole. Sensing the increasing danger of a breakthrough, Martin orders an attack to break up the fanatical assault. He gives his life, but his heroism breaks up a superior force and saves much of his Platoon and Company. At 08:00, Major General James E. Chaney, who had been appointed Commander ETO when established June 8th, 1942, assumes title of Island Commander, concluding the capture and occupation phase of the Iwo campaign. The 5th Marine Division transfers its zone to the 3rd Marine Division and continues to reembark, leaving RCT 9, 3rd Marine Division, and RCT 147 U.S.A., to share responsibility for the island. RCT 21, 3rd Marine Division reembarks for Guam. The approximate 23,000 defenders of the island are almost annihilated; their near impregnable positions have inflicted extremely heavy casualties upon the Americans, which sustain about 5,500 killed out of a total casualty list of over 20,000 men, about 30 percent casualties out of the invasion force of 60,000 men. The capture of this island further seals the fate of the Japanese as it tightens the blockade of Japan and gives the U.S. an Airbase which will now save thousands of additional Airmen as the Air field provides an alternative to crashing in the sea if they run out of fuel or become disabled while returning from bombing missions. **(Pacific-Philippines)** Luzon In the **U.S. Sixth Army** area, **I Corps** sector, subsequent to a blanket bombardment, the 1st Battalion, 161st Regiment, 25th Division commences its final assault against obstinate Knob's Hill along Highway 5. In the **XIV Corps** sector, contingents of the 1st Cavalry Division drive south to Malvar. Meanwhile, the Japanese raise fervent opposition against the 187th Regiment, 11th Airborne as it attempts to reduce Mt. Macalod. In conjunction, its 188th Regiment moves cautiously against Lipa. **Southern Philippines** In the **U.S. Eighth Army** area, contingents of the Americal Division land near Talisay on Cebu; however, the enemy inflicts destruction to eight of the Landing Vehicles, greatly impeding the inland drive. Upon passage of the minefields, the 182nd Regiment pushes through Talisay driving toward Cebu City, scattering an enemy defense force as it moves and gaining crossing sites at the Mananga River and positions in the foothills stretching from Pardo to the Mananga River. Meanwhile, the 132nd Regiment drives to Basak. In other activity, Guerrillas fail to secure a reservoir assigned to them and the responsibility is given to the 182nd Regiment. **(Pacific-Ryukyu Islands)** Operation ICEBERG commences as the 77th Division lands on Kerama Island to seize a Seaplane Base to be used for the main invasion of Okinawa. Following a horrendous Air and Naval bombardment, four Boat Landing Teams assault four of the islands simultaneously and with effective swiftness. The Japanese get some Planes airborne, but the attacks are disorganized and consist primarily of Kamikazes. At 08:04, BLT 3, RCT 305 lands on Aka Island and easily seizes the village of Aka, while securing two thirds of the island. BLT 1, RCT 306 overruns Geruma Island and deploys Artillery to bolster subsequent operations; BLT 1, RCT 305 sweeps and secures about a third of Zamami Island and soon after, handily repulses multiple counterattacks. BLT 2, RCT 306 seizes Hokaji Island without incident and a Reserve BLT (2 RCT 307) is subsequently committed and seizes Yakabi Island after some brief exchanges of fire. Meanwhile, Patrols of Fleet Marine Force Amphibious Reconnaissance Battalion (attached to 77th Division) lands on Keise Island which lies within Artillery range of the majority of southern Okinawa and discovers it undefended. Long-range Naval guns and Aircraft supplement the ground operations, and in conjunction, the Fast Carrier Fleets and Naval Warships continue to pound enemy positions on Okinawa. In other activity, the British Carrier Task Force (TF 57) begins its attacks against Sakishima Island. Off Okinawa, again, Japanese Suicide Planes attack the Fleet causing damage to eight Ships: Battleship *Nevada* (BB-36); Light Cruiser *Biloxi* (CL-80); Destroyers *Porterfield* (DD-682), *O'Brien* (DD-725), and *Callaghan* (DD-792); Destroyer Escort *Foreman* (DE-633); High Speed Minesweeper *Dorsey* (DMS-1); and the Minesweeper *Skirmish* (AM-303). In addition, the Destroyers *Murray* (DD-576) and *Halligan* (DD-DD-584) are damaged by a Dive Bomber and a mine respectively; the Submarine Chaser PC-1133 is damaged by grounding. **(Pacific-ALFSEA)** British General Sir Oliver Leese directs Admiral Mountbatten to formulate plans for a modified DRACULA because the ongoing drive toward Rangoon is not advancing fast enough. **(Atlantic-Western Europe) 21st Army Group** In the **British Second Army** area, the British 30th Corps continues to expand its bridgehead toward the Issel. The 51st Division eliminates the final resistance in Rees, then drives toward Isselburg while the 43rd Division advances to Millingen. In the **XII Corps** sector, the British 15th Division advances to the Issel River at Ringenberg while the British 7th Division deploys to act as vanguard for the assault against Rheine. In the **XVIII (Airborne) Corps** sector, the British 6th and U.S. 17th Airborne Divisions continue driving east against faltering resistance, reaching the next phase line: New York, stretching from Ringenberg on the north to the Lippe River around Krudenberg to the south. In the **U.S. Ninth Army** area, **XVI Corps** sector, progress remains excellent as much ground continues to be secured. The 30th Division extends its bridgehead four miles east against heavy opposition; it secures part of Gahlen. The 79th Division advances as much as two miles, and the 8th Armored Division starts crossing the Rhine. **12th Army Group** In the **U.S. First Army** area, **VII Corps** sector, C.C. Hickey's TF's Doan and Kane on 3rd Armored's right flank drive through German defenses, advancing through Altenkirchen to Hachenburg and Wahlrod. However, the Germans raise stiff opposition on

the left and hinder progress of C.C. Boudinot. Despite Air support, the attack is halted during the afternoon, due to rising casualties. The 1st Division commits contingents of three Regiments and secures the area south of the Sieg River as far east as Eitorf. The 1st Division is being relieved by the 78th Division, permitting it to move behind the Armored as it drives east. The 104th Division speeds forward, gaining about 12 miles as it trails the Armor. In the **III Corps** sector, Armor shoots through Infantry positions, spearheading pursuit of the retreating enemy. In some instances, the Armor moves so quickly it overtakes the disoriented German forces pummeling them severely at Heckholzhausen and Obertiefenbach. The 9th Division seizes crossings of the Holz River near Puderbach. In the **V Corps** sector, the 2nd Division seizes Alsbach, Baumbach, Hilgert, and Ransbach. The 9th Armored Division reinforced by the 38th Regiment, 2nd Division, drives toward Limburg. C.C.B. advances to the Lahn River and gets four Tanks across before the Germans can blow the bridge, clearing Limburg with the Infantry. Meanwhile, C.C.A. makes a quick advance to the Lahn at Diez; however, the bridges are blown. In the **U.S. Third Army** area, **VIII Corps** sector, the bridgehead is expanded. The 347th Regiment, 87th Division eliminates the final resistance in Braubach while the 345th consumes Gemmerich. In the 89th Division sector, an attack across the Rhine is commenced at 02:00, but the Germans react strongly, raising intense opposition. Despite the resistance, the Yanks seize Bornich, Dorscheid, Kestert, Kaub, Lierscheid, Nochern, Weyer, Patersburg, and St. Goarshausen. In other activity, General Patton dispatches a contingent including fifty Vehicles and nineteen Tanks of 4th Armored to liberate a P.O.W. compound at Hammelburg Stalag. The unit, led by Captain Abraham Baum, encounters fierce resistance beyond the Main River at Schweinheim; nevertheless, it pushes on, reaching its destination on the 28th, at a cost of two thirds of its strength. The camp is taken, but the trek back is deadly. Tiger Tanks rush to the scene and at 09:00 on the 29th a fierce battle erupts. The beleaguered survivors run out of gasoline and expend all ammunition, forcing them to surrender. General Patton's son-in-law is reported to have been in the camp; however, Patton makes it clear that he had no knowledge of this until nine days after the attack had been launched. On March 30th, Berlin claims that the entire 4th Armored Division has been killed or captured. In the **XII Corps** sector, the 6th Armored Division powers forward reaching the Main River at Frankfurt, overcoming stiff resistance and entering the city. The 90th Division's C.C.B. drives to the Main and seizes Offenbach. Meanwhile, the 4th Armored Division, manning a small bridgehead at the Main, is struck by intense Air and land attacks, but the enemy is repulsed. In addition, the 5th, 26th, and 90th Divisions drive toward the Main and advance with great speed in the wake of the Armor. The 5th Seizes Raunheim, Kelsterbach, Schwanheim, and the Rhine-Main Airport, in addition to shoving elements into Frankfurt. The 90th overruns Buergel, Muehlheim, and Rumpenheim, clears Offenthal, and propels contingents to Hausen. The 26th Division secures the majorities of its zone and establishes contact with Seventh Army contingents. **6th Army Group** In the **U.S. Seventh Army** area, the Command Post transfers from Sarreguemines to Kaiserlautern. In the **XV Corps** sector, the 3rd and 45th Divisions attack across the Rhine at 02:30, following a carpet bombardment of the opposite shore. The former initially encounters slight opposition, but it quickly builds as the enemy recovers from the thundering bombardment. The 3rd takes Bobstadt, Burstadt, Lamperheim, and Sandhofen, then drives into

Lorcher Wald as it closes on its objective: the Autobahn. The 45th Division advances to the north-south Autobahn outside of Jaegersburger Wald, securing Biblis and Gros Hausen and making contact with the Third Army. **(Atlantic-Eastern Europe)** The Third White Russian Front continues to eliminate the final resistance in East Prussia. The Second White Russian Front is pressing the Germans at both Danzig and Gdynia, having advanced to the final defense line. In Czechoslovakia, contingents of the Second Ukrainian Front take Banska Bystrica, an important communications center. The Third Ukrainian Front maintains its progress in Hungary, seizing Devecser and Papa as it moves toward Austria.

March 27th 1945 — (Pacific-Philippines) Luzon In the **U.S. Sixth Army** area, Burgos is taken by contingents of the 129th Regiment, 37th Division. On the Villa Verde Trail, the 128th Regiment, 32nd Division, attacks to gain Salacsac Pass No. 2, in yet another tedious advance against well-entrenched defenders who are generously spread throughout the area in innumerable intersecting caves. On Norton's Knob, the Yanks seize control and turn back a night counterattack. In the **XI Corps** sector, the 2nd Battalion, 151st Regiment, 38th Division is transported by sea from Corregidor to nearby Caballo Island. Supported by Destroyers, Motor Torpedo Boats, and Aircraft, it lands and attacks toward a strongly entrenched force of about 400 troops. In the **XIV Corps** sector, progress continues as the 1st Cavalry Division drives toward Lipa against moderate opposition; its 8th Cavalry advances to within about 5,000 yards of the objective, Lipa, while the 7th Cavalry gains ground easily as it drives east. In conjunction, the 188th Regiment, 11th Airborne, overruns Lipa Hill and pushes to within about a mile from Lipa. **Southern Philippines** In the **U.S. Eighth Army** area, the Japanese abandon Cebu City, opting for the nearby commanding heights, as the Americal Division takes the city and drives forward. In conjunction, the 182nd Regiment captures a reservoir and hands it over to Guerrillas. Meanwhile, Company G, 132nd Regiment, debarks at Cebu Harbor on Cavit Island and begins a fruitless search for Japanese. **(Pacific-Ryukyu Islands-Kerama Islands)** The Japanese continue to send Suicide Planes against the Fleet offshore. The High Speed Minesweeper *Southard* (DMS-10) and the Light Minesweeper *Adams* (DM-27) are both damaged by Kamikazes. The Carrier *Essex* sustains damage by Aircraft operational casualty. On Zamami Island (Kerama Islands) BLT 1, RCT 305, 77th Division, discovers an enemy stronghold and attacks. On the 29th, it departs the island, its task complete. On Aka Island, a force of about 75 Japanese is scattered by BLT 3, RCT 305. Meanwhile, RCT 306 lands on Tokashiki Island and advances through difficult ground. In addition, Company G, RCT 307 and Company B, RCT 305, seize Kuba Island and Amuro Island respectively. **(Pacific-Japan)** In an effort to totally seal off the islands, B-29s attached to the 313th Bombardment Group commence their first night mining raid. In addition, the Fast Carrier Fleets and Submarines continue to pulverize Japanese Shipping in the sea lanes, virtually decimating the commercial Japanese Merchant Fleet by the middle of Summer. **(Pacific-East China Sea)** The Submarine *Trigger* (SS-237) sinks the Japanese cable layer *Odate*. **(Atlantic-Western Europe) 21st Army Group** in the **British Second Army** 30th Corps sector, the British 51st Division advances to the Issel River at Isselburg, where it is relieved by the British 3rd Division. In the **XII Corps** sector, the British 7th Armored Division seizes Raesfeld In the XVIII (Airborne) Corps sector, and the British 6th Airborne advances to Phase Line Paris before daybreak, then drives east to Erle. The 194th Glider Infantry seizes positions near Erle-Schermbeck while the 6th Guards Armored Brigade, supported by contingents of the 17th Airborne Division, commences a night attack toward Dorsten. Elements of the 194th Glider Regiment, attacking enemy positions near Wesel, are pinned by treacherous fire, prompting Tech Sergeant Clinton M. Hedrick to bolt forward, shooting his automatic weapon from his hip. His men follow and in short order, the obstacle is exterminated. Soon after, another deadly encounter occurs when six Germans suddenly ambush the Yanks. Again, Hedrick springs into action, killing all six with a feverish burst of fire. In conjunction, other enemy troops withdraw across a drawbridge, with Hedrick in pursuit, into Lembeck Castle. A German Soldier offers the Castle's surrender, and Hedrick and four other troops enter the castle yard to accept the surrender; they are met with the fire of a German self-propelled gun, mortally wounding Hedrick. Despite his wounds, Hedrick remains and gives cover fire to allow his men to withdraw. The Castle is overrun on the following day and Hedrick succumbs while being taken back for medical aid; he receives the Medal of Honor posthumously. In the **U.S. Ninth Army** area, General Simpson had been tied to his positions east of the Rhine, to ensure Montgomery's forces under General Dempsey continue to receive priority on all bridges. Now, 9th Army bolts the Rhine and will link with the forces of General Hodges on April 2nd at Lippstadt. In the **XVI Corps** sector, the final resistance in Gahlen is extinguished by the 119th Regiment, 30th Division; it then advances and secures Besten while the 120th Regiment gains positions in the heights near Kirchellen. The 35th Division meets heavy resistance as it attacks. The 79th Division secures Holten, Schmachtendorf, Sterkrade, and Wehofen as it drives south toward the Ruhr; contingents advance to the Emser Canal, some crossing and deploying near Orsey. **12th Army Group** In the **U.S. First Army** area, **VII Corps** sector, the 3rd Armored Division races to the Dill River, striking at Burg and Herborn with Combat Command Hickey, while Combat Command drives rapidly through the night, reaching positions near Heisterberg and Loehnfeld on the following day. The 1st and 103rd Divisions follow behind the Armor, the 1st eliminating final resistance in Breitscheidt, while the 103rd reaches positions less than five miles from the Dill River without incident. In the **III Corps** sector, the 7th Armored advances to the Dill River against sporadic resistance between Herborn and Wetzlar; C.C.R. seizes crossings at Edingen, Katzenfurt, and Sinn while C.C.A. drives across at Asslar and Hermannstein. The 9th and 99th Divisions follow in the shadow of the Armor, the former relieving C.C.R. at the Dill and the latter driving to Sainscheid-Wilsenroth-Friekhofen-Niederzeuzheim. In the **V Corps** sector, the 2nd Division eliminates the remnant resistance in its zone. At Diez, the Germans capitulate to elements of the 9th Armored's C.C.A. while C.C.B. contingents seize a bridge over the Lahn River at Aumenau; in addition they get units to Hadame and to the west bank of the Lahn River at Weilburg. In conjunction, C.C.R. bolts the Lahn and drives down the Cologne-Frankfurt Autobahn toward Niederhausen. Meanwhile, the 69th Division crosses reinforcements over the Rhine and plows into Ehrenbreitstein, seizing the Luftwaffe Citadel, in addition to securing the Lahn River towns of Bad Ems and Nassau. In addition, the 106th Cavalry Reconnaissance Squadron seizes the heights between the Gel and Lahn Rivers. In the **U.S. Third Army** area, **VIII Corps** sector, the 87th Division further extends its Rhine bridgehead and establishes contact with First Army at the Lahn River in addition to advancing to the Bergnassau-Scheurern-Holzhausen road, overrunning about twenty towns and villages as it advances. In the 89th Division sector, the bridgehead is enlarged toward Wiesbaden, seizing Bogel and Strueth and getting other contingents to Lorch. The 78th Division continues progressing east, and the 76th Division gets contingents over the Rhine at Boppard. In the **XII Corps** sector, the 4th and 6th Armored Divisions are relieved by Infantry troops at the Main River bridgeheads, permitting preparation for a breakout attack to the north. The bridging operations are somewhat hampered by a steady flow of enemy fire. The 5th Division assumes responsibility for the Frankfurt bridgehead while simultaneously infusing Frankfurt with additional troops to further the elimination of the remaining resistance there. In conjunction, RCT 11 seizes Wolldorf as it continues clearing the woods south of the Main. In the 90th Division sector, mop-up details are ongoing. In the 26th Division sector, the Hanau bridgehead is being enlarged, but it is an agonizing task as the Germans resist feverishly. Bitter house-to-house fighting develops in Hanau, but Grosskrotzenberg is secured; additional contingents of the 26th Division guard the west bank of the Rhine. The 2nd Cavalry Group, sweeping along the north and south flank of the Corps, encounters friendly forces. In the **XX Corps** sector, the 80th Division deploys for its attack across the Rhine and Main Rivers; some elements cross at Openheim in the XII Corps zone. **6th Army Group** DA ALPS stars to secure the Petit St. Bernard Pass along the Franco-Italian border west of Aosta, Italy. In the **U.S. Seventh Army** area, **XV Corps** sector, the Germans are retreating toward the Main River with the Yanks on their heels the 45th Division drives 16 miles and gets Patrols to the river. Further south, the 3rd Division gains ground at a rapid pace as it closes on the Main. Meanwhile, the 12th Armored and 44th Divisions ford the Rhine, the latter securing the Corps' right flank. **(Atlantic-Eastern Europe)** Heavy close combat erupts in Danzig and Gdynia as elements of the Second White Russian Front pierce the beleaguered German lines along the southern perimeter. The Germans begin fleeing toward the hills outside of Oxhoft. The Germans send in Ferry Boats and begin evacuating the wounded and other troops. Hitler demands that Oxhoft be retained as a strongpoint, but the German forces head toward Hela; by the 1st of April, about 50,000 people are evacuated from the Oxhoft area by the German Navy. In Silesia, the First Ukrainian Front takes Strehlen and Rybnik while troops of the Fourth Ukrainian Front capture Zory and Wodzislaw. In Hungary, contingents of the Second and Third Ukrainian Fronts maintain their westward drive toward Austria. **(Atlantic-Italy)** **15th Army Group** In the **U.S. Fifth Army** area, the 1st Armored Division gets a break; the town of Salvaro is taken without a struggle.

March 28th 1945 — (Pacific-Dutch East Indies) Army Planes sink the Japanese Patrol Boat No. 108 and the Minesweeper No. 11. **(Pacific-Iwo Jima)** The Repair Ship *Agenor* (ARL-3) is damaged by collision. **(Pacific-Japan)** The Japanese lose the Coast Defense Vessel No. 33 to Army Aircraft and the Frigate *Mikura* to the Submarine *Threadfin* (SS-410), off Kyushu. **(Pacific-Philippines)** In the **U.S. Sixth Army I Corps** sector, the 35th Regiment, 25th Division receives orders to suspend its attack on Balete Pass, due to the excellent progress of the 27th Regiment against Mt. Myoko; the 35th is to hold its positions and then to block the eastern entrance to the Putlan Valley. In the **XI Corps** sector, contingents of the 6th Division secure a ridge on Mt. Mataba; however, the attack moves slowly due to tremendous resistance. In the **XIV Corps** sector, the 12th Cavalry secures Mayondon Point. The 187th Regiment, 11th Airborne Division commences a two-pronged assault to seize a saddle between

Bukel Hill and Mt. Macolod, but the Japanese repulse the attempt. **Southern Philippines** In the **U.S. Eighth Army** area, the 182nd Regiment (Americal Division) seizes Lahug Airfield on Cebu with its 2nd and 3rd Battalions while the 1st Battalion takes previously bypassed Hill 30 and attacks Go Chan Hill. The entrenched Japanese retain possession, but 32 pillboxes are exterminated on Guadalupe Road, east of the hill. In other activity, the 132nd Regiment's Company E captures Mactan Island and Opon Airfield without incident. **(Pacific-Ryukyu-Kerama Islands)** Resistance on Aka Island ceases, but some opposition remains on Zamami where the town of Tokashika on Tokashiki Island is seized by RCT 306. The Attack Cargo Vessel *Wyandot* (AM-63) is damaged by a Horizontal Bomber. The Minesweeper *Skylark* (AM-63) is damaged by a mine. **(Pacific-Burma)** The Burma Defense Army, redesignated Burma National Army, revolts against the Japanese in central and south Burma. In other activity, Admiral Mountbatten establishes the Air and Ground Supply Committee to study the Air supply situation. In the **British Fourteenth Army** area, 4th Corps sector, the Japanese under General Kimura begin abandoning their positions in the Meiktila region. **(Atlantic-Western Europe)** Hitler fires General Heinz Guderian as Chief of the Army, replacing him with General Krebs. Guderian is the final General Officer of the original early war Generals to be dismissed. Berlin is no longer the objective of the Allies. General Eisenhower modifies the attack plan, leaving Berlin to the Russians who are closing quickly from the east. Much discussion precipitates the final decision; ultimately, it is based upon former political decisions reached by Stalin, Churchill, and Roosevelt. Leipzig becomes the primary objective and the U.S. 12th Army Group is to execute the main thrust, rather than the British 12th Army Group. The British react vehemently to the decision as they are of the opinion that Berlin should be seized before the Russians can get it; in addition, they are dismayed that Eisenhower is in direct contact with the Russians. However, Roosevelt's health is deteriorating rapidly, thus the decision is backed by Marshall and the Joint Chiefs of Staff. **21st Army Group** The British Second Army commences a breakout attack and drives toward the Elbe. In the **12th Corps** sector, the British 53rd Division plows through Shede and advances toward Bocholt. The British 7th Armored Division drives to Borken. In the **XVIII (Airborne) Corps** area, the British 6th Airborne races rapidly from Erle to Lembeck where it is attached to British 8th Corps. The U.S. 17th Airborne's 507th Paratroop Infantry overpowers the resistance in Wulfen, then drives to Haltern to relieve the 6th Guards Armored Brigade. In the **U.S. Ninth Army** area, the 30th Division drives toward Dorsten and encounters spirited resistance. The 35th Division continues to battle for control of Kirchhellen, and the 79th Division is heavily engaged as it drives south toward the Ruhr, making slight gains on the left; however, on the right, Hamborn and Neumuhl fall. **12th Army Group** The U.S. Fifteenth Army receives responsibility for neutralizing the two bypassed German pockets at Lorient and St. Nazaire in the coastal sector of France; also it receives orders to occupy, organize and govern the Rhine sector of Germany. The Fifteenth Army advances to protect the rear areas. The First and Third U.S. Armies converge north of Idsten. In the **U.S. First Army** area, the VII Corps's 3rd Armored advances eastward against minimal resistance, taking Marburg and Dillenburg before pivoting north to take Bottenhorn and Holzhausen as it closes on Paderborn to complete the investment of the Ruhr in conjunction with Ninth Army. Breitscheidt is seized by the advancing 1st Division while the 104th sweeps as it trails the Armor. In the **III Corps** sector, the 7th Armored Division moves out just after midnight and drives to the Lahn River where it secures crossings between Marburg and Giessen and captures communication centers east of the river; C.C.B. advances to Weismar and seizes it and Grossen Buseck, with TF Erlenbusch. Meanwhile, TF Chappuis overruns Rutterhausen, then crosses the Lahn, capturing Alten Buseck, Lollar, Mainzlar, Stauffenberg, and Daubringen. In the 9th Armored Division sector, V Corps area, contact is made with the Third Army on the Cologne-Frankfurt Autobahn. In other activity, the 69th Division completes its crossing of the Rhine. In the **U.S. Third Army** area, **VIII Corps** sector, traffic congestion arises at the boundary between it and First Army; however, Patton's troops take it in stride and after some evasive maneuvering, contingents of the 87th Division run over Katzenelnbogen as the 87th Drives east. Contingents of the 89th Division secure Hinter Wald and Lorch. In the 80th Division sector, attacks across the Rhine and Main Rivers commence simultaneously at 01:00. By day's end, the bridgehead in the Mainz area is solidly established and includes Auringen, Biebrich, Bierstadt, Delkenheim, Ervenheim, Hochheim, Igstadt, Kastel, Kostheim, Massenheim, Wicker, and Wiesbaden. In conjunction, the 3rd Cavalry Group dispatches the 3rd Squadron to Mainz to protect the bridges. In the **XII Corps** area, contingents of the 90th Division are transported across the Main River in assault boats at 03:00 and vanquish some tough resistance on the left flank as they establish a rigid bridgehead by 12:00, stretching five to six miles. In addition, a footbridge and ferry are put in operation, paving the way for Armor and the remainder of the Division. The 6th Armored Division passes into the 90th bridgehead and drives north, C.C.B. seizing Bergen, Dortelweil, Enkheim, Nieder Erlenbach, Nieder Eschbach, and Vilbel. The 4th Armored Division also attacks at 03:00, crossing at Grossauheim and capturing Ostheim with C.C.A., which then rolls to Grünberg. Meanwhile, C.C.B. drives to the area northeast of Grünberg while C.C.R. converges on Muenzenberg. In the 5th Division sector, the battle for Frankfurt continues to rage; however, most of the city is under control of the Stars and Stripes. The 26th Division maintains its blockade east and south of the Main, reducing the remaining resistance in Hanau during the morning. In other activity, the 45th Division (Seventh Army) assumes responsibility for the bridgehead across the Main at Aschaffenburg. The 5th Infantry and 6th Armored Divisions are transferred to XX Corps. **6th Army Group** In the **U.S. Seventh Army** area, **XV Corps** sector, the 45th Division establishes a bridgehead across the Main in the vicinity of Obernau. The 3rd Division closes on the Main and is passed through by the 12th Armored Division. Meanwhile, the 44th Division drives south along the Rhine and across the Neckar River closing on Mannheim and Heidelberg, the former attempting unsuccessfully to surrender. In the **XXI Corps** sector, initiates its crossing of the Rhine south of the XV Corps positions, getting the 63rd Infantry and 12th Armored Divisions across and into assembly areas for further advance. In the VI Corps sector, the 103rd Division starts to relieve the 71st Division along the Rhine, while the 36th Division continues to hold defensive positions along the river. **(Atlantic-Eastern Europe)** The Germans finally relent at Gydnia, as troops of the Second White Russian Front (Marshal Konstantin Rokossovsky) capture the Naval Base city in addition to securing the western portion of Danzig. Also, Gyoer, east of Budapest along the Danube, falls to the Second Ukrainian Front.

March 29th 1945 — (Pacific-Philippines) Luzon In the U.S.

Sixth Army area, **XI Corps** sector, the 43rd Division seizes positions on Hill 1200, which controls the remaining escape route of the Japanese running northwest from New Bosoboso, while the contingents of 6th Division battle tenaciously against well-entrenched Japanese on Mt. Mataba. In the **XIV Corps** sector, Lipa and its Airdrome are seized by the 8th Calvary, 1st Cavalry Division, which then establishes contact with the 11th Airborne Division. Highway 19 is now clear for Vehicles from Calamba to Batangas. The 7th Cavalry drives to San Andres. Meanwhile, the 187th Regiment, 11th Airborne secures part of Dita as it drives toward Mt. Macolod. **Southern Philippines** In the U.S. Eighth Army area, a reinforced Platoon of Company F, 185th Regiment, 40th Division debarks at Patik in Negros Island and engages in a furious fight with Japanese troops at a bridge across the Bago River; the objective is taken and will become a primary factor in the drive against Macolod. Meanwhile, the remainder of the Regiment debarks unopposed near Pulupandan and uses the bridge to drive to the fringes of Macolod. On Cebu, vicious fighting continues on Go Chan Hill. The 182nd Regiment, Americal Division seizes it after a severe struggle that includes heavy losses when the Japs mine a spur of the hill and blow it, costing the lives of many of the men of Company A. Seventy-two pillboxes are demolished prior to victory. On Mindanao, the 3rd Battalion, 163rd Regiment, 41st Division, forges to the high ground near Mt. Pulungbatu, virtually ending organized resistance in the Zamboanga region; however, the Japanese continue to resist in small groups for quite some time. In other activity, Philippine Guerrilla forces debark at Masbate, following a boisterous bombardment by Gunboats (LCI), and quickly seize the town. **(Pacific-Ryukyu Islands)** The Kerama Islands are in total control of the U.S. 77th Division. Garrison forces remain and the Seaplane Base and Anchorage are immediately utilized. The demolition teams have cleared the landing areas of mines, giving the Warships additional flexibility as they converge on the landing sites and commence close range carpet shelling in conjunction with the Planes which continue to pound Okinawa. Meanwhile, Task Force 58, which has searched futilely for the Japanese Fleet off Japan, directs its fire power against the Kyushu Airfields and upon Japanese Shipping as it returns to the Okinawa area. **(Pacific-Formosa)** Army Aircraft sink the Japanese Submarine Chaser No. 192. **(Pacific-Japan)** Planes from the Task Forces of Rear Admirals J. J. Clark and F. C. Sherman strike Airfields and Shipping in the Kagoshima Bay region, Kyushu, Japan. **(Pacific-South China Sea)** The Submarine Hammerhead (SS-364) sinks the Japanese Coast Defense Vessel No. 84, and Army Planes destroy Coast Defense Vessels No. 18 and No. 130. **(Atlantic-Western Europe)** There is a widening gap in the differences of opinion between the Allies and the British; Eisenhower is determined to destroy the remaining German forces while Churchill wants to reach Berlin before the Russians. The Allies stand at the Rhine, about three hundred miles from Berlin and two hundred miles from the Elbe. However, the Russians are at the Oder River, thirty miles from Berlin. The Russians have pillaged and raped their way through the German-occupied towns. Most women in every conquered town have been raped, while others are literally nailed to barn doors. Soviet troops also roll many women, children, and civilians into barbed wire, sprayed with gasoline and set afire, before sliding the incinerated corpses into the rivers to flow downstream. Ike is also concerned about the possibility of the Germans retiring to the mysterious mountain fortress allegedly stretched through the mountains in southern Bavaria, western Austria, and northern Italy. The legend of a mountain fortress exists only in the minds of a few Germans; however, the Allies have no intelligence to reach that determination. **21st Army Group** The Germans are besieged on all fronts; nevertheless, within their means they continue to resist in many areas. In the **British Second Army** area, 2nd Corps sector the Canadian 3rd Division is encountering heavy resistance as it continues to vanquish Emmerich. The Canadian 2nd Division seizes Netterden. In the 12th Corps sector, the British 7th Armored Division closes on Rheine while the British 53rd Division attacks toward Winterswijk. The 8 Corps grasps the opportunity and commits its 11th Armored and 6th Airborne Divisions on the right flank to make a deeper penetration toward Osnabrueck, the former advancing to Beikelort and the latter driving to Coesfeld. In the **XVIII (Airborne) Corps** sector, the 6th Armored Guards Brigade moves toward Buldern, while the U.S. 194th Glider Infantry is transported by truck to Duelmen. The U.S. 2nd Armored Division (XIX Corps U.S. Ninth Army) comes on the scene and begins to relieve the 11th Airborne Division. In the **U.S. Ninth Army** area, the southwest portion of Dorsten is secured by C.C.A., 8th Armored; contingents of C.C.R. are speeding to the site to assist while other units drive east seizing Feldhausen and Schoven. In the 35th Division sector, the Germans fight tenaciously, holding the Yanks to slim gains, but the 134th Regiment kicks the Krauts to a fare-thee-well at Gladbeck, overpowering the resistance. The 79th Division drives to the Emser Canal near Sterkrade and to the Rhine-Herne Canal on the left and right respectively. The 29th Division is attached to Corps. **12th Army Group** In the **U.S. First Army** area, **VII Corps** sector the 3rd Armored Division rolls forward about fifty miles, pursuing the Germans, who are now completely disorganized and undisciplined, toward Paderborn. The 1st and 104th Divisions are running with the Armor, the former racing on the left and the latter trailing close behind the rumbling cavalcade of Tanks. The 8th Division, which is being relieved west of the Rhine by the 86th Division, starts mop-up operations south of the Sieg, freeing contingents of the 1st Division and 4th Cavalry Group, while the 78th Division is busily engaged defending the south bank of the Sieg and relieving other units of the 4th Cavalry Group. In the **III Corps** sector, the Germans are also coming under extraordinary pressure as the full weight of the advancing 7th Armored begins to blow massive holes in their already deteriorating positions as it drives to the Edersee dam and toward crossing sites at the Eder River; Kirchhain resists with fervor and holds. Amoeneburg and Kleinseelheim defenses collapse easily under the rolling wheels of Task Force Brown; Task Force Beatty rushes to bolster the offensive power of the Yanks at Kirchhain, while Task Force Brown bypasses it and continues toward Bracht. C.C.B. then darts to Kirchhain and assumes command of the troops already there, then pulverizes the defenders, overpowering the city by 18:00. One intrepid Soldier, Staff Sergeant Robert H. Dietz, Company A, 7th Armored Battalion, knocks out a Bazooka team at a bridge, then advances to a second, knocking out several enemy troops with their Panzerfausts and disconnecting the demolitions connected to the structure. Dietz opens the route to the city singlehandedly; however, upon completion of clearing the two bridges, he is slain by another volley. The 9th Division continues to hold its defensive stance along the west bank of the Lahn River, and the 99th Division mops up near Staufenburg and outposts several towns in the area. In the **V Corps** sector, the assault swings from east to north, with the grinding 9th Armored Division as vanguard in the drive to the Eder River. In what could be construed as a

rare treat for the weary Infantry, the 2nd Division is carried by Tanks, Tank Destroyers, and other Vehicles behind the thundering Armor. Meanwhile, the 69th Division remains behind to sweep the rear areas for remnant stragglers. In the **U.S. Third Army** area, the 70th Division, under Major General A.J. Barnett and the 13th Armored Division, commanded by Major General J.B. Wogan are attached to Army. In the **VIII Corps** sector, the attack continues unmercifully. Task Force Sundt, 87th Division, spearheading the assault drives to the Corps boundary, its 345th Regiment severing the Autobahn outside of Niederselters, then taking the town. The 78th Division, in a blistering advance against stiff opposition, seizes Kamberg with its 385th Regiment, while the 417th rolls through Idstein to the Oberems-Kroftel-Wuestems region. The 89th Division's 354th Regiment relieves TF Johnson at Bad Schalbach, then sprints toward the Corps boundary; the 353rd seizes Hausen and secures the surrounding area, while the 355th, supported by a Reconnaissance Troop, secures the area at the Rhine bend west of Wiesbaden. In the **XX Corps** sector, the 6th Armored Division rolls forward, paralleling the Autobahn, its guns almost totally relaxed as opposition is nearly extinct as it drives to the area east of Giessen, passing through many towns. The 80th Division mops up within its Mainz bridgehead and pushes out, extending it to Koenigstein; the attached 16th Cavalry Group bolts acoss the Rhine and drives to the Eltville-Neudorf-Georgenborn line, west of Wiesbaden. The 65th Division converges on the Schwabenheim region and pushes the 260th and 261st Regiments across the Rhine, the latter being attached to 6th Armored. In the 5th Division sector, Frankfurt falls. Meanwhile, the 3rd Cavalry Group crosses the Rhine and in conjunction with 6th Armored, the Autobahn is opened and used as the Main Supply Route for the Corps advance. The Autobahn, planned for extensive use by the Volkswagen (people's car) which had been partially designed by Hitler, is now to be inundated with U.S. Vehicles. In other activity, the 94th Division is transferred to the XXII Corps (Fifteenth Army) and the 71st Division is attached to Corps. In the **XII Corps** sector, the 4th Armored continues its fluid pace thundering through Lauterbach with its C.C.B., seizing it with lightning speed, while C.C.A. overruns Grossenleuder and C.C.R. clears the Main Supply Route by driving to Herbstein; RCT 359 (90th Division) contingents are attached to Division, quickly motorized, and deployed to the right to intercept any enemy interference to the drive. The 11th Armored engines are running full throttle also as it moves through the 26th Division bridgehead at the Main River, driving vigorously toward Fulda: C.C.A. is ordered to stop at Rothenbergen, and the trailing C.C.B. pulls off the road at Ravolzhausen until the following morning. In other activity, the 90th Division mops up in its sector, while the 26th Division starts clearing bypassed areas in the Hanau-Lieblos area, and in both Langendiebach and Rueckingen. To maintain contact between the 26th Division and Seventh Army, the 2nd Cavalry Group begins to cross its 42nd Squadron over the Main during the night. **6th Army Group** In the **U.S. Seventh Army** area, **XV Corps** sector encounters its first rigid opposition east of the Rhine as it attempts to enlarge its Main River bridgehead; vicious house-to-house fighting erupts in Aschaffenburg and Schweinheim as the 157th Regiment starts to secure them; the 179th Regiment, operating near Sulzbach, drives east while the 180th Infantry crosses the Main and plows through Sulzbach. In the 3rd Division sector, preparations are made to cross the Main at Woerth, and in the 12th Armored zone, the eastward attack continues. Meanwhile, the 44th Division enters the abandoned city of Mannheim. In the **XXI Corps** sector, the 10th Armored Division is ordered to prepare to commence an attack south of the Neckar; its sends probing Patrols to search for crossing sites. In other activity, the 63rd Division starts to relieve the 44 Division (XV Corps) and the 101st Cavalry Group assembles east of the Rhine. In the **VI Corps** sector, the 71st Division, relieved by the 103rd Division, moves to Third Army area and is attached; the 101st is taken under Seventh Army jurisdiction. In the 36th Division sector, the 3rd Algerian Division assumes responsibility for the area, and the 36th is assigned to Army control. In addition, the 102nd Cavalry Group is detached from the Corps. In the **French 1st Army** area, the DA ALPS secures most of the Petit St. Bernard Pass, then suspends its assault. **(Atlantic-Eastern Europe)** The besieged and surrounded Germans in the area southwest of Koenigsberg in East Prussia are being mopped up by forces of the Third White Russian Front; however, the persistent Germans attempt to accomplish the impossible by continuing to resist fiercely against insurmountable odds in the remaining strongholds in east Danzig. In Hungary, troops of the Third Ukrainian Front advance to the Austrian frontier and take Kapuva, Koeszeg, and Szombathely.

March 30th 1945 — (Pacific-Philippines) In the **U.S. Sixth Army** area, **I Corps** sector, elements of the 35th Regiment, 25th Division move to cut off the eastern entrance to the Putlan Valley. The 3rd Battalion, 27th Regiment attacks along a ridge and drives toward Mt. Myoko. In the **XI Corps** sector, the 103rd Regiment, 43rd Division is ordered to drive south and establish contact with the XIV Corps. Meanwhile, the elements of the 6th Division continue to encounter fierce resistance which hinders their progress. In addition, the 3rd Battalion, 20th Regiment continues driving toward Mt. Mataba, and the 12th Cavalry, 1st Cavalry Division engages the enemy near Calauan. At Mt. Macolod, the Japanese raise tenacious opposition against the 1st Battalion, 187th Regiment, 11th Airborne. In the **U.S. Eighth Army** area (Southern Philippines), the Japanese withdraw from Macolod, Negros, and move eastward toward the mountains in Patog-Negritos. Contingents of the 40th Reconnaissance Troop discover the Japanese secondary line of defense near Atipuluan. In other activity, the 182nd Regiment secures the balance of Hill 31 (Cebu) and destroys nine pillboxes. **(Pacific-Philippine Sea)** The High Speed Transport *Roper* (APD-20) becomes damaged by collision. **(Pacific-Ryukyu)** The U.S. Fleet continues its pre-invasion bombardment. On land, activity on Kerama Island is restricted to Patrols. At Okinawa, demolition teams continue to clear the way for the assault troops. A Kamikaze damages the Heavy Cruiser *Indianapolis* (CA-35). **(Pacific-Burma)** In the N.C.A.C. area, the British 36th Division reaches Kyaukme and establishes contact with the Chinese 1st Sep Regiment, bringing the operation in the area to its conclusion; Admiral Mountbatten has previously informed Chiang Kai-shek that Chinese forces would not advance beyond the Lashio-Hsipaw-Kyaukme line. In the **British Fourteenth Army** area, 33rd Corps sector, the Indian 20th Division overcomes fierce resistance and seizes Kyaukse. In the **IV Corps** sector, Meiktila is secure, permitting the Indian 17th Division and the 255th Tank Brigade to drive south toward Pyawbwe. By now, the British control most strategic positions between Meiktila and Mandalay. **(Atlantic-Great Britain)** Winston Churchill requests that General Marshall supply U.S. Air Power to assist the British drive against Rangoon. **(Atlantic-Western Europe)** Army Aircraft lambaste enemy Submarine forces, sinking ten U-Boats: the U-2340 at Hamburg;

the U-72, U-329, U-430, U-870, U-884, and the U-886 at Bremen; the U-96, U-429, and the U-3508 at Wilhelmshaven. On the following day, three more are sunk at Hamburg: the U-348, U-350, and the U-1167. **21st Army Group** In the **British Second Army** area, the Canadian 3rd Division reduces remaining resistance in Emmerich, and the Canadian 2nd Division seizes Elten. Meanwhile, the 30th Corps attacks and breaks out of the bridgehead moving toward Lingen. In the 12th Corps sector, the British 53rd Division takes Winterswijk, and the British 7th Armored Division drives to Ahaus. In the 8th Corps sector, the British 6th Airborne and 11th Armored Divisions advance about 14 miles and reach Greven and Ensdetten respectively. In the **XVIII (Airborne) Corps** sector, the 16th Guards Armored Brigade advances to Buldern before dawn. At 06:00, the U.S. 17th Airborne Division is placed under command of the U.S. XIX Corps, and Corps is simultaneously placed within First Allied Airborne Army. In the **U.S. Ninth Army** area, XVI Corps sector the 75th Division prepares to attack east of the Rhine. Contingents of the 8th Armored's C.C.A. seize Polsum, but the Germans pin down some elements outside of Marl; C.C.A. drives to Buer Hassel. The 79th Division terminates its mission by driving to Emser Canal. **12th Army Group** In the **U.S. Fifteenth Army** area, **XXII Corps** is activated and receives responsibility for defending and governing Neuss-Bonn sector along the west bank of the Rhine River. The 95th (Ninth Army) and 86th (First Army) Divisions are temporarily assigned to Corps until Fifteenth Army units arrive. In the **U.S. First Army's VII Corps** sector, advance contingents of the 3rd Armored Division drive to within several miles of Paderborn; C.C. Howze's Task Force Richardson and TF Hogan hit intense resistance and become stalled at Nordborchen and Wewer respectively. To the right, Germans infiltrate the lines of Task Force Welborn in a forest outside of Etteln. In addition, Task Force Doan (C.C. Hickey) attacks to clear passage for the advance. Mean while, TF Lovelady also becomes stalled by heavy fire near Wrexen. Major General Maurice Rose (CG 3rd Armored) is killed by enemy fire as he attempts to reach the front lines. The 3rd Armored encounters fierce resistance; however, the S.S. troops who have vowed to fight to the death are overmatched and will retire toward the Harz Mountains. The 104th Division follows the Armor; its 413th Regiment drives to Adorf and Arolsen, and advance contingents of the 415th Regiment halt outside Heringhausen. The 4th Cavalry Group, relieved by 78th Division, drives north toward Beddelhausen and Markhausen. Meanwhile, the 1st Division attacks with three Regiments and seizes the high ground overlooking Siegen, while the 8th Division operating east of the Rhine attacks and secures ground south of the Sieg River within its sector with its 13th and 28th Regiments. Company K, 18th Regiment, 1st Division, encounters fierce resistance near Eisern. Staff Sergeant George Peterson, braving the machine gun and mortar fire, nudges forward, signaling for the 2nd Platoon to follow. An enemy mortar rips into him, inflicting a grievous wound; nevertheless, he continues the attack, gnawing forward. Despite the agonizing pain and life threatening loss of blood, he continues and knocks out a nest with a grenade. Suddenly, another machine gun begins showering him with fire. With a quick flick of a grenade he destroys the gun and its crew. He darts toward a third machine gun and is again wounded, but he keeps going, pulls himself to his knees, and fires a grenade from his rifle, destroying the obstacle. A medic arrives and begins giving him aid; Peterson peers out and spots one of his wounded men, prompting him to push the Medic away and head for the wounded trooper.

He crawls to within a few yards of the fallen man, but another burst of enemy fire kills the intrepid Sergeant. First Lt. Walter J. Will, also of Company K, knocks out two enemy machine gun nests which have contingents of the Company pinned down, killing several men and capturing nine. Will then attacks a third nest, silencing the gun and killing the crew with the assistance of three grenades. Lt. Will regroups his men and leads a charge to rout the enemy; he is killed during this action and receives the Medal of Honor posthumously. In the **III Corps** sector, the 7th Armored drives north: TF Wolfe (contingent of TF Brown, C.C.R.) seizes Edersee Dam before the Germans can destroy it; in addition, six Eder River crossings are secured by TF Chappuis and its attached TF Beatty (between Bergheim and Hemfurth). In the **V Corps** sector, Armored Divisions pound their way forward with the 2nd Infantry Division trailing closely behind, sweeping the area as they advance. The 9th Armored Division also drives north to the Eder and seizes additional crossings; Bad Wildungen is secured by contingents of C.C.B. Additional contingents drive toward Bergheim to capture another bridge. Meanwhile, C.C.A. drives to Fritzlar and is met by enemy air and land resistance. In addition, the Germans blow the bridge; however, some units cross at a 6th Armored Division bridge at Sennern and come in behind the defenders, while others seize an Airfield south of Fritzlar. In other activity, the 69th Division deploys southwest of Weilburg and sends contingents to relieve III Corps units at Wetzlar. In the **U.S. Third Army** area, **VIII Corps** sector, the 76th Division advances and encounters strong resistance by German Officer candidates at Dorfweil, Finsternathal, and Schmitten, which stalls the drive. TF Fickett pushes contingents to Butzbach, and elements of the 304th Regiment cross the Rhine to guard the Division's right flank along the Cologne-Frankfurt Autobahn. In the **XX Corps** sector, the 6th Armored Division drives explosively north of Frankfurt, reaching the Eder River near Zenner-Wadern, and also advances to the Fulda River outside of Ober Beisheim, knocking over many towns including Alsfeld, Borken, Homberg, Romrod, and Treysa. Meanwhile, contingents of the 65th Division trail the Armor and mop up bypassed resistance. In addition, the 71st Division is transported to Rockenhausen, and the 3rd Cavalry Group drives toward its final objectives in the vicinity of Wallenrode-Hebles. In the **XII Corps** sector, the 4th Armored pivots and drives toward Hersfeld; C.C.B. advances through Asbach, overcoming resistance, but its drive to Hersfeld is halted and it pulls back for the night. Meanwhile, C.C.A. advances to the heights between Hersfeld and Vacha. Most of the 90th Division is transported to positions where it can trail the Armor. The 11th Armored Division gets all contingents across the Main River and maintains its drive toward Fulda; two Regiments of the 26th Division shadow the Armor and mop up. At Gelnhausen, the Germans repulse C.C.A. In conjunction, the 41st Cavalry Reconnaissance Squadron bypasses Gelnhausen to break open a route for C.C.A., while C.C.R. advances to Mittel Gruendau to neutralize Gelnhausen. C.C.B., operating to the right, drives to Nieder Seemen. Meanwhile, the 2nd Cavalry Group relieves the 104th Regiment at Budinger Wald and in addition, gets all elements across the Main River to cover the right flank of the Corps. **6th Army Group** In the **U.S. Seventh Army** area, **XV Corps** sector, the 157th Regiment secures Schweinheim, but it has not been able to overcome German resistance at Aschaffenburg. Meanwhile, the balance of the 45th Division continues to advance steadily. The 12th Armored Division continues to drive east; its C.C.A. advances to the Hardheim region. In addition, the

3rd Division establishes a bridgehead on the Main River across from Woerth. In the **XXI Corps** sector, contact is established between the 12th Armored Division (XV Corps) and the 101st Cavalry Group; a bridgehead line is established. In other activity, the 63rd Division relieves the 44th Division (XV Corps), then fords the Neckar River near Wieblingen. In conjunction, the 10th Armored's C.C.A. and C.C.B. cross the Neckar and drive south. **(Atlantic-Eastern Europe)** Russian General Rokossovsky's force (Second White Russian Front) reduces final resistance and secures Danzig. Meanwhile, General Zhukov's Second Belorussian Front continues to pound the beleaguered and surrounded Germans at Breslau and Glogau in Silesia. In addition, the Second Ukrainian Front initiates an offensive along the Hungarian-Czechoslovakian border; contingents drive across the Hron and Nitra Rivers and push west toward Slovak, Bratislava's capital. In conjunction, other elements engage the besieged Germans along the south bank of the Danube in Hungary. The Third Ukrainian Front pushes contingents from Koeszeg, Hungary, into Austria and sends others southward to the Drava River along the Hungarian-Yugoslavian border; the drive is bolstered by contingents of Bulgarian troops.

March 1945 — Seventh Army crossing the Rhine River near Worms, Germany.

March 31st 1945 — (United States) While the U.S. forces have been swarming across the Rhine River in Germany, the newspaper, *Daily Worker* has been constantly warning of an alleged substantial buildup of German forces in Southern Germany, helping to force an Allied focus on the bogus German Fortress in the Bavarian Alps. Meanwhile, the Russians continue to close on Berlin. On March 25th, Seventh Army G2 had intercepted information concerning supplies ordered by Himmler to equip 100,000 men (supposed elite units) to defend the National (Inner) Redoubt; a map of the area is also displayed. By April 25th, the ruse works to German advantage. At SHEAF, General Walter Bedell Smith will remark: "WE ARE BEGINNING TO THINK IT (FORTRESS WILL BE A LOT MORE THAN WE EXPECT...ESPECIALLY, MORE EXTENSIVE UNDERGROUND INSTALLATIONS THAN ORIGINALLY THOUGHT." **(Central Pacific)** The Seaplane Tender (small) *Coos Bay* (AVP-25) sustains damage by collision. **(Pacific-Philippines)** Luzon In the **U.S. Sixth Army** area, **I Corps** sector, the 128th Regiment, 32nd Division, remains heavily engaged at Salacsac Pass No. 2 on Villa Verdi Trail; it captures one hill and is rebuffed at another. Meanwhile, the 3rd Battalion, 27th Infantry, 25th Division drives along a ridge near Mt. Myoko. In the **XI Corps** sector, advance contingents of the 103rd Regiment, 43rd Division attack into the Santa Maria Valley and establish contact with the 1st Cavalry Division. In the XIV

Corps sector, the 12th Cavalry, 1st Cavalry Division captures Calauan; the Germans have abandoned it. In the Mt. Macolod sector, contingents of the 187th Regiment, 11th Airborne Division, seize ground on Bukel Hill. **Southern Philippines** In the **U.S. Eighth Army** area, the 185th Regiment, 40th Division prepares an attack against Talisay, Negros. On Cebu, the Americal Division fends off night-counterattacks, while preparing to launch its attack against a hill mass which commands Cebu City. **(Pacific-Ryukyu-Okinawa)** The 420th Field Artillery Group, reinforced, lands on four small islands of the Kiese group to support the imminent operations on Okinawa. Meanwhile, the 77th Division withdraws from Kerama Island, which had been a Japanese Suicide Boat Base; however, some troops remain behind to garrison Zamami. During the operation, the Yanks destroy 350 Suicide Boats and kill 530 Japanese. In addition, 121 troops and 1,195 civilians are captured. U.S. losses amount to 31 killed and 81 wounded on the Keramas. Offshore, the Heavy Cruiser *Pensacola* (CA-24) is damaged by collision. The Light Minelayer *Adams* (DM-27), the Attack Transport *Hinsdale* (APA-120), and the LSTs 724 and 884 are damaged by Kamikazes. The Japanese Submarine I-8 is sunk by the U.S. Destroyers *Morrison* (DD-560) and *Stockton* (DD-646). **(Atlantic-Western Europe)** General Eisenhower issues a proclamation to the citizens of Germany, urging them to plant crops, and to the Soldiers, requesting that they surrender to end the conflict. **21st Army Group** In the **British Second Army** area, the Canadian 2nd Corps seizes Hoch Elten feature. In the 30th Corps area, the Guards Armored Division advances to Haaksbergen. In the 12th Corps sector, the British 7th Armored advances to Neunkirchen, and the 53rd Division reaches Alstatte. In the 8 Corps sector, the British 6th Airborne and the 11th Armored Divisions establish bridgeheads across the Ems River. In the **U.S. Ninth Army** area, the **XIII Corps** begins crossing the Rhine at Wesel. In the **XVI Corps** sector, the 75th Division attacks, gaining about four miles. Meanwhile, C.C.R., 8th Armored Division attacks east, reaching positions just short of Langenbochum. Meanwhile, the 35th Division secures several towns and villages as it advances about two miles on the Corps' south flank. **12th Army Group** The U.S. **Fifteenth Army** assumes command of the coastal sector of France and is responsible for neutralizing enemy pockets at Lorient and St. Nazaire. In the **U.S. First Army's VII Corps** sector, 3rd Armored columns approach Paderborn, hitting fierce resistance. C.C. Howze commits Flamethrowers to hasten the capture of both Nordborchen and Wever. In addition, elements of C.C. Boudinot eliminate an enemy pocket which is stalling TF Welborn; the Task Force then advances to Haxtergrund. Meanwhile, the 104th Division races forward behind the Armor; its 413th Regiment advances 35 miles, severing the enemy escape route from Rimbeck. In conjunction, the 415th Regiment halts near Hallenberg-Medebach to intercept any possible German breakout from Willingen and Winterberg. In the 1st Division zone, roadblocks are established southwest of Paderborn and in addition, contact is established with the 3rd Armored Division. The 8th and 78th Divisions deploy defensively; simultaneously, the 8th Division secures Deuz, Grissenbach, Helgersdorf, and Salchendorf with its 121st Regiment; Kirchen is seized by the 13th Regiment. In the **V Corps** sector, the 9th Armored Division establishes a bridgehead across the Diemel River near Warburg. C.C.B. reduces resistance in Wethen, then crosses the river and seizes Menne, Noerde, Ossendorf, and Rimbeck. In conjunction, C.C.R. mops up in Fritzlar, then relieves contingents of C.C.A. which have secured Warbeck and advanced to Daseburg.

Meanwhile, the 2nd Division advances to positions slightly north of Ederstau See. In the **U.S. Third Army** area, VIII Corps sector, Troop Carrier Command delivers desperately needed gasoline; every hour, 60 Planes zoom into Limburg Airfield, each transporting 115 five-gallon cans to forestall Patton's Third Army from becoming immobilized. The 385th Regiment, 76th Division secures part of Usingen; meanwhile, its 417th Regiment overruns heavy German resistance in the Finsternathal-Dorfweil-Schmitten area and drives to positions near the 385th Regiment, battling in Usingen. In the **XX Corps** area, excellent German defenses along the Eder and Fulda Rivers hinder Corps progress toward Kassel; however, the 6th Armored Division establishes a small bridgehead across the Fulda at Malsfeld; other units search for crossings. The resistance prompts the 6th Armored to divert its attention from Leipzig to Weimar, but Mulhaussen remains the primary objective. The 65th and 80th Divisions continue to trail the Armor, the former driving toward Kassel, the latter completing its crossing of the Rhine. In the **XII Corps** sector, the 4th Armored continues to advance, attacking toward Eisenach during the afternoon; C.C.B. seizes Hersfeld and races to Bosserode; C.C.A. advances to Wolfershausen and pauses for the night, but advance contingents outpost Dankmarsheim. General Patton is attempting to replace 4th Armored's loss of the Task Force (one Company of Tanks, and one Company of Armored Infantry, 11 Officers and 282 men) which had been captured at Hammelburg. In conjunction, the 90th Division shadows the Armor, advancing to general line Nieder Jossa-Kruspis-Grossenmoor. In the 11th Armored sector, C.C.B. advances to Grossenlueder, trailed by C.C.R. which halts at Reichlos; in conjunction, the 26th Division trails the Armor toward Fulda. Meanwhile, the 2nd Cavalry Group continues to screen the right flank of the Corps. **6th Army Group** In the **U.S. Seventh Army** area, **XV Corps** sector, the 157th Regiment, 45th Division, gets Air and Artillery support as it continues to reduce resistance in Aschaffenburg. Meanwhile, the balance of the Division advances steadily. In addition, the 3rd Division enlarges its Main River bridgehead. In the **XXI Corps** sector, the newly attached 12th Armored Division (detached from XV Corps) leads the assault against the Wuerzburg-Schweinfurt-Kitzingen area, followed by the 4th and 42nd Divisions on the right and left respectively. Meanwhile, the 10th Armored Division, still pushing south, secures Bammenthal, Leimen, St. Ilgen, and Sandhausen. In addition, the 63rd Division drives to Neckargemund. In the **VI Corps** sector, the 63rd Division (XXI Corps) is relieved by the 100th Division. In the **French 1st Army** area, an assault across the Rhine begins; the 3rd Algerian Division crosses near Speyer while the 2nd Moroccans cross at Germersheim. Resistance is firm, but the Germans have been caught off guard and cannot halt the advance. **(Atlantic-Eastern Europe)** Forces of the First Ukrainian Front seize Ratibor, a Moravian Gap outpost. Contingents of the Second Ukrainian Front seize Nitra, then cross the Vah River and take Galanta. Meanwhile, troops of the Third Ukrainian Front, operating on the right flank, advance toward Sopron, Hungary, and Wiener Neustadt in Austria. Meanwhile, other elements of the Third Front seize Koermend, Szentgotthard, and Vasar, in the Raba River Valley, also in Hungary.

April 1st 1945 — (Pacific-Philippines) Luzon In the U.S. **Sixth Army** area, RCT 158 lands near Legaspi on the Bicol Peninsula without incident, subsequent to a Naval and Air bombardment, seizing the village of Legaspi, its port, and its Airstrip. In addition, the assault force seizes Libog. Meanwhile, the 2nd Battalion encounters resistance near Daraga.

General MacNider comes ashore and assumes command. In the **I Corps** area, the 128th Regiment, 32nd Division regains previously lost ground along the Villa Verde Trail; however, torrential rains hinder operations for several days. The 3rd Battalion, 27th Regiment, 25th Division seizes the ridge leading to Mt. Myoka and begins to secure a spur, west of the crest. In the **XI Corps** area, the 43rd Division whacks the south flank of the Shimbu Line; its 172nd Regiment mops up on Hill 1200 while the majority of the 103rd Regiment in the Maybancal region. In the **XIV Corps** sector, contingents of the 7th Cavalry, 1st Cavalry Division advance to Alaminos. Meanwhile, the 5th Cavalry continues driving east while the 2nd Squadron, 12th Cavalry attacks Imoc Hill, southwest of Calauan. In addition, the 1st Battalion, 187th Regiment, 11th Airborne Division seizes Bukel Hill. In conjunction, the 2nd Battalion, clears Route 416 between Cuenca to Dita. **Southern Philippines** In the **U.S. Eighth Army** area, the 185th Regiment, 40th Division pounds its way to the edge of Talisay on Negros. Granada falls to the 160th Regiment. Meanwhile, on Cebu, the 2nd Battalion, 182nd Regiment, American Division, attacks Bolo Ridge, northwest of Guadalupe, encountering heavily fortified defenses, including caves, tunnels, and pillboxes. **(Pacific-Okinawa)** At 08:30, subsequent to a huge Naval and Air bombardment by Forces of the Fifth Fleet, the Joint Expeditionary Force (TF 51) under Admiral Turner lands the III Amphibious Corps (1st and 6th Marine Divisions) and the XXIV Corps (7th and 96th Divisions), U.S. Tenth Army on the southwest shore of Okinawa near Hagushi, against light opposition. The Northern Attack Force (TF 53), under Rear Admiral Reifsnider, lands the Marines north of the Bishi River, and the Southern Attack Force (TF55), under Rear Admiral J. L. Hall, lands the Infantry south of the river. Both move inland, gaining a beachhead about 15,000 yards long and between 4,000-5,000 yards deep. The XXIV Corps' 7th Division seizes Kadena Airfield while the 96th Division secures the area south and southeast of its beaches, advancing to a river beyond Chatan on the coast. The III Corps seizes Yontan Airfield with its 6th Marine Division while the 1st Marine Division races south in conjunction with the XXIV Corps and breezes through Sobe village. U.S. Naval damages during invasion: Battleship *West Virginia* (BB-48), by Kamikaze; Destroyer *Pritchett* (DD-561), by Dive Bomber; Destroyer Escort *Vammen*, by striking mine; Minesweeper *Skirmish* (AM-303), by Dive Bomber; Attack Cargo Ships *Achernar* (AKA-53) and *Tyrrell* (AKA-80), by Kamikazes. In addition, the Attack Transports *Elmore* (APA-42) and *Alpine* (APA-92) are damaged by a Horizontal Bomber and a Kamikaze respectively. **(Pacific-Japan)** Back on the 17th of April, the Japanese agreed to get packages to the Allied P.O.W.s, claiming it couldn't accomplish the mission because of the Allied blockade. The Japanese are guaranteed safe passage. The *Awa Maru* departed Moji, Japan on April 17th, heading for Singapore and from there she would move to Indonesia and then back to Japan via Hong Kong. The Vessel picks up many Japanese passengers along the route. On April 1st, a Submarine, the U.S.S. *Queenfish*, operating in heavy fog and poor visibility sinks the Vessel. The U.S.S. *Seafish* moves in to help locate any survivors; twelve men are rescued. The *Queenfish* is ordered back to port and her Commanding Officer, Commander Charles E. Laughlin is scheduled for a court martial. The trial is held on Guam. Intelligence sources confirm that the Vessel had picked up ammunition, bombs and Planes and the defense acknowledges that the *Queenfish* had received dispatches concerning the *Awa Maru*, but explains that the Commanding Officer had never received any dispatches concerning the Vessel's route or time schedule. Two of the charges are dismissed, but Laughlin is convicted of "negligence in obeying orders"; he receives a letter of admonition from the Secretary of the Navy as a sentence. **(Pacific-Burma)** In central Burma, the British regroup and simultaneously launch limited attacks while awaiting the 4th Corps (Ind. 5th, and 17th Divisions, and 255th Tank Brigade) to launch a full scale assault down the Mandalay-Rangoon Railroad; the Indian 19th Division is to trail Corps and conduct mop-up operations. Meanwhile, the 33 Corps starts to advance down the Irrawaddy River Valley toward Prome. **(Atlantic-Western Europe) 21st Army Group** Army Group assumes command of the British I Corps which is detached by Canadian First Army. The British Second Army continues to advance from the Rhine toward the Elbe River in the Hamburg-Wittenburg region; advance contingents ford the Dortmund-Ems Canal and encounter the first line of organized German resistance. Meanwhile, the Canadian 2nd Corps expands the Emmerich bridgehead. In addition, the 30th Corps advances toward Dortmund-Ems Canal at Rheine, and the 8 Corps enlarges the bridgeheads at the Dortmund-Ems Canal toward Osnabrueck with its 6th Airborne and 11th Armored Divisions. In the **U.S. Ninth Army** area, contact is made with the U.S. First Army at Lippstadt, encircling the Ruhr industrial region. The linkage traps Army B in its entirety and also corrals two Corps of Army Group H. In the **XIII Corps** area, the U.S. 5th Armored drives toward the Weser River, spearheading the Corps' offensive; it bypasses Muenster. However, it will be assaulted by the 17th Airborne Division; C.C.R. drives to Greffen at the Ems. Meanwhile, C.C.B. advances to Warendorf and sends out Patrols. In the **XIX Corps** sector, C.C.B., 2nd Armored links with elements of the 3rd Armored's Task Force Kane (VII Corps, First Army) at Lippstadt. The U.S. First Army's 3rd Armored Division's C.C.A., takes Cologne-Berlin Autobahn, moving through Teutoburger Wald, but it is unable to pass Augustdorf and Oerlinghausen. The XVI Corps maintains its operation to reduce enemy resistance south of Haltern; the 137th Regiment, 75th Division seizes Recklinghausen as it advances toward the Zweig Canal; the 137th Regiment drives to the Rhein-Herne Canal. Meanwhile, the 320th Regiment mops up along the Rhine-Herne Canal. **12th Army Group** In the **U.S. First Army** area, the 3rd Armored Division attacks Paderborn, sending columns from the south, southwest, and the southeast, seizing it. In conjunction, the 1st Division (minus) pivots southwest of Paderborn to cut off German escape from the Ruhr (Rose) pocket; contingents repulse an enemy breakout attempt in the Winterberg-Medebvach region. In conjunction, the 9th Division drives north, northwest, and west, committing three Regiments to sever enemy escape routes from the Ruhr pocket. In addition, the 8th and 78th Divisions clear the area along the Sieg River line. The XVIII Corps (Airborne) is attached to First Army, detached from First Allied Airborne Army, and also participates in the campaign to terminate resistance in the Ruhr pocket. In the **III Corps** sector, mop-up operations continue while Corps awaits new orders. In the **V Corps** sector, the 9th Armored Division enlarges its Diemel bridgehead, north of Warburg, establishing contact with VII Corps (104th Division) at Rimbeck. **6th Army Group** In the **U.S. Seventh Army** area, German resistance is evaporating in the XXII Corps sector, except at Aschaffenburg where vicious house-by-house fighting ensues; the 1st Battalion, 157th Regiment, 45th Division seizes the high ground northeast of the city, while the remainder of the Battalion clears the city. In the **XXI Corps** sector, the attack continues with the 12th Armored spearheading east and northeast, trailed by the 4th and 42nd Divisions on the right and left respectively. Armored columns close against Koenigshofen and Wuerzburg, initiating an assault against the former. Meanwhile, the VI Corps attacks southeastward, spearheaded by the 10th Armored Division, trailed by the 63rd and 100th Divisions (left and right respectively) encountering unorganized resistance along the Neckar; contact is established with French contingents on the right flank. In the **U.S. Third Army** area, **VIII Corps** sector, the 76th Division concludes its offensive in the sector west of Frankfurt-Bad Nauheim Autobahn after overrunning Ursingen and several other towns. In the **XX Corps** sector, the 80th Division remains behind to clear Kassel while the 6th Armored Division advances east from the Fulda River. Meanwhile, the XII Corps has been getting far out front of the XV and XX Corps; its 4th and 11th Armored Divisions spearhead, trailed by the 26th and 90th Divisions; however, the progress has exposed both flanks. C.C.B., 4th Armored, drives to the Werra River, establishing a small Infantry bridgehead; Engineers construct a pontoon bridge during the night of the 1st. In conjunction, the 11th Armored, driving north, reaches Frankenheim and Kaltensundheim, with C.C.A. and C.C.B. respectively. Elements of C.C.A. also reach Reichenhausen. Meanwhile, the 26th Division's 101st Regiment attacks Fulda. In additional activity, the reserve 71st Division, moves north from Hanau to intercept a bypassed S.S. force. In the **French 1st Army** area, the 2nd Corps severs the Karlsruhe-Frankfurt highway near Mingolsheim and Bruchsal on its left and also drives to Linkenheim on the right. **(Atlantic-Eastern Europe)** The German Garrison at Glogau on the Oder in Silesia is completely destroyed by elements of the First Ukrainian Front. Contingents of the Second Ukrainian Front maintain their western drive along the Danube toward Vienna. Meanwhile, forces of the Third Ukrainian Front seize Soprun in Hungary, then drive toward Vienna (Austria); Bulgarian troops support additional units clearing the region southwest of Lake Balaton in Hungary. **(Atlantic-Italy) 15th Army Group** In the **British Eighth Army**, 5th Corps area the 2nd Commando Brigade launches Operation ROAST; however, as the unit moves by water to secure Comacchio Spit between the lake and the sea, the craft become grounded temporarily in the mud of the shallow lake, hindering the operation.

April 1st 1945 — The Fleet which came to stay off Okinawa.

U.S. Armor moving inland on Okinawa.

Marines advancing on Okinawa.

German Officers surrendering Hersfeld, Germany.

Ernie Pyle, renowned, reporter (dubbed GIs friend), talking with the troops on Okinawa.

April 2nd 1945 — (Pacific-S.E.A.C.) Admiral Mountbatten, subsequent to meeting with Military leaders in Kandy concerning capture of Rangoon, decides on an amphibious invasion to seize it; the attack will be launched from Akayab and Kyaukpyu before the monsoon and not later than May 5th. **(Pacific-Philippines)** Luzon In the **U.S. Sixth Army** area, RCT 158 deploys defensively near Legaspi on the Bicol Peninsula to defend its bridgehead against crack Japanese troops determined to prevent a U.S. advance to Highway 1, running north from the San Bernardino Strait. Severe enemy fire halts movement of the 1st Battalion at Bantog; the 2nd Battalion rescues isolated troops at Daraga, then withdraws. In the **I Corps** sector, elements of the 33rd Division advance along Highway 9 toward Baguio, while elements of the 35th Regiment, 25th Division, attack to secure "Fishhook" Ridge off Highway 5, in the vicinity of Kapintalan. In the **XI Corps** sector, the 1st Infantry, 6th Division reinitiates its northward attack, but heavy resistance hinders progress. In the **XIV Corps** sector, the 5th Cavalry, 1st Cavalry Division drives to San Pablo, as the 7th Cavalry advances toward Mt. Malepunyo. In the **U.S. Eighth Army** area, the 185th Regiment secures Talisay and its Airfield (Negros), then advances toward Silay, halting at the Silay River due to a destroyed bridge. On Cebu, the 2nd Battalion, 182nd Regiment secures a hold on Bolo Ridge and is relieved by the 1st Battalion, 132nd Regiment. Meanwhile, the 3rd Battalion, 132nd Regiment hits strong enemy defenses outside Talamban, pulling back to allow Naval Surface Vessels to bombard the enemy. On the Sulu Archipelago, subsequent to a Air and Naval bombardment of nearby Bongao Island, elements of the 41st Division land on Sanga Sanga Island, in the Tawi Tawi Group, without incident and secure the Airfield. Marine Aircraft fly cover for the landing. Soon after, contact is established with Philippine Guerrillas who control most of the island. The Destroyer U.S.S. *Shaw* (DD-373) becomes damaged by grounding off Leyte. **(Pacific-Ryukyu Islands-Okinawa)** The 2nd Marine Division throws the Japanese main body off guard by feigning an invasion on the eastern side of the island at the Minatoga beaches. Meanwhile, the Japanese still offer only nominal resistance as the U.S. Tenth Army drives inland. Both Kadena and Yontan Airfields are operational for emergency use. Artillery-spotting Planes begin to arrive; the first U.S. Plane to land on the island is one from Marine Observation Squadron 2 which lands on Yontan Airstrip. In the **III Corps** area, the 6th Marine Division drives into the foothills of Yontan-Zan, after securing a peninsula northwest of Hagushi to eradicate entrenched resistance in the ridges and mountains. Meanwhile, the 1st Marine Division's 1st Marines advance on the right; two Battalions of the 1st Marines push to line Ishimmi-Kutoku-Chatan. In the **XXIV Corps** area, the 184th Regiment, 7th Division, closes a gap on the left flank, while the 17th Regiment advances to the high ground dominating Nakagusuku Bay; Patrols move to the east coast, slicing the island in two. In addition, the 32nd Regiment eliminates a strongpoint south of Koza. Meanwhile, the 96th Division drives forward, getting elements beyond Shimabuku and near Futema on the left and right respectively; however, the Japanese stronghold near Mombaru hinders the center thrust of the Divisional advance. In other activity, a Convoy embarking the U.S. 77th Division from the Kerama Islands is attacked by Japanese Planes, including Kamikazes. Naval casualties off the Ryukyu Islands: the Destroyer *Prichett* (DD-561) is damaged by a Horizontal Bomber; the Destroyer *Foreman* (DD-633) is damaged by a Dive Bomber; he Destroyers *Borie* (DD-704) and *Franks* (DD-554) are damaged by collision; the

Attack Transports *Chilton* (APA-38), *Henrico* (APA-45), *Goodbue* (APA-107), and *Telfair* (APA-210); and the LST 599 are damaged by Kamikazes. In addition, the Attack Cargo Ship *Lacerta* (AKA-29) is damaged accidentally by U.S. Naval gunfire. **(Pacific-Yellow Sea)** U.S. Carrier-based Aircraft sink the Japanese Defense Vessel No. 186 and the Transport No. 17. **(Atlantic-Western Europe) 21st Army Group** Headquarters Netherlands District assumes responsibility for sector of British I Corps as Headquarters of I Corps passes to British Second Army command. In the **Canadian First Army** area, I Corps sector, the British 49th Division advances against Arnhem from the Nijmegen bridgehead while the Canadian First Army (attached to Br. Second Army) attacks north toward Doesburg and Zutphen. In the **British Second Army** area, the 30th Corps moves along the Twenthe Canal and Armor continues driving toward Lingen. In the 12th Corps sector, the British 7th Armored Division drives into Rheine; however, German resistance at its Airfields is tenacious. In the **U.S. Ninth Army** area, **XIII Corps** sector, the 17th Airborne Division drives into Muenster, eliminating all resistance except a strong pocket in the middle of the city. The 5th Armored closes on the Weser River; C.C.B. columns nears Borgholzhausen; C.C.R. converges on Herford. In the **XIX Corps** sector, the 2nd Armored Division is still engulfed in combat to secure the Teutoburger Wald passes, but the difficult terrain, defiant roadblocks, and destroyed bridges greatly hinder progress. However, C.C.A., reinforced by contingents of C.C.R., sever the main road from the Autobahn to Bielefeld; other contingents reach the fringes of Oerlinghausen. Meanwhile, C.C.B. plows through Teutoburger Wald advancing to the area near Hiddesen. In other Corps activity, the 83rd Division continues securing the right flank of the Corps along the Lippe, while simultaneously fortifying its bridgehead at Hamm. The 30th Division, minus RCT 119, drives toward Teutoburger Wald to relieve 2nd Armored Division units. In the 8th Armored Division zone, C.C.B. battles viciously at Neuhaus, outside of Paderborn. In the **XVI Corps** sector, the 75th Division advances to Dortmund-Ems Canal; elements relieve the 134th Regiment, 35th Division at Zweig Canal. The 137th and 320th Regiments, 35th Division deploy defensively along the Rhein-Herne Canal. **12th Army Group** In the **U.S. First Army** area, **VII Corps** sector, elements of the 3rd Armored Division enter Dahl without incident. In the 1st Division zone, positions are fortified to intercept any German attempt to penetrate from the west. Rimbach falls to the 413th Regiment, 104th Division; the 415th Regiment handily defeats a German counterattack near Medebach, then drives west to Kuestelberg. The 9th Division seizes Berghausen, Berleberg, Girkhausen, and Neu Astenberg. In other activity, the 8th and 78th Divisions revert to XVIII (Airborne) Corps. In the **XVIII Corps** sector, the area is expanded, encompassing the area bound by the Rhine, Ruhr, Lenne, and Sieg Rivers. The 8th Division is still battling to secure Netphen, Siegen, and the high ground north of the Sieg River. In the **III Corps** sector, C.C.A., 7th Armored Division is attached to VII Corps and moves toward Medebach. In the **V Corps** sector, C.C.B., 9th Armored Division repulses a Tank-Infantry assault against the left flank of the Diemel bridgehead. Meanwhile, the 2nd Division mops up in zone and assumes responsibility for the Eder bridges in the Affoldern region. In addition, the 102nd Cavalry Group screens the right flank of the Corps and maintains contact with Third Army. In the **U.S. Third Army** area, General Patton receives reports that the German 2nd Mountain Division has ambushed a hospital column, killing one Officer and two enlisted men and he is also informed that they have captured an ammunition dump near Frankfurt. Rumors spread that the entire hospital contingent has been wiped out and that all Nurses had been raped. Actually, the three men had been killed during the initial fighting, the ammunition dump had not been detonated and none of the Nurses had been harmed. The Germans merely seize the Vehicles and depart. On the following day, contingents of the 71st Division and the 10th Infantry Regiment, 5th Division (Colonel R.P. Bell) and a Reconnaissance Battalion (Lt. Col. M.W. Frame), 13th Armored capture the Germans. The encounter costs the Germans 500 killed and 800 prisoners; the U.S. troops were still under the impression that the German atrocities had occurred. The **VIII Corps** prepares to attack between the XX and XII Corps. In the **XX Corps** sector, 6th Armored, having crossed the Fulda, drives toward the Werra River from Malsfeld; contingents advance to the Werra near Bad Sooden and search for crossing sites; other elements secure a bridgehead at Reichensachen. The 80th Division repulses strong counterattacks, supported by Tanks, and drives to the edge of Kassel. The 65th Division, driving east from the Fulda along the Corps' right flank, encounters only sporadic resistance, making excellent progress. In the **XII Corps** sector, C.C.B., 4th Armored Division, enlarges the Creuzburg bridgehead to Neukirchen; C.C.A. secures the high ground above Sprichra by use of a pontoon bridge. German ground forces offer slight resistance only, but the Luftwaffe attacks both bridgeheads. The 90th Division crosses the Werra near Berka while the 11th Armored Division drives to the river north and south of Meiningen. C.C.B., 11th Armored Division establishes a small bridgehead at Wasungen, and C.C.A. secures a bridgehead at Grimmenthal and seizes a bridge at Vachdorf. The 26th Division, trailing well behind the Armor, is reducing remaining resistance in the Fulda region. In addition, the 2nd Cavalry Group and the 71st Division battle bypassed enemy forces north of Hanau. Meanwhile, the 71st Division throws its full strength into the Waldensberg area, subsequent to the Germans overrunning the rear of the 2nd Calvary Squadron, seizing the town. **6th Army Group** In the **U.S. Seventh Army** area, **XV Corps** sector, the Germans continue raising heavy resistance against the 157th Regiment, 45th Division; however, the stronghold surrenders on the following day. The 14th Armored Division drives toward Neustadt and Ostheim as the Germans are retreating. In the **XXI Corps** sector, contingents of the 12th Armored, supported by units of the 42nd Division, drive toward Wuerzburg; the 222nd Regiment seizes Marienburg along the Main directly across from the town. In conjunction, the 232nd Regiment, 42nd Division reduces resistance west and north of the Main River in the Wertheim-Marktheidenfeld area. Meanwhile, C.C.R. 12th Armored, bolstered by contingents of the 22nd Regiment, 4th Division seizes Koenigshofen, and the 8th Regiment secures the area southwest of Wuerzburg in addition to establishing a small bridgehead at the Main near Ochsenfurt. In the **VI Corps** sector, the 63rd and 100th Divisions continue mopping up behind the 10th Armored Division which still encounters strong resistance as it closes on Heilbronn. In the **French 1st Army** area, 2nd Corps sector, Bruchsal, Oestringen, and Ubstadt are secured by the 3rd Algerian Division. Meanwhile, the 2nd Moroccan Infantry Division occupies Hochstetten and Karsdorf. **(Atlantic-Italy) 15th Army Group** In the **British Eighth Army** area, 5th Corps sector, elements of the 2nd Commando Brigade establish a bridgehead on the western shore of Comacchio Spit. In conjunction, the 43rd (Royal Marines) Commandos secure the strip of land between Reno and the sea and will assault the spit from the east.

Medical Vehicles crossing the Rhine in Third Army sector.

April 3rd 1945 — (United States) The British get reassurances from the Americans that U.S. Air units will not be withdrawn from assisting them in Burma before June 1st or before the capture of Rangoon. In other activity, the Joint Chiefs of Staff appoint General MacArthur Commander-in-Chief, U.S. Forces, Pacific and in addition designate Admiral Nimitz Commander of all Naval Forces in the Pacific. **(Pacific-Malay Peninsula)** The U.S. Minesweeper YMS-71 sinks after striking a mine off Borneo. **(Pacific-Philippines)** Luzon In the **U.S. Sixth Army** area, RCT 158 still receives stiff resistance as it advances along a ridge near Daraga. In the **XI Corps** sector, the Baldy Force is established (169th Regiment, 43rd Division, and 112th Cavalry) to guard the northern flank of the Corps. After dark, the 103rd Regiment, 43rd Division begins a quiet advance on Mt. Sembrano to make contact with the 1st Cavalry Division. Meanwhile, the 1st Regiment, 6th Division halts its attack to permit heavy bombardment of enemy positions by Artillery and mortars; in addition, Planes support the operation. On Caballo Island, Tanks advance, but they do not reach enemy positions. In the **XIV Corps** sector, the 187th Regiment, 11th Airborne Division drives to Lipa, leaving its 1st Battalion behind to eliminate some previously bypassed resistance on Mt. Macolod. Meanwhile, elements of the 18th Regiment drives into Tiaong without incident. **Southern Philippines** In the **U.S. Eighth Army** area, the 185th Regiment crosses the Guinhalaron River on Negros and advances to the Imbang River. Meanwhile, the 40th Reconnaissance Troop encounters fierce resistance as it advances along the Sila-Guimbalon road when it nears the latter. On Cebu, Bolo Ridge is secured by contingents of the 132nd Regiment, Americal Division; however, elements of the 3rd Battalion have been halted by severe enemy resistance, prompting Air attacks to support the operation. Meanwhile, contingents of the 108th Regiment, 40th Division, land at Masbate on the island of Masbate to bolster Guerrillas attempting to secure the island. In other activity, organized Japanese resistance is terminated on Romblon; the island is turned over to Guerrillas on April 5th. **(Pacific-Okinawa)** In the **III Corps** sector, the 6th Marine Division drives about 7,000 yards securing the Yontan-Zan hill, and in addition, its left flank expands to the Ishikawa Isthmus. Meanwhile, the 1st Marine Division advances to the east coast and sends Patrols which reach Hizaonna on the Katchin Peninsula. In other activity, a disabled F6F makes a successful landing on Yontan Airfield. In the **XXIV Corps** sector, the 7th and 96th Divisions drive south, the former reaching Kuba and the latter advancing to the general line Atanniya-Futema-Chiyunna-Isa on its western flank, but the elements driving on the eastern flank cannot reach Unjo. The

Escort Carrier *Wake Island* (CVE-65) and the High Speed Minesweeper *Hambleton* (DMS-20) are damaged by Kamikazes, and the Destroyer *Sproston* (DD-557) is damaged by a Dive Bomber. In addition, the LST 554 suffers damage from a storm. **(Atlantic-Western Europe)** U.S. Army Aircraft sink the German U-Boats U-1221, U-2542, and U-3505, off Kiel, Germany. **21st Army Group** In the **British Second Army** area, 30th Corps sector, the Guards' Armored Division advances to the Dortmund-Ems Canal near Lingen. In the 12th Corps sector, Rheine is mopped up by the British 52nd Division. In the 8th Corps sector, the British close on Osnabrueck. In the **U.S. Ninth Army** area, **XIII Corps** sector, enemy resistance in Muenster is totally crushed by the 17th Airborne Division, while the 5th Armored Division, followed by the 84th Division, advances to the Weser River. The bridges have been blown; C.C.A. nears Herford, while C.C.R. advances along the Autobahn and accepts surrender of German forces in Bad Oeynhausen. Meanwhile, the 102nd Division is attached to Corps. In the **XIX Corps** sector, the attack against the Ruhr begins as it continues driving east into Germany. Subsequent to relieving the 2nd Armored contingents at Teutoburger Wald, elements of the 30th Division secure part of Forst Berlebeck. Meanwhile, the 2nd Armored Division advances east toward the Weser. C.C.R. severs the Oerlinghausen-Lage road at Mackenbruch. A Task Force from C.C.A., also driving southeast, drives through Osterheide, reaching Lage. Meanwhile, additional C.C.A. units take Oerlinghausen, and with supporting flanking movements of C.C.R., secures the region around Pivitsheide. In addition, C.C.B. seizes Berlebeck. The 83rd Division mops up in Neuhaus subsequent to relieving contingents of the 8th Armored Division; in addition, it continues driving along the Corps right flank, reducing resistance near the Lippe River. The 8th Armored Division begins its drive against the Ruhr pocket; C.C.A. elements advance toward Erwitte; C.C.R. commits contingents against Elsen in support of C.C.B. and also sends columns to Weckinghausen. In addition, the 95th Division relieves the 83rd Division and prepares to attack the Ruhr pocket. In the **XVI Corps** sector, the 75th Division prepares to drive across the Dortmund-Ems Canal. **12th Army Group** The U.S. XVIII and III Corps are ordered to attack in conjunction with the U.S. Ninth Army to eradicate the enemy south of the Ruhr and east of the Rhine. In addition, First Army directs the V and VII Corps to regroup and maintain their eastward drives. In the **VII Corps** sector, the 3rd Armored Division establishes contact with contingents of 8th Armored (XIX Corps). Meanwhile, Hardehausen, Kuestelberg, and Scherfede fall to elements of the 104th Division. Subsequently, C.C.A., 7th Armored Division moves into Kuestelberg, relieves the 415th Regiment, and is attached to the 9th Division. In the 9th Division zone, Oberkirchen is seized by contingents of the 47th Regiment, while the 60th Regiment captures Westfeld. In conjunction, the 39th Regiment secures the area west of Zueschen-Winterberg, but it does pull back slightly at one area. In the **XVIII (Airborne) Corps** sector, the 8th, 78th, and 97th Divisions continue to advance in their sectors. The Germans mount a night attack against a contingent of the 13th Regiment, 8th Division at Birken. P.F.C. Walter C. Wetzel, standing guard, sounds the alarm and his Platoon meets the threat. The Germans close fast, tossing two grenades into the Command Post, but Wetzel blankets both, saving the other men in the outpost. Wetzel gives his life, but the Platoon throws back the attack; he receives the Medal of Honor posthumously. In the **III Corps** sector, preparations are made to attack the sector of the Ruhr pocket between the Lenne and Ruhr Rivers in con-

cert with the XVIII (Airborne) Corps, which is attacking on the left. Meanwhile, the 99th Division drives west toward Schwarzenau. In the **U.S. Third Army** area, **VIII Corps** sector, units assemble to attack the Muhlhausen-Langensalza-Gotha line. In other activity, 4th Armored Division (XII Corps) is attached to VIII Corps. In the **XX Corps** sector, elements (C.C.B.) of 6th Armored Division seize Eschwege and Reichensachen. At Kassel, the fighting continues to rage; the 80th Division seizes part of the city. Meanwhile, the 65th Division drives quickly on the Corps' right flank; however, its 260th Regiment is halted at the Reichensachen-Langenhain line to permit U.S. Armor units to pass. In addition, the 76th Division is transferred to Corps from VIII Corps. The XII Corps receives orders to halt the advance at the Gotha-Suhl line. The 4th Armored Division secures positions which control Gotha with its C.C.B.; C.C.A. drives to positions near Hoerselgau. The 90th Division secures the region Berka-Vacha east of the Werra. Followed by the 26th Division, the 11th Armored Division lunges into Thuringer Wald, a German small arms manufacturing center; C.C.A. secures the south section of Suhl after bitter house-to-house fighting, while C.C.B. drives to Oberhof. In conjunction, contingents of the 26th Division reach Schwarzbach as it nears the Werra. Meanwhile, the 71st Division, contingents of the XX Corps' 5th Division, and the 2nd Cavalry Group nudge the Germans, north of Hanau, into Budinger Wald, trapping them. In conjunction, the 2nd Cavalry Group which is attached to the 71st Division captures a detachment of Germans attempting to reach Wirtheim. In the **U.S. Fifteenth Army** area, **XXII Corps** sector, the 94th Division relieves the 102nd Division at the Rhine; the latter is attached to XIII Corps, U.S. Ninth Army. **6th Army Group** In the **U.S. Seventh Army** area, **XV Corps** sector, Corps continues its northeastern thrust; however, the obstinate Aschaffenburg is taken by the 157th Regiment. Meanwhile, Lohr falls to the 14th Armored's C.C.B. In the **XXI Corps** sector, the 222nd Regiment, 42nd Division, attached to the 12th Armored Division, attacks Wuerzburg, its 2nd Battalion crossing the Main prior to dawn and establishing a bridgehead in the western sector of the town. The 1st Battalion comes in later and expands the bridgehead. Meanwhile, the 8th Regiment, 4th Division crosses the Main at Ochsenfurt, followed by C.C.B. 12th Armored, which is forced to await bridge repairs to support the Vehicles. In the **VI Corps** sector, C.C.R. 10th Armored Division hits fierce resistance north of Heilbronn; it overcomes it to establish a small bridgehead across the Jagst River near Griesheim. In addition, the Germans raise heavy resistance against C.C.A. as it attempts to cross the Neckar River near Heilbronn. Meanwhile, C.C.B. advances to Kirchhausen-Schluchtern, against moderate resistance. In addition, the 63rd Division encounters heavy opposition as it drives on the left flank of Corps, north of the Jagst River. In the **French 1st Army** area, orders are issued to attack Karlsruhe and Pforzheim and to then prepare to secure the Black Forest. In other activity, Detachment d'Armee des Alpes attacks to secure Mt. Cenis pass. **(Atlantic-Eastern Europe)** Contingents of the Second Ukrainian Front continue advancing toward Vienna; elements north of the Danube in Czechoslovakia seize Bratislava, and to the right, elements supported by Rumanian forces capture Kremnica. South of the Danube, contingents of the Third Ukrainian Front in Austria seize Wiener Neustadt, an industrial center, and in addition, sever the rail lines leading to Vienna. Meanwhile, Bulgarian forces and contingents of the Third Ukrainian Front continue battling German forces in Hungary, southwest of Lake Balaton. Some units ford the Drava River, crossing into

Yugoslavia. **(Atlantic-Italy) 15th Army Group** In the **U.S. Fifth Army** area, **IV Corps** sector, contingents of the 96th Division and RCT 442 (Separate 100th Battalion) and the 473rd Regiment pass to Army control to attack along the Ligurian coast toward La Spezia and Massa as a diversion.

April 4th 1945 — (Pacific-Iwo Jima) The 147th Regiment, U.S.A. assumes responsibility for both ground defenses and mop-up operations on the island; the 9th Marines, 3rd Marine Division prepare to depart for Guam. **(Pacific-Philippines) Luzon** In the **U.S. Sixth Army** area, the Japanese resist tenaciously near Daraga; contingents of RCT 158 advance slowly to methodically eradicate the resistance. In the **I Corps** sector, the 129th Regiment, 33rd Division has Patrols out; one encounters intense fire as it approaches Salat, less than four air miles from Burgos. In the **XI Corps** sector, contingents of the 43rd Division take control of the Santa Maria Valley, seizing Famy, Mabitac, and Sinaloan. In conjunction, supporting weapons near the north-south highway interdict, forbidding enemy escape routes. Meanwhile, the 63rd Regiment, 6th Division relieves the 20th Regiment, assuming responsibility for the sector. In the **XIV Corps** sector, Patrols of the 5th Cavalry, 1st Cavalry Division establish contact with the 11th Airborne Division near Tiaong; the linkage totally isolates the remaining Japanese on Mt. Malepunyo. **South Philippines** In the **U.S. Eighth Army** area, the 1st Battalion, 160th Regiment occupies Concepcion on Negros subsequent to Japanese abandonment of the town. In addition, Guimbalon, a primary Japanese supply center, is seized by the 2nd Battalion, 185th Regiment. Meanwhile, on Cebu, the 182nd Regiment seizes Horseshoe Ridge, about 800 yards away from its positions on Go Chan Hill. **(Pacific-Okinawa)** In the **U.S. Tenth Army** area, III Corps Commanding General establishes his Command Post ashore. The 6th Marine Division attacks north, driving up the Ishikawa Peninsula, subsequent to relinquishing responsibility for Yontan Airstrip to the 29th Marines; all three Airstrips are declared operational for Fighter Planes. In addition, the 1st Marine Division occupies the Katchin Peninsula. In the **XXIV Corps** sector, the Japanese offer hardened opposition against the 96th Division as it drives down the west coast toward the hill mass stretching from Urasoe-Mura to Ouki. Also, the 7th Division encounters rigid resistance as it presses forward at the ruins of an ancient fortress castle west of Kuba. Offshore, the High Speed Transport *Dickerson* (APD-21) is damaged by a Kamikaze and subsequently destroyed by U.S. Forces. In addition, the Destroyer *Norman Scott* (DD-690) is damaged by collision. The LSTs 70, 166, 343, 570, 624, 675, 689, 736, 756, and 781 are damaged by grounding. Also, the LST 399 is damaged by collision. **(Atlantic-Western Europe)** Near Kiel, Germany, the German U-Boats U-237, U-749, and U-3003, are destroyed by U.S. Army Planes. **21st Army Group** The British 30th Corps establishes a bridgehead across the Dortmund-Ems Canal outside of Lingen, and the 12th Corps establishes another across the canal at Rheine. Meanwhile, 8th Corps troops enter Osnabrueck, while other contingents advance to the Weser near Minden. **12th Army Group** The U.S. Ninth Army returns to American command, being detached from 21st Army Group. In the **XIII Corps** sector, the 17th Airborne Division bolsters the defenses of Muenster. In the 5th Armored zone, the Germans blow the bridges across the Weser at Minden and Rinteln, before contingents of the British 8th Corps can negotiate surrender of the enemy. The 102nd Division is closely trailing the 5th Armored and mops up remnant pockets. In the **XIX Corps** sector, the 2nd Armored Division moves forcefully; C.C.A. contingents move to Lemgo and beyond to the Weser and

also to Pivitsheide. Meanwhile, C.C.B. drives to Kreuzenstein despite tenacious opposition and extremely difficult terrain. The 30th Division, guarding the left Corps' flank, takes Detmold and also overpowers resistance in Hiddesen, while the 83rd Division pushes feverishly on the right flank. The 95th Division drives south across the Lippe River, initiating its assault against the Ruhr pocket; contingents reach Dinker. In the 8th Armored zone, C.C.A. seizes Erwitte and has additional elements advance to the Mohne River, while C.C.R. roars ahead, capturing Ebbinghausen, Norddorf, Overhagen, Stirpe, and Voellinghausen. In the **XVI Corps** sector, the 75th Division launches an early morning attack, speeding across the Dortmund-Ems Canal, seizing Henrichenburg, Ickern, Waltrop, and some of Brambauer. In the **U.S. First Army's VII Corps** sector, the 8th Armored Division pinches out the 1st Division, while the 3rd Armored Division sets up to drive eastward, reinitiating its offensive. In the **XIX Corps** sector, German resistance begins to further diminish, resulting from strong U.S. pressure; the 104th Division secures its two zones; Forst Hardehausen, Holtheim, and Kleinenberg are secured by the 413th Regiment, and the 415th Regiment, bolstered by the 2nd Cavalry Group, whips through Briloner Stadt-Forst. In the 9th Division zone, C.C.A., 7th Armored seizes Gronebach, Hildfeld, and Niedersfeld. Meanwhile, the 47th Regiment, defending the south flank, is struck by German counterattacks at Oberkirchen; it repulses them. In conjunction, Alt Astenberg is seized by the 60th Regiment, and the 39th Regiment seizes objectives in the Gronebach-Winterberg region. In other activity, the 9th Division forms Task Force Birks, comprising the 47th Regiment and C.C.A., 7th Armored; established at 20:00, the Division and attached units are attached to III Corps. In the **XVIII Corps (Airborne)** area, the 78th Division, which is holding the left flank along the south bank of the Sieg River, is relieved by the 97th Division. Meanwhile, the 8th Division receives heavy counterattacks at both Netphen and Siegen, repelling all, and simultaneously makes some gains at other spots along its lines. In other activity, the **III Corps** is prepared to launch its forces against the Ruhr pocket. The **V Corps** continues its defensive stance, mopping up in its sector. In the **U.S. Third Army** area, **XX Corps** sector, the 6th Armored Division converges on Mulhausen; supported by Air cover, it surrounds the town and pushes strengthened Patrols into the city. C.C.A. plows northward while C.C.B. roars southward, the latter investing Koerner. Meanwhile, the beleaguered Garrison at Kassel capitulates to the 80th Division. The 80th captures a German General (and 400 men) who retains belief that the Germans will end the conflict victoriously; General Patton notes that all other German Generals have concluded that Germany has lost. The 5th Division (detached from Corps) is held in reserve to execute special missions near Frankfurt; the 76th Division moves out toward Langensalza to eliminate bypassed resistance. In other activity, the **VIII Corps** becomes operational in a new area (between the XII and XX Corps) and drives east. Patton visits Corps and notices 29 captured German World War I flags; subsequently, these standards are forwarded to the Adjutant General in Washington. The 4th Armored Division (XII Corps) is attached to Corps; C.C.B. accepts surrender of Germans holding Gotha, then advances to positions near Muehlberg while C.C.A. moves to Ohrdruf. The 65th and 89th Divisions drive east of the Fulda River, trailed by the 6th Cavalry Group, which is eradicating remnant resistance in their wake. In the **XII Corps** sector, the 90th Division gets more than it expects as it advances; the 357th Regiment seizes Marksuhl and Moehra. However, their counterpart, the 358th Regiment, strikes gold when it seizes Merkers and probes in a salt mine containing treasures including gold and Nazi Art pieces. On the 7th, General Eddy notifies Patton that he has entered the German gold reserve vault and that the equivalent of one billion dollars (paper marks) has been discovered. Eddy states that if there is any gold, it is behind a steel door; soon after, 4,500 gold bricks, each weighing 35 pounds (value $57,600,000) are discovered. The 11th Armored's C.C.A. seizes Suhl; its capture rescues many forced laborers and eliminates one more supply center as the town had manufactured small arms. In other activity, the 26th Division gets Regiments across the Werra River near Schmalkalden-Wasungen, and the 71st Division, supported with the 2nd Cavalry Group, reduces a German pocket near Hanau, eradicating a threat to the Main Supply Route. In the **U.S. Fifteenth Army** area, **XXII Corps** sector, the 97th Division is relieved by the 101st Airborne Division. In addition, the 82nd Airborne Division assumes responsibility for the 86th Division's sector. **6th Army Group** In the **U.S. Seventh Army** area, **XV Corps** sector, the ongoing advance continues to move quickly through the Spessart Mountains. Columns of C.C.B., 14th Armored Division drive to the fringes of Gemuenden. In the **XII Corps** sector, smoke screens are laid to assist the 232nd Regiment, 42nd Division and C.C.A., 12th Armored Division force a newly repaired bridge across the Wuerzburg; the 232nd pushes into the city from the east in conjunction with the 222nd Regiment (attached to C.C.A.) which drives into the city and overcomes heated resistance, seizing much of the objective. Meanwhile, C.C.B. enlarges its Ochsenfurt bridgehead to include Erlach. C.C.R., 12th Armored Division seizes Gnoetzheim and Herrnberchtheim, while the 92nd Cavalry Reconnaissance Squadron secures the high ground east of Obernbreit. Meanwhile, the Germans mount fierce resistance in the wooded region around Koenigshofen against the 12th and 22nd Regiments, 4th Division. In the **VI Corps** sector, the German resistance is also fierce at the Jagst and Neckar Rivers, prompting the attack plans against Heilbronn to be modified. The 100th Division's 3rd Battalion, 398th Regiment forces the Neckar before dawn and establishes a small bridgehead at Neckargartach. Soon after, the 100th Division receives the task to maintain the frontal assault while the 10th Armored swivels and attacks Heilbronn from the rear. C.C.A. secures Frankenbach-Neckargartach, and C.C.B. secures the region southwest of Bockingen; meanwhile, C.C.R. withdraws the bridgehead at the Jagst River north of Heilbronn. During the day, the 100th Divisions bolsters its Neckar bridgehead with its 2nd Battalion, 397th Regiment, and its 399th Regiment advances to positions west of Bockingen. In addition, the 63rd Division maintains its eastward drive north of the Jagst; elements establish a bridgehead across the Jagst near Greisheim-Herbolzheim, despite severe resistance. In the **French 1st Army** area, the Valluy Groupement, supported by additional French contingents, have come under heavy German fire near Mt. Cenis, disengaging the operation. **(Atlantic-Eastern Europe)** The beleaguered Germans lose another of their dwindling strongpoints as the Second Ukrainian Front overruns Bratislava in Czechoslovakia. In Austria, contingents of the Third Ukrainian Front converge on Vienna, reaching a point less than three miles from the city. Meanwhile, forces of the Third Ukrainian Front and supporting Bulgarian contingents eliminate the final German resistance in Hungary and pursue the retreating units into Yugoslavia. The Fourth Ukrainian Front and Czechoslovakian forces, pushing west from the Polish-Czechoslovakian border, drive from the vicinity of Nowy Targ, Poland, toward the Moravian Gap. **(Atlantic-Italy) 15th Army Group** In the **British Eighth Army** area, 5 Corps sector, the Germans mount resolute resistance at the Comacchio Spit, stopping the advance of the 2nd Commando Brigade as it approaches the Canale di Valetta; the British 56th Division moves up after dark and relieves the Commandos; however, resistance refuses to relent and subsequent attempts by the 56th also are repulsed. The British disengage. In other activity, the British pull off Operation Fry; troops of the Special Boat Service and of the 28th Garibaldi Brigade occupy four small islands in Lake Comacchio without incident.

April 5th 1945 — (United States) President Roosevelt, having received a repulsive letter from Stalin (April 3rd) fires back a response to clarify an assumed misunderstanding: "FRANKLY, I CANNOT AVOID A FEELING OF BITTER RESENTMENT TOWARD YOUR INFORMANTS, WHOEVER THEY ARE, FOR SUCH VILE MISREPRESENTATIONS OF MY ACTIONS OR THOSE OF MY TRUSTED COMPANIONS." On the 7th, Roosevelt receives another letter from Stalin, however, his tone has been changed; Stalin also dispatches a mellow letter to Winston Churchill. **(Pacific-Japan)** General Koiso's Cabinet resigns; a new Cabinet is formed under Admiral Kantaro Suzuki. **(Pacific-Philippines) Luzon** In the **U.S. Sixth Army** area, **XI Corps** sector, the 63rd Regiment, 6th Division is ordered to seize Mt. Mataba. Meanwhile, the 103rd Regiment, 43rd Division sends out many Patrols, and the 3rd Battalion (motorized) advances to Pagsanjan at Lumban and seizes a bridge. On Caballo Island, the 2nd Battalion, 151st Regiment improvises, using burning diesel oil to eliminate enemy positions. In the **XIV Corps** sector, the 1st Cavalry Division zone becomes less volatile as Japanese resistance has diminished greatly; the 5th Cavalry establishes contact with the 43rd Division near Lumban. Meanwhile, the 12th Cavalry reduces the final resistance on Imoc Hill, and the 7th Cavalry drives toward Mt. Malepunyo. In addition, the 187th Regiment, 11th Airborne Division seizes Talisay and gets elements into the western foothills of Mt. Malepunyo, while the 188th Regiment mops up to the south and east of Mt. Malepunyo. **Southern Philippines** Mop-up continues in the Visayan Passage; however, the U.S. Eighth Army proclaims the Visayan Passage campaign terminated. Guerrillas assume responsibility for Romblon Island; the operation costs the U.S. 17 killed; the Japanese lose 139 killed. On Cebu, the Americal Division fortifies its positions while it awaits reinforcements to launch an attack. On Negros, the 160th Regiment advances toward Hill 3155, subsequently dubbed Dolan Hill. **(Pacific-Ryukyu Islands)** The Fleet Marine Force Reconnaissance Battalion lands on the northern coast of Tsugen Shima, Eastern Islands, the only one of six islands guarding the eastern beaches of Okinawa that is staunchly defended. In the III Amphibious Corps sector, the 22nd Marines, 6th Marine Division advance to the Atsutabaru-Kin line, as it drives up the Ishikawa Isthmus. Meanwhile, the 1st Marine Division dispatches Patrols to the south, while simultaneously mopping up; it checks Yabuci Shima, off the Katchin Peninsula. In other activity, the 96th Division, U.S.A., hits strong opposition in the vicinity of Ginowan and Uchitomari, hindering its advance. The Japanese holding Cactus Ridge repulse the 383rd Regiment, but the 382nd Regiment makes slight progress. In conjunction, the 7th Division advances to positions alongside the 96th Division. Naval damages: Battleship *Nevada* (BB-36) by coastal defense guns; Light Minelayer *Harry F. Bauer* (DM-26) by Aircraft torpedo; Seaplane Tender (Destroyer) *Thornton* (AVD-11) by collision; Oilers *Ashtabula* (AO-70) and *Escalante* (AO-70) by collision; LSTs 273, 810, and 940 and

1,000, by collision; LST 698 by grounding. In other activity, the Destroyer *Hudson* (DD-475) sinks the Japanese Submarine RO-41. **(Pacific-Volcano Islands-Iwo Jima)** A U.S. Advanced Naval Air Base is established on Iwo Jima. The U.S. Repair Ship *Agenor* (ARL-3) and the LST 646 are damaged by collision. **(Pacific-Burma)** The British Fourteenth Army releases the Indian 19th Division to the 4th Corps. **(Atlantic-Western Europe) 21st Army Group** In the **Canadian First Army** area, the area between Nijmegen and the Neder Rijn is totally cleared of enemy resistance by the Canadian I Corps. In the Canadian 2nd Corps sector, contingents establish a bridgehead across the Twenthe Canal and seize Almelo, east of the Ijssel River. In the **British Second Army** area, 30th Corps sector, the British 43rd Division retains control of Hengelo while the British 3rd Division seizes Lingen. Meanwhile, the 12th Corps enlarges its Dortmund-Ems Canal bridgehead while the 8th Corps secures the remainder of Osnabrueck as it nears the Weser River. **12th Army Group** In the **U.S. Ninth Army** area, XIII Corps sector, the 17th Airborne Division (minus RCT 194) is attached to XVI Corps; RCT 194 is serving with XIX Corps. The 102nd Division continues driving east, gaining an average of 20-35 miles a day. In the **XIX Corps** sector, the 2nd Armored Division establishes a beachhead at the Weser south of Hameln. By the end of the day, C.C.B. controls Brockensen, Frenke, Hajen, and Heyen. In conjunction, C.C.A.'s bridgehead stretches from Rohrsen to Voremberg. In addition, the 83rd Division continues to roll over many towns and villages as it closes on the Weser. Meanwhile, the 95th Division enlarges its bridgehead south of the Lippe; its 377th Regiment drives south toward Soest, moving beyond Wiltrop. The 8th Armored Division also is closing on Soest for a combined attack with the 95th. In the **XVI Corps** sector, the remaining resistance in Brambauer is crushed by elements of the 75th Division. In the **U.S. First Army** area, its first elements enter the struggle to gain the Ruhr; the III Corps is committed. The 9th (north) 99th (south) Infantry, and the 7th Armored Divisions (center) advance. Task Force Birks (9th) secures Assinghausen, Bruchhausen, Brunskappel, Elleringhausen, Wiemeringhausen, and Wullmeringhausen. Meanwhile, the 60th Regiment severs the Oberkirchen-Nordenau Road and the 39th Regiment captures Silbach. The 99th Division seizes Aue, Latrop, and Muesse as it drives toward Wingeshausen. Meanwhile the 7th Armored is driving to the fringes of Winkhausen; however, contingents bypass and advance toward Grafschaft. During the heated fighting in the 7th Armored zone, the Germans at Alemert are slicing the 1st Platoon of Company C, 48th Armored Infantry Battalion. Corporal Thomas J. Kelly ignores the menacing enemy opposition and advances to rescue and give aid to wounded troopers, navigating 300 yards of open ground under a thunderclap of intense enemy fire; he runs the gauntlet ten times and each trip brings out a wounded man, saving them from certain death. The agonizing ordeal drains all his strength; nevertheless, he refuses to be evacuated until the objective is taken. His inspired Platoon obliges; Kelly receives the Medal of Honor for his extraordinary courage under fire. In the **VII Corps** sector, the 3rd Armored Division begins an eastward drive, sending four columns abreast against sporadic resistance, gaining over twenty miles. The **V Corps** is ordered to drive to the Duderstadt-Schlotheim line. In addition, the **XVIII (Airborne) Corps** regroups to attack the Ruhr pocket. The 8th Division encounters fierce opposition as it advances north of the Sieg River while maintaining its positions in the vicinity of Siegen and mopping up in Netphen. In the **U.S. Third Army** area, XX Corps sector, C.C.A. and C.C.B., 6th

Armored Division secure Muhlhausen by 09:05; subsequently, C.C.A. attacks Langensalza from the northwest, as the 65th Division closes on the town from the southwest, the latter securing most of the town by evening. The 80th Division opens up an attack east of Kassel, but it is aborted upon orders; the Division is relieved by the 69th Division (V Corps). Meanwhile, the 76th Division is attacking east. The town of Eisenach surrenders to contingents of the 89th Division; however, the Germans begin returning toward the town, compelling the 353rd Regiment to withdraw. In the **XII Corps** sector, regrouping takes place for a southeastward attack; C.C.R., 11th Armored Division seizes Meiningen and its Airport, relinquishing it later to the 101st Regiment, 26th Division. The 328th Regiment, 26th Division seizes Schmalkalden across the Werra River, then establishes contact with the 90th Division at Meiningen. In addition, the 71st Division, guarding the Corps' right flank, begins moving toward the Fulda region. **6th Army Group** In the **U.S. Seventh Army** area, XV Corps sector, Gemuenden falls to elements of the 14th Armored and 3rd Infantry Divisions. In the **XXI Corps** sector, Wuerzburg falls to C.C.A., 12th Armored and contingents of the 42nd Division. C.C.B., secures a bridge at Kitzingen, permitting the 8th Regiment, 4th Division to establish a bridgehead there. Meanwhile, C.C.R. seizes Ippesheim and Seinsheim, and the 12th and 22nd Regiments, 4th Division continue clearing the area east of Koenigshofen. In the **U.S. VI Corps** sector, the 100th Division still pounds Heilbronn from the front while the 10th Armored Division gets elements into the northern portion of the town; C.C.B. passes into reserve subsequent to reducing resistance in Bockingen and encounters French troops as it moves southward along the Neckar River near Lauffen. In the 63rd Division zone, contingents of the 253rd Regiment drive into Moeckmuehl, moving from house to house in bitter fighting; other elements advance along the Jagst River, closing on Hardehauser Wald. Meanwhile, the 254th Regiment consolidates its positions, and the 255th Regiment advances to general line Merchingen-Ober Kessach-Widdern. C.C.R., trailed by C.C.A., 10th Armored Division passes through 63rd Division position as it drives toward Rengershausen-Roth. **(Atlantic-Italy) 15th Army Group** In the **U.S. Fifth Army** area, the 92nd Division initiates a diversionary attack against Massa on the Ligurian coast. The 370th Regiment advances about two miles, but German resistance forces it back after gains of about two miles. Meanwhile, the 442nd Regiment, driving on the left, seizes M. Fragolita and M. Carchio. Also, the 442nd is heavily engaged at Seravezza, where the Germans control the high ground. Company, A, 100th Battalion, 442nd Combat Command is pinned tight. P.F.C. Sadao S. Munemori (Nisei) singlehandedly attacks two machine gun nests, destroying both, then making a fast getaway amidst heavy fire and exploding grenades. As he nears the safety of a friendly crater held by two troops, he is struck in the helmet by an enemy grenade, which bounces from his helmet toward the other men. He instinctively dives on the grenade to save the others. P.F.C. Munemori receives the Medal of Honor posthumously. In the **IV Corps** sector, the 1st Armored Division is attached to Corps. In the **II Corps** sector, the 34th and 91st Division exchange positions, the 34th deploying in the Idice Valley area and the 91st moving near Highway 65. In the British 5th Corps sector, Operation LEVER commences: the British 56th Division attacks across the Reno River to secure the area between it and the southwest shore of Lake Comacchio. **(Atlantic-Russia)** The Soviets inform the Japanese Ambassador that the 5-year neutrality pact signed with the Japanese on April 13th 1941, will be denounced; however, the Russians still do not declare war.

U.S. Fleet under attack off Okinawa.

April 6th 1945 — (Pacific) U.S. Army Forces in the Pacific (AFPAC), under General MacArthur, is established; Headquarters is in Manila. The command incorporates troops formerly assigned to U.S. Army Forces in the Far East and also U.S. Army Forces in P.O.A. **(Pacific-Dutch East Indies)** The Submarine U.S.S. *Besugo* (SS-321) sinks the Japanese Minesweeper No. 12. **(Pacific-Philippines)** Luzon In the **U.S. Sixth Army's Legaspi** area, the 158th Regiment continues driving south near Busay. In the **I Corps** sector, Company G, 129th Regiment (37th Division) under the 33rd Division becomes isolated from the main body of the 2nd Battalion near Highway 9 as it attempts to outflank enemy positions near Salat; the unit holds out until the 10th, when other elements reach it. Hill 519, near Salacsac Pass, falls to the 126th Regiment, 32nd Division. In the **XI Corps** sector, an Artillery barrage precedes an attack by the 2nd Battalion, 63rd Regiment, 6th Division, against Mt. Mataba. The 20th Regiment moves toward Mt. Oro and Mt. Pacawagan. Meanwhile, the Sixth Army solidifies its front in south Luzon as the 103rd Regiment, 43rd Division establishes contact with Troop B, 5th Cavalry, 1st Cavalry Division at Santa Cruz. In the **XIV Corps** area, contingents of the 1st Cavalry and 11th Airborne Divisions drive through the foothills at the north and west approaches of Mt. Malepunyo hill mass. Contingents of the 7th Cavalry retain control of the Mapait hills while others drive to the Onipa River. **Southern Philippines** In the **U.S. Eighth Army** area (Sulu Archipelago), elements of the 41st Division which have secured Bongao Island easily, reembark to Sanga Sanga Island. **(Pacific-Ryukyu Islands)** Japanese Planes strike the Okinawa beachhead and Shipping; however, the Americans are now deeply entrenched and overcome this, the first of ten major Kamikaze attacks. About 300 of the 400 attacking Planes are shot down by a U.S. forces; however, the Japs damage the Fleet. The Destroyer *Bush* (DD-529) and the LST 447 are sunk by Kamikazes, and the Destroyer *Colhoun* (DD-801) and High Speed Minesweeper *Emmons* (DMS-22) are damaged by Kamikazes and subsequently sunk by U.S. forces. The Battleship *North Carolina* (BB-55) and the Light Carrier *Pasadena* (CL-65) are accidentally damaged by U.S. Naval gunfire. Ten Destroyers are damaged by Kamikazes: *Bennett* (DD-473), *Harrison* (DD-573), *Haynesworth* (DD-700), *Howorth* (DD-592), *Hutchings* (DD-476), *Hyman* (DD-732), *Leutze* (DD-481), *Morris* (DD-417), *Mullany* (DD-528), and the *Newcomb* (DD-586). The Destroyer *Taussig* (DD-746) is damaged by a Horizontal Bomber. In addition, the Destroyer Escorts *Fieberling* (DE-640), the *Witter* (DE-636), and the High Speed Minesweeper *Rodman*

(DMS-21) also are damaged by Suicide Planes. Additional Vessels damaged: High Speed Minesweeper *Harding* (DMS-28) by Horizontal Bomber; Minesweepers *Defense* (AM-317), *Devastator* (AM-318), *Facility* (AM-233), and *Ransom* (AM-283) by Kamikazes; Motor Minesweepers YMS 311 and YMS 321, by Kamikazes. In addition, the following Vessels are damaged accidentally by U.S. Naval gunfire: Submarine Chaser PCS-1390; Attack Transport *Barnett* (APA-5); Attack Cargo Ship *Leo* (AKA-60); LSTs 241 and 1,000. The High Speed Transport *Daniel T. Griffin* (APD-38) is damaged by collision. **On Okinawa** In the **U.S. Tenth Army** area, III Amphibious Corps sector, elements of the 6th Marine Division continue moving up Ishikawa Peninsula. In the **XXIV Corps** sector, the 96th Division commences its attack against the Shuri defenses in the southern sector of the island. The 383rd Regiment clears about half of Cactus Ridge after bitter fighting. Meanwhile, the 7th Division's 184th Regiment, operating on the Division's right flank, pounds the enemy with close fire support and extensive use of Flame throwers, reducing resistance at a formidable outpost position about 1,000 yards southwest of Arakachi. In addition, the 32nd Regiment advances through the coastal sector with ease. **(Pacific-China)** Army Aircraft sink the Japanese Destroyer *Amatsukaze* and Japanese Coastal Defense Vessels Nos. 1 and 134. **(Atlantic-Western Europe) 21st Army Group** In the **British Second Army** area, 30th Corps sector, the Guards Armored Division advances from Lingen toward Bremen. Meanwhile, the 12 Corps finalizes the reduction of resistance in the Rheine area. **12th Army Group** In the **U.S. Ninth Army** area, the XIII Corps attacks across the Weser River at 05:00, taking the Germans by surprise. The 335th Regiment, 84th Division gains a bridgehead near Weser Gebirge. In the **XIX Corps** area, C.C.A., 2nd Armored seizes an operational bridge at Schulenberg on the Leine River. Meanwhile, C.C.B. seizes Esperde and Harderode and reduces resistance in the high ground south of Heyen. C.C.R. advances to Elze. The 30th Division trails the 2nd Armored and secures the north flank of the Corps to the Weser and gets elements across the river at Grohnde and Ohr. Resolute German fire pins Company F, 119th Regiment (30th Division) near Hameln. First Lt. Raymond Beaudoin orders his unit to dig in and he takes the forward position, raining fire on the attackers; however, overpowering numbers press the contingent and deplete ammunition. Three men rush for more shells and however, all are felled by Sniper fire. Beaudoin advances singlehandedly to stem the tide, avoiding eight bazooka rounds and other deadly fire which buzz his ears and slash his uniform. He kills three of the occupants and support fire from the Platoon wipes out a fourth, allowing him to race toward a another fortification while simultaneously diverting attention from runners racing for more ammunition. Suddenly, a burst of enemy machine gun fire kills him; nevertheless, the ammunition arrives and the enemy is whipped. Lt. Beaudoin receives the Medal of Honor posthumously. Further right, the 329th Regiment, 83rd Division secures Halle. Meanwhile, the 377th Regiment, 95th Division begins securing Soest in the Ruhr pocket and the 378th Regiment gains part of Hamm. In the **XVI Corps** sector, the 75th Division advances toward the Ruhr River to cut off westward enemy escape routes from Dortmund. In other activity, the 79th Division prepares to attack south toward the Ruhr, while the 29th Division moves eastward and is placed in reserve. In the **U.S. First Army** area, **XVIII** Corps begins to attack toward the Ruhr pocket. At 05:00, the 78th Division drives across the Sieg River and establishes a 6,000 yard (deep) beachhead. Trailing the 78th, the 8th Division jumps off at 06:00, following an Artillery barrage, seizing Seelbach, Weidenau, and German barracks outside of Siegen with its 13th Regiment while Eschenbach and Lutzel fall to the 121st Regiment. In the **III Corps** sector, the 9th Division's 39th Regiment seizes Siedlinghausen while the 60th Regiment seizes several terrain features northeast of Oberkirchen. In addition, Task Force Birch is disbanded subsequent to seizing several towns. Meanwhile, the 99th Division secures Ober Fleckenburg and Wingeshausen. In the **VII Corps** area, the 3rd Armored Division drives against heavy opposition as it nears the Weser River. The 104th Division relieves contingents of the V Corps within its sector, then advances on the right of the 3rd Armored, toward the Weser. In the **V Corps** sector, the 2nd Division establishes a bridgehead at the Weser, and in the 69th Division zone, elements close on Hann Muenden at the confluence of the Werra, Weser and Fulda Rivers. In the **U.S. Third Army** area, Private Harold A. Garman (5th Division), had been awarded the Medal of Honor for gallantry for his actions on August 25th, 1944 near Montereau, France, is decorated by General Patton. In the **XX Corps** sector, Langensalza falls to C.C.A., 6th Armored and contingents of the 65th Division (VIII Corps) by 07:45. The 76th Division's RCT 385 seizes Bad Sooden, Grossalmerode, and Trubenhausen, then fords the Werra and advances near Eschwege. In the 89th Division zone, Eisenach is seized. In the **XII Corps** sector, the 11th Armored Division receives orders to secure an assembly area along line Schleusingen-Hildburghausen, setting up a drive against Bayreuth. Meanwhile, the 26th Division begins relieving the 11th Armored, while the 71st Division advances toward the Fulda area where it relieves the 2nd Cavalry Group and defends the right flank of the Corps from Fulda, eastward. **6th Army Group** The XV Corps continues making great progress as it drives northeast; elements reach positions near Neustadt. In the **XXI Corps** sector, contingents of the 42nd Division and C.C.A., 12th Armored Division advance toward Schweinfurt, while C.C.B. and C.C.R. topple Mainbernheim, Markbreit, and Obernbreit. Meanwhile, the 4th Division's 12th and 22nd Regiments secure the Koenigshofen region, then drive southeast toward Bad Mergentheim. In the **VI Corps** sector, Germans resist bitterly at Heilbronn as the 100th Division drives doggedly against the northeast and western sections of the city, without supporting Armor; at Jagstfeld, contingents of its 398th Regiment struggle to enlarge the Offenau bridgehead south toward the city. Meanwhile, the 63rd Division's 253rd Regiment turns back heavy attacks along the Jagst River and seizes Moeckmuehl while the 254th and 255th Regiments mop up along the northern flank between Bad Mergentheim and Berlichingen. Company A, 253rd Infantry is besieged near Untergriesheim, Germany, for eight hours. The unit, down to 23 Riflemen and several walking wounded, is rallied by Lt. James E. Robinson, Jr. who leads a charge. Ten German troops are in his path, but he personally wipes out the entire contingent. Robinson (861st Field Artillery, attached to 253rd) then leads another assault to seize Kressbach, inspiring his remaining nineteen fatigued men. During the charge, he is struck in the throat by a shell fragment; he continues to attack, despite the mortal wound, until the objective is taken. Robinson, now unable to speak, walks back two miles to receive belated medical attention and succumbs to his wounds; he receives the Medal of Honor posthumously. On the left flank, C.C.R. 10th Armored Division, repulses a heavy German counterattack near Roth. Later, during the night, the Germans pierce the Main Supply Route between Bad Mergentheim and Crailsheim. In the **French 1st Army** area, 2nd Corps sector,

contingents of the French 5th Armored Division and the 3rd Algerian Division advance to the Neckar River at Lauffen; the 3rd Algerian Division starts to secure the Stromberg Forest. Meanwhile, additional 5th Armored contingents and the 2nd Moroccan Division drive to the Enz River at Muehlacker; Koenigsbach and Stein are secured. Meanwhile, the Valluy Groupement seizes Durlach as it maintains its operation to clean out the fortified sector around Karlsruhe. **(Atlantic-Eastern Europe)** Contingents of the Second Ukrainian Front secure the area north of the Danube, advancing to the Morava River line northeast of Vienna, while additional contingents close on the city from the east. Meanwhile, units of the Third Ukrainian Front are engaged against the Germans holding the southern suburbs of Vienna. **(Atlantic-Italy) 15th Army Group** In the **U.S. Fifth Army** area, the Germans continue to resist fiercely. The 442nd Regiment, 92nd Division pounds against the enemy as it drives toward Massa, taking M. Cerreta; however, resolute fire holds the 370th Regiment at bay, unable to advance; the 442nd prepares to attack M. Belvedere. In the **British Eighth Army** area, the British 56th Division stretch their Reno bridgehead to Fossa di Navigazione.

The Yamamoto sinking.

April 7th 1945 — (Pacific) BATTLE OF EAST CHINA SEA — U.S. Planes spot the advancing Japanese Armada, the Special Surface Attack Force (Second Fleet), commanded by Vice Admiral Seiichi Ito, which had departed the Inland Sea to attack the massive American Fleet operating in the Nansei Shotos. The Fleet, which could be dubbed the mosquito fleet, is composed of the Battleship *Yamato*, which has only enough fuel for a one way trip, the Cruiser *Yahagi*, and eight Destroyers. As the puny Flotilla closes from north of Okinawa without Air support, Planes from Task Force 58 pounce upon it, pulverizing the *Yamato*. The decimated Battleship goes under with its giant 18.1-inch guns, which have never been tested in battle. About 2,500 men go down with the Ship; slightly over 250 men survive. Soon after, Mitscher's Pilots devastate the Light Cruiser *Yahagi*, followed by the annihilation of the Destroyers *Asashimo, Hamakaze, Isokaze,* and *Kasumi*. The remaining four battered Destroyers make a frantic dash for home, terminating the final Japanese sortie of the war. Meanwhile, as the Planes wallop the Japanese Navy, the Kamikazes again strike the Fleet, concentrating on the picket Ships (Destroyers); however, U.S. Planes also join the fight, shooting down 54 Planes against a loss of ten. The Carrier U.S.S. *Hancock* (CV-19), the Battleship *Maryland* (BB-46), the Destroyer *Longshaw* (DD-559), and the Destroyer Escort *Wesson* (DE-184) are damaged by Suicide Planes. In addition, the Motor Minesweeper YMS-81 sustains damage by a Kamikaze, and the Motor Minesweeper YMS-427 is damaged by coastal gunfire. The Attack Transport *Audrain* (APA-59) is accidentally struck by U.S. Naval gunfire.

April 7th 1945 — (United States) The Destroyer Escort U.S.S. *Gustafson* (DE-182), patrolling off New England, sinks the German U-Boat U-857 near Cape Cod. **(Pacific-Dutch East Indies)** The Submarines *Gabilian* (SS-252) and *Charr* (SS-328) encounter the Japanese Light Cruiser *Isuzu* and sink it off the Celebes. **(Pacific-Japan)** Army B-29s strike Japan, and for the first time, they are escorted by Land-based Fighters; 80 P-51s, based in Iwo Jima, accompany the flight. As the 29th Bombardment Group (20th Air Force) approaches the target, one of the phosphoresce bombs gets snagged in the chute of one of the Planes in Squadron 52 and springs back into the Aircraft, filling it with smoke; Sgt. Henry E. Erwin gets struck in the face by the exploding bomb, costing his sight, but he locates it and moves through the passage to attempt to discard the bomb before it explodes. All the while, the smoke filled Plane is in an uncontrollable dive. Despite his loss of sight and decimated nose, the bomb is thrown out, but Erwin becomes engulfed in flames as he falls to the deck. The Pilot pulls out of the dive at an altitude of 300 and the crew is saved. Sgt. Erwin receives the Medal of Honor. **(Pacific-Philippines)** In the **U.S. Sixth Army** area, the Airstrip at Legaspi becomes operational. In the **I Corps** sector, Company G, 129th Regiment, remains isolated near Salat. At the Villa Verde Trail, contingents of the 126th Infantry, 32nd Division, overpower the resistance on Hill 518, in the Salacsac Pass area. Meanwhile, the 126th Regiment, bolstered by Air and Artillery support, attacks other Jap positions in the region. In addition, the Japs holding Kapintalan are nearly surrounded by units of the 25th Division. To speed the operation in the north, General Krueger commits the remainder of the 37th Division (less the 145th Regiment) to Corps. In the **XI Corps** sector, the Baldy Force probes in force toward Ipo Dam. In the **XIV Corps** sector, orders come down to drive to Lamon Bay on the east coast and seize Atimonan and Mauban, then to drive southeast into the Bicols. Meanwhile, other contingents maintain pressure against Mt. Malepunyo. In other activity, Malarya Hill falls to the 187th Glider Battalion while the 188th Regiment drive east through Candelaria to make contact with Filipino Guerrillas who are advancing west through Sariaya. **(South Philippines)** In the **U.S. Eighth Army** area on Cebu, elements of the 132nd Regiment, Americal Division drive from Hill 27, advancing about 1,000 yards toward Hill 26; however, a concentrated counterattack pushes them back. On Negros, Paratroop RCT 503 arrives at Pulupandan. **(Pacific-Ryukyu Islands)** In the **U.S. Tenth Army** area, the first F4u Fighter Planes of Marine Aircraft Group 31 arrive on Okinawa at Yontan Airfield. Meanwhile, FMF Reconnaissance Company scouts the remaining Eastern Islands — Takanare, Heanza, Hamahika, and Kutake Shima; Japanese are found on one island. In the III Amphibious Corps sector, the 6th Marine Division advances to line Nago-Taira at the Motobu Peninsula; the battle for it begins on the following day. In the **XXIV Corps** sector, Cactus Ridge falls to the 383rd Regiment, 96th Division. Meanwhile, the 184th Regiment pounds unsuccessfully against the front slopes of a hill about 1,000 yards west of Minami-Uebaru; however, contingents swing around and seize the outpost with a flanking assault. **(Atlantic-Western Europe) 21st Army Group** In the **British Second Army** area, 8th Corps sector, the 6th Airborne establishes a bridgehead across the Weser at Minden while the British 11th Armored establishes one at Stolzenau; both prepare to attack toward the Leine. **12th Army Group** In the **U.S. Ninth Army**

area, the XIII Corps continues to advance from the Weser toward the Leine. In the **XIX Corps** sector, the 2nd Armored Division advances to the line Sarstedt-Hildesheim and terminates offensive operations upon orders. The 83rd Division secures its area west of the Weser; however, one small pocket remains near Polle. Meanwhile, the 377th Regiment, 95th Division, seizes Soest by 07:30, and the 379th pinches out the 377th and drives into Werl. In conjunction, the 378th Regiment reduces the final opposition in Hamm and secures additional areas in the suburbs. In other Corps activity, Task Force Twaddle (Major General Harry L. Twaddle, CG, 95th Division), composing the 8th Armored and 95th Infantry Divisions, plus support attachments, is established to bolster the XVI Corps' operations against the Ruhr pocket. Subsequently, TF Faith, commanded by Brigadier General Don C. Faith, composing 377th Infantry and 194th Glider Infantry, plus support units, is formed from TF Waddle to protect the left flank of the Corps and secure the area between the Mohne and Ruhr Rivers. C.C.A., 8th Armored rolls forward seizing the ground southeast of Soest along the Mohne River while C.C.B. pushes columns toward Werl, advancing to Gerlingen. In the **XVI Corps** sector, the 290th Regiment, 75th Division captures Frohlinde and Kirchline while the 291st Regiment is bitterly engaged at Castrop Rauxel, securing most of it as the Division drives toward the Ruhr. In other activity, at 03:00, the 79th Division drives south across the Emscher and Rhein-Herne Canals, reaching the railway at Katernburg with its 313th and 315th Regiments. Meanwhile, the 35th Division stretches its positions eastward along the Rhein-Herne Canal. The 17th Airborne Division maintains its defensive posture on the right flank of the Corps. In the **U.S. First Army** area, **XVIII (Airborne) Corps** sector, the offensive intensifies. The 95th Division receives its baptism under fire. Following an Artillery bombardment, the 386th Regiment crosses the Sieg River in assault boats and drives about 4,000 yards against nominal resistance. Meanwhile, the 78th Division, operating to the right of the 95th, drives about 5,000 yards against heavy opposition, and in conjunction, the 8th Division drives about 4,000 yards then stands firm against strong counterattacks against Seelbach. In the **III Corps** sector, the 9th Division hammers forward, its 47th Infantry, becoming part of reformed TF Birks, overruns Bestwig, Esshoff, Gevelinghausen, Heringhausen, Nuttlar, and Ostwig. The 39th Regiment seizes Altenfeld, Elpe, and Heinrichsdorf, and the 60th Regiment drives through the woods north of Oberkirchen and secures Ober Sorpe and Mittel Sorpe. In the 7th Armored Division zone, the Germans launch a fierce counterattack against Gleidorf, but it is repulsed by C.C.B., which subsequently, bolstered by Air and Artillery, seizes Schmallenberg. Meanwhile, C.C.R. overruns Holthausen. In the 99th Division zone, the 393rd Regiment takes Oberhundem while the 394th Regiment drives west of Schmallenberg, advancing about 5,000 yards. In other activity, the 28th Division reverts to First Army command at 24:00 (performing security mission). In the **VII Corps** area, the 3rd Armored Division plows along the Weser where the Germans have destroyed the bridges. The Big Red One (1st Division) will ford the river on the left flank of the Corps. RCT 26, less the 1st Battalion plus the 4th Cavalry Group, reinforced, becomes TF Taylor, commanded by Brigadier General Taylor; it is ordered to clear the area east of the Ruhr pocket between the III and XIX Corps. The 104th Division reaches the Weser and gets contingents across. In the **V Corps** sector, the 2nd Division drives across the Weser at Veckerhagen and pushes its bridgehead toward Dransfeld. Engineers lay treadway bridging to permit support Vehicles to cross. In conjunction, the 69th Division driving to the right and bolstered by Planes, Artillery and Armor, reaches the Werra River and establishes contact with the 2nd Division. Its RCT 272 drives to Witzenhausen, arriving in synchronization with the Germans blowing the bridges; assault boats are used while Engineers construct Pontoon bridges. In conjunction, RCT 273 overruns Hann Muenden, then crosses the Werra and secures Altmuenden, Lippoldshausen, and Wiershausen before seizing some high ground northeast of Hann Muenden and bolting to Oberode. In the **U.S. Third Army** area, Army captures its 400,000th prisoner; toward the latter part of the day, 2,000 Germans are snagged between the 87th and 89th Divisions. A contingent of a Quartermaster unit captures German General Lieutenant General Hahm, 82nd German Corps, a Colonel, Major, Lieutenant and seven Privates. General Patton notes: "THE COLORED SOLDIERS CAPTURING THEM WERE THE MOST ELATED SOLDIERS I HAVE EVER SEEN." **XX Corps** sector, elements of the 6th Armored Division move to assist the 76th Division, who is pursuing the Germans which are retreating in droves from the Werra River toward Muhlhausen. In the **VIII Corps** sector, the Germans pound against contingents of the 261st Regiment, 65th Division, at Struth, overrunning their positions; however, reinforcements from XX Corps and Aircraft move in and rectify the situation. In the 89th Division zone, the 353rd Regiment secures the area southeast of Eisenach to line Wutha-Ruhla while the 354th Regiment forces Friedrichroda. In addition, the 355th Regiment spreads out between Seebergen and Woelfis to screen the right flank of the Division. Meanwhile, the 87th Division continues to advance eastward and establishes contact with the 11th Armored Division (XII Corps); a subsequent counterattack is repulsed during the night of the 7th-8th. In other activity, the 6th Cavalry Group moves contingents to Eisenach and Eschwege. In the **XII Corps** sector, the 11th Armored Division prepares to attack Bayreuth, seizing Themar and Schleusingen, trailed by the 26th Division which mops up in its wake. **6th Army Group** In the **U.S. Seventh Army** area, **XV Corps** sector, the Germans offer tenacious resistance against the 14th Armored's right flank; C.C.A. seizes Neustadt on the Saale River without much difficulty. In the **XXI Corps** sector, the 42nd Division and C.C.A., 12th Armored Division receives orders to seize Schweinfurt, the ball-bearing plant which has previously received much attention from the Army Air Corps; the Division gains about ten miles for the day; contingents establish a bridgehead east of the Main River at Volkach. Meanwhile, the 4th Division continues to bolt forward; its 22nd Regiment overruns Bad Mergentheim while its 12th Regiment drives to the Tauber River line. In the **VI Corps** sector, the 100th Division continues to fortify its positions at Heilbronn. Near Untergriesheim, fierce enemy fire holds up a Company of the 100th Division; P.F.C. Mike Colalillo, yells to the others to follow him as he charges through the fire behind a supporting Tank. A German shell puts his weapon out of action, but he then jumps on a Tank and commandeers its machine gun, knocking out about ten enemy troops and destroying their machine gun. As the Tank advances, he continues firing from his exposed position until the gun jams. Soon after, he grabs a submachinegun from the Tankers and reinitiates his foot charge. Eventually, the Armor exhausts its ammunition and is recalled, but Colalillo refuses to retire, choosing to remain with a wounded Soldier. Colalillo, responsible for the elimination of at least 25 enemy troops and the successful rescue of a wounded trooper, receives the Medal of Honor. In conjunction, the 1st Battalion, 398th Regiment moves to the Offenau bridgehead to support

the 2nd Battalion. In the meantime, the 63rd Division, unable to break through German defenses at Hardehauser Wald by frontal attacks, changes strategy and begins to envelop the objective. Additional elements establish a bridgehead across the Jagst at Widdern, and yet others secure several towns along the river Jagst. In other activity, the 10th Armored Division seizes Crailsheim and dispatches others to attack German positions at Heilbronn from the rear in support of the 100th Division and join with it to seal off the enemy embattled with the 63rd Division at Hardehauser-Wald. **(Atlantic-Eastern Europe)** Contingents of the Third Ukrainian Front penetrate the southern portion of Vienna and meet fierce German resistance; house-to-house fighting erupts. **(Atlantic-Italy) 15th Army Group** In the **U.S. Fifth Army** area, M. Belvedere is secured by the 442nd Regiment, 92nd Division after a vicious fight, and the 2nd Battalion, 473rd Regiment is thrown against stiff German resistance which is holding up progress of the units moving on the left flank. In the **British Eighth Army** area, 5th Corps sector, the British 56th Division pushes its Reno bridgehead to Fossa di Navigazione.

April 8th 1945 — (United States) The Destroyer *U.S.S. Turner* (DD834) is christened at Bath, Maine, by the granddaughter (Louise) of Admiral Leahy. The Vessel is named in honor of one of Admiral Perry's Officers who served with him during the War of 1812. **(Pacific-Dutch East Indies)** U.S. Naval Ships sink the Japanese Submarine Chaser No. 101. **(Pacific-Philippines)** Luzon In the **U.S. Sixth Army** area, **I Corps** sector, Major General Inis P. Swift orders the Baguio offensive accelerated; the 37th Division is to drive down Highway 9 while the 33rd Division secures additional routes. Meanwhile, the 32nd Division continues to pound against enemy positions along the Villa Verde Trail at Salacsac Pass and the 25th Division is slugging forward, west of Kapintalan advancing to Crump Hill; its 35th Regiment is securing Kapintalan. In the **XI Corps** sector, the 63rd Infantry, 6th Division awaits cessation of an Artillery an Air bombardment of Mt. Mataba before reinitiating its attack. In the 43rd Division zone, mop-up operations are active. In the **XIV Corps** sector, the 187th Regiment, 11th Airborne Division occupies Sulac in the western foothills of Mt. Mataasna Bundoc. Meanwhile, other Corps contingents drive against Mt. Malepunyo. **Southern Philippines** In the **U.S. Eighth Army** area, the 3rd Battalion, 132nd Regiment seizes a ridge near Hill 27 on Cebu; during the night, the Japanese mount an unsuccessful counterattack. In the meantime, Guerrillas and Company E, 182nd Regiment attack Hill 20, between the Race Course and the Reservoir. On Negros, Aircraft blast enemy positions and in the mountains, U.S. Regiments attack to dislodge the Japanese before they can fortify their positions. **(Pacific-Ryukyu Islands)** Okinawa In the **U.S. Tenth Army** area, the 29th Marines, 6th Marine Division advance across the base of the Motobu Peninsula and occupy Gagusuku and Yamadadobaru, opening the battle for control of the peninsula. In the **XXIV Corps** sector, Air, Artillery, and Naval gunfire supports the attack of the 383rd Regiment, 96th Division as it drives to seize Kakazu Ridge; fierce Japanese resistance holds the line and the Japs pour mortar fire in front of the approaches. Meanwhile, the 7th Division's 184th Regiment hammers against Tomb Hill and Triangulation Hill, seizing the latter. In conjunction, the 32nd Regiment, 7th Division, advances in the coastal sector. Offshore, Japanese fanatics in Suicide Boats damage the U.S.S. *Charles J. Badger* (DD-657) and the Attack Cargo Ship *Starr* (AKA-67). The U.S.S. *Gregory* (DD-802), a Destroyer, is damaged by a Kamikaze. The Motor Minesweeper YMS-92 becomes damaged after striking a mine, and the LSTs 939 and 940 are damaged by collision and grounding respectively. **(Pacific-China)** The Japanese prepare to attack Chihchiang in force. **(Atlantic-Western Europe) 21st Army Group** The Canadian 4th Armored Division drives across the Ems River, advancing toward Oldenburg, while the Canadian 3rd Division seizes Zutphen and advances further toward Deventer. In the **British Second Army** area, 30th Corps sector, the Guards' Armored Division overruns resistance east of Lingen as it drives toward Bremen. In the 12th Corps sector, the British 7th Armored Division nears the Weser. In the 8th Corps sector, Corps advances to the Leine River southeast of Nienburg. **12th Army Group** In the **U.S. Ninth Army** area, **XIII Corps** sector, the 84th Division advances to the Leine River; its 334th Regiment seizes a bridge near Guemmer. In conjunction, C.C.R., 5th Armored Division moves to seize a crossing near Hannover to cut off enemy escape routes; C.C.A. and C.C.R. maintain Minden and deploy around Herford respectively. Meanwhile, the 102nd Division mops up west of the Weser while the 11th Cavalry group crosses the river to guard the north flank of the Corps. In addition, the 29th Division assumes responsibility for the region stretching from the Rhine to the Dortmund Canal; it comes out of Army reserve. In the **XIX Corps** sector, the 2nd Armored Division prepares to attack upon orders; it fortifies defensive positions and probes with limited attacks, trailed by the 30th Infantry Division. The 83rd Division continues advancing, crossing the Leine as it drives east near Alfeld-Greene to line Gandersheim-Westfeld. Bevern is secured by the 3rd Battalion, 331st Regiment, which bolts across the Weser at Heinsen. Meanwhile, TF Waddle continues pounding against the enemy positions in the Ruhr pocket. TF Faith secures the area and seizes the ground between the Mohne and Ruhr Rivers east of the Allengen-Hirschberg-Meschede line. In the 8th Armored sector, C.C.B. overruns Ost Buederich after driving through Werl, while C.C.R. propels westward toward Werl-Wickede road. In the 95th Division zone, many towns are overrun as the Yanks drive west. In the **XVI Corps** sector, the 75th Division, bolstered by effective Air and Artillery support, overpowers Castrop Rauxel, then bursts to the fringes of Luetgendortmund. Meanwhile, the 79th Division enlarges its bridgehead south of Rhein-Herne Canal, supported by the 507th Paratroop Infantry, 11th Airborne Division which advances across the canal and secures the 79th's right flank up to the Berne Canal. In the **U.S. First Army's XVIII Corps (Airborne)** sector, the 97th Division attacks to enlarge its Sieg bridgehead. Contingents of the 78th Division overrun Freudenberg, Lichtenberg, and Waldbrol. Meanwhile, the 8th Division drives rapidly, its 28th Regiment sprinting on the right, and reaches Wurdinghausen-Rinsecke; the 8th Division prepares an attack and the 13th Armored rolls from Homberg to support the attack. In the **III Corps** sector, TF Birks (9th Division) whacks the Germans hard, seizing Halbeswig, Velmede, and Wehrstapel, then drives into Meschede. In conjunction, the 39th Regiment captures Boedefeld, Ramsbeck, Werden, and Westernboedefeld while the 60th Regiment drives tenaciously north and northeast of Fredeburg. In the 7th Armored Division's zone, C.C.B. secures Obringhausen and finds time to pour supporting fire into Fredeburg to bolster the attack of C.C.R., which controls most of the town after a long and bitter fight. In conjunction with the 7th Armored drive, the 99th Division takes Felbecke, Selkentrop, Werntrop, and Wormbach and drives into Saalhausen, securing most of it with the 394th Regiment. The 393rd Regiment overruns Selbecke and crushes bypassed resistance west of Milchenbach. In other activity, the 5th Division (less 11th Regiment) is attached to

Corps. In the **VII Corps** sector, the bridgehead across the Weser is solid; Armor prepares to bolt across and crack the German defenses. The 1st Division forces the river gaining a bridgehead, which includes Derenthal, Fuerstenberg, Lauenfoerde, and Meinbrexen. Also along the Weser, the 104th Division attacks at 04:00, crossing its 413th Regiment at Gieselwerder; C.C.R., 3rd Armored also bolts across and deploys near Imbsen. In other activity, Task Force Taylor is disbanded, as its mission of defending along the Ruhr pocket is now unnecessary. In the **V Corps** sector, the 2nd Division fords the Weser, advancing about ten miles eastward, its 23rd Regiment overpowering Gottingen while the 9th Regiment drives into Forst Reinhausen. Meanwhile, the 38th Regiment deploys east of the Weser to guard the left flank. In the 69th Division sector, elements mop up in Hann Muenden while others advance to Nieder Gandern-Hohengandern and establish a bridgehead at the Leine River. In addition, the 9th Armored Division assembles east of the Weser. In the **U.S. Third Army** area, **XX Corps** sector, RCT 417, 76th Division and C.C.R., 6th Armored Division continue fighting to secure the region north and northeast of Eschwege, while RCT 304 drives northwest and RCT 385 drives to Allendorf and Volkerode. Meanwhile, contingents of the 80th Division drive from Gotha toward Erfurt. In the **VIII Corps** sector, the 87th and 89th Divisions are heavily engaged at Thuringer Wald as the Germans continue to strongly resist, despite being scattered by the overwhelming U.S. force. In the **XII Corps** sector, preparations are made to launch a southeast offensive; it secures the area up to Gehlberg and Stutzenbach on the left and right respectively with the 90th Division. At the same time, the 26th Division drives to the Nahe River, clearing Thuringer Wald and then establishing contact with 11th Armored contingents at Rappelsdorf. In addition, the 71st Division eliminates resistance in its area up to general line Meiningen-Marisfeld-Juchsen, and the 42nd Cavalry Group drives to Juchsen-Nordheim. **6th Army Group** In the **U.S. Seventh Army** area, **XV Corps** sector, the 3rd and 45th Divisions continue to pound the Germans in the hills at Hohe Rhon; C.C.B., 4th Armored supports the 3rd Division drive. In the **XXI Corps** zone, the Germans at Schweinfurt mount tenacious resistance against the 42nd Division; the 242nd Regiment, bolstered by C.C.A., 12th Armored, drives to Ettleben and Volkach in the center, while the 232nd Regiment, operating on the left, advances to the Alt Bessingen-Schwebenried. Meanwhile, the 222nd Regiment holds tight at the Volkach bridgehead and at their positions west of the Main. In addition, the 12th Armored initiates strong reconnaissance and the 4th Division steps up its patrols on the Corps' right flank. In the **VI Corps** area, 100th Division sector, the struggle for Heilbronn continues with viciousness as the troops move from house to house, eliminating the resistance. In conjunction, the 398th Regiment still meets bitter resistance at Jagstfeld as it presses its Offenau bridgehead toward Odheim. Meanwhile, the 10th Armored Division pivots northwest toward the 63rd Division which is driving south on the left flank to eliminate resistance between the Jagst and Kocher Rivers. Compnay C, 383rd Regiment encounters heavy resistance as it moves against Lobenbacherhof. The Platoon Leader is wounded, but Sergeant John R. Crews and two volunteers charge the hill; one man is killed and the other becomes wounded. Sgt. Chews advances and kills two enemy crewmen, then seizes the machine gun from another German. He then charges an automatic rifle position, despite being severely wounded and eliminates it; seven Germans surrender to him and the others make a hasty withdrawal. Chews receives the

Medal of Honor for his heroism under fire. In the **French 1st Army** area, 2nd Corps sector, the 3rd Algerian Infantry Division secures its zone west of the Neckar River as far south as Bissingen on the Enz River. In other activity, Groupements Navarre and Schlesser seize Pforzheim while Valluy Groupement contingents take Dietlingen, Dietenhausen, and Ellmendingen. Meanwhile, the 2nd Moroccan Division establishes a bridgehead near Muehlhausen south of the Enz River. **(Atlantic-Eastern Europe)** The Third White Ukrainian Force commences a full assault against Koenigsberg (East Prussia). The Soviets continue to pound the Germans at Breslau (Silesia), while the Second Ukrainian Front drives through Czechoslovakia toward the Moravian frontier, establishing bridgeheads across the Danube and Morava Rivers near Vienna. Meanwhile, contingents of the Third Ukrainian Front advance on Vienna; however, some contingents bypass the city to drive west toward Linz and others drive south toward Graz. **(Atlantic-Italy) 15th Army Group** In the **U.S. Fifth Army** area, the 473rd Regiment, replaces the 370th Regiment, 92nd Division and continues the attack along Highway 1; the 370th swings to the Serchio Valley to deploy in the vacant lines of the 473rd.

April 9th 1945 — (Pacific-Japan) The Submarine U.S.S. *Parche* (SS-384) sinks the Japanese Minesweeper No. 3. Also, in the Yellow Sea, the U.S.S. *Tirante* sinks the Transport *Nikko Maru.* **(Pacific-Philippines) Luzon** In the **U.S. Sixth Army** area, Legaspi sector, RCT 158 seizes the road junction of Highways 1 and 160, outside of Daraga. In the **I Corps** sector, the 33rd and 37th Divisions prepare to mount a heavy attack against Baguio. Meanwhile, Company G, 129th Regiment, continues to hold on, despite being isolated on the Naguilian-Baguio road. In other activity, the 32nd Division opens an attack against Salacsac Pass, making some gains. The 25th Division reduces final resistance on an obstinate spur west of Mt. Myoko. In the **XI Corps** sector, Japanese positions on Mt. Mataba continue to be pulverized by Air and Artillery bombardment. In the **XIV Corps** sector, contingents of the 1st Cavalry and 11th Airborne Division keep pounding against Mt. Malepunyo; other units of the two Divisions race to the east coast, establishing contact at Lucban. **Southern Philippines** In the **U.S. Eighth Army** area, on Cebu, the Americal Division deploys to commence an enfilade fire upon Jap positions in the mountainous interior. After dark, RCT 164 arrives at Cebu City. On Negros, the 40th Division encounters fierce resistance as it drives against enemy positions in the mountains; the 185th gains about 6,000 yards; the 160th pushes to Hill 3155 (renamed Dolan Hill); the 503rd Paratroop Infantry, on the left, encounters impenetrable fire, halting it as it drives toward Manzanares. Meanwhile, the 41st Division moves to secure the Calamian Islands, north of Palawan; contingents land unopposed on Busuanga Island. In the Sulu Archipelago, RCT 163 (minus 3rd Battalion) lands unopposed on Jolo Island, subsequent to two weeks of relentless bombardment by the U.S. Seventh Fleet; a support Air Team from Marine Aircraft Group 32 accompanies the mission. **(Pacific-Ryukyu Islands)** In the **U.S. Tenth Army** area, **III Amphibious Corps** sector, the 29th Marines, 6th Marine Division, continue probing the Motobu Peninsula. Meanwhile, Kadena Airfield is declared ready to handle Aircraft; Planes from Marine Aircraft Wing 33 begin to operate against the enemy. In the **XXIV Corps** sector, contingents of the 383rd Regiment, 96th Division, launch a predawn surprise attack against Kakazu Ridge in the Shuri defense system; however, intense enemy fire forces a withdrawal; the engagement costs both sides heavy casualties. During the murderous encounter, P.F.C. Edward J. Moskala races through 40 yards of withering fire and knocks

out two machine guns. During his Company's withdrawal, he and eight other Soldiers form a rear guard, forestalling the enemy for three hours; he kills more than 25 Japs before the contingent pulls back. One wounded man is left behind and Moskala runs the gauntlet with other volunteers to rescue him. Soon after, while he is protecting other wounded troops, he kills four infiltrators before getting mortally wounded. P.F.C. Moskala receives the Medal of Honor posthumously. Meanwhile, the 184th Regiment, 7th Division, seizes Tomb Hill. In other activity, the main body of the 27th Division (less RCT 105) debarks on Orange Beach near Kadena to bolster the ground troops. Japanese coastal guns damage the High Speed Transport *Hopping* (APD-51) and the LST 557. In addition, the Destroyer *Sterett* (DD-407) is damaged by a Kamikaze, and the Destroyer *Porterfield* (DD-682) sustains damage after being accidentally struck by U.S. fire. The Escort Carrier U.S.S. *Chenango* (CVE-28) sustains damage when a returning Plane crashes. The Japanese Submarine RO-46 is attacked and sunk by the Destroyers *Mertz* (DD-691) and the *Monssen* (DD-798). **(Pacific-China-Burma-India)** General Wedemeyer confers with Officers of the Tenth Air Force and the India-Burma Theater, discussing the options of transferring Tenth Air Force to China. **(Atlantic-Western Europe)** The Royal Air Force Bombers sink the *Admiral Scheer* while attacking Kiel during the night of the 9th-10th. **21st Army Group** In the **British Second Army** area, 30th Corps moves east and northeast of Lingen. In the 12th Corps area, the British 7th Armored Division drives to the Weser, near Hoya, and establishes a bridgehead. In the 8th Corps sector, elements advance and make contact with U.S. troops, then move toward Celle on the Aller River. **12th Army Group** In the **U.S. Ninth Army** area, **XIII Corps** sector, the 84th Division prepares to mount an attack against Hannover. Contingents of the 5th Armored Division advance and sever the Autobahn near Vohrum. In other activity, the 102nd Division's 407th Regiment begins reducing resistance in the Obernkirchen area. The XVI Corps relieves XIX Corps of responsibility for clearing the Ruhr pocket. It continues the eastward attack (Task Force Twaddle attached). The 75th Division's 290th Regiment seizes Dortsfeld while the 289th secures Luetgendortmund and the 291st Regiment screens the right flank of Corps. The attack is bolstered by Air and Artillery support. The 79th Division blisters through Frillendorf, Kray, and Steele, pushing to the Ruhr and cutting the German forces. In conjunction, the 507th Paratroop Regiment, covering the right flank of the 79th Division, drives to its objective: Berne Canal. Meanwhile, TF Twaddle drives forward toward Unna and Kamen; C.C.B., 8th Armored Division overruns Hemmerde, Holtum, Stockum, and Westhemmerde, while C.C.R. drives west along the Ruhr and C.C.A. deploys at the Mohne River. The 95th Division drives toward Kamen. Contingents make contact with First Army on the left. In the **U.S. First Army** area, the 97th Division fortifies and enlarges its bridgehead along the Sieg. In conjunction, its 303rd Regiment attacks and gains about two-thirds of the objective. Meanwhile, the 86th, and 78th Divisions drive north making good progress, the former gaining about ten miles. In the **III Corps** sector, the 5th Division drives west, its left flank guarded by the 32nd Cavalry Squadron. Task Force Birks, 9th Division eliminates the final resistance in Meschede, then is disbanded, while the 60th Regiment secures Altenilpe and Ober Henneborn. The 7th Armored Division advances to line Mailar-Ober Landenbeck-Kobbenrode, whipping through resistance in several towns and villages. Meanwhile, the 99th Division drives quickly, overrunning Bracht and Saalhausen-Langaner near the Leine.

In the **VII Corps** sector, 3rd Armor pushes across the Weser, trailed by the 104th Division; C.C.B. drives to the Gottingen area and gets contingents across the Leine River; C.C.R. advances to positions near Levershausen and Northeim. Also, the 1st Division completes its crossing of the Weser and drives east; 4th Cavalry Group is attached to Division; Barterode is taken by the 104th. In the **V Corps** sector, the 2nd and 69th Divisions move east against feeble resistance while 9th Armored Division prepares to attack through the Infantry positions, bolstered by units of the 2nd and 9th Divisions. In the **U.S. Third Army** area, **XX Corps** sector, the 3rd Cavalry Group, bolstered by contingents of C.C.R., 6th Armored, reduces resistance on the north flank of Corps. Doellstaedt, Gierstadt, Grossfahner, and Kleinfahner topple to the 76th Division's RCT 385. Meanwhile, C.C.B., 6th Armored Division, seizes Toba while C.C.A., operating on the right flank, encounters friendly forces. In the **VIII Corps** sector, the 87th and 89th Divisions attack abreast, driving east; the 87th, operating on the right, secures the heights east of Oberhof, while the 89th overpowers Finsterbergen, Georgenthal, and Grafenhain. Meanwhile, the XII Corps makes plans to resume its offensive on the 10th. In other activity, the 4th Armored Division is attached to XX Corps. **6th Army Group** In the **U.S. Seventh Army** area, **XV Corps** sector, the 3rd and 45th Divisions seize their objectives in the Hohe Rhon hill mass, permitting Corps to prepare to drive against Nuremberg. In the **XXI Corps** sector, despite being under enormous pressure, the Germans holding Schweinfurt mount rigid resistance against the attacking 42nd Division, which is supported by contingents of the 12th Armored Division. In other activity, the 4th Division confines activity to patrolling along the right flank of the Corps. In the 100th Division sector, heavy fighting continues to ensue around Heilbronn as attempts are still being made to connect both bridgeheads. Meanwhile, the 63rd Division continues to plow forward; on the right flank, the 255th Regiment advances southwest in the Hardehauser Wald region, reaching the Kocher River and establishing a bridgehead at Weissbach, while the 253rd Regiment drives east through the woods, also advancing to the Kocher. Meanwhile, on the left, the 254th drives to the line Ingelfelden-Weldingsfeld and dispatches probing operations toward 10th Armored's area. In the 10th Armored sector, fierce fighting ensues as the Germans attack U.S. positions at Crailsheim, attempting to disrupt the main supply route between it and Bad Mergentheim; however, determined opposition by the Armor and RCT 324, 44th Division repulses the assault. In the **French 1st Army** area, the 2nd Corps advances in the Black Mountains southeast of Ettlingen, while the Valluy Groupement, supported by contingents of the French 1st Armored Division, secures ground south of the town. **(Atlantic-Eastern Europe)** The beleaguered Germans holding at the fortress in Koenigsberg are toppled by the onslaught of the Third White Russian Front, ending organized resistance in East Prussia; the Germans retreat to the Samland Peninsula. Meanwhile, additional Russians pound the exhausted Germans at Vienna. **(Atlantic-Italy) 15th Army Group** In the **U.S. Fifth Army** area, the 92nd Division drives to the edge of Massa. Its 371st Regiment, attached to IV Corps, relieves contingents of the Brazilian Expeditionary Force, permitting the Brazilians to move northeast from M. Belvedere. Meanwhile, the British Eighth Army commences its last offensive in Italy, subsequent to a huge Air and Artillery bombardment of enemy positions at the Senio River. At darkness, the British commit the Polish 2nd Corps' 3rd Carpathian Division, which drives against violent opposition and secures the east bank of the river, while

the British 5 Corps sends the New Zealander 2nd and the Indian 8th Divisions across the Senio where a bridgehead is established near Lugo. As the Poles and New Zealanders are advancing, the British 10th Corps, which contains a Jewish Brigade and the Italian Friuli Group, mounts a diversionary attack; it fights to Cuffiana and establishes a bridgehead by dawn. Meanwhile, the British 13th Corps maintains a defensive posture on Army's left flank.

April 10th 1945 — (Pacific-Philippines) Luzon In the **U.S. Sixth Army** area, RCT 158, having terminated resistance in the Legaspi sector, begins probing missions on the islands in the Albay Gulf and also dispatches units to support the contingents operating near San Francisco. In the **I Corps** area, at Baguio, contingents of the 129th Regiment, 37th Division, reduce the opposition in the Sablan-Salat area; contact is made with isolated Company G. Additional elements drive to within 100 yards of the crest of Three Peaks. Meanwhile, the 1st Battalion, 27th Regiment, 25th Division continues pressing against Mt. Myoko, while the 3rd Battalion reverts to reserve. In addition, the 128th Regiment finally overruns Salacsac Pass, securing an opening to the Cagayan Valley, subsequent to a tedious and expensive campaign. In the **XI Corps** sector, the 63rd Regiment, 6th Division, reinitiates its attack to secure Mt. Mataba and climbs to the summit, but determined resistance lingers for about a week. In the **XIV Corps** sector, contingents reach the coast at Lamon Bay, isolating Japanese troops in the Bicols. Units of the 1st Cavalry Division seize Mauban. Meanwhile, Atimonan falls to contingents of the 11th Airborne Division. **Southern Philippines** In the **U.S. Eighth Army** area, contingents of the 132nd Regiment, Americal Division, seize Hill 26 on Cebu. In other activity, Company E, 182nd Regiment, and Guerrillas overrun Hill 20. Meanwhile, heavy skirmishing continues at Dolan Hill; Japanese fire keeps the 160th Regiment pinned down. On Negros, contingents of the 3rd Battalion, 164th Regiment, Americal Division, land on Tagbilaran to seek native guides and to prepare for an amphibious invasion of Bohol. **(Pacific-Ryukyu Islands)** Carrier Aircraft and Naval Surface Vessels give umbrella coverage to the 3rd Battalion, 105th Regiment, 27th Division, which lands on Tsuken Shima off Okinawa to seek and destroy isolated Japanese forces on this, the only defended island in the Eastern Island. In the **U.S. Tenth Army** area, **III Amphibious Corps** sector on Okinawa, the 29th Marines, 6th Marine Division continues to whack against Jap positions on Yae-Take hill mass on the Motobu Peninsula; the 2nd Battalion captures Unten Ko, a Submarine and Torpedo Boat Base. In the **XXIV Corps** area, the 381st and 383rd Regiments, 96th Division, bolstered by enormous fire support, drives against Kakazu Ridge. Bitter fighting ensues; however, the Japanese are not dislodged, despite gaining territory. Meanwhile, the 7th Division continues advancing toward Ouki. **(Pacific-Burma)** In the **British Fourteenth Army's 4 Corps** sector, contingents of the Indian 17th Division, supported by the 255th Tank Brigade, seize Pyawbwe, along the Mandalay-Rangoon railroad; the assault is supported by Aircraft. **(Atlantic-Western Europe)** About 1,200 U.S. Heavy Bombers are airborne to aid the Russian offensive. The Air Force strikes Jet factories and other installations; this is the final Strategic Bombing of the war. **21st Army Group** In the **Canadian First Army's 2nd Corps** area, Deventer falls to the Canadian 3rd Division as it closes toward Leeuwarden. Meanwhile, the Canadian 2nd Infantry and 4th Armored Divisions drive toward Groningen and Oldenburg respectively while the British Second Army's 30th Corps advances toward Bremen and the British 53rd Division (12th Corps) drives northeast across the Weser toward Soltau. In addition, the 8th Corps moves toward the Celle region of the Aller River. **12th Army Group** In the **U.S. Ninth Army** area, **XIII Corps** sector, fighting is brisk. The 83rd Division captures Hannover, while the 5th Armored Division, which is spearheading the drive to the Elbe, forces the Oker River. The trailing 102nd Division mops up. In the **XIX Corps** sector, units are also fording the Oker; 2nd Armored's C.C.A. drives east, reaching positions near Hallendorf, while C.C.B. reaches the river at Schladen and at Gross Dohren; a bridge is secured at the former. The 30th Division advances on the Corps' left flank to the Fuhse Canal, west of Braunschweig, while the 83rd Division drives on the right, its units pushing north of the Harz Mountains, while others move doggedly through them. In the **XVI Corps** sector, the 75th Division drives south toward the Witten sector of the Ruhr, seizing Dueren and Stockum. Meanwhile, the 79th Division pushes east along the Ruhr, encountering sporadic resistance and seizing Bochum. In addition, the 17th Airborne Division seizes Essen without incident with its 507th Paratroop Infantry, while the 8th Armored's C.C.B. and the 379th Regiment, 95th Division plow through Luernen and Muehlhausen on the left and seize Kamen on the right. Task Force Faith (attached TF Twaddle) reduces opposition in its area except for that at Arnsberg and Neheim. The drive to secure the Rohr Pocket ends on April 18th. General Ridgway will offer Model surrender terms. In the **U.S. First Army** area, **XVIII (Airborne) Corps** sector, the 13th Armored Division pounds forward, its C.C.A. closing on Siegburg, while C.C.B. gets a bridgehead across the Agger River. Meanwhile, the 97th Division finalizes the capture of Sieg and simultaneously supports 13th Armored as it fords the Sieg. The 8th and 78th Divisions move northwest, hitting strong German rear guard activity, reaching general line Nuembrecht-Eckenhage-Hillmicke and the Valbert-Wegeringhausen areas respectively. In addition, the 86th Division propels elements toward Attendorn. In the **III Corps** sector, the 5th Division's RCT 10 secures an intact bridge at the Wenne River near Berge, while RCT 2 establishes a bridgehead across the river in the high ground near Grevenstein. Activity is strong across the balance of the Corps sector. The 9th Division drives forward until pinched out, and the 7th Armored is bulldozing northwestward while the 99th Division moves confidently through Ober Elspe and Odingen, thrusting further into Halberbracht, Kickenbach, and Meggen. In the **VII Corps** sector, the 3rd Armored Division closes fiercely on Nordhausen, trailed by the 1st and 104th Divisions. In the **V Corps** sector, the 9th Armored Division spearheads an eastward attack to finish off the Germans in the area; C.C.B. drives to Hain on the left while C.C.R. topples Schlotheim on the right; C.C.A., pushing down the center, rolls beyond Ebeleben. The rapid-moving Armor is followed by the 2nd and 69th Divisions, which clear the area as they move. In the **U.S. Third Army** area, the XX Corps also drives east, its 76th and 80th Divisions moving on the left and right respectively, while the 4th and 6th Armored Divisions deploy to crash through the Infantry and spearhead the assault. Some 6th Armored units are relieved by contingents of 9th Armored. The Germans holding Efurt are nearly surrounded by the 80th Division. In addition, the 3rd Cavalry Group is to screen the left and right flanks of Corps. In the **VIII Corps** sector, the 87th and 89th Divisions maintain their attacks. Stutzhaus falls to the 345th Regiment, 87th Division, while the 347th Regiment drives to the fringes of Geraberg. The 89th Division reaches the Gera River at several locations. In the **XII Corps** sector, the 11th Armored drives toward Coburg, supported by close Air and Artillery support; C.C.A.

severs the north and northeast escape routes from the city. The 71st Division advances behind the Armor, wiping out remaining resistance. The Yanks pour heavy fire upon the besieged city throughout the night, which helps persuade the defenders to capitulate on the following day. In other activity, the U.S. Fifteenth Army takes control of the 28th Division (less RCT 112). **6th Army Group** In the **U.S. Seventh Army** area, XV Corps prepares to continue its offensive. In the **XXI Corps** sector, the assault to gain Schweinfurt continues, as Medium Bombers are brought to bear upon the targeted city to support the 42nd Division, already bolstered by Armor and Artillery; it drives to within about three miles from the objective. Hambach and Zell fall to the 232nd Regiment, while C.C.A., 12th Armored Division seizes Alitzheim, Ober Spiesheim, and Unter; C.C.B. takes Castell, Klein Langheim, and Stadt-Schwarzach along the east bank of the Main River. Meanwhile, C.C.R. drives to Geckenheim and Weigenheim, followed by the 101st Cavalry Group. In addition, the 4th Division plows ahead, its 22nd Regiment driving southeast to line Bartenstein-Niederstetten and its 12th Infantry advancing on the left to Laudenbach, seizing it. In the **VI Corps** sector, the heavy fighting to connect the two Heilbronn bridgeheads of the 100th Division is nearly complete. In the 63rd Division sector, contingents establish contact with the 10th Armored Division which is ordered to withdraw from its Crailsheim positions and redeploy in the 63rd Division zone. In the **French 1st Army** area, the 2nd Corps bridgehead near the Enz is enlarged on the right to Neuenburg and the Dobel plateau. Meanwhile, the German lines south of Karisruhe are penetrated by the Valluy Groupement, and in addition, the DA ALPS begins attacking l'Aution in the Alpes Maritimes province. **(Atlantic-Italy) 15th Army Group** In the **U.S. Fifth Army** area, the Germans have evacuated Massa, permitting the 92nd Division to occupy it without incident. In the **British Eighth Army** area, Polish 2nd Corps sector, the 3rd Carpathian Division seizes Solarolo and drives beyond to the Lugo Canal. In the 5th Corps sector, the 2nd New Zealand and Indian 8th Divisions advance toward the Santerno. Meanwhile, the British 78th Division fords the Senio, and the British 56th Division attacks toward the flooded coastal region near Bastia, hitting it on the ground with the 167th Regiment, while the 169th Brigade, bolstered by the 40th Royal Marine Commandos, make an amphibious landing in the enemy's rear.

April 11th 1945 — (Pacific-Philippines) In the **U.S. Sixth Army** area, the 158th Regiment moves to attack Cituinan Hill mass; contingents take Camalig without opposition, while additional forces drive to the southwest slopes of Tagaytay Ridge, positioning the Regiment where it can assault Cituinan from the south and north. In the **I Corps** sector, the Japanese resistance on Three Peaks is eliminated by the 129th Regiment, 37th Division. At Salacsac Pass, Japanese resistance remains tenacious. In addition, the 25th Division drives doggedly against Kapintalan with its 35th Regiment while the 161st Regiment retains control of Crump Hill. In the **XI Corps** sector, Japanese dead are piling high. The driving 38th Division has virtually terminated resistance west of Clark Field and at Ft. Stotsenburg, counting over 5,500 dead Japs. In the **XIV Corps** sector, contact is established between the 1st Cavalry and 11th Airborne Divisions along the coast of Lamon Bay. In addition, the Japanese entrenched at Mt. Malepunyo and at Mt. Mataasna remain under severe pressure from additional contingents of the Cavalry and Airborne forces. **Southern Philippines** The U.S. Eighth Army practices landings at Mindoro for the invasion of Malabang-Parang-Cotabato, on

Mindanao. On Cebu, Coconut Hill falls to contingents of the Americal Division. On Bohol, the 3rd Battalion, 164th Regiment lands without incident on Tagbilaran. Meanwhile, on Negros, the Japanese offer stiff resistance against the 40th Division which presses doggedly with coordinated attacks. **(Pacific-Ryukyu Islands)** The Japanese mount another heavy Kamikaze attack against the U.S. Fleet off Okinawa, compelling Task Force 58 to concentrate on destroying the attacking Planes at the expense of the ongoing support missions with the ground troops. The Battleship *Missouri* (BB-63) and the Aircraft Carrier *Enterprise* (CV-6) are struck by Suicide Planes, and the Carrier *Essex* (CV-9) is damaged by a Dive Bomber; the *Enterprise* retires to Ulithi for repairs. In addition, the Destroyers *Bullard* (DD-660) and the *Kidd* (DD-661) are damaged by Kamikazes, the Destroyer *Hank* (DD-702) is hit by aerial strafing, and the Destroyer *Hale* (DD-642) incurs damage by a Dive Bomber. Destroyer Escorts *Manlove* (DE-36) and *Samuel S. Miles* (DE-183) are damaged by aerial strafing and a Kamikaze respectively. During the melee, the Attack Transport *Berrien* (APA-62) is damaged by collision and the Attack Cargo Ship *Leo* (AKA-60) and the Destroyer *Trathen* (DD-530) are accidentally struck by U.S. Naval gunfire. To close out the Navy's damages, the LST 399 suffers damage by grounding. On Tsugen Shima, the 27th Division terminates its two-day mission, counting 234 Japanese dead. The U.S. Tenth Army jumps the schedule slightly, ordering the 77th Division to seize Ie Shima on the 16th (originally set for Phase II of the campaign). In the **III Amphibious Corps** sector, the 6th Marine Division continues grinding forward on the Motobu Peninsula against entrenched Japanese in the mountainous region Yae-Take. In the **XXIV Corps** sector, resolute Japanese resistance prevents the 96th Division from securing Kakazu Ridge. Meanwhile, the 7th Division propels contingents into Ouki; however, the lack of Tanks forces the 32nd Regiment to pull-back. The Japanese resistance has caused stalemate along the entire Corps front at the Shuri approaches. **(Pacific-Burma)** In the **British Fourteenth Army** area, 4th Corps sector, the Indian 5th Division supported by Armor drives to Yamethin. Although the Armor plows through the town, Japanese fire hinders the Infantry advance. **(Atlantic-Western Europe)** Hitler orders the "SCORCHED EARTH POLICY." The order is not obeyed by many of the Generals who realize the cause is lost, but cannot bring themselves to carry out such a plan. **21st Army Group** In the **Canadian First Army** area, the Canadian 1st Division drives across the Ijssel River, moving west toward Apeldoorn in conjunction with Corps which is moving west on a large front. In the **British Second Army** area, 30th Corps maintains its drive toward Bremen, and in the 12th Corps sector, contingents of the British 53rd Division are stalled near Rethem, but other contingents ford the Leine River at Westen. Meanwhile, the 8th Corps pushes forward units to the Celle area along the Aller River line. **12th Army Group** In the **U.S. Ninth Army** area, **XIII Corps** sector, 5th Armored elements advance closer to the Elbe River; C.C.R. advances to Ohrdorf and C.C.A. drives to Poritz. In addition, the majority of the 84th Division also moves toward the Elbe, while the 102nd Division gets contingents to the Leine River outside Hannover. In the **XIX Corps** sector, the racing 2nd Armored Division's C.C.B. advances 57 miles, coming to a halt at the Elbe, south of Magdeburg; C.C.A. drives to Immendorf, Schoppenstedt, and Wolfenbuettel. Meanwhile, the 30th Division jumps off at 02:00, crossing the Fuhse Canal; RCT 117 seizes a German-held Airfield near Braunschweig and gets elements inside the city, while RCT 120 secures a rail bridge over the Oker River

and seals off eastern exits from the city. In conjunction, Cavalry contingents sever the north and northeastern escape routes. Meanwhile, Groeningen and Halberstadt are secured by the 83rd Division. In the **XVI Corps** sector, four Regiments of the 75th Division advance to Witten on the Ruhr and seize two bridges before the Germans can blow them. In addition, the 75th overruns Annen, Brechten, Eichlinghofen, and Witten. The 35th Division advances forcefully, reaching Kettwig and establishing a bridgehead across the Ruhr. The 17th A/B Division sweeps the Mulheim-Duisburg sector of the Ruhr clear; its 507th Paratroop Infantry secures a small bridgehead at Mulheim, then relinquishes it to the 79th Division. Also, TF Twaddle, 8th Armored Division seizes Unna, while the 95th Division pushes two Regiments to the Gahmen-Grevel-Asseln line. Neheim and a pocket northeast of Arnsberg is seized by TF Faith, posturing U.S. forces near enemy held Arnsberg. In the **U.S. First Army** area, **XVIII Corps (A/B)** sector, C.C.B., 13th Armored, trailed by the 97th Division, plows through Urbach and Wahnerheide in addition to powering frontal elements to positions close to Dunnwald; C.C.A. Task Forces move through Lohmar and also sweep the opposition from the Breidt area. In conjunction, C.C.R., 13th Armored fords the Sieg River. The 78th Division continues advancing northwest, overrunning sporadic resistance and reaching Gummersbach, Dummling and the Drabenderderhohe-Bilstein region. In the 8th Division zone, the 28th Regiment speeds to Kierspe (northwest) and the 121st Infantry advances to the Verse River Dam. In addition, Attendorn is swept up by the 86th Division. In the **III Corps** area, the Wenne bridgehead is expanded by the 5th Division; on the right, the 5th Cavalry Reconnaissance Troop, supported by RCT 10 secures Forst Rumbeck to general line Rumbeck-Hellerfeld; in conjunction, RCT seizes Grevenstein, Linnepe, Weninghausen and Westerfeld. The 7th Armored Division drives to positions from where it can bolt across the fronts of the 5th and 99th Divisions. Meanwhile, the 99th Division has advanced to positions near Fretter, Serkenrode and Weringhausen. Also, the 9th Division, being out of action, releases RCT 47 to VII Corps. In the **VII Corps** area, Nordhausen falls to C.C.B., 3rd Armored; the 104th Division then takes responsibility for it. In conjunction, C.C.R., 3rd Armored seizes Bartolfelde, Neuhof, Osterhagen and Tettenborn, while C.C.A. overruns Herzberg and Osterode; these towns are also taken over by the 104th Division. Gudersleben and Obersachswerfen are secured by the 83rd Armored Reconnaissance Battalion. The 104th and the 1st Infantry Divisions are in close proximity to the rapid moving Armor. In the **V Corps** sector, the 9th Armored Division, trailed by the 2nd and 69th Divisions, continues to drive ahead; C.C.A. pushes to Sachsenburg in the center, while C.C.B. plows through Ringleben on the left, reaching the N-S line; in conjunction, C.C.R. operating on the right, drives to the Ropthenberga-Hardishleben region. In the **U.S. Third Army** area, **XX Corps** sector, the 6th and 4th Armored Divisions bolt out in front of the Infantry as the Yanks drive to the Saale River, liberating the Allied P.O.W. camp in Bad Sulza and reaching Buchenwald, one of the infamous concentration camps; about 21,000 people remain at Buchenwald and an additional 30,000 had been recently transported to other locations. At Buchenwald, in addition to the people being killed by gas and in ovens, the S.S. had permitted radical and sadistic medical experiments. One S.S. Soldier named Sommer, would personally kill a prisoner, then peacefully doze off for the night with the corpse near his bed. 6th Armored drives east, crossing the Saale at points southwest of Naumberg with units then moving through Camburg, Kleinheringen and

Koesen. The 4th Armored attacking abreast and to the right of 6th Armored gets C.C.B. to the Ulrichshalben-Schwarbsdorf area, just short of the Saale and C.C.A. drives to the Saale south of Jenna, however, the bridges are blown, forcing it to pull up for the night. Meanwhile, the trailing 76th Division reaches Buttstaedt, while the 80th Division has its 319th Regiment follow 4th Armored as it drives east along the Autobahn; the 317th and 318th Regiments boxes in the Germans at Erfurt. In conjunction, the 3rd Cavalry Group guards the Corps flanks with its 3rd and 43rd Squadrons operating on the left and right respectively. In the **VIII Corps** sector, the 89th Division forms TF Crater subsequent to reaching line Gutendorf-Tonndorf-Kranichfeld-Wilzenben; the unit, composed of motorized contingents of the 1st Bn., 353rd Infantry, 89th Reconnaissance Troop and supporting units prepares to drive to the Saale on the following day. The 87th Division grinds toward Bad Blankenburg and Stadtilm and the 65th Division moves out to the new assembly area at Waltershausen. In conjunction, the 6th Cavalry Group's 28th Squadron works to close a gap between the 87th and 89th Divisions, while simultaneously protecting Corps north flank. In the **XII Corps** area, the 11th Armored Division accepts the surrender of Coburg; RCT 5, 71st Division is attached to 11th Armored and takes control of the captured town. The 11th then prepares to drive to the Hasslach River line. C.C.R., 11th Armored discovers Neustadt free of the enemy. The 71st Division continues moving right behind the 11th Armored, mopping up. Also, the 26th Division seizes Eisfeld without a fight and the 90th Division tears forward as organized resistance is vanishing along the Corps left flank. The 359th Regiment pushes through Gehren and Langenwiesen, while the 358th zips through Gross Breitenbach. Meanwhile, Reconnaissance troops push beyond Konigsee. **6th Army Group** In the **U.S. Seventh Army** area, **XV Corps** sector, the 3rd and 45th Divisions launch a strong attack southeast of Nuremberg at 15:00; the assault has the 106th Cavalry Group operating to the front as a probing action. In the **XXI Corps** area, Schweinfurt, a constant target of the Allied Air forces is seized by the 43rd Division in concert with 12th Armored which is cutting off escape routes heading east along the Schweinfurt-Bamberg highway; C.C.B. advances to Markt Bibart and C.C.R. columns operating with the 101st Cavalry Group tighten the vise on the Germans in the Uffenheim region. Meanwhile, the 4th Division, bolstered by RCT 324, 44th Division drives southeast toward Rothenburg. In the **VI Corps** sector, the 100th Division troops fighting within Heilbronn hook up and secure about three quarters of the contested city; in conjunction, the 398th Regiment seizes Hagenbach and Jagstfeld as it drives to the Kocher River north of Heilbronn near Odheim. Meanwhile, the 10th Armored Division rolls through the positions of the 255th Regiment, 63rd Division, which is experiencing tough opposition as it expands its Kocher bridgehead south of Weissbach; the 254th Regiment establishes a bridgehead across the Kocher near Ingelfingen, then dispatches contingents toward Kunzelsau. In the **French 1st Army** area, the 2nd Corps continues rooting out opposition along the Enz River; while maintaining a bridgehead across the Enz, other contingents reach Calmbach and the valley south of Dobel. Also, Valluy Groupement advances to the Murg River near Rastatt the begins to envelop the town. **(Atlantic-Italy)** **15th Army Group** In the **U.S. Fifth Army** area, abandoned Carrara is seized by the 442nd Regiment, 92nd Division, but the Germans raise tough resistance against the 473rd which is advancing to the left; later in the day, contingents of the 758th Tank Battalion moves up to assist. In the **British Eighth Army** area, the Germans evacuate their positions along the Senio, but the British give chase. In the Polish 2nd Corps sector contingents advance to the Santerno; the 169th Brigade, British 56th Division lands and seizes Menate and Longastrino. In conjunction, the 167th Brigade continues its overland assault, pushing deeper on the right flank.

April 12th 1945 — (United States) President Roosevelt dies of natural causes at Warm Springs, Georgia. Vice President Harry S Truman is sworn in as President. **(Pacific-Philippines) Luzon** General Headquarters, S.W.P.A., establishes a Command Post in Manila. In the **U.S. Sixth Army** area, contingents of RCT 158 attack Cituinan Hill mass; the 2nd Battalion moves south to secure San Francisco. In the **I Corps** sector, heavy enemy fire stalls the 129th Regiment, 37th Division on Highway 9, outside of Monglo. Contingents of the 130th Regiment, 33rd Division drive into Asin, but the Japanese have constructed a complicated system of tunnels in the region which hinder further progress; heavy skirmishes occur along the Pugo Trail as contingents advance to secure it. The 25th Division's 27th Regiment captures Pimple Hill, under the summit of Mt. Myoko; the 2nd Battalion, 35th Regiment relieves the 3rd Battalion on Fishhook. In the **XI Corps** sector, the Baldy Force, which has been probing for enemy positions in the Ipo area, returns to its original lines. In the **XIV Corps** sector, contingents of the 12th Cavalry Brigade, subsequent to relieving the 11th Airborne contingents east of Mt. Malepunyo, advances into the Bicols. **Southern Philippines** In the **U.S. Eighth Army** area, on Cebu, the Americal Division commences its final offensive on Babay Ridge; the 182nd Regiment breaches the enemy trench defenses as it charges toward the Summit of Hill 21; it repulses heavy counterattacks during the night; contingents of the 132nd Regiment drives from Guadalupe Ridge, but the remainder of the Regiment hits the enemy to the right. Meanwhile, the 1st Battalion, 164th Regiment, quietly moves to positions to the rear, about 1,200 yards from the tip of the ridge. On Bohol, the 3rd Battalion, 164th Regiment drives toward Sierra Bullones in central Boholt to engage the primary Japanese forces. **(Pacific-Dutch East Indies)** The U.S. 31st Division is relieved on Morotai by the 93rd Division, U.S. Eighth Army. **(Pacific-Ruukyu Islands)** In the **U.S. Tenth Army** area, **XXIV Corps** sector, contingents of the 96th Division continue fighting for control of Kakazu Ridge, but most activity is confined to mop-up operations and eliminating resistance in bypassed sectors, however, upon darkness, the Japanese mount vicious counterattacks; there is some penetration, but the U.S. holds its positions. In other activity, an Amphibious Battalion of F.M.F. Pacific, scouts Minna Island, south of Ie Shima, finding no enemy troops. Offshore, Japanese Planes attack the U.S. picket Warships and those anchored at Okinawa: the Destroyer U.S.S. *Mennert L. Abele* (DD-733) is sunk by a piloted bomb; the Battleships *Idaho* (BB-42) and Tennessee (BB-43) are damaged by Kamikaze Planes and during the attack, the Battleship *New Mexico* (BB-40) incurs damage from friendly fire; the Destroyer *Stanly* (DD-478) is damaged by a piloted bomb. Also, the Destroyers *Purdy* (DD-734), *Zellars* (DD-777), and *Cassin Young* (DD-793), are damaged by Suicide Planes as well as the Destroyer Escorts Riddle (DE-185), *Rall* (DE-304), *Walter C. Wann* (DE-412) and the Whitehurst (DE-364). The Light Minelayer *Lindsey* (DM-32), Minesweeper *Gladiator* (AM-319) and the Highspeed Minesweeper *Jeffers* (DMS-27) also sustain damage by Kamikaze attacks. In addition, the Gasoline Tanker *Wabash* (AOG-4) and the Attack Cargo Ship *Wyandot* (AKA-92) sustain damage by collision, and the LST 555 is damaged by grounding. **(Pacific-Iwo Jima)** The final elements of the 9th Marines, 3rd Marine Division depart Guam, having concluded its participation in the mop-up operations on the island. **(Pacific-Burma)** In the **British Fourteenth Army** area, 33rd Corps sector, the 33rd Brigade, Indian 7th Division, seizes Kyaukpadaung, between Chauk and Meiktila, costing the Japanese an important communications center. **(Atlantic-Western Europe) 21st Army Group** In the **Canadian First Army** area, the Canadian I Corps opens its attack against Arnhem. The 49th Division shoots across the Ijssel at 22:40 to attack the German rear in conjunction with the other units which commence diversionary attacks from south of Arnem. In the **British Second Army** area, 30th Corps sector, three Divisions attack: the Guards Armored drives up the center with the British 43rd and recently arrived 51st Division on the left and right respectively. In the 12 Corps sector, Rethem is secured by the British 53rd Division, which subsequently establishes a bridgehead across the Leine River at that point. In the 8 Corps sector, the British 15th Division advances into Celle on the Aller River, after moving through the 6th Airborne lines. **12th Army Group** In the **U.S. Ninth Army** area, the 29th Division is released to the operational control of the XVI Corps; it still maintains its security role at Army's rear. In the **XIII Corps** sector, the 5th Armored Division terminates its race to the Elbe, reaching it at Wittenberge and Werben with C.C.R. and at Tangermuende with C.C.A.; it is unable to secure bridges. Meanwhile, the 84th and 102nd Divisions sweep toward the Elbe, while the 11th Cavalry Group screens the Corps northern flank. In the **XIX Corps** sector, C.C.B., 2nd Armored establishes a small Infantry bridgehead across the Elbe outside Randau, south of Magdeburg. The 35th Division tramples over Braunschweig, then drives about 35 miles east, heading for the Elbe. The 83rd Division's 329th Regiment drives to Barbey on the Elbe; the 330th Regiment remains in the Harz Mountains, blocking the primary roads; the 331st Regiment attacks east and seizes Nienburg on the Saale River. In the **XVI Corps** sector, the area between Westhofen and Witten, north of the Ruhr, is being swept by the 75th Division; the 289th Infantry relieves the 137th Regiment, 35th Division. The 134th Regiment, 35th Division fortifies its positions along the Ruhr; the 320th Regiment is relieved by the 75th Reconnaissance Troop and the 95th Division. The 378th Regiment, 95th Division drives into Dortmund from the east and heavy street fighting erupts; the 379th Infantry swings southwest, driving toward the Ruhr; Task Force Faith neutralizes Arnsberg in conjunction with the 5th Division (First Army III Corps), which is attacking it from the south. The 79th Division, operating on the west flank of the Corps north of the Ruhr, is relieved by the 17th Airborne Division; the 507th Paratroop Infantry accepts the formal surrender of Duisburg. Soon after its relief, the 79th pulls back its bridgehead at Kettwig. Meanwhile, TF Twaddle, 8th Armored Division continues mop-up operations around Unna; at 24:00, it passes to Army control as a reserve force. In the **U.S. First Army** area, **XVIII Corps (Airborne)** area, the Germans continue to retreat, speeding up their getaway. prompting disorganization, which causes many more prisoners to be grabbed; as it becomes inevitable that the Ruhr pocket is dissolving rapidly, Corps extends the boundaries of the 8th, 78th, and 97th Divisions, while also instituting a stop line; the plan allows flexibility including alternate plans for advance if the 78th Division advances to the final objective of the Armor, Hueckeswagen-Wipperfuerth region, prior to the culmination of 13th Armored's drive. C.C.A., 13th Armored seizes Altenrath as it closes on Rath; C.C.B., near Dunnwald, followed by

C.C.R., which is mopping up. In the 97th Division zone, Company C, 386th Regiment attacks heavily fortified enemy positions at Drabenderhohe, Germany. P.F.C. Joe R. Hastings eradicates the crews of a 20-mm gun and a machine gun as he dashes through murderous fire through 350 yards of naked terrain, permitting the 1st Platoon to pull back to safer positions. Meanwhile, he notices that the 3rd Platoon is stalled by menacing fire. Hastings charges 150 yards against withering fire by a 40-mm gun, eliminating it, then taking the point of the attack. Roaring forward, he advances another 175 yards, firing his weapon from his hip, knocking out two more machine guns. The heroic Hastings receives the Medal of Honor posthumously, as he is felled on the 16th, while supporting the 3rd Platoon. In conjunction, the 87th Division trails the Armor sweeping up the remnant resistance. The 78th Division drives forward; a contingent plows into the woods near Engelskirchen, while other columns advance toward Wipperfuerth. Also, the 8th Division drives to the Kreuzberg-Oberbruegge region, southwest of Luedenscheid and the 84th Division advances on the right flank of the Corps; at 22:00, TF Pope is formed, composed of 3rd Battalion, 342nd Regiment, reinforced, to drive to Luedenscheid. In the **III Corps** sector, Arnsberg and Wennigloh are seized by RCT 10, 5th Division; RCT 2 advances to the Ruhr in the Hachen-Recklinghausen region and establishes a bridgehead there; the 32nd Cavalry Squadron, moving with RCT 2, secures the area between the Rohr River and Sorpe Staubecken Lake, south to Seidfeld. In the 7th Armored Division sector, C.C.R. overruns Neuenrade, while C.C.A. drives to Hoevel and Balve. The 99th Division advances to general line Rohrenspring-Roenkhausen. In the **VII Corps** sector, C.C.A., 3rd Armored Division seizes Sangerhausen; C.C.B. scoops up Allstedt, and overpowers Holdenstedt and Wolferstedt; C.C.R., overruns seizes Blankenheim, Obersdorf, and Polsfeld. In conjunction, the 83rd Reconnaissance Battalion, driving along right flank, advances to Allstedt, Niederroeblingen, and Oberroeblingen. Also, the 1st Division, and the attached 4th Cavalry Group is cleaning out the remnant resistance in the Harz Mountains, which is now nearly surrounded. The 413th Regiment, 104th Division, drives into Bad Lauterberg, and captures Ellrich and Sachsa; the 415th Regiment gets contingents to Kelbra, Wallhausen, and Oberroeblingen; the 414th Regiment sets up roadblocks to sever the escape routes from the Harz Mountains, northeast of Nordhausen. In the **V Corps** C.C.B., 9th Armored Division, secures ground near the Saale River outside of Delitz and Bad Lauchstaedt and is then ordered to assemble; C.C.A. advances to the Pettstaedt area after crossing the Unstrut River to assemble there; C.C.R. crosses the Saale River and drives toward Zeitz, although some units driving northwest, abandon the drive upon news that the bridge is down at Weissenfels. However, the 2nd and 69th Divisions gain about 30 miles while trailing the Armor. In the **U.S. Third Army** area, General Eisenhower and General Bradley arrive and go with Patton to the salt mine at Merkers to inspect the captured gold, currency and other valuables; after meeting with General Eddy, they head for XII Corps to meet with General Weyland and from there they fly to XX Corps at Gotha. General Walker suggests they and inspect the concentration camp at Ohrdruf. Patton calls it: "THE MOST APPALLING SIGHT IMAGINABLE." THe Germans had forced inmates to exhume recently buried bodies in order to incinerate them to hide the evidence. General Patton states: "THAT ONE COULD NOT HELP BUT THINK OF SOME GIGANTIC CANNIBALISTIC BARBEQUE." Inmates inform the Americans that about 3,000 people have been buried there since January 1st, 1945. In the

XX Corps sector, the 6th Armored Division secures crossings at the Weisse-Elster River; a contingent of C.C.B. discovers blown bridges at Weisse-Elster and pivots north to cross in the V Corps sector to seize a bridge at Pegau and another column rushes to bypass Zeitz to search for a crossing over the Weisse-Elster. C.C.A. hits firm resistance seizes a bridgehead hits tough resistance west of Zeitz, but a column seizes a bridge across the Weisse-Elster at Rossendorf and establishes an Infantry bridgehead; soon after a time bomb blows the bridge. C.C.R., 6th Armored advances to Kretzschau, west of Zeitz, and begins searching for a crossing. In the 4th Armored Division zone, the bridges are blown at the Saale; some elements cross in rubber boats, while others are ferried; the remainder move across later on bridges constructed by Engineers. Meanwhile, C.C.B. crosses the Saale River north of Jena and seizes Kunitz and Laasan, while C.C.A. fords the river south of Jena and drives northeast. Also, the 76th Division, motorized, follows 6th Armored toward Zeitz. In the 80th Division zone, the 319th Regiment takes the surrender of Weimar, then drives toward Jena. The **VIII Corps** advances toward the Saale River, meeting light resistance; the 89th Division's TF Crater leads the attack, reaching the area near Rothenstein, followed by the 355th Regiment which secures Tannroda; the 354th Infantry advances sluggishly, south of Kranichfeld. The 87th Division's TF Sundt drives to the Saale River outside of Rudolstadt; bolstered by the 346th Regiment, Altremda and Ehrenstein are seized; Bad Blankenburg is overpowered by the 347th Regiment. In the **XII Corps** sector, the 11th Armored Division secures bridgeheads at Kronach and Marktzeuln; the 71st Division assumes responsibility for Neustadt, freeing C.C.R. to advance to Ebersdorf. The 71st Division continues trailing the Armor. Meanwhile, the 26th Division roars forward, seizing Lauscha, Oberlind, Sonneberg, and Steinach. Also, the 90th Division speeds ahead, advancing about ten miles, overrunning sporadic light resistance. On the Corps right flank, the 42nd Squadron, 2nd Cavalry Group, gets Reconnaissance Patrols to the Main River and also establishes a small bridgehead at Michelau. **6th Army Group** In the **U.S. Seventh Army** area, **XV Corps** sector, the 3rd and 45th Divisions drive across the Main River and deploy to assault Bamberg. In the **XXI Corps** sector, the 42nd Division eliminates the remnant resistance in Schweinfurt and its attached C.C.A. (12th Armored Division), advances and makes contact with the XV Corps' 5th Division. Also, the Germans at Uffenheim are surrounded by the 101st Cavalry Group and other supporting units. The 4th Division continues driving toward Rothenburg. In the **VI Corps** sector, the 100th Division culminates a hellish nine-day battle, seizing Heilbronn. C.C.A., 10th Armored Division pushes TF Hankins (61st Armored Infantry Battalion) across the Kocher River into the Kocher bridgehead south of Weissbach, then expands it to Neuenstein. In conjunction, the 63rd Division advances along the banks of the Kocher, eliminating remaining enemy positions. In the **French First Army** area, the 2nd Corps completes securing its zone up to the Enz River and bolsters its bridgehead. Baden Baden and Rastatt are secured by the Valluy Groupement. Meanwhile, DA ALPS terminates all resistance at l'Aution, however, the Germans retain the Roya River Valley. **(Atlantic-Italy) 15th Army Group** In the **U.S. Fifth Army** area, the scheduled offensive is postponed for 24 hours due to inclement weather. In other activity, the 92nd Division is plagued with supply problems; Engineers are rushed in to reopen a road along the Carrione Creek, between Carrara and Massa. In the **British Eighth Army** area, Polish 2 Corps sector, establishes a bridgehead

across the Santerno River. In the 5 Corps sector, the German lines along the Santerno fold as the Germans retreat toward positions beyond Massa Lombardo; scores of prisoners are snatched because of the lack of discipline during the retreat. The British 56th Division drives toward Bastia, subsequent to the 167th and 169th Brigades converging on Longastrino. Meanwhile, the British 78th Division is catapulted through the Indian 8th Division bridgehead to pursue the beleaguered retreating Germans; the 36th Brigade swerves west, driving toward the Sillaro River; the 38th Brigade, bolstered with a huge Armor contingent prepares to attack north toward Bastia.

A captured short-range flying bomb on Okinawa.

April 13th 1945 — (Pacific-Philippines) Luzon In the **U.S. Sixth Army** area, RCT 158 contingents continue to struggle for control of Cituinan Hill and surrounding area for the next week, while its 2nd Battalion and AT Company maintain the drive to eliminate the Japs at San Francisco (Sorsogon Province); vicious enemy fire continues to pour down from the hills near the town. In the **I Corps** sector, the 129th Regiment, 37th Division drives to positions about 300 yards west of Monglo, having secured the dominating hills, controlling Highway 9. During the advance, P.F.C. Dexter J. Kerstetter takes his Squad through the Yank lines, the he moves out in front. Taking a circuitous route he gets on top of a Jap position, then suddenly drops down in front of their cave, killing four of the enemy. He gets back to the trail and advances against slicing fire of a machine gun and other small arms; Kerstetter eradicates the gun and its four crewmen. Despite burning his hand severely from the heated fire of his weapon, he routs another group of about twenty Soldiers, but exhausts his ammunition. Undaunted, he returns to get more ammo, then leads another Platoon back to launch a fresh assault. The hill falls to the Americans; P.F.C. Kerstetter receives the Medal of Honor for his indomitable courage. Meanwhile, the 27th Regiment, 25th Division, knocks off a feature known as Wart as it drives toward Mt. Myoko. In addition, the **XI Corps** still jabs against the Japs holding up in the mountains in central Luzon. On Caballo Island, final Japanese resistance is terminated. On El Fraile Island, a Task Force composed of contingents of the 151st Regiment and Engineers destroys Fort Drum by igniting fuel oil. In the **XIV Corps** area, the 5th Cavalry, 1st Cavalry Division drives southeast and encounters fortified but unoccupied enemy positions as it closes on Calauag. Meanwhile, the 8th Cavalry advances close to enemy positions in the Mt. Mataasna Bundoc region while the 11th Airborne sets up for its final assault to secure Mt. Macolod and Mt. Malepunyo. **Southern Philippines** In the **U.S. Eighth**

Army area, on Cebu, heavy fighting continues as the Americal Division still pounds against Babay Ridge. Hill 21 falls to the 182nd Regiment and the 132nd Regiment fights futilely for control of Hill 25, north of Guadalupe Road, spending the next several days blowing pillboxes and sealing caves. By the 16th, the Japanese evacuate their defenses in Cebu city. On Negros, about fifty Japanese mount an unsuccessful predawn counterattack against the 185th Regiment, 40th Division, near San Juan; most die suddenly. In conjunction, the 160th Regiment encounters tenacious resistance at Hill 3155. **(Pacific-Ryukyu Islands)** The Fleet Marine Force Amphibious Reconnaissance Battalion occupies Minna Shima, off the northern coast of Okinawa, in concert with an intensified preinvasion bombardment of Ie Shima; the Battalion lands in preparation for the assault against Ie Shima. In the **U.S. Tenth Army** area, **III Amphibious Corps** sector, final preparations are made by the 6th Marine Division, to eradicate the entrenched positions of the Japanese on the Motobu Peninsula in the Yae-Take hill mass. Contingents of the 22nd Marines drive to the northern tip of the west coast of Okinawa, reaching Hedo. Meanwhile, other contingents maintain reconnaissance operations on the east coast and some head inland. In the **XXIV Corps** sector, Japanese infiltrators which are still alive are being destroyed by mop-up teams; in addition, Corps continues to repulse futile counterattacks. During one nasty attack, the Japanese become acquainted with Beaufort T. Anderson, 381st Infantry, 96th Division; during the predawn hours, the Japs spring a stunning blow against the flank of Company C. Sergeant Anderson directs his men to a time-worn tomb, then shatters the screaming attackers by emptying one magazine at pointblank range, then he tosses one of the enemy mortars, which had not exploded, into their midst, killing several. The Banzai screams diminish further as he hoists U.S. mortar shells, pulls the pins and hurls them at the befuddled enemy between bursts of fire from his carbine. Beaufort Anderson is wounded seriously, but he has decimated the attack and saved the Company flank from collapse. His actions account for the termination of several enemy machine guns, enemy knee mortars and at least 25 enemy Soldiers; he receives the Medal of Honor. Offshore, the Destroyer Escort U.S.S. *Connolly* is damaged by a Japanese Kamikaze. **(Pacific-Burma)** In the **British Fourteenth Army** area, 33 Corps sector, Taungdwingyi falls to the Indian 20th Division. **(Atlantic-Western Europe) 21st Army Group** In the **Canadian First Army** area, heavy fighting continues at Arnhem, as the Canadian I Corps attempts to secure it. Meanwhile, the Canadian 1st Division transfers from the 2nd Corps to I Corps. In the **British Second Army** area, the 30th Corps continues advancing toward Bremen. In the 8th Corps sector, the advance toward Uelzen continues, and in the 12th Corps sector, the Rethem bridgehead stretches toward Soltau. **12th Army Group** In the **U.S. Ninth Army** area, **XIII Corps** sector, the 5th Armored Division secures Tangermuende as it continues to mop up along the Elbe River. Meanwhile, the 84th and 102nd Divisions are closing on the Elbe. In the XIX Corps sector, the 30th Division, driving on the Corps' left flank, gets contingents to the Elbe. The 2nd Armored Division's C.C.B., encounters rigid resistance at its Elbe bridgehead and is compelled to move further south to the Elbenau-Gruenwalde area. At the same time, C.C.A. and C.C.R. neutralize Magdebourg. In other activity, the 83rd Division gets a bridgehead across the Elbe at Barby. In the **XVI Corps** sector, some resistance remains in Herdecke, and the remainder of the 75th Division zone between Witten and Westhofen (north of Ruhr) is clear. In Task Force Twaddle's zone, the 378th Regiment, 95th Division reduces final resistance in Dortmund, now in ruins due to previous Allied air raids. Subsequently, Task Force Twaddle is dissolved at 24:00; however, the 95th Division retains control over 15th Cavalry Group. In the **U.S. First Army** area, **XVIII Corps (A/B)** sector, the Germans continue retreating hastily, with Armor and Infantry in pursuit. The 13th Armored Division, trailed by the 97th Division, makes great progress. The 78th Division seizes the 13th Armored's final objectives, Hueckeswagen and Wipperfuerth, without opposition. The steamroller advance includes the 8th Division, which is speeding northwest, and the 86th Division, operating on the right flank, overrunning Herscheid, Huinghausen, and Plettenberg with its 343rd Regiment; it topples Luedenscheid with its 342nd Regiment. In the **III Corps** sector, the 5th Division advances to line Herdringen-Holzen-Boeingsen, between the Ruhr and Honne Rivers. The 99th Division, trailing 7th Armored, eliminates bypassed resistance on the left flank of Corps in the area south of Sorpe Staubecken Lake. In the **VII Corps** sector, 3rd Armored reaches the Saale River at several locations, crossing dismounted contingents and subsequently laying bridges for Armor. Meanwhile, the 1st Division and attached 4th Cavalry Group start methodical eradication of Japanese in the Harz Mountains. In conjunction, the 104th Division continues running interference on the left along southern perimeter of the Harz Mountains, while also driving east on the right; Task Force Kelleher is organized to spearhead the drive to the Saale. Meanwhile, the 9th Division assembles near Nordhausen. In the **V Corps** sector, the 9th Armored Division continues advancing, trailed by the 2nd Division which reaches the Saale River near Merseburg; C.C.A. deploys defensively at Pegau while C.C.B. halts at Weissenfels until Engineers can construct bridges. In conjunction, C.C.R. seizes a bridge northeast of Zeitz, aborts its attack against the town, and moves to positions south of Leipzig. Meanwhile, the 69th Division, reinforced, gets contingents across the Saale in assault boats, subsequent to securing some of Weissenfels, west of the Saale; contingents of RCT 272 reach Hohenmoelsen. In the **U.S. Third Army** area, **XX Corps** sector, contingents of the 6th Armored Division get additional units across the Weisse-Elster River and acquire more bridges. C.C.B. drives southeast to Lucka while C.C.A. crosses at Rossendorf and at Schkauditz. Meanwhile, C.C.R. and accompanying RCT 304, 76th Division encounter fierce fire as they cross near Zeitz; RCT 304 attacks the town. The 4th Armored Division, also forces the Weisse-Elster, rapidly driving east from the Mulde bridgeheads, establishing additional bridgeheads across the Zwick Mulde River during the 70-mile drive. In the **VIII Corps** sector, mop-up operations continue in the area west of the Saale; all Vehicle bridges have been destroyed by the Germans. The 87th Division reduces enemy resistance in its zone up to the Saale and pushes contingents across the river at several locations by use of foot bridges and by fording. Meanwhile, the 89th Division secures the Rothenstein-Beutelsdorf area west of the Saale, then dissolves TF Crater. In conjunction, the 65th Division drives toward Arnstadt, eradicating stragglers. On the Corps' left flank, the 6th Cavalry Group maintains its defense of the area. In the **XII Corps** sector, the 11th Armored Division, trailed by the 71st Division, races southeast, despite horrible roads, seizes Kulmbach, and severs the Kulmbach-Bayreuth road, prior to being halted by Corps. In conjunction, the 26th and 90th Divisions push forward rapidly, elements of the former seizing a bridge over the Selbitz, southeast of Lichtenberg. In the **U.S. Fifteenth Army** area, **XXII Corps** sector, the 28th Division is attached to Corps and receives responsibility for the Juelich region. **6th Army Group** In the **U.S. Seventh Army** area, **XV Corps** sector, contingents of the 3rd and 45th Divisions crash into Bamberg and begin a vicious fight to secure it; the town falls by the following day, allowing Corps to drive toward Nuremberg. In the **XXI Corps** sector, the 42nd Division prepares to assault Fuerth. The 12th Armored Division's C.C.B. drives toward the Aisch River, southwest of Neustadt, while C.C.R. destroys an enemy pocket in the right portion of its zone; C.C.A., temporarily attached to 42nd Division, reverts to parent unit. In conjunction, the 101st Cavalry Group, operating southeast of the Armor, discovers German forces concentrated along the Adelshofen-Steinach-Burgbernheim line. The 4th Division drives forcefully, making great strides on the right flank of the Corps. In the **VI Corps** sector, German resistance is being crushed all along the front. The 10th Armored crunches through Oehringen, seizing it and thrusting southwest and west, establishing contact with the 100th Division at Heilbronn. The 63rd Division overruns all its assigned objectives easily as it drives on the north flank of the Corps; the 253rd Regiment bolts across the Kocher and propels to the Brettach River; the 255th drives effortlessly to Neuenstadt, and the 254th concentrates around Kunzelsau, advancing southward to general line Kupferzell-Rueblingen. In the **French 1st Army** area, elements of the French 1st Armored Division drives south across the Baden Plain, east of the Rhine, seizing Buehl with little effort; additional contingents in synchronization with 2nd Corps elements plow through the Black Forest driving toward Freudenstadt. **(Atlantic-Eastern Europe)** Vienna falls; the beleaguered German forces lose the city to contingents of the Second and Third Ukrainian Fronts. **(Atlantic-Italy) 15th Army Group** In the **U.S. Fifth Army** area, again inclement weather forces postponement of the offensive. In the **British Eighth Army** area, 5 Corps sector, the New Zealand 2nd Division and the 36th Brigade, British 78th Division drive west in conjunction with the British 56th Division, advancing on the right, moving fast toward Bastia. Meanwhile, the 24th Guards Brigade, 56th Division, and the 9th Commandos launch an amphibious landing against Chiesa del Bando, northeast of Argenta; German resistance along the Fosso Marina is vicious, halting any advance.

April 14th 1945 — (Pacific-Philippines) Luzon In the **U.S. Sixth Army** area, heavy skirmishing continues as contingents of RCT 158 press San Francisco, subsequent to additional Air strikes. In the **I Corps** sector, following an Air strike, the 148th Regiment, 37th Division attacks toward Monglo; contingents reach Hairpin Hill, less than 1,000 yards from the town. Marine SBDs attached to Marine Aircraft Group 24 fly the last Marine Aviation mission on Luzon in support of the 37th Division attack. **(Pacific-Ryukyu Islands)** In the **U.S. Tenth Army** area, **III Amphibious Corps** sector, the 4th Marines and the 29th Marines, 6th Marine Division, bolstered by Air, Naval Surface fire, and Artillery, attack the Yae-Take hill mass on the Motobu Peninsula. The 4th Marines drive east while the 29th Marines drive west and southwest, encountering fierce terrain and tenacious opposition; however, the 4th Marines advance to the initial ridges. In the **XXIV Corps** sector, the Japanese mount another predawn fanatical attack, and again it is repulsed, terminating any further such attempts. Offshore, the Fleet again is struck by suicidal attacks: the Battleship *New York* (BB-34) and the Destroyers *Dashiel* (DD-659), *Hunt* (DD-674), and the *Sigsbee* (DD-502) are damaged. In addition, the Gunboat PGM-11 incurs damage by grounding, and the LST 241 is damaged by collision. **(Pacific-East China Sea)** The Submarine U.S.S. *Tirante*, operating on the surface near Korea, on her first war patrol, encroaches the shoreline at Quelpart Island for a reconnaissance run. The *Tirante* fires two torpedoes at a rotund ammunition Ship igniting a huge fire that exposes the position of the intrepid Submarine. Commander George Levick Street, III, repositions his Submarine and fires additional deadly shots at the Frigate *Nomi* and the Coast Defense Vessel No. 31, sinking both as he makes a quick getaway from the shallow harbor. The *Tirante* still finds time to pick up several downed Japanese Airmen and also captures a few Japanese from a Schooner. Commander Street receives the Medal of Honor and the *Tirante* receives a Presidential citation after returning to Pearl Harbor at the conclusion of its 52 day, 1st War Patrol. **(Pacific-China)** Tokyo orders the China Expeditionary Force to divert four Divisions to central and northern China. The directive forces a withdrawal of Japanese forces from the Hunan-Kwangsi Railroad, a strategic line connecting Hengyang, Kweilin, Liuchow, and Yung-ning, the east China Air Bases. General Ho's Chief of Staff presents a plan to halt the assault by striking the enemy's flanks and employing a double envelopment to terminate the Japanese drive against Chihchiang. The proposition is accepted and the plan becomes effective. **(Atlantic-Western Europe) 21st Army Group** The Canadian I Corps secures Arnhem, but some isolated pockets remain in the town as the Corps continues forward, closing on Apeldoorn. Meanwhile, the Canadian 2nd Corps advances along a wide front, driving north, seizing Zwolle on the left without incident, while advancing to the area around Meppel. In the British Second Army area, Army continues closing on Bremen, Soltau, and Uelzen; contingents of the 8th Corps' 15th Division advances to the fringes of Uelzen. As the British swing north, the U.S. XIII Corps' north flank becomes unprotected, except for the U.S. 11th Cavalry Group. **12th Army Group** In the **U.S. Ninth Army** area, **XIII Corps** sector, the 11th Cavalry Group reaches the Elbe after a quick advance while screening the north flank of the Corps. The 5th Armored Division mops up in its sector; orders to attack across the Elbe had been rescinded. In conjunction, the rapidly advancing 84th and 102nd Divisions dash to the Elbe, overtaking the Armor. During the day, U.S. and political prisoners are liberated at Salzwedel; at Gardelegen, results of massive Nazi atrocities are experienced first hand by conquering U.S. forces. In the **XIX Corps** sector, the 2nd Armored Division's C.C.B. pulls back from its bridgehead at the Elbe after several unsuccessful attempts to place a bridge or use ferry boats to reinforce and supply C.C.B. Infantry, deployed east of the river. Meanwhile, C.C.R. fords the river at Barby and assumes responsibility for the left flank of the 83rd Division's bridgehead and is attached to Division. In addition, the 30th Division secures several towns in its sector west of the Elbe. In the **XVI Corps** sector, operations against the Ruhr pocket are terminated. The 75th Division accepts the surrender of Herdecke and is subsequently relieved by the 79th Division. The 79th Infantry and 17th Airborne Divisions continue their occupation mission, the 17th establishing contact with the 8th Division (VIII Corp, First Army). In addition, contact is established between the 79th and 95th Divisions as the Yanks continue tightening the noose on the besieged German forces still resisting the American advance. The 95th Division relieves the 15th Cavalry Group of its screening operations along the Ruhr; the 15th Cavalry Group is then attached to the 29th Division for Military Government duty. In the **U.S. First Army** area, **XVIII Corps (A/B)** sector, the 13th Armored Division, trailed by the 97th Infantry Division, attacks northeast toward Wipperfuerth; however, this the final phase of the

Ruhr assault must be modified because of the extraordinary progress of the contingents on the right; it is ordered to pivot and move north to establish contact with Ninth Army. Meanwhile, the 78th Division moves into Wermelskirchen, which is declared an open city, as it drives up the center, and it also gets elements to positions near Bursheid and Lennep on the left and right respectively. In the 8th Division sector, Schwelm falls to the 28th Regiment, while the 13th Regiment drives to the Ruhr near Wetter, making contact with Ninth Army. Meanwhile, the 86th Division seizes Hagen with the 341st Regiment; the 343rd Regiment sweeps through many towns and villages along the Lenne River on the right flank, and the 342nd continues driving toward Hohenlimburg. In the **III Corps** sector, the remaining resistance between the Ruhr and Honne Rivers is reduced by RCT 2 and RCT 10, 5th Division. Meanwhile, RCT 11 arrives at Division sector from Frankfurt to bolster the force. In the 7th Armored sector, C.C.A. is prepared to pounce upon Hemer by 12:00. Efforts are made to arrange for a peaceful capitulation, but the Germans turn down the offer, prompting an attack at 20:30 which seizes the town. The 99th Infantry Division, trailing the 7th Armored, eliminates bypassed resistance as it advances to the Neuenrade-Garbeck area where it relieves C.C.R. Meanwhile, subsequent to the successful construction of bridges, bolts across the Saale and drives relentlessly, reaching positions near Dessau at the Elbe and Mulde Rivers. In the Harz Mountains, the 1st Division, disregarding the horrendous terrain and well-fortified roadblocks, penetrates further. In conjunction, the 413th Regiment, 104th Division, also operating around the Harz Mountains, makes contact with the 1st Division. The 9th Division commits two Regiments against German positions in their sector of the Harz Mountains; the 37th and 49th Regiments clear the eastern portion of the mountains. In the **V Corps** sector, C.C.A., 9th Armored Division attacks east, driving from the Weisse-Elster River line at 14:00, advancing toward Lobstadt; it is followed by C.C.B. as soon as bridges are operational. Meanwhile, C.C.R. roars through Breitingen and the factory area at Deutzen. In addition, the 2nd Division gets contingents to the Saale; its 23rd Regiment establishes a bridgehead north of Merseburg, improvising with a damaged railroad bridge. The 38th Regiment, bolstered by the 3rd Battalion, 9th Regiment, launches an attack at 14:00, crossing a bridge at Weissenfels, advancing against horrendous fire raised to forestall loss of the synthetic rubber and gasoline facilities at Merseburg and Leuna. Weissenfels falls to RCT 271, reinforced, 69th Division; in conjunction RCT 272 advances to the Weisse River northeast of Zeitz, at Luetzkewitz. In the **U.S. Third Army** area, **XX Corps** sector, the German defenses crack along the Weisse-Elster River, as the 6th Armored bolts through, driving east bypassing towns and villages to reach the Zwick Mulde River; contingents of C.C.B. establish a bridgehead at Rochlitz, while others halt at the river line near Carsdorf. Meanwhile, C.C.A., also driving in two columns, advances to Spora and Oberkossa, on the left and right respectively. In addition, C.C.R. darts across the river at Zeitz and plows forward destroying many German AA batteries as it romps through Zeitz, which is being cleared by the 76th Division. In the 76th Division zone, RCT 417 takes over the task of mopping up in Zeitz, relieving RCT 304. In the 4th Armored zone, C.C.B. enlarges its Wolkenberg bridgehead and seizes two additional bridges at Penig, while C.C.A., trailed by C.C.R., secures Limbach and Wustenbrand; the Armor is followed by the 318th Regiment, 80th Division. The 319th Regiment, 80th Division seizes Gera as it drives east, leaving the 317th Regiment to control the Gera and Jena areas, until relieved at Weimar by the 5th Ranger Battalion. In the **VIII Corps** sector, the 353rd and 355th Regiments, 89th Division drive east from the Saale, advancing to general line Moeckern-Zwackau-Arnshagen. In the 87th Division sector, TF Sundt spearheads another advance, driving to Peuschen. The 346th Regiment advances east about three miles from an Ettelbach crossing location, while the 347th Regiment pushes to Schmorda. Meanwhile, the 28th Cavalry Group crosses the Saale in the XX Corps zone and advances to Weisse-Elster River in the 89th Division zone near the Gera-Weida region. In the **XII Corps** sector, a Task Force of C.C.B., 11th Armored Division dispatches two columns to seize Bayreuth from the southeast; another attacking force (14th Armored Division, Seventh Army) is converging on the same target, causing some problems. C.C.B. maintains its attack, moving to the north and western fringes of the city to offer an opportunity for the Germans to surrender. The Germans fail to seize the opportunity and again U.S. Planes and Artillery are offered as persuasion as C.C.B. rolls into Beyreuth. In conjunction, the 71st Division is given responsibility for eliminating the German resistance in the town. At 18:30, contingents of RCT 14, bolstered by contingents of the 5th Regiment, charge enemy positions, securing the western section of town and relieving C.C.B. units. In conjunction, the 42nd Squadron, 2nd Cavalry Group, sits patiently at the south and southeast exits from the city, blocking the escape routes. In additional activity, the 26th Division advances reaching the north-south Autobahn west of Hof. The 90th Division nudges against the enemy line of Saale River, Saale Stau Lake, and the Selbitz River, capturing Lobenstein and establishing a bridgehead southeast of Lichtenberg, which had been previously seized by the 90th Reconnaissance Battalion. The 358th Regiment seizes a bridgehead and secures Blankenberg. **6th Army Group** In the **U.S. Seventh Army** area, **XV Corps** sector, the remaining resistance in Bamberg is reduced; Corps drives toward Nuremberg. In the **XXI Corps** sector, the 42nd Division drives southeast in pursuit of retreating German forces which are retiring along the Wuerzburg-Nuremberg Road. To the right, the 12th Armored Division also attacks southeast; C.C.B. pushes up the center followed by C.C.A. and C.C.R. on the left and right respectively; the 101st Cavalry Group, reinforced by the 92nd Cavalry Reconnaissance Squadron, advances intertwined between the Armor. C.C.B. establishes a small bridgehead along the Aisch River at Dietersheim, prior to the bridge collapsing. C.C.R., followed by the 8th Regiment, 4th Division, seizes several towns as it advances on the right flank. Meanwhile, the 101st Cavalry Group establishes a bridgehead across the Aisch, subsequent to crossing at Lenkersheim and Ipsheim. The remainder of the 4th Division closes on Rothenburg. In the **VI Corps** sector, the 100th Division drives from Heilbronn, moving columns east and southeast toward Loewenstein, relieving C.C.A., 10th Armored near Bitzfeld. The 63rd Division relieves C.C.A., 10th Armored near Oehringen and also establishes contact with the 100th Division. The 10th Armored Division has completed its mission of securing its zone, prior to relief. In the **French 1st Army** area, the DA ATL launches an offensive designed to secure the Gironde Estuary. The initial assault targets the Royan sector on the north side of the river. **(Atlantic-Italy) 15th Army Group** In the **U.S. Fifth Army** area, the attack, previously postponed twice, commences in the **IV Corps** sector. The 92nd Division encounters heavy resistance hindering its advance for several days despite matching U.S. firepower against the German guns. The IV corps drives through the region between the Samoggia and Reno Rivers toward the Po Valley, subsequent to an Air and Artillery bombardment. The BEF supports the main thrust of the 10th Mountain Division, seizing Montese. The 10th Mountain Division slugs forward, securing the Pra del Bianca basin, capturing Torre Iussi and Rocca di Roffeno. Also, at Castel d'Aiano, P.F.C. John D. Magrath, Company G, 85th Regiment bolts from his cover after his Company becomes stalled by intense fire; he captures a machine gun and knocks its crew out of action. Transporting the captured gun, he braves more enemy fire and eliminates two additional machine guns. Soon after, the enemy pounds the newly won terrain and Magrath volunteers to make the rounds and get a casualty report, but an enemy shell kills him. Magrath receives the Medal of Honor posthumously. Meanwhile, on the right flank, the 1st Armored Division begins a vicious contest for Vergato, along Highway 64, while simultaneously driving against Suzzano on the left.

In the **British Eighth Army** area, the 10th Corps extends its boundary west to consume the vacated 13 Corps zone, essentially terminating Corps offensive operations due to the lack of manpower; however, contingents cross the Santerno River to support the Polish 2nd Corps, which is fighting hard near Imola. The Jewish Brigade is pinched out as Polish troops advance; it reverts to reserve. Imola falls under the pressure of the Polish 2nd Corps. Meanwhile, the 13th Corps assumes its new zone between the Polish 2nd Corps and the British 5th Corps, leaving six Infantry Battalions behind to help strengthen 10th Corps. Meanwhile, the New Zealand 2nd Division (5th Corps) arrives at the Sillaro River and is attached in place to 13th Corps to bolster the northern drive against Argenta Gap. In the 5 Corps sector, the 36th Brigade, British 78th Division advances to the Sillaro River while the 38th Brigade moves north to the Reno River at Bastia. The Germans still mount enough resistance to hold up the British 56th Division contingents moving northeast of Argenta, but additional elements drive toward Bastia.

April 15th 1945 — (Pacific-Philippines) Luzon In the **U.S. Sixth Army** area, RCT 158 (main body) continues to pound Cituinan Hill mass, striking it repeatedly from the north and south; still the Japanese retain firm control. Meanwhile, the 2nd Battalion, RCT 158, sends two columns against San Francisco, seizing the town. In the **I Corps** sector, the 148th Regiment, 37th Division, supported by Air and Artillery, attacks and seizes Hairpin Hill, then drives down Highway 9 beyond Quioeng. The 130th Regiment, 33rd Division sends contingents against a Jap-held ridge west of the Asin Tunnels, but the well-entrenched enemy holds off the attack. Bombardment becomes necessary to soften positions before launching another assault several days later. Meanwhile, elements of the 27th Regiment, 25th Division lunge from the captured Wart driving across a ravine toward a nearby hill. In addition, the 2nd Battalion, 35th Regiment seizes a hill in its zone. In the **XI Corps** sector, contingents of the 152nd Regiment, 38th Division which has advanced from the west coast establish contact with the 149th Regiment on Mt. Pinatubo area, terminating the long struggle victoriously. In the **XIV Corps** sector, the 511th Regiment, 11th Airborne Division commences an offensive, driving east against the Mt. Malepunyo hill mass. **Southern Philippines** In the **U.S. Eighth Army** area, on Cebu, the Americal Division penetrates deeper to annihilate the Japs holding the high ground at Cebu City. On Bohol, the 3rd Battalion, 164th Regiment, Americal Division encounters Japanese north of Ginopolan. On Negros, Air and Artillery pummel enemy positions in the Negritos-Patog region, while the 40th Division waits to attack; over 170 tons of bombs are dropped by 108 Planes to soften opposition. Meanwhile, the 40th Division is preparing to land on Mindanao, but Major General Franklin C.Sibert, after being informed that Guerrillas have seized Malabang, modifies the attack plan. The 24th Division, minus one Battalion of the 21st Infantry, is to land near Parang. The lone Battalion is to go ashore at Malabang as planned. **(Pacific-Ryukyu Islands)** Artillery comes ashore on Minna Island to bolster the invasion of Ie Shima. Meanwhile, the plastering of Ie Shima by Aircraft and Naval Surface gunfire continues. In the **U.S. Tenth Army** area, **III Amphibious Corps** sector, the Japanese continue resisting bitterly on the Motobu Peninsula, forcing the 6th Marine Division to move forward under extremely heavy fire, eliminating the entrenched Japs methodically in costly fighting. During the brutalizing encounter, P.F.C. Harold Gonsalves, acting as Scout Sergeant, 4th Battalion, 15th Marines, accompanies his Commanding Officer and one other Marine on a mission taking them into heavy fire on Mount Yae Take to coordinate the Artillery fire. As they advance to the front line, an enemy grenade is tossed into their midst. Gonsalves immediately throws his body on the grenade, saving the lives of the other Marines; he receives the Medal of Honor posthumously. On the following day, the Marines launch a full-measured attack to crush the obstinate resistance. Offshore, the Kamikazes strike again; the Destroyers *Wilson* (DD-408) and *Laffey* (DD-724) incur damage. In addition, the Oiler *Taluga* (AO-62) is struck by a Suicide Plane and the Motor Minesweeper YMS-331 is damaged by a fanatical Jap in a Kamikaze Boat. The *Laffey* is commanded by Comander F. Julian Becton. Becton had witnessed the *Laffey's* predecessor, *Laffey* I (DD-459) which had been destroyed during November 13th, 1942 at the Battle of Guadalcanal. The *Laffey's* crew faces attack by 22 Planes; nine are shot from the sky, but seven of them, five of which are still carrying bombs, crash into the valiant Vessel purposely and an eighth Aircraft hits her mast by accident. In addition, a Corsair strikes her mast. If that isn't enough to take her out, add four conventional bombs which strike menacing blows. However, the *Laffey* which came with the Fleet that came to stay, miraculously remained afloat. The Japanese hold her dead in the water, but Commander Becton refuses to give up the fight, stating:" I'LL NEVER ABANDON SHIP AS LONG AS A GUN WILL FIRE!" The Japanese attack against the Fleet lasts eighty minutes and every Vessel puts up a magnificent fight, but the *Laffey* takes an incredible amount of punishment. Although, the beleaguered Ship is towed to safety, within six days she moves toward Saipan under her own power, and from there the crew brings her back to the U.S.A. The *Laffey* still lives as an inspiration to all Americans. She stands proudly at Patriot's Point, near Charleston in Mount Pleasant, South Carolina. **(Pacific-Japan)** Admiral Mitscher's Task Force 58 commences a heavy attack against the Airfields at Kyushu, Japan, to destroy as many Planes on the ground as possible. The Aircraft attack again on the following day. Offshore, the Japanese Submarines RO-64 and RO-67 both sink after striking mines; the Frigate *Mokuto* also sinks after striking a mine. **(Pacific-Southeast Asia)** The Submarine U.S.S. *Charr*, operating off the Malay Peninsula, which extends from Singapore to the Isthmus of Kra, lays mines in Japanese Shipping lanes. **(Atlantic-Western Europe) 21st Army Group** In the **Canadian First Army** area, Canadian I Corps sector, the British 49th Division reduces the final resistance in Arnhem; the Germans abandon the area, heading for their fortified positions in Holland. Eisenhower and Montgomery will concur that the combination of the German defenses in Holland, coupled with the catastrophic burdens already being borne by the civilians there, will cause the impending campaign into Holland to be postponed. The Canadian 5th Armored moves from Arnhem toward Zuider Zee, while the Canadian 1st Division advances toward Apeldoorn. Meanwhile, the Canadian 2nd Corps drives toward the Leeuwarden-Groningen-Oldenburg line; elements start to secure Groningen. In the **British Second Army** area, 30th Corps sector, the Guards Armored Division is now secure. Meanwhile, the British 3rd, 43rd, and 51st Divisions continue driving toward Bremen. In the 12th Corps sector, contingents of the British 53rd Division advance beyond Kirchboitzen. In the 8th Corps sector, heavy fighting continues to ensue at Uelzen. **12th Army Group** In the **U.S. Ninth Army** area, **XIII Corps** sector, 5th Armored units continue mopping up along the Elbe, while additional contingents of the 84th and 102nd Divisions converge on the river. In the **XIX Corps** sector, RCT 134, 35th Division assumes responsibility for the area between Grieben to the area of the Colbitz Forest. Meanwhile, RCTs 117 and 120 finalize the reduction of resistance in the 30th Division zone west of the Elbe. The 2nd Armored retains its defensive deployment in the Magdeburg area. The 83rd Division enlarges its Elbe bridgehead east of Barby. RCT 320, 35th Division is attached to the 83rd Division; it attacks and seizes Tornitz and Werkleitz on the right flank of Corps, then jumps across the Saale to capture Gross Rosenburg. Meanwhile, Engineers await darkness to lay a treadway bridge at Breitenhagen, southeast of the Barby bridgehead, as added support for the positions at Barby. In conjunction, the 330th Regiment, 83rd Division, maintains its mop up operation in the Harz Mountains and establishes contact with the 1st Division (VII Corps, First Army). In the **XVI Corps** sector along the Ruhr, the action decreases during the next several days as the III and XVIII Corps (A/B) mount more pressure on the Ruhr pocket south of the Ruhr River. In the **U.S. First Army** area, **XVIII Corps (A/B)** sector, the 13th Armored Division, less C.C.R., attacks north, driving against fierce resistance toward the Wupper River; C.C.B. seizes Opladen. Close behind the charging Armor is the 97th Division's 303rd Regiment, which snarls the important I.G. Farben chemical facility outside of Leverkusen, then continues advancing to the river. Meanwhile, the 386th and 387th Regiments drive to the Berg Neukirchen-Burscheid railway. The 78th Division advances quickly, overrunning slight resistance, seizing Remscheid and Ronsdorf in addition to capturing Lennep and getting contingents to the fringes of Wuppertal. The 8th Division pushes the 28th Regiment to the Ruhr north of Schwelm. The 13th and 121st Regiments pass through their lines, the former supported by C.C.R., 13th Armored Division, seizes Hattingen and the latter drives about three miles toward Wuelfrath. In addition, the 86th Division finishes eliminating resistance in its sector, along the Lenne as far as the Ruhr, except for a few small pockets. In the **III Corps** sector, the 5th Division concludes its offensive mission in the Ruhr region; RCTs 2 and 10 remain in place while the 11th Regiment secures the area west of Menden between the Ruhr and Iserlohn. The 7th Armored Division moves through the 5th Division lines. C.C.R. drives west toward Kalthof. The 99th Division continues to drive northwest. In the **VII Corps** sector, the 3rd Armored continues to advance. C.C.B. improvises and gets elements across the Mulde River near Torten by way of a damaged bridge to establish a small bridgehead; C.C.R. secures Koethen, except for a pocket in the northeastern part of the town. In other activity, the 83rd Armored Reconnaissance Battalion discovers Bitterfeld and Wolfen strongly fortified, but it seizes Reuden, Sandersdorf, and Thalheim. In the

Harz Mountains, the 1st and 9th Divisions continue slow and steady elimination of obstinate resistance. In the **V Corps** sector, C.C.B., 9th Armored Division seizes Borna without incident; it had been bypassed by C.C.A. which advances northwest of the prize. C.C.R. seizes Grimma, then captures bridges near Colditz-Lastau. Meanwhile, by 08:00, the 2nd Division has secured Leuna and Merseburg; upon darkness it dispatches the 9th Regiment into the 69th Division sector to demolish emplaced German Anti-aircraft batteries. In the **U.S. Third Army** area, General Patton, accompanied by General Walker, visits Buchenwald concentration camp at Weimar. The prisoners have been fed meals which provide 800 calories per day; many of the prisoners are used for slave labor at a nearby factory which manufactured parts for the V-1 bomb. Patton notes that the factory is now: "A MONUMENT TO THE ACCURATE BOMBING OF OUR AIR FORCE, BECAUSE THEY COMPLETELY ELIMINATED THE FACTORY WITHOUT PUTTING A SINGLE BOMB IN THE CAMP, WHICH WAS CONTIGUOUS." General Patton also notes that "ONE OF THE MOST HORRIBLE POINTS ABOUT THIS PLACE (Buchenwald) WAS THAT ALL THESE EXECUTIONS WERE CARRIED ON BY SLAVES." In the **XX Corps** sector, the 6th Armored advances across the Mulde River and drives east to the limiting line, where it is ordered to stop progress and await the Soviet Army. Meanwhile, C.C.A. seizes three bridges across the Zachopau River near Mittweida. The 76th Division moves to relieve the 6th Armored Mulde bridgehead. In the 4th Armored sector, C.C.B. strengthens its lines at Bergstadt while seizing bridges at the Chemnitz River around Draisdorf. Meanwhile, C.C.A. accepts the surrender of Siegmar. The 80th Division moving in the shadow of the Armor secures Grimmitscha and the majority of Glauchau with its 319th Regiment; the 318th will assume responsibility for the bridgehead overlooking Chemnitz. In the **VIII Corps** sector, the 89th Division is ordered to establish a bridgehead over the Zwick Mulde River near Wickau and also is instructed to make contact with the XX Corps. The 87th Division drives southeast, getting contingents to Langenbach. In other activity, the 65th Division is informed that it is being returned to XX Corps. In the **XII Corps** sector, the 11th Armored Division has concluded its mission and remains in the assembly area. At Bayreuth, RCT 14, 71st Division, and contingents of the 2nd Cavalry Group continue mopping up stragglers. The balance of the 71st Division and the 26th Division move to their respective restraining lines. In addition, the 90th Division, keeps moving toward Plauen-Hof road, securing most of Hof. In the **U.S. Fifteenth Army** area, the XXII Corps receives responsibility for the Aachen area. **6th Army Group** In the **U.S. Seventh Army** area, the XV Corps continues to close on Nuremberg. In the **XX Corps** sector, elements of the 42nd Division advance to the Aisch River line. C.C.B., 12th Armored crosses the Aisch and drives toward Scheller and Kotzenaurach; the 101st Cavalry Group drives southeast through Linden, reaching the Zenn River. C.C.R. encounters fierce resistance and is halted near Westheim. Also, the 4th Division attacks southeast with its 8th Regiment, driving in conjunction with C.C.R., 12th Armored toward Ansbach. The 12th and 22nd Regiments, 4th Division close against Rothenburg and also meet tenacious resistance from the Germans who refuse to relent, despite the pressure and insurmountable odds. In the **VI Corps** sector, the attack also heads southeast as the 63rd and 100th Divisions advance abreast. The 63rd advances on a wide front reaching Michelbach and also gets contingents to positions near Goggenbach, Nesselbach, Steinkirchen, Waldenburg, and Westernach. The 100th Division, driving to the

Neuberg-Buchhorn area on the left and Loewenstein in the center, secures Unt Gruppenbach on the right. In the **French 1st Army** area, the 2nd Corps continues driving through the Black Forest, attacking in conjunction with the Valluy Groupement toward the Nagold River. The 1st Corps fords the Rhine north of Kehl without incident, while the Valluy Groupement, bolstered by contingents of the 1st Corps (east of the Rhine contingents), seizes Kehl. In addition, advance contingents secure Offenburg easily as it drives south across the Baden Plain to the suburbs of Lahr; meanwhile, the left flank contingents maintain the thrust through the Black Forest. In the DA ATL sector, Air and Artillery units again bombard the Royan area prior to the attack of the French forces which advance to the fringes of the city. Additional French forces, fighting across the Gironde River in the Pointe de Grave sector, drive a wedge into the German defenses near Vensac. **(Atlantic-Italy) 15th Army Group** In the **U.S. Fifth Army** area, **IV Corps** sector, M. Pigna falls to the 10th Mountain Division and M. Mantino, but no progress is made on the exposed left flank. The 1st Armored Division reduces resistance in Suzzano and continues fighting viciously from house to house for control of Vergato. The II Corps joins the ongoing offensive, attacking east of Highway 64, toward Bologna after dark on the night of the 15th-16th. The 6th South African Division and the U.S. 88th Divisions, both jumping off at 22:30 and followed by the U.S. 34th and 91st Divisions, commence their attack at 03:00. The Germans mount rigid resistance all along the line; however, by 05:30, the 6th South African Division secures M. Sole. In the **British Eighth Army** area, the Polish 2nd Corps advances to the Sillaro River. In the 13th Corps sector, the New Zealand Division spearheads the Corps drive toward Budrio, followed shortly thereafter by the 10th Indian Division. In the 5th Corps sector, British Commandos assume responsibility for British 78th Division zone, freeing it to press against the Argenta Gap. Meanwhile, the Germans hang tough, raising resolute resistance against attacks by the British 56th and 78th Divisions.

April 16th 1945 — U.S.S. Laffey subsequent to attack off Okinawa.

April 16th 1945 — (United States) The Carrier U.S.S. *Boxer* (CV-21) is commissioned at Newport News, Virginia. The Submarine U.S.S. *Kete* (SS-369) is reported missing and presumed lost in the Pacific. **(Pacific-Philippines) Luzon** In the **U.S. Sixth Army** area, the Japanese mount a fierce counterattack against the 2nd Battalion, RCT 158, at San Francisco; however, the Japs are thrown back and the Yanks follow with a counterattack which eradicates resistance in the entire area. With the southern tip of Bicol peninsula secure, Allied Ships can now maneuver the northern exit areas of the San Bernardino Strait free of attack. In the **I Corps** sector, con-

tingents of the 148th Regiment, 37th Division wins a tough fight securing the heights east of Highway 9 outside of Yagyagan. In the **XI Corps** sector, the 1st Regiment, 6th Division attacks "Woodpecker" Ridge near the confluence of the Bosoboso and Mariquina Rivers. Subsequent to two days of softening fire by Aircraft and by Cruisers and Destroyers, the 1st Battalion, 151st Regiment, reinforced, lands on Carabao Island, the final objective in Manila Bay, encountering no opposition. In the **XIV Corps** sector, Mt. Malepunyo and Mt. Dalaga are seized by the 511th Regiment, 11th Airborne Division. In other activity, the 7th and 8th Cavalry, 1st Cavalry Division have German forces bottled up north and northwest of Mt. Mataasna Bundoc. **Southern Philippines** In the **U.S. Eighth Army** area, the Japanese entrenched in the heights above Cebu City continue to staunchly resist the Americal Division, greatly hindering progress; however, the Japanese are preparing to abandon their positions during the night. On Negros, the weather again plagues the Americans, as torrential rains keep all Planes grounded; nevertheless, drenched Artillerymen continue to pound the enemy positions. In the Sulu Archipelago, RCT 163, 41st Division mops up remaining sporadic resistance on Jolo. **(Pacific-Ryukyu Islands)** Subsequent to a Naval and Air bombardment, contingents of the 77th Division hit the south and southwest coast of Ie Shima at 08:00, the 305th and 306th Regiments landing on the right and left respectively. The Regiments race inland, overcoming mines and resistance, seizing about two-thirds of the island and securing the Airfield. After dark, the Japs spring counterattacks against the perimeter of the 305th Regiment, but the Yanks clobber the attackers and hold their ground. The 77th completes capture of the island by the 21st. Marine Aircraft Groups 31 and 33 fly Combat Air Patrol in support of the landing. On **Okinawa**, in the **III Amphibious Corps** sector, the 6th Marine Division throws a powerful blow against the Japs on Motobu Peninsula, striking from three directions. Companies A and C, 1st Battalion, 4th Marines seize Yae Take, the mountain fortress and primary terrain feature on the peninsula, shattering enemy organized resistance. Corporal Richard Earl Bush's Squad (1st Battalion) is the first unit to drive through the squall of fire and reach the summit from where they flush the defenders from their positions. Bush becomes wounded and is being treated by medics when a grenade is thrown among the wounded; Bush instinctively pulls the live grenade to his prone body and absorbs the entire shock, saving many of his buddies. Bush receives the Medal of Honor for his extraordinary bravery. In the **XXIV Corps** sector, regrouping occurs in preparation for a full-strength assault on the 19th. **Offshore**: Despite receiving heavy Air strikes by Task Force 58, Japanese Kamikazes from the Kyushu Airfields again make the one-way trip to strike the Fleet off Okinawa. The Destroyer *Pringle* (DD-477) is sunk by a Suicide Plane. The Carrier *Intrepid* (CV-11), the Battleship *Missouri* (BB-63), the Destroyer *Bryant* (DD-665), the Destroyer Escort *Bowers* (DE-637), and the High Speed Mine Sweepers *Harding* (DMS-28) and *Hobson* (DMS-26) all sustain damage by Kamikazes. In addition, the Minesweeper *Champion* (AM-314) is damaged by a Horizontal Bomber, and the Destroyer Escort *McDermut* (DD-677) is accidentally struck by U.S. Naval gunfire. **(Pacific-Burma)** In the **British Fourteenth Army** area, 4th Corps sector, Shwemyo is occupied by contingents of the Indian 5th Division, after overcoming light opposition; these advance troops are unable to eliminate heavy fire ringing in on them from the Shwemyo Bluff. **(Pacific-Japan)** The Submarine U.S.S. *Sunfish* (SS-281) sinks the Japanese Defense Vessel No. 73 off Honshu. **(North Atlantic)**

The Destroyer Escorts *Frost* (DE-144) and *Stanton* (DE-247) team up and sink the German U-Boats U-180 and U-1235. **(Atlantic-Western Europe)** The German Vessel *Luetzow* is sunk by R.A.F. Planes during a daylight raid against Swinemuende. **21st Army Group** In the **Canadian First Army** area, Leeuwarden and Groningen are seized by elements of the Canadian 2nd Corps. In the **British Second Army** area, 30th Corps forces converge on Bremen; advance contingents of the British 3rd Division advance to Brinkum, slightly south of the objective. In the 12th Corps sector, the British 7th Armored Division advances to Walsrode as it drives toward Soltau. In the 8th Corps sector, the Germans continue to resist violently against the British 15th Division at Uelzen. **12th Army Group** In the **U.S. Ninth Army** area, **XIII Corps** sector, the 5th Armored Division is relieved by the 84th and 102nd Divisions at the Elbe; 5th Armored is directed to clear the rear area of remnant enemy stragglers, which could hinder supply routes. In other activity, the 35th Division, minus RCT 320, is attached to Corps. In the **XIX Corps** sector, RCT 320, 35th Division continues ridding the area between the Elbe and Saale Rivers of enemy resistance. Meanwhile, the Germans continue to mount sporadic nuisance Air raids against the Elbe bridges. In other activity, the 2nd Armored Division keeps its defensive stance; C.C.R. repulses a heavy attack against it. In addition, C.C.A., 2nd Armored, is attached to Corps. In the **U.S. First Army** area, **XVIII Corps (A/B)** sector, 13th Armored maintains its forward advance, followed by the 97th Division. The 97th drives across the Wupper River and makes rapid progress, reaching the general line Hilden-Solingen; however, the Germans retain Solingen. Meanwhile, the 78th Division, seizes several towns including Elberfeld and Wuppertal, totally securing its zone, and is soon pinched out by the 8th Division. In the **III Corps** sector, the Germans, confronted with an insurmountable task, chose to surrender during the early part of the day, folding the resistance in the eastern section of the Ruhr pocket; huge amounts of German troops capitulate. Negotiations for surrender commence at 06:30, bringing C.C.R., 7th Armored Division's attack to a halt. Meanwhile, by 08:50, the attacking 99th Division gives the Germans a reprieve. By day's end, each of the two U.S. Divisions accepts the surrender of over 20,000 prisoners, including the surrender of the Iserlohn Garrison in the 99th Division zone. In the **VII Corps** sector, the orders come down, directing the Corps to halt at the Elbe and Mulde Rivers to greet the Russians when they arrive. 3rd Armored, holding a bridgehead at the Mulde, extends south along the river: C.C.R. reduces all resistance in Bernburg, sealing its Harz Mountain exit and also secures Koethen, Klepzig, and Merzien. In conjunction, C.C.A. whips through Libbesdorf, seizing it and driving beyond toward Dessau; units begin sweeping through Forst Haldeburg. In addition, C.C.B. retains the Mulde bridgehead near Torten and continues bridging while under severe enemy fire. The 104th Division continues fighting for control of Halle and pushes other elements across the Saale. Over on the west flank, the 1st and 9th Divisions keep pressing through the Harz Mountains. In the **V Corps** sector, the 9th Armored's C.C.R. drives to the Mulde in the vicinity of Bennewitz-Grimma and pushes a column across into Colditz, which it seizes. In other activity, the 2nd Division advances about three miles eastward, while the 69th Division drives northeast against Leipzig. In the **U.S. Third Army** area, RCT 304, 76th Division takes over responsibility for the 6th Armored bridgehead over the Zwick Mulde. The 4th Armored Division gives responsibility for the Zwick Mulde bridgehead to elements of the 80th Division. In the **VIII Corps** sector, the

6th Cavalry Group, advancing in front of the 89th Division, captures the bridges over the Weisse-Elster at Berga and at Knottengrund, handing them to the 89th. Meanwhile, the 89th drives to the Pliesse River and immediately assaults Werdau, as well as pushing into Werdauer Wald in the center and pushing to the Weisse-Elster River on the right, reaching the Greiz area. In the 87th Division zone, elements reach the Autobahn; the 346th Regiment seizes Zeulenroda then dashes across the Weisse-Elster toward Brockau. In conjunction, TF Sundt pushes southeast across the river reaching Mechelgruen, and the 347th Regiment, 87th Division overpowers the resistance in Plauen and gets elements to the Autobahn. In the **XII Corps** sector, the 71st Division eliminates the final resistance in Bayreuth. The 90th Division reduces the final opposition and secures Hof. In the **U.S. Fifteenth Army** area, the 422nd and 423rd Regiments, 106th Division are attached to the 66th Division for training. The 106th Division had sustained the initial brunt of the German attack during December 1944 in the Ardennes. **6th Army Group** In the **U.S. Seventh Army** area, **XV Corps** sector, the 3rd and 45th Division close on Nuremberg, the latter penetrating German defenses in the suburbs. In the **XXI Corps** sector, the 42nd Division darts across the Aisch River, seizing Neustadt in a flash prior to driving toward Fuerth. The 12th Armored Division races southeast toward Ansbach. In conjunction, the 8th Regiment, 4th Division closes against Ansbach while the 12th and 22nd Regiments secure positions north and west of Rothenburg respectively. Meanwhile, the 324th Regiment advances southeast on the right flank of the Division. In the **VI Corps** sector, the 10th Armored, trailed by the 63rd and 100th Divisions on the left and right respectively, drives swiftly; C.C.A. reaches Gleichen-Heuholz on the right, while C.C.B., driving on the left, advances toward Schwaebisch. Contingents of the 100th Division advance through Loewenstein. In the **French 1st Army** area, Calw, on the Nagold River to the 2nd Corps. Meanwhile, the 3rd Algerian Division begins clearing the woods south of Pforzheim. In addition, the 1st Corps moves against the Germans in the Black Forest. In the DA ATL area, French troops seize Royan on the north side of the Gironde Estuary and then begin driving northwest, sweeping between the Gironde and Le Seudre Rivers. **(Atlantic-Eastern Europe)** The Soviets launch an immense offensive toward Berlin during the early morning hours, attacking along the Neisse and Oder Rivers. The powerful Russian guns pound the Oder Valley, decimating the villages and farms with spreading fires. Contingents of the Third White Russian Front sweep the Samland Peninsula in East Prussia on the northern front, while the Second Ukrainian Front, driving on the southern front, seizes territory southeast of Bruenn, Czechoslovakia, and also north of Vienna. Meanwhile, forces of the Third Ukrainian Front seize Fuerstenfeld, east of Gratz while advancing west of Vienna. German intelligence had knowledge of the attack. Russian agents had been previously parachuted behind German lines on April 7th with instructions to expect Russian troops on the 20th. Some agents had been captured. Their orders instructed them to scout British and American preparations for attacking the Russians and further ordered: "IN THE EVENT THAT BERLIN IS CAPTURED BY THE BRITISH AND AMERICANS, THE AGENTS ARE TO DESTROY ALL THEIR PAPERS, BUT ON NO ACCOUNT, IDENTIFY THEMSELVES AS AGENTS. Additional information gained from a captured agent identifies the attack date as the 20th, and the Russian anticipation of skirmishes with American troops. The Russians intend to take Berlin before the U.S. and expect to "DRENCH THE

AMERICANS BY ACCIDENT WITH AN ARTILLERY BOM-BARDMENT SO THEY CAN GET A TASTE OF THE RED ARMY'S LASH." **(Atlantic-Italy) 15th Army Group** In the **U.S. Fifth Army** area, **IV Corps** sector, the Germans begin to withdraw, due to enormous pressure. M. Mosco, Monzuno, and Tole are seized by the 10th Mountain Division, while the 1st Armored Division seizes M. Pero and eliminates final resistance in Vergato. In conjunction, the B.E.F. starts relieving contingents of the 10th Mountain Division along the left flank. In the **II Corps** sector, the determined Germans refuse to bend, raising tenacious resistance; the South African 6th Armored Division seizes M. Abelle and M. Caprara. The 88th Division captures Furcoli, but enemy resistance repulses the attempt to seize the crest of M. Monterumici. In addition, the Germans resist fiercely as the 91st Division grinds along Highway 65, toward M. Adone, M. Arnigo, M. Posigliano, and Pianoro. In the 34th Division zone, a well-defended fortification on Gorgognano Ridge is reduced, as the Division jackhammers toward Sevizzano Ridge. In the **British Eighth Army** area, Polish 2nd Corps sector, Medicina is toppled by the Indian 43rd Division. In the 5th Corps sector, Bastia falls to Corps and a vicious struggle begins in the Argenta Gap.

April 17th 1945 — (United States) In twenty days, the war in Europe will cease with the unconditional surrender of Germany to the Allies. Today, the U.S. and the Soviet Government sign the Fourth Protocol for assistance to the Russians, giving them an additional 2 million seven-hundred thousand tons of supplies via the Pacific, and 3 million tons by way of the Atlantic. This figure does not include the Allied German Occupation Marks which Russia will print (initially authorized by Treasury Department, despite strong Military protests) at a cost to the U.S. treasury of $270 million dollars before the practice is finally stopped; the U.S. prints the currency for the other Allies. **(Pacific-Wake Island)** The Submarine U.S.S. *Sea Owl*, lurking off Wake Island for several days for an enemy Submarine she had spotted, becomes impatient and moves in for the attack, sinking the Japanese Submarine RO-56 while it is in anchor. **(Pacific-Philippines) Luzon** In the **U.S. Sixth Army** area, **I Corps** sector, the 148th Regiment, 37th Division drives to the Irisan River, reaching the final defensive positions of the Japanese stretched out in front of Baguio; enemy resistance holds the Regiment in abeyance for a few days at the destroyed bridge. Meanwhile, the 32nd and 33rd Divisions are heavily engaged at Salacsac Pass along the Villa Verde Trail and in the Asin Tunnels area respectively. In addition, the 25th Division encounters fierce resistance as it advances along Highway 5 near Kapintalan. In the **XI Corps** sector, the 63rd Regiment, 6th Division terminates the remaining resistance on the northern tip of Mt. Mataba; the 1st Regiment is stymied at Woodpecker Ridge and cancels its attack. In the **XIV Corps** sector, on the final Japanese stronghold in southern Luzon, the western slopes of Mt. Mataasna Bundoc, the Japanese mount ferocious resistance against the 2nd Cavalry Brigade, 1st Cavalry Division. The 511th Infantry, 11th Airborne Division, pivots north to support the Cavalry. **Southern Philippines** In the **U.S. Eighth Army** area, Victor V Attack Group (TG 78.2), commanded by Rear Admiral Albert G. Noble, commences an Air and Naval gunfire bombardment to soften resistance for elements of the X Corps' 24th Division, awaiting to land on Mindanao. Upon cessation of the attack, the main force lands near Parang and a second contingent lands north of Malabang, each hitting the beach without resistance. As reports had previously indicated, Malabang is controlled by Guerrillas when the 21st Regiment arrives there. The rapid inland advance captures Parang and the high ground above Polloc Harbor. Also, Ground echelons of Marine Aircraft Group 24 participate in the landing. On Bohol, contingents of the 164th Regiment launch an attack against Japanese positions north of Ginopolan; the Japanese are eliminated by the 20th. On Cebu, the Americal Division occupies Hills 22 and 25 effortlessly as the Japanese have abandoned their positions on Babay Ridge. On Negros, the 40th Division reinitiates its attack. The 503rd Paratroop Regiment drives to the outer defenses of the Japanese in front of the lower slopes of Banana Ridge. In conjunction, the 185th Regiment advances about 1,600 yards, but progress is halted by an enemy Tank trap. Also, the 160th Regiment pushes forward, advancing about 1,000 yards. In the Sulu Archipelago, enemy resistance has been eradicated on Jolo Island, except those Japanese compressed on Mt. Daho. The Yanks revert to dispensing enormous punishment into the enemy positions, committing Planes in support of massive Artillery and mortar bombardment, pounding the last remaining stronghold for the next several days. **(Pacific-Ryukyu Islands)** On Ie Shima, the 306th Regiment, 77th Division continues its holding pattern while awaiting the trailing 305th, which is driving east toward the feature which commands the entire island: Iegusugu Mt, dubbed the "Pinnacle." Also, elements advance to the secondary objective, Ie Town. Meanwhile, contingents of the 307th Regiment land on the southern coast and push northeast against menacing resistance from the Japanese holding "Bloody Ridge" and the equally tenacious ridge on it, called "Government House Hill." In other activity, the Destroyer U.S.S. *Benham* (DD-796) incurs damage by a Kamikaze, and it is also struck accidentally by U.S. Naval gunfire. **(Pacific-Burma)** British Admiral Mountbatten modifies plans for Operation DRACULA, specifying amphibious and air operations to seize Rangoon. **(Atlantic-Western Europe) 21st Army Group** In the **Canadian First Army** area, Canadian 1st Corps sector, the Canadian 1st Division seizes Apeldoorn. Meanwhile, the Canadian 5th Armored Division bolts forward, severing the Amersfoort-Apeldoorn Highway. In the **British Second Army** area, the Germans continue their staunch resistance outside of Bremen. In the 12th Corps sector, troops are flowing toward Harburg while others close on Soltau. In the 8th Corps sector, heavy fighting continues at Uelzen. **12th Army Group** In the **U.S. Ninth Army** area, **XIII Corps** sector, a gap has been created between the British and U.S. Forces, prompting the 29th Division to be attached to 5th Armored Division to bolster its drive to the Elbe. C.C.A., 5th Armored initiates action to secure Forst Knesebeck, south of Wittingen and is supported by contingents of the 84th and 102nd Divisions. Meanwhile, C.C.B. establishes roadblocks east of the forest while C.C.R. mops up in its sector near Salzwedel. In the **XIX Corps** sector, German held Magdeburg comes under severe attack at about 15:00, following a heavy Air bombardment. C.C.A., 2nd Armored Division, and the 30th Division converge on the objective from different directions, seizing about two-thirds of it. Meanwhile, the 83rd Division maintains and strengthens its Elbe bridgehead. In the **XVI Corps** sector, the 75th Division assembles around Brambauer. In the **U.S. First Army** area, **XVIII Corps (A/B)** sector, C.C.A., 13th Armored Division plows forward near Mettman, overrunning a German Command Post before halting for the night at Ratingen while C.C.B. drives to Duisburg, establishing contact with elements of the 8th Division near Wuelfrath. Meanwhile, the 97th Division prepares to attack Duesseldorf on the following day, subsequent to securing Solingen. In addition, the 8th Division terminates its offensive mission with the seizure of Werden and the elimination of remaining resistance in its sector south of the Ruhr while the 86th Division mops up while preparing to join the Third Army. Also, in the **III Corps** sector, scores of prisoners are being rounded up as Corps prepares to move to Third Army zone. The 5th Division assumes responsibility for Corps sector. In the **VII Corps** sector, 3rd Armored Division is securing its sector west of the Mulde and south of the Elbe, including the elimination of final resistance in Forst Haldeburg, outside of Dessau. At Halle, the Germans refuse surrender terms, prompting TF Kelleher (104th Regiment) to reinitiate its attack, seizing about two thirds of the city by nightfall. In conjunction, the 413th Regiment seals off escape routes from the city. Meanwhile, the 415th Regiment drives to Sandersdorf and Roitzsch on the left and right respectively. In the Harz Mountains, the 1st and 9th Divisions still pound against the German resistance, the former seizing Braunlage, Tanne, and Zorge. Contingents of the 9th Division are relieved by 1st Division units at Hasselfelde. In the **V Corps** sector, the 9th Armored Division romps along the Mulde, mopping up, and the 2nd and 9th Divisions converge upon Leipzig. In the **U.S. Third Army** area, **XX Corps** sector, preparations are made for the drive into Austria. The 65th Division is attached to Corps. In the **VIII Corps** sector, final resistance in Werdau collapses to the 89th Division, which also seizes Greiz and Reichenbach, receiving Air support with the latter. Meanwhile, elements of the 87th Division get across the Autobahn, reaching Lengenfeld and Treuen; in conjunction, TF Sundt also crosses the Autobahn, advancing to positions near Bergen, while the 347th Regiment occupies Theuma. In the **XII Corps** sector, a defensive posture is maintained while making preparations to attack on the 19th. In other activity, the 11th Armored Division begins to relieve the 14th Armored (XV Corps). **6th Army Group** In the **U.S. Seventh Army** area, the ongoing southeastern drive pivots and attacks southward. In the **XV Corps** sector, the 3rd and 45th Divisions converge on heavily fortified Nuremberg, where the determined German forces fight viciously to forestall the inevitable. First Lt. Frank Burke, 1st Battalion, 15th Regiment (in charge of motor-pool) moves up to search for a motor-pool site, but discovers about ten Germans preparing to attack. Burke, retires and confiscates a light machine gun and an ample supply of ammunition, then he charges the superior force. Enemy return fire is fierce, but Burke neutralizes it and then avoids injury from the withering fire of another machine gun; Burke exterminates the gun crew and scatters the survivors of the original band. Undaunted, Burke procures a rifle and attacks some bombed out buildings to eliminate enemy Infantrymen. As the one-man wrecking crew continues his escapade, a sniper's bullet whizzes from a cellar window and zings past his head, prompting Burke to dash into the cellar and expend an entire clip, terminating the sniper's career. Burke, seemingly forgetting his responsibility is for his Battalion's Vehicles, discards his jammed weapon, scoops up another and stuffs a few grenades into his uniform as he continues the chase. Another exchange of fire erupts, but Burke's marksmanship is not up to par; he pulls the pins on two grenades, charges the enemy position and lets both grenades go. However, simultaneously, the Germans launch a grenade of their own, creating a horrendous triple explosion. When the smoke clears, a stunned Burke emerges, but the Germans have been obliterated. Instead of returning to U.S. lines, Burke advances, killing three more Germans, then he disintegrates the charge of a machine pistolman before concluding his four hour marathon. Burke joins a Platoon and participates in a 30 minute donnybrook which ends in a Yank

victory; Burke singlehandedly kills 11 Germans and wounds three; he receives the Medal of Honor. In other 3rd Division activity at Nuremberg, German fire stalls the advance of a contingent of Company A, 15th Regiment. Lt. Michael J. Daly, singlehandedly advances and destroys the machine gun and kills the crew. Soon after, he is again leading his contingent and encounters a six-man Patrol with an accompanying rocket launcher. Daly moves out and singlehandedly wipes out the enemy contingent. As Daly's unit advances further, an enemy machine gun opens up and again Daly jumps out front. He kills the gunner with his carbine and directs machine gun fire which destroys the remainder of the crew. Lt. Daly then eliminates a third machine gun; he receives the Medal of Honor. Another member of the 3rd Division, Private Joseph F. Merrell, Company I, 15th Regiment receives the Medal of Honor for his bravery near Lohe. Merrell's unit is stalled by heavy fire, but he singlehandedly dashes through 100 yards of blistering fire and annihilates four German machine pistolmen at close range. He advances further and a sniper's bullet destroys his weapon. Undaunted, Merrell, armed with three grenades continues his advance, racing 200 yards through another wall of fire. He destroys the first machine gun with two of his grenades, then jumps in the foxhole and grabs a German Luger, using it to eliminate the survivors of the blasts. Merrell attacks toward the next machine gun, killing four Germans along the way, but he receives a severe wound in the stomach. Disregarding his personal safety, Merrell continues to advance, receiving more enemy fire which shreds his uniform and causes him to bleed more profusely. A staggering Merrell refuses to relent; he tosses his final grenade into the nest and then attempts to charge to kill the survivors, but a burst of fire kills him instantly. Pvt. Merrell receives the Medal of Honor posthumously. In the **XXI Corps** sector, German forces retreat toward Fuerth, pursued by the charging 42nd Division. C.C.A., 12th Armored, and the 232nd Regiment secure Gadolzburg and Zautendorf; C.C.B. captures Heilbronn. In the 4th Division sector, Rothenburg falls to the 12th Regiment while the 8th Regiment drives to Ansbach and also gets units to Ober Felden. In the **VI Corps** sector, Corps is directed to drive to the Swiss border to seal off enemy escape routes from the Black Forest. The 10th Armored, flanked by the 63rd and 100th Divisions on the left and right respectively, drives forward swiftly. C.C.A. reaches Gailsbach, Huetten, and Schuppach. C.C.B. takes Suelz in addition to supporting the 254th Regiment, 63rd Division as it secures the majority of Michelfeld and Bibersfeld, and most of Schwaebisch. The 100th Division drives through the Neckar River Valley, while simultaneously seizing ground in the hills around Loewenstein. In the **French 1st Army** area, the German 19th Army is shattered as the 2nd Corps powers into Freudenstadt. In addition, Horb and Nagold are seized. Meanwhile, 1st Corps attaches Groupement Valluy to bolster the move to surround the Germans in the Black Forest; it seizes Oberkirch subsequent to a violent contest. In the DA ALPS sector, the Germans are also retreating, moving fast out of the Roya River Valley; most of the enemy in the Royan pocket north of the Gironde is eradicated. **(Atlantic-Italy) 15th Army Group** German General Wolf informs the Allies that Mussolini will arrive in Milan today and he is expected to remain there for several days. Wolf pinpoints his exact location and suggests that the U.S. bomb it, but the suggestion is declined because the mission might also kill German General Wolf. In the **U.S. Fifth Army** area, heavy fighting continues as the 92nd Division grinds forward in the Ligurian coastal area. In the **IV Corps** sector, the 10th Mountain Division makes rapid progress, seizing M. Ferra, M. Moscoso, and S. Prospero. In the **II Corps** sector, heavy fighting continues to ensue near Bologna. At M. S. Barbara, the Germans repel the 6th South African Armored Division, but the 88th Division seizes the crest of Monterumici. In other activity, the 91st Division drives slowly against fierce opposition, moving against Pianoro while pressing against the summit of M. Arnigo. Also, the 34th Division hammers against the enemy in the heights in the Sevizzano-Gorgognano region, advancing to the slopes of Dei Mori Hill. In the **British Eighth Army** area, the Germans are retreating; orders come down directing pursuit to the Po River. The 10th Corps drives to the Gaiana River and reinitiates contact with the enemy. In the Polish 2nd Corps sector, contingents of the 2nd New Zealand Division reach the Gaiana River; however, ferocious fire from the opposing bank prevents a crossing. In the 5th Corps sector, contingents converge on the Argenta Gap, encountering tenacious resistance. In conjunction, Argenta village falls to the 78th Division.

Tank flamethrower in action on Okinawa.

April 18th 1945 — **(Pacific-Philippines)** In the **U.S. Sixth Army** area, RCT 158 slugs into Cituinan Hill from the north and south while the 2nd Battalion deploys to attack it from the east. In the **I Corps** sector, heavy fighting ensues in the ridges along Highway 9 as the 148th Regiment, 37th Division, and at Mt. Myoko, contingents of the 27th Regiment, 25th Division are involved in heavy skirmishes in the area around the Wart. In the **XI Corps** sector, preparations are made by the 145th Regiment, 37th Division to assault Mt. Pacawagan on the 21st. Meanwhile, the 6th Division overcomes staunch resistance in the high ground above the Mariquina River. Also, on El Fraile Island, Fort Drum, reduced to near rubble, is occupied by the 38th Division. Sixty-nine German dead remain in the ruins. In the **XIV Corps** sector, the 187th Regiment, 11th Airborne Division attacks Mt. Macolod, pounding forward and seizing positions on the southeastern slope. **Southern Philippines** In the **U.S. Eighth Army** area, **X Corps** sector, General Sibert takes command ashore and establishes a Command Post on Mindanao at Parang. Resorting to amphibious and overland assaults, the 24th Division moves against Fort Pikit. The 2nd Battalion, 21st Regiment, and contingents of the 533rd Engineer Boat and Shore Regiment advance on as two forces along two tributaries of the Mindanao River, seizing Cotabato and Tamontaca without incident. In conjunction, contingents push further up the river, seizing Lomopog. Meanwhile, RCT 19 begins its land attack, advancing after dark, assisted by Naval star shells as it drives along Highway 1. On Negros, Aircraft throw their weight into the

battle, supporting the 40th Division as it drives punishingly against strong opposition. Contingents of the 160th Regiment advance to Hill 3155 where fierce Japanese fire forces it to pull back from the summit. In other activity, Balabac Island, off the southern end of Palawan, is captured by units of Company G, 186th Regiment, 41st Division, which move from Palawan and seize the objective in a quick shore-to-shore operation. **(Pacific-Ryukyu Islands)** On Ie Shima, the 77th Division still battles fiercely to gain control of "Bloody Ridge," striking it from the south and from the west; the Japanese resist tenaciously, making progress difficult. Elements of the 305th Regiment puncture the defenses at Ie Town, but subsequently withdraw to the outskirts. Meanwhile, the 306th Regiment drives to the northeast coast. In other activity, Ernie Pyle, the famous war correspondent, known widely as the Soldiers' best friend, is killed by enemy sniper fire. On Okinawa, in the **U.S. Tenth Army** area, Army opens its Command Post. In the **III Amphibious Corps** sector, Marines drive northward, chasing retreating Japanese. In the **XXIV Corps** sector, Corps continues preparations for a full scale attack to be launched on the 19th. Meanwhile, Company G, 106th Regiment, 27th Division begins a quiet crossing of the Machinato Inlet at 16:30, quickly capturing Machinato village, setting the stage for Engineers who move in and construct a bridge across the inlet by midnight. In other activity, a crippled B-29 lands on Okinawa. Offshore, the Light Cruiser U.S.S. *Mobile* (CL-63) becomes damaged by an explosion, and the Light Minelayer *Tolman* (DM-28) is damaged by grounding. Also, the LST 929 incurs damage by collision. In other sea action, Planes attached to the Light Carrier *Bataan* (CVL-29) join a hunt with the Destroyers *Heermann* (DD-532), *McCord* (DD-534), *Uhlmann* (DD-687), *Mertz* (DD-691), and the *Collett* (DD-730). The combined force destroys the Japanese Submarine I-56. **(Pacific-Burma)** In the **British Fourteenth Army** area, the Indian 5th Division (4th Corps) reduces the final resistance in the Shwemyo Bluff, then advances toward Pyinmana to the south. **(Atlantic-Western Europe) 21st Army Group** In the **Canadian First Army** area, the Canadian 5th Armored Division completes the Corps' offensive mission upon reaching the Zuider Zee and isolating the remaining Germans in the area. In the 2nd Corps sector, German resistance has subsided considerably; the Canadian 4th Armored continues receiving staunch resistance southwest of Oldenburg. In the **British Second Army** area, the 8th Corps seizes Lueneburg and Uelzen with the 11th Armored and 15th Infantry Divisions respectively, while the recently attached 5th Division battles east of Osnabrueck prior to its drive to the Baltic. Meanwhile, contingents of the 12th Corps seize Soltau as they advance toward Harburg. In the 30th Corps sector, preparations for the attack against Bremen continue. **12th Army Group** In the **U.S. Ninth Army XIII Corps** sector, the effects of American pressure are becoming more evident; C.C.A., 5th Armored Division roars through Forst Knesebeck without incident and pulls up at Steimke, releasing attached contingents of the 84th and 102nd Division. Also, organized resistance in the vicinity of Magdeburg is terminated as the 2nd Armored and 30th Infantry Divisions make contact. Meanwhile, contingents of RCT 320, 83rd Division seize Dornbock, west of the Elbe, while the 330th Regiment mops up in the Harz Mountains. The main body of the 83rd fortifies its defensive positions at its bridgehead east of the Elbe while brushing off a counterattack at its Breitenhagen bridge. In addition, C.C.B., 8th Armored Division continues sweeping through the woods south of Derenburg, advancing to the Langenstein-Heimburg Road, while Aircraft scorch Forst Heimburg driving the Germans from their positions. In the **XVI Corps** sector, Corps' operation to protect the right flank of the Ninth Army concludes successfully. In the **U.S. First Army** area, German organized resistance disintegrates in the Ruhr pocket, subsequent to colossal losses suffered by Field Marshal Model's forces. General Ridgway offers Model surrender terms, but he refuses them. Model's Chief of Staff returns with the refusal, but agrees to remain with the Yanks as a prisoner; Model commits suicide. Ridgway has been told that about 150,000 Germans defended the pocket; XVIII Corps scoops up 160,000, including 25 Generals and also overruns 5,000 square miles of German territory. Ridgway also notes that XVIII Corps liberates 5,639 prisoners and 200,000 displaced persons. The **XVIII Corps (A/B)** reduces final resistance and initiates mop-up operations. Over 300,000 Germans have been taken prisoner during the campaign. C.C.A., 13th Armored advances west to the Rhine; C.C.B. stays in Duisburg. In the 97th Division zone, elements of the 97th Division move through Dusseldorf almost without incident. Meanwhile, the 78th Division begins guarding the First Army rear area. In the **XVII Corps** sector, 3rd Armored Division establishes contact with XIX Corps as it clears its zone on the left. C.C.B. finalizes withdrawal of Mulde bridgehead near Torten, while C.C.R., and contingents of C.C.A., reinforced by the 83rd Reconnaissance Battalion drives to Reuden and Thalheim as it advances to secure the Jessnitz-Wolfen-Greppin sector. Meanwhile, TF Kelleher, 104th Division continues vicious house-to-house fighting in the southern portion of Halle, seizing most of the city. Also, the 1st Division establishes contact with the Ninth Army as it continues sweeping east and northeast through the Harz Mountains. In the 9th Division zone, Friedrichsbrunn and Maegdesprung are overrun by the 60th Regiment, while the 47th Infantry takes Meisdorf and Opperode, prior to launching an attack against Ballenstedt. In conjunction, TF X (39th Regiment, and 4th Cavalry Group) drive to Quedlinburg. In the **V Corps** sector, the 2nd and 69th Divisions mount a synchronized attack against Leipzig. Meanwhile, in the 2nd Division zone, RCT 271 is attached; it demolishes resistance in Eythra and then bolts toward Leipzig. In conjunction, the 9th Regiment seizes German Anti-aircraft batteries east of Lutzen. In the **U.S. Third Army** area, units begin maneuvering for the final drive which will lead southeast into Austria and Czechoslovakia. Extensive regrouping occurs. In the **XII Corps** area, the U.S. gets the first Allied contingent of troops into Czechoslovakia; at 09:05, the 358th Regiment, 90th Division propels a Patrol across the border near Prex. In the **U.S. Fifteenth Army** area, **XXII Corps** sector, the 101st Airborne Division prepares to move to Wurzburg, as the 94th Division assumes responsibility for the sector. **6th Army Group** In the **U.S. Seventh Army** area, **XV Corps** sector, the 3rd and 45th Divisions drive a deeper wedge into Nuremberg, against heavy resistance. In the **XXI Corps** the 42nd Division, working in co-ordination with contingents of the XV Corps, seals off exits from Nuremberg, and in addition, enters Fuerth. The 12th Armored Division attacks in the Ansbach region; C.C.B. and C.C.R., drive in to the northern portion of Ansbach. In the **VI Corps** sector, German resistance weakens considerably, permitting the 10th Armored to advance about nine miles. Grab, Mainhardt, and Ob Rot fall to contingents of C.C.A., and the 398th Regiment, 100th Division as they advance and subsequently drive through Hausen. The 397th Regiment reduces resistance near the Murr River at Sulzbach, while the 399th Regiment, encounters formidable opposition as it drives through the heights northeast of Beilstein in the Neckar River Valley. Meanwhile the 63rd Division, bolstered by C.C.B., pulverizes final resistance at Schwaebisch Hall, and also mops up in Bibersfeld and Michelfeld; regrouping occurs and then the units move beyond Gross Altdorf and Fichtenberg on the left and right respectively. In conjunction, the 63rd Division's 254th Regiment sweeps to the general line Ruppertshofen-Croeffellbach, and mops up Schwaebisch Hall; the 255th Regiment secures Eltershofen-Celingen region, and the 253rd Regiment mops up west and southwest of Schwaebisch Hall to line Sanzenbach-Uttenhofen. In the **French 1st Army** area, the 2nd Corps launches an assault against Stuttgart. The French 5th Armored and the 2nd Moroccan Divisions drive northeast, reaching Rottenburg and Herrenberg. In the 1st Corps sector, Black Forest zone, Gengenbach, Lahr, Obertal, and Oppenau are seized. In the DA ATL sector, German resistance in the Royan pocket is eliminated. **(Atlantic-Italy) 15th Army Group** In the **U.S. Fifth Army** area, **IV Corps** sector, about 3,000 prisoners are seized by the 10th Mountain Division as it advances to the Lavino Creek. The 10th Mountain Division then continues to chase the hastily retreating enemy forces. Meanwhile, the 1st Armored Division drives quickly along the Samoggia on the Corps' left flank. In the **II Corps** sector, the Germans are retiring all along the line. The 6th South Armored Division discovers Barbara Ridge abandoned; subsequent Patrols venture to the junction of the Reno River and Setta Creek without opposition. In conjunction, the 88th Division makes rapid progress seizing a ridge west stretching west from Furcoli, while also driving to about a mile from M. Mario. Meanwhile, the 91st Division seizes M. Adone, M. Arnigo, M. Posigliano, and Pianoro, while the 34th Division overruns Dei Mori Hill. In the **British Eighth Army** area, 13th Corps sector, the New Zealand 2nd Division establishes a bridgehead across the Gaiano. In the 5th Corps sector, Argenta Gap is secured.

Army Nurses on Okinawa.

April 19th 1945 — (Pacific) The U.S.M.C. Provisional Air Support Command is disbanded, being replaced by Marine Air Support Control Units, Amphibious Forces, Pacific. **(Pacific-Philippines) Luzon** General MacArthur orders **Sixth Army** to seize the reservoirs northeast of Manila; XI Corps receives responsibility for the operation. In the Bicols, Artillery and Aircraft are brought to bear upon the entrenched enemy on Cituinan hill mass in support of RCT 158, which attacks the strongpoint for the next week against violent opposition. In the **I Corps** sector, in the vicinity of Highway 9, the ridges south and southwest of the Irisan River bridge site are totally secured by the 148th Regiment, 37th Division; however, the Japanese still control ridges to the northeast.

Meanwhile, heavy fighting continues in the Asin tunnels region as the 130th Regiment, 30th Division advances to secure the Galiano-Baguio Road. In the meantime, the 127th Regiment, 32nd Division establishes contact with the 126th Regiment in the vicinity of the Villa Verde Trail near Salacsac Pass. Also, the 2nd Battalion, 27th Regiment, 25th Division repulses a counterattack against its lines on Mt. Myoko, then reinitiates its advance to exterminate the remaining opposition. In the **XI Corps** sector, the 38th Division moves into the 6th Division's sector, permitting the latter to move out and receive some rest after deploying in the vacant 38th's positions. In the **XIV Corps** sector, the Japanese continue holding toughly on Mt. Mataasna Bundoc, despite enormous pressure by contingents of the 1st Cavalry Division and by coordinating elements of the 11th Airborne Division. Meanwhile, the 187th Infantry, 11th Airborne assaults Japanese positions on Mt. Macolod, squeezing the Japanese into a tiny pocket; continued pressure eliminates all resistance except for one pocket by the end of the following day. **Southern Philippines** In the **U.S. Eighth Army** area, the 2nd Battalion, 21st Regiment, remains at Lomopog; Patrols are dispatched toward Highway 1 on Mindanao, and in addition Company F, bolstered by contingents of Boat and Shore Regiment, continues advancing up the Mindanao River, getting elements to Paidu Pulangi where they debark without incident. In conjunction, the 34th Regiment (floating reserve) lands at Parang and embarks up the Mindanao River to reinforce the amphibious attack contingents. On Cebu, the 132nd Regiment, Americal Division, pushes contingents along the east coast road. On Negros, violent fighting continues to ensue. Japanese entrenched near Lantawan and Negritos come under fierce attack by the 40th Division. The 160th Regiment again drives up Hill 3155, only to be pushed back down by fierce resistance. On Bohol, the 3rd Battalion, 164th Regiment maintains its attack against enemy positions; Company I advances from Candijay to bolster the assault. **(Pacific-Ryukyu Islands)** On Ie Shima, the 305th and 307th Regiments, 77th Division continue pounding Bloody Ridge and Ie town without results. P.F.C. Martin O. May places his machine gun in a precarious position to defend his Infantrymen who are struggling to gain control of a hill. He withstands repetitive unsuccessful attempts to dislodge him from his vantage point for three days. On the 21st, the Japanese mount the major assault. Casualties mount near May, but his gun is still giving accurate cover fire to the Yanks in the 307th Regiment. Finally, a mortar knocks May's machine gun out of commission and severely wounds him. He refuses evacuation and begins tossing grenades at the charging Japanese, but becomes mortally wounded; P.F.C. May receives the Medal of Honor posthumously. In the **U.S. Tenth Army** area, a massive preparatory bombardment of enemy positions in the southern sector of the island occurs in co-ordination with a general attack by the **XXIV Corps** against the Shuri defenses; twenty-seven Artillery Battalions participate with the Naval Surface Vessels and the bombardment is further stiffened with the largest single Air attack of the campaign; however, the enemy tunnel systems and caves are basically unscathed by the gargantuan deluge. The Infantry advance meets vehement opposition, and U.S. Tanks also encounter vicious resistance. The 106th Regiment, 27th Division, driving on the west flank, is stopped at the western end of the Urasoe-Mura Escarpment. Meanwhile, subsequent to costly attacks against fervent opposition on Kakazu Ridge, which cost the U.S. 22 Tanks, the 105th Regiment bypasses it to push contingents to the top of the escarpment. The maneuver creates a severe gap between the lines of the 27th and

96th Divisions. On the right, the 7th Division encounters resolute opposition at Skyline Ridge and Rocky Crags on its left and right respectively, halting progress; the 32nd Regiment secures positions on Skyline Ridge, but the ground is untenable, forcing a withdrawal. In conjunction, some progress is made in the center, as the 381st Regiment, 96th Division plows through Kaniku Ridge, seizing positions on the forward slopes of Nishibaru Ridge, while the 382nd, drives between Kaniku and Nishibaru and grabs a hold on N-S Tombstone Ridge. **(Pacific-Burma)** In the **British Fourteenth Army** area, 33rd Corps sector, the Indian 20th Division seizes Magwe and Myingun as it drives to the Irrawaddy. **(North Atlantic)** The Destroyer Escorts *Buckley* (DE-51) and *Reuben James* (DE-153) sink the German U-Boat U-879. **(Atlantic-Western Europe) 21st Army Group** In the **British Second Army** area, the 30th Corps reinforced by the British 52nd Division opens its attack against Bremen. In the 12 Corps sector, the British 7th Armored Division makes swift progress and drives north, severing Bremen-Hamburg Autobahn. Meanwhile, in the 8 Corps sector, the British 11th Armored Division reaches the Elbe near Lauenburg. **12th Army Group** In the **U.S. Ninth Army** area, **XIII Corps** sector, the Germans attempting to evacuate the area are pummeled by Aircraft and Artillery, in addition to the pursuing U.S. 5th Armored Division, decimating their ranks. Meanwhile, the 44th Squadron, 11th Cavalry Group moves to neutralize the Germans attempting to retreat through the Forst Kloetze to reach the Harz Mountains. In the **XIX Corps** sector, defensive positions are fortified while simultaneously searching out the enemy along the Elbe. Also, in the **XVI Corps** sector, regrouping ensues while simultaneously assuming occupational duties and establishing military government within its zone which encompasses all Ninth Army area, west of the Weser. In the **U.S. Ninth Army** area, **XVIII Corps (A/B)** sector, preparations are made by the 13th Armored and 97th Infantry Divisions to join Third Army. Meanwhile, the 78th Division is attached to First Army. Also, the 8th Division extends its territory west to the Rhine. In the **VII Corps** sector, C.C.R., 3rd Armored Division, fighting on the right flank of the Division, drives into Bobbau-Steinfurth and Wolfen, gaining part of both objectives. Meanwhile, C.C.A. and C.C.B. seize territory near Torten; other C.C.A. contingents driving north of Koethen seize several additional towns. Also, TF Kelleher secures Halle prior to 11:00, then lunges into Dieskau and Radewell, seizing both; Petersroda is secured by the 415th Regiment. In the 1st Division area, the advance through the Harz Mountains gains more speed against faltering opposition; Elbingrode and Huettenrode fall to the 16th Regiment, while the 18th seizes the southern portion of Thale. In conjunction with the Big Red One's attack, the 26th Regiment strikes against the dominating hill in the divisional sector. In the 9th Division zone, organized resistance is terminated as the Division reaches its northern boundary and encounters friendly forces, but one enemy pocket still lingers southeast of Ballenstedt. Task Force X is disbanded. In the **V Corps** sector, Leipzig is totally secured by the 2nd and 69th Divisions. In the **U.S. Third Army** area, **VIII Corps** sector, the right boundary is extended along the northern boundary of Bavaria to the Czechoslovakian border. The 6th Cavalry Group sends probing Patrols toward Czechoslovakia. In the **XII Corps** sector, effective Air and Artillery bombardment supports the Corps' southeastern drive. C.C.A. and C.C.B., 11th Armored Division secure Grafenwohr. The 26th Division advances south to general line Trostau-Birk while the 90th Division advancing on the Corps left flank pushes southeast; Rehau is gobbled up by the 358th Re-

U.S. troops advancing toward Austria.

giment, and the 357th pushes advance contingents to Wunsiedel. In the **XX Corps** sector, orders for the final drive to Austria are issued. The attack will be spearheaded by the 65th Division and 71st (temporarily attached to XV Corps) Division, with the 13th Armored and 80th Infantry Divisions held in reserve. In the **III Corps** sector, Corps annexes the 20th Armored Division (First Army) as it continues advancing to Bavaria. In the **U.S. Fifteenth Army** area, the XXIII Corps relieves contingents of the 70th Division at Koblentz and also at Pfalz. **6th Army Group** In the **U.S. Seventh Army** area, **XV Corps** sector, contingents crack through the defenses penetrating the inner walled city of Nuremberg. In conjunction, Fuerth, a suburb on the western side of the city, is seized by the 42nd Division, prior to driving into Nuremberg. Meanwhile, Ansbach is totally secured by C.C.B. and C.C.R., 12th Armored Division, which relieves units of the 4th Division there. 12th Armored then bolts toward Feuchtwangen; C.C.A. establishes roadblocks at Bertholdsdorf and Schwabach. Also, the 4th Division advances to line Bottenweiler-Wildenholz-Theuerbronn while the 4th Reconnaissance Troop secures Rot am See, maintaining contact with the 63rd Division which is sweeping east of the Kocher between Crailsheim and Schwaebisch. In the **VI Corps** sector, the 10th Armored Division is bulldozing forward, advancing south about 20 miles. During the spectacular breakthrough, C.C.A. seizes a bridge at Faurndau outside of Goeppingen while C.C.B. bolts across the Rems River west of Schwaebisch (bypassed), moving east. In conjunction, the 100th Division blasts forward, its 397th Regiment driving to the Murr River at Sulzbach, which it attacks, while the 398th Regiment crosses at Murrhardt. Meanwhile, the 399th Regiment pulverizes Beilstein and Ilsfeld. In addition, the 103rd Division is advancing into Corps sector while the 44th Division mops up behind the Armor. In the **French 1st Army** area, the 2nd Corps continues pressing toward Stuttgart. Meanwhile, the 1st Corps sweeping the western part of the Black Forest advances to the Biberach-Mahlberg region. In the DA ATL sector, Le Verdon in the Pointe de Grave area falls to French contingents. **(Atlantic-Eastern Europe)** The Russians continue closing on Berlin. The Second Polish Army seizes Rothenburg. **(Atlantic-Italy) 15th Army Group** The **U.S. Fifth Army** issues orders to pursue the Germans to the Po River. The 92nd Division is to advance in the Ligurian coastal sector, subsequent to enemy withdrawal, attacking toward La Spezia. The **IV Corps**, instructed to seize crossing sites at the Po between Borgoforte and Ostiglia in addition to securing the Panaro River line west of the Camposanto River, thrusts for-

ward as the enemy is in full retreat. The 10th Mountain Division speeds to the fringes of the Po plain and overruns Mongiorgio, then propels advance units to within three miles of M. S. Michele. In the **II Corps** sector, the beleaguered Germans continue to mount excellent rear-guard actions, covering the retreat. East of the Reno, the 34th and 91st Divisions drive swiftly. The 350th Regiment (88th Division), under jurisdiction of the 91st Division, secures M. Mario, the final objective of the 88th, east of the Reno. In addition, the 34th Division seizes the hills north of M. Arnigo. In conjunction, the Legnano Group attacks along the Idice River to extend the Corps' right flank. In the **British Eighth Army** area, the Polish 2nd Corps crashes through German positions along the Gaiana. Meanwhile, the 13th Corps closes on Budrio and receives orders to continue the attack across the Idice. In the 5th Corps sector, Corps strengthens its positions in the Argenta Gap.

April 20th 1945 — (United States) The Joint Chiefs of Staff direct the O.S.S. to terminate the ongoing surrender talks with the Germans (reference Italy) Allen Dulles (in Switzerland) is to "DISCONTINUE IMMEDIATELY ALL SUCH CONTACT." Dulles is perplexed as he can not contact General Wolf who is in Germany and another contact, Baron Parilli has not been in touch with him. The dilemma also places an O.S.S. agent in Italy, code-named Wally in danger. **(Pacific-Philippines)** The Submarine Chaser SC-737 becomes damaged by grounding in the Sulu Sea, west of the Philippines. **Luzon** In the **U.S. Sixth Army** area, **I Corps** sector, fighting continues to ensue across the area without significant gains; however, the 148th Regiment, 37th Division seizes a ridge northeast of the Irisan bridge site. In the **XI Corps** sector, Artillery continues to thrash enemy positions on Mt. Pacawagan as the 145th Regiment advances prudently. In the **XIV Corps** sector, the Japanese continue to feel the heat at Mt. Mataasna Bundoc as Corps maintains pressure while simultaneously driving against Mt. Macolod, exterminating the resistance on the latter except for one isolated pocket. **Southern Philippines** Marine Aircraft Group 24, having departed Luzon, begins arriving at Malabang, Mindanao. In the **U.S. Eighth Army** area, **X Corps** sector, the 19th Regiment, 24th Division closes quickly on Fort Pikit, encountering a force of about eighty Japanese as it moves; 31 are killed and the balance disperse hurriedly. Meanwhile, the 34th Regiment assumes responsibility for the roadblock at Ulangdang. On Cebu, the 3rd Battalion, 132nd Regiment, Americal Division launches an amphibious attack, embarking from Cebu City and striking Danao; no opposition is encountered as the Japs are in retreat. Patrols move inland quickly to intercept the retiring enemy forces. On Bohol, the 3rd Battalion, 164th Regiment, Americal Division, bolstered by a powerful mortar assault, roars into the area near Ginopolan, scattering the opposition in all directions. On Negros, the 185th Regiment, 40th Division begins securing the Lantawan Plateau. Meanwhile, the 160th Regiment makes repeated unsuccessful attempts to seize Hill 3155. **(Pacific-Dutch East Indies)** The Submarine U.S.S. *Guitarro* (SS-363) lays mines off the northeast coast of Sumatra. **(Pacific-Ryukyu Islands)** On Ie Shima, the 77th Division, which is attacking south, pivots its 306th Regiment to the north. It encircles the Pinnacle (Iegusugu Mountain) while the 305th and 307th Regiments secure positions on Bloody Ridge. In the **U.S. Tenth Army** area, **XXIV Corps** sector, the Japanese continue raising fervent resistance, preventing rapid progress. At an obstinate strongpoint known as "Item Pocket," north of Gusukuma, the battle rages for the following week before the 165th Regiment, 27th Division breaks through. Meanwhile, the 105th and 106th Regiments receive equally fierce resistance as they pound against Urasoe-Mura Escarpment, crashing against the East and West Pinnacles, the dominating features near Iso Village. The 2nd Battalion, 105th Regiment drives a wedge into the escarpment by bypassing the East Pinnacle, but the Japanese surround the unit. Meanwhile, the 1st Battalion, 105th attacks to eliminate the bypassed resistance and progresses rapidly in the Kakazu area; however, after dark the Japanese return to the region in force. In other activity, the 96th Division eradicates remaining resistance, seizing Tombstone Ridge while continuing its contest to secure Nishibaru Ridge. In the meantime, the 7th Division moves punishingly against heavy resistance gaining a slim hold on Ouki Hill, but the Japanese halt its progress in the Rocky Crags region. In the **III Amphibious Corps** sector, final organized resistance on Motobu Peninsula is crushed as the 4th and 29th Marines, 6th Marine Division reach the north coast of the peninsula. Corps zone on Okinawa is secure; nevertheless, mop-up operations continue as a few small groups of Japs are still alive. In Naval activity, the Battleship *Colorado* (BB-45) is damaged by an explosion. The Destroyer *Ammen* (DD-527) is damaged by a Horizontal Bomber. **(Pacific-Burma)** In the **British Fourteenth Army**, 33rd Corps sector, the British 2nd Division and the Indian 268th Brigade encircle the final enemy pocket in the Mt. Popa region, then destroy it. **(Pacific-China)** The Japanese begin to threaten the Chihchiang area; Air-ground liaison units are sped to the region to neutralize the threat. **(Atlantic-Western Europe) 12th Army Group** In the **U.S. Ninth Army** area, **XIII Corps** sector, the 29th Division drives northeast and relieves British contingents near the Elbe. Meanwhile, the U.S. Fifth Armored Division deploys to the right of the 29th and will launch an attack. Contingents of the 11th Cavalry Group contain the Forst Kloetze. In the **XIX Corps** sector, the 8th Armored Division's C.C.A. and C.C.B. drive to secure the eastern fringes of the Harz Mountains, seizing Blankenburg and Heimburg against some resistance. Meanwhile, the 30th Division begins to govern a sector of the Elbe while deploying defensively to protect its area which includes Magdeburg; it also relieves contingents of the 2nd Armored Division. In addition, the 113th Cavalry Group is relieved of its security mission on the flank, due to the fact that First Army's VII Corps has advanced to the Elbe on the right. In the **XVI Corps** sector, the 17th Airborne Division is relieved of responsibility for Duisberg by XVIII Corps (A/B). In the **U.S. First Army** area, **VII Corps** sector, 3rd Armored prepares to attack Dessau. Its C.C.R. secures Greppin, Bobbau-Steinfurth, Wolfen, and the western portion of Jessnitz, then pushes contingents to Klein Kuehnau, slightly west of Dessau. In the 104th Division zone, the 415th Regiment operating on the left launches an attack at 01:30, seizing about a third of Bitterfeld, while the 413th Regiment drives east to Delitzsch and the 414th on the right flank propels beyond Rackwitz and Schladitz. Meanwhile, all organized resistance in the Harz Mountains is crushed; remnant resistance is mopped up by the 1st and 9th Divisions. In the **V Corps** sector, the 9th Armored Division's C.C.B. overruns Klein Krostitz with little effort. 9th Armored is relieved by the 2nd and 69th Divisions on line. **XVIII Corps (A/B)** sector, the Ruhr area is given to the U.S. Ninth and Fifteenth Armies to permit it to move to 21st Army Group to support the British in their drive to the Baltic beginning on the 25th. In the **U.S. Third Army** area, the **VIII Corps** stays in place; nevertheless, Patrols are continually sent out to probe. In the **XII Corps** sector, enormous amounts of enemy supplies and ammunition are found near Grafenwohr by contingents of the 11th Armored Division. The 358th Regiment, 90th Division, attacks Selb, subsequent to an Artillery bombardment, securing it before dashing southeast through Arzberg. In conjunction, the 347th Regiment advances to Fuchsmuehl and to Friedenfels. Meanwhile, the 42nd Squadron, 2nd Cavalry Group seizes the town of As and is joined there by the 2nd Squadron. In addition, the 97th Division begins arriving in the Corps sector to defend the left flank. In the **XX Corps** sector, the 65th and 71st Divisions attack toward the Danube, the latter encountering fiendish terrain and some tough resistance as it drives in the area around Haag and through the woods south of Auerbach in the center. Also, the thrust on the right toward Neuhaus-Velden area is difficult. Meanwhile, the 65th Division gets RCT 260 to line Lauterhofen-Trautmannshofen, and RCT 359 crashes into Neumarkt, securing about one third of the northern sector of the town. In the **III Corps** sector, orders are issued for an attack to be launched on the 22nd. Jump-off will be from a new zone on the Corps' right flank and the attack units are 14th Cavalry Group (left), 86th Division (right), and the 99th Division (center). In the **U.S. Fifteenth Army** area, **XXIII Corps** sector, the relief of the 70th Division contingents in the Hessen area concludes Corps occupation of 12th Army Group zone assignment. **6th Armored Group** In the **U.S. Seventh Army** area, **XV Corps** sector, the 3rd, 42nd, and 45th Divisions strike the fatal blow, toppling Nuremberg. In the **XXI Corps** sector, C.C.R. and C.C.B., 12th Armored Division close on Feuchtwangen, the latter moving in and blowing over the opposition. Meanwhile, C.C.A., deployed near Nuremberg, moves to Feuchtwangen and subsequently to Dinkelsbuehl upon relief by contingents of XX Corps. In the 4th Division zone, German discipline has nearly vanished as Division gains between six-eight miles. The 22nd Regiment drives to the steps of Crailsheim. The 63rd Division, driving on the Corps' right flank, continues to wipe out pockets east and southeast of Schwaebisch Hall. In the **VI Corps** sector, C.C.A. and C.C.B., 10th Armored Division, followed by the 44th Infantry Division, race across the Fils River, driving southwest closing upon Kirchheim, seizing it. The trailing 44th assumes responsibility for the Fils and Rems crossings; its 114th Regiment occupies Schwaebisch Gmuend and deploys to intercept any enemy interference on the exposed left flank facing Gaildorf. The 100th Division operating on the Corps' west flank speeds toward Stuttgart, its 399th advancing to the Winnenden region, while the 398th Regiment drives through Althuette, reaching Eselshalden. In conjunction, the 397th, also driving south, easily topples Backnang and Sulzbach. French troops of the 2nd Corps (French 1st Army) converge on the city to support the attack against Stuttgart; the combined movement nearly encircles the objective. In the **French 1st Army** area, 1st Corps sector, the southward drive to the Danube continues; elements of an Armor unit (Groupement Le Bel) reach the river at Donaueschingen. The final German resistance in Pointe de Grave pocket is eliminated by DA ATL. **(Atlantic-Eastern Europe) (Atlantic-Italy) 15th Army Group** The U.S. Fifteenth Army bursts from the Apennines advancing into the Po plain. In the **IV Corps** sector, the 10th Mountain Division, still spearheading the drive, bolts across Highway 9, near Ponte Samoggia where it crosses the Samoggia River. Meanwhile, 1st Armored Division races to Crespellano on the left while the 85th Division, also trailing the 10th Mountain Division, drives to Gesso on the right. Some units pivot east toward Bologna to establish roadblocks in the suburbs to bar escape from the area. In the **II Corps** sector, the 85th Division, attacking west of the Reno River, advances to positions near Gesso and Casalecchio in conjunction with the 6th South African Armored Division, which crosses to the west side of the Reno and moves toward Casalecchio. Meanwhile, the 34th Division is driving toward Bologna, making rapid progress along Highway 65. Also, the Legnano Group pushes forward along the right flank of the Corps. In the **British Eighth Army** area, 10th Corps sector, the Germans evacuate the area, permitting Corps to advance easily to the Idice River. In the Polish 2nd Corps sector, advance contingents cross the Idice near Highway 9 during the night of the 19th-20th, driving fast toward Bologna. In the 13 Corp sector, the New Zealand 2nd Division establishes a bridgehead across the Idice River. In the 5th Corps sector, the Germans are retiring quickly.

April 21st 1945 — (United States) The Joint Chiefs of Staff approve Operation BETA, created to seize the Canton-Hong Kong area and its strategic port. The operation plan is subsequently modified and renamed RASHNESS and CARBONADO. **(Pacific-Philippines) Luzon** In the U.S. Sixth Army area, **I Corps** sector, the 148th Regiment, 37th Division, advances persistently, seizing the final enemy held ridges, culminating the struggle for the Irisan bridge site; the victors move across a temporary bridge and reinitiate the attack toward Baguio. In the 33rd Division zone, the 130th Regiment opens its assault to secure the Asin tunnel fortifications, pressing from the north. Meanwhile, the 25th Division's 35th Regiment secures Kapintalan, clearing Highway 5 northward to Kapintalan Ridge, while contingents of the 27th Regiment continue battling for control of Mt. Myoko and seize a hill slightly north of the Wart. In the **XI Corps** sector, the Japanese on Mt. Mataba are inundated with Air strikes and huge Artillery barrages prior to being attacked by the 6th Division, including its attached 145th Regiment (37th Division); its 63rd Regiment pours in support fire from the northern tip of Mt. Mataba. In conjunction, the 152nd Regiment, 38th Division relieves the 1st Infantry, 6th Division at the confluence of the Bosoboso and Mariquina Rivers. In the **XIV Corps** sector, Guerrilla forces assume responsibility for the Mt. Macolod region subsequent to the extermination of the final pocket of enemy resistance by the 187th Infantry, 11th Airborne Division. **Southern Philippines** In the **U.S. Eighth Army** area, **X Corps** sector, the Japs have abandoned Fort Pikit on Mindanao giving the 24th Division's 3rd Battalion, 34th Regiment an easy prize; a Gunboat debarks a Patrol which takes the fort and awaits the arrival of the balance of the Regiment which is closing by land. Meanwhile, the 19th Regiment, 24th Division, seizes a road junction along Highway 1, at Dilap. On Bohol, the 3rd Battalion, 164th Regiment, Americal Division continues destroying scattered bands of resistance as it drives north from Ginopolan. On Negros, the 40th Division maintains its assault against enemy forces in the Negritos-Lantawan-Hill 3155 area; its 160th Regiment, making substantial gains, seizes the military summit of Hill 3155. **(Pacific-Ryukyu Islands)** On **Ie Shima**, the Japanese have been thoroughly vanquished by the 77th Division which overruns the Pinnacle and in addition bludgeons the final Japanese attackers that subsequently charge Bloody Ridge. The 77th declares the bloodied island secure at 17:30, culminating a six-day battle which costs the Japanese 4,706 killed; 149 Japanese are captured. On **Okinawa, U.S. Tenth Army** area, **XXIV Corps** sector, the Japanese still mount ferocious resistance on Corps' western flank at Item Pocket, north of Gusukuma, forbidding progress. The persistent 27th Division, which is still pounding against the enemy, succeeds in clearing mines

to allow Armor to advance and support the operation. Meanwhile, the 96th Division still encounters vicious opposition as it drives unsuccessfully against the enemy on the southern slopes of Nishibaru Ridge and also makes no progress against the entrenched positions at Nishibaru village. In the 7th Division zone, the 184th Regiment, bolstered by Company B, 17th Regiment, hammers against Rocky Crags, but the Japanese repel the assault. The 32nd Regiment, operating on the Corps' eastern flank, drives to the northern slope of Skyline Ridge. **(Pacific-Burma)** In the **British Fourteenth Army** area, 33 Corps sector, the Japanese at Yenangyaung are surrounded by the Indian 7th Division; however, while the Japanese attempt to escape toward Allanmyo, rear guard troops are directed to remain and hold off the Allies. In the 4th Corps sector, the Indian 17th Division, assisted by the 9th Brigade, 5th Indian Division, is securing Pyinmana; the main body of the 5th Division has departed for Toungoo. **(Pacific-China)** Operation ROOSTER commences; the Chinese 22nd Division is airlifted to Chihchiang and is trailed several days later by the Chinese 14th Division which is transported by trucks driven by the U.S. 475th Infantry. As the Japanese are advancing west toward Chihchiang, their forward contingents are intercepted in the Keosha-Tungkow region. In conjunction, on the flanks, Japanese retain dominating positions on a Paima Shan Mountain and also are threatening Wukang, northwest of Hsinning. **(Atlantic-Western Europe)** 12th Army Group In the **U.S. Ninth Army** area, **XIII Corps** sector, the 29th Division continues advancing northeast, making rapid progress against slender opposition, reaching general line Guelden-Dalldorf-Salkau-Gielau-Erpensen. Meanwhile, the 5th Armored launches an attack, driving to the right; C.C.A. pushes through violent resistance, reaching positions near Gaddau. The resistance is extremely heavy, compelling C.C.R. to postpone its attack until 17:00. In the meantime, the 84th Division attacks to clear its sector along the Elbe, reaching line Gorleben-Gartow-Kapern. Also, the 175th Regiment, 29th Division and the 11th Cavalry Group eradicate final resistance in the Forst Kloetze. In the **XIX Corps** sector, 8th Armored Division terminates its mop-up operation in the Harz Mountains while the 2nd Armored Division launches units into the Forst Konigslutter to sweep and clear it. In the **U.S. First Army** area, **XVIII Corps (A/B)** sector, orders come down directing Corps to move to positions in the British Second Army area to defend the British left flank. Corps will have the British 6th and the U.S. 82nd Airborne Divisions, as well as the U.S. 8th Infantry and U.S. 7th Armored Divisions for its mission which includes another directive calling for the seizure of a bridge site at the Elbe. The U.S. 13th Armored and 97th Infantry Divisions pass to control of Third Army. In the **VII Corps** sector, fierce house-to-house fighting erupts in Dessau as the 3rd Armored Division pumps continuous rounds into enemy positions in concert with a huge Artillery bombardment; the southwestern sector of the city is secured after bitter fighting. In conjunction, C.C.R. mops up in Klein and also at Gross Kuehnau in the western suburbs. Additional 3rd Armor units continue sweeping along the Mulde on divisional right flank. In other activity, the 1st and 9th Divisions are mopping up remnant resistance in the Harz Mountains. In the **V Corps** sector, the 1st Battalion, 271st Regiment, 69th Division attacks to clear Eilenburg; however, most Corps activity is confined to relief of units and mop-up details. In the **U.S. Third Army** area, although SHAEF still holds the opinion that a German fortress exists, Patton smells a rat, referring to the fortress as a "VERY DUBIOUS NATIONAL REDOUBT." Patton, upon receiving orders to shift his attack to the southeast notes: "THERE WERE THOSE WHO INSISTED THAT A GREAT CONCENTRATION EXISTED TO THE SOUTH." **VIII Corps** sector, the 28th Squadron, 6th Cavalry Group sweeps Corps' right flank clean up to the Czechoslovakian border, then crosses and advances to Rossbach and Gottmannsgruen. In the **XII Corps** sector, Weiden is thrashed throughout the night of the 20th-21st by incessant Artillery bombardment. Meanwhile, the 11th Armored Division is rooting out enemy resistance near Grafenwohr while preparing to assault Weiden and Cham. The 26th Division attacks and gets contingents to Grafenwohr, relieving 11th Armored units there. In other activity, the 90th Division drives southeast with three Regiments, seizing Windischeschenbach with its 357th Regiment, while the 358th drives through Mitterteich, reaching Falkenburg. In conjunction, the 90th Reconnaissance Troop easily tumbles resistance in Tirschenreuth while the 359th Regiment secures Schirnding and Waldsassen. In the **XX Corps** sector, the 71st Division overruns an obstinate enemy pocket on its right flank, in addition to severing the Sulzbach-Nuremberg highway and rail line. At the same time, the 65th Division crunches through many towns and villages and also secures about half of Neumark. In the **III Corps** sector, the 86th Division puts its efforts into the area around Ansbach, and the 20th Armored Division converges on the Oberzenn area. Third Army casualties as of April 21st: killed 21,098; wounded 97,163; missing 16,393; non-battle casualties 106,440. The Rhine campaign cost 17,961 casualties. Enemy losses against Third Army: killed 138,700; wounded 369,700; P.O.W.s 545,800. Third Army equipment losses: Light Tanks 298; Medium Tanks 934; Guns 174. Enemy equipment losses: Medium Tanks 1,492; Panther or Tiger Tanks 857; Guns 3,324. **6th Army Group** In the **U.S. Seventh Army** area, **XV Corps** sector, regrouping takes place in preparation for an assault against Munich. The 3rd Division has responsibility for guarding Nuremberg. In the **XXI Corps** sector, 12th Armored drives toward the Danube. The 4th Division again gains between six-eight miles along its entire southward advance; included in seized ground is the total clearance of Crailsheim by the 22nd Regiment. Meanwhile, the 4th Reconnaissance Troop and supporting contingents drive south toward Aalen. In the 63rd Division zone, motorized Task Forces (attached to 255th Regiment) are sent to seal off exits from Gaildorf and Schwaebisch Gmuend, in coordination with the Division's rapid drive. In the **VI Corps** sector, 10th Armored consolidates in Kirchheim, awaiting relief by the 103rd Division. The 103rd Division nears Corps sector, advancing south behind the Armor, seizing Rems and Schorndorf crossings with its 411th Regiment. On the Corps' western flank, the 100th Division battles to within two miles of Stuttgart, seizing bridges across the Rems along the way. In the **French 1st Army** area, 2nd Corps sector, the French 5th Armored Division moves into Stuttgart and occupies it. In the 1st Corps sector, the French 1st Armored Division reaches the Danube on the left flank of the Corps; one column crosses near Tuttlingen, reaching positions near Lake Constance. Meanwhile, Groupement Le Bel advances to the Swiss frontier at Schaffhausen while contingents of Groupement Valluy seize Emmendingen and Frieburg. Also, additional French contingents cross the Rhine, seizing Vieux Brisach. **(Atlantic-Eastern Europe)** The Soviets continue closing on Berlin as the First White Russian Front bangs into the front of the beleaguered city, now manned by some as young as 13-14 years of age, piercing the defenses and entering the suburbs. In conjunction, contingents of the First Ukrainian Front, attacking on the left,

drive north toward the capital while other units move west toward Dresden and Leipzig. The once-powerful German Army has disintegrated, but still it refuses to relent, offering fierce last-stand resistance in many areas. Hitler still remains in his bunker at the Reich's Chancellery in Berlin with his advisors. On the previous day, Hitler had celebrated his birthday, ignoring the deteriorating circumstances around him. **(Atlantic-Italy) 15th Army Group** In the **U.S. Fifth Army** area, contingents drive into Bologna, sought by Army for several months, then easily bolts toward the Po River. In the **IV Corps** sector, TF Duff (Brigadier General Robinson E. Duff) spearheads the drive of the 10th Mountain Division, using its Tanks, Tank-destroyers, and Engineers to good advantage, getting its Infantry to the Panaro River where they seize an operable bridge at Bomporto. The 1st Armored and 85th Infantry Divisions drive along the 10th Mountain's flanks. In the **II Corps** sector, Tanks, transporting the 3rd Battalion, 133rd Regiment, 34th Division, drive into Bologna, reaching it shortly after the entrance of Polish 2nd Corps forces which had driven well into the city by 06:00. Later, the balance of the 133rd Infantry, Legnano Group (Italian), and units of the 91st Division enter the city. Bologna will be garrisoned by the U.S. 34th Division, under Army control. In conjunction, the 91st Division seizes M. Sabbiuno, south of Bologna, and the 88th Division moves through the 6th South African perimeter and seizes S. Giovanni during the night of the 21st-22nd. In the **British Eighth Army** area, the British 10th Corps is pinched out as a result of the seizure of Bologna, reverting to reserve. In the Polish 2nd Corps sector, the 9th Battalion, 3rd Brigade, 3rd Carpathian Division drives into Bologna, advancing to its center by 06:00. In the 5th Corps sector, the British 6th Armored Division arrives at Poggio Renatico and will advance west as the Indian 8th Division is brought back from reserve to attack Ferrara, freeing the 6th Armored.

April 22nd 1945 — (Pacific-Philippines) The U.S.S. *Winooski*, an Oiler (AO-38), and the Destroyer *Flusser* (DD-368) suffer damage by collision. **Luzon** In the **U.S. Sixth Army** area, **I Corps** sector, the 129th Regiment, 37th Division drives toward Baguio, gaining about 4,000 yards, but the attack is halted to sweep the approaches to ensure the Japanese cannot reinforce the besieged city. The 133rd Regiment, 33rd Division grinds forward at the Asin tunnel systems, seizing the heights above the first tunnel, while other contingents press toward Mt. Mirador, just west of Baguio. Also, the 32nd Division is battling tenaciously to advance through the Jap-infested hills along the Villa Verde Trail. Furious battle also ensues as the 25th Division's 27th Regiment (1st Battalion) exterminates resistance between its positions and a hill to the north, while Company G swings wide in an enveloping maneuver, advancing to the base of Lone Tree Hill, about 2,000 yards from Balete Pass near the junction of Balete and Kapintalan Ridges. In the **XI Corps** sector, the 145th Regiment, 6th Division continues its concentrated assault against Mt. Pacawagan without success. Also, the 149th Regiment, 38th Division attacks enemy positions along a limited pass in the Zambales Mountains. Company B, acting as vanguard is ambushed by Japanese in concealed positions and explosive charges are thrown into their midst. P.F.C. William H. Thomas receives the brunt of one of the charges, which severs both of his legs below the knees. Despite the agonizing pain, he refuses treatment and continues firing his rifle at the enemy positions. An enemy bullet pulverizes his weapon, but Thomas resorts to throwing his last two grenades; the position is overrun by his comrades. Before the day is over, P.F.C. Thomas succumbs to his wounds and becomes a recipient of the Medal of Honor posthumously. The **XIV Corps** assumes control of the Bicols sector as well as RCT 158, heavily engaged there. Meanwhile, the ongoing attack against Cituinan Hill continues to rage, but progress is tedious and sluggish due to fervent resistance. Also, the Japanese on Mt. Mataasna Bundoc are now completely encircled. In other activity, the 11th Airborne Division receives reinforcements to support its drive to secure the Mt. Malepunyo area; the 8th Cavalry and the 2nd Squadron, 7th Cavalry. **Southern Philippines** In the U.S. **Eighth Army** area, **X Corps** sector, the 31st Division (minus 2nd Battalion, 167th Regiment) lands on Mindanao, relieving contingents of the 24th Division, permitting them to drive across the island to Davao Gulf. The 19th Regiment, 24th Division, advances to positions about three miles southeast of Balabac. Meanwhile, the 3rd Battalion, 34th Regiment, advances, seizing the road junction of Highway 1 and Sayre Highway before pushing to the area near Kabacan. The U.S. progress divides the Japanese forces on the island. Marine Aircraft Group 24, based at Malabang, begins support operations, bolstering the advance of the 24th and 31st Army Divisions. In the Sulu Archipelago, on Jolo Island, RCT 163, 41st Division, drives fiercely, seizing Mt. Daho effortlessly, eliminating the final strongpoint on the island, and terminating organized resistance. On Palawan, Company G, 186th Regiment, reinforced, (41st Division) lands without incident on Pandanan Island off the southern end of Palawan, virtually concluding the operation to liberate the Province of Palawan. On Cebu, the 3rd Battalion, 182nd Infantry is transported from Cebu City to Toledo by trucks and from there the Vehicles take them to Tabuclan via the coastal road. On Bohol, the 3rd Battalion, 164th Regiment, Americal Division drives to the vicinity of the barrio of Nanod, regaining contact with the Japanese who have entrenched themselves deeply north of the barrio, preventing further progress. On the following day, a strong assault supplemented by effective Artillery barrages forces the Japs to abandon the positions and withdraw quickly. **(Pacific-Ryukyu Islands)** On Okinawa, in the U.S. **Tenth Army** area, **XXIV Corps** sector, some progress is made through the efforts of the 27th Division on the western flank; however, the determined Japanese retain possession of Item Pocket and Kakazu, in addition to holding most of the Urasoe-Mura Escarpment. To facilitate the destruction of the Kakazu Pocket, Task Force Bradford, composed of contingents of the 7th, 27th, and 96th Divisions, and reinforced by additional supporting units, is formed and is commanded by the Assistant Divisional Commander of the 27th Division, Brigadier General William B. Bradford. In other activity, the 383rd Regiment, 96th Division, subsequent to relieving the exhausted and battle-weary 382nd Regiment, attacks to seize a saddle on Nishibaru Ridge; the assault, bolstered by the 2nd Battalion, 382nd, seizes Nishibaru Village. Meanwhile, the dug-in Japanese at Rocky Crags continue to pour incessant fire in to the Division's right flank, hindering progress. In conjunction, the 32nd Regiment, operating on the left Divisional flank, stays in place on Skyline Ridge, but Patrols are active. Offshore, the Jap Suicide Pilots strike again: the Minesweeper *Swallow* (AM-65) is sunk. In addition, the Kamikazes damage the Destroyers *Hudson* (DD-475), *Wadsworth* (DD-516), and *Isherwood* (DD-520); they also damage the Light Minelayer *Shea* (DM-30) and the Minesweepers *Ransom* (AM-283) and *Gladiator* (AM-319). **(Pacific-Burma)** Japanese forces holding Rangoon receive instructions from Lt. General Kimura to abandon their defenses and move to Pegu and also to Moulmein. In the **British Fourteenth Army** area, 33rd Corps sec-

tor, the Indian 7th Division attacks Yenangyaung, capturing it and gaining control of its oil fields, the largest oil source in Burma. In the 4th Corps sector, the Indian 5th Division advances to Toungoo several days ahead of schedule and pushes advance contingents further south toward Oktwin. **(Pacific-Yucatan Channel)** The Submarine Chaser SC-1019 suffers damage by grounding while operating in the Yucatan Channel. **(North Atlantic)** The Destroyer Escorts U.S.S. *Carter* (DE-112) and the U.S.S. *Neal A. Scott* (DE-769) sink the German U-Boat U-518. **(Atlantic-Western Europe) 12th Army Group** In the U.S. **Ninth Army** area, **XIII Corps** sector, the 5th Armored and 29th Infantry Divisions maintain their swift advance to the Elbe. C.C.A., 5th Armored establishes contact with British forces on the left near Pussade, while C.C.R. swoops into Luechow, accepting its surrender; then it springs toward Dannenberg. Meanwhile, the 84th Division reduces the final resistance in its zone along the Elbe northwest of Wittenberge. In the **XIX Corps** sector, the 2nd Armored clears out the stragglers in Forst Konigslutter. In other activity, Corps is assigned sector of occupation. In the U.S. **First Army** area, **VII Corps** sector, Dessau is secured by the 3rd Armored Division, except for one pocket in the northeastern edge. In the **V Corps** sector, C.C.B., 9th Armored Division begins guarding the factories and utilities in Rotha. The 2nd Division repulses a counterattack near Grimma, east of the Mulde, and subsequently clears the nearby woods. Meanwhile, the 1st Battalion, 271st Regiment, 69th Division continues reducing the resistance in Eilenburg. In other activity, the VIII Corps (Third Army) is transferred to First Army. In the U.S. **Third Army** area, **XII Corps** sector, the 11th Armored Division, trailed by the 26th Division, rolls steadily along; C.C.A. overruns Weiden, then drives to Nabburg; C.C.B. establishes a bridgehead at Schwarzenfeld across the Naab River. In conjunction, C.C.R. pushes to the Naab at Wernberg. In the 90th Division zone, Floss and Ploessberg fall to the 358th Regiment, while the 357th secures the woods and villages east of Weiden. In other activity, the 2nd Cavalry Group pushes its 42nd Squadron into Rossbach and Thonbrunn in Czechoslovakia; it is subsequently relieved by the 97th Division upon attachment to Corps. In the **XX Corps** sector, an attack toward the Danube is launched, spearheaded by the 3rd Cavalry Group, which shoves four columns through the lines of the 65th and 71st Division as it thrusts southeast, seizing a bridge over the Naab at Burglengenfeld with the 3rd Squadron, which also secures a bridgehead. In conjunction, the 43rd Squadron, driving on the right, liberates a concentration camp north of Hohenfels, but it is unable to seize a bridge at Heintzenhofen before it is destroyed by the Germans. The 65th Division drives to general line Kastl-Engelsberg-Wiesenacker-Ob Buchfeld; strong German opposition in the southern portion of Neumarkt holds firmly. In the 71st Division attack zone, Rosenberg and Sulzbach-Rosenberg are seized easily by RCT 5 while motorized contingents of RCT 16 overrun Amberg with the assistance of Tanks. In other activity, 13th Armored is attached to Corps at Eschenau. In the **III Corps** sector, the scheduled attack is postponed to allow additional time for the XV Corps to fully clear its zone. Corps moves southeast to assume zone from XV Corps. **6th Army Group** In the U.S. **Seventh Army** area, **XXI Corps** sector, 12th Armored Division followed by the 101st Cavalry Group advances; elements of C.C.A. seize a bridge (wired for demolition) over the Danube at Dillingen and establish a bridgehead on the south bank. C.C.B. drives to the Danube, near Hoechstadt, but all bridges have been blown. In conjunction, C.C.R., 5th Armored mops up in the Bopfingen-Lauchheim area and makes an unsuccessful attack against staunchly defended Lauchheim. In addition, the 4th and 63rd Divisions continue advancing, the former getting its 8th Regiment to Ellwangen and its 22nd Regiment to the vicinity of Adelmansfelden. Also, the 4th Division's TF Rodwell closes on Aalen. Meanwhile, the 63rd Division seizes a Rems bridge at Unter Boebingen while continuing to secure its zone. In the **VI Corps** sector, units of the 10th Armored drive to the Danube at Ehingen and find the bridges blown. Following close behind and on the flanks of the Armor, the 44th, 100th, and 103rd Divisions plow forward. In the **French 1st Army** area, 1st Corps sector, the French 1st Armored Division advances east astride the Danube toward Ulm. The 2nd Corps consolidates its positions in Stuttgart and initiates action to reduce the remaining resistance at Swabian Jura. Meanwhile, Groupement Le Bel reaches Lake Constance near Stockach while the Groupement Landouzy (9th Colonial Infantry Division) advances to Muhlheim and Neuenburg. **(Atlantic-Eastern Europe)** Heavy fighting continues in the eastern suburbs of Berlin as the First White Russian Front advances further. In conjunction, the First Ukrainian Front still drives north toward Berlin and west toward Dresden. Forces of the Fourth Ukrainian Front seize Troppau, Czechoslovakia, a road center northwest of Moravska Ostrava. **(Atlantic-Italy) 15th Army Area, IV Corps** sector, Task Force Duff moves swiftly to S. Benedetto Po. The 1st Armored Division advances toward the Po, crossing the Panaro near Modena. Meanwhile, the 85th Division seizes a bridge over the Panaro at Camposanto before the Germans can demolish it. Corps prepares to attack across the Po and receives II Corps' bridging equipment to hasten the pace. In the **II Corps** sector, the 6th South African Armored Division closes on the Panaro sending two columns in an effort to seize crossings near Camposanto and Finale and establish contact with the British. Meanwhile, the U.S. 88th Division gets its 351st Regiment to the Panaro where it establishes a bridgehead during the night of the 22nd-23rd between Camposanto and Finale.

Seventh Army troops crossing the Danube.

April 23rd 1945 — (United States) President Truman meets with Soviet representatives. He informs Molotov and Ambassador Gromyko that Russia's treatment of Poland is in absolute disregard to the agreement of Yalta and further tells them that he intends to "accomplish a union of peace-loving nations" with or without the Russians who suggest that the Soviet Union will not cooperate with the United Nations. In other activity, the Gunboat PE-56 sustains an explosion off Portland, Maine, and sinks. **(Pacific-Java Sea)** The Submarine U.S.S. *Besugo* (SS-321), operating between Borneo and Java, sinks the German Submarine U-183. **(Pacific-Philippines) Luzon** In the **U.S. Sixth Army** area, **I Corps** sector, Planes attack Japanese positions in the Mt. Mirador area to soften resistance; however, as the 2nd Battalion, 129th Regiment, 37th Division storms toward the mountain, ravaging rapid-fire originates from a ravine hindering progress as the Yanks reach a cemetery. In the 33rd Division zone, contingents of the 130th Regiment wipe out enemy forces and secure the high ground over the second Asin tunnel system; at the same time, other contingents advance toward Asin, being transported part way by Vehicles. Meanwhile, the 123rd Regiment, advancing doggedly against furious opposition along the Pugo-Tuba Trail, dispatches its 1st Battalion to bolster the 130th Regiment, battling at Mt. Mirador. At Crump Hill, the long struggle terminates with the 161st Regiment, 25th Division emerging the victor subsequent to a vicious fight which began on March 21st. Meanwhile, the 35th Regiment jumps off from the Fishhook attacking north, while simultaneously filling the gap which has existed between it and the 161st Regiment. In the **XI Corps** sector, the Japanese continue mounting fierce opposition, using deadly grid-fire from various positions to forestall the loss of Mt. Pacawagan; nevertheless, RCT 145, 6th Division, gnaws forward systematically eradicating resistance yard by yard. Meanwhile, the **XIV Corps** exploits its encirclement of Mt. Mataasna Bundoc stepping up its pressure. **Southern Philippines** In the **U.S. Eighth Army** area, **X Corps** sector, Kabacan on Mindanao is seized by the 3rd Battalion, 34th Regiment, 24th Division. The 24th is ordered to attack west toward Davao Gulf; contingents at Fort Pikit are relieved by the 19th Regiment. While the 24th Division attacks down Highway 1, the 31st Division will drive north along the Sayre Highway. On Cebu, the 2nd Battalion, 132nd Regiment, American Division is transported by boat to the vicinity of Tooc; it debarks and searches for enemy presence; the 2nd and 3rd Battalions flow into Danao, eliminating the organized resistance. Later actions scour the coastal area to destroy remnant enemy groups. Meanwhile, on the west coast, a contingent of the 182nd Regiment, supported by Guerrilla forces, overcomes resistance and seizes ground near Tabuclan, virtually terminating offensive operations. Mop-up begins while the Guerrillas move north and the 182nd advances east. On Bohol, the 3rd Battalion, 164th Regiment's persistent efforts drive the Japs from their positions north of Nanod. **(Pacific-Ryukyu Islands)** On Okinawa in the **U.S. Tenth Army** area, **XXIV Corps** sector, the 27th Division eliminates the final resistance at Urasoe-Mura Escarpment within its zone and, upon being subsequently attacked, annihilates the assaulting force. In the 96th Division zone, German resistance falters, and the 96th seizes the majority of the high ground in its zone in the Nishibaru-Tanabaru region. Meanwhile, the obstinate Rocky Crags falls to elements of the 17th Regiment, 7th Division, which occupy it with little effort, while the 32nd Regiment incinerates and seals caves on Skyline Ridge. **(Atlantic-Western Europe)** Heinrich Himmler suggests surrendering German forces to the Western Allies during a meeting in Luebeck with the Swedish consulate. The Allies turn down the offer, holding firm for the unconditional surrender of German forces on all fronts. **21st Army Group** In the **British Second Army** area, 12 Corps forces enter Harburg across from Hamburg on the Elbe. **12th Army Group** In the **U.S. Ninth Army** area, **XIII Corps** sector, slight resistance is crunched as the 29th Division closes on the Elbe. Meanwhile, the 5th Armored secures its zone along the Elbe, including the surrender of Dannenberg by C.C.R. subsequent to a victorious skirmish. In the **XVI**

Corps sector, the 75th Division begins relieving the 5th Division at its perimeter south of the Ruhr. In addition, the 55th AAA Brigade assumes responsibility for the northern sector of the 95th Division zone. In the **U.S. First Army** area, the 4th Armored Division is released to the Third Army. In the **VII Corps** sector, 3rd Armored Division reduces final resistance in Dessau and the remainder of its area by 21:00; all resistance in Corps sector is terminated by this time. Meanwhile, the 4th Cavalry Group begins a security mission in the Quedlinburg-Aschersleben-Klostermansfeld region, an operation which lasts until cessation of hostilities. In the **V Corps** sector, elements of the 271st Regiment, 69th Division completes the capture of Eilenburg. In the **U.S. Third Army** area, **XII Corps** sector, C.C.B., 11th Armored Division seizes Cham, concluding Division's present mission. The effectiveness of the U.S. pressure is causing problems as the roads in the entire area are congested and near grid-lock because of thousands of prisoners and slave laborers that have accumulated. In the 26th Division zone, rapid progress is made. The 104th Regiment races unopposed to the Dautersdorf-Neunburg area while the 328th Regiment propels advance contingents to Schoengras. In the 90th Division zone, Flossenburg is easily toppled by the 358th Regiment, which also liberates the town's concentration camp and its Aircraft factory, as well as securing Waldthurn. In conjunction, Albersrieth, Kaimling, and Michldorf fall to the 357th Regiment. The 11th Armored Division, followed by the 26th Division which is advancing on the right rear, receives orders to move southeast to establish contact with the Russians near the German-Austrian border; the 26th is to secure bridges while guarding the right flank. Meanwhile, the 90th and 97th Divisions and the 2nd Cavalry Group are directed to secure the passes along the border while neutralizing the German troops in Czechoslovakia. In the **XX Corps** sector, the 3rd Cavalry Group roars to the Danube, giving responsibility for the Naab River bridgehead to the 71st Division, which is racing southeast. The 5th Regiment, 71st Division, seizes Schwandorf while the 66th Regiment nears Regensburg. In the 65th Division zone, swift progress also occurs as the 261st Regiment overruns Griffenwang and Kittensee on the left and seizes Hardt and See on the right. Meanwhile, the final resistance is reduced at Neumarkt. In the **III Corps** sector, contingents of the 14th Cavalry Group move in to the XX Corps zone to relieve units of the 65th Division embattled on a hill south of Neumarkt. In addition, 14th Armored is attached to Corps to lead an attack, driving south with the 99th Division trailing. Meanwhile, the 86th Division continues advancing southeast on the Corps right flank. In the **U.S. Fifteenth Army** area, Army area of occupation is expanded to encompass First and Ninth Armies' sector of Rheinprovinz east of the Rhine, the 6th Army Group's remaining sections of Hessen, Pfalz, and Saarland. In the **XXIII Corps** sector, the 54th AAA Brigade assumes responsibility for the Koblenz subarea, west of the Rhine, relieving units of the XXII Corps of its sector west of the Rhine and the 8th Division's sector of its portion east of the Rhine. **6th Army Group** In the **U.S. Seventh Army** area, the 20th Armored Division, chosen to spearhead the attack against Munich, is attached to XV Corps. The Armor is to be trailed by the 42nd and 45th Divisions. In the **XXI Corps** sector, C.C.A., 12th Armored Division, bolstered by contingents of C.C.B., enlarges its Dillingen bridgehead. C.C.R. seizes Lauchheim, and the 4th Division continues driving to the Danube; TF Rodwell takes Aalen and Unter Kochen. The 63rd Division also receives orders to drive to the Danube as quickly as possible. The 3rd Division, assigned to garrison duty in Nuremberg, is attached to Corps to bolster the attack against Augsburg. In the **VI Corps** sector, the 10th Armored, trailed by the 44th Division, gets contingents across the Danube near Ehingen and Erbach slightly after midnight, 23rd-24th. Meanwhile, C.C.R., 10th Armored is reinforced for the attack against Ulm. In the 103rd Division sector, the southeast escape routes from Stuttgart are sealed off. The 410th Regiment, fortified by a Battalion of the 409th, grinds toward Urach and Muensingen while the 411th, moving quickly, seizes Honau and Metzingen, as well as overrunning Neuffen, Pfullingen, and Reutlingen. Meanwhile, the 781st Tank Battalion, and the 117th Cavalry Squadron reinforce the 103rd. In the 100th Division zone, mop-up operations ensue north of the Neckar River and east of Stuttgart; in conjunction, the 397th Regiment crosses the Neckar, severing the Autobahn to the west, and secures Koengen. **(Atlantic-Eastern Europe)** German General Reimann is relieved as Commander of Berlin and replaced by Lt. Colonel Barenfanger; within several days he is promoted to Major General. The Germans string the city of Berlin "Berlin Ring" with a few thousand S.S. troops; no one is permitted in or out of the city without a special permit. Also, Generals Keitel and Jodl move to the Chancellery to bolster Hitler, while Konev's troops are wedging into the city. Soviet troops penetrate Berlin; contingents of the First White Russian Front strike from the east, while units of the First Ukrainian Front advance from the south. Also, additional forces of the First White Russian Front seize Oranienburg and Frankfurt-on-Oder, north of Berlin, while units of the First Ukrainian Front seize Cottbus, southeast of the capital; in addition, Pulsnitz, northeast of Dresden, is taken as left flank elements move to the Elbe near Torgau where contact with Allied forces (Western Front) is to occur. **(Atlantic-Italy) 15th Army Group** In the **U.S. Fifth Army** area, **IV Corps** sector, the 10th Mountain Division establishes a bridgehead on the north bank of the Po River after crossing in assault boats. The 1st Armored Division advances C.C.A. to the Po River at both Guastalla and Luzzaro, while C.C.R. drives to the Secchia River south of Highway 9. Also, the 85th Division closes on the Po, reaching it at Quingentole. Meanwhile, the accompanying Brazilian Expeditionary Force, advancing on the right rear of Corps, seizes Marano and Vignola. The U.S. 34th Division is attached to Corps to run interference on the left flank along Highway 9. In the **II Corps** sector, a Task Force of the 6th South African Armored Division, driving on the left, plows through Finale and continues east encountering the British 6th Armored Division. Meanwhile, the 6th Armored secures a bridgehead across the Panaro at Camposanto and then attacks northeast toward the Po, racing with three Regiments abreast. Also, the 88th Division drives to the Po reaching positions near Carbonara, netting large numbers of German troops as they are beginning to retreat across the river. In conjunction, the 91st Division is converging on the Po. In the **British Eighth Army** area, Army boundary is adjusted between the 13th and 5th Corps to extend north from the Reno to the Po River because 5th Corps sector has extended to a width of about fifty miles. In the 13th Corps sector, a bridgehead is established across the Reno River. The British Sixth Armored Division is attached to Corps to attack toward the Po to the right of the New Zealand 2nd Division. Meanwhile, the Indian 10th Division is withdrawn from battle. In the 5th Corps sector, Ferrara is seized by the Indian 8th Division as it drives to the Po, reaching it at Pontelagoscuro. Also, the British 6th Armored Division advances to the Po outside of Bondeno and establishes contact with U.S. troops near Finale. **(Atlantic-Switzerland)** Allen Dulles receives word that Parilli, an Italian intermediary is at the Swiss border and he has brought additional information on the surrender of German troops in Italy. Dulles, still under orders from the Joint Chiefs of Staff to discontinue negotiations, attempts to work the crisis out. It appears that German General Schweinitz has full authority to surrender for Vietinghoff. Generals Wolf and Schweinitz will leave for Caserta; Wolf asks for immediate meeting with Dulles to ensure safe passage to Caserta. After cutting through the red tape, a Captain Waibel, Professor Husmann and two Swiss, smuggle Wolf to Lucerne. By the 25th, Wolf is heading back to Italy, leaving his chief Adjutant, S.S. Major Wenner to continue the talks on his behalf. Soon after Wolf's return, Italian Partisans surround his quarters, but Captain Waibel and another man rescue him and take him to Switzerland. No further discussions occur in Switzerland; the Germans reach Caserta, where General Morgan runs the proceedings. On the 27th, the instrument of surrender (top secret) is signed, effective May 2nd.

April 24th 1945 — (United States) During the Yalta Conference during February, Stalin had agreed to permit U.S. Planes to fly from Airbases within Russia to strike against Japan; Stalin had lied. The Joint Chiefs of Staff agree that further negotiations (ongoing for several months) are useless; they decide to cancel the plans and act independent of the Russians. The Joint Chiefs also decide to abort plans to open a supply route from the Kurile Islands to the Russians who are facing the Japanese. **(Pacific-Philippines) Luzon** In the **U.S. Sixth Army** area, **I Corps** sector, fighting is heavy as the 3rd Battalion, 130th Regiment, 33rd Division bangs forward, reaching positions about 2,000 yards from Baguio. Meanwhile, the 2nd Battalion, 129th Infantry, 37th Division secures the cemetery in front of Mt. Mirador, and the 1st Battalion advances against fierce enemy fire gaining about 300 yards on Highway 9. At Lone Tree Hill, Company G is joined by the main body of its 2nd Battalion, 27th Infantry, 25th Division; on the following day, the 2nd Battalion springs a strong surprise attack, seizing the hill. Meanwhile, the 3rd Battalion, moves through 2nd Battalion lines and continues to pound the Japs on and along Mt. Myoko. **Southern Philippines** In the **U.S. Eighth Army** area, on Mindanao, the 24th Division attacks toward Digos on the Davao Gulf, sending its 34th Regiment as spearhead; it advances to about thirty miles from the objective, reaching Saguing. Meanwhile, the 31st Division receives orders to drive north along the Sayre Highway toward Kibawe-Talomo trail; its 124th Regiment gets the assignment and moves to Kabacan where it will launch the drive. On Bohol, the 3rd Battalion, 164th Regiment is scouring the island attempting to destroy the remaining Japanese stragglers. **(Pacific-Ryukyu Islands)** On Ie Shima, mop-up continues as searchers move about to uncover the elusive enemy stragglers. U.S. casualties to this date total 172 killed, 902 wounded, and 46 missing in action. On Okinawa, in the **U.S. Tenth Army** area, **XXIV Corps** sector, the first line of Japanese Shuri defenses are pierced by Corps with little effort, except for the western flank; the enemy has abandoned their positions during the night of the 23rd-24th. The 96th Division secures Nishibaru Ridge, the Tanabaru Escarpment, plus a ridge to the south, as well as overrunning Hill 143. The 7th Division crushes the final resistance in the Hill 178 area. However, the entrenched Japanese at Item Pocket still resist tenaciously. **(Pacific-Burma)** Japanese General Kimura transfers his Headquarters to Moulmein. In other activity, the first of three Airfields at Toungoo becomes operational. **(Atlantic)** The Destroyer Escort U.S.S. *Frederick C. Davis* (DE-136) is sunk by a Submarine torpedo in the Atlantic. In the North

Atlantic, the U.S. Destroyer Escorts *Pillsbury* (DE-133), *Flaherty* (DE-135), *Chatelain* (DE-149), *Neunzer* (DE-150), *Hubbard* (DE-211), and the *Keith* (DE-241), *Janssen* (DE-396) and *Varian* (DE-798) share credit in the kill, as the combined attack sinks the German U Boat U-546. **(Atlantic-Western Europe) 21st Army Group** In the **British Second Army** area, 30th Corps deploys for attack against Bremen while the 8th Corps converges on the Lauenburg area. **12th Army Group** In the **U.S. Ninth Army** area, **XIII Corps** sector, the 5th Armored Division is relieved along the Elbe by the 29th Division. Meanwhile, the 84th Division stands at the Elbe to meet the Soviets when they arrive. In the **U.S. First Army** area, **VII Corps** sector, the 9th Division assumes responsibility for 3rd Armored sector along the Mulde; it is reinforced by C.C.A. and C.C.R., 3rd Armored Division. In the **V Corps** sector, the 1st Battalion, 273rd Regiment, 69th Division accepts the surrender of Wurzen. In the **VIII Corps** sector, 6th Armored and 76th Infantry Divisions start modifying their defensive positions. In the **U.S. Third Army** area, **XII Corps** sector, aided by Artillery and Air attacks, C.C.B., 11th Armored Division secures Regen. The 26th Division, also driving southeast, gets its 104th Regiment across the Regen River at Roding and pushes its 328th Regiment across the river near Walderbach-Reichenbach. In the 90th Division sector, the 357th Regiment secures Vohenstrauss and seizes a bridge at Burgtreswitz while the 358th Regiment, driving on the right flank, drives toward Eslarn. In the **XX Corps** sector, the 3rd Cavalry Group drives to the Danube, finding the bridges demolished. Meanwhile, the 71st Division speeds contingents to seize the railroad bridge over the Regen River at Regenstauf, but it is also destroyed; RCT 14 seizes Regenstauf, using assault boats and treadway bridging. The 5th Infantry Division follows the 71st; however, lack of Vehicu lar bridges compels it to cross the Regen behind RCT 14 during the night of the 24th-25th. In addition, the 66th Division continues driving southeast against little resistance, and the 65th Division continues closing on the Danube. Its 260th Regiment, secures Bergmatting, Eilsbrunn, and Schoenhofen, while the 261st roars through Hemau, capturing Painten; the 259th Regiment is pinched out. In the **III Corps** sector, an attack is launched southeast toward the Danube. The 14th Cavalry Group, driving on the left, clears Waldorf with its 18th Squadron, while the 32nd Squadron advances to Ludwigs Kanal. Meanwhile, at 06:00, 14th Armored, trailed by the 99th Division, begins its attack in the center of the Corps; contingents reach the Altmuhl River where heavy enemy fire hinders the bridging operation. Also, the 88th Division reaches the Altmuhl near Eichstatt. In the **U.S. Fifteenth Army** area, **XXII Corps** deploys east of the Rhine, relieving the 8th Division (XVIII (A/B) Corps). In conjunction, the 94th Division occupies the Duesseldorf area while Corps Artillery units assume positions in the Cologne area east of the Rhine. In the **XXIII Corps** sector, the 28th Division (officially attached to XXII Corps) moves into Regierungsbezirk Saarland to relieve the 36th Division, 7th Army. **6th Army Group** In the **U.S. Seventh Army** area, **XV Corps** sector, the 42nd and 45th Divisions still drive toward the Danube. In the **XXI Corps** sector, C.C.B., 12th Armored, bolstered by the 15th Regiment, 3rd Division drives against Wertingen, subsequent to seizing Binswangen; C.C.B. bolts the Danube at Dillingen and races south toward Burgau while C.C.R. seeks bridge crossings as it probes southwest along the river. In addition, the 101st Cavalry Group spreads out along the Danube, protecting the Corps' left flank while the 4th Division continues closing on the Danube. Also, the 63rd Division keeps advancing, jumping one Regiment over the other, rapidly heading south to positions near Gerstetten-Geislingen. In the **VI Corps** sector, Ulm, along the Danube, is seized by the joint-attack of C.C.R., 10th Armored Division and the 324th Regiment, 44th Division, while the 114th Regiment, sprints to catch German forces which are retreating toward Ehingen; however, the Germans evade the pursuers. Also, the 71st Regiment, and C.C.A. and C.C.B., 10th Armored speed from the Danube to the Iller River and Canal; as usual the Germans have blown the bridges, preventing a quick crossing. Meanwhile, the 100th Division continues mopping up in Stuttgart vicinity while the 103rd Division crumbles the remaining unorganized resistance in its path, capturing Muensingen, Urach, and Wittlingen. In the **French 1st Army** area, the German forces, caught between the Neckar and the Danube Rivers, find their positions not only surrounded, but now split as the 2nd Corps roars through Swabian Jura, reaching the vicinity of Sigmaringen. In the 1st Corps sector, a French Armored Division column advances to Ulm, which has been seized by U.S. VI Corps troops, while another column moves along the Iller. Meanwhile, the German units still in the Black Forest are being rooted out as Corps advances. In the Groupement Landouzy zone, Loerrach is captured as the drive reaches the Swiss frontier. Meanwhile, contingents of the 10th Military Region ford the Rhine, capturing Kembs Dam unimpaired. **(Atlantic-Eastern Europe)** The Soviets drive deeper into Berlin, signaling the end of the German capital; in conjunction, other Russian contingents seal off German escape routes from the ruined city. The Russian Artillery plasters the city, inflicting more devastation. One German Officer notes: "THE RUSSIANS BURN THEIR WAY INTO THE HOUSES WITH FLAME THROWERS. THE SCREAMS OF THE CHILDREN ARE TERRIBLE." **(Atlantic-Italy) 15th Army Group** In the U.S. **Fifth Army** area, the 92nd Division drives toward Genoa, subsequent to reducing enemy positions along the Gothic Line, except for one strongpoint: Aulla. In the **IV Corps** sector, the 10th Mountain Division drives southwest to seize the Airport at Villafranca, southwest of Verona. Meanwhile, German opposition continues to dwindle. The 85th Division establishes a bridgehead across the Po River at Quingentole, without any German interference. Contingents of the 1st Armored Division eliminate all escape routes east of the Taro River while troops of the 34th Division secure Reggio. In the **II Corps** sector, elements of the 88th Division and the 91st Division cross the Po, the latter near Sermide, at darkness. In the **British Eighth Army** area, 13th Corps sector, the British 6th Armored Division and the 2nd New Zealand Division establish bridgeheads across the Po during the night of the 24th-25th, the former at Stienta and the latter at Gaiaba. In the 5th Corps sector, Corps launches a night-assault across the Po, near Pontelagoscuro, spearheaded by the Indian 8th Division. **(Atlantic-Italy-Air Action)** First Lt. Raymond L. Knight leads a three-Plane mission into the Northern Po Valley to destroy the Airdrome at Ghedi. Knight orders the other Planes to remain at high altitude, but he descends to below tree top level for a grass mowing look at the field and discovers eight enemy Planes nestled safely in a sea of camouflage. Minutes later, three Thunderbolts skirt through the heavy antiaircraft fire, thread the needle and destroy seven of the Aircraft; Knight decimates five of them. Lt. Knight takes the formation back to Base and then leads another raid against Bergamo Airfield, near Ghedi. Knight's Plane becomes damaged as he again swoops down to scoop up some dirt and discovers another hidden Squadron of German Planes. The Thunderbolts strafe the field, but Knight, ignoring the damages to his Thunderbolt, executes ten additional passes and despite being struck two additional times, manages to kill eight more Planes; the mission decimates five other Aircraft. On the 25th, Knight leads another attack against Bergamo; four Planes buzz the Airfield and several more enemy Aircraft are destroyed, however, enemy fire riddles Knight's Plane. Lt. Knight, cognizant of the desperate need for operational Aircraft in the Theater, declines the option of bailing out over Allied lines and attempts to bring his bird in for a safe landing; along the precarious return trip, unyielding air currents batter the crippled Plane and Knight goes down in the Appennines Mountains and is killed upon impact. First Lt. Knight receives the Medal of Honor posthumously.

April 25th 1945 — (United States) In San Francisco, the United Nations Conference on International Organization convenes. In other activity, Churchill informs President Truman that Himmler has agreed to surrender all troops on the Western Front and that Himmler claims Hitler is incapacitated and that he is speaking for the government of Germany. Truman informs Churchill that "America can agree only to an unconditional surrender on all fronts in agreement with Russia and Britain." **(Pacific-Philippines) (Luzon)** In the U.S. **Sixth Army** area, **I Corps** sector, contingents of the 1st Battalion, 129th Regiment, 37th Division, strengthen their defensive positions on Quezon Hill, above Baguio; elements with Tank support penetrate the town. Meanwhile, the 2nd Battalion attacks Mt. Mirador. In conjunction, the 1st Battalion, 130th Regiment, 33rd Division seizes the southernmost peak of Mt. Mirador, then, bolstered by the 1st Battalion, 123rd Regiment, launches an attack against Dominican Hill, which also overlooks Baguio. In other activity, 2nd Battalion, 161st Regiment, 25th Division launches a night attack toward Kembu Plateau about 2,000 yards northwest of Kapintalan. Meanwhile, the Japanese holding Lone Tree Hill lose it to the 2nd Battalion, 27th Regiment, which launches a startling surprise assault. In the 32nd Division zone along the Villa Verde Trail, Company A, receives more than it anticipates from the Japanese who blanket the area of advance with a ring of fire. As the troops seek cover, a Jap Plane deposits a five-hundred pound bomb, which entombs five men. Without hesitation, P.F.C. David M. Gonzales, with his nose hugging the ground, creeps beneath a sheet of murderous fire to help his Commanding Officer extricate the buried Soldiers. The Commanding Officer is riddled with machine gun bullets, but Gonzales reaches the point and begins digging feverishly, detached from the incessant danger. Gonzales stands up to hurry the process and gets two men out of the rubble and then rescues a third, however, enemy fire wounds him mortally; P.F.C. Gonzales receives the Medal of Honor posthumously. In the **XI Corps** sector, RCT 145, maintains its systematic reduction of the Japs on Mt. Pacawagan and vicinity. In the **XIV Corps** the Japanese come under more pressure at the Cituinan Hills and Mt. Mataasna Bundoc. The Japanese receive orders to withdraw to Mt. Banahao, beginning on the 27th. **Southern Philippines** In the U.S. **Eighth Army** area, the 34th Infantry, 24th Division continues driving toward Digos on Mindanao. On Cebu, the 164th Regiment (minus 3rd Battalion), Americal Division embarks for Negros Oriental. **(Pacific-Ryukyu Islands)** In the U.S. **Tenth Army** area, **XXIV Corps** sector, Japanese positions at the Shuri defense come under strong attacks including Air and Artillery, plus Naval Surface Vessel fire, as Corps prepares to drive against the next enemy line of defense. The Japs holding Item Pocket continue being pressed by limited actions by the 27th Division. In other activity, the Escort Carrier *Steamer Bay* (CVE-87) and the Destroyer *Hale* (DD-642) are damaged by collision. **(Pacific)**

The Japanese Submarine RO-109 is sunk in the Philippine Sea by the High Speed Transport *Horace A. Bass* (APD-124), and the Japanese Minesweeper No. 41 is destroyed by the Submarine U.S.S. *Cod* (SS-224), off the coast of China. **(Pacific-Burma)** The final preparations for the attack to seize Rangoon (DRACULA) are complete. In the **British Fourteenth Army** area, 4 Corps sector, Pyu is seized by the Indian 5th Division; the Indian 17th Division moves through the 5th Division's lines to continue the land attack against Rangoon. **(Pacific-China)** As the Japanese continue driving toward Chihchiang, the Chinese 58th Division is compelled to withdraw from its positions on the enemy flank; a small contingent remains at Wukang. In other activity, a radio message from General Marshall is received by General Wedemeyer; it states the adjusted tonnage figures to be delivered by the Air Transport Command. The tonnage is reduced due to the redeployment needs in Europe and is less than previously estimated as necessary for Operation BETA (assault to open port on coast of China). **(Atlantic-Western Europe-English Channel)** The German Submarine U-1107 is sunk by Land-based Naval Aircraft (VPB-103). **(Atlantic-Western Europe)** **21st Army Group** The **British Second Army** assumes control of the U.S. XVIII Corps (A/B), which still controls the 8th Division, to support the British drive from the Elbe to the Baltic. In the 30th Corps sector, contingents enter Bremen and start securing the city. **12th Army Group** In the **U.S. Ninth Army** area, Intelligence Officers interrogate Kurt Dittmar, a radio spokesman for the German Wehrmacht; he had crossed the Elbe to surrender to American forces. Dittmar predicts that Hitler and Goebbels will hold out in Berlin until the very end. In addition he states that the redoubt is a fantasy. The **XIII Corps** terminates its offense, beginning an occupational phase, while simultaneously implementing Patrols. Meanwhile, the 29th, 35th, and 84th Divisions stretch along the Elbe River line; the 5th Armored Division pulls back to the rear. In the **U.S. First Army** area, **V Corps** sector, Patrols of the 69th Division establish contact with the Red Army near Riesa and Torgau. The 1st Battalion, 271st Regiment, begins securing Kultzschau, subsequent to bolting the Mulde at Eilenburg. Meanwhile, the 2nd Division remains in place along the Mulde. In the **VIII Corps** sector, the 6th Armored and 76th Infantry Divisions pull back to the west bank of the Mulde and implement Patrols; some contingents remain on the east side of the river. In the **U.S. Third Army** area, General Patton is informed that the 5,000 White Russian troops (fought on the side of the Germans) who had contacted the 26th Division on the previous day are to be considered P.O.W.s; some confusion had accompanied their request to surrender to the Americans as to whether they should be treated as Allies or P.O.W.s. **XII Corps** sector, C.C.B., 11th Armored Division overruns Perlesreut in addition to capturing bridges across the Ohe River outside Prombach; the balance of the 11th continues advancing, even though bad roads hinder progress. C.C.A., commanded by Brigadier General W. A. Holbrook has been informed that a large contingent of troops (undetermined nationality) is speeding up both banks of the Danube, transporting sizable amounts of horse-drawn Artillery. In the 26th Division sector, contingents reach the Danube; a German Officer points out five barges in the Danube and tells the 26th Division Officers not to bomb it or many people will be killed; upon examination, it is discovered that the five barges contain poison gas. In the 90th Division zone, the attack drives southeast; in conjunction, the 358th Regiment advances along the Czechoslovakian border in the Eslarn-Schoensee region, liberating several Czechoslovakian

villages. Meanwhile, the 97th Division drives northeast toward the Czechoslovakian city of Cheb, seizing the high ground north of the city, then pounding into the city. In the **XX Corps** sector, the 65th and 71st Divisions advance to the Danube, the latter driving across the Danube after dark to support the 65th Division's assault against Regensburg. Its 14th Regiment seizes Donaustauf and Walhalla. In the 65th Division zone, contingents reach the Danube and penetrate Regensburg; an assault across the Danube is scheduled for 02:00 on the 26th. Meanwhile, the 261st Regiment seizes Waldorf and supports the capture of Kelheim which is being assaulted by the 14th Cavalry Group (III Corps). In the **III Corps** sector, the 99th Division seizes Dietfurt and Kinding at the Altmuhl River. The 86th Division's 342nd Regiment seizes Eichstatt, also along the Altmuhl, and establishes a small bridgehead; the 341st Regiment briskly sweeps through the woods near the Gungolding bridge site. In the **U.S. Fifteenth Army** area, regrouping occurs. **6th Army Group** In the **U.S. Seventh Army** area, **XV Corps** sector, the 42nd and 45th Divisions advance to the Danube; the former seizes Donauwoerth. In the **XXI Corps** sector, final resistance in Wertingen is terminated by C.C.A., 12th Armored Division, while C.C.B. seizes Rettenbach and Limbach. In conjunction, some elements of C.C.B. jump to Offingen, but their numbers are too slim to withstand the enemy forces there. Meanwhile, the 3rd Division (less 30th Regiment) moves to the Dillingen bridgehead; the 30th Regiment assumes positions north of the Danube, on the left flank of the Division. The deluge of Yanks continues as forward contingents of the 4th and 63rd Divisions reach the Danube and begin pouring across. The 1st and 2nd Battalions, 254th Regiment, 63rd Division move across a damaged railroad bridge, seizing Leipheim and holding it against a subsequent Tank-supported counterattack. In the **VI Corps** sector, Neu Ulm is seized by C.C.R., 10th Armored and the 324th Regiment, 44th Division after crossing the Danube at Ulm. In conjunction, C.C.R. crosses the Iller River, driving rapidly to the Kellmunz region. C.C.A. encounters heavy resistance preventing it from crossing the Iller at Illerrieden; units divert and cross at Dietenheim, driving north to capture Voehringen. Meanwhile, the 103rd Division speeds southeast, getting forward units to the Danube northeast of Ulm. In the **French 1st Army** area, the 2nd Corps moves to Swabian Jura to eliminate the remaining German resistance there. In the 1st Corps sector, Germans corralled in the Black Forest attempt to break out and escape to the Bavarian Alps. The futile attack thrusts between the Swiss frontier and Villingen; Air support is thrown against the Germans, and in addition, reinforcements arrive quickly, dousing the German effort by the following day. **(Atlantic-Eastern Europe)** Germany is virtually severed in two, as the Soviets get Patrols of the First Ukrainian Front to the Elbe near Torgau where they encounter the U.S. First Army, under orders not to advance beyond the river. In Berlin, the Germans continue to battle the Soviet onslaught; the city is now thoroughly surrounded by the First White Russian Front and the First Ukrainian Front as they converge northwest of Potsdam. In the East Prussian area, Pillau, on the tip of the Samland Peninsula, is seized by forces of the Third White Russian Front. Meanwhile, on the southern front, troops of the Second Ukrainian Front continue battling the Germans at the outskirts of Bruenn in Czechoslovakia. **(Atlantic-Italy)** **15th Army Group** In the **U.S. Fifth Army** area, Aulla falls to the 92nd Division, completely demolishing the enemy defenses of the Gothic Line in the Ligurian coastal sector. In the **IV Corps** sector, a Ranger TF under Colonel William O. Darby moves from Villafranca Airfield, just captured by the 85th Regiment, 10th Mountain Division, toward Verona. Meanwhile, C.C.A., 1st Armored Division races across the Po River in pursuit of the Germans who are retreating west of Lake Garda. In other activity, the 3rd Division seizes Parma, sitting at the junction of Highways 9 and 62. In the **II Corps** sector, the 88th Division drives to Verona and before dawn on the 26th, the remnant resistance is terminated. At Cerea, the Germans are attempting to escape the clutches of the pursuing Yanks; however, effective fire inflicts severe casualties upon the retreating forces. In other activity, the 6th South African Armored Division starts to move across the Po at Felonica. In the **British Eighth Army** area, 5th Corps sector, the Indian 8th Division pushes from its Po bridgehead to the Adige River. Meanwhile, the British 56th Division and the Cremona Group cross the Po near Polesella and in the coastal sector respectively.

April 26th 1945 — (Pacific-Philippines) Luzon In the **U.S. Sixth Army** area, I Corps sector, the 129th Regiment, 37th Division reduces final resistance on Mt. Mirador, seizing it. Also, the Japanese abandon Dominican Hill; contingents of the 33rd Division occupy it. Meanwhile, a contingent of the 25th Division secures the approach to Kembu Plateau. **Southern Philippines** In the **U.S. Eighth Army** area, the 34th Regiment, 24th Division continues driving on Mindanao toward Digos, but progress is slowed due to many obstacles and mines placed by the Japs prior to departing the area. On Negros, RCT 164 (minus 3rd Battalion) lands unopposed on the southeast coast of Negros Oriental, near Looc; the 1st Battalion seizes Dumaguete and its Airfield without a fight. Meanwhile, the 2nd Battalion advances inland to San Antonio and beyond to the Ocoy River. Also, in Negros Occidental, the Japanese still mount fierce resistance on the slopes of Hill 3155, as the 40th Division continues pressing; the 2nd Battalion, 185th Regiment, seizes Lantawan Plateau and releases its 2nd Battalion to augment the ongoing assault against Hill 3155. **(Pacific-Ryukyu Islands)** On Ie Shima, the mop-up operations are terminated. Control of the island is turned over to ISCOM Ie Shima. The **U.S. Tenth Army** is informed that the proposed invasion of Miyako, in the Sakishima Group, by the III Amphibious Corps is shelved, thus permitting it to be committed to battle in southern Okinawa. On **Okinawa** in the **XXIV Corps** sector, the assault against the Japanese second line of defenses at the Shuri defense line commences, subsequent to a strong Artillery bombardment. The 165th Regiment, 27th Division continues wearing down the Item Pocket, while the 105th Regiment drives to Nakama. The 96th Division drives toward the Maeda Escarpment (Big Escarpment), the eastern segment of the Urasoe-Mura Escarpment. The Japanese offer fierce resistance as troops push to the crest of the escarpment, under fire from the reverse slopes. In conjunction, despite the vicious opposition, Armor penetrates and drives in to the village of Maeda. Meanwhile, the 7th Division's 17th Regiment unsuccessfully assaults the east and west sides of Kochi Ridge; however, Company G, secures a slim hold on the east side. In other activity, the Destroyer U.S.S. *Hutchins* is damaged by a depth charge off Okinawa. **(Pacific-Burma)** In the **British Fourteenth Army** 4th Corps sector, the Indian 17th Division reaches Daik-u as it moves toward Rangoon. **(Atlantic-Western Europe) 21st Army Group** In the **Canadian First Army** area, the Canadian 2 Corps proclaims that northeast Holland is secure except for a small pocket on the coast at the Ems estuary. In the **British Second Army** area, Bremen finally falls. In the 12th Corps sector, contingents converge on the Elbe, across from Hamburg. In other activity, the U.S. XVIII Corps (A/B) begins movement to its new sector along the Elbe. **12th Army Group** In the **U.S. Ninth Army** area, the 35th Division, deployed along the Elbe, is relieved by the 102nd Division, permitting it to move to Hannover. In the **U.S. First Army** area, VII Corps sector, a Patrol of the 104th Division makes contact with the Red Army at Pretzsch. In the **V Corps** sector, the Commanding Officer of the 273rd Regiment, 69th Division and the Commanding Officer of the 173rd Regiment, Soviet 58th Guard meet at Torgau. In the **U.S. Third Army** area, **XII Corps** sector, the 11th Armored Division successfully concludes its mission. C.C.A. gets Patrols across the Austrian border near Lackenhausen while C.C.B. seizes Waldkirchen and also advances to the Austrian border near Gollnerberg. Meanwhile, the 90th Division probes along the Czechoslovakian border; the 359th Regiment seizes Waldmuenchen after a vicious contest, and reconnaissance contingents overrun Degelberg, Furth, and Raenkam. Also, the 2nd Cavalry Group extends further in Czechoslovakia, and the 97th Division finishes the reduction of Cheb. In the **XX Corps** sector, an assault is launched at 02:00 as the 260th and 261st Regiments, 65th Division roar across the Danube attacking on the right, seizing ground including Grasslfing, Lengfeld, Matting, Nieder Gebraching, and Oberndorf; a solid bridgehead is also established. The 259th Regiment attacks later in the day. Meanwhile, the 71st Division, commencing its attack at 04:00, crosses the river and seizes several towns. Also, 13th Armored moves to positions near Parsberg to prepare to bolt the Danube. In the **III Corps** sector, the 14th Armored and the 86th Infantry Divisions cross the Altmuhl River and drive rapidly south to the Danube; the 342nd Regiment, 86th Division seizes Ingolstadt prior to crossing. In conjunction, the 99th Division gets its 394th and 395th Regiments to the Danube after pushing from the Altmuhl bridgehead. **6th Army Group** In the **U.S. Seventh Army** area, **XV Corps** sector, the 42nd and 45th Divisions drive across the Danube, establishing strong bridgeheads. In the **XXI Corps** the 3rd Division assumes responsibility for the Dillingen bridgehead, relieving C.C.A., 12th Armored Division; it then proceeds to expand the bridgehead east and southeast, capturing several towns and villages as it stretches toward the Werk Kanal and Augsburg. Meanwhile, C.C.B. makes contact with the 63rd Division, which is moving across the Danube, seizing Bubesheim. Also, the 101st Cavalry Group operating in 12th Armored's zone seizes a bridge at Hiltenfingen over the Wertach River, while the 4th Division jumps from the Danube, advancing south to Dinkelscherben-Horgau region. In the **VI Corps** sector, Engineers complete a bridge across the Iller at Voehringen; soon after, the 71st Regiment, 44th Division and C.C.A., 10th Armored race across the river, the latter moving to Babenhausen and beyond to Mindelheim, followed by C.C.R., which pivots at Babenhausen driving toward Landsberg. The Division's left flank is protected by the 90th Cavalry Reconnaissance Squadron. Meanwhile, C.C.B. 10th Armored, racing south along the Iller Canal, frees the Allied prisoners at Memmingen while the remainder of the 44th Division trails the Armor. Also, the 103rd Division darts across the Danube northeast of Ulm. In the **French 1st Army** area, the 1st Corps places a solid ring around the Germans in the Black Forest, sealing their fate. Meanwhile, the German pocket west of Tutlingen is further reduced. **(Atlantic-Eastern Europe)** In Berlin, the battle-weary Germans fight fiercely against the overwhelming Soviet forces; however, it is a futile endeavor as the end is near. Meanwhile, Stettin and its port are proclaimed seized by Moscow, which states they have been captured by the Second White Russian Front subsequent to overrunning German defenses west of the Oder. Also, contingents of the First White Russian Front are advancing northeast of Berlin, and yet others are pushing west and southwest of Frankfurt. The First Ukrainian Front captures Strehla and Torgau on the west bank of the Elbe. In Silesia, fierce fighting continues to rage in the capital, Breslau. Also, contingents of the Second Ukrainian Front overrun Bruenn, Czechoslovakia, an armament depot. In the Third White Russian Front sector, the Soviets start to secure Frische Nehrung in East Prussia, subsequent to forcing a canal at Pillau to reach the objective. **(Atlantic-Italy) 15th Army Group** In the **U.S. Fifth Army** area, **IV Corps** sector, Task Force Darby, 10th Mountain Division moves into Verona at 06:00, discovering the U.S. 88th Division (II Corps) has the city under control; it then moves to seal German escape routes. The 85th Division establishes a bridgehead across the Adige River near Verona and subsequently reverts to Army control. Meanwhile, the 34th Division drives toward Piacenza, but firm rear-guard actions stop progress in front of the Nure River. In addition, C.C.A., 1st Armored Division heads west along Highway 11 to control escape routes between Lake Como and Lake Garda. In the **II Corps** sector, the 38th Division moves toward Vicenza. The 91st Division starts across the Adige River at Legnago. The 6th South African Armored Division enlarges its Po bridgehead pushing toward the Adige. In the **U.S. Eighth Army** area, 13th Corps sector, the 2nd New Zealand Division establishes a bridgehead at the Adige west of Badia during the night of the 26th-27th. In the 5th Corps sector, the British 56th Division secures a bridgehead over the Adige near Rovigo.

April 27th 1945 — (Pacific-Philippines) Luzon In the **U.S. Sixth Army** area, **I Corps** sector, the 33rd and 37th Divisions finish off the contest for Baguio, seizing the summer capital. Meanwhile, the Japanese continue resisting tenaciously on Mt. Myokyo and along Kapintalan Ridge, as the 25th Division continues pounding against both. Also, contingents of the 25th press strongly against the Japanese near Fishhook. In the **XI Corps** sector, RCT 145 (attached 6th Division) seizes the summit of Mt. Pacawagan with the support of Air and Artillery. In the **XIV Corps** sector, the 1st and 3rd Battalions, RCT 158, each battling on the Cituinan hill mass, establish contact on its dominating ridge. Meanwhile, the 11th Airborne Division, launches a strong attack against Mt. Mataasna Bundoc. It is given umbrella protection by Air and Artillery units as it plows into resolute resistance as the Japanese attempt to hang on to their final strongpoint in southern Luzon. The tenacious assault hinders Japanese plans to abandon the area. **Southern Philippines** In the **U.S. Eighth Army** area, **X Corps** sector, plans are made to eliminate the balance of resistance on Mindanao. Meanwhile, the Japanese seemingly intend to draw a last line of defense in the high ground northwest of Davao City. The 24th, 31st, 40th, and 41st Divisions will participate in the attack which includes a double envelopment of the Davao area. Advance contingents of the 34th Regiment, 24th Division, encounter granite resistance as they reach crossroads near Digos, prompting quick response by support units; Planes and Artillery lambaste the enemy positions. Also, at 22:00, Japanese forces about Battalion strength encounter the 2nd Battalion, 124th Regiment, 31st Division as it drives toward the crossroads of the Sayre Highway and the Kibawe-Talomo Trail; by dawn on the 28th, the Japs are annihilated. On Negros, contingents of the 2nd Battalion, 164th Regiment advance to a ridge which leads to Palimpinon, while the 1st Battalion probes west of Dumaguete City. **(Pa-**cific-Ryukyu Islands)** On Okinawa, in the **U.S. Tenth Army** area, **XXIV Corps** sector, contingents of the 27th Division terminate final resistance within the Item Pocket, while other 27th units seize ground in the Yafusu region. Meanwhile, in the center of the Corps thrust, Flame Throwers and Tanks are committed to strengthen the 96th Division's attack against the Japanese who are defending the Maeda Escarpment ferociously; the determined pressure gains ground on a saddle between two hills and also progresses steadily through Maeda village. Also, the 7th Division continues to be held up at Kochi Ridge; the 1st and 2nd Battalions, meeting curtains of fire, are unable to establish contact with each other. Offshore, the Japanese again attack the Fleet. The Destroyer *Ralph Talbot*, (DD-390), the Destroyer Escort *England* (DE-635), and the High-speed Transport *Rathburne* (APD-25) are damaged by Kamikazes. In addition, the Heavy Cruiser *Wichita* (CA-45) is damaged by enemy coastal gun fire, and the Destroyer *William D. Porter* (DD-579) sustains damage by accidental U.S. Naval gunfire. The Japanese return on the following day to reinitiate the attack. **(Pacific-China)** The Chinese, receiving their supplies by air, continue holding a defensive posture at Ankang and Sian Airbases; however, offensive operations are being implemented slowly. **(Atlantic-Western Europe) 21st Army Group** In the **British Second Army** area, the U.S. XVIII (A/B) Corps establishes a Command Post at Uelzen and begins concentrating in the area. Meanwhile, the 82nd Airborne receives orders to relieve the British 5th Division at their defensive positions along the Elbe, and in addition to completing the operation by the 30th, the Airborne is also ordered to seize a bridgehead near Bleckede. **12th Army Group** The **U.S. First** and **Ninth Armies** adjust their defensive postures. The VII Corps' 1st Division is transferred to VII Corps; it will enlarge the VIII Corps sector and extend into Czechoslovakia and relieve the 97th Division (XII Corps, Third Army). In the **U.S. Third Army** area, **XII Corps** sector, C.C.A., 11th Armored Division sends out a Patrol which moves to the Czechoslovakian border near Bischofsreuth, without encountering any enemy presence. However, many Germans are concentrated north and northeast of Furth and are discovered by the 90th Division as it probes along the Czech border during mop-up operations. Meanwhile, the 26th Division seizes Deggendorf while the 97th Division reduces stragglers in Cheb and the 2nd Cavalry Group fortifies its positions in Czechoslovakia. In the **XX Corps** sector, Regensburg capitulates to the 71st Division without a struggle; it had originally been the objective of the 65th Division, which enlarges its Danube bridgehead to Traubling and Teugn on the left and right respectively, in addition to securing Abbach and Peising by the center assault contingents. The 13th Armored Division moves out to capture an Isar River crossing from which to encounter the Soviets. In the **III Corps** sector, the 14th Armored Division scours its zone along the Danube, eliminating remnant resistance; C.C.R. relieves 86th Division contingents in Ingolstadt. The 86th Division also crosses the Danube. In conjunction, the 99th Division secures a bridgehead across the Danube. Its 393rd Regiment crosses in assault boats, seizing Eining and Straubing, followed later by the 395th Regiment which meets rock resistance near Neustadt and pivots north to cross at Eining. **6th Army Group** In the **U.S. Seventh Army** area, **XV Corps** sector, the 42nd and 45th Divisions maintain their southward momentum. In conjunction, the 20th Armored Division deploys to bolt through the Infantry and drive toward Munich. In the **XXI Corps** sector, 12th Armored, trailed by the 4th and 63rd Infantry Divisions, drives southeast; contingents of Armor reach the west bank of the

Wertach River. In conjunction, the 8th Regiment, 4th Division commits two Companies which seize a bridgehead across the Lech River at Schwabstadl. Meanwhile, the 3rd Division converges on Augsburg while the 36th Division begins relieving the 63rd Division. In the **VI Corps** sector, the Germans are rapidly running for the Austrian border to reach the seclusion of the National Redoubt, alleged to be an impregnable German stronghold. However, the redoubt is non-existent, except in the now obsolete German propaganda circles. U.S. Armor plows forward all across the terrain, followed by the 44th and 103rd Divisions. During the Armored scavenger hunt, units of the 10th Armored establish contact with 12th Armored near Landsberg. Meanwhile, C.C.B., 10th Armored columns pound against retreating Germans; some columns reach Markt Oberdorf and another seizes Kempten without contest. Also, the 411th Regiment, 103rd Division, fighting alongside 10th Armored, starts clearing Landsberg (Hitler spent time in prison here during 1923), while the 409th Regiment charges toward Schongau where it intercepts disorganized retreating German columns. The German contingents, using horse-drawn Vehicles, are demolished by the Yanks. In other activity, the 101st Airborne Division converges on the area around Memmingen, further squeezing the German forces there. In the **French 1st Army** area, German resistance is totally terminated. **(Atlantic-Eastern Europe)** Advance forces of the Second White Russian Front seize Angermuende and Prenzlau as the ongoing offensive sweeps west along the Baltic in Pomerania. Meanwhile, the faltering Germans continue a futile battle within Berlin, having lost nearly three-quarters of the beleaguered city to the Russians. In addition, the First White Russian Front captures Potsdam, Rathenow, and Spandau, a western suburb of the capital. **(Atlantic-Italy) 15th Army Group** In the **U.S. Fifth Army** area, the Germans continue their disorganized retreat with the Yanks in pursuit. Forces of the 92nd Division advance to Genoa on the Ligurian coast. In the **IV Corps** sector, the Germans are on the verge of total defeat; one Division, isolated south of the Po River near Cremona, surrenders while two additional Divisions, lingering south of Highway 9, are being rapidly reduced. In conjunction, elements of the 1st Armored Division force the Po and seal off German escape routes.

April 28th 1945 — (Pacific-Philippines) Luzon In the **U.S. Sixth Army** area, **I Corps** sector, preparations are finalized for the northward drive from Baguio by the 33rd and 37th Divisions. Meanwhile, the 25th Division prepares to move from Lone Tree Hill toward Balete Pass. In the **XI Corps** sector, regrouping occurs prior to a drive against Ipo Dam. In the **XIV Corps** sector, Japanese organized resistance in the Bicols is terminated with the destruction of the remaining defenders in the Cituinan hill mass region. Japanese resistance at Mt. Mataasna Bundoc continues against the systematic advance of the 11th Airborne Division, which makes some progress, but the distance separating the northern and southern forces has created a gap of about two miles between them. **Southern Philippines** In the **U.S. Eighth Army** area, **X Corps** sector, Mindanao is severed as the 2nd Battalion, 34th Regiment, 24th Division overruns Digos. In conjunction, the 19th Regiment drives north toward Davao. Meanwhile, the 31st Division's 2nd Battalion, 124th Regiment drives beyond Atoman, having advanced about four miles along the Sayre Highway. On Negros, the American Division is still heavily active, rooting out remaining opposition; the 165th Regiment's 2nd Battalion sweeps the high ground near Palimpinon in Negros Oriental, while the 160th Regiment, bolstered by the 2nd Battalion, 185th Regiment pounds the Japanese which still hold precariously on the slopes of Hill 3155 in Negros Occidental; the attack is canceled to allow Artillery to begin lambasting enemy positions for the next several days. **(Pacific-Malay Archipelago)** The U.S.S. Motor Minesweeper YMS-329 incurs damage after striking a mine off Tarakan, Borneo. **(Pacific-Ryukyu Islands)** Japanese Suicide Planes launch yet another attack against the U.S. Fleet. The Jap Kamikazes disregard conspicuously identified Hospital Ships, damaging the Hospital Vessel *Comfort* (AH-6) and the Hospital Transport *Pinkney* (APH-2). Also, the Destroyers *Wadsworth* (DD-516), *Daly* (DD-519), *Twiggs* (DD-591), and the *Bennion* (DD-662) suffer damages. In addition, the Destroyer *Lang* becomes damaged by collision. On **Okinawa** in the **U.S. Tenth Army** area, **XXIV Corps** sector, the 27th Division zone is peppered with fire fights in the Yafusu vicinity. One camouflaged pillbox stalls a contingent of the 165th Regiment, by mixing a hail of machine gun bullets with a barrage of grenades. P.F.C. Alejandro Ruiz, clinging to his commandeered automatic rifle, springs to his feet and flies through the maze of the enemy fire, reaching the top of the strongpoint. A Jap bolts forward to engage Ruiz in personal combat and as Ruiz attempts to finish him off, his rifle jams; Ruiz improvises and bludgeons him to death before dashing back for another weapon and ammunition. The conspicuous trooper receives a huge concentration of enemy fire, but he remains unscathed and charges to the top of the fortification, then assuming the role of terminator, he moves imprudently from slot to slot, funneling bursts of fire into each opening. Ruiz's private quarrel culminates with the destruction of the menacing pillbox and the demise of its twelve inhabitants; Ruiz receives the Medal of Honor for his extraordinary courage. In the 96th Division zone, assaults are launched against the Maeda Escarpment, but the Japanese retain possession; in conjunction, the 381st Regiment's Company K sustains severe casualties as it hammers a Jap stronghold called the Apartment House and is compelled to pull back. Meanwhile, in the 7th Division zone, the Japanese repulse attempts by the 3rd Battalion, 17th Regiment to dislodge them near Kochi Ridge and near Kuhazu village the Japanese also repel the advance of the 32nd Regiment, which calls for and receives heated support from Armored Flame Throwers which pour into the village. **(Pacific-Burma)** In ALFSEA's 15th Corps sector, Taungup is occupied by the 82nd West African Division; the capture of the town which had been discovered abandoned during the middle of April concludes the reconquering of the Arakan coast. In the **British Fourteenth Army** area, 33rd Corps sector, the Indian 20th Division seizes Allanmyo. **(Pacific-Japan)** The Submarine U.S.S. *Springer* (SS-414) sinks the Japanese Submarine Chaser No. 17 off Honshu, while the Submarine *Sennet* (SS-408) destroys the Repair Ship *Hatsushima*; the *Trepang* (SS-412), another U.S. Submarine operating in the area, sinks the Japanese Transport No. 146. **(Atlantic-Western Europe) 21st Army Group** In the **Canadian First Army** area, the British 3rd Division joins the Canadian 2nd Corps to support the Corps' task of securing Wilhelmshaven-Emden peninsula and the two cities. In the **British Second Army** area, the 8th Corps makes preparations to launch an assault across the Elbe near Lauenburg, scheduled to commence prior to dawn. In the **U.S. XVIII Corps (A/B)** sector, the 82nd Airborne's 505th Paratroop Infantry and its attached 13th Regiment, 8th Infantry Division, is ordered to establish a bridgehead across the Elbe River near Bleckede. **12th Army Group** In the **U.S. Ninth Army** area, **XIX Corps** sector, Zerbst, east of the Elbe, is occupied by the 329th Regiment, 83rd Division; from here, the 125th Squadron, 113th Cavalry Group heads east to make contact with the Russians. In the **U.S. First Army** area, the **V Corps** sector, is taken over by the VII Corps, which also takes control of the 2nd and 69th Infantry Divisions and the 9th Armored Division at 18:00. In the **U.S. Third Army** area, **XII Corps** sector, the 11th Armored Division pushes Artillery units forward for the attack toward Passau. Meanwhile, the 26th Division continues driving southeast, and the 90th Division maintains its activity around the Czechoslovakian border, seizing Fichtenbach, north of Furth, then establishes a Task Force to attack Nyrsko. In addition, the 2nd Cavalry Group seizes terrain east of Eisendorf in Czechoslovakia while the 387th Regiment, 97th Division captures the Cheb Airfield and nearby villages, terminating offensive action in the region; Division is now getting relieved by the 1st Division (VIII Corps). In the **XX Corps** sector, the 13th Armored continues driving southeast along the Danube; contingents of C.C.B. reach the Isar River at Platting while C.C.A. and C.C.R. cross the Danube in the 65th and 71st Division sectors respectively, with Infantry trailing as the Armor advances to the Isar River. In conjunction, the 16th Armored Division relieves the 80th Division at Nuremberg, freeing it to move behind the Armor and advance to the right of the 71st Division. In the **III Corps** sector, the 14th Cavalry Group moves to cross the Danube in the 99th Division area while the 14th Armored bolts across the river, driving southeast toward the Isar, seizing Steinbach as it advances with its spearheading unit, C.C.A. Meanwhile, the 90th Division enlarges its Danube bridgehead stretching it to line Abensberg-Muehlhausen-Geibenstetten. Also, the 86th Division's 341st Regiment gets across the Danube and with the 343rd Regiment drives forward, getting elements to within five miles of the Isar River by the end of the day. **6th Army Group** In the **U.S. Seventh Army** area, **XV Corps** sector, the 20th Armored Division begins attacking toward Munich, trailed by the 42nd and 45th Infantry Divisions, moving very quickly. In the **XXI Corps** sector, the 101st Cavalry Group (attached to Corps) spearheads the attack of the 12th Armored Division, crossing the Lech River to halt passage of escaping Germans before they can make it to the Bavarian Alps. Meanwhile, the 3rd Division effortlessly seizes Augsburg with its 7th and 15th Regiments; meanwhile, the 30th Regiment crosses the Lech River and drives toward Munich. Also, the 4th Division is swarming around the Lech River: the 8th Regiment maintains the bridgehead at Schwabstadl while the 12th Regiment closes and awaits bridging before crossing; the 22nd, moving southeast, also nears the river. In other activity, the 36th Division assumes responsibility for the 63rd Division sector along the right zone of Corps. In addition, the French 2nd Armored Division is attached to Corps as it nears Corps perimeter. In the **VI Corps** sector, Engineers are doggedly attempting to get bridging across the Lech in co-ordination with 10th Armored which is sweeping the area in search of crossing sites; some right flank contingents cross the Austrian border near Fuessen. C.C.B., moving without rest throughout the night of the 27th-28th, pushes a column into Fuessen during the morning of the 28th. In conjunction, the 44th Division is racing with the Armor, the 71st Regiment supporting the Armor in Fuessen and the 114th Regiment driving across the Austrian border near Steinach; contingents of the 324th Regiment and French forces seize Wertach, west of Fuessen. In the 103rd Division sector, the retreating Germans on the Divisional left flank evade the pursuers; however, Landsberg is totally reduced by the 411th Regiment. In the **French 1st Army** area, the 1st Corps launches its final drive toward Vorarlberg, Austria; the 1st Armored Division drives southeast, trailed by the 2nd Moroc-

can Infantry and the 4th Moroccan Mountain Divisions on the left and right respectively. Also, the 5th Armored Division races right behind the 4th Mountain Division. **(Atlantic-Italy)** Benito Mussolini and his mistress Claretta Petacci attempt to escape from Italy, but he is captured by partisans and hanged in a village on Lake Como. Ironically, this is the same area where Mussolini had initially started his rise to power, tramping through the area instigating trouble, ravaging the citizens, and devastating churches. **15th Army Group** In the **U.S. Fifth Army** area, the 92nd Division seizes Alessandria on Highway 10. In the **IV Corps** sector, Brazilian troops relieve the 34th Division at Piacenza along Highway 9, continuing to mop up the area of isolated German stragglers. The 34th Division drives north toward Brescia while the 1st Armored Division reaches Lake Conio near the Swiss border. Meanwhile, the 10th Mountain Division continues sweeping the eastern shore of Lake Garda and is placed under Army control. In the **II Corps area**, the 88th Division clears Vicenza. The 6th South African Division begins crossing the Adige River at Legnago. In the **British Eighth Army** area, 13th Corps sector, the British 6th Armored Division moves across the Adige River advancing toward Monselice while the 2nd New Zealand Division advances through Monselice to Padua, which is controlled by partisans. In the 5th Corps sector, the British 56th Division launches an attack toward Venice. **(Atlantic-Eastern Germany)** Francis Sampson, a U.S. Army Chaplain who is a P.O.W. at Neubrandenburg (about 75 miles from Berlin) observes the Russians driving into the town about midnight. He states: "THE RUSSIAN TANKS STARTED COMING IN. THE ROAR WAS TERRIFIC. THE GERMAN OPPOSITION WAS ALMOST TOTALLY INEFFECTUAL. THE RUSSIAN INFANTRY RIDING ON THE TANKS KILLED AS MANY OF THEIR OWN MEN AS THEY DID THE GERMANS. THE TOWN IS RAISED, BUT THE CATHOLIC CHURCH, STRANGELY ENOUGH, WAS ALMOST THE ONLY LARGE BUILDING PRESERVED." Chaplain Sampson further states: "THE AMERICANS (P.O.W.s) KEPT CALM AND IN PERFECT ORDER DURING THIS TIME, SOMETHING THAT COULD NOT BE SAID FOR THE FRENCH, ITALIANS AND SERBS, WHO BOLTED FROM THE CAMP IN MOBS AND WENT TO LOOT THE CITY. THE RUSSIAN PRISONERS OF WAR, OF WHOM THERE WERE ONLY 3,000 REMAINING ALIVE OUT OF 21,000...WERE QUITE ODDLY THE ONLY PRISONERS NOT PARTICULARLY HAPPY TO BE LIBERATED." Father Sampson and a French Priest go down town, finding: "SEVERAL GERMAN GIRLS HAD BEEN RAPED AND KILLED. SOME OF THEM HAD BEEN STRUNG UP BY THEIR FEET AND THEIR THROATS SLIT." The pair then go to a church and discover that the Priest there and his father, had been under duress: "TO WATCH THE RUSSIANS RAPE THE PRIEST'S TWO SISTERS (both of whom are Nuns) AND HIS MOTHER." Father Francis Sampson mentions how the Russian Allies treat the Americans: "THE RUSSIANS TAKE THE U.S. P.O.W.s VALUABLES AND FORCE THE AMERICANS TO DIG THEIR LATRINES." He does mention that the Russians are drunk.

April 29th 1945 — (Pacific-Philippines) Luzon In the **U.S. Sixth Army** area, **XIV Corps** sector, RCT 158 drives north, leaving the 3rd Battalion to reduce the remnant enemy troops around Camalig. Meanwhile, the 511th Regiment, 11th Airborne Division seizes Hill 2610 at Mt. Malepunyo hill mass and also captures Hill 2480. **Southern Philippines** In the **U.S. Eighth Army** area, **X Corps** sector, the 19th Regiment 24th Division reaches Darong Airfield (Mindanao). The 34th Regiment's Company K, advances to positions near Guma and begins eliminating a previously bypassed pocket northwest of Digos. In the 31st Division zone, the 3rd Battalion, 124th Regiment, drives forward along Sayre Highway, destroying a Japanese roadblock, while advancing about 7,000 yards, despite the fact that the Japs have destroyed the bridges. On Bohol, the 3rd Battalion, 164th Regiment departs for Cebu. Guerrillas, supported by Company I, assume responsibility for mopping up the area. The Japanese have lost 104 killed and 16 captured. The U.S. suffers seven killed and 14 wounded. On Negros, the 2nd Battalion, 164th Regiment, continues driving through the heights near Palimpinon against intense enemy fire. **(Pacific-Malay Archipelago)** The American Motor Minesweeper YMS-51 becomes damaged off Tarakan, Borneo, after striking a mine. **(Pacific-Philippine Sea)** Planes (VC-92) attached to the Escort Carrier U.S.S. *Tulagi* (CVE-72) sink the Japanese Submarine I-44. **(Pacific-Ryuku Islands)** The Destroyers U.S.S. *Hazelwood* (DD-531) and the *Haggard* are damaged by Suicide Planes. Also, the Light Minelayers *Shannon* (DM-25) and the *Harry F. Bauer* (DM-26) sustain damage by the Kamikazes. On **Okinawa**, in the **U.S. Tenth Army** area, **XXIV Corps** sector, the fierce campaign of the 96th Division against the tenacious Japanese on the Maeda Escarpment has taken a toll on its fighting strength; the 77th Division begins relief of the battle-weary Division. The 307th Regiment, 77th Division advances to the crest of the escarpment, replacing the 381st Regiment, 96th Division. The Japanese give the 1st Battalion, 307th a steaming welcome. An avalanche of artillery, machine gun and mortar fire rips into the advancing Battalion; most pull back, but about 75 men become casualties. One man, P.F.C. Desmond T. Doss (Medical Detachment) refuses to evacuate and risks his life to assist the wounded. One by one, he lugs them to the edge of the escarpment and lowers then in a rope-controlled litter. Doss continues to face death while rescuing the wounded during the next month, often advancing hundreds of yards under severe fire to give aid before transporting them under fire to safety. On the 21st of May, enemy fire forces his Company to take cover during an attack, but again Doss remains exposed to give aid to the wounded. He becomes wounded, but refuses to call for help. Reinforcements arrive to transport Doss to safety about five hours later, but as they move , Doss spots a more seriously wounded man and slides from his litter and orders the bearers to go get him. Another incoming shell hits Doss, shattering his arm; he tapes a rifle butt to it and crawls 300 yards to an aid station. Doss' actions under fire save many troops and his name becomes legend within the 77th Division; he receives the Medal of Honor. Meanwhile, the 96th Division stands firm across its entire front early in the day, repulsing all enemy counterattacks and attempts at infiltrating their lines. The 383rd Regiment drives fero ciously, seizing Hill 138 as it moves toward Shuri. The 7th Division sustains more heavy casualties and is still unable to advance against the wall of enemy fire coming from enemy positions at Kochi Ridge vicinity. In conjunction, the 32nd Regiment strains to get Tanks to Onaga to help reduce the enemy strongpoint on the ridge. **(Pacific-Burma)** In the **British Fourteenth Army** area, 4 Corps sector, the Indian 17th Division drives to the steps of Pegu. **(Pacific-China)** Over 15,600 men of the Chinese New Sixth Army have arrived at Chihchiang. Meanwhile, a contingent of the Chinese 14th Division arrives at Ankiang within the next several days. **(Atlantic-Western Europe) 21st Army Group** In the **British Second Army** area, the 30th Corps has responsibility for securing the Cuxhaven peninsula; it attaches the Guards Armored Division to bolster the task. In the 8 Corps sector, the final Army drive to the Baltic commences as the British 15th Division, rein-

forced by the Canadian 1st Brigade, forces the Elbe at 02:00, establishing a bridgehead near Lauenburg. In the **U.S. XVIII Corps** (A/B) sector, the 505th Paratroop Regiment, 82nd Airborne Division advances to the Elbe and relieves the British 5th Division with its attached 13th Regiment, 8th Division. **12th Army Group** In the **U.S. Ninth Army** area, there is much activity with regrouping and various Corps implementing Patrols within the individual Corps sectors. In the **U.S. Third Army** area, **XII Corps** sector, C.C.B., 11th Armored Division, drives southwest passing through the 26th Division lines while heading toward Passau to secure the area between the Ilz River and north of the Danube. Meanwhile, a Patrol of the 90th Division discovers Nyrsko undefended. Also, the main body of the 2nd Cavalry Group advances to Zwiesel where it will screen along the Czechoslovakian border and also seize control of a pass northeast of Regen. In the **XX Corps** sector, the 13th Armored Division establishes a bridgehead across the Isar River; subsequently, plans are formulated to cross the entire Division over a bridge at Platting. At this point, the 80th Division gets across the Danube. The 71st Division roars over slight resistance advancing to the Isar River and receives orders to secure crossings over the river near Hanau and Zeholfing. In the **III Corps** sector, the 99th Division moves almost without incident to the Isar and secures line Pfettrach-Bruckberg-Moosburg. Meanwhile, the 14th Cavalry Group has crossed the Danube in the 99th Division sector. C.C.A., 14th Armored Division drives to the Isar at Moosburg and dispatches columns to Altdorf; heavy enemy resistance is encountered at Landshut, prompting C.C.B., and C.C.R. to assemble northwest of the strongpoint and attach C.C.A. for a strengthened attack. In other activity, the 86th Division moves across the Amper Kanal and seizes Friesing as it drives to the Isar; the Division begins crossing the Isar in assault boats during the night of the 29th-30th. **6th Army Group** In the **U.S. Seventh Army** area, the XV Corps, spearheaded by the 20th Armored Division, drives to Munich, liberating the infamous Dachau concentration camp as it perches on the outskirts of the city; the 42nd and 45th Divisions take Dachau. About 300 guards attempt to fight it out, but most surrender or attempt to flee. Ohrdrufu, Belsen and Landsberg also contain horror camps. Munich, where riots are breaking out, is the place to which Hitler would always return in time of crisis to regain his composure as he was climbing to power in an attempt to build his dynasty which he expected would last a thousand years. However, it has only lasted about twelve years, and he will not be returning again as he commits suicide on the following day in Berlin. In the **XXI Corps** sector, 12th Armored moves toward Innsbruck, while the 101st Cavalry Group overruns Diessen and Weilheim in addition to seizing bridges across the Ammer River, prior to sending elements to Munich. 12th Armored moves to Weilheim behind the Cavalry and attacks south through their positions, reaching Oberau where it establishes contact with 10th Armored. Meanwhile, the 4th Division gets units across the Lech River and beyond to the Amper River while leaving the 8th Regiment at its Lech bridgehead with orders to relieve contingents of the 3rd Division at Augsburg. Also, the 36th Division attacks southeast to terminate resistance left in the rear of the rolling Armor. In the **VI Corps** sector, 10th Armored drives across the Lech River. In conjunction, the 71st Regiment, 44th Division supports C.C.B., with the seizure of the Vils approach to a narrow pass to Reutte, while the 114th Regiment moves prudently across nasty mountainous terrain toward Gran. Meanwhile, German resistance, although greatly weakened during the closing days of the war, still shows sporadic signs of tremendous tenacity such as that encountered by the 324th Regiment, 44th Division, as it attempts to secure Wertach-Jungholz pass and is halted by resolute opposition. In the 103rd Division zone, the 410th Regiment secures the road between Steingaden and Buching subsequent to forcing the Lech River at Lechbruck while the 409th Regiment advances with C.C.A., 10th Armored. In the **French 1st Army** area, 1st Corps sector, the French 5th Armored Division seizes Friedrichshafen, on Lake Constance, and also pushes columns close to Wangen. Meanwhile, the French 1st Armored Division gets contingents to Kempten and to the fringes of Immenstadt (Iller River Valley). **(Atlantic-Italy)** Two German representatives of the Wehrmacht and S.S. (and Police force) arrive at British General Alexander's Headquarters at Caserta to sign the surrender, making Vietinghoff's unconditional surrender of all German land, sea and air forces in Italy official; the surrender becomes effective on May 2nd. **(Atlantic-Eastern Europe)** The Soviets continue tightening the noose on the remaining German resistance as it advances. Forces of the Second White Russian Front, advancing west along the Baltic, seize Anklan; other contingents move into Mecklenburg. The Germans continue the futile effort to withstand the Russian thrust against Berlin; vicious combat continues to ensue within the city. In Czechoslovakia, forces of the Second Ukrainian Front advance against the beleaguered Germans east of Bruenn and south of Olmuetz. Berlin publicizes the loss of Austerlitz, southeast of Bruenn, and also acknowledges the Soviet offensive northwest of Moravska Ostrava. **(Atlantic-Italy) 15th Army Group** The enduring struggle in Italy is finally concluding victoriously for the Allies. German General Vietinghoff, Commander of German Army Group Southwest, signs an instrument of surrender to become effective on May 2nd, at Caserta. In the **U.S. Fifth Army** area, **IV Corps** sector, the remaining German stragglers still isolated in the Apennines are eliminated by the Brazilian Expeditionary Force which accepts the surrender of two German Division Commanders. Meanwhile, Milan is discovered to be in the hands of partisans. The U.S. 1st Armored Division deploys outside the city and probes to the Ticino River. In the **II Corps** sector, the U.S. 91st Division and the 6th South African Division both cross the Brenta River and drive beyond, the latter advancing far enough to encounter the British Eighth Army at Padua. In the **British Eighth Army** area, 13th Corps sector, the 2nd New Zealand Division drives to the Piave River where the bridge has been blown. In the 5th Corps sector, Venice is seized by the British 56th Division.

April 29th 1945 — U.S. troops capture Dachau, a German concentration camp: note German guards with their hands up.

U.S. Ninth Army troops meet the Russians at Appollensdorf.

April 30th 1945 — (United States) The Destroyer Escorts *Thomas* (DE-102), *Bostwick* (DE-103), *Coffman* (DE-191), and the Frigate *Natchez* (PF-2) sink the German Submarine U-548, off the coast of Virginia. In addition, during the month of April, the following German Submarines are sunk by U.S. Army and R.A.F. Planes: U-677, U-906, U-982, U-3525, in the Baltic area; U-1131, U-1227, U-2516, Kiel, Germany; U-2532 and U-2537, Hamburg, Germany. **(Pacific-Philippines) Luzon** In the **U.S. Sixth Army** area, **XI Corps** sector, the 38th Division and the 6th Division exchange sectors. Meanwhile, on Mt. Pacawagan, RCT 145, 37th Division is attached to 38th Division. Also, the 158th Regiment, 38th Division gets orders to secure Woodpecker Ridge. In the **XIV Corps** sector, some Japanese pockets linger in the vicinity of the Malepunyo Mountain, but organized resistance is exterminated. **Southern Philippines** In the **U.S. Eighth Army** area, **X Corps** sector on Mindanao, Daliao Airstrip and Talomo are seized by the 19th Regiment, 24th Division, as it reaches positions within four miles of Davao. In conjunction, the 21st Regiment prowls confidently, whacking the remaining resistance northwest of the Talomo River. Meanwhile, the 3rd Battalion, 124th Regiment, 31st Division is still trudging steadily along Sayre Highway, despite seemingly never-ending rear-guard opposition, making substantial gains. Meanwhile, on Negros, the 1st Battalion, drives to Malabo to lift pressure against the 164th Regiment, Americal Division, engaged in heavy combat in the high ground near Palimpinon. **(Pacific-Ryukyu Islands)** As of today, the Japanese have lost over 1,100 Aircraft to Naval Forces since the 26th of March, excluding those destroyed by Aircraft and AA guns. Although the Japs have sunk some Ships as well as damaging many others, no capital Warships have been sunk, and in addition, the Fleet is still here to stay. Today's raid by the Kamikazes damage the Destroyer *Bennion* (DD-662) and the Minelayer *Terror* (CM-5). On **Okinawa**, in the **U.S. Tenth Army** area, the 27th Division, operating on the Corps' west flank, begins to be relieved by the 1st Marine Division, which is attached to Corps. The Marines, subsequent to relieving the 165th Regiment, head for the Asa River line. Meanwhile, the bloody struggle for Maeda Escarpment continues to rage as the 77th Division takes over for the 96th Division and continues the furious fight. Also, the Japanese holding Kochi Ridge refuse to relent, despite increasing pressure by the 17th Regiment, 7th Division, however, elements of the 32nd Regiment gain ground on a ridge southwest of Kuhazu. **(Pacific-Dutch East Indies)** The Destroyer U.S.S. *Jenkins* (DD-447) is damaged after striking a mine off Tarakan, Borneo, in the Malay Archipelago. **(Pacific-Burma)** In AL-

FSEA's 15th Corps sector, DRACULA forces (main body) embark for Rangoon. In the **British Fourteenth Army** area, 4th Corps sector, the 17th Indian Division penetrates Japanese resistance and begins securing Pegu. **(Pacific-China)** Japanese pressure compels the Chinese 58th Division to pull back further, retiring to predetermined positions in the Wawu-Tang region. **(Atlantic-Western Europe)** It is reported that Hitler has committed suicide in his bunker at the Reichschancellery in Berlin, but his body is never recovered. German Admiral Karl Doenitz had been selected by Hitler as his successor, and he announces his ascendancy to the position of head of the German state. Some of his advisors, including Martin Bormann, thought by many to be a Soviet spy, escape subsequent capture. Bormann is later reported to have made it safely to the Soviet Union where he lives well. German intelligence had him pinpointed as a direct leak to the Kremlin, although none felt Hitler would believe the astounding story. In other activity, U.S. Land-based Naval Planes (VPB-63) sink the German Submarine U-1055 off the west coast of France. **21st Army Group** In the **British Second Army** area, 8th Corps sector, the Elbe bridgehead is bolstered with the arrival of the British 6th Airborne Division. The U.S. XVIII Corps (A/B) launches its attack from the Elbe to the Baltic Sea, driving on the right flank of the 8 Corps. The Yanks, spearheaded by the 82nd Airborne, cross the Elbe at 01:00 on British Buffaloes of the 4th Royal Tank Regiment and also available ones from the British 79th Armored Division, as well as U.S. Engineer assault boats, driving against sporadic resistance, easily establishing bridgeheads at Bandekow and Stiepelse on the left and right respectively. British General Dempsey makes a request to General Ridgway (subsequent to Patrols of the 82nd getting out front): "IT WOULD MEAN A GREAT DEAL TO BRITISH PRESTIGE IF I COULD ARRANGE MY PLAN OF ATTACK SO THAT THE BRITISH ELEMENTS OF THE CORPS (British 6th Airborne) COULD BE THE FIRST TO MAKE CONTACT WITH THE RUSSIANS." General Ridgway states that such a maneuver would be too complicated, but then, based on his respect for Dempsey, he changes his mind and unleashes the British 6th Airborne. Also, General Ridgway will maintain his Headquarters at Hagenau (Province of Mechlenburg) which contains a concentration camp. Ridgway subsequently states that it is: "SMALL COMPARED TO DACHAU AND BUCHENWALD, BUT EQUAL TO THEM IN GHASTLINESS...THE HORROR OF THESE CAMPS HAS BEEN TOO OFTEN DESCRIBED FOR ME TO REPEAT...NO SCENES OF DEATH ON THE BATTLEFIELD CAN PREPARE A SOLDIER FOR SUCH SIGHT." **12th Army Group** In the **U.S. Ninth Army** area, **XIX Corps** sector, contact with the Red Army is made at Appolensdorf at 13:30 when the 3rd Platoon, Troop C, 125th Cavalry Squadron, 113th Cavalry Group encounters the Soviet 121st Division. In the **U.S. First Army** area, the Commanding General and the Commanding Officer of the Soviet 5th Guard Army speak to each other at the Mulde River in Eilenburg at 13:00 culminating the effort of the two forces to establish contact. In the **U.S. Third Army** area, **XII Corps** sector, the 11th Armored Division reaches the Austrian border; C.C.A. drives into Wegscheid eliminating fierce resistance while C.C.B. soon after propels columns into Crettenbach. In conjunction, C.C.R. scurries to defend the north and west flanks of the Division. In the 26th Division sector, the 104th Regiment moves unopposed to positions beyond Hauzenburg while the 328th Regiment establishes a bridgehead across the Ilz River at Strasskirchen. In the 90th Division zone, heavy skirmishing continues in the woods east of Waldmuenchen, Czechoslovakia. In the **XX Corps** sector, German resistance continues in the 13th Armored area, hindering Armor as it tries to cross the Isar River at Platting. The 71st Division, supported by enormous smoke cover and Artillery, forces the river at 16:45 in modified boats which can better handle the unruly currents and by tramping over damaged railroad bridges. The two committed Regiments (14th and 66th) establish a bridgehead which encompasses Landau, Usterling, Zeholfing, and Zulling. Subsequently, the 80th Division crosses the Isar near Mamming and drives southeast. In the **III Corps** sector, the 14th Armored Division, and the 99th Division, in addition to the 86th Division and the 14th Cavalry Group, all converge on the Isar, continuing their advance to extinguish the final flames of German guns in the region. Many units cross and drive forward. **6th Army Group** In the **U.S. Seventh Army** area, Munich falls to **XV Corps**. In the **XXI Corps** sector, C.C.A., 12th Armored assembles in Murnau while C.C.B. and the 101st Cavalry Group advance to the Loisach River and await Engineers to get bridging across. Meanwhile, the 4th Division gets two Regiments to the Isar, its 12th Infantry seizing bridges across the river in addition to capturing Loisach. Also, the 36th Division continues its southeast advance. In the **VI Corps** sector, elements of C.C.B., 10th Armored drive forward to clear Fern Pass, but German resistance near Fernstein halts its progress. Meanwhile, the 71st Regiment, throws its weight in with C.C.B., and Lermoos and Reutte fall quickly. In conjunction, the 114th Regiment continues advancing southeast driving to Forchach while the 324th Regiment seizes Jungholz. In the 103rd Division zone, C.C.A., 10th Armored is bolstered solidly as it plows east toward Innsbruck. The 103rd and the 44th Infantry Divisions receive orders to pass through 10th Armored and drive to Innsbruck and Imst respectively. Also, the 101st Airborne is to concentrate on policing the Kaufbeuren-Saulgrub-Wertach-Kempten area. In the **French 1st Army** area, the German resistance at Immenstadt remains tenacious against the French 1st Armored Division; however, the French 5th Armored Division is able to burst through its resistance, securing Lindau prior to crossing the Austrian border and reaching positions near Bregenz. In other activity, French forces land on Oleron Island off the Gironde Estuary, meeting disorganized resistance as it moves forward. The operation is bolstered by U.S. and French Aircraft in addition to French Naval units. Later upon darkness, French Commandos land on the east coast and drive toward St. Pierre d'Oleron and Dolus. Meanwhile, on the French mainland, additional French contingents begin marching toward La Rochelle. **(Atlantic-Eastern Europe)** The Moravian Gap, a staunchly fortified strongpoint of the Germans in Moravska Ostrava, is taken by forces of the Fourth Ukrainian Front. **(Atlantic-Italy) 15th Army Group** In the **U.S. Fifth Army** area, abandoned Turin is reached by the 92nd Division; the 473rd Regiment encounters French troops on the Franco-Italian border. The 10th Mountain Division terminates the opposition at the head of Lake Garda, its 85th Regiment advancing beyond to Gargnano without encountering any resistance, then jumps to Riva. The IV Corps occupies Milan with a Task Force. At the same time, the Legnano Group mops up around Brescia while the II Corps is becoming reinforced with the 85th Division. Also, the 91st Division roars into Treviso, north of Venice, culminating the Corps' eastward drive. In the **British Eighth Army** area, 13 Corps sector, the 2nd New Zealand Division crosses the Piave River, moving toward Trieste. Meanwhile, the British 6th Armored Division's pursuit forces continue advancing and establish contact with the Yanks at occupied Treviso, then drive beyond toward Belluno and Udine.

May 1st 1945 — (United States) The Submarine U.S.S. *Trigger* (SS-237), commanded by Commander D. R. Connole, which had departed Guam on her 12th War Patrol on March 11th, is officially reported as missing and presumed lost. The *Trigger* had last made contact with Headquarters on March 26th, but according to other U.S. Ships patrolling near Nansei Shotos, it seems as if the *Trigger* had been lost to enemy Aircraft and depth charges on the afternoon of March 28th, and this possibility is further strengthened by subsequent Japanese reports concerning an attack against a Submarine in that area at the prescribed time. **(Pacific-Philippines) Luzon** In the **U.S. Sixth Army** area, **I Corps** sector, the Kennon Road is plowed open to Baguio as the 136th Regiment, 33rd Division establishes contact with the 123rd Regiment. In the meantime, the 32nd Division sweeps methodically through the high ground in Salacsac Pass, eliminating remaining tough resistance, while the 25th Division, reinforced, prepares to strike a killing blow against the Japanese at Balete Pass; the 161st Regiment, bolstered by Artillery and Aircover, drives against Kembu Plateau. In the **XI Corps** sector, RCT 145, 38th Division tightens its positions on Mt. Pacawagan. Meanwhile, the 43rd Division receives orders to launch an offensive against Ipo on the 7th. In the **XIV Corps** sector, RCT 158, reinforced, advances to Anayan against no opposition and reaches the undefended junction of Highways 1 and 27. **Southern Philippines** In the **U.S. Eighth Army** area, **X Corps** sector, the 19th Regiment, 24th Division, bypasses deadly Hill 550 which dominates the approaches to Davao; however, it contains it in the process of closing upon the city. Meanwhile, elements of the 124th Regiment, 31st Division drive to Misinsman, provoking a fierce fire fight with the Japanese who lose badly and flee quickly from the vicinity. Also, Planes strike Japanese positions around Kibawe. On Negros, the 2nd Battalion, 164th Regiment charges and secures another knob on Cuernos de Negros ridge (Negros Oriental), then throws back a Jap counterattack. Meanwhile, the 185th Regiment, 40th Division, supported by Artillery, attacks Virgne Ridge on Negros Occidental which has sustained severe bombardment for the past few days; the Regiment takes the obstacle with small effort. In conjunction, the 503rd Paratroop Regiment driving on the north flank plunges upon Banana Ridge while the 160th Regiment retains its positions on the slopes of Hill 3155 (renamed Dolan) while Artillery pounds the enemy. **(Pacific-Ryukyu Islands-Okinawa)** In the **U.S. Tenth Army** area, **XXIV Corps** sector, the 1st Marine Division finishes relieving the 27th Division and assumes responsibility for Corps' western flank. Meanwhile, the Japanese raise fervent opposition, greatly hindering the Marines as they advance to the Asa River line. The 77th Division's 1st Battalion, 307th Regiment unsuccessfully attacks the eastern edge of the Maeda Escarpment; contingents scale the difficult slopes using ladders and cargo nets, but the few who hit the top are pushed back by a night counterattack. Also, the Japanese repulse the 3rd Battalion, 307th Regiment at the Apartment House. In other activity, the 7th Division's 32nd Regiment is relieved by the 184th Regiment; however, Jap infiltration complicates the endeavor. Meanwhile, the 184th Regiment's Company L pierces enemy lines on Gaja Ridge during the night of the 1st-2nd, but it pulls back. Also, additional forces continue to secure the paths to Kochi Ridge to permit the 17th Regiment to seize it. **(Pacific-Dutch East Indies)** A naval Attack Force commanded by Vice Admiral D.E. Barbey lands the 26th Brigade, Australian 9th Division on Tarakan Island off Borneo to seize it and its oil resources. **(Pacific-China)** General Wedemeyer chooses General Stratemeyer as Commanding Officer of the Army Air Forces, China Theater; the Tenth and Fourteenth Air Forces come under his jurisdiction. **(Atlantic-Western Europe)** The suicidal death of Hitler is announced over radio in Hamburg. **21st Army Group** In the **British Second Army** area, 8th Corps sector, the 11th Armored Division advances toward Luebeck while the British 15th Division reaches Geesthacht, about sixteen miles from Hamburg. In conjunction, the British 6th Airborne Division is placed under control of the U.S. XVIII Corps (A/B) in place. Meanwhile, the 82nd U.S. Airborne drives into Forst Carrenzien while the U.S. 8th Division seizes Zahrensdorf. **12th Army Group** In the **U.S. Ninth Army** area, offensive actions terminate. Germans surrender in hordes, and the practice continues until the close of hostilities. The Germans prefer capitulating to the U.S. as opposed to the Russians. The 378th Regiment, 97th Division (XVI Corps) shifts to Bremen Enclave Military District, passing to 21st Army Group; it is attached to the British Second Army, 30th Corps. In the **U.S. First Army** area, the front extends 160 miles from the confluence of the Elbe and Mulde Rivers at Dessau on the north to Ronsperk, Czechoslovakia, on the south. It stands in front of a beleaguered and disoriented German force which is no longer qualified to hold off the fast-approaching Soviets. In the **V Corps** sector, the 97th Division stretched along the German-Czechoslovakian border on the Corps' right flank continues bolstering its posture by pumping out limited assaults. In the **U.S. Third Army** area, **XII Corps** sector, the 11th Armored Division probes deeper into Austria, advancing from the border area to the Klein Muehl River; C.C.A. seizes a crossing near Peilstein and pushes contingents to Oepping while the main body of C.C.B. pauses at Lembach until crossings are seized at Krondf; a bridgehead is quickly secured. The 26th Division driving southeast behind the Armor gets elements across the Austrian border while the 41st Cavalry, trailing C.C.B., probes to the Danube in search of crossing sites. Meanwhile, the 5th Division, advancing to the left of the Armor, moves into Czechoslovakia on the left and also gets units across the Austrian border on the right. Also, the 2nd Cavalry Group secures Eisenstein Pass into Czechoslovakia. In the **XX Corps** sector, 13th Armored Division, trailed by the 65th Division, completes crossing the Isar and gets columns to the Inn River; C.C.B. tries unsuccessfully to seize the Marktl bridge. Meanwhile, the 71st Division continues its attack to enlarge its Isar bridgehead and consumes more territory. The 65th Division takes Aldersbach, Osterhofen, Pleinting, and Vilshofen, plus additional towns. In the 80th Division zone, Dingolfing and Reisbach are secured by the 318th Regiment. In the **III Corps** sector, every unit is across the Isar, racing to the Inn River to reach the bridges before the Germans have time to detonate them. In the 86th Division zone, TF Pope is organized to grab a reported intact bridge at Wasserburg. **6th Army Group** In the **U.S. Seventh Army** area, **XV Corps** sector, activity is confined to mopping up stragglers in the Munich area. In the **XXI Corps** sector, 12th Armored also moves toward the Inn River; C.C.R. forces the river at Holzkirchen (4th Division zone) and drives along the Autobahn, its advance contingents reaching the Inn; C.C.A. trails C.C.R. Meanwhile, the 4th Division gets contingents across the Isar. In the 36th Division zone, RCT 141 drives into Bad Toelz and catches a grand prize: Field Marshal von Runstedt. In the **VI Corps** sector, Corps continues moving south through the Alps toward Imst and Innsbruck, its 103rd Division crossing the Austrian border, reaching Seefeld, south of Mittenwald, closing on Innsbruck; the 44th Division prepares an attack against Fern Pass through the Alps. Meanwhile, the 101st Airborne advances to Bavaria near Miesbach. In the **French 1st Army** area, 1st Corps sector, Immenstadt and Sonthofen on the left flank fall while Bregenz on the right is also toppled. Meanwhile, DA ATL concludes its operation in Gironde enclave with the reduction of the final resistance on Oleron Island. Also, the attack to secure La Rochelle is ongoing. **(Atlantic-Eastern Europe)** In Berlin, the Soviets make more progress against the faltering German resistance. Forces of the Second White Russian Front continue swift progress and seize the German Naval Base and communication center at Stralsund along the Baltic coast. **(Atlantic-Italy) 15th Army Group** In the **U.S. Fifth Army** area, **IV Corps** sector, the 1st Division B.E.F. pushes contingents into Alessandria where they encounter the U.S. 92nd Division; however, earlier contact had been made between Corps and the 92nd Division at Pavia. In the **II Corps** sector, the 85th Division starts to secure the Piave Valley which had previously been delegated to the 88th Division, enabling it to clear the Brenta Valley. Also, Corps is directed to sweep Highway 49 clean to ease the drive through Brenner Pass to Austria. In the **British Eighth Army** area, 13th Corps sector, the New Zealand 2nd Division advances to Monfalcone as it drives toward Trieste and encounters Yugoslavian forces commanded by Marshal Tito.

May 2nd 1945 — (Pacific-Philippines) Luzon In the **U.S. Sixth Army** area, **I Corps** sector, the 25th Division is directed to secure Balete Pass, then seize Santa Fe at the junction of Highway 5 and the Villa Verde Trail. The 161st Regiment, 25th Division continues eradicating resistance on the Kembu Plateau, advancing further. In the **XI Corps** sector, the remaining stragglers on Mt. Pacawagan have been eliminated by the 145th Regiment, 37th Division. Meanwhile, subsequent to an Artillery bombardment, the 152nd Regiment, 38th Division drives to the edge of Woodpecker Ridge. In the **XIV Corps** sector, Route 27 in its entirety is clear as the 2nd and 3rd Battalions, RCT 158 converge on Mabatobato and link up. The 1st Battalion, advancing beyond Pili, establishes contact with the 5th Cavalry, 1st Cavalry Division at San Agustin. The U.S. movements now have the remaining Japanese in the Bicols corralled at Mt. Isarog, northeast of Anayan; continuous probing Patrols scour the area for the next two weeks. **Southern Philippines** In the **U.S. Eighth Army** area, **X Corps** sector, heavy fighting continues to ensue as the 19th Regiment, 24th Division tries to cross the Davao River; however, it does establish a small bridgehead despite the fierce resistance. Meanwhile, the 34th Regiment and units of the 2nd Battalion, 21st Regiment secure the majority of Libby Airfield, while the 1st Battalion, 21st Regiment pushes contingents toward Mintal. On Negros, elements of the Americal Division continue the advance, but the Japanese sever the supply line halting progress. Meanwhile, contingents of the 40th Division improve their positions on Virgne Ridge (Negros Occidental), while simultaneously dispatching Patrols; RCT 108 is detached from Division to prepare for an amphibious operation at Macajalar Bay, Mindanao. **(Pacific-Ryukyu Islands-Okinawa)** In the **U.S. Tenth Army** area, **XXIV Corps** sector, the 1st and 5th Marines, 1st Marine Division drive west toward the Asa River, but the Japanese control commanding positions with excellent observation of the Marines and pound them with effective fire, holding progress to a minimum. Japanese infiltrators encroach Marine positions and a deadly exchange of hand grenades commences. An enemy grenade falls into a foxhole and P.F.C. William A. Foster (1st Marines) smothers it with his body, saving his buddy. Despite being mortally wounded, Foster hands his remaining two grenades to the other Marine, stating: "MAKE THEM COUNT." Foster receives the Medal of Honor for his heroism and extraordinary courage under fire. Also, Robert E. Bush, Hospital Apprentice, U.S.N. Reserve receives the Medal of Honor for heroism above and beyond the call of duty while attached to the 5th Marines, 1st Marine Division; Bush advances through walls of enemy fire to give medical aid to the wounded. Upon reaching the crest of the hill to assist a wounded Officer, the Japs counterattack. Undaunted, he calmly continues giving the Officer plasma with one hand and brandishing his pistol with his other hand, expending his ammunition on the attackers. He discards the pistol and clasps a carbine, delivering more fire against the enemy at pointblank range. He becomes wounded, but refuses aid and waits until the Officer is taken to safety; Bush walks to the aid station and collapses, but recovers to receive the Medal of Honor. In the 77th Infantry Division zone, the vicious fight for Maeda Escarpment still rages; still, the Japanese retain control. Meanwhile, the 17th Regiment, 7th Division continues without success to secure a knob on Kochi Ridge; in conjunction, the 184th Regiment takes Gaja Ridge, but soon loses it to a counterattack. However, the consistent pressure has taken its toll on the Japanese as they confer and decide to launch a full scale attack on May 4th. **(Pacific-Dutch East Indies)** Japanese coastal gunfire sinks the Motor Minesweeper YMS-481. Also, the Motor Minesweepers YMS-334 and YMS-364 are damaged by coastal gunfire off Borneo near Tarakan Island, and the Motor Minesweeper YMS-363 becomes damaged by striking a mine. **(Pacific-Burma)** In ALFSEA's area, 15th Corps sector, an Allied Plane lands at Mingaladon Airfield and its Pilot, Group Captain Grandy, goes into Rangoon to confirm a message written on a roof proclaiming the Japanese have withdrawn; the message is fact, permitting the massive Air bombardment of the city, ongoing since April 26th, to cease. Meanwhile, the Airdrop portion of DRACULA drops contingents of the 5th Indian Paratroop Brigade near Elephant Point, lying about 20 miles south of the objective, and moves effortlessly toward Rangoon while the Indian 26th Division lands astride the Rangoon River and advances unopposed toward Rangoon. In the **British Fourteenth Army** area, 33rd Corps sector, Prome is taken by the Indian 20th Division, sealing off the final enemy escape route in the Arakan sector. In the 4th Corps sector, the Indian 17th Division reduces the final resistance in Pegu. **(Pacific-China)** The Chinese 5th Division, Chinese 94th Army clashes with Japanese forces at the entrance to the Wuyang Valley. In other activity, the Japanese Frigate *Ojika* is sunk by the Submarine U.S.S. *Springer* (SS-414) in the Yellow Sea which is part of the China Sea. **(Atlantic-Western Europe) 21st Army Group** Contingents of the **British Second Army** advance to the Baltic, essentially sealing off Denmark and Schleswig-Holstein. In the 12th Corps sector, the British 53rd Division advances through the 8th Corps positions and moves west toward Hamburg. In the 8th Corps sector, the British 11th Armored Division seizes Luebeck while the U.S. XVIII Corps (A/B) gains the final objective, general line Wismar-Schwerin-Ludwigslust-Doemitz. Gadebusch, Labow and Wismar fall to the British 6th Airborne Division as it advances to the Baltic coast, its 3rd Paratroop Brigade establishing contact with the Soviet 1st Motorcycle Battalion, 3rd Tank Corps at the latter (21:00). Meanwhile, the U.S. 8th Division seizes Hagenow and Schwerin without a fight while the 325th Glider Infantry, bolstered by C.C.B., 7th Armored Division, overruns Doemitz, Eldena, and Ludwigslust as it drives east. German Lt. General von Tippelskirch surrenders the Twenty-first Army to the U.S. 82nd Airborne Division at 21:30.

12th Army Group In the **U.S. Ninth Army** area, **XIII Corps** sector, Patrols of the 84th Division encounter the Russians near Balow (16:30) and Abbendorft (17:30). Subsequently, at 21:30 Patrols of the 29th Division meet the Russians. In the **U.S. First Army** area, **V Corps** sector, the 1st and 97th Divisions strengthen their positions along the Czechoslovakian frontier by mounting scaled-down attacks. In the **U.S. Third Army** area, General Patton stops off at the P.O.W. camp at Moosburg, which had confined about 30,000 Allied troops primarily Officers. Also, General Patton calls General Van Fleet and tells him to make a crossing at the Inn River in his sector to ensure control of the road from Wasserburg to Altenmarkt and Salzburg; other units are crossing at Wasserburg. **XII Corps** sector, elements of the 11th Armored Division begin crossing the Muehl River at Neufelden; Tanks transport Infantry contingents across without incident. Meanwhile, the main body of C.C.B. remains at Lembach, hampered by failure of a road net near Krondf that prevents crossing of the Klein Muehl River there; C.C.R. advances to Peilstein. In conjunction, the 26th Division, following the Armor, drives to the Klein Muehl in Austria. In the 5th Division zone, RCT 11 sweeps to the Gross Muehl in Austria and crosses it, while RCT 10 continues advancing in Czechoslovakia. Also, the 90th Division gets contingents close to Vseruby. In the **XX Corps** sector, the 261st Regiment, 65th Division drives to the Inn River; the 2nd Battalion drives into Passau on the left while the 1st Battalion advancing on the right reaches Neuhaus; upon receiving close cover fire, it darts across the river from there; the 259th Regiment reaches the river south of Neuhaus. In the 13th Armored Division zone, bridgeheads are established along the Inn and soon after, C.C.A. convinces the Germans holding Braunau to capitulate. Also, the 71st and 80th Division advance to the Inn, the former capturing dams near Ering and Egglfing with its 5th and 66th Regiments respectively; Division establishes bridgeheads across the Inn at the dams, extending their territory into Austria. In conjunction, the Engineers set to work immediately, constructing bridging to enable Vehicular crossings. In the **III Corps** sector, the advance continues rapidly, but it is ordered to stop at the Inn River. C.C.B., 14th Armored Division captures a bridge intact southeast of Aschau while C.C.A. establishes an Infantry bridgehead near Muehldorf; it is ordered to abandon it and pull back. Corps disengages from attack and assembles north of the Inn River. **6th Army Group** In the **U.S. Seventh Army** area, **XV Corps** sector, the 3rd Division prepares to launch an assault against Salzburg. Also, the 86th Division is attached to Corps. In the **XXI Corps** sector, C.C.A., and C.C.B., 12th Armored Division remain in place, but C.C.R. attacks toward Innsbruck upon orders. Meanwhile, the 101st Cavalry Group covers Armor's north flank. Also, elements of the 36th Division reduce the final resistance in the Bad Toelz region. In the **VI Corps** sector, RCT 409, 103rd Division seizes Auland and Reith while additional contingents are convincing the Germans at Innsbruck to capitulate. In the 44th Division zone, the 71st Regiment secures Fern Pass by sending its 1st Battalion, led by a group of Australian troops, to attack it from the rear in synchronization with the 3rd Battalion's frontal thrust. **(Atlantic-Eastern Europe)** Berlin is under total Soviet control. **(Atlantic-Italy) 15th Army Group** The German surrender of all troops in Italy becomes effective; all hostilities cease. But while the Allies await word that Vietinghoff is carrying out the surrender instructions, word comes in that he has been relieved of command by Kesselring-then the Americans are informed that Generals Herr and Lemelsen have ordered their Tenth and Fourteenth Armies to surrender

(composed of Army Group C, Vietinghoff). In addition, Luftwaffe General von Pohl and General Wolf have ordered their troops to surrender. Kesselring issues orders to arrest the German Generals who surrendered. General Wolf asks for U.S. Paratroop at Bolzano for protection. The U.S. 88th Infantry Division advances as the vanguard of Yanks toward the 1st German Parachute Unit, supposedly blocking entrance to the inner-mountain fortress (National Redoubt). On the 4th, the 88th establishes contact with the Seventh Army at Brenner Pass, then it advances to Bolzano. The Germans, although defeated continue to bear arms and in addition they retain their Vehicles. In essence, they are more arrogant in defeat then when the fighting had been ongoing. The Germans blatantly drive along the roads with girls in the Vehicles, drink profusely and frequently sing "*Hitler is my Fuehrer.*" Often, when the Germans are prodded from their foxholes, they bring their girl friends out with them. The S.S. maintains roadblocks and their Military Police remain active. Between the 5th and 6th of May, the German Army Group G, operating in southeast Germany and Austria also surrender, capitulating to General Devers. In the **British Eighth Army** area, 13th Corps sector, Trieste capitulates to the New Zealand 2nd Division. In other activity, 10th Corps begins moving to Naples for embarkment to the Far East.

German General Wolff in a detention camp.

May 3rd 1945 — (Pacific-Philippines) Luzon In the **U.S. Sixth Army** area, **I Corps** sector, the 3rd Battalion, 161st Regiment, 25th Division gets set for an attack against Mt. Haruna. In the **VI Corps** sector, the 38th Division deploys elements for an assault against Wawa Dam. Also, the 43rd Division moves quietly into position to launch an attack against Ipo while the Fifth Air Force begins pounding the area. Meanwhile, RCT 169 reverts to the 43rd Division as the Baldy Force is disbanded. In the **XIV Corps** sector, RCT 158 prowls in the vicinity of Mt. Isarog to wipe out any remaining Jap stragglers in the Bicols. **Southern Philippines)** In the **U.S. Eighth Army** area, **X Corps** sector on Mindanao, Davao, now a pile of rubble, is swept clean by the 3rd Battalion, 19th Regiment, 24th Division, which then gets Patrols to Santa Ana. Meanwhile, the Japs are pounced upon at Kibawe as the 124th Regiment, 31st Division exterminates the enemy and seizes the Airstrip in addition to gaining control of the junction of Sayre Highway and Talomo Trail. On Negros, heavy indecisive fighting continues at Negros Oriental as the 1st Battalion, 164th Regiment, Americal Division attempts to reestablish its supply line. **(Pacific-Ryukyu Islands-Okinawa)** The Japanese mount a full scale counterattack, the only major offensive of the campaign. Kamikazes strike the Fleet in strength, and later, during the night of the 3rd-4th, two separate amphibious landings are attempted to get behind American lines. The amphibious troops which move to the east and west coasts are met by fierce U.S. reaction, including assistance by Marine Planes, Antiaircraft units, and contingents of the 1st Marine Division. Combined, the Army and Marine forces pulverize the Japs, destroying nearly all the landing craft and killing between 500-800 enemy troops. Some make it to the beaches, but they are annihilated. In other activity, contingents of the 77th Division surge to the crest of Maeda Escarpment; however, incessant fire from the reverse slopes pounds their positions. Also, the Japanese on Kochi Ridge repulse an attack by the 1st and 3rd Battalions, 17th Regiment, 7th Division. Offshore, the Suicide Planes again take a heavy toll, sinking the Destroyers *Luce* (DD-522), *Morrison* (DD-560), and *Little* (DD-803). Also, the Kamikazes damage the Light Cruiser *Birmingham* (CL-62) and the Destroyers *Bache* (DD-470), *Ingraham* (DD-694), and the *Lowry* (DD-770). In addition, the High Speed Minesweeper *Macomb* (DMS-23) and the Light Minelayer *Aaron Ward* (DM-34) are damaged. The Japs also implement piloted bombs and suicide boats, damaging the Light Minelayer *Shea* (DM-30) and the Cargo Ship *Carina* (AK-74) respectively. **(Pacific-Yellow Sea)** The Submarine U.S.S. *Springer* (SS-414) sinks the Japanese Coast Defense Vessel No. 25. **(Pacific-Burma)** In ALFSEA's 15th Corps sector, the Indian 26th Division's 36th and 71st Brigades move into Rangoon and Syriam respectively. **(Atlantic-Western Europe) 21st Army Group** A group of German Soldiers offer to surrender all German forces in the north including those units fighting against the Soviets, but British Field Marshal Montgomery declines the offer of capitulation. In the **British Second Army** area, Hamburg surrenders to 12th Corps; the 7th British Armored Division moves across the Elbe to bolster the 53rd Division's occupation of the city. Meanwhile, the 8th Corps drives toward the Kiel Canal, chasing the retreating Germans. In the **U.S. XVIII Corps (A/B)** sector, the U.S. 7th Armored Division drives along the Baltic on the Corps' left flank establishing contact with the Red Army west of Kluetz. Later, General Ridgway and some of his troops meet with the Russians, trading stories and watching movies. Ridgway relates how one Russian Soldier, after watching Airborne movies, "JUMPS OUT A SECOND STORY WINDOW TO PROVE THE SUPERIORITY OF THE RUSSIAN SOLDIER AND TO SHOW THAT THE RUSSIANS WERE SO TOUGH THAT THEY DIDN'T NEED PARACHUTES." **12th Army Group** In the **U.S. First Army** area, **V Corps** sector, the 2nd Division still converges on Corps' zone and continues relieving the 90th (XII Corps) and 97th (V Corps) Divisions. In the **U.S. Third Army** area, **XII Corps** sector, the 11th Armored Division nears its final objective: Linz. Meanwhile, the 328th Regiment, 26th Division is attached to 11th Armored. Also, the 5th Division concentrates on Patrolling while the 90th Division accepts the surrender of Vseruby. In the **XX Corps** sector, Corps is ordered to halt its southeastern advance and swerve east, moving as rapidly as possible to establish contact with the Soviets expeditiously. The 65th Division crosses most elements over the Inn River, but some contingents are waiting for bridging at Neuhaus. The 261st Regiment reduces final resistance at Passau and also seizes Schaerding before driving toward Linz. In conjunction, the 260th Regiment sweeps the woods between Passau and Sandbach, mopping up stragglers. In the 71st Division zone, the majority of troops move into Austria via the Egglfing and Ering Dams, which are immediately opened for heavy Vehicular traffic. In the 80th Division zone, the 13th Armored is overtaken at Braunau. In the **III Corps** sector, operations

are confined to mopping up with light forces north of the Inn River. **6th Army Group** In the **U.S. Seventh Army** area, **XV Corps** sector, the 3rd Division's 7th Regiment races toward Salzburg. In the **XXI Corps** sector, C.C.R., 12th Armored Division crosses the Austrian border advancing toward Innsbruck. Meanwhile, C.C.V., French 2nd Armored Division, which is following C.C.R., is diverted toward Berchtesgaden with orders to attack it. The 4th Division awaits relief by the 101st Airborne Division and concentrates on mopping up in its zone. In the 36th Division zone, contingents of RCT 141 reach Tegern See and Lenggries on the left and right respectively. In the **VI Corps** sector, the 103rd Division is persuading the German contingents at Innsbruck to capitulate; still, its Regiments are in motion. The 410th Infantry overruns several small towns while RCT 409 advances to the Inn River at Telfs and Zirl, seizing an intact bridge at the former as it continues toward Innsbruck. In conjunction, RCT 411 contingents begin moving from Mittenwald by Vehicles toward Brenner Pass to hook up with Fifth Army forces in Italy. Meanwhile, the 44th Division's 71st Regiment gets elements to Telfs where contact is established with the 103rd Division. In the **French 1st Army** area, the 1st Corps advances along the Iller and the Rhine, reaching Feldkirch on the latter. **(Atlantic-Eastern Europe)** Contingents of the Second White Russian Front, driving on a large front through Brandenburg and Mecklenburg, encounter British troops at the Wismar-Wittenberge line, and to the left, contingents of the First White Russian Front reach the Elbe River, southeast of Wittenberg, and establish contact with the U.S. Army.

May 4th 1945 — (Pacific-Marianas) The U.S. Navy establishes Fleet Air Wing 18 on Guam to bolster operations in the Forward Area, Central Pacific. **(Pacific-Philippines) Luzon** In the **U.S. Sixth Army** area, **I Corps** sector, contingents of the 161st Regiment, 25th Division, overrun Mt. Haruna, slightly west of Balete Pass. Meanwhile, the 2nd Battalion, 27th Regiment moves along Wolfhound Ridge about 3,000 yards from Lone Tree Hill and is relieved by the 3rd Battalion. In the **XI Corps** sector, the 145th Regiment, attacks subsequent to a substantial Artillery bombardment; contingents driving on the left advance half-way to Wawa, but after dark, they pull back to stronger positions at San Isidro; the elements driving up the center and on the right meet stiff opposition and also face terrible terrain. Meanwhile, the 152nd Regiment, 38th Division reinitiates its assault against Woodpecker Ridge; resistance has not faltered, making progress tedious. **Southern Philippines** In the **U.S. Eighth Army** area, the 2nd Battalion, 108th Regiment returns from Masbate to Leyte, having successfully concluded its task; 118 Japanese have been killed during the fighting against the loss of seven Americans; the remaining enemy stragglers will be handled by Filipino Guerrillas. In the **X Corps** sector, the 24th Division continues mopup operations at Davao in Mindanao. Meanwhile, elements of the 31st Division concentrate on Patrol activity. In other activity, a contingent of the 19th Regiment, 24th Division lands on Samal Island to reconnoiter it. Also, the 1st Battalion, 164th Regiment, Americal Division, maintains its pressure to reopen the supply line in Negros Oriental. **(Pacific-Ryukyu Islands-Okinawa)** The Japanese launch another suicidal attack against the U.S. Fleet and also hit land areas including the Yontan Airfield. Japanese Suicide Planes damage the Escort Carrier *Sangamon* (CVE-26), the Destroyer *Cowell* (DD-547), Light Minelayer *Gwin* (DM-33), High Speed Minesweeper *Hopkins* (DMS-13), and the Motor Minesweeper YMS-331. In addition, the Motor Minesweeper YMS-327, is damaged by a Kamikaze and accidentally by U.S. Naval gunfire, and the

Minesweeper *Gayety* (AM-239) is damaged by a Suicide Piloted Bomb. Also, the Motor Minesweeper YMS-311 is accidentally struck by U.S. Naval gunfire, and the Destroyer *Hudson* (DD-475) is damaged by collision. The Motor Gunboat PGM-17 is damaged by grounding. In the **U.S. Tenth Army** area, **III Amphibious Corps** moves south and is replaced in the sector by the 27th Division. In the **XXIV Corps** sector, the 7th Division and the 306th Regiment, 77th Division hold the line against the Japanese onslaught. In conjunction, the 1st Marine Division attacks the enemy west of Machinato Airfield against strong resistance and sustains heavy casualties. Company I, 1st Marines advances up a hill; a Rifle Platoon is surprised by Japanese moving up the reverse slope and a tenacious hand grenade exchange develops. An enemy grenade lands in the midst of a group of Marines and instinctively, Sergeant Elbert L. Kinser dives upon it and receives the full blast to save the other Marines; he receives the Medal of Honor posthumously for his heroism in the face of certain death. The 307th Regiment, 77th Division pounds against resolute opposition on the Maeda Escarpment, and it makes some progress. **(Pacific-Burma)** British Vice Admiral Mountbatten decides to abort Operation ROGER (seizure of Phuket Island, off Kra Isthmus, as a forward Base for ZIPPER, assault on Malaya). He requests the 11th Aircraft Squadron, British Pacific Fleet to provide close-air support for the Malaya attack, but it is denied. Mountbatten is told he will receive one additional Escort Carrier and two general purpose Carriers. **(Pacific-Yellow Sea)** The Submarine *Trepang* (SS-412) sinks the Japanese Minesweeper No. 20. **(Atlantic-Western Europe) 21st Army Group** The Germans sign the instrument of surrender of their Armed Forces in Denmark, Holland, and northwest Germany at 18:20, to become effective on May 5th at 08:00. **12th Army Group** In the **U.S. Ninth Army** area, the XIII Corps Commander and the Soviet III Cavalry Corps Commander meet. In the **U.S. First Army** area, Army Headquarters prepares to embark for the U.S. for redeployment in the Pacific; its contingents are being passed on to other Armies. The **V Corps** is assigned the 9th and 16th Armored Divisions and is then attached to Third Army; it drives toward Karlsbad (Karlovy Vary) and Pilsen (Plzen). In the **VII Corps** sector, contact is made with Soviet troops which close on a wide front. In the **U.S. Third Army** area, the Germans holding at Linz and at Urfahr pour heavy fire upon advancing columns of the 11th Armored Division, prompting a modification of attack plans; instead of attacking Urfahr from the northwest, it pivots to assault from the northeast. In conjunction, the 41st Cavalry drives southeast, seizing Gallneukirchen, and C.C.B., 11th Armored is ordered to stop there and establish contact with the Red Army. Meanwhile, Fighter Bombers support C.C.A., 11th Armored at Linz; the attack lacked support from XIX Tactical Air Command due to heavy AA fire. Also, Artillery is rushed to the area to further lambaste Linz. In other activity, the 5th and 90th Divisions deploy to attack the passes into Czechoslovakia to clear the way for 4th Armored to drive to Prague. In the **XX Corps** sector, the 65th Division is closing on Linz while the 71st Division overruns Lambach and Wels, seizing bridges across the Traun River at both cities. Meanwhile, the 80th Division and the 3rd Cavalry Group are still crossing the Inn River; the 43rd Squadron, which is screening the Corps' right flank, is discussing the surrender of Neumarkt by telephone with the Germans' Garrison; the 3rd Squadron assists elements of the 80th Division eliminate a German stronghold at Voecklabruck. **6th Army Group** In the **U.S. Seventh Army** area, **XV Corps** sector, the 7th Regiment, 3rd Division moves into Austria, then treks through Salzburg

to Berchtesgaden without incident. Meanwhile, the 106th Cavalry Group has already accepted the surrender of Salzburg. In conjunction, additional contingents of Corps advance to Austria's border without encountering opposition. In the **XXI Corps** sector, 12th Armored Division passes into reserve; it releases attached C.C.V., 2nd French Armored and the 101st Cavalry Group. The 36th Division's RCT 141, secures the towns of Tegernsee and Schliersee and also clears the banks of Schlier and Tegern Lakes as it drives south; RCT 142 also maintains its southward attack after relieving C.C.R., 12th Armored at the Inn River. In the **VI Corps** sector, Innsbruck surrenders to the 103rd Division at 10:15; the 410th Regiment garrisons it. Meanwhile, the 411th Regiment enters Brenner Pass by 01:50 and establishes contact with the U.S. 88th Division's (Fifth Army) I and R Platoon, 349th Regiment in Italy at 10:51. Also, the 3rd Battalion, 409th Regiment (103rd Division), bolstered by Tanks, advances rapidly to the Inn River and establishes contact with XII Corps at Worgl. In the 44th Division zone, the 324th Regiment, racing by Vehicles, zooms through Fern Pass, passing the 71st Division at Dollinger and reaching Imst, which it secures; the Regiment continues moving south and seizes Mils and Wenns as it advances to seal the Resia Pass, leading into Italy. In conjunction, German Officers enter U.S. 44th Division lines to discuss terms of surrender. In the **French 1st Army** area, 1st Corps sector, the 2nd Moroccan and the French 5th Armored Divisions are closing on the Inn River near St. Anton from the south and southeast respectively. Meanwhile, DA ATL halts southeast of la Rochelle, awaiting word on surrender negotiations. **(Atlantic-Italy) 15th Army Group** A contingent of the 88th Division makes contact with the U.S. Seventh Army when its 103rd Division's 411th Regiment advances to Vipiteno, south of Brennero on the Austrian-Italian frontier. Also, German General Fridolin von Senger und Etterlin (Rhodes Scholar-Oxford), Commander XIV Panzer Corps and U.S. General Truscott, British General McCreery, and Air Force Major General Benjamin W. Chidlaw are among the Allies at the surrender. Von Senger salutes and asks for Allied orders concerning German Land Forces surrender.

General Wedemeyer (standing) — seated left to right, General Sultan, Br. Admiral Mountbatten and General Donovan during a strategy session in Burma.

May 5th 1945 — (Pacific-Philippines) Luzon In the **U.S. Sixth Army** area, **I Corps** sector, heavy fighting continues at Balete Pass as the 25th Division drills into entrenched enemy positions to destroy them; in conjunction, the 3rd Battalion, 27th Regiment reduces final resistance at Wolfhound Ridge. In the **XI Corps** sector, the 2nd Battalion, 145th Regiment,

37th Division, driving on the Corps' right flank, seizes a hold on the base of Sugar Loaf Hill while the 3rd Battalion reaches the base of Mt. Binicayan. Also, the 152nd Regiment halts its attack against Woodpecker Ridge and regroups. Meanwhile, contingents of the 43rd Division assemble to launch an attack toward Ipo, scheduled to commence on the night of the 6th-7th. **Southern Philippines** In the **U.S. Eighth Army** area, **X Corps** sector, the Japanese holding the heights north of Bancal resist fiercely against the advancing 1st Battalion, 34th Regiment, 24th Division; nevertheless, the Battalion makes some gains. Meanwhile, a Patrol of the 31st Division discovers a Japanese force in the woods (subsequently named Colgan Woods for Captain A.T. Colgan) north of Lake Pinalay. On Negros, the determined efforts of the 1st Battalion, 164th Regiment, Americal Division reopens the supply line in Negros Oriental. The principal body of the 2nd Battalion advances to Badiang to bolster Company G, 1st Battalion in its attempt to destroy a newly discovered strongpoint southeast of Odlumon. **(Pacific-Ryukyu Islands-Okinawa)** Japanese Kamikazes strike again, damaging the Seaplane Tender *St. George* (AV-16) and the Surveying Ship *Pathfinder* (AGS-1). On **Okinawa**, In the **U.S. Tenth Army** area, the Japanese mount additional assaults to penetrate U.S. lines, striking during the early morning hours against the 77th and 7th Division positions; about 450 enemy troops pierce the lines and recapture Tanabaru town and Tanabaru ridge, severing the supply line of the 7th Division. In conjunction, the 77th Division holds off the counterattacks and gains the reverse slopes of Maeda Escarpment. Later, during the night of the 5th-6th, the Japs mount a savage but unsuccessful attack to regain the slopes. Also, in the 7th Divisional zone, contingents of the 17th Regiment are rooting out infiltrators near Tanabaru. **(Pacific-Burma)** The reconquering of Burma is complete as the Indian 26th Division (15th Corps) occupies Rangoon, but the Japanese Burma Area Army has not been destroyed; massive mop-up operations ensue to eliminate the threat. **(Pacific-China)** General Stratemeyer is disenchanted with a suggestion from General Wedemeyer that he should command a smaller Air Force than originally proposed. **(Atlantic-Western Europe)** **21st Army Group** At 08:00, all Group offensive activity ceases, synchronized with effective time of cease-fire. The British establish a Military Government within their zone, and subsequently, on August 25th, 21st Army Group is redesignated British Army of the Rhine. **12th Army Group** In the **U.S. Ninth Army** area, **XIX Corps** sector, the 30th Division encounters Soviet troops at the Elbe River. Meanwhile, the U.S. 83rd Division starts dismantling its Elbe bridgehead and pulling back as the Soviets are closing on their predesignated areas. In the **U.S. Third Army** area, **V Corps** is transferred to Third Army. Major General C.R. Huebner (Corps Commander), while at dinner had been informed of the transfer and makes a prediction: "WELL, I'LL GIVE US JUST ABOUT TWELVE HOURS, BEFORE GENERAL PATTON CALLS UP AND TELLS US TO ATTACK SOMETHING."...Soon after, the phone rings and General Patton is on the phone with Huebner, prompting Huebner to say he had been wrong: "WELL, I MISSED THAT ONE. INSTEAD OF TWELVE HOURS, IT WAS TWELVE MINUTES. WE ATTACK PILSEN AT DAYBREAK." The 1st Division launches a scaled-down attack to strengthen its right flank near Cheb while simultaneously preparing to strike Karlsbad. The 97th Division seizes Bor and Trustenice and secures the Chodova Plana and Plana as it drives toward Pilsen; also, Stribro is surrounded. In the **XII Corps** sector, the 11th Armored Division seizes the Urfahr-Linz industrial center. Urfahr is bombarded heavily by Artil-

lery subsequent to the entrance of C.C.A.'s Task Force Wingard which takes the objective at 11:00, then jumps across the Danube accepting the surrender of Linz at 18:00. These prizes, which include control of the Urfahr-Linz highway and the rail bridges, all having been wired for demolition, virtually forbid escape to the redoubt area by the Germans in Czechoslovakia. Meanwhile, C.C.B. dispatches Patrols (41st Cavalry) far beyond the set boundary (rail line stretching north and south about 12 miles east of Linz) established between the U.S. and Soviets. In conjunction, the elements on the left flank of the Corps prepare to drive against Prague. The 2nd Squadron, 2nd Cavalry Group gallops north into Czechoslovakia; the Garrison at Klatovy capitulates. Meanwhile, to the right, the 5th and 90th Divisions clear Freyung and Regen Passes respectively into Czechoslovakia, paving the way for Armor to burst forth into wide open country. RCT 357, 90th Division bolts through Regen Pass, clearing Zwiesel-Zelezna Ruda-Dobra Voda Road; in conjunction, the 5th Division's RCT 2 and 10 race across the Tepla River driving northeast and north respectively, the former severing the Volary-Kunzvart Road and the latter drilling an opening down the Freyung-Kunzvart-Hor Vltavice Road. Also, 4th Armored scours the area for effective routes to Prague which it will assault on the 6th. In the **XX Corps** sector, a restraining line is established along the Enns River. The 261st Regiment, 65th Division seizes the town of Enns easily while the 71st Division, advancing east from the Traun River, encounters no resistance; contingents of the 5th Regiment drive to the Enns at Steyr, seizing an intact bridge. In conjunction, the 80th Division (minus 318th Regiment and the 1st Battalion, 319th Regiment which is transported by train from Braunau to Voecklabruck) converges on the Enns River to the right of the 71st Division. **6th Army Group** Army Group G, composed of the German First and Nineteenth Armies, accept Allied surrender terms negotiated at Haar, in Bavaria; all hostilities cease. Although the official time for cessation is set for 12:00 on May 6th, both sides order an immediate termination of combat. In the **VI Corps** sector, Landeck is occupied without incident by the 324th Regiment, 44th Division.

May 6th 1945 — (United States) The Destroyer Escort *Atherton* (DE-169) and the Frigate *Moberley* (PF-63) catch the German Submarine U-853 off Cape Cod, Massachusetts, sinking it. **(Pacific-Marshall Islands)** A Naval landing force evacuates about 500 Marshallese from Jaluit Atoll. **(Pacific-Philippines)** **Luzon** In the **U.S. Sixth Army** area, **I Corps** sector, the 161st Regiment, 25th Division reduces the final resistance on Kembu Plateau in addition to capturing the junction of the plateau and Balete Pass Ridge as is tightens its ratchet pressure against the enemy in Balete Pass. In the **XI Corps** sector, the 2nd Battalion, 145th Regiment, seizes the crest of Sugar Loaf Hill while the 3rd Battalion drives to positions just under the summit of Mt. Binicayan. In conjunction, the 3rd Battalion, 149th Infantry moves to Mt. Pacawagan to hold it, freeing the 1st Battalion, 145th Regiment. Later, after dark, the 43rd Division launches an attack against Ipo, the 103rd and 172nd driving on the right and left respectively. In other activity, the Japanese attempt to mount a counterattack; however, U.S. Planes and Artillery lambaste their positions, scattering the troops; the attack is aborted. **Southern Philippines** In the **U.S. Eighth Army** area, **X Corps** sector, a strong attack is mounted by the 3rd Battalion, 34th Regiment, 24th Division to reduce a previously bypassed Jap stronghold in the Guma area of Mindanao, but the entrenched enemy gives no ground. In the 31st Division zone, along the Sayre Highway, Air support is provided the 1st Battalion, 124th Regiment, which is also bolstered by hefty mortar barrages as it attacks the dug-in enemy in the Colgan woods; in conjunction, the 3rd Battalion implementing an outflanking maneuver seizes positions north of the enemy positions. On Negros, the 2nd Battalion, 164th Regiment gains a ridge as preparations are finalized for a major southward drive in Negros Oriental. Meanwhile, in Negros Occidental, the high ground east and south of Virgne Ridge is secured by the 185th Regiment, 40th Division as is continues hammering along the ridge, driving toward Patog Plain. **(Pacific-Okinawa)** In the **U.S. Tenth Army** area, **XXIV Corps** sector, the 1st Marine Division still hits resolute resistance and is unable to gain much terrain. The 1st Marines attack to secure Hill 60, but it holds; however, 200 yards north of the obstinate hill, the Marines repulse Japanese attacks coming from the reverse slopes on Nan Hill. Meanwhile, the Japanese also offer fervent resistance against the 5th Marines in the bulwark defenses in the hills and ridges south of Awacha, preventing progress. In the center of the Corps assault, the 307th Regiment, 77th Division advances from the Maeda Escarpment to the southern slopes of Hill 187. Meanwhile, contingents of the 7th Division's 17th Regiment is heavily engaged at a knob on Kochi Ridge while simultaneously methodically eliminating the infiltrators near Tanabaru. Off Okinawa, the Battleship *South Dakota* incurs damage by an accidental explosion. Also, a Japanese Horizontal Bomber damages the Floating Drydock ARD-28. **(Pacific-Burma)** In the ALFSEA area, 15th Corps sector, the progress of the 71st Brigade, Indian 26th Division is rapid, and contact with the Indian 17th Division occurs along the Rangoon road at Hlegu, virtually isolating the Japanese 28th Army. **(North Atlantic)** The German Submarine U-881 is sunk by the Destroyer Escort *Farquhar* (DE-139). **(Atlantic-Western Europe) 12th Army Group** At 18:00, the U.S. First Army's VII and VIII Corps are attached to Ninth Army. In the **XIX Corps** area, the 30th Division assumes control of the 83rd Division area. Soviet forces make it to the Elbe in 30th Division zone at 17:00. In the **U.S. Third Army** area, **V Corps** sector, the 26th Regiment, 1st Division seizes Schoenbach. In conjunction, the 16th Regiment secures Kynsperk, and the 18th overruns Sangerberg and Mnichov as the 1st Division drives toward Karlsbad. The 9th Armored Division's C.C.A. (attached to 1st Division) drives to Rudolec. Meanwhile, the 16th Armored Division advances through the 97th Division positions, attacking toward Pilsen; its C.C.B., spearheading the effort, bolts into the city and seizes it and its Skoda munitions plant; C.C.R. roars through Pilsen and deploys east of the city in the heights. About 100,000 White Russians attempt to surrender to the Yanks. Soldiers are taken as P.O.W.s and the women and children are considered displaced persons. In the **XII Corps** sector, the 4th Armored Division, trailed by the 5th and 99th Infantry Divisions, drives toward Prague, meeting no opposition as it rolls northeast through the Freyung and Regen Passes into Czechoslovakia; C.C.A. romps to Strakonice where it dispatches a TF east to Pisek; C.C.B., moving on the left, advances to Vel Bor. Meanwhile, the 2nd Cavalry Group drives toward Zinkovy, subsequent to overrunning Planice. On Corps' right flank, the 11th Armored Division sends Patrols into designated Red Army areas; the penetration is deep, but no contact with the Russians occurs. In the **XX Corps** sector, the 65th Division (minus the 260th Regiment) converges on the Enns River; the 260th remained at Linz to police the area. Meanwhile, elements of the 71st Division arrive at the Enns River, relieving contingents of the 80th Division deployed along the west bank. In conjunction, the 5th Regiment, 71st Division secures the Ernsthofen dam and the high ground on

the east bank. **6th Army Group** German Army Group G's capitulation to the Allies becomes official at 12:00 (noon).

May 7th 1945 — The Germans surrendering at Reims.

May 7th 1945 — (Pacific-Philippines) Luzon In the **U.S. Sixth Army** area, the main body of the 145th Regiment concentrates on Patrolling and tightening up its positions; the 1st Battalion attacks, driving from Mt. Pacawagan toward a fortified ridge stretching to Wawa, encountering fierce resistance as it moves. Meanwhile, the 152nd Regiment, bolstered by Air support and Artillery, reinitiates its attack against Woodpecker Ridge and gnaws forward against resolute resistance; the Japanese hold toughly for about a week. Also, the 43rd Division is grinding forward effectively, gaining about 8,000 yards in its quest to take Ipo. **Southern Philippines** In the **U.S. Eighth Army** area, **X Corps** sector (Mindanao), Company C, 21st Regiment, 24th Division races north to intercept the Japanese force near the Talomo River; however, the enemy raises fierce resistance, compelling the contingent to pull back. Planes and Artillery are called in to lambaste the enemy positions. Meanwhile, the firmly entrenched Japanese in the Guma region are saturated with Artillery bombardment and Air strikes, affording the 3rd Battalion, 34th Regiment to commit probing Patrols. In the 31st Division zone along the Sayre Highway, the Japanese continue resisting ferociously in the Colgan woods, hindering progress of the 1st Battalion, 124th Regiment; the 3rd Battalion drives to Maramag Airfield No. 1, southwest of the town. On Negros, Company G, 164th Regiment, Americal Division gets added support from Artillery and Planes, enabling it to thrash the enemy and seize the formidable stronghold southeast of Odlumon in Negros Oriental. Meanwhile, in Negros Occidental, Para RCT 503 plows forward, establishing contact with the 185th Regiment, 40th Division. Patrols are dispatched and discover the Japs have abandoned Patog Plain. **(Pacific-Okinawa)** In the **U.S. Tenth Army** area, Army takes control of operations on southern Okinawa. Lt. General John R, Hodge directs the seizure of line Asa-Dakeshi-Gaja by the following day to clear the way for an Army offensive planned to drive south. In the **III Amphibious Corps** sector, Corps assumes responsibility for the western sector of the Tenth Army front in the southern sector of the island. The 1st Marine Division is still heavily embattled; the 1st Marines continue fending off strong opposition from the reverse slopes of Nan Hill while simultaneously pounding against rock resistance on Hill 60. During one skirmish, the Japanese toss grenades into the midst of a Squad from Company C, 1st Battalion, 1st Marines. Corporal John P. Fardy, in an attempt to save his Marines, jumps on the grenade absorbing its full impact; the others in his group are saved; Fardy receives the Medal of Honor for his devotion to duty and extraordinary heroism while under attack by fanatical Japanese. Also, Private Dale M. Hansen, Company E, 2nd Battalion, 1st Marines goes on the attack and singlehandedly wipes out a machine gun nest with his rocket launcher, then subsequent to the weapon jamming, he confiscates a rifle and continues racing to the crest of the hill, exterminating four of six Japs before his rifle jams. The other two Japs attack him, but he improvises and both are driven off by the butt of his weapon. Soon after, the fearless Corporal procures another rifle and grenades, then he moves out and slays eight more enemy troops and destroys a mortar position in the process. Corporal Hansen receives the Medal of Honor. The Japanese also encounter P.F.C. ALbert E. Schwab, who exceeds the bounds of human endurance during the heated battles with the Japanese; his Company is pinned down by incessant fire and casualties begin to mount. Schwab, transporting his Flame-thrower ascends the steep hill and attacks singlehandedly, knocking out the first stumbling block which permits his troops to seize the ridge. Then a sudden burst of enemy machine gun fire, takes more casualties. Schwab, instantaneously, despite his fuel being at an alarming rate, advances straight into the sheets of fire with his flame-thrower roaring. He becomes wounded, but destroys two more nests and the Company moves forward. Schwab receives the Medal of Honor. Meanwhile, the Japanese mount unyielding resistance south of Awacha, hindering progress of the 5th Marines for the next week. In the **XXIV Corps** sector, the 7th and 77th Divisions, on the left and right respectively, advance prudently against Shuri and Yonabaru. The 17th Regiment, 7th Division concludes the extermination of infiltrators in the Tanabaru region; additional Regimental contingents fortify the perimeter on Kochi Ridge and yet others encounter fierce resistance south of Kochi town as they advance toward Zebra Hill. Meanwhile, the 184th Regiment seizes Gaja Ridge effortlessly. **(Pacific)** The Japanese Minesweeper No. 29 sinks after striking a U.S. mine in the Sea of Japan. **(Atlantic-Western Europe)** Germany surrenders without condition to the Allies. The instrument of surrender is signed by the German High Command at Reims at 01:41 B Central European Time, becoming effective at 00:01 B 9th May. Word spreads rapidly and as it reaches the field, all offensive actions are terminated immediately; defensive postures are begun. In the **Third Army's XX Corps** sector, the Imperial Spanish Riding Academy, which had fled Vienna as the Russians approached and been captured by XX Corps, performs; General Patton and Undersecretary of War, Judge Patterson are in attendance. The Imperial Riding Academy had been performing in Vienna since the days of Charles V of Spain. Also, General Andrei Andreyevich Vlassov (Vlassov's Army) and contingents of his force have avoided capture by the Russians. During mid-May, Vlassov and his Staff depart Third Army Headquarters at Schlusselburg to attend a meeting in a nearby town. Schlusselburg is also occupied by Russian troops. The contingent never makes it to the conference; it is surrounded by Russians and Vlassov and his Staff are seized. About one and a half years later, Vlassov and twelve of his Officers are hanged in Red Square. **(Atlantic-Eastern Europe)** Breslau (Silesia) finally folds under the prolonged pressure of the Red Army. Meanwhile, the Soviets reach the Elbe north and northeast of Magdeburg.

May 8th 1945 — (United States) President Harry S. Truman proclaims May 8th V-E Day (Victory in Europe). **(Pacific-Philippines) Luzon** In the **U.S. Sixth Army** area, **XI Corps** sector, the 145th Regiment, 37th Division reinitiates its offen-

Headline in the STARS AND STRIPES caps the day: "GERMANY QUITS."

sive; the 1st Battalion secures a ridge extending to Wawa, which also opens a blocked trail in the Mariquina (Marikina) River gorge, just south of Wawa; the 2nd Battalion secures Sugar Loaf Hill. Meanwhile, the 3rd Battalion continues its futile attack up the slopes of Mt. Binicayan. During the vicious contest on Hill B, at Balete Pass, a Japanese hand grenade is lobbed into an enemy trench which had been seized by a contingent of Company I, 148th Regiment. P.F.C. Anthony L. Krotiak shoves his four buddies to the side and slams the grenade with the butt of his rifle before smothering it with his body; within minutes Krotiak is dead from the blast, but the others are saved. P.F.C. Krotiak receives the Medal of Honor posthumously. **Southern Philippines** In the **U.S. Eighth Army** area, **X Corps** sector on Mindanao, heavy fighting erupts at the Talomo River north of Mintal as the Japanese attempt to destroy the bridgehead established by contingents of the 21st Regiment, 24th Division. A Japanese sniper pops up from his hole and attempts to throws a grenade into the position of a machine gun crew (Company I); P.F.C. James H. Diamond springs forward and with a sudden burst of submachine gun fire, the Jap is rendered deceased. Diamond then directs the fire from a 105-mm and some machine guns which rips into the enemy, knocking out several more enemy strongpoints. Soon after when two Companies plant a beachhead, Diamond volunteers to commandeer a Vehicle and transport the wounded through a gauntlet of fire. The truck becomes seriously damaged and he becomes wounded but the mission is accomplished; on the following day, Diamond volunteers to go out under fire to help repair a damaged bridge. On the 14th, subsequent to his Battalion encountering fierce opposition which isolates it, Diamond volunteers to transport the wounded back to safety. While dodging machine gun bullets to procure a machine gun, he is struck by enemy fire. Despite being mortally wounded, Diamond intentionally draws more fire upon himself to save the remainder of his Squad. The Patrol reaches safety; P.F.C. Diamond receives the Medal of Honor posthumously. In the Sayre Highway area, fighting continues in the Colgan Woods as the 31st Division maintains pressure as it advances. On Samal, Company K, 19th Regiment lands subsequent to an Artillery bombardment and begins search and destroy operations. On Negros, heavy skirmishing continues to ensue at Negros Oriental as two Battalions of the 164th Regiment gnaw southward, systematically eliminating entrenched enemy troops. **(Pacific-Okinawa)** All Air Ground and Naval operations are hindered by heavy rains. In the **U.S. Tenth Army** area, advance contingents of the 6th Marine Division flow in to the lines on the island's southern front, relieving units of the 7th Marines on the west coast north of the Asa. Also, the 1st

713

Marine Division begins blasting the Japs from their caves on the reverse slopes of Nan Hill, to clear the way for another drive to secure Hill 60. In the **XXIV Corps** sector, vicious fighting erupts as the 305th Regiment, 77th Division pushes further, prompting strong reaction from the enemy. **(Pacific-French Indo China)** The Submarine *Bream* (SS-243) lays mines in the shipping lanes. **(Atlantic-Western Europe) 12th Army Group** The U.S. First Army transfers its remaining contingents to other U.S. Armies. In the **U.S. Third Army** area, **XII Corps** sector, contact is established with Soviet troops when a C.C.A. Patrol (Troop A, 41st Cavalry) encounters them at Amstetten. Also, in the **XX Corps** sector, the 65th Division establishes contact with the Soviets near Strengberg, and the 71st Division makes contact with Soviet contingents at St. Peter; this concludes Corps mission. General Patton has his final press briefing with the war correspondents; one of them asks: "GENERAL, WHY DIDN'T WE TAKE PRAGUE." Patton responds: "I CAN TELL YOU EXACTLY WHY. BECAUSE WE WERE ORDERED NOT TO." Third Army casualties as of May 8th (final report): killed 21,441; wounded 99,224; missing 16,200; non-battle casualties 111,562-total 248,427. Enemy casualties vs. Third Army: killed 144,500; wounded 386,200; P.O.W.s 956,000-total 1,486,700. Third Army equipment losses: Light Tanks 308; Medium Tanks 949; Guns 175. Enemy equipment losses vs. Third Army: Medium Tanks 1,529; Panther and Tiger Tanks 858; Guns 3,454. General Patton soon returns to the United States and gets an opportunity to be reunited with his family for a short time. He has not seen his son, George S. Patton IV (West Point class of 1946), since he departed for North Africa during 1942. General Patton also makes a bond tour before returning to Germany. **(Atlantic-Italy)** General Mark Clark, in Trieste, is informed of Germany's unconditional surrender, effective May 8th; he orders British General McCreery to occupy Southern Austria before the Russians or Yugoslavs can get their forces entrenched. **(Atlantic-Eastern Europe)** In Latvia, fighting ends as the German Sixteenth and Eighteenth Armies begin surrendering to forces of the Leningrad Front. Dresden and Goerlitz are seized by the First Ukrainian Front, which also sends contingents into Czechoslovakia toward Prague. Meanwhile, Olmuetz is seized by forces of the Fourth Ukrainian Front. German Captain Breuninger, at Libau on the Courland Coast, in a letter to his father: "SOME OFFICERS CLAIMED TO KNOW THAT THE BRITISH WOULD SEND SHIPS TO PICK US UP. IT WAS EVEN SAID THAT ENGLISH TROOPS WOULD LAND HERE AND ATTACK THE RUSSIAN FLANK TOGETHER WITH US...WE ONLY KNOW THAT TO THIS DAY WE HAVE FOUGHT BOLSHEVISM, THE ENEMY NOT OF US ALONE BUT OF ALL EUROPE. WE HAVE SEEN BOLSHEVISM IN ACTION AS NO ONE ELSE HAS...AND IF IT IS TRUE THAT THE ENGLISH HAVE KEPT OUR SHIPS FROM LEAVING PORT, THEY WILL REMEMBER IT ONE DAY WHEN THEY SEE AND GO THROUGH WHAT WE HAVE SEEN AND GONE THROUGH."

May 9th 1945 — (Pacific-Philippines) Luzon In the **U.S. Sixth Army** area, **I Corps** sector, the 27th and 161st Regiments, 25th Division have hooked up in the Balete Pass region, signaling the end for the Japanese who still control the pass. In the **XI Corps** sector, Mt. Binicayan falls to the 3rd Battalion, 145th Regiment; in conjunction, the 2nd Battalion fortifies its positions at Sugar Loaf Hill. In the **XIV Corps** sector, a Patrol of the 158th Regiment discovers an enemy contingent in the Bicols; these, the only enemy forces encountered, are wiped out. **Southern Philippines** In the **U.S. Eighth Army** area, **X Corps** RCT 108 departs in separate con-

tingents from Cebu and Leyte, moving by Convoy toward Macajalar Bay, Mindanao, and will land on the following day. In the **X Corps** sector, on Mindanao, the Japanese mount a strong but unsuccessful attack to destroy the Talomo River bridgehead, held by the 1st Battalion, 21st Regiment, 24th Division. Meanwhile, the Japanese abandon the Guma pocket. Also, Mortars, Artillery and Air strikes saturate enemy positions in the Colgan Woods, subsequent to the 124th Regiment, 31st Division halting its attack; the softening up process continues for several days. **(Pacific-Okinawa)** In the **U.S. Tenth Army** area, orders for a general assault to commence on the 11th are handed down by General Buckner. The plan calls for a holding action in the center coordinated with a double envelopment of the Shuri defenses. In the **III Amphibious Corps** sector, the 1st Marines, 1st Marine Division eliminate final resistance on Nan Hill in addition to seizing Hill 60. In the **XXIV Corps** sector, Japanese resistance hinders the 77th Division as it drives toward Shuri. The operation continues to move methodically, implementing a combination of strong support fire bolstering individual Regiments and further ensuring success by committing another Regiment to add its support fire, then move in and mop up the remaining resistance at each stronghold. Meanwhile, most Japanese have been dislodged from their Kochi positions. **Offshore**, the Destroyer Escorts *Oberrender* (DE-344) and the *England* (DE-635) are both damaged by Kamikazes. **(Atlantic-Western Europe)** All hostilities in the European Theater are officially ended at 00:01 B as act of surrender becomes effective. Hermann Goring surrenders to Major General J.A. Dahlquist, 36th Infantry Division. May has not been a good month for German Generals; the Seventh Army had captured von Runstedt in his bath at the Alpenfestung and also, Field Marshals Wilhelm List, Wilhelm Ritter von Leeb, and Kesselring are scooped up. Himmler will attempt to escape from Flensburg (carrying phony papers) on the 21st; he is stopped by the British at Meinstadt. Using cyanide, which is hidden in his mouth, Himmler kills himself on the 23rd, succumbing within twelve minutes after taking the poison. Another German General Reinhardd Gehlen remains in hiding at Elendsalm, Bavaria, near Lake Spitzing, attempting to work out a deal with the Americans for his freedom. His Russian archives are used as bargaining tools. Gehlen's records are the primary source of all information on the Russians and a deal is reached between Gehlen and the U.S. (the arrangement emerges as a forerunner to the CIA) toward the latter part of May. **(Atlantic-Italy)** German Generals Karl Wolff, Heinrich von Vietinghoff, Hans Roettiger and their Staffs arrive at Bolzano by air. Wolff's family will join him. During this enduring operation (SUNRISE) Gero von Schulze (naturalized American-German birth) and Ted Ryan O.S.S., played primary roles in bringing a successful conclusion to the German surrender; using Wolff's car and his chauffeur, they drive to the Tyrolean village of St. Leonhard and become astonished to see the endless pieces of art treasures which had been saved by General Wolff. Himmler had ordered him to ship the treasures to Austria, but he refused stating that he lacked sufficient fuel to transport them. The bonanza is guarded by only a few troops of the U.S. 10th Mountain Division. The treasure include works by Raphael, Botticelli, Bellini, Tintoretto, Rubens and Cranach, as well as sculptures by Donatello and Michelangelo. Wolff had also preserved a multi-million dollar coin collection belonging to the King of Italy. The U.S. Fifth Army returns the treasures to Florence on July 20th. **(Atlantic-Eastern Europe)** Remaining German resistance on the Eastern Front is confined to the Austrian and Czechoslovakia areas, where the Germans are in fast retreat, heading west and southwest, attempting to evade capture by the pursuing Soviets. On the northern front, remaining German forces are beginning to surrender to units of the Second and Third White Russian Fronts in the Gulf of Danzig region. Meanwhile, in Czechoslovakia, the Soviets seize Prague with contingents of the First Ukrainian Front. Also, the Third Ukrainian Front advances to Amstetten and Graz, encountering U.S. troops near the former. German troops holding the Masaryk Railroad surrender to Czechoslovakian Major Count Schwarzenberg, then begin to march across the Moldau bridge-Soviet forces open fire and cut down the Germans. The Russians go on a rampage, again pillaging the area raping the women. The Soviets have begun a practice: "GERMANS DRENCHED WITH GASOLINE, STRUNG FROM FEET, SET ON FIRE-GERMAN MEN AND WOMEN TIED TOGETHER WITH BARBED WIRE, SHOT INTO BUNDLES AND THROWN INTO THE MOLDAU RIVER-DROWN GERMAN CHILDREN IN WATER TROUGHS AND THROW WOMEN AND CHILDREN FROM WINDOWS." The barbarous acts begin at Prague and according to eye witness reports from survivors, happens: "IN EVERY VILLAGE THROUGHOUT CZECHOSLOVAKIA AND SUDETENLAND." On the 20th, a Pastor, Karl Seifort and some elderly peasants, near the Elbe outside Dresden, ask and receive permission from the Russians to bury the corpses that wash ashore. Thousands of people float by (wrapped in barbed wire). One family is nailed to "A WOODEN BED-STEAD,"...THE PEASANTS HALT ITS COURSE AND PULL THE STAKES FROM THE CHILDRENS' HANDS. **(Pacific-Burma)** In the **ALFSEA** area, the West African 82nd Division enters Sandoway.

May 10th 1945 — (Pacific-Philippines) Luzon In the **U.S. Sixth Army** area, **XI Corps** sector, the fighting at Woodpecker Ridge remains fierce; however, the 152nd Regiment, 38th Division is still unable to dislodge the entrenched Japanese. Meanwhile, the 43rd Division reduces gears as it closes on Ipo. In the **U.S. Eighth Army** area, a Naval Attack Group, commanded by Rear Admiral A.D. Struble, lands RCT 108 at Macajalar Bay and with the support of Filipino Guerrillas establishes a bridgehead without incident; the landing had been preceded by Naval and Air bombardment. The 2nd Battalion drives southeast to establish contact with the 31st Division which is advancing north along the Sayre Highway. Meanwhile, Japanese Artillery on Samal Island bombard positions of the 19th Regiment, 24th Division, striking the area near the Command Post; its 2nd Battalion jumps off subsequent to an Artillery barrage to wipe out a bypassed enemy contingent controlling Hill 550, which dominates Davao. The 1st Battalion, 21st Regiment pulls back its Talomo River bridgehead during the evening. **(Pacific-Okinawa)** In the **U.S. Tenth Army** area, **III Amphibious Corps** sector, at 03:00, the 22nd Marines, 6th Marine Division, drive across the Asa Estuary. However, the Japanese destroy the footbridge, forcing the rear contingents to wade across; the Marines advance through Asa and establish a bridgehead extending about one mile wide and 350 yards deep. After dark, a Bailey bridge is constructed to afford passage of heavy weapons. Meanwhile, at fortified Shuri, the Japanese continue to hinder progress of the 1st Marine Division. The 1st Marines are unable to advance because of incessant fire and the 7th Marines storm Dakeshi Ridge, but the Japanese repulse the assault. In the 5th Marines zone, the 2nd Battalion advances against severe fire and becomes stalled. Pharmacist's Mate Second Class William D. Halyburton, Jr., leaps to assist a wounded Marine, despite the unmerciful barrages; while tending to the man,

additional enemy fire strikes the patient. Halyburton, shields the man with his body and continues rendering first aid, but the Japanese fire kills Halyburton, who sacrifices his life that the Marine might live; he receives the Medal of Honor posthumously. In the **XXIV Corps** sector, Japanese deployed north of Shuri are being eliminated position by position and yard by yard in a tedious operation. The 383rd Regiment, drives to the summit of Zebra Hill, digs in, and repulses a subsequent night counterattacks. Meanwhile, the 383rd Regiment, 96th Division prepares to launch an assault against Conical Hill, the eastern bastion of the Shuri defense line. **Offshore** Suicide Planes again strike the Fleet, damaging the Destroyer *Brown* (DD-546) and the Light Minelayer *Harry F. Bauer* (DM-26).

May 11th 1945 — U.S.S. Bunker Hill.

May 11th 1945 — (Pacific-Philippines) Luzon In the **U.S. Sixth Army** area, **I Corps** sector, The 25th Division's 3rd Battalion 27th Regiment, and 1st Battalion, 35th Regiment make contact on Kapintalan Ridge; about 1,000 Japanese bodies are counted, and over 200 caves have been sealed. The 25th Division then advances toward the Villa Verde Trail and Santa Fe. In the 33rd Division zone, about 100 Japanese attack an outpost of Company A, 123rd Regiment near Dingalan Bay. Three Yanks man a machine gun at the point of attack; one man, Pvt. John R. McKinney is slugged on the head by the saber sword of an enemy troop igniting his Irish temper. He plucks a rifle and bashes the Jap, then shoots another Jap who is charging toward him. Meanwhile, enemy fire wounds a member of the detachment and is withdrawn to safety by the third man. The Japanese capture the machine gun, but that does not deter McKinney who singlehandedly attacks ten of the enemy, shooting seven of them at point-blank range before using his rifle butt to exterminate the remaining three. The machine gun is rendered useless during the skirmish, but the indomitable Soldier faces more of the attackers with his rifle. The Japs pour mortars into his position, but still he refuses to relent, choosing to change positions and get more ammunition to mow down the Japanese horde. Reinforcements arrive, but McKinney had the situation well in hand. The Japs had him surrounded, they couldn't get away. Thirty-eight deceased Japanese surround the decimated machine gun and two others are strewn about a silent mortar. Pvt. McKinney, later Sergeant, receives the Medal of Honor for his extraordinary heroism. **XI Corps** sector, contingents of the 43rd Division drive to Hill 815, as it closes on Ipo. **Southern Philippines** In the **U.S. Eighth Army** area, **X Corps** sector on Mindanao, Guerrillas capture Cagayan, and RCT 108, 40th Division nears Del Monte Airfield. Meanwhile, Artillery and Planes support the 2nd Battalion, 19th Regiment, 24th Division as it drives to seize Hill 550; however, progress is slow. In other activity, U.S. positions at Davao, Mindanao, continue to come under fire from concealed enemy positions on Samal; Company K, 19th Regiment is attempting to locate and destroy them. On Negros, the 160th Regiment, 40th Division prepares to renew attack against Dolan Hill; however, there is no pause in pressure as Aircraft and Artillery pound it for the next several days. (Pacific-New Guinea) Wewak is captured by the Australian 6th Division. (Pacific-Okinawa) In the U.S. Tenth Army area, a full measured assault is launched against the inner Shuri defenses following a one-half hour Artillery bombardment. The III Amphibious Corps and the XXIV Corps drive on the right and left respectively. The 6th Marine Division pushes contingents to the northern fringes of Amike, while another contingent seizes a hill lying less than one thousand yards from Asa. Meanwhile, the 7th Marines, 1st Marine Division comes under a wall of fire from Wana Ridge; however, it advances and seizes positions on Dakeshi Ridge. Also, The Japs holding the Shuri Heights pour fire upon the 1st Marines, keeping it pinned. In conjunction, the 2nd Battalion, 5th Marines wipe out the remaining resistance in the Awacha Pocket. In the XXIV Corps sector, Hill 130 (Chocolate Drop Hill) and Flattop Hill, the latter controlling Dick Hill mass, are assaulted by the 306th Regiment, 77th Division, but fierce fire from entrenched positions hinders progress. Meanwhile, the 96th Division's 382nd Regiment attempts to drive to Dick hill mass; however, Japanese resistance halts progress. The 383rd Regiment, 96th Division seizes a hold on some hills at the northwest approaches of Conical Hill. At Zebra Hill, five enemy pillboxes bar advance by Company B, 382nd Regiment, 96th Division. Captain Seymour W. Terry sprints through incessant barrages of fire, grabs a demolition charge on the run and blows the first strongpoint to oblivion. Without pause he dashes from pillbox to pillbox, eliminating the defenders with rifle fire and grenades destroying all four nests, killing twenty enemy troops in the process. Soon after, more enemy fire stalls the Company advance, but Terry, latches on to six charges and attacks, devastating the enemy entrenchments; ten of the twenty enemy killed are attributed to Terry. Company B roars forward until new enemy positions open up and halt progress of two of his Platoons, prompting Terry to race 100 yards to join the support Platoon and lead an assault. The reinforcements thrust forward, scattering the Japanese; quick pursuit annihilates the enemy. Captain Terry then directs his men to reform to guard against a counterattack, however, an enemy mortar rings in and kills him; he receives the Medal of Honor posthumously. Offshore Kamikazes damage the Aircraft Carrier *Bunker Hill* (CV-17) and the Destroyer *Evans* (DD-552). Also, the Destroyer *Hugh W. Hadley* (DD-774) is damaged by a Piloted bomb. (Pacific-China) The Japanese advancing against Chihchiang are intercepted by the ALPHA forces of General Ho, which outflank the enemy and drive them back. The Chinese 18th and 100th Armies neutralize the enemy advance near Paima Shan, the former recapturing Shanmen. Kaosha village, along the Paoching-Chihchiang road, is put ablaze by the Japanese. Meanwhile, the Chinese 94th Army forces the Japanese to swerve its south flank as it closes to within eight miles of Tungkow. (Atlantic-Western Europe) General Patton, in Paris at General Hughes quarters becomes irritated with the situation in Europe. He states: "WELL, BY GOD EVERETT (General Hughes) I'M GOING TO SAY IT NOW. IT'S ALL A GOD-DAMNED SHAME. THAT'S WHAT IT IS." Someone inquires: "ALL WHAT'S A GOD-DAMN SHAME?" Patton: "I'LL TELL YOU. DAY AFTER DAY, SOME POOR BLOODY CZECH, OR

AUSTRIAN, OR HUNGARIAN, EVEN GERMAN OFFICERS COME INTO MY HEADQUARTERS...WITH TEARS IN THEIR EYES THEY SAY, IN THE NAME OF GOD, GENERAL, COME WITH YOUR ARMY THE REST OF THE WAY INTO OUR COUNTRY...GIVE US THIS LAST CHANCE TO LIVE BEFORE IT'S TOO LATE, BEFORE THE RUSSIANS MAKE US SLAVES FOREVER." Patton further states: "EVERY DAMNED ONE OF THEM HAS OFFERED TO FIGHT UNDER MY FLAG AND BRING THEIR MEN WITH THEM...BY GOD, I WOULD LIKE TO TAKE THEM UP ON IT. I'LL FEEL LIKE A TRAITOR IF I DON'T." The room becomes consumed with mild tension, but the General continues without interruption. He admits that it might mean war with the Russians, but adds: "THE THIRD ARMY, ALONE, WITH VERY LITTLE OTHER HELP AND WITH DAMNED FEW CASUALTIES, COULD LICK WHAT'S LEFT OF THE RUSSIANS IN SIX WEEKS." (Atlantic-Eastern Europe) The Red Army concludes its clearing operations in Austria and Czechoslovakia; it initiates mop-up operations. The Soviets meet U.S. troops near Linz, Austria, and also at Chemnitz (Saxony) and Pilsen, Czechoslovakia.

May 12th 1945 — (Pacific-Philippines) Luzon In the **U.S. Sixth Army** area, **XI Corps** sector the 43rd Division closes on Ipo, driving the Japanese from Hill 815 as they near the objective. **Southern Philippines** In the **U.S. Eighth Army** area, **X Corps** sector on Mindanao, Del Monte Airfield is seized by contingents of RCT 108 (40th Division). Meanwhile the 124th Regiment eliminates an enemy strongpoint in the Colgan Woods. In the 24th Division sector, the 21st Regiment, supplemented by Artillery and Air strikes, drives northwest along the Talomo River. Also, the 19th Regiment makes inroads at Hill 550. On Samal, Planes and Artillery lambaste suspected positions of the guns which are still striking U.S. lines on Davao, Mindanao. **(Pacific-Ryukyu Islands-Okinawa) U.S. Tenth Army** area, **III Corps** sector, Company G, 3rd Battalion, 22nd Marines drives to Sugar Loaf Hill, southeast of Amike; however, fierce resistance compels it to pull back. Meanwhile, the 7th Marines, 1st Marine Division gains most of Dakeshi Ridge. In the **XXIV Corps** sector, the 305th Regiment, 77th Division encounters fierce opposition as it grinds forward along Route 5 toward Shuri. In conjunction, the 306th Regiment halts its attack against Hill 130 to pivot and reinforce the 305th Regiment. Meanwhile, heavy resistance hinders the 382nd Regiment, 96th Division which is driving against the Dick Hill mass; elements, however, seize a hill about 600 yards south of Zebra. Also, the 2nd Battalion, 382nd Regiment seizes a fragile hold on a northern spur of Conical Hill, prompting Division to place more heat on the hill by accelerating its frontal assault. **Offshore** Suicide Planes attack the Fleet; the Battleship *New Mexico* (BB-40) sustains damage; the Heavy Cruiser *Wichita* (CA- 45) is accidentally damaged by U.S. Naval gunfire. In other activity, U.S. Destroyers support the landing of Army troops which land on Tori Shima, Ryukyu Islands. **(Pacific-SEAC)** Plans for Operation ZIPPER (Invasion of Malaya) continue. British General O.L. Roberts is to command Force W (amphibious), 15th Corps, 224th Group (air), and the newly established 34 Corps; all are assembled in India. Additional assault forces which will be committed to the operation will be drawn from those in the Rangoon area (Burma), from where the invasion forces will embark. **(Atlantic-Western Europe)** The Russians are at it again. Russian troops enter Prague, but the Communists refuse to permit the entry of U.S. troops for three weeks.

May 13th 1945 — (Pacific-Philippines) Luzon In the **U.S. Sixth Army** area, **I Corps** sector, enemy resistance in Balete

Pass has been vanquished, opening entry to the Cagayan Valley. In the **XI Corps** sector, contingents of the 43rd Division advance to within sight of Ipo Dam. **Southern Philippines** In the **U.S. Eighth Army** area on Mindanao, Japanese resistance emerges fiercely at Mangima Canyon, halting RCT 108 as it drives down the Sayre Highway; the advance is stalled for several days and becomes further hampered by a shortage of supplies. In conjunction, the 31st Division drives north along the Sayre Highway to hook up with RCT 108; meanwhile, on the Talomo Trail contingents of the 167th Regiment drive to the Pulangi River. Also, the 21st Regiment, 24th Division continues its tedious drive along the Talomo Trail, while the 3rd Battalion, 34th Regiment bolts from Guma to supplement the 21st Regiment for its operation to gain the Talomo River Valley. In conjunction the 2nd Battalion, 19th Regiment continues advancing against heavy resistance at Hill 550. On Samal, the Japanese repel an attack by Company K, 19th Regiment. **(Pacific-Okinawa)** In the **U.S. Tenth Army** area, **III Amphibious Corps** sector, Japanese resistance remains resolute as the 6th Marine Division grinds through storms of fire, taking heavy casualties, but maintaining its advance. The 1st Marines, 1st Marine Division attack Hill 55; however, the Japanese holding the strongpoint, which is part of the south wall of the Wana Draw, repulse the attempt. Meanwhile, the 7th Marines extinguish final resistance on Dakeshi Ridge and drive toward Wana Ridge, incurring high casualties as it plows through the village of Dakeshi. In the **XXIV Corps** sector, the 306th Regiment, 77th Division reinitiates its assaults against Chocolate Drop Hill, again encountering vicious resistance, while also driving against Flattop where resistance is rock-hard. Meanwhile, the 382nd Regiment drives against two enemy hills of Dick Hill mass, securing one of them. In conjunction, the 383rd Regiment cracks the eastern tip of the Shuri line, reaching the northeast summit of Conical Hill; the Japanese mount heavy counterattacks, but the Regiment holds firmly. Also, contingents of the 383rd Regiment drive to the slopes of nearby Charlie Hill; however, the Japanese retain the summit. **Offshore** Kamikazes damage the Destroyer *Bache* (DD-470) and the Destroyer Escort *Bright* (DE-747). **(Pacific-Burma)** In the ALFSEA area, the West African 82nd Division concludes its offensive operations in the Arakan sector, reaching Gwa without opposition. **(Pacific-China)** General Wedemeyer informs General Stratemeyer that it is not feasible to accept the Tenth Air Force in China at present; it will be delayed for several months. Meanwhile, General Chennault's Fourteenth Air Force is ordered to move to Chungking to assume control of Air Forces based in China. **(Pacific-Japan)** Planes attached to Admiral M.A. Mitscher's Fast Carrier Task Force attack the Airfields on Kyushu and repeat the strikes on the following day. The Carrier *Enterprise* (CV-6) is damaged by a Kamikaze off Honshu; also, the Light Carrier *Bataan* (CVL-29) is damaged by accidental U.S. Naval gunfire. **(Atlantic-Eastern Europe)** The Soviet Armed Forces conclude offensive operations, eliminating final German resistance in Czechoslovakia.

May 14th 1945 — (Pacific-Philippines) Luzon In the **U.S. Sixth Army** area, **I Corps** sector, the 27th Regiment, 25th Division opens a northward attack, driving from Balete Pass; the advance stalls on the 16th when it encounters heavy resistance at the eastern tip of the Bolong Plateau. In the **XI Corps** the 43rd Division shoves advance contingents to the Ipo Dam, which is strongly defended. Preparations for a massive attack on the 17th are laid. **Southern Philippines** In the **U.S. Eighth Army** area, **X Corps** sector on Mindanao, lack of supplies halts the drive of RCT 108; however, the 31st Division's 155th

German Field Marshal Schroeder with troops of the U.S. 42nd Division.

Hermann Goerring.

Lt. General Alexander Patch, Field Marshal Gerd von Rundstedt and his son, Lt. Hans von Runstedt.

717

Regiment advances north along the Sayre Highway; the 167th Regiment, encounters opposition as it drives over nasty terrain along the Talomo Trail toward the barrio of Sanipon. Meanwhile, contingents of the 34th Regiment, 24th Division advance northward from Bancal toward Mintal, in conjunction with the 21st Infantry which is grinding through the Talomo River Valley. Tenacious resistance rises quickly, halting the 21st Regiment, and in addition, the Japanese also hold Hill 550 against attack by units of the 19th Regiment. **(Pacific-Okinawa)** In the **U.S. Tenth Army** area, **III Amphibious Corps** sector, the 22nd Marines, 6th Marine Division launch an attack, but the effort gains only a slight hold on Sugar Loaf Hill. In the 2nd Battalion zone, Major Henry A. Courtney (Executive Officer) concludes that the enemy will counterattack, details his thoughts to his Marines and moves out to seize the forward slope of Sugar Loaf, followed by every man in the unit. The charge gushes forward and reaches the reverse slope. After acquiring additional ammo and 26 reinforcements, Courtney moves to the point and pounds enemy caves with grenades as he races to the crest, only to discover a huge concentration of enemy troops preparing to attack. Major Courtney charges the Japanese as a one-man wrecking crew, terminating a large number of the foe and chasing the balance into caves. Determined to hold the new ground he orders his unit to dig in for the duration, but as he scampers from man to man, he is struck and killed by an enemy mortar; Major Courtney receives the Medal of Honor posthumously. Meanwhile, heavy fighting develops at Wana Ridge, as the 1st Marines, 1st Marine Division drives to dislodge the enemy and establish contact with the 7th Marines; the Japanese hold, and the 5th Marines move in and relieve the 1st Marines. During the murderous fighting, Japanese fire halts Company C, 1st Battalion's left flank. Corporal Louis J. Hauge, Jr., orders his Squad to afford him cover fire while he attacks the obstacles. Machine gun fire rips into his body as he advances, but he gets off a grenade which exterminates the nest. Enemy fire becomes heavier, but Hauge grinds forward, ignoring his pain until he lobs another grenade which wipes out the second machine gun nest, before a new barrage of enemy fire kills him. Corporal Hauge receives the Medal of Honor posthumously. In the **XXIV Corps** sector, Chocolate Drop and Flattop continue to withstand the pressure of attacks by the 306th Regiment, 77th Division; the Regiment is now greatly reduced in strength. In the 96th Division zone, the 383rd Regiment stretches its control to include Charlie Ridge, while also driving to the summit of King Hill to the south. **(Pacific-China)** The U.S. 5332nd (Provisional) Brigade (Mars Force), which began moving from Burma to China on March 14th, concludes the operation. **(Atlantic-Austria)** The Provincial Republic of Austria under Dr. Karl Renner is formed and is composed of a coalition of Communist, Socialist and Peoples' Parties. Subsequently, General Mark Clark receives word that he is to command U.S. forces in Austria and that he is to become American High Commissioner. Austria is to be occupied by four Powers; British (McCreery); French (Lt. Gen. E.M. Bethouart; Russians (Marshal Ivan S. Koniev). General Mark Clark arrives at Salzburg on August 12th; he chooses the Schloss Klessheim (guest house-Hitler's Eagle's Nest) for his Headquarters.

May 15th 1945 — (Pacific-Philippines) Luzon In the **U.S. Sixth Army** area, **XI Corps** sector, preparations continue for a renewed assault against Ipo Dam and Woodpecker Ridge. **Southern Philippines** In the **U.S. Eighth Army** area, **X Corps** sector on Mindanao, RCT 108 receives Air and Artillery sup-

port and commences another assault against the entrenched Japanese in the Mangima Canyon sector of Sayre Highway. Meanwhile, about 100 Japanese attack the rear lines of the 31st Division, which is protected by contingents of the 124th Regiment; 72 Japs die and the rest scatter. Meanwhile, in the 24th Division zone, the 19th Regiment drives north from Davao to establish contact with Filipino Guerrillas who are advancing southwest, while units of the 21st and 34th Regiments continue the drive through the Talomo River Valley. Also, Company G, 34th Regiment relieves the 2nd Battalion, 19th Regiment at Hill 550. In conjunction, Company F repulses a night counterattack. On Samal, the Japanese have abandoned the island. On Negros, Dolan in Negros Occidental is secured by the 160th Regiment; one small pocket remains on the northern spur. **(Pacific-Ryukyu Islands-Okinawa)** In the **U.S. Tenth Army** area, **III Corps** sector, a small force of Marines composing one Officer and 19 men of the 22nd Marines, 6th Marine Division comes under a storm of fire which compels them to evacuate untenable positions on the Summit of Sugar Loaf. Meanwhile, the 7th Marines, 1st Marine Division halts its advance against Wana Ridge; Air strikes and Artillery lambastes the hill, but the Japanese give no signs of relenting. In the **XXIV Corps** sector, fighting on the right flank of the 77th Division has been grueling; however, the staggered 305th Regiment, fighting at 25 percent of its strength, continues its grinding advance. At one point, Company B is completely stalled by impenetrable fire. Sergeant Joseph E. Muller, snaps from his prone position and darts through the blazing gunfire to rout a group of enemy troops. As they attempt to flee, his Squad eliminates them. Muller spots another unit about to open up with a machine gun. He drives into their midst, wiping the four troops out at point-blank range. Prior to dawn on the 16th, a Japanese counterattack strikes to recapture the lost ground. Singlehandedly, Muller snaps to his feet and drives the attackers off. Sgt. Muller, attempts to rejoin a contingent in a foxhole, but a seemingly dead Jap is playing possum, and as Muller leans into the position a grenade is tossed among the men. Muller instinctively blankets the grenade with his body to save the other Soldiers, succumbing instantly; he receives the Medal of Honor posthumously. On the left flank, the 306th Regiment is passed through by the 307th Regiment, which pounds its way toward Chocolate Drop and also against Flattop, reaching positions close to the summit of the latter. The Japanese mount a night counterattack, but the 307th thwarts it. Meanwhile, violent contests continue on Dick Hill mass and Conical Hill, as the 382nd and 383rd Regiments respectively gnaw forward. **(Pacific-Burma)** In the **British Fourteenth Army** area, the Indian 26th Division, moving north along Rangoon-Prome Road, encounters the Indian 20th Division, which is advancing south. **(Pacific-India)** Base Section No. 1 (Karachi) is deactivated; other sections of S.O.S. receive new designations. **(Atlantic-Germany)** Commander United States Ports and Bases Germany (Rear Admiral A. G. Robinson) is established at Bremen.

May 16th 1945 — (Pacific) The U.S.S. *Snook* (SS-279) is officially reported as lost. The *Snook* had been in contact on the 8th of April with the *Tigrone*; however, there is no communication afterward. The Vessel had been lost somewhere in the Western Pacific. Japanese war records show no sinking of a Submarine in the *Snook's* zone. **(Pacific-Philippines)** Luzon In the **U.S. Sixth Army** area, **I Corps** sector, the 3rd Battalion, 27th Regiment, 25th Division hits heavy opposition at the eastern tip of Bolong Plateau, hindering progress. In the **XI Corps** sector, subsequent to an Artillery bombardment, the

152nd Regiment attacks Woodpecker Ridge, seizing fragile positions on the military crest and forward slopes of Twin Peaks. In the **XIV Corps** sector, General MacNider declares the Bicols secure. On Mindanao, in the **U.S. Eighth Army** area, **X Corps** sector, the 31st Division's 3rd Battalion, 167th Regiment hits fierce resistance along the Talomo Trail about one mile north of Sanipon; the Regiment is unable to advance for over one week. Meanwhile, heavy skirmishing continues as contingents of the 24th Division gnaw forward through the Talomo River. **(Pacific-Okinawa)** In the **U.S. Tenth Army** area, **III Amphibious Corps** sector, the 6th Marine Division attacks entrenched enemy positions on Sugar Loaf, committing two Regiments; the resistance is the fiercest that the Division experiences during the entire Okinawa operation. Violent combat ensues for two days; however, the 29th Marines finally vanquishes the defenders on the 18th. In the 1st Marine Division zone, the 5th Marines, commit M7s and Tank-Infantry teams to counterbalance the enemy holding Wana Draw. In conjunction, the 1st Battalion, 7th Marines drives up Wana Ridge, but unrelenting fire forces a pull-back. In the **XXIV Corps** sector, heavy fighting ensues north of Shuri, as the 7th Division's 305th and 307th Regiments on the right and left respectively press forward; the 307th pounds against Chocolate Drop and Flattop, but the Japanese give no ground. Meanwhile, the 383rd Regiment, 96th Division fortifies positions on the Regiment's left flank and is joined by Tanks which advance to the outskirts of Yonabaru. An effort is made to dislodge the Japanese from Love Hill west of Conical Hill; however, the Japanese repulse the attack. Offshore, the Escort Carrier *Shipley Bay* (CVE-85) is damaged by collision. **(Pacific-China)** General Eaker, A.A.F. Headquarters, informs General Wedemeyer that General Chennault is to be replaced. **(Pacific-Malay Archipelago)** The Submarine U.S.S. *Hawkbill* (SS-366) sinks the Japanese Minelayer *Hatsutaka* off Malaya. The *Hatsutaka* has recently reported sinking an American Submarine on the 3rd of May. The U.S.S. *Lagarto* is in the area of the attack and is subsequently reported as lost on the 24th of May. **(Pacific-Japan)** The Fast Carrier Task Force (Admiral Mitscher) commences a two-day attack against Airfields in southern Kyushu.

May 17th 1945 — (Pacific-Marshalls) Planes attached to Rear Admiral C.A.F. Sprague's Naval Force attack Taroa Island, Maloelap Atoll. **(Pacific-Philippines)** Luzon In the **U.S. Sixth Army** area, **XI Corps** sector, Ipo Dam is seized intact by the 43rd Division; the Japanese retain control of Osboy Ridge. **Mindanao** In the **U.S. Eighth Army** area, **X Corps** sector, Japanese pour heavy fire upon the advancing 2nd Battalion, 21st Regiment, 24th Division near Tugbok; the Yanks call in Artillery and Aircraft which eases the pressure. **(Pacific-Okinawa)** In the **U.S. Tenth Army** area, General Buckner assumes responsibility for all troops ashore, as the Amphibious phase of the operation concludes. He also accepts responsibility for the fortification of all captured enemy positions. Meanwhile, Vice Admiral Richmond K. Turner is relieved by Vice Admiral Harry W. Hill, who assumes the position of Commander TF 51 and will control Naval forces and Air defenses; he is subordinate to General Buckner. Massive Naval Surface Vessel fire, Air strikes, and Artillery precede an assault by the 29th Marines against Sugar Loaf, but still, the Japanese resist feverishly. The 1st and 3rd Battalions hammer from the west end of Crescent Hill while the 2nd Battalion shoots from the east, reaching the summit of Sugar Loaf, until all ammunition is exhausted, forcing a withdrawal. In the 1st Marine Division zone, Hill 55 is assaulted by the 2nd Battalion, 5th Marines, which seizes some ground on the west slope. The

beleaguered 1st Battalion, 7th Marines, pounding against the entrenched Japanese on Wana Ridge, is relieved by the 3rd Battalion; still, the enemy continues to hold against the efforts of the 3rd Battalion. In the **XXIV Corps** sector, Company E, 307th Regiment, 77th Division springs a night surprise attack and lunges to Ishimmi Ridge, outside of Ishimmi village; the positions become untenable as the Japanese interdict, preventing reinforcements from giving assistance. Meanwhile, the 3rd Battalion gains ground around Chocolate Drop and repulses a subsequent counterattack, then pushes to the crest of Flattop; however, severe fire drives it back. Offshore, the Destroyer U.S.S. *Douglas H. Fox* (DD-779) is damaged by a Kamikaze.

Colonel William O. Darby (Darby's Rangers) — Colonel Darby is mortally wounded April 30th 1945 near Lake Garda in Italy when an artillery shell (presumed to be enemy) explodes overhead as he is talking with several other U.S. Officers, including Lt. Colonel Robert L. Cook, Commanding Officer, 10th Mountain Division.

May 18th 1945 — (Pacific-Philippines) Luzon In the **U.S. Eighth Army** area, **X Corps** sector, progress remains tedious on Woodpecker Ridge as the 152nd Regiment renews its assault. Meanwhile, the 43rd Division clears the Metropolitan Road between Bigti and Ipo. On Mindanao, the 1st Battalion, 19th Regiment, 24th Division drives close to the lower end of the Sasa Airfield. Meanwhile RCT 108 destroys the remaining resistance in Mangima Canyon and speeds southward along the Sayre Highway with great ease. Also, the 2nd Battalion, 21st Regiment seizes Tugbok, then pauses for several days, concentrating on regrouping and Patrols. **(Pacific-Okinawa)** In the **U.S. Tenth Army** area, **III Amphibious Corps** sector, the 29th Marines, 6th Marine Division seize Sugar Loaf and also gain part of Horseshoe, a dominating feature slightly southwest of Sugar Loaf. In the 1st Marine Division zone, brutal fighting continues to ensue at Wana Ridge and Wana Draw where 5th Marine M-7s and Tanks continue to pound enemy positions in conjunction with Engineers who are clearing the lower slopes of the ridge. The 3rd Battalion, 7th Marines continues driving against the Japanese on Wana Ridge, but the effort is in vain. In the **XXIV Corps** sector, heavy fighting continues at Flattop and at Chocolate Drop as the 77th Division makes some progress at the latter. In the 96th Division zone, the 382nd Regiment holding Dick Hill comes under a wall of fire from Flattop; nevertheless, its retains the ground, then attacks to secure the reverse slope. Meanwhile, the 3rd Battalion, 381st Regiment commences an assault to seize Sugar Hill. Offshore, the Destroyer U.S.S. *Longshaw* (DD-559) is damaged by enemy coastal gunfire and subsequently sunk by U.S. Naval forces. Also, the High-speed Transport *Sims* (APD-50) is damaged by a Kamikaze, and the LST 808 is damaged by an Aircraft torpedo.

Brigadier General Robert T. Frederick (photo taken while he is a Colonel), Commanding Officer of the 1st Special Service Force, composed of Canadians and American troops. The unit, operating as a Brigade achieves tremendous results and its extensive training nets a bonus as one captured German General dubs them the "Devil's Brigade."

May 19th 1945 — (Pacific-Philippines) Luzon The Motor Gunboat PGM-1 is damaged by an explosion. In the **U.S. Sixth Army** area, **I Corps** the 25th Division begins to sweep the area west of Highway 5 to Imugan and also to clear north and west of Santa Fe; the mop-up operation is reinforced by the 126th Regiment, 32nd Division. In the **XI Corps** sector the 43rd Division terminates remaining enemy resistance in the Ipo area and begins mop-up operations. Meanwhile, at Wood-

pecker Ridge, the 152nd Regiment concentrates on small probing Patrols for the next few days. **Mindanao:** In the **U.S. Eighth Army** area, **X Corps** sector, elements of the 19th Regiment, 24th Division advance to Panacan. **(Pacific-Okinawa)** In the **U.S. Tenth Army** area, **III Amphibious Corps** sector, the 4th Marines relieve the 29th Marines, whose strength is weakened from incessant battle. At Wana Draw, heavy fighting continues as the 5th Marines, 1st Marine Division maintain pressure against the enemy, and at Wana Ridge, the 3rd Battalion, 7th Marines continues pounding against the enemy entrenchments; the 1st Marines move up and relieve the 7th Marines. In the **XXIV Corps** sector, the Japanese mount continued pressure throughout the day to annihilate the exhausted Company E, 307th Regiment, 77th Division, but the effort fails; upon darkness reinforcements rush in and relieve the battered unit. Meanwhile, the Japs on Flattop and Dick Hill are barraged with heavy and direct fire. In conjunction, the 382nd Regiment, 96th Division doggedly stretches its control over the reverse slope of Dick Hill. Meanwhile, contingents of the 383rd Regiment drive to the west end of King Hill, but the Japs drive them off. Also, the 381st Regiment's 3rd Battalion continues closing toward Sugar Hill. **Offshore** the Destroyer Escort *Vammen* (DE-644) is damaged by collision, and the Oiler *Cimarron* (AO-22) incurs damage by grounding. **(Pacific-Kurile Islands)** Destroyers commence a bombardment of Japanese facilities on Paramushiro.

May 20th 1945 — (Pacific-Philippines) Mindanao In the **U.S. Eighth Army** area, **X Corps** sector, the 155th Regiment, 31st Division drills north along Sayre Highway, deploying at positions which dominate the objective: Malaybalay. The Japanese meet the threat with devastating Artillery fire; however, the Regiment withstands the threat and on the following day, effortlessly seizes Malaybalay, a Japanese supply base. The 2nd Battalion, 19th Regiment, 24th Division, advancing along the coastal road, drives to Tibungko; meanwhile, the 3rd Battalion departs Samal Island and returns to Davao. At Hill 550, grueling fighting continues as the 2nd Battalion, 34th Regiment, 24th Division gains ground and then retains it, thwarting several night counterattacks. **Okinawa** In the **U.S. Tenth Army** area, **III Amphibious Corps** sector, the 4th Marines, 6th Marine Division continues to fight vigorously around Sugar Loaf, maintaining attacks to secure the balance of Crescent and Horseshoe features; at the latter, some progress is made and upon nightfall, the Japanese mount night attacks; however, they are thrown back, losing over 200 troops. Meanwhile, Hill 55 is taken by the 5th Marines, 1st Marine Division, which then drives into Wana Draw. Meanwhile, the 1st Marines launch an assault and overrun the summit of Wana Ridge. In the **XXIV Corps** sector, the remaining resistance on Chocolate Drop is eliminated by the 307th Regiment, 77th Division; it also seizes Flattop. Meanwhile, the 382nd Regiment, 96th Division continues grinding on the reverse slope of Dick Hill, seizing more ground. Also, the 3rd Battalion, 381st Regiment moves cautiously as it advances toward Sugar Hill. **Offshore** Again, Japanese Aircraft including Suicide Planes strike the Fleet; a Horizontal Bomber damages the High-speed Transport *Tattnall* (APD-19); the Destroyer *Thatcher* (DD-514), the Destroyer Escort *John C. Butler* (DE-339), the High-speed Transport *Chase* (APD-54), the High-speed Transport *Register* (APD-92), and the LST 808 are damaged by Kamikazes. **(Pacific-China)** The Japanese forces remaining in China are preparing to pull out to defend Japan; they pull out of Ho-chih (Kwangsi Province), moving to Kweiyang.

May 21st 1945 — (Pacific-Philippines) Luzon In the **U.S.**

Sixth Army area, **XI Corps** sector, Patrols of the 149th Regiment, 38th Division discover that the Wawa Dam is defended by Japanese troops. Meanwhile, the Japanese fortifying Woodpecker Ridge receive more pressure as the 3rd Battalion, 152nd Regiment, supported by fire from the 1st and 2nd Battalions, reinitiates its attack, advancing toward Regimental Objective Hill. **Mindanao** In the **U.S. Eighth Army** area, **X Corps** sector, the 155th Regiment, 31st Division seizes Malaybalay. The 1st Battalion, 19th Regiment, 24th Division drives north, advancing to Bunawan. Attempts are made to sever Japanese escape routes in the 34th Regiment zone east of the Talomo River; the 1st and 3rd Battalions cross the river east of Mintal to achieve the objective. Meanwhile, Artillery blasts Hill 550; Company G, 34th Regiment seizes the remainder of it as the Japanese have abandoned their fortifications. **(Pacific-Ryukyus Islands-Okinawa)** Marine Torpedo-Bomber Squadron 131 lands on Ie Shima and will support the ongoing operations of Marine Aircraft Group 22. Also, Marine Fighter Squadrons 113, 314, and 422 (Marine Aircraft Group 22) land on Ie Shima to bolster Marine operations on Okinawa. On **Okinawa** In the **U.S. Tenth Army** area, **III Amphibious Corps** sector, contingents of the 6th Marine Division continue driving toward the Asato River on the western flank of the Corps, hammering against the Sugar Loaf defense system. Some progress is made as Marines move methodically through tunnels within Horseshoe, but the Japanese on Crescent still hold firmly. In the 1st Marine Division sector, furious combat continues to ensue as the advance toward Shuri Ridge bangs forward against fervent opposition raised by the defenders at this final feature protecting Shuri Castle. Progress is tedious on the reverse slope of Wana Ridge; however, Japanese counterattacks to regain the frontal slopes are futile as the Yanks repulse them. In the **XXIV Corps** sector, the 77th Division's Company A, 307th Regiment drives to the base of Jane Hill, southwest of Flattop; the progress places it near untenable positions and it is isolated, coming under fierce fire until the 30th. Meanwhile, the 382nd Regiment, 96th Division advances to Oboe Hill about one thousand yards from Shuri; here also, intense enemy fire halts progress for several days. However, the 3rd Battalion, 381st Regiment seizes Sugar Hill; the prize empties the eastern slopes of Conical Hill and forces the enemy's right flank to turn abruptly. In conjunction, the 184th Regiment, 7th Division jumps off at 19:00, advancing south along the coast road to invest Shuri. The situation for the Japanese is deteriorating rapidly; a decision is reached to withdraw from Shuri. **(Pacific-India-Burma)** S.O.S. merges with Theater Headquarters, IBT G-4, replacing S.O.S. Commander. S.O.S. is inactivated. **(Pacific-Java Sea)** The Submarine U.S.S. *Chub* (SS-329) sinks the Japanese Minesweeper No. 34.

May 22nd 1945 — (Pacific-Philippines) Luzon In the **U.S. Sixth Army** area, **I Corps** sector, contingents of the 27th Regiment, 25th Division reach positions about 2,000 yards southeast of Santa Fe. In the **XI Corps** sector, the Japanese holding Wawa Dam repel an assault by one Platoon of Company A, 149th Regiment, 38th Division. Meanwhile, Flamethrower Tanks are brought to bear upon obstinate resistance near the confluence of the Mariquina and Bosoboso Rivers, bolstering the efforts of the 152nd Regiment, 38th Division, which takes its final objectives. **Mindanao)** RCT 108 closes on Impalutao. Meanwhile, the 155th Regiment, 31st Division finds Kalasungay abandoned by the enemy; it continues driving up the Sayre Highway, where it intercepts an enemy force and thrashes it, inflicting severe casualties. The 2nd Battalion,

19th Regiment, 24th Division launches an assault, driving through the 1st Battalion lines, reaching Tambongan. Meanwhile contingents of the 21st Regiment seize terrain east of the Talomo, but the existing gap between it and the 3rd Battalion, 34th Regiment is not closed. **(Pacific-Okinawa)** In the **U.S. Tenth Army** area, sporadic rains have been hitting the area for several days; the intensity increases and heavy storms move in, lasting until early June, restricting operations. In the **III Amphibious Corps** area, the 4th Marines, 6th Marine Division advance to the northern bank of the Asato River, but supporting Armor is bogged down in the mud; Patrols probe across the river after dark. In the **XXIV Corps** sector, the 383rd Regiment, 96th Division is heavily engaged at Love Hill, west of Conical peak, and fights viciously for several days to eliminate the objective. Meanwhile, the 184th Regiment, 7th Division advances through decimated Yonabaru without incident, driving to the nearby hills. **(Pacific-India-Burma)** General Stratemeyer's Headquarters is surprised to learn that C-54s are heading for India, considering previous information concerning redeployment priorities. **(Pacific-Japan)** Carrier-based Aircraft sink the Japanese Submarine Chasers Nos. 37 and 58 and the Transport No. 173, off southeastern Japan.

May 23rd 1945 — (Pacific-Philippines) Luzon In the **U.S. Sixth Army** area, **I Corps** sector, Tanks are committed to help reduce fierce resistance; however, the determined Japanese continue to halt progress despite the added power. In the **XI Corps** sector, contingents of the 152nd Regiment, 38th Division, drive north closing on the Mariquina River. **Southern Philippines** In the **U.S. Eighth Army** area, **X Corps** sector on Mindanao, the Sayre Highway is open for traffic for its entire length as the 155th Regiment encounters RCT 108 south of Impalutao. Meanwhile, the 2nd Battalion, 19th Regiment, 24th Division encounters Filipino Guerrillas as it arrives at Ising. In conjunction, the 1st Battalion, 21st Regiment pounces upon the enemy north of Talomo bridge, seizing a road junction; Artillery fire is called in and it lambastes the ground between it and the positions of the 34th Regiment. On Negros, the remaining opposition on Dolan Hill in Negros Occidental is wiped out as the 160th Regiment, 40th Division overruns a pocket on the northern spur. Staff Sergeant John C. Sjogren spearheads the drive, knocking out the opposition as the team advances. Sjogren, pauses the advance to run a gauntlet of fire to aid his next in command, darting between grenades, dynamite explosions and small arms fire. Soon after, he bursts forward, killing eight enemy Soldiers in their holes, creeps to a pillbox and flings several grenades through the slit holes; several are tossed back out, wounding him, but he wins the duel with a faster string of tosses. Despite his wounds he leads another assault and eliminates several more strongpoints; at one of the nests, he pulls a light machine gun from the nest before destroying the defenders with grenades; the dauntless Sergeant Sjogren singlehandedly kills 43 Japanese and decimates nine pillboxes; he receives the Medal of Honor. Meanwhile, the 185th Regiment moves prudently, heading south toward the sole remaining Japanese strongpoint in Negros Occidental: Hill 4055. **Okinawa** In the **U.S. Tenth Army** area, **III Amphibious Corps** sector, the 6th Marine Division, deployed near the Asato River, launches a drive toward the Kokuba on the west flank of the Corps. In conjunction, resistance south of the Asato River encounters only sporadic resistance, prompting the 4th Marines to implement smoke screens and push two Battalions across the river. In the **XXIV Corps** sector, the 184th Regiment, 7th Division secures a starting line to permit the 32nd Regiment to drive west and surround Shuri and also guard the rear positions of the 32nd Regiment. Meanwhile, although its Armor is still paralyzed by mud, the 32nd Regiment begins trekking west to positions about one mile southwest of Yonabaru.

May 24th 1945 — (United States) The Submarine U.S.S. *Lagarto* (SS-371) is reported lost. Last point of contact with the Submarine (on its second War Patrol) had been with the Submarine *Baya* on the 3rd of May as discussions by radio occurred to set up strategy for an attack on a Convoy. A Japanese Minelayer, the *Hatsutaka*, reported an attack on a Submarine off Malay in the Gulf of Siam where the *Lagarto* had been on Patrol. **(Pacific-Philippines) Mindanao** In the **U.S. Eighth Army** area, **X Corps** sector, good progress continues to be made. The 2nd Battalion, 19th Regiment, 24th Division and Filipino Guerrillas meet near the Tagum River. Meanwhile, the 21st and 34th Regiments are sweeping the Talomo River Valley while attempting to make contact with each other. **(Pacific-Ryukyu Islands- Okinawa)** In the **U.S. Tenth Army** area, the Japanese launch Air assaults against U.S. Airfields on Ie Shima and Okinawa including dropping Airborne troops on Yontan Field; the Japanese Paratroopers cause damage and destroy some Planes on the ground; however, the Paratroopers are annihilated. Also, the Kamikazes again strike the U.S. Fleet; the Destroyer *Guest* (DD-472), the Destroyer Escort *O'Neill* (DE-663), and the Destroyer Escort *William C. Cole* (DE-641), incur damage. Also, the High-speed Minesweeper *Butler* (DMS-29), Minesweeper *Spectacle* (AM-305), High-speed Transport *Barry* (APD-29), and the High-speed Transport *Sims* (APD-50) suffer damage. In addition, the Escort Carrier *Suwannee* (CVE-27) sustains damage by explosion. The Destroyer *Heywood L. Edwards* (DD-663) is accidentally damaged by U.S. Naval gunfire. In the **III Amphibious Corps** sector, contingents of the 6th Marine Division enter northwest Naha without incident. In the **XXIV Corps** sector, Oboe Hill becomes a seat of fire as the Japanese attack positions of contingents of the 382nd Infantry, 96th Division; two Companies of the 1st Battalion are compelled to withdraw from the hill; however, the Japs retreat, leaving 150 dead. In other activity, Patrols of the 5th Marines, 1st Marine Division probe to Asato, and the 32nd Regiment, 7th Division dispatches Patrols to assess Japanese strength at fortifications which pass the Yonabaru Valley southeast of Shuri. However, after dark, the Japanese mount fierce counterattacks against the Regiment and penetrate the lines.

May 25th 1945 — (United States) The Joint Chiefs of Staff approve plans for Operation OLYMPIC, the invasion of Japan's home islands, scheduled to commence on November 1st, 1945. **(Pacific-Philippines) Mindanao** In the **U.S. Eighth Army** area, **X Corps** sector, the 19th Regiment, 24th Division regroups and makes preparations to attack west, against Mandog. Meanwhile, the 21st and 34th Regiments maintain their sweeping operations in the Talomo River Valley, the latter discovering one obstinate hill now abandoned by the enemy. **Okinawa** The Pilots attached to the Escort Carrier *Gilbert Islands* fly their first combat Air Patrol and close air support missions. In the **U.S. Tenth Army** area, **III Amphibious Corps** sector, the 4th Marines, 6th Marine Division seizes Machishi, then stretch control further, gaining much of the ridge line west of the town. **Offshore** Kamikaze attack the Fleet, sinking the High-speed Transport *Bates* (APD-47) and damaging the Destroyer *Stormes* (DD-547) and the High-speed Transport *Roper* (APD-20). Also, the Destroyer *Cowell* is damaged after being accidentally struck by U.S. Naval gunfire. **(Pacific-**

China) Major General Henry S. Aurand becomes head of S.O.S.

May 26th 1945 — (Pacific-Philippines) Luzon In the **U.S. Sixth Army** area, a Patrol of the 27th Regiment, 25th Division pushes into Santa Fe, subsequent to the clearing of Balete Pass. In the **XI Corps** sector, the 151st Regiment, 38th Division secures a supply route, opening the Wawa Road, while a Platoon of Company A nears Wawa. Heavy fires force the unit to pull-back; the Platoon does seize the barrio on a subsequent attempt. **Okinawa** In the **U.S. Tenth Army** area, the Japanese begin to withdraw their combat forces from Shuri; however, U.S. Artillery and Naval Surface Vessels combine with Aircraft to bombard the escape routes. In the **XXIV Corps** sector, some elements of the 7th Division advance effortlessly along the east coast toward the next ridge line; the 32nd Regiment sustains severe casualties as it futilely attacks Dick Hill lying east of Chan. **Offshore** The Fleet sustains more damage from the dwindling but deadly Kamikaze forces. The Destroyer *Anthony* (DD-515), Destroyer *Braine* (DD-630), the High-speed Minesweeper *Forrest* (DMS-24), the Submarine Chaser PC-1603, and the Survey Ship *Dutton* (AGS-8) suffer damage. **(Pacific-Japan)** The Japanese Submarine Chaser No. 172 is sunk by a U.S. mine near Honshu.

The 5th Marines plant the Colors on a rocky ridge on Shuri.

May 27th 1945 — (Pacific) Admiral Halsey, Third Fleet Commander, assumes control of all Naval Forces attached to Fifth Fleet at midnight 27-28, and the number "5" used in Task Force designations is changed to "3." Vice Admiral John S. McCain succeeds Vice Admiral Marc A. Mitscher as Commander TF 58: it becomes TF 38. **(Pacific-Philippines) Luzon**

In the **U.S. Sixth Army** area, **I Corps** sector, the brutal contest for the Villa Verde Trail concludes successfully as the remainder of the 1st Battalion, 27th Regiment, 25th Division enters Santa Fe; the entrance also terminates the Corps mountain fighting. In the **XI Corps** sector, the Japanese seemingly are abandoning Wawa Dam; the 149th Regiment, 38th Division drives to within 50 yards of the dam; however, intense enemy fire forces it to withdraw to more tenable positions west of the dam; it secures the objective on the following day. **Mindanao** In the **U.S. Eighth Army** area, **X Corps** sector, the 167th Regiment, 31st Division and Filipino Guerrillas establish a bridgehead across the Pulangi River outside Sanipon. Meanwhile, at the Talomo Trail, the Japanese continue resisting fiercely, hindering progress of the 167th Regiment for the next month. In other activity, the battle to secure the Talomo River Valley terminates successfully with the link up of the 21st and 34th Regiments, 24th Division. **(Pacific-Ryukyu Islands-Okinawa)** The Fleet again comes under attack by Japanese Planes off Okinawa. The Destroyer *Drexler* (DD-741) is sunk by a Kamikaze. The Destroyer Escort *Gilligan* (DE-508) is damaged by an Aircraft torpedo, and the Minesweeper *Gayety* (AM-239) is struck by a Horizontal Bomber. The High-speed Minesweeper *Southard* (DMS-10), High-speed Transports *Loy* (APD-56) and *Rednour* (APD-102), the Attack Transport *Sandoval*, and the Ocean Tug *Pakana* (ATF-108) are damaged by Naval gunfire, and the Degaussing Vessel YDG-10 is struck by a Kamikaze.

May 28th 1945 — (Pacific-Philippines) Luzon In the **U.S. Sixth Army** area, **I Corps** sector, Imugan is seized by the 128th Regiment, 32nd Division which also establishes contact with the 126th Regiment which has been attached to the 25th Division. Corps is directed to take advantage of the breakthrough. In conjunction, Filipino Guerrillas revert to Corps control and are directed to seize Cervantes. In the **XI Corps** sector, Wawa Dam falls to the 1st Battalion, 149th Regiment, 38th Division without a fight, gaining Corps its last primary objective east of Manila. On **Negros**, in the **U.S. Eighth Army** area in Negros Oriental, mop-up operations begin subsequent to the 164th Regiment eliminating the final resistance on the ridge positions. **(Pacific-Ryukyu Islands-Okinawa)** The Japanese strike the Fleet off Okinawa, losing over one hundred Planes; the Destroyer *Shubrick* (DD-639) is sunk. The U.S. has finally drained the strength of the Japanese Air strikes as this is the final heavy attack to be launched against Okinawa. In the **U.S. Tenth Army** area, the torrential rains begin to subside, permitting accelerated activity. In the **III Amphibious Corps** sector, contingents of the 22nd Marines, 6th Marine Division move from Naha to the Kokuba estuary effortlessly, but violent enemy reaction emerges as the Marines begin Reconnaissance of Ona-Yama Island in Naha Harbor. Meanwhile, Engineers get bridging across the canal in Naha upon nightfall. Also, the 29th Marines, subsequent to relieving the 4th Marines, drives toward Kokuba. Beehive Hill on the lower portion of Shuri Ridge is seized by the 5th Marines, 1st Marine Division. In the **XXIV Corps** sector, the Japanese mount fierce resistance on Hill 69, north of Karadera village, halting progress of the 184th Regiment, 7th Division. **(Pacific-Burma)** British General Stopford, Commander of the British Twelfth Army, establishes Headquarters in Rangoon and assumes control of all Allied troops in Burma. The 33rd Corps, which is disbanded, had been Stopford's former command. Meanwhile, Headquarters, British Fourteenth Army withdraws to Burma and will assume command of the 15th and 34th Corps for Operation ZIPPER. **(Pacific-Japan)** The Japanese Coast Defense Vessel No. 29 sinks after striking a U.S. mine off Kyushu.

May 29th 1945 — (United States) President Truman authorizes the strength of the Marine Corps to be increased to 503,000. **(Pacific-Philippines) Luzon** In the **U.S. Sixth Army** area, **I Corps** sector, Cagayan Valley becomes the next Corps objective; Aritao is to be seized by the 37th Division, while Filipino Guerrillas take Cervantes, opening the way for both to bolt into the valley. **Mindanao** In the **U.S. Eighth Army** area, **X Corps** sector, Planes support the 19th Regiment, 24th Division as it drivers west toward Mandog, the final Japanese defensive stronghold at the northern fringe of Davao Plain. **(Pacific-Ryukyu Islands-Okinawa)** In the **U.S. Tenth Army** area, **III Amphibious Corps** sector, the 22nd Marines cross into Naha to meet the Japanese who have chosen to stand and fight there. Meanwhile, the 1st Battalion, 5th Marines secures the summit of Shuri Ridge and also takes Shuri Castle, the infrastructure of the Shuri bulwark; the castle in the 77th Division zone has been abandoned. In the **XXIV Corps** sector, the 77th Division closes on Shuri, its 184th Regiment encountering strong opposition at a hill near Karadera. **Offshore** the High-speed Transport *Tatum* (APD-81) is damaged by a Suicide Plane. Also, the Motor Minesweeper YMS-81 and the LST 844 are damaged by grounding. Admiral Halsey is becoming alarmed as Kamikazes are continuing to strike the Fleet and reports are funneling in through Admiral Spruance that Air Corps Planes, based in the Philippines, are destroying sugar mills, railroad trains and other equipment, but not Planes.

May 30th 1945 — (Pacific-Philippine Sea) Planes (VC-13), attached to the Escort Carrier *Anzio* (CVE-57), sink the Japanese Submarine I-12. **(Pacific-Okinawa)** The Japanese 32nd Army has successfully evacuated the majority of its force from the Shuri lines, evading the clutches of the III Amphibious Corps and the XXIV Corps drives, reaching the southernmost part of the island: Kiyamu Peninsula. In the **U.S. Tenth Army** area, **III Amphibious Corps** sector, contingents of the 22nd Marines, 6th Marine Division secure Hill 27 on the southeastern portion of Naha. In the **XXIV Corps** sector, the 77th Division overpowers rear-guard action as it advances, seizing Dorothy, Jane, and Tom Hills, the former containing an extensive cave system. Meanwhile, contingents of the 77th Division pass into the III Amphibious Corps sector and assault 100 Meter Hill, while the 96th Division races forward seizing Hen Hill, which has hindered the Yanks for nine days in addition to capturing the reverse slope of Oboe and Love Hill. Also, the 32nd Regiment, 7th Division secures Ella, June, and Oak Hills southwest of Yonawa; Patrols (184th Regiment) push onto Chinen Peninsula without opposition. **(Pacific)** British Admiral Mountbatten confers in Delhi with the Commanders of Operations Mailfist (Singapore) and Zipper (Malaya). Mountbatten decides that the operations will initially be controlled by 34th Corps and that Headquarters of Fourteenth Army and 15th Corps will be transferred in about D plus 50.

May 31st 1945 — (Pacific-Philippines) Luzon In the **U.S. Sixth Army** area, **I Corps** sector, the 129th Regiment, 37th Division advances along Highway 5, driving from Santa Fe into the Cagayan Valley; contingents gain 6,000 yards north of Santa Fe. Meanwhile, Task Force Connolly, commanded by Major Robert V. Connolly, 143rd Regiment is established and attached to the Guerrillas, U.S. Army Forces in the Philippines (Northern Luzon); the TF, composed of 800 men, drives northeast toward Aparri where it is to be bolstered by a Battalion of Guerrillas. In the **U.S. Eighth Army** area at Occidental Negros, the Japanese abandon positions on Hill 4055, scattering into the mountains, ending organized resistance. On Mindanao, in the **X Corps** sector, the 3rd Battalion, 19th Regiment, 24th Division is bolstered by the 2nd Battalion as it closes on Mandog. **(Pacific-Okinawa)** In the **U.S. Tenth Army** area, **III Amphibious Corps** sector, contingents of the 6th Marine Division encounter tenacious rear-guard action near Hill 46, north of the Kokuba, and call in Tanks and Artillery to ease pressure. Meanwhile, the 1st Marine Division reverts to reserve and will initiate mop-up operations at Shuri. In the **XXIV Corps** sector, the 77th Division overruns 100 Meter Hill, then bursts into the ruins of Shuri, from which the Japanese have made a disciplined evacuation; the city is jointly occupied by the 77th and forces of the 1st Marine Division. The Japanese establish new defensive positions along the Kokuba Gara and at Taukasan. Meanwhile, the 96th Division destroys the remaining resistance in its zone and establishes contact with the 1st Marine Division. During the fighting at Hen Hill, P.F.C. Clarence B. Craft, Company G, 382nd Regiment and five other Soldiers move out in advance of Company G, encountering impenetrable fire. Craft, stands up in conspicuous fashion and advances firing as he moves, knocking out enemy troops with uncanny accuracy as he pushes against a force which has been repulsing attacks of Battalion strength for the past twelve days. Challenging death, he reaches the crest of the hill and defiantly stands as a silhouette from where he casualty lobs grenades which splatter many of the enemy. The extraordinary assault relieves pressure on his Platoon which advances to join him. Forming a human chain, grenades are rapidly passed to the indomitable Private who expends a total of two cases of grenades on the enemy's main trench line, while simultaneously directing the tossing of grenades by his buddies on a lower part of the slopes, slashing more destruction upon the defenders. Private Craft opens up with his rifle, exterminating more of the enemy at point-blank range. As the Japs flee, Craft pursues, driving them down the hill. As he descends, he spots a machine gun pumping shells into the Yanks who are consuming the entire hill. Craft, charges and annihilates the position defenders with rifle fire and another grenade. Many of the fleeing enemy troops seek refuge in a cave, but Craft continues his rampage and slings a large explosive charge into their midst, creating an instant crypt. P.F.C. Craft's actions are greatly responsible for the total collapse of the Naha-Shuri-Yonaburu line; he receives the Medal of Honor. Also, the 7th Division continues its advance, overrunning several hills near Chan, concluding its present mission. **(Pacific-S.E.A.C.)** The interests of the Americans and the British concerning Asia now vary widely, and the U.S. Air Force contingents including the Tenth Air Force and all components of the E.A.C. are withdrawn from S.E.A.C., reverting to operational control of A.A.F. (Army Air Forces). E.A.C. is deactivated. The India-Burma Theater is to support China as a diversion for the Pacific operations. Meanwhile, S.E.A.C. is to concentrate on seizing Singapore and Malaya.

June 1st 1945 — (Pacific-Philippines) Luzon In the **U.S. Sixth Army** area, Japanese resistance is sputtering in the **I Corps** sector, permitting the 129th Regiment, 37th Division to speed northward. **Mindanao** In the **U.S. Eighth Army** area, **X Corps** sector, the 19th Regiment, 24th Division continues driving west toward Mandog and will reach positions from which to launch an attack on the 6th. **(Pacific-Palau Islands)** The U.S. Navy establishes a Naval Air Facility at Peleliu Island. **(Pacific-Ryukyu Islands-Okinawa)** The Japanese have successfully evaded entrapment at Shuri; however, the U.S. Tenth Army is in pursuit, canceling its plans to surround the

enemy. In the **III Amphibious Corps** sector, the 1st and 6th Marine Divisions mount a coordinated assault which gains the high ground dominating the east-west road of the Kokuba Gawa Valley, where the Japanese have drawn new defensive positions. Hill 46 is captured by contingents of the 6th Marine Division; the Division then seizes Shichina and the northern branch of the Kokuba. Subsequent to nightfall, the 6th Marine Division gets Reconnaissance Patrols across the Kokuba estuary to gather intelligence for an imminent assault to secure Oroku Peninsula. In the **XXIV Corps** sector, the 96th Division begins reducing remaining resistance near Chan. In conjunction, the 77th Division protects the rear of the 96th Division and simultaneously mops up in the Shuri area. Meanwhile, the 7th Division exterminates rear-guard opposition at two hills on the Corps' east flank. **Offshore** The Submarine Chaser PC-1599 sustains damage by grounding. **(Pacific-SEAC)** Admiral Mountbatten informs the Chiefs of Staff that he has decided that the invasion of Malaya (ZIPPER) is to be postponed until September instead of the initial schedule calling for an invasion in August. **(Atlantic-Germany)** The U.S. Navy establishes an Advanced Naval Base at Bremerhaven, Germany.

June 2nd 1945 — (Pacific-Philippines) In the **U.S. Sixth Army** area, **XI Corps** sector, the 43rd Division concludes its mop-up operations in Ipo area. **(Pacific-Okinawa)** In the **U.S. Tenth Army** area, the 7th Marines, 1st Marine Division, deploys along the Kokuba, freeing the 6th Marine Division for an amphibious invasion to seize Oroku Peninsula. In the **XXIV Corps** sector, the remaining resistance in Chan is exterminated by the 96th Division; it then drives south rapidly, pursuing the retreating Japanese. Also, the 7th Division is in hot pursuit of the enemy. **(Pacific-Japan)** Vice Admiral J. S. McCain's Fast Carrier Task Force commences a two-day attack against Airfields in southern Kyushu; a sudden typhoon strikes the area on the 4th.

June 3rd 1945 — (United States) The Carrier *Lake Champlain* (CV-39) is commissioned at Norfolk, Virginia. **(Pacific-Philippines)** Luzon In the **U.S. Sixth Army** area, **I Corps** sector, the 129th Regiment, 37th Division continues its advance, reaching positions 9,500 yards north of Santa Fe. **(Pacific-Ryukyu Islands-Okinawa)** A Naval Task Force, commanded by Rear Admiral L. F. Reifsnider, lands Marines on Iheya Shima: the 8th Marines, 2nd Marine Division, clears Iheya and Aguni Shima, west of Okinawa, completing the operation by the 9th of June. The Marines then take added precautions, including installing air warning and Fighter direction facilities to bolster the perimeter of Okinawa. In the **U.S. Tenth Army** area on Okinawa, **XXIV Corps** sector, an existing gap which has developed between the Corps is filled as the 7th and 96th Divisions drive south, elements of the former reaching the southeast coast near Hyakuna, sealing off the Chinen Peninsula. **Offshore**, Japanese Suicide Planes attack the Fleet; the Cargo Ship *Allegan* (AK-225) is damaged.

June 4th 1945 — (Pacific-Java Sea) Army Planes sink the Japanese Submarine Chaser No. 112. **(Pacific-Philippines)** Luzon Patrols of the 129th Regiment, 37th Division reach Aritao. **(Pacific-Okinawa)** In the **U.S. Tenth Army** area, Yaeju-Dake Escarpment (III Amphibious Corps sector) is placed in the XXIV Corps sector as the III Amphibious Corps boundary shifts west. In the **III Amphibious Corps** sector, the 1st Marine Division, operating in a smaller zone, receives responsibility for isolating the Oroku Peninsula; it drives forward seizing Itoman, secures the Kunishi and Mezado Ridges, advancing to Ara Sake, the southernmost point on the island.

Meanwhile, the 4th Marines, 6th Marine Division spearhead an amphibious invasion against Oroku Peninsula on the southwest section of the island; the 29th Marines follow close behind. The Marines drive inland, gaining about half of Naha Airfield. The 6th Reconnaissance Company overruns Ono-Yama in the Naha Inlet, wiping out the few defenders. In the **XXIV Corps** sector, Corps rumbles over crumbling resistance as it races forward, pivoting southwest in accordance with new boundary changes, reaching line Iwa-Minatoga. Meanwhile, in the coastal sector, the 7th Division fords the Minatoga River. **Offshore**, the U.S. Patrol Vessel YP-41 is accidentally damaged during operations.

June 5th 1945 — (Pacific-Philippines) Luzon In the **U.S. Sixth Army** area, **I Corps** sector, Aritao is seized by the 1st Battalion, 129th Regiment, 37th Division during the morning hours. In the **U.S. Eighth Army** area, **X Corps** sector, Japanese assault positions of Company D, 124th Regiment. A grenade detonates in a machine gun position, wounding 2 men and knocking the gun out of action. Other defenders attempt to fix the weapon, but another grenade lands in their midst. Corporal Harry R. Harr smothers it with his body to save the lives of the other four troops; he receives the Medal of Honor posthumously. **(Pacific-Ryukyu Islands-Okinawa)** A violent typhoon slashes across Okinawa, inflicting enormous damage to the Fleet, greatly overshadowing the Suicide Pilots that brave the severe weather to fly to their deaths; Kamikazes damage the Battleship *Mississippi* (BB-41) and the Heavy Cruiser *Louisville* (CA-28). However, the killer storm dwarfs the Jap attack, damaging; 4 Battleships, the *Indiana* (BB-58), *Massachusetts* (BB-59), *Alabama* (BB-60), and the *Missouri* (BB-63); 2 Aircraft Carriers, the *Hornet* (CV-12) and the *Bennington* (CV-20); 2 Light Carriers, *Belleau Wood* (CVL-24) and the *San Jacinto* (CVL-30); 4 Escort Carriers, the *Windham Bay* (CVE92), *Salamaua* (CVE-96), *Bougainville* (CVE-100), and the *Attu* (CVE-102); 3 Heavy Cruisers, *Baltimore* (CA-68), *Quincy* (CA-71), and the *Pittsburg* (CA-72-has its bow torn off); 4 Light Cruisers, *Detroit* (CL-8), *San Juan* (CL-54), *Duluth* (CL-87), and the *Atlanta* (CL-104); 11 Destroyers, *Schroeder* (DD-501), *John Rodgers* (DD-574), *McKee* (DD-575), *Dashiel* (DD-659), *Stockham* (DD-683), *De Haven* (DD-727), *Maddox* (DD-731), *Blue* (DD-744), *Brush* (DD-745), *Taussig* (DD-746), and *Samuel N. Moore* (DD-747); 3 Destroyer Escorts, *Donaldson* (DE-44), *Conklin* (DE-439), and the *Hilbert* (DE-742); 2 Oilers, the *Lackawanna* (AO-40) and the *Millicoma* (AO-73); one ammunition Ship, the *Shasta* (AE-6). Also, the Destroyer *Dyson* (DD-572) is damaged by collision. Miraculously, only six men are lost and no Warships are sunk. In the **U.S. Tenth Army** area, on Okinawa, operations continue; still the supporting Armor is immobilized. In the **III Amphibious Corp** sector, the fighting is ruthless as the 6th Marine Division engages defenders which offer iron resistance at Naha Airfield; despite the grueling opposition, the Marines gnaw forward, seizing most of the Airfield. Meanwhile, the 7th Marines, 1st Marine Division advances southwest to isolate the peninsula while the 1st Marines roars south to positions near Iwa. In the **XXIV Corps** sector, the Japanese have dug in for a last stand at their final defense line on southern Okinawa, deploying from the west to east coast at Guishichan. The Japanese control three dominating features to forestall defeat: Yuza-Dake Escarpment, Yaeju-Dake Escarpment, and Hill 95. **(Pacific-Dutch East Indies)** The Minesweeper *Scuffle* (AM-298) sustains damage after grounding in Brunei Bay. **(Pacific-Volcano Islands)** The Gasoline Tanker *Sheepscot* (AOG-24) incurs damage by grounding near Iwo Jima. **(Atlantic-Europe)** The European Advisory Commission meets to establish German occupation zones.

June 6th 1945 — (Pacific-Philippines) Luzon In the **U.S. Sixth Army** area, **I Corps** sector, the Japanese are now thoroughly disorganized as they retreat toward the Magat River, pursued by Corps forces; rear-guards attempt to delay the Yanks at the River, but they are wiped out. In the 33rd Division zone near Tabio, an inexperienced contingent of Guerrillas fails to commence a scheduled attack. Sergeant Howard E. Woodford volunteers to move out and question the group. Soon after, he discovers the Guerrilla unit is stalled by intense fire. Woodford assumes command of the inexperienced unit and leads an attack, continuously exposing himself to heavy fire to achieve the objective. Woodford's leadership carries the Guerrillas to victory, but despite receiving permission to return to his unit, Woodford decides to remain and support the Guerrillas. Prior to dawn on the 7th, the Japanese launch a fanatical Banzai attack, penetrating the Guerrilla positions. Sergeant Woodford becomes wounded, but remains at his radio calling in mortars, but the Japs knock out the radio. He resorts to his rifle and begins prompting the Guerrillas to hold on. The fearless Sergeant encounters two dead Guerrillas, halts in place and guards the gap. Reinforcements arrive at Woodford's foxhole, discovering Woodford's body; in and around his position are 37 dead Japs; Woodford receives the Medal of Honor posthumously. In the **XIV Corps** sector, the 5th Cavalry reverts to the 1st Cavalry Division. **(Pacific-Okinawa)** In the **U.S. Tenth Army** area, **III Amphibious Corps** sector on the Oroku Peninsula, the remaining resistance on Naha Airfield is crushed by the 6th Marine Division. As it drives beyond ferocious enemy fire originating on Hill 57 in the center of the peninsula, progress is stalled. Meanwhile, the 22nd Marines, 1st Marine Division come out of reserve to form a line of protection for Division's right flank and stretch across the base of the peninsula. The 7th Marines push to positions near Dakiton. In the **XXIV Corps** sector, the enemy's new line of defense is reached. The 1st Battalion, 381st Regiment, 96th Division attacks against Yaeju-Dake Escarpment, encountering incessant fire which compels it to pull back. In conjunction, the 7th Division moves slowly on the right; however, its left flank also receives withering fire which halts progress near a hill which extends northeast from Hill 95. **Offshore** Japanese Suicide Planes continue their futile assaults against the Fleet, inflicting more damage; the Escort Carrier *Natoma Bay* (CVE-62), and the Light Minelayers *Harry F. Bauer* (DM-26) and *J. William Ditter* (DM-31). Also, additional Vessels are damaged by collisions: the Destroyer *Beale* (DD-471), Minesweeper *Requisite* (AM-109), Minesweeper *Spear* (AM-322), and the Gasoline Tanker *Yahara* (AOG-37). **Pacific-Japan** The Japanese Submarine Chaser No. 195 sinks after striking a U.S. mine off Honshu.

June 7th 1945 — (Pacific-Philippines) In Leyte Gulf, an Army P38, buzzing Admiral Sherman's Fleet, misjudges the distance and crashes on the deck of the U.S.S. *Randolf*, killing eleven men and injuring 14 others. The crash also destroys several Planes and inflicts damage to the deck, prompting an incensed Sherman to notify Headquarters that he has authorized the shooting down of the next Plane that buzzes his Warships. However, Admiral Nimitz tempers Sherman's rage. **Luzon** In the **U.S. Sixth Army** area, the 3rd Battalion, 129th Regiment chases the retreating Japanese toward Sonano. **Mindanao** In the **U.S. Eighth Army** area, the 19th Regiment, 24th Division commences its attack against Mandog. **(Pacific-Okinawa)** In the **U.S. Tenth Army** area, **III Amphibious Corps** sector, the 6th Marine Division presses forward, despite the Japanese death wish which prompts feverish resistance; Hill 57 is taken and the defenders decimated with the assistance of Tanks. Pvt. Robert M. McTureous, Jr. 3rd Battalion, 29th Marines spots a contingent of stretcher bearers coming under heavy fire as they attempt to evacuate wounded. He stuffs his uniform with grenades and attacks, charging from cave to cave, incinerating the enemy holes, while simultaneously diverting enemy fire to permit the wounded to reach safe positions. McTureous returns to his lines, scoops up more grenades and reinitiates his thunderous trek, pounding more enemy positions. Many enemy positions are permanently silenced, however, McTureous becomes severely wounded. He crawls about 200 yards to an aid station before calling for help; he receives the Medal of Honor for his extraordinary heroism, while making the ultimate sacrifice for his country. Meanwhile, the 1st Marine Division continues pushing south, the 7th Marines advancing to the coast north of Itoman, isolating the fanatical Japs on the Oroku Peninsula. In the **XXIV Corps** sector, troops await arrival of supplies to bolster a general assault; however, scaled down actions occur as units probe enemy defenses. In conjunction, Artillery and Planes shellac enemy positions. **Offshore** The Destroyer *Anthony* is damaged by a Kamikaze, and the LST 540 incurs damage by grounding. **(Pacific-China)** Brigadier General Robert B. McClure directs the Chinese Armies of the Kwangsi Command (unaffiliated with Alpha Force) to attack to secure the Hong Kong-Canton region (Operation CARBONADO). The Chinese are to assault and seize Fort Bayard. The three Alpha Armies, New First, 8th and 54th, are to participate in the operation. In Hunan Province, the Chinese have successfully pushed the Japanese back from Chihchiang to Paoching where they launched their offensive during May.

June 8th 1945 — (Pacific) Marine Fighter Squadron 112 and 123, the remaining Marine Fighter Squadrons in Task Force 38, depart for Leyte, subsequent to being detached from the force. **(Pacific-Philippines) Luzon** In the **U.S. Sixth Army** area, **I Corps** sector, the main body of the 37th Division closes on Bagabag. The 145th Regiment plows through Solano, reaching the road junction of Highways 4 and 5. **Okinawa** In the **U.S. Tenth Army** area, **III Amphibious Corps** sector, fierce fighting continues as the 6th Marine Division squeezes the noose tighter on the remaining Japanese on the Oroku Peninsula at Tomigusuki. In the 22nd Marines zone, Hospital Apprentice First Class Fred F. Lester attempts to rescue a wounded Marine. He braves incessant fire, reaching the Marine, but while lugging him back to safety, enemy fire rips into him, causing a mortal wound. Lester, realizing his wounds are fatal and unable to give further aid, directs two other members of his Squad as they work on the wounded man. Two additional wounded Marines require aid; Lester refuses treatment and continues to direct the men as they save the lives of the others. Lester succumbs moments later, giving his last breath to save the others; he receives the Medal of Honor posthumously. while directing the Marines. The 1st Marine Division moves south, closing on the enemy's final defense line. In the **XXIV Corps** sector, the Port of Minatoga is opened, greatly aiding the supply system. Heavy resistance continues as the 7th Division gnaws forward on Corps' east flank toward fortified Hill 95, which refuses to relent. **(Pacific-Japan)** Planes attached to Vice Admiral J. S. McCain attack Kanoya Airfield at Kyushi. **(Pacific-Malay Archipelago)** A Cruiser Destroyer Force under Rear Admiral R.S. Berkey commences a two-day bombardment of Japanese positions in the Brunei Bay area, Borneo. Australian troops will invade the area on the 10th. The Minesweeper *Salute* becomes damaged by a mine.

June 9th 1945 — (Pacific-Philippines) Luzon In the **U.S. Sixth Army** area, the I Corps tightens the ratchet, severing escape routes from the Cagayan Valley. Bagabag is seized by the 1st Battalion, 145th Regiment, 37th Division, which also grabs control of a road northwest of the barrio; meanwhile the 3rd Battalion seizes a crossing over the Magat River at Highway 5, east of Bagabag. **Mindanao** In the **U.S. Eighth Army** area, **X Corps** sector, the final Japanese defensive strongpoint on the island is cracked by the 19th Regiment, 24th Division, which overruns Mandog. **(Pacific-Ryukyu Islands-Okinawa)** A Naval Task Force commanded by Rear Admiral L.F. Reifsnider lands a contingent of Marines on Aguni Shima. Also, another Naval Force, commanded by Rear Admiral A.W. Radford, launches Planes in concert with a Surface bombardment of Okino Daito Jima. In the **U.S. Tenth Army** area on Okinawa, **III Amphibious Corps** sector, the 6th Marine Division's 4th and 22nd Marines hook up, unquestionably ending all hopes of the Japanese escaping from the Oroku Peninsula. Meanwhile, the 1st Marine Division advances nearer to the final Japanese strongpoint on Okinawa: Kunishi Ridge. The **XXIV Corps** finalizes preparations for the full-scale attack against the Japanese defense line. Meanwhile, the 7th Division gets contingents to the southeastern tip of Yaeju-Dake Escarpment; the 1st Battalion, 32nd Regiment pounds against Hill 95. Although the effort is in vain, some Japanese positions are eliminated. **Offshore** The Destroyer Escort *Gendreau* (DE-639) is damaged by a coastal defense gun. **(Pacific-Korea)** The Submarine U.S.S. *Sea Owl* (SS-405) sinks the Japanese Coast Defense Vessel No. 41.

June 10th 1945 — (Pacific) (Pacific-Philippines) Luzon In the **U.S. Sixth Army** area, **I Corps** sector, the Japanese continue to resist along Highway 5; entrenched guns in the high ground which dominates Orioung Pass pour fire into the advancing 145th Regiment, hindering progress, nearly pinning it down. Meanwhile, contingents of the 148th Regiment advance to Lantap. **(Pacific-Dutch East Indies)** Rear Admiral R. S. Berkey's Naval Task Force (Seventh Fleet) bombards Brunei Bay area to umbrella the landing of Australians (9th Division) on Borneo and on Labuan and Muara Islands. The landing is also supported by U.S. and Australian Aircraft. **(Pacific-Ryukyu Islands-Okinawa)** A Naval Task Group commanded by Rear Admiral J.J. Clark bombs and bombards a Japanese Airfield and other positions on Minami Daito, Ryukyu Islands. In the **U.S. Tenth Army** area, **III Amphibious Corps** sector on Okinawa, the tenacious Japanese on the Oroku Peninsula are cornered in an area about 1,000 by 2,000 yards by the 6th Marine Division, which is poised for the kill. The Japanese spring a night counterattack expecting to break out; about 200 die swiftly. Meanwhile, the 1st Marine Division buzzes forward. The 7th Marines seize a ridge north of Tera and bolt beyond roaring through Itoman. However, the 1st Marines encounter fierce resistance and sustain heavy casualties while seizing an obstinate hill outside of Yuza. In the **XXIV Corps** sector, improved weather conditions permit sufficient Tank support as a full scale attack is launched against the Japanese line of defense. The 96th Division gets elements toward Yuza and also pushes units to a ledge in a saddle between two peaks: Yaeju-Dake and Yuza-Dake. Meanwhile, the 17th Regiment, 7th Division pumps Artillery fire into its sector of Yaeju-Dake, while the 32nd Regiment, bolstered by Naval Surface Vessel gunfire and Flame-throwing Tanks, attack toward Hill 95, seizing a strategic ridge near the coast line. **Offshore** The Destroyer *William D. Porter* (DD-579) is sunk by a Kamikaze. During rescue attempts, Lt. Richard Miles McCool, Jr., Commanding Officer of the LSC(L)(3)122 receives the Medal of Honor for heroism as his Vessel rescues all survivors of the sinking Destroyer. Kamikazes attack Mc-Cool's Vessel, scoring damage, but the stunned crew responds rapidly, killing one of the attacking Planes and damaging the other; the latter crashes into the conning tower. Lt. McCool receives the Medal of Honor. (Pacific-Burma) In the British Twelfth Army area, Detachment 101-Guerrillas, led by O.S.S. agents, seizes Loilem; the Detachment (101) has been sweeping the Shan Hills since the culmination of the N.C.A.C. campaign. (Pacific-China) Chinese troops overrun I-shan as they pursue the Japanese toward Liuchow; however, the Japanese retake it on the following day. (Pacific-Sea of Japan) The Submarine U.S.S. *Skate* sinks the Japanese Submarine I-22.

June 11th 1945 — (Pacific-Philippines) Luzon In the **U.S. Sixth Army** area, **I Corps** sector, heavy combat ensues at Orioung Pass; nevertheless, the 37th Division's 145th Regiment makes headway. Meanwhile, the 1st Battalion, 148th Regiment nullifies the Japanese strongpoint at Lantap and pushes Patrols into Santa Lucia; some units advance beyond, driving north to the Lamut River. **(Pacific-Okinawa)** Major General Louis E. Woods U.S.M.C. assumes command of the Tactical Air Force and the 2nd Marine Air Wing. In the **U.S. Tenth Army** area, **III Amphibious Corps** sector, the Japanese on Oroku Peninsula are further corralled, as the 6th Marine Division forces them into a square encompassing 1,000 yards. In the 1st Marine Division zone, the 7th Marines encounters impenetrable fire as it attempts to cross open terrain and reach Kunishi Ridge, halting progress; however, at 03:00 on the 12th, it breaks through and seizes positions on the western end of the ridge. Meanwhile, Hill 69, west of Ozato, is seized by the 1st Marines. In the **XXIV Corps** sector, the 383rd Regiment, 96th Division drives to Yuza. The Japanese open up with a wall of fire, forcing a withdrawal; on the following day, it drives into town, again advancing until heavy fire halts it just short of Yuza Peak. Meanwhile, the 1st Battalion, 381st Regiment gets all contingents upon the ledge of the saddle between Yaeju-Dake and Yuza-Dake Peaks and subsequently thwarts a strong early morning counterattack; the Regiment concentrates heavy fire upon Yaeju-Dake counterbalancing the enemy position while the 17th Regiment, 7th Division makes preparations for an attack to seize it. In conjunction, the 32nd Regiment, 7th Division seizes Hill 95 on the east flank ensuring the demise of the Japanese entire Yaeju-Dake Escarpment, which falls on the 17th. **Offshore** The Light Cruiser *Vicksburg* (CL-86) is damaged by collision, and the Landing Ship dock *Lindenwald* (LSD-6) is accidentally damaged by U.S. Naval gunfire. **(Pacific-Kurile Islands)** Cruisers and Destroyers commanded by Rear Admiral J. H. Brown lambaste Japanese facilities on Matsuwa. **(Pacific-Sea of Japan)** U.S. Naval Land-based Aircraft sink the Japanese Submarine Chaser No. 237.

June 12th 1945 — (Pacific-Philippines) Luzon In the **U.S. Sixth Army** area, **I Corps** sector, the responsibility for Highway 5, south of Bayombong, goes to the U.S. 6th Division, freeing up the 37th Division to pinpoint its strength on the Cagayan Valley. The 145th Regiment, 37th Division, maintaining its pace, advances through Orioung Pass and seizes the town of Orioung and bolts beyond, seizing ground north of Balite. **(Pacific-Okinawa)** In the **U.S. Tenth Army** area, **III Amphibious Corps** sector, the Japanese resistance on Oroku Peninsula is faltering and doomed as the 6th Marine Division converges on the dwarfed perimeter of the remaining Japanese; some resist futilely, while the others choose quickly between suicide or surrender, many taking the latter course of action rather than be captured. Meanwhile, in the 1st Marine Division zone, the 1st Marines mop up Hill 69 and push Patrols toward Kunishi Ridge. In the **XXIV Corps** sector, the 381st Regiment, 96th Division, drives to the base of Yaeju-Dake Escarpment, seizing positions on the steepest slope. An early morning attack by the 17th Infantry, 7th Division stuns the Japs and permits the Regiment to seize its assigned part of the escarpment. Yaeju-Dake Peak remains under Japanese control; however, their defenses on the southeastern end of the line have been cracked.

June 13th 1945 — (Pacific-Philippines) Luzon In the **U.S. 6th Army** area, **I Corps** sector, General Beightler reinforces the 145th Infantry, 37th Division, attaching the 37th Reconnaissance Troop and a Platoon of Light Tanks bolstered by a Contingent of Motorized Infantry, to take advantage of the seizure of Orioung Pass. The Armor column drives onto the plain of Cagayan Valley and burst into Cordon, driving beyond to Santiago. Contingents of the 148th Regiment pushes to the Orioung area; however, the Japanese spring a counterattack and establish a roadblock in Orioung Pass, holding it for the night. **(Pacific-Dutch East Indies)** Brunei town falls to Australian troops. **(Pacific-Okinawa)** In the **U.S. Tenth Army** area, **III Amphibious Corps** sector, Major General Lemuel C. Shepherd, Commanding Officer, 6th Marine Division, declares that all organized resistance on Oroku Peninsula has ceased. During the 13th and 14th, a record number of Japanese are captured by the 6th Marine Division: 159. In the 1st Marine Division zone, by dawn, six Companies of the 7th Marines are holding tenuously on Kunishi Ridge coming under ferocious fire; 140 casualties are sustained. Planes and Tanks keep the Marines supplied. In the **XXIV Corps** sector, additional pressure is brought to bear on the Japanese holding cave positions; Armored Flame Throwers systematically incinerate them one-by-one in support of Corps actions. However, the Japanese still hold dominating positions on Yuza-Dake and Yaeju-Dake peaks and also on Hills 115 and 153 from east to west. **Offshore** The Battleship *Idaho* (BB-42) is damaged by grounding. **(Pacific- China)** General Wedemeyer informs General Marshall by letter that Phase 1 of the planned offensive against Canton-Hong Kong is essentially terminated due to the fact that Japanese withdrawals have taken place. New plans are being formulated to use Nanning-Liuchow-Kweilin area as a base for the operation. Although the Japanese still command Kwelin and Liuchow, it is anticipated that the positions are soon to be abandoned. **(Atlantic-France)** Admiral King arrives in Paris and is met by Admirals Stark and Ghormley. King and his contingent depart for Germany on the 14th to attend the Potsdam Conference. Meanwhile, the Russians have seized control of their sector of Berlin and have already begun to harass the Allies. An authorized American Convoy is halted by the Russians and its Officers are told that the Convoy can not proceed. Heated arguments develop between the Americans and the Russians, but the U.S. gives in and agrees to scale down the size of the Convoy. An embarrassed Commanding Officer is compelled by orders, to turn back most of the Convoy to the Russians' delight. On the 14th, in Germany near Potsdam, the Russians harass the Americans again; Charles Cooke, a staff member of King, is threatened as he paddles on a lake near King's quarters and is told that if he does it again he will be shot. The Russians also inform the Americans that if King's Plane strays from the slender air corridor on its approach, it will be knocked out of the air. The U.S. Plane is accompanied by a Fighter escort and the Russians fail to test the skill of the Pilots. The Plane lands unscathed.

June 14th 1945 — **(United States)** The Joint Chiefs of Staff instruct Generals MacArthur and Arnold and Admiral Nimitz to formulate immediate plans to occupy Japan, based on the theory that it might capitulate at any time. **(Pacific-Philippines)** Admiral Halsey anchors his Fleet at Leyte. He joins General MacArthur for lunch and he also takes a flying tour of the area; Halsey is jubilant at the sight of the decimated Jap Warships in the sea. **Luzon** In the **U.S. Sixth Army** area, **I Corps** sector, the enemy defenders on Highway 5 at Orioung Pass are blown away ending the blockage and permitting an Armor column and the 1st Battalion, 145th Regiment, 37th Division to advance through Ipil and beyond to Echague. In conjunction, the 3rd Battalion, 145th Regiment moves from Santiago, taking a circuitous route to Highway 5, while the 148th Regiment deploys units in Cordon and San Louis for security purposes and moves the balance to the Santiago region. In the **XIV Corps** sector, the Bicols are turned over to Filipino Guerrillas. **(Pacific-Ryukyu Islands-Okinawa)** In the **U.S. Tenth Army** area, **III Amphibious Corps** sector, mop-up details are carried out on Oroku Peninsula by contingents of the 6th Marine Division. Also, the 6th Reconnaissance Company secures Senaga Shima, an island off the coast of the Oroku Peninsula. In the 1st Marine Division zone, the 7th Marines continue to hold tight on the western tip of Kunishi Ridge, despite the continuing incessant enemy fire. In an effort to relieve pressure on the ridge, some modifications are implemented to facilitate victory. At 03:00, the 2nd Battalion, 1st Marines attack and seize the eastern end of the ridge and retain control against vicious opposition. The Marines use Tanks and Flame Throwers effectively during the entire Kunishi Ridge contest, the former playing a primary role in keeping the Infantry supplied as well as ferrying the wounded and pulverizing individual entrenched positions. In the **XXIV Corps** sector, the Japs' intricate cave systems are still undergoing methodical scrutiny by Corps which advances and exterminates them as discovered. In conjunction, the Japanese still resist fervently on Yuza peak and Yaeju-Dake peak; the 383rd Regiment, 96th Division claws forward and is stopped in front of the former by a wall of fire; however, the 381st Regiment attacks successfully, climbing to the top of Yaeju-Dake peak. Meanwhile, at Hills 115 and 153 on Corps' eastern flank, the 7th Division maintains its clearing operation, destroying the enemy as it advances. **Offshore** The Motor Gunboat PGM-24 is damaged by collision. **(Pacific-Burma)** In Rangoon, an elaborate victory parade takes place. Admiral Mountbatten attends the festivities and while in the city continues making preparations for Operation ZIPPER (invasion of Malaya) on a scaled down basis; the scheduled invasion date is September 9th.

June 15th 1945 — **(Pacific-Philippines)** **Luzon** In the **U.S. Sixth Army** area, **I Corps** sector, Filipino Guerrillas capture Cervantes on Highway 4 (northern Luzon). Meanwhile, the 145th Regiment drives deeper into the Cagayan Valley, its 1st Battalion driving to the Ganano River. In conjunction, the 3rd Battalion devours an enemy stronghold on the route to Cabatuan about 4,000 yards outside of Santiago. In other activity, the XI Corps assumes responsibility for the XIV Corps area and also takes control of the 11th Airborne Division, 1st Cavalry Division, and RCT 158. Eighth Army orders XIV Corps to make preparations to initiate actions in northern Luzon. **(Pacific-Okinawa)** In the **U.S. Tenth Army** area, **III Amphibious Corps** sector, contingents of the 6th Marine Division probe the infrastructure Headquarters of the enemy tunnel system on Oroku Peninsula and discover about 200 dead Japs, in-

cluding the Commanding Officer and members of his staff who chose death by suicide. In the 1st Marine Division zone, violent fighting continues on Kunishi Ridge, but no progress is made. In other activity, the 8th Marines, 2nd Marine Division lands on Okinawa and are attached to the 1st Marine Division. **Offshore** The Destroyer Escort *O'Flaherty* is damaged by collision. **(Pacific-Dutch East Indies)** Labuan and Maura Islands off the coast of Borneo are now clear of Japanese. **(Pacific-Burma)** In the **British Twelfth Army** area, the 101st Detachment, O.S.S. ends its mission to clear the Shan Hills; the unit is disbanded in July.

June 16th 1945 — **(United States)** A Naval Air Test Center is established at Patuxent River, Maryland. **(Pacific-Philippines)** In the **U.S. Sixth Army** area, **I Corps** sector, contingents of the 37th Division encroach on Cauayan; others advance north toward Naguilian, which will be seized on the following day. **(Pacific-Okinawa)** In the **U.S. Tenth Army** area, **III Amphibious Corps** sector, 1st Marine Division zone, some inroads are gained on Kunishi Ridge as the 7th Marines grind forward, reaching positions from which eye contact is made with the 5th Marines, advancing from the east. In the **XXIV Corps** sector, heavy fighting is ongoing on Yuza-Dake hill mass, continuing as the 96th Division's 382nd Regiment relieves the 383rd Regiment and maintains the attack. Meanwhile, the 381st Regiment finally eliminates the vehement resistance and seizes Yuza-Dake peak. In other combat, the 17th and 32nd Regiments, 7th Division hammer the final dominating ground: Hills 115 and 153. The two stubborn strongpoints fall on the following day in synchronization with the downfall of the Japanese 32nd Army. **Offshore** The Destroyer *Twiggs* (DD-591) is sunk by an Aircraft torpedo. Also, the Escort Carrier *Steamer Bay* (CVE-87) sustains damage by an Aircraft operational casualty.

June 17th 1945 — **(United States)** The Escort Carrier *Vella Gulf*, the fourth Marine Escort Carrier to be commissioned, embarks from San Diego for Pearl Harbor, transporting Marine Carrier Group 3 (VMF-513, VMTB-234, and CASD-3). In other activity, General Henry H. Arnold, by letter to General Albert C. Wedemeyer in China, requests that Major General Chennault be replaced by Lt. General George E. Stratemeyer as head of Air Forces in China. On the 20th, Wedemeyer responds, sending General Marshall his concurrence with the plan. Stratemeyer will command China Theater Air Forces; Major Generals Claire L. Chennault and Brigadier General Howard C. Davidson will be subordinate to him, commanding the SAF and TAF respectively. **(Pacific-Philippines)** In the **U.S. Sixth Army** area, **I Corps** sector, Naguilian falls to the 37th Division. In other activity, the U.S.S. *Chestatee*, a Gasoline Tanker, sustains damage by collision. **(Pacific-Okinawa)** In the **U.S. Tenth Army** area, **III Amphibious Corps** sector, more pressure is applied against resistance on Kunishi Ridge as fresh Marine units are thrown into the battle. In the 4th Marines sector (Oroku Peninsula), Japanese Admiral Minoru Ota, Commander Naval Base Force, is discovered dead in a cave; he is in a ceremonial position (his throat is slashed). In the **XXIV Corps** sector, the Japanese last line of defense folds, its defending 32nd Army thoroughly beaten. Hills 115 and 153 fall to the 7th Division. In other activity, a 7,000 foot runway is completed at Yuntan Airfield.

June 18th 1945 — **(Pacific-Marshall Islands)** Battleships and Destroyers commence a bombardment of Japanese installations on Emidj Island, Jaluit Atoll. **(Pacific-Philippines)** **Luzon** Ilagan Airfield is overrun by Armor and contingents of the 148th Regiment, 37th Division; units bolt across the Ilagan

River. Also, a treadway bridge is thrown across the Cagayan River at Naguilian, permitting Armor and other Vehicles to speed across. On **Mindanao**, in the **U.S. Eighth Army** area, **X Corps** sector, all organized resistance ceases as the 3rd Battalion, 163rd Regiment, 24th Division drives to Calinan, less than ten miles from Tugbok. **(Pacific-Okinawa)** In the **U.S. Tenth Army** area, Lt. General Simon B. Buckner, Jr. is killed by an enemy shell, while on site at a Marine observation post, watching the progress of the first attack on the island by the 8th Marines, 2nd Marine Division. General Bruckner is replaced temporarily by Major General R.S. Geiger, U.S.M.C., senior troop Commander, who assumes command of Tenth Army and directs it for the duration of combat on the island. In the **III Amphibious Corps** sector, the 6th Marine Division continues grinding forward against faltering resistance on the west flank of Corps. In the 1st Marine Division sector, Tank-Infantry teams of the 2nd Battalion, 5th Marines pulverize the final organized resistance on Kunishi Ridge. However, the Japanese resist fervently at Hill 81, west of Medeera, repulsing contingents of the 5th Marines; the obstinate strongpoint is destroyed on the 21st. **Offshore** The Seaplane Tender (small) U.S.S. *Yakutat* incurs damage by collision. **(Pacific-Dutch East Indies)** The Motor Minesweeper YMS-50 is damaged by a mine in the Balikpapan area of Borneo; it is subsequently destroyed by U.S. forces. **(Pacific-Japan)** U.S. B-29 Bombers initiate heavy raids against Japanese cities. The raids continue and increase in intensity, striking such places as Kobe, Osaka, and Tokyo. The precision bombing raids also include striking Airfields and Naval facilities.

June 19th 1945 — (Pacific-Philippines) Luzon In the **U.S. Sixth Army** area, **I Corps** sector, the 1st Battalion, 148th Regiment, 37th Division, out in advance of the Regiment, drives to Moranoa and annihilates a small enemy delaying force; the balance of the Regiment has completed crossing the Cagayan River. In conjunction, the Armor column drives east along the river, seizing five Jap Tanks. **(Pacific-Okinawa)** In the **U.S. Tenth Army** area, efforts to convince the Japanese to surrender have been ongoing and appear to be fruitful as 343 Japanese surrender. The Japanese, since the inception of hostilities, have usually accepted death rather than capitulation. In the **III Amphibious Corps** sector, 6th Marine Division zone, the Japanese resistance is evaporating as forces drive south on the Corps' west flank. In the 1st Marine Division zone, brutal fighting continues at Hill 81 as contingents of the 5th Marines pound it; however, additional units of the 5th Marines and the 8th Marines advance to the island's southern coast. In the **XXIV Corps** sector, the Japanese raise violent opposition against the 96th Division in the Aragachi-Medeera region, forestalling defeat. Meanwhile, to the east, the 7th Division closes on Mabuni and Udo. In the 77th Division zone, heavy fighting breaks out near Ozato. Sergeant John Meagher boards a Tank and begins spotting targets for the gunner. Suddenly, a Japanese Soldier approaches the Tank with an explosive charge. Meagher yells a warning to the gunner then dives from the Tank, killing the Jap with his bayonet, but the explosion knocks him unconscious. Soon after, he is up and with a new weapon in hand, attacks a nearby pillbox, eliminating its six occupants. Meagher moves forward, his uniform becoming more riddled with bullets as he advances. As he reaches the pillbox, his gun runs out of ammunition, but the dauntless Sergeant clasps the barrel, swinging it viciously as he roams the position, eliminating the entire crew; Sergeant Meagher receives the Medal of Honor. **Offshore** The Minesweepers *Device* (AM-220) and *Dour* (AM-223) suffer damage by collision. **(Pacific-Dutch East In-**

dies) The LST 562 incurs damage by collision in Brunei Bay, Borneo. **(Pacific-China Theater)** Final plans for the seizure of Fort Bayard scheduled for August 1st are issued. The Fort is to be utilized as an advance Supply Base to maintain the operations against the Canton-Honk Kong region. The offensive is to be supported by the India-Burma and China Theaters.

June 20th 1945 — (Pacific-Philippines) Luzon In the **U.S. Sixth Army** area, **I Corps** sector, Filipino Guerrillas, operating between Aparri and Ilagan, seize Tuguegarao, lying about midway between the two towns. Meanwhile, Company B, 6th Ranger Battalion, (attached Task Force Connoly) advances during the night of the 20th in to Aparri, finding it abandoned. Also, elements of the 148th Regiment, 37th Division knocks out a Japanese roadblock along Highway 5 about 4,000 yards north of Ilagan. **Southern Philippines** In the **U.S. Eighth Army** area, it is announced that the campaigns to seize Panay-Negros Occidental (Victor 1), Cebu-Bohol-Negros Oriental (Victor II), Palawan (Victor III), and Zamboanga (Victor IV) are officially terminated. **(Pacific-Okinawa)** The Japanese pattern is changing drastically as nearly one thousand additional troops surrender to Tenth Army, a record setting number; however, despite the success of the convincing psychological warfare, other Japanese forces continue fanatical resistance. In the **III Amphibious Corps** sector, 6th Marine Division zone, the Japanese defending in the Kiyamu region mount strong opposition against the 4th Marines; however, the 29th Marines advance to the southern coast against feeble resistance. Meanwhile, in the 1st Marine Division zone, the enemy on Hill 81 resists feverishly, impeding the attempts of the 5th Marines to reduce it. In the **XXIV Corps** sector, defenders on Hill 85 in the Medeera pocket repel attempts by the 96th Division to seize it; Aragachi is overrun. Meanwhile, in the 7th Division zone, Hill 89 outside of Mabuni is reached by the 32nd Regiment; Japanese Headquarters is entrenched underground. **(Pacific-Wake Island)** Rear Admiral R. E. Jennings' Carrier Task Force launches Planes which strike Wake Island. U.S. Naval Forces continue bombarding the island, which has been held by the Japanese since December 1941, until August 9th. **(Pacific-Dutch East Indies)** The Motor Minesweeper YMS-368 sustains damage by a mine near Balikpapan, Borneo.

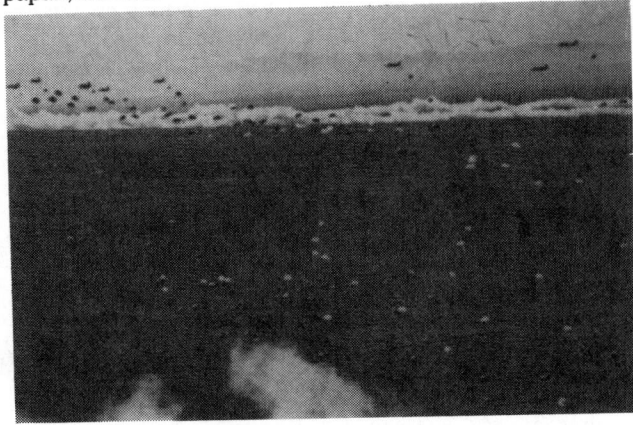

U.S. Paratroopers assaulting Aparri in Northern Luzon, Philippines.

June 21st 1945 — (Pacific-Philippines) Luzon In the **U.S. Sixth Army** area, **XI Corps** sector, Corps is ordered to drop one Paratroop Battalion (TF Gypsy) on the Aparri region to cut off any Japanese attempting to escape from there; the 1st Battalion (reinforced), 511th Paratroop Infantry, 11th Airborne, commanded by Lt. Colonel Henry A. Burgess, receives the task, which takes place on the 23rd. Meanwhile, Ranger detachments, probing from Aparri, establish contact with Filipino Guerrillas. In the 37th Division zone, the 148th Regiment plows deeper into the Cagayan Valley, rumbling over sporadic resistance. Also, the 6th Division continues its advance, the 20th Regiment driving to Pingkian, while the 63rd Regiment moves toward Kiangan. In the 25th Division area, progress continues along Old Spanish Trail as contingents converge from the north and south upon Susuga. **(Pacific-Okinawa)** It has been 82 blood-filled days since the U.S. invasion of Okinawa on Easter Sunday, April 1st, 1945. Despite the agonizing campaign and the fanatical resistance which included mass attacks by Suicide Pilots, the U.S. Fleet remains offshore as the island is declared secure by General R.S. Geiger U.S.M.C., temporary Commanding Officer of the U.S. Tenth Army. Organized resistance is terminated in the **III Amphibious Corps** sector, as Hill 81 is seized by the 1st Marine Division, while the 29th Marines, 6th Marine Division vacuums Ara Sake, the island's southernmost point. In the **XXIV Corps** sector, die-hard resisters continue to hold out on Hill 85 in the Medeera pocket, but the effort is futile as the 96th Division places its final clamps on the hill. Meanwhile, the remaining Japs holding out in a pocket on Hill 89 near Mubini are eliminated by the 7th Division. **Offshore** Japanese Suicide Planes still carry out futile missions; however, damage is inflicted on the Fleet: the Destroyer Escort *Halloran* (DE-305) and the Seaplane Tenders *Curtiss* (AV-4) and *Kenneth Whiting* are struck. **(Pacific-Dutch East Indies)** The Motor Minesweeper YMS-355 is damaged off Balikpapan, Borneo, by a Japanese coastal defense gun.

June 22nd 1945 — (Pacific-Philippines) Luzon In the **U.S. Sixth Army** area, **XI Corps** sector, a small detachment composing eight men is flown north to scout and mark a landing area near Aparri for an impending Paratroop drop. In the **U.S. Sixth Army** area, **XI Corps** sector, contingents of the 148th Regiment, 37th Division seize Tumauini along Highway 5, then bolt north reaching a stream about 9,000 yards southeast of Cabagan. In conjunction, the 149th Regiment assembles in the newly-won town and will take over the northern drive. The towns of Dugo and Camalananiugan sitting in the Aparri region are taken by Task Force Connolly; however, Tuguegarao, which had been seized by Filipino Guerrillas on the 20th is lost again to the Japanese, as strong enemy fire pushes the Guerrillas out of the town. Meanwhile, the 25th Division continues its drive, blowing open the Old Spanish Trail through Susuga Pass. **(Pacific-Okinawa)** Old Glory is officially raised on Okinawa in grand fashion. As the Stars and Stripes signals the end of Japanese domination of the island, the Japanese Commanding Officer exhibits the futility of the Japanese cause; Lt. General Mitsuri Ushijima, Commanding Officer of the decimated 32nd Army and his Chief of Staff commit Hari Kari. With the capitulation of Okinawa, the U.S. sets its sights on the next and final objective in the Pacific; Japan. The U.S. Fleet, which came to stay, sustains grave casualties and severe damage; however, despite the incessant impassioned suicide missions, the Japanese fail to sink one Capital Ship. The U.S. sustains about 49,151 casualties, including 12, 520 missing or killed and 36,631 wounded. The U.S. loses 36 Vessels sunk and 368 damaged. Japanese Suicide Planes continue to strike the Fleet subsequent to the capitulation of the island; today, the high-speed Minesweeper *Ellyson* (DMS-19) and the LST 534 are damaged by a Kamikaze. The Japanese lose about 7,800 Planes during their morbid operation. On the ground, the Japanese lose about 110,000 troops killed; another 7,400 Japs surrender or are captured. **(Pacific-Dutch East Indies)** The Australian troops terminate

organized resistance on Tarakan Island, off Borneo. Offshore, the American Motor Minesweeper YMS-10 is damaged off Balikpapan, Borneo, by an enemy coastal defense gun. **(Pacific-China)** Chinese forces are on the steps of Liuchow, which is set afire by the Japanese as they prepare to abandon it.

June 23rd 1945 — (Pacific-Philippines) Luzon In the **U.S. Sixth Army** area, **I Corps** sector at 09:00, TF Gypsy is dropped by Fifth Air Force Transport Planes over an Airfield just south of Aparri; the Paratroops and their Glider-transported equipment make safe landings without incident, and contact with Guerrillas is quickly established. The Task Force drives south to enjoin the 37th Division, which is rapidly driving north along Highway 5. **(Pacific-Okinawa)** With the total demise of the Japanese on Okinawa complete, the U.S. Army and Marine forces begin mop-up operations, both Corps sweeping northward. On the previous day, the orders to mop up had been given; the operation is to last ten days. General Joseph "Vinegar Joe" Stilwell U.S.A. relieves General Geiger U.S.M.C., as Commanding Officer of the 10th Army. In other activity, the 381st Regiment, 96th Division eliminates the remaining contingents of the Japanese 24th Division in the southern portion of the island. **(Pacific-Java Sea)** The Submarine U.S.S. *Hardhead* (SS-365) sinks the Japanese Submarine Chasers Nos. 42 and 113 and the Shuttleboat No. 833.

June 24th 1945 — (Pacific-Philippines) The Destroyer Escort U.S.S. *Neuendorf* (DE-200) sustains damage by collision. **Luzon** In the **U.S. Sixth Army** area, **I Corps** sector, Task Force Gypsy and the 37th Division continue driving north and south respectively to establish contact. **Southern Philippines** In the **U.S. Eighth Army** area, the 164th Regiment, Americal Division, returns to Cebu from its mission in Negros Oriental. Eighth Army area, except for Mindanao, is now secure. **(Pacific-Dutch East Indies)** The Motor Minesweeper YMS-339 is accidentally damaged by a U.S. Bomber off Balikpapan, Borneo.

June 25th 1945 — (Pacific-Philippines) Luzon In the **U.S. Sixth Army** area, **I Corps** sector, TF Gypsy enters Gattaran, finding it abandoned by the enemy, and keeps moving driving to within 2,000 yards (south) of the Duman River; the advance is supplied by air. Meanwhile, the 37th Division's 129th Regiment seizes Tuguegarao and Penablanca without opposition; the attack had been bolstered by Air and Artillery. **(Pacific-Okinawa)** The U.S. Tenth Army sends its four Divisions north to finish the clean up operation.

June 26th 1945 — (United States) The United Nation Conference concludes in San Francisco and results in the United Nations Charter which is signed by participating nations and subsequently ratified on October 24th. **(Pacific-Philippines) Luzon** In the **U.S. Sixth Army** area, **I Corps** sector, TF Gypsy and the 129th Regiment, 37th Division meet on Highway 5, near Alcala. **Mindanao** In the **U.S. Eighth Army** area, **X Corps** sector, the 167th Regiment, 31st Division, making slow progress along Talomo Trail, advances to Pinamola. **(Pacific-Ryukyu Islands-Okinawa)** A Naval Task Group (TG-31.24), under Captain C. A. Buchanan, lands the Fleet Marine Force Amphibious Reconnaissance Battalion, supported by one reinforced Rifle Company of the 1st Marine Division and a small Naval force, on Kume Island, without opposition. Kume, the final and largest island in the Okinawa Gunto chain, is secure by the 30th. The success of the mission permits implementation of additional air warning systems to ensure the Okinawa perimeter. **Offshore** The Seaplane Tender (small) *Suisun* (AVP-53) is damaged by collision. **(Pacific-Dutch East Indies)** Near Balikpapan, Borneo, the Motor Minesweeper YMS-39 is sunk by a mine, and the Motor Minesweeper YMS-365 is damaged by a mine and subsequently sunk by U.S. forces. **(Pacific-China)** Liuchow Airfield is taken by Chinese troops. **(Pacific-Japan)** Aircraft (B-29s) of the XXI Bomber Command deliver night air strikes against Japanese oil refineries.

June 27th 1945 — (Pacific-Philippines) Luzon In the **U.S. Sixth Army** area, **I Corps** sector, the 129th Regiment, 37th Division concludes its Cagayan Valley offensive, reaching Aparri; the initiative essentially terminates the Luzon campaign. **(Pacific-Dutch East Indies)** The Destroyer *Caldwell* (DD-605) is damaged by a mine in Brunei Bay area, Borneo. **(Pacific-Java Sea)** The Submarine U.S.S. *Blueback* (SS-326) sinks the Japanese Submarine Chaser No. 2. **(Central Pacific)** Naval Land-based Aircraft (VPB-142) sink the Japanese Submarine I-165. **(Pacific-Okinawa)** The bodies of Japanese Lt. General Ushimajima, Lt. General Cho, the Commanding General and Chief of Staff, Japanese Forces Okinawa are discovered; both committed suicide.

June 28th 1945 — (Pacific-Dutch East Indies) The Minesweeper YMS-47 is damaged by a mine in the Balikpapan region off Borneo. Also, the Motor Minesweeper 49 is damaged off Borneo by an enemy coastal gun. **(Pacific-Sea of Japan)** The Japanese Destroyer *Enoki* sinks after striking a mine.

June 29th 1945 — (United States) The Joint Chiefs of Staff decide to step up the air blockade, using Bases in the Marianas and the Philippines and also Aircraft based on Okinawa and Iwo Jima. In addition, it is agreed that an all-out effort is to be made to ensure the security of the Western Pacific sea lanes prior to the invasion of the Japanese mainland and also to secure sea routes to the Russian Pacific ports. Also, the Joint Chiefs of Staff call for total defeat of the Japanese forces remaining in the Philippines. **(Pacific-Ryukyu Islands)** The island of Kume is declared secure.

June 30th 1945 — (United States) At present the Navy has 67,952 Vessels on hand, all types. Personnel: Naval 3,383,196; Marine Corps 474,680 (37,067 Officers and 437,613 enlisted); Coast Guard 171,192. **(Pacific-Philippine Islands)** At midnight 30th June-July 1st, the Luzon Campaign officially ceases. The U.S. Sixth Army transfers responsibility for completing the job of mopping up Luzon to the U.S. Eighth Army, and it immediately begins preparations for its next mission: the invasion of Japan. (Operation OLYMPIC). XIV Corps reverts to Eighth Army and is given assignment of final mop-up of Luzon. The mission, which continues until the cessation of hostilities, will include the elimination of two formidable pockets of resistance still holding in northern Luzon: one in the Sierra Madre Mountains, defended by about 11,000 Japanese, and another defended by about 12,000 Japs in the Kiang-Bontoc region. The XIV Corps contingents are the 6th, 32nd, 37th, and 38th Infantry Divisions, supported by Filipino Guerrillas. Meanwhile, the 24th Division is ordered to make the final amphibious invasion of the Philippines campaign and will land on Mindanao at Sarangani Bay. On **Mindanao**, organized resistance ends. The X Corps's mop-up operations continue until the termination of hostilities. **(Pacific-Ryukyu Islands)** The U.S. Tenth Army completes the mop-up of Okinawa. **(Pacific-Dutch East Indies)** The Destroyer *Smith* (DD-378) is damaged by an enemy coastal gun, and the Minesweeper YMS-314 sustains damage by a mine. **(Pacific-Sea of Japan)** The Japanese Destroyer *Nara* sinks after striking a mine.

July 1st 1945 — (Pacific-Philippines) The final phase of the

Naval war to defeat Japan commences, as the Third Fleet sorties from Leyte Gulf to attack and destroy the remaining Japanese Naval and Air Forces and to pound the home islands of Japan. **(Pacific-Okinawa)** General Joseph Stilwell, Commanding Officer, U.S. Tenth Army, opens Headquarters on Okinawa and becomes responsible for a joint Task Force (directly under CinCPOA) assigned to fortify and develop all captured islands and the surrounding waters within a radius of 25 miles. In other activity, CinCPac disbands Task Force 31; Vice Admiral H.W. Hill, U.S.N. and his Staff embark for Pearl Harbor; Rear Admiral Calvin H. Cobb, U.S.N., assumes command of Naval Forces, Ryukyus, under General Stilwell. Also, Tactical Air Force, Tenth Army, is redesignated Tactical Air Force, Ryukyus. **(Pacific-Dutch East Indies)** The 7th Australian Division lands on Balikpapan, Borneo, supported by a Naval Attack Group (U.S. Seventh Fleet) under Rear Admiral A.G. Noble. The objective has been under Naval bombardment since June 24th and inundated with Air strikes for the past month. The Australians hit the beach against slight resistance; however, the Japanese intensify opposition as the advance drives inland. The objective is seized on the following day and includes the oil facilities. **(Pacific-Yellow Sea)** The Submarine U.S.S. *Haddo* (SS-255) sinks the Japanese Coast Defense Vessel No. 72.

July 2nd 1945 — (Pacific-Philippines) Southern Philippines) In the **U.S. Eighth Army** area, RCT 368, 93rd Division relieves contingents of the 41st Division (Sixth Army) and assumes responsibility for the Zamboanga sector of Mindanao and the islands of Jolo, Palawan, and Sanga Sanga. **(Pacific-Ryuku Is lands)** The campaign for control of the Ryukus is officially terminated. **(Pacific-Japan)** The Japanese Submarine Chaser No. 188 sinks after striking a mine. The Submarine U.S.S. *Barb* (SS-220) is patrolling near Kaihyo Island off the eastern tip of the Karafuto Peninsula where the Japanese operate a seal fishery. As dawn approaches, the *Barb's* commanding Officer notices two beacons, radio antenna, and an observation post at the facility and commences firing, the first successful use of rockets against shore positions by a U.S. Submarine. The radio is knocked out and buildings are set afire as well as Sampans in the dock area. Also, several gun emplacements are destroyed. Return fire fails to hit the *Barb*. On the following day, the *Barb*, under Commander E, B. Fluckey, bombards Shikuka on the western shore of Patience Bay, Karafuto, Peninsula; however, the rockets score no apparent damage. The Submarine continues raiding the Japanese coast, sinking the *Sappore Maru* No. 11, on the 5th. In addition, during the tour, a contingent of Submariners debark on the east coast of Karafuto and sabotage a train to the astonishment of the Japanese who report that a bomb had hit the passenger train.

July 3rd 1945 — (Pacific-Okinawa) The U.S.S. *Ashtabula* (AO-51), an Oiler, is damaged by collision. **(Atlantic-Germany)** Vice Admiral R.L. Ghormley, Commander United States Naval Forces Germany, establishes Headquarters at Frankfurt am Main, Germany.

July 4th 1945 — (Pacific-Philippines) In the **U.S. Tenth Army** area, the U.S. 41st Division prepares to secure the Sarangani Bay area with its Sarangani Task Force, implementing both ground and amphibious operations. In conjunction, a contingent of the 24th Reconnaissance Troop (attached to TF) embark from Talomo to Glan in a shore-to-shore movement and transfers arms to Guerrilla 116th Infantry, 106th Division; in coordinated actions with the Guerrillas, the eastern shore of the bay is being secured.

July 5th 1945 — (Pacific-Philippines) General Douglas MacArthur proclaims the liberation of the Philippine Islands. **(Pacific-Dutch East Indies)** Allied Warships give umbrella protection to the Australian contingents of the 7th Division which land on the western shore of Balikpapan Bay at Penadjim Point without incident. Meanwhile, additional Australians maintain the drive to secure strategic points in Borneo. **Offshore** The Destroyer U.S.S. *Smith (DD-378)* sustains damage by accident (depth charge). Also, the Submarine U.S.S. *Lizardfish* (SS-373) sinks the Japanese Auxiliary Submarine Chaser No. 37, off Java.

July 6th 1945 — (Pacific-China) General Chennault requests permission to retire, and an affirmative response is forthcoming.

July 8th 1945 — (Pacific-Philippines) Mindanao In the U.S. **Eighth Army** area, **X Corps** sector, the Sarangani Task Force continues to advance and sweep the eastern shores of Balikpapan Bay. In conjunction, a Provincial Infantry Battalion, AAA and a Combat Company of the 118th Regiment (Guerrilla 106th Division) drive southeast from Lake Buluan toward Saragani Bay, while contingents of the 108th Guerrilla Division move from Davao, driving southwest toward the bay.

July 9th 1945 — (Pacific-Dutch East Indies) Australian and Dutch troops have totally invested Balikpapan Bay, Borneo. The U.S. Motor Minesweeper YMS-84 sinks after striking a mine. **(Pacific-Malaya)** The Submarine U.S.S. *Bluefish* (SS-222) sinks the Japanese Auxiliary Submarine Chaser No. 50. **(Pacific-Japan)** Admiral Halsey's Fleet is closing to attack Japan. Radar picks up an alleged Submarine near the Armada. Destroyers attack, hoping to eliminate the threat before the enemy Vessel can send an alarm to Japan, but it isn't necessary. a closer observation determines that the intruder had been a whale. It is difficult to differentiate in these waters which are filled with mines and other obstacles. Even porpoises and drifting logs can fool the naked eye.

July 10th 1945 — (United States) The Joint Chiefs of Staff order the activation of the U.S. Army Strategic Air Force in the Pacific, commanded by General Carl A. Spaatz, U.S.A.; it is controlled strategically by the Joint Chiefs of Staff. **(Pacific-Solomons)** The American Submarine Chaser SC-521 sinks by foundering. **(Pacific-Okinawa)** CinCPac orders Major General Louis E. Woods' (U.S.M.C.) Tactical Air Force to conduct coordinated operations with the Eighth Air Force, U.S. Army Strategic Air Force in the Pacific. Also, the LST 1107 is damaged by grounding. **(Pacific-Japan)** Carrier-based Aircraft attached to Vice Admiral J. S. McCain's Fast Carrier Task Force and Land-based Planes strike Airfields in Japan on the Tokyo plain and other targets in the opening shot of a string of powerful blows to soften it for invasion. No Japanese Fighter Planes intercept the attackers over Tokyo; two Reconnaissance Aircraft approach but both are knocked from the sky. Halsey's Airmen report 109 enemy Planes destroyed and 231 damaged; the Pilots also inform Headquarters that the count was difficult because many of the Planes had been degassed. In other activity, the Japanese Destroyer *Sakura* sinks after striking a mine. Also, the Submarine U.S.S. *Runner* (SS-476) sinks the Japanese Minesweeper No. 27, off Honshu. **(Pacific-India)** Naval contingents arrive in India to be flown to China to bolster the effort to seize Fort Bayard.

July 12th 1945 — (Pacific-Philippines) Luzon In the U.S. **Eighth Army** area, **XIV Corps** sector, the 6th Division seizes Kiangan; however, Japanese resistance remains in the region, despite extensive air raids which have deposited thousands of gallons of napalm on Japanese positions in the pocket. Meanwhile, the 32nd Division pushes along Highway 11 to secure the other obstinate pocket remaining in northern Luzon in the Sierra Madre Mountains. On Mindanao, in the **X Corps** sector, the 21st Regiment, 24th Division (attached Sarangani Task Force) lands unopposed on the north shore of Sarangani Bay. Marine Planes support the invasion; this is their final major support mission of the war. Meanwhile, the Provisional Battalion, driving from Lake Buluan, continues closing on the bay in conjunction with the Expeditionary Battalion (Guerrilla 108th Division), reaching positions northwest and northeast respectively. Also, the Guerrilla 116th Regiment secures more of the bay's shore area. The U.S. Submarine Chaser PC-582 is damaged by grounding.

July 13th 1945 — (Pacific-Philippines) Mindanao In the **X Corps** sector, the 1st Battalion, 21st Regiment (24th Division) and the Provisional Battalion converge about 15 miles northwest of Sarangani Bay. **(Southwest Pacific)** The F.E.A.F. is established to execute tactical operations in support of the impending invasion of Japan; on the following day, the Tactical Air Force (Okinawa), having completed its mission, is disbanded and replaced by the F.E.A.F. which assumes responsibility for the attack against Japan.

July 14th 1945 — (Pacific-Dutch East Indies) The Submarine U.S.S. *Bluefish* sinks the Japanese Submarine I-351, off Borneo. **(Pacific-Okinawa)** The LSTs 684 and 826 are damaged by grounding. **(Pacific-Japan)** Japan is struck heavily by Aircraft attached to Vice Admiral J.S. McCain's Fast Carrier Task Force; however, the blow is further supplemented by the Naval Force of Rear Admiral J.F. Shafroth which initiates the first Naval Surface Vessel bombardment of the Japanese homeland. While the Planes splatter Shipping and pound the rail lines and ground facilities in the vicinity of northern Honshu and Hokkaido, the big guns of Shafroth's Armada smash the coastal city of Kamaishi, Honshu (large steel plant located there). The U.S. Surface Ships penetrate shallow mine-infested waters during broad daylight and they are faced by land on three sides when they launch the blistering attack, firing at a distance of 28,000 yards. Also, the Japanese Destroyer *Tachibana* and the Coast Defense Vessels Nos. 65 and 74 are sunk by Carrier-based Planes. No Japanese Planes attack the Fleet, which includes Halsey's U.S.S. *Missouri*. Admiral Halsey remarks: "IT WAS DIFFICULT FOR THEM TO WATCH U.S. WARSHIPS PREVIOUSLY REPORTED SUNK, DESTROYING THEIR WORKPLACE.

The U.S. Third Fleet off Japan.

July 15th 1945 — **(Pacific-Philippines) Mindanao** In the **X Corps** sector, the Guerrilla 116th Regiment and the Expeditionary Battalion, 108th Division establish contact about ten miles northeast of Sarangani Bay; all contingents of the Sarangani Task Force have now hooked up for the final steps to eliminate the few remaining Japanese in the area. **(Pacific-Dutch East Indies)** The Destroyer U.S.S. *Flusser* (DD-368) and the Light Minelayer *Thomas E. Fraser* (DM-24) are damaged by separate collisions. **(Pacific-Japan)** Another Naval Surface Force strikes the mainland; Cruisers, Destroyers, and Battleships, commanded by Rear Admiral O.C. Badger, pummel the iron and steel works at Muroran on the southern coast of Hokkaido. Also, Rear Admiral McCain's Carrier-based Planes return and bombard Honshu and Hokkaido, dealing the Japanese more punishing blows in these final days of the war. The Japanese Minesweeper No. 24 and the Coast Defense Vessel No. 219 are destroyed off Honshu by Carrier-based Aircraft.

July 16th 1945 — **(United States)** The Atomic Bomb is tested successfully at Los Alamos, New Mexico. News of the breakthrough is subdued, but it is determined that its use against Japan will bring the war to an abrupt conclusion and spare enormous casualties. The U.S. anticipates about 1,000,000 casualties if Japan is invaded (Operations Olympic-Coronet). The initial phase (Olympic) is tentatively scheduled for the invasion of Kyushu (southernmost Japanese home island) on November 1st, 1945; the assault force will compose the U.S. Sixth Army and the 5th Marine Division. The second phase (Coronet) is tentatively scheduled for the invasion of Honshu; the assault force will strike at the Plain of Tokyo and be composed of the U.S. 8th and 10th Armies. A Special B-29 Air unit (has been isolated at a secret Base (Wendover, Utah). The Commanding Officer, Colonel Paul W. Tibbets Jr., (509th Composite Group, 313th Wing, 21st Bombing Command, 20th Air Force) has overseen his unit's training until completion, however, even he is not yet aware of the imminent dangerous mission; to deliver the atomic bomb on Japan. Upon arrival at Tinian, in the Marianas, Tibbet's Wing is totally isolated from the remainder of the crews and in fact they never join the daily incendiary bombing raids over Japan. However, Tibbet's Group does fly some separate and often unusual missions over Japan, but never in formations larger than six Planes and always at low altitude. The modified Planes resemble all the others on the surface, but the interiors have been radically changed to accommodate the atomic bomb. As time moves ahead, the other Airmen joke about the mysterious 509th, and question their contribution. Colonel Tibbet will be the only member of the unit to receive advance knowledge of the exact mission that his unit will carry out on August 6th; to deliver the atomic bomb on Hiroshima. Also, today, the Cruiser U.S.S. *Indianapolis* embarks from San Francisco with a secret and precious cargo (atomic bomb), heading for Tinian. Coincidentally, the Japanese Submarine I-58 departs Kure, Japan; the Vessels will collide in the Pacific. SEE JULY 16TH-AUGUST 3RD 1945. **(Pacific-Java Sea)** The Submarine U.S.S. *Baya* (SS-318) sinks the Japanese Torpedo Boat *Kari*. **(Pacific-Japan)** British Task Force 37, composed of one Battleship, four large Carriers (steel decks) six Light Cruisers, 18 Destroyers, commanded by Vice Admiral Sir Bernard Rawlings and Task Group 37.1 under Vice Admiral Sir Philip Vian prepares to join with Admiral Halsey's force. Halsey meets with the British and the encounter is amicable; the British receive the option of operating independently, but choose to work with and under Halsey. Initially, the British had been directed to operate under the U.S., however, subsequent orders from

Leyte offer the options. Later, Halsey remarks about British Admiral Rawlings: "A FINER OFFICER AND FIRMER FRIEND, I HAVE NEVER KNOWN. THE BRITISH, WITH LESSER FUEL CAPACITY ARE NOT EXPECTED TO MATCH TF38 STRIKES OF THREE SUCCESSIVE DAYS, BUT THEY DO." Planes (VC-13) attached to the Escort Carrier *Anzio* and the Destroyer Escort *Lawrence C. Taylor* combine and sink the Japanese Submarine I-13, east of Japan. **(Atlantic-Germany)** The Terminal Conference convenes in Potsdam, Germany, to decide terms for the surrender of Japan and also to discuss Military and political issues tied to the cessation of hostilities. The U.S., Britain, and the Russians attend.

July 16th-August 3rd 1945 — **(United States-Pacific)** Admiral Spruance's Flagship, the U.S.S. *Indianapolis*, (CA-35) sustained serious damage by a Kamikaze off Okinawa on March 30th, but the Ship's stamina and the crew's character forestalls disaster. The *Indianapolis* retires to San Francisco under her own power and is immediately repaired, setting the stage for her next appointment with destiny. Captain Charles Butler McVay receives his final orders at Mare Island; they are short and direct, but nonetheless ambiguous. Admiral William R. Purnell and Captain William Sterling put the situation in perspective without pulling any punches, when they send McVay off to the island of Tinian: "TAKE THE PASSENGERS TO PEARL HARBOR THEN PROCEED TO TINIAN-YOU WILL NOT BE TOLD WHAT THE CARGO IS, BUT IT IS TO BE GUARDED EVEN AFTER THE LIFE OF YOUR VESSEL...SAVE THE CARGO AT ALL COSTS, IN A LIFEBOAT IF NECESSARY..." Captain McVay departs, totally unaware that his cargo is the atomic bomb, but most assuredly pondering the significance of the mission. The *Indianapolis* carries a crew of 1,200 men, but because of a snafu, she inadvertently embarks with 2,500 lifejackets.

The striking Cruiser pulls up anchor at 08:00 and glides smoothly under the Golden Gate Bridge at 08:36. The cruise is uneventful as the *Indianapolis* parts the waves between the West Coast and Pearl Harbor en route to the Marianas. The Ship reaches Tinian on July 26th, after traveling 5,000 miles in ten days. The secret invaluable cargo is delivered and the *Indianapolis* shuffles her way to Guam, still unaware (as is most of the world) that she has delicately deposited the atomic bomb on the island. The *Indianapolis*, expected at Leyte (Philippines) for rendezvous with Admiral McCormick by July 31st, pulls away from Apra Harbor, Guam on the 28th manned by a crew of 81 Officers, 1,114 men and a passenger, Captain Edwin M. Crouch, on what is expected to be a routine cruise through waters which have been docile for months. Sunday, the 29th, turns into an ordinary day, with overcast skies and choppy seas. At about 12:00, there is communication over the TBS (talk between Ships) with a passing LST, heading north to practice antiaircraft firing. Aa night approaches, the weather deteriorates and the visibility diminishes. A message comes in from a Vessel, the *Wild Hunter* which is bound for Manila with supplies, stating that she had fired upon an enemy Submarine on the previous day. The crew takes it in stride as this type of report is not unusual. GUAM RECEIVES THE REPORT AND IT IS DISPATCHED TO ALL SHIPS IN THE AREA. The Navigator, Commander Janney remarks: "WE'RE GOING TO PASS A JAP SUB around midnight" And a fellow Officer retorts: "OH WELL, OUR DESTROYERS WILL TAKE CARE OF THAT." There are no Destroyers within 300 miles of the *Indianapolis*. Later that night, Commander Janney arrives on the bridge with the night orders and some new information.: "WE HAVE A REPORT THAT A PBM AND A DDE ARE SEARCHING FOR AN ENEMY SUBMARINE. WE SHOULD

PASS THE POSITION AT 08:00 TOMORROW." By about 22:30, the moon rises, but the overcast skies shield it and the stars for the better part of the evening as the Vessel (begins non-zigzag course at about dusk) continues moving toward Leyte. Below deck, two men are in the brig, but many of the others are catching some sleep topside; being so close to the equator, the Ship remains hot. One of the men on watch notices an open porthole and a glaring light, etched in the otherwise darkened Ship. The source is located and extinguished.

Meanwhile, the Japanese Submarine I-58 is criss-crossing the Philippine Sea in search of prey. At 00:14 on the 30th, the opposing Vessels which had departed the U.S. and Japan, respectively, on the 16th of July initiate the fateful encounter. The *Indianpolis* is rocked by an explosion, followed by another more devastating blow. The men on the bridge take a shattering blow as the explosions toss the men against the deck and bulkhead again and again, but within seconds after the termination of the explosions, they regain their composure and take action. However, the communications are out and it is not known if messages got through. None have been sent from Guam to the *Indy* since her departure and the *Indy* has dispatched no reports to Guam. The situation is more than critical. There are only two small boats aboard the Vessel, but it is being consumed with choking smoke and rapidly rising water. Commander McVay orders his Vessel abandoned. The crew attempts to escape to safety and await rescue, but it is simply jumping from a bad dream to a horrific nightmare.

Back at the Philippines, Tuesday the 31st arrives without the *Indianapolis* making her rendezvous with Admiral McCormick's Fleet. The no-show is commonplace among Cruisers so no alarm is raised; Admiral McCormick neglects to note the non-arrival. As of Tuesday, the *Indy's* whereabouts are still unknown to anyone except the Japanese Submarine which sunk her and the endangered survivors who are clinging to the flimsiest strands of life in their sea of death and illusion.

On Monday, the survivors had spotted a Plane at about 13:00 and several more a few hours later, but the Aircraft had not noticed the Americans. No Planes appear on Tuesday. Meanwhile, the sea and the weather are taking a heavy toll on the mens' minds and bodies. The lack of survival boats force many of the men to remain in the water, which is permeated with deadly sharks, razor-teethed barracuda that zing through the water at speeds of 75 mph, and an assortment of other deadly fish. The menacing sea monsters strike without warning, ripping limbs and causing relentless pain. By Monday, most of the wounded have succumbed, but the numbers of healthy seamen is dwindling quickly. In addition, the unbearable heat and lack of fresh water begins twisting the minds of the men who are stranded alone and undergoing dehydration.

Also, by Tuesday, the jungle rule of survival sets in as fights erupt over rations in synchronization with the progressive pain of the wounds as they develop ulcers. Wild schemes are dreamed up by some of the men. One believes there is an ice cream store in the hull. Another discovers the *Indianapolis* just under the water line, claiming it has not sunk and another discovers an island with an airstrip and a hotel. Many of the men have become deranged because they disregarded the warnings and have drunk salt water; they soon suffer with anxieties, chills and seizures. The outrageous actions of some of the survivors deteriorate further by Wednesday. More Planes are spotted, but the remaining survivors can not be seen by the Pilots. By darkness, additional men have lost their heads and begin proclaiming that they are being attacked by the Japanese. The unkind clock continues clicking and the remaining swimmers that have outlasted the sharks and barracudas are on the brink of death from exhaustion.

On Thursday, when nearly all hope is gone, a magnificent sight appears overhead when a U.S. Ventura passes over the survivors and plops some rafts and life jackets to them. The Pilot ascends, but continues staying in the area. At about 12:00, another Plane arrives with more life rafts, but keeps flying by. As their luck begins to turn, another Plane, an amphibian zooms in from the south toward dark. Ignoring the 12' swells, he makes a hard landing and scoops up a lone swimmer to ensure he would last the night. The daring action causes some consternation to some other survivors which they vocalize as he flies by. In addition, an Army PBY swoops in then disappears and reappears over a wave. The rescue is on. Some of the men are coming home. Ironically, there are several groups of survivors and each is unaware of the others.

By now rescue Vessels are steaming to the area: the Destroyer Escort *Cecil J. Doyle* races without orders, subsequent to getting the news from a Pilot; the DDE *DuFilho* and several APDs also rush to the area. After dark on Thursday, Commander McVay pulls out some more stops, saying the Lord's Prayer and igniting a smoke pot. Then at 21:30, a glimmering light appears from the south and it keeps closing. No doubt, it is a Ship, but despite having searchlights, his rafts are not sighted. The Ships begin picking up the swimmers. On Friday morning at 10:00, the rafts are still not spotted, but the undaunted McVay still has his old smokepot burning. Ironically, a roving A.P.D. picks up a radar blip; that blip is McVay's smokepot. The remainder of the survivors are rescued, but nine-hundred men are lost: fifteen Officers and 301 enlisted men survive. And of the 39 man Marine contingent, nine are rescued. Had it not been for the fortuitous test flight of LT. Wilbur C. Gwinn, the Pilot (VBD-152) who first discovered the survivors of the *Indianapolis*, thinking a nearby oil slick was an enemy Submarine, all might have been lost. Closer surveillance zooms in on some bobbing heads. Eventually, the draining exhausted saga ends and the Sailors, with a new lease on life, are taken to Peleliu and from there to Guam or to the Philippines. One survivor grapples with the *Bassett's* (APD-73) fantail, getting aboard without any help; he sits down and says: "I CAN'T WALK, A SHARK GOT MY LEG." Other rescue Ships include the *Register* (APD-92), *Madison,*, *Ringness*, *Talbot*, The *Bassett*, *Alvin C.. Cockrell*, *Aylwin* (DD-355) and the *French* (DDE-367), and the *Helm* (DD-388).

The I-58 escapes from the area, but is subsequently sunk by U.S. forces on April 1st 1946. Captain McVay receives a court martial, becoming the only U.S. Naval Officer to be court martialled for losing his Ship during wartime. He is sentenced to lose 100 numbers in his temporary grade of Captain and to lose one hundred numbers in his permanent grade of Commander. The general public is not impressed with the verdict. On December 9th 1946, Secretary Forrestal sends out a letter directing the Chief of Naval Personnel to withdraw the disciplinary letter from McVay's file. There is no press conference.

July 17th 1945 — (Pacific-Japan) Vice Admiral McCain's Fast Carrier Task Force, joined by a British Fast Carrier Task Force under Vice Admiral H.B. Rawlings, RN, launches another attack against Airfields around Tokyo in the first of several joint U.S.-British strikes against Japan's mainland. The British Naval Force operates as part of the U.S. Third Fleet (Admiral Halsey) until war's end. Originally, the British had intended to operate as a separate unit; however, strong objections by the U.S. shelved the idea. In other activity, Japan is also struck again by U.S. Naval Surface Vessels as Rear Admiral O.C. Badger's Battleships, Cruisers, and Destroyers plaster the Mito-Hitachi area of Honshu. The Japanese offer no opposition.

July 18th 1945 — **(Pacific-Guam)** U.S. Army Strategic Air Forces is established at Guam, commanded by General Spaatz. **(Pacific-Okinawa)** The Transport *George F. Elliott* (AP-105) sustains damage cause unknown. **(Pacific-Wake Island)** Aircraft attached to the Third Fleet bomb Wake Island. **(Dutch East Indies)** Sambodja on Borneo is abandoned when Australian troops enter it. **(Pacific-Japan)** Admiral Halsey's Third Fleet sends Planes against Japanese Airfields around Tokyo and against the Yokosuka Naval Base. The Japanese installations at Cape Nojima, Honshu, are struck by Rear Admiral C. F. Holdens' Naval Force, composed of Cruisers and Destroyers. In other activity, the Submarine U.S.S. *Barb* (SS-220) sinks the Japanese Coast Vessel No. 112, off Karafuto.

July 19th 1945 — **(United States)** The Joint Chiefs of Staff order CinCPOA to relinquish control of the U.S.-held areas in the Ryukyu Islands to the CinCAFPAC on or about August 1st; however, CinCPOA retains responsibility for all operations of Naval units and installations there. **(Pacific-Okinawa)** The Destroyer U.S.S. *Thatcher* (DD-514) is damaged by a Kamikaze.

July 20th 1945 — **(Pacific-Philippines)** **Mindanao** In the **U.S. Eighth Army X Corps** sector, Company F, 34th Regiment, 24th Division, lands on Balut Island, hitting the beach at the entrance to Sarangani Bay; however, the operation discovers few Japanese. **(Pacific-Yellow Sea)** The Submarine U.S.S. *Threadfin* (SS-410) sinks the Japanese Minesweeper No. 39. **(Atlantic-Italy)** A well-guarded (U.S. Fifth Army contingents) railroad train of 13 cars departs St. Leonhard heading for Florence. The trip lasting 22 hours finally returns the lost treasures of Italian art; they are presented to the Mayor of Florence by Brigadier General Edgar E. Hume.

July 21st 1945 — **(Pacific-Okinawa)** The Attack Transport *Marathon* (APA-200) is damaged by a Piloted Torpedo. **(Atlantic-Germany)** General Patton having returned to Berlin to observe the absolute devastation, writes in a letter to his wife Beatrice: "WE HAVE DESTROYED WHAT COULD HAVE BEEN A GOOD RACE AND WE ARE ABOUT TO REPLACE THEM WITH THE MONGOLIAN SAVAGES AND ALL EUROPE WITH COMMUNISM."

July 22nd 1945 — **(Pacific)** A Cruiser Destroyer Force Task Force under Rear Admiral J.H. Brown bombards enemy facilities at Suribachi, Paramushiro, in the Kurile Islands.

July 23rd 1945 — **(Pacific-Dutch East Indies)** The Submarine U.S.S. *Hardhead* (SS-365) sinks the Japanese Submarine Chaser No. 117, off Java. **(Pacific-China)** Headquarters, U.S. Tenth Air Force is opened at Kunming. **(Pacific-Japan)** A group of eight volunteers attached to the Submarine *Barb* (SS-220) lands on Karafuto and sabotages a train. Japan later reports that a Plane had bombed the train.

July 24th 1945 — **(Pacific-Philippines)** The Destroyer U.S.S. *Underhill* (DE-682) is damaged by a Piloted torpedo and subsequently sunk by U.S. forces. **(Pacific-Japan)** Admiral W.F. Halsey's Third Fleet commence an attack, launching Aircraft against the Inland Sea area, striking Airfields at Nagoya, Osaka, and Miho and also bombing the Kure Naval Base. The Japanese Battleships *Hyuga*, *Ise*, and *Haruna* are sunk. Also, the Escort Carrier *Kaiyo*, the Heavy Cruiser *Aoba*, and the old Heavy Cruiser *Iwate* are sunk by the Carrier-based Aircraft.

Truman, flanked by Churchill and Stalin at Potsdam.

July 24th-26th 1945 — **(Pacific)** The Marine Escort Carrier *Vella Gulf* launches Planes (VMF-513, VMTB-234, and CASD-3) which strike Pagan and Rota Islands, north of Guam.

July 25th 1945 — **(Pacific-Philippines)** **Mindanao** In the **X Corps** sector, the Japanese resistance folds in Sarangani Bay region, but a few scattered enemy troops remain loose. Patrols search and destroy until August 11th. **(Pacific-Japan)** A Cruiser Destroyer Force under Rear Admiral J. C. Jones bombards Kushimoto Seaplane Base and an Airfield near Shiono Misaki, Honshu, Japan. However, poor weather reduces the power of the air strikes. The weather remains terrible, forcing modification in Halsey's attack itinerary; by the 31st, a typhoon is imminent.

July 26th 1945 — **(Atlantic-Germany)** An ultimatum is issued to the Japanese as directed by the Potsdam Conference, calling for absolute unconditional surrender. **(Pacific-Philippine Sea)** The Destroyer *Lowry* (DD-770) is damaged by an explosion.

July 27th 1945 — **(Pacific-Philippines)** The Cargo Ship *Ganymede* (AK-104) is damaged by collision. **(Pacific-China)** Kweilin is penetrated by Chinese contingents; rear-guard troops are eliminated by the 31st. Also, Tanchuk Airfield is seized by the Chinese. **(Pacific-Japan)** Army Aircraft sink the Japanese Transport No. 176 off southern Kyushu.

July 28th 1945 — **(Pacific-Okinawa)** Kamikazes attack the Fleet and sink the Destroyer *Callaghan* (DD-792) which is the last Allied Vessel lost to a Kamikaze. Also, the Suicide attack damages the Destroyer *Pritchett* (DD-561). **(Pacific-Japan)**

The Third Fleet launches more Aircraft against Japan, pounding the Inland Sea area between Nagoya and Northern Kyushu; however, most pressure is applied on the primary target, Kure Naval Base. The Carrier *Amagi*, Heavy Cruiser *Tone*, old Heavy Cruiser *Izumo* the Light Cruiser *Oyodo*, and the Destroyer *Nashi* are sunk. Also the Japanese Submarine I-372 is sunk. Admiral Halsey reflects about the Japanese situation: "JAPAN HAD TWELVE BATTLESHIPS IN THE WAR; ONLY ONE WAS NOW AFLOAT-THE CRIPPLED *NAGATO* AT YOKOSUKA OF HER 25 AIRCRAFT CARRIERS, FIVE WERE STILL AFLOAT BUT DAMAGED. OF 22 LIGHT CRUISERS, TWO WERE AFLOAT. AND OF 177 DESTROYERS, 42 WERE AFLOAT BUT ONLY FIVE WERE FULLY OPERATIONAL." The attacks started on the 24th and only U.S. Planes hit Kure where the Japanese Ships go to die. Halsey then states: "THE COMMANDER IN CHIEF OF THE COMBINED JAPANESE FLEET COULD REACH HIS CABIN IN HIS FLAGSHIP, THE LIGHT CRUISER *OYODO*, ONLY IN A DIVING SUIT." Halsey speaks on the attacks: "OUR AMERICAN AND BRITISH PILOTS SHOT DOWN OR BURNED UP 306 ENEMY PLANES AND DAMAGED 392. TOGETHER OUR LOSSES FROM ALL CAUSES, OPERATIONS AS WELL AS COMBAT, WERE 102 MEN AND 133 PLANES-ENEMY LOSSES ALSO INCLUDE BUILDINGS, TANKS, SUPPLY DUMPS, MERCHANT VESSELS, AND LOCOMOTIVES." Halsey offers several reasons for striking Kure, including: "THE ONLY APPROPRIATE RETALIATION FOR PEARL HARBOR; ESTABLISH A SECURE SUPPLY LINE FOR THE RUSSIANS; CINPAC HAD ORDERED THE FLEET DESTROYED."

July 29th 1945 — (Pacific-Okinawa) In the **U.S. Eighth Army** area, Japanese stall the advance of two Philippine Companies as they advance in the Cordillera Mountains. Corporal Melvin Mayfield, Company D, 20th Regiment, 6th Division commences a singlehanded assault to relieve the pressure. He darts through fierce fire, advancing near four enemy caves on the ridge, destroying all four and their occupants. During his enduring mission enemy fire destroys his weapon and wounds him, but their action infuriates him and prompts Mayfield to secure more ammunition and extend his attack. He eliminates an enemy outpost, despite facing point-blank fire as he advances. Corporal Mayfield receives the Medal of Honor for his extraordinary courage under fire. The Destroyer *Cassin Young* (DD-793) and the High-speed Transport *Horace A. Bass* (APD-124) are damaged by Kamikazes. **(Pacific-Japan)** The Japanese mainland again is the recipient of an avalanche of U.S. shells, as Battleships, Cruisers, and Destroyers bombard Hamamatsu and Honshu, delivering lethal blows against an Aircraft factory, shops, and other installations. Also, Army Aircraft sink the Japanese Submarine Chaser No. 207, off Kyushu, Japan.

July 30th 1945 — (United States) The Submarine U.S.S. *Bonefish* is officially reported as missing and presumed lost. She had been on her eighth War Patrol, operating in Japanese waters as part of a Submarine Task Group (nine Vessels) designated "Hydeman's Hellcats." The Submarines departed Guam on May 27th. The *Bonefish* had been credited with the sinking of the *Oshukayama*, the biggest Vessel sunk by the pack; however, last communication with the *Bonefish* is on June 18th. Subsequent Japanese reports indicate the sinking of a Submarine in the Toyama Wan, the area which *Bonefish* had requested permission to execute a submerged daylight Patrol. **(Pacific-Japan)** The Allied ultimatum calling for the surrender of Japan is rejected. Generals MacArthur and Wedemeyer and Admiral Nimitz are instructed by General

Marshall (acting on behalf of the Joint Chiefs of Staff) to continue coordinating plans for the capitulation. In other activity, Planes attached to Third Fleet continue striking enemy targets, hitting Airfields and selected industrial targets in central Honshu. The Japanese Frigate *Okinawa* is sunk by Carrier-based Aircraft. Also, the Japanese Destroyer *Hatsushimo* sinks in the Sea of Japan after striking a mine.

July 30th-August 1945 — (Pacific) The Heavy Cruiser *Indianapolis* (CA-35) is sunk by an enemy Submarine torpedo.

July 31st 1945 — (Pacific-Philippines) The Destroyer U.S.S. *Bancroft* (DD-598) is damaged by collision off Luzon. **(Pacific-Japan)** Destroyers commence a bombardment of railroad yards and the industrial sector of Shimuzu.

August 1st 1945 — (Pacific-Philippines) The four SBD Squadrons of Marine Aircraft Group 32 terminate tactical operations in the Philippines and prepare to depart for the U.S. on August 15th. **(Pacific-Wake Island)** The Battleship *Pennsylvania* and Carrier Aircraft pound enemy positions on Wake Island; however, the *Pennsylvania* sustains damage by a coastal defense gun. **(Pacific-Okinawa)** Marine Carrier Group 4, attached to the Marine Escort Carrier *Cape Gloucester* (TG 31.2), embarks from Okinawa to lend cover to the minesweeper operations in the East China Sea and also to attack Shipping in the Saddle and Parker Island Groups near Shanghai.

August 2nd 1945 — (Atlantic-Germany) The TERMINAL Conference ends in Potsdam. It had been attended by President Truman, British Prime Minister Winston Churchill, and Russia's Premier Joseph Stalin. **(Pacific-Japan)** Admiral Halsey still awaits the cessation of a typhoon which has hindered air strikes against the Japanese.

August 3rd 1945 — (Pacific-Philippine Sea) The Destroyer Escort U.S.S. *Earl V. Johnson* (DE-702) sustains damage by an explosion. **(Pacific-Okinawa)** The Attack Cargo Ship U.S.S. *Seminole* (AKA-104) is damaged by collision.

August 4th 1945 — (Pacific-Philippines) The Commander of F.E.A.F. orders the Headquarters, 1st Marine Aircraft Wing and Marine Aircraft Group 61 to be transferred to the Philippines. **(Pacific-Okinawa)** The 27th Division, which had initiated mop-up operations in northern Okinawa on May 17th, concludes the operation, reaching Hedo Misake.

August 5th 1945 — (Pacific-Iwo Jima) The Destroyer U.S.S. *Bristol* (DD-857) is damaged by collision. **(Pacific-China)** Tanchuk is seized by the Chinese 13th Army. Hsinning is retaken by the Chinese 58th Division.

August 6th 1945 — (Pacific-Japan) The Atomic Bomb is dropped on Hiroshima, Honshu, Japan. President Truman is aboard the U.S.S. *Augustus* en route to the States when he receives this message: "THE ATOM BOMB HAS BEEN DROPPED ON HIROSHIMA, JAPAN." The island of Tinian is consumed with activity as usual, however, today, the mysterious group of Superfortresses that have been quite inquisitive about their purpose for being there are in for the flight of their lives. The atomic bomb is loaded aboard the *Enola Gay*, Colonel Tibbett's Plane, and is activated while in flight for fear that if the Plane crashes on take off, it would annihilate the island. Several Planes had crashed while practicing for the mission. The *Enola Gay*, transporting only one bomb, is accompanied by two other Aircraft as observers. At 08:15, from an altitude of over 31,000 feet, the bomb is dropped and with one colossal thud, about five square miles of Hiroshima is decimated. The B-29s are caught in the whirlwind as they race away, rocking them fiercely. Meanwhile, the towering mushroom cloud is ascending, mesmerizing the crews. One crewman manages to speak a few words: "MY GOD." **(Pacific-Guam)** Representatives of the China and Pacific Theaters finalize details for the capture of Fort Bayard. **(Pacific-Wake Island)** Carrier Planes bombard Wake Island. **(Pacific-China)** Planes attached to Vice Admiral J. B. Oldendorf's Naval Task Group attack enemy Shipping in Tinghai Harbor, China. **(Pacific)** The Submarine *Bullhead* departed Fremantle on her third War Patrol on July 31st to patrol in the Java Sea and return to the Philippines on September 5th; however, the *Bullhead*, which reports passing through the Lombok Strait, fails to complete her mission. A Japanese Army Plane indicates an attack against a Submarine on the 6th, off the coast of Bali, which probably had been the *Bullhead* (SS-332), the last U.S. Submarine to be sunk during the war.

August 7th 1945 — (Pacific-Caroline Islands) Army Aircraft sink the Japanese Submarine Chaser No. 66, off Truk. **(Pacific-Sea of Japan)** Army Aircraft sink the Japanese Coast Vessel No. 39. **(Pacific-Philippines)** Luzon Advance detachment of Headquarters, U.S. First Army, arrives for participation in the operation to seize Japan.

August 8th 1945 — (Atlantic-Soviet Union) The Soviet Union declares war on Japan, but it does not become effective until the following day.

August 9th 1945 — (Pacific-Bismarcks) Marine Aircraft fly their final bombing mission against Rabaul; PBJs attached to Marine Bomber Squadron 413, 423, and 443, and Marine Aircraft Group 61, Headquarters, participate. **(Pacific-Japan)** The U.S. drops an Atomic Bomb on Nagasaki. Also, Planes attached to Fast Carrier Task Forces of the Third Fleet strike Airfields and Shipping in northern Honshu and Hokkaaido, Honshu, Japan, while Battleships and Cruisers under Rear Admiral J. F. Shafroth lambaste industrial areas at Kamaishi, Honshu, Japan. The Japanese Frigate *Inagi* is sunk by Carrier Aircraft off Norther Honshu. U.S. and British Carrier Planes sink the Frigate *Inagi* and Army Aircraft sinks the Japanese Minesweeper No. 33. The Destroyer U.S.S. *John W. Weeks* (DD-701) sustains damage by accidental U.S. Naval gunfire, and the Destroyer U.S.S. *Borie* (DD-704) incurs damage by a Kamikaze off Honshu. **(Pacific-Wake Island)** A Battleship, Cruisers, and Destroyers bombard Wake Island. **(Atlantic-Soviet Union)** The Soviet declaration of war against Japan becomes effective as Japan is rocked by a second Atomic Bomb, which has been dropped by the United States. Soviet troops flood into Manchuria.

August 10th 1945 — (Pacific) Fleet Marine Force, Pacific, orders the 6th Marine Division to place a Regimental Combat Team with the Third Fleet in the event that an early occupation of Japan is necessary. Brigadier General William T. Clement, Assistant Division Commander, is assigned command of the Fleet Landing Force. In other activity, Rear Admiral Oscar C. Badger, U.S.N., is assigned Commander, Task Force 31 (Yokosuka Operation Force), and all Ships are instructed to organize and equip Bluejacket and Marine landing forces for the occupation of Japan. **(Pacific-Japan)** The Third Fleet launches Planes which strike Airfields, rail yards, and Shipping in northern Honshu. Halsey reports 175 enemy Planes destroyed and 153 damaged. The Minesweeper No. 1 is sunk by Carrier-based Aircraft, off northern Honshu. The Transport No. 21 is sunk by Army Aircraft in the Inland Sea, Japan. Meanwhile, the Japanese Government sues for peace with the Allies, offering to surrender "without prejudice to the Em-

peror's position." Japanese radio announces a willingness for the Japanese to surrender, provided that "NO DEMAND BE MADE FOR THE EMPEROR (HIROHITO) TO NOT RULE JAPAN." **(Pacific-China)** Major General Charles B. Stone, U.S.A., replaces General Chennault as Commander of the U.S. Fourteenth Air Force.

August 11th 1945 — (United States) President Truman informs Japan that its surrender will be accepted by a Supreme Commander; however, the Emperor and the Japanese High Command must first issue cease fire orders to all Japanese Armed Forces. **(Pacific)** Preliminary plans for the activation of Task Force Able are prepared by the III Amphibious Corps; it will participate in the occupation of Japan and be composed of a small Headquarters Detachment, the 5th Marines reinforced, an Amphibian Tractor Company, and a Medical Company. In conjunction, Major General William T. Clement's (U.S.M.C.) selected Staff Officers initiate planning for Task Force Abel's departure for Japan; a RCT is to be prepared for movement to Japan within 48 hours. **(Pacific-Kurile Islands)** The Destroyer U.S.S. *McDermut* (DD-677) is damaged by Naval gunfire.

August 12th 1945 — (United States) The War Department suspends anticipated operations against Fort Bayard (China) due to the imminent cessation of hostilities. **(Pacific-Okinawa)** The Battleship *Pennsylvania* (BB-38) is damaged by an Aircraft torpedo. **(Pacific-Japan)** A Naval Force, commanded by Rear Admiral J.H. Brown, composed of Cruisers and Destroyers, bombards Japanese facilities on Matsuwa and Paramushiro Islands. **(Pacific-Korea)** The Russians pour troops into Korea, taking advantage of the prone Japanese fighting machine.

August 13th 1945 — (Pacific-United States) Documents for the surrender of Japan are sent to General Douglas MacArthur, subsequent to the approval of President Truman. **(Pacific-Okinawa)** The Attack Transport U.S.S. *Lagrange* (APA-124) is damaged by a Kamikaze. **(Pacific-Wake Island)** Marine Corps Planes attack Japanese positions on Peacock Point Battery; it is the final Air strike against the atoll. **(Pacific-Japan)** Vice Admiral McCain's Fast Carrier Task Force launches Planes which strike Tokyo. The Submarine U.S.S. *Atule* (SS-403) sinks the Japanese Coast Defense Vessel No. 6, off Hokkaido. **(Pacific-China)** The Submarine U.S.S. *Spikefish* (SS-404) fires six torpedoes and sinks a Japanese Submarine off the coast of China, giving the Silent Service the final enemy Submarine destroyed during the war. One survivor is plucked from the sea and he identifies the Ship as the I-373. **(Pacific)** At 01:00, Admiral Halsey receives orders to proceed to Tokyo "with caution." A second order arrives from CinCPac, canceling the first order, permitting Halsey to continue his string of attacks. U.S. Planes visit Tokyo and destroy another 422 Planes, 254 of them on the ground, 149 more are damaged and 19 Aircraft are shot down as they approach the U.S. Fleet.

August 14th 1945 — (United States) President Truman makes an announcement, proclaiming that a cease-fire is in effect and that the war with Japan is over. Admiral William D. Leahy reflects: "WE WERE THE FIRST TO HAVE THIS WEAPON IN OUR POSSESSION, AND THE FIRST TO USE IT. THERE IS A PRACTICAL CERTAINTY THAT POTENTIAL ENEMIES WILL HAVE IT IN THE FUTURE AND THAT ATOMIC BOMBS WILL SOMETIME BE USED AGAINST US."..."EMPLOYMENT OF THE ATOMIC BOMB IN WAR WILL TAKE US BACK IN CRUELTY TOWARD NON-COMBATANTS TO THE DAYS OF GHENGIS KHAN."..."UNTIL THE UNITED NATIONS OR SOME WORLD ORGANIZATION CAN GUARANTEE AND HAVE THE

POWER TO ENFORCE THAT GUARANTEE-THAT THE WORLD WILL BE SPARED THE TERRORS OF ATOMIC WARFARE, THE U.S. MUST HAVE MORE AND BETTER ATOM BOMBS THAN ANY POTENTIAL ENEMY." **(Pacific-Japan)** Japan capitulates, agreeing to the surrender ultimatum issued by the Allies at Potsdam. General of the Army Douglas MacArthur is named Supreme Allied Commander to accept the surrender and initiate the occupation of Japan. Japan's message concerning surrender: WITH REFERENCE TO THE JAPANESE GOVERNMENT'S NOTE OF AUGUST 10TH, REGARDING THE ACCEPTANCE OF THE PROVISIONS OF THE POTSDAM DECLARATION AND THE REPLY OF THE GOVERNMENTS OF THE UNITED STATES, GREAT BRITAIN, THE SOVIET UNION, AND CHINA, SENT BY AMERICAN SECRETARY OF STATE BYRNES UNDER THE DATE OF AUGUST 11TH, THE JAPANESE GOVERNMENT HAVE THE HONOR TO COMMUNICATE TO THE GOVERNMENTS OF THE FOUR POWERS AS FOLLOWS: 1.) HIS MAJESTY THE EMPEROR HAS ISSUED AN IMPERIAL RESCRIPT REGARDING JAPAN'S ACCEPTANCE OF THE POTSDAM DECLARATION. 2.) HIS MAJESTY THE EMPEROR IS PREPARED TO AUTHORIZE AND ENSURE THE SIGNATURE BY HIS GOVERNMENT AND THE IMPERIAL GENERAL HEADQUARTERS OF THE NECESSARY TERMS FOR CARRYING OUT THE PROVISIONS OF THE POTSDAM DECLARATION. HIS MAJESTY IS ALSO PREPARED TO ISSUE HIS COMMANDS TO ALL THE MILITARY, NAVAL, AND AIR AUTHORITIES OF JAPAN AND ALL THE FORCES UNDER THEIR CONTROL WHEREVER LOCATED TO CEASE ACTIVE OPERATIONS, TO SURRENDER ARMS, AND TO ISSUE SUCH ORDERS AS MAY BE REQUIRED BY THE SUPREME COMMANDER OF THE ALLIED FORCES FOR THE EXECUTION OF THE ABOVE MENTIONED TERMS. This culminates the war, having now achieved the unconditional surrender of Italy, Germany, and Japan. It has been three years, eight months, and seven days since the attack against Pearl Harbor. **(Pacific-Sea of Japan)** The Submarine U.S.S. *Torsk* sinks the Japanese Coast Defense Vessels No. 13 and No. 47, the latter becoming the final enemy Vessel sunk by a U.S. Submarine during the war. As the last torpedo is fired, Japan is surrounded by American Submarines, while the Third Fleet stands at the approaches to Tokyo and the skies are inundated with American Planes. **(Pacific-Philippines)** The 11th Airborne Division is transported by Air to Okinawa for further movement to Japan.

August 15th 1945 — (United States) The Joint Chiefs of Staff expound General Order No. 1, calling for the occupation of strategic areas in Japan, Korea, and the China coast. In other activity, the Commandant U.S.M.C. and the Under Secretary of the Navy approve the general plan of the demobilization of the Adjusted Service Rating System of Discharge and Separation: the "Point System." **(Pacific)** All offensive action against Japan is terminated; however, prior to the news of surrender reaching the Fleet, Planes are dispatched from the Fast Carrier Task Force of Vice Admiral J.S. McCain to attack Airfields in the Tokyo vicinity; the raids are strongly opposed by enemy Aircraft. Prior to the announcement of the Japanese surrender reaching the Fleet, Admiral Halsey had launched Planes to strike the Japanese, 103 Aircraft (Able 1) of the first wave hit the mark, but the second wave (Able 2) is recalled about five minutes from the target and Able 3 is held on the flight deck. Admiral Halsey, coincidentally having breakfast with Doug Moulton, the same Officer who was sharing breakfast with him when news arrived about the attack on Pearl Harbor, is informed of the termination of the war. After reading a transcript of President Truman's official proclamation,

Halsey remarks: "I HOPE IT (the world) WILL REMEMBER ALSO THAT WHEN HOSTILITIES ENDED, THE CAPITAL OF THE JAPANESE EMPIRE HAD JUST BEEN BOMBED, STRAFED AND ROCKETED BY PLANES OF THE THIRD FLEET, AND WAS ABOUT TO BE BOMBED, STRAFED, AND ROCKETED AGAIN. LAST, I HOPE IT WILL REMEMBER THAT SEVEN OF THE MEN ON STRIKE ABLE 1 DID NOT RETURN." Also, some Japanese Planes attack the Third Fleet subsequent to the termination of hostilities. At 11:25, a Japanese Dive Bomber closes on the Fleet prompting an announcement: "TALLY HO! ONE BANDIT DIVING." Soon after, another announcement: "SPLASH ONE JUDY." before day's end, eight enemy Planes are knocked out by the Planes and guns of the Third Fleet, with the final kill coming at 1445. During the two campaigns, Third Fleet destroyed 10,355 Planes; 135 Warships; another 90 Warships probably sunk; 150 Warships damaged and 1,000 Merchant Vessels sunk. Admiral Halsey after tallying his figures remarks: "I HOPE NO NATION EVER DARES CHALLENGE THIS RECORD. BUT IF IT DOES, I HOPE THAT THE THIRD FLEET IS THERE TO DEFEND IT." In other activity, a Naval Task Group, commanded by Commodore R.W. Simpson, is formed to tend to the Allied prisoners of war still alive and held by the Japanese; Simpson's Force is to liberate, give medical treatment, and evacuate the troops from Japan. Also, Admiral McCain has been aware that he is to be relieved by Vice Admiral John H. Towers when the Fleet arrives off Eniwetok. As word of Japan's capitulation gets out, McCain requests immediate detachment, but Halsey insists that he remain for the surrender stating: "YOU WERE COMMANDING THIS TASK FORCE WHEN THE WAR ENDED AND I'M MAKING SURE THAT HISTORY GETS IT STRAIGHT." Soon after, Admiral McCain succumbs to a heart attack. **(Pacific-China)** General Wedemeyer has received instructions for the demobilization of the U.S. Armed Forces. He instructs his Officers to establish plans to comply with the orders which initiate a point system. General Wedemeyer, (other Officers share the opinion) is concerned about draining too many specialized troops too fast. General Wedemeyer subsequently states: "MANY CONGRESSMEN WERE URGING THAT THE BOYS BE SENT HOME IN ORDER TO PLEASE THEIR CONSTITUENTS AND ASSURE THEIR RETURN TO OFFICE. THEY WERE FOR THE MOST PART UNMINDFUL OF THE FACT THAT THE COMMUNIST INTERNATIONAL CONSPIRACY CONSTITUTED AN EVEN GREATER DANGER THAN THE NAZIS AND THE JAPANESE WE HAD SOUNDLY DEFEATED." The movement "BRING OUR BOYS BACK," according to General Wedemeyer: "WAS PART OF THE POSTWAR HYSTERIA WHICH THE COMMUNISTS SO CLEVERLY AND WIDELY EXPLOITED."

August 15th 1945 — (Pacific-P.O.W.s) The U.S. Fourteenth Air Force transports O.S.S. "Mercy Teams" to Japanese P.O.W. camps-"Mission Magpie"-Four Airmen from the Doolittle Raid and Commander Winfield S. Scott, the Commander of the Navy and Marines on Wake Island (1941) are discovered near Peking, China. The Plane, troubled with difficulties, lands at Gai Lam, near Hanoi, but it finally gets to its destination. Also, another O.S.S. Mercy Team discovers the survivors of the U.S.S. *Houston*, which was lost at the Battle of the Java Sea during February of 1942. In Thailand, two P.O.W.s had escaped from a camp near Bankok during the summer of 1945 and explained that hundreds more Allied P.O.W.s were still there (Petburi Prison Camp). The team liberates 315 survivors who are still wearing their original Khaki drill uniforms. During the latter part of August, these beleaguered troops are flown to Calcutta to prepare for the long road ahead to restore their dignity and health.

August 16th 1945 — (Pacific-Manchuria) The Americans and other Allied P.O.W.s are reluctantly ready to be packed off to Korea. But a hefty B-29 soars overhead and U.S. Paratroops drop in near the camp at Mukden, Manchuria to save the emaciated prisoners from more bad fate. Major General George M. Parker and Brigadier General Lewis C. Beebe, astonished at the beautiful sight begin to assume order in the camp. Later that night the well-fed Paratroops, under Major J. T. Hennessey (carrying a powerful radio) enter the camp and directly visit the Headquarters. The arrival of the Yanks brings a happy conclusion to the thoughts of the P.O.W.s who according to General Wainright had only one thought: " TO BE DONE WITH THE YEARS OF LIVING UNDER THE JAPS." Also, four Russian Officers enter the camp on the night of the 16th; they allow the Japanese five minutes to line up in formation and drop their weapons on the ground. The Russians tell General Parker to pick twenty men for guards, then he picks up rifles and hands one to each of the P.O.W.s. The Russian authorities will detain a U.S. Plane that arrives in several days to evacuate the P.O.W.s.

August 17th 1945 — (Pacific-Japan) General Prince Higashikuni becomes Prime Minister of Japan and forms a new cabinet.

August 19th 1945 — (Pacific-Philippines) A Japanese contingent arrives in Manila to receive instructions for the formal surrender ceremony. The Japanese representatives depart for Japan on the following day with information and instructions concerning the U.S. occupation of Japan and the Japanese signing of the surrender instrument. The Japanese forces in the Pacific islands south of Japan are to capitulate to CinCPOA or his designated representatives, and the Japanese forces in the Philippines, the southern sector of Korea, and the Japanese mainland are directed to surrender to the CinCSWPA or his designated representatives. **(Pacific-Manchuria)** An American Doctor and a Corporal Leith arrive at Sian P.O.W. camp; both men are Paratroopers.

August 20th 1945 — (Pacific-Marianas) Vice Admiral George D. Murray, U.S.N., Commander Marianas organizes the Marianas Surrender Acceptance and Occupation Command (Task Group 94.3) to ensure the surrender of all enemy troops in the entire area conforms. Rear Admiral Oscar C. Badger, U.S.N., forms the Ships assigned to the Task Force 31 into a separate Tactical Group for the occupation of Japan's Yokosuka Naval Base. In conjunction, the 4th Regimental Combat Team (U.S.M.C.) arrives in Guam to prepare for embarkation to Japan. **(Pacific-Japan)** A blistering typhoon compels Admiral Halsey to postpone the landing of forces at Yokosuka, Japan, scheduled for August 25th until the 28th.

August 21st 1945 — (United States) Asiatic Wing, Naval Air Transport Service is established at Oakland, California. **(Pacific)** Lt. General Robert L. Eichelberger, U.S.A., Commanding Officer, Eighth Army orders that the landing of Task Force 31 be made at the Naval Base at Yokosuka, Japan. The Reserve Battalion, 4th Marines is ordered to land on Futtsu Saki to counterbalance any threat by shore batteries and coastal forts. **(Pacific-Manchuria)** An American Plane, transporting an O.S.S. Mercy Team lands in Manchuria at Mukden (Sian camp) and is informed by the Japanese that the Russians must grant permission for the evacuation of the P.O.W.s. The Russians grant the permission, however, their word means absolutely nothing. General Jonathan M. Wainright, British

General Edward M. Percival (Commander at Malaya) are among the prisoners. The Russian Allies hold up the flight and General Wainright for one week, then to top this audacity, the Russians expel the O.S.S. Mercy Team (Cardinal Mission) and intern the remaining P.O.W.s (most of whom are sickly) until the surrender of Japan. General Wainright had been informed on the 18th that the war was over; on the following morning a Japanese Lieutenant speaks to the P.O.W.s through an interpreter stating: "BY ORDER OF THE EMPEROR, THE WAR HAS BEEN AMICABLY TERMINATED." One of the members of the team, Captain R.F. Hilsman Jr., is convinced his father is being held alive in Manchuria; his determined efforts locate his father at Hoten Prison Camp; Colonel Hilsman had been in command of the Negro Island, Philippines (1942). Another member of the Mercy Teams, John Birch is killed by Communist Chinese as he approaches a P.O.W. camp. The John Birch Society uses his name, however, Birch was not a member of the Society.

August 22nd 1945 — (Pacific-Marshalls) The Japanese on Mili Atoll surrender, becoming the first Jap Garrison in the Pacific Ocean area to do so; the surrender is accepted on the deck of the Destroyer Escort *Levy* (DE-162).

August 23rd 1945 — (Pacific-Okinawa) Aircraft, Fleet Marine Force, Pacific orders Marine Aircraft Group 31 (at Chimu Airfield) to fly to Japan to support the northern occupation operation.

August 24th 1945 — (Pacific-Manchuria) The Sian P.O.W. camp is full of U.S. Jeeps and Trucks, all bearing Russian insignias. The Russian Commanding Officer informs General Wainright and British General Percival: "I'M GOING TO MUKDEN WITH MY DETACHMENT AND THESE JEEPS. IF YOU CAN FURNISH YOUR OWN TRANSPORTATION AND BE READY IN AN HOUR, I'LL TAKE YOU WITH ME." The Convoy departs at about 18:00, but the Russian maps of Manchuria are terribly inaccurate and the Convoy strolls along the wrong roads for five hours.

August 25th 1945 — (Pacific) Task Force 31 is informed that the typhoon threat is holding up U.S. Army Air operations (for 48 hours) and that the Third Fleet will not move into Sagmi Wan (Tokyo Bay's outer bay) until the 28th. **(Pacific-Japan)** Despite the typhoon threat, Carrier-based Aircraft initiate daily sorties over Japan to watch the Airfields and Shipping activity and to locate Allied prisoner of war camps and furnish supplies for them. The flights are maintained until September 2nd 1945.

August 27th 1945 — (Pacific-Philippines) The forward contingents of Marine Bomber Squadron 611 departs for Peleliu to join the 4th Marine Air Wing. **(Pacific-Japan)** General MacArthur requests that no attempts be made to recover P.O.W.s until the Army is ready, but two British P.O.W.s are picked up by Picket Boats and their explicit accounts of Japanese atrocities against the Allies change the plans. On the 29th, Admiral Nimitz arrives at 14:20 and Halsey gets permission to liberate the P.O.W.s. The U.S. Third Fleet, commanded by Admiral W.F. Halsey, moves into Sagami Bay, the outer bay to Tokyo. The Japanese have been directed to send the Destroyer *Hatsuzakuka* to guide the U.S. Warships through the minefields to accept the surrender of the Yokosuku Base. Another Officer, Vice Admiral Mick Carney, standing next to Halsey, watching the beleaguered Destroyer approach remarks: "YOU WANTED THE JAP NAVY, ADMIRAL. WELL THERE IT IS." The fourteen representatives are brought aboard the Destroyer U.S.S. *Nicholas* and processed. They are ordered to take baths before mixing among the Fleet and when they are taken aboard the

Missouri they are again searched, followed by being photographed and marched under guard to Captain Murray's cabin for the surrender ceremony. Meanwhile, two Japanese Submarines surrender to four U.S. Destroyers off Honshu. Vice Admiral Carney remarks after the encounter: "CAPTAIN OTANI, REPRESENTING NAVAL HEADQUARTERS WAS A CARICATURE OF A TREACHEROUS BRUTE. CAPTAIN TAKASAKI, REPRESENTING THE YOKOSUKA COMMAND WAS ALSO A CARICATURE, BUT OF BUGS BUNNY; I HALF EXPECTED HIM TO GREET ME WITH, HIYA DOC!" **(Pacific-China)** General Wainright arrives at a U.S. Airbase at Sian, China (same name as P.O.W. camp). On the following morning, General Wainright gets his first sight of Old Glory being raised at Reveille since his capture during May of 1942; he also hears a new word, GI. Soon after he heads for Chungking, has lunch with General Wedemeyer and then delivers an address that is broadcast in the United States. On the 31st, Wainright has dinner on Okinawa with his old boss, General MacArthur. General Wainright recalls the event. MacArthur: "WELL, I'M GLAD TO SEE YOU." Wainright: " I'M GLAD TO SEE YOU." Wainright then discusses dinner: "WE SAT DOWN AND ATE, SERVED BY BOWED JAP WAITERS. I SKETCHED BRIEFLY THE KIND OF LIVES WE LIVED AS CAPTIVES AND HE TOLD ME OF THE DIFFICULTIES OF GETTING TO WHERE WE SAT THIS NIGHT.."

August 28th 1945 — (Pacific-Japan) U.S. Air Force Technicians land at Atsugi Airdrome, outside of Tokyo, becoming the first U.S. troops to land in Japan. The main occupational force is held back for 48 hours due to the typhoon. Admiral Halsey has a string of Naval Warships protecting the line of flight from Okinawa to protect the incoming 11th Airborne Division. He takes note that one of the first things to get their attention is a sign which a Third Fleet Pilot forced the Japanese to paint; "WELCOME TO THE U.S. ARMY FROM THE THIRD FLEET." In other activity, Administrative and operational control of the Seventh Fleet, under Admiral T. C. Kinkaid, transfers from control of Commander in Chief SWPA (MacArthur) to CinC Pacific Fleet (Nimitz).

August 29th 1945 — (Pacific-Japan) The Submarine U.S.S. *Segundo* (SS-398) accepts the surrender of a Japanese Submarine off the northeastern coast of Honshu. Also, Admiral Nimitz arrives in Tokyo Bay and instructs Admiral Halsey to begin an immediate rescue of Allied prisoners held in Japanese prisoner of war camps. Captain Harold Stassen, U.S.N.: "THOSE ARE OUR BOYS! GO GET THEM." upon arrival at Camp Omori 8, the Japanese bar entrance. A quick reference to Admiral Halsey and the problem ends. At Kawasaki Bunsha, Stassen mentions Halsey's name to a Bluejacket and he responds: "I KNEW IT! I TOLD THOSE JAP BASTARDS THAT ADMIRAL HALSEY WOULD BE HERE AFTER US." By midnight of the 29th, 794 P.O.W.s are evacuated to the Vessel *Benevolence* and within two weeks 19,000 more P.O.W.s are liberated. **(Pacific)** Initial plans for deploying the III Amphibious Corps in North China are issued; the tentative date for implementation is established as September 15th.

August 30th 1945 — (Pacific-Carolines) Brigadier General Robert Blake, U.S.M.C., is appointed Prospective Island Commander, Truk. **(Pacific-Japan)** The occupation of Japan is official as the 11th Airborne Division is flown to Atsugi Airfield, while an amphibious force composed of the 4th Marines, 6th Marine Division, Sailors, British Sailors, and Royal Marine Commandos land at Yokosuka Naval Base and at the harbor forts off Miure Peninsula. The first landing craft debark contingents of the 2nd Battalion, 4th Marines at Futteu Saki;

however, the Marines discover the mortars and coastal guns inoperable and reembark. The main body of the 4th Marines moves ashore at Beaches Red and Green at Yokosuka without incident, advancing inland to establish a defensive perimeter around the Airbase and Naval Base. The Fleet Landing Force's Commanding Officer, Major General William T. Clement U.S.M.C., accepts the surrender of Yokosuka Naval Base area, and Rear Admirals Robert B. Carney and O.C. Badger, U.S.N., receive the surrender of the First Naval District. The Japanese civil Police are permitted to retain their firearms; later, they stop the practice of saluting Allied Officers, incensing Admiral Halsey. He sends Oliver (Scrappy) O. Kessing to see the Mayor of Yokosuka to ensure that the Police salute Allied Officers. The Mayor inquires: "HOW WILL THEY KNOW WHO IS AN OFFICER AND WHO IS NOT?" Kessing makes it easy stating: "IF THEY DON'T KNOW, THEY BETTER PLAY IT SAFE BY SALUTING EVERY FOREIGN UNIFORM." **(Pacific-China)** British troops reoccupy Hong Kong.

August 31st 1945 — (Pacific) The Headquarters and Service Battalion, Fleet Marine Force, Pacific, is disbanded. **(Pacific-Japan)** Company L, 3rd Battalion, 4th Marines, land at Tateyama Naval Air Station on Sagmi Wan (Honshu), initiating reconnaissance of the beach areas and to cover the landing of the 112th Cavalry, U.S.A. scheduled for the 3rd of September; the Base capitulates without incident. **Pacific-Marcus Island)** The Japanese surrender Marcus Island to Rear Admiral F.E.M. Whiting on board the Destroyer U.S.S. *Bagley*.

September 1st 1945 — (Pacific-Japan) Allied troops now control the majority of strategic terrain along the coast of Tokyo Bay, except Tokyo. **(Pacific-Philippines)** Marine Aircraft Groups, Zamboanga is disbanded; operational control of Moret Field and the air defense of Mindanao is assumed by the 13th Fighter Command, U.S.A. **(Atlantic-Cuba)** The Marine Barracks, Naval Operating Base, Guantanamo Bay is redesignated a Marine Corps Base.

September 2nd 1945 — (Pacific-Japan) The official and unconditional surrender of Japan occurs on the decks of the U.S.S. *Missouri* in Tokyo Bay. General of the Army Douglas MacArthur signs for the Allied Powers, and Admiral C.F. Nimitz signs on behalf of the United States. As General MacArthur signs the surrender document, he turns and places his arms around Admiral Halsey and says: "START EM NOW." Halsey responds: "AYE AYE SIR," and 450 Planes soar from the crowded decks of the Carriers and pass over the heads of the Japanese as they officially capitulate aboard the *Mis souri*. Throngs of American Servicemen carpet every available inch of the Vessel to be a part of history. General Wainright gives his observations of the ceremony: "WHEN THE GLUM LITTLE JAP DELEGATION HAD TAKEN ITS PLACE TO FILL THE SQUARE, LED BY FOREIGN MINISTER MAMORU SHINGEMITSU-IN A STOVEPIPE HAT, WHITE GLOVES, AND A DEEP DIP IN HIS ILL-FITTED WOODEN LEG- MacARTHUR MADE HIS ENTRANCE WITH ADMIRAL NIMITZ. IT WAS AN UNFORGETTABLE MOMENT. After the ceremony, General Wainright meets Admiral Halsey in his cabin and is shown a saddle presented to Halsey by the Salinas, California Chamber of Commerce; Halsey had vowed to get to Tokyo to ride the Emperor's white horse. Halsey, stuck by his boast will soon ride a horse, but not the Emperor's. General Wainright also meets with General MacArthur and is offered a command in Japan if he desires; MacArthur also explains that he wants General Wainright in Baguio at the surrender ceremony of the Philippines on the following day. This war involving the United States ends without Congressional approval and without a treaty; the hostilities are finally terminated by a Presidential proclamation by President Truman on December 31st, 1946. Meanwhile, advance contingents of the Eighth Army enter Tokyo harbor, while Ships transporting Headquarters of the XI Corps, U.S.A., and the 1st Cavalry Division move into the docks at Yokohama, debarking the forces; the 112th Cavalry moves to Tateyama. **(Pacific-Carolines)** On Truk Island, the Japanese capitulate, surrendering the largest concentration of Japanese troops in the Pacific. The surrender includes all troops on Truk, Wake, the Palaus, Mortlake (Nomoi), Mille, Ponape, Kusaie, Jaluit, Maloelap, Wotje, Puluwat, Wolesi, Rota, Pagan, Namoluk, Nauru, and Ocean. The Japanese Commanding Officer on Rota Island, Marianas surrenders to Colonel Howard N. Stent, (for Major General Henry L. Larsen, U.S.M.C., Commanding Officer of Guam). Meanwhile, the Japanese Commanding Officer of the Palau Group capitulates to Brigadier General Ford O. Rogers, U.S.M.C., Island Commander, Peleliu; the surrender includes all forces under his command including those on Yap.

Jubilant troops aboard the Missouri observing the surrender ceremony. Note one Sailor perched way up on the yard for a bird's eye view.

Mamoru Shigemitsu, followed by General Umezu, aboard the U.S.S. Missouri for the purpose of signing the surrender document, signifying the capitulation of Japan.

Admiral Nimitz, representing the U.S. signs the surrender document. General MacArthur, Admiral Halsey and Admiral Sherman observe.

September 3rd 1945 — (Pacific-Japan) Company L, 3rd Battalion, 4th Marines, relieved by the 112th Cavalry, U.S.A., at Tateyama Naval Air Station, returns to Yokosuka. Meanwhile, a U.S. Army Task Force attached to 32nd Infantry Division is transported by air to Kanoya to secure an emergency Airfield on the air route to Tokyo from Okinawa and the Philippines. **(Pacific-Volcano-Bonins)** Commodore John H. Magruder, Jr., U.S.N. accepts the surrender of the Japanese forces in the Bonins; the short ceremony takes place on Chichi Jima. While the U.S. was bombing the Bonins, the Japanese captured eight Airmen; four of them were executed. Subsequently, when it became apparent that no reinforcements or supplies would arive, the remaining four Americans were cannibalized. **(Pacific-Philippines)** Major General Edmund H. Leavey, Chief of Staff for Lt. General Styler accepts the surrender of the Japanese forces on the Philippines. Japanese General Yamashita, who had been hiding in the mountains west of the Cagayan Valley had been captured on the previous day. He is accused of being responsible for the atrocities committed in the Philippines, despite the fact that he arrived in the Philippines subsequent to the crimes. He receives a speedy trial and is executed before the end of the year. British General Percival, whom Yamashita had forced to surrender unconditionally at Singapore during February 1942, shows no outward emotion. General Wainright, not surprisingly, asks if Yamashita will be shown courtesy due his rank and receives General Styer's assurances, responding: "HE'LL BE GIVEN EVERYTHING HE'S ENTITLED TO UNDER THE GENEVA CONVENTION. WE DON'T WANT TO BE GUILTY OF TREATING ANYONE AS THE JAPS TREATED YOU AND YOUR MEN." Meanwhile, General Wainright continues to come across new and exciting things which he had missed since his captivity. He comes upon another unusual sight which he describes as "one of the most astonishing sights of my two score years in the Army (a female wearing a feminine version of a uniform)," inquiring: "I BEG YOUR PARDON, BUT WHAT ARE YOU?" and he receives the response: "WHY, I'M A WAC, SIR."

General Wainright reacts, "A WHAT?" Wainright, after several more minutes of conversation with the WAC is still perplexed and asks an accompanying Officer: "WHAT THE DEVIL IS A WAC?" General Wainright, having been imprisoned by the Japanese had no knowledge of the formation of the Women's Army Corps.

September 4th 1945 — (Pacific-Marcus Island) The 11th Military Police Company (Provisional) of the 5th Military Police Battalion arrive to guard the island. **(Pacific-Marianas)** Rota Island is occupied. Colonel Gale T. Cummings, U.S.M.C. is appointed temporary island Commander. The bombed out Airstrip is repaired immediately by Marines and Seabees. **(Pacific-Wake Island)** Brigadier General Lawson H. M. Sanderson, Commanding Officer of the 4th Marine Aircraft Wing, accepts the surrender of the Japanese forces on the island on behalf of the Commander, Marshalls, Gilberts area; the atoll is designated a Naval Air Facility.

September 6th 1945 — (Pacific-Japan) Ships' detachments of Bluejackets and Marines, dispatched to shore for security details, return to their designated Vessels; the Provisional Landing units are deactivated. In other activity, the 4th Marines assumes responsibility for Yokosuka Naval Base, permitting the Sailors, seagoing Marines, and British forces to return to their Vessels. Also, the 32nd Division, U.S.A. replaces the 3rd Marine Division as part of the occupation force. **(Pacific-Bismarcks)** Rabaul surrenders to Australian forces.

September 7th 1945 — (Pacific-Japan) Advance elements of Headquarters, Marine Aircraft Group 31, and Planes of Marine Fighter Squadron 441 arrive from Okinawa at Yokosuka Airfield, becoming the first Aviation unit to operate in Japan. The detachment is under command of the Third Fleet. **(Pacific-Ryuku Islands)** General Joseph J.W. Stilwell, U.S.A. accepts the surrender of the Ryukyus Garrison. **(Pacific-Wake Island)** U.S. occupation forces, including a Marine detachment of two Officers and 54 enlisted men from the Marshalls, begin arriving.

September 8th 1945 — (Pacific) The III Amphibious Corps' order for movement to north China is given. **(Pacific-Japan)** The Commander, Fleet Activities, Yokosuka takes responsibility for the Naval occupation area for S.C.A.P. (Strategic Command Allied Powers); Task Force 31 is simultaneously dissolved. Also, Admiral Halsey is with General MacArthur in Tokyo for the city's formal surrender. About one month prior, an edict is given to the Japanese people demanding that all safes be turned in order to convert them to war supplies. As Halsey moves through Tokyo, it is apparent that few people paid any attention to the Imperial order. U.S. bombing raids against the flimsy Japanese buildings has leveled the houses, but scores of safes lay exposed; Tojo apologizes to the Emperor. During Admiral Halsey's last tour of Tokyo, Major General William C. Chase, Commanding General, 1st Cavalry Division, sends a car, escort and four Tanks to bring Admiral Halsey to camp for a presentation. Halsey arrives to find a waiting stead and the challenge to ride the white horse. When the ride ends, both the Admiral and his stead appear happy. Halsey notes: "GENERAL CHASE SHOWED SOME MERCY. THE WHITE HORSE HAD ONLY TWO SPEEDS, SLOW AND VERY SLOW. Admiral Halsey, always appreciative of his friends, would like to return the favor, stating: "I WANT TO TAKE BILL ACROSS THE NORTH SEA ON A DESTROYER IN MIDWINTER." At about the same time, a directive comes in from Naval Headquarters stating: "THE USE OF INSULTING

EPITHETS IN CONNECTION WITH THE JAPANESE AS A RACE OR AS INDIVIDUALS DOES NOT BECOME OFFICERS OF THE UNITED STATES NAVY." Halsey reacts, stating: "I'LL HAVE TO REFORM, BUT I STILL WOULD LIKE TO KICK THE LITTLE BASTARDS' TEETH IN. THE WAR ENDED TOO SOON. THERE ARE TOO MANY OF THEM LEFT."

September 11th 1945 — (Pacific-Guam) Japanese Lt. Colonel Hideyuki Takeda surrenders the remaining contingent of organized Japanese troops on the island.

September 11th-October 2nd 1945 - (Atlantic-Europe) The London Conference convenes; however, the Allies cannot agree on treaties for the Axis nations involved.

September 14th 1945 — (Pacific-Japan) Colonel Daniel W. Torrey, Commanding Officer Marine Aircraft Group 22, and a reconnaissance detachment lands at Omura Airfield for an inspection; it is selected as the Base for Marine Air operations in southern Japan.

September 16th 1945 — (Pacific-Japan) An advance reconnaissance detachment (V Amphibious Corps), led by Colonel Walter W. Wensinger, Corps Operations Officer arrives at Nagasaki to prepare for the landing of the V Amphibious Corps troops and supporting Army units. In other activity, Marine Aircraft Group 31 at Yokosuka Airfield comes under control of Fifth Air Force.

September 19th 1945 — (Pacific-Japan) Admiral Raymond A. Spruance, U.S.N., Commander Fifth Fleet relieves Admiral Halsey of his responsibilities in the occupation of Japan. Spruance assumes command of all Naval operations in the Japanese Empire.

September 20th 1945 — (Pacific-Japan) Brigadier General William T. Clement, U.S.M.C., Commanding Officer of Task Force Able is relieved by Lt. Colonel Fred D. Beans at Yokohama. Clement and his Staff return to the 6th Marine Division on Guam. Also, another Reconnaissance detachment including V Amphibious Corps Officers and Officers of the 5th Marine Division arrive at Sasebo and finish preparations for the landing of Corps contingents and supporting Army units. Meanwhile, some elements of Marine Aircraft Group 22 arrives at Omura Airfield from Okinawa to bolster the occupation operations.

September 22nd 1945 — (Pacific-Japan) The V Amphibious Corps Headquarters troops and the 5th Marine Division arrive at Sasebo. The 26th Marines (minus 2nd Battalion), supported by the 2nd Battalion, 28th Marines, lands on the beaches at the Naval Air Station. The Marines relieve Japanese guards and take over protection of Base installations as well as the stores in the area. Subsequently, contingents of the 13th and 27th Marines and the 5th Tank Battalion establish guard posts and implement security Patrols ashore. On the following day, Major General Harry Schmidt, V Amphibious Corps Commander, establishes a Command Post at Sasebo and assumes command of the 2nd and 5th Marine Divisions; Major General Thomas E. Bourke (5th Division) also establishes a Command Post there. **(Atlantic-Germany)** General Patton, while speaking to the press responds candidly to some questions and finds himself in trouble with the politicians in Washington. He has been using Germans to keep the rails and other facilities running properly and has been getting heat because of it. When a reporter prods him into asking a flimsy question about comparing Germans joining the National Socialist Party (Nazi) being about equal to Americans joining the Democratic or Republican Party, he wings it and responds affirmatively, jolting the politicians. Coincidentally, while Patton receives heat for using Germans, the U.S. is using captured German Intelligence agents (General Gehlen's men) to prepare intelligence on the Russians. German General Gehlen becomes a top NATO leader. General Patton loses his command of the remnant Third Army after this press conference.

September 23rd 1945 — (Pacific-Japan) The remaining contingents of the 5th Marine Division land at Sasebo. In other activity, the 2nd and 6th Marines, 2nd Marine Division land at Nagasaki, relieving Marine detachments from the U.S.S. *Biloxi* and *Wickita* which had been used for security details.

September 24th 1945 — (Pacific-Japan) General Walter Krueger, Commander U.S. Sixth Army, takes control of all forces ashore. Also, the remaining contingents of the 2nd Marine Division land at Nagasaki. On the following day, the U.S. Sixth Army begins landing at Wakayama.

September 27th 1945 — (Pacific-Japan) Advance elements of the V Amphibious Corps move to Fukuoka, the biggest city in Kyushu. **(Pacific-Carolines)** The Prospective Island Commander, Truk is redesignated the Prospective Commanding General, Occupation Forces, Truk and Central Carolines, under the jurisdiction of Island Commander, Guam.

September 30th 1945 — (Pacific-Japan) The V Amphibious Corps begins arriving at Fukuoka, Kyushu, in strength for occupation duty. Brigadier General Ray A. Robinson, U.S.M.C., Asst. Commander, 5th Marine Division receives command of the Fukuoka Occupation Force, composed of the 28th Marines, reinforced and Army support units. **(Pacific-China)** The III Amphibious Corps arrives at Tangku to implement the occupation of north China. The 3rd Battalion, 7th Marines move by rail to Tientsin, arriving on the following day.

October 1st 1945 — (Pacific-Japan) Kanoya Airfield is occupied by a U.S. Army Task Force, the only major Allied unit ashore other than the 2nd and 5th Marine Divisions. **(Pacific-China)** The 1st Battalion, 7th Marines, reinforced, arrive at Chinwangtao; its Commanding Officer quells ongoing fighting between Communist regular and Guerrilla and former Japanese puppet troops. Marines replace the puppet troops along their perimeter.

October 2nd 1945 — (Pacific-Japan) A Reconnaissance Company of the 5th Marine Division moves north, pushing from Sasebo to Hirado Island.

October 3rd-4th 1945 — (Pacific-China) A Communist Company sized force raids Hsin Ho dump, stealing several cases of ammunition; however, the 1st Battalion, 5th Marines, which is guarding the area, reclaims most of the contraband.

October 6th 1945 — (Pacific-China) Major General Keller E. Rockey, Commanding Officer, III Amphibious Corps accepts the surrender of 50,000 Japanese troops in the area Tientsin-Tangku, Chinwangtao region. Also, Headquarters, 1st Marine Aircraft Wing is established at the French Arsenal located near an Airfield outside of Tientsin. Despite the close of hostilities with Japan, combat is not terminated; Chinese Communists about 40-50 strong attack a contingent of Engineers and their supporting Marine Rifle Platoon which is dispatched to clear a roadblock on the Tientsin-Peiping road, instigating the first major skirmish between Marines and the Chinese Communists in northern China. The roadblocks are cleared on the following day when the Marines receive added support from a Tank Platoon and Carrier Planes.

October 7th 1945 — (Pacific-China) The 29th Marines, 6th Marine Division is scheduled to land at Chefoo, which is held by the Communists, but this is delayed due to anticipated hostility. Toward the latter part of the month, the III Amphibious Corps directs the 6th Marine Division to send a reinforced Infantry Battalion to handle the situation in Chefoo. In other activity, the 5th Marines arrive in Peiping, about 65 miles north of Tientsin.

October 10th 1945 — (Pacific-China) About 50,000 Japanese troops in the area of Peiping surrender to the 11th War Area Commander. **(Pacific-Volcano-Bonins)** Advance contingents of the 1st Battalion, 3rd Marines land on Chichi Jima for occupation duty.

October 11th 1945 — (Pacific-China) The 6th Marine Division lands at Tsingtao; contingents move to Tsangkou Airfield about ten miles outside the town, securing it. On the following day, Observation Planes attached to Marine Observation Squadron 6 arrive at the Airfield.

October 15th 1945 — (Pacific-Japan) Company A (reinforced), 5th Tank Battalion (Oita Occupation Force) begins reconnaissance of the Military installation area in the coastal sector, acting as an advance contingent for the 32nd Infantry Division.

October 18th-19th 1945 — (Pacific-Japan) The 127th Infantry (minus the 1st Battalion) lands at Sasebo and will assume responsibility for the 26th Marines' sector; on the following day, the 26th Marines are detached from the 5th Marine Division and will revert to Fleet Marine Force, Pacific, and subsequently moves to the Palau Islands to oversee the repatriation of the Japanese troops in the Western Carolines.

October 24th 1945 — (Pacific-Japan) The 32nd Infantry Division establishes a Command Post in Fukuoka. In conjunction, the Fukuoka Occupation Force is disbanded, its components assigned support roles in the northern Kyushu area. In other activity, the 27th Marines (minus the 1st Battalion) sets up Headquarters in Kurume and takes responsibility for the sector of the 5th Marine Division.

October 25th 1945 — (Pacific-China) The Japanese officially surrender their Tsingtao Garrison at Shangtung; Major General L. C. Shepherd, U.S.M.C., and Lt. General Chen Pao-Tsang, representing the Chinese Central Government, accept the surrender.

October 26th 1945 — (Pacific-Palaus) The 26th Marines arrive at Peleliu, relieving the 111th Infantry, U.S.A. and assuming responsibility for Garrisoning the island.

October 27th 1945 — (Pacific-Japan) Contingents of the 2nd Marine Division (2nd Battalion, 2nd Marines) arrive at Kanoya, relieving a U.S. Army Task Force.

October 29th 1945 — (Pacific-Japan) Most of the 1st Battalion, 8th Marines, 2nd Marine Division moves from Kumamoto to Kagoshima City and assumes control of western Kagoshima. **(Pacific-China)** The 1st Battalion, 5th Marines, moves to Tangku to protect the railroad there and also moves contingents to Taku, the primary port in North China.

October 30th 1945 — (Pacific-Japan) The 2nd Battalion, 2nd Marines, 2nd Marine Division assumes operational control of the Army Air Force contingent, maintaining the emergency Airfield at Kanoya and freeing a Battalion of the 32nd Division, U.S.A., which returns to Sasebo and rejoins its Regiment.

October 31st 1945 — (Pacific-China) Major General Louis E.

743

Woods arrives at Tientsin and assumes command of the 1st Marine Aircraft Wing from Brigadier General Thomas Larkin. In other activity, the 4th Marines' occupational sector is greatly reduced in size, being confined to the Naval Base, Airfield, and the town of Yokosuka. On the following day, control of the 4th Marines reverts to Commander, U.S. Fleet Activities, passing from U.S. Eighth Army.

November 1945 — (Pacific-China) General Wedemeyer informs Chiang Kai-shek that the U.S. has decided not to send troops to Manchuria to assist the Nationalist Chinese against the Chinese Communists. The message in part: "I AM AUTHORIZED TO ASSIST THE CHINESE IN PLANNING (for occupation of Manchuria) BUT CANNOT SEND AMERICANS TO THAT AREA. THE U.S. FEELS THAT THE ARRANGEMENTS SHOULD BE ACCOMPLISHED BETWEEN THE CHINESE AND SOVIET GOVERNMENTS." There are Soviet Communist and other dissident forces in China and Manchuria. The report is secret, but during the Congressional hearings in Washington, D.C., investigating the Communists, it becomes known that the Communists had a copy of the Wedemeyer report. Also, during 1949, Ching Nu-chi, the Chinese Documents Secretariat turns Communist during 1949; he had worked in General Wedemeyer's office.

November 1st 1945 — (Pacific-Wake Island) The Wake Atoll is commissioned an Island Command and a Naval Base.

November 3rd 1945 — (Pacific-Hawaii) The 4th Marine Division embarks from Hawaii for the United States.

November 14th-15th 1945 — (Pacific-China) Chinese Communist troops clash with Marines assigned to guarding a train transporting the 1st Marine Division Commander, Major General DeWitt Peck; the confrontation occurs near Kuyeh.

November 7th 1945 — (United States) The "Bull," Admiral Halsey is in Elizabeth, N.J. to visit his old school, Pingy School. The city is in its glory. Church bells ring and fire sirens blare as Bill Halsey returns to his hometown as Admiral William Frederick Halsey. After delivering a speech to the multitudes at City Hall, he remarks that he accepts the city's gift of a silver tea set "WITH HUMILITY AND HUMBLENESS AS A REPRESENTATIVE OF THE FINEST FIGHTING MEN IN THE WORLD, WHOM I HAVE BEEN PRIVILEGED TO COMMAND. I CANNOT SAY ENOUGH FOR THEM."

November 20th 1945 — (United States) Admiral Halsey had requested immediate retirement upon his relief by Rear Admiral H. F. Kingman as Commander of Third Fleet, however, his request is denied; he is promoted to Fleet Admiral and does not retire until April 1st 1947. **(Pacific-Japan)** Marine Aircraft Group 22 departs Sasebo for the United States. Also, the 4th Marines are detached from administrative control of the 6th Marine Division and placed under control of Fleet Marine Force Pacific. The Regiment is relieved of its duties in Japan by the end of the year.

November 23rd 1945 — (Pacific-Japan) The V Amphibious Corps starts to relieve the 5th Marine Division, assuming responsibility for its sector and to assign its personnel to the 2nd Marine Division and the 32nd Division, U.S.A.

November 24th 1945 — (Pacific-Japan) Responsibility for Saga and Fukuoka transfers from the 2nd Marine Division to the 32nd Division, U.S.A.

November 25th 1945 — (Pacific-Japan) The remaining Base Command at Fukuoka is disbanded as the 32nd Division assumes its duties. The 5th Tank Battalion and 28th Marines deployed at Fukuoka and Oita Prefectures and Yamaguchi

Prefecture respectively are replaced by Army contingents. **(Pacific-Carolines)** The 2nd Battalion, 21st Marines and the Truk Occupation Force reach Truk Island.

November 27th 1945 — (United States) President Truman selects General of the Army George C. Marshall as Special Representative in China to mediate the crisis developing between the Chinese Nationalists and the Communists.

November 28th 1945 — (United States) The 4th Marine Division is disbanded at Camp Pendleton, California.

November 30th 1945 — (Pacific-Okinawa) The Marine Detachment (Provisional), Naval Operating Base is disbanded.

December 1st 1945 — (Pacific-Japan) All Japanese Army and Navy personnel involved with demobilization operations are given civilian status, in accordance with recently established Government Ministries and Bureaus. Also, the 1st Battalion, 4th Marines, scheduled to be dissolved, sails for the U.S. **(Pacific-Guam)** The 3rd Marines' Headquarters embarks for the U.S. **(Pacific-Volcano-Bonins)** The remnants of the 1st Battalion, 3rd Marine Division arrive at Chichi Jima to participate in the occupational mission.

December 5th 1945 — (Pacific-Japan) The first Transports laden with contingents of the 5th Marine Division depart for the U.S.

December 8th 1945 — (Pacific-Japan) The V Amphibious Corps is informed by the U.S. Sixth Army that effective 30th December, I Corps (Sixth Army) will assume all occupational duties in V Amphibious Corps area. Meanwhile, the 2nd Marine Division takes responsibility for all 5th Marine Division occupation duties.

December 9th 1945 — (Atlantic-Germany) General Patton, while traveling with General Gay in the rear seat of a Staff Car is badly injured after a collision at an intersection on the Frankfurt-Mannheim Autobahn. General Patton becomes nearly totally paralyzed from the neck down. Patton had been scheduled to depart Germany for the U.S. on the following day. There is some speculation that the accident had been an assassination attempt, but all indications, including the subsequent severe depression and sincere sorrow of the driver of the truck which struck the Staff Car, tend to disavow this theory. General Patton's wife rushes to Germany; he an iron-willed man fights a tough battle for twelve days. Doctors note that most men who had suffered such an injury would have succumbed within a few days at best. The Fighting General gets pneumonia, which over stresses his heart. He succumbs on the 21st of December, having noted that: "THIS IS A HELL OF A WAY FOR A SOLDIER TO DIE." General George S. Patton's final words, spoken to his beloved wife Beatrice,:" IT'S TOO DARK, I MEAN TOO LATE." Patton had previously stated that if he died overseas, he wanted to be buried with his troops. He rests at Hamm, Luxembourg next to a colored truck driver. Also, on the 21st, Fred Ayer Jr., an Army Officer and nephew of General Patton was in Boston speaking with two Marines when word of the General's death reached them. Silence followed the tragic news, then one of the Marine Officers (tears in his eyes) speaks extemporaneously: "THERE DIED THE BEST GOD-DAMNED MARINE THE ARMY EVER BRED."

December 10th 1945 — (Pacific-Marshall Islands) The Marine Detachment (Provisional), Eniwetok is dissolved.

December 13th 1945 — (Pacific-China) The Commanding General, China approves of the disbanding of the III Amphibious Corps.

Major General George S. Patton. This photo was taken in Sweden during November 1945 and is displayed through the courtesy of General and Mrs. Patton.

December 15th 1945 — **(United States)** Admiral Nimitz becomes the Chief of Naval Operations, replacing Admiral King. Also, the 3rd Marines arrive at San Diego from Guam and move to Camp Pendleton, California, becoming part of the Marine Training and Replacement Command.

December 19th 1945 — **(Pacific-Japan)** The remaining contingents of the 5th Marine Division depart for the United States. **(Atlantic-Austria)** General Mark Clark attends the opening session of the Austrian Parliament (During the recent elections, the Communists receive only 5 percent of the vote to the Russians' dismay.) The now predictable Russians become more nasty, frequently closing down the primary road leading from the U.S. zone to Vienna. In addition the Russian Allies continually interrupt and harass the U.S. trains which moves between Salzburg and Vienna twice a day. An irritated, but restrained General Clark orders the trains armed to fend off the maliciousness of the Russians. During one appalling episode, two Russian Officers terrorize the people on one of the trains. One Yankee Sergeant terminates the problem instantly; he kills one of the Russians, but only wounds the other. The Russians then demand that the Americans turn the Soldier over to them; they are still waiting.

December 22nd 1945 — **(Pacific-Marcus Island)** The Marine Detachment (Provisional), Marcus Island is activated.

December 24th 1945 — **(Pacific-Japan)** The 3rd Battalion, 4th Marines, reinforced by Regimental units and a Casual Company (established to provide replacements for Ships' detachments) relieves the 2nd Battalion of all guard responsibilities.

December 28th 1945 — **(Pacific-Guam)** The 3rd Marine Division (minus the 1st Battalion in the Bonins and the 2nd Battalion on Truk) is disbanded on Guam.

December 31st 1945 — **(Pacific-Hawaii)** The 3rd Marine Aircraft Wing is decommissioned at the Marine Corps Air Station, Ewa, Hawaiian Islands. **(Pacific-Japan)** The V Amphibious Corps is relieved of all occupation responsibilities as the U.S. Eighth Army relieves the Sixth Army and takes command of all occupation troops in Japan.

1945 Miscellaneous — **(United States-China)** General Wedemeyer had been asked (during 1945) to succeed Ambassador Hurley as Ambassador to China. Wedemeyer informs Secretary of War Patterson that he intends to remain in the U.S. Army. Subsequently, General Marshall persuades General Wedemeyer to accept the post, but during May 1946, Marshall sends a radiogram to President Truman, attempting to abort the appointment. Undersecretary of State Dean Acheson, shows the message to Wedemeyer. It reads: "NEWS CONCERNING WEDEMEYER'S APPOINTMENT TO CHINA HAS LEAKED AND WAS CAUSING HIM CONSIDERABLE EMBARRASSMENT IN HIS NEGOTIATIONS WITH THE COMMUNISTS." Acheson speaks to Wedemeyer: "SORRY, BUT YOUR APPOINTMENT AS AMBASSADOR MUST BE CANCELED." General Wedemeyer had also noted that when the Germans attacked Soviet Russia (June 1941), "THE CHINESE COMMUNISTS STOP DENOUNCING THE BRITISH WAR EFFORT." General Wedemeyer also states that the U.S. Communists had stopped denouncing the war effort when the Germans invaded Russia. Also, General Jonathan Wainright states some of his feelings after his long captivity since the fall of the Philippines: "MY MEN AND I WERE THE VICTIMS OF SHORTSIGHTEDNESS AT HOME AND BLIND TRUST IN THE RESPECTABILITY OF SCHEMING AGGRESSORS. TERRIBLE AS WAS THE ORDEAL OF CAPTIVITY, I OFTEN FEEL THAT WE WERE SPARED CHIEFLY TO WARN AGAINST AN INFINITELY MORE TERRIBLE FATE. THE PRICE OF OUR UNPREPAREDNESS FOR A WORLD WAR III WOULD BE DEATH TO THE MILLIONS OF US AND THE DISAPPEARANCE FROM THE EARTH OF ITS GREATEST NATION." During 1946, Admiral Halsey will make some pointed remarks about the State Department: "PEACETIME SECURITY LIES WITH THE STATE DEPARTMENT, NOT THE ARMY AND NAVY. IT SHOULD BE MADE TO BEAR IT IN THE OPEN...NEITHER THE ARMY OR NAVY EVER STARTED A WAR." Subsequent to the close of hostilities, General Ridgway is offered an appointment as Ambassador to Argentina. He discusses the possibility with President Truman and General Marshall, but turns it down. Ridgway then accepts the position of Commander of Mediterranean Theater, becoming Deputy Supreme Commander to General Sir William Morgan, Supreme Commander, Allied Forces, Mediterranean. Ridgway subsequently states: "DURING THAT PARTICULAR TOUR OF DUTY I HAD THE UNHAPPY RESPONSIBILITY OF TEARING DOWN A GREAT MILITARY ESTABLISHMENT...THE CRY OF BRING THE BOYS HOME WAS RINGING FROM THE U.S., AND WE WERE PLUNGING HEADLONG INTO THE SHAMEFUL DEMOBILIZATION OF ONE OF THE GREATEST MILITARY ORGANIZATIONS THE WORLD HAS EVER SEEN, THE MAGNIFICENT U.S. ARMY THAT HAD DONE ITS FULL SHARE IN BEATING THE GERMAN, ITALIAN AND JAPANESE ARMIES TO THEIR KNEES."

The U.S.S. Arizona Memorial at Pearl Harbor...Lest we Forget.

1941-July 4th 1942 — Prior to the U.S. entrance into World War II, some young Americans (aviators and crewmen) volunteer to go to China to assist in the fight against the Japanese. They become members of an elite aviator group known as the Flying Tigers. The Flying Tigers are officially unsanctioned by the U.S. Government to ensure U.S. neutrality is not breached. To much of the world, these courageous Pilots and their crews, led by a Louisianian, Clare Lee Chennault, are acting as mercenaries, serving under Chiang Kai-shek. Their outmoded equipment is expected to be overmatched by the power of the Japanese, but individual ability reduces the odds.

The Flying Tigers, bolt into action subsequent to the attack against Pearl Harbor and roll up a superb record. Prior to the disbanding of the unit (July 4th 1942), about 296 enemy Planes are destroyed against a loss of four Tiger' Planes. Chennault, who had resigned his commission from the U.S. Army during the 1930's gets recommissioned and becomes elevated to the rank of Lt. General during his tour of duty in the Army Air Corps. During 1945, the men of the Flying Tigers attempt to receive Veterans benefits, but the government refuses the request, stating that they had been volunteers, not Veterans.

Many years later, during 1991, the survivors of the Flying Tigers finally receive the proper recognition. The U.S. Government admits that the Flying Tigers were part of a clandestine operation sponsored by the U.S. Government. The Flying Tigers did receive their pay from the Government of Chiang Kai-shek; however, it is revealed that the operation was subsidized by a large loan from the United States. During 1991, the U.S. Government admits that President Roosevelt, Secretary of the Treasury, Morganthau and the War Department had full knowledge of the operation.

The surviving members, including Pilots and crewmen of the unit finally receive their just due. A Defense Department review board recommends (May 1991) that the Flying Tigers be recognized as Veterans of World War II, having served legitimate active duty while in China. In this instance, better late than never. A word of congratulations is in order to men such as Lts. H.C.K. Spotswood, S.P.M. Kinsey, and the balance of that gallant band of young men who flocked to the call of the Colors without fanfare or hesitation.

1936-1945 — A well disciplined and determined young Colonel named Benjamin Davis is relieved of command of the 99th Pursuit Squadron (Army Air Corps) during 1943 to assume command of the 332nd Fighter Group, which is to be assigned to the Mediterranean Theater (12th Fighter Command). The 332nd flies support missions for the 15th Air Force Bombers, giving them an added edge of well-needed Fighter protection as they lambaste targets in North Africa, Italy and Rumania. The Pilots excel, knocking out scores of enemy Planes in the air and on the ground, gaining the Distinguished Flying Cross for the majority of the men. The capability of this unit had been questioned by many before its entering the scene, but their actions speak loudly and their courage is exemplary.

On the eve of the invasion of southern France (August 1944), the 332nd Fighter Group gets the task of eliminating some key targets to buffer the landing of General Patch's force. In a burst of speed, the Planes destroy much of the enemy's capacity to implement their radar and also sever enemy communication systems. Subsequently, the Infantry rolls inland and the rest is history. Colonel Davis (W.P. 1936 — Cadet No. 10494) who had received his diploma from General John J. Pershing, soon receives a bigger thrill. He is among the Pilots who receive the Distinguished Service Cross; it is pinned by his father, Brigadier General Benjamin Davis Sr.

Thousands of missions are flown by the courageous Pilots before war's end and they perform splendidly for the Stars and Stripes. These men had been pathfinders. The 99th Pursuit Squadron is the first group of colored Pilots to participate in combat for the U.S. Armed Forces. The 332nd Fighter Group had also been composed of colored Pilots. Colonel Davis, like his father, carves a proud career in the military, retiring during 1970 as a Lt. General (Air Force).

GIs pushing a Jeep through Italian mud.

December 1941-December 1945 — As the bombs drop and the Colors call, thousands of young Americans enlist to serve Old Glory. Alongside, are the unsung heroes, the Corpsmen, Doctors, Nurses, Ambulance drivers. No one can accurately calculate how many lives were saved by their devotion to the combat troops, at great risk to their own lives. It is conceivable that no one could really determine why anyone would volunteer to be a Corpsman, but thank God they were there or many more Americans would have never known that tremendous feeling of getting married and being a parent or grandparent. For those who never returned to again enjoy life as an American, or see their families grow, let those of us who carry on the legacy, resolve never to forget their deeds. Last but not least, these gallant warriors had some other unsung heroes to bolster their journey through the hell of war; the Chaplins. It is also impossible to conclude the amount of lives saved by their service to their country. Men of all faiths shared the anguish of the horrors of war as they helped strengthen the moral fiber of our fighting men. In one city, Philadelphia, 75 Catholic priests accompanied the troops. Six of them gave their lives. Father John J. Morley, who returned safely, served some time in the Pacific. In retrospect, he remains firm in his opinion that "it was a necessary war that we didn't start, but had to finish." Reflecting further, he stated that as a Chaplin of the 40th Division, "he was proud of our troops and their Christian values." In closing, Father Morley noted that "God, Liberty and Country are certainly worthy of defense."

Ramage Submarine School, Norfolk Virginia, named in honor of Admiral Lawson "Red" Patterson Ramage.

A young Army Officer, William C. Westmoreland and his new bride, Mrs. Katherine Van Deusen Westmoreland on their wedding day (May 3rd 1947) in Fayetteville, N.C. Many of Americas finest returned from the war to renew their American dream. This young Officer remains in the U.S. Army and climbs to the position of Commanding General, Chief of Staff, United States Army, serving under Presidents Lyndon B. Johnson and Richard M. Nixon, July 1968-June 1972.

Children posing on a Tank at Patton Park, named in honor of General George S. Patton, South Hamilton, Massachusetts.

Marine Recruits preparing for inspection at M.C.R.D., San Diego (after the war).

The author and his wife Barbara with General George S. Patton, U.S.A., during an interview.

The author and his wife Barbara with General William C. Westmoreland, during an interview.

PFC Henry L. "Bud" Shaw Jr. IV Corps signal Battalion; Photo taken Feb. 1946 while Mr. Shaw was stationed in Peiping, North China. Mr. Shaw, Chief Historian, U.S.M.C. 1962-1990.

John Wayne, taking a break during the shooting of "The Sands of Iwo Jima," speaking with Marine Staff Sgt. Rick Spooner (later Major). Major Spooner (Ret.) now spends most of his time with his wife Gloria in Triangle, Virginia, a stone's throw away from the only town in the U.S. which is completely surrounded by U.S. Marines; Quantico. The Spooner's are proprietors of the "Globe and Laurel," a unique Restaurant, known to many as a modern day Tun's Tavern, billed as the only "Museum" in Prince William County, sereving lunch and dinner. Photo courtesy of Major Spooner.

The Long Grey Line — Duty, Honor, Country.

Airmen on the March... Here we go into the Wild Blue Yonder.

Airborne on Parade.

Midshipmen on Parade.

Marines on Parade — Semper Fidelis!

Standing ready for the call; Anchors away.

January 5th 1919 — (Germany) In Berlin, the Army assisted by armed civilians quells Communist riots in Berlin which erupt to forestall elections of a National Constituent Assembly and a constitution for post war-Germany. The leftist Spartacus group is crushed violently, costing the group many casualties by the Germans who despise the growing Bolshevik movement within the country. The elections occur on schedule, January 19th.

January 6th 1919 — Theodore Roosevelt, the 26th President of the United States, dies at the age of 60.

Mid-January 1919 — (France) The Paris Peace Conference convenes in the Palace of Versailles, near Paris. Thirty-two countries participate; however, Germany is not given representation. Rather, it is shunned and the Allied blockade stays in place, preventing necessary supplies from reaching near destitute Germany.

January 21st 1919 — (Ireland) Sinn Fein wins seventy-five percent of the Irish seats in the British Parliament; however, rather than go to England, the group meets in Dublin and declares independence from Great Britain, igniting the Anglo-Irish War, which lasts until 1921.

January 29th 1919 — The 18th Amendment to the Constitution is declared ratified, prohibiting the manufacture or sale of alcoholic beverages, and becomes effective on January 16th of the following year. Subsequently, the amendment is repealed.

February 6th 1919 — (Germany) The Weimar Republic is established in Germany; however, since this government will support the Versailles Treaty, the German populace gives President Friedrich Ebert tepid support, and the government soon fails.

February 23rd 1919 — (Italy) The Fasci del Combattimento is established by Benito Mussolini. The organization is nurtured by the growing anti-Communist sentiments in Italy.

March 1st 1919 — (Korea) Korean nationalists declare independence from Japan, prompting fierce reprisals.

March 10th 1919 — (United States) The U.S. Supreme Court rules that the Espionage Act is constitutional.

Mid-March 1919 — (France) Representatives of the American Expeditionary Force meet in Paris and initiate the founding of the American Legion. It is formed to personify Americanism and to meet the threat of Communism. A previous meeting had occurred during February, and subsequently the American Legion is officially formed in St. Louis, Mo., during May of 1919.

March 25th 1919 — (France) During the ongoing Paris Peace conference, the Covenant of the League of Nations is adopted.

June 1919 — (Germany) The Chancellor, Philipp Scheidemann, resigns in opposition to the treaty imposed upon Germany by the Allies. Also, the German Navy vents its displeasure with the treaty, scuttling the majority of its Vessels which are moored at Great Britain's Naval Base at Scapa Flow. Before the end of the month, representatives of German Republic sign the Versailles Treaty.

June 28th 1919 — (France) The Treaty of Versailles, terminating World War I, is signed at the Palace of Versailles; however, the participating governments must ratify it. Subse-

quently, the U.S. reinitiates trade with Germany during July as the embargo is ended.

July 1919 — (Germany) Germany adopts the Weimar Constitution which establishes the German Republic and approves formation of new German states. Two houses of government, the Reichstag (proportional representation) and the Reichsrat (upper house) which is composed of representatives from the seventeen states.

August 4th 1919 — (Hungary) A Soviet Republic is established in Hungary as Bela Kun, a Communist, assumes power and initiates a reign of terror. Subsequently, Rumanian troops enter Budapest and eliminate the regime. Kun flees to exile in Russia.

August 31st 1919 — (United States) The Socialist Party holds its convention in Chicago, and dissension emerges. A split occurs and a radical wing which caters to the beliefs of the Bolsheviks begins to organize. It subsequently becomes the Communist (Workers) Party.

September 10th 1919 — The Allies sign a peace treaty (Treaty of St. Germain) with Austria. China, which did not sign the Versailles Treaty, becomes a signatory.

September 25th 1919 — President Wilson becomes severely ill while delivering a speech in Pueblo, Colorado. He never fully recovers.

November 19th 1919 — A vote on the Versailles Treaty is defeated by the Senate by a vote of 55 to 39.

December 1919 — The sentiment against Communists in the U.S. rises. Through actions of the Attorney General, 249 Bolshevik sympathizers are deported to Russia.

January 1920 — The nationwide search for Communists continues as the Attorney General Palmer authorizes raids to detain them. Subsequently, during June, Palmer's house is bombed.

January 16th 1920 — The 18th Amendment to the Constitution is ratified, prohibiting the sale of Alcohol. It becomes a most unpopular law which is frequently ignored throughout the Twenties, giving rise to the "speakeasy" as illegal Booze flows profusely. The 18th Amendment is repealed during 1933 and is the only Amendment to receive such action.

February 1920 — (Estonia) Estonia declares its independence and signs a peace treaty with the Soviet Union. Also, Czechoslovakia, in an attempt to maintain independence from the Soviet Union and Germany, embraces a constitution.

February 28th 1920 — (United States) The Esch-Cummins Act is enacted, creating the Railroad Labor Board to control railroad regulation. In addition, the railroads are returned to private industry, having been under government control during the war.

March 1920 — (Syria) Having withstood French efforts to dominate the country, Syria announces that Emir Feisal is king. However, during April, both Lebanon and Syria are placed under France by the Allies.

April 1920 — (Great Britain) The Supreme Allied Council places Mesopotamia and Palestine under British rule.

June 4th 1920 — (United States) The Army Reorganization Act is passed by Congress, mandating a peacetime Army of 300,000 troops. **(Hungary)** The Treaty of Trianon is agreed upon by Hungary which greatly reduces the country in population and square miles, as well as making it a land-locked country.

June 5th 1920 — (United States) The Merchant Marine Act is passed by Congress, extending the wartime Shipping Board. Its new responsibility will be to sell the fleet to private industry and manage those vessels that remain unsold.

July 1920 — A plebiscite vote in East and West Prussia joins them with Germany; however, Poland subsequently receives a part of the latter as a corridor to the sea. Also, Lithuania and the Soviet Union agree to a peace treaty which terminates the ongoing border disputes and leaves Lithuania with its independence.

August 10th 1920 — (Turkey) The Treaty of Sevres, previously signed by Sultan Mohammed VI, is ratified by the Turkish government. Subsequently, it is renounced by the Turkish National Assembly and by Mustafa Kemal.

August 11th 1920 — The Soviet Union and Latvia sign a peace treaty, subsequent to several weeks of fighting which terminated with the Soviets being pushed out of Lettgalen. Also, Italy relinquishes the Dodecanese Islands to Greece.

August 26th 1920 — (United States) Women receive the right to vote as the 19th Amendment is ratified by Congress.

November 2nd 1920 — (United States) Warren G. Harding is elected President, defeating James Cox, whose Vice President on the ticket is Franklin D. Roosevelt. Calvin Coolidge is the Vice President elect.

January 1921 — The United States Supreme Court rules that the Sherman Antitrust Act is applicable to trade unions. Also, Congress overrides President Wilson's veto and reinitiates the War Finance Corporation to assist the nation's farm regions which are badly distressed.

February 9th 1921 — The Soviet Union and Poland sign the Treaty of Riga. Poland relinquishes its claims to the Ukraine, and Russia ceases military aggression into Europe.

February 21st 1921 — The London Conference convenes, opening discussions on the partition of Turkish Asia Minor (Allies Treaty of Sevres 1920).

February 1921 — Treaties are signed by the Soviet Union respecting the sovereignty of Afghanistan and Persia. Also, Mongolia declares independence from China.

March 4th 1921 — Warren G. Harding is inaugurated as the 29th President of the United States.

March 1921 — Great Britain and the Soviet Union sign a trade agreement. Also, the Soviets sign a treaty recognizing the Kemal government in Turkey.

April 20th 1921 — The Thompson-Urrutia Treaty with Columbia is ratified by the U.S. Senate. The agreement grants Columbia the payment of twenty-five million dollars for the loss of Panama and also gives Columbia the right of free access through the Panama Canal.

May 11th 1921 — (Germany) The Allied Supreme Council had threatened occupation of the Ruhr Valley unless reparations are paid; however, on this the eve of the effective occupation date, the Germans reluctantly relent and agree to make payment. The terms are agreed upon during October.

May 19th 1921 — Congress passes the Emergency Quota Act which restricts immigration to three percent of the 1910 figure from any one country on an annual basis, not to exceed a total figure of about 357,000 immigrants per year.

May 21st 1921 — (England) During the Imperial Conference in London, the United Kingdom, the Dominions, and India become the British Commonwealth of Nations.

May 27th 1921 — Congress passes an Emergency Tariff Act increasing the duties on agricultural products, sugar, and wool and also implements an embargo on certain German products.

May 31st 1921 — A Presidential Executive Order transfers the Navy oil reserves at Teapot Dome, Wyoming, and also at Buena Vista Hills and Elk Hills, California, from the jurisdiction of the Navy Department to the Department of the Interior, headed by Albert B. Fall, who urges the President to make the changes. The incident leads to the Teapot Dome Scandal.

June 10th 1921 — Congress passes the National Budget and Accounting Act, establishing the Bureau of the Budget and the General Accounting Office, both of which come under jurisdiction of the Treasury Department.

July 2nd 1921 — Congress declares an end to the war with Austria-Hungary and Germany.

August 15th 1921 — The Packers and Stockyard Act is passed by Congress in an effort to end monopolies in the meatpacking industry and also to eliminate price fixing.

September 1921 — Guatemala, Honduras, and San Salvador agree to form a Central American Union.

October 1921 — Russia agrees to grant the Crimea independence. Also, France and the Turkish government of Mustafa Kemal sign a treaty which defines the Turko-Syrian border.

November 5th 1921 — The Soviets sign a treaty with Mongolia, which gives temporary support to the recently established government against Japan and China.

November 12th 1921 — (United States) The Washington Armament Conference convenes in Washington, D.C. Representatives of the U.S., France, Great Britain, Italy, and Japan confer to formulate agreements concerning limitations on Naval power and also to the right of all the major powers in the Pacific. Although there is much difference of opinion on many items, all concur on banning the use of poison gas. Subsequently, Japan denounces the agreements and invades Manchuria. Also, the Russians are not asked to attend the conference.

December 16th 1921 — (Ireland) Parliament ratifies the Anglo-Irish Treaty, previously agreed upon by British Parliament and Sinn Fein. The accord recognizes the Irish Free State as a British Dominion. It is accepted by Southern Ireland's Parliament during the following month. Northern Ireland (Ulster Ireland) decides to remain as part of Great Britain.

February 9th 1922 — Congress establishes the World War Foreign Debt Commission to untangle the complications of Allied war and postwar loans. The only Ally to completely repay the debt is Finland. France, Great Britain, and Italy are three of the larger debtors.

February 18th 1922 — Congress passes the Capper-Volstead Act, permitting agricultural associations and farmers to purchase and sell farm products cooperatively, shielding the industry from the antitrust laws. The law's intent is also to relieve the beleaguered farmers and their families who are losing their farms at a rapid pace.

February 21st 1922 — Great Britain ceases its protectorate over Egypt, but both Egypt and Great Britain agree to jointly oversee the Sudan. Also, in Ireland, Eamon De Valera calls a convention of Sinn Fein, resulting in a declaration proclaiming the only legitimate government in Ireland: the Republican Government.

March 24th 1922 — The U.S. Congress ratifies the Pacific Treaty, which had been agreed upon by France, Great Britain, Japan, and the United States at the Washington Conference during late 1921.

April 7th 1922 — Subsequent to clandestine negotiations, Secretary of the Interior Albert B. Fall leases the Teapot Dome oil reserves (originally consigned to the U.S. Navy for military use) to Mr. Harry F. Sinclair's oil company (Mammoth). Later, Fall gives leases to two other private companies on the Naval oil reserves on Buena Vista Hills and Elk Hills.

May 30th 1922 — The Lincoln Memorial is dedicated in Washington D.C.

August 1922 — (Ireland) Arthur Griffith, the President of Ireland, succumbs. Soon after, a faction of republicans assassinate Michael Collins, the Commander-in-Chief, inciting civil war.

September 21st 1922 — Congress passes the Fordney-Mc-Cumber Tariff Act, enacted to balance the cost of foreign and U.S. production. The law greatly increases duties on manufacturing products and on farm products.

September 22nd 1922 — Congress passes the Cable Act which assures women that their citizenship is not at risk if they marry an alien; however, the act also makes it clear that a woman who marries an American citizen does not automatically become a citizen.

Late-October 1922 — (Italy) The ongoing intimidation of Mussolini forces the collapse of Luigi Facta's cabinet on the 27th. On the following day, Mussolini's followers enter Rome, followed shortly thereafter by Mussolini who had been perched near the Swiss border in the event of complications. He becomes Prime Minister.

November 1922 — (Germany) Financial experts meet in Berlin to attempt to find solutions for the German currency dilemma.

December 4th 1922 — (United States) The Second Central American Conference convenes in Washington, D.C. The conference results in the reestablishment of a Central American Court of Justice to help resolve differences between neighboring countries. However, the U.S., pointing to the Roosevelt Corollary, emphasizes its intention to maintain its right to intervene in Latin American affairs if it deems it necessary.

December 1922 — (Soviet Union) The Treaty of Union is signed in Moscow, resulting in the Russian Empire becoming the Soviet Union. It is accepted by the Central Executive Committee during July of 1923. The tone emits a strong democracy; however, it is a farce and all power remains with the Bolshevik Communist Party.

January 1923 — (Germany) Under orders of President Harding, the remaining U.S. troops in Germany return to the U.S.

March 3rd 1923 — (United States) The U.S. declines becoming a member nation in the International Court of Justice, preferring to distance itself from foreign affairs.

March 4th 1923 — Congress passes the Agricultural Credits Act in an effort to aid farmers by establishing Federal credit banks to service loans for the agricultural industry.

March 14th 1923 — (Poland) East Galicia and Vilna are given to Poland by the Allies.

May 1st 1923 — (Germany) Communist May Day demonstrations are interrupted by followers of Hitler and Ernst Rohm. The German Army fails to intervene, but Rohm does receive a warning from the Army.

July 1923 — (Italy) All non-Fascist parties are disbanded in Italy by Mussolini.

July 24th 1923 — (Turkey) The Treaty of Lausanne is signed by the Allies and Turkey, which in essence is a revamping of the Treaty of Sevres in favor of Turkey. It receives control of Constantinople, Adalia, Anatolia, Cilicia, Smyrna, and eastern Thrace. Also, the Dodecanese Islands revert to Italy from Greece, and the Straits are demilitarized, becoming international waters.

August 2nd 1923 — (United States) President Harding dies. On the following day, Vice President Calvin Coolidge becomes the thirtieth President of the United States.

September 1923 — (Spain) A military coup occurs which is condoned secretly by King Alfonso who remains on the throne. Miguel Primo de Rivera becomes dictator and declares martial law.

October 25th 1923 — (United States) Public hearings begin in the Senate on the Teapot Dome scandal. Subsequently, during June of 1940, Albert B. Fall, Edward Doheny, and Harry F. Sinclair are indicted on charges of conspiracy and bribery. However, only Fall will be convicted and subsequently given a jail sentence for his activities.

November 8th 1923 — (Germany) A Putsch is attempted by Adolf Hitler in Munich. It fails, but Hitler serves only about nine months in prison despite receiving a sentence of five years. He uses the time to write Mein Kampf, his blueprint for conquering Europe.

January 11th 1924 — (Greece) King George II is ousted. A Republic is proclaimed, with Eleuterios Venizelos becoming Prime Minister of the Greek National Assembly.

January 21st 1924 — (Soviet Union) Nikolai Lenin succumbs. Infighting occurs with Stalin eventually becoming the successor.

January 1924 — (Italy) Under the rule of Mussolini, Fascist trade unions are permitted to flourish; all others are dissolved. Also, in **China**, the Kuomintang (Nationalist) Congress of Sun Yat-sen establishes a government at Canton. Subsequently, it becomes allied with Communist factions, and by June, the Soviets begin to train Chinese troops. Yat-sen dies during March 1925 and is succeeded by Chiang Kai-shek, a staunch anti-Communist, who soon kicks out the Russian advisors.

February 1924 — (Great Britain) Great Britain establishes diplomatic relations with the Soviets.

February 3rd 1924 — (United States) Woodrow Wilson, the 28th President of the United States, dies.

February 9th 1924 — (Italy) The coastal lands of the Adriatic extending to Fiume are annexed by Italy; however, Mussolini makes no additional claims for the Dalmatian coast.

May 19th 1924 — Congress passes the Soldier's Bonus Bill for the Veterans of World War I, garnishing enough votes to override President Coolidge's veto. The House had passed it during March, and the Senate passed it during April.

May 26th 1924 — (United States) Congress passes another immigration law which further reduces the influx of immigrants, limiting admission to two percent of any nationality in the United States during 1890. Canada and Mexico are unaffected by the legislation, but immigrants from Japan can no longer enter the country.

June 15th 1924 — (United States) Congress passes legislation granting citizenship to all native-born American Indians.

November 4th 1924 — (United States) Calvin Coolidge is elected as the 30th President of the United States. He had assumed office subsequent to the death of President Harding during August 1923. His Vice President is Charles G. Dawes.

December 27th 1924 — (United States) A treaty is signed with the Dominican Republic, replacing an earlier treaty signed during the early 1900's.

January 1925 — (U.S.S.R.-Japan) The Soviet Union and Japan reestablish relations.

February 2nd 1925 — A deadly epidemic of diphtheria has gripped Nome, Alaska, threatening the population. An extraordinary effort to get medicine there on time is ongoing by a determined team with dog sleds. Undaunted by a furious blizzard, the serum is delivered, to the jubilation of the nation which is spellbound.

March 4th 1925 — (United States) President Coolidge is inaugurated to a full term of office.

March 13th 1925 — (United States) The U.S. signs a treaty with Cuba which acknowledges Cuba's claim to the Isle of Pines.

October 1925 — Germany and the Soviet Union reach a trade accord; however, at present the Russians are already training German troops. Also, in Iraq the first Parliament convenes under King Feisal. In Persia, Reza Khan (Pahlevi Dynasty) becomes Shah, concluding the Kajar Dynasty which has ruled Persia since 1794.

November 14th 1925 — (United States) The United States, aware of the steep depression (financial) sweeping across Europe, relents and grants huge reductions in foreign war debts and in addition, decreases the rates of interest which are also due.

January 1926 — (Greece) Theodore Pangalos, who had seized power during 1925, becomes a self-appointed dictator. He is deposed during August 1926 and exiled in Crete.

January 27th 1926 — (United States) The Senate adopts a resolution indicating that the U.S. would join the World Court, officially known as the Permanent Court of International Justice. However, the stipulation that the court would have no jurisdiction over disputes involving the U.S. is not acceptable to the other members of the court which convenes in Hague, Netherlands.

May 1926 — (United States) Richard E. Byrd and Floyd Bennett complete the first flight over the North Pole, using a Fokker Aircraft which is heavily laden with additional gasoline. The Plane is equipped with skis and takes off in heavy snow. Byrd, a graduate of Annapolis (1912), had received his Aviation training during WWI. The expedition had sailed from New York to Spitzbergen, a small island off Norway, to execute the 800 mile flight. Upon reaching its destination, the harbor is iced, prompting Byrd to fabricate a raft and guide the Plane to shore rather than abort the mission. On May 6th, another man, Roald Amundsen (Norwegian), arrives in the Dirigible *Norge*, to race Byrd to the North Pole. Incessant work on the part of Byrd's crew has him taking off in a heavily-laden Aircraft (due to additional gasoline). Byrd's Plane,

the *America*, soars over the pristine frozen landscape at 09:02 on May 9th, having safely reached the "top of the world." The success of the mission convinces Byrd that he can conquer the Atlantic and sets his sights on becoming the first man to cross the Atlantic in an Aircraft. Also, Congress passes the Air Commerce Act, which initiates the licensing of Aircraft and Pilots.

July 1926 — The U.S. reaches an accord with Panama, assuring the Panamanians that the U.S. will defend the Panama Canal in the event of a war. Also, Congress establishes the U.S. Army Air Corps.

October 25th 1926 — (United States) The U.S. Supreme Court reverses the Tenure of Office Act which had been passed by Congress during 1867, ruling that the act is unconstitutional; this results in giving the President authority to dismiss Cabinet and other Executive Officers without the approval of the Senate. President Andrew Johnson had defied the act during his Presidency, proclaiming the act unconstitutional and igniting impeachment proceedings. The impeachment vote failed in the Senate by one vote: Edmund G. Ross, a Republican (March 16th, 1868).

December 25th 1926 — (Japan) Hirohito becomes Emperor of Japan, succeeding his father Yoshito who succumbs. Hirohito is on the imperial throne when the Japanese attack Pearl Harbor during 1941 and upon occupation of Japan by the U.S. subsequent to the close of hostilities. He is permitted to remain, but he is obliged to renounce his status as a deity.

Miscellaneous 1926 — (United States) Andrew Higgins has developed a Landing Craft "Eureka LCVP(R)"; it was invented for use in the shallow waters of the Mississippi River. The amphibious innovation is offered to the U.S. Navy during 1927, but the Navy contends that 30' boats are needed and turns down the opportunity. Subsequently, Marine Brigadier General Emile P. Moses and Andrew Higgins improve the craft and install a ramp gate; the new craft (LCM(3) is called Higgins Landing Craft Medium (Landing Craft, Vehicle, Personnel, Ramp), and in 1940 another vehicle, Landing Vehicle Tracked is developed. These Landing Craft eventually lend great assistance to the U.S. Amphibious invasions of WWII. Marine General Holland M. Smith later gives the following credit to these Craft by stating that in his opinion "THE HIGGINS BOAT CONTRIBUTED MORE TO OUR COMMON VICTORY THAN ANY OTHER SINGLE PIECE OF EQUIPMENT USED IN THE WAR." General Smith also notes in his book, *Corals and Brass*, that he writes a letter to Higgins on December 6th 1941, which mentions "WHERE THE HELL WOULD THE AMPHIBIOUS FORCE BE WITHOUT YOUR BOATS?" And then General Smith adds: "HISTORY HAS ANSWERED THAT QUESTION."

January 27th 1927 — (United States) The U.S. and Canada establish diplomatic relations.

April 20th 1927 — (United States) At Roosevelt Field on Long Island, Richard Byrd and his friend and Pilot, Floyd Bennett, prepare to practice for the Trans Atlantic flight. All goes well at first; however, the landing causes disaster and his specially constructed Aircraft, the *America* crashes. Byrd is miraculously unscathed, but Floyd Bennett is seriously hurt and will never fly again. Two other men, Clarence Chamberlain and Charles Lindbergh, are on hand and both expect to give Byrd competition, but the crash cancels the highly anticipated Trans Atlantic Derby. Richard Byrd then offers Charles Lindbergh the use of his customized runway for his historic flight. Byrd will make another attempt on June 30th.

May 21st 1927 — **(United States)** Charles A. Lindbergh makes the first solo flight across the Atlantic when his Plane, the *Spirit of St. Louis*, departs from New York and lands at Orly Airfield at Paris.

June 30th 1927 — **(United States)** Richard Byrd and a crew of three additional men take off from Long Island and complete a flight across the Atlantic in about 40 hours. However, when he reaches the coast, heavy fog forbids landing. The Aircraft circles, then makes an emergency landing near the beach; the Plane is destroyed, but the crew is unharmed.

November 1927 — **(China)** Chiang Kai-shek supports the move to annul the existing extraterritorial treaty with Belgium. He also emphasizes that China will recognize only those treaties and agreements which have been consummated by Nationalist China. During the following month the Soviet Union breaks off diplomatic relations with China because of its staunch anticommunist stand.

January 16th 1928 — **(Cuba)** A Conference of American States convenes in Havana with President Coolidge presiding at the opening session.

February 1928 — **(Great Britain-Transjordan)** Great Britain gives some independence to Transjordan, inhabited by about 300,000 nomadic Arabs led by Emir Abdullah, the brother of Iraq's King Feisal. An elective Assembly and a Council are permitted, but the British retain a High Commissioner of Palestine who is empowered to overrule the Emir. Also, the British maintain the right to commit troops to the area if needed.

March 10th 1928 — **(United States)** President Coolidge signs the Alien Property Act. The legislation authorizes payment of $300,000,000 in compensation to German companies and German nationals whose property had been confiscated from them during World War I.

May 15th 1928 — Congress passes the Flood Control Act, granting $325 million to control flooding along the Mississippi River.

May 22nd 1928 — **(United States)** Congress passes the Jones-White Merchant Marine Act permitting the government to subsidize private Shipping companies; it also permits the companies to purchase surplus U.S. Vessels.

May 27th 1928 — **(United States)** Congress passes the Muscle Shoals Act, allowing the government to own a hydroelectric plant at Muscle Shoals, Tennessee.

June 1928 — **(United States)** Treaties of mutual cooperation are reached between the United States and the countries of Austria and Denmark.

July 1928 — **(Egypt)** King Faud initiates a successful coup against the government and dissolves Parliament.

July 25th 1928 — **(United States-China)** A treaty between the U.S. and China is signed at Peiping (Peking, renamed) which grants China tariff autonomy.

August 27th 1928 — **(France)** The Kellogg-Briand Pact (Pact of Paris) is signed by fifteen nations including the U.S., resulting in a declaration which outlaws war as a means of settling differences. Other nations sign later.

October 6th 1928 — **(China)** Chiang Kai-shek becomes President.

November 6th 1928 — **(United States)** Herbert Hoover, a Republican, is elected President, defeating the Democratic nominee, Alfred Smith (first Catholic to run for the office). The popular vote goes 21,392,000 for Hoover and 15,016,000 for Smith. Hoover receives 444 electoral votes and Smith receives 87.

December 25th 1928 — While most Americans are at home celebrating Christmas in their warm homes, Richard E. Byrd's expedition, which had sailed from the States during autumn, arrives on the fringes of Antarctica. The explorers begin to construct a small compound which they name "Little America." The town, which contains underground dormitories and dining rooms, holds up well through the long sunless winter. Byrd attempts to become the first man to fly over the South Pole. During November 1929, the weather is fine for flying; the Aircraft heads for its objective, but as it approaches high mountain peaks, it can not gain altitude. A life and death decision is made, and the survival gear is tossed out of the Plane. Soon after, as the ragged peaks of the mountains are upon them, the Plane gains the altitude and passes them safely. At 13:14 on Thanksgiving Day, Byrd and his crew fly over the South Pole. While passing over it, Byrd drops a stone which he had brought from Floyd Bennett's grave. The courageous crew starts their return to the U.S. before the end·of the year. Byrd decides that he will return and does so with another expedition during 1933. When he returns, he finds "Little America" unscathed by the elements; it had been protected and covered by the snow and ice. During this mission, Byrd almost dies while spending the winter at an advance weather station about 100 miles away from the other explorers. A dangerous rescue mission saves his life. World War II arrives and delays yet a third trip to Antarctica, but when he does return during 1946, it is with the United States Navy; Admiral Byrd will be a primary factor in the subsequent Treaty of Antarctica, which perpetuates the area for exploration, not conquest. Admiral Byrd makes a final trip to Antarctica during 1955; he succumbs during 1957.

January 1929 — **(South America)** Bolivia and Paraguay place their quarrel with the Pan-American Union.

January 5th 1929 — **(Yugoslavia)** King Alexander I seizes dictatorial power and abolishes the constitution (the nation is still referred to as the Serbo-Croat-Slovene Kingdom).

January 14th 1929 — **(Afghanistan)** Habibullah compels King Amanullah to relinquish the throne, igniting civil war.

January 15th 1929 — **(United States)** The Senate ratifies the Kellogg-Briand Peace Pact.

February 9th 1929 — **(Europe)** The Soviet Union, Estonia, Latvia, Poland, and Rumania sign the Litvinov Protocol, echoing the Western world's Kellogg-Briand Act, which denounces war.

February 11th 1929 — **(Italy)** The Lateran Treaty is signed in Rome, resulting with Mussolini accepting the Vatican as a City State and the Pope as its temporal ruler. Italy agrees to reimburse the Vatican $100 million for confiscated church property.

February 13th 1929 — **(United States)** Congress authorizes the construction of fifteen new Cruisers and one Aircraft Carrier (Cruiser Act).

February 14th 1929 — **(United States)** Prohibition has enhanced criminal gangs throughout the country. Today, the famous "St. Valentine's Massacre" occurs in Chicago when members of the Moran gang are slaughtered by gunfire while lined up against a wall.

March 4th 1929 — **(United States)** Herbert Clark Hoover is inaugurated as the 31st President of the United States. His Vice President is Charles Curtis.

March 1929 — (United States) The U.S. supplies Mexico with some Aircraft and other equipment to assist the government in its attempt to quell insurrections. U.S. troops spread along the border will return to their bases by early-May.

April 16th 1929 — (United States) The U.S. informs the Soviet Union that it will not recognize its Bolshevik government.

May 27th 1929 — (United States) The U.S. Supreme Court rules that a President's use of the "pocket veto" is constitutional.

June 3rd 1929 — (South America) Bolivia, Chile, and Peru sign the Arica Treaty, whereby Chile receives Arica and Tacna is given to Peru. Also, Bolivia settles for railroad rights.

June 15th 1929 — (United States) The Agricultural Marketing Act, which establishes the Federal Farm Relief Board, is signed by President Hoover.

July 1st 1929 — (United States) The Immigration Act of 1924, originally scheduled to become effective on July 1st, 1927, becomes effective today. U.S. population figures for 1920 are utilized as the base for determining national quotas.

July 24th 1929 — (United States) President Hoover announces that the Kellogg-Briand Act is in effect.

October 3rd 1929 — (France) The Serbo-Croat-Slovene Kingdom becomes Yugoslavia.

October 24th 1929 — (United States) The stock market is ready to burst as over 13 million shares are sold, following the sale of over six million shares on Tuesday the 23rd making it at the time the second greatest trading day of the New York Stock Exchange. Today is remembered as "Black Thursday", the prelude to "Black Tuesday."

October 29th 1929 — (United States) The New York Stock Exchange has its worst day ever, as over 16 million shares are sold, debouching the Great Depression. As the year progresses, the situation deteriorates further, wiping out many businesses and personal fortunes. Today is remembered as "Black Tuesday."

November 29th 1929 — (Antarctica) Lt. Commander Richard E. Byrd and Bernt Balchen, an American-Norwegian, complete the first successful flight over the South Pole.

December 6th 1929 — (India) The Viceroy and leaders of India begin discussions on dominion status for India. Meanwhile, the Hindus and Moslems accelerate their fighting.

December 1929 — (United States) President Hoover signs a bill which grants taxpayers a reduction on their 1929 federal taxes. Also, A fire erupts in the Executive Office Building in Washington, D.C.; however, most of the valuable papers are saved.

December 14th 1929 — (United States) The city of Tacoma, Washington, is placed in a state of emergency when the power plant fails; the power outage occurs when the water in the dams freezes. The Carrier U.S.S. *Lexington* (started as a Battle Cruiser with the *Saratoga*, until changed to a Carrier due to the Disarmament Conference of 1922) anchors at Baker Dock and hooks up to the city's power cables; the *Lexington* supplies Tacoma with electricity for about thirty days, while the power plant is repaired.

December 28th 1929 — (China) Chiang Kai-shek proclaims the end of extraterritoriality in China.

January 1930 — (United States) President Hoover reiterates his feelings that crime is the most critical problem facing the U.S., noting that Prohibition, automobile theft, and white slave traffic is overburdening the nation's law enforcement agencies.

January 28th 1930 — (Spain) The dictator Primo de Rivera resigns at the request of King Alfonso, departing for France where he succumbs shortly thereafter.

February 6th 1930 — (Haiti) The U.S. recommends reforms for the island and also suggests that Stenio Vincent become President.

March 12th 1930 — (India) Mohandas Ghandi initiates his campaign for civil disobedience.

March 28th 1930 — (Turkey) Constantinople has its name changed to Istanbul by the Nationalists.

March 31st 1930 — (United States) Congress authorizes $230 million to construct public buildings and on April 4th, authorizes an additional $300 million to subsidize states' highway construction programs all in an effort to help alleviate the growing unemployment in the country brought about by the crash of the stock market. Also, banks throughout the nation are failing. By the end of the year, about 1,300 banks will have closed (since Autumn of 1929).

May 2nd 1930 — (Canada) Canada places high tariffs on U.S. goods.

June 17th 1930 — (United States) President Hoover signs the Hawley-Smoot Tariff, which raises tariffs on many products, some of which are so heavily taxed that they become prohibitive.

June 30th 1930 — (Iraq) Great Britain agrees to recognize Iraq's independence simultaneous to its admission to the League of Nations, which occurs during 1932.

September 3rd 1930 — (United States) Thomas Edison unveils his latest idea; an Electric Train which he designed travels between Hoboken and Montclair, New Jersey, along the Lackawanna rail lines.

September 9th 1930 — (United States) The State Department issues a directive to halt the influx of foreign laborers due to the chronic unemployment spreading across the nation.

October 30th 1930 — (Turkey) Greece and Turkey sign a treaty of friendship at Ankara.

November 2nd 1930 — (Ethiopia) Ras Tafari proclaims himself Emperor and changes his name to Haile Selassie.

November 4th 1930 — (United States) Unemployment rates are becoming more staggering. The President requests that Congress provide an additional $150 million for public works projects. Before the end of the year, Congress authorizes $116 million.

December 11th 1930 — (United States) As the economy continues to falter and unemployment rises, following the collapse of the stock market, the country sustains another grievous blow as another financial institution, the Bank of the United States folds in New York.

January 7th 1931 — (United States) The President's Emergency Committee for Unemployment announces that unemployment is now between four and five million workers and the situation continues to deteriorate. The Commission also emphasizes that the depression is gaining speed throughout the world. Also, soon after, on the 15th of January, in an effort to ease the strain on law enforcement, the President signs a bill which lessens the seriousness of penalties on those arrested for breaking the Prohibition law. Provided the incident involves less than one gallon, the crime becomes a misdemeanor rather than a felony.

March 3rd 1931 — **(United States)** "The Star Spangled Banner," written by Francis Scott Key during the War of 1812 while observing the attack against Fort McHenry (September 1814), is designated the National Anthem by Act of Congress.

March 4th 1931 — **(India)** The Delhi Pact is reached, resulting from discussions between Ghandi and the government. Ghandi promises to end his civil disobedience, and the Congress agrees to acknowledge the London roundtable conferences. Also, Lord Irwin agrees to freeing all political prisoners provided they have not committed any acts of violence.

March 21st 1931 — **(Germany-Austria)** A proposal is raised for a German-Austrian customs union to the consternation of Czechoslovakia, France, and Italy, who proclaim that the proposal is an infringement of Austrian sovereignty. The proposal is withdrawn on September 3rd.

April 14th 1931 — **(Spain)** The Republican leader Niceto Alcala Zamora demands that King Alfonso XIII abdicate. The King departs Spain; however, he does not heed the ultimatum of abdication.

April 22nd 1931 — **(Mideast)** Egypt and Persia sign a treaty of friendship, becoming the first alliance between Egypt and another Moslem nation.

April 22nd 1931 — **(Austria)** Subsequent to a chain of events including the French decision to withdraw short credits to compel the abandonment of the proposed German-Austrian custom union, a primary Austrian financial institution, the Credit-Anstalt fails, despite government attempts to reinforce it. This calamity leads to the domino effect in the economic area, folding financial institutions across the balance of Central Europe. The ramifications of this closure concern President Hoover, and during June he will urge that all nations agree to a one-year suspension on intercountry reparations and debts. His suggestions are subsequently accepted by eighteen nations, including the U.S.

June 16th 1931 — **(Austria)** Although the British are sustaining severe times at home, the Bank of England offers financial help to bolster the national bank of Austria (150,000,000 shillings). The French decline any suggestion of aid.

June 20th 1931 — **(United States)** President Hoover suggests that all nations permit a one-year moratorium on intercountry debts and reparation payments. The President's suggestion is well received, and by July the moratorium is put in place by all major nations. The idea has high ideals, but it is not long-lasting.

July 13th 1931 — **(Germany)** Bankruptcy is declared by the Danatbank, followed by the closing of all banks until August 5th. The financial debacle leads to an unemployment figure in excess of six million Austrians by year's end and sets the stage for the upsurge in Communism and National Socialism in the country.

July 1931 — **(United States)** The financial crisis and the economic situation as a whole continues to deteriorate. Unemployment continues to haunt the nation, and the banks continue to close at alarming rates. President Hoover voluntarily takes a twenty percent cut in pay to exhibit his concern.

August 1st 1931 — **(Great Britain)** The U.S. and France extend credits to bolster the faltering Bank of England to forestall disaster; however, the world wide depression is ever-deepening, and the effort proves to be a short term fix.

August 19th 1931 — **(Switzerland)** Bankers issue the Layton-Wiggin report proposing a six-month extension of credit to beleaguered Germany; however, Germany remains virtually bankrupt. During the following month, a coup d'etat mounted by the Heimwehr, a private Fascist Army, is unsuccessful.

September 1931 — **(Great Britain)** The financial crisis worsens. Actions that have been taken by the British lead to riots in the streets of London and in Glasgow. Problems also develop in the Royal Navy, as a mutiny occurs at Invergordon when Sailors react to a reduction in pay. Before the end of the month, England moves off the gold standard.

October 1931 — **(United States)** The U.S. and France agree to remain on the gold standard after a meeting held in Washington, D.C. The talks between President Hoover and French President Laval also bring agreement that subsequent to the present moratorium on inter-nation debts, new negotiations will have to be undertaken. Also, banks continue to fail around the U.S., and unemployment rises further. By December, civilians are marching on Washington, requesting the President to find them jobs at a minimum wage.

November 1931 — **(China)** Chiang Kai-shek's refusal to cooperate with the Communists has not relented. Mao Tse-tung, who fled the forces of Kai-shek, establishes the first Chinese Soviet Republic in Kiangsi Province.

December 1931 — **(Great Britain)** The British Parliament passes the Statute of Westminster, essentially granting sovereignty to the United Kingdom, Australia, Canada, Ireland, Newfoundland, New Zealand, and South Africa.

January 1932 — **(India)** The Earl of Wellington, recently appointed Viceroy, announces the Indian Congress illegitimate. Ghandi is rearrested and civil strife resumes.

January 22nd 1932 — **(United States)** President Hoover signs a bill into law which establishes a Reconstruction Finance Corporation intended to help extricate the nation from the depression by lending money to institutions such as railroads, banks, insurance companies etc.

February 2nd 1932 — **(Geneva)** A conference convenes in Geneva for the purpose of achieving disarmament and is attended by sixty nations including the United States. The talks continue until July without results; however, the disarmament talks reconvene during February of the following year.

February 27th 1932 — **(United States)** The Glass-Steagall Act is passed by Congress. The law authorizes the Federal Reserve Bank to free government gold to business entities and also permits the bank to allow additional credit.

February 27th 1932 — **(Finland)** A second unsuccessful coup d'etat by the Lapua Group occurs in Finland. Its leaders are arrested, and the organization ceases to exist.

March 1st 1932 — **(United States)** In Hopewell, New Jersey, Charles A. Lindbergh Jr., the son of Charles and Anne Morrow Lindbergh, less than two years old, is kidnaped from the family home; during May, the child's body is discovered about six miles from the Lindbergh home. Subsequently, Bruno Hauptmann is arrested, tried, and executed for the crime. Despite being caught carrying some of the $50 thousand ransom, he maintained his innocence.

March 3rd 1932 — **(United States)** The 20th Amendment, which becomes known as the "Lame Duck Amendment" is circulated to the states for purposes of ratification. Once ratified, the time lapse between a President's election and inauguration day will be shortened; inauguration day will change to January 20th following the election in November.

March 9th 1932 — (Ireland) Eamon de Valera is elected president.

March 13th 1932 — (Germany) Field Marshal Paul von Hindenburg wins the national presidential election. The required majority is not attained, mandating another election during April; von Hindenburg gains 18 million votes versus Adolf Hitler's eleven million votes and Ernst Thalmann (Communist) who receives five million votes.

March 23rd 1932 — (United States) President Hoover signs the Noris-La Guardia Act, limiting the use of injunctions to stop strikes.

May 16th 1932 — (Japan) The Premier of Japan is assassinated, ceasing party government in the country. A nonpartisan government will be established.

May 19th-20th 1932 — (Newfoundland) Amelia Earhart becomes the first woman to fly solo across the Atlantic. She departs Newfoundland for Paris; however, engine difficulties are encountered, forcing her to land in Ireland. She completes the flight in just over fifteen hours.

May 29th 1932 — (United States) Veterans of World War I ("Bonus Army") begin arriving in Washington, D.C., to demand payment on their bonus certificates from World War I. During the following month, the House approves payment; however, on the 17th, the Senate turns down the Patman Bonus Bill, rejecting the Veterans' request, and many depart for their homes. Some remain and are eventually pushed out of D.C. by the military.

June 16th 1932 — (Europe-Switzerland) Representatives of Belgium, France, Germany, Great Britain, Italy, and Japan confer in Lausanne and agree to forgive all of Germany's debts, contingent upon the U.S canceling the debts of the convening nations owed to the United States. The U.S. declines the suggestion.

July 1932 — (Portugal) The minister of finance, Antonio de Oliviera Salazar, becomes premier and he assumes dictatorial powers.

July 9th 1932 — (United States) Congress passes the Wagner-Garner Bill, designed to establish federal employment agencies in states which have state employment agencies of their own; however, the President vetoes the bill on the 11th. On the 18th, the U.S. and Canada sign a treaty agreeing to joint construction of the St. Lawrence Seaway, connecting the Great Lakes with the Atlantic Ocean, at a cost of about $543 million. On the 21st, the President signs the Emergency Relief Act, authorizing $300 million for distribution to states which are in dire need of relief and also providing $3 billion for local and state governments to encourage public works projects. Also, on the 22nd, the Federal Home Loan Bank Act becomes law in an effort to boost the construction of residential homes and create jobs. The law authorizes twelve regional banks which will open during October.

July 25th 1932 — (Soviet Union) A nonaggression pact is reached between the Soviets and the countries of Estonia, Finland, Latvia, and Poland. During November, the Soviets reach a similar accord with France.

September 1st 1932 — (United States) In New York, the Mayor, James J. Walker, resigns, subsequent to several months of scrutiny concerning allegations of corruption and graft in his administration.

November 8th 1932 — (United States) President Hoover is defeated in the Presidential election by Franklin D. Roosevelt who garnishes nearly 23 million votes and receives 472 electoral college votes. Hoover receives nearly 16 million votes, but he gets only 59 electoral votes. Also, the Communist candidate William Foster receives 103,000 votes, and the Socialist candidate Norman Thomas receives 882,000 votes. Subsequent to the election, Roosevelt meets with President Hoover to discuss the war-debt issue.

November 1932 — (Germany) About mid-month, Chancellor von Papen resigns, followed by President Hindenburg offering a limited Chancellorship to Hitler. Hitler declines the offer, preferring to get full powers, something which the President will not concede. Nevertheless, Hitler becomes Chancellor during January 1933.

November 11th 1932 — (United States) At Arlington, Virginia, the Tomb of the Unknown Soldier is officially dedicated.

December 1932 — (United States) The economy continues to decline and unemployment spirals out of control, reaching about 13 million. President Hoover had received much of the blame for the depression; however, years later it is realized that no one man could have caused or stopped the catastrophic economic collapse.

January 1933 — (Spain) Insurrections spring up in Barcelona and subsequently occur in other towns and cities.

January 5th 1933 — (United States) Calvin Coolidge, the 30th President of the United States, dies.

January 13th 1933 — (United States) Congress passes the Howes-Cutting Bill, overriding a Presidential veto, setting the stage for the independence of the Philippines. However, the legislation provides that the U.S. will retain military and naval bases and also stipulates specific tariffs of Philippine goods heading to the U.S. and other articles. Subsequently, the Philippine legislature rejects the plan.

February 1933 — (Switzerland) During a conference in Switzerland, the Little Entente, composed of Czechoslovakia, Rumania, and Yugoslavia, begins to reorganize and bolster the alliance.

February 6th 1933 — (United States) The 20th Amendment, which changes the Presidential inauguration date from March to January immediately following the election, becomes effective.

February 15th 1933 — (United States) President-elect Roosevelt barely escapes assassination while in Miami, Florida. Thanks to a bystander, the assassin's bullets miss Roosevelt, but several others are hit, including Anton Cermak, the Mayor of Chicago, who subsequently dies of his wounds.

February 20th 1933 — (United States) Congress adopts a resolution which will repeal the Prohibition Amendment (18th Amendment), one most unpopular with the nation. The states receive the resolution for ratification.

March 4th 1933 — (United States) Franklin D. Roosevelt is inaugurated as the 32nd President of the U.S. His Vice President is John Nance Garner.

March 5th 1933 — (United States) President Roosevelt asks Congress to convene for a special session on March 9th to deal with the ongoing crisis in the country. The session will become known as Roosevelt's "Hundred Days." Meanwhile, he proclaims a National Bank Holiday and orders the closing of all banks from March 6th through March 9th. Congress will convene and pass the Emergency Banking Relief Act, granting the Treasury Department authorization to control financial transactions. Also, as of May 1st, it will be against the law to own or export gold. However, many citizens refuse to turn in their gold to the Treasury Department.

March 12th 1933 — **(United States)** President Roosevelt talks to the American public by a radio broadcast, explaining his reasons for the bank closures and telling them his plans for finding solutions to the financial dilemma facing the country.

March 20th 1933 — **(United States)** The Economy Act, cutting the salaries of federal employees and reducing payments to veterans, is signed into law by President Roosevelt.

March 22nd 1933 — **(United States)** Congress passes the Beer and Wine Act, effective April 7th. The act, which in essence amends the Volstead Act, legalizes beer and wine with a maximum alcoholic content of 3.2 percent. A tag-along tax goes in with the law assuring a quick influx of revenue.

March 31st 1933 — **(United States)** In an effort to create employment for men between the ages of eighteen and twenty-five, the Civilian Conservation Corps is established.

April 19th 1933 — **(United States)** The President announces that the U.S. is going off the gold standard. Congress will deliver a joint resolution in concurrence with the President during June.

May 12th 1933 — **(United States)** The Federal Emergency Relief Administration is established, another of the President's New Deal programs. It is designed to distribute funds through grants to state and local agencies to provide help to the unemployed. Also, the Agricultural Adjustment Administration (A.A.A.) is established to subsidize farmers for reducing particular crops.

May 18th 1933 — **(United States)** The Tennessee Valley Authority is established by Congress to operate the Muscle Shoals plants on the Tennessee River and also to construct new dams and power plants, in addition to several other economy boosting projects.

May 27th 1933 — **(United States)** Congress passes the Federal Securities Act, which empowers the Federal Trade Commission to supervise all new stock and bond issues.

June 5th 1933 — **(United States)** Congress takes the country off the gold standard in conjunction with the earlier wishes of President Roosevelt. All government and private debts are now payable in "lawful money."

June 13th 1933 — **(United States)** Congress passes the Home Owners' Refinancing Act, which in turn establishes the Home Owners' Loan Corporation (HOLC) which permits bonds in the amount of $2 billion to refinance home mortgages for non-farmers in an effort to halt the alarming number of foreclosures. In many instances, the loans can be used for back-taxes and home repairs.

June 16th 1933 — **(United States)** Congress passes the National Industrial Recovery Act (N.I.R.A.) to create jobs and improve business activity. The act mandates fair business practices and working conditions. A portion of the law provides workers the ability to "organize and bargain collectively." Another section of the act establishes the Public Works Administration (P.W.A.) to initiate large construction projects and the National Recovery Administration, the latter being declared unconstitutional by the Supreme Court during May 1935. Other Congressional legislation passed during this final day of the 100 day session are the Farm Credit Act and the Banking Act of 1933, the latter establishing the Federal

Bank Deposit Insurance.

Mid-July 1933 — **(Germany)** The National Socialist Party is pronounced the only legitimate political party. By now, the Communist and Socialist Parties have already been banned, and the Catholic and Nationalist Parties have disbanded themselves. Also, Germany, France, Italy, and Great Britain sign the Four Power Pact.

August 5th 1933 — **(United States)** The President forms the National Labor Board (N.L.B.) to enforce the collective bargaining provisions of the National Labor Relations Act; the act is signed into law during July 1935.

November 8th 1933 — **(United States)** The Civil Works Administration is established to create jobs, primarily for the country's unskilled workers at minimum wages.

November 16th 1933 — **(United States)** President Roosevelt announces that the U.S. will resume diplomatic relations with the Soviet Union. Relations had been severed during 1919 while the Bolsheviks were seizing power. The agreement, re-initiates trade with the Soviets, and in turn, the Bolsheviks promise to cease Communist propaganda in the U.S.

December 5th 1933 — **(United States)** Utah becomes the 36th State to ratify the repeal of Prohibition (19th Amendment), making it the 21st Amendment to the Constitution.

January 30th 1934 — **(United States)** Congress passes the Gold Reserve Act, giving President Roosevelt authority to compare the value of the dollar in relation to gold "between 50 to 60 cents." The act also gives the President the authority to change the dollar's value which he does, dropping it to 59.06 cents.

January 26th 1934 — **(Europe)** Germany and Poland reach a ten-year nonaggression pact.

February 1934 — **(United States)** The President establishes the Export Import Bank of Washington, formed to bolster commerce between foreign nations and the U.S. and to establish credits for both long and short term periods to assist U.S. exporters. Initially a large effort is put forth to encourage trade with the Soviet Union. Additional banks will follow and the emphasis will be to encourage trade with nations from Latin America. Also, Congress passes the Crop Loan Act on the 23rd to provide funds to the Farm Credit Administration. In other activity, President Roosevelt cancels all private air mail contracts, based on information emerging from a Senate investigation which is investigating alleged bribes accepted by government officials for such contracts. Roosevelt orders the Army to transport the mail until the investigation is concluded.

February 1934 — **(Europe)** In France, riots erupt against the Nationalist government in Paris and some other cities. Measures are taken to try to avert civil war, resulting in a coalition cabinet which excludes Communists, Royalists, and Socialists. **(Balkans)** The Balkan Pact is reached by representatives of Greece, Rumania, Turkey, and Yugoslavia.

March 1934 — **(Europe)** Austria, Hungary, and Italy sign the Rome Protocol to offset France's Little Entente.

March 24th 1934 — **(United States)** Congress passes the Tydings-McDuffie Act, which mandates the independence of the Philippines, effective ten years subsequent to the approval of the Philippine legislature. The event occurs during 1946 on schedule.

April 12th-April 1934 — **(United States)** The Senate forms a committee to probe the actions of the weapons and munitions companies which made extraordinary profits from the sale of munitions during the war.

May 1934 — (Europe) The existing nonaggression pact between the Soviet Union, the Baltic States, and Poland is extended into a ten-year agreement.

May 10th-11th 1934 — (United States) Severe dust storms rip across the country, blowing topsoil from such states as Arkansas, Colorado, Kansas, Texas, and Oklahoma, pushing it as far as the east coast. These continuing catastrophic storms have created what becomes known as the "dust bowl," a direct result of improper farming methods.

May 29th 1934 — (United States) The U.S. signs a treaty with Cuba, ending its status as a U.S. protectorate. During August, a reciprocal trade agreement will be reached between the two countries.

June 6th 1934 — (United States) The Securities and Exchange Commission is established to regulate the stock market and to root out illegal activity.

June 1934 — (United States) On the 12th, Congress enacts the Reciprocal Trades Agreement Act, giving the President authorization to compromise tariff rates with countries willing to lower their tariffs against the U.S. On the 15th, Congress passes the National Guard Act, which attaches the National Guard to the Army in the event of war or in case of a national emergency. On the 19th, the Federal Communications Commission (F.C.C.) is established to regulate the cable, radio, and telegraph communications industry, which the Interstate Commerce Commission has done until now. The Federal Housing Administration (F.H.A.) is established on the 28th to insure mortgage loans granted by banks for housing and farms. Other acts passed by Congress during June are the Silver Purchase Act and the National Labor Relations Board, which replaces the National Labor Board (established 1933). Congress also passes the National Housing Act which establishes the Federal Housing Administration, the Taylor Grazing Act, the Federal Farm Bankruptcy Act (Frazier-Lemke Act), and the Tobacco Control Act.

August 1934 — (Germany) President Hindenburg succumbs and subsequently, a plebiscite is held which chooses Hitler as president.

September 1934 — (Baltic) Estonia, Latvia, and Lithuania sign the Baltic Pact, joining those which had initiated the pact during the previous February.

September 18th 1934 — (Soviet Union) The Bolshevik government, which has publicly renounced the League of Nations, has a change of heart and joins, prompted somewhat by the anticommunism sentiments in Germany.

October 1934 — (France) King Alexander of Yugoslavia and French Foreign Minister Louis Barthou are assassinated in Marseilles by a revolutionary group which is based in Hungary. Intervention by the League of Nations prevents war between Hungary and Yugoslavia.

January 1935 — (Europe) France and Italy sign the Marseilles Pact.

March 22nd 1935 — (Middle East) Persia officially changes its name to Iran.

April 8th 1935 — (United States) Congress passes the Emergency Relief Appropriation Act, which authorizes nearly $5 billion for various public works programs. During May, the Works Progress Administration (W.P.A.) begins putting Americans to work on construction projects. Harry L. Hopkins be-

comes the administrator, and he later becomes heavily involved with lend-lease. Also, during May, the President uses the authority of the law to establish the Resettlement Act (RA) which assists farmers to move to more suitable land and begins to create low cost housing in the suburbs. He also establishes the Rural Electrification Administration on May 11th to make it easier to get electricity to many rural areas. There is much controversy on many of the New Deal programs. Back in 1932, President Hoover had reacted to Roosevelt's ideas as being "state socialism." Now, many industrialists and conservative Democrats are becoming suspicious of Roosevelt's New Deal, claiming he is taking the nation toward Socialism.

May 22nd 1935 — (United States) President Roosevelt addresses a joint session of Congress attempting to clarify his reasons for vetoing the Patman Bonus Bill, denying WWI Veterans their bonus checks. Roosevelt will veto the bill again during January of 1936; however, Congress overrides his veto.

May 27th 1935 — (United States) The U.S. Supreme Court rules that the National Industrial Recovery Act of 1933 is unconstitutional, in essence telling Roosevelt that the Constitution does not give the President the right to make "whatever laws he thinks may be needed or advisable for the rehabilitation and expansion of trade and industry." The Court also admonishes the Roosevelt Administration for attempting to usurp that power and authority reserved for the states by the Constitution.

May 1935 — (France) France concludes an alliance pact with the Soviet Union. Also, the Soviet Union concludes an agreement with Czechoslovakia, offering support if Czechoslovakia is provided similar aid by France.

June 1935 — (England) Great Britain and Germany conclude a naval agreement, whereby Germany agrees to restrict its navy to not more than 35 percent of the British Navy.

June 7th 1935 — (United States) The National Resources Committee is formed to investigate and propose suggestions and plans for the country's resources (human and natural).

July 5th 1935 — (United States) The National Labor Relations Act is signed into law by President Roosevelt.

August 14th 1935 — (United States) President Roosevelt signs the Social Security Act, creating pensions for the elderly and also establishing a national network of social insurance.

August 1935 — (United States) Congress passes the Banking Act of 1935, modifying the Federal Reserve System and enabling it to exert more control over banking and credit. The Public Utilities Act is also passed, and on August 31st, Congress passes the Neutrality Act, prohibiting the shipping of arms to warring nations.

November 1935 — (Greece) King George II returns to Greece after exile in Great Britain.

November 9th 1935 — (United States) The Committee for Industrial Organization is established within the American Federation of Labor, giving unions the right to organize by industry, rather than by employers.

January 6th 1936 — (United States) The U.S. Supreme Court rules that the Agricultural Adjustment Act is unconstitutional. It finds that the assessed tax on food processors to support the subsidies to farmers is improper. During February, the Court rules in favor of the activities of the Tennessee Valley Authority.

January 20th 1936 — (Great Britain) King George V succumbs. He is succeeded by Edward VIII.

761

February 29th 1936 — (United States) Congress enacts the Soil Conservation and Domestic Allotment Act to ensure crop limitation, which ceased with the ruling of the Supreme Court on the Agriculture Adjustment Act (January 1936).

March 2nd 1936 — (United States) The U.S. and Panama sign a treaty which terminates the U.S. obligation to protect the independence of Panama. The U.S. also totally relinquishes its right to intervene in Panama's internal affairs. The Senate ratifies the treaty during July 1939.

April 1936 — (Egypt) King Farouk becomes monarch subsequent to the death of his father King Fuad.

June 1936 — (United States) The Veterans of World War I finally receive their bonus check in the mail, subsequent to Congress overriding a second veto of President Roosevelt during January.

June 30th 1936 — (United States) The Walsh-Healey Government Contracts Act is passed by Congress, compelling all companies engaging in business with the U.S. Government to enact a forty-hour work week, restrict child labor, and conform to a minimum wage.

July 11th 1936 — (Europe) Germany and Austria reach an accord whereby Germany agrees to respect Austria's independence.

August 7th 1936 — (United States) The U.S. declares its neutrality concerning the ongoing civil war in Spain which erupted during July.

September 9th 1936 — (France) France signs a treaty of friendship with Syria.

September 1936 — (Europe) France, the Netherlands, and Sweden go off the gold standard.

October 1936 — (France) The Socialist Government of France devalues the Franc, causing further havoc in the world financial crisis. Action by the U.S. and Great Britain forestalls chaos in the world money market.

October 9th 1936 — (United States) After the completion of Boulder Dam at Boulder City, Nevada, its first generator is activated, delivering electricity to Los Angeles, 260 miles away.

October 25th 1936 — ((Europe) The Berlin-Rome Axis is formed, tightening the relationship between Germany and Italy.

November 3rd 1936 — (United States) President Roosevelt wins the presidential election, defeating Alfred M. Landon. Roosevelt gains over 27,750,000 votes and Landon receives over 16,680,000. The electoral college gives 523 votes to Roosevelt and eight to Landon. Also, the Communist candidate Earl Browder receives about 80,000 votes (during 1932 elections the Communists scored 103,000 votes), and the Socialist candidate Norman Thomas gets about 187,000 votes (during the 1932 elections Thomas received over 880,000 votes). William Lemke, a Populist candidate, receives nearly 900,000 votes.

November 25th 1936 — (Germany-Japan) Japan and Germany sign the Anti-Comintern Pact, an accord directed at an eventual attack against the Soviet Union from the east and the west. Subsequently, Italy joins the agreement.

December 1st-23rd 1936 — (South America) An Inter-American Conference for the Maintenance of Peace convenes in Buenos Aires, Argentina, and concludes with an agreement whereby the nations of the Western Hemisphere will confer with each other if any country is faced with aggression by an adversarial nation.

December 10th 1936 — (Great Britain) King Edward VIII abdicates the throne upon making the decision to marry Wallis Warfield Simpson, an American. He becomes the Duke of Windsor and is succeeded by his brother King George VI.

January 6th 1937 — (United States) Congress passes a resolution barring shipments of arms to either side in the ongoing civil war in Spain.

January 20th 1937 — (United States) Franklin Roosevelt is inaugurated President for his second term of office. His Vice President, John Nance Garner, serves a full second term under Roosevelt.

February 1st 1937 — (United States) The U.S. Supreme Court declines acceptance of an appeal challenging the Social Security Act and subsequently, on the 24th of May, upholds the constitutionality of the act.

February 5th 1937 — (United States) President Roosevelt attempts to manipulate the Supreme Court by increasing its number from nine to 15, by permitting Roosevelt to appoint one new member of the court for every present member over seventy years old with ten years on the Bench. The Senate Judiciary Committee will reject the Presidential plan.

March 25th 1937 — (Europe) Italy and Yugoslavia agree to a five-year nonaggression and neutrality pact.

April 1937 — (India) India's new constitution takes effect, but complications develop as the All-India Congress Party subsequently demands independence from Great Britain.

April 12th 1937 — (United States) The Supreme Court rules that companies which operate on a national scale come under the power of Congress and also the National Labor Relations Board. There are no exceptions even for their specific plants which confine themselves to intrastate manufacturing only.

May 1st 1937 — (United States) The Third Neutrality Act is signed by President Roosevelt, expanding the Neutrality Acts of 1935 and 1936 which expire at midnight.

July 1937 — (Great Britain) In London, the Peel Report, which suggests the termination of the Palestine Mandate, is issued. It recommends the partitioning of the region involved into Arab and Jewish states; however, Britain is to retain control over Bethlehem and Jerusalem. Neither the Arabs or the Jews endorse the idea. Also, Afghanistan, Iran, Iraq, and Turkey sign a nonaggression pact.

July 2nd 1937 — (Pacific-New Guinea) Amelia Earhart, the first woman to cross the Atlantic in a solo flight, departs New Guinea with one passenger as she attempts to fly around the world; however, soon after, the Plane disappears without a trace.

July 22nd 1937 — (United States) The Bankhead-Jones Farm Tenant Act establishes the Farm Security Administration (FSA) in a determined effort to halt the slide in farm ownership.

August 1937 — (China-Soviet Union) The Soviet Union and China reach agreement on a nonaggression pact.

September 1st 1937 — (United States) The U.S. Housing Authority is formed to grant low interest mortgages (long-term) to bolster public agencies which are engaged in cleaning up slums and devoted to creating public housing.

November 15th 1937 — (United States) The President calls Congress into special session to propose legislation on matters such as wages and agriculture concerns. However, Congress remains in session for several weeks without taking any action.

December 1937 — (Turkey) The Turkish Government renounces its treaty of friendship with Syria, in effect since 1926.

January 28th 1938 — (United States) President Roosevelt recommends to Congress that the Armed Forces, especially the Navy, receive additional funding to increase their strength.

March 1938 — (Mexico) The government confiscates U.S. and British oil companies by nationalizing them. Subsequently, Mexico concludes agreements to supply Germany and Italy with oil on a barter type system.

May 11th 1938 — (United States) Congress enacts a law reducing capital gains taxes and also reducing taxes paid by some big Corporations in an attempt to boost the economy by creating additional jobs. President Roosevelt declines to sign or to veto the act, enabling it to become effective on May 27th.

May 17th 1938 — (United States) The Naval Expansion Act (Vinson Naval Act) is enacted by Congress, ensuring funds for a ten-year expansion program to build a formidable two-ocean Navy. Congress authorizes $1,090,656,000. However, Congress turns down pleas for funds to fortify Guam, an advance outpost in the Pacific.

May 26th 1938 — (United States) Congress establishes the House Committee on Un-American Activities (H.U.A.C.). The Chairman is Martin Dies, a Democrat from Texas. Some wonder why the committee is formed; however, Communist organizations and Communist sympathizers are still active within the U.S. despite a previous promise by the Russians to stop their propaganda. The committee is to investigate the left and right groups for illegal activities.

June 25th 1938 — (United States) The Fair Labor Standards Act takes effect, establishing 25 cents an hour as a minimum wage for employees engaged in interstate commerce. The act also forbids child labor.

October 30th 1938 — (United States) On the eve of Halloween, Orson Welles terrifies part of the nation as he convincingly narrates "War of the Worlds," a fictional story about earth being invaded by Martians. Police stations are deluged with calls, especially in New Jersey where the invasion is supposedly taking place. Traffic jams are created on many roads as people flee their houses to escape the invaders. Welles and the additional people involved with the script have no idea of the chaos they are creating. Prior to the radio program it is mentioned that the show is fiction.

November 1938 — (Palestine) The Woodhead Commission reports that the partition of the region is not practical and calls for a gathering of Arabs and Jews to confer on a solution. Subsequently, meetings are held, but no agreement is reached.

December 1938 — (Europe) France and Germany conclude a friendship pact. Also, Italy informs France that the mutually agreed upon pact of 1935 is terminated due to non-ratification. Also, the Italians have been able to break U.S. intelligence in Rome. Commander Max Ponzo, head of Italian Espionage (SIS), has access to records in the Embassy's safe;

an Italian worker with sporadic access to the key to the safe made it possible to duplicate the key. The SIS chooses to collaborate with the British after the outbreak of war, and the secret information never falls into the hands of the Italian Fascists.

December 24th 1938 — (South America-Peru) A conference between twenty-one nations of the Western Hemisphere results in the Declaration of Lima, an ambiguous reaffirmation of mutual consultation if any nation becomes threatened; however, the pact neglects to discuss defense of the offended member. The conference is the Eighth International American Conference.

January 12th 1939 — (United States) Roosevelt attempts to further bolster the Armed Forces, requesting that Congress provide an additional $525 million for defense purposes. The President will again request funds during March and April in an effort to bolster the U.S. in the event of hostilities.

April 3rd 1939 — (United States) Congress passes the Administrative Reorganization Act, something which the President has wanted for about two years to authorize him to reorganize government agencies.

May 16th 1939 — (United States) The U.S. introduces food stamps, starting the program in Rochester, New York, to supplement the incomes of those families on relief.

May 22nd 1939 — (Germany-Italy) As Hitler and Mussolini draw closer together, the two countries conclude the Pact of Steel, an accord that grants mutual cooperation. By this time, the Italians are tapping the phone wires between Rome and Berlin.

May 1939 — (Palestine) Great Britain expects to mandate an independent Palestine State within a time frame of ten years and establish guidelines for both Jewish and Arabic governing bodies, but neither the Arabs nor the Jews concur. British Parliament approves the plan.

June 1939 — (Europe) France, Great Britain, and the Soviet Union spend the next several months attempting to negotiate a three-way peace agreement to forestall German aggression; however, the effort is fruitless due to unreasonable demands by the Russians.

June 1939 — (Turkey) Turkey and France reach an agreement resulting in a pact which includes a mutual aid agreement. Turkey is now considered on the Allied side as she has already concluded agreements with Great Britain.

July 14th 1939 — (United States) President Roosevelt requests that Congress repeal the arms embargo to enable the U.S. to give assistance to the Allies, especially England.

July 18th 1939 — (United States) The President moves further away from the policy of neutrality, asking Congress to revise the present Neutrality Law.

August 1939 — (United States) President Roosevelt receives a letter from Albert Einstein with the startling information that it is possible to create an atomic bomb. The letter, written with the encouragement of other scientists, prompts the Manhattan Project. Einstein had emigrated from Germany during 1933.

August 2nd 1939 — (United States) Congress enacts the Hatch Act, forbidding Federal civil service workers from participating in political campaigns.

November 4th 1939 — (United States) President Roosevelt signs the Neutrality Act of 1939. The new legislation clearly slides the U.S. toward the Allies.

December 11th 1939 — (United States) The Supreme Court rules that wiretapping to gain evidence without the authorization of a warrant is forbidden.

January 1940 — (United States) The trade treaty between the U.S. and Japan ceases, but trade continues between the two countries.

April 12th 1940 — (United States) President Roosevelt signs legislation that extends the Trade Agreement Act of 1937, affording the President the opportunity to continue negotiating tariff reductions with cooperative nations.

April 1940 — (United States) The Supreme Court rules that it is constitutional for the Federal Government to set minimum wage standards for companies conducting business (by contract) with the government.

June 16th 1940 — (United States) Congress passes the Pittman Resolution, authorizing the U.S. to sell arms to South American nations.

June 28th 1940 — (United States) The Alien Registration Act (Smith Act) is enacted, mandating all foreigners to register with the government. Also, the act also forbids persons from belonging to any organizations avowing to the forceful overthrow of the U.S. In other activity, the British have been bolstering their position in the U.S. An agent, William Stephenson (Chief of all British Intelligence, Worldwide), is now operating out of New York from the Rockefeller Center; his organization will control about thirty thousand intelligence personnel who are scattered around the globe; several thousand come under his direct supervision. Stephenson's codename, given to him by Churchill, is "Intrepid." Churchill assures him that he will have President Roosevelt's ear at all times. Stephenson registers with U.S. Immigration authorities as "Passport Control Officer." The clandestine operation works against many U.S. Legislators, including Senator Burton K. Wheeler, who are initially against going to war. The close cooperation between the British Secret Service and the Roosevelt Administration continues throughout the presidency of Roosevelt, but President Truman, soon after taking over the Oval Office, disbands the operation and orders it to leave the U.S. immediately.

July 1940 — (Cuba) At the Pan American Union meeting in Havana, it is announced that the American States will not permit any European Colonies in the Western Hemisphere to come under German control (Declaration of Havana). In Europe, Germany makes strong demands to Sweden to permit German troops to pass through the country by rail; about 300,000 German troops transfer between Finland, Germany, and Norway, until August 1943 when Sweden cancels the transit privilege.

July 4th 1940 — (United States) Chicago hosts an American Negro Exposition to celebrate the 75th anniversary of the Emancipation Proclamation.

July 20th 1940 — (United States) The Hatch Act of 1939 is amended. Congress limits individual contributions to a presidential candidate to a maximum of five thousand dollars and in addition places a ceiling of $3 million on Presidential campaign expenditures.

August 1940 — (United States) Columbia Broadcasting Company introduces color television, demonstrating it in New York; however, it is still a long way from reaching the general public on a grand scale. Subsequent to World War II, television begins to grow widely. During the initial growth of color television, many gadgets hit the market, one of which is a set

of colored plastic discs that fit on the screen and tint the picture. Also, many televisions will be purchased that have small boxes attached to deposit quarters in order to make payment by installment.

September 3rd 1940 — (United States) The U.S. makes arrangements to transfer 50 Destroyers to Great Britain in exchange for permission to establish U.S. Bases on British colonies in the Western Hemisphere.

September 16th 1940 — (United States) Congress enacts the Selective Service Act (Draft).

September 26th 1940 — (United States) The President forbids the export of iron and scrap steel to countries outside of the Western Hemisphere, except for the British, infuriating the Japanese who subsequently protest to no avail.

September 1940 — (United States) The America First Committee is established in opposition to President Roosevelt's position on entering the conflict. Immediate steps are taken to discredit the organization whose members include Charles Lindbergh. Pressure mounts on the organization which is accused of being pro-Germany. The organization questions why similar pressure is not placed upon left wing Communist organizations.

November 5th 1940 — (United States) President Roosevelt wins an unprecedented third term as President; however, his popular vote count is less than his previous two wins. His opponent, Wendell L. Willkie, had run a hard campaign, but toward the end, Roosevelt pulled out front to stay. Roosevelt is inaugurated on the 20th of January, 1941; his Vice President for this term is Henry A. Wallace.

December 1940 — (United States) The Office of Production Management (O.P.M.) is established for the purpose of overseeing and expediting the shipment of arms to the Allies and to regulate the production of defense supplies. The U.S. still maintains a position of neutrality.

December 18th 1940 — Germany Hitler issues Directive No. 21, a secret document which outlines Operation BARBAROSA, the invasion of Russia; nine copies are distributed and within one week, Soviet agents in Berlin receive a copy.

January 6th 1941 — (United States) President Roosevelt delivers his State of the Union Address and in addition to detailing his plans for the Lend-Lease program, he emphasizes that the "four freedoms," speech, worship, want, and fear, are to be preserved in the entire world. Subsequently, upon the conclusion of the Atlantic Charter (August 12th 1941) which results in the Joint Declaration by President Roosevelt and Prime Minister Churchill, the freedoms of speech and religion are dropped from his list.

January 10th 1941 — (United States) President Roosevelt requests that Congress pass the Lend-Lease Act, in essence giving Roosevelt the ability to become involved in the conflict without a declaration of war. Many Americans, including previous Ambassador to England Joseph P. Kennedy (father of the future President), are against this decision. **(England)** Harry Hopkins meets with Winston Churchill, announcing himself as " the closest confidant and personal agent of President Roosevelt." Churchill writes: "WITH GLEAMING EYE AND QUIET CONSTRAINED PASSION HE (Hopkins) SAID": "THE PRESIDENT IS DETERMINED THAT WE SHALL WIN THE WAR TOGETHER. MAKE NO MISTAKE ABOUT IT. HE HAS SENT ME HERE TO TELL YOU THAT AT ALL COSTS AND BY ALL MEANS HE WILL CARRY YOU THROUGH, NO MATTER WHAT HAPPENS TO HIM-THERE IS NOTHING

THAT HE WILL NOT DO SO FAR AS HE HAS POWERS." Churchill also states in his book, *The Great Alliance*, that Hopkins states: "THIS CAUSE WAS TO BE THE DEFEAT, RUIN, AND SLAUGHTER OF HITLER, TO THE EXCLUSION OF ALL OTHER PURPOSES, LOYALTIES, OR AIMS." Subsequently, U.S. General Wedemeyer remarks in his book, *Wedemeyer Reports*: "THUS DID THE PRESIDENT OF THE UNITED STATES THROUGH THE MOUTH OF HARRY HOPKINS RENOUNCE ADHERENCE TO THE CONSTITUTION OF THE UNITED STATES AND REPUDIATE HIS PLEDGED WORD TO THE AMERICAN PEOPLE TO KEEP THEM OUT OF FOREIGN WARS FOR THE SAKE OF AN AIM HE CONCEIVED TO BE HIGHER, NAMELY THE SLAUGHTER OF HITLER."

February 3rd 1941 — (United States) The Supreme Court rules that the Federal Wages and Hours Act (passed during 1938, becoming effective during October 1940) which includes a provision mandating a forty-hour work week, is constitutional. Also, the Supreme Court concludes that the Sherman Antitrust Act does not pertain to labor union disputes.

February 4th 1941 — (United States) The United Service Organization is established. It will become known as the U.S.O. and become a valuable service for all U.S. Service personnel around the world, giving them a welcome place for relaxation and a friend for their other needs. Many of the great Hollywood stars will devote their time freely to roam the world and entertain the troops.

March 11th-12th 1941 — (United States) The President signs the Lend-Lease Act, authorizing the U.S. to supply arms, ammunition, and supplies to its Allies. Congress appropriates $7 billion toward the end of March; however, by 1946, the figure spirals above $50 billion. The British, especially Winston Churchill, are thrilled with the news. Roosevelt had held a press conference on December 17th 1940, and hot nationwide debate ensued; however, Congress passes the act on the 11th with a big majority. Goods are soon on their way to Britain, China, and the Soviet Union. On March 9th 1943, the act is extended by Congress for one year by a vote of 407 to six, and on March 10th (second anniversary of the original act), the Senate votes unanimously 82 to 0 for the extension.

March 19th 1941 — (United States) The National Defense Mediation Board (N.D.M.B.) is formed to act as intermediary between unions and industries engaged in defense work. Crippling strikes have become normal, and they are now beginning to threaten the nation's ability to build its defenses. Communists and their sympathizers have infiltrated many of the labor unions and cause as much confusion as possible.

March 28th 1941 — (United States) The U.S. Antarctic Expedition packs up to return home after a two-year stay at the South Pole. The mission had been led by Admiral Richard Byrd.

Mid-April 1941 — (U.S.S.R.) The Soviets sign a five-year neutrality pact with the Japanese. Also, the Danish Minister to Washington signs a treaty which permits the U.S. to defend Greenland and also permits the U.S. to establish Bases there. However, the Danish Foreign Ministry declares the treaty invalid; U.S. Forces will be sent to Greenland, despite the action of the Foreign Ministry. In addition, President Roosevelt establishes the Office of Price Administration (O.P.A.) to formulate price and wage controls. Almost immediately, the O.P.A. locks the prices of U.S. steel.

April-May 1941 — (England) German Planes have been striking English cities. Coventry received the wrath of the Luftwaffe on the 8th, and London receives a double-blast,

being hit on the 16th and 17th. In addition, Plymouth is struck throughout the latter part of the month. On the 1st of May, Liverpool and Mersey incur severe damage, and thousands of people are left homeless in addition to about 3,000 people killed. On the 10th, London receives a catastrophic blow; incendiary bombs tumble down and ignite about 2,000 fires and smash about 150 water mains, greatly hindering firefighting operations. Several dock areas and many strategic targets including war-effort factories, are demolished; the railroad station entrances also take heavy blows, as all but one station is blocked for several weeks. In addition, the House of Commons is reduced. The German air raids between June 1940 and June 1941 cause over 43,000 civilian deaths and over 50,000 civilians are seriously wounded.

April 23rd-28th 1941 — (United States) Charles Lindbergh delivers a speech predicting tragedy for the entire world if the English Empire collapses. He believes the English are losing the war against Germany and urges a negotiated settlement, fearing the British intend to drag America into the conflict. Lindbergh, in an effort to continue his stance against the President's position, as the nation heads toward conflict, resigns his commission as an Army Air Corps Reserve Officer on the 28th. Lindbergh is deeply involved with the America First movement, which is opposed by Roosevelt. At the outbreak of war, Lindbergh attempts to rejoin the service; however, high sources in the administration prohibit it. Lindbergh takes a position with Ford Motors and becomes involved with the development of U.S. Bombers. Henry Ford, like many other prominent Americans, had been against the U.S. entry into the war. In other activity, a ruling by the U.S. Supreme Court dictates that colored people must receive identical accommodations while traveling on trains as those given to white people. **(Intelligence)** American code-breakers (OP-20) in Washington intercept a top secret message from the German Charge d' Affairs, Washington, D.C., which is en route to his Foreign Ministry: AS COMMUNICATED TO ME BY AN ABSOLUTELY RELIABLE SOURCE, THE STATE DEPARTMENT IS IN POSSESSION OF THE KEY TO THE JAPANESE CODING SYSTEM AND IS THEREFORE ABLE ALSO TO DECIPHER INFORMATION TELEGRAMS FROM TOKYO TO AMBASSADOR NOMURA HERE, REGARDING AMBASSADOR OSHIMA'S REPORTS FROM BERLIN. The Germans subsequently inform the Japanese, but they believe their system (Machine No. 97) is impenetrable and make no changes. (The Germans as well as the Russians and British have reliable intelligence operations in the U.S.

May 9th 1941 — (Ethiopia) Winston Churchill's congratulations reach Haile Selaissie (Emperor of Ethiopia) on his return to the capital: "YOUR MAJESTY WAS THE FIRST OF THE LAWFUL SOVEREIGNS TO BE DRIVEN FROM HIS THRONE AND COUNTRY BY THE FASCIST-NAZI CRIMINALS, AND YOU ARE NOW THE FIRST TO RETURN IN TRIUMPH." When Selaissie had first appeared at the United Nations requesting help after the invasion of the Italian Army, he had been booed by the members, and his pleas had fallen on deaf ears.

May 17th 1941 — (East Africa) The Duke of Aosta, cousin to King of Italy and the Governor-General of East Africa since 1937 (in command of all Italian Armies in these territories), surrenders. Since January, about 220,000 Italians have been captured or killed, but thousands more are still in the mountains of Abyssinia. Subsequently, on the 2nd of July, 4,500 Italians surrender at Debra Tabor to a small British force composed of one Squadron and one Company. Southwest Abyssinia is also secured by contingents of the 11th and 12th

765

African Divisions. Also, native Congo troops move out during the summer and, after completing a journey of about 2,000 miles, participate in the final stages of ousting Mussolini from Africa and shattering his dreams of conquest. Between September and November, 11,500 Italians and about 12,000 local troops are captured.

June 3rd 1941 — (Germany) Japanese Ambassador Oshima, while at Berchtesgaden, is informed by Hitler that Russia is to be attacked "TO ELIMINATE COMMUNISM...FOR THE SAKE OF HUMANITY." On the 5th, the message is transmitted to Japan; it is intercepted and translated by U.S. code-breakers.

June 21st 1941 — (Soviet Union) During early June, the Germans were ordered to begin sending all women, children, and pets home from the German Embassy in Moscow; orders had also been issued to secure their secret archives and make the exit inconspicuous. Today, Ambassador Schulenburg is called to the Kremlin to explain the unexpected movement, and he tells Molotov that it is due to Russia's weather which mandates "vacation leave."

June 22nd 1941 — (United States) Goals of the Communists in the U.S. will begin to swing. With the invasion of Russia by the Germans, which occurs today, the Communists reverse their position. After devoting their previous efforts on keeping the U.S. out of the conflict, as well as having kept up nagging attacks against President Roosevelt, they begin to systematically encourage U.S. participation in the war. Coincidentally, the U.S. does nothing to deter the Communist leading press such as *The Daily Worker*, however, it does attempt to quell other publications which are against U.S. involvement in the war and considered unfavorable to the administration. One in particular is called *Schribner's Commentary*, which has been against America entering the war in Europe.

June 24th 1941 — (United States) In apparent response to Germany's invasion of Russia two days previous, President Roosevelt frees $40 million in credits for the Soviet Union. Subsequently, during July, the President sends Harry L. Hopkins on a clandestine mission to Moscow to inform Stalin that huge quantities of war goods will soon be dispatched to the Soviet Union to bolster their war effort against the Germans. Much of what Hopkins releases for the Soviet Union is desperately needed by U.S. forces, and many other items are in violation of what Lend-Lease authorizes. Ex-President Hoover, while making a speech during 1954, recalls some of his vocal sentiments during this time period: "THE JEST OF ALL HISTORY WOULD BE OUR GIVING AID TO THE SOVIET GOVERNMENT." Hoover also states that such American aid will "SPREAD COMMUNISM OVER THE WORLD."

July 11th 1941 — (United States) William Donovan, a World War I hero, is appointed to lead the Office of Strategic Services (O.S.S.), a new civilian intelligence agency which subsequently becomes the C.I.A. (Central Intelligence Agency).

August 1941 — (United States) The U.S. bars the export of oil and aviation fuel outside the Western Hemisphere, except to Great Britain. Also, some gas rationing becomes effective throughout the Eastern states.

August 14th 1941 — (Atlantic-Newfoundland) President Roosevelt and Prime Minister Churchill meet on a Naval Vessel off Newfoundland and draw up objectives for the postwar period. The agreement becomes the Atlantic Charter. Ironically, the U.S. still maintains neutrality as the President and the Prime Minister of England formulate the plans. The agreement, which fifteen additional nations will join before October, avoids U.S. Senate ratification because it is not a treaty.

August 18th 1941 — (United States) An amendment to the Selective Service Act (draft) of 1940 extends the active duty term for draftees beyond one year. Subsequent to the Japanese attack against Pearl Harbor during December, the President signs a new Selective Service Act which compels all males between the ages of eighteen and sixty-four to register for the draft. It also authorizes the Military to draft all males between the ages of eighteen and forty-four.

October 1941 — (United States) Members of the staff of the *Schribner's Commentary* magazine receive supenas to appear in Washington to give testimony to a Federal Grand Jury to determine if Germans are supplying money to their company. Previously, a Resolution (Clark Resolution) had been passed by Congress authorizing investigation of *Schribner's Commentary* and also several Communist leaning publications (*Daily Worker*, *The New Masses*, and *PM*) to determine where the funding was originating, but the original plan had been derailed; there is to be no investigation of the Communist press. The Prosecutor is William Power Maloney, known for his strong anti-Nazi feelings. *Schribner's Commentary* had welcomed the initial inquiries as the staff believed it would clear them and expose the Communist press. It is noteworthy that the Communist press had been, according to George T. Eggleston, a Schribner Staff member, "demanding the destruction of *Schribner's Commentary*." Many prominent Americans, including ex-President Hoover have been denounced by the left wing press. George Eggleston and other people from the magazine contact Senators Bennett Champ Clark, Gerald P. Nye, and Burton Wheeler only to find out that the original resolution had been "circumvented by the White House clique and that America First Committee, Charles Lindbergh, and *Schribner's Commentary* were to be silenced piecemeal by a Federal Grand Jury." The original "Clark Resolution," according to Eggleston, was scheduled to be a public Congressional hearing; however, it is changed to a private investigation to be held in front of 23 citizens of Washington, D.C. Senator Wheeler remarks to Eggleston during the hearings: "JUST REMEMBER THAT BY ACTUAL VOTE COUNT THERE ARE OVER THREE HUNDRED MEMBERS OF THE HOUSE AND SENATE WHO ENDORSE YOUR STAND ON KEEPING OUT OF THE WAR. AND THERE ARE ANOTHER HUNDRED WHO BELIEVE IN YOUR RIGHT TO EXPRESS YOURSELF." The hearing finds no wrong-doings with the magazine; however, one of its employees, Ralph Townsend, had published a booklet during 1939 condensing his earlier works "arguing for peace between the U.S. and Japan." Copies had been purchased by the Japanese Information Service; he is convicted and imprisoned for violations of the Foreign Agency Registration Act and subsequently released through the determined efforts of Senators Nye, Taft, and Wheeler. Soon after the sneak attack at Pearl Harbor, *Schribner's Commentary* stops publishing and joins the war effort: *Schribner's Commentary* January 1942 has this final issue headline; WIN THE WAR; subscribers are offered refunds or the option, thanks to the generous offer of Dewitt Wallace, to receive *Reader's Digest*.

October 30th 1941 — (United States) President Roosevelt offers the Soviet Union $1 billion in equipment and supplies under the arrangement for the lend-lease program.

November 1941 — (United States) The Supreme Court rules the California Antimigrant Law unconstitutional. It had been enacted to prohibit families forced from the dust bowl states from coming to California to settle.

December 5th 1941 — (United States) Lt. Colonel Albert C. Wedemeyer (later General) receives a copy of the Washington Times Herald, with the headline: "FDR'S WAR PLANS GOAL IS 10 MILLION ARMED MEN; HALF TO FIGHT IN AEF." The story contains many exact parts of a top secret project, the "Victory Program." General Wedemeyer had been working on this project for several months. Copies are only distributed to top echelons of the government. The F.B.I. investigates and General Wedemeyer is among those suspected of leaking the documents; he is of German extraction. After the war breaks out, interest in the investigation begins to diminish. He mentions in retrospect: "MY EFFORTS TO FIX RESPONSIBILITY FOR THIS EPISODE CAME TO NAUGHT. I RETAIN HOWEVER, VIVID RECOLLECTIONS OF THE WASHINGTON SCENE-THE WAR-IMMINENT CLIMATE, THE PROGRESSIVE BUILD-UP BY F.D.R. OF VALID REASONS FOR ENTRANCE INTO THE WAR, AND THE CLEVER CONDITIONING OF THE MINDS OF THE PEOPLE TO SOFTEN THE BLOW OF ANY IRRATIONAL ACT WHICH WOULD PRECIPITATE 135 MILLION AMERICANS INTO THE EUROPEAN CALDRON OF DEATH AND DESTRUCTION." Several of the U.S. top Military leaders, including Eichelberger, Eisenhower, Krueger, Nimitz, Ollendorf, Spaatz, and Stratemeyer come from German heritage. Lt. Colonel Wedemeyer retains his integrity despite the allegations against him; it is Wedemeyer who relieves General Stilwell during 1944 in Burma. Wedemeyer had spent the years 1936-38 at the German War College and during that time had been under constant bombardment with propaganda about, as he calls it, "THE RED MENACE." Subsequently, in his book, General Wedemeyer notes: "UNDERNEATH THE PROPAGANDA, I DISCOVERED A GREAT DEAL OF TRUTH ABOUT THE COMMUNIST AIMS, PRACTICES, AND METHODS UNKNOWN OR IGNORED IN AMERICA."

December 7th 1941 — (United States-Hawaii) The Japanese launch a sneak attack against Pearl Harbor, igniting war with the U.S. On the following day, President Roosevelt asks and receives from Congress a declaration of war against Japan.

December 11th 1941 — (United States) Germany and Italy declare war against the United States, which immediately reciprocates.

December 1941 — (United States) Soon after the beginning of war, the America First Committee disbands as previously predicted by its Chairman, General Robert E. Wood.

January 1st 1942 — (United States) Twenty-six nations are represented at a meeting in Washington, D.C., which results in the Declaration of the United Nations (Allies), proclaiming combined cooperation in opposition to the Axis threat. Also, the Office of Production Management forbids the sale of new cars and trucks throughout the nation.

January 12th-14th 1942 — (United States) On the 12th, President Roosevelt establishes the National War Labor Board (N.W.L.B.) to solve disputes between management and labor. Two days later, the President orders all aliens to register with the U.S. government.

January 1942 — (South America) Twenty-one foreign ministers of American nations confer in Rio de Janeiro, Brazil, and agree to break relations with the Axis. The last to do so is Chile, which severs relations during 1943.

January 1942 — (Great Britain-U.S.S.R.) The British and the Russians sign a treaty with Iran, which grants access through Iran for supplies heading for the Soviets. Also, it assures the Allies Iranian oil.

March 1942 — (United States) Japanese-Americans residing on the west coast and in particular, California, are virtually compelled to leave their homes and relocate to camps for the duration of the conflict. The majority of Japanese are extremely loyal to the U.S., and in fact there are no cases where Japanese Americans are convicted of treason or other similar types of crimes. Some of these Americans (Nisei) join the Armed Forces and their Regiment (442nd) becomes the most decorated unit during the war; it fights only in Europe. There are some exceptions to the rule; some Nisei accompany special missions such as that performed by Merrill's Marauders in Burma, to act as interpreters. American-Germans and American-Italians are not subjected to a similar fate. Also, the Japanese in Hawaii are not interned. Subsequently, during December 1944, the U.S. Army announces that effective January 2nd 1945, American-Japanese will no longer be barred from California.

March 27th 1942 — (United States) The United States Armed Forces receive free mailing privileges for the duration of the war. In related activity, all U.S. mail which arrives in Tokyo for the Embassy is opened by the Japanese, and much of the information therein is passed on to the Germans. Also, the Germans are now capable of intercepting Transatlantic telephone calls between President Roosevelt and Prime Minister Churchill.

April 1942 — (United States) The War Manpower Commission is established to utilize the total effectiveness of the country's workers.

April 8th 1942 — (Great Britain) A formidable group of Americans arrive in London under assumed names; the operation which is initiated to discuss the cross channel invasion with the British is code-named MODICUM. The men who carry out the clandestine meeting are: Colonel H.A. Craig (J.H. Case), Commander James R. Fulton (A.L. Foss), Harry Hopkins (A.H. Hones), George C. Marshall (C.G. Mell) and Lt. Col. A.C. Wedemeyer (J.E. White). Civilian clothes are worn by all members while on this top secret mission. The U.S. entourage departs London on the 18th, stopping at Northern Ireland before jumping to Scotland from where they depart by Seaplane for the U.S.

May 1942 — (Great Britain) The British and the Soviets reach an accord which initiates a twenty-year mutual aid agreement in addition to mutually pursuing the effort to defeat the Germans.

May 1942 — (United States) The country begins to ration sugar. Also, Congress establishes the Women's Auxiliary Army Corps (W.A.A.C.), later becoming the Women's Army Corps (W.A.C.), and the Women's Naval Reserve (WAVES). In addition, Roosevelt establishes the Office of Civilian Defense (O.C.D.).

November 5th 1942 — (United States) George M. (Michael) Cohan dies. Cohan had written many World War I inspirational songs such as: *I'm A Yankee Doodle Dandy*, "*Over There*, and *She's A Grand Ole Flag*. His works become classics. Cohan, born in Providence, Rhode Island during 1878 (claims July 4th) had received a decoration from President Roosevelt during 1942 for his great patriotism and his patriotic songs.

July 22nd 1942 — (United States) The U.S. Government begins to issue gasoline rationing coupons.

November 13th 1942 — (United States) The U.S. lowers the draft age from the minimum of twenty-one years to eighteen.

December 4th 1942 — (United States) Subsequent to over

seven years and an allotted $11 billion, the U.S. closes the Works Progress Administration. Established to aid the unemployed and help boost the economy during the depression, it ceases operations after having provided minimum income for well over eight million unemployed Americans.

February 13th 1943 — (United States) Walter Winchell, who had received a commission as a Lieutenant Commander in the Naval Reserve through the intervention of the White House, is relieved of his commission by Congress which had tired of his contemptuous broadcasts and columns, from which he constantly bombarded many in the Legislature; he wore his Navy uniform while using the media. Upon the termination of Winchell's commission, Congressman Clare Hoffman announces that the Secretary of the Navy, Frank Knox, had assured him that Walter Winchell will not be recalled to active duty.

February-April 1943 — (United States) President Roosevelt states that all U.S. companies engaged in war industry supplies will be required to work a minimum of 48 hours per week. During March, the War Manpower Commission modifies the 4-H deferment, permitting men between the ages of 38 to 45 to be drafted if necessary; it subsequently informs the nation that all able-ready men (not working in defense work) could be drafted before year's end. During May, the President freezes all wages and prices.

May 1st-2nd 1943 — (United States) By the authority of President Roosevelt, the Government is ordered to seize control of the anthracite coal mines in eastern Pennsylvania, which are paralyzed by about 80,000 striking employees. By the following day, the union's leader, John L. Lewis, convinces the strikers to return to the job.

Late-May 1943 — (United States) President Roosevelt prohibits all racial discrimination in all industries working under government contracts.

Early-June 1943 — (United States) In Los Angeles, fights erupt when white servicemen assault colored and Mexican-Americans who are donning what are known as "zoot suits," (fancy suits). Military authorities declare the city off limits to quell the attacks against the civilians.

June 14th 1943 — The U.S. Supreme Court declares that the West Virginia School system's rule, which requires all students to salute the Flag, is unconstitutional.

June 25th 1943 — (United States) Congress overrides President Roosevelt's veto of the Smith-Connally Anti-Strike Act, which forbids strikes in the war industry and also authorizes the government to seize control of the company or companies affected. Also, the law mandates that unions provide a minimum of 30 days notice of any intent to strike.

November 5th 1943 — (United States) The Connally Resolution is passed by Congress, directing the U.S. to support an international peace organization. Several days later, when representatives of forty-four nations meet in Washington, D.C., the U.N. Relief and Rehabilitation Administration is established for the purpose of aiding victims of the war.

December 1943 — (United States) The House Foreign Affairs Committee proclaims that nearly 600,000 persons escaping from German oppression in Europe have entered the United states since 1933.

December 27th 1943 — (United States) The government takes control of the nation's railroads to forestall a threatened strike because of a heated wage dispute, returning them to private industry during mid-January 1944.

February 1944 — (United States) According to information coming from the Office of Price Administration, the "black market" is raking in over $1 billion a year. Since the government ban on many domestic items, the black market has flourished.

March 1944 — (United States) Due to Turkey's refusal to cooperate in the war against the Axis, the U.S. informs the Turkish government on the 2nd that lend-lease aid is being terminated. Two days later, due to Argentina's failure to declare war on the Axis, the U.S. proclaims nonrecognition of that country. Argentina, which has a large German population, has been giving support to the Germans. Subsequently, the President takes additional steps against Argentina, freezing its gold assets (during July) in the U.S. On the 29th, Congress approves a joint-resolution in support of the United Nations Relief and Rehabilitation Agency, authorizing $1,350,000,000.

June 22nd 1944 — (United States) President Roosevelt signs what becomes known as the "GI Bill" (Servicemen's Readjustment Act), giving financial aid for such items as housing and education to veterans upon their return from the war.

July 1944 — (United States) A conference convenes in Bretton Woods, New Hampshire. Representatives from forty-four countries attend. The meeting lasts several weeks and results in the formation of the International Bank for Reconstruction and Development and the International Monetary Fund.

August 1st 1944 — (United States) A nasty strike develops in Philadelphia, Pennsylvania, within the public transit system, prompted by a Presidential order mandating the promotion of colored people. U.S. Army contingents are brought in to quell the trouble.

August-October 1944 — (United States) Steps are taken to establish a world peace organization. Representatives from the U.S., Great Britain, China, and the U.S.S.R. meet in Washington, D.C.. The agreed upon name of the organization will be the United Nations, and its permanent headquarters will be in the U.S.

November 7th 1944 — (United States) President Roosevelt is reelected to his fourth term as President. His running mate is Harry S Truman. The Republican candidate, Thomas Dewey, receives about 22 million votes to Roosevelt's 25 million. The electoral college gives Roosevelt 432 votes while Dewey receives only 99. Roosevelt is inaugurated on January 20th, becoming the first and last President to serve four terms. During 1951, the 22nd Amendment to the Constitution is ratified, limiting Presidential terms to two consecutive elected terms.

January 8th 1945 — (Egypt) Ahmed Pasha is elected premier of Egypt. During February, subsequent to stating that Egypt will declare war on the Axis, he is assassinated.

April 12th 1945 — (United States) President Franklin D. Roosevelt succumbs while on vacation at Warm Springs, Georgia. Within hours, the Vice President, Harry S. Truman, is sworn into office as the 33rd President of the United States.

April 25th 1945 — (United States) A conference among fifty nations convenes in San Francisco to establish the United Nations. The United States, Great Britain, China, France, and the Soviet Union will emerge as permanent nations, each retaining veto powers, while the remainder are to be seated in rotation. The Charter will be signed on June 26th 1945.

July 17th-August 2nd 1945 — (Germany) The Potsdam Conference convenes. President Truman, Churchill, and Stalin confer to continue the discussions of the agreements reached at Yalta.

July 28th 1945 — (United States) The United Nations Charter is ratified by the U.S. Senate.

August 14th 1945 — (China) The Nationalist Chinese and the Soviet Union sign a treaty, whereby the Soviets acknowledge the Nationalist regime and in turn, the Nationalists recognize the independence of Outer Mongolia and agree to some additional concessions.

August 17th 1945 — (Indonesia) Indonesia declares independence from the Dutch; however, the Dutch return to re-initiate their colonial rule, igniting fighting which lasts for several years until the Dutch are pressured by the U.N. to accept the country's independence.

August 18th 1945 — (Indo China-Vietnam) The Communist Nationalists declare independence from the French who will return to regain control of their colony. At this time, the U.S. supports the call for independence. The French drive the Communists under Ho Chi Minh to the jungles, where they revert to guerrilla warfare.

September 8th 1945 — (Korea) U.S. troops land in Korea for occupation duty below the 28th parallel while the Russians occupy northern Korea. The purpose is to keep the peace until elections can be held; however, Korea remains divided.

October 1945 — (China) Talks, which have been occurring since August; between the Nationalists and Communists, collapse. Civil war soon erupts. Meanwhile, during December, General Marshall is dispatched to China to mediate the conflict. The Communists under Mao Tse-tung are greatly outnumbered by the Nationalists under Chiang Kai-shek, ultimately, the Nationalists who receive only tepid support from the U.S. are forced to flee to Formosa.

October 26th 1945 — (United States-International) The United Nations is officially established as twenty-nine nations ratify its charter. It will be based in the United States.

November 3rd 1945 — (Europe-Hungary) National elections are held in Hungary, resulting in the election of an anti-communist Party (Smallholders) led by Zoltan Tildy who establishes a coalition government.

November 11th 1945 — (Yugoslavia) Elections are held. On the 29th, the elected assembly announces a Federal Republic of Yugoslavia; its President is Marshal Tito.

November 18th 1945 — (Europe-Bulgaria) Elections are held in Bulgaria. The Communist-directed Fatherland Front wins the election against no opposition.

November 20th 1945 — (Germany) The Nuremberg War Trials begin as twenty-one German leaders are tried under jurisdiction of international law. The trials conclude during October 1946.

November 25th 1945 — (Austria) The People's Party wins in general elections and subsequently forms a coalition government with the Socialists. On December 20th, Karl Renner is elected President of the Democratic Republic of Austria, which had been reestablished during May.

November 30th 1945 — (Italy) The Christian Democrats win the general election. A new government is formed by its leader, Alcide de Gasperi.

December 2nd 1945 — (Albania) The Communists win in general elections, against no opposition. Its President is Premier Enver Hoxha.

December 4th 1945 — (United States) The Senate agrees to the treaty which has the U.S. joining the United Nations.

December 6th 1945 — (United States) Great Britain receives a loan of $3,700,000,000 from the U.S. and shortly thereafter, the Americans grant Britain another loan of $1,250,000,000.

December 21st 1945 — (Atlantic-Germany) The U.S. loses one of its most brilliant Commanders, as General George S. Patton succumbs. He had sustained serious injuries during an accident with a Military Vehicle on the Autobahn on December 9th. Patton's Staff car and a U.S. Army Vehicle collided in a dense fog during the early morning hours of the ninth. General Patton is buried in Luxembourg during a severe rainstorm with great representation from the Armed Forces. The troops brave the storm as the solemn procession moves. According to a representative of the Big Red One, Sergeant Orville Smith, of Lexington, Virginia, the Commanding Generals, and Mrs. Beatrice Patton arrange for the representatives of each unit to receive a ten-day pass. General Patton had requested (in the event of his death) that he be buried with his men.

December 27th 1945 — (United States) A meeting between representatives of 24 countries which have ratified the agreement establishing the International Bank for Reconstruction and Development (World Bank) convenes in Washington, D.C.

General George S. Patton's gravesite in Luxembourg.

1.

2.

3.

4.

5.

6.

7.

8.

9.

10.

11.

12.

13.

14.

15.

16.

Proper Display of the Stars and Stripes.

1. If the Flag is to be displayed over the middle of the street, the Flag should be suspended vertically with the union pointing to the north in and east and west street. For proper display if the street runs north and south, the union should point east.

2. When displaying the Flag with another Flag from crossed staffs, the United States Flag should always be on the right (the Flag's own right) and the staff of the U.S. Flag should be in front of the staff of the other Flag.

3. When displaying the U.S. Flag at half-staff, the Flag should be hoisted to the peak and then lowered to the position of half staff. Before lowering the Flag for the day, it should first be raised again to the peak. The Flag is at the proper position of half-staff when it is positioned at one half the distance between the top and bottom of the staff (pole). During the Holiday of Memorial Day, the Flag should be flown at half-staff until the hour of 12 noon and at that time be raised to the top of the staff.

4. When it becomes necessary to fly the Flag of a state, city, or a pennant of a society on the same ballyard with the Flag of the United States of America, the U.S. Flag should always be at the peak. If these other Flags are to fly alongside the Stars and Stripes, on adjacent staffs, the U.S. Flag should be raised first and lowered last. No Flag or pennant shall be flown above or to the right of the Stars and Stripes (U.S. Flag) at the same level, except the church pennant. This pennant (church) may be flown above the Flag during religious services at sea.

5. When displaying the Flag over a sidewalk from a rope extending from a house to a pole at the edge of the sidewalk, the Flag should be hoisted out from the building, Union first, towards the pole.

6. When displaying Old Glory from a staff projecting horizontally or at any angle from the window sill, balcony, or front of a building, the Union of the Flag should go to the peak of the staff (unless the Flag is to be flown at half-staff).

7. When the U.S. Flag is to be carried in a procession (parade etc.), with another Flag or Flags, the Stars and Stripes should be on the marching right (two Flags).

8. When there is a line of other Flags, the Stars and Stripes should be out in front and to the center of that line.

9. When the U.S. Flag is displayed with a number of Flags of cities or states or pennants of societies on staffs, the U.S. Flag should be at the center and at the highest point of the group of Flags.

10. When the Stars and Stripes is to be displayed with the Flags of other Nations, the Flags should be flown from separate staffs of equal height and the Flags should be approximately the same size. International usage forbids the display of the Flag of one nation above that of another nation in time of peace.

11. When the Stars and Stripes is displayed in a manner other than by being flown from a staff, it should be displayed flat, whether indoors or out. When displaying the Stars and Stripes either vertically or horizontally against a wall, the Union should be uppermost and to the Flag's own right (to the observers left). When displaying the Stars and Stripes in a window, it should be displayed in the same way (Union or blue field to the left of the observer in the street).

12. When the Stars and Stripes is used to cover a casket, the Flag should be so placed that the Union (blue field) is at the head and over the left shoulder. The Stars and Stripes should never be lowered into the grave or be allowed to touch the ground.

13. When the Stars and Stripes is to be displayed at the unveiling of a statue or monument, it should be distinctive and prominent but should never be used as the covering or veil.

14. When the Stars and Stripes is to be displayed from a staff in a church chapel or speakers platform, the Flag should be placed on the speakers right. If the Flag is displayed elsewhere than on the speakers platform, it should be on the right of the audience as they face the platform. When the Stars and Stripes is displayed flat on a speakers platform, the Flag should be behind and above the speaker with the Union (blue field) to his right. The Union will be above, behind and to the left of the speaker from the audience view.

15. When the Stars and Stripes is passing in parade, being hoisted or lowered, all persons present should face it, stand at attention and salute. Uniformed persons render the military salute; women and uncovered men (no hats) place their right hand over their hearts. Men should remove their hats, holding them over their hearts with their right hands.

16. If the Stars and Stripes is not present during the playing of the National Anthem, all present should stand and face the music. Persons in uniform should salute from the first note and hold it till the last note. Others should stand at attention, men removing their hats. If the Stars and Stripes is displayed, all present should salute.

When reciting the pledge of Allegiance, you should stand at attention with your hand over your heart. Military personnel should salute. The pledge of Allegiance is as follows:

The Pledge of Allegiance to The United States of America.

I Pledge Allegiance to the Flag of The United States of America and to The Republic for which it stands, One Nation under God, Indivisible, with Liberty and Justice For All."

The proper definitions given for the Flag of The United States.

The Flag of the United States of America referred to as the National Flag is also known as the National Ensign, National Color and National Standard. The term "National Flag" is applicable regardless of size or manner of display, but the other terms have certain well-defined usages off long standing within the Armed Services.

1. "National Ensign" is used by the Navy in a general manner, although it actually indicates the National Flag flown by airships, ships and boats.

   The U.S. Navy in addition to displaying Old Glory on its vessels and stations from 8:00 a.m. to sunset, also flies the Flag outside those periods on special occasions:
   a. Ships entering port at night should hoist the Ensign at daylight for a short period to enable port authorities and other vessels to determine her nationality. It is customary for other ships to show their colors in return.
   b. Upon anchoring or getting underway in sufficient light to be seen, the National Ensign should be displayed at the gaff.
   c. Under no circumstances shall an action be commenced or battle fought without display of the National Ensign (chapter V,1920 Navy Regulations).
   d. Custom dictates that when underway, the normal point of display (of the Flag) is at the gaff, while the flagstaff is the point of display at anchor. Prior to 8:00 a.m. or after sunset, the Flag should be hoisted at the gaff.
   e. The U.S. Navy never dips her Colors except to return the compliment. When a vessel registered by a nation formally recognized by the U.S., dips (salutes with colors) her Flag, the U.S. Navy must return the dip. Upon reaching shore, only Battalion or Regimental colors should be dipped in rendering or acknowledging a salute.

2. "National Color" pertains to Flags carried by dismounted units of the landing force and is stubbier than the National Ensign.

3. "National Standard" is carried by mounted, mechanized and motorized units.

   The display of our National Flag is governed by law to insure that it will be treated with the respect due the Flag of a great nation. Public Law 829 enacted by the 77th Congress sets forth rules for the display and care of the Stars and Stripes and prescribes penalties for violations.

Signs of Respect for Our Flag.

The Stars and Stripes should be flown daily from Sunrise to Sunset in good weather from Public Buildings, Schools, Permanent Staffs in the open and near Polling Places on Election Days. The Flag may be flown at night on Special Patriotic Occasions.

The Stars and Stripes should always be flown on National and State Holidays and on those occasions proclaimed by the President. On Memorial Day, the Flag should be half staffed until noon.

The Flag should be raised briskly and lowered ceremoniously. It should never be dipped to any person or thing nor should it ever be displayed with the Union down except as a Signal of Distress.

The Flag should never be allowed to touch anything beneath it, nor should it ever be carried flat or horizontally — always aloft and free. It should never be used as drapery or decoration, for carrying anything, or stored in such a manner that it will be damaged or soiled.

The Stars and Stripes should never be used for advertising purposes in any manner whatsoever, nor should any picture, drawing, insignia or other decoration be placed upon or attached to the Flag, its staff or halyard. The Flag should not be embroidered on personal items nor printed on anything designed for temporary use and then discarded.

When the Flag is so worn or soiled that it is not longer suitable for display, it should be destroyed in a dignified manner, preferably by burning.

The Flag should be displayed on all days, especially on:

1. New Year's Day January 1st.
2. Martin Luther King's Birthday January 15th.
3. Inauguration Day January 20th.
4. Abraham Lincoln's Birthday February 12th.
5. George Washington's Birthday February 22nd (Celebrated 3rd Monday in February).
6. Easter Sunday (Date varies).
7. Mother's Day (Second Sunday in May).
8. Armed Forces Day (Third Saturday in May).
9. Memorial Day (Half Staff until Noon) the Last Monday in May.
10. Flag Day June 14th.
11. Independence Day July 4th.
12. Labor Day First Monday in September.
13. Constitution Day September 17th.
14. Columbus Day Second Monday in October.
15. Navy Day October 27th.
16. Veterans Day November 11th.
17. Thanksgiving Day Fourth Thursday in November.
18. Christmas Day December 25th.
19. Any additional days as may be proclaimed by the President of the United States; the Birthdays of States (Date of Admission); and on State Holidays.

Personal Honors and Salutes.

The Independence of the United States is celebrated by a salute to the Union at 12 noon on the Fourth of July at all military installations where artillery is available. The salute is rendered by the firing of one gun for each state. The United States national salute which is 21 guns is also the salute rendered a National Flag.

A 21 gun salute accompanied by 4 Ruffles and Flourishes is rendered to the President of the United States upon arrival and departure. The identical salute is rendered to an ex-President and to a President elect. Hail To The Chief or the National Anthem is played for the President. The National Anthem is played for an ex-President or a President elect.

If a Soverign or Chief of State of a foreign nation or a member of a reigning Royal Family is visiting, a 21 gun salute with four Ruffles and Flourishes is rendered upon arrival and departure. Immediately following the Ruffles and Flourishes, without pause, the national anthem of his or her country is played.

Listing of the States.

1. Alabama (22nd State) December 14th 1819.
2. Alaska (49th State) January 3rd 1959.
3. Arizona (48th State) February 14th 1912.
4. Arkansas (25th State) June 15th 1836.
5. California (31st State) September 9th 1850.
6. Colorado (38th State) August 1st 1876.
7. Connecticut (5th State) January 9th 1788.
8. Delaware (1st State) December 7th 1787.
9. Florida (27th State) March 3rd 1845.
10. Georgia (4th State) January 2nd 1788.
11. Hawaii (50th State) August 21st 1959.
12. Idaho (43rd State) July 3rd 1890.
13. Illinois (21st State) December 3rd 1818.
14. Indiana (19th State) December 11th 1816.
15. Iowa (29th State) December 28th 1846.
16. Kansas (34th State) January 29th 1861.
17. Kentucky (15th State) June 1st 1792.
18. Louisiana (18th State) April 30th 1812.
19. Maine (23rd State) March 15th 1820.
20. Maryland (7th State) April 28th 1788.
21. Massachusetts (6th State) February 6th 1788.
22. Michigan (26th State) January 26th 1837.
23. Minnesota (32nd State) May 11th 1858.
24. Mississippi (20th State) December 10th 1817.
25. Missouri (24th State) August 10th 1821.
26. Montana (41st State) November 8th 1889.
27. Nebraska (37th State) March 1st 1867.
28. Nevada (36th State) October 31st 1864.
29. New Hampshire (9th State) June 21st 1788.
30. New Jersey (3rd State) December 18th 1787.
31. New Mexico (47th State) January 6th 1912.
32. New York (11th State) July 26th 1788.
33. North Carolina (12th State) November 21st 1879.
34. North Dakota (39th State) November 2nd 1899.
35. Ohio (17th State) March 1st 1803.
36. Oklahoma (46th State) November 16th 1907.
37. Oregon (33rd) February 14th 1859.
38. Pennsylvania (2nd State) December 12th 1787.
39. Rhode Island (13th State) May 29th 1790.
40. South Carolina (8th State) May 23rd 1788.
41. South Dakota (40th State) November 2nd 1889.
42. Tennessee (16th State) June 1st 1796.
43. Texas (28th State) December 29th 1845.
44. Utah (45th State) January 4th 1896.
45. Vermont (14th State) March 4th 1791.
46. Virginia (10th State) June 25th 1788.
47. Washington (42nd State) November 11th 1889.
48. West Virginia (35th State) June 20th 1863.
49. Wisconsin (30th State) May 29th 1848.
50. Wyoming (44th State) July 10th 1890.

Other Possessions of The United States include Guam — claimed by the U.S. June 22nd 1898 and took official control on December 10th 1898 after the signing of the Treaty of Paris at the conclusion of the Spanish American War; **Puerto Rico —** (December 10th 1898 at the signing of the Treaty of Paris; and the **Virgin Islands —** taken over by the United States from Denmark on March 31st 1917. Negotiations for the islands had been completed during August of 1916 with the understanding that possession by the United States would become official on January 1st 1917. The U.S. pays Denmark a sum of $25,000,000 (25 million dollars) for these Islands. In addition, **Washington, D.C.** is part of the United States but not a State in itself. Land had been donated by surrounding States for use as a Federal Capital and designated as The District of Columbia.

Presidents of The United States of America.

1. George Washington (Virginia) April 30th 1789-March 4th 1797. Married to Martha Dandridge Custis Washington.
2. John Adams (Massachusetts) March 4th 1797-March 4th 1801. Married to Abigail Smith Adams.
3. Thomas Jefferson (Virginia) March 4th 1801-March 4th 1809. Married to Martha Wayles Skelton Jefferson.
4. James Madison (Virginia) March 4th 1809-March 4th 1817. Married to Dorothea "Dolley" Payne Todd Madison.
5. James Monroe (Virginia) March 4th 1817-March 4th 1825. Married to Elizabeth Kortright Monroe.
6. John Quincy Adams (Massachusetts) March 4th 1825-March 4th 1829. Married to Louise Catherine Johnson Adams.
7. Andrew Jackson (Tennessee) March 4th 1829-March 4th 1837. Rachel Donelson Robards Jackson.
8. Martin Van Buren (New York) March 4th 1837-March 4th 1841. Married to Hannah Hoes Van Buren.
9. William Henry Harrison (Ohio) March 4th 1841-April 4th 1841 (1 month). Married to Anna Symmes Harrison President Harrison succombs to pneumonia and is replaced by his Vice President John Tyler.
10. John Tyler (Virginia) April 4th 1841-March 4th 1845. President Tyler takes the oath of office on the 6th of April. Married to Letitia Christian Tyler.
11. James Polk (Tennessee) March 4th 1845-March 4th 1849). Married to Sarah Childress Polk.

12. Zachary Taylor (Louisiana) March 4th 1849-July 9th 1850. Married to Margaret Smith Taylor. (President Tyler dies of natural causes). Vice President Millard Fillmore assumes the office and finishes the term.

13. Millard Fillmore (New York) July 9th 1850-March 4th 1853. Married to Abigail Powers Fillmore (dies in 1853) Married for a second time to Caroline Carmichael Fillmore.

14. Franklin Pierce (New Hampshire) March 4th 1853-March 4th 1857. Married to Jane Means Appleton Pierce.

15. James Buchanan (Pennsylvania) March 4th 1857-March 4th 1861. President Buchanan does not marry.

16. Abraham Lincoln (Illinois) March 4th 1861-April 14-15 1865. Married to Mary Todd Lincoln. President Lincoln is assasinated during the evening of the 14th and succombs on the 15th. Vice President Andrew Johnson assumes the office.

17. Andrew Johnson (Tennessee) April 15 1865-March 4th 1869. Married to Eliza McCardle Johnson.

18. Ulysses Simpson Grant (Illinois) March 4th 1869-March 4th 1877. Married to Julia Dent Grant.

19. Rutherford Birchard Hayes (Ohio) March 4th 1877-March 4th 1881. Married to Lucy Ware Webb Hayes.

20. James Abram Garfield (Ohio) March 4th 1881-September 19th 1881 (dies at his home of natural causes. Vice President Chestar A. Arthur assumes the office. President Garfield married Lucretia Rudolf Garfield.

21. Chester Alan Arthur (Vermont) September 20th 1881-March 4th 1885. Married Ellen Lewis Herndon Arthur.

22. Grover Cleveland (New Jersey) March 4th 1885-March 4th 1889. Married to Frances Folsom Cleveland.

23. Benjamin Harrison (Ohio) March 4th 1889-March 4th 1893. Married to Caroline Lavinia Scott Harrison who dies during 1892. President Harrison marries for the second time, Mary Scott Lord Dimmick Harrison.

24. Grover Cleveland (New Jersey) March 4th 1893-March 4th 1897. President Cleveland serves his second term but it is not consecutive.

25. William McKinley (Ohio) March 4th 1897-September 14th 1901. President McKinley dies from wounds suffered when an assassin's bullet struck him on September 6th 1901. Vice President Theodore Roosevelt assumes the Presidency. President McKinley married Ida Saxton.

26. Theodore Roosevelt (New York) September 14th 1901-March 4th 1909. Married Alice Hathaway Lee Roosevelt who dies during 1884. President Roosevelt marries for a second time; Edith Kermit Carow Roosevelt.

27. William Howard Taft (Ohio) March 4th 1909-March 4th 1913. Married Helen Heron Taft.

28. Woodrow Wilson (Virginia) March 4th 1913-March 4th 1921. Married Ellen Louis Axson Wilson.

29. Warren Gamaliel Harding (Ohio) March 4th 1921-August 2nd 1923 (dies in office). Married Florence King DeWolfe Harding. Vice President Calvin Coolidge assumes the Presidency and takes the oath the following day.

30. Calvin Coolidge (Vermont) August 3rd 1923-March 4th 1929. Married Grace Anna Goodhue Coolidge.

31. Herbert Hoover (Iowa) March 4th 1929-March 4th 1933. Married Lou Henry Hoover.

32. Franklin Delano Roosevelt (New York) March 4th 1933-April 12th 1945 dies in office. Married Anna Eleanor Roosevelt Roosevelt. Vice President Harry Truman assumes the Presidency.

33. Harry Truman (Missouri) April 20th 1945-January 20th 1953. Married Bess Wallace Truman.

34. Dwight David Eisenhower (Texas) January 20th 1953-January 20th 1961. Married Mamie Geneva Doud Eisenhower.

35. John Fitzgerald Kennedy (Massachusetts) January 20th 1961-November 22nd 1963. Married Jacqueline Lee Bouvier Kennedy. President Kennedy is assasinated. Vice President Lyndon Baines Johnson assumes the Presidency.

36. Lyndon Baines Johnson (Texas) November 22nd 1963-January 20th 1969. Married Claudia "Lady Bird" Alta Taylor Johnson.

37. Richard Nixon (California) January 20th 1969-August 9th 1974. Married to Thelma Catherine Patricia Ryan Nixon. President Nixon resigns from office on August 9th 1974. Vice President Gerald R. Ford, who had replaced Vice President Spiro Agnew during October of 1973, assumes the Presidency and will nominate Nelson Rockefeller for the Vice Presidency (25th Amendment to Constitution).

38. Gerald R. Ford (Nebraska) August 9th 1974-January 20th 1977. Married Elizabeth "Betty" Bloomer Warren Ford. President Ford is the first non-elected President. President Ford is also the first non-elected Vice President chosen under the guidelines of the 25th Amendment.

39. Jimmy (James Earl) Carter (Georgia) January 20th 1977-January 20th 1981. Married Rosalyn Smith Carter.

40. Ronald Reagan (Illinois) January 20th 1981-(Second term ends January 20th 1989). President Reagan married Anne Frances "Nancy" Robbins Davis Reagan. President Reagan had been married previously to Jane Wyman.

41. George Herbert Walker Bush (Texas) Elected November 8th 1988, will be inaugurated January 1989.

Vice Presidents of the United States.

1. John Adams (Massachusetts) April 1789-March 1797. (Served under President Washington).

2. Thomas Jefferson (Virginia) March 1797-March 1801. (Served under President John Adams).

3. Aaron Burr (New York) March 1801-March 1805. (Served under President Jefferson).

4. George Clinton (New York) March 1805-April 20th 1812 (dies in office). (Served under Presidents Jefferson and Madison).

5. Elbridge Gerry (Massachusetts) March 4th 1813-November 23rd 1814. (Resigns to take a position in the U.S. Senate) (Served under President Madison).

6. Daniel D. Tompkins (New York) March 4th 1817-March 4th 1825. (Served under President Monroe).

7. John C. Calhoun (New York) March 4th 1825-March 4th 1825. (Served under Presidents John Quincy Adams and Andrew Jackson).

8. Martin Van Buren (New York) March 4th 1833-March 4th 1837. (Served under President Jackson).

9. Richard M. Johnson (Kentucky) March 4th 1837-March 4th 1841. (Served under President Van Buren).

10. John Tyler (Virginia) March 4th 1841-April 4th 1841. Becomes President after the death of President Harrison and the Vice Presidency remains vacant.

11. George M. Dallas (Pennsylvania) March 4th 1845-March 4th 1849. (Served under President Polk).

12. Millard Fillmore (New York) March 4th 1849-July 9th 1850. (Becomes President after the death of President Taylor). The Vice Presidency remains vacant.

13. William R. King (North Carolina) King is elected with President Pierce but dies during April of 1853 leaving the Vice Presidency vacant until March of 1857.

14. John C. Breckinridge (Kentucky) March 4th 1857-March 4th 1861. Breckinridge becomes a Confederate General during the Civil War. (Served under President Buchanan).

15. Hannibal Hamlin (Maine) March 4th 1861-March 4th 1865. (Served under President Lincoln).

16. Andrew Johnson (Tennessee) March 4th 1865-April 15th 1865. (Becomes President after the assasination of President Lincoln.

17. Schuyler Colfax (Indiana) March 4th 1879-March 4th 1853. (Served under President U.S. Grant).

18. Henry Wilson (Massachusetts) March 4th 1873-November 22nd 1875. Dies in office (Served under President Grant).

19. William A. Wheeler (New York) March 4th 1877-March 4th 1881. (Served under President Hayes).

20. Chester A. Arthur (New York) March 4th 1881-September 20th 1881. Becomes President after the death of President Garfield.

21. Thomas A. Hendricks (Indiana) March 4th 1885-November 25th 1885. Dies in office (Served under President Cleveland).

22. Levi P. Morton (New York) March 4th 1889-March 4th 1893. (Served under President Harrison).

23. Adlai E. Stephenson (Illinois) March 4th 1893-March 4th 1897. (Served under President Cleveland).

24. Garret A. Hobart (New Jersey) March 4th 1897-November 21st 1899. Dies in office (Served under President McKinley).

25. Theodore Roosevelt (New York) March 4th 1901-September 14th 1901. Becomes President upon death of President McKinley.

26. Charles W. Fairbanks (Indiana) March 4th 1905-March 4th 1909. (Served under President Theodore Roosevelt).

27. James S. Sherman (New York) March 4th 1909-October 30th 1912. Dies in office (Served under President Taft).

28. Thomas R. Marshall (Indiana) March 4th 1913-March 4th 1921. (Served under President Wilson).

29. Calvin Coolidge (Massachusetts) March 13th 1921-August 2nd 1923. Become President after the death of President Harding.
30. Charles G. Dawes (Illinois) March 4th 1929-March 4th 1933. (Served under President Coolidge).
31. Charles Curtis March 4th 1929-March 4th 1933. (Served under President Hoover).
32. John Nance Garner (Texas) March 4th 1933-January 20th 1937. Reelected with President Roosevelt during 1936 and inaugurated on January 20th 1937, becoming first Vice President inaugurated at a time other than March (Due to 20th Amendment to Constitution). Garner serves full second term.
33. Henry Agard Wallace (Iowa) January 20th 1941-January 20th 1945. (Served under President F.D. Roosevelt).
34. Harry S. Truman (Missouri) January 20th 1945-April 12th 1945. Becomes President upon death of President Franklin D. Roosevelt.
35. Alben W. Barkley (Kentucky) January 20th 1949-January 20th 1953. (Served under President Truman).
36. Richard M. Nixon (California) January 20th 1953-1961. (Served under President Eisenhower.
37. Lyndon B. Johnson (Texas) January 20th 1961-November 22nd 1963. Becomes President after the death of President John F. Kennedy.
38. Hubert H. Humphrey (Minnesota) January 20th 1965-January 20th 1969. (Served under President Johnson).
39. Spiro T. Agnew (Maryland) January 20th 1969-November 10th 1973. (Resigns after pleading no contest on tax evasion charges) (Served under President Nixon).
40. Gerald R. Ford (Michigan) Nominated by President Nixon on October 12th 1973 to fill the unexpired term of Spiro Agnew. Gerald Ford is confirmed by Congress and sworn in on the 6th of December 1973 (Authorized by 25th Amendment to the Constitution which spells out process of nominating Vice President for fulfilling unexpired term). Vice President Ford assumes the Presidency after the resignation of President Nixon on August 9th 1974).
41. Nelson Rockefeller (Maine) President Ford nominates Rockefeller on August 20th 1974. He is confirmed by Congress on December 19th 1974 and takes the oath of office on the same day.
42. Walter Mondale (Minnesota) January 4th 1977-January 4th 1981. (Serves under President Carter).
43. George Bush (Texas) January 20th 1981-January 20th 1985. Reelected with President Reagan in 1984. Vice President Bush's term expires on January 20th 1989.
44. J. Danforth Quayle (Indiana) Elected November 8th 1988 will be sworn in January 1989. Serves under President Bush.

CHAIRMAN JOINT CHIEFS OF STAFF

Chief of Staff to the Commander in Chief of the Army and Navy Fleet
Adm. William D. Leahy — 20 Jul 42 to 21 March 49 (At request fo President Truman, Gen. of the Army Dwight D. Eisenhower serves as principal military adviser to the President and the Secretary of Defense, and presiding Officer of the of the Joint Chiefs of Staff, from February to August 1949).

Chairman, Joint Chiefs of Staff General of the Army
Omar N. Bradley, USA- 16 Aug 49 to 15 Aug 53.
Adm. Arthur W. Radford, USN- 15 Aug 53 to 15 Aug 57.
Gen. Nathan F. Twining, USAF- 15 Aug 57 to 30 Sept 60.
Gen. Lyman L. Lemnitzer, USA- 01 Oct 60 to 30 Sept 62.
Gen. Maxwell D. Taylor, USA- 01 Oct 62 to 01 Juyl 64.
Gen. Earle G. Wheeler, USA- 03 Jul 64 to 02 Jul 70.
Adm Thomas H. Moorer, USN- 02 Jul 70 to 01 Jul 74.
Gen. George S. Brown, USAF- 01 Jul 74 to 20 Jun 78.
Gen David C. Jones, USAF- 21 Jun 78 to 18 Jun 82.
Gen John W. Vessey, Jr., USA- 18 Jun 82 to 30 Sept 85.
Gen Colin L. Powell, USA- 01 Oct 89 — .

Chronological List Of Senior Officers Of The United States Army

George Washington (Gen) 15 Jun 1775 — 23 Dec 1783.
Henry Knox (Maj Gen) 23 Dec 1783 — 20 Jun 1784.
John Doughty (Capt) 20 Jun 1784 — 12 Aug 1784.
Josiah Harmar (Bvt Brig Gen) 12 Aug 1784 — 4 Mar 1791.
Arthur St. Clair (Maj Gen) 4 Mar 1791 — 5 Mar 1792.
Anthony Wayne (Maj Gen) 13 Apr 1792 — 15 Dec 1796.
James Wilkinson (Brig Gen) 15 Dec 1796 — 13 Jul 1798.
George Washington (Lt Gen) 13 Jul 1798 — 14 Dec 1799.
Alexander Hamilton (Maj Gen) 14 Dec 1799 — 15 Jun 1800.
James Wilkinson — (Brig Gen) 15 Jun 1800 — 27 Jan 1812.
Henry Dearborn (Maj Gen) 27 Jan 1812 — 15 Jun 1815.
Jacob J. Brown (Maj Gen) 15 Jun 1815 — 24 Feb 1828.
Alexander Macomb (Maj Gen) 29 May 1828 — 25 Jun 1841.
Winfield Scott (Bvt Lt Gen) 5 Jul 1841 — 1 Nov 1861.
George B. McClellan (Maj Gen) 1 Nov 1861 — 11 Mar 1862.
Henry W. Halleck (Maj Gen) 23 Jul 1862 — 9 Mar 1864.
Ulysses S. Grant (Gen) 9 Mar 1864 — 4 Mar 1869.
William T. Sherman (Gen) 8 Mar 1869 — 1 Nov 1883.
Philip H. Sheridan (Gen) 1 Nov 1883 — 5 Aug 1888.

John McA. Schofield (Lt Gen) 14 Aug 1888 — 29 Sep 1895.
Nelson A. Miles (Lt Gen) 5 Oct 1895 — 8 Aug 1903.
Samuel B.M. Young (Lt Gen) 15 Aug 1903 — 8 Jan 1904.
Adna R. Chaffee (Lt Gen) 9 Jan 1904 — 14 Jan 1906.
John C. Bates (Lt Gen) 15 Jan 1906 — 13 Apr 1906.
J. Franklin Bell (Maj Gen) 14 Apr 1906 — 21 Apr 1910.
Leonard Wood (Maj Gen) 22 Apr 1910 — 20 Apr 1914.
William W. Wotherspoon (Maj Gen) 21 Apr 1914 — 15 Nov 1914.
Hugh L. Scott (Maj Gen) 16 Nov 1914 — 21 Sep 1917.
Tasker H. Bliss (Gen) 22 Sep 1917 — 18 May 1918.
Peyton C. March (Gen) 19 May 1918 — 30 Jun 1921.
John J. Pershing (Gen) 1 Jul 1921 — 13 Sep 1924.
John L. Hines (Maj Gen) 14 Sep 1924 — 20 Nov 1926.
Charles P. Summerall (Gen) 21 Nov 1926 — 20 Nov 1930.
Douglas MacArthur (Gen) 21 Nov 1930 — 1 Oct 1935.
Malin Craig (Gen) 2 Oct 1935 — 31 Aug 1939.
George C. Marshall (Gen of Army) 1 Sep 1939 — 18 Nov 1945.
Dwight D. Eisenhower (Gen of Army) 19 Oct 1945 — 7 Feb 1948.
Omar N. Bradley (Gen) 7 Feb 1948 — 16 Aug 1949.
J. Lawton Collins (Gen) 16 Aug 1949 — 5 Aug 1953.
Matthew B. Ridgway (Gen) 16 Aug 1953 — 30 Jun 1955.
Maxwell D. Taylor (Gen) 30 Jun 1955 — 30 Jun 1959.
Lyman L. Lemnitzer (Gen) 1 Jul 1959 — 30 Sep 1960.
George H. Decker (Gen) 1 Oct 1960 — 30 Sep 1962.
Earle G. Wheeler (Gen) 1 Oct 1962 — 2 Jul 1964.
Harold K. Johnson (Gen) 3 Jul 1964 — 2 Jul 1968.
William C. Westmoreland (Gen) 3 Jul 1968 — 30 Jun 1972.
Bruce Palmer, Jr. (Gen) 1 Jul 1972 — 11 Oct 1972.
Creighton W. Abrams, Jr. (Gen) 12 Oct 1972 — 4 Sep 1974.
Frederick C. Weyand (Gen) 3 Oct 1974 — 30 Sep 1976.
Bernard W. Rogers (Gen) 1 Oct 1976 — 21 Jun 1979.
Edward C. Meyer (Gen) 22 Jun 1979 — 21 Jun 1983.
John A. Wickham, Jr. (Gen) 23 Jun 1983 — 23 Jun 1987.
Carl E. Vuono (Gen) 23 Jun 1987 — 23 Jun 1991.
Gordon R. Sullivan (Gen) 23 Jun 1991 — .

U.S. Army Divisions And Commanding Generals In World War II

ARMORED DIVISIONS

1st Armored Division — redesignated from 7th Cavalry Brigade   Jul 40.

Campaigns: Algeria-French Morocco, Tunisia, Naples-Foggia, Anzio, Rome-Arno, North Apennines, Po Valley
Commanders: MG B Magruder — Jul 40
MG O. Ward — Mar 42
MG E.N. Harmon — Apr 43
MG V.E. Prichard — Jul 44
MG R.R. Allen Sep 45

2nd Armored Division — activated   Jul 40.

Campaigns: Algeria-French Morocco, Sicily, Normandy, Northern France, Rhineland, Ardennes-Alsace, Central Europe
Commanders: MG C.L. Scott — Jul 40
MG G.S. Patton Jr. — Jan 41
MG W.D. Crittenberger — Feb 42
MG E.N. Harmon — Jul 42
MG H.J. Gaffey — May 43
MG E.H. Brooks — Apr 44
MG E.N. Harmon — Sep 44
MG I.D. White — Jan 45
BG J.H. Collier — May 45
MG J.M. Devine — Aug 45

3rd Armored Division — activated   Apr 41

Campaigns: Normandy, Northern France, Rhineland, Ardennes-Alsace, Central Europe.
Commanders: MG A.C. Gillem — Apr 41
MG W.H. Walker — Jan 42
MG L.H. Watson — Aug 42
MG M Rose — Aug 44
BG D.O. Hickey — Mar 45
BG T.E. Boudinot — Jun 45
BG F.A. Allen Jr — Jul 45
MG R.W. Grow — Jul 45

4th Armored Division — activated Apr 41.

Campaigns: Normandy, Northern France, Rhineland, Ardennes-Alsace, Central Europe.
Commanders: MG H.W. Baird — Apr 41
MG J.S. Wood — May 42
MG H.J. Gaffey — Dec 44
MG W.M. Hoge — Mar 45
BG B.L. Clarke — Jun 45
BG W.L. Roberts — Jul 45
MG F.B. Prickett — Sep 45

5th Armored Division — activated   Oct 41.

Campaigns: Normandy, Northern France, Rhineland, Ardennes-Alsace, Central Europe.
Commanders: MG J.W. Heard — Oct 41
MG L.E. Oliver — Mar 43
BG M Rose — Jul 45
MG H.E. Dager — Sep 45

6th Armored Division — activated   Feb 42.

Campaings: Normandy, Northern France, Rhineland, Ardennes-Alsace, Central Europe.
Commanders: MG W.H.H. Morris Jr — Feb 42
MG R.W. Grow — May 43
BG G.W. Read Jr — Jul 45

7th Armored Division — activated 1 Mar 42.

Campaigns: Northern France, Rhineland, Ardennes-Alsace, Central Europe.
Commanders: MG L.McD. Silvester — Mar 42
MG R.W. Hasbrouck — Nov 44
BG T.E. Boudinot — Sep 45

8th Armored Division — activated   Apr 42.

Campaigns: Rhineland, Ardennes-Alsace, Central europe.
Commanders: MG W.M. Grimes — Apr 42
MG J.M. Devine — Oct 44
BG C.F. Colson — Aug 45

9th Armored Division — activated   Jul 42.

Campaigns: Rhineland, Ardennes-Alsace, Central Europe. Commanders: MG G. Keyes — Jul 42
MG J.W. Leonard — Oct 42

10th Armored Division — activated   Jul 42.

Campaigns: Rhineland, Central Europe.
Commanders: MG P.W. Newgarden — Jul 42
MG W.H.H. Morris Jr — Jul 44
MG F.B. Prickett- May 45

11th Armored Division — activated   Aug 42.

Campaigns: Rhineland, Ardennes-Alsace, Central Europe.
Commanders: MG E.H. Brooks — Aug 42
MG C.S. Kilburn — Mar 44
MG H.E. Dager — Mar 45

12th Armored Division — activated 15 Sep 42.

Campaigns: Rhineland, Ardennes-Alsace, Central Europe.
Commanders: MG C.E. Brewer — Sep 42
MG D.T. Greene — Aug 44 MG R.R. Allen — Sep 44
BG W.A. Holbrook Jr. — Jul 45

13th Armored Division — activated 15 Oct 42.

Campaigns: Rhineland, Central Europe.
Commanders: MG J.B. Wogan — Oct 42
MG J Millikin — Apr 45

14th Armored Division — activated 15 Nov 42.

Campaigns: Rhineland, Ardennes-Alsace, Central Europe.
Commanders: MG V.E. Prichard — Nov 42
MG A.C. Smith — Jul 44

16th Armored Division — activated 15 Jul 43.

Campaigns: Central Europe.
Commanders: MG D.T. Greene — Jul 43
BG J.L. Pierce — Sep 44

20th Armored Division — activated 15 Mar 43.

Campaigns: Central Europe.
Commanders: MG S.G. Henry — Feb 43
MG R.R. Allen — Oct 43
MG R Ward — Sep 44
MG J.W. Leonard — Aug 45

CAVALRY DIVISIONS

1st Cavalry Division, Special

Campaigns: New Guinea, Bismarck Archipelago, Leyte, Luzon.
Commanders: MG I.P. Swift — Apr 41
MG V.D. Mudge — Aug 44
BG H.F.T. Hoffman — Feb 45
MG W.C. Chase — Jul 45

2nd Cavalry Division (Horse) — activated 1 Apr 41.

Commanders: BG T. de le Mesa Allen — Apr 41
BG J Millikin — Jun 41
BG J.D. Coulter — May 42

2nd Cavalry Division (Horse) (Colored) — activated 25 Feb 43.

Campaigns: European Theater without inscription.
Commander: MG H.H. Johnson — Feb 43

AIRBORNE, INFANTRY, LIGHT, MOTORIZED, AND MOUNTAIN DIVISIONS

1st Infantry Division
Campaigns: Algeria-French Morocco, Tunisia, Sicily, Normandy Northern France, Rhineland, Ardennes-Alsace, Central Europe.
Commanders: MG D Cubbison — Jul 41
MG T. de le Mesa Allen — Jun 42
MG C.R. Huebner — Jul 43
MG C Andrus — Dec 44

2nd Infantry Division
Campaigns: Normandy, Northern France, Rhineland, Ardennes-Alsace, Central Europe.
Commanders: MG J.C.H. Lee — Nov 41
MG W.M. Robertson — May 42
BG W.K. Harrison — Jun 45
MG E.M. Almond — Sep 45

3rd Infantry Division
Campaigns: Algeria-French Morocco, Tunisia, Sicily, Naples-Foggia, Anzio, Rome-Arno, Southern France, Rhineland, Ardennes-Alsace, Central Europe.
Commanders: MG C.F. Thompson — Aug 40
BG C.P. Hall — Aug 41
MG J.P. Lucas — Sep 41
MG J.W. Anderson — Mar 42
MG L.K. Truscott Jr — Apr 43
MG J.W. O'Daniel — Feb 44
MG W.R. Schmidt — Aug 45

4th Infantry Division- activated 1 Jun 40.
Campaigns: Normandy, Northern France, Rhineland, Ardennes-Alsace, Central Europe.
Commanders: MG W.E. Prosser — Jun 40
MG L.R. Fredendall — Oct 40
MG O.W. Griswold — Aug 41
MG H.R. Bull — Oct 41
MG T de la Mesa Allen — Dec 41
MG F.C. Wallace — Jan 42
MG R.O. Barton — Jul 42
MG H.W. Blakeley — Dec 44
MG G.P. Hays — Nov 45

5th Infantry Division — activated Oct 39.

Campaigns: Normandy, Northern France, Rhineland, Ardennes-Alsace, Central Europe.

Commanders: BG C.B. Hodges — Oct 39
MG J.M. Cummins — Sep 40
MG C.H. Bonesteel — Jul 41
MG C Parker — Aug 41
MG S.L. Irwin — Jun 43
MG A.E. Brown — Apr 45

6th Infantry Division — activated Oct 39.

Campaigns: New Guinea, Luzon
Commanders: BG C.A. Trott — Oct 39
BG F.E. Uhl — Oct 40
MG C.S. Ridley — Jan 41
MG D.S. Wilson — Sep 42
MG F.C. Sibert — Oct 42
MG E.D. Patrick — Aug 44
MG C.E. Hurdis — Mar 45

7th Infantry Division — activated Jul 40.

Campaigns: Aleutian Islands, Eastern
   Mandates, Leyte, Ryukyus.
Commanders: BG J.W. Stilwell — Jul 40
MG C.H. White — Aug 41
MG A.E. Brown — Oct 42
MG C.H. Corlett — Apr 43
MG A.V. Arnold — Feb 44

8th Infantry Division — activated Jul 40.
Campaigns: Normandy, Northern France,
   Rhineland, Central Europe.
Commanders: MG P.B. Peyton — Jun 40
MG J.P. Marley — Dec 40
MG W.E. Shedd — Feb 41
MG H Terrell Jr — Mar 41
MG J.P. Marley — Apr 41
MG P.E. Peabody — Aug 42
MG W.C. McMahon — Feb 43
MG D.A. Stroh — Jul 44
MG W.G. Weaver — Dec 44
MG B.E. Moore — Feb 45

9th Infantry Division — activated Aug 40.
Campaigns: Algeria-French Morocco,
   Tunisia, Sicily, Normandy, Northern
   France, Rhineland, Ardennes-Alsace,
   Central Europe.
Commanders: Col. C.B. Elliot — Aug 40
BG F.W. Honeycutt — Sep 40
MG J.L. Devers — Oct 40
MG R.E. DeR. Hoyle — Aug 41
MG M.S. Eddy — Aug 42
MG L.A. Craig — Aug 44
MG J.A. Ladd — May 45

10th Mountain Division — activated Jul
   43.

Campaigns: North Apennines, Po Valley
Commanders: MG L.E. Jones — Jul 42
MG G.P. Hays — Nov 44

11th Airborne Division — activated Feb
   43.

Campaigns: New Guinea, Leyte, Luzon
Commander: MG J.M. Swing — Feb 43

13th Airborne Division — activated Aug
   43.

Campaigns: Central Europe
Commanders: MG G.W. Griner — Aug 43
MG E.G. Chapman Jr — Nov 45

17th Airborne Division — activated Apr
   43.

Campaigns: Rhineland, Ardennes-Alsace,
   Central Europe
Commander: MG W.M. Miley — Apr 43

24th Infantry Division — redesignated
   Oct 41.

Campaigns: Central Pacific, New Guinea,
   Leyte, Southern Philippines, Luzon
Commanders: MG D.S. Wilson — Oct 41
MG F.A. Irving — Aug 42
MG R.B. Woodruff — Nov 44
BG K.F. Cramer — Nov 45

25th Infantry Division — activated Oct 41.

Campaigns: Central Pacific, Northern
   Solomons, Guadalcanal, Luzon
Commanders: MG M Murray — Oct 41
MG J.L. Collins — May 42
MG C.L. Mullins Jr — Jan 44

26th Infantry Division — Massachusetts
   National Guard — inducted into federal
   service Jan 41.

Campaigns: Northern France, Rhineland,
   Ardennes-Alsace, Central Europe
Commanders: MG R.W. Eckfeldt — Jan 41
MG W.S. Paul — Aug 43
MG H.N. Hartness — Jun 45
MG S.E. Reinhart — Jul 45
MG R.W. Grow — Nov 45

27th Infantry Division — New York
   National Guard — inducted into federal
   service Oct 40.

Campaigns: Central Pacific, Western
   Pacific, Ryukyus
Commanders: MG W.N. Haskell — Oct 40
BG R. McT. Pennell — Nov 41
MG R.C. Smith — Nov 42
MG G.W. Griner Jr — Jun 44

28th Infantry Division — Pennsylvania
   National Guard — inducted into federal
   service Feb 41.

Campaigns: Normandy, Northern France,
   Rhineland, Ardennes-Alsace, Central
   Europe
Commanders: MG E Martin — Feb 41
MG J.G. Ord — Jan 42
MG O.N. Bradley — Jun 42
MG L.D. Brown — Jun 43
BG J.E. Wharton — Aug 44
MG N.D. Cota — Aug 44

29th Infantry Division — Virginia,
   Maryland, Pennsylvania, District of
   Columbia National Guard — inducted
   into federal service Feb 41.

Campaigns: Normandy, Northern France,
   Rhineland, Central Europe
Commanders: MG M.A. Reckord — Feb 41
MG L.T. Gerow — Feb 42
MG C.H. Gerhardt — Jul 43

30th Infantry Division — North Carolina,
   South Carolina, Georgia, Tennessee
   National Guard — inducted into federal
   service Sep 40.

Campaigns: Normandy, Northern France,
   Rhineland, Ardennes-Alsace, Central
   Europe
Commanders: MG H.D. Russell — Sep 40
MG W.H. Simpson — May 42
MG L.S. Hobbs — Sep 42
MG A.C. Cowper — Sep 45

31st Infantry Division — Louisiana,
   Mississippi, Alabama, Florida National
   Guard — inducted into federal service
   Nov 40.

Campaigns: New Guinea, Southern
   Philippines

Commanders: MG J.C. Persons — Nov 40
MG C.A. Martin — Sep 44

32nd Infantry Division — Michigan and
   Wisconsin National Guard — inducted
   into federal service Oct 40.

Campaigns: New Guinea, Southern
   Philippines, Luzon Commanders: MG
   I.A. Fish — Oct 40
MG E.F. Harding — Mar 42
MG W.H. Gill — Feb 43

33rd Infantry Division — Illinois National
   Guard — inducted into federal service
   Mar 41.

Campaigns: New Guinea, Luzon
Commanders: MG S.T. Lawton — Mar 41
MG F.C. Mahin — May 42
MG J Millikin — Aug 42
MG P.W. Clarkson — Oct 43
BG W.G. Skelton — Nov 45

34th Infantry Division — North Dakota,
   South Dakota, Iowa, Minnesota National
   Guard — inducted into federal service Feb
   41.

Campaigns: Tunisia, Naples-Foggia, Anzio,
   Rome-Arno, North Apennines, Po Valley
Commanders: MG E.A. Walsh — Feb 41
MG R.P. Hartle — Aug 41
MG C.W. Ryder — May 42
MG C.L. Bolte — Jul 44

35th Infantry Division — Kansas,
   Missouri, Nebraska National Guard —
   inducted into federal service Dec 40.

Campaigns: Normandy, Northern France,
   Rhineland, Ardennes-Alsace, Central
   Europe
Commanders:MG R.E. Truman — Dec 40
MG W.H. Simpson — Oct 41
MG M Murray — May 42
MG P.W. Baade — Jan 43

36th Infantry Division — Texas National
   Guard — inducted into federal service
   Nov 40.

Campaigns: Naples-Foggia, Anzio, Rome-
   Arno, Southern France, Rhineland,
   Ardennes-Alsace, Central Europe
Commanders: MG C.V. Birkhead — Nov 40
MG F.L. Walker — Sep 41
MG J.E. Dahlquist — Jul 44
BG R.I. Stack — Nov 45

37th Infantry Division — Ohio National
   Guard — inducted into federal service Oct
   40.

Campaigns: Northern Solomons, Luzon
Commander: MG R.S. Beightler — Oct 40

38th Infantry Division — Indiana,
   Kentucky, West Virginia National Guard
   — inducted into federal service Jan 41.

Campaigns: New Guinea, Southern
   Philippines, Luzon
Commanders: MG R.H. Tyndall — Jan 41
MG D.I. Sultan — Apr 41
MG H.L.C. Jones — Apr 42
MG W.C. Chase — Feb 45
MG F.A. Irving — Aug 45

40th Infantry Division — California,
   Nevada, Utah National Guard - inducted
   into federal service Mar 41.

Campaigns: Bismarck Archipelago,
   Southern Philippines, Luzon
Commanders: MG W.P. Story — Mar 41

BG E.J. Dawley — Sep 41
MG R Brush — Apr 42
BG D.J. Myers — Jul 45

41st Infantry Division — Washington, Oregon, Idaho, Montana National Guard — inducted into federal service Sep 40.

Campaigns: New Guinea, Luzon, Southern Philippines
Commanders: MG G.A. White — Sep 40
BG C.A. Pennington — Nov 41
MG H.H. Fuller — Dec 41
MG J.A. Doe — Jun 44

42nd Infantry Division — activated Jul 43.

Campaigns: Rhineland, Central Europe
Commander: MG H.J. Collins — Jul 43

43rd Infantry Division — Maine, Vermont, Connecticut, Rhode Island National Guard — inducted into federal service Feb 41.

Campaigns: Guadalcanal, Northern Solomons, New Guinea, Luzon
Commanders: MG M.B. Payne — Feb 41
MG J.H. Hester — Aug 41
MG L.F. Wing — Aug 43

44th Infantry Division — New York and New Jersey National Guard — inducted into federal service Sep 40.

Campaigns: Northern France, Rhineland, Central Europe
Commanders: MG C.R. Powell — Sep 40
MG J.I. Muir — Aug 41
MG R.L. Spragins — Aug 44
MG W.F. Dean — Jan 45
BG W.A. Beiderlinden — Nov 45
BG R.L. Dulaney — Nov 45

45th Infantry Division — Arizona, Colorado, New Mexico, Oklahoma National Guard — inducted into federal service Feb 40.

Campaigns: Sicily, Naples-Foggia, Anzio, Rome-Arno, Southern France, Rhineland, Ardennes-Alsace, Central Europe
Commanders: MG W.S. Key — Sep 40
MG T.H. Middleton — Oct 42
MG W.W. Eagles — Dec 43
MG R.T. Frederick — Dec 44
BG H.J.D. Meyer — Sep 45

63rd Infantry Division — activated Jun 43.

Campaigns: Rhineland, Central Europe
Commanders: MG L.E. Hibbs — Jun 43
BG F.M. Harris — Aug 45
65th Infantry Division — activated Aug 43.

Campaigns: Rhineland, Central Europe
Commanders: MG S.E. Reinhart — Aug 43
BG J.E. Copeland — Aug 45

66th Infantry Division — activated Apr 43.

Campaigns: Northern France
Commanders: MG H.F. Kramer — Apr 43
MG W.E. Lauer — Aug 45

69th Infantry Division — activated May 43.

Campaigns: Rhineland, Central Europe
Commanders: MG C.L. Bolte — May 43
MG E.F. Reinhardt — Sep 44
BG R.V. Maraist — Aug 45

70th Infantry Division — activated Jun 43.

Campaigns: Rhineland, Central Europe
Commanders: MG J.E. Dahlquist — Jun 43
MG A.J. Barnett — Jul 44
BG T.W. Herren — Jul 45

71st Infantry Division — activated Jul 43.

Campaigns: Rhineland, Central Europe
Commanders: BG R.L. Spragins — Jul 43
MG E.M. Landrum — Oct 44
MG W.G. Wyman — Nov 44 BG O.S. Rolfe — Aug 45
MG A.A. White — Oct 45

75th Infantry Division — activated Apr 43.

Campaigns: Rhineland, Ardennes-Alsace, Central Europe
Commanders: MG W.S. Paul — Apr 43
MG F.B. Prickett — Aug 43
MG R.E. Porter — Jan 45
MG A.A. White — Jun 45
BG C.R. Doran — Oct 45

76th Infantry Division — activated Jun 42.

Campaigns: Rhineland, Ardennes-Alsace, Central Europe
Commanders: MG E.F. Reinhardt — Jun 42
MG W.R. Schmidt — Dec 42
BG H.C. Evans — Aug 45

77th Infantry Division — activated Mar 42.

Campaigns: Western Pacific, Leyte, Ryukyus
Commanders: MG R.L. Eichelberger — Mar 42
MG R.B. Woodruff — Jun 42
MG A.D. Bruce — May 43

78th Infantry Division — activated Aug 42.

Campaigns: Rhineland, Ardennes-Alsace, Central Europe
Commanders: MG E.P. Parker Jr — Aug 42
MG R.W. Barker — Sep 45

79th Infantry Division — activated Jun 42.

Campaigns: Normandy, Northern France, Rhineland, Ardennes-Alsace, Central Europe
Commanders: MG I.T. Wyche — Jun 42
BG L.H. Watson — May 45
MG A.C. McAuliffe — Jul 45
BG L.H. Watson — Aug 45

80th Infantry Division — activated Jul 42.

Campaigns: Northern France, Rhineland, Ardennes-Alsace, Central Europe
Commanders: MG J.D. Patch — Jul 42
MG H.L. McBride — Mar 43
MG W.E. Lauer — Oct 45

81st Infantry Division — activated Jun 42.

Campaigns: Western Pacific, Leyte
Commanders: MG G.H. Franke — Jun 42
MG P.J. Mueller — Aug 42

82nd Airborne Division — activated Mar 42.

Campaigns: Sicily, Naples-Foggia, Normandy, Rhineland, Ardennes-Alsace, Central Europe
Commanders: MG O.N. Bradley — Mar 42
MG M.B. Ridgway — Jun 42
MG J.M. Gavin — Aug 44

83rd Infantry Division — activated Aug 42.

Campaigns: Normandy, Northern France, Rhineland, Ardennes-Alsace, Central Europe.
Commanders: MG F.W. Milburn — Aug 42
MG R.C. Macon — Jan 44

84th Infantry Division — activated Oct 42.

Campaigns: Rhineland, Ardennes-Alsace, Central Europe
Commanders: MG J.H. Hildring — Oct 42
MG S Jackson — Feb 43
MG R.B. McClure — Oct 43
MG R.B. Woodruff — Mar 44
MG A.R. Bolling — Jun 44

85th Infantry Division — activated May 42.

Campaigns: Rome-Arno, North Apennines, Po Valley
Commanders: MG W.H. Haislip — May 42
MG J.B. Coulter — Feb 43

86th Infantry Division — activated Dec 42.

Campaigns: Central Europe
Commanders: MG A.E. Anderson — Sep 42
MG H.M. Melasky — Jan 43
MG P.J. Mueller — Jan 46

87th Infantry Division — activated Dec 42.

Campaigns: Rhineland, Ardennes-Alsace, Central Europe
Commanders: MG P.W. Clarkson — Dec 42
MG E.M. Landrum — Oct 43
MG F.L. Culin Jr — Apr 44

88th Infantry Division — activated Jul 42.

Campaigns: Rome-Arno, North Apennines, Po Valley
Commanders: MG J.E. Sloan — Jul 42
MG P.W. Kendall — Sep 44
BG J.C. Fry — Jul 45
MG B.E. Moore — Nov 45

89th Infantry Division — activated Jul 42.

Campaigns: Rhineland, Central Europe
Commanders: MG W.H. Gill — Jul 42
MG T.D. Finley — Feb 43

90th Infantry Division — activated Mar 42.

Campaigns: Normandy, Northern France, Rhineland, Ardennes-Alsace, Central Europe
Commanders: MG H Terrell Jr — Mar 42
BG J.W. MacKelvie — Jan 44
MG E.M. Landrum — Jul 44
MG R.S. McClain — Aug 44
MG J.A. Van Fleet — Oct 44
MG L.W. Rooks — Feb 45
MG H.L. Earnest — Mar 45

91st Infantry Division — activated Aug 42.

Campaigns, Rome-Arno, North Apennines, Po Valley
Commanders: MG C.H. Gerhardt — Aug 42
MG W.G. Livesay — Jul 43

92nd Infantry Division (Colored) — activated Oct 42.

Campaigns: North Apennines, Po Valley
Commanders: MG E.M. Almond — Oct 42
BG J.E. Wood — Aug 45

93rd Infantry Division (Colored) — activated May 42.

Campaigns: Northern Solomons, Bismarck Archipelago, New Guinea
Commanders: MG C.P. Hall — May 42
MG F.W. Miller — Oct 42
MG R.G. Lehman — May 43
MG H.H. Johnson — Aug 44

94th Infantry Division — activated Sep 42.

Campaigns: Northern France, Rhineland, Ardennes-Alsace, Central Europe
Commanders: MG H.J. Malony Sep 42
BG L.J. Fortier — May 45
MG A.J. Barnett — Aug 45

95th Infantry Division — activated Jul 42.

Campaigns: Northern France, Rhineland, Ardennes-Alsace, Central Europe
Commander: MG H.L. Twaddle — Jul 42

96th Infantry Division — activated Aug 42.

Campaigns: Leyte, Ryukyus
Commander: MG J.L. Bradley — Aug 42

97th Infantry Division — activated Feb 43.

Campaigns: Central Europe
Commanders: BG L.A. Craig — Feb 43
BG M.B. Halsey — Jan 44
MG H.F. Kramer — Sep 45

98th Infantry Division — activated Sep 42.

Campaigns: Pacific Theater without inscription.
Commanders: MG P.L. Ransom — Sep 42
MG G.W. Griner Jr — Nov 43
BG J.R. Sheetz — Jun 44
MG R.C. Smith — Jul 44
BG J.R. Sheetz — Aug 44
BG W.C. Zimmerman — Oct 44
MG A.M. Harper — Oct 44

99th Infantry Division — activated Nov 42.

Campaigns: Rhineland, Ardennes-Alsace, Central Europe
Commanders: MG T Lawrence — Nov 42
MG W.E. Lauer — Jul 43
BG F.H. Black — Aug 45

100th Infantry Division — activated Nov 42.

Campaigns: Rhineland, Ardennes-Alsace, Central Europe
Commanders: MG W.A. Burress — Nov 42
BG A.C. Tychsen — Sep 45

101st Airborne Division — activated Aug 42.

Campaigns: Normandy, Rhineland, Ardennes-Alsace, Central Europe
Commanders: MG W.C. Lee — Aug 42
MG M.D. Taylor — Mar 44
BG A.C. McAuliffe — Dec 44
MG M.D. Taylor — Dec 44
BG W.M. Gillmore — Sep 45
BG G. StC. Mickle — Sep 45
BG S Cutler — Oct 45

102nd Infantry Division — activated Sep 42.

Campaigns: Rhineland, Central Europe
Commanders: MG J.B. Anderson Sep 42
MG F.A. Keating — Jan 44

103rd Infantry Division — activated Nov 42.

Campaigns: Rhineland, Ardennes-Alsace, Central Europe
Commanders: MG C.G. Haffner Jr — Nov 42
MG A.C. McAuliffe — Jan 45
BG J.N. Robinson — Aug 45

104th Infantry Division — activated Sep 42.

Campaigns: Northern France, Rhineland, Central Europe
Commanders: MG G.R. Cook — Jun 42
MG T. de la Mesa Allen — Oct 43
BG C.K. Gailey Jr — Nov 45

106th Infantry Division — activated Mar 43.

Campaigns: Rhineland, Ardennes-Alsace, Central Europe
Commanders: MG A.W. Jones — Mar 43
BG H.T. Perrin — Dec 44
MG D.A. Stroh — Feb 45

American Division — organized May 42.

Campaigns: Guadalcanal, Northern Solomons, Leyte, Southern Philippines
Commanders: MG A.M. Patch — May 42
BG E.B. Sebree — Jan 43
MG J.R. Hodge — May 43
MG R.B. McClure — Apr 44
MG W.H. Arnold — Nov 44

Composite Army-Marine Division (CAM)

Campaigns: Guadalcanal

Philippine Division
Campaigns: Philippine Islands
Commanders: MG J.M. Wainwright — Nov 40
BG M.S. Lough — Dec 41

1st Airborne Task Force (Provisional Seventh Army Airborne Division)

Campaigns: Southern France, Rhineland
Commander: MG R.T. Frederick

Listing U.S. Military Academy Graduates who attain rank of Gen. (entering West Point between 1880 and 1939.

The highest rank achieved is listed. Those who serve beyond 1950 are noted as such. In addition, some other West Point Officers who do not achieve the rank of Gen. are also listed. This list is not to be construed as all-encompassing. The number immediately following the name is the year of graduation and this is followed by the Official West Point Cadet Number.

(List starts on page 779)

General Eisenhower in conversation with some troops. General Bradley (right) and Lt. Col. William C. Westmoreland also face the troops. Photo courtesy of General William C. Westmoreland.

Goethals George Washington, Engineer; (W.P. 1880-No. 2828) Major General, 3-4-1915 (Built the Panama Canal).

Chamberlain John Loomis, (W.P. 1880-No. 2831) Artillery: Major General 1917.

Bailey Charles Custin, (W.P. 1880-No. 2834) Artillery: Commanding General 81st Division AEF, Major General 1921.

Aleshire James Buchanan, Cavalry; (W.P. 1880-No. 2844) Frontier Duty 1880-89; USV 1898-99; Cuba 1899-00; Brigadier General QMG USA 07-12; Major General 1912.

Erwin James Brailsford, Cavalry; (W.P. 1880-No. 2848) Frontier Duty 1880-81; Brigadier General, Commanding General Infantry Brigade AEF.

Bell George Jr., Infantry; (W.P. 1880-No. 2869) Frontier Duty 1880-88; Major General, Commanding General 33rd Division AEF.

Biddle John, CE; (W.P. 1881-No. 2880) Major General (NA) 17, CG US RR Regts AEF 17, retire 1920.

Hodges Harry Foote, CE; (W.P. 1881-No. 2882) MG 17; CG 76th Division AEF; retire 1921.

Bartlett George True, Artillery; (W.P. 1881-No. 2888) MG 17; retire 1918.

Gaston Joseph Alfred, Cavalry; (W.P. 1881-No. 2894) Frontier Duty 1881-91, Sioux Indian Wars 1890-91; Cuba 1899-1902; PI 1908-10; PunX; Brigadier General 17; retire 1930.

Carleton Guy, Cavalry; (W.P. 1881-No. 2895) Frontier Duty 1881-86; MG 18; CG Camp Wadsworth 1917-18; retire 1921.

Kernan Francis Joseph, Infantry; (W.P. 1881-No. 2896) Frontier Duty 1881-85, 1887-88; AdC General Arthur McArthur 1900-03; MG 17; Org SOS AEF; retire 1922.

Hodges Henry Clay Jr., Infantry; (W.P. 1881-No. 2901) Frontier Duty 1881-86; AdC General Augur; MG 1917; CG 39th Division AEF; retire 1920.

Dickman Joseph Theodore, Cavalry; (W.P. 1881-No. 2905) Frontier Duty 1883-90; Indian Wars; MG 1917; Division and Corps Comander AEF; CG 3rd Army AGF; MG USA 1919; retire 1921.

Crowder Enoch Herbert, Cavalry; (W.P. 1881-No. 2909) Frontier Duty 1881-84; MG 17.

Kerr James Taggert, Infantry; (W.P. 1881-No. 2906) Frontier Duty 1881-88; Sioux Indian War; BG 1920; retire 1922.

McCarthy Daniel Edward, Infantry; (W.P. 1881-No. 2908) Frontier Duty 1881-94; Sioux Indian War; Wrote the War Department Quartermaster Manual 1901; Chief Quartermaster AEF 1917; retire Colonel.

Rafferty William Carroll, Artillery; (W.P. 1880-No. 2830) Brigadier General, 1917.

Strong Frederick Smith, Artillery; (W.P. 1880-No. 2837) Sioux Indian Wars 1890-91; Major USV 1898-99; Superintendant USMA 1902-04; Major General Commanding General 40th Division, 1917-19.

Sharpe Henry Granville, (W.P. 1880-No. 2872) Brigadier General Comsy General 1905-16; BG QMC 1912-16; MG, QMG 1916-18; Major General USA 1918.

Phillips Charles Leonard, Artillery; (W.P. 1881-No. 2891) Frontier Duty 1881-82, Brigadier General 17, retire 1930.

Townsley Clarence Page (W.P. 1881-No. 2892) Major General 1917, retire 1918.

Morrison John Frank, Infantry, (W.P. 1881-No. 2904) Frontier Duty 1881-83, 1885-87; Observer Jap Army 1904; MG 1917; CG Western Depot 1918-19; retire 1921.

Barth Charles Henry, Infantry; (W.P. 1881-No. 2910) Frontier Duty 1881-82, 1887-89: BG 17: retired 1922.

Stotesenburg John Miller*, (W.P. 1881-No. 2919) Cavalry; Frontier Duty 1881-1891; Sioux Indian Wars 1890-91; Colonel NB Vols. 1898; Killed in the Phln 23 Apr 1899 Comdg Regt a 40; Ft. Stotesenburg PI named in his honor.

Rowan Andrew Summers, (W.P. 1881-No. 2920) Infantry; Frontier Duty 1881-1889; 1st US Off to land in Cuba 1898; Carried message to Garcia; (DSC) LTC USV 1898-1899; MAJ retired 1909.

West Parker Whitney, (W.P. 1881-No. 2921) Cavalry; Frontier Duty 1881-1887; MAJ USV 1898-1899; LTC IG USV 1900-1901; AdC Gen Mac Arthur & Obs Jap Army 1904-1905; MAJ retired dsbl 1909.

Kennon Lyman Walter Vere, (W.P. 1881-No. 2928) Infantry; Frontier Duty 1881-1886; AdC Gen Crook 1886-1890; MAJ USV 1898-1899; Colonel 34 USV Inf in Phln; BG 1917; BG psth 1930.

McDonald John Bacon, (W.P. 1881-No. 2930) Infantry; Frontier Duty 1881-1888; BG 1917; CG 1918; Brig 91 Div AEF (DSC-DSM) BG retired 1923.

Burr Edward, (W.P. 1882-No. 2932) Corps of Engineers; CG 1862 FA Brig AEF; BG retired 1930.

Spencer Eugene Jaccard, (W.P. 1882-No. 2936) Cav-CE; Asst Prof USMA 1887-1889; Resd 1890; LTC USV 1898; BG NGMO 1913; COL 52 Engrs (RR & Bridge Construction) AEF (DSM).

Cronkhite Adelbert, (W.P. 1882-No. 2941) Arty-ARC-CAC; Sioux Indian Wars 1890-1891; MG 1917; CG 80 Div AEF(DSM); MG USA 1920; Retired 1923.

Thompson John Taliaferro, (W.P. 1882-No. 2942) Arty-OD; LTC USV 1898; BG OD 1918; BG retired 1930.

Treat Charles Gould, (W.P. 1882-No. 2944) Arty-ARC-FA; MG 1917; Ch AmMsn to Italy 1918-1919; MG retired 1930.

Young Richard Whitehead, (W.P. 1882-No. 2946) Arty; BG NG Utah 1895-1896; MAJ Comdg Utah Btry in Phln; BG CG 65th FA Brig AEF.

Alvord Benjamin Jr., (W.P. 1882- No. 2948) Arty; BG 1917; AG AEF 1917-1918; BG Asst AG 1922; retired 1924.

McIver George Wilcox, (W.P. 1882-No. 2950) Infantry; Frontier Duty 1882-1891; Sioux Indian Wars 1890-1891; BG 1917; 161st Brig 81st Div AEF; Ret 1922 Col; BG Ret 1930.

Allen Henry Tureman, Cavalry; (W.P. 1882-No. 2951) Cavalry; Frontier Duty 1882-1888; MG 1917; CG 90th Div & 8th Corps AEF; MG USA 1920; CG AFG; Retired 1923.

Sage William-Hampden, (W.P. 1882-No. 2952)Infantry; Frontier Duty 1882-1890; MG 1917; AFG 1919-1920.

Dugan Thomas Buchanan, (W.P. 1882-No. 2962) Cavalry; Frontier Duty 1882-1890; BG CG Inf Brig AEF; Retired 1922.

Allaire William Herbert, (W.P. 1882-No. 2964) Infantry; BG CG Brig AEF; Retired 1921.

Langfitt William Campbell, (W.P. 1883-No. 2970) Corps of Engineers; MG 1917; Ch Engr AEF; Retired 1922.

Haynes Ira Allen (W.P. 1883-No. 2983) Arty ARC CAC; BG 1917; CG 64th FA Brig AEF 1917-1918.

Walke Willoughby, (W.P. 1883-No. 2984) Arty ARC CAC; CO Mid Atlantic CA Dist 1917-1919; BG 1922; Retired 1923.

Kennedy Chase Wilmot, (W.P. 1883-No. 2986) Infantry; Frontier Duty 1883-1895; MG 1917; CG 85th Div AEF; Retired 1922.

Morton Charles Gould, (W.P. 1883-No. 2988) Infantry; Frontier Duty 1883-1888; MG 1917; CG 29th Div AEF; MG Retired 1925.

Littell Isaac William, (W.P. 1883-No. 2996) Infantry QM; Frontier Duty 1884-1890; BG QMC 1918; In charge cantonment const 1917-1918; BG retired 1919.

Cameron George Hamilton, (W.P. 1883-No. 2997) Cavalry; Frontier Duty 1883-1887; MG 1917; CG Div& Corps AEF; Cmdt Cav Sch 1919-1920 MG Retired 1930.

Heard John Wilkinson, (W.P. 1883-No. 3001) Cavalry; Frontier Duty 1883-1890; BG 1918; CG Hawaiian Dept 1918-1919.

Hale Harry Clay, (W.P. 1883-No. 3004) Infantry; Frontier Duty 1887-1890; MG 1917; CG 84th Div AEF; Retired 1921.

Walsh Robert Douglas, (W.P. 1883-No. 3005) Inf-Cav; Frontier Duty 1883-1891; Apache Wars 1886; BG 1917; CG Ports AEF; Col Retired 1919; BG psth .

Read George Windle, (W.P. 1883-No. 3008) Inf-Cav; Frontier Duty 1883-1889; MG 1917; 30th Div & 2nd Corps AEF; MG 1920; CG PI Dept 1922-1924; Retired 1924.

Faison Samson Lane, (W.P. 1883-No. 3009) Infantry; Frontier Duty 1883-1886; BG 1917; 60th Inf Brig AEF; Retired dsbl 1922.

Bundy Omar, (W.P. 1883-No. 3018) Infantry; Frontier Duty 1883-1885; Sioux Wars 1890-1891; MG 1917; CG 2nd Div & 6th Corps AEF; Retired 1925.

Tyson Lawrence Davis, (W.P. 1883-No. 3019) Infantry; Frontier Duty 1883-1887; BG NA 1917; CG 59th Inf Brig AEF.

Edwards Clarence Ransom, (W.P. 1883-No. 3020) Infantry; Frontier Duty 1883-1884; MG 1917; CG 26th Div AEF; MG 1921; CG 1st CA 1921-1922; Retired 1922.

Hale Irving, (W.P. 1884-No. 3021) Corps of Engineers; BG USV 1898-1899; Founded VFW in Denver in 1899.

Chittenden Hiram Martin, (W.P. 1884-No. 3023) Corps of Engineers; River and Harbor duty; BG Retired disabled 1910.

Taylor Harry, (W.P. 1884-No. 3026) Corps of Engineers; Extensive work on rivers and harbors in US and PI; BG 1917; MG C of Engineers USA; Retired 1926.

Sibert William Luther, (W.P. 1884-No. 3027) Corps of Engineers; BG and thanks of Congress 1915; MG 1917; Retired 1920.

Foote Stephen Miller, (W.P. 1884-No. 3030) Arty-ARC-CAC; BG 1917; CG FA Brig AEF; BG psth.

Lewis Isaac Newton, (W.P. 1844-No. 3031) Arty ARC-CAC; Retired disabled 1913; Mfgd Lewis Machine Guns for Allies 1913-1920.

Ladd Eugene Frederick, (W.P. 1884-No. 3032) Cav-AGD; Frontier Duty 1884-1896; Col Retired disabled 1915; BG psth.

Sturgis Samuel Davis Jr, (W.P. 1884-No. 3033) Arty-ARC-FA; MG 1917; CG 87th Div. AEF; MG 1921 CG PC Dept 1921-1924.

Hatch Everard Enos, (W.P. 1884-No. 3035) Infantry; Frontier Duty 1884-1888; BG 1917; Retired 1917.

Cabell DeRosey Carrol, (W.P. 1884-No. 3038) Cavalry; Frontier Duty 1884-1886 BG 1917; MG 1918; CG Border Comd 1917-1918; Retired 1920.

Babbitt Edwin Burr; (W.P. 1884-No. 3039) Arty OD; BG USA 1918; CG 4FA Brig AEF; MG 1923; Retired 1924.

Sayre Farrand, (W.P. 1884-No. 3041) Cavalry; Frontier Duty 1884-1889; Cav Cuba 1898-1899; In charge of Apache POW FT. Sill 1900 1904; Inf & Cav Sch 1904-1906; Author Map Maneuvers; BG 1918; Retired 1925.

Richardson Wilds Preston, (W.P. 1884-No. 3042)Infantry; Frontier Duty 1892-1897; BG in AEF & Russia; Retired 1920.

Gallagher Hugh John, (W.P. 1884-No. 3043) Cav-Comsy-QMC; Frontier Duty 1884-1894; Ch Comsy CRX Ch QM Siberia 1918-1919; Retired 1925.

Dentler Clarence Eugene, (W.P.1884-No. 3044) Infantry; Frontier Duty 1884-1887; Cuba 1906 1907; Tng activities US 1917-1919; Retired 1923; Last surviving member of his class and oldest living graduate USMA 1 Jan to 2 Apr 1955.

Hutcheson Grote, (W.P. 1884-No. 3045) Cavalry; Frontier Duty 1884-1891; Sioux Indian Wars 1890-1891; BG 1917; CG Newport News Port 1917-1918; MG 1918; BG USA 1920; Retired disabled 1924.

Cress George Oscar, (W.P. 1884-No. 3047) 1884 1889; BG 1918; Retired 1926.

Styer Henry Delp, (W.P. 1884-No. 3049) Infantry; Frontier Duty 1884-1892; BG 1917; AEF Siberia 1918-1918; Retired 1919.

Bellinger John, (W.P. 1884-No. 3050) Cav-QMC; Frontier Duty 1884-1888; BG QMD 1922.

Noble Robert Houston, (W.P. 1884-No. 3052) Infantry; Frontier Duty 1884-1886; BG 1918; CG Brig AEF; Retired 1922.

Shanks David Cary, (W.P. 1884-No. 3053) Infantry; Frontier Duty 1894-1898; MAJ VA Vols 1898; Phln; MG 1917; CG Hoboken Port 1918-1920; Retired 1925.

Morse Benjamin Clark, (W.P. 1884-No. 3054) Infantry; AdC Gen Shafter 1900-1901; Cuba 1906-1907; BG 1917; Retired 1920.

Knight John Thornton, (W.P. 1884-No. 3055) Cav-QMC; Frontier Duty 1884-1887; BG 1923; Retired 1925.

Kuhn Joseph Ernst, (W.P. 1885-No. 3058) Corps of Engineers; MG 1917; CG 79th Div AEF; MG & Retired 1925.

Muir Charles Henry, (W.P. 1885-No. 3065) Infantry; Frontier duty 1885-1892; MG 1917; CG 28th Div & 4th Corps AEF; MG 1921; Retired 1924.

Brown Robert Alexander, (W.P. 1885-No. 3068) Cavalry; Frontier Duty 1885-1887; MAJ IG USV 1998-1899 in Cuba; Phln; AcD Gen McArthur 1901-1902; BG 1917; CG Inf Brig AEF; AFG; Retired 1923.

Carson John Miller, (W.P. 1885-No. 3071) Cav-QMC;Adjt USMA 1890-1895; BG 1918; Retired 1922.

Holbrook Willard Ames, (W.P. 1885-No. 3074) Cavalry; Frontier Duty 1885-1889; Crow Indian Wars 1887; AdC Gen Stanley 1991-1892; Cuba 1899; MG 1918; MG C of Cav 1920-1924; Retired 1924.

McCain Henry Pinckney, (W.P. 1885-No. 3077) Inf-ADG; Frontier Duty 1885-1888; BG TAG 1914-1918; MG 1917; Retired 1921.

Michie Robert Edward Lee, (W.P. 1885-No. 3083) Cavalry; Frontier Duty 1885-1893; MAJ USV in Cuba 1898-1899; BG 1917; Died in France 4 June 1918 BG comdg 53rd Inf Brig.

Bullard Robert Lee, (W.P. 1885-No. 3084) Infantry; Frontier Duty 1885-1889; MG 1917; CG 1st Div, 3rd Corps, 2nd Army AEF; LTG 1918; MG USA 1918; CG East Dept Gov Is 1919-1925 MG.

Devore Daniel Bradford, (W.P. 1885-No.

3086) Infantry; AdC Gen Stanley 1891-1892; Phln; MoroX 1903-1904; BG 1917; CG 167th Inf Brig AEF; Retired 1922.

Buck Beaumont Bonaparte, (W.P. 1885-No. 3087) Infantry; Frontier Duty 1885-1889; BG 1917; CG 2nd Inf Brig 1st Div AEF; MG 1918; Retired 1924.

Martin William Franklin, (W.P. 1885-No. 3094) Infantry; Frontier Duty 1888-1891; Cuba 1899; BG 1917; 87th Div AEF; Retired 1927.

Lawton Edward Percival, (W.P. 1885-No. 3096) Infantry; Frontier Duty 1885-1888; Apache Wars 1886; Retired disabled 1908

Newcomer Henry Clay, (W.P. 1886-No. 3097) Corps of Engineers; Asst Dir CWS 1918-1919; BG 1918; Retired 1925.

Patrick Mason Mathews, (W.P. 1886-No. 3098) Corps of Engineers; MG 1918; AEF dir Constr 1917-1918; Ch of AS 1918-1919; MG Ch of AS USA 1921-1927; Retired 1927.

Rees Thomas Henry, (W.P. 1886-No. 3100) Corps of Engineers; BG 1917; AEF 1918; Retired disabled 1922.

Berry Lucien Grant, (W.P. 1886-No. 3105) Arty-ARC-FA; BG 1917; CG FA Brig 35th Div AEF; Retired 1921.

McIntyre Frank, (W.P. 1886-No. 3106) BG Ch BIA 1912; MG Ch BIA 1917-1929; Retired 1929.

McMahon John Eugene, (W.P. 1886-No. 3107) Arty-ARC-FA; AdC Gen McCook 1891-1895; PR 1898-1899; Phln; MG 1917; CG Div AEF; Retired disabled 1919.

Darrow Walter Nicholas Paine, (W.P. 1886-No. 3108) Arty; BG Ch of Engineers Gov's Staff 1900-1904;

Menoher Charles Thomas, (W.P. 1886-No. 3112) Arty-ARC-FA; AdC Gen Williston 1898-1899; Phlm; WDGS 1903-1907; Cuban Pac 1906-1907; MG 1917; CG 42nd Div & Corps AEF; MG Ch of AS USA 1920-1921; MG USA 1921; Retired 1926.

Walcutt Charles Carroll Jr., (W.P. 1886-No. 3123) Cavalry; Frontier Duty 1886-1891; MAJ 44th US Vol Inf 1899-1901; Phln; BG 1918 Actg CH BIA 1918-1920; Asst CH BIA 1920-1924; Retired 1925.

Pershing John Joseph, (W.P. 1886-No. 3126) Cavalry; Frontier Duty 1886-1891; Sioux Indian Wars 189-1891; PMST u of NB 1891-1895; Tac Dept USMA 1897-1898; SanC(SSC); MAJ AG USV in Phln; CO MoroX 1902-1903; MA Japan 1905-1906; BG 1906; Gov Moro Province 1909-1913 & CGPI Div 1910-1911; MG 1916; CG of PunX; Gen 1917; C in C AEF (DSM); Gen of Armies 3 Sept 1919; Thanks of Cong 29 Sept 1919; CS USA 1921-1924; Retired 13 Sept 1924; Many honors and decorations & degrees; Pres Assn of Grads 1924-1926; DSC; D-WRGH 15 July 1948.

Traub Peter Edward, (W.P. 1886-No. 3127) Cavalry; Frontier Duty 1886-1891; Sioux Indian Wars 1890-1891; MG 1918; CG 35th Div AEF(2PH); BG & Retired 1928.

Mott Thomas Bentley, (W.P. 1886-No. 3128) Arty-ARC-FA; AdC Gen Merritt 1896-1898; From 1900 to 1917 MA France Russia Belgium & Switz; Retired disabled 1914; CHQ AEF 1917-1918; MA Paris 1919-1930; BG Retired 1940; Special Asst to Secy ABMC, Paris 1946; D-Bairritz France 17 Dec 1952.

Poore Benjamin Andrew, (W.P. 1886-No. 3129) Infantry; BG 1917; CG 71st Inf Brig AEF; MG 1925; Retired 1927.

Carter Jesse McIlvaine, (W.P. 1886-No. 3133) Cavalry; Frontier Duty 1886-1890; MG 1918; Ch Mil Bu 1917-1918 & 1919-1921; MG

Retired 1930.

Baker Chauncey Brooke, (W.P. 1886-No. 3137) Inf-QMC; Frontier Duty 1886-1887; BG QMC 1917; OCS Ch Embarkation Service 1917-1918; Retired 1921.

Barnun Malvern-Hill, (W.P. 1886-No. 3138) Cavalry; Frontier Duty 1886-1891; BG CG 183rd Inf Brig AEF; MG & Retired 1927.

McRae James Henry, (W.P. 1886-No. 3144) Infantry; Frontier Duty 1886-1888; MG 1918; CG 78th Div AEF; MG 1922; Retired 1922.

Gordon Walter Henry, (W.P. 1886-No. 3148) Infantry Frontier Duty 1887-1890; MG 1918; CG 10th Bde & 6th Div AEF; MG USA 1923; Retired 1923.

Johnson Arthur, (W.P. 1886-No. 3157) Infantry; Frontier Duty 1891-1894; BG 1918; SOS AEF; Retired 1925.

Winn Frank Long, (W.P. 1886-No. 3158) Infantry; Frontier Duty 1886-1889; Sioux Indian Wars 1890-91; AdC Gen MacArthur 1904-09; PunX; MG 1918; CG 89th Div AEF; Retired 1922.

Ballou Charles Clarenden, (W.P. 1886-No. 3159) Infantry; Frontier Duty 1885-91; Sioux Indian Wars 1990-91; MG 1917; CG 1917; CG 92nd Div & 6th Corps AEF; Retired 1926.

Duncan George Brand, (W.P. 1886-No. 3161) Infantry; Frontier Duty 1886-92; MG 1918; CG 1st Bde 1st Div 77th Div & 82nd Div AEF; CG 7th Cav 1922 to retirement 1925.

Durfee Lucius Loyd, (W.P. 1886-No. 3163) Infantry; Frontier Duty 1886-93; Sioux Indian Wars 1890-91; BG 1918; Retired disabled 1920.

Penn Julius Agustus Jr., (W.P. 1886-No. 3165) Infantry; Frontier Duty 1886-89; BG GHQ Brig 38th Div AEF; Retired disabled 1924.

Lewis Edward Mann, (W.P. 1886-No. 3166) Infantry; Frontier Duty 1886-92; MG CG 30th Div AEF; Retired 1927.

Wright William Mason, (W.P. Attendance 1882) LTG CG 35th Div AEF; Retired 1922.

Wheeler Charles Brewster, (W.P. 1887-No. 3177) Arty-OD; BG OD 1917; Retired 1919.

Young Edward Clinton, (W.P. 1887-No. 3178) Inf; NGIL 1890-1914 MG.

Davis Richard Pearse, (W.P.1887-No. 3179) Arty-ARC-CAC; BG 1917; CG FA Brigs AEF; MG 1927; Ret 1929.

Squier George Owen, (W.P.1887-No. 3180) Arty-SC; MG Ch SigO USA 1917-23 Ret 1923.

Hinds Ernest, (W.P.1887-No. 3181) Arty-ARC-FA; BG 1917; MG Cof Arty AEF; Ret.1928.

Jenkins John Murry, (W.P. 1887-No. 3183) Cav.; Frontier Duty 1887-89; CO 11th Cav PunX; CO 30th Inf AEF; BG & Ret 1927.

Russel Edgar, (W.P. 1887-No. 3184) Arty; BG CSO AEF; Ret dsbl 1922.

Wilkins Harry Eugene, (W.P. 1887-No. 3187) Inf-Comsy-QMC; Frontier Duty 1887-89; BG NYQM Dep 1918; Ret 1919.

Martin Charles Henry, (W.P. 1887-No. 3192) Inf; Frontier Duty 1887-93; MG CG 86th Div AEF & CG AFG; Ret 1927; Gov of Ore 1935-39.

Lochridge P. D., (W.P. 1887-No. 3194) Cav; Frontier Duty 1887-88,90-91; Cuba 1899-01; BG 1917; Supreme War Council 1918-19; Ret dsbl 1919; BG Ret 1930.

Slavens Thomas Horace, (W.P. 1887-No. 3195) Cav-QMC-Inf; Frontier Duty 1887-91; Phln(AdC Gen Mac Arthur); Base QM PunX; CO NYQM Dep 1917-18; CO INF Regts AEF 1918; BG 1923; Ret 1927.

McClure Nathaniel Fish, (W.P. 1887-No.

3196) Cav; Frontier Duty 1899-1900; BG CG 69th Bde AEF; Ret 1929.

Rivers William Cannon, (W.P. 1887-No. 3197) Cav; Frontier Duty 1887-91; Ind Wars; BG CG 5th FA Brig AEF; MG IG USA 1927-30; Ret 1930.

Weigel William, (W.P. 1887-No. 3200) Inf; Cuba 1898-99; MG CG 88th Div AEF; MG 1924; CG PIDiv & Dept 1925-27; Ret 1927.

Alexander John Hanks, (W.P. 1887-No. 3205) Cav; Frontier Duty 1887-89; Second Negro graduate of USMA.

Donaldson Thomas Quinton, (W.P. 1887-No. 3207) Cav; Frontier Duty 1887-91; Siuox Ind Wars 1890-91; Cuba 1898-99; BG 1918; IG SOS AEF; MG 1927; Ret 1928.

Hanson Thomas Grafton, (W.P. 1887-No. 3209) Inf; Frontier Duty 1887-89; BG CG 178th Brig 89th Div AEF; Ret 1919.

Hall Herman, (W.P. 1887-No. 3215) Inf; BG PI Constab 1915-17; BG CG Inf Brigs AEF; Ret 1922.

Cronin Marcus Daniel, (W.P. 1887-No. 3218) Inf; Front Dty 1887-93; COL USV in Phln; BG AEF; Ret 1926.

Dade Alexander Lucien, (W.P. 1887-No. 3219) Inf; Front Dty 1887-89; PunX; OCSO (Avation Sect) 1917-18 BG; Ret dsbl 1920.

Farnsworth Charles Stewart, (W.P. 1887-No. 3220) Inf; AdC Gen Chaffee 1898-99; PunX; NG CG 37th Div AEF; 1st Comdt Inf Sch FT Benning 1919-20; MG Ch of Inf 1920-25; Ret 1925.

Gerhardt Charles, (W.P. 1887-No. 3221) Inf; Frnt Dty 1887-94; Sioux Ind Wars 1890-91; BG SOS AEF; Ret 1927.

Dean James Theodore, (W.P. 1887-No. 3225) InfAdC Gen Brooke 1893-95; Cuba 1899; BG CG 156th Brig AEF; Ret 1928.

McAlexander Ulysses Grant, (W.P. 1887-No. 3226) Inf; Frnt Dty 1887-91; CO 38th Inf & BG 180th Brig AEF; BG 1920; Ret dsbl 1924.

Wittenmyer Edmond, (W.P. 1887-No. 3228) Inf; Cuban Pac 1906-09; Cuba 1914-17; BG CG 153rd Brig, MG CG 7th Div AEF; MG ret 1930.

Evans Frederic Dahl, (W.P. 1887-No. 3229) Inf; Frnt Dty 1887-89; BG CG Inf Brigs AEF; Ret 1924.

Lenihan Michael Joseph, (W.P 1887-No. 3230) Inf; Frnt Dty 1887-89; BG CG Brig 42nd & 77th Divs AEF; Ret 1924.

Hersey Mark Leslie, (W.P. 1887-No. 3232) Inf; Frnt Dty 1887-91; MG CG 4th Div AEF; Ret 1924.

Albright Frank Herman, (W.P. 1887-No. 3237) Inf; Frnt Dty 1887-91; BG Inf Brig AEF; Ret 1919.

Jervy Henry, (W.P. 1888-No. 3238) CE; BG 1917; Dir Opns WDGS 1917-21; MG 1918; Ret 1922.

McKinstry Charles Hedges, (W.P. 1888-No. 3239) CE; BG 1917; CG FA Brig & Dir RR's & Roads AEF; Ret 1919.

Judson William Voorhees, (W.P. 1888-No. 3240) CE; Ch Mil Msn to Russia 1917-18; BG 1917; Ret dsbl 1922.

Burr George Washington, (W.P. 1888-No. 3241) Arty; MG Dir Pur Sto & WDGS 19-20; MG psth.

Hayden John Louis, (W.P. 1888-No. 3243) Arty; Sioux Ind Wars 1890-91; BG CG 56th FA Brig AEF; Ret 1922.

Winn John Sheridan, (W.P. 1888-No. 3246) Cav; Frnt Dty 1888-92; Cuba 1899-02; BG CG Inf Brigs AEF; Ret 1922.

March Peyton Conway, (W.P. 1888-No. 3247) Arty; AdC Gen MacArthur 1899; MA Jap Army 1904; BG MG 1917; CG Arty in AEF 1917; Gen CS USA 1918-21; Ret 1921.

McAndrew James William, (W.P. 1888-No. 3249) Inf; Frnt Dty 1888-92; Sioux Ind Wars 1890-91; BG 1917; CS GHQ AEF 1918-19; MG 1920; Cmdt AWC 1919-20.

Hedekin Charles Aloysius, (W.P. 1888-No. 3251) Cav; Frnt Dty 1888-95; Cuba 1898; Phln; WDGS 1918; BG 1918; Ret 1920.

Koester Francis John, (W.P. 1888-No. 3252) Cav; Frnt Dty 1888-93; BG 1917; CG 24th Arty Brig Cp Taylor Ky 1919; Ret 1927.

Hartman John Daniel Leinbach, (W.P. 1888-No. 3257) Cav; Frnt Dty 1888-95; Sioux Ind Wars 1890-91; BG CG TX Tng Cen 1918; Ret 1929.

Howze Robert Lee, (W.P. 1888-No. 3260) Cav; Frnt Dty 1888-91; Sioux Ind Wars 1890-91; Cmdt Cadets USMA 1905-09; PunX; MGCG 38th Div AEF & 3rd Div AFG; MG 1922.

Chrisman Edward Roberts, (W.P. 1888-No. 3261) Inf; Frnt Dty 1888-90; Sioux Ind Wars 1890-91; BG CG Tact Brig CZ 1918; Ret 1921.

Preston Guy Henry, (W.P. 1888-No. 3262) Cav; Frnt Dty 1888-91; Soiux Ind Wars 1890-91; MAJ USV Inf in Phln; BG CG Brig AEF; Ret 1928.

Sample William Roderick, (W.P. 1888-No. 3266) Inf; Frnt Dty 1888-91; BG 1917; CG Adv Sect SOS AEF; Ret 1930 BG.

Anderson Edward, (W.P. 1888-No. 3267) Cav; Frnt Dty 1888-95; Sioux Ind Wars 1890-91; BG 1918; CG Units & Camps in US 1917-20; Ret 1923.

Harris Peter Charles, (W.P. 1888-No. 3268) Inf; Frnt Dty 1888-93; MG TAG 1918-22; Ret 1922.

McFarland Munroe, (W.P. 1888-No. 3269) Inf; Frnt Dty 1888-93; BG CG 162nd Brig 81st Div AEF; Ret 1922.

Hart William Horace, (W.P. 1888-No. 3270) Inf-Cav-QMC; Frnt Dty 1888-94,1896-98; Cuba 1898-1900; MG QMC USA 1922-26.

Dashiell William Robert, (W.P. 1888-No. 3275) Inf; Frnt Dty 1888-91; Sioux Ind Wars 1890-91; BG CG 11th Inf Brig AEF & AFG; Ret 1924.

Helmick Eli Alva, (W.P. 1888-No. 3276) Inf; Frnt Dty 1888-92; Cuba 1899-1901; MG CG 8th Div AEF; CG Base Sec Brest 1918-19; MG IG USA 1921-27; Ret 1927.

Littebrant William Thomas, (W.P. 1888-No. 3278) Inf-Cav; Frnt Dty 1888-92; BG 1918; CG 19th FA Brig Ft. Sill 1918-19; BG psth 1930.

Winslow Eben Eveleth, (W.P. 1889-No. 3282) CE; BG 1917; Asst to C of Engrs 1914-18; Ret disbl 1922.

Flagler Clement A. Finley, (W.P. 1889-No. 3284) CE; BG CG FA Brig AEF; AFG; MG 1918.

Harts William Wright, (W.P. 1889-No. 3286) CE; Aide to Pres Wilson 1913-17; BG 1917; CG Prov Brig w 5th British Army & CG Dist Paris AEF 1918-19; CS AFG 1919-20; BG 1924; CG Arty Def CZ 1924-26; Ret 1930.

Kenley William Lacy, (W.P. 1889-No. 3292) Arty; BG 1917; C of AS AEF 1917-18; MG 1918; Ret 1919.

Haan William George, (W.P. 1889-No. 3293) Arty; MG CG 32nd Div AEF; Ret 1922.

Bethel Walter Augustus, (W.P. 1889-No. 3295) Arty; BG JAG AEF 1917-20; MG JAG USA 1923-24; Ret dsbld 1924.

McGlachlin Edward Fenton Jr., (W.P. 1889-No. 3301) Arty; BG 1917; Corps & Army Cof Arty AEF; MG 1918; CG 1st Div AFG; Cmdt AWC 1921-23; MG USA 1922; Ret 1923.

Campbell Archibald, (W.P. 1889-No. 3302) Arty; CO Ft Screven Ga 1916-19; BG Asst

AG WD 1929; Ret 1929.

Hains John Power, (W.P. 1889-No. 3303) Arty; CO FA Regts & Brig AEF; Ret 1929. Last surviving member of his class and oldest living graduate USMA 15 jul 63 to 25 Mar 64.

Lassiter William, (W.P. 1889-No. 3304) Arty; BG 1917; CG FA Brig, ChArty 1st & 4th Corps & and Army AEF; CG 1932; Div AFG; MG 1918; Ret 1931.

Irwin George LeRoy, (W.P. 1889-No. 3305) Arty; BG CG 57th FA Brig AEF; MG 1928; Cmdt FA Sch 1923-28.

Hagadorn Charles Baldwin, (W.P. 1889-No. 3306) Inf; Wrote USMA texts; CZ 1916-18.

Rhodes Charles Dudley, (W.P. 1889-No. 3307) Cav; Frnt Dty 1889-93; Sioux Ind Wars 1890-91; BG CG FA Brig 82nd Div & MG CG 42nd & 34th Divs AEF; MG 1928; Ret 1929.

Wood Winthrop Samuel, (W.P. 1889-No. 3312) Cav-QMC; Frnt Dty 1889-93; SOS AEF; Ret BG Asst QMC.

Crawford Charles, (W.P. 1889-No. 3322) Inf; Frnt Dty 1889-96; BG CG Inf Brig & SOS AEF; Ret dsbl 1919.

Graves William Sydney, (W.P. 1889-No. 3323) Inf; Frnt Dty 1889-97; BG 1917; MG CG AEF Siberia; Ret 1928.

Webster Frank Daniel, (W.P. 1889-No. 3324) Inf; AdC Gen Wheaton in Phln; BG CG 8th Brig 4th Div AEF May-Nov 1918; Ret dsbld 1918.

Leitch Joseph Dugald, (W.P. 1889-No. 3325) Inf; Frnt Dty 1889-98; MG CS AEF Siberia; BG 1926 MG 1927; Ret 1928.

Young Charles, (W.P. 1889-No. 3330) Cav-Inf-Cav; Frnt Dty 1889-94; MAJ Ohio Colored Inf 1898-94; Haiti 1904-07; Liberia 1912-15; Ret dsbld 1917; Third Negro gradyate of USMA.

Jadwin Edgar, (W.P. 1890-No. 3331) CE; BG Const Projects AEF; BG 1924; MG C of Engrs USA 1926-29; Ret 1929.

Keller Charles, (W.P. 1890-No. 3332) CE; BG 1918; War Industries Bd 1917-18; Ret 1923.

Deakyne Herbert, (W.P. 1890-No. 3333) CE; CO Engr Regts AEF; BG 1918; BG asst Ch Engrs 1926; Ret 1931.

Ruggles Colden I'Hommedieu, (W.P. 1890-No. 3335) Arty-OD; Built Aberdeen PG 1918; BG Asst Ch Ord 1923-30; Ret 1930.

Todd Henry Davis Jr., (W.P. 1890-No. 3337) Arty; BG CG 58th FA AEF; MG 1927.

Heam Clint Calvin, (W.P. 1890-No. 3344) Arty; BG CG 153rd FA Brig 78th Div AEF; Ret dsbld 1927.

Davis William Church, (W.P 1890-No. 3345) Arty; BG CG FA Brigs AEF; Ret 1921.

Lindsay James Robert, (W.P. 1890-No. 3346) Inf; BG CG 97th Div Camp Cody NM 1918-19; Ret 1920.

Marshall Francis Cutler, (W.P. 1890-No. 3349) Cav; With 8th Cav in Sioux Ind Wars 1890-91; BG CG 2nd Inf Brig 1st Div AEF; D-(Air Cr) near San Diego 7 Dec 1922; BG psth.

Maulden Frank Gratin, (W.P. 1890-No. 3350) Arty; Instr USMA 1896-1900; BG 1917; Ret 1917.

Ketcham Daniel Warren, (W.P. 1890-No. 3351) Arty; BG 1918; AEF 1918-19; Ret 1919.

Davis Milton Fennimore, (W.P. 1890-No. 3352) Cav; Phln Secy Inf & Cav Sch 1903-07; Ret dsbld 1909; Col ret BG AC Res 1921.

Mc Nair William Sharp, (W.P. 1890-No. 3353) Arty; MG CG FA Brigs & CH Arty Corps & Army AEF; CS Panama Dept 1020-22; BG 1930; Ret 1932 MG.

Snow William Josiah, (W.P. 1890-No. 3354)

Arty; Org FA Assn & Founded FA Journal 1910; BG 1917; First Ch FA USA 1918-27; MG 1918; Ret dsbld 1927.

Gatley George Grant, (W.P. 1890-No. 3355) Arty; BG CG FA Brig AEF.

Sladen Fred Winchester, (W.P. 1890-No. 3357) Inf; Ind Wars; AdC Gen Otis 1898-1900; BG CG 5th Inf Brig 3rd Div AEF; MG 1924; Ret 1931.

Ryan James Augustin, (W.P. 1890-No. 3358) Cav; BG 1917; Ret 1919.

Bandholtz Harry Hill, (W.P. 1890-No. 3359) Inf; BG CS 27th Div, CG 58th Inf Brig & PMG AEF; MG & Ret dsbld 1923.

Caldwell Frank Merrill, (W.P. 1890-No. 3361) Cav; Cuba 1899; BG CG 75th Inf Brig AEF; AFG; BG 1925; Ret 1930.

Leamard Henry Grant, (W.P. 1890-No. 3362) Inf; BG 1918; AGO 1917-20; Ret 1930.

Hornbrook James Joseph, (W.P. 1890-No. 3363) Cav; PunX; BG 1918; Ret 1929.

Jones Samuel Goode Jr., (W.P. 1890-No. 3365) Cav; Dty with Indians 1891-93; SOS AEF; AFG; Ret1929; BG ret 1940.

Murray Peter, (W.P. 1890-No. 3370) Inf; BG CG 3rd Brig 2nd Div AEF; WDGS 1918-20; Ret 1924; BG ret 1930.

Wolf Paul Alexander, (W.P. 1890-No. 3371) Inf; BG CG 66th Inf Brig 33rd Div AEF; BG 1925; Ret dsbld 1932; MG ret 1942.

Moore George Davis, (W.P. 1890-No. 3373) Inf; BG CG 169th Brig AEF; Ret 1931.

Symmonds Charles Jacobs, (W.P. 1890-No. 3377) Inf-Cav; Cuba 1899; (sick yellow fever); SOS AEF; BG 1923.Ret 1930.

Butts Edmond Luther, (W.P. 1890-No. 3383) Inf; Cuban Occupation 1898-99; CO 7th Inf AEF; Author Butts Manual; Ret 1932; BG ret 1940.

Caldwell Vernon Avondale, (W.P. 1890-No. 3384) Inf; BG CG Inf Brigs AEF; Ret 1919; BG ret 1930.

McIndoe James Francis, (W.P. 1891-No. 3388) CE; SOS AEF & CO 2nd Engrs in combat; BG 1918.

Horney Odus Creamer, (W.P. 1891-No. 3390) Inf; Resd LTC; BG 1918; Reapt LTC 1919; Ret 1930.

Hero Andrew Jr., (W.P. 1891-No. 3392) Arty; Cuba 1899; BG 1917; CG FA Brig 79th Div AEF; MG Cof CAC 1926-30; Ret 1930.

Horn Tiemann Newell, (W.P. 1891-No. 3393) Cav-Arty; BG 1917; CG FA Brig 7th Div AEF; BG psth.

Anderson Edward D., (W.P. 1891-No. 3394) Cav; SanC (wded); MAJ USV Inf in Phln; WDGS 1917-19; BG 1918; Ret 1921.

Winans Edwin Baruch, (W.P. 1891-No. 3403) Cav; BG 1918; CG 64th Inf Brig AEF; AFG; BG 1922; MG 1927; Ret 1933.

Howard Harold Palmer, (W.P. 1891-No. 3407) Cav; AdC Gen Young in Phln; BG 1918; Ret 1920.

Bennet John Bradbury, (W.P. 1891-No. 3412) Inf; BG 1918; CO 11th Inf AEF; Ret 1925.

Glasgow William Jefferson, (W.P. 1891-No. 3414) Cav; Cuban Occupation 1899-1901; BG CG 20th INf Brig Camp Funston 1918-19; BG & ret dsbld 1927; Oldest living graduate USMA 25 Mar 1964 to 4 Aug 1967

Jarvis Melville Shinn, (W.P. 1891-No. 3416) Inf; Cuban Occupation 1898-1900; Organized 17th Inf Brig US 1917-18; Ret 1932.

Heavy John William, (W.P. 1891-No. 3417) Inf; MB 1917-22; BG 1918; Ret 1931.

Upton LaRoy Sunderland, (W.P. 1891-No. 3422) Inf; BG 1918; CO 9th Inf & CG 57th Bde AEF; BG 1823.

Smith Harry Alexander, (W.P. 1891-No. 3423)

Inf; MAJ KS Vols 1898; Phln; VCX; Asst Cmdt GS Sch Langres 1918; BG 1922; Cmdt GSS Ft L Kan 1923-25; MG 1926.

Saffarrans George Coolidge, (W.P. 1891-No. 3425) Inf; BG 1918; Ret dsbld 1919.

Pierce Palmer Eddy, (W.P. 1891-No. 3426) Inf; BG 1917 WDGS & CG 54th Bde AEF; Ret 1920.

Whal Lutz, (W.P. 1891-No. 3427) Inf; WDGS & BG 1918; CG 14th Bde AEF; MG TAG 1927-28.

Jackson William Payne, (W.P. 1891-No. 3428) Inf; BG 1918; CG 74th Bde 37th Div AEF; Ret 1932; MG ret 1942.

Hines John Leonard, (W.P. 1191-No. 3432) Inf; BG 1918; CO Regt & CG Brig Div & Corps AEF; MG 1920; DCS USA 1922-24; Gen CS USA 1924-26; Ret 1932 MG; Gen ret 1940.

Whitman Walter Monteith, (W.P. 1891-No. 3434) Cav; CO 325th Inf 163rd Brig 82nd Div AEF; Ret 1930; BG ret 1940.

Bradley John Jewsbury, (W.P. 1891-No. 3437) Inf; BG 1918; CG Inf Brig 82nd Div AEF; Ret dsbld 1927.

Williams Herbert Owen, (W.P. 1891-No. 3440) Inf; BG 1918; Ret 1930.

Ely Hanson Edward, (W.P. 1891-No. 3447) Inf; MG 1918; CO 28th Inf & CG Brig & 5th Div AEF; BG 1020; MG 1923; Cmdt CGS 1921-23 & AWC 1923-27; CG 2CA 1927-31; Ret 1931.

Blakley George, (W.P. 1892-No. 3453) Arty; BG CG 38th Arty Brig CAC AEF; Ret 1924.

Dickson Tracy Campbell, (W.P. 1892-No. 3455) Arty; BG OD 1918; Ret 1932.

Coe Frank Winston, (W.P. 1892-No. 3457) Arty; BG 1917; CG RR Arty Reserve 1st Army AEF; MG Ch/CAC USA 1918-26; Ret 1926.

Smith William Ruthven, (W.P. 1892-No. 3459) Arty; MG CG 36th Div AEF; BG 1920; MG 1924; Ret 1932.

Whitney Henry Howard, (W.P. 1892-No. 3460) Arty; BG 1917; CS Dist Paris 1918-19; AEF; Ret 1920.

Jamieson Charles Clark, (W.P. 1892-No. 3463) Inf; BG OD; BG ret 1930.

Shipton James Ancil, (W.P. 1892-No. 3464) Arty; BG CG 58th FA Brig & Ch AAA Ser AEF; Ret 1920.

Barnhardt George Columbus, (W.P. 1892-No. 3466) CO 28th Inf & BG CG Inf Brigs AEF; AFG; BG 1927; CG 1922 Brig Sch Bks 1927-30.

Palmer John McAuley, (W.P. 1892-No. 3468) Inf; CG 58th Inf Brig AEF; AdC Gen Pershing 1921-23; BG 1922; Ret dsbl 1926.

Summerall Charles Pelet, (W.P. 1892-No. 3469) MG CG FA Brigs 1st Div 5th & 9th Corps AEF; MG 1920; CS USA 1926-30; Gen 1929; Ret 1931.

Reeves James Haynes, (W.P. 1892-No. 3471) Cav; AdC Gen Joseph Wheeler; AdC Gen Wilson; MA China 1900-02; 1907-12; CO 353rd Inf AEF; BG 1927; CG 1921; Ret 1934.

Lindsey Julian Robert, (W.P. 1892-No. 3481) Cav; BG CG 164th Brig 82nd Div AEF; BG 1932; Ret 1934.

Hickok Howard Russell, (W.P. 1892-No. 3484) Cav; BG 1918; CS 5th Div AEF 1918; CG 19th Inf Brig Camp Funston 1918-19; BG psth.

Stokes Marcus Butler, (W.P. 1892-No. 3496) Inf; CO 311th Inf 78th Div AEF; Ret 1931.

Woodward John Edwin, (W.P. 1892-No. 3500) Inf; CO Depot Units US 1917-19; BG 1918; Ret dsbld 1934.

Mearns Robert Walter, (W.P. 1892-No. 3510) Inf; BG 1918; CG Tng Units US 1917-19; Ret

dsbld 1922; BG ret 1930.

Kutz Charles Willauer, (W.P. 1893-No. 3513) CE; CO Engr Regt AEF; BG 1918; Ret 1929.

Walker Meriwether Lewis, (W.P. 1893-No. 3514) CE; BG 1918; Dir MTC AEF; Ret 1933.

Cruikshank William Mackey, (W.P. 1893-No. 3517) Arty; CO FA Regt & BG CG 3rd Div & Ch of Arty 4th Corps AEF; BG 1925 Comdt FA Sch 1930-34; Ret 1934.

Heiner Gordon Heiner, (W.P. 1893-No. 3518) Arty; BG CG 155th FA Brig AEF; Ret 1929.

McManus George Henry, (W.P. 1893-No. 3520) Arty; Phln; Hoboken Port 1917-19; Ret 1931 BG.

Andrews Lincoln Clark, (W.P. 1893-No. 3524) Cav; MAJ USV in Phln; BG 1918; GHQ AEF & author texts on Training & Leadership; Ret 1929.

Schindel Samuel John Bayard, (W,P. 1892-No. 3526) Arty; BG CG 21st Brig US 1918; BG psth.

Smedberg William Renwick Jr., (W.P. 1893-No. 3527) Cav; AdC Gen Wood in SanC; AdC gen Young in Phln; BG 1918; CO Regt & Brig 77th Div AEF; AFG; Ret 1935.

Laubach Howard Lewis, (W.P. 1893-No. 3528) Inf; BG 1918; CG 14th Div US 1918; Ret 1931.

Babcock Walter Crosby, (W.P. 1893-No. 3536) Cav; CO 310th AEF; Ret 1921; BG ORC 1921.

Smith Mathew Charles, (W.P. 1893-No. 3541) Cav; BG CG 95th Div Camp Sherman 1918; WDGS 1919-24; Ret 1932.

Walker Kenzie Wallace, (W.P. 1893-No. 3544) Cav; Cuban Pac 1906-08; MG 1926; Ret 1928.

Edawrds Arthur Morris, (W.P. 1893-No. 3545) Inf; Phln; Ret dsbld 1911; Merit Medal Air Obsr WW2; Congress appd his Flag data for Natl distribution 1937 & 1949; Poet, Song Writer, Author.

Jamerson George Hairston, (W.P. 1893-No. 3556) Inf; BG 1918; CG 159th Brig 80th Div AEF; Ret 1933.

Williams Clarence Charles, (W.P. 1894-No. 3566) Arty; BG 1917; MG Cof Ord USA 1918-30; Ret 1930.

Joyes John Warren, (W.P. 1894-No. 3568) Arty; BG Asst Cof ORD 1923-27; CO Springfield Armory 1929-33; Ret 1934; BG ret 1940.

Parker Francis Le Jau, (W.P. 1894-No. 3574) Cav; Obsr Rumanian & Russian Armies 1916-17; BG 1918; 86th Div AEF; US Msn Tacna-Arica 1925-26; BG Ch BIA 1929-33; BG 1933; Ret 1936.

Aultman Dwight Edward, (W.P. 1894-No. 3576) Arty; Cuba 1898-1902; AdC Gen Wheaton 1898-99; BG CG FA Brigs & Cof Arty 5th Corps AEF; BG 1921.

Hamilton Alston, (W.P. 1894-No. 3578) Cav-Arty; CO CAC Regt AEF; BG 1927; CG 11th FA Brig Sch Bks 1927-30; Ret 1935.

Malone Paul Bernard, (W.P. 1894-No. 3579) Inf; BG CG 10th Brig 5thDiv AEF 1917-18; MG 1928; CG Phil Div 1928-31; CG 4th Army 1935 to ret 1936.

Hawkins Hamilton Smith, (W.P. 1894-No. 3586) Co 69th Brig 35th Div & CS 35th Div AEF; BG 1928; CG 1st Cav Brig 1929-34; Ret 1936.

Ames Butler, (W.P. 1894-No. 3587) Inf; Resd 1894; MG MA State Gd 1917.

Cocheu Frank Sherwood, (W.P. 1894-No. 3590) Inf; CO Inf Regt & BG CG Inf Brig AEF; BG 1927; CG US Trps in AZ during Mex Rev 1919; MG 1934; Ret 1935.

Hunt Ora Elmer, (W.P. 1894-No. 3591) Inf; BG CG 6th Brig 3rd Div AEF; AFG 1919; CG 3rd Div 1919; Ret 1923.

Parker Frank, (W.P. 1894-No. 3592) Cav; CO 18th Inf, BG CG 1st Bde & 1st Div AEF; BG 1924; Ret 1936.

Rosenbaum Otho Bane, (W.P. 1894-No. 3598) Inf; BG CG Inf Brigs AEF; BG 1927; CG 1934; Ret 1935.

Estes George Hensen, (W.P. 1894-No. 3599) Inf; BG 1929; Ret dsbld 1936.

Vidmer George, (W.P. 1894-No. 3600) Inf-Cav; CO 306th Inf Div AEF; BG 1933; Ret 1935.

Edwards Oliver, (W.P. 1894-No. 3602) Inf; AdC Gen J F Smith in Phln; BG CG Machine Gun Tng Cen US 1918; Hdgrs AEF 1919; BG psth.

Welsh William Ernest, (W.P. 1894-No. 3606) Inf; BG GHQ AEF.

Stritzinger Frederick G. Jr., (W.P. 1894-No. 3607) Inf; CO Inf Regt AEF; Ret dsbld 1928.

Wells Briant Harris, (W.P. 1894-No. 3610) CS 6th & 4th Corps AEF; Cmdt TIS 1923-26; MG 1928; CG HAW Div 1930-31; Ret 1935.

Barker John William, (W.P. 1894-No. 3611) CO Inf Regt AEF; BG 1918; Ret 1920.

Whitworth Pegram, (W.P. 1894-No. 3615) AdC Gen MacArthur in SpW in PI 1898-1900; BG CG 7th Inf Brig AEF; BG 1933; Ret 1935.

Burgess Harry, (W.P. 1895-No. 3618) CE; Gov Panama CZ 1928-32; BG 1932.

Conrad Casper Hauzer Jr., (W.P. 1895-No. 3621) Cav; WDGS 1918-19; CO Adv Embarkation Sec SOS AFG 1919; BG 1928; Ret 1936.

Fleming Adrian Sebastian, (W.P. 1895-No. 3632) Arty; BG 1918; Comdt FAS 1917-18; CG 158th FA Brig 83rd Div AEF; Ret 1921.

Darrah Thomas Walter, (W.P. 1895-No. 3637) Inf; BG CG 55th Brig 28th Div AEF; AFG; BG 1931; Ret 1937.

Miles Perry Lester, (W.P.1895-No. 3639) Inf; CO 371st Inf AEF; CG 1st Div 1936-37; Ret 1937.

Nuttman Louis Meredith, (W.P. 1895-No. 3647) Inf; BG 1918; CO Inf Regt & Bde AEF; Ret 1938 BG.

Bash Louis Hermann, (W.P. 1895-No. 3663) Inf-QMC; SOS AEF; BG ASST QMC 1929; MG QMG USA 1934-36; Ret dsbld 1936.

Watson Frank Bingley, (W.P. 1895-No. 3665) Inf; BG CG Brig & Div US 1918; Ret 1934 BG.

Pearce Thomas Absalom, (W.P. 1895-No. 3667) Inf; CO 323rd Inf AEF; Ret 1934.

Tschappat William Harvey, (W.P. 1896-No. 3673) Arty; Prof Ord & Gun USMA 1912-18; BG Asst Ch Ord 1930-34; MG Ch Ord USA 1934-38; Ret 1938.

Eltinge LeRoy, (W.P. 1896-No. 3678) Cav; Phln wded; Cuban Pac 1906-07; BG GS GHQ AEF.

McNeil Clarence Henry, (W.P. 1896-No. 3679) Arty; BG CG CAC Bde AEF Ret 1922.

Tracy Joseph Powell, (W.P. 1896-No. 3680) Arty; BG 1931; Ch War Plans Div WDGS 1931-32; Comdt CAC Sch 1932-36; Ret 1938.

Hagwood Johnson, (W.P. 1896-No. 3691) Arty; BG CS SOS AEF; BG 1920; MG 1925; Ret 1936.

Drake Charles Bryant, (W.P. 1896-No. 3696) Cav; MoroX 1903-04; PunX; Org MTC 1918 & Ch to 1920- P., 1918: Ret 1922.

Saitzman Charles McKinley, (W.P. 1896-No. 3697) Cav; BG SC 1917; AS 1918; MG CSO USA 1924-28; Ret 1928.

Holbrook Lucius Roy, (W.P. 1896-No. 3703) Cav; CO 7th FA & BG CG 2nd & 54th FA Bdes AEF; BG 1925; CG 1st Div 1930-36; MG 1933; Ret dsbld 1933.

Shelten George Henry, (W.P. 1896-No. 3704) Inf; BG 1918; CS 26th Div, CO 104th Inf, CG 51st Bde 26th Div AEF; BG psth.

Lott Abraham Grant, (W.P. 1896-No. 3711) Cav; BG 1927; Cmdt Cav Sch 1929-35; Ret 1935.

Stewart Merch Bradt, (W.P. 1896-No. 3715) Inf; CS 76th Div & BG CG Inf Bde AEF; Supt USMA 1926-27; BG 1923; Ret 1927.

Lewis Frederick Worthington, (W.P. 1896-No. 3716) Inf; SanC; S & F USMA 1897-1901; PunX; AGO WD 1917-22; Ret dsbld 1923; BG ret 1940.

King Edward Leonard, (W.P. 1896-No. 3717) Cav; BG 1918; CS 28th Div & 65th Inf Bde AEF; MG 1931.

Nolan Dennis Edward, (W.P. 1896-No. 3719) Inf; BG 1918; CG Inf Bde 28th Div; MG 1925; CG 2CA 1931-36; Ret 1936.

Burt Reynolds Johnston, (W.P. 1896-No. 3723) Inf; WDGS & BG 1918; Ret dsbld 1937.

Langdon Russell Creamer, (W.P. 1896-No. 3726) CO 127th Inf 32nd Div AEF; BG ret 1940.

Whitehead Henry Charles, (W.P. 1896-No. 3733) Cav-QMC; Prussian Cav Regt 1912-14; CS AS AEF; BG Asst QMC 1930-34; Ret 1934.

Bolles Frank Crandall, (W.P. 1896-No. 3737) Inf; CO 39th Inf Div AEF; MG 1931 Ret 1936.

Connor William Durward, (W.P. 1897-No. 3742) CE;G4 GHQ, CS 32nd Div, & CG Inf Bde AEF; BG 1918; CG SOS 1919; CG Amer Fcs France 1919-20; BG 1920; CG USA Fcs China 1923-26; MG 1925; Cmdt AWC 1927-32; Ret 1938.

Cheney Sherwood Alfred, (W.P. 1897-No. 3746) CE; MA China 1921-24; Mil Aide to Pres 1925-27; BG 1933; Ret 1937.

Ferguson Harley Bascom, (W.P. 1897-No. 3748) CE; BG Miss Riv Comm 1932-39; MG ret 1939.

Abernathy Robert Swepston, (W.P. 1897-No. 3750) Arty; CO FA Bdes AEF; BG 1932; Ret 1938.

Pope Francis Horton, (W.P. 1897-No. 3752) Cav-MTC-QMC; BG AsstQMC 1927-31; Ret 1940.

Bowley Albert Jesse., (W.P. 1897-No. 3754) Arty; BG CG 2FA Brig AEF; BG 1921; MG 1931; LTG 1939; Ret 1939.

Fiske Harold Benjamin, (W.P. 1897-No. 3766) BG G5 GS GHQ AEF; BG 1922; MG 1933; Ret1933.

Conklin Arthur Stewart, (W.P. 1897-No. 3769) CO 303rd FA 76 Div AEF; BG 1935; Ret 1936.

Smither Henry Carpenter, (W.P. 1897-No. 3770) G4 SOS AEF; BG 1925; Ret 1929.

Hughes John Hendricksen, (W.P. 1897-No. 3772) IG AEF; XO Ch of Inf 1922-25; MG 1936; Ret 1940.

McCoy Frank Ross, (W.P. 1897-No. 3775) CO 165th Inf & CG 63rd Brig AEF; MG 1929; Ret 1938.

Longan Rufus Estes, (W.P. 1897-No. 3778) CS Hoboken Port 1917-18; BG 1918; Ret 1918.

Fassett William Mason, (W.P. 1897-No. 3782) CS 31st Div & CG 73rd Brig AEF; Ret 1924; BG ret 1930.

Dorey Halstead, (W.P. 1897-No. 3784) CO 4th Inf AEF; BG 1922; MG 1933; CG Haw Div Sch Bks 1934-35 Ret dsbld wds 1936.

Conley Edgar Thomas, (W.P. 1897-No. 3792) Phln; AGO WD 1917-18; MG TAG 1935-38; Ret 1938.

Carmichael Roderick Leland, (W.P. 1897-No. 3794) Inf-Arty; CO 162nd FA Brig 87th Div AEF: MG Ch Fin USA 1928-32; Ret dsbld 1932.

Bishop Harry Gore, (W.P. 1897-No. 3795) Inf-Arty; BG CG 3rd FA Brig AEF; MG C of FA 1930-34.

Moses Andrew, (W.P. 1897-No. 3797) Inf-Arty; BG CG 156th FA Brig 81st Div AEF; MG 1935; CG HAW Div 1936-37, HAW Dept 1937 to ret 1938.

Collins Edgar Thomas, (W.P. 1897-No. 3798) Inf; G5 GHQ & CS 6th Corps AEF; BG 1924; Comdt Inf Sch 1926-29; MG 1932.

Ashburn Thomas Quinn, (W.P. 1897-No. 3802) Imf-Arty; CO 324th FA & 158th FA Brig AEF; BG 1924; MG 1927; Ret 1938.

Bridges Charles Higbee, (W.P. 1897-No. 3807) Inf; G1 2nd Div & 6th Corps AEF; MG TAG 1928-33; Ret 1933.

Brown Lytle, (W.P. 1898-No. 3812) CE; BG WDGS 1918-19; BG 1918; MG C of Engr USA 1929-33; Ret 1936.

McCloskey Manus, (W.P. 1898-No. 3816) Arty; CO 12th FA & BG CG 152nd FA Brig AEF; BG 1930; Ret 1938.

Merrill Thomas Emery, (W.P. 1898-No. 3818) Arty; CO 15th FA AEF; CS Haw Div Scho Bks 1928-31; CG 11th FA Brig 1934-37; BG 1933; Ret 1939.

Nugent George Adolphus, (W.P. 1898-No. 3821) Arty; CO 342nd FA AEF; BG CG 23rd & 14th FA Brigs US 1918-19; Ret 1938 bg.

Cole William Edward, (W.P. 1898-No. 3824) Arty; BG 1918; CO FA Regt & Brig AEF; MG 1935; Ret 1938.

Conner Fox, (W.P. 1898-No. 3825) Arty; BG 1918; G3 GHQ AEF; MG 1925; CG HAW Dept1928-30; CG 1st CA 1930-38; Ret dsbld 1938.

Butner Henry Wolf, (W.P. 1898-No. 3826) Arty; BG CG 1st FA Brig AEF; BG 1930; CG FAS 1934-36; MG 1936.

Spinks Marcellus Garner, (W.P. 1898-No. 3828) Arty; Cuban Pac 1906-07; IG 2CA 1934-38; Ret dsbld 1938.

Johnson Jacob Calvin, (W.P. 1898-No. 3830) Arty; IG Cps & 1st Ar AEF; Ret 1936.

Gowen James Bartholemew, (W.P. 1898-No. 3833) Inf; CS 38th Div & GHQ AEF; CO 29th Inf 1925-27; CG 1st & 11th FA Bde, 21st Inf Bde 1929-36; BG 1929; Ret 1936.

Bricker Edwin Dyson, (W.P. 1898-No. 3835) Inf; BG Asst Ch Ord 1930-34; CO Frankford Ars 1934-39; Ret 1939; BG ret 1940.

Scott Ernest Darius, (W.P. 1898-No. 3838) Arty; CO FA Regts & Brigs AEF; AFG; BG 1931; Ret 1936.

Craig Malin, (W,P. 1898-No. 3841) Inf-Cav; CS 41st Div 3rd Ar AEF; AFG; bg 1921; Comdt Cav Sch 1921-23; MG C of Cav 1924-26; CG 9CA 1930-35; Gen CS USA 1935-39; Ret 1939.

Davis Robert Courtney, (W.P. 1898-No. 3844) Inf; BG 1918; MG TAG 1922-27; Ret 1927.

Williams Alexander Elliot, (W.P. 1898-No. 3850) Inf-QMC; BG Asst QMC 1921-25.

Henry Guy Vernor Jr., (W.P. 1898-No. 3853) Inf-Cav; Cof Cav 1930-34; BG Comdt Cav Sch 1935-39; Ret MG 1939.

Babcock Conrad Stanton, (W.P. 1898-No. 3857) Inf-Arty-Cav; CO Inf Regts AEF; CO Regt Victory Parade Paris, London, NY, DC; CS 77th Div NYC 1933-37; Ret dsbld 1937.

Enochs Berkeley, (W.P. 1898-No. 3860) Inf; CS 39th Div, G3 4 Cps AEF; Ret 1929.

Stone David Lamme, (W.P. 1898-No. 3867) Inf; G1 3rd Div & 2nd Ar AEF; AFG; BG 1936; CG 3rd Div Ft Lewis 1936-37; Ret 1940.

Woodruff James Albert, (W.P. 1899-No. 3868) CE; CO 10th Forsrtry Engrs AEF; MG 1938;

CG 1st CA 1939-40; Ret 1941.

Markham Edward Murphy, (W.P. 1899-No. 3872) CE; MG C of Engrs 1933-37; Ret 1938.

Guiney Patrick William, (W.P. 1899-No. 3883) Cav-QMC; QM 78th Div AEF; Asst QMG (Ch Cn Div) 1933-36; D-DC 17 Dec 1936 BG.

Schull Herman Walter, (W.P. 1899-No. 3886) Arty; OC Ord WD 1918-19; BG ASST Ch Ord 1934-38; Ret 1938 BG.

Carter Cliffton Carroll, (W.P. 1899-No. 3888) Arty; Prof Nat & Exp Phi USMA 1917-40; Author; Ret 1940; BG ret 1940.

Kromer Leon Benjamin, (W.P. 1899-No. 3889) Asst CS 82nd Div, 1st Cds & 1st Ar AEF; MG C of Cav 1934-38; Ret 1938.

Simonds George Shermin, (W.P. 1899-No. 3893) Inf; BG CS 2nd Cps AEF; MG 1933; Ret 1938.

Embick Stanley Dunbar, (W.P. 1899-No. 3897) Arty; Mem Amer Sec Supreme War Council 1918-19; BG 1930; MG 1936; Ret 1941.

Ansell Samuel Tilden, (W.P. 1899-No. 3898) Inf; BG 1917; Actg JAG 1917-19; Resd 1919.

Humphrey Evan Harris, (W.P. 1899-No. 3901) Cav; 1st Cav Brig 1935-36; CG 23rd Brig PS & Ft Stotesenburg PI 1936-38; CG NY POE 1938-39; Ret 1939 BG.

Trott Clement Agusta, (W.P. 1899-No. 3903) Inf; BG 1935; CG 6th Div 1939-40; 5CA 1940-41; MG ret 1948.

Moseley George Van Horn, (W.P. 1899-No. 3904) Cav; Conducted negotiations opening Rhine to world traffic; BG 1918 & 21; CG 1st Cav Div 1927-29; Mediator Mex Rev 1929; MG 1930; Dpty CS USA 1930-33; CG 3rd Ar 1936-38.

Burtt Wilson Bryant, (W.P. 1899-No. 3906) Inf; BG 1918; CS 5th Cps AEF; Ret 1938 BG; MG ret 1942.

Bundel Charles Michael, (W.P. 1899-No. 3909) Inf; BG 1934; C & GSS 1936-39; Ret 1939.

Heintzelman Stuart, (W.P. 1899-No. 3910) Cav; BG 1918; Cmdt C & GSS 1929-35; MG 1931; CG 7CA 6th Jul 1935.

Herron Charles Douglas, (W.P. 1899-No. 3916) Inf; CO FA Regt & CS 78th Div AEF; BG 1934; MG 1937; LTG 1940; Ret 1941 MG.

Rhea James Cooper, (W.P. 1899-No. 3921) CS Div AEF; AFG; BG & Ret 1927.

Kerr Frederick Blair, (W.P. 1899-No. 3925) Inf; Phln; BG NG PA 1935-39.

Foy Robert Cherry, (W.P. 1899-No. 3929) Inf-Cac; CO 332nd FA AEF; MA Rumania & Turk 1923-26; WDGS 1928-32; BG 1935, Ret dsbld 1939.

Major Duncan Kennedy Jr., (W.P. 1899-No. 3932) Inf; Phln; CRX; CS 26th Div AEF; BG 1935; WDGS 1932-36; CG 21st Inf Brig Sch Bks 1936-38; Ret 1940.

Peyton Ephriam Geoffrey, (W.P. 1899-No. 3938) Inf; CO 320th Inf 80th Div AEF; MG CG 30th DIv NGGA 1929-32; Ret dsbld 1938.

Pillsbury George Bigelow, (W.P. 1900-No. 3940) CE; 2nd Cps Engrs AEF; BG Asst Ch Engr 1930-37; Ret 1937.

Youngberg Gilbert Albin, (W.P. 1900-No. 3947) Arty-CE; Cuban Pac 1907-08; Inst USMA 1910-14; GHQ AEF; Ret dsbld 1926 LTC; BG ret 1940.

Baer Joseph Augustus, (W.P. 1900-No. 3949) Cav; IG GHQ AEF; CO 7th Cav 1933-35; CS 3rd Cav 1935-39; BG 1943.

Wood Robert Elkington, (W.P. 1900-No. 3952) Cav; BG NA 1918; Actg QMC USA 1918-19; BG ret 1930.

Morris Willis Virlin, (W.P. 1900-No. 3953) Cav; IG AEF Siberia.

Grant Walter Schuyler, (W.P. 1900-No. 3957) Cav; captured insurrecto BG Cabrera 1901; DCS 1st Ar & CS 1st Cps AEF; BG 1936; MG 1938; CG Phil Dept 1939-40; CG 3rd Ca 1940-41; Ret 1942

Kopkins Jay Paul, (W.P. 1900-No. 3959) Arty; Ch AA Ser AEF; G3 Sec Hq 6CA 1924-28; Ret 1930; BG ret 1940.

Wesson Charles Macom, (W.P. 1900-No. 3960) Cav; MG Ch Ord USA 1938-42; Ret 1942; AD to dsbld 1945.

Birnie Upton Jr. (W.P. 1900-No. 3962) Arty; MG C of FA USA 1934-38; Ret 1938.

Sunderland Archibald Henry, (W.P. 1900-No. 3963) Arty; AEF BG 1918; CO CAC Tng Cen 1918-19; MG CAC 1036-40; Ret 1940.

Deems Clarence Jr., (W.P. 1900-No. 3964) Arty; CO 321st FA AEF; Inst C & GSS 1921-25; Ret dsbld 1929; BG ret 1940.

Gleaves Samuel Reid, (W.P. 1900-No. 3977) Cav; G3 42nd Div & G3 Sec GHQ AEF; BG psth 1941.

McIntyre Augustine, (W.P. 1900-No. 3991) Cav-Arty; CG 63rd FA Brig AEF; Cmdt FAS 1936-40; Ret 1940 BG.

Peek Ernest Dichmann, (W.P. 1901-No. 3997) CE; CO 21st Engrs AEF; BG 1937; MG 1941; Ret dsbld 1942.

Spalding George Redfield, (W.P. 1901-No. 3999) CE; Ch Engr V Corps, 1st & 3rd Ar AEF; BG 1936; Ret dsbld 1938.

Jewett Henry Clay, (W.P. 1901-No. 4002) CE; CO 182nd Inf Brig & CS 91st Div AEF; BG psth.

Browning William Stacy, (W.P. 1901-No. 4006) ARC-FA; Mem Supreme War Council 1918-19; Ret dsbld 1939; BG ret 1941.

Smith Walter Driscoll, (W.P. 1901-No. 4012) Cav; GHQ AEF; WDGS 1919-20; Ret BG 39th AD 1941 to ret dsbld 1945.

Ennis William Peirce, (W.P. 1901-No. 4013) ARC-FA; CG 13th FA Brig 1918; Ret dsbld 1941 BG.

Lahm Frank Purdy, (W.P. 1901-No. 4016) Cav; Pioneer Army Avn; Qualified by Wilbur Wright 26 Oct 1909 as one of the two first Military Airplane Pilots; CO AS 2AR AEF; BG Asst Ch AC 1926-30; MAA Paris 1931-35; AirO 1st AR 1936-41; Ret 1941 BG.

Cox Creed Fulton, (W.P. 1901-No. 4022) Cav; CO FA Regt & Brig AEF; BG Ch BIA 1933-37; Ret 1937.

Beck Robert McCandlass, (W.P. 1901-No. 4023) Cav; CS 32nd Div AEF; Inst CGSS 1926-30; BG 1936; MG 1938; Ret 1939 MG.

Currie Dennis Hadley, (W.P. 1901-No. 4024) ARC-FA; BG Cmdt FA Sch 1918-19; Ret dsbld 1922.

Browne Beverlt Fielding, (W.P. 1901-No. 4025) ARC-FA; BG 1918; CG 166th FA Bde & CG 1st Cps Arty AEF; Ret 1928; BG ret 1930.

Shinkle Edward Marsh, (W.P. 1901-No. 4027) ARC-CAC-OD; OCO DC & AEF 1917-18; CO Aberdeen PG 1929-34; BG Asst Ch Ord 1934-38; Ret 1942 BG.

DeArmond Edward Harrison, (W.P. 1901-No. 4040) ARC-FA; CS 32nd Div & Asst Ch Arty AEF; BG 1918; OCh FA 1924-28; Arty Off 2nd Ar 1941-42; Ret 1942 BG.

Haskell William Nawfew, (W.P. 1901-No. 4059) Cav; MG CG NGNY 1926-41; Ret NGNY 1943 LTC.

Hannum Warren Thomas, (W.P. 1902-No. 4069) CE; Col 308th Engrs & GS GHQ AEF; Ret 1942 BG.

Stewart Gilbert Henry, (W.P. 1902-No. 4075) Inf; CO Springfield Armory 1938-42; BG 1940; Ret 1942.

Crissy Myron Sidney, (W.P. 1902-No. 4091) ARC-CAC; Designed first bombs dropped from planes in US Army; Ret dsbld 1934.

Wilson Walter King, (W.P. 1902-No. 4094) ARC-CAC; BG 1937; MG 1941; CG 3rd CPS & Secs WDC 1940-42; Ret dsbld 1944 MG.

McCain William Alexander, (W.P. 1902-No. 4111) Cav-QMC; Dir AIC 1930-34; CO Phil QM Dep 1934-42; BG 1940; Ret 1942.

Herr John Knowles, (W.P. 1902-No. 4112) Cav; MG Ch Cav 1938-42; Ret 1942.

MacArthur Douglas, (W.P. 1903-No. 4122) CE; VCX; BG 1918; CS, Bde CG & CG 42nd Div AEF; Supt USMA 1919-22; MG 1925; CG PI Dept 1928-30; Gen CS USA 1930-35; Field Marshal PA 1936; Ret 1937 Gen; AD 1941; CG US Fcs FE, Supreme Cmdr SW Pac & PAC 1941-45; Gen of Army 1944; Recd surrender Jap 1945; Recd Thanks of US Senate & US House Reps; Mil Gov, CinC FEC & SCAP Jap 1945-51; Restore Act List & exempted from ret for age 48; Many honors, degrees, decorations; Supreme Commander UN Fcs Kor 1950-51.

Tyler Max Clayton, (W.P. 1903-No. 4125) CE; BG Asst Ch Engrs 1936-39; Ret 1944 MG.

Grant Ulysses S. III, (W.P. 1903-No. 4127) CE; GS Supreme War Council 1917-19; Peace Conference 1918-19; Ret dsbld 1943 MG.

Moore Richard Curtis, (W.P. 1903-No. 4133) CE; CO 318th Engrs AEF; MG 1940; Ret 1944 MG.

Smith Frederic Harrison, (W.P. 1903-No. 4136) ARC-CAC; MG & CG 7th Cps 1941; Ret 1943.

Howze Marion William, (W.P. 1903-No. 4138) ARC-CAC; AdC MG Grant 1910-12; G3 77th Div AEF 1918; Ret 1942.

Lynch George Arthur, (W.P. 1903-No. 4142) Inf; MG C of Inf USA 1937-41; Ret 1941.

Jones James Sumner, (W.P 1904-No. 4165) Cav; BG AG ORG 1923.

Johnson Hugh Samuel, (W.P. 1904-No. 4174) Cav; BG Dpty PMG 1918; Resd 1919.

Robins Thomas Matthews, (W.P. 1904-No. 4222) CE; BG Asst Ch Engrs 1939-43; MG 1942 Ret 1945.

Dillon Theodore Harwood, (W.P. 1904-No. 4224) CE; COL CO 37th Engrs & Asst Ch TC 1942-43; Ret 1949 BG AUS.

McNair Lesley James *, (W.P. 1904-No. 4225) ARC-FA; BG GS GHQ AEF; BG GS AGF 1942-44; Wded Tunisia 1943; Kld St Lo 25 July 1944 observing front line units, LTC; GEN psth 1954.

Fenton Chauncey Lee, (W.P. 1904-No. 4229) ARC-CAC; AD to ret dsbld 1946; BG ret 1948.

Allin George R., (W.P. 1904-No. 4231) ARC-FA; BG ExO ChFA 1918; BG 1940; Comdt FA Sch 1941; Ret 1942.

Glassford Pelham Davis, (W.P. 1904-No. 4223) ARC-FA; BG CG FA Brig AEF; Ret 1931.

Bryden William, (W.P. 1904-No. 4233) ARC-FA; CG 4th Sv C 1942-44; Ret 1944 MG.

Richardson Robert Charlwood, (W.P. 1904-No. 4236) Cav; BG 1938; Comdt Cav Sch 1939-40; MG 1940; LTC 1943; CG 7th Cps 1941-43; CG Haw Dept, Mil Gov Hawaii, CG POA & Mid Pac 1943-46; Ret dsbld 1946 LTG.

Honeycutt Francis Webster, (W.P. 1904-No. 4237) ARC-FA; BG 1938; D-GA airacdt 21 Sept 1940 CG 9th Div Ft Bragg.

Benedict Jay Leland, (W.P. 1904-No. 4240) Inf; MG 1940; CG 9th SvC 1941-42; Pres WD Bd 1942 to ret dsbld 1946.

Strong George Veazey, (W.P. 1904-No. 4242) Cav-JA-INF; BG 1938; MG 1941; WD 1942-44; Ret dsbld 1944.

Blakely Charles School, (W.P. 1904-No. 4243) ARC-FA; BG CG Brig Fir Cen 1918; XO OCh FA 1922-25; Ret dsbld 1938.

Hunter George Bowditch, (W.P. 1904-No. 4245) Cav; PunX; Aviation Sec SC 1917-19; BG & ret 1942.

Stilwell Joseph Warren, (W.P. 1904-No. 4246) Inf; Inst USMA 1906-10; 1913-17; GHQ & G2 4th Cps AEF; China 1920-23; 26-29; MA China 1935-39; MG 1940; CG US Forces CBI 1942-44; Gen 1944; CG 10th AR Okinawa 1945; CG 6th AR 1946. D- October 12th 1963.

Danford Robert Melville, (W.P. 1904-No. 4247) ARC-FA; MG Ch of FA USA 1938-42; Ret 1942.

Gillmore Quincy Adams, (W.P. 1904-No. 4251) ARC-CAC; MG CG NGNJ & 44th Div 1924-32.

Crain James Kerr, (W.P. 1904-No. 4252) ARC-CAC; 42nd Div 1st Cps, 2nd Ar AEF; MG & Ret 1942.

Gruber Edmund Louis, (W.P. 1904-No. 4253) ARC-FA; D- Ft Levenworth KS 30 May 1941 BG Comdt C7 GSS; Composed FA Caisson Song at Stotesenburg PI.

Phillipson Irving Joseph, (W.P. 1904-No. 4261) Inf; MG 1941; CG 2CA 1940-42; Ret dsbld 1944 MG.

Gregory Edmund Bristol, (W.P. 1904-No. 4264) Inf QMC; MG QMC USA 1940-46; LTG 1945 Ret dsbld 1946.

Carter William Valux, (W.P. 1904-No. 4268) Cav; Secy Ser Schs 1917-18; BG AGO 1940-42; Ret 1942.

Catts Gordon Rives, (W.P. 1904-No. 4270) Inf; 319th Inf 80th Div AEF; GSC 1935-39; CO 3rd Mil Area NJ-DE 1941-42; Ret 1942.

Pratt Henry Conger, (W.P. 1904-No. 4271) Cav; BG Asst Ch AC 1930-34; MG 1940; CG Trinidad Sec CDC 1942-43; CG WDC 1944-45; Ret dsbld 1946 MG.

Cubbison Donald Cameron, (W.P. 1904-No. 4272) MG 1941; CG 1st Div 1941-42; CG FARTC Ft Bragg 1942-45; Ret dsbld 1946 MG.

Butcher Edwin, (W.P. 1904-No. 4276) Inf; AD as BG CS 3CA & 3SvC 1942-44; BG ret 1948.

Thompson Charles Fullington, (W.P. 1904-No. 4293) Inf; WDGS 1921-24; 26-29; MG 1940; CG 3 Div & 1st Cps 1941-42; CG Allied Forces Fiji IS 1942-44; CG MDW 1944-45; Ret dsbld 1945.

Reilly Henry Joseph, (W.P. 1904-No. 4294) Cav; COL CO 149th FA 42nd Div CO 83rd Inf Brig 1942; Youngest Brig Commdr in US Army WWI; Ret 1948 BG.

Brant Gerald Clark, (W.P. 1904-No. 4316) Cav; AS US 1917-19; WgCdr HawDept1930-34; Comdt AF Schs 1939-40; CG New Findl Base 1941-43; CG Tng Cmd1943-44; Ret dsbld 1944 MG.

Wright Clement Hale, (W.P. 1904-No. 4318) Inf; Ret 1942 Col; AD to Hq 2SvC; BG NYNG & ret 1949.

Swift Innis Palmer, (W.P. 1904-No. 4329) Cav; ACS 86th Div AEF; BG CG 2nd Cav Brig 1939-41; MG 1941; CG 1st Cav Div T-AS 1941-44; CG TF recapture Admiralty Is 1944; CG 1st Cps 6th Ar T-S & Jap 1944-45; Ret dsbld 1946 MG.

Fulton Walter Scott, (W.P. 1904-No. 4332) Inf; AD BG CG Ft Benning 1942-44; BG ret 1948.

Wilby Francis Bowditch, (W.P. 1905-No. 4341) CE; BG 1940; MG 1941; Supt USMA 1942-45; Ret dsbld 1946 MG.

Ridley Clarence Self, (W.P. 1905-No. 4342) CE; BG 1938; MG 1941; Ch Mil Msn Iran 1942-46; Ret 1947 MG.

Hodges John Neal, (W.P. 1905-No. 4351) CE; CO 6th Div Engrs AEF; Ret 1944 BG.

Case Rolland Webster, (W.P. 1905-No. 4354) Inf; BG 1940; CG APG 1941-42; Ret 1942 COL; AD to ret dsbld 1944.

Ramsey Norman Foster, (W.P. 1905-No. 4358) Inf; Ret 1944 COL; AD CG Springfield Armory to 1945; BG ret 1948.

Osborne Thomas Dewey, (W.P. 1905-No. 4361) ARC—FA; CO Brig Fir Cen 1918 COL; Ret dsbld 1940.

Lewis Robert Henry, (W.P. 1905-No. 4390) ARC-FA; BG 1940; MG 1942; CG Sector WDC 1943-46; Ret 1946; MG ret 1948.

Carter Arthur Hazelton, (W.P. 1905-No. 4392) ARC-FA; AUS 1941-46; MG Hq ASF; Ret 1948 MG.

Talbot Ralph Jr., (W.P. 1905-No. 4397) Cav; BG 1940; CG Trinidad Base Cmd 1941-42; CG Utah ASF Dept 1942-45; Ret dsbld 1946 BG.

Manley Frederick Willis, (W.P. 1905-No. 4400) MA Spain 1926-30; Ret 1942 COL; AD to 1943, BG BG CP Rucker AL; BG ret 1948.

Lane Arthur Willis, (W.P. 1905-No. 4401) Inf; BG 1940; Ret 1945 COL; BG ret 1948.

Prosser Walter Evans, (W.P. 1905-No. 4402) ARC-FA; CO 350th FA 92nd Div US & AEF OcSO 1923-34, 26-30; SO 8th CA 1930-37; MG 1941; CZ 1940-42; CG Sig Tng Cen 1942-43; Ret dsbld 1945 MG.

Burgin Henry Tacitius, (W.P. 1905-No. 4403) ARC—CAC; BG 1938; MG 1940 CG Haw Arty Cmd 1942-44; CG Cen Pac Base Cmd 1944-45; Ret dsbld 1946.

Lentz Bernard, (W.P. 1905-No. 4407) Inf; Ret 1942 COL; AD to 1946 Cmdt Tng Schs Ft Slocum; Devised cadence sys of drill.

Corbin Clifford Lee, (W.P.1905-No. 4410) ARC; MA Chile 1915-17; BG Asst QMC 1940-44; MG 1942; Dir Procurement OQMG 1942-46; Ret dsbld 1946 MG.

Miles Sherman, (W.P. 1905-No. 4425) Cav; MA Balkins 1912-14; Obsr Russian Ar 1914-16; Obsr 1st Corps AEF; MA Turkey 1922-25; WDGS 1934-38; BG WD 1940-42; MG 1942; CG 1st SvC 1942-46; Ret dsbld 1946 MG.

Gullion Allen Wyant, (W.P. 1905-No. 4430) Inf; MG JAG USA 1937-41; PMG USA 1941-44; Ret dsbld 1944 MG.

Kunzig Louis Albert, (W.P. 1905-No. 4431) Inf; CG Cp Blanding FL 1941 to ret dsbld 1944 BG.

Barzynski Joseph Edward, (W.P. 1905-No. 4437) Inf-QMC; QM 32nd Div AEF & AFG; BG Asst QMG 1940-44; Ret dsbld 1946 MG.

Daley Edmund Leo, (W.P. 1906-No. 4457) CE; CO 6th Engr 3rd Div AEF; MG 1940; CG PR Dept 1939 & 5th Cps 1941-42; Ret 1942.

Humphreys Frederick Erastus, (W.P. 1906-No. 4460) CE; Qualified by Wilbur Wright 26 Oct 1909 as one of the two first Military Pilots (Lt Lahm the other); Resd 1910 1st Lt.

Williford Forrest Estey, (W.P. 1906-No. 4472) ARC-CAC; CO HD Sandy Hook 1938-40; BG 1940; Ret dsbld 1944.

McFarland Earl, (W.P. 1906-No. 4474) ARC-CAD-OD; XO for Asst Sec War 1931-36; BG Asst Ch Ord 1938-42; CO Springfield Ars 1942-43; Ret 1943 BG.

Green Joseph Andres, (W.P. 1906-No. 4475) ARC-CAC; MG Ch CAC 1940-42; CG AA Cmd 1942-44; Ret 1944; Ret MG.

Wainwright Jonathan Mayhew, (W.P. 1906-No. 4477) Cav; GS 82nd Div & 3rd Ar AEF; AFG; BG 1938; MG 1940; LTG 1942; CG NLuzon Campaign; Bataan Siege of Corregidor 1941-42; POW 1942-45; GEN 1945; CG 4th Ar 1945-47; Ret dsbld 1947.

Chaffee Adna Romanza Jr., (W.P. 1906-No. 4483) Cav; G3 81st Div, 4th Cps, 3rd Cps, AEF COL; BG CG Mecz Brig 1938; MG 1940; CG 1st Armd Cps.

Gillespie Alexander Garfield, (W.P. 1906-No. 4489) ARC-CAC-OD; BG 1940; Watervliet 1940-45; Ret 1943: AD to ret dsbld 1946 BG.

Andrews Frank Maxwell, (W.P. 1906-No. 4494) Cav; CO Kelly Fld 1923-27; MG CG GHQ AF, Langley Fld 1935-39; LTG 1941; CG USFcs ETO 1942 to D-Iceland air acdt 3 May 1943.

Westover Oscar, (W.P. 1906-No. 4495) Inf; BG Asst Ch AC 1932-35; MG ChAC 1935 to D-CA air acdt 21 Sept 1938.

Parker Courtlandt, (W.P. 1906-No. 4498) Cav; COL 6th FA AEF; MA London 1931-35; MG 1942; CG 5th Inf Div Iceland & WDC Sec 1941-45; Ret dsbld 1946 MG.

Pennell Ralph McTyeire, (W.P. 1906-No. 4506) Cav-FA; MG 1942; CG 27th Div 1941-42; Comdt FAS 1944-45; Ret dsbld 1946.

Clagett Henry Black, (W.P. 1906-No. 4508) Inf; CO Kelly Fld 1918-19; Air Off 9th CA 1926-30; BG 1936; Ret dsbld 1944 COL: ret BG 1948.

Abraham Clyde Rush, (W.P. 1906-No. 4509) Inf; IG 81st Div & Asst IG 2nd Ar AEF; BG 1940; Ret dsbld 1943.

Paine George Harris, (W.P. 1906-No. 4514) Inf; BG 1941; CG 46th FA Bde 1940-43; Ret dsbld 1946 BG.

Robinson Donald Allister, (W.P. 1906-No. 4515) Inf-Cav; BG 1941; CS 1st Div 9th Cps & 2nd Ar 1939-41; Ret 1943 COL; BG ret 1948.

Hoyle Rene Edward DeRussy, (W.P. 1906-No. 4516) BG 1940, MG 1942, CG 9th Div 1941-42; Cp Roberts 1942-45; Ret dsbld 1945 MG.

Loughry Howard Kendall, (W.P. 1906-No. 4524) Inf; MG ChFin 1940-44 & Actg to 1945; Ret 1945.

Alexander Roger Gordon, (W.P. 1907-No. 4532) CE; Prof of Drawing USMA 1920-45; BG 1946; Dean 1946-47; Ret 1947 BG.

Oconnor James Alexander, (W.P. 1907-No. 4534) CE; CO 303rd Engr 78th Div AEF; CG NW SvC 1942-43; Engr CBI 1944; Ret dsbld 1946 BG.

Somers Richard Herbert, (W.P. 1907-No. 4538) CAC-OD; OCO 1921-24, 32-36, 40-42; BG 1940; Ret 1942.

Sultan Daniel Isom, (W.P. 1907-No. 4539) CE; Cons fortification Corregidor 1916-18; Nicaragua Canal Survey 1929-31; CG 38th Div & VII Cps 1941-43; CG USFcs CBI 1944-45; IG USA 1945-47.

Rose John Boursiquot, (W.P. 1907-No. 4541) CAC-OD; CO APG 1939-41; BG 1941; CO Frankford Ars 1942-45; Ret 1945.

Harris Charles Tillman Jr., (W.P. 1907-No. 4544) CAC-OD; BG ASST Ch Ord 1938-42; MG 1941; CG Aberdeen PG 1942-46; Ret dsbld 1946.

Murray Maxwell, (W.P. 1907-No. 4545) CAC-FA; CO 5FA 1st Div AEF; MG Haw Div 1941; CG Island Cmds T-S 1944-45; Ret dsbld 1946 MG.

Shedd William Edger, (W.P. 1907-No. 4547) CAC; BG 1940; MG 1941; CG Pan CZ 1940-44; CG 9th SvC 1944-46; Ret dsbld 1948.

Rutherford Harry Kenneth, (W.P. 1907-No. 4553) CAC-OD; Frankford Ars 1919-24; MG 1941; Ret dsbld 1943.

Marley James Preston, (W.P. 1907-No. 4557) FA; CG 8th Div 1940-42; MG 1941; Ret 1942.

Potter Waldo Charles, (W.P. 1907-No. 4563) FA; BG 1941; CG FARTC Ft Sill 1941-43; Ret COL 1946; BG ret 1948.

Drain Jesse Cyrus, (W.P. 1907-No. 4567) Inf; Cuban Pac 1907-09; BG 1941; Ret 1945 COL; BG ret 1948.

Morrison William Eric, (W.P. 1907-No. 4571) Inf; Prof ML USMA 1925-48; Ret dsbld 1948 BG.

McNeil Edwin Colyer, (W.P. 1907-No. 4584) Inf; Prof Law USMA 1923-29; Asst JAG WD 1937-43; Ret 1944: AD to 1947: OJAG ETO 1943-46; WD 1946-47; BG ret 1948; Spec Asst to Secy Army 1950-58.

Lang John Walton, (W.P. 1907-No. 4594) Inf; MA Argentina 1941-45 & Mexico 1945; BG 1943; Ret dsbld 1946.

Arnold Henry Harley, (W.P. 1907-No. 4596) Inf; Pioneer Ar Avn; BG Asst Ch AC 1936-38; MG ChAC 1938-41; Gen of the Army 1944: Built greatest AF in history: Many Honors, decorations,and degrees; Ret dsbld 1946: Gen of the Air Force 1949.

Yount Barton Kyle, (W.P. 1907-No. 4602) Inf; Asst MA (Air) Paris 1925-29; Asst Ch AC 1938-40; CG Flying Tng Cmd 1942-43; CG AAF TngCmd 1943-45; Ret dsbld 1946 LTG.

Christy William Carroll, (W.P. 1907-No. 4610) Cav; BG 1943 IG PCD 1940-41; Ret dsbld 1946 BG.

White Charles Henry, (W.P. 1907-No. 4614) Inf; BG 1940; MG 1941; CG 4CA 1942-44; Sec War Pers Bd 1944-45; Ret dsbld 1946 MG.

Collins James Lawton, (W.P. 1907-No. 4624) Cav; BG 1939; MG 1940; CG PR Dept 1941-43; CG 5th SvC 1944-46; Ret dsbld 1946 MG.

Edgerton Glen Edgar, (W.P. 1908-No. 4642) CE; Gov CZ 1940-44; MG 1942; Ret dsbld 1949 MG.

Sturdevant Clarence Lynn, (W.P. 1908-No. 4647) CE; CG N Guinea Base Sec SOS 1944-45; Ret dsbld 1946 MG.

Burns James Henry, (W P. 1908-No. 4653) FA-OD; MG 1940 Lend Lease Adm 1941-42; Ret dsbld 1944 MG.

Hughes Everett Strait, (W.P. 1908-No. 4654) FA-OD; MG 1943; Dpty CG NATO USA 1943-44; Asst to CinC USFET 1944-45; IG USFET 1945-46; Ch of Ord USA 1946 to ret 1949 MG.

Higby Harvey Douglas, (W.P. 1908-No. 4662) FA; Inst FARD Cp Taylor 1918; AFG 1920-22; BG 1940; Ret dsbld 1941 COL; BG ret 1943.

Smith Rodney Hamilton, (W.P. 1908-No. 4665) CAC; BG Mil Msn Brazil 1936-38; CS AAA EDC 1941-44; Ret 1944 COL: AD 1944-46: BG 1946.

Rodgers Robert Clive, (W.P. 1908-No. 4669) Cav; BG 1940; Comt Cav Sch 1940-42; Ret dsbld 1946 BG.

Jarman Sanderford, (W.P. 1908-No. 4671) CAC; MG 1940; CG CZ CAC Cmd 1939-42; CG Saipan 1944-45; Ret dsbld 1946 MG.

Curry John Francis, (W.P. 1908-No. 4677) Inf; MG 1940; Ret dsbld 1945 MG.

Chaney James Eugene, (W.P. 1908-No. 4678) Inf; Asst MA Air Rome 1919-24; BG Asst Ch AC 1934-38; MG 1940; CG US Fcs Br Isles 1942; 1st AF 1943; Ch US Del Anglo-Amer Msn to Portugal 1944; CG Ar Fcs Iwo Jima 1945 MG USA 1946; Ret dsbld 1947.

Terry Thomas Alexander, (W.P. 1908-No. 4679) CAC; MG 1940; CG New England Sector 1940-42; CG 2nd SvC 1942-45; CG T-1 1945-46; Ret dsbld 1946.

Kennedy John Thomas, (W.P. 1908-No. 4684) Cav; CG Ft Bragg 1942-46; Ret dsbld 1946 BG.

Avery Ray Longfellow, (W.P. 1908-No. 4686)

CAC; CG Edgewood Ars 1939-46; Ret dsbld BG.

Stocton Edw Alexander, (W.P. 1908-No. 4690) CAC; CG AA Repl TC 1942-44; Secy War Sep Bd 1944-46; Ret dsbld 1946 BG.

Groninger Homer McLaughlin, (W.P. 1908-No. 4691) Cav; CG NYPOE 1940-45; CG SFPOE 1945-46; Ret 1946 MG.

Cunningham James Hutchings, (W.P. 1908-No. 4693) CAC; Hv Arty & GHQ AEF; BG 1941; Ret 1946 COL; BG ret 1948.

Buckner Simon Bolivar, (W.P. 1908-No. 4699) Inf; BG 1940; MG 1941, LTG 1943; CG Alaska 1942-44; Kld Okinawa 1945.

Bonesteel Charles Hartwell, (W.P. 1908-No. 4702) Inf; BG 1940; MG 1941; CG Iceland Base Comd 1941-43; Comdt Inf Sch 1943-44; CG WDC 1944; IG GHQ ETO 1945; Ret dsbld 1947 MG.

Hester John Hutchison, (W.P. 1908-No. 4715) Inf; BG USA 1940; MG 1942; CG 43rd Div T-S 1942-43; CG TD Cen 1943-44; CG IRTC 1944-45; Ret dsbld 1946 MG.

Nulsen Charles Kilbourne, (W.P. 1908-No. 4735) Inf; BG 1943; CG Ft SH 1941-46; CG FT Sheridan 1946-47; Ret dsbld 1947 BG.

Watson Edwin Martin, (W.P. 1908-No. 4741) Inf; MA Belg 1927-31; AdC Pres Roosevelt 1933-39 & Secy to Pres 1939-45; MG 1940; Ret dsbld 1944: Died at sea retg from Yalta 20 Feb 1945.

Sneed Albert Lee, (W.P. 1908-No. 4746) Inf; CS Allied Air Cmd T-S 1942; CG Tng Cmd 1944-45; Ret dsbld 1946 BG.

Weaver Walter Reed, (W.P. 1908-No. 4749) Inf; CO Maxwell Fld 1927-31; Cmdt ACTS 1939-40; MG 1941; CG Tech TC 1942-43; Ret dsbld 1943.

Godfrey Stuart Chapin, (W.P. 1909-No. 4750) CE; Air Engr AAF 1942-43; Air Engr HQ CBI 1943-45; Died Spokane air acdt 1945; BG.

Marks Edwin Hall, (W.P. 1909-No. 4757) CE; CG Ft Belvoir 1941-42; Engr SW Div & 8th SvC 1944-46; Engr So Pac Div 1946-47; Ret dsbld 1947: BG ret 1948.

Lee John Clifford Hodges, (W.P. 1909-No. 4761) CE; CG SOS & ComZ ETO 1942-45; CG MTO 1946-47; Ret 1947 LTG.

Ahern Leo James, (W.P. 1909-No. 4767) FA; OIG WD 1940-46; BG 1943; Ret 1946 COL: BG ret 1948.

Oldfield Homer Ray, (W.P. 1909-No. 4770) CAC; MG 1942; CG Pan CAC Cmd 1942-43; CG AAA TC 1943; Asst to CG AAF for AAA 1943-46; Ret 1948 MG.

Van Duesen George Lane, (W.P. 1909-No. 4782) Inf; Asst Cmdt TSS 1921-24,24-29; OCSO 1930-34; MG 1944; CG SC Schs & Tng Cen 1940-44; Ret 1946 COL: MG ret 1948.

Catron Thomas Benton II, (W.P. 1909-No. 4784) Inf; GS AEF; Ret 1936 LTC; AD 1941: CS 3rd SvC; BG 1945; Ret dsbld 1946 BG.

Devers Jacob Loucks, (W.P. 1909-No. 4788) FA; MG 1941; CG 9th Div 1940-41; Ch Armd Fc 1941-43; LTG CG ETO 1943-44; CG NATO USA 1944; CG 6th Ar Grp 1944-45; Gen 1945; CG AGF 1945-47; CG AFF 1947-49; Ret 1949 Gen.

Hayes Phillip, (W.P. 1909-No. 4789) Inf; MG 1944; CG 3rd SvC 1943-46; Ret dsbld 1946 MG.

Baehr Carl Adolph, (W.P. 1909-No. 4793) Inf; CO FA Bn 6th Div AEF; BG 1941; CG 71st FA Brig T-ME 1941-44; CG VI Cps Arty T-ME 1944-46; Ret dsbld 1946 BG.

Patton George Smith Jr., (W.P. 1909-No. 4795) Cav; AdC Gen Pershing in PunX; CO 304th Bde Tk Cps AEF 1918-19; CG 1st Armd Cps, II Cps & 7th Ar T-M 1942-44; CG

3rd Ar T-E 1944-45; Died Heidelberg Ger auto acdt 21 Dec 1945; Gen CG 15th Ar.

Ord James Garesche, (W.P. 1909-No. 4799) Inf; BG 1940; MG 1942; Chrm JBUS DC 1943-45; Ret 1946 COL: MG ret 1948.

Philoon Wallace Copeland, (W.P. 1909-No. 4802) Inf; Dpty CG Alas Dept 1944-45; Ret dsbld 1945 MG.

Stearns Cuthbert Powell, (W.P. 1909-No. 4804) Cav; Org & Cmd Civ Aff Div ETO 1944-45 & G5 ETO 1944-45; BG 1944; Ret dsbld 1946 BG.

Fuller Horace Hayes, (W.P. 1909-No. 4808) Cav; CO 108th FA AEF; Instr C & GSS 1923-27; WDGS 1929-33; MA Paris 1935-40; BG 1938; MG 1941; CG 41st Div T-S 1942-45; Ret dsbld 1946 MG.

Emmons Delos Carleton, (W.P. 1909-No. 4810) Inf; XO to Secy War 1928-31; MG CG GHQ AF 1939-40; LTG 1940; CG Haw Dept 1941-43; CG WDG 1943-44; CG Alaskan Dept 1944-46; Cmdt AFSC 1946-48; Ret dsbld 1948 LTG.

Krogstad Arnold Norman, (W.P. 1909-No. 4811) Inf; CG 1AF 1941-42; CG 2nd & 5th Dist AAF Tech Tng Cmds & Tng Cen 1942-44; Ret dsbld 1944 BG.

Denson Eley Parker, (W.P. 1909-No. 4812) Inf; G3 28th Div AEF; CG Seattle POE 1941-46; Ret dsbld 1946 BG.

Milling Thomas DeWitt, (W.P. 1909-No. 4813) Cav; CS,CO, AS 1st Ar AEF; Ret dsbld 1933 COL; BG ret 1940.

Munnikhuysen Henry Dorsey, (W.P. 1909-No. 4815) Cav; Post QM Ft Meade 1935-38; BG 1940; OQMG WD 1940-46; Ret dsbld 1946 BG.

Gage Phillip Stearns, (W.P. 1909-No. 4816) CAC; BG 1941; CG Harbor Def NY 7 Boston 1940-47; Ret 1946 Col; BG ret 1947.

Eichelberger Robert Lawerence, (W.P. 1909-No. 4817) Inf; AEF Siberia; Adjt USMA 1931-35; Secy WDGS 1935-38; CO 30th Inf 1939-40; Supt USMA 1940-42; MG 1941; CG 77th Div 1942; LTG 1942; CG 1st Cps 1942-44; CG 8th Ar Japan 1945-48 & CG OccJ 1946-48; Ret 1948 LTG; Gen ret 1954.

Harding Edwin Forrest, (W.P. 1909-No. 4823) Inf; CO 27th Inf 1938-40; BG 9th Div 1940-41; MG 1942; CG 32nd Div 1942-43; CZ & Antilles Dept 1943-45; JCS 1945-46; Ret 1946 COL; MG ret 1948.

Sears Robert, Inf; CO IsBase Sec Sicily 1943-44; CO Inf Regt 35th Div 1944-45; Ret 1944 Col; AD to 1946.

Davis Lee Dunnungton, (W.P. 1909-No. 4838) CO Portland OR POE 1942-43; Dpty CO SF POE 1943-44; CO Staging Facility FT Lewis 1945-46; Ret dsbld 1946.

McDowell John May, (W.P. 1909-No. 4844) Inf; CO FA Bn 2nd Div AEF; CO MilDist Buffalo 1942-44; Ret 1944.

Bluemel Clifford, (W.P. 1909-No. 4845) Inf; CO 45th Inf PS 1940-41; CG 31st Div PA Bataan; POW 1942-45; Death March; Hq 6th SvC & CG Ft Benj Harrison 1946-47; Ret dsbld 1947 BG.

Simpson William Hood, (W.P. 1909-No. 4850) Inf; MG 1941; CG 35th Div 12th Cps 1941-43; CG 4th Ar 1943-44; CG 9th Ar T-E 1944-45; CG 2nd Ar 1945; Ret dsbld 1946 LTG; Gen ret 1954.

Strong Frederick Smith Jr., (W.P. 1910-No. 4853) CE-QM; Ch Engr SOS CBI 1943; CG NW SvC 1944-45; CG UK Base 1945.

Garlington Creswell, (W.P. 1910-No. 4854) CE; BG 1942; CG ASF Tng Cen 1943-44; .

Solbert Oscar Nathaniel, (W.P. 1910-No. 4858) CE; MA Norway Denmark 1918-19; AUS 1942-45 BG; SHAEF 1943-45.

Dunn Beverly Charles, (W.P. 1910-No. 4859) CE; BG 1943; Ch Engr SHAEF 1944-45 TD; Ret dsbld 1948 BG.

Connolly Donald Hilary, (W.P. 1910-No. 4860) CE; Admr CAA DC 1940-42; MG 1942; CG Persian Gulf Cmd 1942-44; Ret 1948 MG.

Fowler Raymond Foster, (W.P. 1910-No. 4861) CE; BG 1942; Engr SAtl Div 1943-46; Ret dsbld 1946 BG.

McCoach David Jr., (W.P. 1910-No. 4862) CE; BG Asst ChEngrs 1941-43; MG CG 9th SvC 1943-44; Ch Engr AFHQ T-M 1944-45; CG 6thSvC 1945-46; Ret 1946 COL; MG ret 1948.

Wallace Fred Clute, (W.P. 1910-No. 4867) XO OCH FA 1939-40; MG 1942; CG 5th CA 1942-43; CG Okinawa Base 1945; Ret dsbld 1946.

Lewis Burton Oliver, BG 1940; OCO 1940-42; Asst Ch TC; Ret 1947 Col; BG ret 1948.

Selleck Clyde Andrew, (W.P. 1910-No. 4874) BG 1941; CG 71st Div PA 1941-42; Bataan; POW 1942-45; Death March; Ret dsbld 1947.

Dawley Ernest Joseph, (W.P. 1910-No. 4876) MG CG 40th Div & IV CPS 41-43T-AME; Ret dsbld 1947 BG.

Chamberlin Harry Dwight, (W.P. 1910-No. 4881) Cav; CO Army Horse Show Team 1928-32; BG 1941; CG TF T-S 1942-43.

Muir James Irvin, (W.P. 1910-No. 4882) Inf; MG 1942; Ret 1945 COL; MG ret 1948.

Millikin John, (W.P. 1910-No. 4890) Cav; XO GSSch AEF; Cav S 1933-36; CG 33rd Div T-P 1942-43; CG III Cps & 13th AD T-E 1943-45; CG FARTC 1946-48; Ret 1948 MG.

Wilson Durward Saunders, (W.P. 1910-No. 4893) Inf; MG 1942; CG 24th Div 1940-42; T-AP; Ret dsbld 1946 MG.

Scowden Frank Floyd, (W.P. 1910-No. 4900) Inf-QMC; DQMG 1940-44; OS5 SHAEF 1945; OLiquidation Cmsnr 1945-46; Ret 1946 MG.

Hines Charles, (W.P. 1910-No. 4902) Arty; BG 1941; OUn SW 1938-42; CG 38th AAA Brig 3rd Ar T-E 1944-45; Ret 1946 COl; BG ret 1948.

Heard Jack Whitehead, (W.P. 1910-No. 4903) Cav; Pres Mecz Bd 1938-39; MG 1942; CG 5th AD 1941-43; Ret dsbld 1946 MG.

Frank Walter Hale, (W.P. 1910-No. 4909) Inf; Asst Cmdt ACTS 1926-30; MG 1941; CG ASC T-E 1942; CG ASC AAF 1943-45; Ret dsbld 1945 MG.

Vautsmeirer Walter William, (W.P. 1910-No. 4911) AS US 1917-19; AEF 1919; D-VA Air Acdt dirigible Roma 21 Feb 1922.

Uhl Frederick Elwood, (W.P. 1910-No. 4914) OC Inf WD 1932-35; CG 7th SvC 1941-44 & 4th SvC 1944-45; CG Repl Cmd AFWespac 1945; Ret dsbld 1946 MG.

Griswold Oscar Woolverton, (W.P. 1910-No. 4924) Inf; OCh Inf 1936-39; MG 1941; LTG 1945; CG 14th Cps T-S 1944-45; CG 3rd Ar to ret dsbld 1947 LTG.

Richart Duncan Grant, (W.P. 1910-No. 4926) Cav; BG 1944; CG Ft Jackson 1943-45; Ret dsbld 1946 BG.

Dunlop Robert Horace, (W.P. 1910-No. 4927) Inf; BG 1942; AG Haw Dept 1941-42; Dir Civ Pers Div AGO 1943-45; Ret 1946 COL; BG ret 1948.

Reinhardt Emil Fred, (W.P. 1910-No. 4931) Inf; MG 1942; CG 69th Div made first contact with Russian Ar 25 April 1945; Ret dsbld 1946 MG.

Fleming Phillip Bracken, (W.P. 1911-No. 4936) CE; Dpty Admr PWA 1933-35; BG 1941; MG 1942; Admr Fed Wks Agcy 1941-49; Ret dsbld 1947 MG.

Mehaffey Joseph Cowles, (W.P. 1911-No. 4938) CE; Engr Arlington Mem Bridge 1925-30; MG 1944; Gov PC 1944-48; Ret 1949 MG.

Wheeler Raymond Albert, (W.P. 1911-No. 4940) CE; COL 4th Div Engr AEF; MG 1942; Ch Persian Gulf Msn 1941-42; CG SOS CBI 1942-44; LTG 1944; Dpty Supreme Cmdr SEAC 1944-45; CG CBI 1945; Ch Engrs USA 1945 to ret 1949 LTG.

Kutz Harry Russell, (W.P. 1911-No. 4943) Inf; IGD 1928-31; WDGS 1931-35; AChOrd 1942-46; Ret dsbld 1946 BG.

Lawrence Thompson, (W.P. 1911-No. 4945) Inf; IG 16th Div US 1918-19; Inst AWC 1039-41; MG 1942; CG Repl Tng Centers 1941-42, 43-45; CG 99th Div T-A 1942-43; Ret dsbld 1946 MG.

Franke Gustav Henry, (W.P. 1911-No. 4948) CAC; CO of Btry that fired the first shot of US FA in WWI; MG CG 81st Div T-A 1942; Ret dsbld 1943 MG.

Simpson Bethel Wood, (W.P. 1911-No. 4953) Asst Comdt Ord Sch 1927-32; BG 1942; CG Ord Repl Tcs APG 1941-42; OO AGF 1944-45; JCS 1945-46; Ret 1946 Col; BG ret 1948.

Nichols Harold Floyd, (W.P. 1911-No. 4955) Asst Comdt CASch 1939-40; BG 1941; CG AATC Ft Eustis 1940-41; CG Haw AA Cmd 1941-44; Ret 1947 COL; BG ret 1948.

Hall Charles Phillip, (W.P. 1911-No. 4957) Inf; Instr TIS 1925-29, 32-37; MG 1942; LTG 1945; CG 9th Cps T-S 1942-46; WDGS 1946 to ret dsbld 1948 LTG.

Surles Alexander Day, (W.P. 1911-No. 4958) Cav; BG 1941; MG 1942; Ret dsbld 1946 MG.

Bradford Karl Slaughter, (W.P. 1911-No. 4964) Cav; BG 1941; CG 1st Cav Brig 1941-43; Ret 1946 BG.

Darque Herbert Arthur, (W.P. 1911-No. 4965) CO 1st Aero Sq PunX; BG 1938; Asst Ch AC 1940; MG 1941; CG 1st AF; D- CA air acdt 12 Dec 1941.

Gilbreath Frederick, (W.P. 1911-No. 4967) Cav; QM 4th Div AEF; MG 1942; CG SF POE 1941-44; CG So Pac Base Cmd 1944-45; Ret dsbld 1946 MG.

Crawford James Blanchard, (W.P. 1911-No. 4969) BG 1941; CG AAATC Ft Bliss 1941-43; Sec War Review Bd 1944-45; Ret dsbld 1946 BG.

Shekerjian Haig, (W.P. 1911-No. 4970) Inf; BG CG ASFTC Cp Sibert 1942-45, Ret dsbld 1946 BG.

Lockwood Benjamin Curtis, (W.P. 1911-No. 4972) Inf; CG JFT T-S 1942-43; CG IsBase SWPA 1943; CG AGFRepDep 1943-46; Ret dsbld 1948 BG.

Richards Harrison Henry Cocke, (W.P. 1911-No. 4974) Cav; CO AC-Inf Regt Bataan; POW 1942-45; Death March; Ret 1947.

Ladd Jesse Amos, (W.P. 1911-No. 4983) Inf; PunX; IGD 1918-20; CG Tps AK 1941-43; ETO 1945-46; Ret 1947 COL; BG ret 1948.

Baade Paul William, (W.P. 1911-No. 4984) Inf; WDGS 1935-39; MG 1943; CG 35th Div 1944-45; Ret dsbld 1946 MG.

Weaver James Roy Newman, (W.P. 1911-No. 4987) Inf; WDGS 1933-37; BG 1941; CG Tk Gp Luzon Def & at Bataan; POW 1942-45; CG Spac Tps HQ 6th Ar to ret dsbld 1948 BG.

Lucas John Porter, (W.P. 1911-No. 4990) Cav; WDGS 1032-36; MG 1941; CG 6th Cps T-M 1943-44; CG 4th Ar 1944-46; Ch AAG 1946-48; Dpty CG 5th Ar 1948.

Morris WM. Henry Harrison, (W.P. 1911-No. 4991) Inf; CO Inf Bn 90th Div AEF; MG 1942; CG 6th AD 1942; CG 2nd ACps & 18th Cps 1943; CG 10th AD T-E 1944-45; JBUS DC 1947-49; CinC CarCmd 1949- 52; Ret 1952 LTG.

Kimball Allen Russell, (W.P. 1911-No. 4995) Inf; Asst QM USMA 1921-24; QM USMA 1940-42; BG 1942; CG Jeff Dep 1942-44; HQ Comdt HQ ETO 1944-45; CG Schenectady Gen Sup Dep 1945-46; Ret 1946 COL: BG ret 1948.

Wyche Ira Thomas, (W.P. 1911-No. 5003) Inf; CG 74th FA Bde 1941-42; CG 79th Div T-AE 1944-45; CG 8th Cps, 3rd Cps, 1st SvC 1945-47; TIG USA 1947-48; Ret dsbld 1948 MG.

Homer John Louis, (W.P. 1911-No. 5007) MG 1942; ETO 1940-44; CG AA Cmd SF Cal 1944-45; CG AA 7 GM Cen 1948-50; Ret 1950 MG.

Kuldell Rudolph Charles, (W.P. 1912-No. 5019) CE; AUS 1942-46; BG 1944; Ret Hon List 1949 BG.

Crawford Roscoe Campbell, (W.P. 1912-No. 5020) CE; BG 1941; CO Engr Sch; MG 1948; Ret 1949.

Chynoweth Bradford Grethen, (W.P. 1912-No. 5022) CE-Inf; Resd 1919; Reapt 1920 Maj; BG 1941; CG Visayan Force PA 1941-42; POW 1942-45; Ret dsbld 1947 BG.

Faymonville Phillip Ries, (W.P. 1912-No. 5026) CAC-OD; AEF Siberia; MA Russia 1934-39; BG 1942 Ret 1948.

Maxwell Russell Lamonte, A-CA; MG 1942; CG USAFIME; G4 WD 1943-46; Ret 1946.

Wood John Shirley, (W.P. 1912-No. 5029) CAC-FA; OODiv AEF; CG 4AD T-AE 1942-45; Ret 1946 MG; IRO Austria 1946 (Ch Mission 1947-51): Ch of Mission UN KRA Tokyo 1952, Korea 1952-53, Geneva 1953.

Youngs Wm. Henry Walmsley,(W.P. 1912-No. 5032) Cav; IG 5th SvC 1941-44; IG Hq Island Cmd Okinawa 1945; CO Cp McCoy WI 1947 to ret dsbld 1948.

Crawford David McLean, (W.P. 1912-No. 5033) CAC-SC; BG 1942; CCS 1943-45; Ret dsbld 1946 BG.

Gatchell Oscar James, (W.P. 1912-No. 5034) CAC-OD; Prof Ord & Gun USMA 1938-40; Prof Mech USMA 1940 to ret 1952 BG.

Hayes Thomas Jay, (W.P. 1912-No. 5037) Inf; O Under Secy War 1941-42; MG 1942; Ch Prod Div SOS 1942; Ch Ind Sv OD ASF 1942-45; Ret dsbld 1945 MG.

Fechet d'Alary, (W.P. 1912-No. 5039) Inf; CO Inf Bn 2nd Div AEF; Ret dsbld 1932 MAJ; AD 1940-46; Dpty CS 1st Div & CO 16th Inf NATO 1942-43; Hq 12th Ar Gp & SHAEF 1943-45 Col ret 1948.

Wilbur William Hale, (W.P. 1912-No. 5042) Inf; DCG 36th Div Italy 1943-44; CS 6thCA 1940-41; CS WDC 1945-46; Ret dsbld 1947 BG.

Spalding Sidney Parker, (W.P. 1912-No. 5043) CAC-OD; MG 1944; War prod asgm, Lend Lease activities O UnS War 1940-43; Ch Sup Div Mil Msn USSR 1943-45; Ret 1949.

Jones Byron Quinby, (W.P. 1912-No. 5044) Cav; First Aviator to execute a tail spin Dec 15: CO Air Mail Opns 1934; Ret dsbld 1944.

MacGregor Stephen Harrison, (W.P. 1912-No. 5046) CAC-OD; OCh Inf 1934-38; ChOO USAF Mid Pac 1942-44; Hq TC DC 1944-45; CO Springfield Armory 1945-47; WAA DC 1947 to ret dsbld 1949.

Johnson Davenport, (W.P. 1912-No. 5051) Inf; CO 3 Pursuit Gp AEF; CG 11th AF 1943-45; Ret dsbld 1945 MG.

Kirk James, (W.P. 1912-No. 5052) CAC-OD;

BG 1942; MG 1944; OCO 1943; Ch Fld Ser Ord 1946-52; Ret dsbld 1952 MG.

Littlejohn Robert McGowan, (W.P. 1912-No. 5053) Cav; QM USMA 1934-38; QM Phil Dept 1939-40; Ch Clothing Div OQMG 1940-41; QM ETO 1942-45; MG 1943; CG AGRC 1945-46; Ret dsbld 1946 MG.

Haislip Wade Hampton, (W.P. 1912-No. 5054) Inf; LTC 1918; AEF WDGS 1940-42; LTG 1945; CG 85th Div T-E 1943-44; CG 15th Cps 1944-45; CG 7th Ar 1945; MG USA 1947; DCS Admin Hq DA 1947-48; Gen 1949; Ret 1951 Gen.

Johnson James Harve, (W.P. 1912-No. 5057) CAC; BG 1945; CO 1944-46; Ret 1946 Col; BG ret 1948.

Robertson Walter Melville, (W.P. 1912-No. 5059) Inf; MG 1942; CG 2nd Div T-E 1944-45; CG 15th Cps 1945-46; US Delegate Bulgaria 1946-47; Ret 1950 MG.

Spalding Isaac, (W.P. 1912-No. 5065) Cav; BG 1942; CG FA 77th Div T-P 1943-44; CO Ft Mc Pherson 1946; Ret dsbld 1946 BG.

Malony Harry James, (W.P. 1912-No. 5067) Inf; MG 1942; CG 94th Inf Div 1942-45; CG Internat Fcs Greese 1946; SS USA 1946 to ret 1949 MG.

Cook Gilbert Richard, (W.P. 1912-No. 5073) Inf; MG 1942; T-E CG XII Cps; Ret dsbld 1946 MG.

Sibert Franklin Cummings, (W.P. 1912-No. 5076) Inf; MG 1942 Stff Gen Stillwell Burma 1942; CG 6th Div & X Cps T-PS 1943-45; Ret dsbld 1946 MG.

Arnold Archibald Vincent, (W.P. 1912-No. 5077) Inf; CG 7th Div T-SP 1943-46; Mil Gov Korea 1945-46; US-USSR Comm Kor 1946; Hq AGF 1946-48; Ret dsbld 1948 MG.

Weaver William Gaulbert, (W.P. 1912-No. 5079) Inf; MG 1945; Asst CO 90th Div, CG 8th Div T-E 1942-45; Ret dsbld 1946 MG.

Chamberlin Stephen J., (W.P. 1912-No. 5900) Inf; G3 GHQ T-S 1942-45; DCS USAFPac & SCAP 1945-46; CG 5th Ar 1948; Ret dsbld 1951 LTG.

Hobson William Horace, (W.P. 1912-No. 5082) Inf; CO 30th Inf 1941-42; NMB 1942-43; CG Ft Benning 1943-45; Ret 1946 BG.

Barton Raymond Oscar, (W.P. 1912-No. 5085) Inf; MG 1942; CS 4th Cps 1941-42; CG 4th Div T-E 1942-44; Ret dsbld 1946 MG.

Lewis John Earle, (W.P. 1912-No. 5089) Cav; BG 1942; 30th Div Arty 1943-44; Arty Off ETO 1944; Ret dsbld 1946 BG.

Walker Walton Harris, (W.P. 1912-No. 5090) Inf; CO 13th Mach Gun Bn AEF; LTG 1945; CG XX Cps T-E 1944; MG USA 1947; CG 5th Ar 1946-48; CG 8th Ar, Japan 1948, KW 1950; D-Korea motor acdt Battle Death 23rd Dec 1950; Gen psth.

Harmon Millard Fillmore, (W.P. 1912-No. 5091) Inf; CS AAF 1942; LTG 1943; CG 13th AF, 14th Cps & Cdr Army Fcs Pac T-Sp 1942-44; CG AAF POA & DCG 20th AF 1944-45; Missing Pac Flt 26 Feb 1945.

Kelly John Duncan, (W.P. 1912-No. 5092) Cav; CO Cp Breckinridge KY 1942-43; Ret dsbld 1947.

Brown Albert Eger, (W.P. 1912-No. 5095) Inf; MG 1942; CG 7th Div Aleutians 1943; CG 5th Div T-E 1943-45; Dpty CG & CG USAFK 1947-48; Ret 1949 MG.

Drake Charles Chisholm, (W.P. 1912-No. 5102) Inf-QMC; AEF US AFFE & PI 1941-42; POW 1942-45; Ret dsbld 1946 BG.

Morrissey William Joseph, (W.P. 1912-No. 5105) Inf; 142nd Inf 36th Div AEF LTC; CO 35th Inf 25th Div 1940-42; Dpty G4 WDGS 1942-46; BG 1944; Ret dsbld 1947.

Schneider Frank Victor, (W.P. 1912-No. 5109) Inf; 61st Inf Div AEF; CO SvC New Caldonia 1943-44; Dir Tng TIS 1944-45; Ret dsbld 1946.

Young Gordon Russell, (W.P. 1913-No. 5115) CE; BG 1942; Ch Engr CDC 1942-44; CG Ft Belvoir 1944-45; Ret dsbld 1951 BG.

Nichollas Richard Ulysses, (W.P. 1913-No. 5116) CE; BG Engr 9th Ar ETO 1944-45; Ret dsbld BG.

Dorst James Archer, (W.P. 1913-No. 5120) CE; CO 354th Engr GS Regt T-E 1944-45; Ret 1947.

Oliver Lunsford Errett, (W.P. 1913-No. 5122) CE; MG 1942; CG CCB 1AD NATO 1942; CG 5th AD T-E 1943-45; Ret 1948 MG.

Crane William Carey, (W.P. 1913-No. 5125) BG 1942; CG 4th Cps Arty T-M 1944-45; XG Ft Devens MA 1945-46 Ret 1947.

Rosevear William Bleecker Jr., (W.P. 1913-No. 5126) CO FABn 88th Div AEF; AUS 1941-43; COL AAF Tng Cmd; Ret 1950.

Brewer Carlos, (W.P. 1913-No. 5127) MG 1942; CG 12AD T-S 1942-44; CO 46FA Gp 7th Ar Arty O T-E 1945-46; Ret 1950.

McMahan John Eugene Jr., (W.P. 1913-No. 5129) CG 77th DivArty 1942-43; CG 8th Cps Arty T-E 1943-45; CS SvC 1945; Ret 1950 BG.

Engelhart Francis Augustus, (W.P. 1913-No. 5130) OO CBI 1942; BG 1944; OO USAF Mid Pac 1944-45; Ret dsbld 1946.

Sliney George Wessely, (W.P. 1913-No. 5133) Cav; BG 1944; Arty O Chinese Ar & Tng Units CBI 1941-45; CS AAG 1947; Ret 1947 BG.

Frank Selby Hamey, (W.P. 1913-No. 5134) BG 1945; Ch OO 44-45 T-AME; CG Red Riv Ars 1946; Ret 1951 BG.

Crittenberger Willis Dale, (W.P. 1913-No. 5136) CG 4th Cps 5th Ar Italy 1943-45; CinC Car Cmd 1945-48; CG 1AR 1950-52; Ret 1952.

Van Volkenburgh Robert Heber, (W.P. 1913-No. 5137) BG 1941; CG 40 CA Brig T-S; Comdt AAA Sch 1945-46; Ret 1950 BG.

Jones Junius Wallace, (W.P. 1913-No. 5142) MG 1944; Tech Tng Cmd 1942-43; Air Inspr Hq AAF 1943-48; CG Sacramento Air Mat Area 1948-52; Ret 1952.

Brown Thoburn Kaye, (W.P. 1913-No. 5145) Cav; BG 1942; CG Allied Cmd Rome 1944-45; Ret 1948.

Keyes Geoffrey, (W.P. 1913-No. 5150) Cav; Dpty CG TF 1942-43; Dpty CG 1st Armd Cps NATO & 7th Ar Sicily 1943; CG 3dr Ar 1946-47; High Commissioner USFA 1947-50; Ret 1950.

Greene Douglas Taft, (W.P. 1913-No. 5153) MG 1943; CG 16th & 12th ADs T-E; Dpty CG 2Ar; Ret dsbld 1946.

Perkins Robert Meredith, (W.P. 1913-No. 5157) BG 1942; 53aa Brig 1942-44; CG Haw aa Cmd 1944-45; Ret 1947.

Weeks Lawrence Babbitt, (W.P. 1913-No. 5158) BG 1942; Comdt CA Sch 1942-45; Ret 1948.

Danielson Clarence Hagbart, (W.P. 1913-No. 5159) Inf; AG USMA 1938-41; AG 1st Ar 1941-42; OTAG 1942-43; BG 1943; MG 1944; CG 7th SvC 1944-45; AG USAF Wes Pac 1945-46; Ret dsbld 1946 MG.

Peale James Nixon, (W.P. 1913-No. 5160) CO 306 Inf 77th Div Ft Jackson 1942; Ret dsbld 1944.

Considine John Arthur, (W.P. 1913-No. 5161) Cav; 8th Cav TX 1916-19; Instr USMA 1920-22; BG Guatamalan Army 1930-35; Instr CGSS 1937-40; MA Paraguay 1942-45; SF Cal POE 1945-46; Ret dsbld 1947.

Foote William Cooper, (W.P. 1913-No. 5163) Trinidad BW1 1941-43; Hq ASF 1944-45; G4, Dpty CO, CS, CO Phil Base Sec 1945-47; Ret dsbld 1952.

Fuller Francis Reuel, (W.P. 1913-No. 5165) Inf; Asst to CG 6th Ar Gp T-E 1944-45; Ret 1950.

Russell Clinton Warden, (W.P. 1913-No. 5166) Inf; BG 1940; O Ch AAF 1942; WD LnO Hq of Adm EJ King 1943.

Schmidt William Richard, (W.P. 1913-No. 5166) Inf; MG 1942; CG 76th Div T-AE 1942-45; MG USA 1948; Ar Pers Bd 1947-48; CG 101st Abn Div US 1948-49; OCSA 1949 to ret 1951.

Craig Louis Aleck, MG 1943; CG 9th Div & 20th Cps T-E 1944-45; IG USA 1948-52; Ret 1952.

Lovell George Edward Jr., (W.P. 1913-No. 5170) Cav; CO AAF Bases T-A 1941-45; Ret dsbld 1946.

Ardey John Erskine, (W.P. 1913-No. 5173) G4 6th Div 1939-41; CO 1st Inf 1941-42; CO 131 Inf 1942-45; Cmdr SEBr USDB 1945-46; Ret 1948.

Wash Carlyle Hilton, (W.P. 1913-No. 5175) Cav; CO Wheeler Fld TH 1929-31; BG 1940; CG 3AF Tampa FL 1942; AL air cr 26 Jan 1943.

Perrine Henry Pratt, (W.P. 1913-No. 5176) Inf; BG 1943; Instr, Secy, ExO, CG Sch Tps 1939-44; Ret dsbld 1951.

McCunniff Dennis Edward, (W.P. 1913-No. 5177) BG 1943; CG Cmbt Cmd POA 1943-45; Ret 1943 CG.

Lewis Henry Balding, (W.P. 1913-No. 5178) Inf; BG 1942; AG WDC 1940-42; Asst TAG WD 1942-43; AG & Dpty CS 12 Ar Gp T-E 1943-45; MG AUS 1948; Asst TAG 1946 to ret 1949.

Cheadle Henry Barlow, BG 1942; Asst CG 94th Div T-E 1943-45; Ret 1951 BG.

Newgarden Paul Woolever, (W.P. 1913-No. 5183) BG 1942; MG 1942; D-TN air cr 14 Jul 1944 CG 10AD 1952.

Patch Alexander McCarrell, (W.P. 1913-No. 5187) PunX; LTC 18th AEF; MG 1942; CG Amer Div & 14th Cps 1942-43; LTG 1944; CG 7th Ar T-ME 1944-45.

Lyman Charles Bishop, (W.P. 1913-No. 5188) Inf; CO 21st Inf 24th Div T-S 1942-44; BG 1944; Ret 1946; BG ret 1948.

Spragins Robert Lily, (W.P. 1913-No. 5189) Inf; US Coast Gd Silver; CS 24th Div & XIV Cps T-Sp 1942-43; CG 44th Div T-E 1944-45; Ret dsbld 1945 MG.

Corlett Charles Harrison, (W.P. 1913-No. 5193) Inf; MG 1942; CG TF at Kiska; CG 7th Div Kwajalein; CG 19th Cps T-E; Ret dsbld 1946 MG.

Davidson Howard Calhoun, (W.P. 1913-No. 5197) Inf; CO AS 7Cps AEF; MG 1944; CG 14 Frt WG Hawaii 1940-42; CG 10 AF CBI 1943-45; Ret dsbld 1946.

Roberts William Lynn, (W.P. 1913-No. 5198) Inf; BG 1945; CO Cmbt Cmds 10 AD T-AE 1943-45 & Dpty CG 4th AD 1945-46; MAG Korea 1948; Ret 1950.

McCulloch William Alexander, Inf; CO 119 MGun Bn 32nd Div AEF; CO 27th Inf 25th Div T-S 1941-42; BG 1943; Asst CG Amer Div T-S 1943-44; Ret 1949.

Cress James Bell, (W.P. 1914-No. 5207) CE; AUS 1941-45; CO 333rd Engr & 1056th Engrs T-E 1943-45; MG AUS 1949; Ret dsbld 1951 MG.

Gross CHarles Philip, (W.P. 1914-No. 5208) CE; MG ChTC WD 1942-45; Ret MG 1945;

Bullard Peter Cleary, (W.P. 1914-No. 5210) CE-Inf; G1 Sec SH AEF 1944-46; CO Cp

McCoy 1950-51; Ret 1952.

Somervell Brehon Burke, (W.P. 1914-No. 5211) CE; LTG 1942; CG ASF WD 1942-46; GEN 1945; Ret 1946 MG.

Crawford Robert Walter, (W.P. 1914-No. 5213) CE; MG 1943; SOS USAFIME 1943; DCG SOS ETO 1943-44; G4 SHAEF 1944-45; Ret 1948 MG.

Skinner Frederick Snowden, (W.P. 1914-No. 5214) CE; NGRI & AUS 1941-45; CO 176 EGS Regt 1942-43; G1 Alas Dept 1943-44; Ret 1950.

Elliot Dabnet Otey, (W.P. 1914-No. 5215) CE; BG 1943; CS IXCps 1941-42; Ch Engrs AF Hq NATO 1943-44; CG Engr TC 1944-46; Ret 1950 BG.

Herman Frederick William, (W.P. 1914-No. 5219) CE; CO 1323 EGS Regt T-E 1944-45; Ret 1946

Carruth John Hill, (W.P. 1914-No. 5220) CE; CO 1313th EGS Regt T-E 1944-45; Ret 1950.

Wyeth John Churchill, (W.P. 1914-No. 5223) CO 404 FA Gp 3 Ar T-E 1944-45; Ret dslbd 1946.

Harris Arthur Ringland, (W.P. 1914-No. 5224) BG 1943; G2 1Ar 1941-43; MA Mexico & Argentina 1943-46 Ret dsbld 1948 BG.

Smyth Roy Melvin, (W.P. 1914-No. 5226) Inf; Kid Meuse Argonne 15 Oct 1918 LTC CO Inf Bn 3rd Div.

Stuart La Rhett Livingston, (W.P. 1914-No. 5227) CG 102nd AAA Brig T-S 1945; Ret 1951 BG.

Anderson John Benjamin, (W.P. 1914-No. 5237) BG 1941; MG 1942; CG 102nd Div 1942-43; CG 1th Cps ETO 1944-45; Ret dsld 1946.

Ingles Harry Clyde, (W.P. 1914-No. 5241) Inf; MG 1942; CS CDC 1942-43; Dpty CG ETO 1943; Ret 1947 MG.

Bradley James Lester, (W.P. 1914-No. 5242) Inf; MG 1942; CG 96th Div T-SP 1942-46; Ret dsbld 1947.

Glass Edward Leuffer Nevin, (W.P. 1914-No. 5244) Cav; MA Mexico 1922-26; BG Guatamalan Ar & Mil Advsr to Pres 1939-43; CO Air Ammo Dep Ger 1946-49; Ret 1950.

Burr William Edward, (W.P. 1914-No. 5246) Co Ar Transport 1942-46; CO Mil Dist IA Des Moines to ret 1947.

Villaret Eugene, (W.P. 1914-No. 5247) MA Greece, Rumania & Yugoslavia 1937-39; ComZ ETO 1944-45; Ret 1948.

Rees Thomas Henry, (W.P. 1914-No. 5251) Cav; CO Adv & Base Sect SOS CBI 1942-44; CS 5th Div Ft Jackson 1946-50; Ret 1951.

Waltz Floyd Randall, (W.P. 1914-No. 5252) Inf; CO MGun Bn 41st Inf AEF; GSA 7 CA 1942-43; WD Mpwr Bd 1943-46; Ret dsbld 1946.

Woodberry John Henry, (W.P. 1914-No. 5253) Cav; CO Raritan Ars 1940-43; Ch OO SOS T-S 1944-45; BG 1945; Ret dsbld 1946 BG.

Loomis Harold Francis, (W.P. 1914-No. 5255) LTC 1918; BG 1941; Ret dsbld 1946 BG.

Spaatz Carl, (W.P. 1914-No. 5262) Inf; CG 8th AF ETO 1942; CG Allied AF NATO 1943; CG US STAF ETO 1944-45; GEN 1945; CG US STAF Pacific 1945; CG AAF 1946-47; CS USAF 1947-48; Ret 1948 GEN.

Bull Harold Roe, (W.P. 1914-No. 5263) BG 1941; Asst CG 4th Div; MG 1942; CG 4th Div 1944; CS US FET 1945-46; Ret dsbld 1947.

Milliken Charles Morton, (W.P. 1914-No. 5266) Inf; CG SCR TC 1943-44 & CpCrowder 1944-45; Ret 1948 BG.

Byrom James Fred, (W.P. 1914-No. 5267) Inf-QMC; CO Gen Deps T-E 1942-43; QM West

Point 1943-46; Ret dsbld 1947.

Byron Joseph Wilson, (W.P. 1914-No. 5270) Cav; AUS 1942-46; MG 1944; MG ORC.

Hogan James Patrick, (W.P. 1914-No. 5271) Arty; CO 67th AAA T-AM 1941-43; CO Ft McDowell 1943-46; Ret dsbld 1946.

Paschal Paul Clarence, (W.P. 1914-No. 5272) Inf; BG 1943; Asst CG 1945; CG IRTC Y-A 1944-45; Ret dsbld 1946 BG.

Lim Vicente, (W.P. 1914-No. 5282) Ret dsbld 1936 LTC; BG Dpty CS PA 1039; CO 41st Div PA Bataan; POW (released); Guerrillas; POW 1944; Kld Manila, believed executed Nov 1944-Jan 1945.

Potts Adam Empie, (W.P. 1914-No. 5283) CO 98th CA Haw 1941-42; CO Cp Davis 1942-45; CO Ft Story 1945-46; Ret dsbld 1948; Great grandson Rev Adam Empie 1st Chaplain USMA.

Bratton Rufus Sumter, (W.P. 1914-No. 5286) Inf; CO Sp Tps 3rd Ar ETO 1944-45; G2 Hq Berlin 1945; G2 Sec Hq ASF 1945-46; Ret dsbld 1952.

Downs Sylvester De Witt Jr., (W.P. 1914-No. 5288) Cav; BG 1943; CG Ft Richardson AK 1943-44; Ret dsbld 1946 BG.

Ward Orlando, (W.P. 1914-No. 5290) Cav; 3rdDiv AEF; MG 1942; CG 1AD ETO 1942-43; CG TD Cen 1943; Cmdt FSC 1944; CG20th AD T-E 1944-45; CG 5th Cps 1946; CG 6th Div Korea 1946-49; Ret 1953 MG.

Weir Benjamin Grant, (W.P. 1914-No. 5293) Inf; BG 1945; Ret 1947; BG ret 1948.

Royce Ralph, (W.P. 1914-No. 5294) MG 1942; AAFT-S; CG 1st AF; CG AAF T-D; Dpty CG 9th AFT-E; Ret dsbld 1946 MG.

Ryan William Ord, (W.P. 1914-No. 5295) Cav; CG W Coast ADC 1941-42; CG Pac Div ATC 1943-46; Ret dsbld 1946 MG.

Monroe Thomas Huntington, (W.P. 1914-No. 5297) Inf; CO 15th Inf 3rd Div T-M 1941-43; Ret 1946.

Milburn Frank William, (W.P. 1914-NO.5304) Inf; MG 1942; CG 83rd Div & 21st Cps T-E; CG 1st Div Ger 1948; LTG 1951; CG 1st Cps KW 1950-51; Ret dsbld 1952 LTG.

Thompson John Bellinger, (W.P. 1914-No. 5308) Inf-Cav; BG 1942; CG CCB 7th AD ETO 1942-44; Ret 1946; BG ret 1948.

Doe Jens Anderson, (W.P. 1914-No. 5310) Inf; MG 1944; CO 163rd Inf 1943; CG 41st Div T-S; Ret 1949 MG.

Adler Elmer Edward, (W.P. 1914-Admitted as cadet 1910: non-grad) MG 1945; CG AAF CBI 1942-43; AMC 1943-45; Ret dsbld 1946 MG.

Covell William Edward Raab, (W.P. 1915-No. 5313) CE; Ret 1940 own request: MG AUS 43rd OQMG; CG SOS T-CI; Ret 1948 MG AUS.

Bragdon John Stewart, (W.P. 1915-No. 5317) CE; BG 1943; DivES Atlantic 1941-44; Ret 1951 MG.

Richards George Jacob, (W.P. 1915-No. 5318) 1st Compt USA 1947-48; IG Eucom 1949-50; Ch MAAG Paris France 1950; Ret 1953 MG.

Miller Lehman Wellington, (W.P. 1915-No. 5321) CE; PunX; BG 1941; Ret dsbld 1944.

Weart Douglas Lafayette, (W.P. 1915-No. 5322) CE; BG AsstE Pan Canal 1939-42; CS CDC 1943-44; MG Dpty Comdr T-C 1945; CG TEC 1945-48; Ret dsbld 1951 MG.

Conklin John French, (W.P. 1915-No. 5325) CE; TF 3Ar NATO 1942-43; BG 1945; Ret 1951 BG.

Tompkins William Frazer, (W.P. 1915-No. 5328) CE; BG 1942; MG 1944; Dpty CG & CS Ser Comd T-P 1945; Ret dsbld 1946 MG.

Davison Donald Angus, (W.P. 1915-No. 5331) CE; Inst CGSS 1932-36; Engr Hq SOS

England 1942; Avn Engr 1943-44; MG retroactive to 1944(psth).

Aurand Henry Spiese, (W.P. 1915-No. 5332) CG 6th SvC 1942-44; CG Normandy Base Sec 1945; CG SOS T-C 1945; CG T-M 1946; CG USARPac 1949 to ret 1952.

Larkin Thomas Bernard, (W.P. 1915-No. 5333) CE; CG Base Sec & SOS T-M 1942-44; CG SoloC&DCG ComZ T-E 1944-45; TQMG 1946-49; G4 GSUSA 1949-52; Ret dsbld 1952.

Lester James Allen, (W.P. 1915-No. 5335) CO Btry 7 Bn FA 4th Div AEF; CG 24th Div T-SP 1942-46; CG SF POE 1948 to ret dsbld 1953.

Young Mason James, (W.P. 1915-No. 5336) CE; CG EU COM ComZ Orleans France 1949; Ret dsbld 1953 BG.

Beukema Herman, (W.P. 1915-No. 5338) Prof *MD1*EGH*MD0* Soc Sci USMA 1930 to ret 1954 BG.

Struble Herbert Spencer, ETO 1944-45; ETO 1945; NY POE 1947 to ret 1949.

Zundel Edwin Albert, (W.P. 1915-No. 5341) BG 1944; Arty O, Hq 2 & 11 Cps 1942-43, Hq6 Ar 1943, Hq 41 Div New Guinea & Jap 1944-46; Hq 4th Ar 1946-48; Ch CIC 1948-49; IG GHQ FEC 1949 & UN Cmd KW 1950-52; Ret dsbld 1953 BG.

Howard Clinton Wilbur, (W.P. 1915-No. 5342) BG 1942; CG Sacramento ASC 1943-46; Ret dsbld 1946 BG.

Busbee Charles Manly, (W.P. 1915-No. 5343) CG 102nd Div Arty T-E 1944-46; Ret 1953 BG.

Waldron Albert Whitney, (W.P. 1915-No. 5344) Ret dsbld wds 1946 MG.

Parkinson Parley Doney, (W.P. 1915-No. 5345) BnCO 38th Inf AEF; CO TFA Dutch Guiana 1941-42; Ret dsbld 1942.

Sayler Henry Benton, (W.P. 1915-No. 5349) MG 1944; ChOO ETO 1942-43; Asst Ch Ord USA 1946; Ret 1949 MG.

Swing Joseph May, (W.P. 1915-No. 5350) MG 1943; CG 11th Abn Div T-S 1943-47; CG TAC & Cmdt TAS 1949-50; LTG 1950; CG 6th Ar 1951 to ret dsbld 1954 LTG.

Ryder Charles Wolcot, (W.P. 1915-No. 5351) Inf; 16th Inf Div AEF; Cmdt of Cadets USMA 1937-41; CG 34th Div T-M 1942-44; CG 9th Cps T-S 1944-48; MG USA 1948; Ret dsbld wds 1950 MG.

Irwin Stafford LeRoy, (W.P. 1915-No. 5352) CG Arty 9th Div NATO 1942-43; CG 5th Div T-E 1944-45; CG 12th Cps; LTG 1950; CG USFA 1950; Ret dsbld 1952 Gen.

McNarney Joseph Taggart, (W.P. 1915-No. 5353) Inf; Dpty Supreme Allied Cmdr, CG USA Fcs T-M; Many foreign decorations; CG USAFE & Gov US Zone GER 1945-47; CG AMC 1947-49; OSD 1949; Ret 1952 GEN.

Menoher Pearson, (W.P. 1915-No. Cav); ADC & CG 24th Div KW 1949-50; CG V Cps 1950-52; Ret dsbld 1952 BG.

Bradley Omar Nelson, (W.P. 1915-No. 5356) BG Cmdt Inf Sch; MG CG 82nd & 28th Divs; LTG CG 2nd Cps T-M; CG 1st Ar, 2nd Ar Gp T-E; CS Army 1948-49; Chairman JCS 1949-53; GEN ot the Army 1950.

Mueller John Paul, (W.P. 1915-No. 5357) CS 2nd Ar 1941-42; MG 1942; CG 81st Div T-APS 1942-46; Ret dsbld 1954.

Hobbs Leland Stanford, (W.P. 1915-No. 5358) MG CG 30th Div T-E 1942-45; CG 9th Cps FEC 1949-50; Ch JUS MAG RP Manila 1950-51; Dpty CG 1st Ar 1951-53; Ret 1953 MG.

Kahle John Frederick, (W.P. 1915-No. 5359) CO 107th AAGp T-M 1943-45; Sr Inst NGDC 1949 to ret 1953.

Lyon Edwin Bowman, (W.P. 1915-No. 5360) Cav; CG Antilles Air Cmd 1943; WgCG TngCmd 1944-45; CG AF Mid Pac 1945-46; Ret 1952 MG.

Lindner Clarence Brewster, (W.P. 1915-No. 5362) BnCO 44th Arty CAC AEF; FO Western TF NATO 1942-43; FO 5th Ar NATO & Italy 1943-44; Ret dsbld 1946.

Bank Carl Conrad, (W.P. 1915-No. 5365) Cav; BG 1944; GS Haw Dept 1940-41; Arty OAFHQ NATO 1943-44; CG 13th FA Brig T-ME 1944-45; Ret 1947.

Evans Vernon, (W.P. 1915-No. 5367) Inf; 1st MGun Bn 1st Div AEF; Dpty CS 43-44 of CBI, CS 1944-45; CG 46th of T-I; MG 1945; Ret 1953;

Woodruff Roscoe Barnett, (W.P. 1915-No. 5368) MG 1942; CG 77th Div 1942-43; CG 7th Cps T-E 1943-44; CG 24th Div T-S 1944-45; CG ICps FEC 1945-48; CG XV Cps 1951; Ret 1953 MG.

Eisenhower Dwight David, (W.P. 1915-No. 5373) Inf; Tk Corps 1918-19; CS 3rd Div IX Cps, 3rd Ar 1940-41; Ch WPD WDGS 1942; CG ETO 1942; CINC NATO & Italy 1942-43; CINC AEF, CG USFET, MilGov 1943-45; CS USA 1945-48; Many honors & decorations; Exempted from retirement for age Act of Congress 1948; Pres Columbia U. 1948; SACEUR 1950-52; Ret 1952 Resd 1952; 34th Pres of the U.S. 1953-61; Reapt GEN of Army Mar 1961; Awarded Thayer Medal 1961.

Peabody Hume, (W.P. 1915-No. 5375) Cav; CG AAFTAC 1941-44; CG Eastern FT Comd 1945; Ret dsbld 1946 BG.

Naiden Earl Larue, (W.P. 1915-No. 5380) Cav; BG 1942; CSFerry Cmd 1942, CS 10th AF India 1942.

Summers Iverson Brooks, (W.P. 1915-No. 5383) AG ETO 1942; AG 4th AF 1943; CO Ft Custer 1944; Ret dsbld 1946.

Ellis Edmund De Treville, (W.P. 1915-No. 5384) Cav-QMC; CO Genl Dep ETO 1943; OQMC 1943-46; Ret 1950.

Strong Robert William, (W.P. 1915-No. 5385) Cav; CS USAF Africa 1942; CG RTC 1943-44; Ch USA Msn to Peru 1945; Ret 1950 BG.

Jones Clifford Randall, (W.P. 1915-No. 5386) CO Troops Mid Pac Area 1942-46; Ret 1951.

Wogan John Beugnot, (W.P. 1915-No. 5387) CG 13th AD T-E 1944-45; Ret dsbld wds 1946 MG.

Tenny Clesen Henry, (W.P. 1915-No. 5389) BG Kwajalein 1944; CG 70th AAA Brig 1944; Ret dsbld 1946 BG.

Van Fleet James Alward, (W.P. 1915-No. 5404) CO 81st Inf 4th Div T-E 1941-44; Asst CG 2nd Div 1944; CG 4th Div 1944; CG 90th Div T-E 1944-45; CG 3rd Cps 1945-46; LTG 1948; Dir USA CG 1948-50; CG 2nd Ar 1950-51; CG 8th Ar Kor 1951-53;Ret 1953 GEN.

Sherburne Edward Gill, (W.P. 1915-No. 5406) Inf; CO 118th Inf IBC-ETO 1942-44; Ret dsbld 1946.

Hess Walter Wood Jr., (W.P. 1915-No. 5407) BG 1944; CO 36th FA Brig NATO-Italy 1942-43; CG 36th Div Arty T-MD 1943-45; CG Repl TC Ft Bragg 1945-46; CG Cp Carson 1950; Ret 1952 BG.

Davis Michael Frank, (W.P. 1915-No. 5408) Inf; CG SADPC 1945-46; DCG&LnO 10th & 12th AF 1947-50; Ret dsbld 1950 BG.

Esteves Luis Raul, (W.P. 1915-No. 5409) BG TAG PR 1039; CG PR Mobiles Fcs 1940; MG PRNG 1948 to ret 1957;.

Davis John Fuller, (W.P. 1915-No. 5411) Cav; BG 1943; CS 6th SvC 1942-44; WDGS 1944-45; Ret dsbld 1950 BG.

Harmon Hubert Rielly, (W.P. 1915-No. 5415) CG 6th AF 1943; CG 13th AF 1943-44; CG AF Pers Distribution Cmd 1944-45; LTG 48th AF Repr UNMSC 1947 to ret 1953 LTG.

Ferris Benjamin Greeley, (W.P. 1915-No. 5416) Inf; BG Dpty CS CBI; DCS 1st Ar1948-49.

Hearn Thomas Guerdon, (W.P. 1915-No. 5418) Inf; CS 3rd Cps 1941-42; MG 1943; CS & CG CBI 1942-43; CS T-C 1944; CG IRTC 1945-46; Ret dsbld 1946 MG.

Howell Reese Maughn, (W.P. 1915-No. 5421) Cav; CO 17th FA 13th FA Brig NATO 1942-43; BG 1943; CG 9th Div Arty NATO T-E 1943-46; Ret 1946; BG ret 1948.

Miller Henry Jervis Friese, (W.P. 1915-No. 5422) Cav; BG 1941; MG 1942; Ch AMC England 1943-44; Ret dsbld 1944; BG ret 1948.

McGee Frank D., (W.P. 1915-No. 5425) 126th Inf Div AEF(wded at Fismes) Ret wds 1922; AD JAN 1942 PI; LTC CO 106th Div PA (Mindanao guerrillas); Kld-Davao 7 Aug 1945 operating with US 24th Inf Div LTC.

Boots Norman Jay, (W.P. 1915-No. 5427) Cav; Captured Gen Guttierrez leader Columbus NM raid 1916; First non stop flight Detriot-NYC (distance record): Ret LTC res.

Robinson John Nicholas, (W.P. 1915-No. 5432) Inf; 15th Inf China 1921; BG 1944; Alaska 1941-44; Asst CG 89th Div ETO 1944-45; Ret 1949 BG.

Taylor Victor Vaughn, (W.P. 1915-No. Cav); T-AE 1941-44; BG 1943; Ret dsbld 1944.

Hanley Thomas James, (W.P. 1915-No. 5436) Inf; MG 1943; A4 Hq AF; CG Eastern Fly Tng Cmd; CG ASC-CBI; OTAG 1948 to ret 1952 MG.

Walton Leo Andrew, (W.P. 1915-No. 5440) Cav; BG 1942; CS AAF Tng Cmd 1940-44; CG 14th AF 1946-48; MG OSAF 1948; Ret 1949 MG.

Cousins Ralph Pittman, (W.P. 1915-No. 5441) Cav; MG 1942; CG Western Flying Tng Cmd; Ret dsbld 1946.

Finley Charles Robert, (W.P. 1915-No. 5445) CS Panama CAC Cmd 1940-41; GS 1st Ar T-AE 1941-43; CO 47th AA Bde T-E 1943-45; Ret 1946.

Prichard Vernon Edwin, (W.P. 1915-No. 5446) Inf; AdC GEN Drum 1936-39; MG 1942; CG 14th AD 1943-44; CG 1st AD Italy 1944-45; COM 1946-49; MG USA 1949.

Gilkeson Adlai Howard, (W.P. 1915-No. 5449) Inf; CG Air Def CZ 1939-42; CG Ftr Cmds T-A & CBI 1942-45; OIG Hq DAF 1948-49; Ret 1953 BG.

Stickney Richard Carlton, (W.P. 1915-No. 5451) Inf; Inf BnCo 7th Div AEF; Hq 4thSvC 1943-44; Dpty CS 14th Cps Luzon 1945; AGO WD 1947 to ret dsbld 1948.

Mendenhall John Ross, (W.P. 1915-No. 5456) Inf; Inst 107th Inf NYNG 1930-36; KIA-New Guinea Air Msn 27 Jan 1945.

Randolph Norman, (W.P. 1915-No. 5457) Inf; BG 1942; CS 2nd Ar & 3rd SvC 1942-44; Ret dsbld 1945 BG.

Stratemeyer George Edward, (W.P. 1915-No. 5459) Inf; CG AAF T-CI 1943-46; CG ADC 1946-49; CG FEAF 1949-51; Ret dsbld 1952 LTG.

Boye Frederic William, (W.P. 1915-No. 5462) Cav; CO CavDet, TacDept 1929-33; NGB 1937-40; China 1944-45; BG 1945; Ret 1950 BG.

Watson Leroy Hugh, (W.P. 1915-No. 5463) Inf; MG 1942; CG 3AD 1943-44 T-E; 29th Div 1944-45; CG Ft Lewis & Sr Inst ORC 1950; Ret 1953 MG.

White Arthur Arnim, (W.P. 1915-No. 5470)

Inf-Cav; CS 7th Ar & CG XIV Cps T-E 1944-45; CG 75th Div & CG 71st Div 1945-46; CG VCps Arty 1946-48; CG 9th Div 1948-49; Ret 1949 MG.

Keliher John, (W.P. 1915-No. 5471) Inf; G3 Hq USAF Mid Pac 1942-44; G5 USAF-POA 1944-45; G3 USAF Mid Pac 1946-49; Ret dsbld 1950 BG.

Moses Raymond George, (W.P. 1916-No. 5478) BG 1942; G4 WDGS 1942-43; G4 12th ArGp T-E 1943-45; Ch US Admin O Brit 21st ArGP 1944; DivEngr NewEng 1946 to 1949 BG.

Styer Wilhelm Delp, (W.P. 1916-No. 5479) CE; CnDiv OQMG 1941; Dpty CG & CS ASF WD 1942-45; CG USAF Wes Pac 1945-46; Ret 1947 LTG.

Johns Dwight Frederick, (W.P. 1916-No. 5482) CE; BG 1942; CG Ser Cmd N Guinea 1942-43Cmdt TES 1944-45; Ret 1949 BG.

Finley Thomas Dewees, (W.P. 1916-No. ????) CE-Inf; CG 89th Div T-AE 1943-45; Ret dsbld 1943 MG.

Reinhart Stanley Eric, (W.P. 1916-No. 5487) BG 1942; CG 25th Div Arty T-S 1942-43; CG 65th Div T-AE 1943-45; Ret dsbld 1946 MG.

Worsham Ludson Dixon, (W.P. 1916-No. 5496) CE; E AFWestPac 1945-46; DivE WOcean 1946-48; Ret dsbld 1948 BG.

McBride Horace Logan, (W.P. 1916-No. 5498) MG 1943; CG 80th Div,CG 20th Cps T-E; Ch USA GT 1947; Cmdt CGSC 1950-52; LTG 1952; CinC Car Cmd 1952; Ret 1954.

Neyland Robert Reese Jr., (W.P. 1916-No. 5504) CE; SOS CBI 1944; BG 1944; CG Base Sect SOS T-I 1944-46; BG ret 1948.

Hoge William Morris, (W.P. 1916-No. 5505) CE; MG 1945; CG Alaska Mil Hwy 1942; 9th AD 1942-43; ,44-45; CG 4th AD T-EP 1945; CG 9th Cps KW 1951; CG 4th Ar 1953-53; CG Hq 7th Ar 1953; GEN 1953; CinC USAREUR 1953-55; Ret dsbld 1955 GEN.

Woodward William Roscoe, (W.P. 1916-No. 5506) CG 104th Div Arty T-E 1944-45; CG Amer Div Arty & 104th Div Arty 1942-45; Arty O & G4 6th Ar 1946-50; Ret 1950 BG.

Scott Stanley Lonzo, (W.P. 1916-No. 5507) CE; CS T-G 1942-44; Hq ASF WD 1944-46; WDGS 1944-48; CG USAR AL 1948-50; CG TEC 1951; Ret 1954 MG.

Pickering James Arthur, (W.P. 1916-No. 5517) BG 1942; CG 8th Div Arty T-E 1943-45; Ret 1946 BG.

Spence William, (W.P. 1916-No. 5521) Cav; GS 1st Cav Div 1930-34; CG 93dr Div T-S 1944; CG Arty 38th Div PI 1944-45; Ret 1947.

Chapin Willis McDonald, (W.P. 1916-No. 5523) CO 31st AAA Brig NATO 1943-44; BG 1944; CG 31st AAA Brig ETO 1944-45; Ret 1949 BG.

Inglis Fred Beeler, (W.P 1916-No. 5524) Inf; XO 75th Div Arty & CO 334th Inf T-E 1944-45; Ret 1946.

McBride Robert Bruce Jr., (W.P. 1916-No. 5525) CG 32nd Div Arty T-S 1943-45; CG 32nd Div 1945; Ret 1952 BG.

Kane Paul Vincent, (W.P 1916-No. 5526) CG 3rd Cps ETO 1944-46; Ret dsbld 1949 BG.

Prickett Fay Brink, (W.P. 1916-No. 5533) Cav; CO 4th Div Arty 1942-43; MG 1944; CG 75th Div T-E 1943-46; CG 10th & 4th AD 1945-46; Dpty IG USA 1948 to ret dsbld 1953 MG.

DeWitt Calvin Jr., (W.P 1916-No. 5534) Cav; CS & Dpty Cmdr NY POE & CG Boston POE 1942-45; CG Nagoya & Kobe Bases 1945-46; Dpty CO SF POE 1946-47; Ch Trans Hq Eu Com 1947-50; CG NYPOE 1952-54; Ret dsbld 1954 BG.

Chambers William Earl, (W.P. 1916-No. 5540) Inf; BG 1942; CO SSAC Staff 1943; G3 Sec

GHQ T-S 1944-45; Ret dsbld 1946 BG.

Tully Joseph Merit, (W.P. 1916-No. 5541) Cav; BG 1945; Co 4th Cav, Asst CO 90th Inf Div & CG 80th Inf Div 1943-46; CS 2nd Div Ft Lewis KW 1948-50; Ret dsbld 1951 BG.

Walsh Robert LeGrow, (W.P. 1916-No. 5546) Cav; MG 1943; CG US AFSA 1943-44; Hq AAF 1944-45; Dir Intel Berlin 1947-48; Ret 1953 MG.

Martin Thomas Lyle, (W.P. 1916-No. 5548) Inf; BG 1942; Asst CG 2nd Div 1942-44; Ret 1951 BG.

Baldwin Goeffrey Prescott, (W.P. 1916-No. 5549) Inf; BG 1942; Asst CG 79th Div ETO 1942-43; Ret dsbld 1943 BG.

Bennet John Bennington, (W.P. 1916-No. 5550) Inf; 1st & 77th Divs AEF; GSC Hq CBI 1942 to D-Burma typhus 10 Jun 1944.

Shugg Roland Paget, (W.P. 1916-No. 5555) Cav; CG 13th Cps Arty T-E 1943-45; CG 3rd Div Arty KW 1950-51; Ret 1952 BG.

Krayenbuhl Craigie, (W.P. 1916-No. 5563) Cav; CO 126th ABn & ExO & CO 191st FAGp T-S 1943-45.

Parker Paul Barrows, (W.P. 1916-No. 5565) Inf-CE; AUS 1941-46; Ret dsbld 1944 COL AUS; AD CO Ft Lawton 1944-46.

O'Hare Joseph James, (W.P. 1916-No. 5571) BG 1944; G1 12th ArGp T-E; ArmA Paris France 1949; Ret 1953 BG.

Ellis Arthur Monroe, (W.P. 1916-No. 5572) Inf; XO 101st Inf IBC 1940-42; Ret dsbld 1942 LTC.

Miller Maurice Levi, (W.P. 1916-No. 5573) Inf; BG 1942; Asst CG 100th Div T-E ; CO ASU Ft Benning 1948; Ret dsbld 1950 BG.

Junius Henry Houghton (W.P. 1916-No. 5574) Inf-Cav-Ac: BG 44 (LM): Ret 50 BG:

*Herman Harrison, (W.P. 1916-No. 5581) Cav; CO 7thTD GP ETO 1944 to KIA-Belgium bulge 26 Dec 1944.

Newgarden George Joseph Jr., (W.P. 1916-No. 5583) Inf; CO 262nd Inf, 66th Division 43-44; CO Tng Units 1945-46; Ret dsbld COL 1946.

Goodman John Forest, (W.P. 1916-No. 5586) Inf-Cav; 26th Inf Div AEF; POW; AFG; Inst CGSS 1931-35; CO 364th Inf AK 1944-45; BG 1945; Ret 1946.

Lange Otto Frederick, (W.P. 1916-No. 5592) Inf; ADC 36th Div T-M 1942-43; IRTC Units 1943-47; Ret dsbld 1948 BG.

Mumma Harlan Leslie, (W.P. 1916-No. 5593) Inf-QMC; Dept QM PCD 1941-46; CG Jeffersonville QM Dep 1946-48; Ret 1948 BG.

Weyand Alexander Mathias, (W.P. 1916-No. 5595) Inf; CO MPs DC 1941-42; First PMG ETO 1942-43; Comdt Discip Bks Ft Missoula 1944-46; Ret dsbld 1946.

Heavy William Francis, (W.P. 1917-No. 5604) BG 1942; Engr 4th Cps 1941-42; CG Engr Brig T-SP 1942-46; Ret 1948 BG.

Bathurst Robert Marks, (W.P. 1917-No. 5606) BG 1944; CS WDC 1943-44; CS Alaskan Dept 1944-46; CG USAR Ant 1950; Ret 1953 BG.

Noce Daniel (W.P. 1917-No. 5608) CE; MG 1944; CO Engr Amphib Cmd 1942; G3 ETO 1943-44; G3 AFHQ T-M 1944-45; CS & Dpty CG ASF WD 1945-46; G4 1948-49; IG USA 1952; LTG 1952; Ret dsbld 1954 LTG.

Hurdis Charles Everett, (W.P. 1917-No. 5613) CG 6th Div Arty T-AS 1942-45; MG 1945; CG 6th Div T-S 1945-46; Ret dsbld 1946 MG.

Hutchings Henry Jr., (W.P. 1917-No. 5614) CE; CG 4th ESpBde T-S 1944-45; Ret dsbld 1949 BG.

Devine John Matthew, (W.P. 1917-No. 5617)

CG 90th Div Arty T-E 1943-44; MG CG 8th AD T-E 1944-45; Ret 1952 MG.

Nisley Harold Albert, (W.P. 1917-No. 5618) Ord O Armd Fc 1940-42; BG OrdO 12th Ar Gp T-E 1944-45; Ret dsbld 1948 BG.

Wahl George Douglas, (W.P. 1917-No. 5622) BG CG 79th Div Arty T-E; Ret 1949 BG.

Perry Basil Harrison, (W.P. 1917-No. 5623) BG CG 28th Div Arty T-AE 1942-45; CG Mil Post EU COM 1949; Ret 1953 BG.

Jackson, Harold Rufus, (W.P. 1917-No. 5624) BG 1943; AAO ETO 1944-45; CO Ft McNair 1951 to ret 1953 BG.

Clark Solomom Foote, (W.P. 1917-No. 5627) 1st Div Arty AEF; CO 195th FA Gp 20th Cps Arty T-E 1943-45; Ret 1948.

Gurney Augustus Milton, (W.P. 1917-No. 5628) BG 1942; CS 2nd ArT-A 1944-45; CO USTrps Adak Alas 1946-47; OC AFF 1947-50; GS Hq 1st Ar 1950 to ret dsbld 1954 BG.

Murray John Trott, (W.P. 1917-No. 5629) Inf; BG 1943; Asst CG 40th Div, 6th Div & CS 1st Cps T-S; Ret dsbld 1947; BG ret 1948.

Butler William Ormond, (W.P. 1917-No. 5634) DCG Allied Exped AF T-E 43-44; Ret dsbld 1946 MG.

Beasley Rex Webb, (W.P. 1917-No. 5635) BG 1942; CG 81st B-IN Div Arty T-P; MG 1949; Ret dsbld 1952 MG.

Collins Joseph Lawton, (W.P. 1917-No. 5636) Inf; MG 1942; CG 25th Div T-Sp 1942-43; CG 7th Cps T-E 1944-45; LTG 1945; GEN 1948; CS US Army 1949-53; Ret 1956 GEN.

Ford Elbert Louis, (W.P. 1917-No. 5641) BG 1943; ETO 1942; CS Hq NATO 1943-44; OCO 1944-46; Ch Ord US FET 1946-48; CG APG 1948; Ch USA 1949 to ret 1953 MG.

Cole John Tupper, (W.P. 1917-No. 5648) Cav; CO CCB 5th AD T-E 1943-45; Cmdt Sch Cen EU COM 1945-46; BG 1950; Ch MAAG Thailand 1951-52; CG 3rd AD Ft Knox 1952 to ret 1953 BG.

Beurket George Sampson, (W.P. 1917-No. 5649) CO Ft Jay NY 1943-46; CO 9th Div Arty Ft Dix 1949; Ret dsbld 1953;

Sherrill Stephen Huntting, (W.P. 1917-No. 5650) Cav; BG 1942; CG Air Warning Unit Tng Cen 3AF 1943-44; Ret 1944 BG; AD CG Ft Monmouth 1944-45.

Gerhardt Charles Hunter, (W.P. 1917-No. 5651) Cav; MG 1942; CG 29th Div T-E 1943-46; Ret 1952 MG.

Irving Frederick Augustus, (W.P. 1917-No. 5654) Inf; MG 1942; CG 24th Div & 38th Div T-SP 1942-45; MG USA 1948; Dpty CG 6th Ar 1950-51; Supt USMA 1951 to ret 1954 MG.

Ridgway Matthew Bunker, (W.P. 1917-No. 5657) Inf; CG 82nd Abn Div T-ME 1942-44; CG 18th Abn Corps T-E 1944-45; LTG 1945; CinC Car Cmd 1948-49; DCS Hq DA 1949; CG Eusak 1950-51; GEN 1951; CinC FEC & SCAP 1951-52; SAC EUR 1952; CS USA 1953 to ret 1955 GEN.

Yuill Charles Walter, (W.P. 1917-No. 5662) Inf; CO 11th Inf 5th Div T-E 1942-44; Ret dsbld 1947.

Eagles William Willis, (W.P. 1917-No. 5663) Inf; MG 1943; Asst CG 3rd Div NATO 1942-43; CG 45th Div T-ME 1943-45; CG RY Com 1948; Ret 1953 MG.

Holmes Joel Grant, (W.P. 1917-No. 5666) Picatinny Ars 1926; OCh Ord ETO 1943-45; BG 1950; Ret 1952 BG.

Stanford Albert Charles, (W.P. 1917-No. 5667) Cav; BG CG Arty 34th & 75th Inf Divs T-EM; Ret 1946.

Code James Arthur Jr., (W.P. 1917-No. 5668) MG Asst Ch SigO USA 1941-45; Ch SigO

ETO 1945; Ret 1946.

Sackville William, W.P. 1917-No. 5671) CO TF 1942-43; G2 22Cps T-E 1944-45; G3 Sect ETO USA 1945; CO HD LI Sound 1946-49; Ret 1951.

Harrison William Kelly Jr., (W.P. 1917-No. 5674) BG 1942; Asst CG 30th Div T-AE 1942-45; MG 1949; CG Ft Dix 1950-52; Dpty CG HqAFFE 1952-53; Sr Delegate Truce Team KW 1952-53; CS Hq Fec 1953-54; Ret 1957 LTG.

Harmon Ernest Nason, (W.P. 1917-No. 5677) Cav; CG 2AD NATO 1942-43; CG 1st AD Italy 1943-44; CG 2AD ETO 1944-45; CG 22 Cps OccG 1945-46; CG Con Ger 1946-47; Ret 1948.

Cota Norman Daniel, (W.P. 1917-No. 5680) Inf; Asst CG 29th Div T-E 1943-44; MG CG 28th Div T-E 1944-45; Ret dsbld 1946 MG.

Tate Joseph Scranton, (W.P. 1917-No. 5682) Cav; 80th Div Arty 1942-43; CO 411th FA Gp T-E 1944-45; CO RTC 1947-48; CO 11th Abn Div Arty & G1 I Cps Jap 1948-50; Ret 1951.

Harper Arthur McKinley, (W.P. 1917-No. 5684) Cav; MG 1945; CG 24th Cps Arty & CG 98th Div T-SP 1944-46; CG TAC; Cmdt TAS 1950 to ret dsbld 1953 MG.

Bradshaw Aaron Jr., (W.P. 1917-No. 5686) Ch AAA Def NATO 1941-43; CG AAA 7th Ar & 5th Ar 1943-45; Ret dsbld 1953 MG.

Schwarzkopf Herbert Norman, (W.P. 1917-No. 5689) Cav; Ch Mil Msn to Iran 1942; BG 1946; MG USAR 1954; Ret 1957 MG.

Kilburn Charles Solomon, (W.P. 1917-No. 5693) Cav; CG 11th AD ETO 1944-45; Ret 1946; BG ret 1948.

Slaughter Willis Richardson, (W.P. 1917-No. 5694) Inf; OO Hq 6th Ar 1950-52; BG 1952; CG Ord Tng Cmd APG 1952; Ret 1954 BG.

Weems George Hatton, (W.P. 1917-No. 5695) Inf; BG 1942; Ret BG 1951.

Johnson Charles Radcliffe Jr., (W.P. 1917-No. 5697) Cav; CO 106th Cav 1940-42; MA Morrocco & Algeria 1942; Hq 5th Ar & CO 15th Inf Sicily 1943; Ret 1947.

McMahon William Claude, (W.P. 1917-No. 5698) Inf; Dpty CS 6Ar 1947-49; Ret 1949 MG.

Pierce Harry Russell, (W.P. 1917-No. 5702) CO 2AAA Gp AAA Brigade 9 Ar T-E; Dachau War Crimes Tribunal 1945-46; Ret 1950 COL.

Halsey Milton Baldridge, (W.P. 1917-No. 5705) Inf; MG 1946; CG 97th Inf Div T-E 1944-45 & Jap 1945; CS 9Cps CG Yokohama Cmd, CS 8th Ar Jap 1946-48; CG 6th Ar 1951; Ret 1953 MG.

Mullins Charles Love Jr., (W.P. 1917-No. 5706) Inf; Founder Mil Acad Nicaragua 1939; MG 1944; CG 25th Div T-SP 1943-44; SWP & Far East 1945-48; Dpty CG 2 Ar1948-49; Ret dsbld 1953 MG.

Wooley George Francis Jr., (W.P. 1917-No. 5708) Inf; BG 1945; Sig O 4th Ar 1945; Ret 1949 BG.

Wood Sterling Alexander, (W.P. 1917 — No.) Inf; CO 313 Inf 79th Div T-E 1943-44; FAS ETO 1945-46; BG 1950; Asst CG 5th AD Cp Chaffee 1950-52; Ret 1954 BG.

Clark Mark Wayne, (W.P. 1917-No. 5711) Inf; MG CinC Allied Forces NATO; DCS GHQ & CS ETO 1943; CG 5th Ar Italy 1943-44; GEN 1945; CG 5th Ar & 15th Ar Gp 1943-45 & USFA 1945-47; CG 6th Ar 1947-49; CG AFF 1949-52; CinC FEC & UNCmd 1952-53; Ret 1953 GEN.

Campbell Alexander Hunkins, (W.P. 1917-No. 5713) CO AW Ser PI 1941-42; Bataan; POW 1942-45; Death March; Hq 6th Ar 1950 to ret dsbld 1952.

Rumbough David Sheridan, (W.P. 1917-No. 5714) Inf; BG 1942; XO 34th FA Brig T-E 1944-45; Hq US ARC 1948-50; XO NGB 1951; Ret 1953.

*Swanton Donovan, (W.P. 1917-No. 5717) Inf; CO 51st Inf PA Bataan; POW; Death March; Ret 1951.

Keiser Laurence Bolton, (W.P. 1917-No. 5719) Inf; BG 1944; CS 6th Cps Italy; CS 4th Ar 1945-46; ADC & CG 2nd Div 1948-50 Ft Lewis & KW; MG 1950; CG 5th Div 1951; Ret dsbld 1954 MG.

Brown Homer Caffee, (W.P. 1917-No. 5720) Inf; BG 1944; CG Australia Base Sect 1943-44; CG Spec Tps Manila 1945; G3 4th Ar 1947 to ret dsbld 1948 BG.

Armstrong Clare Hibbs, (W.P. 1917-No. 5721) Inf; BG 1943; CG 50th AA Bde T-E 1943-45; CG Antwerp Def Cmd 1944-45; CG CP Stewart 1950; Ret dsbld 1953.

Melasky Harris Marcy, (W.P. 1917-No. 5722) Inf; MG 1943; CG 86th Div T-EP 1943-45; Ret dsbld 1946 MG.

Sullivan Joseph Pescia, (W.P. 1917-No. 5732) BG 1944; QM 5th Ar T-M 1943-45; Ch QM USFA 1945-47; MG 1948; QM OC AFF 1949-52; Ret dsbld 1953 MG.

Leavey Edmond Harrison, (W.P. 1917-No. 5746) CE; MG 1944; Construction Div OQMG & OCE 1940-42; CS USAF Ireland 1942; CS & CO NATO Base Sect 1942-43; G4 Hq POA 1943-45; Recd Surrender all Jap forces in PI 3 Sep 1945; Ret 1949 MG.

Stamps Thomas Dodson, (W.P. 1917-No. 5747) CE; BG & Dean Academic Bd USMA 1956 to ret 1957 BG.

Reeder William Oliver, (W.P. 1917-No. 5756) SO & G4 Hq CBI 1944-46; MG 1944; Dpty CSO 1947-48; Dpty G4 1948; Ret 1953 MG.

Buechler Theodore Earl, (W.P. 1917-No. 5760) BG 1942; CG 100th Div Arty 1942-43; CG 18th Cps Arty T-E 1943-44; Arty O ETO 1945; Ret 1953 BG.

Futch Theodore Leslie, (W.P. 1917-No. 5766) CG 35th Div Arty T-E 1944-45; Hq 7th Ar 1946; The Citadel 1946; Ret 1954 BG.

Cooney Harold Allum, (W.P. 1917-No. 5769) CO 193rd FA Gp T-E 1944-45; Japan 1945-46; Ret 1954.

Barber Henry Anson, (W.P. 1917-No. 5771) Inf; BG 1943; Asst CG 4th Div T-E T-CP; Asst to Ambassador of Spain 1951.

Cowles Miles Andrew, (W.P. 1917-No. 5772) BG 1943; CG 36th Div Arty T-M 1943-44; Ret dsbld 1953 BG.

*Coffey John Will, (W.P. 1917-No. 5780) BG 1943; Ch Ord O AF Hq Italy 1943-45; CG Ord Dep 1945-47; Prof of Ord USMA 1947 to D-air Accd Ger 8 Mar 1951 BG.

Meade Frank Celestine, (W.P. 1917-No. 5781) BG 1942; OMG US Ger 1944-46; Ret 1947; BG ret 1948.

Willard Robert Alston, (W.P. 1917-No. 5785) Inf; CO SCRTC 1942-43; CO SC Tng Cen 1943-45; SigO 1st Abn Army T-E 1945 & SO Berlin Dist 1945-47; Co Sig TC 1949; Ret dsbld 195 BG.

Hasbrouck Robert Wilson, (W.P. 1917-No. 5789) DCS 12th Ar Gp T-E 1943-44; CG 7th AD T-E 1944-45; Ret dsbld 1947 MG.

Hull Sargent Prentiss, (W.P. 1917-No. 5793) OO AFPG 1941-45; CO Cressona Ord Dep 1946-48; CO Red River Ars 1951-53; Ret dsbld 1953.

Donaldson William Henry Jr., (W.P. 1917-No. 5794) BG 1943; CG SOS N Guinea 1943-44; CG SOS Australia 1944-46; CO Seattle POE 1947.

Heavey Thomas Jackson, (W.P. 1917-No.

5796) Cav; CO TD Cen Cp Hood 1943-44; CBI 1944-45; Ret dsbld 1947.

Black Henry Mans, (W.P. 1917-No. 5797) Opn CWS Arsenals 1941-45; CO CmlC plants 1945-46; CmlC 1946-5; BG 1951; CG CmlC Material Cmd Balt MD 1951 to ret 1953 BG.

*Segundo Fidel Ventura, (W.P. 1917-No. 5804) BG CG 1st Reg Div PA Bataan; POW; Death March; Paroled; Guerrilla underground; Arrested Dec 1944; Kld Manila (executed) about 6Jan 1945 BG.

Williamson Raymond E.S., (W.P. 1917-No. 5805) Cav; BG 1942; G1 Amer Div & CG SvC T-SP 1942-43; Dpty CG 91st Div T-M 1944-45; CG 3rd AD 1950-52; ArmA London 1953 to ret 1954 BG.

Schlenker David Charles George, (W.P. 1917-No. 5806) Cav; Comm O Hq AF 1940-41; ACS Hq 4AF SF Cal 1941-46; Ret dsbld 1953.

Carson Marion, (W.P. 1917-No. 5817) Asst Cmd Cav Sch 1943; AGF Bd T-S 1943-44; CO Sou Land Frontier 1944-45; Ret 195.

Garity Rossiter Hunt, (W.P. 1917-No. 5820) Cav; CO USAF Aitutaki Is; Co 15th Armd Gp; PMST Augusta Mil Acad 1946 to ret 1948.

Bissell John Ter Bush, (W.P. 1917-No. 5834) Inf; BG 1944; CG Arty 89th Inf Div T-E 1944-45; Ret 1946.

Eyster George Senseny, (W.P. 1917-No. 5838) Inf; BG 1944; G3 ETO 1944-45; HqEur Cmd 1946-48; Asst Ch PID SS USA 1948-49; Ret dsbld 1950 BG.

Chapman William McCaskey, (W.P. 1917-No. 5840) Inf; CO 306th Inf 77th Div T-P 1943-44; CO Port Gp Cent Pac Base CMD 1944; CO 389th Inf Div 98th Div T-P 1944-45; Ret dsbld 1946.

McNeil Norman, (W.P. 1917-No. 5843) Inf; Dir US Fcs China 1943-45; CO NCMilDist 1946-49; Ret dsbld 1950.

Glen Henry Anderson (W.P. 1917-No. 5844) CO 46 AInf 5AD T-E (SS-LM-5BSM): Ret dsbl 46 COL:

*Moore Bryant Edward, (W.P. 1917-No. 5845) Inf; CO 164th Inf AmerDiv T-S 1942; BG 1943; MG 1945; DCG 104th Div T-E & CG 8th Div 1945; CG 88th Div & Trust 1945-48; Supt USMA 1949-51; D-Korea battle 24 Feb 1951 MG.

Warner Leo Vincent, (W.P. 1917-No. 5846) Inf; CO MGun Co 3rd Div AEF; AG & G1 8th Cps 1942; BG 1952; Ret 1954 BG.

Bobrink Henry William, (W.P. 1917-No. 5848) Inf; OQMG 1941-44; Asst QM Hq ETO 1945-46; Ret dsbld 1947.

Rolfe Onslow Sherburne, (W.P. 1917-No.) Inf; ADC 71st Div T-E 1945-46; CO 51st Inf USFA 1946; Asst G3 OCAFF 1951-52; CG Northern Cmd 1952; CG Hq & Ser Cmd & Central Cmd 1952-53; Ret dsbld tem 1954 BG.

Matlack Jesse Brooke, (W.P. 1917-No. 5852) Inf; CO Arty 2nd Cav Div & 36th Div T-ME 1943-45; CS 36th Div 1945.

Lewis Parry Weaver, (W.P. 1917-No.) Inf; CO 71st AAA Gp & 31st AAA Brig T-E 1944-45; Ret 1946.

Timberlake Edward Wrenne, (W.P. 1917-No. 5856) Inf; CO 71st AAA & 89th AAA Regts 1942; BG 1943; CG 36th AAA Brig 1943; CG Blandford AAA Tng Cp, CG 49th AAA Brig & AAA 1AR T-E 1944-46; Ret 1950 BG.

Jenna William Wallace, (W.P. 1917-No. 5858) Inf; CO TF Cent Pac; CO 84th Inf 24th Div T-SP 1943-45; CO 3rd Inf 1951-52; Ret 1954.

Cole Paul Wallace, (W.P. 1917-No. 5860) Inf; CO 62nd CA(AA) AF Hq T-M 1943-44; CO

8th AA Gp 7th Ar T-ME 1944-45; Ret dsbld 1954.

Barnes Harry Cooper, (W.P. 1917-No. 5862) Inf; CO AA Gp & Prov AA Brig 1943; Ret dsbld wds 1944.

Goode Paul Ryan, (W.P. 1917-No. 5868) Inf; CO 175th Inf 29th Div & POW Ger 1944-45; Dpty & CO Sch Bks 1947-49; Ret dsbld 1952.

Demuth Henry Cornelius (W.P. 1917-No. 5871) CO & XO Amer Div Arty T-SP 42-43: XO 96 Div Arty T-SP 43-45: DCS & AsstIG HQ USARC 52-53: Ret 53 COL:

Maling Edwin Clark (W.P. 1917-No. 5873) CmlO 12AF 43-44 & SOS T-M 44-45: Ret 47 Col:

Bacon, Robert Lynn (W.P. 1917-No. 5876) CS & CO Regt 90 Div 44 (SS): CO Inf Regt 95 Div 45 (SS-BSM): Ret 47 Col:

House Edwin Jacob, (W.P. 1917-No. 5879) MG 1943; CG Antilles Air Cmd 1941-43; CG 12th Air Support Cmd T-M 1943-44; Ret dsbld 1945 MG.

Wilson Carlisle Brittania, (W.P. 1917-No. 5884) Inf; G1 15th Ar T-E 1944-45; CO 65th Inf Antilles Dept 1946; Ret dsbld 1952.

Whittington William Edward, (W.P. 1917-No. 5885) Inf; Aus 1941-44; Sigo 9th Ftr Cmd 1942-43; T-D XO & CO AFB China 1943-44; Ret 1955.

Harding Horace, (W.P. 1917-No. 5888) Inf; CG 8th Ar Area Cmd & CO 1st Cps Arty T-S 1942-45; CG 8th Ar Area Cmd 1945; CG 40th Div Arty 1951; Ret 1953 BG.

Timothy Patrick Henry, (W.P. 1918-No. 5893) CE; BG 1945; Ch engr 12th Ar T-E 1943-45; Cmdt Engr Sch 1945-46; Ret dsbld 1946 BG.

Casey Hugh John; (W.P. 1918-No. 5894) CE; BG 1942; MG 1944; CG ArSvC T-P 1944-45; Ret dsbld 1949 MG.

Tansey Patrick Henry, (W.P. 1918-No. 5896) CE; BG 1942; OPD WDGS 1942-45; Hq Ser Cmd 8th Ar T-S 1945-46; GHQ FE 1946-49; Ret 1953 MG.

Kramer Hans, (W.P. 1918-No. 5897) CE; BG 1942; Ch Engr Hq USAF Mid Pac 1942-44; Ret dsbld 1945 BG.

Stenzel Roland (W.P. 1918-No. 5907) AUS 42-46 COL; CO 1152 Engr Cmbt Gp 3 Ar 43-5 (PH)

Adcock Clarence Lionel, (W.P. 1918-No. 5909) CE; MG 1945; G4 2Cps T-M 1942; G4 5Ar 1943; G4 AFHQ 1943-44; G4 6Ar Gp T-E 1944-45; Ret 1947, MG ret 1948.

Ward Charles Stuart (W.P. 1918-No. 5911) AUS 42-45 COL; XO 41 Engrs T-D 42-43 (LM): CO 41 Engrs T-M 43-44 Ret 54 COL.

Underwood Henry Morehead (W.P. 1918-No. 5912) CO Engr GS Regt T-E 43-44: Ret dsbl 45 COL:

Newman James Bryan Jr., (W.P. 1918-No. 5913) CE; BG 1943; CG 9th Engr Cmd 9th AF T-E 1944-45; Ret 1946, BG ret 1948.

Clay Lucius Du Bignon, (W.P. 1918-No. 5918) CE; Civil Aero Admin 1940-41; MG 1942; Hq ASF 1941-42; LTG Dpty Mil Gov US Zone Germany 1945-46; Gen inC Eur Cmd & Mil Gov US Zone 1947-49; Ret 1949.

Neilson Alexander Murrey, (W.P. 1918-No. 5921) CE; CO 523rd Boat & Shore Regt, Co 5202 ECnBde & CO 5221 ECnBde T-S 1943-45; Ret 1949.

Sturgis Samuel Davis Jr., (W.P. 1918-No. 5925) CE; CG Ch Engr 6Ar T-S; CG 6th AD Ft L Wood 1951-52; CG USAR EUR ComZ 1952-53; Ch Engrs USA 1953 to ret dsbld 1956 LTG.

Moore Anderson Thomas Wm, (W.P. 1918-

No. 5927) CE; CO 19th EC Regt T-AEM 1942-43; Engr SOS T-M 1943-44; OIC AMBC Paris 1949-53; OCE 1953 to ret 1954.

Caffey Eugene Mead, (W.P. 1918-No. 5929) CE; CO 20th Cmbt Engr NATO 1941-43; CO 1st Engr Spec Brig T-E 1943-45; BG 1953; MG, JAG USA 1954 to ret 1956 MG.

Hoffman Charles Ellicott, (W.P 1918-No. 5933) Inf; Cmdr Warner Robins AB 1943:9th AF ETO 1943-44; Resd 1945.

Barragan Milo Benson (W.P. 1918-No. 5938) XO Arty 36 & 90 Divs US 41-43: Ret Dsbl 43 COL.

Kreber Leo Myron, (W.P. 1918-No. 5942) AUS 1941-46 BG; MG NGUS; CG 37th Div OHNG; Ret 1959 MG OHNG.

Sibert Edwin Luther, (W.P. 1918-No. 5944) BG 1942; CG 99th Div Arty 1942-43; G2 12th Ar Gp T-E 1944-45; G2 USFET 1945-46; CG Cp Edwards 1952; MG 1953; Ret 1954 MG.

Robinson Joseph Stubbs, (W.P. 1918-No. 5948) BG 1945; CG AAA Brig T-E 1944-45; MA Turkey 1948-50; Ret 1950 BG.

Blanchard Charles Clifton, (W. P. 1918-No. 5953) Arty O 14th Cps T-SP 1945; BG 1950; CG Base Sec Comz France 1951-5; CG 15th Cps Arty 1952-53; CG CpGordon 1953 to ret 1954 dsbld BG.

Holt Henry Winston (W.P. 1918-No. 5957) FA: CO 8AD Arty T-E 44-45 (LM) CO Eur Cmd Repl Dep 49-52. ret 54 COL.

Townsley Clarence Page, (W.P. 1918-No. 5959) BG 1942 CG 86th Div Arty 1942-44; CG 36th Cps Arty 1944-45; ETO 1945-46; UNMSC 1948 to ret 1953 BG.

Offley Robert Hilton (W.P. 1918-No. 5960) CO 1st Filipino Inf AUS T-S 42-45 (BSM-CI): CO 45 Inf PS 46. ret 48 COL.

Mesick John (W.P. 1918-No. 5963) FA: FA Units 40-43: CO 250 FA Grp T-AE 44-45: ret 53 COL

Tompkins Francis Parker (W.P. 1918-No. 5966) 1AR Gp 42-44: CO TFc 12Ar Gp & CC 7AD 44-45 (LM-SS-2BSM) Ret 47 Col.

Newman Howard Harvey (W.P. 1918-No. 5973) CO 197 AAA Gp N Guinea 42-44 (LM-CR); Ret dsbl 45 Col.

McKee Richard Gray, (W.P. 1918-No. 5975) CS Hq 7th Cps 1944, CO 8th Inf 4th DivT-E 1944-45; Ret 1954 BG.

Barriger William Lillard, (W.P. 1918-No. 5979) Cav; Dpty G4 12th Ar Gp, G4 15th Ar T-E; BG 1949; MG 1952; CG 2nd Div KW 1953-54; OSD R&d 1954 to ret 1957 MG.

Holman Jonathan Lane, (W.P. 1918-No. 5986) BG 1943; CS SOS T-S 1943-45; WDGS 1945-46; CG APG 1952; Ret dsbld 1956.

Miley William Maynadler, (W.P. 1918-No. 5992) Inf; MG 1943; CG 17th Abn Div T-E 1945; CG USARAL 1952-55; Ret 1955 MG.

Gould Harold Wilbert (W.P. 1918-No. 6003) CO 512TGp T-E (BSM) Ret 46 COL.

Barth George Bittman, (W.P. 1918-No. 6006) Inf; CO 357th Inf 9th Div T-ME; BG 1949; 34th Div 1950; CG 25th Div Arty 1950-51 KW; 5th Div (DCG 51,CG 52) Ch JMAG Greece 1953-55; Dpty CG 1st Ar 1955-57; Ret dsbld 1957 MG.

Sherman Harry Benham, (W.P. 1918-No. 6008) Inf; CO 7th Inf 3rd Div T-M 1943-44; BG 1944; Asst CG 34th & 88th Divs T-M 1944-45; Dpty CG Ry Com 1949-52; CG Ft McClellan 1952; Ret 1953 BG.

Gallagher Phillip Edward, (W.P. 1918-No. 6015) Inf; Cmdt Cadets USMA 1942-43; BG 1943; CG 1st Ar Gp Chinese Cmbt Cmd T-C 1945-46; Eur Cmd 1948-51; MG 1953 CG USAR EUR ComZ 1953-56; CG Ft Gordon 1956 to ret dsbld 1957 MG.

Leeper Carroll Kimball (W.P. 1918-No. 6016) IG 1Armd CPS & 7 Ar T-E 1942-45 (BSM) Ret 1947 COL.

Foster Robert Trueheart (W.P. 1918-No. 6025) CO 330 Inf T-E 1944-46 (SS-LM-3BSM-2PH-CR-CI) Ret 1951 COL.

Kimble Frederick von Harten, (W.P. 1918-No. 6028) Inf; CG 27th FTWg 1942-44; CG Tinian Is 1944-46; CG Aleutions 1947-49; Ret 1953 BG.

Pence Arthur William, (W.P. 1918-No. 6031) BG 1943; CG Base Sects T-M 1943-44; S&F CGSS 1944-48; MG 1953; CG 6th AD Ft L Wood 1953-54; CG TEC 1954.

Groves Leslie Richard, (W.P. 1918-No. 6032) CE; MG 1944; WDGS 1939-40; Coc Div OQ MG & OCE 1940-42; CG MED 1942-46; LTG USA & ret 1948.

Butler Frederic Bates, (W.P. 1918-No. 6036) CE; NATO 1942-44; BG 1944; CG 34th Div, 6th CPS & 45th Div T-ME 1944-45; Ret dsbld 1953 BG.

Ogden David Ayers Depue, (W.P. 1918-No. 6041) CE; BG 1942; CG Engr Brig T-S 1942-45; MG 1953; CG Ry Com & Dpty Gov Ryukyus Is 1953-55; Ret 1957 LTG.

Wanamaker William Wesley, (W.P. 1918-No. 6046) CE; Dist Engr TX 1941-42; BG 1945; Asst Engr 6th Ar & Ch Trans Off T-S 1944-45; Ret 1949 BG.

Peckham Howard Louis, (W.P. 1918-No. 6049) BG 1942; CG 12th AD US 1942-43; OQMG Fuels & Lubricants Div 1943-46; CG GRC EUR Area Paris Fr 1947-49; CG QMPA NY 1950-51; MG 1952; Ch Army AF Exch Ser 1954 to ret 1956 MG.

Niles John Southworth (W.P. 1918-No. 6050) CO 1139 Engr Cmbt Gp T-E 1944-45 (SS-LM-3BSM-PH)

Trower Wendell Phillips (W.P. 1918-No. 6052) CO Engr Regt Gp & Brig T-S 1942-46. (LM-BSM) Ret 55 COL.

Lovett Robert Gilbert, (W.P. 1918-No. 6053) CE; CS 15 Corps T-AE 43-44; CO Engr Cmbt Gp T-E 44; Engr 20 Cps T-E 44-45; BG 51.

Hahn Cornman Louis (W.P. 1918-No. 6054) CO 338 EGS Regt T-AM 1942-45. (LM-CR) Ret 1953 COL.

McReynolds George Brooke (W.P. 1918-No. 6056) XO 69CompWg 14AF 44 (BSM): CO 13Gp Chinese Cmbt Cmd T-C 45 (LM): Ret 1948 COL.

Gilland Morris Williams (W.P. 1918-No. 6057) CE; CS SOS NATO & MTO 43-44; BG 44;S CS SO LOC ComZ T-E 44-45; G4 ComZ ETO 454; ret dsbl BG 48.

*Williams Randolph Piersol (W.P. 1918-No. 6060) CO 84 Ftr Wg T-E: Kld Air Msn St Michel France 5 Sep 1944.

Stevens Frederick Atherton, (W.P. 1918-No. 6065) LTC USMC Res 1942-46; Asst G4 5th Mar Div; Iwo Jima; G4 5th Mar Div Occ Japan; Ret 1959 BG USMC.

Christiansen James George, (W.P. 1918-No. 6067) DCS, CS & AGF 1942-45; MG 1944; CG 2nd AD 1947-49; CG 6th AD Ft l Wood 1952-53; MAAG Italy 1953 to ret 1954 MG.

Twitty Joseph Jones, (W.P. 1918-No. 6071) BG 1944; Magruder Lendlease Msn T-I; CG 2nd Engr Spec Brig Ft Worden 1949; Inchon Hungnam KW 1950-51; CG Cp Rucker 1952; Ret dsbld 1954 BG. CS Base Sec T-M 1944-46; CG Red River Ars TX 1952-53; Ret 1954 BG.

Shaler Harrison (W.P. 1918-No. 6072) CS Base Sec T-M 1944-46 (LM) CG Red River Ars TX 52-53 Ret 1954 BG.

*Searby Edmund Wilson (W.P. 1918-No. 6073) Kld Meurth et Moselle France 14 Sep 1944 BG CG Arty 80 Inf Div 1-48: (SS-LM-PH)

Wicks Roger Manning, (W.P. 1918-No. 6074) BG 1942; CG 103rd Div 1945; CS 6th SvC 1945-46; CG 7th Div Arty Korea 1946-48; OC AFF 1949 to ret 1950 BG.

Chorpening Claude Henry, (W.P. 1918-No. 6081) CS & CO Bases ETO 1943-45; BG 1951; Ret 1956 MG.

Keyser George Vernon, (W.P. 1918-No. 6082) CG XI Cps Arty T-S 1943-45; Ch CIC & CICS 1946-48; CG Cp Carson 1952; Ret 1954 BG.

Bowman Frank Otto, (W.P. 1918-No. 6083) Engr 5th Ar 7 Engr Hq T-M 1943-45; BG 1944; CS & Dpty CG TEC 1949-53; CG Ft L Wood 1956; Ret 1956 MG.

Walsh Orville Ernest, (W.P. 1918-No. 6088) Asst Engr 6th Ar T-S 1943; CO Engr Construction Brig T-SP 1944-45; BG 1951; Ret 1954 BG.

Gullatt Doswell (W.P. 1918-No. 6097) CO 1106 ECGp T-E 1943-44; CO 5 Eng Spec Brig & Port of Antwerp 1944-45 (2LM-BSM): Ret dsbld 1946 COL.

Bixby Lawrence Bradford (W.P. 1918-No. 6099) Arty O 4Ar 1944: Chin CC 1945 (LM-BSM) CO Eta Jima; Ret 1950 COL.

Hinds John Hamilton, (W.P. 1918-No. 6103) BG 1943; CG 71st Div Arty, 13th Cps Arty & 21st Cps Arty T-M 1943-45; Arty O 1st & 2nd Cps Arty & CG 2nd Div Arty T-E 1944-46; KW 1st Cav Div; MG 1951; Ret 1956 MG.

Eddy George Gage, (W.P. 1918-No. 6105) Aberdeen PG 1937-45; CO White Sands PG Feb 1949; BG 1951; Ret dsbld 1954 BG.

Blair William Powell (W.P. 1918-No. 6108) CO Bn18 FA 41-42; WDGS 1942: Hq ASF 1942-43: CO 207 FA Gp US 1944: CO 22 Cps Arty T-AE 44-45: CO TF 12 Ar Gp T-E 45 (LM)Hq AGF 45-46 (CR) Ret 46 COL.

Molitor Eric Spencer, (W.P. 1918-No. 6112) CG 13th Abn Div Arty; S&F TAS 1948-49; MAAG Denmark 1950-51; CG 1st Arty Ger 1951-53; CG 47th Div Arty 1953 to ret dsbld 1954 BG.

Kelly Paul Boyle, (W.P. 1918-No. 6119) BG 1943; AAO 7th Ar T-ME 1944-45; Ret dsbld 1951 BG.

Norman Ernest Calhoun (W.P. 1918-No. 6122) CO 408 FA Gp T-AE 1943-45 (BSM) Ret 1954 COL.

Gildart Charles Rolland (W.P. 1918-No. 6125) CO 12 AD Arty T-E 1944-45 CS 9 Inf Div 1947-48: CO Genl Dep Ft. Buchanan 1949, Ret dsbl 1951 COL

*Cothran Wade Rushton Jr., (W.P. 1918-No. 6128) Inf; MAJFA AUS Dec 1941; AdC Gen King Bataan; POW; Death March; Survivor POW ship 15 Dec 1944; Wded POW ship 9 Jan 1945; D-Jap POW ship enroute to Japan(wds) 24 Jan 1945.

Styron James Clyde, (W.P. 1918-No. 6132) Cav; AD CS 45th Div T-AE 1940-44; MG CG 5th Div NGOK KW 1951-52; Ret 1952 MG NG.

Monroe Hammond McDougal, (W.P. 1918-No. 6134) OCAFE 1949-51; CS VII Cps 1951-53; Dpty CG VII Cps Ger 1953; Ret 1953 BG.

Evans Bryan (W.P. 1918-No. 6135) Arty CO & CO 1Abn TF T-ME 1944 Ret 1960 COL

Fellers Bonner Frank, (W.P. 1918-No. 6136) BG 1942; Staff GEN Mac Arthur 1943-46; BG ret 1948.

Middleton John William, (W.P. 1918-No. 6138) BG 1945; AGF 1942-43; China 1943-46; Ret 1954 BG.

March Francis Andrew, (W.P. 1918-No. 6141) BG 1944; CG Abn Div Arty T-E; Asst CG 82nd Abn Div T-EA 1945-46; Ret dsbld

1953 BG.

Badger George Maurice, (W.P. 1918-No. 6142) BG 1944; CG 56th AAA Brig T-E 1944-45; Treas USMA 1945 to ret 1949 BG.

Winn John Sheridan Jr., (W.P. 1918-No. 6143) BG 1943; Hq AGF 1942-43; CG 79th Div Arty T-E 1945; Ret 1948 BG.

Voorst Marion Van, (W.P. 1918-No. 6144) BG 1945; Asst MA London 1943-46; Ret dsbld 1950 BG.

Conrad Vincent John (W.P. 1918-No. 6159) CO Inf units T-A 1939-43. CO Rep Dep CBI 1944-45. Ret dsbl temp 1953 COL.

Smith Edward Ward, (W.P. 1918-No. 6163) Inf; BG 1945; Hq 7th Ar T-ME 1944-45; Ret dsbld 1946 BG.

Hicks Ronald Austin (W.P. 1918-No. 6164) 4BbCmb 1940-42. A3 AFSC Eng 1942. Ret dsbl 1946 COL.

Moss Joe Davis (W.P. 1918-No. 6168) CO 112 AA Gp 3AR T-AE 1943-45. Ret 1954 COL.

Colson Charles Frederick, (W.P. 1918-No. 6180) BG 1944; CG CCA AD T-E 1944-45; CG Ft Devens 1950-51; Ret 1953 BG.

Holbrook Willard Ames Jr., (W.P. 1918-No. 6185) Cav; BG 1944; CG CCA 11th AD T-E ; Ret 1946; BG ret 1948.

Schow Robert Alwin (W.P. 1918-No. 6188) Asst MA France 1939-44; GS SH AEF 1944-45; G2 15 AR 1945-46 T-E; BG Asst Dir CIA 1949-52; MG USMA 1951: Ret 1958 MG.

Stokes John Harrison Jr., (W.P. 1918-No. 6189) Inf; DCG 2nd Div T-E 1944-45; MG 1953; CG MDW 1954-55; CH Mil Hist DC 1956 to ret 1956 MG.

Graham Jesse Ellis (W.P. 1918-No. 6190) CO TF Aleutians 1942-43; DCS 9 Div 1945: Ret dsbl 1954 COL.

*Baclig Eustaquio, (W.P. 1918-No. 6195) Visayan-Mindanao Force 1942; POW; Death March; Released Jan 1943; Underground; POW 2 Nov 1944; Kld Ft Santiago Manila (executed) 30 Nov 1944.

Brinkley Thomas Markham (W.P. 1918-No. 6198) CO Div Tns 10 AD T-E 1944-45; CO Cmbt Cmd 10 AD 1945; Hq Cmdt 3AR T-E 1945 Ret dsbl tem 1954 COL

Kendall Paul Wilkins, (W.P. 1918-No. 6212) Inf; 27th Inf Siberia 1919-1920; MG CG 88th Div T-ME 1944-45; CG Zone Cmd & Dpty CG USAF 1948-50; LTG 1952; CG 1st Cps KW 1952-53; Dpty CG Hq AFFE 1953-54; CG HALFSEE 1954; Ret dsbl 1957 LTG.

Mackenzie Alexander John (W.P. 1918-No. 6217) CO 395 Inf 99 Div T-E 1942-45: ret dsbl 1946 COL.

Swift Ira Platt, (W.P. 1918-No. 6219) Inf-Cac; Dpty CG 82nd Abn 1944-45; WDGS 1945-47; Dpty CG 2nd Div 1947-48; CG Hq Cmd USAF 1948-51; CG 3rd AD-TARS-TARC 1951; CG 25th Div 1951-52; CG 3rd Cps 1952-53; CG VCps EU Com 1953-54; Ret 1954 MG.

Dunkelberg Wilbur Eugene, (W.P. 1918-No. 6220) Inf; BG 1943; CG Attu 1944-45; Asst CG 24th Jap 1952; Asst CG 3rd Div KW 1952-53; CG 3rd Div 1953: CS 9th Cps Korea 1953; Asst CG 6th Div Ft Ord 1954; Ret 1955 BG.

Pulsifer Arthur (W.P. 1918-No. 6226) SigO 3Ar T-E 1944: SigO 10 Ar T-S 1944-47: SigO 2Ar 1947-50: Asst Ch SO USA 1950: SBG 19 51.

Gillespie Francis James (W.P. 1918-No. 6230) CO CCR&CCB 14AD T-E 1942-45: MAAG Indo China 1950-51. Ret 54 COL

Gibney Jesse Lewis (W.P. 1918-No. 6231) CO 60Inf & CS 28 Div T-E 44-45: CO Ft. Meade 50-52. Ret 53 COL.

*Vesey Robert Hale (W.P. 1918-No. 6232) 31

Inf(PS) 41: Visayan-Mindanao: Kld-Lanao POW Cp 3 Jul 42. LTC a-43:

Hastings Kester Lovejoy, (W.P. 1918-No. 6234) Inf-QMC; OQmg 1940-41,42-49; BG 1948; Dpty QMC USA 1952-54; MG QMG USA 1954-57; Ret 1957 MG.

Williamson George McKnight Jr., (W.P. 1918-No. 6235) CO 6 Div Arty T-S 45-46: Ret dsbl 50 COL

Brimmer Howard Waite (W.P. 1918-No. 6236) CO FABn 78 Div 42-43: CO ReplDeps CBI 44-45: Ret dsbl 53 COL

Muller Walter Joseph, (W.P. 1918-No. 6239) Inf; G4 1st Armd Cps 1942; TF NATO 1942-43; G4 7th Ar T-M 1943-44; BG 1944; G4 3rd Ar T-E 1944-45; Dir OMGG Bavaria 1945-47; G4 AGF 1947-48; CG TC Sch 1948-51; MG 1949; DCS HALF CE 1951-53; CG Bremerhaven POE 1953-55; Dpty CG 6th Ar 1956; Ret 1956 MG.

Murray William Stephen (W.P. 1918-No. 6242) CO 137 Inf 35 Div T-E 44-45: Ret dsbl 46. COL.

Welch James Clyde (W.P. 1918-No. 6245) XO 13 Inf & G2 XVCps T-E 43-46: Ret dsbl 51 COL.

Pence John Perry (W.P. 1918-No. 6247) CO AABn Italy WW2: CO 236 Arty Gp 47: CO 41 Div Arty: BG NG:

Binder John Leo (W.P. 1918-No. 6248) LTC: CO 11AF Retl Dep Alaska 43-45.

AAron Thomas Roswell (W.P. 1918-No. 6254) COSpTps 104 Div 43: Hq USARPac 48-50: Eniwetok 50: Ret dsbl 51 COL

Peck Walter Raymond, (W.P. Non-Grad Class of 1918) 1st LT Inf 1920; AC 1922; BG AUS 1943; Ret dsbld 1948 BG.

Ross David Marshall Ney, (W.P. Non-Grad Class of 1918) 1st LT WWI; 1st LT Inf 1920; BG AUS 1943; Ret 1944.

Stoner Frank Elmer, (W.P. Non-Grad Class of 1918) 1st LT WWI; 1st LT Inf 20; SC26; MG AUS 1944; Ret 1947; MG ret 1948.

Bartlett Boyd Wheeler (W.P. 1919-No. 6258) AUS 42-45 COL: Ret dsbl 61 BG.

Gruenther Alfred Maximillian, (W.P. 1919-No. 6261) MG 1943; CS 3rd Ar T-A 1941-42; CS 5th Ar T-M 1943-44; CS 15th Ar Gp Italy 1944-45; Dpty CG USAF 1945; LTG 1949; GEN 1951; SAC EUR 1953 to ret dsbl 1956 GEN.

Loper Herbert Bernard, (W.P. 1919-No. 6261) CE; BG 1944; OCE 1941-43; Engr USAF T-P 1944-45; MG 1952; Ret dsbld 1955 MG.

Palmer Williston Birkhimer, (W.P. 1919-No. 6264) BG 1942; Arty O 1st Gp T-E 1943-44; CG 7th Cps Arty T-E 1944-45; MG 1950; CG 82nd Abn Div 1949-50; CG X Cps KW 1951-52; LTG 1952 GEN 1955; Ret 1959.

Gard Robert Gibbins, (W.P. 1919-No. 6265) BG 1944; CG 96th Div T-P 1944-45; Trial Comm Jap War Criminals 1945-46; CG 7th Cps Arty 1951-52; MG 1953; Dpty CG 3rd Ar 1954-56; Sr Member UNC MAC Korea 1956; Ch MAAG Korea 1956-57; CG 8th Cps 1957-59; Ret 1959 MG.

Jones Herbert Maury, (W. P. 1919-No. 6269) AG 3AF 1942-43; CS Espiritu Isle Cmd 1943-44; Okinawa Cmd 194446; BG 1951; MG 1954; TAG 57 to ret 1958 MG.

Martin Orville Wells (W.P. 1919-No. 6271) CO 68 FA Bn 1AD T-AEM 41-43: CO 7AD Arty T-E 43-45: CO FA Gp 45-46: CS 9Div 48-50: Ret 50 COL.

Moliter Carl Spencer (W.P. 1919-No. 6279) Lt Cmdr USNR: CO USS PC 1120 T-S 42-46.

Brown Wyburn Dwight, (W.P. 1919-No. 6281) CG 11th Abn Div Arty 1942-44; CG 33rd FABde 1944; Arty O HQ ETO 1944-45; Ret 1951 BG.

Montague Robert Miller, (W.P. 1919-No. 6282) BG 1942; CG 83rd Div Arty T-E 1944-46; CG Sandia Base 1947-51; MG 1949; CG 1st Cps 1955. D-Ancon CZ Feb 20 58 LTG.

McAuliffe Anthony Clement, (W.P. 1919-No. 6284) MG 1945; Dpty CG 101sr Abn Div; CG 103rd Div T-E AGF 1946; Ch CUSA 1949-51; LTG G1 1951-53; CG 7th Ar 1953-55; CinC USAR EUR 1955; Ret 1956 GEN.

Barden Albert Rhett Stuart (W.P. 1919-No. 6287) CO 415 FA Gp T-A 44-45. Ret 53 COL.

Ghingler Don Gilmore, (W.P. 1919-No. 6289) BG 1943; Pioneered Persian Gulf Sup to USSR 1941-43; Ret 1954 BG.

Hartness Harlan Nelson, (W.P. 1919-No. 6290) BG 1942; Hq 26th Div T-E; Asst CG 7th Div Kor 1946-48; Asst Cmdt CGSC 1948-50; CG 4th Div EU Com 1950; MG 1051; Ret 1954 MG.

Slack Julius Easton, (W.P. 1919-No. 6292) BG 1943; CG XX Cps Arty T-AE 1943-45; CO ATL Sec CZ 1950-51; CG 40th Div Arty Jap 1951; Ret 1951 BG.

Hayford Bertram Francis, (W.P. 1919-No. 6293) BG 1945; G4 Sec Hq USAF Mid Pac 1941-43; Hq CinC POA 1943-45; Ch Tran USAR Eur 1950; MG 1954; Ret 1955 MG.

Bixby Ernest Aaron, (W.P. 1919-No. 6294) BG 1944; CG 4th AD Arty T-E 1943-44; CG 90th Div Arty 1944-45; Dpty Post CG Stuttgart 1949-51; CG Nurenberg Mil Post 1951-52; CG Base Sec ComZ France 1952-53; CG 1st Log Cmd Ft Bragg NC 1953-%%; Ret dsbld 1955 BG.

Raymond Robert Rossiter Jr., (W.P. 1919-No. 6295) XO 8 Div Arty T-AE 43-45: Ret 1947 COL.

Scherer Harris Fulford (W.P. 1919-No. 6296) AG 2AF 41-43: AG 8 AFSC T-E 43-44 & US STAF 44-45: AG CAF 45-46; Ret 1954 BG.

Hedekin Thomas Benoit, (W.P. 1919-No. 6300) Arty Sec 12th Ar Gp T-E 1944-45; CG 2nd Div Arty Kor 1953-54; CG IX Cps Arty to D.

Phelps Joseph Vincil, (W.P. 1919-No. 6301) BG 1943; CO 17th Abn Div Arty T-E 1944-45; Ret 1949 BG.

Hardin John Ray, (W.P. 1919-No. 6305) CE; Dpty Ch Engr T-E 1943-45; Asst Ch Engrs 1951-53; MG 1951; Ret 1957 MG.

Tate Foster Joseph, (W.P. 1919-No. 6310) CG 34th Div Arty T-M 1944-45; Ret 1949 BG.

Meyer Henry John Dick, (W.P. 1919-No. 6313) BG 1944; CG 45th Div Arty T-E; CG 2nd Div Arty 1946-48; CG 24th Div Arty Japan-KW 1948-51; CG XV Cps Arty Cp Polk 1951; Ret dsbld 1957.

Hammond Elton Foster, (W.P. 1919-No. 6314) Sig O 7th Ar T-M 1943-44; SigO 3rd Ar T-E 1944-45; XO OG4 1949-51; BG 1951; Ret 1954.

Brannon Ernest Marion, (W.P. 1919-No. 6315) Inf; JAG 1st Ar T-E 1943-45; BG 1947, MG 949; Ret 1954 BG.

Hill Luther Lyons, (W.P. 1919-No. 6318) CO AAF Pers Redistribution Cmd 1943-45; BG 1945.

*Sheehy John Wyville (W.P. 1919-No. 6320) Kld Normandy 15 Jun 44 COL CO 357 Inf 90 Inf Div

Burns John Joseph, (W.P. 1919-No. 6322) CO 425th FAGp T-E 1945; Ret dsbld 1953 BG.

Jacoby Leslie Edgar (W.P. 1919-No. 6323) CO 5 TDGp T-E 44-45: Ret 1953 COL

Ovenshine Richard Powell (W.P. 1919-No. 6326) CO 165 Inf 45: IG 9Cps 46: CO 31 Inf 7 Div Jap-KW 50: Ret 1954 BG.

Kerr Edwin Virgil, (W.P. 1919-No. 6327) BnCO 88th FA PS Bataan; POW; Death

March; Survivor POW Ships 15 Dec 1944, 9 Jan 1945 POW Ship enroute to Japan.

Helberg Harrison How'l Dodge (W.P. 1919-No. 6329) CO 81 Rcn Bn 1AD T-E 42: G3 Sec 1&12 Ar Gps T-E 43-45. Ret 1954 COL.

Kurtz Maurice Keyes (W.P. 1919-No. 6336) CO 14 AD Arty T-AE 43-45: Ret dsbl 1947 COL

*Paquet Leo Clement, (W.P. 1919-No. 6339) POW; Death March; Died from wounds 14 Jan 1945 POW Ship 9 Jan 1945.

McGinley Eugene, (W.P. 1919-No. 6341) Arty O 2nd Ar 1943-44; Arty O 8th Ar T-S 1944-46; DCO Frankford Mil Post 1949-51; Ret 1955 MG (S-WW2).

Flory Lester DeLong, (W.P. 1919-No. 6343) BG 1944; CG 63rd AAA Brig T-A 1943-44; Ret 1949 BG.

Echols Marion Patton (W.P. 1919-No. 6348) CS 102 Div T-a 42-44: CO 417 FA Gp T-AE 44-45: Ret dsbl 1953 COL.

Wood Francis Otis (W.P. 1919-No. 6351) CO 38 CABn 6Ar & CO 144CAGp 10Ar T-P 44-45: Ret 1947 COL.

Hewett Hobart, (W.P. 1919-No. 6352) CG 31st AA Bde T-M 1943-44; CG 31st AA Bde Ft Lewis 1951; Asst Cmdt AAGMS 1952-53; CG 3rd Div Arty & CS UNMAC 1953-54; Ret dsbld 1960 MG.

Phillips James Holden, (W.P. 1919-No. 6355) Cav; G3 Sect AGF 1942-43; CS 3rd Cps T-AE 1943-46; MG 1950; Ret dsbld 1958 MG.

Drury Frederick Weed (W.P. 1919-No. 6358) CO 3CavMecz 3Ar T-AE 43-44: Ret 1953 COL.

Syme Leander Dunbar (W.P. 1919-No. 6359) CO 159 Inf 7 Div Aleutians 43-44: CO262 Inf 66 Div T-E 44-45: Ret 1949 COL.

Williamson Ellis Vern (W.P. 1919-No. 6360) XO 34AA Brig & CO 1st AAGp 42-44: XO & CO 34 Div Arty 45-46. Ret 1950 COL.

Burnell Nathaniel Alanson 2nd, (W.P. 1919-No. 6362) CG 52nd AA Bde 1943-45; CG 52nd AA Bde T-E; MG 1950; MAAG the Hague 1950-51; Ch MAAG Belg 1951-54; CG1 AARgn 1954-57; Ret dsbld 1957 MG.

Parsons Arthur Maxon (W.P. 1919-No. 6370) CO 303Inf 43-44: G3Sec Hq AGF 44-45: Ret 1954 COL

*Perry Howard Rand Jr., (W.P. 1919-No. 6374) Inf; CO 101st Inf 81st Div PA Mindanao 1042; POW; Died 28 Jan 1945 from wounds POW ship 9 Jan 1945.

Mickle Gerald St. Claire, (W.P. 1919-No. 6377) CS Amph Cps Atl Fleet 1940-43; BG 1943; Asst CG 75th Div,CG 101st Abn Div, Asst CG 83rd Div T-E 1943-46; Ret dsbld 1946 BG.

Farrar Benjamin Randolph, (W.P. 1919-No. 6378) XO 127th Inf Buna 1942; Ret totally dsbld from wounds 1944 LTC.

Hoffman Hugh French Thomason (W.P. 1919-No. 6380) BG 44: CG 2Bde 1 Cav Div & 1Cav Div T-S: MG 1951:

Winn Walter Scott Jr., (W.P. 1919-No. 6382) Cav; MG 1944; Asst G3 CBI 1942; Asst G3 AF Hq 1942-43; Dpty CG 1st Div T-E 1943-44; CG 71st Div T-E 1944-45; CG 9th Cps KW 1951-52; LTG 1952; CG 6th Ar 1954-55; CG CON ARC 1956-58; Ret 1958 GEN.

Wyman Willard Gordon (W.P. 1919-No. 6383) MG 44: Asst G3 CBI 42: Asst G3 AFHq 42-43: Dpty CG 1Div T-E 43-44: CG 71 Div T-E 44-45: CG 9Cps KW 51-52: LTG 52: CG 6Ar 54-55: CG CON ARC 56-58. Ret 1958 Gen.

Whitelaw John Leonard, (W.P. 1919-No. 6384) BG 1943; Dpty CG 17th Abn Div T-E 1943-45; Dpty CG Trust 1951-52; Asst CG

10th Div Ft Riley 1952-54; Ret 1955 BG.

*Bowes Edward Henry, (W.P. 1919-No. 6385) Inf; 31st Inf Bataan; POW Death March; Died 24 Jan 1945 from wounds POW ship 9 Jan 1945 LTC.

Sutherland Edwin Malcolm (W.P. 1919-No. 6386) Inf: Amer Msn China 41-43: Sect CO TF9 Kiska 43: CO 119 Inf 30 Div T-E 44-45: Ret dsbl 1953 COL.

Holly Joseph Andrew, (W.P. 1919-No. 6387) Inf; BG 1943; Cmdt TARS 1943-44; Ch Armd Sec ETO 1944-45; Ret 1951 BG.

McNair William Douglas (W.P. 1919-No. 6389) D-Air Cr Australia 20 Oct 43 COL CO Arty 1 Cav Div a-44.

Wilson Charles Forrest (W.P. 1919-No. 6390) CO 414 AA Bn Iceland 42-44: CO CAC Regt 1Ar T-E 44-45: Ret dsbl 1947 COL.

Twining Nathan Farragut, (W.P. 1919-No. 6393) LTG 1945; CG 13th AF T-S 1942-43; CG 15th AF T-M 1944-45; CG 20th AF T-P 1945; CinC Alaskan Cmd 1947-50; GEN 1950; Chrm JCS1947-60; Ret 1960.

Skelton Winfred George, (W.P. 1919-No. 6402) BG 1945; CO 149th Inf Div T-S 1944-45; Asst CG & CG 33rd Div Jap 1945-46; Ret dsbld 1954.

Sebree Edmond Bower, (W.P. 1919-No. 6404) Inf; BG 1944; CG Americal Div T-S 1942-43; MG 1944; Dpty CG 35th Div T-E 1944-45; CG Trust 1951-52; CG 5th AD Cp Chaffe 1952-53; Dpty CG 1st Ar 1953-54; Ret dsbld 1957 MG.

Barlow Raymond Clay (W.P. 1919-No. 6407) Inf: CO85MtnInf T-A 43-45: Ret 1954 COL.

Bean George James, (W.P. 1919-No. 6409) Inf; Cmdt FinS 1942-44; OFiscal Dir OCF 1944-45; CG FinC 1952; Ret 1957 MG.

Collier John Howell, (W.P. 1919-No. 6416) CO 66th ARegt & CG CCA2AD T-ME 1943-45; CG Stuttgart Mil Post 1950-51; MG 1951; CG TARC & Cmdt TARS 1952-54; CG 4th Ar 1955-58; Ret 1958 LTG.

Luce Dean (W.P. 1919-No. 6417) CO 94 AAGp T-S 44-45: Ret 1950 COL.

Elms George Gordon (W.P. 1919-No. 6419) CO 2TD Gp T-E 43-45: Ret 1954 COL.

Armstrong John Dimmick (W.P. 1919-No. 6420) CO 365 Inf 92 Div Italy 45: Ret 1954 COL.

Stearley Ralph Francis, (W.P. 1919-No. 6421) Cav; BG 1943; CG 1st Tac Air Div; A3 9AF T-E 1944; G3 1st Allied Abn Ar T-E 1944-45; ETO 1945-46; MG 1949; CG 14th AF 1948-50; CG 20th AF Okinawa KW 1950-53; Ret 1953 MG.

Hopkins Edward Ora (W.P. 1919-No. 6423) XO & CO 99 & 1 Div Arty T-E 42-47: Ret 1954 COL.

McNary Clarkson Deweese (W.P. 1919-No. 6431) CO Bn 21 Inf Hawaii 7 Dec 41: CO 358 Inf T-E 44: Ret dsbl 1946 COL.

Byrne Bernard Abert (W.P. 1919-No. 6432) Co 320 Inf 35 Div T-AE 43-45: Ret 1954 COL.

Hutchins Robert Barrett (W.P. 1919-No. 6437) CO 179Inf 45 Div T-ME 43-44: Ret dsbl 1946 COL.

Alexander Irvin, (W.P. 1919-No. 6445) Inf; CO 1st Inf PS 71st Div PA Bataan; POW 1942-45; Death March; Ret dsbld 1950.

*Olson Kenneth Sharp, (W.P. 1919-No. 6454) Inf; FO Visayan Fc 1942; Died 24 Jan 1945 from wounds POW ship 9 Jan 1945.

*Nelson Russell John, (W.P. 1919-No. 6457) Inf; CO 102nd Inf 101st Div PA Mindinao; Killed POW ship 15 Dec 1944.

Bradley Joseph Staden, (W.P. 1919-No. 6462) Inf; BG 1944; CO Inf Regt New Guinea 1942-43; G3 Div WDGS; Asst CG 2nd Div

1950-51, CG 25th Div 1951, KW; MG 1951; Ret dsbld 1956 MG.

Crichlow Robert William Jr., (W.P. 1919-No. 6464) CG 57th AABde 1943-44; CG Kobe Base Jap 1946-48; CG 34th AABde Eur 1952; Ret dsbld 1954 COL.

Zimmerman Wayne Cliffton, (W.P. 1919-No. 6470) Inf; BG 1944; MG 1951; WWII CS 7th Div 1942-43; CO 17th Inf Regt 1943-44; Asst Cmdr 98th Div 1944-46; CG 17th Abn Div Cp Pickett 1949-50; Ch US Msn & MAAG Teheran 1951-52; Dpty TIG USA 1953-54; TIG USA 1954; Ret 1956 MG.

Dalbey Josiah Toney, (W.P. 1919-No. 6476) Inf; BG 1944; BG Abn Cent Cp Mackall; Ret dsbld 1952 BG.

Hildebrand Christian (W.P. 1919-No. 6486) CO 342Inf86Div T-E 44-45: CO 305Inf T-S 45: Ret 1949 COL.

Warren Joseph Holleman (W.P. 1919-No. 6487) CO 254Inf T-E 43-45: Ret dsbl 1951 COL.

Frederick John David (W.P. 1919-No. 6489) CO 129 CT 37 Div T-S 42-45: CO TF Bikini 46: Ret 1954 COL.

Kean William Benjamin, (W.P. 1919-No. 6508) CG 5th Div 1947-48; CG 25th Div Jap 1048-50; CG 25th Div Korea 1950-51; CG IIICps 1951-52; CG 5th Ar 1952-54; Ret 1954 LTG.

Moroney William Joseph (W.P. 1919-No. 6511) CO 163Inf & 39OInf T-P 44-46: Ret 1954 COL.

*Keerans Charles Leslie Jr., (W.P. 1919-No. 6513) Inf; Killed Air Msn Sicily 11 Jul 1943 BG 82nd Abn Div.

Morgan Albert Carroll (W.P. 1919-No. 6516) CO 276 Inf 70 Div T-E 45: Ret 1954 COL.

Ferenbaugh Claude Birkett, (W.P. 1919-No. 6520) Inf; WDGS 1943; BG 1944; Asst CG 83rd Div T-E 1944-45; WDGS, CGMDW & CS OpnSanstone 1945-48; CG Schofield Bks 1948-50; CG 5th AD & Cp Chaffee 1950-51; CG 7th Div Kor 1951; DCG 8th Ar Korea 1955; Ret dsbld 1955 LTG.

Wedemeyer Albert Coady, (W.P. 1919-No. 6525) Inf; German War Coll 1936-38; WDGS 1941-43; MG 1943; Dpty CS SE Asia Cmd 1944; LTG 1945; CG US Fcs China 1945-46; MG USA 1948; CG 6th Ar 1949; Ret 1951 LTG.

Porter Frederick Brenton (W.P. 1919-No. 6536) CO 416FAGp T-E 44-45: Ret dsbl 1953 COL.

Bevans James Millikin, (Non-Grad Class 1919) MG AUS 1944; Ret 1951 MG.

Morris Joseph Theodore, (Non-Grad Class 1919) BG AUS 1944; Ret 1953 BG.

O'Neill Merlin, (Non-Grad Class 1919) Coast Guard Acad 1921; Cmdt Cadets CG Acad 1927-30; Amphib Opns POA 1942-44; Rear Admiral Coast Guard 1946; Ret 1954 Admiral Coast Guard.

Holle Charles George, (W.P. 1920-No. 6546) CE; Battle Comm Paris 1939-40: Asst Engr Main PC 1942-44; (SMG).

McCullough Arthur Lee, (W.P. 1920-No. 6553) CE; AUS 1942-46; (SBG).

Partridge Richard Clare, (W.P. 1920-No. 6564) Intered Portugal 1942: AG3 1st ArGp, Hq VII Cps, CO 358th Inf T-E 1943-45: (SMG).

Miller Harold Thomas, (W.P. 1920-No. 6567) CE: G4 & Engr NYPOE 1942-45: G4 SFPOE 1945: (SBG).

Lastyo Edward Haviland, (W.P. 1920-No. 6594) CO 3rd Port & Ch TC MTO 1942-45: (SBG).

Ford William Wallace, (W.P. 1920-No. 6602) BG 1944: Org Flying OP for FA 1941-42: CG

87th Div Arty T-AE 1944-45.

*Vanture George Dewey, (W.P. 1920-No. 6603) CO 91 FA & Arty 0 1st Div PA Bataan: POW: Death March: Killed POW Ship 9 Jan 1945.

*Martelino Pastor, (W.P. 1920-No. 6605) First Supt PI Mil Acad: COL: CS 31st Inf Div PA Bataan: POW: Death March: Released: Underground: POW 22 Dec 1944: Killed Manila (executed) 8 Jan 1945.

Harriman Joseph Eugene, (W.P. 1920-No. 6610) AAO 2nd Cps ETO & NATO 1942-43: BG 1943: CG 52nd AAA Brig & AAA TC CP Edwards 1943-44: MA Turkey 1945.

Fowler Halstead Clotworthy, (W.P. 1920-No. 6623) CO 71st FA PA Luzon & Bataan: POW 1942-45: Death March: Ret dsbld 1946.

Seybold John States, (W.P. 1920-No. 6631) CE: Engr Sect Hq NATO 1943-44 & Hq ETO 1944-45: OCE 1945: (SMG).

Gillette Edward Clinton Jr., (W.P. 1920-No. 6635) Sig Div Hq SHAEF 1944: Ch Sig 0 1st Allied Abn Army 1944-45: Ch Sig 0 Berlin Dist 1945.

Corput Rex Van Jr., (W.P. 1920-No. 6638) Dir SC Labs 1941-44: (SMG).

Kiefer Homer Watson, (W.P. 1920-No. 6639) BG 1945: XO 24th Div Arty, Arty 0 6th Ar T-S 1943-45: (SMG).

Schabacker Clarence Henry, (W.P. 1920-No. 6652) CS AAA Cmd 1944-45: CG 55th AAA Bde T-E 1945. (SBG).

Cassidy John Francis, (W.P. 1920-No. 6656) Hq 6th Cps T-AME 1941-44: DCS 5th Ar T-M 1944-45. (SBG).

Schick Lawrence Edward, (W.P. 1920-No. 6674) AG & DCS Alaskan Dept 1941-44: DCS 10th Ar T-P 1944-45. (SBG).

Hasbrouck Sherman Vitus, (W.P. 1920-No. 6682) CG 97th Div Arty T-EP. (SBG).

Garvin Crump, (W.P. 1920-No. 6684) BG 1944: CS 24th Cps T-S: (SMG).

Harris Frederick Mixon, (W.P. 1920-No. 6688) BG 1943Dpty CG, CG 63rd Div T-AE 1943-45. (SBG).

Carr Lawrence Joseph, (W.P. 1920-No. 6702) BG 1945: 7th Bb Cmd T-P 1943-45. (SBG).

Daniel Maurice Wiley, (W.P. 1920-No. 6704) BG 1944: 1st AD T-M 1942-45, CO Arty 1942-43, CO Cmbt Cmde 1943-45, CG Div 1945. (SBG).

Byers Clovis Ethelbert, (W.P. 1920-No. 6707) CS 1st Cps T-S 1942-44. (SLTG).

Gailey Charles Kenon, (W.P. 1920-No. 6720) BG 1945: XO WPD WDGS 1940-45. (SMG).

Farrell Francis William, (W.P. 1920-No. 6722) BG 1944: CS 11th Abn Div 1943-44: CG 11th Abn Div 1944-45. (SLTG).

McBlain John Ferral, (W.P. 1920-No. 6730) BG 1943: Hq SEAC 1944. (SMG).

Swartz Charles Harlan, (W.P. 1920-No. 6737) BG 1945: CG 25th Div Arty PI-Jap 1945. (SBG).

Honnen George, (W.P. 1920-No. 6756) BG 1942: Cmdt Cadets USMA 1943-45: (SMG).

Williams Edward Thomas, (W.P. 1920-No. 6758) BG 1945: Arty O 3rd Ar T-E 1943-45. (SLTG).

Tully Terence John, (W.P. 1920-No. 6763) SO 2nd Cps T-M 1942-43. Ch Sig 0 US Fcs & Dpty CSO Al Fcs T-M 1943-44. (SBG).

Crist William Earl, (W.P. 1920-No. 6768) CAD 10th Ar T-P 1944-45. (SBG).

McQuarrie Claude Monroe, (W.P. 1920-No. 6770) Inf: CO Regts Amer Div T-SP 1943-45. (SBG).

Mitchell William Lemuel, (W.P. 1920-No. 6772) Hq AGF 1942-45: (SMG).

Dillon Jos Vincent de Paul, (W.P. 1920-No. 6776) OPMG 1941-42: PMG NATO 1943-45.

(SMG).

Hodes Henry Irving, (W.P. 1920-No. 6785) WDAS 1942-44: CO 112th Inf 28th Div T-E 1944: BG 1945.

Hinds Sidney Rae, (W.P. 1920-No. 6791) CO 41st A Inf 2nd AD T-ME 1942-45: CG CCB 2nd AD T-E 1945. (SBG).

Maddox Halley Grey, (W.P. 1920-No. 6793) G3 1st Armd Cps 7th & 3rd Ar T-ME 1942-45. (SMG).

Rush Hugo Peoples, (W.P. 1920-No. 6801) Cdr 98th Bb Gp & 47th Bb Wg T-ME 1942-45. (SMG).

*Ward John Taylor, (W.P. 1920-No. 6806) QM Bataan: POW: Killed Limay on Death March 11 Apr 1942.

Barrett Charles Joseph, (W.P. 1922-No. 6828) CE: BG CG Arty 84th Div T-E 1944-45; (SBG).

Olmstead George Hamden, (W.P. 1922-No. 6829) WDSS 1942-44: BG G5 T-C 1945; (SMG).

Taylor Maxwell Davenport, (W.P. 1922-No. 6831) Asst Secy WDGS 1941-42; BG CG 82nd Abn Div Arty T-M 1942-44; MG CG 101st Abn Div T-E 1944-45 .

Rumaggi Louis Jacob, (W.P. 1922-No. 6833) CO 1311th Engr Regt T-S 1944; XO Dept Ch Engr AF Wes Pac 1945-46; (SMG).

Lynch Edmund Clayton, (W.P. 1922-No. 6834) BG 1944; CG 3rd Tac Air Div 1944-45; (SMG).

Kessler Alfred August, (W.P. 1922-No. 6836) CO 95th BpGp & 13th BgWg 8th AF 1943-44; BG 1944; CG Eastern Cmd USS TAF in Russia 1944.

Strong Paschal Neilson, (W.P. 1922-No. 6837) CE; Engr Channel Base Sec 1944-45; (SBG).

Schuyler Cortlandt Van R., (W.P. 1922-No. 6838) BG CS AAC 1943; Mil Ch Allied Control Com Rumania 1944-47 (SMG).

Gross Mervin Eugene, (W.P. 1922-No. 6840) BG 1943; CS T-C 1945; (SBG).

Stewart LeRoy Judson, (W.P. 1922-No. 6845) CS 7th Div T-ASP 1943-44; (SBG).

Uncles John Francis, (W.P. 1922-No. 6847) WWI Vet; OCFA 1940-42; BG CG 34th FA Bde 9th Ar,CG 32nd FA Bde 7th Ar T-E 1944-46; (SLTG).

Crawford David James, (W.P. 1922-No. 6849) A-Ar; WWI Vet; FA; OCFA 1940-42; BG CG 34th FA Bde 9th Ar, (SLTG).

Lawton William Stevens, (W.P. 1922-No. 6857) Asst G3 & Dpty CS Haw Dept 1941-43; Dpty CS HQAF Mid Pac 1943-46; (SLTG).

*Svihra Albert, (W.P. 1922-No. 6860) JA Phil Div & Security O Bataan; Corregidor POW; Killed — POW ship 24 Oct 1944 LTC.

Kastner Alfred Eugene, (W.P. 1922-No. 6865) CO AD Arty T-AE 1942-45; (SBG).

McClure Mark, (W.P. 1922-No. 6868) BG 1945; CG 95th Div Arty T-E 1944-45;

Chidlaw Benjamin Wiley, (W.P. 1922-No. 6869) BG 1942; (supervised development of first jet aircraft in US) 22nd TAC, 12th AF & Allied AF T-M 1944-45.

Clark Edwin Norman, (W.P. 1922-No. 6874) AUS 1940-45; CO SvCs Eritrea, Libya & ME T-D 1942-44; Dpty ACSSup SHAEF 1944-45; (SBG).

Cook Orval Ray, (W.P. 1922-No. 6884) BG 1943; Ch Procurement Div Air Tech SvC 1944-45; CG Area Cmd FEAF 1945.

Spry James Wrathall, (W.P. 1922-No. 6886) CO Miami Air Dept 1943; CS Air SvCCBI 1943; (SMG).

O'Connell James Dunne, (W.P. 1922-No.

6898) Ch Devl Br, OCSO 1039-44; Sig Sect 12th Ar Gp T-E 1944-45; (SLTG).

Mudgett Gilman Clifford, (W.P. 1922-No. 6899) CO 2A Regt 9th AD 1942-44; G3 Sect 12th Ar Gp T-E 1944-45; (SMG).

Watson Numa Augustin, (W.P. 1922-No. 6901) Co 54th AR 10th AD 1943; CO 13th Inf 8th Div T-E 1944-45; (SMG).

Douglass Robert Wilkins Jr., (W.P. 1922-No. 6905) BG 1942; CG 7th Ftr Cmd T-P 1942-44; MG 1944; CG 7th AF T-P 1944-45; (SMG).

Hughes Oliver Wendell, (W.P. 1922-No. 6907) GS 2nd Cav Div, 6th Mtn Div 2nd Ar 1941-43; CO 337th Inf 85th Inf Div T-ME 1944-45; (SBG).

*Rees James Edward, (W.P. 1922-No. 6911) Inf; CO 1st Inf 6th Div T-S 1942 to KIA-Rizall Luzon 14 Mar 1945.

Pierce James Robinson, (W.P 1922-No. 6912) XO G3 Sec 3rd Ar 1942; CO 194th Gli Inf 17th Abn Div T-AE 1943-45; (SMG).

Mathewson Lemuel, (W.P. 1922-No. 6913) BG 1945; Aide to Pres 1943-44; Asst CO 7th Cps Arty 1944; CG 18 Abn Cps Arty T-E 1944-45; (SLTG).

*Schildroth William Henry, (W.P. 1922-No. 6920) Inf; Killed Corsica 17 Sept 1944 CO CO 133rd Inf 34th Inf Div 1944.

Taylor George Arthur, (W.P. 1922-No. 6925) CO 26th & 16th Inf Div 1943-45; BG 1944; ADC 4th & 1st Inf Divs 1944-45.

McGowan Donald Wilson, (Non Grad Class 1922) WWI Vet; AUS 1941-45; CO 102nd Cav 1941-44; T-E 1942-45; (SMG).

Hayden Gilbert, (W.P. 1922-No. 6933) SO 12th TAC T-E 1944-45; (SBG).

Bryan Blackshear Morrison, (W.P. 1922-No. 6939) BG 1942; OPMG 1942-46; (SLtG).

Newman Oliver Perry, (W.P. 1922-No. 6951) CO 186th Inf 41st Div T-S 1943-45; CS 41st Div Jap 1945-46; (SMG).

*MacDonald Ronald Gorrie, (W.P. 1922-No. 6952) CO Inf Regt & Div PA Bataan; POW Death March; Died-POW Camp Fukuoka Japan 5 Feb 1945.

Lewis Thomas Edward, (W.P. 1922-No. 6955) BG 1943; T-M 1942-45; CG 88th Div Arty; Arty Off 5th Ar 1943-46.

Fry James Clyde, (W.P. 1922-No. 6958) BG 1945; CO 350th Inf, CG 88th Div Italy 1945; (SMG).

Hertford Kenner Fisher, (W.P. 1923-No. 6964) CE; OPD WDGS 1945-46; (SMG).

Reber Miles, (W.P. 1923-No. 6967) CE; BG 1944; Engr Mo Riv Div 1943; DCh Legis Div WD 1943; (SMG).

Noyes John Rutherford, (W.P. 1923-No. 6970) CT SOS NATO & 6th Ar Gp T-E 1943-45; (SBG).

Albrecht Frank McAdams, (W.P. 1923-No. 6975) CE; T-E 1942-45; Hq SOS 1942-43; OMG US 1944-45; (SBG).

Osborne Theodore Morrison, (W.P. 1923-No. 6976) BG 1944; CG 9th Port Persia 1944; Hq ASF 1944-45.

Gjelsteen Einar Bernard, (W.P. 1923-No. 6987) CG 86th Div Arty T-E 1944-46; BG 1945; (SMG).

Carraway William Elgie, (W.P. 1923-No. 6988) CO 261st Inf 65th Div T-E 1944; (SBG).

Galusha Mark Hampton, (W.P. 1923-No. 6991) OPD WDGS 1943-45; (SBG).

Horton John Battle, (W.P. 1923-No. 6994) Asst CO 8th Cps Arty 1944-45; CO 22nd Cps Arty 1945; (SBG).

Magruder Carter Bowie, (W.P. 1923-No. 6999) CS & CG TS FET 1945-46; SGEN.

White Will Walter, (W.P. 1923-No. 7001) AvnO

Petr Admn for War 1942-45; (SBG).

Timberlake Patrick Weston, (W.P. 1923-No. 7009) BG 1942; CG 9th Bmb Cmd; CS Air Cmd T-M; (SLTG).

Rich Clyde Kenneth, (W.P. 1923-No. 7011) CO Is Air Cmd T-P 1942-43; G3 Sect GHQ AFPac 1944; (SBG).

Craigie Laurence Carbee, (W.P. 1923-No. 7014) BG 1943; Cmdr Allied Air Corsica; T-MDESC; (SLTG).

Roper Harry McKenzie, (W.P. 1923-No. 7020) BG 1945; CS 3rd Div NATO; CS Cps T-AS 1943; CG X Cps Arty T-P 1944-46; (SMG).

Biddle William Shepard, (W.P. 1923-No. 7024) CO 113th Cav Gp Mecz T-AE 1943-45; ADC 102nd Div & Gen Bd T-E 1945; (SMG).

Lawrence Charles White, (W.P. 1923-No. 7038) BG 1944; CG Bb Gp & Wg T-M 1943-45; (SMG).

Chandler Rex Eugene, (W.P. 1923-No. 7044) BG 1944; DCS 1st Cps T-S 1942-43; CG 1st Cav Div Arty T-S 1944-45;.

Minty Russell J., (W.P. 1923-No. 7045) Co AFSC 5th AF T-S 1944-45; (SBG).

Binns John Joseph, (W.P. 1923-No. 7051) CO 224th FA Gp 7th Cps T-E 1944-45; (SBG).

Early James Francis Joseph, (W.P. 1923-No. 7056) CO 8th AFSC T-E 1944-45; WDGS 1945; BG 1948.

Vandersluis Howard John, (W.P. 1923-No. 7057) GS HQ ASF 1943-45; (SBG).

*Peoples Ulysses John Jr., (W.P. 1923-No. 7058) POW; Death March; Survivor POW ship 15 Dec 1944; Killed San Fernando by Jap Guard 23 Dec 1944.

Crawford Alden Rudyard, (W.P. 1923-No. 7063) BG 1943; CS Gq AMC 1940-44; (SMG).

Schlatter David Myron, (W.P. 1923-No. 7071) MG 1945; DSCO 9th AF, Sr Air StfO SHAEF, DCG STAF T-E 1944-45; (SLTG).

Myers Charles Trovilla, (W.P. 1923-No. 7072) BG 1943; CG 12th AF; CG AAF T-M 1945; (SLTG).

Ridings Eugene Ware, (W.P. 1923-No. 7074) BG 1944; G3 14th Cps, Asst CG Amer Div T-SP 1942-45; (SMG).

Webber Kenneth Eugene, (W.P. 1923-No. 7076) Fiscal Dir CBI 1944 & T-C 1944-46; (SMG).

Bromley Charles Vinson Jr., (W.P. 1923-No. 7083) CO CCB 12th AD T-E 1944-45; (SBG).

Harmony John William, (W.P. 1923-No. 7084) WWI Vet; Inf; T-E; (SMG).

Post Elwyn Donald, (W.P. 1923-No. 7087) BG 1943; CS Alaskan Dept; CS 10th Ar Okinawa; (SMG).

Hardy Wilfred Henry, (W.P. 1923-No. 7089) Cav; S&f CGSS 1941-43; A4 FEAF T-P 1943-45; (SBG).

Smith Joseph, (W.P. 1923-No. 7093) BG 1944; WDGS 1942-43; JCS 1943; CS 3rd AF 1944;, CS & Dpty CG 20th Bb Cmd CBI 1945; (SLTG).

Sweany Kenneth Shearer, (W.P. 1923-No. 7095) CS 41st Div T-S 1942-45; CG 33rd Div Arty 1945-46 (SBG).

Hicks Joseph Harold, (W.P. 1923-No. 7096) Ch of Sup FE ASC 1944-47; (SMG).

*Stout Warren Cole, (W.P. 1923-No. 7104) Killed Tunisia 29 Nov 1942 LTC CO 5th FA Bn Div.

*Barton David Barbour, (W.P. 1923-No. 7105) Killed Velletri Italy 3 Jun 1944 COL SO 36th Inf Div 5th AR.

Harrison Eugene Lynch, (W.P. 1923-No. 7109) AdC Secy War 1940-42; G3 4th Cps DG3 & G2 6th Ar Gp T-E 1944-45; (SBG).

Oliver Robert Chaffee, (W.P. 1923-No. 7119) BG 1942; CS Air Msn Afr ME & India 1941-42; CG ASC CBI 1942-44; CG Med Bmb CCTC 3rd & 4th AFs US 1944-45.

Dorn Frank, (W.P. 1923-No. 7122) BG 1943; US Msn Burma 1942; CG China Tng & CC 1943-45; CG 11th Abn Div Arty 1945; (SBG).

Weikert John Maurice, (W.P. 1923-No. 7134) BG 1945; CO Stewart Fld 1941-43; Hq CinC Pac 1943-44; (SMG).

Dodd Francis Townsend, (W.P. 1923-No. 7150) Arty Stf IV Cps & Hq 7th Ar T-ME 1943-45; (SBG).

*Breitung Howard Edward C., (W.P. 1923-No. 7158) 60CA Corregidor; Bataan; POW; Killed-Jap POW Camp Cabanataun executed 29 Sept 1942, LTC.

*Garcia Alejandro DuJose, (W.P. 1923-No. 7167) Foreign cadet; FA-PS; CO Div Bataan; Guerilla; POW 15 Dec 1944; Executed Manila 18 Dec 1944 LTC.

Timberman Thomas Sherman, (W.P. 1923-No. 7172) CG ZFce & Cdr USFce SEAC T-IC 1944-46; (SMG).

*Marron Cyril Quentin, (W.P. 1923-No. 7173) Inf; JA Phil Div Bataan; Corregidor; POW; Killed POW ship 15 Dec 1944 LTC.

*Babcock David Sherman, (W.P. 1923-No. 7183) CO FABn Bataan; POW;Death March; Died 23 Jan 1945 from wounds POW ship 9Jan 1945 LTC.

Fitzmaurice James Michael, (W.P. 1923-No. 7190) CO 13th Bmb Cmd, CS 13th AF T-Sp 1943-44; CG 3rd AF Staging Wg, CG 1st Staging Cmd 1944-46; (SBG).

Stewart George Craig, (W.P. 1923-No. 7193) 14th Inf CZ 28;TO MTO & France 1943-45; (SMG).

Dulaney Robert Leroy, (W.P. 1923-No. 7195) BG 1945; Asst CG 44th Div T-E; (SMG).

Vandenberg Hoyt Sanford, (W.P. 1923-No. 7199) BG 1942; MG 1944; LTG 1945; CS 12th AF NATO 1942-43; (SGEN).

*Granberry Hal Clark, (W.P. 1923-No. 7202) Inf; CO 57th Inf PS Bataan; POW; Death March; Died 27 Jan 1945 from wounds POW ship 9Jan 1945 LTC.

Grombach John Valentin, (W.P. 1923-No. 7204) Inf; US Olympic Boxing Team 1924; Asst PM & Asst G2 CZ 1926-27; (SBG).

Howard Edwin Britain, (W.P. 1923-No. 7205) Inf; BG 1944; G2, XI Cps 5th Ar, 15th Ar Gp & G2 USFA T-ME 1942-47.

Jamison Glen Clifford, (W.P. 1923-No. 7217) BG 1943; G3 US Fcs T-S; CS 13th AF; CG 13th Bb Cmd; (SBG).

*Lindsay James Robert Jr., (W.P. 1923-No. 7218) POW; Death March wounded; Survivor POW Ships 15 Dec 1944 & 9 Jan 1945; Died POW ship exposure en route to Japan about 20 Jan 1945 LTC.

Cummings Emerson LeRoy, (W.P. 1924-No. 7224) CE; OCO 1940-42; OCO Detroit 1942-45; OCO Hq ETO 1945 (SLTG).

Partridge Earle Everard, (W.P. 1924-No. 7226) CS & DCG 15th AF, DCG 8th AF, CG 3rd Air Div T-ME 1943-45; (SGEN).

Trudeau Arthur Gilbert, (W.P. 1924-No. 7237) CE-Arm; CS Amph Cmd; G3 AF Wes Pac & CG Base X Manila 1945; (SLTG).

*Brewer John Henry, (W.P. 1924-No. 7238) Killed Msn New Guinea 12 May 1943 Col.

Ker Howard, (W.P. 1924-No. 7242) CO Engr Brig T-E 1944-45; (SMG).

Palmer Charles Day, (W.P. 1924-No. 7243) CS 2nd AD T-E 1944; CS 6th Cps T-E 1944-45; SGEN.

Vogel Herbert Davis, (W.P. 1924-No. 7244) SOS T-SP 1944-45; (SBG).

Textor Gordon Edmund, (W.P. 1924-No. 7249) BG 1945; War Prod 1942-43; WDGS 1943-46.

Robinson Clinton Frederick, (W.P. 1924-No. 7255) MG 1944; OQMG 1940-41; WDGS 1941-42.

*Mitchell Floyd Allen, (W.P. 1924-No. 7260) Corregidor; POW; Killed POW ship 15 Dec 1944 LTC.

Conrad Victor Allen, (W.P. 1924-No. 7271) OCSO 1942-43; Siq Sect AFHQ 1943-44; CO Sig Engr Labs US 1944; (SMG).

Pape Robin Bernard, (W.P. 1924-No. 7272) AMA Tokyo 1938-41; G2 Hq CBI 1942-43; Hq SEAC 1943-45; BG 1944.

Massey Clyde, (W.P. 1924-No. 7276) NATO 1942-43; BG 1944; QM 7th Ar T-ME 1943-45.

Berry Robert Ward, (W.P. 1924-No. 7279) BG 1943; WDGS 1940-45; CG 76th AAA Brig PCD 1945.

Arnold William Howard, (W.P. 1924-No. 7283) MG 1944; CS 14th Cps T-S 1943-44; CG Amer Div 1944-45; (SLTG).

Simon Leslie Earl, (W.P. 1924-No. 7292) Dir Ballistic Research Labs APG 1937-49; (Msns to ETO & NATO 1944-45) (SMG).

Lanham Charles Trueman, (W.P. 1924-No. 7293) CO 22nd Inf & ADC 104th Div T-E 1945; (SMG).

Stephens Richard Warburton, (W.P. 1924-No. 7294) CS 30th Div T-E 1943-45; (SMG).

Dewey Lawrence Russell, (W.P. 1924-No. 7300) (SBG).

Glasgow Ralph Irvin, (W.P. 1924-No. 7301) NY POE 1942-43; S&F AN Stf College 1943-45; SOS T-SP 1945; (SBG).

Loome James Thomas, (W.P. 1924-No. 7309) CO 318th FABn, XO 81st Div Arty, CG 98th Div Arty T-P 1942-44; (SBG).

Richardson William Lloyd, (W.P. 1924-No. 7311) BG 1943; CG 9th Air Def Cmd 9th AF T-E 1943-45; (SMG).

Landon Charles Raeburne, (W.P. 1924-No. 7317) AG SOS ETO 1942-43; AG 12th Ar Gp T-E 1944-45; (SMG).

Ent Uzal Girard, (W.P. 1924-No. 7329) Vet WWI; A-Army; AC; 19th Airship CO 1928; MA Peru 1939-42; CG 9th Bb Cmd 9th AF T-M (led 1st Ploesti Raid) 1943; (SMG).

Willis James Stewart, (W.P. 1924-No. 7332) Sig Sect SHAEFF 1944-45; (SBG).

Stokes Marcus Butler Jr., (W.P. 1924-No. 7338) AF-HQ T-E 1942; OCT 1942-45; (SBG).

Day Francis Marion, (W.P. 1924-No. 7339) Dpty CO 12th Cps Arty, CO 410th FA Gp T-E 1944-45; (SMG).

Stevenson Charles G., (W.P. 1924-No. 7340) G2 Div WDGS 1943-46; (SMG).

Schaefer William Herbert, (W.P. 1924-No. 7341) AGF Obsr NATO 1942-43; CO 1st Bn 180th Inf T-M 1943; POW 1943-45.

Rogers Gordon Byrom, (W.P. 1924-No. 7345) G2 1st Cps T-P 1942-43; G2 AGF 1943-45; (SLTG).

Pence George Dunbar, (W.P. 1924-No. 7354) MG 1945.

*Tacy Lester Joseph, (W.P. 1924-No. 7357) 88th FA Bataan; POW; Death March; Died POW Cmp Fukuoka Japan 9 Feb 1945 malnutrition LTC.

Dasher Charles Lanier, (W.P. 1924-No. 7359) BG 1945; Asst ArtyO 19th Cps T-E 1944; CO 32nd FA Brig 1944-45; CG 75th Div Arty 1945; (SMG).

Boatner Haydon Lemaire, (W.P. 1924-No. 7366) MA in Chinese Lang & Lit CA Coll in China 1943; BG 1942; CBI 1942-45; CG Chinese Area Cmd; CS Chinese Army

India; Dpty CG Cmbt Comd; (SMG).

Moore James Edward, (W.P. 1924-No. 7375) CS 35th Div, 30th Div, 12th Cps, 4th Ar, 9th Ar T-AE 1942-45; (SGEN).

Hains Peter Conover III, (W.P. 1924-No. 7382) CO 1st Armd Regt T-M 1942-43; G3 TD Cen 1944; Hq 1st Ar T-E 1944-45; CO CCA 13th AD T-M 1945; (SMG).

MacCloskey Monro, (W.P. 1924-No. 7383) AUS 1941-46; COL AC; Hq AAF T-M 1943-44; CO Gp 15th AF; (SBG).

Nugent Richard Emmel, (W.P. 1924-No. 7389) BG 1943; CS 1st AF & DCS 9th AF; CG 29th TAC 9th AF T-E 1944-45; (SLTG).

Burger Vonna Fernleigh, (W.P. 1924-No. 7392) COL 1942; (SBG).

*Miller Albert Delmar, (W.P. 1924-No. 7395) FO HD Manila Bay; POW; Killed POW ship 24 Oct 1944 LTC.

Sibley Cleland Charles, (W.P. 1924-No. 7396) CO Ports ETO 1942-46; (SBG).

Kreidel Francis Anthony, (W.P. 1924-No. 7407) NGNY 1941-46; G2 5th SvC 1944-46; (SBG).

Prather Richard Givens, (W.P. 1924-No. 7423) Asst Cmdt TARS 1943-44; CS 100th Div & CO 397th Inf 100th Div T-E 1944-46; (SMG).

Smith Luther Stevens, (W.P. 1924-No. 7431) Dir Mil Msns Hq CDC 1944; (SBG).

Conley Samuel Glenn, (W.P. 1924-No. 7433) Inf; CO 274th Inf 70th Div & Theater Gen Bd T-E 1944-46; (SBG).

*Kirkpatrick Lewis Spencer; (W.P. 1924-No. 7435) Inf; 59th CA & CO Ft Drum PI 1942; POW; Died Jap POW Camp Corregidor 27 Apr 1943 pneumonia LTC.

Nelson Otto Lauren Jr., (W.P. 1924-No. 7439) OCS WD 1942-44; DCG T-M 1945; (SMG).

Harper Robert Wells, (W.P. 1924-No. 7445) Inf; MG 1944; Hq AAF 1944-46; (SLTG).

Turner Howard McMath; (W.P. 1924-No. 7447) MG 1945; CG 13th AF Clark AFB PI; (SMG).

Liebel Willard Koehler, (W.P. 1924-No. 7449) Inf; CS 17th Abn Div; (SMG).

Stadler John Harry Jr., (W.P. 1924-No. 7458) Cav; BG 1945; CO 12th Cav 1st Cav Div T-S 1943-44; (SBG).

Ladue Laurence Knight, (W.P. 1924-No. 7477) Cav; BG 1945; G3 5th Ar & CS 4th Cps 5th Ar Italy 1944-45.

Pulsifer Ralph, (W.P. 1924-No. 7479) Inf; AG Hq ETO 1942-44; BG 1943; Ret dsbld 1945; (SBG).

White Edward Higgins, (W.P. 1924-No. 7490) Budget Off Hq AMC 1941-43; Budget Off Hq AAF 1944-45; (SBG).

Mead Armistead Davis, (W.P. 1924-No. 7496) Inf; G3 4th Ar 1943-44; G3 9th Ar T-E 1944-45; (SMG).

Royce Charles Harold, (W.P. 1924-No. 7498) Inf; CS 9th Cps Japan. (SBG).

Sexton William Thaddeus (W.P. 1924-No. 7506) BG 1944; Asst Secy & Secy WDGS 1940-44; CG 3rd Div Arty T-E 1944-46. (SMG).

*Macklin James Edgar, (W.P. 1924-No. 7512) Inf; QM Bataan 1942; POW; Death March; Died POW Camp Cabanatuan 22 June 1942.

Hart Charles Edward, (W.P. 1924-No. 7517) BG 1944; Arty O 1st Ar T-E 1943-46. (SLTG).

Hill John Gillespie, (W.P. 1924-No. 7526) Inf; G1 Alas 1940-43. (SBG).

Hawkins John Reynolds, (W.P. 1924-No. 7533) BG 1944; CG Ftr Wg 12th AF T-M 1943-44.

Booth Charles Loomis, (W.P. 1924-No. 7535) Hq 8th & 12th AF T-ME 1942-45. (SBG).

Lenzner Emil, (W.P. 1924-No. 7539) BG 1944; SO SOS & 6th Ar Gp 1943-45. (SMG).

Maglin William Henry, (W.P. 1924-No. 7541) Vet WWI; Inf; Cmdt PM Sch 1943-45; OPMG 1945; Dir Nat Police Korea 1945-47. (SMG).

Fisher Ralph Emanuel, (W.P. 1924-No. 7543) A3 1st Tac AF T-E 1944-45; (SBG).

Smythe George Winfered, (W.P. 1924-No. 7545) Inf; BG 1945; CO 47th Inf Div & Dpty CG 80th Div T-ME 1943-45; (SMG).

Traywick Jesse Thomas Sr., (W.P. 1924-No. 7547) Inf; G3 Sect US AFFE 7 Dec 1941; GS Corregidor; POW 1942-45.

Elmore John Archer, (W.P. 1924-No. 7552) Inf; BG 1945.

Eddleman Clyde Davis, (W.P. 1924-No. 7571) Inf; BG 1944;

Stowell James Somers, (W.P. 1924-No. 7578) Inf; BG 1944; CG No Africa Div ATC 1944-45; (SMG).

OConnor William Wheeler, (W. P. 1924-No. 7586) Inf; CS 76th Div T-E 1944-45; (SBG).

Eaton Ralph Parker, (W.P. 1924-No. 7601) Inf; CS 82nd Abn Div & 18th Abn Cps T-ME 1942-45; (SBG).

Hass Martin Frank, (W.P. 1924-No. 7619) Inf; Hq WDC 1942; G4 Div WDGS 1942-44; Hq 12th Ar Gp T-E 1944-45; (SBG).

*Barth Charles Henry Jr., (W.P. 1925-No. 7626) BG 1943; Supervising Engr 3d Locks PC 1940; G4 Hq USAF IME 1942; CS Hq ETO 1943; Died-Air Acdt Iceland 3 May 1943.

Saltzman Charles Eskridge, (W.P. 1925-No. 7629) BG 1945; (SMG) .

Galloway Gerald Edward, (W.P. 1925-No. 7631) CO 543rd Engr Boat Shore Regt T-S 1942-45; (SMG).

Harrold Thomas Leonard, (W.P. 1925-No. 7639) Cav; 9th AD T-E 1943-45; (SLTG).

Esposito Vincent Joseph, (W.P. 1925-No. 7641) BG 1945.

Howze Robert Lee, (W.P. 1925-No. 7643) CO 36A Inf 3AD T-E; (SMG).

Myers Colby Maxwell, (W.P. 1925-No. 7645) CE Cornell 1927; XO & CO 4th Engr Spec Brig T-P 1944-46; (SMG).

*Garver Ralph Tibbs, (W.P. 1925-No. 7646) Cav; Div AG PA; POW; Killed-Lubao on Death March 14 April 1942.

Ritchie William Ludlow, (W.P. 1925-No. 7647) BG 1945; WDGS 1942-45; (SBG).

Clarke Bruce Cooper, (W.P. 1925-No. 7658) BG 1944; CS & Cmbt Cmdr 4th AD & 7th AD T-ES; SGEN.

Tulley David Henry, (W.P. 1925-No. 7665) CE; OCE 1942-43; Engr Sec 3rd Ar T-E 1944-45; (SMG).

Dawson Miles Merrill, (W.P. 1925-No. 7669) OCE GHQ AF Pac 1944-46; (SBG).

Nicholas Charles Parsons, (W.P. 1925-No. 7670) MID WDGS 1943-46; (SBG).

Randall Russell Edward, (W.P. 1925-No. 7671) BG 1942; CZ 1940-42; Dpty CG B-MA CBI 1944;CG West China Raiders 1944-45; (SBG).

Nutter William Henry, (W.P. 1925-No. 7686) Armd Cen 1944-45; (SMG).

Newman Aubrey Strode, (W.P. 1925-No. 7690) CO 34th Inf 1944; (SMG).

Holmes Ernest Victor, (W.P. 1925-No. 7691) 24th Div Arty Haw 1940-42; CS Haw Arty Cmd 1942-44; (SBG).

Babcock C. Stanton, (W.P. 1925-No. 7695) JCS 1944-45; 6th Marine Div T-P 1945; (SMG).

Barlow Ernest Andrew, (W.P. 1925-No. 7707) Inf; CS 32nd Div T-S 1944-45; (SBG).

Cabell Charles Pearre, (W.P. 1925-No. 7712) BG 1944; CO 45th Cmbt Bb Wg T-E; Dir Opns & Int Allied AF T-M; (SGEN).

Wood William Holmes, (W.P. 1925-No. 7726) Cav; CS 13th AD 1944-45; (SBG).

Seleen Paul Maurice, (W.P. 1925-No. 7730) Lend Lease OCO 1939-45; (SBG).

Purdue Branner Pace, (W.P. 1925-No. 7740) Inf; CO 120th Inf 30th Div T-E; (SBG).

Johnson Edwin Lynds, (W.P. 1925-No. 7749) Inf; G3 Hq 1st Ar T-EP 1944-45; (SBG).

Denniston Jos. Cyril Agustin, (W.P. 1925-No. 7768) CO 5th AFSC 1944-45; (SBG).

Kelley Gerard William, (W.P. 1925-No. 7769) Inf; 27th Div T-ASP 1940-45; CO 156th Inf 1943-45; (SBG).

Bird John Franklin, (W.P. 1925-No. 7770).

*Griffith Welborn Barton Jr., (W.P. 1925-No. 7776) Inf; Killed near Paris 16 Aug 1944 leading tanks.

McCormick John Haliday, (W.P. 1925-No. 7786) BG 1944; (SMG).

Gillmore William Nelson, (W.P. 1925-No. 7787) CO Arty 1st AD & 101st Abn Div T-ME 1943-45; (SMG).

Smith Wayne Carleton, (W.P. 1925-No. 7799) Inf; BG 1944; CS Cent Pac Base Cmd 1943-45; (SMG).

*Harper Harry Jean, (W.P. 1925-No. 7801) Arty O 31st Div Bataan; POW; Survivor POW ship 15 Dec 1944; Died-San Fernando 22 Dec 1944 exposure, malnutrition, bronchitis.

*Mack Edward Clement, (W.P. 1925-No. 7805) Inf; 57th Inf Bataan; Died-POW Camp Fukuoko Japan 9 April 1945.

Evans Ira Kenneth, (W.P. 1925-No. 7807) Inf; NY-POE 1942-44; (SBG).

Barnes Earl Walter, (W.P. 1925-No. 7808) BG 1944; CG 13th Ftr Cmd T-S 1944-45; (SLTG).

*Lewis John Llewellyn, (W.P. 1925-No. 7814) Inf; XO 61st FA PA Mindanao; POW; Death March; Died POW ship, 25 Jan 1945.

Keams Edwin Bascum Jr., (W.P. 1925-No. 7816) Inf; OQMG 1943-45; (SBG).

Van Brunt Rinaldo, (W.P. 1925-No. 7817) Inf; CS 83rd Div 1942-44; CS 21st Cps T-E 1944-45; (SMG).

Lynch George Patrick, (W.P. 1925-No. 7818) Inf; CS 102nd Div T-E 1944-46; (SMG).

*Smith Clarence Harwood, (W.P. 1925-No. 7822) Inf; 45th Inf Bataan; POW; Death March; Killed POW ship 24 Oct 1944.

*Smyth Thaddeus Elmer, (W.P. 1925-No. 7824) Inf; Prov Tk Gp Bataan; POW; Death March; Died-POW Camp Fufuoka Japan 5 Mar 1945 malnutrition.

*Damas Waldemar Noya, (W.P. 1925-No. 7825) Inf; Killed Rcn Heidenheim Ger 26 Apr 1945.

Finn Russell Thomas, (W.P. 1925-No. 7829) XO 32nd FA Brig 1st Ar T-E 1942-45; (SBG).

Crandall Harry Wells, (W.P. 1925-No. 7830) FO 13th Cps T-AE 1942-45; (SMG).

Cleland Joseph Pringle, (W.P. 1925-No. 7831) BG 1945; CS Regt CO, Asst CO 43rd Div T-SP 1942-46(SMG).

Peploe George Bateman, (W.P. 1925-No. 7838) Inf; WDGS 1942; G3 13th Cps T-AE 1944-45; (SMG).

Caldwell Charles Henry, (W.P. 1925-No. 7842) BG 1944; 1st AF T-A 1944;(SBG).

Dunford Donald, (W.P. 1925-No. 7858) Inf; XO 88th Div Arty T-M 1944-45; Asst Arty O 5th Ar T-M 1945; (SBG).

Baker William Clyde Jr., (W.P. 1926-No. 7871) XO Engr BD 1939-42; CS 106th Div T-E 1943-45; (SMG).

Bayer William Livingston, (W.P. 1926-No. 7872) Acft Radio Lab 1940-43; OCH Sig O

1943-45; (SBG).

Ehrgott Herbert William, (W.P. 1926-No. 7873) Engr A4 & CS 9th Engr Cmd 9th AF T-DE 1942-45; (SBG).

Sims Turner Ashby Jr., (W.P. 1926-No. 7874) ChAdm Air Tech SvC 1944-45; (SBG).

Ankenbrandt Francis LeRoy, (W.P. 1926-No. 7875) BG 1945; SOT-S 1942-44; Comm Hq AAF Guam 1944-45; (SMG).

Barney Keith Richard, (W.P. 1926-No. 7877) CO 1120th CGP T-E 1943-45; (SMG).

Heiberg Elvin Ragnvald, (W.P. 1926-No. 7878) XO OCE GHQ T-S 1942-43; (SBG).

Maude Raymond Coleman, (W.P. 1926-No. 7882) CommO 9th Bb Cmd 9th AF 1943-44; 29th TAC 9th AF 1944-45; (SMG).

Corderman William Preston, (W.P. 1926-No. 7887) BG 1945; WDGS 1939-42; Asst Dir Censor ship 1941-43; CG Security Agcy 43-46; (SMG).

Smith Clerin Rodney, (W.P. 1926-No. 7888) OCE 1942-43; Hq ASF 1944-45; (SMG).

Johnson Harry Warren, (W.P. 1926-No. 7891) Cav; CS 70th Div; CO Combat Cmd 9th AD T-E (SMG).

Booth Donald Prentice, (W.P. 1926-No. 7895) CG Pers Gulf Cmd 1944-45; (SLTG).

Creasy William Murlin, (W.P. 1926-No. 7897) Pine Bluff Ars 1941-43; O CH CWS 1943; GS DCS CO SOS CBI 1944-45;(SMG).

Johnson Alfred Henry, (W.P. 1926-No. 7898) CO AFProc Dist Detroit 1943-45; Manila Air Dep 1945-46; (SMG).

Osborne Ralph Morris, (W.P. 1926-No. 7899) Dir R&D Div Hq ASF DC 1943-45; G2 Div SHAEF 1945; (SMG).

House William Edward, (W.P. 1926-No. 7906) OO IBC 1941-43; (SBG).

*Andersen James Roy, (W.P. 1926-No. 7907) Inf; Missing Trans Pac flight 26 Feb 1945 BG.

Elliott John Colt Beaumont, (W.P. 1926-No. 7911) CE; Inst USMA 1938-42; AsstE AGF 1942-43; ActgE 6th Ar & CO 5220 ECnBde T-P 1944-46; (SBG).

Harris Samuel Russ Jr., (W.P. 1926-No. 7912) CO Flt Control Cmd Hq AAF 1941-43; CO 499th Bb Gp(VH) 73rd Wg 20th AF T-S 1944-45; (SBG).

Griffing Lewis Sherrill, (W.P. 1926-No. 7913) FA; S&F TAS 1945-46; (SMG).

Laidlaw Waldo Eugene, (W.P. 1926-No. 7914) Inf; OO Overseas Sup NYPE & SFPE 1942-45; (SMG).

Toftoy Holger Nelson, (W.P. 1926-No. 7923) Ch Ord Tech Int Hq ETO 1944-45; (SMG).

Van Syckle David Louis, (W.P. 1926-No. 7926) Inf; OO 12AD&XX Cps T-AE 1942-45; (SBG).

Barnes Wallace Hayden, (W.P. 1926-No. 7927) Cav; 4AD 1941-43; WDGS 1943-44; CS 20th & 12th ADs 1944-45; (SBG).

Doyle John Paul, (W.P. 1926-No. 7929) Cav; BG 1944; Hq 5AF T-S 1943; CS&CG 42 Bb Wg T-ME 1943-45 (SMG).

Johnson Leon William, (W.P. 1926-No. 7930) Inf; MS CA Tech 1936; BG 1943; A3 8AF, CO 44th HvBmb Gp8AF, CG 14th Cmbt Bmb Wg 8AF T-E 1942-45; (MH, Ploesti Raid 1943) (SMG).

Mayo Richard Walden, (W.P. 1926-No. 7931) FA: Fencing, ModPent Olympics 1928 & 1932: Hq 15 Ar T-E 1944-45: (SBG).

Bowen Frank Sayles Jr., (W.P. 1926-No. 7935) Inf: G3 1Cps T-S 1942-44; G3 8Ar T-SP 1944-46; (SMG).

Ennis William Peirce Jr., (W.P. 1926-No. 7937) G1 Sec AF Hq T-M 1942-44; CO 424 FA Gp T-M 1944-45; CO 4Cps Arty T-M 1945; (SMG).

*Conzelman Clair McKinley, (W.P. 1926-No. 7943) Hq HD Manila: POW: Survivor POW Ship 15 Dec 1945: Died 11 Jan 1945 fr wds POW ship 9 Jan 1945 LTC.

Ryan John Lawrence Jr., (W.P. 1926-No. 7952) Cav; CO CCR & CS 7AD T-E 1944-45; (SLTG).

Storke Harry Purnell, (W.P. 1926-No. 7969) Sec. Assn of Grads 1939-42; Arty O 2Cps T-ME 1943-45; NWC 1949; NATOStg Gp 1949. (SLTG).

*Woodbridge John Prichard, (W.P. 1926-No. 7979) CO 81st FA Mindanao 1941-42; Survived sinking POW ship 15 Dec 1944; Killed POW ship 9 Jan 1945 Ltc 1941.

de Shazo Thomas Edward, (W.P. 1926-No. 7980) CO 6th FAGp T-AME 1940-44; Asst Comdt FAS 1944-47; NWC 1947; (SMG).

*O'Connor Richard Edward, (W.P. 1926-No. 7986) GS VCps NATO; Killed Sicily 18 Jul 1943 COL XO 16th Inf Div.

Nelson Morris Robert, (W.P. 1926-No. 7991) BG 1945; CG 305th Ftr Wg 15th AF T-M 1944-45; CG 6th Ftr Wg CZ 1946-47; (SMG).

McNaughton Kenneth Perry, (W.P. 1926-No. 7992) BG 1943; A3 & CS AAF Tng Cmd 1942-45; CS STAF Guam 1945; (SMG).

Canham Charles Draper William, (W.P. 1926-No. 7997) Inf; CO 116th Inf & Asst CG 8th Div T-E 1942-45; Promoted to BG on battlefield 1944; (SMG).

McDaniel Edward Harold, (W.P. 1926-No. 7998) Inf; WDGS & JCS 1941-44; CO 115th Inf & 175th Inf, CS 29th Div T-E 1944-45; (SMG).

Munson Edward Lyman Jr., (W.P. 1926-No. 8004) Inf; BG 1945; Ch Ar PictSer ASF 1941-44; Ch Ar Pict Ser OCSO 1944-45; Ret 1945; (SBG).

Burwell James Bell, (W.P. 1926-No. 8005) G3 Div WDGS 1942-45; CS Hq AAF T-M 1945; (SBG).

Burns John Robert, (W.P. 1926-No. 8010) Inf; CmlO 6th Ar T-P 1944-46; (SBG).

*Horton Thomas Randall, (W.P. 1926-No. 8016) Inf; OQM Manila 1941; POW Bataan; Death March; Died Cabanatuan POW Camp 6 Sep 1942 LTC.

Weyher Theodore Addison, (W.P. 1927-No. 8027) CE-OD; OCO 1940-44; (SBG).

Berrigan Paul Dunn, (W.P. 1927-No. 8030) CE; Engr Sect Hq ETO 1943-45; (SBG).

Johnson Max Sherred, (W.P. 1927-No. 8034) CS 80th Div T-E 1944-45; (SMG).

Washbourne Lee Bird, (W.P. 1927-No. 8035) Engr 6th AF CZ 1942-44; CO 933rd EA Regt T-P 1944-46; (SMG).

McNutt Charles H., (W.P. 1927-No. 8040) T-S 1942-45; CO 5206th Engr SvC 1944; Base X Manila 1945; (SBG).

Garland Elmer Blair, (W.P. 1927-No. 8042) SigO 8th AF T-E 1942-43; SigO Hq 9th TAC T-E 1943-45; (SMG).

Davidson Garrison Holt, (W.P. 1927-No. 8044) BG 1943; Engr Western TF NATO 1942-43; 7th Ar T-ME 1943-45; War Crimes Comm 1945; EBd 15th Ar 1945; (SLTG).

Burgess Woodbury Megrew, (W.P. 1927-No. 8046) Cav; A2Sect Hq AAF 1941-44; DCS 20th Bb Cmd T-1 1945; A2 FEAF 1945; (SBG).

Asensio Manuel Jose, (W.P. 1927-No. 8047) Cav; Engr Brazil 1942; MA Columbia 1942-43; Engr 10th AF T-C 1944-45; Engr AAF T-C 1945; (SLTG).

Brown Frederic Joseph, (W.P. 1927-No. 8050) CO 3rd AD Arty T-E 1942-45; (SLTG).

Chamberlain Edwin William (W.P. 1927-No. 8051) G3 Div WDGS 1942-46; (SBG).

Pachynski Alvin Louis, (W.P. 1927-No. 8052) SigO 5th AFT T-S 1942-44; Air CommO FEAF 1944-45; (SMG).

Paxson Harry Oliver, (W.P. 1927-No. 8053) CE: T-M 1942-45; Engr XO Hq 5th Ar 1943-44; XO G3 Sect 15th Ar Gp 1945; (SBG).

Hoeffer Henry Joseph, (W.P. 1927-No. 8054) Engr 3 Sv Area Cmd, 12th AF Engr Cmd, AAF Engr Cmd T-M 1942-45; (SBG).

Lillard Gerald Francis, (W.P. 1927-No. 8059) ADF Amph TC 1942-43; NATO 5th Ar Invasion TC 1943-44; G3 Sect AGF 1944-45; USN Amph TC PI 1945; (SBG).

Green James Wilson Jr., (W.P. 1927-No. 8063) Cmdt Radar Sch 1942-44; (SBG).

Howard Francis Elliot, (W.P. 1927-No. 8065) Inf; PM CZ 1039-44; PM Hq ETO 1944-45; (SBG).

Kuter Laurence Sherman, (W.P. 1927-No. 8066) WDGS 1941; BG 1942; MG 1944; CG 1Bb Div T-E 1942; NAfr TAF 1943; Hq AAF 1943-44; Dpty CG AAF POA 1945; (SGEN).

Pence William Perry, (W.P. 1927-No. 8068) OCSO; Hq ETO 1944-45; (SBG).

Watlington Thomas Morgan, (W.P. 1927-No. 8069) Exec 3rd Cps Arty US & T-E 1943-45; (SMG).

*Trapnell Thomas John Hall, (W.P. 1927-No. 8071) CO 26th Cav Bataan 1941; POW 1942-45 (Survived 2 POW ship sinkings), Death March; (SLTG).

Curtis Raymond Wiley, (W.P. 1927-No. 8073) Cav; Riding Tm Olympics 1932 & 1936; IV Cps T-M 1944-45; (SMG).

Farrand Edward Gilbert, (W.P. 1927-No. 8077) CS & CO CCA 5th AD T-E; DCS 7th Ar 1945-47; (SMG).

McCoy George Jr., (W.P. 1927-No. 8082) Inf; Hq AAF 1942-43; CG SvC 13th AF T-Sp 1943-44; BG 1943; CS 6th AF CZ 1945. (SBG).

*Bonner Stanley Burton, (W.P. 1927-No. 8086) XO 21st FA Bataan; POW; Death March; Died POW ship 25 Jan 1945 exposure & malnutrition.

Mechling Edward Pont, (W.P. 1927-No. 8087) Cav; A4 Str AF & 15th AF NATO 1943-44; Hq AGF, WDGS & NGB 1945; (SMG).

Martin George Edward, (W.P. 1927-No. 8091) Inf; G3, CS 45th Div Italy 1943-44;. CS 44th Div 1944-45; (SMG).

Holtzworth Bertram Arthur, (W.P. 1927-No. 8093) G4 Sec Hq 12th Ar Gp T-E 1943-45; (SMG).

Bixel Charles Pennoyer, (W.P. 1927-No. 8097) Cav; OCh Cav 1941-42; Hq AGF 1942-43; G2 9th Ar, &th Ar, 3rd Ar T-E 1944-46; (SMG).

Holland Jeremiah Paul, (W.P. 1927-No. 8101) Asst & PM SOS T-S 1942-45; (SBG).

Sterling John Mills, (W.P. 1927-No. 8103) CS 13th AF T-S 1943-45; (SBG).

Collins James Francis, (W.P. 1927-No. 8108) XO 1st Cps Arty 1942-44; DCS & CS 1st Cps 1944-45; (SMG).

Thompson James Virgil, (W.P. 1927-No. 8115) Inf; CO 358th Inf (0th Div T-E 1944; (SBG).

*Coyle Harold James, (W.P. 1927-No. 8117) FA; Btry F 24th FA PA 1941; Cebu Force 1942; POW 16 Apr 1942; Killed Adlaon Cebu exe cuted by Japanese 17 Apr 1942.

Kyster Olaf Helgesen Jr., (W.P. 1927-No. 8119) CS 24th Comp Wg T-E 1943-44; (SMG).

Grover Orrin Leigh, (W.P. 1927-No. 8120) FEAF PI 1941-42; A3 5th AF T-S 1942-43; Air Tng 1943-44; Dpty CO 7th Ftr Wg POA 1944; (SBG).

Johnson Walter Morris, (W.P. 1927-No. 8124) Inf; XO, CO 117th Inf 30th Div T-AE 1943-45; (SBG).

Doan Leander LaChance, (W.P. 1927-No. 8128) Cav; CO 32nd Armd Regt & CCA 3rd AD T-E 1944-45; (SMG).

Verbeck William Jordan, (W.P. 1927-No. 8141) Inf; G2 Alas Dept 1942-43; G2X Cps T-S 1944; CO 21st Inf 24th Div T-S 1944-45.(SMG).

*Ganahl Joseph, (W.P. 1927-No. 8143) N Luzan Force PI; POW; Death March; Survivor 2 POW ship sinkings; Died Camp Fukuoka Japan 11 Feb 1945.

Upthegrove Fay Roscoe, (W.P. 1927-No. 8144) Inf; BG 1944; CG 304th Bb Wg (H) 15th AF T-M 1944-45; (SMG).

Delchelmann Matthew Kemp, (W.P. 1927-No. 8148) 26th Ftr Cmd CZ 1942-43; Hq AAF 1943-45; (SMG).

Stone Charles Bertody 3rd, (W.P. 1927-No. 8151) Inf; MG 1945; CS Hq AAF CBI 1943-45; (SLTG).

Zwicker Ralph Wise, (W.P. 1927-No. 8167) Inf; Hq VCps 1944; CO 38th Inf 2nd Div 1944; CS 2Div T-E 1944-45. (SMG).

Meloy Guy Stanley Jr., (W.P. 1927-No. 8181) Inf; CS 103rd Div T-E 1944-45. (SMG).

Bell Raymond Earle, (W.P. 1927-No. 8186) Inf; CO Cmbt Tms 2nd & 90th Divs T-E 1944-45. (SMG).

Ginder Philip DeWitt, (W.P. 1927-No. 8193) Inf; CO 9th Inf 2nd Div T-E 1944-45. (SMG).

Sink Robert Frederick, (W.P. 1927-No. 8196) Inf; CO 506th Prcht Inf 10st Abn Div T-E 1944-45; (SLTG).

Morin Martin Joseph, (W.P. 1927-No. 8200) Inf; G2 Div WD 1944-46. (SMG).

Aloe Robert Campbell, (W.P. 1927-No. 8205) Inf; CO 354th Inf Div T-E 1945; (SBG).

*McKee Montgomery, (W.P. 1927-No. 8206) Inf; Hq Phil Div Bataan; POW; Death March; Killed POW ship 24 Oct 1944.

*Stark Edgar Daniel, (W.P. 1927-No. 8215) Inf; LTC CO 3Cml Bn; Killed Carassuolo, Italy 12 Jan 1944.

Matthews Willis Small, (W.P. 1927-No. 8221) Inf; G3 82nd & 28th Divs T-A 1942; G3 Sect 6th Ar GHQ & 14th Cps T-S 1943-45; (SMG).

Riggs Theodore Scott, (W.P. 1928-No. 8229) Cav; C/S USA FIME 1942; Jt Log Plans Comm ZI 1943-44 (SMG).

Dau Frederick Jensen, (W.P. 1928-No. 8230) CE; WDGS 1944-45. (SMG).

Hefley William Tell, (W.P. 1928-No. 8232) CE; Dpty CG 8th AF SvC T-E 1944-45. (SMG).

Browning Samuel Roberts, (W.P. 1928-No. 8234) ChTran EUCOM 1945-47. (SMG).

Seeman Lyle Edward, (W.P. 1928-No. 8235) CE; CE Princeton 1934; EBd 1941-43; Air E Hq AAF CBI 1943-45. (SMG).

Van Natta Thomas Fraley 3rd, (W.P. 1928-No. 8239) Cav; MA Paraguay; GS & Cmbt Ln O Hq CBI. (SMG).

Israel Robert Scott Jr., (W.P. 1928-No. 8240) CG 22nd TAC T-M. (SBG).

Smith Donald Bertrand, (W.P. 1928-No. 8242) Inf; AAF Tng Cmds T-A 1943-44; Hq STAF T-E 1945. (SBG).

Heiman David William, (W.P. 1928-No. 8247) CE; CO Engr Gps & Brig 6th Ar T-SP 1943-46. (SBG).

Fleming Robert John Jr., (W.P. 1928-No. 8248) CE; CS Haw SvC & DCS Cent Pac Area 1942-43; Engr 22nd Cps T-E 1944-45. (SMG).

Potter William Everett, (W.P. 1928-No. 8251)

CE; G4 Sec Hq ETO & Hq Com Z ETO 1943-45. (SMG).

Anderson Webster, (W.P. 1928-No. 8254) Inf; OQMG 1941-42; T-EM 1942-45; (SMG).

Briggs James Elbert, (W.P. 1928-No. 8256) A3 8th Ftr Cmd 1942-43; WDGS 1943-45. (SLTG).

Mills John Stewart, (W.P. 1928-No. 8259) CO 450th Bb 15th AF T-M 1943-44; WDSS 1944-46. (SMG).

Traub David William, (W.P. 1928-No. 8263) Dpty Ch Trans 1942-45. (SLTG).

Mundy George Warren, (W.P. 1928-No. 8265) CO 39th Bb Wg T-P 1945-47. (SLTG).

Maxwell Alfred Rockwood, (W.P. 1928-No. 8266) BG 1945; Hq AAF 1942-43; Hq US STAF T-E 1944-45. (SBG).

Wilson Roscoe Charles, (W.P. 1928-No. 8273) AcftLab AAF Mat Cmd 1941-42; AEProjO Hq AAF 1943-44; CS 316th Bb Wg T-P 1944-45. (SLTG).

Todd Walter E., (W.P. 1928-No. 8274) BG 1944; WDGS 1942-44; Hq 8th AF T-E 1944-45; A5 Hq T-S 1945. (SLTG).

Hennig William Henry, (W.P. 1928-No. 8275) Ch US Mil Msn Guatemala 1943-45. (SMG).

Boatner Bryant Lemaire, (W.P. 1928-No. 8276) CO EurWg ATC 1945. (SLTG).

*Forrest Nathan Bedford, (W.P. 1928-No. 8277) Killed Air Msn Ger 13 June 1943 BG CG Wing 8th AF.

Tate Robert Frederick, (W.P. 1928-No. 8281) Cav; 19th Bmb Gp 1941; CO Ferrying Cmd CBI 1942; AirO Hq CBI 1943-44. (SMG).

Brentnall Samuel Robert, (W.P. 1928-No. 8285) ME; Aero Stanford 1938; Test Lab Wright Fld 1039; (SMG).

Born Charles Franklin, (W.P. 1928-No. 8296) Cav; Antilles Air Cmd 1942-43; Opns O & DCG 15th AF T-M. (SMG).

Everest Frank Fort, (W.P. 1928-No. 8298) CO 11th Bb Gp T-Sp 1943. (SGEN).

Coverdale Garrison Barkley, (W.P. 1928-No. 8301) CO FATC T-C 1944-45; CO 5003rd FA Gp T-C 1945; Jap POW 3 days-escaped. (SMG).

Walter Mercer Christie, (W.P. 1928-No. 8304) G2 3rd Div T-M 1941-43; CO 41st FA Bn & G2 2nd Cps 1943-44. (SMG).

Harbold Norris Brown, (W.P. 1928-No. 8312) BG 1943; CO 80th Fly Tng Wg T-A 1943-44; CS & CG 3rd Air Div 8th AF T-E 1944-45; A2 & CG USATAF T-P 1945. (SMG).

Oakes John Cogswell, (W.P. 1928-No. 8313) XO 13th Cps Arty T-AE 1944-45. (SLTG).

*Ross Leslie George, (W.P. 1928-No. 8314) Hq HD Manila; POW Died 5Jan 1945 from wounds POW ship 15 Dec 1944.

*Wilson Russell Alger, (W.P. 1928-No. 8317) Killed Air Msn Berlin 6 Mar 1944 BG CG 4th Bmb Wg 8th AF.

*Goodrich Charles Grant, (W.P. 1928-No. 8319) CO 12th Bmb Gp T-M 1941-42; POW 1942-45.

Gavan Paul Amos, (W.P. 1928-No. 8322) Hq Americal Div T-P 1942-43; (SMG).

Anderson Alvord Van Patten Jr., (W.P. 1928-No. 8325) Cav; CO 23rd Bb Sq TH; (SBG).

Hinrichs John Honeycutt, (W.P. 1928-No. 8327) Och Ord 1943-45; (SMG).

Anderson Frederick Lewis, (W.P. 1928-No. 8328) MG 1943; CG 3rd Div 8th AF & CG 8th Bb Cmd 1943; Dpty Ch Opns STAF ETO 1944-45.(SMG).

Upham John Southworth Jr., (W.P. 1928-No. 8331) Inf; CO 743rd TkBn T-AE 1942-44; Hosps 1944-45. (SLTG).

Myers Samuel Leslie, (W.P. 1928-No. 8333) Cav; GS 2nd Cps NATO 1942-43; DCS 1st Ar

T-E 1943-45. (SLTG).

Travis Robert Falligant, (W.P. 1928-No. 8340) BG 1943; CG 41st Cmbt Bb Wg 8th AF T-E 1943-44. (SBG).

Billingsley John Dabney, (W.P. 1928-No. 8341) WDGS 1943-44; OO 2Cps Italy 1944-45. (SBG).

Butler Robert George, (W.P. 1928-No. 8344) Hq AF Wes Pac 1945; Ord LnO MED 1945. (SMG).

*Daly John Bourke, (W.P. 1928-No. 8347) Killed Normandy 18 Aug 1944 LTC FA 90th Div.

Tunner William Henry, (W.P. 1928-No. 8348) BG 1943; CG India China Div ATC 1944-45. (SLTG).

Frederick Robert Tryon, (W.P. 1928-No. 8349) MG 1944; WDGS 1941-42; CG 1st Spec Ser Fc T-APM 1942-44; CG 1st Abn TF T-ME 1944; CG 45th Div T-E 1944-45.(SMG).

Koon Ralph Edward, (W.P. 1928-No. 8350) Cav; CO 90th Bb Gp 5th Af 1942-43; CO 46th Bb Tng Wg 2nd AF 1944-45. (SBG).

Barnes Verdi Beethoven, (W.P. 1928-No. 8351) (SLTG).

Bunker Howard Graham, (W.P. 1928-No. 8353) Hq ETO & STAF 1943-45; (SMG).

Samford John Alexander, (W.P. 1928-No. 8359) BG 1944; CS 8th AF T-E 1942-44; (SLTG).

Tarrant Legare Kilgore, (W.P. 1928-No. 8361) 1st Ftr Cmd US 1942-44; AAO Hq AAF T-1 Sector 1944-45. (SBG).

Breckinridge William Mattingly, (W.P. 1928-No. 8363) CO Bn 10th Inf 5th Div Iceland 1941-42; XO & CO 10th Inf T-E 1942-45(SMG).

*McNair Douglas Crevier, (W.P. 1928-No. 8370) Killed Guam 6 Aug 1944 COL CS 77th Div.

*Tally Fred Obediah, (W.P. 1928-No. 8371) Hq Phil Dept 1941; POW Death March; Killed POW ship 15 Dec 1944 LTC.

*Morton Powhatan Moncure, (W.P. 1928-No. 8376) Died Canton Is air Acdt 7 Feb 1943 Tran Pac Flight LTC.

McGarr Lionel Charles, (W.P. 1928-No. 8378) CO 30th Inf 3rd Div T-ME 1943-45; (SLTG).

Johnson Wilhelm Paul, (W.P. 1928-No. 8383) CO Res Cmd 1st AD T-M 1944-45. (SMG).

Ramey Roger Maxwell, (W.P. 1928-No. 8385) Inf; BG 1943.

Fritzsche Carl Ferdinand, (W.P. 1928-No. 8388) Inf; Asst Cmdt USMA 1943-44; Dpty G2 12th Ar Gp T-E 1945. (SMG).

Fuller Leigh Austin, (W.P. 1928-No. 8393) Hq 2nd PI Cps Bataan Death March; Died POW Cp Cabanatuan 14 Oct 1942 malaria MAJ.

*Murtha John Thomas Jr., (W.P. 1928-No. 8394) CO 310th Bmb Wg 5th AF; Died hosp ship off Leyte PI 14 Dec 1944 from wounds bombing USS Nashville 13 Dec 1944 COL.

Butchers Ralph Joseph, (W.P. 1928-No. 8396) G4 G3 2nd AD T-AM 1942-43; G3 2nd Cps Italy 1943-45. (SMG).

Anderson Samuel Egbert, (W.P. 1928-No. 8398) MG 1944; WDGS 1942-43; CO 3rd Bb Wg M 8th AF T-E 1943; CG 9th Bb Cmd M 9th AF T-E 1943-45. (SGEN).

Bulger Joseph Arthur, (W.P. 1928-No. 8405) (SBG).

Gilchrist John Raymond, (W.P. 1928-No. 8409) (SMG).

Smith George Ferrow, (W.P. 1928-No. 8412) Hq AAF SvC T-E 1943-45. (SMG).

*Meehan Arthur William, (W.P. 1928-No. 8415) MIA-Air Msn Rabaul 16 Nov 1942.

Landon Truman Hemple, (W.P. 1928-No.

8422) CO Hq Sq 7th Bb Cmd T-P 1943-44. (SGEN).

Spivey Delmar Taft, (W.P. 1928-No. 8432) A3 Air TC 1942-43; 8th AF 1943 (Shot down & POW 1943-45) (SMG).

Kissner August Walter, (W.P. 1928-No. 8436) BG 1944; CS 3rd Bb Div 8th AF T-E 1943-44; CS 21st Bb Cmd 20th AF Guam 1944-45. (SMG).

Saunders LaVerne George, (W.P. 1928-No. 8439) BG 1942; CG 11th Bb Gp(H) 13th AF T-S 1942-43; CG 58th Bb Wg(VH) & 20th Bb Cmd CBI 1943-44. (SMG).

Sherburne Thomas Lilley, (W.P. 1928-No. 8447) (SMG).

Mason Stanhope Brassfield, (W.P. 1928-No.) CS 1st Div & 5th Cps T-E 1942-45. (SMG).

*Thayer Allen, (W.P. 1928-No. 8451) 31st Inf PS 1941; CO 62nd Inf Mindanao 1942; POW; Died 22 Jan 1945 POW ship enroute to Jap from wounds POW ship 9 Jan 1945 LTC.

O'Donnell Emmett Jr., (W.P. 1928-No. 8453) BG 1944; CO 14th Bb Sq 19th Gp PI 1941-42; Hq AAF 1943; CG 73rd Bb Wg 20th AF Saipan 1944-45. (SGEN).

*Williams John Oliver, (W.P. 1928-No. 8454) Inf; Killed Sicily 16 Jul 1943 LTC XO 7th Inf 3rd Div.

Yost Emmett Felix, (W.P. 1928-No. 8457) CO 301st Ftr Wg Oki 1945. (SBG).

Adams Paul DeWitt, (W.P. 1928-No. 8460) CO 143rd Inf Div T-ME 1944-45; Asst CG 45th Div T-E 1945. (SGEN).

Houseman Evan McLaren, (W.P. 1928-No. 8461) CO 3rd Bn 127th Inf 32nd Div T-SP 1945. (SMG).

Nelson Ralph Thomas, (W.P. 1928-No. 8462) Sig Sec 15th Ar T-E 1944-45. (SMG).

Taylor Robert Kinder, (W.P. 1928-No. 8463) CS 15th AF Italy 1944-45; CS 20th AF T-P 1945. (SMG).

*Ivy James Morrow, (W.P. 1928-No. 8464) Inf; 57th Inf Bataan; POW; Killed San Fernando on Death March 15 Apr 1941 LTC.

*Kelly Robert Harper, (W.P. 1928-No. 8472) Inf; Killed Normandy Air Msn 28 Apr 1944 COL CO 100th Bmb Gp 8th AF.

Tarpley Thomas Mason Jr., (W.P. 1928-No. 8479) AG 2nd Phil Cps 1942; POW 1942-45; Death March.

Sirmyer Edgar Alexander, (W.P. 1928-No. 8481) CO 1st AACS Wg 1941-43; CO 5th AACS Wg London 1944-45. (SBG).

Lincoln George Arthur, (W.P. 1929-No. 8490) (SBG).

Nichols Kenneth David, (W.P. 1929-No. 8491) (SMG).

Dent Frederick Rodgers Jr., (W.P. 1929-No. 8497) CO 44th Bb Gp(H) T-E 1943-44; CO 95th Cmbt Bb Wg T-E 1944. (SMG).

Bassett Harold Huntley, (W.P. 1929-No. 8498) Ch WX Div Hq AAF 1942-45; Ch WX Ser & CO 59th WX Wg T-E 1945. (SMG).

Thompson Paul Williams, (W.P. 1929-No. 8499) BG 1945; CO Assault Tng Cen T-E 1943-44; CO 6th Engr Spec Brig 1944; WDGS 1944.

Viney Alvin Galt, (W.P. 1929-No. 8504) Dpty CO & CS Adv Sec ComZ T-E 1944-45. (SMG).

Wilson Walter King Jr., (W.P. 1929-No. 8505) Engr Amph Cps Alt Fleet 1942; Dpty Engr SEAC 1943-45; CG Secs T-I 1945. (SLTG).

Person John Lloyd, (W.P. 1929-No. 8510) Mil Pipeline Const T-E 1944-45. (SBG).

Sands Thomas Jahn, (W.P. 1929-No. 8514) G4 85th Div 1942-43; G4 Div WDGS 1943-44; G2 Sec Hq 12th Ar Gp T-E 1944-45. (SMG).

Browne Roger James, (W.P. 1929-No. 8518) Cav; CS 19th TAC 8th AF T-E 1944-46. (SMG).

Thompson William Jonathan, (W.P. 1929-No. 8523) XO Arty Sect 9th Ar T-E 1944-45. (SBG).

Hannigan James Percy, (W.P. 1929-No. 8524) CO 380th FA Bn 102nd Div T-AE 1942-45. (SBG).

Bryan Thomas Ludwell Jr., (W.P. 1929-No. 8535) CO Radar Sch 1942; Comm O Hq 5th AF T-S 1944-45. (SBG).

Draper Phillip Henry Jr., (W.P. 1929-No. 8537) (SMG).

Scott Richard Lee, (W.P. 1929-No. 8539) XO Sheppard Fld TX 1943-44. (SBG).

Huglin Harold Quiskey, (W.P. 1929-No. 8542) BG 1945.

Guyer Lawrence McIlroy, (W.P. 1929-No. 8547) Haw Sea Arty Cmd 1941-43; Hq AAF 1944-45. (SBG).

Hayes Harold George, (W.P. 1929-No. 8548) Sig Sec AF Hq T-EM 1942-44. (SBG).

Horridge Joseph, (W.P. 1929-No. 8549) Asst OO 3rd Ar T-E 1944-45. (SBG).

Jark Carl Henry, (W.P. 1929-No. 8550) XO Arty 63rd Div T-E 1944-45. (SLTG).

Graul Donald Philip, (W.P. 1929-No. 8551) SO 8th Ftr Cmd T-E 1942-44; Comm O 8th AF T-E 1944-45. (SMG).

Cams Edwin Hugh John, (W.P. 1929-No. 8554) (SMG).

Colby Joseph Milton, (W.P. 1929-No. 8556) Ord Lend Lease T-DGI 1941-42; OCO 1942-44; Sp Msn M26 TK T-E 1945. (SBG).

Theimer John Elliot, (W.P. 1929-No. 8560) CO 695th Armd FA Bn T-AE 1943-45; XO 90th Div Arty 1944; CO 5th FA Gp T-E 1944-45. (SMG).

Horton John Coleman, (W.P. 1929-No. 8562) A3 W Flt TC 1944-45. (SBG).

Mace Ralph Robert, (W.P. 1929-No. 8572) XO 4th Cps Arty T-M 1944-45;DCS 4th Cps 1945; S & F FAS 1941-43. (SMG).

Phillips John David Francis, (W.P. 1929-No. 8578) MA Columbia 1941; G4 94th Div 1942-45. (SBG).

Hall William Evens, (W.P. 1929-No. 8582) BG 1943; Hq AAF 1943-44; Ch Mil Msn Bulgaria 1944-45; Dpty CG 15th AF T-M 1945. (SLTG).

Smith Frederic Harrison Jr., (W.P. 1929-No. 8584) 5th AF T-P 1942-44. (SGEN).

Keirn Donald John, (W.P. 1929-No. 8586) (SMG).

Coolidqe George Waite, (W.P. 1929-No. 8594) (SBG).

*Losey Robert Moffat, (W.P. 1929-No. 8598) Air MA Norway & Sweden 1940; Died Norway 21 Apr 1940 hit during German Bombing. 1st US Officer victim act of war. WW2 CPT.

O'Hara John Jackson, (W.P. 1929-No. 8604) (SMG).

Wetzel Emery Scott, (W.P. 1929-No. 8610) BG 1944; Ch Mil Pers Div Hq AAF: G1 Sect WDGS: SAF Pac. (SLTG).

Fagg William Lafayette, (W.P. 1929-No. 8612) Air G3 9th Ar T-E 1944-45. (SBG).

Hamlin William Darwin, (W.P. 1929-No. 8614) Hq Sig O SHAEF 1943-44. (SMG).

McKenzie Henry Ray, (W.P. 1929-No. 8618) BG 1945. (SMG).

Lasher Edmund Chauncey, (W.P. 1929-No. 8619) (SMG).

Harkins Paul Donal, (W.P. 1929-No. 8620) DCS TF NATO 1942-43; DCS 7th Ar T-M 1943-44; DCS 3rd Ar T-E 1944-45. (SGEN).

McNally Edward Jamet, (W.P. 1929-No. 8624) G2 Chinese Army in India 1942-44.

(SBG).

Svensson Eric Hilmer Frithiof, (W.P. 1929-No. 8625) (SBG).

Bush George Elial, (W.P. 1929-No. 8629) CO 172nd Inf 43rd Div T-S 1943-45. (SMG).

Bullock William Carson, (W.P. 1929-No. 8630) XO 7th Cps Arty T-E 1944-45. (SMG).

Ward Robert William, (W.P. 1929-No. 8632) CO 135th Inf 34th Div T-M 1943-44. (SMG).

Merrill Frank Dow, (W.P. 1929-No. 8633) G3 CBI 1942-43; BG 1943; CG "Merrill's Marauders" 3000 volunteers infiltrating behind enemy lines in Burma, winning all his 5 major & 30 minor engagements 1944: MG 1944.

Keeler George Eldridge Jr., (W.P. 1929-No. 8636) AAO Hq 12th AF T-M 1944-45. (SBG).

Caraway Paul Wyatt, (W.P. 1929-No. 8654) BG 1945; WDGS 1942-44; DC/SHq T-C 1944-45. (SLTG).

McKee William Fulton, (W.P. 1929-No. 8656) BG 1945; Dpty Asst C/AS Hq AAF 1943-45. (SGEN).

*Moseley Eugene Louis, (W.P. 1929-No. 8659) Inf; Killed Casino 26 Jan 1944 Ltc CO 1st Bn 133rd Inf 34th Div.

Conley Edgar Thomas Jr., (W.P. 1929-No. 8660) XX Cps, 11th & fird ADT-E 1943-45. (SBG).

Napier Ezekiel Wimberly, (W.P. 1929-No. 8663) CO 489th Bb Gp(H) 8th AF T-E 1944. (SBG).

Quill James Bernard, (W.P. 1929-No. 8668) DCS 18th Abn Cps T-E 1943-45. (SMG).

Ghormley William Kerr, (W.P. 1929-No. 8669) (SMG).

Cook Robert Little, (W.P. 1929-No. 8670) Inf; 10th Mtn Div US 1941-43; NATO 1943; Hq AGF 1943-44; XO & CO 86th Inf 10th Mtn Div Italy 1944-45. (SBG).

Gavin James Maurice, (W.P. 1929-No. 8671) MG 1944; CO 505th Pcht Inf & CG 82nd Abn Div T-AE . (SLTG).

Sladen Fred Winchester, (W.P. 1929-No. 8672) CO 1st Bn 30th Inf Div T-M 1942-43; G3 36th Div T-ME 1944. (SBG).

Vittrup Russell Lowell, (W.P. 1929-No. 8676) Inf; AFHQ T-M 1943-44; DG3 6th Ar Gp T-E 1944-45. (SLTG).

*Kinnee Dale Joel, (W.P. 1929-No. 8677) Inf; 31st Inf Bataan: Death March: Killed 15 Dec 1944 attempting escape from POW ship MAJ.

Bork Lester Skene, (W.P. 1929-No. 8680) Inf: 98th Div PI Invasion. (SBG).

McDonald Thomas Benton, (W.P. 1929-No. 8689) Mn Div ASC T-A 1943-44. (SMG).

DuBose Thomas Jefferson, (W.P. 1929-No. 8696) Hq AAF 1942-44: 316th Bb Wg 1945. (SBG).

Doubleday Daniel Campbell, (W.P. 1929-No. 8697) Test Pilot Hq AMC 1936-43: Hq AAF T-AE 1943-45. (SMG).

Parks Harlan Clyde, (W.P. 1929-No. 8698) Dmob Plans WDGS 1943-46. (SMG).

Freeman Paul Lamar Jr., (W.P. 1929-No. 8699) (SGEN).

Stubbs Marshall, (W.P. 1929-No. 8701) Hq Adv Sec ComZ ETO 1944: G4 1944-45. (SMG).

Lynch George Edward, (W.P. 1929-No. 8710) CO 142nd Inf 36th Div T-E 1943-45. (SMG).

Mackintosh Hugh, (W.P. 1929-No. 8711) (SMG).

*Bryan John Kauffman, (W.P. 1929-No. 8723) Inf: Died New Guinea auto acdt 5 Jul 1944 LTC CO 251st FA Bn.

*Moody George Putnam, (W.P. 1929-No.

8724) Inf: Flying inst: Airmail Flying: Selected flds for Adv Fly Schs: Died Wichita KS air acdt testing new plane, 5 May 1941 MAJ: Moody Field Named in his honor.

*Smothers Thomas Bolyn Jr., (W.P. 1929-No. 8728) 12th QM Regt & 45th Div PI: POW: Death March: Died POW ship enroute Kor 26 Apr 1945 (pneumonia) MAJ.

Seitz John Francis Regis, (W.P. 1929-No. 8729) Inf: 1st & 69th Divs T-AE 1943-45; 1st contact with Russians 25 Apr 1945. (SMG).

Easley Bruce, (W.P. 1929-No. 8730) Inf: Hq ASF 1943-44: AG SHAEF & OMGUS 1944-45. (SMG).

*Nave William Lester, (W.P. 1929-No. 8732) Inf: Killed Cherbourg 15 Jun 1944 LTC 358th Inf 90th Div.

Cooper Ralph Copeland, (W.P. 1929-No. 8736) CO 36th FA Gp T-E 1944-45. (SMG).

Buchanan David Haytor, (W.P. 1929-No. 8741) Inf: GS,Bn & Regt CO 25th Div T-S 1940-45. (SMG).

Jones Stanley Walker, (W.P. 1929-No. 8742) (SMG).

Herbert John Vander Heide, (W.P. 1929-No. 8749) (SMG).

Costello Normando Antonio, (W.P. 1929-No. 8759) Inf: Italy: GSC 1942-44: OPD WDGS 1944. (SMG).

Griffin Thomas Norfleet, (W.P. 1929-No. 8770) CO 395th Inf T-E 1944-45. (SMG).

*Noble Arthur Knight, (W.P. 1929-No. 8775) 45th Inf Bataan: Guerrilla Leader Luzon to May 1943: POW: Killed Manila 1 Nov 1943 executed LTC.

Yount Paul Frailey, (W.P. 1930-No. 8786) CO Base Sec SOS CBI 1942: bg 1944: Mil Ry Ser Iran 1942-44: CG Mil Ry Ser India, CG Adv Sec SOS T-I 1944-45. (SMG).

Whipple William, (W.P. 1930-No. 8788) SOS ETO 1943-44: G4 Div SHAEF 1944-45. (SBG).

Swofford Ralph Powell Jr., (W.P. 1930-No. 8790) XO, G3 1st Allied Abn Ar T-E 1944-45. (SLTG).

Herbert James Keller, (W.P. 1930-No. 8791) BG 1945: In chg cstr Car Bases 1941-42.

*Castle Frederick Walker, (W.P. 1930-No. 8792) Ch Sup 8th Bb Cmd T-E 1942-43: BG AUS 1944: CG 4th Bb Wg 1943 to Killed Msn Bulge 24 Dec 1944. Took controls and deliberately gave his own life to save his crew (MH).

Ruestow Paul Ernest, (W.P. 1930-No. 8793) A4 Hq AAF 1942-45. (SMG).

Kromer Philip Frederick Jr., (W.P. 1930-No. 8794) (SBG).

*Lothrop Robert Blake, (W.P. 1930-No. 8797) Asst Engr for fortifications HD Manila Bay: POW: Killed off Palawan PI 15 Oct 1944 (attempting escape from ship) MAJ.

Schlatter George Fletcher, (W.P. 1930-No. 8799) Cmdt Stewart Fld 1943-45. (SBG).

*Bosworth Lawrence Arthur, (W.P. 1930-No. 8803) 60th CA Corregidor: POW: Killed POW ship 15 Dec 1944 MAJ.

*Terry Frederick Garside, (W.P. 1930-No. 8808) Killed Saipan air acdt observing fire 24 Jun 1944, LTC Obsr WDGS.

*Schimmelpfennig Irvin Rudolph, (W.P. 1930-No. 8810) CS 11th Abn Div T-AS 1943 to Killed Luzon 4 Feb 1945 COL.

Porter Robert William Jr., (W.P. 1930-No. 8812) G2 1st Div T-EM 1942-43: G3 Sect Hq 2nd Cps T-M 1943-45. (SGEN).

Dudley John Henderson, (W.P. 1930-No. 8813) CO 931st EA Cntr Gp T-S 1944-45. (SBG).

Heath Louis Theilmann, (W.P. 1930-No.

8825) G3 Sect Hq 6th Ar Gp T-E 1944-45. (SMG).

O'Meara Andrew Pick, (W.P. 1930-No. 8827) CO FABns 4th AD 1941-42: S & F TARS 1943-44: Arty Sect Hq 12th Ar Gp T-E 1944: Hq 7th Cps Arty 1944-45. (SGEN).

Wood Robert Jefferson, (W.P. 1930-No. 8829) G3 Sect AF Hq NATO 1942-43 & G3 Sect Hq 5th Ar T-M 1943-44: OPD WDGS 1944-45. (SGEN).

Bradley Mark Edward Jr., (W.P. 1930-No. 8831) Dpty CO Ser Cmd 1st TAC T-E 1945. (SGEN).

Wehle Philip Campbell, (W.P. 1930-No. 8832) 10th Mtn Div T-A 1943-44: Asst Arty O 18th Abn Cps T-E 1944-45. (SMG).

Ganey Wiley Duncan, (W.P. 1930-No. 8834) CO 498th Bb GP VH 20th AF T-P 1944-45. (SMG).

Uhrhane Francis Frederick, (W.P. 1930-No. 8836) Dir Sig Labs TSS 1943-44: OCSO Hq ETO 1944-45. (SMG).

Dodge Charles Granville, (W.P. 1930-No. 8837) CS 8th AD T-E 1944-45. (SLTG).

*Vaughn James Nugent, (W.P. 1930-No. 8839) POW: Killed Bacolor, Luzon, brutally murdered by Japanese during Death March 27 Apr 1942.

Odom Thetus Cayce, (W.P. 1930-No. 8840) CO 452nd Bb Gp 8th AF 1944, DCO Opns STAF T-E 1944-45. (SMG).

Rothschild Jacquard Hirshorn, (W.P. 1930-No. 8842) CO 93rd Cml Bn T-E 1945. (SMG).

Sweeney Walter Campbell Jr., (W.P. 1930-No. 8845) Air TF Midway 1941-42: OPD WDGS 1942-44: 73rd Bn Wg T-P 1944-45. (SGEN).

*Haggerty Robert Foster, (W.P. 1930-No. 8850) 91st CA Corregidor: POW: Killed POW ship 15 Dec 1944.

Howze Hamilton Hawkins, (W.P. 1930-No. 8853) CO 13th AR T-M 1943-44: CO CCA 1st AD Italy 1944-45. (SGEN).

*Packard Harry Brown, (W.P. 1930-No. 8856) G3 II Phil Cps: POW: Death March: Survivor POW ships 15 Dec 1944 and 9 Jan 1945: Died POW ship 27 Jan 1945 (starvation by Japanese captors).

Booth Robert Highman, (W.P. 1930-No. 8859) XO Div Arty & CS 7th Div T-SP 1944-46. (SMG).

Lee Morris John, (W.P. 1930-No. 8865) CO 499th Bb Gp 73rd Wg (VH) Saipan 1944-45. (SMG).

Watson Albert II, (W.P. 1930-No. 8871) Asst Arty O 10th Ar T-SP 1944-45. (SLTG).

Wing Franklin Fearing Jr., (W.P. 1930-No. 8873) XO 7th Cav 1943-44: XO 2nd Cav Brig 1944: CO 5th Cav 1945. (SBG).

Curtis James Owen Jr., (W.P. 1930-No. 8874) G2 Sect AFHQ 1942-43: Hq 1st Div MTO 1943: G2 Div COS SAC 1944: G2 XX Cps T-E 1945. (SBG).

Smith Phillips Waller, (W.P. 1930-No. 8878) Hq ASF T-AMGE 1942-43. (SMG).

Fitch Alva Revista, (W.P. 1930-No. 8879) CO 9th Bn 91st FA (PA) & Btry A 23rd FA PS Bataan: POW 1942-45: Death March. (SLTG).

Baker David Hodge, (W.P. 1930-No. 8886) (SMG).

Lindquist Roy Ernest, (W.P. 1930-No. 8891) CO 508th PIR T-AE 1942-46. (SMG).

Wooten Sidney Clay, (W.P. 1930-No. 8892) CO 51st Inf T-E 1944-46. (SMG).

Wright William Henry Sterling, (W.P. 1930-No. 8895) ADC Secy War 1942-44. (SLTG).

Stuart Archibald William, (W.P. 1930-No. 8896) Inf: G2 Div WDGS 1945. (SMG).

Perry Willis Almeron, (W.P. 1930-No. 8897) CA Bd 1941-43. (SBG).

Taber Alden Pugh, (W.P. 1930-No. 8900) OO 8th AF Comp & Cmds T-E 1942-43. (SBG).

Perrin Edwin Sanders, (W.P. 1930-No. 8902) G4 Allied AF Egypt-Java-Australia 1941-42: BG 1942: CG AFSC Sacramento 1942.

*Millener Raymond Davis, (W.P. 1930-No. 8906) Inf: Died Moumelon-le-Grande France, 7 Dec 1944 COL CS 101st Abn Div.

Hamlett Barksdale, (W.P. 1930-No. 8909) XO 2nd Cps Arty NATO 1942-43: Hq AGF 1943-44: 16th AD Arty T-E 1944-45. (SGEN).

Miller Troup Jr., (W.P. 1930-No. 8911) CO 59th AS Gp 1945: CS 13th Bb Cmd 1945. (SLTG).

Eckert William Dole, (W.P. 1930-No. 8913) XO CG Hq AMC 1941-44: CO 452nd Bb Gp 8th AF T-E 1944: Hq 9th AF T-E 1944-45. (SLTG).

Peterson Arthur Carey, (W.P. 1930-No. 8917) CO AA Gun Bn Bataan & Corregidor: POW 1942-45: Survivor POW ship 15 Dec 1944 & POW ship 9Jan 1945.

Harris William Henry, (W.P. 1930-No. 8921) C4, CS USAF SA 1942-44: WDGS 1944-45. (SBG).

Stoughton Tom Robert, (W.P. 1930-No. 8922) G4 Sect Hq ETO 1943-45. (SMG).

Dunn Thomas Weldon, (W.P. 1930-No. 8923) Arty Sect Hq 6th Ar T-S 1942-46. (SLTG).

Norstad Lauris, (W.P. 1930-No. 8924) Hq AAF CC 1941-44: CS 20th AF T-P 1944-45 (SGEN).

Lewis Millard, (W.P. 1930-No. 8929) CO Bb Gps US 1942-43: CS Bb Cmd & CO Bb Wg & Hq USSTAF T-E 1943-45. (SMG).

Ammerman James Frederick, (W.P. 1930-No. 8931) XO 220th FA Gp 1944: Asst Arty O & Arty O 8th Ar T-S 1945-47. (SMG).

Atkinson Frederick Dwight, (W.P. 1930-No. 8935) 418th FA Gp & Asst Arty O Hq 8th Ar T-S 1944-45. (SBG).

Harris William Warner, (W.P. 1930-No. 8936) (SBG).

Brandt Carl Amandus, (W.P. 1930-No. 8937) Dpty CO 5th AFSC 1943: CO 90th Bb Gp 1944. (SMG).

Hayden John Charles, (W.P. 1930-No. 8940) S5 & XO V Cps Arty T-E 1942-45. (SMG).

Hutton Carl Irven, (W.P. 1930-No. 8943) Co AFA Bns 2nd AD T-E 1943-44. (SBG).

*Hurt Marshall Hill Jr., (W.P. 1930-No. 8953) Inf: 31st Inf & G2 Bataan Force: POW: Died POW Cp Fukuoka Jap 3 Apr 1945 Pneumonia.

*East Joe Clifton, (W.P. 1930-No. 8959) 91st CA Corregidor POW: Died POW ship 15 Jan 1945 (Colitis).

O'Keefe Richard Joseph, (W.P. 1930-No. 8965) CO Accra (W Afr) Air Dep 1944-45: CO 1st ASC T-D 1945. (SMG).

Moore Ned Dalton, (W.P. 1930-No. 8979) Inf: G1 & CS 101st Abn Div T-AE 1942-45. (SMG).

Clarke Christian Hudgins, (W.P. 1930-No. 8980) CO Inf 90th Div T-E 1944. (SMG).

Wilson James Knox Jr., (W.P. 1930-No. 8985) (SBG).

Landon Kurt Martin (W.P. 1930-No. 8988) (SBG).

*Maxwell Winston Rose, (W.P. 1930-No. 8992) Ord Sect Hq Phil Dept: POW: Died 14 Jan 1945 from wounds POW ship 9 Jan 1945.

Guthrie John Simpson, (W.P. 1930-No. 8997) BG 1945: (SMG).

Richardson James Lowell Jr., (W.P. 1930-No.

9001) Xo & G3 70th Div T-AE 1943-45.
(SLTG).

Beauchamp Charles Edward, (W.P. 1930-No.
9007) GS 5 Cpsm & 1st Ar T-AE 1942-44: G3
Sect Hq ETO 1944-45. (SMG).

Smith Sory, (W.P. 1930-No. 9010) A1 9th AF,
CS 9th TAC T-E 1944-45. (SMG).

Bogart Theodore Francis, (W.P. 1930-No.
9014) CO Inf Bn 3rd Div Italy 1943: G2
SHAEF 1943-45. (SMG).

Broom Thad Adolphus, (W.P. 1930-No. 9015)
QM 13th AD 1942-43. (SBG).

*Ohme Herman William, (W.P. 1930-No.
9019) Inf: Killed N. Italy 14 Oct 1944 LTC
Bn CO 35th Inf 88th Div.

Weyrauch Paul Russell, (W.P. 1930-No. 9021)
XO Arty & Asst G3 6th Ar T-S 1943-45.
(SMG).

Townes Morton Elmer, (W.P. 1930-No. 9024)
CO Base New Guinea 1944. (SBG).

*Simpson Frederick James, (W.P. 1930-No.
9025) Inf: Killed Germany 14 Apr 1945 LTC
CO 701st Tk Bn 102nd Div.

McCrimmon Kenneth Adelbert, (W.P. 1931-
No. 9027) G3 Div SHAEF 1943-45. (SBG).

Jewett Richard Lee, (W.P. 1931-No. 9030) XO
364th Engr ComZ T-E 1944-45. (SBG).

Bonesteel Charles Hartwell, (W.P. 1931-No.
9033) G3 Sect 1 & 12th ARGps T-E 1943-44.
(SGEN).

Cassidy William Frederick, (W.P. 1931-No.
9047) CO 815th EA Bn 12th AFSC NATO
1942-43: CO 21st EA Regt & Area Engr Italy
1943-44. (SLTG).

Brown Edward Aloysius Jr., (W.P. 1931-No.
9048) XO OCE GHQ T-S 1944-45. (SBG).

Daley John Phillips, (W.P. 1931-No. 9051)
(SLTG).

Carter Marshall Sylvester, (W.P. 1931-No.
9052) (SLTG).

Sullivan John Barclay, (W.P. 1931-No. 9056)
XO CCB 4th AD T-AE 1942-44. (SBG).

Callahan Daniel Francis, (W.P. 1931-No.
9061) (SMG).

Parker Theodore William, (W.P. 1931-No.
9062) Aide to CG & G3 Sec IBC 1941-43.
(SMG).

Hackett Robert, (W.P. 1931-No. 9073)
(SLTG).

Dick William White Jr., (W.P. 1931-No. 9077)
CO 8th FA 25th Div T-P 1942-43: CS 25th
Div 1943-44: XO 25th Div Arty T-PS
1944-45. (SLTG).

Blake Gordon Aylesworth, (W.P. 1931-No.
9082) CO 7th AACS Wg Hickam Fld & PI
1941-45. (SLTG).

Hall William Charles, (W.P. 1931-No. 9084)
(SBG).

Corbin Frank Pickering Jr., (W.P. 1931-No.
9095) JA 2nd Div US 1943-44. (SBG).

Speidel George Sebastian Jr., (W.P. 1931-No.
9099) (SBG).

Chappell Julian Merritt, (W.P. 1931-No. 9100)
BG 1944: Trp Carrier Gp & Wg T-E.

Harrison Richard Holmes, (W.P. 1931-No.
9102) G4 84th Div 1942-43: XO 89th Div
Arty T-E 1944-45. (SBG).

*Park James William, (W.P.1931-No. 9103) CO
922nd EA Regt T-AE 1943-44: Died
Spokane air acdt 19 Oct 1945.

Train William Frew, (W.P. 1931-No. 9108) XO
109th-112th Inf & G3 28th Div T-E 1944-45.
(SLTG).

Stayton Tom Victor, (W.P. 1931-No. 9110) CO
615th AA Gun Gp CZ 1943-44: Hq ASF 1945.
(SMG).

Yates Donald Norton, (W.P. 1931-No. 9112)
Mil Msn to USSR 1942. (SLTG).

Barclay John Archibald, (W.P. 1931-No. 9113)
(SMG).

Schomburg August, (W.P. 1931-No. 9115) CO
Ord Winter PG 1942-43. (SLTG).

Perry Miller Osborne, (W.P. 1931-No. 9120)
Arty Sect Hq 1st Ar T-EA 1943-45. (SBG).

Smith Charles Coburn Jr., (W.P. 1931-No.
9127) S3 7th Div Arty T-ME. (SBG).

Duff Charles Breckinridge, (W.P. 1931-No.
9131) CO 41st CA Regt Haw 1943-44: Hq Is
Cmd Saipan 1944-45. (SLTG).

Skidmore Wilbur Manly, (W.P. 1931-No.
9133) CO AA Unit Saipan 1944-45. (SBG).

Bell William John, (W.P. 1931-No. 9134) CO
2nd Cmbt Cargo Gp 5th AF T-S 1944-45.
(SMG).

*Blanning James Chester, (W.P. 1931-No.
9135) Cav: CO 2nd Sq 26th Cav: hq Cmdt I
Cps PA: POW: Died POW ship 25 Jan 1945
(exposure, Malnutrition) MAJ.

*Fleeger Harry James, (W.P. 1931-No. 9136)
Cav: CO Sqn 26th Cav PS: POW Death
March: Killed POW ship 24 Oct 1944 MAJ.

Moore Ernest, (W.P. 1931-No. 9138) CS & CG
7th Ftr Cmd 1942-45. (SMG).

Beebe Royden Eugene Jr., (W.P. 1931-No.
9140) BG 1944: Opns Hq 5th AF & Allied
AF T-S 1942-44 & CS FEAF & 5th AF T-SP
1944-45. (SMG).

Bethune Philip Higley, (W.P. 1931-No. 9142)
Cav: G2 Sec GHQ USAF Pac 1945: G2 Sec
GHQ FEC 1945. (SBG).

*Raker John Newlin, (W.P. 1931-No. 9156)
34th Ftr Sq Bataan: POW: Death March:
Killed POW ship 24 Oct 1944 MAJ.

Caraway Forrest, (W.P. 1931-No. 9159) Inf: G1
28th Div T-E 1943-45: G1 23rd Cps 1945:
DCS 21st Cps 1945: EUR Genl Bd 1945.
(SBG).

Young Millard Chester, (W.P. 1931-No. 9165)
CS 5th AF Sv Cmd & ACS /OFEAF Sv Cmd
Australia & New Guinea 1942-45. (SBG).

Berry John Anderson Jr., (W.P. 1931-No.
9166) CO 916th FA Bn 1942-43: XO XI Cps
Arty T-E 1943-45. (SBG).

Magee Mervyn Mackay, (W.P. 1931-No. 9171)
Div Arty, G4, G3 & CS Amer Div T-S
1942-46. (SMG).

Mooney Henry Keppler, (W.P. 1931-No.
9173) CO Bmb Wgs & Gps T-AME 1941-45.
(SMG).

Waters John Knight, (W.P. 1931-No. 9175) CO
1st Bn 1st AD T-EM 1942: XO 1st AR 1st AD
T-M 1943: POW Ger 1943-45. (SGEN).

Lee Robert Merrill, (W.P. 1931-No. 9177) BG
1945: Dpty CG Opns 9th AF T-E 1944-45.

*Donaldson Donald, (W.P. 1931-No. 9180) Inf:
Killed Loue France 7 Aug 1944 LTC CO
749th Tk Bn.

Troxel Orlando Collette Jr., (W.P. 1931-No.
9181) G3 4th Div T-AE 1942-44: G3 7th Cps
T-E 1944-45. (SMG).

Pachler Francis Thomas, (W.P. 1931-No.
9182) G3 7th Div Attu 1943. (SMG).

Strother Dean Coldwell, (W.P. 1931-No. 9189)
BG 1943: CO 13th AFF Tr Carrier T-S 1942-43:
CG 15th AF Ftr Cmd T-M 1944-45; (SGEN).

Hightower Louis Victor, (W.P. 1931-No. 9196)
1st AD Arty T-AE 1942: Bn CO CO 1st Ar 1st
AD NATO Italy 1942-43; (SMG).

Messinger Edwin John, (W.P. 1931-No. 9197)
G3 17th Abn Div T-E 1944-45; (SLTG).

Carlson, Gunnar Carl, (W.P. 1931-No. 9209)
CO Ord Tng Centers US 40-43; OCO
Detroit 43-44; Ord Depot Japan 45-48;
(SMG).

Smart Jacob Edward, (W.P. 1931-No. 9210)
Hq AAF 1942-43: Asst CS 9th AF 1943; CO
97BbGp; POW Ger 44-45; (SGEN).

Harris Hugh Pate, (W.P. 1931-No. 9212) G3
Abn Cmd 1942-43; (SGEN).

Brown Robert Quinney, (W.P. 1931-No. 9214)
CO Sp Tps Hq Cmd AFHQ NATO 1942-44;
(SBG).

Beishline John Robert, (W.P. 1931-No. 9217)
G1 Sec 4th & 9th Armies T-E 1944-45;
(SBG).

Eaton Robert Edward Lee, (W.P. 1931-No.
9223) CO 451st Bb Gp T-AM 1943-44: Hq
STAF T-E 1944-45: Hq AAF 1945; (SMG).

Davis John Joseph, (W.P. 1931-No. 9224) CO
FA Bn 3rd Ar T-ME 1944-45. (SLTG).

King James Irvine, (W.P. 1931-No. 9228) G3
16th AD US 1943-44: AGF Obsr Italy 1943:
Repl & Tng Cond T-M 1944-45. (SBG).

Easterbrook Ernest Fred, (W.P. 1931-No.
9231) Inst China T-1 1942-43: LnO China Ar
Burma 1944: CO 475th US Inf 1944-45.
(SMG).

Herrick Curtis James, (W.P. 1931-No. 9232)
G4 11th AD US 1942-44: G4 Sect Pac Area
1944-46. (SMG).

*Pahl Howard Max, (W.P. 1931-No. 9234) CO
Bn 31st Inf(PS) Bataan: POW: Death
March: Killed POW ship 15 Dec 1944 MAJ.

Decker Charles Lowman, (W.P. 1931-No.
9243) JA 13th Cps T-E 1943-45. (SMG).

Walker Edwin Anderson, (W.P. 1931-No.
9246) CO 3rd Regt 1st Spec Ser Force
Aleutians & Italy 1943-44 & Itlay France
1944-45. (SMG).

Hoy Charles Edward, (W.P. 1931-No. 9250)
CO 334th Inf 84th Div T-E 1944-45. (SMG).

Hardick William Leonard, (W.P. 1931-No.
9252) G3 86th Div T-S 1943-45: OPD WDGS
1945. (SBG).

Steinbach Richard, (W.P. 1931-No. 9254) 2nd
AD 1940-42: AGF 1942-43: G4 2nd A Cps
1943-45: XO DCG ETO 1945. (SMG).

Gordon John Clarence, (W.P. 1931-No. 9265)
BG 1945: A3 ASC CBI 1944-45: Hq AMC
1945 to ret. (SBG).

Adams Andrew Joseph, (W.P. 1931-No. 9273)
CO Units & CS 7th AD T-AM 1942-45.
(SMG).

MacLaughlin Victor James, (W.P. 1931-No.
9274) LnO w British 1st Ar NATO 1942-43:
Dpty QM & QM 5th Ar Italy 1943-45.
(SMG).

Dougher Charles Bowman, (W.P. 1931-No.
9275) CO 94th Bb Gp T-E 1944-45. (SMG).

Woodward William Rogers, (W.P. 1931-No.
9276) G3 81st Div T-S 1943-45: (SBG).

*Humber Charles Ingram Jr., (W.P. 1931-No.
9278) Inf: CO Bn 31st Inf PA Bataan: POW:
Death March: Died POW ship 22 Jan
1945(colitis) LTC.

Hutchinson David William, (W.P. 1931-No.
9279) CO 6th Photo Gp, 91st Rcn Wg,
808th Bb Wg T-SP. (SMG).

*Frederick Charles Elder, (W.P. 1931-No.
9285) Inf: Killed Volturno River Italy 20
Oct 1943, LTC CO Bn 15th Inf 31st Div.

Ruggles John Frank, (W.P. 1931-No. 9290)
Inf: Bn CO, XO, CO 22nd Inf 4th Div T-AEA
1943-46. (SMG).

McGee John Hugh, (W.P. 1931-No. 9294) Inf:
CO Davao Subsector PI: POW 1942-44:
Escaped Jun 1944: CO 169th Inf 43rd Div
1945 (SMG).

Bond Van Hugo, (W.P. 1931-No. 9295) G3 TF
G3 9th Div NATO 1942-43: (SMG).

Leary John Edward, (W.P. 1931-No. 9301) Inf:
G3 & G4 8th & 14th Cps T-SP 1942-44.
(SBG).

*McClellan James Thomas, (W.P. 1931-No.
9306) Inf: Hq II Cps PA: POW: Death
March: Died Jan 1945 from wounds POW
ship 9 Jan 1945 MAJ.

Houser Houston Parks Jr., (W.P. 1931-No.
9309) Inf: G1 1st PI Cps Bataan: POW

1942-45: Death March.

Timberlake Edward Julius, (W.P. 1931-No. 9313) BG 1943: CG Cmbt Bb Wg 1943-44: 20th Combt Bb Wg 1944-45. (SLTG).

Mayo Paul Arthur, (W.P. 1931-No. 9315) FO 6th Ar T-P 1943-46. (SMG).

Elegar Augustus George, (W.P. 1931-No. 9319) CO 2nd Bn 317th Inf 80th Div T-A 1942: G3 80th Div T-AE 1943-45. (SBG).

*Mathews John Hubert, (W.P. 1931-No. 9320) Inf: w 1st Div Invasion N Afr & Sicily: Killed landing Normandy 6 Jun 1944 LTC Bn CO 16 Inf 1st Div.

Lincoln Rush Blodget Jr., (W.P. 1932-No. 9324) OCT ASF T-AMES 1942-45. (SMG).

Wray Stanley Tanner, (W.P. 1932-No. 9325) CO 91st Bb Gp 8th AF T-E 1942-43; A1 Sec HqAAF 43-46; (SMG).

Davis Ellsworth Ingalls, (W.P. 1932-No. 9326) CO 1148th EC Gp T-AE 1944-45. (SMG).

Besson Frank Schaffer Jr., (W.P. 1932-No. 9330) Mi;l RR Ser T-G 1943-45; (SGEN).

*Arnold Richard Roberts, (W.P. 1932-No. 9331) Dpty CS 2nd Cps T-EM: Killed Sedjenae Tunisia 6 Jun 1943 COL CO 20th Cmbt Engr Regt.

Steele John Chandler, (W.P. 1932-No. 9337) CAC Alas 40-43 WDGS 1944; (SBG).

Clark Allen Fraser Jr., (W.P. 1932-No. 9338) CO Engr Units T-A 1942-44: CO 235th EC Bn 2nd Cps Italy 1944. (SBG).

McCormack James Jr., (W.P. 1932-No. 9342) WDGS 1942-43: G4 Sec Hq 12th Ar Gp T-E 1944-45. (SMG).

Russell Sam Carroll, (W.P. 1932-No. 9347) XO CO AA Units T-AE 1943-45. (SMG).

Weber John Henry, (W.P. 1932-No. 9349) (SBG)

*Spengler Daniel Stickley, (W.P. 1932-No. 9353) Killed Normandy 8 Jul 1944 COL CO 110th ECG PI Ar.

Power George Wilson, (W.P. 1932-No. 9361) CO 247th FA Amer Div T-SSP 1943-45. (SMG).

Zitzman Kenneth Frederick, (W.P. 1932-No. 9364) SO 2nd Cps Italy 1943-44: SO 5th Ar Italy 1944-45. (SBG).

Mather George Robinson, (W.P. 1932-No. 9366) XO 110th Inf 28th Div T-E 1944-45. (SGEN).

Gerhardt Harrison Alan, (W.P. 1932-No. 9367) XO OASW 1943-45. (SMG).

Dahl Leo Peter, (W.P. 1932-No. 9369) Ch Opns 12th AF T-M 1943-44. (SMG).

Britton Frank Hamilton, (W.P. 1932-No. 9373) G3 Sect Hq 5th Ar Italy 1943: Hq AGF 1944: G3 Sect GHQ T-S 1944-45. (SMG).

Woolnough James Karrick, (W.P. 1932-No. 9379) WDGS 1942-44: XO 16th Inf Div & CO 393rd Inf 99th Div T-E 1944-45. (SGEN).

Hewitt Robert Augur, (W.P. 1932-No. 9383) Secy GS AGF 1942: G3 2nd Cps T-EM 1942-43: G3 Sect Hq 1st Ar T-EP 1943-45. (SMG).

Webster Benjamin Jepson, (W.P. 1932-No. 9384) XO 67th Ftr Wg 8th Af T-AE 1943-44: Actg CS CO 8th Ftr Cmd 1944-45. (SLTG).

Wheeler Earle Gilmore, (W.P. 1932-No. 9385) Inf: CS 63rd Div T-AE 1943-45. (SGEN).

Hartshorn Edwin Simpson Jr., (W.P. 1932-No. 9386) Obvr 7th Cps Arty DDay: Hq 8th Ar T-SP 1944-45. (SBG).

Baer Charles Michael, (W.P. 1932-No. 9388) SO duties & Sig O Antilles 1941-43: OCSO 1944: Jt Comm Actv Okinawa 1944-45. (SBG).

Johnson Dwight Benjamin, (W.P. 1932-No. 9392) Hq AGF 1943-44: AN St Coll 1944: G3 Div GHQ T-SP 1945.(SMG).

Gill Joseph Edward, (W.P. 1932-No. 9393) (SMG).

Ellery Frederick William, (W.P. 1932-No. 9395) CO 313th FA Bn US 1942-44: (SBG).

McConnell John Paul, (W.P. 1932-No. 9398) BG 1944: CS Tng Cmds & CO AC Units US & China 1940-46. (SGEN).

*Glassburn Robert Douglass, (W.P. 1932-No. 9400) BC 60th CA(AA) Corregidor: POW ships 15 Dec 1944, 9 Jan 1945 & 12 Jan 1945: Died POW Camp Moji Jap 30 Jan 1945 of wounds POW ship MAJ.

Kelly Joe William, (W.P. 1932-No. 9401) CO 386th Bb Gp T-E 1943-45. (SGEN).

*Somerville Erven Charles, (W.P. 1932-No. 9404) Ft Mills, HD Manila Bay: POW: Died POW Cp Fukuoka Jap 11 Feb 1945(enteritis) MAJ.

McCawley John Clifford, (W.P. 1932-No. 9409) Hq AGF 1942-43: ComZ ETO 1933-45. (SBG).

Porter Harry Cecil, (W.P. 1932-No. 9416) OO FEAF PI 1941-42: OO 5th AF T-S 1942. (SMG).

Beach Dwight Edward, (W.P. 1932-No. 9417) CO 167th FA Bn 41st Div T-S 1943-45: XO 24th Div Arty T-Sp 1945. (SGEN).

*Blair Arthur Walter, (W.P. 1932-No. 9420) Killed Luchem Belgium (Bulge) 25 Dec 1944, LTC CO 268th FA Bn 79th FA Gp.

Campbell Daniel Stone, (W.P. 1932-No. 9421) CO Ftr Gp, XO Ftr Cmd Italy 1944-45. (SMG).

Mellnik Stephen Michael, (W.P. 1932-No. 9424) G3 Sect AFFE; G4 Sect Corregidor 1942: Escaped from POW Camp: Guerrilla PI 1943: G2 Sect GHQ T-S 1944-45. (SBG).

Truman Louis Watson, (W.P. 1932-No. 9425) Hq AGF 1942-44: CS 84th Div T-E 1944. (SLTG).

Stecker Ray James, (W.P. 1932-No. 9429) (SBG).

Hobson Kenneth Burton, (W.P. 1932-No. 9433) CO 7th Bb Gp Java Aust 1942: A3, CS 5th Bb Cmd T-S 1942-43: WDGS 1943-45. (SGEN).

Sutherland John Reynolds, (W.P. 1932-No. 9434) A4, CS, A3, Hq 10th AF CBI 1943-44: DCSO 73rd Bb Wg 20th AF T-P 1945. (SMG).

Hardy Donald Linwood, (W.P. 1932-No. 9435) (SMG).

Coiner Richard Tide Jr., (W.P. 1932-No. 9436) O Asst Sec Air 1941-43: CO 397th Bb Gp 9th Af T-E 1944-45. (SMG).

Hansen Floyd Allan, (W.P. 1932-No. 9437) Picatinny Ars 1940-42: OO 8th AD 1943: Ord Sect Hq 1st Ar T-E 1944-45. (SMG).

*McQuade Bernard William, (W.P. 1932-No. 9441) Inf: Killed Normandy 6Jun 1944 LTC CO 58th AFA Bn.

Manhart Ashton Herbert, (W.P. 1932-No. 9443) XO Inf Regt 45th Div, CO 135th Inf 34th Div Italy 1944-45. (SLTG).

Bigelow Horace Freeman, (W.P. 1932-No. 9445) OO Units US 1942-44: AGF Bd T-M 1944. (SMG).

*Jones David Emory, (W.P. 1932-No. 9449) Killed Germany 10 Apr 1945 LTC S3 84th Div Arty.

Anderson Charles Hardin, (W.P. 1932-No. 9455) CO AC Adv Flt Tng Sch T-A 1942-43. (SMG).

*Edison Dwight Drenth, (W.P. 1932-No. 9456) CA Corregidor: POW: Survivor POW ship 15 Dec 1944: Killed San Fernando by Jap Gd 23 Dec 1944 LTC.

Pugh John Ramsey, (W.P. 1932-No. 9460) G2 1st Cps PA Bataan: G2 Corregidor: POW 1942-43. (SMG).

Brucker Wallace Hawn, (W.P. 1932-No. 9463) AA Sec AFHQ, NATO 1943: G3 Div COS SAC 1943-44: AD Div SHAEF 1944-45. (SBG).

Cairns Bogardus Snowden, (W.P. 1932-No. 9468) Bn CO T-M 1943-44: G3 Sec 1st Ar: WDGS 1945. (SMG).

Ondrick John George, (W.P. 1932-No. 9474) Inf: CO 309th Inf 78th Div T-AE 1944-46. (SBG).

Harris Hunter Jr., (W.P. 1932-No. 9478) CO 447th Bb Gp 8th AF 1942-43: DCS Opns 3rd Air Div 8th AF ETO 1944-45. (SGEN).

*Maguire William Halford, (W.P. 1932-No. 9488) Inf: 45th Inf PS Bataan: Died POW Cp Fukuoka Jap 9 Feb 1945 (colitis) LTC.

Kunzig William Bing, (W.P. 1932-No. 9496) G3 Sec Hq 1st Ar T-E 1943-45. (SBG).

Fischer Harvey Herman, (W.P. 1932-No. 9503) WDGS 1942-44: Hq 2nd Cps Italy 1944. (SLTG).

Terrill Robert Haynes, (W.P. 1932-No. 9504) CO 445th Bb Gp 8th AF T-E 1943-44: DC/S Opns 2nd Air Div 8th AF 44-45. (SLTG).

Darcy Thomas Connell, (W.P. 1932-No. 9511) BG 1944: CO Desert Air TF 1943: CS 12th TAC & CG 87th Ftr Wg T-M 1943-44: Dpty CG & CG 22nd TAC T-M 1944-45. (SMG).

Rees Clifford Harcourt, (W.P. 1932-No. 9519) A3 Tech Tng Cmd 1943: DCS AAF Tng Cmd 1944: CO 307th Bb Gp T-P 1944-45. (SMG).

Mussett Eugene Porter, (W.P. 1932-No. 9525) (SBG).

Suarez Edward Willis, (W.P. 1932-No. 9527) DCSO AAF Tng Cmd 1942-44. (SMG).

Schorr David Peter Jr., (W.P. 1932-No. 9533) XO & CO Regt 17th Abn Div T-E 1943-45. (SBG).

Thatcher Herbert Bishop, (W.P. 1932-No. 9537) CO 323rd Bb Gp, CG 99th Bb Wg, A3 SHAEF 1942-45. (SLTG).

D'Orsa Charles Salvatore, (W.P. 1932-No. 9538) G4 TF NATO 1942-43: G4 Sec 5th Ar T-M 1943: G4 Anzio 1944: G4 15th Ar Gp 1944-45. (SLTG).

Landry Robert Broussard, (W.P. 1932-No. 9540) C Cmbt Opns 8th Ftr Cmd T-E 1942-43: CO 56th Ftr Gp 1943-44. (SMG).

Coutts James Winfield, (W.P. 1932-No. 9547) G3 Sect Hq ETO 1942-43: Asst Cmdt Prch Sch 1943-44: CO 513th PIR 17th Abn Div T-E 1944-45. (SBG).

Duncan George Thigpen, (W.P. 1932-No. 9550) G3 65th Div T-E 1943-45. (SMG).

*Thomas William Roy, (W.P. 1932-No. 9560) Inf-FA: 24th FA PS Bataan: POW : Death March: Died POW Cp Fukuoka Jap 12 Feb 1945 malnutrition MAJ.

Cochran Loris Ray, (W.P. 1932-No. 9561) G1 & XO CCA 1st AD NATO 1942-44. (SBG).

Keating John William, (W.P. 1932-No. 9569) CS 66th Div 1944-45 (SBG).

Garland William Madison, (W.P. 1932-No. 9572) Msn to Hq 8th AF T-E 1942-43: A3 Hq 8th AF 1943-44. (SBG).

Bowen John William, (W.P. 1932-No. 9576) CO 26th Inf Div NATO & Sicily 1943-44: WDGS 1944. (SLTG).

Scott Robert Lee Jr., (W.P. 1932-No. 9580) Opns O TF CBI 1942: CO 23rd Ftr Gp & CO Ftr Cmd China 1942-43. (SBG).

Fields Kenneth E., (W.P. 1933-No. 9586) CO 56th AE Bn 11th AD US 1942-43: Inst TIS 1943-44: CO 1159th EC Gp 3rd Cps T-E 1944-45. (SBG).

Hallock Duncan, (W.P. 1933-No. 9589) Engr 92nd Div T-A 1942-44: CO 1127th EC Gp T-EAP 1944-45. (SBG).

Starbird Alfred Dodd, (W.P. 1933-No. 9590)

CO 1135th EC Gp T-E 1944-45: OPD WDGS 1945. (SLTG).

Meyer Richard Davis, (W.P. 1933-No. 9592) Tran Cmd Manila 1945. (SLTG).

Sibley Alden Kingsland, (W.P. 1933-No. 9593) Hq USAF-ME 1941-43: G4 Sec Hq ETO 1943-44: G4 Sec SHAEF 1944-45. (SMG).

Bonner Marshall, (W.P. 1933-No. 9596) MIA-Air Msn Florisdorf Austria 26 Jun 1944(DED 12 Nov 1945) COL CO 464th Bmb Gp 15th AF.

Lincoln Lawrence Joseph, (W.P. 1933-No. 9597) WDGS 1942-43. (SLTG).

Tripp Robert Campbell, (W.P. 1933-No. 9601) COM Z ETO 1943-45. (SBG).

Ely William Jonas, (W.P. 1933-No. 9603) Engr Sec Hq 6th Ar T-S 1943-45. (SLTG).

Honeycutt John Thomas, (W.P. 1933-No. 9604) Asst G3 2nd Cps NATO T-M 1943-44. (SMG).

Harris William Allen, (W.P. 1933-No. 9605) G3 Sec Hq 12th Ar Gp T-E 1943-45. (SMG).

Broshous Charles Russell, (W.P. 1933-No. 9606) Engr & CS Base Secs SOS ETO 1942-44: C/S Adv Sec & DCS ComZ ETO 1942-44. (SBG).

Shinkle John Gardner, (W.P. 1933-No. 9608) Ord PG 1941-44: G4 Div WDGS 1945. (SMG).

Welling Alvin Charles, (W.P. 1933-No. 9612) Sect XO Alcan Hwy 1942-43: Ch Engr 1944-45. (SMG).

*Ball William Harris, (W.P. 1933-No. 9613) 92nd CA Corregidor: CO Bn 155 guns Bataan: POW : Death March: Died POW Cp O'Donnell, 20 May 1942 dysentery MAJ.

Gray David Warren, (W.P. 1933-No. 9617) Hq AGF 1942-44: G3 Sect Hq 6th Ar T-S 1944. (SMG).

Blandford William Orin, (W.P. 1933-No. 9619) G3 Sect Hq 4th Ar T-A 1943-44: CO 3rd Bn 175th Inf 29th Div T-E 1944. (SBG).

McMorrow Francis Joseph, (W.P. 1933-No. 9624) OO Hq 7th AF 1945. (SMG).

Dunn Charles Golding, (W.P. 1933-No. 9625) G1 14th AA Cmd T-S & AF Pac 1944-45. (SBG).

Moorman Thomas Samuel Jr., (W.P. 1933-No. 9627) WXO Hq 9th AF T-E 1943-45. (SLTG).

*Julian Harry, (W.P. 1933-No. 9628) 59th CA Corregidor: POW: Killed POW ship 24 Oct 1944 MAJ.

Sparrow Herbert George, (W.P. 1933-No. 9632) G3 Cen Pac Base Cmd 1944: Obsr 25th Div LO 6th Ar T-P 1944-45. (SMG).

Jensen Walter August, (W.P. 1933-No. 9635) CO 20th A Gp 24th Cps T-P 1944-45. (SMG).

Conway Theodore John, (W.P. 1933-No. 9644) London & N Afr & AdC GEN Alexander British Ar 1942-44: G3 Sect Hq 5th Ar T-M 1944-45. (SGEN).

Dahlen Chester Arthur, (W.P. 1933-No. 9649) Bn & Regt CO 24th Div SWPA 1941-45. (SMG).

Lane John Joseph, (W.P. 1933-No. 9650) CO 438th AAAW Bn 7th Cps T-E 1943-45 (SMG).

Hetherington Travis Monroe, (W.P. 1933-No. 9651) (SBG).

Frentzel William York, (W.P. 1933-No.) CO 383rd FA Bn 103rd Div T-AE 1942-45: CO FA Bn & Arty 45th Div T-AE 1945 (SBG).

*MacNair Thomas Kocher, (W.P. 1933-No. 9656) 60th CA Corregidor: POW: Died Aboard *Oryoku Maru* injuries 14 Dec 1944 MAJ.

Polk James Hilliard, (W.P. 1933-No. 9657) CO

3rd Cav Gp Mecz T-E 1944-45. (SGEN).

*Schenck Harry Winfield, (W.P. 1933-No. 9662) 59th CA Corregidor: POW: Died POW Cp Fukuoka Jap 21 Feb 1945 (colitis) CPT.

Edwards Morris Oswald, (W.P. 1933-No. 9670) G3 63rd Div T-E 1944-45: CO 253rd Inf 63rd Div T-E 1945. (SBG).

Senter William Oscar, (W.P. 1933-No. 9671) CO AAF Wx Wg 1943-44: WxO Hq FEAF &CO FEAF Wx Gp 1945. (SLTG).

Giffin Sidney Francis, (W.P. 1933-No. 9674) Hq AAF 1944-45. (SBG).

Hill Francis, (W.P. 1933-No. 9687) BG 1945: FA Inst China Tng Cen India 1942-43: G3 Hq CBI 1943-44. (SBG).

Thorlin John Frederick, (W.P. 1933-No. 9696) Staff Hq CinC POA 1944-45. (SMG).

Chapman Ethan Allen, (W.P. 1933-No. 9705) (SMG).

Hurlbut Oren Eugene, (W.P. 1933-No. 9706) Asst Cmdt Ord Sch 1943-44: OO So Pac Base Cmd 1944-45. (SLTG).

White George Warren, (W.P. 1933-No. 9708) Ch Mfg OCO Detroit 1942-45. (SBG).

*Hunter Frank Patterson Jr., (W.P. 1933-No. 9712) Killed Air Msn Dusseldorf Ger 23 Jan 1945 COL CO 398th Bmb Gp 8th AF.

*Crawford George Harold, (W.P. 1933-No. 9714) 60th CA Corregidor: POW: Killed POW ship 15 Dec 1944 MAJ.

Maddux Harold Roth, (W.P. 1933-No. 9715) 314th Bb Wg 20th AF Guam 1944-45.

*McReynolds Samuel McF.Jr., (W.P. 1933-No. 9718) Hq HD Manila: POW: Died POW Cp Fukouka Jap 1 Feb 1945 colitis CPT.

Chase Charles Henry, (W.P. 1933-No. 9724) 101st Abn Div T-E 1943-45. (SMG).

*Dalton James Leo 2nd, (W.P. 1933-No. 9729) CO 161st Inf T-Sp 1942-45: Asst Div CO 25th Inf Div SWPA mar 1945 to Killed Balete Pass Luzon 16 May 1945 BG.

Kelley Laurence Browning, (W.P. 1933-No. 9737) CO 494th Bb Gp H T-P 1944-45. (SBG).

Fuqua Stephen Ogden Jr., (W.P. 1933-No. 9738) (SBG).

Neely Robert Benton, (W.P. 1933-No. 9743) 34th Div Arty ETO NATO Italy 1942-44. (SBG).

*Ledward William John, (W.P. 1933-No. 9745) Killed Albano Italy 4 Jun 1944 LTC CO 27th FA Bn 1st Armd Div.

Stilwell Joseph Warren Jr., (W.P. 1933-No. 9746) G2 Sect Hq CBI 1942-44: G2 N Cmbt Area Cmd Burma 1944-45. (SBG).

*Bernd Peter Paul, (W.P. 1933-No. 9747) 745th Ord CO(Avn) & PI Ord Depot: POW: Death March: Killed POW ship 24 Oct 1944 CPT.

Carver George Allen, (W.P. 1933-No. 9751) CO 542nd FA Bn 42nd Div T-AE 1943-45. (SMG).

Whipple Sherburne Jr., (W P. 1933-No. 9759) CO Caw Rcn Sq 12th AD T-E 1944-45. (SBG).

Doleman Edgar Collins, (W.P. 1933-No. 9760) DCS 3rd Div: Bn CO XO 30th Inf T-M 1943-44: CO 6th Ar T-E 1944: Hq 7th Ar 1944-45. (SLTG).

*Darby William Orlando, (W.P. 1933-No. 9762) CO first Am Rangers Landings N Afr, Sicily, Salerno, Anzio: CO 179th CT 451st Inf Div: Killed N Italy 30 Apr 1945 Asst CO 10th Mtn Div 5th Ar.

Powers George Thomas 3rd, (W.P. 1933-No. 9766) CO 337th FA Bn 88th Div Italy 1944: S3 88th Div Arty 1944. (SMG).

Evans Roy Tripp Jr., (W.P. 1933-No. 9769) O Ch QM ETO 1944-45. (SMG).

Ryan William Francis, (W.P. 1933-No. 9771) CO 402nd FA Bn 42nd Div T-E 1943. (SBG).

*Kendall Raymond Emerson, (W.P. 1933-No. 9772) Killed Italy 12 May 1944 LTC.

Carroll Paul Thomas, (W.P. 1933-No. 9775) CO Bns 21st Inf & 10th Inf Div T-E 1944; WDGS; (SBG).

Summerfelt Milton Frederick, (W.P. 1933-No. 9782) CO AC Det APG 1941-42: Hq AAF 1942-44: CO 333rd Bb Gp(H) US & Okinawa 1944-45. (SBG).

Smith Franklin Guest, (W.P. 1933-No. 9783) XO OG1 Hq AF Wes Pac O Manila 1944. (SBG).

Baumer William Henry, (W.P. 1933-No. 9784) (SMG).

Disosway Gabriel Poillon, (W.P. 1933-No. 9785) CO 311th Ftr Gp China 1945. (SGEN).

Bastion Joseph Edward Jr., (W.P. 1933-No. 9791) Asst SGS AFGHQ NATO 1942-43. (SMG).

Beck Thomas Herbert, (W.P. 1933-No. 9793) G3 8th Div T-E 1944-45. (SBG).

Henley Franklin Stone, (W.P. 1933-No. 9798) A4 Base Air Dep Area, Dpty CO Adv Air Dep Area ,& CO 9TCC Ser Wg ETO 1944-45. (SBG).

Dolph Cyrus Abda III, (W.P. 1933-No. 9799) CO 759 Tk Bn Iceland 42-43; CO 102nd Cav G[T-E 1944-45. (SMG).

Breit John Martin, (W.P. 1933-No. 9800) CO 135th Inf 34th Div Italy 1945. (SMG).

*Harrison Charles Fauntleroy, (W.P. 1933-No. 9802) CWS Bataan: POW: Killed by Japs, Mindanao attempting escape 22 May 1944 MAJ.

Evans Thomas Bowes, (W.P. 1933-No. 9803) CO 745th Tk Bn US 1942-43. (SMG).

Johnson Harold Keith, (W.P. 1933-No. 9817) Inf PS Bataan; POW 1942-45: Death March. (SGEN).

Boswell James Orr, (W.P. 1933-No. 9818) G2 90th Division T-E 44-45; (SBG).

Gibbs David Parker, (W.P. 1933-No. 9819) SO 5th Div T-E 1942-45: SO 22nd Cps 1945. (SMG).

Solomon Maddrey Allen, (W.P. 1933-No. 9824) CS 35th Div T-E 1944-45. (SBG).

Engler Jean Evans, (W.P. 1933-No. 9828) (SLTG).

Huntsberry Walter Abner, (W.P. 1933-No. 9830) Asst G4 1st Ar T-AE 1940-45. (SBG).

Vidal Felix Louis, (W.P. 1933-No. 9839) CO 72nd Ftr Wg 1943-44. (SBG).

Zierath Frederick Robert, (W.P. 1933-No. 9841) 24th Div Haw 1940-42: G3 Div CO 1st Bn 19th Inf 24th Div 1942-45. (SMG).

Darnell Carl Jr., (W.P. 1933-No. 9843) (SMG).

Crawford Joseph Brice, (W.P. 1933-No. 9845) Bn CO 1st Div 1940-43, Regt XO 36th & 3rd Div 1943-44. (SBG).

Coleman Frederick William III, (W.P.1933-No. 9846) (SBG).

Gibb Frederick William, (W.P. 1933-No. 9852) 16th Inf 1st Div NATO ETO 1942-45. (SMG).

King Richard Thomas Jr., (W.P. 1933-No. 9862) CO 500th Bb Gp 20th AF Saipan 1944: POW Jap 1944-45. (SBG).

*Berkowitz Paul Henry, (W.P. 1934-No. 9958) Died Air Crash in Solomon Is 26 Jul 1944 LTC CO 648th ET Bn.

*Brugge Byron Elias, (W.P. 1934-No. 9962) MIA-Air Msn Tokyo 3 Dec 1944 COL DCS 73rd Bmb Wg 20th AF: POW: Died POW Cp Fukuoka Jap 4 Mar1945(malnutrition).

*Maury Thompson Brooke 3rd, (W.P. 1934-No. 9964) S3 Prov FA Brig Bataan: POW:

Death March: Killed POW ship 15 Dec 1944, MAJ.

Reynolds Royal Jr., (W.P. 1933-No. 9869) 57th Inf Div (PS) Bataan: Guerrillas 1942-45. (SBG).

Mack Stephen B., (W.P. 1933-No. 9871) Ftr Pilot and ALO 5Ar T-Me; (SBG).

Essman Graydon Casper, (W.P. 1933-No. 9873) GSC SEAC 43-44; G3 Sec Hq 7Cps T-E 44; WDGS 44; OC CmlC 45; (SBG).

Gee Samuel Edward, (W.P. 1933-No. 9883) 25th Div Haw 1942: Amer Div T-S 1943-44. (SMG).

Hartel Frederick Otto, (W.P. 1933-No. 9886) Bn CO 38th Inf 2nd Div US 1941-42: XO361st Inf 91st Div US 1942-43: G3 13th Abn Div T-AE 1943-45. (SBG).

Calhoun William Roberts, (W.P. 1933-No. 9888) CO 50th FA Bn 5th Div T-E 1942-45. (SMG).

Truesdale Karl Jr., (W.P. 1933-No. 9890) AAF Ferry Cmd & ATC 1941-44.(SMG).

deGavre Chester Braddock, (W.P. 1933-No. 9894) CS 1st Abn TF T-ME 1944-45. (SBG).

Grubbs Sydney Dwight Jr., (W.P. 1933-No. 9903) Opns AAF CBI 44; DC/S 10 AF 44-45; CO 80 Ftr Gp 45; CS Air TF Burma 45; (SBG).

Harrell Ben, (W.P. 1933-No. 9908) G3 6 Cps, CO 7th Inf, G3 5th Ar NATO & ETO 1942-45. (SGEN).

*Blatt Richard Churchfield, (W.P. 1933-No. 9909) Died Dieppe France 7 Jun 1944 from wounds 6 Jun 1944 LTC: CO 1st Bn 115th Inf 29th Inf Div.

Risden Richard Allen, (W.P. 1933-No. 9910) Pers O WD 42-45; (SBG).

*Williams Joseph Ermine, (W.P. 1933-No. 9911) Died Liege Belgium 28 Jan 1945 from wounds Cielle Belgium 9 Jan 1945(Bulge) LTC CO 2nd Bn 334th Inf 84th Inf Div.

Blanchard Robert Moore Jr., (W.P. 1933-No. 9914) G2 10th AD 1942-43; G2 Sec Hq 1 Ar; (SBG).

Quinn William Wilson, (W.P. 1933-No. 9915) G2 4 Cps T-AM 42-44; G2 7 Ar T-ME 44-45; (SLTG).

Ehlen Edward Spalding, (W.P. 1933-No. 9918) (SBG).

Montgomery Richard Mattern, (W.P. 1933-No. 9921) CO Basic Sch US 1942-43. (SLTG).

Pottenger Charles Hoffman, (W.P. 1933-No. 9923) Dir Ops TAF Italy 1944-45. (SMG).

*Wood Paul Douglas, (W.P. 1933-No. 9926) Killed Bataan 7 Apr 1942 MAJ, CO Bn 57th Inf.

Tank Charles Francis, (W.P. 1934-No. 9933) G4 Sec Hq 7th Ar Sicily 1943: Engr 3rd Div Italy & ETO 1943-44. (BG).

Rogers Thomas DeForth, (W.P. 1934-No. 9934) CO 1106th EC Gp T-E 1944. (SBG).

Cary John Burroughs, (W.P. 1934-No. 9935) G5 Sect Hq ETO 1943. (SMG).

MacDonnell Robert George, (W.P. 1934-No. 9944) (SMG).

Renfroe Walter Jackson Jr., (W.P. 1934-No. 9947) G3 35th Div T-E 1944-45. (SBG).

Lipscomb Thomas Heber, (W.P. 1934-No. 9954) CO 1131st ECn Gp ETO 1944-45. (SMG).

Betts Austin Wortham, (W.P. 1934-No. 9956) (SLTG).

Stone William Sebastian, (W.P. 1934-No. 9967) Dir WX Ser Hq STAF Guam 1944-45. (SGEN).

Seaman Jonathan Owen, (W.P. 1934-No. 9968) CO 4th FA Bn T-SP 1942-43. (SLTG).

Davis Kermit LeVelle, (W.P. 1934-No. 9969) CO 10th FA Bn 3rd Div T-M 1942-43.

(SMG).

Rogers William Loveland, (W.P. 1934-No. 9971) CO 1141st EC Gp 13th Cps T-E 1944-45. (SMG).

Dany George Bernard, (W.P. 1934-No. 9972) (SMG).

Jablonsky Harvey Julius, (W.P. 1934-No. 9973) WD Obsr Bd ETO 1944CO 515th PIR 13th Abn Div 1945. (SMG).

Moseley Lawson S. Jr., (W.P. 1934-No. 9976) (SBG).

Bunker William Beehler, (W.P. 1934-No. 9985) (SLTG).

*Batson Howard Marshall Jr., (W.P. 1934-No. 9988) 88th FA, PA Bataan: POW: Death March: Died POW Cp Fukuoka Jap 28 Jan 1945 enteritis MAJ.

White Charles Henry Jr., (W.P. 1934-No. 9990) CS 96th Div T-S 1944-45. (SBG).

Stevens John DuVal, (W.P. 1934-No. 9997) (SBG).

Smoller John Farnsworth, (W.P. 1934-No. 9999) CO 497th AFA Bn, XO Div Arty, Actg CO Arty, 13th AD T-E 1945. (SMG).

*Costain James Alexander, (W.P. 1934-No. 10006) Killed Normandy 15 Jun 1944 LTC CO 915th FA Bn 90th Inf Div.

Moorman Frank Willoughby, (W.P. 1934-No. 10027) Sig O 82nd Abn Div T-ME 1942-44. (SMG).

Sanders Horace Lake, (W.P. 1934-No. 10028) 33rd Div Arty 1942-43. (SBG).

DeGuire Merlin Louis, (W.P. 1934-No. 10029) (SBG).

Canterbury William Monte, (W.P. 1934-No. 10034) Ch Radar Br Hq AAF 1943-44. (SMG).

Bondley Charles John Jr., (W.P. 1934-No. 10045) (SMG).

Gross William Milton, (W.P. 1934-No. 10046) BG 1944: CO Cmbt Wg 8th AF T-E 1943-45.

Smith Dale Orville, (W.P. 1934-No. 10048) A4 Anti Sub Cmd 1942-43CO 384th Bb Gp 8th AF T-E 1943-44. (SMG).

Norvell Frank Carter, (W.P. 1934-No. 10054) (SBG).

Adams Robert Hawkins, (W.P. 1934-No. 10057) XO 19th Cps Arty T-E 1944-45. (SMG).

Franklin John Francis Jr., (W.P. 1934-No. 10059) (SMG).

Griffith Perry Bruce, (W.P. 1934-No. 10061) (SMG).

Spivy Berton Everett Jr., (W.P. 1934-No. 10062) (SGEN).

*Meade Lawrence Kent, (W.P. 1934-No. 10065) 92nd CA Corregidor: CO Btry 155s 313th FA PA Bataan(PH): POW: Died POW CP Cabanatuan 24 Sep 1942 (Malaria) CPT.

Winn James Richard, (W.P. 1934-No. 10074) XO 19th Cps Arty T-E 1944-45. (SMG).

Ligon Elvin Seth Jr., (W.P. 1934-No. 10080) CO 466th Bb Gp 8th AF T-E 1945. (SMG).

*Merrill John Wentworth, (W.P. 1934-No. 10083) Killed Cherbourg 24 Jun 1944 LTC Bn CO 12th Inf 4th Div.

Hutchinson John Monroe, (W.P. 1934-No. 10091) (SBG).

*Smith Richard Albert, (W.P. 1934-No. 10095) CA Corregidor: POW: Died 27 Jan 1945 from wounds POW ship 9 Jan 1945 CPT.

Luehman Arno Herman, (W.P. 1934-No. 10096) (SMG).

Barton Paul Lawrence, (W.P. 1934-No. 10097) CO 483rd Bb Gp 15th AF T-M 1944-45. (SBG).

Caufield Frank Joseph, (W.P. 1934-No. 10098) CO Traffic Hq 1st Ar T-E 1944-45. (SBG).

*Forte Floyd Felice, (W.P. 1934-No. 10101)

45th Inf PS: Guerillas: MIA Mindanao Pl May 1942, MAJ Aide to CG 81st Div PA: DED 31 Jul 1944.

*Cleary Joseph Aloysius, (W.P. 1934-No. 10103) CPT 26 Cav PS 1941: Killed Bataan 16 Jan 1942 MAJ Inf PA.

*Van Nostrand William Starr, (W.P. 1934-No. 10105) 26th Cav Luzon: POW ship 9 Jan 1945 COL, psth.

Hillyard Harry Lester, (W.P. 1934-No. 10107) CO 3/67th AR, CO TF 2nd AD NATO T-ME 1942-45. (SMG).

Craig William Hutcheson, (W.P. 1934-No. 10109) G1 4th Cps T-AM 1941-44. (SMG).

Wise William Harvey, (W.P. 1934-No. 10110) CO 8th Ftr Gp 5th AF T-S 1942-43. (SMG).

Higgins Gerald Joseph, (W.P. 1934-No. 10113) BG 1944: ADC 101st Abn Div T-e 1944-45. (SMG).

Alness Harvey Thompson, (W.P. 1934-No. 10115) CO 7th Bb Gp(H) CBI 1944-45. (SLTG).

Johnson Charles Edward, (W.P. 1934-No. 10118) CO 3rd Bn 30th Inf Div NATO 1942-43. (SMG).

Kyser Robert Carson, (W.P. 1934-No. 10119) G4 Sect Hq 12th Ar Gp T-E 1943-44. (SMG).

Lawlor John Dixon, (W.P. 1934-No. 10120) CO 1st Bn 304th Inf 76th Div T-E 1944-45. (SBG).

Volckmann Russell William, (W.P. 1934-No. 10121) XO & CO 11th Inf PS Bataan: Escaped : CO Guerrilla Forces N Luzon 1943-45. (SBG).

*Telford Sidney Thompson, (W.P. 1934-No. 10124) Killed Langfeld Ger 14 Sep 1944 LTC; CO TK Bn 32nd AR, 3rd AD.

Edson Hallet Daniel, (W.P. 1934-No. 10125) EXO & CO 15th Inf 3rd Div T-ME 1934-45. (SBG).

Wilson Albert Theodore Jr., (W.P. 1934-No. 10127) CommO 20th AF 1944-45. (SMG).

White John William, (W.P. 1934-No. 10134) CO Air Flds ATRC US 1942-45. (SMG).

Hayes Thomas Hogan, (W.P. 1934-No. 10141) CO 310th Inf 78th Div T-E 1944-45. (SBG).

*Sanders Robert Herbert, (W.P. 1934-No. 10142) Killed Heel Holland 24 Feb 1945 LTC 1st Bn 291st Inf &5th Inf Div.

Donovan Stanley Joseph, (W.P. 1934-No. 10145) CO 97th Bb Gp T-M 1943. (SLTG).

*Cloud Eugene Harrington, (W.P. 1934-No. 10157) CO Bn 7th Inf N Africa 1942: Died Tunisia auto acdt 29 may 1943 Aide to C in British !st Ar .

Brown Travis Tabor Sr., (W.P. 1934-No. 10159) (SMG).

Cunningham William Alex. Jr., (W.P. 1934-No. 10164) Bn CO 16th Inf 1st Div T-ME 1942-43. (SMG).

*Weber Edward Ernest Bruno, (W.P. 1934-No. 10165) Killed Velletri Italy 30 May 1944 LTC Bn CO 179th Inf 45th Div.

*Robinson Oliver Prescott Jr., (W.P. 1934-No. 10177) Inf-FA-QMC: (Mindanao 1945): Died Honshu Jap 14 Nov 1945 MAJ Hq XCps.

Tyson Robert Nabors, (W.P. 1934-No. 10180) CO 5th FA 1st Div T-AE 1942-45. (SBG).

Frye Arthur Houston Jr., (W.P. 1935-No. 10189) CO 94th Engr GS Regt T-E 1943-45. (SBG).

Davis Leighton Ira, (W.P. 1935-No. 10194) (SLTG).

Dick John Somers Buist, (W.P. 1935-No. 10199) CO 3rd E Bn 24th Div T-S 1944-45. (SMG).

Lapsley William Winston, (W.P. 1935-No. 10200) CO 41st Engr Regt T-ME 1944-45. (SMG).

Throckmorton John Lathrop, (W.P. 1935-No. 10205) (SGEN).

Ruhlen George, (W.P. 1935-No. 10206) CO 3rd FA Bn 9th AD T-E 1943-46. (SMG).

Lang Cornelis de Witt Willcox, (W.P. 1935-No. 10207) CO 63rd FA Bn 24th Div, XO 24th Div Arty T-SP 1943-45. (SBG).

Haug Clarence Carl, (W.P. 1935-No. 10209) (SMG).

Wilson James VanGorder, (W.P. 1935-No. 10217) CO 404th Ftr Bb Gp US 1943-44: Dpty CO 359th Ftr Gp 8th Af T-E 1945. (SBG).

Osmanski Frank Alexander, (W.P. 1935-No. 10218) G4 Sect Hq ETO & Hq COS SAC 1943-44: Log Div Hq SHAEF 1944-45. (SMG).

Waterman Bernard Sanders, (W.P. 1935-No. 10219) CO 532nd FA 3rd Amph Cps, 24th Cps T-S 1944: 419th FA Gp 1945. (SBG).

Cole John Dudley, (W.P. 1935-No. 10222) Engr 85th Div MTO 1942-45. (SBG).

Smyroski Charles Albert, (W.P. 1935-No. 10226) (SBG).

Lemley Harry Jacob, (W.P. 1935-No. 10229) XO 18th FA Brig Italy 1943-44: XO 6th Cps T-E 1944-45. (SLTG).

Stillman Robert Morris, (W.P. 1935-No. 10233) CO 322nd Bb Gp T-E 1943: POW 1943-45. (SMG).

Glass Robert Rigby, (W.P. 1935-No. 10238) CO 748th Tk Bn T-AE 1942-45. (SMG).

Eckhardt George Stafford, (W.P. 1935-No. 10239) Stf 5th Fleet Pac B-KS 1943-44: Asst DCS Ar Fcs POA 1945. (SMG).

Ellsworth Richard Elmer, (W.P. 1935-No. 10240) HQ USAF India 1943-45. (SBG).

Weld Seth Lathrop Jr., (W.P. 1935-No. 10245) Mil Msn Brazil 1942-43: G3 Sect Hq AGF 1943-46. (SBG).

*Harrison Harry John, (W.P. 1935-No. 10246) Killed Wiltz Ger 17 Nov 1944 MAJ 109th Inf 28th Div.

Exton Hugh McClellan, (W.P. 1935-No. 10253) CO 78th FA Bn 2nd AD T-ME 1942-44. (SLTG).

Breakefield Durward Ellsworth, (W.P. 1935-No. 10254) (SBG).

Critz Harry Herndon, (W.P. 1935-No. 10259) XO, CO 32nd FA Bn 1st Div NATO 1942-43: XO 1st Div Arty T-E 1944-45. (SLTG).

Curtis Kenneth Irwin, (W.P. 1935-No. 10263) G3 Div GHQ T-S 1943-44. (SBG).

Bergquist Kenneth Paul, (W.P. 1935-No. 10275) A3 7th Ftr Cmd &th AF T-P 1941-42: Hq AAF 1943-44: A3 73rd Bn Wg 20th AF T-P 1944-45. (SMG).

*Wilson John Newton, (W.P. 1935-No. 10276) Killed Normandy 11 Jul 1944 LTC CO 219th FA Bn 35th Div.

Gibson Elmer John, (W.P. 1935-No. 10295) Ord Sect Hq AGF 1942-44: Ord Sect Hq 10th Ar T-P 1944-45. (SMG).

Walsh James Howard, (W.P. 1935-No. 10297) Bmb Units NATO Italy 1942-45. (SMG).

Leonard Charles Frederick Jr., (W.P. 1935-No. 10302) (SMG).

Chapman Willis Fred, (W.P. 1935-No. 10305) CO 340th Bb Gp 12th AF T-M 1942-45. (SBG).

Totten James Willoughby, (W.P. 1935-No. 10307) CO 69th AFA Bn Italy 1943-44. (SMG).

Twitchell Hamilton Austin, (W.P. 1935-No. 10316) G3 Sect Hq USAF ME 1942-43. (SMG).

Tyer Aaron Warner, (W.P. 1935-No. 10320) CO 45th Ftr Sq 18th Ftr Gp Pearl Harbor 1940-42: CO 18th Ftr Gp Solomons 1943. (SBG).

Alger James Dyce, (W.P. 1935-No. 10321) CO 2nd Bn 1st Armd Regt 1st AD T-EM 1942-43: POE 1943-45. (SLTG).

Haines Ralph Edward Jr., (W. P. 1935-No. 10322) CO 3rd Bn 1st Armd Regt 1st AD 1941-42: CO 88th Rcn Bn & G3 8th AD 1942-44: Asst & Actg G3 2nd Cps MTO 1944-45. (SGEN).

Murdoch Francis Johnstone Jr., (W.P. 1935-No. 10326) Bn CO 1st Div T-E 1943-45. (SMG).

McGoldrick Francis Mark, (W.P. 1935-No. 10330) (SMG).

Russ Joseph Rieber, (W.P. 1935-No. 10333) G3 Sect Alas Dept 1942-43: Bn CO XO CO 346th Inf T-E 1944-45. (SMG).

Maroun Autrey Joseph, (W.P. 1935-No. 10338) CO 2nd Bn 378th Inf 95th Div T-E 1944-46. (SMG).

*Marshall George Frederick, (W.P. 1935-No. 10341) Killed Oran (assault landing), LTC Bn CO A Inf 1st AD.

Caughey John Hart, (W.P. 1935-No. 10359) (SMG).

Schlanser Lawrence Edward, (W.P. 1935-No. 10360) CO 19th Cav Rcn Sq 16th Cav Gp T-E 1945. (SMG).

*Jones Paul Montgomery, (W.P. 1935-No. 10367) CO Hq Tps 26th Cav Bataan 1942: POW: Killed POW ship 24 Oct 1944 MAJ.

Tucker Reuben Henry 3rd, (W.P. 1935-No. 10368) CO 504th PIR 82nd Abn Div T-M 1943-44. (SMG).

Mock Vernon Price, (W.P. 1935-No. 10380) Asst G3 Hq 2nd Ar US 1942-45. (SLTG).

Beall John Allen Jr., (W.P. 1935-No. 10381) CO 702nd TD Bn & 6th TD Gp T-AE 1943-46. (SMG).

Rich Charles Wythe Gleaves, (W.P. 1935-No. 10384) CO 2/19th Inf 24th Div T-P 1942-43: G3 Sect Hq 6th Ar Gp T-E 1944-45. (SLTG).

Musgrave Thomas Cebern Jr., (W.P. 1935-No. 10390) Asst CS Tng Cen 1942: CO 5th Bb Gp 13th AF T-S 1943-44. (SMG).

Sawyer Edward William, (W.P. 1935-No. 10392) 2nd Cav Div 1943, Hq 6th Ar 1944, Hq 1st Cps 1945. (SMG).

*Harold William Lee, (W.P. 1935-No. 10393) Died Normandy 20 Aug 1944 from wounds 19 Aug 1944, LTC CO 610th TD Bn.

Boyle Andrew Jackson, (W.P. 1935-No. 10398) (SLTG).

*Neiger John, (W.P. 1935-No. 10400) Hq II Cps PA Bataan: POW: Death March: Killed POW ship 15 Dec 1944 MAJ.

Gent Thomas Joseph Jr., (W.P. 1935-No. 10401) CO 449th Bb Gp (H) T-M (SMG).

Edwards Norman Basil, (W.P. 1935-No. 10410) G3 Hq ETO 1942-43. (SMG).

Strauss Robert Hollis, (W.P. 1935-No. 10414) CO 312th Bb Gp 5th AF T-S 1942-45. (SBG).

*Harper Ralph Shaffer, (W.P. 1935-No. 10419) Killed Tavigny Belgium 18 Dec 1944 Bulge LTC CO 2nd Tk Bn Armd Div.

Wheeler Lester Lewes, (W.P. 1935-No. 10425) CO 34th Inf 24th Div T-S 1943-45. (SBG).

Jones George Madison, (W.P. 1935-No. 10439) XO & CO 503rd PIR T-S 1942-45. (SBG).

Coburn Melville Brown, (W.P. 1935-No. 10447) (SMG).

*Sellers Harry Franklin, (W.P. 1935-No. 10449) Killed Luzon 19 Jan 1945 LTC CO 2nd Bn 169th Inf 43rd Div.

Haywood Oliver Garfield, (W.P. 1936-No. 10460) G3 Div Hq Ant Dept 1942-43. (SBG).

Harvey Raymond John, (W.P. 1936-No. 10464) CO 863rd EA Bn T-S 1943-44: CO 116th EC Bn 41st Div T-S 1944-45. (SBG).

Palmer Bruce Jr., (W.P. 1936-10465) CS 6th Div T-S 1944-45. (SGEN).

Shuler William Reeves, (W.P. 1936-No. 10466) CO 117th EC Gp 1944-45. (SMG).

Combs Cecil Edward, (W.P. 1936-No. 10469) Led Bb Msn of War on Japs (PI): CO 19th Bb Gp Java 1942: Air TF India 1942-43. (SMG).

Stewart Charles Barnard, (W.P. 1936-No. 10474) CO 318th Ftr Gp 7th Af T-P 1943: A3 7th Ftr Cmd 7th AF T-P 1943-44: CS Marianas Air Def Cmd 1944-45. (SBG).

Monteith Dwight Oliver, (W.P. 1936-No. 10475) CS 58th Bb Wg 20th AF CBI Pac 1944-45. (SMG).

Hayes Thomas Jay III, (W.P. 1936-No. 10482) (SMG).

Connor William Mellard, (W.P. 1936-No. 10485) CO 290th FA Obsn Bn T-E 1945. (SBG).

Morris Howard Allen, (W.P. 1936-No. 10489) Div Engr 4th AD US 1940-44: Dpty Engr Hq 15th Ar T-E 1944-45. (SBG).

Davis Benjamin Oliver Jr., (W. P. 1936-No. 10494) CO 99th Ftr Sq 12th AF, CO 332nd Ftr Gp 15th AF T-ME 1943-45. (SLTG).

Lampert James Benjamin, (W.P. 1936-No. 10495) Engr Sect Hq 14th & 9th Cps T-SP 1944-45. (SLTG).

Kelly John Edward, (W.P. 1936-No. 10504) CO 3rd Bn 378th Inf 95th Div T-E 1944-45. (SLTG).

Austin Gordon Harrison, (W. P. 1936-No. 10509) CO 325th Ftr Gp, CO 319th Bn Gp T-M 1942-45. (SMG).

Persons Howard Pinkney Jr., (W.P. 1936-No. 10515) S3 & XO 34th AA Brig 2nd Cps NATO, 7th Ar Sicily, 5th Ar Italy, 7th Ar Fr 1942-45. (SBG).

Sutherland Edwin Van V. (W.P. 1936-No. 10521) G3 Sec 1st Div T-E 1943: XO, CO 3rd Bn & CO 26th Inf 1st Inf Div T-E 1944-45. (SBG).

Estes Howell Marion Jr., (W P. 1936-No. 10531) AAF Tng Schs US 1942-45. (SGEN).

Hiester David Woodrow, (W.P. 1936-No. 10539) G4 Sec Hq 24th Div 1941-43: G4 Sec Hq AGF 1944-45. (SBG).

*Phelan John James, (W.P. 1936-No. 10541) XO 370th Inf 92nd Div: Bn CO 135th Inf 34th Div Anzio: Bn CO 370th Inf Italy 1944: Killed Italy 15 Apr 1945 LTC Bn CO 473rd Inf 92nd Div.

Smith Selwyn Dyson Jr., (W.P. 1936-No. 10542) CO 976th FA Bn T-ME 1943-45 (SMG).

Carmichael Richard Henry, (W.P. 1936-No. 10551) CO 19th Bb Gp 5th AF T-S 1942 & CO 462nd Bb Gp 20th AF CBI 1943-44. (SMG).

Snyder Howard McCrum Jr., (W.P. 1936-No. 10561) G3 3rd AD 1942-44: G3 XX Cps 1944-45. (SMG).

Landrum James Edward Jr., (W P. 1936-No. 10564) CO Inf Bn 77th Div T-SP 1944-45. (SMG).

Torrey John Davis Jr., (W.P. 1936-No. 10565) (SBG).

Clark Albert Patton, (W.P. 1936-No. 10566) DCO 31st Ftr Gp 8th AF T-E 1942: POW 1942-45. (SLTG).

Grothaus Donald Gilbert, (W.P. 1936-No. 10569) (SBG).

Westmoreland William Childs, (W.P. 1936-No. 10571) CO 34th FA Bm MTO 1942-43: XO 9th Inf Div Arty & CS 9th Div ETO 1944-45. (SGEN).

Dawalt Kenneth Francis, (W.P. 1936-No. 10574) (SBG).

Spencer Norman Calvert Jr., (W.P. 1936-No. 10576) (SBG).

Terrell Frederick Reynolds, (W.P. 1936-No. 10578) CO 47th Bb Gp 12th AF NATO 1942-43. (SMG).

Shea Leonard Copeland, (W.P. 1936-No. 10579) CO Cav Sqs 1942-44. (SMG).

Bell Frederick, (W.P. 1936-No. 10581) (SBG).

Powell Beverley Evans, (W.P. 1936-No. 10585) CO 93rd AFA Bn 5th Ar Italy 1943-44: G1 Hq 2nd Cps T-ME 1944-45. (SLTG).

McCorkle Charles Milton, (W.P. 1936-No. 10587) CO 54th Ftr Gp 11th AF Aleutians 1942: CO 31st Ftr Gp 12th & 15th AF Italy 1943-44. (SMG).

Stafford Robert Hall, (W.P. 1936-No. 10592) CO 310th FA Bn 79th Div T-AE 1942-45. (SBG).

Dunn Edward Clare, (W.P. 1936-No. 10593) CO 4th Cav Rcn Sq T-E 1943-44: XO 4th Cav Gp 1944-45. (SMG).

Steele William Swinton, (W.P. 1936-No. 10608) CO 15th Ftr Gp TH 1942-43: CO 326th Ftr Gp US 1943-44. (SMG).

Haneke William Charles, (W.P. 1936-No. 10611) FO Scott Fld 1941-43, Hq Air Mid Pac 1945. (SMG).

Fergusson Robert George, (W.P. 1936-No. 10615) AdC MG Burgin TH 1941-42: Hq WDC 1942: G2 7th Div T-AP 1943-45. (SMG).

*Oliver Francis McDonald Jr., (W.P. 1936-No. 10616) Killed Sille-Le Guillaume France 9 Aug 1944 LTC CO 106th Cav Rcn Sq 106th Inf Div.

Rogers Turner Clifton, (W.P. 1936-No. 10620) Hq AAF 1941-43: Hq 4th Ftr Cmd US 1943-44. (SMG).

*Baehr Carl Jr., (W.P. 1936-No. 10628) CO 1st Bn 88th FA PA Bataan: POW: Death March : Killed POW ship 15 Dec 1944 MAJ.

Heintges John Arnold, (W.P. 1936-No. 10629) CO 3rd Bn 7th Inf NATO T-M 1943-44. (SLTG).

*Melton Harry Ripley Jr., (W.P. 1936-No. 10631) CO Ftr Bmb Gp (DFC,Burma): MIA-Air Msn Tangoon 25 Nov 1943: POW: Killed Jap POW ship from Singapore 14 Sep 1944 COL.

Daly John Harold, (W.P. 1936-No. 10632) (SBG).

Chiles John Henry, (W.P. 1936-No. 10634) XO & CO 23rd Inf 2nd Div T-E 1945. (SMG).

*Prichard Lawrence Frederick, (W.P. 1936-No. 10640) Inf PS Bataan: POW: Killed POW ship 9 Jan 1945 MAJ.

Abrams Creighton Williams Jr., (W.P. 1936-No. 10644) (SGEN).

Ryder William Thomas, (W.P. 1936-No. 10646) 505 PIR 82nd Abn Div NATO 1942-44. (SBG).

*Priestly William John, (W.P. 1936-No. 10649) AdC H Cmsr PI: Bataan; POW;: Death March: Killed POW ship 15 Dec 1944 MAJ.

*Bauer Karol Anthony, (W.P. 1936-No. 10652) 45th Inf PS Bataan: POW: Death March: Killed POW ship 15 Dec 1944(Pearl Harbor).

*Crowder Robert Thomas, (W.P. 1936-No. 10674) Killed Air Msn Ploesti 15 Apr 1944 COL Cmd Pilot 460th Bb Gp 15th AF.

Michaelis John Hersey, (W.P. 1936-No. 10676) CO 502nd PIR & CS 101st Abn Div T-E 1943-45. (SGEN).

Illig James Michael, (W.P. 1936-No. 10678) (SBG).

Benson Henry Kreitzer Jr., (W.P. 1936-No. 10679) (SMG).

*Bode Augustus Herbert Jr., (W.P. 1936-No. 10680) Killed Cher bourg 26 Jun 1944 LTC CO 2nd Bn 313th Inf 79th Div.

Shores Von Roy, (W.P. 1936-No. 10683) (SMG).

*McGoldrick Peter, (W.P. 1936-No. 10689) Killed Air Msn N Africa 6 Nov 1942 MAJ CO 79th Ftr Gp 9th AF.

*Godfray Leonard Clement, (W.P. 1936-No. 10692) Killed Omaha Beach Normandy 6 Jun 1944 MAJ SupO 16th Inf Div.

*Goldtrap John Clarke, (W.P. 1936-No. 10697) Visayan Military Force: POW: Killed POW ship 15 Dec 1944 MAJ.

Turnage Benjamin Otto Jr., (W.P. 1936-No. 10708) CO 1st Bn 34th Inf 24th Div T-S 1942-44: G3 Sec Hq 6th Ar 1944-45. (SMG).

Yarborough William Pelham, (W.P. 1936-No. 10710) 2nd Cps Italy 1942-43: CO Pchts Bns Italy 1943-44: CO 473rd Inf 5th AR Italy 1945. (SLTG).

Prosser Charles Morgan, (W.P. 1936-No. 10713) (SBG).

Billingslea Charles, (W.P. 1936-No. 10715) XO 504th PIR 82nd Abn Div T-M 1943-44. (SMG).

Evans Benjamin Franklin Jr., (W.P. 1936-No. 10716) S3 27th Inf 25th Div T-S 1942-43: CO 2nd Bn 27th Inf 1943. (SMG).

Necrason Conrad Francis, (W.P. 1936-No. 10733) CO 7th Bb Gp CBI 1942-44. (SMG).

*McBee William Maurice, (W.P. 1936-No.) Died Clarke Fld PI Air Acdt 18 Mar 1938 LT.

Oberbeck Arthur William, (W.P. 1937-No. 10736) CO 3rd Engr 24th Div T-S 1942-44: Engr Sec GHQ USAF PAC 1944-45. (SLTG).

*Snyder Campbell Hodges, (W.P. 1937-No. 10737) 14th Engr Bataan: POW: Death March: Killed POW ship 15 Dec 1944 MAJ.

Parker David Bennett, (W.P. 1937-No. 10738) LnO GHQ to Aus Ar T-S 1942-44: (SMG).

Donohew Jack Norman, (W.P. 1937-No. 10741) CO 28th Comp Gp Aleut 1943. (SMG).

Ohman Nils Olof, (W.P. 1937-No. 10753) Hq AAF 1942-44: CO 97th Bb Gp 15th AF T-ME 1944-45. (SMG).

Hyzer Peter Clarke, (W.P. 1937-No. 10756) CO 3rd Bn 311th Inf 78th Div US 1942-43: G3 Sec Hq 12th Cps T-E 1944-45. (SBG).

*Farrell William Edwin Wilson, (W.P. 1937-No. 10768) Hq 1st Cps PA Bataan: POW-escaped: Recaptured Aug 1942: Died 23 Jan 1945 from wounds POW ship 9 Jan 1945 CPT.

Quandt Douglass Phillip, (W.P. 1937-No. 10772) CO 82nd Abn Div US 1942-43. (SMG).

Schermerhorn John Gamble, (W.P. 1937-No. 10777) CO 15th Engr 9th Div T-ME 1943-45: CO 1120th EC Gp 1st Ar 1945 (SBG)

Walker George Henry, (W.P. 1937-No. 10784) XO 46th EGS Regt T-S 1942-43: CO 1103rd Ec Gp T-E 1944-45. (SMG).

Surles Alexander Day Jr., (W P. 1937-No. 10789) (SLTG).

Spengler Henry Mershon, (W.P. 1937-No. 10804) G3 Sec Y Force China 1943-44: G3 sec Chinese Cmbt Cmd 1944-45. (SBG).

Davisson Horace Greeley, (W.P. 1937-No. 10818) XO OCO Hq ETO 1942-45. (SMG).

Fellows Richard William, (W.P. 1937-No. 10823) DCO 24th Pur Gp Bataan: Dpty & CO 376th Bb Gp 15th AF T-M 1943-44. (SBG).

Cone John Martin, (W.P. 1937-No. 10826) (SMG).

*Baldwin William Perry, (W.P. 1937-No. 10828) 57th Inf & 102nd Inf PA: POW; Killed POW ship 15 Dec 1944 MAJ.

Holloway Bruce Keener, (W.P. 1937-No. 10834) CO 23rd Ftr Gp 14th AF T-C 1943:

Hq AAF 1945. (SGEN).

Preston Maurice Arthur, (W.P. 1937-No. 10843) CO Bb Gp & BBb Wg 8th AF 1943-45: Base CO Salina KS 1945. (SGEN).

Underwood George Vernon, (W.P. 1937-No. 10849) (SMG).

Johnson Chester Lee, (W.P. 1937-No. 10851) Bn XO 24th FA Bataan: POW 1942-45: Death March. (SMG).

O'Malley Charles Stuart Jr., (W.P. 1937-No. 10852) CO 210th AABn 1943-44. (SMG).

Herman Robert Hensey, (W.P. 1937-No. 10856) XO & CO Units 11th AF Aleutians 1943-45. (SBG).

Scherrer Edward C. David, (W.P. 1937-No. 10860) Rcn & Asst Hq USAF SPA 1942-43: XO & CO Cav Units T-e 1944-45. (SMG).

Ostrander Don Richard, (W.P. 1937-No. 10867) Ord Sec Hq 8th Ftr Cmd ETO 1942-44. (SMG).

Connor Albert Ollie, (W.P. 1937-No. 10869) G3 3rd Div Italy 1943-44. (SLTG).

Campbell Fred Pierce, (W.P. 1937- No. 10874) S3 7th Cps Arty T-E 1944-45. (SBG).

Taylor Robert 3rd, (W.P. 1937-No. 10885) (SMG).

*Nelson Richard Ellis, (W.P. 1937-No. 10893) Killed Normandy 28 Jul 1944 LTC: CO Bn 67th Armd Inf Regt 2nd AD.

*Browne Charles Janvrin, (W.P. 1937-No. 10896) 31st Inf PS & 91st Div PA Bataan: POW: Death March: Killed POW ship 9 Jan 1945 MAJ.

Stromberg Woodrow Wilson, (W.P. 1937-No. 10898) (SMG).

Low Curtis Raymond, (W.P. 1937-No. 10902) DCO 12th Bb Gp Mid East 1942-43. (SMG).

Uhger Ferdinand Thomas, (W.P. 1937-No. 10904) CO 718th FA Bn 63rd Div T-AE 1943-45. (SLTG).

Broadhurst Edwin Borden, (W.P. 1937-No. 10916) 19th Bb Gp HI PI 1941-42. (SLTG).

Westover Charles Bainbridge, (W.P. 1937-No. 10918) Div CS & CO Bb Gp 2nd Div 8th AF T-E 1943-45. (SLTG).

*Greeley Horace John, (W.P. 1937-No. 10921) Hq Feaf 1941: Bataan: POW: Death March: Died POW Cp Fukuoka Japan 31 Jan 1945(colitis) MAJ.

Scheidecker Paul William, (W.P. 1937-No. 10936) (SMG).

*Traeger William Henry, (W.P. 1937-No. 10942) 45th Inf & Hq Phil Div Bataan: POW: Death March: Killed POW ship 15 Dec 1944 MAJ.

*Robinson William Leslie, (W.P. 1937-No. 10944) 45th Inf PS & Vvisayan Force: POW: Died POW ship 21 Jan 1945(coloitis) LTC.

Reaves Kelsie Loomis, (W.P. 1937-No. 10949) XO Greenland Base Cmd 1942-43. (SMG).

Taylor Benjamin Franklin, (W.P. 1937-No. 10951) (SMG).

Hipps William Grover, (W.P. 1937-No. 10959) CO 16th Bb Sq 27th Bb Gp PI & Actg A3 feaf 1941. (SBG).

*Wynkoop Hueston Richard, (W.P. 1937-No. 10962) 57th Inf &Hq ICps PA Bataan: POW: Death March: Killed POW ship 15 Dec 1944 Maj.

*Joerg Wood Guice, (W.P. 1937-No. 10965) Killed Rochlinval Belgium(Bulge) 7 Jan 1945 LTC 551st PIR 82nd Abn Div.

Oden Delk McCorkle, (W.P. 1937-No. 10977) CO Tk Bns 4th AD T-AE 1942-45. (SMG).

*Hoyt Charles Sherman Jr., (W.P. 1937-No. 10982) 45th Inf PS Bataan: POW: Killed POW ship 15 Dec 1944 MAJ.

*Kelly Colin Purdie Jr., (W.P. 1937-10983) Killed Air Msn Aparri Luzon, 10 Dec 1941, CPT Bmb Pilot 19th Bb Gp in attack on jap ships : First grad killed in action WW2.

Lemmon Kelley Benjamin Jr., (W.P. 1937-No. 10988) CO units 11th Inf 5th Div T-AE 1941-44. (SMG).

Sanborn Kenneth Oliver, (W.P. 1937-No. 10991) CO Anti sub units 1942-44. (SMG).

Tolson John Jarvis 3rd., (W.P. 1937-No. 10998) (SLTG).

Skeldon James Howard, (W.P. 1937-No. 11003) (SMG).

Graham Ephriam Foster Jr., (W.P. 1937-No. 11010) CO 644th TD Bn T-E 1944-45. (SBG).

Kimbrell Gordon Talmage, (W.P. 1937-No. 11023) CO 3rd/306th Inf 77th Div T-SP 1943-44: CO 305th Inf 77th Div T-SP 1945. (SBG).

Hardaway Eads Graham, (W.P. 1937-No. 11027) Bn CO 89th Div 1943-44CO 2nd Bn 120th Inf 30th Div T-e 1944: POW 1945. (SBG).

Jannarone John Robert, (W.P. 1938-No. 11034) Asst Engr Hq 8th Ar T-SP 1944-45. (SBG).

Breitwieser Robert Allen, (W.P. 1938-No. 11036) A3 Sect Hq SE Tng Cmd 1942-43: A3 68th Comp Wg 14th AF China 1942-45. (SLTG).

Preuss Paul Theodore, (W.P. 1938-11041) (SMG).

Kelsey John Eugene, (W.P. 1938-No. 11042) Sig O 99th Div 1942-44. (SBG).

Stilwell Richard Giles, (W.P. 1938-No. 11046) CO Engr & G3 90th Div T-AE 1942-44. (SGEN).

Kelley Harold Killian, (W.P. 1938-No. 11049) (SBG).

Wickham Kenneth Gregory, (W.P. 1938-No. 11054) (SMG).

Kieffer William Brett, (W.P. 1938-No. 11056) CO 486th Bb Gp 8th AF T-E 1945. (SLTG).

Harvey Clarence Clinton Jr., (W.P. 1938-No. 11057) CO 83rd FA Bn T-E 1944-45. (SBG).

Lotz Walter Edward Jr., (W.P. 1938-No. 11071) XO Dir Comm Hq 9th AF T-E 1944-45. (SLTG).

Skaer William Kenneth, (W.P. 1938-No. 11072) Hq 20th Bb Cmd CBI 1944-45: CO 40th Bb Gp AF T-P 1945. (SBG).

Hutchin Claire Elwood Jr., (W.P. 1938-No. 11073) (SLTG).

Spicer Prescott Miner, (W.P. 1938-No. 11074) Hq 12th AF T-ME 1944-45. (SMG).

Mearns Fillmore Kennady, (W.P. 1938-No. 11087) G3 6th Cps Italy 1942-44: CO 3dr Bn 135th Inf 34th Div Italy 1943-44: Hq 4th Ar 1945. (SLTG).

Beverley William Welby, (W.P. 1938-No.) CO 423rd FA Bn 10th AD T-E 1944-45. (SMG).

Anderson Roland Bennett, (W.P. 1938-No. 11089) CO Ord CO HI 1941-42: OO AA Cmd POA 1942-43. (SMG).

Norris Frank Wade, (W.P. 1938-No. 11091) CO 345th FA Bn 90th Div(1st & 3rd Ar) ETO 1942-45. (SMG).

Brown Burton Robert, (W.P. 1938-No. 11094) CAC: Bataan: Corregidore: POW 1942-45. (SBG).

Ryan John Dale, (W.P. 1938-No. 11099) DCO & CO 2Bb Gp 15th AF Italy 1944-45. (SGEN).

Lough Frederick Charles, (W.P. 1938-No. 11100) CO Sig Bn 5th Ar Italy 1943-45. (SBG).

Latta William Braden, (W.P. 1938-No. 11101) CO 1st Sig Bn T-ME 1942-45: Sig Sect 7th Ar 21st Cps T-E 1945. (SMG).

Lynn William McGregor Jr., (W.P. 1938-No. 11102) XO 8th AD Arty T-E 1945. (SMG).

*Kappes George, (W.P. 1938-No. 11106) CAC:

92nd CA HD Manila: POW: Killed POW ship 24 Oct 1944 CPT.

*Miller Frederick Adam, (W.P. 1938-No. 11108) CO Btry A 60th CA Bataan: POW: Killed POW ship 24 Oct 1944 CPT.

Michelet Howard Edward, (W.P. 1938-No. 11113) (SBG).

Eaton Samuel Knox, (W.P. 1938-No. 11114) S3 13th Cps Arty T-E 1942-45. (SMG).

*Lipps Milton Edward, (W.P. 1938-No. 11116) Inf: Killed Air Msn Mindanao, 9 Mar 1945 LTC Dpty CO 42nd Bb Gp & CO 70th Bb Sq.

Harrison Bertram Cowgill, (W.P. 1938-No. 11134) CO 460th Bb Gp 1944-45. (SLTG).

Coira Louis Edward, (W.P. 1938-No. 11148) DCO 40th Bb Gp & Hq Wg Randolph AFB CBI 1944-45. (SMG).

*Baldwin Lawrence Chandler, (W.P. 1938-No. 11153) 60th CA HD Manila: POW: Died POW Cp Fukuoka Jap 4 Feb 1945(colitis) CPT.

Chesarek Ferdinand Joseph, (W.P. 1938-No. 11159) CO 28th FA Bn 8th Div T-E 1944-45. (SGEN).

Huglin Henry Charles, (W.P. 1938-No. 11170) (SBG).

Folda Jaroslav Thayer Jr., (W.P. 1938-No. 11175) (SMG).

Tillson John Chas. Fremont III, (W.P. 1938-No. 11178) G2 CO Spec Trpd & CO 424nd Inf 42nd Div —1945. (SMG).

Zoller Virgil Lee, (W.P. 1938-No. 11187) A3 Sec Hq 15th AF Italy 1943-44. (SBG).

Van Sickle Neil David, (W.P. 1938-No. 11191) CO Anti sub Sq US 1942-43. (SMG).

Irvin Jefferson Johnson, (W.P. 1938-No. 11199) G3, CS 10th Mtn Div Italy 1943-45. (SBG).

Lynch James Henry, (W.P. 1938-No. 11219) (SBG).

Dean Fred Murray, (W.P. 1938-No. 11227) CO 308th Sq 31st Ftr Gp T-E 1942: CO 31st Ftr Gp T-M 1943. (SLTG).

*Pendleton Alexander Bruce, (W.P. 1938-No. 11228) Died Ecuador Air acdt 3 Jun 1943 LTC.

Finn John Milton, (W.P. 1938-No. 11234) (SMG).

Collins Arthur Sylvester Jr., (W.P. 1938-No. 11242) CO 1st Bn 30th Inf 83rd Div Haw & T-S 1943-44. (SLTG).

Izenour Frank Milton, (W.P. 1938-No. 11245) 7th Inf 3rd Div 1941-44: Bn CO NATO 1942-43: Bn CO Anzio 1944: XO & CO 7th Inf Fr 1944. (SMG).

Miller Frank Dickson, (W.P. 1938-No. 11252) Bn CO & XO 307th Inf, G3 77th Div T-S 1943-45. (SMG).

Sibley Thomas Nelson, (W.P. 1938-No. 11259) XO 343rd Inf 86th Div T-E 1945. (SBG).

Machen Edwin Arthur Jr., (W.P. 1938-No. 11266) G1 Sec IBC 1941-42: Hq 15th Ar 1944-45: G3 Berlin Dist: Hq 1st Allied Abn Army 1945. (SBG).

Sternberg Ben, (W.P. 1938-No. 11268) CO 18th Div NATO 1942-43: XO 18th Inf T-E 1943-45. (SMG).

Denholm Charles Joseph, (W.P. 1938-No. 11275) XO & CO 1st Bn 16th Inf 1st Div NATO 1942-43: Bn CO 16th Inf & 143rd Inf , CO 143rd Inf 36th Div Sicily & Italy 1943-45. (SMG).

Ashworth Robert Leaning, (W.P. 1938-No. 11290) Bn CO 17th Abn Div T-E 1944-45. (SBG).

Corley John Thomas, (W.P. 1938-No. 11307) CO 3rd/26th Inf 1st Div T-ME 1942-45. (SBG).

*Skinner Edward Raymond, (W.P. 1938-No. 11312) Died Tricesimo Italy 31 May 1945 MAJ CO 2nd Bn 85th Mtn Inf.

*Brabson Joe Reese Jr., (W.P. 1938-No. 11318) Killed Air Msn East Indies 1 Jan 1945 LTC DCO 42nd Bb Gp 13th AF.

York Robert Howard, (W.P. 1938-No. 11323) XO & CO 1st Bn 18th Inf 1st Div T-AME 1942-45. (SLTG).

Isbell James Horace, (W.P. 1938-No. 11332) 458th Bb Gp 8th AF T-E 1944-45. (SBG).

Goodpaster Andrew Jackson, (W.P. 1939-No. 11336) CO EC Bn Italy 1943-44(SGEN).

Samuel John Spoor, (W.P. 1939-No. 11339) CO Bb Gp 9th AF T-E. (SMG).

Crawford Roscoe Campbell Jr., (W.P. 1939-No. 11349) A3 Sect 13th AF SWPA 1944-45. (SBG).

Duke Charles Marsden, (W.P. 1939-No. 11350) CO 30th ET Bn Africa & HI 1944-45. (SMG).

Ploger Robert Rils, (W.P. 1939-No. 11357) CO 121st Engr Bn 29th Div T-E 1943-45. (SMG).

Bradley William Thomas, (W.P. 1939-No. 11365) XO, CO 339th WCn Bn T-AS 1942-45. (SMG).

Newcomer Henry Crandall, (W.P. 1939-No. 11367) CO 451st Bb Sq 322nd Bb Gp 9th AF T-E 1944-45. (SBG).

Brinker Walter Evans, (W.P. 1939-No. 11373) Bn CO T-E 1943-45: XO 350th FA Gp 1945. (SMG).

*White Charles Edward, (W.P. 1939-No. 11376) 92nd CA HD Manila: POW: Killed POW ship 7 Sep1944 CPT.

Miller Robert Benjamin, (W.P. 1939-No. 11384) CO 399th Bb Gp 8th AF T-E 1943-44. (SBG).

Collins James Lawton Jr., (W.P. 1939-No. 11385) CO 957th FA Bn 7th Cps 1943-45. (SBG).

Carpenter John Wilson, (W.P. 1939-No. 11387) Bmb Units US 1941; Clark Fld PI 1941: 19th Bb Gp T-S 1941-42: Hq AAF 1943-44: Hq 20th AF 1944-45. (SLTG).

Ewell Julian Johnson, (W.P. 1939-No. 11388) Bn & Regt CO 501st PIR 101st Abn Div T-E 1944-45. (SLTG).

Williams Robert Mabry, (W.P. 1939-No. 11398) CO 604th FA Bn 10th Mtn Div Italy 1945. (SBG).

Vann Walter MacRae, (W.P. 1939-No. 11409) G4 Sec Hq 12th Ar Gp·1945. (SMG).

McDavid John Arthur, (W.P. 1939-No. 11414) Asst SO HQ 7th AF HI 1941-43: SO & Comm O Hq 7th AF T-CP 1943-45. (SBG).

Sullivan Henry Riggs Jr., (W.P. 1939-No. 11427) Sq CO & Dpty Gp CO 20th AF T-I 1943-45: A3 Sect & Gp CO 20th AF T-P 1945. (SMG).

Dickman Joseph Lawrence, (W.P. 1939-No. 11430) XO 78th Ftr Gp 8th AF UK 1943: DCO 82nd Ftr Gp 15th AF Italy 1944-45. (SMG).

*Lehr Phillip Henry, (W.P. 1939-No. 11438) CA HD Manila: POW: Survivor POW ship 15 Dec 1944: Died POW ship 31 Dec 1944(dysentery & starvation) CPT.

Phelan Roger Edwards, (W.P. 1939-No. 11439) CO 22nd Bb Gp 5th AF T-S 1943-44: Hq AAF 1944-45. (SBG).

Kinney Andrew John, (W.P. 1939-No. 11442) (SMG).

*Bowers Charles Russell, (W.P. 1939-No. 11443) Killed North Manila Road 24 Dec 1941 1stLT CO Rcn Patrol 26th Cav.

Mount Charles McNeal Jr., (W.P. 1939-No. 11446) G3 Div Sup Hq AEF 1943-45. (SMG).

Taylor Livingston Nelson Jr., (W.P. 1939-No. 11450) S3 24th Div Arty T-P 1941-45. (SMG).

Keller James Howard, (W.P. 1939-No. 11468) Bn CO 32nd Inf Div T-P 1943-44: G1 7th Div 1944: XO & CO 32nd Inf T-P 1944-45. (SBG).

Curtin Richard Daniel, (W.P. 1939-No. 11486) (SMG).

Knapp James Barclay, (W.P. 1939-No. 11488) CO Sq Bb Sq & CO 451st Bb Gp 15th AF Italy 1944. (SMG).

Boye Frederic William Jr., (W.P. 1939-No. 11489) G3 Sect 2nd Cps AFHQ 5th AR 3rd Div T-M 1942-43: CO 3rd Bn 15th Inf 3rd Div T-ME 1943-44: Hq ASF 1945. (SMG).

Marlin Raymond Bradner, (W.P. 1939-No. 11498) 23rd Inf Div T-AE 1943-44. (SMG).

Price William Herbert Jr., (W.P. 1939-No. 11502) Asst Hq 6th Ar T-S 1944-45. (SBG).

Greer Robert Evans, (W.P. 1939-No. 11509) A4 Hq 20th Bb Cmd CBI 1944-45: DCS Bb Units 20th AF T-P 1945. (SMG).

Lilly Roger Merrill, (W.P. 1939-No. 11525) CO 399th AF A Bn 8th AD T-AE 1942-45. (SMG).

Billups James Sykes Jr., (W.P. 1939-No. 11533) CO Gli FA Bn 1942-43: C) fa Bns T-E 1944-45. (SBG).

Pickett George Edward, (W.P. 1939-No. 11539) (SLTG).

*Breitling George Thaddeus, (W.P. 1939-No. 11550) 43rd Inf PS Bataan: POW: Died 20 Jan 1945 from wounds POW ship 9 Jan 1945 CPT.

Kobes Frank Joseph Jr., (W.P. 1939-No. 11551) Bn XO & CO 15th Inf 3rd Div NATO & Sicily 1942-43. (BG).

*Madison Samuel Alton, (W.P. 1939-No. 11554) 59th CA Corregidor: Died POW Cp Fukuoka Jap 3 Feb 1945(colitis) CPT.

Whitehouse Thomas Bernard, (W.P. 1939-No. 11560) DCO & CO 14th Ftr Gp 15th AF T-ME 1944-45. (SMG).

Kerwin Walter Thomas Jr., (W.P. 1939-No. 11565) (SGEN).

Davidson Phillip Buford Jr., (W.P. 1939-No. 11571) CO Cav Sq & XO Cav Gp T-AE 1943-45. (SLTG).

Richardson Robert Charlwood 3rd, (W.P. 1939-No. 11577) CO Comp Sq So Atl 1942-43: AAF Bd US 1943-44: CO 365th Ftr Gp T-E 1945. 9SBG).

Dolvin Welborn Griffin, (W.P. 1939-No. 11582) CO 191st Tk Bn T-E 1944-45. (SLTG).

*Garnett William Ames, (W.P. 1939-No. 11584) Killed Air Msn Rabaul 18 Apr 1942, CPT 33rd Bb Sq 22nd Bb Gp FEAF.

Crawford Thomas Mull, (W.P. 1939-No. 11585) Bn CO 6th AD T-E 1944-45. (SBG).

Higgins Walter Martin Jr., (W.P. 1939-No. 11589) CO 2nd Bn 9th Inf T-AE 1943-45. (SMG).

Vandevanter Elliott Jr., (W.P. 1939-No. 11591) CO 385th Bb Wg T-E 1943-44. (SBG).

Kinnard Harry Wm. Osborn Jr., (W.P. 1939-No. 11592) 501st PIR 101st Abn Div T-AE 1942-45. (SLTG).

Mildren Frank Thomas, (W.P. 1939-No. 11594) CO 1st Bn 38th Inf 2nd Div T-E 1944-45: XO 38th Inf,CO 23rd Inf,G3 2nd Div 1945. (SGEN).

Schellman Robert Henry, (W.P. 1939-No. 11604) CO 1st Bn 309th Inf 78th Div T-E 1944-45: G3 78th Div 1945. (SMG).

Merrell Jack Gordon, (W.P. 1939-No. 11606) CO Prim Fly Sch 1942-43: DCO & CO Bb Gps 8th AF T-E 1944-45. (SGEN).

Smith William Thomas, (W.P. 1939-No. 11616) CO AAFSch US 1941-43: Trng Cmds US 1943-45. (SMG).

Van Harlingen Wm. Mulford, (W.P. 1939-No. 11618) CO 66th Sig Bn T-E 1944-45. (SBG).

Boles John Keith Jr., (W.P. 1939-No. 11627) Bn CO, XO 32nd Arm 3rd AD T-E 1944-45. (SMG).

Hoisington Perry Milo 2nd, (W.P. 1939-No. 11646) CO Bb Units 20th Bb Cmd 20th AF CBI 1944-45. (SMG).

Davison Michael Shannon (W.P. 1939-No. 11653) CO Inf Bn 45th Div T-ME 1944. (SGEN).

*Turner William LeRoy, (W.P. 1939-No. 11656) Killed Vierville Normandy 7 Jun 1944, LTC CO 1st Bn 506th Pcht Inf 101st Abn Div.

Martin William Kemp, (W.P. 1939 No. 11663) CS, CO Bb Units 8th AF T-E 1943-45. (SLTG).

Smith Edward Paul, (W.P. 1939-No. 11666) Bn CO & XO 17th Inf 7th Div T-P 1942-44. (SMG).

McCaffrey William Joseph, (W.P. 1939-No. 11668) CS 92nd Div Italy 1944-45. (SLTG).

*Bailey Benjamin Mart Jr., (W.P. 1939-No. 11677) Killed St Andre France 23 Aug 1944, LTC XO CCA, 2nd AD.

Wynne Prentiss Davis Jr., (W.P. 1939-No. 11687) Staffs 14th AF, Chinese Amer Comp Wg 10th AF China 1945. (SBG).

*Peterson Raymond Thompson, (W.P. 1939-No. 11690) Killed Air Msn New Guinea 24 Nov 1942 MAJ 90th Bmb Sq 3rd Bmb Gp.

Fredericks Charles George, (W.P. 1939-No. 11696) CO 2nd Bn 32nd Inf 7th Div T-P 1943: G3 7th Div 1944-45. (SBG).

Larsen Stanley Robert, (W.P. 1939-No. 11698) (SLTG).

*Crowell Victor Frederick, (W.P. 1939-No. 11700) Killed Bataan (Acdt gun shot) 31 Dec 1941 1st LT CoD 57th Inf PS.

Whalen Matthew, (W.P. 1939-No. 11706) Killed St Vith(Bulge) 24 Dec 1944, MAJ,S3 CCA 7th AD.

Negley Richard Van Wyck Jr., (W.P. 1939-No. 11712) Killed Air Msn Kangean Isle NEI, 8 Feb 1942, 1st LT 7th Bb Gp FEAF.

Kingsley Joseph Theodore Jr., (W.P. 1939-No. 11716) CO Anti Sub Sq 1942-43: CO Aircraft Rep Unit T-P 1944-45: (SMG).

Smith Charles Bradford, (W.P. 1939-No. 11717) (SBG).

*Eichlin Herbert Henry Jr., (W.P. 1939-No. 11722) 31st Inf Bataan: POW: Death March: Died 27 Jan 1945 from wounds POW ship 9 Jan 1945 CPT.

*Sellars Frank Campbell, (W.P. 1939-No. 11726) Died POW in Ger Hosp 12 Dec 1944 from wounds Saar Union Fr 4 Dec 1944 MAJ Civ Aff O 101st Inf 26th Inf Div.

*Dixon Wiley Lee Jr., (W.P. 1939-No. 11728) Hq 2nd Cps PA Bataan; POW: Death March: Died POW Cp Zentzuji Jap 2 Jan 1943(pneumonia) CPT.

*Brown Harold MacVane, (W.P. 1939-No. 11738) Killed near Rome 19 May 1944 MAJ CO 351st Bn 88th Inf Div.

*Davis John Tyler, (W.P. 1939-No. 11740) Killed Belgium(Bulge) 8 Jan 1945 MAJ Hq 507th PIR 17th Abn Div.

McCoy John Louis, (W.P. 1939-No. 11745) (SMG).

*Coleman George Thomas, (W.P. 1939-No. 11754) Killed Manila 8 Feb 1945, LTC Bn CO 145th Inf 37th Div.

Stocking Lewis Wilson (W.P. 1939-No. 11764) Dpty CO 409th Bb Gp 9th AF T-E 1944-45. (SBG).

*McCray James Oren, (W.P. 1939-No. 11772) Killed Leyte PI 26 Oct 1944 LTC CO 2nd Bn 383rd Inf 96th Div.

Collins Kenneth Wilson, (W.P. 1939-No. 11773) Bn CO 6th Inf 9th AD T-E 1944-45. (SMG).

Wilson James Walter, (W.P. 1939-No. 11778) CO 423rd Bb Sq 8th AF T-E 1942-43: CO 92nd Bb Gp SAF 1944-45. (SLTG).

Adams Milton Bernard, (W.P. 1939-No. 11782) (SMG).

Horner Charles Thompson Jr., (Non Grad) CO 16th Inf 1st Div T-AME 1940-46. (SMG).

Batte James Herbert, (Non Grad) 87th CM Bn, 4th Div T-E 1944-45. (SBG).

Listing Of U.S. Army Generals Who Did Not Attend West Point. Army Air Corps Officers Transfer To The U.S. Air Force During September 1947; USAF Is Noted When Applicable.

GENERAL OF THE ARMY

Marshall, George C., 12-16-44.

GENERAL

Hodges, Courtney H., 4-26-45 — 1-31-49.
Kenney, George C., 3-9-45 — USAF.
Krueger, Walter, 3-5-45 — 7-20-46.

LIEUTENANT GENERAL

Bates, John C., 2-1-06 — 4-14-06.
Brees, Herbert J., 10-1-40 — 6-30-41.
Brereton, Lewis H., 4-28-44 — USAF.
Brett, George H., 1-7-42 — 5-10-46.
Brooks, Edward H., 3-18-49 — 4-30-53.
Cannon, John K., 3-17-45 — USAF.
Chaffee, Adna R., 1-9-04 — 2-1-06.
Corbin, Henry C., 4-15-06 — 9-15-06.
Doolittle, James H., 3-13-44 — 5-22-46.
Drum, Hugh A., 8-5-39 — 9-30-43.
Eaker, Ira C., 9-13-43 — 8-31-47.
Eddy, Manton S., 1-24-48 — 3-31-53.
George, Harold L., 3-16-45 — 12-31-46.
Giles, Barney McK., 4-28-44 — 6-30-46.
Herron, Charles D., 7-31-40 — 3-31-41.
Huebner, Clarence R., 3-28-47 — 11-30-50.
Knudsen, William 1-28-42 — 6-1-45.
Lutes, Leroy, 6-5-45 — 1-31-52.
MacArthur, Arthur, 9-15-06 — 6-2-09.
McLain, Raymond S., 7-6-45 — 4-30-52.
Middleton, Troy H., 6-5-45 — 8-10-45.
Miles, Nelson A., 6-6-00 — 8-8-03.
Paul, Willard S., 1-23-48 — 12-31-48.
Reynold, Eugene 4-15-45 — 1-31-46.
Short, Walter C., 2-8-41 — 12-17-41.
Van Voorhis, Daniel 7-31-40 — 10-31-42.
Washington, George 7-3-1798 — 12-14-1799.
Whitehead, Ennis C., 6-5-45 — USAF.
Young, Samuel B.M., 8-8-03 — 1-9-04.

MAJOR GENERAL

Acheson, George R., 9-11-43 — USAF.
Adams, Emory S., 5-1-38 — 2-28-42.
Ainsworth, Fred C., 4-23-04 — 2-16-12.
Akin, Spencer B., 11-3-43 — 3-31-51.
Alexander, Robert 8-8-18 — 10-17-27.
Allen, Frank A., Jr. 6-20-48 — 11-30-56.
Allen, Robert H., 3-28-25 — 9-7-29.
Allen, Roderick R., 1-17-43 — 5-31-54.
Allen, Wayne R., 9-2-44 — ?
Allison James B., 1-1-35 — 9-30-37.
Anderson, Alexander E., ? — ?
Anderson, Jonathan W., 3-17-42 — 6-30-50.
Anderson, Orvil A., 11-9-44 — USAF
Anderson, Thomas M., 8-13-1898 — 1-21-1900.
Andrus, Clift 8-28-44 — 10-31-52.
Armstrong, George E., 10-12-43 — 7-31-55.
Arnold, William R., 11-7-44 — 10-15-45.
Austin, Fred T., 12-20-27 — 2-15-30.
Back, George I., 8-22-49 — 6-30-55.
Baird, Henry W., 7-11-41 — 11-30-42.
Baker, Walter C., 7-18-37 — 4-30-41.
Baldwin, Frank D., 3-4-15 — 3-4-15.
Barker, Ray W., 6-25-43 — 2-28-47.
Barnes, Gladeon M., 3-11-43 — 8-31-46.
Barnes, Julian F., 1-19-42 — 10-31-47.
Barnett, Allison J., 1-15-44 — 10-31-47.
Barr, David G., 10-15-44 — 2-29-52.
Beach, George C., 1-23-46 — 11-18-48.
Beiderlinden, William A., 8-20-43 — 6-30-55.
Bergin, William E., 10-8-43 — 5-31-54.
Bertrandias, Victor E., 1-6-45 — USAF
Bethea, James A., 4-27-48 — 10-31-49.

Birkhead, Claude V., 8-1-40 — ?
Birnie, Upton, Jr., 3-10-34 — 8-31-38.
Bishop, Percy P., 1-1-38 — 5-31-41.
Bissell, Clayton L., 3-13-43 — USAF
Black, William W., 10-6-17 — 10-31-19.
Blakeley, Harold W., 3-18-45 — 4-30-46.
Blanding, Albert H., 10-15-24 — 6-30-55.
Blatchford, Richard M., 8-5-17 — 12-1-22.
Bliss, Raymond W., 9-13-43 — 6-30-51.
Booth, Ewing E., 12-23-29 — 2-28-34.
Boschen, Frederick W., 4-22-40 — 5-31-40.
Bradley, Follett 2-25-42 — 4-30-44.
Branshaw, Charles E., 6-24-43 — 12-31-44.
Brewster, Andre' W., 11-28-17 — 12-9-25.
Brooke, John R., 5-22-97 — 7-21-02.
Brooks, John B., 3-11-43 — 9-30-46.
Brown, Arthur W., 12-1-33 — 11-30-37.
Brown, Lloyd D., 3-15-43 — 2-17-50.
Brown, Philip E., 12-1-42 — 12-31-45.
Brown, Preston 12-10-25 — 11-30-34.
Brush, Rapp 5-20-42 — 12-31-45.
Bullene, Egbert F., 8-25-49 — 3-31-54.
Bush, Kenneth B., 2-9-44 — 5-31-53.
Campbell, Boniface 3-31-48 — 12-31-56.
Carr, Irving J., 7-1-31- 12-31-34.
Chapman, Elbridge G., Jr. 3-17-43 —11-30-46.
Chauncey, Charles C., 2-25-44 — USAF
Cheatham, B. Frank 1-3-26 — 9-15-30.
Chennault, Clair L., 3-14-43 — USAF
Christmas, John K., 10-31-43 — 1-31-54.
Clarkson, Percy W., 2-25-42 — 12-31-53.
Clem, John L., 8-29-16 — 8-29-16.
Clement, Charles M., 7-15-19 — ?
Colglazier, Robert W., Jr. 8-1-48 —
Collins, Harry J., 3-26-43 — 9-30-54.
Colton, Roger B., 8-7-42 — 1-31-46.
Craig, Howard A., 2-25-44 — USAF
Cramer, Kenneth F., 8-13-47 —
Cramer, Myron C., 12-1-41- 11-30-45.
Crane John A., 9-14-43 — 10-31-46.
Croft, Edward 5-6-33 — 10-31-37.
Cross, Charles P., 8-9-42 — ?
Cross, Thomas J., 7-26-44 — 1-31-53.
Culin, Frank L., Jr. 3-20-45 — 11-30-46.
Cummins, Joseph M., 10-1-40 — 12-31-42.
Cunningham, Julian W., 3-18-49 — 5-31-52.
Curtis, Edward P., 1-5-45 — ?
Dabney, John A., 4-9-48 —
Dager, Holmes E., 5-3-45 --- 10-31-47.

Dalton, Joseph N., 9-21-43 — 11-30-46.
Dean, William F., 7-19-43 — 10-31-55.
Deane, John R., 9-21-43 — 9-30-46.
Denit, Guy B., 9-8-45 — 9-30-53.
Devol, Carroll A., 10-31-16 — 10-31-16.
Donovan, Leo 11-11-44 — 12-31-46.
Donovan William J., 11 —10-44 — ?
Duff, Robinson E., 8-14-43 — 1-31-53.
Dunckel, William C., 1-3-45 — 10-31-45.
Dunham, George C., 2-22-44 — 10-31-45.
Dunton, Delmar H. 3-16-43 — 3-31-45.
Earnest, Herbert L., 5-3-45 — 9-30-47.
Eberle, George L., 8-13-43 — 7-31-54.
Echols, Oliver P., 2-25-42 — USAF
Eckfeldt, Roger W., 11-17-40 — ?
Edmons, James E., 1-12-41 — ?
Edwards, Idwal H., 2-5-43 — USAF
Erickson, Edgar C., 7-1-48 —
Eubank, Eugene L., 7-4-46 — USAF
Evans, Frederick W., 7-3-46 — USAF
Everson, William G., 6-29-29 — 6-29-48.
Fairchild, Muir S., 8-3-42 — USAF
Fales, Eugene W., 9-2-44 — 8-31-46.
Feche't, James E., 12-14-27 — 12-31-31.
Feldman, Herman 10-2-44 — 9-30-51.
Feringa, Peter A., ? — 5-31-39.
Fickel, Jacob E., 10-1-40 — 8-31-46.
Foster, Eugene M., 2-2-47 — 5-31-51.
Foulois, Benjamin D., 12-20-31 — 12-31-35.
Franklin, John M., 6-4-45 — ?

Frink, James L., 9-14-43 — 8-31-46.
Funston, Frederick 4-30-15 — 2-19-17.
Gaffey, Hugh J., 4-28-43 — 6-16-46.
Gaines, Arthur R., 6-1-49 — 5-31-52.
Gardner, Grandison 7-2-46 — USAF
Gasser, Lorenzo D., 1-14-42 — 6-29-43.
Gibbons, Henry 4-1-36 — 3-31-40.
Gibbs, George S., 1-9-28 — 6-30-31.
Gilbert, Harold N., 10-25-45 — 12-31-46.
Giles, Benjamin F., 5-28-44 — 8-31-46.
Gill, William H., 5-24-42 — 5-31-46.
Gillespie, George L., 1-23-04 — 6-17-05.
Goodman, William M., 2-21-44 — 9-30-46.
Gorgas, William C., 3-4-15 — 10-3-18.
Graham, Roy C.L., 12-17-44 —9-30-52.
Grant, David N.W. 9-19-43 — 4-30-46.
Greely, Adolphus W., 2-10-06 — 3-27-08.
Greely, John N., 7-10-41 — 3-1-43.
Green, Thomas H., 12-1-45 — 11-30-49.
Greene, Harry A., 8-5-17 — 11-29-18.
Griffin, Martin E., 7-1-48 — 2-28-58.
Grimes, William M., 5-23-42 — 10-31-46.
Griner, George W., Jr. 9-18-43 — 8-31-46.
Griswold, Francis H., 7-12-46 — USAF
Groom, Joseph A., 4-1-40 — ?
Grow, Malcolm C., 9-17-43 — USAF
Grow, Robert W., 9-17-43 — 1-31-53.
Gulick, John W., 3-20-30 — 11-30-38.
Haffner, Charles C., Jr. 12-1-42 — ?
Hale, Willis H., 6-15-42 — USAF
Hall, Charles B., 3-28-08 — 4-29-08.
Hanley, Thomas L., Jr. 6-24-43 — USAF
Harbord, James G., 6-26-18 — 12-29-22.
Hardigg, Carl A., 11-8-44 — 10-31-46.
Harper, Joseph H., 7-1-48 —
Harries, George H., 8-5-17.
Harrison, William H., 6-24-43 — ?
Hartle, Russell P., 10-31-41 — 6-30-46.
Hase, William F., 3-22-34 — 1-30-35.
Hatcher, Julian S., 11-7-44 — 5-31-46.
Hawley, Paul R., 2-27-44 — 6-30-46.
Hays, Silas B., 8-12-47 —
Hazlett, Harry F., 3-18-43 — 10-31-47.
Heaton, Leonard D., 2-14-44 —
Hegenberger, Albert F., 9-7-45 — USAF
Heileman, Frank A., 1-18-43 — 3-31-53.
Helmick, Charles G., 10-22-44 — 7-31-52.
Helmick, Eli A., 8-8-18 — 9-27-27.
Henry, Stephen G., 3-11-43 — 10-31-46.
Hill, Edmund W., 1-3-45 — 10-31-46.
Hilldring, John H., 9-7-42 — 7-31-46.
Hodges, Charles L., 1-14-11 — 3-13-11.
Hodges, James P., 5-29-44 — USAF
Hoover, Hubert D., ? — 2-29-48.
Horkan, George A., 3-24-43 — 1-31-54.
Hull, John A., 11-16-24 — 11-15-28.
Hume, Edgar E., 4-27-48 — 12-31-51.
Humphrey, Charles F., 7-1-07 — 7-1-07.
Hunter, Frank O'D., 11-3-43 — 3-31-46.
Hyssong, Clyde L., 12-7-44 — 7-31-49.
Ireland, Merritte W., 8-8-18 — 5-31-31.
Irvine, Willard W., 4-30-48 — 4-30-52.
Jackson, Stonewall 3-15-43 — 10-13-43.
Jaynes, Lawrence C., 5-13-43 — 7-31-53.
Johnston, William H., 8-8-18 — 10-19 —25.
Jones, Alan W., 3-16-43 — 10-31-45.
Jones, Albert M., 8-29-44 — 7-31-52.
Jones, Henry L.C., 5-21-42 — 2-28-46.
Jones, Lloyd E., 9-15-43 — 4-30-46.
Joyce, Kenyon A., 11-1-39 — 11-30-43.
Kasten, William H., 7-14-45 — 1-31-49.
Keating, Frank A., 2-6-45 — 8-31-50.
Kells, Clarence H., 1-4-45 — 8-31-46.
Kenner, Albert W., 10-7-43 — 6-30-49.
Kepner, William E., 4-27-43 — USAF
Key, William S., 6-11-40 — ?
Kibler, A. Franklin 11-2-44 — 6-30-52.
King, Campbell, 5-1-32 — 7-31-33.
King, Edward P., Jr. 12-18-41 — 11-30-46.

Kirk, Norman T., 6-1-43 — 7-31-47.
Klein, John A., 4-1-49 — 1231-56.
Knerr, Hugh J., 3-2-44 — USAF
Knight, Harry E., 1-1-37 — 5-31-38.
Kobbe', William A., 1-19-04 — 1-20-04.
Kramer, Herman F., 3-17-43 — 12-31-46.
Kraus, Walter F., 3-16-45 — 4-30-46.
Kreger, Edward A., 11-16-28 — 2-28-31.
Landrum, Eugene M., 3-13-43 — 2-28-51.
Larson, Westside T., 11-3-43 — 6-30-46.
Lauer, Walter E., 1-15-44 — 3-31-46.
Lawton, Kirke B., 10-28-43 — 8-31-54.
Lawton, Samuel T., 1-12-41 — ?
Lee, Jesse M., 9-18-06 — 1-2-07.
Lehman, Raymond G., 6-26-43 — 8-31-45.
LeMay, Curtis E., 3-2-44 — USAF
Lerch, Archer L., 5-31-44 — 9-11-47.
Lewis, Edward M., 6-26-18 — 12-10-27.
Lieber, Albert C., 4-1-49 — 11-9-54.
Lincoln, Rush B., 7-11-41 — 8-31-44.
Livesay, William G., 11-9-42 — 6-30-50.
Love, Walter D., 1-24-48 — 4-30-54.
Lynd, William E., 9-17-43 — 12-31-46.
MacDonald, John C., 4-1-49 — 1-31-57.

MacMorland, Edward E., 5-6-48 — 7-31-52.
Macon, Robert C., 9-19-44 — 7-31-52.
Maddocks, Ray T., 11-6-44 — 6-30-51.
Magee, James C., 5-31-43 — 10-31-43.
Magruder, Bruce 10-1-40 — 5-31-46.
Mahin, Frank C., 5-24-42 — 7-24-42.
Maris, Ward H., 5-1-48 — 11-30-52.
Marquat, William F., 1-27-43 — 9-30-55.
Marshall, Richard J., 8-6-42 — 11-30-46.
Martin, Clarence A., 11-10-44 — 7-31-47.
Martin, Frederick L., 10-1-40 — 7-31-44.
Martin, Joseph I., 9-9-45 — 11-30-55.
Matejka, Jerry V., 3-31-43 — 10-31-55.
Mauborgne, Joseph A., ? — 9-31-41.
Maun, William A., 9-5-17 — ?
McCaskey, William S., 4-15-07 — 10-2-07.
McClelland, Harold L., 6-3-45 — USAF
McClure, Robert B., 4-24-43 — 5-31-54.
McDonald, George C., 7-5-46 — USAF
McFadyen, Bernice M., 6-12-44 — 7-23-54.
McKee, John L., 11-15-43 — 4-30-53.
McKinley, James F., 2-2-33 — 10-31-35.
McMullin, Clements 4-29-43 — USAF
Merriam, Henry C., 5-4-98 — 11-13-01.
Meyer, George R., 3-12-43 — 8-31-46.
Meyers, Bennett E., 2-22-44 — 8-31-45.
Middleswart, William H., 4-12-43 — 2-28-54.
Milburn, Bryan L., 6-11-44 — 11-30-56.
Miller, Fred W., 10-27-42 — 6-30-44.
Miller, Lester T., 6-25-43 — 8-31-46.
Miller, Luther D., 12-20-45 — 11-30-49.
Milliken, John 7-16-41 — 2-29-48.
Mood, Orlando C., 5-24-50 — 5-2-53.
Moore, Cecil R., 3-1-44 — 10-31-46.
Moore, George F., 12-24-41 — 7-31-49.
Noble, Robert E., 8-21-19 — 2-8-25.
Nold, George J., 1-30-44 — 7-31-55.
Noyes, Edward A., 9-6-45 — 4-30-53.
O'Donnell, Emmett 2-2-47 — USAF
Old, William D., 7-8-46 — USAF
O'Reilly, Robert M., 1-14-09 — 1-14-09.
O'Ryan, John F., 8-5-17 — ?
Osterhaus, Peter J., 7-23-04 — 3-17-05.
Parker, Edwin P., 6-1-42 — 1-31-53.
Parker George M., Jr. 12-18-41 — 9-30-46.
Parker, roy H., 8-2-49 — 5-31-52.
Parsons, James K., 6-1-36 — 2-28-41.
Partridge, Frank H., 8-13-47 — 12-31-53.
Patch, Joseph d., 5-24-42 — 12-31-45.
Patrick, Edwin D., 9-5-44 — 3-15-45.
Persons, John C., 11-12-40 — ?
Persons, Wilton B., 11-9-44 — 6-30-49.
Pierson, Albert 11-25-43.
Porter, Ray E., 11-13-42 — 6-30-53.
Porter, William N., 5-1-41 — 3-31-46.

Powell, Clifford R., 4-27-40.
Powers, Edward M., 6-7-40 — ?
Quesada, Elwood R., 4-28-44 — USAF
Quinton, Alfred B., Jr. 10-20-44 — 8-31-52.
Randall, George M., 6-19-05 — 10-8-05.
Randolph, Wallace F., 1-22-04 — 1-23-04.
Ransom, Paul L., 8-9-42 — 5-31-48.
Rawlings, Edwin W., 2-3-47 — USAF
Reckford, Milton A., 7-29-40 — ?
Reed, Walter L., 12-1-35 — 4-30-40.
Reichelderfer, Harry 6-19-48 — 11-30-56.
Reynolds, Charles R., 6-1-35 — 9-30-39.
Reynolds, Russel B., 12-7-44 — 8-31-49.
Rice, George W., 5-8-48 — 10-31-52.
Rice, John K., 10-15-43 — 1-31-53.
Rickard, Roy V., 3-11-49 — 10-30-51.
Rogers, Harry L., 7-22-18 — 8-27-22.
Rooks, Lowell W., 6-3-43 — 12-31-45.
Rose, Maurice 9-5-44 — 3-30-45.
Rose, William C., 9-14-45 — 10-31-46.
Ruffner, David L.,. 11-21-43 — 6-30-53.
Rumbough, William S., 5-24-44 — 5-31-46.
Russell, Henry D., 3-30-40 — ?
Rutledge, Paul W., 11-24-43 — 4-30-56.
Ryan, Cornelius E., 10-3-47 — 6-30-57.
Saltzman, Charles McK., 1-1-24 — 1-8-28.
Sanger, Joseph P., 1-20-04 — 1-21-04.
Sawbridge, Ben M., 8-8-44 — 7-31-52.
Schwan, Theodore 8-29-16 — 8-29-16.
Shambora, William E., 6-8-44 —
Shaw, Franklin P., 8-8-49 — 12-31-53.
Shea, George D., 8-12-43 — 1-31-53.
Sheetz, Josef R., 7-19-49 — 8-31-50.
Shepard, Whitfield P., 8-24-43 — 1-31-56.
Shoe, Robert O., 3-10-49 — 3-31-51.
Sloan, John E., 5-20-42 — 10-31-46.
Smith, Cyrus K., 9-3-44 — ?
Smith, John P., 4-2-41 — 11-30-42.
Smith, Ralph C., 10-26-42 — 10-31-46.
Snyder, Howard McC. (Ret), 11-3-43 —
Soule, Robert H., 3-15-49 — 1-26-52.
Standlee, Earle 10-2-47 — 4-30-57.
Stayer, Morrison C., 11-3-43 — 7-31-46.
Steele, Harry L., 1-21-35 — 3-31-36.
Story, John P., 6-17-05 — 6-19-05.
Story, Walter P., 8-23-40.
Streett, St. Clair, 12-4-42 — USAF
Streit, Paul H., 9-15-43 — 3-31-53.
Stroh, Donald A., 8-24-44 — 11-30-47.
Sumner, Samuel S., 9-7-98 — 2-6-06.
Sverdrup, Leif J., 1-5-45 — ?
Sweeney, Walter C., 12-8-39 — 11-30-40.
Terrell, Henry, Jr. 2-15-42 — 4-30-46.
Thorson, Truman C., 11-5-43 — 1-31-53.
Tinker, Clarence L., 6-14-42 — 6-7-43.
Truesdell, Karl 10-1-40 — 4-30-46.
Truman, Ralph E., 10-3-40 — ?
Twaddle, Harry L., 5-28-42 — 6-30-48.
Van Deman, Ralph 5-27-29 — 9-3-29.
Van Houten, John G., 4-1-49 —
Vaughan, Harry B., Jr. 11-14-44 — 10-31-46.
Wade, James E., 5-4-98 — 4-14-07.
Waitt, Alden H., 11-29-45 — 9-30-49.
Walker, Fred L., 1-15-42 — 4-30-46.
Weaver, Erasmus, M., 7-6-16 — 5-23-18.
Webster, Robert M., 11-9-44 — USAF
Weston, John F., 10-8-05 — 11-13-09.
Weyland, Otto P., 1-5-45 — USAF
Wheaton, Lloyd 6-18-00 — 7-15-02.
White, Miller G., 6-25-43 — ?
Whitlock, Lester J., 3-21-43 — 7-31-54.
Willis, John M., 1-24-48 — 11-30-48.
Willoughby, Charles A., 4-12-45 — 8-31-51.
Wilson, Arthur H., 1-13-44 — 3-31-46.
Wilson, William H., 10-1-38 — 12-31-41.
Wing, Leonard F., 9-14-43 — ?
Winship, Blanton 6-25-39 — ?
Witsell, Edward F., 7-2-45 — 6-30-51.
Wolfe, Kenneth B., 11-8-44 — USAF
Wood, Leonard 12-7-1898 — 10-5-21.

Wood, Walter A., Jr. 8-7-44 — 9-30-46.
Wooten, Ralph H., 5-25-44 — USAF
Wotherspoon, William W., 5-12-12 — 11-16-14.
Wright, Edwin K., 7-31-44 — 9-30-55.
Wurtsmith, Paul B., 3-19-45 — 9-13-46.
York, John Y., Jr. 11-12-44 — 1-31-46.

BRIGADIER GENERAL

Abbott, Frederic V., 4-5-17 — ?
Abbott, Oscar B., 4-26-43 — 10-31-50.
Abraham, Clyde R., 10-1-40 — 7-31-43.
Adams, Claude M., 3-17-43 — 7-31-44.
Adams, Clayton S., 9-8-42 — ?
Adams, Henry H., 4-11-05 — 4-11-05.
Agee, Walter R., 6-16-45 — USAF
Alden, Charles H., 4-23-04 — 4-23-04.
Alexander, Clyde C., 2-3-43 — 7-31-52.
Alfonte, James R., 6-20-42 — 8-31-46.
Allen, Harvey C., 10-1-40 — 8-31-46.
Allen, Hubert A., 8-5-17 — ?
Althaus, Kenneth G., 6-24-43 — 3-31-46.
Anderson, Harry R., 4-5-07 — 4-5-07.
Anderson, Wilhelm A., 10-26-42 — 8-31-45.
Ankcorn, Charles M., 9-15-43 — 12-31-44.
Appleton, John A., 11-13-44 — ?
Arms, Thomas S., 4-27-43 — 9-30-46.
Armstrong, Frank A., Jr. 2-8-43 — USAF
Armstrong, Harry G., 4-27-48 — USAF
Arnold, Calvert P., 2-13-45 — 10-31-49.
Arnolds, Milton W., 6-15-45 — 4-30-46.
Arthur, William H., 8-5-17 — 12-2-18.
] Arrowsmith, John C., 6-25-43 — 5-32-53.
Atkinson, Joseph H., 12-25-42 — USAF
Atterbury, W.W., 8-5-17 — ?
Atwood, Edwin B., 8-2-03 — 8-3-03.
Augur, Wayland B., 12-3-42 — 7-31-53.
Auman, William 4-6-02 — 5-10-02.
Auton, Jesse 3-2-44 — USAF
Ayers, Leonard P., ? — ?
Babcock, Franklin 9-2-44 — 8-31-46.
Babcock, John B., 6-3-1898 — 8-8-03.
Backus, Edward N., 8-17-44 — USAF
Baehr, Carl A., 12-15-41 — 6-30-46.
Bailey, Clarence M., 4-23-04 — 4-23-04.
Baily, Elisha I., 4-23-04 — 4-23-04.
Baird, George W., 2-19-03 — 2-20-03.
Baird, Harry H., 11-9-44 — 3-31-50.
Baker, Frayne 4-5-41 — ?
Baldwin, Frank D., 6-9-02 — 6-26-06.
Baldwin, Theodore A., 4-19-03 — 4-20-03.
Balmer, Jesmond D., 2-22-47 — 1-31-53.
Bamford, Frank E., 8-8-18 — 11-1-21.
Banfill, Charles Y., 2-22-44 — USAF
Barber, Charles W., 8-5-17 — 8-28-18.
Barber, Edward 9-20-43 — ?
Barber, Henry A., 9-17-43 — 12-31-49.
Barcus, Glenn O., 5-3-43 — USAF
Barker, John DeF., 5-25-44 — USAF
Barker, Harold R., 11-7-40 — ?
Barnes, Harold A., 4-27-43 — 5-31-46.
Barnett, James W., 5-23-42 — 6-30-49.
Barnwell, Charles H., Jr. 11-8-44 — 6-30-52.
Barr, Thomas F., 5-21-01 — 5-22-01.
Barron, William A., Jr. 11-16-44 — ?
Bastion, Joseph E., 6-23-43 — 2-28-47.
Battley, Joseph F., 2-22-44 — 7-31-47.
Baylis, James E., 2-18-42 — 10-31-47.
Beach, Maurice M., 4-2-45 — ?
Beacham, Joseph W., Jr. 6-13-40 — 4-30-38.
Beaman, Bartlett 2-29-44 — ?
Beau, Lucas V., Jr. 4-27-43 — USAF
Beck, Clyde McK., 9-7-45 — 6-30-47.
Beebe, Eugene H., 11-11-43 — 11-30-45.
Beebe, Lewis C., 3-17-42 — 9-30-50.
Beebe, Royden E., 5-20-42 — 6-30-42.
Bell, James M., 1-20-00 — 10-1-01.
Bell, Marcus B., 12-3-42 — 10-31-51.
Benham, Daniel W., 4-23-04 — 4-23-04.
Bennett, John B., 10-1-18 — 9-16-25.
Berman, Morris 9-15-43 — 11-11-45.

Berry, Kearie L., 1-21-46 — 6-30-47.
Betts, Edward C., 9-15-43 — 5-6-46.
Betts, Thomas J., 11-3-43 — 7-31-53.
Beverley, George H., 1-25-43 — USAF
Beyette, Hubert W., 9-16-43 — 10-31-46.
Bickelhaupt, Carroll O., 8-7-44 — ?
Biddle, James 4-23-04 — 4-23-04.
Bird, Charles 1-3-01 — 6-17-02.
Birks, Hammond D., 1-7-45 — 11-30-46.
Birmingham, Henry P., 8-5-17 — 3-15-18.
Bisbee, William H., 10-2-01 — 10-1-02.
Bjornstad, Alfred W., 6-26-18 — 8-31-28.
Black, Frederick H., 9-19-42 — 6-30-50.
Black, Garland C., 1-8-45 — 9-30-46.
Blackburn, Thomas W., 12-4-42 — ?
Blackmore, Philip G., 9-16-44 — 1-31-50.
Blakelock, David H., 1-5-45 — 6-30-50.
Bledsoe, William P., 6-24-43 — 6-30-46.
Blesse, Frederick A., 12-4-42 — 10-31-47.
Blount, Roy E., 1-15-44 — 10-31-47.
Boatwright, Walter P., 10-25-40 — 2-28-46.
Boardman, Charles R., 8-5-17 — ?
Bohn, John J., 7-25-42 — 2-28-45.
Boone, Milton O., 1-27-44 — 5-31-48.
Borum, Fred S., 9-16-42 — USAF
Boudinot, Truman E., 9-4-44 — 12-21-45.
Bowen, Charles F., 9-22-40 — ?
Bowman, Alpheus H., 8-12-03 — 8-13-03.
Bowman, Harwood C., 5-28-45 — 6-30-48.
Boyd, Leonard R., 5-23-42 — 11-30-51.
Brach, William L., 8-5-17 — ?
Bradley, Alfred E., 8-5-17 — ?
Brady, Francis M., 2-17-42 — USAF
Brainard, David L., 8-5-17 — 7-25-18.
Bruan, Gustav J., Jr. 1-8-45 — 3-17-45.
Breckinridge, Joseph C., 5-4-1898 — 4-12-03.
Bresnahan, Thomas F., 10-7-43 — 3-31-48.
Brett, Sereno E., 2-15-42 — 10-31-43.
Briggs, Raymond W., ? — 6-30-46.
Brink, Francis G., 4-25-47 — 6-24-52.
Brittingham, James F., 5-24-42 — 6-30-54.
Brock, Ronald C., 3-12-43 — ?
Brooke, Roger 1-29-38 — 12-18-40.
Brougher, William E., 12-24-41 — 2-28-49.
Brown, Ames T., 9-16-40 — ?
Brown, Charles C., 9-4-44 — 3-31-47.
Brown, Everett E., 2-21-44 — 12-31-49.
Browne, Frederick W., 1-28-42 — 11-30-38.
Browning, Albert J., 6-25-43 — ?
Bruton, Philip G., 5-25-44 — 9-30 —46.
Bubb, John W., 4-3-06 — 4-26-07.
Buchanan, James A., 4-14-05 — 5-31-06.
Bucher, Oliver B., 6-24-43 — ?
Bullis, John L., 4-13-05 — 4-14-05.
Burbank, James B., 4-23-04 — 4-23-04.

Burnell, Ray L., 3-17-45 — 2-29-48.
Burns, Robert W., 6-18-45 — USAF
Burpee, Clarence L., 2-24-44 —
Burrows, Paul E., 9-17-43 — ?
Burt, Andrew S., 5-4-1898 — 4-15-02.
Burt, Ernest H., 12-1-42 — 10-31-46.
Burt, William H., 8-8-18 — ?
Burwell, Harvey S., 9-9-42 — 2-29-44.
Buzzell, Reginald W., 7-23-42 — ?
Byrne, Charles C., 4-23-04 — 4-23-04.
Caffey, Benjamin F., Jr. 11-21-42 — 3-31-50.
Califf, Joseph M., 3-24-06 — 3-28-06.
Callender, George R., 3-16-45 — 11-30-46.
Camp, Thomas J., 3-11-42 — 10-31-46.
Campbell, Arthur G., 10-25-40 — 8-31-44.
Campbell, William A., 4-18-42 — 2-29-49.
Campbell, William F., 11-8-44 — 6-30-49.
Candee, Robert C., 6-20-42 — USAF
Carr, Camillo C.C., 8-17-03 — 3-3-06.
Carrington, Gordon DeL., 2-16-42 — 8-31-44.
Carroll, Franklin O., 10-31-42 — USAF
Carroll, Henry 6-8-1898 — 5-6-1899.
Carroll, Percy J., 6-23-43 — 9-30-46.
Carter, Ellerbe W., 3-5-40 — ?
Carter, Warren R., 10-31-42 — USAF

Case, Homer 12-3-42 — 8-31-54.
Castner, Joseph C., 4-12-18 — 11-30-33.
Catlin, Isaac S., 4-23-04 — 4-23-04.
Caziarc, Louis V., 10-1-06 — 10-1-06.
Chance, Jesse C., 8-14-03 — 8-15-03.
Chappell, Sidney L., 9-5-45 — 9-30-46.
Chavin, Raphael S., 12-1-42 — 12-31-52.
Cheshire, Godfrey 5-10-41 — ?
Chickering, William E., 1-16-44 — 2-28-46.
Clark, Frank S., 10-1-40 — 10-31-46.
Clark, Harold L., 9-17-43 — 7-31-46.
Clark, Harvey C., 4-5-17 — ?
Clark, John M., 10-31-42 — 9-30-46.
Clark, Ray H., 2-27-44 — ?
Clarke, Carter W., 11-10-44 — 8-31-54.
Clarkson, Herbert S., 9-14-43 — 5-31-46.
Cleary, Peter J.A., 8-6-03 — 8-7-03.
Cleary, William D., 9-6-45 — 7-31-46.
Clemens, Paul B., 12-22-39 — ?
Clewell, Edgar L., 8-1-42 — 11-30-46.
Clous, John W., 9-21-1898 — 5-24-01.
Coane, Ralph W., 3-17-41 — ?
Coates, Edwin M., 4-23-04 — 4-23-04.
Cobbs, Nicholas H., 5-24-44 — 8-31-46.
Coburn, Henry C., Jr. 4-3-41 — 8-31-43.
Cochran, William B., 10-1-18 — 11-30-22.
Cole, Charles H., 8-15-17 — ?
Cole, Frank L., 4-28-48 — 6-30-50.
Colladay, Edgar B., 10-1-40 — 8-31-46.
Collier, John J., 8-12-44 — ?
Collier, William A., 11-18-44 — 8-31-54.
Collins, Leroy P., 1-29-41 — 3-31-45.
Collins, Vivian B., 9-1-40 — ?
Comba, Richard 9-7-1898 — 7-11-01.
Compere, Ebenezer L., 12-24-40 — ?
Conelly, Ludwig S., 3-24-40 — ?
Connell, Carl W., 6-15-42 — USAF
Connell, Samuel M., 2-28-42 — 11-30-46.
Cook, Henry C., 4-23-04 — 4-23-04.
Cooke, Elliott D., 4-2-43 — 10-31-50.
Cooke, Lorenzo W., 3-9-06 — 3-24-06.
Cooloidge, Charles A., 8-8-03 — 8-9-03.
Cooney, Michael 4-23-04 — 4-23-04.
Cooper, Charles L., 8-16-03 — 8-17-03.
Copeland, John E., 9-10-42 — 4-30-46.
Corliss, Augustus W., 4-23-04 — 4-23-04.
Cort, Hugh 5-1-45 — 8-31-54.
Coulter, Richard 8-15-17 — ?
Coupland, Richard c., 3-18-43 — USAF
Covell, Louis C., 8-5-17 — ?
Cox, Albert L., 2-20-41 — ?
Cox, Richard F., 10-1-40 — 2-29-44.
Coxe, Frank M., 1-23-04 — 1-24-04.
Crabb, Jarred V., 6-5-44 — USAF
Craig, Charles F., 10-30-42 — 9-30-55.
Craig, Daniel F., 10-1-18 — ?
Craigie, David J., 8-12-03 — 8-13-03.
Crawford, Alden R., 11-9-43 — USAF
Crawford, Medorem 1-3-08 — 1-27-08.
Crowell, Evans R., 8-8-44 — 8-31-54.
Culbertson, Albert L., 1-25-41 — ?
Curtis, James W., 4-26-43 — 10-31-48.
Cushman, Horace O., 10-30-42 — 1-31-53.
Cutler, Elliott c., 6-7-45 — ?
Cutler, Stuart 9-15-43 — 11-30-46.
Daggett, Aaron S., 9-21-1898 — 3-2-01.
Dalton, Albert C., 10-1-18 — 7-8-26.
Daly, Cornelius M., 3-15-43 — 11-30-46.
Danforth, Edward C.B., Jr. 1-3-45 — ?
Danielson, Wilmot A., 4-6-41 — 7-31-6.
Darnall, Carl R., 12-5-29 — 12-31-31.
Dart, Raymond O., 4-30-48 — 7-31-50.
Daugherty, Lester A., 6-24-43 — 9-30-51.
Davis, Benjamin O., 10-25-40 — 7-31-41.
Davis, Charles L., 1-26-03 — 2-10-03.
Davis, George A., 3-17-43 — 2-28-46.
Davis, Leonard L., 1-17-44 — 10-31-48.
Davis, Thomas J., 12-4-42 — 10-31-46.

Davison, F. Trubee 6-3-45 — ?
Dawes, Charles G., 8-8-18 — ?
Dean, Herbert R., 4-19-40 — ?
Dear, William R., 4-4-41 — 8-31-46.
DeBevoise, Charles I., 10-1-18 — ?
DeFord, Earl H., 9-17-43 — ?
Delaney, Matthew A., 1-1-32 — 11-30-35.
DeRussy, Isaac D., 4-1-02 — 4-15-02.
Denton, Frank R., 6-8-45 — ?
Devine, James G., 3-17-43 — 8-31-54.
DeVoe, Ralph G., 5-24-44 — 9-30-46.
Devore, Daniel B., 8-5-17 — 4-5-22.
DeWitt, Calvin 8-9-03 — 8-10-03.
Dewitt, Wallace 10-1-40 — 6-30-42.
Diller, LeGrande A., 1-9-45 — 9-30-54.
Dimmick, Eugene D., 4-23-04 — 4-23-04.
Disque, Brice P., 10-1-18 — ?
Ditto, Rollo C., 9-29-41 — 4-30-46.
Dodge, Francis S., 1-23-04 — 9-11-06.
Donnelly, Arthur B., 8-5-17 — ?
Donnelly, Edward T., 4-12-18 — 6-24-26.
Dooling, Henry C., 5-25-44 — 7-31-47.
Doolittle, James H., ? — 7-22-46.
Doran, Charles R., 3-17-43 — 5-31-48.
Doriot, Georges F., 1-11-45 — ?

Dougherty, William E., 1-24-04 — 1-25-04.
Downey, George F., 3-28-21 — 3-7-23.
Draper, William H., Jr. 1-1-45 — ?
Drewry, Guy H., 9-10-42 — 8-31-46.
Dudley, Nathan A.M., 4-23-04 — 4-23-04.
Duggan, Walter T., 6-26-06 — 4-11-07.
Duke, James T., 3-17-43 — 6-30-53.
Duncan, Asa N., 2-26-42 — 11-17-43.
Duncan Earley E.W., 12-2-42 — USAF
Duncan, Joswph W., 1-4-11 — 5-14-12.
Eagan, Charles P., 5-3-1898 — 12-6-1900.
Eager, John M., 9-15-43 — 3-31-46.
Easley, Claudius M., 7-27-42 — 6-19-45.
Easley, Roy W., 7-16-41 — ?
Easterbrook, Arthur E., (Ret) 6-29-43 —
8-21-46.
Eastwood, Harold E., 11-8-44 — 7-31-52.
Edward, Harvey 6-4-45 — ?
Edwards, Jeber L., 2-20-41 — ?
Egan, John F., 3-1-44 — 9-30-46.
Egleston, Nathaniel H., 9-23-40.
Elder, Eugene V., 10-13-50 — 4-30-52.
Elkins, Stephen B., ? — 9-30-54.
Emerson, Gouverneur V., 4-27-48 — 1-31-49.
Emery, Ambrose E., 10-31-41 — 2-20-44.
English, Paul X., 1-30-42 — 7-31-46.
Erickson, Sidney 4-26-43 — 10-31-46.
Estabrook, Merrick G., Jr. 9-17-43 — 8-31-44.
Estes, George H., 1-2-29 — 12-31-36.
Evans, Henry C., 7-22-42 — ?
Eversberg, Eugene A., ? — ?
Ewers, Ezra P., 7-12-1898 — 4-13-01.
Faith, Don C., 12-3-42 — 10-31-48.
Fair, Ford L., 11-17-44 — ?
Farman, Ivan L., 4-2-45 — USAF
Farmer, Archie A., 7-26-42 — 3-31-46.
Farrell, Thomas F., 1-17-44 — ?
Farthing, William E., 4-19-42 — USAF
Farrell, William E., 4-19-42 — USAF
Fenn, Clarence C., 1-7-45 — 2-28-50.
Ferrin, Charles S., 3-30-47 — 11-30-52.
Fielder, Kendall J., 11-8-44 — 7-31-53.
Finney, John M.T., 10-1-18 — ?
Fisher, Henry C., 10-11-29 — 5-31-31.
Fitch, Burdette M., 4-27-47 — 7-31-53.
Fitzgerald, Shepler W., 4-16-42 — USAF
Fleming, Raymond H., 2-11-40 — ?
Flood, William J., 2-6-43 — 5-31-46.
Foote, Morris C., 2-18-03 — 2-19-03.
Forbes, Theodore F., 8-14-03 — 8-15-03.
Forster, George J., 9-14-42 — 4-30-51.
Fortier, Louis J., 8-1-42 — 12-31-50.
Forwood, William H., 6-8-02 — 9-7-02.
Foster, David J., 8-5-17 — ?
Foster, George B., Jr. 5-24-44 — 8-31-46.

813

Foster, Ivan L., 9-14-42 — 7-31-48.
Fox, Leon A., 3-16-43 — 4-30-46.
Franks, John B., 1-8-45 — 11-13-46.
Frazier, Thomas A., 9-2-40 — ?
Freeman, Henry B., 12-16-01 — 1-17-01.
French, Charles A., 11-3-43 — 2-29-48.
Fritch, Donald F., 1-19-45 — USAF
Fritz, Lawrence C., 6-6-44 — ?
Fuller, Howard E., 10-27-42 — ?
Funk, Arnold J., 1-24-42 — 5-31-52.
Furey, John V., 2-24-03 — 2-25-03.
Gaffney, Dale V., 9-17-43 — ?
Gaither, Charles D., 7-25-17 — ?
Galloway, Floyd E., 10-20-42 — USAF
Garrett, Robert C., 10-25-40 — 6-30-46.
George, Charles P., 4-5-41 — 10-31-45.
George, Harold H., 1-25-42 — 4-30-42.
Gerhardt, John K., 1-23-45 — USAF
Gerow, Lee S., 3-15-43 — 7-31-49.
Gibbons, Lloyd H., 3-30-45 — 4-7-45.
Gibson, Herbert D., 8-1-42 — 9-30-46.
Gilmore, John C., 5-27-1898 — 4-18-01.
Girard, Alfred C., 4-6-05 — 4-7-05.
Glancy, Alfred R., 9-20-42 — ?
Gleman, James D., 10-1-18 — ?
Glenn, Charles R., 9-17-43 — ?
Glenn, Edgar E., 12-4-42 — ?
Glennan, James D., 2-9-25 — 3-2-26.
Goldthwaire, Raplh H., 4-25-43 — 5-31-46.
Goodlae, Greenleaf A., 2-23-03 — 2-24-03.
Goodrich, Donald R., 2-22-44 — 7-12-45.
Gorder, Alexander O., 2-15-43 — 5-31-48.
Gorden, David S., 4-23-04 — 4-23-04.
Goss, Wentworth 3-26-45 — USAF
Grahl, Charles H., 6-11-40 — ?
Gravely, William S., 1-17-44 — 9-30-45.
Graves, Davis D., 1-21-44 — 2-8-44.
Gray, Carl R., R. 6-27-42 — ?
] Grayson, Thomas J., 8-30-40 — ?
Greenbaum, Edward S., 3-15-43 — ?
Greenleaf, Charles R., 4-23-04 — 4-23-04.
Greer, Frank U., 6-3-43 — 8-31-46.
Grice, Letcher O., 8-25-48 — 7-31-53.
Grime, George S., 8-12-07 — 8-12-07.
Groesback, Stephen W., 4-16-03 — 4-17-03.
Grower, Roy W., 11-10-44 — 3-31-46.
Gruber, William R., 2-16-42 — 8-31-46.
Guerre, Louis F., 4-13-40 — 8-13-46.
Guest, Wesley T., 3-11-49 —
Gunner, Matthew J., 11-8-44 — 10-31-46.
Guthner, William E., 5-16-40 — ?
Hackett, Frank D., 4-16-42 — ?
Hadden, Julian B., 9-18-42 — 2-28-46.
Hagins, William A., 2-13-45 — 4-30-48.
Haines, Oliver L., 11-3-43 — 8-31-45.
Halloran, George M., 10-27-42 — 7-31-48.
Hamblen, Archelaus L., 12-1-42 — 7-31-54.
Hand, Daniel W., 10-1-18 — ?
Handwek, Morris C., 8-1-42 — 2-28-51.
Haney, Harold 1-7-45 — 7-31-53.
Hansell, Haywood S., Jr. 8-10-42 — 12-31-46.
Harback, Abram A., 5-16-02 — 5-28-02.
Hardaway, Robert M., 9-5-45 — 8-31-48.
Hardin, Thomas O., 1-21-44 — ?
Hardy, David P., 11-5-41 — ?
Hardy, Roswell E., 5-24-42 — 6-30-51.

Hargreaves, John M., 4-27-48 — USAF
Harris, Charles S., 3-15-42 — 7-31-53.
Harris, Harold R., 6-9-45 — ?
Harris, Ray G., 2-4-43 — USAF
Harris, Walter A., 8-5-17 — ?
Hart, W. Lee 3-16-45 — 1-31-45.
Hartman, George E., 4-26-43 — 4-30-54.
Hartmen, Charles D., 8-1-40 — 4-39-43.
Hartshorn, Edwin S., 12-26-35 — 11-30-38.
Hartsuff, Albert 4-23-04.
Harvey, William A., 8-5-17 — ?
Haskell, Harry L., 1-20-04 — 1-31-04.
Haskin, William L., 7-28-03 — 7-29-03.
Hathaway, Forrest H., 1-20-04 — 1-21-04.

Hauseman, David N., 9-4-44 — 9-30-46.
Hawkins, Sion B., 5-20-41 — ?
Hayes, Edward M., 1-15-03 — 1-26-03.
Hayes, Wolcott P., 10-29-42 — 12-31-45.
Haynes, Caleb V., 9-5-42 — USAF
Haynes, Loyal M., 4-20-47 — 7-31-54.
Head, John F., 4-23-04 — 4-23 —4.
Heard, R. Townsend 1-5-45 — 11-30-46.
Hedrick, Lawrence H., 6-19-42 — 11-30-42.
Heflebower, Roy C., 12-15-41 — 8-31-46.
Heger, Anthony 4-23-04 — 4-23-04.
Heiss, Gerson K., 1-21-46 — 9-30-54.
Henning, Frank A., J. 5-29-44 — 7-31-54.
Henninger, Guy 9-8-40 — ?
Hennisee, Argalus G., 4-23-04 — 4-23-04.
Herrick, Hugh N., 11-3-43 — 6-31-41.
Hesketh, William 8-17-42 — 6-30-48.
Hester, Hugh B., 11-10-44 — 8-31-51.
Hewitt, Leland R., 2-4-43 — 3-31-46.
Hickey, Daniel W., Jr. 12-3-42 — 6-30-54.
Hill, Henry R., 7-25-17 — ?
Hill, Milton A., 3-18-45 — 10-31-46.
Hill, Robert B., 5-31-49 — 11-30-50.
Hillman, Charles C., 1-29-42 — 1-31-47.
Hines, Frank T., 4-18-18 — 5-31-44.
Hineman, Dale D., 10-31-41 — 11-30-44.
Hoag, Earl S., 6-25-43 — USAF
Hobbs, Charles W., 4-12-05 — 4-13-05.
Holland, Thomas L., 3-13-43 — ?
Hollar, Gorden C., 12-28-40 — ?
Holmes, Henry B., Jr. 2-16-42 — 8-31-47.
Hood, Charles C., 10-18-02 — 11-25-02.
Hood, Reuben C., Jr. 11-9-43 — USAF
Hooten, Mott 4-15-02 — 4-16-02.
Hoover, Hubert D., 2-27-47 — 2-29-48.
Hopkins, Frederick M., Jr. 9-18-42 — USAF
Hopping, Andrew D., 4-28-47 –– 1-11-51.
Hornsby, Aubrey 2-4-43 — USAF
Horton, William E.. 8-2-27 — 2-1-29.
Hospital, Ralph 2-16-42 — 1-31-51.
Hough, Alfred L., 4-23-04 — 4-23-04.
Hovey, Burton M., Jr. 9-9-44 — USAF
Howe, William F., 11-24-40 — ?
Hoyt, Ross G., 6-24-43 — 4-30-44.
Hubbell, Henry W., 5-20-05 — 5-20-05.
Hueper, Remi P., 9-10-42 — 8-31-46.
Huggins, Eli L., 2-22-03 — 2-23-02.
Hughes, Robert P., 4-1-02 — 4-11-03.
Hulen, John A., 8-5-17 — ?
Humphrey, Evans H., 2-7-35 — 3-31-39.
Hunt, Ora E., 4-12-17 — 9-2-23.
Hurley, Patrick J., 7-24-42 — ?
Hutchings, Henry 8-5-17 — ?
Hutchinson, Donald R., 6-8-44 — USAF
Hutchinson, David W., 4-1-45 — USAF
Hutchinson, Joseph C., 11-25-40 — ?
Hyde, James F.C., 9-12-42 — 8-7-44.
Hyde, John McE., 7-9-04 — 7-10-04.
Ignico, Robert V., 9-15-42 — USAF
Immee, Ralph M., 1-13-44 — ?
Irwin, Bernard J.D., 4-23-04 — 4-23-04.
Irwin, Constant A., 3-15-43 — 3-31-44.
Isreal, Robert S., Jr. 8-17-44 — ?
Jacobs, Fenton S., 11-8-44 — 4-30-52.
Jacobs, Joshua W., 6-25-04 — 6-25-04.
Jamison, Charles C., 10-1-18 — 1-3-19.
Jay, Henry D., ? — 9-30-48.
Jeffe, Ephraim F., 6-2-44 — ?
Jocelyn, Stephen P., 6-16-06 — 3-1-07.
Johnson, Bernhard A., 1-21-45 — ?
Johnson, Evan M., 8-5-17 — ?
Johnson, Harry A., 12-4-42 — USAF
Johnson, James J., 1-2-45 — ?
Johnson, Neal C., 10-15-42 — 1-31-52.
Johnson, Robert W., 4-27-43 — ?
Johnson, William D., 10-1-18 — ?
Johnston, Paul W., 9-3-44 — ?
Jones, Aaron E., 10-31-42 — 5-31-46.
Jones, Edwin W., 7-22-42 — ?
Jones, Thomas H., 7-10-41 — 11-30-46.
Kane, Clarence P., 6-25-43 — 10-31-46.

Karlstad, Charles H., 3-19-45 — 7-31-53.
Kauch, Robert 2-3-43 — USAF
Kean, Jefferson R., 6-26-18 — 6-27-24.
Keefer, Frank R., 2-11-27 — 10-10-29.
Keeler, Maxwell G., 4-10-50 — 11-30-51.
Kelser, Raymond A., 3-9-42 — 1-31-46.
Kennebeck, George R., 4-28-48 — USAF
Kennedy, James M., 3-3-26 — 12-4-29.
Kennedy, John C., 1-8-45 USAF
Kernan, Redmond F., Jr. 1-20-42 —
Kiel, Emil C., 4-27-43 — USAF
Kilbreth, John W., 10-1-18 — 12-15-22.
Kilpatrick, John R., 7-28-42 — ?
Kimball, Amos S., 10-1-02 — 10-2-02.
Kincaid, Alvan C., 2-4-43 — USAF
King, Edgar 10-25-42 — 1-31-46.
King, Henry L.P., 12-3-42 — 6-30-46.
King, Woods 6-3-45 — ?
Kingman, Allen F., 6-20-42 — 5-31-53.
Kline, Jacob 5-27-1898 — 1-23-04.
Knapp, Robert D., 2-20-44 — ?
Koch, Oscar W., ? — 9-30-54.
Koenig, Egmont F., 5-24-44 — 4-30-48.
Krauthoff, Charles R., 10-1-18 — 12-7-22.
Kroner, Hayes A., 5-22-42 — 1-31-47.
Kurtz, Guy O., 8-1-42 — 7-31-53.
Kutschko, Emerick 3-20-45 — 8-31-46.
Lacey, Julius K., 6-4-44 — USAF
Langmead, Edmund C., 5-31-45 — USAF
Lawes, Herbert J., 3-13-43 — 8-31-47.
Lawson, Laurin L., 10-1-18 — 1-28-38.
Lawson, Laurence A., 11-1-42 — 5-31-46.
Layman, Walter G., 5-24-44 — 9-24-44.
Leary, Peter, Jr. 7-7-04 — 7-8-04.
Lebo, Thomas C., 6-22-05 — 6-23-05.

Ledbetter, Louis A., 8-25-40 — ?
Lee, James G.C., 4-23-04 — 4-23-04.
Lee, Raymond E., 10-1-40 — 2-28-46.
Lee, William L., 11-19-44 — ?
Legge, Barnwell R., 5-28-42 — 1-31-48.
Lehner, Charles R., 1-7-45 — 2-28-49.
Lester, James W., 7-16-17 — ?
Lewis, Jpseph H., 4-7-41 — ?
Lieber, G. Norman 1-3-1895 — 5-22-01.
Lincoln, Charles S., 12-1-31 — 10-31-36.
Lincoln, Sumner H., 5-29-02 — 6-9-02.
Lindsay, Richard C., 9-10-44 — USAF
Lindsey, Malcolm F., 11-3-43 — 7-31-51.
Llewellyn, Fred W. (Ret) 7-19-42 — 3-14-44.
Logan, Albert J., 7-15-17 — ?
Longfellow, Newton 10-31-42 — USAF
Longino, Olin R., 1-29-41 — 6-30-45.
Lord, Herbert M., 6-26-18 — 6-30-22.
Lord, Kenneth P., 9-29-41 — 9-30-46.
Lough, Maxon S., 9-29-41 — 8-31-46.
Love, Albert G., 10-1-40 — 8-1-41.
Lovett, Ralph B., 8-3-42 — 2-28-47.
Lowe, Frank E., 7-16-41 — ?
Lowery, Sumter L., Jr. 8-6-40 — ?
Luberoff, George 8-6-41 — 5-31-42.
Ludington, Marshall I., 4-12-03 — 4-13-03.
Luedecke, Alvin R., 8-18-44 — USAF
Lundberg, George G., 9-17-43 — ?
Lyman, Reginald P., ? — 8-31-54.
Lyon, Alfred J., 5-22-42 — 12-1-42.
Lyster, Theodore C., 6-3-18 — 2-28-19.
Mace, Harold L., 11-21-44 — 1-20-46.
MacKelvie, Jay W., 3-14-42 — 9-30-46.
MacNider, Hanford 8-3-42 — ?
Madden, John F., 10-1-18 — 3-31-34.
Maddox, Louis W., 6-4-45 — 8-31-46.
Magruder, David L., 4-23-04 — 4-23-04.
Magruder, Marshall 10-1-40 — 8-31-46.
Mallett, Pierre 2-3-43 — 5-31-50.
Mandell, Harold C., 5-24-44 — 9-30-46.
Manning, Timothy J., 11-21-44 — ?
Maraist, Robert V., 6-2-43 — 2-28-53.
March, William A., 1-19-41 — ?
Marchant, Trelawney E., 3-29-40 — ?
Markey, Alfred C., 3-2-07 — 4-18-07.

Marlin, William L., 7-21-40 — ?
Marriner, Alfred W., 6-25-43 — 4-30-46.
Marshall, Richard C., 6-26-18 — ?
Marston, Morrill W., 4-10-47 — 7-31-53.
Martin, Charles I., 1-21-17 — ?
Matchett, Henry J., 1-9-44 — USAF
Matheny, William A., 11-10-43 — USAF
Matile, Leon A., 8-15-03 — 8-16-03.
Maxwell, Earl 1-19-44 — ?
Mayberry, Hugh T., 10-30-42 — 12-31-52.
Maynard, John B., 4-5-41 — 8-31-44.
McAdams, John P., ? — 6-30-36.
McBride, Allan C, 12-18-41 — 5-9-44.
McCabe, E.R. Warner (Ret) 1-13-44 — 6-30-46.
McCabe, Frederick 10-28-42 — 9-30-47.
McCallam, James A., 1-24-48 — 1-31-53.
McCaw, Walter D., 3-5-19 — 2-10-27.
McChrystal, Arthur J., 2-22-44 — 11-8-46.
McConnell, Frank C., 6-1-47 — 9-30-57.
McCormick, Condon C., 2-20-44 — ?
McCroskey, Samuel L., 6-24-42 — 9-30-50.
McDaniel, Arthur B., 3-27-42 — 12-26-43.
McDaniel, Carl B., 11-10-43 — USAF
McDonald, Robert C., 1-1-45 — 2-28-45.
McDonnell, John C., 10-25-40 — 3-31-43.
McDowell, Rex McK., 1-4-45 — 12-31-48.
McFarland, Andrew J., 5-24-44 — 3-31-47.
McFee, Larry B., 3-1-41 — ?
McGinnis, Harold a., 11-10-44 — ?
McIntyre, Andrew F., 8-11-44 — ?
McIntyre, James D., 9-6-45 — USAF
McKay, Neal H., 12-7-44 — 11-30-48.
McKinley, Edward B., 5-12-43 — 3-31-48.
McMahon, Leo T., 9-17-43 — 2-29-48.
McNaught, Warren H., 6-5-45 — 7-31-51.
McQuillin, Raymond E., 3-10-42 — 2-29-48.
McReynolds. Wilbur R., 11-3-43 — 10-31-47.
McRoberts, Samuel 8-8-18 — ?
McSherry, Frank J., 2-17-42 — 10-31-46.
Means, Lewis M., 9-15-40 — ?
Meloy, Vincent J., 9-17-43 — 4-30-46.
Merriam, Henry C., 5-4-1898 — 11-13-01.

Merrill, Dana T., 12-1-34 — 10-31-40.
Metcalf, Wilder S., 8-5-17 — ?
Metcalfe, Raymond F., 12-15-37 — 5-31-41.
Metzger, Earl H., 2-14-42 — 8-31-49.
Meyer, Vincent 10-31-41 — 12-31-45.
Metzger, Earl H., 2-14-42 — 8-31-49.
Meyer, Vincent 10-31-41 — 12-31-45.
Meyers, Harry F., 1-18-44 — 8-31-54.
Miles, Evan 10-6-1898 — 7-19-1899.
Miller, George A., 6-4-45 — 2-29-48.
Miller, Leland W., 5-24-42 — 5-31-46.
Mills, Samuel M., 6-20-05 — 9-30-06.
Milton, Hugh M. 2d, 6-5-45 — ?
Miltenberger, Butler B., 3-17-45 — ?
Miner, Charles W., 7-29-03 — 7-30-03.
Minton, Hugh C., 1-31-42 — 4-30-46.
Mollison, James A., 11-1-42 — USAF
Montgomery, Edward 10-7-43 — 8-31-49.
Moore, Aubrey L., 2-27-44 — USAF
Moore, Francis 2-25-03 — 4-6-05.
Moore, James M., 4-23-04 — 4-23-04.
Moran, Richard B., 12-2-42 — 4-30-50.
Morgan, Hugh J., 12-4-42 — ?
Morris, Edward M., 9-15-42 — 12-31-45.
Morrisette, James E., 5-24-44 — 8-31-46.
Morrison, William R.C., 9-8-44 — ?
Morse, Winslow C., 8-16-44 — USAF
Moseley, Edward B., 5-10-07 — 5-10-07.
Muhlenberg, John C., 4-7-08 — 4-7-08.
Mundy, George W., 2-3-47 — USAF
Munson, Edward L., 10-11-18 — 12-31-32.
Myer, Albert L., 3-23-07 — 11-14-10.
Myers, Donald J., 9-10-42 — 9-30-46.
Myers, Diller S., 11-12-40 — ?
Myrick, John R., 4-17-03 — 4-18-03.
Naylor, William K., 10-1-18 — 11-3-38.
Neal, Paul LaR., ? — 8-31-54.

Nevins, Arthur S., 12-3-42 — 8-31-46.
Newton, Henry C., 9-19-42 — ?
Nicholson, William J., 8-5-17 — 1-16-20.
Nowland, Bob E., 2-4-43 — USAF
Nutt, Clifford C., 10-25-45 — USAF
O'Brien, John L., 1-5-45 — ?
O'Brien, Maxwell A., 9-6-42 —
O'Dwyer, William 8-3-44 — ?

Offutt, Harry D., 5-4-48 — 3-31-51.
Old, Archie J., Jr. 11-19-44 — USAF
O'Neil, Joseph P., 8-5-17 — 12-27-26.
O'Neil, Christopher 7-15-17 — ?
O'Neill, James H., 1-24-48 — 1-31-52.
O'Neill, Raymond E., 9-10-42 — ?
Opie, Evarts W., 9-7-42 — ?
Osmun, Russell A., 9-14-43 — 9-30-46.
Ostrander, Lester S., 2-3-43 — 12-31-46.
Ostrom, Charles D.Y., 2-16-42 — 4-30-50.
Otis, Elwell S., 5-4-1898 — 3-25-02.
Ott, Edward S., 6-24-42 — USAF
Ott, Isaac W., 3-2-44 — 8-31-46.
Ovenshire, Alexander T., 11-1-33 — 6-30-37.
Owens, Alexander M., 5-24-44 — 2-28-46.
Owens, Ray L., 12-4-42 — 4-30-46.
Page, Charles 4-23-04 — 4-23-04.
Page, John H., 9-21-1898 — 7-27-03.
Page, John W., 10-15-40 — ?
Palmer, Bruce ? — 6-30-42.
Parker, Daingerfield 4-23-04 — 4-23-04.
Paxton, Alexander G., 7-20-42 — ?
Peabody, Paul E., 2-15-43 — 3-31-50.
Pearson, Madison 12-1-42 — 8-31-46.
Peixotto, Eustace M., 2-27-47 — 2-29-48.
Pendleton, Randolph T., 5-22-42 — 8-31-49.
Penington, Carlos A., 5-21-40 — ?
Penn, Julius A., 8-5-17 — 12-5-24.
Penney, Charles G., 8-13-03 — 8-14-03.
Perrin, Herbert T., 3-18-43 — 9-30-46.
Perrine, Nat S., 7-20-42 — ?
Perry, David L., 4-23-04 — 4-23-04.
Philips, Joseph V., 3-18-43 — 5-31-49.
Philips, Joseph L., 7-25-42 — 3-31-46.
Phillips, James F., 1-20-45 — USAF
Phillips, Thomas R., 9-15-43 — 3-31-50.
Piburn, Edwin W., 4-16-47 — 10-31-52.
Pierce, Clinton A., 3-29-47 — 2-28-51.
Pierce, John L., 3-24-43 — 10-31-46.
Pierce, John T., 6-20-42 — 11-30-47.
Pillsbury, Henry C., 4-3-42 — 5-31-45.
Pitman, John 11-12-06 — 11-12-06.
Pope, George Van W., 12-3-42 — 7-31-54.
Porter, John A., 4-25-43 — 6-30-46.
Potts, Ramsay D., 1-31-08 — 4-30-14.
Powell, Carroll A., 11-10-44 — 4-30-47.
Powell, James F., 3-20-45 — USAF
Powell, William D., 10-30-42 — 10-6-43.
Power, Thomas S., 1-22-45 — USAF
Pratt, Don F., 8-1-42 — 6-6-44.
Pratt, Edward B., 11-27-09 — 11-30-09.
Pratt, Richard H., 4-23-04 4-23-04.
Prentiss, Paul H., 9-28-43 — ?
Price, Harrison J., 10-1-18 — ?
Price, William G., 7-3-18 — ?
Putt, Donald L., 2-5-47 — USAF
Pyron, Walter B., 9-28-40 — ?
Quade, Omar H., 5-28-42 — 8-31-48.
Quinton, William 10-6-02 — 10-9-02.
Ramey, Howard K., 9-17-42 — 11-19-45.
Ramey, Rufus S., 9-11-42 — 4-30-53.
Randle, Edwin H., 6-9-43 — 6-30-48.
Randol, Marshall A., 1-29-41 — 10-31-42.
Rank, Fred w., 12-5-42 — ?
Ratay, John P., 5-24-44 — 8-31-46.
Ravdin, Isidor S., 3-31-45 — ?
Ray, P. Henry 5-8-06 — 5-8-06.
Ready, Joseph L., 4-1-42 — 6-30-49.
Read, Henry A., 2-17-06 — 2-19-06.
Rees, Robert I., 10-1-18 — ?
Regnier, Eugene A., 12-3-42 — 9-30-46.
Reimel, Stewart E., 3-17-43 — 2-28-46.

Reinarts, Eugen S., 12-4-42 — 10-31-46.
Reschs, Frederick E., 7-17-17 — ?
Reynolds, Edward 6-17-45 — ?
Reynolds, Royal 5-20-42 — 10-31-45.
Rice, Edmund 8-13-03 — 8-14-03.
Richards, Randolph A., 7-18-17 — ?
Richmond, Adam 3-17-43 — 2-28-47.
Ridenour, Carlyle H., 6-2-43 — 3-31-45.
Rilea, Thomas E., 2-12-40 — ?
Ritter, William L., 8-8-44 — 12-31-50.
Rives, Tom C., 9-4-44 — USAF
Rixey, George F., 11-8-44 — 3-31-48.
Robe, Charles F., 7-31-03 — 8-1-03.
Roberts, Benjamin K., 6-19-05 — 6-20-05.
Roberts, Cyrus S., 8-8-03 — 8-9-03.
Roberts, Edwin H., 6-2-49 — 3-31-50.
Robertson, Ralph K., 7-3-40 — ?
Robinett, Paul McD., 11-20-42 — 8-31-46.
Robinson, Donald B., 1-6-41 — ?
Robinson, Frank U., 4-8-05 — 4-9-05.
Rockenbach, Samuel D., 6-26-18 — 1-31-33.
Rodenbough, Theophilus F., 4-23-04 — 4-23-04.
Roderick, Thomas E., 2-21-44 — 9-21-44.
Rodes, Peter P., 6-25-43 — 10-31-50.
Rodney, George B., 8-4-03 — 8-5-03.
Rpdwell, James S., 11-10-44 — 8-31-46.
Rogers, Arthur H., 1-16-44 — 10-31-46.
Rogers, Arthur J., 11-10-44 — ?
Rogers, John A., 11-10-44 — 11-30-46.
Rogers, Pleas B., 3-16-43 — 1-31-48.
Rogers, William P., 4-20-03 — 4-20-03.
Rollins, Francis W., 9-7-42 — ?
Roosevelt, Elliot 1-20-45 — ?
Roosevelt, Theodore 12-17-41 — ?
Rose, William I., 9-9-40 — ?
Ross, Morrill 8-1-42 — 1-31-50.
Ross, Ogden J., 10-15-40 — ?
Rowan, Hugh W., 5-25-44 — 7-31-53.
Rowe, Guy I., 5-22-42 — 8-31-46.
Royall, Kenneth C., 11-4-43 — ?
Rucker, Casper B., 6-23-43 — 6-30-46.
Rucker, Louis H., 4-18-03 — 4-19-03.
Rudolph, Jacob H., 10-1-40 — 7-31-44.
Russell, Carl A., 12-2-42 — ?
Russell, Edgar 8-5-17 — ?
Sabini, Dominic J., 10-25-45 — 12-31-46.
Sadler, Percy L., 10-30-42 — 11-30-46.
Safay, Fred A., 9-6-42 — ?
Safford, Hermon F., 9-11-42 — 3-31-46.
Saltman, Charles M., 7-24-17 — ?
Sams, Crawford F., 5-12-48 — 7-31-55.
Sanders, Homer L., 8-9-44 — USAF
sanders, Richard C., 6-7-44 — ?
Sands, William H., 11-27-40 — ?
Saville, Gordon P., 11-2-42 — USAF
Sawyer, J. Estcourt 7-3-10 — 7-3-10.
Schindel, S.J.G., 8-8-18 — ?
Schneider, Max F., 1-8-45 — USAF
Schramm, Ned 6-25-43 — USAF
Schulgen, George F., 6-29-43 — USAF
Schwien, Edwin E., 2-2-43 — 10-31-45.
Scott, Don E., 5-25-40 — ?

Scully, James W., 4-23-04 — 4-23-04.
Seals, Carl H., 6-24-42 — 1-31-45.
Seaman, A. Owens 12-18-36 — 7-31-40.
Searcy, Cyrus H., 1-7-45 — 7-31-47.
Shadle, Charles S., 5-25-44 — 10-31-47.
Shaler, Charles 1-19-05 — 1-19-05.
Shaw, Frederick B., 10-1-18 — 6-30-33.
Shaw, George C., 6-25-29 — 3-6-30.
Sheep, William L., 10-1-40 — 10-31-45.
Shelton, Cyrus Q., ? — 8-31-54.
Shelton, George M., 6-26-18 — ?
Sherburne, John H., 6-28-18 — ?
Sheridan, Michael V., 5-27-1898 — 4-16-02.
Shockley, M.A.W., 8-1-35 — 2-28-37.
Sigerfoos, Edward 10-4-18 — ?
Simmons, James S., 3-14-43 — 10-31-46.
Sims, Leonard H., 11-3-43 — 8-31-54.

Singleton, Asa L., 10-1-36 — 8-31-40.
Slocum, LeCount H., 12-8-42 — 7-31-54.
Smedberg, William R., 10-1-18 — ?
Smith, Albert D., (Ret) 3-3-44 — 3-14-47.
Smith, Benjamin M., 8-23-40 — ?
Smith, Frank G., 8-3-03 — 8-04-03.
Smith, Jacob H., 6-1-1900 — 7-16-02.
Smith, Lotha A., 1-8-45 — USAF
Snavely, Ralph A., 11-17-44 — USAF
Sniffin, Culver C., 9-11-06 — 1-1-08.
Snyder, Simon 5-4-1898 — 5-10-02.
Sorenson, Edgar P., 4-26-43 — USAF
Spaulding, Oliver L., 6-26-18 — ?
Speaks, John C., 7-15-17 — ?
Spiller, Oliver L., 10-1-40 — 8-31-45.
Spruit, Charles B., 1-8-45 — 10-31-46.
Stack, Robert I., 6-4-43 — 7-31-53.
Stackpole, Edward J., Jr. 9-8-40 — 12-31-45.
Stanberry, Sanford B., 10-1-18 — ?
Starbird, Alfred A., 4-12-18 — 2-6-30.
Stark, Alexander N., Jr. 3-16-43 — 2-28-46.
Starr, Rupert E., 12-11-42 — 5-31-50.
Steever, Edgar Z., 8-5-12 — 3-27-13.
Steiner, Robert E., 3-19-18 — ?
Stenseth, Martinus 4-27-43 — USAF
Sternberg, George M., 5-30-1893 — 6-8-02.
Stillwell, Frederick W., 7-15-17 — ?
Stockton, Marcellus L., Jr. 2-4-43 — 6-30-44.
Strahm, Victor H., 10-30-42 — USAF
Strickland, Auby C., 8-6-42 — USAF
Strong, Alden G., 9-29-41 — 9-30-46.
Sullivan, Charles W., 11-3-43 — ?
Summers, John E., 4-23-04 — 4-23-04.
Summrs, Owen 9-12-42 — 6-30-47.
Swatland, Donald C., 3-29-45 —
Sweet, Joseph B., 5-12-43 — 6-30-48.
Sweet, owen J., 9-4-09 — 9-4-09.
Sweetzer, E. LeRoy 7-25-17 — ?
Tate, Ralph H., 1-17-44 — 7-31-47.
Taylor, Asher C., 1-21-04 — 1-22-04.
Taylor, Victor V., 9-14-43 — 9-22-44.
Taylor, Willis r., 10-31-42 — ?
Taylor, Yantis H., 6-15-45 — USAF
Thayer, William S., 10-1-18 — ?
Thiele, Claude M., 4-7-41 — 9-30-48.
Thomas, Amos S., 6-26-40 — ?
Thomas, Arthur 2-22-44 — USAF
Thomas, Charles E., Jr. 9-17-43 — USAF
Thomas, Samuel M., 3-28-45 — ?
Thompson, Harry F., 4-26-43 — 6-30-46.
Thompson, j. Milton 8-9-03 — 8-10-03.
Thompson, Orlen N., 6-4-45 — 11-30-46.
Thorp, Frank 2-9-06 — 2-9-06.
Thorpe, Elliott R., 3-19-45 — 11-30-49.
Thrasher, Charles O., 2-22-44 — 8-31-46.
Tiernon, John L., 8-11-03 — 8-12-03.
Tilton, Rollin L., 10-2-40 — 2-29-48.
Tindall, Richard G., 3-26-47 — 4-39-52.
Tobin, Ralph C., 7-22-42 — ?
Tourtellot, George P., 2-4-43 — ?
Townsene, James R., 3-14-42 — 8-31-46.
Townshend, Orval P., 10-1-18 — ?
Tripp. Guy E., 8-8-18 — ?
Troland, Thomas E., 2-6-41 ?
Truby, Albert E., 1-1-33 — 7-31-35.
True, Theodore E., 1-22-04 — 1-23-04.
Tupper, Tristram 11-3-43 — ?
Turrill, Henry S., 3-28-06 — 3-29-06.
Tuthill, Alexander M., 8-5-17 — ?
Tychsen, Andrew C., 3-19-45 — 6-30-53.
Tyner, George P., 10-1-36 — 4-30-40.
Underwood, Edgar H., 3-15-43 — 9-30-46.
Upston, John E., 12-4-42 — USAF
Usher, George L., 2-3-43 — ?
Vachon, Joseph P., 12-18-41 — 8-31-46.
Vanaman, Arthur N., 3-16-42 — USAF
Vanderbilt, Cornelius 6-16-18 ?

Vanderveer, Harold C., 2-14-42 — 8-31-49.
Van Horn, Robert O., 12-1-33 — 8-31-40.
Van Horne, William M., 4-23-04 — 4-23-04.

Vaughan, Cecil C., 8-5-17 — ?
Vaughan, William W., 10-24-45 — 11-30-
Viele, Charles D., 9-21-1898 — 1-23-19.
Vincent, Thomas M., 4-23-04 — 4-23-04.
Vodges, Anthony W., 5-20-04 — 5-20-
Vollrath, Edward 8-5-17 — ?
Vroom, Peter D., 4-11-03 — 4-12-
Waite, Sumner 11-8-44 — 9-30-
Walker, Kenneth N., 6-17-42 — 12-12-
Walker, Nelson M., 9-11-42 — 7-10-
Walker, William G., 3-17-43 — 8-31-
Wallace, William M., 10-2-06 — 10-2-
Wallender, Elmer F., 9-4-44 — 12-31-
Walsh, Roland F., 9-14-43 — 12-31-
Walson, Charles M., 1-3-45 — 8-31-
Ward, Henry C., 10-30-05 — 10-39-
Warden, John A., 4-5-41 — 1-31-
Warfield, Augustus B., 4-1-36 — 6-30-
Warnock, Aln D., 12-2-42 — 5-31-
Waters, Jerome J., Jr. 4-17-42 — 5-31-
Water, William E., 3-21-45 — ?
Weatherred, Preston A., 10-12-40 — ?
Weaver, Theron D., 1-31-46 — 12-31-
Weckerling, John 5-7-47 — 9-30-
Weddington, Leonard D., 6-7-45 — 6-30-
Wedgwood, Edgar A., 8-5-17 — ?
Weed, Frank W., 7-19-42 — ?
Weir, John M., 9-15-43 — 11-30-
Wells, Almond B., 8-5-03 — 8-6-
Welsh, William W., 9-17-42 — 6-30-
Wessels, Henry W., Jr. 4-23-04 — 4-23-04.
Wharton, James E., 3-15-42 — 8-12-
Wheelen, James N., 4-23-04 — 4-23-04.
Wheeler, Daniel D., 8-15-03 — 2-15-12.
Whipple, charles H., 1-1-08 — 2-15-12.
Whisner, Emons B., 1-18-45 — 7-31-53.
Whitall, Samuel R., 6-15-06 — 6-15-06.
White, William R., 9-6-42 — 9-30-46.
Whitney, Courtney 1-14-45 — ?
Whiteside, Samuel M., 1-3-01 — 1-9-02.
Whittaker, Frank L., 2-2-43 — 11-30-46.
Whittaker, Horace L., 7-24-42 — 11-30-46.
Whittemore, James M., 4-23-04 — 4-23-04.
Whitten, Lyman P., 12-11-42 — USAF
Whitworth, Pegram 8-8-18 — 8-31-35.
Wicks, Roger M., 11-9-42 — 5-31-50.
Wilcox, Timothy E., 4-26-04 — 4-26-04.
Wilkins, Paul C., 5-2-43 — 8-31-44.
Wilkey, John P., 9-9-44 — ?
Willey, John P., 9-9-44 — 8-31-54.
Williams, Constant 7-12-04 — 5-25-07.
Williams, Harry C., 6-13-40 — 12-14-27.
Williams, L. Kemper 11-7-44 — ?
Williams, Robert P., 5-27-49 — 8-31-51.
Williams, Roger D., 8-5-17 — ?
Williamson, William J., 9-5-44 — ?
Williston, Edward B., 5-4-1898 — 7-15-1900.
Wilson, Alexander 1-30-42 — 8-31-46.
Wilson, Charles I., 4-23-04 — 4-23-04.
Wilson, John H., 11-8-44 — 9-30-46.
Wilson, Vennard 7-15-48 — 3-30-53.
Wilson, William 7-15-17 — ?
Wingate, George A., 4-12-18 — ?
Wint, Theodore J., 6-9-02 — 3-21-07.
Winter, Francis A., 5-1-18 — 9-1-22.
Wirt, Davis 4-23-04 — 4-23-04.
Wolfe, Henry C., 9-18-42 — 5-31-50.
Wood, Eric F., 2-17-41 — ?
Wood, Henry C., 4-23-04 — 4-23-04.
Wood, Jack W., 11-21-44 — USAF
Wood, John E., 8-3-42 — 7-31-49.
Wood, Myron R., 6-25-43 — 10-29-46.
Wood, Palmer G., 2-16-06 — 2-17-06.
Woodbury, Murray C., 2-29-44 — ?
Woodcock, Amos W.W., 10-11-40 — ?
Woodhull, Alfred A., 4-23-04 — 4-23-04.
Woodruff, Carle A., 8-10-03 — 8-11-03.
Woodward, George A., 4-23-04 — 4-23-04.
Woodward, Samuel L., 7-8-04 — 7-9-04.
Woolfley, Francis A., 3-16-43 — 4-30-53.
Wright, Boykin C., 5-2-43 — ?

Wylie, Robert H., 12-4-42 — 2-28-47.
Wyllie, Robert E., 6-13-40 — 12-30-30.
Yates, Arthur W., 7-9-26 — 8-1-27.
Yates, Donald L., 2-5-47 — USAF
Yeager, Emer 9-17-43 — 9-30-45.
Yenter, Raymond A., 10-24-40 — ?
Young, Laurence W., 9-1-41 — 1-31-44.
Younger, James W., 3-16-45 — 12-31-46.
Zalinski, Moses G., 4-19-25 — 1-23-27.
Zimmerman, Charles X., 7-15-17 — ?

Chief Of Naval Operations.
Office established 11th May, 1915.

1915-1919 Adm William S. Benson 5-11-15 — 9-25-19.
1919-1923 Adm Robert E. Coontz 11-1-19 — 7-21-23.
1923-1927 Adm Edward W. Eberle 7-21-23 — 11-14-27.
1927-1930 Adm Charles F. Hughes 11-14-27 — 9-17-30.
1930-1933 Adm William V. Pratt 9-19-30 — 6-30-33.
1933-1937 Adm William H. Standley 7-1-33 — 1-1-37.
1937-1939 Adm William D. Leahy 1-2-37 — 8-1-39.
1939-1942 Adm Harold R. Stark 8-1-39 — 3-26-42.
1942-1945 Fadm Ernest J. King 3-26-42 — 12-15-45.
1945-1947 Fadm Chester W. Nimitz 12-15-45 — 12-15-47.
1947-1949 Adm Louis E. Denfeld 12-15-47 — 11-2-49.
1949-1951 Adm Forrest P. Sherman 11-2-49 — 7-22-51.
1951-1953 Adm William M. Fechteler 8-16-51 — 8-17-53.
1953-1955 Adm Robert B. Carney 8-17-53 — 8-17-55.
1955-1961 Adm Arleigh A. Burke 8-17-55 — 8-1-61.
1961-1963 Adm George W. Anderson, Jr. 8-1-61 — 8-1-63.
1963-1967 Adm David L. McDonald 8-1-63 — 8-1-67.
1967-1970 Adm Thomas H. Moorer 8-1-67 — 7-1-70.
1970-1974 Adm Elmo R. Zumwalt, Jr. 7-1-70 — 6-29-74.
1974-1978 Adm James L. Holloway III 6-29-74 — 7-1-78.
1978-1982 Adm Thomas B. Hayward 7-1-78 — 6-30-82.
1982-1986 Adm James D. Watkins 6-30-82 — 6-30-86.
1986-1990 Adm Carlisle A. Trost 7-1-86 — 7-30-90.
1990-   Adm Frank B. Kelso, II 8-1-90 —

Principal Civilian Officials And Naval Officers In Command 7 December 1941-2 September 1945

SECRETARY OF THE NAVY
Frank Knox, 7 December 1941-28 April 1944;
James V. Forrestal (A)*, 28 April 1944-19 May 1944; James V. Forrestal, 19 May 1944-2 September 1945.

UNDER SECRETARY OF THE NAVY
James V. Forrestal, 7 December 1941-19 May 1944;
Ralph A. Bard, 24 June 1944-30 June 1945;
Artemus L. Gates, 3 July 1945-2 September 1945.

ASSISTANT SECRETARY OF THE NAVY
Ralph A. Bard, 7 December 1941-24 June 1944;
H. Struve Hensel, 30 January 1945-2 September 1945.

ASSISTANT SECRETARY OF THE NAVY FOR AIR
Artemus L. Gates, 7 December 1941-30 June 1945;
John L. Sullivan, 1 July 1945-2 September 1945.

CHIEF OF NAVAL OPERATIONS
Adm. H.R. Stark 7 December 1941-26 March 1942;
Fleet Adm. E.J. King, 26 March 1942-2 September 1945.

VICE CHIEF OF NAVAL OPERATIONS (Established 12 March 1942.)
Adm. F.J. Horne, 26 March 1942-2 September 1945;

JOINT CHIEFS OF STAFF (Established 9 February 1942.)
Chairman:
Fleet Adm. W.D. Leahy, 20 July 1942-2 September 1945;
Navy: Adm. H.R. Stark, 9 February 1942-26 March 1942;
Fleet Adm. E.J. King, 9 February 1942-2 September 1945.
Army: General of the Army G.C. Marshall, 9 February 1942-2 September 1945.
Army Air Forces:
General of the Army H.H. Arnold, 9 February 1942-2 September 1945.

Chief Of Staff To The Commander In Chief Of The Army And Navy Of The United States (Established 20 July 1942.)
Fleet Adm. W.D. Leahy, 20 July 1942-2 September 1945.

CHAIRMAN OF THE GENERAL BOARD
Rear Adm. W.R. Sexton, 7 December 1941-10 August 1942;
Adm. A.J. Hepburn (Ret.), 11 August 1942-2 September 1945.

COMMANDANT, UNITED STATES MARINE CORPS
Lt. Gen. T. Holcomb, 7 December 1941-31 December 1943;
Gen. A.A. Vandegrift, 1 January 1944-2 September 1945.

COMMANDANT, UNITED STATES COAST GUARD
Adm. R.R. Waesche, 7 December 1941-2 September 1945.

Bureau Chiefs

BUREAU OF AERONAUTICS
Rear Adm. J.H. Towers, 7 December 1941-7 October 1942;
Rear Adm. J.S. McCain, 9 October 1942-6 August 1943;
Rear Adm. D.C. Ramsey, 6 August 1943-1 June 1945;
Rear Adm. H.B. Sallada, 1 June 1945-2 September 1945.

BUREAU OF MEDICINE AND SURGERY
Vice Adm. R.T. McIntyre, 7 December 1941-2 September 1945.

BUREAU OF NAVAL PERSONNEL (Bureau of Navigation until 13 May 1942.)
Rear Adm. C.W. Nimitz, 7 December 1941-19 December 1941;
Vice Adm. R. Jacobs, 19 December 1941-2 September 1945.

BUREAU OF ORDNANCE
Rear Adm. W.H.P. Blandy, 7 December 1941-9 December 1943;
Vice Adm. G.F. Hussey, 10 December 1943-2 September 1945.

BUREAU OF SHIPS
Rear Adm. S.M. Robinson, 7 December 1941-31 January 1942;
Rear Adm. A.H. Van Keuren, 1 February 1942-2 November 1942;
Vice Adm. E.L. Cochrane, 2 November 1942-2 September 1945.

BUREAU OF SUPPLIES AND ACCOUNTS
Rear Adm. R. Spear, 7 December 1941-31 May 1942;
Rear Adm. W.B. Young, 1 June 1942-8 March 1945;
Rear Adm. W.J. Carter, 8 March 1945-2 September 1945.

BUREAU OF YARDS AND DOCKS
Vice Adm. B. Moreell, 7 December 1941-2 September 1945.

Commandants, Naval Districts and River Commands

FIRST NAVAL DISTRICT
Rear Adm. W.T. Tarrant, 7 December 1941-15 July 1942;
Vice Adm. W. Brown, 15 July 1942-8 February 1943;
Rear Adm. R.A. Theobald, 9 February 1943-28 October 1944;
Rear Adm. F.X. Gygax, 28 October 1944-2 September 1945.

THIRD NAVAL DISTRICT
Rear Adm. A. Andrews, 7 December 1941-16 March 1942;
Rear Adm. E.J. Marquart, 17 March 1942-31 March 1944;
Rear Adm. W.R. Munroe, 31 March 1944-6 November 1944;
Rear Adm. M. Kelly, 6 November 1944-2 September 1945.

FOURTH NAVAL DISTRICT
Rear Adm. A.E. Watson, 7 December 1941-30 August 1942;
Rear Adm. M.F. Draemel, 30 August 1942-2 September 1945.

FIFTH NAVAL DISTRICT
Rear Adm. M.H. Simons, 7 December 1941-31 May 1943;
Rear Adm. H.F. Leary, 1 June 1943-30 October 1943;
Rear Adm. D.M. Le Breton 30 October 1943-20 August 1945;
Rear Adm. W.L. Ainsworth, 20 August 1945-2 September 1945.

SIXTH NAVAL DISTRICT
Rear Adm. W.H. Allen, 7 December 1941-2 June 1942;
Rear Adm. W.A. Glassford, 2 June 1942-14 May 1943;
Rear Adm. J. James, 14 May 1943-2 September 1945.

SEVENTH NAVAL DISTRICT (Combined with Sixth until 1 February 1942.)
Capt. R.S. Crenshaw (A), 1 February 1942-3 June 1942;
Rear Adm. J.L. Kauffman, 3 June 1942-3 February 1943;
Capt. H.H.J. Benson (A), 3 February 1943-1 April 1943;
Rear Adm. W.R. Munroe, 1 April 1943-25 March 1944;
Capt. H.H.J. Benson (A), 25 March 1944-17 July 1944;
Vice Adm. W.S. Anderson, 17 July 1944-2 September 1945.

EIGHTH NAVAL DISTRICT
Capt. T.A. Thomson (A), 7 December 1941-22 April 1942;
Rear Adm. F.T. Leighton, 22 April 1942-18 March 1943;
Capt. E.T. Oates (A), 18 March 1943-14 June 1943;
Rear Adm. A.C. Bennett, 14 June 1943-2 September 1945.

NINTH NAVAL DISTRICT
Rear Adm. J. Downes, 7 December 1941-3 January 1944;
Vice Adm. A.S. Carpender, 3 January 1944-2 September 1945.

TENTH NAVAL DISTRICT
Vive Adm. J.H. Hoover, 7 December 1941-12 August 1943;
Vice Adm. A.B. Cook, 12 August 1943-14 May 1944;
Vice Adm. R.C. Giffen, 14 May 1944-20 August 1945;
Vice Adm. W.R. Munroe, 20 August 1945-2 September 1945.

ELEVENTH NAVAL DISTRICT
Rear Adm. C.A. Blakely, 7 December 1941-9 December 1941;
Rear Adm. J.S. McCain (A), 9 December 1941-22 December 1941;
Rear Adm. R.S. Holmes, 22 December 1941-31 December 1942;
Capt. G.M. Ravenscroft (A), 31 December 1942-30 March 1943;
Rear Adm. D.W. Bagley, 30 March 1943-31 January 1944;
Rear Adm. W.L. Freidell, 31 January 1944-2 September 1945.

TWELFTH NAVAL DISTRICT
Vice Adm. J.W. Greenslade, 7 December 1941-1 February 1944;
Rear Adm. C.H. Wright, 1 February 1944-2 September 1945.

THIRTEENTH NAVAL DISTRICT
Vice Adm. C.S. Freeman, 7 December 1941-21 November 1942;
Vice Adm. F.J. Fletcher, 21 November 1942-12 October 1943;
Rear Adm. S.A. Taffinder, 12 October 1943-15 December 1944;
Rear Adm. R.M. Griffin, 15 December 1944-2 September 1945.

FOURTEENTH NAVAL DISTRICT
Rear Adm. C.C. Bloch, 7 December 1941-4 April 1942;
Rear Adm. D.W. Bagley, 4 April 1942-17 February 1943;
Vice Adm. R.L. Ghormley, 17 February 1943-25 October 1944;
Rea Adm. W.R. Furlong (A), 25 October 1944-28 November 1944;
Vice Adm. D.W. Bagley, 28 November 1944-25 July 1945;
Vice Adm. S.A. Taffinder, 25 July 1945-2 September 1945.

FIFTEENTH NAVAL DISTRICT
Rear Adm. F.H. Sadler, 7 December 1941-15 April 1942;
Rear Adm. C.E. Van Hook, 15 April 1942-14 October 1943;
Rear Adm. H.C. Train, 14 October 1943-10 June 1944;
Capt. E.S. Stone (A), 10 June 1944-3 November 1944;
Rear Adm. H.F. Kingman, 3 November 1944-9 July 1945;
Capt. S. Mills (A), 9 July 1945-23 August 1945; Rear Adm. J.R. Beardall, 23 August 1945-2 September 1945.

SIXTEENTH NAVAL DISTRICT (Ceased to exist on 6 May 1942.)
Rear Adm. F.W. Rockwell, 7 December 1941-18 March 1942;
Capt. K.M. Hoeffel, 18 March 1942-6 May 1942.

SEVENTEENTH NAVAL DISTRICT (Created on 15 April 1944)
Rear Adm. F.E.M. Whiting, 15 April 1944-12 August 1944;
Rear Adm. A.E. Smith (T)*, 12 August 1944-24 August 1944;
Rear Adm. R.F. Wood, 24 August 1944-2 September 1945.

POTOMAC RIVER NAVAL COMMAND (Established 8 December 1941.)
Rear Adm. G.I. Pettengill (Ret.), 8 December 1941-15 September 1942;
Rear Adm. F.L. Reichmuth, 15 September 1942-2 September 1945.

SEVERN RIVER NAVAL COMMAND (Established 8 December 1941.)
Rear Adm. R. Willson, 8 December 1941-30 December 1941;
Capt. T.S. King (A), 30 December 1941-31 January 1942;
Rear Adm. J.R. Beardall, 31 January 1942-8 August 1945;
Vice Adm. A.W. Fitch, 8 August 1945-2 September 1945.

Sea Frontier Commanders
ALASKAN (Established 15 April 1944.)
Vice Adm. F.J. Fletcher, 15 April 1944-2 September 1945.

CARIBBEAN (Naval Coastal Frontier until 6 February 1942.)
Vice Adm. J.H. Hoover, 7 December 1941-12 August 1943;
Vice Adm. A.B. Cook, 12 August 1943-14 May 1944;
Vice Adm. R.C. Giffen, 14 May 1944-20 August 1945;
Vice Adm. W.R. Munroe, 20 August 1945-2 September 1945.

EASTERN (North Atlantic Naval Coastal Frontier until 6 February 1942.)
Vice Adm. A. Andrews, 7 December 1941-1 November 1943;
Vice Adm. H.F. Leary, 1 November 1943-2 September 1945.

GULF (Southern Naval Coastal Frontier until 6 February 1942.)
Rear Adm. W.H. Allen, 7 December 1941-3 February 1942;
Capt. R.S. Crenshaw (A), 3 February 1942-3 June 1942;
Rear Adm. J.L. Kauffman, 3 June 1942-3 February 1943;
Capt. H.H.J. Benson (A), 3 February 1943-1 April 1943;
Rear Adm. W.S. Anderson, 17 July 1944-2 September 1945.

HAWAIIAN (Naval Coastal Frontier until 6 February 1942.)
Rear Adm. C.C. Bloch, 7 December 1941-2 April 1942;
Rear Adm. D.W. Bagley, 2 April 1942-17 February 1943;
Vice Adm. R.L. Ghormley, 17 February 1943-25 October 1944;
Commodore M.C. Robertson (A), 25 October 1944-28 November 1944;
Vice Adm. D.W. Bagley, 28 November 1944-25 July 1945;
Vice Adm. S.A. Taffinder, 25 July 1945-2 September 1945.

MOROCCAN (Established 19 November 1942 as Sea Frontier Forces, Western Task Force. Name changed 17 February 1943. Disestablished 1 August 1945.)
Rear Adm. J.L. Hall, 19 November 1942-9 February 1943;
Capt. C.L. Nichols (T), 9 February 1943-19 February 1943;
Rear Adm. F.J. Lowry, 19 February 1943-20 September 1943;
Capt. C.L. Nichols (T), 20 September 1943-13 October 1943;
Commodore B.V. McCandlish, 13 October 1943-1 August 1945.

NORTHWEST (Pacific-Northern Naval Coastal Frontier until 6 February 1942. Disestablished 15 April 1944.)
Vice Adm. C.S. Freeman, 7 December 1941-21 November 1942;
Vice Adm. F.J. Fletcher, 21 November 1942-15 April 1944.

PANAMA (Naval Coastal Frontier until 6 February 1942.)
Rear Adm. F.H. Sadler, 7 December 1941-15 April 1942;
Rear Adm. C.E. Van Hook, 15 April 1942-14 October 1943;
Rear Adm. H.C. Train, 14 October 1943-10 June 1944;
Capt. E.S. Stone (A), 11 June 1944-3 November 1944;
Rear Adm. H.F. Kingman, 3 November 1944-9 July 1945;
Capt. S. Mills (A), 9 July 1945-23 August 1945;
Rear Adm. J.R. Beardall, 23 August 1945-2 September 1945.

PHILIPPINE (Naval Coastal Frontier until 6 February 1942; inactive from 6 May 1942 to 13 November 1944.)
Rear Adm. F.W. Rockwell, 7 December 1941-18 March 1942;
Capt. K.M. Hoeffel, 18 March 1942-6 May 1942;

Vice Adm. J.L. Kauffman, 13 November 1944-2 September 1945.

WESTERN (Pacific-Southern Naval Coastal Frontier until 6 February 1942.)
Vice Adm. J.W. Greenslade, 7 December 1941-1 February 1944;
Vice Adm. D.W. Bagley, 1 February 1944-17 November 1944;
Adm R.E. Ingersoll, 17 November 1944-2 September 1945.

UNITED STATES FLEET (On 20 December 1941, Adm. E.J. King was designated Commander in Chief United States Fleet. He assumed the duties in Washington and established his headquarters in the Navy Department on 30 December 1941.)
Adm. H.E. Kimmel, 7 December 1941-17 December 1941;
Fleet Adm. E.J. King, 30 December 1941-2 September 1945.

ATLANTIC FLEET (Additionally designated Second Fleet, 15 March 1943.)
Adm. E.J. King, 7 December 1941-31 December 1941;
Adm. R.E. Ingersoll, 1 January 1942-15 November 1944;
Adm. J.H. Ingram, 15 November 1944-2 September 1945.

PACIFIC FLEET
Adm. H.E. Kimmel, 7 December 1941-17 December 1941;
Vice Adm. W.S. Pye (T), 17 December 1941-31 December 1941;
Fleet Adm. C.W. Nimitz, 31 December 1941-2 September 1945.

ASIATIC FLEET (Ceased to exist on 4 February 1942.)
Adm. T.C. Hart, 7 December 1941-4 February 1942.

THIRD FLEET (Established 15 March 1943, formerly South Pacific Force.)
South Pacific Force (Established 20 April 1942.)
Vice Adm. R.L. Ghormley, 19 June 1942-18 October 1942;
Adm. W.F. Halsey, 18 October 1942-15 March 1943.
Third Fleet.
Adm. W.F. Halsey, 15 March 1943-2 September 1945.

FOURTH FLEET (Established 15 March 1943, formerly South Atlantic Force, originally Task Force 23, Atlantic Fleet. Disestablished 15 April 1945.)
Task Force 23.
Vice Adm. J.H. Ingram, 7 December 1941-15 September 1942.
South Atlantic Force (Established 15 September 1942).
Vice Adm. J.H. Ingram, 15 September 1942-15 March 1943.
Fourth Fleet.
Vice Adm. J.H. Ingram, 15 March 1943-11 November 1944;
Vice Adm. W.R. Munroe, 11 November 1944-15 April 1945.

FIFTH FLEET (Established 26 April 1944, previously Central Pacific Force which was formed 5 August 1943.)
Adm. R.A. Spruance, 5 August 1943-2 September 1945.

SEVENTH FLEET (Established 19 February 1943, formerly Southwest Pacific Force. Southwest Pacific Force absorbed U.S. Naval Forces, Southwest Pacific, on 20 April 1942, which in turn had succeeded Asiatic Fleet on 4 February 1942.)

United States Naval Forces, Southwest Pacific (Designated 4 February 1942).
Vice Adm. W.A. Glassford, 4 February 1942-2 April 1942;
Rear Adm. W.R. Purnell, 2 April 1942-20 April 1942.

Southwest Pacific Force (Absorbed United States Naval Forces, Southwest Pacific, on 20 April 1942).
Vice Adm. H.F. Leary, 20 April 1942-11 September 1942;
Vice Adm. A.S. Carpender, 11 September 1942-19 February 1943.

Seventh Fleet.
Vice Adm. A.S. Carpender, 19 February 1943-26 November 1943;
Adm. T.C. Kincaid, 26 November 1943-2 September 1945.

EIGHTH FLEET (Established 15 March 1943, and disestablished on 15 April 1945; forces became part of Twelfth Fleet.)
Adm. H.K. Hewitt, 29 March 1943-11 April 1945;
Vice Adm. W.A. Glassford, 11 April 1945-15 April 1945.

TENTH FLEET (All United States antisubmarine activities and forces in Atlantic coordinated and controlled by Tenth Fleet. Established on 20 May 1943, and disestablished on 12 June 1945.)
Fleet Adm. E.J. King, 20 May 1943-12 June 1945.

TWELFTH FLEET (Established 15 March 1943, previously Naval Forces, Europe, which was formed 30 April 1942.)
Adm. H.R. Stark, 15 March 1943-15 August 1945;
Adm. H.K. Hewitt, 16 August 1945-2 September 1945.

AREA COMMANDERS

PACIFIC OCEAN AREAS (Established 3 April 1942.)
Fleet Adm. C.W. Nimitz, 8 May 1942-2 September 1945.

NORTH PACIFIC AREA (Established 17 May 1942.)
Rear Adm. R.A. Theobald, 17 May 1942-4 January 1943;
Vice Adm. T.C. Kinkaid, 4 January 1943-11 October 1943;
Vice Adm. F.J. Fletcher, 11 October 1943-2 September 1945.

SOUTH PACIFIC AREA (Established 20 April 1942.)
Vice Adm. R.L. Ghormley, 19 June 1942-18 October 1942;
Adm. W.F. Halsey, 18 October 1942-15 June 1944;
Vice Adm. J.H. Newton, 15 June 1944-13 March 1945;
Vice Adm. W.L. Calhoun, 13 March 1945-2 September 1945.

SOUTHEAST PACIFIC AREA (Established 8 December 1941.)
Rear Adm. A.T. Bidwell, 8 December 1941-6 January 1942;
Rear Adm. J.F. Shafroth, 6 January 1942-25 December 1942;

Rear Adm. F.E.M. Whiting, 25 December 1942-12 October 1943;
Rear Adm. H.C. Train, 12 October 1943-8 June 1944;
Capt. E.S. Stone (A), 8 June 1944-3 November 1944;
Rear Adm. H.F. Kingman, 3 November 1944-9 July 1945;
Capt. S. Mills (A), 9 July 1945-23 August 1945;
Rear Adm. J.R. Beardall, 23 August 1945-2 September 1945.

SOUTHWEST PACIFIC AREA (Established 18 April 1942.)
General of the Army Douglas MacArthur, 18 April 1942-2 September 1945.

Type Commanders

AIR FORCE, ATLANTIC FLEET (Established 1 January 1943 by combining Carriers, Atlantic Fleet (formerly Aircraft, Atlantic Fleet), with Fleet Air Wings, Atlantic Fleet (formerly Patrol Wings, Atlantic Fleet).)
Aircraft, Atlantic Fleet.
Rear Adm. A.B. Cook, 7 December 1941-6 April 1942.
Carriers, Atlantic Fleet (Established 6 April 1942).
Rear Adm. E.D. McWhorter, 6 April 1942-1 January 1943.
Patrol Wings, Atlantic Fleet.
Rear Admiral E.D. McWhorter, 7 December 1941-3 April 1942;
Rear Adm. A.D. Bernhard, 10 April 1942-1 November 1942.
Fleet Air Wings, Atlantic Fleet (Established 1 November 1942).
Rear Adm. A.D. Bernhard, 1 November 1942-1 January 1943.
Air Force, Atlantic Fleet.
Rear Adm. A.D. Bernhard, 1 January 1943-8 March 1943;
Capt. T.L. Sprague (A), 8 March 1943-20 March 1943;
Vice Adm. P.N.L. Bellinger, 20 March 1943-2 September 1945.

AMPHIBIOUS FORCE, ATLANTIC FLEET (Established 14 March 1942, deleted from Atlantic Fleet organization 18 October 1943.)
Rear Adm. R.M. Brainard, 14 March 1942-18 April 1942;
Capt. R.R.M. Emmett (A), 18 April 1942-28 April 1942;
Vice Adm. H.K. Hewitt, 28 April 1942-28 February 1943;
Rear Adm. A.G. Kirk, 28 February 1943-18 October 1943.

BATTLESHIPS, ATLANTIC FLEET (Functions of type commander transferred on 1 November 1943 to Commander Fleet Operational Training Command, Atlantic Fleet.)
Rear Adm. J.W. Wilcox, 7 December 1941-27 March 1942;
Rear Adm. A. Sharp, 27 March 1942-22 August 1942;
Rear Adm. M. Kelly, 22 August 1942-8 May 1943;
Rear Adm. O.M. Hustvedt, 8 May 1943-1 November 1943.

CRUISERS, ATLANTIC FLEET (No type commander assigned from 18 April 1942 to 1 November 1943 when functions of type commander were assumed by Commander Fleet Operational Training Command, Atlantic Fleet.)

Rear Adm H.K. Hewitt, 7 December 1941-28 April 1942.

DESTROYERS, ATLANTIC FLEET
Rear Adm. F.L. Reichmuth, 7 December 1941-22 December 1941;
Rear Adm. A.S. Carpender, 22 December 1941-3 June 1942;
Rear Adm. O.C. Badger, 3 June 1942-14 December 1942;
Rear Adm. M.L. Deyo, 14 December 1942-1 January 1944;
Rear Adm. J.C. Jones, 1 January 1944-20 September 1944;
Rear Adm. O.M. Rear, 20 September 1944-2 September 1945.

SERVICE FORCE, ATLANTIC FLEET (Established 1 March 1942, formerly Train, Atlantic Fleet.)
Train Atlantic Fleet.
Rear Adm. R. Jacobs, 7 December 1941-17 December 1941;
Vice Adm. F.L. Reichmuth, 17 December 1941-1 March 1942.
Service Force, Atlantic Fleet.
Vice Adm. F.L. Reichmuth, 1 March 1942-22 August 1942;
Vice Adm. A. Sharp, 22 August 1942-11 October 1944;
Commodore C.E. Battle (A), 11 October 1944-23 December 1944; Vice Adm. S.A. Taffinder, 23 December 1944-15 July 1945;
Commodore C.E. Battle (A), 15 July 1945-26 August 1945;
Vice Adm. R.C. Giffen, 26 August 1945-2 September 1945.

SUBMARINES, ATLANTIC FLEET
Rear Adm. R.S. Edwards, 7 December 1941-3 January 1942;
Capt. E.F. Cutts (A), 3 January 1942-30 March 1942;
Rear Adm. F.A. Daubin, 30 March 1942-25 November 1944;
Rear Adm. C.W. Styer, 25 November 1944-2 September 1945.

AIR FORCE, PACIFIC FLEET (Established 1 September 1942 combining Carriers, Pacific Fleet (formerly Aircraft, Battle Force, Pacific Fleet), and Patrol Wings, Pacific Fleet (formerly Aircraft, Scouting Force, Pacific Fleet).)
Aircraft, Battle Force, Pacific Fleet.
Vice Adm. W.F. Halsey, 7 December 1941-10 April 1942.
Carriers, Pacific Fleet (Established 10 April 1942).
Vice Adm. W.F. Halsey, 10 April 1942-11 July 1942;
Rear Adm. A.W. Fitch, 11 July 1942-31 August 1942.
Aircraft, Scouting Force, Pacific Fleet.
Rear Adm. J.S. McCain, 7 December 1941-10 April 1942.
Patrol Wings, Pacific Fleet (Established 10 April 1942).
Rear Adm. J.S. McCain, 10 April 1942-1 May 1942;
Rear Adm. P.N.L. Bellinger, 1 May 1942-9 August 1942;
Rear Adm. A.W. Fitch, 9 August 1942-31 August 1942.

819

Air Force, Pacific Fleet.
Rear Adm. A.W. Fitch, 1 September 1942-15 September 1942;
Rear Adm. L. Noyes (A), 15 September 1942-15 October 1942;
Vice Adm. J.H. Towers, 15 October 1942-28 February 1944;
Rear Adm. C.A. Pownall, 28 February 1944-16 August 1944;
Vice Adm. G.D. Murray, 16 August 1944-20 July 1945;
Vice Adm. A.E. Montgomery, 20 July 1945-2 September 1945.

AMPHIBIOUS FORCE, PACIFIC FLEET (Established 20 February 1942.)
Maj. Gen. C.B. Vogel, USMC, 20 February 1942-10 April 1942;
Vice Adm. W. Brown, 10 April 1942-1 July 1942;
Rear Adm. M.F. Draemel, 1 July 1942-10 August 1942;
Capt. F.A. Braisted (A), 10 August 1942-23 August 1942;
Rear Adm. F.W. Rockwell, 23 August 1942-15 August 1943;
Adm. R.K. Turner, 15 August 1943-2 September 1945.

BATTLESHIPS, PACIFIC FLEET (Established 10 April 1942, formerly Battleships, Battle Force. Type command divided into two Battleship Squadrons on 15 December 1944.)
Battleships, Battle Force.
Rear Adm. W.S. Anderson, 7 December 1941-10 April 1942.
Battleships, Pacific Fleet.
Rear Adm. W.S. Anderson, 10 April 1942-28 September 1942;
Vice Adm. H.F. Leary, 28 September 1942-16 April 1943;
Vice Adm. W.A. Lee, 16 April 1943-15 December 1944.
Battleship Squadron ONE.
Vice Adm. J.B. Oldendorf, 15 December 1944-2 September 1945.
Battleship Squadron TWO.
Vice Adm. W.A. Lee, 15 December 1944-16 June 1945;
Rear Adm. J.F. Shafroth, 16 June 1945-2 September 1945.

CRUISERS, PACIFIC FLEET (Established 10 April 1942 by combining Cruisers, Battle Force, Pacific Fleet, with Cruisers, Scouting Force, Pacific Fleet.)
Cruisers, Battle Force, Pacific Fleet.
Rear Adm. H.F. Leary, 7 December 1941-6 February 1942;
Rear Adm. F.J. Fletcher, 6 February 1942-10 April 1942.
Cruisers, Scouting Force, Pacific Fleet.
Rear Adm. J.H. Newton, 7 December 1941-31 December 1941;
Rear Adm. F.J. Fletcher, 31 December 1941-10 April 1942.
Cruises, Pacific Fleet.
Vice Adm. F.J. Fletcher, 10 April 1942-29 October 1942;
Rear Adm. T.C. Kinkaid, 29 October 1942-31 March 1943;
Rear Adm. M.S. Tisdale, 1 April 1943-2 January 1944;
Rear Adm. J.L. Kauffman, 2 January 1944-31 October 1944;
Rear Adm. W.L. Ainsworth, 31 October 1944-13 July 1945;
Rear Adm. W.H.P. Blandy, 13 July 1945-2 September 1945.

DESTROYERS, PACIFIC FLEET (Established 10 April 1942 from Destroyers, Battle Force, Pacific Fleet.)
Destroyers, Battle Force, Pacific Fleet.
Rear Adm. M.F. Draemel, 7 December 1941-30 December 1941;
Rear Adm. R.A. Theobald, 30 December 1941-10 April 1942.
Destroyers, Pacific Fleet.
Rear Adm. R.A. Theobald, 10 April 1942-4 July 1942;
Rear Adm. W.L. Ainsworth, 4 July 1942-8 January 1943;
Rear Adm. M.S. Tisdale, 8 January 1943-2 January 1944;
Rear Adm. J.L. Kauffman, 2 January 1944-31 October 1944;
Rear Adm. W.L. Ainsworth, 31 October 1944-13 July 1945;
Rear Adm. W.H.P. Blandy, 13 July 1945-2 September 1945;

MINECRAFT, PACIFIC FLEET (Established 15 October 1944).
Rear Adm. A. Sharp, 15 October 1944-30 August 1945;
Rear Adm. A.D. Struble, 30 August 1945-2 September 1945.

MOTOR TORPEDO BOAT SQUADRONS, PACIFIC FLEET (Established 1 February 1944.)
Commodore E.J. Moran, 9 March 1944-3 April 1945;
Commodore R.W. Bates, 20 May 1945-2 September 1945.

SERVICE FORCE, PACIFIC FLEET (Established 27 February 1942, formerly Base Force, Pacific Fleet.)
Base Force, Pacific Fleet.
Rear Adm. W.L. Calhoun, 7 December 1941-27 February 1942.
Service Force, Pacific Fleet.
Vice Adm. W.L. Calhoun, 27 February 1942-6 March 1945;
Vice Adm. W.W. Smith, 6 March 1945-2 September 1945.

SUBMARINE FORCE, PACIFIC FLEET (Established 20 September 1942, formerly Submarines, Pacific Fleet, originally Submarines, Scouting Force, Pacific Fleet.)
Submarines, Scouting Force, Pacific Fleet.
Rear Adm. T. Withers, 7 December 1941-1 January 1942. Submarines, Pacific Fleet (Established 1 January 1942).
Rear Adm. T. Withers, 1 January 1942-14 May 1942;
Rear Adm. R.H. English, 14 May 1942-20 September 1942.
Submarine Force, Pacific Fleet.
Rear Adm. R.H. English, 20 September 1942-21 January 1943;
Capt. J.H. Brown (A), 21 Jaunry 1943-14 February 1943;
Vice Adm. C.A. Lockwood, 14 February 1943-2 September 1945.

Commandants Of The United States Marine Corps: Place Of Birth And Dates Of Service As Commandant; Rank That Appears Is Highest Achieved (Highest rank of any Marine achieved during the American War For Independence was Major).
* Denotes death while serving.

1.) Major Samuel Nicholas (Pennsylvania), Nov. 28 1775-1781.
2.) Lieutenant Colonel William Ward Burrows (South Carolina), Jul. 12 1798-Mar. 6 1804.
3.) Lieutenant Colonel Franklin Wharton * (Pennsylvania), Mar. 7 1804-Sep. 1 1818.
3 A.) Upon the death of Commandant Wharton, Brevet Major Samuel Miller, Adjutant and Inspector serves as Acting Commandant, between Sept. 2-15 — 1818 and Brevet Major Archibald Henderson serves as acting Commandant September 16 1818-March 2 1819.
4.) Lieutenant Colonel Anthony Gale (Ireland), March 3 1819-October 16 1820.
5.) Colonel Archibaald Henderson * (Virginia), Oct. 17 1820-Jan. 6 1859. Col. Henderson achieves the rank of Brevet Brigadier General on March 4th 1843 in recognition for his services during the Florida Indian Wars, however, it is a personal rank and the decoration is for gallantry, having nothing to do with the position of Commandant.
6.) Colonel John Harris, * (Pennsylvania), Jan. 7th. 1859-May 12 1864.
6 A.) Major Agustus S. Nicholson, Adjutant and Inspector, serves as Acting Commandant between the death of Colonel Harris and the appointment of the seventh Commandant; May 13- June 9 1864.
7.) Brigadier General Jacob Zeilin (Pennsylvania), June 10 1864- Oct. 31 1876. Note: By Act of Congress Mar. 2 1867, the Commandant USMC is to receive the rank and pay of a Brigadier General of the Army. A subsequent Act repeals this act (June 6 1874), and stipulates that when a vacancy occurs, the office of Commandant will return to Colonel.
8.) Colonel Charles G. McCawley (Pennsylvania), Nov. 1 1876-Jan. 29 1891.
9.) Major General Charles Heywood (Maine), Jan. 30 1891- Oct. 2 1903. By Act of Congress March 3 1899, the office of Commandant is agaiun raised to Brigadier General and subsequently, by Act of July 1 1902, the Commandant is accorded the rank, pay and allowances of a Major General of the Army; this act stipulates that if a vacancy occurs, the rank will revert back to Brigadier General.
10.) Major General George Elliott (Alabama), Oct. 3 1903-Nov. 30 1910. By Act of Congress, MAy 13 1908, the office of Commandant raises the post of Commandant to that of MAjor General status; General Elliott is promoted on that date.
10 A.) General William P. Biddle is appointed Acting Commandant between the retirement of Elliott and his own permanent appointment.
11.) Major General William P. Biddle (Wisconsin) Feb. 3 1911-Feb. 24 1914.
12.) Major General George Barnett (Wisconsin), February 25 1914-June 30 1920.

13.) Major General John A. Lejeune (Louisiana), Jul. 1 1920-Mar. 4 1929. General Lejeune becomes the first Commandant appointed to a fixed term to be reappointed.

14.) Major General Wendell Neville * (Virginia), Mar. 5 1929-Jul. 8 1930.

15.) Major General Ben H. Fuller (Michigan), Jul. 9 1930-Feb. 28 1934.

16.) Major General John H. Russell (California), Mar. 1 1934-Nov. 30 1936.

17.) Lt. General Thomas Holcomb (Delaware),Dec. 1 1936-Dec. 31 1943. Act of Congress January 20 1942, raises the position of Commandant to the rank of Lieutenant General. The Congressional act also stipulates that the office "henceforth should be known as Commandant of the Marine Corps. Holcomb is raised to the rank of General at time of retirement, becoming the first Marine to attain that rank.

18.) General Alexander A. Vandegrift (Virginia), Jan. 1 1944 Dec. 31 1947. By Act of Congress, March 21, 1945, the President is authorized to raise the Commandant to the rank of General (six months after the close of hostilities WWII); Another Act, of August 7 1947, the rank of General for the Commandant is permanently fixed.

19.) General Clifton B. Cates (Tennessee) January 1 1948-Dec. 31 1951.

20.) General Lemuel C. Shepherd, Jr. (Virginia) January 1 1952-Dec. 31 1955.

21.) General Randolf McCall Pate (South Carolina), Jan 1 1956-Dec. 31 1959.

22.) General M. Schoup (Indiana), Jan. 1 1960-Dec. 31 1963. General Shoup was nominated by the President (Eisenhower) for a two-year term, however, the U.S.Senate invokes the law of 1913 and confirms him for a four-year appointment.

23.) General Wallace M. Greene, Jr. (Vermont), Jan. 1 1964-Dec. 31 1967.

24.) General Leonard P. Chapman, Jr. (Florida), Jan. 1 1968-Dec. 31 1971.

25.) General Robert E. Cushman, Jr. (Minnesota) Jan. 1 1972-Jun 30 1975.

26.) General H.. Wilson (Mississippi), Jul 1 1975-Jun 30 1979.

27.) General Robert H. Barrow (Louisiana), Jul 1 1979-Jun 30 1983.

28.) General Paul X. Kelley (Massachusetts), Jul 1 1983-Jun 30 1987.

29.) General Alfred (AL) M. Gray, N.J. (New Jersey), Jul 1 1987-Jun 30 1991.

30.) General Carl E. Mundy, (Georgia) July 1 1991-.

GENERAL OFFICERS OF THE U.S. MARINE CORPS: JULY 31, 1945 **Generals** — Alexander A. Vandegrift — Commandant of the Marine Corps

Lieutenant Generals — Holland M. Smith — Commanding General, Marine Training and Replacement Command, San Diego Area.

Roy S. Geiger — Commanding General, Fleet Marine Force Pacific.

Major Generals — Allen H. Turnage — Assistant to the Commandant of the Marine Corps.

Field Harris — Assistant Commandant for Air; Director of Marine Corps Aviation.

William P. T. Hill — Quartermaster General.

Thomas E. Watson — Director of Personnel (enroute).

Charles F. B. Price — Commanding General, Fleet Marine Force, San Diego Area.

James L. Underhill — Deputy Commander, Fleet Marine Force Pacific.

Keller E. Rockey — Commanding General, III Amphibious Corps.

Harry Schmidt — Commanding General, V Amphibious Corps.

Pedro del Valle — Commanding General, 1st Marine Division.

Leroy P. Hunt — Commanding General, 2d Marine Division.

Graves B. Erskine — Commanding General, 3d Marine Division.

Clifton B. Coates — Commanding General, 4th Marine Division.

Thomas E. Bourke — Commanding General, 5th Marine Division.

Lemuel C. Shepherd, Jr. — Commanding General, 6th Marine Division.

Claude A. Larkin — Commanding General , 1st Marine Aircraft Wing (enroute).

Louis E. Woods — Commanding General, 2d Marine Aircraft Wing and Tactical Air Force, 10th Army.

Ralph J. Mitchell — Commanding General, Marine Corps Air Bases, Cherry Point, N.C.

Francis P. Mulcahy — Enroute to Headquarters, Marine Corps.

Joseph C. Fegan — At home awaiting retirement.

Dewitt Peck — Enroute to 1st Marine Division.

Julian C. Smith — Commanding General, Department of the Pacific.

Henry L. Larsen — Island Commander, Guam.

Clayton B. Vogel — Commanding General, Marine Barracks Parris Island, S.C.

Philip H. Torrey — Commanding General, Marine Barracks Quantico, Va.

John Marston — Commanding General, Marine Barracks Camp Lejeune, N.C.

Earl C. Long — Commanding General, Marine Corps Base, San Diego, Calif.

Ross E. Rowell — Chief of U.S. Naval Aviation Mission.

Brigadier Generals — William L. McKittrick — Assistant Director of Aviation.

Raymond R. Wright — Paymaster General.

Leonard E. Rea — Executive Officer, Quartermaster Department.

Charles R. Sanderson — Officer in Charge, Purchase Division, Quartermaster Dept.

William C. James — Assistant Director of Personnel (Acting Director).

Elmer E. Hall — Liaison Officer, Personnel Dept.

Gerald C. Thomas — Director, Division of Plans and Policies.

William O. Brice — Executive Officer, Division of Plans and Policies.

Frank Whitehead (Retd) — Attached to Office of Director, Division of Plans and Policies.

Robert L. Denig (Retd) — Director, Division of Public Information.

Merwin H. Silverthorn — Chief of Staff, Fleet Marine Force, Pacific.

Archie F. Howard — Inspector General, Fleet Marine Force Pacific.

Harry K. Pickett — Commanding General, Troop Training Unit, Training Command, Amphibiuos Forces, Pacific Fleet.

Oscar R. Cauldwell — Commanding General, Marine Training Command, San Diego Area.

Merritt A. Edson — Commanding General, Service Command, Fleet Marine Force, Pacific.

Alphonse DeCarre — President, Marine Corps Equipment Board, Quantico, Va.

Andrew, E. Creesy — Director of Supply, Supply Division, Service Command, Fleet Marine Force, Pacific.

Evans, O. Ames — Chief of Staff and Deputy Commander, Supply Service, Fleet Marine Force, Pacific.

William A. Worton — Chief of Staff, III Amphibious Corps.

David R. Nimmer — Commanding General, Corps Artillery III Amphibious Corps.

William W. Rogers — Chief of Staff, V Amphibious Corps.

Robert H. Pepper — Commanding General, Corps Artillery V Amphib ious Corps.

Louis R. Jones — Assistant Division Commander, 1st Marine Division.

John T. Walker — Assistant Division Commander, 2nd Marine Division.

William E. Riley — Assistant Division Commander, 3d Marine Division.

Franklin A. Hart — Assistant Division Commander, 4th Marine Division.

Ray A. Robinson — Assistant Division Commander, 5th Marine Division.

William T. Clement — Assistant Division Commander, 6th Marine Division.

William J. Wallace — Commanding General, Air Defense Command and Fighter Command Tactical Air Force, 10th Army.

Robert Blake — Marine Deputy Chief of Staff, 10th Army.

Omar T. Pfeiffer — Staff Marine Officer, Commander-in-Chief, U.S. Fleet.

Joseph H. Fellows — Staff, Commander-in-Chief, U.S. Fleet and Pacific Ocean Area.

Lewie G. Merritt — Commanding General, 1st Marine Aircraft Wing.

Lawson, H.M. Sanderson — Commanding General, 4th Marine Aircraft Wing and Shore-Based Air Force, Marshalls-Gilberts Area.

Byron F. Johnson — Commanding General, 3d Marine Aircraft Wing.

Littleton W.T. Waller, Jr., Commanding General, Marine Garrison Forces, 14th Naval District.

Walter G. Farrell — Deputy Commander, 11th Naval District Air Bases, El Toro, Calif.

Leo D. Hermle — Deputy Island Commander, Guam.

Christian F. Schilt — Island Commander, Peleliu.

Ivan W. Miller — Commanding General, Marine Fleet Air, West Coast.

Ford O. Rogers — With 1st Marine Aircraft Wing; under orders to duty as Island Commander, Peleliu.

Harold D. Campbell — Commanding General, Marine Corps Air Bases and 9th Marine Aircraft Wing, Cherry Point, N.C.

Thomas J. Cushman — Commanding General, Marine Corps Air Station, Cherry Point, N.C.

Ira L. Kimes (Retd) — Commanding General, U.S. Marine Corps Air Station, Quantico, Va.

Alfred H. Noble — Commanding General, Marine Training Command, Camp Lejeune, N.C.

Samuel C. Cumming — Chief of Staff, Marine Barracks, Quantico, Va.

Oliver P. Smith — Commandant, Marine Corps Schools, Quantico, Va.

Arnold W. Jacobsen — Commanding General, Depot of Supplies, San Francisco, Calif.

Maurice C. Gregory — Depot Quartermaster, Depot of Supplies, Philadelphia, Pa.

Joseph T. Smith — President, Naval Retiring Board.

Listing U.S. Naval Academy Officers who attain rank of ADM (entering Annapolis between 1877 and 1940). The highest rank achieved is listed. Those who serve beyond 1950 or succumb beyond 1950 are noted as such. In addition, some other Annapolis Officers who do not achieve the rank of ADM are also listed. This list is not to be construed as all incompassing.

The number immediately following the name is the year of graduation and this is followed by the Official Midshipman Number.

Benson William Shepherd (1877 — No. 01337) Adm; Ret 9-25-19.

Rodgers Thomas Slidell (1878 — No. 01348) RAdm; Ret 7-19-19.

Glennon James Henry (1878 — No. 01351) RAdm; Ret 2-11-21.

Knapp Harry Shepard (1878 — No. 01352) RAdm; Ret 6-27-20.

Rodgers William Ledyard (1878 — No. 01355) Adm; Ret 2-4-24.

Huse Harry Mclaren, P. (1878 — No. 01357) VAdm; Ret 12-8-22.

Clark George Ramsey (1878 — No. 01372) RAdm; Ret 2-6-21.

Griffin Robert Stanislaus (1878 — No. 01387) RAdm; Ret 9-27-21.

McElroy George Wrightman (1878 — No. 01388) RAdm; Ret 3-19-22.

Burd George Eli (1878 — No. 01396) RAdm; Ret 4-27-21.

Hood John Hayden Edward Everett (1879 — No. 01400) RAdm; Ret 1921.

Hayden Edward Everett (1879 — No. 01400) RAdm; Ret 6-30-21.

Gill William Andrew (1879 — No. 01410) RAdm; Dies 10-10-18.

Snowden Thomas (1879 — No. 01418) RAdm; Ret 8-12-21.

Bryan Benjamin Chambers (1879 — No. 01441) RAdm; Ret 11-4-19.

Carr Clarence Alfred (1879 — No. 01443) RAdm; Ret 7-22-30.

Norton Harold Percival (1879 — No. 01448) RAdm; Ret 11-4-19.

Niblack Albert Parker (1880 — No. 01471) VAdm; Ret 7-25-23.

Simpson Edward Jr. (1880 — No. 01487) RAdm; Ret 9-16-24.

Sims William Sowden (1880 — No. 01493) Adm; Ret 10-15-22.

Rodman Hugh (1880 — No. 01521) Adm; Ret 1-6-23.

Kinkaid Thomas Wright (1880 — No. 01536) RAdm; Dies 8-11-20.

Smith William Strother (1880 — No. 01539) RAdm; Ret 9-15-21.

Hoogewerff John Adrian (1881 — No. 01543) RAdm; Ret 11-27-24.

Wilson Harry Braid (1881 — No. 01560) Adm; Ret 2-23-25.

Kaemmerling Gustave (1881 — No. 01613) RAdm; Ret 5-15-22.

Wood Spencer Shepard (1882 — No. 01637) RAdm; Ret 12-19-21.

Fletcher William Bartlett (1882 — No. 01639) RAdm; Ret 12-31-21.

Johnston Marbury (1882 — No. 01642) RAdm; Ret 12-2-24.

Jayne Joseph Lee (1882 — No. 01647) RAdm; Ret 5-10-21.

Howard William Lauriston (1882 — No. 01652) RAdm; Ret 12-21-19.

Anderson Edwin Alexander (1882 — No. 01654) RAdm; Ret 3-23-24.

Dyson Charles Wilson (1883 — No. 01704) RAdm; Ret 12-2-25.

Halstead Alexander Seaman (1883 — No. 01713) RAdm; Ret 11-12-23.

Field Harry Ashby (1883 — No. 01717) RAdm; Ret 12-31-21.

Williams Clarence Stewart (1884 — No. 01754) Adm; Ret 10-7-27.

Welles Roger Jr. (1884 — No. 01758) RAdm; Ret 12-7-26.

McDonald John Daniel (1884 — No. 01764) VAdm; Ret 11-1-27.

Jones Hilary Pollard (1884 — No. 01766) Adm; Ret 11-14-27.

Shoemaker William Rawle (1884 — No. 01772) RAdm; Ret 2-10-27.

Plunkett Charles Peshall (1884 — No. 01773) RAdm; Ret 2-15-28.

McKean Josiah Slutts (1884 — No. 01778) Adm; Ret 5-30-28.

Crisp Richard Owens (1884 — No. 01794) RAdm; Ret 12-22-25.

Taylor David Watson (1885 — No. 01796) RAdm; Ret 1-16-23.

Tawresey John Godwin (1885 — No. 01798) RAdm; Ret 1-23-26.

Kline George Washington (1885 — No. 01804) RAdm; Ret 6-24-21.

Strauss Joseph (1885 — No. 01809) Adm; Ret 11-26-25.

Eberle Edward Walter (1885 — No. 01816) Adm; Superintendant U.S.N.A. 9-20-15 — 2-12-19; CNO 6-21-23 — 11-14-27; Dies 7-6-29.

Coontz Robert Edward (1885 — No. 01823) Adm; Ret 6-11-28.

Bullard William Hannum, G. (1886 — No. 01634) RAdm; Ret 9-30-22.

Oman Joseph Wallace (1886 — No. 01836) RAdm; Ret 8-31-21.

Andrews Phillip (1886 — No. 01839) RAdm; Ret 3-31-30.

Stocker Robert (1887 — No. 01857) RAdm; Ret 3-1-25.

Snow Elliot (1887 — No. 01859) RAdm; Ret 6-21-26.

Decker, Benton Clark (1887 — No. 01859) RAdm; Ret 12-28-23.

Bristol, Mark Lambert (1887 — No. 01861) RAdm; Ret 5-1-32.

McCully, Newton Alexander Jr (1887 — No. 01863) VAdm; 7-1-31.

Bryan, Henry Francis (1887 — No. 01870) RAdm; Ret 12-31-21.

Long, Andrew Theodore (1887 — No. 01874) RAdm; Ret 4-6-30.

Washington, Thomas (1887 — No. 01877) Adm; Ret 6-6-29.

Scales, Archibald Henderson (1887 — No. 01878) RAdm; Ret 10-5-26.

Blue, Victor (1887 — No. 01885) RAdm; Ret 7-11-19.

Burrage, Guy Hamilton (1887 — No. 01888) VAdm; Ret 7-1-31.

Jackson, Richard Harrison (1887 — No. 01892) Adm; Ret 5-10-30.

Robertson, Ashley Herman (1888 — No. 01904) RAdm; Dies 7-13-30.

Brittain, Carlo Bonaparte (1888 — No. 01905) RAdm; Dies 4-22-20.

Morgan, Casey Bruce (1888 — No. 01906) RAdm; Ret 10-25-23.

Robison, Samuel Shelburne (1888 — No. 01914) Adm; Ret 6-1-31.

Chandler, Loyld Horwitz (1888 — No. 01915) RAdm; Ret 12-17-21.

Hughes, Charles Fredric (1888 — No. 01920) Adm; Ret 11-1-30.

Stickney, Herman Osman (1888 — No. 01929) RAdm; Ret 12-10-67.

Bassett, Frederick B., Jr (1888 — No. 01931) RAdm; Ret 1-4-25.

Wiley, Henery Ariosto (1888 — No. 01934) Adm; Ret 9-30-29.

Hobson, Richard Pearson (1889 — No. 01936) RAdm; Ret 2-6-30.

Rock, George Henry (1889 — No. 01937) RAdm; Ret 10-1-32.

Twining, Nathan Crook (1889 — No. 01939) RAdm; Ret 1-5-23.

Hutchison, Benjamin Franklin (1889 — No. 01940) RAdm; Dies 9-17-27.

Pratt, William Veazie (1889 — No. 01941) Adm; Ret 6-3-33.

Kittele, Summer Ely (1889 — No. 01942) RAdm; Ret 7-1-31.

Marvell, George Ralph (1889 — No. 01943) RAdm; Ret 10-1-33.

Nulton, Louis Mccoy (1889 — No. 01944) Adm; Ret 9-1-33.

MacDougall, William Dugald (1889 — No. 01949) RAdm; Ret 7-1-32.

Magruder, Thomas Pickett (1889 — No. 01951) RAdm; Ret 12-1-31.

De Steiguer, Louis Rudolph (1889 — No. 01953) RAdm; Ret 4-1-31.

Phelps, William Woodward (1889 — No. 01955) RAdm; Ret 7-1-33.

Cole, William Carey (1889 — No. 01958) RAdm; Ret 9-1-32.

Schofield, Frank Herman (1890 — No. 01974) RAdm; Ret 2-1-33.

Chase, Jehu Valentine (1890 — No. 01975) RAdm; Ret 2-1-33.

Ziegemeier, Henry Joseph (1890 — No. 01977) RAdm; Dies 10-15-30.

Taylor, Montgomery Meigs (1890 — No. 01983) Adm; Ret 11-1-33.

Williams, George Washington (1890 — No. 01985) RAdm; Dies 7-17-25.

McVay, Charles Butler Jr (1890 — No. 01988) Adm; Ret 10-1-32.

Vogelgesang, Charles Theodore (1890 — No. 01989) RAdm; Dies 2-16-27.

Dayton, John Havens (1890 — No. 01996) VAdm; Ret 1-6-30.

Bostwick, Lusius Allyn (1890 — No. 01997) RAdm; Ret 3-1-33.

Moffett, William Adger (1890 — No. 02001) RAdm; Dies 4-4-33 (Lost in Akron).

Latimer, Julius Lang (1890 — No. 02002) RAdm; Ret 10-1-30.

Dismukes, Douglas Eugene (1890 — No. 02003) RAdm; Ret 10-1-25.

Gilmor, Horatio Gonzalo (1891 — No. 02006) RAdm; Ret 2-1-34.

Watt, Richard Morgan (1891 — No. 02008) RAdm; Ret 7-1-36.

Belknap, Reginald Rowan (1891 — No. 02009) RAdm; Ret 6-30-26.

Willard, Arthur Lee (1891 — No. 02016) RAdm; Ret 3-1-34.

Christy, Harley Hannibal (1891 — No. 02017) RAdm; Ret 10-1-34.

Hough, Henry Hughes (1891 — No. 02020) RAdm; Ret 2-1-35.

Irwin, Noble Edward (1891 — No. 02021) RAdm; Ret 10-1-33.

Senn, Thomas Jones (1891 — No. 02029) RAdm; Ret 1-1-36.

Leigh, Richard Henry (1891 — No. 02038) Adm; Ret 9-1-34.

Laws, George William (1891 — No. 02047) RAdm; Ret 3-1-34.

Beuret, John Dougall (1892 — No. 02051) RAdm; Ret 11-20-29.

Day, George Calvin (1892 — No. 02054) RAdm; Ret 12-1-35.

McNamee, Luke (1892 — No. 02055) Adm; Ret 9-1-34.

Blakely, John Russell Y. (1892 — No. 02058) RAdm; Ret 7-1-32.

Hussey, Charles Lincoln (1892 — No. 02063) RAdm; Ret 10-1-27.

Stirling, Yates Jr (1892 — No. 02072) RAdm; Ret 5-1-36.

Pringle, Joel Roberts P. (1892 — No. 02076) VAdm; Dies 9-25-32.

Clark, Frank Hodges Jr (1893 — No. 02095) RAdm; Ret 1-1-36.

Crosley, Walter Selwyn (1893 — No. 02100) RAdm; Ret 11-1-35.

Campbell, Edward Hale (1893 — No. 02103) RAdm; Ret 11-1-36.

Upham, Frank Brooks (1893 — No. 02121) RAdm; Ret 10-1-36.

Robert, William Pierre (1894 — No. 02135) RAdm; Ret 8-1-37.

Sellers, David Foote (1894 — No. 02139) Adm; Ret 3-1-38.

Graham, Stephen Victor (1894 — No. 02151) RAdm; Ret 6-30-29.

Hinds, Alfred Walton (1894 — No. 02153) RAdm; Ret 9-1-27.

Scott, William Pitt (1894 — No. 02165) RAdm; Ret 6-30-29.

Reeves, Joseph Mason (1894 — No. 02172) Adm; Ret 12-1-36.

Cone, Hutch Ingham (1894 — No. 02176) RAdm; Ret 7-11-22.

Brumby, Frank Hardeman (1895 — No. 02185) Adm; Ret 10-1-38.

Laning, Harris (1895 — No. 02189) RAdm; Ret 11-1-37.

Butler, Henry Varnum Jr (1895 — No. 02194) VAdm; Ret 3-1-38.

Raby, James Joseph (1895 — No. 02200) RAdm; Dies 1-15-34.

Standley, William Harrison (1895 — No. 02203) Adm; Ret 1-1-37.

Gherardi, Walter Rockwell (1895 — No. 02204) RAdm; Dies 7-24-39.

Johnston, Rufus Zenas (1895 — No. 02217) RAdm; Ret 6-30-30.

Craven, Thomas Tingey (1896 — No. 02226) VAdm; Ret 8-1-37.

Earle, Ralph (1896 — No. 02228) RAdm; Ret 8-25-25.

Cluverius, Wat Tyler Jr (1896 — No. 02237) Adm; Ret 1-1-39.

Marshall, Albert Ware (1896 — No. 02241) RAdm; Ret 5-1-38.

DuBose, William Gunnell (1887 — No. 02261) RAdm; Ret 10-1-40.

Yarnell, Harry Ervin (1897 — No. 02264) RAdm; Ret 11-1-41.

Hepburn, Arthur Japy (1897 — No. 02266) Adm; Ret 11-1-41.

Hart, Thomas Charles (1897 — No. 02273) Adm; Ret 7-30-42.

Murfin, Orin Gould (1897 — No. 02274) Adm; Ret 5-1-40.

White, William Russell (1897 — No. 02279) RAdm; Ret 9-15-23.

Sexton, Walton Roswell (1897 — No. 02283) Adm; Ret 10-1-40.

Smith, Arthur St Clair Jr (1897 — No. 02294) RAdm; Ret 1-1-38.

Leahy, William Daniel (1897 — No. 02295) Fleet Adm; Ret 8-1-39.

Kempff, Clarence Selby (1897 — No. 02306) RAdm; Ret 7-1-38.

Leutze, Trevor William (1897-Non-Graduate — No. 897010) RAdm; Dies 4-25-66.

Halligan, John Jr (1898 — No. 02308) RAdm; Dies 12-11-34.

Williams, Henry (1898 — No. 02309) RAdm; Ret 9-1-41.

Watts, William Carleton (1898 — No. 02310) RAdm; Ret 12-1-40.

Tarrant, William Theodore (1898 — No. 02330) VAdm; Ret 8-1-42.

Williams, Yancey Sullivan (1898 — No. 02334) RAdm; Dies 11-1-38.

Pettengill, George Tifort (1898 — No. 02337) RAdm; Ret 11-1-41.

Schofield, John Anderson (1898 — No. 02338) RAdm; Res 2-1-07.

Nelson, Charles Preston (1898 — No. 02345) RAdm; Ret 6-30-33.

Huntington, Arthur Franklin (1898-Non-Graduate — No. 898017) RAdm; Dies 4-19-54.

Fenner, Edward Blaine (1899 — No. 02350) RAdm.

White, Richard Drace (1899 — No. 02352) RAdm; Ret 7-1-34.

Dungan, Paul Baxter (1899 — No. 02358) RAdm; Ret 1-1-41.

Bloch, Claude Charles (1899 — No. 02360) Adm; Ret 8-1-42.

Lackey, Henry Ellis (1899 — No. 02362) RAdm; Ret 7-1-40.

Taussig, Joseph Knefler (1899 — No. 02363) VAdm; Ret 9-1-41.

Kalbfus, Edward Clifford (1899 — No. 02364) Adm; Ret 12-1-41.

Woodward, Clark Howell (1899 — No. 02365) VAdm; Ret 4-1-47.

Cole, Cyrus Williard (1899 — No. 02367) RAdm; Ret 7-1-40.

Greenslade, John Wills (1899 — No. 02373) VAdm; Ret 2-1-44.

Watson, Adolphus Eugene (1899 — No. 02374) RAdm; Dies 10-3-49.

Brinser, Harry Lerch (1899 — No. 02380) RAdm; Ret 12-1-40.

Courtney, Charles Edward (1899 — No. 02384) VAdm; Ret 7-1-41.

Horne, Frederick Joseph (1899 — No. 02387) Adm; Ret 8-1-46.

Johnson, Alfred Wilkinson (1899 — No. 02388) VAdm; Ret 12-1-40.

Larimer, Edgar Brown (1899 — No. 02389) RAdm; Ret 11-1-34.

Pope, Ralph Elton (1899 — No. 02394) RAdm; Ret 7-30-34.

Snyder, Charles Philip (1900 — No. 02403) Adm; Ret 4-2-47.

Defrees, Joseph Rollie (1900 — No. 02405) RAdm; Ret 7-1-40.

Bryant, Samuel Wood (1900 — No. 02408) RAdm; Ret 3-1-37.

Mannix, Daniel Pratt (1900 — No. 02411) RAdm; Dies 9-1-57.

Wainwright, John Drayton (1900 — No. 02422) RAdm; Ret 7-1-42.

Gannon, Sinclair (1900 — No. 02423) RAdm; Ret 4-1-41.

Freeman, Charles Seymour (1900 — No. 02432) VAdm; Ret 12-1-42.

Cocke, Herbert Claiborne (1900 — No. 02434) RAdm; Ret 6-30-35.

Ellis, Hayne (1900 — No. 02439) RAdm; Ret 9-1-41.

Berrien, Frank Dunn (1900 — No. 02440) RAdm; Ret 6-30-35.

Train, Charles Russell (1900 — No. 02454) RAdm; Ret 7-1-39.

Osterhaus, Hugo Wilson (1900 — No. 02456) RAdm; Ret 6-30-35.

Shea, William H. (1900-Non-Graduate — No. 900019) RAdm; Dies 9-18-58.

Furer, Julius Augustus (1901 — No. 02461) RAdm; Ret 9-30-44.

King, Ernest Joseph (1901 — No. 02464) Fleet Adm; Dies 6-25-56.

Howe, Alfred Graham (1901 — No. 02469) RAdm; Ret 6-30-56.

Fisher, Charles Willis (1901 — No. 02472) RAdm; Ret 8-22-46.

Andrews, Adolphus (1901 — No. 02478) VAdm; Dies 6-19-48.

Simons, Manley Hale (1901 — No. 02489) RAdm; Ret 6-1-43.

Bass, Ivan Ernest (1901 — No. 02491) RAdm; Ret 8-1-41.

Pye, William Satterlee (1901 — No. 02492) VAdm; Ret 7-1-44.

Allen, Burrell Clinton (1901 — No. 02494) RAdm; Ret 6-30-36.

Fairfield, Arthur Philip (1901 — No. 02496) VAdm; Ret 3-1-41.

Vernou, Walter Newhall (1901 — No. 02504) VAdm; Dies 5-23-55.

Foote, Percy Wright (1901 — No. 02506) RAdm; Ret 6-30-36.

Neal, George Franklin (1901 — No. 02511) RAdm; Ret 2-1-41.

Allen, William Henry (1901 — No. 02512) RAdm; Ret 7-1-41.

Downes, John Jr (1901 — No. 02515) RAdm; Ret 12-1-43.

Zogbaum, Rufus Fairchild Jr (1901 — No. 02526) RAdm; Ret 6-30-36.

Roosevelt, Henry Latrobe (1901-Non-Graduate — No. 901017) Dies 2-22-36.

Richardson, James Otto (1902 — No. 02532) Adm; Ret 10-1-42.

Land, Emory Scott (1902 — No. 02532) VAdm; Ret 4-15-37.

Baldridge, Harry Alexander (1902 — No. 02540) RAdm; Ret 2-1-32.

Meyers, George Julian (1902 — No. 02543) RAdm; Dies 12-7-39.

Marquart, Edward John (1902 — No. 02544) RAdm; Ret 4-1-44.

Rowcliff, Gilbert Jonathan (1902 — No. 02553) RAdm; Ret 7-1-45.

Porterfield, Lewis Broughton (1902 — No. 02554) RAdm; Ret 7-1-37.

Lannon, James Patrick (1902 — No. 02558) RAdm; Ret 7-30-37.

Staton, Adolphus (1902 — No. 02562) RAdm; Ret 6-30-37.

Nichols, Neil Ernest (1902 — No. 02565) RAdm; Ret 6-30-37.

Henderson, Robert (1902 — No. 02569) RAdm; Ret 2-12-29.

Townsend, Julius Curtis (1902 — No. 02570) RAdm; Dies 12-28-38.

Brown, Wilson (1902 — No. 02571) VAdm; Ret 12-1-44.

Van Keuren, Alexander H. (1903 — No. 02588) RAdm; Ret 4-1-45.

Anderson, Walter Stratton (1903 — No. 02592) VAdm; Ret 3-1-46.

Ryden, Roy Warren (1903 — No. 02594) RAdm; Ret 8-1-46.

Cooke, Henry David Jr (1903 — No.02595) RAdm; Ret 6-30-39.

Robinson, Samuel Murray (1903 — No. 02597) Adm; Ret 1-1-46.

Holmes, Ralston Smith (1903 — No. 02601) RAdm; Ret 1-1-43.

Leahy, Lamar Richard (1903 — No. 02607) RAdm; Ret 6-30-39.

Blakely, Charles A. (1903 — No. 02613) VAdm; Ret 10-1-42.

Stark, Harold Raynsford (1903 — No. 02616) Adm; Dies 8-20-42.

Metcalf, Martin Kellog (1903 — No. 02621) RAdm; Ret 1-1-38.

Taylor, Thomas Herbert (1903 — No. 02627) RAdm; Ret 6-30-39.

Sadler, Frank Howard (1903 — No. 02628) RAdm; Ret 7-1-43.

LeBreton, David Mcdougal (1904 — No. 02637) RAdm; Ret 10-1-47.

Pickens, Andrew Calhoun (1904 — No. 02638) RAdm; Ret 1-1-43.

Howard, Herbert Seymour (1904 — No. 02648) RAdm; Ret 9-1-46.

Kimmel, Husband Edward (1904 — No. 02649) RAdm; Ret 3-1-42.

Todd, Forde Anderson (1904 — No. 02671) RAdm; Ret 5-1-41.

McMillen, Fred Ewing (1904 — No. 02672) RAdm; Ret 8-1-46.

Halsey, William Frederick Jr (1904 — No. 02679) Fleet Adm; Dies 8-16-59.

Stuart, Harry Allen (1904 — No. 02681) RAdm; Ret 3-1-43.

Johnson, Isaac Cureton (1904 — No. 02690) RAdm; Ret 6-30-39.

Bagley, David Worth (1904 — No. 02693) Adm; Ret 4-1-47.

McCullough, Richard Philip (1904 — No. 02698) RAdm; Ret 1-1-32.

Cox, Ormond Lee (1905 — No. 02701) RAdm; Dies 4-16-68.

Leary, Herbert Fairfax (1905 — No. 02703) VAdm; Dies 12-3-57.

Nimitz, Chester William (1905 — No. 02705) Fleet Adm; Dies 2-10-66.

Church, Albert Thomas (1905 — No. 02710) RAdm; Ret 1-1-43.

Woodson, Walter Browne (1905 — No. 02727) RAdm; Ret 9-1-43.

Furlong, William Rae (1905 — No. 02729) RAdm; Ret 6-1-46.

Cook, Arthur Byron (1905 — No. 02734) VAdm; Ret 1-11-52.

Bowen, Harold Gardiner (1905 — No. 02741) VAdm; Ret 6-1-47.

Spears, William Oscar (1905 — No. 02747) RAdm; Ret 6-30-40.

Hooper, Stanford Caldwell (1905 — No. 02753) RAdm; Ret 1-1-43.

Shoemaker, Harry Earl (1905 — No. 02757) RAdm; Ret 6-30-40.

Newton, John Henry Jr (1905 — No. 02759) RAdm; Ret 5-1-46.

Carter, Andrew Francis (1905 — No. 02762) RAdm; Ret 3-46.

Friedell, Wilhelm Lee (1905 — No. 02774) RAdm; Ret 3-1-46.

McNair, Laurance North (1905 — No. 02780) RAdm; Ret 6-30-41.

Wilcox, John Walter Jr (1905 — No. 02782) RAdm; Dies 3-27-42.

Smeallie, John Morris (1905 — No. 02806) RAdm; Ret 4-1-42.

Chantry, Allan J. Jr (1906 — No. 02813) RAdm; Ret 4-1-46.

Bryan, George Sloan (1906 — No. 02820) RAdm; Ret 6-30-41.

Ghormley, Robert Lee (1906 — No. 02824) VAdm; Ret 8-1-46.

Calhoun, William Lowndes (1906 — No. 02825) Adm; Ret 12-1-46.

Wilson, Russell (1906 — No. 02826) VAdm; Ret 1-1-43.

Noyes, Leigh (1906 — No. 02827) VAdm; Ret 11-1-46.

Glassford, William A. Jr (1906 — No. 02833) VAdm; Ret 3-1-47.

Fletcher, Frank Jack (1906 — No. 02838) Adm; Ret 6-1-47.

Bristol, Arthur Leroy Jr (1906 — No. 02839) VAdm; Dies 4-20-42.

Towers, John Henry (1906 — No. 02843) Adm; Ret 12-1-47.

Draemel, Milo F. (1906 — No. 02846) RAdm; Ret 8-31-46.

Withers, Thomas Jr (1906 — No. 02847) RAdm; Ret 10-1-46.

Smith, Kirby (1906 — No. 02848) RAdm; Res 5-24-20.

Reichmuth, Ferdinand Louis (1906 — No. 02858) VAdm; Ret 8-1-46.

Smith, Norman Murray (1906 — No. 02862) RAdm; Ret 12-1-37.

Kidd, Isaac Campbell (1906 — No. 02865) RAdm; Dies 12-7-41.

Hartigan, Charles Conway (1906 — No. 02882) RAdm; Ret 6-30-41.

Brainard, Roland Munroe (1906 — No. 02889) VAdm; Ret 11-1-43.

McCain, John Sidney (1906 — No. 02892) Adm; Dies 9-6-45.

Sharp, Alexander Jr (1906 — No. 02908) VAdm; Ret 9-1-46.

Taffinder, Sherwoode Ayerst (1906 — No. 02920) VAdm; Ret 1-1-47.

Fitch, Aubrey Wray (1906 — No. 02922) Adm; Ret 7-1-47.

Read, Albert Cushing (1907 — No. 02932) RAdm; Ret 9-1-46.

Theobald, Robert Alfred (1907 — No. 02937) RAdm; Ret 2-1-45.

Schuyler, Garret Lansing (1907 — No. 02939) RAdm; Ret 1-1-47.

Spruance, Raymond Ames (1907 — No. 02953) Adm; Ret 7-1-48.

Gygax, Felix Xerxes (1907 — No. 02956) RAdm; Ret 8-1-46.

Hewitt, Henry Kent (1907 — No. 02958) Adm; Ret 3-1-49.

Cumming, John Whitlow W. (1907 — No. 02960) RAdm; Ret 6-30-35.

Dunn, Charles Alfred (1907 — No. 02968) RAdm; Ret 7-1-47.

Bassett, Claude Oscar (1907 — No. 02969) RAdm; Ret 6-29-48.

Bruce, Bryson (1907 — No. 02978) RAdm; Ret 11-1-46.

Beauregard, Augustin Toutant (1907 — No. 02979) RAdm; Ret 11-1-42.

Jacobs, Randall (1907 — No. 02987) VAdm; Ret 11-1-46.

Edwards, Richard Stanislaus (1907 — No. 02991) Adm; Ret 7-1-47.

Mayfield, Irving Hall (1907 — No. 02293) RAdm; Ret 11-1-46.

Hoover, John Howard (1907 — No. 03001) Adm; Ret 7-1-48.

Jones, Claud Ashton (1907 — No. 03002) RAdm; Ret 6-30-46.

McWhorter, Ernest Doyle (1907 — No. 03009) RAdm; Ret 2-1-44.

Farquhar, Allan Shannon (1907 — No. 03010) RAdm; Ret 10-24-45.

Bemis, Harold Medberry (1907 — No. 03011) RAdm; Ret 8-1-46.

Farber, William Sims (1907 — No. 03019) VAdm; Ret 12-1-46.

Crosse, Charles Washburn (1907 — No. 03029) RAdm; Ret 5-22-45.

Giffen, Robert Carlisle (1907 — No. 03064) VAdm; Ret 9-1-46.

Bratton, Leslie Emmett (1907 — No. 03071) RAdm; Ret 6-4-30.

Allen, Ezra Griffin (1907 — No. 03077) RAdm; Ret 11-1-46.

Ingram, Jonas Howard (1907 — No. 03115) Adm; Ret 4-1-47.

Turner, Richard Kelly (1908 — No. 03142) Adm; Ret 6-30-47.

Charlton, Alexander Mark (1908 — No. 03143) RAdm; Ret 10-1-46.

Bidwell, Abel Trood (1908 — No. 03155) RAdm; Ret 10-1-42.

Broshek, Joseph John (1908 — No. 03156) RAdm; Ret 10-1-46.

Wille, Frank Joseph (1908 — No. 03157) RAdm; Ret 7-1-47.

Kilpatrick, Walter Kenneth (1908 — No. 03159) RAdm; Ret 9-1-46.

Foy, Edward James (1908 — No. 03164) RAdm; Ret 11-1-46.

Kraus, Sydney Moses (1908 — No. 03180) RAdm; Ret 1-1-48.

Rockwell, Francis Warren (1908 — No. 03181) VAdm; Ret 8-1-48.

Taylor, Henry George (1908 — No. 03193) RAdm; Ret 11-1-46.

Kauffman, James Laurence (1908 — No. 03202) VAdm; Ret 5-1-49.

Irish, James McCredie (1908 — No. 03207) RAdm; Ret 11-1-46.

Munroe, William Robert (1908 — No. 03210) VAdm; Ret 10-1-47.

Penn, Albert Miller (1908 — No. 03212) RAdm; Dies 9-19-47.

Bastedo, Paul Henry (1908 — No. 03220) RAdm; Ret 4-1-44.

Shafroth, John Franklin (1908 — No. 03228) VAdm; Ret 4-14-49.

James, Jules (1908 — No. 03236) VAdm; Ret 11-1-46.

Beardall, John Reginald (1908 — No. 03241) RAdm; Ret 11-1-46.

Lee, Willis Augustus Jr. (1908 — No. 03243) VAdm; Dies 8-25-45, aboard Launch transporting him to U.S.S. Wyoming (his Flagship) in Casco Bay, Portland Maine.

Knerr, Hugh Johnston (1908 — No. 03249) becomes Major General in USAF; Ret 4-1-49.

Keleher, Timothy Jerome (1908 — No. 03250) RAdm; Ret 7-1-43.

Pierce, Maurice Rumford (1908 — No. 03252) RAdm; Ret 2-1-32.

Kinkaid, Thomas Assin (1908 — No. 03273) Adm; Ret 5-30-50.

Purnell, William Reynolds (1908 — No. 03227) RAdm; Ret 10-1-46.

Carter, Worrall Reed (1908 — No. 03306) RAdm; Ret 2-1-47.

Emmet, Robert Rutherfurd (1908 — No. 03316) RAdm; Ret 8-2-46.

Janeway, Augustine S. (1908 non-graduate) becomes Brigadier General U.S.A.

Waller, Littleton W Tazewell (1908 non-graduate) becomes Major General USMCR; active duty WWII; Ret 6-1-46.

Wilkinson, Theodore Stark (1909 — No. 03339) VAdm; Receives Mofh; Dies accidently 2-21-46 when automobile is accidently driven off Ferry at Norfolk.

Smith, William Ward (1909 — No. 03341) VAdm; Ret 10-1-46.

Hustvedt, Olaf Mandt (1909 — No. 03346) VAdm; Ret 3-1-45.

Church, Gaylord (1909 — No. 03347) RAdm; Ret 11-1-45.

Smith, Harold Travis (1909 — No. 03349) RAdm; Ret 11-1-46.

Leighton, Frank Thompson (1909 — No. 03357) RAdm; Dies 11-23-43.

Richey, Thomas Beall (1909 — No. 03358) RAdm; Ret 1-1-44.

Bernhard, Alva Douglas (1909 — No. 03359) VAdm; Ret 11-1-46.

Bunkley, Joel William (1909 — No. 03377) RAdm; Ret 7-1-42.

Train, Harold Cecil (1909 — No. 03382) RAdm; Ret 5-1-46.

Kirk, Alan Goodrich (1909 — No. 03383) Adm; Ret 3-1-46.

Kelly, Monroe (1909 — No. 03388) VAdm; Ret 8-1-48.

Robertson, Marion Clinton (1909 — No. 03393) RAdm; Ret 8-1-47.

Daubin, Freeland Allyn (1909 — No. 03401) RAdm; Ret 3-1-48.

Gillette, Claude Sexton (1909 — No. 03403) RAdm; Ret 11-1-46.

Kennedy, Sherman Stewart (1909 — No. 03416) RAdm; Dies 11-4-61.

Platt, Comfort Benedict (1909 — No. 03417) RAdm; Ret 6-30-37.

Chapline, Vance Duncan (1909 — No. 03436) RAdm; Ret 11-1-46.

Van Valkenburgh, Franklin (1909 — No. 03439) Captain; Killed 12-7-41 (Pearl Harbor).

Braisted, Frank Alfred (1909 — No. 03442) RAdm; Ret 3-1-51.

Oldendorf, Jesse Barrett (1909 — No. 03479) Adm; Ret 9-1-48.

Gunther, Ernest Ludolph (1909 — No. 03481) RAdm; Dies 3-27-48.

Van Hook, Clifford Evans (1909 — No. 03491) RAdm; Ret 5-1-48.

Murphy, Joseph Augustine (1909 — No. 03500) Captain; Ret 6-30-37.

Cooke, Charles Maynard (1910 — No. 03514) Adm; Ret 5-1-48.

Bennion, Mervyn (1910 — No. 03515) Captain; 12-7-41.

Gray, Augustine Heard (1910 — No. 03516) RAdm; Ret 1-1-47.

Brand, Charles Lees (1910 — No. 03518) RAdm; Ret 5-1-49.

Sherman, Frederick Carl (1910 — No. 03536) Adm; Ret 3-1-47.

Davidson, Lyal Ament (1910 — No. 03541) VAdm; Ret 6-1-46.

Lee, Robert Corwin (1910 — No. 03545) RAdm; Res 2-1-20.

Beary, Donald Bradford (1910 — No. 03556) VAdm; Dies 10-1-50.

Wills, Bernard Oviatt (1910 — No. 03558) RAdm; Ret 12-1-46.

Moore, Charles Johnes (1910 — No. 03562) RAdm; Ret 1-1-47.

Kelley, Frank Harrison Jr (1910 — No. 03566) RAdm; Ret 12-1-46.

Hancock, Lewis Jr (1910 — No. 03578) Cdr.

Lewis, Spencer Steen (1910 — No. 03583) VAdm; Ret 10-1-47.

Ainsworth, Walden Lee (1910 — No. 03585) VAdm; Ret 12-1-48.

Pownall, Charles Alan (1910 — No. 03593) VAdm; Ret 11-1-49.

Reifsnider, Lawrence Fairfax (1910 — No. 03602) VAdm; Ret 12-1-49.

Flanigan, Howard Adams (1910 — No. 03617) RAdm; Ret 8-1-36.

Mitscher, Marc Andrew (1910 — No. 03620) Adm; Dies 2-3-47.

Weyler, George Lester (1910 — No. 03625) VAdm; Ret 11-1-46.

Bright, Clarkson Joel (1910 — No. 03629) RAdm; Ret 9-1-46.

Griffin, Robert Melville (1911 — No. 03648) VAdm; Ret 6-30-51.

Paine, Roger Warde (1911 — No. 03652) RAdm; Ret 10-1-49.

Merring, Harry Lloyd (1911 — No. 03657) RAdm; Ret 6-30-39.

Lowry, George Maus (1911 — No. 03662) RAdm; Res 3-31-27.

Hill, Harry Wilbur (1911 — No. 03666) Adm; Ret 5-1-52.

Bieri, Bernhard Henry (1911 — No. 03668) VAdm; Ret 6-1-51.

Bruns, Henry Frederick (1911 — No. 03669) RAdm; Dies 1-20-47.

Badger, Oscar Charles (1911 — No. 03671) Adm; Ret 7-1-51.

Hanson, Edward William (1911 — No. 03680) VAdm; Ret 2-1-52.

Callaghan, Daniel Judson (1911 — No. 03681) RAdm; Dies 11-13-42.

Lowry, Frank Jacob (1911 — No. 03684) VAdm; Ret 3-1-50.

Foster, Paul Frederick (1911 — No. 03699) VAdm; Res 3-26-29.

Ashe, George Bamford (1911 — No. 03705) RAdm; Ret 1-1-47.

Wood, Ralph Frederic (1911 — No. 03712) RAdm; Ret 10-1-46.

Reeves, John Walter Jr (1911 — No. 03716) Adm; Ret 5-1-50.

Buchanan, Pat (1911 — No. 03736) RAdm; Ret 8-1-45.

Rood, George Arthur (1911 — No. 03739) RAdm; Ret 1-1-47.

McClaren, John Walter (1911 — No. 03742) RAdm; Ret 3-11-41.

Phillips, Wallace Benjamin (1911 — No. 03750) RAdm; Ret 12-1-46.

Riefkohl, Frederick Louis (1911 — No. 03753) RAdm; Ret 1-1-47.

Cheek, Marion Case (1911 — No. 03778) RAdm; Res 11-1-19.

English, Robert Henry (1911 — No. 03786) RAdm; Dies 1-21-43.

Murray, George Dominic (1911 — No. 03790) Adm; Ret 8-1-51.

Read, Oliver Middleton (1911 — No. 03793) VAdm; Ret 2-1-51.

McMillin, George Johnson (1911 — No. 03795) RAdm; Ret 6-30-49.

Kingman, Howard Fithlan (1911 — No. 03797) VAdm; Ret 2-1-47.

Cobb, Calvin Hayes (1911 — No. 03808) VAdm; Ret 11-1-46.

Simons, Robert Bentham (1911 — No. 03813) RAdm; Ret 1-1-47.

Scott, Norman (1911 — No. 03816) RAdm; Dies 11-13-42.

Deyo, Morton Lyndholm (1911 — No. 03831) VAdm; Ret 8-1-49.

McMorris, Charles Horatio (1912 — No. 03841) VAdm; Ret 9-1-52.

Pace, Ernest Milton Jr (1912 — No. 03842) RAdm; Ret 6-30-48.

Good, Howard Harrison (1912 — No. 03848) VAdm; Ret 9-1-50.

Small, Ernst Gregor (1912 — No. 03850) RAdm; Dies 12-26-44.

Wright, Carleton Herbert (1912 — No. 03851) VAdm; Ret 10-1-48.

Gatch, Thomas Leigh (1912 — No. 03860) VAdm; Ret 9-1-47.

Montgomery, Alfred Eugene (1912 — No. 03864) VAdm; Ret 6-30-51.

Bennett, Andrew Carl (1912 — No. 03865) RAdm; Ret 11-1-46.

McDonnell, Edward Orrick (1912 — No. 03869) VAdm; Res 1-26-20.

Anderson, Anton Bennett (1912 — No. 03881) RAdm; Ret 1-1-47.

Tisdale, Mahlon Street (1912 — No. 03884) VAdm; Ret 11-1-47.

Woodruff, George Lynn (1912 — No. 03885) RAdm; Dies 8-27-50.

Wenzell, Louis Peter (1912 — No. 03896) VAdm; Ret 6-30-33.

Byrd, Richard Evelyn Jr (1912 — No. 03898) RAdm; Ret 3-15-16.

Fort, George Hudson (1912 — No. 03902) VAdm; Ret 9-1-53.

Hunter, Lunsford Lomax (1912 — No. 03903) RAdm; Ret 1-1-47.

Buckmaster, Elliott (1912 — No. 03909) VAdm; Ret 11-1-46.

DeLany, Walter Stanley (1912 — No. 03911) VAdm; Ret 2-1-53.

Zacharias, Ellis Mark (1912 — No. 03914) RAdm; Ret 11-1-46.

Denfeld, Louis Emil (1912 — No. 03923) Adm; Ret 3-1-50.

Barbey, Daniel Edward (1912 — No. 03948) VAdm; Ret 6-30-51.

Mason, Charles Perry (1912 — No. 03952) VAdm; Ret 4-1-46.

Edgar, Campbell Dallas (1912 — No. 03956) RAdm; Ret 1-1-47.

Ramsey, Dewitt Clinton (1912 — No. 03960) Adm; Ret 5-1-49.

Schuirmann, Roscoe Ernest (1912 — No. 03963) RAdm; Ret 6-1-51.

Sowell, Ingram Cecil (1912 — No. 03969) RAdm; Dies 12-21-47.

Whiting, Francis Eliot Maynard (1912 — No. 03970) VAdm; Ret 8-1-47.

Lockwood, Charles Andrews (1912 — No. 03971) VAdm; Ret 9-1-47.

Theiss, Paul Seymour (1912 — No. 03976) RAdm; Ret 6-30-49.

Merrill, Aaron Stanton (1912 — No. 03977) VAdm; Ret 6-1-47.

Blandy, William Henry P. (1913 — No. 03992) Adm; Ret 2-1-50.

Jones, James Cary (1913 — No. 03996) VAdm; Ret 4-1-54.

Davis, Glenn Benson (1913 — No. 04000) VAdm; Ret 6-1-53.

Crisp, Frederick Grafton (1913 — No. 04003) RAdm; Ret 10-1-47.

McFeathers, Charlie Paul (1913 — No. 04007) RAdm; Dies 2-16-47.

Shock, Thomas Macy (1913 — No. 04012) RAdm; Dies 10-4-62.

Mathews, James Thomas (1913 — No. 04002) RAdm; Dies 12-14-47.

Hendren, Paul (1913 — No. 04040) VAdm; Ret 7-1-49.

Du Bose, Laurance Toombs (1913 — No. 04066) Adm; Ret 6-1-55.

Robinson, Arthur Granville (1913 — No. 04068) VAdm; Ret 6-30-51.

Powell, Paulus Prince (1913 — No. 04081) RAdm; Ret 1-1-47.

Moore, Samuel Nobre (1913 — No. 04088) Captain; Dies 8-9-42.

Thebaud, Leo Hewlett (1913 — No. 04098) VAdm; Ret 3-1-52.

Hutchins, Gordon (1913 — No. 04118) RAdm; Ret 5-1-44.

Ard, Ligon Briggs (1913 — No. 04122) RAdm; Res 12-14-19.

Austin, Charles Linnell (1913 — No. 04127) RAdm; Res 8-29-13.

Ellsberg, Edward (1914 — No. 04131) RAdm; Res 12-5-26.

Cochrane, Edward Lull (1914 — No. 04132) VAdm; Ret 11-1-47.

Royce, Donald (1914 — No. 04137) RAdm; Ret 11-30-50.

Jones, Carl Henry (1914 — No. 04140) VAdm; Ret 11-1-46.

Samson, Henry Parsons (1914 — No. 04145) RAdm; Ret 7-1-35.

Bryant, Carleton Fanton (1914 — No. 04147) VAdm; Ret 5-1-46.

Spanagel, Herman Adolph (1914 — No. 04154) RAdm; Ret 6-30-49.

Redman, Joseph Reasor (1914 — No. 04155) RAdm; Ret 6-30-49.

Lowe, Frank Loper (1914 — No. 04156) VAdm; Ret 8-1-45.

Ruddock, Theodore Davis Jr (1914 — No. 04160) VAdm; Ret 12-31-54.

Wilson, George Barry (1914 — No. 04165) RAdm; Ret 11-1-46.

Harrill, William Keene (1914 — No. 04167) VAdm; Ret 6-30-51.

Burrough, Edmund Weidmann (1914 — No. 04175) VAdm; Ret 11-1-52.

Rooks, Albert Harold (1914 — No. 04176) Captain; Dies 3-1-42.

Ray, Herbert James (1914 — No. 04182) RAdm; Ret 7-1-49.

Moyer, John Gould (1914 — No. 04184) RAdm; Ret 7-1-49.

Hayler, Robert Ward (1914 — No. 04185) VAdm; Ret 6-30-53.

Conolly, Richard Lansing (1914 — No. 04189) Adm; Ret 11-1-53.

Corn, William Anderson (1914 — No. 04190) RAdm; Ret 6-1-49.

Short, Edwin Thomas (1914 — No. 04192) RAdm; Ret 6-1-49.

Waller, John Beresford Wynn (1914 — No. 04194) RAdm; Ret 1-1-47.

Early, Alexander Rieman Jr (1914 — No. 04199) RAdm; Ret 7-1-49.

Martin, Charles Franklin (1914 — No. 04200) RAdm; Ret 11-1-46.

Christian, Kemp Catlett (1914 — No. 04202) RAdm; Ret 1-1-47.

Baker, Wilder Dupuy (1914 — No. 04266) VAdm; Ret 8-1-52.

Jalbert, Horace Homer (1914 — No. 04235) RAdm; Res 12-24-20.

Thomas, Frank Pugh (1914 — No. 04240) RAdm; Ret 6-1-47.

Davis, Ralph Otis (1914 — No. 04241) VAdm; Ret 1-1-53.

Cohen, Marion Young (1914 — No. 04245) RAdm; Ret 11-1-46.

Popham, William Sherbrooke Jr (1914 — No. 04251) RAdm; Ret 1-1-47.

Cary, Robert Webster Jr (1914 — No. 04255) RAdm; Ret 12-1-46.

Wiltse, Lloyd Jerome (1914 — No. 04257) VAdm; Ret 4-1-47.

Macgowan, Charles Alton (1914 — No. 04266) RAdm; Ret 6-30-35.

Kessing, Oliver Owen (1914 — No. 04269) RAdm; Ret 6-1-47.

Brown, John Herbert Jr (1914 — No. 04276) VAdm; Ret 2-1-54.

Fox, William Vincent (1914 — No. 04280) RAdm; Ret 6-1-52.

McCormick, Lynde Dupuy (1915 — No. 04286) Adm; Dies 8-16-56.

Davis, Arthur Cayley (1915 — No. 04291) Adm; Ret 11-14-55.

Ritchie, Oliver Henderson (1915 — No. 04294) RAdm; Res 6-14-20.

Struble, Arthur Dewey (1915 — No. 04296) Adm; Ret 7-1-56.

Pennoyer, Fred William Jr (1915 — No. 04302) VAdm; Ret 7-1-50.

Perry, Benjamin Franklin (1915 — No. 04304) RAdm; Ret 6-30-49.

Bates, Richard Walter (1915 — No. 04305) RAdm; Ret 5-1-49.

Kell, Claude Owen (1915 — No. 04309) RAdm; Dies 7-5-55.

Shoemaker, James Marshall (1915 — No. 04311) RAdm; Ret 6-1-48.

Glover, Robert Ogden (1915 — No. 04317) RAdm; Ret 9-1-48.

Vickery, Howard Leroy (1915 — No. 04322) VAdm; Dies 3-21-46.

Umsted, Scott (1915 — No. 04337) RAdm; Ret 1-1-47.

Rhea, Powell McCellan (1915 — No. 04341) RAdm; Ret 11-1-46.

Burnett, Henry Poynter (1915 — No. 04343) RAdm; Ret 1-1-47.

Chandler, Theodore Edson (1915 — No. 04348) RAdm; Dies 1-7-45.

Wiley, Herbert Victor (1915 — No. 04349) RAdm; Ret 1-1-47.

Wagner, Frank Dechant (1915 — No. 04352) VAdm; Ret 7-1-50.

Jenkins, Samuel Power (1915 — No. 04360) RAdm; Dies 6-10-75.

Flynn, Cornelius William (1915 — No. 04361) RAdm; Ret 1-1-47.

Granat, William (1915 — No. 043630) RAdm; Ret 7-1-47.

Small, John Davis (1915 — No. 04375) RAdm; Res 2-1-26.

Low, Francis Stuart (1915 — No. 04381) Adm; Ret 7-2-56.

Wotherspoon, Alex Somerville (1915 — No. 04391) RAdm; Ret 6-30-49.

Fortson, Robert Malcolm (1915 — No. 04393) RAdm; Res 7-26-23.

Royal, Forrest Betton (1915 — No. 04395) RAdm; Dies 6-18-45.

McCrea, John Livingstone (1915 — No. 04396) VAdm; Ret 6-1-53.

Richards, Frederick Gore (1915 — No. 04398) RAdm; Ret 6-30-49.

Shelley, Tully (1915 — No. 04402) RAdm; Ret 6-30-49.

Clarke, Horace Donald (1915 — No. 04408) RAdm; Dies 5-11-57.

Maher, James Edward (1915 — No. 04411) VAdm; Ret 7-1-53.

Smith, Allan Edward (1915 — No. 04414) VAdm; Ret 2-1-54.

Wood, Leighton (1915 — No. 04415) Captain; Dies 6-9-43.

Overesch, Harvey Edward (1915 — No. 04417) VAdm; Ret 5-1-46.

Quynn, Allen George (1915 — No. 04422) RAdm; Ret 6-30-49.

Richardson, Clifford Geer (1915 — No. 04430) RAdm; Ret 6-30-49.

Ring, Morton Loomis (1915 — No. 04441) RAdm; Res 10-7-15.

Mahoney, John Joseph (1915 — No. 04443) RAdm; Ret 6-30-49.

Christie, Ralph Waldo (1915 — No. 04444) VAdm; Ret 8-1-49.

Mullinnix, Henry Maston (1916 — No. 04464) RAdm; Dies 11-25-44.

Davison, Ralph Eugene (1916 — No. 04466) VAdm; Ret 7-1-48.

Moon, Don Pardee (1916 — No. 04467) RAdm; Dies 8-5-44.

Berkey, Russell Stanley (1916 — No. 04468) Adm; Ret 8-31-50.

Hussey, George Frederick Jr (1916 — No. 04470) VAdm; Dies 4-17-83.

Keliher, Thomas Joseph Jr (1916 — No. 04471) RAdm; Ret 6-1-49.

Hardison, Osbourne Bennett (1916 — No. 04472) VAdm; Ret 1-1-55.

Braine, Clinton Elgin Jr (1916 — No. 04475) RAdm; Ret 5-1-49.

Miles, Arthur Clark (1916 — No. 04480) VAdm; Ret 6-1-51.

Fechteler, William Morrow (1916 — No. 04481) Adm; Ret 7-1-56.

Baker, Charles Adams (1916 — No. 04485) RAdm; Ret 7-1-49.

Bogan, Gerald Francis (1916 — No. 04489) VAdm; Ret 2-1-50.

Fiske, Leon Sangster (1916 — No. 04491) VAdm; Ret 7-1-53.

Glutting, Paul Rolland (1916 — No. 04494) RAdm; Ret 6-30-50.

Klein, Grover Cleveland (1916 — No. 04499) RAdm; Ret 11-30-52.

Kitts, Willard Augustus III (1916 — No. 04502) VAdm; Ret 6-30-51.

Rodgers, Bertram Joseph (1916 — No. 04503) VAdm; Ret 4-1-56.

Beatty, Frank Edmund (1916 — No. 04510) VAdm; Ret 5-31-51.

Solberg, Thorwald Arthur (1916 — No. 04515) RAdm; Ret 6-30-51.

Roper, Clifford Harris (1916 — No. 04516) RAdm; Ret 4-1-49.

Sauer, Edward Paul (1916 — No. 04517).

Carlson, Milton Oren (1916 — No. 04520) RAdm; Ret 8-1-47.

Carney, Robert Bostwick (1916 — No. 04521) Adm; Ret 8-17-55.

Radford, Arthur William (1916 — No. 04522) Adm; Ret 8-1-57.

Ryan, Dennis Leo (1916 — No. 04540) RAdm; Ret 8-1-47.

Mayer, Andrew De Graff (1916 — No. 04544) RAdm; Ret 1-1-47.

Joy, Charles Turner (1916 — No. 04547) Adm; Ret 7-1-54.

Wheeler, Charles Julian (1916 — No. 04558) RAdm; Ret 4-1-48.

Ginder, Samuel Paul (1916 — No. 04562) RAdm; Ret 6-30-51.

Ragsdale, Van Hubert (1916 — No. 04565) VAdm; Ret 8-1-48.

Wilkes, John (1916 — No. 04566) VAdm; Ret 6-30-51.

Grosskopf, Homer Louis (1916 — No. 04569) RAdm; Ret 6-30-49.

Burhans, Arthur Daniel (1916 — No. 04582) RAdm; Ret 11-1-44.

Cecil, Charles Purcell (1916 — No. 04589) RAdm; Dies 7-31-44.

Durgin, Calvin Thornton (1916 — No. 04590) VAdm; Ret 8-30-51.

Ziroli, Humbert William (1916 — No. 04591) RAdm; Ret 12-1-47.

Woodward, Douglas Castleberry (1916 — No. 04596) RAdm; Res 6-17-20.

Roberts, John Summerfield (1916 — No. 04599) RAdm; Ret 11-1-44.

Price, John Dale (1916 — No. 04600) Adm; Ret 6-1-54.

Hoover, Gilbert Corwin (1916 — No. 04614) RAdm; Ret 1-1-47.

Cooper, Thomas Valentine (1916 — No. 04615) RAdm; Ret 1-1-47.

Redfield, Heman Judd (1916 — No. 04620) RAdm; Ret 11-1-47.

McFall, Andrew Calhoun (1916 — No. 04624) RAdm; Ret 3-1-46.

Grassie, Herbert John (1916 — No. 04628) RAdm; Ret 6-30-49.

Davis, James Kepler (1916 — No. 04635) RAdm; Ret 7-1-47.

Haeberle, Frederick Edward (1917 — No. 04641) RAdm; Ret 2-1-51.

Maples, Houston Ledbetter (1917 — No. 04644) RAdm; Ret 1-1-48.

McKee, Andrew Irwin (1917 — No. 04646) RAdm; Ret 7-1-47.

Oster, Henry Richard (1917 — No. 04647) RAdm; Dies 8-1-49.

Dees, Randal Euesta (1917 — No. 04648) RAdm; Ret 7-1-49.

Cambell, Colin (1917 — No. 04649) RAdm; 7-1-49.

Fahrion, Frank George (1917 — No. 04654) Adm; Ret 5-1-56.

Noble, Albert Gallatin (1917 — No. 04655) Adm; Ret 10-1-31.

Rawlings, Norborne Lewis (1917 — No. 04656) Adm; Ret 9-1-47.

Kiland, Ingolf Norman (1917 — No. 04657) VAdm; Ret 4-1-57.

Dean, Frank Homewood (1917 — No. 04658) RAdm; Ret 7-1-49.

Mitchell, Edward Alexander (1917 — No. 04659) RAdm; Ret 7-1-49.

Wallin, Homer Norman (1917 — No. 04663) VAdm; Ret 5-1-55.

Duncan, Donald Bradley (1917 — No. 04664) Adm; Ret 2-28-57.

Shepard, Andrew Gilbert (1917 — No. 04671) RAdm; Ret 7-1-49.

Clark, William Price Oliver (1917 — No. 04674) RAdm; Ret 8-1-46.

Tobin, Robert Gibson (1917 — No. 04683) RAdm; Ret 7-1-49.

Waldschmidt, Theodore Max (1917 — No. 04685) RAdm; Ret 12-1-46.

Knowles, Herbert Bain (1917 — No. 04686) RAdm; Ret 9-1-47.

Sallada, Harold Bushnell (1917 — No. 04691) Adm; Ret 10-1-49.

Gregory, Joseph Wesley (1917 — No. 04694) RAdm; Ret 1-1-47.

Denebrink, Francis Compton (1917 — No. 04701) VAdm; Ret 7-1-56.

Stump, Felix Budwell (1917 — No. 04703) Adm; Ret 8-1-58.

Calhoun, Walter Carson (1917 — No. 04706) RAdm; Ret 6-30-49.

Holden, Carl Frederick (1917 — No. 04707) VAdm; Ret 7-1-52.

Hudson, Lester Jay (1917 — No. 04708) RAdm; Ret 6-30-49.

Dietrich, William Francis (1917 — No. 04732) RAdm; Ret 7-1-49.

Heffernan, John Baptist (1917 — No. 04739) RAdm; Ret 6-30-47.

Moran, Edward Joseph (1917 — No. 04740) RAdm; Ret 12-1-47.

Senn, Elliot Marchant (1917 — No. 04743) RAdm; Ret 7-1-49.

Benson, Francis Wyse (1917 — No. 04744) RAdm; Ret 7-1-50.

Cooley, Thomas Ross Jr (1917 — No. 04745) VAdm; Ret 7-1-52.

Porter, Robert Lee Jr (1917 — No. 04754) RAdm; Ret 6-30-49.

Jones, Edward Harral (1917 — No. 04758) RAdm; Ret 1-1-47.

McCann, Allan Rockwell (1917 — No. 04772) VAdm; Ret 5-1-50.

Austin, Leonard Bynner (1917 — No. 04777) RAdm; Ret 7-1-48.

Mack, Andrew Robert (1917 — No. 04787) RAdm; Ret 7-1-49.

Clark, Guy Wheeler (1917 — No. 04791) RAdm; Ret 7-1-49.

Wells, Benjamin Osborne (1917 — No. 04808) RAdm; Ret 7-1-39.

Spencer, Douglas Ancrum (1917 — No. 04811) RAdm; Ret 7-1-49.

Weitzel, Charles William (1917 — No. 04813) RAdm; Ret 4-1-47.

Hoeffel, Kenneth Mortimer (1917 — No. 04822) RAdm; Ret 6-1-47.

Sherman, Forrest Percival (1918 — No. 04824) Adm; Dies 7-22-51.

Fowler, Joseph William (1918 — No. 04827) RAdm; Ret 6-29-49.

Richardson, Laurence Baxter (1918 — No. 04831) RAdm; Ret 12-1-46.

Fife, James Jr (1918 — No. 04832) Adm; Ret 8-1-55.

Dodge, Frank Riley (1918 — No. 04834) RAdm; Ret 6-30-49.

Warlick, William Walter (1918 — No. 04836) RAdm; Ret 11-1-47.

Murphy, Vincent Raphael (1918 — No.04837) VAdm; Ret 11-1-46.

Styer, Charles Wilkes (1918 — No. 04840) RAdm; Ret 6-30-48.

Sprague, Thomas Lamison (1918 — No. 04841) Adm; Ret 4-1-52.

Johnson, Einar Reynold (1918 — No. 04844) RAdm; Ret 7-1-49.

Bennehoff, Olton Rader (1918 — No. 04848) RAdm; Ret 7-17-50.

Inglis, Thomas Browning (1918 — No. 04851) VAdm; Ret 1-1-52.

Stone, Earl Everett (1918 — No. 04852) RAdm; Ret 1-1-58.

Ballentine, John Jennings (1918 — No. 04854) Adm; Ret 5-1-54.

Sullivan, John Raymond (1918 — No. 04857) RAdm; Ret 5-1-49.

Sprague, Clifton Albert F. (1918 — No. 04865) VAdm; Ret 11-1-51.

Clark, Joseph James (1918 — No. 04869) Adm; Ret 12-1-53.

Bledsoe, Albert Mcqueen (1918 — No. 04872) VAdm; Ret 9-1-58.

Biesemier, Harold (1918 — No. 04874) RAdm; Ret 1-1-47.

Browning, Miles Rutherford (1918 — No. 04875) RAdm; Ret 1-1-47.

France, Albert Finley Jr (1918 — No. 04880) RAdm; Dies 6-9-68.

McCaulay, Walter Scott (1918 — No. 04884) RAdm; Ret 2-1-48.

Wilson, Julian Dubois (1918 — No. 04891) RAdm; Ret 6-30-50.

Hurt, Samuel Hansford (1918 — No. 04892) RAdm; Ret 7-1-49.

Johnson, George William (1918 — No. 04897) RAdm; Ret 4-1-46.

Thornhill, Henry Ehrman (1918 — No. 04898) RAdm; Ret 2-1-46.

Pursell, Ion (1918 — No. 04900) RAdm; Ret 12-1-50.

Rowe, Gordon (1918 — No. 04903) RAdm; Ret 11-1-46.

Hartt, William Handy Jr (1918 — No. 04904) RAdm; Ret 6-30-50.

Miller, Christopher Chaffe (1918 — No. 04908) RAdm; Ret 6-30-49.

Loomis, Donald Wood (1918 — No. 04908) RAdm; Ret 6-30-49.

Phillips, John Spinning (1918 — No. 04911) RAdm; Ret 1-1-47.

Wright, Jerauld (1918 — No. 04915) Adm; Ret 1-31-60.

Need, Harry William (1918 — No. 04916) RAdm; Ret 6-1-49.

Leffler, Charles Doyle Jr (1918 — No. 04917) RAdm; Ret 4-1-45.

Mills, Earle Watkins (1918 — No. 04920) VAdm; Ret 3-1-49.

Hoffman, Harry Draper (1918 — No. 04922) RAdm; Ret 6-30-49.

Barringer, Victor Cameron Jr (1918 — No. 04930) RAdm; Ret 6-30-50.

Kendall, Henry Samuel (1918 — No. 04938) VAdm; Ret 7-1-52.

Haight, Stanley Martyn (1918 — No. 04940) RAdm; Ret 1-1-47.

Norton, Stanley Cook (1918 — No. 04945) RAdm; Ret 7-1-47.

Whitfield, James Walter (1918 — No. 04946) RAdm; Ret 1-1-42.

Fischler, Peter Kalsh (1918 — No. 04951) RAdm; Dies 7-14-50.

Moen, Arthur Thomas (1918 — No. 04957) RAdm; Ret 4-1-48.

Whitemarsh, Ross Palmer (1918 — No. 04959) RAdm; Ret 6-30-49.

Duvall, Elmer Ellsworth Jr (1918 — No. 04965) RAdm; Ret 6-30-49.

Sobel, Herbert Russell (1918 — No. 04972) RAdm; Ret 6-30-39.

Duncan, Jack Harlan (1918 — No. 04974) VAdm; Ret 7-1-54.

Bailey, Watson Osgood (1918 — No. 04975) RAdm; Ret 6-30-49.

Lovette, Leland Pearson (1918 — No. 04979) VAdm; Ret 6-30-49.

Dillon, Wallace Myron (1918 — No. 04980) RAdm; Ret 11-1-46.

Busbey, Leroy White Jr (1918 — No. 04983) RAdm; Ret 6-30-49.

Riggs, Ralph Smith (1918 — No. 04986) VAdm; Ret 8-1-51.

Wieber, Carlos Wilhelm (1918 — No. 04987) RAdm; Ret 6-30-49.

Haines, John Meade (1918 — No. 04990) RAdm; Ret 6-1-49.

Macklin, William Alex S. (1918 — No. 04991) RAdm; Ret 1-1-47.

Lewis, Mays Livingston (1918 — No. 05001) RAdm; Ret 11-1-47.

Harrison, Peyton (1918 — No. 05003) RAdm; Res 2-28-29.

Phillips, William Kearney (1918 — No. 05041) Adm; Ret 8-1-55.

Alexander, Ralph Clonts (1918 — No. 05071) RAdm; Ret 6-1-48.

Schoeffel, Malcolm Francis (1919 — No. 05022) RAdm; Ret 2-1-55.

Settle, Thomas Greenhow W. (1919 — No. 05023) VAdm; Ret 12-1-57.

Grant, Lucien McKee (1919 — No. 05024) RAdm; Ret 7-1-54.

Nicholson, Charles Ambrose II (1919 — No. 05029) RAdm; Ret 8-1-51.

Ofstie, Ralph Andrew (1919 — No. 05031) VAdm; Dies 11-18-56.

Hicks, Rex Legrand (1919 — No. 05032) RAdm; Ret 6-30-49.

Gardner, Matthias Bennett (1919 — No. 05034) Adm; Ret 8-1-56.

Stevens, Leslie Clark (1919 — No. 05035) VAdm; Ret 8-1-51.

Wynkoop, Thomas Pilmore (1919 — No. 05043) RAdm; Ret 3-1-49.

Herrmann, Ernest Edward (1919 — No. 05044) RAdm; Dies 11-19-52.

Sprague, Albert Tilden Jr (1919 — No. 05049) RAdm; Dies 4-8-68.

Callaghan, William Mccombe (1919 — No. 05052) VAdm; Ret 3-1-57.

Challenger, Harold Lincoln (1919 — No. 05054) RAdm; Ret 1-1-47.

Jeter, Thomas Powers (1919 — No. 05058) RAdm; Ret 2-1-49.

Clark, David Henderson (1919 — No. 05061) RAdm; Ret 7-1-53.

Metzel, Jeffrey Caswell (1919 — No. 05062) RAdm; Ret 6-30-49.

Roberts, Ralph, Henry (1919 — No. 05067) RAdm; Ret 1-1-47.

Schaeffer, Valentine Hixson (1919 — No. 05068) RAdm; Ret 7-1-49.

Brown, Allen Dudley (1919 — No. 05071) RAdm; Ret 6-30-49.

Roper, John Wesley (1919 — No. 05072) VAdm; Ret 5-1-53.

Vose, William Cecil (1919 — No. 05073) RAdm; Ret 11-1-47.

Slocum, Harry Browning (1919 — No. 05074) RAdm; Ret 5-30-50.

Olsen, Charles Eugene (1919 — No. 05075) RAdm; Ret 1-1-47.

Briscoe, Robert Pearce (1919 — No. 05076) Adm; Ret 1-1-59.

Thurber, Harry Raymond (1919 — No. 05077) VAdm; Ret 7-1-53.

Sykes, James Bennett (1919 — No. 05078) RAdm; Ret 1-1-48.

VonHeimburg, Ernest Herman (1919 — No. 05086) VAdm; Ret 7-1-58.

Updegraff, William Nicholas (1919 — No. 05089) RAdm; Ret 1-1-47.

Murray, Stuart Shadrick (1919 — No. 05090) Adm; Ret 8-1-56.

Sample, William Dodge (1919 — No. 05093) RAdm; Dies 10-3-46.

Ramsey, Logan Carlisle (1919 — No. 05095) RAdm; Dies 8-25-72.

Tuggle, Richard Brittain (1919 — No. 05099) RAdm; Ret 7-1-46.

Cassady, John Howard (1919 — No. 05101) Adm; Ret 5-1-56.

Coney, Charles Edward (1919 — No. 05106) RAdm; Ret 2-1-47.

Colyear, Bayard Henry (1919 — No. 05114) RAdm; Ret 7-1-49.

Andrews, Charles Lee Jr (1919 — No. 05115) RAdm; Ret 11-1-46.

Hunt, Charles Boardman (1919 — No. 05117) RAdm; Ret 7-1-49.

O'R, George McFadden (1919 — No. 05118) RAdm; Ret 7-1-49.

Griggs, John Bradford Jr (1919 — No. 05125) RAdm; Ret 6-30-49.

Bryant, Eliot Hinman (1919 — No. 05126) VAdm; Ret 8-1-48.

Dyer, George Carroll (1919 — No. 05127) VAdm; Ret 2-1-55.

Crawford, David Stolz (1919 — No. 05130) RAdm; Ret 6-30-49.

Staudt, Albert Raymond (1919 — No. 05135) RAdm; Res 6-15-23.

Camp, Chauncey (1919 — No. 05137) Ret 7-1-56.

Lee, Paul Frantz (1919 — No. 05241) RAdm; Ret 7-1-48.

Greer, Marshall Raymond (1919 — No. 05142) VAdm; Ret 7-1-53.

Welch, Philip Pindell (1919 — No. 05143) RAdm; Ret 6-30-49.

Lannom, Joseph Robert (1919 — No. 05146) RAdm; Ret 6-30-49.

Fink, Carl Kenneth (1919 — No. 05152) RAdm; Ret 6-30-49.

Ansel, Walter Charles (1919 — No. 05154) RAdm; Ret 6-30-49.

McGurl, Daniel Michael (1919 — No. 05161) RAdm; Ret 6-30-49.

Talbot, Paul Hopkins (1919 — No. 05168) RAdm; Ret 3-1-48.

Holloway, James Lemuel Jr (1919 — No. 05170) Adm; Ret 7-1-60.

Jennings, Ralph Edward (1919 — No. 05173) VAdm; Ret 7-1-53.

Crawford, John Graybill (1919 — No. 05181) RAdm; Ret 6-1-49.

Atkins, James George (1919 — No. 05183) RAdm; Ret 6-30-49.

Short, Giles Elza (1919 — No. 05192) RAdm; Ret 6-30-49.

Martin, Harold Montgomery (1919 — No. 05198) Adm; Ret 2-1-56.

Redman, John Roland (1919 — No. 05203) VAdm; Ret 10-1-57.

Dierdorff, Ross Ainsworth (1919 — No. 05204) RAdm; Ret 6-30-49.

Mentz, George Francis (1919 — No. 05205) RAdm; Ret 1-1-47.

Allen, Charles (1919 — No. 05209) RAdm; Ret 11-1-45.

Carter, Grayson Birch (1919 — No. 05216) RAdm; Ret 6-30-49.

Hague, Wesley Mclaren (1920 — No. 05221) RAdm; Ret 7-1-56.

Harrison, Lloyd (1920 — No. 05222) RAdm; Ret 8-1-55.

Sylvester, Evander Wallace (1920 — No. 05223) RAdm; Ret 3-1-55.

Good, Roscoe Fletcher (1920 — No. 05224) Adm; Ret 3-1-58.

Robbins, Thomas Hinckley Jr (1920 — No. 05227) RAdm; Ret 1-1-62.

Cowdrey, Roy Thomas (1920 — No. 05231) RAdm; Ret 7-1-56.

Nibecker, Paul Braids (1920 — No. 05235) RAdm; Ret 7-1-54.

Dowd, Wallace Rutherford (1920 — No. 05238) RAdm; Ret 6-1-54.

Forrestel, Emmet Peter (1920 — No. 05239) VAdm; Ret 6-1-59.

Hillenkoetter, Roscoe Henry (1920 — No. 05240) VAdm; Ret 5-1-57.

Holsinger, Raymond Wilson (1920 — No. 05251) RAdm; Ret 11-1-47.

Sinton, William (1920 — No. 05254) RAdm; Ret 6-30-49.

Bolster, Calvin Mathews (1920 — No. 05259) RAdm; Ret 1-1-54.

Mullan, William Evans A. (1920 — No. 05264) RAdm; Ret 7-1-49.

Leahy, William Irving (1920 — No. 05265) RAdm; Ret 12-1-50.

Mullinnix, Allen Prather (1920 — No. 05268) RAdm; Ret 11-1-47.

Goggins, William Bernard (1920 — No. 05272) RAdm; Res 7-1-49.

Sackett, Earl Leroy (1920 — No. 05275) RAdm; Ret 1-1-47.

Reed, Kendall Sturtevant (1920 — No. 05276) RAdm; Ret 6-30-49.

Wooldridge, Edmund Tyler (1920 — No. 05277) Adm; Ret 8-1-58.

Momsen, Charles Bowers (1920 — No. 05278) VAdm; Ret 9-1-55.

Litch, Ernest Wheeler (1920 — No. 05287) VAdm; Ret 7-1-54.

Johnson, Felix Leslie (1920 — No. 05289) VAdm; Ret 9-1-52.

Dupre, Marcy Mathias Jr (1920 — No. 05291) RAdm; Ret 7-1-49.

Kranzfelder, Edgar Paul (1920 — No. 05293) RAdm; Ret 4-1-50.

Tillson, Elwood Morse (1920 — No. 05294) RAdm; Ret 6-30-49.

Decker, Benton Weaver (1920 — No. 05308) RAdm; Ret 7-1-49.

Murphy, Charles Henry (1920 — No. 05312) RAdm; Ret 6-30-50.

Pare, Edward Everett (1920 — No. 05314) RAdm; Ret 6-30-49.

Morse, Richard Swift (1920 — No. 05315) RAdm; Ret 1-1-47.

Beightler, Charles Sprague (1920 — No. 05319) RAdm; Ret 1-1-47.

Perry, John (1920 — No. 05327) VAdm; Ret 2-1-59.

Pearson, Mead Saltonstall (1920 — No. 05328) RAdm; Ret 12-1-50.

Baker, Felix Locke (1920 — No. 05331) RAdm; Ret 7-1-49.

Laird, Oberlin Carter (1920 — No. 05332) RAdm; Ret 6-39-49.

Combs, Thomas Selby (1920 — No. 05335) VAdm; Ret 4-1-60.

Haven, Hugh Elliot (1920 — No. 05342) RAdm; Ret 7-1-54.

Kraker, George Patton (1920 — No. 05343) RAdm; Ret 6-1-48.

Melling, Robert Emmet (1920 — No. 05348) RAdm; Ret 12-1-50.

Fahrney, Delmer Stater (1920 — No. 05357) RAdm; Ret 11-1-50.

Hopwood, Herbert Gladstone (1920 — No. 05365) Adm; Ret 9-1-60.

Christoph, Karl John (1920 — No. 05366) RAdm; Ret 1-1-47.

Mason, Lunsford Yandell Jr (1920 — No. 05369) RAdm; Ret 7-1-49.

Wellings, Augustus Joseph (1920 — No. 05370) RAdm; Ret 7-1-54.

McMahon, Frederick William (1920 — No. 05371) VAdm; Ret 1-1-60.

Weller, Oscar Arthur (1920 — No. 05376) RAdm; Ret 7-1-49.

Hurff, Jack Ellett (1920 — No. 05378) RAdm; Ret 7-1-49.

Brittain, Thomas Baldwin (1920 — No. 05383) VAdm; Ret 2-1-55.

Fitz, Harold Carlton (1920 — No. 05385) RAdm; Ret 7-1-49.

Whelchel, John Esten (1920 — No. 05390) VAdm; Ret 8-1-49.

Hartman, Charles Clifford (1920 — No. 05397) RAdm; Ret 4-1-60.

Hartung, Richard Renwick (1920 — No. 05401) RAdm; Ret 7-1-49.

Dettmann, Frank Carl Lewis (1920 — No. 05407) RAdm; Ret 6-30-50.

Heineman, Paul Ralph (1920 — No. 05414) RAdm; Ret 6-30-49.

Kelley, Bernard Joseph (1920 — No. 05416) RAdm; Res 9-10-23.

McEathron, Ellsworth Dudley (1920 — No. 05421) RAdm; Ret 10-1-47.

Curts, Maurice Edwin (1920 — No. 05423) Adm; Ret 4-1-60.

Cunningham, Winfield Scott (1920 — No. 05426) RAdm; Ret 6-30-50.

Smith, Clyde Wendell (1920 — No. 05442) RAdm; Ret 1-1-47.

Haff, Theodore Germond (1920 — No. 05445) RAdm; Ret 12-3-50.

Graham, Roy William M. (1920 — No. 05451) RAdm; Ret 6-30-50.

Ketcham, Dixwell (1920 — No. 05452) VAdm; Ret 10-1-49.

Glover, Cato Douglas Jr (1920 — No. 05459) Adm; Ret 9-1-57.

Boit, Julian McCarty (1920 — No. 05460) RAdm; Ret 2-1-60.

Fick, Harold Foster (1920 — No. 05461) RAdm; Ret 12-1-46.

Tomlinson, William Gosnell (1920 — No. 05470) VAdm; Ret 5-1-52.

Tillman, Edwin Hord Jr (1920 — No. 05472) RAdm; Ret 11-1-39.

Gingrich, John Edward (1920 — No. 05473) Adm; Ret 10-1-54.

Steinhagen, Paul William (1920 — No. 05485) RAdm; Ret 7-1-49.

Bottom, John Thomas Jr (1920 — No. 05486) RAdm; Ret 7-1-49.

Johnson, Douglass Pollock (1920 — No. 05492) RAdm; Ret 6-30-50.

Old, Francis Paxton (1920 — No. 05493) VAdm; Ret 2-1-54.

Hartt, Beverly Armistead (1920 — No. 05499) RAdm; Ret 12-1-50.

Bassett, Melvin Hughes (1920 — No. 05500) RAdm; Ret 12-1-50.

Browder, Maurice Eugene (1920 — No. 05007) RAdm; Ret 6-30-50.

McVay, Charles Butler III (1920 — No. 05518) RAdm; Ret 6-30-49.

Anderson, Charles Carter (1920 — No. 05519) RAdm; Ret 4-1-50.

Mallard, John Boyd (1920 — No. 05531) RAdm; Ret 7-1-49.

Cruzen, Richard Harold (1920 — No. 05532) VAdm; Ret 6-1-54.

Wilson, James Dudley (1920 — No. 05543) RAdm; Ret 7-1-52.

Turney, Hugh Weber (1920 — No. 05544) RAdm; Ret 6-1-52.

Morrison, George Douglas (1920 — No. 05547) RAdm; Ret 3-1-50.

Power, Harry Douglas (1920 — No. 05552) RAdm; Ret 7-1-49.

Doyle, Austin Kelvin (1920 — No. 05558) Adm; Ret 8-1-58.

Downes, Willard Merrill (1920 — No. 05561) RAdm; Ret 6-30-49.

Brookman, Harold Robert (1920 — No. 05572) RAdm; Res 12-26-23.

Lyon, John Ballachey (1920 — No. 05573) RAdm; Ret 7-1-49.

Doyle, James Henry (1920 — No. 05579) VAdm; Ret 11-1-53.

Brantly, Neill Duncan (1920 — No. 05582) RAdm; Ret 6-30-50.

Murphey, Charles Dresser (1920 — No. 05583) RAdm; Ret 2-1-50.

Hepburn, William Peters (1920 — No. 05589) RAdm; Ret 7-1-47.

Isquith, Solomon Silas (1920 — No. 05597) RAdm; Ret 1-1-47.

Ives, Norman Seaton (1920 — No. 05601) Captain; Dies 8-2-44.

Michael, Stanley John Sr (1920 — No. 05606) RAdm; Ret 7-1-49.

Cope, Harley Francis (1920 — No. 05635) RAdm; Ret 7-1-49.

Binford, Thomas Howell (1920 — No. 05649) VAdm; Ret 8-1-54.

Pendleton, Perley Earl (1920 — No. 05654) RAdm; Ret 6-30-50.

Smith, Walton Wiley (1920 — No. 05656) RAdm; Ret 11-1-46.

Glass, Richard Pollard (1920 — No. 05660) RAdm; Ret 10-1-54.

McElduff, John Vincent (1920 — No. 05667) RAdm; Ret 1-1-47.

Gearing, Hilyer Fulford (1920 — No. 05677) RAdm; Ret 3-31-48.

Watt, Richard Morgan Jr (1921 — No. 05681) RAdm; Ret 6-30-56.

Noble, Kenneth Hill (1921 — No. 05685) RAdm; Ret 9-30-48.

McShane, Ralph Edward (1921 — No. 05686) VAdm; Ret 8-1-54.

Kelley, Marion Russell (1921 — No. 05688) RAdm; Ret 7-1-50.

Wheelock, Charles Delorma (1921 — No. 05690) RAdm; Ret 7-1-53.

Pihl, Paul Edward (1921 — No. 05693) RAdm; Ret 4-1-53.

Moore, Walter Ellery (1921 — No. 05694) VAdm; Ret 3-1-59.

Thompson, Edward Mathew (1921 — No. 05699) RAdm; Ret 6-30-50.

Dodds, Sydney Baltzer (1921 — No. 05702) RAdm; Res 1-15-24.

Wellborn, Charles Jr (1921 — No. 05703) VAdm; Ret 2-1-63.

Granum, Alfred Marcellus (1921 — No. 05705) RAdm; Ret 6-30-51.

Davis, Ransom Kirby (1921 — No. 05710) RAdm; Ret 6-30-50.

Olsen, Clarence Edward (1921 — No. 05716) RAdm; Ret 7-1-59.

Chapin, Nealy Adolphus (1921 — No. 05719) RAdm; Ret 5-1-48.

Ayrault, Arthur Delancey (1921 — No. 05723) RAdm; Dies 9-20-85.

Gallery, Daniel Vincent (1921 — No. 05727) RAdm; Ret 10-1-60.

Switzer, Wendell Gray (1921 — No. 05730) VAdm; Ret 4-1-59.

Fletcher, William Bartlett Jr (1921 — No. 05731) RAdm; Ret 6-30-50.

Williams, Henry Goodman (1921 — No. 05733) RAdm; Ret 7-1-51.

Biggs, Burton Beecher (1921 — No. 05734) VAdm; Ret 10-1-58.

Boone, Walter Frederick (1921 — No. 05735) Adm; Ret 3-1-60.

DeBaun, George Harbord (1921 — No. 05741) RAdm; Ret 7-1-50.

Maquire, Charles Joseph (1921 — No. 05744) RAdm; Ret 7-1-50.

Rees, William Lehigh (1921 — No. 05749) VAdm; Ret 10-1-60.

Lake, Burton Gay (1921 — No. 05751) RAdm; Ret 5-1-51.

Carter, Jesse Hicks (1921 — No. 05752) RAdm; Ret 7-1-50.

Anderson, Bern (1921 — No. 05754) RAdm; Ret 7-1-50.

Conlan, Clarence Vincent (1921 — No. 05756) RAdm; Ret 5-1-47.

Van Deurs, George (1921 — No. 05757) RAdm; Ret 7-1-51.

Erck, Charles Frederick (1921 — No. 05758) RAdm; Ret 7-1-50.

Fullinwider, Edwin Gaines (1921 — No. 05759) RAdm; Ret 7-1-50.

Moebus, Lucian Ancel (1921 — No. 05773) VAdm; Ret 11-1-52.

McLean, Heber Hampton (1921 — No. 05774) VAdm; Ret 12-1-54.

Dudley, James Rogers (1921 — No. 05776) RAdm; Ret 7-1-50.

Bolger, Joseph Francis (1921 — No. 05777) VAdm; Ret 10-1-53.

Tarbuck, Raymond Dombill (1921 — No. 05779) RAdm; Ret 7-1-50.

Zimmerli, Rupert Meyrick (1921 — No. 05780) RAdm; Ret 7-1-50.

Hudson, Roy Clare (1921 — No. 05783) RAdm; Ret 6-30-50.

Colclough, Oswald Symister (1921 — No. 05784) VAdm; Ret 2-1-50.

Jacobi, Leon John (1921 — No. 05786) RAdm; Res 4-30-25.

Thackrey, Lyman Augustus (1921 — No. 05791) VAdm; Ret 9-1-52.

Snackenberg, John Arthur (1921 — No. 05793) RAdm; Dies 12-17-79.

Todd, Carlton Rice (1921 — No. 05794) RAdm; Ret 7-1-50.

Galpin, Gerard Frank (1921 — No. 05796) RAdm; Ret 7-1-50.

Bahm, George Henry (1921 — No. 05809) RAdm; Ret 6-1-50.

McKenna, Francis Joseph (1921 — No. 05813) RAdm; Ret 7-1-50.

Igersoll, Stuart Howe (1921 — No. 05819) VAdm; Ret 7-1-60.

Tompkins, Rutledge Barker (1921 — No. 05823) RAdm; Ret 9-1-47.

Green, Clark Lawrence (1921 — No. 05833) RAdm; Ret 7-1-55.

Jackson, William Bennett Jr (1921 — No. 05843) RAdm; Ret 7-1-50.

Waters, John Augustine Jr (1921 — No. 05844) RAdm; Ret 7-1-50.

O'Brien, Timothy Joseph (1921 — No. 05845) RAdm; Ret 7-1-50.

Harris, John Watts (1921 — No. 05847) RAdm; Ret 6-1-51.

Pace, Leo Leander (1921 — No. 05848) Ret 8-1-46.

Wellings, Timothy Francis (1921 — No. 05851) RAdm; Ret 7-1-52.

Grube, John Franklin (1921 — No. 05853) RAdm; Ret 9-1-45.

Guthrie, Harry Aloysis (1921 — No. 05859) RAdm; Ret 7-1-50.

McInerney, Francis Xavier (1921 — No. 05862) VAdm; Ret 7-1-55.

True, Arnold Ellsworth (1921 — No. 05867) RAdm; Ret 12-1-46.

Hall, Grover Budd H. (1921 — No. 05868) RAdm; Ret 10-1-61.

Cook, Albert George Jr (1921 — No. 05869) RAdm; Ret 7-1-50.

Simpson, Rodger Whitten (1921 — No. 05884) RAdm; Ret 7-1-51.

Kime, Frederick Donald (1921 — No. 05885) RAdm; Ret 7-1-51.

Bowman, Roscoe Leroy (1921 — No. 05897) RAdm; Ret 7-1-50.

Thayer, Rufus Gerard (1921 — No. 05898) RAdm; Ret 1-1-47.

Ryan, Thomas John Jr (1921 — No. 05901) RAdm; Ret 6-1-50.

Fitzgerald, William Francis Jr (1921 — No. 05912) RAdm; Ret 7-1-50.

Kelly, Thomas Joseph (1921 — No. 05913) RAdm; Ret 7-1-50.

Juvenal, William Williams (1921 — No. 05924) RAdm; Ret 5-1-48.

Leggett, Wilson Durward Jr (1921 — No. 05927) RAdm; Ret 4-1-55.

Lalor, William George (1921 — No. 05930) RAdm; Ret 7-1-50.

Womble, John Philip Jr (1921 — No. 05933) RAdm; Dies 10-5-56.

Harper, Bryan Cobb (1921 — No. 05934) RAdm; Ret 7-1-50.

Willis, John Howard (1921 — No. 05945) RAdm; Ret 7-1-51.

Hanlon, Byron Hall (1921 — No. 05953) Adm; Ret 10-1-58.

Abercrombie, Laurence Allen (1921 — No. 05965) RAdm; Ret 7-1-51.

Maderia, Dashiell Livingston (1921 — No. 05969) RAdm; Ret 6-1-51.

Talbot, Frank Russell (1921 — No. 05983) RAdm; Ret 7-1-51.

Braun, Boyton Lewis (1921 — No. 05984) RAdm; Ret 9-1-47.

Cronin, Joseph Campbell (1921 — No. 05985) RAdm; Ret 7-1-51.

Craig, Wyatt (1921 — No. 05987) RAdm; Ret 6-1-51.

Nyquist, Walfrid (1921 — No. 05995) RAdm; Ret 10-1-47.

Callahan, Fort Hammond (1921 — No. 05999) RAdm; Ret 7-1-52.

Taylor, Herbert Watson (1921 — No. 06003) RAdm; Ret 7-1-51.

Freeman, James Shepherd (1921 — No. 06013) RAdm; Ret 6-1-51.

Hamilton, William Van (1921 — No. 06018) RAdm; Ret 7-1-51.

Ames, John Griffith III (1921 — No. 06022) RAdm; Res 2-20-23.

Gray, Charles Wellington Jr (1921 — No. 06026) RAdm; Ret 7-1-52.

Crawford, George Clifford (1921 — No. 06030) RAdm; Ret 4-1-58.

Berry, Robert Wallace (1921 — No. 06031) RAdm; Ret 2-1-51.

Sabin, Lorenzo Sherwood Jr (1921 — No. 06032) VAdm; Ret 3-1-61.

Connolly, Joseph Anthony (1921 — No. 06036) RAdm; Ret 7-1-51.

Cooke, William Robert Jr (1921 — No. 06038) RAdm; Ret 9-1-51.

Kernodle, Micheal Holt (1921 — No. 06039) RAdm; Ret 7-1-51.

Giles, Donald Theodore (1921 — No. 06040) RAdm; Ret 3-2-53.

Emory, Campbell Dallas (1921 — No. 06045) RAdm; Ret 7-1-51.

Lewis, Robert Penniman (1921 — No. 06047) RAdm; Res 11-22-27.

Vanzant, Ralston Birto (1921 — No. 06048) RAdm; Ret 1-1-49.

Firth, Francis Joseph (1921 — No. 06050) RAdm; Ret 7-1-52.

McCollum, Arthur Howard (1921 — No. 06052) RAdm; Ret 7-1-51.

Eaton, Melville Edwin (1921 — No. 06059) RAdm; Ret 7-1-52.

Schindler, Walter Gabriel (1921 — No. 06061) VAdm; Ret 10-1-59.

Moore, Edward Peermen (1921 — No. 06066) RAdm; Ret 11-1-45.

Erwin, Donald Loring (1921 — No. 06068) RAdm; Ret 7-1-52.

Abernethy, Elmer Paul (1921 — No. 06073) RAdm; Ret 7-1-52.

Ewen, Edward Coyle (1921 — No. 06075) VAdm; Ret 2-1-57.

Soucek, Apollo (1921 — No. 06091) VAdm; Ret 7-1-55.

Hanson, Ralph Edward (1921 — No. 06092) RAdm; Ret 7-1-51.

McKee, Logan (1921 — No. 06093) RAdm; Ret 7-1-58.

Carlisle, Harold Avery (1921 — No. 06099) RAdm; Ret 7-1-51.

Aldrich, Clarence Edward (1921 — No. 06103) RAdm; Ret 7-1-51.

Greber, Charles Frederic (1921 — No. 06104) RAdm; Ret 7-1-52.

Russell, George Lucius (1921 — No. 06106) VAdm; Ret 10-1-62.

Crenshaw, John Stewardson (1921 — No. 06107) RAdm; Ret 7-1-52.

Entwistle, Frederick Irving (1921 — No. 06125) RAdm; Ret 5-1-58.

Weidner, Walter Frederick (1921 — No. 06126) RAdm; Ret 7-1-52.

Misson, Clinton Alonzo (1921 — No. 06134) RAdm; Ret 5-1-49.

Johnson, William David Jr (1921 — No. 06140) VAdm; Ret 6-1-56.

Barbaro, Joseph Raphael (1921 — No. 06141) RAdm; Ret 4-1-53.

Nichols, Philip Gardner (1921 — No. 06152) RAdm; Ret 7-1-51.

Swigart, Oral Raymond (1921 — No. 06182) RAdm; Ret 7-1-51.

Houser, Harold Alexander (1921 — No. 06191) RAdm; Ret 8-1-55.

Heath, John Postell (1921 — No. 06194) RAdm; Ret 6-1-51.

Hickey, Robert Ferdinard (1921 — No. 06196) VAdm; Ret 7-1-59.

Cook, Albert Berry (1921 — No. 06197) RAdm; Ret 7-1-57.

Wirth, Theodore Rudolph (1921 — No. 06198) RAdm; Ret 7-1-51.

Brown, Charles Randall (1921 — No. 06206) Adm; Ret 1-1-62.

Hoskins, John Madison (1921 — No. 06207) VAdm; Ret 7-1-57.

Rowe, Lionel Lewis (1921 — No. 06219) RAdm; Ret 7-1-52.

Ferris, Floyd Franklin (1921 — No. 06221) RAdm; Ret 7-1-52.

Beard, Jefferson Davis (1921 — No. 06224) RAdm; Ret 3-1-52.

Libby, Ruthven Elmer (1922 — No. 06229) VAdm; Ret 5-1-60.

Hunter, Robert Nisbet (1922 — No. 06242) RAdm; Ret 7-1-52.

Kniskem, Leslie Albert (1922 — No. 06244) RAdm; Ret 4-1-58.

Walsh, Harvey Thomas (1922 — No. 06252) RAdm; Ret 7-1-52.

Huffman, Leon Joseph (1922 — No. 06253) RAdm; Ret 7-1-57. Died 6-22-74.

Converse, Adelbert Frank (1922 — No. 06261) RAdm; Ret 1-1-48. Died 3-9-58.

Manseau, Bernard Edward (1922 — No. 06263) VAdm; Ret 8-1-57. Died 11-4-57.

Miles, Milton Edward (1922 — No. 06271) VAdm; Ret 2-1-58. Died 3-25-61.

Parsons, William Sterling (1922 — No. 06274) RAdm; Died 12-5-53.

Blue, Robert Eugene (1922 — No. 06277) RAdm; Ret 7-1-52. Died 1-20-57.

Baker, Harold Davies (1922 — No. 06278) VAdm; Ret 11-1-58. Died 10-30-82.

Becker, Adolph Ernest Jr (1922 — No. 06279) RAdm; Ret 7-1-52. Died 7-5-76.

Wallis, Adelbert Vernon (1922 — No. 06281) RAdm; Ret 7-1-55. Died 2-8-72.

Bond, Kener Eldridge (1922 — No. 06286) RAdm; Ret 4-1-44. Died 11-15-86.

Adell, Bruce Byron (1922 — No. 06287) RAdm; Ret 8-25-52.

Hansen, Raymond Alfred (1922 — No. 06288) Cdr. USN; MIA 8-9-42.

Grow, Bradford Ellsworth (1922 — No. 06290) RAdm; Ret 7-1-52.

Malstorm, Alvin Ingersoll (1922 — No. 06294) RAdm; Ret 7-1-52.

Taylor, Edwin Ashby (1922 — No. 06297) RAdm; Ret 7-1-52.

Lester, John Campbell (1922 — No. 06304) RAdm; Ret 1-1-47.

Robertson, Armand James (1922 — No. 06305) RAdm; Ret 7-1-52.

Wells, Maxwell Warnock (1922 — No. 06310) RAdm; Ret 8-1-52.

Shultz, John Henry (1922 — No. 06313) RAdm; Ret 7-1-52.

Nelson, Roger Eastman (1922 — No. 06319) RAdm; Ret 9-1-49.

Dugan, Thomas Buchanan (1922 — No. 06320) RAdm; Ret 7-1-52.

Regan, Herbert Ed (1922 — No. 06321) RAdm; Ret 10-1-53.

Stokes, Thomas Murray (1922 — No. 06322) VAdm; Ret 7-1-56.

Blick, Robert Edwin Jr (1922 — No. 06329) VAdm; Ret 7-1-57.

McCracken, Alan Reed (1922 — No. 06331) RAdm; Ret 1-1-50.

Rickover, Hyman George (1922 — No. 06333) Adm; Ret 1-30-82.

Wiedorn, Paul Hollister (1922 — No. 06334) RAdm; Ret 7-1-53.

Hunter, George Porter (1922 — No. 06338) RAdm; Ret 7-1-52.

Coffman, Raymond Paul (1922 — No. 06339) MGen. USMC; Ret 7-1-55.

Ragonnet, Lucien (1922 — No. 06347) RAdm; Ret 7-1-52.

Pullen, Harold Frederick (1922 — No. 06348) RAdm; Ret 8-31-49.

Murphy, Marion Emerson (1922 — No. 06349) VAdm; Ret 5-1-57.

Uehlinger, Archibald Emil (1922 — No. 06350) RAdm; Ret 7-1-52.

Bauernschmidt, George William (1922 — No. 06357) RAdm; Ret 5-1-55.

Evans, Donald Sidney (1922 — No. 06358) RAdm; Ret 7-1-52.

Watkins, Frank Thomas (1922 — No. 06359) VAdm; Ret 1-1-61.

Cater, Charles John (1922 — No. 06361) RAdm; Ret 10-1-52.

DeWitt, Ralph Birchard (1922 — No. 06363) BGen. USMC; Ret 4-9-30.

Atkeson, Clarence Lee C. Jr (1922 — No. 06366) RAdm; Ret 6-1-57.

Hill, Tom Burbridge (1922 — No. 06367) VAdm; Ret 4-1-55.

Clay, James Powell (1922 — No. 06374) RAdm; Ret 7-1-52.

Adams, Francis Mckee Sr (1922 — No. 06379) RAdm; Ret 8-1-46.

Whitney, John Perry (1922 — No. 06393) VAdm; Ret 3-1-55.

Tucker, William Burns (1922 — No. 06394) RAdm; Ret 7-1-57.

Goodwin, Hubbard Frederick (1922 — No. 06397) RAdm; Ret 7-1-53.

Danis, Anthony Leo (1922 — No. 06399) RAdm; Ret 10-30-52.

Bartlett, Bradford (1922 — No. 06402) RAdm; Ret 7-1-52.

Walker, Frank Robinson (1922 — No. 06413) RAdm; Ret 7-1-52.

Hollowell, John Ambross Jr (1922 — No. 06414) Cdr; MIA 3-1-42.

Goodwin, Hugh Hilton (1922 — No. 06415) VAdm; Ret 6-1-57.

Morse, Robert Wade (1922 — No. 06419) RAdm; Ret 6-30-52.

King, Clyde Whitlock (1922 — No. 06424) RAdm; Ret 10-1-58.

Forsyth, Edward Culligan (1922 — No. 06428) RAdm; Ret 7-1-53.

Sherman, Earl Vincent (1922 — No. 06429) RAdm; Ret 11-1-47.

Jackson, Milton C. (1922 — No. 06432) RAdm; Ret 4-1-55.

Riseley, James Profit (1922 — No. 06441) LGen. USMC; Ret 6-30-59.

Patton, John Williams Jr (1922 — No. 06443) BGen; USAR.

Coleman, Beverly Mosby (1922 — No. 06446) RAdm; Ret 1-59.

Jerome, Clayton Charles (1922 — No. 06451) LGen. USMC; Ret 7-1-58.

Phleger, Charles Clayton (1922 — No. 06453) RAdm; Ret 7-1-52.

Cruise, Edgar Allen (1922 — No. 06458) VAdm; Ret 11-1-59.

Solomons, Edward Alva (1922 — No. 06461) RAdm; Ret 4-1-61.

Duckworth, Herbert Spencer (1922 — No. 06469) VAdm; Ret 9-1-52.

Sutton, Frank Carlin (1922 — No. 06470) RAdm; Ret 7-1-53.

McWhinnie, Charles John (1922 — No. 06485) RAdm; Ret 6-30-52.

Parker, Harold Earl (1922 — No. 06486) RAdm; Ret 12-1-55.

O'Shea, George Joseph (1922 — No. 06489) BGen. USMC; Ret 6-30-52.

Adell, Cecil Clinton (1922 — No. 06502) RAdm; Ret 6-30-52.

Malanaphy, Michael Joseph (1922 — No. 06504) RAdm; Ret 7-1-53.

Little, Marion Nethery (1922 — No. 06505) RAdm; Ret 7-1-52.

Ault, William Bowen (1922 — No. 06506) Cdr; MIA 5-8-42.

Riggs, Whitaker Forcha Jr (1922 — No. 06513) RAdm; Ret 1-1-50.

Smith, Robert Hall (1922 — No. 06514) RAdm; Ret 7-1-52.

Moore, Chauncey (1922 — No. 06517) RAdm; Ret 7-1-53.

Orem, Howard Emery (1922 — No. 06523) VAdm; Ret 5-1-57.

Elmore, Eugene Evans (1922 — No. 06525) LCdr; Died 8-10-43.

Haycock, Warren Elmer (1922 — No. 06531) RAdm; Res 6-1-22.

Fisher, Alvan (1922 — No. 06537) RAdm; Res 6-1-22.

Freseman, William Langfitt (1922 — No. 06552) RAdm; Ret 8-1-47.

Campbell, William Stryker (1922 — No. 06556) RAdm; Ret 7-1-53.

Hylant, Emory Paul (1922 — No. 06565) RAdm; Ret 7-1-52.

Humphreys, Charles Owen (1922 — No. 06575) RAdm; Ret 7-1-52.

Cooper, George Randolph (1922 — No. 06576) VAdm; Ret 4-1-55.

Sinclair, Valvin Robinson (1922 — No. 06583) Capt; Ret 7-1-52.

Comp, Charles Owen (1922 — No. 06586) RAdm; Ret 7-1-52.

Coward, Jesse Grant (1922 — No. 06593) RAdm; Ret 8-1-47.

Huber, Vernon (1922 — No. 06594) RAdm; Ret 7-1-53.

Clark, Sherman Rockwell (1922 — No. 06597) RAdm; Ret 12-1-61.

Butterfield, Horace Bushnell (1922 — No. 06602) RAdm; Ret 7-1-52.

Woods, Edwin Elmore (1922 — No. 06608) RAdm; Ret 7-1-53.

Chanler, Hubert Winthrop (1922 — No. 06615) RAdm; Ret 4-1-50.

Miller, Lyman Gano (1922 — No. 06621) BGen. USMC; Ret 6-1-52.

Akers, Frank (1922 — No. 06625) RAdm; Ret 4-1-63.

Terrell, William Reginald (1922 — No. 06629) RAdm; Ret 7-1-53.

Whaley, William Baynard Jr (1922 — No. 06630) RAdm; Ret 6-30-53.

Furlow, Charles Marvin (1922 — No. 06642) RAdm; Ret 1-1-47.

Durgin, Edward Robison (1922 — No. 06643) RAdm; Ret 7-1-52.

Eckhoff, Frederick John (1922 — No. 06645) RAdm; Ret 7-1-52.

Manees, Leon Jackson (1922 — No. 06647) RAdm; Ret 7-1-52.

Johnson, Rudolph Lincoln (1922 — No. 06655) RAdm; Ret 7-1-52.

Eccles, Henry Effingham (1922 — No. 06660) RAdm; Ret 6-30-52.

Stuart, James Austin Sr (1922 — No. 06661) LGen. USMC; Ret 5-1-55.

Berger, Herbert Everett (1922 — No. 06666) RAdm; Ret 9-1-53.

Kauffman, Roland Phillip (1922 — No. 06668) RAdm; Ret 12-1-52.

Sampson, James Greene (1922 — No. 06669) RAdm; Ret 7-1-53.

Jarrett, Harry Bean (1922 — No. 06670) VAdm; Ret 11-1-54.

Bitler, Worthington Smith (1922 — No. 06671) RAdm; Ret 7-1-53.

Junker, Alexander Foster (1922 — No. 06677) RAdm; Ret 7-1-52.

Cornwell, Delbert Strother (1922 — No. 06680) VAdm; Ret 7-1-57.

English, Robert Allen Joseph (1922 — No. 06687) RAdm; Ret 4-1-50.

Bennington, John Paige (1922 — No. 06694) RAdm; Dies 8-24-57.

Hall, Frederick Sherman (1922 — No. 06695) RAdm; Ret 7-1-53.

Earle, Ralph Jr (1922 — No. 06708) VAdm; Ret 7-1-57.

Pratt, John Lockwood (1922 — No. 06711) RAdm; Ret 4-1-53.

Morehouse, Albert Kellogg (1922 — No. 06722) RAdm; Dies 12-18-55.

Dunn, Joseph Brantley (1922 — No. 06724) RAdm; Ret 2-1-52.

McManes, Kenmore Mathew (1922 — No. 06725) RAdm; Ret 6-1-62.

Menocal, George Lawrence (1922 — No. 06727) RAdm; Ret 3-1-48.

Harrigan, Daniel Ward (1922 — No. 06732) RAdm; Ret 7-1-52.

Hollis, Robert Parker (1922 — No. 06746) MGen. USMC; Ret 10-31-57.

Stevens, Harold Runyan (1922 — No. 06749) RAdm; Ret 7-1-53.

Saunders, William Vincent (1922 — No. 06751) RAdm; Ret 5-1-47.

Mee, Francis James (1922 — No. 06756) RAdm; Ret 7-1-52.

Orr, William Willard (1922 — No. 06763) BGen. USMC; Ret 6-1-52.

Carson, Harry Roberts Jr (1923 — No. 06769) RAdm; Ret 8-1-54.

Pearson, John Bartling Jr (1923 — No. 06770) RAdm; Ret 7-1-57.

Ward, Frank Trenwith (1923 — No. 06773) VAdm; Ret 8-1-58.

Holderness, George Allen Jr (1923 — No. 06774) RAdm; Ret 7-1-58.

Sanders, Harry (1923 — No. 06781) VAdm; Ret 5-1-57.

Parr, Warren Sherman (1923 — No. 06782) RAdm; Ret 11-1-47.

Withington, Frederic Stanton (1923 — No. 06785) RAdm; Ret 4-1-61.

Harris, John Thomas (1923 — No. 06786) Born 4-7-01 MO A-MO USMC Killed 2-21-28 Plane Crash Port-Au-Prince Haiti.

Spangler, Selden Booth (1923 — No. 06787) VAdm; Ret 6-30-58.

Wenger, Joseph Numa (1923 — No. 06793) RAdm; Ret 1-23-58.

McCool, Richard Gunter (1923 — No. 06795) RAdm; Ret 7-1-53.

Murdaugh, Albert Christian (1923 — No. 06797) RAdm; Ret 7-1-53.

O'Regan, William Vincent (1923 — No. 06801) VAdm; Ret 7-1-58.

Crommelin, John Geraerdt Jr (1923 — No. 06803) RAdm; Ret 6-1-50.

Ammon, William Bronley (1923 — No. 06804) RAdm; Dies 8-16-59.

Smoot, Roland Nesbit (1923 — No. 06807) VAdm; Ret 6-1-62.

Wolleson, Henry Dean (1923 — No. 06808) RAdm; Dies 2-5-60.

Dietrich, Neil Kittrell (1923 — No. 06812) RAdm; Ret 7-1-58.

Smellow, Morris (1923 — No. 06816) RAdm; Ret 6-30-54.

Johannesen, John Raymond (1923 — No. 06817) RAdm; Ret 7-1-53.

Olney, Alfred Clarence Jr (1923 — No. 06820) RAdm; Ret 10-1-52.

Keith, Harry H. (1923 — No. 06823) RAdm; Ret 11-1-52.

Strauss, Elliot Bowman (1923 — No. 06827) RAdm; Ret 10-1-55.

Thach, James Harmon Jr (1923 — No. 06828) VAdm; Ret 7-1-57.

Gesen, Carl Glenn (1923 — No. 06829) RAdm; Ret 11-1-53.

Burke, Arleigh Albert (1923 — No. 06836) Adm; Ret 8-1-61.

Crosby, Gordon Josiah (1923 — No. 06848) RAdm; Ret 1-1-49.

Shea, Daniel Francis J. (1923 — No. 06851) RAdm; Ret 1-1-48.

Ageton, Arthur Ainsley (1923 — No. 06853) RAdm; Ret 12-1-47.

Ruble, Richard Waynick (1923 — No. 06854) VAdm; Ret 8-1-55.

Williamson, Thomas Binney (1923 — No. 06855) VAdm; Ret 7-1-58.

Ring, Stanhope Cotton (1923 — No. 06856) VAdm; Ret 11-1-55.

Coe, Charles Frederick (1923 — No. 06860) VAdm; Ret 5-1-54.

Welker, George Washington Jr (1923 — No. 06866) RAdm; Ret 6-1-53.

Rassieur, William Theodore (1923 — No. 06867) RAdm; Ret 5-1-52.

Dugan, Paul Fleming (1923 — No. 06870) RAdm; Ret 12-1-50.

Storrs, Aaron Putnam III (1923 — No. 06872) RAdm; Ret 8-1-57.

McIsacc, John Malcolm (1923 — No. 06873) RAdm; Ret 7-1-53.

Welch, John Lytle (1923 — No. 06876) Lt; KIA 12-15-44 WWII Philippine Isl Enemy Action POW.

Trapnell, Frederick Mackay (1923 — No. 06878) VAdm; Ret 10-1-52.

Mendenhall, William K. Jr (1923 — No. 06881) RAdm; Ret 3-1-62.

Scruggs, Richard Martin (1923 — No. 06882) RAdm; Ret 7-1-53.

Ringle, Kenneth Duval (1923 — No. 06883) RAdm; Ret 7-1-53.

Haas, Peter William Jr (1923 — No. 06888) RAdm; Ret 10-1-55.

Cutts, Richard Malcolm (1923 — No. 06892) BGen. USMC; Ret 9-1-46.

Weir Frank Doudiet (1923 — No. 06893) MGen. USMC; Ret 7-1-53.

Kane, Joseph Lester (1923 — No. 06894) RAdm; Ret 7-1-53.

Kelsey, John Donald (1923 — No. 06900) RAdm; Ret 7-1-53.

Arnold, Ralph Judd (1923 — No. 06905) RAdm; Ret 7-1-60.

Johnson, Henry Charles (1923 — No. 06906) RAdm; Ret 7-1-53.

Schneider, Merlin Frederick (1923 — No. 06913) BGen. USMC; Ret 6-1-48.

Blair, Leon Nelson (1923 — No. 06915) RAdm; Ret 7-1-53.

Felt, Harry Donald (1923 — No. 06917) Adm; Ret 7-1-64.

Will, John Mylin (1923 — No. 06921) Adm; Ret 7-1-59.

Hensel, Karl Goldsmith (1923 — No. 06924) RAdm; Ret 1-31-58.

Wescoat, Herbert Moore (1922 — No. 06925) Lt; BNR Lost 4-4-33 in USS Akron off Barnegat Light NJ.

Rodgers, Robert Henry (1923 — No. 06926) RAdm; Ret 7-1-53.

Fuqua, Samuel Glen (1923 — No. 06932) RAdm; Ret 7-1-53.

Moran, Henry George (1923 — No. 06933) RAdm; Ret 7-1-53.

Kimes, Ira Lafayette (1923 — No. 06934) BGen. USMC; Died 2-4-49.

Moosbrugger, Frederick (1923 — No. 06937) VAdm; Ret 10-1-56.

Hughes, Francis Massie (1923 — No. 06938) RAdm; Dies 12-23-60.

Thayer, William Rudolph (1923 — No. 06939) RAdm; Ret 7-1-53.

Leith Stanley (1923 — No. 06946) RAdm; Ret 7-1-53.

Peck, Edwin Ronald (1923 — No. 06947) RAdm; Ret 7-1-53.

Smiley, Curtis Stanton (1923 — No. 06952) RAdm; Ret 6-1-53.

Young, Howard Leyland (1923 — No. 06960) RAdm; Ret 7-1-53.

Briggs, Josephus Asa (1923 — No. 06965) RAdm; Ret 6-30-53.

Higgins, Ronald Dewolf (1923 — No. 06966) RAdm; Ret 7-1-57.

Good, George Franklin Jr (1923 — No. 06968) RAdm; Ret 7-1-58.

Boyce, Thomas Edward (1923 — No. 06970) RAdm; Ret 1-1-48.

Oliver, Richard Maxey (1923 — No. 06971) RAdm; Ret 2-1-54.

Haynsworth, William McCall Jr (1923 — No. 06977) RAdm; Died 8-23-42.

Lemly, William Conrad (1923 — No. 06978) BGen. USMC; Ret 5-1-47.

Maher, Arthur Laurence (1923 — No. 06982) RAdm; Ret 7-1-53.

Sodergren, Albin Rufus (1923 — No. 06990) RAdm; Ret 5-1-48.

Day, Dwight Harvey (1923 — No. 06999) RAdm; Ret 12-1-47.

Twining, Merrill Barber (1923 — No. 07009) Gen. USMC; Ret 10-1-59.

Koonce, Paul Brogden (1923 — No. 07020) RAdm; Ret 7-1-53.

Drexler, Louis Ashton Jr (1923 — No. 07022) Cdr; Died 5-12-45 Co LSt GR Asia Enemy Action Widow Deceased.

Newton, Frank Herbert Jr (1923 — No. 07023) RAdm; Ret 7-1-54.

Monroe, Frank Jr (1923 — No. 07025) RAdm; Ret 7-1-53.

Lamson-Scribner, Frank H. (1923 — No. 07028) MGen. USMC; Ret 6-1-55.

Peterson, John Valdemar (1923 — No. 07030) RAdm; Ret 7-1-53.

Wright, William Dudley Jr (1923 — No. 07032) RAdm; Ret 6-1-48.

Scheyer, Willaim John (1923 — No. 07034) MGen. USMC; Died 5-14-56.

McCarty, William Penn (1923 — No. 07037) RAdm; Ret 7-1-53.

Manley, William Grant (1923 — No. 07045) MGen. USMC; Ret 7-1-56.

Renn, Joseph Bryan (1923 — No. 07054) RAdm; Ret 7-1-53.

Morris, Robert Melvin (1923 — No. 07055) RAdm; Ret 7-1-53.

White, Thomas Bowman (1923 — No. 07056) BGen. USMC; Ret 9-1-46.

Chandler, Alvin Duke (1923 — No. 07057) VAdm; Ret 11-1-51.

Nelson, Frederick Jens (1923 — No. 07059) RAdm; Ret 7-1-53.

Washburn, George Arthur T. (1923 — No. 07062) RAdm; Ret 5-1-48.

Guillot, James Casimir (1923 — No. 07064) RAdm; Ret 7-1-53.

Anderson, William Donald (1923 — No. 07069) RAdm; Ret 7-1-53.

Arnold, Murr Edward (1923 — No. 07070) RAdm; Ret 1-1-63.

Erwin, Marcus Jr (1923 — No. 07071) Ens; Killed on board USS Mississippi 6-12-24 Explosion near San Pedr.

Burford, William Page (1923 — No. 07079) RAdm; Ret 7-1-53.

Moss, John Broder (1923 — No. 07093) VAdm; Ret 9-1-53.

Hederman, Thomas Henry (1923 — No. 07094) RAdm; Ret 7-1-53.

Pogue, William Grady (1923 — No. 07098) RAdm; Ret 7-1-53.

Lohmann, Philip Daniel (1923 — No. 07100) RAdm; Ret 7-1-53.

Guitar, Wallace Estill (1923 — No. 07101) RAdm; Ret 6-1-54.

Bowers, William Alger (1923 — No. 07107) RAdm; Ret 7-1-53.

Sargent, Walter Shepherd (1923 — No. 07111) RAdm; Res 9-30-25.

McKinney, John Reid (1923 — No. 07114) RAdm; Ret 6-1-54.

Dunn, Harry Albert Jr (1923 — No. 07122) RAdm; Ret 7-1-54.

Brady, John Huston (1923 — No. 07123) RAdm; Dies 11-22-85.

Ridout, Horatio (1923 — No. 07126) RAdm; Ret 1-1-47.

Ginder, John Kenneth B. (1923 — No. 07138) RAdm; Ret 7-1-53.

Woods, Ralph Walter D. (1923 — No. 07146) RAdm; Ret 7-1-53.

Shaw, John Drake (1923 — No. 07157) RAdm; Ret 7-1-53.

Folk, Winston Pilcher (1923 — No. 07171) RAdm; Ret 7-1-54.

Harrison, Beverley Randolph Jr (1923 — No. 07175) RAdm; Ret 7-1-53.

Barrett, John Paul Barker (1923 — No. 07176) RAdm; Ret 4-1-49.

Morgan, Armand Malcolm (1924 — No. 07178) RAdm; Ret 10-1-59.

Hatcher, Robert Stetinius (1924 — No. 07179) RAdm; Ret 7-1-55.

Clexton, Edward William (1924 — No. 07181) VAdm; Ret 7-1-60.

Duke, Irving Terrill (1924 — No. 07182) VAdm; Ret 12-1-57.

Hedding, Truman Johnson (1924 — No. 07183) VAdm; Ret 1-1-59.

Wood, Chester Clark (1924 — No. 07184) VAdm; Ret 7-1-59.

Dockweiler, Edward Vincent (1924 — No. 07187) RAdm; Ret 9-1-49.

Woodyard, Edward Lender (1924 — No. 07191) RAdm; Ret 6-30-54.

Ekstrom, Clarence Eugene (1924 — No. 07192) VAdm; Ret 12-1-62.

Rose, Rufus Edwards (1924 — No. 07199) VAdm; Ret 4-30-64.

Gregor, Orville Francis (1924 — No. 07200) RAdm; Ret 7-1-47.

Wilkins, Charles Warren (1924 — No. 07202) VAdm; Ret 1-1-58.

Campbell, Robert Lord (1924 — No. 07204) RAdm; Ret 10-1-64.

Towner, George Crosby (1924 — No. 07208) VAdm.

Wilson, Ralph Ensign (1924 — No. 07213) VAdm; Ret 6-30-60.

Bachman, Leo Adolph (1924 — No. 07220) RAdm; Ret 7-1-54.

Cole, William Marchant (1924 — No. 07221) RAdm; Ret 7-1-54.

Fines, Clifford Ashton (1924 — No. 07226) RAdm; Ret 7-1-54.

Smith, James Walter (1924 — No. 07228) RAdm; Ret 7-1-48.

Yeomans, Elmer Eugene (1924 — No. 07229) RAdm; Ret 6-1-64.

Grandfield, Francis Joseph (1924 — No. 07234) RAdm; Ret 7-1-55.

Beakley, Wallace Morris (1924 — No. 07235) VAdm; Dies 1-16-75.

Hopping, Hallsted Lubeck (1924 — No. 07238) LCdr; Died 2-1-42 BNR USS Enterprise Kwajalein Atoll enemy action.

Moore, William Thomas (1924 — No. 07240) RAdm; Ret 8-1-53.

Rice, Lester Kimme (1924 — No. 07242) RAdm; Ret 7-1-59.

Becker, Herbert Peter (1924 — No. 07243) BGen. USMC; Ret 6-1-55.

Barchet, Stephen George (1924 — No. 07245) RAdm; Ret 7-1-54.

Kreiser, Alexander Walter Jr (1924 — No. 07247) BGen. USMC; Ret 7-1-56.

Arison, Rae Emmett (1924 — No. 07254) RAdm; Ret 7-1-54.

Mathews, Bob Orr (1924 — No. 07255) RAdm; Ret 10-1-54.

McLean, Ephraim Rankin Jr (1924 — No. 07256) VAdm; Ret 3-1-59.

Bare, Robert Osbourne (1924 — No. 07258) LGen. USMC; Ret 7-1-57.

Vieweg, Walter Victor R. (1924 — No. 07260) RAdm; Ret 7-1-54.

Stout, Richard Farnum (1924 — No. 07263) VAdm; Ret 7-1-59.

Hyman, Willford Milton (1924 — No. 07264) LCdr; Died 5-8-43 BNR USS Sims Battle of Coral Sea.

Austin, Bernard Lige (1924 — No. 07266) VAdm; Dies 9-21-79.

Handly, Albert (1924 — No. 07270) RAdm; Ret 7-1-54.

Pahl, James Robert (1924 — No. 07275) RAdm; Ret 7-1-54.

Griffith, Thomas Richards Jr (1924 — No. 07283) RAdm; Res 9-25-24.

Collins, Howard Lyman (1924 — No. 07284) RAdm; Ret 12-1-58.

Hurst, Adrian Melvin (1924 — No. 07288) RAdm; Ret 7-1-54.

Davis, William Virginius (1924 — No. 07290) VAdm; Ret 4-1-60.

Opie, John Newton III (1924 — No. 07291) RAdm; Ret 7-1-54.

Vosseller, Aurelius Bartlet (1924 — No. 07293) VAdm; Ret 9-1-56.

Smith, Perry Kenneth (1924 — No. 07302) BGen. USMC; Ret 6-1-54.

Tiemroth, Harold Herman (1924 — No. 07306) RAdm; Ret 7-1-55.

Gouin, Marcel Emile Alcan (1924 — No. 07307) VAdm; Ret 8-1-54.

Wilkinson, Edwin Richard (1924 — No. 07319) RAdm; Ret 7-1-48.

Short, Wallace Broughton (1924 — No. 07320) VAdm; Ret 11-1-59.

Wilkin, Warren Dudley (1924 — No. 07328) RAdm; Ret 7-1-54.

Gamet, Wayne Neal (1924 — No. 07331) RAdm; Ret 7-31-54.

Abdill, Everett Woolman (1924 — No. 07334) Capt; Died 12-13-44 USS Clay Asiatic Area Enemy Action.

Weaver, Paul Leister Ford (1924 — No. 07335) RAdm; Ret 7-1-55.

Cleaves, Willis Everett (1924 — No. 07336) RAdm; Ret 11-1-46.

Layton, Edwin Thomas (1924 — No. 07339) RAdm; Ret 11-1-59.

Young, Edward Watson (1924 — No. 07341) RAdm; Ret 7-1-54.

Furth, Frederick Raymond (1924 — No. 07347) RAdm; Ret 1-1-56.

Swart, Robert Lee (1924 — No. 07353) RAdm; Ret 7-1-60.

Ogle, Gerald Barker (1924 — No. 07354) RAdm; Ret 1-1-48.

Layne, Frank Chester (1924 — No. 07356) RAdm; Ret 6-1-54.

Sinclair, George Angus (1924 — No. 07361) RAdm; Ret 3-1-49.

Harris, Dale (1924 — No. 07362) RAdm; Ret 8-1-60.

Ricketts, James Brewerton (1924 — No. 07366) RAdm; Ret 7-1-61.

Hayter, Hubert Montgomery (1924 — No. 07368) Cdr; Died 11-30-42 Pacific Area USS New Orleans.

Calvert, Allen Philip (1924 — No. 07374) RAdm; Ret 7-1-54.

Latimer, Samuel Edwin (1924 — No. 07379) RAdm; Ret 2-1-54.

Miller, Harold Blaine (1924 — No. 07380) RAdm; Ret 12-1-46.

Bailey, William Byron (1924 — No. 07386) RAdm; Ret 9-1-53.

Daniel, Henry Chesley (1924 — No. 07388) VAdm; Ret 3-1-59.

Burroughs, Sherman E. Jr (1924 — No. 07389) RAdm; Ret 7-1-54.

Tichenor, Murray Jones (1924 — No. 07395) RAdm; Ret 2-1-48.

Cromwell, John Philip (1924 — No. 07399) Capt; Died 11-19-43 BNR USS Sculpin Pacific Area.

Fike, Charles Laird (1924 — No. 07411) BGen. USMC; Died 5-3-50.

Hayes, John Daniel (1924 — No. 07428) RAdm; Ret 6-30-54.

Smith, Harold Page (1924 — No. 07434) Adm; Ret 5-1-65.

Magly, Austen Volker (1924 — No. 07436) RAdm; Ret 7-1-54.

Lockhart, Robert Green (1924 — No. 07437) RAdm; Ret 7-1-54.

Ragan, Thomas Cameron (1924 — No. 07439) VAdm; Ret 4-1-59.

Mercer, Preston Virginius (1924 — No. 07440) RAdm; Ret 7-1-54.

Goldwaite, Robert (1924 — No. 07441) VAdm; Died 3-21-79.

Reith, George (1924 — No. 07445) RAdm; Ret 4-1-58.

Cabanillas, Jose Manuel (1924 — No. 07446) RAdm; Ret 7-1-55.

Warburton, Audley Lyne (1924 — No. 07448) RAdm; Ret 7-1-55.

Rucker, Colby Guequierre (1924 — No. 07451) RAdm; Ret 1-1-49.

Brereton, Wilkie Hill (1924 — No. 07456) RAdm; Ret 7-1-48.

Hoffman, Charles Monroe (1924 — No. 07462) RAdm; Ret 7-1-54.

Weeden, William Wager Jr (1924 — No. 07463) RAdm; Ret 7-1-54.

Parker, Elton Council (1924 — No. 07465) RAdm; Ret 7-1-54.

Williams, Roy Dean (1924 — No. 07466) RAdm; Ret 7-1-55.

Watts, Ethelbert (1924 — No. 07467) RAdm; Ret 7-1-54.

Sharp, Louis Dent Jr (1924 — No. 07468) RAdm; Ret 7-1-54.

McPeake, Lawrence John (1924 — 07470) Cdr; BNR missimg in enemy action 3-1-42 USS Pecos Java, pres dead.

Duvall, William Howard (1924 — No. 07473) RAdm; Ret 7-1-54.

Verge, William Ernest (1924 — No. 07474) RAdm; Ret 12-1-47.

Day, Douglas Turner Jr (1924 — No. 07476) RAdm; Ret 7-1-55.

Ramsey, Donald James (1924 — No. 07480) RAdm; Ret 7-1-47.

Creehan, Edward Patrick (1924 — No. 07489) RAdm; Ret 7-1-56.

Callaway, Charles Howard (1924 — No. 07490) Lost in USS Akron 4-4-33 off Barnegat Light NJ.

Hopkins, Howard Vaniman (1924 — No. 07491) RAdm; Ret 7-1-54.

Phillips, Neill (1924 — No. 07495) RAdm; Ret 1-1-48.

Webb, Richard Christopher Jr (1924 — No. 07497) RAdm; Ret 7-1-54.

Lajeunesse, Roy Warren (1924 — No. 07500) RAdm; Ret 12-1-54.

Lillard, Joseph Snell (1924 — No. 07502) RAdm; Ret 8-1-52.

Blanchard, Theodore (1924 — No. 07509) RAdm; Ret 9-1-59.

Taylor, Joseph Irwin Jr (1924 — No. 07512) RAdm; Ret 7-1-55.

Southworth, Harrison Belknap (1924 — No. 07515) RAdm; Ret 7-1-54.

Montgomery, George Cannon (1924 — No. 07516) RAdm; Ret 7-1-54.

Fraser, Thomas Edward (1924 — No. 07519) Cdr; Died 11-16-43 BNR USS Walke Battle of Savo Island.

Cameron, Thomas Stevenson (1924 — No. 07521) RAdm; Ret 7-1-55.

Bellerby, Russell John (1924 — No. 07522) RAdm; Ret Unk, Died 7-2-85.

Ganahl, Richard Gregory (1924 — No. 07523) RAdm; Ret 1-1-48.

Taylor, Edwin James Jr (1924 — No. 07525) RAdm; Ret 7-1-47.

Peterson, Wallis Federick (1924 — No. 07527) RAdm; Ret 11-1-63.

Deutemann, William Vincent (1924 — No. 07533) RAdm; Ret 7-1-55.

Thomas, Lloyd Howden (1924 — No. 07540) RAdm; Ret 6-1-56.

Nunn, Ira Hudson (1924 — No. 07543) RAdm; Ret 4-1-63.

Seay, Erskine Austin (1924 — No. 07546) RAdm; Ret 5-1-48.

Fowler, Joseph William (1924 — No. 07547) RAdm; Ret 7-1-55.

Morrill, John Henry II (1924 — No. 07549) RAdm; Ret 9-1-55.

Shanklin, Elliott West (1924 — No. 07553) RAdm; Ret 2-1-55.

Carroll, Chester Edward (1924 — No. 07561) RAdm; Ret 7-1-54.

Hogle, James Bernhardt (1924 — No. 07565) RAdm; Ret 7-1-54.

Rooney, John Bartholomew (1924 — No. 07566) RAdm; Ret 7-1-54.

Bell, Federick Jackson (1924 — No. 07567) RAdm; Ret 2-1-48.

Evans, William Ashby (1924 — No. 07570) RAdm; Ret 7-1-55.

Stormes, Max Clifford (1924 — No. 07577) Cdr; Died 11-16-43 BNR USS Preston Battle of Savo Island.

Francis, Dennis Larkin (1924 — No. 07583) RAdm; Ret 2-1-55.

Goodall, Henry William (1924 — No. 07586) RAdm; Ret 7-1-54.

Hartwig, Glenn Roy (1924 — No. 07592) RAdm; Ret 7-1-54.

Ferriter, Charles Arthur (1924 — No. 07593) RAdm; Ret 7-1-55.

Temple, Harry Brigham (1924 — No. 07594) RAdm; Ret 4-30-55.

Erdmann, William Lawrence (1924 — No. 07596) RAdm; Ret 4-1-60.

Waller, Raymond Randolph (1924 — No. 07607) RAdm; Ret 6-30-54.

Peterson, George Edmund (1924 — No. 07611) RAdm; Ret 7-1-54.

Baron, Richard Swan (1924 — No. 07613) LCdr; Died 3-15-42 Cebu City PI enemy Action.

Irish, Elija Warriner (1924 — No. 07615) RAdm; Ret 6-1-53.

Herlihy, Joseph Lee (1924 — No. 07617) RAdm; Ret 7-1-59.

Stuart, Walter James (1924 — No. 07622) BGen. USMC; Ret 2-1-49.

Coley, Lewis Elliot (1924 — No. 07626) RAdm; Ret 7-1-54.

Daniel, John Cheshire (1924 — No. 07627) VAdm; Ret 10-1-59.

Wymond, John Ellsworth (1924 — No. 07629) LCdr; Died 9-16-43 BNR Wasp Pacific Area.

Scott, Winfield Wayne (1924 — No. 07636) LCol. USA; KIA 8-1-42 WW II Prisoner of Japanese.

Martin, Hugh Jack (1924 — No. 07638) RAdm; Ret 7-1-54.

Hudnall, James Henry Natt (1924 — No. 07649) BGen. USMC; Ret 7-1-54.

Nichol, Bromfield Bradford (1924 — No. 07655) RAdm; Ret 7-1-54.

Seaward, Eugene Trefethen (1924 — No. 07658) RAdm; Ret 7-1-54.

Warren, John Thompson (1924 — No. 07662) RAdm; Ret 7-1-54.

Gardner, Francis Hartt (1924 — No. 07668) RAdm; Ret 7-1-54.

Landstreet, James Collins (1924 — No. 07670) RAdm; Ret 7-1-55.

Worthington, Joseph Muse (1924 — No. 07672) RAdm; Ret 7-1-54.

Mills, Ralph Erskine (1924 — No. 07699) RAdm; Ret 7-1-57.

Brown, Wilburt Scott (1924-Non-Graduate — No. 924025) MGen. USMC; Ret 12-1-53.

Loomis, Francis Butler Jr (1924-Non-Graduate — No. 924130) MGen; USMC.

Sides, John Harold (1925 — No. 07708) Adm; Ret 10-1-63.

Marshall, William Jefferson (1925 — No. 07715) VAdm; Ret 5-1-59.

Long, Victor Dismukes (1925 — No. 07716) VAdm; Ret 10-1-59.

Crommelin, Henry (1925 — No. 07717) VAdm; Ret 11-1-59.

Robinson, James Marshall (1925 — No. 07718) RAdm; Ret 6-30-55.

Pyne, Schuyler Neilson (1925 — No. 07724) RAdm; Ret 6-1-61.

Tucker, Dundas Preble (1925 — No. 07729) RAdm; Ret 6-30-56.

Loomis, Frederick Kent (1925 — No. 07731) RAdm; Ret 6-1-55.

Harris, Harold Douglas (1925 — No. 07732) BGen. USMC; Ret 1-1-50.

Murphy, John Williams Jr (1925 — No. 07733) RAdm; Ret 7-1-55.

Parker, Edward Nelson (1925 — No. 07736) VAdm; Ret 11-1-63.

Eller, Ernest McNeill (1925 — No. 07738) RAdm; Ret 3-30-55.

Voge, Richard George (1925 — No. 07742) RAdm; Ret 7-1-56.

Brown, Thomas Markham (1925 — No. 07743) RAdm Ret 7-1-56.

Sihler, William (1925 — No. 07745) RAdm; Ret 9-1-59.

Hord, Paul Whitefield (1925 — No. 07748) RAdm; Ret 1-1-47.

Seabury, Claire Clifford (1925 — No. 07749) RAdm; Ret 11-1-47.

Wheelock, Austin Wadsworth (1925 — No. 07752) RAdm; Ret Ukn. Died 12-10-53.

Lent, Wills Ashford (1925 — No. 07753) RAdm; Ret 7-1-55.

Moseley, Stanley Page (1925 — No. 07754) RAdm; Ret 11-1-54.

Walker, Edward Keith (1925 — No. 07757) RAdm; Ret 7-1-55.

Larkin, Richard Alexander (1925 — No. 07760) RAdm; Ret 7-1-55.

Taylor, Edmund Battelle (1925 — No. 07762) VAdm; Ret Ukn. Died 4-30-73.

Melgaard, John Leslie (1925 — No. 07769) RAdm; Ret 7-1-55.

Cronin, Robert Emmet (1925 — No. 07771) RAdm; Ret 7-1-61.

Smith, James Stuart Jr (1925 — No. 07772) Cdr; 11-13-42 BNR USS Atlanta Battle of Solomon Isl.

Buerkle, Elmer Charles (1925 — No. 07773) Cdr; 7-6-43 BNR USS Helena Kula Gulf Pacific Area.

Warder, Federick Burdett (1925 — No. 07777) RAdm; Ret 7-1-62.

Thomas, Francis James (1925 — No. 07780) RAdm; Ret 11-1-53.

Stryker, Joe Warren (1925 — No. 07785) RAdm; Ret 7-1-55.

Powell, Morgan Allen (1925 — No. 07786) RAdm; Ret Ukn. Died 6-21-79.

Paro, Eugene Edward (1925 — No. 07788) Radm; Ret 7-1-49.

Phillips, George Lincoln (1925 — No. 07793) RAdm; Ret Ukn. Died 7-10-86.

McNally, James Anthony (1925 — No. 07794) RAdm; Ret 7-1-56.

Mumma, Morton Claire Jr (1925 — No. 07805) RAdm; Ret 4-1-53.

Hogaboom, Robert Edward (1925 — No. 07806) Gen. USMC; Ret 11-1-59.

Smith, Stirling Patterson (1925 — No. 07809) RAdm; Ret 6-30-55.

Clark Jeane R. (1925 — No. 07810) RAdm; Ret 6-30-55.

Rorschach, Anthony Lawless (1925 — No. 07813) RAdm; Ret 7-1-55.

Smith, Chester Carl (1925 — No. 07814) VAdm; Ret 1-1-59.

Wright, George Charles (1925 — No. 07815) VAdm; Ret 3-1-58.

Tyree, David Merrill (1925 — No. 07816) RAdm; Ret 8-1-63.

Lyon, Harry Nelson (1925 — No. 07817) BGen. USMCR; Res 7-7-28.

Gibbs, Robert Henry (1925 — No. 07821) RAdm; Ret 7-1-55.

Von Kleeck, Ernest St Clair Jr (1925 — No. 07823) RAdm; Ret 7-1-55.

Champlin, Jackson Selover (1925 — No. 07826) RAdm; Ret 7-1-55.

Ray, Clarence (1925 — No. 07829) RAdm; Ret 7-1-55.

Brink, Francis Harry (1925 — No. 07832) BGen. USMC; Ret 7-1-55.

Jackson, Alexander Jr (1925 — No. 07833) RAdm; Ret 9-30-59.

Snedeker, James (1925 — No. 07835) BGen. USMC: Ret 5-1-48.

Smith, Rodman Davis (1925 — No. 07837) RAdm; Ret 7-1-55.

Parks, Lewis Smith (1925 — No. 07840) RAdm; Ret 1-1-60.

Bell, Harman Brown (1925 — No. 07842) RAdm; Ret 7-1-55.

Dawson, Kenneth Vernon (1925 — No. 07844) RAdm; Ret 7-1-55.

Nickerson, Roger Brown (1925 — No. 07851) RAdm; Ret 7-1-55.

Goodney, Willard Kinsman (1925 — No. 07852) RAdm; Ret 8-1-57.

Ludewig, Joseph William (1925 — No. 07856) RAdm; Ret 1-1-47.

Van Metre, Merle (1925 — No. 07858) RAdm; Ret 7-1-55.

Hart, John Neely (1925 — No. 07864) MGen. USMC; Ret 6-30-55.

Briggs, Cameron (1925 — No. 07873) RAdm; Ret 7-1-55.

Messmer, William Le Roy (1925 — No. 07875) RAdm; Ret 7-1-55.

Sima, Frederick Frank (1925 — No. 07882) RAdm; Res 10-31-30.

Kivette, Frederick Norman (1925 — No. 07890) VAdm; Ret 10-1-61.

Sowell, Jesse Clyburn (1925 — No. 07891) RAdm; Ret 7-1-55.

Hobbs, Ira Earl (1925 — No. 07892) VAdm; Ret 5-1-59.

Gallery, William Onahan (1925 — No. 07897) RAdm; Ret 7-1-55.

Larson, Harold Oscar (1925 — No. 07899) VAdm; Ret 11-1-59.

Miller, Harry Fanker (1925 — No. 07902) RAdm; Dies 4-1-52.

Burrowes, Thomas (1925 — No. 07904) RAdm; Ret 7-1-60.

Varian, Donald Cord (1925 — No. 07905) RAdm; Ret 8-1-61.

Hoffner, Carleton Crosby (1925 — No. 07906) RAdm; Ret 7-1-55.

Henderson, Harry Havelock (1925 — No. 07908) RAdm; Ret 5-1-60.

Weeks, Charles Stillman (1925 — No. 07910) RAdm; Ret 8-1-55.

Hurd, Kenneth Charles (1925 — No. 07913) RAdm; Ret 7-1-55.

Goudeau, Lionel Claudius (1925 — No. 07914) BGen. USMC; Ret 6-1-55.

Wright, William Leslie (1925 — No. 07915) RAdm; Ret 4-1-47.

Smith, Russell Simonds (1925 — No. 07921) RAdm; Ret 7-31-55.

Sylvester, Malcolm Duncan (1925 — No. 07922) RAdm; Ret 1-1-48.

Pefley, Alfred Reed (1925 — No. 07923) BGen. USMC; Ret 7-1-55.

Jarrell, Albert Edmondson (1925 — No. 07924) VAdm; Ret 10-1-59.

Naquin, Oliver Francis (1925 — No. 07927) RAdm; Ret 7-1-55.

Haviland, James William III (1925 — No. 07933) RAdm; Ret 7-1-56.

Benson, William Lewis (1925 — No. 07938) RAdm; Ret 7-1-55.

Laffan, John James (1925 — No. 07945) RAdm; Ret 6-30-55.

Vanasse, Roland Benjamin (1925 — No. 07947) RAdm; Res 8-1-48.

Wellings, Joseph Harold (1925 — No. 07948) RAdm; Ret 8-1-63.

Headden, William Ramon (1925 — No. 07949) RAdm; Ret 7-1-55.

Bacon, Barton Elijah Jr (1925 — No. 07950) RAdm; Ret 7-1-56.

Dufek, George John (1925 — No. 07962) RAdm; Ret 9-1-59.

Beck, Edward Louis (1925 — No. 07968) RAdm; Ret 11-1-46.

Leahey, George Aloysius Jr (1925 — No. 07969) RAdm; Dies 11-22-48.

Lyons, Raymond Richard (1925 — No. 07971) RAdm; Ret 1-1-49.

Standley, William Harrison Jr (1925 — No. 07980) RAdm; Ret 7-1-60.

Mayer, Walter Scott Jr (1925 — No. 07990) RAdm; Ret 7-1-55.

Jordan, Julian Bethune (1925 — No. 07993) Lt; Died 12-7-41 BNR USS Oklahoma Pearl Harbor.

Reynolds, Carroll Dayne (1925 — No. 08004) RAdm; Ret 7-1-49.

Thorington, Alexander Clark (1925 — No. 08010) RAdm; Ret 7-1-55.

Hourihan, John Joseph (1925 — No. 08015) RAdm; Ret 7-1-56.

Beecher, William Gordon Jr (1925 — No. 08021) VAdm; Ret 8-1-55.

Davidson, Walter Bunn (1925 — No. 08025) RAdm; Ret 5-1-56.

Carson, Joseph Malcolm (1925 — No. 08027) RAdm; Ret 7-1-63.

Schonland, Herbert Emery (1925 — No. 08031) RAdm; Ret 1-1-47.

Chillingworth, Charles F. Jr (1925 — No. 08041) VAdm; Ret 8-1-56.

Veeder, William Schuetze (1925 — No. 08042) RAdm; Ret 7-1-55.

Nevins, Joseph Henry Jr (1925 — No. 08045) RAdm; Ret 7-1-55.

King, George Joseph (1925 — No. 08048) RAdm; Ret 5-1-48.

McFall, Edward Alspaugh (1925 — No. 08054) RAdm; Ret 2-1-57.

Williams, Frederick Paul (1925 — No. 08057) RAdm; Ret 7-1-55.

Fitz-Gerald, Phillip Henry (1925 — No. 08058) RAdm; Ret 7-1-55.

Florance, John Edwards (1925 — No. 08067) RAdm; Ret 7-1-55.

Swinburne, Edwin Robinson (1925 — No. 08070) RAdm; Ret 7-1-55.

Delaney, John Francis Jr (1925 — No. 08076) RAdm; Ret 7-1-56.

Drury, Martin Joseph (1925 — No. 08077) RAdm; Ret 7-1-55.

MacIntyre, Alezander (1925 — No. 08080) RAdm; Ret 7-1-56.

Gordinier, Virgil Francis (1925 — No. 08081) RAdm; Ret 7-1-56.

Johns, John Graham (1925 — No. 08083) RAdm; Ret 7-1-56.

Sims, Gelzer Loyall (1925 — No. 08084) RAdm; Ret 6-1-47.

Thomson, Hugh Pollard (1925 — No. 08088) RAdm; Ret 7-1-52.

Smith, James McDonald (1925 — No. 08096) RAdm; Ret 9-1-48.

Hickey, Thomas Joseph (1925 — No. 08098) RAdm; Ret 10-1-48.

Hank, William Edwin (1925 — No. 08100) LCdr; Died 11-14-43 BNR USS Laffey Battle of Savo Island.

Phelan, George Richardson (1925 — No. 08103) RAdm; Dies 5-25-75.

Sears, Norman Walker (1925 — No. 08104) RAdm; Ret 7-1-55.

Davis, Ernest Judson (1925 — No. 08109) RAdm; Ret 1-1-48.

Ford, Walter Chilcott (1925 — No. 08118) RAdm; Ret 7-1-61.

Copping, Bennett Smith (1925 — No. 08120) RAdm; Ret 7-1-56.

Markham, Lewis Merrill Jr (1925 — No. 08130) RAdm; Ret 7-1-55.

Fenno, Frank Wesley (1925 — No. 08141) RAdm; Ret 4-1-61.

Ashton, Robert Kyle (1925-Non-Graduate — No. 925010) RAdm. USNR; Res 7-1-58.

Jackson, Robert Slaughter (1925-Non-Graduate — No. 925127) Died 9-8-34 Asbury Park NJ Officer SS Morro Castle Burned and Sank.

Sylvester, John (1926 — No. 08148) VAdm; Ret 10-1-64.

Strain, Charles Lynn (1926 — No. 08150) RAdm; Ret 7-1-58.

Floyd, William Orrin (1926 — No. 08151) RAdm; Ret 7-1-56.

Lyman, Charles Huntington III (1926 — No. 08153) RAdm; Ret 12-1-65.

Brown, Bert Franklin (1926 — No. 08156) RAdm; Ret 3-1-55.

Weaver, George Calvin (1926 — No. 08159) RAdm; Ret 7-30-56.

Taylor, John McNay (1926 — No. 08160) VAdm; Ret 7-1-67.

Meade, Robert Heber (1926 — No. 08161) RAdm; CEC Ret 8-1-59.

Russell, James Sargent (1926 — No. 08162) Adm.

Phares, Jesse Lewis (1926 — No. 08163) RAdm; Dies 6-16-53.

Mumma, Albert Girard (1926 — No. 08165) RAdm; Ret 5-1-59.

Stroop, Paul David (1926 — No. 08167) VAdm; Ret 11-1-65.

Lovett, Benjamin Barnes C. (1926 — No. 08168) RAdm; Ret 1-1-58.

Bruton, Henry Chester (1926 — No. 08170) RAdm; Ret 8-1-60.

Mundorff, George Theodore (1926 — No. 08171) RAdm; Ret 8-1-56.

Goldman, Robert Boggs (1926 — No. 08173) RAdm; Ret 9-1-47.

Sullivan, Dennis Joseph (1926 — No. 08174) RAdm; Ret 6-30-56.

Whipple, Walter Jones (1926 — No. 08175) RAdm; Ret 7-1-56.

Smith, Sidney Layton (1926 — No. 08176) LCdr; MIA 3-1-42 USS Houston Sunk in Enemy Action Java Sea.

Evenson, Marvin Pabodie (1926 — No. 08179) RAdm; Ret 7-1-59.

Ward, James Henry (1926 — No. 08180) VAdm; Ret 7-1-59.

Whiteside, William Smith (1926 — No. 08184) RAdm; Ret 7-1-56.

Stout, Herald Franklin (1926 — No. 08186) RAdm; Ret 7-1-56.

Pirie, Robert Burns (1926 — No. 08189) VAdm; Ret 11-1-62.

Lee, Fitzhugh (1926 — No. 08191) VAdm; Ret 8-1-67.

Dunlap, Stanton Baldwin (1926 — No. 08192) RAdm; Ret Ukn. Died 12-27-70.

Prime, Nathaniel Scudder (1926 — No. 08202) RAdm; Ret 12-1-46.

Wright, Wesley Arnold (1926 — No. 08203) Capt; Ret 7-1-57.

Niekum, Philip Jr (1926 — No. 08204) RAdm; Ret 10-1-41.

Snedeker, Edward Walter (1926 — No. 08211) LGen. USMC.

Horne, Charles Frederick Jr (1926 — No. 08212) RAdm; Ret 5-1-51.

O'Beime, Frank (1926 — No. 08213) VAdm; Ret 10-1-63.

Linaweaver, Walter Ellsworth (1926 — No. 08217) Radm; Ret 5-3-56.

Morgan, Philip Sidney (1926 — No. 08222) RAdm; Ret 7-1-56.

Benner, Kenneth Wachter (1926 — No. 08227) BGen. USMC; Ret 6-1-56.

Whiteside, William Joseph (1926 — No. 08229) RAdm; Ret 12-1-47.

Rodee, Walter Fred (1926 — No. 08230) RAdm; Ret 7-1-61.

McCorkle, Francis Douglas (1926 — No. 08233) RAdm; Ret 12-1-60.

Cavenagh, Robert William (1926 — No. 08236) RAdm; Ret 12-1-66.

Grenfell, Elton Watters (1926 — No. 08240) VAdm; Ret 9-11-64.

Strother, John Almon (1926 — No. 08244) RAdm; Ret 12-1-55.

McLean, John Boyd (1926 — No. 08247) RAdm; Ret 8-1-56.

Wolverton, Thomas Michael (1926 — No. 08248) RAdm; Ret 11-1-48.

Blinn, Welford Charles (1926 — No. 08249) RAdm; Ret 6-30-48.

Buchanan, Charles Allen (1926 — No. 08251) RAdm; Ret 6-1-64.

Biederman, Karl Joseph (1926 — No. 08254) RAdm; Ret 7-1-56.

Newman, John Francis Jr (1926 — No. 08257) RAdm; Ret 5-1-56.

Busck, Vilhelm Klein (1926 — No. 08259) RAdm; Ret 7-1-56.

Adair, Charles (1926 — No. 08260) RAdm; Ret 7-1-56.

Brewer, James Theodore (1926 — No. 08261) RAdm; Ret 1-1-52.

Sweetser, Willard Merton (1926 — No. 08265) RAdm; Ret 7-1-56.

Broussard, Clarence (1926 — No. 08266) RAdm; Ret 11-1-56.

Parish, Herman Oliff (1926 — No. 08267) RAdm; Ret 7-1-56.

Poehlmann, Karl Frederick (1926 — No. 08270) RAdm; Ret 7-1-56.

Young, John Somerville E. (1926 — No. 08272) BGen. USMC; Ret 4-1-53.

Armstrong, Justus Morris B. (1926 — No. 08281) RAdm; Ret 1-1-48.

Gallaher, John Francis (1926 — No. 08282) RAdm; Ret 8-1-56.

Byrne, James Francis (1926 — No. 08286) RAdm; Ret 7-1-56.

Barker, Nathaniel Charles (1926 — No. 08288) RAdm; Ret 11-1-47.

Cooper, William Goodwin (1926 — No. 08291) VAdm; Ret 2-1-60.

Butler, Arthur Howard (1926 — No. 08292) MGen. USMC; Ret 7-1-56.

Fox, Douglas Harold (1926 — No. 08295) LCdr; Died 11-14-43 BNR USS Barton Battle of Savo Island.

Anderson, William Lovett (1926 — No. 08303) RAdm; Ret 7-1-56.

Withers, Hartnall Jackman (1926 — No. 08304) BGen. USMC; Ret 5-1-48.

Grant, Etheridge (1926 — No. 08305) RAdm; Ret 7-1-56.

McClusky, Clarence Wade Jr (1926 — No. 08306) RAdm; Ret 7-1-56.

Halloran, Thomas Francis (1926 — No. 08308) RAdm; Ret 1-1-48.

Nelson, Nels Herning (1926 — No. 08312) MGen. USMC; Ret 7-1-56.

Henderson, Loften Russell (1926 — No. 08316) Maj. USMC; Died 6-5-43 Midway Island.

Tucker, Samuel Marion (1926 — No. 08319) RAdm; Ret 7-1-56.

Duerfeldt, Clifford Henderson (1926 — No. 08320) RAdm; Ret 5-31-64.

Jordahl, Russell Nelton (1926 — No. 08322) BGen. USMC; 7-1-58.

Watson, Paul Wesley, (1926 — No. 08323) RAdm; Ret 7-1-56.

Joyce, Allen Raymond (1926 — No. 08324) RAdm; Ret 1-1-48.

Taff, Clarence Orvill (1926 — No. 08328) RAdm; Ret 8-1-49.

Greytak, John Joseph (1926 — No. 08330) RAdm; Ret 7-1-57.

Graham, Chester Baird (1926 — No. 08333) BGen. USMC; Ret 4-1-50.

Pederson, Oscar (1926 — No. 08334) RAdm; Ret 7-1-56.

Hull, Jesse Lyle (1926 — No. 08335) RAdm; Ret 7-1-56.

Shepard, Seth Armstrong (1926 — No. 08341) RAdm; Ret 9-1-56.

Greenslade, John Francis (1926 — No. 08345) RAdm; Ret 7-1-56.

Frederick, Theodore Ridenour (1926 — No. 08350) RAdm; Ret 7-1-56.

Dolan, William Augustine Jr (1926 — No. 08351) RAdm; Ret 7-21-62.

Aylward, Theodore Charles (1926 — No. 08353) RAdm; Ret 7-1-56.

Kunz, Chester Arthur (1926 — No. 08355) RAdm; Ret 6-1-57.

May, Eugene Franklin (1926 — No. 08356) RAdm.

Jones, William Thomas (1926 — No. 08358) RAdm; Ret 4-1-57.

Katz, Benjamin (1926 — No. 08363) RAdm; Ret 6-30-57.

Rozendal, Henry Dirk (1926 — No. 08364) RAdm; Ret 7-1-56.

Wilfong, John Lester (1926 — No. 08365) RAdm; Ret 2-1-57.

Miller, William (1926 — No. 08366) RAdm; Ret 4-1-60.

Smedberg, William Renwick III (1926 — No. 08367) RAdm; Ret 4-1-64.

Schanze, Edwin Stansbury (1926 — No. 08369) RAdm; Ret 7-1-56.

Edwards, Heywood Lane (1926 — No. 08372) LCdr; Died 10-31-41 BNR USS Reuben James North Atlantic.

Reich, Herman (1926 — No. 08376) RAdm; Ret Ukn. Died 6-28-82.

Salzman, Elmer Henry (1926 — No. 08378) MGen. USMC; Ret 8-1-49.

Hollingsworth, William Right (1926 — No. 08385) RAdm; Ret 7-1-56.

Leeper, James Edward (1926 — No. 08388) RAdm; Ret 6-30-56.

Taylor, Ford Newton Jr (1926 — No. 08389) RAdm; Ret 7-1-56.

Wornham, Thomas Andrews (1926 — No. 08390) LGen. USMC; Died 12-17-84.

Rimer, Theodore Wesley (1926 — No. 08398) RAdm; Ret 8-17-56.

Gano, Roy Alexander (1926 — No. 08399) VAdm; Ret 7-1-64.

Johnson, Robert Ruffin (1926 — No. 08400) RAdm; 2-1-57.

Olsen, Earl Kenneth (1926 — No. 08402) Cdr; Died 11-30-42 USS Pensacola.

Romoser, William Kilian (1926 — No. 08406) RAdm; Ret 7-1-61.

Weimer, Edward Loomis B. (1926 — No. 08409) RAdm; Ret 7-1-56.

Russell, Benjamin Van Meter (1926 — No. 08410) RAdm; Ret 6-1-48.

Fradd, John Ernest (1926 — No. 08411) RAdm; Ret 6-30-57.

Ellis, Robert Beaman (1926 — No. 08412) RAdm; Ret 12-1-59.

Clark, Ralph Sperry (1926 — No. 08414) RAdm; Ret 7-1-67.

Havard, Valery Jr (1926 — No. 08416) RAdm; Ret 6-30-56.

Moses, Charles, William (1926 — No. 08420) RAdm; Ret 7-1-56.

Strange, Hubert Ellis (1926 — No. 08421) RAdm; Ret 2-1-47.

Sweeney, Daniel Joseph (1926 No. 08422) RAdm; Ret 7-1-56.

Gulick, Roy Moyer (1926 — No. 08424) MGen. USMC; Died 9-27-76.

Hains, Hamilton (1926 — No. 08427) RAdm; Ret 12-1-46.

Purvis, Robert Selden Jr (1926 — No. 08429) RAdm; Ret 7-1-53.

Reybold, John Keane (1926 — No. 08430) LCdr; KIA 3-19-42 WW II USS Dickerson Atlantic Area.

Tedder, Fondville Lee (1926 — No. 08433) RAdm; Ret 7-1-56.

Fleming, Morton Klyne Jr (1926 — No. 08437) RAdm; Ret 11-1-49.

Zurmuehlen, Gerald Dale (1926 — No. 08438) RAdm; Ret 7-1-56.

Glick, John Albert (1926 — No. 08442) RAdm; Ret 7-1-56.

McLean, Gordon Alexander (1926 — No. 08443) RAdm; Ret 7-1-56.

Armstrong, Robert Gordon (1926 — No. 08449) RAdm; Ret 7-1-56.

Ruth, Ernst August (1926 — No. 08450) RAdm; Ret 8-1-59.

Foster, John Golden Jr (1926 — No. 08451) RAdm; Ret 7-1-56.

Paschal, Joe Bennett (1926 — No. 08453) RAdm; Ret 7-1-56.

Kobey, Theodore Hertzel (1926 — No. 08455) RAdm; Ret 2-1-52.

Armentrout, Erasmus Wilson Jr (1926 — No. 08456) RAdm; Ret 6-30-56.

Fullinwider, Ranson (1926 — No. 08460) RAdm; Ret 7-1-56.

Dyer, Walter Leo (1926 — No. 08468) RAdm; Ret 7-1-56.

Hutchinson, Edward Shillingford (1926 — No. 08473) RAdm; Ret 7-1-56.

Craig, Kenneth (1926 — No. 08474) RAdm; Ret Ukn.

Singleton, Charles Tod Jr (1926 — No. 08477) RAdm; Ret 7-1-56.

Frost, Laurence Hugh (1926 — No. 08483) VAdm; Ret 7-1-64.

Dow, Leonard James (1926 — No. 08486) RAdm; Ret 7-1-56.

Stelter, Frederick Carl Jr (1926 — No. 08487) RAdm; Ret 2-1-61.

Shane, Louis Jr (1926 — No. 08489) LCdr; Died 2-16-43 BNR Asiatic area USS Shark Enemy Action.

Dudley, Paul Lee (1926 — No. 08492) RAdm; Ret 7-1-61.

Cooper, Jacob Elliott (1926 — No. 08500) RAdm; Ret 5-1-52.

Conley, Thomas Francis Jr (1926 — No. 08501) RAdm; Ret 7-1-56.

Westbrook, Ralph Edward (1926 — No. 08503) RAdm; Ret 8-1-54.

Livdahl, Orlin Lester (1926 — No. 08506) RAdm; Ret 7-1-56.

Hufty, Malcolm Alexander (1926 — No. 08508) RAdm; Ret 9-1-48.

Reynolds, Luther Kendrick (1926 — No. 08509) RAdm; Ret 7-1-56.

Whiting, Charles Jonathan (1926 — No. 08513) RAdm; Ret 7-1-56.

Helmick, Guy Benton (1926 — No. 08515) RAdm; Ret 7-1-56.

Miller, Wallace Joseph (1926 — No. 08524) RAdm; Ret Ukn. Died 11-22-51.

Cochran, Joe Brice (1926 — No. 08539) Radm; Ret 7-1-56.

Howe, Hamilton Wilcox (1926 — No. 08544) RAdm; Ret 7-15-56.

Taylor, John Barrett (1926 — No. 08545) RAdm; Ret 7-1-56.

McGregor, Donald (1926 — No. 08546) RAdm; Ret 7-1-56.

Willingham, Solomon David (1926 — No. 08547) RAdm; Ret 1-1-52.

Custer, Benjamin Scott (1926 — No. 08549) RAdm; Ret 7-1-57.

Johnston, Harry Darlington (1926 — No. 08552) RAdm; Ret 6-30-56.

Sweeney, John Driscoll (1926 — No. 08554) RAdm; Ret 6-30-56.

Miller, Daniel Byrd (1926 — No. 08558) RAdm; Ret 7-1-57.

MacMillan, Duncan Calvin (1926 — No. 08562) RAdm; Ret 2-1-55.

Hamberger, Dewitt Clinton E. (1926 — No. 08567) RAdm; Ret 12-1-56.

Lamb, Raymond Starr (1926 — No. 08568) RAdm; Ret 7-1-56.

Callahan, Joseph William (1926 — No. 08569) RAdm; Ret 6-30-56.

Agnew, Dwight Merle (1926 — No. 08571) RAdm; Ret 7-1-56.

Tompkins, Benjamin Francis (1926 — No. 08572) RAdm; Ret Ukn.

Griggs, Gale Emerson (1926 — No. 08574) Radm; Ret 7-1-56.

Carpenter, Charles Lorain (1926 — No. 08583) RAdm; Ret 7-1-56.

Groff, Rowland Haverstick (1926 — No. 08585) RAdm; Ret 7-1-57.

Walsh, John Franklin (1926 — No. 08586) RAdm; 6-30-56.

Jones, Carroll Burgess (1926 — No. 08595) RAdm; Ret 7-1-56.

Shane, George Leonard (1926 — No. 08599) RAdm; Ret 3-1-57.

Leslie, Maxwell Franklin (1926 — No. 08601) RAdm; Ret 6-30-56.

Bays, John William (1927 — No. 08610) RAdm; Ret 12-1-46.

Jelley, Joseph Franklin Jr (1927 — No. 08614) RAdm; Ret 6-39-57.

Davey, Thomas Leo (1927 — No. 08615) RAdm; Ret 5-1-49.

Daspit, Lawrence Randall (1927 — No. 08616) RAdm; Ret Ukn. Died 5-19-79.

Crittenden, Samuel Hallett Jr (1927 — No. 08617) RAdm; Ret 1-7-57.

Hesser, Frederic William (1927 — No. 08621) RAdm; Ret Ukn. Died 4-2-54.

McCoy, Melvyn Harvey (1927 — No. 08626) RAdm; Ret 7-1-57.

Hogg, James Henry (1927 — No. 08628) RAdm; Ret 7-1-57.

Ramsey, Paul Hubert (1927 — No. 08629) VAdm; Ret Ukn. Died 2-15-82.

Anderson, George Whelan Jr (1927 — No. 08631) Adm; Ret 8-1-63.

Scoles, Albert Buddy (1927 — No. 08634) RAdm; Ret 11-1-47.

Olsen, Eliot (1927 — No. 08638) RAdm; Ret 7-1-57.

Miller, Shirley Snow (1927 — No. 08643) RAdm; Ret 5-1-56.

Jack, Samuel Sloan (1927 — No. 08647) MGen. USMC; Ret 7-1-61.

Phillips, Richard Helsden (1927 — No. 08650) RAdm; Ret 7-1-62.

Mewhinney, Leonard Sparks (1927 — No. 08651) RAdm; Ret 7-1-57.

Cooper, Clifford Steele (1927 — No. 08653) RAdm; Ret 7-1-62.

Chilton, William Pierce (1927 — No. 08654) RAdm; Ret 7-1-57.

Nation, William Millage (1927 — No. 08655) RAdm; Ret 7-1-62.

Organ, William Hugh (1927 — No. 08656) RAdm; Ret 7-1-56.

McGarry, William Thomas (1927 No. 08657) RAdm; Ret 1-1-50.

Bowling, Selman Stewart (1927 — No. 08658) RAdm; Ret 3-1-57.

Caldwell, Henry Howard (1927 — No. 08666) RAdm; Ret 11-1-67.

Caufield, Cecil Thilman (1927 — No. 08668) RAdm; Ret 7-1-57.

Hamley, Joseph Ronald (1927 — No. 08669) RAdm; Ret 6-30-55.

Murphy, Joseph Nathaniel (1927 — No. 08670) RAdm; Ret 4-1-62.

Honsinger, Leroy Vernon (1927 — No. 08672) RAdm; Ret 4-1-62.

Harnly, Harold Shepard (1927 — No. 08679) RAdm; Ret 7-1-57.

Leahy, William Harrington (1927 — No. 08682) RAdm; Ret 6-1-61.

Rice, Robert Henry (1927 — No. 08683) VAdm; Ret 8-1-57.

Paige, Henry Reid (1927 — No. 08685) MGen. USMC; Ret 7-1-61.

Stillman, Carl Frederic (1927 — No. 08693) RAdm; Ret 7-1-57.

Moore, Benjamin Eugene Jr (1927 — No. 08694) RAdm; Ret 8-1-66.

Chamberlin, Leonard Cornelius (1927 — No. 08695) RAdm; Ret 7-1-57.

Williamson, Delbert Fred (1927 — No. 08696) RAdm; Ret 7-1-57.

Hamilton, Thomas James (1927 — No. 08700) RAdm; Ret 2-1-49.

Earnshaw, Joseph Wayne (1927 — No. 08701) BGen. USMC; Ret 7-1-57.

Bayler, Walter Lewis John (1927 — No. 08703) BGen. USMC; Ret 6-1-57.

Allan, Halle Charles Jr (1927 — No. 08706) RAdm; Ret 7-1-57.

Berry, Frederic Aroyce (1927 — No. 08708) RAdm; Ret 7-1-57.

Pfingstag, Carl Jesse (1927 — No. 08712) RAdm; Ret 5-1-60.

Dawson, Marion Lindsay (1927 — No. 08715) MGen. USMC; Ret 6-30-62.

Scott, Roger Frederick (1927 — No. 08717) RAdm; Ret 7-1-57.

Murphy, John William (1927 — No. 08721) RAdm; Ret 7-1-57.

Specht, William Carl (1927 — No. 08722) RAdm; Ret 7-1-49.

Hubbard, Miles Hunter (1927 — No. 08728) RAdm; Ret 6-15-62.

Heath, George Lucius (1927 — No. 08729) RAdm; Ret 3-1-57.

Zahm, John Crawford (1927 — No. 08730) RAdm; Ret 7-1-57.

DeKay, Charles Gordon (1927 — No. 08732) RAdm; Ret 12-1-59.

Eddy, Daniel Thomas (1927 — No. 08734) RAdm; Ret 2-1-49.

Griffin, Charles Donald (1927 — No. 08735) Adm; Ret 2-1-68.

Eckelmeyer, Edward Herman Jr (1927 — No. 08738) RAdm; Ret 7-1-57.

Potter, George Hubbard (1927 — No. 08741) BGen. USMC; Ret 8-1-48.

Schumm, Brooke (1927 — No. 08742) RAdm; Ret 7-1-59.

Smith, Richard Wilder (1927 — No. 08747) RAdm; Ret 7-1-57.

Fraser, George Kittrell (1927 — No. 08748) RAdm; Ret 6-1-57.

Piper, Earl Sanford (1927 — No. 08750) BGen. USMC; Ret 6-30-57.

Born, Arthur Stephen (1927 — No. 08754) RAdm; Ret 8-1-55.

Smith, Allen Jr (1927 — No. 08755) RAdm; Ret 3-1-66.

Klakring, Thomas Burton (1927 — No. 08756) RAdm; Ret 6-1-49.

Kowalzyk, Alexander Martin Jr (1927 — No. 08758) RAdm; Ret 7-1-57.

Donohue, Timothy Francis (1927 — No. 08760) RAdm; Ret 8-1-53.

Schwarz, Alden Delbert (1927 — No. 08762) RAdm; Ret 7-1-57.

Bennett, Rawson II (1927 — No. 08766) RAdm; Ret 2-1-61.

Briggs, Harold Melvin (1927 — No. 08772) RAdm; Ret 7-1-61.

Hammond, Wellington Anthony (1927 — No. 08776) RAdm; Ret 3-1-48.

Hottel, Martin Perry (1927 — No. 08780) RAdm; Ret 2-1-49.

Gleim, Fritz Jr (1927 — No. 08781) RAdm; Ret 7-1-57.

McCormick, James Rhorer (1927 — No. 08790) RAdm; Ret 6-30-57.

Bowling, Jack Frank Jr (1927 — No. 08795) RAdm; Ret 10-1-47.

Ferrall, William Edward (1927 — No. 08797) RAdm; Ret 10-1-67.

Lawrence, Martin Jay (1927 — No. 08798) RAdm; Ret Unknown.

Quackenbush, Robert Stewart Jr (1927 — No. 08799) RAdm; Ret 7-1-57.

Price, Walter Harold (1927 — No. 08801) RAdm; Ret Unknown.

Stone, Martin Robert (1927 — No. 08803) RAdm; Ret 7-1-55.

McAlister, Francis Marion (1927 — No. 08802) MGen. USMC; Ret 6-30-60.

Juhan, Jack Philip (1927 — No. 08804) MGen. USMC; Ret 6-1-58.

Weintraub, Daniel Jacob (1927 — No. 08805) RAdm; Ret 7-1-56.

Lampman, Leland Ralph (1927 — No. 08808) RAdm; Ret 7-1-57.

Parks, Joel Dodson (1927 — No. 08808) RAdm; Ret 7-1-62.

Monroe, Jack Pendleton (1927 — No. 08810) RAdm; Ret 6-30-6.

Hoerner, Herbert Lisle (1927 — No. 08811) RAdm; Ret 6-1-57.

Bauer, Harry Frederick (1927 — No. 08816) Cdr; Died 9-5-42 Pacific Area BNR — USS Gregory.

Henkel, John Fisher (1927 — No. 08817) RAdm; Ret 7-1-57.

Richardson, Gill Macdonald (1927 — No. 08820) RAdm; Ret 6-30-57.

Beasley, Charles Black (1927 — No. 08823) RAdm; Ret 7-1-57.

Corwin, John Thomas (1927 — No. 08824) RAdm; Ret 7-1-57.

Dudley, Clayton Rodes (1927 — No. 08825) RAdm; Ret 7-1-57.

Zern, Richard Dewey (1927 — No. 08828) RAdm; Ret 7-1-57.

Bailey, Leonard William (1927 — No. 08833) RAdm; Ret 1-1-49.

Evans, Myron Thomas (1927 — No. 08835) RAdm; Ret 7-1-57.

Knickerbocker, William Lane (1927 — No. 08838) RAdm; Ret 11-1-63.

Prichard, James Alexander (1927 — No. 08839) RAdm; Ret 6-2-57.

Hines, John Fore Jr (1927 — No. 08844) RAdm; Ret 9-1-48.

Gordon, Howard Wright Jr (1927 — No. 08845) RAdm; Ret 7-1-57.

Davis, Eugene Edward (1927 — No. 08848) Lt; Died 5-23-41 BNR Declared Officially dead 5-23-41, disappearance of British Plane.

Burlingame, Creed Cardwell (1927 — No. 08849) RAdm; Ret 7-1-57.

Speck, Robert Hursey (1927 — No. 08850) RAdm; Ret 12-1-68.

Hansen, Harold Dale (1927 — No. 08852) BGen. USMC; Died 1-4-87.

Blanchard, James Williams (1927 — No. 08854) RAdm; Ret 7-1-57.

Schmidt, John William (1927 — No. 08859) RAdm; Ret 7-1-57.

Cook, Jesse Strother Jr (1927 — No. 08861) BGen. USMC; Ret 7-1-57. Died 7-30-70.

Deutermann, Harold Thomas (1927 — No. 08862) VAdm; Ret Unknown.

Melson, Charles Leroy (1927 — No. 08864) VAdm; Dies 9-14-81.

Herron, Edwin Warren (1927 — No. 08865) RAdm; Ret 7-1-57.

Oberrender, Thomas Olin Jr (1927 — No. 08866) LCdr; 11-13-42 BNR KIA WW II USS Juneau Solomon Islands.

Osborn, Wendell Gullefer (1926 — No. 08868) LCdr; 11-13-42 BNR KIA WW II USS Juneau Solomon Islands.

McKechnie, Arnold Wilfred (1927 — No. 08869) RAdm; Ret 11-1-61.

Newton, Miles Stanley (1927 — No. 08877) BGen. USMC; Ret 5-1-54.

Dahl, Theodore Oscar (1927 — No. 08878) RAdm; Ret 7-1-57.

Creighton, Liles Walker (1927 — No. 08879) RAdm; Ret 7-1-57.

White, David Charles (1927 — No. 08880) RAdm; Ret 7-1-49.

Boulware, Joe Wood (1927 — No. 08885) RAdm; Ret 7-1-57.

Bergin, Charles Kniese (1927 — No. 08887) RAdm; Dies 12-6-64.

Dixon, Robert Ellington (1927 — No. 08888) RAdm; Ret 12-1-60.

Sharp, Ulysses S. Grant Jr (1927 — No. 08892) Adm; Ret 8-1-68.

Lindsey, Eugene Elbert (1927 — No. 08895) LCdr; Died 6-5-43 USS Enterprise Battle of Midway Pacific Area BNR Shot Down COM VT-6.

Nilon, Leo William (1927 — No. 08898) RAdm; Ret 4-1-49.

Riker, Monro Marvin (1927 — No. 08902) RAdm; Ret 7-1-57.

Brodie, Robert Jr (1927 — No. 08906) RAdm; Ret 6-1-57.

Habecker, Frederic Shrom (1927 — No. 08907) RAdm; Ret 7-1-57.

Martin, Farar Benjamin C. (1927 — No. 08910) RAdm; Ret 7-1-57.

High, Paul Laverne (1927 — No. 08914) RAdm; Ret 11-1-47.

Cooper, Hysell Prater (1927 — No. 08918) RAdm; Ret 11-1-52.

Dyson, Howell Jesse (1927 — No. 08920) RAdm; Ret 7-1-57.

Collins, Richard Charles (1927 — No. 08921) Lt; Died 11-23-34 Pearl Harbor.

Saunders, Willard Arthur (1927 — No. 08927) RAdm; Ret 7-1-57.

Van Mater, Blinn (1927 — No. 08928) RAdm; Ret 7-1-57.

Royall, William Freeman (1927 — No. 08934) RAdm; Ret 7-1-57.

Neblett, Thomas Barbee (1927 — No. 08935) RAdm; Ret 7-1-57.

Dykers, Thomas Michael (1927 — No. 08938) RAdm; Ret 9-1-49.

Ashford, William Henry Jr (1927 — No. 08942) RAdm; Ret 6-1-56.

Matthews, Mitchell Dudley (1927 — No. 08944) RAdm; Ret 7-1-57.

Coffin, Clarence Emmet (1927 — No. 08945) RAdm; Ret 7-1-57.

McKinney, Eugene B. (1927 — No. 08948) RAdm; Ret Ukn. Died 8-15-86.

Flynn, Thomas Joseph (1927 — No. 08949) RAdm; Ret 7-1-57.

Winn, Walter Coulter (1927 — No. 08954) RAdm; Ret 7-1-57.

Jennings, William Croft (1927 — No. 08955) RAdm; Ret 7-1-53.

Nation, Milton Adolphus (1927 — No. 08958) RAdm; Ret 6-30-57.

Eldridge, John Jr (1927 — No. 08960) LCdr; Died 11-2-42 Pacific Area BNR USS Wasp Plane Crash.

Garcia, Edmund Ernest (1927 — No. 08961) RAdm; Ret 4-1-58.

McIlhenny, Harry Haywood (1927 — No. 08962) RAdm; Ret 7-1-57.

Heckey, Albert Rossville (1927 — No. 08963) RAdm; Ret 7-1-57.

Chappell, Lucius Henry (1927 — No. 08966) RAdm; Ret 7-1-57.

Fitzgibbon, John Edmondson (1927 — No. 08967) RAdm; Ret 7-1-52.

Carey, Joseph L. (1927 — No. 08969) RAdm; Ret 6-30-57.

Loud, Wayne Rowe (1927 — No. 08970) RAdm; Ret 7-1-62.

Waterman, John Randolph (1927 — No. 08972) RAdm; Ret 10-1-49.

McDaniel, Eugene Field (1927 — No. 08973) RAdm; Ret 7-1-57.

Hunte, Louis Henry (1927 — No. 08974) RAdm; Ret 8-1-47.

Shands, Courtney (1927 — No. 08976) RAdm; Ret 12-1-61.

Duffill, Monroe Barrows (1927 — No. 08977) RAdm; Ret 7-1-57.

Riley, Herbert Douglas (1927 — No. 08980) VAdm; Ret 4-1-64.

O'Neil, Archie Edward (1927 — No. 08988) BGen. USMC; Ret 7-1-57.

Drew, Edward John (1927 — No. 08992) RAdm; Ret 7-1-57.

Fitzwilliam, Albert Eisner (1927 — No. 08997) RAdm; Ret 7-1-57.

Taylor, Joe (1927 — No. 09004) RAdm; Ret 1-1-30.

Clendening, Cyrus Turner (1927 — No. 09008) Lt; Died 4-4-33 BNR lost in Akron 4-4-33 Barnegat NJ.

Ross, Philip Harold (1927 — No. 09010) RAdm; Ret 7-1-57.

Southerland, Leonard Bradshaw (1927 — No. 09016) RAdm; Ret Ukn. Died 11-15-58.

Virden, Frank (1927 — No. 09018) RAdm; Ret 7-1-63.

Nickelson, William Richardson D. Jr (1927 — No. 09019) RAdm; Ret 7-1-57.

Winterhaler, Emile Reeves (1927 — No. 09021) RAdm; Ret 7-1-57.

Foley, Robert Joseph (1927 — No. 09023) RAdm; Ret 7-1-57.

Blake, Ernest (1927 — No. 09024) RAdm; Ret 7-1-57.

Shapley, Alan (1927 — No. 09027) LGen. USMC; Ret 7-1-62.

Coleman, David Buncombe (1927 — No. 09028) RAdm; Ret 7-1-48.

Armstrong, Henry Jacques Jr (1927 — No. 09029) RAdm; Ret 7-1-57.

O'Neill, David Ferguson (1927 — No. 09036) MGen. USMC; Ret 7-1-58.

Harris, William Stephen (1927 — No. 09037) RAdm; Ret 7-1-57.

Dalton, Carl Malcolm (1927 — No. 09038) RAdm; Ret 7-1-57.

Duke, Claren Emmett (1927 — No. 09041) RAdm; Ret 7-1-50.

Brockman, William Herman Jr (1927 — No. 09043) RAdm; Ret 11-1-47.

McClaughry, John Glenn (1927 — No. 09046) RAdm; Ret 7-1-57.

Wev, Bosquet N. (1927 — No. 09048) RAdm; Ret 6-30-57.

Yeager, Howard Austin (1927 — No. 09050) VAdm; Ret Ukn. Died 3-11-67.

Taylor, Arthur Howard (1927 — No. 09052) RAdm; Ret 7-12-65.

Kaitner, William Eugene (1927 — No. 09054) RAdm; Ret 12-31-57.

Pancoast, Leonidas Walthall (1927 — No. 09058) RAdm; Ret 9-1-48.

Montgomery, Alan Robert (1927 — No. 09060) RAdm; Ret 7-1-49.

Durski, Malen (1927 — No. 09065) RAdm; Ret 7-1-57.

Cooper, Joshua Winfred (1927 — No. 09067) RAdm; Ret 7-1-62.

Russillo, Michael Peter (1927 — No. 09069) RAdm; Ret 7-1-57.

Moore, Granville Alexander (1927 — No. 09072) RAdm; Ret 7-1-57.

Lofberg, Gus Brynolf Jr (1927 — No. 09073) LCdr; Died 8-5-42 BNR KIA 8-5-42 WW II USS Little Pacific area.

Maher, Joseph Benedict (1927 — No. 09076) RAdm; Ret 10-1-57.

Southwick, Edward Page (1927 — No. 09078) RAdm; Ret 7-1-57.

Everett, Gordon Stafford (1927 — No. 09080) RAdm; Ret 1-1-50.

Atkeson, John Conner (1927 — No. 09082) RAdm; Ret 7-1-57.

Clark, John Edward (1927 — No. 09086) RAdm; Dies 9-30-79.

Hummer, Harry Reid Jr (1927 — No. 09090) RAdm; Ret 7-1-57.

Sutherland, William A. Jr (1927 — No. 09093) RAdm; Dies 8-31-83.

Green, Thomas Chandler (1927 — No. 09094) RAdm; Ret 11-1-47.

Thach, John Smith (1927 — No. 09097) Adm; Ret 5-1-67.

Marshall, Henry Morris (1927 — No. 09099) RAdm; Ret 7-1-56.

McCune, Francis Creith Brewer (1927 — No. 09106) RAdm; Ret 9-1-57.

Tracy, John Steuert (1927 — No. 09108) RAdm; Ret 1-1-56.

Stallings, George B.H. (1927 — No. 09109) RAdm; Ret 7-1-57.

Irvin, William Davis (1927 — No. 09110) RAdm; Ret Ukn.

Munn, John Calvin (1927 — No. 09116) LGen. USMC; Ret 7-1-64.

Parker, Charles William (1927 — No. 09117) RAdm; Ret 7-1-57.

Patterson, Alex Mcleod (1927 — No. 09119) RAdm; Ret 6-30-58.

Caswell, Gordon Leonard (1927 — No. 09125) RAdm; Ret 7-1-57.

Braddy, Robert Edgar Jr (1927 — No. 09126) RAdm; Ret 10-1-51.

Outerbridge, William Woodward (1927 — No. 09127) RAdm; Ret 7-1-57.

Dayton, Milton Theodore (1927 — No. 09130) RAdm; Ret 7-1-57.

Way, Julius Frederick (1927 — No. 09131) RAdm; Ret 11-1-47.

Lange, George Adam (1927 — No. 09135) RAdm; Ret 7-1-55.

Burch, William Oscar Jr (1927 — No. 09140) RAdm; Ret 7-1-62.

Donaho, Glynn Robert (1927 — No. 09141) VAdm; Ret 4-1-67.

Ramsay, Alston (1927 — No. 09143) RAdm; Ret 1-1-56.

Dodson, Oscar Henry (1927 — No. 09147) RAdm; Ret 7-1-57.

Walker, James Paul (1927 — No. 09151) RAdm; Ret 7-1-57.

Ross, Richard Potts Jr (1927 — No. 09152) BGen USMC; Ret 7-1-57.

Johnston, Paul Fisher (1927 — No. 09159) RAdm; Ret 9-1-55.

Gullett, William Mayo (1927 — No. 09162) RAdm; Ret 7-1-58.

Myers, Richard Edwin (1927 — No. 09166) RAdm; Ret 7-1-57.

Heald, Wilton Stewart (1927 — No. 09167) RAdm; Ret 7-1-57.

Ford, Robert Stephens (1927 — No. 09170) RAdm; Ret 7-1-58.

McKinney, Joseph Dwight (1927 — No. 09175) RAdm; Dies 2-17-81.

Rubins, Joseph Russell (1927 — No. 09176) RAdm; Ret 9-1-48.

Giambattista, Frank Daniel (1927 — No. 09178) RAdm; Ret 7-1-58.

Clark, Thurston Booth (1927 — No. 09179) RAdm; Ret 7-1-62.

Carter, Albert Samuel (1927 — No. 09181) RAdm; Ret 8-1-55.

Van Orden, George Owen (1927-Non-Graduate — No. 927225) BGen. USMC; Res 9-1-49.

Lee, James Richard (1928 — No. 09185) RAdm; Ret 9-1-65.

Howard, William Eager Jr (1928 — No. 09186) RAdm; Ret 7-1-63.

Ballance, Robert Green (1928 — No. 09188) BGen. USMC; Ret 10-1-59.

James, Ralph Kirk (1928 — No. 09190) RAdm; Ret 6-30-63.

Quinn, John (1928 — No. 09191) RAdm; Dies 9-15-66.

Fay, Albert James (1928 — No. 09192) VAdm; Ret 6-30-59.

Sears, Harry Edward (1928 — No. 09194) VAdm; Ret 8-16-58.

Ahroon, Thomas Andrew (1928 — No. 09202) RAdm; Dies 1-26-72.

Nieman, Hugh Robert Jr (1928 — No. 09247) RAdm; Ret 2-1-58.

Parmelee, Perry Ormiston (1928 — No. 09248) BGen. USMC; Ret 4-1-54.

Wagner, Daniel Jacob (1928 — No. 09249) RAdm; Ret 7-1-58.

Heil, John Joseph (1928 — No. 09251) Maj. USMC; Large BNR KIA 1-25-45 WW II Bombing of POW ship enroute to Japan.

Smith, Thurmond Augustus (1928 — No. 09252) RAdm; Ret 7-1-58.

Dexter, Edwin Boardman (1928 — No. 09254) RAdm; Ret 3-1-49.

Ambruster, Stephen Henry (1928 — No. 09256) RAdm; Ret 7-1-58.

Flaherty, Michael Francis D. (1928 — No. 09258) RAdm; Ret Ukn.

Schaeffer, Max William (1928 — No. 09259) LCol. USMC; KIA 1-29-45 WW II POW Killed During Transport to Japan.

Norgaard, Rollo Niel (1928 — No. 09260) RAdm; Ret 4-1-58.

Archer, Robert John (1928 — No. 09261) RAdm; Ret 7-1-58.

Fritschmann, George (1928 — No. 09271) RAdm; Died 8-20-80.

Mullaney, Baron Joseph (1928 — No. 09277) RAdm; Ret 8-1-58.

Brown, Chesford (1928 — No. 09278) RAdm; Ret 8-1-47.

Hannegan, Edward Allen (1928 — No. 09279) RAdm; Ret 7-1-63.

Freiburghouse, Leonard (1928 — No. 09280) RAdm; Ret 7-1-58.

Curtin, Neale Roland (1928 — No. 09282) RAdm; Ret 7-1-58.

Young, Edwin James (1928 — No. 09283) RAdm; Ret 7-1-58.

Bowley, Clarence Matheson (1928 — No. 09285) RAdm; Ret 6-30-58.

Donovan, Thomas Alton (1928 — No. 09286) RAdm; Ret 7-1-58.

Morris, Robert Lee (1928 — No. 09294) RAdm; Ret 7-1-58.

Banister, Alan Boyd (1928 — No. 09295) RAdm; Ret 7-1-58.

Ennis, Thomas Gates (1928 — No. 09297) MGen. USMC; Ret 6-30-62.

Iderman, John Clement (1928 — No. 09299) RAdm; Ret 7-1-58.

Burke, John Edward (1928 — No. 09304) LCdr; Died 11-15-42 USS South Dakota Battle of Solomons.

Renard, Jack Clayton (1928 — No. 09311) RAdm; Ret 7-1-58.

Anderson, Paul Ramseur (1928 — No. 09312) RAdm; Ret 7-1-58.

Gallery, Philip Daly (1928 — No. 09316) RAdm; Ret 7-1-58.

Tackney, Stephen Noel (1928 — No. 09317) RAdm; Ret 7-1-58.

Raborn, William Francis Jr (1928 No. 09322) VAdm; Ret 10-1-63.

Keith, Robert Taylor (1928 — No. 09323) VAdm; Ret 7-1-64.

Wood, Robert Winthrop (1928 — No. 09327) RAdm; Ret 2-1-57.

Thomas, William Dow (1928 — No. 09330) RAdm; Ret 3-1-47.

Rittenhouse, Basil Norris Jr (1928 — No. 09334) RAdm; Ret 1-1-62.

Lovelace, Donald Alexander (1928 — No. 09336) LCdr; BNR KIA 6-2-42 WW II USS Yorkown Midway Plane Crash.

Stokes, Phillip Gaines (1928 — No. 09346) RAdm; Ret 7-1-58.

Scott, John Addison (1928 — No. 09350) RAdm; Ret 7-1-58.

Batterton, Boeker Charles (1928 — No. 09351) BGen. USMC; Died 7-17-87.

Farrin, James Moore Jr (1929 — No. 09358) RAdm; Ret 7-1-65.

Keatley, John Hancock (1929 — No. 09360) RAdm; Ret 9-1-49.

Wales, George Herrick (1929 — No. 09365) RAdm; Ret 7-1-64.

Adamson, Frank Marshall (1929 No. 09367) RAdm; Ret 7-1-59.

Weakley, Charles Enright (1929 — No. 09368) VAdm; Ret 1-1-68.

Wait, Delos E. (1929 — No. 09369) RAdm; Ret 6-1-48.

Persons, Henry Stanford (1929 — No. 09371) RAdm; Ret 6-1-67.

Coleman, William Francis (1929 — No. 09381) BGen. USMC; Ret 6-1-53.

Miller, Clair Lemoine (1929 — No. 09382) Cdr; Died 1-21-45 USS Ticonderoga Asiatic Area.

Moore, John Raymond (1929 — No. 09388) RAdm; Ret 8-1-58.

Kabler, William Leverette (1929 — No. 09389) RAdm; Ret 11-1-57.

Bacher, Edward Johnson (1929 — No. 09393) RAdm; Res 6-1-30.

Laning, Caleb Barrett (1929 — No. 09394) RAdm; Ret 5-1-59.

Canty, Joseph Patrick (1929 — No. 09396) RAdm; Ret 4-1-55.

Foley, Paul Jr (1929 — No. 09397) RAdm; Ret 7-1-59.

Ricketts, Claude Vernon (1929 — No. 09399) Adm; Died 7-6-64.

Duborg, Francis Rahr (1929 — No. 09401) RAdm; Ret 7-1-59.

Ashford, George Woodson (1929 — No. 09411) RAdm; Ret 6-1-59.

Baldauf, Laurence Charles (1929 — No. 09413) RAdm; Ret 4-1-59.

Lynch, Ralph Clinton Jr (1929 — No. 09417) RAdm; Ret 7-1-59.

Waterhouse, Jacob Wilson (1929 — No. 09421) RAdm; Ret 7-1-59.

Kennedy, Marvin Granville (1929 — No. 09422) RAdm; Ret 10-1-52.

Ray, Herman Lamar (1929 — No. 09425) RAdm; Ret 6-30-59.

Carver, Lamar Peyton (1929 — No. 09426) RAdm; Ret 7-1-59.

Kirk, Oliver Grafton (1929 — No. 09428) RAdm; Ret 7-1-59.

McGinnis, Robert Devore (1929 — No. 09430) RAdm; Ret 9-1-49.

Schreiber, Earl Tobias (1929 — No. 09433) RAdm; Ret 7-1-59.

Johnson, Roy Lee (1929 — No. 09434) Adm; Ret 1-1-68.

O'Donnell, Edward Joseph (1929 — No. 09437) RAdm; Ret 8-1-67.

Collett, John Austin (1929 — No. 09438) LCdr; BNR KIA 10-27-43 WW II COM TORP RON 10 Pacific Area.

Davidson, John Frederick (1929 — No. 09439) RAdm; Ret 4-1-64.

Van Voorhis, Bruce Avery (1929 — No. 09440) Cdr; KIA 7-6-43 COMBOMSQD 102 Asiatic Area.

Schwable, Frank Hawse (1929 — No. 09441) BGen. USMC; Ret 7-1-59.

Rodimon, Warner Scott (1929 — No. 09422) RAdm; Ret 7-1-59.

Triebel, Charles Otto (1929 — No. 09433) RAdm; Ret 8-1-62.

Hogle, Reynold Delos (1929 — No. 09446) VAdm; Ret 6-1-68.

Patrick, G. Serpell (1929 — No. 09456) RAdm; Ret 7-1-64.

Coe, Benjamin (1929 — No. 09457) RAdm; Ret 9-1-50.

Benson, Roy Stanley (1929 — No. 09458) RAdm; Ret 12-31-68.

Dyer, Edward Colston (1929 — No. 09464) BGen. USMC; Ret 2-1-49.

Stone, Lowell Thornton (1929 — No. 09465) RAdm; Ret 7-1-59.

Beardsley, George Francis (1929 — No. 09468) VAdm; Ret 6-1-63.

Ballinger, Richard Robert (1929 — No. 09469) RAdm; Ret 6-30-59.

Crichton, Charles Helmick (1929 — No. 09473) RAdm; Ret 5-1-59.

Curry, Manley Lamar (1929 — No. 09474) BGen. USMC; Ret 7-1-59.

Frankel, Samuel Benjamin (1929 — No. 09475) RAdm; Ret 7-1-64.

Tolley, Kemp (1929 — No. 09479) RAdm; Ret 6-30-59.

Keeler, Frederic Seward (1929 — No. 09482) RAdm; Ret 7-1-59.

Clark Robert Nicholson S. (1929 — No. 09486) RAdm; Ret 6-1-59.

Galbraith, William Jackson (1929 — No. 09488) RAdm; Ret 7-1-59.

Coffin, Harry Nelson (1929 — No. 09495) RAdm; Ret 7-1-59.

Welsh, David James (1929 — No. 09499) RAdm; Ret 5-1-64.

Eller, Donald Temple (1929 — No. 09502) RAdm; Ret 7-1-64.

Johansen, Gustave Norman (1929 — No. 09503) RAdm; Ret 2-1-59.

Carmichael, George Kennedy (1929 — No. 09505) RAdm; Ret 6-1-59.

Mitchell, Frank Paul Jr (1929 — No. 09507) RAdm; Ret 8-1-59.

McGregor, Rob Roy (1929 — No. 09508) RAdm; Ret 2-1-58.

Wilkinson, Robert Holden (1929 — No. 09510) RAdm; Ret 5-1-57.

Carlson, Daniel (1929 — No. 09511) RAdm; Ret 5-1-59.

Frank, Nickolas John Jr (1929 — No. 09512) RAdm; Ret 7-1-59.

Burke, Edward Joseph (1929 — No. 09514) RAdm; Ret 7-1-59.

Dennett, Erie Van Emburgh (1929 — No. 09516) RAdm; Ret 7-1-59.

Rembert, John Patrick Jr (1929 — No. 09518) RAdm; Ret 9-1-57.

Loomis, Almon Ellsworth (1929 — No. 09522) RAdm; Ret 7-1-64.

Denbo, Robert Wayne (1929 — No. 09523) RAdm; Ret 7-1-59.

Raby, John (1929 — No. 09525) RAdm; Ret 5-1-49.

Stephan, Edward Clark (1929 — No. 09523) RAdm; Ret 3-31-64. Recalled to Active Duty on 7-1-63. Ret 3-31-64.

Rooney, Roderick Shanahan (1929 — No. 09529) Cdr; BNR Missing in enemy action 11-30-43 USS Corvina Western Pacific Ocean Presumed Dead 1-9-46.

Griffith, Samuel Blair II (1929 — No. 09531) BGen. USMC; Ret 4-1-56.

Crist, Raymond Fowler Jr (1929 — No. 09535) BGen. USMC; Ret 9-1-55.

Fenton, Charles Rudolph (1929 — No. 09540) RAdm; Ret 7-1-59.

Butts, Whitmore Spencer (1929 — No. 09548) RAdm; Died 12-24-59.

Brunton, Charles Edward (1929 — No. 09551) RAdm; Ret 7-1-59.

Johnson, Francis Joseph (1929 — No. 09554) RAdm; Ret 7-1-59.

Flatley, James Henry Jr (1929 — No. 09556) RAdm; Ret 6-2-58.

Sharp, George Arthur (1929 — No. 09558) RAdm; Ret 8-1-57.

Stovall, William S. Jr (1929 — No. 09560) RAdm; Ret 7-1-59.

Simpler, Leroy Coard (1929 — No. 09562) RAdm; Ret 6-30-59.

Davison, Thurlow Weed (1929 — No. 09563) RAdm; Ret 3-1-58.

Lang, Harry Cox (1929 — No. 09565) Maj. USMC; KIA 5-6-42 WW II Capitulation of Corregidor.

St Angelo, Augustus Robert (1929 — No. 09569) RAdm; Ret 7-1-59.

Cone, Henry Shipman (1929 — No. 09572) RAdm; Ret 3-10-54.

Brandley, Frank Albin (1929 — No. 09576) RAdm; Ret 9-1-67.

Visser, Richard Gerben (1929 — No. 09577) RAdm; 7-1-59.

Mattie, Dominic Lewis (1929 — No. 09588) RAdm; Ret 3-1-47.

Duffy, Leonard Vincent (1929 — No. 09591) Lt; Died 4-5-44 BNR USS Atix Island area.

White, Albert Francis (1929 — No. 09595) RAdm; Ret 8-1-58.

Jackson, Andrew Mcburney Jr (1930 — No. 09596) VAdm; Ret 3-31-69.

Hines, Wellington T. (1930 — No. 09597) RAdm; Ret 7-1-65.

Hean, James Halleck (1930 — No. 09602) RAdm; Died 8-20-51.

Hughes, Thomas Brandenburg (1930 — No. 09605) BGen. USMC; Ret 7-1-49.

Horn, Peter Harry (1930 — No. 09606) RAdm; Ret 9-30-59.

Martell, Charles Bowling (1930 — No. 09610) VAdm; Died 11-11-78, Chief Anti-Sub WRFRE Program In '60S.

Howard, James Hampden (1930 — No. 09611) RAdm; Ret 10-29-59.

Gladney, Donald Wesley Jr (1930 — No. 09615) RAdm; Ret 11-1-59.

Gentner, William Ellis Jr (1930 — No. 09619) VAdm; Ret 6-30-60.

Hilles, Frederick Vantyne H. (1930 — No. 09620) RAdm; Ret 7-1-65.

Simons, Manley Hale Jr (1930 — No. 09622) RAdm; Ret 9-1-59.

Coates, Leonidas Dixon Jr (1930 — No. 09625) RAdm; 7-1-64.

Masterson, Kleber Sandlin (1930 — No. 09628) VAdm.

Dornin, Marshall Edgar (1930 — No. 09634) RAdm.

Adkins, James Alvin (1930 — No. 09643) RAdm; Ret 11-1-59.

Holmes, Ephraim Paul (1930 — No. 09644) Adm.

Walter, Wilfred Aves (1930 — No. 09645) RAdm.

Foster, Walter Manly (1930 — No. 09646) RAdm; Ret 11-1-59.

Butler, William Clayton Jr (1930 — No. 09647) RAdm; Ret 11-1-59.

Moore, Robert Lee (1930 — No. 09650) RAdm; Ret 7-1-65.

Hayward, John Tucker (1930 — No. 09653) VAdm.

Johnson, Frank Lesher (1930 — No. 09654) RAdm; Died 8-7-84.

Bauer, Harold William (1930 — No. 09655) LCol. USMC; MIA 11-14-42 Solomon Islands area South Pac. Presumed dead 1-8-46.

Nelson, William Thackeray (1930 — No. 09659) RAdm; Ret 6-30-65.

McKean William Baggarley (1930 — No. 09660) BGen. USMC; Ret 7-1-56.

Beans, Fred Dale (1930 — No. 09666) BGen; Ret 7-1-48.

Pieczentkowski, Herman Arnold (1930 — No. 09668) RAdm; Ret 6-30-57.

Peterson, Mell Andrew (1930 — No. 09672) RAdm; Ret 11-1-59.

Allen, Burrell Clinton Jr (1930 — No. 09673) RAdm; Ret 11-1-59.

Brook, Charles Bates (1930 — No. 09674) RAdm; Ret 6-24-46.

Heyward, Alexander Salley Jr (1930 — No. 09677) VAdm.

Kinert, John Oscar (1930 — No. 09678) RAdm; Ret 5-31-59.

Knoll, Denys William (1930 — No. 09679) RAdm; Ret 5-1-67.

Burns, Martin Charles (1930 — No. 09682) RAdm; Ret 8-21-48.

Ailes, John William III (1930 — No. 09686) RAdm; Died 7-30-74.

Carmick, Edward Seabury (1930 — No. 09688) RAdm; Ret 7-1-56.

Seay, George Cameron (1930 — No. 09689) RAdm; Ret 11-1-59.

Sanders, Eddie Reuel (1930 — No. 09692) RAdm; Ret 1-1-59.

Morton, Dudley Walker (1930 — No. 09693) Capt; BNR lost in USS Wahoo 10-11-43 Japanese area enemy action.

McKnight, John Rowland Jr (1930 — No. 09695) RAdm; Ret 11-1-59.

Quiggle, Lynne Cline (1930 — No. 09696) RAdm; Died 7-23-58. BNR lost overboard USS Cleveland.

Dennis, Jefferson Rice (1930 — No. 09698) RAdm; Died 2-17-58.

Stroh, Robert Joseph (1930 — No. 09699) VAdm.

Lee, John Elwood (1930 — No. 09700) RAdm; Ret 10-1-57.

Corbus, John (1930 — No. 09703) RAdm; Ret 3-1-58.

Dorsey, Jack Sidney (1930 — No. 09706) RAdm; Died 11-8-74.

Greene, Wallace Martin Jr (1930 — No. 09714) Gen. USMC; Ret 1-1-68. Comd't US Marine Corps 1-1-64 — 1-1-68.

Corey, Howard Grant (1930 — No. 09716) RAdm; Ret 11-1-59.

Sands, Eugene Thomas (1930 — No. 09720) RAdm; Ret 10-1-59.

Ross, Russell Roosevelt (1930 — No. 09721) Lt; 6-5-43 BNR POW in Thailand USS Houston-KIA.

Davis, James White (1930 — No. 09722) RAdm; Ret 7-1-65.

Stevens, Clyde Benjamin Jr (1930 — No. 09726) RAdm; Ret 8-1-59.

Burden, Harvey Paul (1930 — No. 09727) RAdm; Ret 10-1-59.

Esslinger, Robert John (1930 — No. 09733) RAdm; Ret 11-1-59.

Marshall, Thomas Worth Jr (1930 — No. 09735) LDcr; KIA 2-28-42 WW II Torpedoing of USS Jacob Jones Off Cape May NJ.

Dodson, Joseph Edward (1930 — No. 09740) RAdm; Ret 2-1-64.

Miller, Frank Blake (1930 — No. 09742) RAdm; Died 5-31-62.

Kyes, James Elsworth (1930 — No. 09743) Cdr; Died 12-25-44 BNR Missing in enemy action 12-24-43 USS Leary.

Clark, Henry Garner (1930 — No. 09746) RAdm; Ret 6-1-63.

Macgregor, Edgar John III (1930 — No. 09748) RAdm; Ret 11-1-59.

Blackburn, Paul Prichard Jr (1930 — No. 09750) VAdm; Ret 3-1-68.

Brady, Parke Howle (1930 — No. 09751) RAdm; Ret 11-1-59.

Renfro, Edward Clark (1930 — No. 09752) RAdm; Ret 11-1-59.

Canaday, Harry Ridge (1930 — No. 09753) RAdm; Ret 6-4-30.

Craighill, Robert Rutherford (1930 — No. 09760) RAdm; 9-30-59.

Bourgeois, Aubrey Joseph (1930 — No. 09761) RAdm; Ret 11-1-63.

Armstrong, John Hord Jr (1930 — No. 09762) LCdr; Died 7-12-45 BNR USS Jarvis enemy action.

McGregor, Louis Darby Jr (1930 — No. 09763) RAdm; Died 1-22-83.

Malpass, Ray Edward (1930 — No. 09765) RAdm; Ret 8-1-59.

Palmer, George Goldston (1930 — No. 09766) RAdm; Ret 11-1-59.

Marshall, Edmund Sylvester L. (1930 — No. 09768) RAdm; Ret 6-1-57.

McCombs, Charles Edward (1930 — No. 09769) RAdm; Ret 11-1-59.

Miller, Theodore Taft (1930 — No. 09772) RAdm; Ret 4-1-58.

Williams, Francis Hubert (1930 — No. 09783) Maj. USMC; KIA 3-6-45 WW II POW Maji Japan.

Lang, James Graeme (1930 — No. 09785) RAdm; Ret 7-1-59.

Chambers, George Mitchell (1930 — 09788) RAdm; Ret 12-1-55.

Shaffer, John Jackson III (1930 — No. 09794) Cdr; KIA 4-8-44 WW II Atlantic Area enemy action.

House, Herschel Austin (1930 — No. 09797) RAdm; Ret 4-1-55. Army War College Graduate.

McCready, George Thomas Jr (1930 — No. 09798) RAdm; Ret 8-1-58.

Hulme, John (1930 — No. 09800) RAdm; Ret 11-1-59.

Bauer, Rudolph Charles (1930 — No. 09802) RAdm; Ret 2-1-55.

Wylie, William Naylor (1930 — No. 09804) RAdm; Ret 12-1-55.

Adams, Carlton Rolla (1930 — No. 09805) RAdm; Ret 11-1-59.

Sharp, Raymond Neil (1930 — No. 09806) RAdm; Ret 1-1-68.

O'Beirne, Emmet (1930 — No. 09809) RAdm; Ret 12-1-64.

Lowrance, Vernon Long (1930 — No. 09814) VAdm; Ret 11-1-69.

Snead, William Overton P. Jr (1930 — No. 09821) RAdm; Ret 11-1-59.

Colestock, Edward Emerson (1930 — No. 09823) RAdm; Ret 7-1-65.

Reinecke, Frank Mills (1930 — No. 09824) BGen. USMC; Ret 6-1-58.

Ostrom, Charles Howard (1930 — No. 09827) Cdr; Died 11-25-44 BNR USS Liscombe Bay sunk in Pacific enemy action.

Ruff, Lawrence Ernest (1930 — No. 09830) RAdm; Ret 11-1-58.

McMillian, Ira Ellis (1930 — No. 09833) RAdm; Died 4-22-87.

Allen, William Young Jr (1930 — No. 09836) RAdm; Died 11-5-73.

Bisson, John Kenneth (1930 — No. 09839) LCdr; BNR KIA 9-8-42 USS Vincennes sunk in Battle of Savo Island enemy action.

Grantham, Elonzo Bowden Jr (1930 — No. 09843) RAdm; Ret 1-31-65.

Whitfield, James Dickson (1930 — No. 09844) RAdm; Ret 4-1-59.

Andrews, Charles Herbert (1930 — No. 09845) RAdm; Ret 10-1-59.

Fromhold, Walfried Halton (1930 — No. 09846) BGen. USMC; Ret 1-1-49.

Hayes, Charles Harold (1930 — No. 09851) LGen. USMC; Ret 6-30-65.

Ebert, Walter Gale (1930 — No. 09856) RAdm; Ret 8-1-50.

Weller, Donald Mcpherrin (1930 — No. 09857) MGen. USMC; Ret 8-30-63.

Sheeley, William Robert (1930 — No. 09859) RAdm; Ret 8-1-61.

Montgomery, Edward A. (1930 — No. 09866) BGen. USMC.

Hawkins, David Delos (1930 — No. 09869) RAdm; Ret 3-1-55.

Coe, James Wiggins, (1930 — No. 09874) Cdr; MIA 11-6-43 USS Cisco S. China Sea Pres dead 1-8-46.

Rosasco, Robert Adrian (1930 — No. 09881) RAdm; Ret 10-1-46.

Wakefield, Ellis Kerr (1930 — No. 09882) RAdm; Ret 1-1-59.

Van Metre, Thaddeus Johnson (1930 — No. 09887) RAdm; Ret 11-1-59.

Brokenshire, Douglas Best (1930 — No. 09888) RAdm; Ret 7-1-59.

Ellis, William Edward (1930 — No. 09889) VAdm; Died 9-26-82.

Roby, Allan Barkhurst (1930 — No. 09890) RAdm; Ret 11-1-59.

Gross, Royce Lawrence (1930 — No. 09893) RAdm; Ret 6-30-47.

Mayo, Raymond Leon (1930 — No. 09894) Cdr; KIA 3-28-44 WW II USS Grayback.

Post, William Schuyler Jr (1930 — No. 09895) RAdm; Ret 6-1-65.

Doyle, William Thomas Jr (1930 — No. 09898) RAdm; Ret 3-30-59.

Smith, Philip Thomas Jr (1930 — No. 09902) LCdr; KIA 11-13-42 WW II USS Atlanta Battle of Solomons Islands.

Sanchez, Henry Gabriel (1930 — No. 09907) RAdm; Ret 11-1-59.

Moffett, William Adger Jr (1930 — No. 09909) RAdm.

Hill, Robert Edward (1930 — No. 09911) BGen. USMC; Ret 10-1-59.

Robbins, Josephus Amberg (1930 — No. 09912) RAdm; Ret 8-1-57. Died 9-29-84.

Sanders, William Henry Jr (1930 — No. 09917) RAdm; Ret 7-1-59.

Westhofen, Charles Louis (1930 — No. 09918) RAdm; Ret 11-1-59.

Daly, James Michael (1930 — No. 09919) BGen. USMC; Ret 6-1-58.

Farmer, William Howard (1930 — No. 09920) RAdm; Ret 11-1-58.

Nix, Joshua James (1930 — No. 09922) LCdr; Died 11-25-45 BNR MIA 3-1-42 USS Edsall vicinity of Java.

Salmon, Ronald Dean (1930 — No. 09925) BGen. USMC; Died 8-26-74.

Dimmick, John Bagley (1930 — No. 09926) RAdm; Ret 10-1-59.

Smith, Harry (1930 — No. 09931) RAdm; Ret 7-1-65.

LLoyd, Russell (1930 — No. 09943) BGen. USMC; Ret 8-1-59.

Ruddy, Joseph Aloysius Jr (1930 — No. 09947) RAdm; Ret 10-1-59.

Bristol, John Morgan (1930 — No. 09948) RAdm; Ret 10-1-53.

Wilbourne, William Wilkerson (1930 — No. 09949) RAdm; Ret 10-1-59.

Hanson, Burton S. Jr (1930 — No. 09950) RAdm; Ret 6-1-59.

Eddy, Ian Crawford (1930 — No. 09954) RAdm; Ret 9-1-54.

Haynsworth, Hugh Charles Jr (1930 — No.09956) RAdm; Ret 7-1-64.

Stevenson, Harry Clinton (1930 — No. 09959) RAdm; Ret 10-1-47.

Williams, Macpherson Berrien (1930 — No. 09964) RAdm; Ret 11-1-59.

Wygant, Henry Sollett Jr (1930 — No. 09965) Cdr; Died 1-3-44 BNR CO USS Turner Vessel Exploded.

Spring, Arthur Finn (1930 — No. 09968) RAdm; Died 11-14-60.

Lidstone, Nicholas Adair (1930 — No. 09976) RAdm; Ret 11-1-59.

Over, George Russell (1930 — No. 09977) RAdm; Ret 9-1-58.

Chapple, Wreford Goss (1930 — No. 09979) RAdm; Ret 11-1-59.

Reeder, Frederick Martin (1930 — No. 09982) RAdm; Ret 10-31-46.

Clifton, Joseph Clinton (1930 — No. 09984) RAdm; Ret 12-24-67.

Edwards, John Ellis (1930 — No. 09986) RAdm; Ret 10-1-59.

Howerton, Charles Cabaness (1930 — No. 09992) RAdm; Ret 10-1-59.

Wright, Thomas Kenneth (1930 — No. 09993) RAdm; Ret 1-11-59.

Barrett, Arthur Jenkins (1930 — No. 09995) RAdm; Ret 2-1-58.

Connor, Ray Russell (1930 — No. 09997) RAdm; Ret 10-1-59.

Rivero, Horacio Jr (1931 — No. 10000) Adm; Apptd AMB to Spain — Aug '72-Dec '74.

Reed, Allan Lorentz (1931 — No. 10002) RAdm; Ret 6-30-66.

Colwell, John Barr (1931 — No. 10003) VAdm.

Holtzworth, Ernest Charles (1931 — No. 10009) RAdm; Ret 11-1-64.

Roeder, Bernard Franklin (1931 — No. 10019) VAdm; Died 9-3-71.

Brunelli, Austin Roger (1931 — No. 10023) BGen. USMC; Ret 8-1-65.

Moulton, Horace Douglass (1931 — No. 10026) RAdm.

Booth, Charles Thomas II (1931 — No. 10033) VAdm; Ret 2-1-69.

Needham, Ray Cannon (1931 — No. 10034) VAdm; Ret 8-1-69.

Wright, Edward Alvey (1931 — No. 10035) RAdm.

Webster, John Alden (1931 — No. 10036) Capt. 2-10-61.

Foley, Joseph Ferrall (1931 — No. 10040) RAdm; Ret 11-1-59.

Brossy, Henry Earl (1931 — No. 10042) LCdr; Died 2-13-43 BNR Loss of USS Amberjack So Pacific.

Robbins, Berton Aldrich Jr (1931 — No. 10047) RAdm; Ret 11-1-59.

Hooper, Edwin Bickford (1931 — No. 10049) VAdm; Died 9-12-86.

Keller, Albert James (1931 — No. 10054) BGen. USMC; Ret 8-31-59.

Weatherwax, Hazlett Paul (1931 — No. 10061) RAdm; Died 5-26-67.

Schoeni, Walter Paul (1931 — No. 10074) RAdm; Ret 10-31-59.

Mackenzie, George Kenneth Jr (1931 — No. 10075) LCdr; KIA 4-9-44 WW II Loss of USS Triton in SW Pacific.

Wulff, John Thayer (1931 — No. 10081) RAdm; Ret 11-1-59.

MacDonald, Donald John (1931 — No. 10082) RAdm; Ret 10-1-59.

Janz, Clifford Thurston (1931 — No. 10099) Lt. USN KIA 12-7-41 WW II USS Arizona.

Renken, Henry Algemon (1931 — No. 10103) RAdm; Ret 6-30-70.

Ramage, Lawson Paterson (1931 — No. 10104) VAdm.

Bater, Harold (1931 — No. 10105) RAdm; Ret 7-1-57.

Miner, John Odgers (1931 — No. 10110) RAdm.

Lewellen, Bafford Edward (1931 — No. 10111) RAdm; Ret 11-1-59.

Reynolds, James Richard Z. (1931 — No. 10116) RAdm; Ret 2-1-58.

Fellows, John Benjamin (1931 — No. 10121) RAdm; Ret 11-1-59.

Fraser, Archie Donald (1931 — No. 10122) RAdm; Ret 10-1-56.

Peckham, George Edward (1931 — No. 10123) RAdm; Ret 10-1-59.

Hunter, Raymond Paul (1931 — No. 10130) RAdm; Ret 11-1-59.

Peters, James McClellan (1931 — No. 10131) RAdm; Ret 1-1-55.

Carr, Bruce Lewis (1931 — No. 10133) RAdm; Ret 9-1-59.

Williams, Russell Champion (1931 — No. 10134) RAdm; Ret 11-1-59.

Brooks, Charles Ballance Jr (1931 — No. 10135) RAdm; Ret 11-1-62.

Kurtz, Thomas Richardson Jr (1931 — No. 10138) RAdm; Ret 9-1-63.

Torgerson, Theodore Adolph (1931 — No. 10147) RAdm.

Bronson, Ward (1931 — No. 10150) Cdr; Died 1-30-44 USS Chicago.

Kirkpatrick, Charles Cochran (1931 — No. 10157) RAdm; Ret 6-1-64.

Fiala, Reid Puryear (1931 — No. 10159) RAdm; Ret 11-1-59.

Sieglaff, William Bernard (1931 — No. 10162) RAdm; Ret 7-1-66.

Metsger, Alfred Bowne (1931 — No. 10164) RAdm; Ret 11-1-59.

Brown, Nelson Kenyon (1931 — No. 10169) BGen. USMC; Ret 10-1-55.

Miles, Lion Tyler (1931 — No. 10170) Lt; MIA 3-1-42 USS Asheville enroute Java-Australia Presumed dead 11-25-45.

Harper, John Frank Jr (1931 — No. 10171) RAdm; Ret 10-1-59.

Putnam, Frank Rowell (1931 — No. 10175) RAdm; Ret 10-1-56.

Madden, George Bernard (1931 — No. 10182) RAdm; Ret 8-1-55.

Shuey, Clifford Henry (1931 — No. 10183) BGen. USMC; Ret 1-31-56.

Fitzgerald, John Allison (1931 — No. 10186) RAdm: Ret 11-1-59.

Adams, Wayne Horace (1931 — No. 10187) BGen. USMC; Ret 11-30-57.

Cook, John Henry Jr (1931 — No. 10189) BGen. USMC; Ret 5-1-59.

Lawrence, Sidney Jack (1931 — No. 10191) RAdm; Ret 11-1-59.

Hughes, John Nelson (1931 — No. 10200) RAdm; Ret 11-1-59.

McMahon, Bernard Francis (1931 — No. 10202) RAdm; Ret 11-1-59.

Smith, James Thomas (1931 — No. 10207) RAdm; Ret 9-1-58.

Ketchum, Gerald Lyle (1931 — No. 10211) RAdm; Ret 11-1-59.

Johnsen, William Harry (1931 — No. 10215) RAdm; Ret 11-1-59.

Antrim, Richard Nott (1931 — No. 10217) RAdm; Ret 4-1-54.

Johnson, Harlan Thode (1931 — No. 10222) RAdm; Ret 10-31-59.

Forney, Edward Hanna Jr (1931 — No. 10226) BGen. USMC; Ret 6-1-59.

Gallaher, Wilmer Earl (1931 — No. 10234) RAdm; Ret 11-1-59.

Allen, Robbins Woodhouse (1931 — No. 10244) RAdm; Ret 5-1-59.

Ellsworth, Ernest Bradford Jr (1931 — No. 10245) RAdm.

Grant, James Dorr (1931 — No. 10258) RAdm; Ret 11-1-59.

Werts, Charles Luther (1931 — No. 10261) RAdm; Ret 11-1-59.

Taxis, Samuel G. (1931 — No. 10262) BGen. USMC; Died 11-22-84.

Dillon, Edward James (1931 — No. 10264) BGen. USMC; Died 1-9-78.

Leverton, Joseph Wilson Jr (1931 — No. 10273) RAdm; Ret 1-1-65.

Jensen, Marvin John (1931 — No. 10275) RAdm; Ret 11-1-59.

Walpole, Kinlock Chafee (1931 — No. 10276) RAdm; Ret 10-31-59.

Kirkpatrick, John Elson (1931 — No. 10277) RAdm; Ret 8-1-55.

Dempsey, James Charles (1931 — No. 10279) RAdm; Ret 9-1-70.

Crumpacker, John Webber (1931 — No. 10294) RAdm.

Weiler, James Buchanan (1931 — No. 10295) RAdm; Ret 8-1-58.

Shaffer, Leland Griffith (1931 — No. 10304) RAdm; Ret 11-1-59.

Parham, John Calhoun Jr (1931 — No. 10305) RAdm; Ret 1-1-59.

Richardson, Alvin Franklin (1931 — No. 10311) RAdm; Ret 10-1-53.

Roscoe, David Livingston Jr (1931 — No. 10312) RAdm; Ret 11-1-59.

King, Robert Donovan (1931 — No. 10316) RAdm; Ret 3-1-58.

Byng, John Weston (1931 — No. 10317) RAdm; Ret 6-2-62.

Hollingsworth, John Christie (1931 — No. 10319) Cdr; Died 11-11-44 BNR USS Scamp Sunk by mine off Tokyo Bay.

Evans, Ernest Edwin (1931 — No. 10320) Cdr; Died 10-25-44 USS Johnston.

Andrews, Richard Stottko (1931 — No. 10322) RAdm; Ret 11-30-59.

Lyon, Hylan Benton (1931 — No. 10324) RAdm; Ret 12-31-57.

Black, Joseph Dean (1931 — No. 10326) RAdm.

Hill, Andrew Jewel Jr (1931 — No. 10327) RAdm; Ret 6-1-66.

Holcomb, Bankson Taylor (1931 — No. 10330) BGen. USMC; Ret 12-31-58.

Wieseman, Frederick Leonard (1931 — No. 10335) LGen. USMC; Ret 7-1-66, Recalled to ACDU 2-69 to 7-70.

Dunn, William Archer, (1931 — No. 10343) RAdm; Ret 3-1-59.

O'Neill, Edward Joseph (1931 — No. 10345) RAdm; Ret 2-1-57.

Cassedy, Hiram (1931 — No. 10347) RAdm; Ret 4-1-56.

Brown, Robert Samuel (1931 — No. 10348) Maj. USMC; Died 9-14-42 Guadalcanal Pac Area.

Gillespie, Thomas Evan (1931 — No. 10351) RAdm; Ret 2-1-52.

Smith, Norman Ernest (1931 — No. 10354) RAdm; Ret 11-1-58.

South, Jerry Curtis (1931 — No. 10358) RAdm; Ret 6-1-59.

Phifer, Thomas Carson (1931 — No. 10360) RAdm; Ret 10-1-59.

Woodaman, Ronald Joseph (1931 — No. 10364) RAdm; Ret 11-1-59.

Yancey, Evan White (1931 — No. 10365) RAdm; Ret 7-1-57.

Peterson, Richard Ward (1931 — No. 10366) RAdm; Ret 11-1-59.

Bass, Raymond Henry (1931 — No. 10376) RAdm; Ret 10-31-59.

Massey, Forsyth (1931 — No. 10377) RAdm; Ret 6-30-69.

Becton, Frederick Julian (1931 — No. 10386) RAdm.

Williamson, Francis Thomas (1931 — No. 10391) RAdm; Ret 1-1-65.

Fojt, Robert Edward (1931 — No. 10394) BGen. USMC; Ret 10-31-59.

Brush, Frederick James (1931 — No. 10402) RAdm.

O'Connor, Michael Gallighan (1931 — No. 10406) RAdm; Ret 11-1-59.

Norvell, William Clanton (1931 — No. 10420) RAdm; Ret 9-1-59.

McCain, John Sidney Jr (1931 — No. 10421) Adm; Ret 11-1-72.

Gardiner, Josef Marshall (1931 — No. 10426) RAdm; Ret 1-1-55.

Wood, Paul douglas (1931-Non-Graduate — No. 931128) Maj; Died 4-7-42 BNR Graduate U.S. Military Academy Killed in Action Bantaan PI While Commanding Battalion 57T.

Mandelkorn, Richard Shai (1932 — No. 10439) RAdm; Ret 8-1-57.

Fawkes, Emerson Evans (1932 — No. 10440) RAdm; Ret 7-1-67.

Ruckner, Edward Aberle (1932 — No. 10441) RAdm.

Schultz, Floyd Bernard (1932 — No. 10442) RAdm; Ret 4-1-67.

Waters, Odale Dabney Jr (1932 — No. 10447) RAdm; Died 5-7-86.

Ward, Alfred Gustave (1932 — No. 10451) Adm; Ret 9-1-68.

Horner, John Stuart (1932 — No. 10455) RAdm; Ret 11-1-59.

Mustin, Lloyd Montague (1932 — No. 10456) VAdm; Ret 8-1-71.

Jaap, Joseph Abraham (1932 — No. 10459) RAdm; Ret 7-1-67.

Bryan, Louis Allen (1932 — No. 10461) RAdm; Died 2-27-66.

Lewis, Porter (1932 — No. 10462) RAdm; Ret 11-1-59.

Hull, Harry (1932 — No. 10463) RAdm; Ret 7-1-67.

Palmer, Charles Joseph (1932 — No. 10466) RAdm.

Hodge, Ernest Debbes (1932 — No. 10467) Lt; KIA USS Houston Battle of Sunda Strait.

Weeks, Robert Harper (1932 — No. 10468) RAdm; Ret 7-1-71.

Reiter, Harry L. Jr (1932 — No. 10472) RAdm; 6-30-67.

Kinert, David Frederic (1932 — No. 10477) RAdm; Ret 11-1-59.

Frakes, Dale Roderick (1932 — No. 10478) RAdm; Ret 1-1-57.

Hummer, Harry Cessna (1932 — No. 10487) RAdm; Died 8-27-79.

Coleman, Herbert Mcclellan (1932 — No. 10492) LCdr; KIA USS Barton Third Battle of Savo Islands.

Wellings, Albert Aloysius (1932 — No. 10505) RAdm; Ret 7-1-56.

Fulton, Robert Burwell II (1932 — No. 10511) RAdm; Ret 7-1-68.

Kintberger, Leon Sameul (1932 — No. 10515) RAdm; Ret 10-31-59.

Pavlic, Milton Frank (9132 — No. 10518) LCdr; Died 11-14-42 USS South Dakota.

Denig, Robert Livingston Jr (1932 — No. 10521) BGen. USMC; Ret 10-1-59.

Wylie, Joseph Caldwell Jr (1932 — No. 10533) RAdm; Ret 7-1-72.

Munholland, John (1932 — No. 10535) RAdm; Ret 7-1-58.

Kaufman, John Holladay (1932 — No. 10540) RAdm; Ret 9-1-55.

Foley, Francis Drake (1932 — No. 10544) RAdm.

Kirn, Louis Joseph (1932 — No. 10545) RAdm; Ret 7-1-70.

Williams, Richard Claggett Jr (1932 — No. 10564) RAdm; Ret 11-1-52.

Zink, William Talbott Jr (1932 — No. 10567) RAdm; Ret 11-1-59.

Murphy, Charlton Lewis Jr (1932 — No. 10569) Ret 11-1-59.

Schroeder, William Paul (1932 — No. 10571) RAdm; Ret 9-1-55.

Perkins, William Beckwith (1932 — No. 10578) RAdm; Ret 11-1-59.

Craighill, Richard Starr (1932 — No. 10581) RAdm; Died 2-7-80.

Beer, Robert Oakley (1932 — No. 10602) RAdm; Ret 11-1-59.

Eastwold, Earl Russell (1932 — No. 10603) RAdm; Died 10-8-87.

Kemper, James Lawson (1932 — No. 10606) LCdr; Died 11-14-43 USS Monssen Battle of Guadalcanal.

Warfield, Thomas Glover, (1932 — No. 10611) RAdm; Ret 9-1-56.

Parker, Frank Mahlon (1932 — No. 10613) RAdm; Ret 11-1-59.

Johnson, Ralph Clarence (1932 — No. 10614) RAdm; Ret 1-1-67.

Atkins, Barry Kennedy (1932 — No. 10615) RAdm; Ret 11-1-59.

Tagg, William Leonard (1932 — No. 10623) RAdm; Ret 4-1-56.

Stuart, William Aurand (1932 — No. 10625) RAdm; Ret 7-1-67.

Snowden, Ernest Maynard (1932 — No. 10626) RAdm; Ret 10-1-59.

Groverman, William Heald Jr (1932 — No. 10636) RAdm.

Matter, Alfred Richard (1932 — No. 10639) RAdm.

Nuessle, Francis Edward (1932 — No. 10640) RAdm; Ret 7-1-67.

Andrew, John Douglas (1932 — No. 10642) RAdm; Ret 1-1-59.

Lewis, John Stephen (1932 — No. 10643) RAdm; Ret 3-1-57.

Bowser, Alpha Lyons (1932 — No. 10650) LGen. USMC; Ret 6-30-67.

Shinn, Allen Mayhew (1932 — No. 10655) VAdm; Ret 5-1-70.

Luker, George Robert (1932 — No. 10660) RAdm.

Pressey, George Washington (1932 — No. 10663) RAdm; Ret 4-20-66.

Konrad, Edmond George (1932 — No. 10672) RAdm; Ret 11-1-59.

Cox, William Ruffin (1932 — No. 10678) RAdm; Ret 11-1-59.

Hutchings, Charles Slack (1932 — No. 10679) RAdm; Ret 11-1-59.

Seely, Harry Woodworth (1932 — No. 10681) RAdm; Ret 4-1-56.

McCandless, Bruce (1932 — No. 10687) RAdm; Ret 9-1-52.

Garrison, Malcolm Everett (1932 — No. 10691) RAdm; Ret 11-1-58.

Billingsley, Edward B. (1932 — No. 10694) RAdm; Ret 10-1-59.

Pierce, George Ellis (1932 — No. 10695) RAdm; Ret 10-1-59.

Hutchinson, George Leland (1932 — No. 10710) Lt; KIA 1-21-42 WW II Piloting Catalina Plane enemy Aircraft Salamau New Guinea.

Connaway, Fred (1932 — No. 10711) Cdr; KIA 11-19-43 USS Sculpin.

Wolsieffer, Frederick (1932 — No. 10716) RAdm; Ret 10-1-56.

Ottinger, George Malone (1932 — No. 10721) Cdr; Died 3-24-45 BNR KIA USS Bunker Hill.

Winter, William Jr (1932 — No. 10724) RAdm; Ret 10-1-55.

Enright, William Keith (1932 — No. 10725) Ret 11-1-59.

Ramey, John William (1932 — No. 10726) RAdm; Died 3-5-58.

Tschirgi, Harvey Curtis (1932 — No. 10727) BGen; USMC.

Innis, Walter Deane (1932 — No. 10730) RAdm; Ret 9-30-59.

McCornock, Samuel Aldo (1932 — No. 10733) RAdm; Ret 1-1-55.

Bisson, Robert Omer (1932 — No. 10734) BGen. USMC; Died 3-19-59.

Thompson, Forest Carson (1932 — No. 10742) BGen. USMC; Died 10-11-70.

Smiley, Clare Brown (1932 — No. 10748) RAdm; Ret 5-1-53.

Phares, Everett Lang (1932 — No. 10749) RAdm; Ret 12-1-55.

Harral, Brooks Jared (1932 — No. 10758) RAdm; Ret 8-1-59.

Moore, Robert Brevard (1932 — No. 10761) RAdm; Ret 3-15-67.

Thomas, James Alfred (1932 — No. 10765) RAdm; Ret 10-1-58.

Smith, Daniel Fletcher Jr (1932 — No. 10778) RAdm; Died 10-5-71.

Jonson, William Crawford Jr (1932 — No. 10784) RAdm; Ret 7-1-59.

Flenniken, James Alexander (1932 — No. 10786) RAdm; Ret 11-1-59.

McCrea, Victor B. (1932 — No. 10790) RAdm; Ret 11-1-58.

McCarley, Henry Harris (1932 — No. 10796) RAdm; Ret 10-1-59.

Raymond, William Henry Jr (1932 — No. 10800) RAdm; Ret 11-1-59.

McGoldrick, Joseph Aloysius (1932 — No. 10805) RAdm; Ret 11-1-59.

Catlett, William Jackson Jr (1932 — No. 10808) RAdm; Ret 7-1-58.

Jukes, Herbert Lollis (1932 — No. 10809) RAdm; Ret 11-1-59.

Chase, Irwin Jr (1932 — No. 10813) RAdm; Ret 1-1-59.

Scherini, Otto Axel (1932 — No. 10818) RAdm; Ret 11-1-59.

Owens, Hinton Allen (1932 — No. 10820) RAdm; Ret 11-1-59.

Lanman, Charles Burrows (1932 — No. 10821) RAdm; Died 11-27-57.

Porter, George Egbert Jr (1932 — No. 10830) RAdm; Ret 4-1-53.

Tennent, John Gardner.III (1932 — No. 10832) Cdr; Died 1-30-44 KIA USS Anderson, Marshall Islands.

Lyons, Charles Malaher Jr (1932 — No. 10833) RAdm; Ret 11-1-59.

Smith, James Gene (1932 — No. 10834) BGen. USMC; Ret 5-1-59.

Tuttle, Magruder Hill (1932 — No. 10841) RAdm; Ret 6-1-67.

Short, Wallace Clark Jr (1932 — No. 10846) RAdm; Ret 7-1-59.

Smith, Charles Hubert (1932 — No. 10850) RAdm; Ret 11-1-59.

Perkins, Charles Elliott (1932 — No. 10853) RAdm; Ret 12-1-56.

Adams, Richard Donald (1932 — No. 10857) RAdm; Ret RAdm. USNR 7-3-69.

Bowen, Harold Gardiner Jr (1933 — No. 10863) RAdm; Ret 10-1-72.

MacKenzie, Dewitt Clinton (1933 — No. 10867) RAdm; Ret 10-1-59.

Raymond, Reginald Marbury (1933 — No. 10874) LCdr; KIA 4-29-43 WW II USS Scorpion.

Morton, Thomas Howard (1933 — No. 10877) RAdm; Ret 4-1-64.

Lambert, David (1933 — No. 10878) RAdm.

Curtze, Charles August (1933 — No. 10882) RAdm; Ret 12-1-65.

Heinz, Luther Carl (1933 — No. 10883) VAdm; Ret 2-1-71.

Dietz, James Stratton (1933 — No. 10905) RAdm; Ret 6-1-68.

Drustrup, Norman James (1933 — No. 10909) RAdm; Ret 1-1-67

Connolly, Thomas Francis (1933 — No. 10912) VAdm; Ret 9-19-71.

Sherrill, Wallace Andrew (1933 — No. 10915) RAdm; Ret 1-1-59.

Bullock, James Earl (1933 — No. 10917) Lt; KIA 6-30-42 WW II By Japanese POW Philippine Islands.

Wade, Sidney Scott (1933 — No. 10918) MGen; USMC.

Wendt, Waldemar Frederick A. (1933 — No. 10923) Adm; Ret 5-30-71.

Miller, Edwin Swain (1933 — No. 10924) RAdm; Ret 8-1-68.

Lane, Richard (1933 — No. 10926) RAdm; Ret 12-1-57.

Loveland, Kenneth (1933 — No. 10927) RAdm; Ret 2-1-59.

Haskins, Enrique D'hamel (1933 — No. 10930) RAdm; Ret 1-1-59.

Duncan Charles Kenney (1933 — No. 10931) Adm; Ret 11-1-72.

Vogeley, Theodore Robert (1933 — No. 10932) RAdm; Ret 11-1-59.

Shifley, Ralph Louis (1933 — No. 10937) VAdm; Ret 3-1-71.

Purdy, Frederick Warren (1933 — No. 10951) LCdr; Died 7-5-43 BNR USS Strong Kulä, Gulf Pac Area.

Tyree, John Augustine Jr (1933 — No. 10953) VAdm; Ret 11-1-71.

Burton, Paul Willits (1933 — No. 10962) LCdr; Died 2-13-44 BNR Grounding and loss of USS Macaw.

Schwartz, Frank Dewey (1933 — No. 10963) RAdm; Ret 11-1-59.

Wagstaff, Ruben Eli (1933 — No. 10966) RAdm; Ret 12-1-54.

Wallace, Paul Eugene (1933 — No. 10976) BGen. USMC; Ret 10-1-59.

Coye, John Starr Jr (1933 — No. 10983) RAdm.

Ashworth, Frederick Lincoln (1933 — No. 10994) VAdm; Ret 9-1-68.

Williams, Joseph Warford Jr (1933 — No. 10996) RAdm; Died 12-20-85.

Kimball, Leland Porter Jr (1933 — No. 10997) RAdm; Ret 10-1-59.

Keating, Robert Allen Jr (1933 — No. 10998) RAdm; Ret 10-1-59.

Tyler, Marshall Alvin (1933 — No. 11007) MGen USMC; Ret 9-1-55.

Loughlin, Charles Elliott (1933 — No. 11008) RAdm; Ret 7-31-68.

Thomas, Millener Weaver (1933 — No. 11011) Lt; USN Loss of USS Grunion August '42.

Davenport, Roy Milton (1933 — No. 11012) RAdm; Ret 11-1-59.

Fair, Robert Eli (1933 — No. 11016) Cdr; Died 1-9-45 USS Colorado air attack.

Bird, Horace Virgil (1933 — No. 11022) RAdm; Died 11-6-84.

Strean, Horace Max (1933 — No. 11024) VAdm; Ret 7-23-71.

Leach, Robert William (1933 — No. 11025) RAdm; Ret 9-1-58.

Manning, Joseph Ignatius (1933 — No. 11026) RAdm; Ret 11-1-59.

Lord, Edwin Elmer (1933 — No. 11028) RAdm; Ret 11-1-57.

Martineau, David Louis (1933 — No. 11029) RAdm; Ret 11-1-59.

Jackson, Charles B. Jr (1933 — No. 11031) RAdm; Ret 11-1-59.

Moorer, Thomas Hinman (1933 — No. 11041) Adm; Ret 7-1-74.

Schade, Arnold Frederic (1933 — No. 11047) VAdm; Ret 9-1-71.

Lee, Lamar Jr (1933 — No. 11048) RAdm; Ret 2-1-57.

Vaughan, James (1933 — No. 11053) RAdm; Ret 11-1-59.

Miller, George Harold (1933 — No. 11056) RAdm.

Macpherson, Robert Anthony (1933 — No. 11073) RAdm; Ret 6-1-72.

Cobb, James Outterson (1933 — No. 11076) RAdm.

McNenny, Wilbur James (1933 — No. 11079) BGen. USMC; Ret 9-1-55.

Jones, Carlton Benton (1933 — No. 11094) RAdm; Ret 6-1-68.

Clementson, Merrill Kinsell (1933 — No. 11097) RAdm; Died 12-17-79.

Masters, James M. Sr (1933 — No. 11098) LGen; USMC.

McCormack, John Joseph Jr (1933 — No. 11099) LCdr; MIA 12-13-43 Plane bombing Sqn 108.

Blouin, Francis Joseph (1933 — No. 11101) VAdm; Ret 7-1-71.

Barnum, Robert Hudson (1933 — No. 11102) RAdm; Res 6-1-34.

Masterton, Paul (1933 — No. 11108) VAdm; Ret 2-1-71.

Mott, William Chamberlain (1933 — No. 11110) RAdm; Ret 4-1-64.

Fuller, Donald Walker (1933 — No. 11115) BGen. USMC; Ret 10-1-56.

Fulton, Raymond Lester (1933 — No. 11120) RAdm; Ret 9-1-59.

Copeland, Richard Goodwin (1933 — No. 11124) RAdm; Ret 7-1-59.

Jackson, Edward Frank (1933 — No. 11132) RAdm; Ret 11-1-59.

Buie, Paul Douglas (1933 — No. 11137) RAdm; Died 4-16-72.

Costello, Joseph Patrick (1933 — No. 11138) RAdm; Ret 11-1-59.

Newton, Walter Hughes (1933 — No. 11141) RAdm; Ret 5-1-56.

Fulmer, Herbert Samuel Jr (1932 — No. 11142) Cdr; Died 1-21-45 BNR USS Ticonderoga.

Reedy, James Robert (1933 — No. 11149) RAdm; Ret 8-1-68.

Blick, Charles Augustus (1933 — No. 11161) RAdm; Ret 9-1-68.

Koch, George Price (1933 — No. 11170) RAdm; Died 9-17-72.

Poor, Richard Longstreet (1933 — No. 11185) RAdm; Res 10-1-66.

Kefauver, Russell (1933 — No. 11196) RAdm; Died 8-1-80.

Keller, Clarence Armstrong Jr (1933 — No. 11197) RAdm; Ret 9-1-59.

Grimm, Edward Elias (1933 — No. 11203) RAdm; Ret 8-1-69.

Metzger, Edward Francis (1933 — No. 11204) RAdm; Ret 6-1-68.

Neville, Lawrence Robert (1933 — No. 11210) RAdm; Ret 11-1-59.

Barker, Christopher S. Jr (1933 — No. 11225) RAdm; Ret 11-1-60.

Taylor, Rufus Lackland (1933 — No. 11239) VAdm; Died 9-14-78.

Monroe, Henry Stone (1933 — No. 11244) RAdm; Ret 8-1-68.

Bulkeley, John Duncan (1933 — No. 11254) RAdm; Ret 2-1-64.

Kauffman, Draper Laurence (1933 — No. 11257) RAdm; Res 6-33. Died 8-18-79 Budapest Hungary.

Kuehl, Howard Frank (1933 — No. 11263) RAdm; Ret 7-1-69.

Rakow, William Magnus (1933 — No. 11265) RAdm; Ret 6-1-56.

Long, Thomas Albert (1933 — No. 11269) RAdm.

Drescher, Carl George (1933 — No. 11273) RAdm; Ret 9-1-56.

Mandarich, Steve (1933 — No. 11277) RAdm; Ret 11-1-59.

Selby, Frank Gordon (1933 — No. 11281) RAdm; Ret 8-1-59.

Cundiff, Charles Reed (1933-Non-Graduate — No. 933027) RAdm; Res 10-1-59.

Oren, John Birdsell (1933-Non-Graduate — No. 933093) RAdm; Res 1-1-68.

Wilson, John Murray (1934 — No. 11295) Lt. USNR; Res 5-31-34. Died 9-5-42 USS Gregory.

Gralla, Arthur Robert (1934 — No. 11300) VAdm; Ret 12-1-71.

Fahy, Edward Joseph (1934 — No. 11303) RAdm; Ret 8-1-69.

Batcheller, Edgar Hadley (1934 — No. 11306) RAdm; Ret 7-1-69.

Brockett, William Alden (1934 — No. 11311) RAdm; Ret 2-1-66.

Pinney, Frank Lucius Jr (1934 — No. 11313) RAdm; Ret 6-20-69.

Browne, George Henry (1934 — No. 11318) RAdm; Ret 11-1-59.

Pittard, George Franklin (1934 — No. 11321) RAdm; Ret 1-1-68.

Smith, John Victor (1934 — No. 11323) VAdm; Ret 7-1-73.

Smith, William Robinson III (1934 — No. 11324) RAdm; Ret 7-31-57.

Chambers, Lester Smith (1934 — No. 11334) RAdm; Ret 8-1-66.

Davis, James Robert (1934 — No. 11338) RAdm; Ret 2-1-66.

Hyland, John Joseph (1934 — No. 11348) Adm; Ret 1-1-71.

Schulz, Lester Robert (1934 — No. 11352) RAdm; Ret 6-30-68.

Ingersoll, Royal Rodney II (1934 — No. 11363) Lt; Died 6-4-42 USS Hornet Pacific area Battle of Miday.

Townsend, Robert Lee (1934 — No. 11370) VAdm.

Church, William C.G. (1934 — No. 11373) RAdm; Ret 6-1-64.

Van Arsdall, Clyde James Jr (1934 — No. 11377) RAdm; Ret 7-1-73.

Condon, John Pomeroy (1934 — No. 11389) MGen. USMC; Ret 10-1-62.

Mann, Charles Clark (1934 — No. 11396) RAdm; Ret 7-1-57. Died 1-29-87.

Christensen, Ernest Edward (1934 — No. 11399) RAdm; Ret 2-1-72.

Rottet, Ralph Kasper (1934 — No. 11405) LGen. USMC; Died 11-26-71 USNH Camp Lejeune.

Pesante, Juan Bautista (1934 — No. 11406) Lt; Died 11-15-42 BNR USS Preston Battle of Solomons Islands.

Griffith, Walter Thomas (1934 — No. 11408) RAdm; Ret 1-31-57.

Sweeney, William Edward (1934 — No. 11412) RAdm; Ret 10-1-67.

Robertson, Robert Neal (1934 — No. 11422) Lt; Died 1-11-44 BNR USS Argonaut.

Whitaker, Reuben Thornton (1934 — No. 11427) RAdm; Ret 7-31-69.

Newman, Arthur Lester (1934 — No. 11428) Lt; Died 2-18-42 at sea near St Lawrence NewFoundland USS Truxton.

Thompson, Harry Leroy Jr (1934 — No. 11435) RAdm; Ret 11-1-59.

Tibbets, Joseph Bonafield (1934 — No. 11441) RAdm.

Nichols, Richard Eugene (1934 — No. 11465) RAdm; Ret 11-1-59.

Dickinson, Clarence Earle (1934 — No. 11483) RAdm; Ret 11-1-59.

Blakely, Edward Noe (1934 — No. 11485) Died 2-11-42 China Sea BNR - Enemy Action USS Shark.

Joachim, Paul Lamar (1934 — No. 11492) RAdm; Ret 7-1-54.

Baumberger, Walter Harlen (1934 — No. 11496) VAdm; Ret 1-1-73.

Johnson, Nels Clarence (1934 — No. 11502) VAdm; Ret 8-31-72.

Harllee, John (1934 — No. 11508) RAdm; Ret 10-1-59.

Semmes, Benedict Joseph (1934 — No. 11511) VAdm; Ret 7-1-72.

Deakin, Harold Osborne (1934 — No. 11512) BGen. USMC; Ret 7-1-57.

Buse, Henry William Jr (1934 — No. 11524) LGen. USMC; Ret 1-7-70.

Shaw, Samuel Robert (1934 — No. 11525) BGen. USMC; Ret 3-1-62.

Hommel, Robert Emerson (1934 — No. 11527) BGen. USMC; Died 8-24-83.

Price, Lowell Scherich (1934 — No. 11530) RAdm; Ret 9-1-59.

Daunis, Stanley Stephen (1934 — No. 11540) RAdm; Ret 11-1-59.

Hutchings, Curtis Howell (1934 — No. 11541) RAdm; Ret 11-1-59.

Sapp, John Wesley Jr (1934 — No. 11545) BGen. USMC; Ret 8-1-57.

White, Marshall William (1934 — No. 11548) RAdm; Ret 6-30-69.

O'Kane, Richard Hetherington (1934 — No. 11555) RAdm; MH. Ret 7-1-57. Awarded Medal Of Honor 3-27-46 By Pres. Truman.

Arnold, Jackson Dominick (1934 — No. 11565) Adm; Ret 12-1-71.

Clarey, Bernard Ambrose (1934 — No. 11569) Adm; Ret 9-30-73.

Graham, Robert Wallace (1934 — No. 11570) RAdm; Res 5-31-34. Ret 8-57.

Swift, Douglas McKean (1934 — No. 11571) RAdm; Ret 12-1-54.

Tharin, Frank Cunnington (1934 — No. 11573) LGen. USMC; Ret 7-1-70.

Savidge, Paul Sheppard (1934 — No. 11574) RAdm; Ret 10-1-64.

Miller, Henry Louis (1934 — No. 11580) RAdm; Ret 9-1-71.

Whitaker, Frank Melvin (1934 — No. 11585) LCdr; KIA 2-2-44 Eniwetok Atoll Air Attack Pacific.

Zeiler, Samuel Francis (1934 — No. 11587) BGen. USMCR; Ret 11-1-46.

Boyle, Francis Dennis (1934 — No. 11589) RAdm; Ret 8-1-68.

Ray, Martin Hasset Jr (1934 — No. 11594) Lt; Died 6-7-43 Loss of USS Hammann Battle of Midway.

Martin, William Inman (1934 — No. 11610) VAdm; Ret 2-1-71.

Weber, John Edmund (1934 — No. 11611) BGen. USMC; Ret 10-1-56.

Kossler, Herman Joseph (1934 — No. 11612) RAdm; Ret 6-30-73.

Kinsella, William Thomas (1934 — No. 11617) RAdm; Ret 6-30-57.

Brown, Samuel Robbins Jr (1934 — No. 11621) RAdm; Ret 7-1-69.

Ashley, James Henry Jr (1934 — No. 11641) RAdm; Ret 11-1-59.

Gunn, Frederick Arthur (1934 — No. 11666) RAdm; Ret 11-1-59.

South, Thomas Winfield II (1934 — No. 11668) RAdm; Ret 10-15-64.

Reeves, Malcolm Clephane (1934 — No. 11676) RAdm; Ret 7-1-57.

Fleck, Francis Edward Jr (1934 — No. 11702) RAdm; Ret 11-1-59.

Coffin, Albert Peyton (1934 — No. 11727) RAdm; Ret 11-1-59.

Stone, Archibald Jr (1932 — No. 11728) Died 2-28-42 BNR USS Pecos South of Java.

Chung-Hoon, Gordon Paiea (1934 — No. 11733) RAdm; Ret 10-1-59.

Avise, John Ellsworth (1934 — No. 11734) KIA 10-17-42 WW II Flying Officer RCAF Air Operations in Middleast.

Allen, Russell Bowes (1934 — No. 11738) RAdm; Ret 11-1-59.

Worthington, Edward Hicks (1934 — No. 11740) Lt; Died 1-31-42 BNR Missing on Patrol Duty in Pacific Area.

Johnston, Dewey George (1934 — No. 11742) Lt; KIA about 10-31-41 WW II USS Reuben James at North Atlantic.

DuBois, Thomas Hodgskin (1934 — No. 11754) RAdm.

Payne, Frederick Rounsville Jr (1934-Non-Graduate — No. 934099) BGen; USMC.

Medal Of Honor Recipients 1919-1945

Note: Whenever Possible, We Have Crossed Referenced The Recipients' Actions Within The Text. The Date Or Dates On Which The Action Occurred Can Be Checked Within The Text. Frequently, The Individual's Action Is Chronicled On The Corresponding Date, Or The Action In Which The Recipient Received The Medal Is Detailed.

HAITIAN CAMPAIGN-1919 TO 1920

Button, William Robert, Corporal, USMC, 31 October-1 November 1919, Grande Riviere, Haiti.

Hanneken, Herman Henry, Second Lieutenant, USMC, 31 October-1 November 1919, Grande Riviere, Haiti.

SECOND NICARAGUAN CAMPAIGN

Schilt, Christian Frank, First Lieutenant, USMC, 6, 7, and 8 January 1928, Quilali, Nicaragua.

Truesdell, Donald LeRoy (name officially changed to Truesdale), Corporal, USMC, Guardia Nacional Patrol; 25 April 1932, Constancia, near Coco River.

INTERIM 1920 TO 1940

Badders, William, Chief Machinist's Mate, USN, 13 May 1939, rescue and salvage operations following the sinking of the U.S.S Submarine *Squalus.*

Bennett, Floyd, Machinist, USN, Byrd Arctic Expedition May 8th-9th 1926.

Breault, Henry, Torpedoman, Second Class, USN, U.S. submarine O-5; 28 October 1923.

Byrd, Richard Evelyn, Jr., Commander, USN, Arctic Expedition May 8th-9th 1926.

*Cholister, George Robert, Boatswain's Mate First Class, USN, U.S.S. *Trenton*; 20 October 1924.

*Corry, William Merrill, Jr., Lieutenant Commander U.S. Navy, 2 October 1920, air crash near Hartford Conn.

Crandall, Orson L., Chief Boatswain's Mate, USN, 1 May 1939, rescue and salvage operation following sinking of the U.S.. *Squalus.*

*Drexler, Henry Clay, Ensign USN, U.S.S. *Trenton*; 20 October 1924, explosion of powder bags.

Eadie Thomas, Chief Gunner's Mate, USN, 18 December 1927, Off Provincetown, Mass. during the sinking of the U.S.S. Submarine S-4.

Edwards, Walter Atlee, Lieutenant Commander USN, 16 December 1922, Sea of Marmora, Turkey during the U.S.S. *Bainbridge's* rescue operations near the French Military Transport *Vinh-Long.*

Greely, Adolphus W., Major General, USA, 21 March 1935, service 27 March 1844 to 10 February 1906 for exemplary service since his enlistment in the U.S. Army on July 26th, 1861 until retirement February 10th 1906 by Act of Congress March 21st 1935.

Huber, William Russel, Machinist's Mate, USN, 11 June 1928, Aboard the U.S.S. *Bruce* at the Naval Shipyard, Norfolk, Va.

*Hutchins, Carlton Barmore, Lieutenant, USN, U.S.Navy Seaplane PBY-2 No. 0463 (11-P-3); Off California coast February 2nd 1938.

Lindbergh, Charles A., Captain, USA Air Corps Reserve, 20-21 May 1927, First non-stop Transatlantic flight by an AirPlane when the *Spirit of St. Louis* travels from New York to Paris.

McDonald, James Harper, Chief Metalsmith, USN, 23 May 1939, Area at sea during sinking of the U.S.S. *Squalus.*

Mihalowski, John, Torpedoman First Class, USN, 23 May 1939, Area at sea during the sinking of the U.S.S. *Squalus.*

Ryan, Thomas John, Ensign, USN, 1 September 1923, Yokohama, Japan.

Smith, Albert Joseph, Private, USMC, 11 February 1921, Marine Barracks, Naval Air Station, Pensacola, Florida.

MEDAL OF HONOR RECIPIENTS WORLD WAR II

Adams, Lucian, Staff Sergeant, USA, 30th Infantry, 3rd Infantry Division; 28th October, near St Die, France.

*Agerholm, Harold Christ, PFC, 4th Battalion, 10th Marines, 2nd Marine division, 7 July 1944, Saipan, Marianas Islands.

Anderson, Beaufort T., Tech. Sergeant, USA, 381st Infantry, 96th Infantry Division; 13 April 1945, Okinawa.

*Anderson, Richard Beatty, PFC, 4th Marine Division; 1 February 1944, Roi Island, Kwajalein Atoll, Marshall Islands.

*Antolak, Sylvester, Sergeant USA, Company B, 15th Infantry, 3rd Infantry Division; 24th May 1944, Near Cisterna di Littoria, Italy.

Antrim, Richard Nott, Commander, USN, April 1942, Makasser, Celebes, Netherlands East Indies.

Atkins, Thomas E., PFC, USA, Company A, 127th Infantry, 32nd Infantry Division; 10th March 1945, Villa Verde Trail, Luzon, Philippine Islands.

*Bailey Kenneth D., Major, U.S. Marine Corps., Company C, 1st Marine Raider Battalion; 12-13 September 1942, Henderson Field, Guadalcanal, Solomon Islands.

*Baker, Addison E., Lt. Col., USA, Air Corps., 93rd Heavy Bombardment Group; 1 August 1943, Ploesti Raid, Rumania.

*Baker, Thomas A., Sergeant, USA, Company A, 105th Infantry, 27th Infantry Division; 19 June to 7 July 1944, Saipan, Mariana Islands.

Barfoot Van T., 2nd Lt., USA, 17th Infantry, 45th Infantry Division; 23 May 1944, Near Carano Italy.

Barrett, Carlton W., Pvt, USA, 18th Infantry, 1st Infantry Divi sion; 6 June 1944, Near Laurent-sur-Mer, France.

Basilone, John, Sgt., USMC, 1st Battalion, 7th Marines, 1st Marine Division; 24 and 25 October 1942, Lunga Area, Guadalcanal, Solomon Islands.

*Bauer, Harold William, Lt. Col., USMC, Squadron Commander Fighting Squadron 212 ; 10 May to 14 November 1942, South Pacific Area.

*Bausell, Lewis Kenneth, Corporal, USMC, 1st Battalion, 5th Marines 1st Marine Division; 15 September 1944, Peleliu Island, Palau Group.

*Beaudoin, Raymond O., 1st Lt., USA, Company F, 119 Infantry, 30th Infantry Division; 6 April 1945, Hamelin, Germany.

Bell, Bernard P., Tech. Sergeant, USA, Company I, 142nd Infantry, 36th Infantry Division; 18 December 1944, Mittelwihr, France.

Bender, Stanley, Staff Sergeant, USA, Company E, 7th Infantry, 3rd Infantry Division; 17 August 1944, Near La Lande, France.

*Benjamin, George, Jr., PFC, USA, Company A, 306th Infantry, 77th Infantry Division; 21 December 1944, Leyte, Philippine Islands.

Bennett, Edward A., Corporal, USA, Company B, 358th Infantry, 90th Infantry Division; 1 February 1945, Heckhuscheid, Germany.

*Bennion, Mervyn Sharp, Captain, USN, Commanding Officer of the U.S.S. *West Virginia*; During the attack of the Fleet at Pearl Harbor December 7th, 1941.

*Berry, Charles Joseph, Corporal USMC, 1st Battalion, 26th Marines, 5th Marine Division; 3 March 1945, Iwo Jima, Volcano Islands.

Bertoldo, Vito R., Master Sergeant, USA, Company A, 242nd Infantry, 42nd Infantry Division; 9-10 January 1945, Hatten France.

Beyer, Arthur O., Corporal, USA, Company C, 603rd Tank Destroyer Battalion; 15 January 1945, Near Arloncourt, Belgium.

Bianchi, Willibald C., 1st Lt., USA, 45th Infantry, Philippine Scouts; 3 February 1942, Near Bagac, Bataan Province, Philippine Islands.

Biddle, Melvin E., PFC, USA, Company B, 517th Parachute Infantry Regiment; 23-24 December 1944, Near Soy, Belgium.

*Bigelow, Elmer Charles, Wartertender 1st Class, USN Reserve, U.S.S. *Fletcher*; 14 February 1945, Off Corregidor Island, Philippine Islands.

Bjorklund, Arnold L., 1st Lt., USA, 36th Infantry Division; 13 September 1943, Near Altavilla, Italy.

Bloch, Orville Emil, 1st Lt., USA, Company E, 338th Infantry, 85th Infantry Division; 22 September 1944, Near Firenzoula, Italy.

Bolden, Paul L., Staff Sergeant, USA, Company I, 120th Infantry, 30th Infantry Division; 23 December 1944, Petit-Coo, Belgium.

Bolton, Cecil H., 1st Lt., USA, Company E, 413th Infantry, 104th Infantry Division; 2 November 1944, Mark River Holland.

Bong, Richard I., Major, USA Air Corps., 10 October to 15 November 1944, (Air Mission) Southwest Pacific.

*Bonnyman, Alexander, Jr., 1st Lt., USMC Reserves, 2nd Battalion Shore Party, 8th Marines, 2nd Marine Division; 20-22 November 1943, Tarawa, Gilbert Islands.

*Booker, Robert D., Pvt., USA, 34th Infantry Division; 9 April 1943, Near Fondouk, Tunisia.

*Bordelon, William James, Staff Sergeant, USMC, 1st Battalion, 18th Marines, attached to 2nd Marine Division; 20 November 1943, Tarawa, Gilbert Islands.

*Boyce, George W. G. Jr., 2nd Lt., USA, 112th Calvary Regimental Combat Team; 23 July 1944, Near Afua, New Guinea.

Boyington, Gregory, Major, USMC Reserve, Marine Squadron; 12 September 1943 to 3 January 1944, Central Solomons.

Briles, Herschel F., Staff Sergeant, USA, Company C, 899th Tank Destroyer Battalion; 20 November 1944, Near Scherpenseel, Germany.

Britt, Maurice L., Captain (then Lieutenant), USA, 3rd Infantry Division; 10 November 1943, North of Mignano, Italy.

*Brostrom, Leonard C., PFC, USA, Company F, 17th Infantry Division; 28 October 1944, Near Dagami, Leyte, Philippine Islands.

Brown, Bobbie E., Captain, USA, Company, 18th Infantry, 1st Infantry Division; 8 October 1944, Crucifix Hill, Aachen, Germany.

Bulkeley, John Duncan, Lieutenant Commander, USN, Commander of Torpedo Boat Squadron 3; 7 December 1941 to 10 April 1942, Philippine waters.

Burke, Frank (also known as Francis X. Burke), 1st Lieutenant, USA, 15th Infantry 3rd Infantry Division; 17 April 1945, Nuremberg, Germany.

*Burr, Elmer J., First Sergeant, USA, Company I, 127th Infantry, 32nd Infantry Division; 24 December 1942, Buna New Guinea.

Burr Herbert H., Staff Sergeant, USA, Company C, 41st Tank Battalion, 11th Armored Division; 19 March 1945, Near Dorrmoshel Germany.

Burt, James M., Captain, USA, Company B, 66th Armored Regiment, 2nd Armored Division; 13 October 1944, Near Wurselen, Germany.

Bush, Richard Earl Corporal, USMC Reserve, 1st Battalion, 4th Marines, 6th Marine Division; 16 April 1945, Mount Yaetake on Okinawa, Ryukyu Islands.

Bush, Robert Eugene, Hospital Apprentice First Class, U.S. Naval Reserve, 2nd Battalion, 5th Marines, 1st Marine Division; 2 May 1945, Okinawa Jima, Ryukyu Islands.

*Butts, John E., Second Lieutenant, USA, Company E, 60th Infantry, 9th Infantry Division; 14, 16, and 23 June 1944, Normandy, France.

*Caddy, William Robert, PFC, USMC Reserve, Company I, 3rd Marines, 5th Marine Division; 3 March 1945, Iwo Jima, Volcano Islands.

*Callaghan, Daniel Judson, Rear Admiral USN, 12-13 November 1942, off Savo Island.

Calugas, Jose, Sergeant, USA, Battery B, 88th Field Artillery, Philippine Scouts; 16 January 1942, Culis, Bataan Province, Philippine Islands.

Cannon, George Ham, First Lieutenant, USMC, Battery Commander of Battery H, 6th Defense Battalion, Fleet Marine Force; 7 December 1941, Sand Island, Midway Islands.

*Carey, Alvin P., Staff Sergeant, USA, 38th Infantry, 2nd Infantry Division; 23 August 1944, Near Plougastel, France.

*Carey, Charles F., Jr, Technical Sergeant, USA, 379th Infantry, 100th Infantry Division; 8-9 January 1945, Rimling, France.

Carr, Chris (name legally hanged from Christos H. Karaberis, under which name the medal was awarded), Sergeant, USA, Company L, 337th Infantry, 85th Infantry Division; 1-2 October 1944, Near Guignola, Italy.

*Carswell, Horace S., Jr., (Air Mission), Major, U.S.Army Air Corps, 308th Bombardment Group; 26 October 1944, Over South China Sea.

*Castle, Frederick W. (Air Mission), Brigadier General, U.S. Army Air Corps, Assistant Commander, 4th Bomber Wing; 24 December 1944, Germany.

Chambers, Justice M., Colonel, USMC Reserve, 3rd Assault Battalion Landing Team, 25th Marines, 4th Marine Division; 19 to 22 February 1945, Iwo Jima, Volcano Islands.

*Cheli, Ralph (Air Mission), Major, USA Air Corps; 18 August 1943, Near Wewak, New Guinea.

Childers, Ernest, Second Lieutenant, USA, 45th Infantry Division; 22 September 1943, Oliveto, Italy.

Choate, Clyde L., Staff Sergeant, USA, Company C, 601st Tank Destroyer

Battalion; 25 October 1944, Near Bruyeres, France.

*Christensen, Dale Eldon, Second Lieutenant, USA, Troop E, 112th Calvary Regiment; 16-19 July 1944, Driniumor River, New Guinea.

*Christian, Herbert F., PFC, USA, 15th Infantry 3rd Infantry Division; 2-3 June 1944, Near Valmontone, Italy.

*Cicchetti, Joseph J., PFC, USA, Company A, 148th Infantry, 37th Infantry Division; 9 February 1945, South Manila, Luzon, Philippine Islands.

Clark, Francis J., Technical Sergeant, USA, Company K, 109th Infantry, 28th Infantry Division; 12 September 1944, Near Kalborn, Luxembourg.

Colalillo, Mike, PFC, USA, Company, 398th Infantry, 100th Infantry Division; 7 April 1945, Near Untergriesheim, Germany.

*Cole, Darrell Samuel, Sergeant, USMC Reserve, Machinegun Section of Company B, 1st Battalion, 23rd Marines, 4th Marine Division, 19 February 1945, Iwo Jima, Volcano Islands.

*Cole, Robert G., Lt. Colonel, USA, 101st Airborne Division; 11 June 1944, Near Carentan, France.

Conner, James P., Sergeant, USA, 7th Infantry, 3rd Infantry Division; 15 August 1944, Cape Cavalaire, southern France.

Cooley, Raymond H., Staff Sergeant, USA, Company B, 27th Infantry, 25th Infantry Division; 24 February 1945, Near Lumboy, Luzon, Philippine Islands.

Coolidge, Charles H., Technical Sergeant, USA, Company M, 141st Infantry, 36th Infantry Division; 24-27 October 1944, East of Belmont sur Buttant, France.

*Courtney, Henry Alexius, Jr., Major, USMC Reserve, Executive Officer 2nd Battalion, 22nd Marines, 6th Marine Division; 14 and 15 May 1945, Okinawa Shima, Ryukyu Islands.

Cowan, Richard Eller, PFC, USA, Company M, 23rd Infantry, 2nd Infantry Division; 17 December 1944, Near Krinkelter Wald, Belgium.

Craft, Clarence B. PFC, USA, Company G, 382nd Infantry, 96th Infantry Division; 31 May 1945, Hen Hill, Okinawa, Ryukyu Islands.

*Craig, Robert, Second Lieutenant, USA, 15th Infantry, 3rd Infantry Division; 11 July 1943, Near Faoratta, Sicily.

*Crain, Morris E., Technical Sergeant, USA, Company E, 141st Infantry, 36th Infantry Division; 13 March 1945, Haguenau, France.

*Craw, Demas T., Colonel, USA Air Corps, 8 November 1942, Near Port Lyautey, French Morocco.

Crawford, William J., Pvt., USA, 36th Infantry Division; 13 September 1943, Near Altavilla, Italy.

Crews, John R., Staff Sergeant, USA, Company F, 253rd Infantry, 63rd Infantry Division; 8 April 1945, Near Lobenbacherhof, Germany.

*Cromwell, John Philip, Captain, USN, 19 November 1943, waters off Truk Island while aboard U.S.S. Sculpin.

Currey, Francis S., Sergeant, USA, Company K, 120th Infantry, 30th Infantry Division; 21 December 1944, Malmedy, Belgium.

Dahlgren, Edward C., Second Lieutenant, (then sergeant) USA, Company E, 142nd Infantry, 36th Infantry Division; 11 February 1945, Oberhoffen, France.

Dalessondro, Peter J., Technical Sergeant, USA, Company E, 39th Infantry, 9th Infantry Division; 22 December 1944, Near Kalterherberg, Germany.

Daly, Michael J., Captain (then Lieutenant), USA, Company A, 15th Infantry, 3rd Infantry Division; 18 April 1945, Nuremberg, Germany.

*Damato, Anthony Peter, Corporal, USMC, 19-20 February 1944, Engebi Island, Eniwetok Atoll, Marshall Islands.

*David, Albert Leroy, Lieutenant Jr. Grade, USN, 4 June 1944, Off French West Africa while attached to U.S.S. Pillsbury.

Davis, Charles W., Major, USA, 25th Infantry Division; 12 January 1943, Guadalcanal.

*Davis, George Fleming, Commander, USN, Commanding Officer of the U.S.S. Walke, 6 January 1945, Lingayen Gulf; Luzon, Philippine Islands.

*Dealey, Samuel David, Commander, USN, Commanding Officer of the U.S.S. Harder, 23 —24 August 1944, Off west coast of Luzon, Philippine Islands.

DeBlanc, Jefferson Joseph, Captain, USMC, Reserve, 31 January 1943, Kolombangara Island in the Solomon Group.

*DeFranzo, Arthur F., Staff Sergeant, USA, 1st Infantry Division; 10 June 1944, Near Vaubadon, France.

*DeGlopper, Charles N., PFC, USA, Company, 325th Glider Infantry, 82nd Airborne Division; 9 June 1944, Merderet River at La Fiere, France.

*Deleau, Emile, Jr., Sergeant, USA, Company A, 142nd Infantry, 36th Infantry Division; 1-2 February 1945, Oberhoffen, France.

Dervishian, Ernest H., Second Lieutenant, USA, 34th Infantry Division; 23 May 1944, Near Cisterna, Italy.

*Diamond, James H., PFC, USA, Company D 21st Infantry, 24th Infantry Division; 8-14 May 1945, Mintal, Mindanao, Philippine Islands.

*Dietz, Robert H. Staff Sergeant, USA, Company A, 38th Armored Infantry Battalion, 7th Armored Division; 29 March 1945, Kirchain, Germany.

Doolittle, James H. (Air Mission), Brigadier General, USA Air Corps., 18 April 1942, Over Japan.

Doss, Desmond T., PFC, USA, Medical Detachment, 307th Infantry, 77th Infantry Division; 29 April-21 May 1945, Okinawa, Ryukyu Islands.

Drowley, Jesse R. Staff Sergeant, USA, Americal Infantry Division; 30 January 1944, Bougainville, Solomon Islands.

Dunham, Russell E., Technician Sergeant, USA, Company I, 30th Infantry, 3rd Infantry Division; 8 January 1945, Near Kayserberg, France.

Dunlap, Robert Hugo, Captain, USA Reserve, Company C, 1st Battalion, 26th Marines, 5th Marine Division; 20 and 21 February 1945, Iwo Jima, Volcano Islands.

*Dutko, John W., PFC, USA, 3rd Infantry Division; 23 May 1944, Near Ponte Rotto, Italy.

*Dyess, Aquilla James, Lieutenant Colonel, USMC Reserve, 1 and 2 February 1944, Commanding Officer of the 1st Battalion, 24th Marines, (rein.) 4th Marine Division, Namur Island, Kwajalein Atoll, Marshall Islands.

Edson, Merritt Austin, Colonel, USMC, Commanding Officer of the 1st Marine Raider Battalion, 13-14 September 1942, Solomon Islands.

Ehlers, Walter D., Staff Sergeant, USA, 18th Infantry, 1st Infantry Division, 9-10 June 1944, Near Goville, France.

*Elrod, Henry Talmage, Captain, USMC, Marine Fighting Squadron 211; 8 to 23 December 1941, Wake Island.

*Endl, Gerard L., Staff Sergeant, USA, 32nd Infantry Division; 11 July 1944, Near Anamo, New Guinea.

*Epperson, Harold Glenn, PFC, USMC Reserve, 1st Battalion, 6th Marines, 2nd Marine Division; 25 June 1944, Saipan in the Marianas.

Erwin, Henry E. (Air Mission), Staff Sergeant, USA Air Corps., 52nd Bombardment Squadron, 29th Bombardment Group, 20th Air Force; 12 April 1945, Koriyama, Japan.

*Eubanks, Ray E., Sergeant, USA, Company D, 503rd Parachute Infantry; 23 July 1944, Noemfoor Island, Dutch New Guinea.

*Evans, Ernest Edwin, Commander, USN, Commanding Officer of the U.S.S. Johnston; 25 October 1944, Off Samar, Philippine Islands.

Everhart, Forrest E., Technical Sergeant, USA, Company H, 359th Infantry, 90th Infantry Division; 12 November 1944, Near Kerling, France.

*Fardy, John Peter, Corporal, USMC, Company C, 1st Battalion, 1st Marines, 1st Marine Division; 7 May 1945, Okinawa Shima, in the Ryukyu Islands.

*Femoyer, Robert E. (Air Mission), Second Lieutenant, 711th Bombing Squadron, 447th Bomber Group, USA Air Corps.; 2 November 1944, Over Merseburg, Germany.

Fields, James H., First Lieutenant, USA, 10th Armored Infantry, 4th Armored Division; 27 September 1944, Rechicourt, France.

Finn, John William, Lieutenant, USN, 7 December 1941, Naval Air Station, Kaneohe Bay, Territory of Hawaii.

Fisher, Almond E., Second Lieutenant, USA, Company E, 157th Infantry, 45th Infantry Division; 12-13 September 1944, Near Gramont, France.

*Flaherty, Francis C., Ensign, US Naval Reserve, 7 December 1941, Pearl Harbor.

*Fleming, Richard E., Captain, USMC Reserve, Flight Officer Marine Scout-Bombing Squadron 241; 4-5 June 1942, Battle of Midway.

Fluckey, Eugene Bennett, Commander, USN, Commanding U.S.S. Barb; 19 December 1944, Along coast of China.

Foss, Joseph Jacob, Captain, USMC Reserve, Fighting Squadron 121, 1st Marine Aircraft Wing; 9 October to 19 November 1942, Over Guadalcanal.

*Foster, William Adelbert, PFC, USMC, 3rd Battalion, 1st Marines, 1st Marine Division; 2 May 1945, Okinawa Shima in the Ryukyu Chain.

*Fournier, William G., Sergeant, USA, Company M, 35th Infantry, 25th Infantry Division; 10 January 1943, Mount Austen, Guadalcanal, Solomon Islands.

*Fowler, Thomas W., Second Lieutenant USA, 1st Armored Division; 23 May 1944, Near Carano, Italy.

*Fryar, Elmer E., Private, USA, Company E, 11th Parachute Infantry, 11th Airborne Division; 8 December 1944, Leyte, Philippine Islands.

Funk, Leonard A., Jr., First Sergeant, USA, Company C, 508th Parachute Infantry, 82nd Airborne Division; 29 January 1945, Holzheim, Belgium.

Fuqua, Samuel Glenn, Captain, USN, U.S.S. Arizona; 7 December 1941, Pearl Harbor, Territory of Hawaii.

Galer, Robert Edward, Major, USMC, Commander Marine Fighter Squadron 244, Solomon Island Campaign. During a 29 day period Major Galer knocks down eleven enemy Planes; total kill for his Squadron 27 Planes.

*Galt, William Wylie, Captain, USA, 168th Infantry, 34th Infantry Division; 29 May 1944, At Villa Crocetta, Italy.

"Gammon, Archer T., Staff Sergeant, USA, Company A, 9th Armored Infantry Battalion, 6th Armored Division; 11 January 1945, Near Bastogne, Belgium.

Garcia, Marcario, Staff Sergeant, USA, Company B, 22nd Infantry, 4th Infantry Division; 27 November 1944, Near Grosshau, Germany.

Garman, Harold A., Private, USA, Company B, 5th Medical Battalion, 5th Infantry Division; 25 August 1944, Near Montereau, France.

Gary, Donald Arthur, Lieutenant Junior Grade, USN, U.S.S. Franklin; 19 March 1945, Japanese Home Islands near Kobe, Japan.

Gerstung Robert E. Technical Sergeant, USA, Company H, 3313th Infantry, 79th Infantry Division; 19 December 1944, Siegfried Line near Berg Germany.

*Gibson, Eric G., Technician Fifth Grade, USA, 3rd Infantry Division 28 January 1944, Near Isola Bella, Italy.

*Gilmore, Howard Walter, Commander, USN, Commanding Officer U.S.S. Growler; 10 January to 7 February 1943, Southwest Pacific. remembered for his immortal words: "TAKE HER DOWN."

*Gonsalves, Harold, PFC, USMC, 4th Battalion, 15th Marines, 6th Marine Division; 15 April 1945, Okinawa Shima in the Ryukyu Chain.

*Gonzales, David M., PFC, USA, Company A, 127th Infantry, 32nd Infantry Division; 25 April 1945, Villa Verde Trail, Luzon, Philippine Islands.

Gordon, Nathan Green, Lieutenant, USN, Commander of Catalina Patrol Plane; 15 February 1944, Bismarck Sea.

*Gott, Donald J.(Air Mission), First Lieutenant, USA Air Corps., 729th Bomber Squadron, 42nd Bombardment Group; 9 November 1944, Saarbrucken, Germany.

*Grabiarz, William J., PFC, USA, Troop E, 5th Cavalry Division; 23 February 1945, Manila, Luzon, Philippine Islands.

*Gray, Ross Franklin, Sergeant, USMC Reserve, Company A, 1st Battalion, 25th Marines, 4th Marine Division; 21 February 1945, Iwo Jima, Volcano Islands.

Gregg, Stephen R., Second Lieutenant, USA, 142nd Infantry, 36th Infantry Division; 27 August 1944, Near Montelimar, France.

*Gruennert, Kenneth E., Sergeant, USA, Company L, 127th Infantry, 32nd Infantry Division; 24 December 1942, Near Buna, New Guinea.

*Gurke, Henry, PFC, USMC, 3rd Marine Raider Battalion; 9 November 1943, Solomon Islands.

Hall, George J., Staff Sergeant USA, 135th Infantry, 43th Infantry Division; 23 May 1944, Near Anzio, Italy.

Hall, Lewis, Technician Fifth Grade, USA, Company M, 35th Infantry, 25th Infantry Division; 10 January 1943, Mount Austen, Guadalcanal, Solomon Islands.

Hall, William E., Lieutenant, Junior Grade, US Naval Reserve, 7 and 8 May 1942, Coral Sea.

*Hallman, Sherwood H., Staff Sergeant, USA, 175th Infantry, 29th Infantry Division; 13 September 1944, Brest Brittany, France.

*Halyburton, William David, Jr., Pharmacist's Mate Second Class, US Naval Reserve, 2nd Battalion, 5th Marines, 1st Marine Division; 10 May 1945, Okinawa Shima in the Ryukyu Chain.

Hamilton, Pierpont M., Major, USA Air Corps., 8 November 1942, Near Port Lyautey, French Morocco.

*Hammerberg, Owen Francis Patrick, Boatswain's Mate Second Class, USN, 17 February 1945, West Loch, Pearl Harbor.

*Hansen, Dale Merlin, Company E, 2nd Battalion, 1st Marines, 1st Marine Division; 7 May 1945, Okinawa Shima in the Ryukyu Chain.

*Hanson, Robert Murray, First Lieutenant, USMC Reserve; Marine Fighting Squadron 215; 1 November 1943 , Bougainville Island, and 24 January 1944, New Britain Island.

*Harmon, Roy W. Sergeant USA, Company C, 362nd Infantry, 91st Infantry Division; 12 July 1944, Near Cassaglia, Italy.

*Harr, Harry R., Corporal, USA, Company D, 124th Infantry, 31st Infantry Division; 5 June 1945, Near Maglamin, Mindanao, Philippine Islands.

Harrell, William George, Sergeant, USMC, 1st Battalion, 28th Marines, 5th Marine Division; 3 March 1945, Iwo Jima, Volcano Islands.

*Harris, James L., Second Lieutenant, USA, 756th Tank Battalion; 7 October 1944, At Vagney, France.

*Hastings, Joe R., PFC, USA, Company C., 386th Infantry, 97th Infantry Division; 12 April 1945, Drabenderhohe, Germany.

*Hauge, Louis James, Jr., Corporal, USMC Reserve, Company C, 1st Battalion, 1st Marines, 1st Marine Division; 14 May 1945, Okinawa Shima.

Hawk, John D., Sergeant, USA, Company E, 359th Infantry, 90th Infantry Division; 2 August 1944, Near Chambois, France.

*Hawkins, William Dean, First Lieutenant, USMC, Scout Sniper Platoon; 20 and 21 November 1943, Tarawa, Gilbert Islands.

Hawks, LLoyd C. PFC, USA, Army Medical Detachment, 30th Infantry, 3rd Infantry Division; 30 January 1944, Near Carano, Italy.

*Hedrick, Clinton M., Technical Sergeant, USA, Company I, 194th Glider Infantry, 17th Airborne Division; 27-28 March 1945, Near Lembek, Germany.

Hendrix, James R., Private, USA, Company C, 53rd Armored Infantry Battalion, 4th Armored Division; 26 December 1944, Near Assenois, Belgium.

*Henry, Robert T., Private, USA, 6th Infantry, 1st Infantry Division; 3 December 1944, Luchem, Germany.

Herrera, Silvestre S., PFC, USA, Company E, 142 Infantry, 36th Infantry Division; 15 March 1945, Near Mertzwiller, Germany.

Herring, Rufus G. Lieutenant, US Naval Reserve, LCI (G) 449; 17 February 1945, Iwo Jima.

*Hill Edwin Joseph, Chief Boatswain, USN, U.S.S Nevada; 7 December 1941, Pearl Harbor.

Horner, Freeman V., Staff Sergeant, USA, Company K, 19th Infantry, 30th Infantry Division; 16 November 1944, Wurselen, Germany.

Howard, James H. (Air Mission), Colonel, USA Air Corps., 11 January 1944, Over Oshersleben, Germany.

Huff, Paul B., Corporal, USA, 509th Parachute Infantry Battalion; 8 February 1944, Near Carano, Italy.

*Hughes, LLoyd H. (Air Mission), Second Lieutenant, US Army Air Corps., 564th Bomber Squadron, 389th Bomber Group, 9th Air Force; 1 August 1943, Ploesti Raid, Rumania.

*Hutchins, Johnnie David, Seaman First Class, US Naval Reserve, serving aboard a Landing Ship, Tank; 4 September 1943, Lae, New Guinea.

*Jachman, Isadore S. Staff Sergeant, USA, Company B, 513th Parachute Infantry Regiment; 4 January 1945, Flaierge, Belgium.

Jackson, Arthur J., PFC, USMC, 3rd Battalion, 7th Marines, 1st Marine Division; 18 September 1944, Island of Peleliu in the Palau Group.

Jacobson, Douglas Thomas, PFC, USMC Reserve, 3rd Battalion, 23rd Marines, 4th Marine Division; 26 February 1945, Iwo Jima, Volcano Islands.

*Jerstad, John L. (Air Mission), Major, USA Air Corps., 9th Air Force; 1 August 1943, Ploesti Raid, Rumania.

*Johnson, Elden H., Private, USA, 15th Infantry, 3rd Infantry Division; 3 June 1944, Near Valmontone, Italy.

Johnson, Leon W. (Air Mission), Colonel, USA Air Corps., 44th Bomber Group, 9th Air Force; 1 August 1943 Ploesti Raid, Rumania.

Johnson Leroy, Sergeant, USA, Company K, 126th Infantry, 32nd Infantry Division; 15 December 1944, Near Limon, Leyte, Philippine Islands.

Johnson, Oscar G., Sergeant, USA, Company B, 363rd Infantry, 91st Infantry Division; 16-18 September 1944, Near Scarperia, Italy.

Johnston, William J., PFC, USA, Company G, 180th Infantry, 45th Division; 17-19 February 1944, Near Padiglione, Italy.

*Jones, Herbert Charpoit, Ensign, US Naval Reserve, U.S.S. California; 7 December 1941, Pearl Harbor.

*Julian, Joseph Rodolph, Platoon Sergeant, USMC, 1st Battalion, 27th Marines, 5th Marine Division; 9 March 1945, Iwo Jima, in the Volcano Islands.

*Kandle, Victor L., First Lieutenant, USA, 15th Infantry, 3rd Infantry Division; 9 October 1944, Ner La Forge, France.

Kane, John R. (Air Mission), Colonel, USA Air Corps., 9th Air Force; 1 August 1943, Ploesti Raid, Rumania.

Kearby, Neel E (Air Mission), Colonel, USA Air Corps., 11 October 1943, Near Wewak, New Guinea.

*Keathley, George D., Staff Sergeant, USA, 85th Infantry Division; 14 September 1944, Mt. Altuzzo, Italy.

Kefurt, Gus, Staff Sergeant, USA, Company K, 15th Infantry, 3rd Infantry Division; 23-24 December 1944, Near Bennwihr, France

*Kelley, Jonah E., Staff Sergeant, USA, 311th Infantry, 78th Infantry Division; 30-31 January 1945, Kesternich, Germany.

*Kelley, Ova A. Private, USA, Company A, 382nd Infantry, 96th Infantry Division; 8 December 1944, Leyte, Philippine Islands.

Kelly, Charles E. Corporal, USA, Company L, 143rd Infantry, 36th Infantry Division; 13 September 1943, Near Altvilla, Italy.

*Kelly, John D. Technical Sergeant (then Corporal), USA, Company E, 314th Infantry, 79th Infantry Division; 25 June

1944, Fort du Roule, Cherbourg, France.

Kelly, Thomas J., Corporal, USA, Medical Detachment, 48th Infantry Battalion, 7th Armored Division; 5 April 1945, Alemert, Germany.

*Keppler, Reinhardt John, Boatswain's Mate First Class, USN, U.S.S. San Francisco; 12-13 November 1942, Solomon Islands.

Kerstetter, Dexter, PFC, USA, Company C, 130th Infantry, 33rd Infantry Division; 13 April 1945, Near Galiano, Italy.

*Kessler, Patrick L., PFC, USA, Company K, 30th Infantry, 3rd Infantry Division; 23 May 1944, Near Ponte Rotto, Italy.

*Kidd, Isaac Campbell, Rear Admiral, USA, U.S.S. Arizona; 7 December 1941, Pearl Harbor.

*Kimbro, Truman, Technician Fourth Grade, USA, Company C, 2nd Engineer Combat Battalion, 2nd Infantry Division; 19 December 1942, Near Rocherath, Belgium.

*Kiner, Harold G., Private, USA, Company F, 117th Infantry, 30th Infantry Division; 2 October 1944, Near Palenberg, Germany.

*Kingsley, David R. (Air Mission), Second Lieutenant, USA Air Corps., 97th Bombardment Group, 15th Air Force; 23 June 1944, Ploesti Raid, Rumania.

*Kinser, Elbert Luther, Sergeant, USMC Reserve, Company I, 3rd Battalion, 1st Marines, 1st Marine Division; 4 May 1944, Okinawa Shima in the Ryukyu Chain.

Kisters, Gerry H., Second Lieutenant (then Sergeant), USA, 2nd Armored Division; 31 July 1943, Near Gagliano, Italy.

Knappenberger, Alton W., PFC, USA, 3rd Infantry Division; 1 February 1944, Near Littoria, Italy.

*Knight, Jack L. First Lieutenant, USA, 124th Cavalry Regiment, Mars Task Force; 2 February 1945, Near Loi-Kang Burma.

*Knight, Raymond L. Air Mission), First Lieutenant, USA Air Corps. 24-25 April 1945, In Northern Po Valley, Italy.

*Kraus, Richard Edward, PFC, USMC, 8th Amphibious Tractor Battalion, Fleet Marine Force; 5 October 1944, Peleliu, Palau Islands.

*Krotiak, Anthony L., PFC, USA, Company L, 148th Infantry, 37th Infantry Division; 8 May 1945, Balete Pass, Luzon, Philippine Islands.

*La Belle, James Dennis, PFC, USMC, 27th Marines, 5th Marine Division; 8 March 1945, Iwo Jima, Volcano Islands.

Lawley, William R., Jr. (Air Mission), First Lieutenant USA Air Corps., 364th Bomber Squadron, 305th Bomber Group; 20 February 1944 Over Europe.

Laws, Robert E., Staff Sergeant, USA, Company G, 169th Infantry, 43rd Infantry Division; 12 January 1945, Pangasinan Province, Luzon, Philippine Islands.

Lee, Daniel W. First Lieutenant, USA, Troop A, 117th Cavalry Reconnaissance Squadron; 2 September 1944, Montreval, France.

Leims, John Harold, Second Lieutenant, USMC Reserve, Company B, 1st Battalion, 9th Marines, 3rd Marine Division; 7 March 1945, Iwo Jima, Volcano Islands.

*Leonard, Turney W., First Lieutenant USA Company C, 893rd Tank Destroyer Battalion; 4-6 November 1944, Kommerscheidt, Germany.

Lester Fred Faulkner, Hospital Apprentice First Class, USN, 1st Battalion, 22nd Marines, 6th Marine Division; 8 June 1945, Okinawa Shima in the Ryukyu Chain.

*Lindsey, Darrell R. (Air Mission), Captain, USA Air Corps. 9 August 1944, LIsle Adam railroad bridge over the Seine in occupied France.

Lindsey, Jake W., Technical Sergeant, USA, 16th Infantry, 1st Infantry Division; 16 November 1945, Near Hamich, Germany

*Lindstrom, Floyd K., PFC, USA, 3rd Infantry Division; 11 November 1943, Near Mignano, Italy.

*Lloyd, Edgar H., First Lieutenant, USA, Company E, 319th Infantry 80th Infantry Division; 14 September 1944, Near Pompey France.

*Lobauch, Donald R., Private USA, 127th Infantry, 32nd Infantry Division; 22 July 1944; Near Afua, New Guinea.

Logan, James M., Sergeant, USA, 36th Infantry Division; 9 September 1943, Near Salerno, Italy.

Lopez, Jose M., Sergeant, USA, 23rd Infantry, 2nd Infantry Division; 17 December 1944, Near Krinkelt, Belgium.

Lucas, Jacklyn Harold, PFC, USMC Reserve, 1st Battalion, 26th Marines, 5th Marine Division; 20 February 1945, Iwo Jima, Volcano Islands.

*Lummus, Jack, First Lieutenant ,USA Reserve, 2nd Battalion, 27th Marine Division; 8 March 1945, Iwo Jima, Volcano Islands.

Mabry, George L., Jr, Lieutenant Colonel, USA, 2nd Battalion, 8th Infantry, 4th Infantry Division; 20 November 1944; Huertgen Forest Near Schevenhutte, Germany.

MacArthur, Douglas, General, USA, commanding U.S. Army Forces in the Far East; April 1942; Bataan Peninsula

MacGillivray, Charles A., Sergeant, USA, Company I, 7th Infantry, 44th Infantry Division; 1 January 1945, Near Woelfing, France.

*Magrath, John D., PFC, USA, Company G, 85th Infantry, 10th Mountain Division; 14 April 1945, Near astel d'Aiano Italy.

*Mann, Joe E, PFC, USA, Company H, 502nd Parachute Infantry, 101st Airborne Division; 18 September 1944, Best, Holland.

*Martin, Harry Linn, First Lieutenant USMC Reserve, Company C, 5th Pioneer Battalion, 5th Marine Division; 26 March 1945, Iwo Jima, Volcano Island.

*Martinez, Joe ,P., Private, USA, Company K, 32nd Infantry, 7th Infantry Division; 26 May 1943 On Attu, Aleutians.

*Mason Leonard Foster, PFC, USMC, 2nd Battalion 3rd Marines, 3rd Marine Division; 22 July 1944, Asan-Adelup Beachhead, Guam.

*Mathies, Archibald (Air Mission), Sergeant, USA Air Corps. 510th Bomber Squadron 351st Bomber Group; 20 February 1944, Over Europe.

*Mathis Jack W. (Air Mission), First Lieutenant, USA Air Corps. 359th Bomber Squadron, 303rd Bomber Group; 18 March 1943, Over Vegesack, Germany.

Maxwell, Robert D., Technician Fifth Grade, USA, 7th Infantry, 3rd Infantry Division; 7 September 1944, Near Besancon, France.

*May, Martin O. PFC, USA, 307th Infantry, 77th Infantry Division; 19-21 April 1945 Iegusuku-Yama, Ie Shima, Ryukyu Islands.

Mayfield Melvin, Corporal, USA, Company D, 20th Infantry, 6th Infantry Division; 29 July 1945, Cordillera Mountains, Luzon, Philippine Islands.

McCall Thomas E., Staff Sergeant, USA Company F, 143rd Infantry, 36th Infantry Division; 22 January 1944, Near San Angelo Italy.

McCampbell, David, Commander USN, Air Group 15; 19 June 1944, 1st and 2nd battles of the Philippine Sea.

McCandless, Bruce, Commander, USN, U.S.S. San Francisco; 12-13 November 1942, Battle off Savo Island.

*McCard Robert Howard, Gunnery Sergeant, USMC, Company A, 4th Tank Battalion 4th Marine Division; 16 June 1944 Saipan, Marianas Islands.

McCarter, Lloyd G. Private, USA, 503rd Parachute Infantry Regiment; 16-19 February 1945, Corregidor, Philippine Islands.

McCarthy Joseph Jeremiah, Captain USMC Reserve, 2nd Battalion, 24th Marines 4th Marine Division; 21 February 1945, Iwo Jima Volcano Islands.

McCool, Richard Miles, Jr. Lieutenant, USN, U.S.S. LSC(L)(3)122; 10-11 June 1945, Off Okinawa.

McGaha Charles L., Master Sergeant USA, Company G, 5th Infantry, 25th Infantry Division; 7 February 1945, Near Lupao, Luzon Philippine Islands.

McGarity, Vernon, Technical Sergeant USA, Company L, 93rd Infantry Division; 16 December 1944, Near Krinkelt, Belgium.

*McGee, William D. Private, USA, Medical Detachment 304th Infantry, 76th Infantry Division; 18 March 1945, Near Mulheim, Germany.

McGill, Troy A. Sergeant, USA, Troop G, 5th Cavalry Regiment, 1st Cavalry Division; 4 March 1944, Los Negros Islands, Admiralty Group.

*McGraw, Francis X. PFC, USA, Company H, 26th Infantry, 1st Infantry Division; 19 November 1944, Near Schevenhutte, Germany.

*McGuire Thomas B., Jr. (Air Mission), Major, USA Air Corps, 5th Air Force; 25-26 December 1944, Over Luzon, Philippine Islands.

McKinney, John R.,Sergeant, (then Private) U.S. Army, Company A, 123rd Infantry, 33rd Infantry Division; 11 May 1945, Tayabas Province, Luzon, Philippines.

*McTureous, Robert Miller, Jr., Private, USMC, 3rd Battalion, 29th Marines, 6th Marine Division; Okinawa.

*McVeigh John J., Sergeant, USA, Company H, 23rd Infantry, 2nd Infantry Division; 29 August 1944, Near Brest, France.

*McWhorter, William A., PFC, USA, Company M, 126th Infantry, 32nd Infantry Division; 5 December 1944, Leyte, Philippine Islands.

Meagher, John, Technical Sergeant, USA, Company E, 305th Infantry, 77th Infantry Division; 19 June 1945, Near Ozato, Okinawa.

Merli, Gino J. Pfc, USA, 18th Infantry 1st Infantry Division; 4-5 September 1944, Near Sars la Bruyere, Belgium.

*Merrell, Joseph F., Private, USA, Company I, 15th Infantry, 3rd Infantry Division; April 1945, Near Lohe, Germany.

*Messerschmidt, Harold O. Sergeant, USA Company L, 30th Infantry, 3rd Infantry Division; 17 September 1944, Near Radden, France.

*Metzger, William E., Jr. (Air Mission), Second Lieutenant, USA Air Corps; 729th Bomber Squadron, 452nd Bombardment Group; 9 November 1944, Saarbrucken, Germany.

848

Michael, Edward S. (Air Mission), First Lieutenant, USA Air Corps, 364th Bomber Squadron, 305th Bomber Group; 1 April 1944, Over Germany.

*Michael, Harry J.Second Lieutenant, USA, Company L, 318th Infantry, 80th Infantry Division; 14 March 1945, Near Neiderzerf, Germany.

*Miller, Andrew, Staff Sergeant USA Company G, 377th Infantry, 95th Infantry Division;16-29 November 1944, From Woippy, France, through Metz to Kerprich Hemmersdorf, Germany.

Mills, James H. Private, USA, Company F, 15th Infantry, 3rd Infantry Division; 24 May 1944, Near Cisterna Di Littoria, Italy.

*Minick, John W., Staff Sergeant, USA, Company I, 121st Infantry, 8th Infantry Division; 21 November 1944, Near Huertgen, Germany.

*Minue, Nicholas, Private USA, Company A, 6th Armored Infantry, 1st Armored Division; 28 April 1943, Near Medjez-el Bab, Tunisia.

*Monteith Jimmie W., Jr. First Lieutenant, US, 16th Infantry, 1st Infantry Division; 6 June 1944, Near Colleville-sur-Mer, France.

Montgomery, Jack C. First Lieutenant, USA, 45th Infantry Division; 22 February 1944, Near Padiglione, Italy.

*Moon, Harold H., Jr. Private USA, Company G, 34th Infantry, 24th Infantry Division; 2 October 944, Pawig Leyte, Philippine Islands.

Morgan, John C. (Air Mission), Second Lieutenant, USA Air Corps, 326th Bomber Squadron, 92nd Bomber Group; 28 July 1943, Over Europe.

*Moskala, Edward J., PFC, USA Company C, 383rd Infantry, 96th Infantry Division; 9 April 1945 Kakazu Ridge Okinawa, Ryukyu Islands.

*Mower, Charles E. Sergeant, USA, Company A, 34th Infantry, 24th Infantry Division; 3 November 1944, Near Capoocan, Leyte, Philippine Islands.

*Muller, Joseph E. Sergeant, USA, Company B, 305th Infantry, 77th Infantry Division; 15-16 May 1945 , Near Ishimmi, Okinawa, Ryukyu Islands.

*Munemori, Sadao S. PFC, USA, Company A, 100th Infantry, 442nd Combat Team; 5 April 1945, Near Servezza, Italy.

*Munro, Douglas Albert, Signalman First Class, U.S. Coast Guard, 27 September 1942, Point Cruz, Guadalcanal.

Murphy, Audie L., Second Lieutenant, USA, Company B, 15th Infantry, 3rd Infantry Division; 6 January 1945, Near Holtzwihr, France.

*Murphy Frederic K. PFC, USA, Medical Detachment, 259th Infantry, 65th Infantry Division; 18 March 1945, Siegfried Line at Saarlautern, Germany.

Murray, Charles P. Jr., First Lieutenant, USA, Company C 30th Infantry, 3rd Infantry Division; 6 December 1944, Near Kaysersberg, France.

*Nelson, William L. Sergeant, USA, 60th Infantry, 9th Infantry Division; 4 April 1943, At Djebel Dardys, Northwest of Sedjenane, Tunisia.

Neppel, Ralph G., Sergeant, USA, Company M, 329th Infantry, 83rd Infantry Division; 14 December 1944, Birgel Germany.

Nett, Robert P. Captain (then Lieutenant), USA, Company E, 305th Infantry, 77th Infantry Division; 14 December 1944, Near Cognon, Leyte, Philippine Islands.

*New, John Dury, PFC, USMC, 2nd Battalion, 7th Marines, 1st Marine Division; 25 September 1944, Peleliu Island, Palau Group.

Newman, Beryl R., First Lieutenant, USA, 133rd Infantry, 34th Infantry Division; 26 May 1944, Near Cisterna, Italy.

*Nininger, Alexander R., Jr. Second Lieutenant, USA, 57th Infantry, Philippine Scouts; 12 January 1942, Near Abucay, Bataan, Philippine Islands.

*O'Brien, William J., Lieutenant Colonel, USA, 1st Battalion, 105th Infantry, 27th Infantry Division; 20 June through 7 July 1944, Saipan, Marianas Islands.

O'Callahan, Joseph Timothy, Commander (Chaplain Corps), U.S. Naval Reserve, U.S.S. Franklin; 19 March 1945, Near Kobe, Japan.

Ogden, Carlos C., First Lieutenant, USA, Company K, 314th Infantry, 79th Infantry Division; 25 June 1944, Near Fort du Roule, France.

O'Hare, Edward Henry, USN, Lieutenant, Fighting Squadron 3; 20 February 1942, Pacific.

O'Kane, Richard Hetherington, Commander, USN, U.S.S. *Tang*; 23 and 24 October 1944, Vicinity Philippine Islands

*Olson, Arlo L., Captain, USA. 15th Infantry, 3rd Infantry Division; 13 October 1943, Crossing of the Volturno River, Italy.

*Olson, Truman O. Sergeant, USA, Company B, 7th Infantry, 3rd Infantry Division; 30-31 January 1944, Near Cisterna di Littoria, Italy.

Oresko, Nicholas, Master Sergeant, USA, Company C, 302nd Infantry, 94th Infantry Division; 23 January 1945, Near Tetting ton, Germany.

*Owens, Robert Allen, Sergeant, USMC, 1 November 1943 Cape Torokina Bougainville, Solomon Islands.

*Ozbourn, Joseph William, Private, USMC, 1st Battalion, 23rd Marines, 4th Marine Division; 30 July 1944, Tinian Island, Marianas.

Paige, Mitchell, Platoon Sergeant, USMC, 26 October 1942, Solomons.

*Parle John Joseph, Ensign, U.S. Naval Reserve, U.S.S. LST 375; 9-10 July 1943, Sicily.

*Parrish, Laverne, Technician 4th Class, USA, Medical Detachment; 161st Infantry, 25th Infantry Division; 18-24 January 1945, Binalonan, Luzon, Philippine Islands.

*Pease, Harl, Jr. (Air Mission), Captain, USA Air Corps, Heavy Bomber Squadron; 6-7 August 1942, Near Rabaul, New Britain.

*Peden, Forrest E., Technician 5th Grade, USA, Battery C, 10th Field Artillery Battalion, 3rd Infantry Division; 3 February 1945 Near Beisheim, France.

*Pendleton, Jack J. Staff Sergeant, USA, Company I 120th Infantry, 30th Infantry Division; 12 October 1944, Bardenberg, Germany.

*Peregory Frank D. Technical Sergeant, USA, Company K, 116th Infantry, 29th Infantry Division; 8 June 1944, Grandecampee, France.

*Perez Manuel, Jr., PFC USA,Company A, 511th Parachute Infantry, 11th Airborne Division; 13 February 1945, Fort William McKinley, Luzon, Philippine Islands.

*Peters, George J., Private, USA, Company G, 507th Parachute Infantry, 17th Airborne Division; 24 March 1945, Near Fluren, Germany.

*Peterson, George, Staff Sergeant, USA, Company K, 18th Infantry, 1st Infantry Division; 30 March 1945, Near Eisern, Germany.

*Peterson, Oscar Verner, Chief Watertender, USN, U.S.S. Neosho; 7 May 1942, Battle of the Coral Sea.

*Petrarca, Frank J., PFC, USA, Medical Detachment, 145th Infantry, 37th Infantry Division; 27 July 1943, At Horseshoe Hill, New Georgia, Solomon Islands.

Pharris, Jackson Charles, Lieutenant, USN, U.S.S. California 7 December 1941, Pearl Harbor, Territory of Hawaii.

*Phelps Wesley, Private, USMC Reserve, 3rd Battalion, 7th Marines, 1st Marine Division; Peleliu Island, Palau Group.

*Phillips, George, Private, USMC Reserve, 2nd Battalion, 28th Marines, 5th Marine Division; 14 March 194 Iwo Jima in the Volcano Islands.

Pierce, Francis Junior, Pharmacist's Mate First Class, 2nd Battalion, 24th Marines, 4th Marine Division; 15 and 16 March 1945, Iwo Jima.

*Pinder, John J., Jr., Technician Fifth Grade, USA, 16th Infantry, 1st Infantry Division; 6 June 1944, Near Colleville-sur-Mer, France.

Pope, Everett Parker, Captain USMC, Company C, 1st Battalion, 1st Marines 1st Marine Division; 19-20 September 1944, Peleliu Island, Palau Group.

*Power, John Vincent, First Lieutenant USMC, 4th Marine Division; Namur Island, Kwajalein Atoll, Marshall Islands.

*Powers, John James, Lieutenant, USN, Bombing Squadron 5, May 4th-8th 1942, Coral Sea area.

Powers, Leo J. PFC, USA, 133rd Infantry 34th Infantry Division; 3 February 1944, Northwest of Cassino, Italy.

Preston, Arthur Murray, Lieutenant, USN Reserve, Torpedo Boat Squadron 3; 16 September 1944, Wasile Bay, Halmahera Island.

*Prussman, Ernest W., PFC, USA 13th Infantry 8th Infantry Division; 8 September 1944 Near Les Brittany France.

*Pucket, Donald D. (Air Mission), First Lieutenant USA Air Corps, 98th Bombardment Group; 9 July 1944, Ploesti Raid, Rumania.

Ramage, Lawson Paterson, Commander, USN, U.S.S. Parche; 31 July 1944, Pacific.

*Ray, Bernard J., First Lieutenant, USA, Company F, 8th Infantry, 4th Infantry Division; 17 November 1944, Huertgen Forrest near Schevenhutte, Germany.

*Reese, James W., Private, USA, 26th Infantry, 1st Infantry Division; 5 August 1943, At Mt. Vassillo, Sicily.

*Reese, John N., Jr. PFC, USA, Company B, 14th Infantry, 37th Infantry Division; 9 February 1945, Paco Railroad Station, Philippine Islands.

*Reeves, Thomas James, Radio Electrician (Warrant Officer), USN, U.S.S. California; 7 December 1941, Pearl Harbor.

*Ricketts, Milton Ernest Lieutenant, USN, U.S.S. Yorktown; 8 May 1942, Battle of the Coral Sea.

*Riordan, Paul F., Second Lieutenant,USA, 34th Infantry Division; 3-8 February 1944, Near Cassino, Italy.

*Roan, Charles Howard, PFC, USMC, 2nd Battalion, 7th Marines, 1st Marine Division; 18 September 1944, Peleliu, Palau Islands.

*Robinson, James E., Jr. First Lieutenant, USA, Batter A, 861st Field Artillery Battalion, 63rd Infantry Division; 6 April 1945, Near Untergriesheim, Germany.

Rodriguez, Cleto, Technical Sergeant (then Private), USA, Company B, 148th Infantry 37th Infantry Division; 9 February 1945, Paco Railrad Station Manila, Philippine Islands.

*Roeder, Robert E.,Captain USA, Company G, 50th Infantry, 88th Infantry Division; 27-28 September 1944, Mt.Battaglia, Italy.

*Rooks Albert Harold, Captain, USN, U.S.S. Houston; 4 to 27 February 1942, Battle of the Java Sea.

*Roosevelt, Theodore, Jr., Brigadier General, USA, 6 June 1944, Normandy Invasion.

Ross, Donald Kirby, Machinist, USA, U.S.S. Nevada; 7 December 1941, Pearl Harbor.

Ross, Wilburn K., Private, USA, Company G 350th Infantry, 3rd Infantry Division; 30 October 1944, Near St. Jacques, France.

Rouh, Carlton Robert, First Lieutenant, USMC Reserve, 1st Battalion, 5th Marines, 1st Marine Division; 15 September 1944, Peleliu Island, Palau Group.

Rudolph Donald E., Second Lieutenant, USA, Company E, 20th Infantry, 6th Infantry Division; 5 February 1945, Munoz, Luzon, Philippine Islands.

*Ruhl, Donald Jack, PFC, USMC, Company E, 28th Marines, 5th Marine Division; 21 February 1945, Iwo Jima, Volcano Islands.

Ruiz, Alejandro R. Renteria, PFC, 165th Infantry, 27th Infantry Division; 28 April 1945, Okinawa, Ryukyu Islands.

*Sadowski, Joseph J. Sergeant USA, 37th Tank Battalion, 4th Armored Division; 14 September 1944 at Valhey, France.

*Sarnoski, Joseph R. (Air Mission), Second Lieutenant, USA Air Corps, 43rd Bomber Group; 16 June 1943, Over Buka Area, Solomon Islands.

*Sayers, Foster J., PFC, USA, Company L, 357th Infantry, 90th Infantry Division; 12 November 1944, Near Thionville, France.

Schaefer, Joseph E. Staff Sergeant USA, Company I, 18th Infantry, 1st Infantry Division; 24 September 1944, Near Stolberg, Germany.

Schauer, Henry, PFC, USA, 3rd Infantry Division; 23-24 May 1944, Near Cisterna, Italy.

Schonland, Herbert Emery, Commander, USN, U.S.S. San Francisco; 12-13 November 1943, Savo Islands.

*Schwab, Albert Earnest, PFC, USMC Reserve, 7 May 1945, Okinawa Shima in the Ryukyu Islands.

*Scott, Norman, Rear Admiral, USN, 11-12 October and 12-13 November 1942, Off Savo Island.

*Scott Robert R. Machinist's Mate First Class, USN, U.S.S. California; 7 December 1941, Pearl Harbor.

Scott, Robert S., Captain (then Lieutenant), USA, 172nd Infantry, 43rd Infantry Division; 29 July 1943, Near Munda Air Strip, New Georgia, Solomon Islands.

Shea, Charles W., Second Lieutenant, USA, Company F, 350th Infantry, 88th Infantry Division; 12 May 1944, Near Mount Damian, Italy.

*Sheridan, Carl V. PFC, USA, Company K, 47th Infantry, 9th Infantry Division; 26 November 1944, Frenzenberg Castle, Weisweiler, German.

*Shockley, William R., PFC, USA, Company L, 128th Infantry, 32nd Infantry Division:

31 March 1945, Villa Verde Trail, Luzon, Philippine Islands.

Shomo, William A. (Air Mission), Major, USA Air Corps, 82nd Tactical Reconnaissance Squadron; 11 January 1945, Over Luzon, Philippine Islands.

*Shoup, Curtis F. Staff Sergeant, USA, Company I, 46th Infantry, 87th Infantry Division; 7 January 1945, Near Tillet, Belgium.

Shoup, David Monroe, Colonel, USMC, Commanding Officer of all USMC troops on Betio Island, Tarawa Atoll, and Gilbert Islands; 20 to 22 November 1943.

Sigler, Franklin Earl, Private, USMC Reserve, 2nd Battalion, 26th Marines 5th Marine Division; 14 March 1945, Iwo Jima, Volcano Islands.

Silk, Edward A. First Lieutenant, USA, Company E, 398th Infantry, 100th Infantry Division; 23 November 1944 Near St. Pravel, France.

Sjogren, John C., Staff Sergeant, USA, Company I, 160th Infantry, 40th Infantry Division; 23 May 1945, Near San Jose Hacienda, Negros, Philippine Islands.

Skaggs, Luther, Jr. PFC USMC Reserve, 3rd Battalion, 3rd Marines, 3rd Marine Division; 21-22 July 1944, Asan-Adelup Beachhead, Guam, Marianas Islands.

Slaton, James D., Corporal, USA, 157th Infantry, 45th Infantry Division; 23 September 1943, Near Oliveto, Italy

*Smith, Furman L., Private, USA, 135th Infantry, 4th Infantry Division; 31 May 1944, Near Lanuvio, Italy.

Smith, John Lucian, Major, USMC, Marine Fighting Squadron 223; August-September 1942, Solomon Islands.

Smith, Maynard H. (Air Mission), Sergeant, USA Air Corps, 423rd Bombardment Squadron, 306th Bomber Group; 1 May 1943, Over Europe.

Soderman, William A., PFC, USA, Company K, 9th Infantry, 2nd Infantry Division; 17 December 1944, Near Rocherath, Belgium.

Sorenson, Richard Keith, Private USMC Reserve, 4th Marine Division; Namur Island, Kwajalein Atoll, Marshall Islands.

*Specker, Joe C. Sergeant, USA, 488th Engineer Combat Battalion; 7 January 1944, At Mount Porchia, Italy.

Spurrier, Junior J. Staff Sergeant, USA, Company G, 134th Infantry 35th Infantry Division; 13 November 1944, Achian, France.

*Squires, John C. Sergeant (then PFC), USA, Company A, 30th Infantry, 3rd Infantry Division; 23-24 April 1944, Near Padiglione, Italy.

*Stein, Tony Corporal, USMC Reserve, Company A, 1st Battalion, 28th Marines, 5th Marine Division; 19 February 1945, Iwo Jima.

Street, George Levick, III, Commander, USN, U.S.S. Tirante; 14 April 1945, Harbor of Quelpart Island, off the coast of Korea.

*Stryker, Stuart S., PFC, USA, Company E, 513th Parachute Infantry, 17th Airborne Division; 24 March 1944 Near Wesel, Germany.

Swett, James Elms, First Lieutenant, USMC Reserve, Marine Fighting Squadron 221, with Marine Aircraft Group 12, 1st Marine Aircraft Wing; 7 April 1943, Solomon Islands area.

*Terry, Seymour W., Captain, USA, Company B, 382nd Infantry, 96th Infantry Division; 11 May 1945, Zebra Hill, Okinawa, Ryukyu Islands.

*Thomas, Herbert Joseph, USMC Reserve, 3rd Marines, 3rd Marine Division; 7 November 1943, Battle at Koromokina River, Bougainville Islands, Solomon Islands.

*Thomas, William H., PFC, USA, 149th Infantry 38th Infantry Division; 22 April 1945 Zambales Mountains, Luzon, Philippine Islands.

*Thomason, Clyde, Sergeant, USMC Reserve, Marine Raider Expedition; 17-18 August 1942, Makin Island.

Thompson, Max, Sergeant, USA, Company K, 18th Infantry, 1st Infantry Division; 18 October 1944, Near Haaren Germany.

*Thorne, Horace M., Corporal, USA, Troop D, 89th Cavalry Reconnaissance Squadron, 9th Armored Division; 21 December 1944, Near Grufflingen, Belgium.

*Thorson, John F., PFC, USA, Company G, 17th Infantry, 7th Infantry Division; 28 October 1944, Dagami, Leyte, Philippine Islands.

*Timmerman, Grant Frederick, Sergeant, USMC, 2nd Battalion, 6th Marines 2nd Marine Division; 8 July 1944, Saipan, Marianas Islands.

*Tomich, Peter, Chief Watertender, USN, U.S.S. Utah; 7 December 1941, Pearl Harbor.

Tominac John J. First Lieutenant, USA, Company I, 15th Infantry, 3rd Infantry Division; 12 September 1944, Saulx de Vesoul, France.

*Towle, John R., Private USA, Company 504th Parachute Infantry, 82nd Airborne Division; 21 September 1944, Near Oosterhout, Holland.

Traedwell, Jack L., Captain, USA, Company F, 180th Infantry, 45th Infantry Division; 18 March 1945, Near Nieder-Wurzbach, Germany.

*Truemper, Walter E. (Air Mission), Second Lieutenant USA Air Corps, 510th Bomber Squadron, 351st Bomber Group; 20 February 1944, Over Europe.

Turner, Day G., Sergeant, USA, Company B, 319th Infantry, 80th Infantry Division; 8 January 1945, At Dahl, Luxembourg.

Turner, George B., PFC, USA, Battery C, 499th Armored Field Artillery Battalion, 14th Armored Division; 33 January 1945, Philippsbourg, France.

Urban, Matthew, Captain (later Lt. Colonel) Company F, 9th Regiment, 2nd Division; 14 June — 3 September 1944 Normandy, St. Lo. Lt. Colonel Urban of Holland, Michigan receives his Medal of Honor during the year 1988; it is presented to him by President Jimmy Carter.

*Valdez, Jose F., PFC, USA, Company B, 7th Infantry, 3rd Infantry Division; 25 January 1945, Near Rosenkrantz, France.

*Vance, Leon R., Jr. (Air Mission), Lieutenant Colonel, USA Air Corps, 489th Bomber Group; 5 June 1944, Over Wimereaux, France.

Vandegrift, Alexander Archer, Major General, USMC, Commanding Officer 1st Marine Division; 7 August to 9 December 1942, Solomon Islands.

*Van Noy, Junior, Private, USA, Headquarters Company, Shore Battalion, Engineer Boat and Shore Regiment; 17 October 1943, Near Finschafen, New Guinea.

*Van Valkenburgh, Franklin, Captain, USN, 7 December 1941, Pearl Harbor.

*Van Voorhis, Bruce Avery, Lieutenant Commander, USN, Squadron Commander, Bombing Squadron 102 and Plane Commander of a PB4Y-1 Bomber; 6 July 1943, Solomon Islands.

*Vaile, Robert M., Second Lieutenant, USA, Company K, 148th Infantry, 37th Infantry Division; 5 February 1945, Manila, Luzon, Philippine Islands.

*Villegas Ysmael R. Staff Sergeant, USA, Company F, 127th Infantry, 32nd Infantry Division; 20 March 1945, Villa Verde Trail, Luzon, Philippine Islands.

Vlug, Dirk J., PFC, USA, 126th Infantry, 32nd Infantry Division; 15 December 1944, Near Limom, Leyte, Philippine Islands.

Vosler, Forrest T. (Air Mission), Technical Sergeant, USA Air Corps, 358th Bomber Squadron, 303rd Bomber Group; 20 December 1943, Over Bremen, Germany.

Wahlen, George Edward, Pharmacist's Mate Second Class, USN, 2nd Battalion, 26th Marines, 5th Marine Division; March 1945, Iwo Jima, Volcano Islands.

Wainwright Jonathan M., General, Commanding U.S. Army Forces in the Philippine Islands; 12 March to 7 May 1942.

*Waler, Kenneth N. (Air Mission), Brigadier General, USA Air Corps, Commander of V Bomber Group; 5 January 1943, Rabaul, New Britain.

*Wallace, Herman C. PFC, USA, Company B, 301st Engineer Combat Infantry Battalion, 76th Infantry Division; 27 February 1945, Near Prumzurley, Germany.

Walsh, Kenneth Ambrose, First Lieutenant, Pilot in Marine Fighter Squadron 124; 15 and 30 August 1943, Solomon Islands.

*Walsh William Gary, Gunnery Sergeant, USMC Reserve, Company G, 3rd Battalion, 27th Marines, 5th Marine Division; 27 February 1945, Iwo Jima, Volcano Islands.

*Ward, James Richard, Seaman First Class, USN, U.S.S. Oklahoma; 7 December 1941, Pearl Harbor.

Ware, Keith L. Lieutenant Colonel, USA, 1st Battalion 15th Infantry 3rd Infantry Division; 26 December 1944 Near Sigolsheim France.

*Warner, Henry F., Corporal, USA Antitank Company, 2nd Battalion, 26th Infantry, 1st Infantry Division; 20-21 December 1944, Near Dom Butgenbach, Belgium.

Watson, Wilson Douglas, Private, USMC Reserve, 2nd Battalion, 9th Marine, 3rd Marine Division; 26 and 27 February 1945, Iwo Jima, Volcano Islands.

*Waugh, Robert T. First Lieutenant, USA, 339th Infantry, 85th Infantry Division; 11-14 May 1944, Near Tremensucli, Italy.

Waybur, David C., First Lieutenant, USA, 3rd Reconnaissance Troop, 3rd Infantry Division; 17 July 1943, Near Agrigento, Sicily, Italy.

*Weicht, Ellis R., Sergeant, USA, Company F, 142nd Infantry Division; 3 December 1944, St. Hippolyte, France.

*Wetzel, Walter C., PFC, USA, 13th Infantry 8th Infantry Division; 3 April 1945, Birken, Germany.

Whiteley, Eli, First Lieutenant, USA, Company L, 15th Infantry, 3rd Infantry Division; 27 December 1944, Sigolsheim, France.

Whittington, Hulon B., Sergeant, USA, 41st Armored Infantry, 2nd Armored Division; 29 July 1944, Near Grimesnil, France.(EP Wiedorfer, Paul J., Staff Sergeant (then Private) USA, Company G, 318th Infantry, 80th Infantry Division; 25 December 1944, Near Chaumont, France.

*Wigle, Thomas W., Second Lieutenant, USA, Company K, 135th Infantry, 34th Infantry Division; 14 September 1944, Monte Frassino, Italy.

Wilbur William H., Colonel, USA, Western Task Force, North Africa; 8 November 1942, Fedala, North Africa.

*Wilken, Edward G., Corporal, USA, Company C, 157th Infantry, 45th Infantry Division; 18 March 1945, Seigfried Line in Germany.

*Wilkens, Raymond H. (Air Mission), Major, USA Air Corps, 24 March 1944, Rabaul, New Britain.

*Will Walter J., First Lieutenant, USA, Company K 18th Infantry, 1st Infantry Division; 30 March 1945, Near Eisern, Germany.

Williams, Hershel Woodrow, Corporal, USMC Reserve, 21st Marines, 3rd Marine Division; 23 February 1945, Iwo Jima, Volcano Islands.

*Williams, Jack, Pharmacist's Mate Third Class, US Naval Reserve, 3d Battalion, 28th Marines, 5th Marine Division; 3 March 1945, Iwo Jima, Volcano Islands.

*Willis, John Harlan, Pharmacist's Mate First Class, USN, 3rd Battalion, 27th Marines, 5th Marine Division; 28 February 1945, Iwo Jima, Volcano Islands.

*Wilson, Alfred L. Technician Fifth Grade, USA, Medical Detachment, 328th Infantry, 26th Infantry Division; 8 November 1944, Naer Bezange la Petite, France.

Wilson Louis Hugh, Jr., Captain, USMC, Commanding Rifle Company, 2nd Battalion 9th Marines, 3rd Marine Division; 25-26 July 1944, Fonte Hill, Guam.

*Wilson, Robert Lee, PFC, USMC, 2nd Battalion, 6th Marines, 2nd Marine Division; 4 August 1944, Tinian Island, Marianas Group.

Wise, Homer L., Staff Sergeant, USA, Company L, 142nd Infantry, 36th Infantry Division; 14 June 1944, Magliano, Italy.

*Witek, Frank Peter, PFC, USMC Reserve, 1st Battalion, 9th Marines, 3rd Marine Division; 3 August 1944, Battle of Finegayen at Guam, Marianas.

*Woodford, Howard E., Staff Sergeant, USA, Company I, 130th Infantry, 33rd Infantry Division; 6 June 1945, Near Tabio, Luzon, Philippine Islands.

Young, Cassin, Commander, USN, U.S.S. Vestal; 7 December 1941, Pearl Harbor.

*Young, Rodger W. Private, USA, 148th Infantry, 37th Infantry Division; 31 July 1943, New Georgia, Solomon Islands.

Zeamer, Jay Jr. (Air Mission), Major, USA Air Corps; 16 June 1943, Over Buka, Solomon Islands.

*Zussman, Raymond, Second Lieutenant, USA, 756th Tank Battalion; 12 September 1944, Noroy le Bourg, France.

*Mitchell, William, Colonel, USA, Be it enacted by the Senate and House of Representatives of the United States of America in Congress assembled: "That the President of the United States is requested to cause a gold medal to be struck, with suitable emblems, devices and inscriptions, to be presented to the late William Mitchell, formerly a Colonel, United States Army, in recognition of his outstanding service and foresight in the field of American military aviation."

GLOSSARY OF ABBREVIATIONS

A — Armored, Assistant, Army, Appointed, Attache.

AA — antiaircraft.

AADC — Army Armament Development Center, Picatinny Arsenal.

AAA — antiaircraft artillery.

AAF — Army Air Force.

AAFEC — Army Air Force Engineer Command.

AAFSC — Army Air Force Service Command.

AAI — Allied Armies in Italy.

AASC — Allied Air Support Command (Mediterranean).

ABDA — Australian-British-Dutch-American.

ABMC — Amrican Battle Monuments Commission, Wash., D.C.

Abn — Airborne.

ABTF — airborne task force.

AC — Army Air Corps (Act of 2 July 1926. Became US Air Force Act of 26 July 1947).

Acad — Academy.

ACC — Army Communications Command; replaces STRATCOM.

ACR — Armored Cavalry Regiment.

ACMF — Allied Central Mediterranean Force.

ACS — Asst. Chief of Staff.

Actg — Accounting.

ACTS — Air Corps Tactical School.

ADC — assistant division commander.

Air Defense Command
Aero (Air Defense Command)

Adjt — Adjutant.

Admr — Admiral.

AEAF — Allied Expeditionary Air Force (Europe).

AEF — American Expeditionary Forces (6 Apr 1917**11 Nov 1918).**

AF — American Force (meaning USAF. Act of 26 July 1947).
Air Forces
Allied Forces
Army Forces

AFABn — Armored Fielld Artillery Bn.

AFFE — Army Forces Far East.

AFG — American Forces in Germany Dec 1918**Jan 1923.**

AFHQ — Allied Force Headquarters (Mediterranean).

AFPAC — U.S.FORCES in the PACIFIC.

AFPG — Air Force Proving Ground.

AFR — Africa.

AFWesPac — Army Forces Western Pacific.

AG — Adjutant General.

AGD — Adjutant General's Department (became AGC, Act of 28 June 1950).

AGF — Army Ground Forces.

AGO — Adjutant General's Office.

AirAcdt — air accident.

Alas — Alaska.

ALFcs — Allied Land Forces.

AM — Air Medal.

AMER Div — Americal Division.

AMET — Africa**Middle East Theater.**

AMGE — American Military Government.

AMLG — Allied Military Headquarters, Greece.

AMMISCA — American Military Mission to China.

Ammo — ammunition.

amph — amphibious.

amphib — amphibian.

amtrac — tractor.

ANG — Air National Guard.

AP — transport.

AP — transport, high speed.

APG — Aberdeen Proving Ground, MD.

Ar — Army.

ARC — Arty Cps to 1907**Amer Red Cross.**

armd — armored.

Arty — Artillery (regiments from 1 June 1821 to 2 Feb 1901).

AS — Air Service (Act of 4 June 1920. Became Army Air Corps AC, Act 2 July 1926, and US Air Force, AF, Act of 26 July 1947).

ASC — Air Support Command.

ASF — Army Service Forces.

Assn — association.

Asst — Assistant.

AT — antitank.

ATC — Air Transport Command.

Aus — Australian.

AUS — Army of the United States.

Aust — Australia.

AVG — American Volunteer Group (China).

AVnS — Aviation School, Ft. Ruckner, Al.

AW — Acft warning.
automatic weapons.

AWC — Army War College Carlisle Bks Pa since 30 June 1951.

B — born.

BB — battleship.

BC — bomber command.

BCT — battalion combat team.

Bd — Board.

BEF — Brazilian Expeditionary Force.

BG — Brigadier General, Battle Group.

BLT — boat landing team.

bn — battalion.

Br — British.

brig — brigade.

BTE — British Troops in Egypt.

Btry — Battery.

BW1 — British West Indies.

C — Chief, Combat, College.

CA — heavy cruiser, Coast Artillery, Corps Area, Civil Afairs.

CAA — Concepts Analysis Agency, Bethesda, MD; replaces STAG.

CAC — Coast Artillery Corps (4 May 1907 to Act of 28 June 1950).

CACW — Chinese-American Composite Wing.

CAD — Civil Affairs Division, General Staff.

CAI — Chinese Army in India.

CAM — Composite Army-Marine.

CarCmd — Carribbean Command, Quarry Heights, CZ.

CATF — Chinese Air Task Force.

Cav — Cavalry.

CAWS — Cannon Artillery Weapons system.

CBI — China-Burma-India.

CC — combat command.

CCA — Combat Command A.

CCB — Combat Command B.

CCC — Combat Command C.

CCD — Combat Command D.

CCL — Combat Command L.

CCR — Combat Command R.

CCV — Combat Command V.

CC1 — Combat Command 1.

CC2 — Combat Command 2.

CDC — Caribbean Defense Command.

cdo(s) — commando (s).

Cdr — Commander.

CE — Corps of Engineers.

Cen — Center, Central.

CG — commanding general.

Ch — Chinese.

Ch Am Msn — China American Mission.

Ch Mil Bu — Chinese Military Bureau.

Chrm — Chairman.

CI — Combat Infantry Badge.

CinC — Commander in Chief.

CINCPAC — Commander in Chief, Pacific Fleet.

CINCPOA — Commander in Chief, Pacific Ocean Areas.

Civ — Civil, Civilian.

CL — light cruiser.

Cmbt — Combat.

Cmd — Command.

Cmdt — Commandant.

CMF — Citizen Military Forces (New Guinea).

co — company.

CO — commanding officer.

COMAIRSOLS — Commander Air Forces, Solomons.

COMCENPAC –– Commander Central Pacific.

Comdg — commanding.

COMINCH — Commander in Chief.

Comm — Commissioner, Commission, Committee, Communications.

Compt — Comptroller.

COMSOPAC — Commander South Pacific.

ComZ — Communications Zone.

Con — Constabulary.

Cong — Congress.

Const — Construction.

COSC — Combined Operational Service Command.

COSSAC — Chief of Staff to the Supreme Allied Commander (designate).

CP — command post.

Cps — Corps.

Cpsm — Corpsman.

CRX — China Relief Expedition (entry indicates service within the period 6 July 1900-1 May 1901).

CS — Congressional Surplus.

CSO — Chief Signal Officer.

CT — China Theater, combat team.

CTF — commander, task force.

CV — aircraft carrier.

CVE — aircraft carrier, escort.

CWS — Chemical Warfare Service. Became Chemical Corps (CmlC) Act of Aug 2, 1946.

CZ — Canal Zone.

CofEngin — Corps of Engineers.

D — Died, Deputy.

DA — Department of the Army, Washington, DC.

DA ALPS — Detachment d' Armee des Aples

DA ATL — Detachment d' Armee de l'Atlantique

DAF — Department of the Air Force, Washington, DC.

DC — Dental Corps.

DCS — Deputy Chief of Staff.

DD — destroyer.

DDay — Invasion of France 6 June 1944.

DED — Officially Declared Dead.

Dept — Department.

Dir — Director.

Dist — Distinguished, District.

div — division.

Dsbl — disabled.

DSC — Distinguished Service Cross.

DSM — Distinguished Service Medal.

DTY — Duty.

E — Engineer, east, eastern.

EAC — Eastern Air Command (CBI).

EAM — Ethniko Apeleftherotiko Metopo (National Liberation Front, Greece).

EBn — Engineer Battalion.

EGS — Engineer General Service.

engr(s) — engineer(s).

ETO — European Theatre of Operations.

ETOUSA — European Theater of Operations, USA.
EuCom — European Command.
ExO — Executive Officer (also XO).
FA — field artillery.
FAS(C) — Field Artillery School (Cen), Ft Sill, OK, unless otherwise indicated.
FC — Finance Corps (FD before Act of 28 June 1950).
FEAF — Far East Air Force.
FEC — French Expeditionary Force**Far East Command.**
FF — Free French.
FFI — Forces Francaises de l'Interieur.
FFO — Forces Francaises de l'Ouest.
Findl — Finland.
FMF — Fleet Marine Force.
FO — field order.
Fr — French.
FRNT — Front.
FT — Fort.
Ftr — Frontier.
Gd — Guard.
Gds — Guards.
Gen — General.
Ger — German, Germany.
GHQ — General Headquarters.
gli — glider.
GMT — Greenwich mean time.
GO — general orders.
Gov — Government.
gp — group.
GRC — Group Command.
GRP — Group.
GS — General Staff.
HALFSEE — Hdqrs Allied Land Forces Southeastern Europe, Izmir Turkey.
HALPRO — Air operation against Rumanian oil fields,1942.
H — Heavy Bombers.
HD — Harbor Defense.
Hon — Honor.
hq — headquarters.
Hwy — Highway.
I — Island.
IBT — India-Burma Theater.
IG — Inspector General.
Il — Illinois.
Ind — Indian.
Inf — Infantry.
Inst — Instructor.
Instr — same as Inst above.

Internat — International.
IRTC — Inf Replacement Tng Cen.
Is. — Islands.
ISCOM — Island Commander.
JAG — Judge Advocate General.
Jap — Japan.
JBUSDC — Joint Brazil-U.S. Defense Commission, Brasila.
JCS — Joint Chiefs of Staff.
JTF — Joint Task Force.
JWPC — Joint War Plans Committee.
KIA — Killed in Action.
Kld — Killed.
LANDFOR — landing force.
LCI — landing craft, infantry.
LCI(G) — landing craft, infantry, gunboat.
LCM — landing craft, mechanized.
LCVP — landing craft, vehicle and personnel.
LOC — line of communications.
LOGC — Logistics Center, Ft. Lee, Va.
LRP — long-range penetration.
LST — landing ship, tank.
LTC — Lieutenant Colonel.
LTG — Lieutenant General.
M. — Mont, Monte, etc. (Italy and Sicily only).

MA — Military Attache, Military Airlift.
MAAF — Mediterranean Allied Air Forces.
MAAG — Mil. Assistance Advisory Gp.
MAC — Marine Amphibious Corps.
Mach — machine.
MAG — Marine Aviation Group.
Maj — Major.
Mar — Marine.
MATAF — Mediterranean Allied Tactical Air Force.
MD — Maryland.
MDW — Military District of Washington, DC.
ME — Middle East.
Mecz — Mechanized.
MEF — Middle East Forces.
Mem — Memorial.
MG — machine gun.
Mgun — machine gun.
MLR — main lin eof resistance.
MoroX — Expedition against the Moros (combat).
MP — military police.
Mpwr — manpower.
MSR — main supply route.
MTB — motor torpedo boat.
MTC — Motor Transport Corps.
mtn — mountain.
MTOUSA — Mediterranean Theater of Operations, USA.
N — north, northern.
NA — National Army 1917-1919, Nuclear Agency.
NAAF — Northwest African Air Force.
NAfr — North Africa.
Nat — National.
NATO — North African Theater of Operations.
NCAC — Northern Combat Area Command (Burma).
NEI — Netherlands East Indies.
NG — National Guard.
NGVR — New Guinea Volunteer Reserve.
NMB — National Munitions Board, DC.
NTLF — Northern Troops and Landing Force.
NW — northwest, northwestern.
NZ — New Zealand.
Obs — observer.
OC — Ordinance Corps (OD before Act of 28 June 1950).
OCAFE — Office Chief of Army Field Forces, Ft Monroe, Va.
OccG — Occupation of Germany.
Occj — Occupation of Japan.
OCE — Office Chief of Engineers, U.S. Army, Washington, DC unless otherwise indicated.
OCS — Office Chief of Staff.
OCSO — Office Chief Signal Officer (US Army, Wash DC unless otherwise indicated).
OD — Ordinance Department (becomes OC, Act of 28 June 1950).
OF — Office Officer.
OIG — Office Inspector General.
OK — Oklahoma.

OMGG — Office of Military Gov't. for Germany.
OMGUS — Office of Military Gov't. United States.
OO — Ordinance Officer.
OPD — Operations Division (General Staff).
OPL — outpost line.
OPLR — outpost line of resistance.
OPNS — operations.
OR — Organized Reserves.
ORC — Officers Reserve Corps.
ORG — organization, organic.

OSAF — Office Secretary of the Air Force.
OSS — Office Strategic Services.
OTAG — Ordnance Tank Automotive Command.
PA — Philippine Army.
Pac — Pacific.
Para — parachute.
PBM — patrol search plane.
PC — Philippine Constabulary.
Pers — personnel.
PG — patrol vessel, gunboat.
PGC — Persian Gulf Command.
PGSC — Persian Gulf Service Command.
Phi — Philippines.
Phln — Philippine Insurrection (entry indicates service within the period of combat 4 Feb 1899 to 4 July 1902).
P.I. — Philippine Islands.
PIB — Papuan Infantry Battalion.
PID — Public Information Division.
PIR — Parachute Infantry Regiment.
PMG — Provost Marshal General.
PMST — Professor of Military Science and Tactics.
POA — Pacific Ocean Areas.
Pol — Polish.
POW — Prisoner of War.
PR — Puerto Rico.
Prch — purchasing.
Pres — President.
Proc — proclamation.
Prof — professor.
prov — provisional.
PS — Philippine Scouts.
Psth — Posthumously.
pt — point.
PT — patrol vessel, motor torpedo boat.
PunX — Punitive Expedition into Mexico (Entry indicates service within the period 15 Mar 1916-7 February 1917).
Pur — purchasing.
Pz — Panzer.
QM — quartermaster.
QMC — Quartermaster corps.
QMD — Quartermaster's Department.
QMG — Quartermaster General.
R — river.
RAAF — Royal Australian Air Force.
RAF — Royal Air Force.
rcn — reconnaissance.
RCT — regimental combat team.
Reapt — reappointment.
regt — regiment.
reinf — reinforced.
Rep — representative.
Repl — replacement (s).
Resd — resigned.
RI — Rhode Island.
Riv — river.
RN — Royal Navy.
RR — railroad.
RTC — Replacement Training Center.
R&d — Research and development.
S — south, southern.
S. — San, Sant, Santa, etc. (Italy and Sicily only).
SAC — Strategic Air Command, Offutt AFB, NB.
SACEUR — Strategic Air Command Europe.
SACMED — Supreme Allied Commander, Mediterranean.
SAF — Strategic Air Force.
SanC — Santiago de Cuba Campaign (Service within the period of combat 22 June 1917 July 1898).
SAtl — South Atlantic.
SBD — "Dauntless" single-engine Navy scout-bomber.
SC — Signal Corps.
SCAP — Supreme Commander for Allied Powers.

Sch — School.
SEAC — Southeast Asia Command.
Sect — sector, section.
Secy — Secretary.
sep — seperate.
SHAEF — Supreme Headquarters, Allied Expeditionary Force.
SO — Signal Officer or Office.
SOPAC — South Pacific.
SOS — Services of Supply.
SPM — self-propelled mount.
Sq — squadron
SS — Schutzstaffel (Elite Guard).
SS — Silver Star.
SSC — Silver Star Citation (earlier award, same as SS.
SSF — Special Service Force.
STAF — Strategic Air Force.
Stff — Staff.
STLF — Southern Troops and Landing Force.
SBGen — Brigadier General subsequent to WWII.
SMGEN — Major General subsequent to WWII.
SLTGEN — Lt. GEN subsequent to WWII.
SGEN — General subsequent to WWII.
Sup — Superintendent.
SvC — Service Command.
Switz — Switzerland.
SWPA — Southwest Pacific Area.
SYS — system.
T — Theatre or area of operations World War II (is followed by one or more of the following letters indicating the particular theatre or area).
TA — American Theater.
TA — Tactical Air.
TAC — Tactical Air Command, Langley AFB, Va. unless otherwise indicated.
TAF — Tactical Air Force.
TAG — The Adjutant General of the Army.
TARC(s) — The Armored Center (Sch), Ft. Knox, Ky.
TC — Transportation Corps
Training Center
Troop Carrier.
TD — tank destroyer.
TEC(S) — The Engineer Center (Sch), Ft. Belvoir, Va.
Tech — Technical, Technician.
TF — task force.
TH — Territory of Hawaii.
TIG — The Inspector General, US Army.
Tk — truck.
Tng — training.
TOT — time on target.
TP(s) — troop(s).
tr — troop.
TSS(C) — The Signal School (Center), Ft. Gordon, Ga.
Turk — Turkey.
U.K. — United Kingdom.
UNMSC — United Nations Millitary Staff Committee (US Delegate thereto).
U.S. — United States.
USA — U.S. Army.
USAAF — U.S. Army Air Force.
USAAFUK — U.S. Army Air Forces in the United Kingdom.
USAFBI — U.S. Army Forces, British Isles.
USAFFE — U.S. Army Forces, Far East.
USAFIA — U.S. Army Forces in Australia.
USAFICPA — U.S. Army Forces in Central Pacific Area.
USAFIME — U.S. Army Forces in the Middle East.
USAFISPA — U.S. Army Forces in the South Pacific Area.

USARPac — US Army, Pacific, Fort Shafter, Hawaii.
USASOS — U.S. Army Services of Supply.
USCG — United States Coast Guard.
USFET — United States Forces European Theatre.
USFIA — U.S. Forces in Australia.
USFIP — U.S. Forces in the Philippines.
USMA — United States Millitary Academy.
USMC — U.S. Marine Corps.
USN — U.S.Navy.
USSAFE — U.S. Strategic Air Forces in Europe.
USSR — Union of Soviet Socialist Republics.
USSTAF — U.S. Strategic Air Forces.
UStrps — US troops.
USV — United States Volunteers.
V — Veteran (s).
VAC — V Amphibious Corps.
VET — Veteran (s).
VFW — Vets of Foreign Wars.
W — west, western.
WD — Western Desert.
WDAF — Western Desert Air Force.
Wded — wounded.
WDGS — War Department General Staff.
Wds — wounds.
WPD — War Plans Division (General Staff).
WRGH — Walter Reed General Hospital.
WW — World War.
XO — Executive Officer.
ZFce — Z Force.

GLOSSARY OF CODE NAMES
ABERDEEN — Chindit stronghold near Manhton, Burma.
ALAMO — Code for U.S. Sixth Army while operating as a special ground task force headquarters directly under GHQ SWPA.
ALPHA — Plan to defend Kunming and Chungking.
ALPHA — U.S. 3rd Division force for southern France operation.
ANIKIM — Plan for recapture of Burma.
ANVIL — Early plan for invasion of southern France.
ARCADIA — U.S.-British conference held in Washington, December 1941-January 1942.
ARGONAUT — International conference held at Malta and Yalta, January-February 1945.
ARGUMENT — USSTAF air operations against German aircraft factories, February 1944.
AVALANCH — Invasion of Italy at Salerno.
AXIOM — Mission sent by SEAC to Washington and London in February 1944 to urge Culverin.
BACKHANDER — Task force for operations on Cape Gloucester, New Britain.
BARBAROSSA — German offensive against USSR, 1941.
BAYTOWN — British invasion of Italy on Calabrian coast.
BETA — Plan to open port on coast of China.
BLACKCOCK — British 12th Corps operation to clear enemy salient between the Meuse and Roer-Wurm Rivers from Roermond southward.
BLACKPOOL — Chindit roadblock on railroad near Namkwin, Burma.
BLOCKBUSTER — Canadian 2nd Corps offensive in Calcar-Udem-Xanten area.

BOLERO — Build-up of U.S. forces and supplies in United Kingdom for cross-Channel attack.
BRASSARD — Operations against the island of Elba.
BREWER — Operations in the Admiralties.
BRIMSTONE — Plan for capture of Sardinia. Canceled.
BROADWAY — Drop site for Chindits, about fifty miles northwest of Indaw, Burma.
BUCCANEER — Plan for amphibious operation in Andaman Islands. Canceled.
BUFFALO — Operations to break out of Anzio(Italy) beachhead.
BUTTRESS — British operation against toe of Italy.
CAMEL — U.S. 36th Division force for southern France.
CAPITAL — Attack across the Chindwin River to Mandalay.
CARBONADO — Revised Beta.
CARPETBAGGER — Air operation from United Kingdom to drop supplies to patriot forces in Western Europe.
CARTWHEEL — Converging drives on Rabaul by South Pacific and SWPA forces.
CASANOVA — U.S. 95th Division diversionary action during operations against Metz.
CATCHPOLE — Operations against Eniwetok and Ujelang Atolls, Marshall Islands.
CHAMPION — Late 1943 plan for general offensive in Burma.
CHATTANOOGA CHOO CHOO — AEAF operations against enemy train movements in France and Germany.
CLEANSLATE — Invasion of Russell Islands.
CLIPPER — British 30th Corps offensive to reduce Geilenkirchen salient.
COBRA — U.S. First Army operation designed to penetrate the German defenses west of St Lo and secure Coutances,France.
CORKSCREW — Conquest of Pantelleria.
COTTAGE — Invasion of Kiska, 1943.
CRICKET — Malta portion of Argonaut Conference.
CROSSBOW — RAF operations against German V-weapons experimental bases.
CUDGEL — Planned small-scale operation on Arakon coast, Burma. Canceled.
CULVERIN — Plan for Assault on Sumatra.
CYCLONE — Task force for Noemfoor.
DELTA — U.S. 45th Division force for southern France.
DEXTERITY — Operations against Cape Gloucester, New Britain.
DIRECTOR — Task force for invasion of Arawe, New Britain.
DIXIE — Mission of U.S observers to Chinese communists.
DRACULA — Plan for attack on Rangoon, 1944.
DRAGOON — Final code for invasion of southern France.
ELKTON — Plan for seizure of New Britain, New Guinea, and New Ireland area.
END RUN — Task force of GALAHAD survivors used in drive on Myitkyina, Burma.
EUREKA — International conference at Teheran, November 1943.
FIREBRAND — Invasion of Corsica, 1943.
FLAX — Air operation to disrupt flow of German air transports from Italy to Sicily and Tunisia.

FLINTLOCK — Operations in the Marshall Islands.

FORAGER — Operations in the Marianas.

FRANTIC — AAF shuttle bombing of Axis-controlled Europe from bases in United Kingdom, Italy, and USSR.

FRY — Occupation of four islands in Lake Comacchio, Italy.

GALAHAD — American long range penetration groups (Burma).

GALVANIC — Operations in Gilbert Islands.

GOBLET — Invasion of Italy at Cotrone canceled.

GOLD — Normandy beach assaulted by troops of British 30th Corps, 6 June 1944.

GOLDFLAKE — Movement of Canadian I Corps from Italy to ETO.

GRANITE — Plan for operations in POA in 1944.

GRENADE — 21st Army Group large-scale offensive from the Roer to the Rhine.

GYMNAST — Early plan for Allied invasion of northwest Africa.

HERCULES — German plan to invade Malta. Canceled.

HURRICANE — Assault force for Biak, New Guinea.

HUSKY — Allied invasion of Sicily, July 1943.

ICEBERG — Invasion of the Ryukyu Islands.

ICHIGO — Japanese operation to take U.S. air bases in east China.

INDEPENDENCE — French offensive toward Belfort, France.

INTERLUDE — Rehearsal for Morotai operation.

JUNO — Normandy beach assaulted by troops of Canadian 3rd Division, 6 June 1944.

LEVER — Operation to clear area between Reno and southwest shore of Lake Comacchio, Italy.

LONDON — XVIII Corps (A/B) phase line near Wesel, Germany.

MAGNET — Movement of first U.S. forces to Northern Ireland.

MAILFIST — Capture of Singapore, 1945.

MALLORY MAJOR — Air offensive against Po River bridges, Italy.

MANNA — British occupation of southern Greece.

MARKET-GARDEN — Operation to secure bridgehead over Rhine River.

MARS — U.S. task force (533rd Brigade (Provisional)), CBI.

MICHAELMAS — Task force for seizure of Saidor, New Guinea.

MUSKET — Projected landing on heel of Italy near Taranto, 1943.

NEPTUNE — Actual 1944 operations within OVERLORD. Used for security reasons about September 1943 on all OVERLORD planning papers that referred to target area and date.

NEW GALAHAD — American long range penetration groups (Burma).

NEW YORK — XVIII Corps (A/B) phase line in Ringenberg-Krudenberg area Germany.

NORDWIND — German offensive against U.S. Seventh Army, January 1945.

OCTAGON — U.S.-British conference at Quebec, September 1944.

OLIVE — Attack on Gothic Line, Italy.

OLYMPIC — Plan for March 1946 invasion of Kyushu, Japan.

OMAHA — Normandy beach assaulted by troops of U.S. V Corps, 6 June 1944.

OVERLORD — Allied cross-Channel invasion of northwest Europe, June 1944.

PANTHER — British 10th Corps drive across the Garigliano, Italy.

PARIS — XVIII Corps (A/B) phase line west of Erle, Germany.

PERSECUTION — Assault force for Aitape operations, New Guinea.

PICCADILLY — Drop site for Chindits, Burma.

PIGSTICK — Limited operation on south Mayu Peninsula. Canceled.

PLUNDER — 21st Army Group assault across the Rhine north of the Ruhr.

POINTBLANK — Combined bomber offensive against Germany.

PROVIDENCE — Occupation of Burma area, New Guinea, 1942. Canceled.

PUGILIST — Attack on Mareth Line, Tunisia, 1943.

QUADRANT — U.S.-British conference at Quebec, August 1943.

QUEEN — 12th Army Group operation on Roer Plain between Wurm and Roer Rivers.

RAINCOAT — Assault on Camino hill mass, Italy.

RASHNESS — Revised CARBONADO plan.

RAVENOUS — 4th Corps plan for recapture of northern Burma.

RECKLESS — Assault force for Hollandia operation.

RENO — SWPA plan for operations in the Bismarck Archipelago, along northern coast of New Guinea and thence to Mindanao, P.I.

RO — Japanese air operation to augment Rabaul air forces and delay Allied offenses.

ROAST — Operation to clear Comacchio Spit, Italy.

ROGER — Capture of Phuket Island, off Kra Isthmus, Burma.

ROMEO — French commando force that lands at Cap Negre, Mediterranean.

ROMULUS — Arakan part of Capital plan.

ROOSTER — Operation to fly Chinese 22nd Division to Cannes.

ROSE — Ruhr pocket, April 1945.

ROSIE — French naval force that lands southwest of Cannes.

ROUNDUP — Plan for major U.S.-British cross-Channel operation in 1943.

RUGBY — Airborne force that drops to rear of southern France assault beaches.

SATIN — Plan for U.S. II Corps operation against Sfax, Tunisia. Canceled.

SAUCY — Limited offensive to open land route from Burma to China.

SEA LION — Planned German invasion of United Kingdom. Canceled.

SEXTANT — International conference at Cairo, November and December 1943.

SHINGLE — Amphibious operation at Anzio, Italy.

SHO — Japanese plan to counterattack U.S. forces in Western Pacific.

SITKA — Force that takes islands of Levant and Port Cros, Mediterranean.

SLAPSTICK — Airborne drop at Taranto, Italy.

SLEDGEHAMMER — Plan for limited cross-Channel attack in 1942.

STALEMATE — Invasion of the Palaus.

STRANGLE — Air operation to interdict movement of enemy supplies in Italy.

SUPERCHARGE — British 30th Corps breakout, Egypt, 1942.

SUPERCHARGE — Revised plan of assault on Mereth Line, March 1943.

SWORD — Normandy beach assaulted by troops of British 3rd Division, 6 June 1944.

TALON — Akyab part of CAPITAL plan.

TARZAN — India-based portion of general offensive in Burma.

TED — Task force in Aitape area, New Guinea.

TERMINAL — International conference, Potsdam, Germany, 16 July-2 August 1945.

THUNDERBOLT — Offensive in Metz area.

TIDALWAVE — Low-level heavy bomber attack on Ploesti, Rumania, 1943.

TIGER — One of the rehearsal exercises for OVERLORD.

TOGO — Second phase of ICHIGO operation.

TORCH — Allied invasion of northwest Africa.

TOREADOR — Airborne assault on Mandalay.

TORNADO — Assault force for Wakde-Sarmi area, New Guinea.

TRADEWIND — Force for Morotai.

TRANSFIGURE — Plan to drop troops west of Seine River to block enemy escape routes.

TRIDENT — U.S.-British conference held at Washington, May 1943.

TULSA — GHQ SWPA's first outline plan for operations directed at the capture of Rabaul.

TWILIGHT — Plan to base B-29's in CBI.

TYPHOON — Task force for Sansapor-Mar operation, New Guinea.

UNDERTONE — U.S. Third and Seventh Army offensive to break through West Wall and clear the Saar-Palitinate triangle, within the confines of the Rhine Moselle, and Lauter-Sarre.

UTAH — Normandy beach assaulted by troops of U.S. VII Corps, 6 June 1944.

VARSITY — Airborne drop east of the Rhine.

VERTIBLE — Canadian First Army operation to clear area between Maas and Rhine Rivers.

VICTOR I — Panay and Negros Occidental operation.

VICTOR II — Cebu, Bohol, and Negros Oriental operation.

VICTOR III — U.S. Eighth Army operations against Sulu Archipelago and Zamboanga area of Mindanao.

VICTOR V — U.S. Eighth Army operations against western Mindanao.

VULCAN — Final ground offensive to clear Tunisia, 1943.

WEBFOOT — Rehearsal for SHINGLE.

YOKE — All U.S. organizations working with Y-Force, CBI.

ZEBRA — U.S. sponsored Chinese division in east China.

ZIPPER — Plan for assault on Malaya, 1945.

Bibliography
Listing Of Primary Reference Sources.

-U.S.M.C. Historical Division, Washington, D.C.

-U.S. Army War College, Carlisle, Pa.

-U.S. Army, Historical Division, Washington, D.C.

-U.S. Navy, Historical Division, Washington, D.C.

-U.S. Navy Historical Foundation, Washington, D.C.

-U.S. Coast Guard, Public Affairs Division, Groton, Ct.

-U.S. Government Official records concerning Medal of Honor recipients.

-Official records, United States Military Academy, West Point, N.Y.

-United States Naval Academy, Annapolis, Md., Official records.

-United States Naval Academy, Annapolis, Md. Public Affairs Dept.

-U.S. Marine Corps, Public Affairs Dept, Washington, D.C.

-U.S.S. Nautilus Memorial Submarine Force Library & Museum, Groton, Ct.

-U.S. Military Academy, Public Affairs Division, West Point, N.Y.

-Freedoms Foundation, Valley Forge, Pa. (MofH) reference material.

—The US Army in WWII: Multiple Volumes, Office of Chief of Military History, Wash., D.C...all Theaters & special volumes including Engineers.

-A Chronology of the U.S. Marine Corps 1935-1946, U.S.M.C. Historical Division, Washington, D.C.

-U.S. Navy Chronology WWII-U.S. Naval Historical Division, Washington, D.C.

-U.S. Army Chronology WWII, Office Chief of Military History, Washington, D.C.

-Various video & audio tapes & papers, concerning official Army, Navy & Marine Corps history, (note, during World War II, the Air Force was the Army Air Corps). - interviews with participants of W.W. II.

-War As I Knew It, General George S. Patton, Jr., Houghton Mifflin, 1947.

-General Wainright's Story, General Jonathan Wainright, Doubleday & Co. Inc. Garden City N.Y., 1945.

-Coral & Brass, General Holl& M. Smith & Percy Finch, Charles Scribner's Sons, New York, 1949.

-The Stilwell Papers, General Joseph W. Stilwell, William Sloane Assoc. Inc., New York, 1948.

-Crusade In Europe, General Dwight D. Eisenhower, Doubleday & Co., New York. 1948.

-I Was There, Fleet Admiral William D. Leahy, Whittlesey House, New York, 1950.

-A Soldier's Story, General Omar N. Bradley, Henry Holt & Co Inc., 1951.

-Admiral Kimmel's Story, Admiral Husb& E. Kimmel, Henry Regmery Company, Chicago, 1955.

-Soldier, General Matthew B. Ridgway, Harper & Brothers, New York 1956.

-Reminiscences, General Douglas MacArthur, McGraw Hill Publishing Co. 1964.

-Wedemeyer Reports, General Albert C. Wedemeyer, Henry Holt & Co., N.Y., 1958.

-A Soldier Reports, General William C. Westmorel&, Doubleday & Co., Garden City, N.Y., 1976.

-Admiral Halsey's Story, Admiral Wiliam F. Halsey & J. Bryan, III, Whittlesey House, McGraw Hill Book Co. Inc., N.Y. &

London, 1947.

-Walkout (with Stilwell), Frank Dorn, Thomas Y. Corwell Co., New York 1971.

-The Service: The Memoirs of General Reinhard Gehlen, George Bailey, The World Publishing Co., New York 1972.

-Born to Fight, Ralf B. Jordan, David McKay Co., Phila., 1946.

-Major Jordan's Diaries, George Racey Jordan, Harcourt, Brace & Co., New York, 1952.

-Roosevelt, Churchill, & The WWII Opposition, George Eggleston, Devin-Adair Co., Old Greenwich, 1979.

-America & Germany 1918-1925, Sidney Speer, The Macmillan Co., New York, 1925.

-The Dreadful Decade, Don C. Seitz, The Bobbs-Merrill Company, USA, 1926.

-The Martial Spirit, Walter Millis, The Riverside Press Cambridge Mass., 1931.

-Merchants of Death, H.C. Engelbrecht & F. C. Hanighen, Dodd, Mead & Co., N.Y., 1934.

-And So To War, Hubert Herrong, Yale University Press, New Haven, 1938.

-Beans Bullets and Black Oil, Rear Admiral Worrall Reed Carter, U.S. Government Printing Office, 1953.

-The Goebbels Diaries, Louis P. Lochner, Doubleday & Co. Inc., Garden City, N.Y. 1948.

-Our Maginot Line, Livingston Harley, Carrick & Evans Co., New York, 1939.

-Armies Of Spies, Joseph Gollomb, The MacMillan Co., New York, 1939.

-Through the Diplomatic Looking Glass, Oliver Benson, University of Oklahoma Press, Norman, 1939.

-Inside Europe, John Gunther, Harper & Brothers, New York, War Edition, 1940.

-S-2 in Action, Shipley Thomas, The Military Publishing Service Publishing Co., Harrisburg, 1940.

-Suicide of a Democracy, Hienz Pol, Reynal & Hitchcock, New York, 1940.

-The American Cause, Archibald MacLeish, Duell, Sloan & Pearce, New York, 1941.

-Invasion In The Snow, John Langdon, Davies Houghton Mifflin Co., Boston 1941.

-Engl&'s Hour, Vera Brittain, The MacMillan Company, New York, 1941.

-Union Now With Britain, Clarence K. Streit, Harper & Brothers Publishers, 1941.

-Stalin, Leon Trotsky, Harper & Bros. Publishers, N.Y., London 1941.

-America at War, (Geographical Analysis), Van Nalkenburg, Prentice Hall, New York, 1942.

-The Valor of Ignorance, Homer Lea, Harper & Bros., New York, London, Curtis Publishing Co., 1942 (Orig published 1909).

-They Were Expendable, W. L. White, Harcourt, Brace & Co., N.Y. 1942.

-America in the New Pacific, George Taylor, The MacMillan Co., 1943.

-I Saw The Fall of The Philippines, Colonel Carlos P. Romulo, Doubleday Doran & Co. Inc., Garden City, N.Y. 1943.

-Iwo Jima, A Legacy of Valor, Bill Ross.

-America's Navy In World War II, Gilbert Gant, The John Day Co., New York 1943.

-Retreat With Stilwell, Jack Belden, Alfred A. Knoff, N.Y. 1943

-Vertical Warfare, Francis Vivian Drake, Doubleday, Doran & Co. Inc., Garden City, New York 1943.

-Combined Operations, The MacMillan Co.,

New York 1943.

-Wildcats Over Casablanca, Lieut. M.T. Wordell & Lieut. E.N. Seller, Little, Brown & Co., Boston 1943.

-The Battle for the Solomons, Ira Wolfert, Houghton Mifflin Company, Boston, 1943.

-Betrayal from the East, Alan Hynd, Robert M. McBride & Company, 1943.

-Britain in the World Front, R. Palme Dutt, New York International Publishers, 1943.

-Dress Rehersal, Quentin Reynolds, Random House, New York, 1943.

-Here is Your War, Ernie Pyle, The World Publishing Co., Henry Holt & Co., 1943.

-Guadalcanal Diary, Richard Tregaskis, Blue Ribbon Books, Garden City, New York, 1943.

-Mein Kamph, Adolf Hitler, Houghton Mifflin Company, Boston, 1943.

-Seven Came Through, Cpt. Edward V. Rickenbacker, Doubleday, Doran & Co. Inc., New York, 1943.

-Brave Men, Ernie Pyle, Scripps Howard Newspaper Alliance 1943-44, Henry Holt, New York, 1944.

-Solution In Asia, Owen Lattimore, Little Brown & Co., Boston, 1944.

Der Fuehrer, Konrad Heiden, Hooughton Mifflin Co., Boston 1944.

-As We Go Marching, John T. Flynn, Doubleday, Doran & Co. Inc., 1944.

-Balkan Journal, Laird Archer, W.W. Norton Company Inc., New York, 1944.

-Triumph of Treason, Pierre Cot, Ziff Davis Publishing Co., New York 1944.

-Lend-Lease, Edward R. Stettinius Jr., The MacMillan Co., 1944.

-Pacific Victory 1945, Joseph Driscoll, J.B. Lippincott Company Publishers, Phila. & New York, 1944.

- When Johnny Comes Marching Home, Dixon Wecter, Houghton Mifflin Co. 1944.

-Ten Years in Japan, Joseph C. Grew, Simon & Schuster, New York 1944.

-General Ike, Alden Hatch, Consolidated Book Publishers, Chicago 1944.

-Story Of A Secret State, John Karski, Houghton Mifflin Co., Boston, 1944.

-Tarawa, The Story of Battle, Robert Sherrod, Duell, Sloan & Pearce, 1944.

-Who's Who 1944, The Macmillan Co., New York, 1944.

-Chungking, Listening Post, Mark Tennien, Creative Age Press,Inc., New York, 1945.

-A Ribbon & a Star, John Monks Jr., & John Falter, Henry Holt Co. Inc. 1945.

-WACS At Work, Fjeril Hess, MacMillan Co., N.Y. 1945.

-Robinson Crusoe USN, Blake Clarke, McGraw Hill Book Co. New York-London, 1945.

-Solution in Asia, Owen Lattimore, Little, Brown & Co., Boston 1945.

-Sea, Surf & Hell, Arch A. Mercey & Lee Grove, Prentice-Hall Inc., New York, 1945.

-Women in Aviation, Betty Peckham, Thomas Nelson & Sons, New York, 1945.

-The U.S. Marines on Iwo Jima, Capt. Raymond Henri(PR 3rd Div) 1st Lt. Jim G. Lucas Asst P.R. 4th Div T-Sarg W. Keyes Beech Combat Corres 5th Div T-Sarg David K. Dempsey Combat Corres 4th Div T-Sarg Alvin M. Josephy Jr. Combat Corres 3rd Div Dial Press & Infantry Journal Inc., 1945.

-Wartime Mission in Spain 1942-1945, Carlton J. H. Hayes, MacMillan Company, New York, 1945.

-The Ciano Diaries 1939-1943, Count Ciano,

Doubleday & Company Inc., Garden City, New York, 1945,1946.

-Builders for Battle, David O. Woodbury, E.P. Dutton & Co. Inc., New York, 1946.

-Last Chapter, Ernie Pyle, Henry Holt & Co., New York, 1946.

-Montgomery, Alan Moorehead, Coward-McCann, Inc., New York, 1946.

-My Three Years With Eisenhower, Captain Harry C. Butcher, USNR, Simon & Shuster, New York, 1946.

Secret Missions, Captain Ellis M. Zacharias, USN, G.P. Putnam Sons, N.Y., 1946

-The United States In The Second World War, Marc Harris, Barnes & Noble Inc., New York, 1946.

-Pearl Harbor, George Morgenstern, The Devin-Adair Co., New York, 1947.

-Home Country, Ernie Pyle, William Sloane Assoc. Inc., New York, 1947.

-The German Generals Talk, B.H. Liddell Hart, William Morrow & Co., 1948.

-Last Days of Europe, Grifore Gafencu, Yale University Press , New Haven 1948.

-Israel, A History of The Jewish People, Rufus Learsi, The World Publishing Company, 1949.

-Great Mistakes Of the War, Hanson W. Baldwin, Harper & Brothers Publishing, New York 1949.

-Submarine Operations in World War II, Theodore Roscoe, Naval Institute Press, Annapolis Maryl&, 1949.

-Their Finest Hour, Winston S. Churchill, Houghton Mifflin Co., Boston, 1949.

-The Riddle of MacArthur, John Gunther, Harper & Brothers, New York 1950.

-Operation Cicero, L.C. Moyzisch, Coward-McCann Inc., New York, 1950.

-This is Your Navy, Theodore Roscoe, United States Naval Institute, Annapolis, Md., 1950.

-Clear the Decks, Daniel V. Gallery, William Morrow & Company, New York, 1951.

-Flight In The Winter, Juergen Thorwald, Pantheon Books, N.Y. 1951.

-Closing The Ring, Winston S. Churchill, Houghton Mifflin Co. Boston, 1951.

-The Gr& Alliance, Winston S. Churchill, Houghton Mifflin Co. Boston, 1951.

-History of Marine Corps Aviation in WWII, Robert Sherrod, Association of the U.S. Army, Combat Force Press, Wash., D.C., 1952.

-Spies, Dupes & Diplomats, Ralph de Toledo, Duell, Sloan & Pearce Inc., Little Brown Co. 1952.

-The Man Who Never Was, Ewen Montague, J.B. Lippincott Company, Phila., New York, 1953.

-U.S. Destroyer Operations in World War II, Theodore Roscoe, Naval Institute Press, Annapolis Maryl&, 1953.

-Triumph & Tragedy, Winston S. Churchill, Houghton Mifflin Co., Boston, 1953.

-Assignment to Catastrophe Vol. I Prelude To Dunkirk, MGen. Sir Edwards Spears, A.A. Wyn, Inc., 1954.

-Ships, Salvage & Sinews of War, Worrall Reed Carter & Elmer Ellisworth Duvall, Washingtomn 1954.

-MacArthur 1941-1945, Major General Charles A. Willoughby & John Chamberlain, McGraw Hill Book Co. Inc., N.Y., & London, 1954.

-A History of United States Foreign Policy, Julius Pratt, Prentice Hall Inc., New York 1955.

-Memoirs, Harry S. Truman Vol I — Year of Decisions, Doubleday & Company Inc.,

1955.

-Midway, Mitsio Fuchida & Mastake Okumiya, United States Naval Institute, Annapolis, Md., 1955.

-The Kersten Memoirs, Felix Kersten, The MacMillan Co., New York, 1956.

-Death in the South Atlantic: The Last Voyage of the Gaff Spee, Michael Powell, Rinehart & Co. Inc., New York 1956.

-MacArthur: His Rendezvous with History, MGen. Courtney Whitney, Alfred A. Knopf, New York 1956.

-Eisenhower's Six Great Decisions, General Walter Bedell Smith, Longmans Green & Co., N.Y., London, Toronto, 1956.

-The Naked Warriors, Comm&er Francis Douglas Appleton, Century-Crofts, Inc., New York 1956.

-20 July, Constantine Fitzgibbon, W.W. Norton & Co. Inc., 1956.

-The Marauders, Charles Ogburn, Jr. Harper & Brothers, N.Y. 1956.

-The Battle of Cassino, Fred Majdalny, Houghton Mifflin Company, Boston, 1957.

-Operation Sea Lion, Peter Fleming, Simon & Schuster, New York 1957.

-Samurai, Saburo Sakai & Martin Caidin & Fred Saito, E.P. Dutton & Co. Inc., New York 1957.

-The Sledge Patrol, David Howarth, The MacMillan Co., New York 1957.

-Ab&on Ship, Richard F. Newcomb, Henry Holt & Company, 1958.

-The Divine Wind, Capt. Rikihei Inoguchi, U.S. Naval Institute, Md. 1958.

-The Clay Pigeons of St. Lo, Glover S. Johms Jr., Miliary Service Publishing Co., Harrisburg, Pa., 1958.

-Lost Victories, Field Marshal Erich von Manstein, Ed. & Trans. by Anthony G. Powell, Methuen & Co. Ltd., 1958.

-The Memoirs of Field Marshall Montgomery, World Publishing Co., New York, 1958.

-The Battle for the Atlantic, Jay Williams, R&om House, New York, 1959.

-Destroyers & Destroyermen, Brock Yates, Harper & Bros., New York, 1959.

-Triumph in the West, Arthur Bryant, Doubleday & Co. Inc., New York 1959.

-Memoirs, Admiral Karl Doenitz, The World Publishing Co., New York, 1959.

-The United Nations, Lel& M. Goodrich, Thomas Y. Crowell Company, New York, 1959.

-Salvation, War Memoirs of Charles DeGaulle, Simon & Schuster, New York, 1960.

-My Life, Gr& Admiral Erich Raeder, U.S. Naval Institute, Annapolis, 1960.

-Wake of the Wahoo, Forest J. Sterling, Chilton Co., Book Division, Phila., New York, 1960.

-The Far Shore, James MacDonald, Dodd, Mead, & Co., New York 1961.

-The Rome Escape Line, Sam Derry, W.W. Norton & Co., Inc., New York 1960.

-The Bombing of Germany, Hans Rumf, Holt, Rinehart & Winston, New York 1961.

-The Man With The Miraculous H&s, Joseph Kessel, 1961.

-The Rise And Fall of Adolf Hitler, William L. Shirer, World L&mark Books — R&om House, New York, 1961.

-Pearl Harbor, Roberta Wahlstetter, Stanford Univ. Press, Calif., 1962.

-A Spy in Rome, Peter Tompkins, Simon & Schuster New York 1962.

-Pearl Harbor Warning & Decision, Roberta

Wohlstetter, Stanford Univ. Press, Cal. 1962.

-Hell at 50 Fathoms, Charles Lockwood & Hans Christion Adamson, Chilton Co., Phila-New York, 1962.

-The Uninvited Envoy, James Leasor, McGraw- Hill Book Co., Inc., New York 1962.

-Admiral Arleigh (31 knot) Burke, Ken Junes & Hubert Kelley Jr., Chilton Books, New York-Phila., 1962.

-Room 3603, H. Montgomery Hyde, Farrar, Straus & Co., New York 1962.

-The Brutal Friendship, F.W. Deakin, Harper & Row Publishers, New York 1962.

-Death In The Forest, J. K. Zawodny, Univ. of Notre Dame Press, Ind. 1962.

-Yanks Don't Cry, Martin Boyle, Bernard Geis Assoc., 1963.

-Illusion & Necessity, John L. Snell, Houghton, Mifflin, Co., Boston 1963.

-Sixty Days That Shook The West, Jacques Benoist-Mechin, G.P. Putnam's Sons, New York 1963.

-On Valor's Side, T. Grady Gallant, Doubleday & Co., Inc., Garden City, New Jersey 1963.

-Front-Line General, Jules Archer, Julian Messner, Inc., New York 1963.

-The Year That Changed the World, Brian Gardner, Coward-Mccann, Inc., New York, 1963.

-Ordeal by Sea, Thomas Helm, Dodd, Mead & Company, New York, 1963.

-A Night Before Christmas, Jacquin S&ers, G.P. Putnam's Sons, New York, 1963.

-The Two Ocean War, Samuel Eliot Morison, Little Brown & Co. Boston, Toronto, 1963.

-LaVal, Hubert Cole, G. P. Putnam's Sons, N.Y., 1963.

-The Fortress That Never Was, Rodney G. Minott, Holt, Rhinehart & Winston, 1964.

-Blitzkrieg To Defeat, H. R. Trevor-Roper, Holt, Rinehart & Winston, N.Y., Chicago, San Francisco, 1964.

-Rum War at Sea, Malcolm F. Willoughby, Gov't Printing Office, Washington, 1964.

-Before the Colors Fade, Fred Ayer Jr., Houghton Mifflin Co., Boston 1964.

-The Invasion of Europe, Allon A Michie, Dodd, Mead & Co., New York 1964.

-The Minute Man in Peace & War, Jim Dan Hill, The Stackpole Co., Pennsylvania, 1964.

-Neither Fear Nor Hope, German General Frido von Senger und Etterlin, E.P. Dutton & Co. Inc., N.Y. 1964.

-Secrets & Spies, Readers Digest, The Readers Digest & Associations, 1964.

-Portrait of Patton, Harry H. Semmes, 1964.

-The Battle of El Alamein, Fred Majdalany, J.B. Lippincott & Company, Phila., New York, 1965.

-Iwo Jima, Richard F. Newcomb, Nelson Doubleday, Inc. Garden City, N.Y. 1965.

-A History of the Jewish People, Max Margolis *MD1*Alex*MD0*er Marx, Harper & Row Publishers, New York, 1965.

-The Honorable Conquerers, Weil Sheldon, The MacMillan Co., New York, 1965.

-The Nazi Seizure of Power, William Sheridan Allen, Chicage Quadrangle Books, 1965.

-Flying Fortress, Edward Jablonski, Doubleday & Company Inc., Garden City, N.Y., 1965.

-With MacArthur in Japan, Ambassador William J. Sebald, with Russell Brines,

W.W. Norton & Co., Inc., New York 1965.
-Challenge for the Pacific, Robert Leckie, Doubleday & Co., Inc., 1965.
-The Nazi Seizure of Power, William Sheridan Allen, Quadrangle Books, Chicago, 1965.
-The Murder of Admiral Darlan, Peter Tompkins, Simon & Schuster, N.Y. 1965.
-Hostile Allies, Milton Viorst, The MacMillan Co., New York 1965.
-The Secret Surrender, Allen Dulles, Harper & Row Publishers, Inc., New York 1966.
-Hitler's Last Offensive, Peter Elstob, The MacMillan Co., 1967.
-Berlin '45, Richard Brett-Smith, St. Martin's Press, New York, 1967.
-The Fall of Japan, William Craig, The Dial Press, 1967.
-The GI War, Ralph G. Martin, Little, Brown & Co., Boston-Toronto 1967.
-Bloody Winter, Cpt. John M Waters Jr., D. Van Nostr& Co., Inc., New Jersey 1967.
-Tarawa A Legend IS Born, Henry I. Shaw, Jr. Ballantine Books, Inc., N.Y. 1968.
-The Battle of Cape Esperance, Charles Cook, Thomas Y. Crowell Co. 1968.
-Rome Fell Today, Robert H. Adelman & Colonel George Walton, Little, Brown & Company, 1968.
-The Battle of North Africa, John Strawson, Charles Scribner's Sons, New York, 1969.
-Iron Coffins, Herbert A. Werner, Holt, Rinehart & Winston, New York 1969.
-Get Yamamoto, Burke Davis, R&om House, New York 1969.
-Darkness Over Europe, Tony March, McNally & Co., New York, 1969.
-Luftwaffe, Birth, Life, & Death of an Airforce, Alfred Price, Ballantine Books, (Book No. 10), 1969.
-In Review, D.D. Eisenhower, Doubleday & Co., Garden City, N.Y., 1969.
-Bloody River, Martin Blumerson, Houghton Mifflin Co., Boston, 1970.
-Inside The Third Reich, Albert Speer, The MacMillan Company, New York, 1970.
-The German Dictatorship, Karl Dietrich Bracher, Praeger Publishers, 1970.
-The Rising Sun Vol I, John Tol&, R&om House, New York, 1970.
-The Rising Sun Vol II, John Tol&, R&om House, New York, 1970.
-The Trials of the Germans Nuremburg 1945-1946, Eugene Davidson, MacMillan Company, 1970.
-The Fall Of Eben Emael, Col. James E. Mrazek, 1970.
-Roosevelt: The Soldier of Freedom, James MacGregor Burns, Harcourt Brace Jovanovich, Inc., New York 1970.
-Donovan, OSS, Corey Ford, Little Brown & Company, Canada, 1970.
-Stilwell & American Expedition in China 1911-45, Barbara Tuchman, MacMillan Co., New York, 1970-71.
-Air War, Edward Jablonski, Doubleday & Company, Garden City, N.Y., 1971.
-The Case of General Yamishita, A. Frank Reel, Octagon Books, 1971.
-The General Was A Spy, Heinz, Hohne & Herman Zolling, Coward, McCann & Geoghegan Inc., New York 1971.
-The Inner Circle, Joan Bright Astley, Little, Brown & Co., Canada 1971.
-Japan's Imperial Conspiracy Volume I, David Bergamini, William Morrow & Company Inc., New York, 1971.
-Japan's Imperial Conspiracy Volume II, David Bergamini, William Morrow & Company Inc., New York, 1971.

-Why Hitler, Amos E. Simpson, Houghton Mifflin Company, 1971.
-The Patton Papers 1885 — 1940 Vol I, Martin Blumenson, Houghton Mifflin Company, 1972.
-The Patton Papers 1885 — 1940 Vol II, Martin Blumenson, Houghton Mifflin Company, 1972.
-The Double-Cross System in the War of 1939-1945, J.C. Masterman, Yale University Press, New Haven & London, 1972.
-Days of Sadness, Years of Triumph, Geoffrey Perrett, Coward, McCann & Geoghegan Inc., New York, 1973.
-Codeword Barbarossa, Barton Whaley, MIT Press, Cambridge, Mass. & London, 1973.
-The Darkest Year Britain Alone June 1940-June 1941, Herbert Agar, Doubleday & Company Inc., 1973.
-Crisis Convoy, Vice Admiral Sir Peter Gretton, Naval Institute Press, 1974.
-Meeting At Potsdam, Charles L. Mee, Jr., M Evans & Co., Inc., New York 1975.
-Silent Victory, Clay Blair, Jr., J.B. Lippincott Co., New York 1975.
-Line of Departure, Tarawa, Martin Russ, Doubleday & Company Inc., 1975.
-Special Envoy (to Churchill & Stalin), W. Averell Harriman & Elie Abel, R&om House 1975.
-The G.I.'s, The Americans in Britain — 1942-1945, Norman Langmate, Charles Scribner's Sons, 1975.
-WWII, James Jones, Grosset & Dunlap, New York, 1975.
-Adolf Hitler, John Tol&, Doubleday & Company Inc., 1976.
-A Man Called Intrepid, William Stevenson, Howard Brace Jovanovich, New York, 1976.
-The Soviet Air Force Since 1918, Stein & Day, New York, 1977.
-Churchill And Eden At War, Elisabeth Barker, St. Martin's, 1978.
-American Caesar, William Manchester, Dell Publishing Co. Inc., New York, 1978.
-The Four-Front War, William R. Peri, Crown Publishers Inc., 1978,79.
-Deadly Magic, Edward VanDer Rhoer, Robert Hale, London, 1978.
-Naples 1944, Norman Lewis, Pantheon Press, New York, 1978.
-U-Boats Offshore, Edwin P. Hoyt, Stein & Day, New York, 1978.
-Who Financed Hitler, James Pool & Suzanne Pool, The Dial Press, New York 1978.
-The Enigma War, Jozef Garlinski, Charles Scribner & Sons, New York, 1979.
-United States Marines, Thomas A. Siefring, Cartwell Books, Bison Books, Secaucus, N.J., 1979.
-Batfish, Hughston E. Lowder with Jack Scott, Prentice-Hall Inc., Englewood Cliffs, N.J., 1980.
-Death of a Division, Charles Whiting, Stein & Day, Briarcliff Manor, New York, 1980.
-The Victory That Never Was, John Grigg, Hill & Wang, New York, 1980.
-Master of Seapower, Thomas B. Buell, Little Brown & Co., Boston, Toronto, 1980.
-World War II, Ed. Brugadier Peter Young, Bison Books Ltd., London, 1981.
-The Impossible Victory, Brian Harpur, Hippocrene Books Inc., N.Y. 1981.
-The Pacific War, John Costello, Rawson, Wade Publishers, Inc., New York 1981.
-Hap, Thomas M. Coffey, The Viking Press,

1982.
-Above And Beyond 1941-1945, Wilbur H. Morrison, St. Martin's Press, New York, 1983.
-Almanac of American History, Arthur M. Schlesinger Jr., Bison Books, 1983.
-History of The United States Marines, Jack Murphy, Bison Books Corp., Greenwich, Ct., 1984.
-Mark C. Clark, Martin Blumenson, Congdon & Weed, New York, 1984.
-The Rise & Fall of Imperial Japan 1894-1945, S.L. Mayer, The Military Press, Bison Books Ltd 1976, Bison Books Corp., 1984.
-American Headlines Year By Year, Thomas Nelson Publishers, Nashville, Tn. 1985.
-Petain: Hero or Traitor: The Unknown Story, Herbert R. Lottman, William Morrow & Co. Inc., New York, 1985.
-Scabby, Lel& Cunningham, Nicholas Christodoulu Jr., Nashville, Tennessee, 1985.
-Surrender & Survival, E. Bartlett Kerr, William Morrow & Company Inc. New York, 1985.
-Pearl Harbor, The Verdict of History, Gordon W. Prange W/Donald M. Goldstein & Katherine V. Dillon, McGraw-Hill Book Company, 1986.
-Retaking The Philippines, William B. Breuer, St. Martin's Press New York, 1986.
-Thank You Uncle Sam, Eugenia M. Kielar, Dorrance & Company Inc., 1987.
-The Franco Regime 1936-1975, Stanley G. Payne, Univ. of Wisconsin Press, London, Engl& 1987.
-Bushmasters, Anthony Arthur, St. Martin's Press, N.Y. 1987.
-War At Sea (Pearl Harbor to Midway), Jack Greene, Gallery Books, New York, Combined Books, 1988.
-The Second World War, West Point Military History of World War II, (Three Volumes), 1989.
-West Point Military Campaign Atlas, Thomas E. Griess, Avery Publishing Group Inc., Wayne, N.J., 1989.

Photo Credits: Photos are from the National Archives, U.S. Army, U.S. Navy, U.S. Air Force, U.S. Coast Guard, U.S. Marine Corps, U.S. Naval Historical Foundation & U.S. Army War College, Carlisle, Pa, U.S. Naval Academy. However, several are from personal collections & are so noted. Our thanks to Major General George S. Patton, USA (Ret.) & General William C. Westmoreland, USA (Ret.) for their permission to use some personal photos.

Also, we would like to thank Mrs. Joann Patton, Mr. Henry I. Shaw, Jr. and Mrs. Ramage for their permission to use personal photographs.

Illustrations, courtesy of Justin Grecescu.

SUMMARY

Battle casualties by type of casualty and disposition, type of
personnel, and theater: 7 December 1941 - 31 December 1946

Line No.	Type of battle casualty and disposition	Total	Type of personnel		Theater			
			Officers	Enlisted	European Theater	Mediterranean Theater	Pacific Theaters a/	All other theaters b/
1	Total c/	936,259	95,998	840,261	586,628	175,107	157,938	16,586
2	Deaths among battle casualties . . .	234,874	35,984	198,890	135,576	40,455	50,385	8,458
3	Killed in action d/	192,798	31,057	161,741	117,215	35,377	33,011	7,195
4	Died of wounds and injuries e/ . .	26,762	2,309	24,453	16,458	4,056	5,889	359
5	Declared dead	6,058	1,974	4,084	1,361	978	2,889	359
6	Died of other causes (nonbattle) f/	9,256	644	8,612	542	44	8,596	830
7	Other battle casualties g/	701,385	60,014	641,371	451,052	134,652	107,553	74
8	Killed in action . . . . ✓	189,696	30,157	159,539	116,991	35,313	30,538	8,128
9	Wounded and injured in action . .	592,170	38,504	553,666	381,350	111,125	95,021	6,854
10	Died of wounds and injuries overseas . .	26,225	2,109	24,116	16,264	3,993	5,707	4,674
11	Returned to duty overseas	383,196	23,747	359,449	239,669	80,853	59,391	261
12	Evacuated to the United States	182,749	12,648	170,101	125,417	26,279	29,923	3,283
13	Died of wounds and injuries	84	11	73	0	0	0	1,130
14	Returned to duty, discharged, etc. . .	182,665	12,637	170,028	125,417	26,279	29,923	84
15	Captured and interned	124,079	21,593	102,486	73,759	20,182	27,465	1,046
16	Killed in action	3,102	900	2,202	224	64	2,473	2,673
17	Died of wounds and injuries	453	189	264	194	63	182	341
18	Died of other causes (nonbattle)	9,098	637	8,461	532	44	8,452	14
19	Returned to military control	111,426	19,867	91,559	72,809	20,011	16,358	70
20	Missing in action	30,314	5,744	24,570	14,528	8,487	4,914	2,248
21	Declared dead	6,058	1,974	4,084	1,361	978	2,889	2,385
22	Died of other causes (nonbattle)	158	7	151	10	0	144	830
23	Returned to duty	24,098	3,763	20,335	13,157	7,509	1,881	4
								1,551

For footnotes see table below.

Battle casualties by type of casualty and disposition, and duty branch:
7 December 1941 - 31 December 1946

Line No.	Type of battle casualty and disposition	Total	Air Corps (incl. flight officers)	Other branches				
				Total	Infantry	Field Artillery	Corps of Engineers	All other h/
1	Total c/	936,259	115,382	820,877	661,059	42,692	29,806	87,320
2	Deaths among battle casualties . . .	234,874	52,173	182,701	142,962	9,585	7,691	22,463
3	Killed in action d/	192,798	45,520	147,278	118,376	6,979	5,920	16,003
4	Died of wounds and injuries e/ . .	26,762	1,140	25,622	19,799	1,701	1,149	2,973
5	Declared dead	6,058	3,603	2,455	1,735	176	137	407
6	Died of other causes (nonbattle) f/	9,256	1,910	7,346	3,052	729	485	3,080
7	Other battle casualties g/	701,385	63,209	638,176	518,097	33,107	22,115	64,857
8	Killed in action	189,696	44,785	144,911	117,641	6,868	5,773	14,629
9	Wounded and injured in action . .	592,170	18,364	573,806	471,376	29,068	20,006	53,356
10	Died of wounds and injuries overseas . .	26,225	1,004	25,221	19,545	1,680	1,124	2,872
11	Returned to duty overseas	383,196	12,661	370,535	304,521	18,731	12,985	34,298
12	Evacuated to the United States	182,749	4,699	178,050	147,310	8,657	5,897	16,186
13	Died of wounds and injuries	84	1	83	68	3	5	7
14	Returned to duty, discharged, etc. . .	182,665	4,698	177,967	147,242	8,654	5,892	16,179
15	Captured and interned	124,079	41,057	83,022	56,212	5,966	3,518	17,326
16	Killed in action	3,102	735	2,367	735	111	147	1,374
17	Died of wounds and injuries	453	135	318	186	18	20	94
18	Died of other causes (nonbattle)	9,098	1,893	7,205	2,992	706	472	3,035
19	Returned to military control	111,426	38,294	73,132	52,299	5,131	2,879	12,823
20	Missing in action	30,314	11,176	19,138	15,830	790	509	2,009
21	Declared dead	6,058	3,603	2,455	1,735	176	137	407
22	Died of other causes (nonbattle)	158	17	141	60	23	13	45
23	Returned to duty	24,098	7,556	16,542	14,035	591	359	1,557

a/ Excludes Alaskan Department, U. S. Army Strategic Air Forces, and Burma, China, and India Theaters.
b/ Includes unreported theaters (theater unknown), and enroute personnel not chargeable to any command.
c/ Sum of lines 8, 9, 15, and 20.
d/ Sum of lines 8 and 16.
e/ Sum of lines 10, 13, and 17.
f/ Sum of lines 18 and 22. Excludes 83,400 nonbattle deaths of persons not in a battle casualty status.
g/ Sum of lines 11, 14, 19, and 23.
h/ Includes general officers, warrant officers and female personnel.

SUMMARY

Battle casualties by month of occurrence, duty branch, and theater
group: 7 December 1941 – 31 December 1946

Year and month of occurrence	Total	Duty branch		Theater group		
		Air Corps branch (including flight officers)	All other branches a/	Atlantic area theaters b/	Pacific area theaters c/	Theater unknown and enroute (not chargeable to any command)
Total	936,259	115,382	820,877	765,751	169,635	873
1941 December . . .	1,093	762	331	11	1,080	2
1942	40,042	7,044	32,998	4,028	35,822	192
January . . .	860	98	762	42	818	0
February . . .	1,055	192	863	50	1,005	0
March	220	63	157	8	212	0
April	1,165	142	1,023	7	1,157	1
May	29,159	4,704	24,455	47	28,966	146
June	318	139	179	69	231	18
July	189	109	80	34	152	3
August	208	169	39	52	156	0
September . .	249	214	35	96	153	0
October . . .	315	225	90	140	168	7
November . . .	3,110	426	2,684	2,060	1,046	4
December . . .	3,194	563	2,631	1,423	1,758	13
1943	73,952	21,071	52,881	60,217	13,206	529
January . . .	3,353	968	2,385	1,529	1,821	3
February . . .	6,674	1,125	5,549	5,942	320	412
March	4,583	710	3,873	4,297	282	4
April	5,310	935	4,375	5,061	245	4
May	4,088	1,356	2,732	2,638	1,415	35
June	1,597	1,311	286	1,204	383	10
July	10,466	2,381	8,085	6,783	3,679	4
August	7,153	2,605	4,548	5,419	1,692	42
September . .	6,810	1,634	5,176	5,930	879	1
October . . .	6,640	2,751	3,889	6,157	476	7
November . . .	9,471	2,596	6,875	8,200	1,269	2
December . . .	7,807	2,699	5,108	7,057	745	5
1944	521,390	66,290	455,100	478,389	42,893	108
January . . .	13,815	3,486	10,329	12,707	1,106	2
February . . .	17,735	4,896	12,839	15,837	1,890	8
March	12,345	5,024	7,321	9,005	3,337	3
April	11,454	7,651	3,803	10,054	1,394	6
May	23,061	6,543	16,518	21,239	1,819	3
June	55,320	6,785	48,535	49,061	6,247	12
July	65,906	6,769	59,137	61,454	4,439	13
August	51,577	6,101	45,476	49,458	2,107	12
September . .	57,150	5,014	52,136	54,937	2,206	7
October . . .	53,788	3,957	49,831	47,725	6,058	5
November . . .	71,704	4,874	66,830	65,918	5,777	9
December . . .	87,535	5,190	82,345	80,994	6,513	28
1945	298,714	19,836	278,878	222,548	76,136	30
January . . .	78,828	3,797	75,031	70,568	8,252	8
February . . .	56,348	4,068	52,280	43,603	12,744	1
March	65,367	5,505	59,862	56,282	9,077	8
April	69,980	3,536	66,444	49,706	20,266	8
May	18,081	1,273	16,808	2,201	15,879	1
June	7,913	796	7,117	82	7,830	1
July	1,369	546	823	36	1,332	1
August	697	294	403	13	683	1
September . .	58	10	48	12	46	0
October . . .	21	4	17	11	10	0
November . . .	24	5	19	11	13	0
December . . .	28	2	26	23	4	1
1946	10	6	4	5	5	0
Date unknown . . .	1,058	373	685	553	493	12

a/ Includes general officers, warrant officers, and female personnel.
b/ Africa – Middle East Theater, Caribbean Defense Command and South Atlantic, European Theater, and Mediterranean Theater.
c/ Alaskan Department, China – Burma – India Theater, China Theater, India – Burma Theater, Pacific Theaters, and U. S. Army Strategic Air Forces.

SUMMARY

Battle casualties by grade in which serving and duty branch:
7 December 1941 - 31 December 1946

Grade in which serving	Battle casualties a/			Deaths among battle casualties		
	Total	Air Corps branch	All other branches b/	Total	Air Corps branch	All other branches b/
Total	936,259	115,382	820,877	234,874	52,173	182,701
Officers	95,998	49,385	46,613	35,984	23,174	12,810
Commissioned	93,074	46,769	46,305	34,710	22,022	12,688
General	72	c/	c/ 72	25	c/	c/ 25
Colonel	403	111	292	121	44	77
Lieutenant colonel	1,192	214	978	440	102	338
Major	1,978	644	1,334	824	358	466
Captain	9,669	2,581	7,088	3,501	1,386	2,115
First Lieutenant	35,003	15,673	19,330	13,240	8,072	5,168
Second Lieutenant	44,757	27,546	17,211	16,559	12,060	4,499
Warrant and flight	2,924	2,616	303	1,274	1,152	122
Chief warrant officer	90	0	90	45	0	45
Warrant officer, junior grade	218	0	218	77	0	77
Flight officer	2,616	2,616	0	1,152	1,152	0
Enlisted personnel	840,261	65,997	774,264	198,890	28,999	169,891
Master and first sergeant	3,870	375	3,495	1,077	199	878
Technical sergeant	24,614	11,171	13,443	7,748	4,717	3,031
Staff sergeant and technician 3rd grade .	83,540	29,538	54,002	24,717	12,527	12,190
Sergeant and technician 4th grade	92,487	16,159	76,328	24,777	7,154	17,623
Corporal and technician 5th grade	54,250	4,163	50,087	18,086	2,132	15,954
Private first class	302,558	1,922	300,636	65,662	919	64,743
Private	278,942	2,669	276,273	56,823	1,351	55,472

a/ Includes deaths among battle casualties.
b/ Includes female personnel.
c/ Recorded as "General officers" in branch tables of this report regardless of duty branch.

Battle and nonbattle deaths by type of death and duty branch:
7 December 1941 - 31 December 1946

Type of death	Total	Air Corps branch (including flight officers)	All other branches a/
Total	318,274	88,119	230,155
Deaths among battle casualties	234,874	52,173	182,701
Battle deaths	225,618	50,263	175,355
Killed in action	192,798	45,520	147,278
Died of wounds and injuries received in action	26,762	1,140	25,622
Declared dead from missing in action	6,058	3,603	2,455
Nonbattle deaths	9,256	1,910	7,346
Died of other causes (nonbattle) while captured or interned .	9,098	1,893	7,205
Died of other causes (nonbattle) while missing in action . .	158	17	141
Other nonbattle deaths b/	83,400	35,946	47,454

a/ Includes general officers, warrant officers, and female personnel.
b/ Consists of nonbattle deaths of personnel not in a battle casualty status.

Battle casualties by duty branch, and by grade in which serving for officers: 7 December 1941 - 31 December 1946 a/

| Duty branch | Total battle casualties | Total officers | Officers | | | | | | | | | | Warrant and flight | Enlisted personnel |
| | | | Commissioned | | | | | | | | | | | |
			Total	General	Colonel	Lieutenant colonel	Major	Captain	First lieutenant	Second lieutenant			
Total	936,259	95,998	93,074	72	403	1,192	1,978	9,669	35,003	44,757		2,924	840,261
Male	936,113	95,864	92,940	72	403	1,192	1,978	9,668	34,977	44,650		2,924	840,249
General officers	72	72	72	72	0	0	0	0	0	0		0	0
General Staff Corps . . .	56	56	56	0	21	27	6	2	0	0		0	0
Inspector General's Dept.	5	5	5	0	1	3	1	0	0	0		0	0
Military Intelligence . .	21	21	21	0	0	2	3	3	9	4		0	0
Air Corps	112,766	46,769	46,769	0	111	214	644	2,581	15,673	27,546		0	65,997
Armored Force	6,827	0	0	0	0	0	0	0	0	0		0	6,827
Cavalry	21,703	2,054	2,054	0	25	59	89	322	865	694		0	19,649
Coast Artillery Corps . .	15,277	896	896	0	16	33	52	227	363	205		0	14,381
Field Artillery	42,692	4,798	4,798	0	27	129	177	867	2,097	1,501		0	37,894
Infantry	661,059	33,538	33,538	0	148	564	721	4,275	14,159	13,671		0	627,521
Adjutant General's Dept.	74	34	34	0	3	7	5	8	6	5		0	40
Chemical Corps	3,499	266	266	0	2	5	5	34	130	90		0	3,233
Corps of Chaplains . . .	204	204	204	0	0	5	7	132	60	0		0	0
Corps of Engineers . . .	29,806	1,931	1,931	0	12	48	81	356	880	554		0	27,875
Corps of Military Police	1,294	60	60	0	0	3	6	11	26	14		0	1,234
Finance Department . . .	76	20	20	0	1	8	3	4	4	0		0	56
Judge Advocate Gen's Dept	9	9	9	0	1	2	4	0	1	1		0	0
Medical Department . . .	23,828	1,205	1,205	0	14	34	127	660	297	73		0	22,623
Dental Corps	117	117	117	0	1	1	8	90	17	0		0	0
Medical Admin. Corps .	192	192	192	0	0	1	4	15	99	73		0	0
Medical Corps	884	884	884	0	12	32	110	550	180	0		0	0
Sanitary Corps	2	2	2	0	0	0	0	2	0	0		0	0
Veterinary Corps . . .	10	10	10	0	1	0	5	3	1	0		0	0
Medical Dept. - other .	22,623	0	0	0	0	0	0	0	0	0		0	22,623
Ordnance Department . . .	3,245	214	214	0	3	10	10	54	84	53		0	3,031
Quartermaster Corps . . .	4,823	266	266	0	11	26	18	65	89	57		0	4,557
Signal Corps	3,993	282	282	0	6	10	15	42	119	90		0	3,711
Transportation Corps . .	1,124	71	71	0	1	1	2	11	29	27		0	1,053
Detached enl. men's list	228	0	0	0	0	0	0	0	0	0		0	228
No branch assigned . . .	508	169	169	0	0	2	2	14	86	65		0	339
Chief warrant officers .	90	90	0	0	0	0	0	0	0	0		90	0
Warrant officers, j. g.	218	218	0	0	0	0	0	0	0	0		218	0
Flight officers	2,616	2,616	0	0	0	0	0	0	0	0		2,616	0
Female	146	134	134	0	0	0	0	1	26	107		0	12
Army Nurse Corps	134	134	134	0	0	0	0	1	26	107		0	0
Women's Army Corps . . .	12	0	0	0	0	0	0	0	0	0		0	12

BATTLE CASUALTIES

Battle casualties, by theater, type, and disposition:
7 December 1941 - 31 December 1946 a/

Theater	Total battle cas- ualties	Total deaths among battle cas- ualties b/	Killed in action	Wounded and injured in action				
				Total	Died of wounds and injuries	Evacuated to U.S.		Returned to duty
						Died of wounds and injuries	Returned to duty, discharged etc.	
(1)	(2)	(3)	(4)	(5)	(6)	(7)	(8)	(9)
Total	936,259	234,874	189,696	592,170	26,225	84	182,665	383,196
Atlantic area theaters	765,751	177,100	153,270	493,020	20,276	0	151,814	320,930
Africa - Middle East Theater . . .	3,959	1,031	930	536	17	0	117	402
Caribbean Defense Command and South Atlantic	57	38	36	9	2	0	1	6
European Theater	586,628	135,576	116,991	381,350	16,264	0	125,417	239,669
Mediterranean Theater	175,107	40,455	35,313	111,125	3,993	0	26,279	80,853
Pacific area theaters	169,635	57,137	35,909	98,958	5,928	0	30,821	62,209
Alaskan Department	1,875	877	853	933	16	0	179	738
Burma, China, and India Theaters .	6,925	3,727	2,723	2,597	192	0	617	1,788
China - Burma - India Theater .	4,595	2,479	1,739	1,787	127	0	418	1,242
China Theater	500	227	167	106	10	0	26	70
India - Burma Theater	1,830	1,021	817	704	55	0	173	476
Pacific Theaters	157,938	50,385	30,538	95,021	5,707	0	29,923	59,391
U. S. Army Strategic Air Forces . .	2,897	2,148	1,795	407	13	0	102	292
Theater unknown	148	146	42	92	8	84	0	0
Enroute (not chargeable to any command)	725	491	475	100	13	0	30	57

See footnotes on next page.

Continued on next page

THEATER

	Captured and interned					Missing in action				
		Died					Died			
Total	Killed in action	Wounds and injuries	Other causes (non-battle)	Returned to military control	Total	Declared dead	Other causes (non-battle)	Returned to duty	Theater
(10)	(11)	(12)	(13)	(14)	(15)	(16)	(17)	(18)	(19)
124,079	3,102	453	9,098	111,426	30,314	6,058	158	24,098	Total
95,532	290	257	577	94,408	23,929	2,420	10	21,499	Atlantic area theaters
1,590	2	0	1	1,587	903	81	0	822	Africa - Middle East Theater
1	0	0	0	1	11	0	0	11	Caribbean Defense Command and South Atlantic
73,759	224	194	532	72,809	14,528	1,361	10	13,157	European Theater
20,182	64	63	44	20,011	8,487	978	0	7,509	Mediterranean Theater
28,526	2,805	194	8,517	17,010	6,242	3,637	147	2,458	Pacific area theaters
48	0	0	0	48	41	8	0	33	Alaskan Department
679	274	4	59	342	926	473	2	451	Burma, China, and India Theaters
539	262	3	59	215	530	289	0	241	China - Burma - India Theater
37	2	0	0	35	190	47	1	142	China Theater
103	10	1	0	92	206	137	1	68	India - Burma Theater
27,465	2,473	182	8,452	16,358	4,914	2,889	144	1,881	Pacific Theaters
334	58	8	6	262	361	267	1	93	U. S. Army Strategic Air Forces
12	7	2	2	1	2	0	1	1	Theater unknown
9	0	0	2	7	141	1	0	140	Enroute (not chargeable to any command)

a/ See Introduction for sources and coverage.
b/ Represents sum of battle deaths (columns 4, 6, 7, 11, 12, and 16) and nonbattle deaths (columns 13 and 17). Excludes nonbattle deaths of personnel not in a battle casualty status. See pages 96 through 118 for all Army deaths.

Battle casualties in Air Corps and all other branches, by place, type,
and disposition: 7 December 1941 - 31 December 1946 a/

Branch and place of occurrence	Total battle casualties	Total deaths among battle casualties b/	Killed in action	Wounded and injured in action		Evacuated to U.S.		Returned to duty
				Total	Died of wounds and injuries	Died of wounds and injuries	Returned to duty, discharged etc.	
(1)	(2)	(3)	(4)	(5)	(6)	(7)	(8)	(9)
All branches	936,259	234,874	189,696	592,170	26,225	84	182,665	383,196
Atlantic area	766,181	177,549	153,639	493,032	20,290	68	151,792	320,882
Algeria	1,735	1,130	1,038	663	88	0	90	485
Austria	5,972	1,846	1,736	979	38	0	308	633
Belgium	55,257	10,900	9,100	38,004	1,600	2	12,146	24,256
Czechoslovakia	1,230	351	337	417	9	0	178	230
English Channel and North Sea	3,088	3,088	3,052	17	17	0	0	0
France (including Corsica)	241,137	57,530	48,962	169,776	7,906	25	49,037	112,808
Germany	249,762	57,610	50,133	152,055	6,029	13	57,313	88,700
Hungary	1,518	406	389	123	11	0	37	75
Italy (including Sicily and Sardinia) .	123,522	30,050	25,900	84,058	3,440	8	19,213	61,397
Netherlands	11,889	3,201	2,699	7,488	445	1	2,153	4,889
Romania	2,381	758	723	248	10	0	69	169
Tunisia	17,464	3,711	3,155	9,038	356	8	2,266	6,408
United Kingdom	4,215	2,866	2,635	1,527	222	0	298	1,007
Yugoslavia	2,619	714	643	264	7	0	58	199
Other reported places	3,220	1,048	948	457	54	0	151	252
Place unknown	41,172	2,340	2,189	27,918	58	11	8,475	19,374
Pacific area	169,936	57,286	36,023	99,052	5,932	16	30,845	62,259
Admiralty Islands	2,393	396	314	2,048	71	0	611	1,366
Alaska	1,773	829	810	935	16	1	180	738
Burma	3,253	1,466	1,121	1,832	123	0	402	1,307
Caroline Islands	3,167	962	637	2,324	145	0	524	1,655
China	1,840	1,204	983	251	23	0	70	158
Japan (incl. Ryukyu and Kuril Islands)	23,832	7,040	5,381	17,445	1,068	0	5,997	10,380
Marianas Islands	5,968	2,202	1,858	3,982	319	0	989	2,674
Marshall Islands	1,640	512	336	1,190	67	0	157	966
New Guinea	12,405	4,868	3,682	7,974	500	4	1,974	5,496
Philippine Islands	90,454	30,424	15,050	46,405	3,048	7	15,138	28,212
Solomon Islands	8,227	2,667	2,127	5,843	315	0	1,955	3,573
Other reported places	6,345	3,496	2,706	2,216	181	1	625	1,409
Place unknown	8,639	1,220	1,018	6,607	56	3	2,223	4,325
Area unknown	142	39	34	86	3	0	28	55
Air Corps branch (including flight officers)	115,382	52,173	44,785	18,364	1,004	1	4,698	12,661
Atlantic area	91,105	36,461	34,362	13,708	748	1	3,548	9,411
Algeria	532	459	436	89	21	0	8	60
Austria	5,413	1,728	1,633	558	24	0	156	378
Belgium	1,052	482	450	260	19	0	88	153
Czechoslovakia	697	235	230	57	2	0	24	31
English Channel and North Sea	1,797	1,797	1,768	10	10	0	0	0
France (including Corsica)	10,129	4,686	4,349	2,101	126	0	521	1,454
Germany	38,584	14,695	14,047	4,510	206	0	1,314	2,990
Hungary	1,491	406	389	113	11	0	30	72
Italy (including Sicily and Sardinia) .	8,204	4,097	3,696	1,882	121	1	417	1,343
Netherlands	1,491	733	705	235	13	0	64	158
Romania	2,373	755	720	248	10	0	69	169
Tunisia	1,154	658	542	362	43	0	59	260
United Kingdom	3,427	2,498	2,394	987	95	0	228	664
Yugoslavia	2,579	707	638	240	7	0	55	178
Other reported places	2,591	808	746	218	21	0	45	152
Place unknown	9,591	1,717	1,619	1,838	19	0	470	1,349

Continued on next page

Battle casualties in Air Corps and all other branches, by place, type, and disposition: 7 December 1941 - 31 December 1946 a/ - continued

	Captured and interned					Missing in action			
Total	Died			Returned to military control	Total	Died		Returned to duty
	Killed in action	Wounds and injuries	Other causes (non-battle)			De-clared dead	Other causes (non-battle)	
(10)	(11)	(12)	(13)	(14)	(15)	(16)	(17)	(18)
124,079	3,102	453	9,098	111,426	30,314	6,058	158	24,098
95,495	290	257	575	94,373	24,015	2,418	12	21,585
12	0	0	0	12	22	4	0	18
2,527	2	8	4	2,513	730	58	0	672
6,318	17	18	82	6,201	1,835	78	3	1,754
381	2	0	2	377	95	1	0	94
0	0	0	0	0	19	19	0	0
16,423	34	44	37	16,308	5,976	522	0	5,454
41,447	188	132	415	40,712	6,127	694	6	5,427
718	1	1	1	715	288	2	1	285
9,195	26	26	12	9,131	4,369	638	0	3,731
1,428	2	5	0	1,421	274	49	0	225
878	1	5	0	872	532	19	0	513
4,796	16	12	18	4,750	475	146	0	329
33	0	1	0	32	20	8	0	12
735	0	1	0	734	977	63	0	914
1,411	1	3	2	1,405	404	39	1	364
9,193	0	1	2	9,190	1,872	78	1	1,793
28,570	2,812	196	8,522	17,040	6,291	3,639	146	2,506
7	1	0	0	6	24	10	0	14
4	0	0	0	4	24	2	0	22
106	1	2	46	57	194	173	0	21
0	0	0	0	0	206	180	0	26
149	6	1	53	89	457	138	0	319
473	83	12	186	192	533	309	1	223
103	7	1	1	94	25	16	0	9
3	2	0	0	1	111	107	0	4
18	6	2	0	10	731	674	0	57
26,424	2,622	164	8,169	15,469	2,575	1,223	141	1,211
6	3	0	2	1	251	219	1	31
732	54	7	59	612	691	485	3	203
545	27	7	6	505	469	103	0	366
14	0	0	1	13	8	1	0	7
41,057	735	135	1,893	38,294	11,176	3,603	17	7,556
35,621	68	92	46	35,415	7,414	1,143	1	6,270
2	0	0	0	2	5	2	0	3
2,496	2	8	3	2,483	726	58	0	668
270	0	2	1	267	72	10	0	62
326	0	0	2	324	84	1	0	83
0	0	0	0	0	19	19	0	0
2,520	3	10	1	2,506	1,159	197	0	962
18,431	54	51	34	18,292	1,596	303	0	1,293
702	1	1	1	699	287	2	1	284
1,787	5	8	1	1,773	839	265	0	574
469	0	1	0	468	82	14	0	68
873	1	5	0	867	532	19	0	513
164	1	1	0	162	86	71	0	15
28	0	1	0	27	18	8	0	10
728	0	1	0	727	973	61	0	912
1,358	1	2	2	1,353	269	36	0	233
5,467	0	1	1	5,465	667	77	0	590

Continued on next page

BATTLE CASUALTIES

Battle casualties by theater, organization, type, and disposition:
7 December 1941 - 31 December 1946 a/

Theater and organization	Total battle casualties	Total deaths among battle casualties b/	Killed in action	Wounded and injured in action				
				Total	Died of wounds and injuries	Evacuated to U.S.		Returned to duty
						Died of wounds and injuries	Returned to duty, discharged etc.	
(1)	(2)	(3)	(4)	(5)	(6)	(7)	(8)	(9)
All theaters	936,259	234,874	189,696	592,170	26,225	84	182,665	383,196
Combat divisions	664,024	140,175	117,891	482,416	20,371	0	152,165	309,880
Airborne divisions	27,577	6,161	5,070	19,778	967	0	5,207	13,604
11th	2,431	620	494	1,926	120	0	659	1,147
17th	6,745	1,394	1,191	4,904	191	0	1,432	3,281
82nd	9,073	1,992	1,619	6,560	332	0	1,477	4,751
101st	9,328	2,155	1,766	6,388	324	0	1,639	4,425
Armored divisions	62,334	13,143	10,851	45,958	2,096	0	15,384	28,478
1st	7,096	1,467	1,194	5,168	234	0	1,198	3,736
2nd	5,864	1,196	981	4,557	202	0	1,397	2,958
3rd	9,243	2,147	1,810	6,963	316	0	2,239	4,408
4th	6,212	1,366	1,143	4,551	213	0	1,641	2,697
5th	3,075	716	570	2,442	140	0	770	1,532
6th	4,670	993	833	3,666	156	0	1,294	2,216
7th	5,799	1,138	898	3,811	200	0	1,416	2,195
8th	2,011	469	393	1,572	73	0	621	878
9th	3,845	728	570	2,280	123	0	848	1,309
10th	4,031	784	642	3,109	132	0	1,159	1,818
11th	2,877	524	432	2,394	90	0	810	1,494
12th	3,527	732	616	2,416	109	0	906	1,401
13th	1,176	253	214	912	39	0	308	565
14th	2,690	566	505	1,955	55	0	710	1,190
16th	32	5	4	28	1	0	13	14
20th	186	59	46	134	13	0	54	67
Cavalry divisions	4,055	971	734	3,311	236	0	961	2,114
1st	4,055	971	734	3,311	236	0	961	2,114
Infantry divisions	565,986	118,945	100,364	410,235	16,991	0	129,625	263,619
1st	20,659	4,365	3,616	15,208	664	0	4,899	9,645
2nd	16,795	3,512	3,031	12,785	457	0	3,834	8,494
3rd	25,977	5,634	4,922	18,766	636	0	4,996	13,134
4th	22,660	4,907	4,097	17,371	757	0	5,389	11,225
5th	12,818	2,684	2,298	9,549	358	0	3,129	6,062
6th	2,370	517	410	1,957	104	0	586	1,267
7th	9,212	2,337	1,948	7,258	386	0	2,133	4,739
8th	13,986	2,852	2,532	10,057	288	0	3,493	6,276
9th	23,277	4,550	3,856	17,416	648	0	5,227	11,541
24th	7,012	1,691	1,374	5,621	315	0	2,040	3,266
25th	5,432	1,500	1,235	4,190	262	0	1,441	2,487
26th	10,701	2,136	1,850	7,886	262	0	2,921	4,703
27th	6,533	1,849	1,512	4,980	332	0	1,416	3,232
28th	16,762	2,873	2,316	9,609	367	0	3,331	5,911
29th	20,620	4,824	3,887	15,541	899	0	4,256	10,386
30th	18,446	3,547	3,003	13,376	513	0	4,245	8,618
31st	1,733	415	340	1,392	74	0	445	873
32nd	7,268	2,002	1,613	5,627	372	0	1,860	3,395
33rd	2,426	524	396	2,024	128	0	616	1,280
34th	16,401	3,408	2,866	11,545	484	0	2,675	8,386
35th	15,822	2,997	2,485	11,526	462	0	3,539	7,525
36th	19,466	3,717	3,131	13,191	506	0	3,583	9,102
37th	5,960	1,348	1,094	4,861	250	0	1,386	3,225

Continued on next page

Battle casualties by theater, organization, type, and disposition:
7 December 1941 - 31 December 1946 a/ - continued

Captured and interned					Missing in action			
Total	Died			Returned to military control	Total	Died		Returned to duty
	Killed in action	Wounds and injuries	Other causes (non-battle)			De-clared dead	Other causes (non-battle)	
(10)	(11)	(12)	(13)	(14)	(15)	(16)	(17)	(18)
124,079	3,102	453	9,098	111,426	30,314	6,058	158	24,098
48,919	169	129	441	48,180	14,798	1,167	7	13,624
2,008	15	6	16	1,971	721	86	1	634
0	0	0	0	0	11	6	0	5
426	1	2	4	419	224	5	0	219
615	3	0	4	608	279	34	0	245
967	11	4	8	944	207	41	1	165
4,567	12	19	58	4,478	958	106	1	851
518	3	2	14	499	216	20	0	196
266	0	0	1	265	60	12	0	48
366	0	2	2	362	104	17	0	87
453	1	4	2	446	65	3	0	62
22	0	0	0	22	41	6	0	35
83	0	0	1	82	88	3	0	85
925	2	3	11	909	165	24	0	141
41	0	0	0	41	5	3	0	2
908	4	2	24	878	87	4	1	82
216	0	2	1	213	64	7	0	57
40	0	0	2	38	11	0	0	11
478	0	2	0	476	17	5	0	12
34	0	0	0	34	16	0	0	16
212	2	2	0	208	18	2	0	16
0	0	0	0	0	0	0	0	0
5	0	0	0	5	1	0	0	1
1	0	0	0	1	9	1	0	8
1	0	0	0	1	9	1	0	8
42,315	142	104	367	41,702	13,072	972	5	12,095
1,336	8	5	6	1,317	499	66	0	433
786	1	2	6	777	193	15	0	178
1,735	3	4	4	1,724	554	65	0	489
731	5	2	.	720	461	42	0	419
683	1	1	1	680	288	25	0	263
0	0	0	0	0	3	3	0	0
2	1	0	1	0	4	1	0	3
668	1	2	2	663	729	27	0	702
1,648	10	1	2	1,635	357	33	0	324
6	1	0	0	5	11	1	0	10
2	0	0	0	2	5	3	0	2
806	4	6	7	789	159	7	0	152
1	0	0	0	1	40	5	0	35
3,953	14	15	58	3,866	884	103	0	781
845	0	2	4	839	347	32	0	315
1,164	3	3	2	1,156	903	23	0	880
1	0	0	1	0	0	0	0	0
1	0	0	0	1	27	17	0	10
1	0	0	0	1	5	0	0	5
1,368	7	4	9	1,348	622	38	0	584
1,471	2	4	20	1,445	340	23	1	316
2,650	8	5	5	2,632	494	62	0	432
1	0	0	0	1	4	4	0	0

Continued on next page

BATTLE CASUALTIES

Battle casualties by campaign and type of organization:
7 December 1941 - 31 December 1946 a/

Campaign and type of organization	Total battle casualties	Total deaths among battle casualties b/	Killed in action	Wounded and injured in action		Captured and interned		Missing in action	
				Total	Died c/	Total	Died c/	Total	Died c/
Total	936,259	234,874	189,696	592,170	26,309	124,079	12,653	30,314	6,216
Atlantic area campaigns	749,832	174,090	150,701	485,020	19,905	90,597	1,074	23,514	2,410
Air Offensive, Europe (4 July 1942 to 5 June 1944)	23,931	7,504	7,143	2,940	148	13,048	55	800	158
Combat divisions	0	0	0	0	0	0	0	0	0
Air Force units	23,931	7,504	7,143	2,940	148	13,048	55	800	158
Other units	0	0	0	0	0	0	0	0	0
Algeria - French Morocco (8 to 11 November 1942)	1,254	479	449	720	24	24	2	61	4
Combat divisions	874	253	233	579	18	8	0	54	2
Air Force units	39	23	22	11	1	4	0	2	0
Other units	341	203	194	130	5	12	2	5	2
Anzio (22 January to 24 May 1944)	23,173	5,538	4,668	15,558	720	2,468	15	479	135
Combat divisions	19,976	4,520	3,817	13,462	572	2,254	11	443	120
Air Force units	0	0	0	0	0	0	0	0	0
Other units	3,197	1,018	851	2,096	148	214	4	36	15
Ardennes - Alsace (16 December 1944 to 25 January 1945)	105,102	19,246	16,001	62,489	2,439	23,554	572	3,058	234
Combat divisions	88,323	14,973	12,359	53,333	1,958	20,102	482	2,529	174
Air Force units	2,793	1,314	1,249	605	27	872	7	67	31
Other units	13,986	2,959	2,393	8,551	454	2,580	83	462	29
Central Europe (22 March to 11 May 1945)	62,704	15,009	13,016	44,475	1,907	3,722	8	1,491	78
Combat divisions	53,244	11,843	10,178	39,271	1,628	2,509	6	1,286	31
Air Force units	3,265	1,633	1,564	623	28	962	0	116	41
Other units	6,195	1,533	1,274	4,581	251	251	2	89	6
Egypt - Libya (11 June 1942 to 12 February 1943)	3,712	997	902	442	13	1,490	3	878	79
Combat divisions	0	0	0	0	0	0	0	0	0
Air Force units	3,712	997	902	442	13	1,490	3	878	79
Other units	0	0	0	0	0	0	0	0	0
Naples - Foggia (18 August 1943 - air, 9 September 1943 - ground, to 21 January 1944)	23,364	6,266	5,398	15,411	769	1,999	15	556	84
Combat divisions	11,930	2,604	2,191	8,171	378	1,323	10	245	25
Air Force units	2,519	1,599	1,476	493	68	394	2	156	53
Other units	8,915	2,063	1,731	6,747	323	282	3	155	6
Normandy (6 June to 24 July 1944)	63,360	16,293	13,959	43,221	2,170	5,087	42	1,093	122
Combat divisions	54,099	12,923	10,812	40,621	2,034	2,148	15	518	62
Air Force units	6,706	2,506	2,362	1,129	62	2,690	25	525	57
Other units	2,555	864	785	1,471	74	249	2	50	3
North Apennines (10 September 1944 to 4 April 1945)	36,820	8,486	7,563	21,592	647	4,017	23	3,648	253
Combat divisions	25,465	4,903	4,314	18,384	504	1,208	6	1,559	79
Air Force units	8,861	3,070	2,847	1,310	63	2,656	12	2,048	148
Other units	2,494	513	402	1,898	80	153	5	41	26
Northern France (25 July to 14 September 1944)	72,014	17,844	15,239	49,919	2,450	4,931	41	1,925	114
Combat divisions	59,501	13,850	11,704	43,882	2,057	2,473	17	1,442	72
Air Force units	5,559	2,261	2,144	906	63	2,138	21	371	33
Other units	6,954	1,733	1,391	5,131	330	320	3	112	9

CAMPAIGN AND TYPE OF ORGANIZATION

Battle casualties by campaign and type of organization:
7 December 1941 – 31 December 1946 a/ – continued

Campaign and type of organization	Total battle casualties	Total deaths among battle casualties b/	Killed in action	Wounded and injured in action — Total	Wounded and injured in action — Died c/	Captured and interned — Total	Captured and interned — Died c/	Missing in action — Total	Missing in action — Died c/
Atlantic area campaigns – concluded									
Po Valley (5 April to 8 May 1945)	8,639	1,914	1,719	6,345	185	373	1	202	9
Combat divisions	6,066	1,297	1,161	4,690	133	127	0	88	3
Air Force units	704	258	241	140	10	217	1	106	6
Other units	1,869	359	317	1,515	42	29	0	8	0
Rhineland (15 September 1944 to 21 March 1945)	240,082	50,410	43,258	172,450	6,485	19,060	168	5,314	499
Combat divisions	204,046	40,293	34,370	151,850	5,397	13,084	135	4,742	391
Air Force units	11,635	4,761	4,581	1,876	90	4,775	14	403	76
Other units	24,401	5,356	4,307	18,724	998	1,201	19	169	32
Rome – Arno (22 January to 9 September 1944)	46,924	11,393	10,087	29,131	1,007	5,409	58	2,297	241
Combat divisions	27,166	5,032	4,331	20,755	637	1,062	16	1,018	48
Air Force units	11,020	4,808	4,495	1,668	104	3,723	36	1,134	173
Other units	8,738	1,553	1,261	6,708	266	624	6	145	20
Sicily (14 May 1943 – air, 9 July 1943 – ground, to 17 August 1943)	9,195	2,572	2,237	5,946	200	598	10	414	125
Combat divisions	6,119	1,434	1,269	4,319	130	331	7	200	28
Air Force units	1,492	753	638	528	20	190	2	136	93
Other units	1,584	385	330	1,099	50	77	1	78	4
Southern France (15 August to 14 September 1944)	15,574	7,301	6,672	5,804	443	2,257	26	841	160
Combat divisions	2,251	961	818	1,045	139	362	2	26	2
Air Force units	7,500	4,524	4,280	1,117	83	1,540	20	563	141
Other units	5,823	1,816	1,574	3,642	221	355	4	252	17
Tunisia (12 November 1942 – air, 17 November 1942 – ground, to 13 May 1943) . . .	13,984	2,838	2,390	8,577	298	2,560	35	457	115
Combat divisions	10,954	1,993	1,668	7,046	234	1,902	28	338	63
Air Force units	730	309	256	259	8	157	1	58	44
Other units	2,300	536	466	1,272	56	501	6	61	8
Pacific area campaigns	160,276	55,145	34,568	92,664	5,712	27,181	11,163	5,863	3,702
Air Offensive, Japan (17 April 1942 to 2 September 1945)	4,578	3,602	3,076	581	37	437	99	484	390
Combat divisions	0	0	0	0	0	0	0	0	0
Air Force units	4,578	3,602	3,076	581	37	437	99	484	390
Other units	0	0	0	0	0	0	0	0	0
Aleutian Islands (3 June 1942 to 24 August 1943)	1,736	818	793	875	17	47	0	21	8
Combat divisions	1,110	457	443	666	14	0	0	1	0
Air Force units	343	239	229	49	2	47	0	18	8
Other units	283	122	121	160	1	0	0	2	0
Bismarck Archipelago (15 December 1943 to 27 November 1944)	945	346	240	615	20	7	3	83	83
Combat divisions	493	64	52	441	12	0	0	0	0
Air Force units	375	264	172	113	6	7	3	83	83
Other units	77	18	16	61	2	0	0	0	0
Burma, 1942 and India – Burma (7 December 1941 to 28 January 1945) d/	5,110	2,797	2,030	1,833	142	621	266	626	359
Combat divisions	0	0	0	0	0	0	0	0	0
Air Force units	2,712	1,922	1,466	354	41	305	91	587	324
Other units	2,398	875	564	1,479	101	316	175	39	35

BATTLE CASUALTIES

Battle casualties by campaign and type of organization:
7 December 1941 - 31 December 1946 a/ - continued

Campaign and type of organization	Total battle casualties	Total deaths among battle casualties b/	Killed in action	Wounded and injured in action		Captured and interned		Missing in action	
				Total	Died c/	Total	Died c/	Total	Died c/
Pacific area campaigns - continued									
Central Burma (29 January to 15 July 1945)	960	552	446	344	35	89	17	81	54
Combat divisions	0	0	0	0	0	0	0	0	0
Air Force units	498	357	283	82	7	56	16	77	51
Other units	462	195	163	262	28	33	1	4	3
Central Pacific (7 December 1941 to 6 December 1943)	1,710	517	464	1,100	26	47	11	99	16
Combat divisions	276	41	36	238	5	0	0	2	0
Air Force units	1,117	360	326	668	18	30	0	93	16
Other units	317	116	102	194	3	17	11	4	0
China Defensive (4 July 1942 to 4 May 1945)	487	194	137	167	8	28	6	155	43
Combat divisions	0	0	0	0	0	0	0	0	0
Air Force units	365	192	137	49	6	25	6	154	43
Other units	122	2	0	118	2	3	0	1	0
China Offensive (5 May to 2 September 1945)	74	47	37	6	2	8	4	23	4
Combat divisions	0	0	0	0	0	0	0	0	0
Air Force units	69	44	35	4	2	7	3	23	4
Other units	5	3	2	2	0	1	1	0	0
East Indies (1 January to 22 July 1942) . .	605	461	305	118	8	22	1	160	147
Combat divisions	0	0	0	0	0	0	0	0	0
Air Force units	492	427	277	34	3	22	1	159	146
Other units	113	34	28	84	5	0	0	1	1
Eastern Mandates (Air, 7 December 1943 to 16 April 1944; ground, 31 January to 14 June 1944)	1,490	434	281	1,101	45	2	2	106	106
Combat divisions	1,067	175	144	923	31	0	0	0	0
Air Force units	275	218	107	60	3	2	2	106	106
Other units	148	41	30	118	11	0	0	0	0
Guadalcanal (7 August 1942 to 21 February 1943)	1,434	712	586	755	45	0	0	93	81
Combat divisions	1,095	527	479	601	38	0	0	15	10
Air Force units	166	150	79	9	0	0	0	78	71
Other units	173	35	28	145	7	0	0	0	0
Leyte, Luzon, and Southern Philippines (17 October 1944 to 4 July 1945) e/ . . .	60,717	16,233	13,106	47,166	2,934	96	44	349	149
Combat divisions	51,327	12,679	10,144	41,087	2,503	18	4	78	28
Air Force units	2,392	1,539	1,366	728	52	45	7	253	114
Other units	6,998	2,015	1,596	5,351	379	33	33	18	7
New Guinea (24 January 1943 to 31 December 1944)	12,291	4,684	3,455	7,997	511	50	12	789	706
Combat divisions	6,435	1,585	1,212	5,183	356	3	0	37	17
Air Force units	3,689	2,533	1,778	1,133	62	39	10	739	683
Other units	2,167	566	465	1,681	93	8	2	13	6
Northern Solomons (22 February 1943 to 21 November 1944)	6,593	1,774	1,378	5,057	258	6	5	152	133
Combat divisions	5,685	1,285	1,050	4,627	228	1	0	7	7
Air Force units	587	406	262	175	13	5	5	145	126
Other units	321	83	66	255	17	0	0	0	0

CAMPAIGN AND TYPE OF ORGANIZATION

Battle casualties by campaign and type of organization:
7 December 1941 - 31 December 1946 a/ - concluded

Campaign and type of organization	Total battle casualties	Total deaths among battle casualties b/	Killed in action	Wounded and injured in action		Captured and interned		Missing in action	
				Total	Died c/	Total	Died c/	Total	Died c/
Pacific area campaigns - concluded									
Papua (23 July 1942 to 23 January 1943) . .	947	343	273	614	21	3	3	57	46
Combat divisions	762	218	201	559	17	0	0	2	0
Air Force units	130	104	57	19	2	2	2	52	43
Other units	55	21	15	36	2	1	1	3	3
Philippine Islands (7 December 1941 to 10 May 1942)	30,838	13,847	1,909	1,231	120	25,580	10,650	2,118	1,168
Combat divisions	0	0	0	0	0	0	0	0	0
Air Force units	6,521	3,387	316	338	26	5,560	2,951	307	94
Other units	24,317	10,460	1,593	893	94	20,020	7,699	1,811	1,074
Ryukyus (26 March to 2 July 1945)	19,929	4,718	3,672	16,027	995	58	37	172	14
Combat divisions	18,492	4,320	3,392	14,943	919	4	0	153	9
Air Force units	60	18	12	46	4	0	0	2	2
Other units	1,377	380	268	1,038	72	54	37	17	3
Western Pacific (17 April 1944 - air, 15 June 1944 - ground, to 2 September 1945)	9,832	3,066	2,380	7,077	488	80	3	295	195
Combat divisions	7,268	1,945	1,513	5,740	429	0	0	15	3
Air Force units	1,699	925	711	629	19	79	3	280	192
Other units	865	196	156	708	40	1	0	0	0
Campaigns not identifiable	26,151	5,639	4,427	14,486	692	6,301	416	937	104
Combat divisions	0	0	0	0	0	0	0	0	0
Air Force units	1,105	815	772	197	18	84	19	52	6
Other units	13,249	3,643	2,848	7,994	622	1,982	110	425	63
Organizations undetermined	11,797	1,181	807	6,295	52	4,235	287	460	35

a/ See Introduction for sources and coverage.
b/ Represents sum of battle deaths (columns 4, 6, 7, 11, 12, and 16 of pages 8 through 91) and nonbattle deaths of personnel in a battle casualty status (columns 13 and 17 of pages 8 through 91). Excludes nonbattle deaths of personnel not in a battle casualty status. See pages 96 through 118 for all Army deaths.
c/ Included in "Total deaths among battle casualties."
d/ Consists of battle casualties in the following campaigns for which the data cannot be identified separately: Burma, 1942 (7 December 1941 to 26 May 1942), and India - Burma (2 April 1942 to 28 January 1945).
e/ Consists of battle casualties in the following campaigns for which the data cannot be identified separately: Leyte (17 October 1944 to 1 July 1945), Luzon (15 December 1944 to 4 July 1945), Southern Philippines (27 February to 4 July 1945).

BATTLE CASUALTIES AND NONBATTLE DEATHS

Battle casualties and deaths, by geographic area of residence:
7 December 1941 - 31 December 1946 a/

Geographic area of residence	Battle casualties b/	Deaths				
		Total deaths	Deaths among battle casualties			Other nonbattle e/
			Total	Battle c/	Nonbattle d/	
Total	936,259	318,274	234,874	225,618	9,256	83,400
Alabama	.14,715	5,215	3,468	3,409	59	1,747
Arizona	4,043	1,553	1,150	1,112	38	403
Arkansas	10,699	3,918	2,773	2,704	69	1,145
California	39,978	17,428	12,139	11,509	630	5,289
Colorado	5,995	2,776	1,998	1,913	85	778
Connecticut	13,093	4,422	3,373	3,312	61	1,049
Delaware	1,820	563	425	420	5	138
District of Columbia	3,261	1,485	903	874	29	582
Florida	8,928	3,646	2,315	2,258	57	1,331
Georgia	16,211	5.810	3,916	3,829	87	1,894
Idaho	3,543	1,423	1,052	991	61	371
Illinois	52,208	18,850	14,065	13,750	315	4,785
Indiana	23,939	8,270	6,219	6,122	97	2,051
Iowa	15,979	5,800	4,364	4,255	109	1,436
Kansas	11,592	4,629	3,430	3,357	73	1,199
Kentucky	21,670	6,909	5,174	5,073	101	1,735
Louisiana	10,812	4,032	2,707	2,636	71	1,325
Maine	6,181	2,184	1,687	1,624	63	497
Maryland	12,951	4,457	3,278	3,240	38	1,179
Massachusetts	29,117	10,198	7,602	7,393	209	2,596
Michigan	38,739	13,057	9,996	9,826	170	3,061
Minnesota	17,798	6,533	4,980	4,834	146	1,553
Mississippi	9,711	3,622	2,403	2,341	62	1,219
Missouri	22,720	8,100	6,025	5,871	154	2,075
Montana	3,664	1,575	1,197	1,064	133	378
Nebraska	7,716	3,044	2,290	2,194	96	754
Nevada	880	350	238	225	13	112
New Hampshire	3,276	1,219	912	877	35	307
New Jersey	30,421	10,536	7,904	7,799	105	2,632
New Mexico	5,372	2,109	1,720	1,245	475	389
New York	89,183	31,522	23,322	22,992	330	8,200
North Carolina	21,469	7,271	5,158	5,073	85	2,113
North Dakota	4,644	1,640	1,285	1,254	31	355
Ohio	48,198	17,168	12,835	12,616	219	4,333
Oklahoma	14,782	5,582	4,067	3,937	130	1,515
Oregon	7,119	2,836	2,053	1,909	144	783
Pennsylvania	82,395	26,971	20,597	20,182	415	6,374
Rhode Island	4,913	1,687	1,276	1,239	37	411
South Carolina	10,081	3,443	2,438	2,385	53	1,005
South Dakota	3,810	1,479	1,103	1,076	27	376
Tennessee	20,553	6,704	4,982	4,914	68	1,722
Texas	42,001	16,286	11,374	10,898	476	4,912
Utah	3,287	1,463	1,069	1,031	38	394
Vermont	2,518	861	664	642	22	197
Virginia	17,745	6,179	4,356	4,276	80	1,823
Washington	9,413	4,043	2,927	2,760	167	1,116
West Virginia	16,321	4,937	3,836	3,767	69	1,101
Wisconsin	19,399	7,122	5,402	5,193	209	1,720
Wyoming	1,560	706	520	492	28	186
Alaska	232	48	35	32	3	13
Hawaii	2,593	722	584	584	0	138
Panama Canal Zone	1,576	17	8	8	0	9
Puerto Rico	165	346	23	23	0	323
Philippines	10,808	5,337	5,135	2,161	2,974	202
United States - area not specified	1,966	25	18	14	4	7
United States possessions	12	4	0	0	0	4
Other countries	2,566	162	104	103	1	58
Geographic area unknown	49,818	0	0	0	0	0

b/ Includes deaths among battle casualties.
c/ Consists of deaths of personnel in a battle casualty status of killed in action, died of wounds and injuries received in action, or declared dead from missing in action (columns 4, 6, 7, 11, 12, and 16 of pages 8 through 91).
d/ Consists of nonbattle deaths of personnel in a battle casualty status of captured and interned, or missing in action (columns 13 and 17 of pages 8 through 91)
e/ Consists of nonbattle deaths of personnel not in a battle casualty status at time of death.

NAVAL PERSONNEL [1]
ACTIVE SERVICE CASUALTIES — WORLD WAR II—BY AREA
(ESTIMATED)

AREA	GRAND TOTAL	TOTAL OFFICERS	OFFICERS ENEMY ACTION TOTAL	DEATHS	WOUNDED	NON-ENEMY ACTION DEATHS	TOTAL ENLISTED	ENLISTED ENEMY ACTION TOTAL	DEATHS	WOUNDED	NON-ENEMY ACTION DEATHS
GRAND TOTAL	100,392	13,208	7,325	4,025	3,300	5,883	87,184	67,403	32,925	34,478	19,781
1941 (OCT & DEC) 2/	3,338	223	204	116	88	19	3,115	3,057	2,101	956	58
1942	15,379	1,722	1,234	810	424	488	13,657	12,005	8,329	3,676	1,652
1943	16,476	2,368	1,073	608	465	1,295	14,108	10,044	5,912	4,132	4,064
1944	30,926	4,188	2,325	1,212	1,113	1,863	26,738	19,889	7,530	12,359	6,849
1945	31,857	4,139	2,489	1,279	1,210	1,650	27,718	22,408	9,053	13,355	5,310
1946	2,416	568	0	0	0	568	1,848	0	0	0	1,848
ATLANTIC – TOTAL	10,966	1,219	615	306	309	604	9,747	6,919	3,674	3,245	2,828
1941 (OCT & DEC) 2/	165	18	10	7	3	8	147	140	104	36	7
1942	1,366	151	77	32	45	74	1,215	761	294	467	454
1943	2,226	299	92	56	36	207	1,927	1,072	804	268	855
1944	5,876	583	365	158	207	218	5,293	4,187	1,910	2,277	1,106
1945	1,241	138	71	53	18	67	1,103	759	562	197	344
1946	92	30	0	0	0	30	62	0	0	0	62
ASIATIC – TOTAL	40,920	4,166	3,779	2,080	1,699	387	36,754	34,712	15,960	18,752	2,042
1941 (DEC)	194	23	23	10	13	0	171	167	97	70	4
1942	2,948	307	305	254	51	2	2,641	2,592	2,288	304	49
1943	2,042	177	177	169	8	0	1,865	1,853	1,842	11	12
1944	10,972	1,244	1,159	703	456	85	9,728	8,941	3,571	5,370	787
1945	24,450	2,343	2,115	944	1,171	228	22,107	21,159	8,162	12,997	948
1946	314	72	0	0	0	72	242	0	0	0	242
PACIFIC – TOTAL	30,765	3,945	2,588	1,508	1,080	1,357	26,820	21,779	11,609	10,170	5,041
1941 (DEC)	2,944	177	171	99	72	6	2,767	2,750	1,900	850	17
1942	9,903	952	845	524	321	107	8,951	8,553	5,736	2,857	358
1943	7,201	937	655	350	305	282	6,264	5,212	2,781	2,431	1,052
1944	8,033	1,156	635	273	362	521	6,877	4,875	991	3,884	2,002
1945	2,353	661	282	262	20	379	1,692	349	201	148	1,343
1946	331	62	0	0	0	62	269	0	0	0	269
MEDITERRANEAN – TOTAL	4,597	398	341	129	212	57	4,199	3,973	1,672	2,301	226
1941 (DEC)	0	0	0	0	0	0	0	0	0	0	0
1942	63	7	7	0	7	0	56	54	8	46	2
1943	2,128	160	149	33	116	11	1,968	1,900	485	1,415	68
1944	2,180	192	165	77	88	27	1,988	1,883	1,056	827	105
1945	211	34	20	19	1	14	177	136	123	13	41
1946	15	5	0	0	0	5	10	0	0	0	10
UNITED STATES – TOTAL	13,144	3,480	2	2	0	3,478	9,664	20	10	10	9,644
1941 (DEC)	35	5	0	0	0	5	30	0	0	0	30
1942	1,099	305	0	0	0	305	794	5	3	2	789
1943	2,879	795	0	0	0	795	2,084	7	0	7	2,077
1944	3,865	1,013	1	1	0	1,012	2,852	3	2	1	2,849
1945	3,602	963	1	1	0	962	2,639	5	5	0	2,634
1946	1,664	399	0	0	0	399	1,265	0	0	0	1,265

1/ EXCLUDES MARINE CORPS AND COAST GUARD

2/ INCLUDES HOSTILE ACTION OCCURRING OCTOBER 1941

DEATHS — WORLD WAR II — DUE TO ENEMY ACTION
NAVAL PERSONNEL 1/

TYPE OF CASUALTY	GRAND TOTAL	OFFICERS								ENLISTED						TOTAL OFFICER CANDIDATES INCLUDED WITH ENLISTED USNR
		TOTAL OFFICERS	MEN		RETIRED		WOMEN	NURSES		TOTAL ENLISTED	MEN				WOMEN	
			USN	USNR	USN	USNR	WAVES USNR	USN	USNR		USN	USNR	USN-I	FLEET RESERVE	WAVES V-10	
TOTAL COMBAT DEATHS	36,950	4,025	1,038	2,982	5	-	0	0	0	32,925	14,296	18,136	276	217	0	5
KILLED IN ACTION	30,891	2,148	737	1,407	4	-	-	-	-	28,663	12,540	15,766	240	137	0	4
*1941	2,155	104	49	55	0					2,051	1,965	61	0	25		0
1942	2,809	205	106	98	1					2,604	1,862	726	0	16		0
1943	4,524	277	115	161	1					4,247	2,900	1,713	7	27		0
1944	7,685	515	117	397	1					7,170	1,998	5,087	66	19		1
1945	11,446	828	244	583	1					10,618	3,335	7,078	157	48		3
1946	2,212	219	106	113	0					1,993	880	1,101	10	2		0
KILLED IN ACTION (AIR COMBAT)	3,173	1,514	172	1,341	1					1,659	627	1,015	17	0	0	1
1941	26	9	4	5	0					17	16	1	0			1
1942	81	41	12	29	0					40	35	5	0			
1943	315	143	47	96	0					172	128	44	0			
1944	502	244	20	224	0					258	74	181	3			
1945	1,071	516	53	462	1					555	198	353	4			
1946	1,178	561	36	525	0					617	176	431	10			
DIED OF WOUNDS	1,837	151	29	122	0					1,686	432	1,233	15	6	0	0
1941	36	3	2	1	0					33	31	2	0	0		
1942	181	26	11	15						155	106	46	0	3		
1943	251	26	3	23						225	66	159	0	0		
1944	677	44	5	39						633	126	499	6	2		
1945	692	52	8	44						640	103	527	9	1		
1946	0	0	0	0						0	0	0	0	0		
DIED PRISONER OF WAR	919	180	96	84	0					739	673	0	0	66	0	0
1941	0	0	0	0						0	0			0		
1942	187	15	10	5						172	129			43		
1943	143	7	3	4						136	132			4		
1944	414	78	47	31						336	321			15		
1945	172	77	35	42						95	91			4		
1946	3	3	1	2						0	0			0		
OTHER DEATHS DUE ENEMY ACTION	190	32	4	28	0					158	24	122	4	8	0	0
1941	0	0	0	0						0	0	0	0	0		
1942	20	9	3	6						11	4	4	0	3		
1943	18	1	0	1						17	2	14	0	1		
1944	70	4	0	4						66	13	51	1	1		
1945	48	8	0	8						40	4	31	2	3		
1946	34	10	1	9						24	1	22	1	0		

* INCLUDES USS REUBEN JAMES & USS KEARNEY OCT 1941

DEATHS — WORLD WAR II — DUE TO OTHER THAN ENEMY ACTION

TYPE OF CASUALTY	GRAND TOTAL	OFFICERS								ENLISTED						OFFICER CANDIDATES				
		TOTAL OFFICERS	MEN		RETIRED		WOMEN	NURSES		TOTAL ENLISTED	MEN				WOMEN	TOTAL OFF. CAND.	V-5	V-7	V-12	NAV. ACAD. MIDN.
			USN	USNR	USN	USNR	WAVES USNR	USN	USNR		USN	USNR	USN-I	FLEET RESERVE	WAVES V-10					
TOTAL DEATHS NON-COMBAT	25,664	5,883	828	4,859	147	-	10	12	27	19,095	5,056	13,117	433	394	95	635	573	9	95	9
NATURAL CAUSES	5,533	841	247	452	129		3	4	6	4,601	907	3,201	143	311	39	91	32	6	49	4
1941	9	3	1	0	2		0	0	0	6	5	0	0	1	0	0	0	0	0	0
1942	498	74	28	31	15		0	0	0	419	173	176	0	70	0	5	3	1	0	1
1943	1,146	139	31	89	16		0	1	2	985	191	698	16	76	4	22	14	2	5	1
1944	1,619	237	58	137	38		0	3	1	1,344	182	1,010	47	90	15	38	10	1	27	0
1945	1,591	237	69	121	43		2	0	2	1,331	173	1,017	70	56	15	23	4	2	15	2
1946	670	151	60	74	15		1	0	1	516	183	300	10	18	5	3	1	0	2	0
AVIATION ACCIDENTS	8,164	4,142	373	3,756	1		3	3	6	3,515	1,162	2,304	35	2	11	527	516	0	9	2
1941	38	15	7	8	0		0	0	0	20	19	1	0	0	0	3	3	0	0	0
1942	722	347	43	303	1		0	0	0	278	212	66	0	0	0	97	97	0	0	0
1943	2,171	1,010	98	910	0		1	1	0	922	363	555	2	2	0	239	235	0	4	2
1944	2,590	1,304	81	1,216	0		0	2	5	1,161	286	850	19	0	6	125	122	0	1	2
1945	2,126	1,164	89	1,073	0		2	0	0	910	153	741	12	0	4	52	49	0	3	0
1946	537	302	55	246	0		0	0	1	224	129	91	3	0	1	11	10	0	1	0
OTHER DEATHS	11,947	900	208	651	17		4	5	15	10,979	2,987	7,612	254	81	45	68	25	3	37	3
1941	30	1	0	1	0		0	0	0	29	21	8	0	0	0	0	0	0	0	0
1942	920	67	27	39	1		0	0	0	848	474	346	0	28	0	5	3	1	0	1
1943	2,041	145	34	102	3		1	2	3	1,878	684	1,156	13	19	6	18	12	0	5	1
1944	4,504	323	66	246	6		0	2	3	4,155	755	3,281	88	14	17	26	6	1	19	0
1945	3,243	249	39	196	5		3	0	6	2,978	472	2,342	132	18	14	16	3	1	12	0
1946	2,209	115	42	67	2		0	1	3	1,091	581	479	21	2	8	3	1	0	1	1

Marine Casualties[1]

Location and date	KIA		DOW		WIA		MIAPD		KDPOW		TOTAL	
	Officer	Enlisted	Officer	Enlisted	Officer	Enlisted	Officer	Enlisted	Officer	Enlisted	Officer	Enlisted
Marines												
Guam (7–10 Dec 41)	----	4	----	1	----	13	----	------	----	5	----	23
Wake Atoll (7–23 Dec 41)	4	46	----	------	6	38	----	6	----	13	10	103
Philippines (7 Dec 41–6 May 42)	43	267	----	5	33	324	----	16	14	225	90	837
Midway Islands (7 Dec 41–6 Jun 42)	2	8	1	------	14	25	23	14	----	------	40	47
Makin (17–18 Aug 42)	1	17	----	------	2	14	----	12	----	------	3	43
Guadalcanal (7 Aug 42–8 Feb 43)	71	1,026	11	98	223	2,693	52	246	----	------	357	4,063
Naval Medical Personnel Organic to Marine Units												
Philippines (7 Dec 41–6 May 42)	----	------	----	------	2	------	----	------	3	25	5	25
Guadalcanal (7 Aug 42–8 Feb 43)	8	23	1	4	15	86	----	------	----	------	24	113

[1] These final Marine casualty figures were compiled from records furnished by Statistics Unit, PersAcctSec, (RecsBr, PersDept, HQMS. They are audited to include 26 Aug 52. Naval casualties were taken from NavMed P-5021, *The History of the Medical Department of the Navy in World War II*, 2 vols (Washington: Government Printing Office, 1943), II. 1–84. The key to the abbreviations used at the head of columns in the table follows: KIA, Killed in Action; DOW, Died of Wounds; WIA, Wounded in Action; MIAPD, Missing in Action, Presumed Dead; KDPOW, Killed or Died while a Prisoner of War. Because of the method used in reporting casualties during World War II a substantial number of DOW figures are also included in the WIA column.

Marine Casualties [1]

Location and date	KIA		DOW		WIA		MIAPD		POW [2]		TOTAL	
	Offi-cer	En-listed	Offi-cer	En-listed	Offi-cer	En-listed	Offi-cer	En-listed	Offi-cer	En-listed	Offi-cer	En-listed
Marines												
New Georgia [3] (20Jun–16Oct43)	8	145	0	10	31	384	1	57	0	0	40	596
Bougainville [4] (28Oct43–15Jun44)	18	334	7	81	77	1,172	6	286	0	0	108	1,873
Cape Gloucester (26Dec43–1Mar44)	19	245	1	49	40	775	0	124	0	0	60	1,193
Talasea	2	10	0	16	8	125	0	9	0	0	10	160
Aviation [5]	92	104	1	15	108	114	232	339	17	5	452	577
Sea-duty	1	19	0	5	8	87	3	58	0	0	12	169
Miscellaneous [6]	0	1	1	0	5	1	0	0	0	0	6	2
Total Marines	140	858	10	176	277	2,658	242	873	17	5	688	4,570
Naval Medical Personnel Organic to Marine Units [1]												
New Georgia	0	3	0	0	0	11	0	0	0	0	0	14
Bougainville	1	8	1	2	1	29	0	0	0	0	2	39
Cape Gloucester	1	8	1	2	1	29	0	0	0	0	2	39
Talasea	0	0	0	0	0	4	0	0	0	0	0	4
Marine Aviation	1	2	0	0	0	2	0	0	0	0	1	4
Total Navy	2	21	1	4	2	86	0	0	0	0	5	111
Grand Total	142	879	11	180	279	2,744	242	287	17	5	693	4,681

[1] These final Marine casualty figures were compiled from records furnished by Statistics Unit, Personnel Accounting Section, Records Branch, Personnel Department, HQMC. They are audited to include 26 August 1952. Naval casualties were taken from NavMed P-5021, *The History of the Medical Department of the Navy in World War II*, 2 vols (Washington: Government Printing Office, 1953), II, pp. 1-84. The key to the abbreviations used at the head of columns in the table follows: KIA, Killed in Action; DOW, Died of Wounds; WIA, Wounded in Action; MIAPD, Missing in Action, Presumed Dead; POW, Prisoner of War. Because of the casualty reporting method used during World War II, a substantial number of DOW figures are also included in the WIA column.

[2] Included are 4 officers who died while POWs, and 2 who escaped.

[3] Includes: Rendova, Arundel, Vella Lavella, Enogai, and Vangunu operations.

[4] Includes: Choiseul operation and consolidation of Northern Solomons.

[5] Includes: All operations in Solomons-New Britain area during period 9Feb43–15Mar45.

[6] Includes: Arawe, Russell Islands, and Treasury Islands operations.

Marine Casualties[1]

Location and Date	KIA Officer	KIA Enlisted	DOW Officer	DOW Enlisted	WIA Officer	WIA Enlisted	MIAPD Officer	MIAPD Enlisted	Total Officer	Total Enlisted
Marines										
Tarawa[2] (20Nov–8Dec43)	51	853	9	84	109	2,124	------	88	169	3,149
Kwajalein/Majuro (29Jan–8Feb44)	13	162	1	30	41	590	------	181	55	963
Eniwetok (17Feb–2Mar44)	4	177	1	37	27	541	2	37	34	792
Saipan (11Jun–10Jul44)	137	1,940	18	349	493	8,082	------	708	648	11,079
Guam (21Jul–15Aug44)	80	1,076	15	380	288	5,077	------	17	383	6,550
Tinian (24Jul–1Aug44)	22	278	4	61	97	1,824	1	2	124	2,165
Aviation[3]	19	18	------	6	30	90	7	15	56	129
Sea-duty[3]	------	13	------	2	1	57	------	4	1	76
Total Marines	326	4,517	48	949	1,086	18,385	10	1,052	1,470	24,903
Naval Medical Personnel Organic to Marine Units[4]										
Tarawa	2	28	------	------	2	57	------	------	4	85
Marshalls[5]	------	5	------	1	2	34	------	------	2	40
Saipan	1	70	------	6	7	330	------	------	8	406
Guam	3	43	1	4	11	195	------	------	15	242
Tinian	1	23	------	2	------	40	------	------	1	65
Marine Aviation	------	5	------	------	1	4	------	------	1	9
Total Navy	7	174	1	13	23	660	------	------	31	847
Grand Total	333	4,691	49	962	1,109	19,045	10	1,052	1,501	25,750

See footnote at end of table.

[1] These final Marine casualty figures were compiled from records furnished by Statistics Unit, Personnel Accounting Section, Records Branch, Personnel Department, HQMC. They are audited to include 26 August 1952. Naval casualties were taken from NavMed P–5021, *The History of the Medical Department of the Navy in World War II*, 2 vols (Washington: Government Printing Office, 1953), II, pp. 1-84. The key to the abbreviations used at the head of columns in the table follows: KIA, Killed in Action; DOW, Died of Wounds; WIA, Wounded in Action; MIAPD, Missing in Action, Presumed Dead. Because of the casualty reporting method used during World War II, a substantial number of DOW figures are also included in the WIA column.

[2] Includes Apamama.

[3] Includes operations in Gilberts, Marshalls, and Marianas during periods indicated above.

[4] See Footnote (1) above.

[5] Includes Kwajalein/Majuro and Eniwetok during periods indicated above.

Marine Casualties[1]

Location and Date	KIA		DOW		WIA		MIAPD		TOTAL	
	Offi-cer	En-listed	Offi-cer	En-listed	Offi-cer	En-listed	Offi-cer	En-listed	Offi-cer	En-listed
Marines										
Peleliu[2] (6Sep–14Oct44)	66	984	18	232	301	5,149	0	36	385	6,401
Iwo Jima (19Feb–26Mar45)	215	4,339	60	1,271	826	16,446	3	43	1,104	22,099
Aviation[3]	66	49	3	6	91	212	44	32	204	299
Sea-duty	4	61	0	9	8	142	0	63	12	275
Total Marines	351	5,433	81	1,518	1,226	21,949	47	174	1,705	29,074
Naval Medical Personnel Organic to Marine Units[4]										
Peleliu	1	49	0	11	11	238	0	0	12	298
Iwo Jima	4	183	0	22	19	622	0	0	23	827
Marine Aviation[5]	0	2	0	0	2	10	0	0	4	10
Total Navy	5	234	0	33	32	870	0	0	39	1,135
Grand Total	356	5,667	0	1,551	1,258	22,817	47	174	1,744	30,209

[1] These final Marine casualty figures were compiled from records furnished by Statistics Unit, Personnel Accounting Section, Records Branch, Personnel Department, HQMC. Figures for the Peleliu Operation were certified and released on 1 June 1950; those for Iwo Jima in August 1952. Naval casualties were taken from NavMed P-5021, *The History of the Medical Department of the Navy in World War II* (Washington: Government Printing Office, 1953). The key to the abbreviations used at the head of columns in the table follows: KIA, Killed in Action; DOW, Died of Wounds; WIA, Wounded in Action; MIAPD, Missing in Action, Presumed Dead. Because of the casualty reporting method used during World War II, a substantial number of DOW figures are also included in the WIA column.

[2] Includes Ngesebus.

[3] Includes bypassed Marshalls, Carolines, Palau, Philippines, and Volcano Bonin Islands, overall period covering February 1944 - June 1945.

[4] See Footnote (1) above.

[5] Time frame identical to (3) above.

Marine Casualties [1]

Okinawa (1Apr–22Jun45)	KIA Officer	KIA En-listed	DOW Officer	DOW En-listed	WIA Officer	WIA En-listed	MIAPD Officer	MIAPD En-listed	TOTAL Officer	TOTAL En-listed
ReconBn, FMFPac	0	3	0	0	3	10	0	0	2	13
IIIAC Troops	0	18	1	4	14	148	0	0	15	170
IIIAC Artillery	1	10	1	11	11	458	1	1	14	480
1st Marine Division	56	1,036	13	149	311	6,094	0	6	380	7,285
RCT-8	1	36	0	11	11	317	0	0	12	364
6th Marine Division	27	1,337	18	274	388	7,041	1	10	434	8,662
2d Marine Aircraft Wing	24	21	0	9	51	162	28	3	103	195
Replacement Drafts[2]	1	157	1	28	9	735	0	1	11	921
Miscellaneous Air[3]	4	0	1	0	9	11	4	0	18	11
Miscellaneous Ground[4]	0	16	0	8	0	117	0	0	0	141
Total Casualties	114	2,634	35	494	806	15,093	34	21	989	18,242
Marine Ships Detachments	1	47	0	1	8	97	0	10	9	155
Marine Carrier Air Detachments	10	40	0	0	7	6	2	0	19	46
Grand Total Marine Casualties	125	2,721	35	495	821	15,196	36	31	1,017	18,443
Naval Medical Personnel[5] Organic to Marine Units	1	108	0	9	12	430	0	0	13	547
Grand Total	126	2,829	35	504	833	15,626	36	31	1,030	18,990

[1] These final Marine casualty figures were compiled from records furnished by Statistics Unit, Personnel Accounting Section, Records Branch, Personnel Department, HQMC. They are audited to include 26 August 1952. The key to the abbreviations used at the head of columns in the table follows: KIA, Killed in Action; DOW, Died of Wounds; WIA, Wounded in Action; MIAPD, Missing in Action, Presumed dead. Because of the casualty reporting method used during World War II, a substantial number of DOW figures are also included in the WIA column.

[2] Most members of replacement drafts who became casualties did so as member of regular combat units. In many instances, these men were hit before official notice of their transfer reached Headquarters Marine Corps, and therefore, they are carried on the casualty rolls as members of the various drafts.

[3] Included in the miscellaneous categories are those men whose personnel records still showed them as members of units not part of Tenth Army when the report of their becoming a casualty reached Headquarters Marine Corps.

[4] This category includes the casualties suffered by the 2d Marine Division while it was in the Okinawa area.

[5] Compiled from NavMed P-5021, *The History of the Medical Department of the Navy in World War II*, 2 vols (Washington: Government Printing Office, 1953), II, pp. 1–84.

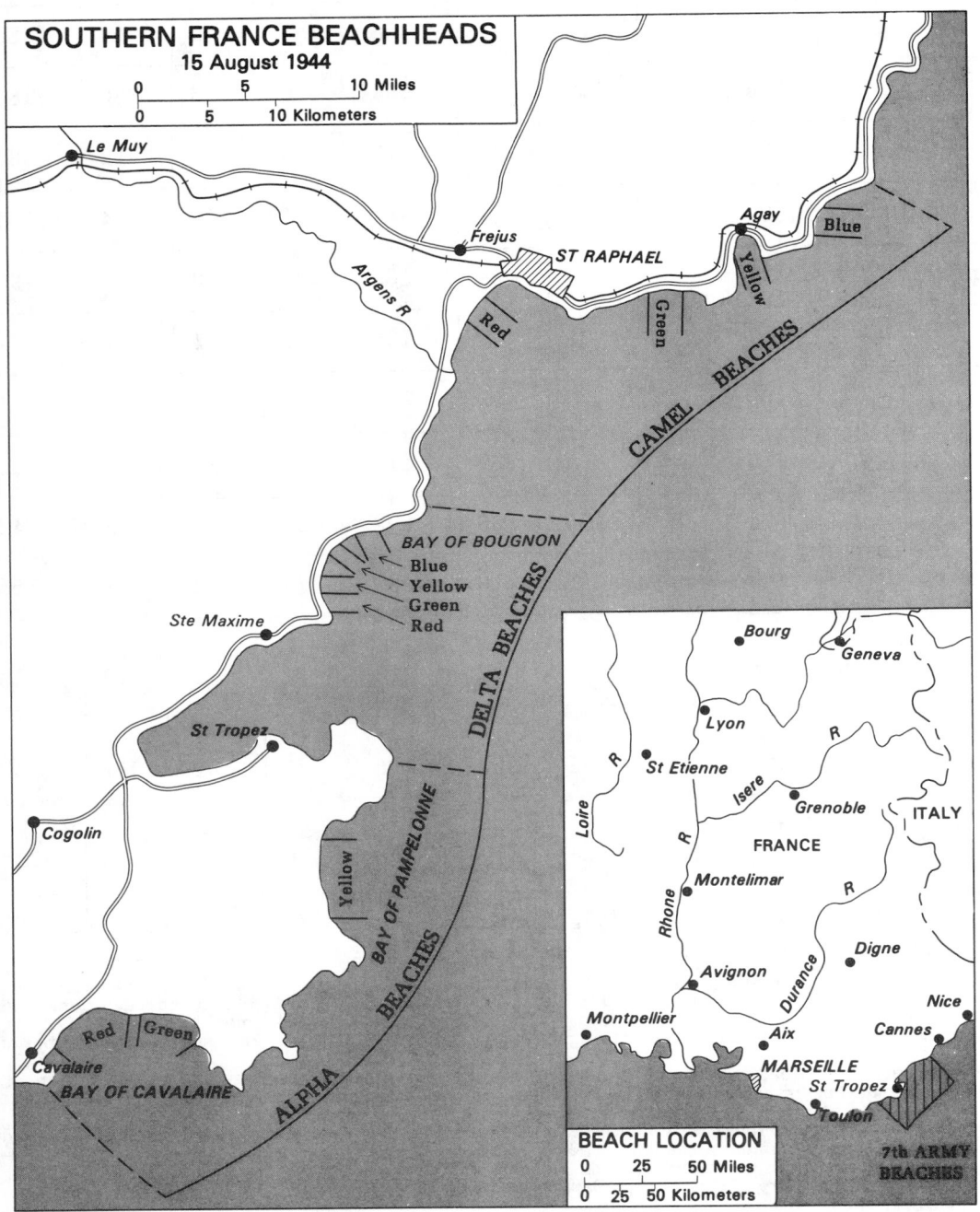

SOUTHERN FRANCE BEACHHEADS
15 August 1944

0 — 5 — 10 Miles
0 — 5 — 10 Kilometers

Le Muy

Argens R

Frejus

ST RAPHAEL

Agay

Blue

Yellow

Red

Green

CAMEL BEACHES

BAY OF BOUGNON

Blue
Yellow
Green
Red

DELTA BEACHES

Ste Maxime

St Tropez

Cogolin

Yellow

BAY OF PAMPELONNE

ALPHA BEACHES

Red   Green

Cavalaire

BAY OF CAVALAIRE

BEACH LOCATION

Bourg

Geneva

Lyon

St Etienne

Loire R

Isere R

Grenoble

ITALY

Rhone R

FRANCE

Montelimar

Durance R

Avignon

Digne

Montpellier

Nice

Aix

Cannes

MARSEILLE

St Tropez

Toulon

0 — 25 — 50 Miles
0 — 25 — 50 Kilometers

7th ARMY BEACHES

880

Manus I.
Los Negros I.
ADMIRALTY IS.

NEW IRELAND

BISMARK ARCHIPELAGO

Rabaul

Madang

Cape Glaucester

NEW BRITAIN

Finschhafen
Lae
Salamaua

TROBRIAND IS.
Kiriwina I.

Gona
Buna
Dobodura
Jaure

Woodlark I.

Gulf
of Papua

Port Moresby

Owen Stanley Range

Milne Bay

881

8" Howitzers in action in the Pacific.

Index

886

890

892

894

910

918

939

940

941